A Treasury of
LITERARY MASTERPIECES

the novels, plays, poems, and other works of the most
celebrated and historic writers in all lands and times

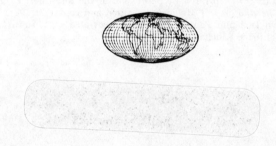

Edited by ALBERT H. MOREHEAD
Executive editor HAROLD J. BLUM
Drawings by RAFAELLO BUSONI
Portraits by CLAUDE PONSOT
Designed by DONALD D. WOLF and MARGOT L. WOLF

First published as LITERARY TREASURES

Publishers   GROSSET & DUNLAP   New York

The outlines for *Literary Treasures* were written by Elizabeth Mac-Lean, Howard Barnes, Harold J. Blum, Dina Dellalé, Paul Grillo. Lorimer Hammond, Hanz Holzer, Martin Keen, Princess Alexandra Kropotkin, Anne Richardson, James Wilhelm, Janet Wilson, Nancy Starrels, Bruce Brown, Muriel Claeke, Robert Condon, Grace Egan, Henry Engel, Sylvia Plapinger, Marion Segal, Susan Margulies, Thomas Stamm, Gerard Meyer, Patricia Secord, Nicholas Bela, Sue G. Walcutt, Joe Caldwell, Robert Condon, Grace Shaw, Jeanne Rosenthal, Phyllis Pollard, Robert P. Miller, Sheila Haker, Ernst Schlochaeur, James E. Tobin, Mary Louise Birmingham, Adrienne Foulke, Rosalind Lawson, Stockman Barner, Christopher Lazare, Mildred Lee Marmur, and the Editors. Outlines of *Barnaby Rudge* and *Bleak House* are adapted from *The Dickens Dictionary* by Gilbert A. Pierce and William A. Wheeler. Illustrations by George Herriman from *archy and mehitabel* by Don Marquis, copyright 1927 by Double-day & Co., Inc., reprinted by permission of the publisher. Excerpts from *The Anatomy of Melancholy*, edited and copyright 1927, 1955 by Floyd Dell and Paul Jordan-Smith, reprinted by permission of the publishers, Rinehart & Co., Inc.

First published as LITERARY TREASURES

How to Get the Most from
"Literary Treasures"

THIS WORK IS A SUMMARY OF THE GREATEST LITERATURE of all kinds that is or should be read and known by cultivated and educated people of the English-speaking world. It has five main purposes:

1. To select the literature of greatest interest and usefulness, whether novels, plays, poems, stories, or works of scholarship and opinion, and whether written originally in English or made familiar to English readers through translation from another language.

2. To "tell the story"—that is, to give an outline or summary of the plot and action of every fiction work and to give the gist or basic conclusion of every nonfiction work.

3. To give the historical background of each book: Who wrote it, and in what circumstances; when it was written and published; what its purpose and effect were.

4. To add any facts of interest relating to the book: Why its author selected its title, what it means, and where he got it; how popular or unpopular the book was when it was published; what characters or quotations from the book became noteworthy; when a play was first produced and what famous actors and actresses may have played in it.

5. To supply a critical appraisal of the book: How it ranks among other works of its kind, and among other works of the same author; how it should be read and understood today.

LITERARY TREASURES is essentially a reference book, that is, a "question-answerer," just as an encyclopedia or dictionary is. It is designed to refresh the memory of those who have already read a particular book; to make reading and understanding much easier for those who are about to read the book or perhaps see a dramatization on television, in the theater, or in the opera house; to point up the outstanding features of a book so that the reader may pay special attention to them; to give an adult the information he needs in social conversation about a book with which a well-educated person is expected to be familiar; and to give a student the basic information he will be expected to know in his school work.

There is no substitute for reading the book itself. For that reason, we have made every outline show the chapters (or other divisions of the book) in which each particular part of the action appears. The reader can then turn without difficulty to the desired part of the book and read the section that most interests him at the moment.

That is only one feature of LITERARY TREASURES that makes it different and superior to other reference works of the same kind. Other advantages are: Fuller treatment; all the plots in correct sequence; a more general selection of titles to be included; and much greater accuracy.

HOW WE SELECTED THE TITLES TO BE TREATED IN THIS WORK

Our first criterion in selection was, of course, literary excellence. We selected the "great books," including those that are standard on the required and recommended reading lists of schools and colleges.

But these are not the only books we selected.

There are many books that are important because they have contributed to our language or culture, or because they aroused controversy, or that have become famous for some other reason. Such books may have, but do not necessarily have, literary excellence. For example, no one can call *Uncle Tom's Cabin* a great work of literature, but it is so important a book historically that every educated American should be familiar with its story and characters. Many children's books have no claim to recognition except their remarkable (and in some cases inexplicable) appeal to children; but they are important because they have shaped the attitudes of millions of people in their most formative ages, and therefore we have considered them worth treating in LITERARY TREASURES.

We have not rejected any book simply because it is controversial. In many cases we have felt that fact to be all the more reason to include it. Thomas Paine's *Age of Reason* and Charles Darwin's *Descent of Man* have been attacked on religious grounds, Karl Marx's *Capital* on political grounds, James Joyce's *Ulysses* and dozens of other novels on moral grounds, but when such books are historically important you will find them here.

In every case we give the outline of the book as the author wrote it. We do not, *ever,* necessarily agree with the author's ideas or vouch for the correctness of statements the author makes. Of course, the outlines are written so as not to offend good taste, and when an author's statement is palpably a factual error or has been proved one since, we usually comment on that fact.

THE MEANINGS OF MARKINGS IN THIS WORK

The following typographic styles and marks have special meanings:

SMALL CAPITALS are used for the names of principal characters in a story, the first time they appear. If later in the outline the reader encounters the name of a character and cannot recall who he is, he should look back and pick out that character's name in SMALL CAPITALS, and there he will find the character clearly identified.

Parentheses are used for explanatory remarks taken from the book being outlined, but not necessarily from the chapter or section being treated at that point. For example: "Joshua (who was heavily indebted to his cousin) tried to stop her . . ." The fact that Joshua was heavily indebted may not be revealed, in the actual book, until many chapters later.

Brackets are used for comments, corrections or explanatory remarks by the editors; statements made in brackets are *not* to be found in the book itself. For example: "After the Peace of Tilsit [July 7–9, 1807] . . ." The author does not give the date, but the editors thought it well to supply it.

IMPORTANCE OF USING THE INDEX

This work is fully indexed.   To derive the greatest benefit from LITERARY TREASURES, the reader is urged to use the index.

One reason for this is that many works of literature are known by various titles. For example, the famous English book *Anatomy of Wit* is nearly always called simply *Euphues* (the name of its key character) and the editors have chosen to put it in alphabetical order as *Euphues.* Often a novel and its sequel or sequels are treated together, and to find the sequel one must look in the index, which will guide him to the first novel of the series. A trilogy such as *The Forsyte Saga* includes three novels that were originally published under different titles.

Contents

Especially in the case of books published within the last fifty or sixty years, the name and city of the publisher are usually given. Such books may most conveniently be obtained through bookstores, which either have them in stock or can promptly obtain them from the publishers.

As an extra service to readers, the editors have usually listed the cases in which books are available in low-priced editions, many of them paperbound. Such editions are noted by "key" numbers and letters. They may often be obtained from bookstores, or may be ordered direct from the publishers. Following is a list of the key letters and their meanings.

ML The Modern Library, 457 Madison Avenue, New York 22, N.Y. When the number of the book is preceded by G, for example G38, the book is a Modern Library Giant, having perhaps 1,000 pages; other numbers indicate shorter books, mostly clothbound, some paperbound.

PB Pocket Books, Inc., 630 Fifth Avenue, New York 20, N.Y. All are paperbound, but the numbers are often preceded by letters such as C, CG, or PL, indicating a particular series of books of which the desired book is part.

NAL New American Library of World Literature, Inc., 1301 Ave. of the Americas N.Y. 19, N.Y. All books so listed are paperbound but their numbers may be preceded by letters giving the size (for example T, a triple-length book) or series (for example M, a Mentor book, one of a group of very serious books).

Ban. Bantam Books, Inc. 271 Madison Ave. N.Y. 16, N.Y. All books paperbound.

Dell Dell Publishing Co., Inc., 750 Third Ave., N.Y. 17, N.Y. All books paperbound.

RE Rinehart Editions, published by Rinehart & Co., 430 Park Avenue, New York 22, N.Y. Paperbound editions of books used in school and college work.

Complete catalogs are available from all these publishers and from others noted throughout this book.

Abe Lincoln in Illinois

Play by Robert Sherwood, 1896–1955. Produced in New York, Oct. 16, 1938. Published by Charles Scribner's Sons, New York. © 1937, 1938, 1939 by Robert Emmet Sherwood.

IN *Abe Lincoln in Illinois* Sherwood covers Lincoln's life from the time he was 22 years old, and newly come to Illinois, to early 1861, when he had been elected to the Presidency. In many cases Sherwood uses poetic license and he fully credits the doubtful story of Lincoln's love for Ann Rutledge; but in the main the play is historically accurate. In its first New York production Raymond Massey played the title rôle with such effect as to become permanently Lincoln to playgoers.

Act I. 1. ABE LINCOLN is 22 years old, living in the village of New Salem, Illinois, of which he is postmaster. As the first scene opens, he is studying with MENTOR GRAHAM, the village schoolmaster, who is trying to improve Abe's knowledge of English grammar. Abe mentions that the store he owns in partnership with a man named Berry is unprofitable because Berry drinks the whisky instead of selling it. The first scene establishes the unsettled, wandering, and rather unhappy life that Abe had known as a boy, and emphasizes his eagerness for learning. **2.** It is a few months later, and the store has failed. Abe has assumed responsibility for all of the partnership's debts, although he need not have done so. On this day, the Fourth of July, Abe enters the Rutledge Tavern just in time to prevent a most unequal fight between three of the town bullies and NINIAN EDWARDS, son of the Governor of Illinois and a man who is to prove most influential in Lincoln's political life. Edwards offers Abe a place on the Whig ticket as candidate for the state Assembly. Abe does not accept immediately, but after a conversation with ANN RUTLEDGE, the tavern-owner's daughter, he decides to run. During that conversation, he declares his love for Ann and she agrees to let him become her suitor. **3.** A year later, Abe has been elected to the Assembly and is visiting his old friends, Judge BOWLING GREEN and his wife NANCY. Abe has come down from Springfield because Ann is very ill. Bowling Green and Nancy are waiting for him, but when he arrives he announces that Ann died as he stood by her bedside.

Act II. 1. It is five years later, and Abe is now a lawyer in Springfield, Illinois. BILLY HERNDON, who later becomes Lincoln's law partner, is in the office when Abe returns from a trip around the circuit. Their conversation indicates Herndon's Abolitionist sympathy. Lincoln agrees but fears that the agitation of the Abolitionists may cause fighting and bloodshed, to which he is even more strongly opposed. As Abe and Herndon are talking, Abe's old friends Bowling Green and JOSHUA SPEED, of New Salem, enter, and a few minutes later Ninian Edwards enters. Edwards says that his wife's sister, MARY TODD of Kentucky, is visiting them and he would like Abe to meet her. He includes Bowling Green and Josh Speed in his invitation to his house, and Abe and Josh accept but Green cannot. **2.** Six months later, in the living room of the Edwards house, Elizabeth Todd Edwards is expressing to Ninian her violent disapproval of the idea that her sister Mary might marry Abe. As she and Ninian are talking, Mary enters and announces her intention to do just that —and that she plans to receive a proposal that very evening. Abe enters, and Ninian takes his wife from the room. Abe and Mary are left alone. **3.** It is New Year's Day, a few weeks later. Abe and Josh are sitting in Abe's office and Josh has just finished reading a letter Abe has written to Mary Todd, on their planned wedding day, asking her to release him from their engagement. Josh is unwilling to deliver the letter, as Abe wants him to do. He proposes that Abe tell his fiancée in person, rather than hide behind a written communication delivered by an impersonal go-between. While the two men argue (and Abe expresses his doubts as to his own sanity) Ninian Edwards appears and presents Abe with a cane as a wedding present. Edwards wonders why Abe is looking like a man who has been to a funeral—and learns that Abe has just returned from the funeral of Bowling Green. Herndon then enters, somewhat under the influence of alcohol and in time to hear Ninian attempt to cheer Abe by telling him that Mary Todd had always declared she would some day be married to the President of the United States. Ninian says she is an ambitious woman and warns Abe not to allow her to prod him too far. When Ninian leaves the office, Herndon says he doubts the possibility of cordial relations between himself and Mary Todd, but if she can stir up Abe and make him do something with himself, then Billy's blessing—and best wishes! —are hers. Billy then suggests toasts—and drinks them himself. His last toast is "To the President of the United States"—and Mrs. Lincoln. This causes Abe to tell Herndon that there will be no wedding, and Abe tries to give the letter to Herndon for delivery, but Josh throws it in the fire. Herndon accuses Abe of deserting not only his bride-to-be but all the people of the United States. Josh urges Abe to talk to Mary Todd as a man should. Lincoln at length agrees. **4.** The next scene takes place on the prairie, near New Salem, almost two years later. Beside a covered wagon SETH GALE, an old and dear friend of Abe's, is holding his feverish and very sick son, Jimmy. They are waiting for Abe to arrive with a doctor. Abe arrives soon, but the doctor is not with him. Abe tells the worried parents that he must go in another direction to notify the doctor, and bring him back. The Gales ask Abe if he will pray for their son, and although Abe admits that he is not much for praying, the sight of the child and the tone of Seth's voice seem to inspire him, and he utters a beautiful prayer. Something about this experience alters Lincoln's whole attitude, and he returns to beg Mary Todd to marry him. She consents willingly.

Act III. 1. It is the scene of one of the Lincoln-Douglas debates, in an Illinois town, 1858. The two men are running for United States Senator, and after Stephen A. Douglas has stated his belief that each state should be allowed to decide for itself whether to be slave or free, Lincoln makes the famous concluding speech in which he says, "'A house divided against itself cannot stand.' This government cannot endure permanently, half slave and half free!" **2.**

Young Abe Lincoln prays for the recovery of Jimmy Gale

Two years after this debate, the Lincoln family is sitting in the parlor of the Edwards house, where they now live, and Abe is telling his youngest son about the little son of Seth Gale, who is now a grown man with a son of his own. Josh Speed is present and reminds Abe that the men from the East should arrive at any moment. Mary is horrified that important Eastern politicians are coming to her house without her having been told of it. It seems that Abe forgot to mention it. He remarks that they are coming to look him over to see if he is worth being nominated for President of the United States. Mary scolds him, and continues her scolding because Abe's suit is not his best one and his shoes are not shined. After Abe goes out to shine the shoes, Mary hysterically complains of her husband's lack of ambition throughout the eighteen years of their marriage. She leaves to prepare refreshments for the visitors, who soon appear and start questioning Abe on his views. When Abe leaves to help Mary with the food, the men make it quite clear that they intend to nominate Lincoln on the Republican Party ticket. 3. It is the evening of Election Day, November 6, 1860. Lincoln, Mary, their son Robert, and several others are watching the results as they are posted on the bulletin board. The strain of the election, and her driving ambition, cause Mary to start berating her husband—accusing him of not caring whether he is elected or not, and generally abusing him. Lincoln becomes violently angry; he will not tolerate such treatment in public. He sends Mary home and remains to learn the election results. Soon it is announced to the crowd outside the campaign headquarters that Lincoln has won. He makes a short speech to the people, and says he must go home and tell Mary. 4. The play closes with the Lincoln family aboard the Presidential train, en route to Washington. All their friends are present to see them off, and a great crowd of townspeople and visitors. Lincoln speaks briefly from the platform of the train, and as it pulls away the crowd is heard singing—"... his soul goes marching on."

Abraham Lincoln

Play by John Drinkwater, 1882–1937. Produced in London, 1918. Published 1918 by Sedgwick and Jackson, Ltd., London.

THE FACT that one of the most famous plays about Abraham Lincoln was the work of an Englishman is a good indication of Lincoln's international fame. Drinkwater, noted as a poet, introduced each of his six scenes with rhymed prologues spoken by two "Chroniclers," who also delivered a brief epilogue after the last scene. Drinkwater's play covers Lincoln's Presidency only (see *Abe Lincoln in Illinois*, which was written to cover the earlier period of Lincoln's life). Only the Chroniclers' speeches are in poetry, the play itself being in regular dialogue.

1. The scene is ABRAHAM LINCOLN'S house in Springfield, Illinois, early in 1860. Mrs. Lincoln receives local political friends of her husband; they discuss John Brown and their opposition to slavery; the split among the Democrats, which seems to assure a Republican victory in the Presidential election; and Lincoln's carelessness about his personal appearance. Lincoln joins them. The guests leave and a delegation of Republicans—William Tucker, Henry Hind, Elias Price, James Macintosh—enter and ask if Lincoln will accept the Republican nomination. They discuss the fact that WILLIAM H. SEWARD and BURNETT HOOK may be more logical candidates and also difficult to handle as subordinates in the administration. Lincoln states his position: No force to be used against slavery, but no approval of it and no extension of it. The delegation renews its invitation and Lincoln accepts.

2. Seward, now Secretary of State in Lincoln's cabinet, meets with the Confederate commissioners, JOHNSON WHITE and CALEB JENNINGS. The commissioners want Union troops to withdraw from Fort Sumter and say slavery can be settled by negotiation but the South wants states' rights established. Lincoln enters and joins the conference. He makes it clear that slavery is the issue but he will not permit secession. The commissioners leave to communicate with their government. Lincoln and Seward have a brief conversation in which Lincoln wins Seward over to his point of view but also affirms his confidence in Seward. A messenger brings news of the imminent fall of Sumter. White and Jennings re-enter to say that there can be no compromise; they leave, and Lincoln and Seward face the prospect of war. Other cabinet members arrive and there is a meeting. The majority votes to withdraw from Sumter. Lincoln overrules them and invites resignations but there are none. He sends the messenger back to Sumter with a mesage that no men can be sent but that provisions will be sent; the import is that the fort will not be abandoned willingly.

3. It is nearly two years later. In the White House, the Lincolns have guests for tea. They are served by the same maid, Susan, that they had in Springfield. Their guests are Mrs. Goliath Blow, wife of a war profiteer, and Mrs. Otherly, who disapproves of war and whose son just been killed. Lincoln expresses his political philosophy but grieves with Mrs. Otherly even though they disagree on the war. When they leave, a freed slave, William Custis, comes in and discusses the problems of the present slaves; Custis favors vengeful action, Lincoln opposes it.

4. A cabinet meeting in the same year. The proposed Emancipation Proclamation is under discussion. Lincoln delays the business somewhat by reading a humorous article by Artemus Ward. But when the proclamation is discussed he is firm, though at the end Hook resigns and refuses to shake hands with Lincoln on leaving.

5. A farmhouse near Appomattox Courthouse, shortly before Lee's surrender. General Grant is told that Lincoln has arrived and ushers him in; Lincoln is attended by his secretary, JOHN HAY. Lincoln counsels mercy when the surrender comes. On leaving, Lincoln pardons a soldier found asleep at the post and sentenced to be shot. The next day Lincoln reads Grant's terms of surrender, finds them generous, and thanks Grant. After Lincoln leaves, the surrender of Lee is shown: Lee finds Grant's terms magnanimous. Grant refuses to accept Lee's sword.

6. Ford's Theatre in Washington on April 14, 1865. Lincoln, on entering, makes a short speech to the audience. The play itself is not shown; John Wilkes Booth enters the Lincolns' box from the rear and Lincoln is shot; Susan sobs and Secretary Edwin Stanton ends the play with the words "Now he belongs to the ages."

John Wilkes Booth enters the Lincolns' box at the Ford Theatre

Absalom, Absalom

Novel by William Faulkner, 1897-1961.
Published 1936. © 1936 by William
Faulkner. Published by Random
House, New York. (ML, 271)

EVEN FOR A Faulkner novel, *Absalom,
Absalom* is complex. It is set, like most
Faulkner novels, in the imaginary
town of Jefferson and county of Yoknapatawpha, Mississippi. The story
concerns a legendary figure in the
county's history and the tragic lives of
him and his offspring. All the story is
told through a young man, Quentin
Compson. Another Faulkner novel
(*The Sound and the Fury*, 1929) tells
us that Quentin later committed suicide. In *Absalom, Absalom*, the story
develops piecemeal and disjointedly
through reminiscences that Quentin
hears; perhaps for this reason, Faulkner appended a chronology and descriptive index of the principal characters. The outline that follows below is
preceded by a similar chronology. The
title of the book is from 2 Samuel
18:33 and alludes to a theme of the
novel, Thomas Sutpen's longing for a
son to extend his own participation in
life. Despite its complexity, *Absalom,
Absalom,* is a powerful novel, one of
the greatest works of a great artist and
by some critics considered his best.

Chronological outline. THOMAS SUT-
PEN, born 1807 in West Virginia mountains, of poor whites, at 14 runs away and
goes to Haiti, where in 1827 he marries
Eulalia Bon. Their son CHARLES BON is
born 1829. In 1831 Sutpen learns his wife
has Negro blood, repudiates marriage,
leaves her and child; in 1833 he reaches
Jefferson, buys "Sutpen's Hundred" (100
sq. mi.) from Indians, builds mansion. His
various illegitimate children by slave
women include Clytemnestra (CLYTIE),
born 1834. In 1838 Sutpen marries ELLEN
COLDFIELD, born in 1818 in Tennessee,
daughter of GOODHUE COLDFIELD, who
moved to Jefferson in 1828. Children of
Sutpen and Ellen: HENRY SUTPEN, born
1839; JUDITH, born 1841. ROSA COLD-
FIELD, Ellen's sister, born 1846—younger
than her nephew and niece. Henry Sutpen
goes to University of Mississippi in 1859,
meets Charles Bon, they become friends;
Charles has a son by a Negro (octoroon)
mistress in New Orleans, CHARLES
ETIENNE DE ST. VELERY BON, born that
year. Charles meets Judith, they become engaged in 1860; Sutpen forbids marriage
and sends Charles away. Henry sides with
Charles and leaves with him. All three go
to war in 1861; Sutpen becomes a colonel.
In 1862 Ellen dies, charging her sister Rosa

to care for Judith; in 1864 Rosa moves to
Sutpen's Hundred. In 1865 Henry and
Charles return to Sutpen's Hundred; when
Charles persists in plans to marry Judith,
Henry kills him and disappears. Sutpen returns in 1866 and he and Rosa become engaged but quarrel and she returns to Jefferson. Sutpen takes as mistress Milly Jones,
14-year-old granddaughter of Wash Jones,
a former squatter and now handy man on
Sutpen's Hundred. When a child is born
to Milly in 1869, Wash kills Sutpen, then
kills both Milly and child. Charles E. St. V.
Bon (aged about 11) comes to Sutpen's
Hundred in 1870; in 1879 he marries a
Negress, and in 1881 he brings her to Sutpen's hundred; their son JIM BOND is born
1882. In 1884 Judith Sutpen and Charles
E. St. V. Bon die of smallpox. In September
1910 Rosa Coldfield, accompanied by
QUENTIN COMPSON, goes to Sutpen's
Hundred and finds Henry Sutpen living
there, hidden in the house and cared for by
Clytie; Jim Bond also is there. In December Miss Rosa goes again, intending to take
Henry back with her; Clytie sets fire to the
house and she and Henry die. Jim Bond disappears.

1. Quentin Compson, 18 years old and
due to go to Harvard that same month of
September, 1909, is summoned by Miss
Rosa Coldfield to hear the story of Colonel
Sutpen ("a demon who came out of nowhere, built a plantation, married Miss
Rosa's sister Ellen and without gentleness
begot two children, who destroyed him or
whom he destroyed, and died without regret—save by her [Miss Rosa]"). Quentin
already knew much of the story, by local
tradition. —How did Sutpen marry Ellen?
He might have won her at cards from her
father. Why did Miss Rosa later want, and
become engaged to, Sutpen? She does not
know. Miss Rosa remembers from her early
childhood: Ellen alone with her two young
children; Sutpen engaged always at his wild
pleasures including violent fights between
his wild Negroes in the stable and often he
with them, while a crowd of men, white
and black, watched and bet; little Henry
watching them and even little Judith hiding to watch.

2. Quentin recalls the story of Thomas
Sutpen as Jefferson knows it: How Sutpen
came to Jefferson in 1833, a young man of
25 with a short reddish beard, powerfully
built but now gaunt from illness, to record
his purchase of 100 square miles from the
Chickasaws, paid for with Spanish gold
coins. He brought in a crew of strange, wild
Negro slaves and built a fine big mansion
and formal gardens, completing everything
that did not have to be bought with money.
GENERAL COMPSON, Quentin's grandfather, was the only man who knew Sutpen was wholly out of money; the General
lent Sutpen seed cotton and offered to lend
him money to finish the house, but Sutpen
refused this. For three years Sutpen lived
in the mansion without windows, hard-
ware, etc. He entertained men from Jeffer-

son for hunting, fishing, and to see his
wild Negroes fight; and the men slept on
the floors, rolled in blankets. Then (Quentin's father adds details): Sutpen left town
temporarily and returned with a tremendous load of windows, chandeliers, etc.,
which his slaves installed in the house. The
townspeople suspected him of having stolen
them and treated him as a public enemy;
he was even arrested but Goodhue Coldfield signed his bail. Two months later,
Sutpen married Ellen Coldfield. The townspeople threw mud at them as they left the
church.

3. Mr. Compson continues his reminiscence, but on later events: When Sutpen
returned from the war in 1866 he found
Miss Rosa living there. During the war
Goodhue Coldfield, refusing to fight, had
hidden in his house while Rosa secretly
fed him; he died in 1864. All her life Rosa
had looked upon Sutpen as an ogre; he
never would enter the Coldfield house after
the marriage and he never told but one
man (the General) what had been his true
hold on Coldfield. For years Rosa did not
see him; but she saw Ellen, who had
achieved a placid and sometimes gay existence as a mother, including the time in
the summer of 1860 when Ellen passed by
on the way to Memphis to buy Judith a
trousseau for her marriage to Charles Bon,
whom Henry had met at the University
and brought home with him. (But Rosa
never met Charles Bon, and she only heard
how, on Christmas Eve, Sutpen quarreled
with Charles, and Henry renounced his
father and rode away with Charles.) Then
came war and Sutpen rode off, second in
command of the regiment. During the war,
though food was so scarce, Rosa fed her
father till his death and deprived herself.

4. Quentin receives a letter from Miss
Rosa. Before he reads it, his father continues: Henry loved Charles Bon, yet killed
him to prevent his marrying Judith—
though Charles loved Judith and Judith
loved him. The courtship was strange:
Judith saw Charles only about twelve
times, an hour at a time, over a period of
1½ years, but waited four years for him.
Henry knew Charles had gone through a
marriage ceremony (legally meaningless)
with an octoroon woman in New Orleans
and a son was born to them; Henry considered the marriage binding. And Henry
knew of the blood relationship, though
Judith did not—and it would not have
stopped her anyway. So Henry shot and
killed Charles.

5. Miss Rosa tells Quentin how after the
shooting she went to the mansion; was
shocked when Clytie greeted her familiarly,
and so was insulting to Clytie; found Judith
completely self-controlled. Two years later
Rosa moved to the mansion, as had been
her dead sister Ellen's request. There Sutpen found and proposed to her, and she
accepted. But for months she scarcely saw
him. He had financial reverses and lost almost all his land. She returned to the Coldfield house in Jefferson, and, penniless, al-

most starved. . . . And she tells Quentin she is sure there is someone now, 43 years later, hidden and living in the mansion.

6. Quentin at college has told the whole story as he knows it to his roommate, Shrevlin McCannon. On Jan. 10, 1910, his father writes to him that Miss Rosa is dead. Quentin and Shreve discuss the case at length, Shreve often patronizing or sarcastic about Southern mores and customs. Quentin tells of how, after Rosa left, Sutpen seduced the 15-year-old granddaughter of Wash Jones, Sutpen's handy man and intimate, and how Jones killed Sutpen with a scythe. And Judith, now 30 but looking older, stayed on and she and Clytie did the plowing, Jones having died later in the same day he killed Sutpen. And how Charles Bon's son had come to Sutpen's Hundred and was welcomed by Judith. He and Judith died in 1884—he leaving a son.by a fullblooded Negress, a feeble-minded boy, Jim Bond, who lived in a slave cabin near the mansion for 26 years.

7. Quentin tells Shreve of things Sutpen had confided to General Compson: Sutpen's birth in the mountains of western Virginia, in a log cabin; how as a boy he was impressed by the rich whites and baffled by Negro attitudes, and acquired a desire for literacy; how he went to the West Indies. Also, how Sutpen persuaded Coldfield to enter with him into a shady transaction, which gave him his hold on Coldfield. And why Miss Rosa broke the engagement: Because Sutpen suggested that they try first, and if they had a boy they would be married. And more about Sutpen's death at the hands of Wash Jones; and how Jones actually killed his granddaughter and her baby by cutting their throats, then with the scythe attacked the sheriff, Major De Spain, who had come to arrest him, and was shot by De Spain.

8. Quentin and Shreve continue. Shreve analyzes the case: All Sutpen really wanted was a son, but he lost Henry and though he wanted to he could not bring himself to accept Charles, because of the Negro blood; Sutpen's first father-in-law had told him Charles's mother was a Spaniard, but she was not wholly so. And Henry's relationship with Charles Bon: Henry accepted him as an older brother but would not accept incest, Charles marrying Judith. And how Miss Rosa and Quentin went out to the mansion in 1910 and Miss Rosa found Henry, though she had to knock Clytie down to get upstairs.

9. Quentin tells more details of how he went with Miss Rosa to the mansion and they broke into the house with a hatchet, and first Miss Rosa and then Quentin saw Henry Sutpen, who had come four years before, to die at home. And then how Miss Rosa had gone back three months later with an ambulance, to bring Henry to her house, and Clytie set the house on fire. Jim Bond ran away. Miss Rosa had to be restrained from going into the burning house, and it was she who was taken back to town in the ambulance, to die. So the

Sutpens had killed themselves off—all but Jim Bond, the only one left. ——And tell me one thing, Shreve says finally, Why do you hate the South? And Quentin says quickly, *I don't. I don't! I don't hate it!*

Jones kills Sutpen with a scythe

Adam Bede

> *Novel by* George Eliot (Mary Ann Evans Cross, 1819–1880).
> Published 1859. (PB, PL507; RE, 32)
>
> BY MANY *Adam Bede* is considered George Eliot's best novel. Its characters, though humble people by the standards of those who read novels in 19th-century England, are real and familiar. The novel is an excellent picture of life in an English village at the end of the 18th century and contains many revealing sidelights on the prejudices and convictions of English country people of the time. The novel is quite short and partly for that reason has long been a school favorite.

Books 1–2. ADAM BEDE and his brother, SETH, work in the shop of JONATHAN BURGE, a carpenter. Jonathan would like Adam as a son-in-law, but Adam has eyes only for HETTY SORREL. Hetty, in her turn, has eyes only for Captain DONNITHORNE, heir to the estate of Squire Donnithorne. Seth believes himself to be in love with DINAH MORRIS, a young woman who is a

traveling Methodist preacher and a devoted follower of John Wesley. She has a certain magnetic charm and appeal that draw audiences in a section where the Church of England has great power.

Adam Bede is known about his neighborhood for his outstanding strength and physical power, and also for his skill as a woodworker. His superb physique attracts the attention of a man riding through the countryside—who says that this is the kind of man England could use as a soldier to fight the French.

Seth attends the open-air Methodist meeting conducted by Dinah Morris, and afterward walks with her back to the Poyser home, where she is visiting. He declares his love, but Dinah says her devotion to her religion and her duties are much more important than any personal life of her own, and she cannot think of marriage. Perhaps never, but at least not at the present.

When Seth arrives back at his own house, dejected and unhappy, he finds Adam busily at work making a coffin that his father is supposed to have made and delivered to a bereaved family. THIAS BEDE, father of Adam and Seth, is addicted to drink, and his wife, LISBETH, assumes that he is drunk somewhere away from home. Adam and Seth find him drowned in a nearby brook, however, and the death of her husband makes Lisbeth more than ever dependent upon Adam, who is the most important person in her life. She believes that no woman is quite good enough for him—and most certainly not Hetty Sorrel, whose infatuation for Captain Donnithorne is well known locally.

Books 3–5. Hetty leaves in search of Captain Donnithorne, only to learn that his regiment has been transferred. She soon bears his child, but leaves the baby' in the woods. Remorse for what she has done makes her return for the child, but it is dead. She is accused of murder and serves some time in prison, although she was innocent of that crime. After her release she leaves the country, and soon afterward she dies.

After Hetty's death, Adam devotes himself energetically to his work, putting aside all thoughts of marriage. In this his mother encourages him. She occupies most of his time and attention when he is not working.

Book 6. Eventually Dinah Morris makes Adam realize that he wants a wife and a home of his own. Even then Adam's life does not proceed smoothly and easily. Although Dinah is unquestionably fond of Adam, she still feels that continuing her work as a Methodist preacher is more important than getting married, and she leaves the village of Hayslope.

Adam remains with his mother, becoming more and more resigned to a life of bachelorhood. Finally his mother realizes his need for a wife, and she comments on the fine character and gentle ways of Dinah. Adam takes matters into his own hands and sets out to court Dinah—at long last settling upon a life of his own, with the woman he loves.

The Admirable Crichton

Play by James M. Barrie, 1860–1937.
Produced in London 1902, in New York
1903. Published by Charles Scribner's
Sons, New York.

CRICHTON is a delightful satire on the
social and class distinctions of England
in the early part of the 20th century.

Though the butler, Crichton, is a man
of parts and his master, the Earl of
Loam, is pointedly depicted as pompous, inept, and more than slightly
stupid, neither questions the traditional master-and-servant relationship.
But then on a desert island . . . The
movie of it was called *Male and Female.*

Act I. The play opens in the Mayfair
(London) town house of the Earl of LOAM.
It is the day of his monthly tea party, at
which family and servants sit down together
as equals. CRICHTON, the butler, has just
arranged the tea things when ERNEST
WOOLLEY, Lord Loam's nephew, enters the
main hall of the house. Ernest and Crichton
discuss briefly Lord Loam's eccentricity, but
Crichton refuses to be maneuvered into expressing any criticism of the earl's "radical"
ways. It is not his place to criticise or disapprove. Ernest starts rehearsing a speech
he has prepared—"in case I should be asked
to say a few words to the servants"—and
Crichton leaves the room. Almost immediately two of Lord Loam's daughters, CATH-
ERINE and AGATHA, come in, followed soon
by his third daughter, Lady MARY. The
entire group is clearly bored with the function. They mention that the servants also
hate it. Another guest arrives—a young
clergyman named TREHERNE, whose hope
of advancing in the Church seems based on
his ability to play a good game of cricket.
Lady Mary expresses weariness from trying
on engagement rings; she is wearing one.
Her fiancé, Lord Brocklehurst, enters with
Lord Loam, and it is time for the party to
begin. Crichton announces each of the servants, and each grimly greets the master of
the house and his family, obviously miserable and uncomfortable. The family is stiff
and unnatural also, with the single exception of Lord Loam. Throughout the stiff
conversation that follows, it is made quite
clear that the servants do not consider themselves equal among themselves. One of the
ladies' maids is indignant because a kitchen
maid was offered a second cup of tea before
she was given hers.

The discussion of a yachting trip, planned
to start in two days, brings up considerable
dissension. Lord Loam has decided that one
servant must serve all three of his daughters,
but none of the maids is willing to do the
work of three and they resign in anger, one
by one. The next problem is that of Lord
Loam's valet, ROLLESTON. It is beneath
Rolleston's dignity to undertake a cruise
without the proper number of servants present, and he resigns. The problem of a ladies'
maid is temporarily solved by Crichton, who
offers TWEENY, the kitchen maid. She is
willing until she learns that Crichton is not
going, then she firmly rejects the offer, even
though the elevation in her servant's social
standing would have made it far more likely

that she might one day marry Crichton.
Eventually Lady Mary persuades Crichton
to go along as Lord Loam's valet, pointing
out that he could scarcely dare let his master
out of his sight for the period of the cruise,
in view of His Lordship's dangerously radical ideas about equality.

Act II. The family has been shipwrecked
on a desert island. Lord Loam is not
with them. He tried madly to be the first
in the lifeboat, and as a result was swept
overboard and presumably lost. On the
island are Crichton, Ernest, Treherne,
Tweeny, and the three young ladies, Mary,
Agatha, and Catherine. Ernest writes a
vague and somewhat inaccurate description
of their shipwreck, in case he ever has an
opportunity to present it to the British press
for publication.

Crichton is busy cutting down trees for
a shelter. He seems to be the only one of the
group who knows anything about getting
along in these primitive surroundings. He
explains to Mary—who does not really understand what he means—that equality is
impossible anywhere in a group of people,
because it is "against nature." In England
it was against nature for him to be the equal
of Lord Loam, and here on the island it is
against nature for Ernest to be his equal. To
Mary's comment—and question—about
Ernest's utter loathing of work, Crichton
replies that Ernest will work if it is a case
of no work, no food. Crichton becomes
the natural leader and chief of the island
group, and when Lord Loam appears, after

being washed ashore on some wreckage,
Crichton remains in charge. Lord Loam is
wholly unable to understand immediately
that his position and Crichton's are reversed.
In fact, when Crichton ventures to express
his regret that His Lordship has discarded
a single hairpin which might have been
made into a needle for sewing necessary
garments, Lord Loam discharges Crichton—
quite forgetting that they are marooned on
an island. When this is pointed out, he
haughtily declares that there is another part
of the island, and the family will occupy a
different section. The matter of food, and
the aroma of the cooking pot which Crichton has placed over a fire of twigs, brings
the family trickling back, and eventually
Crichton is conceded to be the chief.

Act III. Two years later, there is a substantial house, and Crichton's ingenuity has
even put a flowing stream to work for the
production of electricity. Crichton is now
called "The Gov" and Lord Loam has become merely "Daddy." Ernest works—and
when he makes a poor joke that bores Crichton (and bored him in England, although
he never allowed it to show) Crichton ducks
Ernest's head in a bucket of water.

Lady Mary is now called Polly. Tweeny
issues orders to Catherine—now called
Kitty—and Agatha has become Aggie.
Crichton has allowed himself to become romantically attracted to Lady Mary, and she
to him. He asks her to become his wife, and
she humbly and adoringly consents. After
the entire group has been informed—and
Tweeny is made utterly miserable by the
news—as rescue becomes certain, Crichton
detaches himself from what would have been
a romantic scene with Mary.

"My Lady," he says; it is the speech of his
life.

Act IV. Back in England, a fantastic story
of Ernest's prowess and heroism on the island has appeared in the papers. Crichton

Crichton addresses the shipwrecked party

is unmentioned. Lady Mary—no longer Polly—renews her engagement to the dull and uninteresting Lord Brocklehurst, in spite of his mother's suspicion that a girl who has been shipwrecked on an island for so long can scarcely be a suitable wife for her son. Mary attempts to wring from Crichton an admission that there is something wrong with the system that makes him a servant and her a superior being, but Crichton says only that this is the English way. At Mary's vehement declaration that then there must be something wrong with England, Crichton declares that even from her he cannot listen to any comment or remark against England—and the play closes.

Adventures

There are many books whose titles begin with the words "Adventures of." In many cases this part of the title has become unfamiliar to most readers and has even been dropped by the publishers of the books. Examples are *The Adventures of Tom Sawyer, The Adventures of Huckleberry Finn, The Adventures of Sherlock Holmes.* In this work all such books will be treated in the alphabetical order of the names in their titles, for example "Tom Sawyer," "Huckleberry Finn," "Sherlock Holmes," etc.

The Aeneid

Poem by Virgil (Publius Vergilius Maro, 70–19 B.C.)
Published 29 to 19 B.C. Many translations. (ML, 75; ML, T39)

VIRGIL has by many scholars been considered the greatest of all poets and the *Aeneid* was his greatest work. It is the story of Aeneas, a prince of Troy, who appears also in Homer's Iliad and in various myths and legends, both Greek and Roman. Aeneas was the son of Anchises, a Trojan prince, and Venus (or Aphrodite), the goddess of love; he was hated by Juno, the queen of heaven. He fought for Troy, and after the Trojan Wars ended in Greek victory he escaped and eventually became king of Latium in Italy and founder of what became the Roman Empire. ❡ Virgil wrote in the classical Latin of the Golden Age. The *Aeneid* is very long, consisting of twelve books of about one thousand lines each. The meter is dactyllic hexameter, exemplified by the famous first line of the poem: *Arma virumque cano, Troiae qui primus ab urbis* . . . ("Arms and the man I sing who first from the walls of Troy . . .").

The Trojans drag the wooden horse of the Greeks into the city

Book 1. AENEAS leaves Troy, fleeing from Fate, to go to Italy; but cruel Juno causes Aeolus, god of the winds, to create a great storm at sea. Aeneas loses one ship and fears all is lost, but Neptune, god of the sea, befriends him and stills the storm. Aeneas lands on the coast of Africa near Carthage, and aided by ACHATES, his lieutenant and faithful friend, he rallies his men but mourns his comrades lost at sea. Meanwhile Venus, grieving for her son, appeals to Jupiter, the lord of heaven. Jupiter promises that Aeneas will found a Trojan dynasty in Italy; that a member of this dynasty, Romulus, will found Rome; and that Rome will become very great; and Jupiter sends Mercury, messenger of the gods, to cause DIDO, queen of Africa, to befriend Aeneas. Venus then appears in disguise (as a nymph) to Aeneas and Achates and reassures them; at the end she momentarily assumes her true form and vanishes. Aeneas and Achates approach Carthage, which is being built as a great city. On the walls of the temple they see scenes from the Trojan Wars: Priam, the king of Troy; Achilles, the Greek hero, and Hector dead after Achilles killed him. Then Dido enters, and they see ILEONEUS and others of their Trojan party, whom they had thought lost at sea, appearing before the queen. They had thought Aeneas and his group dead, but Aeneas appears and is welcomed by the queen. He sends for his son ASCANIUS, but instead Venus has her son Cupid impersonate Ascanius so that he can cause Dido to fall in love with Aeneas. Dido gives a great feast for the Trojans. Already in love with Aeneas, she asks him to tell her of his seven years of wanderings since Troy fell.

Book 2. Aeneas tells his story. The Danaans (Greeks), unsuccessful in the war, build a huge wooden horse and a group of their best warriors hide in it. The Greeks pretend to sail home but actually stop at the nearby island of Tenedos. Most of the Trojans want to take the horse into their temple and worship it, but some, led by the priest

LAOCOÖN, warn against it, and Laocoön utters the famous line *Timeo Danaos et. dona ferentes,* "I fear the Greeks even when bearing gifts." A Greek named Sinon pretends to allow himself to be captured as a fugitive from the Greeks and persuades the king, Priam, that the horse should be taken into the city and if it is not the gods will not favor Troy. Laocoön still opposes it, but while he is sacrificing a bull two great serpents come out of the sea and kill Laocoön and his two young sons. This seems to be an omen that Laocoön was wrong and the Trojans drag the horse into the city; Cassandra, Trojan princess and prophetess, warns against it but is not believed. That night the Greek ships sail back. Sinon opens the horse and lets out the Greek warriors. The ghost of Hector appears to Aeneas and tells him to flee, but already the Greeks are sacking and burning the city. Aeneas and others disguise themselves in the armor of dead Greeks and fight, but vainly. The Greek leader PYRRHUS, son of Achilles, kills Priam, stabbing him at an altar. Aeneas sees HELEN, cause of the war, and is about to kill her when Venus appears to him and sends him instead to his father ANCHISES. He prepares to flee with his wife Creusa, son Ascanius, and father; but Anchises prefers to stay and die in the city. But a flame appears on Ascanius's head and Anchises, accepting it as a sign, agrees to go. Aeneas puts a lion skin over his shoulders and carries Anchises. They become separated from Creusa and Aeneas looks for her, but she is already dead and her ghost appears to tell him so. Then Aeneas leads the survivors to refuge in the mountains.

Book 3. Aeneas continues his story. The Trojan refugees build a fleet and sail to Thrace; but the ghost of Polydorus, Priam's youngest son, appears to Aeneas and says he was betrayed and murdered by the king of Thrace, to whom he had been sent for aid. They sail again, to Anius, the city of Apollo, where Apollo tells Aeneas the Trojans must return to the land from which their ancestors came originally. They believe

6

The ship bearing Aeneas sails from Carthage, leaving Dido behind

this to be Crete and go there, but cannot remain because of a blight and plague. They land briefly at the Strophades islands but are attacked by Harpies led by their queen, CELAENO, who prophesies many dire events for the Trojans. Next they reach Actium on the Greek mainland, where they hold the traditional athletic games of the Trojans. Next they go to Buthrotum, in Épirus, and to their amazement find it ruled by HELENUS (brother of Hector), who is married to ANDROMACHE, Hector's widow. She had been taken as a slave by Pyrrhus and had borne him a child. When Pyrrhus was killed, Helenus inherited part of the kingdom and Andromache married him. Aeneas and his party sail on, sight Italy, land on Sicily, and make burnt offerings to Juno. They meet Achemenides, a Greek living there in fear of Polyphemus, a Cyclops, who has been blinded by Ulysses. They take Achemenides with them, and at Drepanum, another point on Sicily that they touch in their wandering, Anchises dies. Then, when next they sailed, came the storm that had driven them to Africa.

Book 4. Dido tells her sister Anna that she loves Aeneas but after the murder of her first husband, Sychaeus, she resolved never to remarry. Anna urges her to marry Aeneas and together the sisters sacrifice to the gods, especially Juno, who rules over marriage. Juno now speaks to Venus, proposing that Aeneas marry Dido and that she (Juno) and Venus share control of Carthage. Venus recognizes this as Juno's plot to become supreme in Italy, but pretends to agree if Juno can get Jupiter's consent. But Fame spreads the story throughout African cities, causing Iarbas, son of Jupiter, who himself wants to marry Dido, to intercede with his father. Jupiter sends Mercury to remind Aeneas that Italy is his destiny. Aeneas is afraid to disappoint Dido but even more afraid to defy the gods and prepares to sail away stealthily, but Dido catches him. She makes an impassioned speech to him, a mixture of pleas and threats, and also sends her sister to plead, but Aeneas sails. When Dido learns that he has gone, she kills herself with a sword.

Book 5. Aeneas, sailing from Carthage, sees Dido's great funeral pyre but does not know what it is. A threatening storm persuades the pilot, PALINURUS, not to try to reach Italy and they stop at Sicily, in the domain of ACESTES. Aeneas decrees games to mark the anniversary of Anchises' death. There is a boat race, won by Cloanthus; a foot race, won by EURYALUS; and wrestling, won by Entellus. The archery contest is won by Acestes when his arrow disappears, blazing, which is taken as an omen of the gods' wishes. Finally there is an exhibition of horsemanship led by Ascanius, which Romans still (40 B.C.) call the Trojan Ride. But Juno, still strongly against Aeneas, agitates among the Trojan women, who were not permitted to go to the games, and they set fire to the Trojan ships. Aeneas prays to Jupiter, who sends a heavy rain and saves all but four ships. Aeneas fears to remain in Sicily. Nautes, an aged and wise member of his people, advises leaving behind the infirm members, and Aeneas leaves them to be ruled by Acestes and to build their own city, to be named Acesta. Venus appeals to Neptune to spare the Trojans as they sail to Italy, and Neptune agrees that they will lose only one man, who proves to be Palinurus. Aeneas himself then steers safely to Italy.

Book 6. Aeneas lands his fleet at Cumae. He visits the famous Sibyl in her cave and she prophesies many more trials for him but ultimate success if he does not yield. Aeneas prays to her to let him visit his father Anchises in the Underworld, which is entered through her cave. She agrees but warns him that to come back he must pluck a golden spray from the tree given to the Underworld by Pluto's wife (Proserpine) and must give burial to a dead comrade there. Accompanied by Achates, Aeneas finds the friend (Misenus) and makes a funeral pile for him, then plucks the golden bough. They proceed, led by the Sibyl; meet unburied dead who must wander for one hundred years without a home; and cross the river on Charon's ferry. They meet Palinurus, who begs for burial, and Dido, of whom Aeneas asks forgiveness but who will not speak to him. They go to Elysium, where Aeneas finds Anchises. Anchises explains that the waiting souls seen by Aeneas drink

the waters of Lethe, to find oblivion, and wait until other bodies are available for them. Anchises also delivers a long prophecy on the future history of Rome. Then he sends Aeneas and the Sibyl through the gates of Sleep back into the world.

Book 7. Aeneas sails up the coast of Italy, then up the Tiber into Latium. LATINUS, king of Latium, has no son but has one daughter, LAVINIA, whose hand is sought by many princes, among them TURNUS, king of the Rutuli, to whom Lavinia has been promised. But an oracle tells Latinus that his daughter must marry a foreign prince and is destined to found an imperial dynasty. The Trojans, having landed, fulfill a prophecy by "eating their tables"—bread baked in the form of plates. Ileoneus leads an embassy of Trojans to Latinus, who recognizes Aeneas as the prophesied foreign prince and proposes marriage between Lavinia and Aeneas. Juno is chagrined that Aeneas seems likely to defeat her despite all her efforts. She enlists the aid of Alecto, one of the Furies. First Alecto goes to AMATA, wife of Latinus and kinswoman of Turnus; then she goes to Ardea, the city of Turnus; and she incites both to oppose the Trojans. Turnus leads his Rutuli against the Trojans and there is a battle. The nations of Latium are now aroused and assemble to go to war against the Trojans.

Book 8. Turnus organizes the warriors of Latium to fight Aeneas. The spirit of the Tiber appears to Aeneas, prophesies that he will find success on her banks and that his son Ascanius will found Alba Longa, and tells him to win over EVANDER, king of Pallanteum, the city on whose site Rome will rise. Aeneas goes to Evander and is well received; they feast together, and Aeneas hears the story of Cacus, a giant, son of Vulcan; Cacus was killed by Hercules. Venus goes to her husband, Vulcan, god of fire, and uses her physical charms to arouse passion in him and win his aid for Aeneas. Vulcan has his servants make divine armor for Aeneas. The next morning Evander promises aid to Aeneas, designating his son PALLAS to lead his forces, and forecasts aid from TARCHON, leader of the Tuscans. Omens—lightning and thunder—confirm the decision. Venus brings Aeneas the armor from Vulcan. On the shield Aeneas sees a pictorial record of Rome's growth and triumphs, up to the time of Augustus Caesar.

Book 9. Juno sends word to Turnus that Aeneas is not in the Trojan camp and that he should attack. Turnus attacks; the Trojans will not come out and fight and he besieges them. He seeks to burn their fleet but the Berecynthian goddess (Cybele) has promised them protection and despite opposition by her son he turns the ships into sea-nymphs, which swim away safely. Nisus proposes to seek Aeneas and persuades Euryalus to undertake the mission with him. They attack the enemy but are killed; their heads are shown on the points of spears to the Trojan camp, and the mother of Euryalus delivers a mother's lament. The Volsci, one of the nations of Latium, attack the Trojans. They succeed in burning a tower. Ascanius fights, urged on by Apollo. Two brothers, Pandarus and Bitias, open the gates of their fort so that the enemy can enter and be killed; Turnus enters and is shut in by Pandarus. He kills Pandarus but receives a message from Jupiter that he must flee, so he jumps into the Tiber and swims back to his own camp.

Book 10. Jupiter summons the gods to a meeting on the Italian conflict. Venus supports the Trojans, Juno the Latins. Jupiter rules that the war must continue until Fate decides the winner. Turnus's forces continue to besiege the Trojan camp. Aeneas leaves Evander, calls on Tarchon and wins the support of the Tuscans, and sails down the Tiber with various allies. He lands near the Trojan camp and there is a battle led by Pallas for the Trojan side and Lausus, son of Mezentius, for the Latins. Turnus takes Lausus's place, challenges Pallas to single combat, and kills him. Aeneas then pursues Turnus. Jupiter foresees death for Turnus unless he withdraws, so Juno assumes the form of Aeneas and lures Turnus into a ship that carries him to safety. Mezentius replaces Turnus and fights bravely but is wounded by Aeneas and withdraws; Lausus, assisting him, is killed by Aeneas. Mezentius returns to avenge his son but is killed by Aeneas.

Book 11. Aeneas, triumphantly but also as a gesture of respect, makes a display of Mezentius's armor. He grieves over Palias, whose body he sends back to Evander. Latin emissaries ask for a truce while the dead are buried. Aeneas agrees but reproaches the Latins for warring against him, when he came peacefully. Drances, a Latin warrior who does not like Turnus, speaks favorably of Aeneas's cause. He suggests settlement by single combat between Aeneas and Turnus. Latinus now realizes that Aeneas has been chosen by the gods, and also he is advised by the neighboring king Diomedes to end the war. Latinus advises letting the Trojans remain in peace, and Drances speaks in support of Latinus, but Turnus insists on continuing the fight and offers to meet Aeneas in single combat. CAMILLA, a warlike woman allied with Turnus, assists him. She is a follower of the goddess Diana, and Diana sends a nymph, Opis, to protect Camilla or avenge her if she falls. There is a battle at the city of Latinus. Camilla is killed by Aruns, who in turn is killed by Opis. The Trojans put the Latins to rout. When the news is brought to Turnus he sets forth to meet Aeneas, who is seeking him.

Book 12. Turnus announces his intention to fight Aeneas, both for honor and for the hand of Lavinia. Juno sends the nymph JUTURNA to spoil the plans and Juturna inspires a Latin to attack and kill a Trojan. Aeneas tries but fails to prevent a general fight. He is wounded and the fight continues. Venus heals the wound. Aeneas seeks Turnus but he is hidden by Juturna.

Now Venus tells Aeneas to attack the city and he does so. Amata, seeing the Latin forces return without Turnus, thinks him dead and hangs herself. Turnus returns and

The armor of Mezentius

engages Aeneas in single combat. His sword breaks and he flees, but Juturna gives him another sword and they face each other to renew the fight. At this time Jupiter tells Juno that Turnus will be killed, Aeneas will marry Lavinia and merge his Trojans and the Latins into a new kingdom of Latium. Juno is satisfied. Jupiter recalls Juturna. Aeneas vanquishes Turnus and would spare his life except he remembers that Turnus killed Pallas; so Aeneas kills him.

Aesop's Fables

FOR SO MANY YEARS all fables were called "Aesop's Fables" that none can be definitely attributed to Aesop himself, who lived early in the 6th century B.C. For literary purposes *Aesopian* is a better word than *Aesop's* and two criteria should be applied to the fables: Each must have sentient animals as characters and must lead to a "moral" as a conclusion; and each must have been included in the collection made by Phaedrus, first-century Latin poet. This is not to say that all or even any of the fables in Phaedrus's collection were necessarily written by Aesop.

THE DOG AND HIS REFLECTION

A dog carrying a piece of meat in his mouth walked across a bridge over a stream. He saw his reflection in the water and thought there was another dog with another piece of meat. The dog was greedy, and snapped his jaws to seize the meat in the water, so his own meat fell into the stream and was lost.

MORAL: *Don't lose the good things at hand in greed for something more.*

THE CITY MOUSE AND THE COUNTRY MOUSE

A city mouse visited his cousin in the country. The country mouse gave him a piece of cheese, fresh country bread, and bacon. The city mouse was very scornful of such plain, simple things. "You must come to visit me in the city," he said, "and I will give you some real dainties." The country mouse accepted the invitation. In the house where the city mouse lived, there was a big table with the remains of a fine feast upon it. The two mice were enjoying themselves thoroughly when suddenly they heard dogs snarling. Both mice lost no time diving into a convenient mouse hole. They just barely got out of the dog's way in time.

"I don't like it here!" exclaimed the country mouse. "I'm going home, where there are no horrible dogs that try to kill me while I'm enjoying my food!"

MORAL: *Better to have simple foods in peace than the most costly delicacies in fear and hunger.*

THE LION AND THE MOUSE

A little mouse came upon a sleeping lion and boldly ran up and down its back. Suddenly the lion awoke and placed a huge paw on the mouse.

"Oh, please don't kill me!" the mouse begged. "Let me go, and some day perhaps I can do something to help you."

The lion was amused—what could a tiny little mouse ever do to help him?—but he released the mouse. Some time later the lion was caught in a trap, tied with heavy cord. The little mouse came by and chewed through the ropes, setting the lion free.

MORAL: *Help in time of need can come from any source.*

ANDROCLES AND THE LION

Androcles was an escaped slave. Hiding in the woods, he came upon a lion that was whining and licking its paw. Androcles found that a large thorn was stuck in the lion's paw, and Androcles removed it. Some time later both Androcles and the lion were captured. The slave was sentenced to be thrown to the lion. But when Androcles was thrown to the lion, instead of devouring the slave the lion licked his hand. The king gave Androcles his freedom, and set the lion free.

MORAL: *Gratitude is a sign of greatness.*

THE LIONESS

There was a great stir made among all the Beasts, which could boast of the largest family. So they came to the Lioness. "And how many," said they, "do you have at a birth?" "One," said she, grimly, "but that one is a Lion."

MORAL: Quality comes before quantity.

THE FOX AND THE CROW

A fox saw a crow sitting on a branch with a large piece of cheese in her mouth. The fox wanted the cheese.

"If your voice is as beautiful as your plumage, you must be the finest singer in the forest," he said. "Won't you sing for me?"

The crow opened its mouth to caw, and the cheese fell to the ground, where the fox snapped it up.

MORAL: The words of a flatterer are uttered only to benefit himself.

THE GOOSE WITH THE GOLDEN EGGS

A certain man had the good fortune to possess a Goose that laid him a Golden Egg every day. But dissatisfied with so slow an income, and thinking to seize the whole treasure at once, he killed the Goose; and cutting her open, found her—just what any other goose would be!

MORAL: Much wants more and loses all.

THE BOY WHO CRIED "WOLF"

Once there was a shepherd boy who watched over a flock of sheep near a forest. Because he grew lonely, he sometimes shouted "Wolf! Wolf!" because he knew it brought other people running to help him.

One day a real wolf appeared, but when the boy shouted no one paid any attention, supposing that it was merely another trick. The wolf ate several sheep (and in some versions of the story, killed the boy).

MORAL: When a man is known to have been a liar, no one believes him when he tells the truth.

THE LION AND THE FOUR OXEN

Once there were four oxen in a field. A lion passed that way frequently and wanted very much to eat one of the oxen, but they stood together, tail to tail, so that from whichever side the lion approached he was barred by a pair of horns. One day the oxen quarreled among themselves, and each went to a different part of the field. When the lion approached, it was easy for him to kill them, one at a time.

MORAL: In unity there is strength.

THE ANT AND THE GRASSHOPPER

On a cold frosty day an Ant was dragging out some of the corn which he had laid up in summer time, to dry it. A Grasshopper, half-perished with hunger, besought the Ant to give him a morsel of it to preserve his life. "What were you doing," said the Ant, "this last summer?" "Oh," said the Grasshopper, "I was not

The lion and the four oxen

idle. I kept singing all summer long." Said the Ant, laughing and shutting up his granary, "Since you could sing all summer, you may dance all winter."

MORAL: Winter finds out what Summer lays by.

SOUR GRAPES

A hungry fox stole one day into a vineyard where many bunches of grapes hung ripe and ready for eating. But as luck would have it, they were fastened upon a tall trellis, just too high for Reynard to reach. He jumped, and paused, and jumped again, in the attempt to get at them. But it was all in vain. At last he was fairly tired out, and thereupon, "Take them who will," he cried, *"the grapes are sour!"*

The Age of Innocence

Novel by Edith Wharton, 1862–1937. Published 1920 by Appleton-Century-Crofts, New York. © 1920, 1947 by Frederic King. (ML, 229)

EDITH WHARTON wrote of life as she herself knew it personally—the life of rich and socially prominent families in New York City at the turn of the 20th century. Her depiction of the manners and mores of the times is accurate, revealing, and often exasperating to those whose lives began later than the lives of the characters in her books. Standardization of living and aims in living characterized the people of the class described in *The Age of Innocence*. Edith Wharton has contrived to render both actions and characters thoroughly believable, and the course of events inexorable and inevitable. It is not a light novel and demands a modicum of understanding and sympathy from the reader—but it is an excellent portrait of life and persons in its time.

Chaps. 1–5. MAY WELLAND is the beautiful daughter of a wealthy and rigidly conventional New York family in the late 1800s. Her parents and most of her relatives live by inflexible social standards and have equally set ideas and convictions as to what is "suitable" and what is not "suitable" for persons of their particular social position.

May's cool beauty—and her family's impeccable social position—completely charm the eligible young bachelor and attorney, NEWLAND ARCHER, and at length May permits him to know that she "cares," as a properly reared young lady of the day states such matters.

Archer is a bit taken aback to learn that their engagement is to be announced at a party in honor of May's cousin the Countess ELLEN OLENSKA. This is not entirely consistent with the conventionality of the Wellands and their set, inasmuch as Ellen is a problem and a trial to the family. She has been foolish enough to marry a ne'er-do-well Polish count, and her marriage has failed. Worse, she does not behave as the Wellands' tenets set forth for a women whose marriage is a failure. She even contemplates obtaining a divorce, which is almost too much for her relatives to bear. This is one of the many things that are just "not done."

At the party, however, the engagement of May Welland and Newland Archer is duly announced, and Archer finds himself strongly attracted to Ellen. He is not the only man to feel her personal magnetism and charm. Among her other admirers is JULIUS BEAUFORT, a relative of the Wellands by marriage, tacitly recognized by all who know him as a man of few scruples. His wife is among those who have no illusions about his self-indulgences outside his home.

Chaps. 6–18. Newland Archer begins to call on Ellen and take her flowers, on the pretext of making her feel at home in New York. The very unconventionality that is such a trial to the Wellands lends her charm in Newland's eyes, and often he finds himself defending her.

Chaps. 19–24. May and Newland are married and settle down into a fixed and stiff pattern of living. Newland is discontented with it but drifts along because there does not seem much else to do—and perhaps because he lacks courage. At one time, in a period of sharp disgust at himself for submitting to the deadly conventionality of his existence, he asks Ellen to go away with him—but she has the maturity and wisdom to convince him that this would be a most unsatisfactory solution, and their friendship continues without increase in their intimacy.

Chaps. 25–29. Circumstances beyond Archer's control throw him and Ellen together some years later, when Julius Beaufort—whose speculations have often been less than ethical—finds himself ruined financially with the collapse of a business built upon false claims. Many innocent investors suffer with him, and the scandal causes Mrs. MINGOTT, matriarch of the Welland family, to have a stroke. She sends for Ellen to return and live with her.

Chaps. 30–34. Archer again sees a great deal of Ellen, and certain signs tell him that both his wife and their circle of friends and relatives are aware of their friendship. When Ellen learns that May is going to have a child, she leaves New York and moves to Paris, thus effectively putting an end to the source of gossip.

Life continues in the same even tenor for Archer and his family, which eventually consists of a son, Dallas, and a daughter, Mary.

May dies when Archer is in his fifties, and eventually Dallas is about to be married. He suggests that he and his father take a trip to Europe as their last outing together before the wedding, and Archer agrees. He agrees also to Dallas's suggestion that they call on his mother's cousin, Ellen, who is living in Paris—but when they reach the building in which Ellen lives, Archer sends Dallas ahead and tells him to make some excuse for the fact that Newland will be a bit late. Laughingly, Dallas says that he will tell Ellen his father prefers to climb the five flights of stairs, rather than ride in the lift, and that this naturally takes more time.

Newland seats himself on a bench across the street, and sees the light in Ellen's apartment windows. He remains seated until a servant comes to draw the blinds, and then Newland Archer arises from the bench and walks slowly home to his own hotel room. Newland is cut off from the past.

Age of Reason

Monograph by Thomas Paine, 1737–1809.
Published 1795.

THOMAS PAINE wrote Age of Reason in 1793 and 1794, when he was in France participating in the French Revolution (and considered himself a citizen of France). The book is of historical importance because it created such a furor, especially in the United States, where it was published. Even today there will be those who disapprove its being summarized here. At the time, Age of Reason was called "atheistic"; but this was a misuse of the word, because in the book Paine affirms belief in one God and in human immortality. Rather than being an attack on religion, the book is an attack on literal interpretation of the Bible, specifically the Authorized ("King James") version.

Part 1. France having abolished the priesthood and compulsory religion, I set down my ideas on religion lest we lose sight of humanity, morality, and the theology that is true.

I believe in one God, and I hope for a life hereafter, but I do not believe in the Jewish, Christian or Turkish [Mohammedan] religions. Each of these churches is based on revelation, but revelation is the direct word of God to a man, and when that man tells another it becomes hearsay, which one is not obliged to believe. The Christian Church derived from mythology, from fables more ancient than the Jewish traditions. The early prophets were merely magicians and poets. The New Testament was all written after Christ's death. Furthermore, without a universal language there can be no written word of God, for translations are inaccurate. The only true revelation of God is the creation [universe and all natural things] we behold. It shows God's power, wisdom, mercy, etc. The Christian Church has always opposed science, as though dreading the result. The three principal means used by religions in all ages to impose upon mankind are Mystery, Miracle, and Prophecy. To summarize: 1, There can be no written word of God. 2, The Creation proclaims God's power, wisdom, goodness. 3, The moral duty of man is to imitate God's moral goodness. The Power that gave me existence is capable of continuing it, and I think it likely that I shall exist hereafter. Every man has a right to follow his own religion.

Part 2. When [one year before] I wrote Part 1, I had no Bible. Now I have, and on reading it I have found it to be a much worse book than I thought before. It is said that anything may be proved from the Bible; but not unless one accepts the Bible as true. In the Bible much is done by express command of God that is so shocking to humanity that to believe them we must unbelieve the goodness of God. The books of the Bible are testimony of men and we cannot believe them unless we believe these men and believe that they wrote the books. But Moses, Joshua, Samuel, etc. (and all others whose names are given to books of the Old Testament) did not write them personally. There are many errors and inconsistencies in the Bible. Isaiah's prophecy of the virgin birth was to be fulfilled in the same period and not seven hundred years after. I see no reason not to believe in the existence of Mary, Joseph, and Jesus, but the Gospels are inconsistent collections of anecdotes written long afterward. If the Bible is someday rejected, I will not have been responsible; each reader may judge for himself as I have done. In conclusion: Christianity has been spread by the sword. There is no need for it. Deism is the only natural religion. All invented religions have actually blasphemed God. The Creation is God.

Agnes Grey

Novel by Anne Brontë, 1820–1849.
Published 1847.

ANNE was the least-read and -admired of the remarkable Brontë sisters, but the fact remains that she was one of the remarkable Brontë sisters and her novels are brilliant in spots, competent elsewhere. Agnes Grey was published in 1847 as part of a three-volume set, the first two volumes being sister Emily's Wuthering Heights. Anne's pseudonym was "Acton Bell." Agnes Grey has a large autobiographical background, of course: Anne, like her heroine Agnes, was a poor clergyman's daughter, was docile to a fault, and worked as a governess. But unlike the novel, Anne's life had no happy ending —not even in a literary sense, for Agnes Grey was never well received during her lifetime. But then, neither was its celebrated companion, Wuthering Heights. ¶ Agnes Grey is quite a short novel, under 150,000 words.

Chaps. 1–4. My father, RICHARD GREY, was a north-of-England clergyman; my mother was a squire's daughter who sacrificed many luxuries to marry him. They were very happy. My older sister MARY and I were brought up almost in seclusion. Because of my parents' poverty I decided to become a governess and engaged to teach the two older children of Mrs. BLOOMFIELD. They were TOM, 7, and MARY ANN, 6; they had younger sisters, FANNY, 4, and HARRIET, 2. Tom was a possessive, domineering boy and cruel—he liked to pull the wings off live birds; Mary Ann was contrary and usually mean. Mr. Bloomfield was arrogant—though he was a retired tradesman— and rude and complaining. Together with Mrs. Bloomfield's mother, who visited them regularly, the parents indulged the children and blamed me; I was not permitted to punish my charges and I could not control them.

Chap. 5. The children's uncle, Mr. ROBSON, encouraged Tom's cruelty. He helped Tom find a nest of young birds to torture. I forbade it and killed the birds mercifully. Mrs. Bloomfield rebuked me for interfering with "the dear boy's amusement." As the year neared an end I was told that I would be replaced—since the children's behavior showed so little improvement; and I returned home.

Chaps. 6–7. My father was in ill health and the need for money acute, so I advertised my qualifications—"music, singing, drawing, French, Latin, German"—and accepted a position at £50 a year in the home of Mr. MURRAY, a country squire of Horton Lodge. My pupils were ROSALIE, 16, vain and selfish, rapidly becoming beautiful; MATILDA, 14, a hoyden who could swear like a trooper, usually ill-tempered with me; JOHN, 11, a healthy, boisterous boy but unteachable; and CHARLES, 10, mother's darling, cowardly and malicious. All were too spoiled to teach, though in the course of the next two years Rosalie came to apply herself to everything that would make her more charming to men. I was mistreated by the children and neglected by the servants, but I bore it for the sake of my family; and soon both boys went away to school and it was better.

Chaps. 8–12. At 18 Miss Murray (Rosalie) made her debut with a ball at home. (I was 23.) It occurred during my four weeks' winter holidays at home, at which time my sister Mary married the vicar of a nearby parish, Mr. Richardson. On my return Rosalie told me glowingly of her success at the ball and how many suitors she had, including Sir THOMAS ASHBY and the handsome, snobbish rector, Mr. HATFIELD. Also, the parish had a new curate, EDWARD WESTON. I learned that Mr. Weston was kind to the lowly cottagers, as Mr. Hatfield had never been—especially to an old widow, NANCY BROWN, who lived in fear that the squire's dogs would kill her cat.

Chaps. 13–15. Walking back from church I stopped to pick some flowers. Mr. Weston happened along and helped me,

Mr. Weston joins Agnes in picking flowers after church

then we walked together. I learned he had recently lost his mother and had no permanent home. Rosalie had taken to afternoon walks, and at Mrs. Murray's request I went with her so she could not secretly meet Mr. Hatfield; her mother was determined to marry her to Ashby. Rosalie assured me she would never marry a poor man; one day she contrived to avoid me, did meet Hatfield, and enticed him to propose—whereupon she rejected him contemptuously. Then she boasted to me about it. I was disgusted by her vanity, selfishness, and unkindness. Mr. Weston continued to be very courteous to me and I had another opportunity to walk and talk with him while Rosalie talked to

two of her friends who had never spoken to me; then to my surprise Rosalie joined us and talked very attentively with Mr. Weston. When he parted from us, she boasted that now he adored her. For his sake, I prayed she was wrong; and when I reached my room I wanted to cry. Rosalie told me she would soon have to marry Ashby and did not want Hatfield to have been her only victim, so she had picked Weston as the next.

Chaps. 16–18. At the next ball, Ashby proposed to Rosalie and they were married on June 1. In parting from me, Rosalie unexpectedly kissed me and had tears in her eyes, which surprised me. I was now reproached by Mrs. Murray because Matilda, my one remaining charge, remained interested only in horses, dogs, and hunting. I seldom saw Mr. Weston but when I did it made my life bright.

Chaps. 19–20. My father died, leaving my mother without support. Her father wrote, offering to restore her to fortune if she would confess that she was wrong in marrying my father; but she refused, a decision applauded by Mary and me. My mother and I decided to rent a house at a fashionable watering place, furnish it from my small savings, and open a young ladies' seminary. In the meantime I returned to Horton Lodge for a final six weeks. To my sorrow I saw Mr. Weston only twice, though I thought of him constantly.

Chaps. 21–25. Our school did well enough. I did not hear from Mr. Weston, but toward the end of the year I received a warm letter from Lady Ashby (Rosalie) insisting that I visit her "as a *friend*." I did so and was cordially received but Rosalie was thoroughly relieved when I preferred not to take my meals with the family. I learned that Rosalie hated her new husband, who was dissolute and neglectful. Soon I returned home, and while out walking one day I met Mr. Weston, who had been made vicar of a parish near us. The next day he called and proposed, having already obtained my mother's consent. I happily accepted, and here my diary ends, for that was long ago and our marriage has been everything we could wish.

Ah, Wilderness!

Play by Eugene O'Neill, 1888–1953. Produced Oct. 2, 1933, in New York. Published by Random House, New York. © 1933 by Eugene O'Neill.

AMONG O'NEILL'S most popular plays, *Ah, Wilderness!* deserves a special place as the easiest for any amateur group to produce. Its characters and sets are conventional and it is over at a convenient hour. It has a happy ending. The import of the title (from the *Rubaiyat*) is that happiness requires little more than to be in love. George M. Cohan played Nat Miller in the first New York production.

Act I. The scene is the sitting room of the Miller house in a "large small town" in Connecticut. It is just after breakfast on the Fourth of July, 1906, and the family is making plans for the day. NAT MILLER, newspaper publisher, invites his wife's brother, SID DAVIS (who sometimes drinks too much), to the picnic of his men's club that afternoon. Nat's wife, ESSIE, and Nat's sister LILY MILLER, who lives with them, have no plans till evening, when Sid has invited Lily to the fireworks. TOMMY, 11 years old, the youngest of their four children, dashes out to shoot off firecrackers; ARTHUR, the oldest, who is at Yale, and MILDRED, the teenage daughter, have dates and tease each other about them. That leaves

Sid and Nat plan their outing

only RICHARD, the second son, who is overcome by revolutionary feeling and does not want even to recognize the Fourth. His mother is apprehensive about the wicked books he is reading: Carlyle's *French Revolution;* books by Shaw, one of whose plays [*Mrs. Warren's Profession*] was banned in New York, and by Wilde, who was arrested for immorality; Swinburne's love poems; and the *Rubaiyat,* from which Richard quotes "A Book of Verses underneath the Bough . . ." not quite reaching the line that begins "Ah, wilderness . . ." Miller and Davis are amused but not shocked.

"Old Man McComber"—DAVID MC-COMBER—is seen coming up the walk and everyone but Miller hastens out, to avoid him. McComber—thin, dried-up, like Miller in his late fifties but older looking—accuses Richard of trying to corrupt his daughter MURIEL by writing her letters that are very radical. He threatens to stop advertising his store in Miller's *Evening Globe.* Miller calls him a damned old fool and sends him off. McComber leaves a letter from Muriel to Richard, breaking off. Richard, in love with Muriel, is devastated.

Act II. About 6 o'clock the same day. While NORAH, the "Second Girl," sets the table, Essie and Lily talk. Essie knows Lily loves Sid, but Lily will not marry a man who drinks. WINT SELBY, who is at Yale with Arthur, invites Richard out on a date with "two hot babes" that night, since Arthur is not available. Miller, tipsy, and Sid, drunk, come home and dinner begins. The conversation is pleasant at first but Lily is upset about Sid and leaves and at the end Miller snaps at Richard and all ends unpleasantly.

Act III. 1. In a bar in a small hotel, at 10 o'clock that night, Richard is at a table with BELLE, who is about 20 and a typical college "tart." They are drinking and smok-

ing. Belle sits on his lap and makes him kiss her, but he will not go upstairs with her—to her disgust. A salesman in the bar joins in their conversation. Richard becomes drunk, recites poetry, and becomes belligerent. The bartender throws him out, then becomes fearful when told Richard is Nat Miller's son.

2. The Millers, with Lily, Mildred, and Tommy, are in the Miller sitting room. It is 11 o'clock and they are worried because Richard is not home. Arthur and Sid come in, and Lily forgives Sid. Richard comes in, dirty (from landing on the sidewalk outside the bar) and still drunk. Sid takes him upstairs.

Act IV. 1. It is one o'clock the next day; Miller has come home from the office to have a talk with Richard, but goes back because Richard is reported still asleep. He looks fine and is not contrite, but sulks when his mother scolds him. Mildred brings him a letter from Muriel, saying that she did not mean anything in the letter her father made her write, and Richard is happy again.

2. On the beach, about 9 o'clock that night, Richard is waiting for Muriel. He plans not to let her know, at first, how tickled he is. She comes; they have a long talk on life and love, including their love. At first she will not let him kiss her, but finally she does. They plan their marriage

and honeymoon, years later.

3. At 10 o'clock, Nat and Essie are discussing the disciplining of Richard—but neither seems very confident. Richard returns, glassy-eyed with love. Essie goes out to the porch. Miller laboriously talks to Richard about desires of the flesh, but Richard indignantly states his love for Muriel and his intention to be faithful. Miller is proud of him. Essie comes in and before leaving for bed, Richard impulsively kisses his father—"First time he's done that in years," says Miller huskily—and then Nat and Essie happily turn out the lights and retire.

Alexander's Bridge

Novel by Willa Cather, 1876–1947. Published 1912 by Houghton Mifflin Co., Boston. © 1912, 1922, 1930, 1940 by Willa Cather.

THE FIRST PUBLISHED NOVEL of Willa Cather is in length little more than a novelette. It was not a commercial success, as first novels usually are not, but it foreshadowed her later work: The writing is quiet, restrained—no surprises, no suspense. There is no contrived plot. The characters are conventional or at least self-controlled. Yet without evident effort she makes them real—a quality of her writing that within a few years was to win Willa Cather recognition as a major novelist. Especially because it is so short, *Alexander's Bridge* is a proper introduction to the writing of Willa Cather.

Chap. 1. Prof. LUCIUS WILSON, on one of his infrequent trips to Boston, calls to see his friend and former pupil BARTLEY ALEXANDER, who at 43 is an internationally famous engineer and builder of bridges. Wilson is received by Mrs. (Winifred) Alexander, a tall, beautiful woman of one of the best families and very rich. Alexander arrives shortly after, a vital and open person, large and blond and handsome. The Alexanders are happy, their marriage ideal.

Chaps. 2–4. Alexander, on a trip to London, is taken by his acquaintance Maurice Mainhall, a well connected literary dilettante, to a play in which the actress HILDA BURGOYNE has made her first great success. She is a principal topic of conversation in London, for her beauty, popularity, and genuinely admirable qualities; she is not married and Mainhall has heard privately that she has not recovered from an early love affair with an American student that ended badly. Alexander muses on his early courtship of Hilda (for he was that American student); it had seemed perfect, yet when he had first met Winifred 12 years before, in Canada where he was building a bridge, he had written to Hilda telling her he intended to marry Winifred if she would have him and Hilda had never replied. Alexander also muses on the new Moorlock Bridge, a cantilever so long that it is an engineering departure, that he is now building in Canada and for which, undoubtedly, he will chiefly be remembered. Mostly he thinks of Hilda; day after day he walks near her house and visits places they used to go together, but he cannot quite bring himself to call on her. He meets her at a party and she is quite formal but invites him to call on Sunday afternoons, when she always has a crowd at her house, and he does so. Finally she invites him to dinner alone. They are still formally friendly until the very end, when he takes her in his arms and she breaks down with love of him.

Chaps. 5–9. Wilson visits the Alexanders the following Christmas and finds them the same contented couple. But actually Alexander is suffering from his dual feelings. He is soon leaving for England and is determined to end his relationship with Hilda, yet on shipboard he is overcome by anticipatory excitement. In London he and Hilda are happily reunited, but still he tells her of his misgivings and asks her to help by refusing to see him again. She refuses; it must be up to him, for she can love only one

man all her life. He relinquishes his resolve and again they live wholly in love. When he returns to Boston he writes to Hilda, telling her how much he is suffering and again asking her to help. That same spring Hilda's play comes to New York for a six weeks' engagement. He purposely stays out of town, but the engagement is extended and he goes to New York before it ends. He does not seek out Hilda, but she comes to him, unannounced; and in the irresistible renewal of their love he decides he must cling to Hilda and leave Winifred. He writes Winifred a letter, but does not mail it.

Chap. 10. Alexander is summoned to Canada; despite the careful calculations, the Moorlock Bridge is in danger of collapsing. He goes and has the construction work stopped, but it is too late. The bridge begins to collapse while he is on it. He jumps into the river and could have swum to safety without trouble, but a number of workmen fall into the water around him and drag him down with them, and he is drowned.

In an Epilogue, Prof. Wilson, living in London the previous six years and now 70, is calling on Hilda; they have become good friends. They speak of Alexander and of the dignified way in which Winifred is bearing her grief. He still lives, with as much vitality as ever, in their minds too.

The Alhambra

Stories by Washington Irving, 1783–1859.
Published 1832.

IN *The Alhambra* Irving told of his visit to that historic castle and, far more importantly, recounted the tales of the Alhambra that he heard while he was there. The book earned the special distinction of becoming popular in Spain. It is a typical work of North America's first man of letters— good writing but seldom superlative.

The Alhambra, fortress and royal palace of the Moorish kings (in Spain), is almost as much an object of devotion to Moslems as is the Caaba. Within its walls, studded by towers, it could contain 40,000 or more men. After the Moors, Christian kings used the Alhambra as a palace into the 18th century; then it was maintained as a military post, but was allowed to become partly ruins. When the French recently invaded Spain they restored much of the artistic quality but on their departure they blew up enough of the walls and towers to leave no military value. [There follows a physical description.] Our *cicerone,* showing us around, told of how a former caretaker had encountered the ghosts of four Moorish soldiers and had run away and never returned. Our female guide, Dolores, showed us (indignantly) how the Moorish kings kept their

wives shut up. At the invitation of the Spanish governor, we [Mr. and Mrs. Irving] took up our quarters in the Alhambra, where I cannot help imagining myself back in the past, in the days of its glory. (There follow "Tales of the Alhambra.")

THE TWO INDISCREET STATUES

LOPE SANCHEZ lived in the Alhambra and worked in its gardens; he was a merry fellow who liked to play the guitar and sing,

or play for dancing. He had a buxom, strapping wife and one child, a 12-year-old daughter, SANCHICA. At play one day, Sanchica found a little hand carved of jet. Lope's friends told him tales of magical powers the Moors attributed to such talismans, and Lope hung the little hand around his daughter's neck.

Not long after Sanchica daringly explored ruins in the nearby mountains and penetrated into its depths. The Alhambra's bell tolled midnight and she returned, to see a pageant of living Moorish princes and courtiers, magnificently arrayed, riding by, including the great king BOABDIL EL CHICO. She wandered about and saw a fine lady—a Gothic princess of legend, imprisoned in the Alhambra—and because it was the Eve of St. John her talisman released the lady for that one night and the lady showed her the Alhambra just as it was in the days of its glory. The lady gave her an adornment of gold and emeralds in the form of a myrtle wreath. At first cockcrow all vanished and Sanchica returned home, still having the myrtle wreath.

When Lope saw the wreath, though he could not imagine its real value, it convinced him that there were treasures in the Alhambra. He ventured into the vault, "guarded" by two statues, alabaster nymphs whose faces were turned discreetly away from the entrance. He found great porcelain jars filled with Moorish gold pieces and precious stones. Now he was rich, if he could find a way to remove and use the treasure.

Lope's wife confessed all this to Brother Simon, a friar, who insisted that since it was infidel treasure it should belong to the Church. At the start Brother Simon took only the wreath and a purseful of gold, but time after time he returned for more pursefuls. Lope, not a religious man, objected to his wife's confessions but could not stop them. Eventually he procured a mule and planned to pack the remaining treasure on it and leave for another part of the king-

The Alhambra, with the Sierra Nevada of Spain in the background

dom. That night Brother Simon (who had been informed of Lope's intention) came and mounted what he thought was the pack-mule, loaded with treasure; but instead his mount was BELLUDO, the goblin-horse of Moorish legend, which gave him a rough ride and then threw him off, after which he found that his treasure had vanished and even the myrtle wreath had turned to withered leaves of no value.

Some years later, when Lope was almost forgotten, an old acquaintance of his who was traveling saw at Malaga a sumptuous wedding procession for Sanchica, with Lope and Dame Sanchez, richly dressed and be-jeweled, riding in their carriage.

THE ADVENTURE OF THE MASON

A poor mason in Granada was aroused one night by a priest, who asked him to do a job at night, blindfolded, for good pay. The mason found mortar and bricks pro-vided for him, then helped the priest "bury" in the vault four jars evidently full of money. Years later, a rich old curmudgeon bought the house and sought to hire the mason, at an insufficient fee, to make some repairs on a house that had belonged to a rich and miserly priest. The mason agreed to do the work free, even though the house was said to be haunted by the clinking of coins in the priest's former room—if he could live there rent-free in the meantime. The rich man ac-cepted, and somehow the mason came to be one of the richest men in Granada.

LEGEND OF PRINCE AHMED AL KAMEL

AHMED AL KAMEL ("Ahmed the Per-fect") was a prince of Granada for whom the astrologers predicted a great life, except that he had an unusual passion for love. The king, his father, built him a palace overlook-ing the Alhambra and put him there with a wise tutor, EBEN BONABBEN, who was instructed to teach him everything except about love, and let him know nothing of that. Robbed of normal love, the prince lavished his affection on flowers and birds—with which he learned to talk.

A dove that the prince rescues from a hawk finally tells the prince about love and then flies off, risking death to be with its mate.

Later the dove tells the prince of a beauti-ful princess in a far-off land. The prince writes her a letter, "To the Unknown Beauty," which the dove carries; and long after, when the prince has almost given up hope, the dove returns with the princess's picture hung on a chain of pearls around its neck. The dove dies from the flight, but the prince consults his friend the owl, who sends him to a raven at Seville, a soothsayer and conjurer; the raven sends him to a wise parrot at Cordova; and the parrot identifies the picture as the Princess ALDEGONDA, daughter of the Christian king of Toledo, who is shut up until her seventeenth birth-day so that she cannot fall in love. Accom-panied by the parrot and the owl, the prince sets out for Toledo. The parrot, sent ahead to talk to the princess, finds that she loves

14

Ahmed but her hand is to be awarded on the result of a tournament the next day, which several princes are entering. Ahmed despairs, for he knows nothing of chivalry; but the owl knows where there is hidden, in a cave, a suit of magic armor and a spell-bound steed. The prince procures the armor and steed and rides to the tournament.

At the tournament, Ahmed is first barred because only princes can compete; then, when he proves he is a prince, it is even worse because he is a Moslem. Enraged, he charges the Christian princes and knights and defeats them all, even the king. But exactly at noon the magic spell ends, the steed dashes away to the cave, and Ahmed

The picture brought by the dove

is left on foot and helpless. The parrot re-ports that the princess has fallen under some kind of spell and has been shut up in a high tower. A great prize awaits the man who can effect a cure.

The owl knows of a talisman dating from the time of Solomon, a magic carpet that can fly, now held in the king's treasury in To-ledo. Disguised as a poor Bedouin, Ahmed approaches the king and offers to save the princess if he may have the sandalwood box in which the carpet is kept. The princess is brought forth and the prince arouses her by chanting lines from the letter he first wrote to her. He is rewarded with the magic car-pet, for the Christians do not know its magi-cal qualities. He spreads it under the otto-man on which the princess lies, and they fly away together. The king of Toledo makes war on Granada to recover his daughter, but when he finds that Ahmed is now the king of Granada and the princess his sultana, and that she has not been forced to change her religion, he is reconciled to the marriage. Ahmed appoints the owl his prime minister and the parrot his master of ceremonies and has a wise and successful reign.

THE MOOR'S LEGACY

In Granada there was a sturdy little water-carrier, Pedro Gil, called PEREGIL. He was a henpecked husband but devoted to his wife and children.

One night Peregil encounters a poor

Moorish traveler, whom he befriends and takes home. The traveler dies during the night and Peregil buries him secretly, be-cause his wife fears entanglement with the law; but a barber across the street has seen all and tells the alcalde (magistrate), who arrests Peregil. But Peregil explains truly that the traveler left nothing but a small box in which there is a scroll of writing and a wax taper; and the alcalde lets Peregil go and keep the box, taking instead Peregil's donkey—the poor man's means of liveli-hood. But a merchant who can read Arabic translates the scroll and Peregil learns that it is a secret incantation to open the way to en-chanted buried treasure—so long as the taper is kept burning. When the taper's flame dies, the cave will close again and any-one inside will be trapped forever.

Peregil and the merchant find the buried treasure and take away pockets full of gold. When they spend it, the barber again in-forms the alcalde, to whom Peregil and the merchant are forced to reveal the entire story. The alcalde agrees to share everything with them, actually intending to kill them later and take all. When all go to the cave, Peregil and the merchant first take large quantities of the treasure, and go out while the others are taking theirs. At this point Peregil extinguishes the flame of the taper, and the villains are left imprisoned for all time while Peregil and the merchant live their remaining lives as rich men.

THE THREE BEAUTIFUL PRINCESSES

In old times there was a Moorish king of Granada called MOHAMMED EL HAYZARI ("the left-handed"). He captured a beauti-ful Christian princess and wooed her un-successfully until he enlisted the assistance of her duenna, who persuaded the princess

Peregil secretly buries the body

Wooing the Christian captive

to marry the king and become a Moslem, and who herself also became a Moslem under the name KADIGA. The queen gave birth to triplet daughters, for whom the astrologers prophesied no trouble until they reached marriageable age; and the king shut them up in the castle of Salobreña with Kadiga as their nurse.

All three were beautiful as they grew older. They were ZAYDA, the oldest, bold and curious; ZORAYDA, vain and preoccupied with her beauty; and ZORAHAYDA, the youngest, timid and sensitive. From their castle one day they saw three Castilian noblemen who had been taken prisoner, and grew to love them. When the princesses reached marriageable age, the king came to take them to the Alhambra. On the way they passed a convoy of prisoners, including the three Castilians; the entire convoy bowed low except these three, who were too proud, but when the king was going to put them to death for their insolence the intercession of the three princesses saved them, besides which they came of noble families and would bring big ransoms. Instead the king sentenced them to hard labor and Kadiga contrived to have them work at a place under the windows of the princesses' quarters.

Finally the noblemen were ransomed, and as the time approached for them to leave Kadiga arranged for them to carry with them the three princesses and also herself; all were willing to become Christians, the princesses because of their Christian mother and Kadiga because she had once been a Christian before. When the time of escape came, Kadiga and the two older princesses went down the ladder from the castle but Zorahayda became too frightened and stayed. There was a great chase and a desperate fording of a river, in which Kadiga was swept away from the party, but the cavaliers and princesses reached Cordova safely; Kadiga survived but never ventured near the territory of the Moslems again; and Zorahayda stayed with her father but died young and is now buried in a vault beneath the Alhambra's tower.

THE LEGEND OF THE ENCHANTED SOLDIER

In old times, in the Cave of St. Cyprian at Salamanca the "dark and damnable arts" such as necromancy and chiromancy were secretly taught. Attending this school was a penniless student, Don VICENTE, who made out by playing on his guitar.

One day as Don Vicente set out on his wanderings he saw and picked up a ring marked with the seal of Solomon, which is powerful against enchantments. In one town he saw a fat priest being served by a maid who appealed greatly to him; but the priest lived too lavishly for him to approach the house. Then he met an old soldier, lavishly but quaintly dressed, who proved to be several hundred years old and forced by an enchantment to guard a treasure left in the times of Ferdinand and Isabella. To lift the enchantment, a Christian priest and a Christian maid were necessary. Don Vicente was now able to obtain the help of the priest and his young servant. With some pain, for he was very self-indulgent, the priest fasted long enough to make himself pure and be able to exorcise the spirits that held the treasure secure. The damsel touched Don

Vicente's seal of Solomon to the coffer and it opened, making available the treasure, with which the student and soldier began stuffing their pockets. But the priest, famished and seeing some food available, began to stuff himself, which broke his fast too soon. Also, he gave his maid a chaste kiss in gratitude for something she served him. As a result, the spell was reëstablished and they found themselves transported outside; nor could they reënter, for the maid had dropped the ring with Solomon's seal. In some versions (there are many), the student keeps enough of the treasure to make himself prosperous for life, and marries the damsel.

THE ROSE OF THE ALHAMBRA

Eventually Granada (and the Alhambra) fell to the Christian kings of Spain, but none visited there until Philip V made a state visit. In the tower previously occupied by The Three Beautiful Princesses lived JACINTA, a girl only 15 years old but so beautiful that the peasants called her "the Rose of the Alhambra," and her maiden aunt, FREDEGONDA. During the visit of the king, a youth named RUYZ DE ALARCON, a page of Queen Isabella (or Elizabetta), had a gerfalcon fly into the tower. Pursuing it, he met Jacinta and they fell in love, but Fredegonda's watch was so strict that they could not meet again.

One night the apparition of the Princess Zorahayda visited Jacinta and asked to be baptized by a true Christian, so as to be released from evil genii. Jacinta baptized her and as a reward was left a silver lute, which produced the most beautiful music ever heard. At this time the king became ill and enjoyed nothing but fine music, so Jacinta was called to his seat to play for him. Her music was so beautiful that it restored the king, and in gratitude the queen took Jacinta as her ward. This made easy the marriage of Jacinta to Ruyz de Alarcon, whose noble father had previously opposed his marrying a penniless girl. The silver lute became one of the crown treasures until it was stolen and taken to Italy, where it was melted down for the value of the silver; but the strings (this is a great secret) became the strings on the violin of Paganini.

Jacinta's music cures the king and wins her a husband

Alice Adams

Novel by Booth Tarkington, 1869–1946.
Published 1921 by Doubleday & Co., New York. © 1949 (renewal) by R. Susannah Tarkington.

ALICE ADAMS is one of the several characters through whom Booth Tarkington's readers were admitted to his keen appreciation of human embarrassments, especially those of the adolescent. To the sensitive reader, some of Alice's experiences are excruciating. The novel is short, about 100,000 words. It is not ranked with *The Magnificent Ambersons* and *Penrod* but remains important because of its bits of insight that are scarcely exceeded anywhere.

Chaps. 1–8. VIRGIL ADAMS, 55 years old, who has worked many years for J. A. LAMB & Co., wholesale druggists, is convalescing from an illness. His wife is nagging him to go into business for himself, to improve their social standing and income. ALICE ADAMS, their daughter, 22 years old, partly agrees because she is no longer fully accepted by the girls of the better families, girls who went away to school and college when she could not afford to; but she sympathizes with her father and does not like to see him nagged. The Adams live in a distinctly lower-middle-class house with typical furnishings. Alice walks two miles to the house of Mildred Palmer, daughter of one of the rich families, whom she mistakenly considers a "close friend," to learn what Mildred will be wearing to her own party that night (to which Alice is invited). Alice and her mother work all day making a presentable dress for Alice; and Alice's brother WALTER, 20 years old, who long ago gave up going with the rich set and chose companions nearer his family's income range, is bullied into escorting Alice to the party in a rented Ford. Alice is ashamed of the car and will not let Walter drive it up to the door, insisting that they park it outside and walk to the house in the rain with an unconvincing story about their car's having broken down. At the party no one dances with Alice except Frank Dowling, an occasional but not wholly welcome suitor; Walter, under pressure; and once ARTHUR RUSSELL, a rich young man, a cousin of Mildred's and reputedly engaged to her, who (Alice is sure) was sent by Mildred to rescue her. When she returns home she bursts into tears.

Chaps. 9–12. Alice continues to live in a dream world. On a walk downtown she passes, as always, a sign "Frincke's Business College" and as always it has some strange effect on her, but she rejects the whole idea. She meets Arthur Russell, who is very attentive and asks to call on her, to which she

agrees. At home, Mrs. Adams continues to nag Virgil Adams; she wants him to leave his job and open a glue factory. Many years before, J. A. Lamb assigned Virgil and another employee to develop a liquid glue and they did so, but Mr. Lamb never got around to opening that branch of his business and the other man died, so only Virgil now knows the formula. Old Mr. Lamb calls on Virgil, as he does every week, which greatly pleases Virgil but causes Mrs. Adams to renew her nagging. Arthur Russell begins to come to see Alice almost every night, and they sit and talk on the front porch, with Alice telling him all kinds of lies to make her social position seem better than it is.

Chaps. 13–18. Mr. Adams does determine to open the glue factory. He asks Walter, who has a job at Lamb's company, to come with him but Walter refuses unless he is given $300 cash. This Mr. Adams refuses, because he needs all he has and can raise by mortgaging his house to open the factory. Mr. Adams has not the courage to resign his job but sends a friend in the company, Charley Lohr, with a letter to Mr. Lamb—who receives and reads the letter without comment. Mr. Adams proceeds with his glue factory; meanwhile a mysterious large factory is being built across the street.

Chaps. 19–22. Arthur Russell has continued to call regularly and Mrs. Adams thinks he should be invited to dinner. The invitation is issued and accepted; and Mrs. Adams plans everything, including hired servants, to make it seem that the Adams live much better than they actually do. Meanwhile Walter urgently asks his father for $350 and is refused. At dinner at the Palmers' (whom he has neglected while spending most of his time with Alice) Russell learns that the Lambs consider Mr. Adams a thief of the glue formula and that even Mildred has never thought much of Alice. When Arthur Russell comes to dinner at the Adams house it is an unusually hot day but a hot and formal dinner has been prepared and it is a failure; when Alice and Russell part that night, both know it is final. Next it is discovered that Walter has defalcated with $350 of Lamb & Co.'s money, and Mr. Adams is determined to find the money and make good, though he is overmortgaged already and does not know exactly how to do it.

Chaps. 23–25. Mr. Adams discovers that the big factory across the street will be occupied by the J. A. Lamb Liquid Glue Co. This ends his last hope of raising money. He meets Mr. Lamb, who proves never to have known about Walter's defalcation (or even that Walter was his employee), but generously he offers to buy out the Adams glue factory for $9350. When Mr. Adams has another attack, Mr. Lamb takes him home. The offer has to be accepted. Alice, as often on a morning, dresses to go downtown; she meets Arthur Russell and is only polite when he suggests calling again; and as though by fate she finds her steps guided to the door and up the stairs of Frincke's Business College.

Alice's Adventures in Wonderland
and
Through the Looking-Glass

Children's books by Lewis Carroll (Charles Lewis Dodgson, 1832–1898).
Published 1865 & 1872. Available in many editions. (ML, 79; PB, 835)

THESE ARE two separate books, but they are so much more of a unit than the usual book-and-sequel that they are almost always published together. They constitute the most generally admired children's book ever written. The first (almost always called simply *Alice in Wonderland*) is a child's dream based on a pack of playing cards; the second (whose full title is *Through the Looking-Glass, and What Alice Found There*) is based on a set of chessman and a game of chess. Many of the characters and incidents in both works are related to familiar nursery rhymes, and both sparkle with the author's parodies and original nonsense verses. The eminence of the Alice books derives from the delicious satire on conservative Victorian customs and attitudes and on the peculiarities of the English language. The original illustrations by Sir John Tenniel are almost inseparable from the text. The usual sulphitic criticism of *Alice* is that children can't appreciate it.

Alice in Wonderland

Chaps. 1–3. ALICE is sitting outside with her sister when she sees a WHITE RABBIT dart by—and take a watch from his pocket. She follows him down the rabbit hole, which is very long and lined with cupboards and bookshelves. At the bottom, the

Left: The animals after the caucus race. The mouse tells a "long and sad tale"; in the book it is printed so as to look tail-shaped. It is about a dog named Fury who kills a mouse. Below: Curiouser and curiouser!

White Rabbit dashes off, down a passage, and disappears around a corner. Alice is left facing three locked doors. There is a tiny gold key on a table; it fits the lock on a very small door that leads to a garden; but Alice is much too big for the doorway. She sees a small bottle with a label that says "Drink Me." Alice does so and begins to shrink. She grows small enough to get through the door but now is too small to reach the key. Then she sees a small cake marked "Eat Me." She eats it and suddenly grows more than 9 feet tall. "Curiouser and curiouser!" Alice exclaims. She starts to cry and sheds gallons of tears. The White Rabbit dashes by again, late for an appointment. Alice picks up his fan and gloves, which he dropped, and starts to grow small again, until she is a few inches high. Suddenly she finds herself swimming in a lake of the tears she shed before, and there are many other animals swimming with her. She meets a mouse but frightens him by mentioning her cat, Dinah. They all reach shore. The Dodo, one of the animals, suggests a "Caucus-race" to get dry. It consists of running around in circles.

Chaps. 4–5. The White Rabbit returns for his gloves. He mistakes Alice for his maid, Mary Ann, and sends her to his house for a pair of gloves and a fan. She finds the gloves and fan, and also a bottle. She takes a sip from the bottle and grows so large she fills the entire room. The White Rabbit sends Bill (a lizard) down the chimney to get her out, but she kicks him back up. Then they throw pebbles through the window at her and the pebbles turn to cake. She eats

some and becomes so small (3 inches tall) that she can get out of the White Rabbit's house and run away into the woods. There she meets a playful puppy who seems huge to her. Next she encounters a CATERPILLAR sitting on a large mushroom smoking a hookah. After some conversation he tells her to recite "You Are Old, Father William." She tries, but the words come out wrong. [Here follows a parody of Southey's poem.] The Caterpillar tells Alice that one side of the mushroom will make her larger, the other side smaller. Alice nibbles on pieces of mushroom, growing short and tall with alarming speed, until she makes herself 9 inches tall—just the right size for a house she sees nearby.

Chap. 6. At the house she sees a Fish-Footman (a fish dressed in footman's livery) deliver to a Frog-Footman an invitation from the QUEEN to the DUCHESS to play croquet. Alice goes into the house, and in the kitchen she finds the Duchess holding a crying baby, while the cook is making soup with so much pepper that everybody is sneezing. A cat by the hearth doesn't sneeze, but grins; it is a CHESHIRE CAT, the Duchess explains. The Duchess hands Alice the baby and Alice carries the baby outside, where it turns into a little pig. She sets it down and it trots into the woods. Alice is startled at seeing the Cheshire Cat sitting in a tree near her. The Cat directs her to the homes of a MAD HATTER and a MARCH HARE, then vanishes gradually, the grin last.

Chaps. 7–10. Alice walks to the house

of the March Hare. At a table set under a tree outside, the March Hare, the Mad Hatter and a Dormouse are having tea. (The Dormouse is asleep and the other two are using it as a pillow.) Alice sits down and joins them. They have a conversation, with many rude or strange remarks. The Hatter has a watch that tells the date, not the time. The table is set for many persons, for it is always tea-time there and occasionally they all move to fresh places. The Dormouse wakes and tells a story about three sisters who live in a treacle-well and draw things that begin with M. At length Alice walks away. She sees a tree with a little door in the trunk, and she goes through the garden side of the same tiny door that she had seen so long before. In the garden three gardeners are painting a white rosebush with red paint. Their names are Two, Five, and Seven, and they are playing-cards. The Queen of Hearts had ordered a red rosebush and a white one had been put in by mistake. The KING and QUEEN of HEARTS appear with a great procession of courtiers, soldiers, children, and royalty—all of whom are playing-cards. The Queen orders Alice into the croquet game. The mallets are flamingoes, the croquet balls are live hedgehogs, and the wickets are soldiers who double themselves up, standing on their hands and feet. It is very difficult to play. Every few minutes the Queen becomes angry at someone and cries "Off with his head!" The Cheshire Cat appears—only its head, the grin appearing first. The King and Queen come by and talk

The mad tea-party: Alice, the March Hare, the Dormouse, the Mad Hatter. A riddle is asked: Why is a raven like a writing-desk? The author never tells the answer.

17

rises up into the air and falls down on her. She gives a little cry; and as she is trying to brush the cards away, Alice wakes up and finds her sister brushing away a handful of leaves that had blown down over her face as she slept.

to it but soon the Queen orders its head to be cut off, which creates a difficulty because there is nothing to cut it off of. The Duchess then arrives, but after she and Alice talk for a while the reappearance of the Queen makes the Duchess run off quickly. The Queen takes Alice to meet the GRYPHON and the MOCK TURTLE, and leaves Alice with them. The Gryphon, a monster, looks fierce but is very friendly. He tells Alice that the Queen's executions are never actually carried out, then he takes Alice to the Mock Turtle, a turtle with a calf's head, who is sighing sadly—but the Gryphon says the Mock Turtle isn't sad as he pretends to be. The Mock Turtle's sorrow is that he once was a real turtle and went to school in the sea, under the direction of a tortoise ("because he taught us"). At school they learned Reeling, Writhing, and Arithmetic (Ambition, Distraction, Uglification, Derision) plus Mystery, Seaography, and Drawling, Stretching and Fainting in Coils. The Gryphon and Mock Turtle dance the Lobster Quadrille for Alice and the Mock Turtle sings the song that goes with it. Alice recites a poem (all wrong again) and the Mock Turtle sings another song, "Beautiful Soup." But a cry in the distance tells them that the trial is beginning. Alice does not have the least idea what the trial is about, but with the Gryphon she rushes to it.

Chaps. 11–12. The Knave of Hearts is being tried for stealing some tarts. The King is the judge; the jury is composed of animals and birds. Witnesses include the Mad Hatter, March Hare, and Dormouse, who never seem to get to the point, and one by one they run away or are thrown out of court. Meanwhile Alice finds herself growing large again. By the time she is called as a witness she is her normal size again. The Queen says "Sentence first—verdict afterward," and Alice calls this nonsense. The Queen shouts "Off with her head!" but Alice says, "Who cares for you? You're nothing but a pack of cards!" With that the whole pack of cards

18

Through the Looking-Glass

Chap. 1. ALICE is playing with her two little kittens, one black and one white, and playing "Let's pretend" about "Looking-glass house," which one sees in the mirror. The glass in the mirror suddenly becomes a mist and she walks through it. The pieces of a chess set are walking about on the hearth. Alice sees the RED KING, RED QUEEN, WHITE KING, and WHITE QUEEN (who is wailing for her child Lily, a White Pawn, which is on the table and screaming quite loudly). Alice picks up the White Queen and sets her beside her noisy little daughter, and the Queen thinks she has been blown up by a volcano. (Alice is invisible to the chess pieces.) Alice looks at a book on the table but cannot read it until she realizes that it is mirror writing. Then she holds it up to a mirror and reads a poem called "Jabberwocky," but most of the words are still so strange that she cannot understand them.

Tweedledum and Tweedledee (note their collars.) Alice has just come upon them.

Chap. 2. Alice goes into the garden, though for a long time she has trouble walking to where she wants to be. The flowers are able to talk, and though they make some uncomplimentary remarks they do at least tell Alice that she must walk away from something in order to reach it. Alice finds this is true when she sees the Red Queen approaching and walks away; she meets the Queen face to face. The last time Alice had seen her, the Red Queen had been three inches tall; now she is half a head taller than Alice herself. The Red Queen is friendly but always contradicts whatever Alice says. Everything in this country seems to be backward; Alice and the Red Queen run fast, for a long time, and stay in the same place. The Red Queen explains, "Here it takes all the running you can do to stay in the same place." Together they walk to the top of a hill and Alice sees that the countryside is marked out in squares, like a chessboard. The Red Queen tells Alice she may play as the White Queen's pawn, since Lily is too young to play. Alice must journey through all the squares until she comes to the Eighth Square, where she will become a queen. The Red Queen vanishes.

Chap. 3. Alice, knowing that little brooks separate the squares, jumps over the first brook, into the Third Square. Suddenly she is in a train and the Guard is asking for her ticket. The train is filled with a remarkable assortment of passengers; a gentleman dressed all in white paper, a goat, a beetle, a horse, and a tiny gnat that keeps whispering in Alice's ear. Soon the train jumps over a brook. Alice is frightened but at least the jump takes her rapidly into the Fourth Square. Now she finds herself sitting under a tree with the Gnat, grown to about the size of a chicken. It points out three of the Looking-Glass insects: the Rocking-horse-fly, the Snap-dragon-fly, and the Bread-and-butter-fly. The Gnat disappears and Alice walks into the woods, where she meets a Fawn. She and the Fawn have both forgotten their names. They are very friendly until they reach a place where they remember again; then, realizing that Alice is a human being, the Fawn becomes frightened and runs away. Alice sees a pair of signposts, pointing in the same direction. One says "To TWEEDLEDUM'S house" and the other says "To the house of TWEEDLEDEE." She follows them and comes upon two little fat men who look exactly alike.

Chap. 4. The only noticeable difference is the name "Dee" on the collar of one and the name "Dum" on the other. Almost every time Tweedledum speaks he ends his sentence with "Nohow," while Tweedledee says "Contrariwise." Suddenly they are dancing, and singing "Here we go round the Mulberry bush." Then Tweedledee recites a long poem called "The Walrus and the Carpenter." It tells how these two invite oysters from the sea to walk with them,

The walrus, the carpenter, and the oysters. "I weep for you," the walrus told the oysters; "I deeply sympathize." With sobs and tears he sorted out those of the largest size.

then eat the oysters. Part of this poem is often quoted:

"The time has come," the Walrus said,
"To talk of many things;
Of shoes—and ships—and sealing-wax—
Of cabbages—and kings—
And why the sea is boiling hot—
And whether pigs have wings."

Alice hears a noise like a steam engine's puffing. Tweedledum and Tweedledee tell her it is the Red King snoring, that the King is dreaming about Alice, and if he wakes up Alice will "go out—*bang!*—like a candle." Then Tweedledum accuses Tweedledee of breaking his rattle, and the brothers prepare to fight; but the sky darkens, a giant crow flies up, and both brothers run away.

Chap. 5. The White Queen comes running wildly toward Alice, with her shawl flying, her hair in a dreadful, untidy state, and all her clothes on wrong. Alice straightens her out a bit. Suddenly the White Queen starts to scream that her finger is bleeding. It is already bandaged. After a few minutes the Queen pricks her finger and does not utter a sound; she explains that she has done all her screaming already. The White Queen asks how old Alice is. Alice answers 7½. Together they cross a brook and suddenly the Queen becomes a Sheep. Alice is no longer in the woods but in a little shop. The sheep is knitting, and every few moments she picks up another pair of knitting needles, until at last she is using fourteen pairs at once. Strangely, Alice finds herself in a rowboat with the sheep, with herself rowing. Then they are back in the shop and Alice asks if she might buy an egg. The sheep sells her the egg and sets it on a shelf, standing it upright on one end. Alice must go and fetch it herself, said the sheep.

Chap. 6. As Alice walks toward the egg, it becomes larger and larger, and finally Alice sees it is HUMPTY DUMPTY. The shelf is a high, narrow wall. Alice and Humpty Dumpty have a long talk. He is very critical of Alice but explains to her what some of the strange words in the "Jabberwocky" meant. Some of them he calls "portmanteau" words, for example *slithy*, which means "lithe and slimy." Humpty Dumpty recites a poem that makes no sense at all. He then stops talking, and closes his eyes. As Alice walks away there is a great crash.

Chap. 7. Many soldiers come running through the woods, then many horses. They are all the King's soldiers and all but two of his horses, coming to try to put Humpty Dumpty together again. (The missing horses, or knights, are needed in the chess game.) Alice meets the White King, too. He is waiting for one of his two Messengers, Haigha and Hatta. Haigha arrives and says the LION and UNICORN are fighting again. Alice remembers the rhyme about the Lion and the Unicorn fighting for the Crown. The two fighters come into the clearing and are given white and brown bread. Alice learns that the Unicorn had never believed human children really existed, but thought they were fabulous monsters. Next plum cake is served, and Alice has to pass it around first and cut it later; then drums begin beating and the Lion and Unicorn leave.

Chap. 8. After the noise of the drums stops, Alice is alone briefly. Then a Red Knight rides up and claims her as his prisoner. The WHITE KNIGHT rides up to rescue her, and the two knights have a battle in which each of them seems to fall off his horse many times and land on his head every time. Alice does not understand the fight, but after it the Red Knight gallops off and the White Knight claims a glorious vic- When at last the White Knight has to leave her, Alice is beside a brook. She jumps over—and she is wearing a golden crown.

Chaps. 9–12. At last Alice is a queen. The Red Queen and White Queen are there. They ask Alice all kinds of questions, most tory. The White Knight escorts Alice to the end of the square, and he explains to her the many odd contraptions he has on his horse. He always says, "It's my own invention." Also he sings Alice a long song. His "inventions" all seem utterly foolish and quite useless to Alice but she does not say so. of which have queer answers. Then they both go to sleep and soon disappear. Alice finds herself at a doorway marked QUEEN ALICE. A Frog dressed as a footman finally opens the door for her and she is at a banquet in her honor. Everyone cheers Queen Alice and sings songs about her. Alice is introduced formally to the roast of mutton, and to the pudding, after which she may not eat them. The dishes and utensils start walking and flying about, everything becomes very confused, and Alice begins to shake the Red Queen. She wakes up and finds she is shaking her own black kitten.

Alison's House

Play by Susan Glaspell, 1882-1948. Performed Dec. 1, 1930, in New York. Published by Samuel French, New York. © 1930, 1958 by Susan Glaspell.

ALISON'S HOUSE won the Pulitzer Prize for 1931. It was first produced at the Civic Repertory Theatre in New York City, a venture headed by Eva Le Gallienne; Miss Le Gallienne directed and played one of the important rôles, that of Elsa. The character of Alison Stanhope is certainly suggested by Emily Dickinson but the play is not otherwise biographical of Emily Dickinson.

Act I. The scene is the library of the old Stanhope house in Iowa, on the Mississippi. It is Dec. 31, 1899, which the characters in the play (like most of the world) treat as the last day of the 19th century. Alison Stanhope, a maiden poetess whose few, posthumously published poems made her famous, has been dead 18 years. Miss AGATHA, Alison's aged sister, has been living alone in the house; Mr. STANHOPE, Alison's brother, a lawyer in the nearby big city, is closing the house and will take Miss Agatha home with him. His secretary, young ANN LESLIE, is typing as the curtain rises; JENNIE, the maid, announces RICHARD KNOWLES, a reporter from Chicago. He wishes to write a feature on Alison Stanhope. Ann likes him, and TED, Mr. Stanhope's younger son, a college student, shows him through the house. LOUISE, Mr. Stanhope's snobbish daughter-in-law (married to his older son, EBEN), objects to any notoriety but Mr. Stanhope does not care; he proceeds with inventory-taking and moving plans. Miss Agatha enters and also objects to the intrusion on their privacy; she is disturbed by Knowles' question as to whether any other papers of Alison's have been found. He leaves. Ted also is pressing for additional information about Alison, with which he can persuade his English professor at Harvard to give him a passing grade. Eben arrives and proves to be as liberal as his father, and not in sympathy with his wife Louise. The conversation develops the fact that ELSA, Mr. Stanhope's daughter, has disgraced the family by running off to live in sin with the husband of one of her friends; and that Alison too was in love with a married man but gave him up so as not to embarrass her family and lived the rest of her life as an unhappy recluse.

19

Elsa arrives; Louise snubs her but the others do not. There is a brief flurry when fire breaks out upstairs, but it is put out. It develops that Miss Agatha set it intentionally, and she mutters something about "trying to burn them."

Act II. The apportionment of property and keepsakes among the family continues. Mr. and Mrs. HODGES are shown in; they are a vulgar couple who want to buy the house for use as a summer hotel, and though all the family finds the prospect distasteful a deal is made. Knowles comes back, frankly to see Ann; Stanhope encourages her to take a walk with him. The conversation develops how kind Alison was to the children, Eben and Elsa, and how much they loved her. Miss Agatha wants to burn a portfolio she is carrying, but cannot bring herself to do it and in the emotional turmoil has a stroke and dies.

Act III. The scene is Alison's bedroom, the same night. It has been maintained unchanged by Miss Agatha all these years. Elsa and Eben reminisce about Alison. Stanhope comes in and they propose to open the portfolio; Jennie desperately tries to obtain it and burn it, saying she promised Miss Agatha to do so, but she is persuaded not to. In the portfolio they find many unpublished poems of Alison's. Stanhope decides he must burn them, in accordance with his dead sisters' wishes; Ted, for selfish purposes, insists that the poems must not be burned and even snatches a handful and runs out of the room. Stanhope, Eben and Elsa debate the destroying of the poems. Knowles comes in, having seen a poem taken downstairs by Ted. He protests robbing the world of these poems. Stanhope finally decides the poems belong to the world. He gives them to Elsa, as her rightful gift from Alison, as the bells toll midnight and the passing of the century.

All For Love or, The World Well Lost

Play by John Dryden, 1631–1700. Produced 1678.

IN THIS PLAY Dryden dared to take the same theme that Shakespeare had so recently covered in *Antony and Cleopatra*. His self-confidence was justified: *All for Love* is considered his best play and one of the finest in English literature. Dryden covers a much smaller portion of the Antony-Cleopatra romance than Shakespeare did. The action of the play begins after

Antony and Cleopatra have lost the Battle of Actium to Octavian (Octavius Caesar, soon to become the Emperor Augustus). Antony fled with his fleet, not from cowardice but to follow Cleopatra in her retreat with her fleet. He reproaches himself not only for this but also for his previous desertion of his wife to be with Cleopatra. The entire play emphasizes the great love of Antony and Cleopatra and how the downfall of both is attributable to it.

Act I. In the Temple of Isis, SERAPION, Priest of Isis, tells MYRSIS, another priest, that he has dreamed of Egypt's downfall. ALEXAS, the Queen's (Cleopatra's) chief eunuch, and later VENTIDIUS, Antony's general, enters; the conversation reveals that Antony, having been beaten by Caesar (Octavian) in war, stays in retirement and does not even see Cleopatra. CLEOPATRA has decreed a holiday in honor of Antony's birthday. ANTONY enters, he is disconsolate, and Ventidius has difficulty arousing his ambition again, but finally succeeds: Antony will take the field against Caesar once more.

Act II. Cleopatra, with her ladies IRAS and (later) CHARMION, and with Alexas, sorrows that Antony—whom she loves more than Egypt and her throne—is going to war without even consenting to see her. Alexas assures her that Antony loves her but must assert his independence of his love. Alexas takes to Antony jewels as gifts from Cleopatra, and gifts also to Ventidius, who refuses them and urges Antony to do the same. But Antony accepts the gifts and agrees to see Cleopatra, to say goodbye. In the leave-taking, Antony learns that Cleopatra could have sold him out to Caesar but loved him too much. Antony, impressed by such devotion, is reconciled to Cleopatra.

Act III. Antony returns from a successful battle and Cleopatra crowns him with a laurel wreath. Ventidius urges negotiation with Caesar but Antony considers it fruitless. DOLABELLA, Antony's friend, who previously left him because he too loved Cleopatra, and has been in Caesar's camp, returns with conditions from Caesar. With him has come Antony's wife OCTAVIA, who is Caesar's sister and has interceded with her brother. Antony is offered the rule of the East, and Octavia does not even demand restoration to her full place as Antony's wife. Under pressure from everyone including his two young daughters, Antony agrees to accept. Octavia and Cleopatra meet briefly and exchange reproaches.

Act IV. Antony cannot bear to tell Cleopatra his decision and sends Dolabella to do so. Cleopatra is overcome with grief but asks for a final interview with Antony. Ventidius deceives Antony by saying that Cleopatra accepted the news cheerfully and let Dolabella make love to her. This seems to be confirmed when Alexas (who wants to separate Antony and Cleopatra) suggests to Antony that his mistress's grief might be less if Dolabella is left with her. Antony, encountering Cleopatra and Dolabella at the same time, bitterly reproaches both and will not believe them despite their true protestations.

Act V. Serapion informs Cleopatra that her fleet has deserted her and joined Caesar's fleet. Antony learns that he is betrayed by Caesar, who intends to overcome and kill him. Alexas, still lying in an effort to save his own life, tells Antony that Cleopatra has killed herself with a dagger, for love of him. Antony then determines to kill himself and asks Ventidius to help him; but Ventidius cannot do this and instead kills himself. Antony then kills himself by falling on his sword. When Cleopatra hears of this she kills herself by letting an asp bite her.

Antony takes his leave of Cleopatra before going out to battle

All God's Chillun Got Wings

Play by Eugene O'Neill, 1888–1953. Produced 1932 in New York. Published by Random House, New York. © 1932 by Eugene O'Neill.

THIS IS A penetrating study of a controversial subject. A white girl, Ella, marries a Negro man, Jim, and she loses her mental balance. It is a foreseeable consequence in psychology and is not subject to controversy. On the message of the play, however, the United States divides on sectional lines. Generations of Northern students have been taught that the play is a protest against our culture, in its implanting of ineradicable prejudices. Southerners rather see in it a warning against the natural perils of miscegenation; and of course the warning is there, protest or no. The title is from a Negro spiritual.

Act I. 1. On a corner on the streets of lower New York, eight children are playing marbles: Two white boys, two white girls, two Negro boys, two Negro girls. SHORTY and MICKEY are the white boys, JIM HARRIS and JOE the Negro boys. ELLA DOWNEY, one of the white girls, is a blonde with a beautiful complexion but they call her Painty Face, which she dislikes. She likes Jim and tells him she wishes she were black; she will be his girl. She is 8 years old. Jim loves her.

2. Nine years later on the same corner; graduation time at high school. Mickey is a successful young prizefighter. Joe and Shorty are talking; they and Mickey did not continue through high school. Jim Harris, who failed the year before, is graduating this year; so is Ella, who now hates Negroes and is Mickey's girl. Jim, who still loves her, asks Mickey not to treat her as he has treated other girls; Mickey is too scornful to hit him, and Ella, when she comes to meet Mickey, is rude to Jim.

3. On the same corner, five years later, a poorly dressed, gaunt Ella meets Shorty, now a gangster type. He has brought her some money from Mickey, who some years before deserted her and his illegitimate child, Ella refuses the money (because the child has died) and also Shorty's offer to "work" for him. She works in a factory and Jim Harris has been her only friend. Shorty throws the money at her and leaves; she gives it to a passing Salvation Army troupe. Jim comes in. He has worked for years to be a lawyer but has failed his exams each time; he knows the answers but freezes up and cannot answer. Ella and Jim agree to marry and go to a foreign country where there is no color consciousness.

4. A street, facing a brick church; a Negro tenor is heard singing, from the street at the right. Jim and Ella come out of the church, married and on their way to the boat; she is trembling and he tries to cheer her up but is on the verge of collapse himself.

Act II. 1. In the Harrises' flat in the same neighborhood, two years later, Jim's mother and his sister HATTIE are waiting for Jim and Ella, who are returning from France. Hattie, a teacher, who got through college and post-graduate schools with the greatest ease, does not like the interracial marriage; Mrs. Harris will not condemn it. When the doorbell rings, Mrs. Harris goes out and Jim then comes in alone; Ella did not stand the trip well and Mrs. Harris is taking care of her. Jim tells Hattie how Ella was at first happy in France but got so she could not stand to see people, even though there was no sign of prejudice. And Jim decided he must come back, study, and pass his bar examination, to prove himself. Ella and Mrs. Harris come in. Ella is hostile and patronizing; she is repelled by a Congo mask, a fine example of African art; and finally she insults Hattie and Mrs. Harris. She makes "among their own people."

2. Six months later, Jim is wearing himself out studying. Hattie is with him, to give him the doctor's report on Ella, who has broken down mentally and physically.

Jim will not hear of Ella's going to a sanitarium. Ella raves, "Black! Black!" and called Hattie "a dirty nigger," but Hattie now knows that Ella really loves Jim and her trouble is the prejudices she cannot overcome. After Hattie leaves, Ella comes in briefly, childlike and not wholly lucid—but at one point she turns vicious and is vituperative toward Jim.

3. Ella, alone in the flat six months later, is railing at the Congo mask—and raving in her fear that Jim has passed his examinations. Jim comes in, haggard, looking crushed, holding a letter. With irony, almost with hysteria, he reveals that he did not pass. Ella is joyous; she takes the Congo mask and plunges a knife through it. Jim finally turns on her in a rage, but she soon subsides into childlike simplicity. She wants Jim and her to be children again, playing marbles. Jim feels an ecstasy of religious humility; he has lost Ella the woman but is given back Ella the child. He humors her. it clear—though only Hattie understands—that she does not want Jim to pass his examinations. Finally Mrs. Harris and Hattie are forced to leave—and they explain that they are giving Jim this house anyway, as a gift, and have taken a flat in Harlem

Ella in hysterical ecstasy plunges the knife into the Congo mask

All Quiet on the Western Front

Novel by Erich Maria Remarque, 1897– Published 1929 (Germany). English translation by A. W. Wheen. © 1929 by Little, Brown & Co., Boston.

ONE OF THE LATEST BUT BEST of the World War I novels, *All Quiet on the Western Front* (original German title, *Im Westen nichts Neues*) had the dual function of establishing its author as a major novelist and introducing to the English-speaking reader the German soldier as a human being and not a bestial Boche. The story is told in the first person and present tense by one of the principal characters, Paul Bäumer, who is 19 years old and a recent recruit in the German Army when the action begins. The diary style permits Remarque to use the clipped sentences, brief paragraphs and unadorned descriptive language that have proved so effective in the novels of James M. Cain. (Unlike Cain, Remarque departs from this technique in other of his novels.) The original German title is based on a communiqué from the High Command at a time when it reported daily on the two fronts, west and east, and a more faithful rendering into English would be, "nothing to report in the West."

Paul carries Kat back

PAUL BAUMER is one of four boys who enlisted in the German Army at the age of 18, just out of school. The others are ALBERT KROPP, MÜLLER, and LEER. Their friends in the same company are TJADEN, a locksmith; HAIE WESTHUS, a peat-digger; DETERING, a peasant, and STANISLAUS KATCZINSKY, 40 years old and the leader. They are now front-line veterans and are happy because they have extra food and tobacco rations: These were prepared for 150 men but casualties were unexpectedly heavy and only 80 are left. The schoolmates speak often of KANTOREK, their former schoolmaster, who had persuaded them to volunteer before being called.

The friends go to see a wounded comrade, KEMMERICH. Müller covets Kemmerich's fine boots, but they cannot bring themselves to tell Kemmerich that his leg has been amputated and he will soon die. (But before Kemmerich does die, he realizes that he will and Müller gets the boots.) In training camp the schoolmates were under a Corporal HIMMELSTOSS, a tyrant who abuses his authority as drillmaster; in civilian life, a postman. Most drillmasters in the training camp are overly strict, fearing that if their discipline is lax they may be sent to the front themselves. Tjaden hates Himmelstoss most, because Himmelstoss used a cruel method in trying to cure him of bedwetting. To the

schoolmates' delight, Himmelstoss is sent to the front. They waylay him at night, throw a bed-cover over his head so that he cannot recognize them, and give him a thorough whipping.

The war proceeds as usual: The men dodge enemy shells, lay barbed wire, survive gas attacks (which often kill the recruits who have not learned that gas lingers longest in the shell holes), catch and kill their lice, and talk about the war—how neither they nor the enemy's common soldiers really have any part in it. At the front, where discipline is less strict, Tjaden defies Himmelstoss and receives the mild sentence of three days' arrest. Paul and Kat (Katczinsky) catch and roast a goose. Much time is spent fighting the many rats, which get at the men's bread.

Preparations are made for an advance. The veterans teach the recruits not to carry saw-edged bayonets, for the enemy mercilessly kills and often tortures any soldier carrying one. Actually, sharpened spades have been found by the veterans to be better weapons. In waiting through a bombardment the recruits often get claustrophobia and try to rush out to what would be sure death; they are forcibly restrained and even beaten by the veterans in the dugout. Paul sees all the horrors of death and mutilation.

Also he finds Himmelstoss hiding in a corner of a dugout, afraid to go into the battle; he forces Himmelstoss out. Once out, Himmelstoss fights well and also bring back Haie Westhus, who is wounded (and later dies). After the battle Himmelstoss tries to make friends and gives them extra food and better assignments for duty; especially because of Haie, all accept him except Tjaden, who is still reserved.

In a quiet period, stationed on the side of a canal, they see two young Frenchwomen on the other side. Paul, Kropp and Leer make a date with them, by sign language; that night they swim across the canal with food and cigarettes. They are naked but the French girls give them enough clothing to cover themselves and they have a happy night.

Paul receives a 14-day leave, plus traveling time, and goes home. His mother is dying of cancer, but he is joyously received by her, his elder sisters, his former schoolmasters, and others. Nevertheless he is not comfortable at home. Once he is called down for failure to salute a major on the street, and after that he wears civilian clothes. He goes to a training camp to see Mittelstaedt, a schoolmate who became an officer; their teacher Kantorek has been called up and Mittelstaedt persecutes him in ways that Paul finds humorous. Paul has the uncomfortable duty of calling on Franz Kemmerich's mother and telling her of Kemmerich's death; he lies and tells her that her son died instantly, and swears to the truth of this without a qualm.

Instead of returning to the front at once, Paul is sent to a training camp. Here he sees a camp of the many Russian prisoners, who are almost starving because even for the army and civilian population Germany does not have enough food. Paul feels pity for the prisoners and kinship with them. He travels again to the front, where his company is issued new uniforms to be reviewed by the Kaiser, after which it goes into battle again. On patrol in No Man's Land, Paul finds himself alone. A French soldier jumps into the same shell hole and Paul kills him with his bayonet, then is overcome by remorse and talks at length to the dead man. He is rescued by Kat and Albert Kropp.

Paul is one of eight, all the friends, detailed to guard an abandoned village in which there is a supply dump. They eat well from the supplies and even catch and roast two suckling pigs. It does not bother them that the village is under constant bombardment. But on the next assignment both Paul and Albert are wounded, Paul in the arm, Albert in the leg. They contrive to stay together and are sent by train to a Catholic hospital. Albert's leg is amputated. Paul is sent home on convalescent leave, then is returned to the front. Detering has died madly, trying to find and shoot a wounded horse; Müller has been killed and

Paul gets the boots. Westhus had died long before. It is the summer of 1918 and an armistice is rumored but does not come, though now the Allies have five planes to one, five fresh men to one, fifty times as much food. The German soldiers are better because they are more experienced, but the enemy superiority is overwhelming. Knowledge that the end is near makes life seem more desirable than ever.

Paul and Kat are out alone. Kat is wounded and Paul begins to carry him back. They talk; yet when Paul reaches his own lines, Kat is dead. A shell splinter has hit his head and killed him while Paul was carrying him.

Now it is the fall of 1918. Paul knows that the war has ruined him, even if he retains his life; his friends are gone, his generation will have nothing in common with the ones before it and after it. But Paul himself is killed on a day in October, 1918, a day so uneventful that the army report said: All quiet on the Western front.

All's Well That Ends Well

Play by William Shakespeare, 1564–1616.

Produced 1602 or 1603.

THIS COMEDY is set in France and in Florence in the late 15th century, when France often supported Florence and other Italian cities in their nearly constant wars. The French scenes are at the seat of the Count of Rousillon and at the King's court in Paris, plus one scene in Marseilles; there are several scenes in Florence. *All's Well That Ends Well* was first performed in 1602 or 1603. The themes of the switched bedmates and the ring are very old.

Act I. 1. BERTRAM, Count of Rousillon, takes leave of his mother, the COUNTESS, to go to the court of the KING OF FRANCE. The king is dying; the Countess expresses regret that the great physician Gerard de Narbon is not still alive to cure the king. HELENA, daughter of Gerard, is living with the Countess, and the Countess considers her an adopted daughter. Helena loves Bertram and confesses her love to PAROLLES, one of Bertram's followers, but Helena cannot aspire to marry a count. 2. Bertram reaches court and is well received by the King. The current war between Florence and Senoy (the Sienese) is discussed. 3. The Countess tells Helena that she would be welcome as a daughter-in-law, but Helena still cannot aspire so high. Helena says she is sure there is a remedy for the King among the prescriptions her father left, and re-

ceives permission to go to court and try to save the King.

Act II. 1. The King sends off some of his young lords to fight for Florence. LAFEU, an old lord of Bertram's train, tells the King that Helena has come. She persuades the King to let her try to cure him, and asks as her reward if she succeeds that she be allowed to select as a husband any noble lord in the King's service. The King agrees. 2. The Countess sends a CLOWN to court with a message to Helena. 3. Helena has cured the King. The King lines up various lords; Helena speaks to several but selects Bertram, who pleads with the King not to force him to marry so low-born a person as the daughter of a physician. The King forces him to marry her, but Bertram swears he will not take her to bed. He decides to go off to war. 4. Parolles tells Helena that Bertram is going to war and wishes her to return home. 5. Helena sees Bertram but he rejects her and sends her home.

Act III. 1. The Duke of Florence is promised some aid by French envoys. 2. Helena receives a letter from Bertram: Until she can get from his finger his ring "which never shall come off," and also bear him a child, he will not act as her husband. 3. Bertram enters the service of the Duke. 4. The Countess receives a note from Helena saying that Helena has gone to Italy. 5. Helena, disguised as a pilgrim, arrives in Florence and meets DIANA, who is being wooed by Bertram but does not want him. Diana's mother, an old WIDOW, invites Helena to their house. 6. Bertram and others discuss war plans. Bertram mentions his unsuccessful wooing of Diana. 7. Helena arranges with the Widow to have Diana get Bertram's ring from him. Diana agrees to try.

Act IV. 1. The war continues. 2. Diana obtains Bertram's ring from him and arranges to have him come secretly into her room and into her bed at midnight. 3. Bertram returns to the Florentine camp after midnight; he has been to bed with the woman he thought, in the dark, was Diana but actually was Helena. He thinks Helena is dead, having misunderstood a message from the Countess. The Duke is sending him back to France with a message to the King. 4–5. Helena thanks Diana and the Widow, and leaves Florence, taking them with her; Bertram returns to Rousillon.

Act V. 1. Diana learns that the King has gone to Rousillon. 2–3. The King is visiting Rousillon. He asks Bertram to marry the daughter of Lafeu and Bertram agrees. Bertram gives Lafeu, as a token, his ring. He is told that Helena was seen wearing the ring, but refuses to believe it. Diana arrives and claims Bertram as a husband; he denies his promise, but now she produces his ring, actually a copy bought from a jeweler. The King, confused, is almost determined to throw everyone in prison when Helena is brought in and the whole plot revealed: She fulfilled Bertram's conditions, for she obtained the ring and she is bearing Bertram's child. Bertram's heart has changed and he loves her dearly.

The old widow welcomes the supposed pilgrim, actually Helena, to her house

All the King's Men

Novel by Robert Penn Warren, 1905–
Published and © 1946 by Harcourt
Brace & Co., New York. (Ban., A939)
ROBERT PENN WARREN won the
1947 Pulitzer Prize with *All the
King's Men*. The novel was inspired
by the career and to some extent by
the personality of Huey Long, the
Louisiana governor and senator, but
in its details it is in no way a biography of Huey Long. The title, of
course, is from the "Humpty Dumpty"
nursery rhyme: All the king's horses
and all the king's men could not restore the subject character, Willie
Stark, once he was dead. The novel is
fairly long, about 250,000 words. It
sees Southern political life (which
Warren knows thoroughly) through
the newspaperman Jack Burden, who
must in many cases express Warren's
own attitudes yet is undeniably an
individual on his own, one of the
most sharply and effectively drawn
characters in American literature.
Warren, born in Kentucky of Southern families on both sides, has lived
most of his life in the deeper South.
All of his many fine novels are set in
the South.

Chap. 1. JACK BURDEN, who is the narrator throughout the book, is riding in a
car with WILLIE STARK, governor and political boss of the state; they are going to
Mason City, Willie's original home town,
for a visit to his father (chiefly for publicity purposes). Jack is a general assistant
to Willie. In the car are LUCY, Willie's
wife, a former school-teacher; "TINY"
DUFFY, Willie's political henchman and
at present the lieutenant governor; and
"SUGAR-BOY" O'SHEAN, Willie's chauffeur (a daredevil driver) and bodyguard.
A retinue of newspapermen follows in
other cars. The year is 1936. Jack thinks
back to 1922, when he was a newspaperman and he and Duffy first met Willie,
who was County Treasurer in Mason City,
a country boy ignorant of politics. Now
Willie is a local hero. He makes a brief impromptu speech to a crowd that assembles,
then visits his father on the small family
farm and poses for publicity pictures.

But Willie is upset by some news given
to him by SADIE BURKE, his press-relations
assistant and incidentally his mistress. She
tells him that Judge IRWIN, former Attorney General of the state and a man of
great and irreproachable reputation, has
come out for Callahan, who is running for
the Senate against Willie's candidate,
Masters. Willie and Jack drive down to
Burden's Landing, where Judge Irwin lives.
The judge is an old family friend of Jack's;
Jack comes of an old and fine family and
his playmates in childhood were the children of Governor Stanton: ADAM STAN-
TON, who has become an eminent surgeon,
and ANNE STANTON, with whom Jack has
long been in love.

Judge Irwin is cordial with Jack but unfriendly toward Willie (of whom all the
"better element" disapprove). Willie cannot persuade Judge Irwin to withdraw his
endorsement of Callahan. When Willie and
Jack leave, Willie tells Jack to dig up some
disgraceful episode in the judge's life that
can be used for pressure. Jack warns that
this is probably impossible.

Chap. 2. Jack recalls how Willie became
the state Boss. As County Treasurer, Willie
knew there was big graft in the building of
a new school at Mason City. Prodded by
Lucy, he tried to stop the graft; but the
county political organization defeated him
easily and even made him a laughingstock.
Willie holed up at the farm, fed the pigs,
studied law and became a lawyer. Then,
during a fire drill about two years later, part
of the school collapsed and several children
were killed or crippled. Willie was vindicated and became a local hero, the honest
politician. He did not try to cash in on it
but not long afterward one of the two rival
political factions in the state, the one led
by MACMURFEE, decided to use him as a
tool. They persuaded him to become a candidate for governor, hoping he would split
the vote of their opposition. Willie did not
have a chance but did not know it. Duffy
and Sadie Burke, who actually were of Mac-
Murfee's party, pretended to be working
for Willie. Late in the campaign, Willie
found out from Sadie and from Jack, who
was covering the campaign, that he was
simply being used by MacMurfee. This
made him so heartsick and angry that he
withdrew from the campaign but continued
to lecture throughout the state, telling the
truth about the political maneuvering that
went on. This made him popular with the
farming element and two years later he was
able to run for governor and win. During
this campaign, Jack resigned his newspaper job because he disagreed politically
with his paper. When Willie became gov-

ernor he called Jack in and hired him, the
job Jack still has. Sadie and Duffy had already joined Willie's following, and Sadie
was by now in love with him.

Chap. 3. Jack reminisces about his own
home and early life. His mother is quite
rich, chiefly through having been married
several times. Her first husband, Jack's
father, was a successful lawyer who inexplicably left his profession and his home
and became a religious worker in the slums
of the capital. Jack classifies his mother's
husbands by types: the Scholarly Attorney
(his father), the Tycoon, the Count, and
the present one, the Young Executive. In
1915, the year Jack went away to college,
he fell in love with Anne Stanton, but they
drifted apart and he married Lois, with
whom he had too little in common; after
some years they were divorced.

The rest of the chapter is episodes pic-
turing Willie Stark's life as governor: His
curbing the graft of a political associate,
but letting the honest Attorney General resign rather than let him take action against
that associate; Sadie's violent jealousy when
Willie has a few wild nights on a trip to
Chicago; Lucy's more or less leaving Willie
and retiring to the farm, but publicly maintaining their marriage for the sake of their
son, TOM, a football hero in high school
and college.

Chap. 4. When Jack Burden was in college, he almost finished work for his Ph.D.
—all he had to do was finish his dissertation, or written thesis. But he never finished
it. The dissertation was based on the old,
Civil-War-period memoirs of Jack's great-
uncle, CASS MASTERN, and the rest of the
chapter tells the story of Cass Mastern, who
died of a wound while serving in the Confederate Army. Cass Mastern and his older
brother Gilbert (who became a multimil-
lionaire) were born in a log cabin in the
Georgia hills. Gilbert grew up, prospered,
and helped Cass to go to Transylvania College in Lexington, Ky. There Cass had an
affair with Annabelle Trice, wife of Duncan Trice, a prominent young banker. It
was in the middle 1850s. Both suffered
from guilt but their passion was irresistible.
Duncan Trice shot himself—accidentally,
according to the newspapers—and died.
Annabelle sold her maid Phebe—an attractive, light-colored slave girl—because she
could not bear the real or fancied look of
accusation in the girl's eyes. Cass tried to
find the girl to buy her back and free her.
He was unsuccessful, but in the process
learned enough about the slave trade to repel him. He returned to the plantation his
brother had given him in Georgia, freed
his slaves, and tried to run the plantation
by hiring them as free men, but it did not
work. When war broke out he refused a
commission and enlisted as a private,
fought through several campaigns, and
finally was mortally wounded. But Jack
Burden found that he still did not know
Cass Mastern well enough to be satisfied
with the result, so with the dissertation
nearly finished he stopped and left college.

Sadie and Willie

Chap. 5. As instructed by Willie, Jack begins to dig into the past of Judge Irwin. First, Jack goes to see "the Scholarly Attorney," living in squalor, preaching and ministering to unfortunates. Jack asks if Judge Irwin was ever in great need of money, but learns nothing. Then he goes to see Anne Stanton (and incidentally learns that she has been to see Willie to get support for a Children's Home). Anne remembers a time when, as a child, she heard something about the judge's being in money trouble. Later Anne calls him to say she has learned from her old Cousin Mathilde that Judge Irwin was "broke" but saved himself by marrying money.

Jack checks the county records and finds recorded a $42,000 mortgage on the judge's house, due but not paid in 1910; but in 1914, when foreclosure proceedings were under way, it was suddenly paid in full. Jack goes to Savannah, Ga., where the judge's wife came from. He finds that she had once been rich but had thrown away her money and, when she married the judge, actually thought she was marrying a rich man for his money—so both were fooled. Next Jack learns that in 1915 the judge resigned as Attorney General and became vice-president of the American Electric Power Company, at $20,000 a year, and also received and sold a large block of the company's stock. This company had previously been in danger of prosecution by the state, but proceedings were dropped. A man named Mortimer L. Littlepaugh, whom the company dropped to make room for Judge Irwin, committed suicide. Littlepaugh had a sister, Miss Lily Mae Littlepaugh, whom Jack tracks down living in poverty in Memphis. Jack bribes her to tell him all she knows, and she shows him an old letter from her brother, telling her that Judge Irwin accepted a bribe and Governor Stanton refused to take action when Littlepaugh went to him. Now Jack knows that not only the judge but also Governor Stanton (now dead) had been guilty of improper acts.

Chap. 6. Willie Stark's great ambition is to build a great free hospital for the state. He will permit no graft in its construction or management, despite Duffy's pressure on him to give the construction contract to LARSON, a supporter of MacMurfee, who will pay graft. Willie tells Jack to get Adam Stanton to accept the directorship of the hospital, promising that there will be no political interference or graft. Adam is reluctant to believe Willie, but for some reason Anne helps to persuade him to accept.

Jack tells Anne that Judge Irwin was guilty of past corruption and that her father covered up for him. He proves it to her, but she makes him promise that before he uses the information he will give Judge Irwin a chance to clear himself. Not long afterward, Jack learns both indirectly and from the jealous Sadie Burke that Anne has

become one of Willie's mistresses.

Chap. 7. Jack is so unhappy about Anne that he runs away to California, drinking and thinking of the past for about eight days. He thinks of what a great friend Judge Irwin had been to him when he was a boy; and of his first love affair, with Anne, who said she loved him too but would not marry him; and of his married life with Lois, who wanted to live a fashionable social life that was distasteful to him, so he left her and she divorced him.

Chap. 8. Adam, as director-designate of the hospital, is offered a bribe by Hubert Coffee, representing Larson. Adam hits Coffee and wants to resign, but Jack persuades him that Willie had nothing to do with it and actually will have Coffee prosecuted if Adam will sign a complaint. But then Jack persaudes Adam to refrain voluntarily from signing the complaint, because Anne would be a witness and would become involved in the unpleasantness of a political scandal.

Meanwhile Willie has decided that he will have himself elected senator, instead of remaining governor. MacMurfee, his political opponent, brings pressure through Tom Stark, who is accused of violating a girl named SIBYL, daughter of a small-town barber named Marvin Frey. MacMurfee controls Frey and will prevent him from prosecuting, but the price is that MacMurfee and not Willie goes to the Senate. Now Willie insists that Jack bring pressure on Judge Irwin, who has great influence on MacMurfee. Jack goes to see the judge and confronts him with the evidence. The judge admits it. Jack is to go back to see him the next morning. That night Judge Irwin shoots himself. Jack learns from his mother, who is hysterical, that Judge Irwin was his father—that was why the Scholarly

Attorney left her. When the judge's will is read, Jack finds that he is the judge's heir.

Chap. 9. Unable to bring pressure through Judge Irwin, Willie gives up. To protect Tom and still prevent MacMurfee from being senator, Willie agrees to give the hospital construction contract to Larson. But in a football game not long after, Tom Stark is injured; two vertebrae in his neck are fractured and at best he will be paralyzed for the rest of his life, which probably will not be very long.

Willie Irwin calls off the deal with Larson, telling him to do his worst. He breaks off with both Sadie and Anne, announcing that he is going back to Lucy.

Anne tells Jack that Adam has learned about her affair with Willie and has made wild and reproachful accusations. Jack tries to find Adam but cannot. Then Adam shows up at the capitol as Willie is entering, and he shoots and kills Willie. Sugar-Boy kills Adam.

Chap. 10. Sadie has gone to a sanitarium. Jack sees her there and learns that Duffy told Adam about Anne and Willie; but that it was Sadie who, in jealous anger, suggested it to Duffy. Jack sees Duffy, who is now governor and who wants to keep Jack in the same job; but Jack intends to give out the news of Duffy's scheme to inspire Adam to assassinate Willie. However, Sadie writes to Jack and says she is going away and she thinks such things should be kept private, if only for Anne's sake; and Jack decides to do nothing. Tom Stark dies of pneumonia and Lucy gives all the money she has to Sibyl Frey. Jack settles down in Judge Irwin's house, is reconciled with his mother, marries Anne, and takes into the house the Scholarly Attorney, his supposed father. He plans, however, to sell the house and move away from Burden's Landing.

Amelia

Novel by Henry Fielding, 1707–1754. Published 1752.

AMELIA was Fielding's last novel. While neither as good nor as historic as *Tom Jones*, it is a good novel and remarkably readable, fitting the 20th-century taste better than nearly any other novel of its century. It is comparatively short for a Fielding novel (about 200,000 words) and the action is fast despite the many delightful passing essays in the Fielding tradition. Included are famous satirical descriptions of 18th-century British law and justice. Fielding himself was a barrister and later a justice of the peace, or judge.

Book 1. Jonathan Thrasher, justice of the peace, is holding court in Westminster. A young man named Booth [Captain WILLIAM BOOTH] is charged with beating a watchman (policeman). Booth is "shabbily drest" but tells a convincing story of

how he was only trying to help a man being beaten by two others, and that he never attacked the watchman; the two offenders got liberty by bribery and he too was offered liberty if he could have paid half a crown, but he had no money. Nevertheless the judge sends him to prison. Here, unable to bribe the keeper or the prisoners, he is at the mercy of the many criminals and at once they steal his coat. During the day he sees a beautiful, well-dressed woman brought in as a prisoner and thinks he recognizes her as a Miss FANNY MATTHEWS; she has a full purse and bribes the keeper to give her a private room. Soon afterward Booth mysteriously receives a guinea wrapped in paper, with no way to tell whence it came. He uses part of it to redeem his coat but loses the rest at cards to another prisoner, a Mr. ROBINSON, who had previously seemed friendly. The next day he is summoned to the private room of the beautiful lady, who turns out to be Miss Matthews and who had sent him the guinea.

Miss Matthews (now known as Mrs. Vin-

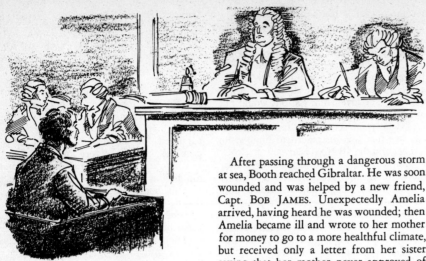

Booth before Judge Thrasher

cent) tells her story: She was first seduced by a handsome officer named Hebbers, whom she at first disliked but then encouraged out of jealousy for her sister and another woman, the widow Carey, to whom he was paying his attentions. Hebbers evaded marrying her and she learned it was because he was already married; nevertheless she lived with him for a year and bore him a child, which died. But later he deserted her and when she heard that he had married Mrs. Carey she sought him out and stabbed him with a penknife—the offense for which she is now in prison. Miss Matthews has twenty guineas left and persuades Booth to accept two. The keeper and Miss Matthews' lawyer, Mr. MURPHY, were vying as to which could get more of the remaining guineas.

Books 2–3. Booth tells Miss Matthews his story, beginning with his wooing of AMELIA HARRIS, now his wife. He had not loved her when she was beautiful, but after her face was disfigured in an accident and her friends deserted her, he came to love her. He won her by pretending to be in love with another woman and asking Amelia to help him in his courtship. He and Amelia wanted to marry and were befriended by a kind clergyman, Dr. R. HARRISON, but Amelia's mother insisted on marrying her to a rich man. Despite this opposition, Dr. Harrison eventually married them. For a time he even reconciled them with Mrs. Harris, who agreed to buy Booth a better army commission than the one he had. But Amelia was pregnant and Mrs. Harris repudiated her agreement so as to keep Booth at home—instead of which, he soon had to go to Gibraltar with his old regiment. When he left he discovered that Amelia's sister BETTY, who he had thought liked him, had spitefully taken the picture of Amelia that he carried. (Miss Matthews agreed that Betty was an unlikeable woman.) Booth's attendant on his trip was Amelia's foster-brother, Sergeant ATKINSON.

After passing through a dangerous storm at sea, Booth reached Gibraltar. He was soon wounded and was helped by a new friend, Capt. BOB JAMES. Unexpectedly Amelia arrived, having heard he was wounded; then Amelia became ill and wrote to her mother for money to go to a more healthful climate, but received only a letter from her sister saying that her mother never approved of the marriage and would not help her. Nevertheless the Booths managed to reach Montpelier, where they became friends with another English officer, Major BATH, and his sister, Miss Jenny Bath. A Frenchman, M. Bragillard, disappointed Miss Bath in love and Bath fought and killed him. The Booths had run out of money, and appeals to Mrs. Harris were unavailing, but James appeared and helped them. They then received a letter from Dr. Harrison saying that Mrs. Harris had died and left all her money to Betty. When the Booths returned to England they called on Betty, who blamed Amelia for their mother's death and drove the Booths away. Booth, with a wife and now two children, had only £40 a year, but Dr. Harrison gave him a small estate to farm. But Booth had been unsuccessful and had run heavily into debt, so a few days before his arrest he had come to London to seek better fortune, with his family left behind to join him later. This ended Booth's story.

Book 4. Miss Matthews wishes Booth to share her room in the jail with her; which the governor of the jail permits for half a guinea a day, and they live together illicitly for a week. An admirer of Miss Matthews sends her a £100 banknote, and she is offered release from prison, but she refuses to leave without Booth, whom now she loves. She buys his release, but before they leave the jail Amelia appears. She accepts Miss Matthews as a friend of her husband's, and she is happily reunited with her husband. Booth, Amelia, and their two children live in London. Miss Matthews seeks to continue her illicit relationship with Booth, and her letters embarrass him but Amelia is not suspicious or jealous. Booth meets James, now a colonel, who has married Miss Bath but has tired of her; James becomes enamored of Miss Matthews but still she prefers Booth. Booth is harassed by his creditors, even Dr. Harrison. The Booths become friendly not only with the Jameses but with their landlady, Mrs. ELLISON, who is the cousin of a rich lord; Mrs. MOLLY BENNET, a young woman who also has

lodgings at Mrs. Ellison's; and Sergeant Joe Atkinson, the foster-brother of Amelia. Mrs. Ellison recommends Booth to the lord, who tells her to have Booth call on him.

Book 5. Booth runs into Bath, now a colonel; when Booth says he seems to have lost James's friendship (through jealousy about Miss Matthews), Bath recommends a duel. Atkinson meets Mrs. Ellison, who likes him; and soon afterward he accepts the position of porter in the Booths' household, ostensibly at least to guard Booth against arrest for debt. But the lord temporarily satisfies Booth's creditors. Booth again meets Bath, who first ignores and then insults him; they have a duel, in which Booth's behavior wins Bath over and Bath explains that he was turned against Booth by his brother-in-law James. Atkinson tells Booth he is to marry; he will not reveal the woman's name, but Booth is convinced it is Mrs. Ellison. Soon Booth and James become reconciled.

Book 6. When Amelia mentions Mrs. Ellison's prospective marriage, Mrs. Ellison seems horrified that she should marry a sergeant. Mrs. Ellison and Amelia are invited by the lord to a masquerade, and Booth becomes suspicious of the lord's intentions toward Amelia, who herself is always oblivious to any evil intent on the part of anyone. Mrs. Bennet asks Amelia to call on her, and Amelia does so.

Book 7. Mrs. Bennet tells Amelia her story. She was the daughter of a clergyman. On her sixteenth birthday her mother was drowned, and she alienated her father's affection by opposing his remarriage, so she went to live with an aunt. There she met and married a poor young clergyman, Tom Bennet. But this cost her the friendship of her aunt, who had wanted to marry Bennet; and Bennet's debts cost him his place and made them become fugitives. In one lodging they met the lord, Mrs. Ellison's cousin, who seemed to befriend them; but once when Bennet was away, Mrs. Ellison took Mrs. Bennet to a masquerade, at the lord's invitation, and after it Mrs. Bennet drank some drugged wine and under its influence yielded to the lord. Bennet learned of it, hit Mrs. Bennet with a heavy book, and tried to kill himself. He seemed to recover, and forgave Mrs. Bennet, but died not long after. Mrs. Bennet ends her story by saying she believes Amelia is marked by Mrs. Ellison for the same experience. Mrs. Bennet then confesses that she, not Mrs. Ellison, is the new wife of Atkinson. At the end of the interview Atkinson comes in and tells Amelia that Booth has been imprisoned for debt; the complainant is Dr. Harrison.

Book 8. Booth is in prison. Mrs. Atkinson (Mrs. Bennet) befriends Amelia. James calls on Amelia and offers any necessary amount of money, then goes to the jail to bail Booth out, but cannot do so before morning. James is revealed to have designs on Amelia, and tries to get Atkinson to help him. Mrs. Atkinson tells Amelia, who learns that James had no real intention of effecting

Booth's release on bail. But Dr. Harrison arranges for Booth's release.

Book 9. Released from jail, Booth tells Amelia that James has promised to get him a commission and has offered to care for Amelia and the children while Booth is away. Booth praises James so highly that Amelia does not tell him she has contrary suspicions. Amelia is determined to go with Booth and asks Dr. Harrison to help her. He solves the problem by deciding she must visit him in the country while Booth is away.

Book 10. Amelia, in distress, tells Dr. Harrison that James has given Booth tickets to a masquerade for them and Booth insists on going. Mrs. Atkinson comes in and tells Amelia she is sure two women can handle one man. The Booths go to the masquerade, and Booth is disturbed when Amelia remains beside the lord who tried to lure her to a masquerade before. But on their return he finds that Amelia has been at home all evening and that Mrs. Atkinson has been masquerading as her. Booth plays cards and loses £50—far more than he can afford—which his friend Captain TRENT presses on him. While Booth is frantic with worry about the debt, Trent calls on him and Booth gets the impression that Trent is speaking on behalf of the lord, who will lend Booth limitless sums if Booth will make it possible for him to see Amelia. At this time also Amelia receives a letter she thinks is from James, declaring his love for her, but it turns out to be from the lord. The letter promises a commission for Atkinson—which Mrs. Atkinson, posing as Amelia, wheedled from him at the masquerade, for "her friend." Amelia is furious and refuses to be a party to this; they quarrel and Mrs. Atkinson leaves angrily.

Book 11. Col. and Mrs. James have a very intimate talk. She knows he likes Amelia, and for 200 guineas and other concessions she agrees to help him. She advises James not to get Booth a foreign commission (for Amelia would go with him) but a local one, so that Amelia cannot go when Booth is ordered to Scotland for short periods. Trent, who is revealed as being an unscrupulous accomplice of the lord in London, now demands repayment of the £50. Booth is almost driven mad. At this point Booth meets Fanny Matthews, who compels him to have supper alone with her by threatening to tell Amelia of their relationship in prison. Booth does so, and afterwards he is arrested and jailed for debt on Trent's complaint. A messenger delivers a letter to Booth from James that night; Amelia reads it. It is a challenge to a duel, because Booth supped alone with Fanny.

Book 12. Amelia goes to the bailiff's, where Booth is being held. Booth learns from her that she knew all about his affair with Fanny, and had forgiven it without even mentioning it. Dr. Harrison calls on James and prevails on him to withdraw the challenge. He then goes to see Booth; and while he is there, the bailiff asks for a clergyman to hear a dying man's confession. The dying man is Robinson, the card sharp, whom Booth met in the prison so long before. Robinson confesses to Dr. Harrison that he and the lawyer Murphy helped Amelia's sister Elizabeth to forge a new will when Mrs. Harris died, for Mrs. Harris's real will had left everything to Amelia. Dr. Harrison dashes out and with some difficulty has Murphy brought before a magistrate. Amelia is not vengeful toward her sister, but writes to warn her to flee, which Elizabeth does, to France; and Amelia promises to give her an income. James and his lady separate; the lord and Mrs. Ellison both die; Murphy is convicted and hanged; Elizabeth dies of chagrin after three years; and Dr. Harrison and the Booths live happily.

The American

Novel by Henry James, 1843–1916. Published 1877. (RE, 16)

THE AMERICAN belongs to Henry James's earlier period. In it he portrays the old French aristocracy and their attitude toward the rich American. Though often accused of snobbishness in his writing, of too great preoccupation with titles and antiquity of breeding, James in this novel puts his aristocrats in a bad light throughout—and in later years he went even farther and acknowledged a mistake in having had them stick to their principles rather than sell out for American dollars. *The American* is not overlong, about 135,000 words.

Chaps. 1–4. In May 1868 an American, CHRISTOPHER NEWMAN is resting in the Louvre. He sees a pretty little copyist with a boyish coiffure copying a Murillo Madonna, and though he does not speak French he arranges with her to buy the copy when it is finished. She is Mlle. NOÉMIE NIOCHE, and when her father comes for her she arranges for him to teach Newman French. He is a man formerly rich but in reduced circumstances. Then Newman meets an American friend, TRISTRAM, whom he tells how he happens to be there: One day he was on his way to his Wall Street office, where that day he would make $60,000 at someone else's expense. The whole thing suddenly became distasteful to him, he had his carriage drive on, and he retired. In Paris he wishes to meet the best society and find a wife. He begins to see much of the Tristrams. Mrs. Tristram introduces him to young Mme. CLAIRE CINTRÉ, whom she wants him to marry. Claire, a member of one of the most noble families, was married at 18 to a rich old man and is a widow at 25. Newman tries to call on Claire. Her younger brother, Count VALENTIN DE BELLEGARDE, is polite but her older brother, the Marquis URBAIN DE BELLEGARDE, will not let him see her. In his first French lesson, Newman learns from M. Nioche that since there is no dowry for Noémie, he fears she may become a rich man's mistress. Newman offers to supply the desired dowry, 15,000 francs, for six or eight more copies by Noémie. But later, talking to Noémie, he learns that she would not be satisfied with a husband such a dowry would bring, and also that she is an accomplished coquette.

Chaps. 5–10. Mrs. Tristram urges Newman not to be discouraged about Claire, but to "see Europe" and wait. He travels that summer. When he returns Mrs. Tristram tells him that Claire is persecuted by her wicked old mother and Grand Turk of a brother. They want her to marry wealth, for example some old duke. Newman calls on Claire again and this time is received by Claire and her brother Valentin, who is cordial and invites him to come again. A week later Valentin calls on Newman. They see each other often and become friends. Newman tells Valentin he wants to marry Claire. Valentin tells him frankly that an untitled person is not considered good enough for Claire, but he is personally sympathetic and agrees to help. The next day Newman is fortunate enough to see Claire alone. She is friendly but when he speaks of marriage she says she should not remarry and if he wishes to remain welcome he must not speak of it again. He promises, but only for the next six months. Through Valentin, Newman now meets the dowager marquise, Claire's mother, and her brother the marquis and his wife, whom he had met before. The marquis congratulates Newman on having made a fortune but is less pleased at learning that Newman began work at ten, leaving school to do so, and is self-educated. Claire's mother is impressed by Newman's wealth but still not favorable to his marrying Claire.

Chaps. 11–17. Newman introduces Valentin to Noémie. He is invited to dinner at the Bellegardes', with only the family there. He learns that he is accepted as a candidate for the hand of Claire; their decision was difficult, to accept a man of business into the family. That night Newman learns from Valentin that Noémie has left her father's house and is being kept by a man, not Valentin. Newman calls on Claire often in the following weeks. While waiting for Claire one day he meets Mrs. BREAD, an English servant who had come to France 40 years before with Claire's English grandmother. She tells him to be patient in his suit and he has a good chance. At the Bellegardes' he also meets Lord Deepmere, a rich English cousin of Claire's, whom the marquis seems to relish as a rival candidate. After six months Newman proposes, and though Claire cries, she accepts, because she loves him. The Bellegardes accept the decision gracefully and plan a large ball to introduce him to their friends. Newman spends the happiest days of his life. The Bellegardes' party seems successful. At the opera, two days later, Newman sees Noémie with a young man; he discovers that Valentin, despite protestations to the contrary, is disturbed by this and is infatuated with Noémie. Valentin gets into a quarrel with the man beside Noémie, who is a rich brewer's son, Stanislas Kapp, and they are to have a duel in Switzerland.

Chaps. 18–20. Newman calls on Claire the next morning. As he is admitted to the house Mrs. Bread comes to him, hands him a letter from Claire, and says Claire has gone away. On his insistence, Mrs. Bread admits Claire is still in the house and takes him to her. Claire's mother and the marquis are also in the room. Claire tells him she cannot marry him and does not want to see him—because she is ashamed. Her mother has commanded her to give Newman up, and she obeys. She leaves the room and Newman has an angry conversation with the mother and brother. He learns that the ball, which he had thought so successful, confirmed their early belief that they should not accept into their family one of different antecedents. He leaves, telling them he will follow Claire. But a telegram from Valentin, seriously "ill," summons him to Switzerland; he writes Claire a note and leaves for Geneva. There he finds Valentin wounded and dying. He does not intend to tell Valentin of the broken engagement, but Valentin worms the information from him and then tells him to go to Mrs. Bread, who knows about some foul play connected with his father's death. Valentin dies and Newman goes at once to Claire. She cannot explain her reasons, but she will not change her decision and she is going into a convent. He is aghast and pleads with her not to do that, but he cannot sway her.

Chaps. 21–26. Newman goes to see Mrs. Bread. She makes an appointment to see him privately. He then sees Claire's mother and brother and urges them to release Claire and save her from her decision; when they refuse, he tells them he knows they have committed a crime, and he sees they are shaken. He leaves to let them decide and notify him if they will yield. That afternoon a note from the marquis tells him they will not. Mrs. Bread meets Newman and tells him the marquise and marquis actually murdered Claire's father so he could not prevent her marriage to Cintré. She gives him a

deathbed note by the old marquis that affirms this. Mrs. Bread becomes housekeeper for Newman. With Mrs. Tristram's help he receives permission from the abbé, a friend of hers, to see Claire; but Claire will not see him. He shows a copy of the letter to the marquise and marquis and threatens to reveal it to their friends, as his revenge. The marquis calls to try to get the letter; Newman quickly stops any suggestion of money, and the marquis will not withdraw from his position about Claire. Newman calls on a duchess, planning to start with her in making his revelation, but cannot bring himself to do it. He runs into Noémie, who is now with Lord Deepmere, who met her through Valentin. Newman makes a trip to America, travels in England, and finally returns to Paris. Mrs. Tristram has written to him that Claire finally, on her 27th birthday, took the veil. He decides to burn the letter, while at the Tristrams', and drops it into the fireplace, at the same time telling Mrs. Tristram the story of it. She is sure the Bellegardes, after consulting, had simply decided to rely on Newman's good nature, and they were right. This idea makes Newman look to the fireplace, but the paper is wholly consumed.

The Americanization of Edward Bok

Autobiography by Edward Bok, 1863–1930.

Published and © 1920 by Charles Scribner's Sons, New York.

NO FICTION could supply a better inspirational story for boys than this true account of the remarkable rise of a poor immigrant boy to international fame as a journalist. Success was Edward Bok's god; he worshiped it devoutly and served it with unflagging devotion. He permitted himself no human weaknesses; even as a child of seven he was strong. His autobiography was a runaway best-seller and won the Pulitzer Prize in 1921. Except for some personal comments in the closing chapter it is written in the third person, as though it were a biography instead of an autobiography— the method that Henry Adams used. There is no great writing here, but it is good, straightforward journalistic prose befitting an editor who was a pioneer in creating the mass magazine.

Chaps. 1–2. The Bok family emigrated to the United States in 1870: the father, 42 years old; the mother; the elder son, William, 8½; and Edward William Bok, almost 7, later known simply as Edward Bok. They had been prosperous at home, then had lost all their money by unwise investments. They settled in Brooklyn. The boys, though they knew no English, were sent to the public school at once. The other children teased them until Edward fought and trounced the ringleader. That same first year Edward was beaten by his teacher because he would not write the fancy Spencerian script then taught, which he did not consider practical; the principal of the school later agreed with him and a simpler method was substituted. Edward's father did not flourish and Edward devised ways of making money: Washing a baker's windows at 50 cents a week; then acting as salesclerk in the bakery for another dollar; delivering newspapers; and even selling ice water on the horse-cars, at a cent a glass. Then he went to a party, and afterward he wrote it up and took the account to the Brooklyn *Eagle,* where he was promptly offered a job reporting such parties at $3 a column. At 13 he left school and became an office boy for Western Union, at $6.25 a week.

Chaps. 3–6. Hungry for education, Edward saved until he could buy a set of Appleton's Encyclopedia. He got the idea of writing to famous men, asking them questions. He was amazed when the greatest men answered promptly and fully: President Garfield, Generals Grant, Sherman, and Early, Longfellow and Whittier and Tennyson and many others. Then Edward began to call on the personages with whom he had correspondence, when they were in New York. His reception was amazing, including the time the Grants had him to dinner and Jefferson Davis got him an autograph letter from each member of the Confederate cabinet. One day, noticing one of the pictures of actresses that were packed in cigarette boxes, Edward went to the printers and suggested a brief biography on the back of each picture. One hundred biographies were ordered from him at $10 each, then another hundred and another, until he had five writers supplying them to him at $5, while he edited and sold them. He decided to learn stenography, and through that was assigned to report a speech by President Hayes. He impressed the President and Mrs. Hayes because he had the wineglasses removed from his place at the banquet table, and that created a friendship that lasted for years. He made a pilgrimage to Boston and was cordially received by Holmes, Longfellow, Emerson, Miss Alcott, and others. He was 16 years old.

Chaps. 7–14. Edward's father died when Edward was 18, so Edward and his brother had the household to support. Edward, noting how unwieldly and ugly theater programs were, offered to supply them free to theaters in exchange for the exclusive rights. He took a friend (FREDERIC L. COLVER) as his partner and they prospered, selling advertising and supplying the kind of program that is used today. They expanded, founding *The Brooklyn Magazine,* to which so many of Edward's famous friends (including President Hayes) contributed that the public was amazed. Edward still worked for Western Union, where he had become a protegé of Clarence Cary, the company counsel, and often he took stenography from Jay Gould, who controlled the company. By following what Gould did, he plunged in Wall Street and multiplied his small investment. Gould wanted him to come to Wall Street, but Edward preferred editing; and besides, his one experience had been so nervewracking that he never again speculated in stocks. Edward next became a stenographer for Henry Holt's publishing firm and also started syndicating newspaper articles by Henry Ward Beecher. This led to a long, close association with Beecher. With his brother, Edward expanded the Bok syndicate with a woman's page and later a literary article. Edward was now 21. He left Holt and went to Scribner's publishing house, still as a stenographer. He learned much about the publishing business and he worked very hard, which was noticed and rewarded. He was moved into the advertising department. He continued his outside writing, including his literary letter, which now appeared in 45 newspapers. Cyrus H. K. Curtis, seeking a new editor for *The Ladies' Home Journal* (which Mrs. Curtis was then editing, but unwillingly), was impressed by the literary letter and offered the job to Bok. The decision was a difficult one, but Bok finally decided to accept and move to Philadelphia. On Oct. 20, 1889, aged 26, he became the new editor.

Chaps. 15–20. There is nothing to the popular notion that the editor of a woman's magazine should be a woman, not a man. Bok planned a department of confidential talks to women, answering their personal questions, and wrote the first ones himself. They were so successful that there was a mass of letters, which his mother looked at first and told him he had no right to read; soon he found a capable woman author for the department. While the *Journal* was already very successful when he took over, with a circulation of 440,000, he increased it rapidly and made it the first magazine to pass the million point. Curtis worked with him almost as father and son (as they later became) and supported him with a great deal of advertising to build circulation. He had many interesting experiences with famous writers and with famous men whom he prevailed upon to write for him—including President Benjamin Harrison, who made him smoke his first cigar (which made him sick). Bok paid high prices when necessary —$10,000 for William Dean Howell's autobiography (and Curtis spent $50,000 advertising it); $15,000 for Harrison's 12 articles. Bok published a book on his autograph collection. He pleased Frances Willard by cutting out nearly all references to drinking; and in all ways he was careful not to publish anything thought improper for children. On a trip to England, though his

old friend Kipling and others received him well, he met some reverses; C. L. Dodgson would not even admit he was Lewis Carroll, and Florence Nightingale would not see Bok at all.

Chaps. 21–32. At Bok's suggestion, Curtis bought the magazine *Country Life;* but he also bought *The Saturday Evening Post* and decided to put all his new effort into it, so Bok gave *Country Life* to Frank Doubleday, his old friend at school and at Scribner's. Bok used his magazine to improve American taste in art and architecture, employing the best artists and architects, publishing designs for houses and interiors, and publishing reproductions of great art masterpieces. In 1896 Bok married Mary Louise Curtis, daughter of Cyrus Curtis, after an engagement of four years. In 1906 he persuaded President Roosevelt to let an interview with him on matters of current interest be published each month; they were called "the shaving interviews" because Roosevelt jokingly said the only spare time he had was while shaving. Later Roosevelt wrote a series of anonymous articles for the *Journal,* addressed to men. All this time Bok had maintained the syndicate in New York and his weekly literary letter, but now he was too busy and discontinued them. He became interested in women's clubs and woman suffrage, and worked on ending the

abuses of patent medicines (whose advertising the *Journal* had stopped accepting in 1892). He started an educational campaign for good music and supported the Philadelphia orchestra.

Chaps. 33–39. Bok wanted to buy the *Century Magazine* for himself, put in another editor, and supervise it; but Curtis talked him out of it. Bok comments on the fact that the greatest writers and men— Kipling, Mark Twain, Roosevelt, Woodrow Wilson—never objected to having their work edited or even rejected. His previous dealings with Wilson gave him some advance warning of the U.S. entry into World War I and he made the *Journal* the semi-official mouthpiece of the various government war-work bodies, for example in support of the Liberty Loan drives, war thrift, and aid to Belgium. Bok visited the battlefronts late in 1918. On his way back he decided to retire in 1919, at the end of 30 years as editor. His last issue set a record, the first magazine to pass two million circulation. He closes with general comments on success. In some ways he criticizes America—its emphasis on quantity and speed rather than quality. He was never able to give an American writer an assignment calling for long, faithful research. But he owes a great deal to America, the greatest land of opportunity, idealism, and fair play.

An American Tragedy

Novel by Theodore Dreiser, 1871–1945.
Published 1925. © 1925, 1953 by Mrs. Theodore Dreiser. Published by The World Publishing Co., Cleveland. (ML, G80)

THIS IS GENERALLY considered Dreiser's greatest work, but perhaps because of its length—it is a *very* long book, originally published in two volumes—or because of its unremitting pessimism, it was not as popular with the book-buying public as were other great American novels of its decade. *An American Tragedy* did not shock readers as Dreiser's earlier works did. Readers were almost beyond shock by 1925. The themes are social and economic inequality and man's helplessness before the force of circumstances.

Book I. Chaps. 1–6. CLYDE GRIFFITHS is the son of two evangelists who run shabby missions and sing hymns on the street with their eldest daughter, ESTA, as organist. Clyde hates the life they lead and is a solitary child. He is ashamed to take friends home to the dreary place where the family lives behind the mission. Poverty and constant moving hinder the education of the children, and Clyde is only about 14 years old when he realizes that he has no trade and no apparent opportunity to acquire one. At 15 he obtains a job in a soda shop, working there for a while at five dollars a week, and

then he transfers to a better job as a bellhop in a large hotel. This gives him his first glimpse of what seems to him the height of luxury. He sees young people enjoying themselves at parties, travelers from all parts of the country, glamorous women who wear jewels and paint their lips. To live in luxury of this kind becomes Clyde's dream of his own future.

Chaps. 7–16. Working at the hotel does more than make Clyde aware of luxuries and a way of living that are new to him. His clothes are now of better quality. He puts hair-cream on his hair, he drinks hard liquor, he goes out with women who are willing to exchange a kiss for a small gift and more than a kiss for a larger gift. He is particularly fascinated by HORTENSE BRIGGS. In the course of four months during which he hopefully woos Hortense, his sister Esta, who had run away with an actor who promised to marry her, returns to town, abandoned and pregnant. Mrs. Griffiths asks Clyde if he can lend her a hundred dollars— which he afterwards learns was to help Esta. However, at this time Clyde is far more interested in buying an expensive coat for Hortense, believing that she will give herself to him if he does so, and evades making the loan.

Chaps. 17–19. A group of bellhops and their girls with whom Clyde often goes out on parties decides to undertake an automobile trip out of town. The day is a great success for the most part, but Clyde becomes jealous of the manner in which Hortense flirts with the other men on the party. On

Clyde and Roberta's outing

the way home, in a borrowed Packard, they suddenly realize that it is later than they had realized, and the driver starts to put on speed. If they are late in arriving at the hotel for duty, they will all be discharged. He drives faster and faster, and at one point suddenly a small girl runs out at a corner and the car hits her. Rather than stop to be questioned, the driver puts on more speed, and there ensues a wild chase by the police, which the Packard eventually succeeds in outdistancing. Careening along the snowy road, the driver finally takes one too many chances, and the borrowed car is wrecked. Hastily, all the occupants leap out and run from the site of the accident. Clyde Griffiths leaps out with the others and hides himself by crawling on hands and knees in the snow to escape. He is successful.

Book II. Chaps. 1–4. After his escape from the scene of the accident, Clyde moves from place to place in menial jobs, under a false name, and for three years fears the police. After many moves, Clyde reaches Chicago and there encounters another of the boys who had been in the accident; he obtains a job for Clyde in the Great Northern Hotel. From there Clyde transfers to the Union League Club, where one day he meets his father's brother, SAMUEL GRIFFITHS, a rich collar-manufacturer from Lycurgus, New York. His uncle gives him a job in the factory, and Clyde is started on a new kind of life. GILBERT, Samuel's son, is instantly jealous and unfriendly—for several reasons. Clyde bears a strong family resemblance to him, and is a relative. Up to now, Gilbert has been the unquestioned heir to all the important parts of his father's estate. Clyde settles himself quietly and unobtrusively in town.

Chaps. 5–14. The people Clyde meets are impressed by the fact that his name is Griffiths. He meets many people and is treated almost like visiting royalty. Some of the girls he meets are attractive to him, but he is doubtful about entering into any intimate relationship with them, because he must keep an eye on his future. When a dinner invitation to the Griffiths house arrives, and he attends, he meets the type of girl whom he knows is acceptable in the social circle to which he wishes to belong. SONDRA FINCHLEY excites and attracts Clyde as no young woman has before. Soon Clyde is given a promotion, and a position of some responsibility in the firm, against Gilbert's opposition. Clyde acquires a new dignity, as well as higher pay. The new job is demanding, because of his total inexperience, but he is proceeding with a reasonable degree of success when he meets ROBERTA

ALDEN, a young woman of a middle-class, respectable background, whom Clyde hires to work in the shop. Orders are stern that no executive or foreman may mix socially with any of the female employees, but Clyde meets Roberta secretly and falls in love with her. She is in love with him.

Chaps. 15–21. Day after day for some months, Roberta and Clyde meet surreptitiously. On several occasions they are seen together, but fortunately not by persons who could identify Clyde as a foreman at the shop. Still Roberta does not bring herself to yield fully to Clyde, in spite of his earnest pleas, and in spite of the fact that she loves him deeply. It is only when Clyde declares that he is going to stop seeing her that Roberta capitulates. Their joyous and yet frighteningly guilty relationship terrifies Roberta, even while her love overwhelms her. At first both are ecstatically happy. The problem of Sondra Finchley re-enters Clyde's thinking very soon. Her social position and her beauty have an irresistible appeal for Clyde, and he envisions her as his wife—an eminently suitable and lovely wife. His fascination for Sondra is sufficient to make him break more and more engagements with Roberta.

Chaps. 22–33. The social life of Clyde becomes more and more pleasurable, and he finds more reasons weekly for spending time with his friends of the higher echelons. Roberta is aware that he is seeing other girls—she even sees notes about him in the society columns. After a vacation away from town, Roberta finds Clyde more remote than ever. He is absorbed with Sondra. Marriage into the Finchley family will secure his future. When Roberta at length informs him that she is pregnant, he is helpless and at a loss.

Chaps. 34–42. Clyde knows nothing of what may or can be done in such cases. He visits a drug store and obtains pills, which produce no effect. Roberta visits a doctor and is advised to bear the child. Clyde meanwhile has become more and more deeply involved with Sondra, and his desperation increases day by day. Even Roberta's offer to marry him and then allow him to leave her makes no impression. All he can think of is the irremediable damage to his prospects for a marriage with Sondra if the scandal of Roberta and her pregnancy should become known. Wild thoughts go through his head —and a newspaper item about a drowning accident strikes him with horror, as he con-

siders the implications and possibilities. To kill—to murder! The thought is abhorrent and terrifying. But the longer he thinks of it, the more inevitable it seems.

Chaps. 43–47. Clyde's plans are made. He persuades Roberta to go away with him to a resort at a lake, allowing her to think that they will remain together for a time. His plans are carefully laid. He knows that he can upset the boat in which he plans to take her out, and that she will drown if he does not make any effort to save her. His confusion and inner turmoil are such that he believes that she is driving him to this terrible deed. Carefully, he plans the trip. They must go separately to the train, sit in different parts of the coach, remain completely aloof from each other so that there will be no association of memories with them together. Roberta is unsuspicious, and indescribably happy. She sees him and pretends no recognition in the railroad station —on the train—none until they reach their destination, where Clyde will marry her, and everything will be all right. Clyde plans to take her out in a boat after they have registered under an assumed name. After interminable delays and interruptions in the sequence of events, they are at last on the water. Roberta is happy, and Clyde is steeling himself for the work he must do. The spell of quiet waters reaches his mind, and he realizes that he cannot kill her. He need only step abruptly on one side of the boat— or rock it violently—or push her slightly— No! He cannot do it.

The strange, iron expression on his face and the position of his body, tense and stiff, frighten Roberta, and she cries out to him and moves toward him, trying to put aside the camera tripod Clyde is carrying. Quite accidentally, the camera hits her and what Clyde had been steeling himself to do is done by a freak of fate. He sees her floundering in the water as the boat becomes overbalanced and he too falls in.

Book III. Chaps. 48–60. Clyde goes back alone; but foul play is suspected and Clyde is found from letters Roberta had. The circumstantial evidence against him is overwhelming. Despite good defense by a lawyer —hired by Clyde's uncle—who tells the jury Clyde was weak but not a murderer, Clyde is found guilty and sentenced to electrocution. He is in the death house at Auburn Prison for more than a year while appeals on his behalf fail one by one. He suffers most because he has heard nothing from Sondra. His mother visits him. One of the worst features is the open cells in the death house, so that the convicted murderers come to know one another and suffer as each in his turn is led away to die. At last, after a year, a note reaches him—unsigned and in disguised handwriting, but he knows it is from Sondra. She says she still cannot understand, but is not without sorrow and sympathy. It is worse than nothing for him. Finally in winter the day comes; the chaplain reads from the Bible; Clyde exchanges goodbyes with the other prisoners and shuffles on toward the last door.

Aesop
6th Century B.C.

George Gordon, Lord Byron
1788–1824

Amphitryon

Play by Plautus, 254–184 B.C.
Written about 200 B.C. Outline based on
translation by Sir Robert Allison.

WHEN THE FRENCH playwright Jean
Giraudoux wrote a modern version, in
1937, of the old story of Amphitryon
and how Jupiter became father of Alcmena's miraculous son Hercules, he
called it *Amphitryon 38.* There may
not have been quite thirty-seven versions before, but Giraudoux cannot
have been far from the mark. Before
Plautus's classic Roman rendition the
story had occupied Greek dramatists
including Euripides, and outstanding
among later versions are Molière's in
1668 and Dryden's in 1690. Molière
introduced a new and welcome character, Cleanthus, to be Sosia's shrewish
wife; he also gave Sosia the best lines
and played the rôle himself. Dryden's
script was frowned upon by later critics as being unduly coarse, but so was
all English drama in his day. ❨ Giraudoux took the most liberties with the
original story—or used his imagination
best. His No. 38, when produced on
Broadway in its English translation by
S. N. Behrman and with Alfred Lunt
as Jupiter and Lynn Fontanne as Alcmena, was a smash hit. The story's
vitality seems to be endless and every
version is well worth reading. The following outline follows the Plautus
treatment, the simplest.

Prologue. MERCURY, on a street in
Thebes before the house of AMPHITRYON,
general of the Theban army (the scene
throughout the play), gives the theme:
Amphitryon went to war, leaving his wife
ALCMENA pregnant. Mercury's father JUP-
ITER disguised himself as Amphitryon and
has been living with Alcmena; he has made
her doubly pregnant. Mercury has disguised
himself as SOSIA, Amphitryon's slave. But
today the real Amphitryon and Sosia are
due back.

Act I. 1. Sosia enters. Before he notices
the presence of Mercury, he talks about how
Amphitryon, having won a great victory,
has sent him ahead from the ship to prepare
Alcmena for her lord's arrival. Mercury
and Sosia talk; Mercury convinces him that
he, Mercury, is actually Sosia. Sosia, bewildered at the loss of his identity, returns
to the harbor. **2.** Mercury, alone, muses on
the fact that Alcmena will that day give
birth to two sons: Amphitryon's a ten-
month baby, and Jupiter's a seven-month
baby. **3.** Jupiter (disguised as Amphitryon)
and Alcmena come out of the house. Mercury retires but listens. Alcmena complains
because her supposed husband is leaving
after so short a visit. Jupiter pacifies her
and promises to return soon. Mercury butts
in with arguments to support Jupiter but is
rebuffed.

Act II. 1. Amphitryon and Sosia come in;
Sosia is trying to convince Amphitryon
that there is really another Sosia, but
Amphitryon is sure he is drunk or a liar. **2.**
Alcmena enters, not seeing them, and speaks
of her love for Amphitryon; pleased, he reveals himself. But then there is complete
confusion because she cannot understand his
pretending not to have seen her earlier, and
he cannot understand the purpose of her
statements—or how she knows things (told
to her by Jupiter) that no one but he could
have told her. She produces a gold cup given
him by King Pterela as a reward of victory,
and (she says) given to her by him; he has
Sosia open the sealed container for the cup
and it has vanished. Amphitryon concludes
she is bewitched. He is especially appalled
to learn that the substitute husband has
been sharing her bed. He proposes to bring
proof of his absence and then divorce her.

Act III. 1. Jupiter announces his intention of helping Alcmena. **2.** Alcmena comes
from the house, planning to leave rather
than be unjustly accused. Jupiter, as Amphitryon, asks forgiveness. **3.** Sosia enters and
Jupiter sends him to the ship to bring back
the pilot, Blepharo, from the ship. Alcmena
goes inside. Jupiter summons Mercury to
keep the real Amphitryon out of the house.
4. Mercury returns to do Jupiter's bidding.

Act IV. 1. Amphitryon enters, finds the
door locked, and knocks. **2.** Mercury, as
Sosia, appears on the roof of the house and
insults Amphitryon in a very unslavelike
way. [Here the manuscript is lost, but in
this scene or scenes the true and false Amphitryon confront one another. Blepharo
cannot tell which is which.] Alcmena's time
comes and she goes into the house. Jupiter,
still maintaining he is Amphitryon, goes in
to join her; Amphitryon plans to complain
to the king against the "sorcerer" but Jupiter
knocks him senseless with a thunderbolt.

Act V. 1. BROMIA, Alcmena's maid,
comes from the house; Alcmena has just
had twin sons. Amphitryon recovers consciousness. Bromia assures him she recognizes him. She tells him of the twin
birth, and how one of the babies, when
two snakes attacked the cradle, leaped out
and strangled one with each hand. Then
Jupiter reveals himself and says this is his
son, the other Amphitryon's. Amphitryon,
hearing this, is satisfied. **2–3.** Jupiter appears, confirms the report, and commends
Alcmena as a faithful wife. Amphitryon
goes into the house.

Mercury, posing as the slave Sosia, insults Amphitryon from the rooftop

The Anatomy of Melancholy

Treatise by Robert Burton, 1576–1640. Published in 1628. Edition edited and © 1927, 1955 by Floyd Dell and Paul Jordan-Smith, published by Rinehart & Co., New York.

FEW BOOKS HAVE HAD greater influence on English literature than this, the masterpiece of a well-born Oxonian clergyman of the Church of England. Robert Burton probably started out to write a quasi-medical treatise; but, a man enormously well-read, he finished by delving into nearly every phase of human thought and behavior in more than half a million remarkably cogent and readable words, copiously sprinkled with quotations from the (chiefly Latin) classics and allusions to history, legend, and literature that summed man's knowledge. The editors (Dell and Jordan-Smith) of the edition used here have opined that in this Freudian age the book would be called *An Analysis of Morbid Psychology.* ❡ The book, signed "by Democritus Junior" in tribute to the most rational of the ancient Greek philosophers (incidentally, the one who first conceived of the atom), was a best-seller of its time and remained for two centuries a chief inspiration of English writers, vying with the Holy Bible and Spenser's *Faerie Queen* in their affections. Byron called it more rewarding than any twenty other books he knew; Dr. Johnson said it was the only book he would rise two hours early to read; the book inspired Sterne in *Tristram Shandy,* Fielding in *Tom Jones,* Lamb and Keats and perhaps even Milton (*Il Penseroso*). ❡ Burton organized his material thoroughly. The work was divided into three *Partitions.* Each Partition was divided into *Sections,* each Section into *Members,* each Member into *Subsections;* and he prefaced each of the three Partitions with a Synopsis.

1ST PARTITION: MELANCHOLY

Sec. I. Memb. I. In diseases consider: **1,** their causes; they may be *impulsive* (sin, concupiscence, etc.) or *instrumental* (intemperance, all second causes, etc.). **2–5,** their definition and classification. Of the body there are 300 diseases [Pliny's count]; they are *epidemical* (plague, plica, etc.) or *particular* (gout, dropsy, etc.). Diseases of the mind or head may be in *disposition,* as all perturbations, evil affection, etc.; or *habits,* as dotage, frenzy, madness, ecstasy, lycanthropia, chorus sancti viti, hydrophobia, possession or obsession of devils, and Melancholy. Temporary melancholy afflicts everyone; it comes and goes on every occasion of sorrow, need, sickness, trouble, fear, etc. But the melancholy of which we will treat is a habit, a serious ailment, a chronic disease.

Memb. II. 1–11. First a disgression on anatomy. The body has parts, contained as *humors* (blood, phlegm, etc.) and *spirits* (natural, from the liver; vital, from the heart; and animal, from the brain). The *similar* parts of the body are flesh, bones, nerves, arteries, etc; the *dissimilar* or organic parts may be outward, as the face, buttocks, joints, etc., or inward, as the heart, brain, liver. There are also the soul and her faculties: vegetal, sensible, and rational. The vegetal faculty includes nutrition, generation, etc.; the sensible faculty includes the five senses plus the inner senses (common sense, fantasy, memory); and the rational faculty includes understanding and the exercise of the will.

Memb. III. 1. Melancholy is defined as a kind of dotage, or anguish of the mind, without a fever and without any apparent cause. **2.** Various parts of the body may be affected, as by hypochondriacal, or windy melancholy (gas in the stomach), or the whole body; or it may be indefinite, as love-melancholy. **3–4.** It may be natural or unnatural.

Sec. II. Causes of Melancholy. Memb. I. 1–4. The causes may be *supernatural,* proceeding directly from God or the devil, or caused by magicians, witches, the stars, etc. **5–6.** *Natural* causes include old age; heredity (it being inherited from parents); and outward causes discussed in the following Members.

Memb. II. 1–3. Bad diet is a cause, either in *substance* (the kind of food eaten), *quality* of food eaten, or *quantity* of food eaten. **4.** Retention and evacuation, including sweating, Venus in excess, phlebotomy (blood-letting), etc., are causes; also: **5.** Bad air. **6.** Immoderate exercise; solitariness; idleness. **7.** Sleeping overmuch, overlittle, etc.

Memb. III. 1–3. How passions and perturbations of the mind cause melancholy; the force of imagination. *Irascible* causes are: **4.** Sorrow. **5.** Fear. **6.** Shame, repulse, disgrace. **7–9.** Envy, malice; ambition, hatred; anger. **10.** Discontents, cares, miseries, etc. *Concupiscible* causes are: **11–12,** Vehement desires; covetousness. **13.** Love of pleasures, gaming in excess, etc. **14.** Pride, vainglory, etc. **15.** Love of learning; why scholars are melancholy.

Memb. IV. Non-necessary causes of melancholy. 1. It can begin with the child's nurse. **2.** Education is a cause of melancholy as is lack of education. Others are: **3.** Terrors and affrights. **4.** Scoffs, calumnies, bitter jests (directed at one). **5.** Loss of liberty, servitude, imprisonment. **6.** Poverty and want. **7.** A heap of other accidents, such as death of friends, loss of goods, and such things as cause sorrow, fear, curiosity.

Memb. V. 1. Indirect causes of melancholy; how the body works on the mind. **2–4.** Effect of particular diseases, as of the brain, heart, spleen, liver, stomach, etc.; also effects of a hot sun, a blow on the head, etc. **5–6.** Possible causes of hypochondriacal melancholy; effect of the whole body.

Sec. III. Symptoms of Melancholy. Memb. I. 1. General symptoms include those of the body, such as ill digestion, thick blood, much waking, etc.; or **2.** Those of the mind, as fear and sorrow without a just cause, suspicion, jealousy, restless thoughts, vain imaginations, etc. **3.** Influences of the stars, parts of the body, etc. **4.** Symptoms applying to particular individuals, according to their education, custom, condition, etc.: ambitious, thinks himself a king, a lord, etc.; covetous, runs on his money; lascivious on his mistress; religious, has revelations, is a Prophet; a scholar on his book; etc.

Memb. II. 1. Symptoms of head melancholy: heaviness of the head, fixed and hollow eyes, etc. **2.** Symptoms of windy hypochondriacal melancholy: belching, wind and rumbling, vehement griping. **3.** Symptoms abounding in the whole body. **4.** Maids', nuns' and widows' melancholy; similar symptoms in males, as monks and friars.

Memb. III. Causes of these symptoms: Why they are so fearful, sad, suspicious without a cause; why solitary; why melancholy men are witty; why they suppose they hear and see strange voices, visions, apparitions. Why they prophesy and speak strange languages, whence comes their rumbling, convulsions, fearful dreams. etc.

Sec. IV. Prognostics of Melancholy. Memb. I. Melancholy can be cured if not hereditary. If it can get out, as in scabs, leprosy, morphew, it can be cured. But inveterate melancholy is incurable; if cold it often degenerates into epilepsy, apoplexy, dotage, or blindness, and if hot into madness, despair, and violent death. The diseases of the mind are more grievous than those of the body. Is it lawful for a man suffering from melancholy to offer violence to himself? No.

2ND PARTITION: THE CURE OF MELANCHOLY

Sec. I. Membs. I–III. Unlawful means of cure are from the devil, witches, magicians, etc., by charms, incantations, etc. It is held that they can effect a cure but it is better to endure misery than to forfeit one's soul. Lawful means is by recourse to God, through prayer, etc. Can saints, reliques, etc., effect a cure, and is it lawful to sue to them for aid? No, the intercession of Christ Himself should be sought by prayer. **Memb. IV. 1–3.** Lawful also is a cure by Nature, which works through the physician, who must have science, confidence, honesty, etc.; the patient, who must have obedience, constancy, patience, confidence, etc.; and physick or medicine, which may be dietetical, pharmaceutical, or surgical.

Sect. II. Dietetical Cures. Memb. I. 1. The diet should be rectified first in *substance,* or the nature of what is eaten; recommended are such meats as are easy of digestion, well-dressed, hot, young, moist, nourishing, etc; bread of pure wheat, well baked; water clear from the fountain; wine and drink not too strong. **2.** In *quantity:* eat at seasonable and usual times of repast, sparing, not overmuch of one dish.

Memb. II. Rectification of retention and evacuation, as costiveness (constipation), Venery, bleeding at nose, months (menstruation) stopped, etc.

Memb. III. Air rectified, naturally by choice of our dwelling place (to be hot, moist, light, wholesome, etc.), and artificially by frequent change of air, opening windows, avoiding winds, fogs, perfumes, etc.

Memb. IV. Exercise: of body, but moderately, by hunting, riding, bowling, fishing, walking, tennis, etc.; of mind, by chess, cards, seeing plays, reading, serious studies, all honest recreations.

Memb. V. Rectify waking and terrible dreams by sleep: The proper time is two or three hours after supper, lying on the side, not the back; seven or eight hours are a competent time.

Memb. VI. 1-2. Passions and perturbations of the mind to be rectified by resisting to the utmost, confessing grief to a friend, seeking counsel from friends. **3.** Music is a remedy. **4.** Mirth and merry companions are a remedy, but not to the neglect of business or duty—or one might as well be melancholy.

Sec. II. Membs. I-VIII. A consolatory digression, containing remedies to all discontents and passions of the mind. The redeeming features of: I. General discontents and grievances. II. Deformity of body, sickness, baseness of birth, etc. III. Poverty and want. IV. Servitude, loss of liberty, banishment. V. Sorrows for the death of friends, vain fears, etc. VI. Envy, hatred, malice, ambition, self-love, etc. VII. Abuses, injuries, contempts, slanders, etc. VIII. All other symptoms of the disease melancholy.

Sec. IV. Pharmaceutics, or curing with medicines. **Membs. I & II** contain listing and discussion of drugs and pharmaceuticals of many kinds. **Memb. III** discusses chirurgical physick (surgery): phlebotomy or blood-letting, with knife or leeches; cupping-glasses; cauteries, and searing with hot irons; borings and lancings.

Sec. V. Cure of Head Melancholy. **Memb. I. 1.** Moderate diet, good air, sleep more than ordinary, void excrements daily, exercise. **2.** Blood-letting if need be. **3.** Preparatives and purgers, with recipes for compounds. **4.** Averters. **5.** Cordials and various drugs. **6.** Various drugs, including those to produce sleep; to prevent terrible dreams, do not sup late and do not eat peas, cabbage,

venison, or meats hard to digest.

Memb. II. Cure of melancholy of the body. Diet and various medicines as before; phlebotomy more necessary and more frequent; certain specific drugs to correct and cleanse the blood.

Memb. III. Cure of hydrochondriacal or windy melancholy. **1.** Diet, medicines, etc. as before but not so vehement; drugs to provoke urine; use treacle now and then in winter; vomit after meals sometimes. **2.** Drugs to expel wind.

3RD PARTITION: LOVE-MELANCHOLY

Sec. I. Memb. I. 1. Preface or introduction: Love's definition, pedigree, object: fair, amiable, gracious, and pleasant, from which come beauty, grace, which all desire and love; parts affected. **2.** Division or kinds of love: It is *natural,* in things without life, and *sensible* (felt) in living things, for pleasure, preservation of kind, mutual advantage, custom, etc. Love is Desire, or enjoyment of the fruits of desire; this may be either virtue or vice. A second kind of love is heroical love, religious love, etc. A third kind is rational love, or intellectual love. God is love itself, the fountain of love.

Memb. II. 1-3. Man's love. Love is profitable, bringing health, wealth, and honor. Pleasant and honest objects of love: beauty, art; men themselves, as friends, children, kinsmen; virtue, learning, eloquence, etc.

Memb. III. Charity is composed of all three kinds: pleasant, profitable, honest.

Sec. II. Memb. I. 1. Heroical love causing melancholy. **2.** How it tyrannizes men. Love that causes melancholy is immoderate. It cannot be satisfied by marriage or apply to one object.

Memb. II. Causes: **1.** Stars; temperature; full diet; place, country, clime, condition, idleness. **2.** Natural allurements as causes of love: Beauty, grace, resulting from parts such as face, hair, hands, etc. **3.** Artificial allurements, provocations of lust and love: Gestures, apparel, dowry, money, etc. Does beauty owe more to art or nature? **4.** Opportunity of time and place; music, singing, dancing; amorous tales, lascivious objects, familiarity, gifts, promises, etc. **5.** Bawds and philters.

Memb. II. Symptoms and signs, of body and mind. Dryness, paleness, leanness, waking, sighing, etc. Bad effects, as fear, sorrow, suspicion, anxiety, etc.; dotage, slavery, neglect of business. Good effects, as spruceness, courage, music, singing, poetry, etc.

Memb. IV. Prognostics: Despair, madness, frenzy, death.

Memb. V. Cures: **1.** By labor, diet, medicine, abstinence. **2.** To withstand the beginnings, avoid occasions; fair and foul means; change of place, contrary passion. **3.** Cure by good counsel. **4.** Cure by philters; magical and poetical cures. **5.** Whether to let lovers have their desire. Reasons for removing impediments. Arguments for and against marriage.

Sec. III. Jealousy. **Memb. I. 1.** Definition: Jealousy is eager desire to enjoy some beauty alone, and a fear of sharing it. Jealousy is improper to many beasts, as swans, cocks, bulls; to kings and princes, as applied to their subjects or successors; to friends, parents, tutors over children. It is proper to bachelors and husbands, before and after marriage, but is an intolerable burden. **2.** Causes in the parties themselves: Idleness, impotency, long absence; unkindness, wantonness, inequality of years or fortunes. Outward enticements and provocations of others.

Memb. II. Symptoms: Fear, sorrow, suspicion, anguish of mind; strange actions, gestures, looks, speeches. Laws and other means of preventing jealousy or insuring chastity.

Memb. III. Prognostics: Despair, madness; the killing of oneself or others.

Memb. IV. Cures: **1.** By avoiding occasions; by not being idle; by good counsel. **2.** Preventions before marriage; marry one equal in years, fortune, beauty, family, etc., and use them well.

Sec. IV. Religious melancholy. **Memb. I. 1.** A proof that there is such a species of melancholy (though some may disagree), the object of love being God. How this allures. Excessive religious love. **2.** Causes: The devil's allurements; false miracles. Politicians, to keep men in obedience. Simplicity, fear, ignorance, solitariness, curiosity, pride. **3.** Symptoms: Zeal without knowledge; obstinacy, superstition, strange devotion, stupidity, stiff defense of their tenets, mutual love and hate of other sects, belief in incredibilities, impossibilities. Fasting, sacrifices, oblations, prayers, vows, pseudo-martyrdom, mad and ridiculous customs. Visions, revelations, dreams, prophecies, new doctrines, etc. **4.** Prognostics: New doctrines, paradoxes, blasphemies, madness, stupidity, despair, damnation. **5.** Cures: By conference, good counsel, persuasion; by correction or punishment.

Memb. II. Religious melancholy in defect (too little religious love). **1.** Who is affected: Epicures, atheists, magicians, hypocrites; such as have cauterized consciences or are in a reprobate state; some philosophers; impenitent sinners, etc. **2.** Causes: The devil and his allurements; rigid preachers that wound the conscience; melancholy, contemplation, solitariness. Distrust, weakness of faith; guilty conscience; misunderstanding Scripture. **3.** Symptoms: Fear, sorrow, anguish of mind, extreme tortures and horror of conscience, fearful dreams, illusions, visions, etc. **4.** Prognostics: Blasphemy, violent death. **5.** Cures: Conference; not to be idle or alone. Good counsel, good company, all comforts and contents.

Andersen's Fairy Tales

Stories by Hans Christian Andersen, 1805–1875.

Published in several volumes, beginning in 1835.

ANDERSEN'S FAIRY TALES are too familiar and too classic to demand comment. He represented them at first as being folk tales remembered from his childhood, and no doubt some of them were; but at the peak of his output Andersen was producing a volume a year and that makes too many to remember. Besides, some—such as *The Snow Queen*—were built up from stories so bare that the telling might requie a paragraph. All the rest was Andersen's invention, for which he had an incomparable gift. ❡ Of the stories that follow, two—"The Ugly Duckling" and "The Emperor's New Clothes"—have become proverbial. *The Snow Queen,* a play, is often performed by children's groups.

THE LITTLE MERMAID

The little mermaid of this story is the youngest of five sisters, living in the palace of the king, their father, and she waits impatiently for her fifteenth birthday, when she may go up to the surface and see the land of mortals. She knows that men die if they sink below the waves, and she knows that mortals have two strange-looking things upon which they move about on the land, instead of a graceful fishtail. She does not know the word "legs" because mermaids have no word for them. At last her fifteenth birthday comes and she swims to the surface, where she sees a brightly-lighted ship on which the people are having a party in honor of a young prince's birthday. When she sees the prince, she immediately falls in love with him.

Suddenly a dreadful storm comes up, and the ship is wrecked. She realizes that the prince will die in the water, and swims until she finds him. He is almost drowned, but she carries him safely to shore. He is unconscious, however, and does not know who has saved him.

Afterward, she is unhappy in her underwater home and wants to go to the prince, but she realizes that first she must exchange her fishtail for the legs of a mortal. An old witch mermaid agrees to perform the necessary magic, in exchange for the mermaid's lovely voice, but she warns that the new legs and feet will always hurt terribly. Furthermore, if the prince should marry someone else the little mermaid would die on his wedding day and become foam on the water. The mermaid agrees to all the conditions and the old witch cuts out her tongue and performs the magic. When the mermaid awakens she has two human legs and the prince is standing beside her. She is happy in his land for a time, although of course she cannot speak to tell him of her love, but one day the prince tells her that he is going to marry a beautiful princess. The little mermaid knows that on his wedding day she must die.

Her sisters come and tell her that if she will stab the prince through the heart before his wedding, she can be a mermaid again, and go home. However, she cannot kill him, even to save her own life. After the wedding she starts to fade away and become foam on the sea, but the gentle breezes of the air come and tell her that she is going to join them, and she becomes a sweet breeze, giving comfort to many for hundreds of years.

THE LITTLE MATCH GIRL

A poor little barefoot girl on a bitterly cold winter night is trying to sell matches to obtain a few pennies. It is New Year's Eve, but nobody stops to buy matches from the little girl, and she sits down in the shelter of a building. She decides that she will warm her cold hands with one of the matches, and in its glow she thinks she can see through the wall of the house, and inside there is a table piled high with rich food. When the match goes out the vision disappears, and she lights another match. This time she sees a beautiful Christmas tree, with hundreds of candles burning brightly, but this too disappears when the match goes out. With the third match, she sees her grandmother, who has been dead for some time. The little girl loves her grandmother very much, and lights the rest of her bundle of matches, begging her grandmother not to go away. The grandmother says that she will take the little girl with her, and they will both go to heaven, where the grandmother has just come from. She takes the little girl, and everything is very beautiful.

In the morning people passing on the street see the little girl's frozen body where she had been sitting, and they see the burned bundle of matches.

"Poor child," someone murmurs. "She was trying to keep warm with matches, and she has frozen to death."

THE EMPEROR'S NEW CLOTHES

A certain emperor, a very vain man who thinks more about handsome clothes than anything else, is approached by two merchants. They offer to make him the most beautiful clothes in the world. But, they say, these will be magic clothes, woven of magic cloth. A worthy man will be able to see the clothes in all their splendor; but to a man who is stupid and is not fit for his job, the clothes will be invisible.

The emperor commissions the merchants to make the clothes. He supplies them with unlimited gold and silk and fine things for weaving the magic cloth. At length the emperor sends one of his ministers to see how the work is progressing. The minister sees only an empty loom; but the merchants pretend to handle and feel the fine cloth and the minister is afraid to admit he can see nothing, or to confess this to the emperor. He returns and reports that the cloth is beautiful. Some weeks later, the emperor sends another minister to see how the cutting and sewing of the clothes progresses, and again the minister is afraid to say the clothes are invisible to him.

Finally the merchants announce that the clothes are ready. They very elaborately "clothe" the emperor in his magic clothes; and the emperor cannot dare admit he cannot see the clothes. for that would brand him as unfit to rule. With his supposed new clothes on, the emperor parades through the crowded streets and every man and woman watching pretends to see the beautiful new clothes. But one little child cries out, "Why, the emperor has no clothes on at all!"—and so he had not.

THUMBELINA

An old woman who wants a tiny little girl very badly goes to a witch and obtains a seed of magic barleycorn, which grows immediately to a large tulip plant. In the middle of the tulip sits a tiny, beautiful little girl, about half the size of a thumb. She is called Thumbelina.

One night as Thumbelina is sleeping an old toad hops through the window and kidnaps her to be her son's bride. Thumbelina escapes, but is caught by a huge beetle and carried off again. After the beetles let her go, she wanders alone in the woods. She is happy until winter comes and she is cold. A friendly field mouse takes her and arranges for her to marry a mole.

Thumbelina befriends a swallow lying almost dead in the mole's tunnel, helping him to get out. As the time for her wedding to the mole approaches, she goes outside to see the beautiful sun, for moles never go about in daylight and she dreads the thought of remaining always in the cold, dark house of the mole, underground. The swallow she befriended comes by and carries Thumbelina to a beautiful, warm, flower-filled land where the sun always shines. There she meets the king of the Angels of the Flowers, a tiny person like herself, and Thumbelina becomes his queen, with a golden crown and a pair of white butterfly wings to wear.

THE SNOW QUEEN

Part 1. An evil demon makes a magic mirror that causes the bad part of everything to stand out and the good part to shrink to almost nothing. Bad goblins fly up into the sky, carrying the mirror, but they drop it and it shatters. Pieces fly about. They turn to ice any heart that they strike, and they make eyes they strike see only evil and ugliness in everything.

Part 2. In a small town, a little boy named KAY and a little girl named GERDA live next door to each other and play happily

Greta rides the reindeer toward the North Pole

together. When the snow comes, the boy's grandmother tells him that the snowflakes are bees and the queen bee is the SNOW QUEEN. At night Kay sees a snowflake grow larger and larger, and finally it becomes the Snow Queen before his eyes. Next day he feels something fly into his eye, and it is a splinter of the evil mirror. Another hits his heart, and it begins to become ice. He is no longer a kind boy, but sees ugliness everywhere. The Snow Queen comes and takes him away in her carriage to the northlands, where it is dark all winter long.

Part 3. Gerda misses Kay and determines to look for him. She floats down the river in a boat and is rescued by an old woman with a beautiful flower garden. She stays there for a while, and asks all the flowers where Kay might be. None can tell her, and she goes away to continue her search. But now it is winter again.

Parts 4–6. She meets a friendly crow and tells her story. He thinks he may know where Kay is, but warns Gerda that he is married to a beautiful princess, and living in the palace. The crow's sweetheart—a tame crow who lives in the palace—arranges for Gerda to get in, but when she sees the prince it is not Kay. The prince and princess hear the story and give Gerda a golden coach with driver and horses to continue her search, and she leaves the palace. On its way through a forest, the coach is stopped by robbers. A little robber girl decides to keep Gerda as a friend. Among her caged bird and animal pets are two wood doves who tell Gerda that Kay is with the Snow Queen, and a reindeer agrees that this is true. The little robber girl frees Gerda and gives her the reindeer to ride north, where Kay and the Snow Queen are staying. Gerda and the reindeer move swiftly toward the North Pole. First they stop at the hut of a woman in Finland, where Gerda warms herself and is given a note for a woman they will see later in Lapland. They travel on, and the Lapland woman directs them further. Finally they reach a point where the reindeer must leave Gerda, and she is alone in the far north. Huge snowflakes turn into animals and threaten her, but the frosty breath she breathes becomes angels and they drive away the snowflake guard of the

Snow Queen. Gerda goes on alone.

Part 7. Kay is in the palace, working a puzzle with ice crystals, trying to form the word "Eternity" with the pieces, for the Snow Queen has promised him his freedom if he can do it. She bids him goodbye as he works, and she leaves to take winter to the lands where it is time for it. Gerda arrives, and seeing Kay sitting stiff and cold, she weeps. Her tears melt the ice in his heart, and he weeps. His own tears wash out the splinter of the evil mirror in his eye, and he leaps with joy, shaking the ice splinters so that they fall quite by accident into the form of the word "Eternity," and Kay is free. They go home, and find that they are grown-up, and everything is beautiful again, and they are together.

BIG CLAUS AND LITTLE CLAUS

Two farmers named Claus live in a small village. One has four horses and the other only one. The villagers call the one with four horses Big Claus, and the other Little Claus. Once a week Little Claus plows with all five horses, and he likes to call them his own five horses as he works; but Big Claus becomes angry and says he will kill the horse of Little Claus if he says it again. Little Claus forgets this warning and Big Claus kills the horse.

Little Claus skins his dead horse and goes away to sell the hide. At a cottage a woman refuses to give him food or shelter. Later he peeks into the cottage and sees a fine meal prepared, and the woman and a clerk are about to eat. The woman's husband appears, and the woman hides everything. Her husband hates clerks, so the clerk is hidden too, in a large chest.

With his horsehide in a bag, Little Claus enters the cottage and is invited by the husband to eat. He pretends that his horsehide is a wizard, and he says that the wizard has conjured up a fine meal in the oven (for the wife had fed them only porridge). Of course, Little Claus saw her hide the food there, and also some fine wine in another place. Finally he pretends that his wizard has conjured a clerk in the chest. The man gives him a bushel of money for this "wizard" and asks him to take the chest and the clerk away. Little Claus fools the clerk and makes him think he will be thrown into the river, and the clerk buys his free-

dom with another bushel of money.

Little Claus is now rich. When he tells Big Claus that he has sold his horsehide for all that money, Big Claus kills his four horses and tries to sell their hides. Everyone laughs at him when he says the price is two bushels of money for each one. He comes back and determines to kill Little Claus.

Little Claus's old grandmother has died, and Little Claus puts her in his own bed till morning, while he sleeps in a chair. Big Claus comes with an axe and strikes the dead grandmother, thinking it is Little Claus. Next day Little Claus places his grandmother upright in a carriage and drives to an inn, where he asks the host to take a glass of mead to his grandmother sitting in the carriage. When she pays no attention, the host throws the glass in her face. Little Claus accuses him of killing the old woman. The host pays Claus a bushel of money to be quiet, and promises to bury the grandmother in fine style. Claus goes home and tells Big Claus he got all that money by selling his grandmother's body. Big Claus immediately kills his own grandmother, and goes out to sell her body. People think him mad and tell him how wicked his deed was.

Big Claus goes home to be revenged on Little Claus. He throws Little Claus into a sack, preparing to drown him in the river. He passes a church, and goes inside. Little Claus changes places with a very old man who wants to go to heaven, and drives the old man's fine flock of cattle and sheep back to his own house, where Big Claus finds him. He tells Big Claus that he got the cattle from the river, and that there are many more farther downstream. Big Claus asks to be tied up in a bag so that he may get some river cattle, and Little Claus ties him up and throws him in the river, with a rock in the bag to make sure it will sink. Big Claus is gone for good.

THE UGLY DUCKLING

A duck in a farmyard is sitting upon her eggs, waiting impatiently for them to hatch, and at last they do—all except one egg that is larger than the others. She finally hatches that one, but the duckling is larger than it ought to be, and most ugly. All the other ducks tell her that she has made a bad mistake with this one, and it is probably a turkey. One of them had hatched a turkey egg once by mistake, and it had been dreadful. The creature would not go in the water!

The Ugly Duckling goes in the water, however, so the mother knows it is not a turkey. She decides it is just another duckling that is not handsome like her others. The hens in the barnyard peck at it, the ducks make fun of it, and its life is miserable. Finally it flies away. It almost joins with some wild geese, but a hunter shoots the geese and the Ugly Duckling goes on to a small farmhouse. Immediately it upsets everything; it spills milk, and tips over the flour, and the people are very angry. It travels on, and the weather becomes cold.

Finally it reaches a tiny, broken-down hut, where an old woman lives with her tomcat and an old hen. The duckling is allowed to stay, but the hen is unkind to it. She scoffs at it because it cannot lay eggs. The cat scoffs because it cannot arch its back, or purr, or give off sparks when its fur is rubbed the wrong way, as the cat can.

At last the Ugly Duckling is too unhappy to stay there any longer, and it flies away. It reaches a little lake and dives down into the cool water. Swimming in the lake are some beautiful white swans, and the Ugly Duckling is filled with a feeling of love for them. He does not understand why he should feel as he does, but sadly realizes that these beautiful creatures will undoubtedly hate him as everyone else has hated him, because he is so ugly. Still, he would rather be killed by them than pecked by hens, or scorned by ducks, or kicked by people. He calls out to them to kill him, and bows down his head for the death blow. The sight of his reflection in the water is the most amazing thing that could ever happen to anyone. He suddenly sees that he too is a beautiful white swan, with a lovely, curved neck like the others. They come to greet him, and love him immediately, because he is the most beautiful of them all. The Ugly Duckling is no more—but in his place is a beautiful swan, and great happiness fills him.

Andersonville

Jonas and family, despite Ira's misgivings, leave to seek Mr. Linkum's heaven

Novel by MacKinlay Kantor, 1904– Published 1955 by World Publishing Co., Cleveland. © 1955 by MacKinlay Kantor. (NAL, T1388)

THE FORTE OF MacKinlay Kantor is tender pathos, sentiment such as all men feel and only the Nordics seem to consider shameful. In *Andersonville*, a historical novel of admirable scholarship and authenticity, there are occasional displays of Kantor's greatest gift but chiefly the tone is more conventionally impersonal. Therefore Kantor may be longer remembered for some of his shorter works. ❡ The major character, Ira Claffey, who loved his fellow men, has seemed to some critics to be overidealized. He is not. He existed, and he is no less typical because there were and are unfortunately too few of him. ❡ Andersonville is a very long novel, more than 400,000 words.

1–14. IRA CLAFFEY lives on his plantation in Sumter County, Georgia, with his wife VERONICA, whose mind is gone; his daughter LUCY; and only a handful of slaves, COFFEE, JEM, JONAS, their wives, and the very old and very young. Claffey's two sons and Lucy's fiancé have died in the war. Claffey sold his other slaves for their sake when it became clear he could not long continue to feed so many. The slaves are being requisitioned to work on a prison camp nearby, officially Camp Sumter, near the village of Anderson, which will be known as Andersonville. The Rev. CATO DILLARD, a saintly man, and his wife, after visiting the Claffeys, pay a charitable visit to the nearby shack of the Widow TEBBS, who sells her favors and whose children CORAL (who has lost a foot in the war), FLORAL, LAUREL and ZORAL all have different, unknown fathers. The Claffeys' distant cousin HARRELL (Harry) ELKINS, Surgeon in the Confederate Army, is sent to be stationed at the prison and they like him; he is the right age for Lucy, but officially she is in mourning. Claffey opposed secession and the war but is aghast at the thought of the plight of the Negroes if slavery were suddenly ended.

The first prisoners in the camp include WILLIE COLLINS, a totally ruthless and cruel man, and some of the followers with whom he terrorized the camp at Belle Isle (Richmond) from which he was shipped. He is from the Five Points section of New York City.

15–17. Gen. JOHN WINDER, Confederate provost-marshal, callous and greedy, sends Capt. HENRY WIRZ, of Swiss origin, to command the camp, with orders not to pamper the prisoners. Wirz suffers constantly from pain in an arm wounded some years before, and takes morphine. Capt. SID WINDER, the general's son, was in charge of building the camp, and his arrogance, stupidity and dishonesty combined to produce an unsuitable one. Another son, DICK WINDER, is made quartermaster.

18–33. Willie Collins organizes his brigands within the camp. He forces EDWARD BLAMEY, a sharp-eyed little man, to join him and report on newcomers who have anything valuable; then the Collins gang robs them. Among the prisoners too shrewd or formidable to be Collins' victims are NATHAN DREYFOOS, member of a rich Philadelphia Jewish family, a master of fencing and boxing; and SENECA MAC-BEAN, a sergeant from Illinois, six-four and rangy. Dreyfoos becomes a barber, MacBean runs a laundry, to gain income by barter. Even with only 12,000 prisoners, the camp is inadequate—insufficient water, no sewage facilities, rotten food, no shelter, stupid and unfeeling guards (including Floral, who is 14 and enlists). A persecuted, cowardly little man called CHICKAMAUGA steps over the barrier line and is shot to death by a young guard. The depredations of Willie Collins grow worse and Dreyfoos and Mac-Bean begin to organize a group of vigilantes among the prisoners. LEROY KEY is elected commander. There are other gangs of raiders, but Collins' are worst. When all the gangs fall on a newly arrived West Virginia group and beat and rob it, the vigilantes act. Wirz agrees to let them have clubs, rope, and a place by the gate to hold trials. The vigilantes lead crowds of other decent prisoners against the raiders, who are captured and tied up to await trial. Collins and five others are sentenced to be hanged; Blamey is killed trying to escape; many others are punished.

34–49. Harry Elkins is away but corresponds with Lucy. Veronica dies. Amid conditions of unbelievable filth, disease, starvation, and death, Wirz makes routine reports. In July there are 33,000 prisoners in the camp and 1,700 die. Elkins asks Claffey to provide some food to help the prisoners and Claffey takes it to the camp but the guards get it instead, pleading equally great need.

The Union soldiers believe that any guard who shoots a prisoner gets a month furlough; Floral shoots a prisoner, then runs. He is put in jail, not for shooting the prisoner but for deserting. In August 3,000 prisoners die.

50–55. Lt. Col. ALEXANDER PERSONS, commander of the garrison, proposes to close the prison as a nuisance to the landholders of the neighborhood (knowing an appeal on grounds of humanity would not succeed). He is reprimanded by Gen. Howell Cobb for seeking to discredit his own government. The medical officers report on the condition of 30,000 men crowded onto 27 acres of land with one small stream for water. Ira Claffey decides he must go to Richmond and appeal directly to Jefferson Davis. The fall comes; Sherman's army leaves Atlanta on its march to the sea. Claffey's train is commandeered by the Confederate Army. He walks back home, through conditions of anarchy. Elkins proposes to Lucy and they are married. Gen. Winder has a stroke and dies.

56–59. NAZARETH STRICKER, who has lost a hand, escapes and in the woods encounters Coral Tebbs, embittered by his lost foot and hating all Yankees; yet a strange friendship grows between them. Coral hides and feeds Stricker and Stricker carves a fine wooden foot for Coral. Ira Claffey discovers Stricker and gives him money to help him work his way northward. Lucy is pregnant. The war is lost. Lincoln is dead. The slaves are free and Jonas wants to leave, taking his wife and children, because of the legends he has heard of the blessings of Linkum's kingdom; Claffey tries to dissuade him but cannot and finally gives him a horse and wagon and a note saying Jonas and his family are under Claffey's protection. Then, with misgivings, Claffey sees the family leave.

60–61. Union cavalry arrives at the prison camp; Wirz is arrested. He does not understand; he was kind to the prisoners.

And Quiet Flows the Don

Novel by Mikhail Sholakhov, 1905– Published 1928; English translation by Stephen Garry published 1934, © 1934 by Alfred A. Knopf, Inc.

THIS LONG (250,000-word) novel and its sequel, *The Don Flows Home to the Sea*, which makes a unit with it, are by many considered the outstanding work of Russian fiction produced under the Soviet regime. (They have been published together, under the title *The Silent Don.*) Though both were published during the reign of Stalin, they were not distorted in the manner usually associated with that reign. ❡ The Cossacks of whom Sholakhov writes were a unique group in Czarist Russia. Even the poorest Cossacks were free and most of them owned their own small farms; they looked down on peasants and even on relatively rich merchants of peasant stock. Most of them were literate. They elected their own leader, or ataman. In the Russian Army they were traditionally cavalrymen and each owned and rode his own horse. There were, of course, Cossack nobility and gentry, represented in this book by the Listnitsky family. The Cossacks' family life was communal in the Russian fashion, the head of each family, his sons, their wives and children, and his unmarried children all living together and working the family farm.

Part 1. The Melekhovs are Don Cossacks who have a small farm near the village of Tatarsk. They are known for their Turkish blood and appearance, Prokoffey Melekhov having captured and brought home a Turkish wife from the Russo-Turkish wars of the 1870s. Now, in 1913, Prokoffey's son PANTALEIMAN MELEKHOV is head of the family, living with his wife ILINICHNA; their sons PIOTRA and GREGOR (or GRISHKA) and daughter DUNIA; and Piotra's wife DARIA. All work the farm. Gregor has been flirting with AKSINIA, wife of their neighbor STEPAN ASTAKHOV. Aksinia was raped by her father and has been abused and overworked by Stepan, but still she resists Gregor until Stepan is called up for a brief army training period; then she yields and soon loves Gregor passionately. Their affair becomes generally known. Stepan hears of it in camp. The Melekhovs are scandalized and Pantaleiman arranges to marry Gregor to NATALIA KORSHUNOVA, daughter of a more prosperous Cossack and sister of Gregor's friend MITKA. On his return, Stepan beats Aksinia daily and brutally, yet finds that he loves her; he vows to kill Gregor one day. Gregor and Natalia are married and his affair with Aksinia ends temporarily.

Mitka seduces ELIZABIETA, daughter of the rich merchant SERGEI MOKHOV; but his offer of marriage is refused by Mokhov, who sends Elizabieta to school. A stranger, OSIP STOCKMAN, comes to Tatarsk as a locksmith; actually he is a Bolshevik agent sent to work for revolution.

Gregor, finding Natalia physically unresponsive compared to Aksinia, believes he does not love her. His family sides with Natalia and he leaves home. A young officer, EUGENE LISTNITSKY, son of a retired general, offers Gregor a job as coachman on their estate at Yagodnoe. Aksinia willingly leaves Stepan and goes with Gregor, becoming a servant in the Listnitsky household. Natalia, heartbroken, goes home to her father's house and soon afterward tries to kill herself by cutting her throat; she recovers but her head is permanently askew. She goes back to live with the Melekhovs. Aksinia has a daughter, whom she insists is Gregor's; he is not sure. Gregor is called up for four years' military service and becomes partly reconciled with his father. Stockman is arrested and taken off by the Czar's police.

Part 2. War breaks out. Gregor's regiment is on the Austrian border and sees action at once. Piotra and Stepan are called up as reserves and are assigned to the same unit as Gregor. Piotra reminds Gregor of Stepan's vow. The Melekhovs receive official notification of Gregor's death in battle, but twelve days later Piotra writes that Gregor is alive and has been decorated and promoted to corporal. Tatarsk is very proud of him. Later, wounded, he is sent to Moscow for treatment.

Aksinia's daughter dies of diphtheria. Eugene is wounded and returns home to convalesce. He enters into an affair with Aksinia. Gregor, when discharged from the hospital, goes to Yagodnoe. He hears of Aksinia's affair with Eugene. Volunteering to drive Eugene in the droshky, he waits till they are out of sight of the house then beats Eugene very severely with his knout and boots. He returns and whips Aksinia, then despite her pleas he leaves and returns to his father's house and Natalia.

In 1916 Eugene is back at the front. There is much talk of revolution; in his unit one of the officers, ILIA BUNCHUK, is a Socialist. Eugene informs on him, but Bunchuk deserts. Meanwhile, in a 1915 battle, Stepan has shot at Gregor from behind but missed, and later Gregor saves his life; at home in Tatarsk, Natalia has had twins. Daria has not been faithful to Piotra, who knows it and also knows that Stepan has been among her lovers, when he was home on leave. Piotra plans to kill him, but Stepan is lost on a patrol. In Tatarsk most of the wives, starved for men, take what men are available.

Part 3. In March 1918 the Czar abdicates. The Kerensky government takes over. Many of the Cossacks favor the Bolsheviks, but the officers follow their commander, General KORNILOV, when he attempts to set up an independent Cossack state. Some Cossacks follow their officers, some do not, and civil war breaks out among troops retreating from the forces of the Central Powers; there are the revolutionary forces, favoring the Bolsheviks who have seized power in Petrograd, and the counter-revolutionary forces led by Kornilov. Gregor, who was promoted to officer's rank in January 1917, joins the Bolsheviks.

Part 4. Civil war continues, centered in Rostov. Bunchuk is among the revolutionary leaders; he meets and loves ANNA POGOODKO, a Jewish girl sent to him as a machine gunner. The men of Tatarsk join the counter-revolutionaries—except Mitka, who declines to fight any more. Gregor commands two revolutionary companies but disapproves the bloodthirsty attitudes

39

of PODTIELKOV and other revolutionary leaders; the counter-revolutionists gain the upper hand and Gregor, his side defeated, returns to Tatarsk with his neighbors.

The revolutionary forces gradually regain the ascendancy. The Cossacks of Tatarsk mobilize to fight them. Some want to make Gregor their commander, but he has been in the Red Army so they elect Piotra; but Gregor goes with them. In the battle that follows, Anna is killed and Bunchuk grieves. The counter-revolutionaries win; Podtielkov surrenders, and Bunchuk must reluctantly surrender with him. The counter-revolutionaries nevertheless condemn all to death, and when Podtielkov reproaches Gregor for this inhumanity, Gregor reminds him of how he, Podtielkov, had opposing officers shot in the same way. Podtielkov dies predicting the ultimate victory of the revolution. Gregor and his townsmen return to Tatarsk.

The Animal Kingdom

Play by Philip Barry, 1896–1949. Produced January 12, 1932, in New York City. © 1931 by Philip Barry.

THE PLAYS OF Philip Barry are of so many different types that perhaps none can be called typical of his work. He experimented with religion, mysticism, fantasy, and social protest, all the while making his biggest successes with modern drama and comedy. *The Animal Kingdom,* a serious but not oppressive drama of modern married life, has a typical Barry hero: A lover of beauty trapped in a world of Philistines. It was a big success on Broadway. ¶ Philip Barry was born in Rochester, N.Y., and was one of many playwrights-to-be who studied in the "English 47 Workshop" of George P. Baker; he attended it at Harvard after graduating from Yale, to which the Workshop later moved. His many other plays include *The Philadelphia Story.* He died untimely, a relatively young man.

Act I. 1. In the living room of a comfortable but not fashionable house in Connecticut, a group of people are waiting for TOM COLLIER, a publisher, who is to be their host for the evening. RUFUS COLLIER, Tom's father, comments that Tom's lateness is no surprise; Tom has always been careless, Bohemian, and improvident. Others there are OWEN ARTHUR, a lawyer and friend of Tom's; RICHARD REGAN, Tom's butler; and CECILIA HENRY, Tom's new fiancée and the reason for the assem-

bly, although the others do not know it. Rufus mentions scathingly a woman Tom has been living with for three years; Owen says she is a fine person. Cecilia announces that Tom is going to marry her. Regan brings in a radio message for Tom and sets it on the table. Rufus finally picks it up; it says that DAISY SAGE (the woman with whom Tom has been living) is docking that very evening in New York.

Tom arrives, and the formal announcement is made that he and Cecilia are to be married. As they are having cocktails, Tom reads the cablegram. He contrives to have Owen take his father outside, then tells Cecilia about Daisy: He is very fond of Daisy and always will be, but marriage never occurred to either of them. Cecilia says she understands. Tom tells Cecilia he must go to New York to inform Daisy immediately, since she must have left Paris before his cable to her could be delivered. Cecilia agrees and Tom tells Rufus and Owen he must go to New York. Rufus is furiously angry, but Tom kisses Cecilia goodbye, and leaves.

2. In the studio apartment of Daisy Sage in New York, Tom is seated with JOE FISK, a novelist, listening to FRANC SCHMIDT, a young woman German violinist. After 2 A.M., Joe and Franc leave, and Daisy is bubbling over with happiness and excitement. She tells Tom that at last she really believes she can paint seriously. She wants Tom to spend about three months in Mexico with her. Before he has a chance to say that he plans to be married, she bursts forth with a statement that she loves him madly and wants to have a baby—so much that she wants him to marry her right away. The shock that this gives Tom is nothing to the shock his news gives her. He wants them to remain good friends, but she wants a break. She goes to the other room to pick up a package of his shirts and socks, and he slips out. The curtain falls with Daisy holding the package and gazing blankly at the door.

Tom and Regan talk it over

Act II. 1. The next January, on a bitterly cold evening, Cecilia and her friend GRACE MACOMBER are having after-dinner coffee in the Collier living room, in which Cecilia has made a number of changes. They are discussing the first concert of Tom's friend, Franc Schmidt; Tom insists they must attend, but Cecilia suggests slyly to Grace that she may persuade him otherwise but it will seem to be his own idea. Grace admires Cecilia's subtle skill; she also thinks it perfectly beastly of Tom's father not to loosen his hold on the Collier pursestrings. Tom comes in, and Grace compliments him on the latest book he has published; Tom says it is tripe, at which point Cecilia mentions that she persuaded him to publish it.

It would produce funds for publishing at least ten books of the kind he likes. After Grace leaves, Cecilia pleads a bad headache as an excuse not to attend the concert. She also repeats what she has obviously said many times before—that Tom is doing a wicked thing to Regan in keeping him on, when he could make something of himself. When Regan gets home, the two men sit down with a bottle of beer, and Regan tells Tom he has accepted a job at a training gym, because he knows the Missus doesn't like him. He leaves. Cecilia has appeared, seductively garbed in the dressing gown she wore on their honeymoon. She urges Tom to go to the concert alone, kisses him passionately, and goes upstairs. Tom starts for the door, then turns, picks up the telephone, and sends a telegram of congratulations to Franc instead of attending.

2. Joe and Franc are waiting for Tom in Daisy's apartment; Tom believes that he is going to meet Joe alone. Daisy comes in; she has just closed her first exhibition of paintings, and is talking with great animation of going to Nova Scotia. Tom arrives, and in utter honesty tells Daisy that she was not ready for an exhibit. But gradually Daisy softens and as Joe and Franc slip out quietly, she and Tom are once again on their old footing. Happy, at ease, and natural for the first time in months, Tom makes a date for lunch and dinner the next day. After he leaves, Daisy realizes suddenly that this would be impossible. The only thing she can do is to run away, and never see him again. She starts packing furiously.

Act III. 1. The former library at the Colliers' house is now a formal dining room. Owen, Grace and Cecilia are at breakfast. Tom is upstairs still, recuperating from the celebration of his birthday the night before. Daisy and Joe have been there but left to accompany Franc Schmidt to the railroad station. Cecilia mentions that Tom's father has sent him a check for his birthday. Tom has had an offer from a publishing firm that specializes in sensationalism to buy into his business, but does not want to sell and so has set the price unreasonably high. Cecilia is determined that they pay Tom's price and coaxes Owen to use his influence, hinting that then she might be willing to have an affair with him. Owen capitulates.

Regan has returned. His new job was not a success, and he has been ill, so Tom made him come back.

Daisy and Joe, who have returned from the station, are alone for a few moments. They agree that Cecilia has managed to twist Tom into a replica of what she thinks a proper husband and businessman ought to be. They are sorry for him, but don't want to stay and observe the process any longer; they leave.

2. That night Cecilia has arranged an intimate supper for two, and she is dressed seductively in a negligee, awaiting Tom's return from the interview with the publisher. Tom arrives and tells her that they agreed to pay his price. Cecilia does not understand why he is unhappy. Tom analyzes Cecilia coldly and intensely, for the first time, and sees a woman who is selfish,

calculating, and devious. Cecilia asks him why he so foolishly refuses to cash the check his father sent him. She also urges him to go and live in the city in his father's house, as they have been invited to do. She has no idea of what is going through Tom's mind, and attempts to lure him again.

After their supper is finished, she goes upstairs. Tom says he will be along directly, but instead he takes the check from his pocket, endorses it over to Cecilia, and places it on the mantelpiece. He then calls Regan, who announces that he is quitting, and this time he means it. Tom says they

will go together, that he is going to his wife. Regan glances up the stairs toward the lighted bedroom with its open door, but Tom repeats what he said—he is going to his wife—and they walk out of the house together.

Anna and the King of Siam

Narrative by Margaret Landon, 1903– Published 1944 by the John Day Co., New York. © 1943, 1944 by Margaret Mortenson Landon. (PB, C222, abridged; available also in children's edition, The John Day Co.)

THIS BEST-SELLING BOOK is described by its author as 75% true; the other 25% is the author's conjecture of what must have happened. The main sources are the writings of Anna Leonowens herself, *The English Governess at the Siamese Court*, 1870, and *The Romance of the Harem*, 1872, plus articles and letters. However, Siamese history of the times is well enough documented. Anna's king Somdetch Phra Paramendr Maha Mongkut, whom Western histories know as Rama IV, was Siam's first enlightened king; Anna's Prince Chulalongkorn, or Rama V, carried the modernization much farther. Their descendants still reign in Siam or Thailand. ❡ *Anna* made the successful musical play *The King and I*, by Rodgers and Hammerstein.

Chaps. 1–3. Mrs. ANNA LEONOWENS went from Singapore to Bangkok on the ship *Chow Phya*, in 1862, to teach English to the children and women of the king of Siam. She was accompanied by her son LOUIS, 6; her Hindustani maid, Miriam BEEBE, and Beebe's husband, MOONSHEE, a Persian. Anna was young (28) and pretty but would not consider proposals from Capt. Orton of the *Chow Phya* or others. She had been born in Wales in 1834, daughter of an army officer. He was killed in India, where Anna went to join her mother, who had remarried. Anna married a young officer, Leonowens, in 1851, and traveled much with him, learning several languages of the East. Leonowens died of sunstroke in 1860 and after running a school for officers' children in Singapore Anna accepted the offer of King MONGKUT at $100 a month and a brick house.

Chaps. 4–6. Some hours after the *Chow Phya* reached Bangkok an officer boarded it. He was the KRALAHOME, or Prime Minis-

ter. His dozen attendants were prone, like toads, crawling to him when he called; all Asiatics on the ship also prostrated themselves when he appeared. He was rude and indifferent to Anna and would not even help her to find lodging for the night, but the English harbormaster, Capt. JOHN BUSH, and his wife took her in. The next day the Kralahome sent for Anna and moved her into rooms in his palace; he was polite (calling her "sir") but still cold. His interpreter (and half-brother) became overfamiliar with Anna, who spurned him in disgust; thereby making an enemy. Anna met various members of the Kralahome's harem including the KHUN YING (Lady) PHAN, his head wife, a cultivated woman of 40 who managed the big household of several hundred members and slaves. Also she met ROBERT HUNTER, a Eurasian, the Kralahome's English secretary, who was polite and helpful.

Chaps. 7–9. Anna met Mr. and Mrs. MATTSON, American missionaries, who told her that the king was very learned, having been a priest, scholar and astronomer for 30 years before succeeding to the throne, but was dictatorial, unpredictable, and difficult. After about three weeks she was presented to the king (by Capt. Bush). She was permitted to remain in a half-kneeling crouch in place of prostration. The king's English was fluent but weirdly un-

Anna's first audience

idiomatic. He said her duties would be to teach his 67 children and a number of his wives and to help him in English correspondence and translation of letters he received—much more work than she expected. She met his new wife, Lady TALAP, who would be among her pupils. Nothing happened for several more weeks, then the Kralahome's sister, Lady PLAM, took her to the king's harem, where she met some more wives and saw the king again. He wanted her to live in his palace; when she insisted on the house she had been promised, he flew into a rage and she left. A week later she was escorted to her house—an unlivable, filthy hut in the fish market. She refused it and was sick of a fever for more than a week. Weeks later, Lady Phan found her a livable house on the river and she moved in.

Chaps. 10–11. Finally the King opened the school. Pupils in the morning were the royal children, 5 to 10 years old, and in the afternoons the wives and concubines, 15 or older. The best pupils included the favorite prince, CHULALONGKORN, about 10, whom the king wished to succeed him; and his younger sister, Princess Chantara Monthon, the FA-YING (Celestial Princess), the king's favorite child. Also Lady SON KLIN (Hidden Perfume), who had once been the favorite concubine but for some reason was in disgrace. All had many slaves; even the older children were carried to and from the schoolroom by slaves.

Chap. 12. The Palace was a walled city covering more than a square mile and divided in three parts by inner walls. In two of these were government buildings, temples, theaters, and other public places. The third part, where Anna taught, was the city of women, guarded by Amazons (woman soldiers). No man could enter except the king and, to conduct religious services, Buddhist priests. Nine thousand women lived there—the king's wives and concubines, present and former, nearly all of royal or noble families; and his female relatives; and his young children (of both sexes); all with their female slaves. With rare exceptions, the women never left its confines. Lady THIANG, an "elderly" woman (about 40), the king's most influential wife, and Anna became friends.

41

Teaching the wives and concubines, aged 15 and up

Chap. 13. The king and his council, the Senabodi (which also elected the king), were pressed by the imperialism of European countries, France especially, and were trying with great difficulty to avoid losing their country. Anna participated in much of the king's political correspondence. She won a compromise by which she did not have to kneel in the king's presence; but she had to do whatever he did, stand, sit, etc., and his favorite posture was stretched out on his stomach on the floor. The king conducted correspondence with Queen Victoria and wrote to President Lincoln to offer elephants for breeding in the U.S.; Lincoln had to refuse because the climate was not right. When Lord John Hay paid a state visit with a British fleet, the king had Anna dress six of the prettiest women in European fashion and train them in European manners so Hay would not think the Siamese barbarians. All went well until Hay put his monocle to his eye to see the pretty girls better; they were so frightened of the evil eye that they threw their skirts over their heads and fled.

Chaps. 14–19. Despite some clashes, Anna became friendly and very influential with the king. No one else had the courage to oppose him as she did. Anna's hatred of slavery and oppression caused her to intercede often for sufferers, sometimes through the Kralahome (whom she found to be cold but fair) and sometimes direct to the king. She won the release of Son Klin when the king unfairly had her beaten and put in a dungeon, and she arranged for a mistreated slave, L'ORE, to buy her freedom. Anna was beloved by her pupils and the women of the harem; and by the slaves and common people of Bangkok she was almost treated as a goddess. The death of the little Fa-ying, of cholera, brought the king and Anna closer in their grief. He gave her a noble title and an estate far away. (He also began to send her presents, which later included a very valuable diamond ring; but this Anna sent back when she surmised that the king

thought she might become one of his harem.) The king once flew into a rage when a Singapore paper described him as a spare man; he thought it meant "a man who can be spared," and on his 59th birthday he had Anna give a European-type banquet for the entire foreign colony, so they could see how vigorous he was.

Chaps. 20–24. The interpreter, who had been waiting for vengeance, began to harass Anna. He had Moonshee beaten, and the old man insisted on going back to Singapore, but Beebe stayed. Then a stone thrown through a window hit Anna. Finally Hunter arranged for the Kralahome to protect Anna. The king provided a better house, nearer the palace. Lady Son Klin became entranced with *Uncle Tom's Cabin*, translated it into Siamese, and changed her name to Son Klin Harriet Beecher Stowe. (Later she freed all her own slaves.) With Lady Thiang and the KHUN THAO AP, the chief woman judge, Anna conspired to save many women in danger of unfair punishment. But there was a concubine addicted to gambling who had lost almost all her possessions except a slave MAE NOI, who was devoted to the concubine's little daughter, Princess WANI, one of Anna's favorite pupils; and when this slave too was gambled away, Anna could not deter the king from having the concubine savagely beaten. Anna bought back the slave for Wani. The king at this time was worried by the arrogance and impossible demands of the French consul, M. AUBARET; France seized Cambodia from the king and he was afraid they would attack Siam and annex it by conquest.

Chaps. 25–26. The king's new favorite concubine, TUPTIM, did not like her position. She ran away and was found at a monastery, disguised as a young man and serving a young priest, KHUN PHRA KALAT. Both were condemned by the court. Anna interceded with the king and he promised her he would release them, but when he learned the evidence against them

he had them tortured to death on a scaffold built under Anna's window. Then he relented and had a monument built to them.

Chaps. 27–30. Over New Year's Eve, 1865–66, Chulalongkorn, almost 14, left Anna's classes to serve his novitiate in the priesthood and become a man. Anna had instilled in him principles of humanity and freedom and hoped that she would influence his reign for the better. The SECOND KING, the king's brother, who was the Siamese most admired by foreign officials, died early in 1866. He had recently married, in a love match, the beautiful Princess of CHIENG-MAI, daughter of a rich and powerful Lao prince, a tributary of Siam's. Soon after the Second King's death she seemed to vanish. At this time Anna became sick and almost died. When she recovered, the king was having trouble with M. Aubaret again; and when she refused to take the blame for an unwise move the king had made he dismissed her in a rage and drew up a list of accusations against her—all trivial and some false. The Kralahome sent her a message advising her to resign, but she refused. While Anna was shut up in her own house, in danger of reprisals, a woman sneaked in—MAE PIA, slave of the Princess of Chiengmai, who told Anna the princess was a prisoner in the king's harem and begged Anna to carry a letter to her.

Chaps. 31–32. When Anna went back to the Palace the soldiers at the gate attacked her, but a mass of slaves interposed their own bodies to protect her. She returned home but soon she easily disproved the king's accusations and besides he recovered from his rage and they resumed work together. With the help of Lady Thiang, Anna delivered the letter to the princess and learned that the princess was a prisoner because she had refused to shift to the king. A few weeks later the princess mysteriously disappeared from her cell and in her place was found a slave, unable to talk. Even the court had to accept sorcery as the only explanation, and no one was punished. Anna discovered that Mae Pia had accomplished the whole thing by perfectly natural means and had cut out her own tongue so she could not be made to talk. The princess was safe with her father.

Chaps. 33–34. With difficulty Anna obtained leave of absence from the king to take Louis to England and put him in school. Before she could return the king died, Oct. 1, 1868. He remembered Anna and Louis generously in his will, but his executors refused to pay them. Chulalongkorn was elected king, and when he came of age he ended slavery and the custom of prostration. Anna wrote, lectured and taught until she retired in 1878 to live with her married daughter Avis. Louis returned to Siam as a man and became an officer in Chulalongkorn's army. Anna had letters from her friends in Siam and in 1897 she had a reunion with the new king in London. He credited much of his successful reign to her teaching.

Anna Christie

Play by Eugene O'Neill, 1888–1953. Produced Nov. 2, 1921, in New York City. © 1921, 1949 by Eugene O'Neill. Published by Random House, New York. (ML, 146)

O'NEILL WROTE THIS play first under the title *Chris Christopherson*. It was produced in 1920 and failed. He rewrote it for production as *Anna Christie* the following year and it received the Pulitzer Prize in 1922. Anna was played by Pauline Lord, a fine actress who unluckily was in fewer successful plays than she deserved.

Act I. In Johnny the Priest's saloon near the waterfront in New York City, a letter arrives for CHRIS CHRISTOPHERSON, father of the girl known as ANNA CHRISTIE, and captain of a coal barge. Chris comes in with a tough, uneducated woman who lives with him on the barge—MARTHY OWEN. The letter is from Anna, whom he has not seen in many years, saying that she is coming to town. She has been living in the Middle West—as a nursemaid, her father thinks; actually, she has been a prostitute. Chris celebrates her pending arrival by getting drunk, and goes out for something to eat. While he is gone Anna arrives and asks Marthy what kind of man Chris is. Marthy describes him as kind, good, and thoroughly fine, although rough, as a barge captain would naturally be. Marthy immediately recognizes Anna for what she is, and Anna makes no attempt to conceal or deny it. Chris returns, and is overflowing with happiness when he greets his daughter. Marthy leaves to remove all trace of her residence on the barge before Anna goes there. As the first act closes, Chris toasts Anna in beer, and she drinks a glass of port wine, which Chris suggests as not being too strong.

Act II. On the stern deck of the barge *Simeon Winthrop*, Anna is standing alone wrapped in the mysterious spell of a heavy fog. Chris comes out and urges her to go inside. He has no understanding of how the fog affects Anna, but angrily denounces fog as one of the worst tricks of that old devil, the sea. He often berates the sea, and blames the sea for the fact that his wife left him. He blames the sea also for the fact that Anna grew up far away from him. He declares vehemently that a sailor is no good for any girl to marry. On the deck, Anna learns that all the men in her father's family have always been sailors, and that the daughters of the family have almost invariably married sailors as well. Anna tries to explain the feeling of peace and relaxation that she experiences on the water, and the feeling of having been cleansed. As they are talking, a lifeboat from a wrecked ship pulls alongside and the exhausted sailors are brought on board the barge. One of them, MAT BURKE, sits down on the deck with Anna while Chris goes off to tend the others, who are unable to walk. Mat is a virile, boastful Irishman who recounts with considerable vigor and relish the story of the wreck, emphasizing the fact that the lifeboat would never have made shore if he had not been able to do the work of three men.

Mat assumes that Anna is living with Chris as his mistress, and tries to kiss her, at which point she accidentally knocks him down. Striking his head on the deck causes him to lose consciousness for a moment, but when he comes to he learns that Chris is Anna's father, and apologizes for even daring to think what he had, when anyone could certainly see that she wasn't that kind at all. No, indeed! She was a fine, decent, lovely girl—and it was Fate that had thrown them together—for he's going to marry her. Anna does not take him seriously, and helps him to walk unsteadily to the cabin.

Act III. The barge is moored at Boston, and for about a week Anna has been going out every night with Mat. Mat is in love with her, and she with him—and the situation is very strained. Chris is uneasy at seeing his daughter becoming obviously interested in a sailor, and swears he won't let it happen. Anna wishes aloud that they could leave and return to New York, which seems strange to Chris, if she's having such a good time where she is. He accuses her of being in love with Mat, and she admits it. Tiring of his rantings against the sea, and sailors in general, she goes out, leaving word for Mat that she is on the dock.

When Mat arrives, he is dressed in a brand-new suit and is generally polished and slicked from head to toe. He announces to Chris that he intends to marry Anna that very day, and they quarrel violently—Chris declaring hotly that Anna will never marry him. Anna returns and realizes that something has happened between the two men. Finally they admit that they quarreled over her, and Mat forces an admission from her that she loves him and that she has never loved anyone before in her life. She kisses him, and says goodbye. Mat is so blissful he fails to hear the word. Chris, however, heard Anna say that she would never marry him, and almost immediately both men are fighting over which one Anna will remain with. Anna becomes angry at hearing herself discussed like a chattel, and bursts in with her reason for refusing to marry Mat, blurting forth the entire story in a rush. Both Mat and Chris are stunned, and Mat in his hurt rage is almost ready to kill her. Finally he rushes out, declaring that he is going to get drunk, and telling her that she has torn his very heart out. Soon afterward Chris goes out also, with the same purpose, leaving Anna alone, staring at nothing as the curtain falls.

Act IV. About two days later, Anna is sitting in the cabin of the barge, suitcase beside her—just waiting. Chris appears and tells Anna that he has arranged things so that she won't ever have to go back to that other life, as she has dully declared her intention of doing. He has signed up to ship out to sea again, and his pay will be sent directly to her. He begs Anna to forgive him for everything, and she comments wearily that it isn't his fault that things worked out as they did—nor is it hers, nor Mat's. They just got all mixed up. Chris blames the old devil sea once again, and goes off to bed. Anna waits a bit longer, hopefully, and hears Mat's footsteps. He comes in and tells her that no matter how much he drank, he could forget nothing, and her face kept appearing before him. He begs her to tell him that what she said two days before was all a lie. Miserable, she says that it was all true. He becomes violently angry again, but in spite of his hurt and anger his love for her won't let him go. If she would swear a terrible oath that she has never loved anyone before him, he could forget everything, he says. Anna swears, with her happiness almost too much to bear. They'll be married in the morning, Mat says, and Chris returns to hear the news and is almost as happy as they are when the curtain falls.

Anna is packed and ready to leave, to go back to her former life

Anna Karenina

Novel by Leo Tolstoy, 1828–1910.
Published 1875–1877. Several translations. (ML,G23; ML, 37)

TODAY *War and Peace* is generally considered the world's greatest novel and *ipso facto* Tolstoy's best; but there was a time when *Anna Karenina* was by many ranked ahead of it. Tolstoy wrote *Anna Karenina* in emulation of Pushkin's simple, direct style. The parts were published serially and there were long gaps between, so that publication was not completed for two years. The novel is not nearly so long as *War and Peace,* but it is by no means short; it has more than 350,000 words. It is usually described as essentially the story of a woman whose love is so great that she scorns all consequences; but, artistically, Tolstoy records the qualms and misgivings that assail but do not stop her. Equally it would be the story of a man in love, except that Vronsky's sacrifice cannot be so great as Anna's. Within the story of the principal characters, given below, run the usual side issues of Russian political and social life in the 1870s and the stories of numerous subsidiary characters.

Part I. Chaps. 1–4. There is a crisis in the house of Prince STEPAN OBLONSKY, a rich and prominent government official in Moscow. His wife DARYA (or DOLLY) has learned of his affair with a former French governess of their five children, and refuses to forgive him. He has asked his sister, ANNA KARENINA, wife of ALEXEI KARENIN, in St. Petersburg, to come to Moscow.

Chaps. 5–16. At his office Stepan sees an old friend, KONSTANTIN LEVIN, a rich landowner, who has come to Moscow with the intention of courting CATHERINE (KITTY) SHTCHERBATSKY, Dolly's youngest sister, 18 years old. Stepan predicts that Kitty will marry him, but Kitty fancies herself in love with handsome young Count ALEXEY VRONSKY. When Levin proposes later that evening, she tells him that this cannot be. The look on her face when Vronsky arrives tells Levin the whole story.

Chaps. 17–23. Vronsky's mother arrives in Moscow on the same train with Anna Karenina. The two women have met and become friends. At the railroad station there is a bad accident; a man falls in front of the train and is killed. Anna and Vronsky feel an immediate attraction for each other, merely as they meet in the railroad station. Anna reaches her brother's house and her genuine sympathy softens Dolly somewhat. After dinner that evening Stepan goes to his wife's room at Anna's signal and a reconciliation is effected.

There is an impressive ball scheduled. Anna does not want to attend, but must. On the night of the ball Kitty is blissful—certain that tonight Vronsky will ask her to marry him. Vronsky hasn't the slightest intention of marrying Kitty, or anyone, but he enjoys Kitty's company and is pleased to squire a beautiful girl. When Vronsky dances with Kitty, she gazes adoringly at him. She is to remember for a long time, with bitter shame, that he made not the slightest response. Then she sees Anna and Vronsky dancing and she knows instantly that they are in love. Her misery is complete; she has refused the proposal of the man she may really love, expecting a proposal that will never be.

Chaps. 24–28. Konstantin Levin goes to visit his brother NIKOLAI and finds him living with a woman and "as good as married." The woman, MARYA, tells Levin she is troubled by the amount of vodka Nikolai is drinking. Nikolai is poor and has become interested in coöperative organizations that make no sense to Levin. Levin returns to his country home, filled with confusion about the social conditions of his country.

Chaps. 29–32. Soon after the day of the ball, Anna's husband summons her home and she returns to Petersburg. Alexei Karenin is a cold, uncompromising man, and Anna feels stiffly uncomfortable in his presence. On the train, in another compartment, was Vronsky—completely infatuated with Anna. He watches the greeting of husband and wife and reassures himself that Anna does not care for Karenin. He goes to his rooms, and Anna slips naturally back into the routine of family life.

Part II. Chaps. 1–7. In Petersburg, Vronsky contrives to be at almost all the theater and dinner parties that Anna attends, and she in turn attends more than ever in the past. She first tells herself that Vronsky's attentions are irritating, but one day she realizes suddenly that she more than welcomes them. The fashionable circle in which they move is quite aware that Vronsky is wooing Anna, and they feel it will be just a matter of time until she becomes his mistress.

Chaps. 8–11. When Alexei becomes aware of the gossip he warns Anna that she must do nothing to reflect on his dignity. Anna realizes that it is merely the appearance of things that concerns him. This makes her move more quickly toward the inevitable. She becomes Vronsky's mistress a year after they met.

Chaps. 12–17. Konstantin Levin throws himself into work about his farm, to put into the back of his mind the pain Kitty caused him. One day he is surprised by a visit from Stepan Oblonsky, who brings him up to date on events among their acquaintances in Moscow. Levin learns that Kitty has been very ill and is now convalescing abroad. She has not been married. Levin pretends no interest, but shortly thereafter he decides to go back and ask Kitty again to marry him. He feels certain that she loves him.

Chaps. 18–23. Anna and Vronsky are together, as often as it can be arranged, and all their friends are aware of the *liaison.* Vronsky's mother is rather pleased at first, but when she hears that her son has refused a promotion in his regiment, to stay near Anna, she becomes irritated. On the day when Vronsky's regiment is to hold its annual races and steeplechase, Anna informs him that she is pregnant. He wants to elope at once; she refuses because of the disgrace (and her son), divorce being impossible.

Chaps. 24–29. During the race in which Vronsky rides, his horse falls; Vronsky is unhurt, but Anna cannot conceal her dreadful fear. Her husband once again reminds her to be more careful of appearances. Anna can endure the pretense no longer and tells him that she loves Vronsky and is his mistress. Karenin's reaction is cold, and his concern is still solely for his reputation.

Chaps. 30–35. Kitty and her family are at Soden, a little German watering place, for Kitty's health. Kitty makes a friend, VARENKA, the companion and adopted daughter of Madame STAHL, a philanthropic widow. Kitty admires Varenka's faculty for helping others, and tries to emulate her, but trouble with a jealous wife who misunderstands Kitty's friendly gestures toward her tubercular husband puts an end to this.

Part III. Chaps. 1–6. Konstantin Levin's half-brother, SERGEI KOZNUISHEF, visits him at his country estate. The two men discuss social conditions; they have widely disparate ideas about the peasantry. Sergei wants a medical center and schools to be established in their district. Levin sees no particular reason for schools, since the peasants would not send their children anyway, and a medical center seems to him impractical, because bogs in warm weather and ice in cold weather prevent fast transportation. He does not say so, but he concludes that two kinds of people are interested in social welfare: those who hope to further their own self-interests, and those who have heard it is a worthy career and have nothing much else to do. To relieve his inner tension, Levin goes out in the meadows and works on the mowing, swinging a scythe. It is hard for him to keep up with the sturdy peasants. A letter from Stepan Oblonsky tells him that Dolly is having difficulty at their summer lodge, and Levin goes to help her out.

Chaps. 7–12. Levin learns that Kitty is still unattached, but though he admitted long since to himself that pride stood in his way, he finds that his pride is still a problem. Some time later he glimpses Kitty in a carriage, heading toward Dolly's lodge. He knows that nothing else is good enough. He loves Kitty.

Chaps. 13–23. The situation between Anna and her husband becomes constantly more unpleasant. Alexei considers divorce, but dreads the vileness of court evidence and knows also that it would be highly damaging to his social and political standing. Anna has not yet told him that she is pregnant.

Chaps. 24–32. Levin works hard at his estate and with great pain devises a scheme for profit-sharing among the peasants on the land. They are not enthusiastic, for many reasons, and the scheme does not go well. The arrival of Nikolai, in an advanced state of tuberculosis, creates extra tensions, and Levin recognizes that he is confronted with something that puzzles and confuses him. Levin is struggling with a social conscience, although he does not so define it.

Part IV. Chaps. 1–16. Against Alexei's orders Anna invites Vronsky to the house, and the two men meet on the doorstep. Alexei goes on to the meeting he was to attend, and Vronsky visits briefly with Anna. On his return, Alexei in a rage says that he is going to send SEROZHA, their son, to an aunt. Anna begs him to leave the boy; she now tells him that she will soon have another baby. Her husband visits a lawyer to start proceedings for a divorce, but later changes his mind because of the sordid publicity and evidence. Meanwhile, Levin and Kitty have been reconciled, and they are to be married—both of them blissfully happy, and very much in love.

Chaps. 17–19. Anna's baby—a little girl —is born, and Anna very nearly dies. She summons Alexei to the hospital, seeking forgiveness. The closeness of death briefly brings Vronsky and Karenin together in sympathetic understanding. Alexie decides he must remain with Anna. Vronsky's misery leads him to attempt suicide, but he recovers from the self-inflicted gunshot wound.

Chaps. 20–33. Stepan Oblonsky, Anna's brother, does his best to persuade Alexei that a divorce would be the best possible thing for everyone, and at long last Alexei concurs. In a burst of noble sentiment he agrees to give up his son, his wife, his pride. A friend rushes to tell Vronsky the news, and he in turn hurries to Anna's side. They are both as deeply in love as ever, but Anna's strange pride will not allow her to accept the apparent generosity of Alexei, and now she does not think it makes any difference whether she and Vronsky are married or not, so long as they are together. With the baby girl, they leave Russia.

Part V. Chaps. 1–6. With much fuss and confusion, the preparations for Kitty's wedding to Levin are completed. The greatest confusion was that of Levin himself, who was still in a state of delirious happiness and excitement. He forgets to go to confession until Stepan reminds him that he must have a certificate to that effect before the priest will perform the ceremony. The final disaster occurs when Levin discovers that his servant has packed all his clean shirts. Late and breathless, Levin does at length reach the church, and he and Kitty are married.

Chaps. 7–13. Vronsky and Anna have been traveling in southern Europe for three months. Vronsky is bored, with no job

to occupy him (he had resigned from the army). Their life in Europe is strained. Vronsky becomes interested in painting and painters, but soon tires of it. They return to Russia.

Chaps. 14–20. Levin's brother Nikolai dies, but Kitty's presence saves him from despair. Kitty discovers she is pregnant.

Chaps. 21–30. Anna had not been permitted to see Serozha since she had the baby; Alexei was persuaded by his friend Countess Lidia Ivanovna, who disliked Anna, not to let her see the boy. When Anna returned to Moscow she went anyway, on Serozha's birthday, with gifts. He had been told she was dead but refused to believe it, and their reunion is joyous.

Chaps. 31–33. The relationship between Anna and Vronsky becomes more and more difficult. Their love is as great as ever, but the fact that they are not married is a severe handicap, particularly to Vronsky. Anna suspects that Vronsky no longer loves her— even that he is in love with another woman. Her unreasonableness increases, and with it Vronsky's ill temper.

Part VI. Chaps. 1–15. The Levins, very happy, are at their summer place while Kitty waits for her baby. The Oblonskys visit them. They speak of Vronsky and Anna, living together on Vronsky's great estate, and the Oblonskys plan to go to see Anna.

Chaps. 16–24. Dolly visits Anna, who says she is "unpardonably happy." But Vronsky talks privately to Dolly, says that Anna's position in society is hell, he is discontented by being idle, and he wants Anna to write to Karenin and ask for a divorce. Dolly promises to urge Anna to do so. But Anna hesitates to humiliate herself by asking, and fears she will not get custody of Serozha anyway.

Chaps. 25–32. Election time in Kashin (their district) occupies Levin, Oblonsky, and Vronsky. Anna, increasingly sensitive,

hates to have Vronsky leave but resolves not to make a scene as usual. But she is irritable and all is not well between them. When he leaves, she writes to Alexei and asks for the divorce. Before he replies, Anna and Vronsky go to Moscow for the winter, living as if they were married.

Part VII. Chaps. 1–15. The Levins are in Moscow. Kitty's baby is late. Levin goes with Stepan to call on Anna. When he returns home and tells Kitty, she is jealous and accuses him of having fallen in love with Anna. It takes him hours to pacify her. The next morning a son is born to her.

Chaps. 16–22. Stepan sees Alexei in Petersburg; Alexei will not give a definite answer on the divorce.

Chaps. 23–31. An atmosphere of suspicion and irritation grows between Anna and Vronsky. It increases when Stepan telegraphs that Alexei is still undecided. Anna and Vronsky quarrel and he leaves the house in anger. Anna becomes filled with a desire to punish Vronsky for all the pain he has caused her. She sends him a note, asking him to return. When he replies that he cannot return before ten that night, brooding, she goes to the railroad station and takes a train—hardly caring where it will go. She gets out of the train, and suddenly she remembers the man who was run over on the day she first met Vronsky. Now she knows what she must do. She throws herself in front of an approaching train; at that moment she regrets her act, but it is too late.

Part VIII. After Anna's death, Vronsky feels that his life is empty. She was all in the world to him, in spite of her suspicions. He goes back to the army and is sent to Serbia, to the Turkish frontier. Levin, though he muses and puzzles much about social and religious dilemmas, settles with Kitty into a life of happy domesticity.

Anthony Adverse

Novel by Hervey Allen, 1889–1949. Published 1932, © 1933 by Hervey Allen. Published by Rinehart & Co., New York.

IT WOULD NOT BE far wrong to call *Anthony Adverse* a historic as well as a historical novel. It was the first of a type of novel—overlong, high-priced, sexy, romantic, swashbuckling, and quasi-historical—that went like wildfire for ten full years and brightened the Great Depression for every publisher who

had one. Whether *Anthony Adverse* started the trend or merely heralded it, it is impossible to say. Hervey Allen was not well known when *Anthony Adverse* began to break all sales records, but neither was he unknown; he had the distinction of having collaborated with DuBose Heyward and he had written an excellent popular biography of Poe, *Israfel*, 1926. *Anthony Adverse* may not be his best book but needless to say it is easy and great fun to read.

Chaps. 1–11. When young MARIA BONNYFEATHER, daughter of the rich merchant ANGUS BONNYFEATHER, marries Don LUIS, Marquis da VINCITATA, a man many years her senior, the Marquis is under medical care and for many months it is a marriage in name only. During this time Maria falls in love with DENIS MOORE, who is to become Anthony's father. Don Luis learns of the affair when a friend comments

that only prospective motherhood can give a woman's eyes the glow he sees in Maria's. Don Luis accepts congratulations in seething inner fury, and takes Maria away to a retreat high in the Alps. Denis attempts to follow his beloved Maria, and Don Luis kills him. Maria dies in childbirth, and Don Luis abandons the baby boy at the gate of a convent, leaving with him a cape and the statue of a Madonna that had belonged to

Maria. The nuns take him in, and baptize him ANTHONY, but as a foundling he has no last name.

Chaps. 12–26. When Anthony is ten Father XAVIER, who has been his guardian at the convent, makes arrangements for him to be apprenticed to Mr. Bonnyfeather, who realizes that this is Maria's son when he sees the cape and the statue of the Madonna. Maria always carried it with her. Mr. Bonnyfeather's housekeeper, FAITH PALEOLOGUS, knows the Madonna well, for she had given it to Maria; she called it the "Luck of the Paleologus." It is Mr. Bonnyfeather who gives Anthony the last name of "Adverse," because he declares that the boy's life is indeed one of adversity. Without telling Anthony that he is related to him, Mr. Bonnyfeather gives the boy a fine education and allows him to understand that some day he will inherit the Bonnyfeather business.

While he is still in his teens, Anthony has an affair with ANGELA, the cook's daughter, who soon goes away. Anthony does not know it, but she bore his child—a son. Angela becomes a popular and famous singer eventually. Anthony, meanwhile, falls in love with FLORENCE UDNEY, whom he is to marry many years later, but her mother—wife of the English consul—disapproves heartily of any association with a mere merchant's apprentice and makes it clear that Anthony's attention is unwelcome. Over the years, Anthony continues to love Florence.

At this time Napoleon is moving toward Leghorn, where Bonnyfeather has his business, and the shrewd Scotsman turns his assets gradually into cash, which he sends out of the country for safe-keeping. Anthony is given passage aboard the *Wampanoag*, a ship bound for Cuba, to collect an old debt of his grandfather's. The ship makes port at Genoa, and there Anthony learns from Father Xavier who his parents had been, and that Mr. Bonnyfeather is his grandfather.

Chaps. 27–32. When Anthony arrives in Cuba, he finds that GALLEGO, the man from whom Anthony was to collect Mr. Bonnyfeather's debt, has gone to Africa as a slave-trader. Don LUIS DE LA CASAS, the captain-general, gives Anthony a position as government agent, and thus the authority to go to Africa in an official capacity and seize one of Gallego's cargoes, to be shipped back to Cuba and there sold to discharge the debt, and incidentally to enrich Don Luis, who would share in the profits.

Chaps. 33–35. Anthony falls in love with DOLORES DE LA FUENTE, a relative of Don Luis, and with an idea of increasing his prospects for marrying her some day, agrees to remain at the slave-trading post and ship a few more groups of slaves back for sale.

Chaps. 36–45. Aboard ship, Anthony nurses a priest, Father ANTOINE, who contracts yellow fever and very nearly dies. Fear of contagion and hatred of the ship's captain cause the crew to become mutinous, and Anthony finds himself forced to take

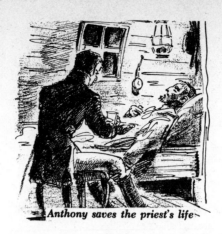
Anthony saves the priest's life

command in order to complete the voyage. Finally the ship is docked in the Rio Pongo, at the Gallego slave-trading post. Gallego has died and the post is in charge of his foreman, Ferdinando. Father Antoine sets up a small mission and erects a large wooden cross. Anthony takes Ferdinando's sister, a half-breed named NELETA, as his mistress, and for three years he ships cargoes of slaves to Cuba, although his conscience is never at ease concerning this traffic in human beings. One day Anthony returns from a business trip to find that Father Antoine has been nailed to his own cross, crucified by a native witch doctor who has long resented him.

Chaps. 46–53. Mr. Bonnyfeather has died during Anthony's long absence, and Anthony decides to return to Leghorn and settle the estate. He arrives in that city at the same time as Don Luis da Vincitata, who hates him viciously as a reminder of Maria and her betrayal of him. Faith Paleologus is now Don Luis's mistress, and she too hates Anthony, but for far different reasons. She felt herself the woman scorned, years before, when Anthony had refused to have an affair with her after one extremely youthful experience.

VINCENT NOLTE, whom Anthony knew at about the same time he first met Florence Udney, has become a banker. Anthony goes to him for the settlement of his grandfather's affairs. Vincent proposes that Anthony go to New Orleans and take charge of a complicated financial manipulation by which a French financier plans to exchange French money and food for Mexican silver, to be transferred through the presently bankrupt Spanish government. Anthony learns that Florence Udney's husband, DAVID PARRISH, is in Philadelphia and will receive the money that Anthony will ship from New Orleans, after the silver reaches there from the mines at Vera Cruz. Anthony will have considerable silver to invest for himself and can conceivably make excellent profits with the arrangement. Anthony and Vincent leave for Paris to complete the necessary negotiations with OUVRARD, the French financier who is manipulating the entire affair.

Meanwhile, Faith Paleologus and Don

Luis have conspired to kill Anthony and Vincent, knowing that they must travel by coach over a treacherous pass in the Alps on their way from Leghorn to Paris. They plan to force Anthony's carriage off the road, thus making him crash to his death in the ravine below. Faith and Don Luis get out of their own carriage to enjoy the spectacle of Anthony's death; but their plans misfire and the Marquis's coach and coachman plummet off the road, leaving the two conspirators to descend the mountain on foot.

Chaps. 54–62. In Paris, Anthony learns that Angela has borne him a son, whom she named Anthony. Angela is now a famous singer and is the mistress of Napoleon. Anthony begs her to marry him and go to New Orleans with him but she firmly refuses. She feels that he ought to be given his son, however, and Anthony learns to his astonishment that fatherhood is a deeply satisfying thing. He wonders why only motherhood is credited with the warmth and love that he as a father feels so powerfully. The boy is left with Vincent's cousin, Anna, at Angela's request, and Anthony willingly accepts responsibility for all of his expenses.

When David Parrish dies, Anthony marries Florence, whom he finds he still loves deeply. He has been most successful in his investments and is now a rich man. He has built a beautiful house to which he takes Florence, and they have a little girl, named MARIA.

Chaps. 63–64. While Dr. TERRY MITCHELL is paying them a visit, Anthony has to absent himself on business that keeps him away overnight. During the night a spark flies out of the fireplace and ignites the floor. Soon the house is a raging inferno, with no chance of escape for the two-year-old Maria, Florence, or Terry. Three revolver shots are the only comfort Anthony has—the knowledge that at least his wife and child did not suffer the agonies of burning to death.

Chaps. 65–68. Anthony goes west and is captured by soldiers of his old enemy, Don Luis, who sentences him to prison in Mexico City, achieving vengeful satisfaction at last. Don Luis's satisfaction is short-lived, however, for he dies of a stroke on that very day. Faith goes back to Spain—as a widow, for Don Luis had married at last.

Dolores de la Fuente, now the widow of a plantation owner, finds Anthony in prison two years later and arranges for his release. They marry and have two children. As Anthony is cutting down a tree one day, the axe slips and cuts him so deeply that he bleeds to death before anyone knows that he has been hurt.

Epilogue. Years later, a little girl finds the statue of the Madonna in the ruins of an old chapel. She thinks it beautiful, but her family is certain it must be an idol of some kind and they forbid her to keep it. Instead, it is used as a target and is shattered to bits.

Antigone

Tragedy by Sophocles, 495–406 B.C. Produced about 440 B.C. Many translations. (ML, T30; NAL, MT238; RE, 29)

THE STORY OF Antigone is traditional in Greek legend. The Sophocles classic has been translated innumerable times and there have been many other versions. Most notable among modern versions is a French one by Jean Anouilh, which was adapted for the English stage by Lewis Galantiere, and produced in New York in 1946 by Katharine Cornell. Miss Cornell played Antigone and Sir Cedric Hardwick played Creon. Guthrie McClintic (Miss Cornell's husband) directed. The production did not make money. ❡ The Sophocles play is on the plan of the ancient Greek drama. The theater is circular. Throughout the play the chorus comments on the story and on the actors' speeches and makes suggestions to the characters. *Antigone* is one of seven Sophocles plays (of the hundred-odd he wrote) that survive complete.

As the play opens, the scene is an open place before the palace of the King of Thebes. ANTIGONE and her sister ISMENE, daughters of the deposed king EDIPUS of Thebes, are bewailing the fact that the body of their brother POLYNICES is unburied. The new king of Thebes, CREON, has issued orders that no one give Polynices a funeral; Creon's reason is that Polynices plotted against him and also that Polynices died in a duel with his own brother, ETEOCLES, who remained loyal to Creon after the banishment of Edipus.

Antigone declares her intention of burying the body of Polynices. Ismene refuses to take part in this defiance of the king's edict.

Meanwhile, Creon learns that the people of the city are angry at his edict, because they feel that no one should be denied funeral rites. When news comes that someone has covered the body with dust and twigs, Creon threatens to execute the guards (who had been ordered to see that no one buried Polynices) unless they produce the guilty one. The guards then remove the dust and twigs and leave the body exposed again. They keep vigilant watch and eventually see Antigone return. Finding that her work has been undone, she again buries her brother's body. She is captured and taken to Creon and Creon sentences her to death, although she is the fiancée of his son, HAEMON. Antigone is to be entombed alive in a cave and left to die there.

When Haemon appears, he tries to convince his father that the people will be angry at this stern reprisal for violation of an order that they disapproved of in the first place. Creon refuses to listen, and Haemon leaves.

The opinion of Haemon is confirmed by a blind sorcerer upon whom Creon has relied often in the past. Once again Creon refuses to listen. The elders of the chorus warn Creon that the sorcerer has never been known to advise anyone badly, but still Creon is reluctant to countermand his sentence or to allow the body of Polynices to be buried.

Finally, however, he consents to listen to the advice of others and is about to set forth to release Antigone from the cave. A messenger comes in at this point to inform Creon that Haemon has learned of Antigone's death and has gone to the cave himself.

Antigone has hanged herself in the cave. Just as Creon arrives, Haemon stabs himself and dies by the body of Antigone. Creon carries his son's body back to the palace. There he finds that his wife, EURIDICE, upon learning of her son's death, was so filled with grief that she went home and killed herself. Now Creon has three deaths on his conscience—Antigone's, Haemon's, and Euridice's. It is too much for him to bear, and he gives himself over to his servants, ordering that he himself be killed. As the play ends, he is led away.

Antony and Cleopatra

Play by William Shakespeare, 1564–1616. Produced about 1606.

IT IS ACKNOWLEDGED that *Antony and Cleopatra* is one of Shakespeare's greatest tragedies, both as poetry and as drama. It covers a period of some eleven years, 40 to 30 B.C., but the incidental history of the times is sufficiently passed over or contracted to make the period seem much shorter. For his history, Shakespeare seems to have relied on Plutarch. The principal other play about Antony and Cleopatra is Dryden's *All for Love*. ❡ As the play opens, Rome is officially ruled by the triumvirate of Octavius Caesar in the West, Antony in the East, and Lepidus in Africa; but Antony's wife Fulvia and her brother are warring with Caesar for control of Italy, and Antony (though not supporting them) is also on the point of war against Caesar. Sextus Pompeius (called Pompey in the play), son of Pompey the Great, is to be feared. Antony has been luxuriating idly in Alexandria, Egypt's capital, as the lover of Cleopatra.

Act I. 1. Antony, living in Cleopatra's palace in Alexandria, is told that a messenger arrived from Rome. Antony is reluctant to see him. Cleopatra sarcastically advises Antony to hear the messenger, who may have brought orders from his wife Fulvia or from [Octavius] CAESAR. They talk lovers' talk and embrace. 2. In another room, CHARMIAN, the queen's principal female attendant, and IRAS, another, with ALEXAS, the queen's principal male attendant, and ENOBARBUS, one of Antony's generals, hear a Soothsayer predict their fortunes. Cleopatra enters and asks them to find Antony; but when Antony approaches, they all leave. A messenger from Rome tells Antony that his wife Fulvia and brother Lucius first fought each other, then combined forces against Caesar. Another messenger brings word that Fulvia has died and that Sextus Pompeius, commanding the naval forces, is threatening Caesar. Antony announces to Enobarbus his intention to return to Rome. 3. Cleopatra sends for Antony, and when he comes she scolds jealously about Fulvia; but he tells her he must leave for Rome, and that Fulvia is dead. Her jealousy and grief subside gradually and she sends him off with love. 4. In Caesar's house in Rome, Caesar is in conference with the third triumvir, LEPIDUS. Caesar tells of the reports of Antony's life wasted in revels in Alexandria. A messenger brings news that Pompey's revolt is thriving. Caesar hopes Antony will return to join him and fight Pompey. 5. Cleopatra grieves over the absence of Antony, expresses her great love for him, and writes to him every day.

Act II. 1. Pompey, in his house in Messina, is told that Antony is returning to Rome. 2–4. Antony, Caesar and Lepidus meet in Lepidus's house. Antony and Caesar exchange reproaches, but Antony denies having inspired or approved her brother's uprising against Caesar. Enobarbus and Caesar's general MECAENAS seek conciliation, and AGRIPPA, who becomes Caesar's chief general, suggests that Antony marry Caesar's sister OCTAVIA, to make them brothers. Antony and Caesar agree. Antony meets Octavia and pledges fidelity. (Enobarbus nevertheless predicts, privately, that Antony will return to Cleopatra, of whom he says, "Age cannot wither her, nor custom stale her infinite variety.") The men prepare for a campaign against Pompey. 5. In Alexandria, Cleopatra receives a messenger from Italy; when he tells her Antony has married Octavia, she strikes him down and threatens even to kill him; but she subsides, though still devastated by grief, and accepts the news. She sends an order to Alexas to give her a complete report on Octavia's appearance and character. 6–7. Caesar, Antony and Lepidus meet with Pompey near Misenum. The triumvirs have offered Sicily and

Sardinia to Pompey if he will rid the sea of pirates and will pay an annual tax. Pompey accepts. To seal the treaty the triumvirs attend a banquet on one of Pompey's ships.

Act III. 1. VENTIDIUS, one of Antony's generals, has conquered Parthia for Antony. He is bound for Athens, where he expects to meet Antony. 2. Antony and Octavia part from Caesar, Antony giving assurances of continued friendship. 3. Cleopatra receives a messenger who reports to her on Octavia's appearance: about 30 years old, not so tall as Cleopatra, with a low voice, round face, low forehead, and brown hair. Cleopatra tells Charmian that Antony will soon tire of his new wife. 4–5. In Athens, Antony tells Octavia of his grievances against Caesar. She tries to pacify Antony, saying she is torn between love of her husband and love of her brother. Antony consents to let her try to reconcile them, and tells her to go to Rome for that purpose; but says that in the meantime he must prepare for war. Enobarbus is told by EROS, another of Antony's followers, that Caesar and Lepidus have made war on Pompey, who is dead, and that now Caesar has deposed Lepidus, who has no more power. 6. In Rome, Caesar tells Agrippa and Mecaenas of Antony's crimes: Antony has had himself enthroned beside Cleopatra and has given to her and to her children by Antony many kingdoms of the Eastern empire. Octavia comes in and announces her mission. Caesar makes her unhappy by telling her that Antony has gone back to Alexandria and Cleopatra and that he is rallying the kings of the East for war against Caesar. But Caesar welcomes his sister lovingly. 7–10. The opposing forces of Antony and Caesar have gathered for battle at Actium. Cleopatra is with Antony; Enobarbus urges Cleopatra to return to Egypt but she insists that as a ruler she must stay. Antony determines to fight Caesar at sea, his fleet aided by Cleopatra's sixty ships. He tells CANIDIUS, who commands his ground forces, to hold off Caesar on land while they fight at sea. Caesar, meanwhile, is advised by his general TAURUS not to attack by land until the sea battle is decided. From a hill overlooking the battle, Enobarbus sees the Egyptian fleet of sixty ships flee from the battle; and he hears from Scarus, one of Antony's followers, that Antony has also fled with his ships. Canidius announces his intention of surrendering to Caesar, but Enobarbus decides to remain faithful to Antony, though he knows it is unwise. 11. In Cleopatra's palace, Antony is lost in shame that he fled from the battle. He sees Cleopatra, who is remorseful but says she did not know he would follow her. He tells her she should have known how his heart was tied to her. Now he is helpless before Caesar; and if he wishes to survive, he who once ruled half the world must humiliate himself before Caesar. 12. Caesar receives Euphronius, sent as ambassador by Antony. With Caesar is DOLABELLA, who deserted Antony and joined Caesar. Through Euphronius, Antony declares submission to

Caesar and asks to be allowed to live in Egypt, or, if Caesar refuses this, to live as a private citizen in Athens. Cleopatra also submits and asks that her heirs continue to rule Egypt. Caesar refuses to grant anything to Antony, but says he will grant Cleopatra's plea if she banishes or kills Antony. Euphronius leaves and Caesar sends his own representative, THYREUS, to offer Cleopatra even more if she will betray Antony. 13. Euphronius returns to Alexandria with Caesar's reply. Cleopatra then receives Thyreus, and tells him she submits to Caesar's wish; but Antony enters, becomes enraged, and has Thyreus taken off to be brutally whipped. He then sends Thyreus back to Caesar with a message of defiance. Cleopatra now affirms her love for Antony and applauds his determination to fight.

Act IV. 1. Caesar receives Antony's defiance and prepares to fight "the last of many battles." He scorns Antony's challenge to personal combat; he has "many other ways to die." 2–5. Antony prepares for battle. In his camp he learns from a soldier that Enobarbus has deserted to Caesar. Antony sends all Enobarbus's treasure and personal belongings to him, with a letter that does not reproach him. Antony grieves only that his bad fortune has corrupted honest men. 6. The battle has begun. Enobarbus is told that Antony has sent him his treasure, and more. His remorse is great and he goes off to kill himself. 7–9. At first the battle goes well for Antony. Cleopatra visits him in the field, with expressions of devotion. Caesar retreats. In Caesar's camp, Enobarbus kills himself. 10–13. Unsuccessful by land, Caesar prepares to fight Antony at sea. Antony prepares too, then learns that his fleet has surrendered to Caesar without a fight. He thinks Cleopatra is responsible, and when she comes to the field to see him he flies into a rage at her, despite her denial and protestation of love. In his rage he warns her that Caesar will take her to Rome as a captive and parade her before the plebeians. Cleopatra returns to her palace, thinking him mad. 14. She sends her servant Mardian, a eunuch, to tell Antony she has killed herself. Mardian finds Antony talking to Eros, still railing against Cleopatra's treachery; but when Mardian tells

Antony that Cleopatra always loved him, and has killed herself, Antony resolves also to kill himself and ask her pardon in the afterworld. He asks Eros to kill him, but instead Eros kills himself. Antony weeps for Eros, and then stabs himself with his own sword. He does not die at once and begs friends and members of the guard to dispatch him, but none will. Then, learning that Cleopatra is not dead, he asks to be taken to her and is carried off in his dying condition. 15. Antony is brought to Cleopatra. "I am dying, Egypt, dying," he tells her; and he wishes only to kiss her once more. He does so. She expresses her love; he advises her to seek safety with Caesar. He dies, and she grieves and faints.

Act V. 1. Caesar sends Dolabella to bid Antony yield; then Dercetas, one of Antony's followers, enters with Antony's sword and the information that he is dead. Caesar does not exult but says it is cause for weeping. An envoy from Cleopatra enters to say that Cleopatra asks instructions from Caesar. Caesar sends her a message to wait for instructions. Then he sends Proculeius, one of his men, to Cleopatra with the treacherous message that she is safe; for Caesar fears that she may kill herself and thwart his intention to parade her in Rome. 2. Proculeius gives Cleopatra Caesar's insincere message, but when he instructs the guard to watch her, she draws a dagger to stab herself. He stops her and reassures her. Caesar makes his entry and she kneels to him. He tells her not to kneel, and he too reassures her. Then he leaves. Dolabella comes to Cleopatra and tells her of Caesar's intention to send her and her children to Rome. After he is gone, Cleopatra has her best robes brought, to dress herself as befits a queen. A farmer brings her a basket, supposedly figs but actually containing asps. Cleopatra puts on her state robes and crown. She kisses Charmian and Iras, giving them poison. Iras dies. Cleopatra applies an asp to her breast, then another. She dies, then Charmian dies. When Caesar enters again, he learns that his plans have been thwarted as he feared, but he orders that Cleopatra and Antony be buried side by side, saying that no grave on earth shall hold a pair so famous.

The sea battle at Actium

The Apostle

Historical novel by Sholem Asch, 1880–1957.
Published 1943 by G. P. Putnam's Sons, New York. © 1943 by Sholem Asch. Translated by Maurice Samuel.

THE STORY OF ST. PAUL has been told in many forms and almost innumerable times. It is the best-documented personal story in the Bible and is supported by masses of collateral history. To his treatment of it Sholem Asch brought also an unusual knowledge of the Jewish customs that shaped Paul's youth and young manhood. ¶ Sholem Asch was born in Poland and came to the United States in 1914. He continued to write in German and Yiddish and his books were translated. *The Apostle* is one of his best novels.

Part I. Chaps. 1–6. Seven weeks after the crucifixion of Jesus of Nazareth, the Jews of all the area for many miles from Jerusalem are coming to the city on the feast of Pentecost, the feast that celebrates the giving of the Ten Commandments to Moses. For this feast they bring the first fruits of their gardens, as an offering to the God of Israel. This time, however, there is another element present. Whispers and loud affirmations tell of the strange and wonderful thing that has happened. The Jesus who was crucified has reappeared, with scars and wounds still upon his body. He has talked with his followers and has instructed them to take his Word to the entire world, gentiles as well as Jews. This reaches the ears of SAUL, in Tarsus, and offends him greatly, for he believes it is blasphemy. His friend JOSEPH of Cyprus seems doubtful that it will be easy to suppress this movement. Too many people are convinced that the Messiah promised by Isaiah has indeed come. The next day STEPHEN, a rabbi, declares his conviction that Jesus was the Messiah. The words of Stephen impress Joseph, who had known Jesus during his lifetime, and he becomes a convert. Joseph's turning is a bitter blow to Saul. Joseph frees his slaves and sells all his worldly goods, and gives the gold to SIMON, the chief disciple of the Messianists. He is then baptized.

Simon, called Peter, causes further disturbance by the performance of a miracle in the name of Jesus. He heals a lame beggar who has been crippled for many years. This is considered evil by the High Priests of the Jews, because it was performed in the name of Jesus rather than in the name of the God of Israel. When Simon refuses to be intimidated by the High Priest, the priest realizes that he must be magnanimous and forgiving, and Simon is released with a warning. The release of Simon and his follower, JOCHANAN, makes many people wonder if these men are protected by some higher power than that of the priests.

Chaps. 7–9. Saul of Tarsus lives in a city filled with wickedness and evil. He talks to the Rabbi GAMALIEL, and from the Master hears words of tolerance and spiritual understanding that to him seem almost a denial of the words of the Torah. Still, the words are an important influence that will eventually lead to his embracing the faith of the Messianists—or, as they come later to be known, Christians.

There is a second arrest of Simon and Jochanan. They are imprisoned, with a powerful guard, and still are free in the morning. The High Priest of Jerusalem hesitates to admit that they have escaped by supernatural means, and yet there is no other logical explanation—unless there are treacherous Christian sympathizers among the prison guard. The two disciples are arrested for a third time, and it is the Rabbi Gamaliel who declares that they have committed no evil that is punishable by law, and they are therefore released.

Chaps. 10–17. Saul, in his vigorously religious convictions, devotes himself to the elimination of the Messianists and Galileans. He becomes an official spy of the High Priests in Jerusalem. He takes the disciple STEPHEN into custody and sentences him to be stoned to death. Stephen is the first Christian martyr, and as he dies he prays for the people who caused his agony. Even Saul is troubled by this demonstration of faith.

News comes that there are followers of Jesus in Damascus, and Saul offers to search them out. On the road to Damascus a vision appears to him and there is heard a voice that says "Saul, Saul, why do you persecute me?" Saul asks who is speaking, and the same voice says that it is Jesus of Nazareth. Saul asks what he should do and is told that he should go to Damascus and there he will learn what he must do. When the vision is over, Saul has been blinded and must be led into Damascus.

In Damascus Saul visits Chananyah, an old priest who he has heard is a Messianist. A talk with Chananyah convinces Saul. He is baptized into the Christian faith and his blindness is healed.

Chaps. 18–20. Saul has difficulty in convincing the Messianists that he has realized the rightness of their beliefs. For a long time he remains in Jerusalem, waiting for the sign that will tell him what he must do. Joseph is happy and prays that Saul receive his sign. Finally the sign comes. Saul hears a voice that tells him to leave Jerusalem and go far away. Joseph watches his friend depart, and prays that the fulfillment of God's will will direct Saul to the place where he must go.

Part II. Chaps. 1–5. Unrest and conflict between Jews and Gentiles arise in Alexandria when Agrippa, a Jew, becomes king. The Greeks and Egyptians resent him, but his influence in Rome was great. The unrest turns into riots and concerted persecutions of Jews. In Rome, the Emperor Caligula in his madness has proclaimed himself a god and orders all countries in the Roman Empire to worship him as such. The crowning affront is his command that a statue of himself be placed in the Holy of Holies, the innermost chamber of the Temple at Jerusalem. PETRONIUS, a Roman officer, is sent to Jerusalem to place the statue in the temple, and his soldiers are met by a solid wall of Jews who refuse to yield, although they raise no hand against the soldiers. Petronius halts the soldiers and sends a message to Caligula to report this strange behavior. Caligula sends back a command for Petronius to commit suicide for having failed to carry out his orders. Caligula himself, however, is murdered before this command reaches Petronius, and Claudius becomes emperor.

Simon Peter travels widely, teaching of the Messiah everywhere. He receives a vision in the night, wherein a voice tells him that the food taboos of the Mosaic law should be forgotten. Jew and Gentile must sit at table together. It is while they are doing so that the Holy Ghost descends upon them.

Chaps. 6–11. Saul's first convert to the faith is a young man named Titus, and Titus travels with him. After Saul has received his sign—the blinding of an evil sorcerer by the angel of the Lord at Saul's behest—he changes his name to PAUL. When the Jewish congregation of a synagogue rejects him, he knows that he must take the word of the Savior to Gentiles.

Chaps. 10–27. Paul travels to Antioch, and to Philippi in Macedonia, and establishes congregations. He goes to Corinth, to Athens, to other cities in Greece, and to Ephesus. In Ephesus Paul wins many converts. Diana's images are destroyed by her former worshipers and the inner temple of her shrine is burned.

Chaps. 28–35. Paul's travels are beset with trouble. In some places he is recognized and hated as the Saul who persecuted Messianists. In other places he is accused of betrayal of the faith of Israel. A silversmith accuses him falsely of desecrating the temple by carrying dead bones into the inner sanctum, and by taking Gentiles inside it. This accusation inflames the people, and Paul is seized and taken to the field of stoning. He reminds the mob of his Roman citizenship and demands a trial. Later he insists on his right to a trial before the emperor, and eventually is put aboard a prison ship—after two long years of being held prisoner. He is on his way to Rome when a shipwreck occurs, and Paul calms the frightened sailors and prisoners by assuring them that he has been informed that none will die. This proves true, and they are washed ashore. They finally reach the capital, and Paul is surrounded by devoted followers as he enters prison.

Part III. Chaps. 1–22. Paul is imprisoned

in Rome, but even in prison his work continues. Peter meanwhile is teaching Christianity in the Jewish section of the city and is winning converts in great numbers. Among the slaves the new faith takes hold rapidly, and Rome begins to fear the movement. Nero is now emperor of Rome, and his empress is Sabina Poppeia.

Through Poppeia, Nero agrees to give Paul a long-delayed trial, but he himself is too busy to trouble himself with affairs of state. He sends a judge to hear the trial, and Paul is set free. Nero in his boredom decides to set fire to the city of Rome and rebuild it according to his own fancies. One night Nero's servants execute his orders to burn the city. Although Nero thought it a fine idea at the time, he now seeks a scapegoat and a whispering campaign is started to make the people believe it was the Christians. The lies spread swiftly and the Romans begin to abuse Jews and Christians alike. The culmination is Nero's great spectacle in the arena, when thousands of men, women, and children die horribly for the crime of having a religious faith. Paul is not among these thousands, but remains in prison, where he has once again been thrown in to await a hearing. The hearing is brief and a mere matter of form, and Paul is sentenced to death. Among the other condemned prisoners he finds Simon Peter. Paul is a Roman citizen and is beheaded. Simon Peter is crucified.

The Roman people are filled with wonder at the ways of the Christians. No matter how many they execute, the number increases like an avalanche. And they begin to fear and to ask themselves if perhaps they have been wrong.

Appointment in Samarra

Novel by John O'Hara, 1905– Published 1934. © 1934 by John O'Hara. Published by Harcourt, Brace & Co., New York. (ML, 42; NAL, S1437)

JOHN O'HARA'S qualifications as a novelist are rated higher and higher as the years pass, but as to one of them there has never been any doubt. His ear for American conversation has always been superlative, perhaps even matchless; and it was already at its best in his first big success, *Appointment in Samarra*. This novel also is almost sure to be the one for which O'Hara is best remembered, though he himself rates it only as "tied for second" among his works. ❧ *Appointment in Samarra* is a tragedy, covering a period of less than three days in which its protagonist, Julian English, degenerates from a respected citizen and human being to a wreck for whom the only solution is suicide. The setting is Gibbsville (always said to be modeled on Harrisburg), Pennsylvania, as are so many of O'Hara's later stories. The book is fairly short, about 75,000 words, and very readable; the character portrayals are good, especially that of Caroline English, Julian's wife.

The title is from a story told by W. Somerset Maugham in his play *Sheppey* (1913): A merchant in Baghdad sends his servant to market, where the servant sees Death. Frightened, the servant borrows his master's horse and flees to Samarra. Later in the day the merchant meets Death and asks, Why did you threaten my servant? Death replies, I did not threaten him; I only showed surprise at seeing him in Baghdad, when I have an appointment with him tonight in Samarra.

1. On Christmas morning, 1930, Luther FLIEGLER and his wife IRMA are awake in the middle of the night. LUTE is a salesman for the Cadillac agency in Gibbsville. Irma, lying awake, thinks of how the Christmas Eve dance at the Lantenengo Country Club is just getting good, at 3:20 A.M., and how she and Lute expect to be members by next year. At the club, the usual set of young married couples, of Gibbsville's best society, are assembled in the "smoking room," drinking heavily. HARRY REILLY, very rich, middle-aged, and a social climber, is sitting with them telling his usual Irish stories. JULIAN ENGLISH and his wife CAROLINE, a young couple of 30 who "belong" in every way, are among those at the table. Julian is president of the Cadillac agency—but Harry Reilly, having helped him out financially, practically owns it. Julian feels annoyed and has an impulse to throw his highball in Reilly's face, but he knows he won't. However, he gets drunker and drunker—and he does. After an embarrassing half hour, the Englishes go home. AL GRECCO (real name Tony Murascho), young ex-convict and now a driver for ED CHARNEY, Gibbsville's principal bootlegger, driving back from Philadelphia with champagne for a party at the Englishes' the day after Christmas, is passed on the road by Julian, driving wildly. He surmises that Julian is very drunk and Caroline very angry.

2. Julian wakes up with a hangover. He dresses carefully, for Christmas dinner at his parents', and goes downstairs. Caroline has already been out, delivering presents. She wants Julian to take back the bracelet he got her for Christmas; Harry Reilly is vengeful and powerful, the story is already all over town, and they won't be able to afford it when Harry gets through. She thinks Julian's real reason was jealousy—suspicion of her with Reilly. Julian denies it, but not wholly. Caroline begins to cry, because she is used to love Julian so much and he has changed so much.

3. Gibbsville, primarily an anthracite town, still has much wealth despite the depression. Dr. WILLIAM ENGLISH, Julian's father, is very prominent and prosperous. He is head of the hospital but is not actually a good physician and is small in many ways. Dr. and Mrs. English and Julian and Caroline have a typical, dull, family Christmas dinner. On the way home, largely to appease Caroline, Julian goes to Harry Reilly's to apologize but Reilly refuses to see him. That night, Al Grecco goes to the Stage Coach, a roadhouse owned by Charney, to keep an eye on HELENE HOLMAN, the singer with the band there, who is Charney's girl; she drinks, and when drunk she cheats. Charney cannot be there because one of his children has broken a leg.

4. The Englishes drive to the club to a dinner dance; they are reconciled and talk about having a baby, for which they have intentionally waited almost five years. Caroline urges Julian not to drink too much tonight. At the club Julian is kidded by everyone. Harry Reilly is not there (because he has a black eye, from an ice cube in the drink) but his sister, Mrs. GORMON, has a dinner party for a group of leading Catholics including Monsignor CREEDON, principal local priest. Julian gets an opportunity to speak privately to Father Creedon, who is friendly and says he does not like Reilly either; but he offers no good suggestion on how Julian can make up with Reilly. Julian dances with Caroline and they intermittently quarrel and make up; he is oversensitive when anything she says seem like a reproach. They go out and sit in their car but when he becomes amorous she is cold and goes back in. Julian goes to the locker room to get drunk.

5. How Caroline came to marry Julian: She had known him well all her life, but had never thought of him seriously; she had only thought she was in love once, and only briefly. That was a young man named Joe Montgomery whom she met in New York on her way to Europe. She returned to Gibbsville and dated various men including Julian. Then in 1926, when she was 27, she found herself madly in love with Julian and he with her, and they were married.

6. At the Stage Coach, the Flieglers are in a party of couples in a similar income and social group. Al Grecco and Helene, who chafes at being watched by him, have angry words. The Englishes come in with friends—WHITNEY HOFMAN and his wife KITTY, and CARTER DAVIS, the club party is over and Julian is very drunk. He goes over to the Flieglers' table, where everyone is flattered by the attention from a society man, and he stays to drink. Then he goes to the table where Helene is sitting with Al Grecco. Al warns Julian that Helene is Ed Charney's, but Julian is not impressed. He and Helene dance, then he takes her outside to his car. There he falls asleep, Helene goes

Julian goes home to drink alone

back in alone, and Julian's friends find him sleeping when they come out to go home.

7. Julian wakes at 9:30 the next morning; Caroline has been down for breakfast and has gone back to bed. Julian has breakfast and snaps at Mrs. GRADY, the cook. Then he goes to Harry Reilly's office, but Reilly is dashing out to make a train, so Julian goes to his office. Lute Fliegler tells him they may have lost a sale to a Catholic, who like most Catholics in town thinks there was a religious basis to his throwing the highball in Harry Reilly's face, and also that their best customer, Ed Charney, may be lost because of Julian's behavior with Helene. Julian starts to go over his finances and thinks about the $20,000 he borrowed from Harry Reilly; it is all gone and at least half he spent unwisely. Meanwhile Caroline is suffering, for she is convinced that Julian was unfaithful, just because he was annoyed at her; Al Grecco is thinking murderous thoughts because Ed Charney bawled him out; and Helene is taking a train for New York.

8. Julian has finished going over his figures for the year. He finds he needs $2000 to stay in business; but he tells himself he needs $5000 because it is just as easy to get five as two. He broods about what it will mean to have Harry Reilly as an enemy and he takes his .25 automatic from the drawer, but after going so far as to put the barrel in his mouth he has a drink instead. Caroline calls and says that if he insults Mrs. Grady again she will leave him. Julian goes to the Gibbsville Club for lunch, and is joined by FROGGY OGDEN, Caroline's cousin and supposedly his close friend, who lost an arm in the war. Ogden wants to talk to Julian about his recent behavior; Julian takes offense and is insulting. Ogden vainly tries to make Julian fight and eventually

swings at him; Julian wards off the blows and other members, just becoming aware of the fight, think Julian has attacked the one-armed war hero. Julian loses his temper completely, knocks down one of the other members, hits Ogden, and leaves.

Caroline has a long talk with her mother, but gets no help because her mother cannot understand (or Caroline cannot express) her real problem. When Caroline comes out of her mother's house, Julian has driven there and is waiting for her. He tells her he is now in trouble at the second club; he is pugnacious and sarcastic and they quarrel. Their party for that night is to be postponed. Though Caroline warns that it will be final, they part on the street.

9. Julian goes home alone and begins to drink. A girl reporter from the society section comes to get a story about the party, learns it is off, but stays to drink; when she and Julian become dangerously amorous, she leaves. Julian sees a hopeless, lonely future in store for him. He goes to the garage, closes it, starts the car, and within half an hour is dead.

10. Julian is officially adjudged a suicide, though Caroline's mother is shocked when Caroline does not seem interested in trying for a different verdict. But Caroline cannot sleep. Harry Reilly assures his sister that Julian's act cannot be connected with him; why, Julian dropped in at his office that very day. Lute Fliegler pretends not to be worrying about who will be made head of the company, and Irma expresses confidence that he will.

Archy and Mehitabel

Humorous stories by Don Marquis, 1878–1937.
Published 1927 by Doubleday & Co., New York.

THE FOLLOWING OF Archy and Mehitabel (properly, archy and mehitabel) was numbered in the millions. The idea was the happiest of Don Marquis's many happy ideas. Archy, a cockroach in his present incarnation, could use the typewriter only by jumping from key to key, so of course he could not hold down a shift key, and there are no capital letters (or punctuation, either) in the stories. The earliest stories were published in Don Marquis's newspaper column "The Sun Dial," in the New York *Sun*. Three books were published: *archy and mehitabel*, *archy's life of mehitabel*, and *archy does his part*. Our illustrations are two of the original, famous ones by George Herriman, the Krazy Kat man.

One day, the author says, he entered the room where his typewriter reposed a little earlier than usual, and found a huge cockroach jumping from key to key of the machine. It was apparently very difficult for the cockroach, but he achieved results. Thereafter a sheet of paper was left in the typewriter for his use each night.

ARCHY the cockroach explains—on paper —how it happens that he is such a literate cockroach. He was once a free-verse poet, but he died and his soul went into the body of a cockroach. He thanks the writer— whom he always addresses as "boss"—for the apple peelings in the waste basket, but complains that the paste is too stale for him to eat. He then comments on a cat named MEHITABEL, about whom he has two complaints: She almost ate him a few nights before, and she is neglecting her job of catching rats—a rat named Freddy in particular, who was also a poet in a former life. Freddy is jealous of Archy's poetry, and every time Archy leaves a new poem in the typewriter, Freddy reads it, sneers at it, and then eats the paper. Archy's first letter ends on a wistful note. He wonders if the boss doesn't ever eat sandwiches in his office. He hasn't had a bit of bread or a morsel of ham since he can remember. Nothing but apple peel and paste.

Mehitabel the cat declares that she was once Cleopatra—among others. She sings of her life, and every time she remarks on one of her misadventures she follows it with a casual "wotthehell" or "toujours gai." Archy comments that he sometimes thinks that our Mehitabel is *too* gay.

Mehitabel returns from a visit to the suburbs, relieved to be back. She has had an adventure and it did not please her. A slicker tomcat named Fluffy struck up acquaintance with her and invited her to his house, where he assured her there was an ample supply of delicacies to delight the palate, including some excellent cream. According to Mehitabel's report to Archy, he promised her a little love nest, and a red ribbon with silver bells, not to mention a life of ease and luxury. They had barely managed to open the refrigerator door when Fluffy's mistress appeared and demanded to know what on earth he was doing, associating with such a disreputable type of alley cat. As Mehitabel explains to Archy, this was bad enough, but when Fluffy turned on her, and literally chased her out, she became furiously angry. For two days she lurked about the house, but not too close to the house, of course, and finally she caught him. Emphatically she announced her intention of removing one of his eyes, and with her skilled

claws did so. An ear in shreds seemed like a fine idea, too, and Fluffy's ear was shredded. A brisk stroke lacerated his nose, and another his back. Mehitabel then explained politely that it was fortunate he had not made her *really* angry, and fortunate also that she always behaves like a lady. She then warned Fluffy never again to trifle with another young woman's confidence, and deposited him on the doormat. She assures Archy that she has been abducted many times before by much better cats than he would ever be. Still, her motto is "Toujours gai!"

In another of Archy's notes to the boss, he says that Mehitabel is back, after a brief absence, with a family of three kittens. She says she does not know what she has done to deserve all these kittens. Her life has just been one batch of kittens after another, as long as she can remember. Not that she doesn't love the little things, of course! She is not like some cats she knows who would simply abandon their kittens. She has made a home for them in an old, empty garbage pail. Of course, it might rain hard, and in that case they would naturally drown. On the other hand, if she were the kind of cat that lived in a house with people, they would probably be drowned anyway. Archy remarks that it did rain, but philosophically notes that it's an old garbage pail and probably leaks. So the kittens probably aren't drowned.

One day Archy hears a spider and a fly talking, and he listens. The fly begs the spider not to eat him because he is very useful in the world. The spider doubts this, and asks for some proof. The fly explains that he scampers around all sorts of dirty places—such as trash heaps, garbage dumps, and dirty barns—and then when he has collected a fine assortment of germs on his feet, he carries them into people's houses and gives them diseases. This may not sound like a useful service to mankind, but the fly explains why it is. All the people who have lived good, clean lives get well, but all the people who have lived bad lives and have weakened their bodies with alcohol get sicker and sicker, and finally die. In this way, the fly says, he helps to get rid of the wicked.

The spider agrees that in a plodding sort of way the fly is useful, after a fashion. However, the spider is an artist, and creative. The webs of the spider are things of beauty—woven with skill and artistry, of gossamer filaments. It is foolish to ask a spider to deny himself the food he needs to keep up his strength for his artistic endeavors. It is foolish also for that food to make a request not to be eaten. The fly is convinced, and resigns himself to becoming the spider's meal. However, he thinks he could have made out a better argument in his own favor if he had really tried. The spider agrees, but says that it really wouldn't have made any difference anyway. In fact, if neither one of them had said a word, the same exact thing would have happened—so why worry?

This last comment gives Archy something to think about. He wonders seriously if words and writing are not more or less a waste of time, if people are going to do the same thing anyway.

Archy hears two fleas talking together one day. One invites the other to lunch, saying that he knows where there is a pedigreed dog available. The second flea answers that he doesn't care in the least whether the dog is pedigreed or not. All he is concerned about is whether the dog is wearing a muzzle. Frankly, he has found that millionaires taste just about the same as hoboes.

Arms and the Man

Comedy by George Bernard Shaw, 1856–1950.
Produced in London, 1894.

THIS IS PERHAPS closest to a straight farce of all Shaw's plays; in Broadway parlance, it has the most belly laughs, or buffos. The characters duck in and out of closets and at times all depends on the concealment of some prop or other. The plot is strong and the theme is timeless; it can amuse audiences of the late 20th century as well as it amused audiences of the Nineties. The title comes from the traditional translation of the first words of the *Aeneid*. *Arms and the Man* became an equally successful operetta, *The Chocolate Soldier,* with music by Oscar Straus.

Act I. In the bedchamber of RAINA PETKOFF in her father's mansion, a showplace in Bulgaria, Raina is admiring the night sky when CATHERINE, her mother, bursts into the room with news of a battle and a victory. At Slivnitza, the Bulgarian troops have been victorious over the Serbians, and the hero of the cavalry charge that won the victory is Raina's fiancé, SERGIUS SARANOFF. Raina is overcome with remorse that she ever doubted the

dows must be shuttered and bolted. Several Serbian fugitives have escaped. Catherine leaves to check on the windows of the lower floor. Louka shows Raina how to open and close the shutters if she wants to enjoy the beauty of the evening.

Raina prepares for bed, but goes to the window for another few moments. Suddenly there is the sound of shooting. She hastily runs to extinguish the candles in her bedroom and forgets about closing the shutters. Almost immediately a soldier appears on the balcony outside her window. He is disheveled and dirty, and extremely tired. He is a Serbian officer, and he threatens to shoot Raina if she makes any disturbance. He tells her of the ridiculous cavalry charge that routed the Serbian forces—because they were out of ammunition, and the Bulgarian officer doubtless knew about it. Raina is furious and refuses to believe him.

The soldiers of the town come to search for the fugitive, and Raina hides him. The maid, Louka, hears them talking and knows that someone has been concealed in Raina's bedchamber. Catherine knows it too. As Act I ends, The Man has fallen asleep on Raina's bed—impervious to the fact that Catherine is shaking his arm violently.

Act II. In the garden of the Petkoff establishment, NICOLA, the head manservant, is talking with Louka, warning her that she is far too disrespectful in her attitude toward the mistress. Louka is unrepentant and declares that she knows something about Miss Raina that would ruin her engagement to Sergius. They are interrupted by a hail from Major PETKOFF, returned from the war. Catherine appears, moderately pleased to have her husband at home again. Major Sergius Saranoff appears next.

The two men talk of a Swiss officer in the Serbian Army who outbargained them in an exchange of horses for prisoners. Further, he had told them an amusing tale of how he escaped the rout after the battle of Slivnitza, taking refuge in the bedroom of a Bulgarian lady—a young lady, at that. She and her mother had sheltered him, and had sent him on his way in the morning wearing a coat that belonged to the master of the house.

Major Petkoff remarks that he must send three calvary regiments to Philippopolis and he does not know the best route. Will Sergius please come to the library with him and help out? Catherine tactfully says that she will help instead, leaving Sergius and Raina together. Their protestations of love are on a very loftly level, and when Raina leaves to get her hat, preparatory to taking a walk, Sergius descends abruptly to a more earthy level with Louka, the maid. Raina

Bluntschli on his first appearance at the Petkoff house—Catherine tries to wake him

comes back, but the Major badly needs help in routing those three regiments, so Sergius goes to render assistance.

Raina and her mother leap to the subject of the tattletale Swiss officer. But Louka announces that a Serbian officer named Captain BLUNTSCHLI—a Swiss, she thinks—is calling and wishes to see the lady of the house. The officer is carrying a big carpet bag, which makes Catherine jump to the conclusion that it is The Man and that he has come to return the coat. She orders Louka to bring the man to the garden and to tell Nicola to come later with the carpet-bag.

Captain Bluntschli steps out into the garden, and before Catherine can spirit him out of sight and out of the vicinity, Major Petkoff comes bounding out, delighted to see the Captain and eager for his help in routing the three regiments. Between Sergius and the Major, Bluntschli is prevailed upon to become a house guest.

Act III. In the library, Bluntschli, Petkoff and Sergius are working on the orders for the calvary. That is, Petkoff is asking if he can help, Sergius is signing the completed documents as they come up, and Bluntschli is doing all the work.

The orders are at last completed, and Sergius and Major Petkoff go to deliver them. As an afterthought, the Major asks his wife to accompany them, feeling that they will be more likely to obey orders implicitly if she lends her disciplinary strength; they'll be more afraid of her than of him.

Bluntschli and Raina are left alone. For the first time in her life, Raina realizes that here is a man who sees through her dramatizations of herself. As they are talking, Louka brings in some mail to the Captain, and he learns that his father has died, leaving him several hotels. He leaves to instruct his man concerning the necessary trip to Switzerland.

Sergius comes in and finds Louka alone. Louka taunts him with the declaration that he would not be brave enough to marry her even if he loved her, because he would fear to face the people of his own rank. She tells him that Raina will never marry him, because now the Swiss has come back—the one whom Raina had sheltered in her room during the past war. Sergius is furious, and

when Bluntschli comes in, Sergius challenges him to a duel. Raina overhears, and Bluntschli assures her that he will do his best not to hurt her fiancé. There follows a bit of confusion, which is resolved when it becomes clear that Sergius and Louka wish to be married and so do Bluntschli and Raina.

The appearance of Major Petkoff and Catherine, and their bewilderment concerning the sudden alteration in engaged couples, leads to a brisk comparison of worldly possessions. Bluntschli is victor by a large margin, thanks to his new inheritance. He leaves for Switzerland, asking Sergius not to get married until at least a week from Friday, when he will be back. The play closes with Sergius's comment that this is indeed a man!

Around the World in 80 Days

> *Novel by* Jules Verne, 1825–1905. Published 1873.
>
> AMONG THE MANY imaginative novels of Jules Verne, two have always been uppermost in public favor, this one and *Twenty Thousand Leagues under the Sea.* The fact that *Around the World in Eighty Days* was based on sound reasoning—as were so many of Verne's books—was almost immediately proved when a young New York newspaperwoman named Nellie Bly promptly set off to see if she could make the trip in eighty days and beat par by three days. Verne was not a great writer but his books were interesting and the content was usually more than enough to compensate for the deficiencies in style.

Chaps. 1–4. PHILEAS FOGG, a rich bachelor in London and a member of the Reform Club, was almost superhumanly prompt and regular. Having just discharged his valet for bringing him shaving water at 84° instead

of 86°, on Oct. 2 he employed a new French valet, JEAN PASSEPARTOUT, who had lived an adventurous life including experience as a circus rider and gymnast and who now wanted a quiet existence. At his club, Fogg found there were two main topics of conversation: A well-dressed gentleman had calmly picked up £55,000 in the Bank of England and walked out with it; and the *Daily Telegraph* had estimated that with the opening of a new rail connection in India the world could be circled in 80 days, thus:

London to Suez, rail and steamboats . 7 days
Suez to Bombay, steamer . . . . 13 days
Bombay to Calcutta, rail . . . . 3 days
Calcutta to Hong Kong, steamer . . . . 13 days
Hong Kong to Yokohama, steamer . . 6 days
Yokohama to San Francisco, steamer . 22 days
San Francisco to New York, rail . . . . 7 days
New York to London, steamer and
    rail . . . . 9 days

Fogg's whist-playing friends scoffed at this; Fogg believed it correct and bet them £20,000 he could do it. It was then 7 P.M. He finished the whist game, picked up Passepartout and a bag containing £20,000 in cash, and took an 8:45 P.M. train for Dover. In the rush Passepartout forgot to turn off the gas light in his room and Fogg said he would have to pay for it.

Chaps. 5–10. In London betting on and against Fogg was brisk; "Phileas Fogg bonds" were traded on 'Change. But on Oct. 9 Scotland Yard received a telegram from Mr. FIX, a detective, saying he had located the bank robber and a warrant for his arrest should be sent to Bombay. Fix had seen Fogg in Suez and Fogg fitted the description. Fix took the boat for Bombay to stay with Fogg and struck up an acquaintanceship with Passepartout. The great amount of cash Fogg had with him seemed to confirm the suspicion. Fogg paid the engineer of the steamer, *Mongolia,* to keep steam up and they arrived at Bombay a day early. The warrant had not arrived so Fix wired to have the warrant sent ahead and took the Calcutta train with Fogg.

Chaps. 11–14. After about two days the railroad stopped at a hamlet, Kholby, and discharged all passengers: The report in the London newspaper had been incorrect and 50 miles of the line had not yet been laid. Imperturbably, Fogg found an elephant, Kiouni. Its owner would not rent or sell it until Fogg virtually forced him to sell for the incredibly high price of £2,000. With Sir Francis CROMARTY, a British general, they set off for Allahabad, where the rail line resumed. On the way they passed a suttee procession: The young widow of a rajah was to be burned to death to join her dead husband. Fogg calculated he could spare 12 hours and must save her. It seemed hopeless, when suddenly at the last minute the dead rajah came to life and sat up. The crowds, overcome with dread, prostrated themselves; and the dead rajah seized the woman and joined Fogg and Cromarty. It was Passepartout, in disguise. They set off, eluded the vengeful Indians, and reached Allahabad.

The rescued woman was the most beautiful ever seen by any, and equally charming; her English was perfect. Her name was AOUDA. Fogg reached Calcutta on schedule, Oct. 25, having lost back two days he had gained before.

Chaps. 15–17. At Calcutta Fogg and Passepartout were arrested—not, as they first thought, because of the suttee rescue but on a trumped-up charge arranged by Fix to delay them. Fogg put up £1,000 bail for each of them and they jumped bail and took the steamer *Rangoon* for Hong Kong. Fix, aghast at such expenditures, took it with them. Heavy weather delayed the *Rangoon* disastrously.

Chaps. 18–21. The *Rangoon* was a day late but the *Carnatic* for Yokohama had been delayed for repairs and would not sail till the next day. Fogg sent Passepartout to get tickets and Passepartout learned that the repairs had been made earlier than expected and the ship would sail that night. But Fix enticed Passepartout into a bar and drugged him, so he did not return with the news and Fogg missed the boat. Fogg chartered a 20-ton boat to take him to Shanghai, where he could catch the same steamer to San Francisco. He tried to find Passepartout but could not, and he and Aouda sailed without him. Fix represented himself as being in the same predicament and Fogg took him along.

Chaps. 22–24. Passepartout sailed on the *Carnatic* because he recovered from his drugged state just enough to remember and stagger to it. But he arrived in Yokohama penniless. To eat, he got a job with a troupe of acrobats, replacing a man who held up a pyramid of men on his nose. But before Passepartout could do this act he caught sight of Fogg and deserted the troupe. They sailed as scheduled on the *General Grant* for

The superstructure was used as fuel

An elephant serves in place of the railroad and only two days are lost

San Francisco. Fix's warrant had finally reached him but now they were no longer on British soil, so he went along to follow till they reached England.

Chaps. 25–29. In San Francisco a political campaign was in full swing, and in the heat of it Fogg chanced to trade insults with a Col. STAMP PROCTOR. Fogg's party took the train for New York. They passed through Mormon territory and an unsuccessful effort was made to convert them. Proctor happened to be on the same train but at first Fogg did not know it. The train stopped because a bridge ahead was dangerous; finally the passengers decided to take a chance on crossing and the train got a flying start and made it but the bridge collapsed the next moment. Fogg encountered Proctor and they prepared to fight a duel—in the train, for the conductor refused to stop it—but just then the train was boarded by Sioux Indians and a fight began. A U.S. Cavalry detachment was near by but could not catch up with the train. Fogg managed to slip to the platform and uncouple the train from the locomotive and apply the brakes. The cavalry arrived and the Sioux fled.

Chaps. 30–31. But three passengers, including Passepartout, had disappeared. Fogg let the train go without him, to stay and try to rescue Passepartout; the cavalry, impressed by his bravery, sent 30 volunteers with him. Passepartout was rescued but the goal seemed lost. Fix, who too had stayed behind, found a man with a sledge propelled by sails (the land was covered with snow). The sledge sailed at 40 miles per hour and they reached Omaha, got a train for Chicago, and then a fast train for New York. But they arrived 45 minutes after the boat for Liverpool had sailed.

Chaps. 32–33. Fogg chartered a freighter, the *Henrietta*, from Capt. ANDREW SPEEDY, paying an exorbitant price. At sea, weather was bad and fuel ran low, but Fogg bribed the engineer to use all the fuel to keep up full speed; then, when fuel ran out 770 miles from Liverpool, he bought the ship from Speedy for $60,000, or £12,000—nearly all he had left, but 50% more than the ship was worth—and burned its superstructure and decks to keep going. He arrived at Liverpool at noon on the 80th day, only six hours from London and with eight hours and forty-five minutes to win his bet. At this point Fix arrested him and he was put in jail.

Chaps. 34–36. At 2:33 Fix dashed in—the real bank robber had been found three days ago and Fogg was free. Fogg knocked him down but was too late for the train. He sadly returned to London, where he told Aouda that the £20,000 he spent and the £20,000 to pay the bet were all he had—he was now a poor man. But she wished to marry him anyway and Passepartout went out to arrange for the wedding the next day, Monday. Yet at exactly 8:45 on the 80th day, with only a second to spare, Phileas Fogg walked into the Reform Club and won his bet.

Chap. 37. When Passepartout went out to arrange the wedding, he found that the next day was Sunday, not Monday. Traveling eastward, Fogg had gained a full day and only 80 days had elapsed in London. With ten minutes left, Fogg took a cab, offered the driver £100 bonus to get him there in time, and just made it. He was rich again. He divided the cash he had left, nearly £1,000, between Fix and Passepartout, but from the latter's share he deducted the cost of the burning gas.

Arrowsmith

Novel by Sinclair Lewis, 1885–1951.
Published 1925 by Harcourt, Brace &
Co., New York. © 1925 by Sinclair
Lewis, renewal © 1953.

THE NOVELS OF Sinclair Lewis were
usually a form of social criticism,
pointing out elements of imbalance
or hypocrisy in various walks of life.
In *Arrowsmith* Lewis scrutinized the
medical profession and found examples
of political corruption in public health
services, and limitations in medical
clinics, but also he deplored the lack of
public interest in true dedication to the
science of medicine. The novel won the
Pulitzer Prize in 1926.

Chaps. 1–18. MARTIN ARROWSMITH
grew up in the little town of Elk Hills, in
the state of Winnemac, a descendant of
hardy pioneers. During his teens he spent
much of his time in the office of the town
general practitioner, Doc Vickerson. Although the Doc was rarely sober, he instilled a deep interest in medicine in the
mind of young Arrowsmith, and the result
was that Martin entered the University of
Winnemac, taking a course that would prepare him for medical school. He became
very interested in chemistry and in general
was an earnest student. From chemistry it
was a short step to interest in bacteriology,
and on his first day in medical school he
approached Dr. MAX GOTTLIEB, a brilliant
research scientist, and asked permission to
enroll in his bacteriology course. Dr. Gottlieb refused, saying he was not ready, with
only organic chemistry as a background.

The first year passes, with basic courses
in anatomy, physiology, and general subjects connected with the medical-profession.
Martin goes to his first concert, and learns
the magic of listening to great music. He
sees again a girl whom he knew in college
—MADELINE FOX—and becomes engaged
to her. During the summer he works as a
lineman for the telephone company. He
returns for his second year thinking of
Madeline, Max Gottlieb, and bacteriology.

The second year brings the longed-for
course in bacteriology with Professor Gottlieb. The experience of watching guinea
pigs injected with anthrax germs, then the
examination of their organs when the disease had killed them, cements Martin's determination to go seriously into the research
side of medicine.

Max Gottlieb sees in Martin a young man
who may by-pass the practice of medicine
for a large income in favor of research and
the possibility of important discoveries,
and appoints Martin his student assistant.

While Martin is serving as undergraduate
assistant he is sent on an errand to the
Zenith General Hospital, and there he meets
LEORA TOZER, who is to become his wife.
At the time she is only a young probationer,
training to become a nurse. Her humor and
natural freshness, totally devoid of affection, delight Martin, and he falls in love
with her. On their second date, he becomes
engaged to her, creating an awkward situation. He is now engaged to two girls, and
in order to settle it takes them both to lunch,
when he announces the situation. Madeline
Fox is furious and leaves the restaurant,
yielding completely to Leora, who is merely
amused, and assures Martin that it will do
him no good to get engaged to anyone else.
She intends to keep him.

For a time Martin works hard and grows
more deeply interested in working out research problems for himself, which pleases
Gottlieb immensely. However, Leora is
called home because her mother is sick, one
of Martin's best friends leaves after trouble
with the Dean of the Medical School, and
Martin's mind is so filled with his personal
problems that he makes a mistake in Dr.
Gottlieb's laboratory. It is enough to make
Gottlieb angry, and ordinarily Martin would
not have minded too much, but this time
his patience is short, and he walks out.
This results in his suspension from school,
and he travels westward to Wheatsylvania,
where Leora's family lives, in North Dakota.
On arriving there he finds the family most
unsympathetic to the idea of his marriage
to their daughter, but he elopes with Leora
nevertheless. It is finally agreed that he will
go back to school, finish his medical course
and fulfill his internship, and then return
to Wheatsylvania to practice. He returns
to school, but devotes his time to general
medicine rather than research courses. He
is eventually graduated, and Leora's family
sets him up in an office in Wheatsylvania.
As a general practitioner he is quite successful, although he is frequently infuriated
by the attitudes of people whom he treats.

Leora becomes pregnant, but she loses the
baby. They know now that they can never
have a child, and life goes on in its dull
routine until Martin finds an opportunity
to do some practical research. The cattle of
the region have been dying of blackleg, and
the vaccine used has been ineffectual.
Martin discovers that it contains no living
organisms, which makes it worthless. He
laboriously manufactures some of his own,
and the cattle inoculated with it recover.
This reawakens his interest in research.
When there is an announcement that
GUSTAVE SONDELIUS, a famous research
expert, is to lecture in Minneapolis, Martin
makes arrangements to go and hear him.

As a result of listening to Sondelius, and
spending an entire evening talking with
him after the lecture, Martin's interest
centers on a combination of bacteriology
and public health, and he becomes acting
head of the Department of Health in
Wheatsylvania. Almost immediately he
incurs the enmity of many people in the
section. A series of typhoid cases puzzles
him and he sets out to find the source. The
townspeople have decided on their own
that a group of squatters some distance up
the river are responsible. Martin manages
to localize the cause, however, in a spinster
seamstress, who had suffered from the disease four years earlier. To his statement
that she was the cause, he receives only
ridicule. The seamstress, however, is a
chronic carrier of typhoid and Martin has
her confined in a county institution. He
has bacteriological proof, and his decision
stands.

He becomes the laughingstock of the
county when he campaigns for vaccination
against smallpox, with one case proved, and
several suspected cases which turn out to be
chicken pox. When a genuine epidemic of
diphtheria occurs later, his pleas for im-
munization are similarly ridiculed, although
several children die for lack of it.

After this, Martin can stand no more of
Wheatsylvania and obtains a public health
job in Nautilus, Iowa, with Dr. ALMUS
PICKERBAUGH, through the good offices of
Sondelius, now in Boston. With the well-
wishing citizenry of the town cheering
them, the Arrowsmiths are off.

Chaps. 19–25. In Nautilus, Martin and
Leora find that Dr. Pickerbaugh is a slogan-
writer and a naïve composer of verses in
praise of health. He sets up "Weeks" for
everything, from Better Babies to Toughen
the Teeth, and seems to think that sufficient
slogan-posting and jingle-writing will auto-
matically eliminate all violations of health
regulations and put a stop to epidemics and
infections. Martin becomes acting head of
the department when Pickerbaugh campaigns for the United States Senate. He
incurs considerable enmity by closing the
cleanest and most sanitary dairy in the
county because he has found streptococcus
germs in the udders of a few of the cows.
From this point, his popularity drops lower
and lower, simply because of his insistence
on sanitation where the regulations demand
it. His burning a disease-infested block of
decrepit tenements is almost the final straw,
although there was a court order authorizing it. With all the influential factions in
town lined up against him, Martin resigns
and joins the Rouncefield Clinic in Chicago,
which is partly owned by his friend, Angus
Duer. The clinic prematurely releases news
of a bacteria-destroying material that Martin has developed. This indicates to Martin
that even a fine clinic can be more interested
in publicity than in efficient research, and
eventually Martin leaves Chicago to join
the McGurk Institute of Biology, with his
old idol, Max Gottlieb.

Chaps. 26–29. For a hectic and exciting period, Martin works on an important
experiment, hoping to isolate a substance
that will destroy all kinds of germs—or at
least, many kinds. After months of work,
and a heavy schedule of study and experi-
mentation, he believes he has discovered
a miraculous "X-Principle" that will do

55

Martin Arrowsmith finally finds happiness in his first love, laboratory research

everything that he and Gottlieb have hoped for.

His triumph is quashed when Gottlieb reads in a French medical journal that the Pasteur Institute has already announced the same discovery, calling it instead a "bacteriophage." Martin continues to work with the "phage," as he calls it now, and when Gustave Sondelius appears at McGurk the two men become close associates in practical experiments directed toward a cure for bubonic plague, using the phage.

A plague epidemic strikes the island of St. Hubert and it is not long before Martin and Sondelius undertake to test the phage there. Gottlieb begs Martin never to forget the importance of scientific tests, and to divide his patients into two groups, so that one will receive the phage, the other a neutral solution. This is the only scientific approach, the only way to determine whether or not the phage is effective.

On the island the terror is mounting. People are dying every minute. Rats are plentiful, carrying plague from street to street and from house to house. Sondelius works indefatigably, and he and Martin carefully maintain the control group of un-immunized patients, but Sondelius himself becomes infected, and dies. Martin and Leora continue to work day and night. Martin goes to another island where there are also many cases. While he is gone, Leora smokes a cigarette on which there has been spilled a test tube of plague germs in culture, and she dies of the plague before Martin's return. Finding her dead, he gives up all scientific experimental ideas and orders the phage given to everyone, including the control group.

When the plague has abated and is ap-parently under control, Martin returns to New York. He eventually marries JOYCE LANYON, a woman whom he met at St. Swithin's at the time of Leora's death, but the marriage is not successful and he goes with his friend TERRY WICKETT, of Mc-Gurk Institute, to work in pure research in backwoods Vermont. He feels that his life has begun.

As The Earth Turns

Novel by Gladys Hasty Carroll, 1904– Published 1933 by The Macmillan Company, New York. © 1933 by Gladys Hasty Carroll.

IN THIS VERY SUCCESSFUL and very fine novel, Mrs. Carroll carries a Maine farm family through the year 1932. Not once does she attempt to inject artificial drama or unusual events into the noiseless tenor of their ways, yet the people live and are interesting as well as real. The central character, Jen, is an admirable creation. The entire novel richly deserves its great success.

Winter. 1. Since she was 8 years old, JEN SHAW has been housekeeper, extraordinary cook, and mother to the younger children, for her father MARK SHAW—first when he was widowed by the death of his wife MIN-NIE FOOTE but even after he married his present wife, CORA, who was a widow with two daughters, LOIS MAY, now 16, and Bernice or BUN, now about 9. Jen is now 19 and is the center and strength of the household. JOHN, almost 6, is the youngest, Mark Shaw's one child by Cora. Mark Shaw is a Maine farmer. At supper, he muses on his family: GEORGE, oldest son, married (to MIL), with several children, is a farmer on land nearby; RALPH and Eliza or LIZE, twins, are both away from home, Ralph an airplane pilot and Lize a stenographer in the city of Rumfret; ED, who is soon to marry MARGARET, Mil's sister and the local school-teacher; then Jen, then OLLY, away in his first year in college, and finally John. There is some conversation at supper: The farm next door, which former owner "Old Joe" let become run down, has been bought by a Polish family named JANOWSKI; there is no house and they will live in the barn. **2–6.** Mark Shaw and various neighbors dig out the snowed-in road. Margaret's school now has two Polish students. Ed and Margaret, when married, will occupy the former Searles farmhouse, fine and big but very dirty; he asks Jen to help him clean it and she easily combines it with her full-time home work. **7.** Mr. KEELE, the peddler, makes his annual call. Cora, who does the family sewing, buys goods for some dresses for Lois May, it being hoped they can afford to send her to secretarial school in Rumfret. They consider some cloth that would make a coat for Lois May but decide not to spend the money. Mr. Keele, mentioning their new Polish neighbors, reveals that he was originally Polish. As he leaves, he gives the cloth for the coat to Lois May and asks Bun and John to be nice to the Polish children. **8.** Lize and Olly come home for Washington's Birthday. Lize is Lois May's heroine, for her style consciousness and city polish; Lize likes Lois May as much. Olly, slight and different from his husky father and brothers, has made alternate on the college debating team. **9.** Ed is in a rage because Lize asked him to contribute $25 for Lois May's registration at secretarial school and he refused; he has money because he has worked hard for long hours since he was 14. Lize is going to house and feed Lois May and is bitter at Ed's penury. Lois May is in tears and so is Cora. **10–11.** Lize and Olly go back. Ed, after talking it over with Margaret, sends a $25 money order.

Spring. 1. Ralph unexpectedly comes home for Ed's wedding, landing his little plane in one of Mark's fields. Mark has expressed disapproval of Ralph but has taken pains to make this field especially level. Friends and family assemble for the wedding. Ed and Margaret go to Boston for their honeymoon. (Mark has never been; it is 90 miles away.) **2.** Stan Janowski, the young man in the neighboring Polish household, comes at night to use the telephone; a child is sick. The Shaws have no telephone but Jen goes to the Janowskis' and knows what to do. **3–4.** There is a new heifer; it is given to John. It looks like a good year for crops. **5.** Mark encounters Stan doing heavy work with his father; Janowski is not up to it. Mark takes his place. Mark learns that Ja-nowski is a tailor and has come to the farm only because Stan wanted it so much; the other Janowskis want to go back to the city.

Jen goes to the Janowskis'
and knows what to do

6. Ed objects to his wife's working and Margaret promises not to teach after the current year. 7. George, a hard-working but inept and careless farmer, loses a cow (which breaks her leg and must be shot); without it he cannot supply his butter customers and he is already fully mortgaged. Mark Shaw lends him a cow and Cora is resentful because the income from that cow went to Lois May's fund. 8. Margaret is to have a baby. 9. Lois May has to leave secretarial school, not because of the cow but because there is not enough money from all sources to keep her in it; she gets a job in Rumfret at $15 a week and can stay on with Lize.

Summer. 1–3. School is out; Margaret's children give her as a present a paper written by each on "My Teacher." Olly comes home and works on haying; he keeps up with his father though he is not accustomed to the work and his hands are covered with blisters. He has spoken on the debating team, the first freshman ever to do so. He is physically attracted by Doris Carpenter, who works in the general store. 4. Mil confides to Jen that she is so unhappy with George she is thinking of leaving him. Without telling George, Jen lets him know that he should make circumstances more pleasant for Mil. 5. Olly becomes friendly with Stan and is often at the Janowskis' in the evening. 6–8. There are Fourth of July celebrations. Jen is in charge of refreshments for the Ladies' Aid. Afterwards Doris wants Olly to take her home and stop on the way, but he becomes conscious of his distaste for her and breaks off with her. 9–10. Ralph is killed in an airplane accident. Undemonstrative though he always is, Mark Shaw shows his grief.

Fall. 1. Stan begins to be a visitor at the Shaws', talking to Jen. 2. The apples are ripe. 3. Bun brings the four little Janowskis home and Cora snubs them; Bun is greatly disturbed, also because they are persecuted by the other children at school. Olly is sent to California with the debating team and Mark Shaw is very proud of this and of the fact that Olly is going to be a lawyer. 4. Potatoes are harvested. Mark waits for the best

pregnant again. She is reconciled to George and asks Jen to forget what she said about leaving him. 5. Janowski gets a job in Lynn as a tailor. He and his wife and the four children leave. Stan stays on to farm the place alone. 6. Mark Shaw, with Jen's consent, suggests that Stan move into the Shaw house, work for Mark four days a week, and in return receive Mark's help two days. Stan accepts. Cora is delighted by the music Stan plays on his violin. All the Shaws like him. He is in love with Jen but has said nothing.

Winter Again. 1. Margaret has her baby; Jen helps and washes the baby. Ed indirectly treats Stan as his future brother-in-law. 2. At Christmas, the family is assembled, the stockings are hung for the children. All is serene in Mark Shaw's household.

As You Desire Me

Play by Luigi Pirandello, 1867–1936
Produced in New York Jan. 28, 1931.
    Published 1931 by E. P. Dutton & Co.,
    New York.

THE SUCCESS OF this play can perhaps be attributed to the great rôle it offers an actress. Greta Garbo played it famously in a motion picture success after the play had been successful on Broadway. Next to *Six Characters in Search of an Author*, it was Pirandello's most popular play in America. Pirandello won the Nobel Prize for Literature shortly afterward (1934).

Act I. In the house of CARL SALTER, a writer, in Berlin, he and his daughter GRETA (called MOP) are awaiting the return of the STRANGE LADY, who is living with Salter. (The Strange Lady is never given a definite name throughout the play, although she is the central character.) She is a victim of amnesia. Mop and Salter look out the window and see the Strange Lady approaching with a group of gay, tipsy young men. She is a professional dancer and has been giving her nightly performance. Following the

tipsy crowd is BOFFI, who has appointed himself a kind of guardian over the Strange Lady. He is convinced that she is really Lucia, the wife of BRUNO PIERI. Lucia disappeared ten years before, during World War I.

Salter scoffs at Boffi, and Mop thinks that the whole idea is ridiculous. The Strange Lady seems to be quite indifferent, but also seems to recall a few scattered incidents of a past life that might possibly have been that of Signora Lucia Pieri.

Boffi announces that he has brought Pieri to Berlin. He leaves to summon Pieri and the Strange Lady is left alone. She wonders aloud who she really is. Sadly she murmurs that she is merely a "body without a name."

Act II. Four months later, the Strange Lady is living as Signora Pieri. She has accepted her identity as "CIA." Aunt LENA and Uncle SALESIO, Bruno's relatives by marriage who live in the house, have apparently accepted her also. The Strange Lady seems to think sometimes that she is Lucia, and sometimes that perhaps she is not. She loves Bruno unstintingly and is molding her life to Bruno's pattern. Today she is to see her (or Lucia's) sister and the sister's husband for the first time. She talks to Bruno; she knows he is not yet entirely sure she is Lucia. She wants only to have him accept her as Cia on faith—because no one could be more truly Cia than she is now. Lucia's sister had taken the necessary legal steps to have Lucia declared legally dead. Now the procedure must be annulled.

The life that the Strange Lady has lived since the war is the subject of chattering tongues in town, and she is aware of it. There is a villa that Lucia had taken to her husband as a dowry. With Lucia declared legally dead, the dowry would revert to her family. This would deprive Bruno of the villa, on which he has spent large sums of money. She cannot fail to wonder how much this has influenced Bruno to accept her as his wife.

Bruno gets home before Lucia's sister and brother-in-law arrive. He has a letter from Salter, whose fury and jealousy over the Strange Lady's leaving him for her "husband" have led him on a search for revenge. Salter is on his way with an insane woman, her doctor, and a nurse.—Salter says the woman is the real Lucia Pieri. The Strange Lady says that the evidence will make no difference, for doubt will never die. She mentions a mole she had had removed from her side, but reminds Bruno that he has only her word for its removal. She goes upstairs to change clothes.

Act III. The family is assembled, waiting for the Strange Lady to come downstairs. They discuss the annulment of the death certificate, the return of the villa, the uncertainty of the woman they call Cia, and her sordid career since the war. They hear a car outside and see Boffi arrive with two other men, a nurse, and a strange woman. It is the insane woman, and one of the men is her doctor from the sanatorium. The other man is Salter.

The family looks with revulsion but also with doubt at the poor creature Salter declares to be Cia. The Strange Lady observes them all for a moment as she descends the stairs. She realizes that never can she be certain of their belief in her. Doubt will exist for the rest of her life. She tells them to find out if the insane woman has a mole on her side. A notebook written by Cia years before says that there should be a mole, red and protruding, on her side. The doctor says the woman has a mole, but it is black, not red, and it is not exactly on her side. On this note of general uncertainty, the Strange Lady declares that she is going away. She is going back to Salter—back to Berlin—back to dancing. No one will ever really know the truth.

As You Like It

> Play by William Shakespeare, 1564–1616.
> Produced about 1599.
>
> THE IMMEDIATE SOURCE of *As You Like It* is a 1590 romance, *Rosalynde*, by Thomas Lodge, of which it is almost a straight dramatization; but beyond that the story goes back to the *Tale of Gamelyn*, a narrative poem of about 1350. Chaucer also apparently intended to rewrite this poem, as one of the Canterbury Tales, but he did not. The action of *As You Like It* is probably intended to take place in the early
> 14th or perhaps the 13th century—later, at least, than the time of Robin Hood. ¶ *As You Like It* is one of Shakespeare's best comedies and the part of Rosalind is one of the best and most difficult of the female rôles he created. In Act II, Scene 7 occurs the famous speech of the character Jaques, "All the world's a stage/And all the men and women merely players . . ." The songs in the play include some of Shakespeare's best-liked lyrics: "Under the greenwood tree," "Blow, blow, thou winter wind," and "It was a lover and his lass."

Act I. 1. ORLANDO, youngest son of the late Sir Rowland de Boys, complains to the old servant ADAM that the eldest brother and heir, OLIVER, treats him like an animal instead of a brother, will not educate him, and will not give him his inheritance. Orlando makes the same accusation to Oliver, and they quarrel. Later, Oliver receives CHARLES, the duke's wrestler. Charles tells him the current news from court: The old (and rightful) DUKE has been banished by his younger brother, FREDERICK, who now reigns as duke; the old Duke, with a few faithful noblemen, is hiding in the forest of Arden. Charles tells Oliver that he has heard that Orlando, in disguise, plans to challenge him in the wrestling matches at the palace tomorrow. For Oliver's sake, Charles offers to spare Orlando; but Oliver tells him to do his worst, even if Orlando is killed. **2.** CELIA, Frederick's daughter, has kept with her ROSALIND, the old Duke's daughter, because of their love for each other. At the palace, Celia is trying to cheer up Rosalind. They banter somewhat with TOUCHSTONE, the clown. Then they are summoned to the wrestling matches, where Charles has already broken the first three challengers so badly that they may not live. At the wrestling matches, Frederick has warned Orlando against wrestling with Charles; when the girls arrive and see how slight Orlando looks in comparison with Charles, they add their entreaties. But Orlando persists in fighting Charles, and defeats him. Frederick congratulates Orlando, but on learning that he is the son of Sir Rowland de Boys, a close friend of the old Duke's but Frederick's enemy, he is less pleased. This fact, however, makes Rosalind love Orlando, as her father loved his father. **3.** Frederick orders Rosalind out of his palace. Celia loves Rosalind so much that she goes along. For safety along the lawless way, Celia disguises herself as a poor maid and takes the name ALIENA; Rosalind disguises herself as a young soldier and takes the name GANYMEDE. They take along Touchstone, for company and comfort, and slip out of the palace.

Act II. 1–3. The Duke and his attendants are in the forest of Arden, living a rough

The practice wooing in Arden Forest

but not unhappy life. Meanwhile Frederick has discovered Celia's departure, and it is rumored that the girls have gone with Orlando; so he sends to have Orlando brought to him, or Oliver if Orlando cannot be found. Orlando has gone home, but Adam meets him outside and warns that Oliver intends to kill him; so Orlando and Adam go off together. **4–7.** The disguised girls arrive at the forest and meet two shepherds, an old one, CORIN, and a young one, SILVIUS, who is in love with a shepherdess, PHEBE. In another part of the forest two of the Duke's noblemen, AMIENS and JAQUES, are singing and talking. In still another part, Adam's strength gives out from hunger and Orlando begins to carry him. Orlando leaves Adam and seeks to take food by force from the Duke; when the Duke kindly invites him to eat, he puts up his sword and apologizes, saying he thought all would be savage in the forest. He brings back Adam and they eat. The Duke learns that Orlando is the son of his old friend and takes him among his followers.

Act III. 1. Frederick gives Oliver one year to deliver Orlando, his lands to be forfeit if he fails. **2–5.** Orlando, who thinks only of Rosalind, writes love poems to her and leaves them scattered through the forest; Rosalind finds them and learns from Celia that Orlando is in the forest and is writing them. In her disguise as Ganymede, Rosalind meets Orlando and suggests that he pretend Ganymede is Rosalind and practice wooing her; Orlando agrees. Also Rosalind, as Ganymede, is coaching Silvius on how to woo Phebe; but Phebe thinks herself in love with "Ganymede."

Act IV. 1–3. The practice wooing continues. Oliver reaches the forest, seeking Orlando. He pauses for sleep and while he sleeps he is attacked by a snake and threatened by a lioness, but Orlando saves him from both and is wounded in the process. Oliver repents of his previous behavior and the brothers are reconciled. "Ganymede" faints on hearing that Orlando is hurt, which Oliver considers most unmanly.

Act V. 1. Touchstone wishes to marry a country girl, Audrey, and talks her previous suitor, William, out of continuing his suit. **2–3.** Oliver tells Orlando he has fallen in love with Aliena (Celia); and thinking her to be a shepherdess, he plans to marry her and remain in the forest as a shepherd, endowing the estate on Orlando. All the lovers find themselves together and Rosalind promises to give each his heart's desire the next day. **4.** Before the Duke, Rosalind reveals herself as his daughter, and ready to marry Orlando; therefore Phebe cannot marry her and will marry Silvius, and Oliver gets a duke's daughter and niece instead of a shepherdess. Orlando's other brother, Jacques de Boys, enters to say that Frederick met a religious man who converted him, and that he has turned to a religious life, restoring to the old Duke his former place.

Atalanta in Calydon

> *Poetic drama by* Algernon Charles Swinburne, 1837–1909.
> Published 1865.
>
> THE STORY OF Atalanta was a Greek favorite. After taking part in the Calydonian boar hunt, the topic of Swinburne's poem, the young lady returned home and offered her hand in marriage to any young man who could beat her in a race. She lost, it may be remembered, to the young man who carried three golden apples and at intervals tossed one behind him, gaining ground when she paused to pick it up. ❡ Swinburne's poem is not a drama for modern performance. It is fashioned on the Greek drama, with recitatives and the burden on the chorus. The opening chorus, "When the hounds of spring are on winter's traces," has appeared in many anthologies for the simple reason that *Atalanta* is an early Swinburne poem and the copyrights ran out in time to print it free.

While ALTHEA, Queen of Calydon, is with child, she dreams that the three Fates prophesy three things for her son: He will have great strength in his hands; he will have good fortune in life; but he will live no longer than it takes for a brand burning in the fire to be consumed. Althea then takes the brand from the fire, quenches its flame, and keeps it.

The son is born and grows to manhood; his name is MELEAGER. He is one of the heroes who sail with Jason for the golden fleece. The goddess ARTEMIS is offended by OENIUS, king of Calydon, Meleager's father, because he worshiped other gods but not her. She causes northern tribes to invade his land but Meleager, along with his uncles, Althea's brothers TOXEUS and PLEXIPPUS, scatters the invaders.

Artemis now sends into Calydon a wild boar, which kills many and ravages the land. Many try to kill the boar but are killed by it. The chief warriors of Greece assemble to hunt the boar, and among them is one woman, the beautiful ATALANTA, a maiden, daughter of Iasius, king of Arcady. Meleager loves Atalanta; and Artemis, who favors Atalanta greatly, lets her wound the boar, whereupon Meleager dispatches it.

Meleager gives the spoils of the hunt to Atalanta, because of his love for her. Toxeus and Plexippus, among others, object that the maiden should get the praise when many shared the work. They lay in wait for Atalanta to take away her prize, and Meleager fights them and kills both his uncles.

When Althea hears this, she is made mad by rage and sorrow. She takes the brand and throws it in the fire; and as it burns, Meleager's life is consumed with it. He is carried back to his father's house and dies, forgiving his mother and asking her forgiveness. Atalanta sadly returns home.

Aucassin and Nicolette

> *Medieval romance* in prose and poetry. Probably 12th century, perhaps 13th.
>
> IN THIS UNIQUE song-story, the minstrel or troubadour told a bit of the tale in prose, then sang a brief song, told a bit more and sang a bit more, alternating in this way to the end. There may have been other romances on the same form, but no other has survived. The action is set in the south of France, in Provence, probably midway of the 12th century. The story is told chiefly by the prose portions, which are short (a few hundred words at most) and terse. Most of the songs, which have some twenty lines of seven syllables each, comment on but do not add to the narrative; but there are a few exceptions. There are several translations; the following is from the translation by Andrew Lang.

Count BOUGARS DE VALENCE makes war on Count GARIN DE BIAUCAIRE and presses him hard. Garin is old and cannot lead his men; his only child is a son, AUCASSIN, who is handsome and strong but who refuses to become a knight and go to battle because he loves NICOLETTE and his father will not let him marry her. Nicolette is a slave girl whom the captain of the town captured from the Saracens and has brought up as a Christian and as his adopted daughter. Garin offers his son any king's or count's daughter, but Aucassin will not yield.

Garin protests to the Captain, and threatens him; so the Captain seals Nicolette into an upper chamber of one of his palaces, with an old woman to keep her company. Aucassin then agrees with his father that he will take up arms if, on his return, he be permitted to see Nicolette long enough for "two words or three, and one kiss." Garin promises, and Aucassin goes to battle. But his mind is on Nicolette, not on war; and while he dreams, the enemy seizes his spear and shield and takes him prisoner. Aucassin, now aware that death is in store for him and fearful chiefly of never seeing Nicolette again, draws his sword and lays about him so vigorously that he kills ten and wounds seven of the enemy, takes Count Bougars captive, and returns home. Garin breaks his word and will not let Aucassin see Nicolette, so Aucassin frees Count Bougars, first extracting Bougars' promise not to war on Garin any more. But Garin casts Aucassin into a dungeon.

While the old woman is asleep, Nicolette escapes from her chamber with knotted sheets and napkins. She goes to Garin's castle and hears Aucassin wailing for love of her. They speak together of their love and she cuts and gives him her golden curls. Garin's guard approaches to arrest her, but the sentinel on the castle warns her and she escapes over the moat and the wall into the forest outside. Here the danger is great from wild beasts, but Nicolette survives. She meets some shepherds and pays them to take a message to Aucassin: That there is a beast in the forest, which if he could take it he would not give one of its limbs for five hundred marks of gold; but he must come within three days to find it. Then she builds herself a lodge of boughs woven with flowers and leaves, and waits for Aucassin.

When Nicolette is known to have fled, and perhaps died, Garin releases his son and gives a great feast in his honor. But Aucassin is sad. A knight advises him to ride out into the forest, and he does so and meets the shepherds and hears Nicolette's message; but though he rides all day he cannot find her. He meets a countryman who has lost an ox and cannot find it, and Aucassin gives him twenty sols to buy a new ox. He rides on and that night finds Nicolette's lodge, but falls and dislocates his shoulder. Nicolette heals it and they ride off together lest the Count's men find them the next day. At the seashore they see a merchants' ship and are taken aboard.

A storm drives them to the land of the King of Torelore, where Aucassin and Nicolette leave the ship and ride to the King's castle. They learn that a war is going on. The Queen is leading the Army. The King they find in bed, about to be delivered of a child. Aucassin beats the King and makes him promise that men will bear no more children in Torelore. Then the King leads Aucassin to the battle, where men are fighting with baked apples, eggs, and fresh cheeses. Aucassin wins the war for the King, but is not permitted to put the enemy to the sword because it is not the custom of the country to kill in warfare.

Aucassin and Nicolette live in the King's castle until Saracens attack and overcome it. Aucassin is bound and put into one ship, Nicolette in another. Aucassin's ship is wrecked at the castle of Biaucaire, where he learns that Garin is dead and he is now the count. Nicolette is taken to Carthage. Actually, the King of Carthage is her father, from whom she was captured as a child; and when she reveals this and is recognized, there is great joy. But her father wants to marry her to a Paynim (Moslem) king. She learns to play the viol, then she stains her face brown, disguises herself as a minstrel, and makes her way over the sea to Biaucaire. Here she sings the story of Nicolette, her escape, and her love for Aucassin.

Aucassin hears her and asks her to lead him to Nicolette. She promises to deliver Nicolette. Then she goes to the Captain's house, cleans the stain from her face with a herb until she is as fair as ever, clothes herself richly, and sends for Aucassin. "And Aucassin was right glad." He marries her, makes her countess of Biaucaire; and they live for many years in delight and with no regret.

Aurora Leigh

Narrative poem by Elizabeth Barrett Browning, 1806–1861.
Published 1857.

THIS LONG POEM was written about ten years after Elizabeth Barrett married Robert Browning. They were living in Italy. The poem is a novel in verse—unrhymed iambic pentameter. It has been criticized as much too long, and it is very long; and also the good poetry is often lost between unadorned narrative that should be in prose and is forced into metrical verses. But in most ways *Aurora Leigh* is both good poetry and an interesting novel.

Book 1. AURORA LEIGH'S mother was Florentine; she died when Aurora was 4 years old. Aurora's father was an austere Englishman who loved her mother very much; he tried, with the help of the old nurse, Assunta, to bring up Aurora, but he could only teach her what was in books. He

died when Aurora was 13 and she went to England to the home of her father's sister, a frozen spinster who had lived a harmless —she would call it a virtuous—life within the confines of the church, its charities, and formal upper-class society in the county. Aurora's aunt brought her up and taught her dutifully, but could not win her affection because she disapproved, even hated, Aurora's mother. Aurora was a good child, meek and manageable—and studious. She learned much. Her friend in this period was her cousin, ROMNEY LEIGH, a few years older, who had inherited the estate (Leigh Hall) at an early age. He was cold, shy, and absent—but tender when, rarely, he thought of it. Sometimes his friend VINCENT CARRINGTON, a young painter, joined them. Aurora wrote poetry, not good, but she liked to dream and muse, and her aunt would bring her back to reality and her tasks —reading, crocheting. But Aurora came to love England.

Book 2. When Aurora was 20, Romney found a book in which she had been writing poetry. He returned it to her (without having read any of it) and they had a long conversation. He thought such efforts as writing poetry were not befitting a woman; women should be wives and mothers. He offered his love and wanted to marry her. But Aurora disagreed; a woman is entitled to an independent life and she would not be a man's handmaid. She said Farewell. He thought she must be joking, but she insisted. Her aunt joined them; Romney told her that his suit had been rejected, and he left bitterly. The aunt was incredulous that Aurora could have refused such an offer. Aurora affirmed her rejection of him, but later wept because she had lost a friend. Romney wrote to her, repeating his offer and expressing his love; she wrote that she liked him but did not love him enough to wed him.

Aurora's aunt died not long afterward. Romney told Aurora she had inherited more than 30,000 pounds; she did not believe her aunt had so much money and accused Romney of trying to make her a disguised gift. He denied this, but finally had to admit that the aunt got the money by a deed of gift from him, made very shortly before her death. Aurora then refused the money, taking only 300 pounds that her aunt actually left her. She went off to London to write. (She mentions that she is writing this seven years later.)

Book 3. Three years later, Aurora was in London, a recognized and published author but barely making a living—which was better than many writers she knew. A letter from Vincent Carrington mentioned Romney's activities in politics. Aurora had worked hard and enjoyed work. She did not see or hear from Romney. One day a Lady WALDEMAR called on her, expressed admiration for her work, and confessed love for Romney; Aurora said her own love for Romney was only cousinly. Lady Waldemar was very anxious to be friends with

Aurora and told Aurora that Romney seemed likely to make an unsuitable marriage. She wanted Aurora to go to see the girl, MARIAN ERLE, and Aurora went and met the girl.

Marian Erle's story is told: She was born in a hut, an outcast by birth, the daughter of a squatter. As a child she begged torn books from a pedlar so she could read. She was a strange, sickly child. She wandered with her parents. One day her mother wanted to sell her to the squire where they were; she ran away, running till she fainted from exhaustion. A waggoner found her and took her to a hospital in town. On her last day in the hospital, Romney Leigh came through as a visitor. He sent her to London to learn to be a seamstress.

Book 4. Marian Erle's story continues. About a year later she met Romney again. Lucy Gresham, a sick girl who sewed in the chair next to Marian's, swooned in the street and was taken home, dying. When Marian heard, she moved into Lucy's apartment and nursed her. Lucy died and a charitable gentleman visited the place; it was Romney. She and Romney both agreed not to part again, and later he proposed that she be his wife.

Marian loved Romney in all humility— content to love without demanding anything. While Aurora and Marian were talking, Romney came in and Aurora expressed approval of his choice. During the next month Aurora did not see Marian again. She did not really disapprove of the marriage, but somehow it jarred. Then the announcement of the wedding came. Aurora went; it was attended by a very highborn crowd, gossiping while they waited—partly about how Lady Waldemar helped the bride prepare herself to be Leigh's wife. They waited and waited; the bride did not appear. Aurora asked Lord HOWE, Romney's friend, what was wrong; eventually he told her that the bride was not coming, there would be no wedding. Romney's face was terrible to behold, calm and hurt, as he announced that the wedding was off. The lowerclass people in the church, thinking Marian had been forced out of the marriage because of her class, started a riot. Later, Romney sent to Aurora the letter Marian had sent to him at the church. In the letter Marian asked forgiveness but said the marriage would not be right and she knew Romney did not really love her. She would not let Romney lose his place in the social world because of her.

Romney looked for Marian everywhere. Now and then he went to see Aurora and talked to her in his unhappiness.

Book 5. Aurora's poetry did fairly well. She did not see Romney for two years; she heard he had turned Leigh Hall into an almshouse. Aurora saw Lord Howe and his wife, and at their house heard Romney's socialist ideas discussed by guests. There also she met Lady Waldemar again; Lady Waldemar was sure Romney never loved Marian. Aurora learned that Romney was to marry Lady Waldemar, and she wrote Lady Waldemar a note of good wishes, but she was strongly disturbed.

Book 6. Aurora went to France. Walking one day she was sure she saw Marian, but lost her in the crowd. She was fairly sure Marian had a child in her arms. She started to write and tell Romney, but thought better of it. Many weeks later Aurora saw Marian again and this time caught her. Marian did not want to be recognized, but Aurora insisted and urged Marian to come live with her—just the two of them. Marian refused and asked Aurora to go, for Romney's sake, but Aurora insisted on going home with her. There Aurora saw Marian's year-old baby. Marian did not defend herself or apologize for her fatherless child and Aurora did not condemn her. But Marian insisted she must be considered dead. When Marian heard that Romney was to marry Lady Waldemar she said she would have expected it before, since Romney loved Lady Waldemar so. This statement surprised Aurora. In the conversation that followed, Aurora learned that Lady Waldemar had indirectly but deliberately persuaded Marian to call off the wedding. Lady Waldemar offered to send Marian to the colonies, in care of one of her former maids, and Marian thanked her. But the former maid drugged Marian (in which condition Marian was raped) and sent her on a boat only to France, so as to keep the rest of the money Lady Waldemar had provided.

Book 7–8. In France Marian got a job as a maid, but her mistress—though she had lovers—dismissed her indignantly when Marian's pregnancy became apparent. Marian became a seamstress again. This ended Marian's story.

Aurora now renewed her invitation to Marian to live with her and Marian gave in; Aurora took Marian and the child home with her. She wrote a letter to Lord Howe, telling him Marian's story and charging him to tell Romney if he was not yet married but otherwise to tell Romney only that Marian was found and living with Aurora. Then Aurora wrote an angry letter to Lady Waldemar, saying that if she was already married to Romney she must make him a good wife or Aurora would tell him all.

Aurora took a house in Florence and lived there with Marian and the baby. A letter from Vincent Carrington told her that Romney had been dangerously ill with the fever and that Lady Waldemar had nursed him. Aurora thought constantly of Romney. Then one day Romney came to her house in Italy. They had a long talk, in the course of which he confessed that he had gone too far in his efforts to be all-charitable and reform the world. Almost until the end of the conversation, Aurora thought he was married to Lady Waldemar. Then she learned that he had not married.

Book 9. Romney delivered a letter to Aurora from Lady Waldemar, who states that she did not willfully spoil Marian's marriage, that she is sorry she did not win

Romney's love (as she would have, except for Aurora), but that she does not forgive Aurora. After this surprise, Aurora was again surprised when Romney announced that he considered himself married to Marian in the eyes of God and came to claim her and would accept the child with her.

But Marian would not accept Romney, and now at last Aurora confessed her love for him and convinced him that she had changed and it was genuine love. And as he had always loved her, they were happy in the conclusion.

Autobiography

The full title of any autobiography usually begins with the words "Autobiography of . . ." In this work, all autobiographies will be treated in alphabetical order under the *last* name of the writer. Thus, the *Autobiography of Benvenuto Cellini* will be found under "Cellini," the *Autobiography of Benjamin Franklin* under "Franklin," etc. An exception is made in the case of the *Autobiography of Alice B. Toklas,* which follows, for there the word "autobiography" is a notable part of the title, the book actually being the autobiography not of Alice B. Toklas but of Gertrude Stein.

Autobiography of Alice B. Toklas

Autobiography by Gertrude Stein, 1874–1946.
Published 1933 by Harcourt, Brace & Co., New York. © 1933 by Gertrude Stein. (ML, P 12)

THOSE WHO DO NOT READ Gertrude Stein because they cannot understand her need have no fears of this book. It is simple, direct writing that a child can understand—and find rewarding, for this is an important book. Gertrude Stein saw and influenced the emergence of a new generation, almost a new species, in art and literature; in literature especially it might be said that no one had a greater influence. The book is rich in anecdote and in its trenchant expressions of Gertrude Stein's critical opinions, including a famous opinion of Ernest Hemingway (whom she liked and admired, but not unreservedly). *The Autobiography of Alice B. Toklas* is a short book, about 75,000 words, and can easily be read in one long or two shorter sittings.

1–2. I (Alice B. Toklas) was born in San Francisco [in 1881]. My father was of Polish patriotic stock, my mother the daughter of a Forty-niner. As a child I led a gently bred existence. After the San Francisco fire of 1906 Gertrude Stein's brother and his wife came back to San Francisco and I met them, so when I went to Paris in 1907 I called on them and met GERTRUDE STEIN. She had just privately printed her *Three Lives* and was working on her long *The Making of Americans;* Picasso had just finished his portrait of her. She lived then, as now [1932], at 27 rue de Fleurus, in a home with a big studio, four tiny rooms, kitchen and bath. The cubism movement was at its height. I had dinner at Miss Stein's and met PICASSO and MATISSE. Picasso was her dearest friend, and after him JUAN GRIS [whom she met much later].

3. Gertrude Stein went to Paris in 1903, after attending Johns Hopkins Medical School. She lived with her [younger, unmarried] brother, and both became interested in the work of Cezanne and bought some of his paintings from the dealer Volland; one, a portrait of a woman, caused Gertrude Stein to write *Three Lives.* Then they met Matisse through offering 400 francs for his "La Femme au Chapeau," for which he was asking 500; he refused the offer and they met him to negotiate and became close friends. Gertrude Stein and her brother often disagreed on paintings, including their first Picasso, which she did not like but he did. Gertrude Stein made many friends but most important to her was her sister-in-law. Others were Miss Etta Cone, from Baltimore, who typed her first manuscript; Guillaume Appollinaire, and Marie Laurencin, who went with Guillaume.

4. Gertrude Stein was born in Allegheny, Pennsylvania (now part of Pittsburgh) but was taken to Europe when she was six months old. She lived in Vienna and Paris until she was four, then her family returned to America, lived briefly in New York and Baltimore, and finally settled in Oakland, California. When Gertrude Stein was 17, her father and mother having died, she returned to Baltimore with a sister and brother. She went to Radcliffe, where William James had the greatest influence on her, then to medical school, where she finished the course but did not graduate; she did very well her first two years but then got bored. She was interested only in pathological psychology. Then she and her brother lived for a few months in London, and then moved to Paris.

5. Paris, 1907–1914. At first I lived in a hotel or apartment with a friend, but then I joined Gertrude Stein in the rue de Fleurus. I had been there every Saturday evening, when Gertrude Stein entertained many people, and very often on other days. We traveled together, including trips to Spain and England. At that time Gertrude Stein wore a brown corduroy suit, a small crocheted straw cap, and sandals, and carried an amber-headed cane. One of her friends who impressed me most was MILDRED

ALDRICH, who was then arranging to put Maeterlinck's *Blue Bird* on the stage. There were many artists and writers. We met the famous publisher JOHN LANE of the Bodley Head, in London. (Although no publisher would take Gertrude Stein's first book, it had aroused attention and good reviews.)

6. The War. We had been in England since July 5, 1914, and were there when the war broke out. We stayed, visiting Dr. and Mrs. (North and Evelyn) WHITEHEAD until, on Oct. 15, we were told we could go back to Paris. Lytton Strachey and Bertrand Russell were among those we saw at the Whiteheads'. Paris did not have many people in it. There were some Zeppelin attacks, one while Picasso was dining with us. That was when the friendship between Gertrude Stein and Juan began. He was a melancholy, tormented character in those days. In the spring [1915] we wanted to go to Palma [Mallorca] to forget the war a little. The embassy did not want to give us passports but Gertrude Stein insisted. We stayed in Palma till the following spring. When we got back to Paris we saw a sign, American Fund for French Wounded, and we volunteered. Gertrude Stein ordered a Ford truck from America and our friend William Cook taught her to drive in an old taxi. It took the Ford months to arrive. The winter in Paris was bitterly cold and there was no coal. Finally the Ford came and we were useful. We called it Auntie. Much of the time we were at Nîmes, where the AFFW had a hospital. We had a great many military godsons; our duty was to write them letters and send them packages. Gertrude Stein got the idea of writing a history of the United States telling how the states differ, but she only wrote a little of it. The armistice came, and the next morning we were summoned to Alsace. Gertrude Stein drove to Strasbourg through the mud. Our work there was with refugees. We stayed until late in May. Back in Paris, Gertrude Stein began to work very hard; she wrote *Accents in Alsace* and other plays. She had a quarrel with Picasso—neither knew quite what it was about—and it lasted two years.

7. After the War: 1919–1932. The old crowd had disappeared. We began to meet new people all the time. . . . Gertrude Stein liked Ezra Pound but did not find him amusing. Lady Rothermore brought T. S. Eliot and Gertrude Stein wrote a portrait of him and sent it to him but he did not print it (in his magazine *The Criterion*). Gertrude Stein was trying to get Mildred Aldrich the Legion of Honor, for her pro-French propaganda, and finally succeeded. Gertrude Stein wrote a great deal, and had several books published. Picasso did not like Juan Gris, but when Juan died Picasso came and spent all day with her. *The Life and Death of Juan Gris* is the most moving thing she has ever written. Hemingway, 23 years old, came with a letter of introduction from Sherwood Anderson. He was extraordinarily good-looking. We visited him at his apartment and Gertrude Stein saw the novel he had begun and some poems. She liked the poems but advised him to begin again on the novel. When the Hemingways had a baby Gertrude Stein and I were godmothers; for a time we were very active godparents. Gertrude Stein and Sherwood Anderson are very funny when they talk about Hemingway, who was formed by the two of them. Hemingway credited his first book, *In Our Time,* to *The Making of Americans,* which he and others were anxious to get published —as, at last, it was. It is 1,000 pages long and has 565,000 words and was written in 1906 to 1908, all in manuscript. My eyes gave out in proofreading and Gertrude Stein had to finish alone. George Antheil brought Virgil Thomson, who had put a number of Gertrude Stein's things to music, to the house and they became friends. He asked her to write an opera and she wrote *Four Saints [in Three Acts].* In 1926 we went to London. Edith and Osbert Sitwell gave parties for us and Gertrude Stein lectured at Cambridge and Oxford. That winter (in Paris) we gave many parties. Carl Van Vechten sent Paul Robeson to us and we saw much of him, and also of Elliott Paul. The song "The Trail of the Lonesome Pine" appealed to Gertrude Stein; she played it over and over on the phonograph. We bought a country house and Gertrude Stein was radiantly happy when we were invited to lunch by the Bromfields because he knows all about gardens. Gertrude Stein had been after me to write my autobiography and I promised I would if I had time but about six weeks ago Gertrude Stein said I would never write it so she would write it for me. And she has and this is it.

The Autocrat of the Breakfast Table

Sketches by Oliver Wendell Holmes, 1809–1894.

Published serially in *Atlantic Monthly,* 1857–58; published in book form 1858.

"THE AUTOCRAT" is generally considered Holmes's masterpiece. He imagines himself as one of the boarders in a Boston boarding house and reports on the conversations there and his own thoughts and impressions. He takes the opportunity to introduce much of his poetry, both serious and doggerel, often attributing it to "his friend the Professor" (who also is himself). In No. 4 appears his most quoted serious poem, "The Chambered Nautilus," and in No. 11 his best-known humorous poem, "The Deacon's Masterpiece, or, The Wonderful 'One-Hoss-Shay.'" The humor, urbanity, iconoclasm and scholarship of the essays are almost unique for their times and are timeless, being as good reading today as then. Holmes continued the series with *The Professor at the Breakfast Table* (1860), followed some years after (1872) by *The Poet at the Breakfast Table.* Both were popular, but not so much as the first.

1. Holmes approves of the "Society of Mutual Admiration" and of both self-admiration and mutual admiration among men of genius or superiority. Great literature and art have resulted from the consorting of the great. Included in the conversation are the landlady, her 19-year-old daughter (a tender-eyed blonde with long ringlets), and "the old gentleman who sits opposite." 2. Why can we beat England at trotting but not horse-racing? Horse-racing is not a republican institution and race horses are gambling implements, as much as a roulette wheel, while trotting horses are useful. Some remarks on the mutilating of literature, especially poems, to fit editorial or conventional preferences. Here appears one of Holmes' most famous humorous poems, an ode to good wine as altered by a teetotaler. 3. Introduces "the Schoolmistress," a boarder of whom the Autocrat becomes enamored. 4. Introduces "the Divinity Student . . . a rather nice young man," with whom there are occasional debates and colloquies. Here the Divinity Student reproaches the Autocrat for abusing other people's beliefs and the Autocrat expresses his own (Unitarian) belief as consisting of two words, "Our Father." Here appears "The Chambered Nautilus." 5. He quotes his friend the Poet on the onset of inspiration leading to the composition of a poem. Holmes burlesques a typical newspaper report "From Our Foreign Correspondent," this one being on Sumatra. 6. General conversation with the Divinity Student and the Schoolmistress. 7. Contains a paper "by the Professor" on old age. 8. Spring has come, a fact leading to various musings. 9. Having previously warned away young readers when he discussed old age, he now addresses himself to the young—ages 12 to 90. One of the conclusions: All men love all women. 10. The Schoolmistress has a rose in her hair, which inspires the Autocrat to pretty phrases. Flowers and the great trees of New England are discussed. The Autocrat takes his first walk with the Schoolmistress. He points out to her a house: "My friend, the Professor, lived in that house for years and years. He died out of it, the other day." The Professor is still alive, but we die out of houses just as we die out of our bodies. Privately, the Autocrat is becoming convinced that he loves the Schoolmistress. 11. Here appears "The Deacon's Masterpiece," plus some spoofing of those who display their knowledge of Latin. The walks with the Schoolmistress have continued, and finally the Autocrat proposes by asking, "Will you take the long path with me?" She accepts. 12. The Professor, while inebriated, produces a sequel to "The Deacon's Masterpiece"; this one is "Parson Turell's Legacy, or, The President's Old Arm-Chair." (The President of Harvard.) The Autocrat and the Schoolmistress have married; she is no longer a schoolmistress and he no longer a boarder.

The Awkward Age

Novel by Henry James, 1843–1916. Published 1899. Available in Doubleday Anchor Books (Doubleday & Co., New York) and in other editions.

DURING HIS "later period" Henry James wrote several novels about the complexities of social life in the upper classes. The group of novels in general is considered his best and *The Awkward Age* is often considered the best of the group. The novel is very skillfully — and intricately — constructed.

The reader's knowledge of what happens must usually be abstracted from devious and indirect social conversation. "Mrs. Brook," the master of social contrivance and intrigue, is the dominating character and is clearly portrayed. Her daughter Nanda, the other principal character — and the more important one — is made enough of a mystery to be subject to every reader's interpretation. To the student of the novel almost no novel can be more important than *The Awkward Age*.

Book I. 1–3. In London GUSTAVUS ("Van") VANDERBANK, a young man 34 years old with an important civil service position, at dinner at the house of another civil servant, EDWARD BROOKENHAM, meets and likes an older man, Mr. LONGDON. In a long conversation Vanderbank learns that Longdon was once in love with his mother and also with Lady Julia, the mother of Mrs. Brookenham (Fernanda, or "MRS. BROOK"). Their conversation includes: How the Brookenhams can afford to live so elaborately, with a fine town house in Buckingham Crescent; the current project of the Brookenhams to marry their 19-year-old daughter NANDA well, and the similar project of the DUCHESS (an Italian duchess) on behalf of her niece Agnesina (AGGIE).

Book II. 4. Mrs. Brookenham insists that her son HAROLD go to visit at Brander; he objects that he has no written invitation and wonders why his mother always wants him to be away visiting, but he submits and goes. The Brookenhams' expensive living is so carefully managed that every pound counts. **5.** Jane, the Duchess, calls on Mrs. Brookenham, who tells her (and later will tell her husband) that Harold did receive a written invitation. They discuss the rich Mr. MITCHETT, who may be interested in Nanda; Lord PETHERTON, whom the Duchess likes, and who lives on Mitchett; TISHY GRENSON, a young married woman, Nanda's best friend, of whom the Duchess disapproves. **6–7.** Edward fears that Harold is borrowing from their friends. (He is.) Mitchett tells Mrs. Brook that Nanda is in love with Van. **8–9.** The Duchess brings the demure Aggie to call. The Duchess asks Petherton to help switch Mitchett's attention to Aggie.

Book III. 10–12. Van invites Mitchett, Longdon and Mrs. Brook for tea; Mrs. Brook sends Nanda, alone, in her place. She hopes Longdon will like Nanda (who does remind him of Lady Julia). Longdon is elderly and has no heir. Nanda, unaware of any intrigue, genuinely likes Longdon.

Book IV. 13. Harold borrows £5 from Mr. CASHMORE, whose wife, Lady FANNY, is Petherton's sister. Cashmore is rumored to have a liaison with CARRIE DONNER, who is Tishy Grendon's sister. He tells Mrs. Brook it is not so and that actually he likes Nanda, which proves his purity. **14–15.** Mrs. Brook admits to Van her interest in Longdon's money, but Nanda does not think Longdon liked — or at least approved of — her. No one is really sure Longdon is rich.

Book V. 16–17. At Mertle, Mitchett's estate, Nanda and Van meet and talk alone; he acts properly as a much older man (and she calls him "Mr. Van"). Longdon appears and sends Van to the rest of the party; Nanda correctly surmises that Mrs. Brook asked him to do so. Nanda tells Longdon she will never marry Mitchett — and not because he is the son of a bootmaker who made a fortune. She thinks Aggie and Mitchett should marry. **18–20.** Longdon tells Van that he has settled a large sum on Nanda, which neither she nor anyone else knows about — or will know about, till she marries. Longdon is anxious to have Van propose to Nanda; he thinks Nanda's only rival for Van is Mrs. Brook herself. Van promises to think it over.

Book VI. 21–22. Van tells Mrs. Brook that Longdon wants him to marry Nanda. She guesses the rest — that Longdon thinks she wants Van herself, and that he offered a settlement on Nanda. Van admits it. Mrs. Brook at once tells Mitchett. She is convinced Van will not propose to Nanda. Mitchett has considered marrying Aggie "to please Nanda." **23.** Nanda sees much of Longdon. She tells her mother she thinks she will never marry.

Book VII. 24–25. Nanda is visiting Mr. Longdon and is in effect his hostess. Van and Mitchett are guests. She persuades Mitchett to ask for Aggie as his wife. Van still has not brought himself to accept Longdon's proposal; he is even unwilling to know how much money is involved.

Book VIII. 26–30. Van, accepting an invitation to Tishy Grendon's, finds Nanda staying there. All concerned — the Brookenhams, the Duchess and Aggie, the Cashmores, and Mitchett — are there for dinner. Nothing is settled, but Mrs. Brook works for Mitchett's marrying Aggie.

Book IX. 31. After staying away for months, Van has tea with Mrs. Brook. Mitchett has married Aggie. Mrs. Brook has "called in" Nanda, who is living at home again. Van leaves, deliberately, without seeing Nanda (but Mrs. Brook is sure he wanted to). **32.** Edward Brookenham wonders if he should "ask Van his intentions"; Mrs. Brook forbids any such vulgarity. She has Edward tell Nanda how Van avoided her. **33–34.** Mitchett calls that afternoon, shortly afterward. Mrs. Brook tells him Nanda is always waiting for Van, and that Van now hates her (Mrs. Brook). Longdon, who has been away, comes to see Nanda but is intercepted by Mitchett — a step carefully planned by Mrs. Brook. Longdon has heard nothing from Van. Mitchett agrees to help him toward the marriage of Van to Nanda.

Book X. 35–36. Van calls on Nanda, who finally wrote him a note asking him to. He still acts the part of her "older friend." She asks him not to be unfriendly toward her mother; to be "charming" to her again. As he leaves, he asks her to influence Longdon not to think bad of him. They part as friends but, on the surface at least, no more than friends. **37.** Mitchett calls next; since his marriage, he and Nanda are close friends. Longdon is due after Mitchett, to learn if Nanda will leave her parents and be, in effect, his daughter. Nanda implies that she knows about Longdon's intended settlement. She does not know about his efforts with Van. **38.** Longdon arrives. Nanda intercedes for Van, as she promised. Longdon says he is hurt only for Nanda, because she loves Van so; the matter has never been brought out in the open by them before. Nanda sobs for a while, then says she wrote to Van only so that Longdon could see for himself how easily Van could resist her. Van does not approve of her or of the social atmosphere and in his way he is right, though he does not know everything has become different. Nanda agrees to go away with Longdon, tomorrow.

Charles Dickens
1812–1870

Edgar Allen Poe
1809–1849

Babbitt

Novel by Sinclair Lewis, 1885–1951.
Published 1922 by Harcourt, Brace &
Co., New York.

MAIN STREET WAS Sinclair Lewis's
first and biggest success on the subject
of small-town quasi-culture, but *Babbitt,* which came two years later, was a
better book on the same subject. If it
is not Lewis's best novel (a rank that
is usually accorded to *Arrowsmith* or
Dodsworth), it is not far from it. ❶
Even more than *Main Street,* the title
of *Babbitt* added a standard word to
the American language.

Chaps. 1–9. George F. Babbitt is a successful real estate operator (he insists on
Realtor) in Zenith, a small city. His life is
devoted to admiration of his city, worship of
business sense and drive, and the enrichment of George F. Babbitt. He lives as befits a man who makes $7,000 a year—a
proper house, a six-cylinder car with a self-
starter. It is a touring car, because he likes to
get plenty of good fresh air on his Sunday
afternoon drives. He belongs to the Zenith
Athletic Club, and eats lunch there every
day in a special group that calls itself the
Roughnecks, all very successful men, all
completely standardized. They talk of important things: the weather, a little politics
(agreeing that what this country needs is a
good business administration in Washington), the outrageous extravagance of their
wives.

At breakfast, George reads the real estate
page to his wife, MYRA (whom he really
didn't intend to marry; he just drifted or
was trapped into it one night in the porch
swing at her house). He speaks fondly to
the 10-year-old girl, TINKA. VERONA, his
22-year-old daughter, is just out of Bryn
Mawr and filled with an urge to Serve Mankind. Until she decides how, she is spending
endless hours in serious conversation and
bridge with her friends. There is a daily
squabble as to which may have the family
car that evening, Verona or TED, who is 18
and in college, much against his will.

Babbitt is not particularly ethical in his
real-estate deals, though he would be horrified to think so. He is a God-fearing church
member, Presbyterian.

At lunch in the Zenith Athletic Club one
day with his dear friend, PAUL REISLING,
Babbitt wonders for a brief moment
whether his life is as satisfactory as he has
supposed. Paul is miserable with his shrewish wife, ZILLA, and is discontented with
his business of selling tar roofing materials,
when all his life he had wanted to be a
violinist. Babbitt agrees; what they both
need is a vacation from their respective
wives. He will arrange it so that they can go
to Maine alone for a few days before their
wives join them. Paul wishes him luck but
doubts that he can do it.

The Babbitts give a dinner party for
twelve people. Two full weeks of frantic
preparation have gone into it, including the
little touches that Myra found in a woman's
magazine. When at last the great day arrives,
Myra is nervous and exhausted. Of course,
George must wear his dinner jacket, which
he persists in calling a Tux in spite of Myra's
anguished correction. Myra reminds George
not to forget the ice cream from Vecchia's.
Vecchia is *the* caterer for Zenith. At all
parties, the guests must be able to recognize
the standard Vecchia sandwiches and pas-
tries, and the three standard Vecchia molds
for Vecchia's Neapolitan ice cream. George
promises not to forget, but Myra reminds
him three times more, and telephones him
at his office in the afternoon to remind him
for the fourth time. George goes forth to
purchase material for cocktails—a daring
thing in this Prohibition era. The party is a
great success. Everybody drinks illegal cocktails with a feeling of great daring and
sophistication, everybody eats too much and
becomes very uncomfortable, and everybody
wants the party to be over long before anyone has the courage to break it up. After the
guests have gone, George tells Myra that he
and Paul want to go away without their
wives for a few days. After Myra's incom-
prehension turns to hurt feelings and then
to understanding, George knows that he has
won a modicum of freedom, and goes to
sleep wondering what he should do with
such a terrifying thing as freedom.

Chaps. 10–20. The day after the dinner,
George and Myra go to call on the Reislings.
Zilla launches almost immediately into a
vicious tirade against Paul, and George's
control snaps. He tells her she is an evil,
nagging, ugly woman. In spite of this, Paul
and George at length reach Maine alone.
The north woods have a soothing effect.
Shortly thereafter, George attends a state
convention of Realtors. He scores a great
success as a terrific mixer, a grand booster of
home industry, and a Really Great Guy. His
speech before the convention is printed in
the Zenith paper, along with a large and
impressive picture. Soon he has an opportunity to use his oratorical faculty again.
One SENECA DOANE is running for mayor of
Zenith on a most alarmingly liberal labor
ticket. Right-thinking Republicans and
Democrats support LUCAS PROUT, a manufacturer of mattresses. George makes a
speech in praise of practical business, the
idealistic attitudes of businessmen, and the
importance of keeping Zenith ahead as a
zippy, fast-growing community of looking-
ahead people with Vision and Ideals. Prout
is elected. There are several patronage jobs
available for any relatives or friends George
might wish to help out, but George suggests
that he would find more useful a bit of
advance information as to where the new
trolley lines will be routed.

Helping a publicity campaign for the
Sunday school, George is instrumental in
hiring a young man to act as press agent and
the young man becomes attracted to Verona.
The two young people have many long and
serious conversations on weighty subjects.
Ted and Eunice Littlefield, the girl next
door, are beginning to feel the stirrings of
young love. Babbitt is far too busy to pay
any particular attention, though he does not
approve of his son's parties and he suspects
strongly that Eunice smokes.

There is a crisis in the office. One of his
salesmen has decided he is through with the
crooked deals that Babbitt engineers—deals
which Babbitt considers merely "shrewd"
and "good business." The young man is
fired.

On a trip to Chicago, Babbitt is shocked
to see Paul Reisling having dinner with a
woman in a hotel. He lectures Paul for being
unfaithful, but eventually agrees to tell
Zilla he saw Paul in Akron. It was a dreadful shock to George.

Chaps. 21–34. The Booster's Club annual elections make George vice-president.
He is so overwhelmed at this signal honor

Babbitt is embarrassed to see Reisling with a strange woman

66

that he can hardly follow an urgent telephone call from Myra. At length she manages to tell him that Paul has shot Zilla and she may not live. But actually the bullet had gone through Zilla's shoulder and she recovers almost without incident. Paul is tried and convicted, pleading guilty, and refusing to have any evidence given that would reflect on his wife. He receives a sentence of three years.

George Babbitt realizes suddenly that without Paul his world has no particular meaning. He changes his political, social and general attitudes. He becomes a liberal and defends loudly the things he has always declared to be opposed to Hard Business Sense. He no longer thinks the heavy jests of his friends at the Zenith Athletic Club are funny.

A young widow, Mrs. Daniel JUDIQUE, who is looking for a flat, attracts him enormously. She eventually becomes his mistress and George starts going about with her and her friends. He begins to drink heavily and "eats one cigarette after another." He even approves of some of the liberal ideas expressed by his old arch-enemy, Seneca Doane. He grows closer to his children during this period of humanness, but his businessman friends drop him. When Myra becomes ill he realizes that he is at heart just the same as he has always been. He concludes his affair with Mrs. Judique and gradually returns to all the old clichés that have been his life—and vocabulary—for so long. His acceptance again as one of the Regular Fellows and the hearty enthusiasm of his fellow Boosters make George a Solid Citizen again. When Ted elopes with Eunice Littlefield, and the families are torn between anger and shock, George takes Ted aside and wishes him luck—hoping that his son may be able to do what he wants to do with his life. Still, George is a success.

Back Street

Novel by Fannie Hurst, 1889-1968. Published 1930 by Rinehart & Co., New York. © 1930 by Fannie Hurst. (NAL, 3961)

THIS HAS BEEN one of the most successful of Fannie Hurst's novels and the only one that critics have treated as significant literature. The heroine, Ray Schmidt, forgoes proffered wealth and respectability to be the "kept woman" of the man she loves. The man who is object of her overpowering love Miss Hurst paints as selfish as her heroine is selfless. Both are true portraits except that Ray Schmidt seems to have unnatural immunity to even occasional outbursts of rebellion and avarice. Fannie Hurst, born of a Jewish family in St. Louis, wrote *Back Street* with peculiar knowledge of the wholly similar German and upper-class Jewish communities of Cincinnati at the turn of the century.

Chaps. 1–3. Traveling salesmen who called on ADOLPH SCHMIDT's notion store, in the Cincinnati of the '90s, had trouble figuring out RAY SCHMIDT, his pretty 19-year-old daughter. She caused gossip because she would go with them "Over-the-Rhine" to eat late suppers in beer gardens. All men flirted with her. But was she really fast? One of the drummers, WALTER PROTHERO, finds out when he asks her to be his mistress; she slaps him. Actually Ray is "good," but easy-going. She has always let boys kiss and touch her because she enjoys giving them pleasure, but she has never felt passion. Her father, equally innocent, has given Ray unlimited freedom; Ray's stepmother, formerly the widow CORA TAGENHORST with a son, MARSHALL, and a daughter, FREDA, who is Ray's age, permits Freda no such privileges. One night Adolph Schmidt dies in his sleep.

Chaps. 4–9. Schmidt never made a will, so the widow gets everything. Ray continues to work at the store until she can show its operation to the new owner, HERMAN HEYMANN. She receives a proposal from KURT SHENDLER, a bright young man interested in a new invention, a motorbicycle, but she refuses because she does not love him, though she likes him and knows he loves her. Through a salesman Ray meets WALTER SAXEL, from nearby Hamilton, a bank teller and a member of a conservative Jewish family, who officially is courting CORINNE TRAUER, a girl whose family is connected with the great banking family of Friedlander. Ray is strangely drawn to Walter.

Chaps. 10–14. Ray begins to see Walter almost daily—as often as he will see her; but he does not tell his mother about her and it never occurs to him that he might marry any girl who is not Jewish. Finally Walter plans an "accidental" encounter at the zoo where his mother can meet Ray. But Ray does not get there; for on that morning she discovers that Freda is pregnant and suicidal, having been seduced by HUGO HANCK, an unsavory young man who expects to inherit much from a rich uncle, a brewer. Ray goes to Hugo and forces him, much against his will, to marry Freda. That same night Walter becomes engaged to Corinne Trauer.

Chaps. 15–19. Ray makes a buying trip to New York for Heymann and is offered a job by Ledbetter & Scope, ribbon manufacturers. She cannot get Walter out of her mind and knows she never will; she stops going out with men. She discovers that Freda faked her pregnancy, just to make Ray help her. The Schmidt house is sold and Ray takes the New York job. She makes a good salary and attracts men as much as ever, having a good time but remaining virginal. Some of her salary she sends to Freda, for Hugo's uncle Herman Hanck has remarried and thrown Hugo out and Hugo cannot get or keep a good job. In her seventh year in New York Ray runs into Walter Saxel on the street.

Chaps. 20–27. Walter has been living in New York; he is a junior partner in Friedlander-Kurz; he has two children (RICHARD and IRMA). Ray breaks a date to eat with him on their first meeting and inevitably they become lovers with a small flat where Ray lives and waits for such times as Walter can see her. She quits her job and calls herself Mrs. Schmidt. Walter admits freely that he loves his wife, but in a different way. It is Ray to whom he can talk business and who helps him with encouragement and even advice. The money he gives Ray is barely enough to support the flat but she hates to ask for more, though HATTIE DIXON, the woman across the hall, whose circumstances are similar, thinks Ray is crazy not to. Ray takes up china-painting. Walter's firm sends him to France; he forgets to leave money and Ray cannot pay the rent and runs out of food. Providentially, Kurt comes to town, takes her out often, and lends her $60—all she will accept. He is starting in the automobile business. It is 1903.

Chaps. 28–35. Walter returns. Ray learns that he did leave $500—tucked away where he thought she would see it, but she never did. The years pass. Ray's entire life is to please Walter, who takes this for granted; once, when she speaks of traveling "the back streets of his life" he sulks. Walter becomes an important figure in finance and big charities. Ray's stepmother dies; Ray's niece, EMMA HANCK, gives her an extra interest. When Walter goes to Europe Ray often goes too, staying at hotels near his. She comes to like the casinos more and more. She also goes to the resorts where the Saxels go in the summer. One summer at Mount Clemens, near Detroit, she meets Kurt again. He is a millionaire automobile manufacturer, and still unmarried. Upset by the news that Corinne, after some 14 years, is to have another baby (a son, ARNOLD), Ray confides everything to Kurt. He still wants to marry her. Ray goes to

Freda's for a visit and to think it over, and writes a note to Walter breaking off their relationship. Ray has not enough money for very long, yet she cannot reconcile herself to marrying Kurt despite his millions, for she still does not love him. Then Walter comes to town to find her.

Chaps. 36–53. Ray resumes her life with Walter, in the same flat. Again the years pass. Richard comes of age. Irma becomes engaged. In Europe, Ray can again indulge her love of gambling. One day Richard comes to see her and asks her to stop seeing his father, because the gossip might affect Irma's marriage. She agrees, but during the interview Walter comes in, makes Richard leave, and makes Ray promise not to go. Back in New York, Ray wants to go to Emma's graduation from college but Walter becomes ill in her apartment and again she promises not to leave him.

Chap. 54. Walter and Ray manage to spend some time together in the Black Forest. They are growing old and Walter thinks of providing for Ray in his will. But the next day he dies suddenly. Richard later comes to Ray; he wishes to continue the allowance made by his father and is aghast to learn it was only $200 a month. Then Richard is killed in a polo match. For some time Ray makes a precarious living betting on horse races. Then Emma needs an operation to prevent blindness and almost all Ray's money goes for that. She goes to Europe and for a time makes out by gambling; but finally her money is gone. She sells her possessions one by one. In the casino she catches 500 francs tossed aside by a young man; she discovers he is Arnold, Walter's last son. She cannot spend this last link with Walter and she dies of starvation, clutching the 500-franc note.

Balder Dead

Poem by Matthew Arnold, 1822–1888. Published 1855.

THE STORY OF BALDER (or Baldur) is a favorite in Norse mythology. Balder the Good was the son of Odin and Frigga or Frea (whose day is our Friday). Balder's mother made every substance and plant promise not to hurt him, but she overlooked mistletoe. Now the other gods, thinking Balder invulnerable, liked to amuse themselves by casting spears and darts at him and he was always unharmed until the mischievous Loki persuaded the blind god Hoder to throw a sprig of mistletoe. Balder was hit and killed, and his soul went to Hel. He was a beloved god and the other gods were anxious to bring him back. Arnold's narrative poem takes up the story there. William Morris was another English poet who wrote of Balder.

1. Sending. All the gods and heros of Valhalla are mourning the death of BALDER when ODIN, father of the gods, tells them they must prepare the funeral pyre by piling Balder's ship high with firewood, which will be ignited and set off to sea. HODER, ostracized by the gods, seeks out FREA, mother of the gods, and asks her if there is any way he can bring Balder back to life and thereby vindicate his error. She tells him that if he sends the first person he sees out on the hazardous journey to HELA'S realm, the hell where the souls of the gods go after death, Hela might be persuaded to give back Balder. Hoder leaves Frea and encounters HERMOD, another god. He tells Hermod to make the trip to Hela, riding Odin's own horse, SLEIPNER. Meanwhile, Balder's ghost visits his sleeping wife NANNA; and to ease his painful mourning and his loneliness, Balder has Frea bring Nanna's soul to him in Hela.

2. Journey to the Dead. The next day, the gods all prepare the funeral pyre for Balder. Hermod, taking advantage of their absence from home, saddles Sleipner and rides toward Hela. After a long and arduous journey, Hermod arrives before the throne of Hela. He declares his mission and she tells him that she will give Balder back if she can be convinced that everything on earth mourns the hero's death. If just one thing fails to grieve, then Balder will never leave her realm. Hermod agrees to her terms and asks to see Balder. He speaks with Balder, who gives him a ring to take back to Odin as a memorial. Hermod leaves Hela's kingdom and, repeating his difficult journey, returns to Valhalla, where the gods are still working on Balder's funeral pyre.

3. Funeral. Hermod tells Odin and the gods of Hela's terms and they agree to them. First they bury Balder. The lovely goddess Freya cries a eulogy to Balder, followed by several others. Then Balder, Nanna and Hoder (who has meanwhile committed suicide) are all put aboard the ship. It is set fire to and sent out to sea. Later, Odin speaks to the gods about Hela's demands. He suggests that instead of accepting they all ride into her kingdom, devastate it, and bring back Balder that way. Odin's wife Frea tells him that he would be doing wrong; because in the beginning he gave Hela that kingdom and he must not invade it now. Convinced by Frea, Odin orders the gods to roam the world and ask everything in sight to weep for Balder, in the hope that Balder might be brought back to them. The gods do so. Soon, "through the world was heard a dripping noise/of all things, weeping to bring Balder back." Hermod is riding with Niord, the god of storms, when they encounter an old hag who is in reality the evil LOK. The old woman greets their tale of Balder's death with laughter, and the gods return to Valhalla to announce the failure of the plan, realizing now that Lok was behind it. Hermod returns to Hela's land. He en-

counters the ghost of Hoder, who tells him that Balder has forgiven his (Hoder's) mistake with the mistletoe. Hermod realizes that the gods were wrong in blaming Hoder, that "when they have woe, they blame the nearest cause." Hermod then encounters Balder, who tells him that he is quite happy with Nanna by his side and with the respect and affection of the dead around him. Then he tells Hermod that he is luckier than the rest of the gods, who must someday see their kingdom fall and be replaced by a far happier one where gods do not fight among themselves and joy reigns everywhere. He tells Hermod that when that new land comes, then he will return. Hermod parts from the three ghosts and, sorely tempted to stay with them, sighs sadly and returns to Valhalla.

Bambi

Children's story by Felix Salten, 1869–1945.

Published and © 1929. Published by Simon and Schuster, New York. Translated by Whittaker Chambers.

BAMBI IS A charming story for children that is also an educational exposition of the ways and nature of the deer. Parents enjoy reading it to children below the reading ages. The story appears in editions for younger ages. It made one of Walt Disney's most effective full-length cartoon films.

Chaps. 1–4. In a small sheltered glade in the forest, BAMBI, the baby deer, is born. His mother loves him as all mothers love their babies, and she takes care of him as all good mothers take care of their babies. After a while, she takes him to the meadow. She teaches him the proper way to enter the meadow free from danger. He cannot yet understand what danger is.

In the meadow Bambi discovers many wonderful things: The butterflies, like flying flowers; the scurrying ants; the great leap of the grasshopper. Bambi hears a tiny squeak and his mother explains that a ferret has killed a mouse. He asks if they will kill something, and his mother explains that deers never kill anything. He is relieved at that.

Another mother deer and her two fawns come to the meadow. They are Bambi's Aunt ENA and her twins, FALINE and

Bambi and the Old Prince

GOBO. The three young deer become friends immediately and play together until it is time to go home. A few days later Bambi's mother introduces him to the HARE, whose stiff whiskers and wiggly nose and big ears fascinate Bambi. That day Bambi is thrilled at the sight of two beautiful Princes—stags, with wonderful antlers. The stags enter the meadow majestically, saying not a word to the two mothers with their children, and disappear crashing off into the underbrush of the forest. Bambi learns that they are the fathers of the twins and himself, and that stags speak to the family only at times. He learns too that some day, if he avoids danger, he will have beautiful antlers and look like his father. Bambi is very proud.

Chaps. 5–10. Bambi learns quickly to recognize the sounds and scents of the forest. His mother no longer stays by his side all the time and sometimes she even pushes him away, reminding Bambi that he is not a baby any more.

One day Bambi cannot find his mother and he is terribly frightened and begins to cry. Suddenly a huge majestic stag appears and tells him sternly he should be ashamed of himself for crying like a foolish little baby. And just as suddenly as the stag appeared he vanishes. After that, Bambi no longer cries for his mother when she is away.

One night Bambi is in the glade with his mother when suddenly there is a great pounding of hoofs and three enormous creatures gallop past. Their antlers are gigantic. Bambi's mother starts to bleat, and Bambi finds himself bleating, too. When the great beasts have gone, Bambi's mother explains that they are their cousins, the Elk. She does not know of their ever having hurt one of the deer, but she is not certain that they wouldn't. Bambi does not understand why a cousin should hurt a relative, and says so to the screech owl. The screech owl says that relatives are not nearly as reliable as friends.

On a beautiful day, Bambi strolls to the meadow. There are many other deer there. One of the Princes is in the meadow. The sound of thunder fills the air with a great explosion, and the Prince falls down to the ground. The other deer run swiftly away. In the safety of their little glade, Bambi's mother tells him that the Prince is dead because no one heard Him coming. *He* is everybody's enemy, because He kills what He wants, and no one can stop Him.

Autumn comes, and the leaves fall one by one from the trees. Tiny, cold, white, feathery things fall from the sky, and it is snowing. At first Bambi loves the snow and plays happily, but he soon finds out that it is harder to find food than it used to be. He has to dig through the snow quite hard in order to find even one tiny blade of grass. It hurts his foot, and he is afraid of cutting himself. Gobo, who always has any misfortune that is about, cuts himself quite badly.

As the winter grows colder, some of the Princes come and graze with the mothers and children. One young Prince has been wounded by Him and limps quite badly. Although all agree that He is terribly dangerous, only a crow seems certain what makes him dangerous. It is the extra arm that he sometimes carries over his shoulder, she declares. Without that extra arm, He hurts no one. Most of the animals are doubtful of this, but they all agree that He is loathsome and that His scent is maddening and terrifying at the same time.

One day the terrifying scent reaches them and they know that He is there. Madly they try to run away, but there are too many of Him and His thunder-making arm speaks again and again. Pheasants, hares, deer, and almost every kind of bird and animal die from that evil arm. At last the deer who have been able to escape meet in a clearing

far away. Gobo is missing, and Bambi's mother is missing. He never sees her again.

Chaps. 11–19. Bambi has grown, and his antlers are beautiful. A young squirrel admires them and assures Bambi that he is going to be an extremely handsome stag. Bambi is pleased but lonely. The other young bucks won't let him come near. A strange feeling comes over him. He does not know what is the matter, but when he sees the outline of another buck in the woods he feels that he must charge and fight him. He rushes toward the other, but in a single motion the stag fends him off and Bambi realizes to his horror that it is the old Prince, who spoke to him so long before. The old Prince is understanding and compliments Bambi on having grown so well.

In the summer, when it is very hot, Bambi has a strange feeling that he cannot understand at all. He is unhappy. Then he sees Faline and they are delighted to talk over old times. Suddenly Bambi realizes that he loves Faline, and asks her if she can love him. But Faline is a girl, and she must flirt a bit before she confesses her love. They run off on a playful chase, and suddenly there is another young buck, who also loves Faline. He orders Bambi away, but Bambi is not to be commanded now. In a furious charge he knocks over the other young stag, and after three or four times his rival runs away. Still he cannot resume his courting of Faline, for the lame young buck comes along, and he too is determined that Faline shall be his. Another fight, and Bambi is once more the victor. Faline congratulates him on his wonderful fighting and confesses that she loves him.

One day Bambi is sleeping in the glade. He wakes up and finds Faline gone but the old stag is beside him. Bambi hears Faline's voice calling to him. The old stag tells him that it is not Faline, but Bambi refuses to believe him. The old stag cleverly and skillfully leads Bambi toward the sound of the voice. The skill and silence of the old stag are most wonderful. Not a twig breaks under his feet, not a leaf crackles. Suddenly, there He is. It had been He, imitating the voice of Faline. Silently, the two deer retrace their steps, and the old stag has saved Bambi's life.

Faline must flirt a bit before she confesses her love

69

A young buck comes who does not trouble to look for danger, but walks boldly about. It is Gobo. He was picked up by one of the hunters on that dreadful day, and has been kept in a very fine place where it is warm even in winter and where the rain never touched him. He was fed on delicious fresh-mown hay. Gobo is no longer afraid of Him or His dogs. Ena is happy to see her son again. Only the old stag, who comes to call one day, notices a band on Gobo's neck. Gobo explains that this is His halter. The old stag murmurs that Gobo is a "poor thing."

Gobo has forgotten the meaning of danger signals given by birds and other animals. One day, in spite of the crow's and the magpie's warning, he goes out in the open meadow to graze. There is a shot and Gobo comes back to the woods, mortally wounded. The other deer run away in terror, and they hear Gobo's death shriek.

Chaps. 20–25. Bambi is alone now, and wandering about in search of something, but he does not know what it is. He meets the old stag and learns that He has other methods than the arm for killing animals. They find the Hare caught in a trap noose, and the old stag frees him. As they walk onward together, He appears from nowhere and Bambi feels a terrible pain in his shoulder. The old stag will not let him stop, but cleverly outwits Him and his dogs and leads Bambi to a place where he can recover from his wound.

Long afterward, Bambi and the old stag meet again. They hear the dreaded thunder that comes from His extra arm, but this time the old stag takes Bambi in the direction of the hated scent and they find a dead man lying on the ground. The old stag explains to Bambi that there is a force that is even more powerful than He is, for He can also die. Then the old stag tells Bambi that he must go away, alone, for his time has come, and for this everyone must be alone.

Bambi is wandering about in the springtime, and he comes upon a pair of twin fawns crying for their mother. Just as the Old Prince before him, he asks them sternly if they cannot stay by themselves. As he moves away, he thinks that he would like to know that young male when he becomes a fine stag. And the girl fawn is quite nice, too.

Bambi goes back into the woods.

Barabbas

Novel by Pär Lagerkvist, 1891–1950.

Published 1950; in the U.S. published and © 1951 by Random House, New York, in a translation from the Swedish by Alan Blair. (ML, P13)

TWO NOTABLE JEWS awaited crucifixion in Jerusalem, Jesus and a bandit and revolutionist named Barabbas. As was the Passover custom, Pontius Pilate offered to release either. The people—impelled to do so by the priests—demanded that Barabbas be released and Jesus be crucified. That is all the Gospels tell. The challenge to novelists is apparent and dozens of them have drawn on their imaginations to give the fuller story of Barabbas—where he had come from, what he had done, what became of him. This is the most distinguished of the many efforts. It has, of course, a Swedish and Protestant outlook. It is very short, some 50,000 words. The English translation by Alan Blair is superb. Lagerkvist received the Nobel Prize in 1951, the year after the novel was published.

When Jesus was crucified on Golgotha, BARABBAS stood by and watched to the end. Barabbas was about 30, powerfully built, with black hair and a reddish beard that almost hid a deep scar under one eye. He watched the passion and burial and saw the big stone rolled in front of the tomb. Then he went back to Jerusalem. On the street he met the GIRL WITH THE HARE-LIP (whom he had known, and owned, before his arrest) and with her he went to the place of the FAT WOMAN. The others there welcomed him gaily, as the man who had been sentenced to crucifixion and then spared; but Barabbas was chiefly interested in questioning the girl with the hare-lip about the crucified rabbi, whom she knew about and believed in: What were his miracles? what did he preach? It was incredible to him that the man was the Messiah. The others went to sleep. Barabbas slept on the roof with the fat woman.

The next day Barabbas met a man [Peter] who told him about the Master, how he died for men, was the Son of God, would rise from the dead. Barabbas was still inwardly incredulous; would the Son of God let himself be crucified? Peter did not recognize Barabbas, but other Christians came up, recognized him, and drove him away.

The girl with the hare-lip slept down outside the Dung Gate, where the refuse of Jerusalem lived, many of them living on garbage. The lepers lived nearby. She remembered her one meeting with the Son of God. He had stroked her cheek and had told her she would bear witness for him.

Barabbas returned to the place of the tomb before dawn. When it was light he saw that the stone had been rolled away and the body was gone. The girl with the hare-lip was kneeling in the tomb. She told him of the angel that had come, but he had not seen the angel. And she told him of the preacher's doctrine: *Love one another.*

Barabbas thought always of the crucified man. He mixed with Christians in Potter's Lane and they took him on a short journey to meet a man [Lazarus] whom the Master had raised from the dead. But Barabbas could not quite believe. He mooned constantly. The fat woman, with whom he was still living, found herself lonely even when he was with her.

Barabbas went to a secret meeting of Christians. The girl with the hare-lip was among those who confessed their faith (though because of her deformity she could hardly be understood). When the persecution of Christians began she was denounced to the Sanhedrin and sentenced to be stoned to death. After the stoning Barabbas took her broken body and carried it many miles to bury it in the grave of the child she had once borne.

Instead of returning to Jerusalem, Barabbas went on to his original home and to the band of brigands that he had led (after killing the powerful but aged Eliahu, whom he did not know was his father). Now his people found him changed and very strange in his constant musing, and they were relieved when one morning he had suddenly disappeared.

There are only legends, no certain knowledge, of what happened to Barabbas then; but when he was in his 50's he appeared as a slave of the Roman governor of Cyprus. He had spent several years in the Cyprian copper mines, the worst sentence possible for a criminal. The slaves were shackled together in pairs and Barabbas's mate, in the mines and then at the governor's, was SAHAK, an Armenian; they had become also soulmates because Sahak was a Christian and Barabbas had seen the Saviour. At the governor's they were harnessed together to pull a plow. Sahak had the Saviour's name—*Christos Iesus*—engraved on the back of his slave's disk, and Barabbas asked him to engrave it also on his own disk. One day, to everyone's amazement, Sahak and Barabbas were summoned to an audience with the governor, who questioned them on the engraved words. Sahak said he believed in Christ; Barabbas said he did not, but had the words on his disk because he wanted to believe. The governor tried to persuade Sahak to recant. Sahak would not and the governor reluctantly had him crucified, for that was the law. Barabbas was not punished, for he did not believe, but the governor took a dagger and crossed out the words on his disk. The governor had Barabbas given lighter work. Once again "Barabbas the acquitted" watched a man—this time Sahak—being crucified.

When the governor returned to Rome, Barabbas was one of the slaves he took with him. In Rome Barabbas found there were many Christians, especially slaves; and he went into the catacombs where they met, though his life in the mines had given him great fear of underground places and also he had great fear of death. When fire began to consume Rome [under Nero, A.D. 64] and Barabbas heard the spreading report that the Christians were doing it, he went around setting fires more enthusiastically than anyone else. He was captured, confessed everything, and was thrown into prison. The many Christians there could not believe Barabbas was one of them, for a Christian would not have set fires; but a venerable old man, the most revered among them [Peter], finally recognized him as Barabbas.

As he sat there with the others, waiting for crucifixion, Barabbas finally became able to believe; and when dying on the cross he spoke the words he had heard Jesus say, "To Thee I deliver up my soul."

The Barber of Seville

Comedy by Pierre Caron de Beaumarchais, 1732–1799.

Produced in Paris 1775. Translated many times.

THE BARBER OF SEVILLE is now best known in the history books, though it was only a symptom and not a contributing factor in the last mad years of the French kingdom. In its own right it is a prime example of playmaking craft and its dialogue sparkles with wit. The play is no longer revived, but of course it survives in the Rossini opera.

Act I. In front of the house of Dr. BARTHOLO in Seville, Count ALMAVIVA is standing, hoping for a glimpse of the beautiful ROSINA. FIGARO, a former servant of Almaviva's, enters, singing gaily. Almaviva learns that Figaro is now a barber. Rosina appears on a balcony, with Bartholo. She pretends to drop a "song" she is holding, and before Bartholo can run downstairs to recover it Figaro gets it. It is a note to Almaviva, whose loitering around the house has aroused Rosina's curiosity. She tells Almaviva to come and sing under the balcony as soon as Bartholo goes out. Almaviva and Figaro hide while Bartholo looks for the "song" and discovers he has been tricked; he goes back and locks Rosina into her room. Almaviva has thought Rosina was Bartholo's wife, but Figaro, who is Bartholo's barber, tells him that she is Bartholo's ward; however, Bartholo is planning to marry her the next day. First Figaro proposes to get Almaviva into the house by drugging everyone in it (except Rosina);

then he suggests that Almaviva pose as a soldier and get his friend the colonel to billet him in Bartholo's house. Bartholo leaves the house to call on Don BAZILE,

Rosina's singing teacher. Almaviva decides he will pose as LINDOR, a poor scholar, hoping Rosina will love him for himself alone.

Act II. Rosina, in her apartment, is writing a letter to her unknown lover. Figaro comes in and tells her the man is Lindor, who will come to see her that night; this frightens Rosina. She gives Figaro her letter just as Bartholo comes in. Figaro hides. Bartholo is enraged because Figaro has drugged the servants. Rosina leaves; Bazile comes in and tells Bartholo that Rosina's admirer is Count Almaviva. Bartholo decides he must marry Rosina before she finds this out. The trouble is that Rosina does not want to marry him. Bazile offers to arrange it, for a fee, and Bartholo agrees. After Bazile leaves, Almaviva comes in, dressed as a cavalry officer and feigning drunkenness. He has a letter billeting him there for the night, and since the name Lindor is used in it Rosina knows it is her admirer. But Bartholo has an official exemption from the billeting of soldiers on him, and orders Almaviva thrown out. Almaviva has contrived to slip Rosina a note (from "Lindor"), and though Bartholo suspects Rosina she fools him by substituting another, innocent note she has received.

Act III. Almaviva returns to Bartholo's house the next day, this time disguised as a singing master, ALONZO, and saying Bazile is ill and has sent him. He wins Bartholo's confidence by discussing Bazile's plans to persuade Rosina to marry her guardian; to which end he shows Bartholo Rosina's letter to "Lindor" and says Rosina must be made to think Lindor betrayed her by giving it to another woman, from whom Alonzo had it. Then Rosina will not refuse

to marry Bartholo. Rosina comes in to say she will have no more singing lessons, but recognizing "Lindor" she changes her mind. During the singing lesson Figaro comes in, to shave Bartholo. Bartholo will not leave the room, but insists on being shaved there. He gives Figaro his keys to get his shaving things and this permits Figaro to abstract the key to Rosina's window. Bazile comes in, and though Almaviva and Figaro cleverly talk themselves out of exposure and Almaviva gives Bazile money to persuade him to leave, Bartholo detects Alonzo's imposture.

Act IV. Bazile has arranged for a notary to come and marry Bartholo and Rosina. Bartholo shows Rosina the letter she wrote to Lindor, and persuades her that Lindor gave it to a certain Count Almaviva and actually is only Almaviva's agent. Rosina is convinced that Lindor's arrangement to carry her off that night is only to deliver her to Almaviva. Overcome by this treachery, she promises to marry Bartholo. While Bartholo goes for the police to arrest Lindor and Figaro when they appear, they do come in. Almaviva now reveals his true identity to Rosina. The notary and Bazile arrive. Almaviva bribes Bazile, and Almaviva and Figaro persuade the notary to marry Rosina to Almaviva at once. Bazile and Figaro act as witnesses. Bartholo returns with the police, but they will not touch Almaviva because of his high rank. Bartholo can still block the marriage by refusing to give his assent as guardian, but then he is reminded that an accounting of what he has done with Rosina's property may be embarrassing; so he signs. Figaro reminds him that love will find a way.

Almaviva poses as a singing-master; Bartholo waits to be shaved

71

Barnaby Rudge

Novel by Charles Dickens, 1812–1870. Published 1841. Available in many editions.

THOUGH IT IS NOT celebrated as one of Dickens' best novels, *Barnaby Rudge* contains some of Dickens' most effective writing and best-drawn characters. It is a book of moods—the ghostly slinking of the villain Rudge, the eery voice of Barnaby's pet raven Grip—and of dramatic and suspenseful scenes. It is historical in its portrayal of the anti-Catholic riots led by Lord George Gordon in 1780. ¶ *Barnaby Rudge* was the second and last novel of a series that Dickens had started with *Master Humphrey's Clock* and continued with *The Old Curiosity Shop;* he had devised the series to help the serial sales of installments of his novels, but since people were standing in line to get the latest installment no device to stimulate sales was needed.

Chap. 1. On the 19th of March, 1775, it being a cold and stormy night, a little group of people are gathered in the Maypole Inn, on the borders of Epping Forest, about 12 miles from London. There are old JOHN WILLET, the innkeeper; SOLOMON DAISY, the sexton; and a few other cronies; JOE WILLET, old John's son; and two guests. One of the guests is EDWARD CHESTER, a handsome young man, who has ridden down from London to see Miss EMMA HAREDALE, the niece of GEOFFREY HAREDALE, a country gentleman in the vicinity; he presently sets off for London. The other guest is a morose, shabby man, who sits apart from the others. Solomon Daisy relates how, on that very day of the month, 22 years before, a double murder occurred, at dead of night, in Mr. Haredale's house, called the Warren. His only brother, Reuben Haredale, was found dead in his room. The steward and the gardener were both missing; but months afterward a body, supposed to be that of RUDGE, the steward, was found in a pond nearby, stabbed with a knife. It was concluded, therefore, that the gardener was the guilty person.

Chaps. 2–3. This story being finished, the ill-looking stranger hastily rises, mounts his horse, and gallops away with such recklessness that he runs into the chaise of GABRIEL VARDEN, a locksmith from London. Gabriel Varden calls at the Maypole to replace his lantern, which was broken. When he leaves, Joe Willet brings around his horse and confides his intention of running away to seek his fortune, since his father treats him like a child. Gabriel, on his way to London, finds BARNABY RUDGE waving a torch over young Chester, stabbed and robbed by a highwayman. Barnaby is the son of the widow Rudge, whose husband was the murdered steward. Barnaby, born after that terrible event, is of a disordered intellect. His long red hair hangs in disorder about his face and shoulders, giving him an unearthly expression. With Barnaby's assistance, Gabriel carries Chester (not seriously wounded) to the house of Barnaby's mother.

Chaps. 4–6. The locksmith's family consists of his wife; his beautiful and bewitching daughter, DOLLY; Miss MIGGS, a cantankerous maidservant; and SIMON TAPPERTIT, his apprentice, a thin-faced, sleek-haired, sharp-nosed, small-eyed little fellow, not much more than 5 feet high. He is in love with his master's daughter.

Chaps. 7–9. When all is quiet, Simon Tappertit steals out of the house to a dingy cellar, where a secret club of apprentices, headed by Simon himself, hold their meetings, plotting insurrection, rebellion, and death to their masters.

Chaps. 10–15. The Maypole Inn has another notable guest: Mr. Chester, senior, the father of Edward. It is well known that Mr. Chester and Mr. Haredale were for many years bitter enemies. Mr. Haredale arrives and is ushered upstairs. The gentlemen for the first time in their lives come to an agreement: by fair means or foul, the engagement between Mr. Chester's son and Mr. Haredale's niece shall be broken. Joe Willet has gone to London, hoping to see the charming Dolly. But Dolly is just setting out for an evening party. Edward Chester calls at the Warren; a lovely girl appears, and her dark hair, next moment, is resting on Edward's breast. Mr. Haredale steps between them, thrusts Edward away, and forbids him the house. The next day Edward is informed by his father that he is expected to retrieve the family fortunes by marrying an heiress. When Edward indignantly declines, Mr. Chester senior coolly and politely disowns him.

Chaps. 16–18. Among the worst vagrants and criminals who haunt the dark places of London, there is one who has a pale, wild face and is never seen without a slouch hat pulled over his brows. This man forces his way into the widow Rudge's house early one evening. "The very marrow of my bones," he says, "is cold with wet and hunger. I must have warmth and food, and I will have them here." The widow gives him food. Barnaby comes home and the man seizes a knife from the table and slinks into the closet. When Barnaby falls asleep, the fellow creeps out of his hiding place, gazes intently at the face of the sleeper, and says in a hoarse whisper to the widow, "Observe. In him, I have you in my power." Then he goes out into the darkness.

Chaps. 19–22. Edward Chester goes to the locksmith's with a note for Miss Haredale, to be taken by Dolly, who is a sort of companion for the young lady. Mrs. Varden joins her husband and daughter in an excursion to the Maypole Inn. After dinner Dolly trips over the fields to deliver her letter to Miss Haredale; and in return she receives a reply for Edward and a bracelet for herself. On the way back to the inn she meets Maypole HUGH, a tall, rough, handsome fellow in a savage way, the hostler of the inn. He snatches away the letter, the bracelet, and a kiss. Joe Willet, in answer to her shriek, comes to the rescue. Hugh has disappeared when Joe arrives; and terrified by threats he made, Dolly does not dare to say who robbed her.

Chaps. 23–24. Hugh's misdeed, so far at least as the letter was concerned, was directly incited by Mr. Chester senior, to whom the letter for his son is delivered by Hugh. The theft of the bracelet was a little affair of his own; and Mr. Chester, learning of it, holds it over Hugh as a whip, for in those days men were hanged for crimes no greater. Mr. Chester has another visitor the same day, Simon Tappertit, who suggests that Mr. Chester call upon Mrs. Varden, "flatter her up a bit," and through her stop Dolly's acting as a messenger between Edward Chester and Miss Haredale. Mr. Tappertit also has a word to say about Joe Willet, calling him a villain and warning that he will arrange a marriage between Edward and Miss Haredale unless Mr. Chester gets rid of him.

Chaps. 25–32. Meanwhile Mrs. Rudge, without giving any explanation, renounces the pension that Mr. Haredale has paid her since the double murder at the Warren, and disappears. Hugh gives Mr. Chester information which leads him to seek out Miss Haredale and tell her a false story of his son's inconstancy to her. As Mr. Chester is about to leave the Maypole the next morning, Joe comes out to hold his stirrup. Seeing this, old John comes diving out of the porch, collars his son, and sends him back inside. This crowning humiliation is too much for poor Joe; that night he goes to London. After a farewell visit to Dolly, who pretends not to care but bursts into tears as soon as he is gone, Joe enlists in the Army for foreign service. Edward Chester, too, has a final parting with his father, and, like Joe, disappears from England for five long years.

Chaps. 33–49. The 19th of March 1780 comes around at the Maypole. After midnight, Solomon Daisy comes in, the image of fright and horror. He has seen in the churchyard the bareheaded figure of a man—which he took to be a ghost—in the likeness of Rudge, the former steward. Three persons, who are Lord GEORGE GORDON, his secretary, and his servant, put up at the Maypole. That night GASHFORD, the secretary, places in the inn yard a printed handbill adjuring "every Protestant into whose hands this shall come," "to join without delay the friends of Lord George Gordon." This paper is found by Hugh, who, within a few days, follows the party to London and joins the mob of "No Popery" rioters whom Lord George Gordon stirs up. At London Hugh makes two friends, one DENNIS, a mysterious person whose calling is not known to his associates, but who is really the common hangman, and our old friend

Simon Tappertit, both ardent "No Popery" men. Hugh is amused to be under the leadership of Simon, a little man whom he might crush with one hand. Sir John Chester—for Edward Chester's father has now become Sir John—had a hand in Hugh's conversion to "No Popery," his motive being one of revenge upon his old enemy, Mr. Haredale, who is a Catholic; because of him Mrs. Varden also became an enthusiast for the faith, greatly to the disgust of Gabriel, who is a staunch upholder of law and order. Another person who hates Mr. Haredale and has determined to use Hugh and the "No Popery" mob to injure him is Gashford. Just as these events are happening Mrs. Rudge flees to London, hoping to hide herself and Barnaby from her terrible visitor. On Westminster Bridge they meet the "No Popery" mob and Barnaby, recognizing in the crowd his old friend Hugh, is drawn along with the rest, leaving his poor mother almost distracted. Hugh gives Barnaby the banner to carry—an honor which pleases him immensely.

The mob breaks up old John Willet's inn while he watches helplessly

Chaps. 50–53. Simon Tappertit returns late at night to his master's house, much the worse for liquor and fighting. He hands a dirty piece of paper to Mrs. Varden; on this paper, in the handwriting of Lord George Gordon himself, is written a protection for the house. Varden, to his wife's dismay, tears the paper into fragments. For the next two days the rioters have their way in the streets of London: Catholic chapels are pillaged and burned; the houses of Catholics are plundered and pulled down, and many are cruelly beaten and misused. Hugh posts Barnaby as a sentry at the Boot Inn, while he and the rest are off marauding.

Chaps. 54–55. The mob is on the road. Old John Willet, who is alone in the bar that evening, hears them coming. The mob rushes at the Maypole pell mell, and in a few seconds John is bandied from hand to hand. The crowd help themselves; the neat and cheerful bar is wrecked and gutted, and everything breakable is destroyed. After this diversion the mob proposes to knock Old John in the head, but Hugh does not consent. Instead, the landlord is bound fast to his chair, and the mob departs for the Warren. They have been gone but a short time when Mr. Willet has a strange caller, a man wearing a slouch hat pulled low on his forehead. He devours the fragments of bread and meat that are left. The loud sound of an alarm bell is heard, and the bright glare of a fire appears in the sky. The rioters have set fire to the Warren, and Miss Haredale and Dolly are carried off as prisoners by Hugh and Simon Tappertit.

Chap. 56. Mr. Haredale gallops up with Solomon Daisy clinging on behind him. He dismounts and searches the ruins. Some of the ashes in the high tower slip and roll down, and Mr. Haredale with drawn sword steals into the turret. A figure is briefly visible. The little sexton, Solomon Daisy, is frozen with terror at the sight and screams,

"The ghost! The ghost!" Mr. Haredale leaps on the man and seizes him. It is Rudge, the

double murderer—captured.

Chaps. 57–62. Meanwhile Barnaby is captured by a company of soldiers and taken to Newgate. Hugh returns to the Boot Inn after depositing Miss Haredale and Dolly in an obscure house in London, where they are guarded by a group of Hugh's followers. Rudge the murderer is also taken to Newgate, and there Barnaby and his father meet for the first time in their lives.

Chaps. 63–65. The mob is determined to free the prisoners in Newgate. They seek Gabriel Varden, the locksmith, who made the great lock on the prison door. He appears at an upper window, gun in hand, but Miggs calls from another window that she has poured beer in the barrel of the gun so that it will not fire. The mob thereupon breaks through the doors and Gabriel is carried off to Newgate. He bravely refuses to pick the lock of the prison, and he is severely beaten. A tall fellow raises a pole-axe and aims it at the old man's uncovered head, but at that very instant he falls himself, and over his body a one-armed man leaps to the locksmith's side. Another man joins him, and they fight their way back through the crowd, carrying the locksmith with them. Now the mob sets fire to the building, then pours in and frees the prisoners, Barnaby and his father among them.

Chaps. 66–70. Quite unaware that the murderer is at liberty again, Mr. Haredale finds himself homeless in London, for even the tavernkeepers dare not take in a Catholic. He is rescued by the vintner, a Catholic, who supplies the cellars of the Maypole Inn. It is night again, and the streets are a dreadful spectacle. The leader of one mob is Hugh, mad with liquor and excitement. Seeing Mr. Haredale by the light of the burning buildings, he swears to have his life. But just as the mob pours in at the front of the vintner's house, the same one-armed man, with his companion, enter the house from the rear and take the vintner and Mr. Haredale to a place of safety. These two men are Joe Willet, returned from the wars with the loss of an arm, and Edward Chester.

Hugh is wounded and falls from his horse. Barnaby carries Hugh off to the Boot Inn, where his father, the murderer, is already lodged. Here they all remain until the

soldiers come for them—guided by Dennis, who has turned traitor. They are all taken to prison.

Chaps. 71–82. The mob is, by this time, thoroughly put down. Miss Haredale and Dolly are found in the wretched house where they have been kept prisoners; Mr. Haredale, the locksmith, Joe, and Edward burst in together and knock down all who stand in their way—and there is such a meeting of friends, relatives, and lovers as is seldom seen. The reunion of poor Mrs. Rudge with her son takes place in the prison, where Barnaby, his father, Hugh, and Dennis are all under sentence of death. The locksmith makes an effort to save Hugh. He has been told that Hugh is really the illegitimate son of Sir John Chester by a gypsy woman. Sir John pretends not to believe it, and abandons Hugh to his fate. Great efforts are made also to save Barnaby, but nothing comes of them. On the day of the execution Dennis, the hangman, falls upon his knees and howls for mercy—a pitiable sight. Hugh and Barnaby are quite brave and calm. Barnaby is scheduled to hang an hour later than the others.

Hugh, Dennis, and Rudge the murderer are all hanged, but Barnaby is reprieved at the last moment and for the rest of his life he and his mother live peaceably and happily at the Maypole. Joe marries Dolly, and restores the old inn. Mr. Haredale kills Sir John Chester in a duel and spends the remainder of his life in a monastery on the continent. Edward Chester marries Miss Haredale and rebuilds the Warren. Old John Willet, whose mind never quite recovers from the shock of the riot, is installed in a little cottage near the Maypole, where a miniature bar is fitted up for him and he entertains—as before—Solomon Daisy and his other cronies. The score that he adds up against them for pipes of tobacco and glasses of grog is of enormous size.

Barren Ground

Novel by Ellen Glasgow, 1874–1945. Published & © 1926 by Doubleday & Co., New York.

ELLEN GLASGOW's reputation was already good and her novels many, but the publication of *Barren Ground* in 1926 was what chiefly made it clear that she was a major novelist. Mrs. Glasgow wrote not about her own upper-class circles—though later she proved she could do so with equal success—but about the rural people of the countryside near her native Richmond, Virginia. Like fine poetry or music *Barren Ground* in its writing reflects the temperament of the action depicted, dull or emotional or brisk as the case may be.

Part I. Chaps. 1–10. In a dreary, unproductive section of the South, in the 1890s, DORINDA OAKLEY works for $10 a week at the store of NATHAN PEDLAR, an honest but poverty-ridden farmer-storekeeper. His tubercular wife, ROSE EMILY, is rapidly dying but has unquenchable optimism. Nathan is far ahead of his time in farming methods and soil conservation. He is considered unpractical and foolish.

EUDORA OAKLEY, Dorinda's mother, suffers constantly from neuralgia and is totally absorbed in her religion. She works unceasingly. Her husband, Joshua Oakley, is an uncommunicative and stolid man. Before she married him she was in love with a young missionary but she received news of his death in Africa. She tells Dorinda that it is no use to expect anything of marriage but pain and hard work. Dorinda is young enough to disagree. She falls in love with JASON GREYLOCK, the son of ·the former town physician. Jason's father is a hopeless alcoholic and flails about with his whip when he is drunk, striking anyone in reach. Young Jason has studied medicine in New York and has returned only at the urging of his father, who wrote that he was ill.

Dorinda travels two miles each way on foot to Pedlar's store. She fell in love with Jason after he picked her up accidentally one afternoon. One day he lightly suggests that she get a dress exactly the same shade of blue as her eyes. Dorinda has thirty dollars, saved painstakingly over a long period of time, with which she had planned to buy a cow so that the family might have milk and butter. She determines instead to buy a dress and a hat for Easter, as she hears that GENEVA ELLGOOD, a young woman whose family is comparatively rich, is doing. On Easter Sunday, Dorinda wears her new blue dress and hat to church, to see Jason sitting with Geneva Ellgood in the Ellgood pew. She decides not to meet Jason that night at Gooseneck Creek. Soon afterward, however, Jason proposes. Preparations for the wedding absorb Dorinda—except for the blissful evenings she spends with Jason by Gooseneck Creek. She laughs at a rumor that Geneva Ellgood and Jason are to be married.

Chaps. 11–16. Jason goes to New York to buy surgical instruments. The wedding is to take place when he returns, in a week. More than two weeks pass and there is no word from Jason. Dorinda walks the many miles through the woods to AUNT MEHITABLE's cabin. Aunt Mehitable is an old Negress who is believed to have some supernatural powers as a "conjure woman." When Dorinda reaches Aunt Mehitable's cabin, after walking through a drenching rain for a long time, she faints. Aunt Mehitable says that no one will know that the baby is already on the way. Dorinda thus learns that she is pregnant. Desperately she heads for Five Oaks, the home of Jason and his father. She finds the old man and his house both in a state of incredible filth. She is horrified. The old doctor tells her that he wishes Jason had married her, but Jason was always lily-livered and Geneva's father and brother had threatened him. Dorinda learns that Jason and Geneva have indeed been married and are expected back that night. She gradually realizes that Jason is a weak, spineless man. When she sees him again, and he protests that he could do nothing else, she feels only contempt and loathing and wonders how she could ever have imagined that she loved him.

Dorinda packs an old carpet bag with her wedding finery and takes a train. By the merest chance, she gets a northbound train, sending her to New York. She has $50 in savings and a $20 wedding present. The last person she sees is Nathan Pedlar, waving goodbye from the railroad station.

Part II. Chaps. 1–10. Dorinda arrives in New York. She roams about inquiring in stores whether they need an extra clerk, on the basis of her experience at Nathan Pedlar's store. She has no luck, and tries being a waitress for a few days. The odor nauseates her. As she is walking, Dorinda faints and is struck by a cab. She recovers consciousness somewhat later in the hospital, to learn that she has lost her baby, but that she will be all right. Dr. FARADAY, who treats her, takes her home to work in his office and help his wife with their six children. She stays with the Faradays for two years, then returns home when her father has a stroke.

Meanwhile Dorinda has studied every book she could find on scientific dairy farming, crop rotation, soil conservation, and modern farming methods in general. She has determined to farm her family land and farm it properly. Dr. Faraday lends her a substantial sum of money. While Dorinda has been away, Rose Emily Pedlar has died, her small daughter MINNIE MAY has become the young mother of the family, and Nathan has prospered in his store.

Dorinda busies herself in plans to make Oak Farm productive and sees a great deal of Nathan. She wonders how she ever thought him repulsively ugly. When she encounters Jason Greylock she wonders even more strongly how she could ever have imagined herself in love with him. He is dissolute, shaky, whining, and weak. Geneva, though she is only Dorinda's age, is a faded, middle-aged woman.

Dorinda buys seven Jersey cows from BOB ELLGOOD, Geneva's brother, and through Nathan hires some Negro field hands. Jason tries to talk with her; he says she will be responsible if he goes straight to the devil, as he will unless she relents. She is disgusted.

Dorinda's father dies. Her younger brother RUFUS wants to leave the farm. He has always hated farming. Her married brother JOSIAH and his wife offer weakly to take Mrs. Oakley, but Dorinda refuses. Her mother and she will stay and work Old Farm.

Chaps. 11–19. Dorinda has been working her farm successfully for more than six months. One day Rufus comes running home, in obvious terror. He demands of his mother that she swear he has been at home all afternoon. That evening the sheriff calls and tells them that a man has been shot and his brother accuses Rufus of the murder. Mrs. Oakley tells the sheriff that Rufus has been at home all afternoon. At the court hearing next day, Mrs. Oakley reiterates her lie and is believed. Rufus is free, and leaves for New York. Dorinda is glad to see him go. Mrs. Oakley takes to her bed, unable to stand or walk. She dies after a year. Nathan and his children come to visit each Sunday. Dorinda is especially fond of one of them, a boy who was born with a club foot, JOHN ABNER. At length Dorinda agrees to marry Nathan, after many proposals on his part. On the day of the wedding, Geneva (who has become mentally deranged) drowns herself in the mill pond. Dorinda continues to

Dorinda is struck by a cab

74

prosper and when a tax sale puts the old Greylock place up for auction, Dorinda buys it. She is 38 and a handsome woman. Hard work has kept her muscles and her flesh firm. The only real affection she has is directed toward John Abner. She still cannot express any affection for Nathan, good and kind as he always is.

Part III. Chaps. 1–11. For the next few years Dorinda is occupied with her family farm and the recently acquired Five Oaks. Everything prospers. Jason is living in a little shack in the woods, drinking himself to death in squalor. Nathan must go to the city to have a tooth pulled. It is a snowy day and the train is wrecked. Nathan tries heroically to save others, and dies himself. Now Dorinda is left alone with John Abner to help her. As usual, she carries on.

One day Jason is found sick and helpless in the woods, and the neighbors carry him to Dorinda's house, assuming she will take care of him. She does so, although she feels only pity for him. After several months Jason dies and another part of Dorinda's life is irrevocably closed.

Dorinda realizes now that life is never what one expects it to be, and rarely what one desires, but it is a continuing adventure. She is at peace with herself.

The Barsetshire Chronicles

Novels by Anthony Trollope, 1815–1882.
Published 1855 (*The Warden*) and 1857 (*Barchester Towers*). (ML, T37; ML, 41; RE, 21)

THERE WERE SIX NOVELS in the series called the Barsetshire Chronicles, which Trollope wrote about the imaginary town of Barchester near London. *The Warden* was the first and *Barchester Towers* the second, and together they are considered the best work Trollope did. With gentle humor and satire he examines the good men and bad men of the Church, and his principal good man, Mr. Harding, is an excellent creation. Though many of the titles and allusions may be strange to American readers who do not know the complex organization and interior politics—ecclesiastical, theological, and doctrinal—of the Church of England, the novels are easy to follow and reading them is a rewarding experience. ¶ *The Warden* is a short novel, barely 100,000 words; *Barchester Towers* is somewhat more than twice as long.

The Warden

Chaps. 1–2. The Rev. SEPTIMUS HARDING at the age of 60 was precentor (leader in chanting the service) at the cathedral in a town we shall call Barchester, and also a clergyman with a benefice, or living, in a parish nearby. His elder daughter, SUSAN, was married to Dr. THEOPHILUS GRANTLY, archdeacon of Barchester and son of the bishop. Mr. Harding had also an unmarried daughter, ELEANOR. Mr. Harding was also warden of Hiram's Hospital. In 1434 a man named John Hiram had left an estate to provide an almshouse for twelve aged woolcarders, and as he loved music he willed that the precentor be the warden if he chose. The estate's income had grown greatly. The twelve old men got their lodging and one shilling fourpence a day; Mr. Harding as warden got £800 a year, compared to £80 he received as precentor. There had been murmurs that the income was not fairly divided, but Mr. Harding's popularity and high repute had kept the murmurs down. He did add twopence per man daily, in all £62/11/4 per year, from his own income.

When Mr. Harding had been the warden for ten years, a young surgeon, JOHN BOLD, 27 years old, rich enough so that he did not practice much, a dissenter and mild radical, a reformer at heart, took an interest in the Hiram income. John was in love with Eleanor, and she with him (though she had not agreed to marry him) and Mr. Harding approved, John being his close friend. Yet John took a course that could hurt Mr. Harding. He studied Hiram's will; he called on CHADWICK, steward of the diocese, for a statement of the property's income; and when Chadwick refused he engaged a lawyer, FINNEY, to sue (on behalf of the bedesmen, the twelve old men).

Chaps. 3–6. But first John called to tell Mr. Harding what he planned to do. Mr. Harding was playing his cello for ten of the old men. Afterwards John tried to tell Mr. Harding, but the warden would not hear him; he said John must do what he considered right and nothing could affect their friendship. Mr. Harding then called on his old friend BISHOP GRANTLY, who was over 80 but a fine, keen old man; and he confessed some misgivings as to his right to so much income as warden. He also told the bishop that John was his prospective son-in-law. The bishop advised him to talk to Dr. Grantly. Finney got eleven of the twelve bedesmen to sign a petition to the bishop asking for £100 a year each; only old BUNCE, who was convinced the Church could do no wrong, refused to sign. Dr. Grantly went to see the warden, to convince him that there was nothing wrong and that the handling of the case should be left to Chadwick; then Dr. Grantly addressed the bedesmen and tried to bully them into withdrawing the petition. But the warden was

unconvinced and the petition reached the bishop, who signed a refusal written by his son. To show his good feelings toward John Bold, Mr. Harding gave a party for Eleanor and invited John and his sister MARY BOLD, but John made Mary refuse on his behalf. John's absence from the party was so strange that Eleanor asked and found out what he planned to do. When she met him on the street next day she told him she could not have a high opinion of anyone who damaged her father, then curtseyed and walked off.

Chaps. 7–10. The daily *Jupiter*, the powerful and widely read London newspaper, attacked the disposition of the Hiram funds, with an implied accusation of guilt or greed on Mr. Harding's part. Chadwick called on Dr. Grantly at Plumstead Episcopi, the parish of which Dr. Grantly was rector, with advice from their counsel, Sir ABRAHAM HAPHAZARD, that Bold's suit on behalf of the bedesmen was directed at the wrong persons, since Mr. Harding and Chadwick were only paid servants and did not control the funds. The bishop invited Mr. Harding to the palace, where Dr. Grantly explained Haphazard's opinion; but Mr. Harding insisted that he could not continue to accept the money if he had no moral right to it. He returned home, where he pondered the problem at great length. Seeing his worry, Eleanor learned from him what was troubling him, then urged him to give up the income, or at least not to keep it for her sake.

Chaps. 11–12. The next morning Eleanor resolved to go to John and plead with him to stop the attack on her father. John was out and she talked first to Mary. She would not admit to Mary that she loved John, but she wept on Mary's bosom. When Eleanor then talked to John she was resolved not to let the question of love enter into it. John assured her that no one could think ill of her father, but she told how he suffered from the implied slurs. John promised to withdraw the case; and then he pleaded his love so vehemently that eventually Eleanor had to capitulate and confess hers. John then went to Plumstead Episcopi to tell Dr. Grantly that he was discontinuing the suit, but Dr. Grantly obviously wanted the suit continued (since he was sure the Church would win) and on various pretexts refused. John left, thinking Dr. Grantly was a devil. But Mr. Harding solved his own problem. He told Eleanor he would go to London, see Haphazard, and resign. He and Eleanor would retire to his little church at Crabtree Parma, where the income was about £80 a year. Eleanor was very glad.

Chaps. 13–15. John tried to get his friend TOM TOWERS, of the *Jupiter*, to have the articles about Hiram's Hospital discontinued. Towers, though confident that he had the power to do so, excused himself on the grounds that he had not. All the almshouses were being looked into by the *Jupiter* and it was too good a story to drop.

Chaps. 16–19. In London Mr. Harding tried to make himself unattainable so he

John pleads his love to Eleanor

could not be found (by Dr. Grantly) and dissuaded from his course. He could not see Haphazard until 10 P.M. When they met, Haphazard congratulated him on the fact that the opposing attorneys had dropped their case; but Mr. Harding insisted on resigning. Haphazard was amazed, especially when he learned that Mr. Harding had no private income. Haphazard assured him that no one questioned the justice of the warden's income; Mr. Harding replied that one did: He himself. Then Mr. Harding went to see Dr. Grantly and Susan, who tried but could not sway him. The next morning he wrote to the bishop, resigning the wardenship. His act was bewildering to everyone.

Chaps. 20–21. The bishop summoned Mr. Harding, promising not to try to dissuade him. The bishop tried to press £6,000 on Mr. Harding, but it was refused. So Mr. Harding settled down to his new life as precentor and rector only. At his leavetaking the twelve old men were very sad—and poorer besides, for now they would not get the extra twopence a day. Mr. Harding took modest lodgings in Barchester, and officially he still lives there, but actually he spends most of his time at Eleanor's—who soon married John Bold—and at the palace, where at least three times a week the bishop insists that he come to dinner, and that means 3 to 10 o'clock.

Barchester Towers

Chaps. 1–2. The Bishop of Barchester is dying; his son Dr. Grantly, the archdeacon, and his dear friend the precentor, Septimus Harding, are by his bedside. The archdeacon has mixed feelings. The present prime minister would appoint him bishop, and it is his last chance; he is in his fifties. But the present ministry has five days at most to last.

The bishop dies but it is too late for Dr. Grantly. The ministry has already fallen and the new prime minister appoints Dr. PROUDIE bishop. Meanwhile there has been a change in the status of Hiram's Hospital, where the lucrative post of warden was resigned some years before by Mr. Harding. By Act of Parliament, the stipend of the warden has been set at £450 a year. But no warden has been appointed and Mr. Harding still lives in modest lodgings, often visiting his daughter, Eleanor Bolt, a widow whose husband's untimely death left her with a posthumous child, John Bold Jr., and a large annual income.

Chaps. 3–8. Dr. Proudie, the new bishop, has risen through his great toler-

ance, which made him politically a good negotiator. He has not great ability. Mrs. Proudie rules him despotically. The Rev. Mr. SLOPE, who has come with him as chaplain, is ambitious and at one time thought of advancing himself by wedding the bishop's daughter OLIVIA, but nothing came of it; now he expects to be the actual bishop by controlling Mrs. Proudie.

When Dr. Grantly and Mr. Harding call formally on the bishop upon his arrival, they find Mrs. Proudie present—an unprecedented thing—and also Mr. Slope. Mrs. Proudie leads the conversation and does not hesitate to be critical, abetted by Mr. Slope. Upon leaving, Dr. Grantly and Mr. Harding are united in their dislike of both Mrs. Proudie and Mr. Slope; Mr. Harding thinks Mrs. Proudie the worst. On the first Sunday after the bishop's arrival, Mr. Slope delivers the sermon in the cathedral. He speaks against High Church practices such as chanting. Not only the Barchester clergy but all the parishioners are disturbed. There are meetings and gossip and it is agreed that Mr. Slope must be debarred from preaching in the cathedral. Meanwhile

Mr. Harding is happily preparing to resume his old job as warden, since his appointment seems sure.

Chaps. 9–14. In the diocese there were several absentee clergymen who took the income without working, for old Bishop Grantly had been very lenient; and the worst offender was Dr. VESEY STANHOPE, who is rector of two prosperous parishes but has been in Italy for 12 years. Now he is summoned home. With him come his daughter CHARLOTTE, unmarried, about 35; his younger daughter, MADELINE NERONI, who was a great beauty but is now wholly crippled and is separated from her husband; and his son, ETHELBERT ("BERTIE"), who has a great distaste for work and who once offended his father by being converted to Judaism. At a large party given by the Proudies soon afterward, Madeline, carried in by four men, is a sensation. Bertie is impudent as usual, even to the bishop. A few days after the party Mr. Harding is told by Mr. Slope that an appointment to the wardenship would entail many new clerical duties Mr. Harding did not have previously. Mr. Harding hesitates to accept on this basis and Mr. Slope recommends to the bishop the appointment of Mr. QUIVERFUL, a rector in the diocese. Dr. Grantly obtains a living in the diocese for the Rev. FRANCIS ARABIN, a friend of his at Oxford.

Chaps. 15–21. Learning of Eleanor's fortune, Mr. Slope becomes a suitor. Bertie's sisters consider Eleanor a good catch for Bertie. Some trouble arises because the wardenship has been promised to Mr. Quiverful and Mrs. Proudie insists that he get it, while the bishop (now with Mr. Slope's support because of Eleanor) feels that Mr. Harding is legally entitled to it and failure to appoint him will cause public resentment. Mrs. Proudie is annoyed at Mr. Slope because of this and also because he paid too much attention to Madeline at the party. She forces the bishop to stand by the promise to Quiverful, but the bishop is afraid to tell Dr. Grantly this and feigns illness so that Mr. Slope can tell him. Bertie is piling up ruinous debts. Eleanor meets

Mr. Harding lives in retirement

Mr. Arabin, who is an attractive bachelor, and finds his conversation interesting.

Chaps. 22–30. WILFRID THORNE of Ullathorne is the principal squire of St. Ewold's, Mr. Arabin's new parish. The Thornes are a proud and rich family. Fortunately Thorne approves of Arabin and his daughter becomes friendly toward Eleanor. Mr. Quiverful is dismayed when he hears that he may not get the wardenship, for he has fourteen children and needs the income; and Mrs. Quiverful cites an absolute promise made to her by Mrs. Proudie. Mrs. Proudie makes an issue of it with the bishop, who chooses for once to side with Mr. Slope against her.

Though Mr. Slope has his eye on Eleanor, he is actually in love with Madeline and finally declares his love to her—fruitlessly, for her husband is still alive. Eleanor's family greatly fear the possibility of her marriage to Mr. Slope and work on her to prevent it; even Mr. Arabin joins with them, which offends Eleanor, but actually she has come to love Mr. Arabin, and he her.

Chaps. 31–34. The dean of Barchester, Dr. Trefoil, has a stroke; he is over 70 and his death is assumed. Mr. Slope asks the bishop for the preferment, but hardly anyone including the bishop can imagine him as dean. Mrs. Proudie, who is now Mr. Slope's bitter enemy, finally is the victor over him, successfully demanding that the bishop not only refuse Mr. Slope the deanship but also replace him as chaplain.

Chaps. 35–42. Miss Thorne gives a party. Because Eleanor rides to it with Mr. Slope, her father is more fearful than ever; but she tells him that she finds Mr. Slope odious. In the course of the party Mr. Slope tries to make love to Eleanor and she slaps him. Madeline finds Mr. Arabin very attractive but nobly (as she feels) resolves to give him up to the woman he loves. Bertie tells Eleanor that his sisters have urged him to woo her, and though Eleanor has been very friendly toward the Stanhopes and on terms of confidential friendship with Charlotte, she is angered by this and turned against the whole Stanhope family. Bertie's debts finally are too much for his father to countenance, and he is sent away.

Chaps. 43–49. Mr. Harding having decided not to accept reappointment as warden of Hiram's Hospital, Mr. Quiverful gets the appointment after all. Tom Towers, in the *Jupiter,* supports Mr. Slope for appointment as dean. Madeline asks Eleanor to call on her. When Eleanor does so, Madeline advises her to marry Mr. Arabin; she warns that Mr. Arabin may hesitate to express his love but she knows he feels it. The deanship is offered to Mr. Harding, to everyone's surprise; but he refuses it because he is more satisfied with his simple life. Mr. Arabin, encouraged by Miss Thorne, finally proposes to Eleanor and is accepted. Mr. Harding is delighted to hear of Eleanor's engagement and decides to try to have Mr. Arabin made dean.

Chaps. 50–53. With Dr. Grantly's help, Mr. Arabin is made dean. Mr. Slope leaves Barchester, after bitterly reproaching Mrs. Proudie for her treatment of him. Eleanor and Mr. Arabin are married, and Dr. Grantly is pleased because Mr. Arabin is a High Churchman—in fact, two degrees higher than himself. Mr. Harding is still precentor of Barchester.

Beau Geste

Novel by Percival Christopher Wren, 1885–1941.
Published 1924.

BEAU GESTE IS FAMOUS for its ingenious plot and its interesting picture of the French Foreign Legion, at least as it existed before World War I. Wren was by no means a good writer, and among other things his effort to render American conversation was ludicrous even for an Englishman, but he had been in the Legion himself. *Beau Geste* made a most successful silent movie of 1926, starring Ronald Colman. It was one of a series of novels Wren wrote about the same characters; the best of the others was *Beau Sabreur,* of which Major de Beaujolais was the hero.

Part I. Chap. 1. GEORGE LAWRENCE, a British diplomatic officer stationed in Nigeria, is returning home on leave. In Kano he is happy to run into Major HENRI DE BEAUJOLAIS of the French Spahis (cavalry recruited in Algeria), for they are old friends and have mutual friends in England, particularly PATRICIA, Lady BRANDON, the wife of Sir HECTOR BRANDON of Brandon Abbas. Lawrence and Major de Beaujolais ("Jolly") take the long ride to the seaport of Lagos together and on the way de Beaujolais tells Lawrence of a remarkable mystery he has just encountered:

An Arab messenger brought word to de Beaujolais at his headquarters that the Foreign Legion's little desert post of Zinderneuf had been attacked by a large force of Touaregs, Arab bandits of the desert. De Beaujolais at once set out with a large relief force. When he reached the fort, no attackers were in evidence and the tricolor was flying over the fort. He observed that the lookout's perch was empty, something unheard of, but also that men with rifles manned every embrasure of the parapet. Two shots were heard from inside the fort, but after that, silence. Then he saw the men at the embrasures were all dead.

The trumpeter volunteered to go in and investigate. He did not return. Then de Beaujolais went in himself, alone. All the men, shot in battle, were at the embrasures but two: The commanding officer, who lay stabbed by a French bayonet, and lying beside him a Legionnaire who had been shot. There was no clue to who had fired the two shots and no sign of the trumpeter. The dead officer held in one hand his pistol and in the other a crumpled letter. De Beaujolais left to bring back his sergeant-major while he investigated further. He found that the letter was addressed to Scotland Yard and was a confession to having stolen the "Blue Water," fabulously valuable sapphire belonging to the Brandons. It was signed by MICHAEL GESTE, Lady Brandon's nephew.

Now Lawrence became excited, for he had been in love with Lady Brandon all his life. De Beaujolais continued:

He decided to post a guard inside the fort, but the men threatened mutiny rather than brave the "ghosts." However, two Americans (who addressed each other as BUDDY and HANK) volunteered, then others volunteered. When de Beaujolais led the party inside the fort, he discovered that the bodies of the stabbed officer and the Legionnaire beside him had disappeared, nor could they be found. That night, mysteriously still, while the entire relief party camped outside, the fort began to burn and was consumed by flames. While it was still burning some rapid rifle fire warned that Arabs were about to attack. De Beaujolais decided to send for reinforcements and the two Americans were selected. They were never seen again, yet the Arabs did not follow up their attack.

Lawrence could not help solve the mystery. He did offer to take the confession letter to Lady Brandon, since de Beaujolais had other engagements.

Chap. 2. Lawrence visited Brandon Abbas. Lady Brandon was lovely as always. Sir Hector, as always, was away hunting in some far-off land; he was a selfish, cruel man and she had never loved him. Lady Brandon heard the story with interest but would say nothing about whether the sapphire had been stolen and said she did not know where Michael Geste was. Lawrence could not press her for information and he did not see "the CHAPLAIN," the Rev. MAURICE FFOLLIOT, whom Lady Brandon had taken into her home when he became afflicted with mild mental illness. So Lawrence learned nothing to tell his French friend.

Part II. Chaps. 1–2. Michael Geste, called "BEAU" Geste, was always the leader of the band of children at Brandon Abbas, which included Beau's twin brother, DIGBY; the third Geste brother, JOHN, only a year younger (who is the narrator throughout Part II); Lady Brandon's niece ISOBEL RIVERS; Sir Hector's nephew AUGUSTUS, whom they called "Ghastly Gustus" and despised generally; and CLAUDIA, a distant cousin. Beau was the Captain and they had a system of strict military discipline and many traditions, including that of giving any of them a "Viking's funeral" (by setting a toy boat afire) when he bore injury courageously. One feature of the Viking funeral, always, was that the "dead" hero was consigned to the flames with a dog at his feet, the dead dog being represented by a toy or some other effigy. Usually the hero was also given a special name. In their youthful play, Isobel always was inclined toward John, while Beau had a decided feeling for Claudia.

One of the most memorable points of their youth was when the dashing French officer de Beaujolais visited and told them of the Foreign Legion; Michael dreamed aloud of some day being in it. Another was the time when Michael encased himself in one of the suits of armor in the great hall. The children were surprised when Lady Brandon and a guest entered the hall and almost caught them. The others fled but Michael could not, so he stood completely still till the guest and his aunt had left. And it was always a high point when occasionally the Blue Water was brought out of its hiding place, the "Priest's Hole," and displayed.

Chap. 2. One night when the children were grown to young manhood and womanhood, all were at dinner. After dinner Claudia suggested looking at the Blue Water and Lady Brandon got it. Suddenly the lights failed and when they came on again after a moment the jewel had disappeared. It soon became clear that it was not simply a joke. Lady Brandon passed from indignation to anger. The Geste brothers could not suspect one another, nor would John suspect Isobel—or, in fact, anyone but Gus, and Isobel cleared Gus by saying she was beside him while the lights were out. In the stress, John and Isobel confessed their long-standing and undying love for each other. Then Michael runs away. Digby, sure Michael has done this as an act of sacrifice, goes the next day. And John knows he must go too.

Chap. 3. By selling his personal possessions, John is able to make his way to Paris and enlist for five years in the Foreign Legion, calling himself John Smith. As he

suspected and hoped, Michael and Digby had also enlisted and this reunited them. Their sergeant-major, LEJAUNE, is tyrannical and cruel. A Legionnaire who has just reënlisted, BOLDINI, overhears joking talk by the brothers and believes they have actually stolen a jewel worth £30,000; from that time on there are plots, led chiefly by Boldini, to steal the supposed jewel. The Gestes make good friends in two Americans—HANK, a giant of a man, the strongest they have ever seen; and BUDDY, small but well able to take care of himself, a former Texas Ranger. The Gestes learn Arabic— just in case they become generals some day. They are excellent soldiers, which is fortunate because Lejaune is prejudiced against them (as gentlemen) and would punish them if possible.

Chaps. 4–5. The Gestes' unit has one battle in the desert and the Gestes acquit themselves well. Then, to their sorrow, they are separated. Digby, with Hank and Buddy, are sent for training as mounted infantry. Michael and John are sent in Lejaune's troop to Zinderneuf. Conditions here are oppressive. There are many cases of *cafard* (a kind of berserk madness brought on by desert conditions). The captain commits suicide; the lieutenant becomes ill and dies. This leaves Lejaune the ranking officer and his rule is so cruel that a mutiny is planned, led by a German Legionnaire, SCHMIDT. Michael and John, and a handful of others, cannot be mutineers and murderers, yet they hear that Lejaune is plotting to kill them, whatever happens, to get the supposed jewel. Just when their dilemma comes to a head, the Touaregs attack. Now all is forgotten while the men defend the fort. Lejaune drives the men who are alive and props them up in the embrasures as a bluff when they die. The Touaregs finally retire, but their parting shots fell Michael and now John and Lejaune are the only men alive. Lejaune begins to search Michael's body. John stops him and Lejaune starts to shoot but Michael has enough life left to trip him and then John stabs him.

Chaps. 6–7. John finds several letters Michael has prepared for Lady Brandon, Digby, and himself. The letter to him urges him to have the formal confession published. He sees a French force riding up and fires two shots, then slips out at the rear of the fort and hides. He later sees the fort begin to burn—and he is joined by Digby, who was the trumpeter. Digby hid the bodies, then gave Michael a "Viking's funeral." He even laid out Lejaune's body below Michael's, so that Michael would be burned "with a dog at his feet."

Soon the Gestes are joined by Hank and Buddy, who have camels to ride and who want to join them in making their way out of French territory. The trip, through the desert, is long and hard, and there are many hostile Arabs to fight. Without the desert knowledge and skills of the Americans, both Westerners, they would have had no chance. Digby is killed in one fight. Then Hank sacrifices himself to save Buddy and John,

who finally get through. Lawrence takes care of John but Buddy insists on going back to look for Hank.

At last John is lovingly reunited with Isobel at Brandon Abbas, and he delivers Michael's letter to Lady Brandon, who reads it aloud: While encased in the suit of armor, Michael heard Lady Brandon sell the Blue Water to a maharajah. (She needed the money because Sir Hector was nearly starving his tenants to get money for his extravagances.) Michael stole the imitation so Sir Hector would not catch her. Now Sir Hector had died on one of his hunting trips and the story could be told. "A *beau geste* indeed," said Lady Brandon. So John marries Isobel and Lady Brandon finally marries Lawrence.

The Beaux' Stratagem

Comedy by George Farquhar, 1677–1707.

Produced in London, 1707. Edition edited by William Archer published by A. A. Wyn, New York.

THIS WAS THE LAST PLAY Farquhar wrote; he was sick and in the utmost poverty when he wrote it—for money to pay his creditors—and he died on the night of its third performance. It was one of his most successful plays and has been the longest-lived. The comedy is broad but very effective, even to a reader of today. The landlord's name, Boniface, added a word to the English language.

Act I. To the inn of the landlord WILL BONIFACE, at Lichfield, come Mr. AIMWELL, as a gentleman, and Mr. ARCHER, as his servant, using the name MARTIN. They are received by the landlord's beautiful daughter, CHERRY. From the landlord they hear of Lady BOUNTIFUL, living in the neighborhood, very rich and very charitable, who knows many remedies for illnesses and treats the entire countryside. Lady Bountiful has a daughter (DORINDA) and a son, Squire SULLEN, a brutish man, who has a fashionable wife from London.

When Aimwell and Archer are left alone, their conversation reveals that they are two nearly impoverished gentlemen (with only £200 left) who are fortune-hunting, traveling about and taking turns at acting as gentleman and servant. Aimwell gives Boniface the £200 to keep safe. Boniface talks to Cherry, who thinks Aimwell must be a highwayman; greedily Boniface plots to betray him for the reward. He tells Cherry to seduce Archer, to find out. Cherry, left alone, muses that she must not be the landlord's daughter, but of better blood.

Archer comes in. She likes him, and they flirt. He kisses her.

Act II. 1. At Lady Bountiful's house, Mrs. Sullen and Dorinda talk of Sullen's drunkenness and neglect of his wife. Sullen comes in briefly, but only to decline to go to church and to order his servant SCRUB to set out drink. Mrs. Sullen considers distracting herself with other gallants; a French count, one of numerous captured French officers paroled at Lichfield, has shown interest in her. [Britain is at war with France.] **2–3.** At the inn, Boniface and Cherry receive Mr. GIBBET, a highwayman, with whom they work. He gives them his latest stolen money and other treasure to keep. Archer comes in, feigning drunkenness; Gibbet is represented to him as a captain. Archer and Cherry are left alone and flirt again. Cherry suspects, from his speech, that Archer is only pretending to be a servant. She offers to bring him a dowry of £2,000 if he will marry her at once, and when he refuses she knows she was right, for no servant could refuse such a dowry.

Act III. 1. Dorinda and Mrs. Sullen tell Scrub to invite Aimwell's servant over for a bottle of ale and perhaps he can find out about the mysterious gentleman at the inn (Aimwell). The maid GIPSY announces dinner. **2.** At the inn, Aimwell and Archer discuss winning Dorinda for Aimwell; she has £10,000 dowry. Aimwell meets "Captain" Gibbet and a French priest, FOIGARD. **3.** Archer visits Scrub. He represents his "master" as Viscount Aimwell. Scrub confesses his love for Gipsy. Dorinda and Mrs. Sullen happen by; Mrs. Sullen is struck by Archer's handsomeness and he by her beauty. They talk. Both ladies like Archer and are impressed by his manners. He sings a song for them but refuses a tip. When he and Scrub leave, they conjecture that Aimwell is hiding from the consequences of a duel and Archer is a gentleman who was his second and is posing as his valet to hide. The French Count BELLAIR calls and flatters Mrs. Sullen. Sullen enters with his sword drawn to attack the count, but Mrs. Sullen prevents this with a pistol. The two men threaten each other when they meet again.

Act IV. 1. As Lady Bountiful is treating an old countrywoman, Archer runs in to implore help for his master, who has had an attack outside: Archer says he is subject to such fits. Aimwell is carried in. It is a subterfuge to meet Dorinda. With Dorinda holding his hand, under Lady Bountiful's ministrations he "recovers." Archer addresses him as "my lord." The ladies lead them all out to show Aimwell the house. Foigard bribes Gipsy to hide the count in Mrs. Sullen's closet that night. Aimwell and Dorinda pass through; he is already wooing her. Scrub tells Archer about Gipsy's acceptance of the bribe, which he overheard. Mrs. Sullen and Dorinda discuss Aimwell and Archer; Dorinda likes the idea of marrying a lord, while Mrs. Sullen thinks Archer an even "prettier fellow." **2.** Aimwell and Archer plan to use the priest's intrigue to help their own ends. They trick

the priest into confessing that he is an Irishman, posing as French, and they force him to agree to take Archer instead of the count to Mrs. Sullen's room. Meanwhile, Gibbet with two accomplices are planning to burglarize Lady Bountiful's house.

Act V. 1. Sir CHARLES FREEMAN arrives at the inn from London. Sullen is there, drinking heavily. They talk about Sullen's

Mrs. Sullen promises anything—later

marriage; Sullen would like to end it but not to give back Mrs. Sullen's dowry (£10,-000), though he is very rich. **2.** Cherry tells Aimwell of the plan to rob Lady Bountiful. She is in distress, for she loves Lady Bountiful (her godmother) and Dorinda. **3.** Archer, hidden in Mrs. Sullen's room, reveals himself to her. She shrieks, though actually she is afraid she will be unable to resist

giving in to him. She promises him anything at another time, if he will leave now. Her shriek brings Scrub, who is running from the robbers and thinks Archer is one of them. Hearing of the robbery, Archer catches Gibbet and overcomes him. Scrub brings Foigard and while they guard Gibbet, Archer goes to seek the other robbers. Mrs. Sullen lovingly goes with him. **4.** The other thieves are robbing Lady Bountiful and Dorinda when Aimwell arrives with Cherry. Archer comes in and he and Aimwell engage and overcome the thieves. At this point Aimwell resolves to propose to Dorinda at once, and Archer to make as much headway as possible with Mrs. Sullen. A servant announces that Freeman is calling on Mrs. Sullen, who is his sister; and Freeman is an acquaintance of Archer's. **5.** Dorinda has accepted Aimwell's proposal. Now he confesses that he is poor and no lord; it is his brother who is Lord Aimwell. Dorinda is actually happier than ever; but when Aimwell tells Archer, privately, that the marriage is off because he has confessed, Archer reproaches him for breaking their bargain. Now Freeman comes in with his sister; he has brought the news that Aimwell's brother has died and that he is now truly a rich lord. The marriage of Aimwell to Dorinda is happily agreed upon. Archer claims his half of her dowry, under his agreement with Aimwell, and is instead promised all of it. Bellair brings word that Boniface,. fearing for himself when Gibbet was caught, has fled, taking with him his guests' money; Archer regrets only that this means losing Cherry. But Aimwell's £200 are delivered to him with a note from Cherry, and he persuades Dorinda to take Cherry into her service. Sullen comes in and it is finally agreed between him and Freeman that he and Mrs. Sullen will divorce and he will give back the dowry. But at the end it is not sure whether Archer will marry Mrs. Sullen or be drawn back to Cherry.

The Beaver Coat

Play by Gerhart Hauptmann, 1862–1946.
Produced in Berlin, 1893. Translated from the German by Horst Frenz and Miles Waggoner. (RE, 52)

THE BEAVER COAT is a comedy, almost a farce, but is also a serious play and a major work of literature. Four years after production of his sensational but less than mature play *Before Dawn* (outlined next after this) and thirty years before the first "Hays code" established the principle that crime may not go unpunished in motion pictures, Hauptmann remained a rebel. The kindest thing one can say about his principal character in *The Beaver Coat*, the washwoman Mrs. Wolff, is that she is amoral. She steals, lies, connives, and even masterminds the criminal acts of others—the worst crime in the book, since the advent of Fagin. But Hauptmann has made her so winning that any audience would groan if she had to suffer the consequences. So she does not. ⟨ With ever an eye to his main theme, Hauptmann contrives still to be effectively satirical—of the Junker, the courts of law, the bureaucracy, the "scholar" whose only qualification is his degree—and realistic, of the working man and the working-class household. The Hauptmann who won the Nobel Prize (in 1912) was at his best in *The Beaver Coat*.

Act I. Early morning in the Wolff flat near Berlin. Mrs. WOLFF has a sackful of venison from a poached deer. She finds her 17-year-old daughter LEONTINE at home; Leontine has run away from her job as a servant at the KRUEGERS', who she says "abuse" (overwork) her. They told her to carry in a load of wood late the night before. Mrs. Wolff scolds her, then sets her to helping dress the venison. JULIUS WOLFF, a ship's carpenter, 43 years old, comes in. His daughters fear his beatings but he himself cringes with fright when he thinks a ranger (game warden) has come to arrest them for having the venison. The younger daughter, ADELHEID, returns, having been out very early. She is 13-going-on-14 but already shows signs of depravity. Mrs. Wolff is severe with her daughters but protects them against their father; she sees prospects of family fortune in their beauty, has "educated" them (to speak and act like ladies), and aspires to have them actresses, but they need more money to launch them. A smuggling boatman, WULKOW, comes to buy the contraband deer and does so, after much haggling; in the course of the conversation Mrs. Wolff hears that Krueger has a new beaver coat for which Wulkow would pay 70 thalers (about $250 today). After he leaves with the venison Mr. and Mrs Motes, who have been lodgers in the Kruegers' home but after a quarrel have left, come and buy some eggs and bread from Mrs. Wolff. MITTELDORF, a bailiff or minor court official, comes to say the judge's wife wants Mrs. Wolff to do her washing the next day. The judge has just fired him, because he was not hard enough on people. Then Mrs. Wolff takes Julius and Mitteldorf and goes off to steal the load of wood that must be still standing outside the Kruegers' home.

Act II. Judge VON WEHRHAHN, a baron, with his clerk GLASENAPP and Mitteldorf, discusses various cases including that of Dr. FLEISCHER, who boards at the Kruegers'. He [Krueger, though the text makes it Fleischer] is a chronic complainer. There is gossip that a load of wood has been stolen from Krueger. Motes, having been summoned, appears to testify to the dangerously democratic talk he heard when he lived at Krueger's house. Then Krueger, a little old man, comes in to report the theft of his wood. Von Wehrhahn sends for Mrs. Wolff, whom he knows as a washerwoman and considers very respectable. When Mrs. Wolff comes, Krueger demands that she pay for his wood because her daughter's failure to bring it in caused the loss; Mrs. Wolff defends Leontine and says she will not return to the Kruegers'; and the judge, after vainly trying to keep peace, himself ends up in a quarrel with Krueger.

Act III. At home, Mrs. Wolff is counting her hoarded money and gloating over it, but pauses to urge Adelheid to get the wood into the house faster. Julius is still frightened by the possibility of going to jail. Adelheid says she knows the wood is the stolen wood and Mrs. Wolff slaps her. Dr. Fleischer, a young scholar about 27, enters with his 5-year-old son, PHILIPP. Mrs. Wolff offers Adelheid to Fleischer as his servant (she is actually thinking of the girl's continued education). Fleischer mentions the new loss

at the Kruegers': A new coat has been stolen. Adelheid calls that Krueger is coming; Fleischer leaves and Mrs. Wolff frantically assists Adelheid in getting the wood out of sight, but when Krueger arrives he is conciliatory and his purpose is only to have Leontine sent back to him. He sees some of the wood that is still in evidence, compliments Mrs. Wolff on the quality of it, and swears to find the thieves who took his wood. He is not suspicious.

Act IV. Mrs. Wolff and Adelheid are in the courtroom waiting for the judge, who is late. Adelheid is to testify that she found a package. Wulkow comes in, to register the birth certificate of a child born to his wife. Mrs. Wolff rebukes him for having appeared publicly in the beaver coat. The judge arrives and Adelheid tells him about the package she found; in it is an old green vest of Krueger's. Motes is still pressing his charges that Fleischer has made subversive statements. Fleischer rushes in, excited, with information bearing on the theft of the beaver coat: He has seen a boatman (Wulkow) wearing a fine beaver coat, and that is cause for suspicion. Von Wehrhahn sees no cause for suspicion. Wulkow testifies that numerous boatmen, including himself, have fur coats, even beaver coats. Krueger expresses the opinion that the package containing the green vest was planted by someone to confuse the investigation of the theft of the beaver coat. Von Wehrhahn is talked out of any suspicion by Mrs. Wolff's glibness. He is more interested in the accusations that Fleischer is a radical.

Before Dawn

Play by Gerhart Hauptmann, 1862–1946.
Produced at Berlin, Oct. 20, 1889. Translation by Ludwig Lewisohn published 1923 by B. W. Huebsch, New York.

THE RECEPTION OF Hauptmann's first produced play was "tumultuous," according to Lewisohn; literary historians agree that it was "sensational." Today the play reads like an adolescent effort to be impressive by being shockingly different. It protests a bit too much the grievances of labor, the perils of alcohol, and the righteousness of the Icarians (one of a spate of Utopian colonies in America during the mid-19th century). But it was written by Hauptmann and Hauptmann could already write.

Act I. The living room of KRAUSE, a rich farmer, in Witzdorf. MIELE, the maid, is letting in ALFRED LOTH. He has come to see HOFFMANN, husband of Krause's daughter, MARTHA; they were at the university together. At that time they were

radicals, dreaming of starting an ideal community in America. In the ten years since, Hoffmann has become an engineer—successful, unscrupulous, ruthless. Loth has remained a radical and was once jailed for two years. Loth has come to borrow 100 crowns; Hoffmann lends it without argument and makes Loth stay to eat. Loth is interested by Hoffmann's pretty, 21-year-old sister-in-law HELEN, Martha's sister. At dinner Loth meets Mrs. Krause, the second wife, lowborn and vulgar and addicted to drink; her nephew WILLIAM KAHL, coarsely attentive to Helen, whom he disgusts; and her companion Mrs. SPILLER, who encourages her mistress's bad habits. EDWARD, Hoffmann's servant, serves wine. Loth does not drink, which astonishes the others; he explains in a brief lecture on temperance, quoting American temperance dogma (Everett). Martha is not at dinner (she is expecting a child) nor is Krause. Kahl becomes drunk and Mrs. Krause insulting. Helen is in tears as the act ends.

Act II. In the farmyard at 4 A.M. Krause—as usual the last to leave the inn—staggers along drunkenly. He is about 50 and though rich is poorly dressed, dirty, and coarse. Helen tries to help him into the house; he is indecent toward her and she calls him a swine and weeps. BEIPST, a laborer on the farm, comes and helps get Krause inside. Kahl then comes smashing out of the house; he bribes Beipst not to have seen him. Loth appears. He converses with Beipst, to whom he explains the Icarians in the U.S. Two other maids, GUSTE and LIESE, appear, going to work. Kahl returns. Loth says he deserves to be beaten for shooting larks, and they almost fight. Kahl goes. Helen returns and she and Loth talk, partly about abuses suffered by workingmen. Suddenly Mrs. Krause appears, screaming, cursing and beating at MARIE, another maid; it seems Marie has misbehaved with the hired man. Helen threatens to tell her father that Mrs. Krause has been doing the same with Kahl; she saw Kahl leaving Mrs. Krause's room that morning. Mrs. Krause, very frightened, agrees not to dismiss Marie.

Act III. In the living room, a few minutes later. Dr. SCHIMMELPFENNIG is reporting to Hoffmann on Martha's condition. She is well enough. The doctor says healthy development of a child requires that it be separated from its mother. He suggests Hoffmann and Martha live apart after the birth, the child with Hoffmann; and that Helen be persuaded to bring the child up, instead of its mother. He leaves and Helen enters. Hoffmann remarks that she weeps so often and she says she could scarcely fail to—her father is a drunkard and her stepmother evil. Hoffmann, pretending to comfort her, tries to make love to her. This merely arouses her loathing, which she does not conceal. He then becomes haughty and warns her against Loth, a dangerous radical. She is not convinced. Loth comes in and they have breakfast. In the conversation it develops that Loth has come chiefly to get information; he is going to write a pam-

Miele brings news of Helen's suicide but Krause is too drunk to understand

phlet about local working conditions, especially among the miners. Hoffmann is outraged. They quarrel. Loth tears up Hoffmann's check and goes. Helen runs after him and declares her esteem—almost love— begging him to stay.

Act IV. The farmyard, 15 minutes later. Loth is leaving, but Hoffmann apologizes. He persuades Loth to stay at least until Monday. They go in. Mrs. Spiller warns Kahl—who supposedly is Helen's betrothed —against Loth. Marie leaves, despite Mrs. Krause's offer to raise her pay. Loth and Helen have a love scene. They are now happily pledged to each other, with or without the Krause family's approval. At the end of the act Mrs. Krause calls to her maids to run for the doctor; Martha's time has come.

Act V. Living room, about 2 o'clock the next morning. Edward reports to Loth: No birth yet, after 15 hours of labor. Dr. Schimmelpfennig proves to be an old friend of Loth's and they share some secrets. They talk. The doctor and then Helen, when she comes in, seem to see something wrong with Loth—paleness, wildness. Helen and Loth agree to leave and marry at once, that night. Loth tells Dr. Schimmelpfennig, who tries to dissuade him and finally reveals that drinking is hereditary in the Krause family. The doctor also says that Helen has been seduced by Hoffmann. Loth agrees he must break with Helen; he will go visit Dr. Schimmelpfennig, as the doctor urges. He writes Helen a note, takes his leave of Hoffmann, and goes. Helen comes in with sad news for Hoffmann—the baby was stillborn. Then she seeks Loth but he is gone. Krause comes home drunk. Helen finds

Loth's letter. Edward assures her Loth went with Dr. Schimmelpfennig. Helen takes a big hunting knife from the wall. The play ends as Miele, seeking Helen, finds her a suicide offstage and runs back on screaming, while Krause crows drunkenly.

The Beggar's Opera

Play, with music, by John Gay, 1685–1732.

Produced at London, 1728. (NAL, MD216)

THE SOCIETY OF BEGGARS was England's term for what is now called the underworld; it included beggars, but also cutpurses, pickpockets, housebreakers, highwaymen, and the variety of criminals. *The Beggar's Opera* was a burlesque upon the operas that had recently become popular on the continent. It was also a satire on upper-class manners and morals of the time, all spoken through the lips of the "debased and criminal classes." (There is no respectable character in the play.) *The Beggar's Opera* was the first ballad opera—its lyrics were set to popular London tunes of the day. It has lasted remarkably well; a London revival of 1920 was an outstanding success and an adaptation, *The Threepenny Opera,* with new music by Kurt Weill, had a short Broadway run in 1933 and then became a smash hit in a 1955 revival.

Prologue. A BEGGAR admits himself such, but asks is not poverty a title to write poetry? A PLAYER agrees. The Beggar assures the Player that except for the absence of recitatif, this is an opera in every respect.

Act I. 1–6. The scene is in the house of PEACHUM, a receiver of stolen goods. Peachum muses that his is an honest employment, like a lawyer's; for he, like the lawyer, acts both for and against rogues. Peachum sends FILCH, the pickpocket, to Newgate prison to tell various prisoners which ones he (Peachum) will free by bribery, which he will let hang, which he will let be transported. Peachum then goes over his bookkeeping records. He profits from thieves while they are useful, then again when he informs on them for a reward. Mrs. Peachum enters and discusses a thief, Bob Booty, whom she likes but whom Peachum has down for death; she does not object, for she will not meddle. Then she speaks of Captain MACHEATH, the highwayman, who seems to like the Peachums' daughter, POLLY, and she him. Peachum objects to any thought of marriage, for Macheath loves women and gambling too well to become rich, and also Macheath would get information from Polly and have power over them.

7–13. Mrs. Peachum gets from Filch the information that Polly has secretly married Macheath. Polly admits this to her parents, who scold her for doing anything so immoral as to marry. Besides, a highwayman's habits are so dissolute and extravagant that Polly will be as badly off as if she had married a lord. They are even more horrified when Polly tells them she loves Macheath, for that is ill-bred. Peachum decides that the only solution is to inform on Macheath; he will get the reward and Polly will inherit Macheath's money. But Mrs. Peachum cannot reconcile Polly to the advantages of widowhood. Polly tells Macheath of the plot and after a love scene between them it is agreed that he must hide.

Act II. 1–6. At a tavern near Newgate, Macheath drinks and talks with the gang of thieves. Then a number of women come in, thieves and street women. Macheath enjoys conversation with them, until they take his pistols and hold him for Peachum and the constables, who enter and take him off to Newgate. The women remain and there are envious remarks by those who were not permitted to help betray Macheath and share the reward money. 7–9. LOCKIT, the jailer at Newgate, receives from Macheath the customary garnish (bribe) to assign a light set of fetters. Lockit's daughter, LUCY, is bitter toward Macheath, because after their affair he did not marry her; but Macheath cajoles her by calling her his wife and promising to marry her. 10–12. Peachum and Lockit agree to divide the reward for Macheath. They quarrel briefly because Lockit accepted bribes from Peachum's customers and did not make good, but they

The two girls, Polly and Lucy, start to quarrel

are reconciled. Lucy appeals to Lockit to save Macheath but he simply tells her to do as other women do, buy widow's weeds and be cheerful. **13–15.** Polly comes to see Macheath and addresses him as husband in Lucy's presence. Lucy is enraged but Macheath persuades her that Polly is distracted. He tries to send Polly away, but she will not go until Peachum appears and forces her. Lucy, appeased by Macheath, steals her father's keys and Macheath escapes.

Act III. 1–3. Lockit reproaches Lucy for helping Macheath to escape; and she, being now convinced that he is married to Polly, repents having done so. Lockit suspects that Peachum intends to cheat him. **4.** Macheath meets with other highwaymen and plans to rob gamblers on the road. **5–6.** Lockit finds Peachum at his lock (warehouse, or repository for stolen goods). From one of the thieves they learn where Macheath is hiding. **7–12.** Polly goes to Newgate and sees Lucy. They exchange barbed comments. Lucy offers Polly a drink, which is poisoned. Polly accepts the drink but is suspicious and does not drink it. Macheath, recaptured, is brought in; the two girls start to quarrel again but Macheath stops them, for he is to die today. **13–15.** Macheath is in the condemned hold. He tells other thieves in the prison to see to it that Peachum and Lockit also go to the gallows. Lucy and Polly come to say farewell. Then a jailer announces that four more of Macheath's wives have come to see him, each with a child. Macheath says this is too much and asks to be taken out to die at once.

16. Here the play is interrupted for an apparent Epilogue by the Beggar and Player. The Beggar says Macheath must die, and all the criminals must be hanged or transported, for the sake of morality. The Player objects that an opera must have a happy ending. So the Beggar agrees that a rabble will demonstrate and Macheath, reprieved, will be brought back to his wives in triumph.

17. Macheath is brought back. He says Polly is his only legal wife. All sing and dance.

A Bell for Adano

Novel by John Hersey, 1914–
Published and © 1944 by Alfred A. Knopf, New York.

A SENTIMENTALIST with a hardboiled style, John Hersey wrote a real tearjerker in *A Bell for Adano*. It was both a best-seller and a critical success. The hero is an overidealized second-generation American; the villain, General Marvin, is based on the swashbuckling George Patton, who alternated between public disfavor (as when he slapped a soldier from Brooklyn) and favor (as when his armored division won the race into Germany). At the time Hersey wrote *Adano* Patton was in disfavor and Hersey may have overpainted him just a bit. Hersey's later novel *The Wall* must be ranked ahead of this one, but *Adano* still best typifies Hersey's style and is fast, engrossing reading.

Chaps. 1–6. When the American forces invade the town of Adano in Italy, Major VICTOR JOPPOLO is in charge of the occupation forces. With Sergeant BORTH he sets up his office in the city hall, where he is soon visited by a delegation of important local citizens. He asks the town's most important needs. All agree that food is most necessary, but there is another serious problem. The town bell has been taken, to be melted down for ammunition, and the town is almost helpless without the bell that has rung there for 700 years. By it the farmers milked their cows, the women fed the hens, the children knew when it was time to eat. Everyone for miles around regulated his life on the tolling of Adano's bell.

The Major appoints a local interpreter, RIBAUDO GIUSEPPE, a former resident of Cleveland who was deported from the U.S. for illegal entry. Joppolo speaks Italian fluently but needs the interpreter for help in local dialects. He also keeps the town hall usher, ZITO GIUSEPPE, but surprises him by insisting that seven in the morning means seven; and he retains the town crier, MERCURIO SALVATORE, who has an incurable habit of inserting personal comments —usually uncomplimentary—between the lines of his shouted communiqués.

Adano learns that the streets must be kept clean—with water, although this is quite unheard of. Women chatter about the fact that one may go to the office of the Major without waiting two weeks for an appointment. Further, the Major rises when a visitor enters the room! At a line at the bakery, the former Fascist captain of police forces his way to the head of the line, as in the past. The woman there shrieks and is taken by the irate captain to the Major for suitable punishment. The Major makes the incident a source for a lesson in democracy.

Word that the Major will attend mass at San Angelo fills the church to capacity. He arrives late, causing the expectant priest no end of anxiety. In the pew before him Joppolo sees a blonde girl, TINA, sitting next to Giuseppe. He learns that she is the daughter of Tomasino, a fisherman, and asks Giuseppe to arrange a meeting with her father, thinking to augment the food supply with fish if he can persuade the Navy to let the boat go out. Giuseppe is sure the Major is interested in the daughter.

Outside of town, General MARVIN is irritated by slow-moving carts on the road and loses control of his temper completely when in one cart the driver is asleep and the mule cannot be urged to one side. He orders the cart thrown into the ditch and the mule shot. On reaching the city hall he arbitrarily commands that no more carts be allowed to enter Adano. In one quarter hour he has undone all that has been accomplished in nine days. Joppolo knows the town cannot live without the mule carts that bring in food and water. He promises to do what he can. It turns out that the only thing he can do is to countermand the general's order, which he does—at risk of being court-martialed. The people are delighted and once more the occupation forces are their beloved friends.

Chaps. 7–12. Captain PURVIS, the officer

to whom Major Joppolo gave his order countermanding the General's instructions, is determined to protect himself. He writes a note to be sent to Division Headquarters, describing both the original and the second orders. Sergeant TRAPANI places the note in a heap of seldom-noticed papers on the Captain's desk, hoping it will be lost.

Giuseppe reports sheepishly that the fisherman, Tomasino, will not come to the office. Tomasino hates authority and all people in authority. The Major electrifies the townspeople by going to see Tomasino. A great crowd follows the Major and Giuseppe to the fisherman's dock. It is very difficult to convince Tomasino that he will not be taxed or cheated and will not have to pay graft. Finally he is convinced and is overjoyed to be able to go out fishing again.

A day or so later, a jeering crowd in the street heralds the reappearance of the former Fascist mayor, NASTA, who has been hiding out in the hills. Joppolo places him on probation, to report each day to Sergeant Borth. Borth devises an original system of penance: The Fascist official must confess and repent publicly each day for one of the sins he committed while in office. Finally the mayor has to repent one more time for offering to be a spy for the Americans if Borth would let him stop repenting.

The Major learns that Adano's bell was melted down in a foundry in Milan. He goes to Tomasino's house and finds Purvis and Guiseppe there—Purvis to see the daughters and Guiseppe as interpreter. The Major is reminded of his wife by the daughter named Tina, and realizes that he misses the Bronx and his wife. Purvis goes away irritated because the Major interrupted a promising evening. He suddenly decides to sort the papers on his desk, and finds the note that was never sent to Division Headquarters. He orders the note sent off immediately, but the sergeant addresses it to the wrong person to gain a bit more time.

Chaps. 13–18. CACOPARDO, aged 80, the master of the local sulphur works, gets some information on a German counterattack. Joppolo sends him, with a pass, to General Marvin. After great difficulty, Cacopardo reaches General Marvin. He has expressed his contempt for persons who will play mumblety-peg on the surface of a 300-year-old mahogany table. The General orders him thrown out, without troubling to hear his message.

Purvis has a great personal interest in the daughters of Tomasino. He gets Joppolo to join him in an unannounced visit to Tomasino's home. Joppolo learns that Tina, the blonde daughter, is far more interested in the whereabouts of her fiancé, Giorgio, than in the American major. Though he misses his wife badly, this injures his pride. Meanwhile, two enlisted men who think the Major is undoubtedly the finest and best officer that ever existed decide they will give him a going-away present. Very drunk, the soldiers decide they can doubtless find the best possible present in the villa in which they are bil-

leted. They shatter several thousand dollars' worth of priceless *objets d'art*. Next day Major Joppolo is confronted by the owner of the villa. The enlisted men are punished by being told that they must repent for the sorrow they have caused the owner of the villa. The boys repent enthusiastically.

Cacopardo reports some dealings in the black market which he considers irregu-

The general rebuffs Cacopardo

lar. Investigation of the black market indicates that it has developed quite innocently. To American soldiers, two fingers meant two dollars. To the local peasants, it meant two lira, one-twentieth as much as the boys had offered. So the peasants would not sell to the natives. Joppolo corrected the situation.

Meanwhile the letter containing the memorandum to Division Headquarters reaches the wrong person, as it was intended to. The wrong person understands. He sends it on by as slow and unreliable a route as possible, a mail pouch that would travel by way of Algiers. On this route much mail has been lost. Perhaps this will be lost—accidentally. His conscience is clear.

Chaps. 19–25. The Fascist ex-mayor Nasta spreads rumors that there will be a German counterattack on the 23rd of the month, and also that Joppolo has been having affairs of the heart with young ladies of the town. Borth, a systematic man, waits until he has substantial evidence and then confronts the Fascist ex-mayor with damning facts concerning his activities. As a result Nasta is incarcerated in the prisoner-of-war cage. He escapes, but is recaptured very soon. The only possible sentence is exile in Africa. Major Joppolo so directs.

Fishing is resumed and the catch is good. News comes that Italian prisoners of war are to be returned, and Tina wonders if her fiancé will be back.

Chaps. 26–28. The people of Adano insist that the Mister Major have his photograph taken and he goes where they send him, though it seems foolish. The sunken freighter *Anzio* is being salvaged by the Navy, at the Major's instigation, to produce revenue for the town by the sale of its cargo. The Navy is getting the credit, also at Joppolo's instigation.

Meanwhile the memorandum reaches Algiers and a zealous mail clerk redirects it to the front.

Chaps. 29–37. By playing on the pride of the Navy officers, Joppolo arranges for them to get a ship's bell for Adano. The townspeople have a portrait painted from the Major's new photograph and plan to present it on the night a grand party is to be given in the Major's honor. On the day of the party, orders come through for Major Joppolo to proceed at once to be reassigned elsewhere. The letter has at last reached its destination. Only Sergeant Borth knows about it, and he keeps the news to himself until he becomes drunk at the party and blurts it out to the Major. The last thing Joppolo notes is the sound of the great bell, as he is being driven toward Vicinamare, away from Adano.

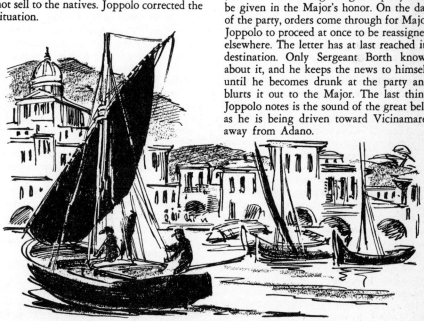

Through Major Joppolo's efforts fishing is resumed at Adano

Ben Hur

Novel by Lew Wallace, 1827–1905.

Published 1880 by Harper & Brothers, New York.

BEN HUR IS ONE of the biggest-selling books of all time. It is not great literature but it would be hard to imagine anyone's packing more action into a single volume. Its versatile author was a successful Union general in the Civil War. It was his idiosyncrasy to prefer his nickname Lew to his full name Lewis even in formal presentation as author, officer, or diplomat (he was Arthur's minister to Turkey). Wallace's other novels were successful enough but are now forgotten. *Ben Hur's* subtitle is *A Tale of the Christ* and it is concerned with the life and especially the times of Jesus.

Book I. Chaps. 1–5. Three men meet in the desert, each in response to a sign given him that a star will lead them to the place where a babe is lying—one who is born to be king of the Jews. The three men are BALTHASAR, the Egyptian; GASPAR, the Greek; and MELCHIOR, the Hindu. They prepare for their journey.

Chaps. 6–11. People from every part of the country are assembling for the census. Among those heading for Bethlehem are the carpenter Joseph of Nazareth and his betrothed, Mary. They cannot find shelter when they reach Bethlehem, even when Joseph tells the innkeeper that they are of the house of David. Another family makes their acquaintance and the innkeeper finds a stable in which they can stay. Outside the town, some people see a strange light in the sky. It is wide where it approaches the earth, and tapers off to a far distant point. One man declares it is Jacob's ladder. Out in the fields, an angel's voice tells the shepherds that tonight a child is born to bring peace. They see the star and start for the place to which it guides them.

Chaps. 12–14. The three men from the desert have followed the star. As they approach Bethlehem an angel tells them that the child is lying in a manger, wrapped in swaddling clothes. They will find the child in Bethlehem. At Jerusalem they see Herod and ask where they may find this child. Herod knows nothing of such a babe and thinks that they mean "king" in the sense that he is king. He asks them to seek out the babe, then come and tell him about it.

Book II. Twenty-one years later, two young men meet after a long separation. They look very much alike, though one, MESSALA, is a Roman, and the other, BEN HUR, is a Jew. The Roman, trained in war, has become cold and heartless. The Jew is still kind and gentle, and later he tells his mother how much he regrets the change in his former friend. The sound of a parade outside draws him and his sister, TIRZAH, to the flat roof of the house to watch. It is to celebrate the arrival of VALERIUS GRATUS, new prefect of Jerusalem.

As Ben Hur leans forward to see better, a fragment of tile is loosened by his hand and falls on the prefect. Valerius accuses Ben Hur of attempting to assassinate him. Messala joins in the persecution. Ben Hur is hauled away and his mother and sister are thrown in prison. The fortune of the Hur family is confiscated in the name of the emperor. Ben Hur is sentenced to be a galley slave for life, without a trial. As he is being forced along in the heat by his guards, he passes a well and a kind young man gives him water. This is Ben Hur's first encounter with the Nazarene.

Book III. Ben Hur is rowing in the galley of a trireme. His grace and skill attract the attention of ARRIUS QUINTUS, newly appointed Roman tribune. The crew leader tells him this boy has asked to be changed from side to side of the ship, because men who rowed always on the same side became misshapen. The boy suggested that some day, in a battle, it might be necessary to transfer him to the other side and if he could not row on that side he would be of no use.

Pirate ships attack. The slaves are chained to their seats, all except Ben Hur, who is left free at the order of Arrius. The ship is sunk; Ben Hur, floating on a plank, sees and rescues Arrius. Gratitude and a genuine liking make Arrius adopt Ben Hur as his son, and Ben Hur starts to live in the fashion of a wealthy Roman, heir to a fortune.

Book IV. Chaps. 1–10. Some years later, in Antioch, Syria, Ben Hur learns about a man named SIMONIDES who is a rich merchant and shipowner. This is the same name as one of his father's most trusted servants, the steward of his property. Ben Hur finds out that the fortune of his family has never been found by the Romans, though Simonides has been tortured and broken on the rack for his refusal to reveal the secret. He is crippled and can only sit in a heap of cushions. Ben Hur goes to see Simonides and meets his beautiful daughter, ESTHER. He tries to convince the merchant of his identity. Simonides is almost certain but sends his servant, MALLUCH, to follow Ben Hur and find out what sort of man he is. Malluch strikes up a "chance acquaintance" with him and offers to guide him to the stadium. A magnificent white camel, on which are riding an elderly man and his daughter, is endangered by a careless charioteer. Ben Hur leaps forward and turns away the horses of the chariot. The chariot is driven by Messala.

In the stadium, Ben Hur meets Sheik ILDERIM, owner of a beautiful team of Arabs that he wishes to race in the games. He mistrusts Romans with horses. Ben Hur learns that the old man on the camel was the Egyptian Balthazar and the young woman was his daughter, IRAS—perhaps the most beautiful girl Ben Hur has ever seen. He offers to drive Ilderim's team in the chariot race, because he wishes to beat Messala publicly.

Chaps. 11–12. Malluch reports to Simonides that Ben Hur seems to be all that he claims. At Messala's headquarters, a wild party is going on. The rumor of a young man who resembles Messala, although he is Jew, not Roman, disturbs Messala. He suspects strongly who this Jew with the Roman name really is.

Chaps. 13–17. Ben Hur sees the beautiful team of four horses for which the Sheik wants a driver. Balthazar is there, and commends the skill and bravery of the young man who saved him.

Book V. Chaps. 1–11. Sheik Ilderim is advised by Simonides to intercept messages going toward Jerusalem, because someone is plotting danger. The sheik intercepts a letter signed by Messala. Something in the letter makes Ben Hur think there is hope his mother and sister are living still.

Tremendous wagers are made on the coming race, with Messala and Ben Hur the favorites. Eventually all of Messala's fortune is at stake. Simonides has furnished tremendous amounts to bet on Ben Hur.

Chaps. 11–14. The race begins. According to custom, the chariots start several hundred yards before the actual starting line, to be lined up properly. Ben Hur and Messala keep close together with Ben Hur slightly behind. Messala reaches out with his long whip and lashes Ben Hur's team. The sound from thousands of throats indicates disapproval. Ben Hur drives a magnificent race. In the last stretch he accidentally catches the wheel of Messala's chariot, wrecking it. Messala is crippled. Ben Hur wins the race. Messala's friends protest that the bets should not be paid because of the accident, but the judges merely laugh and remind them of Messala's earlier foul.

A messenger who purports to come from Iras asks Ben Hur to meet her. He goes and finds it is a trap to kill him. Instead, he kills one of the two men, gives the other a sum of money, and changes clothes with the dead man. This way, he can be reported dead and be free to go off in search of his mother and sister.

Book VI. Valerius Gratus has been succeeded by Pontius Pilate. The tribune in command of the prison learns that in a cell in which there were supposedly three men there is actually only one man and in a cell beyond him are two women. They are Ben Hur's mother and sister, who were purposely thrown into a cell infected with leprosy. They are lepers, but still living. They are released but have to be put outside the town limits, for that is the law. Ben Hur arrives in Jerusalem and goes to his own family house, where the old servant AMRAH is still living. The mother and sister creep toward the house under cover of darkness, just to look once more upon their old home, and see Ben Hur sleeping on the doorstep. Amrah goes each day to the hills where the lepers must stay and takes food and drink.

She is made to swear she will never tell Ben Hur his mother and sister are lepers.

Book VII. Ben Hur meets again the Egyptian, Balthazar, traveling with his daughter. The old man seeks a certain prophet. At a stream they find John the Baptist, who declares that he is to be followed by another and far greater man. Almost immediately, a slender young man is seen, and John the Baptist points dramatically toward him, declaring him to be the Son of God. Ben Hur recognizes the young man who so many years ago had given him a drink of water while he was prisoner. Balthazar knows this is the Redeemer for whom he has waited so many years.

Book VIII. The Hur house is now occupied by Simonides, Esther, Malluch, Balthazar, and Iras. Ben Hur has bought it secretly and has had it restored to perfect condition. He awaits the sign of what he should do for the Nazarene, whose works he watches with awe and reverence. Iras taunts Esther, implying that Ben Hur will marry her instead of Esther, who loves him. When Ben Hur arrives, he seats himself and tells about

Nazarene. When he tells of how lepers have been cleansed by this man, Amrah listens eagerly. When she takes food to Ben Hur's mother and sister, she leads them to the Messiah and he heals them. Ben Hur witnesses the transformation as the two lepers become clean and he recognizes his mother and his sister.

Events move swiftly to the condemnation of the Nazarene, and to his crucifixion. Ben Hur and Balthazar witness the crucifixion, and at the moment of the Nazarene's death old Balthazar dies on his litter. Ben Hur wonders where Iras is and why she has not come to watch with her father's body. She has gone to Messala, the Roman. Years later she returns to see Esther, who long since has been married to Ben Hur, and she shows the evil of her life in her features. Esther is still beautiful, but Iras is coarse and ugly. Ben Hur is heir to the riches of Shiek Ilderim and is now the richest man in the country. He asks what can be done to help the cause of Christianity and is told that he should give his wealth to making tombs for Christians, for even the Romans

respect the dwelling place of the dead. Ben Hur accepts the suggestion and even today the catacombs he caused to be built can be seen by the visitor to Rome.

Beowulf

Traditional 9th-century Anglo-Saxon epic, author unknown. From a translation by Strafford Riggs, published and © 1933 by Appleton-Century-Crofts, New York.

The literary value of Beowulf can be known only to students of Old English; to the modern reader this aspect depends on the translation. But Beowulf is important as folklore and the educated man is supposed to have read it.

Part I. It is between 500 and 600 A.D. In the far north of Europe there is a kingdom named Geatsland, a rugged country of high mountains and narrow valleys, rocky and harsh, with forests of enormous trees. The coastline of Geatsland is long and twisting, with hundreds of coves, harbors, and inlets. The people are as rugged as the country itself, and the warriors are noted for bravery and strength on land and sea. Not only do they fight against invaders, but they must also be ever on the alert against monsters that live in great caves along the seacoast and vicious creatures that inhabit the forests.

For many years the king of Geatsland has been HYGELAC, a just and kindly monarch. His queen is HYGD, the Wise and Fair. The kingdom has been at peace for some time.

News comes from across the sea that the land of the Danes is suffering the most dreadful time in the memory of man. Each night a fearsome dragon named GRENDEL bursts into the hall where the young warriors of the king are sleeping and devours fifteen of them. Then, while all are made helpless to move by the magic of the dragon, he seizes fifteen more and carries them off to his den by the sea. This has gone on for 12 years and there are almost no young warriors left. The kingdom of HROTHGAR, king of the Danes, is weak and broken.

All this is told in the songs of minstrels. One who hears the tale of Grendel is a young nobleman who has just reached manhood. He is BEOWULF, nephew of King Hygelac and the strongest youth in the land. He has never been active in the games of the youths and has acquired a reputation for laziness. But as he listens to the minstrels' tales he is fired with zeal to slay the dreadful Grendel. He declares that he has a right to go, for his father, ECGTHEOW, was a war-brother of Hrothgar. Hygelac grants permission to leave and tells him to select

Ben Hur and Messala race their chariots in the arena at Rome

The viking ship weathers the storm

fourteen strong young earls to accompany him.

The young men set sail for Daneland. A violent storm threatens their ship, but they weather it and beach the ship on Daneland's shore. They are met by the Guardian of the Beach, who makes them welcome and directs them to the palace of Hrothgar.

Part II. The effect of 12 years of terror is seen sharply. Farms are idle, the land is neglected, houses are abandoned and falling down. The great banquet hall of Hrothgar is dank and dismal.

Hrothgar makes Beowulf welcome and blesses his mission. The great banquet hall is swiftly made ready for a feast. Then the king and his entourage depart and Beowulf's party settles down to sleep. Beowulf determines to remain awake. A young warrior named HONDSCIO lies near the door, ready to battle the monster if he should come. Soon all save Beowulf are sleeping. Suddenly the fog outside parts and a hideous shadow falls on the doorway. It is the monster, Grendel, and with him comes a magic spell that makes the warriors sleep. Beowulf is only half asleep and the spell does not hold him as fully as the others. In a nightmare of horror, he sees Grendel seize young Hondscio in his huge hands and tear him to pieces. Beowulf is horrorstruck and lies frozen in his place while Grendel devours the body of poor Hondscio. Grendel looks about for another young man and his milky-white eyes discern Beowulf.

Beowulf suddenly throws off the remainder of the spell that is on him. Silently, Grendel and Beowulf fight. Still none of the sleeping warriors awaken. Beowulf at last manages to get a firm grip on the monster's arm. So powerful is Beowulf that fear strikes Grendel and he attempts to escape. Beowulf's grip on the monster's arm does not slacken, and Grendel's arm is torn from his body. At this moment the spell on the sleeping warriors is broken and they wake. Grendel gives a long, unearthly wail and flees into the night. His arm is hung for all to see in the great hall, and there is joyous celebration in Daneland.

The joy is shortlived. The king's most trusted and beloved lord, Aescher, is killed by another fiend, Grendel's mother, to avenge her son. She too must be killed! Beowulf makes ready immediately. The warrior UNFERTH steps forward and offers Beowulf his magic sword, Hrunting. Beowulf embraces Unferth, and they set out. Hunting dogs follow the scent of Grendel and his mother to a small, evil-looking lake. Beowulf insists on going down into the lake alone, and brandishing Unferth's sword he leaps into the water. At one time he is attacked by a swarm of poisonous jellyfish, and again by a hundred-armed monster which he swiftly kills. He reaches the lair of Grendel's mother. She is the most hideous sight imaginable, with live snakes instead of hair on her head, horrid green fangs in her mouth, and huge, hairy arms that try to crush Beowulf. In a single glance, Beowulf sees a fire on the hearth—for this is a dry, waterless cave in the bottom of the lake—and sees also Grendel's massive body lying on the floor.

The fight is swift and violent. Beowulf finds that the magic of the monster is too powerful for Unferth's sword. Barehanded he fights her. He is gradually weakened, until the hag feels so sure of her victory that she relaxes her grip for a moment. At that moment, Beowulf finds his hand upon the hilt of a sword driven in the wall, and he seizes it with his mighty strength. With one tremendous stroke, he cuts through the body of Grendel's mother, and she dies instantly. Quickly he cuts off Grendel's head and throws both bodies in the fire. Carrying the head and the sword he found, he rises to the surface. He notices that this time he is not attacked by the creatures swimming about in the water. As Beowulf rises through the waves, the sword melts away until only the hilt is left.

Beowulf and his earls are heaped high with costly gifts of jewels and treasure, and at last they set sail for Geatsland.

Part III. For many years Geatsland enjoys peace and prosperity. The old king Hygelac dies and is succeeded by his son, Heardred, who reigns only a short time, and Beowulf becomes king. He reigns for many years.

Then one night a ragged man comes to the door of the banquet hall. He has stumbled upon the lair of a great dragon that guards such treasures as no man has ever seen. To prove his story, he presents Beowulf with a gorgeous jeweled cup of solid gold—beautiful beyond description.

The dragon learns through his magic that plans are being made to slay him and take his treasure. Great is his rage, and great is the destruction he wreaks upon the land. Beowulf assembles eleven trusted earls and they set out to destroy the dragon. Among the earls is WIGLAF, Beowulf's best and most trusted lord. As they approach the cave, all the earls save Wiglaf are suddenly seized with unreasoning terror and flee for their lives to the surrounding forest. Beowulf does not see their flight, for his eyes are directed to the entrance of the cave. He shouts a challenge. With a mighty roar, and breathing flames, the dragon rushes forth. The heat of the dragon's fiery breath is enough to burn Beowulf to death, if he fails to keep his shield between himself and the dragon. In vain Beowulf seeks the vulnerable spot in the dragon's armor. Wiglaf, the true friend, joins in the fight, and gradually the two great warriors force the dragon back. Before they can vanquish him, a sweep of his huge tail strikes Beowulf, and the old warrior falls to the ground, mortally injured. Wiglaf deals the death blow to the dragon. The cowardly earls now emerge from the forest and crowd about Beowulf as he lies dying. Wiglaf lashes out at them for their cowardice, but the dying Beowulf forgives them.

The body of Beowulf is placed upon his great shield and carried to the part of the country called the Whale's Headland, for the funeral rites. There a great funeral pyre is built and all the treasure of the dragon's cave is placed on the pyre to honor the man who died to save his countrymen. Fifty barons and fifty musicians march around the pyre, on which Beowulf's body lies in state, and after they have circled it three times, Wiglaf sets fire to the mound. The march goes on until daylight, when the flames have died down. And this is the manner in which Beowulf enters into his last, unbroken sleep.

The Betrothed

Novel by Alessandro Manzoni, 1785–1873.
Published 1825 to 1827.

MANZONI WAS ITALY'S first great novelist and this is his greatest novel. Sir Walter Scott called it the best novel he had ever read. (By coincidence, Scott wrote a novel titled *The Betrothed* that was published in 1825, the year the first part of Manzoni's novel appeared; but the coincidence ends there, for the actual name of Manzoni's novel is *I Promessi Sposi,* "the promised spouse.") The novel is set in the early 17th century, which fact gave Manzoni opportunity for some heroic historical writing on the Thirty Years War, a war so ruthless and destructive that its like was not seen again for 300 years; the Black Death that all but depopulated Europe; the dying gasp of medieval lawlessness; and miscellaneous turmoil such as bread riots and a famine. The novel is a long one, consistent with the custom of the times.

Chaps. 1–2. In a village near Milan, Italy, in November 1628, Don ABBONDIO, the parish priest, on his daily stroll is accosted by two *bravos,* or hired ruffians. The *bravos* command Don Abbondio not to perform a marriage that has been scheduled for the next day between LORENZO TRAMAGLINO and LUCIA MONDELLA. The command has been ordered by the local baron, Don RODRIGO. The priest is warned that he will not live if he ignores the command and is warned also to mention it to no one. Frightened, he goes home and tells his housekeeper, PERPETUA. Next day he tells RENZO (Lorenzo) that certain impediments prevent the marriage. Angrily, Renzo queries Perpetua and the priest and learns eventually that Don Rodrigo is behind everything. He then proceeds to Lucia's house and informs her.

Chaps. 3–4. Lucia tells Renzo that Don Rodrigo has attempted to strike up intimate conversations with her, and that she overheard him mention a wager concerning her. AGNESE, Lucia's mother, suggests that Renzo consult a wise lawyer in Lecca for his advice, and Renzo goes. The lawyer refuses to credit his story. Lucia tells Father CRISTOFORO at the Capuchin monastery.

Chaps. 5–10. Father Cristoforo calls on Don Rodrigo, planning to attempt persuasion, but Don Rodrigo becomes violently angry and asks the priest to leave. Agnese suggests marriage by a traditional method: If they appear with two witnesses in the priest's presence, and utter two sentences: "Father, this is my husband," and "Father, this is my wife," they are married in the eyes of the church. Lucia protests that it is not right, but Renzo wants to do it. Father Cristoforo reports his failure with Don Rodrigo and tells Renzo to visit the monastery next day, or send a trusted friend, for more news. Renzo frightens Lucia with threats to kill Don Rodrigo, and she finally agrees to marry him as he wishes, though she thinks it wrong. Don Rodrigo, meanwhile, conspires with his *bravos* to abduct Lucia. Renzo and Lucia go to Don Abbondio's house with their witnesses, but only Renzo's sentence is spoken. Don Abbondio throws a table scarf over Lucia's head to stop her speech, and then shrieks for help. But Lucia and Renzo receive a message to go quickly to the monastery, to avoid capture. Father Cristoforo has a boat ready to take them out of Don Rodrigo's reach. Renzo proceeds to Milan, and a priest escorts the two women to the Convent of Monza, where they are given protection and a place to sleep by a nun known as HER LADYSHIP. This nun is the daughter of a noble, who forced her to take the veil against her will. As a nun she had a clandestine affair with a man, then murdered another nun who found her out. The dead nun was thought to have run away and Her Ladyship was not detected.

Chaps. 11–19. Don Rodrigo, hearing of his *bravos'* failure, sends GRISO, their leader, to find out what has happened to his quarry. Griso learns from village gossip and is dispatched to Monza to plot Lucia's capture. To make sure Renzo will never return, Don Rodrigo obtains a warrant of expatriation on a charge that would mean life imprisonment or execution should Renzo come back. In Milan Renzo finds rioting in the streets, due to a shortage of bread. There have been bad harvests for two successive years, and the people believe that bakers and the local officers are hoarding. Renzo follows the crowd and eventually reaches a tavern in which he becomes drunk and loudly declaims that nobles and petty officials are despicable rascals generally. The landlord reports him to the police, fearing for himself if he harbors one who speaks against the nobles, and Renzo is arrested. He escapes and flees to Bergamo, where his cousin, BARTOLO CASTAGNERI, finds him a job in a silk mill.

Chaps. 19–20. Don Rodrigo convinces his uncle, a count, that Father Cristoforo should be transferred to some distant spot. The count confers with the father-provincial of the Capuchins, and Father Cristoforo is sent to Rimini. One of Don Rodrigo's *bravos* knows the man with whom Her Ladyship had the clandestine romance, and Her Ladyship is forced to enter into a conspiracy; she sends Lucia on a fictitious errand that will take her past a waiting carriage. It takes her to the castle of a robber baron (called merely THE UNNAMED throughout the book). Don Rodrigo has made a bargain with him to kidnap the young woman. At the robber baron's castle an old hag is sent to wait on Lucia and keep her company.

Chaps. 21–24. To the Unnamed's astonishment, his callous *bravo* who escorted Lucia in the carriage admits that she has quite touched his heart. Lucia spends a night in mortal terror, too frightened to eat or to go to bed. During the night she prays to the Madonna to rescue her and makes a solemn vow to remain a virgin all her life, and to forswear all thought of marrying Renzo, whom she loves. The robber baron too has a sleepless night, his heart inexplicably touched by the young woman; his remorse reaches such a peak that he contemplates suicide. Toward morning he hears many voices outside, and the noise of marchers in the road. He learns that the cardinal, FEDERIGO BARROMEO, Archbishop of Milan, is expected that day. The robber baron goes to see him. Before leaving, he gives the old hag a message for Lucia: that later in the day all her wishes will be granted. The Unnamed calls on the cardinal, who greets him warmly. Then the Unnamed's pent-up remorse breaks forth: He weeps unashamedly and swears to spend the rest of his life in atonement. Don Abbondio is summoned. Plans are made to escort Lucia back to her mother. Don Abbondio is convinced that either the baron or one of his hired brigands will do away with him before morning. Next day the cavalcade starts Lucia toward her village. Lucia remembers her sacred vow of the night before and realizes that the Madonna has answered her prayer and she can never marry Renzo. The robber baron informs his henchmen of his conversion and reformation. Over a period of some time, many of them become converts, others remain brigands and move on to other employers.

Chaps. 25–27. Don Rodrigo finds that the story of his villainy has become common knowledge. He leaves for Milan. A rich and philanthropic woman, Donna PRASSEDE, takes Lucia into her home. A messenger from the Unnamed arrives with a purse of 100 gold crowns for Agnese, to be used for Lucia's dowry; this is vast wealth to her, and she hurriedly travels to the Prassede villa to tell Lucia. Lucia now tells her mother of the vow she made. Agnese promises to

Lucia makes a vow to the Madonna

The plague strikes Milan

seek Renzo and explain to him all that has happened, and to give him half of the gold. The cardinal tries to obtain news of Renzo, and learns only that he has left the house of his cousin and no one knows where he went. Actually he is working in a silk mill not far from Bergamo, under another name, because the police of Milan are still seeking him. Since Renzo cannot write, he has a scribe write a letter to Lucia for him, and eventually it is delivered. The answering letter from her reaches him at length, and so a slow but constant correspondence is established. Neither is ever quite certain what the other wishes to say, for the scribes alter sentences and even ideas and the readers at the other end lend their own interpretations.

Chaps. 28–30. There is famine in Milan. Thousands starve to death; thousands more die of contagion attacking bodies weakened by malnutrition. The famine ends with the next harvest, but war brings new horror. Twenty regiments pass through, plundering, devastating, and raping. Perpetua and Don Abbondio flee with Agnese to the castle of the Unnamed. They are warmly welcomed by the baron and remain safely for 24 days. When the danger ends and they return home, their houses are in a state of filth and disorder beyond description and the invaders have taken the treasured silver that Perpetua buried.

Chaps. 31–36. The year 1630 is even worse. The bubonic plague strikes, having been left by the troops as they passed through. Many are the causes attributed to the deaths, including witchcraft or sorcery. The most popular fantasy is that of the "anointers," or persons who travel about smearing persons and places with evil substances that cause the illness. Don Rodrigo, returning home one evening, burns with fever. He sends Griso to fetch a doctor, but Griso instead summons a team of attendants that carry plague victims to the *lazaretto,* a half jail, half isolation hospital. The attendants and Griso divide Don Rodrigo's valuables. Griso picks up Don Rodrigo's contaminated clothing, unthinkingly, and

next day dies on the way to the *lazaretto.* In Bergamo, Renzo has contracted the plague but has recovered. He returns home to look for Lucia and encounters Don Abbondio, who also has survived and who tells him that Agnese is staying with cousins in another town, while Lucia is in Milan, if she is still alive. Renzo proceeds to Milan, where two-thirds of the population has died. He finds the house where Lucia has been living, but is told that she is in the *lazaretto.* There he sees Father Cristoforo, who knows nothing of Lucia but tells Renzo to seek her in the women's area. Renzo finds her there; she has survived and is convalescent. Now she is compelled to explain the sad fact of her vow. Renzo goes to Father Cristoforo and explains the situation. The good priest explains to Lucia that she had pledged to the Madonna a life that was not hers to pledge. She was already betrothed, and her vow of betrothal came first. Formally, he absolves her of the other vow, and the young couple are happy at the prospect of marrying at last. Don Rodrigo is in the *lazaretto,* dying, and in their happiness they pray for him and forgive him. But Don Rodrigo dies. Renzo goes to seek Agnese.

Chap. 37. As Renzo leaves the *lazaretto,* a rain starts, gentle at first, becoming a raging torrent. He does not realize it, but that rain is washing away the contamination of the plague; the epidemic is over. He finds Agnese well, and tells her all the good news. They wait impatiently for the time when Lucia will arrive.

(During this eventful period, "Her Ladyship" became a true penitent. She was eventually suspected of her crimes, but she reached a point where her conscience made her confess and enter into a life of expiation. And Father Cristoforo contracted the plague and his dearest prayer was granted: He died while serving his fellow man.)

Chap. 38. Lucia arrives at last. Don Abbondio is still timorous and protests that the ban on Renzo—the warrant issued so long ago—must first be lifted. This is merely a device on his part; he fears the

wrath of Don Rodrigo, who he does not know is dead. When Don Rodrigo's successor arrives, Don Abbondio yields gracefully. The successor tries to make amends for what Don Rodrigo did to the young couple by giving Renzo a large sum of money with which to establish his business. He does not do it openly, but instead buys Renzo's old cottage at an exorbitantly high price. He also uses his influence to have the ban on Renzo erased. Renzo and Lucia are duly married, and within a year their first child is born, a little girl, whom they name Mary in honor of the Madonna.

Beyond the Horizon

Play by Eugene O'Neill, 1888–1953.

Produced 1920 in New York. © 1920 by Eugene O'Neill, 1925 by Horace Liveright. Published by Random House, New York.

THIS WAS O'NEILL'S first big success. It won the Pulitzer Prize in the year it was produced. O'Neill was never more effective dramatically; his scenes rise to breathtaking peaks, fall into breathing-spell valleys, and finally, almost imperceptibly, lead into the subdued tone of an ending that is the more effective by its contrast.

Act I. 1. ROBERT MAYO is talking with his brother, ANDREW MAYO, about Robert's forthcoming voyage on the bark *Sunda,* under the captaincy of their uncle, DICK SCOTT—a voyage that will take Robert to places throughout the world. Robert has always longed to go "beyond the horizon," and this is his great opportunity. Andrew thinks in terms of Robert's chance to make a financial success as a result of the voyage—either by becoming a qualified ship's mate or by finding an opportunity for "a big chance" in a foreign land. Andrew is a born farmer and asks nothing more than to work on the family farm, an occupation at which he is good and which he enjoys. Robert dislikes the farm, much to the disgust of his father, JAMES MAYO. Robert has always been sickly. It is somehow understood that Andrew will eventually marry a neighbor's daughter, RUTH ATKINS, whose mother, confined to a wheelchair for many years, makes life miserable for her daughter. When Andrew departs on an errand, Ruth appears, and in the ensuing conversation admits her love for Robert—not Andrew, as both families had supposed. Swiftly on the heels of this mutual recognition, Ruth begs him not to go on the three-year voyage, and he assents happily. They start back for the house. **2.** After dinner, James Mayo and his wife, KATE, are talking with Dick

Scott about the voyage. The ship is to sail on the tide in the morning, which is sooner than expected. Robert has wheeled Mrs. Atkins, Ruth's mother, home after dinner. Andy goes out to attend to chores, and while he is gone Robert returns to report that he has decided to stay at home after all, and tells them of his love for Ruth. Andy is shocked when he overhears this but gives his brother hearty congratulations. As for Robert's decision to abjure the voyage, Scott becomes angry but is appeased when Andy says that he has decided to go in Robert's place. James swears never to speak to Andy again if he goes. A later conversation between the brothers convinces Robert that it would be too difficult for Andy to remain at home, because of his love for Ruth.

Act II. 1. It is three years later, and James Mayo has been dead for two of the three. Robert and Ruth have a little girl named Mary, two years old, and sickly. Kate and Mrs. Atkins are discussing the imminent return of Andy, whom they expect within a day or so. Mrs. Atkins complains about the slovenly way in which the farm is managed and prophesies even such dire things as a mortgage. She complains also that Robert is never on time for dinner. Mrs. Mayo pushes her wheelchair out as Robert appears. He and Ruth quarrel bitterly after the farmhand, Ben, quits his job because he is suffering ridicule in the town for working at such a rundown, badly managed farm. Ruth tells Robert she has always loved Andy, not him. When Andy comes, the farm will come to life again. As she finishes her tirade, Andy appears at the door. 2. Andrew and Robert are talking. Robert learns that his brother is going to Buenos Aires to enter the wheat business. Andrew says he realized long ago that he never really loved Ruth. Later he tells Ruth the same thing, to her distress. He plans to stay for a while, but Captain Dick brings news of a ship leaving for the Argentine next day and Andrew ships on as first mate.

Act III. 1. Five years later, the farm is shabby and poverty-stricken, little Mary is dead, as is Mrs. Mayo, and Robert is extremely ill. He is tubercular. Once again Andrew is expected to arrive at any moment. Ruth sent him a cablegram some time ago telling of Robert's illness, and Andrew is bringing a doctor from the city. They arrive and the doctor examines Robert. Both lungs are badly affected and Robert may live a few hours or a few weeks, no longer. Nothing can be done at this stage. Robert comes out of the bedroom after the doctor has left and tells them he knows the whole story. He begs Andrew to marry Ruth later. When he is finally persuaded to go back to his bed, Andrew asks Ruth why Robert wants his promise to marry her. Ruth apathetically remarks that she told Robert she still loved his brother, about five years before. Andrew is horrified and compels Ruth to promise she will convince Robert she loves him before he dies. They go into the bedroom, only to find the window open and Robert gone. 2. They find Robert on a hill where he had loved to go all his life, waiting to watch the sunrise. He is happy, for he realizes that the horizons he has never passed will no longer hem him in, and he is to have an eternity of wonders. He dies, happy—and Ruth has not had the opportunity to tell him her final lie. Pathetically, she pleads that it is better so. At least, Robert was happy this way.

Robert on his deathbed

The Big Sky

Novel by A. B. Guthrie, Jr., 1901–
Published 1947. © 1947 by A. B. Guthrie, Jr. Published by Houghton Mifflin Co., Boston. (PB, C-52)

THIS IS A MINOR CLASSIC. Set against a geographical and historical background that is depicted with great fidelity are characters that live and action that is never slow or obscure. *The Big Sky* is both educational and interesting, a rewarding experience for every reader. ❡ The outline that follows may at times make the principal character, Boone Caudill, seem like a belligerent and callous man. He is not. He is peaceable and conscientious, and he never violates the rights of others. But he is quick-tempered, and if he seems to defend his own rights somewhat violently it must be remembered that the times and the country were violent.

Part I. Chaps. 1–4. In 1830 BOONE CAUDILL is just 17. He lives in central Kentucky with his Pap, his mother SERENA, and his brother DAN. A neighbor boy, MOSE NAPIER, tries to bully Dan, who beats him badly. Mose's father swears out a warrant. When Pap tries to whip Boone, Boone knocks him out and leaves home, taking Pap's fine cap-and-ball rifle. Boone heads for the Northwest, where his uncle ZEB CALLOWAY is a hunter. On the road to Louisville he meets JIM DEAKINS, a good-natured redhead a few years older than Boone. Jim decides to go along to the Northwest. Pap follows Boone to Louisville but Boone escapes by swimming the Ohio River to Indiana.

Chaps. 5–8. Tramping toward St. Louis, Boone stops to eat and sleep. He is joined by JONATHAN BEDWELL, who during the night steals his rifle and rides off. Boone follows and finds Bedwell, but while they fight the sheriff, MARK YORK, comes on them. Boone's story is not believed and he is sentenced to jail for a week. In jail the sheriff beats him with a whip. Jim Deakins, riding after him, helps him to escape. Boone takes a horse hitched outside (the sheriff's or Bedwell's) and they ride to St. Louis.

Part II. Chaps. 9–19. Boone and Jim ship on the riverboat *Mandan,* which the master, JOURDONNAIS, and his partner, the hunter DICK SUMMERS, plan to take all the way up the Missouri to trade liquor to the warlike Blackfeet. Most of the crew are French. The work is hard, rowing, poling or towing against the current. The liquor in the cargo has to be sneaked by government authorities at Leavenworth. On board is a pretty Indian girl, 10 or 12 years old, whom they call TEAL EYE because of her soft, bluish eyes; she is the daughter of a Blackfoot chief and was lost, and they hope to win the Blackfeet's friendship by returning her. Food is poor until they reach buffalo country, where hunting is good. When Boone becomes slightly ill, Summers takes him to help in hunting, to spare him the heavy work; Boone was already a good shot but learns much. Summers and Boone are attacked by Indians but fight their way out; later the entire boat and crew are attacked, but the boat carries a small cannon, which saves them. The monopolistic American Fur Co. sends two men to scuttle the ship, but Boone catches them sneaking on board. The men are turned loose, naked, in hostile country hundreds of miles from their post. Finally, after months, the *Mandan* reaches Fort Union. MCKENZIE, the company manager there, tries to discourage them from going farther; he offers to buy their cargo for double its value, then he threatens cut-price competition. But they insist on going on. Here Boone meets his Uncle Zeb, who hunts for the company by day and is a drunkard at night. The *Mandan* goes on. In Blackfoot country, Teal Eye runs away one night. Then the Blackfeet attack unexpectedly and all are killed but Boone, Jim, and Summers.

Part 3. Chaps. 20–23. It is 1837. Boone, Jim and Summers have lived in the mountains since the massacre, trapping beaver and hunting. They go to the winter rendezvous of mountain men on the Powder River. On the way they meet a POORDEVIL (lone)

Indian who speaks some English, and they take him into their party. Boone begins to learn the Blackfoot language from him. At the rendezvous the mountain men sell their furs, drink, and trade with the Crows for their young squaws. Boone takes it on himself to protect Poordevil against abuse and fights STREAK, a man who hates Blackfeet. Streak pulls a knife but Boone gets it and kills him.

Chaps. 24–30. Summers decides to retire to some farmland he has near Independence, Mo. Boone decides to go north and look for Teal Eye, whose beauty even as a child still allures him. Jim and Poordevil go with him. Boone kills a Crow for his scalp, which will please the Blackfeet (the Crows' enemies), and his horse, to be a gift to Heavy Otter, Teal Eye's father. They pass a Blackfoot village wiped out by smallpox. They go on and on the Teton River they find Teal Eye's tribe, who are Piegans. Heavy Otter is dead and Teal Eye's brother, RED HORN, is chief. Boone gives Red Horn the presents. Teal Eye has never been given to a man. She makes the sign of love to Boone, then runs.

Part IV. Chaps. 31–34. In 1842, Boone has lived happily with Teal Eye in the Piegan village for five years. They have no children. Boone's Indian name is STRONG ARM. Jim (who is called RED HAIR) often lives there, often goes off on long trips. Dick Summers is married and is farming in Missouri. Jim returns from one trip with an offer from a government man, ELISHA PEABODY, who wants to find a pass through the mountains suitable for wagons, so settlers can be brought up the Missouri and then down the Columbia Rivers. Red Horn and the Piegan braves object to showing their secret passes to white men, but Boone stubbornly agrees to go with Jim and Peabody. Teal Eye tells Boone she is pregnant: "Strong Arm will have a son."

Chaps. 35–51. They leave as winter is coming on: Boone, Jim, Peabody, and two Frenchmen, ZENON and BEAUCHAMP. As they go on, Boone begins to feel strongly that Red Horn will try to stop them. This impression is sadly confirmed when Indians attack them, wounding Jim badly and leaving the party without horses and equipment. Hunting is almost impossible in the snow, but Boone braves death to go out and shoot two mountain goats. Somehow they get through the winter, see Peabody across the mountains, and return to the Piegans' camp in the spring. Teal Eye has had her son, but it was born blind.

Chap. 52. Boone broods about the baby. Then he hears the old men's gossip that the child is not his but Jim's, because it has reddish hair. He pretends to go away, then returns unexpectedly and finds Teal Eye in Jim's arms. Actually Jim was only comforting her while she wept about Boone, but Boone does not know this. He shoots and kills Jim. Jim had just brought a letter from Boone's mother (saying his pap was dead and she wanted to see him before she died). Boone decides to go. Teal Eye knows he will not return.

90

Part V. Chaps. 53–57. Boone travels by boat down the Missouri and Mississippi, then walks home across country. He goes by the Indiana town where he was arrested and asks for Sheriff York, but York is dead; asked why he wanted York, Boone replies that he "aimed to kill him." Boone arrives home. His mother tells him his pap died "of the phthisic." Dan has married a girl named CORA and they have two boys. One is redheaded and Boone learns that the red hair comes from his family, not Cora's. Boone has a brief affair with a neighbor girl, NANCY LITSEY, who wants him to marry her, but he goes off abruptly.

Chap. 58. Boone goes to see Summers, settled down as a farmer. They drink and talk. Boone tells Summers he shot Jim, and that his whole life, even Teal Eye, is ruined for him. He leaves Summers' house, half drunk, and walks off wearily.

The Birds

Play by Aristophanes, 448–385 B.C. Date unknown. Various translations.

THE BIRDS is one of the most admired satires of Aristophanes. This one is on governments and men in government: How universal and inevitable is the course of power, pride, and ambition.

Two old Athenian gentlemen, EUELPIDES and PISTHETAERUS, have become so disgusted with the interminable lawsuits and the insincerity of people in their country they have decided to leave it and seek the domain of the birds. Long before their time, a king of Thrace was punished by being transmuted into the form of a bird. The one-time king of Thrace is now the king of the birds. He is EPOPS, and it is he whom the old men seek. As guides to this bird kingdom, they have bought a raven and a jay. Each carries his bird gingerly because the birds resent captivity and frequently slash at their jailers' hands with unfriendly beaks. The two old men, however, are convinced that the king of the birds, with his wide

knowledge of the world over which he has made his flights, can tell them of a place where there is no sycophancy, no hypocrisy, no litigation for sheer love of display and oratory.

Neither of the birds seems to have any inclination to guide them, but Pisthetaerus notices that his crow is pointing to a certain point, and Euelpides notes that his jay is craning his neck in the same direction. There must be other birds thereabouts. They therefore shout "Epops!"—to which they receive a response from a servant, TROCHILUS. He is a slavebird, he explains, who had to join the bird kingdom when his master did so. The voice of Epops is soon heard. Epops is naked, save for his crest. It is the moulting season.

The two old Athenians tell Epops they are seeking a city—or a place to found a city—where the faults of Athens will not prevail. Epops suggests several places, none of which is acceptable to the Athenians. Pisthetaerus is soon inspired with an idea. The kingdom of birds should establish its own city—between the heavens and the earth—where only birds can reach and where the people of earth must ask permission before their sacrificial fires can send their smoke to the gods on Mount Olympus.

Before the two old Athenians can truly join the kingdom of the birds, they must have wings with which to fly. This is conveniently arranged by the eating of an herb. Soon on the shoulders of both men appear the beginnings of wings, which develop to an effectual size.

With great enthusiasm, the birds commence construction of their city, and the two Athenians are astounded at the speed and skill with which it is done. Next comes the problem of a name. Pisthetaerus suggests Nephelococcygia—a made-up name that is a combination of two Greek words meaning cloud and cuckoo. This name meets with general approval.

Scarcely is the new land of the birds established when outsiders begin to appear, each in search of some gain to himself. First there is a poet, who insists upon reciting verses until he is bribed to leave by the gift of a cloak. Next a prophet appears and demands a reward for his prophecy, but he is denounced and driven away as an imposter. There is a man who wants to measure the reaches of the air and divide it into lots. One man declares he is an inspector sent from Athens. A dealer in decrees wants to sell the city a group of new laws to be posted in a public place. Each of them is driven away unceremoniously.

A messenger rushes in with the news that a god from Olympus has slipped past the guards. It is the goddess IRIS, who refuses to be convinced that the birds are now the gods to whom mortals offer sacrifices. She too is driven out. Soon a herald from the earth appears, saying that thousands of people wish to join the birds and there is great need for a large supply of wings. Pisthetaerus hastens to order them. The first mortal to arrive is a young man who detests his father and who has heard that among the birds it is permitted a son to fight and kill his own father without shame. The old Athenian tells him that there is another custom in the land of birds. A son must support his father when the son is grown. This information is enough to change the young man's mind, and he leaves.

Prometheus comes next, and tells of the terrible straits in which the gods on Olympus find themselves, since no longer is there any smoke from sacrifices reaching them.

He urges Pisthetaerus to press his advantage quickly and demand the hand of BASILEIA in marriage. Basileia is the handmaid of Zeus and it is she who makes his lightning for him, among other useful services. From Olympus Heracles is sent to negotiate terms, accompanied by Poseidon and a barbarian god from a distant place. The Olympians eventually yield to the superior power of the birds, and Pisthetaerus is wed to Basileia. They go toward the throne of Zeus, where the king of the birds will now reign.

Black Beauty

Children's story by Anna Sewell, 1820–1878.
Published 1877. Available in many editions.

THIS IS THE ONLY BOOK Miss Sewell wrote. Like other gentlewomen of her time she was a reformer and *Black Beauty* is sheer propaganda *pro* humane treatment of animals and, wherever possible, *anti* dat ole debbil alcohol. Since Miss Sewell was a spiritual cousin german to schoolteachers and children's librarians everywhere, her book necessarily became recommended reading and a standard children's classic; but surprisingly enough, it really is a classic and now with the horse-and-buggy era long past it is more educational than ever. It is written in the first person with the horse, Black Beauty, the narrator.

Chaps. 1–3. I (the horse) was born on an estate where there were many horses. Most of them were carthorses. I had better breeding. My grandfather won the cup twice at the Newmarket races. My first master was kind, but like the other horses I did not like it when, in a chase after a hare, a rider was thrown and killed and a horse broke his leg and was shot; it seemed silly, for one little hare. I was broken in skillfully, and kindly too, but I could never like wearing a bit in my mouth. My master had a wonderful way to teach horses not to fear trains. He sent me to a neighboring farmer and had me pastured beside the railway until I was used to it.

Chaps. 4–10. When I was almost four, I was sold to Squire Gordon. I had been called Darkie, but the Gordons renamed me Black Beauty. In the stable I met MERRYLEGS, a 12-year-old horse, who was in the next stall; and GINGER, a mare who had a reputation for biting. The coachman, JOHN MANLY, was kind and skillful and he found me perfectly trained. I got to know Ginger, and when we were harnessed together she was an excellent partner. She told me how ill-treatment by previous owners had made her bitter, so that she bit and kicked. I observed that now, with kind treatment, she became much more gentle. Sir Oliver, a horse whose tail had been cropped, and Ginger, whose head had been strapped up and held high with checkreins, told me how

horses are abused in the name of "fashion."

Chaps. 11–17. I was very happy at Birtwick (the Gordons' estate). I won praise when, drawing the dogcart, I felt something unsafe about a bridge and would not go on it; we found the bridge was broken in the middle, by a storm. JAMES, the stableboy, was recommended by the master as coachman at his brother-in-law's, and Ginger and I had much practice in drawing the carriage while James was practicing to be a coachman. While taking the Gordons on a visit to some friends, we stopped at a hotel. That night there was a fire in the hotel's stable. We were rescued by the bravery of James.

Chaps. 18–20. One night I was wakened by John, and saddled, and John was told we must ride for our lives to bring the doctor to our mistress. I carried John to the doctor's, and the doctor back to the Hall, as fast as I could. Afterward the master told me I had saved the mistress's life. But my lungs were inflamed and I was ill for a long time. After I recovered, once when the new stableboy, JOE GREEN, was riding me we saw a man flogging two horses cruelly. Joe told John, who reported the man to the authorities. Now I had spent three happy years at this happy place; but the mistress remained ill and the master took her to Europe, closing the estate. Ginger and I were sold to the Earl of W——.

Chaps. 22–24. The earl's coachman was Mr. YORK. We learned that the earl was reasonable about horses but the countess, his wife, insisted on the checkrein. York tried to do this gradually, but my lady forced him to put our heads higher and higher. I found it almost intolerable and Ginger began to kick. The countess could not use the car-

riage that day. Ginger was turned into a saddle horse but for four months I continued to be a carriage horse and wear the checkrein. In the spring Lady Anne, Lord W——'s daughter, had a horse run away with her. With a gentleman named Blantyre on me I chased and caught them, but Lady Anne was thrown. I carried a workman to get the doctor and she was saved.

Chaps. 25–31. When the W——s went to London, York went with them and REUBEN SMITH was in charge of the stables. He was a drinking man. One day he rode me to the tavern and I had a loose nail in one shoe. Smith would not let the hostler fix it, saying it would do till we got home. That night he rode me too fast, the shoe came off, I stumbled, and he was flung off. He did not rise and I stood by until two men came. The fall had killed Reuben. My knees were so torn that even after they healed they showed the blemish and the earl would not keep me. I was sold to a livery stable. Many of the people who rented us "job horses" did not know how to drive. There were tight-rein drivers, loose-rein drivers, and "steam-engine" drivers who thought a horse was a machine. One customer of the stable liked me so much that he recommended me to a friend, a Mr. Barry, who bought me. He lodged me at a nearby stable, but the groom he hired was stealing the feed and I nearly starved. A farmer warned my new master and the thief was arrested. The next groom he hired was lazy and ignorant; he did not exercise me or feed me properly and soon I was ill. I recovered but was sent to a horse fair to be sold.

Chaps. 32–38. My new owner was JERE-

James rescues the horses

MIAH BARKER, who paid £24/10 for me to use me as a cab horse in London. His was the happiest, merriest family I have ever known, with his wife POLLY, their 12-year-old son and their 8-year-old daughter, DOLLY. They all petted me and made much of me, and they gave me a new name, JACK. Jerry owned his cab and two horses, one of which, CAPTAIN, was now quite old. Captain drew the cab in the morning and I in the afternoon. I was kindly treated and properly driven. Captain told me of his life as an army horse in the Crimean War, and what it was like when horses and men were shot down in battle. A Mr. BRIGGS wanted Jerry to drive his wife to church every Sunday morning but Jerry did not work on Sundays, partly because seven days' work was too much for the horses and partly because he did not think it right. Briggs was angry at first and tried other cabs, but finally he came back to Jerry to drive Mrs. Briggs on weekdays.

Chap. 39. I was very well off for a cab horse, being driven by my owner. One miserable-looking driver called "SEEDY SAM" told what it was like to work for a master who fixed the cab rates low and the rentals high; Sam had to pay 18 shillings a day rent before any of the income belonged to him, and with a wife and six children he had to work fourteen to sixteen hours a day, seven days a week, and still could not afford the overcoat or raincoat he needed. The week before he had to pawn his clock because he had not taken in the 18 shillings to pay his master. A few days later Sam became sick with a fever and died.

Chaps. 40–45. One day to my surprise I encountered Ginger as a cab horse. She was no longer beautiful or well kept and her spirit was broken; she no longer fought back when abused. I think it was Ginger I saw not long after, a dead horse being carted away. There was an election. Jerry would not let one of the candidates hire his cab, to put placards on it and make the horses carry drunken voters from taverns to polls; besides, he disapproved of this candidate's policy toward workingmen. On New Year's Eve Jerry and I were kept waiting in the cold for more than two hours by two gentlemen at a card party, and Jerry almost died of bronchitis [bronchial pneumonia?]. He had to move to the country to recover and the horses were sold.

Chaps. 46–49. I was sold to a corn (wheat) dealer and baker. The loads were heavy and the work almost beyond my strength. When I could not easily get up a hill I was badly whipped. A lady intervened and persuaded the driver to take off my checkrein. Then I could pull better and got up the hill. But the work weakened my sight and a younger horse was bought. I was sold to a large cab owner, Nicholas Skinner, for whom Seedy Sam had worked. He was the cruelest master I ever knew, and the driver was just as cruel with the whip. I did the best I could, but one day I fell. The farrier told Skinner I was simply overworked and would recover with six months'

rest, but Skinner would not do this. He rested me for ten days and sent me to a horse sale. Here a kind farmer, Mr. THOROUGHGOOD, was persuaded by his grandson WILLIE to take a chance on me for £5, for both saw that I had seen better days. I had my six months' rest, cared for by Willie, and I began to feel young and strong again. In the summer Mr. Thoroughgood sold me to three ladies, the Misses Blomefield, and to my delight their coachman was Joe Green, who had been stableboy at the Gordons'. I got back my old name Black Beauty, and I have now been in this happy place a year.

Black Oxen

Novel by Gertrude Atherton, 1857–1948.
Published 1923. © 1923 by Gertrude Atherton.

USUALLY MRS. ATHERTON set her novels in and near her native San Francisco, but in this, perhaps the one most widely read, she wrote of people in the upper social levels of New York and the Continent. *Black Oxen* was a kind of science fiction. When it was written there was new knowledge of the effect of the endocrine glands on the body and personality and there was much speculation on the possibility of rejuvenation by transplanting "monkey glands" into the human body. *Black Oxen* is no work of art but its characters are interesting. The title is from Yeats' play *Countess Cathleen:* "The years like black oxen tread the world/ And God the herdsman goads them on behind." It alludes to the differences in age that are important to the story.

Chaps. 1–3. LEE CLAVERING, 34 years old, a successful drama critic and columnist for a New York newspaper, at the theater sees and is struck by the beauty and distinguished bearing of a young woman, a blonde, who seems to be about 28. At the same performance he runs into his cousin CHARLES DINWIDDIE, a considerably older man; Dinwiddie is considerably shaken because, he says, he has "seen a ghost." The young woman who so impressed Clavering is, according to Dinwiddie, an exact replica of MARY OGDEN, who had been the principal New York belle about 35 years before. Dinwiddie had been in love with her and hard hit when she married Count ZATTIANY of Hungary, who has since died. However, Dinwiddie saw the former Mary Ogden at the opera in Paris about ten years before and she was very aged and withered. The girl at the theater, despite the resemblance, cannot be Mary's daughter because the Zattianys had no children—unless Mary had had, and skillfully concealed, an earlier illegitimate daughter.

Chaps. 4–11. Dinwiddie asks Mary's lawyer, Judge TRENT, whom he knows well, if any relation of Mary's is in the country. Trent says there is none, but Dinwiddie is sure he is lying. Mary's friend Mrs. JANE OGLETHORPE calls on the stranger but is rebuffed by her. Meanwhile Clavering sees the same young woman at every first night. He hungers to meet her but knows no way to get an introduction. One night he even follows her from the theater to her limousine, and he is sure she laughs at him as she enters it. Then he follows her to the Ogden mansion on New York's upper East Side, which has been reopened since she came to New York. Here, fortunately, he finds her helplessly before her door; she has forgotten her key and cannot rouse the servants. He offers to help and climbs in a window to let her in. He finds that she knows who he is. She introduces herself as Countess MARIE ZATTIANY, a cousin of Mary Ogden's who met and married Count Zattiany's nephew. She says the former Mary Ogden is in a sanitarium in Vienna. In her talk with Clavering it becomes apparent that she is bitter toward men, perhaps from a disillusioning experience in her past. She invites Clavering to come to dinner and bring Dinwiddie.

Chaps. 12–22. Alone, Countess Zattiany muses on the strange attraction the young man Clavering has for her. It is incredible that she could be interested in a romantic affair, for she has been obsessed by her plan to use her wealth and charm to help Austria reëstablish itself politically. But for the past month she has had this feeling for Clavering and she thinks perhaps love has come to her at last. Meanwhile Clavering is feeling much the same way and deliberately stays away from the countess. Then he gets a note saying she has been sick but inviting him to dinner alone. He goes and confesses his love. She will not say whether or not she reciprocates or will marry him, and tells him he must wait.

Chaps. 23–29. Clavering receives a note from the countess, telling him to come to see her Saturday; she has a revelation to make and after that it will be up to him whether he wants to see her again. When he calls on her, she tells him her strange story. She is actually the Mary Ogden that Dinwiddie knew. She is 58 years old. Thirty-four years before, she met the handsome young Count Otto Zattiany in Paris, married him in New York, and had not since returned to the United States before the present visit. She never loved Zattiany, nor did he love her for long; she had had affairs, including a long one with one of the most important Austrian statesmen, but she came to the conclusion that men were not capable of more than physical love. But the war (World War I) gave her an interest in life—nursing and rehabilitation work—and since then international politics had become an engrossing interest to her. After the war, collapsing with fatigue, she entered a sanitarium in Vienna and while there she was persuaded by the doctors to let them try a new rejuvenating process on her. It consisted of restoring the endocrine glands with special x-ray treatments. Obviously, it had worked; and the doctors said the present effect would last ten years and then could be renewed once. But she could not have children. After telling this, the countess left Clavering, telling him to think about it till Monday at least.

Chaps. 30–43. Clavering's decision is painful but he reaches the conclusion that he loves Mary too much to give her up. However, he will not live on her money and will not go to live with her in Europe, at least until he has established himself as a successful playwright. She agrees to his conditions but will not marry him for two months, and he determines that during the two months he will complete the play he has planned. The writing of the play proceeds well and his friends are enthusiastic, predicting great fame for him. But he has some strange premonition when he reads in the paper that Prince HOHENHAUER, the Austrian statesman, has come to New York. Intuitively he knows this is the man who was Mary's principal love, and also that the arrival of the prince is dangerous to him.

Chaps. 44–56. Dinwiddie has a house party in the Adirondacks, with Clavering and Mary among the guests. (Actually the party was at Clavering's suggestion.) Here the feeling of love reaches its peak in Mary and she even tells Clavering she will give up all other plans and live in New York as simply his wife. But then a telegram comes from Trent to say that Prince Hohenhauer is taking a train up to the nearest town to see her, and urging her to see him. She does so, meeting Hohenhauer in the hotel. He proposes bluntly that she give up her plan to marry Clavering and instead marry him, simply because together they can do so much for Austria. He reminds her—something she had not thought of—that if she marries Clavering she will be an American citizen,

no longer a Hungarian countess, and she can never have any influence in European politics again. She is swayed by what he says and runs away to New York to think it over, not returning to the house party.

Chaps. 57–59. Clavering returns to New York and sees Mary. He knows, and tells her, that she must marry him at once or they can never marry. She knows this too; but she is now convinced that her dream of love was only a dream. She is too old and too wedded to her previous ambitions. Clavering recognizes the truth of this and they part.

Mary Ogden at the theater

Bleak House

Novel by Charles Dickens, 1812–1870
Published 1852–53. Available in many editions.

AS IS NOT UNUSUAL with Dickens, his novel *Bleak House* is notable chiefly for its minor characterizations. The heroine Esther is neither quite true nor quite sympathetic by modern tastes, and the admirable John Jarndyce leaves today's reader cold. Tulkinghorn the lawyer is a stereotype. But Mrs. Jellyby the overdevoted philanthropist and Mrs. Pardiggle the malevolent one, Miss Flite the fluttery maiden lady and the overproper Turveydrop, and at least half a dozen others, are drawn with consummate skill. The book was popular chiefly because Dickens wrote it. His "message"—the need for reform in England's courts of chancery (equivalent to courts of equity in the United States)—meant little to the public because too few were affected.

Chaps. 1–2. There is a notable case in Chancery—the case of JARNDYCE and

JARNDYCE—which stretches far back in time and involves countless people. Sir LEICESTER DEDLOCK and Lady Dedlock, of Lincolnshire and London, are among those in it. Mr. TULKINGHORN, one of the lawyers, is reading them some of the latest documents when Lady Dedlock is overcome with sudden faintness, and the reading is interrupted.

Chaps. 3–7. ADA CLARE and RICHARD CARSTONE are two wards in Chancery in the case. JOHN JARNDYCE of Bleak House, who is their guardian, has provided a companion for Ada in ESTHER SUMMERSON, a girl of unknown parentage in charge of Kenge and Carboy, solicitors. Esther, who was a governess, met Ada in court and also met Miss FLITE, who has some dim, remote connection with the case. Richard, Ada and Esther are taken by Mr. GUPPY, a young man from Kenge and Carboy, to the house of Mr. and Mrs. JELLYBY and their daughter CADDY in Thavies' Inn, to spend the night before starting for Bleak House. Mrs. Jellyby's chief interest seems to be the hard lot of African natives. The three young people run across Miss Flite and visit her in her rooms, in the upper part of the building in which KROOK maintains a shop. Krook lives alone with his cat, Lady Jane. He gives the young people gruesome accounts of people who have been concerned with the case of Jarndyce and Jarndyce. All seem to have appallingly bad luck.

After breakfast they set out for Bleak House, where they are met by John Jarndyce. His companion is HAROLD SKIMPOLE, a pleasant, likable young man but selfish and lazy. The other country house in which Jarndyce and Jarndyce are interested is Chesney Wold in Lincolnshire, the house of the Dedlocks. The housekeeper, Mrs. ROUNCEWELL, who for 50 years has been connected with the estate, is in charge there. Her companion is ROSA, a pretty young girl from the village. Her grandson, WATT ROUNCEWELL, is visiting. He is the son of a well-to-do manufacturer. Mrs. Rouncewell had another son, a wild vagrant who went off as a soldier.

Guppy and TONY JOBLING of the law office obtain leave to see Chesney Wold and are shown the picture gallery. Guppy, seeing Lady Dedlock's portrait, is astounded at the resemblance to someone he knows.

Chaps. 8–12. At Bleak House, Esther Summerson is established as a sort of housekeeper. John Jarndyce makes a confidante of her. She is drawn by his kindness. Esther and Ada discover that he is set upon by many people asking for help, especially money. One of these charitable beggars is Mrs. PARDIGGLE, who insists on taking Ada and Esther with her on one of her charity expeditions. They see what cold comfort she distributes.

On the evening when Lady Dedlock fainted, Tulkinghorn noticed that the sight of certain handwriting on one of the documents seemed to bring on the spell. He determines to find out why. Mr. SNAGSBY, the law stationer, takes him to see NEMO, the copyist, a poor writer who lives at Krook's. When Tulkinghorn reaches Nemo's room, the man is dead of an overdose of opium. No one seems to know anything about Nemo except a young streetsweeper named JO, who was the only mourner for him. Tulkinghorn mentions in a letter to Sir Leicester that he can tell Lady Dedlock something about the copyist. The Dedlocks are on their way to Chesney Wold, returning from Paris. Lady Dedlock has brought a French maid with her—HORTENSE—who is jealous of the preference shown to the village maid, Rosa. Later Tulkinghorn, visiting the Dedlocks, manages to mention casually—but taking care that he is heard—the fact that the copyist left no papers or identification.

Chaps. 13–16. Richard Carstone should find some means of livelihood and it is decided that he should take up medicine, but the only thing in which he has ever shown any interest is Ada. Richard is to study with BAYHAM BADGER, who seems to be identified most frequently as the third husband of Mrs. Bayham Badger. For the sake of Richard's career, all the young people go to town. Guppy worships Esther from afar, but she makes it clear that she does not welcome his attentions. Now that Richard is launched on a career, he becomes engaged to Ada. Another young man joins the group, a young surgeon, Mr. WOODCOURT. Caddy Jellyby comes to see them with news of her engagement to a dancing master, Prince Turveydrop, whom she met at Miss Flite's.

A lady disguised as a servant speaks to Jo, the streetsweeper, and asks him to take her to the neglected churchyard where the poor writer is buried.

Chaps. 17–24. Richard's study of medicine is short-lived and he tries studying the law, but his real hope is to obtain a fortune from a favorable decision in the Chancery case. Woodcourt bids them all goodbye and leaves to practice in the East. Jarndyce, with the girls and Skimpole, pays a visit to LAWRENCE BOYTHORN, another man concerned in the case.

Mrs. Snagsby gives a tea party. It is interrupted by the arrival of a constable who has poor Jo, the sweeper, in custody for failing to move on when told to do so. Jo has related a fantastic story about a strange woman who gave him a sovereign. Guppy, determined to distinguish himself, cross-examines everyone who will reply to his questions. He learns that Esther was given into the custody of a Mr. and Mrs. Chadband by the firm of Kenge and Carboy, years before. This indicates a definite connection between Esther and one of the groups in the Jarndyce and Jarndyce case. Tulkinghorn also is eager to get information. He has Snagsby in his rooms and also Jo. There Jo sees the person who gave him the sovereign. It is Hortense, Lady Dedlock's maid, recently discharged. Hortense applies as maid to Esther, but Jarndyce sends little 12-year-old CHARLEY to fill the position. Charley

is an orphaned girl. Caddy Jellyby marries Prince Turveydrop. Richard Carstone cannot get away from the fascination of the Chancery case, but he can and does get away from Kenge and Carboy and joins the army. He practices one detail of his new profession in Mr. GEORGE's shooting gallery. Jarndyce calls off Richard's engagement to Ada.

Chaps. 25–29. George in his shooting gallery is visited by Grandfather SMALLWEED. The old gentleman wants to show a lawyer a sample of the handwriting of one Captain HAWDON, whom George has befriended. They prepare to visit Tulkinghorn but the visit is postponed. At Chesney Wold, Rosa is to marry young Rouncewell. Guppy calls on Lady Dedlock, and lets her know that he has discovered a likeness between her and Esther Summerson, that Esther's real name is Esther Hawdon, and that Guppy will next day have a bundle of letters belonging to the late Captain Hawdon.

Chaps. 30–34. Charley brings Esther word that tramps (who turn out to be brickmakers) have taken poor Jo, who has been taken ill, to a loft in one of the buildings near Jarndyce's place. After a short time Jo disappears mysteriously. Charley becomes ill, evidently of a disease she contracted from the brickmakers. Esther nurses Charley, then develops the disease herself. She recovers her strength somewhat but is blind. Tony Jobling, as Guppy's spy, has gone to live at Krook's under the name of Mr. Weevle. He discovers that Krook has a bundle of letters of the late Captain Hawdon. One night Guppy comes to the shop to collect the bundle, but finds that there has been a fire, Krook is dead, and the letters are destroyed. Next morning they learn that Krook was the brother of Mrs. Smallweed. George of the shooting gallery owes money to old Smallweed, and the old miser suddenly demands it. The paper that George has refused to give up becomes the price of clearing up his debt.

Chaps. 35–42. Esther Summerson's blindness gradually passes away but her face is left marked by the illness. She learns that Richard has broken with his guardians and learns also of the heroism of Allan Woodcourt in a shipwreck. She realizes that she is in love with Woodcourt. Also she learns from Lady Dedlock the secret of her birth—Lady Dedlock is her mother. Esther persuades Guppy to stop his prying into the secret of her parentage. Tulkinghorn continues to pry, hoping to find something in favor of his client, Boythorn. Lady Dedlock informs him that she plans to leave her home and husband secretly, because her shameful secret is now known. He dissuades her, on the ground that this would cause a complete collapse of Sir Leicester.

Chaps. 43–49. Esther confides the secret of her parentage to Jarndyce, and he proposes marriage. Although Esther knows that she loves Woodcourt, she accepts. Richard has become so possessed with his hope of an inheritance that he has gone completely to pieces. He is penniless. Esther finds him, and finds Allan Woodcourt as well. Woodcourt promises to look after Richard. Woodcourt comes across Jo, who is still very ill, and at Miss Flite's suggestion takes him to George's, but Jo dies.

Tulkinghorn lets it be known that he has power over Lady Dedlock (because he knows of her secret and can tell Sir Leicester). That very night Tulkinghorn is shot to death in his room.

Chaps. 50–65. After vast confusion and many false accusations, the murder is brought home to Hortense, Lady Dedlock's French maid. The story of Lady Dedlock's former lover is told to Sir Leicester. Lady Dedlock flees from the house. Esther, the

Lady Dedlock's body is found on top of Captain Hawdon's grave

police officer and Woodcourt engage in a wild search during the night. In the cemetery where the starving writer—the former Captain Hawdon—is buried, on top of his grave, they find Lady Dedlock, dead.

Esther becomes very ill after this shock and Woodcourt is attentive throughout her illness. At length he tells her he loves her,

only to hear that she is betrothed to Jarndyce. Suddenly there is news of great import to the case in Chancery. Among Krook's papers has been found an ancient document that turns out to be a will that settles the entire dispute. The case is closed, but all the years of litigation have consumed the entire estate. With all hope of an in-

heritance gone, Richard Carstone dies. Jarndyce proves himself kind and generous as usual. He gives Esther Bleak House, along with his blessing on her marriage to Woodcourt. For a little longer Sir Leicester Dedlock lives on at Chesney Wold then he dies. Esther Woodcourt lives a happy lifetime at Bleak House.

A Blot in the 'Scutcheon

Play by Robert Browning, 1812–1889. Produced 1843 in London, published 1843 as Volume V of the *Bells and Pomegranates* series. Available in several editions.

As "THEATER" AT LEAST, this was the most successful of Browning's plays and justly so. It has the best plot and the best dramatic structure and in it Browning best resisted the urge to divagate into poetical passages that do not advance the plot. *All* the characters are really wonderful. A modern version or an operatic version might be a great success. ¶ The play is a tragedy, the principal characters dying at the end. It has been compared to the far greater tragedy *Romeo and Juliet,* but the only real similarity is in the fact that Browning's heroine Mildred was 14 years old, only a few months older than Shakespeare's Juliet. ¶ As for the title: The scutcheon or escutcheon was the coat of arms of the Treshams. By a blot in or on it is meant a disgrace in the family history, a skeleton in the closet.

this; she is not a good enough actress. They agree that Mertoun will come again the next night. He is sure he is always undetected.

Act II. Gerard tells Tresham he has seen covers. Then, when left alone with Mildred, Guendolen surmises that the mysterious lover and Mertoun are the same man. Guendolen calls Austin back in and learns that Tresham has left the house, presumably to lie in wait for Mildred's lover.

Act III. 1. That night, Tresham waits in the garden under Mildred's window. Mertoun, cloaked as before, enters and is stopped by Tresham. He reveals himself but Tresham insists that they fight. Mertoun draws but does not resist and falls, mortally wounded. He states his great love for Mildred and asks forgiveness. Tresham forgives him and begins to feel very guilty. Mertoun dies, asking Tresham to tell Mildred that he loved her. Led by Gerard, Guendolen and Austin arrive, horrified because they are too late. Austin and Gerard carry out Mertoun's body. Guendolen warns Tresham that the news will kill Mildred. **2.** Tresham goes to Mildred's chamber. His changed attitude makes her suspicious and his empty scabbard tells her what he has done, even before he reveals it. Bitterly, Mildred pardons Tresham, then dies. Austin and Guendolen enter as Mildred dies and Tresham swallows poison. With his dying breath, Tresham says that the blood has washed away this blot on the 'scutcheon. Austin and Guendolen will be lord and lady now, and Austin promises there will be no blot on the 'scutcheon.

Act I. 1. In the lodge on the estate of THOROLD, Lord TRESHAM, the warrener GERARD and other retainers look out the window for the arrival of HENRY, Earl MERTOUN, who comes to ask the hand of Tresham's sister MILDRED (who is only 14). The retainers poke fun at Gerard for his apparent calm, it being known that he has a special regard for Mildred, who has shown him special attention. **2.** Mertoun arrives and Tresham welcomes him in the mansion, pleased with the prospect of joining their two noble families by marriage. Tresham introduces Mertoun to his brother AUSTIN and cousin GUENDOLEN, who are engaged. Mertoun expresses great love for Mildred. After showering Mertoun with compliments and promising to tell Mildred of his wish for the marriage, Tresham sees him out and asks Austin and Guendolen for their opinions of the young earl. Guendolen chides her cousin for his effusive display of affection for Mertoun—who, she implies, is perhaps too young and lacking in wit. Tresham defends his prospective brother-in-law, in whom he sees no fault. **3.** Guendolen visits Mildred in her chamber and tells her of Tresham's adulatory reception of Mertoun; Tresham considers his family spotless and wishes to prolong it by bringing in a spotless noble. Guendolen suggests, however, that there may be a flaw in the earl's family at that, for one of his ancestresses was the woman whose garter so famously fell off. After Guendolen leaves a voice is heard singing outside Mildred's window and then Mertoun enters, wrapped in a mantle. Their conversation reveals that they are lovers, that they have often met like this, and that Mildred is no longer virginal. Mildred does not see how she can go through the meeting of Mertoun as a stranger, and the formal wedding, in view of

a stranger enter Mildred's window nearly every night for a month, with Mildred's assent and aid. Tresham next sees Guendolen. She finds him looking in a large book and teases him about the possibility that it has revealed "some blot in the Earl's 'scutcheon." Tresham asks her to send Mildred to him. Mildred comes shortly after Guendolen leaves. Tresham confronts her with the information he has about her nightly visitor. She does not deny it but will not name the man. At Mildred's instructions Tresham sent word to Mertoun, the night before, that his suit would find favor with Mildred; now he proposes to countermand this message but Mildred insists that she will still receive the earl, as planned, to discuss the marriage. Tresham considers this so dishonorable that he denounces her before Guendolen and Austin, who enter on his call. Mildred faints. Austin first sides with Tresham, but Guendolen makes him wait and comfort Mildred when she re-

Mildred faints when her brother confronts her with her guilty secret

95

The Blue Bird

Play by Maurice Maeterlinck, 1862–1949.

Produced 1907. Translation by Alexander Teixeira de Mattos, published by Dodd, Mead & Co., New York.

A FAIRY-TALE PLAY FOR CHILDREN is the best-known and most surely immortal work of the Belgian Nobellian. It gave the world a phrase, "the blue bird of happiness," and its moral is that the blue bird is to be found at home, be it ever so humble. The play is excellent for performance by schoolchildren in large schools because it offers an almost unlimited number of parts, costume parts at that. It can easily accommodate 200 performers. But it demands elaborate sets and machinery for professional performance. When it is properly produced it is quite a spectacle. ❊ Originally the play had only five acts. Act IV in the following outline was written in for a revival in 1910, in New York.

Act I. The scene is in the cottage of TYL the woodcutter. The little boy TYLTYL and little girl MYTYL are supposed to be asleep but are not. They look through the window at guests arriving for a Christmas Eve party being given by the children of their rich neighbors; they talk greedily of the food that will be eaten there and can hardly understand that there are people who are not always hungry. There is little prospect that Father Christmas will bring them anything the next day.

There is a knock at the door of the cottage. They admit a humpbacked, lame, ugly old woman; it is the FAIRY BÉRYLUNE. (She looks somewhat like their neighbor, Madame BERLINGOT.) The Fairy is looking for a BLUE BIRD, which will cure her little daughter, who is ill. Tyltyl has a bird but it is not blue. The Fairy gives Tyltyl a hat on which there is a big diamond; turning the diamond releases the souls of animals and of inanimate substances such as sugar and water. Tyltyl turns the diamond.

The cottage becomes beautiful; TYLO, the DOG, and TYLETTE, the CAT, and also BREAD, FIRE, LIGHT, WATER, SUGAR, and MILK, come to life, talk, and act characteristically. All leave together for the Fairy's house.

Act II. 1. They are in the Fairy's beautiful palace. At a private meeting of the things, the elements, and the animals, the Cat says they must prevent the finding of the Blue Bird, for if it is found mankind will learn about their souls and will have them at his mercy. Only the Dog is faithful to man, whom he worships (Tyltyl is his god). **2.** The Fairy takes Tyltyl and Mytyl to the Land of Memory. Here they meet their dead grandparents, GRANNY TYL and GAFFER TYL, who look and act just as they remember them; and they meet their three little brothers and four little sisters who died as children. Their grandparents' old blackbird is, to their delight, now blue. They put it in a cage to take to the Fairy. But as they leave the Land of Memory they see that the bird has become black again.

Act III. 1. The scene is the palace of NIGHT, who is a very old woman. The Cat has come to warn her that Tyltyl will come seeking the Blue Bird; they plot to prevent his finding it. Tyltyl, Mytyl, the Dog, and some of the spirits come in. Night reluctantly gives Tyltyl the key to the chambers that hold her secrets, but warns him that there are evils in them, plagues, sicknesses, and other enemies of man. Tyltyl enters several chambers and meets the evils; the others are afraid but the Dog will not desert him. Finally he comes upon thousands of blue birds and captures many, but when they leave the palace all have died.

2. The scene is a forest. The Cat is there to warn the trees and animals that Tyltyl is coming. They agree that Tyltyl and Mytyl must die. When the children enter, the Cat flatters and cajoles them and even prejudices Tyltyl against the Dog. The trees hold court; the fact that Tyltyl's father is a woodcutter, and has done them much damage, is a point against him. Tyltyl sees the Blue Bird on a young oak tree but the trees will not let him have it; if man should get the Blue Bird, the secret of the mysteries of life and of happiness, he would use it to oppress them even more. Tyltyl and Mytyl are condemned to death; then the trees and various animals such as the BULL and ASS argue about how they are to be put to death. Tyltyl has a knife and resists, and the Dog helps him. They are losing until Light comes and reminds Tyltyl to turn the diamond. He does and his enemies' souls vanish. The Cat now pretends to have been on the children's side all the time, and they believe her.

The blue bird flies away

Act IV. 1. The children and all their attendants have a conference in front of the curtain. They have reached the Palace of Happiness, where the Blue Bird should be found. But there is danger, for the Miseries live in adjoining caves. **2.** In the vulgarly ornate and luxurious Palace of Happiness, the children meet the LUXURIES; their host is the biggest Luxury, the Luxury of Being Rich. Some of Tyltyl's attendants, even the Dog, succumb to the pleasures offered by the Luxuries. At Light's suggestion, Tyltyl turns the diamond; the garishness fades away and the palace becomes tasteful. The HAPPINESSES come in and the children meet many of them: The Happiness of Being Well, of Maternal Love, of Understanding, and so on. But the Happinesses do not have the Blue Bird.

Act V. 1. The group assembles again before the curtain. They are now at the gates of the graveyard, where the Blue Bird may be found. **2.** In the graveyard they are frightened, though Tyltyl will not admit that he is. Tyltyl turns the diamond and the graves open, but they see no dead; there are no dead. **3.** They are in the Kingdom of the Future. Here they meet the souls of children who have not yet been born. Here everyone is blue, so if they find the bird it is sure to be blue. The unborn children tell them some of the things they are destined to do on earth, such as great inventions they will make. The doorkeeper is TIME, who catches some unborn children who try to sneak out and be born before their time. Tyltyl and Mytyl meet a brother who is yet to be born. Light comes to Tyltyl to say she has the Blue Bird, hidden under her cloak. Tyltyl turns the diamond and they leave.

Act VI. 1. They are all again outside the woodcutter's cottage; Light tells the children that they left just a year ago that day. The children are to part from their spirit friends. The Fairy is coming the next morning to ask for the Blue Bird. They do not have the Blue Bird, but it is not their fault, for they tried. [What happened to Light's bird is not explained.] The Dog and Cat fight; the Dog is aware of the Cat's treachery throughout. The children sadly part from their friends. **2.** The children are asleep in the bedroom in the woodcutter's cottage. Mummy Tyl comes in and they wake. They tell her about their long journey but she thinks they were only dreaming and when Daddy Tyl comes in, that is what she tells him. Then Mme. Berlingot, who looks so much like the Fairy, arrives. The children insist she is the Fairy, but she does not understand. Her little daughter is still sick and she thinks a Christmas gift might cure her. The little girl likes Tyltyl's pet dove, and Tyltyl gets its cage, to send it to her. He sees that the dove is blue. He sends it as a gift to the little girl and soon afterward she comes in, cured. But as they are petting the dove it flies away. The little girl cries, but Tyltyl reassures her: He will find the bird for her again. And he asks the audience to help him.

Robert Browning
1812–1889
Elizabeth Barrett Browning
1806–1861

Fedor Dostoevski
1821–1881

Bonds of Interest

Play by Jacinto Benavente y Martinez, 1866–1954.

Produced 1907 (in U.S.A., in translation by John Garrett Underhill, 1917).

SPAIN'S NOBEL PRIZE dramatist (he won the prize in 1922) wrote this play as a farce along the traditional lines of the Italian comedy. The Spanish title was *Los intereses creados*. It was not produced in English until Benavente followed it with a second part in 1916—*La ciudad allegre y confiada*, The Gay and Confident City. *Bonds of Interest* is set in the 17th century and uses an old theme (its similarity to Farquhar's *The Beaux' Stratagem* is immediately apparent). It has survived as Benavente's most successful play.

Act. I. LEANDER and CRISPIN, two penniless young gentlemen, have just arrived in the city. Crispin explains that here there are really two different cities, one for the poor and one for the rich. To be able to live the life of the rich they can choose between robbing on the highway or using their intelligence to obtain the keys to the city. With Crispin posing as Leander's servant, they enter a fashionable inn. Crispin arrogantly demands the best service for his master and boasts that their baggage (they have nothing) is coming in 8 carts. Crispin tells the INNKEEPER that Leander is on a secret mission in the city. Leander strikes Crispin with his sword for disclosing this information and accidentally hits the innkeeper, who is so impressed by the manner of his guests that he asks for neither money nor identification. They go to their rooms.

HARLEQUIN, a poet, and the CAPTAIN enter. They, too, are without money for a meal. Harlequin cannot sell his poetry; the army is out of favor with the government, which sent the soldiers into an unjust war then made a disastrous peace to serve the commercial interests. They knock at the innkeeper's door. He refuses to let them in or extend them any further credit. The captain flies at the innkeeper with his sword and the poet threatens him with a deadly satire. The noise brings Leander and Crispin to the scene. Crispin takes the side of the poet and soldier, and speaking for the benevolence of his master assures Harlequin and the Captain that they will not want for anything. Crispin pretends to know the sonnets of the poet and the brave deeds of the captain. He insists that the innkeeper give the new guests 50 crowns on Leander's account. The party dines on good food and wine.

Act II. Doña SIRENA, a lady in reduced circumstances, and her young attendant COLUMBINE enter a garden before a fine house. Sirena is in distress; Columbine has just told her that none of the merchants will extend further credit. Sirena is to give a party that evening but the musicians and servants will not attend unless they are paid. Sirena wishes she were still young and could attract wealthy lovers. She reproaches Columbine for wasting time with the ragged Harlequin. Sirena is distressed because the rich merchant Signor POLICHINELLE is coming to her house to dine, with his wife and daughter SILVIA. Some impecunious nobles are also expected and if one can marry Silvia and secure the dowry, Sirena will be well rewarded. Columbine promises that Harlequin will provide the music and the service. Columbine goes to meet her lover in the corner of the garden but finds Crispin. Crispin assures Columbine that the evening party will be brilliantly taken care of if his master, the noble Leander, is invited. He offers a tremendous reward to Sirena if a match between his master and Silvia is arranged.

The party begins; the first guests, Laura and Risela, talk about the arrival in the city of a mysterious personage [Leander], who everyone thinks is an ambassador. Polichinelle comes, with his wife and daughter; he complains that his daughter is too interested in poetry and should think about making a practical marriage to a wealthy merchant. The mother and daughter will settle only for a nobleman. Crispin calls Polichinelle aside and identifies himself as one who knows the merchant's criminal past and who was in the galleys with him. Crispin tells Polichinelle to separate his daughter from Leander, as Leander is as much a rogue as he, Crispin. Polichinelle storms into the house, pulling Silvia away from Leander. Later Leander confesses to Crispin his real love for Silvia. Crispin tells Leander that he has made the father oppose the match in order to intensify Silvia's love for Leander and win the mother's support. Silvia slips into the garden and meets Leander. They talk of love as Harlequin plays a song in the background.

Act III. Crispin has started a rumor that Leander was set upon by a dozen ruffians (hired, he implies, by Polichinelle). Silvia leaves her father's house and goes to Sirena's, where she insists she will stay until she has married Leander. Harlequin and the captain spread the false story of Polichinelle's assault. Crispin explains that intelligence, if used to its fullest extent, can win the world.

Sirena comes to the inn and asks Crispin for half of the money promised her. When he refuses, because he hasn't the money, she promises to see that the marriage will be performed before evening. Silvia believes Leander to be badly wounded and comes to the inn. Leander, who really loves Silvia, tells her that he and Crispin are penniless frauds. He wants to give her back to her father, feeling that he is unworthy. Polichinelle arrives with a doctor of law (LAWYER) and a crowd of angry people who have discovered that Leander and Crispin have no money. Leander hides Silvia in a back room, climbs out the window, and leaves Crispin to face the crowd. They are angry creditors roaring for justice. The lawyer insists on writing everything down and slows the proceedings with all the trivia of jurisprudence. Crispin explains that the creditors will be better off letting the marriage take place so that Leander can pay all his debts. If the creditors send Leander and Crispin to the galleys, they will get no money. The crowd agrees that Leander be allowed to marry Silvia. Crispin pulls away the tapestry on the back wall, revealing Silvia, Leander, Sirena, Columbine, and the wife of Polichinelle. Silvia and Leander say that they do not want the dowry money, but will live on pure love. The crowd insists that Polichinelle give them the dowry. Everything settled, Crispin leaves Leander, to go on to other adventures. He plans to become a success in politics. Silvia speaks to the audience, saying that love, among all the passions of man, has dignified the farce and makes us think something eternal remains when the farce of life is over.

Bonjour Tristesse

Novel by Françoise Sagan, 1938– Published and © 1955 by E. P. Dutton & Co., New York. Translated from the French by Irene Ash.

THE TREMENDOUS INTEREST aroused by this very short novel, and its big sale, can perhaps be attributed chiefly to the interest in its youthful author, who was 16 when she wrote it. Mlle. Sagan is the contemporary and authentic voice of the "beat generation," in her native France affected by existentialism and living in shameless pursuit of thrills, speed in sport cars and rhythm in music. Nevertheless Mlle. Sagan has undoubted genius as a writer. She became the idol of teenage Paris and fulfilled her promise by almost killing herself in a motor accident. John Steinbeck satirized her in passing in his novel *The Short Reign of Pippin IV*.

Part 1. CECILE, spoiled and 17, vacations with her father, RAYMOND, and his mistress, ELSA MACKENBOURG, in a remote, white villa on the Mediterranean. Though cynical about love from the influence of this gay widowed father with his many affairs, Cecile starts a serious summer flirtation with CYRIL, a young college student. ANN LARSEN, a friend of Cecile's mother, arrives at the invitation of Raymond. She is 40, glamorous, serious, and intelligent, with high standards of good taste and fastidiousness. With good manners she hides her disapproval of the open situation of Elsa and Raymond, treating the mistress with gentleness. It soon becomes apparent that Elsa is no match for Ann's intelligence and refinement and after a drunken scene at the Casino she will not return to the villa, though she and Cecile were always friends in spite of the situation with Raymond. The next morning Ann tells Cecile that she is going to marry her father. An abrupt change comes over their pattern of life. Respectability is now her companion. Ann begins to organize Cecile's days, after catching her in a compromising position with Cyril. Sophisticated beyond her years, Cecile vows to destroy Ann in order to bring back the gaiety of the past two years with her father.

Part 2. Little by little the obsession to part Ann and her father develops in Cecile. She can think of nothing else. Elsa returns to the villa for her clothes and is encouraged by Cecile to think that Raymond is in love with her and is only trapped by Ann. Elsa agrees to Cecile's plan to stay at Cyril's and to pretend to be in love with him. Cyril and Elsa play their parts so well that even Cecile is slightly jealous. Raymond notices how Elsa is glowing and his possessive instinct is aroused. Cecile is so pleased that she is nicer to Cyril than ever before and they become lovers. Step by step the discord to be sown between the engaged couple is planned by the three plotters. A chance meeting is arranged at a bar in the

Cecile plans to destroy Ann, to restore the old days

village where Raymond and Ann are entertaining old friends. As Elsa passes, the old friends exclaim at her fresh beauty. Ann is hurt by Raymond's ready agreement to this remark, and Cecile with feelings of guilt praises Ann. As the elaborately planned chance meetings increase, Elsa blooms at the hope of recapturing her exlover. Cecile is torn between her desire to accomplish the break between her father and Ann, and a creeping sense of guilt at hurting the one woman she really respects and likes. She knows her father well, that he will be haunted until he gets the new desire for Elsa out of his blood even though he really loves Ann. Fate assumes a strange form. After what he considers successful maneuvering, Raymond finally is alone with Elsa and embraces and kisses her. Ann accidentally sees them. Uncontrollably hurt, Ann runs for her car; but Cecile, running

beside her, confesses her part in the whole mess and begs her not to leave. Ann does not believe Cecile and after a gesture of sincere affection drives off, with tears blinding her eyes. Raymond is frantic when he learns that Ann has left, and he and Cecile write her long, loving letters imploring forgiveness. Momentarily they are soothed, sure of Ann's final acceptance of their real feelings for her; but a telephone message informs them that Ann has met with a serious automobile accident on a treacherous stretch of road. She is dead. Dazed with shock, they return to Paris. Only Cecile realizes that it was no accident but was Ann's way of committing suicide. It does not take long for the fickle, pleasure-loving Raymond and his counterpart, Cecile, to return to their useless gaiety and they go back to their previous life, haunted only for brief moments.

The Book of Snobs

Humorous essays by William Makepeace Thackeray, 1811–1863.
Published serially 1846–47, in book form 1848.

THE BOOK OF SNOBS arose from a single sarcastic essay or sketch that Thackeray wrote for *Punch.* Popular (or at least editorial) demand caused him to expand it into a long series on "Snobs of England." The separate sketches were later called chapters when the whole was collected for publication in book form as *The Book of Snobs.* Thackeray enjoyed writing humor and fancied himself as a humorist but was not so good in the field as he supposed. *The Book of Snobs* is his best humorous writing but is not in a class with his novels.

Chaps. 1–8. History claims great men for

great moments and I have been so chosen to write the History of Snobs. Chosen because I know snobs, have an Eye for them, in every class. I am one of them. First I turn my attention to the Manners Snob. Once I was revolted by my dear friend GEORGE MARROWFAT, who ate peas with a knife, a custom that should be reserved to foreign nobility. Then one day I saw him use his fork and I was happy once again to recognize him in polite society. The Snob Royal is a flunkey who admires snobs and has an impressive awe of titles. Snobs Royal are those who pretend to have contact with the nobility, and those who seek contact with the ranks above them. The lords and ladies who pride themselves on their titles and who carry themselves as if the universe were theirs for the mere beckoning are also snobs. They surround themselves with admirers and flatterers and forget that they might achieve something of worth if they tried. They do not feel called upon to show their hand. The ladies preen themselves like pea-

cocks and the gentlemen, like prize stud horses, merely paw the ground. Many of them are feebleminded but hide their paltry wits behind the family crests. A lady of my acquaintance once fell in love with a young lord whom she knew only from hearsay. Being a merchant's daughter she could never meet the object of her affection, but this did not in the least prevent her from pining away in her chamber. She turned down several suitors who admired the affected airs she wore, and scared away several more young men who were unwilling to approach a woman with such advanced aspirations. She is now 45 and her beloved lord has been married twice. She has remained true to her first love, though I understand she is nasty to those who must live with her and she weeps in her room all the time. It is amazing how many people imagining themselves to be grand will stand in the rain to watch a duke's marriage and later his funeral. Merit, of course, has little to do with the matter. What a temptation to cringe we all have, and how we practice lordolatry. We are either arrogant or mean according to our fortune. A lord may be an ass and yet be respected. Excuses will be found for him. The piously respectable are also snobs. They think the church will fall if they fail to attend. These self-righteous snobs give to the poor and look down on those who don't. They talk about social matters as if without their attention the world would stop. They find all kinds of outrages everywhere but continue to live in comfort and style. They feel superior because of their goodness and use the word sin frequently when talking about others. They are close to the reverend and give, if not generously, conspicuously to his various projects.

Chaps. 9–17. We must not omit the Snob Clerical from our attention. Some members of this category are only as bad as everyone else. But others grow rich and fat on a sense of self-importance. One of the commonest clerical vices is leaving the service of ordinary folk at the bid of royalty. I know a parson once who left a wedding party and the young people standing hours by an altar waiting for him to complete the ceremony while he comforted a duke who had suffered a mild attack of gout. The clergy like to attend the mighty and often refer to their ministrations in the next week's sermon. I admit that I would jump out of my skin if two dukes would walk down Pall Mall with me. But nevertheless I think such temptations should be removed from the clergy. Among the Clerical Snobs the University Snob must be remembered. Universities are the last places to be reached by reform. Class distinctions according to wealth are as blatant as in feudal times. Students who are on scholarship are forced to wear garments of a certain color and eat together, apart from the more fortunate of their contemporaries. This makes matters more convenient for the student who wishes to make important contacts during his academic years. He can see at a glance whom to avoid. Among students there are Drinking Snobs, Dressing Snobs, Philosophical Snobs, and those who go to "rack and ruin aping their betters." University dons are a most remarkable type of snob. These gentlemen, who should be devoted to the various branches of learning, are in fact more involved in their petty powers. I have myself

seen a don keep nine students standing in his elaborately comfortable study while he himself relaxed and smoked in a large chair. This he did not to teach the students manners, but to exercise the full power of his position. I have also known University Snobs who will curry favor with their noble pupils and be totally indifferent even to the most intelligent of the lowerborn. They will spend hours in the evening writing to the parents of their noble charges and attempt to gain their permission for an interview with these people, whom the dons respect despite the fact that their learning may be as negligible as their interest in their offspring.

Chaps. 18–26. As the Season draws to a close a great many Social Snobs have left London. The Party-giving Snobs are those who give parties in order to be invited in return. Dining-out Snobs are those who pretend to be richer and grander than they are. It is appalling how all the honesty of society is tainted by fashion-worship. Another form of snob is the Nationality Snob. Who has not sensed that calm British confidence that the British are the absolute center of the world? One of the dullest creatures under heaven, the Englishman, goes to every city of Europe being snobbish about what he sees. When he goes into churches in Italy he thinks about how superior his altar is to theirs. He looks down on the foreign religion without noticing its beautiful surroundings. He finds the food bad and the people dirty, though he cannot speak their language. He finds the trains and boats inferior and forgets the inconveniences of his native transportation. In the museums he says he prefers the painting over his own fireplace. His tastes for the new are dulled by his inordinate pride in his own.

Chaps. 27–35. In the country the situation is the same. I paid a visit to some country friends and found them eager for some news of the royalty. Guests would arrive in carriages, bearing their family colors. Everyone pretended connections in high places. Snobbishness is at war with love and human kindness and ruins many marriages. So many lives are spent in loneliness because of quarrels over a dowry. Bachelors rot in singleness and spinster women dry up like lemon peels, because the snob-walls prevent them from reaching each other.

Chaps. 36–43. In the final chapters we malign the Club Snobs. Clubs provide shelter for the moneyed, yet there are some clubs where no one speaks to anyone else. Club members are grave and concise in their speech. Their manner is weary. This is the Englishman relaxing. Actually the only men

who belong in clubs are married men who have no profession or occupation. They are a nuisance to have around the house. The children want to practice their music. The chambermaid must clean and the wife wants to entertain. This sort of man belongs in the club, where he can waste his time at cards and conversation without really being in anyone's way. Other club members are all snobs of one sort or another. They will brag about their exploits with women, even repeating glorious details that never happened. They will boast of their boyhood pranks or military exploits, which also have a fictional basis. They will collect odd leather boxes or buttons from foreign lands and feel themselves distinguished because of their exclusive good taste. Without their clubs they would feel lost in the social structure, but with them they feel bloated with importance and immediately let strangers know how valuable they are by mentioning the names of their clubs. Wiggle and Waggle are two types of men found in the clubs. They like second-rate pleasures and fourth-rate women. They drop names of people and places. They are not precisely rogues, but see if they won't marry a fortune, ugly and old as she may be. Bacchus is the divinity whom they worship. Wine-amateurship is the distinctive mark of the Club Snob. It is next in boringness to food-amateurship. Captain Shindy has been known to destroy everyone's evening, creating a tremendous scene over a mutton chop. At the club he has ten servants to attend him while poor Mrs. Shindy and the six children are waiting in dingy lodgings for the wash to dry. Snobs despise their neighbors while they themselves lead small lives, following those that appear to have attained a higher degree. "Those who are proud of their pedigree and their wealth, they are the Snobs that Mr. Punch will laugh at. Hitting no foul blow, with his broadest grin, he will never forget that fun is good, truth is still better, and love best of all."

Boris Godunov

Play by Aleksandr Pushkin, 1799–1837. Published 1831 (written 1825). Various translations from the Russian; translation by Alfred Hayes © 1936 by Random House, New York.

WHEN PUSHKIN WROTE *Boris Godunov* in 1825 he was living under police surveillance, suspected of atheism. Pushkin is called the Russian Byron (because he was a contemporary of Byron's, was of similarly aristocratic birth, had similar poetic talent, and died similarly untimely) and he was influenced by Byron, but in this "dramatic poem" he was influenced chiefly by Shakespeare. *Boris* is based on events of the years 1598–1605 and is semi-historical. Its publication was delayed for six years after Pushkin wrote it and it was not performed on the stage until 35 years after his death in 1837. Then it was unsuccessful as a play. Nevertheless it proved to be the Pushkin work that brought him his most lasting international fame, because of the Moussorgsky opera based on it.

Palace of the Kremlin. Prince SHUISKY and Prince VOROTYNSKY discuss the treachery of privy councillor BORIS GODUNOV, who schemes to usurp the throne after having secretly contrived the assassination of Czarevitch DIMITRI, son and heir of Ivan the Terrible. Shuisky tells how the actual assassins were caught and killed by a mob,

101

Waiting for news at the Kremlin

without any suspicion involving Boris. Laconically sly, Shuisky admits he parroted Boris Godunov's version of the murder, which he had been sent by Boris to investigate. Just between themselves, Shuisky and Vorotynsky contend that the succession to the throne should not go to Boris but to a member of their own family, the Ruriks.

The Red Square. SHCHELKALOV, secretary of the Council of Boyars, announces to the Moscow populace that the Patriarch of the Russian Orthodox Church will petition the widowed Czarina to have the crown rulership bestowed upon Boris Godunov.

The Maiden Field. Peasants and people of Moscow kneel in crowds as they wait anxiously for news that Boris has accepted the crown.

The Kremlin Palace. With a solemnly hypocritical display of humility and hesitation, Boris accepts the crown. The Boyar nobles pledge allegiance to him. Shuisky and Vorotynsky agree surreptitiously not to denounce Boris until a safer opportunity occurs.

Cell in the Chudov Monastery. An aged monk, Father PIMEN, is writing an historical account of Russia's contemporary troubles. GRIGORY OTREPYEV, a young monk who sleeps in the same cell with Pimen, is disturbed by dreams of grandeur. Grigory dreams he is looking down over the whole city of Moscow from the top of a great stairway. Old Pimen tells Grigory that worldly power is an illusion not worth considering. Grigory discounts this, saying Pimen is merely tired of life from having had his fill of it when he was young and a soldier.

Beside the Monastery Wall. A wicked monk intrigues Grigory with the idea that Grigory could pretend to be Dimitri, the murdered czarevitch, because Grigory and Dimitri were the same age. Grigory is tempted.

Palace of the Patriarch. The abbot of the Chudrov Monastery informs the Patriarch of the Russian Church that Grigory has run away. At the Patriarch's demand, the abbot recites Grigory's family history and tells of Grigory's claim to the identity of the Czarevitch. The Patriarch calls Grigory a tool of the devil and will have his iniquity reported to the political police.

Palace of the Czar. Two courtiers are commenting on the curious extent to which Boris has fallen under the influence of magicians and fortune-tellers since he acquired the crown. Boris delivers a bitter soliloquy expressing the disappointments of his reign as czar, his fears, and his constant pangs of guilty conscience.

Tavern on the Lithuanian Frontier. Grigory is here on his way to seek Lithuanian support for his claim to the throne of Russia. He is traveling with two beggar monks, disguised as their companion. But Boris has discovered Grigory's rôle as an impostor and has sent agents to arrest him. At dagger's point Grigory escapes from the czar's officers, who try to seize him in the tavern.

Moscow—Shuisky's House. AFANASY PUSHKIN tells Shuisky there is news from Cracow that Czarevitch Dimitri, son of Ivan the Terrible, was not actually assassinated but is alive. Pushkin and Shuisky, both enemies of Boris, determine to support the new Dimitri, even if he is an impostor.

Palace of the Czar. Having been informed by his spies of the news given to Shuisky by Pushkin, Boris doubts Shuisky's loyalty and questions him as to the identity of the pretender. Boris reminds Shuisky that it was he whom Boris had sent to investigate the murder of the genuine Dimitri. Shuisky is under suspicion. Boris is gravely alarmed.

Cracow, House of Wisniowiecki. Grigory wins strong support from Polish nobles who hate the Muscovites, and from Russian foes of Boris. A Jesuit priest, Father CZERNIKOWSKI, also joins Grigory's conspiracy, offering to bring the influence of Rome to bear on behalf of the pretender. Grigory plans to march against Moscow at the head of a rebel army, menacing Boris with downfall and death.

Castle of Governor Mniszech in Sambor. MARYNA, daughter of Governor MNISZECH, is urged by her lady's maid to encourage the ardor of Grigory, who has fallen in love with Maryna. The possibility of becoming empress of Russia inflames Maryna's imagination.

Another Room in the Sambor Castle. The governor expresses gratification at seeing Grigory infatuated by his daughter.

Night. The Garden. The Fountain. In this romantic setting Maryna asks Grigory pointblank whether he really is Czarevitch Dimitri or merely an unfrocked monk pretending to be Dimitri, as she had heard rumored. The lovesick Grigory confesses his true origin to Maryna, whereupon she arrogantly refuses to consider his plebeian bid for her noble hand in marriage. She threatens to denounce him. He retaliates by insisting that he will be czar, then threatens to punish her for her disloyalty when he comes into power. His forcefulness impresses her. She promises to be his wife despite his lowly birth. She urges him not to delay his military campaign against Boris. Grigory declares he will march his men to war at daybreak.

The Lithuanian Frontier. Leading his rebel troops across the border into Russia, Grigory, the pretender, voices patriotic regret for the necessity of using foreigners to fight Russians.

The Council of the Czar. In Moscow, menaced by the rebellion, Boris asks the Patriarch what can be done. The Patriarch tells him that Dimitri's tomb has become a shrine of miracle-healing for the sick, the lame, and the blind, so the Patriarch advises Boris to have Dimitri's remains brought to the Kremlin for the performance of a public miracle. This would prove to the populace that Dimitri is dead and that Grigory is an impostor. Boris refuses to mix religion with politics; he declares he trusts the people to

Maryna is ambitious

reject Grigory when they learn the truth directly from Boris himslf.

A Plain near Novgorod-Seversk. Foreign officers serving Boris discuss the trend of the fighting. They speak in French and German as well as in Russian. They praise the military talent of BASMANOV, one of Boris's generals.

Square in Front of the Moscow Cathedral. A street crowd waits to see Boris come from a requiem mass being offered in the cathedral in memory of the murdered Dimitri. When Boris appears, an idiot boy calls him "Herod," accusing him of having had Dimitri assassinated. Boris prevents his retinue of nobles from arresting the idiot.

Sevsk. Questioning a prisoner, Grigory learns that Basmanov has been made a member of the Czar's council and that Boris now has an army of 50,000 troops in the field against Grigory's 15,000.

A Forest. Grigory admits he is losing his last battle. He upbraids his Cossack followers for their inferior fighting and praises the German troops in the army of Boris. Afanasy Pushkin declares that Grigory's cause is not yet lost.

Moscow, Palace of the Czar. Boris gives supreme command of his army to Basmanov, remarking that brains are worth more than noble birth in a soldier, for Basmanov is of plebeian origin. Basmanov declares he has no sympathy for court intrigues, nor for the wavering sentiments of the populace. Boris goes to receive a delegation of foreign merchants. Soon after he leaves the room there is an outcry that he has been mortally stricken by a sudden illness and is bleeding to death from the mouth and ears. Boris, dying, is carried in on a chair. He names his son, FEODOR, to succeed him as czar, instructing Feodor to retain Basmanov as chief commander of the army and to observe all the traditional dignities of the court and the church. The Patriarch and prelates administer last rites to Boris Godunov as he dies.

Army Headquarters. Afanasy Pushkin, supporter of Grigory the pretender, makes a political bargain with Basmanov, persuading Basmanov to help put Grigory on the throne instead of Feodor. Basmanov hesitates, but finally agrees when convinced that Feodor's succession would be hopelessly defeated by popular acclaim for Grigory, because Grigory represents himself under the great, honored name of Dimitri. Basmanov proclaims his decision to lead the army in favor of Grigory.

Place of Execution, Red Square, Moscow. Afanasy Pushkin, in a public address to the townspeople of Moscow, denounces the harsh rule of Boris and makes an eloquent appeal for the acceptance of Grigory. The mob roars approval. Riotous peasants shout their determination to invade the Kremlin and kill Feodor. They yell, "Crush the race of Godunov!"

The Kremlin, House of Boris. Guards on the steps try to turn the mob back. Feodor is seen looking out through a window. From the crowd a few voices pity him but they are howled down. The Boyar nobles force their way past the guards. It is said they will make Feodor swear allegiance to Grigory, the false Dimitri. Screams are then heard from inside the house. A Boyar nobleman opens the door and announces that Feodor and the queen have committed suicide by taking poison. The Boyar says he has seen their dead bodies. He urges the mob to acclaim Dimitri, meaning Grigory. But the people stand silent, shocked speechless.

The Bostonians

Novel by Henry James, 1843–1916. Published 1886. (ML, 16)

THE BOSTONIANS is a novel of James's "middle period." He was in the realm of high society as usual, this time in the very starched Boston of the late 19th century. The novel was not successful when published and James was very unhappy. Among other things, it was considered wicked. Perhaps it was and still is, but it is among his most important works.

Chaps. 1–3. Miss OLIVE CHANCELLOR, an active feminist, dines in her fashionable Boston home with her cousin BASIL RANSOM. This is the first time they have met and mutual interest grows with mutual dislike. Olive, a tragic, morbid figure, broods on the sufferings of women; she longs to die for some ideal, so intensely does she find opposition to the world pleasurable. Basil, a handsome young man, has left the ruins of his Southern aristocratic family and settled in New York to make his fortune as a lawyer. Basil loves the Southern tradition and seeks everywhere a counterpart to the grace and order he knew as a child on his family's plantation. He also has the good sense to see that the South as he knew it is dead, and that he must go on to new challenges. Olive feels aggressive and angry in the presence of any man but finds Basil's indifference to the crimes against womanhood particularly unpleasant. Basil meets Olive's visiting sister, the flirtatious Mrs. LUNA, who is despised by the ascetic Olive. Mrs. Luna is struggling into a long pair of gloves and prepares to leave for a party. She loves the underprivileged position of women and thinks it is all very just. She criticizes Olive's hideous black bonnet and simple black dress. Olive decides to try to convince Basil of her side of the feminist issue and takes him to a suffragette meeting, especially to meet the famous feminist Miss BIRDSEYE and Mrs. FARRINDER. He goes out of curiosity and an amiable willingness to let life show him.

Chaps. 4–9. At the meeting Basil finds hundreds of black-bonneted women, most of them very unattractive, and their conversation seems humorless and silly, for to the end they take their agitations seriously. Basil does meet a wonderful woman doctor who is taciturn and cross because she believes women should do what they want, but not talk about it like hens in the coop. At the meeting, with her parents, is pretty, red-haired young VERENA TARRANT. Mrs. Farrinder, the expected speaker, refuses out of temperament to address the waiting audience. She says she has too much humility to speak before her sisters. After a disappointed silence, Verena is asked to speak. She claims to pronounce on vital issues only by means of another voice entering her body; everyone in the room must be very silent and she needs her father, a Mesmeric healer, to bring the spirits to her. After this mystic preamble she speaks on women's rights with purity and imagination. She still has a child's innocence when she reproves the terrible adult world. Ransom is enchanted by her manner and Olive is overwhelmed by the girl's eloquence and charm. Olive invites Verena to visit her and speaks to her parents, urging them to send Verena to her. The Tarrants have made money on all the mystic frauds, from séances to fortune-telling, but they are socially ambitious for their daughter and insist that she visit Olive on the very next day.

Chaps. 10–15. Olive, whose mind has become obsessed by Verena, greets the girl with open arms and insists that she devote her gift with words permanently to the feminist cause. She demands that Verena come to visit often and indicates that she wants to take the girl over and make her into a private possession. In the midst of this strange, subdued yet frightening conversation, Ransom enters. Again he is delighted with Verena, but Olive's cold reception and obvious dislike of his company forces him to leave. His business in Boston over, he returns to New York; but

to take tea at her house. Verena seems to enjoy the company of some young men also at the tea, which produces a panic in Olive that blinds her to all else. As Olive leaves the tea she calls Verena out to the porch and standing in the snow tries to elicit a promise from Verena never to marry. The girl is very anxious to please her patroness but is frightened by the intensity of the request. She cannot really promise so great a thing. Olive rides home slumped in her carriage, for the first time afraid of some great grief that lies in her future. The next day Verena, seeing how tortured her friend is, gives the desired promise. As proof of her loyalty, Verena immediately turns down a journalist who wished to be her husband and to make money by taking her on lecture tours all through the country.

Verena is frightened as Olive rides home alone

Chaps. 16–19. Verena and Olive continue to see each other constantly. Olive takes Verena to several feminist meetings and has her speak to the public. Verena gradually attains a reputation in Boston and a certain sort of fame follows. Verena develops a friendship with a Harvard student, HENRY BURRAGE. Henry is an amiable dilettante who simply wants to enjoy life in the manner of his New York social family. He has been captivated by a certain charm of Verena's and has proposed marriage. Verena takes Olive to tea with Henry at Harvard in hopes that Olive will approve of Henry and release her from her promise. Mrs. BURRAGE, Henry's mother, is also at the tea and she turns out to be very sympathetic to the feminist cause. Despite this, Olive suffers in the company and tells Verena that Henry is worth nothing and merely wants to exploit her, as do all men with their women. Verena acquiesces and breaks off her relationship with Henry, but she wishes that Olive did not always force her to think of the evilness in men. Out of affection for Olive she follows her completely in all her

arguments and agrees to devote her own life to an oratorical career.

Chaps. 20–24. The winter season in New York goes badly for Basil. He has not succeeded as a lawyer and is living in rather extreme poverty. Besides that, he has grown to doubt his own ability to master the world. He has been plagued by Mrs. Luna, who first hired him as a tutor for her incorrigible son and then began to flirt with him in an embarrassing way. In Boston, Olive writes out a large check to Dr. Tarrant, who then permits Verena to live with Olive in her big house. The Tarrants are the kind of people who will let Verena go if they are paid. Henry Burrage refuses to take no for an answer; he comes to Olive's house one day and repeats his proposal. Verena again turns him down but Olive becomes frightened that his persistence will win Verena over. She decides to take Verena to Europe for several months. In Europe they visit feminist meetings and Verena gives speeches that are well attended and well received. At the end of this time Basil pays a long-overdue visit to Mrs. Luna and he learns that Olive and Verena have come back to Boston. His enthusiasm for life is rekindled as he thinks of Verena and he determines to go to see her. Mrs. Luna becomes jealous of his interest in Verena and warns him that Olive will never let him near her friend.

Chaps. 25–32. Basil goes to Boston on business and spends many hours searching for Verena. He finds her when he visits her parents and induces her to go walking with him. They argue; she tries to convince him of the justice of the feminist cause and he tries to explain to her his concept of the woman as a thing of grace and beauty that supports a man in all his efforts and bears him children to continue his love. These are all arguments Olive has taught Verena to despise and she tries to tell Basil that they have nothing to share and will never agree on the important things. But he feels differently. He is certain Verena really wants to believe in what he is saying and he tells her that he will stay near her for as long as she will allow him the honor. Verena becomes frightened of Basil as the conversation grows obliquely personal. She leaves him quickly, but unknown to Olive she sends him an invitation to a lecture to be given at Mrs. Burrage's party in New York some weeks later. At the party, despite Olive's entreaties, Basil seeks out Verena. However, the girl becomes really frightened by his threat to her way of life and promises Olive to remain with her forever.

Chaps. 33–40. But the next day Verena goes out with Basil. He tells her he wishes to save his own sex, to bring back order and grace into the world. Verena leaves New York and goes to the country. Basil follows her there and proposes marriage. He has just published an article and he feels encouraged. He believes his future will be brilliant if Verena will just aid him in his work. She has fallen in love with him and finds his plans of more interest than her feminist duties. But again she runs away from him because of Olive and the life to which she has already been committed.

Chaps. 41–42. Basil hears that Verena is again in Boston, where she is about to give an important lecture to a large audience. Basil comes to the stage door and Verena, sensing that he is there, refuses to begin her lecture. At last he convinces a policeman, posted by Olive, to let him through. Basil and Verena leave the hall together. Olive remains behind, suffering deeply as she faces the silent and disappointed crowd.

Basil finds a large crowd assembled for Verena's lecture

The Bourgeois Gentleman

Play by Molière, 1622–1673.
Produced 1670. (ML, 78)

THIS IS ONE OF Molière's two or three most popular plays with American readers. There are many translations and it is the title that has given the translators the most trouble. Among the efforts are "The Citizen-Gentleman," "The Middle-Class Gentleman," "The Citizen Who Would Be a Lord," and "The Citizen Who Apes the Nobleman." The last is perhaps most accurate, for Jourdain was not a gentleman, did not become one, and hardly aspired to become one; he merely wanted to associate with "the quality," act like them, and be thought one of them— not necessarily by them, but by others. His failures make a broad farce. In Molière's time was just beginning the 200-year process by which the rich middle classes pulled up to terms of equality with the gentry. In the first performances Molière himself played the part of M. Jourdain.

Act. I. 1. In the living room of Monsieur JOURDAIN, the MUSIC-MASTER and DANCING-MASTER discuss their services to Jourdain. The dancing-master is dissatisfied to work for a man who has no knowledge or appreciation of their arts, but the music-master finds that the large fees they collect are ample reward and the dancing-master agrees at least partly. 2. Jourdain enters, preening himself in a dressing-gown that his tailor has told him is a must for all men of quality. The two masters discuss with him the significance of music and dancing in life and current affairs and finally convince him that, to really be a man of the world, he must learn both. The act ends with a composition sung by a trio, followed by a ballet.

Act II. 1. Jourdain asks the two masters to prepare musical festivities for the afternoon, as he is entertaining a person of quality. Then he executes a few dance steps he has been learning and has the dancing master show him how to bow to a marquise because he expects one, DORIMÈNE, that afternoon. 2–3. The FENCING-MASTER arrives and Jourdain goes through some exercises after which the fencing-master gets into a dispute with the other two masters: He contends that fencing is far superior to dancing and music. The masters of fencing and dancing then insult each other violently. Jourdain tries to separate them. 4. A PHILOSOPHER whom Jourdain has hired to teach him logic enters and is asked by Jourdain to settle the dispute. The philosopher tries to reason but finds himself in the fight when the others all insist

that their professions are more important than his. Despite Jourdain's pleas, they continue fighting and exit fighting. 5–6. The philosopher returns and prepares for the lesson. Jourdain wants none of logic, ethics, or physics, not understanding them; he wishes to be taught spelling. The philosopher tells him about the five vowels and demonstrates carefully how each is made, much to Jourdain's surprise and excitement. Then Jourdain asks to be taught how to compose a love letter. When told he must choose either prose or verse, he is amazed; he is then completely overcome when he learns that he has been speaking prose all his life. After a brief discussion of the love letter itself, the philosopher leaves. 7–9. Jourdain's MASTER TAILOR enters with a suit that has just been made for Jourdain. With orchestral accompaniment, which is how persons of quality do it, Jourdain is dressed in his new suit. To flatter Jourdain into tipping, the tailor and his men address him as Noble Sir, My Lord, and Your Grace, after each of which he is so overcome that he tips heavily, almost depleting his purse. The ballet at the end of this act consists of dancing while Jourdain is being dressed and then more dancing by way of rejoicing over his liberality.

Act III. 1–3. Jourdain, the maid, NICOLE, and Mme. JOURDAIN engage in a lengthy argument about his behavior in recent weeks. He is outraged when both women ridicule his new suit and he explains that it is necessary to impress persons of quality. Mme. Jourdain states that he should be more concerned about getting his daughter LUCILE married but he insists that what he is doing is more important. He explains his discovery that he has been speaking prose all his life and with the fencing foils he tries to show Nicole that he is learning how not to be killed, but she bests him in a practice duel. Mme. Jourdain is mostly annoyed by his extravagant loans to Count DORANTE, who gives nothing in return. Jourdain explains that it is a very great honor to know the count and have him for a friend. 4–9. Dorante enters and, after flattering Jourdain, asks for more money. As Jourdain leaves to get it, Dorante tries without success to have a friendly conversation with Mme. Jourdain. Jourdain returns with the money and Dorante whispers to him that he has finally persuaded the Marquise Dorimène to accept Jourdain's gift and invitation to his house. Nicole overhears some of their conversation and reports to Mme. Jourdain, who lets it pass because she is more anxious about getting her daughter married. Mme. Jourdain dispatches Nicole to tell CLEONTE, who has been interested in Lucile, that she is ready to discuss marriage plans. Nicole gives Cleonte and his valet COVIELLE, who incidentally is interested in Nicole, her mistress's good news. But they are unfriendly toward Nicole and she leaves to tell Lucile. Their pride is hurt because they suspect that over the last few days both young women have been shunning them; Lucile snubbed Cleonte that morning. Cleonte suspects that

Lucile is interested in Dorante, who has been visiting the Jourdains so often. 10–11. Lucile and Nicole come back together to try to discover what has so angered the two young men. The men still refuse to speak. In their turn, the women refuse to continue asking, at which the young men begin pleading with them to explain. Finally, Lucile explains that Cleonte was snubbed that morning because an old aunt was visiting who has very strict ideas about young ladies' speaking to men. Mme. Jourdain arrives to tell Cleonte that Jourdain is coming and he should ask for Lucile's hand. Jourdain enters and refuses to give his daughter to Cleonte because he must have a nobleman for a son-in-law. Mme. Jourdain is furious at his pose and, after he is gone, tells Cleonte not to be discouraged. Once alone, the two young men ponder Cleonte's problem and Coville gets an idea, which involves a masquerade (imposture) that might work. 15–21. Dorante arrives at Jourdain's, escorting Dorimène. Their conversation quickly reveals that Cleonte himself is courting Dorimène, giving her in his own name the gifts that Jourdain has been sending her. They greet Jourdain, who impresses Dorimène as a fool. Then they go in to dinner, which is introduced by an interlude ballet of the six cooks.

Act IV. 1–4. The dinner begins, with Dorante trying to hide from Jourdain the fact that Dorimène is not in the least interested in him (Jourdain). Three musicians with orchestra sing a drinking song, after which Dorante tries to quell Jourdain's ardor for the unsuspecting Dorimène. Mme. Jourdain arrives in a jealous rage and Jourdain is grateful to Dorante for explaining that the lady is not interested in Jourdain. But Mme. Jourdain insults Dorimène and the two guests leave. After a brief dispute Mme. Jourdain also leaves. 5–13. Coville, in disguise, comes in to tell Jourdain that he knew his father, who was a gentleman. Amazed and delighted, Jourdain is set up

M. Jourdain explains

for further deception; namely, Covielle's report that the Grand Turk's son wants to marry Lucile and is arriving. Cleonte, disguised as a Turk, arrives, babbling incoherently in what Jourdain believes to be Turkish and which Covielle translates as the highest compliments. Dorante arrives and Covielle tells him privately about the masquerade. Jourdain undergoes a comic ceremony that makes him a "Mamamouchi," a fictitious Turkish title. This is part of the ballet, danced by Turks.

Act V. 1–7. Mme Jourdain enters and is stupified by the spectacle confronting her. Completely taken in by the rigamarole, Jourdain explains to her that he is a Mamamouchi and goes on babbling incoherently, which convinces her that he is mad. He leaves, followed shortly afterward by his distraught wife, discussing the absurdity of Jourdain's position. Dorimène decides to marry Dorante. Lucile arrives and, recognizing the "Grand Turk's son" as Cleonte, accepts her father's order to marry him. Mme.

Jourdain refuses to allow her daughter to marry a Turk, but after Covielle explains the ruse, she consents. Jourdain, learning of Dorante's intent to marry Dorimène, is pleased because he believes it is being done to hide his own great love for the woman from his wife. Jourdain gives Nicole's hand to the "Dragoman" (Covielle). The final curtain falls with the company waiting for the notary who is to perform the double ceremony. An extravagant ballet ends the play.

Box and Cox

Play by John Maddison Morton, 1811–1891.
Produced 1847.

CHIEFLY, THIS FARCE deserves its immortality because it is a classic idea. It is not, however, merely a dramatic idea. Lodging houses in industrial cities—in the U.S., notably Pittsburgh—used to rent rooms in sleeping shifts, two or three each twenty-four hours, when the steel mills were busy. The idea made a musical show for Sir Arthur Sullivan in 1867; there the title was *Cox and Box.* The librettist was not Gilbert but Francis Burnand. It is very short and is usually produced in a double bill with a short Gilbert and Sullivan operetta.

Act. I. COX, preparing to go to work one morning, is complaining aloud that his hair has been cut too short when Mrs. BOUNCER, the landlady, enters. Cox complains to her that his candles and coals are being pilfered and his room smells of tobacco. Mrs. Bouncer answers that the gentleman upstairs smokes a pipe and the smoke must

come down the chimney to Cox's room. Cox is skeptical, but leaves for his job (he is a hatter). The landlady has actually rented the same room to a Mr. BOX, who has a night job on a newspaper. The landlady is thus receiving double rent. She is busy rearranging the room for her daytime guest when Box enters. He responds angrily to her suggestion that he should not smoke. He, too, finds his candles missing and complains. He puts some bacon on the fire. Then, still wondering about the mystery, he falls asleep. Cox returns because the owner of his shop has given him a holiday. He finds the fire going and the bacon cooking. Surprised, he puts his mutton chop on the grid and goes out for some rolls. Box wakes and throws Cox's chop out the window. Cox reënters and they confront each other with loud threats. Mrs. Bouncer comes in and explains the duplicity, promising another room for the following day. In the meantime Box and Cox begin a conversation. Cox admits that he has a fiancée who operates bathing machines at a resort. Box confesses that he was friendly with a young widow

who wished to marry him and he, to avoid this drastic end, pretended to drown, leaving his clothes and a suicide note on the shore. It turns out that the same woman who chased Box is now pursuing Cox. Cox tries to make Box go back to the woman, PENELOPE ANN, so that he himself can slip out of their arrangement. They argue and call for pistols. Deciding that dueling is too dangerous they play at dice and then toss coins. The loser will have to take Penelope Ann. They both cheat and argue until Mrs. Bouncer brings in a letter saying that Penelope has drowned and wills her estate to her intended. Now Box and Cox, reversing themselves, argue over which of them is the heir. But another letter is delivered saying that Penelope is well and will arrive soon. Box and Cox now revert to their previous attitudes and both try to escape till they find out that Penelope has decided to marry a third party named Knox. This resolves the difference between Box and Cox and they decide they are long-lost brothers. They will continue to share the room.

Brave New World

Novel by Aldous Huxley, 1894-1963.
Published 1932 by Harper & Bros., New York. © 1932 by Aldous Huxley.
(ML, 48; Ban., AC1)

MIRANDA SAID IT, in *The Tempest:* "How beauteous mankind is! O brave new world, that has such people in it!" She was speaking ironically, so her words were an apt title for Huxley's satirical Utopia. In a 1946 Foreword to a new printing, Huxley apologizes for not foreseeing the atomic age (as he might have; Wells did, before the turn of the century). But no one ever said *Brave New World* is good science fiction. It is enough to be good satire.

Chaps. 1–2. In the year 632 A.F. (After Ford) the D.H.C., or Director of Hatcheries and Conditioning, shows a group of students through the small (34-story) building. All human beings are hatched in bottles. The lower orders (Gammas, Deltas, and Epsilons) are made as much alike as possible by the Bokanovsky process of splitting eggs to

create as many as 96 identical-twin types. The Alphas and Betas are bred as individuals. The castes are carefully conditioned so that Alphas will have great intelligence, graded down to Epsilons of low intelligence to do the menial work. The highest are Alpha-Plus. Neo-Pavlovian conditioning trains the lower castes to dislike books, the beauty of nature, etc., but to consume manufactured goods and keep the economy going. While the children sleep they are conditioned by *hypnopaedia,* subliminal messages that among other effects make each caste contented with its station. "Mother" has become a very obscene word, "parent" and "father" only slightly less so. "Ford" is the god, used even in mild oaths such as "My Ford!"

Chap. 3. His fordship Mustapha Mond, Resident Controller for Western Europe, is in the garden where the children amuse themselves with sex play. He benignly talks to the students about ancient times when Ford and Shaw were on earth. In the Alpha Girls' Dressing Room LENINA CROWNE, a

nurse, shocks her friend FANNY CROWNE (no relation, but there are only 600 surnames on earth) because she, Lenina, is going out again with HENRY FOSTER; she has seen almost no one else for months, which outrages the dogma that "Everyone belongs to everyone else" and that men and women both should be as promiscuous as possible. Lenina partly excuses herself by saying she is considering a trip with BERNARD MARX, who is Alpha but unseemingly short and also, more or less secretly, sensitive about the blatant promiscuity around him. The great entertainment medium of the age is the "feelies," which are like the movies or talkies except that the spectators grasp knobs and feel every sensation portrayed on the screen.

Chap. 4. Bernard visits his friend HELMHOLTZ, one of the few men with whom he feels comfortable because Helmholtz, a writer, also disapproves of some of the dogmatic rules of living.

Chap. 5. 1. Foster and Lenina fly (everyone flies everywhere) to the standardized fun of dining and dancing, then go to bed together. 2. Bernard attends a meeting of a singing group to which he belongs, and after the singing beds conventionally with one of the girls, but finds little enjoyment in it.

Chap. 6. 1. Bernard has a preliminary date with Lenina, who talks only in clichés reflecting her conditioning and is at ease only when he brings himself to become conventionally amorous. 2. The Director calls Bernard in; when he hears that Bernard is taking a girl to the New Mexican Reservation where the Indians still live as in prehistoric times, the Director reminisces a bit about a trip he took there once with a Beta-Minus girl, who got lost and whom he left there; then warns Bernard about the reports he has been hearing of Bernard's unconventional behavior. 3. Bernard and Lenina fly to Santa Fe (6½ hours from London). In the Reservation are about 60,000 savages and half-breeds, retaining all the old customs: marriage, families, Christianity, totemism, extinct languages, wild beasts, infectious diseases, priests, and no air-conditioning.

Chaps. 7-9. In the Reservation Bernard and Lenina see a [Hopi] Indian snake dance where a young man is whipped, and they meet JOHN, a young white man who to their amazement wishes he had been the young man in the ceremony and also knows much from the civilized world though he has been brought up as an Indian. Bernard learns that John's mother, LINDA, was lost in the Reservation long ago (and undoubtedly was the Director's girl, making the Director John's father). Linda taught him much, but also he learned much of the Indian and Christian philosophy. Lenina, on their return to Santa Fe, loses herself in the pleasant sleep induced by the drug *soma*. Bernard calls the Controller and is authorized to bring back John and Linda for scientific study. John, wandering into the room where Lenina is sleeping, falls in love with her.

Chaps. 10-13. When Bernard returns he is in disgrace with the Director and slated for a post on a remote island, but he turns the tables and makes the Director a laughingstock by bringing in John, who emotionally greets the Director as "Father." John then becomes the lionized curiosity of the entire civilized world and Bernard and Lenina (separately) are important personages by reason of the reflected glory. All the important people want to attend their parties and have sexual intercourse with them. John still nurses romantic love for Lenina, which she cannot understand. When once he begins to reveal it, she is reassured by the sign of normality and starts to go to bed with him, but he throws her out of his room. Then John ("the savage") disgraces Bernard by refusing to appear at a party attended by various important personages who have come only to see John; and once again Bernard is a nobody.

Chaps. 14-17. Linda dies in the hospital and John amazes everyone with his show of grief. He almost goes berserk afterwards and tries to start a rebellion of Deltas. Bernard and Helmholtz, from genuine friendship, take him away. The Controller and John have a talk in which the Controller tries to explain why the present system is best, as the least of evils, but John is not convinced.

Chap. 18. Bernard and Helmholtz are sent away to assignments in isolated places. John retreats to an old lighthouse and sets up an Indian-style home with various observances of worship. Some wayfarer observes him and then sightseers by the thousands come in helicopters to watch, especially after reporters write about his strange actions in the London papers. So John hangs himself.

Bread and Wine

Novel by Ignazio Silone (Secondo Tranquilli, 1900–   ).
Published and © 1937 by Harper & Bros., New York. Translated from the Italian by Gwenda David and Eric Mosbacher.

A NOVEL of almost straight antifascist propaganda, *Bread and Wine* was written while its author was living in exile from Fascist Italy. Silone's preoccupation with his message did not reduce the quality of the novel, which is generally considered a major work and his best. The English title is a literal rendering of the Italian, *Pano e vino*.

Chaps. 1-3. Old Don BENEDETTO, priest of the Italian village of Rocca, celebrates his 75th birthday with some of his former students. Only three have come, for many have died or been alienated by the priest's outspoken ways in the cause of liberty. One asks who was his favorite pupil and he replies PIETRO SPINA. There is a silence, for Spina has been expelled from Mussolini's Italy for championing the cause of the oppressed and now there is a rumor that he has returned surreptitiously.

One morning, Dr. NUNZIO SACCA, a classmate of Spina's, is called to the bedside of a sick man. He suspects it is the political agitator, Spina, and is fearful about attending him. When he finds Spina a prematurely old man (having disfigured his face with iodine), he is ashamed and not only heals him but obtains the clothes of a priest for his use in escaping and also chooses a name, Don PAOLO SPADA, for Spina to use in his disguise. Spina goes back to Fossa, the region of his birth, and stays at the Girasole Hotel. The next morning he is called to the bedside of a young girl, BIANCHINA GIRASOLE, who is thought to be dying as a result of a self abortion. He comforts her—uneasily—in his guise of a priest and prepares to leave the region to search for members of his party.

Chaps. 4-7. In Pietrasecca, Spina as Don Paolo rests and begins the recuperation necessary to go on his way to free the oppressed. He has great trouble avoiding priestly duties among the women of the valley. One morning Bianchina of Fossa appears to see

John sees Lenina asleep and falls in love with her

him and tells him she is sure he is a saint for having saved her life. Her aunt has thrown her out, and having no place to go she puts her problems at his feet. A school-friend of hers, CRISTINA COLAMARTINI, who wishes to become a nun, lives nearby and gives her shelter. ALBERTO, Cristina's brother, falls in love with Bianchina and they go to live in an old deserted house of the Colamartinis without the benefit of marriage. Cristina comes often to see Don Paolo and they discuss liberty and God.

Don Paolo begins to go more among the peasants. There is a wild, destructive storm and he goes with the parish priest to see if Alberto and Bianchina are alive in their deserted house. They are alive but starving and with only a forlorn hope of marrying. Don Paolo speaks to Alberto's father, Don PASQUALE, in the hope of obtaining his consent. Before Pasquale can answer, Cristina, with her peasant pride, refuses the marriage because a Colamartini would lose caste by marrying a lowly Girasole. Don Paolo is appalled by Cristina's hardness and loses his respect for her. As Don Paolo's health improves, he goes more among the peasants and enters into their daily lives and conversations. It soon becomes apparent to him that he will not have success here in turning their minds toward his cause of liberty, for their intellects are too limited. He decides to leave the valley.

Don Paolo goes back to Fossa and begins his search for those interested in bringing about the revolution against Fascism. He feels that he is beginning to lay his cornerstone when he comes across Bianchina and Alberto again. They bring a young friend, POMPEO, to meet Don Paolo. Pompeo wholeheartedly joins in their ideas and plans and becomes one of them.

Chaps. 8–10. In Rome, where Don Paolo next goes, the clerical garb is cast aside and again Spina emerges. He meets ROMEO, his main contact with the anti-Fascists. Spina is distressed at the air of despair in the great city. He fights the futility of Romeo, who feels they are fighting a lost cause. Spina now believes that words alone are of no value, but that they must show others the way by living the deeds of which they speak. He is disillusioned when students demonstrate in favor of the Ethiopian war. He leaves Rome and returns to the Hotel Girasole again as the priest, Don Paolo. He can hardly believe the enthusiasm throughout the countryside for the victory over Ethiopia. His days are spent writing anti-war slogans on every available wall. His heart is broken when he discovers that Pompeo, his early convert, has been captivated by the war hysteria and has enlisted to fight. The people of the valley, steeped in victory, are furious with the writings on the walls but Don Paolo's identity as the instigator is kept secret by Bianchina's pleas to Pompeo, who knows of his activity.

Chaps. 10–12. Don Paolo as himself, Spina, goes to visit his old teacher, Don Benedetto. They find that their thoughts and ideals are similar and they determine not to compromise them in any way. Don Benedetto exhorts Cristina to be of aid to Don Paolo and to find a more tolerant attitude in her feelings toward him. The peasants are enraged at the candid statements of the old priest. They fear he will bring harm to their village. He is poisoned when, offering Mass, he drinks the sacramental wine.

Don Paolo has given Bianchina money to go to Rome and she sends word to him that Romeo has been placed under arrest. He goes to Rome and finds that Bianchina is now a prostitute but she protests her great and pure affection for the priest, Don Paolo, whom she considered a saint. Spina now takes over all Romeo's revolutionary activities in Rome and soon finds that the situation is hopeless, with exposure imminent. He rushes back to the valley to destroy all the evidence he hid there during his recuperation period. While he is doing this he receives a warning that his true identity has been discovered and he is about to be arrested. He flees to the snow-covered mountains, hoping to lose his pursuers in the coming blizzard. Hearing of his plight, Cristina, true to her promise to the dead Don Benedetto, hurries to gather food and warm clothes and starts to follow his tracks to help him escape. The snow mists become blinding and she loses her way. Realizing that she is hopelessly lost and that night has fallen, she knows that she will not survive and with religious fervor she sinks slowly to her knees and makes the sign of the cross as she waits for certain death from the wolves.

The Bride of Lammermoor

Novel by Sir Walter Scott, 1771–1832. Published 1819.

WHEN SCOTT WROTE THIS NOVEL he was still using the pseudonym Waverley; and his creation "Waverley" had become the world's most popular novelist. *The Bride of Lammermoor* is typical of the Waverley novels, neither better nor worse than the others. Its more lasting fame is due to the Donizetti opera *Lucia di Lammermoor,* based on it.

Chaps. 1–2. An impoverished artist who traveled in the Lammermoor section of Scotland came upon a strange legend, notes of which he has given to the writer of this tale. Out of these notes comes the story of the bride of Lammermoor.

The impoverished noble family of Ravenswood is deposed from its ancestral castle by a man appointed "King's Keeper" at the time when James VI of Scotland left to become James I of England. The new Keeper is Sir WILLIAM ASHTON. He is the father of LUCY ASHTON, a beautiful and sensitive young woman of 19. His wife, Lady Ashton, is a domineering, determined matron who brooks no insubordination from anyone, including her husband. The Ashtons are Presbyterians and are rigidly opposed to the Church of England. When Lord Ravenswood (who has been a bitter enemy toward Ashton) dies, his Church of England burial service is interrupted by an official sent by Ashton's authority to stop it. EDGAR RAVENSWOOD, now Master of Ravenswood, holds the officer off with a sword so that his father's remains may be properly interred.

Chaps. 3–5. Lucy Ashton takes her father for a walk to see old BLIND ALICE, a former servitor of the Ravenswoods. Blind Alice is possessed of acute perceptions. She warns Sir William that a Ravenswood means great danger to him, and Sir William is impressed by the warning, having heard of the legend concerning Ravenswood vengeance in the past. He is preoccupied on the homeward walk and is quite unprepared when one of the wild cattle that roam the vicinity charges him and Lucy. A shot from an unknown source saves them, and Lucy faints. The young man who fired the shot remains with Lucy as her father goes to seek help. It is Edgar, as Sir William learns on his return. Sir William then alters his report of Edgar's offense at his father's funeral.

Chaps. 6–11. In a tavern not far from the dreary tower where Edgar Ravenswood now lives, two men are awaiting him. They are Captain CRAIGENGELT, a soldier of fortune, and Mr. HAYSON OF BUCKLAW, an impoverished young man whose only hope of wealth is through an inheritance from his aunt, Lady GIRNINGTON. With Ravenswood, they had expected to leave for France and commissions in the French army. Ravenswood appears and tell them he has decided not to go. Craigengelt is angry and Bucklaw offended. In the resulting conversation Bucklaw considers himself insulted.

Consulting Blind Alice

He follows Ravenswood and they have a brief duel: Ravenswood wins easily and spares Bucklaw's life. This cements their friendship and Bucklaw goes to Wolf's Head, Ravenswood's castle, for refuge; for Craigengelt has been arrested for his political activity and it is probable that Bucklaw is in danger. While he is at the tower there is a festive hunt. Ravenswood attends, as do a young lady and her father, both masked, as is the custom. When a violent thunderstorm breaks out, the elderly man asks for shelter and Ravenswood takes them to the tower. He learns that his guests are Lucy Ashton and her father, Sir William, the sworn enemies of the House of Ravenswood. The tense situation is relieved by the ridiculous pretenses of CALEB BALDERSTONE, the old butler of the Ravenswoods, who wails that the storm has destroyed the sumptuous repast they might have had. He will never admit to anyone that a Ravenswood is suffering from poverty.

Chaps. 12–18. Caleb goes to the hamlet of Wolf's Hope to obtain food and there meets LOCKHARD, Sir William's servant. At length—through some considerable chicanery—he has supplies for a meal and returns to the tower. The news that Sir William is at Wolf's Crag astounds the people, and Caleb has implied a possible romance between Ravenswood and Miss Ashton. Back at the tower, a fine meal is enjoyed, and all retire for the night, but not until Sir William has made some overtures of friendship toward Ravenswood. Edgar is puzzled, but is attracted to Lucy. Sir William is aware that there may be some political changes soon that would make it advantageous to him to have Ravenswood's friendship. The time soon comes when the Ashtons must return to Ravenswood and Edgar decides to go with them to return their visit. Caleb is horrified and reminds Edgar of the prophecy concerning the last Laird of Ravenswood. The old verse says that the last Laird will win a dead maiden to be his bride, and will disappear then in the quicksand that is named after the water sprite, Kelpie. Edgar scoffs, and makes the journey. Lucy's younger brother HENRY interjects an ominous note when he refuses fearfully to approach Edgar when introduced. He declares to his sister that Edgar is the same man who is pictured in an old portrait of Sir Malise of Ravenswood—famous for dealing murderous vengeance upon his enemies.

Chaps. 19–26. The visit of Edgar is pleasant and free of contention. Lucy takes him to visit old Blind Alice, who warns him, privately, that only ill can come of his staying at Ravenswood. She tells him that without question Lucy loves him, but that this can never be good for either of them. Edgar is to meet Lucy at the Mermaiden's Well, which according to legend has always been a fatal spot for Ravenswoods. At the well Edgar finds Lucy alone, Henry having gone off to wander through the woodlands. Soon his love and hers are openly avowed, and they pledge their troth in a sacred oath, commemorated by breaking a thin gold coin in two pieces, one of which each would keep until their marriage. Lucy ties hers on a ribbon about her neck. When Sir William tells Edgar that the Marquis of A——, Edgar's kinsman and politically differing from Sir William, is about to pay a visit to Ravenswood, Edgar accepts his host's invitation to remain longer. Bucklaw, who by now has inherited both his aunt's fortune and the title of Laird, disapproves of the friendly connection between Ashton and Ravenswood. He has reason to suppose that his own suit for Lucy Ashton's hand is welcome, and Ravenswood's, if it exists, is not. Lady Ashton is the reason for this supposition, and Lady Ashton will as ever make all important family decisions. Craigengelt calls on Lady Ashton, who is in Edinburgh, and insidiously lets it be known that Edgar has been visiting a considerable time at Ravenswood and that a marriage is rumored. Lady Ashton seethes in fury and hastens to get home. The result is a near-race between her coach and the coach of the Marquis, which she concedes at the last moment, so that the noble guest enters the gate first. Inside, there is confusion and trepidation. Lady Ashton demands that her husband evict Ravenswood, which he refuses to do. She herself then writes him a note, and he leaves immediately. He rides toward the house of old Blind Alice, and as he approaches the Mermaiden's Fountain along the way, he sees Blind Alice—or her apparition—standing before him, silently mouthing words he cannot make out. Proceeding to the hut, he finds that Blind Alice has died. Shortly thereafter Edgar meets the Marquis and learns that there is a mission for him in a foreign land. They plan to go to Wolf's Crag, and a message is sent ahead to Caleb. As they approach the tower, a tremendous glow fills the sky. The tower is afire. Caleb meets them and conducts them to the inn at Wolf's Hope, where he has contrived to establish the notion that the Marquis is about to select those who will receive lucrative and dignified offices when the political picture clarifies. The Marquis

Lucy is seen holding a dagger

and Edgar are received and treated royally. Ravenswood elicits from Caleb the information that he set the fire to prevent the arrival of the Marquis in a castle lacking in food, furnishings, and comfort. The tower itself did not burn, only some tinder.

Chaps. 27–32. Edgar and the Marquis reach Edinburgh without incident and go to the nobleman's house. Political events put the Marquis in power and Sir William out of favor. A letter from Edgar to Lady Ashton elicits a scathing reply, one to Sir William is answered in most ambiguous legal terms, and one to Lucy is answered merely by a note that affirms her fidelity but pleads the danger of further communication for the present. Bucklaw still believes that his suit is favored by Lady Ashton and attributes Lucy's lack of eagerness to her vow to Edgar, which she cannot in good conscience break. Her letters to Edgar, and Edgar's to her, are intercepted by her mother and burned. Lucy thinks Edgar has not tried to communicate with her but refuses to violate her oath until he releases her. Even the intervention of the local minister finds her obdurate, but he persuades her that a reasonable length of time without a reply would constitute a release by implication and he promises that nothing will interfere with the delivery of at least one letter. The date approaches when the official agreements for Lucy's marriage to the Laird of Bucklaw are to be signed. Lady Ashton has hired the services of one known locally as a witch, to influence the mind of her daughter. Lucy suffers, and gradually her mental condition becomes intolerable. Still no answer comes to her last letter to Edgar. Finally she can wait no longer; the day arrives and Lucy signs. No sooner have the contracts been completed than there is a sound of hoofbeats, and Lucy cries aloud that Edgar has come.

Chaps. 33–35. Edgar asks Lucy to tell him if the handwriting in a letter he carries is hers. The letter was dictated by Lady Ashton and expresses nothing of Lucy's feelings, but she must admit that it is her hand. Edgar gives her his half of the coin and releases her from her oath. He departs. Four days later, the wedding takes place. While the guests are celebrating, horrible screams come from the bridal apartment. Bucklaw is found unconscious and bleeding from a dozen wounds; Lucy is covered with blood, and in her hand is a dagger. She is completely mad and dies without recovering her sanity. On the challenge of Colonel DOUGLAS ASHTON, Lucy's elder brother, Edgar agrees to meet him in a duel. At dawn on the day set, Edgar rides toward the point of rendezvous. The Colonel sees him approach and Caleb, watching from Wolf's Crag, sees him go forth. He disappears from the sight of both watchers, and when they seek him there is no trace. The prophecy of long ago has been fulfilled. Edgar, the last Laird of Ravenswood, has "stabled his horse in the Kelpie's flow." He has sunk in the quicksand.

Brideshead Revisited

Novel by Evelyn Waugh, 1903-1966. Published 1945 by Little, Brown & Co., Boston. © 1944, 1945 by Evelyn Waugh. (Dell, D163)

ANYONE WHO HAS KNOWN the younger upper classes of London after either World War can testify that Evelyn Waugh did not overpaint their wildness, their excesses, for they could hardly be overpainted. In fact, in *Brideshead Revisited* Waugh was quite moderate. As a novel it is great. When all the arguments about Waugh's other works are ended, *Brideshead Revisited* will remain to testify that the man could write. The ambivalence produced by Catholicism in Englishmen, a favorite theme of Waugh's, is accented in this novel.

Prologue. The entire story is told in the first person by Captain CHARLES RYDER. During World War II Ryder, a captain in the (British) Reserves, at 39 old for a captain, moves his company with the rest of the regiment to a new billet in England. He is preoccupied with military matters—the unreasonable new colonel; the untrained young lieutenant, HOOPER. Then the regiment arrives and he finds that their new place is the estate Brideshead; and his whole life is recalled to his memory.

Book I. Chap. 1. Charles went to Oxford in 1923, when he was not quite 19. His father, who had not noticed the world very much since Charles' mother died, and who lived alone with Charles in a large house in London and confined his attention to scholarly pursuits, gave Charles £550 and little advice. Charles got good advice from his Oxonian cousin JASPER but nevertheless found himself drawn into a group of aesthetes, dissolute and in some cases degenerate, of whom Jasper and the solid Oxford community disapproved. One was ANTHONY BLANCHE, world-traveled scion of a rich South American family, a brilliant (though often outrageous) conversationalist despite his slight stutter. The principal one was Lord SEBASTIAN FLYTE, younger son of the Marquis of MARCHMAIN, whose houses were Marchmain House ("Marchers") in London and Brideshead (a former tremendous castle that had been moved physically more than 100 years before to a new location nearby). The Marchmains were very rich. Sebastian affected to make his best friend and confidant a Teddy-bear that he called ALOYSIUS. Sebastian took Charles one day to Brideshead to see his old nurse, NANNY HAWKINS. Charles discovered that Sebastian did not like his family, and though his sister JULIA—about a year older—was there, Charles did not meet her.

Chaps. 2-4. Despite Jasper's disapproval, Charles and Sebastian became inseparable friends. Like the rest of their group they drank too much—Charles from youthful unrest but Sebastian because he was an incipient alcoholic. Charles discovered that Lord and Lady Marchmain were separated, Marchmain living in Italy with his mistress. They were Catholics, Marchmain having become one to marry Lady Marchmain, who was very devout and was considered saintly. Lord BRIDESHEAD (by his familiars called BRIDEY), the elder son, was unlike Sebastian, very conservative and very Catholic. When Charles returned home for the summer his father, disliking having his solitude disturbed, made his life unpleasant and Charles was glad when Sebastian sent a telegram saying he had been seriously injured and asking Charles to come at once. Charles found that the injury was minor and Sebastian just wanted company, but he spent the rest of the summer with Sebastian. He briefly met the beautiful Julia and saw much of the younger sister, 12-year-old CORDELIA, who like Bridey was very devout. Charles became almost a member of the family to the servants, headed by WILCOX, the butler. Then Sebastian and Charles visited Lord Marchmain in Venice. Marchmain's mistress, CARA, a middle-aged woman who was accepted in good society, was very outspoken and told Charles that Marchmain did not really love her, his principal emotion being his hatred of his wife.

Chap. 5. In the new term at Oxford, Anthony Blanche did not return, the former group of aesthetes was broken up, and usually Charles and Sebastian had only each other's company. Charles met Lady Marchmain when she visited Oxford briefly, trying to arrange for Sebastian to live with Monsignor BELL and redeem himself for the escapades that had got him in trouble at Oxford. Charles was struck by Lady Marchmain's beauty and charm, which however did not captivate him as much as most. Julia also visited Oxford, bringing REX MOTTRAM, a rich Canadian and now an M.P. Charles, Sebastian, and an Oxford friend, Viscount "Boy" MULCASTER, went to a party given by Rex in London and later were arrested for drunkenness. The result was small fines but unpleasant publicity and a black mark at Oxford. At Brideshead, Sebastian's drinking disturbed his family. Sebastian was unwilling to move in with Monsignor Bell and Oxford would not have him otherwise, so he was sent abroad with his Oxford tutor, a don, Mr. SAMGRASS.

Chap. 6. Charles went to Brideshead for Christmas. Sebastian and Samgrass were back from their tour. Sebastian persisted in drinking, and when Lady Marchmain learned that Charles had lent him money she was vigorous in her condemnation and Charles left. Cordelia wrote him a loving letter saying that she too was in disgrace for stealing Wilcox's keys and giving Sebastian whiskey. Charles saw Rex in London and learned that Rex and Julia would probably marry and that the Marchmains were living far beyond their means.

Chap. 7. A digression on information about Julia that Charles learned from Julia much later: Rex's political career had been furthered by his being a favorite lover of the influential Mrs. BRENDA CHAMPION, but he knew the proper kind of wife was necessary and was determined to marry Julia. In the meantime Julia fell in love with him. Rex was totally pliable about family conditions—becoming a Catholic, marriage settlement, etc.—treating it all as unimportant. Just before the wedding, Bridey discovered that Rex had been married and divorced. Rex could not understand how this made the marriage seem impossible to the Catholic family; but when they persisted, he appealed to Lord Marchmain, who authorized a Protestant wedding, being sure this would displease his wife. They were married without the family present. Then Julia discovered that Rex was not quite a complete human being—unaware of everything except power, money and politics (and also he continued his affair with Brenda Champion).

Chap. 8. Instead of continuing at Oxford, Charles studied art in Paris. He returned to London for the general strike of 1926, falsely thinking it an emergency in which his help would be needed. Julia told him Lady Marchmain was dying and wanted to see Sebastian, who was living in degradation in Morocco. Charles volunteered to get him and went to Fez, where he found Sebastian in the hospital, temporarily, as a result of his alcoholism, but regularly living with a German émigré, KURT. Sebastian found some solace in waiting on Kurt and being mistreated by him. Charles returned to London, where Bridey asked him to make some paintings of Marchers (which was to be torn down); these paintings were the start of Charles' reputation as an artist. While painting he saw Cordelia, now 15, and they talked about why Lady Marchmain, who had died, had been so loved by all others but had failed to be loved by her husband and children.

Book II. Chaps. 1-2. Ten years later, Charles was an established artist. Finishing a painting trip of about two years in Central America, he was joined in New York by his wife, Lady CELIA, sister of Mulcaster. They had been married almost ten years and had two children, the second of whom Charles had never seen. He had not been happy in marriage, though his wife was always very dutiful (except for her infidelities). On the ship taking them to Europe Julia was also a passenger. She was still married to Rex but her trip to America was to chase another man she believed she loved but found out she did not. On the ship a storm made most of the passengers seasick but not Charles and Julia, who became intimate for the first time and discovered they were in love. In London Celia continued to be a helpful wife, working to make Charles' exhibition a success (as it was). Anthony showed up at it and he and Charles briefly renewed their acquaintanceship. Charles refused to go home with Celia, even to see the daughter he had never seen. Instead he "visited" Julia and Rex at Brideshead, and stayed there.

Chaps. 3–4. Bridey came to Brideshead and told Julia and Charles that he was going to marry a widow, Mrs. BERYL MUSPRATT, whom he met because her husband, like Bridey, collected match boxes. Beryl, a Catholic of course and very proper, would not visit Brideshead while Charles and Julia were there in their sinful relationship; Julia was not only offended but disturbed. Charles and Julia both decided to get divorces so they could marry. Rex was puzzled at the necessity; he did not object to their present relationship. Cordelia, now 26, had been nursing in Spain (where the Civil War was on). She came back for the wedding and told what had happened to Sebastian: Kurt went back to Germany and pretended to be an enthusiastic Nazi. Sebastian followed him and finally convinced him that he did not like it and should escape; but Kurt was caught. Sebastian then retired to a monastery in Tunis, back to the faith.

Chap. 5. Lord Marchmain came back to Brideshead to die. He had a bad heart. Cara was with him. A compromise had to be worked out between Wilcox and Marchmain's chief servant, PLENDER; both were made *grooms of the household,* with equal rank. Bridey, Beryl and Cordelia all wanted Marchmain to have final rites, when the time came, from Father MACKAY; Marchmain at first objected and Charles and Julia fought about it, Charles thinking the priest should not be forced on Marchmain. Marchmain decided not to leave Brideshead to Bridey, largely because he disliked Beryl so much. Marchmain's impending death made Julia feel more and more guilty about her own departure from the faith, of which she was reminded by her father's case. Marchmain finally died, and almost as he died, though he was unable to speak or nod, he managed to make the sign of the cross. After his death, Julia told Charles she could never marry him; it was an act of penance on her part. It was no surprise to him, for he had seen it coming during the preceding weeks. He told her he hoped her heart would break, but that he understood.

Epilogue. So the reminiscence ends. Charles, the reserve captain, is with his troops at Brideshead. Lady Julia, the owner, is abroad, and so is her sister Cordelia, but Charles sees Nanny Hawkins. She is impressed by the fact that Rex Mottram is now a cabinet minister and many of the friends he used to bring up are similarly important in the government. Charles goes about his duties.

The Bridge of San Luis Rey

Novel by Thornton Wilder, 1879–

Published 1927. © 1928 by A. & C. Boni, Inc. (PB, PL 36)

THORNTON WILDER made his first great success with *The Bridge of San Luis Rey.* It is very short, not 35,000 words—hardly a novel at all by most standards—but it ranks with such magnificent miniatures as *A Christmas Carol* and *Of Mice and Men.* It won a Pulitzer Prize.

Part I. On July 20, 1714, the Bridge of San Luis Rey in Peru suddenly collapsed and five persons dropped to their deaths in the deep gorge below. The bridge was old and famous, and to those who used it it was unthinkable that the bridge could ever collapse. The people of Peru considered the disaster an act of God. One person, Brother JUNIPER, determined to find out if possible why those particular five people were selected by God for death at that particular moment. He investigated the life of each of the five.

Part II. The Marquesa de Montemayor was one of those thrown to their deaths. Today the letters of Doña MARIA, Marquesa DE MONTEMAYOR, are classics of Spanish literature, but at that time Brother Juniper had a difficult research. He learned that she had been an ugly, unprepossessing child, the despair of her mother. To compensate for her homeliness and her habit of stuttering, her mother decked her in costly jewels. Doña Maria was very unhappy. She resolved never to marry but was eventually forced into marriage with an impoverished nobleman and bore him an exquisite daughter, Doña CLARA. The girl was like her father, cold and selfish, and from an early age was contemptuous of her mother. The Marquesa, however, formed an almost worshipful love for her daughter. Their relationship was never pleasant. At last Doña Clara accepted a proposal of marriage that took her to

Spain. The Marquesa started her immortal letter-writing at this time. She combed the city for anecdotes and sketches. Doña Clara scarcely glanced at the painstakingly penned epistles, but her husband delighted in them.

In her loneliness, the Marquesa took to drink and remained in a semi-conscious state for the greater part of each month, sobering herself only to produce one of her elaborate letters. As a companion she had taken in an orphan girl named PEPITA, whose life she made miserable with her selfishness and bitterness.

When news came that Doña Clara was to have a child, the old Marquesa began using all manner of magic charms to help her daughter and to protect the unborn child. One of these observances was a visit to a shrine across the famous Bridge of San Luis Rey from Lima. On this journey she read a letter that little Pepita had written to the Abbess of the convent where she had been reared. The girl's misery and bravery touched the Marquesa as nothing else ever had. The masterpiece of all of her letters was written then. In this letter, she poured out her heart with love—but a truly selfless love in this case. Two days later, she and Pepita died in the collapse of the bridge.

Part III. Twin baby boys were left in the foundling basket at the convent at Santa Maria Rosa de las Rosas. The nuns named them Manuel and Esteban and brought them up. No one ever devised a method of telling one brother from the other. They lived apart from the world, close to each other but to no one else. They even devised a secret language in which they spoke when alone. At one time a professor and priest determined to probe into their language and discover its source; he failed.

The boys worked at many different jobs. The education the nuns had given them made it possible for them to become scribes and write letters for the more ignorant people. They also wrote theater programs. One day Manuel was asked to write a letter for a beautiful and popular actress in town, LA PERICHOLE. He fell in love with her, creating for the first time a barrier between him-

Julia was a passenger on the ship

self and his brother. Esteban assured Manuel that he need not be troubled about having another love; Manuel tried to pretend that he cared nothing for La Perichole. He wrote letters for her to her various lovers, which made him violently angry. When he cut his leg and developed blood poisoning, his delirium revealed that he did love her. Manuel died. Esteban pretended that it was he and not his brother who died. He took Manuel's name and lived an aimless, deranged life. He accepted a job aboard a ship setting forth on a world trip; on the way he had to cross the Bridge of San Luis Rey and went down with it.

Part IV. Uncle Pio had encountered a young girl singing in a tavern, long ago when he first came to Peru, and had groomed and coached her until she became one of the most famous names in the country—La Perichole, the great actress. She was beautiful and gay and the toast of Peruvian gallants. She had many love affairs, as Manuel well knew—and resented—but the one that most influenced her was with the viceroy, during which time she decided loftily that the stage was unfit for one of her station and withdrew from such a life. All was well until she contracted smallpox and lost her beauty. She withdrew to a small farm and refused even to see Uncle Pio, but at length he tricked her into opening the door by engaging the services of a young girl for whom he felt sure the door would be opened. He begged her to let him take Jaime, her illegitimate son, away so that he might be educated as a gentleman, and at length she agreed. Like the others, Pio and Jaime set out to cross the Bridge of San Luis Rey, and like the others they fell to their deaths.

Part V. Long after the mass funeral for the victims, events were still evolving out of the accident. Brother Juniper was accused of heresy in attempting to interpret the will of God, and after a trial with the usual amount of bigotry and superstition he was sentenced to be burned at the stake. He tried to interpret the will of God in this, still convinced that everything happens when it does as an act of God. La Perichole abandoned her resentment over her lost beauty and became a friend of the Abbess of the Convent. Doña Clara, remorseful, also became the Abbess's friend.

The Brothers Karamazov

Novel by Fedor Mikhailovich Dostoevski, 1821–1881.
Published 1880. Translated from the Russian by Constance Garnett. (ML, G36 & T12; NAL, T1488)

SEVERAL OF Dostoevski's novels have been nominated as his greatest, but despite its defects in novel-construction and literary finesse *The Brothers Karamazov*, his last work, should have unchallenged position also as his best. Neither Dostoevski nor any other novelist ever explored the souls of his characters so completely as Dostoevski did in this novel, traveling the full range from the depths of depravity to the heights of exaltation, from the meanness to the nobility of which the ambivalent human spirit is capable. The characters are Russian and their emotions may seem unreal or exaggerated to English-language readers, but these readers would be better advised to accept the characters as the novelist portrays them. *The Brothers* is a long novel, overlong in fact; it is one of those Somerset Maugham named as the world's greatest but said were candidates for "artful skipping." Also enjoyment of *The Brothers* in English is lessened by the fact that there is only one translation and it is a very poorly written one, though it may be quite faithful in sense. There is an excellent revision of the Garnett translation by Princess Alexandra Kropotkin, but it is published only in a "cut" version.

Part I. Book I. 1–4. FYODOR PAVLOVITCH KARAMAZOV is a well-to-do landowner but known as a dissolute man, a toady in his youth, a man who will clown to make an impression. Somehow he managed to marry a beautiful heiress but she ran away, leaving her 3-year-old son DMITRI (MITYA), who is now 27. By his second wife, whom he abused, and who became insane and died, Fyodor has two other sons, IVAN, who is 23, and ALEXEY (ALYOSHA), who is 20 and has recently entered the monastery to study and perhaps become a monk. Mitya has been a cavalry officer. Ivan is studious, intellectual. Alyosha loves everyone and everyone loves him. Mitya and Ivan hate their father—Ivan for mistreating his mother, and Mitya for all but abandoning him and for having stolen the fortune his mother left him. Mitya is living in lodgings, not at home, and is all but penniless. **5.** It is arranged for all four Karamazovs, along with a friend, PETER MIÜSOV, to visit the elder of the monastery, the saintly Father ZOSSIMA, to seek reconciliation.

Book II. 1–2. They assemble at Father Zossima's cell. Fyodor, acting the buffoon, exaggerates his piety. **3–4.** They wait while Father Zossima goes to see other visitors who have come for his blessing. Among these are the young, wealthy widow Mme. HOHLAKOV and her crippled 14-year-old daughter LISE. (Both are just a bit unbalanced mentally.) Mme. Hohlakov gives Alyosha a message that KATERINA IVANOVNA (a rich, beautiful young woman who is ostensibly engaged to Mitya), wants Alyosha to come to see her. Lise has a crush on Alyosha. **5–8.** The Karamazovs' interview with Father Zossima fails, ending in a loud quarrel between Mitya and his father. The principal issue between them is a woman, an "enchantress" (named AGRAFENA ALEXANDROVNA and nicknamed GRUSHENKA), whom apparently both want. RAKITIN, a fellow-student of Alyosha's who is poor and jealous of the Karamazovs' wealth, chides Alyosha on the sensuality of the Karamazovs—for example Mitya, who could marry Katerina and be rich, but instead pursues Grushenka.

Book III. 1–2. The Karamazovs' big house is served by three servants: GRIGORY, old, faithful, honest; his wife MARFA; and a young man, SMERDYAKOV ("the stinking one"), who is generally supposed to be the illegitimate son of Fyodor and a half-witted girl of the town. **3–4.** Alyosha starts out to call on Katerina. He encounters Mitya. In

Uncle Pio encountered the girl when she was singing in a tavern

112

a long conversation, Mitya tells him the history of his relationship with Katerina. Mitya was a young officer; Katerina, the colonel's daughter, was aloof to him. The colonel became 4,500 rubles short in his accounts and was threatened with disgrace. Mitya told Katerina's sister he would supply the money if Katerina came to him. Katerina came, ready to sacrifice herself; but Mitya, after humiliating her with words only, gave her the money and would not touch her. Soon afterward they became betrothed. Now she wants to marry him—in gratitude, Mitya believes; Mitya says she is an angel, he is unworthy of her, and he thinks she should marry Ivan, who loves her. **5.** Mitya also reveals that he owes Katerina 3,000 rubles that he virtually stole from her, and he is desperate to repay it and save his honor. Yet his father, who stole most of his fortune, will not give him even that. Instead, Fyodor keeps 3,000 rubles in an envelope for Grushenka if she will come to him. Mitya sends Alyosha on to Katerina to "give her his compliments"—in effect, break his engagement to her. **6–8.** Alyosha first goes home to dinner, at which Fyodor carouses and makes outrageous and irreverent assertions. **9.** Suddenly Mitya rushes in wildly; he has a false notion that Grushenka has come to see Fyodor. Fyodor is afraid for his life, but Mitya leaves. **10.** Alyosha calls on Katerina. She says Mitya owes her nothing; also, that Grushenka (whom she calls an "angel") has promised to give Mitya up. Katerina brings into the room Grushenka herself, who was calling on her when Alyosha arrived. Grushenka changes completely, mocks Katerina, says she was only fooling and will take Mitya again if she wishes. She reveals also that Mitya has told her about Katerina's first visit to him. Katerina becomes like a tigress and throws Grushenka out. **11.** Mitya confesses to Alyosha that he did dishonorably tell Grushenka that secret; he calls himself a scoundrel. Alyosha receives a love letter from Lise insisting that he come to see her.

Part II. Book IV. 1–2. Alyosha returns to the monastery, then goes to his father's house, where he asks his father to give Mitya the 3,000 rubles. Fyodor refuses, fearing that Mitya will use the money to buy Grushenka. **3.** On the street Alyosha sees a group of schoolboys, about 10 or 11, defied by a lone schoolboy of 9; they are throwing stones at one another. He stops them but the lone boy is unfriendly to him too and bites him. **4–5.** At Mme. Hohlakov's Alyosha finds both Katerina and Ivan. He can tell they are in love with each other, but Katerina will not relinquish her self-imposed obligation to Mitya. Katerina asks Alyosha to take 200 rubles from her to an improvised captain whom Mitya insulted. **6–7.** Now Alyosha understands why the boy bit him—the boy is the son of this Captain NICOLAY SNEGIRYOV—and the boy fights the other boys because they tease him about the captain's beard, which Mitya pulled. Alyosha offers the captain the money; he first takes it, then is revolted by shame and gives it back.

Book V. 1. Alyosha goes to see Lise. Mme. Hohlakov tells him Katerina had hysterics after they left and is still delirious. **2–5.** Going home, Alyosha enters through the back alley and the summer house, where Smerdyakov is playing his guitar to a neighboring girl. Inside, Alyosha has a long talk with Ivan, who expounds on the conflict of faith (Christian) and natural skepticism. **6–7.** Smerdyakov speaks very cryptically to Ivan, advising that he be out of town for a while and adding that "a word to the wise is sufficient." Ivan does not understand, but the implication is that this will give him an alibi while Mitya kills his father.

Book VI. 1–3. Father Zossima is dying. Alyosha has written down notes on his life, constituting a fairly long autobiography: Zossima was born of a good family. His father died and his mother put him in a cadet corps. He lived the usual wild life and became involved in a duel. His adversary fired first and wounded him slightly; then Zossima, over whom a complete change of heart had come, threw his pistol away. A man confessed to him an old murder for which he could never be caught but which he was impelled by conscience to confess publicly; however, all thought him merely mad. Father Zossima then expresses his faith and exhorts others to faith, good works, and prayer.

Part III. Book VII. 1–3. After Father Zossima's funeral, Rakitin asks Alyosha to go to Grushenka's with him and Alyosha goes. He discovers that Grushenka has promised to pay Rakitin if he would bring Alyosha to her. Grushenka expresses love (the pure kind) for Alyosha. Grushenka was deserted by her first love (a Polish officer) and was befriended by a very rich old merchant, KUZMA SAMSONOV, who has guided her investments so well that she is now financially secure. Grushenka tells Alyosha that she has seen Mitya lately only because she is afraid of his violence if she does not. Her officer, after several years, has reappeared and summoned her and she is joyously going to him.

Book VIII. 1–3. Mitya, desperate for the 3,000 rubles, has been to Samsonov to try to borrow against the inheritance he expects he will legally recover from his father. Samsonov, who actually is unfriendly, sends Mitya on a trip to see a peasant who has a woodland to sell, on which a large profit can be made. Mitya finds it is a wild goose chase. He returns and tries to borrow from Mme. Hohlakov, who leads him on with apparent promises but in the end merely advises him to go off gold-prospecting. Half-mad by this time, Mitya goes by Grushenka's, makes threatening remarks when he finds she is not at home, and dashes off to his father's house. **4–5.** Grigory tries to stop Mitya, who seizes a brass pestle and knocks the old man out, then rushes inside. Later Mitya returns to Grushenka's. His hands are bloody. Grushenka's terrified maid, FENYA, tells him Grushenka has gone to Mokroe to meet "her officer." With a bundle of 100-ruble notes in his hands, Mitya goes to PETER PERHOTIN, a young official, to redeem a pair of dueling pistols on which Perhotin lent

him money. Then Mitya buys a load of champagne and fine foods, hires an expensive carriage, and sets off for Mokroe. **6–8.** After a wild ride, Mitya arrives at the inn at Mokroe and finds Grushenka with the Polish officer, Pan (Mr., or Sir) MUSSYALOVITCH, and Pan VRUBLEVSKY, his Polish friend. Also there are Mitya's friend KALGANOV and an older man, MAXIMOV. Mitya soon discovers that the Poles are deadbeats, seeking merely to win some money with marked cards and get money from Grushenka. Mitya privately offers them 3,000 rubles to leave Grushenka to him and they accept, but then they refuse when they find that Mitya can pay no more than 700 in cash and the rest is a promise. Mitya then spends his money recklessly on a party, including gypsy girls for singing and dancing. But Grushenka does admit she loves him, and lets him kiss her, but pleads with him to do no more till they are married. She will repay Katerina, of whom her jealousy is extreme. Their love scene is interrupted by the arrival of officers who have come to arrest Mitya for murder. Fyodor has been murdered that night.

Book IX. 1–6. Perhotin, suspicious when Mitya showed up with so much money, promptly investigated, which led to Mitya's arrest. The prosecutor, IPPOLIT KIRILLOVITCH, and the investigating attorney, NIKOLAY PARFENOVITCH, have excellent circumstantial evidence against Mitya, though there is no evidence from Smerdyakov, who has had an epileptic fit (to which he is subject) and is unconscious. Mitya indignantly denies being a parricide but refuses to explain how he so suddenly became possessed of so much money. Grushenka clings to Mitya and says "Punish us together!" Mitya is overemotional and distraught when examined and he can not or will not give lucid or convincing answers. **7–9.** Finally Mitya admits that he had kept 1,500 of the 3,000 rubles of Katerina's, in a bag around his neck, and this was the money he spent. But he had spent so wildly that he cannot prove he did not spend 3,000 rubles—the amount Fyodor had in the envelope for Grushenka, which has disappeared. Protesting his innocence, Mitya is put in jail.

Part IV. Book X. 1–4. Alyosha becomes friendly with the schoolboys—KOLYA KRASSOTKIN, one of the group of boys who were throwing stones; ILUSHA, Snegiryov's son, whom the other boys were persecuting; and the others. **5–7.** Ilusha is very ill, probably dying. Alyosha comforts him and inspires Kolya to do the same.

Book XI. 1. Ivan goes to see Grushenka. She has taken in the old man, Maximov, because he is destitute, and she has received regular begging letters from the two Poles, to whom she has given a few rubles—largely because of her happiness at the end of her dream that she still loved the Polish officer. She loves Mitya and Ivan assures her that Mitya loves her. **2–3.** Lise gives Alyosha a private letter for Ivan. **4.** Alyosha goes to the prison to visit Mitya. Both Grushenka and Katerina visit him, and

113

Dmitri in jail

Katerina is active in his defense, which makes Grushenka jealous. Mitya wants to marry Grushenka in prison if the authorities will permit it. Grushenka wants to follow Mitya to Siberia. Katerina is trying to have Mitya declared insane and Ivan is working on escape plans. Ivan thinks Mitya is guilty. **5.** Alyosha next drops by Katerina's. Ivan is there. He seems to think Smerdyakov was the murderer; yet Alyosha has heard Ivan say, in delirium, that he—Ivan—actually killed their father. **6.** Ivan goes to see Smerdyakov, in the hospital, and grills him, but Smerdyakov admits nothing—not even that his fit was a sham. **7–10.** When Smerdyakov is released, Ivan goes to see him at home. This time Smerdyakov says he knows Ivan wanted Fyodor dead but wanted Mitya to kill him, to increase his own inheritance. Ivan is aghast at this thought. Meanwhile Ivan reads the letter—a letter Mitya wrote to Katerina, the day of the murder, promising to have the money "tomorrow"; and at last Ivan thinks Mitya guilty. But then Ivan has a third interview with Smerdyakov, and this time Smerdyakov confesses that he faked the fit and murdered Fyodor, expecting to be rewarded by Ivan; and Smerdyakov proves it by showing Ivan the 3,000 rubles he took from Fyodor. Ivan goes home, knowing that the next day he can prove Mitya's innocence. But when he wakes the next morning he learns that Smerdyakov hanged himself during the night. Now Ivan has only his own testimony as to Mitya's innocence, and it will not be believed.

Book XII. 1–3. The trial of Mitya begins. The first evidence builds a case against Mitya. **4–5.** Katerina's testimony creates sympathy for Mitya. Ivan, ill and distraught, gives his true testimony and produces the money Smerdyakov stole, but of course it is unconvincing; and Katerina is so distressed by what she considers Ivan's sacrifice for his brother that she has herself recalled to the stand and this time she shows the damning letter. **6–9.** Ippolit Kirillovitch delivers an eloquent summation, skillfully directed at the prejudice of the peasants on the jury against the excesses of the nobility. **10–14.** Mitya's lawyer, the great orator FETYUKOVITCH, delivers an eloquent and persuasive summation, but the peasants cannot be swayed. They find Mitya guilty

and he is in for at least a sentence of 20 years in the mines.

Epilogue. 1–2. Katerina has collapsed after the trial, from remorse at her vengeful act that led to Mitya's conviction. Ivan also is unconscious, in a high fever. When she is able, Katerina goes to the prison hospital—for Mitya also has collapsed. Mitya now considers escaping, with Grushenka, though America seems to him as bad an exile as Siberia. When Katerina comes he and she ask each other's forgiveness. Then Grushenka comes, and she is venomous toward Katerina. Katerina flees and Mitya, still forgiving, sends Alyosha to comfort her. **3.** Ilusha has died. At his funeral Alyosha tells the boys to be good and have faith, as he will, despite his grief.

Buddenbrooks

Novel by Thomas Mann, 1875–1955. Published 1901. English translation by H. T. Lowe-Porter published and © 1924 by Alfred A. Knopf, New York. (PB, C 60; GC 3)

MANN'S FIRST NOVEL is still ranked among his best. It pictures the high-bourgeois business family of which Germany's commercial cities have had a superabundance for at least a century and it portrays the problems of the monster or mutant of artistic soul born into such a family. The novel is wholly authentic because Thomas Mann was such a person born into such a family.

Part I. The Buddenbrook family in 1835 is solidly prosperous and solidly united—with the exception of JOHANN BUDDENBROOK's eldest son, GOTTHOLD, offspring of his first marriage. JOHANN Junior, upon reading a letter from his half-brother, in which Gotthold demands a third interest in his father's estate, advises old Johann to give nothing. Gotthold married against his father's wishes, voluntarily cutting himself

off. Old Johann agrees, and the subject of Gotthold and his demands is dismissed.

Part II. The Buddenbrook business continues to thrive. Old Frau Buddenbrook, Johann's second wife, dies about two years after the day when Gotthold's demands were denied, and shortly thereafter Johann signs over the business to his son Johann, whom most people call JEAN. The old man dies and Jean's children start to mature. TOM, Jean's eldest son, leaves school at 16 and enters the business with his father. The younger boy, CHRISTIAN, is quite unbusinesslike and most unlike the stolidly practical family. The youngest child, ANTONIE—nicknamed TONY—shows signs of growing up, and when she goes so far as to take afternoon strolls with a boy, she is packed off to boarding school. She is 15.

Part III. Tony is 20. She has a suitor that her family approves but she finds detestable. Herr GRUNLICH, the suitor, is an eminently respectable business man. Tony avoids him as much as possible. She goes to the seashore to avoid him, and there she becomes attached to a young medical student, MORTEN SCHWARTZKOPF. She writes her family that she has fallen in love. Grunlich goes to Morten's father, declaring that the boy has infringed on his prior claim. The elder Schwartzkopf sends his son away to punish him for this violation of convention, and Tony's family takes her home. She submits at last to the betrothal, and Herr Grunlich acquires a dowry from her father of 80,000 marks.

Part IV. Tony is married to Grunlich. Her letters to her family complain that he is very trying and unreasonable, miserly and asserting his will upon her in everything. She soon bears him a child, a daughter. She wants to name her daughter Meta but Grunlich insists on ERICA.

Things go from bad to worse with Grunlich, and his creditors finally force him to ask his father-in-law for additional funds, to spare Johann's daughter and grandchild the humiliation of bankruptcy. In the course of his pleas to Johann, Grunlich is uncovered as an unscrupulous cheat by the drunken boasts of a friend who happens to be present. Grunlich had sought Tony's hand solely for the dowry. Johann takes Tony and Erica back home and arranges for a divorce.

The Buddenbrook business is enriched further with the death of Johann's mother-in-law, who left a substantial sum. Tony lives a useful domestic life and feels that there is nothing amiss that a good second marriage would not cure. Johann Buddenbrook dies suddenly and the business falls into the capable hands of his elder son, Tom.

Part V. Tony, still of the opinion that she should remarry, speaks to Tom. The proper social and financial level is a most important point with the Buddenbrook family. The result is that each marries someone almost exactly like himself, insuring the standardization of offspring. Tom marries the statuesque GERDA, whom Tom had known in boarding school. Christian is still unconventional, by Buddenbrook standards, and is sickly.

Part VI. Tony sets out to travel and broaden her interests. There is little chance that she will meet an eligible male in her mother's house.

She meets a hop-dealer from Munich—Herr PERMANEDER—who calls when she returns home. Permaneder proves to be a substantial, reliable, well-to-do businessman—all the Buddenbrook qualifications. Tony marries him, which seems to settle her domestic situation. This does not endure for long. Permaneder, after an exceedingly profitable investment of Tony's dowry, is most willing to relax and live on income. He has enough money and is not a mercenary man. Tony, conditioned to a completely mercenary way of life, is bewildered by Permaneder's attitude.

The knowledge that she is going to have a baby gives Tony cause for rejoicing, but the baby, a little girl, lives only a few minutes. Her relationship with Permaneder becomes worse. After a brief period of mourning, Permaneder returns to his tavern friends each evening. One night Tony finds her husband and the maid, BABETTE, in an amorous embrace. She goes home again, taking Erica, and demands a second divorce. The reaction of Herr Permaneder astounds everyone. He does not contest either the divorce or the restitution of the dowry.

Part VII. Gerda and Tom have a son to carry on the name of Buddenbrook. JUSTUS JOHANN KARPAR BUDDENBROOK is christened at a gala celebration. Christian returns from his latest business venture, at which he has failed again, and this time he is sent to London. A senator dies and Tom is elected to fill his place. Tom works harder than ever, in spite of the doctor's warning. Old Frau Buddenbrook does something unthinkable: At the request of her youngest daughter, CLARA, who is dying of tuberculosis, she signs over Clara's dowry and inheritance to Clara's minister husband.

The fortunes of war in 1865 cause the total bankruptcy of a wholesale firm in Frankfort, and the firm of Johann Buddenbrook is involved and loses at one stroke 20,000 thaler.

Little Johann Buddenbrook, called Hanno, is a quiet, shy child of about 4½ years.

shows great talent as a pianist, but Tom is bewildered by the shy, imaginative child. Weinschenk is involved with shady manipulations of insurance and is sent to jail for 3½ years. The Buddenbrooks are deflated only temporarily; the man was an outsider away.

Part VIII. Erica is now 20 years old. She becomes engaged to HUGO WEINSCHENK, a director of an insurance company. Though not outstandingly rich in the merchant world of the Buddenbrooks, he holds a respected position and is found suitable for Erica. They are married and Tony goes to live with them and manage their house. Erica has a daughter, a frail and delicate child. Tom's son, Hanno, is also frail. He

Part IX. Old Frau Buddenbrook dies of pneumonia. A violent argument occurs between the three heirs. Tom and Christian quarrel bitterly and Tom refuses to agree to Christian's marrying—not so much because Christian wants to marry his mistress, ALINE, as because Christian's inheritance would eventually pass to Aline's children, out of the reach of all true Buddenbrooks.

The dissolution of the family is emphasized when the old home is sold. Tony sees the new name over the door and weeps unashamedly in the street.

Part X. Tom watches little Johann (Hanno) hopefully for signs that the boy is developing interest in the Buddenbrook firm. Tom fears he is heading swiftly toward his end. Christian has a similar premonition. An excruciating toothache takes Tom to the dentist. The attempted extraction fails. On his way home Tom falls in the snow, after a sudden and violent seizure of dizziness, and dies later.

Part XI. With Tom's death, and the permanent disappearance of Erica's husband, there seems little to cause concern in the family when Christian marries Aline and is later committed by her to a mental institution. Hanno dies of typhoid, and Gerda departs for America. Tony reviews her life and finds that everything is gone. The family of Buddenbrook has descended the implacable slope to oblivion.

Bulfinch's Mythology

Stories (retold) by Thomas Bulfinch, 1796–1867.
Published 1855; republished with additions by Edward Everett Hale, 1894.

THIS IS ONLY ONE of many retellings of the classical myths and legends for young readers, but it has been the most successful book of its kind (except for Hawthorne's *Wonder Book* and *Tanglewood Tales* in their day) and it has survived as the standard book on the subject. ❡ Bulfinch devotes most of the book to the Greek mythology, which however he takes chiefly from the Roman poets Virgil and Ovid and in which he uses the Roman rather than the Greek names of the gods and goddesses. Then come chapters on Eastern (Persian and Hindu) myths; and Norse mythology; the Druids of the ancient Celtic nations; and Greek sculpture. There are many quotations from English poets such as Milton and Shakespeare, giving their allusions to the mythological stories and characters.

The Greeks, Romans and Germans all belonged to the Aryan race or stock and their stories often bore much resemblance though found in different forms.

The (ancient) Greeks believed the world to be flat and circular, with Greece (especially Mount Olympus) in the center and the "River Ocean" flowing all around. The Dawn, Sun and Moon were supposed to rise out of the Ocean. The gods lived on Mt. Olympus, and when summoned they assembled in the palace of Jupiter, where they ate ambrosia and drank nectar. The Roman names of the Greek gods were not mere translations; in many cases there were equivalent gods among the two peoples. JUPITER (in Greek, ZEUS), the chief god, was the father of many gods and goddesses; he himself was the son of SATURN (or, in Greek, KRONOS, or Time) and OPS (in Greek, RHEA), who were Titans, the original race that came before the gods. Jupiter and his brothers and sisters rebelled against the Titans and conquered them. They im-

Tony sets out to travel and broaden her interests

115

prisoned some and punished others; for example ATLAS, a Titan, was condemned to bear the heavens on his shoulders. Then Jupiter and two of his brothers divided the universe: Jupiter got the heavens, NEPTUNE the seas, and PLUTO the underworld. Jupiter was the king of gods and men. His wife Juno was queen of the gods.

The chief gods and goddesses who were children of Jupiter were: VULCAN, artist of the heavens; MARS, god of war; PHOEBUS APOLLO (a Greek name), god of the sun, and his sister DIANA, goddess of the moon; VENUS, goddess of love and beauty, mother of CUPID, the god of love; MINERVA (in Greek, PALLAS ATHENE), goddess of wisdom; MERCURY, Jupiter's messenger; the nine Muses; and BACCHUS, the god of wine. Others, not children of Jupiter, were: CERES, Jupiter's sister, goddess of agriculture; JUNO, wife of Jupiter; the three Graces, the three Fates, and the three Furies, all goddesses; NEMESIS, the avenging goddess; PAN, the god of shepherds; MOMUS, the god of laughter, and PLUTUS, the god of wealth. There were many others. All the foregoing were recognized by both Greeks and Romans. In addition the Romans had gods unknown to the Greeks: SATURN; JANUS, the two-headed porter of heaven; and the household gods, Penates who guarded the family and Lares who were the spirits of dead ancestors.

The creation. Ovid tells the story of creation: First there was CHAOS, all the elements of nature in a disordered jumble. God and Nature separated earth and sea, and the fiery part, being lightest, sprang up and formed the skies. The Titan EPIMETHEUS made men and animals, and his brother PROMETHEUS went up to the sun, stole fire, and brought it down to man. Woman was not yet made; Jupiter made her and sent her to Prometheus to punish him for stealing fire. The first woman was named PANDORA. Curiosity caused her to open a jar in which Epimetheus had confined all unpleasant things such as disease and envy; they escaped to plague men forever, but Pandora managed to put back the top of the lid in time to save Hope, which accordingly never leaves man.

Stories of gods and goddesses. Apollo slew with his arrows a terrible serpent, PYTHON, which appeared at the time of the creation. At Delphi, Apollo founded the Delphic oracle, which all nations came to consult.

Apollo offended Cupid, who thereupon shot Apollo with an arrow that made him love the nymph DAPHNE and shot Daphne with an arrow that made her abhor Apollo. When Apollo pursued her, she ran; and when she was almost caught, she cried for help to her father Peneus, the river god, and he changed her to a laurel tree. Apollo adopted the laurel as his tree and victors at the Pythian games, founded by Apollo, were crowned with laurel wreaths.

PYRAMUS, a handsome youth, loved THISBE, a beautiful maiden, but their parents would not let them marry. They arranged to meet secretly. Thisbe arrived first but was frightened away by a lioness, dropping her veil as she ran. The lioness rent the veil with her jaws, bloody from a previous kill. When Pyramus arrived he saw the lion's footprints and the bloody veil; and thinking Thisbe was dead, he plunged his sword into his heart. Thisbe found him dying and killed herself with his sword. Their parents acceded to Thisbe's dying wish and buried them together.

CEPHALUS, a youth fond of hunting, was loved by the goddess AURORA, the Dawn; but he loved his wife PROCRIS, who had been given a never-failing javelin by Diana, who also was goddess of hunting. Cephalus had the habit of speaking to "the sweet breeze" when he was alone. Someone heard him and told Procris he was wooing another woman. She hid to hear for herself, and Cephalus heard the rustling in the bushes, thought it was game, and threw his magic javelin, which killed Procris.

IO was a maiden loved by Jupiter; when JUNO spied on him, he changed Io to a heifer to deceive her. Juno took the heifer and assigned ARGUS, who had a hundred eyes, to guard it. Jupiter sent Mercury to kill Arbus and liberate Io. Mercury had trouble doing this, for he could not get Argus to sleep so soundly that all his hundred eyes were closed; but finally he put Argus wholly to sleep by telling him a long story. Then he cut Argus's head off. Juno took Argus's hundred eyes and put them in the tail of her peacock. Juno then sent a gadfly to torment Io, who swam all over the world to get away; finally Jupiter promised he would not see Io again and Juno changed her back to a woman.

CALLISTO was another maiden of whom Juno was jealous. Juno changed her to a bear. Callisto's son, when hunting, encountered this bear and was about to kill it, but Jupiter stopped him by changing them both to stars, the Great and Little Bear.

ACTAEON, a son of King Cadmus, was resting in the course of a hunting expedition when he happened to see the goddess Diana being dressed by her nymphs. Diana changed him to a stag so that he could tell no one; and his own dogs pursued and killed him.

PHAETON, son of Phoebus Apollo (the sun), was boasting to Epaphus, son of Jupiter and Io. Epaphus would not believe him. So Phaeton went to his father and asked to be allowed, for one day, to drive the chariot of the sun through the heavens. Apollo urged him not to attempt this, and offered him anything else, but Phaeton persisted and Apollo gave in. Phaeton set off but could not control the fiery horses; the chariot of the sun through the heavens. Jupiter finally averted total disaster by killing Phaeton with lightning.

MIDAS, a king, befriended Silenus, the foster-father of Bacchus. As a reward Bacchus offered Midas whatever he might wish and Midas asked that everything he touched might turn to gold. Bacchus granted the wish, but now even Midas's food and drink turned to gold. He prayed for relief to Bacchus, who allowed him to rid himself of the unwanted gift by plunging into the River Pactolus.

BAUCIS, a pious old dame, and her husband PHILEMON had grown old together. They lived in a hut in Phrygia. Jupiter and Mercury, journeying in that land and seeking shelter for the night, were turned away at one house after another; but Baucis and Philemon received them hospitably, and placed all they had to eat before them. As a reward, the gods built a fine temple in which Baucis and Philemon lived the rest of their lives, and in accordance with their wish Baucis and Philemon died together, being changed to a linden and an oak tree; but the rest of the village, for its inhospitality, was sunk beneath a lake.

PROSERPINE, daughter of Ceres, was loved by Pluto, who carried her off to the underworld. Ceres searched for her daughter all over the world; embittered when she could not find her, Ceres withheld agriculture from the earth and all plants died. The fountain Arethusa, at the entrance to the underworld, then told Ceres that Proserpine was the bride of Pluto and was queen of Erebus (the underworld). Ceres appealed to Jupiter, who agreed to have Proserpine released—on one condition, that Proserpine should not have eaten any food while she was in the underworld. But Proserpine had sucked a few seeds of a pomegranate that Pluto had given her. So a compromise was made, by which Proserpine would spend half of each year with her mother and half with her husband. This story is an allegory of the planting of seed underground and the emergence of the plant in the spring.

GLAUCUS, a fisherman, ate some grass that affected him strangely, drawing him irresistibly into the water. There he was welcomed by the sea-gods, changed in form, and became one of them. From the water he saw and loved the maiden SCYLLA, but she would not have him. He appealed for advice to the enchantress Circe, who advised him to abandon Scylla; but he refused to do this. Circe found this an occasion to persecute Scylla, rooting her in the water with serpents and monsters attached to her. Scylla's temper grew as ugly as her form and she devoured all mariners who came within her grasp. Later she was changed to a rock.

PYGMALION saw so much to blame in women that he came to hate them. He was a sculptor and made an ivory statue of a woman, so beautiful that he fell in love with it. (He named it Galatea.) He prayed to Venus for a wife just like the statue; but Venus knew that he really wanted the statue itself, and she caused the statue to come to life.

Venus, playing one day with her boy Cupid, wounded her bosom with one of his arrows. Before the wound healed she saw and fell in love with ADONIS. She loved to hunt with Adonis, but warned him to be careful. He was too noble to heed her counsel, and soon after this he was slain by a boar. Venus changed his blood to a flower, the anemone, which blooms briefly each

116

year. Another flower story is: Apollo was passionately fond of a youth named HYACINTHUS. One day when they were playing quoits the god threw one with too much strength and it bounced back from earth and killed Hyacinthus. Apollo in his grief changed the youth's blood to a flower.

PSYCHE, the youngest of a king's three daughters, was so beautiful that Venus became jealous. Venus commanded her son Cupid to make Psyche fall in love with some mean, unworthy being. Cupid obediently touched Psyche with one of his arrows; but accidentally he also touched himself with the arrow. An oracle told Psyche's parents that she must marry a god—but a monster—who lived on a mountaintop. Obediently they took her to the mountain and left her. She fell asleep and awoke to find herself in the garden of a beautiful palace. A voice told her that she had a host of invisible servants and might have anything she desired. So she lived in luxury but never saw her husband, who came to her only in the darkness and fled before dawn. Her husband allowed her to visit her sisters, who reminded her that her husband was supposed to be a hideous monster. Filled with suspicion, she armed herself with a knife. The next time her husband visited her, when he fell asleep, she uncovered her lamp and looked at him. She saw not a monster but a beautiful god, Cupid. But Cupid, waking, reproached her for her suspicion. He said she could go back to her sisters; then he left her, and the next morning the palace had vanished.

Psyche wandered day and night trying to find her husband again. She prayed at the temple of Ceres, who sent her to Venus, so she prayed at the temple of Venus. Venus gave her a series of impossible tasks, but (unknowingly helped by Cupid) Psyche was able to accomplish them all. Then Cupid asked Jupiter to help him and Jupiter persuaded Venus to relent. Psyche was made a goddess and married Cupid, and they had a daughter, Pleasure.

CADMUS was a son of Agenor, King of Phoenicia. Jupiter, disguised as a bull, had carried away Cadmus's sister, EUROPA, to Crete; and Cadmus went there in search of her. Failing to find her, he consulted the oracle of Apollo and it told him to follow a cow he would see; and when it stopped, he should build a city and call it Thebes. The cow stopped and Cadmus sent his men to find water. They encountered a horrid serpent (or dragon), which killed them. Cadmus, discovering this, managed to kill the serpent. Then Cadmus heard a voice commanding him to sow the dragon's teeth in the earth. He did so and armed warriors grew from them. The great crop of warriors fought one another until only five were left; these were peaceful and joined Cadmus, helping him to build Thebes.

ECHO, a beautiful nymph but too fond of talking, offended Juno. As punishment, Juno took away Echo's power ever to speak first, leaving her only the power to reply, as she had always liked to have the last word. Echo saw and loved the beautiful youth NARCISSUS, and had a conversation with him, repeating his words; but he spurned her and she grieved until she lost her beauty and faded away. Her bones were changed to rocks. But she is still ready to reply to anyone. Narcissus fell in love with his own image in a fountain and he too lost his beauty and died of unrequited love.

LEANDER was a youth of Abydos, a town on the Asian side of the strait between Asia and Europe, and on the opposite shore, in the town of Sestos, lived the maiden HERO. Leander loved her and used to swim the strait nightly to see her. One night, in a tempest, he was drowned; and Hero in her despair cast herself from a tower into the sea and perished.

Minerva, who is said to have sprung forth from Jupiter's brain fully grown and clad in complete armor, was a warlike goddess. Athens was her own city, awarded to her for winning a contest with Neptune. Once a mortal maiden, ARACHNE, dared to challenge Minerva to a contest at needlework, of which Minerva was the goddess. Both wove magnificent work; Minerva had to admire Arachne's, but still punished Arachne for her presumption and impiety. She transformed Arachne into a spider.

Niobe, queen of Thebes, also presumed to challenge a goddess, Latona, mother of Apollo and Diana; Niobe thought she had a right to be prouder of her own fourteen children. Latona complained to her children, who slew Niobe's children one by one. Niobe at the end cried, "Spare me one!" but that last one was killed too.

The king of Argos, Acrisius, was told by an oracle that he would be slain by the child of his daughter DANAE. He shut Danaë up in a tower but Jupiter went to her there and they had a son, PERSEUS. Unwilling to kill his daughter and grandchild, Acrisius placed them in a chest and sent them floating out to sea. They reached an island, Seriphus, when Perseus was brought up by a fisherman. When Perseus was grown, the king of Seriphus sent him to bring back the head of MEDUSA, one of the three GORGONS, whose hair was coiled serpents that would turn to stone anyone who looked at it. (Minerva had turned the hair to serpents, to punish Medusa for vying with her beauty.) Minerva and Mercury helped Perseus: Minerva lent him her shield and Mercury lent him his winged shoes and sword. Perseus saw Medusa's reflection in the shield and killed her by cutting off her head, which he put in a bag.

On his way home, Perseus arrived in Ethiopia, of which CEPHEUS was king and CASSIOPEIA queen. Cassiopeia's vanity had offended the sea nymphs, who sent a prodigious sea-monster to ravage the coast. An oracle told Cepheus he must sacrifice his daughter, ANDROMEDA, to this serpent; so Cepheus chained her to a rock by the sea. Perseus, flying over, saw the monster approach. He killed the monster and so was awarded the hand of Andromeda. But PHINEAS, her betrothed, objected and attacked. Outnumbered, Perseus told his friends to turn their faces away and then took from his bag the head of Medusa, turning all his enemies to stone.

OEDIPUS was the son of LAIUS, king of Thebes. An oracle warned Laius that his newborn son was dangerous to him and Laius gave the infant to a herdsman to destroy; but the herdsman pitied the child and simply abandoned him, and he was found and raised to manhood by another herdsman. When Oedipus was a young man, the Delphic oracle prophesied that he would kill his father and marry his mother.

Jupiter, disguised as a bull, carries away Europa (see next page)

117

Oedipus resolved to leave the country. On his way, he encountered Laius driving to Oedipus; there was not room for two chariots to pass and in a quarrel that ensued Oedipus killed Laius, his own father. Oedipus journeyed on toward Thebes, which was afflicted by a monster, the SPHINX, which had the body of a lion but the head and torso of a woman. The Sphinx blocked the road and killed all travelers who not could answer "the Riddle of the Sphinx": What animal is that which in the morning goes on four feet, at noon on two, and in the evening on three? Oedipus gave the correct answer: Man, who creeps as a child, walks in manhood, and uses a staff in old age. The Sphinx, mortified, killed herself. The people of Thebes were so grateful to Oedipus that they gave him their widowed queen, JOCASTA, as his wife; and so he married his mother. When later this was discovered, Jocasta killed herself and Oedipus tore out his eyes and wandered till he died, accompanied however by his faithful daughters.

PEGASUS was a winged horse that grew from the blood of Medusa, when Perseus cut off her head. The CHIMAERA was a fearful monster, breathing fire; its fore part was lion and goat and its rear part was dragon. BELLEROPHON, a gallant young warrior, was charged with the task of killing the Chimaera. With the aid of Minerva, who gave him a magic bridle, Bellerophon found Pegasus drinking at the well of Pirene, tamed him, and by riding him was able to kill the Chimaera. Bellerophon and Pegasus together performed many other feats until Bellerophon became so proud that Jupiter sent a gadfly to sting Pegasus and make him throw Bellerophon. Bellerophon became lame and blind and wandered miserably until his death.

NEPHELE, a queen in Thessaly who had been put away by her husband, feared for the lives of her two children. Mercury gave her a ram that had golden fleece and could fly, and she set her children on it. The girl, HELLE, fell off; but the boy, PHRYXUS, safely reached the kingdom of Colchis and was welcomed by its king, AETES. The ram was sacrificed to Jupiter and the golden fleece was hung in a consecrated grove guarded by a dragon. JASON, the prince of another kingdom, was sent in quest of the golden fleece by his uncle PELIAS, who actually wanted to get rid of him. Jason employed Argus (not the monster) to build a ship that would carry fifty men (at that time considered a gigantic undertaking). The ship was called the *Argo* and Jason and his men, including such heroes as Hercules, Theseus, Orpheus and Nestor, were called Argonauts. The Argonauts had various adventures in sailing to Colchis, which was on the Black Sea.

The king of Colchis, AETES, consented to give up the golden fleece if Jason would yoke to the plow two fire-breathing bulls and also would sow the dragon's teeth as Cadmus had done. Jason had already become engaged to marry MEDEA, the king's

daughter, who was a potent sorceress. With the help of her magic he yoked the fire-breathing bulls; then he sowed the dragon's teeth and when the warriors sprang up and rushed to attack him he threw a stone in their midst, which set them fighting among themselves until all were killed. Aetes promised the golden fleece the next day, but that night Medea told Jason that actually her father planned to attack him. They went to the grove, where Medea put the dragon to sleep with a magic potion. Then with the golden fleece they sailed back to Thessaly. Medea had other adventures: With her magic she restored Jason's aged father, Aeson, to youth; then, under pretext

The riddle of the Sphinx

of doing the same for Pelias, she killed Pelias and fled to Athens, where she married the king, Aegeus.

HERCULES (in Greek, HERACLES) was the son Jupiter and ALCMENA. Juno, jealous as always, sent two serpents to destroy him in his cradle but he strangled them with his hands. However, under Juno's curse Hercules had to undertake the twelve "Labors of Hercules," set for him by his cousin Eurystheus. The chief ones were: 1, to kill the terrible Nemean lion; Hercules strangled it. 2, to kill the Hydra, a nine-headed monster. Each time Hercules cut off a head, two others grew. Eventually Hercules burned away all heads but one, which was immortal, and this one he buried. 3, to clean the Augean stables, which housed three thousand oxen and had not been cleaned for thirty years. Hercules turned two rivers through them and cleansed them in one day. 4, to procure the girdle of HIPPOLYTA, queen of the Amazons, a nation of warlike women. Hippolyta was willing to give Hercules the girdle; but Juno spread the rumor that Hercules was carrying off the queen and the Amazons attacked Hercules. Thinking Hippolyta treacherous, Hercules slew her and sailed off with the girdle. 5, to bring home the oxen belonging to Geryon, a three-headed monster; to do this Hercules had to kill a giant, Eurytion, and a two-headed dog, who guarded the oxen. 6, to to get the golden apples of the Hesperides,

which had been Juno's wedding present. Hercules did not know where they were, but he persuaded the giant Atlas to get them for him while he held up the heavens in Atlas's place.

Other exploits of Hercules included killing the giant ANTAEUS, son of Terra (the Earth), who forced all strangers to wrestle with him. Hercules found it was of no avail to throw Antaeus, who rose with renewed strength from every fall; so Hercules lifted him from the earth and strangled him in the air.

THESEUS, son of AEGEUS, king of Athens, after various exploits, went to Crete to save Athens from paying a terrible annual tribute: Seven youths and seven maidens had to be sent each year to feed the MINOTAUR, a monster with a bull's body and human head, which belonged to MINOS, king of Crete. The Minotaur was kept in a labyrinth built by Daedalus, so artfully that no one in it could find his way out. Theseus won the heart of ARIADNE, daughter of Minos, and she gave him a thread of which she held one end, to guide him out. Theseus entered the labyrinth, slew the Minotaur, escaped from the labyrinth, and sailed back home, taking Ariadne with him. Then he treacherously abandoned her on the island of Naxos. But he had promised his father to fly white sails instead of black if he succeeded, and he forgot; so when the old king, watching from the coast, saw the ship approach with black sails he thought his son had perished and he killed himself.

PROCRUSTES was one of the evil-doers that Theseus overcame in his journeyings. Procrustes had an iron bedstead on which he tied all travelers who fell into his hands. If they were shorter than the bed, he stretched them; if they were longer, he lopped them off. Theseus served him as he had served others.

DAEDALUS, a most skillful artificer, made wings for himself and his young son ICARUS; the wings were made of feathers held together by wax. Daedalus warned Icarus not to fly too high, but Icarus disregarded this and flew too near to the sun. The wax melted, the wings fell apart, and Icarus fell into the sea and died.

ORPHEUS was the son of Apollo and Calliope, the Muse of music. He was the greatest musician. He married EURYDICE, but soon afterward she killed by a snake bite. Orpheus followed her to the underworld, where his music so charmed the gods that Pluto consented to let him take Eurydice back to earth—with one condition, that Orpheus should not look back at her until they reached the upper air. But Orpheus forgot and looked back and lost her forever.

THE NORTHERN MYTHOLOGY

The mythological records of the Scandinavians are contained in two collections called the *Eddas,* of which the oldest, in poetry, dates back to 1065, and the more modern or prose Edda is dated 1640.

Once there was no earth or heaven but only a mist, in which flowed a fountain. From the fountain twelve rivers issued and froze. The vapors in the air formed clouds, from which sprang the giant YMIR, the Frost, and his progeny; and the cow AUDHUMBLA, whose milk nourished the giant. The cow licked the hoar frost and salt off the ice, revealing a god, whose children were three brothers, ODIN, VILI, and VE. They slew Ymir and made the earth from his body and the seas from his blood. They made a man, Aske, from an ash tree and a woman, Embla, from an alder.

A mighty ash tree, Ygddrasil, was supposed to support the whole universe. It had three immense roots, one extending into Asgard, the abode of the gods; another into Jotunheim, the abode of the giants; and the third into Niffleheim, the regions of darkness and cold.

The root that extends into Asgard is guarded by the NORNS, three goddesses who dispense fate; they are URDUR, the past, VERDANI, the present, and SKULD, the future. Access to Asgard is only by crossing the bridge Bifrost, the rainbow. Asgard consists of golden and silver palaces, the most beautiful being Valhalla, the residence of Odin. Here he feasts with his chosen heroes, those who have fallen bravely in battle. The Valkyrior [Valkyries] are warlike virgins, mounted on horses and armed, whom Odin sends to every battlefield to choose those to be slain; the Aurora Borealis is the reflection from their armor as they ride.

THOR, the thunderer, Odin's eldest son, is the strongest of gods. He has three precious possessions: his hammer, Miölnir; his belt of strength, which when worn doubles his strength; and his iron gloves. The god FREY presides over rain, sunshine, and the fruits of the earth; his sister FREYA is the goddess of love, music, spring, and flowers. BRAGI is the god of poetry and HEIMDALL is the watchman of the gods and guards the bridge Bifrost. LOKI is the god of fraud and mischief.

THOR, with his servant THIALFI and with Loki, set out on a journey to Jotunheim, the abode of the giants. At nightfall they were in an immense forest with no shelter until they found a large hall, where they slept. At dawn they discovered that the supposed building was the glove of a giant, who said his name was Skrymir and proposed that they travel together. That night, while Skrymir slept under a tree, Thor tried three times to kill him with mighty blows of his mallet; but each time the giant seemed to think merely that a leaf, or some moss, or an acorn had fallen on his head. They journeyed on and came to the city of King UTGARD-LOKI. The city was peopled by giants. Loki, Trialfi and Thor tried feats of strength and of eating and drinking with the giants but were easily beaten. Thor lost a wrestling match to an old crone, could not lift the king's cat, and failed to drain a horn of liquor in three tries. When they left the city, Utgard-Loki confessed to Thor that all their defeats were illusions and in reality Thor was the strongest god he could imagine: The old crone was Old Age; the cat was the earth; and the horn was connected with the oceans. Thor angrily tried to kill Utgard-Loki, but he vanished.

BALDUR THE GOOD dreamed that his life was in peril and told the other gods. Then Frigga, wife of Odin, made fire, water, metals, disease, all animals, and poisons promise not to harm Baldur. But she forgot to exact the promise from mistletoe. Loki, learning this, took a twig of mistletoe. The gods were amusing themselves by casting things at Baldur, to prove his immortality. Loki suggested that Hodur, a blind god, cast the twig at Baldur; Hodur did so, and Bladur fell lifeless.

Frigga offered a reward to anyone who would go to Hel, in Niffleheim, the abode of HELA, daughter of Loki, and ransom Baldur. HERMOD undertook the journey. He reached Hel, but Hela refused to release Baldur unless all things on earth, alive and lifeless, wept for him. Hermod returned with the message and all things did weep for Baldur except one old hag, Thaukt, who refused. So Baldur had to remain dead.

Loki fled the vengeance of the other gods and turned himself into a salmon. As he was trying to escape, Thor caught him by the tail; so salmon have very thin tails.

The ELVES were lesser gods. The white elves lived in Alfheim. They loved the light and were kindly disposed toward men. The black or night elves were ugly, long-nosed dwarfs. They were the most skillful artificers of things in metal and wood, making among other things Thor's hammer and the ship Skidbladnir, large enough to hold all the gods and their possessions but so skillfully wrought that it could be folded and put into a side pocket.

Ragnarok, or the Twilight of the Gods, was a prophesied time when all the gods and the universe would burn up, the earth would sink into the ocean, and time would be no more. Then ALFADUR, the Almighty, would create a new world in which there would be no wickedness and misery.

THE DRUIDS

The Druids were the priests of the ancient Celtic nations in Gaul, Britain, and Germany. They taught the existence of one god, named Be' al, identified with the sun. Fire was a symbol of the divinity. They had no temples, their sacred place being a circle of great stones 20 to 30 yards in diameter; the most celebrated of those remaining is Stonehenge, in England. They also worshiped at piles of stone, called cairns, on the summits of hills.

The Druids offered sacrifices to their deity, and according to Roman writers these were sometimes human sacrifices.

There were two festivals each year. The first, at the beginning of May, was called Beltane or "fire of God." The other was called Samh' in, or "fire of peace," and was held the first of November. At this time the Druids acted as judges, settling all questions and crimes.

The Bards were part of the Druidical hierarchy. They preserved the history and genealogy of the people in songs and stories. They were thought to be inspired.

The Valkyrie ride

119

The Cabala

Novel by Thornton Wilder, 1897–
Published 1926 by A. & C. Boni, New York. © 1926, 1954 by Thornton Wilder.

THIS IS Thornton Wilder's first published novel. It did not create much of a stir at the time, but after he made his great success less than two years later with *The Bridge of San Luis Rey* readers went back to *The Cabala* and found it good. ❡ The original cabala was an occult religious system, but also any principal group or council of scholars considered authoritative on the system was known collectively as "the Cabala."

Book 1. The narrator of the story, a young American writer (SAMUELE), arrives in Rome a couple of years after the end of World War I. He is accompanied by his friend JAMES BLAIR, a classical scholar, and through Blair meets a group of rich and talented people. This group, known as the Cabala, are absorbed in antiquarian lore and they attempt to create the present in terms of the long-dead past. Blair takes the narrator to the home of Miss ELIZABETH GRIER, an American member of the Cabala, who entertains lavishly. She has her own private orchestra and stays awake all night. She is constantly inviting favored guests to tea, dinner, and late supper. The members of the Cabala accept the narrator and call him SAMUELE. He meets other members of the group at Miss Grier's and finds them a fascinating group. There is Cardinal VAINI, who has been a missionary in China. The Cardinal is concerned with the inner affairs of the Church, but also, as the friend and counselor of the Duchessa D'AGUILANERA, he is worried about her 16-year-old son MARCANTONIO, who is living a wild and dissolute life. Samuele also meets ASTRÉE-LUCE DE MONFONTAINE, a religious fanatic who as a French royalist believes in the divine right of kings; Mme. BERNSTEIN, the daughter of a German banker, and the

Princess ALIX D'ESPOLI, who has beauty and charm but not enough intelligence to hold the man she is attracted to.

Book 2. Samuele has tea and dinner at Elizabeth Grier's, leaves, and returns later in the evening for a late supper. The Duchessa d'Aguilanera begs him to come to her home and talk to Marcantonio. She thinks Samuele can influence the boy to change his wayward life. Samuele agrees and goes to the duchessa's Renaissance villa for study and rest. There he spends much time listening to Mme. Bernstein play the

piano. The Cardinal has told Samuele that Marcantonio is completely dissolute, immoral in character, and habituated to his evil life with older companions. This shocks but does not deter Samuele from undertaking the reformation of Marcantonio. The boy tells him that he likes to drive fast cars, but that also he has an ambition to run in the Olympic games. Samuele agrees to coach him, but soon becomes disgusted by the boy's way of life and castigates him with a torrent of Puritan invective. Marcantonio is deeply affected and in a state of religious frenzy jumps from a balcony and kills himself.

Book 3. Samuele becomes the intimate friend of the Princess Alix d'Espoli and he introduces her to James Blair. The princess falls madly in love with Blair, but as is usual with her the love is not reciprocated. She mistakes Blair's friendly attitude and begins to visit him uninvited. Blair is annoyed and leaves Rome to escape her insistent demands on him. The princess pours out her grief to Samuele and plunges into the weird life of the artistic colony of Rome. Blair returns a month later and he and Samuele visit a Rosicrucian seer. At a public séance they encounter Alix. They try to avoid her but she sees them, and evidently realizing that Blair is through with her she leaves the place in a fit of anger. Samuele later hears that she has left Rome for Greece, but has returned and is once more the subject of gossip for her attempts to snare a man.

Book 4. Samuele next becomes involved with Astrée-Luce de Monfontaine and finds that the deeply religious woman is shy and full of goodness. She wants Samuele to intercede with Cardinal Vaini and persuade him to use his influence to establish the Divine Right of Kings as a dogma of the Church. She wants the Bourbons restored to the throne of France to help save Europe from destruction. Samuele visits her at her villa and at Anzio and he agrees to approach the Cardinal with her plan. The Cardinal, instead of agreeing to Astrée-Luce's royalist schemes and joining forces with her in this impossible venture, rebukes her for her exaggerated faith in prayer. Astrée-Luce is disturbed and when the Cardinal visits her at her villa she cries out to her other guests that "the devil is here" and takes a shot with a pistol at the Cardinal. He is not hurt, but

he cannot be reconciled to her. He decides to return to missionary work in China, but en route he falls ill and dies and is buried at sea.

Book 5. As Samuele prepares to leave Rome he visits places where strange events with members of the Cabala occurred. He makes a last call on Elizabeth Grier, who tells him that the members of the Cabala are in reality the reincarnation of the pagan gods of antiquity. Despite this ancient knowledge they are lost in the complexities of the modern world. She shows Samuele a document written by a Hollander who in-

sisted his body had been entered by the god Mercury. Samuele leaves Rome to return to America. On board ship he invokes the shade of the poet Virgil and it appears to him in mid-air, telling him, "hurry and die."

Cabbages and Kings

Novel by O. Henry (William Sidney Porter, 1867–1910)
Published 1899.

THIS IS ABOUT AS CLOSE to a novel as O. Henry ever wrote. It is a series of short stories, but they are tied together by the same characters and they reach a conclusion as though they had been written as a novel. The quality of O. Henry's work was so uniform that it is hard to pick his best, but he was at his best in *Cabbages and Kings*. The title is from the poem "The Walrus and the Carpenter," in *Through the Looking-Glass*: "The time has come, the walrus said,/To talk of many things—/Of shoes—and ships—and sealing-wax—/Of cabbages, and kings . . ."

The Proem. A little love, plus plotting and counterplotting with warm U.S. dollars, begins the tale of Doña ISABEL GUILBERT, young American opera singer, who only once gave the key to her heart and then to President MIRAFLORES, the brilliant but now dead President of the volatile Latin republic of Anchuria. It is said there that he died by his own hand while fleeing with Doña Isabel and a valise filled with a hundred thousand dollars. The valise disappeared but Isabel quickly married FRANK GOODWIN, an American resident of the coast town of Coralio.

Fox-in-the-Morning and **The Lotus and the Bottle.** A telegram to Goodwin, who is secretly allied to the Out Party, revolutionary in its attempt to overthrow the In Party, is a delight; for it brings the news of the flight of President Miraflores. It advises Goodwin to be sure to retrieve the valise; the money will be needed when the new party takes over. His reward for these endeavors is many thousands of coffee-bearing acres. To pass the days that must elapse before the departing Miraflores reaches Coralio, Goodwin calls frequently on WILLARD GEDDIE, the consul for the United States. Geddie is a young man escaping from a lover's quarrel with the beautiful Miss IDA PAYNE of New York.

120

His year in Coralio has greatly eased his heart's pain and he has definitely decided to marry PAULA BRANNIGAN, a most delectable native girl with a tinge of Indian blood and a very rich Irish father. Though his attentions have not been voiced, he is confident of his decision until he reads in a newspaper that Ida is cruising on a yacht in his vicinity. Trying to analyze his feelings, he walks along the beach, where absentmindedly he picks up a bottle washed ashore. There is a note inside and he perceives that it is from Ida. Resisting the temptation to remove and read it, he goes immediately to Paula and proposes. He is accepted and returns to the sea to throw the bottle as far as he can—only to halfdrown while swimming to recover it again!

Meanwhile Frank Goodwin quietly prepares to take all the precautions necessary to keep the fleeing president from making good his escape. By chance, the barber ESTEBÁN DELGADO tells Goodwin he has just shaved off the president's whiskers. He takes Goodwin to where Miraflores is staying for the night. First Goodwin enters Doña Isabel's room and she, in anger at allegation of money stolen from the treasury, brings the valise and opens it. Her astonishment when she sees the money is vocal and brings Miraflores into the room. He immediately grasps the situation and with a farewell kiss to Isabel goes into his room and shoots himself. It is said in Coralio that they still search for that valise with its dollars. No one has ever seen it, but Mr. and Mrs. Frank Goodwin have a paradise of a home and Doña Isabel has forgotten her waywardness and Miraflores to become a happy and perfect wife.

Cupid's Exile Number Two. The Phonograph and The Graft. Mr. JOHN DE GRAFFENREID ATWOOD is the successor to the consulship when Geddie resigns to go into his future father-in-law's business. Atwood, too, is a fugitive from a shattered romance. He proceeds to do absolutely nothing as consul, but he does it very charmingly. BILLY KEOGH becomes his boon companion and one still, alcoholic evening tells him how he introduced the first phonograph to South America. Keogh and a partner had set up their one machine in the small town of Solitas, where they were immediately wined and dined by the American secretary to the President, HOMER P. MELLINGER, a man proud of his honesty in a country of graft. Mellinger invited Keogh and his Indian partner, HENRY HORSECOLLAR, to demonstrate the novelty at his reception. A district governor was coming and Mellinger knew the governor was about to offer him a bribe to betray the President. When the bribe came it was so enormous that Mellinger faltered; but just at that moment Keogh played a record of "Home Sweet Home" and Mellinger resisted the temptation and stayed honest. The next day Mellinger insisted on buying the phonograph for many times what it was worth. He put the cost on his expense account because it was worth that much to the government to

Clancy works with pick and shovel

keep him honest.

Money Maze and **The Admiral.** The new administration that takes over now in Anchuria has one major concern, to recover the Miraflores valise with its monetary content. The secretary to the new President, Colonel EMILIO FALCON, comes to Coralio to investigate, and all clues lead to Frank Goodwin. It is surprising that privately Goodwin and his wife, Doña Isabel, admit taking the money but both being of such honest mien, the reason is a mystery, the more so since Goodwin denies it to the Colonel. In jest, the new government appoints that fine sailor but half a man, FELIPE CARRERA, Admiral of the Navy of the Republic. It seems fitting, since Carrera is half-witted, for him to have this appointment, for there is no navy. Carrera proceeds to do the best he can with one small freighter, and waits and waits for government orders.

The Flag Paramount. One morning orders finally come for the faithful "loco" admiral and he rushes his small boat to the River Ruiz, where instead of beef and provisions he finds three men who board his ship. He recognizes the leader, Don SABAS PLACIDO; who, being exceedingly talented, plays with revolutions and collects naval flags. The admiràl knows Don Sabas for a traitor to the In government and reveals that he will have him shot. Don Sabas regretfully kills the admiral and turns the small craft towards the ship that is waiting to take him into exile and safety. He does not forget, however, to take the admiral's flag to complete his collection.

The Shamrock and the Palm. In the heat of a relaxed evening CLANCY tells Johnny Atwood the story of his fight for liberty in Guatemala. He is shanghaied under false pretenses by General DE VEGA to build a railroad that is politically needed, and he spends months hard at work with a pick and shovel instead of fighting in the glorious cause. He finally escapes, and he discovers that the general has just staged an unsuccessful *coup d'état* and has stowed away penniless on the same freighter to New Orleans. In New Orleans Clancy gets his revenge by turning the general in as a vagrant and watching him serve his sentence with a rake and shovel in front of the Irishman's favorite saloon.

The Remnants of the Code. BEELZEBUB BLYTHE, Coralio's town drunk and former U.S. gentleman, awakes one morning with all his credit exhausted and not one cent to his name. When he is refused his reviving morning drink everywhere, he is faced with his last resource, to blackmail Frank Goodwin about the lost valise with the hundred thousand dollars. Because he likes Goodwin, it is with great regret that he tells him he was the only witness to Goodwin's stealing the valuable valise and asks for a thousand dollars. Goodwin agrees, with no explanation, and says he will deliver the money when Blythe boards the afternoon ship to leave for the States. Blythe refuses brandy, though he desires it desperately; for one does not drink with the man one blackmails.

Shoes and **Ships.** The same evening the heartsick American consul and Billy Keogh are leisurely passing the time by ignoring all the consulate's mail. Keogh spies a letter from Atwood's home town. The letter seriously asks if a first-rate shoe store would be profitable in Coralio. Hysterical with laughter at the thought of a shoe store in this village of barefoot natives, they draft a jesting reply praising such a venture to the hilt. Never dreaming anyone would take them seriously, they are surprised weeks later when the would-be storekeeper arrives accompanied by packing cases of shoes and his beautiful daughter. In horror Atwood discovers that the daughter is his lost love ROSINE HEMSTETTER. He discovers also that she loves him and not his hated former rival, PINK DAWSON. Atwood is frantic. He solves his problem by cabling his rival, Dawson, to send thorny cockleburrs. These he and Keogh, secretly at night, spread on all the roads and streets. The natives are forced to buy shoes and Atwood confesses his love to Rosine. He resigns and returns to the U.S. to live in marital bliss.

Masters of Arts. Keogh decides to strike it rich with the aid and concert of the new dictator of Anchuria, President LOSADA. He goes to New York and enlists the aid of an old friend, CAROLUS WHITE, a down-and-out portrait painter. They return to Coralio during the only weeks of the year when it is a popular resort, and Losada is relaxing there. In no time, White is demeaning his art by painting the dictator to look like Washington and Napoleon combined. When he is finished and is paid $10,000 for his efforts he cannot bear what he has done and tears the check to pieces. Keogh is

121

furious. He goes about taking pictures with his camera. There is a brief flurry of revolution over an English money deal. Losada quashes it quickly, but not before Keogh has taken an incriminating picture of him negotiating with the Britisher. Losada pays him $20,000 without a murmur and Keogh, impressed by his good sportsmanship, is as big a fool as White and rejects the money.

Dicky. DICKY MALONEY drops from the clouds into Coralio to add to its odd fish. He is gay and compatible with a free-and-easy style. Soon he opens a small tobacco and sweet shop and meets, woos and marries PASA, the beautiful daughter of Madame ORTIZ. The Commandante flirts with Pasa and Dicky teaches him a painful lesson with his fists. Dicky· is put into jail and being temporarily without funds he languishes for three days. Pasa's fidelity weakens slowly with the absence of his love. But an American ship arrives in the harbor and its captain hurries to supply Maloney with all the funds he needs, so he and Pasa are reunited.

Rouge et Noir. Two Recalls. Dictator Losada antagonizes the Vesuvius Fruit Company, mighty in American dollars, by trying to shake them down for additional graft. The company gets busy at replacing this annoying President, who placed an extra cent on the price of bananas. A startling thing happens when the people are whipped into a frenzy of remembering their poor honest President, OLIVARRA. Dick Maloney jumps to the high steps, tears off his red wig, and reveals himself as the son of the dead Olivarra. He is proclaimed President and he lovingly draws Pasa with him to his future and Anchuria's future.

Caesar and Cleopatra

Play by George Bernard Shaw, 1856–1950.
Produced 1900. (ML, 19)

TO SHAW THERE WAS nothing temerarious about approaching one of Shakespeare's major characters. In a preface to the play, Shaw deprecates Shakespeare as well as Bardolatry and explains why his Julius Caesar is far superior to Shakespeare's. Many readers have agreed with him. *Caesar and Cleopatra* is masterful historical drama as well as magnificent comedy. Caesar is wholly believable as he transforms Cleopatra from a convincing juvenile into a convincing woman prepared to conquer Antony. The characters speak in modern language and the frequent anachronisms Shaw treats with the disdain they deserve. A sly touch is Britannus, Caesar's Briton henchman, Shaw's portrayal of the timeless Englishman in his conservatism and doggedness.

Prologue. The first act is preceded by a prologue and an alternative to the prologue. In the first, the Egyptian god Ra, arrogant and cynical, gives a brief history of Caesar's conquest over Pompey and Pompey's flight to Egypt and death. Caesar, following Pompey, enters Egypt to set up a Roman governor of his own and settle the dispute between young Queen Cleopatra and her younger brother Ptolemy. The *alternative to the prologue* is a brief dramatic section introducing the audience to Cleopatra's chief nurse FTATATEETA, an imperious battle-axe; the captain of the palace guards, BELZANOR, a gruff warrior; a sly Persian recruit; and the proud Egyptian soldier, BEL AFFRIS. They discuss the imminent arrival of the Romans and plan to sell Cleopatra to her brother so that when Caesar comes they can join him in her rescue and remain as palace guards to the joint rule of the Roman and Cleopatra. Cleopatra and a sacred white cat have disappeared, however, and the prologue ends with panic.

Act I. In the desert, by a sphinx, CLEOPATRA is found by an old stranger and they talk about the approaching Romans. The old man, in reality CAESAR himself, tells her she must be brave to meet the Roman conqueror. Together, they go to her palace just before the Roman soldiers arrive and hail their leader. Cleopatra is stunned but relieved to find that her friend turns out to be the man she had feared so.

Act II. At Alexandria, PTOLEMY is in the palace attended by his tutor, THEODOTUS; the chief of his army, ACHILLAS; and his guardian, POTHINUS. The boy is being encouraged to fight his sister and the Romans. At that instant, Caesar enters accompanied by his officer, RUFIO, and his secretary, BRITANNUS. Caesar decides to settle the dispute over Egypt's throne by calling out Cleopatra and declaring that the two young people will rule jointly, which dismays the court. When Caesar learns of Pompey's brutal assassination he is horrorstricken. He sends Ptolemy and his entourage away and makes plans to set up Cleopatra's court. He tells her about Mark Antony, whom she met when she was younger, and with whom she is deeply infatuated, and promises her that he will bring Antony back to her. Learning that Achillas has brought the Egyptian army into the city and incited riots against his men, Caesar prepares to withdraw his troops to a lighthouse and the quay by the palace. Pothinus returns to offer Caesar an ultimatum and is warned by Caesar to stop the rioting. Theodotus enters, hysterical because the library is burning from the fire spreading from Caesar's burning ships. Caesar remains unruffled and gets dressed for battle, with the help of Cleopatra. Then he leaves for the refuge of the lighthouse.

Act III. APOLLODORUS the Sicilian, a dapper young nobleman, confronts a Roman sentinel on the shore by Caesar's island lighthouse. He has some carpets for Cleopatra's palace but the sentinel refuses to let him pass. Ftatateeta arrives to ask that Apollo-

Caesar and Cleopatra

dorus may pass and after some angry debate the Roman allows the merchant and the nurse to go to the palace. Cleopatra runs out, asking for a boat to go to the lighthouse, and, once again a fight ensues. She is not permitted to go and decides to send Caesar a present of a carpet. She retires in the palace to make her choice, asking Apollodorus to take the gift to Caesar for her. The carpet is then brought out, with Ftatateeta's warning to Apollodorus that it is very fragile and must be handled with care, and he sails off with it toward the lighthouse. Meanwhile, at the lighthouse, Rufio and Caesar discuss the progress of the battle. Britannus brings Caesar a bagful of letters which could reveal the names of all Roman traitors and Caesar throws the sack into the sea, not wishing to waste time suspecting and condemning people. Apollodorus arrives, angry because his boat was destroyed by the falling bag of letters, but his carpet is safe and Caesar has it brought up to him by a crane. The present is opened, revealing Cleopatra. During this action the Egyptian army has cut them off from the Roman troops and they must escape. Following Apollodorus's lead, Caesar, Rufio and a reluctant Cleopatra dive into the water to swim to the safety of their incoming ships, leaving Britannus to be rescued later.

Act IV. Six months later, Cleopatra is with the women of the palace. She has grown older and wiser under Caesar's guidance. Pothinus arrives, angry because she has apparently sold her country to the Romans—who, though outnumbered, still hold the

Egyptian troops at bay. A sumptuous dinner is set for Caesar, who arrives with Rufio. Pothinus, now a prisoner, comes to warn Caesar against the treachery of Cleopatra. He is interrupted by her arrival. Caesar makes him speak in her presence and is not at all surprised at his news; Caesar shrugs it off as a natural and inevitable course of affairs, and one he expected. Cleopatra denies everything hotly but Caesar, amused, tells her that it is true. Left alone to compose herself, Cleopatra sends for Ftatateeta to kill Pothinus. The nurse leaves and the men return to eat and chat. They hear the dying scream of Pothinus; and Caesar, suspecting the truth, questions Cleopatra. The people in the streets, enraged by the assassination. rise up against the palace. Caesar, disgusted, prepares to leave Cleopatra. Just as the situation grows desperate outside, a Roman relief army approaches, to Caesar's great joy. Caesar leaves to join the incoming army. Rufio, staying behind, warns Cleopatra against further murder. Suspecting Ftatateeta of having committed the crime, he slits her throat and departs.

Act V. The conflict over, Caesar prepares to embark for Rome. He sets up Rufio as governor and promises once again to Cleopatra that he will send Mark Antony to her. Amid great pomp and celebration, Caesar departs; Cleopatra cries at the loss of her great old friend but awaits the arrival of the young Antony.

Caesar's Commentaries

History by Julius Caesar, 100–44 B.C. Written: *The Gallic Wars*, about 50 B.C.; *The Civil War*, about 47 B.C. (ML, 295)

CAESAR WAS ONE of history's remarkably versatile men and among other gifts he was a great stylist in classical Latin. This gift is perhaps inadequately appreciated by the generations of schoolboys who have had to learn the first line of *The Gallic Wars*: "*Gallia est omnis divisa in partes tres, quarum unum incolunt Acquitaniae . . .*" It is unfortunate that an outline necessarily cannot include any of the details of strategy, tactics and military engineering so painstakingly described by Caesar. There are many good translations and it would amaze many ten-o'clock Latin scholars to read one and find themselves enjoying it.

The Gallic Wars

Book I. 58 B.C. Gaul was divided into three major tribes, the Belgians, the Aquitanians, and the Gauls (Celts). The Helvetians were the bravest of the Gauls. They were constantly at war with the Germans and attempted to gain supremacy over the rest of Gaul. The leader of the Helvetians died and the tribe, wishing independence from Rome, attempted a march through the Province. The Helvetians tried to force their way across the Rhone. CAESAR built a barricade and pushed the Helvetians back. The Romans with their organized phalanx and superior discipline destroyed the enemy's army. The barbarians could not withstand the pikes and artillery of the Roman legions. The Helvetians fled and attempted to find safety in neighboring villages, but the vastly depleted army was captured and returned to their territory. Chiefs of the other tribes came to Caesar and thanked him for vanquishing the Helvetians. They asked the Roman general's protection against the German Sequanians, who, under the leadership of the tyrannical ARIOVISTUS, had moved into Gaul. Caesar sent overtures of friendship to the Sequanians but was curtly rebuffed. At a battlefield near Mulhausen, Caesar's army thoroughly defeated the German force.

Book II. 57 B.C. Caesar brought his army to Cisalpine Gaul to spend the winter. After they were installed in camp he learned that the Belgians had attacked the Roman garrison at Bibrax. The barbarians, with a multitude of soldiers, had surrounded the fortification and cast stones to knock down the Romans from the top wall. Holding their shields over their heads, they advanced on the garrison. The line of Belgians with shields raised looked like a giant tortoise to the men in the garrison. Caesar came to Bibrax and attacked the Belgians. They were forced to retreat from the garrison but later that day stormed Caesar's camp across the Sambre river. The Roman soldiers fought the Belgians in the river and the blood of both armies ran in the water. In the evening the Belgians decided to retreat and fight Caesar in their own territory, but he surprised them on their midnight march, killing and capturing many. The battle ended with the rout of the tribes and their survivors surrendered to Caesar. Caesar settled his legions in winter quarters and sent word of his victory to Rome and the Senate declared 15 days of thanksgiving.

Book III. 57-56 B.C. Caesar sent SERVIUS GALBA, with the 12th Legion, to open a pass through the Alps, which the Nantuates, Veragrians and Sedunians were holding. Caesar wanted this pass to be opened for Roman merchants. Galba, despite one defeat, fought a successful campaign and established a garrison. Caesar at last believed Gaul to be under Roman control, but a coastal tribe, the Venetians, protested a grain duty and gathered the other seacoast tribes together in a new rebellion. Caesar depended, in this battle, upon his well-equipped and skillful navy. The Roman fleet was victorious and the defeat of the Venetians was accomplished. Caesar decided to punish the tribe and killed or sold as slaves the members of its Senate. Caesar then campaigned against the mutinous tribes of Morini and Menappi. He chased them from their homes into the hills and ravaged the countryside.

Book IV. 55 B.C. The German tribes, hungry for land and war, moved across the Rhine. Their strength was extraordinary but their discipline weak, and the individual fighters were pushed back by the Roman line. Caesar decided to chase the Germans across the Rhine, but feeling that boats were an undignified means of transportation for the Roman army, he built a bridge to carry his men and supplies into German territory.

Caesar made an expedition to Britain. There he made a landing and despite the loss of ships and supplies brought some of the Britons under his control. Since Caesar's horses had been lost at sea he was unable to pursue the Britons after the battle. He wished to stop them from sending aid to Gaul. Back in Gaul, Caesar again vanquished the erring Morinians and Menapians, and when he sent word of his triumphs to the capital, the Senate decreed 20 days of thanksgiving.

Book V. 54 B.C. Caesar planned the preparation of his fleet for a second expedition to Britain, and left with hopes of a brilliant success. The landing was unopposed and the following day the Britons were again defeated. Caesar had to return to Gaul because of several new rebellions. He demanded hostages from the Britons and fixed a tribute that they were forced to pay to Rome each year. Britain was milder in climate than Gaul. Its people were settled in small agricultural communities and had the strange custom of painting themselves blue, which made them frightening in battle. In Gaul, Cicero had been attacked and surrounded by the Nervians. Caesar, back in Gaul, rescued the Romans and his soldiers brought in the head of the Gallic leader, INDUTIOMARUS.

Book VI. 53 B.C. There was a new revolt in Gaul. Caesar moved his legions against the Nervians, Senones, Carnates, and Menapians. He crossed the Rhine to prevent the warring tribes from obtaining asylum in Germany. The Gauls were very religious. They were Druids and led an elaborate ritual life. The Druid priests were the leaders of the society, along with some powerful nobles. Most of the people were slaves. The Germans were not as religious as the Druids. They recognized only the useful gods, such as Sun and Water. The Germans were better fighters and stronger people.

Book VII. 52 B.C. Another conspiracy of the Gauls was formed under the able leadership of VERCINGETORIX. His personal power and ability with words brought many tribes into the rebellion. Vercingetorix spoke of freedom and liberty and the rights of the people who tilled the land. After several minor battles Caesar managed to end the rebellion at the town of Alesia. The town was besieged and women and children ran terrified in the streets. The men were

Caesar's strength was in his Roman legions

cornered and killed and their houses burned. Vercingetorix, a brave and intelligent leader, was captured and the tribes who had followed him were punished and forced into submission. Caesar went on to subdue the Aeduians and the Avernians, and 20 days of thanksgiving were decreed in Rome.

Book VIII. 51–50 B.C. The final book of the Gallic war was written not by Caesar but by GALUS HIRTIUS, who was one of Caesar's officers. A successful campaign against the Bellouacians was described, and Caesar's glorious welcome on his return to Italy.

The Civil War

Book I. 50–49 B.C. Caesar has crossed the Rubicon into Italy, which precipitates the Civil War.

Chaps. 1–13. Caesar sent a letter offering to resign if POMPEY also would resign. Consuls refused to have the letter read in the Senate. SCIPIO, who spoke for Pompey, said that he would stand by the Senate if they were firm, but if they were irresolute he would not support them in a future crisis. Pompey's army was near Rome and his spokesmen in the Senate were loud and aggressive. It was decided to demand that Caesar disband his army by a specific date or be considered a traitor. In the evening the session was adjourned and Pompey's friends rallied to him and new soldiers came to his side. Caesar's enemies CATO and Scipio bore him ancient grudges and desired more power for themselves. They turned Pompey against Caesar even though he had once been Caesar's son-in-law. After an election in which Caesar's enemies were placed in control, Caesar's friends and members of the tribune came to Caesar at Ravenna. In Rome, Pompey and his friends divided the control of the Roman Empire. All rights of the people, sacred and secular, were taken away. On hearing of this, Caesar

addressed his troops and told them of the wrongs done him. They promised to defend him and the liberty of the Roman citizens. ROSCIUS and LUCIUS CAESAR came to Caesar at Rimini, where he had advanced with his soldiers, and entreated him to disband his army for the sake of unity within the state. Caesar asked the messengers to request a conference for Caesar with Pompey. They did, but Pompey refused to see Caesar until he disbanded his army. Caesar took several towns around Rimini. He heard that one of Pompey's generals had taken Gubbio but that the townspeople were for Caesar, so he sent several cohorts there under the charge of CURIO. Pompey's men withdrew and the townspeople cheered Caesar's troops.

Chaps. 13–25. Caesar marched to Osimo. The people let him into the town and Pompey's forces fled. News of this created panic in Rome, where Pompey's government was sitting. From Osimo Caesar moved swiftly through the entire region of Picenum. He was provided with supplies and welcomed by all the towns. Caesar surrounded the town of Sulmo and then the town of Corfinium. He forced these towns to surrender and absorbed Pompey's cohorts into his own army. He did not punish in any way those in the town who had conspired against him.

Chaps. 26–50. Caesar again demanded an interview with Pompey and designated Brindisi for the meeting. Caesar put floats into the harbors to prevent Pompey from attacking. As a countermeasure Pompey fitted large freighters with armed three-story towers. He drove the freighters against Caesar's works. Caesar decided to abandon all attempts at negotiation and concentrate on war. Pompey and his troops left the harbor and escaped to Asia. Caesar proceeded to Spain.

Chaps. 50–86. AFRANIUS, an officer of Pompey's, almost conquered Caesar in a battle at Lerida, because Caesar had lost important bridges in a rainstorm and could not attack or retreat. But he was ultimately able to cross the river and attack. There was

a naval battle at Marseilles, in which Caesar's fleet vanquished the enemy. Caesar forced Afranius's army up a hill and cut off their food supply. Some of the enemy soldiers deserted to Caesar's camp but there was a fierce battle, which Caesar won, taking Afranius's army and releasing the soldiers to return to their own homes.

Book II. 49 B.C. BRUTUS led Caesar's fleet against a second unsuccessful attack by the Massilians, and Marseilles capitulated to Brutus. Curio, one of Caesar's generals, went to Africa to fight Pompey's forces under the leadership of VARUS. Curio underestimated his opponent and took too small an army. Caesar's legions were badly defeated. Many of the men were killed and others taken prisoners. Curio declared that he would never face Caesar after losing so many of his men and he was killed on the battlefield. Caesar maintained control of Italy and Europe while Pompey's forces gathered strength in Africa.

Book III. 49–48 B.C. Pompey had assembled a large fleet from Asia and borrowed large sums from the various potentates of Asia and Syria. But Caesar transported his men and supplies from Brindisi and landed in Asia. He sent a message to Pompey, asking again for a peace conference. Pompey refused to accept and his army panicked, many of the men deserting to their homes. Pompey's fleet was unable to reach the mainland and in many areas his men were starving. He asked for a truce only in order to force Caesar to release his blockade, and Caesar, perceiving this, went on with his plans for war. Caesar was waiting for ships from Rome, bringing more men and supplies. MARK ANTONY came from Rome to aid Caesar. Pompey planned to ambush Antony's forces as they marched to join Caesar, but Antony was informed of the plan and kept his men in camp until Caesar had joined him. Scipio was notified of Antony's arrival by Pompey and brought his forces out of Syria to join Pompey. Pompey's army was down in the swamplands and Caesar in the mountains. Caesar built dams to prevent the clear mountain water from reaching Pompey. Pompey's army was forced to charge uphill because the men were starving. Due to a sudden panic among Caesar's soldiers, they were successful in splitting the army in two and killing many men. Caesar withdrew and spoke to his soldiers to uplift their morale.

At the decisive battle some weeks later the Pompeians were overconfident and fanciful in their battle plans. Caesar's army broke into Pompey's camp and Pompey fled. Caesar chased his opponent to prevent him from securing new soldiers and arms. Pompey was assassinated by the generals of PTOLEMY'S army. Caesar followed to Alexandria, where he tried to settle an inheritance quarrel between CLEOPATRA and her brother Ptolemy. Ptolemy's forces, under the rule of a regent, marched on Caesar in Alexandria, and this was the beginning of the Alexandrine War and the end of the Civil War between Pompey and Caesar.

The Caine Mutiny

Novel by Herman Wouk, 1915–
Published 1951 by Doubleday & Co.,
New York. © 1951 by Herman
Wouk.

IN THIS, HIS SECOND NOVEL, Wouk
fulfilled the promise of his earlier work
and was rewarded by one of history's
biggest best-sellers, plus a successful
Broadway play and Hollywood movie
(*The Caine-Mutiny Trial*). *The Caine
Mutiny* is perhaps not a "war novel,"
for its principal characters see no battle action, but it is an excellent novel
about men in the war. It won the Pulitzer Prize for 1952.

Chaps. 1–5. WILLIE SEWARD KEITH, a
young man of wealthy family whose mother
tries to spoil him, is admitted to midshipman school during World War II, mainly
to escape the Army for the Navy. He is
billeted with a young Southerner named
KEEFER and a pessimistic young man named
KEGGS. Willie has been in love with MAE
WYNN, a nightclub singer whose real name
is Marie Minotti, and he plans that their
romance will come to a natural end when
he is shipped out to sea after his four months
in midshipman school. The experience he
receives in training has a profound effect
upon him and he finds that he wants genuinely to succeed in the naval service. After
many vicissitudes, and near expulsion for
excessive demerits, he is at length graduated
and assigned to Destroyer Minesweeper 22,
U.S.S. *Caine*. He is now Ensign Keith.

Chaps. 6–8. While Willie is in San
Francisco awaiting orders to board the
Caine, he learns of his father's death. He
fails to make connections in Hawaii with
the ship, because of an error in his orders,
and at a party attracts the attention of an
admiral, through his piano playing. He is
given a part in the officers' pool that will
keep him ashore for some time, but he
seeks a means of reaching the *Caine*, with
no success. After several months, Willie is
awakened early one morning by Ensign
PAYNTER, a member of the *Caine's* complement, and learns that Keefer's brother
TOM is on the same ship. On boarding the
ship, Willie receives an impression that is to
remain with him indefinitely: The *Caine* is
a "pile of junk in the last hours of decay."
Life aboard the *Caine* is uncomfortable and
dull. Willie thinks that Captain DE VRIESS
is responsible for the slovenly condition of
the ship and is delighted when an order arrives to transfer him elsewhere and put in
command instead one Lieutenant Commander PHILIP F. QUEEG.

Chaps. 9–14. At first Captain Queeg is
pleasant and agreeable. He holds a meeting
of his officers and tells them that everything
aboard the *Caine* is henceforth to be done
with rigid obedience and conformity to
regulations, and with no deviations permitted. Soon the meaning of "conformity" becomes painfully clear. The free-and-easy
days under Captain de Vriess are over.
Every smallest detail is checked and enforced by Captain Queeg, and soon an
atmosphere of tension develops aboard the
Caine. The first evidence of Queeg's incompetence in handling a ship comes when
orders arrive to send the *Caine* to tow
targets for ship's gunnery practice drills.
Queeg botches his orders for getting the
ship clear of the dock, and in his report of
the resultant grounding of the propeller
in the harbor mud, he blames failure on the
part of the engine tenders to respond to
his commands. The entire ship knows that
the fault was solely Queeg's. Next, the captain appoints Willie Keith as morale officer, with instruction that all officers and
crew keep their shirts tucked in the trouser
bands at all times. Queeg's habit of constantly rolling steel balls between his fingers
has been noted by all his staff. An incident
concerning the manner of giving orders to
the helmsman causes Queeg to run down
the wrong side of a channel. Although they
barely miss a battleship, Queeg refuses to
admit that they are on the wrong side of
the channel. The next unpleasant incident
occurs when Queeg spends so long berating a sailor for having a shirttail out that he
forgets to give the orders to straighten out
after a turn. Before he corrects this the ship
has made two complete circles and has
severed the tow-rope attached to the target.
Queeg refuses to send out a boat to retrieve
the valuable target, and heads for home,
blaming a defective tow-rope for his own
stupidity. Returning to the *Caine*, he finds
young STILWELL, the helmsman of the day
before, reading while on watch, which has
been permitted in the past, but which Queeg
sternly forbids. Stilwell is given six months'
restriction to the ship for it. Word comes
that the *Caine* is to go to the States for general overhaul, and everyone is pleased.

Chaps. 15–18. Queeg buys all the unused liquor rations of the officers, having in
mind the far higher cost of liquor in the
States. It is against regulations, but he
orders a crate to be made to hold his loot.
He takes the ship out of its way to debark
the liquor, and the extremely heavy weight
causes the crate to slip from the handlers
into the harbor. Queeg blames Willie, and
withholds shore leave until Willie gives him
the cost of the lost liquor. When the ship
finally docks, both Mrs. Keith and Mae are
waiting for Willie. The *Caine* stays in port
a shorter time than was expected, but Willie and Mae go skiing at Yosemite and see
a great deal of each other. Mrs. Keith hopes
they will not marry.

Chaps. 19–23. Orders come, sending
Caine in advance of an attack force on
Kwajalein. The DMS is supposed to steam
ahead on the proper course, so that the attack force will know exactly where to go.
Queeg hurries toward the point too fast for
the attack boats to keep up, and drops a
yellow dye marker by the spot, turning and
getting away as quickly as possible. This
earns him the nickname of "Old Yellow-
stain," which sticks. A day later orders
come to detach Lieutenant RABBIT, and
Queeg attempts to procrastinate. He is
foiled when the captain of the ship to which
Rabbit is transferred comes aboard the
Caine. Queeg's frustration puts him in a vile
temper, and he cuts off all water for bathing
and drinking, as he learns that on the day
of the Kwajalein operation water consumption increased ten percent. Forty-eight hours
of sweltering tropic heat without water has
a powerful effect on officers and crew. Queeg
extends the officers' water ban for an extra
48 hours when he catches an ensign taking
a shower with the water left standing in the
pipes. Shortly after the water famine, a
court-martial is scheduled for Stilwell, accusing him of falsifying a report of his
mother's illness in order to see his wife. The
officers who judge are forced to find him
guilty, but they deliberately insult Queeg by
ordering as punishment the loss of a few
days' leave.

Chaps. 24–27. STEVE MARYK, executive
officer, has listed the strange and eccentric
behavior of Captain Queeg in a "medical
log," on the basis of Tom Keefer's earlier
and emphatic declaration that Queeg is on
the verge of a psychological disorder. Keefer
is prevented from seeing his brother, Roland, on a carrier moored nearby. Queeg
refuses to let him leave because of some unimportant filing that is incomplete. Next
day Roland is killed as the result of a Japanese suicide plane that crashes the carrier.
One of the other ships in the group is a
tender, and Ensign JORGENSEN acquires a
gallon of frozen strawberries from a friend
aboard. There is a feast of strawberries and
ice cream, but late that night the Captain
sends for more, only to be told that the
strawberries are gone. In a rage, he summons a meeting and goes through a wild
and furious investigation to account for the
missing strawberries—which he calculates
must be about a quart. No one admits eating them, and Queeg becomes violent. The
scene verges on farcical madness as he demands an inspection of every man aboard, in
possession of every man aboard, determined
to uncover the extra—but nonexistent—
key to the supply room. The frantic and
senseless search leads Tom Keefer to
remark to Maryk that this seems like the behavior of a raving lunatic. Subtly, he asks
Maryk if he has read Article 184 of *Navy
Regulations*, which states that the commanding officer of a ship may be "relieved"
if he is completely unable, because of illness, to continue in his command. Queeg
seems at least mentally "unfit" as he insists
on continuing a fruitless search for a key
that does not exist, even after two witnesses
have declared they saw the mess boys scraping out the strawberry can.

Chaps. 28–30. During a typhoon, Queeg
indicates general incompetence, and in the

opinion of the ship's personnel he does not know what to do. The danger seems imminent when Maryk assumes command and brings the *Caine* through safely. After the storm, the *Caine* picks up three survivors of a ship they see floating bottom-up. Queeg would not have troubled to look for survivors, he says.

Chaps. 31–33. Maryk is to be court-martialed, but not on a charge of actual mutiny. The charge is "Conduct to the Prejudice of Good Order and Discipline." Before the trial, Willie has time to go East for a brief visit with his mother, and an even briefer visit with Mae, at which time he tells her that their romance is finished. Meanwhile, the defense for Maryk encounters some difficulty in finding a lawyer to represent him. At length BARNEY GRUENWALD, a young Jewish lawyer from Albuquerque, agrees to take on the task, after he learns from Maryk that Tom Keefer was the source of all the rumors of Queeg's mental unbalance. Maryk was Keefer's victim, and Gruenwald declares that he can unquestionably get an acquittal.

Chaps. 34–37. The trial produces the recounting of all the events that have taken place on the *Caine* since Queeg took command. Queeg often tells direct untruths, but it is his word against that of one officer or sailor in each case, and only his contradictory statements can be challenged. At length he becomes so excited and so angry that he speaks incoherently and shrilly, for far too long. He is not insane, but merely stupid, disagreeable, and inept. However, Barney Gruenwald wins his case by emphazing that at the times noted, Queeg *was* mentally ill, for it is quite inconceivable for an officer

Cakes and Ale

Novel by W. Somerset Maugham, 1874–1966.

Published 1930 by Doubleday & Co., New York. © 1930 by W. Somerset Maugham. (ML, 270)

ASHENDEN THE WRITER has been used by Maugham as narrator in many stories, notably his excellent stories of spying and intrigue during World War I. *Cakes and Ale* is considered one of Maugham's major novels.

Chaps. 1–3. My name is WILLIAM ASHENDEN and I am a writer by profession. When I learn that ALROY KEAR wishes to see me, I assume that he has in mind some purpose advantageous to himself, for he does almost nothing without such a motive. His talent for advancing himself has won him great fame as a novelist, and great personal popularity as well. He likes people in general, and in general they like him. I lunch with Roy at his club. I do not learn the reason for his seeking me out, but our conversation is guided skillfully by him to the subject of the late EDWARD DRIFFIELD, who at this time is acknowledged to have been one of the best of Victorian novelists. I knew Driffield and his wife when I was a boy living with my aunt and uncle in Blackstable, a Kentish town near the sea. My opinion of Driffield's work is not very high, and Kear seems somewhat irritated by that. He leaves without asking the favor —whatever it may be—that I am certain he has in mind. His mention of Driffield recalls to my mind the first time I had heard of him. He was considered rather common in Blackstable, and socially unacceptable. Worse, his then wife, ROSIE, was a former barmaid!

Chaps. 4–10. I receive a note from AMY DRIFFIELD, the writer's second wife, now his widow. It invites me to call. I remember the only time I met the second Mrs. Driffield. She had been the nurse who attended Driffield during a long and serious illness some time before. At the time when I met her, in the United States Navy to be either incompetent or a coward. Maryk is acquitted. Tom Keefer comes rushing up to him with the news that he has sold his novel, which he worked on aboard the *Caine,* and that he is giving a grand dinner party that night. Maryk and Gruenwald must attend, as guests of honor. Gruenwald arrives late, already half intoxicated. He makes a speech, when asked to propose a toast, in which he excoriates the "sensitive civilians" who scoff at regular Navy procedure and personnel, when it is the regulars who give the

A kamikaze strikes the ship

civilians freedom in which to scoff if they wish.

Chaps. 38–40. Tom Keefer is captain of the *Caine,* and when a Kamikaze plane strikes the ship, setting fire to one engine room, Keefer jumps overboard, leaving Willie, his executive officer, to save the ship and take charge of extinguishing the fire. Soon the war is over, and Keefer is in line for a fast discharge on the point system. Willie becomes the last captain of the *Caine* and takes the ship from Okinawa to Bayonne, New Jersey, for de-commissioning. He then goes to find Mae, knowing that she is the woman he will always want to have beside him. After some difficulty he locates her and convinces her of his sincerity. Both Mae and Mrs. Keith realize that he is not the same boy who joined the Navy so long ago. Willie Seward Keith has become a man.

Driffield was an acknowledged personage in the literary world, and something of a celebrity. He mentioned that he had taught me to ride a bicycle, and the associations with that incident recalled events of earlier times. My aunt and uncle were most scornful of Driffield and his wife and disapproved heartily of my seeing them. I thought also of Rosie, who had been a most disarmingly likable person. My aunt's maid, Mary Ann, had known Rosie from childhood, and mentioned to me that Rosie had "carried on" with many different men while employed as a barmaid. One of these was GEORGE KEMP, our local coal merchant and occasional dealer in real estate. I myself observed positive evidence that Rosie and George had not ceased their friendship with her marriage. I saw them slip away into the fields for a romantic tryst, which shocked me deeply. My acquaintance with Rosie and Edward Driffield continued through my holidays from school. It was at Easter holiday that I learned suddenly of their departure, leaving behind them many debts. All the shock of this discovery sweeps over me again as I am reminded by Amy Driffield's note of those times so long before.

Chaps. 11–16. In a conversation with Roy, I learn that he is to write Edward Driffield's biography. He seems to think that there are many things about Driffield's life that should be touched upon only lightly and subtly, if at all. Rosie, for example— who Roy says has been dead for years—is one of the "unfortunate" parts of the great man's life. So also are his dislike of bathing, and his regrettable habit of conversing with all manner of common persons at the local pub, a place that he visited far too regularly. In short, the biography of Edward Driffield is to paint an artist, a genius, and a solemnly important literary figure, with little trace of the man himself. I do not contemplate with relish a visit with the second Mrs. Driffield and I agree to go to Blackstable only if I may stay at the inn and enjoy complete privacy whenever I wish. Some whim to recall the past sends me to my former lodging house in town, where Mrs. HUDSON, my former landlady, is still the humorous, likable, warm-hearted woman I remember. So much has happened since I lived in her house! It was after two years there that I met the Driffields in London. Quite accidentally I encountered Mrs. (Rosie) Driffield and realized for the first time that she was very pretty. I went to their flat, and found Driffield as hospitable as ever. Soon I developed the habit of dropping in every Saturday, when various and assorted groups of people congregated there. Eventually Mrs. BARTON TRAFFORD, a socially prominent and influential woman, took Driffield under her competent wing and set out to make him famous in what she termed "the right circles." That she succeeded most admirably is a matter of history. Mrs. Trafford was, incidentally, the only person I ever knew Rosie to dislike—heartily and uncompromisingly. The indescribable charm and very real beauty of Rosie impressed itself more deeply on me each time I saw her, and before long I was occasionally escorting her to the theater or to the interesting occasions of the day. Driffield worked at night, and there was no reason for Rosie to sit alone in their flat while he worked. One night after attending a popular play we sat down for a moment in the park. It was a beautiful night. Suddenly we were hungry and stopped for fish and chips at a small place I knew. Heading back toward her flat, we passed my lodgings and I invited Rosie in to see them. She spent the night with me.

Chaps. 17–18. I suspected that she might be sleeping with some of the other men who took her out, but chose to deny the suspicion to myself. I was able to continue my self-deception until the episode of a rich Dutch Jew named JACK KUYPER. He squired Rosie for some time, and just before returning to Amsterdam gave her a sable cape and muff that cost more than I earned in two years. Then I knew. Still, Rosie was warmly sweet and human, and she somehow made it seem utterly unimportant. It was at about this time that Driffield in *Cup of Life* caused a major sensation. Critics said that it was shocking, dreadful, and wicked—should be banned. Not a word in it would even ruffle the modern reader, but this was the Victorian era. Driffield simply shrugged and continued to write.

Chaps. 19–21. (Still reminiscing.) A telegram from Mrs. Trafford asked me to call and I obeyed the summons. I learned that Rosie had left Driffield and had run away with George Kemp. At the exhortation of the Traffords, I went to Blackstable and found ample confirmation of the report. Kemp had left his wife and two sons, and a mountain of debt. The scandal rocked the town, but I personally was merely hurt and angry that Rosie should prefer George Kemp, as a lover, to me. Back in London, Driffield was staying with the Traffords and was not well. Time passed, and I lost touch with him. Money from America was forthcoming to Rosie's mother, but never with a message or a return address. When her mother died, no more was heard of Rosie.

Chaps. 22–25. This was all in my recollection. On Friday, Alroy Kear and I meet as scheduled in Victoria Station, en route to Blackstable. From him I learn that Isabel Trafford tended Driffield for some time and as a reward was honored by a dedication in his novel *By Their Fruits*. He became very ill with pneumonia shortly thereafter, and since he was away from London Mrs. Trafford hired a nurse for him. Three weeks later she learned that he had married his nurse by special license. This was Amy. We reach Blackstable and I find things much changed. A former schoolmate of mine is a grandfather three times over, which is somehow a shock. The second Mrs. Driffield is more than a shock. She obviously ruled the home life of Edward Driffield with a velvet-clad iron hand. She made over his appearance, his house and his manner of living into what she considered proper for one of his eminence. At that meeting with Roy and Amy, I feel constrained to dispute their coarse conclusions with regard to Rosie. I know better. Amy never told Driffield when she heard from one of Kemp's sons that Rosie was dead. She did not want to disturb the great man with a sordid note out of the past!

Chap. 26. Alroy wants material for his biography of Edward Driffield, but he wants only the sugar-coatings. I could give him far more than he suspects to exist—for Rosie Driffield Iggulden is very much alive. I know, for I saw her not long ago in New York, where I received considerable publicity in connection with the opening of one of my plays. She and George Kemp had changed their name to Iggulden, and George was dead. Rosie was then about 70, but still vital and appealing, and still filled with love of life. I learned from her that Driffield had completely understood his infidelities and had accepted them. Her attraction to George Kemp she summed up most succinctly: "He was always such a perfect gentleman."

The Call of the Wild

Novel by Jack London, 1876–1916. Published 1903. Copyright 1903, 1931 by The Macmillan Co., New York. Published by Grosset & Dunlap, New York. (PB, 593)

PERHAPS TO PROVE the doctrine that dog books are the surest successes and the longest-lived in the world of books, *The Call of the Wild* has long been the most popular of Jack London's books. It is one of the best-written of the dog stories and has several emotional high points. It is written from the dog's point of view.

Chap. 1. From a house in the Santa Clara valley the dog BUCK is stolen, to be sold for use as a sled dog in the Alaska gold rush of 1897. Buck is a magnificent large dog with luxuriant fur. His father was a St. Bernard and his mother a shepherd. Buck is treated cruelly by the man who is taking him to his new owner. He fights angrily against each new outrage, from the strangling rope about his neck to the cramped cage in which he eventually rides. He learns that a man with a club is not to be disputed. Soon he is resold —this time to a French Canadian named PERREAULT, who with another man, FRANÇOIS, is commissioned to purchase sled dogs for carrying government dispatches. CURLY, a Newfoundland; a large white dog from Spitzbergen called SPITZ; a sullen, unfriendly dog called DAVE, and Buck are all taken aboard ship and transported to the coast of Alaska, where Buck sees his first snow.

Chap. 2. Buck learns quickly that he is in a land where the only law is the law of club and fang. Curly is killed swiftly in a brief fight with a husky and his body is torn to pieces by the circle of dogs that witness the battle. Buck learns that once a fighter goes down, the pack closes in to finish him off. Spitz has a way of rolling out his tongue and laughing, and he laughs as he sees the end of Curly. Buck suddenly hates the big white dog with an undying hatred. Almost immediately he is introduced to the sled harness. Dave is impatient with mistakes, nipping him sharply to correct him. Spitz is the lead dog. Buck learns fast, and François is delighted with him. Sleeping in the bitter cold poses a problem until Buck sees one of his teammates curled in a hollow dug in a snowdrift. He proceeds to dig one for himself. The warmth of his body quickly heats the tiny area and he sleeps comfortably. Instincts long buried under domestication come to life again and Buck swiftly hardens into a cunning, powerful, resourceful dog of the north.

Chap. 3. Buck's hatred for Spitz continues. One night they begin a fight but a pack of starving huskies raid the camp and precipitate a free-for-all. Buck's feet are not as hard as those of the other dogs and a set of boots is made for him by François. Shortly afterward, one of the dogs bitten in the fight with the huskies goes mad, and it is Buck that she chases. He is saved when François' club hits his pursuer, and he sinks exhausted to the ground. Spitz, seeing Buck's weakness, attacks viciously but is beaten by François, who says that some day Buck will kill Spitz. Buck is now an accomplished sled dog and resents the fact that Spitz is the leader. One day the dogs are chasing a snowshoe rabbit, filled with the thrill of the chase. Spitz cuts across a curve and seizes the rabbit, which Buck felt to be his legitimate prey. He flies at Spitz and the long-awaited battle is on. Spitz has killed many another

127

rival but goes down at last to be torn to pieces by the circle of huskies, while Buck looks on—triumphantly victorious.

Chap. 4. Buck steps into the lead dog's place next day, but the dog drivers put him out and place another in the traces. Buck drives the interloper away three times, until he is threatened with a club. He keeps his distance, but refuses to go into the old place. The drivers at length acknowledge defeat and put him in the lead dog's place. François and Perreault receive orders to go elsewhere and the team is turned over to a mail train group. This is hard, gruelling work and soon the dogs are in poor condition—badly in need of a rest period. Dave is obviously in pain but refuses to be taken out of harness, as is the way with true sled dogs. It is more merciful to let him die in the traces; he would die anyway, of a broken heart, if he were not allowed to work. Finally Dave is shot.

Chap. 5. When the team reaches Skaguay, both drivers and dogs are in a state of utter exhaustion. The team is sold to two greenhorns named HAL and CHARLIE. With them is MERCEDES, Charlie's wife and Hal's sister. They overload the sled, they pack it improperly, they carry dozens of unnecessary things. The two men think to lighten the load with a team of fourteen dogs. Fourteen is too many, because a single sled cannot carry enough food for fourteen dogs. Hal and Charlie mismanage what food they have. One by one, dogs begin to starve to death. The five left reach the camp of JOHN THORNTON with the beginning of the spring thaw. Thornton warns them against the rotting ice ahead. Hal sneers at him, determined to continue despite the warning. Buck refuses to move and Hal takes the club

to him. Buck is beaten unmercifully, until he is only a quarter conscious. Thornton warns grimly that if another blow falls on the dog, he will kill Hal. He takes Buck out of the traces, and the remaining dogs drag the sled away. Dogs, sled and the three humans disappear in an ice hole. John Thornton is Buck's new master.

Chap. 6. Buck learns for the first time the meaning of true love for a man. He adores John Thornton. HANS and PETE, Thornton's associates, remark that they would not like to be the man who attempted to lay hands on John Thornton. In Circle City Thornton good-naturedly steps between two quarreling men and BLACK BURTON, an ill-tempered man, strikes out with his fist. Buck goes for him but is driven off by the crowd. The opinion of the miners is that Buck was within his rights. Later Buck saves Thornton from certain death in the rapids of the river—breaking three of his own ribs in the act. Still later, he enables Thornton to win a substantial bet by the unheard-of feat of pulling by himself a load of one thousand pounds on a sled frozen in the snow—breaking it out unaided. This achievement earns $1,600 for John Thornton. A famous passage in the book occurs when Thornton refuses to sell Buck.

The dogs are turned over to a mail train group

Chap. 7. The money won by Thornton makes it possible for him to seek a certain lost mine, and with Pete and Hans he sets out. For months they travel, and after many hundreds of miles, they come upon a shallow basin in which the gold is so plentiful that it can be seen gleaming through the water. Day after day, they fill sacks with gold dust and nuggets. There is nothing for the dogs to do. Buck becomes aware of a call that seems to come from the depths of the forest. It is the call of the primitive—and of the wild. One night he awakens with a start at the sound of a certain call in the forest. He approaches the source of the sound and at length sees the lean form of a timber wolf, muzzle pointed skyward, and howling. The wolf dashes away and Buck follows. At length the wolf is cornered and turns to snarl and snap at him. Buck circles about, making friendly advances, but the wolf is fearful. At length they sniff noses, then they run together through the night. But Buck remembers John Thornton and returns to Thornton's camp. On another of Buck's lonely prowls he encounters a herd of buffalo—with one old bull that has an arrow protruding from his shoulder. Buck stalks the beast for four days until at last he closes in for the kill. Four days more of eating and sleeping beside his prey, and Buck is ready to go back to the camp. Doom seems to hang over him as he lopes along. At the approach to the camp it is suddenly clarified. The body of Hans is lying with many arrows protruding from it. Strange men are moving about rhythmically, chanting strange sing-song chants. An over-powering fury possesses Buck, and with no warning he leaps into the circle of men, slashing and killing with lightning speed. So vicious and so fast are his movements that the Indians—Yeehats—flee in panic. Buck follows the trail of John Thornton to the edge of the pool—and there the trail stops. Buck raises his nose and howls. Pete he has already found dead in his blanket roll. Buck remains near the camp and hears timber wolves approaching. He stands and awaits them, motionless. When the boldest attacks, Buck breaks its neck. Three others try, but withdraw slashed and bleeding. Now Buck must fight the whole pack. He fights so powerfully that at length the wolves stand back, uncertain. One of their number moves forward slowly, the wild brother with whom Buck ran in the woods, and they touch noses. An older wolf moves up next, and after a warning snarl, Buck sniffs noses with him also. The old wolf sits down and howls, and the rest of the pack follows his example. Buck then does the same thing—and when the pack yelps and courses away, Buck runs with them.

As the years go on, the Yeehats notice a change in the breed of timber wolves—and they tell tales of a Ghost Dog that runs with the pack. The Yeehats do not visit the valley where John Thornton's camp was once located, but each summer a great wolf visits the valley, sits quietly there for a while, then lifts his muzzle to the sky and howls just once.

Camille

(The Lady of the Camellias)

Novel by Alexandre Dumas *fils*, 1824–1895.
Published 1848. (ML, 69)

IN THIS CASE the fame of the novel is as nothing compared to the fame of the play that Dumas *fils* made of it. The play appeared in 1852 with Eleonora Duse in the title rôle. The part is one of the best ever made available for an actress. The title of both novel and play (*La Dame aux Camélias*, The Lady of the Camellias) and the name of the heroine have been all but forgotten in the survival of her sobriquet, Camille. The novel is short and the play introduces new scenes and characters.

Chaps. 1–2. I learn that at an apartment at 9, Rue Lantin, the furniture is to be sold at public auction some days hence. The owner, a woman of ill repute, died in debt. I follow the curious crowds of sightseers and learn that this was the apartment of a MARGUERITE GAUTIER (Margherita Gauthier), whom I knew by name and sight only. I knew also the story of Marguerite's daughterly relationship with a wealthy and elderly duke, who had been entranced by her resemblance to his dead daughter and asked her to allow him a father's interest in her, not knowing of her profession. Even when he became aware of her past, and she herself resumed her gay life between his visits, he refused to reject the girl so like his daughter. Marguerite was seen and known everywhere. She always wore camellias.

Chaps 3–4. At the sale of Marguerite's effects, I buy a copy of *Manon Lescaut*, inscribed in front "Armand Duval." Some days later, Armand Duval himself appears at my house to ask if I will sell him the book. I give it to him willingly. From him I begin to learn what a wonderful woman Marguerite Gautier really was.

Chaps. 5–7. I seek the grave of Marguerite, for a reason I cannot explain even to myself, and find that it is kept covered perpetually with fresh camellias, at the order of Armand Duval. I learn also that Armand has gone to obtain permission from Marguerite's sister to have the body removed and placed in another grave. This entails an identification of the uncovered corpse, and Armand provides it, nearly fainting in horror at the sight. He becomes ill and is confined to his bed for several weeks. I remain with him, and he tells me the story of the love between him and Marguerite Gautier.

Chaps. 7–13. Armand tells me of the first time he saw Marguerite and of the tremendous attraction she exerted toward him. He did not see her often, and always at a distance. Suddenly he failed to see her at all, and learned that she was ill. She was consumptive and had gone to Bagneres for her health. There she met an elderly duke, rich and kind, whose daughter died of tuberculosis a few days after Marguerite's arrival. In his grief, the startling resemblance between Marguerite and his daughter caused him to ask her if she would take his daughter's place in his life, and she agreed. He visited her regularly, and it was during this period that Armand met and fell in love with her. He called at her apartment in the company of her next-door neighbor, PRUDENCE DUVERNOY, and another young man, GASTON. He learned that she was very ill with tuberculosis and could not expect to live very long. They became lovers, and the next day Marguerite told him of her plan for them to spend the summer in the country, far from Paris and the life she lived there.

Chaps. 14–15. A jealous quarrel separated Armand from his love, but reconciliation was swift, for both were truly in love. NANINE, Marguerite's maid, prepared them a supper and they were happy together again.

Chaps. 16–18. Armand and Marguerite spent the day in the country at Bongival and saw a cottage that delighted them. Marguerite determined to ask the old duke to rent it for her, and he did so. Armand moved to a suite in an inn nearby. The old duke, who had been so generous, suddenly stopped supplying Marguerite with money, and Armand's income was inadequate. Marguerite sold and pawned her possessions, to pay some debts, and Armand determined to help somehow.

Chaps. 19–22. Armand's father came to Paris, arriving just after Marguerite and Armand had taken a small house in town. Armand had started making arrangements for an income left him to be turned over to Marguerite. Monsieur Duval was angry and distressed over his son's relationship with Marguerite, whose past he knew. He could not convince Armand, however, and instead approached Marguerite with a plea that she give up Armand so that his sister's engagement would not be endangered by a scandal. Her fiancé was of a stern and unbending family. Marguerite's sympathy for another woman's love caused her to tell Armand that all was over between them. He did not know of his father's responsibility.

Chaps. 23–24. Armand, in his hurt, was intentionally cruel and appeared with a new mistress in all the places where he was sure to see Marguerite. At length she could stand no more and went to England. Armand also was miserable and went to Alexandria, where he learned that Marguerite was dying.

Chaps. 25–26. Armand did not reach her in time to see her before she died, but her letters told him the entire story of her great sacrifice and told him also how great was her love. His father confessed that Marguerite was indeed a great and noble woman.

Geoffrey Chaucer
1340?–1400

William Butler Yeats
1865–1939

Candide

Novel by Voltaire (François-Marie Arouet, 1694–1778).
Published 1759.

AMID HIS LARGE CATALOG of major works and for all his timeless prestige, Voltaire left precisely one book that is still widely read by Americans. This is it. *Candide* is a satire, chiefly on the optimistic philosophies (the subtitle of the book is "Optimism") but also on whatever struck Voltaire's fancy in passing. Much of the action is extravagant or fantastic. The best-remembered phrase of the book, "the best of all possible worlds," was uttered not by Candide but by the almost equally well-remembered tutor, Doctor Pangloss. Candide is naughty in spots but it should be read.

Chaps. 1–7. CANDIDE is a pleasant young man who lives with Baron THUNDER-TEN-TRONCKH and is secretly enamored of the baron's beautiful daughter CUNEGONDE. Dr. PANGLOSS, tutor to Cunegonde's brother, introduces Candide to his optimistic doctrines of sufficient reason and a perfect world, and Candide is the happiest of men until one day he is surprised by the Baron in the act of embracing Cunegonde. Candide is rudely kicked out, penniless. Wandering about, starving, Candide is shanghaied by two men into the Bulgar army, where he is flogged 4,000 times for trying to escape his imprisonment. He is witness to a great battle with 30,000 casualties. He passes through a ravished village and leaves the army for good. After some rough treatment at the hands of some religious zealots he befriends a kindly Anabaptist, JAMES, who feeds him and gives him some money. Continuing his wanderings, Candide encounters a decrepit, diseased beggar who turns out to be Pangloss. From him Candide learns that Cunegonde was ravished and disemboweled by the enemy and that Pangloss caught his terrible disease from a servant girl. Candide gets James to cure Pangloss and then all three sail to Lisbon on business. They run into a tempest that kills everyone but Candide and the Doctor, who get to shore just as an earthquake strikes. They barely escape this, only to be captured for a sacrificial offering to prevent further earthquakes. Pangloss is hanged and Candide flogged mercilessly. Staggering half-conscious, Candide is led by an old woman to her humble home, where she feeds him and brings him back to health. Then Candide meets his real benefactor, who had sent the woman to get him. Cunegonde, who lived through her ordeal, explains how both her parents and brother were butchered and then, after listening to Candide's story, relates her own.

Chaps. 8–14. Cunegonde describes her ordeal with the soldiers and how she was sold to a JEW who owns the house she presently lives in. Her situation was complicated when the Grand Inquisitor became interested in her and arranged to share the house and her with the Jew. When she recognized Candide as a victim of the Grand Inquisitor's persecution, she had him rescued. Cunegonde's story is interrupted by the arrival first of the Jew and then of the Grand Inquisitor. Both are slain by Candide. The young lovers escape with the old servant woman. Cunegonde is robbed on the way but they all manage to travel by horse to Cadiz. Candide joins a ship bound for Paraguay as an army captain. On the trip, Cunegonde and Candide listen to the old woman tell her story. She was the daughter of a Pope and engaged to a man who shortly was poisoned by a jealous mistress. Mother and daughter escaped in a yacht and were boarded by pirates, captured as slaves, and taken to Morocco where they were ravished and everyone murdered except the narrator. She was rescued by a young Italian eunuch, who then sold her to the governor of Algiers, where she got the plague and was sold again. After several changes of owners, she was bought by a Turkish captain who took her with him to war. When supplies ran out, the entire harem of women lost one buttock each to stave off starvation. Shortly afterward, everyone was killed but the women, who were sold again. After still more transfers of ownership, the old woman arrived as a servant at the house of Cunegonde's Jew.

Their ship arrives in Paraguay. Candide loses Cunegonde to the Governor and flees to a Jesuit camp. Here he meets Cunegonde's brother, alive after all.

Chap. 15–19. Cunegonde's brother tells Candide how a Jesuit saved him after the slaughter of his family and how he came to Paraguay to fight the Spanish. Candide slays him when he ridicules him for wanting to marry Cunegonde. Candide and his servant CACAMBO escape the Jesuit camp, then are captured by savages who plan to eat them. Cacambo convinces the cannibals that the two mean no harm and they escape once more, wander through the South American jungle, and finally, by chance, stumble onto the country of Eldorado, where everything is truly perfect. The people are happy, wealth abounds, and Candide is convinced that this must be what Pangloss was referring to when he said "the best of all possible worlds." After a month of leisure the two men, with the assistance of the king, leave with a great fortune. They come to Surinam and Candide tells Cacambo to get Cunegonde back for him and rejoin him in Venice. After Cacambo's departure, Candide is robbed of most of his possessions by a sly Dutch captain whose ship he chartered for his trip to Venice. Desperate, he charters a French ship going to Bordeaux and hires a French scholar named MARTIN to accompany him on the trip.

Chaps. 20–24. On the voyage to Bordeaux, Candide finds his companion to be a cynical and very pessimistic young man who in a long discussion explains to Candide that man was created by evil forces, not good forces. Before reaching their destination, they witness the sinking of the Dutch ship that carries his stolen wealth and Candide recovers some of his fortune. At Bordeaux they board a carriage for Paris, where Candide falls ill and almost dies. After recovering, he is escorted with Martin to a theater by a mercenary abbot. Candide wants to meet the leading actress and after he has lost some money to her friends gambling, she seduces him. The abbot arranges for Candide's arrest and only his wealth saves him from the materialistic clutches of Paris. He leaves for Portsmouth, England, where he witnesses the shooting of an admiral as an example to discipline others. Thoroughly disgusted, Candide and Martin sail for Venice and spend months searching for Cunegonde. He encounters PACQUETTE, the girl who gave Pangloss his disease, who is now with a young monk named Brother GIROFLÉE. Determined to find someone happy and good in the world, Candide asks Martin to join him in a visit to Count POCOCURANTE, a Venetian nobleman.

Chaps. 25–30. Count Pococurante proves to be a man of great wealth whose great cultural knowledge has only served to displease him with everything. Too sophisticated to enjoy anything, he tells the naïve Candide about the great disillusionment which the world's great literature is to him. Candide leaves, impressed with the count's critical genius and convinced that he must be "the happiest man alive, because he is superior to all he possesses." Candide finally finds Cacambo while dining at an inn with six strangers who prove to be dethroned kings. Candide and Martin board the ship on which Cacambo is a galley slave and together they head for Constantinople to find Cunegonde, who is now very ugly and washing dishes. Much to Candide's surprise (but no longer to the reader's) he finds Cunegonde's

The embrace discovered

brother and Pangloss are galley slaves on the same ship. The young baron relates how he was cured of Candide's wounding shot and then, after several adventures, was lashed 100 times and condemned to the galleys because he, a Christian, was found bathing naked with a young Mussulman in Constantinople. Pangloss did not die of his hanging but suffered a severe autopsy operation; recovered, and went to Constantinople where he got 100 lashes and was condemned to the galleys for flirting with a young girl in a mosque. But Pangloss still holds onto his original philosophy. They all find Cunegonde and the old woman. Candide is once more rebuked by the baron for wanting to marry his horribly ugly sister. They marry and all settle on a little farm, where Pacquette and Brother Giroflée join them. Finally, they all conclude that the only way to find happiness is to work in their own garden, though Pangloss stubbornly maintains that they could not have found this happiness had they not gone through the terrible chain of events that preceded it in this best of all possible worlds.

The Canterbury Tales

Poem by Geoffrey Chaucer, 1340?–1400. Published 1378 and later (exact dates unknown). (ML, 161; RE, 65)

A MAN NAMED DUNBAR, who wrote poetry not much later than Chaucer, called him "the noble Chaucer, flower of poets." Chaucer's stature has not suffered in the meantime. He is acknowledged to have been the greatest English poet before Shakespeare and worthy of a place beside any who has come since. But today's reader can read him only in translation, as though he had written in a foreign language. ❡ *The Canterbury Tales* is Chaucer's masterpiece and cannot be exceeded in importance by anything in English literature. It is very long, more than 17,000 lines of verse in heroic couplets (rhyming ten-syllable lines) plus the equivalent of some 3,000 more lines in prose. The theme of the poem is simple. A group of pilgrims are to amuse one another by telling stories. Long though it is, the poem is not nearly so long as Chaucer apparently intended to make it. He listed 31 pilgrims, each of whom was to tell four tales. Ultimately he wrote 23 tales, some unfinished. He drew the stories chiefly from French tradition or from such other sources as fed Boccaccio's Decameron. Few if any of the stories were original. Not the stories but Chaucer's way of writing them makes *The Canterbury Tales* great.

Prologue. As Chaucer lay in the Tabard Inn outside of London in the month of April, preparing to go on pilgrimage to see the bones of the martyr St. Thomas à Becket at Canterbury, a group of 29 pilgrims arrived at the inn. Chaucer decided to join their merry company, and with them the next day rose early and departed. To relieve the long horseback journey, the HOST proposed that everyone tell two stories to and from Canterbury, which would make four stories each. [Actually no pilgrim tells more than one story and not every pilgrim tells a story, for the work was left unfinished.] The KNIGHT volunteered to speak first and told an epic tale of courtly love:

THE KNIGHT'S TALE

Duke THESEUS of Athens, returning home after his conquest of the female warriors, the Amazons, rides with his bride, HIPPOLYTA, the Amazon queen, and her beautiful young sister, EMILY. As they near Athens, they see women clad in black standing in pairs by the side of the road and lamenting loudly. The women tell Theseus that their husbands have fallen in the famous Revolt against Thebes and cruel King CREON forbids burial of their dead bodies. Theseus, taking pity on the women, rides off to Thebes and conquers the city. Among the dead Thebans the Athenians find two young nobles named PALAMON and ARCITE, who are not quite dead. Theseus takes these nobles with him to Athens and casts them into a strong prison near his palace. One morning the two friends peer out the window and spy the lovely Emily walking in the garden. Both men fall desperately in love with the girl, endangering their friendship.

By a stroke of luck Theseus's good friend PIRITHOUS comes to Athens on a visit and learns that his comrade Arcite is imprisoned. Pirithous persuades Theseus to free Arcite, but he does not know Palamon, who is left behind bars. Theseus warns the liberated Arcite that he must never again set foot inside the Athenian realm. Arcite is stricken by these words, which would mean he can never see Emily again. He disguises himself, calls himself Philostratus, and takes a job as an assistant to the chamberlain in the royal palace. Meanwhile Palamon succeeds in breaking out of the prison and escapes into a nearby forest. Arcite, riding in the same woods, is overheard by Palamon while he laments his inability to marry Emily. Palamon threatens to expose him to Duke Theseus, and they fight. The duke and his followers come upon them in time to separate them and learn of the deception. Hippolyta persuades Theseus to allow the rivals to fight a duel for the hand of Emily.

Palamon goes to the Temple of Love, presided over by Venus, and offers a gentle prayer for his lady's love. Venus's statue shakes and Palamon interprets this as a sign of approval. Arcite goes to the Temple of War and prays for success from the god Mars. The statue of Mars murmurs, amid frightful shakings of the temple, "Victorie!" Emily prays to Diana, the goddess of chastity, and Diana tells her that she must abandon the virgin's life and be possessed by one of the men. The quarrel between Mars and Venus in Heaven is settled by Saturn, father of the Olympian gods, who assures Venus that Palamon will win.

All of Athens turns out for the exciting tourney. At the beginning of the list Palamon seems to have the upper hand, but then Arcite begins to overpower him. Venus rages in Heaven, and Saturn sends "a furie infernal" from Hell to frighten Arcite's horse. The horse upsets its rider and tramples him. As Arcite dies he tells Emily to marry Palamon, for he is a worthy man. For a long time Emily stays in mourning. Duke Theseus finally summons her and Palamon and delivers an eloquent plea on rights of the living as opposed to the rights of the dead. Emily is prevailed upon to marry Palamon, and Love (Venus) wins out over War (Mars).

MILLER'S, REEVE'S, COOK'S TALES

The coarse MILLER objected to the courteous Knight's tale. His own tale was a ribald one about a foolish old CARPENTER whose beautiful wife ALISOUN is seduced by a young clerk (Scholar) named NICHOLAS. Nicholas persuades the old man that the world is going to be flooded and the Carpenter goes to spend the night in a tub on the roof. Another of Alisoun's admirers, ABSALON, the church clerk, comes to the window but is rudely treated by the girl. Absalon returns with a hot poker and when Nicholas tries to repeat the indignity, Absalon burns him. In the confusion, the old Carpenter falls off the roof. Thus all were punished.

The REEVE (village magistrate) had once been a carpenter, so he did not like the Miller's making a carpenter the butt of his story. He countered with a story in which a Miller's wife and daughter are seduced by two clerks. The COOK began a similar story (left unfinished).

THE MAN OF LAW'S TALE

The three preceding stories having been indelicate at the very least, the MAN OF LAW (lawyer) told a more proper one. CONSTANCE (or Custance), daughter of the Roman emperor Tiberius Constantius, agrees to marry the Sultan ALLAH of Syria if he will become a Christian. The Sultan agrees but his mother contrives to have Constance sent in a ship out to sea to drift and die. After many adventures Constance is reunited with her father. The tale personifies Constance as an example of fortitude.

133

The hag asks if her husband would prefer a young wife

THE WIFE OF BATH'S TALE

Dame Alice, the WIFE OF BATH, then spoke loud and long about her five husbands and how men mistreat women. She spoke of her own clever devices for getting around her husbands and in so doing justified the love of men for women, which the Church seemed to frown upon. Her tale was an Arthurian legend about a certain knight of King Arthur's court who ravishes a maid and is committed for sentence to the hands of the court's women, headed by Queen GUINEVERE. She commands him to go out into the world and find out what all women most desire; if he fails he will be beheaded. The knight does not find the answer until he meets an old hag, who promises to tell him if he will marry her. The knight agrees. He returns to court and gives the hag's answer. All women most desire sovereignty, that is, the right to rule their husbands. The answer is correct and he is freed, but Guinevere rules that he must keep his promise and marry the hag. On the wedding night the hag asks him if he would rather have a young, beautiful wife who is stupid, or an old, wise wife like herself. When he says she can make the choice for him better than himself, it is evidence that she will rule his life. Forthwith she transforms herself into a beautiful young woman. This proves the Wife of Bath's contention that women should rule their husbands.

FRIAR'S, SUMMONER'S, CLERK'S TALES

The debate about women and the nature of marriage continued after the greedy FRIAR told a tale about an evil SUMMONER, or official of the church court (for at that time the Church had its own courts, which were independent of courts of law) and the Summoner told a brief story about a wicked begging friar. The knowledge-loving CLERK of Oxford ("gladly wolde he lerne and gladly teche") almost went out of his way to appease the Wife of Bath by telling the tale of GRISELDA, who was an allegorical figure of Patience. Griselda was severely tried by her husband WALTER, who took away her children and eventually divorced

134

her and pretended to remarry simply to see if she would remain true to him. [See the story of "The Patient Griselda," in Boccaccio's *Decameron*.] The tale ends with a poem by Chaucer, who says that such patience was "buried in Italy."

MERCHANT'S AND SQUIRE'S TALES

The MERCHANT countered with a tale about a feeble old dotard named JANUARY who was deceived by his frisky wife MAY. The Knight's SQUIRE began a traditional gaudy tale about a knight of Cambuscan, but he did not finish. The FRANKLIN ended the marriage discussion with an unresolved tale:

THE FRANKLIN'S TALE

In the land of Amorica, or Brittany, on the bleak coast of northern France, lives a gentle knight named ARVIRAGUS. He is very much in love with his wife DORIGEN, but his duties often call him far away from home. During one of these enforced absences, a squire named AURELIUS sees Dorigen brooding by herself on the seashore and praying to God to deliver her husband safely back to her. Aurelius falls so deeply in love with the beautiful woman that he makes a foolish promise to grant her whatever her heart desires. Dorigen looks at the black rocks along the coast and says that to win her he must remove those rocks one by one. Dorigen believes that she has put him permanently aside; but Aurelius recalls a book of natural magic he read when he was a student at Orleans. Aurelius rides away to the town and there encounters a very skilled magician, who offers to perform the task for an enormous sum of money. No amount of money seems excessive to the passionate Aurelius, and a compact is signed. The miracle is accomplished and all the Brittany rocks disappear. Aurelius rides proudly back to Dorigen's house to claim her. At first Dorigen proposes to commit suicide, but her husband returns and she pours out her troubles to him. Arviragus decides that honor demands that he offer his wife to Aurelius. Dorigen goes to Aurelius, who is so astonished by

her husband's noble act that he cannot claim his reward. He dismisses Dorigen and receives her blessing. However, Aurelius has the huge debt of 1,000 pounds to the magician. He has no recourse but to go to the man and confess the whole story. When the magician hears his tale, he likewise discharges the debt. Then, asks the Franklin, which of the three men was the noblest?

THE PHYSICIAN'S TALE

The PHYSICIAN told a very moral tale about a Roman knight VIRGINIUS whose daughter VIRGINIA is awarded to a man named CLAUDIUS by the connivings of a "false judge" APPIUS. Rather than give herself over to a life of lechery, Virginia offers her life to her father, who slays her. The Romans then rise up and hang the evil legislators. The next tale was told by the wise, witty PARDONER, who duped the ignorant people by selling them Church pardons for their sins and charging them admission prices to use his hastily concocted bones and relics of long-dead saints. Like the Wife of Bath, the Pardoner is one of Chaucers' masterfully drawn characters. The Pardoner's Tale is equally brilliant and has been called the world's first short story.

THE PARDONER'S TALE

Three rioters who live in Flanders are drinking merrily in a tavern when their revels are suddenly interrupted by the toll of a funeral bell. One of their friends has died and the thought angers them because they want to spend the rest of their lives drinking. When they ask who has slain the man, a pallbearer replies that it is a foul thief called DEATH, who has been ravishing the countryside recently. One of the rioters rises up and proposes that they kill Death, and the plan appeals to the other two. They rush drunkenly from the tavern down the highway until they suddenly come upon an old man (possibly Death himself). They ask the old man where Death is, and he replies sadly that he does not know, for he is condemned to wander the world without ever lying in the arms of Mother Earth. When the rioters insist on an answer, the old man points to a thicket and tells them he left Death there, under a tree. They rush toward the tree, where instead of finding Death they find heaps of gold florins. Eager to celebrate, they send their youngest to town to buy some wine. As soon as he disappears, the other two plot his murder so that they can split the money between them. Meanwhile the young man has the same thought. He buys some poison from an apothecary and drops it into two of the bottles. As soon as the young man returns to the grove, he is seized and slain. The other two rioters drink the poisoned wine and die too. Thus they who went foolishly in search of Death found him but could not slay him.

SHIPMAN'S AND PRIORESS'S TALES

After finishing the tale, the Pardoner asked if anyone would like to see his relics, but the indignant Knight silenced him.

The brawny SHIPMAN (Sailor) told a brief bawdy tale like the Miller's but this was offset by the PRIORESS'S tale about a singing Christian boy whose throat is cut in the Jewish quarter of a large Asiatic city. The boy's mother searches the city in vain for his body, then hears the boy's voice rising from a pit into which he had been thrown. The boy has been killed, yet a miracle wrought by Jesus gives him life long enough to sing the hymn *Alma Redemptoris Mater,* not only in the well but also when his body is taken to the church and placed upon a bier. Then he gives up the ghost and the people praise the miracle. [This story is strikingly unique because of the way the elegant, dainty Prioress handles the details of violence. It is also an ancient calumny on Jews—that they murdered Christian children—that persisted even in this century in the propaganda of Russia under the czars and Germany under Hitler.]

CHAUCER'S AND THE MONK'S TALES

The pilgrim CHAUCER was next asked to speak, and he began a silly tale about a knight called Sir THOPAS, but was quickly silenced by the Host. Trying again, Chaucer told a long, dull, philosophical debate between MELIBEE and Dame PRUDENCE, a prose translation from a French tract. Strangely enough he was allowed to finish it and was complimented by the Host. The virtuous MONK then told a series of brief tragedies or stories of great men who had toppled "out of prosperitee," such as Adam, Lucifer, Hercules, Nero, and Julius Caesar. The Knight interrupted him, complaining of all that "hevynesse."

THE NUN'S PRIEST'S TALE

When the Monk refused to tell another tale, the NUN'S PRIEST offered a beast-fable about a rooster named CHANTICLEER who is troubled by dreams of destruction that his hen-wife PERTELOTE cannot pacify. Their learned discussion about the nature of dreams and their meanings is interrupted by Don Russell, a FOX, who frightens Chanticleer up a tree. Then by flattering him about his singing ability, the Fox makes Chanticleer lose his balance so that he topples and falls into Don Russell's mouth. As the Fox is bearing him away, Chanticleer tells him to curse against the men who pursue him. The Fox does so, opening his mouth so that Chanticleer can escape again into a tree. The Priest thus lectured against false pride and flattery.

THE FINAL TALES

The SECOND NUN recounted a typical medieval saint's life, the life of St. CECILIA and how she suffered martyrdom. Suddenly, at the town of Boughton under Blee, a CANON'S YEOMAN rode up and joined the company. He had just run away from an alchemist for whom he worked, because he had uncovered some of the man's deceptions. The Yeoman told a tale about a swindling alchemist; this tale contains one of the most complete descriptions of that ancient craft in medieval literature. It is also one of Chaucer's most bitterly satiric tales. The MANCIPLE (steward of a court) next recited a tale about a tell-tale nightingale that informs its master, the Greek god Phoebus Apollo, about his unnamed wife's deception. Phoebus kills his wife, but then thanklessly turns the nightingale into a crow. The Manciple said that all evil tongues were thus rewarded. The last tale, told by the simple humble PARSON, is really a sermon on the Seven Deadly Sins. It is in prose, like Chaucer's *Tale of Melibee.*

The Canterbury Tales end with a famous leave-taking from Chaucer, who begs the reader to attribute any virtues of the book to Jesus Christ and any faults to himself.

He names his other works, such as the *House of Fame, Book of the Duchess, Troilus and Cressida,* and *Legend of Good Women,* and excuses himself for any of their indelicacies. In his last words he hopes that he will sit with Christ on Judgment Day among the redeemed.

Capital

Treatise by Karl Marx, 1818–1883. Published 1859 to 1889 and later. (ML, 202; ML, G26)

AMID ALL THE CONTROVERSY aroused by the writings of Karl Marx and their extreme political effects it should perhaps be remembered that Marx was not a political figure, a reformer, or a crusader. He was an economist and a scholar. It is not strange that so many millions disagree with the conclusions that Marx reached or that have been reached in his name. Almost no two economists can agree with each other. ❡ *Capital,* or *Das Kapital* (for the book is better known by its untranslated name), is not an easy book to delimit. It may have been planned as a unit, but Marx was afflicted by poverty when he was writing its various parts, he sold for serial publication any part that was salable, and he did not live to see a unified treatise assembled and published, much less to do the work of assembly and selection himself. Others, notably Engels and Lenin, ultimately had more to say than Marx about what should be collected and combined as his *major opus.* The outline that follows is taken from the first published edition of *Das Kapital* but does not cover at least two of his most notable contributions to economic theory, the concept of *the crisis* with the boom-depression cycle he considered inescapable in a capitalistic economy, and the prediction of the inevitable collapse of capitalism. Let it be hastily said here that the foregoing are *theories* of Marxist economics. They have not been proved and the majority of economists think they will not or need not be.

Part I. Commodities and Money. 1. A commodity is an object that by its properties satisfies human wants. A commodity may have either (1) use-value, or (2) substance of value and magnitude of value. Use-values become a reality only by use or consumption; they also constitute the substance of all wealth. Exchange value is independent of use-value. Exchange-value is the only form in which the value of commodities can be expressed. The only reason a commodity has use-value is because human labor in the abstract has been embodied or materialized in it. If a thing is useless, so is the labor contained in it; the labor does not count as labor, and therefore creates no value. The mode of production in which the product takes the form of a commodity, or is produced directly for exchange, is the most general and most embryonic form of bourgeois production. It therefore makes its appearance at an early date in history. **2–3.** The use-value of the money commodity becomes twofold. In addition to its special use-value as a commodity (gold, for instance, serving to fill teeth, to form the raw material of articles of luxury, etc.), it acquires a formal use-value, originating in its specific social function. All commodities become merely particular equivalents of money. The first chief function of money is to serve as a *universal measure of value.* Price is the money-name of the labor realized in a commodity. Price, like relative value, expresses the value of a commodity (e.g., a ton of iron), by stating that a given quantity of the equivalent (e.g., an ounce of gold), is directly exchangeable for iron.

Part II. The Transformation of Money (M) into Capital (C). 4–5. Money, the final product of the circulation of commodities, is the first form of capital. The formula (1) C-M-C' is that of the circulation of commodities. But this formula also implies (2) M-C-M' the formula for capitalistic circulation. All money moving in this latter circle is, potentially, capital. The aim of (1) is use-value; the aim of (2) is exchange value. In (2), $M' = M + \triangle M$, i.e. M' is equal to the original sum advanced, M, + an increase, $\triangle M$. This increase $\triangle M$ is surplus value. *Surplus value cannot be created by simple circulation of commodities.* **6.** The essentials of capitalist production are (1) that use-value and exchange-value are distinct; (2) that the stages of (a) barter and (b) the circulation of commodities is past; (3) that the capitalist, the possessor of the means of subsistence and production, meets in the market the free laborer possessing only his labor-power. The value of labor-power, as the value of all commodities, is determined by the labor-time necessary for its production and reproduction, i.e., by the labor-time necessary for the production of the means of subsistence of the laborer. And the use-value of the commodity, labor-power is advanced to the capitalist.

Part III. The Production of Absolute Surplus-Value. 7. Labor-power in use is labor. The capitalist sets the laborer to produce a particular use-value. When the labor-process becomes the capitalistic-process, two things occur: (1) the laborer works under the control of the capitalist; (2) the product becomes the property of the capitalist. The capitalist has in view the production of a use-value that has an exchange-value (i.e., the production of a commodity), and the production of a commodity whose value is greater than the sum of the values of the labor-power used in its production. In the production process, labor-power not only creates value for the capitalist but more value than the labor power has itself. Thus, the labor-power creates surplus value for the capitalist. 8. The capitalist-owned means of production are not the source of surplus-value. *Surplus-value is the difference between the value of means of production and labor-power taken together, and the value of the product.* 9. The laborer during the first part of the day produces only the value of his labor-power, the value of his means of subsistence. After the expiration of the time necessary for the production of subsistence value, the laborer is producing surplus value for the capitalist. 10. The working conditions in England today [1850s] reflect the desire of the capitalists to obtain as much surplus-value from labor-power as they possibly can. The working day is as much as 14 hours. Women, and children as young as 8, work these heartlessly long hours. Some women and children work long night hours. Women, some of them mothers and some pregnant, haul coal and cars underground in the coal mines. Children work at the breakers in the foul and unhealthy conditions of the mines. So far, remedial legislation has been sidetracked or has proved futile. 11. The capitalist (1) becomes master of the labor-power; (2) sees that it works properly, and with sufficient zeal; (3) compels the laborer to work surplus-labor-time so as to produce surplus-value. From the point of view of the creation of surplus-value, the laborer does not employ the means of production; it employs him.

Part IV. Production of Relative Surplus-Value. 12. The object of all development in the productiveness of labor for the capitalist is to shorten necessary labor-time, lengthen surplus-labor-time, and result in

more relative surplus value. (Surplus value due to the shortening of necessary labor-time, as the result of increased productiveness of labor, is relative surplus value.) 13. The working together of many laborers at the same time, in the same place, is the starting-point of capitalist production. The collective labor-power is not only a quantitative labor gain but also a qualitative one. One man in one day may make one pair of trousers while three men in one day can make 12 pairs of trousers. By paying the cost of three independent labor-powers the capitalist receives the combined labor-powers, which equal 12 labor-powers. 14. Manufacture, i.e., coöperation based on division of labor, is only a particular form of getting surplus-value, and under it the national wealth, the domination of the capitalist, the productiveness of labor, all increase. In the manufacturing period of a nation's economy, the number of unskilled laborers is small. When manufacture produces machines, we pass to modern industry. 15. Machinery shortens the necessary labor time in the working day, lengthens the surplus labor time. A machine is a tool with motive power other than manpower. A factory is a workshop in which machinery is used. In the product of machinery, the value due to labor increases relatively but decreases absolutely. That is, the value to the laborer is less in proportion to the value of the product, though the same amount of labor produces a more valuable product. The productiveness of a machine is measured by the amount of human labor-power that it replaces. The difference between the price of machinery and the price of the labor-

power it displaces may vary, but the difference between the labor required to produce the machine and the total labor-power replaced by it remains constant.

The fact that machinery replaces muscle-

power makes it possible for large numbers of women and children to enter the ranks of labor. This weakens the resistance that men could once show their masters in the matter of wages and working conditions. The result is the prolongation of the working day, lower wages, poorer working conditions. The setting free of laborers that are supplanted by machinery gives rise to a surplus labor population.

In manufacture the workman uses a tool. In machinery, the workman is used by a machine. In manufacture the movements of the tool proceed from the workman; in machinery, he follows the movements of the machine. In manufacture, the workman is part of a living mechanism; in machinery, he is the living appendage of a lifeless mechanism. This situation results in loss of bodily and mental activity of the workman, monotony, and consequent debility and danger.

Craftsmen looked upon the advent of machinery as inimical to their welfare; they were right. Machinery is not only their competitor, it is the most powerful of weapons upon the side of the autocracy of capital. And certainly one of the worst features of the use of the machine in a capitalist economy is that the machine's great productiveness causes overproduction and consequent unemployment with its attendant miseries to the laborer. Machinery has transformed the peasant into a wage-laborer and has broken the bond between agriculture and industry.

Part V. The Production of Absolute and of Relative Surplus-Value. 16. The prolongation of the working day leads to the production of surplus value. *This is the basis of the capitalistic system and the starting point for the production of relative surplus value.* The working day is divided into two parts, necessary labor-time and surplus labor-time. Any expedient that shortens the necessary labor-time increases the surplus labor-time. The production of absolute surplus-value depends exclusively on the length of the working day; the production of relative surplus value revolutionizes out and out the technical process of labor and the

Child labor was the rule in England in the time of Marx

136

composition of society. It therefore presupposes a specific mode, the capitalist mode of production. **17.** The value of labor power depends upon three things: (1) the value of the means of subsistence; (2) the expense of developing the labor-power, varying with the mode of production; (3) the natural diversity of the labor-power of men, women, and children. **18.** The Socialist formula for the rate of surplus-value is surplus labor time divided by necessary labor time. The ordinary formula for the rate of surplus-value is the surplus product divided by the total product. This latter formula does not express the degree of exploitation of labor. The capitalist pays only for labor-power during the necessary labor-time but benefits from both the necessary labor-time and the surplus labor-time (for which he has not paid). Capital is not only the command over labor, it is the command over unpaid labor, the labor that produces surplus value.

Part VI. Wages. 19. The wage of the laborer is not the value of labor but the price of labor-power. The value of the laborer's labor-power varies with the value of the means of subsistence; its price may vary with conditions of supply and demand. **20.** Wages take many forms. Time wages are the converted form under which the value of labor-power presents itself. The distinction between nominal and real wages is the distinction between the exchange value of labor-power and the sum of the necessaries of life into which this exchange value can be converted. The longer the working day in any branch of industry, the lower the wages. Competition among workers (unemployed or fearful of being unemployed) enables the capitalist to beat down the price of labor, and the same conditions enable him to lengthen the working time. **21.** Piece-wages are only a modified form of time-wages, just as time-wages are a modified form of labor-power. **22.** When the wages of different nations are compared, all the factors must be considered: cost of the means of subsistence; cost of training the laborer; woman- and child-labor.

Part VII. The Accumulation of Capital. First, the conversion of a sum of money into money-power and labor-power. Second, the turning of money-power into commodities containing surplus value. When these commodities are put in circulation and sold, their value is realized as money, and this money is again turned into capital. **23.** Capitalist production reproduces the separation between labor-power and the means of labor; reproduces the conditions necessary for the exploitation of the worker; and reproduces the capitalist-labor relation. **24.** The employment of surplus-value as capital result in accumulation of capital, or property, which in turn results in the right of the capitalist to appropriate the unpaid labor of the worker, that is, the product. The worker cannot appropriate his own product. As the accumulation of capital goes on, *the difference between the capital em-ployed and the capital actually consumed in a given time increases.* **25.** The very nature of the process of accumulation of capital excludes any reduction of the exploitation of the worker, for example a rise in wages that could increase the relative power of labor in the capitalist-labor relation. Centralization of capital proceeds; the large capitalists swallow the small. The general law of capitalistic accumulation is that *the greater the social wealth, the greater the industrial reserve army—the employable unemployed.*

Part VIII. The So-Called Primitive Accumulation. 26. Money becomes capital. Capital begets surplus-value. Surplus-value in turn begets more capital. Tracing it backwards, accumulation of capital presupposes surplus-value; surplus-value presupposes capitalist production; and capitalist production presupposes an original primitive accumulation of money power. The basis of the whole process of primitive accumulation is the expropriation of the agricultural laborer from that upon which he works—the soil. **27.** By the end of the 14th century serfdom had all but vanished. The mass of the people were free peasant proprietors. But in the 15th century, the breaking up of the bands of feudal retainers gave rise to the first proletariat. Feudal lords drove the peasants from the land and stole the common lands. Arable land was enclosed and turned into pasture. The spoliation of the Church property under the Reformation, the abolition of feudal tenure under the Restoration, the theft of state lands under the Revolution, the theft of common lands by feudal lords, the clearing of peasants from estates, are the chief phases in the primitive accumulation. **28.** The expropriated "free" proletariat could not be absorbed by the nascent industrialization as rapidly as it was set free. Hence, through the 15th and 16th centuries the increase of vagabonds and of laws against vagabonds. These laws were very cruel. **29.** The usurpation of the common lands was the greatest boost in the rise of the farmer-capitalist. In the farm commodity exchange relationship, the lion's share always falls to the middlemen: financiers, merchants, shopkeepers, lawyers, M.P.'s, priests. **30.** With the expropriation and the separation of the expropriated from money-power, rural domestic industry is destroyed and the process of separation between agriculture and manufacture begins. **31.** The Middle Ages handed down two distinct forms of capital—usurer's and merchant's. This capital could not become industrial capital until the feudal system was destroyed. The mercantile system was a method of hurrying the transition from feudal to capitalistic means of production. **32.** At the beginning of industrialization, the worker was expropriated. The inexorable laws of history will see the capitalist expropriated. The inevitable causes of this result are immanent in capitalistic production: (1) Overcentral-ization of capital; (2) socialization of labor; (3) internationalization of capital; (4) increase of misery; (5) class consciousness of the workers; (6) their revolt. **33.** The political economist can see still going on in the colonies the whole process of capitalist expropriation of labor, annihilation of self-earned private property, and the capitalist mode of production and accumulation.

Captains Courageous

Novel by Rudyard Kipling, 1865–1936. Published 1897.

KIPLING WROTE *Captains Courageous* for boys. When he wrote it he was living in Vermont, which accounts for his selecting a New England fishing boat to rescue his young hero; but his knowledge and love of the sea were not new. The value of the book is largely in its technical details of life on a fishing boat, and despite the passing of more than half a century there are still boats that sail and fish just as the *We're Here* did.

Chap. 1. HARVEY CHEYNE, spoiled 15-year-old only son of an American millionaire, is traveling with his mother to Europe, where he is to be educated. Aboard the ship, all the passengers consider him a nuisance whose attitude can only lead him to a meaningless and worthless playboy life. Offered a strong cigar by one of the passengers, Harvey gets sick and while leaning over the rail, gets washed overboard. When he recovers, he is aboard the *We're Here,* a fishing schooner from Gloucester. The weather-beaten and shrewd skipper, DISKO TROOP, tells the boy they will not return to land for six months and that, despite his protestations and offers of money, he will have to stay aboard. He meets MANUEL, a Portuguese fisherman, and DAN, Disko's son, about his own age. Bitter, disgusted, scared, Harvey resigns himself to the humiliation of his surroundings.

Chap. 2. Dan listens to Harvey's tale about his rich background and, though impressionable, tends to discredit it and is merely amused. Harvey apologizes to Disko for his previous rash words and they become friends. The dories from the schooner return, laden with fish, and Harvey meets the rest of the men as he and Dan work cleaning up the boats. Later, Harvey helps the crew "dress down" the fish, cleaning and salting them for storage. Then the boys go on watch and end the day by falling dead asleep.

Chap. 3. The next morning Harvey wakes to see many schooners surrounding the *We're Here,* all of them watching the movements of Troop, who has a reputation for knowing where to find the fish. Dan and

Harvey row out in a dory and Harvey catches a huge halibut. The schooner calls them back and on the way they help PENN disentangle his anchor. Dan tells Harvey that Penn is a displaced farmer brought onto the schooner by Disko's brother, UNCLE SALTERS, who also was a farmer once. A heavy fog settles and Harvey gets a lesson in seamanship from LONG JACK with the assistance of slightly senile TOM PLATT, who is often ridiculed for his reminiscences of the old days on the man o' war *Ohio*. After several depth soundings, the schooner arrives at a great fish area where Dan catches a big fish with his line, over the side. The boys then go below to bait fish for a coming trawling expedition.

Chap. 4. The ocean is too rough for trawling and the crew sits around singing fishing songs. There is some discussion of the fisherman's superstition, the Jonah (any person or thing that brings bad luck). As the fog lifts slightly they see the run-down schooner of UNCLE ABISHAI, a notorious Jonah. Instants later, Uncle Abishai's ship sinks into the ocean.

Chaps. 5–7. Dan and Harvey are now very close friends and Harvey is a well-liked working crew member on the schooner. While Harvey and Manuel are out in a dory taking depth and bottom samples, they see a huge passing iceberg. Harvey learns how to handle the helm of the schooner. He is all over the ship, learning how everything works and what everything means. He picks up information from the crew's stories and conversations. Gradually the schooner's hold fills with fish. One day they encounter a French schooner and trade food for tobacco. A meeting with another New England fishing schooner ends up in embarrassment for Disko at Salters' expense. The crew tries to settle the dispute and only when Long Jack, the peacemaker, tells a story of a similar situation does the dispute end. The next day, they run into a school of squid and catch some for cod-bait. Another schooner tries to trade some squid from them but Disko refuses. In heavy fog, the *We're Here* just misses being cut in half by an ocean liner. Moments later, another schooner is crushed by the liner and the *We're Here* rescues the sole survivor of the wreck, the skipper, who is hysterical with the loss of his summer's work, his source of livelihood, and his son. Penn, in

Dan and Harvey fish

a strange fit, prays with the old man and shortly afterward another schooner draws up, announcing the recovery of the skipper's son. Penn is credited with a miracle. The next few days bring many fish and finally the schooner arrives through the fog at its destination.

Chap. 8. The destination is a shoal area that is prize fishing grounds. When the schooner arrives, the region is dotted with other schooners. Working elbow to elbow, all the dories hit the water and pull in fish as the men exchange insults, pleasantries, and general news. The next day, over a rough sea, the fleet moves off to find a better school of fish, leaving the *We're Here* behind; in the night the fleet returns from a stormy and fruitless search while the *We're Here*, by staying back, had a successful catch. On the following day the French ship passes by, holding a funeral for a dead crew member. Harvey and Dan go aboard to an auction of the sailor's belongings and Dan buys a sheathknife in a belt. Back in their dory, the boys are fishing in the fog when Dan gives Harvey the knife as a present and an instant later, Harvey's line pulls up the dead French sailor. Terrified, the boys throw away the knife, disentangle the dead man, and get back to the schooner with their tale. Now full of fish, the *We're Here* sails for home. On shore they are greeted like heroes and Harvey stays with the Troops while waiting word from his parents.

Chaps. 9–10. In the office of Harvey's father, the telegram arrives announcing his son's safety. The parents, having thought the boy drowned, are overjoyed and reach Gloucester in record time. Harvey's father, knowing that Disko will not accept money as thanks, offers Dan a place on one of the Pacific ships he owns. Disko and Dan are overjoyed. Harvey's mother thanks Manuel, who first rescued Harvey, by a donation to his church. The *We're Here's* cook is hired by the Cheynes as personal valet for Harvey. A father-son talk ensues in which Harvey is persuaded to go to college so that he will be able to take over the leadership of his father's shipping. A few years later, Harvey has graduated and, as owner of his father's Pacific ship-holdings, meets Dan, now first mate on one of the Cheyne ships.

The Captain's Daughter

Novel by Aleksandr Pushkin, 1799–1837.
Published 1836. (ML, P33)

PUSHKIN WROTE THIS NOVEL after his appointment to the office of Crown Historian under Catherine II gave him access to the state archives and private papers. This fact is considered sufficient to give the work exemplary authenticity. *The Captain's Daughter* has been called the first Russian novel. Its most august admirer was Tolstoy [see the note on *Anna Karenina*]. The action of the novel is set about 1774. The novel is well plotted and is consistently interesting. It should be read more than it is.

Chap. 1. PETER GRINYOV is nearing his 17th birthday when the story opens. He is living on the country estate of his wealthy landowner father, spending gay, carefree days wenching with the maids and sporting with peasant boys. He has had almost no education at all. His manservant, old devoted SAVELYICH, has taught him to read, write, and count. ANDREY GRINYOV, Peter's father, decides that now is the time for Peter to enter the army. Peter is delighted. He knows that at birth he was attached to the famous Guards regiment, the Semenovsky, in St. Petersburg. He sees himself having a glorious time in the great city, member of a fashionable regiment, a crony of all the gay young blades and their girls. His father sits down to write a letter, but he writes it not to his relative in the Semenovsky regiment but to an old army crony now posted in the remote small town of Orenburg, an outpost set in the Kirghiz steppes, ringed with wild and rebellious Tatars. Peter is horrified; his mother pleads to no avail. The autocratic old Grinyov orders immediate preparation for Peter's departure. Peter leaves with his faithful Savelyich, laden with hastily prepared provisions, warm coats, pillows, featherbeds, and all the paraphernalia with which people traveled by chaise. On the route to Orenburg he puts up for the night at a posting inn in Simbirsk. While Savelyich (who is in charge of all funds) goes to make some purchases, Peter is inveigled into playing billiards with a fellow-soldier, ZOURIN, who gets Peter tipsy, makes him play for money, and fleeces him of 100 rubles, a large sum of money for the young man.

The Cossacks are in control

When Savelyich returns he refuses at first to pay this sum, but Peter orders him to hand over the money and they leave the inn.

Chap. 2. They travel all day across the seemingly endless snow-covered steppes, without a village in sight, and find themselves in a blinding blizzard at sundown. They are faced with the prospect of being buried in the snowdrifts and freezing to death. Suddenly a man appears. They hail him and he guides them to an inn. They spend the night at the inn and in gratitude Peter gives the man who saved them, and who has no warm clothes, his own jacket, lined with rabbit fur. Without further adventure they reach Orenburg and Peter goes at once to present himself to the general in command, his father's old crony. The general assigns Peter to the isolated fortress garrison of Belogorsk, under the command of Capt. MIRONOV, where Peter will be safe from temptations and dissipations.

Chaps. 3–4. Belogorsk, a tiny village surrounded by a log fence, is at the very edge of the Kirghiz steppes, subject to unexpected raids by the natives. Mironov, a kindly but ineffectual soul, is managed, as is the entire fortress, by his energetic, lively wife, VASSILISSA EGOROVNA. Here in the fortress Peter meets the meek and shy MARIA, the Mironovs' daughter. Peter makes friends with his fellow officer SHVABRIN, who was exiled to this outpost from a smart regiment for fighting a duel. Peter becomes an intimate of the Mironov family and is already in love with Maria. He keeps his sentiments to himself except that he writes a sentimental poem, which he shows to Shvabrin. Shvabrin is secretly in love with Maria and makes derogatory remarks about her. Peter calls him a liar and Shvabrin challenges him to a duel. Vassilissa stops the duel and the two young men are forced to reconcile in public, but the next day they duel secretly and Peter is wounded in the breast. He is taken to the Mironov home, where he lies uncon-

scious for five days. When he recovers he asks Maria to marry him. Shvabrin is put in jail. Peter receives a letter from his father disapproving his marriage to Maria, and Peter is certain that Shvabrin is the one who informed his father.

Chaps. 5–7. Peter writes at length to his father, begging permission to marry Maria, but to no avail. Maria avoids him, and Peter is sunk in despair, until dangerous events threaten the lives of all in the garrison: Yaikian Cossacks, led by a man known as EMELYAN POUGACHEV, have sacked a number of fortresses and committed unbelievable atrocities. Pougachev claims to be the Emperor Peter III, long since known to be dead. The news of the rebellion spreads like wildfire and many people in the small town side with Pougachev. Mironov receives an ultimatum from the Cossack leader to surrender the garrison. It is decided to send Maria to Orenburg; but before she can leave, the fortress is attacked and despite valiant efforts to defend it, traitors within the walls surrender and Pougachev is master. He promptly has Mironov executed in the public square and Vassilissa Egorovna murdered at the foot of the gallows. Shvabrin deserts to the rebels. Peter is in danger of being executed but old Savelyich pleads with Pougachev, whom he recognizes as the man who saved them in the snowstorm on the steppe. Pougachev spares Peter for the sake of the warm coat Peter gave him. He even takes Peter with him when he rides to inspect the fortress.

Chaps. 8–11. Peter begins his search for Maria and finds that she has been hidden by the wife of the local priest. Pougachev tries to persuade Peter to join the Cossack rebels, but finally grants Peter's request to join his own forces in Orenburg. Pougachev gives Peter and Savelyich a safe-conduct, a horse, and a sheepskin coat for Peter, since all Peter's possessions were lost in the looting of the Belogorsky fortress. Some days later Orenburg is attacked and one of the Cossacks who was in the Belogorsky fortress gives Peter the news that Shvabrin is holding Maria prisoner and trying to force her to marry him. Peter and Savelyich start out without the general's permission to reach Belogorsky; they are waylaid by rebels and taken before Pougachev, who insists that Peter feast with him. Then he discovers that Maria is Peter's betrothed. Next morning he sets off with Peter and Savelyich and his own men to rescue Maria from Shvabrin.

Chaps. 12–15. They find Maria under lock and key, sitting on the floor, with a pitcher of water and a piece of bread; this after Shvabrin has lied to Pougachev, saying Maria is dangerously sick. Pougachev frees her and orders passes for Peter and Maria through rebel territory. Peter makes arrangements for Maria, with her faithful maid, to travel to his father's estate. Once again disaster overtakes Peter and Maria. They are arrested, for Peter is supposedly the favorite of the False Tsar. However, the commanding officer turns out to be Zourin, who gambled with Peter when he was on his way to Orenburg on his first journey from home. Zourin lets Maria leave with her maid and Savelyich, but insists that Peter stay as officer with his detachment. Just before Peter is finally due to leave for his father's estate and reunion with his beloved Maria, Zourin receives an order to deliver Peter under escort to Kazan for inquiry into his participation in the Pougachev rebellion.

Peter is tried and is condemned and put in chains. He is charged with having been sent to Orenburg as a spy by Pougachev. He knows he can clear himself by summoning Maria as a witness but he cannot bring himself to submit her to this. Rather will he spend his life in exile in Siberia. In the meantime news reaches him that his parents have taken Maria to their hearts. She decides to lay a petition before the empress to establish Peter's innocence. Maria goes to Petersburg and thence to Tsarskoë Selo, where the empress is in residence. Maria stays with a lady who has a connection with the court. Early in the morning after her arrival, she goes for a stroll in the beautiful palace gardens and meets a lady with a little white dog, which barks at Maria. The lady reassures her, invites her to sit down on a bench, and in kindly fashion asks her who she is. Maria explains that she is an orphan, daughter of the Captain Mironov who was so cruelly murdered, and she tells of her petition to the Empress. The unknown lady tells Maria that she goes to court at times and will present Maria's petition. The same day Maria is summoned to the imperial presence and discovers that her acquaintance of that morning is the great Empress herself. Peter is pardoned and the empress even tells Maria that she will "provide for her" as she knows the poor orphan has nothing. Shortly after this Peter marries the captain's daughter.

Carmen

> *Novelette by* Prosper Mérimée, 1803–1870.
>
> Published 1846 (serially in 1845). Translated from the French by T. B. Peterson; also in other translations.
>
> THE CONTINUED FAME of Mérimée's *Carmen* rests wholly on the operatic version, with music by Bizet, which is easily the most popular opera in the United States. Without the opera the book would probably be forgotten, partly because it is only a *nouvelle,* or very short novel of the kind now often called a novelette. But to one who knows only the story of the opera, which is simplified and somewhat altered, the original book should have special interest and be worth reading.

Chap. 1. The story is written in the first person. The author is on an archaeological expedition in the environs of Montilla, Spain, in the autumn of 1830, looking for evidence that Caesar waged a final campaign against enemies of the Republic in the region. With a guide he enters the hills of the Calera Sierra and discovers a fine spring where a Spaniard is encamped. He offers the stranger cigars and food and thereby makes him his friend, although his guide ANTONIO tries to signal him that the stranger is not the sort of person to consort with, particularly after the stranger confesses that he has made a wild and hasty trip to Córdova. In spite of the guide's disquietude, the stranger joins them and they proceed to an inn at Cuerva, meanwhile discussing a notorious bandit, JOSÉ MARIA. At the inn, an old woman greets the Spaniard as Señor Don José, but the author is unperturbed and they have dinner together, after which Don José accompanies himself in some Basque songs. Antonio tries to speak to his master and warn him that this is the outlaw but Don José settles himself in the author's room and it is only when he is asleep that the Frenchman can rejoin his guide. Antonio tells him that Don José has threatened to kill him (Antonio) if he informs on him; but Antonio purposes to go to the police anyway to tell them where the bandit is and collect a 200-ducat reward. The author tries to dissuade Antonio, and when he cannot do so he wakes Don José and tells him to escape while he can. Thereupon the author resumes his archaeological researches, although Antonio is angry with him, suspecting that he allowed Don José to escape and thereby did him out of the 200 ducats.

140

Chap. 2. The author spends several days at Córdova looking through Dominican manuscripts. In the evenings he frequents the Guadalquiver River, where the young ladies make their bath-toilet. On one occasion, when it is nearly dark, a woman ascends the stairs from the river and sits down beside him, accepting a papelito. He offers to buy her an ince at a nearby cafe and it is then that she tells him she is a gypsy, CARMENCITA, and offers to tell his fortune. The girl has a strange, wild beauty, particularly in the expression of her eyes, "eye of gypsy, eye of wolf" according to a Spanish expression. The author suggests that they visit her home to have his fortune told and she consents after asking him the time, for which he consults his gold repeating watch. In her room Carmen uses cards and a dried chameleon to tell his fortune. They are interrupted by the arrival of an angry man with a cloak drawn around his face, who upbraids the woman in a mysterious language. The strange man then reveals his face to the author, who recognizes him as Don José. Then Carmen and Don José quarrel again and Don José leads the author to the street and directs him to his inn. When he arrives there he finds that his gold watch is missing. Passing through Córdova again after several months of rambling in Andalusia, he visits the Dominican convent and there he is informed that his gold repeating watch has been found on a murderer, who is to be executed in two days. The man is known as JOSÉ NAVARRO. A Dominican father escorts the author to the doomed man's cell, where he recognizes the same man he has met twice before. From him the author learns a sad history.

Chap. 3. Don José tells the author of his first meeting with Carmen while he was stationed in Seville as the corporal in a military unit. In a cigar factory nearby, 400 or 500 women are employed. The soldiers gather to watch them return to work after dinner, calling out particularly to "GITANELLA" (gypsy). This is Carmen, who wears

José is on sentry duty

a short scarlet skirt and silk stockings full of holes. Don José is attracted to her and she asks him for a chain he is making. She then taunts and ridicules him, but throws a cassia flower at his feet, which he picks up and places in his jacket. He is still thinking of her and the holes in her stockings two or three hours later when the quartermaster orders him to investigate a supposed assassination in the factory. He finds Carmen has attacked another girl with a knife and has cut a cross on her face. Don José has to arrest Carmen for the crime. On their way to the barracks she begs him to allow her to escape, speaking in Basque to him; and he arranges this, even keeping his dragoons from pursuing her. For this he is demoted and put into prison for a month. In the prison he receives a loaf of bread containing a file and a gold piece, supposedly from a cousin but actually from Carmen. On being discharged from prison he is posted as sentinel at a colonel's quarters. Here he sees Carmen enter, dressed in a spangled gown with gold lace. She persuades him to leave his post and she tells him to meet her in Triana at the house of a friend. Carmen is there when he arrives and takes him on a shopping tour, spending the gold piece (which he has returned to her) and everything else he has. They pass the day together. By now Don José is madly in love with her and she confesses that she loves him a little. He returns to quarters for roll call and is ordered to do extra guard duty. While he is on sentry duty Carmen approaches with a group of smugglers, whom he permits to pass through with English goods. She meets him next day and makes fun of him, but he continues to seek her out and she is sometimes affectionate and sometimes disdainful. He is in her room one night when a lieutenant who also loves Carmen comes in; the lieutenant draws a sword and cuts Don José on the forehead. Don José runs the officer through with his sword and Carmen arranges his escape, dressing him in a striped mantle and putting him in touch with a smuggling band led by DANCAIRE. Carmen and he join the band and he finds that she acts as a spy for the smugglers, who receive goods in Gibraltar and on the coast. He gives Carmen presents but Dancaire confides that Carmen is married to GARCIA, a hideous one-eyed monster of a man who has escaped from the galleys and prison through Carmen's efforts. The smugglers are pursued by troopers but they escape and Carmen gives them information on rich travelers, whom they rob. Don José goes to Gilbraltar, looking for the gypsy girl, and finds her consorting with an Englishman in scarlet uniform. Carmen has Don José invited into the Englishman's house. Don José upbraids her as a shameless jade but she retorts that she is only working for the gang. They talk together in Basque, which the Englishman does not understand, and she asks Don José back to rob their host. Returning to the smugglers' camp, more infatuated with Carmen than ever, Don José picks a quarrel with Garcia and clubs him to death. With Dancaire he robs the Englishman, and in the course of this Carmen saves his life by pushing the victim's arm. Don José and Carmen are happy together for several months, until Carmen visits several bullfights at Cordova and frequently speaks of a toreador named ESCAMILLO. Don José forbids her to speak to the bullfighter but she defies him and refuses to be restricted. (It was at this time, while smuggling bales of cotton, that they met the author, Don José tells him, and Car-

men stole his gold watch.) The lovers quarrel and are once more reconciled but Carmen goes to a fête at Córdova. Don José follows her and watches Escamillo's feats in the arena. He finds Carmen and asks her if she loves the bullfighter and she admits that she did, briefly. "You intend to kill me," she says quietly, "but I will live with you no longer." He stabs her twice and buries her in a grave he digs in the woods.

Chap. 4. The author discusses the nomads of Europe known as Bohemians, Gitanos,

Gypsies, or Zigeuner, many of them living in Catalonia. The men for the most part are tall, slender, and agile. In Germany the women are often very pretty, but this is not so in Spain. It is unheard of for a gypsy to have a love affair with a man foreign to her race. As a whole the gypsies are indifferent to religion and even superstitions. They speak of Egypt as their original country but Orientalists believe they were originally from India. A great gypsy proverb is "Into the closed mouth no fly enters," with which the author concludes.

The Memoirs of Casanova

Autobiography by Jacques Casanova, 1725–1798.
Published 1822–37, and since, in various editions and versions. (ML, 165)

CASANOVA'S MEMOIRS have never been published complete and perhaps never will be, for the original manuscript describes the author's carnal acts in too great detail to be legally publishable and the original publishers are a respectable house that does not publish pornography. As it is, the book is largely a succession of amorous adventures leading from one woman's name to another's; but interspersed with these adventures are descriptions of Casanova's times and the great men and women of them, giving the book considerable value to historians and scholars. ¶ No one does or can believe all of what Casanova wrote. Many or most of the love affairs he recounts in such detail are probably an old man's daydreaming, written simply to excite himself, and his social successes are no doubt similarly overpainted. He usually represents himself as a honorable man, albeit an adventurer by calling. Contemporary accounts written by others make it clear that he was largely a scoundrel. Nevertheless this is one of the most famous books of all time, and not only because of its wickedness.

Chaps. 1–5. JACQUES (GIACOMO) CASANOVA, the offspring of an actor and a shoemaker's daughter, was born in Venice in 1725. The mother became an actress also and supported her children by this profession after the father died. Three Venetian noblemen named GRIMANI became the Casanova family's patrons at the request of the dying father. By one of these, the Abbé Grimani, Casanova at the age of 9 was placed in a boarding home where he slept in an attic dormitory, with rats and insects running over him. He became the favorite of the schoolmaster, Dr. GOZZI, and was taken into his home and treated well. At 16 Casanova was made to begin study for a doctorate in law, though he would have preferred medicine. Now he planned to become an ecclesiastical lawyer, but he lived a wild life among the students and fell into debt. An elegant and well-dressed young man, he found himself very attractive to the ladies. He had various loves. One of the first was BETTINA, daughter of a shoemaker. Then, when he visited the Countess of Mont-Réal at her estate Paséan, the concierge's 14-year-old daughter LUCY appointed herself his servant and was devoted to him, but he did not violate her youthful chastity and he was as shocked as anyone when she eloped. Casanova went to Rome, did not like it, and went on to Naples, then to Calabria to enter the service of the Bishop of Martorano. In an inn at Ancona Casanova met a boy singer called BELLINO and correctly guessed it was a girl posing as a boy;

he proved to be right. Her name was TERESA and she traveled with him as his wife until she began to earn so much as a singer that his pride would not let him live on her.

[One of his early loves was ANGELA, the daughter of a vicar. She was too chaste and he was forced to discover the merits of her friends, the sisters NANNETTA and MARTINA, who consented to be his joint mistresses.]

In order to advance his career Casanova entered the service of a Cardinal ACQUAVIVA in Rome and made many important contacts.

[He had a clandestine affair with the wife of a distinguished lawyer, LUCREZIA, and also with her maiden sister, ANGELICA. Some news of scandal reached the Cardinal's ears and he dismissed Casanova from his service.]

Chaps. 6–9. Casanova went to Constantinople as an officer, with the rank of ensign, to carry some dispatches for Cardinal Acquaviva. There he exposed an impostor posing as a French duke, fought him, and was placed under arrest; he escaped but was recaptured and put in chains in Corfu, but the friendship of other officers got him back safely to Venice. Here he gambled successfully, lived the life of a rich young man, and had an affair with ANCILLA, the city's most famous courtesan. When Count MEDINI cheated him in gambling, Casanova fought the Count and won; but the Count won so much from him that soon

Casanova was penniless. He met the rich and beautiful CRISTINA, the niece of a priest, and though he loved her he arranged her marriage to a noble friend. He next met and traveled with HENRIETTE, Frenchwoman, who finally had to leave him because of other commitments but who gave him a large sum of money when they parted.

[When unsuccessful as a gambler, Casanova turned to playing the violin in an orchestra. One night, while playing at a fashionable wedding, Casanova saw a wealthy senator who had suffered a stroke. Pretending to be a physician with divine knowledge, Casanova was taken into the nobleman's house and when the elderly man recovered Casanova was adopted as his son. He continued to live a free life, now amply supplied with money. But Casanova was accused of raping a young lady and the scandal forced him to flee to Verona. Casanova in his next caprice pretended to be a magician and offered to find the buried money of a simple man. He pretended to need the aid of the man's daughter, then with magic mumbling he violated her.]

Chaps. 10–11. Casanova went for the first time to Paris. He met members of the fashionable world and became medical adviser to the young Duchess of Chartres, winning her favor when he prescribed an ointment that improved her complexion. He visited Dresden and Vienna, then returned to Venice.

[In Paris Casanova went to Fontainebleau to the court of Louis XII. He met the Maréchal de Richelieu. He had an affair with the 15-year-old daughter of his landlady. The mother, on finding the girl pregnant, hauled Casanova into court. Glibly he lied out of the situation but decided it was time to return to Venice. Once there, he gambled, drank, and started an affair with the beautiful CATRINA, who intended to become his bride; but her father sent her off to a convent for four years till she became old enough for marriage. While visiting Catrina in the convent he met a beautiful nun, MARIA, who agreed to meet him at night. He continued to make love to Catrina, but conducted an affair with the passionate and lusty Maria at the same time.]

Casanova again encounters Theresa, now leading lady of the Opera

Chaps. 12–16. Back in Venice Casanova got into trouble with the Inquisition by writing about occult matters and was jailed as a "magician." He was 31. His friend and adopted father, the French nobleman M. DE BRAGADIN, interceded and saved his life but he stayed in the jail—"the Leads," a garret in an old house—until he managed to cut a hole through the roof and, with a fellow prisoner named MARIN BALBI, escaped and got to Paris. Here he won favor with the government with a plan for a lottery to raise money, which also richly rewarded him and various men in the government, since it was not honestly operated. The rich Mlle. DE LA MEURE proposed marriage to him but as always he was fearful of wedding, though he loved her and grieved when—on his advice—she married a rich merchant. It was now 1760. He met Voltaire. He journeyed to Italy. He again encountered Teresa, who was the leading singer of the opera in Florence, and who could delude her husband enough for them to resume their affair. Casanova also met his own 15-year-old son, whom Teresa had had by him but whom she called her brother.

Casanova went on to Rome and had an audience with Pope Benedict XIV, who helped him to get a pardon in Venice.

[In Paris he met the Count LA TOUR-D'AUVERGNE, who introduced him to many fashionable courtesans, among them the famous CAMILLE. One evening in a dark carriage he determined to kiss the Count's young Lady BABET. In the dark he accidentally kissed the Count. The incident caused much amusement to the gay people of Paris. Casanova started a business venture of printing pictures on silk cloth. He hired 20 young

working girls to sew the materials. This business was almost ruined because he had to buy the favors of his girls and found them so pleasing that he needed all twenty of them every day. They all demanded a house, furniture and jewels from him. Casanova then developed a special passion for a shop girl and contrived to deceive the young girl's husband. Later his business collapsed and he left Paris in debt. In Holland he fought a duel with a man who insulted a lady of his acquaintance. He wounded the man with his sword. In Holland Casanova found a pretty Bourgemaster's wife. She let him into her house at night through a little staircase leading from a church next door. In his next adventure, in Stuttgart, he found nothing but trouble. He was rebuffed by a famous actress and held in confinement in his rooms by orders of the Duke, accused of cheating three officers out of a gambling debt. He escaped from his room by getting the sentry drunk. He was afraid of being murdered by a hired assassin so he fled to Switzerland. In Zurich he went to a beautiful old church and met a kindly abbot. He was disgusted with all the misfortunes life had brought him and conceived an overwhelming desire to become a monk. On seeing a lady back at the inn, who was traveling to visit the church, he changed his mind abruptly and followed his new desire, the Baroness ROLL. He disguised himself as a waiter to be near her. Then he rented a house from the baron, hoping to make it a second home for the baroness. His housekeeper, Mme. DUBOIS, was also a charming woman willing to allow him every liberty. An ugly woman who was in love with Casanova hid in the baroness's antechamber when she was visiting and Casa-

nova made love to her, thinking she was the baroness. In the morning the ugly lady left a note, threatening to make the story public, disgracing the baroness as well as her host; Casanova outwitted her by contending it was his valet who made love to her. Casanova then went to Bern with his housekeeper. He found real happiness with Mme. Dubois and planned to keep her as his mistress for the rest of his life, but a letter arrived offering the woman a good marriage and she was forced to accept. Casanova then went on to Naples, where he met a beautiful 17-year-old girl, LEONIDA. He fell in love with her and, determined to end his miserable wanderings, proposed marriage. The young girl accepted and the nuptials were being arranged when Leonida's mother arrived. She was Lucrezia, the woman Casanova had known in Rome at the start of his career. They recognized each other and Lucrezia told him that he was the father of the beautiful Leonida. This cancelled the marriage plans, but Casanova recovered from his depression when he realized that Lucrezia was still a beautiful woman.]

Chaps. 17–19. In Turin Casanova (who by this time called himself by the title Chevalier DE SEINGALT) loved and gambled expensively. He had a tender affair with AGATHA, a dancer in the opera company. An English earl, Lord PERCY, fancied Agatha and offered to trade his own mistress, REDEGONDE, plus cash for her. Casanova refused, but Percy got Agatha anyway by supplying money to an impresario to pay her an exorbitant price as a dancer. Percy was friendly and gave Casanova a letter of introduction to his mother in England. Casanova wooed the Spanish Countess A.B., who coveted a sable robe he had but was insulted by his offer to give it to her in return for her favors. Her husband, Count A.B., undertook to arrange matters for 1,000 sequins (15,000 francs), which he needed. A Venetian, BARBARO, proposed a gambling alliance with Casanova and implied that he could cheat skillfully. Casanova refused. The Countess finally offered herself and he avenged himself by rejecting her but leaving the money for which he had sold his robe.

A little staircase let him in

Chaps. 20–25. While Casanova was in Genoa his youngest brother came to him, penniless and in disgrace. The brother was a priest but had succumbed to love of a woman, MARCOLINA. Casanova paid his bills and sent him to Paris. Casanova started for Marseilles, taking Marcolina with him, but with the intent of sending her home at the first opportunity. His carriage broke down and they spent the night at the house of a countess, who would not let Casanova see her but revealed in a note, which Marcolina gave him later, that she was Henriette. Casanova then met QUERINI, the Venetian ambassador, who sent him on a mission to England. He was presented to George III and the queen, and also met Percy's mother, the Duchess of Northumberland. With the aid of his housekeeper, Casanova advertised for a mistress—by placing a placard in the window of the house. An apparently "ideal" lodger applied, Miss PAULINE. She was very mysterious but finally revealed that she was Portuguese, the daughter of a count. She had rejected a marriage her grandfather planned for her, and risking the displeasure of a royal princess she had come to England, disguised as a man, with the young Count Al——, the man she loved (who was disguised as her wife). He was returned to Portugal and she was waiting until she might be permitted to rejoin him in Lisbon. Casanova fell in love with Pauline but languished unsatisfied while she remained faithful to Count Al——, though she was quite friendly. Finally she yielded to him, but they had only three weeks, then Pauline returned to Lisbon. Casanova would not let the housekeeper put out the placard again.

[In Paris again, Casanova picked up a dancer of some fame and took her to dinner in Clichy. They met some Portuguese adventurers, who stole Casanova's ring. When he accused them of the theft they denied it and one escaped while his friend dueled with the angry Casanova. The Portuguese was killed by Casanova's sword and Casanova left Paris quickly. He went to Munich with a dancer; she spent most of his money and he lost the rest gambling.]

Chaps. 26–27. Casanova met a Miss MARIANNE CHARPILLON, a great beauty. Lord Pembroke warned him that she was an adventuress, and when Casanova met her mother he recognized a woman who had swindled him in Italy. Despite these warnings, Casanova courted the girl. Miss Charpillon proposed that Casanova back her aunt in a venture to market an "elixir of life." Miss Charpillon coquettishly evaded all of Casanova's advances but the three women lured him with promises so he would give them money. Finally, in a rage, he beat Miss Charpillon, whose mother threatened legal action, but Miss Charpillon pretended remorse, again led him on enough to get more money, and again refused her favors. His infatuation was such that this was several times repeated. When Miss Charpillon feigned serious illness and death, Casanova actually planned to kill himself. Then he

was arrested and jailed on Miss Charpillon's complaint that he was seeking to disfigure her. He was released and he bought a parrot and trained it to say insulting things about Miss Charpillon. Then he had the bird sold in the public marketplace, where a friend of Miss Charpillon's bought it for 50 guineas. By this time Casanova was over his infatuation but it had cost him all his money.

[Casanova was moving quickly toward financial ruin and physical exhaustion. He gambled with the Baron STENAU and won. The baron gave him a large note to exchange. Casanova was to take out his gambling winnings and return the rest. He did this but the note turned out to be a forgery and Casanova was in debt for the entire amount. He could have lost his life in an English court on a forgery charge. Casanova fled from England.]

Chaps. 28–35. Casanova went to Germany. He was befriended by the Duke of Brunswick, and was received by Frederick II of Prussia at his palace at Sans Souci. Then he went to Riga and saw Catherine the Great when she visited there. He went on to St. Petersburg, where he bought a peasant girl as a servant, for 100 rubles; this gave him the right to do anything with her but kill her. He renamed her ZAIRA. She came to love him so much that she was violently jealous. Casanova was presented to Catherine and had several conversations with her. He left Zaira in Russia and traveled to Warsaw, to France, and into Spain. There, with some difficulty, he won the favors of Dona IGNAZIA, a cobbler's daughter. He was imprisoned for secretly having weapons, despite the efforts of his friend the Chevalier MENGS, a painter. Mengs became unfriendly when Casanova's name was posted on the church door for not having fulfilled his

Easter duties—an omission Casanova promptly made good by going to Communion and confession. But Casanova's downfall came in Spain. A Baron DE FRAITURE came to Madrid. Casanova knew him only slightly and refused to lend him money. In revenge, Fraiture maligned Casanova enough to lose him his friends. All doors were closed to him. Then LA NINA, a dancer, mistress of the captain-general of Barcelona, took a fancy to Casanova. When Casanova was attacked by ruffians in the street, he killed one of them with his sword. The captain-general invented charges against Casanova and he was banished. He went to Aix in Provence, and he tried to get in touch with Henriette but she would not see him, though she offered him whatever money he might need. (It was 22 years since their romance and she had grown fat.) Casanova did some writing to earn money. He was now 55. In Rome he found himself enamored again, this girl being ARMELLINA, not quite 16. The result of this romance is not reported, nor the next, which caused Casanova much sorrow: He was not yet reconciled to the disadvantages of old age.

But Casanova's eclipse continued; he was banished from Florence, persecuted by the same man who had sent him from Spain. He lived for a time in Trieste, directing an amateur theatrical group; he had a brief romance with a peasant widow and almost had a duel with the count, her landlord, when he protected her against a beating by the count.

[The memoirs end here. Casanova later was pardoned and returned to Venice. He lived there for some years, in poverty. Then the Count Wallenstein (or Waldstein) gave him a position as librarian in his castle in Bohemia and Casanova lived there the last 12 to 14 years of his life, writing.]

The Case of Sergeant Grischa

Novel by Arnold Zweig, 1887– Published 1927. In U.S. published & © 1928 by Viking Press, New York, in a translation from the German by Eric Sutton.

EITHER THIS IS the best-written German novel (in style) of its decade or the translation by Eric Sutton is the best translation of its decade. The American reader can expect no better reward than a reading of *The Case of Sergeant Grischa*. The novel's theme is the German approach to the niceties

of a person's legal rights. The American may find that the German sense of legal form and abstract justice is a bit finer than his ingrained English sense of the same, but he will be reassured by the contrast of this German sense of justice with some practical applications of it that he has seen in his lifetime. ❡ *The Case of Sergeant Grischa* was the first-published of Arnold Zweig's tetralogy, or series of four novels, about World War I. The others did not come up to the reasonable expectations of those who had read the first.

Book 1. In the winter of 1917, GRISCHA ILJITCH PAPROTKIN is a Russian prisoner of war behind the German lines. He is determined to escape in order to see his wife and family once more. He constructs a coffinlike compartment, just large enough

to hold himself, in a load of lumber scheduled to move in the general direction of Russia. In his hiding place he feels the train start up and move, but he does not know that it is heading south rather than east. He does not know where he is when the train stops and he emerges from his hiding place, but with the aid of a compass he makes his way generally eastward. An umbrella he finds provides material to make a bow and arrows, and he is able to kill rabbits and other small game to sustain him en route. His campfire attracts the attention of two strangers, whom he fears to be German spies, or members of a party seeking escaped prisoners such as himself. They are Russians, however: KOLJA, a large man, and BABKA, a young woman of about twenty who looks like a boy, except for her snow-white hair—the result of four years of war and hardship—which gives her he nickname Babka, "grandmother." Her real name is ANNA KYRILLOVNA, and she is a Lithuanian whose father and brothers were shot by invading Germans for retaining possession of a gun. She is immensely attracted to Grischa and soon loves him deeply. He responds with a strange and violent kind of affection for her, and they become lovers in the refugee camp to which Kolja and Babka take him. When it is time for the refugees to move on, as German patrols approach their vicinity, Babka provides Grischa with a new identity, complete with papers and identification tags. He is now Ilja Pavlovitsch Bjuscheff, a Russian deserter on his way home. He floats down the Niemen River on a raft with two other refugees, then separates from them to make his way eastward as best he can. He reaches the town of Bialystok, where is situated the office of Lt. Gen. ALBERT SCHIEFFENZAHN of the German Army, a man who is to become the most important influence in Grischa's life.

Book II. Grischa finds refuge in a wooden hut at Mervinsk and is befriended by DEBORAH SUSSKIND and her cousin ALEXANDER, known as SASCHA. At Mervinsk, His Excellency Gen. OTTO VON LYCHOW is in command of German forces. Schieffenzahn is his military subordinate but has been in Mervinsk so long that he has assumed great authority. Schieffenzahn posts a notice to the effect that all Russian soldiers or deserters wandering about the neighborhood must give themselves up or face execution as spies, but Grischa cannot read and merely wonders what the proclamation says. He is captured in his wooden hut when field police chance to pass by and glance in.

His trial is brief, and when the report reaches von Lychow it seems like a clear case of espionage, with its inevitable death sentence. Grischa cannot believe that he will be convicted of something of which he is so obviously innocent. However, in the prison where he is confined he receives formal notice that he is to be shot. In his incredulity, it bursts upon him that the man they wish to shoot is Bjuscheff—not Grischa—and he sets out to convince them of his true identity. The information as to the labor camp from which he escaped is duly checked and proved correct. When two guards from the labor camp confirm his identity, it seems that the matter is closed,

and there remains only the question of which court now has the authority to decide his case. An advocate aide of von Lychow's, PONSANSKI, convinces von Lychow that Grischa should not be executed.

Book III. While Grischa is waiting for a decision, and working at odd jobs about the prison where he is still held, Babka is walking toward Mervinsk to find him. She has learned that he is imprisoned and she determines to do something about it. Meanwhile the dossier (file record) of Grischa has been sent to the Department of Justice at Bialystok, where it rests unnoticed in a pigeonhole with other papers. The courier who delivered it did not trouble to obtain the personal interview with the chief, though he had been warned that such an interview was very important. He merely left the dossier in the hands of a soldier-clerk in the outer office. Eventually the dossier reaches the desk of the man for whom it was originally intended, but he is distracted at the time by his courtship of a young woman in his office staff and once again it is put aside.

Book IV. Babka arrives at the prison and enters as an innocent vendor of berries. She looks harmless, like an ignorant, penniless peasant woman, and soon she is a familiar sight, walking unchallenged in and out of the prison compounds with her baskets. Grischa learns that the "raspberry woman" is Babka when she appears unexpectedly in the doorway of the shop where he is working, and he nearly gives away his acquaintance with her in spite of her warning finger upon her lips. Exhausted, she falls asleep in the shop, before she can tell Grischa that she is to bear his child. Shortly thereafter an order from Schieffenzahn arrives. The order upholds the decision of the first court-martial and states that Grischa must be executed. Grischa is bewildered but is phlegmatically resigned. Babka is not, and sets out to find poisonous herbs and mushrooms with which to poison the schnapps of the prison guards, so that Grischa may escape. Grischa is not in accord with this suggestion. In one way he seems to be resigned to his fate, but on the other hand he does not really believe that he will be executed, for he has talked to von Lychow and knows that the general has committed himself to upholding the obvious proof of Grischa's innocence. Through the early part of the autumn the matter of the death sentence continues to hang fire—not executed, but not rescinded. Babka tells

Grischa that their baby will be born in December.

Book V. Von Lychow goes on leave. First he makes an appointment to see Schieffenzahn and warns him that if Grischa's order of execution is not countermanded, the Kaiser will hear of the situation and Schieffenzahn's glowing future will be dimmed. Schieffenzahn suspects the first part of von Lychow's purpose, and to forestall him orders a wire sent directing that Grischa be executed at once and that confirmation be sent to him within 24 hours. The receipt of the telegram disturbs the officers, but they are sure that after von Lychow's call even Schieffenzahn will back down and will send a countermanding order. A severe and heavy snowstorm has disrupted communications, however, and there is no possibility of repair—therefore no possibility of reprieve for Grischa—before the next morning, which will be too late.

Book VI. Babka is stunned by the news that Grischa is to be shot, but she makes a last desperate effort to save him. She prepares a bottle of poisoned liquor for the guards, and she thinks she has persuaded Grischa to give it to them. Lieut. WIN-FRIED, a young officer who has taken a great interest in the legal aspects of Grischa's case, is also trying to contrive a postponement at least until communications are restored. Grischa pours the poisoned liquor down the sink when Babka has left. The shock of learning that her "silly soldier man" is definitely going to die in the morning, in spite of her efforts, brings on Babka's labor. She is taken to the hospital, and Grischa goes to sleep.

Book VII. Winfried is still hopeful that the reprieve telegram may arrive in time, and Grischa himself is sleeping in his cell. Instead of a firing squad from the local soldiery, one is recruited from another company. Grischa goes with four guards to dig his own grave in the Russian soldiers' cemetery. He welcomes the activity; it is better than sitting alone and thinking. He faces his executioners like a soldier and dies like one. Babka's baby—a girl—is born within half an hour after his death. When von Lychow learns that the execution was carried out, at Schieffenzahn's command, he appeals to the Kaiser, who promises to punish the younger general. However, just at this time the Kaiser receives the gift of a jeweled box and this distracts him, so he delivers only a light reprimand and the matter is closed forever.

Grischa faces his executioners and dies like a soldier

Indolence

Poem by James Thomson, 1700–1748. Published 1748.

THERE WERE TWO Scottish poets named James Thomson. *The Castle of Indolence* was written by the earlier and more respectable one, the one who wrote the more ambitious *The Seasons* and also the poem "Rule, Britannia." *The Castle of Indolence* is an allegory. It is written in Spenserian stanzas. Critics have generally considered it Thomson's best poetry, and this is true of the first canto, in which he paints the perils of indolence. In the second canto, in which he seeks a happy and moral ending, the writing is more pompous and less poetical. The writing of the various parts was widely separated. Thomson started the poem in 1733 and it was not published until 1748.

Canto 1. The WIZARD OF INDOLENCE lives in a beautiful valley beside a flowing river. In this valley there are quiet, sunny lawns and cool shady groves, soothing green hills and bright flowers. Gentle breezes rustle the leaves of trees and the murmur of brooks mingles with the sound of gently lowing herds. It is never too hot or too cold and nothing annoying ever happens to disturb the peace. At the entrance to this lovely land the wicked wizard waits, playing his lute. As pilgrims from all parts of the world pause to admire the valley, the wizard sings a song: "Come and live here with me. Why get up early and work hard all day? Why worry and struggle? Here you can forget everything and live a life of ease. It is foolish 'To toil for what you here untoiling may obtain.'" Then the wizard suddenly leaps towards the listening pilgrims and pulls them through the gate.

Everything in the valley seems to be as fine as the wizard promised. Each person receives a comfortable flowing robe to wear and the life of easy pleasure begins. The inhabitants walk on the softest carpets and lie on beds piled high with pillows. They eat the richest food and drink rare wines. The one rule in the valley is that no one must think of pleasing anyone but himself. Sometimes the inhabitants amuse themselves by gazing into a crystal ball, a mirror of vanity, where they view the struggles of the earth. They see people plodding about their daily chores, fighting and cheating and hurting others. They see nations warring against other nations and "Then sit down, just where they were before." Among the persons here are some of the famous literary and political figures of the poet's day, and, in fact, he himself is one of the occupants of the castle. Life in the valley is delightful. "But not e'en pleasure to excess is good," the poet observes.

This pampered existence gradually enfeebles the inhabitants of the castle until they are too weak to do anything but lie on couches and sigh with weariness. At this point, they are thrown into a dark and terrible place underground and abandoned. "Fierce fiends, and hags of hell, their only nurses were." Some of the hideous monsters who rule this foul place are Lethargy, Hypochondria, and Intemperance. Gnawing wolves and stinging serpents are their companions.

Canto 2. A rough and daring Knight meets Dame Poverty in the forest. They have a child, the KNIGHT OF ARTS AND INDUSTRY, who is destined to overthrow the Castle of Indolence. The gods favor this child and give him strength and cunning, wisdom and talent. His aim in life is to civilize the world, which has, until now, been a wild and savage place. The Knight of Arts and Industry sets sail for Britain, where he begins his great work. At last, satisfied that he has done his task well, the worthy Knight retires to a farm to spend his old age in peace and joy. News reaches him that Indolence is spoiling all his good work. The Knight, in righteous anger, vows to destroy the wizard of Indolence. He starts at once upon a journey to the Castle of Indolence, accompanied by a trusted friend, the BARD.

When the Knight and the bard reach the valley, they are charmed by the beauty of the view and marvel at the crafty way the wizard mingles wrong and right in his song so that no one can detect his evil purpose. The wizard tries to grab the Knight but after a fierce struggle the Knight ensnares the wizard in his Net of Woe. At this, all the demons of the valley begin to howl, "And lightning flash'd, and horror rock'd the ground." The brave Knight orders the bard to sing a song that will reach the souls of those who are still in the valley. The bard sings a praise of honest toil and assures his listeners that it is not too late to save themselves. They have the great gift of reason and can change. Some persons heed the bard but most do not. The Knight, seeing this, grows angry and waves a magic wand. The lovely landscape sinks from view, leaving in its place foul marshes crawling with snakes and toads and other loathsome creatures.

The Knight throws open the underground dungeon and assures the pitiful beings there that when they have fully repented, they will have a new life. He promises to stand by them until that great day comes. They, however, are impatient and *pretend* to repent. Now they lose their chance to be saved. A vast desert suddenly stretches before them, strewn with carcasses. They must travel from this desert through a foul-smelling land of bogs to a land of snow and ice, and back to the desert again. The cruel fiends Gaunt Beggary and Scorn drive the lost souls on this fearful ceaseless journey, as a ruthless driver goads a herd of cattle through a muddy town.

The knight and the bard

The Castle of Otranto

Novel by Horace Walpole, 1717–1797.
Published 1764.

TOWARD THE END of the 18th century there arose a vogue for "horror stories," usually set in castles and punctuated by mysterious occurrences that were supposed to have rational explanations but were occasionally left with no explanation other than the occult or supernatural. Walpole's *Castle of Otranto* may have set the fashion. He subtitled it *A Gothic Story* and as a result all novels of its kind came to be called gothic stories. In the first edition Walpole presented the novel as a translation from the Italian. The action is set in the 12th century or earlier.

Horace Walpole was the fourth son of Sir Robert Walpole, first English prime minister, and eventually inherited his father's title of Earl of Orford.

Chap. 1. MANFRED, Prince of Otranto, has arranged a marriage between his son, CONRAD, and the Princess ISABELLA, daughter of the Marquis FREDERIC DE VICENZA. The princess's father has been away from home for several years and is believed by many to have been killed in the Holy Land; her guardians arranged the match. The wedding is to take place on Conrad's 16th birthday. The day comes and all is ready. Suddenly a tremendous crash is heard, and terrified servants can say only incoherent words about a helmet. A gigantic helmet has fallen from no known place and has killed Conrad. HIPPOLITA, Manfred's wife, and MATILDA, their beautiful 18-year-old daughter, are prostrated and retire. A peasant in the crowd remarks that the helmet resembles the one on a marble statue of ALFONSE THE GOOD in the church. When an excited servant reports that the helmet is mysteriously missing from that statue, the peasant is accused of sorcery and blamed for the tragedy. Manfred commands that he be imprisoned under the iron helmet that killed Conrad, and left to starve.

Manfred then seeks out the Princess Isabella and informs her of his intention to divorce his wife and marry her. The suggestion so terrifies Isabella that she flees toward some passages that will lead her to sanctuary in a convent—if she can find the opening and escape. She is helped by a stranger and learns that he is the peasant. He was imprisoned under the giant casque in the courtyard which just happened to be set on a trapdoor through which he entered the passages below. Isabella escapes, but Manfred catches her benefactor and locks him in a small room outside Manfred's own quarters.

Chap. 2. during the night, Matilda hears a voice speaking to her from a nearby casement. It is the imprisoned peasant. He tells her that he loves the beautiful princess, and she believes he means Isabella. It is Matilda whom he loves, however, having seen her at the wedding that never took place. He could not see the face of Isabella in the cavern, and he mistakenly believes it was Matilda who fled, after he hears from the servants that "the princess" is gone.

The arrival of Father JEROME, from the monastery to which Isabella has fled, next creates excitement. Father Jerome reports that Isabella has sought sanctuary there but that she begs permission to go home, where she will find out whether her father is dead or alive. If he is dead she will allow her guardians to arrange a suitable marriage for her. Manfred is determined to marry her himself and is angry that Father Jerome has been told the reason for the girl's terror and flight. When it seems there is little he can do to dissuade Manfred, Father Jerome suggests that perhaps Isabella and the peasant who saved her are lovers, and Manfred is wild with jealousy and rage. He orders the peasant removed from where he is confined, and almost immediately he convinces himself of the young man's guilt. He condemns him to be beheaded, but just as the ax is about to fall the young man asks for a priest. Father Jerome is summoned and recognizes his son, Theodore, product of a marriage that ended tragically when pirates kidnapped his wife and child years before.

It was after this tragedy that Father Jerome entered the priesthood. Manfred bargains. He will spare the boy's life if Father Jerome will return Isabella to Castle Otranto and will help in furthering Manfred's schemes.

Chap. 3. The sound of a trumpet is heard, and the plumes on the miraculous casque are agitated violently. Manfred is terrified. He thinks this must be a sign from heaven, though he cannot imagine what kind of sign it may be. It proves to be a herald from Frederic of Vicenza, who demands that his daughter be returned and demands also the return of the Castle of Otranto, which Manfred has usurped from the true heir of Alfonso the Good. Manfred trembles with fear and fury, and asks where is the knight that represents the Marquis of Vicenza. When he learns that the entire cortege is but a league away from the castle, he sends the herald to invite all for the night. The herald reports that he is also instructed to challenge Manfred to a duel with the knight in the morning, and Manfred says that if the knight still wishes the combat after talking with him, he will of course take up his sword in the morn.

The tremendous company enters the castle gate, and the knights partake of a banquet in silence. The chief knight does not allow his face to be seen. Meanwhile Matilda has released Theodore, begging him to be gone. He leaves, reluctantly, but encounters Isabella in the woods, where by now a searching party of the Marquis of Vicenza and soldiers from the castle are also beating the grounds. Theodore defends Isabella from one whom he thinks to be Manfred's deputy, only to learn from the mouth of the sorely wounded knight that he is of the other group and is determined not to let Isabella be taken by Manfred. To everyone's astonishment and horror, the wounded man proves to be Isabella's father. A sorry procession bears him to the castle for help.

Chap. 4. At the castle, the surgeon reports that Frederic's wounds are not serious, and that he will recover. Frederic then tells of an experience he had in the Holy Land, which led him to find the gigantic sword his bearers carried to Otranto. Manfred had wondered about that sword, which was too large for any single man to wield. On it was engraved a verse predicting that one day a casque of corresponding size would appear, and on that day the daughter of the house of Vicenza would be surrounded by dangers indescribable. The casque is the miraculous helmet that killed Conrad. With no explanation to account for these phenomena, Matilda and Isabella retire, each in a strange state of confusion and love, and a touch of jealousy. They are both in love with Theodore, and each believes that Theodore is in love with the other. Matilda determines to sacrifice her love, but then Hippolita appears with the news that Manfred has agreed to the marriage of his daughter Matilda to Frederic. Hippolita, at the same time, has agreed to a correct church divorce from Manfred, so that he may marry Isabella. Both girls are horrified at this, but there is little that they can do. Matilda begs to be allowed to enter a convent with her mother.

Chap. 5. Matilda's maid, BIANCA, comes rushing from another part of the castle to tell Frederic and Manfred in trembling tones that she has seen a giant hand in armor—of a size large enough to wield the giant sword brought by Frederic. She is terrified, and this third apparition seems to Frederic to be a sufficient sign that his family should never marry with the family of Manfred. He refuses his daughter and declares that he on his part will not marry Matilda. It has been noted again by several persons that there is a strange and startling resemblance between young Theodore and Alfonso the Good, a resemblance that none can account for, for it is known that Alfonso died without issue.

Frederic sees Hippolita in the chapel and is there accosted by the specter of the hermit who guided him to the giant sword in the Holy Land. The hermit now adjures him to forget Matilda. Frederic returns to his apartments, rejecting Manfred's invitation to an evening of revelry. Manfred is infuriated. He believes that Isabella and Theodore are meeting secretly, and when he hears a feminine voice saying that Manfred would never permit their union, he stabs toward the voice. His dagger pierces the breast of Matilda with a mortal thrust. As Matilda lies dying, Theodore declares his love for her and begs his father to marry them while life remains. In the midst of his supplication, Matilda breathes her last.

Now it is made known why Theodore bears such a striking resemblance to Alfonso the Good. In the Crusade during which Alfonso was lost, he met and fell in love with a fair young woman of Sicily named VICTORIA. He married her, and left her pregnant, and it was her daughter whom the present Father Jerome married. Their son, Theodore, is therefore the rightful heir to the estates and title of Alfonso the Good. Manfred and Hippolita see nothing in life for them but devotion to the Church, and both enter missions. It is a long time before Theodore can bear to face the thought of marriage, but eventually he weds Isabella, feeling that it is most suitable that two who so loved Matilda be joined in holy wedlock. The houses of Otranto and Vicenza are at last joined, by proxy at least.

Cathleen ni Houlihan

One-act play by William Butler Yeats, 1865–1939.
Produced at Dublin, 1902.

THIS IS A skillfully wrought allegory and remains one of Yeats' most popular works. In the 18th century "Cathleen ni Houlihan" was one of the names by which the Irish poets called Ireland when they wrote of the independence movement. Yeats set his play at Killalla in 1798, when there was an attempted French invasion of Ireland. Lady Augusta Gregory, who with Yeats was in the group that revived the Irish theater (and founded the Abbey Theatre), declared herself virtually co-author of *Cathleen ni Houlihan;* Yeats explained that the idea came to him in a dream and he called on Lady Gregory to help him with the country speech.

The play is set in a small country cottage where PETER and BRIDGET are waiting for the return of their son MICHAEL, who is to be married and is coming home with his betrothed's dowry. As they wait, PATRICK, Michael's younger brother, hears cheering outside and sees an old woman wandering around. Michael comes home with the money and Patrick leaves to find out why everyone is cheering. The old woman comes to the cottage and is welcomed inside, where she describes her troubles. Her land was taken from her and there is a crowd of strangers in her house. Michael suspects her true identity and asks her to tell him more. She describes all the men who have died for love of her over the years. Peter believes she is mad. Bridget is uneasy and frightened for Michael, who is listening very attentively to the old woman. Asking her what she would like, Peter learns that it is not money, food, or shelter. She says simply, "If anyone would give me help he must give me himself, he must give me all." Her only hope is to retrieve her beautiful stolen lands and to oust the strangers from her house. Now everyone knows who she is and Peter tries to keep Michael from going with her as she goes out. Bridget tries to make him forget the old woman by showing him his wedding clothes. But at that moment Patrick returns to explain that all the shouting is caused by the French invasion nearby. Michael, now determined, follows the old woman out. Patrick, asked if he saw an old woman outside, says that he saw only a young girl, "and she had the walk of a queen."

Autobiography of Benvenuto Cellini

Autobiography by Benvenuto Cellini, 1500–1571.
Published 1559. (PB, 42; ML, 150)

CELLINI WAS a great artist, an irascible man, and a compulsive writer. With the combination of the three qualities he was able to give the world one of its great books. There are several translations of Cellini's self-centered rantings and none can be bad. Such a book can be an inspiration to a young man. It tells how a great artist really feels.

Book I. 1. All men who have done anything of excellence should write their lives, but not till they are over 40. I am 58 and at the peak of my career. **2–15.** I am Benvenuto ("welcome") Cellini, a Florentine. My ancestors owned large estates. My father, Cristofano Cellini, was musician to the Medicis and faithful to them even after they were banished and Florence came to be ruled by the EIGHT (a council of magistrates). My father began to teach me music (flute and cornet) when I was only a child and I showed great talent. But when I was 15 I put myself under a master goldsmith and continued to work under several masters in various cities, becoming very skilled. I earned very good money.

16–18. I had criticized some goldsmiths for unfair dealing; when they abused me in the streets, I slapped one of them (GHERARDO) and was fined by the magistrates. A friend who was deeply indebted to my family refused to bail me, and being high-tempered by nature I became generally enraged, seized a dagger, and attacked the household of Gherardo. By God's grace I did no harm, but I had to flee town or the Eight would have had my life.

19–25. In Rome I worked in the shop of LUCAGNOLO. I redesigned a fine jeweled piece for the rich Madonna PORZIA, who had taken a fancy to me; Lucagnolo was making a large vase. He thought it a waste of time to work on so small a piece as mine, but I produced such a masterpiece that I was paid twice as much as he was. He was so jealous that he became unfriendly. The Bishop of Salamanca commissioned me to make a pair of large water-vessels. While I was working on them, Pope Clement VII (a Medici and friendly to the Cellinis) asked me to join his band of Musicians. I did not want to accept, but I dreamed that my father would curse me if I did not. The music cut into my working time and I was late with the Bishop's vase. When I delivered it, he said he would delay payment. But a Spaniard in his house broke the vase and brought it to me for repair. I decided to hold it till I was paid. The Spaniard brought back a gang to take it, but I scared them off with a musket. The Bishop paid. The Pope was amused. With Madonna Porzia's help I opened my own shop. I had one helper, PAULINO, a 14-year-old boy, admirable in every way.

26–31. A young Roman dandy made insulting remarks about Florentines; I slapped him and he challenged me, but then he apologized and there was no fight. The plague broke out in Rome and thousands died daily. I escaped, but did have an illness of boils. I took to hunting pigeons for sport and health and became a remarkable shot. Meanwhile I was doing much work of many kinds. Most artists specialize but I tried every form of the goldsmith's art and excelled in all.

32–38. The talented singer Luigi Pulci came to me in Rome and asked my help in curing him of a foul disease. The young man was cured but became involved with Messer GIOVANNI and sank into sin. He courted Pantasilea, a strumpet. I made him swear he would have nothing to do with her, but he must have broken his oath to me because he fell off his horse and died. Pope Clement waged war against his enemies and I gained great favor by acting as his head artilleryman. The Pope was afraid he would lose the gold jewels in his possession. I took the gems and melted the gold, forming it into an open dish.

39–46. When the siege was over I returned to Florence, where I was reconciled

Cellini's brother is killed in a fight with his lord's enemies

with the Eight through the good offices of my father. Plague had broken out in Florence and I went to Mantua to be safe. The Prince commissioned me to make a model for a reliquary. The Prince was so pleased with the object that he took me into his service. But I fell ill with a fever and went back to Florence. I found my father and sisters had died of the plague. I opened a shop in Florence and made many gold medals and plates. MICHELANGELO saw my work and praised it highly. Pope Clement declared war on Florence and I was summoned by the Pope to join his army. I made a fine button of gold and diamonds for the Pope, with which he was very pleased. The King of France, receiving one of my medals as a gift, desired to know me. A beautiful girl of my acquaintance was suffering from a bone disease in her hand. I brought a doctor to her. While he was operating, I realized his instruments were too clumsy. I quickly went to my shop and made him some fine, delicate tools that made his work easy.

47–75. My brother came to Rome to serve a noble lord. In a fight with the lord's enemies, he was killed. I determined to avenge him and made a magnificent emblem for his tomb. A robber entered my shop planning to steal the Pope's jewels, but my dog delayed him and he did not find the chest where they were hidden. Later my dog attacked the man in the streets and the silver he had taken from me fell from his cape. I had the man arrested and he was hanged. I was commissioned to make a chalice for the Pope, but was delayed in my work by an inflammation of the eyes. The Pope became angry with me, and only after a friend spoke to him was I able to continue my work and receive my pay. I later got into trouble with the Pope in an argument. I accidentally killed a rival goldsmith. But when all the facts of the case were heard I was forgiven again and commissioned to

do more work. I went to Naples and there had an affair with the beautiful ANGELICA. I wanted to take her back to Rome with me but her mother demanded too much recompense and I was forced to leave the girl behind. I gave the Pope the medals I had been working on and he was very pleased. He said the ancients did not have such fine gold work. The Pope died but my coins had gained such a reputation that the new Pope brought me into his service and promised to protect me from the new trouble I was in. (I had killed an enemy of mine in a sword fight.)

76–127. I took a leave and went to Florence, where I was employed by the Duke to design his coins and make a portrait of him in gold. I was paid handsomely and stayed in Florence several months. In Rome my pride was always making enemies for me, and they had me placed in prison, but the Pope needed my art and I was released. I fell ill in Rome and everyone despaired of my life. They made my shroud but I recovered and went to Florence to rest at my sisters' house. There I found myself falsely accused of another crime and I had to return to Rome. When my health was restored I made a golden crucifix for the [Holy Roman] Emperor, as a gift from the Pope. I delivered this gift to the Emperor myself and was received with honor at his court. But when I returned to Rome I found that lying tongues had turned the Pope against me and I went to France. I could not obtain an audience with the king there and returned to Italy, where I was imprisoned on a false charge, accused of stealing jewels. I managed to escape and made my way without money or friends to Florence. There I obtained the protection of the Duke's wife, who admired my art.

Book II. 1–83. I found refuge with the Cardinal of Ferrara, who bade me make a statue of Venus with Cupid. The King of

France came to Italy and now took me into his service. I made a large bronze statue of Jupiter for him and some silver vases. He was pleased with my work and assured me I would always have his favor. I made him a fountain for his palace at Fontainebleau and he commissioned me to do more work for him. In Florence I made statues for the Duchess and was given lavish rooms in her castle. I planned a great statue of Perseus and one of Medusa. I took a side trip to Venice and was warmly received by LORENZO DE MEDICI. I returned to Florence and made a statue of Ganymede and one of Narcissus. I had to defend my work against slanderers who tried to convince everyone that my concept of anatomy was wrong. I demonstrated that I was right with many drawings and my adversaries were vanquished. Michelangelo approved my work and I was filled with the joy of executing my plans. I had an accident in my shop and my furnace exploded. My men were terrified by the hot liquid that flowed everywhere. But I managed to control the fire and successfully fill my molds.

84–113. Some antique statues were found around the gates of Florence and I restored them and the Duke enjoyed helping me in my work. My statue of Perseus was set up in the plaza and the people immediately greeted it. Sonnets in praise of the statue were placed all over the plaza. A rival tried to poison the Duke's mind against me by saying that the statue looked badly when seen from the rear, but the public praise grew and pleased the lord and he paid me a very large sum of money. All the people marveled at me in the streets and many came to kiss my hand. I fell out of favor with the Duchess because I had made her a necklace with inferior pearls. She persuaded the Duke to give a piece of marble and a commission for a statue of Neptune to a rival. I made a gold crucifix and gave it to her as a gift. She rewarded my work by restoring me to favor. I took leave of my noble patrons and went to Pisa to do some work there. [Here, in 1762, the autobiography is discontinued.]

The Charterhouse of Parma

Novel by Stendhal (Marie Henri Beyle, 1783–1842).
Published 1839. Many translations from the French.

STENDHAL'S GREAT NOVEL in today's estimation is *The Red and the Black,* but there have been many critics who considered *The Charterhouse of Parma* the greatest. While those critics were undoubtedly wrong, it should be sufficient for a book to be the second-best of one of the all-time best novelists, and Stendhal was that. *The Charterhouse of Parma* should be read. Its title, incidentally, has less connection with the action of the novel than might be expected. A charterhouse is a kind of city hall, and in the novel the city hall of Parma figures not too importantly.

Giletti himself is killed

Chaps. 1–4. The Marchese (Marquis) DEL DONGO, rabid leader of the anti-Napoleon party in Italy, chooses voluntary exile to his estate of Grianta rather than submit to the Frenchman's victorious rule. His sister, the beautiful GINA, married to the Conte PIETRANERA, is the leader of that very society the marchese hates. She develops and fosters a great affection for FABRIZIO, the second son of her brother, and sponsors his education until he is recalled home. Life is sad and dreary there and his timid, beautiful mother is so cowed by her stingy husband that there is little she can do for Fabrizio, though he is her favorite son. After the Conte Pietranera is killed in a pointless duel, Gina returns to the castle at Grianta to live, having no funds, and life becomes gayer for Fabrizio. When Napoleon escapes from Elba, Fabrizio is in a hurry to go and fight with him. His aunt, to whom he confides this, tells him there is no chance for victory but that it will be a wonderful thing for him. She gives him the last of her jewels and sends him on his way. With a false passport obtained from a friend, he goes to Paris. There, conspicuous

in his youthful zeal, he is thrown into jail as a spy for Napoleon. The wife of the jailer, with a keen eye for his remaining francs, helps him to escape and he rides on to find himself at the edge of the Battle of Waterloo. His adventures at this great battle are many and he emerges from it a real soldier, an escort of generals; but he is wounded in the debacle that follows the defeat of Napoleon.

Chaps. 5–8. Fabrizio is betrayed by his elder brother, who is jealous of him. In danger of being denounced as a conspirator, Fabrizio is helped by his enterprising aunt and mother. They find a way to keep him from being imprisoned, and the three

go to Milan in the aunt's carriage. Enroute, the carriage is stopped by constables looking for General CONTI, who is to be put under arrest. Other constables bring the general and his 12-year-old daughter, CLELIA, out of the woods. She attracts Fabrizio with her great beauty and warmth. Clelia is allowed to ride in the carriage and the general is given a horse. In Milan, while Gina is trying to settle Fabrizio's maze of difficulties, Fabrizio hears he may be imprisoned and he escapes and goes into exile at an estate owned by his mother near the town of Homagnano.

Count MOSCA, Prime Minister of Parma, falls completely in love with Gina and she finds herself returning his feelings, even though she has a deep love in her heart for Fabrizio. The count wants her with him at the court of Parma and since he is a married man living apart from his wife, it seems advisable to make the happy arrangement of marrying her to the very old Duke SANSEVERINO, who goes out of the country as an ambassador to another country. Mosca is so content with Gina and her influence with his prince that there is nothing he will not do for her. He undertakes to set the future course of Fabrizio, her most beloved nephew, and it is decided to send the young man to study theology for three years, after which time he will be given a place at the Parma court. Though still wishing to be a soldier, Fabrizio agrees.

After four years Fabrizio comes to Parma, now a strikingly handsome young man; and Mosca, in his fifties, is plagued with jealous fears that his beloved Gina will fall in love with him. The fear haunts him day and night and he is inflamed further by an anonymous letter, which he traces directly to the prince. The count has Fabrizio's every move spied upon and is greatly relieved when he is informed of the young

man's infatuation for a young actress, MARIETTA VALSERA. Her protector, GILETTI, becomes ragingly jealous and Mosca arranges for Fabrizio to visit his mother, to avert any mishap. Gina learns of Mosca's suspicions and is saddened; for though she loves him, there is an element of truth in his jealousy.

Chaps. 9–12. One day while Fabrizio is hunting, a carriage passes him in which Giletti and the actress Marietta are riding. Thinking that a trap has been set and that Marietta will be taken from him, Giletti tries to stab Fabrizio but is himself killed in the abortive attempt. Fabrizio takes Giletti's passport to thwart the consequences of his act and with the willing Marietta he flees to exile in Bologna. He immediately informs his aunt of his whereabouts, and also the Archbishop of Parma. Both beg him to stay away for the time being and they see to it that he has plenty of money. Exile is pleasant with the charming actress, who loves him greatly, but in his heart Fabrizio knows this is only a temporary attachment.

Chaps. 13–16. The attraction to Marietta vanishes when Fabrizio meets and pursues FAUSTA, a charming singer, who enjoys the difficulties they must overcome to be able to come together. These difficulties lead them back to Parma, pursued by Fausta's jealous lover. Mosca and Gina are again involved in trying to save Fabrizio from imprisonment. This time they are not successful, even with all the influence that the Prime Minister can bring to bear. Gina, assured of her power over the prince, threatens to leave Parma forever if Fabrizio is not immediately set free. The prince, after a noble struggle, tells her it will be so. But as soon as she leaves, he signs the order sentencing Fabrizio to 12 years in a fortress. There is now nothing Mosca can do to help the nephew of the woman he has loved so devotedly and long.

The general in charge of the fort where Fabrizio is imprisoned is the father of little Clelia, whom Fabrizio encountered many years ago. When Clelia and Fabrizio meet he

is again enraptured by her beauty and she in turn has never forgotten the handsome young man. That same evening Clelia meets Gina at a reception and they become friends and allies in the cause of Fabrizio. Mosca is frantically trying to see Gina, who has refused to see him because of his cowardice in not standing up to the prince. Then Gina, recalling their long years together, relents and agrees to see him; but only to inform him that she wishes to part from him forever and that her life now will be devoted to revenge for what has been done to her nephew.

Chaps. 17-20. By clever manipulation of his prince, Mosca averts the death sentence that now hangs over Fabrizio's head. Still Gina avoids Mosca and goes her own way, squandering huge sums of gold trying to make a contact inside the fortress. From his cell with its small barred window, Fabrizio is able to gaze upon Clelia in her aviary. Soon she is conscious of his presence and they arrange to communicate by signals. She is rapidly falling in love with him. With Clelia's help, Gina lays elaborate plans for Fabrizio's escape. At first Fabrizio is reluctant to leave, for fear that Clelia, his true love, will marry another while he is fleeing; but she extracts his promise to help in every way with their plans, and she agrees to remain true to her heart, which has been given to him. Mosca also joins in the plans.

Chaps. 21-24. Gina forms an alliance with the mad poet, FERRANTE, who agrees to effect her nephew's escape with the aid of rope ladders. Clelia carries them to him and the escape is successful. Fabrizio flees with his aunt to Piedmont. The poet, who is in love with Gina, also poisons the Prince of Parma on her instructions. When the new prince assumes power, both return to Parma, where not only is Fabrizio pardoned for his crime of killing in self-defense but also he receives an illustrious appointment from his old friend, the Archbishop. His joy is short-lived, for he hears of Clelia's marriage to a rich nobleman. Mosca finds many ways to prove again and again his lasting love for Gina and she now decides she will marry him, since they are both free and rich. They plan to retire together, for their quiet years, to Naples.

Chaps. 25-28. Fabrizio becomes a changed man, even with all his honors. His grief at losing Clelia is inconsolable. He wishes for nothing but the sight of her.

150

One evening, at a reception of the new Prince of Parma, they meet; and to both it is obvious that their love is forever. Clelia tries to remain true to her marriage vows but is unable to resist the urgency of her love and finally they become lovers. Clelia bears Fabrizio's child; then, being involved in controversy with her husband, she entrusts the child to the care of Fabrizio, visiting them both frequently. The baby dies. Clelia feels it is her penance for the sin of loving outside her marriage, and she grieves and soon dies. When he loses her, Fabrizio no longer wishes to remain at court and resigns all his offices to go into retreat at the Charterhouse of Parma, a monastery, where he plans to spend his remaining days thinking quietly of those he has loved.

Gina marries Mosca and it is a good alliance; but their retirement is brief. Mosca returns to Parma, and to all his former power, to rule with greater tolerance and understanding.

The Cherry Orchard

Play by Anton Pavlovich Chekhov, 1860-1904.
Produced 1904.

CHEKHOV IS ACKNOWLEDGED to have been a great writer. To those whose interest is primarily in reading, his reputation rests upon his short stories and is secure. He also wrote plays, and among these *The Cherry Orchard* is considered his masterpiece. The reason is probably clear to those who judge plays and have contributed to the majority opinion. ❡ In 1951 a modern version of *The Cherry Orchard* was produced in New York. The title was *The Wisteria Trees*. It was an adaptation by Joshua Logan. Helen Hayes played the leading part, equivalent to that of Mme. Ranevsky in *The Cherry Orchard*.

Act I. The scene is a room formerly used as a nursery, in the main house on the country estate of Mme. RANEVSKY, also called LYUBOV. It is very early morning in the month of May. LOPAHIN, a well-to-do merchant, and DUNYASHA, a maid on the

estate, discuss the impending arrival of Mme. Ranevsky, who has been abroad for five years. EPIHODOV, a clerk who has a habit of bemoaning his misfortunes, brings some flowers. Dunyasha confesses to Lopahin that Epihodov has proposed to her. The party arrives from the station: Lyubov; her 17-year-old daughter, ANYA; CHARLOTTA, Anya's governess; VARYA, Lyubov's 24-year-old adopted daughter; Lyubov's brother GAEV; and SEMYONOV-PISHTCHIK, a landowner friend. Anya and Varya discuss Lyubov's blindness to her own desperate financial position. She has lost her villa in the south of France, and they have come home without any funds, yet Lyubov wants to continue living in the grand manner. In August the estate, including its famous cherry orchard, must be sold at auction to satisfy overdue mortgage payments. Anya asks if Lopahin has proposed to Varya yet; Varya doubts he ever will. Marrying Anya to a wealthy man could save them. To complicate matters, PETYA TROFIMOV, once tutor to Lyubov's little son who drowned several years before, is present on the estate and the girls are afraid his presence might recall the tragedy to their mother. But as FIRS, the old retainer, serves them coffee, they forget their worries in their happiness at their reunion. Lopahin, however, reminds Lyubov of the impending auction sale and suggests that she break up the estate into small lots to be rented to summer visitors. Lyubov and Gaev are shocked at the idea of cutting down the cherry trees. Old Firs suggests canning the cherries, but he is silenced by Gaev. Varya hands Lyubov two telegrams from Paris, but Lyubov tears them up unread. She is through with her Paris past. Lopahin offers to lend Lyubov 50,000 rubles if she consents to his plan; then he leaves, saying he will return in three weeks to hear her decision. The moment he is gone, Pishtchik asks Lyubov for a loan to pay the interest on his own mortgage. Lyubov refuses. Trofimov, the tutor, enters to pay his respects and Lyubov breaks down when she remembers her dead son. Pishtchik asks her again for the loan and she tells Gaev to give it to him despite their own desperate situation. Lyubov leaves the room and Gaev and Varya talk. There is a rich aunt in a nearby town, but she looks with disfavor on Lyubov's "immoral behavior." Anya comes in, she has overheard the conversation. Varya promises to go to see the rich aunt. Old Firs comes to fetch the talkative Gaev off to bed. As they all leave, the sun starts to rise over the cherry orchard. Trofimov appears at the door and, unheard by Anya, calls her his sunshine, his spring.

Act II. Near an old shrine in the open country on the estate, the servants sit with their thoughts. Charlotta muses on the fact that she does not know who her parents were, even how old she is; she recalls her early childhood with a circus, and how she was brought up by a German lady to become a governess. Epihodov is playing sad songs on a guitar. He sings of his unrequited love for Dunyasha, but she is fascinated with YASHA, the valet, who has just returned with Lyubov from Paris. Epihodov is not sure whether he wants to live or kill himself, and he carries a revolver at all times. Now he wants to speak to Dunyasha alone, and reluctantly she agrees, but she sends him to fetch her coat first. When Epihodov is out of earshot, she and Yasha embrace. Hearing people approach, Yasha sends her off by herself. The arrivals are Lopahin, Lyubov, and Gaev. Lopahin is pressing for an immediate answer to his proposal to break up the estate and chop down the cherry orchard. Yasha is sent away by Lyubov. She feels that she is being punished for the immoral life she has led, but Lopahin denies this. Lyubov suggests he marry her daughter Varya, who loves him. He is willing, but no action is taken. Gaev says he has been offered a good job in a bank, but Lyubov does not think it will be good for him. Trofimov and the two girls join the group and there is a philosophical discussion of the state of humanity and its lack of culture. A beggar comes by and Lyubov, not finding anything in her purse but a gold coin, gives him that. Varya reproaches her and Lyubov promises to turn all she has over to Varya. Lopahin promises to lend her more money. Varya is informed that they have made a match for her with Lopahin. They return to the house, leaving Anya and Trofimov behind. He succeeds in painting rather a terrifying picture of the cherry orchard to her, comparing each tree to the hundreds of serfs or slaves her ancestors owned in bygone days. As the moon rises, Epihodov is heard again playing a mournful song on the guitar, and Varya's voice is heard in the distance as she looks for her sister, but Trofimov and Anya want to be alone and go down to the river.

Act III. In the drawing room of the old house a dance is in progress, while Lyubov and the others await word from the town, where the auction is taking place. Varya hopes Gaev will be able to buy the estate, with the help of their rich aunt; Lyubov is doubtful. Trofimov teases Varya about Lopahin and Lyubov wonders why she won't marry him. Varya would, but as yet he has not asked her. When Varya leaves the room, Lyubov speaks of her sentimental ties to the place. Her lover in Paris keeps sending for her; he is ill and needs her, and although he has betrayed her she is thinking of going back to him. Anya reports that someone has said the cherry orchard has been sold, but not to whom. After minor action at the party, Gaev and Lopahin return from the auction. Lopahin has bought the cherry orchard. On hearing the news, Varya takes the keys and throws them on the floor in front of Lopahin, who is in ecstasy at the thought of now owning the estate where his ancestors were serfs. He will chop down every tree in the orchard and will build houses. Lyubov is crushed. Anya beseeches Lyubov to go away with her and start afresh.

Act IV. The room once used as the nursery is now almost bare of furniture and packed trunks are in evidence. The peasants come to say good-bye to Lyubov, who gives them her purse. Lopahin offers Lyubov a farewell drink, but she refuses. Trofimov will ride with the women and Gaev as far as the town, then go on to Moscow. He is offered financial assistance by Lopahin, but refuses it. The first trees are already being chopped down, and Anya asks Lopahin to defer the chopping at least until they have gone. Old Firs has been taken to the hospital. Yasha is going to Paris with Lyubov, jilting a crying Dunyasha. Lyubov finds new hope in her children, and Gaev, who has taken the job in the bank, expresses a feeling of relief that the decision has been made. Lyubov will leave for Paris without Anya, who must complete her schooling. Pishtchik comes to repay his debts; valuable white clay has been found on his land. Once more, Lyubov tries to make a match between her daughter Varya and Lopahin, and again he is willing but nothing happens and the chance passes. Lopahin is off on a trip, leaving the house in the hands of Epihodov until spring. As the travelers go out to the waiting coach, Lyubov and Gaev remain for a moment for one last look at their home; then they too leave, weeping. After they have left old Firs appears at the door. Mumbling incoherently, he lies down to die, as the ax of the woodman is heard in the distance.

Childe Harold

Poem by Lord Byron, 1788–1824. Published 1812 (first two cantos), 1816 (third canto), 1818 (fourth canto).

"I AWOKE ONE MORNING," Byron recalled, "and found myself famous." The first two cantos of Childe Harold's Pilgrimage had just been published. Ultimately there were four cantos comprising 495 Spenserian stanzas, 4,455 lines. The vehicle did not fit Byron's genius best, the poem lags more often than it rises to heights, and critics vastly prefer Don Juan and other Byronic efforts; yet here and there in Childe Harold Byron produced his noblest poetry, including his final apostrophic stanzas to the ocean. Class-conscious as always, Byron first cast himself as a childe (young nobleman), but soon he all but forgot his hero Harold and resumed his own identity as the narrator. The poem was begun in 1809 and matured along with Byron, becoming better canto by canto.

Canto 1. Childe Harold, bored with England and having lived the life of a wastrel, decided to abandon his native land and see the world. He left his loving mother and departed by ship for Portugal, singing a Scottish song, "Good Night." Immediately the sensuous land of the south brought him new interest in living, although the sight of the Portuguese city of Cintra reminded him of the scourge of Napoleon Bonaparte, for the British troops had abandoned the Iberian Peninsula there. Beautiful Spain also lay slave to conquering France and Childe Harold mourned the death of chivalry. Everywhere he could see monuments of a glorious past, but that glory was dead, except for the colorful pageantry of bullfighting. In Cadiz he wrote the love song of a dying bullfighter to his lady, called "To Inez."

Canto 2. Sailing on to Greece, Byron begins to tell the story from his own point of view. He sings a song to Athena, the ancient goddess of wisdom. Greece, however, depresses him, for it is held by the Turks and only ruins of the past seem magnificent. Byron summons the character of Childe Harold again, but from this point he becomes the self-exiled wanderer himself. In Albania he finds respite from the corrupt societies of men and the tormenting beauties of the past. He expresses the idea central to all romantic poets that man is born uncorrupted but is twisted by society. Only nature itself remains pure: "Dear Nature is the kindest mother still." He wanders among the monasteries of the wild Albanian mountains and decides that the life of contemplation and communion with nature is most profitable. True solitude or loneliness exists in the midst of men. The primitive natural Albanians appeal to him more than the sophisticated Britons. Sailing south again to Greece, he finds that the battlefield of Marathon, where ancient Greeks drove back the Persian armies, is a sad reminder of Greece's slavery under Turkey. He adjures France and England to free the cradle of democracy, thus forever endearing himself to the cause of Greek independence. He concludes that "Art, Glory, Freedom fail, but Nature still is fair."

Canto 3. Byron dedicates this canto to Ada, his daughter by Lady Milbanke Byron. He and Lady Byron have ended a brief and stormy marriage, and again Byron leaves England for the Continent. His first visit is to the "place of skulls . . . the deadly Waterloo!" where another empire has collapsed—that of the once-mighty Napoleon who had cast his shadow over Spain and Portugal and the rest of Europe. Byron muses on how transitory are the achievements of man, reliving the moment when the clash of cannon interrupted the stately balls at nearby Brussels. Here occur the celebrated lines called "The Eve of Waterloo," beginning "There was a sound of revelry by night" and including the line "On with the dance! Let joy be unconfined!" Next he visits the "majestic Rhine" where the castles remind him of once-violent human life that disturbed the now quiet river. He then goes to

Byron in Venice relives the lives of the Venetian merchants

"the palaces of Nature," the Swiss Alps, where he can look down on France, Germany, and Italy. Here he ponders the very different lives of the strict moralist Calvin and the French Romantic philosopher Jean-Jacques Rousseau, whom he most admires. He echoes Rousseau's own doctrines when he says "Are not the mountains, waves, and skies, a part/Of me and of my soul, as I of them?" He walks the old familiar haunts of Rousseau at Lake Leman, and ends the canto again thinking of his daughter back in England and his unfortunate marriage. He says, "I have not loved the world, nor the world me—/But let us part fair foes . . ."

Canto 4. Byron goes to Venice and stands on the Bridge of Sighs, recalling the abundant lives that were lived in this now quiet town. He re-imagines the exotic lives of Venetian merchants who traded throughout the East and richly decorated the Cathedral of St. Mark. Then he goes on to "ungrateful Florence," which exiled Dante, the great Italian poet. At the Church of Santa Croce he thinks, above the grave of Galileo, about the glorious writing of Boccaccio and Machiavelli. Then he goes on to Rome, "city of the soul!" That city, like Athens, wounds him deeply, for he sees indolence, poverty and greed in the shadows of the Coliseum. He quotes Gibbon: "While stands the Coliseum, Rome shall stand . . ." After tributes to many famous Roman writers and historical figures, he turns to the Vatican. Instead of admiring the great palace of Roman Catholicism, however, he admires the pagan Greek statue, the *Laocoön.* Concluding that only Time can avenge mens' wrongs, he prepares to return once more to England, again summoning

the figure of Childe Harold. The poem ends with an address to the Ocean, one of the few parts of the world that are not sullied by men's conquests and wars: "Roll on, thou deep and dark blue Ocean, roll! Ten thousand fleets sweep over thee in vain." Then Byron bids farewell.

Christabel

Poem by Samuel Taylor Coleridge, 1772–1834.
Written 1797 (Part I) and 1800 (Part II). Published 1816.

THESE ARE TWO PARTS of a projected five-part poem that Coleridge never finished. The importance of "Christabel," apart from the fact that it is very beautiful poetry, is that it is an early Coleridge effort to reduce the monotony of a regular meter—a principle that Coleridge expounded with authority years afterward when his fame was established. His notes say that the meter of Christabel is not "irregular," for while the syllables in a line may vary from seven to twelve, in each line there are four accents.

Part I. The opening section of the poem establishes the setting in the days of knighthood at the castle of the rich baron, Sir LEOLINE, whose daughter, the pure and lovely CHRISTABEL, has gone to the neighboring woods in the middle of the night to pray for the safe return of her knight. She hears a low moan behind a tree and discovers a beautiful woman, GERALDINE, who

tells Christabel of her plight. She was captured, the day before, by five villains, who left her by the tree and told her they would return shortly. Desperate, she pleads with Christabel to help her. Christabel takes her home with her, telling her that Sir Leonine will send her safely back to her own home with an escort the next morning. At Christabel's castle, the two women enter the courtyard and the large sleeping dog that guards the place reacts with strange ominous groans. In Christabel's chambers, the two women prepare for bed and Christabel tells her friend about her dead mother, who is her guardian spirit. In a strange voice, Geraldine whispers to the mother's ghost to be gone, adding "I have power to bid thee flee." Christabel is puzzled by Geraldine's behavior and assumes that the difficult trials Geraldine has gone through accounts for it. After undressing, Geraldine lies down with Christabel and hints to her that she has strange powers that can completely captivate Christabel.

Conclusion to Part I. This brief passage is a detached comment on Christabel's fate now that she has been beguiled by Geraldine's spell and lies powerless in her arms. Christabel dreams uneasily, cries, and wonders if her mother's guarding spirit is near.

Part II. The next morning, the castle bell mourning Christabel's mother's death rings and wakes up Geraldine and Christabel. Christabel guiltily remembers her fears and doubts of the night before; but seeing the seemingly innocent Geraldine, she attributes everything to her dreams. The two greet Sir Leoline, who grows pale when he learns that Geraldine's father is Lord ROLAND DE VAUX of Tryermaine. The two men had been close boyhood friends but then had parted enemies. Seeing the beautiful Geraldine, Sir Leoline remembers the friendship and decides to attempt a reconciliation. As Geraldine and Sir Leoline embrace, Christabel senses again the evil she felt the night before. Sir Leoline dispatches BRACY THE BARD to Lord Roland's castle to tell him that his daughter is safe and that Sir Leoline wishes to renew the old friendship. But Bracy tells Sir Leoline of a dream he had the night before in which he saw Christabel as a dove crying fearfully in the forest. Investigating, he found (in his dream) that a green snake was coiled around Christabel. He woke just as midnight struck. Sir Leoline decides to postpone Geraldine's return until the evil in the forest is found and destroyed. Geraldine glances at Christabel with small serpent eyes and Christabel is entranced by her spell. When she comes out of her trance, Christabel implores Sir Leoline to get rid of Geraldine but Sir Leoline is pained and enraged at his daughter's apparent loss of hospitality and friendship. Furious with Christabel, he turns from her and walks away with Geraldine.

Conclusion to Part II. This passage is the poet's reflection on the kind of twist in fate that can turn a father against daughter, love into hate.

The Christian

Novel by Sir Thomas Henry Hall Caine, 1853–1931.
Published 1905.

HALL CAINE (as he billed himself until such doubles became obsolete) never fulfilled his ambition to please the intellectuals. In the course of trying he made himself the darling, or at least one of the darlings, of the general reading public. He was good for a novel a year, at his peak, and every one was gobbled up. *The Christian* may and should be read by those who have not read Hall Caine, who is worth reading if only because any novelist is worth reading who has brought pleasure to so many millions.

Book I. Chaps. 1–5. GLORY QUALE is on the boat to Liverpool from the Isle of Man. Her grandfather, Pastor Quale, takes her to the boat and asks a young clergyman, JOHN STORM, to watch over her in London. Glory is leaving her home to become a nurse in a London hospital. Her father, a missionary in Africa, died just after she was born; her mother, a lively Frenchwoman, daughter of an actress, died a few years later. Glory grew up to be a red-haired pagan despite the religious atmosphere about her. When she was 12 she met John Storm, then 22 years old, son of Lord Storm. He was her first love. She longs for the riches of the great world beyond her island and she was disappointed when John defied his father to enter the church. Now he has been appointed chaplain of the hospital where she will work. Glory is fed up with poverty. She wants to become a singer and have all the luxuries of the world. She wishes John would share her views. He fell in love with Glory as a young man and because she was poor he wanted to be poor also. He discovered religion and Christian Socialism as a means of being near Glory, while she wants the wealth and position he has abandoned. John hopes to convince Glory that the Kingdom of God is with the poor.

Chaps. 6–31. In London John is assigned to aid the corrupt Canon WEALTHY. The canon reproves John for riding in a third-class carriage and for bringing a poor sick woman to his rooms. Glory is ashamed for John. On her first day off from the hospital she goes to see a parade with a new friend, POLLY LOVE, and falls in love with the grandeur of London. It is hard for her to go back to her dreary life at the hospital. Polly takes Glory to a nurses' ball a few days later. There she meets DRAKE, a rich, handsome dilettante. They spend the evening together and Glory is excited at being with a man of the world. The next week he takes her to the theater and she is enchanted by the play. She decides to become an actress and tells John that she will not remain a nurse for long. John preaches a sermon against wealthy families that sell their daughters for titles and to men they do not love. He offends many people in Canon Wealthy's congregation and is given a month's enforced vacation. He decides to visit a small Catholic monastery, although he is a member of the Anglican Church. He hopes the Catholics will be less worldly than the clergy in his own faith. Polly Love becomes pregnant by a lord who is a member of Canon Wealthy's congregation. Polly is expelled from the hospital and called a prostitute by the Canon, but no action is taken against the frightened lord. John renounces the world and decides to join the Catholic monastery. Glory pays a forbidden call on Polly and her baby and is also dismissed from the hospital.

Book II. Chaps. 1–6. John finds peace with the brothers in the Society of the Holy Gethsemane. He says farewell to life, liberty, and love, though he always hears Glory's voice whispering in the corner. He takes the vows for three years. Glory is determined to make her way as an actress in London. She obtains lodgings and pays her little savings to an agent. She runs out of money and is forced to work in a tobacco shop, but she writes a letter to her grandfather telling him that work is wonderful and she has no respect for people who run away from it.

Chaps. 7–11. John discovers that the man

Glory is found at a music hall

in the next cell at the monastery is Polly's brother, PAUL. Paul, learning that John was in Polly's hospital, begs for news about her. When John tells him of Polly's fate, the brother falls ill. John agrees to help Paul slip in and out of the monastery to look for his sister and attempt to save her soul. Glory, unable to get work on the stage, takes a job as an usher. She has been avoiding Drake but at the theater he offers to use his connections to help her.

Chaps. 12–17. Brother Paul, who absented himself from the monastery the preceding night, does not come back in the morning. John learns from the Father Superior that Paul murdered the man who ruined his other sister, and John fears that Paul might murder again. But Paul returns later to the monastery, having harmed no one. Months later, Paul becomes ill of consumption (tuberculosis). John has passed several months in solitary contemplation in his cell. He eats frugally, speaks to no one, and strives, like all ascetics, for spiritual purity. He does not achieve his spiritual goal; and when Paul dies, John is still haunted by memories of Glory and can no longer stand the monastic rule. He resolves to leave.

Book III. 1–5. In the meantime Glory has begun to find success. A former patient of hers gives her singing lessons and introduces her at a society function. Drake is proud of Glory and plans a luncheon in her honor. John leaves the monastery and goes in search of Glory. He cannot find her at the hospital, and no one can tell him where she has gone. He sees the name Gloria on the posters outside a music hall, and he goes in and watches as she sings and dances. His religious sense is horrified. He later goes to see her at her lodgings. Glory is overjoyed to see John again, because she has always really loved him, but he plans only to save her from the wicked world she seems to love. Glory tells him all about life at the music hall and how men send her flowers and presents. John tries to convince her that this is sinful and shameful, but she likes the attention and adulation she is receiving and she tells John she will not see him again.

Chaps. 6–12. Polly Love commits suicide at the wedding of her lover to a fashionable lady. John Storm buries Polly and Glory is the only mourner. She is so upset by Polly's death and John's moving sermon at the grave that she decides to go home for a vacation. John takes the orders of an Anglican priest and determines to save the ruined women of London. His love of God is still confused with his love for Glory. She writes him from home, telling him that she is bored on the island. John takes a poor parish and begins a crusade to help unwed mothers and their babies. Glory, unable to resist temptation, returns to London after the death of her grandfather, and her name is in all the newspapers. She plans to act in Shakespearean plays as well as the usual musical revues. John gets into a fight with the Catholic hierarchy because of his work, and he is forced to give up his parish. He uses his inheritance to continue the home for unwed mothers. He is determined to obliterate Glory from his life and he hates Drake.

Chaps. 13–14. The Father Superior of the monastery asks John to return but John refuses, saying there is too much work to be done in the streets of London. Glory writes John a friendly letter and he visits her. He admits to her that he has loved her for years, but he says their different natures will always keep them apart. Glory starts to rehearse a part in a new play.

153

Book IV. Chaps. 1–14. John Storm preaches that a great calamity will befall London; he says that the time of God's justice has come. His sermon creates a panic among his listeners. Some influential men have John arrested on a charge of sedition and inciting to riot. While in jail John learns his father has died and he has succeeded to the earlship. Drake, out of kindness, has John released on bail. Glory, seeing John in court, with crowds of jeering people around him, runs away from her theater circle and none of her friends can find her. The night John is released he walks through a low neighborhood and is attacked and given a merciless beating by some hoodlums who bear him a grudge. Glory finds him as he lies close to death. She insists that they marry so that she can bear his name and continue with his work. She wants him to feel his life has not been useless. They take the marriage vows, at his deathbed.

Chaps. 15–17. On the night John is to leave his church, Glory comes to him and discloses her love. She throws herself into his arms and they kiss. Glory resolves to give up the stage and to go with John, but the next morning her resolution weakens when John takes her to see his new parish. She is sickened by the sights and smells of the slum. At the end of the day she writes to John to tell him she cannot stay in London with him. Here the glamorous world of the theater is too near to her, and she feels she can only be with him away from the city. John accepts a missionary post in a leper colony on a tropical island. Glory, after many struggles with her soul, decides that she cannot live with John. His idea of love is too pure for her and she wants all the fame that awaits her in London. When John receives her first letter of refusal he goes back to the Holy Society of Gethsemane and once again takes the monastic vows, this time for life.

A Christmas Carol

Novelette by Charles Dickens, 1812–70.
Published 1843. Many editions available.

DICKENS WROTE many "Christmas stories"; *A Christmas Carol* was the first and is the classic. It has been called the greatest short story ever written, but actually it is nearly as long—about 25,000 words—as many works classed as novels. However else it is described, it is the finest thing of its kind that exists in the English language.

Stave 1. JACOB MARLEY has been dead as a doornail for 7 years but his partner EBENEZER SCROOGE carries on the firm of Scrooge and Marley on London's 'Change (stock exchange). Scrooge is known as the most tight-fisted, most pitiless man in the city. The day before Christmas, Scrooge's nephew FRED drops in to wish him merry Christmas and invite him to Christmas dinner; Scrooge refuses, saying Christmas is a humbug. Two GENTLEMEN come in to ask contributions for the poor, but Scrooge recommends that the poor go to prisons or workhouses—or else die and decrease the surplus population. Reluctantly, Scrooge gives his poor, underpaid, overworked clerk, BOB CRATCHIT, Christmas Day off. Then Scrooge goes home to his lonely house. That night the ghost of Jacob Marley appears to him, dragging the heavy chains it wears for Marley's sins. The ghost is making one effort to save Scrooge from its own fate. It promises to send three spirits to Scrooge, the first to appear at the stroke of one the following night; the second at the same time the next night; the third the next night on the last stroke of twelve. Scrooge would rather not, but the ghost leaves and Scrooge uneasily goes to bed.

Stave 2. The clock strikes one and the SPIRIT (or GHOST) OF CHRISTMAS PAST appears. He takes Scrooge back to Christmases in Scrooge's past: The time Scrooge was left, as a boy, at school—the only boy not to go home for Christmas; but his beloved sister FAN, who became Fred's mother, came and took him home. The gay Christmas parties when Scrooge was a young man, apprenticed to jovial old FEZZIWIG. The day when BELLE broke her engagement to him because she had been replaced in his heart by a Golden Idol. Scrooge, gradually more and more overcome, begs the Spirit to show him no more, but one more scene he must see: When Belle's husband comes home, to a happy home, and tells Belle he caught a glimpse of Scrooge in his office—quite alone in the world. Scrooge drops into unconsciousness.

Stave 3. Scrooge awakes on the stroke of one and the GHOST OF CHRISTMAS PRESENT is in the adjoining room, surrounded by turkeys, plum puddings, and other Christmas dainties. This Spirit takes Scrooge first to the house of Bob Cratchit. Despite their poverty, the Cratchits are having a gay Christmas. Their eldest daughter MARTHA has the day off from work and is home, delighting the younger daughter BELINDA and son PETER. Bob comes in from church, carrying the crippled youngest child, TINY TIM, on his shoulders. Dinner begins with a fine goose. Afterward the first toast is to a Merry Christmas, and Tiny Tim adds, "God bless us every one!" The Spirit warns Scrooge that unless something is done, Tiny Tim will not live long; so, says the Spirit, he had better die "and decrease the surplus population." Bob then proposes "Mr. Scrooge, the Founder of the Feast," and Mrs. Cratchit objects, but relents

because it is Christmas Day. After briefly visiting some miners, who despite their terrible working conditions are charitable and happy on Christmas Day, Scrooge is taken by the Spirit to his nephew's house. This is a jolly gathering, made especially so by Fred's wife, of whom Scrooge disapproves because she brought Fred no dowry. They play a guessing game in which a bear is described, and the answer is "Scrooge." But Fred drinks a toast to his uncle, for it is Christmas. The Spirit shows Scrooge an emaciated boy and girl, representing Ignorance and Want, spawn of man's folly and heedlessness. Scrooge, horrified, asks if there is no remedy. "Are there no prisons?" the Spirit asks. "Are there no workhouses?" The clock strikes 12 and the Spirit is gone.

Stave 4. The GHOST OF CHRISTMAS YET TO COME is the last. He takes Scrooge to 'Change on the day after he (Scrooge) dies; no one cares. Scrooge's servants hasten to steal his loose effects and take them to sell to a fence. No one has a kind word for Scrooge. The Spirit takes him to one house where a man and wife cannot help being glad Scrooge has died, for Scrooge was about to ruin the man financially. Then, for contrast, the Spirit shows Scrooge the genuine grief at the death of Tiny Tim. Finally Scrooge is allowed to see his own uncared-for grave. Scrooge pleads with the Spirit to tell him there is still time to change. He is on his knees as the Spirit departs.

Stave 5. Scrooge wakes in his own bed, his own bedroom. He flings open the window and calls to a boy in the street, who tells him it is Christmas Day—Scrooge has not missed it. He is so happy he acts crazy. He sends the boy to buy the prize turkey at the butcher's and have it sent to Bob Cratchit's house. Scrooge dresses and goes out; happening to encounter one of the two gentlemen, he stops him and makes a con-

Scrooge sees his own grave

154

tribution so large it makes the man gasp. Then Scrooge goes to his nephew's house and asks if he may come to dinner after all. He is joyously welcomed. The next morning he goes to the office early, hoping to catch Bob Cratchit late. Bob is late, so Scrooge has the pleasure of seeing his surprise when he receives not a scolding but a wage increase. And for the rest of his life Scrooge is a kind man, a second father to Tiny Tim (who did not die), and a man who knows how to keep Christmas well if anyone does.

Cicero's Orations Against Catiline

Speeches by Marcus Tullius Cicero, 106–43 B.C.
Delivered 63 B.C.

NOT EVEN CAESAR can be more unpopular in the United States than Cicero, whose orations against Catiline have been rammed down the throats of tens of millions of high-school students. As in the case of Caesar, it would amaze most of Cicero's unwilling audience if they would read him in an adequate translation and find out what actually it was all about. ⁋ But it should not be expected that Cicero in a clear translation would win the sympathy of most of his erstwhile enemies. Cicero was a representative of the patrician or conservative segment of Rome. He was one of the two consuls (prime ministers) when he delivered his orations against Catiline, who in turn represented the common people. If today's reader could hear both sides, he might very likely vote for Catiline. ⁋ There were four orations in the Catiline series. All four qualify as excellent writing. But in the first and fourth, Cicero was talking to the Roman senate, where he knew he had a clear majority. In the second and third he was talking to the public, as though on a coast-to-coast television network, and here his skill was most apparent. ⁋ Cicero's most quoted words, *O tempora, O mores* ("Oh, what an age! oh, what customs!"), occur early in the first oration.

THE FIRST ORATION
(TO THE SENATE)

1. How much longer, Catiline, must we suffer your threats, your reckless temper, your uncontrolled audacity? Do not the extra sentinels in the city and the guards on the Palatine mean anything to you? Are you not aware of the temper of the loyal citizens? Do you believe that there is one of us here in this well-guarded senate who does not know your bloody plans, your intrigues? Do you, who have had the temerity to attend this convening of the senate, think we do not know that even as you sit here, you mark every single one of us down for massacre? No, Catiline, long ago, you yourself should have been led to execution. Our city's past is filled with executions of men whose crimes against it were much less than yours. 2. In many instances of the past, when the senate voted that the consul should provide protection for the city against harm, just punishment was swiftly taken against the city's enemies. Yet we here have been hesitating for twenty days upon the resolution of the senate—which remains an unpublished document; were it rightly understood, it would require your immediate execution. In the meantime you live and increase your crimes against the city. If I do not order your immediate arrest and execution, it is not because I fear that my act will be judged too harshly. It is because I will take this action only when there will not be one citizen so base, so shameless, so much your counterpart as to call your execution unjust. As long as there is one person to defend you, you will live; but you will be constantly watched by the eyes and ears I have posted all around the city. 3. And what are you waiting for, Catiline, if even the dark of night does not conceal from us your plotting? Have I not predicted your every move? Did I not tell you, on the 21st of October, just what you planned? 4. Review with me, Catiline, the events of the night before last, and I will show you that my watchfulness to secure the safety of the city is more thorough and diligent than your designs to ruin it. Listen, while I tell you every street you traversed, every house you stopped in, every evil deed you plotted. 5. Under these circumstances I urge you, Catiline, to pursue the course you have begun. Leave the city and go to the camp of Manlius, your desperate fellow-conspirator. The gates are open. Leave and take with you the foul band of your followers. I am taking this mild line because if I order you executed, your evil co-conspirators will go, too, and the city's political sewers will have been flushed. Do you hesitate to do at my command what you had intended to do of your own free will? Simply leave the city. Go! 6. What is there to keep you in the city, Catiline? Do you not know that, aside from your band of plotters, there is not a man who does not fear you and hate you? Is there any scandal or any form of personal immorality that has not been stained your life? How many times have I, when I was consul-elect, escaped by the very narrowest margin your attempts to kill me? 7. Perhaps I should feel pity for you, Catiline. When you came today to the senate did a single member give you any sort of welcome? Does anyone now sit near you? Catiline, your country pleads with you thus: "For years there has not been a crime or a scandal in which you have not had some part. And you have gone scotfree. These were personal crimes, and I was able to overlook them. But now you threaten me, and I can no longer ignore your evil ways. Leave, now! If my fears are well founded, withdraw so that I may not be destroyed; if they are groundless, leave so that I may be freed of apprehension. 8. Have you, Catiline, not had the temerity to come to my house, to ask me to keep you safe there, so that you would be above suspicion? If you are deserving of such confinement in a private house, are you not really deserving of confinement in the state prison? "No," you say, "the question must be put to the senate." Does not the silence of this august body tell you its wishes? If I spoke of one of our honorable citizens as I speak of you, how long do you think the senators would remain silent? They would lay harsh words on even me, the consul. I can hardly hold back the hands that would slay you. 9. But if you wish to harm me, go into exile. I shall, then, barely be able to endure the crushing ill opinion men will have of me. But if you wish to make a hero of me, leave the town with your evil pack, join Manlius, and then turn to make war upon your city. Then you will show clearly that I did not throw you to the unfriendly arms of strangers, but merely sent you to your friends. 10. When I defeated your efforts to obtain the consulship, I obliged you to attack Rome from without in the rôle of an exile, and not to strike against her from within as a consul. I changed your criminal schemes to brigandage rather than civil war. 11. But I have to answer a question that I am sure Rome addresses to me: "Why, when you have such overwhelming proof of this man's crime against the city, do you hesitate to order him put in chains and executed?" 12. My answer to this just question is this: There are yet those who do not believe that we have in our midst so evil a man as Catiline, so foul a band as are his fellow conspirators. If, however, Catiline leaves the city and joins his fellow plotter, Manlius, and then threatens to march against us, none will then doubt me. 13. Too long, O senators, have we been surrounded with this dangerous conspiracy. If Catiline leaves, it will be only one among many who would harm the city. The danger will be driven underground. Yet, my colleague [the other consul] and I shall find such energy, you shall find such resolution, the Roman Knights such courage, and all loyal men such singleness of purpose, that with Catiline's departure from Rome, the evil shall be brought to light, and punished, and crushed.

With this word of warning, Catiline, get you gone to your evil friends and begin your unholy and treasonable campaign.

Cicero speaks to the people

THE SECOND ORATION
(TO THE PEOPLE)

1. At last we have cast out of our city Lucius Catiline. He departed full of audacity, blazing with anger, threatening this city and all of us with destruction by word and fire. No longer will that misbegotten monster plot from within the very city walls destruction of them, and of us. No longer do we need to fear when we are in the Campus Martius, or in the Forum, or in the senate-chamber, or in our own homes. He did not carry with him a word stained in our blood, and now he looks back on this city and mourns that it has been snatched from his jaws. 2. Do not blame me for not having arrested our deadly enemy, but rather having simply driven him away. The fault is one of circumstances, not one of mine. He should have been slain long ago, but, sadly, too many among us were too stupid or too wicked to believe my report on him, and thus too many would have disapproved his death. 3. I utterly despise that army of his, that gang of high-livers, boors, spendthrifts, and ruined old men. Their leader has fled. What are these men waiting for? 4. I have long waited for this hour when all may see that a conspiracy has been made against the state. Or do some of you still disbelieve and still fail to feel relief? 5. Now we may mark his varied crimes, his wantonness, his grief, his indulgence in murder, arson, pillage. There is not a criminal or a desperate ruined man in the city who did not participate in Catiline's evils. Why don't they leave the city too? If they persist among us, let them expect the punishment they deserve. 6. Catiline did not flee simply because I gave the word. No, it was yesterday, when I had almost been killed in my own home, that I went to the senate and exposed Catiline's plotting,

while he himself, was present—it was only then that he fled. 7. I am willing to have it said he was driven out by me, if only he goes into exile. But he will not do this. He is on his way to the camp of Manlius, his co-conspirator, and from there he plans to march upon us. 8. From what classes are his troops procured? First, those who, although greatly in debt, still have their property. How foolish they are to believe they will be able to keep what they have if Catiline triumphs in war. 9. Second, those who, though hard-pressed by debts, still expect to rule. Let these persons (and the others) know that I am on guard, alert, protecting the state. Also, let them know that the honest citizens have great courage, and moreover a great force of soldiers. The third class is of old men, mostly from the colonies, whose grand scale of living has ruined them. These madmen hope for proscriptions and dictatorships. 10. The fourth class is that varied, turbulent and promiscuous group of ne'er-do-wells who, worn out by summonses, bail, judgments, and attachments of their goods, hope for renewed well-being by joining Catiline. The fifth class is made up of parricides, assassins, and all sorts of other criminals. 11. On our side fights modesty, on theirs shamelessness; on ours chastity, on theirs wantonness; on ours honor, on theirs fraud; on ours righteousness, on theirs crime. How can we but believe that the gods themselves are on our side? 12. Good citizens, defend your homes against the evil men Catiline has left behind in the city. Do this, and leave the rest to the senate. Let me warn again those Catilinians in our midst, I will see the honest citizens avenged. 13. I will see to your safety, dear citizens. I, your commander, wearing the garb of peace, will triumph. Go, you, to the temples and pray to the immortal gods for the final deliverance of this,

the most beautiful, most powerful, most flourishing.

THE THIRD ORATION
(TO THE PEOPLE)

1. On this day my own efforts, my plans and my perils have delivered you from fire and sword, almost from the jaws of death. I have informed the senate of how this was done; now I shall inform you (the people). 2. At first I thought that when Catiline left the city he would take with him his gang of co-conspirators. But when I saw that they did not leave with him, I spent my days and nights watching their every move. When I heard that Catiline's man, Publius Lentulus, had tampered with the envoys of the Allobroges, with the idea of starting an insurrection in Gaul—when I heard this I saw my opportunity. When the envoys of the Allobroges were leaving the city I had two picked detachments fall upon them, at the Mulvian Bridge. 3. Then the praetors, Lucius Flaccus and Gaius Pomptinus, intervened and stopped the fighting and they obtained the letters the Allobroges carried. 4. The next morning, in the senate, Volturcius, leader of the Allobroges, under the pledge of public protection, told of the conspiracy of Lentulus and his allies Cathagus and Statilius to put the city to fire and sword. 5. We then opened the letters. They further implicated Catiline's allies. Suddenly Lentulus, who had been putting up a bold front of denial, confessed all. The other conspirators followed suit. 6. When all evidence had been duly given, the senate voted several measures. First, thanks were bestowed upon me because my courage, counsel and forethought had saved the republic. Then the praetors Lucius Flaccus and Gaius Pomptinus were praised. Then all the conspirators were given into custody. And thanksgiving was decreed to the god in my honor—an honor which I am the first man in civil capacity to receive since the founding of the city. 7. Actually, citizens, the conspirators Catiline left behind him were not very dangerous. Catiline was the capable and energetic one, and if he had remained in the city we should have had to fight. 8. I have conducted matters so well that they can hardly seem to have been done by a mortal; surely we must see that the immortal gods had a hand in them. Were not portents seen—torches in the night, thunderbolts, earthquakes during my consulship? 9. Who can be so blind as not to see the rule of the gods, and their protection of this city? Why would the envoys of the Allobroges, men of Gaul, the only nation now remaining that can challenge Rome, spurn the hope of empire offered to them by men of noble birth, and set your safety before their own? Why but for the immortal gods? 10. Others have in the past acted as Catiline wished to: Lucius Sulla, Gnaeus Octavius, Marcus Lepidus. The streets ran with blood and corpses were piled in the market places. Catiline threatened to do this once again, but I saved you without the

Cicero speaks before the Roman Senate

spilling of a drop of blood. 11. For these great services I ask no rewards, no insignia, no monument. I only wish for eternal peace for our city, so that men may talk of my deeds and enhance them by their words. 12. Since I have served you, dear citizens, you must take it upon yourselves to see to my safety. You must guard me from revenge taken by the enemies I have made in your defense. The defense of loyal men counts for much, and that is mine forever.

THE FOURTH ORATION
(TO THE SENATE)

1. I perceive, my lords, by your glances, that you are not only anxious about your safety but also about mine, that of your consul. 2. Take thought for yourselves, your city, your loved ones, your properties. Do not think of me; if I die I shall die contented that as consul I have served my fatherland well. Think of those you have seized, those left behind by Catiline to burn down the city, to massacre us all, to welcome Catiline, their leader. You have all the evidence against them. You know that even now they are appealing to the Allobroges, are trying to raise the slaves, are calling for the return of their leader. 3. You have shown by your acts yesterday that you understand the seriousness of the situation. The persons seized have been declared guilty without hesitation. But I have decided to consult you upon the punishment to be given. I have never imagined that Roman citizens could be engaged in a conspiracy so vast and so evil as this. It endangers not only Rome but all of Italy, and even the provinces. 4. I see that there are two motions before us: One of D. Silanus who proposes the death penalty; one of C. Caesar who

omits the death penalty but includes all other severe modes of punishment. Caesar's motion understands that death is not necessarily severe; the gods have ordained it as the natural end of existence, or as a peaceful release from troubles and toil. But imprisonment, especially life imprisonment, is an exceptionally severe punishment. 5. I see my way clearly in this matter. The proposal of C. Caesar is certainly the more popular. 6. If you decide in favor of Caesar's motion you will provide me, when I address the people, with a colleague who is a popular favorite. If you decide in favor of Silanus's proposal, you will free me from any possible imputation of barbarity. My opinion is set by my own feelings. I believe that anyone who kills or plots the death of another deserves death himself. And those

you have taken into custody have plotted not only our deaths but also those of our wives and children. Although we may consider death to be the less severe of the two punishments, this is probably not the popular sentiment. But how can you fear to be unpopular in dealing with a crime so horrible as that before us? 7. Let us not fear for our personal safety. Every precaution has been taken. The Forum and all the approaches to this temple are filled with loyal citizens ready to defend us. The whole mass of freeborn citizens are present. 8. Do not fear a rising of the slaves. There is not one of them that does not fear the violence of the aroused citizens. And do not be disturbed by rumors of Lentulus's agents' arousing the shopkeepers. No, the whole shopkeeping class is loyal and profoundly desires peace and order. You have the open

support of the Roman people. 9. I, your consul, have been preserved from death in order to promote the general welfare. I only wish to provide, this day, that all of us may never again have to face so terrible a threat to our city. 10. The conqueror of external foes is better off than the conqueror of internal enemies. The former crushes and reduces to slavery his country's enemies, and they may be made friends. But those members of the community who have been led astray to become enemies of their own country can never be reconciled. Hence, I know I have entered into an endless war with some among us. But with your support, I do not fear for myself. 11. From you, from the rest of the loyal citizens, from the provinces, all of whom I have delivered from ruin, I ask nothing but that you remember this crisis and the whole of my consulship. But if you do not agree with me in this matter before us today, I commend to you my infant son for protection and even for advance to honor. Think of him as the son of a man who bought your safety alone, at his own expense and risk. Come to your decision with care, thinking only of the welfare of the Roman people. Your consul will faithfully carry out your instructions.

The Cid

Traditional epic and ballads of Spain, collected in 13th century.

Play by Pierre Corneille, 1606–1684, produced 1636. Translation from the old Spanish into English by Robert Southey, 1774–1843.

DON RODRIGO DIAZ DE VIVAR was a historical as well as a legendary Spanish character, a notable warrior and conqueror who earned the sobriquet *el Cid Campeador,* the leader-champion. The legend accumulated in Spanish ballads of the 12th century, and in the 13th King Alfonso the Good had them assembled into a unified epic. The stories of the Cid have inspired several playwrights and poets: In English literature principally Robert Southey, who translated the ballads into English and contributed from his own genius to the result; in France, the playwright Corneille. ❡ The French drama of Corneille's time was bound by formalities as rigid as the elaborate rhyme-schemes of earlier French poetry. A play had to depict one action at one place, in one day. Accordingly Corneille in *Le Cid* tried to compress the events of a lifetime into one day. Transcending its artificialities, the play was and remains one of the greatest and most popular known to the French stage.

The Legends

The kingdoms of Leon and Castile have been united, in 1037, by Don FERDINAND, King of Castile, but their borders are constantly threatened by the Moors. In Castile there is a feud between two counts, Don GOMEZ and Don DIEGO. Don Diego is old and cannot do personal battle with Don Gomez, so Don Diego's son, RODRIGO (or Roderick) of Vivar (or Bivar) fights and slays Don Gomez. For this, Don Diego places his son at the head of the table.

Five Moorish kings invade Castile. Don Rodrigo vanquishes them and captures all five. Then he releases them to return home, by which he wins their respect and friendship. Now he is known as the CID.

Dona XIMENA (or Chimena), daughter of Don Gomez, appeals to the King to give her the Cid as her husband, in recompense for his killing her father. The King summons the Cid, who agrees, so the Cid and Ximena are espoused; but the Cid swears to win five battles before consummating the marriage.

First the Cid makes a pilgrimage to Compostella, leading 20 knights. On the way the Cid befriends a leper, who in the night breathes warmly on the Cid's shoulders, then disappears. It is a miracle and a sign of God's favor, and thereafter whenever the Cid feels the warmth on his shoulders it will mean he will win in battle.

Some counts try to conspire with the Moors against the Cid, but the Moorish kings the Cid befriended warn him and he fights and subdues the counts. Then the Cid leads a victorious battle against an army of Moors invading Portugal. In one battle against the Moors the Cid ravages some territory of the King of Toledo, which angers the new king of Castile and Leon (Don ALFONSO, son of Don Ferdinand). As a result, the Cid is exiled. He parts sadly from his wife Ximena and the son she has borne him. Then he goes into exile, accompanied by 700 faithful followers.

In the lands of the Moors, the Cid wins many places and much booty by conquest, and he always sends gifts back to King Alfonso to prove his continued allegiance. At last the Cid conquers the great city of Valencia, which at the time is ruled by a despot who murdered the previous king and usurped the throne. The Cid stays as king of Valencia. After long years he is reunited with his family.

Two powerful brothers who are counts of Carrion ask in marriage the two daughters of the Cid and Ximena, Dona Elvira and Dona Sol. The King supports the brothers' suit and the Cid and Ximena dutifully obey the King's command, though they know the brothers are wicked. After the double marriage the brothers abuse their wives, beating them till they are nearly dead. The Cid complains to the King, who forces the brothers to meet in battle champions for the Cid, and one brother is killed and the other beaten.

BUCAR, Emperor of Morocco, comes with 29 kings to attack Valencia. The Cid attacks the Moorish camp while all sleep and routs them. The Emperor goes back to Morocco, but he assembles a greater force and comes to attack Valencia again. The Cid is now old and it is time for him to die. His reported death emboldens the Moors to attack, but his dead body is mounted on a horse and behind this leadership the Christian knights win a victory over the Moors, but then they go on to Castile and leave Valencia to the Moors.

The Play

Act I. ELVIRE tells her mistress CHIMENE that Chimene's father, the COUNT, has consented to let Chimene marry Don RODERICK, which overjoys her. The INFANTA and her maid, meanwhile, are discussing the young lovers, Chimene and Roderick. The Infanta loves Roderick but since she is a princess and cannot marry a cavalier, she wants the two to be married quickly so that her love for Roderick can be quenched. During this action, the Count and Don DIEGUE, father of Roderick, are arguing about their respective merits. The Count is angry because the king chose Diegue, instead of himself, to tutor the prince. Their dispute is climaxed when the Count challenges Diegue to a duel and the latter is too feeble to respond. Alone, Diegue is mortified by his inability to fight back and, summoning Roderick his son, he asks him to fight and protect the honor of their name. Roderick, left alone, bemoans his fate. Is he to protect his family's honor by killing Chimene's father, and so lose her? or should he refuse to fight the Count and thereby have Chimene believe him a coward? Finally he places duty above love and prepares to duel the Count.

Act II. A messenger from the king pleads with the Count to apologize to Diegue and forget the quarrel but the Count sees his honor as more important than compliance with the King's wish. The Count and Roderick meet and prepare to duel. The Infanta tells Chimene not to worry about her father or her lover, for she promises to hold Roderick in capitivity until the quarrel is forgotten; but she is too late. The two men have left the palace to duel. Alone with her maid, the Infanta feels strangely happy at the turn of events, since Roderick's behavior means his separation from Chimene. But she changes her mind shortly, realizing that she was only momentarily succumbing to a base passion. The King meanwhile receives word of the Count's disobedience and plans some punishment. Then the king learns that Roderick has killed the Count, so he feels that justice has been done. He is visited then by Chimene and Diegue. She wants the hasty youth, Roderick, punished. Diegue offers his own life instead of his son's because he feels that he alone is to blame. The king promises he will settle the argument after a conference with his council.

Act III. Roderick goes to Chimene's home. He is told by Elvire to leave, lest he create a scandal by having people believe

Trial of the wicked brothers

158

Chimene has offered refuge to her father's murderer. Roderick, however, has come to die at her hands and only agrees to conceal himself temporarily. Don SANCHO, in love with Chimene, vows to kill Roderick for her but she will have no one do it but herself. Chimene then tells Elvire of her grief at the thought of killing the one she loves, for honor's sake. Roderick confronts her and asks her to kill him; she refuses to be handed an easy victory and tells him that she will pursue him and kill him thus. Roderick leaves. Outside he runs into his father, who tells him that if he will lead an armed force against the invading Moors, he will be vindicated; and if he does die in the process it will be no more than he is asking now.

Act IV. Elvire brings Chimene the news that Roderick has won a glorious victory and is acclaimed in all Spain for driving off the Moors. Then the Infanta arrives to tell Chimene to forget her vow against Roderick because she would deprive the country of a hero and savior. But Chimene does not relent, feeling still that she must avenge her father's death. At the King's palace, Roderick describes how he led his small force against the Moors and, by ambushing them, won. He also captured two kings who call him the Cid, which is a great honor. Roderick leaves and Chimene enters. The King plans a ruse to test her love for Roderick by pretending Roderick died in battle. Chimene faints but explains it is because battle robbed her of her revenge. The King tells her that Roderick lives and she vows once more to avenge her father. She promises that the man who kills Roderick will have her hand in marriage. Roderick's father asks that his son be challenged alone and by a man chosen by Chimene. Sancho volunteers and is accepted.

Act V. Roderick confronts Chimene before the fight to tell her he will not defend himself, because death will be just punishment. Finally breaking down, Chimene tells him to fight because she abhors the thought of marriage to Sancho and still adores Roderick. Hearing this, Roderick is ready to fight mountains. The Infanta meanwhile is in a quandary. Roderick's becoming the Cid gives him equal standing with her royal position and now there is no bar to her marrying him. But once more she decides to overcome her own desires to help Chimene gain Roderick. Chimene is also in a difficult position because, as she puts it, "Whoever wins, I must accept a husband stained with the blood of him I most adore." Sancho arrives and Chimene, thinking him the victor, calls him a murderer and vows never to marry him. As it turns out, however, Roderick won the affair by rendering Sancho defenseless. Since he had to rush to the King for orders, he sent Sancho to tell Chimene of the outcome of the fight. The King tells Chimene that she has promised to marry the winner, so she must marry Roderick; but he tells her to wait a year so that she may forget her momentary grief and pledge of honor. Roderick will meanwhile invade the realm of the Moors and return an even more illustrious hero and claim her as his wife.

The Citadel

Novel by A. J. Cronin, 1896–
Published 1937 by Little, Brown & Co., Boston. © 1937 by A. J. Cronin.

BOOKS ABOUT OR BY DOCTORS are traditionally popular in America. Cronin, a practicing physician who became an author of novels about physicians, fulfilled both parts of the formula and became predictably successful. *The Citadel* is one of his best and most popular novels. After its publication, for several years, it was said that A. J. Cronin's name on the cover of a magazine would sell more copies at the newsstands than any other novelist's name. The theme of *The Citadel* had been worked almost to death before the novel was published but the doctor-and-wife relationship expertly treated by Cronin proved to be enough to rescue it.

Book 1. Dr. ANDREW MANSON, a very recent medical graduate, arrives in South Wales to be assistant to Dr. EDWARD PAGE. He finds Dr. Page has just had a serious stroke and is completely unable to attend to his patients. After his first professional call, aided by a sarcastic hint of Dr. PHILIP DENNY, he uncovers an epidemic of typhoid. Dr. Denny, who is cynical but devoted to medicine, finds the cause, an infected old sewer. Unable to get any help from the authorities, the two doctors join together to blow up the sewer with dynamite and this quickly brings about the building of a new one.

CHRISTINE BARLOW, a softly attractive schoolmistress, makes a decided impression on Manson and he begins to see her frequently, sharing with her many of his confidences and problems concerning his medical career. As time passes he knows he loves her but is dismayed at the thought of marrying on an assistant's small salary. Dr. Page continues to be an invalid and his wife runs all their affairs in a miserly fashion. She has an argument with Manson over five pounds and he gives her his notice. Through Dr. Denny, he is appointed to a very lucrative post at the Aberalaw Medical Aid Society. A house goes with his salary and at last he feels he can ask Christine to marry him. She accepts.

Book 2. Christine and Andrew are married and settle in their new home in Aberalaw. While they are happy together there, the going is rough with the miners, who resent a doctor who is ethical. There is another irritant; the head doctor, Dr. LLEWELLYN, takes a fifth of all assistants' salaries on the pretext of consultations. To equip himself to be professionally on the same level as Llewellyn, Andrey begins studying the necessary languages to get further degrees.

Christine becomes pregnant but loses her baby in a freak accident and will never be able to bear a child again. Research becomes the absorbing interest of Manson and his paper on dust inhalation wins him the degree he sought. He is anxious to better the lot of his patients in the mines and experiments harmlessly on guinea pigs, but there is a strong element in the community against his progressive methods and they try to get him dismissed by the Committee. They fail, but he no longer wants to stay and resigns. He and Christine leave happily for France and a well-earned holiday, which is interrupted with the news that he is appointed medical officer to the Coal Mines and Metaliferous Fatigue Board, as a direct result of his scientific paper on dust inhalation.

Books 3–4. Unfortunately for Andrew, the Board is a political instrument and there is no opportunity to carry on his research. After six months of doing nothing, he resigns, deciding to find his own practice. With their small savings, he and Christine buy a practice in the unfashionable part of London. It is not long before Andrew realizes that he will never make money there and he yearns after "good" patients. With his diagnostic skill he relieves a new patient of a troubling skin disease and her

Fearing for Roderick's life, Chimena tells him to fight

gratitude starts a chain of prosperous patients. This builds the practice into a solid success, but Andrew's strict medical honesty is compromised to earn the large fees and gradually this causes estrangement from Christine. Money becomes Andrew's absorbing interest and he cultivates those who can lead him to it. He finds himself lying to Christine about his friends and his appointments to see them. In a desperate effort to revive his strict medical interest, Christine invites his old colleagues, Dr. Denny and Dr. HOPE, for dinner. She is rewarded by a temporary return on Andrew's part to all his deeply-felt ethical opinions. But this interest is short-lived and he continues pandering to those who can send him rich patients. An unnecessary operation by one of his fee-splitting surgeon friends fails and the patient dies. Andrew becomes aware of how far he has fallen from his former strict standards. Abruptly he returns to his past and denounces all his new money-making medical partners. This brings about a reconciliation with Christine and they are happier than ever, planning the future. Confident with her at his side, Andrew evolves a striking idea of coördinating his knowledge with those of his two friends, Denny and Hope, the three to join together in establishing a clinic in a vicinity that needs them, with charges based on the patients' ability to pay. His friends are excited by the idea and agree to join him. Christine is delighted. While walking in the street, absorbed with thoughts of Andrew and the future, she is struck by a bus and killed. Andrew almost goes out of his mind with grief and has no desire to go on with his plans. Denny comes to him and is his constant companion. Grief is interrupted by charges brought against Andrew for removing a patient from Andrew's hospital to the clinic of a man who is famous for healing tuberculosis but who does not have a physician's degree. The patient recovers but still there are those who dislike Andrew and who wish to see him disgraced and barred from the practice of medicine. After Andrew makes an impassioned plea for the rights of the sick, he is acquitted. He leaves with his two staunch friends to start his clinic, devoted entirely to the welfare of its patients. A last visit to the grave of Christine gives him the courage to face what is ahead. He feels her close beside him, with her gentle hands pushing him along the way.

The mother appeals to Lincoln

The Clansman

Novel by Thomas Dixon, 1864–1924. Published 1905.

THE PRINCIPAL CLAIM for recognition of *The Clansman* is that from it was made the motion picture "The Birth of a Nation," which was rather special in its day (1914–1920, and perhaps longer). The novel as a novel is worth reading only for those who are interested in what kind of literature has occupied the reading attention of the American people and extended itself notably into collateral media of public expression.

Book 1. On the day news is brought to Washington of Lee's surrender and the end of the Civil War, ELSIE STONEMAN, the daughter of the Honorable AUSTIN STONEMAN, is attending wounded Confederate soldiers in a prison hospital. One of her patients, BEN CAMERON, has been unjustly sentenced to be executed for guerrilla activities. Elsie is struck by his appearance and manner. When his mother comes to visit him, she cannot tell the woman that her son had been condemned. Fearing that her father will be of no help to her, she decides to bring the matter to the attention of President Lincoln and ask him to pardon the young soldier. The following day Elsie goes to Mrs. Cameron's lodgings and tells her Ben is to be executed. Then she proposes that they both visit President Lincoln to petition for Ben's release. Because Elsie is the daughter of the influential Austin Stoneman, no one challenges the two women and when Mrs. Cameron asks for her son's life, Lincoln, only too happy to avoid further bloodshed, grants her request. Elsie and Mrs. Cameron deliver the written pardon to Secretary of War Stanton. He refuses to recognize it and declares that the death sentence will be carried out. Frightened by this threat, the two women return to the President's

office and inform him of the Secretary's defiance. He promises them that everything will be arranged, then he summons Stanton and demands that his order be followed. The Secretary threatens to resign, but Lincoln refuses to accept his resignation and orders him to put through the pardon of Ben Cameron. Lincoln returns to his office and finds Elsie again waiting for him. While he is reassuring her on the matter of Ben Cameron's freedom, the arrival of Elsie's father is announced. Not wanting him to know of her visit, Elsie asks the President to say nothing and then leaves by a side door. Stoneman, called the "Great Commoner," enters Mr. Lincoln's office in a rage. He is incensed that the President does not wish to take harsh reprisals on the South. A bitter abolitionist, he demands that the Negro be accorded full suffrage privileges and, in effect, be made the ruler of the southern states. Lincoln does not think the white Southerners who fought so valiantly in the war deserve such humiliating treatment. Elsie overhears this exchange and is hurt and disappointed in her father. The next day she secures the pardon and takes it to Mrs. Cameron at the prisoners' hospital. That afternoon she and her brother, PHIL, visit Mrs. Cameron at her lodgings. Phil, a captain in the Union Army and the very man who held Ben Cameron in his arms after Ben was wounded, is struck by the dignity and beauty of Mrs. Cameron's daughter, MARGARET. In happy spirits over Ben's coming release, they plan an evening at the theater. The city of Washington is aglow with the celebration of the North's victory, and President Lincoln, in his first public appearance since the war's end, goes to the same theater, where are also the Camerons, Elsie, and Phil. He receives a magnificent ovation from the audience, but during the play John Wilkes Booth, a fanatic, enters the box and assassinates him. This act inflames the North with hatred of all things southern. Reprisals are promised and Mrs. Cameron fears that the dead President's pardon of her son will no longer be honored. Adding to her worries is the news that her husband, Dr. RICHARD CAMERON, has been accused of involvement in the assassination.

Book II. With Lincoln dead, Stoneman no longer has a serious opponent in the government who can block his desire for extreme reprisals against the South. At a meeting in his home, attended by Colonel HOWLE, a dishonorably discharged Army officer, LYDIA, his mulatto housekeeper, and SILAS LYNCH, a Negro missionary, Stoneman reveals his plan to take all property out of the hands of southern landowners and redistribute it among the Negroes and those loyal to his cause. Ben has received a pardon but still has not fully recovered from his wounds. Meanwhile, some six months after her husband was imprisoned, Mrs. Cameron is still trying to obtain permission to visit him. She finally asks Elsie to request her father to intercede on her behalf. Though fearful that he will refuse, Elsie goes to him. Because his own weakness is a deep love for her and Phil, her father agrees to write President Johnson a note. With this written support from such an influential figure, Mrs. Cameron obtains the President's consent to visit her husband. She sees him and is assured he is well. Mrs. Cameron and Margaret leave Ben in Elsie's care and go to their home in the South. Ben is released from the hospital and goes about seeking a fair trial for his father. Elsie helps him in every way and soon the two are in love with each other. Elsie is apprehensive about her father, who is devoting all his energies to the establishment of a Reconstruction government for the South, and she postpones any talk of marriage. Stoneman continues his battle to enforce Negro rule in the South. He ruthlessly removes all obstacles to his plan, not stopping at the President himself. However, his scheme to impeach Johnson fails and, his health broken, he agrees to go South for a period of recuperation. Both Elsie and Phil suggest Piedmont, South Carolina, as a suitable place because Ben and his father, who has been released from prison, have joined Mrs. Cameron and Margaret there. Grumbling over the delay in his plans and still threatening to carry out his reconstruction proposals, Stoneman departs with his family for the South.

Book III. Mrs. Cameron, not having sufficient room for the Stonemans, makes arrangements with Mrs. LENOIR and her daughter MARION to house the Northern guests in their small cottage. No sooner have they arrived than Silas Lynch, the Negro organizer, comes to visit Stoneman. Elsie receives him coolly, but her father demands he be admitted. They discuss plans for giving the Negro full power in the South. When Lynch leaves, the exhausted, sick Stoneman falls into a deep coma. Meanwhile Ben Cameron, feeling that the South must be saved from Negro rule, has begun attending secret clan (Ku Klux Klan) meetings. On his way home from one of these gatherings he sees AUGUSTUS CAESAR, a former slave, and now a trouble-maker, loitering in front of his mother's house. After telling him to leave and receiving an insolent reply, Ben strikes Caesar. Ben is arrested because of this and is sent to Columbia to stand trial. Phil, pretending to be a Reconstruction sympathizer from the north, finds out where his friend is and

engineers his escape. Dr. Cameron writes an article in the Piedmont paper, protesting the seizure of his son, and the military government puts him under arrest. He is placed in chains and forced to march through the town while the Yankee in charge tells his former slaves that they are now the equal of their one-time master. Old JAKE, one of Dr. Cameron's faithful former slaves, goes to the prison in Columbia, sees Colonel Howle, and asks that the doctor be released since he is needed to attend his patients. Howle is worried about the Southerners' reaction to the rough treatment of Dr. Cameron; anxious to insure their acceptance of the first Negro election,

he releases the doctor. A week later Ben and Phil watch the first election under the Reconstruction government. Appalled by the conduct of the Negro voters, Ben proposes to his father that they join the secret League of Southerners, whose members have sworn to overthrow the Negro government by violence if necessary. Dr. Cameron is not anxious to employ arms against the lawful government, but when, some weeks later, he sees the new Negro legislature in action and hears their threats and boasts, he realizes that no conservative measures can prevent the Negro's domination and destruction of the South. Dr. Cameron solicits Stoneman's aid, but failing to receive it he joins his son in the secret movement. However, the doctor's words have softened "the Old Commoner" somewhat; when Stoneman learns that Elsie and Phil are in love with Ben and Margaret Cameron, he reacts with kindness and sympathy. He even promises to buy Mrs. Lenoir's cabin, which is soon to be confiscated for taxes. Mrs. Lenoir and Marion are overjoyed by his offer, but their happiness is shortlived. One night, caught unprotected by a group of Negro soldiers, Marion, only 16, is raped by Augustus Caesar, the former slave whom Ben Cameron struck. Mrs. Lenoir is forced to witness the scene, and when her daughter regains consciousness the mother is near madness. Filled with shame, Marion tells her mother that they must both commit suicide, and they jump to death from a mountain ridge called "Lover's Leap."

Book IV. Enraged by this crime, Ben organizes the local Ku Klux Klan and captures Caesar. Under Dr. Cameron's hypnotic gaze, the Negro confesses his crime and the clansmen execute him. That night they throw his body on Silas Lynch's lawn, and the following day they openly proclaim their resistance to the Reconstruction government. This defiance infuriates Stoneman, who demands that Elsie and Phil break off their engagements with the Camerons. Phil refuses, but Elsie, moved by her father's plea, asks Ben to give up his leadership of the clan. Ben refuses and continues to take action against the Negro garrison in Piedmont. Stoneman calls for more troops to be sent to the region and tries to have Ben arrested. No one will testify against Ben and Stoneman is forced to have martial law declared. In the ensuing confusion, two Negroes attack Margaret Cameron. Phil comes upon them, and he shoots and kills one. Ben helps him escape and then finds himself accused of the deed. A military court sentences him to be shot. By a ruse, Phil takes his place in the prison and tells Ben to go to his father, Stoneman, and tell the truth about the shooting. However, the old man is not to be found and, as the moment of execution nears, Ben returns to the prison and tries to persuade the commander that they have the wrong man. The commander suspects a ruse and refuses to listen. Stoneman is finally located and comes to demand the release of his son. The commander confesses that Phil has been taken

from the prison to be executed in the surrounding woods. Stoneman is grief-stricken and confesses to Dr. Cameron the error of his cause. Stoneman is certain that he has condemned his own son and he is near death when Phil arrives, escorted by Ben and several other clansmen who rescued him. The following day a new election is held throughout the South and the Negro government is overthrown. Ben, his work accomplished, tells Elsie he will give up the clan if she will marry him. She consents and Margaret agrees to marry Phil.

Clarissa

Novel by Samuel Richardson, 1689–1761.
Published 1747–48. (ML, 10)

SEVEN VOLUMES WERE REQUIRED to publish *Clarissa* (*or, The History of a Young Lady*) in the first place, and it takes a good afternoon to thumb through it. Is it still worth reading? Mr. W. S. Maugham would say yes, it is, for him who has the knack of skipping. Eighteenth-century England delivered a resounding Yes, for *Clarissa* was more popular in its times than its contemporary Fielding novels such as *Tom Jones,* which we can still read with pleasure. At any rate, *Clarissa* is historic from the standpoint of technique, for it is a novel developed in letters. The technique has since proved too slow for the general reader or (with some exceptions) too difficult for the modern novelist.

Letters 1–94. The well-born ROBERT LOVELACE is ostensibly the suitor of CLARISSA HARLOWE's sister ARABELLA, and is sponsored by Clarissa's uncle, but turns against the latter's wishes by falling in love with Clarissa instead of Arabella. Clarissa does not return his passion, but she is unalterably opposed to the plan of her brother JAMES to marry her to Mr. SOLMES, a rich old man for whom she has no regard or affection. James and Arabella, in turn, are jealous of Clarissa because they did not share with her in a bequest left by their grandfather. Clarissa refuses to have anything to do with the elderly bore Solmes and is accused of being uncivil to him. Her statement that she will not marry against her will causes the Harlowes to think she is in love with Lovelace, whom they consider a bounder. Lovelace had incurred James's disfavor when the two matriculated at Oxford. Clarissa is locked in her room by her indignant father when she refuses to entertain Solmes and she is further

161

Clarissa writing in her room

humiliated (as she writes to her friend, Miss HOWE) by having her loyal maid replaced by a rude and spying servant in the confidence of her brother. Miss Howe urges her to flee from her hated family with the aid of Lovelace, who is more than eager to aid the scheme after the insolent treatment he has received from Clarissa's relatives. He is able to meet Clarissa secretly in the garden of the Harlowe home and he urges her to go away with him. Actually he is intent on seducing her.

Letters 95–130. After due consideration Clarissa elopes with Lovelace, feeling certain of his honorable intentions, particularly when he tells her that she will be taken to the house of his cousin, a Lord M——, to stay until their marriage can be effected with the blessing of her family. This, Lovelace assures her, will be arranged by her cousin, Colonel MORDEN, who is on the continent at the time of the elopement. Instead of finding herself in a lordly castle, Clarissa discovers that she has been tricked into entering a house of assignation, presided over by a Mrs. SINCLAIR. Clarissa permits Lovelace to tell Mrs. Sinclair that she is his wife but that their marriage cannot be consummated until arrangements and settlements have been concluded. She agrees to this subterfuge in order to elude pursuit by her family, but soon she finds that she is not free to leave Mrs. Sinclair's house. When her family does discover her whereabouts, her father disowns her and refuses to aid her financially. Meanwhile Lovelace repudiates his promise of marriage though he continues to make violent love to her. The distraught Clarissa escapes and rushes off to Hampstead. There Lovelace finds her and arranges with two girls to pretend they are his cousins. Reassured, Clarissa accompanies them, only to find herself back in Mrs. Sinclair's house. Here Lovelace drugs and seduces her. A letter from Miss Howe is scarcely necessary, as it merely tells her the true nature of the place in which she is being held. Having been warned by Miss Howe, who has followed the

162

whole affair with Lovelace by means of a lengthy interchange of letters with the heroine, Clarissa realizes that her situation with Mrs. Sinclair, who is actually operating a house of ill-repute, is far worse than was her virtual imprisonment by her father and her brother James. She resolves, in an answer to Miss Howe's letter of information about Mrs. Sinclair, to escape the harridan's clutches at all costs. Several attempts at escape are made by Clarissa and on one occasion she is almost successful when she attracts the attention of a passer-by from an open window. Hearing of this state of affairs, Lovelace becomes afraid that his nefarious scheme of seduction will be discovered and he promises to leave Clarissa untouched until he is able to get in touch with Miss Howe or her traveling cousin, Colonel Morden. The latter is ignorant of the rape to which Clarissa was forced to submit, but the promise of his intercession in her behalf calms Clarissa's fears momentarily and she is resigned to mourning over the terrible mistake she made by eloping in the first place.

Letters 131–152. When Lovelace leaves for a visit to his noble cousin in London, Clarissa disguises herself in a maid's uniform and escapes briefly, but Mrs. Sinclair follows her and has her jailed for a supposed debt. Now a correspondent of Lovelace, JOHN BELFORD, discovers Clarissa's plight, proves that the arrest was fraudulent, and turns over the poor girl to the friendly attentions of a shopkeeper and his wife, who summon a doctor to attend her. Clarissa has had too much, however, and she pines away, all the while writing letters to friends in an effort to have her true situation revealed to her family. She spurns Lovelace, but he, finding that he truly loves her, beseeches her to marry him. Since her letters do not have any effect in causing a reconciliation with her family, Clarissa plans quite deliberately

to die, giving the date of death as the day she left home, even ordering her coffin.

Letters 153–176. Colonel Morden returns to England and tries to win forgiveness for Clarissa from the immediate members of her family, but to no avail. To them, Clarissa is already dead. Then Morden tries to have Clarissa accept Lovelace's (by now) honorable intentions, but despite the pleading of Lovelace's noble relative, Lord M——, Clarissa refuses to accept her seducer as a husband. Finally Clarissa's family decide that Clarissa is really adamant in her desire to depart this world and they agree on forgiveness and reconciliation with the unhappy creature, each upbraiding himself, or herself, as the case may be, for cruelty and lack of understanding. Clarissa's father, the stern Mr. Harlowe, and her brother James, promise to lift the ban on her returning to her home and urge her to do it. The father retracts his denial of her as a daughter and his earlier exposed hope that she would have a terrible life on earth and be condemned to suffer in the hereafter as well. Arabella admits in her letter that she persecuted Clarissa because Lovelace had deserted her for Clarissa, her younger and more beautiful sister. Clarissa's mother begs her forgiveness, taking full blame herself for not having cared properly for Clarissa, for not having protected her from the cruel world and particularly Lovelace, and for not having brought Clarissa's father and brother to their senses after they disowned the girl. The letters all express the hope that Clarissa will forget her transgressions and rally her strength for a healthy and happy family reunion. The letters unfortunately are delivered after Clarissa has breathed her last, and the heroine of the novel is given a fine funeral in her father's house, the nearest thing to a reconciliation possible after this sad turn of affairs. Lovelace is stricken by remorse when he hears she has been buried at the feet of the grandfather whose bequest to her originally caused the envy and hate of James and Arabella, and he goes off to the continent with the noble kinsman who was to have befriended Clarissa on her elopement eve. Lovelace gets his just deserts, for Colonel Morden tracks him down and kills him in a duel.

The concluding episodes, including a description of Lovelace's dying repentance for the mischief he has caused, are related in a very long letter written by Belford. The author has appended a justification of his unrelenting tragic climax, pointing out that it would have been easy for him to have Clarissa marry Lovelace in a conventional happy ending, in spite of the dire deeds that had brought her to her sorry pass, but that the actual ending was foreordained on moral and classical grounds.

The Cloister and the Hearth

Novel by Charles Reade, 1814–1884. Published 1861. (ML, 62)

THIS CELEBRATED NOVEL has been ranked as an English classic almost since its publication. It is set in the 15th century and the author instills in it the flavor of medieval writing without making it unpalatable to the modern reader. The great surprise to many readers comes at the end, when suddenly it appears that the entire novel was leading up to the birth of the great Erasmus. The novel is not unreasonably long, especially for the times when it was written.

Chaps. 1–8. Life is hard in 15th-century Holland, where ELIAS and his wife CATHERINE are living with their nine children, in Tergou. Elias is a merchant who never has quite enough money for his large family. Two of the older children leave home to become merchants in Rotterdam. The dwarf GILES and the cripple KATE are doomed to live on in their parents' home. Two of Elias's other sons refuse to go anywhere and also pass their time by his fireside, waiting for him to die, hoping to inherit some money. The favorite child is GERARD. The anxious parents do not worry about his future, for he has been promised to the Church and the Church always supports its own. Gerard has a great talent for penmanship and illuminating manuscripts, which he learned from the neighboring monks. At home his family calls him a dreamer because he is always copying or painting. But the monks respect his work and send him to study with MARGARET VAN EYCK, sister to the famous artists. She admires his talent and becomes his patroness as well as his teacher. She is a kind woman and a friend to all the Dutch artists and scholars of her time. She suggests to Gerard that he go to Rotterdam to compete in an art contest being held by the royal court. Gerard persuades his family to give him the money and leaves for the big city. On the road he sees an old man and his lovely daughter carrying wood. They are PETER and MARGARET BRANDT, on their way to Rotterdam to borrow money from a wealthy cousin. Gerard stops to help the weary and ragged couple and quickly falls in love with the red-haired Margaret. The Brandts are poor because GHYSBRECHT VAN SWEITEN, the burgomaster of Tergou has cheated them out of their rightful inheritance. The burgomaster is riding on the road to Rotterdam, and when he sees Gerard with the people he has betrayed he fears that Gerard will discover the theft and expose him. From that instant on Ghysbrecht becomes Gerard's mortal enemy.

Gerard declares his love to Margaret Brandt and learns that she loves him, but not wishing to impede his church career she refuses to reveal her address. Margaret Van Eyck has given Gerard a letter of introduction to the powerful Princess Marie, who receives him cordially and admires his work. She promises he will have a benefice as soon as he is ordained. This is a privilege usually reserved only for the children of noble families. It assures Gerard of a position far beyond the modest hopes of his family. Gerard wins a prize in the competition and goes joyfully home to tell his parents of his good fortune.

Chaps. 9–17. The burgomaster questions Gerard to find out how much he knows about the Brandts. He inadvertently confides that Margaret and her father live in Sevenbergen. Gerard goes there and finds Margaret. Now he is sure he no longer wants the clerical life; he prefers to forfeit the benefice and marry Margaret. The burgomaster, still afraid of Gerard, discloses to Catherine and Elias the young man's love for the penniless girl. There follows a terrible quarrel and the favored son is denounced as ungrateful. Elias threatens to place Gerard in jail if he persists in marrying against his father's command. Margaret Van Eyck, proving her friendship, gives Gerard some money and suggests that he and his love go where he can learn art from great masters. But as the young couple wait at the Church altar for the marriage ceremony to begin, Gerard is taken in custody for disobeying his father. When he refuses to take an oath that he will never see Margaret again, he is locked in the high tower of Tergou. His sister Kate and brother Giles, who are very fond of him, go to the tower to help him escape. Their crippled shadows frighten Margaret and Peter Brandt, who have also come to the tower to help Gerard. Gerard climbs down, bringing with him some city deeds he has found in his cell. He does not know they contain evidence of Ghysbrecht's theft from Peter Brandt. He hides in Margaret's house. His escape is soon discovered and Ghysbrecht also sees that the deeds are gone. He and his men chase Gerard to Sevenbergen and almost catch him but he and Margaret flee into the woods. There they bury the deeds, still unaware of their importance.

Chaps. 18–24. Gerard and Margaret flee toward Germany, pursued by the mayor's men. Fortunately they have with them an old soldier friend, MARTIN, who is brave and knowledgeable. The mayor and his men surprise the escape party as they are sleeping and almost take them, but Gerard manages to run away with Margaret. Martin knocks down Ghysbrecht, avoids the pursuers, and rejoins his friends. When at last they reach the border Margaret is slightly wounded and weak from her adventures. Martin escorts her back to her father and Gerard continues. He finds the people of Germany hostile and is often unable to obtain food or lodging. He longs for his sweetheart and for his home, but bravely walks farther into Germany every day.

Chaps. 23–35. While staying at a lowly inn, Gerard finds himself sleeping next to a tough and lusty Burgundian soldier, DENYS. They develop a fast friendship and become traveling companions. Denys almost drowns in the Rhine and Gerard rescues him. In the forest they are attacked by a bear. Gerard is knocked to the ground and wounded but Denys kills the bear and nurses Gerard's wound and his fever. They stay at a monastery, where Gerard meets Father ANSELM and Father JEROME. He illuminates a manuscript for them and Denys give the vagabonds food and comfort. Denys tells Gerard amusing stories of the wickedness of some monks and the orgies they carry on in their chapel. They go to Burgundy because Denys has a longing to see his old country and hear the sound of his harsh language. In Burgundy they discover a group of men and wailing women being driven along by constables armed with spears. The constables are forcing these citizens to move to another town, which has been depleted by plague. Denys and Gerard see many acts of cruelty typical of a time when human life is cheap and most men are living under some distant authority. Denys's favorite expression is "The Devil is dead." Traveling through Burgundy they come across a troop of soldiers, who order Denys to ride with them to Flanders to help quell a rebellion. When Denys refuses to leave his friend, the soldiers draw their bows and threaten to shoot. Denys mounts a horse and tearfully rides away. Gerard goes on alone, mourning the loss of his friend. Later that day some wealthy men send their servants to rob Gerard for amusement. Gerard tries to fight but is overpowered by the robbers. He is bleeding and penniless in the snow.

Chaps. 36–42. In Sevenbergen Margaret Brandt becomes sick and Elias and Catherine repent their cruelty. Margaret Van Eyck comes to visit the sick girl and is very kind to her. Martin obtains pardon for himself and Gerard from Philip the Good. Then Margaret Van Eyck sends a letter, written by the young Margaret, with HANS MEMLING, to Gerard in Italy. Ghysbrecht, who is afraid Gerard has discovered his theft of Margaret's property, hears of this later and manages to substitute a false note saying that Margaret Brandt has died. He hopes to keep Gerard in Italy.

Chaps. 43–50. Denys is released from the army and goes to Holland, where he is welcomed by Gerard's parents. He discovers that Margaret, finding herself pregnant, has disappeared with her father. Denys searches for them. He finds Margaret taking in laundry in Rotterdam and brings her back to Gerard's parents. There the family listens to a letter from Gerard telling of his adventures on his way to Venice. He describes saving a Roman lady and her child from a shipwreck.

Chaps. 51–58. In Rome Gerard cannot find work and eventually paints playing cards in a poor lodging. The Roman lady whom he saved obtains a job for him illuminating manuscripts. He meets the Princess CAELIA, who tries to seduce him. When he rejects her, the royal lady hires an assassin to kill him.

Gerard is saved by the assassin who was following him

Chaps. 59–65. Hans Memling finds Gerard and delivers the false letter. Gerard, learning that Margaret is dead, falls into a terrible sickness. Then he abandons the Church and turns to a life of debauchery. Finally, in despair, Gerard throws himself into the Tiber. He is saved by the assassin, who has followed him everywhere. The assassin is the husband of the lady Gerard saved in the shipwreck and is unable to bring himself to murder his wife's savior. Gerard is taken to a monastery and there he becomes Brother CLEMENT of the Dominican order.

Chaps. 66–78. In Holland Margaret has given birth to Gerard's son. Brother Clement, known for his oratory and his holiness, gives a sermon in Rotterdam. Margaret hears the sermon without recognizing Gerard. He sees her but thinks it is a vision. At last Gerard realizes that she is alive but he cannot go to her now, as he is committed to God. He goes to Tergou, where the dying Ghysbrecht confesses to Gerard his crime and at last restores Margaret's fortune. Gerard, seeing that Margaret is wealthy, retires to a hermit's cave in Gouda, where he has been assigned a vicarage. Margaret, with the help of Gerard's dwarf brother, Giles, finds Brother Clement in Gouda. He is mortifying his flesh in hatred at human existence and the irony of life. He is out of his mind with rage and sorrow. When he first sees Margaret he thinks she is a spirit of Satan. Only when Margaret brings his son before him is he restored to reason. He and Margaret live apart in Gouda, devoting their lives to the needy. She helps him daily in his work

164

and they find peace together. Ten years later Margaret dies of the plague and Gerard follows directly after her. Their son, Gerard, vows to enter the Church and take the name of Erasmus. He becomes the great Biblical scholar and literary figure of the Renaissance.

A Comedy of Errors

Play by William Shakespeare, 1564–1616.
Produced about 1592.

THIS RANKS AMONG Shakespeare's best-known plays principally because it is so "different." It is a farce of the most extreme kind, its comedy based on confusion and little else. The play is set in pre-Christian Ephesus, some 200 years before St. Paul got there to establish the Church. The Roman Plautus wrote a play, *Menechmus*, on a similar theme and Shakespeare borrowed from it but also greatly elaborated it. The best comedy comes in the early scenes and is provided by the confused slaves. Shakespeare was always as much a classist as a classicist.

Act I. 1. SOLINUS, Duke of Ephesus, grants an audience to AEGEON, a merchant from Syracuse, whose life is forfeited under Ephesian law. The law forbids anyone of Syracusian birth to enter Ephesus. Aegeon must die unless he can pay 1,000 marks

ransom, and the goods he has with him are worth no more than 100. Solinus asks Aegeon why, knowing the danger, he came to Ephesus. Aegon tells how his wife had identical twin sons and he bought another pair of twins to be their slaves. In a shipwreck, one of each pair of twins was lost, along with Aegeon's wife. Aegeon himself and one of each pair of twins was saved. When the boys reached 18, Aegeon, his son ANTIPHOLUS of Syracuse, and the slave twin DROMIO of Syracuse, set out to seek the lost twins. They have risked even their lives to come to Syracuse in the hope their brothers are there. The duke expresses sympathy and hopes Aegeon can save his life by raising the ransom money. Meanwhile Aegeon is sent back to jail. **2.** In the marketplace at Ephesus, Antipholus of Syracuse and his attendant Dromio of Syracuse are advised by a local merchant to say that they are from Epidamnum, lest they be apprehended as Syracusians. Antipholus sends his purse with Dromio to the Centaur Inn, to wait his return. DROMIO of Ephesus approaches. Antipholus mistakes him for the other Dromio and asks what he has done with the money; Dromio mistakes Antipholus for his master ANTIPHOLUS of Ephesus and asks why he has not returned home, where his wife is alone waiting and getting very hungry. Antipholus does not understand and starts to manhandle Dromio of Ephesus, who escapes him and runs away.

Act II. 1. At the house of Antipholus of Ephesus, ADRIANA his wife and her sister LUCIANA are wondering what is keeping him. Luciana counsels that they eat alone and not wait, as a man is master of his liberty and all through nature the male is superior to the female. Adriana remarks that this attitude must be the reason for Luciana's single status. Dromio, marked by the beating he received, comes and explains that his master is out of his mind, but Adriana sends him back to fetch her husband. **2.** Antipholus of Syracuse encounters his Dromio, but thinks it is the same Dromio as before. When Dromio of Syracuse proclaims his ignorance of the whole thing, Antipholus beats him. Adriana and Luciana enter. Adriana reproaches him and he claims not to know her. Dromio also denies ever having seen either of the sisters. The women think that Antipholus and Dromio are plotting against them. The two men decide to humor the women and go off to dinner with them.

Act III. 1. In front of the house of Antipholus of Ephesus, the rightful owner is returning with his Dromio, ANGELO the goldsmith, and a merchant named BALTHAZAR. Antipholus, worried about being late for dinner, asks the goldsmith to explain to his wife that he lingered at his shop, selecting a piece of jewelry (a gold chain) he had promised her. Dromio puzzles him with the tale of being asked for 1,000 marks in gold. They try to get into the house, but the other Antipholus and Dromio will not open the door. Antipholus of Ephesus decides to get a crowbar and force the door open, but the merchant Balthazar thinks it will cause a scandal in the town. Antipholus of Ephesus then decides to dine at the house of a COURTESAN he knows well, and to spite his wife he plans to give the courtesan the chain he had intended for his wife. 2. Inside, Luciana berates the dumbstruck Antipholus of Syracuse for neglecting Adriana. Antipholus assures her he is not married to Adriana, and what is more, he is in love with her, Luciana, and wants to marry her. Dromio of Syracuse has similar problems; a kitchen maid named NELL has mistaken him for her husband. Master and servant come to the conclusion that their hostesses are mad. Angelo arrives with the gold chain and gives it to the wrong Antipholus, who has no idea why.

Act IV. 1. Angelo is being pressed for payment of a debt and comes to collect for the chain from Antipholus of Ephesus. Meanwhile Antipholus of Ephesus sends his Dromio off to buy a "rope's end" as a "gift" for his wife (to beat her with, for locking him out). Antipholus of Ephesus then meets Angelo. He denies having received the chain and refuses to pay for it, and Angelo has him arrested. Dromio of Syracuse returns and again mistakes Antipholus of Ephesus for his own master. He has found passage for them on a ship bound for Epidamnus. Antipholus of Ephesus thinks he is mad and sends him instead to bring bail money from his wife. 2. At home, Adriana and her sister discuss Antipholus of Syracuse's love for Luciana (thinking of course it is Adriana's husband). Adriana will not give up her husband. Dromio arrives and asks for the bail money, which Adriana gives him. 3. In a public place, Antipholus of Syracuse is surprised that the people of the town seem to know him. Dromio brings him the bail money but of course Antipholus of Syracuse has no idea what it is all about. Next the courtesan appears and asks for the chain Antipholus of Ephesus promised her, and for the return of a valuable ring. When Antipholus indignantly denies knowing her, she thinks he is mad and decides to tell all to his wife. 4. In the street, Antipholus of Ephesus, with the arresting officer, runs into Dromio of Ephesus, who brings the rope. He knows nothing of having been sent for bail money. They are joined by Adriana, Luciana, the courtesan, and PINCH, a schoolmaster, whom Adriana has engaged to cure her "mad" husband. When he gets angry, they tie him up and the schoolmaster takes him away. He is hardly gone when the other Antipholus and the other Dromio appear. Sword drawn, Antipholus of Syracuse orders his Dromio to get their belongings from the inn and get aboard their ship immediately.

Act V. 1. Angelo the goldsmith and a second merchant discuss the financial responsibility of Antipholus. Angelo sees Antipholus of Syracuse wearing the chain. Angelo denies swearing he did not receive

it. There is an argument and the men draw swords. Adriana enters and tries to have the two men taken to her house; they escape into an abbey. The ABBESS questions the pursuers as to what is happening. Adriana explains that her husband is mad. The abbess refuses to deliver him until she brings him back to his senses. Adriana appeals to the duke, who is passing the abbey on his way to the execution of Aegeon. A servant girl appears and informs Adriana that "her husband" and Dromio have broken loose again, but Adriana thinks she lies. Antipholus of Ephesus appears, with his Dromio, and he too asks the duke for justice. While Antipholus is accusing Adriana of mistreating him, Aegeon recognizes him as his son. The testimony is so contradictory that the duke thinks they are all drunk. Then the abbess brings on the other pair. The abbess turns out to be Aegeon's missing wife, AMELIA. The duke then disentangles their lives, and also spares Aegeon's life.

The Compleat Angler

Monograph by Izaak Walton, 1593–1683.
Published 1653, and later, with portions added, 1655 to 1676.

FISHING IS SAID TO BE the most popular of all outdoor diversions, but man's love of fishing has not been the principal factor in making this book loved through the ages. The author had great wit and an agreeable style in writing that would make his descriptions, arguments and philosophical diversions wonderful reading today even without the extra enjoyment of his archaic expressions. *The Compleat Angler* is very short, a fact that removes the last excuse for not having read it. ❡ Walton wrote only Part I. The second part was written, and added to later editions, by his self-appointed "adopted son," Charles Cotton. It does not really matter whether one reads or likes Part II. Cotton made his own immortality, free of anyone else's sponsorship, when he wrote *The Compleat Gamester*, another classic of his age but without so readymade a following.

Chap. 1. *First Day.* The PISCATOR (ANGLER, or Fisherman) on the road overtakes the VENATOR (HUNTER) and the AUCEPS (HAWKER, or Faulkner, who hunts birds with falcons or similar hawks). The latter two have just met each other on the road. The three men converse, each defending his own sport. The hunter praises hunting as both a business and a pleasure, in which the excitement of the chase satisfies the appetite for adventure. He is on his way to hunt otters and he loves otterdogs; he hunts foxes, also, and loves hounds. The hawker boasts that the element he trades in is the Air, which exceeds both Earth and Water. He praises the birds he hunts with his hawks, and he enumerates the hawks, 29 kinds, plus some others. The hunter counters with an enumeration of beasts. Hunting, he says, is a game for princes. The angler now defends fishing, with allusions to history and quotations from classical and modern poetry. Fishing is a quiet and a simple pastime, fit for simple and humble people, whereas hunting is a sport for men of pretense, such as kings and judges. Water is the element in which a fisherman finds his quarry, and water is one of the most sacred materials in the universe. Fishing is of great antiquity and the prophet Amos mentioned fishhooks. Furthermore, Christ himself fished at various times and several of his disciples, such as St. Peter, were fishermen. The fish has always been an animal that is sacred to Christianity and therefore fishing has religious sanction as a worthwhile pastime. The fisherman claims that fishing is an art. "For angling is somewhat like Poetry." It requires patience, hope, love and craft. Fishing is furthermore conducive to contemplation, for the fisherman can sit on a riverbank and gather his thoughts while pursuing his sport. Also, fishing leads one to a worship of the beauties of nature, because it takes him into lovely secluded valleys. Since times immemorial, poets have sung the praises of fish and philosophers have acknowledged their importance. In the course of the debate the angler has walked with the hunter all the way to the hunter's destination. The hunter invites the angler to hunt the next day, and promises in return to fish for two days. The angler accepts.

Chaps. 2–3. *Second and Third Days.* The two men hunt together and the dogs get an otter; the next day they fish and the angler seeks a chub. The hunter regrets that it is not a trout, for he considers chub the worst of fish; but the angler shows him how to dress a chub so that it is most edible.

Chaps. 4–5. The angler describes in poetic terms how a trout breeds and what is the best way to catch one. After the day's activity the friends retire to a nearby house where a MILKMAID sings Christopher Marlowe's poem, "Come live with me, and be my Love," itself a eulogy of the pastoral

165

The fishermen spend the evening in song and conversation

life, and the milkmaid's mother sings the reply by Sir Walter Raleigh. The angler then embarks on a discourse about catching trout with artificial minnows and flies. The discussion is enlivened by the appearance of PETER, a friend of the angler's and CORIDON, a simple young man of the country. Songs are exchanged and the evening is passed in merriment.

Chaps. 5–16. *Fourth Day.* Up bright and early, the two debaters again embark on a fishing trip. The angler describes various fish and their characteristics. The angler lectures the hunter on how to raise fat, juicy worms by adding milk to their soil—a suggestion that is still used today. He then enumerates the various kinds of fly that may be used for special types of fish, and compares the effects of minnows, flies and worms with relation to catching particular fish. Gradually the hunter begins to incline toward the fisherman's viewpoint that his sport is ideally suited for happiness. The angler says: "There is no life, my honest Scholar, no life so happy and so pleasant as the life of a well-governed angler." The angler then embarks on an interesting discussion of the salmon, "King of the fresh-water fish" and its strange breeding habits. The pike is considered to be a tyrant among fishes because it preys on others and broods alone among shoals. The angler gives explicit explanations of how to catch these two fish, and adds pointers on catching carp, perch, and eels. The hunter recites a parody on Marlowe's poem, written by Dr. John Donne in praise of fishing. That night all four fishermen convene again at an ale-house, where they sing the song, "O, the gallant fisher's life, It is the best of any. . ."

Chaps. 17–21. *Fifth Day.* The angler discourses briefly on caddis flies, minnows, and sticklebags, giving the hunter directions on how to make a line and how to color both the rod and line for catching particular fish. At the end of that day the hunter thanks his friend for his assistance and concedes that fishing is a sport for gentlemen and scholars. Again the angler stresses that virtue and knowledge are qualities

166

particularly suited to fishermen because the silence of the sport and contemplation of nature help to build a better man.

Part II of *The Compleat Angler* [written as an expansion of the first part by Charles Cotton, and often published with Part I] continues the dialogue form by introducing a WAYFARER who speaks to the angler. The first part of the book is discussed briefly. The dialogues are held during a three-day period, and the most valuable is probably the discussion of the second day, in which flies are discussed and their uses related to the monthly calendar.

Confessions of an English Opium-Eater

Memoirs by Thomas De Quincey, 1785–1859.
Published 1821–22. (Enlarged edition published 1856.)

THOMAS DE QUINCEY LIVED at a time when fine writing was admired for its own sake. His most lasting work, the *Confessions*, qualifies if only on the grounds of its fine writing. The book has three main sections: Autobiographical; apologetic; descriptive (of the effects of drug-taking). The drug that De Quincey took, but also other opium derivatives, were in his times usually called laudanum. ❧ If De Quincey's *Confessions* are authentic, they are a valuable scientific document; but are they? The man was a professional and not unsuccessful journalist. He wrote the *Confessions* for publication in a journal. If he was merely a reporter, using his imagination to improve and fill as myriad reporters have done before and will do again, much of the first-person validity is lost. In the medical profession there has been little disposition to credit De Quincey with a more valuable contribution than having written a very good book.

1. Autobiographical. De Quincey writes in the first person. At the start he confesses that he was once an "opium-eater," or drug addict. He first resorted to the drug to relieve the pain of a rheumatic condition that had plagued him for many years. He believes this must have been in 1804. He asserts opium's ability to soothe the irritations of the nervous system, to stimulate one's capacity for enjoyment, and to sustain flagging energies.

Probably the ultimate reason why De Quincey turned finally to opium, as a habitual rather than an occasional user, was his unhappy youth. His father having died when De Quincey was only 7 years old, the boy was placed under the tutelage of the Reverend Mr. H. for classical instruction. He was put to live with a happily married couple in Manchester, but the wife died. De Quincey was moved around, attending several different schools. When he was 15 his guardians sent him to the Manchester Grammar School. Here he lived in the house of the headmaster, Mr. Lawson, along with a group of boys in the elder school. He found their collective knowledge of literature a cause for admiration.

Unfortunately his health, never good, began to fail as a result of the rigorous schedule imposed by Mr. Lawson and also the absence of adequate medical care. His liver was not good (he was constipated) and melancholy overtook him. He pleaded with his guardians to let him leave the school but they refused. Just before his 17th birthday he ran away. He borrowed ten guineas from a friend, Lady Caberry, wrote a letter of farewell to the school, and set off on foot. His first plan was to go to the Lakes District, because there lived Wordsworth, whom he admired. Instead he went to North Wales to see his mother, stayed briefly, and went on to London.

For seven or eight weeks in London he lived in cheap lodgings. He calculated that he needed 200 pounds and tried to borrow it from moneylenders. This led to his meeting Mr. BRUNELL, whom he describes as "a practitioner in the lower departments of the law." Though he suspects Mr. Brunell of unscrupulousness, De Quincey admits that the man was kind and generous to him. Mr. Brunell took him into his house, where was also living at the time a poor waif, a destitute 10-year-old girl.

During this period De Quincey was in poor health. A twitching sensation made it difficult for him to rest comfortably and his dreams were "tumultuous." Sleeplessness gave him the habit of walking through the streets at night. One bright spot of the period was his meeting a family friend who lent him 10 pounds. (He had not sought family aid because he feared that if his guardians knew his whereabouts they would make him return to school.) Another feature of his nocturnal wanderings was his meeting with ANN, a girl scarcely 16 years old, whose poor circumstances had forced her to a prostitute's life. De Quincey found her a sympathetic and sincere person and still thinks of her with tenderness.

Continuing his efforts to borrow money, De Quincey showed a letter he had received from his school friend the Earl of Altamont. The moneylenders told him that if Altamont would guarantee payment, upon reaching his majority, they would lend him (De Quincey) 200 or 300 pounds. De Quincey set out for Eton to get Altamont's guarantee. He arranged to meet Ann a week later on the street where they always met. He did not know her last name and did not ask it because it did not occur to him that they would not meet as scheduled and that he would never find her again.

When De Quincey reached Eton he found that Altamont had gone to Cambridge. Instead he got a guarantee from the Earl of Desert, but the moneylenders would not accept this. At this point De Quincey was destitute, but much more grievous to him was the fact that he could not find Ann. At this point he became reconciled with his guardians and left London, with his ultimate destination Oxford.

2. The Pleasures of Opium. De Quincey

Ann waits at night

first took opium on the advice of a college friend, whom he met accidentally on the streets of London and to whom he spoke of the racking pains that assailed him. In a druggist's shop on Oxford Street he bought laudanum and when he returned to his lodgings he took some. The relief came within an hour. In the place of pain he felt a heady happiness. De Quincey compares opium with wine and concludes that wine produces rapidly mounting pleasure that quickly declines, while opium produces a steady glow for eight or ten hours. Wine also disorders the mental faculties while

opium introduces "exquisite order." Opium did not produce in De Quincey the supposed feeling of torpor. He used to fix his times for taking opium beforehand, usually once every three weeks and on a Tuesday or a Saturday night when he could go to the opera and hear the beautiful voice of Grassini [a diva of those times]. On Saturday nights he liked almost as much to visit the markets, where the laboring classes spent their only free time during the week. His sympathies are with these people and he felt with them most keenly when under the influence of opium. He has a preference for silence and solitude, especially when under the spell of opium, but to avoid the consequences of melancholy he forces himself into society.

By 1812 De Quincey had left the academic world and was living in solitude in a cottage deep in the mountains. He had not married. He continued to take opium, but only on Saturday nights. He was in good health, though he knows that according to all medical opinion he should have been very ill. Then, in 1813, he was stricken with the same kind of stomach trouble that

had afflicted him in youth. As a result, he became a regular and confirmed daily opium-eater.

3. The Pains of Opium. De Quincey emphasizes, as the connecting link of his confessions, his conviction that opium was the only means of easing the miseries that had resulted from his youthful privations. He is certain he would have lost his sanity without the drug. He denies any lasting deleterious effects. It is quite possible to rid oneself of the opium habit.

The main consequence of opium-eating is the dream, which De Quincey describes in great detail. In his dreams space and time were distorted. Gloom and horror often pervaded the dreams. His brain became phantom-haunted by phenomena such as crocodiles, seas paved with innumerable faces, weird chattering birds. All stages of delirium were undergone. In a dream of 1820, he heard unearthly music filling vast vaulted spaces.

He began to suffer violent internal palpitations, and out of concern for his family he finally gave up the use of opium.

The Confessions of St. Augustine

Autobiography by Augustine, Bishop of Hippo, 354–430.
Written 399. Translation by F. J. Sheed published and © 1942 by Sheed and Ward, New York. Various other translations. (ML, 263)

THE WORD CONFESSIONS is used in a double sense by St. Augustine. In the most popular present sense it is a recounting of sins and an admission of guilt. It has also the sense of a declaration of faith and belief. St. Augustine's *Confessions* serve a triple purpose as an autobiography—one of the greatest of all time—and a book of theology and philosophy. The book was of tremendous importance in the early Christian Church, for in it a wise and devout but human man, who himself had been prey to heresy, tells other doubtful men how he himself was drawn back to Catholicism. The book is written in the first person and is addressed directly to God. It contains many apostrophes of praise and some of prayer. Incidentally it constitutes a superb brief biography and character study of St. Monica, Augustine's mother.

Book 1. Augustine praises God's greatness and infinite wisdom. [It is generally considered that the theme of the book and of Augustine's philosophy is:] "Thou madest us for Thyself, and our heart is restless until it repose in Thee." God gave Augustine his faith through Jesus and through St. Ambrose (who baptized Augustine). Augustine fell ill in his infancy and his mother MONICA (St. Monica) postposed his baptism, for she was a Christian although her husband was pagan. Augustine detested his father at that time and does not mention his name at this point, declaring that God is everyone's true father. Augustine wasted the first fifteen years of his life by listless studying, love of sport, and idle habits. He read Latin, his native tongue, with relish but scorned Greek. He loved Latin grammar chiefly, though he wept over dead Dido (in the *Aeneid*). He hated Greek, he thinks because it was a strange language and so difficult for him. But while he wept over

Dido, he did not think to weep for himself, though his own soul was dying for lack of love for God. He disliked arithmetic, the singsong of the multiplication tables. He cautions the people of his day not to become too bound up in pagan classical studies, and thanks God for his early aversion to them. As a boy he was not aware of the sins he committed—lying to deceive his tutor, teachers, parents; love of play and shows; thefts from his parents' cellar and table; ambition for preëminence among boys. Was this the innocence of boyhood? No, it was genuine sin.

Book 2. Augustine now recalls his past carnal corruptions; the recollection pains him but he does it to love God more. It is good for a man not to touch a woman, for the unmarried man thinks of God but the married man of his wife and how to please her. Augustine as a boy had been at school at Madaura. His father was resolved to send him for further study to Carthage, which not many men of his father's limited means would have done. His 16th year he spent in his parents' home, at Thagaste. He was maturing sexually, which pleased his father because it promised grandchildren. His mother urged him not to commit fornication, and especially not adultery—advice he dismissed as "woman's words," not then knowing they were God's teaching. Augustine was easily seduced and lived a dissolute life. He recalls when in a group of "lewd young fellows" he helped rob a pear tree, carrying away many pears, though the pears themselves were not worth having and he could have had as many pears as he wished, of better quality, that appealed to them; it was theft for theft's sake. He thanks God that he is free from such temptations, for they made him "a barren land."

Book 3. Augustine spent his 17th to 19th years at Carthage, the capital and metropolis of the province. He lived in a bubbling "cauldron of unholy loves." He studied rhetoric and learned books of eloquence; a book of Cicero's turned his thoughts to God, though the book was not so intended. His father had died when Augustine was 16. Augustine prepared to become a lawyer or teacher. Augustine fell into the error of Manicheanism because that religion, preaching that the universe was divided between Good and Evil, seemed logical. Christianity seemed unable to explain how Evil arose in a universe created by an omniscient, loving God. At the age of 17 Augustine did not understand what he later knew: that Evil is not a substance that has been, but is non-being or lack of being, and thus has no Devil Creator to rival God. Monica was heartbroken by her son's blasphemy, but was comforted by a dream in which a shining youth told her that the "son of your tears" would be saved. Nevertheless, for nine years Augustine clung to Manicheanism.

Book 4. At the age of 18 Augustine settled down to teach rhetoric in his native Thagaste. He took a mistress, but only one, to whom he was faithful. (He kept her 15 years.) Once he entered himself for a theatrical prize (as an orator); a wizard asked him what he would pay to win and he replied that he would not let any living creature, even a fly, be sacrificed so he could win. When he was 20 he read Aristotle; others did not understand the book but he did, though at the time it did not help him to understand God and may even have hindered him. When Augustine was 26 or 27 he wrote two or three books "On the Beautiful and the Fitting" and dedicated them to Hierius, an orator of Rome, whom he did not know personally but whose learning he admired. At that time he admired men whom men admired, not yet knowing that only God's judgment is infallible. His closest friend, a pagan, died and grief drove Augustine back to Carthage. Augustine ponders the nature of death and friendship, concluding that only in God are all things eternal.

Book 5. In Augustine's 29th year a great bishop of the Manichees, FAUSTUS, came to Carthage. Augustine had been a Manichean since he was about 20 and had been eager for Faustus's arrival for years. The accuracy of certain calculations and predictions in astronomy he had read were very impressive and he wanted to compare the Manicheans' calculations. But Faustus could tell him nothing, and though Augustine liked Faustus he decided to go no further in Manicheanism. Bored with the sophisticated orators of Carthage called Overturners, Augustine deceived his mother and left to teach at Rome, where he fell violently ill. Again seized by restlessness, Augustine went to Milan to hear (St.) AMBROSE lecture on the *Bible*. The Bishop of Milan spoke so poetically and forcefully that Augustine decided to undertake catechism.

Book 6. Monica joined her son in Milan, but Augustine still had doubts about Christianity and craved honors. He saw a drunken beggar in the street and realized that he himself was drunk with ambition, but he could not take a decisive step. At Milan Augustine had two friends from Africa, ALYPIUS and NEBRIDIUS, who likewise dabbled with religion. Augustine decided to end his lustful ways by sending his mistress back to Africa and intending to marry a very young girl. But lust, though he has now forsworn it, was then a habit with him. Despairing over the two years he would have to wait for marriage, Augustine abandoned the idea and took another mistress.

Book 7. At 30 Augustine read a great deal of Plato's philosophy and understood at last that God is pure spirit and is everywhere by the power of that spirit. Christianity later taught him that God also became matter in the body of Christ. Thus God is both matter and spirit, and the human body is likewise a combination of the eternal and transient, with the eternal predominating. One of Augustine's prime contributions to Christianity was his introduction and enlargement of these neo-Platonic ideas.

Book 8. At 31 Augustine went to SIMPLICIANUS, who had converted Ambrose, for help. Simplicianus told him the inspiring story of a Roman professor named VICTORINUS who had sacrificed his career to become a Christian. Another friend from Africa, PONTICIANUS, told Augustine how

He heard a child singing

two Roman officials were persuaded toward Christianity after hearing about the life of St. Francis. At last one day while sitting in a garden Augustine heard a child sing, "Take up and read, take up and read." He opened the Bible at random to Romans, Chapter XIII, verse 13, and read the exhortation against drunkenness and lust. Augustine told his friend Alypius about the moving incident and together they went to Monica and told her that they wanted to become Christians.

Book 9. Augustine, Alypius and Augustine's illegitimate son ADEODATUS, 15 years old, were received into the Church with joy and Augustine gave up his career of rhetoric. Later other friends such as Nebridius also took up the religion. Augustine composed a dialogue between himself and his son called *On Teaching,* and the words spoken by the son were literally transcribed. Augustine also supported Ambrose, who was being threatened by the Emperor Valentinian's mother Justina, who favored the Arian heresy. Hymns were introduced into Christian services while the people barricaded themselves in the churches. Augustine decided to return to Carthage and on the way Monica died at Ostia. Augustine reviews her life. She was an obedient and devoted daughter. She was a good influence on the maids, teaching them not to drink wine (though in later years she confessed that she had liked it herself—but took only a sip when she drew a flagon for her parents). (Monica had also opposed the use of wine in church, and several bishops agreed with her.) When Monica was of marriageable age she was given to PATRICIUS, Augustine's father, and she served him as her lord. Though he was violent in lust and in temper, she got along well with him by a simple system: Whether she was right or wrong she never defended herself while he was in a temper, waiting until he was tranquil. The same method, which she recommended to other wives, served her well with her mother-in-law, who had been prejudiced against her (by false gossip) at the start but was completely won over. Eventually Monica converted her husband to Christianity, at the very end of his life. May she rest in peace and may many remember her at God's altar.

Books 10–13. Augustine reviews his sins, previously confessed, and the doubts of himself and others about Christianity and the answers to these doubts. He closes with prayers to God and Christ from one who "loved Thee late."

A Connecticut Yankee at the Court of King Arthur

Novel by Mark Twain (Samuel Clemens, 1835–1910).

Published 1889 by Harper & Bros., New York.

THE CONNECTICUT YANKEE was one of Mark Twain's best creations. He was inspired by Mark Twain's admiration for the ingenuity of the Hartford neighbors he acquired when he became a New Englander. Actually very little of New England ever rubbed off on him. Until recently a new movie of *Connecticut Yankee* could be made every few years and there would be enough new inventions to add a twist here and there and still keep it pleasant, but in the atomic age it becomes more difficult.

The "princesses" were pigs

Preface. Mark Twain met a man at Warwick Castle who seemed to have an intimate knowledge of the days of King Arthur in the 6th century. At the man's invitation, Twain went to his room and was shown a manuscript called *The Stranger's History,* which told of the man's experiences thirteen centuries before. Twain could not believe his eyes. As he read, the stranger fell asleep.

The manuscript said that the stranger (afterward called the YANKEE) hailed from Hartford, Connecticut. After a crowbar fight with a brawny neighbor, he fell asleep under a tree. When he came to, he saw a horseman in armor riding toward him. The Yankee asked if the horseman, whose name was CLARENCE, was going to Bridgeport. Clarence replied that he was going to King Arthur's castle Camelot and he took the Yankee as his hostage.

Chaps. 1–9. The Yankee was amazed to find himself at romantic Camelot in the midst of Arthur's famous knights and their Round Table in the year 528. He saw Sirs LANCELOT, GALAHAD, MODRED, and DINADAN, and the magician MERLIN. After Arthur and his queen GUENEVER (usually spelled Guinevere) had examined the Yankee, they sentenced him to death for the following day, the 20th of June. The Yankee had a little vest-pocket reference book whose miscellaneous information included a list of dates on which there were total eclipses of the sun. June 20, 528, was one of the days. So he told Clarence, who was fast becoming his friend, that he was going to stop the sun the next day. Word spread around and the whole court was first apprehensive, then shocked to see the boast come true, and badly frightened. The magician Merlin was so jealous that the

Yankee ordered him thrown into prison and no one dared disobey. The King named the Yankee his chief minister, and after the Yankee mixed some gunpowder and blew up a tower his power was complete and he took the title of "The Boss." The Yankee was appalled by the filth, the suppression of the masses and the idle lives of the knights. He stirred the enmity of a leading jouster named Sir SAGRAMOR, who proposed a duel on horse three years in the future. Sagramor could not fight the duel at that time because he was going off to claim the Holy Grail.

Chaps. 10–20. The Yankee set about to modernize England by building factories. He manufactured soap and tried to popularize bathing. He and his right-hand man Clarence built a network of telephones and telegraphs. Much to the Yankee's discomfort, the King appointed him the chivalric savior of a girl named Alisande la Carteloise (SANDY). Sandy said that her mistress and 44 beautiful princesses were kept in a castle guarded by monstrous ogres. The Yankee thought it was all a lie, but he promised to save them. As he and the girl rode out together, the Yankee was bored by her long epic tales (lifted to a great extent from Sir Thomas Malory's *Morte d'Arthur*), annoyed by her awkward armor, and again upset by the injustice of monarchy and a strong church. Eventually they stopped at the castle of an evil noblewoman named MORGAN LE FAY, the wife of King URIENS. These two hosts tried to enslave the wanderers, but when they realized that "the Boss" was their guest, changed their minds. The Yankee forced them to free many prisoners from their dungeon and rode on to the bewitched castle. The castle was simply a pigsty, the ogres were swineherds, and the princesses were pigs. The Yankee freed the pigs and then upbraided Sandy for a too vivid imagination.

Chaps. 21–24. On the way home they met a band of pilgrims traveling to the Valley of Holiness, to a sacred fountain.

Sandy and the Yankee followed and found that the fountain had gone dry. The monks pleaded with "the Boss" to fix it, and he called Clarence at Camelot to tell him to rush over with some plumbing materials. Soon the fountain worked again and the miraculous legend of the Yankee spread, much to the (now released) Merlin's hatred. The Yankee also embarrassed another rival magician who claimed to know what King Arthur was doing at a particular moment. This magician said that Arthur was sleeping, but after telephoning Camelot, the Yankee learned that Arthur was riding to that very place.

Chaps. 25–26. When the King arrived, the Yankee was universally acclaimed. He tried to persuade Arthur to institute civil service examinations in selecting his knights. When the King balked out of fear, the Yankee recruited his personal corps on merit. He also established a weekly newspaper.

Chaps. 27–34. The Yankee took the King on a long journey around the realm, traveling incognito so that they could observe the standards of living. On the way, the Yankee prophesied to the King the world's future for the next 13 centuries (an easy task for a 19th-century New Englander). The Yankee taught the King how to act humbly so he could go unrecognized. After witnessing a heartbreaking scene at a manor ravaged by smallpox, Arthur and the King took up with a lowly man named MARCO. They treated Marco and his family as if they were nobles, and so incurred the jealousy and suspicion of Marco's neighbors that they rushed upon the wandering pair. A noble fortunately drove away their lowly attackers, but instead of restoring the Yankee and King, he sold them to a slavedriver without knowing who they were.

Chaps. 35–38. After a miserable journey to London, the Yankee escaped but got involved in a brawl and was cast into jail.

On being released, he found one of his telephones hidden in a butcher's shop, called Clarence for help, and tried to rejoin the King and other slaves. The slaves had risen up and killed their master, but they had all been put in jail. The Yankee rejoined them and marched with them to the place of execution. Suddenly Sir Lancelot and the knights, summoned by Clarence, rode onto the scene and freed everyone.

Chaps. 39–43. Back at Camelot, the Yankee had to fight his long-standing duel with Sir Sagramor, for the three years had elapsed. He overcame Sagramor first with a lasso and then with a revolver. He shot nine men before the knights accepted him as champion, and thus he ended knight-errantry. After three more years, the Yankee had succeeded in abolishing slavery and making men equal before the law. Knights were employed, and railroads coursed the whole of England. The Yankee and Sandy had married and their daughter was named HELLO CENTRAL by Sandy. The Yankee did not like the name and assured Sandy that people would always use it in speaking over the telephone out of respect for his deeds. The Yankee also introduced baseball and seemed ready to establish England as a republic, when suddenly the scandal of Lancelot's attachment for Queen Guenever broke out. Arthur and Modred

fought to the death and the land was seized with civil war. The Church put an interdict on all parties and claimed control. The Yankee and Clarence recruited 52 prize young soldiers, established a retreat at Merlin's cave with electric wire, and laid dynamite throughout the land. The nation refused to accept a republican form of government after years of monarchy, so the Yankee blew up most of England merely by pressing buttons. After annihilating thousands at the Battle of the Sand-Belt, the Yankee and his few supporters staved off flank after flank of attackers inside their electrified fortress.

Chap. 44. Clarence wrote the last entry of the manuscript, telling how the Yankee was stabbed by one of the electrified soldiers, Sir MELIAGRAUNCE, who had not died. While recovering, the Yankee was attended by a woman nurse who turned out to be Merlin in disguise. Merlin put him in a trance to last 13 centuries and thus the Yankee's body was left in the cave near Warwick Castle.

As Mark Twain finished reading the stranger's manuscript, he saw with horror that the man was mumbling in his sleep, calling Twain "Sandy." Twain watched helplessly as the man slowly died, talking wildly about drawbridges, castles, and knights.

The Conquest of Granada

Play by John Dryden, 1631–1700. Produced 1670.

THE CONQUEST OF GRANADA is really two plays, but they were produced in the same year and are treated as one. Medieval legend made much of the feud between the two noble houses of Moorish Spain, the Abencerrages and

the Zegrys (both of which names are spelled in other ways), and Dryden fashioned his play or plays on this Romeo-and-Juliet theme. The play(s) has (have) been criticized as drama, but as English literature they rank high. The time, being that of Ferdinand and Isabella of Spain, is the very late 1400s.

PART I

Act I. BOABDELIN, King of Granada, speaks with ABENAMAR, the father of his intended bride, and ABDELMELECH, chief of the ABENCERRAGES (one of the noble Moorish families). The alarm bell rings: the ZEGRYS (another noble family) and the Abencerrages are fighting again. Boabdelin determines to bring peace, so all can unite against the Christians. But the fight cannot be stopped and a man is killed. His assassin is a noble foreigner, ALMANZOR, who has great prestige and persuades the families to give up fighting and support their king. The Duke of ARCOS enters, bearing a message from the monarchs of Castile and Aragon, FERDINAND and ISABELLA. They demand the city of Granada. The duke reminds the king that once, having been captured in battle, he signed away his crown in return for his life. Boabdelin, supported by Almanzor, denies the contract.

Act II. The men of Granada return triumphant from the day's battle, praising Almanzor, whose bravery and skill led them to victory. Almanzor has taken the Duke of Arcos prisoner. When they leave, LYNDARAXA, a Zegry maiden, enters with Prince ABDALLA, brother of Boabdelin. The prince declares his love but she wants to be queen and will marry him only when he becomes king. He resolves to take the throne from his brother.

Act III. Almanzor has asked Boabdelin to release Arcos, but the king has refused. For this reason, when Abdalla asks Almanzor's help in the fight to make him king, Almanzor agrees. Abdelmelech comes to warn the prince against the fickle charms of Lyndaraxa. Abdalla refuses to listen. Abdelmelech loves the girl too, and declares he will fight for her. Abdalla leaves and Lyndaraxa enters and taunts Abdelmelech. He weeps at her cruelty and begs her to

music and dancing. News is brought that Abdalla has won the battle. The Duke of Arcos is freed. Almanzor enters the castle and Almahide kneels before him and pleads for mercy and protection. As she talks, Almanzor falls in love with her; he tells her, but she protests that she is betrothed to Boabdelin. Almanzor sends her to her chamber, assuring her of safety. Abdalla, now the king, enters and gives Almahide to Almanzor as a captive. Almanzor tells the new king that he will set her free and win her love. ZULEMA, a supporter of Abdalla and a leader of the Moors, enters and demands Almahide as his prize. Abdalla is forced to take his gift away from Almanzor and give the lady to the powerful Zulema. Almanzor says his destiny is stronger than any crown. Abdalla summons Lyndaraxa to offer her the queen's crown.

Act IV. 1. Almanzor visits Boabdelin in prison and says he will now change sides, since Abdalla has denied him his one wish. He promises to win back Boabdelin's kingdom. 2. Abdelmelech bribes one of his guards and goes to visit Lyndaraxa. She tells him she loves him, but she refuses to run away with him as she wants to be queen. Abdalla approaches and she shows Abdelmelech out through a back exit. Abdalla asks Lyndaraxa to become his bride but she demands that he bring her his brother's head so she will know his crown is secure. Almanzor tells Almahide she is free and that he loves her above all else. She says he must have a kingdom before her father will permit her to marry him. He resolves to win a throne.

Act V. 1. Abdalla, pursued by Almanzor and Boabdelin, comes to the walls of the fortress Albayzyn. He has given the keys to Lyndaraxa. Now that he is alone and hunted she will not open the gates. Abdalla decides to fly to the Christian king and ask his protection. BENZAYDA, a Zegry girl, saves the life of OZMYN, an Abencerrage. They fall in love and are banished by their families. 2. Boabdelin is again king and for Abdelmelech's sake he frees the brothers of Lyndaraxa. The king sends Abdelmelech in pursuit of Abdalla. Almanzor promises Boabdelin that he will fight the Spaniards and bring him the head of Ferdinand. Almanzor then asks the king for Almahide. Boabdelin refuses and Almanzor boasts that he will take Almahide away with him. Boabdelin's guards fall on Almanzor and take him captive. Almahide weeps. She refuses to marry the king and threatens to kill herself. Boabdelin is forced to release Almanzor, to placate Almahide. Almanzor leaves the city. Abdelmelech returns with the news that Ferdinand will wage war to place Abdalla on the throne.

PART II

Act I. 1. In Ferdinand's camp, Benzayda and Ozmyn are brought in as prisoners. Ozmyn has killed a Spanish leader and Ferdinand orders his execution, but Benzayda tells the story of their love and Queen Isabella spares Ozmyn. 2. Boabdelin has

170

The Constant Nymph

The exiled young lovers are brought before Ferdinand

Novel by Margaret Kennedy, 1896–
Published and © 1924 by Doubleday &
  Co., New York.

THIS WAS Margaret Kennedy's first novel. It was greeted with enthusiasm by critics and especially by young (college age) readers; with the young women it rivaled Galsworthy's *Forsyte* books in popularity. The novel was dramatized in 1926 and was produced successfully in London and New York. Margaret Kennedy's later novels did not prove so pleasing to critics and did not hold her youthful following. *The Constant Nymph* deserves its preëminent place among her works. It is a warm, sensitive portrayal of very interesting people.

suffered heavy losses. The people are rebellious and demand that he surrender to the Spaniards or else call back Almanzor. Boabdelin knows Almanzor will return if asked by Almahide. She tells the king she will do as he asks and that she no longer loves Almanzor because her virtue will not permit it. But when the king is gone she admits to herself that she still longs for Almanzor.

Act II. In the woods outside the Spanish camp, Ozmyn and Benzayda meet Benzayda's father, SELIN. Ozmyn's father enters and tries to kill Selin. Ozmyn protects Selin, thus winning his affection. Abdalla learns that Lyndaraxa, following the winds of fortune, favors him again. He decides to lead the Spanish forces to her fortress. **2.** Abdelmelech enters the fortress in triumph and takes Lyndaraxa prisoner. But she flatters him into believing she was holding the fortress for him, and he releases her, again declaring his love for her. Abdalla and the Spanish soldiers arrive and quickly defeat the forces of Abdelmelech. Lyndaraxa is reconciled with Abdalla. **3.** Almanzor enters Granada to the cheers of the people and makes his way to the palace. Almahide tells him she can never love him but asks him to save Boabdelin's throne. He asks only that she give him her scarf to wear into battle.

Act III. 1. Boabdelin grieves in jealousy and will not be consoled by Almahide's assurance of love. When he sees Almanzor wearing Almahide's scarf, he rages. Almahide makes Almanzor return the scarf, which she places around the king. Almanzor curses the king and refuses to fight for the town. The Spaniards attack; Boabdelin is taken prisoner by the Duke of Arcos. Almanzor, when bitterly reproached by Almahide, resumes fighting for Boabdelin and captures Abdalla. **2.** The two sides agree to exchange the captive princes. **3.** Lyndaraxa tries to persuade Almanzor to change

sides, saying Almahide does not love him, but he stands firm.

Act IV. 1–2. Almanzor, fighting on Boabdelin's side, is victorious. Abdelmelech fights Abdalla and wounds him. Lyndaraxa enters as Abdalla dies. She scorns him and praises Abdelmelech, but he at last is disgusted and declares his love for her is over. He takes her prisoner. **3.** Almanzor waits to beg Almahide for her love. The ghost of his mother appears, telling him that he is a Christian and must not break the laws of God. Almanzor entreats Almahide for her love and she threatens to kill herself. He leaves, promising never to disturb her again. Abdelmelech brings in Lyndaraxa and is about to kill her when Almahide runs in, screaming for help. Zulema, whom she has previously repulsed, is trying to seize her. Abdelmelech follows Zulema to protect Almahide. Lyndaraxa takes the opportunity to run to Boabdelin and say that she and Zulema saw Almahide making love to Abdelmelech. Boabdelin orders both his wife and his friend killed, but Almanzor refuses to believe the tale and it is agreed that he shall defend Almahide at her trial.

Act V. 1–2. The trial turns into a fight between Almanzor and Almahide's false accuser, Zulema. Almanzor fatally wounds Zulema, who confesses that he lied. Almahide and Abdelmelech are freed. Almahide tells Boabdelin she now loathes him for his lack of trust. He determines to kill Almanzor, but the Spaniards attack again and Boabdelin needs Almanzor. **3.** In the battle Boabdelin is killed. Almanzor is about to kill the Duke of Arcos when the ghost of his mother intervenes, telling him that the duke is his lost father. They embrace. The battle is finally won by the Spaniards. Ozmyn, Benzayda, Almanzor and Almahide all vow to become Christians. Queen Isabella decrees that Almahide shall become the bride of Almanzor and wear a Spanish coronet.

Chaps. 1–7. ALBERT SANGER is a musician known to the *avant-garde*. He has a large family acquired through several marriages. He travels through Europe with his brilliant and sensitive brood of children, spending the summers at a chalet in the Austrian Alps. He is now living with a voluptuous, stupid woman, LINDA. She lolls around indolently while Albert's oldest children, KATE and CARYL, take care of the family. Kate is studying to be a singer and Caryl a musician. They are the stable children born of his first wife, kind and long-suffering VERA BRADY. The next four children have the talent and romantic longings of their society mother ELEANOR CHURCHILL. They are ANTONIA, TERESA, PAULINA, and SEBASTIAN. They live in a world of fantasy created through the freedom given them by their genius father and his many bohemian friends. The youngest child, SUSAN, is Linda's daughter and she is stupid and whines continually like her mother. LEWIS DODD, a young composer friend of Sanger's, is on his way to the house in the Alps when he meets TRIGORIN, a ballet impresario, who admires Sanger and is also coming to visit him. Trigorin is a lover of music but has no talent himself. He is always being rejected by real artists and defensively hides his wounds behind an air of wealthy smugness. Teresa, 14 years old, and Paulina, 10 years old, meet the two travelers on their way to the mountaintop house. They tell them the news of the family and describe Sebastian's adventures when he was lost for two weeks and traveled around by himself. The children are animated and excited by seeing Lewis again. When the two men arrive at the house they find Kate very disturbed because 16-year-old Antonia has run off to Munich to live for a week with a Jewish concert impresario, JACOB BIRNBAUM. Sanger is working on a concerto and has spoken to nobody for days. The sensitive Teresa has a long, intimate conversation with Lewis, whom she loves. They have known each other many years and have a secret rapport. On this visit Lewis suddenly realizes that Teresa is growing up and may become as wild and difficult as Antonia. He cannot stand this idea. He wants her to be pure and innocent forever. In a sense he wants her to exist only for him. She seems to him fragile and tender, with an impudence and intensity that he senses could bring disaster to her. He is afraid she will be betrayed by another man. Antonia comes back from Munich, bringing Jacob with her. She is hysterical and afraid of what she has done. She loves Jacob but treats him as if she despises him because he has seduced her. During the next few days Sanger comes down to dinner occasionally. The conversation is brilliant but everyone is rude to Trigorin, who consoles himself in an affair with the simple Linda. The children and Lewis propose a surprise for Sanger's birthday, an opera written by Lewis to be performed by the family. Jacob thinks Lewis's opera is brilliant. Sanger also appreciates it. When Trigorin tries to express his pleasure in the work the others mock him with their cruel intellectual superiority. One night the children hear groans from Sanger's room. They enter and find their father dead. They are left without money and with no one to look after them. Teresa and Sebastian become sick with grief.

Chaps. 8–14. Lewis writes to EVELYN'S brother CHARLES (Evelyn was Sanger's second wife), telling him of the children's difficulties. Charles sends his brother ROBERT and Charles' daughter FLORENCE to Austria. They are very proper English society people and find the Sanger household impossibly wild. They are scandalized by Antonia's admitted relationship with Jacob. Antonia finally tells Jacob that she loves him and he, who has not dared tell her of his feelings because she is so beautiful and socially superior, proposes marriage. The couple plan to be married in Vienna. Lewis Dodd falls in love with Florence despite the fact that she symbolizes the society of his family, from which he has run away. She loves him for his rebellious nature and his art, and they spend many hours together walking through the countryside. Florence has none of the Sanger family's "traveling circus" air. She has the simplicity and honesty of Teresa and a certain calm intelligence that attracts Lewis like a perfect bar of music, and he looks on her as an ideal of womanhood. Teresa sees their love growing and becomes pale and worried. Paulina tries to console her with the impossibility of Lewis's ever really loving Florence, but Teresa knows different and sees that such a union will have serious and unhappy consequences for them all. The whole family takes a trip to Innsbruck to see Antonia, Jacob, and Uncle Robert, who is chaperoning the young couple. After the goodbyes are said the children go off to a movie and Florence and Lewis go into a church. In the sanctity of the church Lewis kisses Florence and proposes marriage.

172

They loved to walk together

When Teresa hears the news she faints and becomes ill. In Vienna, Antonia and Jacob find the interim before their marriage difficult because Robert will not let them stay at the same hotel. News comes to them of Florence and Lewis's engagement. Robert is appalled and hurries back to try to prevent the marriage.

Chaps. 15–16. Florence and Lewis are married and Kate and Caryl go off to jobs in the theater. Teresa, Paulina and Sebastian are sent to English boarding schools. There they are ridiculed by the teachers and students because of their individualistic behavior and their unwillingness to join in sports. In their lonely misery they write to Lewis to take them out of the schools. But Lewis cannot help them because Florence disapproves of his coddling them. He finds Florence more worldly and cold than he had supposed. Florence is trying to force Lewis into society to aid his career. He tries to hold on to the free way of life he found with Sanger and his children. Sebastian runs away from his school, where he could get no musical training. He comes to his sisters' school, and finding them unhappy, insists they run away with him. They go to Florence and Lewis. Lewis is overjoyed to see them. He feels especially alive at being with Teresa again. But Florence wants to send them back to school immediately. The principals refuse to take them so they must stay indefinitely.

Chaps. 17–18. Florence has a party to promote Lewis's musical career. Lewis hates all the guests and is rude. He goes upstairs and talks with Teresa, where he finds warmth and companionship. Florence has

become jealous and wants to send Teresa back to school. Sebastian has obtained a scholarship at a music school. Paulina has decided to study acting in Paris, which leaves Teresa undecided and alone. Florence's father, Charles, comes to visit the Dodd household. He realizes that Lewis is in love with Teresa. He tries to talk Teresa into going back to school but he is charmed by her quick mind and nymphlike qualities. He tries but cannot prevent his daughter from hurting the sensitive Teresa.

Chaps. 19–22. Lewis realizes that he only loved Florence because he imagined her to be Teresa. He asks Teresa to run away with him. Teresa confesses her love for him but refuses to destroy his home and insists that she will go to the school. Lewis, on receiving her refusal, runs off alone without letting anyone know where he has gone. Sebastian and Teresa find him when they visit their sister Antonia, who has just had a baby. There they all enjoy concerts and picnics. Lewis's sister MILDRED reveals to Florence that she has seen Lewis at the Birnbaums. Florence goes to Antonia's and prevails on Lewis to return home with her, but he thinks incessantly about Teresa. Florence can no longer control her hatred for Teresa, with whom she has a savage verbal fight just before Lewis's concert. Teresa runs down to the river, weeping. There she meets Sanger's old manservant, who is now in the Dodd employ, and he takes a note from her to Lewis backstage, telling him she will meet him on the first boat train the following day. She goes to the concert with Florence, as had been planned. Florence is fiercely proud when she sees all the fine people coming to listen to her husband's work. She will not give up the pleasure of being Lewis Dodd's wife. The symphony composed by Lewis is not understood and is rejected by the audience, but his conducting of two classical works is considered brilliant.

Chap. 23. Lewis barely makes the boat train. He finds Teresa standing, pale and tense, by a post and takes her in his arms. They have a bad crossing and Teresa is very sick. In France they stay at the home of a Mme. MARXSE, who was an old friend of Sanger's. Mme. Marxse makes several lewd remarks but in her French manner accepts the couple and gives them a large double room. Teresa, trying to open a window, exerts great effort, has a stroke, and dies within seconds. Lewis is in a total daze and unable to think for himself. Florence insists that he come back to England, to their home. He has at least temporarily lost his will and acquiesces in everything, but it is clear that the death of Teresa meant the loss of the one person he could ever have loved.

Coriolanus

Play by William Shakespeare, 1564–1616.

Produced about 1608.

THE SIMPLEST WAY to describe *Coriolanus* is to say that it is a play Shakespeare wrote when he was at his peak. There are more memorable snatches of poetry in the earlier plays, but in the later plays such as *Coriolanus* is found the memorable philosophy, sometimes so deep that rumination is required to appreciate it. The story of Coriolanus is from Plutarch. Coriolanus was of the days of the early republic, close to 500 B.C. His story having passed through Plutarch and Shakespeare, it is doubtful that much remains in the play that is truly historical.

Act I. 1. A group of mutinous citizens assembles with the intention of killing CAIUS MARCIUS (later known as CORIOLANUS), the leader of the aristocracy. He was formerly a hero, but now grain prices are too high. Five tribunes have been named to air the grievances of the commoners. Two of these tribunes are JUNIUS BRUTUS and SICINIUS VELUTUS. Marcius is afraid this will give the mob too much power in the future. A messenger brings Marcius a report that the Volsces are up in arms. A group of senators, including the consul, COMINIUS, and a general, TITUS LARTIUS, ask Marcius to take command against the Volscians, who are led by TULLUS AUFIDIUS. He is respected by Marcius. The tribunes Brutus and Sicinius discuss Marcius's great pride and arrogance. 2. At the senate building in Corioli, Volscian capital, Aufidius tells the senators he is prepared to fight and he departs with the blessings of the senators. 3. In Marcius's house in Rome, Marcius's mother VOLUMNIA berates her daughter-in-law VIRGILIA for complaining about Marcius's absence, when he is fighting for glory. VALERIA, friend of Virgilia, brings news that Marcius's army is laying siege to the city of Corioli. 4. Before Corioli, Marcius and Lartius hear that the Roman and Volscian armies face one another but have not yet met in batttle. Marcius calls for a conference with the beleaguered enemy and the Volscian senators taunt him. The noise of fighting is heard. The Romans are pushed back and Marcius curses his troops and rallies them. They advance once more to the open gates and Marcius is among the first to enter. The gates close and Marcius is trapped inside. He is presumed lost, but reappears wounded, and his example spurs the others to fight their way into the city. 5. Marcius leaves Lartius to hold the city

and goes outside to seek out his personal enemy Aufidius. 6. In the camp of Cominius there is a lull between battles. Marcius selects four volunteers and departs to seek Aufidius. 7. Lartius, leaving a guard behind, sets out for the field. 8. Aufidius and Marcius meet and fight. When other Volscians come to Aufidius's aid he feels shamed and breaks off the fight. 9. Cominius offers Marcius a special bonus of a tenth of the booty, but Marcius refuses. Cominius then crowns him CORIOLANUS (that is, "Marcius of Corioli") for his victory in that city. 10. At the Volscian camp, Aufidius swears to fight Coriolanus again.

Act II. 1. In Rome, the two tribunes, Brutus and Sicinius, tell MENENIUS the commoners will not be happy about Coriolanus's victory. They accuse Coriolanus of insufferable pride. The victorious generals, Cominius, Lartius, and Coriolanus, arrive. Coriolanus goes to make his report to the senate. The tribunes are sure he will try to become consul. 2. At the Capitol there are three candidates for consul, but only Coriolanus seems to have a chance. Coriolanus leaves temporarily. When he returns, Menenius offers him the consulship, which Coriolanus in affected modesty at first turns down, but finally accepts. 3. Some citizens are still distrustful of Coriolanus; others, impressed by his newly shown humility, now favor him. In small groups the citizens approach Coriolanus, who manages to win

Coriolanus leaves for exile

their support. Brutus and Sicinius change the minds of the crowd, which leaves for the Capitol to change their votes and vote against Coriolanus.

Act III. 1. In a Roman street, Lartius reports to Coriolanus that the Volsces are a beaten people. Aufidius has retired to Antium, but hopes for a return fight with Coriolanus. The tribunes stop Coriolanus from going to the marketplace. Coriolanus, incensed, repeats his attacks upon them, despite the efforts of Menenius and other senators to calm him. There is a skirmish as the tribunes try to seize Coriolanus and

throw him from the rock of Tarpeia. The patricians manage to fight off the mob, which finds its victim gone. Menenius promises to bring Coriolanus to the marketplace to answer all charges. 2. Coriolanus is at home. Menenius chides him for being too rough, and advises him to mend his ways, to prevent civil war. Cominius reports that the marketplace is full of angry people. Coriolanus reluctantly agrees to go and talk to them. 3. At the Forum the tribunes plan the strategy of their accusations against Coriolanus. They plan to get him angry. Coriolanus and his friends arrive and he promises to submit to the judgment of the people. Sicinius then accuses him of attempted tyranny. Coriolanus forgets his promise and answers in anger. Gleefully Sicinius asks for his death but Coriolanus is sentenced to banishment from the city.

Act IV. 1. Coriolanus takes leave of his mother and goes into exile. 2. The tribunes, Brutus and Sicinius, decide to show more humility with the nobility, now that Coriolanus is out of the way. 3–4. Coriolanus, disguised as a Roman beggar, learns that the Volscians intend to strike at Rome. 5. A feast is in progress inside the house of Aufidius. The servants try to keep the beggar out but he insists on seeing their master. Coriolanus throws himself on the mercy of his erstwhile enemy and to his surprise Aufidius welcomes him and offers him half of his army to lead against Rome. 6. In Rome, Sicinius and Brutus hear that Coriolanus and Aufidius are joined. 7. In camp not far from Rome, Aufidius and his lieutenant discuss their campaign. The lieutenant is perturbed by Coriolanus's leadership, which seems to overshadow that of Aufidius. Aufidius calms his officer's fears, saying that once Rome is taken, Coriolanus will be his.

Act V. 1. Cominius has returned from an unsuccessful mission to Coriolanus, who refused to talk to him. The tribunes send Menenius to reason with him. 2. Menenius arrives at the camp of the Volscians and is refused admission by the guards. Coriolanus and Aufidius arrive. Coriolanus refuses to talk to Menenius, but gives him a letter of safe conduct. 3. Virgilia, with Coriolanus's young son Marcius, his mother Volumnia, and Valeria, arrive in mourning clothes to plead with him. They say that by making peace he can be a greater hero in Rome than by conquering. Coriolanus is swayed by is mother's plea and wins the consent of Aufidius. 4. In Rome, the mob is threatening to kill Brutus if the women are unsuccessful in obtaining peace. A messenger brings word that the women have won; The Volscians are gone. Volumnia is the day's heroine. 5. In Antium, Aufidius summons the city fathers to the marketplace. He intends to take revenge on Coriolanus. Aufidius calls him a traitor. The lords of Antium defend Coriolanus, but Aufidius's hirelings kill him. Aufidius then regrets what he has done and promises to honor the memory of Coriolanus.

The Counterfeiters

Novel by André Gide, 1869–1951.
Published 1925. Published in the U.S.
and © 1927 by Alfred A. Knopf,
New York, in a translation from the
French by Dorothy Bussy.

THE COUNTERFEITERS is ranked
among the best works of Gide, who
won the Nobel Prize for Literature in
1947. In the United States it has been
his most popular book. Though counterfeiting is mentioned in the book,
the title alludes chiefly to false or
"counterfeit" standards and motives.
The novel stresses the emotional relationships of men with men.

1ST PART—PARIS

Chap. 1. BERNARD PROFITENDIEU, a
young man, is at home cramming for his
baccalaureate examination. Upon discovering a 17-year-old love letter addressed to his
mother, he learns that he is the son of his
mother's former lover. He plans to run
away from home, but first goes to seek help
from his young friend, OLIVIER MOLINIER,
who promises to let him sleep at his house
that night.

Chap. 2. M. Profitendieu, a judge, walking home with M. Molinier, Olivier's father,
discusses a scandal involving a number of
minors. Molinier advises his colleague not
to act hastily. On reaching home, Profitendieu finds a letter from Bernard bidding him
goodbye. The letter reveals that Bernard is,
in a way, relieved to know he is not his real
father since he never really liked him anyway. Now that he knows, Bernard says he
can no longer allow the elder man to support him as a son. Profitendieu is deeply
saddened, since he actually loves Bernard
better than his own children. His wife and
children are told of Bernard's departure;
Mme. Profitendieu at first thinks he has
forced Bernard to leave. The unfortunate
circumstances of Bernard's birth had been
forgiven and forgotten, although Profitendieu is inclined to think Bernard's action is
just retribution for the sin committed. Mme.
Profitendieu is resentful of her husband's
feelings and would actually like to run away
too.

Chaps. 3–4. Bernard spends the night at
Olivier's house, where Olivier tells him that
his brother VINCENT, a recently graduated
medical student, has a mistress, whom he
sees every night. In reality, it is to the house
of Count ROBERT DE PASSAVANT that Vincent goes. Passavant is a wealthy writer,
though of questionable character, who has
introduced Vincent to gambling. Vincent
loses all of the 5,000 francs his mother has
given him to set up a medical practice. He
was actually planning to give this money to
his mistress, LAURA DOUVIERS, a married
woman whom he met while both were
patients at a tuberculosis sanitarium. She

has become pregnant and cannot face returning to her husband. Laura is desperate
and begs him not to leave her. Passavant
offers Vincent 5,000 francs to use trying to
win back the money he lost.

Chaps. 5–7. Visiting at the home of Lady
LILIAN GRIFFITH, Passavant reveals that
he is actually bored by, and dislikes, Vincent.
Lilian, a rich, demanding woman who must
have her own way, fancies she is in love
with Vincent. Vincent returns from gambling, having won 50,000 francs, and is
exuberant. He becomes Lilian's lover and
gives in to her demands that he abandon
Laura. Lilian tells him she cannot stand a
moody and anxious person, that with her
help he can become a success.

Chaps. 8–9. The reader is introduced to
Olivier's uncle EDOUARD, a writer, who is
on a train coming to Paris to help his good
friend, Laura, who has written to him for
assistance. Edouard is reading Passavant's
latest book, a big literary success, and decides that he hates Passavant's work.
Edouard meets Olivier at the railroad station. The two are strangely attracted to each
other and are overjoyed to see one another,
though they are not well acquainted. But
each is afraid to let the other know his feelings, so their conversation is strained.
Edouard absent-mindedly throws away his
cloakroom ticket and it is picked up by
Bernard, who has also come to the train
station.

Bernard begins to read through Edouard's journal

Chaps. 10–13. Bernard claims Edouard's
suitcase, intending to return it to the older
man after he has looked it over. Finding a
bundle of banknotes, he checks into a hotel
and begins to read through Edouard's
journal. The journal discusses Edouard's
plans for a proposed novel to be called *The
Counterfeiters*. It also reveals Edouard's
deep fondness for Olivier, which he says he
tries to hide by affecting an air of detachment. Edouard has also written about an
old friend, M. LA PEROUSE, whose son's
mistress has given birth to a boy, BORIS,
whom he loves but has never seen.

Chap. 14. Having found Laura's letter in
the suitcase, Bernard goes to her to offer
his help. Edouard arrives while he is there
and confronts him with the theft of the
suitcase. Bernard says he planned to return
it all along and used it merely as a way to
introduce himself to Edouard. He asks
Edouard for a position as his secretary, and
Edouard finally agrees.

Chaps. 15–17. Passavant has developed
a fondness for Olivier and asks Vincent to
influence his parents to allow Olivier to go
away for the summer with Passavant. Passavant also offers Olivier the position of editor
on a literary review he is financing, but
Olivier is hesitant. Vincent, now under
Lilian's influence, has forced himself to be
cold toward Laura. Lilian is to subsidize
him while he does scientific research.

Chap. 18. Edouard's journal reveals that
he has visited old La Perouse, who is tired
of life and planning to kill himself. The old
man asks Edouard to try to look up his
grandson Boris in Switzerland.

2ND PART—SAAS FEE

Chaps. 1–2. In a letter to Olivier, Bernard reveals that he has gone to Switzerland
with Edouard and Laura. They are staying at
the same place where Boris is being treated
for a nervous illness by a Polish woman
doctor, Mme. SOPHRONISKA.

Chap. 3. Edouard and Bernard are not
getting along particularly well, and Laura
is uncomfortable in the position circumstances have forced her to take. She has no

174

choice but to accept Edouard's help, but is uncomfortable because she was once in love with him and only married her husband Douviers because Edouard always evaded her love. Edouard discusses his proposed novel, *The Counterfeiters,* which will depict the struggle between facts presented by reality and the ideal reality.

Chaps. 4–6. Bernard confesses to Laura his love for her. She is planning to return to her husband, who has written forgiving her for her sins. Bernard realizes that he has been ungrateful to his father, Profitendieu, and expresses hope that he will act honorably in life. Edouard discusses his novel with Madame Sophroniska, and also suggests that Boris go back to Paris to Azais school, which is run by Laura's father. In a letter to Bernard, Olivier reveals he has accepted Passavant's offer and is now traveling with him. Olivier accepted Passavant's offer only because he was jealous of Bernard and Edouard and their close association, but that association is coming to an end because the two are not particularly congenial. Bernard plans to assist at the Azais school as Boris' tutor.

3RD PART—PARIS

Chaps. 1–3. Edouard takes Boris to visit his grandfather, La Perouse. Molinier tells Edouard about a case involving a number of young schoolboys who are mixed up in an organized ring of prostitution. Edouard visits the Azais school and asks M. VEDEL, the headmaster, to give old La Perouse a job there.

Chap. 4. Boris, having a sensitive nature, is terrified of his schoolmates. It is revealed that Olivier's young brother, GEORGE, and several other classmates are involved in the prostitution ring.

Chap. 5. Olivier has returned to Paris with Passavant. He goes to visit Bernard. George has also become involved in passing off counterfeit coins, which are given to him by a classmate, LEON GHERINDANISOL, an unscrupulus young man whose cousin, VICTOR STROUVILHOU, is head of the counterfeiting ring. Olivier is unhappy because Bernard disapproves of his close association with Passavant. Bernard promises to attend Passavant's dinner party, and to bring Edouard if he'll come.

Chaps. 6–8. Mme. Molinier expresses her concern about George's behavior, and reveals to Edouard that she knows her husband has a mistress. Olivier's friend, ARMAND, refuses an invitation to Passavant's dinner, but suggests that Bernard take his sister, SARAH. At dinner, Olivier becomes upset, realizing that both Edouard and Bernard are disappointed in him and his association with Passavant. An argument arises between two of the guests, and Olivier himself gets involved in a scuffle. He almost faints and begs Edouard to take him away from Passavant. After the dinner, Bernard escorts Sarah home, with Armand maneuvering it so that they spend the night together in her room.

Chaps. 9–12. Olivier tries to commit suicide, but is revived by Edouard. Bernard visits him, and decides to resign his position so that Edouard may have Olivier as his secretary. Edouard calls on Passavant to get Olivier's belongings. Passavant has convinced himself he is tired of Olivier anyway.

Chap. 13. Edouard, now that Olivier is with him, is exhilarated and begins work on his book. M. Profitendieu tells Edouard to warn George about getting mixed up in a second scandal by passing counterfeit coins. Actually, Profitendieu wants to talk about Bernard, whom he really loves.

Chaps. 14–15. Bernard passes his baccalaureate examination. He is followed by an "angel" who struggles to set him on the right path in life. Bernard leaves the Azais school because Sarah's sister, RACHEL, has learned about their affair and has requested his departure. His struggle with the angel has matured him.

Chaps. 16–17. La Perouse is getting on poorly at his new duties, being unable to keep discipline in the classroom. He regrets that Boris does not show more affection. Armand has become Passavant's new secretary. In a letter from Armand's brother, it is revealed that Vincent, who went away with Lilian, has gone insane and probably has killed her.

Chaps. 18–20. Boris is teased by his classmates and is talked into joining their organization, their intention being to taunt him. Gherindanisol has stolen a gun from La Perouse, and Boris is to hold it to his temple and pull the trigger. Unknown to all the boys except Gherindanisol, the pistol is loaded. On the appointed day, in the classroom, Boris pulls the trigger and is killed instantly. Gherindanisol maintains his innocence. George is horrified at this monstrous act of his friend, and is reconciled with his mother. The Vedel family is almost in ruins because of the scandal to the school, and La Perouse, of course, is grief-stricken. However, Bernard has been reconciled with his father.

Countess Cathleen

Play by William Butler Yeats, 1865–1939.
Published 1892, produced 1899, in Dublin.

THIS WAS THE FIRST PLAY produced by the Irish National Theatre. In it will be found some of Yeats' greatest writing, though it is not as striking (in the purest, bludgeoning sense of that word) as Yeats' other, shorter Cathleen play, *Cathleen ni Houlihan.* The public of the turn of the century picked *Countess Cathleen* to be Yeats' best-read work and later generations could do worse than follow them.

Scene 1. MARY, a 40-year-old peasant, is grinding meal. She sees the gray hen flutter and wonders what the hen has seen or heard. Her son TEIQUE, a boy of 14, comes in with peat. People are saying that the land is blighted by famine and the dead are walking; Teique says his father believes that God and the Mother of God have dropped asleep, abandoning the world. Mary worries about the safety of her husband, SHEMUS. He comes in from hunting but has brought no dinner because all the animals have died in the drought. There is no food in the house. Countess CATHLEEN, with OONA, her former nurse, and ALEEL, a poet, enter the hut. Cathleen and Oona are looking for an abandoned castle that was Cathleen's childhood home. They found the poet on the edge of the wood, singing about the terrible things he had seen. Cathleen gives Shemus the little money she has left and her empty purse to Teique. She has been giving to beggars all day and she is dying with grief for the land. When Cathleen and her party leave, Shemus decides to conjure up a devil in the form of a white bird. When you dig where the bird scratches you find gold. Mary objects; Shemus hits her and calls on the devils. Mary prays. Two demons dressed as Eastern merchants enter the hut. They sit on a little carpet they have brought with them. They take money out of their purses and arrange it on the carpet. They tell Shemus and Teique that they will pay high prices for people's souls. Shemus and Teique decide to sell their souls. The demons tell them they must become the devil's agents and go to every door where poverty lives, offering gold for souls. Shemus and Teique take a bag of gold and go out into the night. Mary faints. The demons sit by the fire and prepare to praise their master

Scene 2. Approaching Cathleen's castle in the woods, Aleel tells Cathleen the story of MAEVE the queen of fairies, who weeps, when the moon is full, for a mortal lover who died. She weeps because she cannot remember the man's name. Cathleen asks if fairies live forever because they have such short memories. Oona warns that Aleel has not been baptized and is not a Christian. The steward of Cathleen's castle comes and tells her starving men have broken in to steal some cabbages. Cathleen says that for a starving man to take what he needs cannot be a sin. Shemus and Teique enter and tell the group that souls can be sold for money. Cathleen, horrified, offers to buy back the peasants' souls from the merchants, but Shemus and his son are not interested and rush off to tell the world the good news. Cathleen sends Oona and Aleel to bring them back. She commissions her steward to sell the castle and buy cattle and meal to distribute. Aleel is wounded by Shemus when he tries to stop him.

Scene 3. In the hall of Cathleen's great

Countess Cathleen agrees to sell her soul for her people

house Aleel tells Cathleen he has been warned in a dream, by something like an angel, that Cathleen must go to the hills until the trouble has passed. Cathleen refuses to go because Aleel's warning came from a pagan god. Aleel holds out his arms to the countess in love, but she tells him she can love only in heaven and now must save her people. She sends him away. The demons, still disguised as merchants, come to tell Cathleen that her cattle are dead and the wheat has dried up (the cattle and wheat for which she traded her castle). They rob her treasury but suggest that she can sell her soul for enough money to feed all the starving. She sends the peasants out to hunt for the stolen treasure and instructs everyone to pray to God.

Scene 4. The peasants in the woods are talking about the beauty of gold; how it shines and what it can buy. The demon merchants follow them silently. Aleel comes by singing of his sad love that God has willed should not be fulfilled.

Scene 5. The demons talk in Shemus's house. Mary is dead. The demons rejoice in their lies to Cathleen; the food is, in truth, only three days away. The peasants enter and begin to sell their souls. The more virtuous get a higher price. Aleel offers his soul to the demons for nothing. He is tired of his life and his love for Countess Cathleen haunts him. But the demons have no power to take Aleel's soul because it belongs to Cathleen. They offer a thousand crowns to any old woman who was always ugly. When a peasant steps forward to claim the money, they give it to her and she says "God bless you." Then she screams in pain. The demons explain that the name of God is like a fire to all damned souls. Countess Cathleen enters and offers the demons her soul in return for 500,000 crowns and the release of the souls already purchased. She wants the money to feed the people.

The demons agree to the price and ask her to sign a contract. They offer her a quill made from the feather of the cock that crowed when Peter denied Christ. As she is about to sign, Aleel rushes in and takes the pen away. In a vision he has seen her grain arrive safely. But Shemus drags Aleel

away and Cathleen signs. She goes to distribute the money. Aleel and Ooona pray for Cathleen. As they kneel, peasants enter carrying Cathleen. There is a great storm outside the house. Cathleen dies and Aleel begs to die with her. He curses Time, Fate, and Change. Lightning is followed by thunder and Aleel says he can see the angels fighting the demons. The peasants look up and see a band of armed angels in battle formation, looking downward. The peasants lie prostrate on the ground. An angel tells Aleel that Cathleen has been taken into heaven and kissed by the Mother of God: The Light of Lights looks always on the motive, not the deed. Oona tells the angel she is weary of the world and wants to join Cathleen.

The Count of Monte Cristo

Novel by Alexandre Dumas, 1803–1870.
Published 1844. (Ban., F1570)

THIS IS PRIME DUMAS, matched only by *The Three Musketeers,* exceeded by nothing. Millions of boys have loved it and it is recommended to millions of others. It is just as good reading as any mystery, and better than most, for bedtime reading. None of the numerous translations is a work of art, but neither was the original. The story is of a man who was wronged, sought revenge, and achieved it. The character of the Count of Monte Cristo has made series for both movies and television.

Chaps. 1–10. Early in 1815 the ship *Pharaon* arrives in Marseilles, the captain having died enroute from Smyrna. The owner of the ship, M. MORREL, wants to make the mate, EDMOND DANTÈS, the new captain. The supercargo of the ship, DANGLARS, plots against Dantès. Danglars is aided by FERNAND, the rejected

suitor of Dantès' sweetheart MERCÉDÈS. The plot is to accuse Edmond of bearing a letter from Napoleon in Elba to the Bonapartist Committee in Paris. Danglars writes an anonymous letter with his left hand and Fernand has it delivered to the deputy procurer (prosecuting attorney) of the king, VILLEFORT. Dantès is placed under arrest and Villefort discovers that Dantès is innocent; but Dantès did bring from Elba a letter that would incriminate Villefort's father, NOIRTIER, and ruin Villefort's career. Therefore Villefort has Dantès secretly escorted to the prison of the Chateau d'If, where he is thrown into a dungeon. Villefort visits the Marquis DE ST. MERAN, to whose daughter he is betrothed, in Marseilles, and there finds high approval of what he has done. Then he has an audience in Paris with Louis XVIII, who tells him he will be rewarded for having prevented the Bonapartist plot.

Chaps. 11–20. Noirtier tells his son that Napoleon is on his way to Paris, having escaped from Elba. Napoleon does arrive to reign for his Hundred Days. The shipowner, Morrel, intercedes with Villefort to have Dantès released. Villefort promises, now that Napoleon is back in power, but does nothing. An inspector visits Edmond in the dungeon and promises to review his case, but he finds a notation on the register, added by Villefort after Napoleon's defeat at Waterloo, accusing Dantès of being a violent Bonapartist. Years pass. Edmond thinks of himself only as Number 34. He resolves to starve himself to death, but one night he hears the sound of digging and realizes that another prisoner is trying to escape. A few days later, after Edmond has also begun to work for his escape with a crude pick made from the handle of a saucepan, the floor under him moves and the other prisoner, Number 27, appears out of a subterranean passageway. He is the Abbé FARIA, imprisoned on political grounds for having desired the unification of Italy. He has misjudged his way in his underground escape. By means of the passage dug by the Abbé, the two visit each other constantly and Faria gives Edmond a liberal education, teaching him languages, history, and mathematics. He tells Edmond of a vast treasure, worth 13,000,000 francs, hidden on the island of Monte Cristo by the great Spada family. The two plan to escape together, but Faria is stricken with a fatal illness. Edmond conceives a new method of escape: He substitutes himself in the Abbé's burial sack, supposing he will be buried in the prison cemetery and then can dig his way out of the grave with a knife. Instead he is thrown into the sea with a 36-pound weight attached to his feet. He cuts his way loose with his knife and swims to the deserted island of Tiboulen.

Chaps. 21–30. On Tiboulen Dantés watches a shipwreck during a terrible storm. He tries to rescue a sailor but only retrieves his red cap. Then, pretending that he is a member of the ill-fated crew, he intercepts a passing ship, *The Young Amelia.* It is manned by a gang of smugglers and he becomes one of them. He finds himself quite unrecognizable after his 14 years of imprisonment. In the course of avoiding customs men the smugglers' boat puts in at the island of Monte Cristo. Dantès pretends to have hurt himself in a fall and is left alone by the smugglers for six days. During this time he finds the secret grotto where Spada secreted his great treasure, hidden by undergrowth and a huge rock, which he dislodges with a charge of powder. He takes some jewels with him and converts them into money in Marseilles. There he finds that his father has died and Mercédès has disappeared. With his new wealth he buys the house his father lived in and he builds a fast yacht with secret compartments to hold the immense treasure. Dantes disguises himself as the Abbé BUSONI and visits the drunken tailor CADEROUSSE, who has become a measly innkeeper. As the abbé, he bribes Caderousse with a diamond worth 50,000 francs, which he says was entrusted to him by the dying Dantès to divide among his true friends. In return for the jewel, Caderousse tells him that Villefort has earned fame and fortune by his turncoat tactics; that Danglars is a rich banker; and that Fernand has won a title, Count DE MORCERF, and acquired great wealth. Fernand married Mercédès, who has borne him a son, ALBERT. Edmond also hears that M. Morrel, who befriended Edmond's starving father before he died, is on the verge of bankruptcy. Impersonating an English broker, Dantès saves Morrel from immediate ruin. Then, just as Morrel is about to commit suicide because the *Pharaon* is lost at sea, Edmond turns over a large sum of money to Morrel's daughter and saves him from ruin. He even has a replica of the *Pharaon* sail into Marseilles harbor.

Chaps. 31–40. In 1838 Edmond has taken the name COUNT OF MONTE CRISTO from his island, which he has bought. He also calls himself "Sinbad the Sailor," the name he took when he gave money to Morrel's daughter. He is visited on his island redoubt by a priest, FRANZ, a close friend of Albert, the son of Mercedes. The priest is overwhelmed by the magnificence of the appointments in the grotto and the loyal service of the Nubian servant, ALI. Franz joins Albert in a series of adventures in Italy and in a brush with Roman bandits, from which Dantès extricates them. In the meantime the "Count of Monte Cristo" has gone to Paris, where he has caused a sensation with his great wealth, his background and learning, and his mysterious woman companion, HAIDÉE. Edmond boasts that she is no mere mistress but that he bought her outright during his travels in the Near East. All the time he is slowly plotting revenge on the man who caused his imprisonment.

Chaps. 41–50. As Count of Monte Cristo, Edmond is introduced to his former fiancée, Mercédès, who thanks him for rescuing

Albert from the bandits. Edmond wins the confidence of Danglars, by posing as a wealthy broker connected with a British firm. He also discovers that Villefort's wife dabbles in poisons and that she covets the fortune of her stepdaughter, VALENTINE, who loves M. Morrel's son, MAXIMILIAN. (Valentine's ambitious father insists that she marry Baron Franz d'Epinay. Edmond introduces to Paris society the rich young Count ANDREA CAVALCANTI and Villefort accepts him in place of d'Epinay as Valen-

Edmond disguised as Busoni

tine's suitor.) Morrel has died and his children are living comfortably but in simple style in Paris. The little ex-tailor, Caderousse, tries to rob Dantès and is shot to death by his accomplice BENEDETTO, with whom he once served time in prison. (Benedetto is actually the illegitimate son of Villefort and Mme. Danglars. These two had thought they had killed the boy as an infant, but Dantès found their guilty secret out and also found the boy alive and had him pose as Count Cavalcanti.)

Chaps. 51–75. The count trains Mme. Villefort in the use of poisons, having learned chemistry from the Abbé Faria in prison. She finally stoops to poisoning her stepdaughter Valentine, but Edmond sees

to it that the poison is merely a sleeping potion. His revenge on Villefort is consummated when Villefort discovers the crimes of his wife and the true identity of Benedetto. Villefort goes mad, just after discovering that Dantès is still alive in the person of the Count of Monte Cristo.

Chaps. 75–90. Edmond discovers that Fernand gained most of his wealth in Greece by betraying ALI PASHA during the revolution there in 1823. He persuades Danglars to send to Greece to confirm this report and it is found to be true. In the ensuing exposé, Albert believes that his father has been unjustly accused and challenges the Count of Monte Cristo to a duel. Haidée, however, reveals herself as the daughter of Ali Pasha and confronts Fernand with proof.

Edmond wishes to make his revenge complete by killing the son of Fernand, but Mercédès, who has discovered he is Edmond Dantès, begs him not to kill the boy. At the scene of the duel Albert, who has learned the truth from his mother, publicly denounces his father and declares that his ruin by the count was amply justified. Mercédès and Albert leave Paris and Fernand kills himself with a pistol. Danglars, through the financial manipulations of the Count of Monte Cristo, is brought to bankruptcy; his daughter EUGÉNIE runs off to seek her fortune; and Danglars is deserted by his wife.

Chaps. 91–107. Monte Cristo, having disposed of all the enemies who stole 14 years of his life, now dedicates himself to the happiness of the son of his one benefactor, Maximilian Morrel. He reunites the young man with his sweetheart Valentine, who, as noted above, was not fatally poisoned by Mme. Villefort but merely drugged. The two lovers meet on the island of Monte Cristo and there, in a noble gesture, Edmond gives them what is left of the huge Spada fortune, presumably to live happily ever after. Edmond bids them adieu and sails away in his yacht with Haidée. In the postscript of a letter to Morrel he writes, "There is neither happiness nor misery in the world; there is only the comparison of one state with another—nothing more. We must have felt what it is to die, Morrel, that we may appreciate the enjoyment of living."

Fernand, ruined, kills himself with a pistol

The Country of the Pointed Firs

Novel by Sarah Orne Jewett, 1849–1909.
Published 1896.

PERHAPS, STRICTLY SPEAKING, this book is not a novel. It is a series of related stories about the same characters—an approach to writing that once was popular and has lost its popularity. Such series were often more closely knit than many books called novels. This is one of Sarah Orne Jewett's two great story-sequences (the other is *Deephaven*) in which she examines down-east New Englanders through the eyes of a furriner who loves them, and this is the better of the two, the one book by Miss Jewett to read if only one of her books is to be read.

Chaps. 1–4. In Dunnet Landing on the coast of Maine, a woman writer boards with ALMIRA TODD (the widowed Mrs. Nathan Todd), seeking solitude for some writing she wants to finish during the summer. Mrs. Todd deals in herbs, both wild and cultivated. While she is in the woods and fields gathering them, the boarder obligingly takes care of customers who drop in, serving them the spruce beer for which Mrs. Todd is famous. At the end of July, the writer realizes she must be alone to write. She rents the schoolhouse at 50 cents a week.

Chaps. 5–7. The boarder receives a visit from Captain LITTLEPAGE, an octagenarian and retired sea captain. He is a man of breeding and education, extremely well versed in classic English poetry. He tells the boarder a strange story: In his seagoing days he was shipwrecked on a small island in the Arctic on which there was a Moravian mission. Its only other white inhabitant was a Scotsman named GAVETT, who had been shipwrecked on an island farther north than any white man had gone before. This island, Gavett declared, was peopled exclusively by ghosts, and he was convinced that it was a stopping place for souls on their way from this world to the next. The story stops as the old man's mind apparently wanders to something else, and the boarder never learns of his conclusions.

Chaps. 8–11. Mrs. Todd's mother, Mrs. BLACKETT, is still living, at the age of 86, and keeps house for her unmarried son, WILLIAM, on Green Island, a short distance from the mainland. The boarder and Mrs. Todd visit Mrs. Blackett. A boy helps with the rowing. On the way, Mrs. Todd catches a large haddock to take along. Old Mrs. Blackett is brisk, wiry, and full of life. William is not at home, and the boarder is told that he is so painfully shy that he avoids meeting people. However, when the boarder

178

goes for a walk, she meets William and finds him most pleasant. Later in the day Mrs. Todd and the boarder go out to gather herbs and Mrs. Todd points out the spot where her husband's ship went down. She had not loved him as he loved her, but he died before he found out that her heart had been given to another man long before she married him. The boarder gathers that the man was of much higher social station than that of Mrs. Todd and his family opposed the match. Back at the cottage, William and Mrs. Blackett sing for the boarder. Their voices are unusually fine.

Chaps. 12–14. Mrs Susan FOSDICK comes to visit Mrs. Todd and they reminisce. Mrs. Fosdick has traveled widely and at one time even went to sea with her parents and brothers and sisters. The boarder hears the story of JOANNA TODD, a cousin of Nathan Todd. Joanna was a woman disappointed in love who left her home on the mainland and went to live alone on a tiny island called "Shell-heap," from the heap of Indian shells that could still be seen there. No one thought that she would stick it out through winter, but Joanna never returned to the mainland. Fishing boats, and boats of townspeople who were sorry for the lonely woman, often left packages of useful articles for her. Once Mrs. Todd took the minister to persuade Joanna to come back, but the call was a failure. Joanna died on the island and at her own request was buried there.

The expert knitter

Chaps. 15–19. Mrs. Blackett was a Bowden by birth, and at the family reunion she is the honored guest, because of her age. The boarder hears much of the Bowden family, which is of French Huguenot extraction. Apparently almost everyone in the vicinity is related either directly or by marriage with a Bowden. William does not attend.

Chap. 20. The boarder meets ELIJAH

TILLEY, a very old fisherman who has been widowed for eight years. He has never accepted the loss of "poor dear" (his late wife) and tries to keep his house exactly as she loved it. He lives by himself and is a meticulous housekeeper. All the while the boarder is talking with him, he is expertly knitting on a blue sock. He explains that during the winter, when it is too cold to go fishing, he stays at home and knits socks. The Dunnet sock has become quite famous, even as far down as Boston. Many of the villagers knit in the winter.

Chap. 21. To the boarder's surprise, she is invited to go trout-fishing with William. Delighted, she accepts, and they set off in the wagon for the trout stream. On the way they stop at a farmhouse, where William leaves a package of dried fish on the doorstep. He says nothing, no one comes to the door, no one greets him—but when the boarder looks back at a turn in the road a moment later, the package has disappeared. Apparently William knows of some need in this house, and quietly helps out occasionally. At the trout stream William is quiet, as usual, and acutely aware of the small animals and birds. He occasionally gestures in the direction of a small owl or wood duck. The boarder finds that there is little need for verbal communication between them. Each seems to understand the other's unspoken thoughts. There are no trout that day and William suggests that they look in on Mrs. THANKFUL HIGHT, who is confined to a wheelchair and cared for by her daughter, ESTHER. Another gift of dried fish is made at the Hight farmhouse. William goes out to seek Esther. She is a shepherdess with a most successful flock of sheep that well supports herself and her mother. The boarder remains in the farmhouse talking to old Mrs. Hight, who at first is somewhat querulous but mellows as she is brought up to date on the news and gossip of the town. William and Esther return and the boarder observes that they are in love—yet apparently content to see each other only about once a year, fully aware that Esther cannot neglect her mother or the sheep.

Chap. 22. Mrs. Todd goes out one day, and for some strange reason the boarder feels unfairly deserted. It is unlike Mrs. Todd to go anywhere without announcing her route, destination, purpose, and probable time of return. When she comes home this time, she seems mysteriously pleased with herself. The boarder learns that Almira has just paid a visit to the "Queen's Twin." This is an old woman who lives alone, Mrs. ABBY MARTIN, widow of Albert. She was born on the same day and at the same hour as Queen Victoria. Mrs. Todd is especially pleased because Mrs. Martin has consented to receive Almira and the boarder day after tomorrow. The boarder sheepishly realizes that this somehow seems like a royal audience. When they reach the old woman's house, the feeling of a formal encounter with majesty lingers. Mrs. Martin is beautiful, in spite of her age, and charmingly gracious. She has lived in the dream of being the twin of Queen Victoria, in spirit if not in fact, for so many years that the queen seems very close to her. One time, about 40 years before, Mrs. Martin visited London when the queen was visible on a state occasion, and the wonder of seeing Victoria is still fresh and beautiful in the old woman's mind. Her husband was Albert, just like Victoria's, and her children were born at the same times as Victoria's. She even gave them the same names. Her one disappointment was in failing to have a little girl at the last, as Victoria did, to stay at home and keep her company, like Victoria's last daughter. The boarder leaves after tea with a feeling of tenderness and sympathy for Mrs. Martin.

Chap. 23. The boarder returns to the city but can scarcely wait for the next summer and her return to Dunnet's Landing. At last it is May and she once again enters Mrs. Todd's little house. The news is startling, and quickly told. The Lord has seen fit to take old Mrs. Hight, as Almira puts it, and now after forty years of annual courting disguised as trout-fishing expeditions William can marry Esther. The happy couple are married and stop at the cottage to greet everyone and enjoy the cakes and wine that Almira has provided. William seems to be in complete control of his shyness and speaks to everyone until at last it is time to take his bride to the boat for Green Island. The boarder thinks no young girl could look more radiant than Esther. Almira and the boarder say nothing to each other on the walk back from the dock to the cottage, but silently they hold each other's hands all the way.

The Courtship of Miles Standish

Poem by Henry Wadsworth Longfellow, 1807–1882.
Published 1858.

LONGFELLOW IS NO LONGER so admired as he was in the last century, and even if he were, this poem would not deserve to be among his most admired efforts; but it is a standard classic in American literature and for another century or so, at least, it must continue to be read and known. John Alden and Priscilla Mullins have even greater distinction than was endowed upon them by Longfellow's poem. They are said to have more known descendants than any other couple of history, some millions in all. Longfellow was one of them.

1–2. During the early days of Puritan settlement in Plymouth Colony, Massachusetts, Captain MILES STANDISH, a stern and rugged military leader of the small colony, had a close friend named JOHN ALDEN. Alden was the opposite of Standish, for he was bookish, sensitive, and scholarly. Both men were secretly in love with a young orphan named PRISCILLA MULLINS, who had recently arrived from England. One night while they were seated together in Standish's house, the Captain expressed his favorite moral sentiment: "You must do it yourself, you must not leave it to others!" Then, surprisingly, he violated this doctrine by asking Alden to court the young girl on his behalf. Standish was lonely because his wife Rose had been the first person to die after leaving the *Mayflower*. Alden was dismayed by Standish's request and tried to shirk it, but Standish implored him because he knew that John was an eloquent speaker. At last, seeing no way out, Alden consented to take on the strange mission.

3. At the house where Priscilla was living, Alden gave her a bouquet of flowers, finding himself speechless because of her beauty and his desire. Then in a halting way he made his friend's offer of marriage. Priscilla replied: "Why does he not come himself, and take the trouble to wed me?" Alden replied that the Captain was too busy—a fatal remark. Priscilla brushed aside Standish's proposal; but looking at Alden's face she could see that the scholar loved her just as the soldier did. She then said, "Why don't you speak for yourself, John?"

4. Alden went raging, confused and hurt, from the house. His deep Puritan sense of guilt was aroused for he felt that he had undermined his best friend and had soiled himself by embarking on such a dubious mission. At last he found the strength to return to Standish and tell him the whole affair. Standish erupted in a fit of rage, accusing Alden of treachery, and thus ended their friendship. He strode to the Town Council, where the elders were debating conciliatory peace with nearby savages, and proclaimed that war was the only means of ending their threat.

5–6. Standish departed with the friendly Indian guide HOBOMOK and a small army to fight the Indians. The *Mayflower* left the harbor at Plymouth, returning to England.

Alden and Priscilla watched its sails disappear on the horizon, knowing they were imprisoned in the lonely, dangerous colony. Priscilla walked over to John and apologized for her words, saying that she had grown tired of the silent rôle imposed upon women. She said that Standish was fearsome to her and she much preferred the quiet, gentle ways of Alden. From that time, the two lovers resolved to be close friends.

7–8. Standish, burning with jealousy, and his men hacked their way through the dense forests of New England. They met astonishing success, for Standish killed the Pecksuot brave WATTAWAMAT. The Indians fled with their bows and arrows, which were no match for the white man's guns. Back at Plymouth, the whole colony was overjoyed at the news of Standish's conquests. Then suddenly a messenger arrived saying that the brave Captain had been killed in ambush by a poison arrow. Fear swept over the tiny community, but two people stood together unafraid. For months John Alden had gone regularly to Priscilla's house. He had sat and watched her weaving cloth on her spinning wheel. Alden had already built his own house and thus was prepared to ask Priscilla to marry him. When at last he worked up the courage, Priscilla readily consented.

9. The day of the marriage was one of great blessing to the community. The ceremony was simple and brief, and when John and Priscilla stood as man and wife, the threatening specter of Captain Standish seemed to have receded completely. Suddenly into the midst of the celebration strode the Captain, like a ghost returning to haunt those who had wronged him. At first Priscilla and John were amazed at the sight, but Standish quickly made his purpose known. Taking John's hand he begged forgiveness for his cruelty, saying that he had contradicted his prime maxim in asking his friend to undertake a task that should have been his own. Thus Plymouth had double reason to rejoice. Their leader had returned after all had thought him dead, and the two lovers were inseparably united. The poem closes with a description of John leading his wife, on a snow-white palfrey to their new home, with the blessing of their friend Miles Standish.

John leading Priscilla

Cousin Bette

> Novel by Honoré de Balzac, 1799–1850.
> Published 1847.
>
> LA COUSINE BETTE is always ranked among the best of the network of novels that make up Balzac's vast "Human Comedy." Some place it first, some put it on a par or almost with *Père Goriot*. In this novel Balzac's primary characters are unsympathetic ones, a condition that often proves the writer's skill more than it pleases the reader.

Chaps. 1–3. Monsieur MARNEFFE visits the office of a capable official of state, Baron HULOT D'EURY. Marneffe wants a job as chief of his Bureau. He threatens to use a political influence inimical to the baron if he is not raised immediately. The baron is afraid of Marneffe's power. He is also in love with Marneffe's wife VALERIE, despite his 72 years. Valerie is a beautiful but evil woman who has attracted and ruined many men of talent and fortune. The baron receives in his office a letter from Valerie describing the jealous rage of her husband when he learned of their relationship. She says she must never receive him again in her home and suggests that they run away together. She reminds the baron that she is expecting his child and asks him for money. He writes her a letter saying that he adores her and they will run away together and start a new life. He decides not to give Marneffe the promotion, depending upon the continued patronage of the Prince DE WEISSEMBOURG to protect his own position. He has been in the ministry for many years, despite the enemies he has gathered, due to the protection of the Prince, who has taken an interest in the Hulot family because he and Hulot's older brother were generals together in Napoleon's army and share a code of honor and a style of life. On leaving the office the baron tries to see Valerie but Marneffe threatens him with a pistol and he is forced to leave. Valerie waves to him from the window and he determines to find a way to see her.

Chap. 4. Lisbeth (Cousin BETTE) is the old-maid sister of ADELINE, the Baron's beautiful and dignified wife. The old maid has been jealous of her sister's title and money and hates the whole family for their good fortune. She tries to encourage the Baron's infidelities and to destroy the happiness of the family in every possible way. At this time Cousin Bette is planning to become the bride of Baron Hulot's elder brother, who is a MARQUIS. She has promised to support Hulot's family with her money if the Baron and his wife will encourage the marquis to marry her; but actually she intends to inherit the marquis's money and to watch her sister and her sister's family starve, in revenge for all the years she has been the poor relation. When the baron goes home he finds his wife upset at his infidelities, but because she so loves her errant husband she is forgiving. She tells her children that a man's passion for women is not like the other vices. It will come to an end with age. In this she is wrong, because the baron's lust for young beauties is incurable. The baron's son VICTORIN and his wife CELESTINE have come for dinner. Celestine's father, Monsieur CREVEL, was once in love with Adeline, but her insistent virtue made a liason impossible. Now he is in love with Valerie and is courting her with expensive gifts. Crevel is the Mayor of Paris and a very wealthy man. HORTENSE and her child are also part of the dinner party. Hortense is the daughter of the baron and Adeline. She is married to Count STEINBOCK, an artist of promise. He has deserted her to conduct, in total freedom, his romance with Valerie. Cousin Bette has become Valerie's best friend and confidante, partly out of admiration of the beautiful woman's charms and partly because of her destructive effects on the Baron Hulot's household. At dinner the baron is contrite and promises fidelity to his wife, who wonders why her husband admires the seductive charms of other women, when she herself is still beautiful and can give him love and forgiveness. But the baron seeks the excitement of the unvirtuous woman. After a short period of chastity he arranges, with Cousin Bette's help, to meet Valerie at a beautiful little house that has been given to her, for the purpose of their own illicit meetings, by Crevel. He seeks Valerie often and she encourages him to lose his heart to her completely. One evening Valerie postpones their meeting to a later hour, pretending her husband is ill; but as they lie sleeping in the early hours of the morning, Marneffe bursts into the room accompanied by two police officers. Valerie acts as if she is going mad with shame while Marneffe threatens to take out a warrant against the baron if his promotion is not secured and if the baron does not give him 2,000 francs. The baron gives him the money, which takes all of the family's savings and leaves the baron only the income of his job in the ministry. The following day Hulot visits his patron, the Prince de Weissembourg, and secures Marneffe's appointment. The Prince warns the baron that the appointment of Marneffe will further jeopardize Hulot's position in the ministry, because it is a bad appointment and will indicate a lack of competency on Hulot's part. It will also make it impossible for the baron ever to become a deputy chief. The baron learns through the police officer that Valerie was in league with her husband and established the late meeting in order to trap him and obtain the money. The baron is destroyed by this revelation because he really believed that Valerie loved him. She had been so tender to him and had never, except in her letters to him at the ministry, asked for money. Cousin Bette learns what has happened and is delighted because she is about to triumph over the family she despises. Her marriage banns with the marquis are posted.

Chap. 5. A letter arrives from Algiers from Adeline's uncle JACOB, who has been appointed head of a French commissary by Hulot. He and Hulot have been stealing funds from the government, and the scandal is about to break open. They will both be discovered if 2,000 francs are not sent immediately to cover the discrepancy. The baron becomes desperate at this news, as he has given the 2,000 francs to Valerie. He falls, as if dead, on the couch. Adeline finds him staring vacantly at the floor. She reads the letter. She sees there is no purpose in reproaching her husband and summons all of her strength to try to help him. First she tries to obtain the money by offering herself to Crevel, but he no longer wants her; he is too much in love with Valerie. When Adeline fails as a seductress she falls at Crevel's feet, weeping, and he becomes compassionate and offers to give her the money. Unfortunately, on his way to the bank he stops to see Valerie and she will not allow him to give the money to Adeline, out of meanness and avarice.

Chap. 6. Meanwhile the scandal in Algiers has broken and the Prince has received a letter informing him that Adeline's uncle is in jail. The baron is summoned to the Prince's chambers and the Prince withdraws his patronage, dismissing Hulot from the ministry. The baron's brother, the marquis, bursts into the meeting. He is very distraught and offers to replace the 2,000 francs, but it is too late to hide the theft. The Prince regrets the shame that has come to the marquis, his old comrade-in-arms. He asks that the marquis take care of the family and tells Hulot he never wants to see him again, because he is a coward. He instructs Hulot to blot himself out of the memory of the ministry and disappear from the world. The Prince tries to extract the 2,000 francs from Marneffe, but that shameless gentleman explains that his wife has spent all the money giving parties every night. Marneffe is demoted to a government post in Algeria. The marquis goes home in his carriage and refuses to sit next to his brother. He dies from shame three days later. Uncle Jacob dies in jail and the baron, in despair over what he has done to his family, despite the loving pardon by his wife, runs away from his home. Cousin Bette is left without money or a title by the death of the marquis. Her hatred for the family increases. The Prince, finding that he can cover the scandal without returning the money to the commissary in Algiers, gives the 2,000 francs, returned to the government by the marquis, to Hulot's son Victorin. Victorin pays off the mortgage on his house and establishes his position as a lawyer. He moves his mother, his sister and his sister's child, along with Cousin Bette, into his house. Adeline falls ill and from this time on suffers from constant trembling fits. But with the tender nursing of her family she is returned to health. The baron runs to a former lover of his, the courtesan and singer JOSEPHA. She finds a young girl to live with him and buys the pair an embroidery shop, which he operates under the assumed name of PETER THOUL. Cousin Bette traces the baron and gloats over her knowledge of his hiding place. Meanwhile Marneffe becomes ill and dies, and Crevel plans to marry Valerie. This distresses Victorin and his wife, both because they detest the lady who ruined the baron and because they do not want Crevel's fortune to fall into other hands. In spite of their opposition and Adeline's entreaties, Valerie becomes Mme. Crevel. This also distresses Count Steinbock, but Valerie promises him that their affair will go on after her new marriage and he is mollified. Valerie has actually fallen in love with Steinbock; it is her first real passion and she suffers as the baron suffered in loving her.

Chap. 7. The singer Josepha comes to visit Adeline and tells her that the baron is safe and well. She is a kind, good woman bringing comfort to the forsaken wife. A ragged, hideous old woman, Madame SAINT-ESTEVE, visits Victorin and asks for a huge sum of money to murder Valerie. At first Victorin refuses, as he is not a murderer, but he promises he will give the gold to the first beggar who comes after Valerie's death to ask alms for a project of God's; then he agrees, but tries to find the old woman's identity. By checking with the police he discovers that she is the leader of a group of Paris criminals. Shortly after Victorin's interview with the old woman, Valerie and Crevel come down with a terrifying illness. They lose their skin and their nails and develop running sores. The doctors believe it to be a tropical disease or an unknown form of poisoning. Valerie becomes hideous and, after a week of agony, dies. Crevel follows two days later. The inheritance goes to Victorin and his wife and children, and the Hulot family is restored to great fortune. A beggar comes to Victorin asking money for a missionary development and he gives him the agreed-upon amount.

Chap. 8. Adeline joins a Catholic organization that proselytizes among the poor, attempting to effect marriages among those couples who are living together in sin. The baron has been abandoned by the young girl brought to him by Josepha, but he has found another girl, ATALA JUDIC, who is 15 years old and very happy to live with the kind old gentleman. Adeline is told about Atala by a neighbor and takes to the girl. She finds her innocent and willing to marry. She decides to visit the elderly man (not knowing he is her husband) and convince him to marry the girl. She finds the baron, living in poor surroundings. After recovering from her initial shock she persuades him to return home. He becomes the baron once more, the dignified head of his family. Steinbock comes back to Hortense. Cousin Bette, who grieved over the restored happi-

ness of the family, falls ill and dies, keeping the secret of her hate even on her deathbed. The family lives in harmony for some time, but the baron develops a passion for a peasant scullery maid. One night Adeline wakes up, finds him gone, and discovers him in the attic with the maid, promising marriage to the young girl. Adeline succumbs to grief and dies. The unrepentant baron moves away from his family and marries the vulgar girl, making her a baroness.

The baron with the maid

Cranford

Novel by Elizabeth Cleghorn Gaskell, 1810–1865.
Published 1853.

CRANFORD IS A CLASSIC, by Mark Twain's definition a book you wish you had read. It was not written as a unified novel but as a series of stories about the same or related characters. When collected, these stories proved to have the required length to make them a novel. In the late 1800s no maiden lady or dowager in comfortable circumstances was without *Cranford* on her bookshelves. For him who dares read it despite these indisputable facts a pleasant surprise is in store. He will enjoy it.

Chaps. 1–2. The narrator, who never names herself, is a woman who lives near the sleepy town of Cranford and frequently goes there to visit her old friend Miss MATILDA (MATTY) JENKYNS, daughter of the Cranford rector (now dead). The narrator warns the reader that Cranford is dominated

by willful old women and seldom does a man dare challenge their community rule. The most virtuous and the strongest woman of Cranford is Matty, who binds various factions together. She and her older sister DEBORAH, who has since died, long presided over the taste and morals of Cranford; now Matty does so alone. There has been one challenge, from a retired Captain BROWN and his daughters, Miss Brown and Miss JESSIE. Captain Brown became memorable by his participation in the case of Miss BETSY BARKER'S cow. Miss Betsy Barker loved the cow as a daughter. The cow fell into a lime-pit and while Capt. Brown recommended its destruction, he did tell Miss Betsy she could save it by outfitting it in flannel drawers and flannel waistcoat, and accordingly Cranford was treated to the sight of a cow dressed in flannel. Miss Jenkyns (Deborah) had a feud with Capt. Brown over the relative merits of Dr. Samuel Johnson (whose *Rasselas* was held up as an ideal by Miss Jenkyns), and Dickens (whose *Pickwick Papers* Capt. Brown preferred). Then Capt. Brown was killed by a train while he was reading *Pickwick Papers*. Miss Jenkyns relented, and when Miss Brown died shortly after her father Miss Jenkyns took the 18-year-old Miss Jessie into her house and fostered her romance with and marriage to Major GORDON. After that Miss Jenkyns died and Matty succeeded to the position and the tidy family fortune.

Chaps. 3–4. The author returns to Cranford after Deborah's death and visits both Matty and their mutual friend, Miss POLE. While walking in the street one day, Matty meets one of Miss Pole's cousins, Mr. HOLBROOK, who invites the three ladies to a tea at his house. During the course of this get-together the author realizes that Matty once was in love with Mr. Holbrook and the whole experience is very painful to her now. Before the ladies leave, they hear with mixed emotions that Mr. Holbrook intends to go to Paris; and when he dies soon after, they are sure that it is because he had "gone to that wicked Paris." Matty's somewhat solitary home life is meanwhile enlivened by an affair between her maid MARTHA and a man named JEM HEARN. Matty, with noble sentiments, gives her approval to the match.

Chaps. 5–6. On another visit to Cranford the author learns that Matty once had a brother named PETER, who ran away from home at an early age after his father beat him for wearing his mother's clothes. Matty reads aloud some old letters that tell of those early years. Then she reads the only letter from Peter himself, wishing the family luck from his new home in India. Matty believes that her brother is dead "among the heathens" and weeps.

Chaps. 7–8. The world of Cranford is excited by the arrival of some new faces of importance. A former maid, Miss BARKER, has risen far in the world of fashion and makes a determined effort to change Matty's cap style. She succeeds, but only after long

A strange gentleman is seen on the streets of Cranford

effort. Miss Barker invites all her former social betters to a party, including the aristocratic Mrs. JAMIESON, the lonely widow Mrs. FORRESTER, and Mrs. FITZADAM, whom Mrs. Jamieson detests and studiously ignores. The women are thrown into a state of confusion by Mrs. Jamieson's announcement soon after that her sister-in-law, Lady GLENMIRE, is coming to reside in the town. The resentful Mrs. Jamieson forbids everyone to attend Lady Glenmire's receptions, and thus further tension is created. The women are too possessed by curiosity to pass up the invitation, however, and soon Lady Glenmire is more respected (for her down-to-earth ways) than Mrs. Jamieson herself.

Chaps. 9–11. Cranford is delighted by the sudden appearance of an Italian magician, Signor BRUNONI—or, as the town later learns through his wife, SAM BROWN. At first Mr. Brunoni's appearance is greeted with enthusiasm, but Miss Pole soon dispels the man's glamor by reading up on tricks and showing others how they are performed. Mr. Brunoni falls ill and is placed under Dr. HOGGINS' care. The author chats with Brown's disgruntled wife and learns that they spent a long time in India, where they met a certain mogul named Aga JENKYNS.

The author, convinced that the Aga is Peter, Matty's long lost brother, dispatches a letter in haste to the Aga's palace. In the meantime the whole town is thrown into a state of shock by testimonies concerning ghosts. After a time everyone is convinced that the widow Mrs. Forrester is responsible for most of these apparitions. The incident drives Mrs. Jamieson away from the town for a time, and during that time her hated sister-in-law Lady Glenmire suddenly announces her engagement to the commoner, Dr. Hoggins. The incident only strengthens Mrs. Jamieson's resentment toward Lady Glenmire.

Chaps. 12–16. The greatest crisis of Cranford breaks suddenly when Matty Jenkyns learns that her bank has failed and she is penniless. Forced to sell her possessions and abandon her proud family home, she retires with her maid Martha and Jem into a small apartment. The ladies of Cranford are so touched by this sudden change of fortune that they decide to contribute funds for Matty's support, thanks to the leadership of Miss Pole. The author meanwhile waits expectantly for a reply from India, but none arrives. At last the author is surprised to see a strange gentleman walking the streets of Cranford, searching for the Jenkyns residence. She greets him and learns that he is the missing Peter. A joyful reunion takes place and Peter explains how he passed from a life of obscurity into a life of courage, wisdom and wealth "among the heathens." Besides restoring Matty to her rightful place in society, Peter brings peace to the passion-torn community. He personally throws a massive party that unites Mrs. Jamieson and her relative Mrs. Hoggins. There were even rumors that Peter might marry Mrs. Jamieson. The town of Cranford thanks Peter for his miraculous appearance, but everyone, including the author, is aware that Matty's endurance and friendship, even in her tribulations, enabled all to live within the bonds of love.

The Crescent Moon

Poems by Rabindranath Tagore, 1861–1941.
Published 1913 by The Macmillan Company, London.

TAGORE WAS AWARDED the Nobel Prize for Literature in 1913 by a committee of which no member had ever read any of his works except in translation. His reputation in India was sufficient evidence that the originals as well as the translations earned the prize. This collection has seemed to many readers to be the most appealing.

The first twelve poems in the collection see children and babies through the eyes of the poet and the mother. Tagore writes of the Indian farmland, which is the setting for most of his observations; then he raises some questions about children in general, their innocence and their playfulness in contrast to the dangers around them. He muses on the origin of a baby's eyes, on his smile as he sleeps, and on his fresh complexion, concluding that these come from fairyland, from the crescent moon, and from mother love. He fancies that there are many things a baby knows and can do, but will not reveal because he would then cease living in his mother's arms. The carefree day of a child is described, and the mother's anger when mysterious causes disturb a baby's sleep. The baby's origin is the accumulated love of the mother and of God. Every mother desires to enter the baby's world and thoughts. She knows that the beautiful and the good of the world were placed there for her baby. Tagore voices the anger of the mother at all who chastise her child for behaving childishly and defends her rôle as sole judge of her child. He ends with ironic comment on the embarrassment of all adults who waste life in meaningless work instead of with the playthings of children.

The second group, twenty poems, deals with the child's own view of the world and his parents. Tagore begins with the voracious curiosity of a child and the adult's inability to comprehend or appreciate the child's questions; and also the child's sense of duty and love for his mother. He gives illustrations of the imagination of children and their great dependence on the world of fantasy. There follows a section that treats of water and its meaning for children. Rain can be a prison, rivers can be part of a game, and boats hint of faraway lands and adventure. Tagore shows the immense imaginative power of children as a mother is told by her child about the world of flowers, which go to school underground and go home in the sky with the stars. The child then dreams of the variety of fantastic gifts he could bring to his mother if he could travel far away. The strange mind of children is demonstrated in the child who imagines he is something else and gets angry at his mother when he imagines her reaction to him in his new form. Again, the child daydreams about some exciting occupations such as carnival hawker, gardener, and watchman, who all have a beautiful and mysterious aura for the child. Now Tagore subtly attacks the narrow mind that considers a child's imagination, its fears and beliefs, silly. The child is then shown to imagine he is his father's age, and to see this as a means of being free to do everything he is forbidden to do as a child. The strange logic of a child is made to ask "If twelve o'clock can come once in the night, why can't the night come when it is twelve o'clock?" and to criticize the grown man's occupation of authorship as meaningless and "spoiling sheets and sheets of paper with black marks all over both sides." Once more, the child's logic reassures the worried mother when no mail comes from her husband and the child explains that the postman keeps these letters to read himself. The child tells his mother he will protect her from all the most fantastic perils he imagines could befall her. When the time comes for the child to grow up or to die, he reassures his mother by explaining that "I shall become a delicate draught of air and caress you; and I shall be ripples in the water when you bathe, and kiss you and kiss you again."

Once again Tagore leaves the child's mind and enters the adult's in the concluding eight poems. A mother laments for her absent child. The adult is reminded to remember the things the child knew long ago. Tagore quietly reminisces, blessing the child who in some mysterious way came to bless the home. The child is ordained to be a messenger of purity and truth in the cruel and doubting and despairing world. The last poem tells how the poet, in his wanderings, was offered power, wealth, pleasure, for his gifts but only bargained with the innocent child who said smilingly, "I hire you with nothing."

Crime and Punishment

Novel by Fedor Mikhailovich Dostoevski, 1821–1881.
Published 1866. Translated from the Russian by Constance Garnett. (ML, 199 & T11)

THIS NOVEL is ranked high among Dostoevski's works, sometimes at the very top. Perhaps the reason is that its theme is a traditionally popular one—the perfect crime. However, the criminal and chief character, the murderer Raskolnikov, represents only the pathological criminal who suffers pangs of conscience, makes every possible slip, and ends up to the complete satisfaction of "crime doesn't pay" moralists. Fortunately the novel is saved by its inclusion of Sonia, as well-drawn a character as any novelist can boast.

Chaps. 1–3. RODION RASKOLNIKOV, an impoverished young research student living in St. Petersburg about 1850, dreams of committing a perfect crime. He plans to kill and rob an elderly widow who is a pawnbroker and from whom he has borrowed money that he cannot repay. He has heard that she keeps a large amount of cash and valuables hidden in her rooms. On the pretext of wanting to pawn his watch, he goes to her apartment to calculate every detail of his crime in advance. He leaves and in a reaction of self-disgust goes to drink in a basement dive, where he becomes acquainted with MARMELADOV, a drunken government clerk. Raskolnikov's desperation increases the next day, when he receives a letter from his mother, PULCHERIA, telling him that his beloved sister DOUNIA has consented, because of their destitution, to marry LOOSHIN, an uncouth but successful old businessman who is heartless and stingy. Dounia has had to give up a position as a governess because her employer, SVIDRIGAILOV, tried to seduce her.

Chaps. 4–6. Raskolnikov interferes on behalf of an unknown girl, apparently drunk or drugged, who is being molested by the dissolute Svidrigailov, who has come to St. Petersburg. Raskolnikov then sees an exhausted old horse being beaten to death by a brutal peasant, and he feels he cannot nerve himself to murder the old woman moneylender. But he then overhears the old woman's stepsister, ELIZABETH, say the old woman will be alone at a certain hour tomorrow, and he resolves anew to do the deed. The following day, at the opportune hour, he goes furtively to the old woman's house, armed with a hatchet.

Chaps. 7–11. Raskolnikov hacks the old woman to death with the hatchet, takes her keys from her dead body, ransacks her rooms, and under her bed finds a trunk full of pawned jewelry. He stuffs the jewelry into his pockets, but he fails to find any hidden money. Elizabeth walks in on the bloodsplashed scene and Raskolnikov kills her also with the hatchet. He hides the stolen jewels in a hole in the wall of his room. He is summoned to the police station and first believes the double killing has already been traced to him, but the summons is merely for the collection of unpaid rent he owes his landlady, the widow ZARNITZIN. Guilt tempts Raskolnikov to confess to police officer NICODEMUS THOMICH, but he resists the temptation. Then he faints upon hearing that two young men, Koch and Pestryakov, are suspects in the murder case. Raskolnikov fears the stolen jewelry may be found in his room and he buries the loot under a stone behind a shed. He visits his former classmate, RAZOUMIKHIN, and he behaves so strangely that Razoumikhin doubts his sanity. Razoumikhin brings a police inspector, ZAMETOV, to see Raskolnikov, who has become delirious with fever. Zametov, a personal friend of Razoumikhin, considers Raskolnikov slightly demented from illness. A friendly doctor, ZOSIMOV, examines Raskolnikov, who is further disturbed by the news that a housepainter has

been arrested for the killings. Raskolnikov receives 20 rubles from his mother in the mail.

Chaps. 12–16. Raskolnikov quarrels with Looshin, who comes to his room to tell him his mother and sister will arrive next day in St. Petersburg, where Looshin has rented cheap, squalid rooms for them. In a cafe, Raskolnikov's unbalanced talk on the subject of criminals arouses Zametov's suspicion. Raskolnikov contemplates suicide but is dissuaded by witnessing the rescue of a drowning woman. He revisits the house where he committed his crime. Presently he goes to the aid of the drunkard, Marmeladov, who has been knocked down and critically injured by a carriage on the street. Marmeladov dies and Raskolnikov consoles his widow, Catherine, and gives her the 20 rubles his mother sent him. Zosimov and Zametov, from their observations of Raskolnikov, say he is probably insane. Raskolnikov returns to his room and finds his mother and sister there. Razoumikhin meets Dounia and at once feels passionately attracted to her, and she reciprocates his feeling. After hearing Raskolnikov declare that his landlady is in love with him, his mother and sister surmise that he shows symptoms of mental disease. Looshin forbids the mother and sister to let Raskolnikov visit them in their rooms.

Chap. 17. In defiance of Looshin, Dounia and her mother ask Raskolnikov to visit them. Dounia also invites Razoumikhin. Raskolnikov admits that the 20 rubles he received from his mother have been given to Catherine Marmeladov to pay for her husband's funeral. Raskolnikov's mother tells him that the brutal Svidrigailov has beaten his wife Marfa so badly as to cause her death. Sonia Marmeladov, who is Catherine's stepdaughter, brings Raskolnikov an invitation to attend her father's wake. She is beginning to regard Raskolnikov with affection. A strange man speaks to Sonia in the hallway of the tenement house where she lives. The encounter leaves her inexplicably frightened. The man is Svidrigailov, who now lives in the house where Sonia has a furnished room. Raskolnikov's mental condition seems to get worse. He can scarcely remember a girl whom he had thought of marrying only a year ago. In a hysterical temper he threatens to break all ties with his sister if she marries Looshin against his wishes. Raskolnikov tells Razoumikhin about the small loans he had obtained from the old woman pawnbroker before she was killed. He is worried that this might be traced by Magistrate PORPHYRIUS, a legal expert now investigating the crime. Razoumikhin takes Raskolnikov to consult the magistrate, who is a relative of Razoumikhin's. Porphyrius discusses a magazine article written the previous year by Raskolnikov, in which he theorized that any criminal is always mentally unhinged at the moment he commits a crime, but that there are some individuals of such masterly character (Napoleon, for example) that any wickedness of theirs should be con-

183

sidered above the law. Zametov, who is present, significantly hints that the old woman was perhaps killed by some future Napoleon. Zametov and Porphyrius catch Raskolnikov off guard with tricky questions. His answers lack convincing candor. His friend Razoumikhin fears Raskolnikov may have laid himself open to sharp suspicion. Raskolnikov later is terrified when he cannot be sure whether he hears or dreams that he hears an unknown man, a peasant, call him a murderer. He falls into a trancelike sleep and awakes to discover Svidrigailov sitting beside his bed. They have never met before. Svidrigailov asks Raskolnikov to help him prevent the match between Looshin and Dounia. He wants to give Dounia 10,000 rubles, and he says she has a legacy of 3,000 from Marfa, his dead wife.

Chaps. 22–27. In a letter to Raskolnikov's mother, Looshin has unjustly accused Raskolnikov of giving the 20 rubles to Sonia for an unmoral purpose. Dounia, incensed by this slandering of her brother, breaks off her betrothal to Looshin. Razoumikhin, in love with Dounia, arranges for the girl and her mother to occupy an apartment in a building where he is about to establish a new publishing business with capital lent by a prosperous uncle of his. Raskolnikov, conscious of the net of murder evidence now tightening around him, and anxious not to involve his mother and sister, tells them that henceforth he wants them to leave him entirely alone. They attribute his attitude to sheer insanity, as does Razoumikhin. Raskolnikov goes to Sonia and tells her she may never see him again. He finds a Bible that was given to Sonia by the murdered Elizabeth. This prompts him to tell Sonia he knows who killed Elizabeth. He says he will soon reveal the identity of the murderer to Sonia alone. Raskolnikov is overheard by Svidrigailov, who is lurking outside the door of Sonia's room. At the office of Magistrate Porphyrius, Raskolnikov frenziedly insists on being officially informed whether or not he is regarded as a

Porphurius warns Raskolnikov

murder suspect. He is tricked into listening to a false confession of the murder by a poor young workman named NIKOLA, whom the police have seemingly intimidated. Porphyrius, playing cat-and-mouse with Raskolnikov, then has him hear that Nikola's confession is a fake. To Raskolnikov comes the unknown man who, on the street, had called him a murderer, and whom Raskolnikov thought was merely a dream. In reality he is the handyman at the house where the double murder took place. He grew suspicious when Raskolnikov revisited the scene and he reported the fact to Porphyrius. He has since considered his suspicion unfounded and he has also reported this to Porphyrius. The handyman now apologizes to Raskolnikov, who rejoices in the notion that all this has absolved him in the eyes of the police. Looshin, in the meantime, learns that Sonia has become a prostitute, and he pretends to befriend her and her consumptive stepmother, Catherine, giving them ten rubles and hinting at substantial aid.

Chaps. 28–32. In a scatterbrained folly of social pretensions, Catherine Marmeladov

squanders her pitifully few rubles to give a big funeral banquet after burying her husband. At this dinner Looshin accuses Sonia of stealing a 100-ruble note from him. She submits to search and a 100-ruble note drops out of her pocket. But Looshin was seen to slip the note into her pocket himself, and he is denounced for his act. Raskolnikov says Looshin did it for revenge, because of Sonia's friendliness toward him, the brother of Dounia, who broke her betrothal to Looshin. Raskolnikov accompanies Sonia to her furnished room, where he tells her in detail that he murdered the two women. Sonia amazes him by kissing him passionately and vowing she will stay with him through whatever may happen to him. She begs him to surrender himself to the police and to make atonement for his crime. He refuses to give up voluntarily, although he expects to be arrested. Svidrigailov, again eavesdropping at Sonia's door, now knows all the facts of Raskolnikov's guilt from Raskolnikov's own mouth. Catherine and her young children, Poletchka and Kolia, are evicted by their landlady and Sonia sees the children dancing in the street for kopeks, with Catherine drumming the rhythm for them on a frying pan. Catherine is hurt by a fall on the pavement and is carried to Sonia's room and dies there. Svidrigailov offers to pay the funeral expenses and get the children into an orphanage. But he insinuates that he knows all about Raskolnikov's crime. Raskolnikov hears that Porphyrius has induced another man, a workman, to confess the double murder. Raskolnikov turns so secretive that Razoumikhin surmises he is a political conspirator. This gives Raskolnikov a sense of security. But presently he is dismayed by an unannounced visit from Porphyrius.

Chaps. 33–38. Porphyrius coolly informs Raskolnikov that he now has evidence enough to convict him of the murders but hopes Raskolnikov will surrender himself voluntarily to the police, which would lighten the penalty. He warns Raskolnikov of impending arrest and politely asks him to leave an explanatory note if he should commit suicide. Raskolnikov rejects the advice to confess and surrender. He is now gravely concerned over Svidrigailov's knowledge of his guilt, and fears Svidrigailov may use that knowledge to impose his attentions on Dounia. Svidrigailov tells Raskolnikov pointblank that he knows all about his crime and offers to finance an escape to America. Svidrigailov tells Dounia that her brother has confessed the murders to the prostitute Sonia, and that unless Dounia will consent to his dishonorable advances he will report her brother's crime to the police. When Svidrigailov threatens to rape her, Dounia stops him with a pistol that was given to her by his dead wife. He nevertheless seizes Dounia. She cannot steel herself to shoot him, but he only takes the pistol from her and lets her go. Later that night he gives Sonia money enough to provide a decent livelihood for herself and Catherine's orphaned children. He pretends

Raskolnikov goes to Sonia and tells her everything

184

he plans to emigrate to America. Then, after spending a night of misery in which he sees himself with contempt, he goes out into the street and blows his brains out with his dead wife's pistol. Raskolnikov bids farewell to his mother and says he is going away but does not say where. Dounia pleads with him to give himself up and expiate his crime. Despite his haunting guilt, he clings to the theory that it was not really a crime for him to kill the two wretched women, whom he describes as vermin. Once more he goes to Sonia. He tells her the influence of her God-fearing counsel has persuaded him to confess. Around his neck she hangs a cross of cypress wood, a symbol of humility. Following Sonia's advice, but not letting her come with him, he goes to a public marketplace, kneels in the midst of the people, and humbly kisses the earth after loudly declaring "I am a murderer." The people believe he is crazy. At police headquarters he writes and signs a full confession.

Epilogue. Raskolnikov is sentenced to eight years' hard labor in Siberia. His mother dies, but not before Dounia marries Razoumikhin. Sonia follows Raskolnikov to Siberia, where she works as a seamstress and is permitted to talk with Raskolnikov only on holidays. Her kindness endears her to all the prisoners. She and Raskolnikov are deeply in love and they can now look forward to a regenerated life together in the future. Raskolnikov will be only 32 years old at the end of his prison term.

The Crime of Sylvestre Bonnard

Novel by Anatole France (François Anatole Thibault, 1844–1924). Published 1881.

THIS NOVEL, WRITTEN when Anatole France was 36, established his reputation. It is still one of his two or three best-read works. It may be his best, for in it he was at his most sympathetic. If his later work had been bad instead of good, this one novel would have been sufficient to make him a distinguished one-book author. It is worth reading.

Part I. The Log. SYLVESTRE BONNARD, elderly bachelor devoted to the science of philology, is a learned member of the French Institute who lives a retiring life among his books of obscure history concerning the ancient Paris churches. Absorbed in antique lore, he is indifferent to current activities. His crusty old housekeeper, THÉRÈSE, is the real ruler of his home and his habits. An impoverished book-dealer, nerve-wracked and emaciated by ill health, brings some cheap books to Bonnard, desperately hoping to sell them. Bonnard does not buy them, but his pity for the man's condition prompts him to ask Thérèse what she knows about him. She tells Bonnard that the man's name is COCCOZ, and that he and his wife and newborn baby occupy an attic room at the top of the house where Bonnard lives. Thérèse says the attic is unheated and is damp because of the leaking roof. Sorry for the Coccoz family, Bonnard has some firewood delivered to their cold attic. Not long after this, Bonnard learns of the death of Coccoz. Thérèse is somewhat scandalized to observe that the widow of Coccoz appears to be having a gay time with more than a few friends. On the stairs one day, Bonnard meets the attractive widow and her little child. Mme. Coccoz expresses her gratitude for Bonnard's gift of the firewood. Bonnard does not see Mme. Coccoz again during the next ten years. Meanwhile he has become absorbed in a search for a manuscript of the *Golden Legend,* a rare volume he has seen mentioned in a catalog and is extremely eager to add to his library. At length he discovers that it belongs to a Signor POLIZZI in Sicily. Polizzi refuses to part with the manuscript but will be happy to let Bonnard study it thoroughly if Bonnard will come to Sicily. Bonnard is appalled at the prospect of the difficult journey to a foreign land but he compels himself to brave the trip. In Sicily he is introduced to TREPOF, a Russian prince who has married the former Mme. Coccoz. Bonnard does not recognize Princess Trepof as the widow he saw but once, years ago, in Paris. He sees the Trepofs merely as rich dilettante tourists. The prince collects matchboxes. The princess seems devoted to her husband. She would prefer home life, it seems, to traveling. Bonnard has a hard time locating Polizzi, whose abode is so remotely situated that Bonnard can get there only by mule. After the difficult journey, he finds Polizzi is a shifty ne'er-do-well who does not have the *Golden Legend* manuscript in his possession in Sicily. It is in Paris, in a bookshop quite near the street where Bonnard lives. The bookshop, recently opened, belongs to Polizzi's son, to whom Polizzi sent the manuscript without informing Bonnard that he had done so. Princess Trepof listens sympathetically when Bonnard, bitterly indignant, tells her how cruelly he has been mistreated by Polizzi. On his return to Paris, Bonnard examines the *Golden Legend* in the shop owned by Polizzi's son, who declines to set a price on it because it is to be sold at auction. At the sale, Bonnard, in high hopes of acquiring the manuscript, goes along with the bidding up to 6,000 francs, but is continually outbid by an unidentified bidder. Presently Bonnard is dismayed to find that Pollizi himself has made the winning bid on behalf of a mysterious client who will pay any price to regain possession of the manuscript. Sorely disappointed, Bonnard is back in his apartment when a boy arrives with a package for him. The boy will tell nothing beyond saying the package contains a present from his mother. Thérèse, however, sees a carriage standing at the door, and has recognized the occupant as the former Mme. Coccoz. Bonnard unwraps the package and finds in it a hollow imitation log of firewood. The hollow log is filled with fresh violets. There is a card bearing the name of Princess Trepof. Beneath the violets Bonnard finds the manuscript of the *Golden Legend.* Thérèse can't understand how Mme. Coccoz came to be waiting at their door after all these years, and in such a luxurious carriage.

Part II. The Daughter of Clementine. Bonnard is asked to catalog the library at the newly inherited country estate of a M. DE GABRY. The country house is dilapidated but the library is a large one, so Bonnard begins the lengthy job with pleasure.

The Fairy Elf. He falls asleep at his work and dreams that a wee elf is mocking his stuffy bookishness and showering him with ink. Bonnard suddenly wakes up and sees that his inkpot has tipped over. He describes his dream to Mme. de Gabry, who is impressed by it. Some days pass, then to Bonnard's bewilderment his dream elf appears on a table in the hall. Mme. de Gabry introduces Bonnard to JEANNE ALEXANDRE, a shy girl whose hands are peculiarly reddened. She modeled the little statuette of Bonnard's elf as a gift for him. He is delighted with it, but touching memories from bygone years are revived when he hears who Jeanne is. Her grandmother, whose name was CLEMENTINE, was Bonnard's sweetheart many years ago. Jeanne now has no living relatives. Out of love for her dead grandmother, Bonnard decides to take care of Jeanne.

The Little Saint-George. At Clementine's grave in a Paris cemetery, Bonnard confides the story of his youthful romance with Clementine. Her father, a widower, was a cartographer by trade and a man of violent temper. Clementine dwelt for a short time in a rented apartment owned by Bonnard's father. Bonnard fell in love with her, and she understood this, though he dared not say so openly. A fierce conflict occurred one night between Clementine's royalist father and an uncle of Bonnard, who was a Bonapartist. As a result, Clementine's father left the Bonnard house and took Clementine with him. Bonnard never saw her again. Mme. de Gabry informs Bonnard there is a Maitre MOUCHE, a notary, who is Jeanne's legal guardian. He must be consulted about any assistance Bonnard may offer the girl. Mouche, a slippery type of lawyer, agrees to let Bonnard visit Jeanne once a week, on Thursdays, at the Mlle. PRÉFÈRE'S exclusive school for girls, where Jeanne is a charity pupil. Mlle. Préfère distrusts Bonnard's motives until she hears that he is a member of the Institute, after which she becomes obsequious and her treatment of Jeanne improves at once. The schoolmistress frequently brings Jeanne to see Bonnard at his apartment during school vacations. Mlle. Préfère establishes herself firmly in Bonnard's rooms, selecting a permanent chair for herself and a place she reserves for her knitting. She contrives to be alone with Bonnard, and to his shocked amazement she makes him a proposal of marriage, which he rejects. Mlle. Préfère retaliates by shutting the door of her school to him and declaring that he will not be allowed to have any further association with Jeanne. Bonnard appeals to Maitre Mouche, who sides with Mlle. Préfère. Bonnard then astonishes himself by having the temerity to abduct Jeanne. By trickery he gets her out through the school gate during a rainstorm and takes her to the home of Mme. de Gabry. Maitre Mouche has embezzled money entrusted to him and has vanished, as Mme. de Gabry discovers when she seeks him to intercede for Bonnard. Now Bonnard becomes the legal guardian of Jeanne and she comes to live at his house. HENRI GELIS, a student, comes to Bonnard for advice in writing a thesis. Gelis and Jeanne fall in love, and he asks her hand in marriage despite the fact that no dowry has been provided for her. Bonnard prepares to sell his beloved collection of rare books in order to set the young couple up financially. He browses through his books for the last time and cannot resist the temptation to hide one of them to keep it from being sold. He feels guilty of committing a crime by withholding this one cherished book. Following the marriage of Jeanne and Gelis, Bonnard moves from Paris to the village of Brolles. Jeanne and her husband come to see him about twice a year. They have a baby boy, Sylvestre, named after Bonnard, but the child dies in infancy. Bonnard has the dead baby's cradle in his village home. Though deeply touched by the loss of his

little namesake, Sylvestre Bonnard optimistically expects that Jeanne and Gelis will have other children, for their health is sound and they are young.

The Crisis

Novel by Winston Churchill, 1871–1947.
Published 1901.

FOR A LONG TIME there was one sure way to tell Winston Churchill the American novelist from Winston Churchill the British statesman: Whatever the American novelist Churchill wrote went immediately to the top of the best-seller lists. In recent years Sir Winston Churchill as an author has been doing almost as well, but not quite. *The Crisis* was no exception among the American Churchill's works; it was Number One in its day. It is the best remembered of all his novels.

Book I. Chaps. 1–13. When STEPHEN BRICE and his widowed mother settle in St. Louis, most of the townsfolk expect them to possess all the pretensions of Boston aristocrats; but they find that the Brices are modest people who hope only to recoup the fortune that Stephen's late father lost

Sylvestre Bonnard browses through his books for the last time

the year before in the panic of 1857. Stephen enters the law firm of a distant relative, Judge SILAS WHIPPLE, a staunch abolitionist like himself. Judge Whipple is tireless in his condemnation of slavery, often arguing bitterly with his closest friend, Colonel CARVEL. Stephen soon falls in love with Carvel's handsome daughter, VIRGINIA. His pursuit of Virginia is without great success, however, for she cannot tolerate "Black Republican Yankees" in her company. Instead, Virginia encourages the advances of her cousin and fellow Southerner, CLARENCE COLFAX. Nevertheless, life runs along pleasantly for Stephen in St. Louis. He buys his mother a small house and soon they are well settled into the social activities of the town.

Book II. Chaps. 1–14. In August 1858 Judge Whipple sends Stephen as a messenger to Springfield, Illinois. Stephen is to deliver a letter to Mr. ABRAHAM LINCOLN, a young lawyer who has entered the race against STEPHEN A. DOUGLAS for a seat in the U.S. Senate. Stephen's first meeting with Lincoln is disturbing. Stephen is both confused and impressed. Stephen asks Stephen to spend a few extra days in Springfield. Stephen agrees, now swept away by the power of personality and sensibility he finds in Lincoln. Attending a Lincoln-Douglas debate, Stephen suddenly sees the very "Crisis of America" emerging before his eyes. Inspired by Lincoln's arguments in favor of the abolition of slavery, Stephen becomes the devoted "Black Republican" that Virginia once called him. Back in St. Louis, Stephen dabbles casually in local politics. He also continues his pursuit of Virginia, receiving some slight encouragement. But when he begins to voice his political opinions openly, Virginia rejects him completely.

Two years pass. Stephen is now an established lawyer and also contributes to an abolitionist paper, *The Missouri Democrat*. Virginia has become engaged to Colfax. The entire nation is bubbling with political unrest. When Abraham Lincoln is nominated for the Presidency, and wins, all St. Louis begins to rumble. Stephen is thoroughly committed to the Republican cause; he often spoke politically during Lincoln's campaign for the Presidency, earning either admiration or contempt among his neighbors. Both Virginia and her fiancé, Clarence, are strong in their defense of the rights of the South, going so far as to wish the exclusion of "Black Republicans" from St. Louis's social functions. As the months pass and relations between the North and the South become more strained, even friendships begin to crack and fall apart. Judge Whipple tells Carvel he thinks it would be better if they no longer see each other, ending an association of 20 years.

Chaps. 15–23. As the year 1861 begins, the prospect for peace has all but vanished. St. Louis is at war with itself, a town divided into two camps, those for and against the South. The attack on Fort Sumter comes. A voluntary draft is announced, and North

Virginia and Stephen's mother attended the judge's bedside

and South prepare for a bitter struggle. War is finally declared; Missouri does not actively join the South, but the streets of St. Louis are filled with fighting. Union troops arrive to restore order. Among the soldiers, Stephen meets a captain who had been in the regular army for 9 years. Although 40 years old and unsuccessful, the captain thinks he should be given a regiment to command. His fellow officers treat him with ridicule. "He's worn out," they say, "this man who calls himself Ulysses Grant." During these days, Stephen also meets an old army officer named SHERMAN.

On May 10, 1861, a brisk skirmish between the adherents of the North and the South takes place, the Southerners being defeated. Clarence Colfax is placed in prison as a potential enemy agent. Virginia learns that Clarence's life was saved by Stephen during the battle. She begins to feel remorse about her behavior toward Stephen. Clarence refuses to take the parole from prison offered by the Union forces, but he manages to break out. His loyalty to the South fills Virginia with admiration.

Book III. Chaps. 1–9. As the war progresses, times grow harder. The quick end to the conflict, which had been optimistically forecast, does not come. Before long Carvel finds himself bankrupt. With nowhere else to turn, he decides to flee to the South and join its armies. Stephen has not yet joined the Union Army, because of his obligations to both his mother and Judge Whipple, but he decides now (with some encouragement from General Sherman) to enlist. Stephen is soon promoted to lieutenant in the Sixth Missouri division under Sherman. By the time of the Battle of Vicksburg, Stephen is a captain. When Vicksburg falls to the Union forces, Stephen comes across Clarence Colfax, now a captain in the Confederate Army. Clarence is wounded. Stephen arranges for Sherman to send Clarence back to St. Louis to receive medical attention, though he knows that

Virginia will undoubtedly fall into Clarence's arms once more. Clarence is aware of Stephen's kindness, and he tells Virginia how much he has begun to admire Stephen. Virginia becomes distraught, and Clarence asks her if she wants to marry Stephen. She answers angrily that she will never marry a Yankee.

Chaps. 10–16. In the meantime, Judge Whipple has become seriously ill. Forgetting differences of opinion, Virginia, with Stephen's mother, has attended the judge's bedside day after day. As the judge's condition grows worse, he says that he would like to see Virginia's father just once more before he dies. Virginia gets word to her father, who rushes back to St. Louis in civilian clothes. Carvel, Clarence Colfax and Stephen are with the judge when he dies. Suddenly, all the political hostilities and personal animosities fade. The lives of all three men are in danger; they could all be shot on suspicion of being in a Confederate conspiracy. It is at this moment that Virginia sees Stephen's true qualities and knows that she is in love with him.

Stephen returns to Sherman's army. He participates in the march through Georgia. This time Colfax has been caught in civilian clothes and has been denounced as a spy. Stephen intercedes again with Sherman, temporarily saving Clarence's life. Before long, Stephen is promoted to major, being sent with dispatches to Grant in Virginia. Stephen recognizes Grant as the man whom the officers scorned in St. Louis in 1861. During his conference with Grant, Stephen meets Lincoln again. Lincoln wants to hear at first hand about the Georgia campaign. Stephen gives him all the details he desires, making, in return, a single request. He begs a full pardon for Colfax. Lincoln agrees to consider the matter.

Meanwhile, Virginia Carvel travels to Washington to see Lincoln. She intends to ask Lincoln to spare Clarence's life. When

she finally is admitted to the President's office, she is amazed to see Stephen there. Lincoln grants the pardon, observing that clemency must be shown if peace is ever to be accomplished. He leaves Virginia and Stephen alone. They declare their love for each other and arrange to be married the next day. Immediately after the wedding, they travel to Annapolis, Virginia's family home. They are at Annapolis only two days when they receive the news of Lincoln's assassination.

The Critic

Play by Richard Brinsley Sheridan, 1751–1816.
Produced 1779 at Drury Lane Theatre, London.

EVEN THE OUTLINE of *The Critic* will indicate how much vitriol Sheridan poured out through it. The play is a satire that satirizes everyone connected with the theater of his times. The full play better rewards the reader, for every page sparkles with wit.

Act I. 1. Mr. and Mrs. DANGLE are at breakfast. He notes in the newspaper the rehearsal of a new tragedy called *The Spanish Armada,* said to be written by Mr. PUFF, a friend of the Dangles. His wife upbraids him for affecting the character of a critic; she tells him he gets the plague and trouble of theatrical activity without the profit. He reminds her that she gets first-night seats and that at his request an author dedicated his farce to her. She retorts that her home is becoming the rendezvous for lackeys of literature and would-be actors. Mr. SNEER is announced and gives Dangle two plays, which he wants him to place with managers. Sneer assures Mrs. Dangle that the theater, in proper hands, might be made the school of morality. One of Sneer's manuscripts is *The Reformed Housebreaker,* in which housebreaking is put in such a ridiculous light that Sneer expects bolts and bars will be discarded if the play has a proper run. They are interrupted by Sir FRETFUL PLAGIARY, whom Sneer describes as envious, petulant, and so covetous of popularity that he would rather be abused than not mentioned at all. Sir Fretful complains bitterly about other writers' stealing from him. Sneer, after making fun of him and his charges of plagiarism, proceeds to criticize his tragedy. Sir Fretful is indignant. He calls upon Mrs. Dangle for approval which she gives but adds that his play is a little too long. He says he will read the whole work to her in three hours and a half. On prompting from Dangle, Sir Fretful launches into an attack on the newspapers, calling them villainous and abominable, adding that on that account he never reads them. A servant announces the arrival of an Italian gentleman with a French interpreter, three young ladies and a family of a dozen musicians sent by Lady RODEAU and Mr. FUGUE. 2. In the drawing room of Dangle's house the interpreter struggles to make the Italians understood by Mrs. Dangle; he translates their conversation into French, which she does not understand either. Dangle essays a word or two of French and Italian and beats out time as the visitors sing trios. Puff arrives and the musical family goes off. Puff starts to eulogize Sneer. Dangle assures Sneer that Puff is only talking in the style of his profession—that of puffing. Puff writes for the papers, manufacturing complimentary paragraphs about authors, for which the authors pay him. Puff explains that he contracted a debt to help a friend, a widow with dropsy and consumption, who had six helpless children and was eight months gone with child. He was imprisoned for debt but succeeded in collecting contributions to get out. With such success and a handsome sum to show for it, he quit his previous unethical business of doctor and attorney to engage in puffing. Puff describes types and methods of puffing, such as letters to the editor.

Act II. 1. Puff, Sneer and Dangle are in the theater before the curtain rises. Puff is describing his tragedy, *The Spanish Armada*, the scene of which is laid before Tilbury Fort. He has contrived to introduce a romance by supposing the governor of Tilbury Fort's daughter to be in love with the son of a Spanish admiral. Dangle asks if this is not improbable. Puff says that Don Ferolo Whiskerandos, the lover, might have been at Tilbury Fort in the train of the Spanish ambassador or that Tilburnia, the heroine, might have seen his picture and fallen in love with him because he was the last man in the world she should have cared

for or for any other good female reason. The Under Prompter tells Puff he may find the piece rather short, since the performers have followed his suggestion to omit, very liberally, heavy or unnecessary portions of the plot. 2. The play opens. Two sentinels are discovered asleep as a clock strikes four o'clock in the morning. Puff points out that two great men are coming on scene and probably would not open their mouths if they thought they were being overheard. Sir Walter Raleigh and Sir Christopher Hatton enter and discuss the Armada launched by Philip of Spain. Dangle asks why, if Sir Christopher knows all this, Sir Walter goes on telling him about it. Puff points out that the audience has to be let in on the events. When the morning gun goes off the property man, liking the sound, fires it a couple of times more. There is soft music as Tilburnia and her confidante come on stage. Tilburnia recites a catalog of flowers and birds. Then she weeps for her lover. Her father comes on and she envisages the battle with the Armada. Puff justifies this poetical second sight by pointing out that a heroine, in consideration of being often obliged to overlook things that are on the stage, should be allowed to see things that are not. Tilburnia proposes to her father that her lover, Whiskerandos, be

released from prison. Due to extensive cutting, Don Ferolo Whiskerandos himself appears and the lovers bid farewell forever. Puff refers to his underplot, which he has contrived to have as little connection with the main plot as possible.

Act III. 1. Puff announces the appearance of the justices and constable in the action as the curtain rises again. One of the justices discovers that a conscript is his long-lost son. Sneer objects to the fine language they

use but Puff insists that he is not for making slavish distinctions and giving all the fine language to the upper classes. Sir Christopher and Sir Walter engage in sword play with Don Ferolo Whiskerandos. A lounging beefeater (English guardsman) discloses himself as the man who captured Whiskerandos. The two pick up discarded swords and have a duel in which the Spaniard is killed. Tilburnia comes on stark mad in white satin, and her confidante comes on stark mad in white linen; Puff explains that a confidante always does everything her mistress does. Tilburnia has a

mad scene. Puff tells Sneer and Dangle she is going to throw herself into the sea where the great battle occurs. "Thames" and two attendants enter. Puff cries, "There's a river for you, blending a little of the masque with my tragedy—a new fancy." When Sneer asks who the two attendants are Puff says they are the banks of the river. There is a flourish of drums, trumpets, cannon, etc., then martial music; the procession of English rivers takes place and Handel's water music is played, together with a chorus of the march in *Judas Maccabeus*, as Puff directs and applauds everything.

Gathered to watch the play

188

Narrative of the Life of David Crockett

Autobiography by David Crockett, 1786–1836.
Published 1834 and after, in many and varying editions.

THERE IS MUCH DOUBT as to whether Davy Crockett himself wrote all or any of the different versions of the autobiography attributed to him in various editions. It can be assumed that he wrote much that appears in them, for he was a writing man. He was also an interesting man, in his lifetime and after, and he was a man of action. A Walt Disney motion picture made Davy Crockett a hero to children in the 1950s, but perhaps the tasseled coonskin cap supposedly worn by Davy appealed to them more than the man himself. In any version Davy Crockett's book is a standard item in Americana.

Chaps. 1–2. As the public seems to feel some interest in an individual so humble to no other person living as to myself, I have at last determined to put before the world a narrative which it may at least rely on as being true. My father, John Crockett, who fought in the Revolutionary War, was of Irish birth; my mother was born in Maryland. According to the best information I have received on the subject, I was born on the 17th of August, 1786. My father was by profession a farmer but turned his hand to other ventures to support his family of six boys and three girls. When I was about 9 years old he moved to Jefferson County, now in the State of Tennessee, where he opened a tavern on the road from Abbingdon to Knoxville. Times were hard and he hired me out to a Dutchman, with whom I walked the 400 miles to Rockbridge, in Virginia. This perfect stranger treated me well enough, but I became homesick and ran away. I reached home and my father put me in school, but on the first day I had a fight with another boy and was afraid to go back. I ran away and hired myself out to a neighbor. I soon left him and hired out to a wagoner. I then worked for other wagoners. One night I stopped at my father's tavern, where no one recognized me because I was now almost 15. But when I sat down to supper with my family one of my sisters then recognized me, and my whole family was so happy to see me it made me weep.

Chaps. 3–4. After working out a debt of $36 for my father, I hired out to an old Quaker. He had a married son who kept a school, and I made a bargain with him to go to school four days and work for him the other two. I fell in love with the Quaker's niece, who disappointed me, and then with another lass, who jilted me. I was very heartsick, but it was not too long before I met a girl of Irish parents, and although her mother first opposed me I was finally married to this lass and we settled down to housekeeping, while I farmed some rented land. But after a few years I found this work not what it was cracked up to be, so I packed my wife and two young sons to the newly-opened country along the Elk River in Lincoln County. I lived there during the years 1809 and '10, and in that rich country I became quite a hunter of game. Then we moved to Beans Creek in Franklin County.

Chaps. 5–8. When the Creek Indian War began we were living 10 miles from Winchester. When I told my wife I was going to volunteer she begged me to stay with her and the children, as she was a stranger in the county, but I felt that if the Creeks were not put down they would soon take to killing and scalping women and children. So I fought through the whole Creek War under General Jackson, being in at the battles of Beaty's Spring, Taladega, and Horseshoe Bend. Then I came home for a few days, but set right out again to join the army for the Florida campaign and I was at the Battle of Pensacola. Then I made my way home, hunting as I went. I found my wife and children quite well, and I was deeply moved at how happy they were to see me. Much as I was eager to be in the war, I was even more happy to have come out of it alive.

Chap. 9. I continued at home now, working my farm for two years. In this time I met with the hardest trial that ever falls to the lot of man. Death entered my humble cottage and took from my children an affectionate good mother and from me a tender and loving wife. I was left with three children; the two eldest were sons, the youngest a daughter. I could not bear the thought of scattering my children among my kin, so I got my youngest brother and his family to live with me; but, good people though they were, I soon realized that I must have another wife. There lived near me the widow of a man killed in the war. She had two young children about as old as my own, and I thought that since we were in the same situation we might be able to do something for each other. We were soon married, and we lived in peace and raised our first crop of children quite successfully. The next fall after this marriage, three of my neighbors and I decided to explore the Creek country. I came down with a sickness and was lucky to get home. I tried exploring again and found the country near Shoal Creek to be so good we moved there. Soon I was appointed magistrate, and I handed out justice on the principles of honesty between man and man, relying on natural-born sense, for I had never read a page in a law book all my life.

Chap. 10. I soon found myself in politics, somewhat against my will, but I got myself elected colonel of my regiment, and I found that this had gone so well I got myself elected to the Legislature. Here I met Colonel JAMES POLK, who asked me if I didn't think we'd have an extensive change in the judiciary. "Very likely, sir," I said, and lit out, for if I knowed what the judiciary were may I be shot. At the Legislature I

got the bad news that the grist mill and powder mill, with the attached distillery, all of which I had built, mostly on borrowed money—all this had been washed away in a large freshet. I returned home and had to give up all I owned to my creditors.

Chaps. 11–13. Having lost all I had, I decided to move out by the Obion. I explored that country with my eldest son and found it rich with game. One day I killed a big bear, which, on my honor, I believe weighed 600 pounds. This provided my family with plenty of meat. And I found that I could easily keep supplying my family with food and clothing by hunting, selling some of the meat and peltry. About this time I was urged to run again for the Legislature, but as I lived 40 miles from any white settlement I decided I just couldn't run. But I soon found out that I had been put up and advertised as a candidate without my knowledge or consent. This got my dander up and I decided to run. We had a three-cornered race, and I won handily. I then served the years 1823 and 1824 in the Legislature. Then they put me up for Congress, but I lost this one by just *two* votes.

Chaps. 14–16. In the fall of 1825, I concluded to build two large boats and load them with pipe-staves for market. I hired some hands and worked at boat-building until the bears got fat. Then I commenced bear-hunting in earnest, and within less than a year I killed 105 bears. I returned to my boats and staves. We put out into the Mississippi and started downstream. It turned out that navigation was mighty difficult, and though we tried hard we ended by being swamped and losing the boats and staves and everything.

Chap. 17. I had no money and no prospects, so I entered a canvass for Congress and was elected. I served out the end of President (John Quincy) Adams' administration. Then I got myself reëlected and went back to Congress in President Jackson's first term. But I voted against the president's Indian Bill and got myself on his blacklist. The politicians went after me, claiming I was too often absent from the voting and was not giving the government its money's worth. They got me licked the next time I ran for Congress, and then they changed my district to keep me out again,

but the people began to cry for fair play and I was sent back to Congress the next time.

Chaps. 18–22. During this session of Congress, I decided to take a travel through the northern states. So I went up through Baltimore to Philadelphia, where there was a grand reception for Colonel Crockett. Then I met all kinds of distinguished citizens and visited the theater, the mint, and the insane asylum. Then I went to New York, where things went pretty much like in Philadelphia, and in addition I got to make a speech at the Exchange. But to me the city is a miserable place to live, especially for poor people who are always crowded up and half starved. I moved on to Boston, where I was shown every honor and met the famous persons from the oldest families. I was invited to Harvard University, but I did not go for fear that they might make me a Doctor of Laws, and I did not want to exchange "Member of the House of Representatives of the United States" for LL.D., which my constituents would have trans-

The bear weighed 600 pounds

David Crockett and son

lated as "lazy lounging dunce." Upon leaving Boston, I made my way south through Providence, New York, Philadelphia, Camden, New Jersey—where I lost my purse—and Baltimore, and landed back in Washington. When the Congress of 1834 broke up I was invited back to Philadelphia, where I was presented by some young men who liked my political views with a rifle they had had made especially for me. Then I visited Pittsburgh, and headed home by way of Cincinnati and Louisville. I was very happy to return to the confines of my humble home with its ocean of love and affection, which neither time nor circumstances can dry up. Soon I entered a target shoot for prizes from a prime beef. I tried out my new rifle and found it excellent.

Chaps. 23–24. In 1835 I was settled at Weakley County, Tennessee. Wanting to be back in Washington for the next Congress, I mounted the stump and bushwhacked all over the district in the most approved style. But the Administration was strong against me and sent some of their biggest men and lots of money into the district for my opponent; and I was beaten by 237 votes. Since they wouldn't let me serve my country in Congress, I made up my mind that I'd serve her anyhow, and I determined to go down to Texas to give the Texans a helping hand on the road to freedom.

Chaps. 25–31. On the way down, I stopped at Little Rock, on the Arkansas, where I was given a public dinner and made a fine speech. At Fulton, on the Red River, I took a boat for Natchitoches, in Louisiana. On the boat I met a man running a game of thimblerig, outwitted him, and finally talked him into joining me for the fight in Texas. At Natchitoches I met up with a fine, handsome young man who was a BEE HUNTER. He joined me and THIMBLERIG for our venture in Texas. But first we went with our new recruit to Nacogdoches, where he took a most tender leave of his lady-love.

Chaps. 32–33. The Bee-hunter, Thimblerig and I set out on what proved to be a most enjoyable journey. My two companions were good sports, and we three had much fun playing tricks on each other. We encountered a large herd of buffalo, among which I saw a huge bull. I shot him, but he ran off, and the rest of the herd after him. I pursued them for two hours but finally had to give up. I then found I was lost. I entered the prairie and came upon a herd of mustangs, with which the mustang I was riding entered into a long and breathtaking race. He ran himself right to the ground and my best efforts failed to revive him. Night was coming on and I decided to spend it in a large fallen tree. But the tree already had an occupant—a large cougar. We got into quite a disputation over the tree and I finally had to stab the critter to death. The next day I met up with a party of Indians. At first I was worried that they might rob me, but when they found the cougar's carcass, and I told them how

I had killed it, they called me a great hunter and gave me back my mustang, now recovered, which they had found. Soon I was reunited with my companions. The next morning we headed for the Alamo, which was our destination.

Chaps. 34–36. When we arrived at the Alamo, I made the acquaintance of Colonel BOWIE, inventor of the Bowie knife. And I learned about the Mexican general, SANTA ANNA, who seems to be a tough and acute customer. Later in February, he and about 1,600 men marched our way. Our little army of 150 men decided to make a stand in the Alamo, and we were promptly beseiged. We got a message to Col. FANNING for reinforcements, but the Mexicans did their own reinforcing at a faster clip. Our little band of men fought bravely, but we wanted greatly for provisions and ammunition. Our little garrison was thinned out more each day. The poor Bee-hunter died with the name of his lady-love, Kate of Nacogdoches, on his lips.

[Here ends Colonel Crockett's manuscript with the words: "*March 5.* Pop, pop, pop! Bom, bom bom! throughout the day. No time for memorandums now. Go ahead! Liberty and independence forever!" The Alamo fell the next day, March 6, 1836.]

Crock of Gold

Novel by James Stephens, 1882–1950. Published 1912 by the Macmillan Co. © 1912, 1940 by James Stephens.

STEPHENS WAS A POET and could not escape poetry even in his prose. This fact has helped make his works much loved. *Crock of Gold* is his best-known work and was his first major success. It reflects the spiritual whimsy (or whimsical spirituality) of Irish folklore as effectively as the following outline implies.

Book I. In the center of a pine wood called Coilla Doraca live the two wisest PHILOSOPHERS in the world. There is no difficulty submitted to them, even by women, that they cannot instantly resolve. Both of them are married, one to the GREY WOMAN OF DUN GORTIN, the other to the THIN WOMAN OF INIS MAGRATH. Both have children, who were born on the same day in the same hour. The only difference between the children is that one is a boy and the other a girl. They all live to-

gether in a small house in the very center of Coilla Doraca. Each of the two mothers hates her own child but loves the other, so they are constantly swapping children in order to live in peace and harmony.

As the years go by, both Philosophers busy themselves by composing sage maxims, which their wives try to disprove by deliberately holding contrary opinions. At the end of ten years, one of the Philosophers dies. He has decided that he has now learned all he can possibly learn and it is his time to go. It is unfortunate, he observes, that he is robust and in excellent health, but death does not depend upon health. And so he must go. His wife, the Grey Woman, applauds his resolution. The Philosopher bids his friends and child farewell and advises them to remove all the furniture to the sides of the room. For twenty full minutes he spins himself like a top, then he drops in a heap on the floor. Seeing her husband dead, the Grey Woman decides that she, too, must die, for she has no knowledge at all. After three-quarters of an hour (she was very tough) she falls beside her dead husband. The Thin Woman buries them both under the hearth, having smacked the two children into bed.

The next day MEEHAWL MACMURRACHU comes to the Philosophers to learn who has stolen his wife's washing board. He is disturbed to discover that only one Philosopher remains to help him, but he is even more disturbed about his wife's board: It is brand new, since it has been used for only three or four years. The Philosopher decides that the leprechauns have gone off with the washing board, and he advises Meehawl to take revenge by stealing the Crock of Gold that belongs to the LEPRECHAUNS OF GORT NA CLOCA MORA. It has taken the Leprechauns thousands of years to amass the crock of gold and they are furious with the Philosopher when it disappears. They are shrewd little people and they know who originated the scheme against them. The gold is very special because it is used as ransom money whenever a leprechaun falls into human hands. The leprechauns cannot do without it. They try to make Meehawl return the gold by sending plagues against him and his wife, but this does not work. One leprechaun also appeals to the Thin Woman of Inis Magrath, but she cannot help. The leprechauns lure the Philosophers' children down under the roots of a tree. When the Thin Woman tells the Philosopher what has happened, he replies that it is all very well, for kidnapping is an age-old custom even among ants and bees. The Thin Woman frightens the leprechauns into returning their children. The little people now decide to capture Meehawl's daughter, CAITILIN. They send the GREAT GOD PAN to coax the girl away with his pipes. The Philosopher sends his children to persuade Pan to let Caitilin go. The children fail.

Books II–IV. The Philosopher is very angry when he hears that Pan will not release Caitilin. Putting some cakes into his wallet, the Philosopher sets off to see Pan himself. The Philosopher discovers that Caitilin is happy with Pan, and he leaves in a fury, saying that she does not deserve to be rescued. Nevertheless the Philosopher goes to ANGUS OG for help. Angus Og is one of the old gods and is very powerful. Angus Og goes to see Caitilin, asking her to choose between him and Pan. Angus Og tells Caitilin that Divine Imagination is the greatest thing in the world. With him, she will find Divine Imagination. After much indecision, Caitilin concludes that real happiness can be found only with Divine Imagination. Happiness with Pan is merely pleasure, and so it is a kind of hunger. Caitilin leaves with Angus Og. The Philosopher returns home and delivers many messages for the god. The messages say that the old gods will soon return and there will be a golden age again. The Philosopher is no sooner home than three policemen break down his front door. The leprechauns, still angry because their gold has not been returned, have told the police that two dead bodies lie under the Philosopher's hearthstone. The police suspect the Philosopher of murder and put him in jail.

Books V–VI. During the time that the Philosopher is having trouble with the

Caitilin is happy with Pan

police, the two children find the place where Meehawl has hidden the crock of gold. They dig it up and return it to the Leprechauns of Gort Na Cloca Mora. But it is too late to save the Philosopher from jail. The leprechauns cannot help him get out. The Thin Woman is outraged by the behavior of the police and she spends a great deal of time before her fire muttering imprecations and calling down violent curses upon their heads. The Philosopher is taken away in a car to the city to await trial and the ultimate punishment, hanging. The Thin Woman is wildly incensed. Before she undertakes to redeem the Philosopher through the sheer power of hatred, she embraces all the Leprechauns of Gort and forgives them for their

unthinking crime against her husband. Then she bakes three cakes and prepares for a journey to Angus Og, hoping to win his intercession on behalf of the Philosopher. The Thin Woman gives a cake to each of the children and the three begin their rigorous journey. Along their route the Thin Woman advises the children on many matters, so that their journey becomes an intensely moral one. After they are on the road for several days, they encounter the THREE ABSOLUTES—The Most Beautiful Man, the Strongest Man, and the Ugliest Man. These detain the Thin Woman, insisting that she choose one of them to be her husband. She replies that she is already well married. To this they answer that her being married does not matter. The Thin Woman enters into a debate with all three, swiftly defeating each man as he attempts to press his point. Through the use of her logic and her rhetoric, she secures her freedom. Immediately upon departing from the Three Absolutes, the Thin Woman and her children arrive at the Brugh of Angus Mac an Og, the great god. She tells him what has happened and implores his assistance. This is readily granted, for it is the business of the gods to give protection and assistance to those who require it. But they cannot give it until it is demanded—that is why Angus Og has not already acted in behalf

of the Philosopher. In the Brugh of Angus Og, the Thin Woman finds Caitilin. Caitilin is happy now, for she has learned the great lesson of Divine Imagination. She has discovered that happiness is not laughter or satisfaction, and that no person can be happy for himself alone. Caitilin's happiness has grown out of being both happy and sad for Angus Og. Angus Og tells Caitilin that they will take a trip to the world of men. Caitilin consents. They begin their journey to the city, coming across great clans of fairies that the Thin Woman of Inis Magrath has assembled to greet the god and his wife. There is tremendous joy among all the little peoples, and jubilant dancing takes place. Caitilin and Angus Og are in an ecstasy of delight. They join hands and run down the mountainside surrounded by the fairies, who never cease their singing and dancing for an instant. They pass through groves of trees and over grasslands. Finally they reach the city and enter it, still dancing and singing. Rushing through the streets, they pay no attention to the cold stores and grumbling voices of the townsfolk. They sweep straight up to the prison and take the Philosopher from the hands of doctors, and lawyers, and priests, and from the professors and merchants. And then they return, dancing and singing, to the magic country of the gods.

Cymbeline

Play by William Shakespeare, 1564–1616.
Produced about 1610.

CYMBELINE IS NOT a play about Cymbeline. It is a play about his daughter Imogen. She has one of the best, though not one of the most difficult, parts Shakespeare wrote for a woman. Cymbeline is merely a symbol; as King of Britain he first resists infringement on British rights, then, having fought and won, he generously yields to the demands of international amity. Imogen is a woman of any country, and in her great scene (Act III, Scene 4) she is as wholly womanly as any man could imagine or wish. The scene should be read. ❧ The play is set in the times when the actual Cymbeline of England supposedly lived (about 40 A.D.) and is anachronistic because in those times England was not yet a colony of Rome and was not so Romanized as the play would have it.

Act I. **1.** A conversation between two Gentlemen gives the background: IMOGEN, the daughter of Cymbeline, King of Britain, is his sole heir because his two sons were kidnapped 20 years before when they were infants. Cymbeline's present QUEEN has a son, CLOTEN, and the king desires his daughter to marry his stepson, but Imogen has married POSTHUMUS LEONATUS. Cymbeline banishes Posthumus from the land and puts Imogen in the queen's custody. The queen allows the newlyweds to live together, secretly. Imogen gives Posthumus a diamond ring to give to another wife should she die, and he gives her a bracelet to wear. Cymbeline, finding them together, banishes Posthumus. PISANIO, Posthumus's servant, reports a sword fight between Cloten and Posthumus; courtiers separated

them. Pisanio has been left behind to serve Imogen. **2.** In a public place, Cloten and two lords discuss the duel. **3.** Imogen and Pisanio discuss Posthumus's departure. **4.** Posthumus comes to the house of PHILARIO in Rome. A friend, IACHIMO, bets a large sum of money against Posthumus's ring that he can seduce Imogen. **5.** CORNELIUS, a physician, brings the queen some poisonous substances, prepared at her request; but unknown to her he has given her drugs that induce a coma, not death. The queen, telling Pisanio the medications are for the king's illness, gives him the box to deliver. She tries to induce Pisanio to change masters, but he will not betray Posthumus. **6.** Pisanio brings Iachimo to Imogen with letters from her husband in Rome. Iachimo proceeds to create doubt about her husband's fidelity. When he sees her perturbed he follows with an attempt to win her for himself. When she refuses him, he confesses that he has spoken falsely only to try her, and that she is indeed all Posthumus said she was. She forgives him and he asks her to keep for him a trunk of valuable silver he has bought as a gift for the emperor. He plans to leave the next day.

Act II. 1. Cloten and his companions discuss the arrival of the stranger from Italy. **2.** Imogen falls asleep in her room. Iachimo, who has been hiding in the trunk he sent her for safekeeping, comes out of it, takes off Imogen's bracelet, and observes her birthmark and what she has been reading, to use this information as proof of his success. He then returns to the trunk. **3.** Cymbeline advises Cloten to be patient, that Imogen has not yet gotten over her love for Posthumus. A messenger tells of the arrival of CAIUS LUCIUS, a Roman general, and the king leaves to receive him. Cloten goes to Imogen and she again turns him down, saying she will never betray her husband. **4.** Iachimo returns to Rome, claiming he has won the ring. He describes Imogen's bedchamber in detail, shows him the bracelet, and mentions the birthmark. Posthumus is convinced and gives him the ring. In a rage, Posthumus decides to seek revenge in Britain. **5.** Posthumus bemoans his lack of family background and bitterly denounces his wife.

Act III. 1. Cymbeline, accompanied by the queen and Cloten, receives the Roman ambassador, Caius Lucius. The Roman wants the tribute Caesar has extracted from Britain. Cymbeline refuses to pay it, and Lucius pronounces a declaration of war against Britain. **2.** Pisanio receives a letter from Posthumus and is not convinced by his master's accusations against Imogen. Imogen also receives a letter, telling her he has landed in England. She immediately

plans to join him at Milford-Haven. **3.** In a Welsh mountain cave, BELARIUS and two young men, GUIDERIUS and ARVIRAGUS, discuss Belarius's banishment from court on false charges of complicity with the enemy. The two boys leave and Belarius muses on the fact that they do not know they are the sons of Cymbeline, nor does Cymbeline know they are still alive. The boys think Belarius is their father. **4.** Imogen and

Pisanio are looking for Posthumus. Pisanio shows her the letter he received from his master, ordering him to kill her. Imogen insists he kill her. Instead Pisanio suggests that she hide and he report to Posthumus that he has killed her. He suggests that she go to Milford-Haven and attach herself to the party of the Roman ambassador, disguised as a man. She agrees and Pisanio leaves her, giving her the box of "medications" the queen gave him, for her use if she is ill at sea. **5.** Lucius leaves London bound for Rome. The king misses Imogen and sends for her, but she is gone. The queen thinks that perhaps the distraught Imogen has taken the poison, but the queen does not care, so long as she is free to name a new heir to the throne. Pisanio shows Cloten Posthumus's letter to Imogen and Cloten immediately asks him to serve him instead of Posthumus. To this Pisanio pretends to agree. Cloten plans to go to Milford-Haven, dressed in Posthumus's clothes, and to kill Posthumus and humiliate Imogen. **6.** Imogen, dressed as a man, arrives at the cave of Belarius, exhausted and hungry. She addresses Belarius and the two boys, who are really her brothers, and offers them money to feed her. They bid her welcome. **7.** In Rome two senators inform two tribunes that the emperor plans to use the gentry for the campaign against Britain, since the common soldiery is too busy elsewhere. Lucius will lead the armies.

Cyrano de Bergerac

Act I. At a theatrical performance at the Hotel de Bourgogne, a large and fashionable crowd has assembled to see a performance by the celebrated actor MONTFLEURY. Among those present is the beautiful maiden ROXANE. One of her admirers, the young guardsman CHRISTIAN DE NEUVILLETTE, is there, and Montfleury is another of her admirers. Just as Montfleury appears, a guardsman named CYRANO DE BERGERAC, Roxane's cousin, who has a great reputation as a swordsman, poet, and philosopher, and who is the unproud possessor of a grotesquely large nose, loudly insults Montfleury. The performance is stopped; the crowd is scandalized at Cyrano's audacity. Cyrano eloquently rebukes a meddler for staring too long at his nose. The Count DE GUICHE, who is in love with Roxane but is trying to marry her to his friend VALVERT because he himself is married, incites Valvert to insult Cyrano's nose. Cyrano launches into a soliloquy on how much more effectively the insult might have been given;

Act IV. 1. Cloten nears the cave of Belarius in Wales, searching for both Posthumus and Imogen. **2.** At the cave, Imogen feels ill and takes some of the drugs Pisanio gave her. Cloten arrives. Belarius and Arviragus go looking to see if Cloten has more men with him. Guiderius and Cloten fight. Belarius and Arviragus return, then Guiderius comes back with Cloten's head, having killed him. He decides to throw the head into a stream. When he returns, Imogen lies as if dead and they consult on how to bury her. Belarius leaves Cloten's body beside Imogen. She wakes, and seeing Cloten's headless body, in Posthumus's clothing, she thinks it is Posthumus who is dead. Lucius and his officers arrive. He offers to take the disguised Imogen with him and she accepts. **3.** Cymbeline threatens Pisanio with torture to find the whereabouts of Imogen. The queen is ill; Cloten to save Posthumus. The jailers come to fetch Posthumus for execution but a messenger appears just in time, summoning Posthumus to the king. **5.** Cymbeline, in his tent, thanks Belarius for the rescue, creating him and the two boys knights. Cornelius, the physician, reports that the queen is dead. She admitted on her deathbed that she tried to poison Cymbeline. Lucius, Iachimo, and Roman prisoners, including Posthumus and Imogen, are brought before the king. Iachimo confesses his deception and praises Posthumus's valor and Imogen's chastity. Posthumus, hearing the account, advances toward him, but is restrained by Imogen, whom he strikes without recognizing her. Pisanio tells them all the truth. Guiderius confesses that he killed Cloten. Belarius tells the king that the two boys are really his own sons. Posthumus is recognized as the soldier who fought so well for Britain. Cymbeline accepts him as son-in-law. Also Cymbeline, though victorious, decides to pay Caesar tribute, blaming his insubordination upon his dead queen.

has disappeared; there is news of Roman landings. **4.** At the cave, the three fugitives decide to join the army of the Britons, for in the heat of battle no one will question them.

Act V. 1. Posthumus, in the Roman camp in Britain, holds the bloody handkerchief Pisanio has sent him as alleged proof of Imogen's death. Now he is sorry and he decides to change to British clothes and die for Imogen's country. **2.** In battle Posthumus defeats Iachimo. The Britons are defeated. Cymbeline is taken prisoner, then is rescued by Belarius, Guiderius, and Arviragus. Imogen, still disguised, is with Lucius. **3.** In another part of the battlefield, two British captains report that Lucius is taken prisoner, thanks to Belarius and his two boys. Posthumus, challenged, calls himself a Roman and is taken prisoner also. **4.** In a British prison, Posthumus is content to die for having taken Imogen's life. As he sleeps, he has a vision of his father, his mother, and his two dead brothers, asking the gods to save him. Jupiter appears and promises

Play by Edmond Rostand, 1868–1918. Produced in 1897.

ROSTAND'S MOST POPULAR PLAY was written when the new realism of Ibsen was in fashion, but good romantic and swashbuckling comedy transcends all fashions. Cyrano de Bergerac was an actual minor poet and hero of the 17th century, but there is little attempt to be biographical in the play. The most famous point in the action comes when Cyrano composes a ballade—one of the strict French forms in romantic poetry—while fighting a duel. Rostand wrote the ballade into his play because Théodore de Banville had made such a great success in the Comédie Francaise with the play *Gringoire,* which had a ballade in it. Rostand's ballade turned out to be far inferior to de Banville's, but the play as a whole is fine literature and fine theater.

then he challenges Valvert and there is swordplay between them. As they fight Cyrano composes a ballade with the refrain line "À la fin de l'envoi, je touche": "At the end of the envoy [a short final stanza] I shall hit." Good to his word, he wounds Valvert just at that point. Cyrano is a hero and the crowd disperses. Cyrano talks to his friend LE BRET and confesses his secret love for Roxane and his terrible fear that she is not interested in him because of his nose. Roxane's duenna comes with a message that Roxane wishes to see Cyrano on an urgent private matter. Cyrano's hopes soar. He arranges to meet Roxane the next day at the bakery shop of the patriot RAGUENEAU. Then, surging with love and power, Cyrano goes off to escort his friend LIGNIÈRE, who had been threatened with an ambush of 100 men.

Act II. Cyrano arrives at Ragueneau's shop for the rendezvous, bearing a letter of love he has composed to Roxane. She comes and tells him she loves Christian. Though heartbroken, Cyrano promises to protect the young man for her and she leaves. Cyrano's cadets arrive to celebrate his great victory of the night before against 100 men. De Guiche arrives to praise Cyrano and ask him to join his entourage. Cyrano refuses because he disdains the rôle of follower. The count leaves, promising revenge for the insult, and Cyrano begins the story of his battle of the previous night. Christian, though he has been warned that to mention noses is extremely dangerous in Cyrano's presence, proceeds to taunt him as he tells the story. Cyrano cannot harm the man he swore to protect for Roxane. After dismissing the crowd, he explains to Christian that he is her cousin. Christian, afraid to declare his love because he is clumsy with words, goes into collaboration with Cyrano. Roxane will be courted by his face and figure but with the words of Cyrano.

Act III. Later, at her home, Roxane, describes to Cyrano Christian's great love and praises Christian's eloquent words. De Guiche arrives to declare his love before he leaves for the front with his regiment, which includes Christian and Cyrano. Roxane convinces him that the best way to insult Cyrano would be to keep the regiment here while the rest went to war, because Cyrano loves action. The count agrees and tells her he is coming back later, masked, with a Capuchin friar to marry them that night. He leaves and Christian arrives to see Roxane alone and tell her of his love, but he is inarticulate and calls on Cyrano to aid him. With Christian hidden under the balcony, Cyrano woos Roxane and, when she is dazzled by the words, sends Christian up to kiss her. The Capuchin arrives and is fooled into believing he was sent to marry Roxane to Christian. While the ceremony is performed inside, Cyrano detains de Guiche, who has just arrived, by pretending to be a voyager from the moon. The two lovers are married. The count, furious, sends Christian off with the rest of the regiment to the front, where he hopes to get even with Cyrano.

Act IV. At the front, the cadets are besieging Arras but starving, and Cyrano tries to cheer them up. De Guiche comes up to announce that the enemy will attack their position in an hour and they are to die fighting. Cyrano has been writing to Roxane every day, under the name of Christian, but cannot bring himself to send the last letter because it says he will die that day. Roxane arrives by surprise in a carriage laden with food, and the men eat. She tells Christian that she had to come because his letters revealed the true beauty of his being, his soul, and that she would love him even if he were ugly. Christian tells Cyrano this, convinced that she does not really mean it and planning to reveal himself. The battle is engaged and Christian dies. Cyrano, rather than crush Christian's love, assures the dying man that Roxane really loves him. Roxane cries over the dying Christian and retrieves his last letter from his body.

Act V. At a convent in Paris 15 years later, Roxane, who has been living there since Christian's death, relinquishing all her worldly surroundings, awaits the weekly visit from Cyrano. He always comes to tell her the news of the week. Cyrano comes, despite a fatal head injury suffered in a murderous attack that was made on him while he was on the way. He is bandaged but covers his wound with his hat to keep Roxane from seeing his condition. He tells her the week's happenings, trying to hide his condition. Finally, he asks her to let him read Christian's letter. As he reads, it grows dark and suddenly she realizes that Cyrano wrote it and that he has always loved her. He denies it at first, but then admits all and bitterly describes his life of frustrated happiness. Even his writing is stolen in part by Molière. Delirious, he does not hear Roxane's declaration of her love for him, and in a final imaginary duel with coming death, he challenges anyone who would take from him his freedom, his independence, his "white plume"; and he dies.

Cyrano composes a ballade during the swordplay

193

William Shakespeare
1564–1616

Dante Alighieri
1265–1321

Darkness at Noon

Novel by Arthur Koestler, 1905–
Published & © 1941 by The Macmillan
Co., New York. Translation from the
German by Daphne Hardy. (NAL,
S1220)

HERE IS ONE of the great classics of the
century; the very top rank can be withheld if at all only by the fact that it is
timely rather than timeless. In the
middle 1930s Stalin was ruthlessly
purging his Soviet realm of all who
were or might become dangerous to
him. Inexplicably and in the presence
of the foreign press old revolutionaries
of known character and proved valor
came before public tribunals and
confessed abjectly to what was patently
false. An international mystery grew up
around their confessions. Was it a new
mesmeric drug? Were they sacrificing
themselves to save their loved ones?
Were they simply men of flesh, subject
to the weaknesses of the flesh, scared
of future consequences if they did not
comply? Arthur Koestler, himself a
disillusioned Communist, in this novel
supplied the most—the *only*—persuasive answer that has yet been advanced. In his brief preface to his
wonderful book he as much as said so.

The First Hearing. 1. NICOLAS SALMAN-
OVITCH RUBASHOV, former Commissar of
the People, is cast into a cell. It is brick-
walled, with a window that overlooks the
prison courtyard, a washbasin, a can, and a
bunk with a straw mattress and two
blankets. It is 5 a.m. Rubashov goes to
sleep. 2–5. He was arrested in the middle
of the night by two young men bred in the
Party and naturally brutal. The porter, WAS-
SILIJ, admitted them; he did not care much
for the Party but feared his Communist
daughter. 6–7. Rubashov is in cell 404
(even numbers on his side, odd numbers on
the other, and he can see cells 401-3-5-7).
He recognizes his cell as an isolation cell
and assumes he will be shot. The warder
comes and he complains of his bad toothache, so he is reported ill and gets no
breakfast. He thinks of various Party inconsistencies; he thinks of No. 1 (the
Party leader); he thinks of torture, expects
to be tortured, hopes he will not scream—
he did not when tortured before. He craves
only a newspaper and a pencil and paper.
8. Rubashov hears a tapping on the drainpipe that runs through the cells. Tapping
back with his pince-nez on the pipe, he
begins a prison-code conversation with the
prisoner in cell 402, a czarist who first con-
temns him but whose loneliness makes him
converse; 402 craves only women and wants

196

to be told about Rubashov's recent sex experiences. 9. Rubashov reminisces. He was
in Germany in 1933. The Nazis had just
come to power and had brutally suppressed
the Communists. The young Communist
RICHARD and his wife ANNY had not distributed the official Party literature, which
insisted there had been no defeat, because
it would appear so absurd to German Communists who had seen the defeat for themselves. The boy won Rubashov's sympathy
in every way, but Rubashov carried out
Party orders by expelling him from the
party and then informing on him so he
would be arrested and executed. A week
later Rubashov himself was arrested in Germany. 10–11. Rubashov's neighbor tells
him the other prisoners in the block are
also political and that one, HARE-LIP (a
harelipped man Rubashov has noticed in
the courtyard), sends greetings but will not
reveal his name. Hare-lip was tortured
yesterday. Rubashov craves a smoke; 402 is
not allowed to send him tobacco nor can
Rubashov buy any. 12. Memories overwhelm Rubashov, especially the memory of
LITTLE LOEWY in Belgium. After two years
of prison and torture in Germany, in which
he admitted nothing, Rubashov had been
released. He had returned as a hero to Russia. Now he was on a mission to Belgium.
The Spanish Civil War was on. The Party
had urged the labor unions not to unload
war supplies for Franco's forces. The Belgian dock-workers, led by Little Loewy, had
enthusiastically coöperated. Now The Country of the Revolution itself was sending
gasoline for Franco, and Rubashov's job
was to get it unloaded. Little Loewy had had
the same experience once before—Russia
had sent war materials to the Nazis after
urging everyone else not to. Little Loewy
refused to do it again. Rubashov had him
expelled and denounced as an *agent pro-
vacateur,* and Little Loewy hanged himself.
13. The toothache is worse but the prison
dentist will extract the tooth only as a form
of torture. Rubashov refuses. 14. Rubashov
has his first examination. The examiner is
IVANOV, his old college friend and battalion
commander. Ivanov tries to be friendly and
informal. Rubashov admits that he has disapproved the trend of the Party in recent
years; Ivanov reminds him of the many
times he (Rubashov) has been ruthless in
betrayals and murders, and has abjectly expressed allegiance to No. 1, even as recently
as six months ago. Ivanov offers Rubashov
his life—perhaps 20 years imprisonment,
with parole after two or three years—in
return for a limited confession. Rubashov
declines.

The Second Hearing. 1. In his diary (for
now he has pencil and paper) Rubashov
muses upon—and approves—the fact that
in history right and wrong are judged by
success and failure. 2. Ivanov discusses the
Rubashov case with his colleague GLETKIN.
Ivanov is sure Rubashov, being a man of
logic, if left in peace will come logically to
the conclusion that he must capitulate.
Gletkin believes in force and torture. 3.

Rubashov muses in his cell: First, on the
"grammatical fiction," the first person
singular, *I* [in life no one is singular; everyone exists in relation to the whole]. Then
on ARLOVA. He was head of the Trade
Commission in a foreign city. She was
his secretary, a big, well-formed, sleepy,
acquiescent girl who was undemonstratively
in love with him. She became his mistress.
But her brother and his wife, in Russia, were
arrested. This made her tainted and she was
dismissed from her job and sent home. He
did nothing to help her. 4. Rubashov is
taken to the barber to be shaved. Back in
his cell, he finds that the barber has slipped
into his collar a message, "Die in silence."
5–6. Rubashov is given more and more
comforts and is taken for walks. One day
402 signals that 380 is to be executed.
Rubashov learns from 402 that 380 is
MICHAEL BOGROV, a pioneer of the Revolution. (Bogrov has been under torture for
some time.) Bogrov screams and fights as
they take him out, and his final cry is
"Rubashov!" Complying with custom, all
the prisoners including Rubashov stand at
their cell doors and drum as the death march
goes by. 7. Ivanov comes to Rubashov's
cell. He brings brandy. Rubashov scorns the
offer of comfort; Ivanov assures him that
the obvious psychology of having Bogrov
led by his cell was a device of Gletkin, who
advocates hard treatment. Bogrov was
tortured and executed because he advocated
building big submarines when the Party
decision was to build small ones. Then
Ivanov reminds Rubashov how, on his return
to Russia, he joined in the denunciation of
Arlova and let her be executed when his
recommendation would have saved her but
would perhaps have subjected him to
suspicion. Ivanov and Rubashov philoso-
phize on the sacrifice of the individual to
the whole, of the present to the future.
When Ivanov leaves, he drops in on Gletkin
and tells him he is sure Rubashov will sign
the confession tomorrow. Gletkin is unfriendly.

The Third Hearing. 1. In his diary,
Rubashov concludes that the individual
must be sacrificed and that personal pride
is a crime when it conflicts with the inexorable event. 2. Rubashov taps out to 402
the message "I am capitulating." He writes
out a formal statement agreeing to renounce
publicly his errors. 3–6. Rubashov is taken
to another examination, but this time the
examiner is Gletkin and there is no in-
formality: The bright light shines in
Rubashov's face; Gletkin is coldly hostile.
Gletkin will not accept Rubashov's confession or offer of public recantation. He
reads a statement to be signed by Rubashov,
confessing to a long series of deliberate
acts of sabotage and incidents of plotting
against the government. The statements are
so untrue that Rubashov thinks Gletkin is
mad. At first Rubashov insists he cannot
confess to crimes he has not committed.
He is confronted with a witness—Hare-lip,
who proves to be the son of his old friend
and fellow-revolutionary KIEFFER. Kieffer

has already been purged, for writing a biography that turned out to be criminal because the Party's version of history had changed in the meantime. Hare-lip, wholly broken by torture, confronts Rubashov with untrue testimony that is nevertheless cleverly fashioned on some frank statements Rubashov privately made from time to time. Hare-lip is to testify that Rubashov plotted against No. 1. From this time on Rubashov's life is a series of examinations. He is never permitted enough sleep or rest. His power of arguing is weakened by fatigue and one by one he grants the Party's accusations, based on the Party's interpretations of casual statements and acts, in each of which there is a germ of heresy. These are the accusations he previously considered so absurd. At one of the later examinations Rubashov faints. Almost immediately afterward, Gletkin makes him more comfortable during the examination and speaks to him more reasonably. Gletkin proposes that Rubashov confess everything in a public trial—that he do this as a service to the Party, in the cause of the world revolution.

For this Gletkin offers nothing. Rubashov consents. He signs the statement. Asked if he has any special wish, he states only one: to sleep. Gletkin's secretary compliments Gletkin on the successful conclusion; Gletkin attributes it solely to the bright lamp, lack of sleep, and physical exhaustion.

The Grammatical Fiction. 1. The porter Wassilij's daughter reads aloud to her father the newspaper account of Rubashov's trial: How he confessed everything, condemned himself, asked no mercy, and was sentenced to death by shooting. Fearing his daughter, the porter signs a petition she has been told to circulate, demanding extermination of all such traitors. **2–3.** Hare-lip is led out to be executed first. Through 402 he sends Rubashov his greetings. Rubashov drums on the door with the others. Then comes Rubashov's turn. He must go down a dark, spiral staircase. His pince-nez drops off and smashes. He receives a blow on the head from behind; he has half-conscious, disjointed thoughts for some seconds, then comes the second blow and all becomes quiet.

Rubashov is confronted with Hare-lip's untrue testimony

David Copperfield

Novel by Charles Dickens, 1812–1870. Published 1850. (ML, 110 & T10; PB, PL751)

THE FULL TITLE IS *The Personal History of David Copperfield.* It is the best novel Dickens wrote, a good candidate for the best in the English language, one of the best in any language. Its cast of characters is matchless. Its first chapter, especially if skillfully truncated, is the best short story in English literature. It has the two primary qualities of greatness, universality and longevity; it grows on one; it is more impressive the second time it is read than the first, and the third time than the second. Yet from the standpoint of technical novel-construction *David Copperfield* is slipshod even for Dickens. He wrote it for publication in installments of rigid length, and sometimes he had to cut off short when space ran out and sometimes he had to pad to fill. In the latter cases his pathos tended to become bathos. His moralizing at times was too artificial for anyone but a Victorian old maid. His overwriting was often indefensible; it has been said that one could cut out every second sentence without destroying the sense. The ending is so weak and abrupt that it almost seems Dickens had grown tired of the book, and maybe he had. But no one else is likely to. ❡ *David Copperfield* is written in the first person and surely has an autobiographical background. Dickens, like his hero David, in his boyhood endured poverty and did menial work that he considered unbefitting his station. His father, who is supposed partly to have inspired the character of Mr. Micawber, was in a debtors' prison as Mr. Micawber was. ❡ Robert Graves wrote a novel, *The Real David Copperfield,* purporting to be *David Copperfield* as Dickens would have written it if he had been emancipated from Victorian shibboleths. Graves may have been wrong, but his novel is a good one too. ❡ *David Copperfield* is quite long, more than 250,000 words.

Chaps. 1–2. I was born six months after the death of my father; and the fact that I was a boy was so exasperating to my father's aunt, Miss BETSEY TROTWOOD, that she left the house in a fury and never entered it again. My earliest recollections are of my poor widowed mother, with her pretty hair and youthful shape, and PEGGOTTY (her first name was CLARA, which was also my mother's), our maidservant, the most affectionate and devoted woman that ever lived. We were very happy until Mr. MURDSTONE began to be often at our house.

Chaps. 3–5. Peggotty took me to Yarmouth to visit her brother, whose house was a superannuated schooner snugly anchored in the sand. Mr. Peggotty's household included Mrs. GUMMIDGE, the widow of his former partner; his nephew HAM PEGGOTTY; and his niece, "Little EM'LY," a beautiful child. We returned home. Mr. Murdstone and my mother had been married. I wept. My mother tried to comfort me, but Mr. Murdstone sent her away and gave me to understand that if I proved obstinate he would beat me. Mr. Murdstone's sister, who was to live with us, arrived the next morning. Miss Murdstone disliked me from the start. The Murdstones set about to form my mother's character and to correct my faults. One day when Mr. Murdstone beat me I bit him through the hand. I was forthwith sent, as an incorrigible, to a boarding-school near London. On the way to Yarmouth the driver, Mr. BARKIS, asked me to include a message from him in my next letter to Peggotty. The message was simply, "Barkis is willin'."

Chaps. 6–7. At school I was made to

carry a sign on my back, "Take care! he bites!" Seeing this, the boys teased me, pretending I was a dog. The master, Mr. CREAKLE, flogged me so ferociously that often half the school would be writhing and crying in their seats. The only boy he did not beat was STEERFORTH, a handsome, extremely clever lad, who took me under his wing. I could not understand the arrogant way in which Mr. Creakle treated poor Mr. MELL (one of the teachers). Another boy I particularly liked was TRADDLES, a chubby, jolly fellow, who was perpetually being caned. Mr. Creakle seemed to like beating chubby boys. I was chubby myself, and I know.

Chaps. 8–9. When the term was over I returned home and found my dear mother very pale and anxious looking, with a new baby at her breast. The Murdstones made life miserable for me and for her. I went back to school. Three weeks later my mother died, and the baby died the next day.

Chaps. 10–12. After my mother's death I went with Peggotty (whom the Murdstones had dismissed) on another visit to Yarmouth. Little Em'ly was getting to be a beautiful girl. Peggotty married Barkis, and I was sent by Mr. Murdstone to London, to earn my living by washing bottles in a wine store he partly owned. Thus, at the age of 10, I was launched upon the world. A lodging was provided for me in the house of a bankrupt but irrepressibly optimistic gentleman, WILKINS MICAWBER, whose family consisted of himself, his wife, and their young children. The Micawbers had no visitors except creditors, but these came at all hours of the day and night. At length Mr. Micawber was put into a debtors' prison and the Micawbers' furniture was sold. I took lodgings near the prison so I could continue to see them. The Micawbers were my only friends and they left London for Plymouth, to try to improve their fortunes, as soon as Mr. Micawber was released.

Chaps. 13–16. I was so disheartened at parting with the Micawbers, and so shamed at being a common workman, that I traveled to Dover on foot and presented myself, ragged, dirty, and tired, to my aunt, Miss Betsey Trotwood. Miss Betsey was a tall, rather hard-featured, but handsome woman, of a stern, resolute character but kind and generous. There were two other occupants of her house, JANET, a pretty maidservant, and Mr. DICK, a gray-headed half-mad gentleman, good-natured and smiling. My aunt received me kindly and washed, fed and clothed me. She made herself and Mr. Dick my guardians and soon she sent me to school at Canterbury. There I lived with Mr. WICKFIELD, a lawyer and a friend of my aunt's. He had a beautiful daughter, AGNES, of about my own age. Mr. Wickfield's clerk was URIAH HEEP, a pale, bloodless fellow, with no eyebrows or eyelashes to speak of and cold, clammy hands. Uriah Heep was, he frequently said, a very "'umble" person; but he had a sly manner that was not quite pleasant.

Chaps. 17–20. I found friends in the master of the school, Dr. STRONG, an absent-minded, learned, and very kindly man, nearly 60 years old, and his young and lovely wife. Uriah Heep once took me to tea with his mother in their "'umble abode," and very cleverly they wormed out of me much information about myself and Mr. Wickfield that I never intended to reveal. On this occasion Mr. Micawber showed up, on a flying visit to Canterbury in an unsuccessful search for employment, and I was obliged to introduce him to Uriah. At Canterbury I spent five peaceful, happy years. Then, at my dear aunt's suggestion, I started off for London, where I met my old schoolmate Steerforth. I arranged to take him with me on a visit to Yarmouth, but first I stayed with him for a few days at his mother's house in Highgate. There were two other persons there. One was Miss ROSA DARTLE, a dark woman of about 30. She had a red scar on her upper lip, made by a hammer Steerforth had thrown at her in a fit of anger, when he was a boy. The other person was LITTIMER, Steerforth's valet, a smooth, wholly self-possessed man, whom I could not quite trust.

Chaps. 21–23. We reached Mr. Peggotty's cottage just after Little Em'ly had given her word to marry Ham, who had been her faithful suitor for many years. Steerforth took his place in the family circle so easily and naturally that he charmed them all. We stayed there for two weeks. I visited Mrs. Barkis and her husband, he being now incapacitated by rheumatism. Steerforth bought a lugger, christened it the "Little

Em'ly," and placed it under the command of Mr. Peggotty. Littimer came to oversee the repairing and outfitting of it.

Chaps. 24–26. Going up to London, I met my aunt and became an articled clerk to Messrs. SPENLOW and JORKINS, Proctors, my aunt generously agreeing to pay the £1,000 for my training. I was installed in very comfortable little chambers in the Adelphi. At the theater I met the woman whom I liked and respected most, Agnes

Wickfield. The next day I called on her. She warned me, very unjustly as I thought, against Steerforth and his influence. Also she told me that Uriah Heep had acquired some mysterious power over her father and was about to become his partner. Soon afterward I was invited to Mr. Spenlow's country place. His only daughter, DORA, had lately returned from school in Paris. Dora Spenlow was a slight, blond girl, with the most delightful little voice, the gayest little laugh, the pleasantest and most fascinating little ways that ever led a lost youth into hopeless slavery. I fell madly in love with her at first sight.

Chaps. 27–29. I looked up my old friend, Traddles, who lived in the upper story of the same house where the Micawbers were then tenants. Traddles worked for a man who was compiling an encyclopedia. He was in love and engaged—to Sophy, "the most darling girl in the world," whom he wanted to marry as soon as he could afford it. Their watchword was "Wait and hope." I met Mr. Micawber, who was bitter because the water works had turned off his supply, for lack of payment. The next day, in response to an invitation, I called on Steerforth. Rosa Dartle asked me what occupied his attention so much of late, but I could only answer that I did not know. She sang for us—most beautifully—and when Steerforth complimented her and put his arm about her, she struck him and burst angrily from the room.

Chap. 30. Steerforth brought me a message from Peggotty that Barkis was ill and not expected to recover; so I went down to Yarmouth. "He's a-going out with the tide," said Mr. Peggotty to me. At one point Barkis opened his eyes. He said to me distinctly, with a pleasant smile, "Barkis is willin'!" And, it being low water, he went out with the tide.

Chap. 31. Barkis left several thousand pounds to Peggotty. I stayed at Yarmouth for the funeral. Ham and Little Em'ly were to be married the next day. Presently there was a knock at the door, and there was Ham, alone, pale as a sheet, with wild eyes. "She's gone" he groaned. He gave me a letter. In it, Em'ly prayed the forgiveness of all and said she would not be back unless "he" brought her back a lady, mentioning no name. Mr. Peggotty demanded, "Who's the man?" I felt a shock, for I felt that the man was Steerforth. I was right, as Ham admitted. Mr. Peggotty pulled down his rough coat from its peg in a corner. Grimly, he declared his intention to seek his niece throughout the world.

Chaps. 32–33. During all these trials I had gone on loving Dora Spenlow harder than ever. It was not many days before I declared my passion, on my knees—while Jip, her little dog, barked. The more I raved, the more Jip barked. But by and by Dora and I were sitting on the sofa quietly enough, and Jip was lying in her lap, peacefully winking at me. We were engaged.

Chaps. 34–36. One night I went home to my chambers and found my aunt and Mr.

Dick encamped there. My aunt told me calmly and courageously that she had lost all her property. Agnes Wickfield, with her father and Uriah Heep, was in London at this time, and Agnes came to see my aunt. Agnes evidently had some fears that my aunt's property had been lost while in her father's hands for investment, but my aunt declared she had taken charge of it herself and had made disastrous investments. The firm was now Wickfield and Heep, and a new clerk had been engaged, my old friend Micawber. With Traddles I passed an evening with the Micawbers and Mr. Micawber, after calculating the total of two debts Traddles had paid for him, solemnly made out an I.O.U. and handed it to Traddles with a flourish, saying that now he could hold his head up, having discharged his financial obligation to his dear friend. I am certain that this was quite the same to Mr. Micawber as paying the money.

Chaps. 37–44. I bestirred myself to earn what money I could, and was engaged by Dr. Strong, to assist in the production of a long-deferred dictionary. I told Dora of my altered prospects and quite alarmed her by calling myself a beggar. "Don't talk about being poor," said Dora, nestling close to me. But Spenlow sternly forbade me the house. A few days later he fell from his carriage and died. Dora was taken in charge by her two maiden aunts at Putney. Going to Canterbury at this time, I found Agnes very unhappy about her father, who seemed to be getting more and more under Uriah Heep's thumb, and Uriah himself beginning to display a sort of triumphant insolence. Back in London I saw Mr. Peggotty, still on his fruitless search for Little Em'ly. He had missed her by a few days here and there in Europe and was now just setting out for a town on the upper Rhine. But brighter days were in store for me. Dora's maiden aunts consented to receive me as an acknowledged suitor. I was practicing shorthand, with the hope of fitting myself to be a parliamentary reporter. I added a third industry, that of writing short stories. Between them all I acquired an income sufficient to be married, and Dora and I were installed as husband and wife in a miniature house, where Jip had a pagoda to sleep in. We had our little troubles, with the cook and otherwise, but Dora was the prettiest, most affectionate, most lovable child in the world.

Chap. 45. Mr. Dick had, through me, become intimate with Dr. Strong and his young and lovely wife. The doctor loved his wife, but feared she found him dull and unattractive. She loved him, but feared he considered her mercenary. Mr. Dick divined the trouble by sheer force of sympathy, and brought husband and wife most happily together.

Chaps. 46–48. I had been married about a year when one day I was summoned to Mrs. Steerforth's house. There I saw Littimer and heard from him that Steerforth had abandoned Little Em'ly, meaning to have her marry Littimer; but Little Em'ly

had fled from the house and had not been heard of since. I told Mr. Peggotty, and we arranged with a woman whom Little Em'ly had once befriended to be on the lookout for her in London. Dora and I encountered so many difficulties in housekeeping that we finally gave up the task and let the house keep itself. During the second year of our marriage, Dora seemed to lose her strength, and finally she became ill and bedridden. She looked very pretty, and was very merry; but she and Jip danced together no longer.

Chap. 49. Mr. Micawber, in a state of mysterious agitation, made an appointment to meet my aunt, Traddles, and me at Canterbury a week afterward.

Chaps. 50–51. At last Mr. Peggotty found Little Em'ly in London. She had come back to England, but she felt her disgrace so keenly that she would not go home. Mr. Peggotty proposed that he and she should emigrate to Australia. First he went down to Yarmouth, and I accompanied him. I saw Ham, and walked with him on the beach. Through me he sent Em'ly a message that it was not a matter of his forgiving her; he wanted her to forgive him, for having pressed his affections on her.

Chap. 52. We met Mr. Micawber at Canterbury. He read a long indictment against Uriah Heep, showing how Mr. Wickfield had been deluded and cheated; how, by taking advantage of Mr. Micawber's pecuniary difficulties, Heep had made a tool of him; and finally Mr. Micawber proved that Uriah had forged Mr. Wickfield's name. Confronted by this proof, Uriah Heep surrendered to Traddles (who produced a power of attorney from Mr. Wickfield) and disgorged money (including my aunt's fortune). My aunt proposed to Mr. Micawber that he should emigrate to Australia, and offered him the necessary capital. Mr. Micawber declared that to emigrate had been the dream of his youth, though I am sure that he had never thought of it.

Chap. 53. Day by day Dora became weaker. One night she told me that perhaps it was better that she should die; that she had been too young and inexperienced to become my wife. She asked me to send Agnes to her; and I did. I sat downstairs alone with Jip. Jip crawled into my house, lay down at my feet, stretched himself out as if to sleep, and with a plaintive cry was dead. Almost at the same moment, his little mistress passed away in sleep, her head resting upon the bosom of Agnes.

Chaps. 54–57. The Micawbers and Mr. Peggotty, with Little Em'ly, were to sail on the same ship. I had a note of farewell from Little Em'ly to deliver to Ham. I went down to Yarmouth. The night before I arrived there had been a terrible gale, and I heard that a ship had come ashore and was fast breaking up. I hurried to the beach. One mast was standing, and to that there clung four men. Even as I watched them, three were swept away and there remained only one. Suddenly Ham appeared on the scene. With a rope around his waist he plunged into the sea. But a great, green hillside of water swept away the wreck and

cast ashore the dead body of Ham, and the dead body of the other man—who was Steerforth. I had the dreadful task of telling Mrs. Steerforth. Rosa Dartle became frantic with grief and passion. "I loved him," she cried to his mother. Mrs. Steerforth lay back in her chair like a statue. I left them.

Chaps. 58–60. I went abroad and roamed about for a year. Then, stirred to action by a letter from Agnes, I began to work patiently and hard. I wrote a story that brought me some fame. After an absence of three years I came back to England. Traddles was established with his wife in his chambers at Gray's Inn. My dear aunt and Mr. Dick were well and happy. Then I saw Agnes and her father at Canterbury. She was the same sweet, noble, sympathetic girl as ever, but it seemed to me that her smile was more sad than it used to be.

Chaps. 61–63. One day Traddles and I, at the invitation of our old schoolmaster and tyrant, Creakle, paid a visit to a model prison in which Creakle was much interested. It appeared that in this prison all the inmates were good and religious men. The very best and most religious were, it was said, No. 27 and No. 28. When we came to their cells, who should step out but Uriah Heep and Littimer, Uriah with a hymn book in his hand and Littimer with an air of pious resignation. Christmas Day I spent with Agnes; and now at last we came to understand each other.

Ten years after we were married, there came one night to our house Mr. Peggotty, an old man now, but ruddy and vigorous. He had come back to England for a short visit only. He reported that all our friends in Australia were doing well; Mr. Micawber was a magistrate and a prominent man, and Em'ly quiet and retiring.

Chap. 64. It remains only to take a last retrospect. I see my aunt and Peggotty, both in spectacles, but still upright and sturdy. I see Mrs. Steerforth, a querulous, imbecile woman, and Rosa Dartle, a worn and withered figure with a white scar upon her lip. I see Traddles, busy with a large and growing practice, about to be made a judge. Above all, I see one beautiful face, shining on me like a heavenly light. O Agnes, when realities are melting from me like the shadows which I now dismiss, may I still see thee beside me!

Uriah Heep   David

Micawber   Traddles

David Harum

Novel by Edward Noyes Westcott, 1846–1898.
Published 1898.

ED WESTCOTT anticipated Ed Streeter in proving that an American banker could make history as a writer. Westcott's David Harum is such a natural character that people have always liked him and always will, when given the chance—by reading the book, for instance. David Harum has done his bit in movies, too.

Chaps. 1–2. In the town of Homeville, Freeland County, DAVID HARUM, the town banker, is talking with his sister, Mrs. BIXBEE, who is usually addressed as AUNT POLLY by the townspeople, though none of them are relatives of hers. David tells how he has outwitted the deacon in a horse trade. Mrs. Bixbee is somewhat shocked to learn that the deacon deserved the trick because of a shabby trade some time before in which he fleeced David. Now they are even. David informs Aunt Polly that he has hired a new clerk who should arrive next day—JOHN LENOX—and laughingly mentions his intention of testing the young man's fortitude by letting him live for a time at the Eagle Tavern, which is notably uncomfortable and shabby.

Chaps. 3–11. Before he was hired by David Harum, John Lenox spent the greater part of his life in enjoying himself. He attended Princeton for two years, then worked for a time in a brokerage house, where he learned the rudiments of accounting. Soon he regretted having given up college, and suggested to his father that he be allowed to spend a year or two in Europe, taking occasional courses at one of the universities there. His father agreed, and John did exactly that. On his return voyage he encountered MARY BLAKE, a wealthy young woman traveling with her sister and brother-in-law, whom John had known briefly when they were children. John fell in love with Mary but said nothing to her about it. At home once again, John learned that his father's business had been going downhill. John went to work in a law office as a minor clerk. He was not enthusiastic about the work, and after his father's death by suicide he decided to accept the job that a friend, General WOLSEY, told him about. This was the job in David Harum's bank. Mary Blake had written him a note but it was not delivered—because her nephew, JACKIE CARLING, forgot to mail it.

Chaps. 12–16. John arrives in Homeville and is taken to his hotel—the Eagle—by a local cab driver, who immediately decides that John is "stuck-up" and passes the word to that effect. At the Eagle, John tries to get something substantial to eat but settles for the only things available, pie and dough-nuts. The hotel is worse than unprepossessing. The sheets and pillowcases are dirty and the room is dismal, with a mattress that is "conducive to early rising." At the bank, John meets CHESTER TIMSON, who assures him that Dave does almost nothing but horse-trading and expects miracles of industry and efficiency from his clerk. Dave soon corrects this distorted report, without showing any rancor toward Timson, whom he indicates to be rather stupid but with delusions of grandeur. Dave has arranged for Timson's new job, but Timson believes his own reputation and worth attracted the attention of his new employers. John soon discovers that Timson's work has been very slipshod and there is much to be done in order to bring all records up to date. This work keeps him busy for a time, and Dave is pleased with his new assistant. He tests John's honesty with two counterfeit bills, and learns that the young man is highly ethical. His sister rebukes him for doing this and Dave admits he may have been wrong.

Chaps. 17–21. Shortly before Christmas, Dave tells John that he holds a mortgage on the property of the Widow CULLOM and he intends to clear it up once and for all on Christmas morning. The widow has not been able to pay the interest for some time. Dave tells John to write Mrs. Cullom a note asking her to call at the bank on Christmas so that they can execute the necessary documents. John is to be there too, as a witness, which is a prospect most distasteful to him. He thinks it is unnecessarily cruel of Dave to set such a date. In a note to Mrs. Cullom John expresses personal regret. When Christmas comes, the three meet in Dave's office and Dave once more declares his intention of clearing up the entire matter. Without apparent reason, he launches into a long story of his own youth, which was miserable and indescribably poor. Hard work, no love, no tenderness, no recreation—this had been Dave's early youth, with his sister Polly his only comfort. While mending a fence one day, he slipped away to watch the roustabouts and handlers pitch the tents for a circus, thrilled and excited beyond description. Bareback riders, clowns, elephants, wild animals, trapeze artists, sideshows—these were all part of a world of wonders and magic that the shabby, barefoot boy could only dream of. He had not the least hope of seeing the show, but merely watching the preparations was a highlight in his drab existence. Suddenly a fine gentleman spoke to him and asked if he didn't want to go to the circus. Up to that moment, going to the circus had been so far out of Dave's reach that he had not even formed the thought—but suddenly he realized that he wanted to see that circus more than he had ever wanted anything. The fine gentleman was Billy P. Cullom, the late husband of the Widow Cullom. With him Dave saw the circus, with peanuts and soda pop and everything that makes a circus wonderful for a small boy. Billy P. even gave him a dime of his own to spend. The widow's eyes fill with tears as she listens, and she declares that this was just like her husband—always good and kind and thoughtful. Dave then says that perhaps the Widow Cullom didn't know it, but her husband left a small investment that has paid substantial interest over the years and now has reached a size sufficient to pay off her mortgage. Therewith he proceeds to mark the mortgage paid in full, getting the astonished John to sign as a witness. Dave has even written to the widow's married son—who has been struggling unsuccessfully to make a living out West—to come home and work the family land. The widow is so happy she cannot speak, John is ashamed of his previous thoughts about Dave, and Dave is calmly amused at John's chagrin. They all go to Dave's house for Christmas dinner, where Polly is expecting them.

Chaps. 22–29. Arriving at Dave's house, John is astonished and delighted to discover that Dave has surreptitiously moved all of his belongings out of the dreary Eagle Tavern into Aunt Polly's best bedroom. John is to live with Dave and his sister from then on, as long as he wants to remain. Dinner is plentiful and delicious, and the Widow Cullom looks quite different from the dejected, defeated creature whom John saw that morning at the bank. The day is a great success, and Dave recounts a few anecdotes, as is his custom.

Chaps. 30–34. John's life goes on in much the same routine and at the end of a full year nothing notable has happened. He has become friendly with Mr. EUSTON, rector of the Episcopal church in town, but not on a familiar footing. He buys a piano and enjoys frequent musical evenings at home with Aunt Polly and Dave. Mr. Euston learns of his playing and asks him to take charge of the church choir, which he reluctantly agrees to do, so gradually he becomes a part of Homeville's somewhat limited social life. During this time John has learned that Dave is far from being a sharp trader or a stingy man. John thinks often of Mary Blake, whom he still loves, but he does not attempt to find her or write to her.

Chaps. 35–40. John owns a piece of property in Pennsylvania that Dave thinks might prove valuable some day, for there may be oil in that section. Dave also thinks it would be a fine thing if John "teamed up" with Miss CLARA VERJOOS, an attractive young woman whose family spends summers in Homeville. Shortly after this, Clara invites John to a musical evening at the Verjoos house, at which a well-known Boston pianist and a good violinist will perform. She warns John that he will be asked to sing, and he is. He sings several numbers and soon the entire party joins in. The affair is most enjoyable—the first such gathering he has attended in more than two years. On a drive with Dave, John learns that Dave has been married and had a son. His wife died when the boy was only a month old, and Dave never remarried. His son died when he was seven.

Chaps. 41–44. John has been in Homeville for nearly five years when Dave tells him of an opportunity to speculate in the stock market. They invest in pork shares and after a period of tense watching and waiting they sell at a most satisfactory profit. Shortly afterward, David tells John he has decided to make him a partner in the bank. John is happy in Homeville and feels as if Dave and Aunt Polly were his own people. Not long after this John becomes ill with influenza and it lingers an unusually long time, leaving him with a bad cough. The doctor tells Dave that John should go away on a trip, and Dave insists that he do so. Reluctantly, John agrees and arrangements are made for a trip to Europe. Before John leaves he gives David a deed so he can sell his Pennsylvania property.

Chaps. 45–48. John sails on the *Vaterland*. To his astonishment he sees Mary Blake on board. She is with a married couple whom John hears addressed as Mr. and Mrs. Ruggles. On the passenger list he sees their names and a Mrs. EDWARD RUGGLES as well. John assumes that Mary is married and is lost to him. He tells her of his love, almost in the same breath declaring that he knows he should not speak to a married woman in such a manner. Mary lets him think he is correct, for a femininely perverse reason. John's vacation loses its savor, and when news comes that Dave has arranged a very lucrative contract with oil interests John merely feels that his comparative wealth has come too late. He meets Mary again in Italy and she confesses that she is single. The real Mrs. Ruggles was unable to make the trip and Mary took over the reservation, too late for correction on the passenger list. Quickly the lovers make up for lost time and are married. Their son is named for David Harum, about a year later, back in Homeville, where Dave and Aunt Polly have dinner each Sunday with John and Mary Lenox.

Dead Souls

Novel by Nikolai Gogol, 1809–1852. Published 1842. Translated from the Russian by Constance Garnett. (ML, 40)

GOGOL DID NOT FINISH this book. The second "volume" was not developed beyond outline form and parts of the manuscript are missing. Yet *Dead Souls* has become Gogol's most notable work, at least in its English translation. The idea is an amusing one, a scheme to take dishonest advantage of an old law whereby Russian landowners had to pay a head-tax on serfs as of the preceding census, so they were taxed not only on living serfs but on serfs who had died in the meantime. The serfs (who were slaves, except for a few legal rights that were seldom honored) were called "souls." ❡ The novel, incomplete as it is, is quite short, some 60,000 words.

Vol. I. Chap. 1. PAVEL IVANOVITCH TCHITCHIKOV, a collegiate councillor and landowner traveling on private business, drives his little carriage up to the hotel in the provincial town of N., where he is entirely unknown. He is not handsome but he has a solid respectable manner. After a good meal he goes out to look the town over and appears satisfied with the look of it. Next day he calls on the town dignitaries—the governor, the public prosecutor, and others. He attends an evening party at the governor's residence and takes great care to be very well groomed and well dressed. At the party he makes the acquaintance of two landowners, MANILOV and SOBAKEVITCH, the former an affable person, the latter a clumsy yokel. At the first opportunity he quietly questions the postmaster about the two landowners, especially their financial condition. Before long he has Manilov and Sobakevitch completely fascinated. Tchitchikov meets another landowner, NOZDRYOV, a jolly fellow of 30, with whom he quickly establishes himself on familiar terms. Tchitchikov cultivates all the officials and all are pleased with him; he is so gentlemanly, so well-educated.

Chap. 2. Tchitchikov drives out to call on Manilov and Sobakevitch at their country estates. Driving into Manilov's village, which is called Manilovka, Tchitchikov counts 200 huts, dwellings for serfs. Near the Manilov manor-house he sees a garden pavilion with the words "*temple of solitary meditation*" inscribed on it. Manilov greets Tchitchikov with a kiss and takes him inside to introduce him to his wife. Manilov is a careless, easygoing man. Married for eight years, he and his wife are affectionately satisfied with each other. The guest stays for dinner, a simple family meal consisting chiefly of cabbage soup. The two Manilov children are little boys, Themistoclus, 8 years old, and Alkides, 6. In Manilov's study, after dinner, Tchitchikov in a strange tone of voice asks Manilov how long it has been since he made out a census report, and how many of his serfs have died since then. Manilov does not remember. He calls his steward to give the information. The lazy, insincere steward, his head shaved absolutely bare, says a good many serfs have died, but the number has not been counted. Tchitchikov tells him to count them and give him an accurate list of all the serfs who have died since the last census. Manilov asks Tchitchikov why he wants such a list. Tchitchikov hesitates before answering. Finally he tells Manilov he wants to buy the dead serfs. Manilov thinks Tchitchikov must be insane. Tchitchikov gives a vague explanation, intimating that he buys dead serfs—dead souls, he calls them—for some unspecified charitable purpose "in aid of widows and orphans." Manilov is convinced though bewildered and offers to let him have the dead souls free of charge, but Tchitchikov insists on making it a business transaction with a legal bill of sale. Tchitchikov drives off to call on Sobakevitch.

Chap. 3. Tchitchikov's serf coachman, SELIFAN, has been drinking; they are caught in a thunderstorm and the carriage tips over, dumping Tchitchikov out in the mud. He ineffectually threatens to thrash Selifan, who is not at all afraid of him. They seek shelter at a small house nearby. The lady of the house, talkative old Mme. KOROBOTCHKA, invites them to stay overnight because of the rain. Tchitchikov's muddy clothes are cleaned by her serving woman, FETINYA. Tchitchikov sleeps badly. The next morning he learns that the old lady knows nothing of Sobakevitch or where his estate is located. He learns also that 18 of her own serfs have died. He asks her to sell him her dead serfs; he argues that she will reduce her taxes by selling them to him, at 15 rubles apiece, and he pretends that he merely wants to help her because she is old and not very well-off. At his request she signs a letter to the town clerk of her village listing the names of the serfs Tchitchikov is buying from her. The letter is written by Tchitchikov on paper bearing a legal stamp. He omits the fact that every one of the listed serfs is dead.

Chap. 4. At the village tavern Tchitchikov picks up a little information about the personality of Sobakevitch. The young landowner Nozdryov comes to the tavern. He has been drinking and gambling at a fair, and he tells Tchitchikov he has been fleeced by dishonest gamblers and has lost all the money he had with him. Tchitchikov goes home with Nozdryov but refuses to drink or play cards. Nozdryov scoffs at Tchitchikov's offer to buy his dead serfs. Tchitchikov tells a romantic lie. He says he wants to marry a rich young woman whose ambitious parents will not betroth her to any man who owns fewer than 300 serfs, and that he is 150 short. Nozdryov proposes a game of checkers. Tchitchikov is to stake 100 rubles against all of Nozdryov's dead serfs. The game begins and Tchitchikov soons sees that Nozdryov is cheating. He accuses Nozdryov, who becomes violently insulting and summons two of his house serfs, Porfiry and Pavlushka, both of them huge, rough fellows, commanding them to trounce Tchitchikov. Nozdryov is about to assault Tchitchikov when a police captain comes to arrest Nozdryov on charges of committing a drunken assault on a gentleman named Maximov. Tchitchikov gets quickly out of the house.

Chaps. 5–8. Tchitchikov finds Sobakevitch to be as cunning as a fox in money matters. Sobakevitch, taking it for granted that Tchitchikov has some profitable use for the names of dead serfs, is not interested in the motive, only in the price. He raises Tchitchikov's bid from one ruble per dead soul to 2½. Sobakevitch tries to sell him female souls, but Tchitchikov buys male souls exclusively. At an evening party in town, Sobakevitch stirs up curiosity by mentioning his sale to Tchitchikov; he quickly tries to cover up, but Nozdryov, tipsy as usual, loudly discloses Tchitchikov's mysterious business to the governor. Nobody pays serious attention to the alcoholic talk of Nozdryov, but it worries Tchitchikov. The women of the vicinity start gossiping about Tchitchikov. Some say his dead-soul project is a myth to hide his plan to elope with the governor's daughter. Another rumor says it is to hide his activities as a counterfeiter. The postmaster intimates that Tchitchikov is a wounded veteran with a wooden leg, who has turned to highway robbery. One official is almost positive that Tchitchikov is Napoleon wandering about Russia in disguise. Tchitchikov is ill and knows nothing of these rumors and farfetched theories, but he wonders why the town officials have not come to visit him. He recovers and goes to the governor's, but the porter refuses to admit him. He visits the other officials in turn, and they, too, refuse to see him. He meets Nozdryov, who confesses that he started some of the rumors from spite. Tchitchikov decides to leave town.

Chap. 11. Now we take a retrospective look at the origin of Tchitchikov and his interest in dead souls. Raised in genteel poverty, with no inheritance, he became a poorly-paid clerk in the Department of Justice. He won promotion to the post of head clerk. He was next appointed to a committee in charge of a public construction enterprise, at which he prospered no less than his fellow committeemen from pilfering materials. He transferred to the customs department for the advantages offered in dealing with smugglers. Then he shifted to the work of mortgaging serfs to a trustee organization. At this point he conceived his

brilliant scheme for mortgaging dead serfs at 100 rubles each. (Serf owners in Russia could mortgage their serfs as well as any other kind of property.)

Vol. II. Chaps. 1–5. Some years later Tchitchikov pays a visit to ANDREY TYENTYETNIKOV, a progressive young landowner. Tchitchikov now says not a word about dead souls. He learns that Tyentyetnikov regrets a misunderstanding that has alienated him from General BETRISHTCHEV. Tchitchikov goes to the general's estate, unbeknownst to Tyentyetnikov, and endeavors to patch up the trouble. The general is delighted with Tchitchikov and the latter launches his scheme again. He tells the general he has a senile old uncle who is likely to marry

his housekeeper and leave his money to her, but that the uncle will give Tchitchikov his inheritance now if he shows the uncle that he has bought a large number of serfs. When Tchitchikov offers to buy the general's dead serfs, the general roars with laughter at the prank being played on the senile uncle, and volunteers to give Tchitchikov the dead souls for nothing.

[Here there is a gap in the manuscript.]

At the estate of a Colonel KOSHKARYOV, Tchitchikov comes in contact with a group of landowners whose familiarity with economics and finance leads him to think that projects for land development may be more profitable than his dead souls. Koshkaryov, who is addicted to dogmatic statements, declares that no one could be accused of trafficking in dead souls, because dead souls cannot exist, the soul being immortal.

[Two manuscript pages are missing here.]

Tchitchikov is imprisoned on complicated charges of forgery, smuggling, and purchasing dead souls to cheat the government tax bureau. His lawyer convinces the governor that the evidence against Tchitchikov came from disguised persons using false names. Tchitchikov is released but is ordered to get out of town immediately.

Dear Brutus

Play by James M. Barrie, 1860–1937. Produced 1917.

THE FAULT, DEAR BRUTUS, remarked Cassius, is not in our stars but in ourselves, that we are underlings. Cassius said it in Shakespeare's *Julius Caesar* and it was a successful remark. It helped persuade Brutus to assassinate Caesar. Barrie was similarly successful when he devised a fantasy to prove Cassius right. As literature the play is one of his best. As theater it was very successful. But it is seldom revived, perhaps because it has no one part that is sufficiently outstanding.

Act I. The scene is in the country home of an eccentric old gentleman, LOB, who has invited a group of people to visit him for Midsummer's Week. As the play opens, the five women guests enter the drawing-room. The oldest, Mrs. COADE, is the nicest and most gentle. Mrs. ALICE DEARTH is an embittered woman of strong emotions. Mrs. MABEL PURDIE is of a soft, pleading nature. Lady CAROLINE LANEY is a disdainful

snob. Miss JOANNA TROUT is a young woman to whom love is all-important. The ladies are plotting to uncover the secret of why Lob has invited them. They summon the butler, MATEY, and confront him with a telegram they are planning to send the police; it reveals that he has stolen some rings from them. Matey confesses and returns the rings. The ladies agree not to have Matey arrested if he will tell why Lob has invited them and also Lob's age. Matey says the age is a deep mystery, but some villagers remember that he looked exactly the same as long ago as 70 years. Joanna recalls that Lob is another name for Puck, the mischievous sprite known also as Robin Goodfellow.

For years it has been Lob's custom to invite guests for Midsummer's Week. This is Midsummer Eve, and Matey says the villagers always stay indoors this night because they are afraid of Lob's powers. He warns the ladies that they may go out into the garden but no further, especially not into the wood. Mrs. Purdie exclaims that there is no wood within miles, but Matey mysteriously repeats his warning.

Lob enters, accompanied by two male guests. Mr. Coade is a sweet, gentle man whose only regret is that he has not lived a useful life, which he blames on the fact that he has never been in want of money. The other guest is Mr. Purdie, whose one mistake in life, he believes, was his marriage to Mabel, who does not understand him. (There is another male guest, Mr. Dearth, not with them.) Coade suggests looking for the mysterious wood. Joanna insists that there is no wood, but Coade maintains that strange things can happen on Midsummer's Eve. Villagers have seen a wood that appears each year in a different place. Lob first insists there is no wood, then says that some villagers have never returned from the wood. This dampens the group's enthusiasm for the adventure. Now Lob is disappointed and begins to cry, so to soothe him almost everyone agrees to go.

Joanna and Purdie, left alone while the others ready themselves, are in love with each other. Joanna is afraid Mrs. Purdie suspects them, and her suspicions are confirmed when Mrs. Purdie enters, saying she is looking for something—her husband's love. Purdie says Joanna is the one woman in the world for him. Mrs. Dearth enters, looking for her husband; Purdie agrees to look for him. Joanna retires and Dearth enters, a shadow of what was once a fine man and a good artist. He drinks too much and his wife despises him. He speculates on why he is a failure and wonders if it is too late; his wife assures him it is. She speaks regretfully of her lost opportunity to marry Freddy Finch-Fallowe.

The group is ready to look for the wood. Dearth declines their invitation to go along but asks Lob what they will find in the wood. Lob says it will be what each of them secretly desires—a second chance in life. The women realize that this is the thing they all have in common that prompted Lob's invitation. Dearth draws back the curtains to reveal an endless wood of large trees. He goes first and soon disappears from view, followed by everyone else except Mrs. Coade. Lob is left alone as Matey enters with coffee. Lob then pushes his butler out into the wood.

Act II. The scene opens in the depths of the wood. Lady Caroline and Matey, under the wood's spell, have been transformed into a devoted husband and wife. Matey, instead of becoming a butler, has begun his life as a clerk and has achieved wealth. As they leave the glade they encounter Joanna, who is now unknown to them. She seeks her husband, but they have seen only an old man in gala costume frolicking among the trees. This is Coade, though none recognize him. Each has become a stranger to the others. Joanna waits behind a tree for her husband. Soon Purdie appears with Mabel. In the wood, however, Purdie and Joanna have become man and wife, and Purdie's illicit love is for Mabel. Their conversation is exactly like the previous love talk between Purdie and Joanna.

In another part of the wood are Dearth, looking radiantly happy and healthy, and a young girl who it appears is his daughter, MARGARET. Dearth is painting. He and the girl are very fond of each other and very gay. Margaret fears that someone will take her father away from her, as beautiful things cannot last. She asks what is a "might-have-been," and Dearth explains that it is a ghost; that he might have taken the wrong path in life and wound up without his lovely daughter. A vagrant woman enters, a stranger to both yet in actuality his wife Alice. She is searching the ground for food. Margaret, taking pity on her, offers her money. Alice introduces herself as Mrs. Finch-Fallowe and adds proudly that once she had wealth. They see the light of a house and Dearth goes there to get food for the hungry woman. Margaret does not want him to go. The wood grows dark and she calls out for her father to come back. She does not want to be a "might-have-been."

Act III. Lob's drawing-room. Mabel and Purdie enter, still under the spell of the mysterious wood. They do not recognize the house or Lob, who lies asleep. Joanna enters, and the three begin to argue. The spell wears off. They realize who they really are and Purdie knows he is just a philanderer who could not be faithful to any woman. His supposed mistake in life was not the work of fate, because given a second chance he did exactly the same thing.

Next to enter are Matey and Lady Caroline, who also remain under the spell. Matey, still the great financier, lets slip the fact that he has been stealing large sums of money from various companies. Joanna observes that Matey, too, has remained the same person—a thief. The spell wears off and Lady Caroline is horrified at the thought of being married to a lower-class person. Coade appears next, gaily whistling. Mrs. Coade, who has not gone into the wood, is

afraid; but Coade demonstrates his deep love for her, saying he would have married her even if given a second chance in life. However, he has proved still an idle person who will never be useful. Mrs. Dearth enters, followed by Dearth. They realize their true identities; he becomes the shaky, defeated man he was before.

Breakfast is served by Matey, who reveals that the experiment rarely succeeds. Given a second chance, few people are able to change their natures. Just before the curtain falls, Lob is seen walking in his garden.

Dearth's daughter loves his work

Death Comes for the Archbishop

Novel by Willa Cather, 1876–1947. Published 1927 by Alfred A. Knopf, New York. © 1926 by Willa Cather.

AFTER ESTABLISHING HERSELF as a great writer with her studies of commonplace persons such as one meets, Willa Cather turned to history, projected herself into the American past, and again proved herself a great writer with her historical novels. Among these *Death Comes to the Archbishop* is always rated high and often highest. Among other things, it is an illuminating picture of many facets of the Southwest that exist and appeal to tourists today.

Prologue. In the summer of 1848 three Cardinals and an American bishop assemble in Rome to select a bishop for the sprawling territory of New Mexico, recently annexed to the United States. They select a vigorous young parish priest, Father JEAN MARIE LATOUR, to preside over the new bishopric of Santa Fe. They have only a vague idea of the hardships and dangers to which they are exposing the priest, a recent seminary graduate.

Book I. Father Latour sets out on his rigorous journey accompanied by his boyhood friend from France, Father JOSEPH VAILLANT. Together they cross the rugged American continent, finally arriving in Santa Fe, where they find an environment totally unlike any they have ever known before. Slowly Father Latour begins to reshape his church, which has been under Mexican control. He finds it difficult to accustom the easygoing Spanish aristocrats and poor, lax Indians to his demands for a high level of morality. He and Father Vaillant quickly master the Spanish language. They furnish their main church in Santa Fe with a bell and dream of a future cathedral.

Book II. The stocky, hard-working Father Vaillant begins the first of his many missionary journeys, going to Albuquerque. He cultivates the friendship of a rancher named

MANUEL LUJON, whom he persuades to donate two mules to the Christian cause. These animals, Contento and Angelifa, carry the two priests on most of their future journeys. On one of these journeys, to the Indian town of Mora, the two priests intend to spend the night in the house of a shiftless American pioneer named SCALES, but are ostensibly driven out by his young Mexican wife, MAGDALENA. Later they learn that Scales has deliberately killed his children to avoid responsibility. The two priests rescue Magdalena and send her to a nunnery. Father Latour becomes friendly with the famous American scout KIT CARSON, who assists him when a little strong intervention is needed to supplement Christian persuasion.

Book III. On a trip to Albuquerque the priests are shocked by learning that Padre GALLEGOS, a holdover from Mexican administration, is openly carrying on an affair with a woman of the town. They continue to the wild but romantic Pueblo Indian village of Acoma, where they hear a tale about the dissolute FRAY BALTAZAR, who was thrown over a cliff after accidentally killing one of his servant boys. The priests find life in the region full of violence and immorality.

Book IV. On returning to Santa Fe, Father Latour quietly replaces Padre Gallegos with Father Vaillant as administrator of the important parish of Albuquerque. Strangely enough, the Mexicans do not resent the stern Frenchman's preachings, and they take to morality as passionately as they have previously taken to vice. One bitter winter night, on a long packtrip, Father Latour and his faithful Indian servant JACINTO are in danger of freezing and seek shelter. The Indian boy takes him to an immense cave where a fire is kept burning as part of some mysterious Indian rite. Father Latour thus escapes death, and he promises Jacinto to never mention the night in the cave, though memory of that strange place and the primitive nature of the Indian religion often sends chills through his heart.

Father Vaillant is sent to take the Faith to Arizona

Book V. Father Latour encounters strong resistance from the obstinate Indian priest of Taos, Padre ANTONIO MARTINEZ, who is reputed to have grown wealthy by inspiring an Indian revolt and confiscating the property of the murdered rebels. When he visits Padre Martinez, Father Latour is astounded by the casual way in which the Padre introduces his sons and attacks celibacy in the priesthood. Martinez says, "You cannot introduce French fashions here," and the thought haunts Father Latour, who does not dare displace the man for fear of another bloody revolt. At last the Bishop (Father Latour) is called to Rome for a year. While there he appoints a new Spanish priest, Father TALADRID, to succeed Padre Martinez. The Church at Taos is split into factions as the two priests contend for control. Padre Martinez falls ill and dies but leaves his friend Father LUCERO to carry on his struggle against the new order. Father Lucero dies soon afterward in a ghastly delirium in which he relives an incident in which he murdered a thief. A small fortune in gold and silver is discovered in his cellar.

Book VI. Father Latour gradually wins over the rich ranchers, who contribute to his ever-growing Cathedral fund. He is especially loved by the powerful Don ANTONIO OLIVARES and his wife ISABELLA. Don Antonio dies and Isabella and her daughter are left his entire estate, but the rancher's brothers try to prove that Isabella is too young to be the mother of Antonio's child. Father Latour, with the help of Kit Carson, persuades Doña Isabella to confess her age, which she does with great dignity.

Book VII. Three years after Father Latour's arrival at Santa Fe, the great diocese is further enlarged by the addition of territory gained through the Gadsden Purchase. Father Vaillant is sent off to Arizona to survey the new land, while Father Latour continues his work at Santa Fe. He sees Magdalena, the girl whom he and Father Vaillant rescued from the evil American, Scales, and who has now blossomed into a beautifully mature woman. He works desperately to bring comfort and the word of God to an old Indian woman who is held as a slave by a family newly emigrated from Georgia. Finally, he reviews his past life

204

and especially his long-standing friendship with Father Vaillant. He sorely misses his old friend's companionship, and he dispatches messengers to call Father Vaillant back to Santa Fe.

Book VIII. When Father Vaillant arrives, Father Latour shows him the realization of their dreams—the completed cathedral of Santa Fe. Its clean white lines and unpretentious façade reflect the spirit that has regulated the two holy men's good works. The humble Father Vaillant admires the building but never quite understands why the Bishop has called him home from the more important job of saving men's souls. Bishop Latour receives a letter from the Bishop of Leavenworth, saying that the new Colorado Territory must be covered by the Church. Lawlessness and vice prevail there. Bishop Latour sends Father Vaillant on the mission. Father Vaillant builds himself an impressive wagon and heads north to Colorado, where "his strange Episcopal carriage" comes to be known throughout "that rugged granite world." Against incredible hardships Father Vaillant establishes parishes in the wild mountain towns and camps. He becomes the first Bishop of

Colorado. He returns to Santa Fe only once, after a severe accident that lames him for the rest of his life, and has a final and touching reunion with Bishop Latour. The old missionary priest Father Vaillant dies and as the Bishop of Colorado he is given an impressive burial.

Book IX. In his last years, Father Latour becomes Archbishop of an enormous territory with thousands of Mexicans, Indians, and Americans within its folds. He learns the English language, the better to serve the thousands of Americans who keep pouring into the Southwest. He instructs a group of new priests and missionaries who arrive from his native France. He spends his time in his house near Santa Fe, attended by a young seminarian named BERNARD DU-CROT, the favored companion of his last years. In the fall of 1888, the Archbishop says the midnight mass in his cathedral. He falls ill of a cold shortly thereafter and is confined to his bed for several days. Bernard expresses the confident hope that he will not die of a cold, and the Archbishop replies, "I shall not die of a cold, my son. I shall die of having lived." Then the Archbishop reviews his life from the monastery days in France to the past few years. He still feels the presence of his old and dear friend Father Vaillant. The Archbishop also remembers the way that the Indians, who were being cheated out of their best lands by the United States government, pleaded with him to intercede, and how he refused to do so out of respect for the American separation of Church and State. Yet he lived to see the government retract and allow the Indians to return to their sacred lands. At last, vanquishing time itself by his presence in time past, present, and future, the Archbishop dies and the next morning "lay before the high altar in the church he had built."

The Decameron

Stories by Giovanni Boccaccio, 1313–1375.
Published 1353–58. Available in several translations from the Italian. (ML, 71; also, abridged, PB, PL43)

IN THE DECAMERON there are 100 stories. Some were probably original with Boccaccio, but the great majority were already known. The collection is notorious for its impropriety, in some places obscenity; illicit and especially adulterous love is a constantly recurring theme, and even when the stories are "clean" they are often anticlerical. But literature like conversation was bawdy in those earlier centuries. The *Decameron* is one of history's greatest and most important literary works—great because of the story-telling skill and high good humor of the writing, important because of the dozens of poets and playwrights including Chaucer and Shakespeare who have drawn on it for story material. No other work of literature has had greater influence on later authors. While the Decameron is very long, it is not so long as to discourage reading, being about 325,000 words. Many modern novels are longer.

Preface. In the spring of 1348 a devastating plague is ravaging the city of Florence.

In order to escape the death that lies everywhere, seven young noblewomen who gather at the Church of Santa Maria Novella decide to flee into the countryside. Realizing that they need male companionship for protection, they invite three noblemen, PAMFILO, FILOSTRATO, and DIONEO, to attend them. When the ten nobles assemble at a manor house with their servants, they decide to establish a miniature court and elect one person to rule every day. In order to pass the time, each will tell a story each day and the ruling king or queen will choose the day's theme. They remain outside of Florence for 15 days, but tell stories on only 10 of these. The collection of their tales is thus called the *Decameron* (from the Greek, "ten days").

THE FIRST DAY

On the first day, Queen PAMPINEA says that everyone may tell any story he pleases, and Pamfilo tells the tale of a certain notary from Italy named CEPPARELLO who went to France to work for the powerful knight MUSCIATTO FRANZESI. In France Cepparello was called CIAPPERELLO ("chaplet") and was much detested because he was a usurer. For years Ciapperello waxed fat and rich, but when he grew sick in old age, his two brothers were fearful about his last confession. Surely that would undo them all, they felt. Ciapperello overheard their doubts and persuaded them to fetch him a priest. The FRIAR appeared and began to question the evil man about his past. Ciapperello claimed that he was as virgin pure as the day he was born, that he had never known ambition and had never missed a Sunday sermon in his life. He did confess that he had spat in church once, and when the Friar dismissed the sin, Ciapperello reproached the Friar. Before the confession had ended, Ciapperello was lecturing the Friar on moral virtues. A short time later Ciapperello died and the two brothers commissioned a sumptuous funeral. They then cannily called upon the Friar to deliver the last sermon. The Friar praised the usurer so highly that all the French people in the church tore off the dead man's clothes in the hope of salvaging a relic from that "pious" man. Soon afterward the usurer was canonized, and is now known as Saint Ciapperello. Pamfilo warns the listeners to beware of all people who are diabolically clever as Ciapperello.

THE SECOND DAY

On the second day FILOMENA is queen and the ten stories told all concern people who meet with unhappy adventures but are finally restored to good fortune. The second tale, recounted by Filostrato, concerns a merchant named RINALDO D'ASTI who had gone to Bologna on business and was returning home to Ferrara. He and his servant fell in with three affable men whom they believed to be merchants, but who were actually robbers. One of the robbers asked Rinaldo if he was a pious man, and Rinaldo answered that he prayed every day to St. Julien. The robbers then fell upon the merchant, stripped him of everything but his shirt and told him to pray to St. Julien for help. Abandoned by his cowardly servant, Rinaldo scampered freezing through a heavy snowstorm toward the little town of Guglielmo, but the city gates were closed for the night. He huddled outside a door, wailing and rubbing himself furiously to prevent freezing to death. Inside the door a beautiful WIDOW had been waiting for a secret visit from the Marquis AZZO of Ferrara, who was unable to keep his appointment. While bathing alone, she heard the miserable Rinaldo's lament and ordered her maid to see what was happening. The maid admitted the half-dead Rinaldo into the house, and the widow rushed him into a warm bath. That night the widow did not resent the Marquis' absence, for Rinaldo was an excellent companion. The next morning the widow sent him on his way under a vow of silence with money and new clothes. Just as he was leaving the gates of Guglielmo, Rinaldo spied the three robbers, who had been arrested for another offense. He got back all his money and clothes (except a pair of garters) and continued home while the brigands dangled from the ends of ropes in the town square.

THE THIRD DAY

NEIFILE was elected queen for the third day, but since this was Friday, she proposed that no stories be told until they had moved to another place. On the third day of storytelling, Neifile ordered everyone to speak of someone who obtained or rewon something he wanted very badly. The fourth story-teller was Pamfilo, who told about a rich but simple-minded merchant named PUCCIO, who became such a devout lay friar that he was renowned as Brother Puccio. Because of his religious zeal, his young wife ISABELLA was lonely and disheartened. One day a worldly young monk named FELICE returned to their small town from Paris and became friendly with Brother Puccio. He soon came to intimate terms with the lonely Isabella. Finally Felice proposed to Brother Puccio that if he were really desirous of becoming a holy man, he should extend himself at night on a plank as if he were being crucified and should repeat prayers until the dawn. Brother Puccio eagerly consented, and while he was carrying out his plan to reach heaven, Felice accomplished his goal of seeing Isabella. One

night Brother Puccio heard his wife making a great deal of noise and asked what she was doing. Isabella shouted merrily back that she was "flopping about" from having fasted too long. Thus Brother Puccio achieved the penance that he so zealously hoped for, while Felice and Isabella settled for a more earthly pleasure.

THE FOURTH DAY

On the fourth day King Pamfilo decreed that everyone should tell a tale of someone's woe. Filomena told the famous story of the unfortunate lover ISABETTA of Messina, Sicily [later told by the English poet John Keats in *Isabella*]. Isabetta lived with her three brothers in Messina and was especially attracted to a young man named LORENZO, who worked for them. The two lovers contrived to see each other often, but one night one of the brothers spied Isabetta and informed the others of her potential disgrace. Secretly the brothers waylaid Lorenzo, killed him, and buried his body. They then told Isabetta that he had gone away on a business errand. When Lorenzo did not return, Isabetta plied her brothers with questions, but could learn nothing. Then one night Lorenzo's ghost came to her in a dream and told her where his body was lying. She hurried to that place, found the corpse (which had not been corrupted), and carried the head back home wrapped in linen. Then she wept constantly over the head, which she placed in a pot in which she planted sweet basil. A beautiful plant sprang up, watered by her tears. Soon her brothers noticed that she was visibly wasting away and so they stole the pot from her. On digging up the plant, they found Lorenzo's head. They fled Sicily for fear their murder might be uncovered. Isabetta, abandoned, slowly pined away to her death.

THE FIFTH DAY

FIAMMETTA, queen for the fifth day, proposes that everyone tell a story about lovers who are united after much suffering. She herself tells the much celebrated tale of FEDERIGO and his falcon. [Longfellow used this story in his *Tales of a Wayside Inn*.] Federigo degli Alberighi was one of the most courteous cavaliers of Florence. He was hopelessly in love with a woman named GIOVANNA, who was already married, and he squandered his entire fortune vainly trying to win her approval. When the last of his money was gone, he retired to a small farm at Campi, where his only valuable possession was a beautiful black falcon. As time passed, Giovanna's husband died and she was left a widow with a frail, delicate son. She retired to an estate near Federigo's miserable dwelling, where her son often went to watch the falcon. Eventually the son fell ill and when Giovanna promised him whatever he wanted, the son demanded Federigo's beautiful bird. The poor woman was dismayed, for she felt that she had no right to demand anything from Federigo. Nevertheless she went to his farmhouse, prepared to beg. When Federigo saw her there he was overjoyed, but likewise dismayed, for he had nothing suitable to offer Giovanna for a meal—except the falcon. With a gesture of supreme generosity, he roasted the handsome bird and served it for dinner. When the meal had ended, Giovanna at last worked up enough courage to make her strange request. Immediately Federigo broke into tears and explained that he had just given her the thing she wanted. Giovanna was overcome by his sacrifice but returned home sadly, knowing that her son would be broken-hearted. In no time at all, the son's condition grew worse and he died. Now Giovanna was more alone than ever, but she had never forgotten Federigo's honorable act. She summoned him to her house, over the protest of her brothers, and offered him her hand in marriage. Thus Federigo, who had sacrificed everything he had for her, was raised back to nobility by his beloved Giovanna.

THE SIXTH DAY

On the sixth day of the story-telling, ELISA orders her companions to recite tales in which a person's glibness got him out of danger. Neifile tells the story of a cook named CHICHIBIO, who was employed by the noble Florentine CURRADO GIANFIGLI-AZZI. Currado was fond of hunting and one day captured a crane, which he gave to his cook to roast for an important dinner. While Chichibio was going about his duty, his sweetheart BRUNETTA came into the kitchen and demanded one of the drumsticks. Chichibio, knowing how dangerous it was to change the shape of the bird, nevertheless did as she asked and then carried the one-legged crane to the dining table. Currado was outraged when he saw that the fine bird had been mutilated, but Chichibio insisted almost maniacally that all cranes had only one leg. The next morning Currado took his cook to the hunting ground, promising him dire consequences if his foolish statement did not prove to be true. Fortunately for the cook, some of the cranes were asleep, and so were standing on one leg. However, Currado shouted "Ho, ho!" and the birds dropped their raised legs and flew away. The quick-thinking cook, undaunted by this proof, replied, "Well, if you'd yelled 'ho ho' to that crane on the plate, he might have dropped the other leg too." Thus he escaped punishment by using his wits.

THE SEVENTH DAY

Under the order of Dioneo to speak about women who cleverly deceived their husbands, Filostrato told of a young Neapolitan wife named PERONELLA who was married to an old MASON. Peronella caught the eye of a handsome youth called GIANNELLO, and they met each other every day in Peronella's house while the mason was off at

206

work. One day, however, the trusting mason returned early and thumped at the door, shortly after Giannello had entered the house. In their frenzy, Peronella pushed Giannello into a large wine vat and then admitted her husband. She berated him viciously for not working, but the mason said that he had brought along a friend who wanted to purchase their wine vat for five florins. Using her wits, Peronella said that she already had a prospective customer inside the vat who had offered seven. The mason dismissed his buyer and greeted Giannello, who then insisted that the vat be cleaned out before he took it. The mason changed places inside the vat and while he scraped away, his wife directed his work from above at the same time she enjoyed Giannello's love.

THE EIGHTH DAY

Under the reign of LAURETTA, who demands stories concerning tricks that men played on women or on other men, Pampinea tells a tale about a Florentine widow, HELEN, who loved a young man and was loved in turn by a scholar named RINIERI. When the young man grew jealous of her, Helen offered to play a trick on Rinieri in order to prove her fidelity. She invited the scholar to her house on the night after Christmas. There she kept him waiting out in the snow-filled courtyard while she and her lover disported upstairs. All night long the maid called to Rinieri, reassuring him that he would be admitted. When Rinieri finally realized that he had been duped, he crept home half-crippled by the chill. It took him months to regain his strength, but in the spring he found a wonderful opportunity for revenge. Helen's maid came to him, saying that the young lover had deserted her mistress. The mistress, knowing that Rinieri was skilled in magic and lore, begged him to employ sorcery to win back the young man's love for her. Rinieri went to Helen and, pretending to be still in love with her himself, told her to go off to some deserted place and perform a strange rite. He supplied her with an effigy of the lover and some incantations. Helen went to a nearby estate in the Arno Valley, left her maid at the main house, and then went alone to a stream and bathed. She climbed naked with her effigy up into a stone watchtower and there recited Rinieri's magic words. Then she waited for fairies to appear and work her will. Meanwhile Rinieri had followed her to the tower and taken away the ladder. When dawn broke, he saw Helen striding about naked up above

and then directed a malicious harangue against her. Helen begged and pleaded, offering to give him whatever he wanted, but Rinieri refused to let her down—despite her obvious beauty and his continuing desire. All during that hot July day Helen

was exposed to sun, flies, and mosquitoes, until she was baked to a crisp. Finally Rinieri took pity on her. He gathered up her clothes and carried them back to her maid, whom he told where Helen was imprisoned. The maid darted to the tower and there she and a straying herdman rescued her mistress. After long, careful treatment Helen was restored to her former beauty, but never again did she dare to cross a scholar and gentleman.

THE NINTH DAY

EMILIA tells her subjects that they may recite any tale they wish, and most of them narrate anecdotes. Neifile tells how the famous humorous poet and contemporary of Dante Alighieri, CECCO ANGIOLIERI of Siena, left for the south, with his friend Cecco FORTARRIGO attending him as valet. Angiolieri was decked out in his finest clothes on a magnificent horse—all farewell presents from his father. The two stopped at an inn. Angiolieri went to sleep but Fortarrigo gambled with people at the inn and lost all his money. He then crept up to Angiolieri's room, stole his money, and returned to his gambling. Toward dawn Angiolieri arose. He was shocked when he tried to pay the inn bill and found his gold gone. Then he spied Fortarrigo sneaking upstairs in his shirt. His valet had lost all his clothes and was going up to steal his master's garments. Enraged, Angiolieri decided to abandon Fortarrigo to his fate. He set off on horseback. Fortarrigo ran out of the inn, leaped on another horse, and rode after him, crying, "Thief! thief!" When the peasants saw the half-naked Fortarrigo they believed he had been robbed and they stopped Angiolieri, stripped him to his shirt, and gave everything to Fortarrigo. Thus the valet's craft got the better of his master's kind intentions.

On the last day of the story-telling and the fourteenth day after their departure from Florence, the nobles accepted Pamfilo's order to tell a story about someone who had distinguished himself greatly in love, war, or any other endeavor. Dioneo was the last story-teller, and he recounted the amazing tale of "the patient Griselda" [which Chaucer adapted in his *Clerk's Tale*]. Lord GUALTIERI of Saluzzo was a young man who had never wed. When his subjects clamored for his marriage, he chose a peasant girl named GRISELDA, daughter of the poor farmer GIANNUCOLO. Griselda bore him a son and daughter and proved to be a model wife, but Gualtieri toyed with the idea of testing her. First he sent a servant to deprive her of her daughter, making his wife believe that the little girl was being murdered at his command. Instead, Gualtieri sent the girl to Count PANAGO in Bologna. Then he did the same thing with the son. Finally he told Griselda that his subjects demanded a noblewoman as ruler rather than a peasant girl (though actually the populace now thought of him as a monster). He sent Griselda back to her wretched hut and pretended that Count Panago was bringing his young daughter for marriage. Gualtieri faked a divorce decree from the Pope and then summoned Griselda to clean the house for the new marriage and to superintend the ceremony in her rags. When Panago appeared with the young girl, Gualtieri dined all his subjects and finally, overcome by his wife's fidelity, announced that the girl whom Panago had brought was actually his and Griselda's daughter. He remarried Griselda at that very feast and his wife lived on in people's memory as a model of patience.

On the next day, the ten story-tellers returned to Florence, ending their brief idyll of story and romance.

Conclusion. Boccaccio begs his readers to excuse him for any breach of good taste, insisting that morals have been imbedded in even the naughtiest tales. Besides, says Boccaccio, the tales are frank portrayals of human nature and will not harm those who believe good deeds are more important than good words. Also the book does not beg anyone to read it. He concludes by thanking God for having directed his pen through 100 tales and by praying that the women of the world may benefit from them.

Delphine

Novel by Mme. [Germaine] de Stael, 1766–1817.
Published 1802.

DELPHINE was Mme. de Stael's first successful work. French critics do not rate her a major novelist, but her first-hand knowledge of the highest French politics and politicians during the Revolution and early Napoleonic years make her novels important as sidelights on history. *Delphine* is also an interesting, well-constructed novel. It is not nearly so naughty as its reputation once made it out to be; there are allusions to scandals, but the heroine is entirely virtuous.

Part I. DELPHINE D'ALBÉMAR is a rich, talented and amiable widow of 21. She was married to her childhood tutor, who gave her the passion of a younger man and the tenderness of an older one. He also instilled in her a love of freedom and intelligence, something unusual for a woman of the 18th century. Although she is a member of the French nobility, she sympathizes with the revolutionary thinking that is growing more prevalent in the circles of scholars and creative minds. Delphine writes to her cousin MATILDE, an 18-year-old girl, and offers a large part of her fortune so that Matilde will be in a position to marry the Spanish nobleman LÉONCE MONDEVILLE. Matilde is anxious to consummate this marriage despite the fact that no one has met Léonce, who has been away for many years. The marriage is being arranged by ested in securing an advantageous marriage for her daughter. She determines to turn Mondeville against Delphine. M. de Serbellane is seen one night entering Delphine's house. He is keeping a tryst with Mme. d'Ervin but scandal associates him with Delphine. A short time later M. d'Ervin, alerted by Mme. de Vernon, surprises the lovers in Delphine's house. There is a duel and de Serbellane kills M. d'Ervin. The fashionable world whispers that Delphine was the subject of the quarrel. Delphine, unwilling to destroy her friend's honor by vindicating her own, does not tell people the real cause of the duel. Delphine is afraid, however, that Mondeville will believe the current story. She asks her aunt,

Matilde's mother (and Delphine's aunt), Mme. DE VERNON, who has long been a close friend of Mondeville's mother. Delphine assures Matilde that she would inherit Delphine's fortune if Delphine should die, and Delphine prefers to confer happiness while she lives. Matilde accepts the gift but reproaches Delphine for her views on politics and accuses her of being a poor Catholic. Mlle. D'ALBÉMAR, Delphine's sister-in-law, writes to her that Mme. de Vernon is a treacherous woman and warns Delphine of the consequences of her generous gift, but Delphine disregards the warning. In Paris Delphine becomes involved in the romance of Mme. D'ERVIN and her lover, the Portuguese DE SERBELLANE. Delphine helps Mme. d'Ervin find happiness away from her selfish husband, by permitting the lovers to meet in her house. Mondeville arrives in Paris and meets his future wife. Delphine, unable to control herself, falls in love with Léonce and prays that he will prefer her to Matilde. She is caught in a situation of her own making, since she has already given her cousin the money that will enable her to marry Léonce. Aware of the ironies of fate, Delphine despairs of ever finding happiness. She thinks of death.

Part II. Léonce regrets that he must marry Matilde. He seeks a solution by asking his mother to let him marry Delphine. Delphine tries to find a way out of her difficulty by confiding in Mme. de Vernon; but she, though fond of Delphine, is more interested.

Mme. de Vernon, to serve as her friend and tell the Spanish nobleman the truth. Mme. de Vernon uses this opportunity to poison Mondeville's mind against Delphine. She tells him that de Serbellane is Delphine's lover and that Delphine plans to join him in Italy. Léonce writes to his mother that Delphine is false and that he is now ready to marry Matilde, though he will never love her. They marry but Léonce is unhappy with Matilde. He finds no joy in life except in the moments he can see Delphine from a distance. Delphine learns that the treachery of Mme. de Vernon turned her lover against her.

Part III. Delphine hears that Matilde loves her husband. Resolved not to hurt her young cousin, Delphine promises herself not to see Mondeville, and to subdue her passion for him. Unfortunately, neither Léonce nor Delphine can control their love. Mme. de Vernon becomes ill and on her deathbed confesses her duplicity to Léonce. The lovers feel that they have been denied their lawful happiness and decide to continue seeing each other in secret. People see them together and this creates a new scandal. Actually the lovers do not permit themselves the liberties of love, but the talk increases and Delphine is placed in a compromising situation.

Part IV. DE VALORBE, a friend of Delphine's husband, has known and admired Delphine for many years. He determines to marry her to save her from scandal. His attentions to Delphine and his announced desire to marry her cause Mondeville to become jealous. Delphine insists that she does not care for de Valorbe and does not intend to marry him. De Valorbe, in trouble with the police on political questions, tries to hide in Delphine's house. Mondeville sees him there and challenges him to a duel. De Valorbe fears the scandal of a duel will cause him to be imprisoned, and he refuses to fight. A witness reports the scene and society delights in the new tale of two men who had appointments with Delphine at the same time. De Valorbe's refusal to answer Léonce's challenge brings him into dishonor in the eyes of the world. Matilde hears the gossip that her husband is in love with Delphine. She has long known that Léonce does not love her but she did not know his real love. She visits Delphine and reveals the fact that she is soon to have a child. Delphine, moved by conscience and by the entreaties of her young cousin, decides to leave France.

Part V. Delphine goes to Switzerland and enters a convent as a boarder. The convent is under the direction of Mondeville's aunt, who pretends to be sympathetic to Delphine but actually dislikes her for bringing scandal to her nephew. De Valorbe follows Delphine to Switzerland and pays so much attention to her that everyone talks about her again. De Valorbe offers to clear her name by marrying her but she refuses out of pride and lack of love. De Valorbe is shaken with grief and takes his own life. Before he dies, he manages to clear Delphine's name with Mondeville, who now knows that Delphine loves no one but him and has always been innocent.

Part VI. Word comes to Mondeville's aunt ·that Matilde is dying. Mondeville's mother is anxious lest her son marry Delphine, whose reputation is dubious and whose fortune is now small. She enlists the aid of her sister in the convent, who convinces Delphine that the only good thing to do with the rest of her life is to take the vows of a nun. So that Delphine can become a nun before she learns of Matilde's death, the aunt petitions the Pope to waive the required year's novitiate. Matilde dies. Mondeville comes to claim Delphine in the convent, but finds that she has already taken the unbreakable vow. Meanwhile the French Revolution of 1789 has taken place. In France the validity of religious vows is repudiated. Mlle. d'Albémar persuades Delphine to renounce her vows and return to France to marry Léonce. But Delphine discovers in France that public opinion is against her and she has become a social outcast. She does not want Léonce to share her lonely life and she refuses to marry him. Mondeville, in a state of despair and confusion, leaves to join the royalist forces fighting against the Republican government. On his way he is captured by the Republicans and is sentenced to death.

Conclusion. Delphine, who has some influence because of her early liberal views, tries to obtain a pardon for her lover, but she is ignored by the bloodthirsty members of the government, who distrust all members of the nobility. When Delphine real-

Matilde goes to see Delphine

izes that all hope is gone, she takes a slow poison and joins Léonce as he walks with the Republican soldiers to the execution ground. There she dies, confessing her eternal love for Léonce. At first the soldiers, moved by Delphine's dying words, refuse to kill Mondeville but he is weary of life and taunts them into raising their muskets and shooting him. Friends bury Delphine and her lover in the same grave.

Desert of Love

Novel by François Mauriac, 1885–Published 1925. Translated from the French by Gerard Hopkins.

MAURIAC, a major French novelist of this century and a Nobel prize winner (1952), is known for the strong flavor of Christian and specifically Roman Catholic sentiment in his books. *Desert of Love,* one of his most popular novels, pursues the familiar theme of a father and his young son in love with the same woman, and it reaches a conclusion in which faith and the help of God are the solution. It is in many respects a profound book.

Chap. 1. One evening in a Paris bar RAYMOND COURRÉGES, a man of 35, prematurely jaded by a dissolute life, comes unexpectedly face to face with MARIA CROSS, after 17 years of vengeful memories of her. He has blamed Maria for an emotional crisis that diverted him from the promising seriousness of his youth to a life of lechery. The crisis occurred when he was an adolescent schoolboy in Bordeaux, their home town. She was then known to local

scandal as the mistress of a prosperous Bordeaux widower, VICTOR LAROUSSELLE. Here in the Paris bar, Larousselle is still with her. Raymond's father, Dr. PAUL COURRÉGES, played a painful part in Raymond's involvement with Maria Cross. Raymond has just received a curt note from his father, who has come to attend a medical congress in Paris. Five years ago Raymond broke with his parents when he was refused a cash advance on his inheritance. He has not seen his father in three years and does not intend to see him now. Raymond is impressed by how little Maria has changed. She is still beautiful, while Larousselle has become a noisy, hard-drinking, crimson-faced fat man.

Chaps. 2–5. In Raymond's memories he is back in the past in Bordeaux. His mother is a nagging scold; his sister MADELEINE seems to dislike him; and Madeleine's husband, GASTON BASQUE, blames Raymond's boyhood faults on the weakness of Raymond's father, who is enfeebled by recurrent heart attacks. Raymond's paternal grandfather, a brilliant surgeon, had squandered his more than ample income on disreputable women. Raymond's father tries to develop a comradely relationship with Raymond but is rebuffed by the boy's unwillingness to show or accept affection. One of the doctor's patients is Maria Cross, who broods over the recent death (from polio) of her illegitimate son. She is in her middle twenties. Raymond's father is secretly in love with her but in a torment of self-guilt fights desperately to control his passion for her. Maria is said to have had numerous affairs with men and to have been a servant girl. Local ladies refer to her as "that woman." She lives in a house owned by Larousselle, ostensibly as a caretaker. His son BERTRAND is a schoolmate of Raymond's. The doctor does not permit himself to give way to his mania for Maria. He contemplates suicide with a revolver but he never can find any cartridges in the house. At length he cannot resist the temptation of touching Maria while he is at her bedside as her physician. She pretends not to notice. Maria has relinquished the luxury of Larousselle's chauffeured automobile and rides on streetcars. Here, one day, Raymond sees her for the first time. Neither knows who the other is. Her loveliness bewitches Raymond, and she is attracted by his boyish admiration. She wants him to speak to her but he does not dare.

Chaps. 6–10. One day Maria gets a chance to talk to Raymond because the car breaks down. Raymond's advances are clumsily juvenile, but their very awkwardness delights and excites Maria. He tells her who he is. Now she has father and son captivated; the spicy situation stirs her. At home that evening, Raymond cannot resist the impulse to say he has seen Maria. "Was she alone?" his father asks. An unrecognized bond of secret interest draws Raymond and his father together, but they come to the point of quarreling over her reputation. Maria can think of nothing but the moment when she will see Raymond again. Waiting for him in a park, she is terrified by the idea that she has roused him from childish purity to bold lust. He wonders if she would go to a hotel room with him, but he does not ask her. She toys with the idea of asking him to her house, but she will not destroy his innocence. The doctor is now tortured by jealousy, because Raymond has falsely implied that Maria has several lovers. Raymond's father tries to quiet his jealousy by assuring himself that Maria Cross is more romantic than sensual. Larousselle, during a blood-pressure examination, once confided to the doctor that Maria does not really enjoy physical love. Maria meets Raymond in the park and persuades him to come to her house the following Sunday. He makes boorish hints about her status as a "kept woman." Humiliated, she tells Raymond she originally went to live in Larousselle's villa for the sake of her little boy, who since has died. That evening she writes to Raymond, saying he had better not come to her house on Sunday. He goes nevertheless. A school friend has advised him to make abrupt, insistent love to her. She deters Raymond by talking pathetically of her dead child. A few days later he returns to her house. This time he quickly attempts intimate advances. She cannot sidetrack Raymond this time. He lays rude, clumsy hands on her. She gently resists; then she stares at his sweaty young face and the blackheads on his nose and fights him off. She laughingly pretends the struggle is not serious and gets him out of the house as fast as she can. She feels disgust at his callow attempt and does not realize that by leading him on, then resisting him, she has let loose upon the world a young man whose mania it will be thereafter to prove himself irresistible to women. Raymond walks home, where his father is in bed recovering from a mild heart attack. Raymond intends to relieve his spite by reviling Maria to his father, but he is touched by the tenderness with which his father greets him. To his own amazement, Raymond tells his father he has found out after all that Maria is not promiscuous. This makes the doctor happy. Late that night the doctor is called to attend Maria, who has fallen and is seriously injured. He leaves his sickbed against the protests of his wife. Although never confirmed, the supposition is that Maria has nearly killed herself in a suicidal leap from a window of her house. Examining her, the doctor forces himself to remember that he is there to heal her body, not to possess it. Slightly delirious, Maria says, "Only by the embrace of the flesh can we really communicate." Very ill himself, the doctor contemplates Maria's injured body and realizes that his desire for her would be dead if she were married to him. He stumbles from the room.

Chaps. 11–12. The story returns to the Paris bar. Raymond no longer wishes to avenge himself. He only wants her to know of his amorous career, the countless women he has had, including an American woman whose gigolo he has been. Larousselle, very drunk and very rude to Maria, brings Raymond to their table although she asks him not to. At first she is icily silent. Raymond is astonished to learn that she and Larousselle have been married for some years. Larousselle goes to drink with two Russian girls at the bar and Raymond asks Maria if she remembers their last meeting. She says that there is nothing serious to remember about it. He says it was serious for him. Still fighting to get the best of this inaccessible woman, he tells her he probably has had more women than any young man of his age—and not just tarts, he adds insinuatingly. Maria says she presumes that sort of filth is the only thing he cares for. Then Larousselle, blind drunk, falls off his bar stool and cuts himself severely when his glass breaks. Raymond and Maria take him home. Larousselle is in an alcoholic coma. Raymond telephones to his father, who comes to give Larousselle medical attention. Raymond is shocked to see how old his father looks. The doctor cannot take his eyes from Maria's face. She faces up to the situation and bids goodbye to her two frustrated lovers of bygone days, father and son. It is the beginning of a new and close accord between Raymond and his father. Raymond resolves to mend his ways, to work hard and lead a worthwhile life. He understands now that he carries within himself a frantic capacity for passion, inherited from his father. Raymond and his father part affectionately and the doctor takes the train back home to Bordeaux.

Desire Under the Elms

Play by Eugene O'Neill, 1888–1953. Produced 1924. Published by Random House, New York. (NAL, S1502)

THOUGH A WORTHY and successful play, Desire Under the Elms is marred for reading by its author's attempt to transliterate New England country dialogue into syllables of the English alphabet, for instance yewr for your. Such sniping aside, it is one of the best plays of America's greatest playwright. Each of his plays emphasized the universality of something human. In this play passion thrives in a farmhouse surrounded by a rocky New England farm. Deferring to a vagary of the author's, the play must be divided into "parts," not "acts."

Part I. 1. EBEN CABOT is admiring the sunset on the porch of a New England farmhouse in 1850 when he is joined by his older half-brothers, SIMEON and PETER. They speculate on the possible death of their slave-driving father EPHRAIM, who has been gone from the farm for two months. Peter thinks they might be able to commit the old man, but the three decide that they must wait until he dies before there is any future for them. 2. The older brothers upbraid Eben for praying that the elder Cabot die, but he reminds them that the old man drove Eben's mother to death. After dinner Eben leaves to visit the Scarlet Woman, Minnie. His brothers taunt him but this does not deter Eben. 3. Just before dawn, Eben returns and wakes Simeon and Peter to tell them their father has remarried, a pretty woman of 35 from New Dover. The older brothers agree that this is the last straw and decide to join the gold rush to California. Eben offers to give them $300 each to get there in return for their shares of the farm. When they ask where he got the money he tells them his mother found the hiding place where their father had secreted the amount he got for her farm.

4. Simeon and Peter sign the papers for Eben and receive their money in $20 gold pieces. They are like a couple of youngsters with delight, but they stiffen like statues when Ephraim Cabot and his new wife, ABBIE, appear. The new maw is introduced to Simeon and Peter, who sarcastically warn her that Eben thinks it is his home. They insult their father and throw rocks through the parlor window and go off singing a song of the gold-seekers, "I'm off to California with my washbowl on my knee." When Abbie meets Eben he curses her but she says they have a lot in common. They quarrel about ownership of the farm.

Part II. 1. Eben and Abbie confront each other outside the farmhouse two months later. He accuses her of having sold herself to his father for the farm and she upbraids him for visiting Minnie. Cabot appears and asks if they have been quarreling again and Abbie, in a rage at Eben, tells the old man that his son was making love to her. Then, frightened, she takes it back and reminds Cabot that he needs the boy to work the farm. Cabot is worried about what will happen to the farm when he dies but Abbie says "Mebbe the Lord'll give us a son." Cabot promises to will the farm to her if this happens. 2. Cabot is upbraiding Abbie for not bearing him a son and he stalks out to sleep in the barn. Abbie runs into Eben's room, kisses him, and declares her love for him. He affects to scorn her and threatens to murder her, but she knows he wants her. She tells him she will be waiting for him in the parlor.

3. Eben goes to the parlor, where Abbie is waiting. She says she thought someone was there when she entered the room. He assures her that it is his mother's spirit (which he has often seen there). Abbie says she will take his mother's place. She proceeds to the idea that the spirit feels kindly toward her because she loves Eben, and she admits it may be his mother's vengeance on his father, so that she can rest quietly in the grave. They declare their passion. 4. Abbie and Eben kiss lovingly at dawn as he goes off to work the farm. Cabot

209

Abbie separates Eben and his father

accuses Eben of drinking and becomes suspicious when the boy offers to shake hands with him. Then, scornfully, he puts down Eben's gaiety to the old charge of his being "soft-headed, like his maw."

Part III. 1. A dance is being held in the farmhouse kitchen a year later. Abbie asks her neighbor where Eben is. The neighbor says, meaningly, that she hasn't seen him since Abbie came to the farm. When Abbie asks others the same question they answer with innuendoes. Abbie looks at Cabot, but he has not heard; when told the guests are waiting for Eben, Cabot says: "Eben's done for now! I got a new son!" The party gets in full swing and Cabot takes over the floor, proving to his guests that a man of 76 can beat the youngsters. He even wears out the fiddler before he is through. In an upstairs room Eben is at the cradle of a newborn child and Abbie, as though sensing something, tells Cabot she is going upstairs to see the baby. A woman declares that what has happened in the house is "as plain as the nose on yer face." In the upstairs room Abbie throws herself into Eben's arms and asks to be kissed, pledging him to secrecy about the paternity of the baby. **2.** Cabot asks Eben why he has not been dancing with the pretty girls, reminding him that if he marries he could earn a share of the farm. Eben retorts that this is his farm. Cabot tells him he will never own stick or stone of the farm because it is now Abbie's and her son's, and that Abbie has told him how Eben tried to get around her by making love to her. The young man is petrified with rage and threatens to murder Abbie. Cabot struggles to restrain him. Abbie appears and separates them, then falls on her knees beside Eben as Cabot leaves them. The boy accuses Abbie of lying to make the old man promise her the farm, and she admits it but says it was before they loved each other and asks forgiveness. Eben threatens to join his half-brothers in California and Abbie pleads with him to stay with her for her sake and the sake of their son. Then she says she will prove she loves him. **3.** Eben is sitting in the kitchen, his carpetbag on the floor beside him. Abbie comes and tells him she has proved her love for him. When she tells Eben she has killed "him," he thinks she means his father; but it is the baby she killed, by holding a pillow over his face. Eben rushes off to get the sheriff and tell everything before he leaves for California.

4. Abbie tells Cabot the baby is dead; that she has killed it. The old man asks why and she tells him the truth about her affair with Eben. Cabot starts to go for the sheriff but Abbie says Eben has already gone for him. Eben rushes in and Cabot threatens to kill him, but he stalks off as Eben tells Abbie he is going to share responsibility for the baby's death, because he really loves her. Abbie and Eben have a tender scene, with Abbie mothering him. Cabot returns from the barn to tell them he has let the stock loose and is going to burn up the house as soon as the sheriff takes them away. Then he will go to California. He looks for the hidden money and discovers that Eben has already taken it. The sheriff appears and arrests Eben and Abbie. Then, looking around the farm, he says to a companion, "Wished I owned it!"

Diana of the Crossways

Novel by George Meredith, 1828–1909. Published 1885.

EARLIER NOVELS BY George Meredith (especially *Richard Feverel*) are now ranked ahead of *Diana*, but *Diana* was his first success with the book-buying public. It is in fact easier to read than most Meredith novels (see the note on *The Egoist*). *Diana* is based on a celebrated English scandal, the case of Caroline Norton and Lord Melbourne, the British prime minister, who are respectively represented in the novel by Diana and Lord Dannisburgh. In 1836 Mrs. Norton's husband sued her for divorce, naming Melbourne, a man nearly thirty years older than she. Mrs. Norton won the case, and a later accusation that she had sold state secrets was also proved false. Meredith's novel makes this latter accusation true but he absolves his heroine of blame.

Chap. 1. The diary of HENRY WILMERS, which begins with events of the period 1825–50, praises the beautiful and witty

Mrs. WARWICK but not Wilmers' enemy Lord DANNISBURGH, who was involved in the famous Warwick-Dannisburgh affair. The novelist will tell the story free from prejudice.

Chaps. 2–3. At a ball in Dublin, DIANA ANTONIA MERION attracts the attention of all the men with her charm and beauty. She is the daughter of the late Dan Merion, and her family home is known as "The Crossways." At the ball Diana meets THOMAS REDWORTH, a friend of the husband of EMMA, Lady Dunstane, Diana's dear friend and protector (whose pet name for Diana is TONY). One of the others present is SULLIVAN SMITH, an Irishman. Smith overhears a certain Mr. MALKIN, a harmless and inconsequential young man, declare that the popular Diana had broken her promise to give him a dance. This, in Smith's mind, constitutes calling the young lady a jilt—an insult. He declares his intention to challenge Malkin. Redworth attempts to dissuade him, with the result that Smith considers it his duty to duel Redworth as well. With rare diplomacy and tact, Redworth persuades Smith that neither duel is necessary, and that the connection could not fail to tarnish the young lady's name. Smith is convinced.

Chaps. 4–5. Visiting at Copsley, the Dunstanes' country home in England, Diana is concerned over Emma's health. Emma's husband, Sir LUKIN, seems to be devoted but on one occasion as he and Diana are walking through the woodlands he attempts to make love to her. Her shock is such that she will not remain at Copsley. She plans to return to The Crossways for a time. She and Sir Lukin, returning to London together, meet Redworth, who tells them he has invested all of his resources in railway stocks. This, to Sir Lukin, seems a dangerously risky speculation. Diana leaves in the coach, and Redworth is to remember the sight of that departing coach for many a year. His investment prospers and soon he has considerable wealth. He visits Emma at Copsley to tell her of his good fortune and to ask where he may reach Diana, whose hand he wishes to ask in marriage. He has procrastinated this long only because he wanted to have ample means to sustain her as one of her birth and standing deserves. Emma is distressed; Diana has just written that she has accepted AUGUSTUS WARWICK, a promising public official, so Redworth's proposal has come too late. Lady Emma is chagrined partly because she believes Redworth would be a better match and partly because Diana's letter indicates that Diana is making a loveless match for the sake of retaining her beloved Crossways and to avoid the defenseless position of an unmarried orphan.

Chaps. 6–14. The marriage of Diana and Warwick is not happy. Warwick is concerned only with his political career. He is convinced of the superiority of the English. He scorns Crossways, and though before their marriage he promised Diana never to ask her to sell it, now he does propose this, and she refuses. They live in lodgings in London that he considers below their station. Among their good friends in London is the elderly Lord Dannisburgh, a Cabinet member and most influential politically. He takes a fancy to the charming Mrs. Warwick, and Warwick is not averse to profiting from this attraction. A pleasantly lucrative political appointment results, but tongues begin to wag. Indiscreetly, Diana selects Lord Dannisburgh to accompany her on a visit to Lady Dunstane at Copsley. The tongue-wagging becomes a matter of public scandal when Warwick serves Diana with a summons to appear in court to answer to charges of adultery. Diana disappears, writing to Emma that she has decided to leave England. Emma realizes that this is tantamount to an admission of guilt, which she is certain does not exist. Knowing Diana so well, Emma is sure she has gone to the Crossways for a last farewell to the place she loves so well. Sir Lukin is not at home, or Emma would have made him go to persuade Diana to return and face the charges. Providentially, Redworth appears, just back from a trip to America. Emma asks him to go to the Crossways, carrying her letter to Diana. He sets out immediately. He reaches Diana's house, and though he has a bit of difficulty he convinces her of the wisdom of returning.

Chaps. 14–18. When Diana is back in London awaiting trial, Emma wages a battle to have her accepted in the best society as usual, and is successful; even the influential Mrs. CRAMBORNE WATHIN (soon to be Lady Wathin) goes to dinner with Diana, but takes a dislike to her through jealousy of her wit and popularity. On the same day, Redworth is elected to Parliament; Dannisburgh's nephew, PERCY DACIER, whom Diana has noticed but not met, makes a good speech in Commons; a novel *The Princess Egeria*, which Diana wrote under the name Antonia, is readied for publication; the Crossways is let at a good price; and Diana wins the case Warwick brought against her. But she is still bound legally to Warwick and helpless to act independently of him, under English law. She spends some time nursing Lady Emma through a serious illness, then leaves England for a cruise of the Mediterranean with some friends, Lord and Lady ESQUART.

In her travels Diana meets Dacier. He is not formally betrothed, but is is generally assumed that he will marry the very rich Miss CONSTANCE ASPER. Dacier falls in love with Diana, however, and defers matrimony with Miss Asper. His uncle is reported to be seriously ill and he returns to England. Redworth has been busily engaged in stimulating interest in Diana's book, with the result that it is immediately a tremendous success. He knows that Diana needs the money. Diana is not deceived by the success of her first book but she enjoys her success, which establishes her in London.

Chaps. 19–20. Diana is visiting at Copsley when news comes that Dannisburgh has died. He made a dying request that

Diana come and sit by his body for one hour. His family is shocked at the request, but all feel that it must be fulfilled. Diana sets out for Dannisburgh's house immediately and sits with the dead man through the night. Dacier is there and expresses his admiration for Diana's fidelity to her friendships. He knows, as Diana does not, that Dannisburgh has left her a legacy.

Chaps. 21–26. In the months that follow, Diana writes a new book, *Young Man of State,* and it is very successful. It is the kind of book that stirs gossip about its writer and

Diana is victor in court

its characters, who resemble individuals in real life. *Young Man of State* is very obviously about Percy Dacier, and gossip is heavy. Diana finds Dacier's company pleasant and sees him often. Her husband is ill, and Lady Wathin asks Diana to return to him in his trouble. Diana refuses flatly, increasing Lady Wathin's animosity. Diana goes to France for a brief holiday on the seacoast and Dacier visits her there, much to her surprise. They are, as ever, on most formal terms, and do not address each other by their first names; Dacier once suggested this, tentatively and diffidently, but Diana insisted that they would do well to keep matters on the more formal basis. Now Diana wonders if she may have fallen unwittingly in love with him. Dacier gives Diana some news he received from Lady Wathin; Warwick is instituting a "process of law" to force Diana to return to him. Dacier then declares his love and begs Diana to elope with him and avoid Warwick forever. Diana realizes that she loves him and agrees to his proposal. They are to be married later, when she is legally free of her husband. She is saved from this ultimate indiscretion by the unexpected appearance of Redworth with the news that Emma is seriously ill and Diana must return with him immediately. Emma undergoes an operation, and the ordeal serves to bring both Diana and Dacier back to reality. The reckless plan for elopement is as if it had never been.

Chaps. 27–34. Diana continues to see Dacier but permits no mention of love. She also sees Tom Redworth frequently. Her

thirst for information on political situations intrigues him. Diana's financial condition becomes so bad that she has to sell the Crossways, much as she loves it. She becomes almost a secretary to Dacier, helping him in every possible way and holding gay soirées to gather influential men about him. One night Dacier returns after a party and tells Diana some secret news of further political developments. At the same time he importunes her to allow him to become her lover. Diana knows she cannot have him as a friend if she will not have him as a lover, yet this she cannot envision. Later that night, Diana goes to the editor of a paper that opposes Dacier's group and sells him the secret news. When Dacier reads the article the next morning, he is aghast and incredulous. Diana is desperately unhappy when she learns she has seriously damaged the cause of her beloved; she merely needed the money and thought that providing a news item to the papers was a legitimate way to earn it. Dacier does not understand and in his anger he leaves her—both as hopeful lover and as friend. Diana is cold in her heart. She is sincerely penitent, but now it matters not one bit. She is once again alone.

Chaps. 35–36. Dacier swiftly becomes engaged to Constance Asper. A bulky letter from Diana is tossed into the fireplace unopened. The check sent her in payment for the secret was enclosed. Some days after the episode of the secret, Warwick is struck by a cab and dies. Diana is now free.

Chaps. 37–40. The story of Diana's revelation of the secret has made her an object of recrimination. Dacier has married Constance, and Sullivan Smith courts Diana. She refuses his suit and goes again to visit Emma in the country. Copsley is soothing to her spirit, and her composure becomes such that she can face Dacier and his bride with equanimity.

Chaps. 41–43. Emma is still the staunch friend, and Diana visits her again. This time she meets Redworth there. He is most successful and is also one of the more distinguished members of Parliament. He invites Emma and Diana to visit him at the Crossways. This is the first inkling Diana has had of the fact that he was the purchaser of her family estate when she had to sell it. He has furnished it with such of her possessions as remained and has prepared it for her—in the hope that she will one day become his wife and live there with him. Diana hesitates, fearing that her reputation and the ancient scandal might damage his political and business careers. She knows, however, that she loves him, and that he loves her; and with the encouragement of Emma she overcomes her fears for the future and ecstatically accepts his proposal of marriage.

The Divine Comedy

Poem by Dante Alighieri, 1265–1321. Written about 1300 to 1321. Several translations from the Italian. (ML, 208; ML, T7; RE, 72)

ALMOST WITHOUT DISSENT, Dante's *Divine Comedy* is classed as one of the world's greatest poems along with the *Aeneid, Iliad,* and *Odyssey,* and Dante as one of the world's greatest poets along with Shakespeare, Virgil, and Homer. The poem is a vision in which Dante is admitted to the mysteries of Hell, Purgatory, and Heaven; he sees and names hundreds of persons, some Biblical or historical, some mythological, some personal acquaintances. His plan of the places he sees and his scheme for punishments and rewards were intricately wrought and have engaged the study of scholars for centuries. Dante's Hell is a funnel-shaped succession of circles or rings into the earth; his Purgatory, a mountain simi-larly devised; his Heaven, the planets and the sun. Sinners, penitents and saints occupy different circles or stages according to a careful system of classi-fication. ❡ The principal characters, other than Dante, are the poet Virgil, who leads him through Hell and Pur-gatory; and Beatrice, whom Dante un-questioningly places in Heaven. She is the Florentine lady for whom, as a child, he developed a love-from-afar that long survived her death in 1290, when Dante was 25. ❡ As poetry, the *Divine Comedy* is devised with simi-lar care as to form. There are 100 cantos—an introductory one, then 33 each for three main divisions. Each canto ends with the word "stars." The rhyme scheme is *terza rima,* the suc-cession *ababcbcdc . . .* The lines have eleven syllables each. Shelley used this form in his "Ode to the West Wind," but with a longer stanza.

INFERNO

Cantos 1–2. "Midway in the journey of my life" (at the age of 35), I found myself lost in a dark wood. I stumbled upon a hill and suddenly spied a leopard (standing for Worldly Pleasure and Florence) who almost made me turn back. Then I saw a lion (Ambition; France) and a ferocious she-wolf (Avarice; Rome). I was about to turn back when the Roman poet VIRGIL ap-peared and offered to show me Hell, prom-ising me that someone else would guide me through Purgatory and Heaven. The first day of my adventure thus ended and on Thursday evening before Good Friday in the year 1300 we set out. Again I was seized by doubts, but Virgil assured me, saying that a lady in heaven whom I once loved (BEATRICE) had willed my salvation. Ac-cordingly I accepted my lofty mission.

Cantos 3–5. We started into Hell by pass-ing a fearful gate that was inscribed "Aban-don all hope ye who enter here." Entering a dark plain, we saw Trimmers (people who had done neither good nor evil in life) pursued by hornets and wasps. Then Virgil forced Charon, the horrid boatman on the river around the Inferno, to carry us into the first circle of Hell, called Limbo. There I saw those who died unbaptized, including Homer and hundreds of other pagans. The great Greek and Roman poets lived in a noble castle here, which was also Virgil's home. In the second circle, where King Minos judges the carnal sinners, I saw in-famous lovers such as Helen of Troy and Dido. Francesca de Rimini, blown around and around in circles by the wind, paused to tell me how she and her brother-in-law Paolo Malatesta were surprised at love by her husband Gianciotto.

Cantos 6–11. I swooned at her story and Virgil carried me down to the third circle, composed of gluttons. There I saw the fat Ciacco ("Hog"), who told me how our native city Florence would be torn by fights between the Black and White Guelphs. I left him torn by hail and bitten by the three-headed dog Cerberus. In the fourth circle, ruled by the money-god Plutus, I saw the prodigal and the avaricious rolling stones endlessly toward each other. Most were high officials of the Church, but I have forgotten their names. Deeper in the fifth circle, called the Marsh of Styx, I saw the wrath-ful and gloomy souls. The ferryman Phleg-yas took us through this dismal swamp to the towered gates of the City of Dis, home of Lucifer. Some fallen angels tried to pre-vent us from entering, but a heavenly angel appeared and opened the gates. Thus we entered the sixth circle, where heretics are tortured in burning tombs. There I saw Cavalcante de' Cavalcanti, father of my best friend Guido, and Guido's father-in-law, Farinata Degli Uberti. They were suf-fering because they believed in Epicurean philosophy, and my heart was torn when Father Cavalcanti asked me about his son. As we progressed downward, Virgil told me we were entering Lower Hell, where sins were made graver by violence and sim-ple or treacherous fraud.

Cantos 12–17. Among the many divi-sions of the seventh circle, where the violent who have committed crimes are kept, I saw in descending order: murderers and tyrants such as Alexander the Great; suicides such as the Sicilian poet Pier delle Vigne, who had changed into a stunted tree; rebels against God, such as Capaneus, one of the Seven against Thebes, who lay on burning sand; and rebels against nature, such as Brunetto Latini, my old professor at Bologna, who ran in vain across the burn-ing sands. The deepest inhabitants of this circle were the usurers, who abused both nature and art. They sat without any iden-tity, with purses dangling from their necks. I did not even speak to them. The monster Geryon carried us downward on his back.

Cantos 18–30. Then I entered the eighth circle, which holds those guilty of simple fraud. It is called *Malebolge* and is divided into ten bolgias or chasms. First I saw pan-ders scourged by horned devils. Secondly I saw flatterers such as Thais lying in filth. Thirdly I saw simonists or sellers of divine offices such as the present pope, Boniface VIII (whose soul is already in Hell), with their heads wedged in stones. Fourthly I saw false prophets and magicians such as Tiresias walking backwards for eternity. Fifthly I saw barrators (sellers of public offices) boiled in blood by Centaurs. Sixthly I saw hypocrites carrying leaden cloaks. Seventh I saw thieves in snake-filled caves, and learned from one of them, Vanni Fucci, that I would soon be exiled from Florence. In the eighth chasm of evil counselors I heard Ulysses speak about his last voyage before he drowned at sea. I also exchanged moving words with Guido da Montefeltro,

The ferryman Phlegyas took us through the dismal swamp

Pope Boniface's advisor. In the ninth chasm I saw sowers of discord hacking at each other, such as Mohammed, who founded Islam on misunderstood Christian principles. In the dark, disease-ridden tenth chasm I saw falsifiers of every description, such as Simon, who persuaded the Trojans to receive the Trojan Horse into their city.

Cantos 31–34. At last we reached the last circle or bottom pit of Hell, which contains those guilty of treacherous fraud. Hell's bottom is not filled with fire but is an icy swamp called Cocytus. There I saw traitors such as Count Ugolino della Gherardesca, who betrayed his own brother in Pisa and devoured his four sons in prison. At the very bottom, I saw Judas Iscariot and the Arch-Traitor SATAN imbedded in ice. We climbed Satan's back and started to ascend through the other side of the world, coming out at Mount Purgatory, where I was glad to see the stars.

PURGATORY

Cantos 1–9. Virgil and I began to ascend the foothills of the enormous mountain, which lies at the opposite end of the world from Jerusalem, on the morning of Easter Sunday. An angel carried us across a river into Antepurgatory, where the souls are divided among the excommunicated and late repentants. With earthly prayers these people have hope of ascending the mount and reaching the Garden of Eden or Earthly Paradise on top. The moral Roman senator Cato sternly welcomed me and ushered us on among such excommunicated souls as King Manfred of Sicily. Next I saw late repenters such as my slothful musician friend Belacqua and the lovely La Pia of Siena, murdered by her husband before she fully accepted Christ. The great Italian troubadour Sordello showed us many kings who waited here too for salvation. While I slept that night St. Lucia bore me to the gate of Purgatory, where an angel carved seven P's (for *peccato,* sin) on my brow. One P would be erased on each of the seven rungs of the mountain.

Cantos 10–12. On the first rung I saw the proud, such as the famous illuminator of manuscripts Oderisi of Gubbio, carrying stones on their backs and listening to the Angel of Humility.

Cantos 13–17. On the second I saw the envious, leaning on one another like blind beggars. I spoke with the once restless Guido del Duca, who labored there under the care of the Angel of Brotherly Love. Among the wrathful of the third rung I spoke with Marco Lombardo, the Venetian courtier, and we mourned the dissension throughout Italy. I left Marco with the Angel of Meekness.

Cantos 18–22. I saw the slothful, pursued by the Angel of Zeal, on the fifth rung. I slept and then passed to the sixth, where Pope Adrian V addressed me on behalf of the greedy and prodigal, who lay bound to the earth and were lectured to by the Angel of Liberality. Then we met the Roman poet, Statius, author of the epic *Thebaid*

[the story of the Seven against Thebes], who had wisely become a Christian convert and thus was saved, although he was suffering for prodigality. Statius said he had learned the truth from Virgil's *Fourth Eclogue* about a "child soon to be born" (Christ). Statius became the third poet of our little group.

Cantos 23–26. On the sixth rung, of the gluttonous, I met my friend Forese Donati, who told me to comfort his wife back in Florence. I left Forese, who had been changed into a thin tree, and then heard my writings praised by the older poet Bonagiunta of Lucca. On my third day on the mount I saw the lustful souls who were purified by fire and the Angel of Chastity on the seventh rung. I spoke with two great poets there whom I have always admired: Guido Guinicelli of Bologna and the French troubadour Arnaut Daniel, who "returned to the fire that refines him."

Cantos 27–33. Just before reaching the Earthly Paradise, I fell asleep; and when I woke, Virgil bade me farewell, for he could accompany me no farther. I was welcomed by Matilda into the beautiful garden, for the seven P's were erased from my brow. Inside I saw seven pennants and seven candlesticks at the beginning of a grand procession and a chariot drawn by a griffin. This procession brought to me my beloved Beatrice, whom I had not seen for ten years but whom I had loved even after she died. After Matilda baptized me in the River Lethe, Beatrice unveiled her brilliant eyes. I fell asleep under a mystic tree and dreamed about beasts and harlots. When I awoke Beatrice reminded me of my unworthy manhood, spoke to me of the seven virtues, gave Statius and me water from the Eunoë spring, and made me "pure and ready to climb to the stars."

PARADISE

Cantos 1–5. With Beatrice beside me I began flying away from Earth toward the first Planetary Heaven, the Moon, where the inconstant dwell. There I saw Piccarda Donati, sister of Forese in the sixth rung of Purgatory, and Constance, who had inherited the Kingdom of the Two Sicilies and abandoned her life as a nun. Since they had broken their vows, they were content with their places, but if God chose, they would be happy to move closer to His essence.

Cantos 6–9. In the second Heaven, Mercury, abode of the honor-seekers, I met Emperor Justinian, who gave civil law to the Romans, and Beatrice told me about the greater divine law. Leaving the triumphal hymns behind, I reached the third Heaven, Venus, home of the loving, where I spoke with Charles Martel, who drove back the Moors, and Cunizza da Romano, whom everyone had falsely condemned for her elopement with the poet Sordello. The troubadour Folco told me that God allows us to sin only so that He can redeem us with His love.

Cantos 10–14. In the fourth Heaven, the Sun, home of the prudent, I saw St. Thomas

Aquinas revolving on a bright wheel to the accompaniment of incredible music. He pointed out other great philosophers such as Albertus Magnus, and told me the inspiring life of St. Francis. Then St. Bonaventura told me the life of St. Dominic and how the Dominican Order arose. Solomon told me how angels are freed from the flesh, and hearing a beautiful hymn, I moved on to the fifth Heaven, Mars.

Cantos 15–17. Approaching the home of the courageous, I saw an immense white cross appear over the red planet and heard a victory hymn. My distant forefather, Cacciaguida, who was killed on Crusade, told me the history of Florence in all its past glory and present deprivation, warning me about my future fate.

Cantos 18–22. Approaching the sixth Heaven, Jupiter, I saw the white planet transform itself into a Roman eagle. The souls of the just sang to me about all the evil kings of the world, and then I saw the good kings there, such as David of Israel, Trajan of Rome, and William the Good of Sicily. On the seventh planet, Saturn, home of the contemplative, I saw Jacob's Ladder stretching beyond into the heavens. Peter Damian, the hermit, and Benedict who founded Monte Cassino, told me not to press God's inscrutable ways.

Cantos 23–27. Next I entered the Starry Heavens, home of the redeemed. After Beatrice's long instruction, I was questioned about faith by St. Peter, who circled me three times in approval. Next St. James tested me about hope and St. John about love, and both admitted me to the True Heaven beyond space and time.

Cantos 28–33. I entered the Empyrean, home of the Angels, whose nine ranks lead to the still center of the Universe, God, Who encompasses all. We passed through the angelic orders as if over the petals of a beautiful rose. Then St. Bernard kindly came and took me out of Beatrice's care to show the "true order of things." I saw countless saints and angels of varied beautiful shapes, and all the virtuous people of the Bible such as Moses and the redeemed Adam. As we sped on to the bosom of God, the light grew brighter, the music increased, and the whole universe seemed to engage in a stately dance. Then I saw the Virgin Mary rising like the dawn over the Church Triumphant, and I sang a hymn to her, beginning "Virgin mother . . ." At last I looked upon God, the ineffable Three in One, where all harmony and order join in indescribable stillness. I had looked at the center of the cosmic circle, but a flash covered my eyes and I can remember no more. All I can do is proclaim to the world that I reached the point where my desire and will were one, and that I revolved as a wheel, rolled "by that Love that moves the sun and other stars."

Dr. Jekyll and Mr. Hyde

Novel by Robert Louis Stevenson, 1850–1894.
Published 1886. (PB, 123)

THE COMPLETE TITLE is *The Strange Case of Dr. Jekyll and Mr. Hyde.* This short novel (only 30,000 words) shares with *Treasure Island* the honor of being the longest-lived of Stevenson's works and both have a chronic appeal to motion-picture producers, who bring out a new version about once per decade. When Stevenson wrote *Dr. Jekyll* science was beginning to surmise the existence of schizophrenia and the disease epilepsy was thought to produce split personalities of good and evil, but Stevenson chose to make drug rather than disease accomplish the cleavage. Stevenson's widow, in her notes to this novel, says it is allegorical and that Stevenson wrote his first draft in three days, found he had not made the allegory strong enough, tore it up, and wrote an entirely new draft in another three days—60,000 words in six days.

Chaps. 1–2. It is the custom of the lawyer, Mr. UTTERSON, to stroll the streets of London with his kinsman, Mr. ENFIELD. One evening Mr. Enfield recounts this story: Once he was walking along the street when a little girl came dashing out of a doorway into the road. She got in the way of a man who was approaching, and instead of avoiding her he continued like a Juggernaut and trampled on her. Her family and a neighboring doctor came out and he merely stood silent and unmoving. His face as he stood there was the embodiment of all evil. The man seemed oddly misshapen, yet without any actual deformity that one could define. He stated quite coldly that he would pay for any damages he had caused. He paid with a check, and while Enfield discreetly refrains from mentioning the well-known name on the check, Utterson knows as soon as he hears the name of the evil one, EDWARD HYDE. Reposing in a safe in Utterson's office is a strange will, that of Dr. HENRY JEKYLL. Dr. Jekyll bequeaths his entire estate and property, apart from some small legacies to his servants, to that same Edward Hyde. Further, there is specific instruction that if Dr. Jekyll should at any time disappear for longer than three calendar months, Edward Hyde is to assume full, unquestioned possession and control of all Jekyll's wordly goods. Utterson determines to stalk Edward Hyde until he can look upon the face that so horrified others. At length his patience is rewarded; he encounters and speaks to Hyde, who becomes violently angry at the idea that Jekyll might have mentioned him. He accuses Utterson of lying. At Dr. Jekyll's residence, Utterson learns that Hyde has full freedom to come and go as he wishes. Utterson convinces himself that Hyde is holding a youthful indiscretion over the doctor's head.

Chaps. 3–5. After a small dinner party at the house of Dr. Jekyll, Utterson lingers to chat a while. He mentions his distaste for the doctor's will and Jekyll pleads with him to honor it. Utterson is mystified but he promises to safeguard Hyde's rights. Nearly a year later an event occurs that shakes all of London. An elderly statesman, Sir DANVERS CAREW, is brutally murdered in the street. The deed is witnessed by a serving maid who chances to be looking out of a window. The old man was merely walking slowly along the street when he chanced to collide lightly with a man who was proceeding in the opposite direction. When the stranger then trampled and beat the old man unmercifully, ·the maid fainted; but not before she had seen the assailant with clarity enough to identify him as Edward Hyde. Now Hyde is sought by the police as a murderer. Utterson calls on Dr. Jekyll, hoping the doctor will at last see the folly of his will. He is happy to hear Dr. Jekyll declare that he too is utterly horrified and is quite done with Hyde. He gives Utterson a letter he says was delivered by messenger that morning. The letter, signed by Hyde, expresses concern for Dr. Jekyll. Hyde seems very certain that he is safe from the police. Utterson's clerk, Mr. GUEST, is his confidant in most matters, and he shows Guest the letter. The handwriting is angular and slopes backward. Guest happens to compare it with a sample of Dr. Jekyll's writing. Reluctantly but positively he declares that the handwriting is the same. Utterson is horrified to think Dr. Jekyll has forged a note for a murderer.

Chaps. 6–8. After the disappearance of Hyde, Dr. Jekyll becomes more like his old self. He sees his friends Utterson and Dr. LANYON. After a time, however, Jekyll becomes more and more retiring. On one occasion he pays a call on Dr. Lanyon. This call so unnerves Dr. Lanyon that he begins almost immediately to fail in health. Utterson assumes an incurable malady has seized Lanyon, who is obviously very near death and knows it. Lanyon gives Utterson a sealed packet, not to be opened until after Lanyon's death; and if Utterson should die first, it is to be destroyed unopened. Lanyon dies and Utterson opens his mysterious packet, but inside is another sealed envelope, to be opened only upon the death of Dr. Jekyll, or upon his permanent disappearance. Jekyll becomes more and more a recluse. POOLE, Dr. Jekyll's butler, comes to Utterson's house one evening pleading for help. Poole says the doctor's time has been taken exclusively with preparing medication of some kind in his laboratory, but the ingredients seem always to be wrong for his purpose. Poole has sent many times for the chemicals that are needed, but each time the voice in the laboratory shouts that the ones purchased are impure. He must have the same kind he purchased several years before from a certain drug firm. Utterson accompanies Poole to the door of the laboratory. They knock, and the lawyer calls out to his friend. The voice that answers is the voice of Hyde. Fearing that Hyde has murdered Jekyll, they decide to break down the door. The wrecked door falls and they see the body of a man dead on the floor of the laboratory. The odor of almonds tells Utterson that this has been a suicide. They turn the body over and see the face of Edward Hyde, as hideous in death as it had been in life. There is no sign of Jekyll. Utterson finds a note addressed to him, dated at noon of the same day, in Jekyll's handwriting. It says that if Utterson ever sees it, it will be because Jekyll has disappeared forever. It begs Utterson to read the narrative Lanyon gave him and one that he himself leaves.

Chaps. 9–10. Utterson reads first through Lanyon's narrative. Lanyon had received one day a cryptic request from Dr. Jekyll to visit his laboratory, accompanied by a locksmith and a strong man to force the door. The servants had been instructed to admit them. From the laboratory Lanyon was to take the entire drawer marked "E" and go back to his office, there to await the arrival of someone to whom he was asked to turn over the drawer, its contents undisturbed. Lanyon did as he was asked. Late in the evening a strangely evil-looking man appeared, asked for the drawer, and immediately started to blend certain ingredients from the phials in it. A pungent, bubbling liquid resulted, and the misshapen creature drank it hastily. He was seized with convulsive spasms; then the face and body of Dr. Jekyll evolved out of the face and body of the man sought for the murder of Sir Danvers Carew: Edward Hyde. The horror of the realization that the two personalities occupied the same body unhinged Dr. Lanyon so that he knew he would never recover. Next Utterson reads Jekyll's narrative. Jekyll had been sure that in each individual there are at least two—one good and one evil. This led Jekyll to experiment with drugs to suppress the one and bring out the other. He succeeded and became two men. As Edward Hyde, he could indulge in depravities that Henry Jekyll would never have countenanced. Then he need only swallow a draught of his drug and become again the kindly, philanthropic physician that everyone knew. This continued for years, but gradually the draught had to be made more powerful. Finally it failed entirely and Jekyll became desperate. He feared that he might find himself permanently trapped in his identity as Mr. Hyde. Hence his strange will. Henry Jekyll merely begged forgiveness and understanding. Jekyll hated Hyde for his depravity, and Hyde hated Jekyll for his power of life and death. At the time this letter was written, Dr. Jekyll was under the control of the last dose of the successful formula. He did not know how long its effects would endure.

214

Dodsworth

Novel by Sinclair Lewis, 1885–1951.
Published and © 1929 by Harcourt,
Brace & Co., New York. (Dell, F63)

DODSWORTH IS RANKED as one of
Lewis's two or three best novels (along
with *Arrowsmith* and *Babbitt*). To
nearly every reader's surprise, Lewis
seemed actually to like his title character, a retired and quite typical American businessman in Europe. The Nobel
Prize for Literature was awarded to
Lewis soon after the publication of
Dodsworth; and though this prize is
given to the writer, not to a particular
work, it has usually followed hard upon
publication of a book that is at least a
critical success. Therefore the Nobel
award was to some extent a favorable
criticism of *Dodsworth.*

Chaps. 1. In 1903, at a dance in Zenith,
SAMUEL DODSWORTH—Yale 1896, football
hero, engineer at the locomotive works, 28
years old—meets again a high-school friend,
FRANCES VOELKER, daughter of a millionaire brewer. He courts her and they are
married, though he warns him that she is
ambitious and "wants the whole world."

Chaps. 2–10. At 50, Sam Dodsworth is
the epitome of the American captain of
industry. He is a Republican, an Episcopa-
lian, and president of the Revelation Motor
Company. He sells out to the mighty Unit
Automotive Company. He turns down their
offer of a vice-presidency to spend the next
year traveling around in Europe, partly
because Fran insists, but he also wants a
rest. There is nothing to stop them, for their
daughter EMILY will be married in a short
while and their son BRENT is at college.
Sam hopes that after 23 years of marriage,
being alone with Fran will break through
her cold affection and bring them close together again. He is an intelligent, likable
man and quickly makes friends on the ship
going to England. He meets Major CLYDE
LOCKERT and introduces him to Fran.

Lockert is attracted to Fran and in his
bumptious way takes charge of their stay
in London. Sam is bewildered by the surroundings. Like many who have not traveled
abroad before, he finds it difficult to
believe that there are people who live in
environments so unlike the one he knows.
Fran is an intolerable snob. Bored with
America and Sam, she glows at the idea of
being the week-end guest of General Lord
HERNDON, who is Lockert's cousin. Sam
is lost and lonely at first but this phase
passes and he is fascinated with the English
countryside and Lord Herndon's house,
which is just what he imagined it would

be. He is happy and he tries not to be concerned by Fran's attention to Lockert.

Chaps. 11–14. The Dodsworths return to
London and attend a dinner party given by
Sir FRANCIS and Lady OUSTON. She is a
British snob, born in Nashville, Tenn. Sam
vigorously defends America against the
sneers of the British. Fran backs him up,
though at the risk of her social career in
London, and he becomes more hopeful
about the success of their year's vacation.
Sam feels at home in England and seriously
thinks of living there permanently. Lockert
returns from a trip to the Riviera and takes
them on a tour of luncheons and dinners,
which Fran enjoys. Sam is given a stag din-
don and Fran dines alone with Lockert and
goes to the opera with him. Sam comes
home and finds her in tears because Lockert
has tried to seduce her. She tells Sam the
whole story. They have a mild quarrel when
he is not furious with Lockert, but he feels
that she has led Lockert on with her flirting. However, neither is he angry at her.
Fran wants to run away from England, the
England that Dodsworth now loves dearly,
and in four days they are in France. Paris
at first is lonely for the Dodsworths, but
Fran is happy and contented to accompany
Sam on his sightseeing expeditions. She has
a snobbish illusion of culture and is less
impressed by the art galleries and museums
than is her husband. He really enjoys them,
somewhat to his surprise. They meet an

Dodsworth and Fernande

acquaintance from Zenith, JERRY WATTS,
and gradually they meet others. Finally they
meet some members of the International
Set and Fran is launched on a round of
social activities.

Chap 15. Fran's days are completely
devoted to the pursuit of social pleasure.
Sam finds himself alone a great deal of the
time and he often goes to the New York
Bar to talk with Americans. He becomes
friendly with ROSS IRELAND, a correspondent for one of America's big news

agencies. Sam hears Ross is sailing for New
York in a month and he decides he wants to
go home for a time and then travel to the
Orient. Before broaching the subject to
Fran, he trails along with all her new friends
and makes himself as affable as he can. He
does not like them and tells Fran so. One
night he tells her of his plans and they have
a bitter quarrel during which Fran uses the
words "If we're going on together." Sam
is frightened at the idea of losing her and
tries to do all he can to please her. Finally
Fran suggests that he return home alone for
a few months and come back in the late
summer to join her for the trip to the
Orient. She is cool and distant until the day
he leaves, when she breaks down and cries.

Chaps. 16–19. Sam and Ross arrive in
New York and Sam finds he is unused to
the city's rapid tempo of living. He is lost
and lonely and yearns for Fran. He attends
his 30th reunion at Yale and then returns
to Zenith to stay with his daughter Emily.
Sam is unhappy at home. There is no business to occupy him and no one needs him
around the house. His sense of loneliness
increases. Fran writes that she has a charming villa in Switzerland with a friend. Her
next letters are filled with references to a
young man named ARNOLD ISRAEL. Sam
has an uneasy feeling that Fran is having
a flirtation, if not something more. He is
jealous but recovers his temper in the
peacefulness of the voyage that takes him
back to Europe.

Chaps. 20–26. Sam meets Fran in Paris.
They have a showdown. It is obvious to Sam
that Fran has been having an affair with
Israel, and while she protests that she does
not want a divorce, Sam issues an ultimatum,
that she either get a divorce or never see
Arnold Israel again. Fran is humiliated by
his attitude, but she agrees and they leave
together for Italy to see if they can pick
up the pieces of their marriage. They meet
EDITH CORTRIGHT in Venice. She is a
charming widow about Fran's age and she
greatly impresses Sam with her softness and
lovely sense of ease. The Dodsworths leave
Italy and go to Berlin. They meet Count
KURT VON OBERSDORF at a dinner given
by Fran's cousins. Kurt is extremely handsome, charming, and only a few years
younger than Fran. He exerts all his energies
to making their stay pleasant. His attentions
to Fran are polished and subtle and she is
drawn to him in a serious way. Sam learns
of her new love interest when she forbids
him to tell Kurt that she is a grandmother
since Emily has had a baby. Sam is beginning to see the shallowness of his wife and
for the first time in his life he is aware that
other women find him attractive. It disturbs
him. His closest friend in Zenith, TUB
PEARSON, arrives in Paris and Dodsworth
hurries there to greet him but Fran refuses
to leave Berlin. Sam gets a boyish pleasure
out of taking Tub and his wife, MATEY, to
all the places where he is known by name.
Sam and Tub get drunk together. Sam has
a premonition that his marriage is coming
to an end. Fran's letters from Berlin are full

of Kurt. He goes alone to a cafe and picks up an American girl, ELSA. He knows she is a gold-digger and he plans to spend the night with her, but after making him buy drinks for all her friends she sneaks out.

Chaps. 27–29. Sam flies to Berlin and goes to his hotel. He is told that Mrs. Dodsworth is out for the evening. She returns five hours later with Kurt and she informs her husband that she wishes an immediate divorce so that she may marry Kurt. Sam is disconsolate but agrees and leaves with all his luggage for Paris to make all the financial arrangements.

Chaps. 30–35. The rest of the summer is horrible for him. He constantly sees Fran's face before him. He finds NANDE (Fernande) AZEREDO, an uninhibited, 25-year-old artist's model, and is passionately untrue to Fran for the first time. It is a short-lived affair, ending after three days. Dodsworth leaves for Italy. He runs into Edith Cortright again and his spirit is refreshed by her warmth and understanding. He tells her the whole story of his imminent divorce. Then he begins to see her daily. They go to Naples together to visit friends of Edith's, the Baron and Baroness ERCOLE, and there Sam discovers that Edith is not only a soft, cultured woman but also a vigorous outdoor girl. They explore Capri and Sorrento and Sam realizes that he has previously seen only the indoors of Europe. He realizes that he is definitely and positively happy and wonders if it is because he is in love. His tranquillity is spoiled by a letter from Fran asking him to take her back. Kurt's mother disapproved of their marriage and Kurt would not go through with it until they had won her over. Fran says she is through with Kurt forever and begs Sam's forgiveness. He calls Fran in Berlin and tells her to get ready to sail for home and then tells Edith he is going back to Fran. His parting with Edith is heartbreaking for both of them. They love each other, but Sam feels that Fran is a child and needs him now more than ever.

Chap. 36. The Dodsworths sail for New York. Fran is brittle and gay but Sam is depressed at parting from the woman he loves. He is finally unable to stand it any longer and cables Edith that he will return to Naples in three weeks. Sam tells Fran that he is through and cannot continue with the reconciliation. She is panicked at being left alone. Sam rejoins Edith and finds the only real happiness he has known in years. In fact, once she makes him forget Fran for almost two days.

A Doll's House

Play by Henrik Ibsen, 1828–1906. Produced 1879.

THE MESSAGE OF *A Doll's House* is still valid but in 1879 it was sensational. In the play the wife, Nora, is the strong member of the family, especially when a crisis comes; but it does not occur to her husband that she is or should be, and she is sufficiently enslaved by the conventions of her times to feel guilt to the point of planning suicide. At the end it occurs to her that this point of view is wrong and that a wife should be a partner in the family, not merely an implement for the husband's convenience and pleasure. Family situations such as Ibsen described were the rule in 1879. For this reason his play was not only an example of "the new theater" but also a much-discussed plea for the "emancipation" of married women.

Act 1. It is just before Christmas and TORVALD HELMER'S young wife NORA is just returning from a shopping spree. Helmer calls her a spendthrift. When he asks what she wants for Christmas, she asks him to give her money. He reminds her that his salary increase will not be due for three months. He speaks to her sternly but indulgently, as though she were a child, and she assumes a childlike manner. It seems she is not allowed to eat too much candy and she insists she has not. They are expecting Dr. RANK, a friend, for dinner. HELENE, the maid, brings in a visitor, Mrs. LINDE. Dr. Rank has also arrived and Helmer goes to join him. Nora first does not recognize Mrs. Linde but then she sees it is her old friend KRISTINE, whom she has not seen for 10 years. Nora gloats over her husband's new position as bank president. She tells Mrs. Linde how Helmer fell ill from overwork and they went to Italy for a year on an inheritance from her father. Mrs. Linde says she married only for money, but her husband's business failed and she is left with nothing. After her husband died, Mrs. Linde tried running a school, but that failed. She has come to town to look for a job. Nora confides to Mrs. Linde something she does not want her husband to know: It was not her father's legacy that paid for the trip to Italy, but money borrowed by her. She has repaid some of it with money given her by Helmer and from low-paid odd jobs. Helene shows in KROGSTAD, the attorney for the bank of which Helmer is to be president, who goes to Helmer's study. Mrs. Linde recognizes him, saying she has heard he has a reputation for shady business deals. Nora changes the subject. Dr. Rank enters and is introduced to Mrs. Linde. He says Krogstad is a wretched person, and Nora pretends to be surprised. Helmer is introduced to Mrs. Linde and Nora asks him to find her a job. He questions Mrs. Linde and promises to try to get her a position at the bank. Helmer, Dr. Rank and Mrs. Linde leave together. ANNE-MARIE, the nurse, comes in with the children. Nora occupies herself with the children, playing with them on the floor. There is a knock at the door and Krogstad returns. Nora seems frightened and sends the children out of the room. She thinks he wants the money—for it is to him she owes it—but he has not come for money. He says that keeping his position in the bank is a matter of life and death for him. Many years ago he got into trouble, all doors were closed to him, and he was forced to become a money-lender. Now he wants to regain his former respectability and the small position in the bank was to be the first step. He asks Nora to influence her husband to keep him. She insists she has no influence over her husband. Krogstad threatens to expose her to Helmer; also, he knows she forged her father's counter-signature to the note when she borrowed the money. This could send her to jail. He leaves and the children return; Nora asks them not to tell Helmer about the visitor. But Helmer has seen Krogstad leaving and Nora admits he came to ask her to use her good influence with Helmer. Nora talks about the fancy-dress ball they will attend on Christmas and asks Helmer to help her select her costume. Helmer tells her Krogstad committed forgery, but never was punished for it; Helmer feels he cannot work with such a man.

Act II. Christmas Day finds Nora still worried about what Krogstad may do. Mrs. Linde arrives, summoned by Nora to help with the costume. Mrs. Linde suspects that Nora is in trouble and wants to know about it. Helmer enters and Nora sends her friend out of the room. Again she asks her husband not to dismiss Krogstad, but Helmer says he has already let it be known that Krogstad will be dismissed and to change his mind now would seem foolish. Nora calls him petty and he gets angry and immediately dispatches the letter of dismissal to Krogstad. Nora is terror stricken. Dr. Rank calls on them. He tells her he will die in a month, of an inherited illness of the spine caused by his father's excesses. Nora asks him to do her a favor and he confesses he would give his life for her; that he has always loved her. Now Nora is shocked and does not want to ask him the favor (to lend her the money). Helene announces a visitor and Dr. Rank goes to Helmer's study. Nora then locks Helmer's door and receives the visitor, Krogstad. She offers to somehow get the money, but he does not want any money. He wants a chance at a new start. He has written to her husband, telling everything and demanding not merely reinstatement but a better position in the bank. Krogstad leaves and Nora peers out after him and watches him drop the letter into their mailbox. She collapses just as Mrs. Linde brings in the repaired costume. She tells Mrs. Linde that it was Krogstad who lent her the money. Mrs. Linde offers to intercede with

Nora is now suicidal

Krogstad, for there was a time when he would have done anything in the world for her. Mrs. Linde goes to see Krogstad, who lives nearby. Rank and Helmer enter, surprised not to find Nora in costume. To prevent Helmer from looking in the mailbox, Nora starts to rehearse her little act for the fancy-dress ball with him and Helmer dutifully sits down at the piano and plays for her. Mrs. Linde returns. Helmer suspects that Krogstad left a letter in the mailbox, but Nora makes him promise not to look until after the party. Mrs. Linde brings Nora the bad news that Krogstad is out of town for the day but that she has left a note for him. Nora thinks nothing can prevent the catastrophe now.

Act III. Mrs. Linde meets Krogstad at the party. She confesses she broke off with him to marry a man with money. Now that Krogstad is a widower and needs a mother for his children, she has come to the city to seek him out. Krogstad, at first unable to believe her, is finally convinced and happy. Now Krogstad wants to get back the letter he has written to Helmer. For a moment he thinks Mrs. Linde is coming back to him to save Nora, but she convinces him it is for her own sake. To his amazement, she does not want him to recover the letter and end the crisis for Nora; Mrs. Linde wants Helmer to know the truth about his wife. Mrs. Linde tells Nora that she has nothing to fear from Krogstad but must tell her husband the truth just the same. The party over, Helmer goes to empty the mailbox. He finds a card with Rank's name and a black cross, and Nora explains its sad meaning. Helmer starts to read his mail. Nora has determined to drown herself if he finds out, and she prepares to do so. Helmer reads the letter from Krogstad; Nora admits she knows the contents and confirms them. He accuses her of having ruined his career, but he wants her to keep on living with him to keep up appearances. Just then there is another letter for Nora. It is from Krogstad and contains the forged note and his apologies and his promise never to bother her again. Helmer is jubilant; they are saved and it was all a bad dream. He burns the note and both letters. Helmer turns to Nora and tells her he has forgiven her everything. He excuses everything she has done as an act of love for him. Nora changes her costume to a daytime dress. Then she has a serious talk with him and recapitulates her life for the past eight years. In her father's house she was always treated like a toy. Now she is Helmer's doll-wife, always playing games. Therefore she will leave Helmer and go home to what was her father's house. She wants to find herself first, before being anything else to anyone. She does not love Helmer any more, because at the time of the crisis, when he knew the contents of the letter, he did not fight for her but was only afraid for his own future. Helmer is saddened and promises to change for her, but she frees him of any responsibility for her, gives him back his ring, and demands hers in return. Only a miracle can turn their lives into a real marriage, and she no longer believes in miracles. When she has gone, Helmer realizes how empty his house will be henceforth.

Don Juan

Narrative poem by George Gordon, Lord Byron, 1788–1824.
Published: First five cantos, 1819–1820; 6th canto, 1821; 7th to 16th cantos, 1821–1824.

LATER CRITICISM has made *Don Juan* Byron's masterpiece, though it was not so acknowledged while he was alive. The later appraisal is based on the fact that it is more mature than his earlier work (notably *Childe Harold*, the readiest basis for comparison), and also, of course, on the fact that *Don Juan* is his longest work (exceeding 15,000 lines). Volume always has a favorable effect on criticism. But most of *Don Juan* is written in either a light or a prosaically narrative vein. Even the serious portions are unemotional and to that extent cannot appeal to the reader's senses as do the best parts of the "immature" *Childe Harold*. However, some of Byron's loveliest short lyrics are interpolated in *Don Juan*. ¶ Of the sixteen cantos of *Don Juan,* the last nine or ten are considered inferior to the first six or seven. *Don Juan* is written in a verse-form called *ottava rima*, eight-lined stanzas in iambic pentameter, rhymed *ababababcc*.

Dedication and Canto 1. Byron begins by berating his popular contemporaries such as Coleridge, Wordsworth, and Southey, who have replaced Milton, Dryden, and Pope. Then he announces his grand intention of writing an epic and says that he has chosen Don Juan as his hero simply because "I want a hero."

Juan is the son of a Spanish nobleman named Don JOSÉ and his overly learned wife Donna INEZ, who closely resembles Byron's wife, Lady Milbanke Byron. José dies when Juan is small and Juan is reared by his disciplined mother in the romantic city of Seville. When he is 16 years old he attracts the eye of a beautiful noblewoman, Donna JULIA, who is married to old, proud

Don ALFONSO. Both Juan and Donna Julia are conscious of the probable consequences of their illicit attachment, but they nevertheless spend a great deal of time reading and talking together. Eventually Juan decides to spend the night at Donna Julia's house. They are aroused by the shouts of Donna Julia's maid, who informs them that Don Alfonso has come home unexpectedly. Juan hides under the bedclothes while Donna Julia bravely persuades her husband that his jealously is ill-grounded. Don Alfonso leaves but returns and finds Juan, who barely escapes murder by fleeing naked into the night.

Byron then digresses to inform the reader that his epic will be divided into 12 or 24 books and will have love, war, a storm at sea, and lists of soldiers, just like the *Aeneid* and *Iliad*.

Cantos 2–4. Resuming the story, Byron tells how Juan is forced to flee Spain and Alfonso's revenge. Juan's mother gives him money to make a sea voyage, but on the way a great tempest swells and the ship is wrecked. Juan enters a lifeboat with his tutor PEDRILLO and other shipmen. While they float about the Mediterranean Sea, they draw lots to decide who must offer his body as food for the others. Pedrillo loses the draw and is eaten. At last the shipwrecked men are cast upon a Grecian island owned by a shrewd merchant named LAMBRO, who has a gorgeous 17-year-old daughter, HAIDEE. Haidee finds the embattered Juan and sneaks him into a cave where she

and her maid ZOE nurse him back to life. For a long time Lambro remains away from the island, and Juan and Haidee enjoy an idyllic romance. Haidee is "nature's bride," the typical island-princess heroine of 19th-century literature, unspoiled by learning and society. She teaches Juan her language and eventually takes him to her palatial home, where they prepare a magnificent nuptial feast. While the marriage banquet is going on, Lambro steals back to the island into the midst of the guests. A minstrel is singing a lovely Byronic poem, "The Isles of Greece," but Lambro shatters the bliss. Haidee begs to die in place of Juan, but

Don Juan falls in love with Greece

Lambro turns his pistol upon the illicit lover. Lambro shoots Juan and orders his wounded body to be carried down to the ships. Juan is thrown into a galley and carried off to a slave market in Constantinople (Istanbul), while poor Haidee pines away and dies after 12 days of mourning.

Cantos 5–6. Don Juan is bought at the slave market by a Negro eunuch named BABA, who carries him off in a gilded boat to the palace of the sultan. There Juan is dressed, despite his protests, in female clothes. He learns that the sultan's beautiful fourth wife, GULBAYEZ, is interested in him but is forced to clothe him thus because the sultan might discover her plot and kill them both. Juan refuses the advances of the bold Gulbayez. The sultan meets and falls in love with "Juanna," as Juan is called in his disguise. Juan is taken to the harem, where the sultan's other wives receive him with great pomp. The "mother" of the harem decides to put Juan under the care of a wife named DUDÚ. Juan struggles through many embarrassing incidents but never reveals his real sex. When Juan snores loudly at night and keeps Dudú from sleeping, the harem-mother places him under the care of another wife, LOLAH. Jealous because she cannot see him, Gulbayez orders Baba to bring both Juan and Dudú before her. [At this point the most famous portion of the poem ends. The later cantos never received the notice, whether favorable or unfavorable, that greeted the previous sections.]

Cantos 7–8. Byron begins by describing the Russian siege of the Turkish city of Ismail, completely abandoning the harem scene. He informs the reader that this is the epic account of war that he promised previously. In lines that are bitter as well as amusing, he subjects the whole 19th-century attitude toward the glory of war to scathing criticism. The incidents are particularly remembered for their intricate rhymes on Russian names, such as that of the leader SUWARROW. In the midst of the furious assault on Ismail, two persons emerge from the smoke—Juan, who has escaped from the harem, and an English companion of his, JOHN JOHNSON. Together they join the Russian army of Empress Catherine the Great, distinguishing themselves with such heroism that Juan is admitted into the exclusive order of St. Vladimir. Actually their heroism consists of cleverly avoiding any risk. Juan's finest act is rescuing a little Turkish orphan girl, LEILA, whom he takes with him on his journey to Russia, where he is accorded the honors of a national hero.

Cantos 9–10. In St. Petersburg (Leningrad), Juan soon becomes Catherine's favorite and is elevated to wealth and Russian nobility. He reports this to his mother, Donna Inez, in Spain and receives her blessing. But Juan is infected by the decadent life of the court and his only true love is the little girl Leila, whom he treats like a sister. Eventually the chilly north makes Juan ill and doctors advise him to seek warmer climates. He leaves "Russia's royal harlot" and travels with Leila westward across Europe to England.

Cantos 11–15. Byron presents a particularly caustic picture of smoky London, where winter ends in July. He describes the high-society existence of Lord HENRY and Lady ADELINE AMUNDEVILLE, who invite Juan to their manor. There all guests are divided into two tribes, the Bores and the Bored. One of the most crushing bores is the stuffy Lady FITZ-FULKE. Lady Adeline warns Juan about getting too close to other men's wives but then finds herself falling in love with him. Lady Adeline contrives to marry Juan off to a young woman so that they can consort without suspicion. She chooses one of her guests, AURORA RABY, for this honor.

Cantos 16–17. One night on retiring, Juan is startled by a noise and sees what looks like a monk in dark robes walking by him. All that night he does not sleep. The next day Lady Adeline tells him the monk was a famous ghost called the Black Friar, who has haunted the Amundeville estate for centuries. That night Juan goes to his room with foreboding, but when the door creaks open he sees not a monk but Lady Fitz-Fulke. In the brief lines of Canto 17 Byron refuses to say what happened that night, except that Juan looked sleepless at breakfast the next day. With these words, the poem ends abruptly.

Don Quixote

Novel by Miguel de Cervantes Saavedra, 1547–1616.
Published 1605 (Part I) and 1615 (Part II). (PB, PL517; NAL, MD207; ML, 174; ML, T6)

INDISPUTABLY SPAIN'S GREATEST, *Don Quixote de la Mancha* has been beloved by centuries of readers. Cervantes apparently began the novel as a simple satire on the chivalric romances that were sop to the vulgar reading appetite of his day; but once he was writing, his wise, penetrating and humorous studies of eternal mankind had to make themselves evident and within a few chapters this aspect became the important one. Cervantes may not have intended to write beyond Part I; but another writer published a spurious "Further Adventures of Don Quixote" and in self-defense Cervantes then wrote his own continuation. There are many translations. Seldom is the book published entire in an English edition and the numbering of the chapters varies among the different editions, serving the preference and convenience of each translator or editor. The 1700 translation by Motteux probably best reflects the flavor of the original but is said to be among the least accurate.

Part I. Chaps. 1–6. An old gentleman about the age of 50, living in the village of La Mancha, Spain, with his 20-year-old NIECE and 40-year-old HOUSEKEEPER, spends so much time reading the popular romances of his day and previous ages that he begins to believe chivalry is not dead. His real surname is Quixada or Quesada, but he calls himself by the noble name of Don QUIXOTE de la Mancha. Don Quixote vows that he will go out into the world as a modern knight. He collects a batch of rusty armor and an old nag called Rosinante. He knows that every knight must have a fair lady to whom he pledges obedience, and Don Quixote selects a humble farm-girl, DULCINEA DEL TOBOSO. One July day Quixote embarks boldly on his new life of adventure. He chances upon a common inn by the side of the road, and pretends it is a castle. He regards the innkeeper as a lord and asks that the befuddled man confer the honors of knighthood upon him. The innkeeper informs his guests about the lunatic staying under his roof and they begin to tease Quixote. The old man pelts them and drives them away with his sword, and for the sake of peace the innkeeper performs a mock ceremony of knighting Quixote. On leaving the inn Quixote sets free a herding-boy who is being beaten by his master, but he himself is mishandled by a troupe of muleteers. Quixote, bruised and beaten, is found by a fellow resident of La Mancha and carried home, where the town priest or CURATE and the BARBER burn all the romances in his library and order Quixote's niece and housekeeper not to let the man out of their sight.

Chaps. 7–10. Quixote stays at home for 15 days, but is restless. He sells some of his dearest possessions and buys a new suit of armor. Then, realizing that he needs a squire, he approaches the crafty peasant SANCHO PANZA and his wife TERESA. At first Sancho is not enthusiastic about going off in the company of a madman, but he is shrewd enough to realize that he may possibly pick up some spare booty by cultivating Quixote's friendship. Furthermore, Quixote glibly promises Sancho an island. The two companions ride off together. They come to some windmills on the plains, which Quixote mistakes for large, many-handed giants. Quixote charges the wheels with his lance. He is swept from his saddle by one of the turning vanes. He tells Sancho that the giants have been turned into windmills by sorcery. On the second day Quixote spies two Benedictine monks followed by a Basque lady in a coach, and believes that the monks are enchanters who have captured a princess. Quixote attacks one of the monks and strips him of his goods. Sancho takes to his heels when the Basque lady's squire prepares to defend her, but Quixote bravely rushes the squire and overcomes him. He frees the man at the plea of the lady and orders his victim to go seek the mercy of Dulcinea del Toboso.

Chaps. 11–17. Sancho and Quixote fall in with a pack of goatherds and spend the night in their company, listening to the lament of the shepherd Chrysostome who died for the love of the witch-girl Marcella. They then part company, and Quixote once again encounters rough treatment from a band of herders from the town of Yanguas. These men attack Rosinante when the horse begins to assail their mares, and they also beat Don Quixote. Sancho is disconsolate, but Quixote persuades him to carry on and the pair reach another "inn-castle." That night a maid named MARITORNES comes to their room for a rendezvous with a carrier who is also sleeping there. Quixote grabs her, believing the girl to be Dulcinea, and suffers another beating from the disgruntled lover. Quixote's wounds are healed with balsam and when the innkeeper demands payment of his bill, Quixote tells him that he will not pay his bill because the innkeeper pretended to own a castle, and rides away. Sancho does not escape in time, however, and loses their money-bags and most of his clothes.

Chaps. 18–21. Quixote sees some dust clouds raised by flocks of sheep, and is sure that two armies are engaged in battle. He charges into the dust and is stoned by the irate shepherds for scattering the sheep. Quixote meets some clergymen bearing a corpse on the highway and mistakes them for monsters. He attacks and robs their leader because of his insolence. After this famous exploit Sancho calls him "The Knight of the Sad Countenance." They meet a barber wearing his brass bowl on his head to protect himself from the rain. Quixote snatches the bowl and claims it is the magic golden helmet of Mambrino.

Chaps. 22–32. Quixote comes upon a band of galley slaves being led to the king's palace and frees them by attacking their sergeant and orders them to go to Dulcinea. The convicts turn on him and Sancho, rob them, and then flee in haste. Sancho loses his ass Dapple and is forced to carry burdens on his back. Quixote and Sancho wander the Sierra Morena Mountains, coming upon a wild-looking hermit whom they call The Knight of the Wood. The hermit says his name is CARDENIO and starts a long story of his love for a girl named LUCINDA, but he does not finish his tale because he argues with Quixote about the *Amadis of Gaul*, Quixote's favorite romance. Quixote and Sancho come to a remote part of the mountains where Quixote prepares to do penance for Dulcinea. He writes his lady a love letter and sends Pancho on Rosinante back to Toboso to deliver it to her. Sancho goes instead to La Mancha and informs the barber and curate of his master's whereabouts and they decide to rescue Quixote. Their plan is to disguise the curate as a damsel-errant and the barber as her squire, and have Quixote follow the damsel home. In their disguises they set out. They encounter Cardenio, who finishes his tale of his love for Lucinda, who has probably married another man. The three men hear someone nearby and discover DOROTHEA, a friend of Cardenio, disguised as a boy. Dorothea and Cardenio have a happy reunion, for Dorothea tells him that Lucinda must still be unmarried. Dorothea herself is wedded to Don FERNANDO, Cardenio's rival. Next they hear Sancho's cry that he has found Quixote, and they persuade the knight to abandon his strange penitence by calling his attention to "Princess" Dorothea. Everyone then amuses himself by teasing the old knight, including Dorothea, who pretends she is the Princess Micomicona. On their way home, Sancho spies one of the convicts who stole his ass and retrieves it. Quixote also meets the boy whom he saved from a beating on his first skirmish, and the boy tells him that he was beaten worse after being saved. At last Quixote and his large entourage pull up at an inn, the very same one where Quixote had his adventure with Maritornes.

Chaps. 33–41. The curate reads an old romantic tale of the group, *The Tale of Foolish Curiosity.* It is precisely the sort of thing that Quixote has been reading in great quantities. The tale is interrupted by the sudden appearance of Sancho, who cries for everyone to see Quixote attacking some dragons. They all rush out of the room and see the poor knight assailing some wine-skins and dripping wine as if it were blood. The innkeeper and his wife are furious, but the curate quiets Quixote and puts him to bed. The curate finishes his tale, and there is a clatter of horses' hoofs. Cardenio and Dorothea are shocked to find that Lucinda and her suitor Don Fernando have arrived at the inn. After many entreaties from the curate, Fernando consents to reunite Cardenio and Lucinda, and acknowledges the lowly-born Dorothea as his true wife. Dorothea, out of kindness to Quixote, continues to pretend that she is a princess. Events are complicated by the arrival of a man who was held captive by the Turks and was assisted in his escape by a lovely Moslem girl named ZORAIDA. The man is searching for both Zoraida and his long absent brother. A judge arrives at the inn and turns out to be the captive's brother, while Zoraida is discovered to be a mysterious veiled woman who entered the inn earlier. Thus all three are united and Zoraida promises conversion to Christianity so that she can marry the ex-captive.

Chaps. 43–52. Quixote serenades the innkeeper's daughter, thinking that she is Dulcinea. The daughter lures him into a trap and he is trussed over his horse for the night, with the assistance of the maid Maritornes. When freed, Quixote goes wild and attacks many of the guests. Finally the curate and barber "enchant" him; they put him in a cage and prepare to take him back to La Mancha. On the journey home, Sancho consoles his master through the bars of the cage, while the curate and a newcomer, the CANON of Toledo, debate the harmful effects of too much imagination. They free Quixote to perform some vital functions. A goatherd joins their company and tells of his love for the maiden LEANDRA, who spurned all affections and entered a nunnery. Quixote takes offense at some of the goatherd's words and fights with him. Their fight is interrupted by a procession wending its way to a church. Quixote mistakes the image of a saint for a captive princess and attacks the procession. He is finally restrained and put back in the cage while the curate settles for the damages. After a six-day journey, the entourage at last reaches La Mancha, where everyone gathers in the streets to hail the returning "knight-errant." Sancho is set upon by his wife, who demands some of the spoils he has gathered, but the unfortunate man has nothing to give her. Quixote is handed back to the care of his niece and housekeeper.

Part II. Chaps. 1–7. Sancho clamors for Quixote to return to their quest for fortune, because he still wants an island. The pair entertain a young bachelor, SAMSON CARRASCO, who criticizes Part I of their story, especially certain inaccuracies about Sancho's ass, but these errors are defended. Don Quixote is first incredulous, then pleased that a history of his adventures has been written. Sancho comforts his wife by promising he will make another journey with Quixote and this time return overflowing with wealth. With the help of Carrasco, he and Quixote make plans to go off in quest of Dulcinea. Carrasco leaves them after helping Quixote elude his niece and housekeeper.

Chaps. 8–15. Sancho and Quixote proceed to Toboso to see Dulcinea, but when Sancho is sent to find her, he merely pretends to make a real effort. He sees a band of village peasant girls, and calls Quixote out to view Dulcinea and her court. Quixote believes that Dulcinea has been changed into a peasant girl by some evil spell, and Sancho persuades him to continue on his quest for fortune in the hope of transforming the girl back into a princess. They do not go far before meeting the KNIGHT OF THE MIRRORS and his Squire, who challenge them both to duels. During the combat Sancho arranges with the other squire to only pretend they are fighting, but Don Quixote goes at the other knight with such vengeance that he easily overcomes him. The knight turns out to be Carrasco and the squire is Sancho's friend THOMAS CECIAL, whom the curate and barber persuaded to trap Quixote in this ruse, hoping they could discourage him from future travels. Carrasco and Cecial go back to La Mancha, and Quixote and Panza continue their quest for adventure.

Chaps. 16–21. Quixote next meets a gentleman from La Mancha named Don DIEGO, whom he insists on calling the Knight of the Green Coat. He confounds Diego by offering to fight some caged lions. Fortunately the lions will not leave their cages, but from that time on Quixote insists on being called "The Knight of the Lions" instead of "The Sad Countenance." At Don Diego's house, Quixote reveals a further strange blend of vision and insanity by the way in which he talks to Diego's young son. They next go to a village where CAMACHO, a wealthy man, is about to marry a girl named QUITERIA despite the pleas of a fervent gallant named BASILIO. Basilio dashes into the wedding ceremony, plunges a knife into his breast, and falls dying to the floor. Quiteria runs over to him and promises to marry him before he dies. As soon as the ceremony is performed, Basilio leaps up from the floor and reveals that the whole scene was a trick. Thanks to Quixote's timely intervention, peace is restored and everyone, including Camacho, celebrates the wedding. Quixote is entertained like a visiting prince.

Chaps. 22–31. Quixote descends into the Cave of Montesinos, and when he comes out he says he saw a marvelous vision in which Dulcinea's enchantment was explained to him. Sancho regards this vision with a certain skepticism. As they travel on to an inn,

Don Quixote believes Dulcinea has been changed into a peasant girl

they fall in with a magician, Master PETER, who has a prophetic ape. The ape asserts that Quixote's cave vision was a hoax and Quixote smashes Master Peter's puppets in revenge. Master Peter is actually one of the galley slaves whom Quixote freed and who stole Sancho's ass. Quixote and Sancho continue their wanderings, coming upon a boat by the River Ebro that Quixote believes to be enchanted. They cross the river on the boat but are surrounded by nearby millers to whom the skiff belongs. The boat crashes into a windmill and is destroyed, and the two adventurers spend most of their money paying for the destroyed bark.

Chaps. 32–41. Sancho and Quixote's luck changes radically when they come upon a DUKE and DUCHESS riding in the woods. These nobles have read the First Part of Quixote's adventure and eagerly invite the knight and squire to their palace. The invitation is extended as a means of providing humor for the court, and almost immediately Sancho and Quixote are bedeviled by all the servants and nobility. The duke and duchess provide a mock-devil and a girl who impersonates Dulcinea. She tells Quixote that to free her from enchantment Sancho Panza must lash himself of his own free will 3,000 times on the buttocks. Sancho protests violently, but is offered the governorship of his much-coveted island if he will agree. Meanwhile the duke and duchess dream up an even more amusing scheme. They introduce a mysterious beautiful lady called the Countess of TRIFALDI who has come from the remote land of Candaya seeking the help of the illustrious Don Quixote. The countess asks Sancho and his knight to fly to her land on the winged horse Clavileno and break the spell of the giant enchanter Malambruno. The adventurers consent and mount a strange wooden horse that is brought into the palace garden. With the help of numerous sound and lighting effects they are made to believe that they are moving through space for the whole night, but in the morning when they awake they find they are back in the same garden. A parchment dangling on cords states that they have accomplished the dangerous mission and also freed Dulcinea from her enchantment. At last Pancho is rewarded with his island.

Chaps. 42–54. Before Sancho departs, Don Quixote gives him a great deal of sound advice about government—so sound that it makes the duke, who wastes time in luxury and in tricking fools, look ridiculous. Sancho immediately distinguishes himself with great wisdom in governing the island and acquires the reputation for being a King Solomon, despite several pitfalls and inconveniences rigged up for him by the duke. Meanwhile Don Quixote, still at the palace, is visited nightly by the Duchess's serving woman, Doña RODRIGUEZ, who begs him to fight to redeem her daughter's ravished honor. He is also visited by various "phantoms," which are fond of pinching him. The duchess writes to Sancho's wife and informs her of her husband's good luck. On his island,

Sancho almost dies of hunger and on the seventh day of his rule he is attacked late at night by assassins. They eventually let him go free, but Sancho renounces all attempts to try to rise beyond his class and returns on his ass to the Duke's palace. On the way he meets a pilgrim, who is his old friend RICOTE, and when Sancho tells him that he has been governing the island of Barratria, Ricote informs him that Barratria is about as far inland as one can get in Spain.

Chaps. 55–57. Quixote prepares to fight the Duke's steward TOSILOS, who is impersonating the ravisher of Doña Rodriguez' daughter, but Tosilos draws short in the charge and declares that he will marry the girl gladly. A maid named ALTISIDORA makes bold advances to Quixote and he escapes her by leaving for Saragossa with Sancho.

Chaps. 58–71. At an inn they find a bogus novel about their adventures, and they start for Barcelona to confront the author. There they are received by a nobleman, Don ANTONIO MORENO. While visiting Moreno's galleys they find a slave boy about to be put to death, who turns out to be a girl named ANNA FELIX. The pilgrim Ricote enters the ship and recognizes Anna as his daughter. Plans are made to rescue her husband Don GREGORIO from the Turks. Meanwhile a mysterious KNIGHT OF THE WHITE MOON challenges Quixote to a bat-

tle and defeats him. For days Quixote lies in bed, unaware that his rival is his old nemesis Carrasco. This defeat shakes Quixote a great deal and he promises to return home for a year. On the journey home, he and Sancho are herded by strange troops to the duke's palace once again, and there they see Altisidora laid out on a bier. As music plays, Altisidora rises and again begs love from Quixote, but the old knight refuses and leaves in disgust. Don Quixote is slowly regaining his senses, but as a last act he asks his friend Sancho to flog himself in order to restore the enchanted Dulcinea. Sancho agrees, if paid about three halfpence each for the 3,300 lashes required. Quixote accepts the offer.

Chaps. 72–74. They return to La Mancha, where Sancho's happy wife is eagerly waiting to share the money he gained as a governor. Quixote falls willingly under the care of his niece and housekeeper, promising to obey the Knight of the White Moon's injunction to stay home for one year. Quixote falls sick and all his friends gather around his bed and try to humor him with news of Dulcinea's disenchantment. Quixote tells them to stop lying and says that his real name is Alonso Quixano the Good. He makes his niece Antonia his heiress, but she must marry a man who has never read tales of adventure and imagination. The old man, restored to his senses, dies peacefully.

Double Indemnity

Novel by James M. Cain, 1892– Published 1943 by Alfred A. Knopf, New York. © 1936, 1943 by James M. Cain. (NAL, 1427)

DOUBLE INDEMNITY was written as a so-called "book-length" novel for magazine publication, so it is quite short, little more than 30,000 words. It is one

of the best examples of Cain's very effective, truly excellent style of writing, which so many American writers have emulated: Short, simple sentences, almost staccato; authentic American conversation; no waste words, no waste action. *Double Indemnity* is also highly dramatic and made a most successful motion picture.

Chap. 1. When the maid at H. S. NIRDLINGER'S house insists on knowing what I want before she'll let me in, I tell her my name is WALTER HUFF—which it is—and that my business is personal—which it is, to me at least. Nirdlinger's automobile insurance is about to run out. It takes a little more to give the maid the idea that I'm an old friend without actually saying so, but she finally lets me in. Next thing I know Mrs. PHYLLIS NIRDLINGER appears. Her husband is not at home. I tell her why I'm there, but she don't seem too interested in the car. She asks me if we handle accident insurance, and this gives me the creeps. When a wife starts thinking about accident insurance for the old man, you kind of wonder what's on her mind. At least you do if you've been in this insurance racket as long as I have. I make up my mind that I'll clip a little warning on the policy if she ever gets around to actually buying it. This pays off for the agent's reputation if any

funny business comes up later. The manager in our office, KEYES, can smell a phony claim from sixty yards. He's the top claims man on the Coast.

Chaps. 2–3. Mrs. Nirdlinger calls me three days later to say I should come to the house at 3:30. She's wearing a white sailor suit and her figure is something you don't see often. She hasn't said anything to her husband about accident insurance—and I know why. But there's something about her that gets me, and when I kiss her goodbye she says she'll call me. She does better. She comes down to my place that same night, and pretty soon we've got it all laid out on the line. She puts on an act, pretending she couldn't think of such a thing, but she knows it doesn't fool me a little bit—especially when I tell her that she hasn't a prayer of doing it by herself. You have to know how insurance companies and police work on accident cases. She has a lot of crazy ideas about how she can rig up an accident, and all of them would get her just exactly no-

where—except into the death house. I tell her the set-up on railroad accidents, because insurance companies pay double indemnity on railroad accidents. It isn't hard to make Nirdlinger sign an application for an accident policy. He thinks he's signing papers for his automobile insurance renewals. I get to talking about accident policies and Phyllis talks against them—like I told her to do—and she has her 19-year-old stepdaughter, LOLA, there to be a witness. I've made friends with Lola by doing a favor—arranging a loan—for her boy friend, BENIAMINO (NINO) SACHETTI, who is studying for his doctorate in chemistry. I rig a couple more details, just so there won't be any loose ends. Now all we have to do is wait till we can get Nirdlinger on a train.

Chaps. 4–7. We got our chance—or thought we did—when Nirdlinger decided to go to his class reunion at Palo Alto. He says he wants the car, though, so he can get around to picnics and things. Then he breaks his leg. It comes to me that even if a guy can't drive a car, he can still get to his class reunion on a train. The night of the big deal comes. I have a beautiful alibi worked out. I rig myself up to look pretty much like Nirdlinger. I meet Phyllis's car on schedule, and everything goes off without a hitch. I get myself hidden in the back seat and when Nirdlinger gets the bar of a crutch hooked under his chin, he doesn't even know what hit him. Phyllis leaves me to get on the train by myself, and she drives to the spot I told her. I let plenty of people see me hobbling along on Nirdlinger's crutches, till I get to the observation platform at the end of the train. I drop off exactly where I was supposed to. Phyllis is there, and she carries Nirdlinger's body to the right spot so it will look like he fell off the train and broke his neck. We get out of there fast, and I mean fast. Phyllis drops me at my car, and I get out and go home to finish fixing up my alibi. She yells at me and I yell at her all the way, and suddenly I know I have killed a man for a woman I hate. Fear! That's what does it. One word from her, and I could hang!

Chaps. 8–9. The newspaper story next day tells about the accident to a prominent oil man. If it *is* an accident, the company stands to lose $50,000. NORTON, the president, hopes it can be made to look like a suicide. Keyes knows it's no accident, and he knows it's no suicide. His statistics show that people just don't kill themselves by jumping off the back of a train. Keyes wants Norton to have Mrs. Nirdlinger arrested and held incommunicado for 48 hours so that she'll lose her nerve and spill the whole story, but Norton says it's against company practice. They decide the company is not going to pay the claim unless the beneficiary sues. They aren't going to let Mrs. Nirdlinger out of their sight in the meanwhile. Keyes figures out that there must have been someone else on the train masquerading as Nirdlinger. He comes so close to the whole

221

answer that I get a creepy feeling up my spine. Phyllis calls me from a drug store and I tell her she's got to sue for payment, because if she doesn't they'll be more suspicious. She says that Lola is pretty hysterical. This doesn't ring any bells with me right away, but then Lola comes to see me in the office and tells me about how her mother died. She was at the family camp at Lake Arrowhead with her dearest friend, and suddenly she got pneumonia. Before the doctor could arrive, she was too far gone to be helped. And who was the dearest friend? None other than Phyllis—who was a brilliant nurse specializing in pulmonary diseases. Phyllis could be sufficiently cold-blooded to lock Lola's mother out in the cold just too long. Lola feels sure of it. So do I, but I can't say so. I know I have been taken when Lola tells me Phyllis is going out with Sachetti. She made me kill a man to get her another man. I look at Lola, and something hits me. I'm in love with the kid!

Chaps. 10–12. I start seeing quite a lot of Lola. Phyllis isn't worrying me much right now. She filed a claim, the company refused to pay it, and she started suit to collect. She's sore. As long as she feels that way, they can put her on the stand and she won't be any problem. Lola is something else. All this time she has been kind of afraid that Sachetti killed her father, in cahoots with Phyllis. She has followed them and listened to their conversations, and she is sure now that Sachetti didn't do it. She has some more ideas, and she has a couple of things on Phyllis that don't sound so good to me. A few days before Nirdlinger's death, Phyllis was shopping for black dresses in a shop in town, and Lola saw and heard her. Lola says that she's going to tell the lawyers for the insurance company a couple of things to ask Phyllis. Why did she wrap herself up in a red silk thing that looks like a shroud, paint her face all dead white, put on flaming red lipstick, and stand in front of the mirror with a dagger in her hand, making horrible faces at herself? Lola is ready to stand up in the courtroom and shout out her questions if the lawyers won't put her on the stand. I listen, and I know I have to kill Phyllis. The world isn't big enough to hold two people with a secret like ours. I plan it very carefully. I'll meet her on one of the observation parking spaces in Griffith Park—one without a guard rail—and I'll be driving Sachetti's car—a key to which I can get because he had to leave one at the finance company when he borrowed money on it. My car will be handy, and when Phyllis and the coupé are pushed over the bank I'll be gone in a minute. Fine. I even have an alibi fixed up. Everything works out except for one tiny item. Phyllis doesn't show up. Somebody else does, though, and the first thing I know I hear a shot and feel something hit me in the chest. Next I'm in a hospital—and Keyes is there with the doc. He knows all about the murder of Nirdlinger, and he has Sachetti and Lola in jail to prove it.

A little workout with a rubber hose and the girl will break, he says. End of suit, end of claim, end of story. This I can't take. I tell him who really killed the guy.

Chaps. 13–14. Keyes gives me a break. Or does he? He says I'll write a statement and mail him the whole thing—registered —and the day he gets the return receipt in person I get on a boat for Balboa and points south. Next day the police get the statement, and I take my chances on being picked up. A funny thing happens, though. Lola

Something hits me in the chest

comes to see me in the hospital—and begs me not to prosecute Nino for shooting at me! He's hot-tempered and just jealous, she says. I can't laugh. It hurts too much. Well, Keyes comes back, and I learn plenty about that Phyllis babe. She is a psycho, and a real one. She has killed something like eight children, and a couple of other people, including the first Mrs. Nirdlinger, for the sake of some small properties or legacies. Completely cold-blooded. She killed three kids just to throw the trail away from the fact that she wanted one of them dead!

And so this is the statement I write for Keyes. I'm on the boat now, and this is what you might call an addition. Because on deck I just saw Phyllis. She knows what we have to do. I know too. She calls it a kind of marriage—when we both go into the ocean together, in the wake of the ship. For a marriage we need a moon, she says. I guess she's right. We saw a shark following the ship a little while ago. Phyllis is in the stateroom doorway now. She's wearing a queer-looking piece of red silk with no armholes or sleeves, just sort of wrapped around her. Her face is all painted dead white, with black circles under her eyes—and her mouth and cheeks all daubed with bright red.

There's the moon.

Dracula

Novel by Bram Stoker, 1847–1912. Published 1897. (ML, 31)

AMONG HORROR NOVELS *Dracula* must rank either first or second (to *Frankenstein*) in longevity and in influence on later writers. In writing it Stoker drew on the standard legends of medieval demonology: There are vampires, the living ghosts of dead persons, who walk by night and sustain their bodies by sucking the blood of living persons, whose throats they puncture for the purpose with two sharp, tubular teeth. They steal and devour human children. They fear daylight, garlic, the crucifix, and any blessed object or substance. They are closely allied to bats and wolves (whose form they often take, as in lycanthropy). ❡ Stoker told his tale by the medium of contemporary diaries, letters, newspaper accounts, and so on. He took the opportunity to introduce the new phonograph as a means of keeping a spoken diary.

Chaps. 1–4. On May 3, JONATHAN HARKER, a young English lawyer, is traveling through central Europe on his way to the castle of Count Dracula, a famous and mysterious Transylvanian nobleman. Harker carries the deed to an English estate his firm has bought on behalf of the count. In Bistritz, a town not far from Dracula's castle, the elderly landlady of the inn tries to persuade Harker to proceed no further. She insists on placing a crucifix around his neck. Harker hears talk of werewolves and vampires. He continues on his way in a coach sent by Dracula to fetch him. When the coach is surrounded by howling wolves, a signal from the coachman disperses them, and Harker arrives safely at the castle. Count Dracula appears to be an exceedingly hospitable and civilized old man. His face is pale and bloodless and his features worn. Harker soon surmises that he and the count are alone in the great castle and that all the doors are locked. One morning while shaving, he feels Dracula's hand on his shoulder, but he cannot see Dracula's reflection in the shaving mirror. Harker is so startled that he cuts his cheek with his razor. He hears Dracula speak politely, but when he turns to answer and Dracula sees the blood where he has cut himself, a look of insane fury comes on the nobleman's face. Dracula clutches at Harker's throat, but abruptly stops when his hand brushes against the crucifix that Harker is still wearing. Dracula then seizes Harker's shaving mirror and throws it out the window and it smashes on the ground. Harker is gripped by fear. That night he sees Dracula crawl through a window and go down the stone walls of the castle like a great bat or lizard. The next night, Harker is attacked in his sleep by three voluptuous women. One tries to caress him, and touches his throat with two sharp teeth. Count Dracula enters and drives them away, giving them instead a sack that contains some moving, moaning thing. It sounds like a human child and later Harker hears a peasant woman at the gate curse Dracula and demand her child back. He sets the wolves on her and they kill her. Harker is terrified for his life and writes letters that he unsuccessfully tries to sneak out of the castle into the hands of peasants or gipsies. He searches the castle when alone and comes across an old room filled with coffins. In one of the coffins is Dracula, lying in fresh earth, obviously dead. He is so appalled that he runs back to his room. Harker knows now he is among vampires waiting to suck his blood and he expects to die; but to his surprise, a few lays later Dracula tells him it is time for him to return to England; Dracula, too, is to leave the castle. Harker, suspicious, asks to leave at once, that night, and Dracula promptly agrees; but when they reach the gates the wolves are so thick and fierce that Harker is frightened back to his room. The next morning Harker goes back to the coffin where he had seen Dracula lying. Dracula is there again, but strangely restored—more flesh and color, even more color in his hair, and on his lips flecks of blood. He reminds Harker of a gorged leech. Half mad, Harker moves to destroy the corpse, but it turns and looks at him and he cannot. During the morning peasants come, nail the boxes shut, and carry them off. Harker is left alone in the castle with the three awful women. He schemes to escape. The last entry in his diary is June 30.

Chaps. 5–12. In England, MINA MURRAY, Harker's fiancée, goes to visit her best friend, LUCY WESTENRA, in the country. Lucy has three suiters: ARTHUR HOLMWOOD, a lord's son; Arthur's American friend QUINCEY P. MORRIS; and a young physician, Dr. JOHN SEWARD. She loves Arthur and accepts his proposal. The other two remain her friends. Mina worries greatly when she has not heard from Harker for weeks. On Aug. 8 a derelict Russian ship, the *Demeter*, is grounded on the coast near Lucy's home. It has a strange cargo—50 coffinlike boxes of earth. They are consigned to a lawyer, who has them delivered to their destination. Soon afterwards, Lucy shows signs of a strange illness—sleepwalking, paleness, fatigue, weakness. On Aug. 19 Mina is overjoyed to hear that Harker is found; he is in a hospital in Budapest and can return after some weeks' convalescence. Mina goes to Budapest and they are married there. Meanwhile Seward discovers that a patient of his, RENFIELD, with symptoms similar to Lucy's, makes strange night visits to the graveyard and meets someone he addresses as "Master." Seward calls in the great Dutch specialist ABRAHAM VAN HESLING from Amsterdam to help with Lucy. Seward has diagnosed her illness as

anemia. He and Van Helsing see on her throat two strange, small puncture-wounds just over the jugular vein. Lucy receives constant transfusions but the condition always returns. Van Helsing puts garlic flowers in the room and hangs them around Lucy's neck; he is greatly disturbed when Lucy's mother removes them, and the next morning Lucy needs another transfusion. On Sept. 17 a big gray wolf escapes from the zoo, then strangely returns of its own accord. It has been to Lucy's, where its appearance causes Mrs. Westenra to die of a heart attack; but meanwhile Mrs. Westenra has torn away the garlic flowers from Lucy's throat. The next morning Lucy is almost dead from loss of blood. Lucy dies on Sept. 20. Van Helsing says it is not the end, but only the beginning.

Chaps. 13–16. Van Helsing discovers that a gold crucifix he had placed on Lucy's mouth, to be buried with her, was stolen from the body. He had wanted to operate after death—to cut off Lucy's head and take out her heart—but says it is now too late. Children begin to disappear in the neighborhood of Lucy's home, after a strange "Woman in Black" has been seen. Harker has returned to England and tells Van Helsing of his experiences with Dracula. Van Helsing explains to Seward about vampires, who live after death by sucking blood from the living; those they kill become vampires also. Lucy has become one of these Un-Dead. They stealthily go to Lucy's coffin at night and open it. It is empty. Van Helsing proves to Arthur (who is now Lord GODALMING) and Quincey that Lucy is in the coffin by day and away at night. They encounter Lucy, walking, and she tries to entice Arthur to become a vampire with her. Van Helsing and Seward then perform the necessary operation: They drive a stake through Lucy's heart, then cut off her head and fill the mouth with garlic. Now her

soul is saved.

Chaps. 17–21. Renfield tries to persuade Seward to release him from the asylum in which Seward has placed him. Though he seems sane, Seward refuses. Renfield warns of dire consequences. Van Helsing, leading Arthur, Quincey, Harker, and Seward, breaks into Dracula's London house. Only 29 of the boxes are still there. Mina Harker wakes one morning strangely weak and spiritless. Seward gives her a sleeping draught. Renfield is found dead in his room, his body smashed and broken. Van Helsing and his group break into the Harkers' room at night and find Dracula there, kneeling beside Mina. Dracula shows fight until they confront him with crucifixes and a blessed Sacred Wafer Van Helsing has brought from Amsterdam. Then he flees. Mina is well on her way to becoming a vampire.

Chaps. 22–23. Van Helsing and his group break into Dracula's house in Piccadilly. Van Helsing destroys the usefulness of the earth-filled boxes (as a resting-place for vampires) by breaking a bit of the Sacred Wafer into each. They find Dracula and attack him, but he escapes, taking with him a large amount of cash; he has provided one earth-filled box on shipboard for his return home.

Chaps. 24–27. Van Helsing and the entire party pursue Dracula to Transylvania; Mina insists on going too. The journey is hazardous and beset by obstacles, which they overcome. Fought by the wolves, peasants, and gipsies, they attack the cart bearing the box in which Dracula lies. Quincey Morris is killed but not before he has plunged his bowie knife into Dracula's heart, while Harker's knife cuts through Dracula's throat. The body of Dracula crumbles into dust. Seven years later, there has been no further trouble with vampires.

The Education of Henry Adams

Autobiography by Henry Adams, 1838–1918.

Privately printed 1907, published 1918 by Houghton, Mifflin Co., Boston. © 1918 by the Massachusetts Historical Society. (ML, 76)

THIS IS JUSTLY one of the most famous and most admired of all autobiographies. Its author, however, was right in not calling it an autobiography, for it does not tell the whole story of a man (for example, it never mentions his wife) but only the story of this man's lifetime quest of an explanation of man's purpose in life. To this end he treated himself as "a manikin on which an education is to be draped" and he wrote the book in the third person, about this "manikin" Henry Adams. His tone throughout is one of

self-depreciation. Adams felt that his formal education was a failure, his empirical education not much better, and he himself a failure (which is never true). But he did eventually reach a theory of man's unity with the world and the effect of this on history, which he expressed partly in the closing chapters of this book and partly in his almost equally famous *Mont-Saint-Michel and Chartres*. He concluded that modern man had drifted too far from such unity. ¶ Henry Adams was born into the most prominent American family of his century, and except for his father, Charles Francis Adams, no one ever had a better opportunity to see the inner workings of world events from boyhood on. Much of this advantage Henry Adams put to use in his autobiography, thus adding greatly to its interest and importance.

The yard at Harvard when Henry Adams was a student there

Chap. 1. Quincy (1838–48). Henry Adams began his lifelong education with his birth Feb. 16, 1838, in Boston, under the shadow of the State House. The society into which he was born was still colonial, revolutionary, financially solid, and on the highest social level. The outstanding memories of the boy's first decade were of Quincy and the home of his grandfather, President JOHN QUINCY ADAMS, where Henry spent his summers and vacations.

Chaps. 2–3. Boston (1848–54). He remembered his father, CHARLES FRANCIS ADAMS, as the only member of the Adams family to possess a perfectly balanced mind. His father's three close friends were Dr. John G. Palfrey, Richard H. Dana, and CHARLES SUMNER (young Henry's boyhood hero). The boy took for granted his place among the leaders of his time, and looked forward without qualms to a leading rôle in politics. He hated school and never mastered the subjects taught him. He was almost completely without religious training, and had no religious emotions. Henry's father took him to Washington to visit his grandmother. He was taken to the floor of the Senate and introduced to several senators; and later he was taken to the White House to visit President Taylor.

Chap. 4. (1854–58). Henry took his years at Harvard with little seriousness, but no Boston student took them seriously. He did not admire Harvard much or consider that it contributed much to his education. The most educational experience at this time was the presence at Harvard of three Virginians, the leader of whom was "Rooney" Lee, son of the then Colonel Robert E. Lee. So different from the New Englanders were these three that Henry was continually measuring himself against them.

Chap. 5. Berlin (1858–59). Henry went to study civil law at Berlin. The new sights, and particularly new smells and sounds, impressed him vividly. He could not master the language and attended but one lecture

on law, meanwhile enjoying himself as well as he could in stuffy Berlin society.

Chap. 6. Rome (1859–60). In the spring Henry, with three companions, moved to Dresden. His sister was staying in Italy and he went to visit her, then on to Rome, which fascinated him. A year later, with no formal education to show, he returned, by way of Paris, to Boston and Quincy.

Chap. 7. (1860–61). On the same day in 1860, Henry voted for Abraham Lincoln and began the study of law. However, he soon accompanied his father, who was a Congressman, to Washington, as private secretary. In this city torn by pro- and anti-slavery emotions, Henry found his attempts at education floundering in confusion. When secession came, he turned to Senator Sumner for counsel and received one of the great shocks of his life upon learning that Sumner had accused C. F. Adams of betraying his principles and had broken off with the Adams family.

Chaps. 8–13. (1861–1864). Charles Francis Adams was appointed Minister to England. Henry put away his law books for a second and last time and went to London as private secretary. On the day the Adamses landed in Liverpool, England recognized the belligerency of the Confederacy. The elder Adams concealed his reaction with equanimity; Henry was terribly shocked and perplexed. His father's position was difficult. Henry became absorbed in watching the careful battle his father was waging with the inner circle. Henry was able to watch the political maneuvering of the highest English statesmen—Palmerston, Russell, Gladstone—and he concluded that his education had progressed when he became aware that politics is rough, and its judgments rougher, and the level of its morality is not what he had been taught it should be. Henry Adams trembled as the English directed diplomatic blasts at his father, but the elder Adams remained steadfast and gave back more than he re-

ceived. He forced Russell and Palmerston to recognize his ability and they prevented the sailing of the two ironclad ships the Confederacy had bought in England. Henry Adams came to believe that a knowledge of the English mind was of no use outside England; that the English mind was one-sided, eccentric, systematically unsystematic, and illogically logical. He concluded that eccentricity is a sign of weakness.

The triumph of C. F. Adams in stopping the English government's aid to the Confederacy by boldly threatening war caused him to be lionized by the English, who admire a strong man. The doors of English society opened wide to the Adamses and 26-year-old Henry became a young man about town. Not being able to hunt, race, fish, shoot, or gamble or to earn a dollar, and not being marriageable, he belonged to no set.

Chaps. 14–15. (1865–1866). C. F. Adams remained in his post after Lincoln's assassination and President Johnson was too busy at home to recall him. So Henry realized he must now look to his own career. Diplomacy had unfitted him for the law; and being at the most sensitive and exciting diplomatic post for four years had unfitted him for a diplomatic career because he could not now take a post in some back-water consulate. He decided to try journalism but sold a single article after taking most of two years in getting around to writing it. Darwinism was making its full impact, and the bored and lonely Henry Adams took it up enthusiastically. He read much and did some digging for fossils, but found the matter too confusing for one not trained to handle facts, and gave it up. He wrote an article on British finance of 1816 and another on the Bank Restrictions of 1797 and to his surprise sold them to the *North American Review*. In 1868 the Adamses at last turned homeward. Henry found that leaving England caused him a painful wrench.

Chaps. 16–18. (1868–1870). After a few months of visiting old acquaintances, Adams decided to try to earn a living as a journalist. He went to Washington, under the protection and sponsorship of William Evarts, then Attorney General. He furthered his career by the sale of a few articles to the *Nation* and *North American Review*. He had a chance meeting with Charles Sumner and was the more urbane of the two; Sumner was unable to conceal his uneasiness about his quarrel with Charles Francis Adams. The atmosphere in Washington was a lazy one, and Adams did little work but did sell some writing on financial subjects. He joined about four-fifths of the American people in electing Grant to the presidency, believing the general to be somewhat like George Washington, a firm man who represented order; he was shortly appalled at the mess Grant made in Washington. He wrote an article on Jay Gould's conspiracy to corner the gold market and took it to London for publication in the *Edinburgh Review*.

Chap. 19. (1870). Adams was glad to be back in London society. He found the very much wanted rest, pleasure, entertainment. But the *Edinburgh Review* and other journals refused his article for fear of libel suits. Henry received word that his sister had been thrown from a cab and injured. He hurried to Italy and arrived in time to watch her suffer and die from lockjaw. This was the sheltered young man's first experience with the harshest side of life and he was very shaken. As he traveled slowly northward from Italy, he heard the news of Bismarck's ultimatum to France and the beginning of the Franco-Prussian war. He returned to the United States to find that some of his articles had received very favorable publicity. Although he was still far from making a living, he felt he was now on his way. However, his family seemed to think his activities were not socially acceptable and urged him to accept an offer from President CHARLES W. ELIOT of Harvard to become an assistant professor of American history. Adams balked a bit but finally accepted, at a salary of $4 a day.

Chap. 20. Failure. (1871). Adams at first worked very hard, just trying to keep ahead of each day's assignments. Later he concluded that he was failing to teach his students in a properly inspired manner. He felt that a novel by Walter Scott or Alexander Dumas taught history better than a college. Yet he was humiliated to think that only Harvard, in all the world, had offered him a job with a living wage. In 1877 he quit and was genuinely surprised when his work was praised. His post at Harvard had carried with it the editorship of the *North American Review.* Editing, too, was a great disillusionment to him; he had no time to do any writing of his own and he had to drudge to meet his deadlines. In 1869 Adams' friend FRANK EMMONS, geologist with the Fortieth Parallel Survey, had invited him to go West with the survey teams. Adams had gone in the summer of 1871 and had enjoyed the grandeur of the West and some aspects of prairie life. While at Estes Park, Colorado, he met geologist CLARENCE KING, whom he worshiped all the rest of his life.

Chaps. 21–23. Twenty Years Later. (1892–98). Upon quitting Harvard, Adams felt that his education, formal and otherwise,

had substantially come to an end and henceforward he must get along with what he had learned. He went to Washington, mingled with the leading politicians and statesmen, and wrote much. After nearly experiencing bankruptcy in the panic of 1893, Adams went to Chicago to visit the Centennial Exposition. It caused Adams to ponder the direction our civilization was taking. He felt that America's energies were being wasted. This problem intrigued him and he felt that his education was beginning again. The panic of 1893 had bankrupted Clarence King and had undermined his health. He and Adams traveled to Cuba, then to Yellowstone Park. Adams found no joy in the West this time. He then went to

Europe as a sort of chaperone to Mrs. Cabot Lodge and her sons. He became immersed in his theories of history and sought verification for them in Europe.

Chaps. 24–27. (1898–1901). Adams drifted, pursuing things that interested him but moving without purpose. He sought to build a theory of history that had a basis in the conditions of the stellar universe, but without success. He visited the Paris Exposition with SAMUEL LANGLEY, who attempted to explain to him the workings of the exhibits. Adams came to feel about the dynamo much as early Christians felt about the Cross—as a symbol of a new age. Yet he saw that the dynamo, a symbol of America, would build an age very different from the Cross. America would build no cathedrals; America could do but not feel; it needed to worship a Virgin or a Venus if it were to find meaning. In 1901 Adams went again to Europe, seeking evidence to bolster his theory of history. This time he traveled to the Scandinavian countries and to Russia.

Chaps. 28–29. (1902). Adams returned to Washington and closely watched his friend JOHN HAY function as Secretary of State. And thanks to Hay, Adams had under his eyes the whole workings of the government at a time when it was at the height of its activity and influence. Education could be carried no farther yet Adams felt that he was being carried further and further into ignorance. Needing unity more than ever, he turned to writing his *Mont-Saint-Michel and Chartres.*

Chaps. 30–31. (1903). Adams felt that he owed more to the help of women during his life than to any other source. He saw in the United States the New Woman, the suffragette, and he predicted that by 1940 her influence would be profound. He heard of the book *The Grammar of Science,* by Karl Pearson, and tried to master it; but his ignorance of mathematics thwarted him. However, he felt he did discern that the new science had brought an understanding of a kind of unity in multiplicity, and that the child born in 1900 would not be bothered with seeking the sort of unity that Adams with his 18th-century mind sought. He wished he had lived in the world of his Calvinist ancestors, when God was a father and nature a mother.

Chap 32. (1903–04). The Russo-Japanese War began. Adams felt as ignorant as to its significance as any statesman. He felt more than ever drawn toward the Virgin, and looked upon her as an adorable mistress who should lead him to the ONE he had so long and so diligently sought.

Chaps. 33–35. (1904–1905). Adams' dynamic theory of history demanded a theory of Progress, the development and economy of forces. Energy, in one form or other, was

the key. As the supply of energy increased, and was expended, so did the fortunes of a civilization ebb and flow. The vast expenditure of energy of western civilization was hastening the rate of progress of that civilization at an unprecedented speed; but the means of creating energy were also increasing. This posed a problem too complex for Adams. In November 1904, Adams persuaded Hay to go to Europe for a desperately needed rest. Hay revived a bit, but in July 1905 he died. Adams felt completely alone. He saw no reason now to continue his lifelong education, and he went to Washington to await the end.

The Egoist

> *Novel by* George Meredith, 1828–1909. Published 1879. (ML, 253)
>
> ARTFUL SKIPPING is said to be the soul of novel-reading, but when reading George Meredith's novels one dare not skip. Too often matters of essential importance to the plot are dropped casually into the center of a paragraph while the bulk of the long novel (usually more than 200,000 words) is devoted to character development and side issues. All this makes Meredith hard reading, and *The Egoist* demands especially careful reading. But it is one of the best and most skillfully constructed novels Meredith wrote, if not the very best, and having read it one is likely to consider the investment of time and attention well worth while.

Chaps. 1–3. At a party celebrating his 21st birthday, Sir WILLOUGHBY PATTERNE announced his engagement to CONSTANTIA DURHAM. On that same day, in the presence of Miss Durham, he refused to receive his cousin Lieut. CROSSWAY PATTERNE, whom he scorned as a Marine; and he excused himself by saying to Miss Durham, "I shall send him a cheque." This began the feelings that caused Miss Durham to elope, ten days before the scheduled marriage, with Col. HARRY OXFORD. Willoughby's female connection Lady BUSSHE had favored his marrying Constantia, but another female connection, Mrs. MOUNTSTUART JENKINSON, favored LAETITIA DALE, a lovely shy violet, who lived in the neighborhood with her aged father and who had loved Willoughby for years. Willoughby had seemed attracted to her before his engagement, and after being jilted he again seemed to court her

for some months. Then he left for a trip around the world, which lasted three years.

Chaps. 4–10. Willoughby returns, aged 24. His cousin, VERNON WHITFORD, a would-be writer, will live with him; also young CROSSJAY, 12-year-old son of the cousin he snubbed three years before. Laetitia's hopes rise again, only to be dashed once more when Willoughby becomes engaged to CLARA, 18-year-old daughter of Dr. MIDDLETON, a noted scholar. The girl is in no hurry to become Lady Willoughby and begs for time to know the world and herself. She and her father come to the estate for a few weeks and Clara finds her fiancé's excesses in words and manner rather frightening. She constantly contrives to keep from being left alone with him. She becomes attached to young Crossjay and spends hours with the boy. She talks with Vernon Whitford about Crossjay's future and agrees to persuade Willoughby to help financially in preparing him for the navy. The more Clara sees of Willoughby and the more she learns of his nature, the more she longs to escape from him forever. He tells her his side of the break-up with Constantia and how she eloped with another man. Clara envies Constantia with all her heart and her thoughts are constantly absorbed with possible ways to end her engagement, but she realizes with regret that in her case there is no gallant gentleman to rescue her. Willoughby jocularly advises her not to marry an Egoist and suddenly she realizes he is one himself.

Chaps. 11–24. Vernon wishes to leave Willoughby's estate and go to London to write. The Egoist begins to spin his web to stop Vernon. He decides that Vernon must marry Laetitia, thereby keeping both of them within his reach and power, for he needs the admiration and worshipful love of Laetitia as well as the companionship of Vernon. Clara asks Vernon's advice, indirectly, by getting his opinion of the propriety of what Constantia Durham did; she finds he approves. Clara then goes to the Egoist to tell him that he and Laetitia are meant for each other. Clara begs him to release her from their engagement but he evades the subject as if she were not serious, telling her he could never marry Laetitia. She then appeals to her father to go with her to the Alps, where she hopes to be able to

turn him to her way of thinking. Willoughby persuades her father to stay. More forcibly Clara asks Willoughby to release her; this time he refuses outright. Laetitia and Clara become friends and Clara confides in Laetitia. Her unhappiness grows daily and when Colonel HORACE DE CRAYE arrives, to be best man at the wedding, it is not long before he discovers her unhappiness. Her desperation increases when her beloved father is won over by Willoughby after Willoughby gives him an ample opportunity to drink some rare old port. Clara, in despair, writes to her London friend, LUCY DARLETON; she asks Lucy to cancel plans to be a bridesmaid at Clara's wedding and begs Lucy to invite her to London for a visit. De Craye is so enamored of Clara that he is instinctively aware of her plans and vows to himself to help her in any way he can.

Chaps. 25–28. Clara receives Lucy's invitation to come to London and she makes her plans to leave immediately. Young Crossjay walks with her to the station and gives his word to say absolutely nothing about her destination. He keeps his word, even when he is severely questioned by Vernon, and it is only accidentally that Vernon finds Clara at the station. She feels very close to Vernon and listens to his pleas to return and arrange her parting from Willoughby in another way. He begs her to consider what the Egoist will do to Crossjay's future when he discovers the boy has aided her to leave. Vernon fails to sway Clara and he leaves her at the station. De Craye comes by in his carriage and offers to accompany her to London. Clara hesitates, then steps into the carriage without knowing why she does it, instead of taking the train for London. She and De Craye return to the estate.

Chaps. 29–40. Willoughby can no longer fool himself. He knows that Clara is trying to escape and will probably be successful. For a brief moment his egoism recedes and he really feels his love for her. The mood does not last long and he begins planning what he will do to soothe his pride. Late one night he asks Laetitia to come and talk with him. He feels she will listen to whatever he says and accept it. He tells her how Clara has deceived him and puts himself in a good light. His story touches Laetitia deeply and

the Egoist again feels secure in having established himself as the most perfect being in one woman's eyes. A few days later he asks Laetitia to be his wife. She is shocked to find herself refusing him, but she discovers she no longer loves him. Willoughby asks her to promise not to tell of his proposal, and she promises. Crossjay, who earlier fell asleep in the room, now is awake, and being hidden, overhears as the Egoist makes his impassioned plea to Laetitia. He is puzzled as to what to do and at first cannot bring himself to reveal what he has overheard. When Laetitia and Willoughby leave the room Crossjay runs into De Craye, in whose room he spends the night, not yet telling.

Chaps. 41–45. Willoughby broods on the disgrace of being twice jilted. Clara again pleads with her father, and with Willoughby, for release, but both refuse. Crossjay tells De Craye what he overheard. De Craye hastens to tell Clara. Now Clara has a weapon to win her father's support. She knows her father will not consider her bound by her promise when Willoughby himself has made a proposal of marriage to another woman while affianced to her; but she cannot tell her father the true circumstances, for he would consider it only womanly jealousy. She talks to her father and Willoughby together and she drops hints that should make it clear that she knows, hoping Willoughby will be frightened at the prospect of disclosure and will release her voluntarily. Willoughby ignores the hints. Clara accuses him of proposing to Laetitia and he says it was on behalf of Vernon. But Vernon comes in and Clara perceives that he knows the truth. Dr. Middleton shifts sides and supports Clara; Willoughby gives up and releases her. Mr. Dale calls; so also do the various ladies attached to the Patterne family, Mrs. Mountstuart, Lady Busshe, and Willoughby's Aunts ISABEL and ELEANOR. Dr. Middleton encourages Vernon now to try to win Clara for himself, and offers him a father's support.

Chaps. 46–48. Willoughby must still be the general and have every event the result of his generalship. He wishes Clara to marry Vernon and the match to have been arranged by him. He asks Clara if she would marry Vernon; she confesses that she would marry no one else. (She has long known she loves Vernon.) Then she learns that Willoughby is sending Crossjay away. Clara tells Laetitia Vernon tried to propose and could not, despite her encouragement. Then Vernon comes to Clara and does propose and she accepts, for she has long loved him. She is going with her father to the Alps and he will meet them there and he and Clara will be married.

Chaps. 49–50. Willoughby now proposes insistently to Laetitia. She accepts on certain conditions: He must know she does not love him. He must take back Crossjay. With Willoughby's consent, Laetitia calls in all the ladies and describes him openly as an Egoist. On these terms, the marriage is agreed upon. Willoughby, humbly accepting all the censure, still is proud of himself. He has won the best of all brides.

Crossjay hears the Egoist's proposal to Laetitia

226

Jane Austen
1775–1817

John Keats
1795–1821

Elizabeth and Her German Garden

Novel by "Elizabeth" (Mary, Countess Russell, 1866–1941)
Published 1898.

BY HER FIRST MARRIAGE Australian-born Mary Annette Beauchamp became the German Countess von Arnim and went to live in Germany. This, the first of her numerous books (all signed "Elizabeth"), is in diary form and probably is the genuine diary of an Englishwoman transplanted to the manor of a modest German estate where some vestiges of feudalism persisted. The book was a tremendous success. Elizabeth was the darling of leisure-class readers, mostly women, who had good taste but little serious interest in literature. Perhaps the best word to describe her books is "charming." *Elizabeth and Her German Garden* has acquired additional interest since the style of living it depicts has vanished. It is quite short. Elizabeth's literary connections were impeccable: Katherine Mansfield was her cousin and Bertrand Russell, by her second marriage, her brother-in-law.

May 7. I am sitting in my garden just after a rainstorm. The leaves are lovely and there are two owls speaking to each other. No one has lived in this house for the past 25 years. It is spring and I am happy. Last year, despite my many children and my age, I danced in the snow. Now it is warm and I am peaceful, living most of my life in the garden. We came to the house five years after we were married, and I spent six weeks supervising the workmen as they changed the old barracks into our home. I was alone here for a time and passed the days in the sun among the daisies and the dandelions. My husband, the MAN OF WRATH, visited the house and accused me of being happy without him or the children. My garden was at first a wilderness. The years of neglect had killed the lilacs and the tea-roses, but now they are growing back and there are sweet-peas and hollyhocks. Every day I walk in the garden and see the new colors that have added their beauty to the scene. May 14. Today I am in the garden with my three babies playing beside me in the sun. I can see nothing but sun-bonnets, pinafores, and little legs, among the flowers. My friends in town pity me and wonder how I can live, buried in this house out in the country. I am happier than ever before in my life. My oldest child is 5, my youngest 3. They all helped me this afternoon when some neighboring cows broke into our garden and almost trampled the flowers. We beat them back with sticks

and repaired the damage. I discovered three infant owls on the ground. I put them in a cage on a branch because my husband had always wanted to train an owl. May 15–16. Regret having tried to keep the owls. This morning I found one of them dead. The other two had broken out of the cage with the help of the parent owls. My babies are digging a grave for the dead owl and preparing a wreath of dandelions. Today I went walking with the children in a little wood called Hirschwald. We found a bed of cowslips and made them into chains. We went wading in the tiny stream that flows through the wood. I often dream of building a little cottage in this wood, with daisies on the doorstep. Sometimes, it is true, I wish I had a friend with whom to share the loveliness of my garden.

June 3. My neighbor and his wife are casual friends of mine. They live busy lives. The wife supervises the children and the making of the sausage. Her flaxen-haired children are clean and industrious, but I prefer the haphazard life of my children and my reading of poetry and writing. Sometimes strangers come to visit and I find that we share no common interests and when they leave I am always depressed. The rockets and the azaleas have come out in my garden. My gardener insisted on planting them in rows when they should have been arranged more naturally, as if they were wild. But they are beautiful, and my garden has taken on the dominant color of mauve. July 11. The garden has not done as well as I had hoped. The rockets have all withered to sticks, but still I love the place. We have had too many visitors, reading our books and sitting in our chairs. One visitor, IRAIS, remains. She is a singer and makes up songs as she practices. We are glad she is here. My babies just came and showed me some newborn kittens. They insisted I tell them a story about the *lieber Gott* (dear God). I told them the stories of Adam and Eve and Noah and the Ark. My oldest girl insisted on rewriting the stories with a happy ending.

The sleigh-ride to the church

Sept. 15. This is the month of crimson and blackberries. The Man of Wrath shoots partridges. My garden flowers are beginning to die. Nov. 10. Last night we had a frost. It did not kill the tea-roses as I had feared. I like plants that will grow in health in God's sunshine. My assistant gardener is a Russian. There are many Russian workers here who go back to Russia in the winter. The women work too, but are not paid as much as the men. The women go right back to work the moment after they have had a baby. I think this is barbaric but my husband, the Man of Wrath, thinks that peasant women know their vocation and are happy. Dec. 7. I have been to my home in England and my Man of Wrath and my babies welcomed me back with love. I was especially happy to see my library again. It is a gay room in yellow and white with all the books we have ever read and many that await our attention. I am reading a book on the life of Luther that was lent to me by our parson. Our parson is a sensitive, studious man who devotes the better part of his time to the peasants of the parish, but they do not understand or like him and his life is hard. His predecessor was a man who drank beer all week and never worked. He was dismissed and preached a final sermon howling invectives against the Man of Wrath.

Dec. 22. I am very busy preparing for Christmas but I often take time out to study the seed catalogue and plan my spring garden. My babies have a new governess, Miss JONES. She is English and dislikes us because we are not. She is always teaching the children and never playing with them. She has a dark line of hair over her upper-lip. The Man of Wrath says this happens to all unmarried women. I had to invite Irais for Christmas, and also MINORA, a strange girl who my mother insisted is lonely. Minora told us that she writes books. Irais and I decided to snub her. Dec. 27. Christmas is a lovely poetic occasion for us. We have a great tree and presents and good things to eat for everyone including the servants. They are really big children and enjoy the day in the same way as do my babies. We have a party for all the peasants and the overseers. I believe people are meant to be happy and it is good to see them rejoicing in their life. Minora struck up a friendship with Miss Jones but Miss Jones left us suddenly and Minora is now moping.

Jan. 1. Last night we rode in our sleigh to the New Year's Eve service in our little church. The wind was howling and the dark church evoked sad thoughts. At midnight we sipped wine made by the Man of Wrath. Minora tried to teach us a popular English dance. The Man of Wrath was moved to make a speech about women. He classed them with children and idiots. At the end of his lecture he insisted a woman should be concerned only with dressing well and cooking. He is a remarkable man. Jan. 15. This morning the bills for my seeds came. I have to pay for them out of my clothing money because the Man of Wrath is not interested in rosebushes or marigolds. Our gardener is gone because he was in love with the cook and the cook left because she saw a ghost. Minora is afraid of ghosts and grows friendly about bedtime, hoping to keep us up for a while. We must hire another governess or the school inspector will take us to court. Minora has been studying the children so that she may write about them. She takes her notebook outside and watches a dog pull the children around on a large sled. Minora writes down everything we say. She plans to take a man's name when she becomes an author. That is as close as she will ever get to a man. Jan. 28. It is very cold and clear and I feel buoyant and happy. The two guests have announced their departure and I intend to whitewash the house as soon as they have gone. Minora has painted my portrait and she is now doing one of Irais for her husband's birthday. Yesterday we hitched the horses to a sleigh and went on a winter picnic. We skated for a while and then drove home with the bells jangling from the horses' bridles. We were perfectly happy except for Minora, who was afraid the driver would fall asleep and smash us against a tree.

April 18. Since Irais and Minora left I have been busy, seeding my garden. Now there is the first coat of green. I brought some primroses with me from England but I fear they have died in the cold. The winter is over and I could dance and sing with delight. I have spent the whole of this Easter day out of doors. I took the babies for a walk in the Hirschwald. I trust that I may grow in grace and patience and cheerfulness, just like the happy flowers I so love.

Emma

Novel by Jane Austen, 1775–1817.
Published 1816.

JANE AUSTEN WROTE an unbroken succession of masterful novels, always constructed with the utmost skill, and *Emma* is one of the two or three best. Miss Austen feared that readers might not like her heroine, but there is no reason why they should not, for Emma may often be unwise but she is never mean. Virtually everything about *Emma* is good—characters, story development, sustained interest. At about 175,000 words it is not overly long, especially for the times when it was written. It deserves a place among the world's masterpieces.

Chaps. 1–5. EMMA is the second daughter of Mr. WOODHOUSE, a gentleman whose estate and village, Hartfield, is part of the large town of Highbury, 16 miles from London. Emma, besides being rich, is beautiful and clever, and also is likable; but she has a disposition to tamper with other people's lives. When she is about 20 her dear friend and governess, Miss ANNE TAYLOR, marries Mr. WESTON, a lonely widower in very comfortable circumstances. Emma, though she favored the match and even gives herself credit for having promoted it, is desolated by the thought of her impending loneliness without her friend. Mr. Weston has a son named FRANK CHURCHILL (he uses his mother's maiden name because it represents a more aristocratic family than Weston). Frank lives with, and is the heir of, his mother's rich brother. One of Emma's friends is GEORGE KNIGHTLEY, a rich bachelor of 38, owner of Donwell Abbey, the largest estate of the district; George's younger brother, JOHN KNIGHTLEY, is married to Emma's sister ISABELLA. Another of Emma's friends is the new rector, young Mr. ELTON, recently come to Hartfield. Emma is determined to arrange some suitable marriage for him. Emma meets HARRIET SMITH, a 17-year-old pupil at Mrs. Goddard's school. Though Harriet is the "parlour-boarder" (the girl with the best and most expensive room), she is the object of everyone's silent pity because she is the illegitimate daughter of some mysterious person. Harriet is interested in 24-year-old ROBERT MARTIN, whose family farms a large portion of George Knightley's estate. Emma decides that Harriet will be a perfect wife for Mr. Elton and talks Harriet out of her attachment to Robert Martin. George Knightley advises Emma against her matchmaking efforts and confides to Mrs. Weston that Emma is treading on dangerous ground with her meddling.

Chaps. 6–9. Emma is gratified when Mr. Elton calls frequently and seems interested in Harriet. Emma paints a portrait of Harriet and gives it to Mr. Elton to take to London for framing. George Knightley stops by the house and warns Emma that Harriet ought to marry Robert Martin, who is a more suitable husband for the parentless girl than Elton. Emma dismisses this warning, and when Mr. Elton returns with the framed portrait she begs him to compose some interesting charades. Elton is extremely unskilled at charade-writing, but offers one that a friend of his composed to a lover. Emma gives the charade to Harriet, saying that Elton wrote it expressly for her.

Chaps. 10–16. Isabella and John Knightley come from London to spend Christmas with the family, and they are all invited to the Westons'. Emma does not want to go when she learns that Harriet is sick, but she has no choice and attends the gathering with Mr. Elton, who does not seem at all upset about Harriet's illness. Instead, Elton seems to enjoy Emma's company a great deal more. Mrs. Weston accounts for the absence of Frank Churchill by saying he is living with an aunt. Emma thinks Frank may be a more likely suitor for Harriet than Mr. Elton. On the drive back home Emma is alone in a carriage with Mr. Elton, who proceeds to make violent love to her. Emma repulses him and accuses him of being unfaithful to Harriet. Elton rages that he never gave a thought to Harriet, and leaves Emma without even saying goodnight. Emma is pleased by the thought that Elton loves her, but she feels he is not of sufficiently high social standing to wed a Woodhouse.

Chaps. 17–22. Isabella and John return to London after Christmas and Mr. Elton hastens away to visit friends at Bath. Emma learns from the Westons that Frank Churchill will not visit them, so her desire to see the young man is frustrated. Emma and Harriet visit a talkative townswoman, Miss BATES, and her mother, Mrs. Bates, whose orphaned 19-year-old grandchild, JANE FAIRFAX, rivals Emma in beauty and talent. Jane Fairfax comes to live with Mrs. Bates. At a reception held in Jane's honor, George Knightley breaks the news that Mr. Elton is engaged to a Miss AUGUSTA HAWKINS. With Elton off her hands, Emma now tries to keep Harriet from seeing Robert Martin, particularly when she hears that Frank Churchill has actually condescended to visit the Westons.

Chaps. 23–28. Emma meets Frank and each is favorably impressed by the other, but Emma worries about Frank's eagerness for holding elegant balls. She is also a bit perturbed by the fact that Frank knows Jane Fairfax, although he seems to agree with Emma's subtle criticisms of her "friend." At a party held by the wealthy but lowborn Coles family, Emma sings a duet with Frank, while Jane, an accomplished songstress, sings alone. During the party Emma has a slight quarrel with Mrs. Weston, who hints that Knightley is courting Jane. Emma is slightly surprised at her own jealousy, but rationalizes it by the fact that Knightley is her brother-in-law and she does not want her family connected with orphans. She leaves the Coles' party with Frank's compliments still ringing in her ears. The next day Emma's suspicions of Knightley's attachment to Jane are confirmed by a conversation she overhears between Mrs. Bates and Knightley.

Chaps. 29–37. Plans for another ball are cut short by Frank's announcement that he cannot overstay his planned visit of two weeks. He parts with Emma on warm terms, and Emma feels lonely, for she has now jeopardized her friendship with Jane Fairfax by undercutting the girl to Frank. Emma is sure she is in love with Frank, but wonders how much; she does not plan to marry him. Her romantic feelings are jolted only slightly by Frank's thank-you letter to Mrs. Weston, in which he ends by offering his best respects to Emma's "beautiful little friend" Harriet. Mr. Elton marries and brings home the new Mrs. Elton, whom Emma finds crude and pretentious. Emma's main concern at this time is George Knightley's affection for Jane Fairfax, and she confronts him openly about his involvement with Jane. The sophisticated Knightley insists that there is nothing to the whole story. Emma hears that Frank Churchill is due to return to Hartfield, after a two months' absence. The plans for the cancelled ball are resumed.

Chaps. 38–44. The second ball is not at all as satisfying as the first, for Frank's feelings toward Emma have obviously cooled. Mr. Elton rudely avoids Harriet Smith and this makes her completely lose any trace of affection she once had for him. Only Knightley acts civilized and for once he does not criticize Emma for misconduct. The next day Harriet comes to tell Emma an incredible story about being surrounded by gypsies on the highway and being miraculously rescued by Frank Churchill. Emma accepts the girl's story, although no trace of the gypsies in the vicinity is ever found. A few days later Harriet returns to confess that she is in love with Frank, and Emma gladly bestows her blessings upon her. May and June are celebrated with numerous picnics but Emma flounders in despair at the almost hopeless confusion of her matchmaking plans. During a picnic at which almost all her friends are present, Emma insults Mrs. Bates openly, for which she is later admonished by Knightley. Emma feels genuine grief when she learns a few days later that the frail Jane has fallen ill.

Chaps. 45–48. Mrs. Churchill, Frank's aunt and guardian, dies and everyone realizes that Frank is now free to marry anyone he chooses. Emma is convinced that he will propose to Harriet. Emma is shocked when Mrs. Weston tells her that Frank has been engaged to Jane for months. Emma is further shocked when Harriet says she is not at all perturbed by the news of Frank's engagement. Harriet says she has long since become disenchanted with Frank's foppish ways and that she has pinned her hopes instead upon George Knightley. Only then does Emma realize how much she herself loves the kind, sensitive Knightley, who has always been a kindly, moral guide to her in her self-created muddles. Emma also realizes that she will have to hurt Harriet because she will fight for Knightley's love.

Chaps. 49–55. Emma does not have to struggle at all for Knightley's attention, because she has had it throughout her escapades. Knightley is so overcome by what he feels is Frank's deception toward Emma that he hurries to her side and confesses his love. Emma announces this latest development in a gently worded letter to Harriet. Harriet reacts reasonably, but with a slight note of resentment in her reply. Jane recovers from her illness and has a reconciliation with Emma. Frank likewise apologizes to Emma, through Mrs. Weston, and regrets that his intentions may have been misinterpreted. Emma feels that her father may be upset by her marriage to Knightley, but Mr. Woodhouse gives his consent after the couple assure him they will live in his house. Emma's muddlings are rectified completely when Knightley announces that Harriet has at last consented to marry her very first suitor, Robert Martin, whom Emma

once scorned. Furthermore, Harriet learns that her father is a fairly well-to-do merchant but without high social standing. Emma attends Harriet's wedding in September and makes plans to attend that of Jane and Frank in November. In the intervening month she and Knightley find happiness in their union, and she feels that everything has finally turned out well for all concerned.

The Emperor Jones

Play by Eugene O'Neill, 1888–1953. Produced 1920. Published by Random House, New York. © 1921 by Eugene O'Neill. (ML, 276 & 146; RE, 90)

EVERYTHING O'NEILL WROTE is important as literature, though not all his plays had the public appeal to be successful when staged. *The Emperor Jones,* written in his early and most productive years, succeeded in both respects. Its themes, developed by fantasies, are the power of conscience on even the conscienceless and the irony of retributive forces, with a doff of the hat to the occult.

Scene 1. HENRY SMITHERS, a cockney trader, is in the palace of BRUTUS JONES, self-styled Emperor of an island in the West Indies "as yet not self-determined by white Marines." As the scene opens Smithers detains an old Negro woman who is fleeing the palace with a bundle. He accuses her of stealing. She tells him, in effect, that the palace has been deserted except for Jones. Smithers understands; this means revolution, and they will soon hear the tom-toms. He adds vindictively that it serves Jones right for putting on airs. The old woman escapes. Jones, a powerfully built Negro of middle age, appears; he wears a fancy, braided light blue uniform coat; bright red pants; patent leather lace boots with brass spurs; and a long-barreled, pearl-handled revolver in a holster. He has a way of carrying off his grandeur. Smithers recalls the day he first met Jones and hired him, though he had heard it rumored that Jones had broken jail in the States. Jones boasts about going from stowaway to emperor in two years. He says he gave the natives a big

circus show for their money even though he squeezed them dry with taxes. Jones had told the natives that only a silver bullet could kill him; now he is playing out his bluff by having a real silver bullet in his pistol, with which he will shoot himself when his time comes. He tells Smithers he will resign in six months and make his getaway. Jones repeats the runout story: that he went to jail while working as a Pullman porter, after getting into an argument over a crap game; that he got 20 years when his opponent died; that he then had an argument with a prison guard overseer and split his head with a shovel; that he filed off his chains and escaped. He says maybe the story is true and maybe not and asks what Smithers is going to do about it. The trader, terrified, says he is Jones's friend but tells him it is time now to resign. Jones has planned an escape through the forest. By dawn tomorrow, he says, he will be on the coast, where a French gunboat is waiting, and he will go on to Martinique, where his money is waiting for him. The two men hear the tom-tom begin to beat. Jones reaches under his throne, pulls out an expensive Panama hat, and starts off without any luggage, telling Smithers he has canned food hidden at the edge of the forest. Smithers tries to keep him from leaving by the front door but Jones says "I'se emperor yet, ain't I?"

Scene 2. Jones, alone, approaches the end of the plain where the Great Forest begins. The tom-toms are still beating. Jones throws himself on the ground and in a soliliquy complains that the emperor's soft job was no training for a long hike in the broiling sun. He starts looking for a white stone under which he has hidden his food. He cannot find it and starts lighting matches, then upbraids himself for showing his pursuers where he is. Shapeless little "formless fears" with little glittering eyes creep out from the deeper blackness of the forest. Jones pulls out his revolver and, in a panic, fires; then accuses himself again of making it easier for his pursuers. He plunges into the forest.

Scene 3. A moon has risen. The tom-tom continues. In a clearing the figure of JEFF, dressed in a Pullman porter's uniform, appears, crouching on his haunches. He is middle-aged and thin and is throwing a pair of dice on the ground before him. Jones

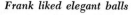

Frank liked elegant balls

The soldiers bring the body of Jones out of the forest

approaches along the trail. He has lost his Panama hat, his face is scratched, and his uniform is torn. He tries to cheer himself up by thinking of the bankroll waiting for him. He hears a clickety sound from the clearing and sees the figure of Jeff rolling the dice. Jeff is the man he killed. His first instinct is to rush over and congratulate Jeff for not having died from the razor wounds. Then he recoils in horror. He jerks at his revolver, yelling that he killed the man once and will do it again. He fires and the figure disappears. The tom-tom becomes perceptibly louder. Forgetting the path, Jones plunges wildly into the underbrush.

Scene 4. Jones stumbles into a clearing, ragged and torn. To his surprise he sees a well-defined road in the forest. He reassures himself by remembering his Baptist upbringing and the fact that there are no such things as "ha'nts." From the background a chaingang of Negroes enters. They are followed by a white guard with a Winchester slung across his shoulders and a heavy whip in his hand. The guard cracks his whip and the convicts start work on the road. He points sternly at Jones with his whip and Jones goes through motions, as though digging. The guard approaches him angrily and lashes him with the whip. Jones makes as though crushing the guard's skull with a shovel. Then he tugs frantically at his revolver and fires pointblank at the guard.

Scene 5. Jones finds himself in a large circular clearing. A crowd of figures silently gathers and a slave auction takes place. Jones clambers to the top of a stump and finds himself being sold to a planter. He fires in rapid succession at the auctioneer and planter and rushes into the forest.

Scene 6. Jones comes to a clear place in the forest and sinks to the ground exhausted. Gradually it grows lighter and he sees Negroes in loincloths, in despairing attitudes, shackled to the forest walls. A wail rises and he joins in it. Then he rushes off, as the tom-tom beats louder.

Scene 7. At the foot of a gigantic tree at the end of a river Jones confronts a witch doctor. The latter prances about, indicating that Jones is to be a human sacrifice. Jones hypnotically crawls toward a waiting crocodile; then, remembering his final, silver bullet, he shoots at the monster.

Scene 8. Smithers and a group of natives are gathered at the dividing line of plain and forest. The leader of the soldiers, LEM, says, "We cotch him." Smithers insists that Jones has escaped but Lem merely repeats the phrase. Lem says his soldiers have silver bullets. Lem made them of silver money. The soldiers come out of the forest, carrying Jones's body.

Endymion

Poem by John Keats, 1795–1821.
Published 1818.

ENDYMION WAS SO savagely attacked by reviewers that a story sprang up and persists that Keats' heart was broken, leading to his early death. This legend was fostered by Keats' eminent admirers, including Byron ("Who killed John Keats?/I, said the Quarterly,/So savage and Tartarly,/'Twas one of my feats.") Probably the review did Keats no more damage than any bad review does any artist. *Endymion* is very long—about 4,250 lines—and was a youthful effort, so it is not surprising that Keats could not sustain high quality throughout; but it contains some of the world's best poetry, including the celebrated opening line, "A thing of beauty is a joy forever." The heavy dependence on classical mythology, on which the characters and stories of *Endymion* are based, shows that Keats was still strongly influenced by his boyhood idol, the Spenser of the *Faerie Queen.*

Book I. In a forest grove on Mount Latmos numerous shepherds and woodsmen are gathered for a ceremony dedicated to the Greek nature god, PAN. The handsome Prince of the shepherds, ENDYMION, is dressed in the clothes of a chieftain king. The worshipers of Pan assemble in a large circle. A venerable priest offers a prayer for fertile lands. A chorus of shepherds and shepherdesses sing a hymn to Pan. The worshipers then pass the time in talk and the pursuit of love. Endymion, however, sits quietly with the priest, oblivious to the mortal happiness. His eyes close and he falls into a trance brought on by a "cankering venom." His sister PEONA steals up behind him and helps to carry him to her favorite island bower. There he quietly sleeps.

Endymion wakes and says he has had a strange dream in which the most beautiful moon he had ever seen took him on a journey through outer space, but his senses failed him and he woke. Now the earth holds no charms for him. Peona struggles against criticizing her brother for his wild imagination but she suggests that dreams are immaterial and should not be taken too seriously. Endymion will not accept her argument. He tells his sister of his ideal of participating in the "clear religion of heaven," where order is maintained like the notes of a beautiful melody in the bonds of love. He tells Peona he will never smile again. They then leave their island bower.

Book II. Endymion wanders widely over the world, sick with love and unable to satisfy his desire. A fountain rises up in the form of a nymph and tells him he must continue his wanderings before he will be accepted by his lover. Endymion prays to CYNTHIA, the moon, to rescue him. A voice issues from a cavern, telling Endymion to descend "into the fearful deep." He enters a strange underworld of twisted fantasy, where he sees temples, groves, and a beautiful statue of DIANA, the Greek goddess of chastity and of the hunt, who is also known as Cynthia. In the dark underworld of his passions, Endymion learns the "deadly feel of solitude." He spies a handsome youth lying asleep in the forest. The young man is ADONIS, the beloved of VENUS. Adonis was slain by a boar and now spends half of the year in the Underworld and half with his goddess lover. Adonis wakes and heartens Endymion by his kind words, and Venus herself appears and tells him, "Endymion! one day thou wilt be blest." Endymion starts back to earth with a renewed passion, for Adonis has shown him that a mortal can possess the love of a goddess. Endymion hears the voice of his beloved goddess calling him. Cynthia tells him she would like to keep his love forever but she fears the envy of the gods. She vanishes and Endymion finds that he has awakened from a dream. He wanders madly in the midst of frightening visions. He hears the trees whisper the sad tale of the unrequited love of the River Alpheus for the fountain nymph Arethusa. This tale warns him about the dangers of his love. Endymion finds himself standing beneath the Ocean and the sea roars above his head.

Book III. The Moon feels lonely and heartsick. She sends her lover a moonbeam, down to the "deep, deep water-world." Endymion receives her ray of hope. Wandering along the Ocean's bottom he meets an old man named GLAUCUS, who says Endymion is fated to free him from his imprisonment. Glaucus was a fisher on the sea who fell in love with the beautiful SCYLLA. She would not listen to his plaints and the sorceress CIRCE, of whom he asked aid, offered him her own love instead. Glaucus accepted but soon desired his freedom. The vengeful Circe changed him into an old man who is destined to live 10,000 years. She then slew Scylla, whose dead body drifted down to Glaucus. A prophecy told Glaucus to change his shape constantly, to gather all the corpses of tempest-tossed lovers, and to await the arrival of a young man who is loved by a goddess. Endymion realizes that he is their savior and promises to perform the rites that Glaucus teaches him. They carry out the ceremonies. Scylla and the other corpses arise and a magnificent feast is held in the watery palace. Father Ocean and all the other sea gods and nymphs attend, as well as Venus. The love goddess sees Endymion still a wanderer but she promises it will not be long. Endymion hears a voice from the moon telling him that his act of kindness has won them immortal bliss. The moon orders him to awake, and he finds himself "happy once again in grassy nest."

Book IV. Endymion reaches the earth's surface and offers prayers to PHOEBE (another name for the Moon, or Cynthia) to lift him into the heavens. He proclaims that he has a triple soul, for he has wandered through the dark earth and the seas, and now would enter the air. He sees a beautiful maiden who is singing a song of sorrow. She tells how the wine-god Bacchus came and carried her off into the heavens. Endymion is tempted by the girl's beauty but the messenger-god Mercury appears with two steeds. Endymion and the maiden mount and ride through space. They fall asleep. After a miraculous journey among the gods and stars, Endymion turns to kiss the maiden's hand. Instead he kisses his own and finds himself falling out of his high imaginative trance, back to the earth and reality. He awakes on a green hill. He feels embittered when the Moon tells him that fate forbids their love. Then the Moon says farewell. Endymion wanders into a forest and sits beneath a tree and cries. Two women appear. One is Peona, his sister. Endymion tells her he has loved but lost the Moon and vows he will live the rest of his life in a mossy cave, allowing only Peona to visit him. Peona says that already all his Latmian friends are mourning his death. Endymion orders his sister to go to a nearby shrine of Diana at twilight and wait for him. He sleeps for the rest of the day and wakes when the evening star appears in the night

Phoebe takes Endymion skyward

sky. He finds Peona with another maiden, whose face becomes constantly more radiant. The other maiden is Phoebe, the Moon, who has changed the decrees of fate by transforming her lover into a spiritual state. They can be together every night, but Endymion must sleep during the day. Peona watches in amazement as Phoebe gathers Endymion into her arms, kisses him three times, and swoops him away into the starry evening sky.

Enoch Arden

Poem by Lord Tennyson, 1809–1892. Published 1864.

THE FAME AND WIDE READING given to *Enoch Arden* when it was published were undoubtedly due to the popularity of Tennyson, who was then at his peak, and not to any outstanding poetical qualities of the work. But the interesting plot makes the poem readable as a story apart from its value as poetry. *Enoch Arden* became a standard English term and laws governing the presumption of death are still called Enoch Arden laws. In the Victorian tradition, Tennyson made every sympathetic character act only in accordance with conventionally moral and noble motives—which unrealistic approach causes some of Tennyson's poetry to be contemned today much more vigorously than it deserves to be. The poem is of moderate length, about 500 lines.

Two boys and a girl grow up in an idyllic atmosphere on a British seacoast near a small, bustling port filled with sailors and fishermen. The girl, ANNIE, divides her attentions evenly between a strong, noble youngster named ENOCH ARDEN and a shy, more sensitive boy named PHILIP RAY, son of the local miller. The children mature and Annie is faced with the problem of which she shall marry. Philip seems to be the one, but secretly Annie favors the stronger Enoch. One day Philip accidentally eavesdrops on the two lovers and can tell that his love is doomed. Shortly after, Enoch and Annie wed. Their married life seems blessed at first, for a son and daughter are born to them. Then misfortunes begin to fall. A third, sickly child is born. Enoch suffers an accident while working on a ship and appears to be deprived forever of his livelihood at sea. An old seafaring friend offers to hire Enoch as a boatswain on a long voyage to the Orient. Enoch hesitates, but the threat of poverty impels him to embark on the long voyage. When Enoch tells Annie she protests, fearing both for his safety and for the welfare of the children, but her protests are of no avail.

At their farewell, Annie speaks words of ominous premonition. She fears that she may never again set eyes upon her beloved husband. Enoch remains strong in his determination and expresses his confidence in the bounty of God. Annie bears up well under the strain of her loneliness until the sickly child dies. Annie tries to eke out a decent existence for herself and her children. Shortly after the burial of the child, Philip Ray works up enough courage to pay a call on Annie, whom he still loves very deeply. Philip has taken over his father's mill and has won himself a respected place in the community. He begs Annie to accept money for the two children's schooling and says that Enoch would want her to. Annie is overcome by Philip's generosity and accepts, with the promise that the money will be repaid on Enoch's return. Philip calls often at the Arden household but remains a little aloof from Annie, whose mind he cannot begin to penetrate. He becomes a second father for the children, who call him Father Philip. Enoch has been away now for the strangely long period of ten years and the children have no recollection of him.

Thoughts that have long lain dormant in Philip's mind finally are expressed. He asks Annie if it seems reasonable to suppose that Enoch is still alive. Annie struggles against the mere suggestion of Enoch's death, but when she hears Philip's proposal of marriage she is moved by his longstanding devotion. She begs Philip to wait just one more year. If her husband does not appear then, it will be safe to assume that he has died. The year passes quickly and Annie, who has lived too long in solitude, cannot put Philip off any longer. From a phrase in the Bible Annie has conjured a vision of Enoch sitting in Paradise beneath a palm, singing praises to the Lord. Annie and Philip are wed, putting an end to the gossip.

Meanwhile Enoch has suffered a great

deal. He is stranded on a lonely island where he took refuge after a shipwreck. The island is a miniature Paradise, just as Annie saw in her vision, and Enoch has erected a small hut beneath a palm-tree. All of his fellow seamen are dead, but Enoch perseveres by heeding the divine warning, "Wait." After his years of solitude a ship blown off its course approaches the island in search of water. The crew rescues Enoch and takes him back to England, but the poor man has been driven almost out of his mind by his grueling experience. His firm, strong body has become bent and his face is weather-beaten and wrinkled. Enoch returns to the town of his youth. His former house has a bill of sale attached to the door. He is certain his wife and children are dead. Enoch rents a room in an almost deserted inn run by an old widow named MIRIAM LANE. She tells Enoch the story of his wife's remarriage and immediately one word creeps into his mind: "Lost!"

Enoch is now faced with a difficult choice: Should he make his presence known to Annie or should he live the rest of his years in isolation? Nobody in the town recognizes him. He is finally driven by the desire to take one last look at Annie's face and he steals at night to Philip Ray's house and mill. He peers through a window and sees the children, who have grown into beautiful maturity, and Annie and Philip moving happily around the family hearth. Enoch sees that Philip is holding a baby on his knee, the child of this second marriage. The scene is too tragic for Enoch to bear. He keeps from shrieking aloud and steals quietly away from the house.

Enoch prays to God to give him fortitude to endure his newest, deepest crisis. After long thought and prayer he resolves "Not to tell her, never to let her know." With fortitude derived from his faith, Enoch lives happily as a cooper and carpenter in the port. He is seized a year later by a grave illness, and knowing he will die he calls Miriam Lane and confesses all. He makes the widow promise on the Bible not to reveal anything until he dies. Miriam sees a child's lock of hair that Annie gave to Enoch before his departure and she realizes that the story is true. Miriam sits constantly at the side of the dying Enoch. On the third night of his illness, he rises up in bed, stretching his arms toward the heavens, and exclaims, "A Sail! A Sail!—I am saved" and the "strong heroic soul" passes away.

The Enormous Room

Novel by E. E. Cummings, 1894-1962. Published 1922. © 1922, 1949 by E. E. Cummings. (ML, 214)

THIS WAS CUMMINGS' first book and, by his own testimony, his most successful. It is based on his true experience as a prisoner in France during World War 1, unjustly put in prison and unjustly kept there by bureaucratic abuses and inadequacies. In his introduction to a 1934 Modern Library edition, Cummings describes *The Enormous Room* as a novel about the individual, "something more unimaginably huge than the most prodigious of all universes." ❡ E. E. Cummings has been a controversial figure in American letters. He strives for special effects with both words and spellings (for example, he will use capitals for some purposes but not for conventional ones; his name is e. e. cummings), and picture-writing, in which the set-up of the words contributes to the intended impression. He has written mostly poetry and though his poems are not always easy to read at first, they include many of the finest of the century. When he wrote *The Enormous Room*, Cummings was just beginning to explore such fields. The book is conventionally written and printed and he even spelled his name with capital letters or used his full name, Edward Estlin Cummings.

1. CUMMINGS and his friend W. S. B. are working in an American unit of the French ambulance corps under the command of a detested Lieutenant, A. Cummings and B. are summoned before a French board of officers and questioned about a certain unspecified "crime" that they have committed. Cummings asks what this crime was and is told that B. has written certain indiscreet letters to people in America. Cummings swears to his love of France, but will not say that he detests Germany, and he is summarily jailed in the little town of Noyon. 2. Cummings finds the jail a relief from the highly regimented army life that he has been leading, despite the incredible filth of the prison. The next day he is put on a train and taken to a new jail. 3. Cummings takes another train trip—this time with two guards, THE YOUNGER and THE OLDER. The guards are at first indifferent to the American's plight, but gradually they warm up to him because of his capable French. The train stops at Paris, where the three men transfer to another train. Cummings ask where he is going, and the reply is "Mah-say," which he interprets as Marseilles. His destination actually is the detention camp of Ferté Macé, where traitors and suspicious foreigners await trial. Cummings and his guards leave the train and walk from a dark, cheerless station to the prison camp. Cummings hands over his valuables, registers his name, and is taken to the Enormous Room where male prisoners are segregated. He is so fatigued that he falls asleep and can remember only ghostlike movements about him.

4. The next day Cummings sees Macé's Enormous Room in the full light of day. It is a dirty, squalid cell with a huge line of windows along one side; more than twenty prisoners live in the cold room, which is lined with pillars so that it resembles the nave of a Gothic church. The prisoners, who come from all over the world, sleep on straw mats behind the pillars. Cummings is overjoyed to be reunited with his friend B. and to be free of the nagging presence of Lieutenant A. Cummings learns that as a *nouveau* (new prisoner) he is subject to a great deal of attention. There are many prisoners in the Enormous Room and gradually he meets the more important: a pathetic Russian named Monsieur Auguste, who is married to a French woman: a crazy Dutchman, Harry, and a preposterous Britisher with a somewhat Cockney accent, who calls himself COUNT BRAGARD. Cummings accustoms himself to the routine procedure of meals, washing cells, peeling potatoes, and exercising in the open court, from which the woman prisoners can be seen over a wall. Communication between unmarried men and women is strictly forbidden and is punished by the painful experience of *cabinot* or solitary confinement in a dank cell. Cummings also learns that the biweekly bath is an event to be avoided at any cost, once he has felt the ice-cold water. The bath is administered by a German named Richard, and strangely enough the cook, washwoman and *Gestionnaire* or Treasurer are also Germans.

5. Cummings describes a number of assorted prisoners, including two named The Young Russian and The Barber, who manage to escape. He is especially fond of hardy men-of-the-world, such as the Dutch Skipper and the strange, brown Silent Man. He calls the people whom he admires most "Delectable Mountains" (a term drawn from *Pilgrim's Progress*). He calls the director of the camp APOLLYON, a traditional name for the Devil. 6. Cummings is especially bitter toward Apollyon because of the way he handles the women. He permits the guards to molest them openly but he rigidly prevents them from mixing socially with

The director Apollyon

the male prisoners. The two sexes can meet only on Sunday at chapel and then under careful surveillance. Cummings salutes the bravery of those who defy the petty tyrant and praises the courage of four prostitutes named Celina, Lena, Lily, and Renée. This foursome repeatedly breaks the laws against talking to men and drinking, and the tortures of the *cabinot* in no way break their spirits. The girls get drunk on Lily's birthday and sing in the *cabinot* despite repeated warnings. The guards stick straw in the door and burn it to keep the girls quiet. They are almost overcome by smoke, but they still sing when they are rescued by the horrified director.

7. Cummings begins to sketch a few of his favorite Delectable Mountains. One of them is a vagabond Mexican boy, MEXIQUE, who is stranded in France. Mexique has a childlike way of talking about the Mexican Revolution that deepens Cummings' sense of the futility of war. One of the few persons he dislikes in the whole group is the FIGHTING SHEENEY, who arrives as a general factotum for a wealthy Rumanian whom everyone calls ROCKYFELLER. The Fighting Sheeney terrifies people such as the YOUNG POLE, who likes to sing obscene songs to the women prisoners. The Sheeney and Rockyfeller evidently have bribed the officials, for they are allowed to chat all night on an enormous bed that is brought into the cell. The other prisoners rebel and, by staging an all-night howling session, force them to follow regulations. Count Bragard announces that he is about to be set free and Cummings manages to slip him a note to send to his family in the United States. 8. One of the most sympathetic persons in the Enormous Room is the WANDERER, a Gypsy who has been incarcerated with his wife and baby boy. Cummings is enchanted with this strange man, who has wandered all over the civilized world without ever learning to read or write. The Wanderer's child, whom everyone calls the Imp, is beloved by all the women prisoners. The Wanderer is shipped on to the dreaded prison of Precigne. 9–10. ZULU is a Polish farmer who migrated to Paris with his friend, the Young Pole. He is a strangely taciturn person who has no communication with Cummings until they conspire with the German washerwoman Marghareite to raise a bucket of food from the kitchen by means of a rope constructed of handkerchiefs and sheets. A guard spies them in the act and is ordered to shoot the bucket and those who are pulling it up into the Enormous Room, but he is too cowardly to pull the trigger. The guard is punished and the prisoners go scotfree. Cummings admires the simple, humble Zulu for his courage in this tiny drama. 10. Another Delectable Mountain is a strangely religious man called SURPLICE. The prisoners tease him with a false accusation of having had syphilis, but Surplice earns their admiration by his skill in playing the harmonica. Surplice is sentenced to the terrible prison of Precigne, and everyone donates clothing to him. 11. The last Delectable Mountain is a

huge, strapping Negro named JEAN LE NÈGRE. He has been arrested for impersonating a British colonel yet cannot speak a word of English. Jean le Nègre is almost immediately the hero of the whole prison, for he single-handedly disposes of six guards when he is being put into the *cabinot*. Then, after earning a reputation for being a powerful giant, Jean shows moments of extreme humility and childlike innocence. A girl named LULU, with whom he has illicitly corresponded, is moved to another camp, and Jean's spirit is broken. Cummings sees in the Negro the indomitable human strength that no bureaucratic injustice can quite stamp out.

12. In November a panel of three judges comes to Macé to review the cases and decide who shall be freed and who shipped on to prison for the duration of the war. Cummings' friend B. is one of the unfortunates destined for Precigne. Cummings himself is allowed to stay on at Macé, but he must bid farewell to most of his friends.

13. Cummings' stay at the detention camp is terminated in January 1918, when he receives word from Apollyon that he may go south to paint. Then a second letter arrives telling him to report to the American Embassy in Paris. After numerous insults from Apollyon, Cummings leaves the world of Macé behind and finds himself once more in civilization. In Paris he receives profuse apologies from the American and French Governments for their "oversights," but is told that his friend B.'s letters were truly indiscreet. Cummings returns home.

Erewhon

Novel by Samuel Butler, 1835–1902. Published 1872. (ML, 136)

INEVITABLY BUTLER'S *Erewhon* is listed among the Utopia books, but like the majority of the Utopias and quasi-Utopias it is a satire. Butler wrote it to draw attention to inconsistencies in the conventional criteria of respectability, which were not much different in 1872 from today. His title *Erewhon* is "nowhere" spelled phonetically backwards, and his subtitle, *Over the Range*, places his imaginary empire in the (then) not fully explored antipodes, undoubtedly Australia. Like most Utopians, Butler could not resist following up with a sequel, *Erewhon Revisited*, nearly 30 years later (1901). The sequel was not really needed.

Chaps. 1–6. Young Mr. STRONG, 22 years old, an Englishman of good family, is learning about the vast sheep industry in (probably) Australia in 1870. He

ventures to explore a territory not then known and braves various natural obstacles, in the process being deserted by his native attendant CHOWBOK. He reaches the isolated land of Erewhon and tries to identify the origin of the natives he encounters; they are Caucasian but do not speak Greek or Hebrew, and they may be the Ten Lost Tribes of Israel.

Chaps 7–8. Strong is jailed as a trespasser. In jail he is waited upon by YRAM (Mary, backwards), an attractive girl; she is very kind to him except once, when he feels ill. All the men are handsome and the women comely.

Chaps. 9–13. Strong reaches the metropolis of the country and becomes a guest at the house of SENOJ NOSNIBOR (Jones Robinson, backwards). He learns that in Erewhon crime is considered a distressing malady to be pitied but not condemned, while illness is disgraceful and respectable persons will not associate with one who is ill; in fact, illness can be severely punished. Death is not feared. Childbirth is not a subject for conversation in polite society. The counterpart of the Western World's doctor is the *straightener*, who prescribes curatives such as flogging for such unfortunate maladies as embezzlement (but the person who has been defrauded may be imprisoned or executed).

Chaps. 14–16. The Nosnibors' elder daughter is ZULORA, who does not appeal to Strong. Strong is introduced to the Erewhonian system of Musical Banks, which issue money that has value measured in music (that is, aesthetic value) but no purchasing power. There is another system of currency that is less admired but that controls the country's actual economy. Strong admires and aspires to win the hand of AROWHENA, the Nosnibors' younger daughter. The Nosnibors consider Strong very eligible as a son-in-law, especially since he is a blond, but Zulora's claims take precedence and she wants Strong, so Strong can see Arowhena only surreptitiously; and besides, he has trouble swaying her preconceptions of matters of custom and religion. (Eventually he succeeds and she is baptized in the Church of England.)

Chaps. 17–27. In Erewhon there is worship of the goddess YDGRUN (Grundy, or conventional respectability). The Erewhonians believe that man goes through life backwards, the child is older than the man, the soul is most mature before one is born. Strong becomes acquainted with the Colleges of Unreason, where only useless scholarship is taught. Machines are considered evil *per se* and were outlawed in Erewhon in ancient times. Animals are conceded to have inherent rights including especially the right not to be eaten—or at least not to be killed for food; but since similar philosophical arguments can be applied to the rights of vegetables, Erewhonians resign themselves to the eating of meat.

Chaps. 28–29. Strong plans to escape by

balloon. He has been presented to the king and queen and the queen is so consumed by curiosity that she sanctions the plan but the king (who distrusts Strong because he brought into the country a watch, which is a machine) warns that failure will be a crime. Strong's greatest problem is to get Arowhena into the balloon. Arowhena disguises herself as her maid, slips out of her house, and is secreted in the balloon. Strong gets the balloon filled with gas and into the air, and manages to get himself and Arowhena over the range, onto a ship, and back to England. Once there, he spends his time planning a way to open trade with the Erewhonians, to his own profit, and also to convert the Erewhonians to the true, i.e. English, civilization.

[In *Erewhon Revisited*, the son of Strong and Arowhena tells how his father contrived to reach Erewhon again. Strong found he was now worshiped as the SUN-CHILD, a god who visited the country briefly and then was taken to heaven in a kind of Assumption. All the English ideas of Strong have become the new religion, Sunchildism. Strong meets a son he did not know he had, GEORGE, his son by Yram. Strong's English son later reaches Erewhon and meets George, but George stays in Erewhon and arranges for it to become part of the British Empire.]

Essays of Elia

Essays by Charles Lamb, 1775–1834. Written 1820 to 1825, published in *The London Magazine,* first collected in 1824.

LAMB WAS THE IDEAL essayist, with universal interests, unfailing good humor, and a vast store of miscellaneous knowledge. His essays by Elia (he pronounced it *ellia*) are among the world's best and several, notably the Dissertation on Roast Pig, have never lost one bit of their interest and popularity. The good humor is the more remarkable when one considers the tragic life he endured and the fact that even while writing he was working as a bookkeeper on subsistence pay.

TWO RACES OF MEN

There are two kinds of men; those who borrow and those who lend. It is easy to tell by their appearance that the borrowers belong to "the great race." They are open and generous, while the lenders have a lean and suspicious look. Borrowers have a kind of grand carelessness and a cheerful light-heartedness, as if every day were Christmas.

These are thoughts that arise because of the death of RALPH BIGOD, Esq., an old friend of the author, who died "as he lived, without much trouble." This fine gentleman had an enormous number of acquaintances and friends from whom he had borrowed money. It was remarkable that with so many resources he should be so often without funds. Ralph Bigod would often repeat an old saying: "Money kept longer than three days stinks," and he tried to live accordingly. "A good part he drank away (for he was an excellent tosspot), some he gave away, the rest he threw away, literally tossing and hurling it violently from him—as boys do burrs." Now that he has gone, one must be content with the company of lenders, "little men."

There are those, and the author is one, whose treasures are books. What a plague are the borrowers of books, "those mutilators of collections, spoilers of the symmetry of shelves, and creators of odd volumes." The author's friend S. T. Coleridge is, however, an exception. When this great man borrows a book, he returns it in even better condition than before, because he makes such interesting notations in the margins. Therefore, "I counsel thee, shut not thy heart, nor thy library, against S.T.C."

NEW YEAR'S EVE

There are two days every year when a man pauses to think about time and how quickly it passes; one such occasion is a birthday, the other is New Year's Eve. The author is not so fond of new faces, new books and new years. He prefers the past and would not change it if he could. He does not even care so much for himself as he is now; but when he thinks of the boy he was, he is filled with admiration and sympathy for this little fellow who exists no more.

Until the age of 30, a man cannot believe he will ever die. But at the age of 45 the shortness of life seems all too real. The author longs to stop the wheel of time just where it is. "I am in love with this green earth." If it were only possible to remain just as old as he is now! There are so many things to enjoy; candlelight and good conversation and the "delicious juices of meats and fishes, and society." Whatever happens afterwards, these things will be no more. In the winter the author is especially subject to these sad musings and cannot be comforted by any of the things people say to dispel the fear of death. Meantime, life can be enjoyed.

DREAM-CHILDREN: A REVERIE

Children love to hear grown-ups tell about how it was when they were children. The author tells his "children," little Alice and John, about the great house where his grandmother Field was housekeeper. Grandmother Field was such a good kind person that everyone loved her. When she slept alone sometimes in the great house, two small ghosts would come at midnight and glide softly up the stairs. Grandmother Field knew that they were her friends and she was never afraid. At Christmas and other holidays she would invite all her grandchildren to the great house and this was always a wonderful time for the author. He would gaze at the marble statues and walk in the beautiful gardens and was very happy. Grandmother Field was good to all her grandchildren but her favorite was John, who was very handsome and lively. Sometimes John would carry the author, who had a lame foot, on his back, and they had many fine times together. Many years later John became lame too and sometimes he would be very cross and mean because his foot pained him. When John died, the author "missed him all day long, and knew not till then how much I had loved him." At this the children begin to cry and beg the author not to tell any more sad stories but to tell about their pretty mother who is dead. "Then I told how for seven long years, in hope sometimes, sometimes in despair, yet persisting ever, I courted the fair Alice W——." [Lamb was in love with her but never married because he had to care for his sister, who was subject to fits of insanity. In one of these seizures Mary Lamb had killed their mother.]

As the author tells the children about their pretty mother, they seem to disappear in the distance. The author awakes to find himself "quietly seated in my bachelor armchair, where I had fallen asleep, with the faithful Bridget (his sister Mary) unchanged by my side."

A DISSERTATION UPON ROAST PIG

According to a Chinese manuscript, which the author's friend has explained to him, it seems that for the first 70,000 ages man ate his meat raw. The manuscript explains how quite by accident this custom changed. One day HO-TI, a swineherd, went out into the forest and left his son BO-BO alone at home. Bo-bo liked to play with fire and soon the hut caught fire and quickly burned down. There were some pigs in the hut and of course they were burned to death. Bo-bo happened to touch one of these burned pigs and then put his fingers into his mouth. He could not at first understand why his fingers tasted so good. When he realized that it was the burned pig that was delicious, he stuffed himself with as much of the pig's flesh as he could eat. When his father found out what had happened he was very angry but when he tasted the burned pig he was no longer angry. When the neighbors found out about the roast pig, Ho-ti and Bo-bo had to go to Peking to stand trial, since in these days to eat meat in any form different from the way God had sent it was considered a crime. The roast pig was brought into court and when the judge and jury tasted it they were so delighted that Ho-ti and Bo-bo were declared innocent. Soon the whole neighborhood was aglow with the flames of burning huts and everyone was feasting on the delicious new food. Finally people learned how to roast pig without having to burn down their

The neighbors are scandalized by the eating of roast pig

homes. "By such slow degrees . . . do the most useful and seemingly the most obvious arts, make their way among mankind."

The author believes that of all the wonderful things in the world to eat, roast pig, when it is properly prepared, is the finest. He likes to share good things with his friends, but generosity has to stop somewhere and when it comes to roast pig, this is where generosity ends. When he was a schoolboy, the author gave a delicious plum-cake, made by his aunt, to a beggar. He regretted it afterwards. The author recalls many student debates on the subject of whether a pig that has been whipped to death is more tender than a pig that dies in a natural way, and whether its tenderness justifies the cruelty to the animal. He does not remember the decision. Sauce for the pig is very important. Onions are too strong for it; the pig "is a weakling—a flower" and must be treated with care.

MY FIRST PLAY

There is a door, now the entrance to a printing office, that "I never pass without shaking some forty years from off my shoulders," for it was through this door the author went to see his first play. He was 6 years old and his godfather, who was friendly with one of the actors of that day, secured the tickets. The green curtain, the handsome and finely-dressed women in the boxes, the cry of the vendor of oranges, nonpareils (candy) and playbills, the glittering lights—all this is as bright as ever it was. The enchantment was so great that "No such pleasure has since visited me but in dreams." Two other plays followed in that same season, 1781–82, and then the author did not return to the theater until he was 16. "In that interval what had I not lost!" Fortunately, after a while the author was able to recapture some of his earlier

feeling about the theater so that it became again "the most delightful of recreations."

OLD CHINA

For a reason he cannot explain the author has "an almost feminine partiality for old china" and after the picture gallery in any great house he visits, the most fascinating thing to him is the china closet. There is something so delightful in the way little figures seem to be suspended in air, yet firmly anchored to their base; the sweet faces of these figures, men and women alike, a dainty foot, tiny animals, all of these things make up a fascinating world.

The author points some of these wonders out to Bridget (his sister Mary) as they have tea. Bridget takes the occasion to comment that she wishes they were not so rich. "A thing was worth buying then when we felt the money that we paid for it." Bridget recalls how they planned and discussed and saved and wore old clothes to buy a book they longed for, and how much more precious the book seemed. She remembers the little lunches they took with them and searched for a proper eatinghouse where they could, without embarrassment, buy only a glass of ale. How good it was to enjoy a play from the cheapest seats and never worry about what anyone might think. Then there were the special treats—strawberries or a dish of peas when peas were expensive. "I see no harm in people making much of themselves. . . . It may give them a hint how to make much of others. But now—what I mean by the word—we never do make much of ourselves. None but the poor can do it."

Bridget, usually so quiet, must not be interrupted, but the author smiles at her notion of them as wealthy. He thinks to himself that when they were young, they were strong, could meet the struggles of life and be better for them. To be young and as they were—for this he would give all the wealth in the world.

Emerson's Essays

Essays by Ralph Waldo Emerson, 1803–1882.
Published: First Series, 1841; Second Series, 1844.

IT IS PERHAPS unfortunate that schoolboys of an earlier generation were forced to read essays by Emerson; for the words were often beyond them and the thoughts could not compete with baseball, so what the starched educators selected to be inspiring was rather repellent. The result was a national prejudice against Emerson's Essays and the prejudice will long be felt. But even for the unprejudiced, Emerson is seldom a writer to read for relaxation. He wrote beautifully but this very virtue permitted him to pack into a sentence too much meaning to be captured at a glance. Throughout his essays runs his doctrine of Transcendentalism, his insistence that man can master the natural, the supernatural, and even himself. Too often, then, he seems to demand of us a strength of character that we consider it unrealistic to attempt.

First Series

HISTORY

There is one mind common to all individual men. Every man's mind partakes of the universal mind. What Plato thought, each man may think; what a saint has felt, he may feel; what at any time has befallen any man, he can understand. Of the works of this mind, History is the record. Man is explicable by nothing less than all his history. It is the universal nature that gives worth to particular men and things. The student is to read history actively, to esteem his own life the text and books the commentary. The world exists for the education of each man. There is no age or state or society or mode of action in history to which something in his own life does not correspond. We are always coming up with the emphatic facts of history in our private experience and

237

verifying them there. I have seen a chain of summer lightning in the sky that at once showed me that the Greeks drew from nature when they painted the thunderbolt in the hand of Jove. Everything the individual sees around him corresponds to his states of mind, and everything is in turn intelligible to him, as his onward thinking leads him into the truth to which that fact or series belongs. In the light of these two facts, namely, that the mind is One, and that nature is its correlative, history is to be read and written.

SELF-RELIANCE

To believe your own thought, to believe that what is true for you in your own private heart is true for all men—that is genius. Trust thyself: Every heart vibrates to that iron string. Accept the place the Divine Providence has found for you, the society of contemporaries, the connection of events. These are the voices we hear in solitude, but they grow faint and inaudible as we enter into the world. Society everywhere is a conspiracy against the manhood of every one of its members. No law can be sacred to me but that of my nature. What I must do is all that concerns me, not what people think. The world whips you for noncomformity, with its displeasure. The other terror that scares us from self-trust is our consistency. A foolish consistency is the hobgoblin of little minds. With consistence a great soul has simply nothing to do. Speak what you think now in hard words and tomorrow speak what tomorrow thinks in hard words again, though it contradict everything you said today. The relations of the soul to the divine spirit are so pure that it is profane to seek to interpose helps. Let a man then know his worth, and keep things under his own feet. Insist on yourself; never imitate. Nothing can bring you peace but yourself. Nothing can bring you peace but the triumph of your principles.

COMPENSATION

Polarity, or action and reaction, we meet in every part of nature; in darkness and light; in heat and cold; in the ebb and flow of waters; in male and female; in the inspiration of animals, An inevitable dualism bisects nature, so that each thing is a half and suggests another thing to make it whole; as spirit, matter; man, woman; odd, even; in, out; motion, rest; yea, nay. There is something that resembles the ebb and flow of the sea, day and night, man and woman, in a single needle of pine, in each individual of every animal tribe. A certain compensation balances every gift and every defect. If the good is there, so is the evil; if the affinity, so the repulsion; if the force, so the limitation. A perfect equity adjusts its balance in all parts of life. Every act rewards itself. You cannot do wrong without suffering wrong. Men call this retribution. But there is a deeper fact than compensation in the soul, to wit, its own nature. The soul is not a compensation, but a life. The soul *is*.

SPIRITUAL LAWS

The intellectual life may be kept clean and healthful if man will live the life of nature and not import into his mind difficulties that are none of his. Nature will not have us fret and fume. When we come out of the caucus, or the bank, or the Abolition-convention, or the temperance meeting, or the Transcendental Club, into the fields and woods, she (Nature) says to us "So hot? my little Sir." A little consideration of what takes place around us every day would show us that a higher law than that of our will regulates events; that our painful labors are unnecessary and fruitless; that only in our easy, simple, spontaneous action are we strong. Not in nature but in man is all the beauty and worth he sees. The lesson these observations convey is, Be, and not seem.

LOVE

Love expands the sentiment; it makes the clown gentle and gives the coward heart. In the most pitiful and abject it will infuse a heart and courage to defy the world, if only it have the countenance of the beloved object. In giving him to another it still more gives him to himself. He is a new man, with new perceptions, new and keener purposes, and a religious solemnity of character and aims. He does not any longer appertain to his family and society; *he* is somewhat; *he* is a person; *he* is a soul. And beholding in many souls the traits of the divine beauty, and separating in each soul that which is divine from the taint it has contracted in the world, the lover ascends to the highest beauty, to the love and knowledge of the Divinity.

FRIENDSHIP

In poetry and in common speech the emotions of benevolence and complacency that are felt toward others are likened to the material effects of fire; so swift, or much more swift, more active, more cheering are these fine inward irradiations. From the highest degree of passionate love to the lowest degree of good will, these emotions make the sweetness of life. When they are real, they are not glass threads or frostwork, but the most solid thing we know. I who see nothing in nature whose existence I can confirm with equal evidence to my own, behold in a true friend the semblance of my being in all its height, variety, and curiosity, reiterated in a foreign form; so that a friend may well be reckoned the masterpiece of nature.

PRUDENCE

Prudence is the virtue of the senses. It is the science of appearances. It is the outmost action of the inward life. It is God taking thought for oxen. The spurious prudence is the god of sots and cowards and is the subject of all comedy. It is nature's joke, and therefore literature's. The true prudence limits this sensualism by admitting the knowledge of an internal and real world. Prudence does not go behind nature and ask whence it is. True prudence concerns the present time, persons, property, and existing forms. But as every fact has its roots in the soul, and if the soul were changed would cease to be, or would become some other thing, prudence that secures outward well-being achieves its stability from the changelessness of the soul in which it is rooted.

HEROISM

Heroism is an obedience to a secret impulse of an individual's character. Self-trust is the essence of heroism. It is the state of the soul at war, and its ultimate objects are the last defiance of falsehood and wrong and the power to bear all that can be inflicted by evil agents. It speaks the truth and it is just, generous, hospitable, temperate, scornful of petty calculations, and scornful of being scorned. The characteristic of heroism is persistence. All men have wandering impulses, fits and starts of generosity. But when you have chosen your part, abide by it, and do not weakly try to reconcile yourself with the world. The heroic cannot be common, nor the common heroic. Adhere to your own act, and congratulate yourself if you have done something strange and extravagant and have broken the monotony of a decorous age.

THE OVER-SOUL

Within man is the soul of the whole; the wise silence; the universal beauty, to which every part and particle is equally related; the eternal ONE. The soul in man is not an organ but animates and exercises all the organs. It is not a function like the power of memory, of calculation, of comparison, but uses these as hands and feet; it is not a faculty but a light; it is not the intellect or the will, but the master of these; it is the background of our being in which all these lie. The soul contradicts all experience; it abolishes time and space. The soul is superior to its knowledge, wiser than any of its works. Great is the soul, and plain. Let man then learn the revelation of all nature and all thoughts to his heart; that the Highest dwells within him; that the sources of nature are within his own mind. This inner spiritual essence is the Over-Soul.

CIRCLES

Our life is an apprenticeship to the truth that around every circle another can be drawn; that there is no end in nature, but every end is a beginning. Every ultimate fact is only the first of a new series, every general law only a particular fact of some more general law which will presently disclose itself. The natural world may be conceived of as a system of concentric

238

circles. The naturalist or chemist has not learned his craft who has not explored the gravity of atoms, and who has not yet discerned the deeper law whereof the natural law is only a partial or approximate statement. The incessant movement and progression in which all things are involved could never become sensible to us but by contrast to some principle of fixity or stability in the soul. Whilst the eternal generation of circles proceeds, the eternal generator abides.

INTELLECT

Intellect lies behind genius, which is constructive intellect. Intellect is the simple power behind all action or construction. Intellect and intellection signify to the common ear consideration of abstract truth. The intellect always ponders the problem of existence. Nature shows all things formed and bounded. The intellect pierces the form, overleaps the wall, detects intrinsic likenesses between remote things, and reduces all things to a few principles. The intellect is a whole and demands integrity in every work. This is resisted equally by a man's devotion to a single thought and by his ambition to combine too many. Neither by detachment nor by aggregation is the integrity of the intellect transmitted to its works, but by a vigilance that brings the intellect in its greatness and best state to operate every moment. It must have the same wholeness which nature has.

ART

Because the soul is progressive, it never quite repeats itself but in every act attempts the production of a new and fairer whole. This appears in works of both the useful and the fine arts. It has been the office of art to educate the perception of beauty. We are immersed in beauty, but our eyes have no clear vision. Art needs, by the exhibition of single traits, to assist and lead the dormant taste. The reference of all production at last to an aboriginal Power explains the traits common to all works of the highest art—that they are universally intelligible; that they restore to us the simplest states of mind, and are religious. Though we travel the world over to find the beautiful, we must carry it within us or we find it not.

Second Series

THE POET

The poet, surrounded by partial men, stands for the complete man, and apprises us not of his wealth but of the common wealth. The poet is the person in whom the powers of apprehension, understanding and expression are in balance. He is the man without impediment, who sees and handles that which others dream of, traverses the whole scale of experience, and is representative of man. He is the sayer, the namer, and represents beauty. The sign and credentials of the poet are that he announces what no man foretold. For it is not metres, but a metre-making argument that makes a poem —a thought so passionate and alive that like the spirit of a plant or an animal it has an architecture of its own and adorns nature with a new thing. Man, ever so often deceived, still watches for the arrival of a brother who can hold him steady to a truth until he has made it his own. For as it is the dislocation and detachment from the life of God that makes things ugly, it is the poet who reattaches things to nature and the Whole and disposes very easily of the most disagreeable facts. It is the poet who can articulate things, for he stands nearer to them than do other men.

EXPERIENCE

We find ourselves in a series of which we do not know the extremes, and believe that there are none. All things swim and glitter. I take this evanescence and lubricity of all objects, which lets them slip most easily through our fingers when we clutch the hardest, to be the most unhandsome part of our condition. Nature does not like to be observed, and likes that we should be her fools and playmates. Dream follows dream, and there is no end to illusion. Gladly we would anchor, but the anchorage is quicksand. Life is a series of surprises, and would not be worth having or keeping if it were not. If I have described life as a flux of moods, I must now add that there is that in us which changes not and which outranks all sensations and states of mind. The consciousness in each man is a sliding scale that identifies him now with the First Cause, and now with the flesh of his body.

CHARACTER

I have read that those who listened to Lord Chatham felt there was something finer in the man than in anything he said. This is what we call Character—a reserved force, which acts directly by presence and without means. It lies in the man; that is all anybody can tell you about it. Character is centrality, the impossibility of being displaced or overturned. Character is nature in the highest form. It is of no use to ape it or to contend with it. There is something in it possible of resistance, and of persistence, and of creation, which will foil all emulation.

What fact is more conspicuous in modern history than the creation of the gentleman? The gentleman is a man of truth, lord of his own actions, and expresses that lordship in his behavior; not in any manner dependent and servile, either on persons, or opinions, or possessions. My gentleman gives the law where he is; he will outpray saints in chapel, outgeneral veterans in the field, and outshine all courtesy in the hall. He is good company for pirates and good with academicians; so that it is useless to fortify yourself against him; he has the private entrance to all minds. The famous gentlemen of Asia and Europe have been of this strong type; Saladin, Sapor, The Cid, Julius, Scipio, Alexander, Pericles, and the lordliest personages. They sat very carelessly in their chairs, and were too excellent themselves to value any condition at a high rate.

GIFTS

He is a good man who can receive a gift well. We are either glad or sorry at a gift, and both emotions are unbecoming. Some violence I think is done, some degradation borne, when I rejoice or grieve at a gift. The gift, to be true, must be the flowing of the giver unto me, correspondent to my flowing unto him. When the waters are at level, then my goods pass to him and his to me. I admire the Buddhist, who never thanks, and who says, "Do not flatter your benefactors."

NATURE

Nature is the circumstance that dwarfs every other circumstance and judges like a goddess all men that come to her. We nestle in nature and draw our living as parasites from her roots and grains. The beauty of nature is supreme. Art and luxury have early learned that they must work as enhancement and a sequel to this original beauty. The difference between landscape and landscape is small, but there is great difference in the beholders. There is nothing as wonderful in any particular landscape as the necessity of being beautiful under which every landscape lies. Nature is always consistent, though she feigns to contravene her own laws. She keeps her laws and seems to transcend them. She arms and equips an animal to find its place and living on the earth, and at the same time she arms and equips another to destroy it.

239

POLITICS

In dealing with the State we ought to remember that its institutions are not aboriginal, though they existed before we were born; that they are not superior to the citizen; that every one of them was once the act of a single man; every law and usage was a man's expediency to meet a particular case; they are all imitable, all alterable; we may make as good; we may make better. The theory of politics that has possessed the minds of men, and that they have expressed the best they could in their laws and in their revolutions, considers persons and property as the two objects for whose protection government exists. All persons have equal rights, in virtue of being identical in nature. This interest, of course, with its whole power demands a democracy. Born democrats though we may be, we are nowise qualified to judge of monarchy, which, to our fathers living in the monarchial idea, was also relatively right. But our institutions, though coincident with the spirit of the age, have not any exemption from the practical defects that have discredited other forms. Hence, the less government we have the better—the fewer laws, and the less confided power. The antidote to the abuse of formal government is the influence of private character, the growth of the Individual. The power of love as the basis of the state has never been tried.

NOMINALIST AND REALIST

I cannot say often enough that a man is only a relative and representative nature. Each man is a hint of the truth, but far enough from being that truth which yet he quite newly and inevitably suggests to us. The man momentarily stands for the thought, but will not bear examination; and a society of men will in a cursory way well enough represent a certain quality and culture, for example, chivalry or beauty of manners; but separate them and there is no gentleman and no lady in the group. In the famous dispute with the Nominalists, the realists had a good deal of reason. General ideas are essences. They are our gods; they round and ennoble the most partial and sordid way of living. Our proclivity to details cannot quite degrade our life and divest it of poetry. If we cannot make voluntary and conscious steps in the admirable science of universals, let us see the parts wisely and infer the genius of nature from the best particulars with a becoming charity. What is best in each kind is an index of what should be the average of that thing.

man learned from nature. Cities and different kinds of governments grew. Religion and government have a source in common. Self-love gives rise to ambition and lust, but self-love is also what restrains Man and gives birth to government and law.

Epistle 4 deals with Man's relation to happiness. Happiness is attainable, but it lies not in the good of one, but in the good of all. Though there are seeming inequalities among men, "Bliss is the same in subject or in king." Man's happiness is bound up with his hopes and fears as to some future condition, not the present moment only. Fortune and nature should not be confused with virtue. In fact, too many outward honors are threatening to virtue, which comes from being true to oneself. Nobility, greatness, fame—these things do not bring happiness. Happiness is not a narrow individual matter, but spreads to everything. Happiness lies in seeing that *Whatever is, is right,* that reason and passion have one purpose, and that self-love and social living are one thing. The only true happiness in this world comes from virtue. The purpose of knowledge is to know ourselves.

Essay on Man

Poem by Alexander Pope, 1688–1744. Published 1732–1734.

POPE DEDICATED this poem to Henry St. John, Lord Bolingbroke, whose essays had expressed a similar philosophy. The poem is written in heroic couplets (ten-syllable lines, rhyming two by two) and over the centuries has been so quoted that nearly every line sounds like a cliché. There are 1,304 lines. The whole adds up to a fervent statement of faith in man and God. It is Pope's most famous poem and probably his best, though it has suffered in critical esteem from its too great popularity.

Epistle 1. The nature of Man is described, and his relation to the universe. Man can reason only about what he knows. He does not know the relation that he, on earth, has to the whole universe. Man is presumptuous to seek the reason. Man is actually perfectly suited to his place in the whole scheme of the universe. His happiness is based on the fact that he cannot know what the future holds, including all the bad things that may befall him; and at the same time "Hope springs eternal in the human breast:/Man never Is, but always To be blest." Pride makes Man rebel against the laws of order. This is sinful. Pride causes Man to think that all things in nature exist just for him, and then he complains because everything is not just as he wishes. Though

Man complains because he cannot do everything and be everything, he has no cause to complain; he has reason, and reason includes all other powers. If Man could see it, he would know that what appears to be chance really has direction; discord is really harmony; nature is really art and "One truth is clear, WHATEVER IS, IS RIGHT."

Epistle 2 deals with man in relation to himself. "Know then thyself, presume not God to scan;/The proper study of Mankind is Man." In Man there are two principles, self-love and reason. Both of these are necessary and they can work together for the good of Man, though self-love is stronger than reason. All of the passions can work together in man for his good or they can destroy him. Each man has one ruling passion and reason should become a friend to this passion in every person. Virtue and vice exist together in Man, just as black and white exist together in a painting. Every man wants to be himself. Even such mean passions as self-love can be turned to good ends. For example, through love of self we can discover the desires of others. "Though Man's a fool, yet GOD IS WISE."

Epistle 3 is concerned with Man's relation to society. There is a something, the *universal cause,* that is present in everything. Nothing exists for itself alone. There is a benevolent interaction and relation between things. Reason and instinct both can lead Man to good. Society benefits from both but receives the greatest benefit from reason. Art developed as reason copied instinct and

Esther Waters

Novel by George Moore, 1852–1933. Published 1894.

GEORGE MOORE, with youthful bravery, was one of the first English novelists to defy the conventional morality of Victorian critics and sympathize with sinful characters in his books. *Esther Waters* has been generally rated his best novel. His heroine is one of the Plymouth Brethren, one of the strictest of the new Puritan sects, and the novel is an admirable portrayal of one who is genuinely good and who nevertheless errs humanly.

Chaps. 1–3. ESTHER WATERS, a 17-year-old English girl, is forced by her brutal stepfather to leave home; he says he can no longer afford to provide for her. She is faced with going to the workhouse, but secures a job as kitchen maid at Woodview, the mansion of the BARFIELD family. The main interest at Woodview is the racing stable, and even the servants frequently bet on the Woodview horses entered in races. Esther works hard but gets little approval or sympathy from the other servants. She meets WILLIAM LATCH, the son of the cook, and is attracted to him because he shows her more kindness than the others. William's mother wants him to work elsewhere but he is interested in gambling and

Mrs. Barfield's Sunday service

wants to be around the racing stable. SARAH TUCKER, one of the maids, discovers that Esther cannot read or write and taunts her. Mrs. BARFIELD, an intensely religious woman, holds Sunday services for the domestics, and she is attracted by Esther's piety. The mistress takes an interest in the girl and starts to teach her to read and write. Esther worships her mistress and feels more secure at Woodview.

Chaps. 4–10. William pays a great deal of attention to Esther and tells her of his plan to make money by betting on horses. They go to a servants' ball together and Esther looks lovely in a dress she has borrowed from Mrs. Barfield's daughter. William tells Esther he loves her and for the first time in her life she is really happy. Sarah Tucker resents the attention that William shows Esther and makes nasty comments about Esther. Soon after, all the servants bet on a Woodview horse and they win nice little sums of money when the horse comes in first.

Chaps. 11–12. Esther and William take a walk one night and he leads her to a lonely spot and seduces her. He tells her he wants to marry her but must wait until he has more money. Esther, humiliated and shocked, refuses to have anything more to do with her betrayer. He tries to reason with her and convinces her of his good intention, but she is adamant. William becomes enamored of PEGGY BARFIELD, a young cousin of the master's who is visiting Woodview, and elopes with her several weeks later. Needless to say, he is discharged for his indiscretion. Esther still secretly loves William and she is crushed by his going off with another woman. A few months later, Esther discovers she is pregnant. She knows she will have to leave Woodview. Mrs. Barfield kindly gives her references and some extra money and joins Esther in prayer. The other servants regret their past unkindnesses to Esther and even Sarah gives her a warm embrace when the poor girl leaves the estate.

Chaps. 13–16. Esther goes home to her family. She is seven months pregnant, but her stepfather wants to throw her out. He

relents when he finds she has money. Esther's mother also is pregnant. She is gaunt and ill and fears she will not survive another birth. Esther's stepfather tries to take all her money but she finds lodgings near a hospital. When her time comes she is delivered by a group of mocking medical students in a public room. Esther forgets everything in the joy of having given birth to a son, JACKIE. Her sister JENNY comes to the hospital and tells Esther that their mother has died in childbirth and the baby was stillborn. Jenny says that the stepfather plans to take the family to Australia, but that he will leave Jenny behind because she is old enough to fend for herself and he cannot afford to take her. Esther gives Jenny the money Jenny needs to accompany the family. When they go she is left alone in the world, except for her infant son.

Chaps. 17–22. Esther gets a job as a wet-nurse and boards her son with a Mrs. SPIRES. Esther wants to see her son, but her new mistress forbids her to go to the boy. She tells Esther she may not leave the house, and if she does she may never come back. Esther flees from this form of bondage and is terrified when she learns that Mrs. Spires is planning to murder Jackie. Esther saves him and tries to support herself and the baby, but is unsuccessful and seeks refuge in the workhouse. Esther hears that the Barfields have lost all their money on racing, and that all the servants were dis-

At the Derby

missed. This further depresses the girl but her life is brightened by Miss RICE, a kindly woman who writes novels. Miss Rice often sends Esther to the stationer's, where she meets a clerk, FRED PARSONS. He is a deeply religious man of 35, and when Esther tells him of her sin he is forgiving. He loves her and wants to marry her, but though Esther is grateful to him for his kindness she does not love him. She is pleased, however, when he and Jackie become good friends.

Chaps. 23–39. Fred takes Esther to visit his aged parents in the country, and she finally agrees to marry him in the spring. But she meets William Latch again, and he tells her that he now owns a half share in a tavern and that he has left his wife and is getting a divorce. William learns that he has a son, and when he meets Jackie the two are attracted to each other. William asks Esther to marry him, and she realizes that she cannot deny Jackie the right of living with his own father. She knows she would be better off with Fred, but she sacrifices herself for her son's happiness. Esther and Jackie go to live with William and after his divorce she marries William. Her one-time affection for him is reborn and for a time they are happy.

Chaps. 30–39. Esther now has a servant of her own and a real home for Jackie, but William has been making book on the horses and every time a favorite wins he loses a great deal of money. They go down to the Derby and Esther wears a new dress, but the day is spoiled for her when Fred appears with a religious group, carrying placards denouncing racing. Fred sees Esther and tries to persuade her to return to the good religious life. William gets a lung infection and Esther worries about his health. He gets worse and coughs so badly he can hardly conduct his business and Esther learns how to take the bets and pay off the losses. Fred joins the Salvation Army and determines to end the betting in William's tavern. Meanwhile Sarah Tucker, who has a position nearby, has stolen a plate to help her boy friend place a bet on a horse. The horse does not win and Sarah gets drunk. William promises to buy the plate back for her, but before they can do anything two policemen come and arrest Sarah for robbery. Sarah is sentenced to 18 months at hard labor.

Chaps. 40–44. William is always careful about not taking bets from strangers, but he forgets this rule and takes a bet from a man who turns out to be a policeman. Several hours later the tavern is raided and William is fined 100 pounds. William gets thinner and coughs more often. He is afraid to use the tavern to take bets so he stands out in all weather on the race course. After there is a fight in the bar, William loses his license and sells the house. They move to poorer lodgings. William dips heavily into their savings and loses the money on the horses. The doctor tells him he has an advanced case of consumption (tuberculosis) and that he must go to Egypt for the winter.

241

William bets the remainder of their savings on a horse at 18-to-1 odds, trying to make enough money to live easily in Egypt for several months. William enters a hospital with all his hopes pinned on the longshot. The horse loses and with the loss goes the chance for William's life. William, in his last days, reads the Bible and finds beauty and comfort in its words. He regrets all the wrong he has done to people through his gambling and he apologizes to Esther for the life he has given her and for the fact that he has nothing to leave her.

Chaps. 45–46. William insists on dying at home. He calls for his son. He tells him that his death is a punishment for the way he has treated Esther. After his death, Esther tries scrubbing floors but finds that she and Jackie cannot make ends meet. She writes to Mrs. Barfield, who asks her to come and stay with her at Woodview. Mrs. Barfield is alone in the large house. Her husband and daughter are dead. The two women live as friends, not as mistress and maid. They share the same religious beliefs and hold prayer meetings in the grand house. They think about the beginning of their lives and resign themselves to destiny. Mrs. Barfield helps support Jackie, who has not been able to find employment in London.

Chap. 47. Mrs. Barfield grieves because her son Arthur has become a racing man. He will have nothing to do with his mother or with Woodview. She is keeping the house going in the futile hope that one day Arthur will marry and come back to live in his first home. Esther is gratified when one day Jackie visits her. He is a soldier and he is handsome and strong in his uniform. He has nothing but love and admiration for his mother and he is proud of her life's work when he sees her. She has finally come to know true joy and peace in her life.

Ethan Frome

Novel by Edith Wharton, 1862–1937. Published and © 1911 by Charles Scribner's Sons, New York.

IT MAY HAVE BEEN only surprise that Edith Wharton, whose life was one of wealth in New York's excessively formal society, could write so well about poverty and simplicity on a New England farm where only poverty and simplicity were known; but for whatever reason, critics acclaimed this novel when it was published and have generally rated it her best work. That is a high rating, for Edith Wharton was one of the most important American novelists of her times.

Introduction. The author of the book goes to the typical New England town of Starkfield, Massachusetts. At the post office she first sees the striking figure of ETHAN FROME. She is fascinated, as anyone who sees him must be, by this large, gaunt farmer and woodcutter, "the ruin of a man" and surprisingly only 52 years old. He is badly crippled but still carries an air of pride, despite his misfortune and his poverty. The author is staying with a widow, Mrs. HALE, who is very friendly; but neither Mrs. Hale nor the other townspeople will divulge the story of Ethan's life to a "foreigner." The author makes daily trips to Corbury Flats to take a train and she hires Ethan to drive her there. Ethan's interest is aroused when he learns that the author studies science, for he himself once studied scientific subjects at Worcester. But he is uncommunicative about himself.

One winter night, when the author has known Ethan for several months, she finds herself stranded with him in a snowstorm while he is driving her back from Corbury Flats. They are near Ethan's farm and their only recourse is to take shelter there. The author meets the two strange women who share Ethan's household with him. The story that follows is pieced together from her night's stay at the Frome house and from bits of town gossip.

Zeena is waiting when Ethan and Mattie return home

Chaps. 1–2. Ethan Frome, dogged by misfortune from his youth, is forced to abandon his schooling to help his crippled mother and father operate their farm in Starkfield. His parents die and at the age of 28 he marries ZENOBIA PIERCE (ZEENA), whose sickly nature is worsened by her tendency to hypochondria. It is a loveless marriage. Ethan struggles to make the farm pay. His hopes for a better, more meaningful life fade, and Zeena is no help to him at all. She cannot even take proper care of the house and Ethan is forced to hire a girl to assist his wife. Zeena has an orphaned cousin named MATTIE who needs a home and is willing to work for nothing. The young, laughing Mattie is a welcome addition to the barren farmhouse where Zeena's whinings and complaints are constantly heard. One night Ethan drives the sleigh into town to pick up Mattie at a dance, to which she was escorted by DENIS EADY, son of the rather prosperous town grocer. Ethan cannot help feeling jealous of the way they dance together and linger in each other's company, but as he drives Mattie home he has the feeling that the girl's true affections were not for the foolish Denis. They get back to the farm and Ethan gropes around the doorway, trying to find the key. Zeena appears with a candle to admit them and stands there in a quiet brooding way, like some ghost of the Puritan past. Mattie hurries up to bed and Ethan retires to spend the rest of the night reading.

Chaps. 3–6. The querulous Zeena decides to seek the advice of a new doctor in a nearby town and demands that Ethan take her there. Ethan demurs and proposes that a neighbor, JOTHAM POWELL, make the trip, because Ethan has to sell some lumber to Mr. Hale. Actually Ethan is contriving to spend some time alone with Mattie, to experience a form of friendly companionship that he has never known before. Zeena grumbles but goes off with Powell, hoping that Frome's sale of lumber may pay her new doctor's bills. Ethan hurries into town and sells the lumber, but Mr. Hale is unable to pay cash because one of his children is soon to be married. Ethan and Mattie live a brief but idyllic existence without Zeena's continuous harping. Ethan never so much as kisses the girl, but merely being alone with her is enough. The only accident to mar their happiness is the breaking of Zeena's most prized pickle dish by a cat. Ethan offers to glue the dish together and protect Mattie, who let the cat use it. That night they contemplate a wild sleigh ride down the dangerous hill near Corbury Flats, but instead they part company without so much as holding hands. The next morning Powell brings back Zeena, who goes directly to bed without saying a word.

Chap. 7. Ethan learns that Zeena must have an operation. Zeena further demands a new serving girl, whom she has already hired. She says that Mattie will then be free to leave and marry. Ethan is enraged and tells his wife that Mr. Hale has not given him any money and that a new serving girl is out of the question. Zeena retracts somewhat, but then informs Ethan that she has also made plans to send Mattie's luggage to the railroad station. Ethan watches his wife's face in the candlelight and feels that he is looking into the heart of evil. He can see the frustration and cruelty of a life cut off from a world of knowledge and beauty. He then breaks the news to Mattie, who weeps unrestrainedly. Both feel hopelessly consigned to their fates. At dinner that night Zeena discovers the broken dish, her most prized possession. She limps out of the room after upbraiding Mattie, whom she accuses of much deeper guilt.

Chaps. 8–9. Ethan struggles hard within himself and tries in vain to find some scheme for freeing himself and Mattie from Zeena's clutch. He ponders their running away to the West, but lack of funds makes this impossible. After a sleepless night, he decides that they must yield to fate. His last gesture of independence is to insist on taking Mattie to the station. He helps Mattie with her trunk, and both are in despair and under great tension. Ethan imagines terrible things that may happen to the girl when she is alone in some large city. His hatred for Zeena deepens when Zeena does not even bother to say goodbye to her cousin. The ride to Corbury Flats is a painful experience, especially when they sight a small lake where they had a picnic the previous year. At last on the steep Corbury Hill they see a sled that has been abandoned by some youngsters and both are seized by the idea of taking a brief ride down the hill as a gesture of independence. Ethan manipulates the dangerous course with great skill, carefully avoiding the big elm tree midway down the slope. They climb back up the hill, and Mattie can no longer restrain her passion. They kiss and then she makes one last desperate plea to be with him. She tells him to take her for another ride, but this time to strike the tree and kill them both, for at least that way they can be together forever. The lovers mount the sled, speed down the long hill, and ram the tree. Ethan hears the whinny of his horse, and he knows he has failed. Neither Ethan nor Mattie is killed by the fateful ride. Both are carried back to the farmhouse, where they are left to the mercy of Zeena to tend them. Zeena snaps out of her illness and bears her burden with surprising patience and strength. Mattie has been so crippled by the accident that she cannot move from a chair. Ethan recovers but still walks with a limp. The three of them live on in the bleak farmhouse in a terrible snare of hatred, distrust, and frustration. Mattie herself is so embittered by the accident that she loses all her girlish charm. Only Ethan manages to hoard a little pride and dignity through the long years.

Eugene Onegin

Poem by Aleksandr Pushkin, 1799–1837.

Published 1831. Published 1936 by Random House, New York, in a new translation from the Russian by Babette Deutsch.

THE COLUMBIA ENCYCLOPEDIA says flatly that Pushkin was Russia's greatest poet and that *Eugene Onegin* was his masterpiece. Princess Alexandra Kropotkin says of the poem: "While Pushkin was undoubtedly influenced by Byron and the form of *Eugene Onegin* somewhat resembles *Childe Harold*, actually the content and magnificent lyrical quality of Pushkin's poem are entirely original. ⦿ "*Eugene Onegin* is the best known of all Pushkin's works. It is known outside Russia, better even than *Boris Godunov*. It is more than a great poem, it actually marks the 'coming of age' of the written Russian language. The sentiments and dialogue are infinitely more natural, warmer, nearer the Russian heart, than the stilted language used by writers who preceded Pushkin. Many of these were strongly influenced by French (and in some cases German) writers." Princess Kropotkin goes on to say that much in the drama of Eugene Onegin is autobiographical: "Pushkin identifies himself over and over again with Onegin. Onegin's exile is the parallel of Pushkin's own banishment at one time." ⦿ There are many unfinished stanzas in the poem. Some critics have held that Pushkin intended to revise them, others that parts were deleted by government censorship. The popularity of the poem is helped by the Tchaikovsky opera based on it.

EUGENE ONEGIN is a spoiled, fashionable fop. He is wealthy, willful and inclined to show himself superior to acquaintances and even friends. His life is the sybarite life of the very rich young men of aristocratic birth, enjoying all the pleasures of St. Petersburg. For the summer, Onegin, tired of city amusements, retires to his country estate. Here he finds a new friend in a neighbor, VLADIMIR LENSKY, who is the complete opposite of Onegin. He is a budding poet, strongly influenced by German literature and philosophy. Sentimental, with lofty ideals, Lensky becomes devoted to Onegin, who himself has aspired to write verse. Through Lensky, Onegin becomes acquainted with a neighboring widow and her two lovely daughters. They are of noble birth but not rich. They are hospitable, unspoiled people. The two daughters are as much of a contrast in character as Onegin and Lensky. TATIANA, the older girl, is serious-minded, with high ideals and dreamy aspirations to a more interesting life than she leads in the country. OLGA, the younger girl, is gay, frivolous, happy and thoughtless. She is the one who attracts Lensky. Tatiana falls hopelessly in love with Onegin, who pays her very little attention. He who has had many conquests—even at the early age of 19—has assumed a pose of disillusion with society, flirtations, and even love. The pure love of a naïve young country lady means nothing to him. He lectures Tatiana when she writes a pathetic letter declaring her love. Lensky and Olga in the meantime are about to be betrothed.

All is suddenly changed when the young people attend a dance. Olga loses her head when the aloof Onegin, moved by some evil spirit of mischief, begins to flirt with her. They dance many dances together, drawing attention by their gay flirting. Lensky is livid. He accuses Onegin of cruel betrayal and challenges him to a duel. They fight and Onegin kills his friend Lensky. For this act Onegin has to leave the country.

Several years pass. Tatiana suffers a severe illness; finally, at her mother's insistence, she agrees to go to Moscow. There she meets and marries a wealthy, elderly general who has a prominent social position in court circles. Onegin returns from exile and meets Tatiana, now a worldly, beautiful woman. He hardly recognizes her as the child who once declared her love for him so artlessly. Now Onegin falls madly in love with Tatiana and pursues her constantly, but without success. She refuses to see him; his letters remain unanswered. Finally Onegin goes to Tatiana's house and manages to be shown into her presence. He finds her reading his letters, her eyes full of tears. He declares his passionate love for her. [Here follows one of the most beautiful lyrical scenes in Russian literature.] She tells him that she loved him, as he knows, but that he was not interested in the pure love of an unsophisticated girl. But why now does he pursue her? Is it because she is rich now and belongs to the highest society? "Is it," says Tatiana, "because my fall, in such condition, would be noted everywhere, and bring to you an envied reputation?" Tatiana tells Onegin that she would once have gone anywhere with him and would have lived in simple circumstances. But now it is too late. She sends Onegin away and he goes back to his meaningless life of the jaded aristocrat.

Eugénie Grandet

Novel by Honoré de Balzac, 1799–1850. Published 1833. Several translations. (ML, 245; T2)

THE SUSTAINED EXCELLENCE in Balzac's series of short novels and stories that he called "The Human Comedy" is so remarkable that it is almost impossible to select any one as the best; nearly every one is great. *Eugénie Grandet* is usually on any critic's list of the best. Its title character, the girl Eugénie, is just another character in fiction, but her father, the miser, is a tremendous creation. English literature's classic miser, Silas Marner, by comparison is a wooden creature. *Eugénie Grandet* is short, reaching not quite 75,000 words. In the original French it is easy reading for a student, but the student should keep a good translation at hand to avoid missing the sense of the colloquial French in many passages.

Chap. 1. After the Revolution of 1789 in France, much of the property of the Church was confiscated and sold to the highest bidder. In the town and district of Saumur, M. GRANDET, a 40-year-old master cooper, combined his wife's dowry and his own savings to buy at a very low price the abbey, a few farms, and some of the best wine-growing land of the district. This translation was the cornerstone of his great fortune; though no one is ever sure how much money Grandet has, for he is miserly beyond belief.

Over the years, Grandet has improved his lands and the quality of the wines, and has continued to prosper as a cooper. He serves his village as mayor and instigates many improvements, for example good roads (each of which happens to pass by one or more of his own properties). M. Grandet is respected as a rich man, but he is very unsociable. He never visits, never has visitors, rarely speaks unless it is absolutely necessary.

Napoleon comes to power and places a nobleman in the office of mayor. Grandet inherits three fortunes to console him—his wife's mother dies, then her father, and finally his own grandmother. By this time Grandet is the richest man in town. The obsequious attention of the banker, M. DES GRASSINS, and the town notary, M. CRUCHOT, hint at vast wealth. By the time he is 57 years old, in 1806, he is popularly believed to be the richest man in France. He is looked upon as an old man and he stutters badly. His daughter EUGÉNIE is 10 years old. His wife has had no other children, although she is 19 years younger than he. Their life is frugal and austere. The only things on which Grandet spends actual cash are taxes; wages to BIG NANON, the Grandets' one maidservant; church contributions; and clothing for his wife and daughter. Mme. Grandet is totally submissive to her husband. He even doles out the food for each day, and grudgingly allows one candle to be used for illumination in the evening. No matter how cold the weather may be, no fire is permitted on the hearth until the middle of November. Even Eugénie, who is regarded by Grandet as a most important part of his life because she will doubtless inherit his vast wealth, is not permitted an extra candle to work on some embroidery for herself in the evening. Her daytime hours are of course well filled with helping her mother with the housework and sewing. Grandet's own clothing is worn until it can be repaired no longer. He gives his worn-out shoes to Nanon, whose feet are the same size as his; but by the time he considers them worn out, they are hopeless. Nanon wears them, nevertheless, and uncomplainingly. She is still, after 35 years, grateful to him for having hired her in the first place when no one else would, for she was unbelievably ugly.

The townspeople speculate freely on whom Eugénie will marry, for her husband will eventually control Grandet's millions. There is probable competition between the nephew of Cruchot and ADOLPHE DES GRASSINS, the banker's son. On the heiress's 23rd birthday, all gather in the Grandet parlor to celebrate the event. Grandet gives her on her birthday each year a gold coin, and another on her saint's day. Altogether her annual income is not inconsiderable; and she spends nothing, she merely collects the gold coins in a box where her father can gloat over them frequently. Grandet does not feel that he is losing anything by giving her this gold. It is merely a case of taking it out of one box and placing it in another.

Chap. 2. The conversation in the parlor is interrupted by a sharp knock at the door. CHARLES GRANDET, Grandet's nephew, has come from Paris on his father's instructions. Charles has arrayed himself like a peacock, in the latest Paris styles for a young man of 22, with the deliberate intention of impressing these provincials. He succeeds and they jump to the conclusion that here is dangerous competition for Eugénie's hand, for surely Grandet would prefer to have his money still in the possession of a Grandet. They do not know the contents of the letter brought to Grandet by his nephew. In that letter, GUILLAUME GRANDET confesses that he is ruined, and inextricably in debt, and plans to kill himself. He appeals to the conscience of his brother to give Charles a hope for the future and a home.

Chap. 3. Eugénie rises early the next morning and takes unusual pains with her toilette. She has felt the first awakenings of love with her meeting with Charles. She sighs to herself that he will never notice her, for she is too ugly. It does not occur to her that her father would deny her happiness until she overhears him telling Cruchot he would sooner throw her in the Loire than give her to Charles. A short while later the news of Charles's father's suicide becomes known and Charles bursts into sobs and retires to his room, where he remains for a long time. During this period, Grandet has gone to the village and negotiated a shrewd but underhanded deal to dispose of large quantities of his wine, at the expense of other vintners in the village. He is gleeful with his triumph but furious when his daughter calculates his large profit and comments that now he can certainly help Charles. Grandet has no intention of spending one sou for his nephew, but he knows the world of business and devises a scheme by which he will win himself a reputation for honor and still make a profit. He commissions des Grassins to go to Paris and buy up at a large discount all the outstanding debts of the late Guillaume Grandet. Des Grassins does this and the collectible value of Guillaume Grandet's assets is larger than the discounted debts.

Chap. 4. Eugénie has been falling more irrevocably in love with Charles. She is jealous of a woman, ANNETTE, to whom he has written a letter; she reads the letter and to her joy Charles is breaking off with Annette. Eugénie and Charles confess their mutual love, but actually to Charles it is an expedient to further his own ends. Eugénie begs him to accept her little store of gold pieces, which total in value about 2,000 francs, and after feigning reluctance Charles takes the

244

Eugénie defies Grandet

money. They pledge their love, and Charles leaves for the Indies to make his fortune.

Chap. 5. One of Grandet's greatest pleasures was to count with Eugénie the total in francs that her birthday and saint's day gold pieces reached. On the next New Year's Day after Charles's departure, Grandet asks her to bring out her gold. He is furious when Eugénie defies him and refuses to tell what she has done with her little hoard. He is certain that it was given to Charles. As punishment for her defiance, he locks her in her room and orders that she be given nothing but bread and water to eat. Nanon smuggles extra food to her as often as she can, but the miserly dole of Grandet leaves nothing unaccounted for and Nanon must use her own money and the favors of friends. Mme. Grandet becomes seriously ill and is dying. This leads the notary, Cruchot, to warn Grandet about the laws of inheritance. Eugénie is her mother's heiress and on Mme. Grandet's death can force an inventory and an auction of her father's properties to satisfy her rightful claims. This so terrifies Grandet that he magnanimously forgives his wife and daughter, and barely in time, for Mme. Grandet dies soon thereafter. Eugénie is shown how to manage Grandet's affairs, and when her father suffers a paralytic stroke she is able to take over. He never recovers, and Eugénie is left alone with Nanon, upon whom she settles a sum of money. This enables Nanon to make an advantageous marriage with Antoine Cornoiller. Eugénie makes him manager of her estates.

Chap. 6. Eugénie, now 30, finally hears from Charles. He wants to marry a titled Parisienne and asks for release from his old pledge to Eugénie. He has been successful in the Indies, and has lost the few scruples he may have had. He is still responsible for his father's remaining debts, however, and Eugénie pays them for him—2,000,000

francs. She has 17 million left and an income of 800,000 francs a year. She then marries Monsieur Cruchot, who has been her suitor for many years, but on the condition that he accept her as wife in name only. He consents, and for a few years he advances rapidly in politics, due to her wealth, and is in line for a peerage, but he dies suddenly. Eugénie lives on, lonely and listless. The faithful Nanon remains her only companion. All of Grandet's jealously hoarded wealth fails to bring happiness to his daughter, who except for it would have made a wonderful wife and mother.

Euphues

Novel by John Lyly, 1554–1606. Published 1578–79.

Euphues is doubly famous in English literature: As one of the earliest examples of the English novel, and for its ornate style that has given the English language the word *euphuism*. Lyly was better known at the time as a playwright but he is best remembered for *Euphues*. The euphuistic style makes much use of apothegms or maxims, allusions to historical and mythological characters, and various rhetorical devices to vary straightforward English expression. This did not prevent the book from being a most effective and amusing satire on the social conventions of Lyly's century, and the book took England by storm.

The Anatomy of Wit. A wealthy and learned young man named Euphues decides to leave his native Athens for a more luxurious life in Italy. He goes to Naples, where he immediately falls in with some companions who devote all their time to gratifying their sensual desires. One day an old man named Eubulus encounters Euphues on the street and delivers a long lecture against worldly living. Eubulus tells Euphues that he must not forsake his university training to indulge himself in these excesses. The young man listens attentively to the eloquent Eubulus, who says that "fairest silk is soonest soiled." Nevertheless, Euphues promptly refutes Eubulus's arguments in equally eloquent terms by attributing the old man's virtue to senility. Euphues insists that all love is not lust, nor is every pleasure a vice. He rushes away, leaving the old man to pray for his safe conduct. Euphues later makes the acquaintance of a young Italian noble called Philautus. The two young men get along so well together that they exchange elaborate vows of eternal friendship. Philautus confides that he is in love with Lucilla, the daughter of his business partner Don Ferardo. Since Don Ferardo is away in Venice on business, Philautus feels free to take Euphues along to visit his beloved. At first Lucilla greets the two men coldly, but Philautus explains that Euphues is his "shadow." At last Lucilla accepts the fact that the two friends are indivisible. She then calls upon Euphues to deliver an after-dinner address on love so that she and her noble friends can be amused. Euphues proceeds to "show every wrinkle of woman's disposition" in a most thorough but unflattering way. Instead of alienating the ladies by his words, Euphues causes them to look upon him as an accomplished lover who understands the ways of women. Lucilla becomes especially enamored of the Greek. When Euphues leaves, the girl throws herself upon her bed and bewails the day she ever caused Philautus to hope for her hand. Euphues is now the only man she will consider for marriage.

The friendship between Euphues and Philautus is now endangered. Euphues decides that "where love beareth away, friendship can have no show." Consequently he decides to abandon his former friend in pursuit of his new attachment. Philautus, however, is aware that his courtship is not succeeding and he comes to Euphues and demands to know his friend's true feelings. Instead of confessing his love bravely, Euphues pretends to be in love with Livia, one of Lucilla's friends. Philautus is deceived by this pretense and is content. The two men return to Lucilla's house and the ladies beg Euphues to continue his discourse on women. This time the crafty Greek praises them to the skies. In the midst of his eulogy, Don Ferardo returns home and demands that Philautus accompany him north to Venice to redeem some mortgaged lands. The time is now ripe for Euphues and Lucilla to enjoy each other's company unattended. Each professes to love the other just as the famous lovers of antiquity have done. Lucilla says she is willing to throw over her patrimony to marry Euphues, if her father stands in the way of their marriage.

Don Ferardo and Philautus return from

Venice and immediately the father tells his daughter that she must marry his business partner. Lucilla first tries to avoid the marriage by using philosophical arguments, but at last she is forced to confess that she loves Euphues and not Philautus. Don Ferardo is outraged but fights down his anger. He tries every kind of persuasion but cannot sway Lucilla from her decision. He informs Philautus and Philautus writes an acid letter to Euphues, accusing him of hiding his true evil desires under the cloak of friendship. Philautus says he will never again share Euphues' company. Euphues is not at all dismayed by these words and writes a gallant retort in which he states the principle of courtly love: "He that cannot dissemble in love is not worthy to live." The two friends are therefore parted.

For a time Euphues stays away from his beloved's house, but when he hears that Don Ferardo and Philautus have gone to Venice again he goes there at once. Lucilla receives him coldly, for she is now welcoming the courtship of a Neapolitan noble named CURIO. Euphues is stricken by this sudden change of attitude and he curses both her and Curio. Then he returns home, moaning the fact that he has lost both a lover and a best friend. He vows that he will leave Italy and return to his studies in Greece. In a short time, Don Ferardo comes back from Venice and is further dismayed to find his daughter infatuated with the poor, witless Curio. Again he begs her to accept Philautus, but once more the self-willed girl refuses. Ferardo is so shattered by her obstinacy that he dies soon after, leaving Lucilla his money and Curio the management of his estates. When the news circulates around Naples, Euphues and Philautus forget their old griefs in the face of this fresher woe. The fickle cruelty of their loved one brings them together in a stronger bond of friendship. The two men shakes hands, consigning Lucilla to her proper fate, and Euphues plans to return to his studies in Greece. Before departing for Athens, Euphues writes a "cooling card for Philautus and all fond lovers," in which he bares all the wiles of women. He proclaims that since "the very blossom of love is sour, the bud cannot be sweet." He exhorts men to follow the rigorous lives of great generals or philosophers instead of pursuing the combats of love. Then, in a postcript written to the "grave matrons and honest maidens of Italy," he apologizes for his bitterness. Euphues says that he will not blame all women because of the fickleness of one. The author Lyly concludes the story by promising to account at some later time the wisdom that Euphues gained in his struggle for virtue.

Euphues and his Ephoebus. The second section of the novel presents Euphues' conclusions about the rearing of children. There is no action in this part, for it is written as a philosophical tract. (*Ephoebusis* is a Greek word meaning "young man.") Most of the ideas are taken from the Greek writer

Lucilla is cold to Euphues

Plutarch's *On the Education of Boys*. Euphues first suggests that children should be born in legitimate marriages. He then advises men to teach perfection to their sons by showing them how to use nature, reason, and exercise. He advises them to hold philosophy superior to all other arts, for the speculative life brings the greatest rewards. The section concludes with a bitter attack on universities, in which Lyly points direct criticism to his *alma mater,* Oxford. [After the book was published, Lyly was forced to tone down some of his satire in the face of fierce rebuttals.]

Euphues and Atheos. The third section of *Euphues* is a brief dialogue modeled after the famous discussions of the Greek philosopher Plato. In this dialogue Euphues persuades a Greek named Atheos (Godless, or Atheist) to believe in the intimate nature of Christ and God the Father. Atheos is tempted to interpret God as the whole universe, but Euphues successfully argues that their divine natures are much more personal. In the end both men praise Christ for man's inheritance of everlasting life.

Letters of Euphues. The last section of the novel includes various letters written by Euphues from Athens to his friends in Italy. In the first letter, to Philautus, Euphues praises the scholarly life he is leading in Greece and urges Philautus to forgo some of his pleasures and think about life in the afterworld. Then in a letter to Eubulus, Euphues excuses the harsh way he greeted the old man's sane advice. He also offers Eubulus consolation on the death of his daughter and hope for a future life after death. Euphues writes a second letter to Philautus on hearing of Lucilla's untimely death. Euphues says that the end justly punished the life that the girl had led. He also counsels Philautus to take this sudden death as a warning to repent. In closing, Euphues expresses sorrow on learning of the illness of Lucilla's friend Livia. Euphues receives a letter from Livia in which she states that she has abandoned common pleasures to dedicate herself to a life of devotion to religion. Euphues replies that she is much to be praised for her action and that she should also try to reform Philautus. He promises to visit Livia on his way to England, where he is going to see "a woman that in all qualities excelleth any man." With this tribute to Queen Elizabeth the novel closes. It was followed in later years by a sequel called *Euphues and his England.*

Evangeline

Poem by Henry Wadsworth Longfellow, 1807–1882.
Published 1847.

AFTER THE French and Indian Wars, the French settlement called Acadie in eastern Canada became British property and some 6,000 of its French residents were required to leave and settle elsewhere. A preacher who was friendly with both Longfellow and Nathaniel Hawthorne heard and told them a story of two young lovers who were separated in the exodus. Hawthorne rejected the story as a plot for a novel and of it Longfellow made his long (about 1,200 lines) poem *Evangeline, A Tale of Acadia.* He wrote *Evangeline* in dactyllic hexameter, the meter of the *Aeneid* and a meter of which Longfellow had recently become enamored for English verse. *Evangeline* is the most celebrated example of dactyllic hexameter in English poetry and its opening line, "This is the forest primeval. The murmuring pines and the hemlocks," is especially famous. Dr. Oliver Wendell Holmes considered *Evangeline* unquestionably Longfellow's masterpiece.

The tale begins in Newfoundland, where a "forest primeval" trades whispers with the resounding sighs of the sea. The story they tell is one of "woman's devotion," when the land was settled by Frenchmen and called Acadie, or Acadia, "home of the happy."

Part I. 1. In the little village of Grand-Pré the many farmers of nearby fields gather in a happy, secluded society. There, far from the rest of the world, they worship as they did back in their native France. It does not matter to them that the King of England has taken over Canada, for their land is not particularly wealthy. In the shadow of Father FELICIAN's Catholic church they live honest, stalwart Christian lives. One of the wealthiest farmers in the vicinity is BENE-

DICT BELLEFONTAINE, father of the beautiful EVANGELINE. Evangeline is courted by all the young men of Grand-Pré, but only one appeals to her—GABRIEL LAJEUNESSE, son of the blacksmith BASIL. Gabriel and Evangeline grow up almost as brother and sister, attending church together and frisking over the broad meadows near the ocean. As time passes by and they ripen to maturity, Gabriel and Evangeline seemed predestined for happy married lives.

2. The seasons pass quickly, and after the harvests of autumn comes the long winter spell. One winter night while Benedict sits at home alone with his daughter, Basil and his son come to sign the contract that will enable the happy children to wed the following day. In the midst of the joy of the household, few words are spoken about another event of the next day—a proclamation in the church from the King of England. 3. The notary, RENÉ LEBLANG, arrives with the contract. All the complications of dowry are arranged. René tells his favorite story to correct the indifferent blacksmith, who does not like the mention of God or justice. René tells how a French girl was once beheaded for having stolen a necklace, and after her death a storm blew down the Statue of Justice in her village's square, revealing the missing jewels. The notary cautions the happy celebrators that "man is unjust, but God is just and finally justice triumphs." These words go unheeded as the lovers hold hands and whisper farewell on the eve of their marriage.

4. The next morning the whole town convenes for the ceremony, and MICHAEL the fiddler makes everyone gay with his music. The martial sound of a drum interrupts the festivities and agents of the British king startle the crowd with a dread proclamation. The French Catholic residents of Acadie having defied the king (to cling to their religion), their lands are confiscated and they are to be exiled from their homes. They must seek refuge in what is now the United States. The whole village threatens revolt but is quieted by Father Felician, who counsels submission and Christian forgiveness. All that day Evangeline waits for her wedding, but at last she falls asleep, praying to God and his inscrutable justice. 5. Five days after the proclamation, the townspeople gather at the harbor to be transported to new dwellings. In the rush for the ships, Evangeline and her father are separated from Basil and Gabriel, with only a brief goodbye. As Evangeline watches the village of Grand-Pré being burned by the king's soldiers, she turns to find her father dead. With Father Felician's help the good farmer is buried on the shore, and Evangeline is left alone with the priest.

Part II. 1–3. Evangeline begins a long search for her lost lover. It takes her to New England, then down the Ohio and Mississippi Rivers to Louisiana, where many Acadians (called Cajuns) have settled. Everywhere she and Father Felician go, they are told that Gabriel has just departed. At last in the lush bayou country of Louisi-

ana they approach a place where Gabriel and Basil are believed to have settled. When they arrive at the farmhouse in the swamps, only Basil greets them. He reassures Evangeline, saying that his restless son, who has gone to make a fortune in the West, can be easily overtaken. After a grand reunion with Michael and other people of Grand-Pré, Evangeline sets out the next morning with Basil, trying to follow Gabriel's path to the Ozarks. 4. Together the two penetrate the dangerous Indian country and at last arrive at a Jesuit mission in the Shawnee country, where a priest tells them that Gabriel left six days before, heading for the Great Lakes. Similarly year after year goes by and Evangeline grows old, never finding her elusive lover. 5. At last in old age Evangeline settles in Philadelphia and becomes a Sister of Mercy among the sick and homeless. A plague falls on the city and the hospitals are filled with the bodies of the dying. One Sunday morning as Evangeline moves through the crowded wards, she sees an aged face and knows at once it is Gabriel. She calls his name and drops to his side, but the man is so close to death that her name dies on his lips. Evangeline murmurs "Father, I thank thee!" and thus God's justice is done.

This tale is still told by the forest primeval, and "the neighboring ocean/Speaks, and in accents disconsolate answers the wail of the forest."

Evelina

Novel by Fanny Burney (Mme. d'Arblay, 1752–1840).
Published 1778.

EVELINA IS ONE of many novels of its era in which the story is told in a series of letters. Fanny Burney was perhaps not a major novelist but her novels were popular and *Evelina* is easy to read (not as badly overwritten as many novels of its kind) and is a most interesting picture of the manners and attitudes of highborn Londoners at the time when America was breaking away from their control.

Letters 1–5. Lady HOWARD, who had been friendly toward the late Lady Belmont, receives a letter from Mme. DUVAL, Lady Belmont's mother. Mme. Duval knows her daughter is dead, but she has heard that she may have a grandchild. If so, she offers to take the child and care for it. Lady Howard writes to the Rev. ARTHUR VILLARS for information and he replies in full. Villars had been the tutor of Mr. EVELYN,

Mme. Duval's first husband. He had opposed Evelyn's marriage to Mme. Duval, who was only a common waitress in a French tavern. However, Evelyn defied him and he and his French wife had a daughter. Evelyn died two years after, leaving the baby girl in Villars'. Villars cared for the young Miss Evelyn until she was 17. Then Miss Evelyn's mother—who meanwhile had married Duval—sent for her and tried to force her into an unwelcome marriage. To escape this marriage and her mother's abuse, Miss Evelyn eloped with a young Englishman, Sir JOHN BELMONT, of good birth but profligate habits. Mme. Duval, enraged, disinherited her daughter; and Belmont, feeling cheated of the fortune he thought his wife would bring him, tore up the marriage certificate and disavowed his marriage. His disavowed wife, Lady Belmont, returned to Villars' loving care but died giving birth to Belmont's child, a daughter, EVELINA, whom Villars has brought up. (She is called Miss Evelina Anville, for her relationship to Belmont is not acknowledged.) Villars tells Lady Howard he will not make the same mistake twice but will keep the girl, whom he has grown to love as a daughter, and whom he has adopted. At Lady Howard's urgent request, Villars agrees to send his ward to Howard Grove, Lady Howard's estate, in the care of Mrs. MIRVAN, Lady Howard's daughter.

Letters 6–20. Lady Howard writes that she finds Evelina angelic in her beauty and her manner, and reports a friendship between Evelina and her own granddaughter, MARIA MIRVAN. Evelina goes to London and writes to her adopted father and tells him of her excitement at being in the city. She writes him about a grand ball she attended at Mrs. STANLEY's. She describes her shyness with the young Lord ORVILLE, who was her partner. She fears he must think her stupid. Maria tells her that another young man of fashion, Sir CLEMENT WILLOUGHBY, thought her beautiful. At the opera Evelina accidentally meets her grandmother, Mme. Duval, who insists that she visit her. Evelina wants to return to Villars. Lord Orville visits Evelina several times. She meets some of her grandmother's friends and abhors them, finding them crude. She goes to the theater and begins to enjoy the company of Lord Orville.

Letters 21–24. Mme. Duval forces Evelina to go with her to the opera on a night when the girl is looking forward to seeing Lord Orville. She manages to escape from her vulgar grandmother and rides home in a carriage with Willoughby, who admires her so much that he has been following the Howard party around London seeking her company. The party plans to return to Howard's Grove and Mme. Duval has been invited to join them. Evelina confesses her disappointment and her desire to go back to Villars. He writes to her, warning her not to become infatuated with the vices of town life. He wants her to lead a simple, good life in the country, for which he has spent years preparing her.

Letters 23–24. Mme. Duval conceives the plan of going into the law courts and establishing Evelina's rights to the Belmont name and fortune. Evelina is ashamed at the crudeness of this action and does not want the wealth or position it would bring her, but Lady Howard writes to Villars favoring the plan, suggesting that it might be a good idea to obtain for Evelina her correct place in society. Villars replies that he has often thought of this but does not want the pure Evelina to associate with her corrupt father. He thinks a lawsuit is too violent an action, but gives his permission for Lady Howard to write to Belmont and make a private attempt to secure Evelina's just inheritance. Mrs. Mirvan's husband and the visiting Sir Clement plan a cruel trick on Mme. Duval. They send her out in her carriage on a wild goose chase to a friend, who they have told her is in trouble. They disguise themselves as robbers, stop her coach, cut off her curls, and bind her to a tree. Though the lady deserves this treatment Evelina finds it unnecessarily harsh. She asks Lady Howard to dissuade the gentlemen from such further pranks.

Letters 35–49. John Belmont writes a cordial note to Lady Howard, protesting that he has no claim on Evelina. Evelina writes Villars that she is sad at being rejected but turns to him in her need. She feels sorry for her father. Mme. Duval plans to take her granddaughter to Paris and make Belmont receive her. Evelina dreads the trip and tries to dissuade Mme. Duval. Villars writes to Evelina and refuses to permit her to go to Paris. Mme. Duval visits Villars and threatens to cut Evelina out of her will if he will not at least permit the girl to visit her in London for a month. He reluctantly gives this permission. In London, Evelina learns that Mme. Duval intends to take her to Paris without telling anyone. She resolves never to leave town with the vulgar old woman. Mme. Duval forces Evelina to associate with her cousins, the shopkeeper, BRAUGHTON, and his family. They have a lodger, Mr. MACARTNEY, a Scottish poet. The family mocks him because he is poor. Evelina saves him from committing suicide and feels bad that he has to live among such crude people.

Letters 50–54. Mme. Duval insists that Evelina go to a ball with a vulgar young man, Mr. SMITH. Evelina despises the company at the ball. She is embarrassed when her grandmother in a "showy dress" and paint on her face dances the minuet and creates a sensation. Evelina recalls the elegant parties she attended with Lady Howard and the perfect manners of Lord Orville. Evelina refuses to dance with Smith or to listen to his words of admiration. On another evening with the Braughtons, Evelina meets Lord Orville. She is ashamed that he should find her in such company. He is very kind to her and seems concerned with her obvious unhappiness. Evelina longs to go away from Mme. Duval, who is increasingly rude to her. Lord Orville visits Evelina and seems concerned about her. They have

a warm conversation and as he leaves he kisses her hand. Mme. Duval informs Evelina that she thinks it would be a good idea for her to marry her cousin, TOM BRAUGHTON. Evelina loathes him, but the older woman says she will insist on the marriage if nothing better turns up. In the park the Braughtons see Lord Orville's coach, and knowing that Evelina knows the

Evelina will not dance

lord, they use her name to persuade the coachman to give them a ride. Evelina is embarrassed by such rudeness and writes Orville a note of apology.

Letters 55–64. Evelina reports to Villars that Mme. Duval is angry with her for refusing to go to Paris or to marry Tom. Evelina returns to Villars' house at Berry Hill. She writes to her friend Maria Mirvan at Howard's Grove and tells her about a letter she has received from Lord Orville. At first Evelina was proud to receive what she takes to be a love letter but then she became angry at the tone of freedom the letter assumes and she concludes that he meant no affection. Evelina grieves over the loss of her idol. She falls ill and Villars sends her to the shore to recover her health. She writes that Lord Orville's sister, Lady LOUISA, is about to marry and that Orville is coming to the shore. She longs to see him, despite her offense at his letter. He arrives and she meets him and finds him charming and polite. Her delight in the world returns and with it her health. Evelina admires Lord Orville more and more.

Letters 65–77. Evelina and her companion, Mrs. SELWYN, a rich neighbor at Berry Hill who has befriended her, have been asked to stay with Lord Orville and his sister. Louisa, her fiancé and the other company are very rude to Evelina because she has no title, but Lord Orville engages her in pleasant conversation. Mr. Macartney comes to Bristol and tells Evelina that he is the illegitimate son of Sir John Belmont. She realizes that they are sister and brother. Villars sends Evelina a letter that her dead mother had written to John Belmont, demanding that he recognize the child as legally his. While Evelina waits, trying to decide how to present herself to her real father, Sir Clement Willoughby arrives and asks her hand in marriage, but she refuses him. Next Orville confesses his love for Evelina and she tells him that she worships him. He wants to know whom to ask for her hand. She promises to tell him after her

trip to London (where she intends to present herself to Belmont). But that gentleman makes an unexpected trip to Bristol. Evelina sends Mrs. Selwyn there to plead for her. Mrs. Selwyn is rebuffed by Belmont. He says he has found his daughter and has brought her to London.

Letter 78. The next day Mrs. Selwyn takes Evelina to see her father. When he is forced to look at the girl he is overcome with emotion, because he sees the face of his dead wife. A nurse of Evelina's had brought her own child to Belmont, claiming it was his. The nurse is found and she confesses. The father acknowledges his rightful daughter and gives his permission for Evelina to marry happy Orville. Belmont promises to give his rightful daughter all the honor possible and to the mistaken daughter, POLLY GREEN, he gives his son, Macartney, and promises to aid the young couple. Evelina is married to Lord Orville and she writes to Villars that she is on her way to visit him and present her husband to him.

Everyman

Drama in poetry. Author unknown. Written in late 15th century. (RE, 45)

EVERYMAN CAME somewhat later than the mystery and morality plays that were the earliest English theater. It is a morality play but in form approaches the plays that not long afterward developed and flourished in Elizabethan England. Since the theme of *Everyman* is eternal, it has remained popular as reading and often for production throughout the intervening centuries and into the present day. It is an allegory in which Everyman, representing anyone, must die and finds that he can take with him nothing but his good deeds.

Lines 1–84. A MESSENGER steps forward onto the stage of the world. He declares that he is about to present a moral play called "The Summoning of Everyman." The play will show how brief life is; that consequently, man must mend his wicked ways. The messenger departs. GOD speaks from above. He says He has become aware that EVERYMAN is unfaithful to Him, and lives sinfully and for material gain. Therefore God must execute justice upon Everyman living without fear of Him. He calls for His personal messenger, DEATH. He commands Death to go to Everyman, in God's name, and show him a pilgrimage that he must take. God withdraws.

Lines 85–402. Death meets Everyman and tells him he must make a long journey and that he must give a reckoning of his good and bad deeds. Everyman asks for some time to consider the matter, but Death says there can be no delay. Everyman offers Death money—a thousand pounds—to defer the trip until another day, but Death refuses the bribe. Death departs, telling Everyman he can take on his journey any friend who is willing to go with him but to be ready at the end of the day. Everyman starts alone, wondering if he can possibly find anyone to make the journey with him. FELLOWSHIP comes up to Everyman and asks what is wrong. Everyman replies that he is in grave danger. Fellowship promises to do all he can to aid Everyman, even till the day he dies. Everyman reports that the highest judge of all has commanded him to make a reckoning. Everyman asks for Fellowship's company on the journey. Fellowship asks when they will return. Everyman sadly replies "Never." Fellowship is appalled and immediately asserts that he will not go with Everyman. Everyman reminds Fellowship that he has made a promise. Fellowship admits this, but says he will accompany Everyman in eating, drinking, and marching, but not in dying. Everyman says Fellowship should at least stay with him and escort him to the city gate, but Fellowship will not and bids Everyman farewell. KINDRED and COUSIN appear and Everyman tells them of his plight. They also refuse to accompany him on his journey, and depart abruptly. Everyman, who has been fond of riches, wonders if his possessions will at least go with him, and he calls to GOODS, who replies unseen from a corner. Everyman implores Goods to go with him but Goods says that it would be impossible. Goods says it is because of him that Everyman's record is blotted and that moreover he cannot travel, for he is too brittle. Everyman denounces Goods as a thief of sorts and a traitor to God. Goods laughs, telling Everyman he has only himself to blame.

Lines 463–921. Everyman summons GOOD DEEDS and she speaks, in answer, from the ground. She says that she lies in the ground bound by the sins of Everyman and she cannot rise to accompany him. She tells Everyman to summon her sister, KNOWLEDGE. Knowledge steps up to Everyman and tells him that she will be his guide. Everyman rejoices. Good Deeds tells Everyman that once Knowledge has guided him safely to the end of his journey, his Good Deeds can be with him. Knowledge leads Everyman to CONFESSION, the cleansing river. Knowledge orders Everyman to kneel down and Everyman does so, asking Confession to wash him clean of vice and sin. Confession tells Everyman to remember that Christ died for the world and that Everyman should implore God's mercy and be scourged by PENANCE. Everyman asks to be drubbed with the scourge of Penance. He receives the scourge from Knowledge and flagellates himself. When he is done, Good Deeds rises from the ground, saying that now she can go with him. Knowledge gives Everyman a garment and bids him wear it when he must go before God. It is

the garment of Sorrow. Everyman says he is ready to begin his journey with Knowledge and Good Deeds but Good Deeds tells him that he must take some other friends with him: BEAUTY, STRENGTH, DISCRETION, and FIVE WITS. All four appear. Knowledge tells Everyman to receive communion and extreme unction and as Five Wits speaks of the virtues of the priesthood, Everyman goes to receive the last sacrament. Knowledge tells Five Wits that there are sinful priests, who give sinners bad examples. Everyman returns exultant, and all arrive at the edge of his grave. Everyman feels so faint that he cannot stand. Everyman calls upon his new friends to remain with him, but Beauty says she cannot enter the grave and bids Everyman farewell. Everyman is disillusioned. Now Strength also departs. Every-

man swoons. Discretion leaves next and Everyman is stunned. Five Wits goes. Everyman calls for help, crying that all have forsaken him. But Good Deeds speaks up and says she has not forsaken him. Everyman learns that Knowledge, too, must leave him, but not until the final moment. Good Deeds tells Everyman that all earthly things are vanity: Beauty, Strength, Discretion, Five Wits, friends, kindred—every one flees except Good Deeds. Pleading for mercy, Everyman commends his soul to God. He sinks into his grave. An Angel calls his soul to God's side. In an epilogue, a DOCTOR (scholarly clergyman) speaks the moral of Everyman: Good Deeds alone remain with man; after death, amends may not be made. Therefore let man live by the word of God, with holy charity in his heart.

The Faerie Queen

Poem by Edmund Spenser, 1552–1599. Published 1590 (first three books) and 1596 (second three books).

BLISS PERRY, professor of English at Yale, estimated at one time that there were no more than a dozen men living who had read *The Faerie Queen* through, though it is acknowledged to be one of the greatest works in English poetry. The sheer bulk of the work is hard to visualize. It contains more than 3,800 stanzas of nine lines each—some 34,000 lines of poetry. Furthermore, Spenser planned to write twelve books and finished only six, plus a small fragment of a seventh. ❡ *The Faerie Queen* is an allegory. The plan of it is given in an introductory letter that Spenser was careful to send to Sir Walter Raleigh, who at the time was in favor with Queen Elizabeth I. (In that Golden Age it might cost a poet his head if his allegory were misunderstood.) The Faerie Queen, called also Gloriana, is Elizabeth herself, representing Glory; but her womanly qualities are also represented in part by the character Belphoebe, a fairy princess. The proposed twelve books were de-

signed to fit the twelve days of Elizabeth's annual festival. On each day a knight allegorically representing some admirable quality was to undertake an adventure or quest. Throughout the whole appears the figure of Prince Arthur, pictured as the young man who would one day be King Arthur of the Round Table. English history and politics are worked into many parts of the allegory. ❡ English poets well into the 19th century doted on *The Faerie Queen* above all other poems and its influence on English poetry has been tremendous. Among its contributions is the *Spenserian* stanza in which the entire poem is written. This stanza is the *huitain*, or stanza of eight lines rhyming *ababbcbc*, which appears in many sonnets and in the French ballade, plus a ninth line with one extra foot, two extra syllables, having the *c* rhyme. The Spenserian stanza has been used by many later poets, including Byron in *Childe Harold*. ❡ The first two books are considered most important (perhaps because so few readers get any farther) and they are outlined below somewhat more fully than the others.

Book I. Cantos 1–2. The REDCROSSE KNIGHT, who stands for Holiness, is introduced by the famous line: "A gentle knight was pricking on the plaine." His fair damsel UNA (Truth) rides close behind him on a snow-white donkey and behind her lags a dwarf. The Knight is going out at the behest of GLORIANA (The Faerie Queene) to slay a dragon for the sake of Una. As the three ride along, they meet a foul half-monster, half-woman, called ERROR, who gives birth to scores of ugly toadlike children. The Redcrosse Knight cuts off Error's head and watches her children devour her and one another. The little group next encounters a more fearful temptation, HYPOCRISIE, who appears as an

"aged sire, in long blacke weedes yclad." The Knight is deceived by Hypocrisie's glowing words and they all go to Hypocrisie's house. While they are sleeping, Hypocrisie sends a messenger to the Cave of Sleep, ruled by the pagan god MORPHEUS. Sleep sends the Knight a "fit dreame" in which a temptress impersonates Una and tries to seduce the Knight. Deceived by this and disheartened by Una's action, the Knight rides off alone the next morning, leaving Una behind with Hypocrisie (also called ARCHIMAGO). Hypocrisie then changes his shape into the figure of the Redcrosse Knight. Meanwhile the true Knight comes upon a Saracen named SANSFOY (Faithless), whom he kills. Sansfoy has a lady companion who calls herself FIDESSA (but is actually the witch DUESSA). She persuades the Knight that she is helpless and innocent. The Knight promises to protect her and pulls a branch from a tree to make a garland for her head, but the tree cries out in pain and says that it was formerly the man FRADUBIO, who fell victim to Duessa's wiles. One day he spied Duessa bathing and saw that she was a monster, and she changed him into his present shape. Not heeding the tree's words and Fidessa's sudden faint, the Knight proceeds on his way.

Canto 3. The abandoned Una wanders aimlessly through forests and deserts, but her beauty and gentleness subdue even wild lions. At last she comes upon the disguised Archimago and mistakes him for the Redcrosse Knight. They ride off together. A Saracen named SANSLOY (Lawless) mistakes Archimago for Una's true protector and charges at him. The cowardly Hypocrisie flees, leaving Una in Sansloy's hands.

Cantos 4–5. Duessa leads the Redcrosse Knight to the House of Pride, ruled by Queen LUCIFERA. There they behold a mighty spectacle in which LECHERY, SLOTH, ENVY, WRATH, AVARICE and GLUTTONY appear in a funeral cortege. Satan rides behind them and urges them on. The Knight is amazed at the splendor of the House of Pride. He does not know that it is a castle built on sand. A Saracen named SANSJOY, brother of the slain Sansfoy, rides into their midst and challenges the Redcrosse Knight to combat the following day. A dark cloud envelops Sansjoy during the battle and the Redcrosse Knight is proclaimed victor. Duessa cannot conceal her grief at Sansjoy's fate and she hastens off to MOTHER NIGHT for a magic potion to restore her true lover to life. Duessa and Night go down to Hell, where they plead with the Greek physician-god AESCULAPIUS to restore the Saracen. "Her words prevailed," but when Duessa returns to the House of Pride, she finds that the Redcrosse Knight has vanished. The dwarf has seen numerous corpses strewn around the palace and the Knight at last has realized that he is stranded in an evil place.

Canto 6. Una, who has fallen into Sansloy's clutches, is assailed by the passionate Saracen but is rescued through Divine Providence when a troop of nearby satyrs drives off her captor. One of the satyrs, SATYRANE, becomes especially enamored of her, and Una finds herself reigning almost like a queen among the woodland creatures. In her heart she mourns the absence of the Redcrosse Knight. Her idyllic existence is shattered when another Saracen tries to capture her. Satyrane engages him in combat and Una rushes off into the forest, followed by Archimago's evil eye.

Cantos 7–9. Duessa finds the Redcrosse Knight sitting near a stream. The false temptress effects a reconciliation, but as they ride off together they encounter a huge giant named ORGOGLIO (Pride). Orgoglio engages the Redcrosse Knight in battle and defeats him. The faithless Duessa immedi-

ately promises to be the giant's wife. The dwarf sees that his master has been bettered and rushes off to find Una and tells her the sad tale. The two are desperate and hopelessly wander along until they meet a knight in shining armor, the famous Prince ARTHUR. Arthur (who stands for the Whole Man or Magnificence) promises to fight the giant on behalf of Una and the Redcrosse Knight. Arthur's magic shield and sword enable him to defeat the monster in an earth-shaking battle. He reconciles

Lions will not attack Una

Una and her Knight and forever shames Duessa by stripping her and exposing her true ugliness to the whole world. Arthur warns the Knight and his lady that they must henceforth be very cautious, and tells them about his past. He is descended from Timon of Athens and was predestined to rule Britain from early childhood, as he was told by the magician Merlin. His life has been one of many adventures and loves, in which he has always battled on the side of virtue. Arthur bids his friends goodbye. He gives the Redcrosse Knight a diamond and receives in return a beautiful embossed Bible. Arthur disappears in the woods and a breathless knight comes charging upon the united couple. It is Sir TREVISAN, who tells a terrible tale about a friend of his who fell into the clutches of the old man DESPAIR. The Redcrosse Knight decides that he must vanquish this dangerous enemy, and he rides off to the old man's cave. The Redcrosse Knight then engages in a long debate with Despair, in which he tries hard to prove that life is worth living. Despair argues that suicide is the better choice. The Knight successfully resists the instruments for suicide that Despair places before him, and the old man hangs himself because of his failure.

Canto 10. The Redcrosse Knight and Una proceed to the House of Holiness, ruled by Dame CAELIA and her three daughters: FIDELIA (Faith), SPERANZA (Hope), and CHARISSA (Charity). The Knight hears instructive words about virtue from the three beautiful girls and then is subjected to torture by Penance and Remorse.

Through the aid of Patience, he survives and is carried to a hospital where seven men (corresponding to the seven virtues and contrasting with the Seven Deadly Sins) nurse him back to health. Caelia then takes the Knight to a hill and shows him a vision of Cleopolis, the perfect city, and the future. Caelia tells the Knight that he shall be known as St. George to succeeding generations of Britons. The Redcrosse Knight leaves the holy house with her blessing to complete the mission on which he departed—to slay the dragon for Una.

Cantos 11–12. The battle is a titanic affair that rages for two whole days, but finally on the third day the dragon is slain and falls downward into Hell. The Redcrosse Knight returns with his beloved Una to her father, the King of the Fairies, to claim her hand. The Knight is received with great pomp and celebration as a returning hero. A messenger interrupts the wedding and reads aloud a letter from Duessa, who claims that the Redcrosse Knight is her husband. Una and the Knight explain this dastardly deed to the King, who forgives the Knight for his past rashness and permits the marriage. Una, however, points to the messenger and claims that he is the false Archimago, who has engineered most of their troubles. The King has Archimago seized and placed in a deep dark dungeon where he will not interfere with anyone's life again. The Redcrosse Knight (Holiness) and Una (Truth) are wedded.

Book II. Canto 1. Archimago succeeds in breaking loose from his bonds and escapes down a highway, where he meets a stern, well-controlled knight called Sir GUYON or the Knight of Temperaunce. Archimago tells Guyon about a chaste lady who has been violated and the Knight offers to assist the poor woman. The woman turns out to be the false Duessa in disguise, but the Redcrosse Knight happens on the scene in time to warn his friend. The Redcrosse Knight and Guyon become companions in arms and as they wander through the forest they spy a dying woman with a child in her arms, beside her dead husband. The woman, AMAVIA, says that her husband became enamored of the arch temptress, ACRASIA, who lives in the Bower of Bliss. Acrasia undid the man so thoroughly that he died for lack of virtue. Amavia says she is dying of grief and Sir Guyon comforts her by saying that he will destroy Acrasia and her Bower. Amavia dies.

Cantos 2–3. Sir Guyon takes Amavia's baby with him but finds that he cannot wash the infant's hands clean of the family's sinful blood. He arrives at a castle ruled by three sisters: the excessively severe and ascetic ELISSA, whose lover was Sir HUDDIBRAS; the moderate MEDINA (or Golden Mean); and the very wild PERISSA and her lord, the Saracen Sansfoy who had tried to violate Una. Sir Guyon avoids the severe self-denial on one side and the rioting on the other, by keeping company with Medina, in whose hands he leaves the baby RUDDYMANE. He rides on and meets two vainglorious braggarts named TROMPART and BRAGGADOCHIO, who try to impress him with accounts of their marvelous exploits. A huntress much like the Greek goddess Diana appears in the woods, and the two men give way to her in the most cowardly manner.

Canto 4. Next Sir Guyon comes upon an aged hag named OCCASION and her ugly demented son FUROR, who are dragging an unfortunate victim called PHEDON down the road. Sir Guyon succeeds in overcoming Furor and binds him with iron chains. He next attaches an iron lock to Occasion's mouth to keep her quiet. Phedon tells Sir Guyon how he killed his beloved because of his false suspicions about her fidelity, aroused by his best friend, PHILEMON. Phedon poisoned Philemon and thus heaped crime on crime. Sir Guyon lectures the tormented man on the virtues of temperance, but is interrupted by a squire who dashes into their midst. The squire is ATTIN, or STRIFE. He is carrying a message to Occasion from the two hateful brothers CYMOCHLES and PYROCHLES. When he learns what Sir Guyon has done to Occasion and her son, Strife hurls a dart at Guyon and flees.

Canto 5. Strife warns his lord, Pyrochles, about Guyon's deeds and Pyrochles rushes into battle against the Knight. Guyon's clear-headedness helps him to win the battle easily and he graciously spares Pyrochles' life. Pyrochles, on being released, frees both Furor and Occasion. The old hag berates both her son and her savior for the cowardice, impelling them both to fight once more. Pyrochles again rushes at the Knight and when Pyrochles falls to the ground Strife believes his lord to be dead. He rushes away to summon Cymochles, the other brother, who is resting in the Bower of Bliss with Acrasia in the midst of every conceivable delight. Cymochles rushes off to avenge what he believes is his brother's death.

Canto 6. Cymochles comes to the Idle Lake, where PHAEDRIA (or Immodest Mirth) skims over the waters in a beautiful bark, enchanting men after the manner of the ancient Sirens. Cymochles falls under her spell and forgets entirely about his brother, falling into a deep slumber. Sir Guyon and his guide Phedon come to the shore of the lake and Guyon calls to Phaedria to take him across the water. Phaedria agrees but Phedon will not enter her boat. Guyon enters and falls victim to her spell. When Cymochles awakes he is furious about his rival, but Phaedria's soothing words quiet him. The peace is dispelled by the sudden appearance of Pyrochles, who cries, "I burne!" He shouts to his brother that it is Furor who has undone him, but Cymochles will not come to his aid. Pyrochles plunges into the lake to soothe his wounds and Strife plunges in to prevent his master from drowning. The tempter Archimago happens upon the scene and rescues them both.

Cantos 7–8. Weakened by his sojourn with Phaedria, Sir Guyon next stumbles into the lair of MAMMON, the god of wealth. Mammon casts a spell over the Knight by taking him down into the bowels of Earth and showing him all the riches that have seduced mankind from the very beginning. Sir Guyon sees Ambition and Disdain, as well as all the other vengeful gods who ally themselves to gold. He returns to earth and falls into a sleep. He is spied by his former guide, Phedon. Pyrochles and Cymochles appear on the scene. Sir Guyon still lies deep in his enchanted sleep. Phedon makes a valiant effort to defend himself and the Knight, but is weakening, when Prince Arthur comes and defeats the two brothers after a long and bloody battle. Sir Guyon rises out of his sleep and thanks the Prince.

Cantos 9–10. Prince Arthur sends the Knight to the House of Temperance, where he must purify himself if he wishes to destroy Acrasia and the Bower of Bliss. The House of Temperance is ruled by Queen ALMA (The Soul), who instructs the Knight about the ways that one may keep his castle (or body) free from outside ravages. The Knight sees a book, *Antiquitee of Faery Land,* and Alma reads him some passages about the early history of British kings and all the rulers of the Faeries down to the reign of Gloriana, the Faerie Queene, to whom there is a eulogy at the end.

Canto 11. The House of Temperance is suddenly besieged by various ragged armies of monsters who attack successively the Sight, Hearing, Smell, Taste, and other sensations. Prince Arthur leaps to the defense of the castle against the forces of MALEGER, and he is joined by Sir Guyon, who acquits himself splendidly. They rout the enemy but Guyon is badly wounded and must be carried by his squire Phedon to Alma, who nurses him carefully back to health.

Canto 12. Sir Guyon is ready to set out on the last phase of his journey to the Bower of Bliss. He sails on a boat with Phedon as his guide, and together they endure many hardships at sea but manage to avoid the Rock of Reproach, Sirens, mermaids, and the onslaught of rapacious birds. They encounter Phaedria again but this time Sir Guyon ignores her. They finally arrive at their destination, the beautiful Bower of Acrasia. Sir Guyon and his friend steal upon Acrasia, who lies in a silken bed with a youth, and together they ensnare the lovers. Then they destroy the entire garden and transform many of the men whom Acrasia has changed to pigs back into human beings—except for one named GRYLL, who prefers to be a pig. With their mission completed, Sir Guyon and his friend return home.

Book III. Cantos 1–3. Prince Arthur, his squire TIMIAS, and Sir Guyon ride on. They meet BRITOMART, or Britomartis (Chastity), a warlike princess disguised as a knight. Sir Guyon rides against her and she unhorses him. Prince Arthur recognizes Britomart and has Guyon desist. A maiden (FLORIMELL) rides by, chased by a forester. Arthur, Guyon and Timias ride after them. Britomart rides on alone and comes to Castle Joyous, where any passer-by must fight six knights or else serve MALECASTA (Unchastity), the beautiful lady of the castle. She fights and overcomes the six knights and now Malecasta loves her, thinking her a man. Britomart frees the Redcrosse Knight, who had not been able to overcome the six knights. Britomart is seeking ARTEGALL or Arthegall (Justice), whom she has seen only in a magic mirror made by MERLIN. The magic mirror shows that Britomart and Artegall will marry and from them will spring a line of British kings. Cantos 4–7. Britomart encounters and overcomes Sir MARINELL. Prince Arthur learns that

The two braggarts flee when the huntress appears

Florimell loves Marinell but he will not have her. Timias fights three foresters and kills them, but is wounded almost to death. BELPHOEBE rescues and nurses him. Belphoebe and her twin sister AMORETTA or Amoret are fairy princesses. Amoretta loves the noble knight Sir SCUDAMOUR. **Cantos 8–10.** Florimell is loved and pursued by a witch's son. She flees to the sea god PROTEUS. Britomart jousts with PARIDELL, a softspoken but false knight, and overthrows him. Paridell rapes HELLENORE, wife of MALBECCO (Jealousy). Malbecco throws himself from a cliff. **Cantos 11–12.** Britomart is riding with the good knight Sir SATYRANE. They meet Sir Scudamour and learn that Amoret has been stolen by the enchanter BUSIRANE. Britomart frees Amoret.

Book IV. Canto 1. Sir Scudamour has given up waiting for Britomart. The evil Duessa, along with ATÉ (Dissension), cause the thoughtless Sir BLANDAMOUR to make Scudamour think Britomart (whom he thinks a man) has seduced Amoretta. **Cantos 2–3.** Blandamour and Paridell compete for Florimell. She prefers Blandamour. CAMBELL, brother of the fair CANACE, undertakes to fight three brothers who compete for Canace's hand, the victor to have her. He vanquishes the first two but the third, TRIAMOND, fights him to a standstill. CAMBINA, Triamond's sister, reconciles them. Triamond marries Canace and Cambell marries Cambina. **Cantos 4–6.** Sir Satyrane has a tournament to see who will win Florimell. Britomart, still disguised as a man, enters the tournament and wins. (Among those she vanquishes are Scudamour and her love, Arthegall.) Then the ladies have a beauty contest to see which will have Florimell's magic girdle and Amoret wins. Artegall sees Britomart's face and falls in love with her. He woos her and she consents to marry him but he has to leave her for an unfinished mission. **Cantos 7–9.** Amoret is abducted by CORFLAMBO (Lust). Prince Arthur kills him and rescues her. Timias, healed by Belphoebe, is in love with her. He suffers greatly but recovers and marries PAEANA, Corflambo's daughter. **Canto 10.** Scudamour tells how he won Amoret by fighting for the magic shield of Love that carried with it her heart. **Cantos 11–12.** Marinell finds that he does love Florimell. He goes to the underseas palace of Proteus. His mother persuades Neptune to intercede and Florimell is espoused to Marinell.

Book V. Cantos 1–3. Artegall rides on with his squire, TALUS. Artegall destroys the pagan robber POLLENTÉ and his greedy daughter MUNERA. The wedding of Florimell is celebrated by a tournament. **Cantos 4–7.** Artegall reconciles two fighting brothers. He saves Sir TERPIN, a victim of the disguised Amazon RADIGUND. Then he fights Radigund and overcomes her but desists when he sees she is a woman; whereupon she captures him. Talus carries the news to Britomart, who sets out to free him. Britomart kills Radigund and frees Artegall.

252

Cantos 8–12. Prince Arthur and Sir Artegall defeat a series of enemies (representing enemies of Queen Elizabeth I or the English realm), including Soudan, or Philip II of Spain; and Artegall rescues Irena (Ireland) by killing the monster GRANTORTO.

Book VI. Cantos 1–4. Sir CALIDORE, the Knight of Courtesy, hails Artegall on his successful return, then rides forth. He saves a damsel from cruel MALEFFORT. When Sir Calidore sees young TRISTRAM slay a discourteous knight, he makes Tristram his squire. Sir Calidore pursues the BLATANT BEAST (representing enemies of the Church). He saves the lady SERENA from the blatant beast, but her lover, Sir CALEPINE, is captured by the wicked Sir TURPINE. A "savage," or "wyld man," rescues Sir Calepine, but stopping to rescue an infant threatened by a bear, Sir Calepine fails to meet Sir Calidore and Serena again. **Cantos 5–8.** Serena meets Prince Arthur. He leaves her and his squire with a HERMIT, then overcomes Turpine. Serena falls into the hands of savages but is freed by Calepine. **Cantos 9–11.** Sir Calidore sees and loves fair PASTORELL, a shepherd girl loved by all the shepherd swains. Calidore rescues Pastorell from the attack of a tiger. But while Calidore is hunting, brigands attack and carry away Pastorell, among others. The brigands fight over Pastorell, which saves her until Calidore comes and rescues her and the other captives. **Canto 12.** Calidore fights the blatant beast, subdues it, and binds it in bands. A mark on Pastorell's bosom shows that she is the lost daughter of Lady Claribell, so she and Calidore are espoused.

A Farewell to Arms

Novel by Ernest Hemingway, 1898–1961.
Published and © 1929 by Charles Scribner's Sons, New York.

THIS IS Ernest Hemingway's best novel, one of the greatest of the century, one of the greatest in the English language. It is honest, tender, often profound, and unexcelled not only as a love story but also as a war novel. Some of the love scenes were daring when the novel was published and perhaps are still so, but they are never in bad taste. The novel is not overlong and there is no reason not to read it.

Book I. FREDERIC HENRY is an American who volunteered for duty in the Ambulance Corps of the Italian Army in World War I. He is a lieutenant. He has been on leave and he returns to his unit at Gorizia just as the Austrians launch a spring offensive. Henry gets along well with the Italians he serves with, and he is particularly friendly with Lt. RINALDI, an able surgeon who likes to drink and has an eye for beautiful women.

Rinaldi tells Henry that an English hospital unit has been established in Gorizia during Henry's leave, and that a corps of British nurses is on duty there. Rinaldi describes the charms of his latest love, one of the newly-arrived nurses, named CATHERINE BARKLEY. He takes Henry to meet her, and she is indeed beautiful. It is soon obvious that Catherine prefers Henry to Rinaldi. Henry is attracted to her and sees her on several occasions, but he is not in love with her and considers her a good prospect for a casual affair. The front has erupted and Henry tells Catherine he has to drive his ambulance there to pick up wounded soldiers. She gives him a St. Anthony's medal to keep him safe. Henry gets to the front and a shell hits near his dugout. Henry is severely wounded in the legs and is completely immobile. While he is in the field hospital waiting removal to the hospital in Milan, Rinaldi comes to visit him with a bottle of cognac and says that Catherine has been transferred to Milan. The next morning Henry is driven to Milan and reaches there after a tiring and rough trip. He finds that Catherine is not yet there.

Book II. In the hospital in Milan, Henry is the first patient and the resident doctor has not yet arrived. Henry has a run-in with Miss VAN CAMPEN, the superintendent, about obtaining wine. She refuses to get him any but he is able to bribe the porter to bring him a bottle of brandy, which he carefully hides under his bed. Catherine arrives before the doctor, and as soon as he sees her Henry knows that he is in love and it is nothing casual. He begs her to arrange to stay on at this base so that they can be together during his convalescence. Three rather inexperienced doctors hold a consultation about the wounds in his legs and inform Henry that he will have to stay in bed for six months before an operation can be performed. Henry refuses to believe them and calls for the top-ranking surgeon,

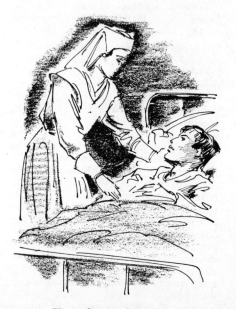

Henry knows this is love

Dr. VALENTINI, who examines him briefly and says with complete confidence that he will operate successfully in the morning. Catherine manages to spend the entire night with Henry and when morning dawns they are both happy and in love. The operation is successful. Henry recovers slowly but Catherine is with him constantly. She has arranged to be on night duty and is able to be with him in the quiet of the night. He wants very much to marry her but she asks him to wait, for they would send her home if she were a married woman. Henry finally is able to get around on crutches and he and Catherine enjoy sightseeing in an open carriage. The summer passes idyllically except for one rainy night when Catherine weeps because she says she sees herself or Henry dead in the rain. As soon as Henry is well enough they plan to spend his convalescent leave together. One evening he notices that Catherine does not look well and seems nervous. She tells him that she is three-months pregnant but not to worry; that they will work everything out. For a moment he feels trapped, then his love for her conquers this feeling. They are not able to go off on his leave because Henry gets jaundice and his old enemy, Miss Van Campen, finds empty brandy bottles in his room and accuses him of bringing on the attack of jaundice by drinking, so he will not have to return to the front. Henry recovers from the jaundice and he and Catherine spend a last evening together in a hotel room before he returns to the front. At first the red-plush aspect of the room makes Catherine ashamed, but not for long. They part at the station the next day.

Book III. Morale is low at the front and Rinaldi has a hard time making jokes with Henry. Henry loads his ambulance with hospital supplies and goes south to the Po Valley. The Italians have suffered a great defeat from the combination of German and Austrian forces; it is the famous retreat from Caporetto. The going is rough and in an effort to reach his destination, Udine, Henry tries to use side roads to avoid the retreating army and the civilians fleeing from the enemy. The ambulance is stuck in the mud and with his companions he begins to walk to Udine. The Italian Army is in panic. Everyone is trying to escape at once, without any regard for discipline or order. Murder is wholesale and officers are being shot by their men. Drumhead courts-martial give out summary death sentences without listening to evidence. Henry is detained by drunken *carabinieri*. Faced with death if he is taken to the court-martial, he realizes that he must make a run for it. The night is dark and when the opportunity presents itself he jumps into the swirling Tagliamento River and manages to get across. He makes his way on foot until he reaches a station, where he jumps a freight train. His only thought is to get to Catherine at the hospital at Milan.

Book IV. Henry reaches the hospital but finds that the English nurses have gone to Stresa. He has definitely decided to desert from the Italian Army and he goes to a friend and borrows civilian clothing. He then goes to Stresa and finds Catherine and stays with her in a hotel. Life is pleasant in the hotel and their thoughts are not on escape until one night the bartender, who has befriended Henry in the past, knocks on their door and tells them Henry will be arrested in the morning. The bartender offers them his rowboat and explains what course they are to take on the lake to get to Switzerland in the morning. Henry rows hard through the night but in the morning his hands are so blistered that he can hardly handle an oar. Catherine insists upon rowing part of the way despite her condition. They finally reach the Swiss shore, where they indulge in a huge breakfast in anticipation of their arrest by the authorities. The authorities treat them with respect and courtesy because they have valid passports and sufficient money.

Book V. They spend the early winter and Christmas at the little village of Montreux. On their long walks they often talk of their marriage, but Catherine refuses to have the ceremony performed until she is thin again. In February they move to Lausanne to be near the hospital where the baby will be delivered. The night that Catherine wakes with her first pains, both of them feel exhilarated and sure that the ordeal will be over in a short time. In the hospital her suffering is intense and it is necessary to give her the anesthetic gas frequently. The doctor insists that a Caesarian section be performed. She is delivered of a dead baby. It is a boy. Worn out, Catherine urges Henry to go out and eat while she rests. He fears Catherine is dying, but he walks in the rain to a little cafe and has supper. While he is gone, Catherine has a hemorrhage. She is still alive when he returns. The thought of dying frightens her and she clings to Henry, telling him again and again of her love. She dies and the doctors and nurses try to take him from the room, but he insists on staying to say a private good-bye. Then he walks back to his hotel in the rain.

The Father

Play by August Strindberg, 1849–1912. Produced 1887, in English 1907. Translation from the Swedish by Edwin Bjorkman and N. Ericksen published by Charles Scribner's Sons, New York; several other translations.

STRINDBERG WAS a pioneer in the psychological drama based on the new psychology of the late 19th century. *The Father,* which is probably his best-known play in the English-speaking world, combines a treatment of morbid marital psychology with an indirect attack on the ignorance and bigotry of the conservative medical profession, hardly any of whose members were conversant with the theories of psychology that were then new. The validity of the psychological background of *The Father* has stood up. Unfortunately the play is an unrelieved succession of unpleasant scenes and the fact that they are dramatically effective serves often to make them terrifying.

Act I. Captain ADOLF informs his brother-in-law the PASTOR that NÖJD, an enlisted man, has gotten a servant girl into trouble. Nöjd, called in, counters by saying one can never be sure about the paternity of a child in a case like this. The Pastor insists that Nöjd should contribute to the support of the child, but the man observes that it would be terrible to be compelled to support someone else's child. Nöjd leaves. Adolf tells the Pastor that bringing up a child is no easy matter and he is having difficulty with his daughter, BERTHA. His wife, LAURA, wants Bertha to be an artist; her governess wants to make her a Methodist; her grandmother insists that she become a spiritualist. Adolf complains that his house is full of women and he seems to have less and less authority. The Pastor sympathizes and leaves. Laura enters and asks for household money. Adolf says he would like to see the accounts and she becomes belligerent. Then, when Adolf says that Bertha will be sent to boarding school, Laura is furious and berates him. She asks what will be done about the "villainous" Nöjd. Adolf says nothing will be done, because paternity can never be definitely proved. Laura says that if this is so, then paternity can also never be certain in a legitimate marriage. Adolf goes out; Adolf's new doctor arrives. Laura tells the doctor that she suspects her husband is mad. Her reasons are that the captain is always buying books he never reads and that he claims to see life on other planets when he peers through a microscope. The doctor interviews Adolf and Laura's observations seem to be confirmed. Adolf is so distracted that he does not make a great deal of sense. The doctor leaves and Adolf thinks his wife is plotting against him. He is further disturbed when Laura darkly hints that he is not Bertha's real father.

Act II. The doctor tells Laura that Adolf does not stare through a microscope, but through a spectroscope, an instrument that can help determine the elemental composition of other planets. Laura then tells the doctor that Adolf is suffering paranoid delusions. He suspects that he is not the father of their child. Adolf does begin to fret over Bertha's paternity, and his old nurse MARGARET tries to comfort him. He decides to have matters out with his wife. He accuses her of intercepting his mail and circulating rumors that he is insane. She denies both charges. Adolf then appeals to her self-interest. He confesses that he has begun to doubt his own sanity and observes that it is important for him to remain sane; for if he should commit suicide, Laura would be in sorry financial circumstances. He asks Laura to confirm that Bertha is not his child because the suspicion is driving him mad. Laura will not confess that Bertha is illegitimate, but Adolf refuses to believe her. He recalls the circumstances of Bertha's birth. He had been ill and a lawyer had told Laura she had no rights of inheritance unless a child were born to her. A short time later Bertha was born. Adolf breaks down completely and begins to cry. He accuses Laura of having made their entire marriage a long term of penal servitude. Laura tells him that now he is undoubtedly mad. She tries again to convince him that he is Bertha's father, but he will not listen. Laura tells him that he is unmanly, that she has always thought of him as a child, and that the minute he became her lover she detested him. She shows Adolf a forged letter in which he supposedly admits that he is insane and she tells him she has sent a copy of it to the Lunacy Commission. Adolf snatches a lighted lamp and hurls it at Laura but she escapes through the door.

Act III. Laura barricades the door to Adolf's study and ransacks his desk in search of papers. The Pastor arrives and asks Laura to explain how the trouble began. He says he knows she is the troublemaker but he will remain silent because he is her brother. The doctor arrives with a straitjacket. He asks Laura whether she thinks Adolf ought to be arrested for assault or institutionalized for insanity. She refuses to answer. The doctor explains that if Adolf is sent to prison, he will be out again soon. He and Laura then agree that it would be better to treat the captain as a madman. The doctor tries to get Nöjd to put Adolf in the straitjacket. The old nurse protests and says she will do it gently. Adolf forces the barricaded door and enters with a pile of books under his arm. Each book makes a reference to some historical case in which paternity is doubtful. Adolf becomes hysterical. The doctor cautions him but Adolf will not listen. The Pastor tells Adolf he must be insane, and Adolf agrees and asks what they want with him. Bertha comes in and accuses her father of abusing Laura and says that he cannot be her father if he treats her mother so badly. Adolf tells Bertha that she has two souls—one that loves him and one that hates him. He insists that she have only one soul, a loving one. He grabs a revolver to destroy Bertha's unloving soul. The revolver, however, is empty. Bertha runs out of the room in a panic. The nurse comes up to Adolf and takes the revolver out of his hand. She speaks to him soothingly, as though he were a little boy, and slowly helps him with the straitjacket. Adolf does not resist until the jacket is strapped tight, when he begins to scream that he has been trapped

and outwitted. The nurse begs forgiveness. Adolf orders Nöjd to fling the nurse into the street, but Nöjd refuses to lay violent hands on a woman. Laura implores Adolf not to believe she is his enemy, but Adolf says his experience has proved all women are insane—his mother, his first lover, his wife, his nurse, and his child. All have been abusive and cruel. Laura, trying to soothe him, says sincerely that Bertha is his child. Adolf suddenly becomes ill and falls back unconscious, a victim of a stroke, his head in the nurse's lap. Bertha runs to her mother, who holds her, saying "My child, my own child!"

Father of the Bride

Novel by Ed Streeter, 1891–
Published 1949 by Simon and Schuster, New York. © 1949 by Edward Streeter.

THE NOVELS OF Ed Streeter are never merely novels. They are accounts of the personal experiences of one of the keenest observers and best gentle humorists America has produced. The excellence of the books is all the more remarkable considering the fact that when Streeter wrote his principal successes he was a full-time working banker. His first success, *Dere Mabel*, the letters of a soldier in World War I, was a much more slapstick kind of humor than the produce of his mature years, and not nearly so good. *Father of the Bride* had a tremendous effect on American life: For several years after it was published, nearly every American father-of-a-bride in comfortable circumstances offered his daughter some sum ranging from one to five thousand dollars to elope. The practice continues but not quite so generally. Hardly ever does a daughter accept.

Chap. 1. STANLEY BANKS is very fond of his first-born child, KAY. He is jealous of all the crew-cut adolescents who come to take her to football games and dances. One day Banks notices that his daughter, now 24, looks especially radiant. He worries that she may be in love with some cavalier. For the next weeks he hears the name BUCKLEY in all his daughter's conversation. He is alarmed. She tells the family at dinner one night that she is going to spend the weekend with Buckley's family. Banks forces her to admit that she plans to marry the young man. He learns that Buckley's last name is DUNSTON and that he is in some strange business. Kay is vague about everything but Buckley's wonderful qualities and her love for him. Banks promises to love Buckley, but he begins to brood and he resents the man who plans to snatch his child away.

Chaps. 2–4. The Dunstons invite Mr. and Mrs. Banks to dinner. Banks has to be dragged to the dinner and he says that the Dunstons must live in a shack. The shack turns out to be a large white brick house, twice the size of his own. Banks, fortified by some martinis, becomes friendly and talkative. Kay gives a cocktail party to announce her engagement and Banks finds himself mixing drinks for 50 people. The party is such a success that the exhausted host forgets to announce Kay's engagement.

Chaps 5–7. Banks sends an announcement of the engagement to the newspaper. He has made many drafts of it, but the paper prints Kay's name with a "C" instead of "K". Kay insists she wants a small wedding but when all the necessary guests are listed there are more than 300 names. Banks envisions 300 people drinking his champagne and feels that he will be ruined economically. After a sleepless night he goes to Kay and offers her $1,500 cash to elope. She refuses. Buckley sends his list over and it is clear that the Banks house will burst at the seams. Compromises are made and the final list is only twice the size of the estimated maximum the house can hold. The clothes carnival begins. Banks and his two sons are lost in the welter of trousseau talk. Banks wonders why Kay must buy as if she had never been anything but naked. His weak attempts to save money are brushed aside by Mrs. Banks and Kay. Buckley becomes alarmed when Banks tells him it costs a million dollars to clothe a woman and the bond of friendship between them deepens. Mysterious boxes begin to arrive. Everything in them is unsuitable for the house in which the newlyweds plan to live. Mr. Banks takes out the formal clothes he bought in the '20's. He struggles into them and calls the effect snug, but he looks like a sausage. Banks goes to buy the champagne and almost has a heart attack when he learns the price. He brings home three different brands to sample and invites some friends over to help him choose the best. He finally picks the brand with the most impressive label.

Chap. 8. Caterers, photographers, florists and others start calling. Banks feels as if

254

he were the sole customer of a highly organized industry. He learns he must buy Kay silver and linen. He resents the fact that the Dunstons do not buy anything, but is consoled when he looks at his two handsome sons. He will have revenge when they get married. When Banks hears about the dresses he has to buy for the bridesmaids he considers lying on the floor, making queer noises, and frothing at the mouth.

Chap. 9. Banks rejoices over the few refusals they receive but almost everyone accepts the invitation. He dreams that he is walking down the aisle of a great cathedral and everyone is laughing at him because his clothes do not fit. The next day he goes to the church and learns from the sexton that all fathers are nervous and shaky before weddings. Kay comes to him that evening and confesses that she is scared of walking down the aisle. He tells her it is silly to worry, because he will be right beside her.

Chaps. 10–12. Kay receives more wedding presents. A horrid china figure arrives and she begins to criticize the gifts and plans to return most of them. Women come to look at Kay's gifts. Banks and the visiting husbands drink and hide in the living room until the women are through. The Buckingham Caterers come and look at the house. The caterer, Mr. MASSOULA, implies that the Banks house is small and dingy. He insists that they clear out all the furniture and take down the doors between rooms. Mr. and Mrs. Banks are overwhelmed by his imperious manner and submit.

Chap. 12. The day before the wedding Banks goes to his office but he is constantly bothered by phone calls from his wife and by his partners' and clients' humorous indifference to the great event. He leaves at noon. At 6 P.M. he and his family go to the wedding rehearsal. Everyone else is very late. The preacher assures the anxious father that all will go well. They go off to the country club, where Banks drinks more than he should.

Chap. 13. He wakes the next morning feeling as though he had been run over. Several men begin to put up a tent in the back yard. Banks wants them to take the tent down, as it is a beautiful day, but the men insist that they are going to do the work they were paid for. Banks takes a walk to calm his nerves. By the time he returns his house is swarming with relations. The phone rings continuously. He goes upstairs and finds Kay crying on her bed. He comforts her. There is a huge luncheon for the bridal party. Kay looks radiant and her father eats only hot soup. Banks puts on his formal clothes and feels rather pleased with himself. Mrs. Banks enters the room and her husband is startled into shyness by her beauty. She is as lovely as she was on their own wedding day. Banks goes to see his daughter, who is finished dressing. She is wearing her mother's bridal dress and looks so much like a princess that his eyes fill with tears. He kisses her gently and after a short, anxious wait the hired limousines arrive and they drive off to the church.

Chap. 14. In the car Banks feels like a small boy being taken to dancing school. Miraculously everyone seems to know just what to do, and the wedding begins without any of the catastrophes he had imagined. He feels his daughter beside him, a strange, beautiful woman. The bridesmaids begin to cry and the music plays. Kay and her father start down the aisle. Banks begins on the wrong foot. Just as he manages a quick change, the procession changes the other way and he shifts back again. Pride in Kay removes all other thoughts from his mind. He responds to the question "Who giveth this woman?" with a weak "I do" and steps back into the pew besides Mrs. Banks. He feels as if he has parted irrevocably with his dearest possession. The wedding is over in a few minutes and he wonders why the preparations took so long.

Chap. 15. At home, Mr. Massoula has everything under control. The receiving line seems endless. Kay finally throws the bouquet into the arms of her maid of honor. Banks sees the triumphant expression on Kay's face and feels that women marry men as part of a large plot against the male sex.

Chap. 16. The last guest has gone. The Bankses are left alone with the wreckage of their house. They start to clear the floors but stop and drink a glass of champagne together.

All the women come to look at Kay's wedding presents

Fathers and Sons

Novel by Ivan Turgenev, 1818–1883. Published 1862. Several translations. (ML, 21; T38)

LIKE MOST RUSSIAN NOVELS of its times, *Fathers and Sons* was written about the nobility; but it pictured them in a changing world, not long before the serfs were declared technically free men. Turgenev gently mocked the nihilism of his most significant character, the young doctor, Bazarov, but he treated the ideas respectfully. Turgenev coined the term *nihilism*. He later told Prince Peter Kropotkin, the pioneer Russian anarchist who spent most of his life in exile for his beliefs, that he thought "revolutionary" was a more accurate term but he did not want to use it because it might bring the law down on those who held such beliefs.

Chaps. 1–3. NIKOLAI PETROVITCH KIRSANOV, a provincial landowner, waits at a posting house, in May 1859, to meet his son, ARKADY, who is arriving by coach from St. Petersburg, where he has just been graduated from the university. With Arkady is his friend BAZAROV, a student in the medical school of the university. Kirsanov greets his son very affectionately and Arkady returns the affection. The father, with much embarrassment, tells his son that he has taken a mistress, THENICHKA, a young woman Arkady met on a previous visit home. Arkady laughs at his father's embarrassment and tells him to make nothing more of the matter.

Chaps. 4–10. At Kirsanov's mansion, Marino, they meet PAUL PETROVITCH KIRSANOV, Arkady's uncle. Handsome, capable, and charming, he gave promise of a brilliant career until he fell in love with the famous and eccentric beauty Princess R. After a 10-year-long, stormy affair, the princess died; Paul withdrew from society and came to live at his brother's estate. Bazarov upsets the two elder Kirsanovs with his scornful, direct, almost rude manner. Arkady explains that he and Bazarov are nihilists, "who decline to bow to authority, or to accept any principle on trust, however sanctified it may be." During the next two weeks the two young men take life easy at Marino. However, because of several discussions on the subject of nihilism, tension grows between the elder Kirsanovs and Bazarov, especially between him and Paul. Bazarov's continual sneering at those things the elder men hold dear, and his repeated assertions that he denies everything, the

Kirsanovs find particularly obnoxious. Nikolai Petrovitch is particularly unhappy because nihilism symbolizes a division between him and his beloved Arkady.

Chaps. 11–15. Bazarov suggests to Arkady that the two of them accept an invitation to visit a relative of the Kirsanovs, even though the older men have no desire to go. He says it will be a diversion; and then after a few days he will go on and visit his parents, who live a bit farther in the same direction. Arkady is delighted with the idea, but agrees indifferently because to show enthusiasm is unnihilistic. The relative, MATVEI ILYITCH KOLIAZIN, welcomes the two young men warmly but puts them up in a hotel, where Bazarov meets a young woman, EVDOKSIA KUKSHINA, who shares their nihilistic beliefs. Toward the end of a discussion in their advanced manner, which becomes too inane for Arkady, she tells them about Mme. ODINTSOV, a rich, clever young widow who lives nearby. A few days later, at the Governor's ball, they meet Mme. Odintsov. She is a stately, beautiful woman. When she is introduced to Arkady, she finds that his mother and her mother were dear friends. She invites Arkady to visit her and to bring Bazarov with him.

Chaps. 16–19. ANNA SERGIEVNA (Mme. Odintsov) lives on a large estate, Nikolskoe, nearby. The two young men are captivated by the beautiful and truly intelligent Mme. Odintsov, but pay court to her in the somewhat indifferent manner their nihilism requires them to affect. Arkady is divided in his attentions because he finds himself more and more attracted to Madam Odintsov's younger sister, KATIA. Bazarov is upset because he finds himself falling in love with Mme. Odintsov, and he is chagrined at learning that so commonplace an emotion can influence a nihilist. His indifferent attitude piques Mme. Odintsov, and she seems to him to be sharing his feelings. His reserve breaks down and he blurts out his love for her. She is clearly moved but firmly discourages him. That night Bazarov and Arkady have a bitter quarrel over nothing. The next morning Bazarov leaves for his parents' estate, and at the last minute Arkady asks if he may come along.

Chaps. 20–21. At the Bazarovs' small estate the travelers are warmly welcomed by the elder Bazarov, a retired army doctor, and his wife. Despite young Bazarov's professed philosophy of life he is genuinely touched by his parents' affection for him and responds to it. Soon the quiet country life bores the two young men so much that they quarrel. The next day both leave.

Chaps. 22–23. Arkady has said he was going back to Marino, and Bazarov is ostensibly going back to St. Petersburg, but when they arrive at the road that leads to Mme. Odintsov's establishment they look at each other sheepishly and belligerently and head for Nikolskoe. Mme. Odintsov receives them with reserve, says she is feeling out of sorts, and bids them return soon. They both head for Marino. They find the estate going to seed with labor troubles and

deterioration of the stock and the buildings, and Kirsanov seems helpless before his misfortunes. Arkady digs up some letters that his mother wrote to the mother of Mme. Odintsov and ten days later he uses them as an excuse to go back to Nikolskoe. At Marino, Bazarov busies himself with dissecting frogs and arguing with Paul. One day, in the garden, he impulsively kisses Thenichka. Paul sees the kiss and challenges Bazarov to a duel with pistols. Paul aims at Bazarov's head and misses; Bazarov fires blindly and wounds his antagonist in the flesh near the hip. He doctors his erstwhile assailant. Paul confronts Thenichka with what he saw in the garden, and he realizes the fault was not hers. He urges his brother to marry Thenichka, and Kirsanov agrees.

Chaps. 24–26. At Nikolskoe, Arkady finds it is pleasant to talk romantically to Katia, though he feels a bit guilty at thus forsaking nihilism. Before long, Bazarov shows up at Nikolskoe. He picks a jealous quarrel with Arkady, but soon realizes his mistake. He then engages in an intellectual disputation with Mme. Odintsov. Arkady, after much stumbling and a few false starts, blurts out his love for Katia. She accepts him. Bazarov and Mme. Odintsov continue their polite quarrelsome discussion, which ends with neither surrendering. Bazarov, bitter, prepares to leave. In saying to Arkady what both know will be goodbye forever, he speaks sentimentally in a most un-

nihilistic manner. Then he remembers himself, reverts to form, and castigates Arkady for his failings as a nihilist. When he has gone, Mme. Odintsov fears that the happiness of Arkady and Katia will be too much for her, but she finds she can view them cynically, somewhat as Bazarov might.

Chaps. 27–28. Bazarov goes home and mopes about for some time. Then he takes some interest in local affairs, doing a little medical work. He cuts his finger while handling the corpse of a typhus-stricken patient, and becomes critically ill. When he believes he is dying, he sends a messenger to Mme. Odintsov to tell her of his plight, calling the message a "greeting." She arrives the following day, bringing with her a German doctor. After the doctor has seen Bazarov, Mme. Odintsov comes to the sickroom. Bazarov thanks her for coming to see him. She is deeply moved and tries to comfort him. He speaks grandiloquently and acidly about his approaching end. That night he dies.

Arkady and Katia marry; so do Nikolai Petrovitch and Thenichka. Paul leaves Marino to settle in Dresden, because there is a large English colony there and he worships the English. Mme. Odintsov marries a cold, practical man-of-affairs. The two Kirsanovs, father and son, manage to rehabilitate the crumbling estate, mainly because of Arkady's good practical sense and ability.

Faust

Medieval legend, told in dramatic poem, *Faust,* by Johann Wolfgang von Goethe, 1749–1832, and in play, *Doctor Faustus,* by Christopher Marlowe, 1564–1593.

Faust: Published, in parts, 1790 to 1831; standard version published 1808. Various translations. (ML, 177 & T19; RE, 75)

Doctor Faustus: Produced about 1588, published 1604. (ML, 94; RE, 45)

THE STORY OF FAUST is the story of a scholar who deliberately sells his soul to the devil—a theme so timeless and provocative that it is no accident that it produced two of the greatest works in world literature. ❡ Goethe's *Faust* is generally conceded to be the greatest poem in the German language and worthy of a place with the masterpieces of Homer, Virgil, Dante, and Shakespeare. Among educated Germans it is more quoted than anything comparable in English, even *Hamlet.*

Goethe's *Faust* is so profound that one might study it for a lifetime without plumbing its depths, but essentially it is a debate between the noble mind of the scholar Faust and the cynicism of the devil Mephistopheles. ❡ Marlowe's *Doctor Faustus* is by most critics accounted as good as anything Shakespeare did in the same period. Marlowe embellishes the theme with many supernatural excursions in the Fourth Dimension and when Faustus nearly achieves his earthly reward with Helen of Troy the play's most-quoted lines occur, beginning "Was this the face that launched a thousand ships?" In *Doctor Faustus* the numbering of scenes varies in different editions, according to the preference of the editor. ❡ Marlowe consigned his hero's soul to perdition; Goethe at the end saved his hero's soul, but Goethe had created a soul worth saving.

Faust

Prologue. The Lord says that not all men are miserable and cites Doctor Faust as an example of a noble, worthy soul. Mephistopheles says Faust has ambitions that soar beyond human abilities, a condition that

makes him susceptible to temptation. The Lord says Faust is incorruptible. Mephistopheles bets the Lord that he can win Faust's soul for the Devil. The Lord accepts the challenge.

Part I. Scenes 1–14. FAUST is seated in his study at a desk. Thinking about his life as a scholar, he concludes that he has really learned very little. He is discontent and reflects how intensely insignificant he (like every human being) is. Faust's servant WAGNER enters and Faust confesses to him that he longs for a new, genuinely creative life. Faust and Wagner decide to walk through the city. Mephistopheles determines that the time is right for his assault upon Faust's virtue. He assumes the form of a poodle and follows Faust home. Faust picks up the Bible and has no sooner begun to study the holy text than Mephistopheles throws off his canine form and steps forward as a student. Mephistopheles unsuccessfully tries to win Faust's soul by promising him great powers but Faust makes a wager with Mephistopheles. He is willing to have Mephistopheles show him luxury and pleasure but he denies that he will be greatly affected. He tells Mephistopheles that he will consign his soul to hell if Mephistopheles can show him any single moment in life that is so pleasurable that he would wish it to endure eternally. Mephistopheles gladly takes on the challenge and is convinced that he has Faust trapped at last. Mephistopheles tries to tempt Faust with scenes of common debauchery. Faust scorns them all. Mephistopheles now notices Faust's admiration for beautiful women. He offers Faust the love of MARGARET, a girl whom Faust passionately admires. Faust accepts and asks that his youth be restored. His request is fulfilled. Mephistopheles now tempts Margaret in Faust's name, sending her a beautiful casket of jewels. She adorns herself with the jewels and completely surrenders her heart to Faust.

Scenes 15–25. Faust arranges to spend a night with Margaret and she breathlessly agrees. However, she is filled with remorse when she learns that she is going to bear Faust's child. Margaret observes how easy it is to lapse from virtue, and that we must learn not to scorn others. VALENTINE, Margaret's brother, discovers her condition and determines to kill Faust. But Faust, with Mephistopheles' help, kills Valentine instead. Valentine dies with a curse for Margaret upon his lips. She is wild with grief and burdened by a sense of her own sin, and she kills her newborn child. Faust has already begun to forget her. Mephistopheles tries to tax him further with more scenes of violent debauchery and voluptuousness, but Faust still has not found a living moment or experience that he would wish to endure forever. Faust hears of Margaret's wretched condition—she has been placed in prison for the murder of her child. Faust is overwhelmed with remorse and rushes to the dungeon where Margaret is confined. Mephistopheles promises to help set Margaret free. Margaret is near death, but she refuses to leave with Faust and Mephistopheles. She looks toward heaven and offers her soul to God. Mephistopheles is furious. A voice from above announces that Margaret is saved. Mephistopheles and Faust disappear at the moment of Margaret's immortal triumph.

Part II. Act 1. Mephistopheles transports Faust to the EMPEROR'S palace. The Emperor and his retainers engage in a long debate with Mephistopheles. The courtiers all complain that the world is in disorder. No one is trustworthy and danger lurks everywhere. Mephistopheles comments that there never has been a time or place in which something was not wrong. The Emperor tells Faust that to be bankrupt is the worst malady in the world. Mephistopheles promises to give the Emperor great sums of money. The Emperor is skeptical and orders Mephistopheles to produce the money under pain of death. The pleasure-loving Emperor is bored and asks Faust to perform an entertaining stunt. Faust decides to produce a vision of Helen of Troy, reportedly the most beautiful woman who has ever lived. To find Helen he must journey to the supernatural realm of "Mothers," where the spirit of Helen exists in eternity. In the meantime, Mephistopheles presents the Emperor with as much wealth as he can ever use. The Emperor grants Mephistopheles the privilege of bringing all his lands into accord with the principles of Hell. Faust returns to the court with an image of Helen. Mephistopheles is not impressed by Helen's beauty but Faust desires her madly. He seizes her but there is an explosion as all the spirits produced by Faust, including Helen, disappear. Faust faints.

Act II. Mephistopheles carries the unconscious Faust back to his old study and finds Faust's servant, Wagner, busily manufacturing something in a furnace. Wagner tells him that he is making a "HOMUNCULUS" that has superior powers of perception. Wagner succeeds in creating the homunculus, who slips out of his hands and hovers over the head of Faust. The homunculus looks into Faust's brain and tells Mephistopheles that Faust craves Helen. The homunculus then offers to guide Mephistopheles and Faust to Greece, where they may witness all the classical demons of the past gathered together. Mephistopheles sees this as a per-

fect opportunity to tempt Faust once again with a more substantial incarnation of Helen. In Greece, Methistopheles assumes the guise of PHORCYCES, a monster in Greek mythology. Faust searches for Helen and the homunculus destroys himself in a demoniac orgy.

Act. III. Faust finally finds Helen in her native Sparta. With Mephistopheles' help he has acquired a castle near Helen's palace. Helen is terrified of Mephistopheles and turns to Faust for help. Faust says she must marry him in return for his assistance. Helen consents. Their only child, EUPHORION, attempts to fly but plunges to a horrible death. Helen is sick with grief. She tells Faust that she must follow Euphorion and dissolves away, leaving behind only her veil. There is now no doubt in Faust's mind that no beauty is enduring. Methistopheles has still not trapped him into losing his soul. Faust now thinks of true beauty as being spiritual, and he sees a vision of Margaret.

Act. IV. Faust returns to his own country with new knowledge of himself and with a clearer understanding of the nature of the universe. Methistopheles once again offers Faust the satisfactions of lust and carnal pleasure, but Faust scorns them. He is not even moved by the promise of fame. His attempt to possess Helen has taught him the necessity for heroic action. He wants to become a fully creative human being. He uses the magical powers that Mephistopheles has given him and defeats an enemy of the Emperor's and is given a barren strip of swampland as a reward. This is exactly what Faust desires. This is the perfect opportunity for him to create something out of nothing, to produce something of great value for man.

Act V. Faust is more than 100 years old. He can see before him the great terraces and palaces, rich orchards and gardens, that cover the once barren swamp. There is still one small settlement on his land, however, that is not under his control. He orders Mephistopheles to move the ageing couple

Helena tells Faust he must follow, then she dissolves

257

who live there. Mephistopheles oversteps himself and destroys them. Faust, at last completely appalled by Mephistopheles' diabolical behavior, rejects him for good. Faust also rejects "magic," knowing it to be useless in a truly moral life. Near death, Faust suddenly sees the real beauty of the community he has created out of the swamp. He wishes that the moment of this new truth could last forever, and so finally he loses his soul to Mephistopheles. But the Lord intervenes and does not let Mephistopheles carry away Faust's soul. Faust is lifted by angels to heaven, where he will achieve "the beautiful" eternally.

Doctor Faustus

Scene 1. The middle-aged Doctor JOHN FAUSTUS of Wittenberg, in his study, questions aloud the value of his great learning and wonders what the aim of life should be. He decides to turn to magic for an answer. A GOOD ANGEL exhorts Faustus to lay aside the book of magic and to read the Scriptures; an EVIL ANGEL urges Faustus to go forward with his magic. Faustus decides to go on with his magic. VALDES and CORNELIUS, friends of Faustus, enter and Faustus asks their advice. Both encourage the magic and promise to instruct him. Two SCHOLARS, seeking Faustus, meet WAGNER, Faustus's servant, who tells them his master is consulting with Valdes and Cornelius. The scholars fear Faustus has fallen into evil and decide to inform the Rector.

Scene 2. Faustus conjures up MEPHISTOPHELES, who appears as a devil. He is too ugly and Faustus commands him to leave and return as an old Franciscan friar. Mephistopheles does this and asks Faustus what he commands. He tells Faustus that in the nether world, when the fiends hear the Scriptures reviled they fly quickly to try to get the sacrilegious one's soul. Faustus boasts that he is not afraid of LUCIFER and he bids Mephistopheles return to Hell and tell Lucifer that he, Faustus, wishes to accept eternal torture in return for 24 years of voluptuous living, including the binding of Mephistopheles as his servant. Mephistopheles agrees to do this and to return at midnight with Lucifer's decision. Faustus daydreams about what a powerful personage he will become.

Scene 3. Wagner and a CLOWN engage in much merry horseplay in farcical imitation of Doctor Faustus and Mephistopheles. Two devils, BALIOL and BELCHER, enter and frighten the clown, who runs up and down crying. Wagner orders the devils away, and they go. The clown, very impressed, promises to serve Wagner.

Scene 4. Faustus debates with his conscience. The Good Angel and the Evil Angel appear and exhort Faustus. Faustus decides that with great wealth he will be beyond harm. Mephistopheles returns and says that Lucifer has instructed him to wait on Faustus, and thereby purchase his soul. Faustus must write in his own blood a solemn deed of sale. Faustus asks what good his soul will do Lucifer and is told that it

will enlarge Hell. Faustus draws blood from his arm and writes the deed: First, Faustus shall be a spirit in form and substance; second, Mephistopeles shall be Faustus's servant; third, Mephistopheles shall do for Faustus and bring him whatever he desires; fourth, Mephistopheles shall remain invisible in Faustus's chamber or house; and last, he shall appear to Faustus in whatever shape or form Faustus shall desire. In return for these things, Faustus agrees to give his body and soul to Lucifer, at the end of 24 years. Faustus delivers the deed to Mephistopheles, and scoffs that there is no Hell and that pain after death is a delusion. Then he asks Mephistopheles to bring him a wife. Mephistopheles brings a devil dressed as a woman. Faustus does not like Mephistopheles' choice. He and Mephistopheles get into an argument, and Faustus threatens to break his deed, renounce magic, and repent. The Good and Evil Angels appear and again each calls Faustus to its way of thinking. Faustus and Mephistopheles engage in a long metaphysical argument. Finally, Faustus asks Mephistopheles who made the world. Mephistopheles refuses to utter the name of God, and Faustus consigns him to Hell. The Good Angel and Evil Angel appear and have another go at Faustus's soul. Faustus calls on Christ to save him. Lucifer, the devil BELZEBUB and Mephistopheles come in. Lucifer chides Faustus for attempting to break their compact. Frightened, Faustus says he will never speak the name of God or call on Him. Lucifer is satisfied. He then displays to Faustus the Seven Deadly Sins: Pride, Covetousness, Wrath, Envy, Gluttony, Lechery, and Sloth. Each of these describes his or her birth and each tells how he or she acts in the world. Faustus thanks Lucifer.

Scene 5. Faustus bids Mephistopheles whisk him away to Rome. Mephistopheles accuses Faustus of wanting to see the Pope and enter into some holy rites. Faustus denies this and bids Mephistopheles make him invisible. This is done. The invisible Faustus attends a banquet at which are the Pope, the Cardinal of Lorrain, and attendant friars. Faustus snatches away the Pope's dish and cup and boxes the Pope's ear.

Scene 6. ROBIN, the ostler, steals one of Faustus's books on magic. He is joined by his friend RALPH, who has just stolen a silver goblet from the VINTNER. The Vintner enters and searches the two for his

goblet. Robin reads some Latin words from the book, hoping to put a spell on the Vintner. The invisible Mephistopheles enters and ties firecrackers to the backs of the three, so frightening them that Robin promises never to attempt magic again. Mephistopheles transforms Robin into an ape and Ralph into a dog.

Scene 7. The Emperor, Faustus, a Knight, and attendants enter. The Emperor says he has heard of Faustus's skill in the black art of sorcery and asks to be shown his ancestors. Faustus, via Mephistopheles, conjures up the spirits of Alexander and his paramour. He also puts horns on the Knight. The Emperor and retinue leave. Faustus goes home to sleep.

Scene 8. A HORSE-COURSER comes to Faustus's house and tells Mephistopheles he bought a horse from Faustus which Faustus bade him never to ride into water. The horse-courser rode the horse into water and it disappeared. He now wants his money back. The horse-courser rushes to Faustus and yanks his leg, which comes off. The frightened horse-courser flees. The equally frightened Faustus cries for his leg, which magically returns to place.

Scene 9. Wagner announces the Duke and Duchess of VANHOLT. They thank Faustus for entertaining them. Faustus has Mephistopheles bring a bunch of grapes, astounding the noble couple, for it is midwinter. For some scholars Faustus conjures up Helen of Troy. The scholars leave after praising Helen's beauty. An old man enters and abjures Faustus to repent. Faustus says he will, but Mephistopheles threatens him. Faustus weakens and asks Mephistopheles to produce Helen of Troy again. Helen is conjured up and Faustus asks her to make him immortal with a kiss. He kisses her and declaims her praises. The old man enters and curses Faustus. Devils enter and tell Faustus his hour is near. All leave.

Scene 10. Faustus returns in the company of scholars. They observe his distressed mien and attribute it to too much studying. Faustus confesses to them his compact with Lucifer. The scholars promise to pray for Faustus. As the clock strikes 11, they leave. For the last hour of his life, Faustus writhes in fear of his imminent fate, cries for help to God, and curses himself. When the clock strikes 12, thunder and lightning are heard and a band of devils carry Faustus away.

At the stroke of twelve a band of devils carry Faustus away

Fingal

Poetic prose epic by Ossian, 3rd-century Gaelic poet, or James MacPherson, 1736–1796.
Published 1762.

PUBLICATION OF the poems of Ossian created a raging literary controversy in the 18th century. James MacPherson, a man of substance as well as literary ability, said that he had collected old Gaelic manuscripts and translated them. Dr. Samuel Johnson was one of many writers and critics who charged a complete hoax. A committee of scholars finally decided that MacPherson had used some traditional Gaelic poems but had invented the rest. Probably this is true, in which case MacPherson deserves all the more credit; the "translations" are stirring and beautiful. They were called prose when they were published, but that was before Walt Whitman had demonstrated the fact that true poetry requires neither rhyme nor regular meter. The tales seem, at least to a nonexpert (and rather famously to some experts), to have the authentic Gaelic flavor of old Ireland and Scotland. Whoever wrote them, they are worth reading.

Book I. CUCHULLIN (spelled *Cuthullin* by MacPherson) sits under a tree near a castle in Ulster, Ireland. Because the true monarch, King CORMAC, is too young, Cuchullin must direct the army against the invading King SWARAN from the country of Lochlin. A scout named MORAN runs up to tell Cuchullin that Swaran and his forces have landed on the coast. Cuchullin calls a general council, where the men debate the advantages of waging war directly against Swaran. Cuchullin's good friend CONNAL advises the general to put off combat until the famous Scottish hero FINGAL arrives to join them. Another chief, CALMAR of Connaught, urges Cuchullin to give immediate battle and the headstrong Cuchullin accepts. Three of his bravest men are missing and one of them, FERGUS, rides up to tell about the deaths of the other two, DUCHOMAR and CATHBA. Both were in love with a beautiful girl named MORNA. They fought a duel and Duchomar slew Cathba. But Morna loved Cathba and in revenge she stabbed Duchomar. Duchomar in turn killed Morna.

Meanwhile King Swaran draws up his forces in a suitable battle formation. A scout tells Swaran of Cuchullin's frightening appearance: "His hair flies from his head like a flame, as bending forward he wields the spear. He comes, like a storm, along the streamy vale!" Swaran, undaunted, plunges into combat. Night falls and both sides withdraw. In accord with an ancient Celtic custom, Cuchullin invites his enemy Swaran to come to a banquet at his tent. The message is delivered by CARRIL, the bard or poet of Cuchullin's army. Swaran rudely refuses. That night at the banquet Carril sings about two young men named CAIRBAR and GRUDAR who fought for a spotted bull. Cairbar killed Grudar, then learned that his own sister BRASSOLIS loved Grudar. Brassolis died of grief by her lover's side and two beautiful yew trees sprang up from their corpses.

Book II. As Connal sleeps, he sees the apparition of CRUGAL, a hero who fell at the hand of Swaran. Crugal tells Connal that their cause is lost, for only the great Fingal can defeat Swaran. He urges Connal to make Cuchullin sue for peace. Connal tries but Cuchullin spurns such a cowardly act. As the armies again stand ready for combat, Swaran offers his enemies a peace pact with harsh terms. Cuchullin refuses. For a time the fighting is close but Cuchullin's forces weaken and are driven back in a rout. Most of the soldiers escape to a high hill. Cuchullin joins them and is heartened by the appearance of a sail on the horizon. It is Fingal's fleet coming from Scotland. Night falls and the fleet is lost in the darkness. Cuchullin blames his defeat on his murder of his friend Ferda long ago. The bard Carril will not accept this and tells a tale to prove that accidental murders do not bring ill fortune. A hero named COMAL killed his beloved GALBINA when she donned armor and walked in the woods. In desperation Comal threw away his shield and allowed an arrow to pierce his breast. The lovers' tombs stand side by side in northern Ireland, where they live together in death.

Book III. Calmar brings warning that Swaran is planning a sudden ambush. Calmar offers to sacrifice his life by guarding the rear. Cuchullin commends Calmar and vows to stand guard with him. He tells Carril to lead the retreat. The next morning Calmar is wounded but Cuchullin manages to escape. Fingal lands and Swaran turns back to the beach to repel him. The mighty Fingal and his men are more than a match for Swaran's army, but again night prevents a decisive action. As Fingal camps with his men he extols the bravery of his grandson OSCAR, son of the poet OSSIAN. He tells Oscar: "Never search thou for battle; nor shun it when it comes." Then Fingal tells of his ward, the maiden FAINASOLLIS, who was beloved by her childhood sweetheart SORA, a god of the sea. Sora came to claim Fainasollis, whom Fingal had promised to protect. Despite Fingal's bravery, Sora shot the girl with an arrow. In retaliation, Fingal slew the sea god against almost impossible odds. Fingal promises the brave warrior GAUL he may take command in the next day's battle.

Book IV. That night Ossian sees the ghost of his dead wife EVERALLIN, mother of Oscar, who tells him that their son was almost killed while scouting. Ossian relieves his son of that duty. In the morning Swaran attacks. Fingal allows Gaul to lead the forces and himself withdraws to a nearby hill. Gaul makes some foolish moves and Swaran's army bears down upon his flank. Fingal sends his bard ULLIN to rally their forces, but Swaran drives back Gaul's side of the forward line. Fingal must resume command. Swaran quickly retreats to a hill, where he awaits the onslaught of the hero. Cuchullin and Carril, who have been lurking in a nearby cave, appear on another hill to watch the outcome of the battle. Cuchullin sends Carril into the thick of the fight to congratulate the Scottish hero, for Fingal appears to have won.

Book V. Fingal and Swaran clash in the decisive combat and Fingal easily emerges as victor. He binds the defeated general and hands him over to Gaul and Ossian. Then Fingal and Oscar pursue the retreating flanks of the enemy. Fingal kills the noble chief ORLA in battle, then ends the pursuit. He then learns to his great grief that his youngest son RYKO is dead. After mourning this loss, Fingal goes back to the spot where he left Swaran. There he meets the bard Carril and receives his congratulations. Carril then hails the poet Ossian, who "best can raise the song." Ossian salutes the Irish bard with affectionate words: "Hail, Carril of other times! Thy voice is like the harp in the halls of Tara."

Book VI. As night approaches, Fingal holds the customary victory celebration. He asks Ullin to sing a traditional song of peace. Ullin sings about Fingal's great-grandfather, TRENMOR of Scandinavia, who married INIBACA, ancestress of Swaran. The song reminds Fingal that he is related by blood ties to his enemy. The hero then promises to free Swaran on condition that he never return to Ireland from Lochlin again. The rest of the night is spent in joyous feasting and song. In the morning Swaran departs. Fingal hunts in the woods and stumbles upon the cave where Cuchullin is hiding. The hero comforts the general for his ill fortune and then prepares his men for the return journey to Scotland. Glad to be returning to his home, Ossian says, "We rushed, with joy, through the foam of the deep."

Ernest Hemingway
1898–1961

Christopher Marlowe
1564–1593

The Fisher Lass

Novel by Björnstjerne Björnson, 1832–1910.
Published 1868. Several translations.

THE IMPORTANCE OF this novel is in its debates on the rigid doctrines of Norwegian Christianity, especially as applied to the theater and to music; but there is also much of life in a Norwegian fishing village that must interest the reader. Björnson is one of the great names in Norwegian literature. This short novel (about 60,000 words) has been his most popular in English but there are several other of his novels and plays that have had a wide audience. He was awarded the Nobel prize in literature in 1903.

Chap. 1. PER OLSEN, a peddler and a fiddler, comes from the country to a quiet fishing town. There he opens a shop, prospers, and marries, and soon he has a son, PETER. The boy grows up and is sent to grammar school but he is beaten by the other boys because he is the son of Per Olsen, the ex-peddler. He runs home and his father beats him to make him return to school. Peter becomes an indifferent scholar because of this and Per permits him to work in the shop. He becomes an excellent businessman and in time enlarges his father's business. He marries and has a son called PEDRO. Old Per retires. He finds time heavy on his hands and his wish for a speedy death is soon fulfilled. Pedro is a delicate child, abused by his parents because all he cares for is music. He turns for companionship to the poor children of the town. The leader of their band is GUNLAUG, an independent girl who helps her father, a fisherman. She is called the FISHER LASS. She allows Pedro to play his flute in her boat. She takes him on her fishing expeditions and repeats the tales that sailors have told her. Several years pass happily. Gunlaug's father dies one winter and she goes away. Pedro's father dies also and his mother sells the shop. Pedro plays the flute and idles away his time. Summer comes and Pedro buys a boat and goes to an island he visited with Gunlaug. She appears there one day. She has become a tall, strong woman. She loves Pedro, but because he is so weak her love dies and she leaves him. He goes back to town a beaten man and lives as an eccentric, afraid to leave his house because of the taunts of small boys. Gunlaug later comes back to town with an 8-year-old daughter, PETRA. Gunlaug opens a tavern for sailors and becomes the most influential person in the town. Her daughter now is called the Fisher Lass.

Chaps. 2–4. Petra, a mischievous child, leads the town boys in a raid on Pedro's orchard and is caught by Pedro. He learns she is the daughter of Gunlaug and he lets her go. Gunlaug makes the child promise to stay away from Pedro's house. Petra sits and sobs on the doorstep and HANS OEDEGAARD, the son of the minister, comforts her. Hans is a fine young man, but because he accidentally killed his best friend he thinks himself unfit to follow his father in the pulpit. He is appalled when he learns Petra cannot read. Gunlaug reluctantly gives him permission to teach the child. Pedro meets Petra one day and gives her a present. She receives other presents from him but never lets Gunlaug know about them. Petra is confirmed and is a grown-up lass. Hans goes away. His sisters and Petra go to a sewing school, where Petra hears other girls talk about romance. Petra sets her cap for GUNNAR, a young sailor, then meets YNGVE VOLD, a young shipowner who tells her fanciful tales of Spain and gives her a gold chain. He sails away and she impatiently waits for his return. He comes back and promises he will marry her and take her away. She dreams of being a fine lady. The next day she receives a letter from Gunnar, who is in a French port, asking her to marry him. Petra is confused and goes to her mother for advice. Gunlaug tells her that Hans has come home and Petra joyfully rushes to him. They embrace and each enjoys a first kiss. They admit their love for each other.

Petra reciting in her room

Chap. 5. Yngve Vold tells Hans that he is bewitched by Petra, the fisher lass, and wants to marry her. Hans is outraged and drives Yngve from his house. Hans goes to Petra and bitterly denounces her for having deceived him. He leaves Petra and she faints. Gunlaug puts her to bed and then hears the whole story of her daughter's attraction for three men. Hans becomes seriously ill and is cared for by his father. Gunnar returns from his voyage and finds that Yngve had been attentive to Petra. He attacks Yngve and their battle sets the town in an uproar. The gossips blame everything on Petra and a mob stones Gunlaug's tavern and sings a bawdy song to the Fisher Lass.

Chap. 6. The crowd returns the following night and becomes dangerous. Petra fears for her mother's safety and determines to run away. Gunlaug dresses her in sailor's clothes and takes her to Pedro, to whom she has not spoken in many years. Pedro puts Petra on a ship sailing to Bergen and gives her 100 thalers. Gunlaug waits several weeks and then reopens her tavern. Her customers are ashamed of what they have done and gladly come back to the bar.

Chap. 7. Petra goes to the theater in Bergen. She has never known of it before and is overwhelmed by its beauty. She is so excited that she wants to talk to the actors and join in the play. She decides that she must become an actress. She goes to the theater the next day and is interviewed by the director. She does not understand what he wants of her, and she reads badly when he gives her a book. When he learns who she is he turns her out. Her reputation has reached Bergen. She resolves to go inland, where she is not known.

Chap. 8. Near Bergen, Petra sees a beautiful parish house. She is tired and lonely and she goes to the door and asks to be allowed to rest. The parson's lovely daughter SIGNE is warm and sweet to Petra, who begs the parson to let her stay. At first he refuses, but when he learns that she is the Fisher Lass he relents. He is a friend of Hans Oedegaard. Petra confides her whole story to Signe, who writes to Hans from time to time.

Chap. 9. Two years later Petra is still staying with the pastor and Signe. A sailor brings word that Gunlaug is living with Pedro. Petra has been studying hard and has learned several languages. She still dreams of being an actress and each night, alone in her room, she recites scenes from great literature. The pastor and his daughter believe that Petra is meeting someone secretly. They are relieved when they discover that Petra is reciting to herself, but the pastor has often spoken about the wickedness of acting and he berates Petra for her secret desire. Signe is upset by the altercation. She goes to her room and refuses to answer Petra. In desperation, Petra climbs out on the window ledge to see if Signe is in her room. Signe sees Petra's figure in the moonlight and screams with fear. Petra lets go of the window ledge and falls into the bushes. She is found unconscious by the pastor, who carries her to her room.

Chap. 10. Petra recovers from the fall and goes to church to find peace. She feels the infinite mercy of God and is uplifted. But the parson, at home, is stern and unforgiving. Petra is thinking of running away, when Hans arrives in a sleigh. Petra greets him with embarrassment and then goes to her room. Three members of the parish come to ask the pastor to give up his playing of the violin. They believe that music, dancing and song are sins against God. The pastor replies that his music is a necessary relaxation and enables him to think more purely about God. Hans asks the people what activity they do not consider a sin. They reply that "work" is the only activity that does not tempt man into sin. Hans forces them to agreee that work for profit tempts man away from God. He says that a life of work and prayer with no love or lightness makes the world a prison and that God does not feel glorified by men living in prison. They say that the early Christians abandoned music and dance, but Hans insists that the New Testament must be interpreted according to the spirit, not the letter. He also argues that the Bible uses imagery, therefore it cannot be sinful for man to give comfort to others through the images of song or stage. The three parishioners are convinced by this and the pastor too sees things in a new light.

Chap. 11. The pastor's original prejudices against the theater have been severely shaken by Han's arguments. Hans has discovered through Signe's letters that Petra is an artist as an actress and he feels that God has meant us to develop our potential. Pedro dies and leaves Petra a large amount of money on condition that Gunlaug tell her Pedro was her father. Gunlaug does this and Petra decides to go to the city with her money and start her acting career. Hans finds he loves Signe and he comes to the parish and opens a school.

Chap. 12. Petra makes her debut as an actress in the capital. Her past and her future are gathered together in the theater. Yngve Vold has come and so has Gunnar. Signe is now married to Hans and is there with her husband. Gunlaug is there too, although she knows nothing about the theater and cannot even read or write. The pastor sits in the audience, confident of Petra's success. He has entrusted her cause to God. The curtain rises. The life of a Fisher Lass is over. The life of an artist begins.

Flowering Judas

Short stories by Katherine Anne Porter, 1894–
Published 1930 by Harcourt, Brace & Co., New York. © 1930, 1935 by Katherine Anne Porter.

THE REPUTATION OF Katherine Anne Porter is most firmly established on her short stories, many of which are works of art. They seldom rely on plot but the writer's skill makes them as dramatic and suspenseful as though they did. Most of them belong to the "stark" school of the short story in which no human being is ever permitted to have a wholly happy moment.

FLOWERING JUDAS

LAURA is working as a Revolutionist in Mexico City. Each day when she goes home she is awaited by BRAGGIONI, an enormously fat man, a powerful and dedicated Revolutionist. Since Braggioni is her superior in the Revolutionary movement, she must listen to him sing each evening. His voice is dreadful and his guitar-playing evokes sounds of anguish from the tortured instrument, but Laura listens politely. She knows what Braggioni wants and she knows she must resist while appearing not to resist. Braggioni is patient. He waits as one waits for the inevitable. To keep Braggioni at arm's length; to deliver messages to and from political inmates of the prison; to acquire money for those who must get away or face a firing squad; to maintain her position as a young woman not to be molested day or night; this is Laura's life. She tells Braggioni that she has seen EUGENIO, one of their workers, verging upon a stupor. She had taken him a bottle of sleeping pills, and he swallowed all of them at once. Braggioni says that Eugenio is a fool and the movement would be better off without him. That night Laura dreams that Eugenio comes to her and leads her on the road toward death. It is a long journey. She is faint and he plucks blossoms from the Judas tree for her to eat. The blossoms appear to be bleeding, and Eugenio shouts at her that she is a murderess and a cannibal. The sound of her own voice shouting the word "Not!" awakens her, and she is afraid to go to sleep again.

MARIA CONCEPCION

MARIA CONCEPCION is 19 and she is married to JUAN VILLEGAS. Juan works for an American archaeologist, and each day Maria, on her way to sell her chickens in the village, takes lunch to the men at the excavation. The archaeologist shudders at the sight of Maria coolly cutting the throat of a chicken. He tells Juan that one day Maria will catch him in one of his infidelities and will slit his throat as if it were a chicken's. But Juan merely laughs. One day after leaving the archaeologist, Maria Concepcion passes the house of Maria Rosa, who keeps bees, and she decides that she would like a crust of honey. She is pregnant, and she tells herself that if she does not eat some honey she will mark her child. She hears masculine and feminine laughter, and through a gap in the hedge sees her husband and Maria Rosa. They run away to the war together that day. Maria Concepcion shows no signs of grief. Her baby dies when he is only 4 days old, and still she shows no grief. The village comments that she is indeed a cold one. Juan and Maria Rosa tire of army life and come back to the village. Maria Rosa is expecting a baby, which is born the next day. The military

police pick up Juan as a deserter, but the archaeologist rescues him and he goes home. He attempts to resume his authority in the house by beating Maria Concepcion, but she fights back. He is tired and falls asleep. When he awakens in the morning, his wife has already left for the market with her chickens. He goes back to sleep and when he awakens again he sees her coming through the doorway, mumbling incoherently, in her hand the bloodstained butcher knife. She prostrates herself on the floor and her mutterings become unintelligible. Juan realizes what has happened. He washes the bloody knife and tells Maria Concepcion to remove her bloodstained clothes and start cooking dinner. She obeys, and when the gendarmes arrive they come upon a family scene of husband and wife at table. Still an inquiry must be made. A woman has been killed. Questions are asked, but no answer is sufficient to constitute a scrap of evidence. All are certain that Maria Concepcion killed her rival, but none will say so and the police go away. Maria Concepcion takes Maria Rosa's baby, stating calmly that he belongs to her, and goes home with her husband. Juan goes to sleep, and she and the baby sleep.

MAGIC

A woman is dressing the hair of Mme. BLANCHARD. Mme. Blanchard casually remarks that her linens must be bewitched, they are so full of holes when they come back from the laundry. This reminds the woman of another story of magic. Once she had worked in a "fancy house" where one girl, NINETTE, and the madam were constantly fighting. Ninette complained that she was not getting her full earnings; but she could not go away, because she always owed the madam money and she could not discharge the debt when she did not receive her full pay. One day Ninette suddenly produced $40 and threw it at the madam, saying that now she had paid her debt and could leave. The madam flew into a rage and accused Ninette of robbing the men customers. She then beat Ninette unmercifully and threw her out. Soon afterward the madam wanted Ninette back, because so many customers asked for her, but no one knew where to find the girl. The cook was well versed in magic and offered to concoct a special New Orleans charm that would surely bring Ninette back. The charm was concocted of all the relics of Ninette that could be found—strands of hair, nail clippings, and powder from her puff. All were combined and the magic pronounced. Just as the cook had predicted, in seven days Ninette was back, and from that day on there was never trouble between her and the madam.

Folly or Saintliness

Play by José Echegaray, 1832–1916.
Written 1876. Several translations.

THE GREAT SPANISH playwright Echegaray, who won the Nobel prize for literature in 1904, here posed a question that can cause as many unresolvable arguments as *Hamlet*. His chief character, a rich nobleman, discovers he is not by actual birth entitled to his name and fortune. No one need know if he remains silent. Does honor demand him to expose himself? The playwright and some of his disinterested characters seem to feel that to do so is so highly honorable as to be called saintly. To most others it would probably seem folly or madness, the other half of the title. (The English title selected for one translation, *Madman or Saint*, better expresses the idea.) The setting is clear from the outline that follows.

Act I. DON LORENZO DE AVENDAÑA is concerned about the health of his daughter INES. His physician, Dr. TOMAS, says Ines is not medically ill but sick with love. She is actually in danger of dying of despair if she is not permitted to marry EDWARD, the son of the Duchess of ALMONTE. Don Lorenzo's wife, Doña ANGELA, begs him to ask the duchess not to block the marriage, but he replies that he is of an ancient family, he has great wealth, and he need not humble himself before anyone. Doña Angela determines to go to the duchess herself. Don Lorenzo then consents to go himself, though it is the duchess's duty to ask for Ines's hand. Ines, learning that her father intends to arrange her marriage, swoons with emotion. Dr. Tomas tells Don Lorenzo that he has just seen a dying old woman called JUANA. She is Don Lorenzo's former nurse and once was accused of stealing his dead mother's locket but he secured her release from the police. Don Lorenzo declares his old nurse will not die in loneliness. Edward arrives with exciting news: He has persuaded his mother to visit Don Lorenzo and propose their marriage. Juana, close to death, is brought to the house and privately confesses to Don Lorenzo that she did steal the locket—because it contained something his mother had written and Juana did not want him to see. Juana now gives him his mother's message. It says Don Lorenzo is not really his parents' child. They had to have an heir to secure the family fortune; therefore they pretended that Juana's child was their own. Don Lorenzo is overwhelmed. The broken old woman with him is his mother. He is a fraud, enjoying a fortune and name that are not justly his. At this very moment the Duchess of Almonte comes into the room. She asks Don Lorenzo's consent to the marriage and he replies that he cannot give it because both he and his child are nameless and without fortune. He says he must redress all the wrongs he has committed while living on other men's wealth. The duchess and Doña Angela are shocked. Ines falls fainting into a chair.

Act II. Edward feels certain that Don Lorenzo has gone mad. The duchess tells Edward he must give Ines up; Edward refuses. He suggests that Don Lorenzo is reveling in his daughter's misfortune and that scandal can be avoided by silence: The fortune can be returned to the proper heirs discreetly. The duchess is shocked but agrees. She confesses that she suspects Don Lorenzo is mad. She and Edward tell Doña Angela of their plan to maintain the strictest silence and proceed with the marriage. Doña Angela tells Don Lorenzo he must hold his tongue for the sake of them all; he replies that doing such a thing would be infamous. Doña Angela points out that by exposing the scandal Don Lorenzo will expose Juana to arrest for a major crime. For the time being, Doña Angela seems to win her point. Don Lorenzo asks her to leave him in peace for awhile. Juana comes into the room and Don Lorenzo tells her he will tell the whole truth tomorrow. He shouts angrily that she has obliged him to break his daughter's heart. When he goes out, Juana takes the letter in which Don Lorenzo's supposed mother confessed the truth and substitutes a blank sheet of paper in the original envelope. Then she faints. Don Lorenzo hears her moaning and rushes to her side. He presses her to his chest so hard that Doña Angela thinks he is strangling her. With her dying breaths, Juana denies to Doña Angela and the duchess that she is Don Lorenzo's mother. She dies.

Act III. The next day Dr. Tomas arrives with Dr. BERMUDEZ, an expert on mental diseases, to observe Don Lorenzo. Doña Angela is sure Don Lorenzo smothered Juana to death. Bermudez says if Don Lorenzo is able to present proof that Juana was his mother he cannot be accused of insanity. Don Lorenzo enters and takes out the envelope that contained the confession. Dr. Tomas remarks that Don Lorenzo is a saint if he possesses incontestable proof, a madman if he does not. The paper is examined. It is blank. Don Lorenzo begins to rage. Ines tells her father she is full of remorse and really believes him. But it is too late. Everyone is afraid that Don Lorenzo will become violently mad and injure Ines. Dr. Tomas prevents Don Lorenzo from embracing her. Ines rushes to her father's side and tries to protect him. Don Lorenzo strikes his forehead, scarcely able to believe what is happening. Two keepers enter the room to escort Don Lorenzo out. Ines swears to save her father. He replies that not even God has seen fit to do that.

Foma Gordyeeff

Novel by Maxim Gorki, 1868–1936.
Published 1899. Translation from the Russian by Isabel F. Hapgood published 1901 by Charles Scribner's Sons, New York. Other translations.

THOUGH ONE of Gorki's early works, *Foma Gordyeeff* remains one of his most popular and is surely very close to his best. It is a warning against materialism and it has pleased Communists to construe it as a warning against capitalism, which (though indirectly) it may well be. Few novelists in any language have succeeded in one novel in drawing so many characters so effectively as did Gorki in *Foma Gordyeeff*. The action is set in the Volga region that Gorki knew and described so well. Everything about this book makes it worth reading.

Chap. 1. The gigantic, handsome IGNAT GORDYEEFF has risen from water-pumper on a river barge to a rich merchant. He owns steamers on the Volga, granaries, and freighters. He is a man of three sides, one avaricious, with an indomitable passion for work, trading, and cheating; the second philosophical, so that he can watch one of his barges crushed by an icepack and be on the side of the strong, ruthless river; the third reckless, with a taste for drinking and carousing and fighting until a period of profound penance sets in. In every phase he is never free from one profound passion—to have a son to whom he may leave his riches and power. His wife bears him four daughters, all of whom die in childhood. She dies and he takes a handsome young Kazak woman, NATALYA, as a bride. She is from the sect of the Molokani (milk drinkers) from the Urals, and is strangely withdrawn from the world. She is quite unafraid when Ignat threatens to beat her. "If you touch me, you will never come near me again," she cries. He knows she is as powerful and wild as he, and it kindles in him an insane desire to tame the woman. Before his campaign starts she tells him she is pregnant and in due time she bears him a son. Even as he is celebrating, Natalya dies. Ignat names his son FOMA and places him with an old friend, MAYAKIN, whose wife also has just borne a child.

Chap. 2. Foma grows up in a strange household. Mayakin, a shopowner, prides himself on his business, the antiquity of his

The boat on the Volga

family, and his brains. Foma's first six years are a succession of long, monotonous days, enlivened by beatings he administers to Mayakin's daughter, LIUBA, prayers, and reading from the Bible. In Foma's 7th year Ignat takes him home. Ignat's sister, ANFISA, has come to live with him and care for Foma. A new world opens up to Foma. His aunt gives him affection, which he has never known. His father he fears and respects. He grows accustomed to his father's drunken spells and accompanies him on the ship *Yermak,* down the Volga to the Caspian Sea. When he overhears the pilot and engineer call Ignat a greedy curmudgeon, he tells his father, who dismisses the pilot and engineer. This delights Foma and he boasts about the triumph to a friendly sailor. From then on he is shunned by the crew, who before had played with him. One sailor, EFIM, complains about being made a porter and Ignat smashes him to the deck. This disturbs the boy but Ignat talks for a long time about his own youth and the two grow closer in their relationship. One night Foma is awakened by shouts and sees the deckhands push a body away from the ship. Terrified, he wakes his father, who tells him it was a drowned man he saw, and comforts him.

Chap. 3. Foma goes to school and makes two friends, SMOLIN AFRIKAN and EZHOFF NIKOLAI. Smolin is the slow, redheaded son of a rich merchant. Ezhoff is a very bright son of a janitor. Ezhoff helps Foma with his lessons in return for sweets that Foma brings from home. They join in boy's pranks. When Foma has spent five years in the district school his godfather Mayakin urges Ignat to send him out on his own, having in mind a marriage of the lad to his daughter Liuba. Foma is sent off on the steam tug *Diligent* with Efim as captain. They anchor at a village to unload grain and Foma is attracted to PELEGAYA, a black-eyed woman 30 years old. She comes aboard that night and seduces him. Foma insists on taking her to Perm. Efim chides him but Foma soon makes it clear who is the master of the *Diligent*. At Perm he receives an urgent summons from Mayakin to come home as his father is drinking heavily and has lost his mind. Foma asks Pelegaya to return with him and offers to marry her. She laughingly says she has a husband and leaves Foma. He goes home and finds that Mme. MEDYNSKY, the wife of an architect, has persuaded his father to contribute a large sum to the build-

ing of a lodging house and library for the poor. Mayakin hates to see Foma's inheritance dissipated. Foma refuses to listen to Mayakin's warnings. He and his father get along very well, with no criticism of each other. Soon after, the old man dies.

Chap. 4. Mayakin takes charge of the funeral. Foma is so stunned with grief that he insults the guests. At an aristocratic gathering to celebrate the building of the lodging house he becomes infatuated with Mme. Medynsky but he feels very much out of place with her elegant friends. He avoids Liuba, knowing he is supposed to marry her, but she disarms him by her frank appraisal of her father and the merchant class, to which he now belongs. With the

death of his father, Foma is lonely and seeks out Mayakin and Liuba for companionship. The old man gives him long philosophical dissertations. His is a defeatist idea, a conception of the merchants toiling desperately for money but finding that it does not bring them any real power and that it banishes Christ.

Chap. 5. Mayakin tells Foma to hold honey in one hand and a knife in the other, "bite everybody or lie in the mud." These harangues have a subtle effect on Foma. His vanity is aroused and he patterns his business life on that of Mayakin. At the same time he falls more and more under the spell of Mme. Medynsky, who keeps him at arm's length and enjoys playing with him to the point of torturing him. He declares his love for her and while she lets him kiss her hand, she immediately puts him in his place with comparisons of his merchant class and her aristocratic class. Mayakin warns Foma that she will ruin him if she can. He suggests that the young man offer himself as her lover but that he should be careful that she does not charge him too much. Foma is wildly indignant and upbraids Mayakin.

Chap. 6. Foma tells Mme. Medynsky he knows all about her and she must deal with him in a straightforward manner. She tells him he will have a difficult time in life, since he won't be satisfied with the pursuit of the ruble, and he may never find out what he really longs for. Foma hoped his abrupt statement would bring her into his arms, but she merely calls him ridiculous and says he should find a woman friend of a different sort, a healthy-souled creature,

simple, merry, and lively. Their meeting ends with a dramatic farewell on his part and a resolution to marry. Even this is tempered by an uncertainty about life.

Chap. 7. For a week Foma pines for his beloved but refuses to go to her. His godfather commissions him to get an extension on money he owes a rich old dealer in lumber named SHTCHUROFF, who is said to have been a counterfeiter and probably a murderer. The man attracts Foma mightily, particularly when he divines that Foma knows very little about himself. He also urges Foma to marry Mayakin's daughter and thus increase his riches when his godfather dies. Shtchuroff has little hope for

the merchant class. When Foma challenges the idea that money gives power, Shtchuroff immediately demands payment of his notes. He changes from an understanding and sympathetic old philosopher into a hard and pitiless trader and finally drives a hard bargain with Foma. Foma confesses to Liuba that he is in love with Mme. Medynsky. He goes to the club, where he thrashes a member who refers to his beloved as a cocotte.

Chap. 8. After the episode at the club, Foma has spent three days in debauchery and revelry. He and his companions are on a huge raft in the Volga. As the party breaks up it becomes acrimonious. Foma, intoxicated, resents being called a peasant by his well-born companions. He goes ashore and cuts loose the moorings of the raft. He watches the raft careen down the river and smash against the rocks. A little later, Foma pulls SASHA, one of the girls, from the water. He does not know what has happened to the others.

Chap. 9. Mayakin is visited by Efim, who reports that Foma came aboard drunk, had him bound hand and foot and stowed under the hatch, then in his drunken state allowed two chains of barges to collide so that a barge was sunk, a man lost, and several men badly hurt. Efim adds that Foma, when he became sober, took over salvage operations. At this time Foma is staying with Sasha. Mayakin confronts Foma when he returns. Foma tries to dismiss him but the old man warns him he will have to stop playing the fool or stern measures will be taken to prevent his squandering his inheritance and ruining himself.

Chap. 10. After his quarrel with his godfather, Foma carouses heavily with many companions of both sexes. Sasha leaves him. He becomes delirious and sees all the people who have influenced his life. Mayakin, furious with Foma, hears that his long-lost son, TARAS, is engaged in business. He has Liuba write to Taras. Foma runs into his boyhood friend Ezhoff, who has become a drunken journalist, and the two have wild parties together and curse their diverse fates.

Chap. 11. Mayakin, despairing of having Foma for a son-in-law, chooses Smolin as the husband of Liuba and she finds the young redhaired merchant attractive. He talks to her of the theater, music, and books —and business. The old man questions him about drinking and he says he takes just a glass or two in case of illness or fatigue; there are other pleasures far more worthy of a cultivated man. Mayakin leaves his daughter and her suitor, who loses no time in pressing his suit.

Chap. 12. On his steamer Foma meets a pilgrim from the Shrine of St. Stephen and thinks he recognizes him as MIKHAIL, the son of Shtchuroff. The pilgrim denies that he is Mikhail but goes to Foma's cabin and tells him about retiring from the world.

Foma is moved. The pilgrim tells him his only salvation is to withdraw, deliver himself to the Lord, and gaze upon the world with freedom—from afar. Returning to town, Foma learns that Mayakin's son, Taras, has returned and that Liuba is going to marry Smolin. He hears that Taras is rich through having plundered his father-in-law. In despair, Foma goes to Ezhoff, who tells him to go away and leave him to his own self-destruction.

Chap. 13. A shipowner is launching a new steamer and all the merchants are aboard for the maiden voyage, including Foma and his godfather. Mayakin makes an

eloquent toast to the merchant-class but Foma harangues the gathering, calling each to task for his sins. When they can take no more, the merchants leap on Foma, beat him and bind him. When the vessel docks, Mayakin takes Foma to a hospital. He is discharged from the hospital soon after and Mayakin sends him off to his mother's relatives in the Urals. Three years later Mayakin dies and Foma reappears in town. He wanders about in a constant state of dishevelment and intoxication. He avoids people but they constantly jeer at him and shout "Hey, you—prophet—say a few words to us about doomsday!"

Forever Amber

Novel by Kathleen Winsor, 1916– Published 1944 by The Macmillan Co., New York. © 1944 by Kathleen Winsor.

THIS WAS A FOLLOW-UP to the successful *Gone with the Wind* and a rival to it in success. *Forever Amber* is very long, about half a million words. One of its unique distinctions is that its author was a young glamor girl capable of being one of the wives of Artie Shaw, along with Lana Turner and other movie stars. The critics were patronizing at best and usually treated the book as just another hack job dashed off for dollars. They overlooked one distinctive aspect of *Forever Amber* when it is compared to genuine hack jobs: The novelist was always trying to be a good novelist, and occasionally she succeeded. Her description of the plague in London would grace any novel. The novel is great fun to read, as any novel that sells in the millions must be.

Part 1. Chaps. 1–6. AMBER ST. CLARE, the illegitimate daughter of JOHN MAINWARING and of JUDITH, daughter of Lord WILLIAM MARSH, flaunts her young, fiery beauty before the townspeople of Marygreen. Her foster parents wish to marry her off before she gets into trouble, but Amber has other ideas. Lord BRUCE CARLTON passes through the village with his noble friends and she manages to catch his eye and completely captivates him. He seduces her and finds that she is a virgin. Amber loves him and accompanies him to London, despite his declaration that he will never marry her. She falls in love with London at first sight and in a very short time changes from a bold and pretty country girl into a ravishingly beautiful woman. She and Bruce live together for many months, while he seeks the favor of King CHARLES II, who has returned to his throne after the death of Cromwell. With the aid of the King's mistress, BARBARA PALMER, Bruce receives letters of marque as a privateer. Amber, truly in love, is torn with grief at the thought of his departure, the more so since she has

discovered that she is pregnant. But he finally sails, leaving her well provided with money for several years.

Chaps. 7–8. Amber moves to another part of London as soon as Bruce leaves, so that she will not be reminded of him. She is lonely and worried about the coming child, and accepts the friendship of SALLY GOODMAN. Sally has a nephew, LUKE CHANNEL, who is a lout and personally repulsive to Amber, but she marries him to assure the legitimacy of her expected child. Sally and Luke turn out to be a pair of conniving thieves who steal all Amber's money and possessions and leave her destitute.

Part II. Chaps. 9–16. Amber is thrown into Newgate Prison for her debts, which amount to nearly 400 pounds. She writes an appeal to Lord ALMSBURY, Bruce's close friend, but her appeal is unanswered. Her one thought is not to have her child in prison, and with this in mind she accepts the attentions of BLACK JACK MALLARD, a highwayman, who ranks among the elite of his profession. She is intimate with him in prison and escapes with him. They take shelter with MOTHER REDCAP, a pawnbroker, and Amber's son, BRUCE, is born. Black Jack trains Amber to assist him and he hires MICHAEL GODFREY to teach her the ways of ladies of fashion and rid her of her country accent, so that she may pass as a lady. Charles II is preparing for his coronation. His infatuation with Barbara Palmer has reached a point where she believes she might tease him into marrying her. She is greatly disappointed when Charles refuses, but she holds on to the honors and attention she is getting as the acknowledged mistress of the king. Amber sees Mrs. Palmer ride past in a carriage and she jealously remembers Barbara's association with Bruce. Amber determines to be just such a woman herself. In order to do this, she helps with Black Jack's schemes to get money to pay her debts and buy her way to freedom. Black Jack is caught on one of their forays, but Amber escapes and is rescued by Michael Godfrey, who is in love with her. He safely hides her in his rooms. Black Jack is hanged and Amber feels free.

Life with Michael is very pleasant. Amber begins to lose her fear of being arrested and gets about. She is drawn to the stage and

finally is hired for small parts. Though a beginner's salary is slight, the great inducement for her is that all actors are servants of the king and cannot be arrested without his direct warrant. Amber feels safe from prison at last. She has some success and develops a following among the young blades. She accepts none of their offers, deciding to remain with Michael until she can acquire a gentleman who can really afford to keep her. Michael's father forces him to leave Amber just as she finds a man she feels she can use as a stepping-stone for her ambitions. Capt. REX MORGAN sets her up in luxurious style but she continues with her career on the stage, where she feels she may attract an even better proposal.

Chaps. 17–21. King Charles marries the Infanta Catherine of Portugal. The new queen refuses to receive Barbara Palmer, who is now Lady CASTLEMAINE. The King had intended to part with Barbara, but his wife's attitude drives him back to her. One day Amber meets Almsbury, who tells her Bruce is still on the high seas. She realizes that though she is happy with Rex, she still loves Bruce. She is unfaithful to Rex for the first time with Almsbury, who pays her £200. Rex wishes to marry her but her bad experience with Luke Channel has soured her on marriage. She also hears rumors at the theater that the king has seen her and wishes to meet her. The king sends for her twice and seems well pleased, but Lady Castlemaine finds out and he drops Amber to avoid a quarrel. When Amber realizes that the king will not be summoning her again, she makes up her mind to marry Rex. But Almsbury brings Bruce to visit her and Amber knows there is no one but Bruce in her heart. They go to the country to see their son and spend five days together, with Amber scheming how to keep Bruce from returning to Jamaica. When she finds she cannot persuade him to stay, she returns to Rex. She finds that he knows everything and is wild with jealousy. He challenges Bruce to a duel and is killed by Bruce.

Parts III–IV. Chaps. 22–32. The queen is pregnant and Lady Castlemaine no longer commands the attention of the king. She is worried and fearful but is reassured when her astrologer tells her the royal child will be born dead. The queen lies near death and Barbara, more frightened of what the next

Amber and Buckingham

queen may do to her, prays hard for her recovery. Amber, meanwhile, is shopping for a new protector. She is singled out by the Duke of Buckingham and spends the night with him for a large sum of money. She is currently the vogue of the dandies because of the duel between Bruce and Rex. But she is pregnant again and with her faithful maid, NAN, she leaves town for Tunbridge Wells. The ride is very hard on her and she suffers a miscarriage. At Tunbridge Wells she meets SAMUEL DANGERFIELD, 60, widowed, and one of the richest men in England. Amber passes herself off as a lonely young widow with ample funds. She marries Samuel and goes with him to his imposing house in London to meet his large family. His children all dislike her, largely because she has become entitled to a third of their father's fortune when he dies. Amber plays the role of a young, devoted wife to perfection, but Henry, the youngest son, discovers that she has been an actress and her secret is revealed to the family.

Through JEMIMA, Samuel's youngest and prettiest daughter, Amber discovers that Bruce does business with Samuel. She is not surprised when she meets him in the Dangerfield offices and her heart again tells her that he is the only man in the world for her. They manage often to be alone together during his month's stay in London. Samuel is not well and Amber affectionately nurses him: Jemima has fallen in love with Bruce, but Amber settles that by having her father marry her off quickly to her affianced, JOSEPH CUTTLE. Samuel Dangerfield dies, happy in the knowledge that Amber is to bear his child. Amber delays her removal from Dangerfield House until her daughter is born. She then takes fashionable quarters and awaits Bruce's return. Now that she is a rich woman, she firmly believes he will marry her.

Chaps. 32–38. London is devastated by the plague, and thousands flee the city. Amber refuses to leave, because Bruce has not yet returned. Bruce arrives but is stricken with the plague. Amber, deserted by her servants, nurses him herself. Bruce lies near death for ten days; then he passes the crisis. His recovery is slow but the time is happy for Amber. His eyes follow her every move with love and gratitude. They prepare to flee the city but Amber is stricken by the plague. Bruce nurses her slowly back to health. He is gentle and kind and tells her that he loves her. When strength returns to both of them they manage to reach Almsbury's house in the country. Amber regains her beauty and hope grows in her heart that finally Bruce will marry her.

Chaps. 38–45. Bruce stands firm in his refusal to marry her, and he leaves for America again without saying goodbye. Amber marries the 57-year-old Earl of RADCLYFFE. She wants to be a countess so that Bruce, only a baron, will regard her more highly. Amber and her husband hate each other. Radclyffe forces Amber to give him what money he demands. Her only compensation comes when her dream of being presented at court is fulfilled. She is an immediate success with the king and Radclyffe, furious, takes her by force to his country estate, where he plans to keep her unless she turns over all her money to him. Amber refuses and amuses herself by making his oldest son, PHILIP, fall in love with her. She seduces him. Radclyffe finds out and attempts to poison them both. Philip dies, but Amber miraculously escapes. Determined to rid herself of this sadistic man, Amber has him murdered. Fortuitously a great fire sweeps the city and destroys Radclyffe House and her husband's body.

Part V. Chaps. 46–52. Amber returns to court and becomes the mistress of the king, with as much power as Lady Castlemaine had. When she finds herself pregnant once again the king seems pleased but insists that she marry young GEORGE STANHOPE, who is made Earl of DANFORTH by the king. Stanhope is a weakling and does not interfere with the life Amber leads. Bruce returns from Jamaica and he and Amber are reunited in their passion, but he tells her he has married an earl's daughter in the colonies and wishes to take their son back with him. Amber is hurt but agrees.

Chaps. 52–59. Amber considers herself the most fortunate woman on earth. King Charles continues her as his favorite and makes her husband the Duke of Ravenspur, so Amber is a duchess. Bruce is expected back in England early the following month.

Part VI. Chaps. 60–69. Lord and Lady Bruce Carlton arrive in London and the court finds CORINNA (Lady Carlton) is a beauty and very much in love with her husband. Amber is more madly in love with Bruce than ever and he reciprocates. They resume their affair despite his marriage. Lady Carlton hears what is going on and Bruce stops seeing Amber, but not for long. The lovers begin to meet in secret, but Amber becomes dissatisfied. Angry, Amber goes to see Corinna and tells her everything. Bruce comes in and, enraged by what Amber has done, attacks her. Amber's life is saved when Corinna begins to have labor pains. As soon as Corinna is able to travel she and Bruce leave for America. Amber's enemies at court tell her that Corinna died on the journey. Amber immediately makes preparations to leave for America. Those who know that Corinna is alive and well in Virginia laugh.

The Forsyte Saga

Trilogy of novels by John Galsworthy, 1867–1933.

Published (*The Man of Property*, 1906; *In Chancery*, 1920; *To Let*, 1922) by Charles Scribner's Sons, New York.

GALSWORTHY WAS A major novelist and playwright; his Forsyte novels were enough to secure him in that position. During the 1920s, when Sinclair Lewis and Ernest Hemingway and other American giants had emerged, Galsworthy was the only major novelist England had left. (Hardy and Kipling were superannuated, and Conrad was a Pole.) *The Forsyte Saga* is important literature by all standards. Its three novels are concerned with a social phenomenon of primary importance, the rise of the "upper middle class," the moneyed merchant and professional classes, to parity with the nobility and gentry. The movement was first observed in France, where Molière's *The Bourgeois Gentleman* of 1670 satirized its start, but it came first to fruition in the new United States (1770–1800) and only second in France (1800–1850). Next came Germany, Austria-Hungary, and —surprisingly—Russia, where the process was well under way before it had its halting start in England in the 1860s. In England the transition period was six or seven decades. In the earliest phase (1860–1900), the aspirations of the middle class were conscious; midway (1900–1920), a distinction was still felt; by the end of the 1920s the upper middle classes and the upper classes had become so blended by emulation and intermarriage as to be indistinguishable. Galsworthy recorded every phase of the process with skill, sympathy, and fidelity. In the course of doing so he created characters who seemed alive to his readers. Few English novels have won a more admiring audience than Galsworthy's Forsyte novels. He continued the series in a second trilogy, *A Modern Comedy,* in which he displayed as much skill but had a much less significant message.

The Man of Property

Part I. It is June 1886. Old JOLYON FORSYTE calls the members of his family together at his house in London, to announce the engagement of JUNE, his granddaughter, to PHILIP BOSINNEY, a promising but impoverished architect. Most of the family, including Old Jolyon, are opposed to the marriage because Bosinney has neither income nor property. June has agreed not to marry until Bosinney makes at least £400 a year. Unlike her father, Young JOLYON, June tries to follow Forsyte principles. Fifteen years before, Young Jolyon ran away with June's foreign governess. He married her nine years later when June's mother died. Young Jolyon is not at his daughter's engagement party—he has, as the Forsytes see it, forfeited his right to be there. June goes away for a brief visit and Old Jolyon is overcome by loneliness. He is suddenly desperately anxious to see his estranged son and he finds Young Jolyon at his club and invites him to his house. Young Jolyon is touched by the old man's loneliness. It seems to him that his father has been so absorbed in the love of property that he has become almost a machine.

Others of the Forsytes are unhappy. SOAMES, Old Jolyon's nephew, is troubled by the total indifference of his beautiful wife, IRENE, who refused his first five proposals of marriage and then consented only after Soames promised to restore her freedom if their marriage should prove a failure. Soames's greatest fault is that he is a Forsyte at heart—his chief interest is money. Soames decides to try to capture his wife's love by building a country house for her. He buys a substantial site at Robin Hill and hires Bosinney to design the house. Bosinney and Soames argue about where the house should stand. Bosinney's idea prevails, and Soames cannot understand how he can let this architect, whom he secretly despises, overrule his opinions. Bosinney seems to get along well with Irene, and Soames takes this to mean that his wife is coming around to the idea of having a country house. At the end of September, ANN FORSYTE, Old Jolyon's sister, dies.

and the older Forsytes live in fear of a scandal. June and Old Jolyon return from their trip. June is in better spirits. Old Jolyon is annoyed with Soames for suing Bosinney: such a thing is not becoming to a "man of property." Distraught by his love for Irene and the impending lawsuit, Bosinney begins wandering the foggy London streets at night. The lawsuit is tried and Soames easily wins a judgment that will bankrupt Bosinney. Soames arrives home and finds that Irene has left him. June goes to Bosinney's rooms and finds Irene there waiting for him. The women argue and Irene runs away. That very evening Bosinney is run down and killed by a carriage in the fog. Suicide is suspected. Because she now has no other place to go,

Irene returns to Soames, who is broken with despair. Old Jolyon buys Robin Hill from Soames and plans to give it to Young Jolyon, to whom he is now fully reconciled.

INTERLUDE:
INDIAN SUMMER OF A FORSYTE

Irene has left Soames for good and gives piano lessons to earn her living. Old Jolyon, with June and Young Jolyon, lives at Robin Hill. One spring day in the early '90s, Old Jolyon encounters Irene on the grounds of Robin Hill. The old man is delighted to see her and she visits and entertains him. Old Jolyon visits Irene in London and they grow very close. He decides to leave Irene £15,000 in his will, not caring what the other Forsytes will think. Toward the end of July he begins to fail in health. June is due to return soon, so Irene no longer visits Robin Hill. Old Jolyon writes to Irene, telling her that he misses the pleasure she gave him. She telegraphs that she will come to see him. Old Jolyon dies that afternoon.

In Chancery

Part I. Several years have passed. Many of the older Forsytes are dead. (Young) Jolyon, now a widower, is trustee of Irene's inheritance from Old Jolyon. Soames has amassed greater and greater wealth. Lonely, he has been paying attention to a French girl, ANNETTE LAMOTTE. But Soames is not divorced. His sister WINIFRED is also having trouble; her husband, MONTAGUE DARTIE, has stolen her pearls and run off with a Spanish dancer. Soames recommends a divorce to Winifred, who is confused. Soames wants to introduce Winifred's son VAL to Jolyon's son Jolly; both of them will soon be at Oxford. Soames decides that he, too, must seek a divorce, and Jolyon says he will speak to Irene and see what can be arranged (until now Jolyon has seen Irene only three times in his life). Val meets Holly and is impressed by her. They make a date for the next day. Jolyon goes to see Irene, who tells him she has been leading an exemplary life and can provide no grounds for divorce. Soames becomes enraged and accuses Jolyon of having a special interest in Irene, as Old Jolyon had had before him. Soames is determined to be free and marry Annette, but a few days later Soames visits Irene and realizes he is still in love with her. Irene treats him coolly and asks him to leave.

The Boer War begins and the Forsytes worry about their South African investments. Irene tells Jolyon that Soames has been to see her and she is now afraid to be alone; Soames tells Jolyon he is thinking of re-exercising his rights as Irene's husband. Soames now will do anything Irene wishes, if she will only return.

Part II. Val and Jolly meet at Oxford and are not attracted to each other. Val disapproves of Jolly's "pro-Boer" sentiments. This upsets Holly, who loves Val. Meanwhile, in London, Soames calls on Irene again, this time taking with him an expen-

sive diamond brooch. It is Irene's 37th birthday. Soames has not changed much; just as he had expected to gain her love by building a house, he now assumes he can do it with jewelry. Irene repulses his advances. Soames leaves humiliated, certain she has a lover. Jolyon and June visit Irene and both tell her she must never give in to Soames. Irene determines to go abroad. Jolyon encourages her. He muses that his pity for her is akin to love. Soames, in no way daunted by Irene's departure, hires detectives to dog her steps. Winifred writes to her husband, who is in Buenos Aires, and tells him that everything will be forgiven if he will only come back. Soames, however, is set upon getting a divorce for his sister.

Part II. The following April Soames's house is half finished. Soames thinks the cost exorbitant and protests to Bosinney, who goes into a rage. Soames, afraid that Bosinney will abandon the house, is conciliatory. One night when Bosinney goes to Soames's London house to meet June she has not finished dressing and he spends time with Irene. June overhears them and is disturbed. The next Sunday Irene persuades Uncle SWITHIN FORSYTE to drive to Robin Hill. Swithin is tired when they arrive and falls asleep, leaving Bosinney and Irene alone. Bosinney kisses Irene and confesses his love for her. Irene becomes distraught. On the way home, she tells Swithin she does not care if she ever gets home.

The house is completed. Bosinney asks Soames for a free hand in decorating it and Soames consents, up to £12,000. Old Jolyon has been seeing Young Jolyon from time to time. Younger Jolyon has two children born of his second marriage, JOLLY, a boy, and HOLLY, a girl. Old Jolyon confides to Young Jolyon that he thinks Bosinney is behaving badly toward June. June, suspicious of Irene, no longer sees much of her, but at a ball given by ROGER FORSYTE, June catches sight of Bosinney and Irene gazing at each other lovingly. She feels ill and goes home. Soames also notices it and is disturbed. June, heartsick, goes off with Old Jolyon on a holiday, and Old Jolyon asks Young Jolyon to ask Bosinney about his intentions. Young Jolyon does so but accomplishes nothing. Irene asks Soames to let her go, but he refuses, contending that she is his property. The house at Robin Hill is finished. Soames tells his father, JAMES FORSYTE, that Irene does not intend to live in it. James tries to interfere and Irene rebukes him. Bosinney sends Soames the final bill and once again Soames says it is excessive. Soames decides to sue Bosinney, and also he accuses Irene of carrying on with Bosinney. Irene locks Soames out of their bedroom. One night Soames breaks in and takes Irene by force, which disgusts her.

Part III. The house at Robin Hill remains uninhabited. Soames sues Bosinney for the cost in excess of the estimate. Irene has a separate bedroom and refuses to have anything to do with Soames. London gossip has linked the names of Irene and Bosinney

Irene and Old Jolyon

Jolly and Val have a violent disagreement about the war in South Africa. Jolyon visits Irene in Paris, but his trip is cut short by a message from Jolly, who has enlisted to fight in the Boer War. Winifred's divorce suit comes to trial and Val is disgusted at having his name bandied about in court. He asks Holly to marry him, which Jolly overhears. Holly accepts and Jolly steps forward and challenges Val to go to war with him. Val accepts the challenge. Soames is now vaguely suspicious of Jolyon. Montague returns to Winifred and Soames is furious, for Winifred's divorce would have made a precedent for his own.

Part III. Soames goes to Paris, meets Irene, and begs her again to return to him—all he wants is a child. He promises her a separate house, but nothing can sway her hatred. Soames, sick with anger, returns to England and visits Annette, whom he tells he is seeking a divorce. Jolyon learns that Jolly, in the army, is down with enteric fever. Both June and Holly have left Robin Hill to join the Red Cross. Irene returns from Paris and Jolyon is overcome by a feeling of love for her, but he says nothing because of his anguish about Jolly. Jolyon does not know that Jolly is already dead. Soames' detectives have traced Irene and reported her meetings with Jolyon. Soames serves papers on both of them. He is delighted by this chance to disgrace both Irene and Jolyon. Just as Irene and Jolyon are preparing to leave England and live abroad, they receive news of Jolly's death. Val and Holly are married. Soames wins his divorce and proposes to Annette Lamotte. They are married in Paris in January, 1901. Jolyon and Irene are married and she gives birth to a son. They name him JON. Annette is due to have a baby in November. When the baby is about to be born, Soames is told he will have to choose between saving the mother or the child. The doctor says he cannot save both. Soames chooses to save the life of the child—he still wants

an heir to his property. Fortunately, both mother and child survive. Soames now has a daughter, whom he names FLEUR. Shortly after this, Soames old father, James, dies. The Forsytes are going one by one.

INTERLUDE: AWAKENING

Irene is now middle-aged, but she is happier than she has ever been before. She is a warm and loving mother to her 8-year-old Jon. It is 1909.

To Let

Part I. On May 12, 1920, Soames Forsyte visits a small art gallery off Cook Street. He meets a young man named MICHAEL MONT and invites him to his house to see his picture collection. At the exhibit Soames becomes conscious of a woman and young man near him and realizes they are Irene and her son Jon, who is six months older than Fleur, his daughter, whom he expects at any moment. Fleur arives and Soames observes Jon admiring her. Fleur and Soames leave and she tells him that Val and Holly have decided to start training race horses. Fleur has her heart set on visiting them and Soames is unhappy about it. They go to a tea house, where they encounter Irene and Jon once again. Fleur has dropped her handkerchief in the gallery and Jon now returns it to her. They are alone for a moment and they learn that they have the same surname. Soames hurries Fleur away. Fleur questions her father and learns there has been a family feud. Jon knows nothing of it. He continues to see Fleur and she and Jon are convinced of their love for each other. While Fleur is away, Michael Mont comes to see Soames's pictures and brings PROSPER PROFOND, who is Annette's secret lover. Fleur runs across Michael Mont, who shows great interest in her. Soames begins to worry about his daughter, though he knows nothing of her meeting with Jon.

Part II. Irene takes Jon to Spain for a short holiday. Jon is lovesick away from

Fleur. Irene has a sense of what is wrong, but they never discuss the matter. At home, June reproaches Jolyon for concealing the truth about the family from Jon. June meets Fleur, who forthrightly asks why there has been a feud. June will not answer, but she warns Fleur of the danger of loving Jon. Fleur learns about the famimly feud from Prosper Profond and her aunt Winifred. Fleur declares to herself that she does not care—she means to have Jon. She, too, is a Forsyte, with a sense of property. Michael Mont asks Soames's permission to court Fleur. Soames gives a half-hearted consent. Soames is shocked when he learns of Annette's infidelity with Prosper Profond from an anonymous letter. He confronts her and she admits it but promises there will be no scandal. Fleur tries to rush Jon into marriage, but he fears he will hurt his parents. Fleur tells Soames she is in love with Jon and suggests that the past be buried. Soames is angry; he says Fleur will have only herself to blame if her life turns to misery. Michael Mont tries to court Fleur but she ignores him. Annette returns to Paris to live with her mother. Fleur is all Soames has left.

Part III. Jolyon writes Jon a letter that reveals the full story of the family's past, but he hesitates to give the letter to Jon. Jon tells his father that he has become engaged to Fleur. Jolyon, who is now 72, says he will not live much longer and Jon becomes upset. Jolyon gives his son the letter. Jon reads it and cannot believe that Soames ever looked upon a woman as "property." Jolyon dies and Jon is in an emotional turmoil about Fleur. He accuses Fleur of having concealed the truth about Irene and Soames from him. She says she lied because of her love and begs him not to give her up. Jon now feels that Fleur comes from the enemy camp—that she, like her father, is hostile to him and his mother Irene. Soames sees Irene and they decide that the decision rests with Jon. After struggling with himself, Jon feels he owes too much to his mother and announces that he cannot marry Fleur. Fleur is hysterical when Soames reports Jon's decision. Jon goes to America. Irene promises to follow him. On the rebound Fleur marries Michael Mont, an excellent match in Forsyte terms, for Mont is the heir to an ancient baronetcy. Fleur still loves Jon and she seeks counsel from June. June tells her she must fight life and the pain of living will be less. Not long after, Soames's last uncle, old Timothy Forsyte, dies. For Soames this marks the end of an age, the Forsyte age. He feels as though the Forsyte way of life was more like an empty house with a "To Let" sign on it.

The Forty Days of Musa Dagh

Novel by Franz Werfel, 1890–1945. Published and © 1934 by Viking Press, New York. Translation from the German by Geoffrey Dunlop.

THIS FIRST BIG SUCCESS by Franz Werfel was, like his later and greater success *The Song of Bernadette*, a novel formed on a historical incident. It tells how a small number of Christian Armenians, made desperate by ingrained recollection of a century of persecution by the Moslem Turks, fought a brave but hopeless fight in a mountain fastness. Werfel, himself a Jew, had an emotional sense of oneness with any person or people striving for spiritual freedom. His sincerity helps to make this well-written novel appealing.

Book I. GABRIEL BAGRADIAN has lived in Paris for 23 years and has almost forgotten his native village of Yoghonoluk, Syria. Now, in 1915, he must return to handle the business affairs of his dying brother, AVETIS. Gabriel takes with him his wife JULIETTE and his son STEPHAN. The land seems strange to Gabriel, for he has become more French than Armenian, but Stephan is delighted to be in his father's homeland. Gabriel wants to send his wife and child to Switzerland, but Stephan says he will not go. Gabriel concedes that it would be better for Juliette and the child to remain with him. World War I is raging across Europe and life seems safer in the small Syrian village. Avetis dies and Gabriel settles down to wait out the war.

Representatives of the Caliph of the Ottoman Empire come to the village to collect all foreign passports. Gabriel protests to the officials in Antioch, saying that he has lived a great part of his life in France and is not used to the deprivation of liberty. He is told that he is overconcerned, that the collection of the passports is merely a wartime precaution. Gabriel later hears that the War Ministry has decreed that all Armenians within the Ottoman Empire be deprived of weapons and subjected to forced labor. A short time later Gabriel also hears that all rich and distinguished Armenian families will be persecuted and liquidated. His influential Moslem friend the Agha RIFAAT BEREKET promises Gabriel that he will do all he can to prevent the persecutions, but Gabriel is still very disturbed. He rides back to Yoghonoluk and begins to gather information about the number of Armenian men who are old enough to fight. Several days later Gabriel learns from TER HAIGASUN, the Catholic pastor of Yoghonoluk, that mass arrests of Armenians have already been made in Antioch and Istanbul. All Armenian newspapers have been shut down, all Armenian shops and businesses have been closed, and fifteen Armenians have been hanged as an example to the entire population. Gabriel knows there is no time to lose. The Turkish government is clearly planning a purge of all Christians. Gabriel is determined not to be exiled or exterminated by the Turkish Government. He begins a geographic survey of Musa Dagh, a great mountain that rises like a wall between the Armenian communities of the Ottoman Empire and the sea. Gabriel goes to map the mountain and when he comes down he feels certain it is a perfect natural stronghold, a place of asylum for the Armenian people.

The Turkish government has been busy rounding up Armenians throughout the land. Gabriel hears a report that Turkish troops will enter Yoghonoluk within a few days. Gabriel calls a meeting of all the inhabitants of Yoghonoluk and and the surrounding villages. He presents his plan to occupy and defend Musa Dagh and asks the villagers for their approval. Many of them say they would prefer to fight the Turks at their own doorsteps, that they would rather die defending the houses in which they have always lived than retreat to a remote mountaintop. Pastor NOKHUDIAN, the Protestant minister, says that neither fighting nor fleeing to Musa Dagh is sensible.

He urges the villagers to apply for internment in a concentration camp. The votes are counted. Pastor Nokhudian's congregation has chosen exile. The rest of the people support Gabriel. Ter Haigasun is elected the leader of the villagers who will depart for Musa Dagh. Food and medical supplies are secretly carried to the mountain, under cover of night. Gabriel also arranges with Pastor Nokhudian to tell the Turks that the Armenians going to Musa Dagh have packed their belongings and set out into exile. Also Pastor Nokhudian is to tell the Turks that he cannot say exactly

Gabriel captured by the Turks

which road the exiles took, that they set out in small bands in every conceivable direction. Ter Haigasum strips his church of all its sacred objects and places them in wooden boxes. Even the bells of the church are taken down. A huge burial ceremony of the objects and the bells is held, and to the assembled Armenians it is like the burial of their race. Gabriel knows that the defense of Musa Dagh will not be as easy as it first seemed. The Armenians have almost no weapons of defense. In fact, there are only a few hundred armed men to protect a community of 5,000. The Armenians make their solemn journey to Musa Dagh in the darkness of night.

Book II. Food is rationed on Musa Dagh and daily tasks are assigned to each person. Ter Haigasun sets up a small tent with an altar, which becomes the spiritual center of the community. Gabriel insists that the strictest discipline be enforced and a 24-hour vigilance set. For five days life on Musa Dagh is a bustle of activity. Trenches are dug and weapons are prepared for immediate use. The Turks attack but they are repulsed and a considerable amount of ammunition and other supplies is captured from them. Some Turkish soldiers also fall into the hands of the defenders, and Gabriel can do nothing to prevent the Armenians from killing their captives. The Turks defer their next attack for several days. Gabriel uses this period of grace to complete his defenses. Just as his work is done, Turkish shells begin falling all about the enclosure. The grain warehouse is set on fire and destroyed—a major catastrophe—and six noncombatants are wounded. The defenders are running low on ammunition and one of the commanders hits upon the idea of catapulting huge stones at the Turks. The Armenians set up catapults and rain stones upon the western group of the Turkish besiegers. The stones start an avalanche, and more than half the Turkish troops are killed or wounded. The Turks attack again in a few days, this time with more than 2,000 highly trained men. They make grave breaches in the defense system of Musa Dagh. The first line of trenches is overrun and captured, but it is regained by Gabriel's troops during a nighttime skirmish. Gabriel starts a brushfire on the side of the mountain and it races downward toward the valley, driving the Turks before it. Gabriel is having difficulty with his wife, who no longer wishes to stay on Musa Dagh. She knows that capture and death are only a matter of time. Gabriel is too distracted to appease Juliette and she becomes ill. Gabriel finds her in another man's tent. He has not recovered from this shock when he learns that Stephan has run away with another boy to seek the help of the American consul, Mr. MORGENTHAU.

Book III. Stephan tries to return to Musa Dagh but falls into the hands of Turkish soldiers. He is taken to a Turkoman village square and stripped naked. He refuses to tell his name, but someone in the crowd recognizes him as Gabriel's son. The Turks fall upon him like wild dogs. That night his body is found, mangled and torn, lying in the Yoghonoluk churchyard. Gabriel is given the body of his son. The end of Musa Dagh is close. Turkish soldiers have succeeded in capturing all of the Armenians' domestic animals. Every sheep, every lamb, every goat, even all the donkeys, have disappeared. The food supplies can now last only three or four days. After that, famine! A fever epidemic has begun to spread within the community on Musa Dagh. The Agha Rifaat Bereket comes to see Gabriel on Musa Dagh. He urges Gabriel to think of

the future and give up the defense of the mountain. Gabriel listens patiently, but he replies that he cannot abandon his people. The agha has brought grain and sugar and tobacco as his gift and tribute to the refugees on Musa Dagh. The provisions are distributed in the village square. On the 34th day of exile on Musa Dagh, 200 people are down with fever. By nightfall, 43 die. On the 40th day there is total famine. Gabriel plans a last attack. His plan is aborted when deserters set fire to the build-

ings holding all the refugees' ammunition. The Turks capture the whole southern half of the mountain. In the morning, a French warship begins shelling the Turks in the valley. The Turks beat a quick retreat. Gabriel takes advantage of the Turkish confusion to lead the Armenians from Musa Dagh to the seacoast, where they are all taken aboard French ships. Gabriel then returns to the mountain. He wishes to see Stephan's grave. He reaches the grave and a Turkish soldier spies him and fells him with a single bullet in the temple. Now two Bagradians lie dead on Musa Dagh.

For Whom the Bell Tolls

Novel by Ernest Hemingway, 1898–1961.

Published 1940 by Charles Scribner's Sons, New York. © 1940 by Ernest Hemingway.

THE SPANISH GOVERNMENT takes the official position that everyone who fought for the Loyalists (or Nationalists) in the Spanish Civil War of 1936–38 was *ipso facto* a Communist. No exceptions. Hemingway's novel of that war is eloquent refutation of that position. The novel may not be the best Hemingway on record, and some critics were unkind enough to say it never would have been a best-seller without the sleeping bag, but it is still a great novel. The title is from a passage by the revered and reverend Dr. John Donne, quoted in the book, affirming man's racial unity where the "racial" applies to the human race, not one of its subdivisions. Beginning with "No man is an iland," Donne goes on to warn, "Do not send to ask for whom the bell tolls. It tolls for thee."

Chaps. 1–6. ROBERT JORDAN, an American, is given the assignment of blowing up a bridge for the Spanish Loyalist guerrillas before they begin an attack. He is led by the old man ANSELMO up a long road to join Anselmo's compatriots. On the way they meet PABLO, the leader of the guerrilla band, who takes them to the gypsy camp where they make their headquarters. There Jordan is fed by MARIA, a refugee from the prison at Valladolid, who is a very beautiful girl despite her close-cropped head. PILAR, the wife of Pablo, is stronger than her husband and more of a leader. She greets the American as a comrade but warns him to be easy with Maria, whom she guards with strange affection. Jordan goes to see the bridge and finds the problem of its demolition not a difficult one. Orders were that this bridge must be blown up with split-second timing. Anselmo warns Jordan to be wary of Pablo, who was once a brave man but now drinks and is a coward. Returning to the cave, Jordan finds that Pablo does not want the bridge blown up as it will bring the enemy on them. Pablo is overruled by Pilar, who cruelly reminds him that it is she that the men trust and obey. For a moment, Jordan feels that he must kill Pablo, but decides rather to spare his life but watch him carefully.

Chaps. 7–11. The girl, Maria, comes to Jordan in the middle of the night to share his sleeping bag. She tells him that she loves him and that her feeling for him will erase all the horrible things that were done to her in prison. Jordan is soothed by her childlike tenderness and they become bound to each other in their love.

The next morning there is a concentration of the enemy's planes in their vicinity. Jordan goes with Pilar and Maria to see EL SORDO, another guerrilla leader, who is going to aid them. It is a long walk and while they rest Pilar tells of the civil strife in her village when the Civil War began. Her unadorned recounting of the cruelties is horrifying. They go on to meet El Sordo, who is large, strong, and deaf. When he realizes that it will be his responsibility to organize the retreat in daylight after the work has been done, he is worried. Both he and Pilar ask about Jordan's nerves. El Sordo agrees to supply not only men but also the horses for their retreat.

Chaps. 12–17. On their way back to the cave after the visit to El Sordo, Pilar becomes ill. Maria attends her gently and with love. Pilar begs them to be together and happy. Her illness, she says, is due to her jealousy of what is before them. She goes on alone, leaving them to have a few precious moments of privacy. Fear enters Jordan when he realizes that his life is beginning to matter to him, for he wishes to marry Maria and take her back to the United States. He is worried about the reaction in his home town of Missoula, Montana; the people there may think he is a Red because he is trying to better the ways of the world. Not knowing how long life will be for them, he resolves to live each hour with Maria as much as possible.

By the time they reach camp it is snowing. Pablo is drunk and there is the odor of treachery around him. He knows that as long as the snow falls they will all have to stay in the cave. He baits Jordan and be-

comes so objectionable that Pilar drives him from the cave. They all now agree that Pablo is no longer trustworthy and must be killed.

Chaps. 18–23. Jordan completes his planning for the demolition while Pablo pretends to work on his plans for the retreat. Jordan's mind dreams of living in Madrid with Maria when all this is finished. The snowstorm ends during the night and while Maria sleeps on Jordan's shoulder in the sleeping bag, Jordan becomes aware that something is happening. He goes out and discovers that Pablo has destroyed the explosives and detonators.

Chaps. 24–30. El Sordo is attacked but Jordan will allow none of his band to go to his aid, as it is hopeless. In the preparations for the blast, each has his specific job. Jordan and Anselmo hate their task, which is to kill the young sentry who guards the opposite side of the bridge. Jordan does not deceive himself any longer about his beliefs. He knows that he is not a real Marxist holding life cheaply. He believes in liberty, equality, and fraternity. His love for Maria has cut away the illusions of "live today, die tomorrow" for the cause.

Sordo puts up a strong fight by using all his peasant ingenuity. He places his men in strategic places among the rocks. Sordo knows that he will in all probability be able to kill just one, but he promises himself that it will be the leader. The enemy climb the hill and all is quiet, but at the first crack of Sordo's rifle they are alert. It is too late, for the shot kills their leader. They pour bullets into the hillside, killing Sordo and all his men. To prove what they have done, they cut off the heads of the dead and fasten them to the horses as they start back to their headquarters. Pablo returns, penitent. He tells Jordan that all is not lost, as he can do more for them now that he is convinced of the necessity of blowing the bridge.

Chaps. 30–36. The night before the blowing comes and all orders are given. Everyone knows exactly what he must do in the morning. Jordan lies quietly with Maria in their sleeping bag and they talk not of the morrow but of their future together. He tells her that he would like them to be married. Maria tells him that Pilar has told her that they will all be dead the next day. Jordan reassures her. He says they will marry themselves before they go to sleep, and she is no longer afraid. Peace comes to Maria, but there is no sleep for Jordan. He knows Pilar is right and there is little chance that they will come out alive.

Chaps. 37–42. To show his confidence in Jordan, Pablo arrives the next morning with five new men and fresh horses. Pablo leads his men in an attack on the Fascists approaching the bridge, to prevent their crossing before the bridge is destroyed. The time for the demolition is the beginning of the Loyalists' air attack on the Fascist lines. Lying deep in a bed of pine needles, Jordan waits to pull the pins from the hand grenades. The noise of the exploding bombs gives him his signal and he sets the plans in motion. The bridge shoots high into the air. He escapes the flying debris but the old man Anselmo is killed by one of the steel girders. Jordan knows Pablo's treacherous destruction of the detonators is to blame for this unnecessary death.

Chap. 43. Maria is waiting for news of Robert's safety and has their horses with her. She prays until she hears Pilar shouting to her that the bridge has been blown and Jordan is safe. As she thanks God for this news, a squadron of Fascist planes flies over. The remnants of the guerrilla band wait for Pablo. When Pablo finally runs to meet them, Jordan realizes that he is late because he has killed his men and taken their horses. Jordan accuses him of having done this, but Pablo shrugs it off because the men were not part of his band and he needed the horses. They begin their retreat across the road, which may at any moment be swept with enemy fire. Jordan chooses Pablo to lead the way. He is determined that nothing happen to Maria and puts her on the second horse. Pilar follows with the remaining two men. Jordan brings up the rear to insure the safety of those before him. They are strafed by enemy fire and Jordan's horse is hit. It swerves and falls on Jordan's leg. The leg is badly broken and the others drag him across the road. He knows that he will not be able to ride a horse to safety. Jordan knows Maria will insist on staying with him and he tells Pablo that when he gives the signal they are to take Maria with them by force if necessary.

Maria comes to him to do what she can for his leg and he prepares her for their separation. He tells her that she must go on for his sake and they will meet somewhere, sometime, for man does not know what lies beyond this life. She listens silently but refuses to go. Pilar and Pablo lift her, crying and struggling, onto her horse and they ride away.

Now at last there are no problems. Jordan drags himself to a tree and props himself up to wait. He tries to believe what he has told Maria, that he will always be with her. His thoughts review all he has done in Spain and the fight for a cause he believes is right. Pilar, he knows, will take care of Maria and Pablo will see that they get away to a safe place. As for the war, he knows it will be many years before the little people win, and the struggle will go until one day peace will come to the world. The thought of ending his agony by shooting himself enters his mind, but he rejects it because he wants to kill at least one of the approaching Fascists. Finally he sees them over the slope and knows that his minutes are few. He finds that he is calm—the fight has been worth while and his luck held until the very end. He puts the sights of his rifle on the nearest approaching Fascist.

Jordan's work is effective and the bridge is blown up

The Fountain

Novel by Charles Morgan, 1894-1958. Published 1932 by Alfred A. Knopf, New York. © 1932 by Charles Morgan.

CHARLES MORGAN WROTE a succession of excellent novels, of which *The Fountain* is often ranked as his best. Through his character Alison he certainly expresses much of his own feeling toward the beauties of a life of scholarship and contemplation, and the love affair, though conceivably introduced to satisfy public demand, is treated with the utmost skill.

Book 1. LEWIS ALISON, an English army officer in World War I, is in a German prisoner-of-war camp in an old fortress in Holland. His fellow officers and the men in his barracks chafe at the monotony but Alison is happy, for the first time in his life, to have to make no decisions. He is an idealist and in civilian life is a publisher. He plans to read continually and then write a history of the contemplative life. The commandant invites Alison and his friend BALLATER to lunch in his quarters. There Alison meets his old friends the Dutch Baron and Baroness VAN LEYDEN. The baroness's first husband was an Englishman named QUILLAN and Alison tutored their daughter JULIE when he was a student at Oxford. He hears that Julie is now married to a German, RUPERT NARWITZ. General parole is granted to the prisoners after several months of internment and Ballater makes arrangements for Alison and himself to live in a cottage at Enkendaal, the van Leydens' estate. They arrive there and are made welcome.

Book 2. Alison clearly remembers Julie as a child, but he is not prepared for her beauty as a young woman. She has been married for three months but she is tortured by the fact that her husband is a German officer at the front while her English blood makes her urgently desire a victory for Britain. Alison and Julie find themselves drawn together and they establish secret intimacy. Alison finds his reading and research constantly interrupted by his unexpressed thoughts of love for Julie. The old baron gives Alison free run of his famous library and the key to the unpublished papers of his dead uncle, DIRK VAN LEYDEN. The papers are filled with wonderful philosophical thoughts expressed in eloquent prose, and Alison starts to prepare them for publication. This is with the approval of the baron. Julie is rarely alone with him but even when they are with others they manage to communicate their unspoken feelings. News comes that the

English fleet has been severely beaten and the neutral Dutch assume the war will quickly end. Julie is frantic at the thought that England will lose the war and she will have to return to the husband she now knows she does not love. She entreats Alison to take her somewhere where they can be alone. They go off together and she tells him of her deep love for him. Alison returns her love with a greater depth and passion than she had believed possible and this frightens her, for she is sure that Alison will try to make her into another person to fit his idea of perfection. They return to the castle and she writes him begging him to leave Enkendaal and forget her, since she is half English and half Dutch and is married to a dedicated German.

Book 3. Alison immediately leaves, and weeks pass before he writes to Julie and tells her she is the only love of his life. They engage in a long and frequent correspondence. Julie is finally convinced that Alison understands that no matter how strong her love for him, she will never upset the long-established pattern of her parents' and her husband's lives. She suggests that she and Alison can be together as lovers until it is time for her to return and face her responsibilities. Julie goes to The Hague with her stepfather and expects Alison to meet her there. He confuses the date of their arrival and arrives the day Julie is leaving, but the baron invites him to return with them to the castle.

Book 4. Alison and Julie return to the castle together and soon they become lovers. In the warmth of their love the winter passes quickly. Then the abdication of the czar in Russia indicates that the war may soon end, and Julie is again faced with the thought of living without Alison. She now knows she cannot part from him. Alison has finished editing the Dirk van Leyden papers and he and Julie agree to withhold this fact from the baron so that their idyll may continue at Enkendaal. One afternoon Julie announces to her assembled family that Rupert, her husband, will arrive in three days. He has written to Julie that he is extremely ill and incapacitated by the loss of his right arm and right leg, and that he is really coming to Enkendaal to die. He says that the only thing that now means anything to him is to be with her when he dies. Alison is shocked at the news and announces that he has finished the van Leyden papers and will be leaving the castle to live in the cottage. Later, when they are alone, Julie tells Alison that she needs him more than ever now and though they will be parted for a short while when Rupert comes, she loves him and will not give him up.

Book 5. Julie is astonished, when she sees Rupert, by the extent of her compassion for him. He has grown greatly in spirit and wisdom and his love for her is the strength that keeps him alive. Rupert hears that Alison is a scholar and asks to meet him. They find themselves in accord and they become friends. Julie becomes Ru-

pert's slave and sees that his every wish is granted, but she cannot bring herself to show him physical affection and Rupert finally realizes that there is love between Julie and Alison. This knowledge robs him of his last desire to live and he sinks rapidly. Hovering between life and death, he is no longer affected by jealousy and he wishes only to die in peace. He calls Julie and Alison to him and tells them he is aware of their love and does not wish a feeling of guilt to part them. Death comes to Rupert as he cries out the name of Julie.

Books 6–7. Alison is one of the British prisoners in Holland who are given amnesty by the Germans and allowed to return to England. He is affected by Rupert's death and he leaves Enkendaal without having a last meeting with Julie. Julie, dazed by her husband's death, does not notice an intrigue that is developing around her: Her mother is anxious for the baron not to know about Julie's affair with Alison. She seeks to persuade Julie that any remarriage must be with a rich man, not with Alison, who is poor. The baron's children by his first wife hate Julie and her mother. They tell the old man what has been going on. The baron is shocked but he loves his stepdaughter and at first refuses to believe. He asks Julie and she tells him the truth. His visible hurt causes Julie to leave the castle and join Alison in The Hague, where he is waiting to be transferred to England. Julie leaves with him on the transport. As they leave the coast of Holland they know that in their marriage they will hold the enchantment of their first days of love.

The Four Horsemen of the Apocalypse

Novel by Vicente Blasco Ibáñez, 1867–1928.
Published 1916. In English translation by Charlotte Brewster Jordan, published & © 1918 by E. P. Dutton, New York.

THE SPANISH NOVELIST Blasco Ibáñez scored his greatest international success with *The Four Horsemen*. In the United States the book's popularity was helped greatly by the silent motion picture made of it. Among other things, the motion picture introduced to stardom Rudolph Valentino, who became the most adulated star of all time. Blasco Ibáñez, a social-ist, was exiled from Spain and lived in South America, which gave him the background for this combined epic of an Argentine family and war novel about World War I. The Apocalypse, in Roman Catholic Bibles, is the name of the last book of the New Testament, which in Protestant Bibles is called the Revelation of St. John the Divine. The "four horsemen" are described in Chapter 6. Death rides a pale horse; the riders of the other three horses—white, red, and black—are not named and their exact allegorical representations are disputed. Blasco Ibáñez called them War, Pestilence (or Disease), and Famine.

Part I. MARCELO DESNOYER flees his native France to avoid military service in the war of 1870 and goes to Argentina. He stays in Buenos Aires for a time and then goes to work for JULIO MADARIAGA, a wealthy Spanish rancher. Don Julio, an eccentric and often tyrannical employer, is attacked by a frenzied peon, and Marcelo saves his life. Don Julio rewards him by making him manager of his vast estates and admits him into the family circle, which consists of Madariaga's wife CHINA and their two daughters, LUISA and ELENA. Luisa and Marcelo fall in love and Don Julio consents to their marriage because he admires Desnoyer's serious nature and ability. Soon after, Don Julio hires KARL HARTROTT, a young German, to assist Marcelo. Karl incurs Don Julio's wrath by running away with Elena. Marcelo secretly supports them until the death of China, when they are permitted to return home; but Don Julio ignores them and their four sons and is not happy until Luisa and Marcelo present him with a grandson, who he insists bear his name JULIO. He spoils and pampers the child. When death finally claims the old man, he leaves everyone rich, even Karl and Elena (to their surprise) but young Julio Desnoyer is the only grand-child made independently wealthy in his own right. The Desnoyers move to Buenos Aires and Karl and Elena Hartrott liquidate their Argentine holdings and take their large family to Berlin.

Julio Desnoyer and his younger sister, CHICHI, bored with life in Buenos Aires, persuade their father to return to Paris to make their home there. Marcelo, now wealthy, finds Paris one large bargain center and he spends his days tracking down treasures to be bought for a third of their value. Young Julio decides to become an artist and takes a large comfortable studio that immediately becomes the center for a group of lazy, dissolute companions. Julio does little painting but pays the bills for his companions' pleasures. Marcelo, disgusted, cuts off his son's funds. Just as Julio's creditors are beginning to catch up with him, the tango becomes all the rage in Paris. Julio, skilled at this dance, becomes the social pet of the hour. Even old, respectable Senator LACOUR is delighted to have him as a guest at the engagement party of his son, RENÉ, to Chichi, though Julio has been estranged from his father. Lacour and Marcelo have neighboring estates in the country and have become staunch friends.

273

Julio meets MARGUERITE LAURIER at the Lacours'. She is young, beautiful, middle-class, and bored with her marriage to an upright, honest, dull gentleman who makes motor cars. She is delighted to play at love with Julio. After a few months they are passionately involved. They are discovered in Julio's studio by the husband, who demands a divorce. Julio decides to marry Marguerite after her divorce and returns to Argentina to raise money on his holdings, as his father opposes the match and refuses to aid them. When Julio returns to Paris Europe is on the brink of war. The eldest of his German cousins arrives to warn Julio to leave Paris, as he is sure Germany will rule the world. Julio is depressed, because he loves France. He is a republican at heart and he is sure the four horsemen of the Apocalypse, the four scourges of the earth, War, Famine, Disease, and Death, will sweep brutally over the world. France mobilizes and World War I begins.

Part II. Marcelo Desnoyer is frightened by the war but wishes he were not 70 so he could join in the defense of his native land against the oncoming Boche. Julio Desnoyer finds he is no longer an idol with his dancing. Uniforms and somber war bulletins have replaced the gaiety of Paris. Even his beloved, frivolous Marguerite trains to be a nurse. Julio feels out of things, and not at all lucky that he is an Argentinian and safe from conscription. His money is hard to get now because bank withdrawals are restricted. Luisa Desnoyer is frantic as the Germans make progress toward Paris. Her sister Elena is in the house, separated from her German family, and is constantly in hysterics. Marcelo sends the women to the north of Spain, where they will be safe, but he refuses to go and wanders daily through the city, giving tobacco to soldiers. The Germans press perilously near and Marcelo decides he must go to protect his rich belongings at his country estate at Villeblanche. Lacour tries to dissuade him, confiding that the French government is leaving Paris within hours and that he will surely be killed if he ventures north, but despite the warning and the rigors of the trip Marcelo goes. The French army retreats on the road surrounding Marcelo's land and he raids his wine cellar to give his rare vintages to the bedraggled soldiers.

Julio receives a hurried note from Marguerite, saying only that she is going South. He leaves Paris to search for her all through the crowded refugee cities. Finally he discovers her near Lourdes, dressed in her nurse's uniform and leading a blind man. The blind man is her husband. Though the divorce was in process, she now feels it her duty to care for her husband. It is an expression of her patriotism, even though her love for Julio is deeper. She begs Julio never to see her again. Julio feels useless and cowardly, and resolves to return to Paris and become a volunteer. He feels he will personally be fighting his German cousins, whom he has always despised.

The estate at Villeblanche has been taken

274

Julio leaves Paris with the refugees

over by the German army. They ruthlessly kill innocent people and burn the entire village. Marcelo hides in a hut but is discovered by a German officer, who proves to be the second son of his brother-in-law Karl. He is brought back to his castle and told he will be treated courteously if he remains quiet. He prefers to be a prisoner in the cellar of his own house rather than witness the German atrocities. When Paris escapes capture, Marcelo leaves the ruins of his estate and goes back. Julio visits him in uniform and Marcelo is overcome with emotion. He warns Julio to forget any family ties with his German cousins and shoot to kill.

Part III. The Desnoyer family returns to

Paris, which is considered out of danger and turns back to normal. Julio is wounded and comes home a hero on sick leave. Old Marcelo, proud of his son, can hardly bear to have him out of sight. One day while they are walking they pass Marguerite, who refuses to recognize Julio; but the old man sees the longing and love in her face and forgives her for making his son unhappy. After Julio has returned to the front, René Lacour is seriously wounded and brought to a hospital in Paris. He and Chichi are married before he leaves the hospital and she devotes herself entirely to his recovery.

Senator Lacour takes Marcelo on a tour of the front so that he may see Julio. Julio is popular with his men and is respected for his leadership and courage. It is obvious to Marcelo that his son has become a man.

Elena is still with the Desnoyers in Paris and receives news of her family in Germany by way of Switzerland. Two of her soldier sons are dead and a third is seriously wounded. Both her daughters have lost the men they love. Elena becomes distracted and Luisa lives in constant fear that Julio will be killed. When news comes that Julio has been killed in action, Marcelo collapses. As soon as they are permitted, the entire family make the trip to the battlefield and Julio's grave, on which there is a simple marker with the name Desnoyer. Marcelo realizes it is the end of that name. As he kneels at the grave of his son, his mind goes back to the four horsemen of the Apocalypse, of which Julio had spoken. Marcelo has a flash of intuition that the four horsemen are the eternal scourge of mankind. No matter how long they remain in hiding they eventually reappear. He feels that in his lifetime they will ride again over the earth.

Anne Frank:
The Diary of a Young Girl

Diary by Anne Frank, 1929–1944. Published 1952 by Doubleday & Co., New York. © 1952 by Otto H. Frank; © 1952 by The American Jewish Committee. Translated from the Dutch by B. M. Mooyaart-Doubleday. (PB, C317)

ANNE FRANK had aspirations to be a writer when she grew up. Her aspirations would surely have been realized had her life not been cut off, when she was 14, by the genocidal German terror. She wrote her diary while she and her family, Jews sought for destruction by German occupation forces in the Netherlands, were being hidden by civilized Dutch Christians (of whom there were many who did the same). The diary became one of the principal World War II books through its dissemination as a best-selling book, a hit Broadway play, and a major motion picture. But even without the suspenseful setting that intensified its interest, it would have been well worth reading as a remarkable baring of an adolescent girl's soul.

June 14—July 5, 1942. ANNE'S 13th birthday was two days ago. She received many presents but best of all is this Diary. Here is the friend she has been waiting for. She will call this new friend KITTY and write letters to it. She will begin with a short history of her life.

Anne and her sister MARGOT (3 years older) were born in Germany but the Frank family fled to Amsterdam to escape the German persecution of the Jews. For the last two years Jews have found life in Poland very hard. All Jews must wear yellow stars; they are not permitted to ride on trains, must stay indoors after 8 P.M., and are subjected to countless painful humiliations. In spite of these things, Anne enjoys life. LIES is her best friend and she has a special boy friend, HARRY. She likes school and ping-pong and jokes and her cat Moortje. She does complain because the weather is very hot.

July 1942–Jan. 1943. Margot Frank is "called up" (to be taken to a German concentration camp) but the Franks have made careful preparations to disappear (go into hiding). Sunday morning, July 5, they leave their house. All of them are wearing as many skirts, sweaters and other articles of clothing as possible, since Jews carrying suitcases would be stopped immediately. Daddy (Mr. Frank, called PIM) explains that they will hide in some rooms (the "Secret Annexe") behind the building where he had his office. His Dutch business associates Mr. KRALER and Mr. KOOPHUIS, and MIEP and her husband HENK, and ELLI, the secretary, will bring them food and other necessary supplies. Another Jewish family, the VAN DAANS, will join them. The Franks will have two bedrooms and there will be a room with a gas burner for Mr. and Mrs. Van Daan and a small attic room for their 16-year-old son PETER. In the daytime they must all speak in whispers and walk softly so that the men working in the office and warehouse will not know they are there. At night, when all the working people have gone home, they can go downstairs and listen to the news on the radio. A week later the Van Daans arrive, including Peter's cat MOUSCHI. One of the hardest and most important things to do is to keep busy. Anne, Margot and Peter try to keep up with their schoolwork and read books. Anne does not get along very well with Mummy, her mother. Mummy and Margot seem to be good friends but Anne cannot be sweet and good as Margot is, and though Mummy tries, she cannot understand Anne. Anne loves to talk and has been given the nickname "Miss Quack-Quack." Peter is lazy and unsociable most of the time. Daddy is the one comfort, but sometimes even he doesn't understand.

In November the Secret Annexe gets a new member and Anne a new roommate, Mr. DUSSEL, a dentist. Anne finds him a difficult roommate. He is always telling her to be quiet and he does exercises in the morning and does not understand young people. But the adult members felt that as long as there was room for one more they could not refuse refuge to a person in danger.

Jan. 1943–July 1943. Sometimes at night there are bombings. Anne is so frightened that she crawls into bed with Pim for comfort. Everyone waits for the invasion [of Europe by the Allies] that must be coming soon. Anne has grown so much that her clothes are much too small for her. There is not much food. Still there are good times.

For her 14th birthday Anne receives a poem from Daddy and a fat book on her favorite subject, Greek mythology, and everyone manages to produce some sweets for her.

July 1943–Jan. 1944. One night there are burglars downstairs. The Secret Annexe is frightened but the police do not catch them. Anne tells Kitty what a routine day is like in the Annexe. You can tell, she thinks, a lot about people from the way they behave at mealtime. Mr. Van Daan is always the first one served. He eats a lot and thinks his opinion is the only one that matters. Mrs. Van Daan complains that she is not getting her share. Peter eats quietly and never gets enough. Mr. Dussel does not like to talk at meals, except about the food. Margot is silent and eats like a bird. Mummy is talkative and polite and has a good appetite. Daddy is unselfish and "the perfect example." Anne tries to pretend that whatever the food, she is eating something delicious. The Van Daan parents quarrel a great deal. Anne begins to read the Bible and studies a lot. At Christmas she receives her first Christmas present. Miep brings a cake with "Peace 1944" written on it. Everyone is in good spirits.

Jan. 1944–July 1944. Anne reads over her past letters to Kitty and is shocked at how much she complains, especially about Mummy. She pities herself much too much, she thinks. However, she is beginning to see many things differently. There are some wonderful changes going on in her body that make her feel happy and proud. She is lonely and longs for someone to talk to. She chooses Peter. Peter and she have, she discovers, much in common. Both of them are lonely and want to love something or some-

one. Anne now feels her life has an object—to see Peter, and all day long she waits for the next meeting. She begins to visit Peter in his little attic room. Anne worries that Margot is hurt by her new friendship with Peter. The sisters write each other letters on this subject and Margot assures Anne that she could never care for Peter except as a brother. Everyone waits for the invasion. Anne is writing stories. She is very interested in genealogy, especially of royal families. She loves history and pictures of film stars. There is another burglary.

April 16, 1944, is a date Anne wants to remember always. It is the day she receives her first kiss. Mummy has forbidden her to spend so much time with Peter and Anne worries about whether it is right for a girl of 14 to allow a boy of 16 to kiss her. She feels it is so lovely that it can't be wrong. Should she tell Daddy about it? She writes a letter to Daddy about it. At first he is hurt but they talk and both feel better; Anne continues to visit Peter.

June 6, 1944, is D-Day, and with the invasion hope comes to Secret Annexe. Margot says that by September Anne may be able to go back to school. Anne continues to question her true feelings about Peter and his for her. She thinks maybe Peter is too dependent on her and that this is not really love, but she isn't sure. Anne sees that there are really two Annes. One is gay and cheerful, always making jokes, the other is quieter and deeper; but the lighter side always seems to win out.

[The last Diary entry is August 1, 1944. Three days later, August 4, the Secret Annexe was raided by the Gestapo. All its inhabitants were sent to concentration camps, and all died but Otto Frank ("Pim" in the book). Anne died in March 1945 in the dreadful Bergen-Belsen concentration camp, two months before Holland was liberated. The Diary was discovered in a pile of rubbish on the floor when the Gestapo had gone.]

All the inhabitants of the Secret Annexe were sent to concentration camps

Frankenstein

Novel by Mary Godwin Shelley, 1797–1851.
Published 1818.

BY FAR THE most famous and longest-lived of the "Gothic" or horror novels, and by many critics considered the best of them, *Frankenstein, or The Modern Prometheus*, was written by a 20-year-old girl. Mary Wollstonecraft Godwin had eloped with Shelley when she was 17, and without benefit of clergy (for his wife was still living). They were married in 1816 and she wrote *Frankenstein* in 1817, more or less for the purpose of joining in a friendly writing competition between Shelley and Byron. Though the characters in *Frankenstein* (except the monster) are stilted and unreal, the melodrama and suspense are executed with a touch of genius. Motion pictures and television have made Frankenstein and his monster known to far more millions than ever read anything by—or even heard of—Shelley and Byron.

Prologue. ROBERT WALTON, an English explorer, is aboard a ship heading for the North Pole. The ship is frozen in the polar ice, and Walton and the crew see a hulking man on a dogsled pass the ship on his way north. Later that day, a second dogsled is brought close to the ship by an ice floe and a man in weakened condition is seen on the sled. The man, a European, refuses to come aboard until he is assured that the vessel is northward bound. After resting for several days and partly regaining his strength, the man tells Walton that he is in pursuit of someone. When he hears that a sled and driver were spotted on the day he came aboard, the man becomes agitated. He tells Walton the following tale.

Chaps. 1–4. The stranger, VICTOR FRANKENSTEIN, is a Swiss of an old and distinguished family. As a boy Victor showed extraordinary ability in natural sciences and was absorbed in the works of ancient mystics and alchemists, though his father told him that such things are obsolete and trash. At 17, Victor's parents entered him in the University of Ingolstadt. His mother, having personally nursed his foster-sister, ELIZABETH, through an attack of scarlet fever, caught the disease and died. Victor was deeply saddened. At the university, his father's statements about alchemy were confirmed but M. WALMAN, a professor of chemistry, told him that modern science owed much to the early alchemists. Victor soon assimilated all the professor could teach him. He continued his research alone and accidentally discovered what he hoped was the basic principle of life. He was now driven by a compulsive desire to create a human being and he haunted meat shops, dissecting rooms, and graveyards, collecting the materials he needed. In his laboratory, Victor fashioned the first man-created being, a hideous monster 8 feet tall, into which he infused life. Victor then had strange misgivings. That night the monster entered Victor's room and stood by his bed. Victor screamed and frightened the monster away. The next morning Victor roamed the streets of Ingolstadt in fever and delirium. HENRY CLERVAL, a friend of his, nursed him back to health. Victor could not tell Clerval the cause of his illness.

Chaps. 5–9. Victor received a letter from his father saying that Victor's younger brother, WILLIAM, had been brutally murdered. Victor hastened to Geneva and went out to visit the spot where William's body was found. A fierce storm arose and Victor saw, in a flash of lightning, the monster he had created. Victor knew the monster had murdered William and wanted to tell the authorities but knew they would think him insane. JUSTINE, a devoted family servant, was charged with the crime. A miniature that William wore was found in her pocket, and it provided sufficient evidence for the court to condemn her to death. Victor, greatly depressed by these events, went on a walking tour in the mountains. Here he once again saw the monster and he set out in pursuit. The monster eluded him and Victor was forced to give up the chase and rest, but then the monster came to him and demanded that he listen to his story and explanation.

Chaps. 10–15. When he left Victor's chambers in Ingolstadt, the monster began to adapt himself to the necessities of survival and to find food. All humans he encountered were terrified of him, and their screams confused him so he took shelter in an abandoned hovel adjoining a cottage. He hid by day and spent the nights foraging for food and studying the ways of human beings, the creatures he felt himself closest to. Lonely and desiring friendship, he listened to the people in the cottage and acquired the ability to speak. He saw that the people in the cottage did not have sufficient food for themselves and he stopped stealing their provisions and nourished himself on the berries of the forest. He also brought wood to their cottage door at night, but when he showed himself they were horrorstruck. The monster vowed eternal hatred of all men. He set off for Geneva and on the way he met and killed William. Having acquired the cunning he discovered necessary for life among men, he removed the miniature from the boy's neck and when he saw Justine later that night he put it into her pocket.

Chap. 16–23. The monster finished his story and threatened that unless Victor created a mate for him he would continue his murderous attacks; but promised that if Victor would give him a mate he would take her to the vast South American plains and they would lead a harmless life alone. Victor was revolted by the idea of creating another monster but felt he must do it. He went to England to see an English philosopher who had made certain discoveries along the same lines. After a pleasant visit with his friend Clerval, Victor went to the remote Orkney Islands to begin his work. But then, revolted at the thought of providing the means for a race of monsters to appear on earth, he decided he could not continue and destroyed his work. The monster was watching through a window. Enraged by Victor's betrayal, he forced his way into the house and demanded that Victor make good his promise. Victor refused and the monster threatened to punish his maker on his wedding night. Some time later, he killed Clerval. Victor was suspected of the crime but, due to lack of evidence, was released. He returned to Geneva, plagued by his feeling of guilt, and was consoled by Elizabeth. She was his sister only by adoption and they planned to marry. On the night

The monster watches Frankenstein through a window

276

following the wedding ceremony, the monster made good his threat and murdered Elizabeth. Victor, in his terrible anguish, made a full confession to the authorities but, as he feared, his story was not believed. He now vowed to track down and destroy the monster.

Chap. 24. Victor finishes his story. He refuses to tell Walton what the secret principle of life is, saying that such things should remain beyond man's knowledge.

Several days later Victor dies. On the night of his death the monster comes to seek Victor's body and Walton discovers the creature weeping over his creator. He realizes that the monster has suffered perhaps greater injustices than has Victor. The monster admits his crimes but contends that the man who created him was the greater criminal. With this the monster flees and Walton watches him disappear, alone, across the icy wastes.

Autobiography of Benjamin Franklin

Autobiography by Benjamin Franklin, 1706–1790.
Published 1818 (in part), 1867 in full. (PB, PL18; ML, 39 & T18; RE, 12)

BENJAMIN FRANKLIN was the greatest American and one of the world's greatest intellectuals in a century of great intellectuals. Because he raised himself to eminence solely by his own efforts and by a determined self-discipline, his autobiography has always ranked highest among American books of inspiration. It is also intensely interesting. Unfortunately it stops in 1757, with his

greatest glories yet to come. Franklin began the autobiography in 1771, more or less as a letter to his son. The first part, written in England, carries his career up to 1730. The second, written in Paris, is rather a description of his rules for morality and self-improvement than a recounting of events. The third part, written in Philadelphia in 1788–89, records the events of his life from 1732 to 1757. Though parts of it were published abroad earlier, the autobiography was not published in America until 1818 and some parts were not included until 1867.

Part I. Franklin addresses his son and expresses his desire to retell his family history. He has learned that his people stem from the town of Ecton, England, where Franklins are contained in the birth registers dating back to the year 1555. His grandfather THOMAS, who was born in 1598, had four sons. JOSIAH, Benjamin's father, was a Dissenter and had to leave England, with his first wife, about 1682. They settled in Boston, Mass. Benjamin was the youngest son born to Josiah and his second wife, ABIAH FOLGER, daughter of an early New England settler. Benjamin was first destined by his father to become a clergyman, for Josiah rigidly administered the lives of his 17 children. Benjamin failed arithmetic, however, and was forced to assist Josiah in his trade as a tallow-chandler and soap-boiler. Benjamin disliked this labor intensely. In 1717, at the age of 12, Benjamin was indentured as an apprentice to his brother JAMES, who was beginning to publish a newspaper in Boston called *The New England Courant*. Benjamin meanwhile was a constant reader of such moral works as Bunyan's *Pilgrim's Progress*, his favorite book. He spent much time debating philosophical points with his young friend JOHN COLLINS. At 16 Benjamin was so concerned with temperance that he became a vegetarian. He also perfected his knowledge of arithmetic and tried to develop a sound writing style by studying the works of Alexander Pope. Benjamin's work with James did not proceed happily, as his older brother tended to

ignore his achievements. Benjamin was already concerned with colonial affairs and submitted anonymous letters to the newspaper. He received no praise from James, though the letters were attributed to certain wise old men. James incurred the disapproval of the British governor of Boston and was imprisoned. For a time Benjamin put out the newspaper under his own name, but eventually he decided to leave Boston for a more tolerant and progressive city. He sailed to New York and called on WILLIAM BRADFORD, one of America's first printers. Bradford sent him on to Philadelphia to see his son ANDREW BRADFORD. Benjamin took to sea again and after a storm-tossed passage arrived in Philadelphia. Walking on Market Street with only a Dutch dollar and a copper shilling in his pockets, he first bought three "great puffy rolls" and then fell asleep in a Quaker meetinghouse. He also passed the door of Mr. READ, little knowing that the man's daughter, who ridiculed his "awkward, ridiculous appearance," would later become his wife. Benjamin found a room and went to see Andrew Bradford. Andrew had no opening but took Benjamin to another printer, a recent immigrant named KEIMER, who gave him a job. Soon the British governor, Sir WILLIAM KEITH, summoned Benjamin and promised to set him up in business, because Philadelphia was badly in need of a good printer. Benjamin returned to Boston to ask his family's permission and his father yielded only after much pleading. Young Franklin returned to Philadelphia with his friend Collins,

after narrowly escaping the company of some dubious ladies from New York. Collins, who proved to be a burden because of his excessive drinking, soon left. To finance his return trip to Philadelphia Benjamin had used money that his father's friend Vernon had sent to Boston in repayment of a loan. He calls this "one of the first great errata of my life," and he rectified it later by paying back the sum in full. On this trip Franklin also abandoned his vegetarian diet by eating some cod. Benjamin began to court Miss Read. He made a journey to England, under the sponsorship of Sir William, to buy some printing equipment. One of his close friends, the poetic JAMES RALPH, went with Franklin. Sir William never supplied the financial assistance he had promised. Franklin was told by a new friend, Mr. DENHAM, that the governor was irresponsible. To support themselves, Benjamin and Ralph had to find jobs in London printing houses. While he worked in England, Benjamin forgot to write to Miss Read. He published a paper called *A Dissertation on Liberty and Necessity, Pleasure and Pain*. He also established a reputation as a swimmer and thought of opening a swimming school. His friend Ralph, meanwhile, fell in love with a Mrs. T——, and eventually wandered off into the English countryside to become a teacher. Franklin erred by courting the lady—unsuccessfully—in Ralph's absence and thereby lost a good friend. After spending 18 months abroad, Franklin returned to Philadelphia with Denham, whom he joined in a small business. Miss Read had married, but she soon abandoned her worthless husband. In 1730 Franklin rectified his previous neglect by taking the girl as his wife.

Denham died shortly after his return to America and Franklin became manager for Keimer, who had another assistant named HUGH MEREDITH. Conditions became intolerable with Keimer and Franklin joined Meredith in founding a private printing establishment. He began to meet many important people in Philadelphia and his business flourished. He bought out Keimer's failing newspaper. Keimer went off to the West Indies and Meredith joined him there later. Franklin's *Pennsylvania Gazette* was now unchallenged in Philadelphia except for the elderly Bradford's paper. Franklin widened his social life by forming the Junto, a club for mutual improvement. Some of the more prominent members were WILLIAM COLEMAN, THOMAS GODFREY, and ROBERT GRACE. Franklin and Grace pushed the need for paper money to replace coins and Franklin was commissioned to print the first paper money used in the colony. Franklin and his friends also established the first public lending library in North America.

[At this point, the first half of the *Autobiography* ends, covering events up to the year 1730.]

Part II. At the instigation of two friends, ABEL JAMES and BENJAMIN VAUGHAN,

Franklin in his own print shop

Franklin undertakes to enlarge his life story at Passy, France, in 1784. Vaughan has requested especially that Franklin write about the acquisition of moral virtues. Franklin mentions that he was educated according to Presbyterian doctrines. He has always felt that "doing good" is man's highest act. Although he seldom attends any church, he is a strong believer in the existence of God and the immortality of the soul. Once he went to church and heard a preacher deliver a sermon on basic Christian acts, such as attending church and reading the Scriptures. Franklin found this woefully inadequate, so he drew up his own code of beliefs, which he called *Articles of Belief and Acts of Religion*. His most important belief was: "*Temperance*. Eat not to dullness; drink not to elevation." He also sought to practice the following virtues in order of descending importance: Silence, Order, Resolution, Frugality, Industry, Sincerity, Justice, Moderation, Cleanliness, Tranquillity, and Humility. His rule of humility was: "Imitate Jesus and Socrates." Equipped with these standards of behavior, Franklin tried every day to improve his conduct. He drew up a weekly chart with the virtues placed vertically and the days of the week horizontally. Every day he placed a black ink mark beside some of the virtues that he felt he had violated. The purpose of this daily examination was to accustom himself to the "habitude" or constant action of a moral life. Franklin never achieved perfection, of course, but he improved himself immensely.

Franklin rose at 5 in the morning and recited a prayer beginning *Powerful Goodness!* At this time he asked himself the question: "What good shall I do this day?" From 8 A.M. to 5 in the evening he worked. At 6 he returned home and about 9 he retired after asking himself, "What good have I done today?" Franklin remarks that even in his 79th year, while composing the *Autobiography*, he heeds the articles of his private faith. Humility was one of the vir-

tues he added to his list later in life, through the friendship of a Quaker. Franklin states frankly that even if he did not acquire virtue in reality, he acquired it in appearance. Furthermore, the self-assurance that he was behaving rationally helped him greatly in his attitude toward life. [After this famous discussion, Franklin put aside his life history for another four years.]

Part III. In August 1788 Franklin resumes his writing at home in Philadelphia. Many of his papers were lost during the Revolutionary War, but he has preserved enough to refresh his memory to the year 1730. He begins by quoting something he wrote in 1731 expressing skepticism about the virtue of political leaders, all of whom are motivated by "their present general interest." Also he reaffirms his belief in the immortality of the soul.

In 1732 Franklin first published the famous *Poor Richard's Almanac,* under the pseudonym of RICHARD SAUNDERS. His purpose was to disseminate bits of wisdom from many cultures, but especially American proverbs. The Almanac proved to be so popular that it was widely distributed in England and translated into French. He also used the paper to spread the current opinions of the Junto Club. In 1733 Franklin enlarged his journalistic enterprises by sending a journeyman to Charleston, S.C., to publish a newspaper, which eventually became a profitable venture. In 1734 Philadelphia and the rest of America thrilled to the open-air sermons of a young preacher named HEMPHILL, but Franklin's respect for the man was dimmed when he learned that Hemphill's sermons were copied from other sources. At this time Franklin was perfecting his knowledge of foreign languages, which were later to prove very useful. He learned French, Italian, and Spanish, besides keeping up his grammar-school Latin. He also returned to Boston and became reconciled with his brothers.

The year 1736 was an eventful one in

Franklin's life, for he lost a son by smallpox and received his first political appointment, clerk of the Pennsylvania Assembly. The following year the governor of Virginia, Colonel SPOTSWOOD, appointed him deputy postmaster-general in Philadelphia. Franklin began earnest campaigns for civic improvements. With the assistance of the Junto Club, he transformed the disorganized police force of the city into a highly efficient unit. Through his constant efforts, Philadelphia also established the Union Fire Company, a pioneering fire-fighting group that made the city one of the safest in the world.

In 1739 the city was visited by the Rev. Mr. WHITEFIELD, a brilliant Methodist evangelist from Ireland. Because there was no Methodist church at that time in Philadelphia, Whitefield had to speak in the streets or open fields. Franklin attended a few sermons, and though he vowed not to make the voluntary contribution he found himself emptying his pockets at the conclusion. In 1744 Franklin proposed a philosophical society and dreamed of founding an academy in the city. Meanwhile France and Britain were at war, and Franklin was worried about the defenseless state of America. He wrote a phamphlet called *Plain Truth* in which he pleaded for defense measures. As a result, a Philadelphia regiment was formed and cannons were bought. His proposals were opposed at first by peace-loving Quakers such as JAMES MORRIS, but eventually many Quakers declined to vote and the resolution was passed. Numerous Quakers withdrew from public life because they would not surrender their principles against war.

In 1742 Franklin invented a stove that he called a Pennsylvania fireplace (later called the Franklin Stove) which provided adequate ventilation to the fire. He and the Junto Club set to work founding the University of Pennsylvania, which opened its doors to scholars in 1749. Franklin was one of the original trustees. During the 1740s he also began a series of electrical experiments and negotiated a peace treaty with some Indian tribes at Carlisle, Penna. In 1751 he and his friend Dr. THOMAS BOND promoted the idea for a hospital, which was built soon afterward through public donations. Franklin was also instrumental in building a town meetinghouse. In 1757 he saw his dream of paved streets and street lighting come true.

In 1753 Franklin was appointed postmaster-general of the colonies. By sacrificing his own salary he saw that no profits reached England. Harvard and Yale both awarded him the degree of Master of Arts. War was again breaking out between France and England and the welfare of the colonies was endangered. Franklin was sent to Frederictown, Md., to greet the recently arrived British General BRADDOCK. The general intended to make a quick assault on Fort Duquesne (now Pittsburgh) and acted very haughty when Franklin mentioned the dangers. Franklin was not at all surprised to learn later that Braddock had died of wounds and his army had fled. Governor Morris of Pennsylvania charged Franklin with the duty of erecting forts against French and Indian invasions. Franklin and his men built a fort at the ruined settlement of Gnadenhut, where numerous Moravian dwellers had been massacred. When he returned to Philadelphia, Franklin was appointed commander of his regiment and he held frequent parades.

Franklin interrupts his account of political events to mention his electrical experiments by which he proved the "sameness of lightning with electricity." He mentions his famous kite experiment and the published papers that brought him the British Royal Society medal for the year 1753. He also mentions his old friend James Ralph, who distinguished himself by writing prose histories. Ralph is more famous however, for being attacked by Alexander Pope in his *Dunciad*. In 1757 the Pennsylvania Assembly finally decided to send Franklin to England with a signed protest against royal intervention in economic and political affairs. This was the first of many missions by Franklin. After a long delay he sailed, arriving in London on July 27, 1757. In England Franklin had no success with the British lords who received him. The British government decided that their taxes were equitable and that the colonies must bear their financial burdens.

[At this strategic point in his career, the *Autobiography* ends.]

Freckles

Novel by Gene Stratton-Porter, 1868–1924.
Published 1904. © 1904 by Doubleday & Co., New York. Published by Grosset & Dunlap, New York.

IN HER DAY Mrs. Porter, *née* Miss Stratton, could sell more millions of books than any other novelist. They never appealed to the literati but seekers of vicarious romance adored them. *Freckles* was one of the two biggest sellers, along with *Girl of the Limberlost*. They may have been the first two novels to sell two million copies. The plot outlined below was amplified by descriptions of the Michigan timberland and the natural life in it.

Chaps. 1–3. FRECKLES, a young, redhaired, freckled boy, comes to the Grand Rapids lumber camp seeking work. McLEAN, the owner, is a kind man who loves the forest and, despite his millions, shares the camp life of the lumber gangs. Freckles has only one hand and seems frail, but McLean is impressed by him and hires him to guard 2,000 acres of timber. The forest is half swampland and is crawling with snakes. JOHN CARTER, nicknamed BLACK JACK, a former employee of McLean's, is plotting to cut and steal some of the trees (which are worth up to $1,000 each). Freckles tells McLean that he does not know his last name. He was beaten as a baby, one hand was cut off, and he was left bleeding and bruised on the steps of a charity home. McLean decides to give the boy his own father's name, JAMES ROSS McLEAN. Freckles is sent to board with DUNCAN, the head teamster. He learns how to use a rifle, works hard in the forest and comes to know it well, and turns to the birds and beasts of the swamp for friendship. Duncan's wife, SARAH, takes good care of Freckles and tells him she will be his mother. The lonely boy cries in his happiness.

Chaps. 3–4. Duncan tells Freckles the men are betting that Freckles will betray McLean and let Carter and his gang into the forest. Out of loyalty to Freckles, McLean offers $1,000 to any man who can find a fresh stump when the camp moves into the forest. One day WESSNER, a friend of Black Jack's, comes to the swamp and offers Freckles $500 if he will ignore Black Jack when he comes to take some timber. McLean has followed Wessner. Hiding in the brush, he hears Freckles condemn Wessner for disloyalty. They fight and Freckles beats Wessner and runs him off the property. McLean takes Freckles to Mrs Duncan, who gives him a hot bath and puts him to bed. Freckles finds a nest with a baby bird and one of the men suggests they call a nature photographer known as the BIRD WOMAN to take pictures of the nest.

Chaps. 4–5. A girl comes through the brush and tells Freckles she is with the Bird Woman. Freckles admires her beauty and courage; she is not afraid of rattlesnakes and seems at home in the forest. Freckles calls her his swamp ANGEL. McLean says he loves Freckles and wants him to be his own son. A few days later the Angel and the Bird Woman come back to the swamp. Freckles tells the girl all about birds and their eggs and the two walk together, singing gaily. The Bird Woman calls to Freckles that two men have begun to saw down a tree. He runs to the spot and starts shooting at the men, who are Wessner and Black Jack. The Bird Woman fires at them also. The pair are chased out of the forest.

Chaps. 7–9. McLean is disappointed that the thieves left no evidence and there is no way of arresting them. McLean buys Freckles a bicycle so that he can race for help should Black Jack return. McLean wants to put another guard on the property but Freckles refuses aid. Freckles goes into town to deliver a hat the Angel left in the forest. He meets her father, who likes him.

Chaps. 9–12. While Freckles was in town Sarah took over his post in the woods and when he goes back he finds Sarah lying in the mud. She was frightened by a rattlesnake and fainted. Freckles revives her. The next day the Bird Woman, Angel and McLean come to the forest. While McLean goes off with the Bird Woman to watch her take pictures, Angel and Freckles sing together. Angel kisses Freckles on his forehead and tells him he will be a great singer and have everything in the world he wants. Later he asks Sarah if kisses wash off. She says they do not if they come from someone you love. One morning Freckles has a feeling he is being watched. Black Jack, Wessner and two other men grab him and tie him to a tree. They gag Freckles and start to cut down the great trees. Wessner starts to torture the helpless boy. Black Jack stops Wessner, but agrees to let him continue later; he does not want to watch the torture himself. Freckles, his mind swimming, looks up the trail and sees Angel staring at the scene. She and the Bird Woman have come to see the butterflies. Angel disappears and Freckles is not sure whether she was really there or he had a vision, but then he hears Angel's voice. The men untie him, hoping they can fool Angel into going away. She pretends to be unsuspicious and flirts gaily with Black Jack. Freckles cannot believe his ears, then he decides that she is stalling for him and he must trust her. She has so completely captivated Black Jack that when the other men urge him to kill her and Freckles, he cannot bring himself to do so. He sees her safely to the trail. Angel finds Freckles' bicycle and pedals as fast as she can to Duncan's cabin. She tells Sarah to go into the swamp and tell the Bird Woman what has happened. Sarah is terrified of the swamp but conquers her fears and sets off. Angel continues to McLean's camp. A wheel of the bicycle is broken off but Duncan finds her and lends her one of his horses to go for help. She rides into the camp and screams. A gang of lumberjacks leap onto their horses and race to the swamp. McLean leads the procession, with Angel riding beside him. They find the Bird Woman hiding in the brush with her small revolver aimed at Black Jack's head. They surprise the lumber pirates. Angel runs to Freckles and falls into his arms. Black Jack swears he will kill both Freckles and Angel and then escapes into the swamp. The next day McLean finds Freckles on the trail, hunting for Black Jack. McLean and the boy see a group of vultures circling, then they find a giant rattlesnake coiled beside the dead body of Black Jack.

Chaps. 13–18. The Angel and Freckles find one of the valuable trees that Black Jack had marked. It is their reward. Angel plans to have a dining-room table made from her share and Freckles decides to use his share for singing lessons. When the men fell the tree they lose control and it starts to fall near Angel. She is in danger of being smashed but Freckles runs and throws her free of its limbs. He is caught and pinned beneath a branch and is badly hurt.

279

McLean takes him to Chicago to get expert medical care. Angel tells Freckles she loves him and this knowledge, coupled with the expert surgical care, speeds his recovery. He still broods about whether it was his mother who cut off his hand, and he feels he must know about his family before he can marry anyone as fine as Angel. Angel goes to the charity home in Chicago where Freckles was abandoned as a baby. She learns that a man claiming to be Freckles' uncle has been looking for him, but has given up the search and is sailing back to Ireland that same day. Angel catches him in his hotel just as he is about to leave. She finds out that he is an Irish lord and she takes him and his wife to the hospital to meet Freckles. The boy learns that his father was the youngest son of a lord. He married without permission and ran away to America, where the young couple were killed in an accident and their baby, Freckles, was maimed. A friend wrote to the grandfather in Ireland, but he never tried to find the child. He has recently died and his eldest son, finding the letter, came to America to locate the boy. Freckles, restored to health, decides to marry Angel and stay with McLean and become his

partner in the lumber business, instead of going to Ireland with his uncle.

The men who fell the tree lose control of it and Angel is endangered

Lectures by Sigmund Freud, 1856–1939.
Published 1910. English translation © 1920 by Edward L. Bernays.

THIS BASIC WORK was divided into a series of lectures and published as *A General Introduction to Psychoanalysis.* It contains all the fundamentals that have come to be called Freudian. The importance of Freud's contribution to psychology and psychiatry is never questioned, and this work must be accepted as one of the most significant in the history of human thought; but also it is one of the most controversial. For many, Freudianism is like a religion and has its dogmas like any other religion. The dissenters claim the right to accept or reject at will.

Freud's Introduction to Psychoanalysis

THE PSYCHOLOGY OF ERRORS

I. Introduction. In approaching psychoanalysis, one must first learn two fundamentals: (1) that psychic processes are inherently unconscious; those which are conscious are isolated acts and part of the total psychic process; (2) instinctive impulses, particularly the sexual (in either the narrower or the broader sense of the term) play a major rôle in determining our psychic life.

2–4. Errors are caused by the influence of unconscious psychic processes. For example, an engineer damaged some equipment which he knew full well how to use and which he was testing in preparation for a lecture the following day. He later admitted that he disliked the thought of giving the lecture, and the strength of this dislike had caused the confusion that led him to turn a valve in the wrong direction, although, as a conscientious man, he intended to deliver the lecture. Slips of the tongue, such as, "Let us *roast* our esteemed colleague," instead of "Let us *toast* our esteemed colleague," are the result of failure to suppress the word one unconsciously wishes to say. The same is true of slips such as saying "He is a *grave* man," when one had begun to say "good" and then in mid-word felt impelled to change the adjective to "brave."

THE DREAM

5–7. The dream is our psychic life during sleep. The biological intention of sleep is recuperation; its psychological use is suspension of interest in the external world. Dreams are influenced by both external and internal situations. I dream I am riding in an outboard motorboat, and awaken to the sound of the lawnmower's motor; or I am hungry and dream of food. It is important to compare sleeping dreams with daydreams. In daydreams we straightforwardly know we are creating a fantasy world that satisfies our wishes and ambitions; the reason for the content of a sleeping dream is not at all clear. Thinking hard about the meaning of a dream will produce no results, but a technique that will produce results is *free association*—simply allowing one's thoughts to follow where they will and saying whatever comes into one's mind. This is not a simple matter, for soon we find we are rejecting certain thoughts that occur to us, calling them too ridiculous, trivial, or inappropriate. Obviously, we *resist* the process of free association as it uncovers facts about our dreams. But *without exception* the thoughts we resist are the most important in dream interpretation. A man dreams his brother is in a closet. The first association is "clothes-press." He thinks this to be ridiculous, but immediately remembers that his brother is *close-pressed* for money. Evidently the unconscious part of the mind, from which the associations as well as the dreams stem, has a logic of its own.

8–10. Distortion is *not* inherent in a dream. We know this from investigating children's dreams; these dreams are straightforward fulfillments of wishes. A child away from home is homesick and dreams he is home. Adult dreams, too, are in a modified way wish fulfillments. From this fact we can learn that dreams are not disturbers of sleep, but rather guardians of sleep. They present us with satisfactions of our desires in order to quell disturbances. Why then are most dreams not straightforward wish fulfillments, as are little children's? Because as we grow older we learn about right and wrong, and since much of our basic desires involve those things which are taboo or modified by moral precepts, especially sexual desires and desires to commit hostile and violent acts, we find that these things are not allowed to appear directly in our dreams. Instead, they are modified by regrouping, substitution, displacement, and other devices that disguise them; and the psychic mechanism that causes such changes is the *dream censor*. It is our inhibitions, based on moral precepts, that hold back the meanings of a dream as we try to probe it by means of free association. Also, if the dream censor did not operate to disguise our raw desires, their fulfillment in a dream would not allow the dream to function as a sleep preserver but would shock us into wakefulness. Since there is a direct connection between the original impulse and its form as modified in the dream by the dream censor, the modified material is symbolic in nature. For example, elongated objects—pencils, nails, guns, swords, etc.—may be symbols for the male genital organ; while concave objects—caves, pits, boxes, closets, etc.—may be symbols of the female genital organ.

11–13. The process of distorting a dream is called *dream work*. One of the methods of distortion is *condensation*, by which ideas or pictures are run together, as in the slip of the tongue when "good" and "brave" were condensed to "grave." Another process is *displacement*, by which the true psychic element is replaced by a seemingly unimportant element, so that the dream centers elsewhere. A third process is *translation*, by which ideas are translated into visual images. Upon interpreting dreams successfully, we find that the unconscious psychic life that is the site of our latent dreams is that of our infantile years—direct, violent, selfish.

14–15. If dreams are wish fulfillments, why are some of them painful? One reason is that the dream work is incompletely done. However, it can be demonstrated that painful as the manifest dream may be, the latent material from which it was fashioned was even more painful. Another reason is that the dreamer's moral precepts get in the way and condemn as an unpleasant situation that which his more primitive instincts desired. In this latter case, if the dream censorship fails, and painful material gets into the manifest dream, the censor destroys sleep—but not before some of the tabooed material has entered the awakening sleeper's consciousness. In fabricating a dream, the latent dream thoughts residing in the unconscious make use of thoughts the sleeper had very recently, usually the day before, and called "day-remnants," as vehicles for its material.

GENERAL THEORY OF NEUROSES

16–17. The understanding of the unconscious psychic activity of an individual enables psychoanalysis to deal with neurotic symptoms that classical psychiatry cannot master. As an example, take the malady known as compulsion neurosis—the overpowering need felt by an individual to perform some task over and over, in a strict ritualistic fashion. An instance might be the possession and continual ceremonial winding of several clocks. Psychoanalysis has shown that such activity is due to the need to assuage an unconsciously-motivated anxiety.

18–19. Patients who have compulsion neuroses are found to be *fixated* upon a very definite part of their past. Psychoanalysis demonstrates that the patient is wholly unconscious of what part of the past is responsible for the fixation. In other words, the fixation is in the unconscious mind. In trying to uncover the cause of the fixation, psychoanalysis makes use of the same technique used in dream interpretation—free association. Soon it is found that the patient is strongly resisting the discovery of the cause of his difficulty. The unconscious thought that has the power to cause this antagonism is said to be *repressed*. This repression is a necessary preliminary condition for formation of symptoms. When a repressed thought attempts to enter the conscious and is prevented by the psychic censor, it is said to be *suppressed*.

20–21. Psychoanalysis includes in the meaning of the term *sexual* the contrast between the sexes, the attainment of sexual excitement, the function of reproduction, and the indecency that must be kept concealed. Herein it is not too far from the concepts of classical psychiatry. However, it includes two other things in which it is unique: sexual perversion, and infantile sexuality. In the latter, it uses the term in a broader sense than is usual; it includes all infantile gratification that comes from stimulation of the body's erogenous zones, e.g., sucking. In the development of the sexual life, the child first experiences a pregenital period in which satisfaction is attained through stimulation of anal and oral areas. As the child matures, it then enters an *Oedipal* period in which it has suppressed desires for the parent of the opposite sex. Upon reaching puberty, the child enters the *sexual* stage.

22–23. When for some reason, the course of sexual development turns back in its path, and the objects of sexual gratification become those of an earlier period, we say *regression* has taken place. Regression must not be confused with suppression; the latter is a local matter, including only single thoughts, while regression involves the whole psychic life. Patients who manifest regression, and its consequent fixation, have contradictory personalities of which one part has one set of desires, an-other part other desires. Such a situation is said to be a psychic *conflict*. Psychoanalysis calls the sexual life the *libido* and the consciousness the *ego*. Conflict between new forms of gratifying the libido and the dictates of the ego is the cause of neurosis. Since the neurotic cannot actually regress in time, he does so through the medium of fantasy. For a neurotic, fantasy possesses psychological reality (as contrasted to physical reality); and for the neurotic, psychological reality is the determining factor. The return of the libido to fantasy has been given by C. G. Jung the name *introversion*. In attempting to avoid conflict, the libido may turn from tabooed goals to socially acceptable ones; if it does this it is said to have *sublimated* successfully.

24–25. A person begins to suffer from a neurosis when his ego loses its ability to cope with the libido. There are real fear and neurotic fear. Real fear is fear justified by dangerous situations; it must be learned. When, on the other hand, fear is manifested in situations of no real danger, it is neurotic fear. Such is the case in fear of spiders, darkness, high places, blood, caterpillars, crowds, solitude, etc. Neurotic fear is expectant fear. In the case of real fear, the ego prepares to escape from, or to overcome, the danger. In the case of neurotic fear, the ego is attempting to escape the claims of the fixated libido. Since the ego cannot really escape its counterpart, the neurotic cannot ever overcome his own fears, unless the libido fixation is relieved by psychoanalysis.

26–27. When, in neurotic regression, the libido turns back on itself, making itself its own object of gratification, the neurosis called *narcissism* exists. In its extreme manifestation it is *dementia praecox*. Narcissism makes homosexual choice of object easier than heterosexual. Before the psychoanalyst can successfully help the patient pry into his own unconscious, the patient must transfer the object of his libido from its neurotic pseudo-object to the psychoanalyst. This takes the form of falling in love with the psychoanalyst and looking upon him as a father, husband, or lover, if the patient is a woman, or as a father, if the patient is a man. The patient thus puts herself or himself in a dependent relation to the psychoanalyst. It is the task of the analyst to aid the patient in strengthening his ego so that this dependent relationship no longer need exist. The act of taking the psychoanalyst for a libidinous object is called *transference*.

28. The work of psychoanalytic therapy falls into two phases: first, the libido is forced from the neurotic's symptoms into the transference and is concentrated there; second, the struggle over the new object is carried on and the libido is set free from its fixated situation. In doing this, the psychoanalyst makes use of the paths to the unconscious; dreams, slips of the tongue, and free association.

Friar Bacon and Friar Bungay

Play by Robert Greene, 1560–1592. Produced 1590, published 1594. (RE, 45)

GREENE DIED BEFORE he was 34. Had he lived longer, he might have achieved a far greater degree of immortality. This is his best-known play and is probably his best, for the debates on black magic are great *tours de force*. The originally published name of the play is, *The Honorable Historie of frier Bacon and frier Bungay*.

Act I. 1. Prince EDWARD (later King Edward I) is in love with a farm girl named MARGARET whom he has seen in the village of Fressingfield. He tells his friends LACY, Earl of LINCOLN, and JOHN WARREN, Earl of SUSSEX. The court jester, RALPH, proposes that they go to Oxford and ask the famous necromancer, ROGER BACON, to make Ralph look like the prince so that King HENRY III will not miss his son when Edward goes off to court Margaret. Edward sends Lacy to a fair at Fressingfield to prepare the way. 2. Three doctors (scholars) named BURDEN, MASON, and CLEMENT have gathered in Friar Bacon's cell to see a magic brass head that Bacon has made. Bacon says the head will someday foretell the future. When Burden mocks him, Bacon causes an inn hostess to appear magically. She declares that Burden spends every night in her company. Bacon dismisses the maiden and the devil who brought her, and cautions the doctors against ridicule. 3. Lacy meets Margaret at the fair. She is charmed by Lacy's bearing and consents to share his company. Lacy says he is a poor farmer. He soon forgets the prince's cause and advances his own.

Act II. 1. King Henry receives the King of Castile and his daughter ELINOR, who has come to England to marry Prince Edward. The Holy Roman Emperor, who has come to England for the marriage, wishes to go to Oxford because a scholar with him, JACQUES VANDERMAST, would like to debate with the famous Bacon. The royal party all go to Oxford. 2. Edward arrives in Oxford. Ralph is wearing Edward's clothes. Lord WARREN and a gentleman named ERMSBY are with the prince. The group accidentally encounter Friar Bacon and his ignorant assistant MILES, who angers the nobles by his insolence. Friar Bacon protects Miles with magic powers, then miraculously reveals Edward's plans for courting Margaret. He takes Edward alone into his study. 3. In Bacon's magic glass Edward watches Lacy courting Margaret in Fressingfield. A priest of that town, Friar BUNGAY, has told Margaret who Lacy really is. The two lovers ask Friar Bungay to marry them. Through his magic

glass Friar Bacon bewitches Friar Bungay and whisks him off to Oxford on the back of a devil. Lacy and Margaret run away. 4. Edward's friends and Miles are arrested by the town constable for riotous conduct. On their way to jail they encounter Bacon's three doctor friends. Ralph, still dressed as a prince, tries to exert royal power but is mocked. Finally the men are freed.

Act III. 1–2. Edward goes to Fressingfield to punish the deceitful Lacy but Margaret pleads so eloquently that the prince gives the lovers his blessing. Edward rides back to Oxford and Elinor, his future wife. Lacy leaves Margaret to attend the royal wedding. The scholar Vandermast is pitted against Friar Bungay to determine which is the wiser. The two men hold a learned dispute on the relative powers of fiery and earthly spirits. Friar Bungay summons the mythical tree with the Golden Apples that Hercules stole. Vandermast summons Hercules himself and orders him to rip off the precious branch. King Henry is discouraged because his English scholar has failed, but Friar Bacon appears and commands Hercules to disobey Vandermast. He wins the contest by sending Vandermast back to Germany. Edward arrives and meets the gracious Elinor. Friar Bacon invites all the royalty to dinner. Miles carries in a poor meal but Bacon uses magic to fill the table with the world's most luxurious foods. 3. In Fressingfield, two squires, LAMBERT and SERLSBY, court Margaret and vow to fight a duel, not knowing she is engaged. A messenger brings Margaret a letter from Lacy saying that he has changed his mind and is going to marry Elinor's chief lady-in-waiting. Margaret is so stricken that she decides to go off to a nunnery.

Act IV. 1. Friar Bacon orders Miles to watch the magic brass head. Bacon believes it will speak soon and when it does he will

become the most powerful man on earth. His first project will be to construct a bronze wall around the entire length of England. Bacon falls asleep and Miles hears the head say, "Time is." These words confuse him, as do the following words, "Time was." Finally the head says, "Time is past." Then lightning flashes out of the heavens and the head is broken. The uproar wakens Friar Bacon, who discharges Miles. When the head said "Time is," it was ready to make its prophecies. 2. Edward tells his father he will marry Elinor, and Elinor consents. Lacy tells the King of Castile he knows the most virtuous girl in the world. King Henry offers horses and Lacy rides off to fetch Margaret. 3. Friar Bacon broods in his cell, telling Friar Bungay how Miles destroyed his head. Two young Oxford scholars ask to look at Bacon's magic mirror. They see their fathers, Lambert and Serlsby, duel and stab each other to death. Friar Bacon, appalled at the evil that has come about through his magic, decides to abandon his pursuits and live a virtuous religious life.

Act V. 1. Lacy finds Margaret already clothed in nun's attire, but persuades her that his letter was merely a test of his devotion. 2. The dismissed Miles wanders straight into the path of a devil, sent to claim Miles as a last act of magic by Friar Bacon. Miles is charmed by the devil and intrigued by his invitation to go to Hell. He asks to be a "tapster" or bartender there, for he has heard that it is a hot, dry place. The devil promises him the job and carries Miles off on his back. 3. Edward marries Elinor and Lacy marries Margaret. King Henry asks Friar Bacon's benediction on the ceremonies. Bacon says he has abandoned his magic craft but prophesies that both couples will be blessed with happiness and that ultimately England will be ruled by the world's most glorious queen (Elizabeth I, in whose honor the play was first enacted).

Miles is instructed to watch the brass head and wait for it to speak

The Frogs

Play by Aristophanes, 448–385 B.C.
Produced 405 B.C. Many translations.
(ML, T30; RE, 68; also Doubleday
Anchor Books)

THIS IS PROBABLY the favorite today among Aristophanes' comedies and in his lifetime it was the most successful. It not only won the prize for the best comedy of its year in the annual competition in ancient Athens but was presented a second time, which was a rare honor. Besides its intrinsic worth as a witty comedy, it has lasting value in its study of the relative merits of the tragedies of Aeschylus and Euripides.

The wine-god DIONYSUS (or BACCHUS) and his slave XANTHIAS call on the Greek hero HERACLES (or HERCULES). Dionysus not only wears his usual yellow robe and sandals but also has a stout club and a lion skin, which disguise him as Hercules. As the patron god of Athenian drama, Dionysus deplores the bad plays that are being written and plans to go to the Underworld and restore the great tragedian EURIPIDES, who has been dead only a few months. Hercules agrees that the modern playwrights are atrocious and the dead Euripides was admirable. Dionysus has disguised himself as Hercules because Hercules once descended into the Underworld (to bring back the three-headed dog Cerberus), and he asks Hercules for tourist information on the best hotels and restaurants. He also asks Hercules how to get there speedily. Hercules suggests hanging, but Dionysus considers it too stifling. Dionysus also rejects hemlock and leaping from a tower. Hercules then tells him to go to the Acherusian Lake and get the ferryman CHARON to take him across.

Dionysus and Xanthias see a funeral procession and follow it because the corpse must lead them to the Underworld. Dionysus asks the corpse to carry their luggage but the corpse demands two drachmas, which is exorbitant. At the Acherusian Lake Charon refuses to take the slave aboard, and Xanthias has to walk around the lake. Charon takes Dionysus but makes him help row the ferryboat. On the way across the god is annoyed by the CHORUS OF FROGS with their persistent song, "Brekekekekex, ko-ax, ko-ax," but finally succumbs to it and joins in. On the other side he pays his fare and is joined by Xanthias.

Dionysus and Xanthias timidly proceed downward. Xanthias asks if Dionysus has seen any of the sinners of Hades and Dionysus says he has—and points to the audience. The travelers encounter a few monsters and Dionysus displays ungodly timidity while Xanthias is brave. A MYSTIC CHORUS approaches with sacrifice to the grain goddess Proserpina (Persephone) and to Bacchus—that is, to Dionysus himself. Dionysus feels famished but does not dare claim the sacrifices, for that would mean relinquishing his disguise as Hercules. At PLUTO'S palace the door is opened by AEACUS, the porter, who is unfriendly because he thinks Dionysus is the man who stole his dog. Aeacus goes off to bring reinforcements of vengeful monsters and Dionysus, terrified, makes Xanthias change clothes with him. A beautiful girl then approaches Xanthias and says, "Welcome, sweetheart!" Hercules had been her lover. She goes to prepare a feast with dancing girls, and Dionysus makes Xanthias change back. Then the priestess of a pastry shop and her daughter Plathane appear and threaten Dionysus (in Hercules guise) for leaving unpaid bills, and they go to summon the souls of dead tyrants for revenge. Dionysus makes Xanthias change back again.

Aeacus returns with his monsters and bids them seize "Hercules." He is confused when Dionysus, dressed as a slave, claims to be a god, while Xanthias, dressed as Hercules, orders Aeacus's men to torture his "slave." Aeacus decides to test both by beating them, to see if the mortality of either makes them cry out. Xanthias, accustomed to beatings, does not flinch; nor does Dionysus. The intensity of the beatings is increased and both cry out the names of gods, but each quickly covers himself by quoting a line of poetry that includes the god's name. Aeacus decides to take both men to King Pluto and Queen Proserpina for a decision, for they are gods themselves. As all go out, the Mystic Chorus assails modern Athenians for lack of unity and criticizes some of the leaders of the state for selfishness.

Aeacus and Xanthias reappear alone and chuckle over ways in which a servant can deceive his master. They hear a great uproar and Aeacus explains that there is a contest over who shall have the Chair of Tragedy in King Pluto's court. AESCHYLUS, who has long held it, is now challenged by Euripides. There is to be a debate, with scales and measuring rods to determine the winner. The Chorus sings the praise of Aeschylus against the upstart Euripides, whose plays appeal to persons of less refined taste. As Aeacus and Xanthias enter the great hall, Euripides is accusing Aeschylus of being an old-fashioned rhetorical windbag, while Aeschylus says Euripides is a panderer to low tastes. Dionysus, now recognized as a god, says he will judge their contest though he is prejudiced in favor of Aeschylus.

Aeschylus defends idealism, conservative religion, and traditional forms. Euripides supports realism, liberalism, and *avant garde* art. Dionysus causes each to quote a line of his poetry, and the lines are put on the scales. Aeschylus's line includes the word "river" and Euripides' line the word "winged," so Aeschylus wins, since a river weighs more than a wing. Again and again Aeschylus wins, but Dionysus refuses to make a decision because both are good poets and good poets are rare. But Pluto demands a decision. Dionysus chooses Aeschylus and the Chorus approves, for Aeschylus represents the glorious past. Dionysus prepares to take Aeschylus back to earth with him and Pluto warns Dionysus not to send any of the prominent Athenians of that day to the Underworld. Aeschylus tells Pluto to let Sophocles, not Euripides, sit in the Chair of Tragedy during his absence. Dionysus and Aeschylus leave for earth while the Chorus sings a song of praise to them.

Dionysus, as the judge, causes Aeschylus and Euripides to recite their poetry

From Here to Eternity

Novel by James Jones, 1921–
Published 1951 by Charles Scribner's
Sons, New York. © 1951 by James
Jones. (NAL, T1075)

THERE IS UNDOUBTEDLY great writing in this novel, but critics have not agreed on how much. The novel is very long, more than 400,000 words. It is the most thorough, the most outspoken and the most accurate novel about enlisted men in the regular U.S. Army in the years between the two World Wars. Too often Jones writes like a little boy with a "you'll be sorry" attitude, as when his character Sergeant Warden just can't bear the disgrace of becoming a commissioned officer, but despite such minor flaws the net result is an important book. The title is from a line in a Rudyard Kipling ballad, the one now called the Whiffenpoof Song: "Gentlemen-rankers out on a spree, damned from here to eternity."

Book I. Chaps. 1–2. PREW (ROBERT E. LEE PREWITT) is a Pfc. in the Regular U.S. Army, stationed at Schofield Barracks near Honolulu, Hawaii. Disgruntled when another man is made First Bugler of his outfit, Prew, a "hard head," has himself transferred—with a lower rating—to an infantry battalion. Prew grew up in the coal-mine area of the Kentucky mountains. The first time he blew a bugle he knew he had the "call." He enlisted when he was 17. Every company wanted him because he was a good boxer, but the bugle was his real love. He reënlisted once and rose to a sergeantry when he won the welterweight championship, but one of the men he knocked out was in a coma for a week and came out blind, and Prew quit boxing despite great pressure from his superiors.

Chaps. 3–4. First Sergeant MILTON WARDEN, the topkick of Company C, is a demon for work and keeps the company at top efficiency, but the captain, DANA ("Dynamite") HOLMES, makes him tolerate inept men like O'HAYER, the supply sergeant, because they are boxers. One day Warden sees Capt. Holmes's wife, KAREN on the company grounds. Warden likes her looks but has contempt for her because he has heard she is promiscuous. He meets her one day and decides she is cold or snobbish. Prewitt reports and Holmes offers him the job of company bugler and a stripe if he will come out for the boxing squad, but Prew turns him down. Holmes hints at unpleasant consequences but Prew is adamant. Warden assigns Prew to Cpl. CHOATE's squad.

Chaps. 5–6. The regimental commander, Lt. Col. DELBERT, subtly but firmly advises Holmes to see to it that Prew comes out for the team. Holmes goes home in a nasty mood, has a fight with Karen, and is reproached by her once again, as he has been for 8 years, for being responsible for a long, ugly scar on her abdomen. She tells him to attend a general's party alone and rejects his hints that it would help if she were "nice" to Col. Delbert.

Chaps. 7–8. Choate is a huge, full-blooded Choctaw Indian, an easygoing athlete who performs few other duties. Prew actually gets his orders from Sgt. GALOVICH, an apelike taskmaster who revels in drilling his men hard. Because Prew refused to box, Galovich (under orders from Holmes, through Warden) persecutes Prew and keeps him from going into Haleiwa to see his native girl. Prew asks her to move closer to Schofield Barracks so that he can see her more often, but she refuses unless he marries her. He will not do this and leaves her.

Book II. Chap. 9. Holmes presses Warden to break Prew down and Warden suddenly knows why he hates Holmes—the man is a typical regular army officer who doesn't give a damn about the individual man. One day, when he knows Holmes is off the base, Warden goes to see Karen. He bluntly tells her what he wants. She agrees almost indifferently. He does not know she is merely seeking revenge on Holmes, and she knows that he is, but in the end they achieve a feeling of great tenderness.

Chaps. 10–11. Prew becomes friendly with ANGELO MAGGIO, a scrawny little Italian from Brooklyn. During a poker game IKE BLOOM, one of Holmes's boxers, threatens to whip Maggio and Prew goes for Bloom. The fight is broken up.

Chaps. 12–13. Warden takes Karen to a secluded beach where they swim nude in the moonlight. Karen gets a chill and they drive back. Warden is offended when she

Prew and Lorene talk

refuses him in the car, but she feels it would be degrading. When he leaves her he gets drunk and goes to a house of prostitution. The next day MAHLON STARK reports for duty as a cook by request of Holmes, under whom he served at Fort Bliss. Stark says he had an affair with Karen at Fort Bliss and Warden feels like smashing him, but he shows no emotion. Warden is tortured by his thoughts of Karen in bed with Stark, but Stark makes good as expected and in less than two weeks he is mess sergeant.

Chaps. 14–15. Prew learns that Stark and Warden are decent guys, along with Maggio, and that Bloom is not—but Bloom is due for promotion to corporal. Stark wants Prew as a permanent kitchen worker and advises Prew to take the job if he's smart, unless he wants to go out for boxing. Prew says he can't take this easy way out. That night Prew is prevailed upon to blow taps. All his hurt and despair goes into the horn. In the hush that follows every man within hearing knows that Prew was the bugler.

Book III. Chaps. 16–19. Prew and Stark go to town, get drunk, and go to Mrs. KIPFER's New Congress Hotel, a name that covers up the activity within. Mrs. Kipfer introduces Prew to a new girl, a slight brunette much in demand, called LORENE. Prew does not treat Lorene like a prostitute; he talks with her, and looks into her eyes, and in a semi-drunken dream state tells her he loves her. The memory of her does not leave him, and from that time on he pursues a plan to win Lorene exclusively for himself. At camp, Galovich rides him hard. He suddenly rebels and Capt. Holmes hears him. Holmes orders him to apologize to Galovich and Prew refuses. Prew is subjected to one punishment after another but still will not apologize. Holmes orders Warden to prepare court-martial papers for Prew. Warden skillfully talks Holmes out of the court martial. Company punishment is substituted and Warden "forgets" to enter Prew's name in the company punishment book.

Chaps. 20–22. After paying his debts, Prew has exactly $12 left on payday. He needs more to court Lorene and goes to the gambling shed run by O'Hayer. He runs his money up to $200 but does not know when to quit, loses a big pot to Warden, and finally has to borrow $20 at usurious interest from one of the sergeant-sharpers. Warden meets Karen and takes her to a beachfront hotel. He accuses her of having slept with Stark and other men. She says his accusations are true but that she loathed the men and herself. She then tells Warden how she got the scar on her abdomen: Her husband gave her a venereal infection and she had a hysterectomy. It made her feel she was not a woman any longer and, disgusted with her husband, she tried to find herself with other men. Warden cries and tells her he loves her.

Chap. 23. Holmes senses that Karen is having an affair with another man. Col. Delbert asks how Holmes is making out

Galovich pulls a knife on Prew, who knocks him cold

with Prewitt and the captain says they are giving him "the treatment." The senior officers present approve of anything that will break an enlisted man's spirit, but stress the fact that an officer must be successful—he must never let the man make him back down.

Chaps. 24–27. At Mrs. Kipfer's Lorene greets Prew as if he were just another soldier. When she comes to his room he cannot bring himself to go to bed with her. He leaves her, outraged, and he and Maggio drink up most of Prew's money. They get a ride to Waikiki and allow a couple of homosexuals to buy them drinks. They see Bloom and other men from their outfit with other homosexuals. Prew and Maggio go to a homosexual's apartment to drink. When Maggio leaves angrily, the homosexuals are frightened and give Prew $40 to find Maggio and take him away. Maggio is arrested by two M.P.'s, who club him to the ground. Prew starts to help, but Maggio shouts at him to run and Prew dives behind some bushes. The M.P.'s drag Maggio, insanely cursing, away.

Book IV. Chap. 28. Maggio is courtmartialed and sentenced to six months of hard labor. The police and FBI start an investigation of soldiers involved with homosexuals. Prew and Bloom are in the truckloads of soldiers taken to be questioned. The men are examined individually and Prew has no trouble; only Bloom seems troubled when he rejoins his mates.

Chaps. 29–34. Prew's campaign to win Lorene succeeds. Her real name is ALMA SCHMIDT, and she shares a cottage with another prostitute, GEORGETTE, in a respectable section of Honolulu. Once Prew makes the mistake of telling Alma he loves her, but at once he senses his mistake and pretends he was joking. He goes to the cottage every week-end and they spend many happy hours together. Alma says she could never marry him because he is not respectable enough. Georgette explains that Alma must marry a man of such respectability that nobody can ever suspect she has been a prostitute. Warden and Stark get drunk one

night and have a violent fight about Karen.

Chaps. 34–35. Prew gets into an argument with Bloom and they have a bloody battle, which is broken up by the chaplain. That night Galovich taunts Prew for not going out for the boxing team and works himself into such a rage that he pulls a knife on Prew, who knocks him cold. Prew is placed in the guardhouse. Warden promises to help and Prew asks him to call Alma and tell her what happened. Prew is sentenced to three months at hard labor.

Chaps. 36–37. Prew begins his sentence in the stockade, where the regimen is so cruel that John Dillinger, when he left there, vowed to get even with the whole United States. The commanding officer and fat Sgt. JUDSON are equally sadistic. The guards beat the prisoners at their whim. Prew meets Maggio on the rock pile and learns about "The Hole," where prisoners are put in solitary confinement. Maggio is in Number Two barracks with the most hardened prisoners. Prew wants to be moved to Number Two, to be with his buddy, but Maggio tells him he can only get there by being insubordinate and taking three days in the Hole.

Chap. 38. Bloom has been promoted to corporal and feels more lonely and disliked than before. He broods on his latent homosexuality and his consciousness of the fact that he is a Jew. He toys with the idea of shooting himself; that would make them take notice. He puts his rifle in his mouth and pulls the trigger.

Chap. 39. Prew complains about the food. Judson gives him a large dose of castor oil, then two guards beat him severely and put him in the Hole. He manages to endure the three solitary days without cracking up, then he is put in Number Two, where he meets the toughest men in the stockade. He hears about Bloom's suicide and wishes he could have blown Taps at Bloom's burial. Maggio has a plan to get out of the stockade, by feigning insanity.

Chaps. 40–41. Warden sees Karen as often as he can. They discuss the future and she tells him she will divorce Holmes and

marry him if he takes an extension course and becomes an officer (as Holmes has insistently urged him to do). The idea of being an officer is repugnant to Warden, but the thought of having Karen makes him change his mind. But for some reason he delays sending in his application. He and Karen quarrel about it but make up and plan a trip together. Warden puts in his application and also talks Holmes out of a two-week furlough, two months later.

Chaps. 42–44. Maggio attacks a guard and is beaten with the butt of a gun. After being in the Hole for 24 days, with daily torture, he succeeds in his plan and is discharged from the Army. Shortly after that, Judson has one of the prisoners beaten to death in front of the others. Prew grimly determines to kill Judson. He serves out his term and returns to his company. There have been several changes. Holmes has moved to a higher job and Warden is on leave. Prew buys a knife and gets Judson in an alley in town. Judson's knife slashes a gash in Prew's back but Prew kills Judson. Prew staggers through side streets to Alma's cottage, where he collapses as she opens the door.

Book V. Chaps. 45–47. Alma and Georgette nurse Prew back to health. He is AWOL—he had intended to go back to camp after the fight, but feared the wound would give him away. Warden and Karen are at an elite hotel, some distance from the base, and they swim, drive through the lovely countryside, and make love, but both feel guilty and they quarrel, so the idyl ends on a sour note. Warden gets back and finds that Prew has been missing for two days but the men have covered up for him. Warden continues to carry Prew as present for duty. He hears that Judson was killed and knows nothing much will be done about finding the killer, but wonders if Prew is the killer. He sees Karen again and tells her all about Prew, including his affair with Lorene and his being AWOL. Warden can no longer cover up for Prew and has to report him AWOL. The outfit goes on maneuvers and sets up camp on a beach near Waikiki.

Chaps. 48–49. Alma and Prew quarrel, chiefly because she is so worried about what might happen to him. Prew makes advances to Georgette but she will not have him. Prew puts on civilian clothes, takes a revolver that Alma keeps in the house, and goes into town to find Warden. Warden tells him he is not suspected of killing Judson but that he is marked AWOL. Faced with another stay in the stockade, Prew will not go back to camp. He goes to Mrs. Kipfer's, asks for Georgette, and takes her to a room. Then he goes back to the cottage, but Georgette has told Alma what happened and Alma will not go near him again.

Chap. 50. On Dec. 7 the Japanese attack Pearl Harbor and strafe Schofield. Warden organizes his men and they shoot down two enemy planes and do not suffer a single casualty. In the dead silence after the attack, they move out to the beach defenses they built and set up camp. Everybody is there except one man, Prewitt.

Chaps. 51–52. Eight days after the attack Prew reads that all prisoners in the stockade have been released to fight and he makes up his mind to rejoin his outfit. Alma and Georgette are planning to leave for the States in a few days, but Alma fears for Prew and says she will stay if he will. She becomes hysterical when he says he must leave because he is a soldier. He leaves the sobbing Alma and reaches the highway to the beach where his outfit is stationed. A patrol car stops him and he has no pass, but he begs them to take him to his outfit. When the soldiers say they must take him to headquarters, he slugs one of them and runs off. A spotlight picks him out and a machine gun cuts him down. Warden is called to identify the body and he talks an officer into marking the death as killed in action. Warden knows he must go to tell Lorene.

Chaps. 53–57. The order making Warden a second lieutenant comes through, but after Prew's death he has no taste for becoming an officer. He gets drunk and tears up the orders. Karen is soon to leave for the States and they have a last meeting. They spend several hours together without sexual passion but in a keen understanding of their love. Several days later, Warden and Stark get roaring drunk, fight with some other soldiers in a tavern, flee the M.P.s, and wind up in an all-night orgy at Mrs. Kipfer's. Karen boards her ship to the States and meets a lovely girl who says her fiance was killed on Dec. 7, dying a hero. The girl tells Karen her name was Robert E. Lee Prewitt and he came from an old Virginia family. Karen is amused but sad. She can recognize the girl as Lorene.

The Front Page

Play by Charles MacArthur, 1895–1956, and Ben Hecht, 1894– Produced Aug. 14, 1928, in New York.

BOTH AUTHORS OF this comedy worked in Chicago in the years of hot—often violent—competition for newspaper headlines and circulation, and the frantic pace of the play is hardly an exaggeration. *The Front Page* is one of the best, funniest and most successful of modern American comedies and it is a favorite with amateur and repertory groups. The principal characters, Hildy Johnson and Walter Burns, had real-life counterparts on Chicago newspapers. The action of the play covers a period of only a few hours and has two themes, the scramble for news beats and the unprincipled methods used by Burns to avoid losing his star reporter.

Courts Building in Chicago. EARL WILLIAMS, a murderer (of a Negro policeman) is to be hanged the next morning. One reporter, HILDY JOHNSON, is not there and it is rumored that he has quit his job—against the wishes of his managing editor, WALTER BURNS, who is trying to track him down. BENSINGER of the *Tribune* complains of the unsanitary conditions; he is nicknamed "Listerine." Hildy comes in, all dressed up, to say goodbye; he is marrying the boss's daughter, PEGGY, and going to New York to work for an advertising agency. They are leaving that night. When Burns calls again, Hildy tells him off. Then he waltzes the charwoman, JENNIE, out of the room. A tart, MOLLIE MOLLOY, comes in to complain of the press treatment of Williams, whom she has just visited in the death house. The SHERIFF comes in and tells the reporters that Williams is being seen by an alienist. Hildy is leaving finally when there is pandemonium: Williams has broken out. The other reporters dash out of the room and Hildy calls Burns and says, "Don't worry, I'm on the job."

Act 2. Reporters rush in and out, phoning in brief communiques to their papers. It appears that while the alienist was ex-

The mayor with the reporters

amining him, Williams acquired a gun, shot his way out of the office, and slid down a drainpipe to the street. But when the room is empty Hildy phones the true story to Burns: The alienist asked for a reënactment of the crime and the sheriff himself handed his gun to Williams. Hildy paid out $260 for this information and demands that Burns send the money at once. Peggy has appeared in the doorway, and she is enraged to learn that Hildy is still working and has spent their transportation money to New York. Peggy's mother, Mrs. GRANT, comes in after her. The reporters bring in the MAYOR for an interview and quiz him on the effect Williams' escape will have on the Negro vote. The Sheriff comes in, the reporters go out, and a man named PINCUS arrives with a reprieve for Williams from the governor. The mayor and sheriff offer Pincus a high-paying city job to say he never delivered the reprieve, then the sheriff orders his deputies to shoot to kill. Hildy phones his office and learns that Burns has not sent the $260, so he borrows $150 from LOUIE, a flashy gangster. Louie leaves and Hildy is alone. Earl Williams, gun in hand, comes through the window into the press room. He hands Hildy the gun and collapses. Hildy drags him into the toilet to hide him from Mollie, who is coming in, but Williams recovers enough to stagger out and Mollie sees him. Hildy hides Williams in a big rolltop desk, which he closes. It is Bensinger's desk, but when Bensinger comes in Hildy coughs in his face and Bensinger dashes off to gargle. Walter Burns arrives. He calls his office and tells them to send him ten huskies from the circulation department to carry the desk out. Hildy sits down to write his story and Peggy comes back and berates both him and Burns.

Act 3. Hildy is still typing furiously; Burns paces the floor. Bensinger comes back and this time Burns intercepts him and pretends to phone to someone to get him a job at twice his *Tribune* salary. Then he sends Bensinger off on a wild goose chase for the job. Burns tries to talk Hildy out of getting married, saying all women are double-crossers. Louie comes in, disheveled; he has been in an accident with a police car, and he says Mrs. Grant was injured in the same accident. Hildy starts out but the sheriff and deputies burst in, overpower Hildy, and find on him the gun Williams had. The sheriff sends for the mayor. Mrs. Grant comes in and accuses Burns of having her kidnapped. Williams is found in the desk and the mayor and sheriff threaten Hildy and Burns for obstructing justice, but Hildy and Burns find out about the attempt to bribe Pincus and the mayor and sheriff have to back down. Peggy comes back. She and Hildy are reconciled, and Walter Burns not only gives them his blessing but gives Hildy his watch as a wedding present. Then, after they have left, Burns sends a wire to the chief of police at LaPorte, Indiana, to stop and detain Hildy: "He stole my watch."

Gammer Gurton's Needle

Early English drama, probably by William Stevenson, d. 1575.
Published 1575; year of first production estimated at 1553 to 1566. (RE, 45)

THIS IS THE earliest or next-earliest (to *Ralph Roister Doister*) English comedy. It still makes good reading, in an edition in which the Early Modern English has been more or less translated to equivalent modern words and the antique spelling has been simplified. Like many medieval comedies, it involves a confused situation deliberately created by a prankster. The importance of the lost needle can be better understood when one remembers how carefully handmade, and how expensive, needles were at that time— a time when a wife's "pin money" had to be a considerable allowance.

Act I. 1. A Bedlam (released inmate of Bethlehem hospital for the insane) stands before GAMMER GURTON's house. There is great commotion inside. **2.** HODGE, Gammer Gurton's servant, comes from the fields to have a tear in his breeches repaired. **3.** TIB, Gammer's maid, comes out of the house. She explains that in the midst of a commotion caused by the cat, GYB, Gammer Gurton dropped and lost her needle— her one needle, a dire loss. **4.** Gammer comes out and bewails her great loss. Hodge reproaches her. Tib is sent to sift over all trash in the house and COCK, Gammer's boy, is sent to find a candle to give her light. **5.** Tib returns; she could find nothing. Cock returns, laughing: Looking for a glowing coal to light the candle, he blew on what he thought were two sparks, but they were Gyb's eyes. When he blew, the cat shut its eyes and the sparks went out; when he stopped blowing, the sparks appeared again. All agree to wait for morning light to continue the search.

Act II. 1. DICCON comes from Dame CHAT's alehouse. Hodge complains of hunger; in Gammer Gurton's house there was only a morsel of bread, no bacon (as Diccon knows, for he stole the bacon). Diccon undertakes to conjure up a devil to find the lost needle, but when he begins, Hodge runs away. **2.** Dame Chat comes from her alehouse, some playing cards in her hand (she has been in a game and has left her maid DOLL to play for her). Diccon tells her that Gammer's red rooster has been stolen and that Gammer thinks Dame Chat has roasted and eaten it. **3.** Hodge fearfully returns. Diccon tells him the devil spoke of a cat, a rat, and a chat—but did he mean the cat Gyb, the curate Dr. RAT, and

Dame Chat? He promises more information the next day. Hodge goes for string to mend his breeches. **4.** Diccon tells Gammer he saw Dame Chat pick up something, perhaps a needle or pin. Gammer rushes off to claim her needle. **5.** Diccon anticipates, with great enjoyment, seeing a battle between the two women.

Act III. 1. Hodge returns with an awl and thongs to mend his breeches. **2.** Gammer, who has gone inside for a clean apron, meets Hodge and tells him Dame Chat has her needle. Hodge now pretends he saw the devil, who gave him the same information. **3.** Gammer goes to Dame Chat and demands her property. Dame Chat thinks she means the rooster. The women fight, with violent language and blows, and both take a beating. When the fighting ends, Gammer sends Cock to bring Dr. Rat, the curate. **4.** The cat Gyb chokes and, thinking it may have swallowed the needle, they shake it violently but find nothing.

Act IV. 1–2. Dr. Rat enters and delivers a soliloquy on a curate's unhappy life. Everyone sends for him at the least sign of trouble. Gammer and Hodge tell him of the loss of the needle and refer him to Diccon, who is approaching, for testimony that Dame Chat has it. Diccon will not commit himself but offers to see Dame Chat and meet them later. **3.** Diccon does see Dame Chat, but he tells her that Hodge plans to steal her hens. She decides to welcome Hodge with boiling water. **4.** Diccon tells Dr. Rat he has seen Dame Chat with the needle in her hand, but he warns that Dr. Rat must sneak into her house very quietly to catch her with it. He sends Dr. Rat in the way Dame Chat expects Hodge to come for the hens. Dr. Rat gets the bath of boiling water.

Act V. 1. Dr. Rat asks Master BAILY to find out why Dame Chat was so well prepared for him. Master Baily considers it quite natural for a woman to greet a prowler thus. **2.** Master Baily sees Dame Chat, who insists she did not hit Dr. Rat. (She still is sure it was Hodge.) Gammer Gurton comes in and resents the accusation of Hodge. Hodge himself appears, with no mark on him, and obviously he was not the man she hit. Gradually the confusion is cleared up and Diccon is identified as the villain. Diccon is summoned. Dr. Rat is for hanging him, but Master Baily reduces the punishment: Diccon must swear, on Hodge's breeches, always to let Dr. Rat pay for any refreshment they have; never to offer a second time to pay Dame Chat for her ale if she refuses payment the first time; never to take Hodge for a fine gentlemen; always to be kind to the cat; and to help Gammer Gurton find her needle. In swearing, Diccon slaps Hodge smartly on the buttock and Hodge shrieks. The needle has been found.

The Garden of Allah

Novel by Robert Hichens, 1864–1950.
Published 1905. © 1904 by Frederick A. Stokes Co., New York.

SOME CONSIDERED Robert Hichens a novelist of great stature, others dismissed him as just another novelist. His novels lean so heavily on the spiritual and the introspective that they are bound to be dull to readers who feel no kinship to the particular characters. *The Garden of Allah* is his best-known work and, whether or not it is his best, is quite typical. It should probably be read first among his works.

Book I. Chaps. 1–3. DOMINI ENFILDEN, 32 years old, is an unmarried English woman. Her father, Lord RENS, has died and left her a small fortune. Because her mother, a Catholic, ran off with a Hungarian musician, Domini has mistrusted love and has lived an independent and lonely life. She has remained true to the Catholic Church, largely through the love and intellectual guidance of an uncle who is a priest. She goes to Africa and is on her way to the town of Beni-Mora, accompanied only by her personal maid, hoping in the immense solitude of the African desert to

find herself. On the train to Beni-Mora, Domini notices a powerfully built man with a gentleman's face and a laborer's hands. He is rude to her and she tries to ignore him, but she sees sadness in his face and suffering in his eyes.

Chaps. 4–6. Domini is met by BATOUCHE, an Arab guide, who also claims to be a poet. He takes her to the hotel and tells her that her traveling companion is an Englishman and will stay at the same hotel. Domini visits the little church and meets the parish priest. She then orders a horse so that she can ride into the desert. Batouche takes her to the beautiful gardens of an Italian Count ANTEONI. She meets the count, who shows her his many treasures and invites her to return.

Book II. Chaps. 7–9. At dusk Domini looks out over the village from a high tower. The English stranger is there but seems afraid to speak to her. That evening she goes with Batouche to a dancing house. The stranger is there also. Later Domini meets the man in a crowd and allows him to take her back to the hotel. He introduces himself at last. He is BORIS ANDROVSKY. The next day Domini invites him to go riding with her. He cannot ride but mounts a horse anyway. He is thrown but gets on again and goes off with her. She admires his courage. They ride to a village miles

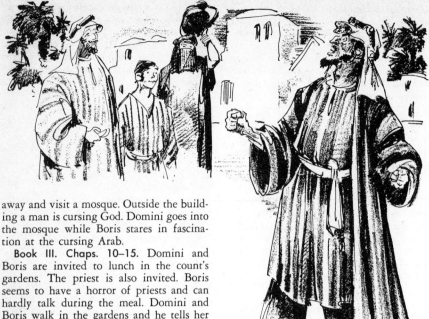

Boris sees the cursing Arab

away and visit a mosque. Outside the building a man is cursing God. Domini goes into the mosque while Boris stares in fascination at the cursing Arab.

Book III. Chaps. 10–15. Domini and Boris are invited to lunch in the count's gardens. The priest is also invited. Boris seems to have a horror of priests and can hardly talk during the meal. Domini and Boris walk in the gardens and he tells her he is afraid of feeling deeply about anything. She says she has come to Africa to learn how to feel emotion. The count takes Domini to a diviner, who goes into a trance and tells her that her life will come to full bloom in the desert. The count is interested in Boris because he seems like a man who has defied Allah in Allah's Garden (the Arabs' name for the desert). The count sets off on a journey into the desert. Domini grows restless and afraid of the strange sensations that are mounting within her. She watches an Arab dance in which two scorpions are mesmerized and the dancers eat the insects at the height of their frenzy. After the dance she rides into the moonlit desert with Batouche. Boris follows and insists that she send Batouche back. In the desert they come across a dead Arab woman and Domini suddenly has a sense of impending tragedy. Boris plans a trip into the desert next day. When he says he is leaving, Domini realizes that she loves him. In the morning Boris comes to her and declares his love.

Chaps. 16–20. The day of Domini's marriage to Boris there is a sandstorm in the desert. Domini is very happy; the priest cannot help disliking something in Boris, but for Domini's sake he controls his feeling. Boris and Domini start their trip into the desert despite the storm. The first night they spend in an oasis. The wind dies down and they lie peacefully in their tent. They determine to forget the past and live only in the present. A French officer, DE TREVIGNAC, and his men come to the Androvsky camp. They have just escaped death in the desert. Domini greets them warmly and invites de Trevignac to dinner. Boris is out hunting gazelle; when he returns and hears about the invitation he becomes moody, and when he hears the name of the officer he is frozen with fear. At dinner the conversation is pleasant enough but when Domini slips out of the tent for a moment,

Boris sends the officer away. The officer has recognized Boris and knows his secret. Later when de Trevignac meets Domini on a road he rides over to her and makes the sign of the cross above her head.

Chaps. 21–24. Boris and Domini go to the desert city of Amara. Boris wants to stay in the desert but Domini has a longing for human companionship. While Boris is out walking, the priest of Amara, Father BERET, comes to the tent. Domini offers him a certain wine, which he tells her was made in a Trappist monastery at El-Largani. The one monk who was entrusted with the secret formula for making the wine has left the monastery. He had

been a monk for 20 years before he broke his vows. Domini tells Boris the story when he returns from the desert. Boris is moved by the tale and by Domini's comment that God forgives everything. Domini is troubled by the fact that her husband has some secret; she feels their love is incomplete. On a ride through Amara Domini meets Count Anteoni, who tells her he has become a Mohammedan. He has found peace in the faith of the land he loves.

Chaps. 25–30. That night, after a second visit to the priest, Boris tells his wife his awful secret. He is the Trappist monk who broke his vows. He entered the monastery when he was 17, mostly because his mother wished it, and he lived there for 19 years in peace and happiness. But he was placed

in charge of the cemetery and from the hill he saw the minarets of the town and began to wonder about the world outside. He was then placed in charge of the monastery guests and for the first time in years spoke to other men. One man in particular told him about many adventures and about a woman he loved, who had forsaken him. The woman followed her lover to the monastery. When Boris saw them reunited he could no longer stand the silence of the Trappist community and ran away. After Boris tells his story, Domini and he leave Amara. Domini insists that they sleep in separate tents. She wants to take some of the guilt from him. They go back to Beni-Mora, where Boris confesses to the priest. Then they agree that Boris must return to the monastery and expiate his sin. Boris says he will always love Domini and she knows that, though alone in the world, she will always be near to him.

Chap. 31. Many years later Domini is the mistress of the count's home and gardens. She has a little boy named Boris, born soon after his father went back to the monastery. Domini does not rebel against her fate, because she knows Boris, her husband, is at peace with God.

Gargantua and Pantagruel

Novel by François Rabelais, *c.*1490–1553.

Published 1532 to 1562, in five books. Various translations. (ML, G65)

WORLD LITERATURE hardly contains anything greater than this lusty, bawdy, irreverent book. Though very long (more than 400,000 words) it is worth reading through for sheer pleasure and it can be opened and read anywhere. Its humor is positively delicious. Rabelais was a clergyman but had enough wit and resourcefulness to escape the condemnation of the Church, which condemnation in his times was notoriously quick and usually fatal. The classic translation, the one that best captures the flavor of the original, is that of the Scotsman

Thomas Urquhart (1611–1660), who translated at least the first two books and whose translation was completed by a Frenchborn Englishman, Pierre Le Motteux (1660–1718); but this translation is archaic in vocabulary and there are several translations into more modern English that are easier to read. The outline below is based on one of these, that of Jacques Leclercq—the translation used in the Modern Library edition—which skillfully combines the archaic flavor with the modern senses of words. Actually, since Rabelais wrote in early modern French, the original French is possible to read as regards spellings and constructions, but many words and more connotations are bound to baffle the reader.

Book I. 1–7. In order to tell the history of the great giant GARGANTUA, the author must retell certain episodes from the *Chronicle of Pantagruel*, his son. [Book II.] Both father and son are descended from a famous race of massive beings whose exact genealogy is uncertain; still they are definitely related to many great heroes of the past, such as Hercules. Gargantua is the son of the giant GRANGOUSIER ("Greatgullet") and GARGAMELLE, the daughter of the King of Butterflies. Gargamelle labors 11 months before giving birth to Gargantua after eating too much tripe for dinner. She delivers the baby in a meadow in the midst of a Bacchic wine celebration. The child issues out of his mother's left ear and immediately clamors for wine instead of milk. As a result he is named Gargantua, a corruption of the French phrase for "what a big gullet you have!" **8–15.** The tailors in Gargantua's realm go to great pains to assemble yards of elaborate cloths for the enormous child's clothing. The most striking features of his dress are an ostrich plume and a jeweled codpiece. His colors are white, which stands for joy, and blue, for strength. During the first 5 years of his life, Gargantua delights everyone with his sense of humor and mischievousness. Finally his father, impressed by the boy's decision that geese make the finest toilet paper, decides to begin his education. After experimenting with various Latin doctors, Grangousier decides to send him off to Paris to study under the learned PONOCRATES. **16–24.** Upon entering the city, Gargantua is met by a crowd of Parisians, who welcome him. Believing that the people expect some entertainment, Gargantua drives them away by urinating upon them. He remarks that he has done this *par ris* ("for a laugh"). Thousands of people perish in the flood, however, and the survivors take his sporting words as the new name for the city of Paris. For a time Gargantua speaks with the various members of the Sorbonne University, but finally he decides to leave the city. On departing, he takes the bells of Notre Dame Cathedral and ties them around his gigantic mare's head. The Parisians are so annoyed by the loss of the bells that they send the learned JANOTUS DE BRAGMODO to reclaim them. Janotus delivers a windy, Latinate appeal for their restoration, and finally is rewarded by a present of cloth and the bells. Meanwhile Gargantua spends all of his time pursuing countless games and sports. (The long catalogue of these games in Chapter 22 is one of the most famous passages in the book.) Finally the tutor Ponocrates attempts to reform Gargantua's habits by teaching him swimming and weight-lifting. They also study numerous ancient tracts on good dieting. By varying these activities, Gargantua makes excellent strides in his education. **25–58.** The peace of Gargantua's country is suddenly sundered by a war with the land of Lerné, ruled by King PICROCHOLE. The war begins when some Gargantuan shepherds demand the fine wares of some Lerné bakers who are passing through

their hills. When King Picrochole strikes back, a brave monk named Friar JOHN rises up to lead the Gargantuans to some triumphs. Grangousier sends a letter demanding that Gargantua lead the army. Gargantua restores the stolen cakes, but King Picrochole accepts the bad counsel of his advisors and rejects a bid for peace. With the help of the valiant Gymnastes, Gargantua forces Picrochole back. Simply by combing his hair, Gargantua bombards the enemy forces. At last he confers with

Friar John about strategy. The two men discuss the reasons why a monastic life is generally condemned. Finally the friar and Gargantua rout the enemy army and drive Picrochole into a life of obscurity. Gargantua delivers a noble address to the vanquished people of Lerné, but then divides up the country among his friends. When Friar John refuses to accept any of the established monasteries as his reward, Gargantua builds the ideal new Abbey of Thélème. There women are admitted on an equal status with men, and life is spent in a round of merry entertainment. The only law is: "Do as thou wilt."

Book II. 1–9. (After recounting a long genealogy of giants from Biblical and Grecian times, Rabelais mentions that) Gargantua "begat his son PANTAGRUEL upon his wife named Badebac," who died in the pangs of childbirth. Pantagruel's size and temperament are much like his father's, but he profits from Gargantua's close supervision of his education. In his adolescence, Pantagruel goes to Paris to study, and there meets his lifelong friend, PANURGE. Panurge, who speaks numerous languages, says only that he has recently escaped from the Turks. Pantagruel studies the countless, pointless books on witchcraft and alchemy that fill the Library of St. Victor. He also receives a loving letter filled with good advice from his father Gargantua. **10–22.** Heeding his father's suggestions that he put his knowledge to a test, Pantagruel decides to settle a debate between Lords Kissarse and Bumfondle. Throwing aside all books of law, Pantagruel pronounces a

judgment that is as obscure as the point in question. He commands the two men to be friends and they accept eagerly. The fact that both sides greet a decision cordially is so strange that Pantagruel is hailed as a genius. His friend Panurge is also widely acclaimed for his suggestion that the walls of Paris be built of women, since they are cheaper than stone. Panurge proves his special worth to his master when he successfully defeats an English scholar named THAUMASTES who has come to challenge the giant. The Englishman refuses to debate with words, but Panurge uses such a wide variety of difficult signs and gestures that Thaumastes is forced to acknowledge defeat. He then goes off to compile an enormous explanatory tract. Panurge revenges himself on a Parisian woman who has spurned his love, by covering her with a scent that attracts dogs. **23–34.** When Gargantua dies, his realm of Utopia is suddenly invaded by King Anarchus and the men called Dipsodes (or Thirsty People). Together with Panurge, CARPALIM, EUSTHENES and EPISTEMON, the new king Pantagruel rides away from Paris to wage war. For a time Pantagruel's men sail off to exotic lands in the south, where Pantagruel fathers a race of pygmies. He drowns the greater part of the Dipsodes' army by urinating upon them. Then he uses their leader WEREWOLF as a battering ram and finally throws his corpse into the city of Amaurotes. Throughout the epic battle, Pantagruel's forces suffer only the loss of Epistemon. Pantagruel finds Epistemon's dying body and revives it with applications of magic drugs. Then Epistemon tells his friends of his quick journey to hell. He mentions the many popes and famous heroes who dwell in the underworld despite their great reputations on earth. Pantagruel enters the city of Amaurotes and forces King ANARCHUS to marry a prostitute; Anarchus spends the rest of his life peddling sauces. On returning from the war, Pantagruel falls sick and the various liquids he voids from his body form the world-famous spas of the Mediterranean region. Eventually some miners armed with pickaxes are sent down into his stomach. They hack out the harmful germs and the giant is quickly cured. The author promises to continue the giant's adventures in a future book.

Book III. 1–15. After the war Pantagruel transports thousands of Utopians into the ravished land of Dipsody. He also makes Panurge ruler of Salmagundi in that land. Then he visits Panurge and is exasperated to learn of his friend's enormous debts. The two men debate the advisability of falling into debt. Pantagruel finds himself unable to dissuade his friend. Finally Panurge sells his costly jeweled codpiece and pays off all his creditors. He then drapes himself with a blanket and informs Pantagruel that he wants to marry. The giant insists that this step is very serious and must not be undertaken without wise guidance, because men are often cuckolded by unfaithful wives. Pantagruel takes a copy of Virgil's *Aeneid*

Pantagruel summons a deaf-mute to talk to Panurge in sign language

and asks Panurge to open at random to a verse. When Panurge does so, the verse is so ambiguous that both men can argue equally well for and against marriage. Since the ardent Panurge will not give in, Pantagruel takes him to Friar John's abbey at Thélème to consult about dreams. After taking drugs, Panurge is visited by a strange dream that promises happiness but ends with his being transformed into a drum. Again Panurge refuses to accept Pantagruel's ill-omened interpretation.

16–28. Panurge visits the Sibyl of Panzoult. He finds an oracular message foretelling unhappiness in marriage, but he remains obstinate. Next Pantagruel summons a deaf-mute, who talks to Panurge in signs that forebode ill fortune. Panurge tries to strike the man and is held back by the giant. He encounters similar bad luck when he seeks advice from an old poet named Raminagrobis and an astronomer named Herr Tripa. Finally Panurge is encouraged when he visits Friar John alone. The friar tells him that the only way to insure the constant faithfulness of a woman is to make constant love to her. **29–47.** Panurge holds a lavish banquet, to which he invites several learned men for advice. The theologian Hippothadeus tells him to marry one of the wise women from the Bible, but Panurge insists that they are all dead. Dr. Rondibilis counsels him to feed his wife drugs, work her to death, or make constant love, to insure her fidelity. The philosopher Skeinwinder quibbles so cleverly that Panurge never does learn his advice. At last Pantagruel persuades Panurge to consult the great fool Triboulet, an advisor to kings. Before doing so, Panurge visits a town where his friend, the lawyer BRIDLEGOOSE, is being tried. For years Bridlegoose has decided cases at court by throwing dice, and he has only recently been caught. Panurge frees his friend by pleading old age and by promising to make restitution for any bad de-

cisions. The fool Triboulet arrives and speaks some insane words. Pantagruel and Panurge argue their meaning. Triboulet hands Panurge a bottle and Panurge decides that he must make a pilgrimage to the place of the Holy Bottle. **48–52.** Pantagruel, Panurge, Friar John and others prepare for a sea voyage. The author describes the marvelous plant called pantagruelion or hemp. He gives a learned summary of its growing conditions and uses, remarking that it is best used for hanging criminals.

Book IV. 1–32. (In the last two books of the novel, Rabelais describes a mock-epic voyage that satirizes traditional medieval crusades, particularly the quest for the Holy Grail.) On the island of Medamothy or Nowhere, Pantagruel buys some relics from ancient times that he sends to his father

Pantagruel prepares a sea voyage

Gargantua. He also writes his father about the great adventures that the group is encountering. Panurge meets some returning pilgrims from Lanternland and tries to bargain for one of their sheep. When he fails, he causes the whole flock to run madly into the sea. Friar John informs him that he has put a curse upon their voyage. The travelers visit the island of Ennasin, where all relatives intermarry; Cheli, where perpetual peace proves to be a great bore; and the Land of Pettifogging, where the hospitable Lord Basché is hard put to discipline his dishonest servants. A raging storm then causes everyone to make his will. After it quiets down, Friar John reproves Panurge for his cowardice with the proverb: "Danger past, God forgot." In the islands of the Macreons, Pantagruel encounters the great heroes of the past, for heroes never die. On Sneaks Island, the voyagers are appalled by the ghostlike appearance of King Lent and his ascetic friends. **33–67.** On nearby Wild Island, Pantagruel learns that the inhabitants, called Chitterlings or Sausages, wage constant war against King Lent. When the Chitterlings prove hostile to the voyagers, several are caught, cooked and eaten. Friar John defends the Chitterlings. The sausages are saved when a flying pig appears in the air and warns them to retreat. Eventually Pantagruel signs a truce with their queen, Niphleseth. Soon afterward the voyagers land on Popefiggery Island, where the inhabitants detest all popes and are thus leagued with the devil. On nearby Papimania Island, the inhabitants worship the decrees of the popes and long to see the current pope's face. Stoutmoron, the Bishop of Papimania, receives the voyagers cordially when they profess to have visited Rome. He bores the pilgrims with longwinded accounts of miracles effected by papal decrees. Traveling onward, they visit the land of Gaster or Belly, who is responsible for all human arts and crafts. Gaster recites many events from history and claims that noble deeds were done "all for the sake of their guts!" Pantagruel and his friends are soon cloyed by the great feasts on the island and push onward. The pilgrims wisely skirt the islands of Robbers and Hypocrites. Pantagruel orders the men to shoot a salute near the island of Muses, and the explosion causes Panurge to lose control of his body.

Book V. 1–17. The voyagers next land on Ringing Island, where all mortals have become birds. The chief bird is the Popehawk, but the pilgrims do not have a chance to hear him sing. Pantagruel remarks that this island seems to be a paradise, because no one ever does any work except singing. The pilgrims soon learn, however, that food is provided only in payment for song. The birds are happy and look forward to an even better life in the Elysian Fields. Next, the voyagers pass Wicket Island, inhabited by Furry Lawcats led by the Archduke Graspall. They manage to elude these corrupt men, whom Friar John drives away with a sword. **18–48.** In the land of Quintessence, the pilgrims watch the queen miraculously cure diseased persons with music. Life on this island is so philosophical that the queen eats only pre-chewed abstractions. When the pilgrims are invited to a ball, they are surprised to find that the dance proceeds according to a chess game. The court is divided into gold and silver sides, and the queen's side is gold. The voyagers are shocked when the queen is defeated in the game and a new silver queen is chosen to replace her. The pilgrims scurry back to their ships and later land at Sandal Island, where untalkative monks called Demisemiquavers reside. Panurge questions a monk about the whereabouts of prostitutes. He learns that the Demisemiquavers speak only in monosyllables.

Next the voyagers visit the land of Satin, which is filled with exotic creatures and works of art. At last they arrive at their destination, Lanternland. Equipped with a Lantern to guide them, they go underground to the Temple of the Holy Bottle. Before they are received by the priestess BACBUC, the pilgrims inspect murals showing Bacchus's triumph over the Indians. The priestess allows them to drink from a splendid fountain, and the pilgrims are sure that the liquid is wine. At last Panurge stands before the magic bottle, waiting for advice. The bottle utters a single word: Trinc. The priestess tells Panurge that the word means Drink! Soon the whole party breaks out into a festive celebration. As the pilgrims prepare to leave, Bacbuc tells them that they are protected by "that intellectual sphere, whose center is everywhere, whose circumference is nowhere, and whom we call God."

The Gentleman from San Francisco

Story by Ivan Bunin, 1870-1953. Published 1916.

BUNIN, AN EMIGRÉ from Red Russia, was awarded the Nobel Prize in 1933. His story about the gentleman from San Francisco shares with his novel *The Well of Days* position as his best-known works. The story has a familiar theme, the workings of fate to upset the best-laid schemes; the natural popularity of this theme and the virtuosity with which it is executed in this story have combined to give the story its eminence.

The GENTLEMAN FROM SAN FRANCISCO has amassed a large fortune and desires to enjoy the pleasures and luxuries of a trip to Europe. With his rather plain wife and pretty but unsophisticated daughter he embarks on the great liner *Atlantis,* sailing from New York for Mediterranean ports.

The Gentleman and his family are ensconced in a sumptuous suite and they partake of the rich fare and entertainment afforded first-class passengers. An Eastern prince boards the ship at a Mediterranean port and the Gentleman's daughter is thrilled when he deigns to chat with her. The Gentleman and his family disembark at Naples, where they engage rooms in the best hotel.

The Gentleman has promised himself the pleasures of that city including "the love of young Neapolitan women conferred—let us admit—with wholly disinterested motives." He also looks forward to mingling with the most select society gathered in the most exclusive spots in Italy and on the French Riviera.

The weather is unseasonably cold in Naples, and the Gentleman takes his wife and daughter first to Sorrento and then across the bay to the Isle of Capri. They arrive on the island after a short but rough voyage on a small ship, and are installed in the very best hotel suite. The Gentleman keeps the servants hopping and the room-service waiter jokes with his colleagues about the frequency with which the Gentleman rings for service. The Gentleman requests a good table in the dining salon and orders with the proper savoir-faire. He finishes dressing before his wife and daughter are ready and descends to the reading room to wait for them. He lights a fine cigar, then suddenly suffers a stroke and slumps unconscious in his chair. A doctor attempts to revive him, but the Gentleman dies.

No coffin is available and the Gentleman's body is taken back to Naples in an oblong packing case.

The Gentleman's wife and daughter board the *Atlantis* for the return trip to New York and deep in the hold of the ship, surrounded by general cargo, the body of the Gentleman from San Francisco lies in a plain coffin.

He has made his trip to Europe and now he is returning home.

Gentlemen Prefer Blondes

Novel by Anita Loos, 1893– Published 1925 by Boni & Liveright, New York. © 1925 by Anita Loos.

NO MORE HILARIOUS book than this has been written in the United States and the fortune it must single-handed have brought to its author—what with a play, a musical comedy, motion pictures, and by-products—is richly deserved. One strange, and to most readers incredible fact about the book is that the blonde, Lorelei, is not greatly exaggerated. She existed in considerable numbers, just as Miss Loos pictured her. The subtitle of the book is *The Illuminating Diary of a Professional Lady,* and as it says, the book is in diary form. It is quite short, about 40,000 words.

Chap. 1. LORELEI LEE, a blond chorus girl with sex appeal, is short on education but long on her taste for the more expensive things of life. Her current gentleman friend in the opulent 1920s is GUS EISMAN, the Button King from Chicago. He is interested in furthering Lorelei's education and gives her books to read and even persuades her to keep a diary. She feels she is justifying the faith her family in Little Rock has in her talent. Lorelei and her friend DOROTHY always manage to have dates with rich and generous men. Mr. Eisman gives Lorelei a diamond ring for her birthday and when she is obviously disappointed at its smallness, he buys her a beautiful diamond bracelet. While he is away, Lorelei becomes friendly with GERALD LAMSON, an English author, who likes her more for her soul than for her beauty. Lorelei does not think this sort of affection pays off, but she really tries to improve her mind for his sake. Lamson tries to get her to stop seeing Eisman and promises he will divorce his English wife and marry Lorelei. The thought of spending years in serious discussions with Gerald depresses her and when Mr. Eisman suggests a trip to Europe at his expense, with Dorothy as a traveling companion, she readily agrees.

Chaps. 2. Thanks to Mr. Eisman, the girls have a lavish stateroom loaded with flowers. Dorothy snares a rich Englishman, Major FALCON, but Lorelei fears her friend's slang will not get her very far with the major, who she thinks is delightful for an Englishman because he spends money freely. Lorelei sees a familiar-looking man and is distressed to learn that he is Mr. BARTLETT, the former District Attorney in Little Rock, who once tried her for the murder of a Mr. Jennings. Bartlett was the only one at the trial who was not smitten with Lorelei, but his efforts to convict her were in vain, as the jury took but three minutes to acquit her and the judge took her to dinner and got her a job in Hollywood. Falcon tells Lorelei that Bartlett is going to Vienna on a mission for the U.S. Government, and he asks her to find out what the mission is. Lorelei uses her usual charms and soon finds out that Bartlett is going to buy some new airplanes that other countries, especially England, want to buy. She is sore at Bartlett for some of the things he said about her seven years ago in Little Rock, and Falcon has been showering her with gifts, so she tells him what Bartlett's mission is. Lorelei looks forward to the end of the voyage because there is no jewelry shop aboard the ship and she has too many bottles of perfume and too many stuffed dogs.

Chap. 3. Lorelei and Dorothy arrive in London and stay at the Ritz. They like the hotel because it is filled with rich, free-spending American men. The girls make the rounds of tea parties, dinners, balls and country homes. Lorelei is entranced by an old dowager's diamond tiara, which can be bought for $7,500. She gives the dowager a deposit of $100 and cables Mr. Eisman for more money. Eisman sends her only $1,000 and Lorelei decides she will have to find and train an Englishman to buy the tiara for her. She picks out Sir FRANCIS BEEKMAN, despite his reputation for tightness, and before Sir Francis knows what has happened to him he is mad about Lorelei and has bought the tiara for her. She promises that she will always stay in London and will always be friendly with him. But she and Dorothy are soon bored with London and head for Paris.

Chap. 4. The girls are slightly off stride until they become accustomed to the rate of exchange, but they soon find Paris a most educational place. They improve their minds with visits to the ancient city's famous landmarks such as Cartier's and Coty's. Dorothy is entranced by the gallantry of the Frenchmen, but Lorelei observes that they are more gallant than giving. The large and determined wife of Sir Francis appears and demands that Lorelei return the tiara to her husband or she will ruin Lorelei's reputation. The threat is meaningless. The next day two French attorneys, M. BROUSSARD and his son LOUIS, call on the girls. They have been retained by Lady Beekman to get back the tiara. In no time at all the father and son are smitten by the girls' charms and the foursome make a grand tour of Paris. Lorelei has a paste imitation of the tiara made and has Dorothy sell it to Louis. She gets it back from Louis and sells it to his father. She then lifts it from his pocket and he accuses Louis of having stolen it. Lorelei tells him the truth and they decide to have another paste duplicate made and give it to Lady Beekman. They are sure she will not know the difference, and the two lawyers charge the cost of it to her as part of their expenses.

Chap. 5. Mr. Eisman arrives in Paris, then goes to Vienna to buy a button factory. He sends for the girls and they take the Oriental Express. On the train Lorelei meets a delightful American gentleman named HENRY SPOFFARD. He is of a very fine old family and is a reformer. He is in Europe looking at all the things that spoil peoples' morals. Lorelei is intrigued with him and convinces Spoffard that she is an old-fashioned girl. She doesn't want Spoffard to meet Eisman, so they get off the train at Munich. Spoffard takes Lorelei to the museums, where she gets full of culture, but Dorothy finds a German gentleman who takes her to the "Half Brow" House

where she gets full of beer. They go on to Vienna. Mr. Eisman is busy with the button profession and tells Lorelei to run around with Dorothy. But she runs around with Spoffard instead, and sees Mr. Eisman at night. Spoffard brings his mother to meet Lorelei, who is wearing a simple dress for the occasion. The two women get along beautifully and the mother gets giddy on champagne. Spoffard and his mother go to Budapest, but he writes to Lorelei and says he wants to marry her. She wires back her acceptance of the proposal, but then ponders the wisdom of her decision and decides to go back to New York.

Chap. 6. Lorelei decides to have nothing to do with men on the ship, but she meets a dealer in unset diamonds. She spends some time with him, but they quarrel the night before the ship docks and Lorelei is left with some unset diamonds, which she puts in her handbag so that she will not have to declare them to customs. Spoffard meets her at the dock and reporters question the two, find they are engaged, and listen to Lorelei's story of her background as a society girl in Little Rock. They ask her when she made her debut and Dorothy tells them it was at an Elks' carnival when she was 15. This upsets Lorelei and Dorothy decides to throw a debutante party for her. The whole Racquet Club turns out for the party, plus various and sundry characters including the members of the Silver Spray Social Club of Brooklyn. Three days later the party breaks up, but it is properly noted in the newspapers with headlines such as "Lorelei's Debut a Wow!" Spoffard takes Lorelei to his home in Pennsylvania to meet his family. His aged father jumps out of his wheelchair and fawns all over the girl, but Lorelei finds the atmosphere dull and goes back to New York. The prospect of a life with Spoffard no longer seems to appeal to her and she plans to break the engagement by charging vast purchases to Spoffard. Dorothy tells him about Lorelei's extravagances and he leaves in a panic. Lorelei changes her mind and finds Spoffard at Penn Station. She tells him the whole thing was a plot to test his love for her, and they are married.

Lorelei promises that she will always stay in London

The Brothers Grimm

Jakob, 1785–1863, and Wilhelm, 1786–1859

Nathaniel Hawthorne
1804–1864

Ghosts

Play by Henrik Ibsen, 1828–1906.
Produced 1881. Several translations.
(RE, 4)

IN GHOSTS, IBSEN typically dramatized an aspect of the new scientific knowledge that was rising to a´peak late in the 19th century. Here his peg is the congenital aspects of syphilis [a forbidden word in those times] and the dire later consequences of the disease, such as paresis. In the playwright's art Ibsen was never better, especially in his skillful recounting of past events in the dialogue without slowing down the tempo of the current events.

Act I. ENGSTRAND, a crippled carpenter, visits his daughter REGINE, who works for the widowed Mrs. ALVING. Engstrand, having saved money he earned working on a new orphanage, intends to open a home for seamen and wants her help him run the tavern. Regine refuses because she intends to work in the orphanage and because her father is a drunkard. Pastor MANDERS, then Mrs. Alving, come in as Engstrand leaves. Mrs. Alving's son OSVALD has come home to spend the winter. Manders wonders if the new orphanage, which has been named in honor of Mrs. Alving's late husband, should be insured; some people might consider insurance a lack of faith in Divine Providence. Mrs. Alving says there was a small fire at the orphanage the day before, due to Engstrand's carelessness, and Manders says that Engstrand drinks only to relieve his pains. He asks Mrs. Alving to let Regine live with her father, but Mrs. Alving refuses. Osvald enters and Manders berates him for being an artist and having artist friends, who are immoral. Osvald denies this and leaves. Manders reminds Mrs Alving that she once left her dissolute husband and that he, Manders, persuaded her to go back, as her husband had´reformed. Mrs. Alving says that her husband never reformed; he seduced one of their serving girls, who then gave birth to Regine. Mrs. Alving built the orphanage only to counteract the talk about her husband's immorality. Osvald is heard making advances to Regine in the adjoining room and Mrs. Alving thinks she is hearing ghosts—the ghosts of those who carried on in the same room years before.

Act II. After dinner, Osvald leaves. Mrs. Alving and Manders decide that Regine cannot remain in the house, as she is the illegitimate daughter of the late Alving. Manders is furious that Engstrand married the servant girl knowing she was pregnant, and fraudulently pretended to be Regine's real father. Mrs. Alving regrets not having told Osvald about his father's true nature. She speaks of the ghosts that keep haunting her and wishes she had the courage to banish them by letting the light in on them. She berates Manders for not taking her in when she left her husband—she loved the pastor, but now she feels there is no understanding between them. Engstrand comes in and asks Manders to conduct an evening service at the orphanage. Manders accuses him of concealing the truth about Regine's parentage. Engstrand admits it but says he was not paid to marry the pregnant girl, and Manders forgives him. The two men leave and Osvald returns. He tells his mother he has had a nervous breakdown and a doctor told him his constitution was undermined due to the sins of his father. He wants to take Regine with him to Paris, where they can live joyfully. Before Mrs. Alving can say anything, Manders returns and says he wants Regine to help her father run his home for seamen. They hear shouts that the orphanage is on fire and all rush out.

Act III. The orphanage has burned. Engstrand accuses Manders of having set fire to it, but the pastor knows he will be under public attack for having opposed insurance.

Mrs. Alving feels that the fire was all for the best—the orphanage was a false memorial and would never have brought any good to anyone. Engstrand offers to take the blame for the fire and Manders promises to help him with funds for his home for seamen. Mrs. Alving tells Osvald about his father's dissolute life and that Regine is his half-sister. Regine also is told and then will not accept Mrs. Alving's offer of a home. She leaves to find Engstrand and Manders. Mrs. Alving tries to console Osvald and is almost happy that he is ill, for now she will be able to care for him. She talks to him of the future and how he will be able to paint again when his depression and illness are cured. But Osvald tells her his illness is mental and that the doctor has told him it will gradually grow worse. He has saved enough morphine to kill himself. Mrs. Alving wants to run for a doctor, but Osvald makes her promise she will help him to die when it becomes necessary. She calms him. The sun rises and Osvald begs her to give him the sun, over and over again. He is insane.

The Adventures of
Gil Blas of Santillane

Novel by Alain René Le Sage, 1668–1747.
Published from 1715 to 1735. Translation from the French by Tobias Smollett published 1749; several other translations.

PART OF THE great reputation of *Gil Blas* stems from the fact that it has been called the first picaresque novel —that is, a novel about rogues or adventurers. It was not that, since the literary treatment of rogues goes all the way back to Cervantes and Rabelais and besides Le Sage's hero was disqualified by having a conscience; but undoubtedly *Gil Blas* was a great work worthy of its fame and the appreciation of it by English readers was helped along greatly by the fact that a major English novelist, Smollett, translated and sponsored it. The book is very long, more than 300,000 words, but it is amusing from start to finish. It is set in the early 1600s.

Chaps. 1–15. GIL BLAS, the son of a former soldier, is sent to school in the town of Oviedo by his uncle, GIL PEREZ, who then sends him to Salamanca to make his own way, giving him some money and a mule. During the journey, he sells the mule to buy a dinner for a fop who flatters him at an inn. Gil Blas resumes his journey in the company of a newly married couple. The wife is plump and comely and the muleteer resolves to seduce her. To get rid of his other passengers he accuses them of having robbed him and threatens them. They flee to the woods. Gil starts back to rescue the woman but is intercepted by two horsemen, who take him to an underground cave. The cave is the sanctuary of a wealthy thieving order called The Brotherhood. The cook, LEONARDA, is made Gil Blas' superior with full power over him. At first he waits on table. He attempts to escape but is caught and beaten by a Negro servant and in time by the entire band. In the days that follow Gil Blas wins the confidence of his captors and asks to join the thieves on their raids. The captain, ROLANDO, gives consent and after six months in the cave Gil Blas is outfitted in a manner befitting a gentleman-thief. The bandits attack a coach, rob and kill four men, and take a girl captive. Gil Blas feigns illness to be excused from the next day's expedition. He gets the key from the cook and escapes, taking the girl with him. They ride to Astorga and put up at an inn, where the girl, Donna MENCIA, tells Gil Blas she was married; thought her husband was dead; became engaged to another man; and was reclaimed by her husband, who reappeared. The thieves killed her husband when they captured her. Donna Mencia's story is interrupted by officers who arrest Gil Blas.

The girl is not arrested. Gil Blas is freed when a passenger who was on the coach with him vouches for him. He proceeds to Burgos, where he finds Donna Mencia at a convent. She gives him 100 ducats to buy clothes and hints that her gratitude is far greater than a handful of ducats. Later he visits Donna Mencia and receives a present of 1,000 ducats from her. He leaves Burgos for Madrid.

Chaps. 16–21. At Valladolid, Gil Blas meets Donna CAMILLA, who says she is Donna Mencia's cousin. She and her brother, Don RAPHAEL, entertain Gil Blas and the girl persuades him to exchange rings. He believes the ring he gets to be very valuable and is smugly certain he has made a conquest. In the morning he finds the two dubious "cousins" gone and his portmanteau with them. Leaving the apartment, Gil Blas meets FABRICIUS, a friend from his native village, who gets him a job as footman in the house of SEDILLO, a boor and glutton. Gil Blas finds his work disagreeable but manages to conceal the fact and soon Sedillo dies and leaves Gil Blas his library, but it consists of worthless books. Gil Blas seeks out the doctor, SANGRADO, who treated Sedillo and becomes both his servant and his pupil. One day Gil Blas is called by an old lady to attend her niece, who turns out to be Donna Camilla. With the aid of Fabricius, Gil Blas gets back his ring but she declares her accomplice ran off with the money. She offers her personal jewelry and that of her aunt and Gil Blas and Fabricius take all of it and depart.

Chaps. 22–30. The aunt tells the story to the police and Gil Blas is once again in jail. Fabricius's master effects their release but the authorities confiscated Gil Blas' ring and the other jewelry. Gil Blas is now practicing medicine feverishly, but Dr. Sangrado's bloodletting and water cure seem only to result in swift death for all the patients. Gil Blas treats a handsome widow who is betrothed to a fiery Latin and when the widow dies Gil Blas is forced to flee the city to escape the Latin's wrath. He goes to Madrid and secures a position as valet to a mysterious man whose name and occupation are unknown. The authorities investigate the man and he wins their confidence by showing them a trunk filled with gold. On the street one day Gil Blas meets Captain Rolando, who invites him to rejoin the band of thieves. Gil Blas refuses, but his master saw him with Rolando and dismisses him. Gil Blas is next employed in the home of a playboy lord of Spain, whose household is ruled by a diabolical steward. The young lord lives a dissolute and Gil Blas leads the same life, but one scale down. They drink the same wine and while the young fop is entertained by the mistress Gil Blas is entertained by her maid. During this time the valets de chambre of the other lords are schooling him in superciliousness.

Chaps. 31–35. On the advice of his colleagues, Gil Blas steals some of his master's

fine clothes and goes forth to seek an intrigue with a lady of quality. He meets one, sets an assignation, and tells her he is a cousin to the man he actually serves as valet. That night he accompanies his master to the home of an actress and the actress's maid, LAURA, is the "lady of quality" he met that afternoon. But they spend a pleasant evening together. Gil Blas now takes over duties as secretary to the lord. His work consists of forging letters from

The maid entertains Gil Blas

beautiful young ladies of Madrid. The lord reads these at dinner parties to amuse his companions, saying, of course, that they are genuine. But the lord is killed in a duel and Gil Blas is unemployed again.

Chaps. 36–40. Laura gets Gil Blas a position as steward in the home of her own mistress, the famous actress, where he will handle all household affairs, including the financial accounts. He succumbs to the general air of debauchery in the house, but soon he becomes satiated and disgusted. He quits and the steward of his deceased lord places him in the service of Don VINCENT, an old nobleman and widower, solely dedicated to raising his daughter, AURORA. One day the girl's duenna whispers to him of an assignation at midnight in the garden. Gil Blas meets Aurora, but contrary to his expectations Aurora confesses she is in love with a handsome cavalier she has never met. She wishes Gil Blas to quietly investigate the man, Don LEWIS. Gil Blas gets the required information, and though his report to Aurora is unfavorable she rewards him.

Chaps. 41–45. Don Vincent dies. Aurora inherits the estate and moves to a small castle in the country. She tells Gil Blas she cannot forget Don Lewis. She plans to go to Salamanca, where he is studying, disguise herself as a cavalier, meet Don Lewis, and extol the virtues and beauty of her "cousin" Aurora. She will engage two apartments and live in one as Aurora and in the other as the cavalier, "Don FELIX." Aurora and Gil Blas go to Salamanca. "Don Felix" intercepts a letter sent to Don Lewis

by his latest mistress and shows it to Don Lewis, pretending it was written to herself. He reads it and believes the girl guilty. Aurora proposes they write abusive letters to the girl. They do so and she gives them to Gil Blas, who delivers only the note from Don Lewis. The affair is broken up and the undisguised Aurora is brought "onstage" the next day. The deception, with much dashing about, is accomplished and Don Lewis asks for Aurora's hand in marriage. Aurora reveals the deception to him but they are married and now Aurora places Gil Blas in the service of her husband's uncle, Don GONZALES DE PACHECO. The old man is decrepit in health and wasted of body but has a young mistress, EUPHRASIA, who enlists Gil Blas' aid in a conspiracy to win her full favor in the old nobleman's will. Gil Blas pretends to accept but one day he discovers a young man concealed in Euphrasia's quarters and tells his master. Don Gonzales forgives Euphrasia, and dismisses Gil Blas as proof of his forgiveness, but does introduce Gil Blas to the home of the Marchioness DE CHAVES, where he is accepted for service.

Chaps. 46–55. The Marchioness entertains a daily gathering in her salon, the wits and intellectuals of Madrid. Gil Blas is attracted to a housemaid named PORTIA but the secretary to the Marchioness also favors the girl. A duel is fought and Gil Blas' life is spared on condition he leave Madrid immediately. At an inn Gil Blas hears of a fugitive the police are seeking and on the road he encounters Don ALPHONSO, the fugitive. A thunderstorm is brewing and they find shelter in a hermit's grotto. In the morning the hermit is recognized as the rascally Don Raphael. He and his valet beg Gil Blas and Don Alphonso to join them as wanderers living by their wits, and all agree. They go to Valencia, disguise themselves as police and church authorities, and terrorize a converted Jew, whose strongbox they rob. Gil Blas and Don Alphonso suffer remorse and leave. They set out for Italy but on the road they stop at a castle, where Alphonso finds his true love, SERAPHINA. They are married and Gil Blas becomes steward of the household. He enters into a flirtation with a lady-in-waiting, but then he hears gossip of a young surgeon's nocturnal visits to her. Gil Blas challenges the surgeon to a duel but the doctor talks him out of it. He no longer cares for the lady and she, scorned, loathes him with a passion that causes him to leave.

Chaps. 56–65. The brother-in-law of Don Alphonso secures Gil Blas a position with the Archbishop of Grenada, copying manuscripts. The Archbishop suffers an attack of apoplexy and though he recovers he can no longer write coherently. He instructs Gil Blas to criticize but when Gil Blas does so he is castigated for his bad taste and dismissed. Gil Blas goes to the theater and the favorite actress turns out to be Laura. He determines to see her even though her "patron" is a wealthy Portu-

Gil Blas flees to Toledo

guese nobleman, the Marquis de MARI-ALVA. Laura deceives the marquis by addressing Gil Blas as her brother, and Gil Blas is invited by the marquis to become his personal secretary. His first assignment is to visit Laura and make apologies for the marquis, taking a gift. He spends the morning with the actress. That night Gil Blas learns his true identity is known and he flees to Toledo to seek sanctuary with the father-in-law of Don Alphonso. He cannot find him and goes to Madrid to seek favor at the court.

Chaps. 66–75. In Madrid Gil Blas encounters his old friend Fabricius, who is now a poet in the favor of a nobleman. Fabricius obtains a position for Gil Blas as secretary to Count GILIANO, a Sicilian. His duties are to spy on the servants and reduce household expenses. He does this and becomes the steward, hated by the rest of the staff. Gil Blas falls sick. The count returns to Sicily and the butler robs Gil Blas. His next job is with the Duke of Lerma as a rent collector. The Duke makes him a confidante and a messenger to the Duke's nephew, the Count DE LEMOS. His position is important, he even meets the King, but unfortunately he has not been paid nor has there been any mention of salary. He is poverty-stricken amidst splendor.

Chaps. 76–85. A colleague of Gil Blas warns him that he now knows too much to be dismissed and will most certainly go to jail by the Duke's order, but Gil Blas is summoned before the Duke and given a year's salary. In addition, he is permitted to take bribes from rich persons who desire favors from the Duke. He moves into a fine apartment, buys expensive clothes, and hires a valet. The valet, SCIPIO, schooled in intrigue, brings to Gil Blas a nobleman who killed a man in a duel and seeks a royal pardon. Gil Blas manages this and gets a cash reward. He shares his bribes with the Duke. He buys a house with a full staff and entertains nightly. He is summoned to the Count de Lemos and told to procure a young beauty for the Prince. Scipio finds one, named CATALINA, and the Prince is overjoyed with her charms, but Gil Blas suspects the girl and her duenna and learns that they own two

houses, connected by a tunnel, and in the other house Catalina is the mistress of the Duke's chief secretary. He tells the Duke, but matters stand as they are. Scipio finds Gil Blas a bride with an enormous dowry. Gil Blas and SOLERO, his prospective father-in-law, agree to terms. Gil Blas remembers his old friend Don Alphonso and through the good offices of the Duke secures for him the governorship of Valencia.

Chaps. 86–95. The preparations for the wedding are well under way when suddenly Gil Blas is arrested, transported to the tower of Segovia, and thrown into a bare cell, with no charges against him. After two days the warden, whom Gil Blas befriended when he was in the service of the Archbishop, moves him to a room in the tower and feeds him fine foods and wine. Gil Blas has been imprisoned because the king has heard of his complicity in procuring a mistress for the Prince. The warden thinks the king's wrath will be dispelled in a couple of months. Scipio reports that soldiers and servants have ransacked his house, except for two bags of coins. Scipio insists on living at the prison. He says the Duke does not know of Gil Blas' fate and Gil Blas and Scipio decide to write to the Duke. Scipio delivers the letter but is rebuffed by the Duke. Gil Blas becomes very ill and when he recovers he is released from prison but is banished from Castile. He and Scipio buy mules and set out for Aragon. Solero has given his daughter in marriage to a rich merchant. Gil Blas visits Don Alphonso, now governor of Valencia, who rewards him with an estate at Luria in Valencia. Gil Blas goes to Oviedo to see his parents and arrives home in time to be at his father's bedside as he dies. He buries his father ostentatiously but is reviled by the townspeople, who think the money would have been better spent feeding the father while he lived. Gil Blas provides for his mother and leaves for his new estate.

Chaps. 96–105. Gil Blas and Scipio find their new home staffed with servants on the payroll of the governor but Gil Blas insists on hiring his own staff. In the city Gil Blas encounters the old bandit Don Raphael, dressed as a Carpathian monk. He tells Don Alphonso, but a few days later Raphael absconds with the monastery strongbox. Gil Blas meets and marries ANTONIA, the daughter of a neighboring farmer. The governor is host at the wedding and at his house. During the feast Scipio finds that one of Seraphina's maids, BEATRICE, is his wife, whom he deserted ten years before. They are reconciled and there is a double celebration.

Chaps. 106–115. Both Gil Blas and Scipio become fathers, but Gil Blas' wife and child die soon after. The King dies and the Prince succeeds to the throne. On the advice of Don Alphonso and Scipio, Gil Blas returns to Madrid and presents himself at Court. The new king recalls the service Gil Blas rendered him and orders the PRIME MINISTER to find suitable employment for Gil Blas. The Prime Minister sets Gil Blas up in great style and tells him to prepare propaganda to inform the people of Spain about the bad financial standing of the country and the fine efforts of the new king and Prime Minister to straighten matters out. In so doing, Gil Blas is forced to malign his former master, the Duke of Lerma, which he does without compunction. The propaganda is published and is very successful. Gil Blas roams the streets listening to the mood of the people, which he reports to his employer. Gil Blas' mother and uncle (Gil Perez) die. Gil Blas meets Fabricius, who now has a sponsor for his writings; his tragedy is presented and is practically hissed off the stage but the sponsor is so enraged at the audience that he doubles Fabricius's salary.

Chaps. 116–120. Scipio now having a family to provide for, Gil Blas supplies him with money for trade in the Indies on one of the Prime Minister's ships. Don Alphonso loses his governorship and is in trouble, because the Duke of Lerma is now a cardinal, but Gil Blas tells the Prime Minister how Alphonso got his post and the Prime Minister not only pardons Alphonso but makes him Viceroy of Aragon. The Prime Minister sends Gil Blas to Toledo incognito to watch a young actress named LUCRETIA. Gil Blas arrives on the eve of the *auto da fe* (burning of heretics), which he watches the following morning. He is horrified to see Don Raphael among the wretched awaiting execution. He goes to the theater and sees Lucretia; his old sweetheart Laura is her "aunt," actually her mother, and Gil Blas is not too sure but that he is the father.

Chaps. 121–125. Lucretia is called from Toledo and performs for the King. The King is smitten with Lucretia and Gil Blas is told to produce Lucretia as the King's mistress. Laura is willing; the girl has a virtue previously unassailable but after two or three meetings with the King she submits. Then she is so overcome with remorse that she enters a convent and soon dies of grief. Laura, to repent, enters the same convent. The King is peeved, the Prime Minister chagrined, and Gil Blas weighted with guilt. The Prime Minister has an illegitimate son in Genoa and sends Gil Blas to find the boy and educate him so that the Prime Minister can elevate him to a title and make him his heir. Gil Blas rents a house, staffs it, hires various tutors, and trains the boy well. Scipio returns from a most successful voyage and Gil Blas appoints him valet to the young man. All goes so well that the Prime Minister makes a very advantageous marriage for the boy. The Prime Minister presents Gil Blas with a king's patent raising him to noble rank. He is now Don Gil Blas.

Chaps. 126–130. Gil Blas again befriends Fabricius, who warns Gil Blas that the Prime Minister is losing favor and his days are numbered. The Prime Minister manages to avoid the conspiracy for some time, but then the Portuguese revolt and set up the Duke of Braganza as their king. The revolt is blamed on the Prime Minister, who has to resign. He takes up residence at Loeches and Gil Blas accompanies him. The Prime Minister is overcome with a strange melancholy and soon dies. Gil Blas is genuinely griefstricken.

Chaps. 131–133. Gil Blas is remembered handsomely in the will. He toys with the idea of entering a monastery but Scipio persuades him to return to his estate in Valencia. Scipio leaves the service of the Prime Minister's son and returns also. Scipio's daughter is being courted by a young man, Don JUAN, and Gil Blas meets Don Juan's sister, DOROTHEA, and falls insanely in love. He marries Dorothea and his life is serene and is blessed with two children.

God's Little Acre

Novel by Erskine Caldwell, 1903– Published 1933 by Viking Press, New York. © 1933 by Erskine Caldwell. (NAL, S581; ML, 51)

IT IS NOT NECESSARILY the highest praise for a book to cite its sales records, but in the case of *God's Little Acre* the record is so outstanding that it must serve. In its paperbound Signet Books edition, *God's Little Acre* has been the most popular novel ever published and may have outsold its nearest competitor among all books by two to one. At last reports the total was 12,000,000 and going strong. The earthily sexy passages may have helped more than Mr. Caldwell would have wished, but he may take comfort in the general opinion that *God's Little Acre* is a great novel, sufficient to insure his literary immortality. His character Ty Ty is as fine a homely philosopher as any novelist would wish to create. God's little acre may be vile, but every other aspect pleases. The novel is quite short, about 65,000 words.

Chap. 1. TY TY WALDEN, two of his sons, BUCK and SHAW, one of his daughters, DARLING JILL, and Buck's wife, GRISELDA, live together in an old, ramshackle farmhouse in Georgia. They do little farming. For 15 years they have spent most of their time digging for gold and the land around the farmhouse is pockmarked with holes. In that part of Georgia a few nuggets have been found and many people, especially the Negroes, hopefully dig and dig. PLUTO, a fat man, who is running for sheriff because he has nothing else to do, tells Ty Ty about an albino "all-white" man down near the swamp who is supposed to be able to divine the location of gold.

Chap. 2. Ty Ty's other daughter, ROSAMOND, "loved off" to a mill town and married a mill man. His third son, JIM LESLEY, has moved off to Augusta and become a rich broker and refuses to speak to his family. Ty Ty has set aside one acre, which he calls "God's little acre"—just so God will know that Ty Ty has a little of Him in his heart. But whenever the family digs in this acre Ty Ty dedicates a different acre to God, for Ty Ty has promised to give any proceeds coming from God's little acre

to God and he does not want to risk striking gold on God's plot.

Pluto asks Ty Ty if he can marry Darling Jill. Ty Ty says it would be all right with him but he doubts if the girl wants fat and lazy old Pluto.

Chaps. 3–4. When Pluto is ready to leave he finds his car has been swiped by the wild Darling Jill. He and Ty Ty plan to rope the albino and bring him back. Ty Ty suggests that Pluto drive over to Horse Creek Valley to get Rosamond and her husband, WILL THOMPSON, to help with the big gold-dig coming up. Ty Ty tells Pluto about the amazing beauty and modesty of his daughter-in-law, Griselda. Two Negro workers on the farm come up and say they are hungry and have nothing to eat. Ty Ty waves them off. He, Buck and Shaw leave in the old family car to capture the albino. Darling Jill returns and Pluto comes upon her taking a bath in the back yard. He stands staring at her ripe nudity, and she blows soap in his eyes.

Chap. 5. Darling Jill and Pluto go for Rosamond and Will. They find Rosamond in tears because Will is off drinking somewhere. He soon returns drunk and growls about how he intends, sometime, to have the lush Griselda. He talks about how the mill has been closed down for 18 months and people are practically starving but won't go back to work for $1.10 a day. He wants to break into the mill and turn the power on.

Chap. 6. The following morning Rosamond goes out to shop and Darling Jill seduces Will. Rosamond catches them. She beats Darling Jill and grabs a gun, which she shoots at Will's feet. She misses and then Will runs out of the house, naked. Rosamond and Darling Jill weep and console each other. Pluto holds Darling Jill naked, while Rosamond applies salve to her welts. Darling Jill wiggles and teases Pluto and runs off.

Chap. 7. Will manages a reconciliation with Rosamond. He still has a fierce impulse to turn the power on in the mill. He hates the union, which wants only useless and endless arbitration.

Chaps. 8–9. Ty Ty's place is full of ex-

Pluto comes upon Darling Jill taking a bath in the back yard

citement. The albino has been caught and everybody has been digging furiously at the spot where his divining indicated gold. The albino is young and handsome and flirts with Darling Jill. She drags him out into the yard and they make love. Ty Ty again lauds the beauty of Griselda, who blushes and hides her face.

Chaps. 10–13. The next morning the men are digging in the pit. Will taunts Buck and Shaw and a fight breaks out. The men go at each other with shovels. They are torn apart by Ty Ty, who knows that the real source of the conflict is Griselda. Ty Ty has not planted enough cotton to support the family the coming winter, so the whole family piles into the car and heads for Augusta to get money from Jim Lesley. In the city everyone but Ty Ty, Griselda and Darling Jill gets out of the car, being unwilling to face Jim Lesley. While the car is stopped prostitutes call down to Ty Ty from balconies. He wavers, but does not give in. They drive on to Jim Lesley's big white house on the hill, where they are rudely greeted. Jim Lesley's wife does not appear, as she is sick. Jim Lesley fixes a lecherous eye upon Griselda and Ty Ty immediately begins to praise Griselda's beauty. Ty Ty eventually gets the money he came for, and he and the girls get into the car. Jim Lesley leans in and puts his hands on Griselda, saying he will drag her from the car. Darling Jill starts the car. Jim Lesley's hands tear Griselda's dress as his arm is jerked from the car.

Chaps. 14–16. The following day everybody is back digging in the sweltering pit. Tension bristles between Buck and Will, and Will decides he wants to return home. Darling Jill persuades Pluto to take Will and Rosamond home in his car and she and Griselda go along for the ride. Buck is highly displeased. At Horse Creek Valley Will jumps out of the car and disappears for several hours. When he reappears he is agitated and says he and his friends have decided to break into the mill the following morning. Will feels like "God Almighty Himself." He tells Griselda he is going to tear all the clothes off her back. He does so, violently, passionately, in front of the others, and carries her off to another room. Rosamond remains silent and composed. Darling Jill is frantic with excitement;

Pluto is speechless. All of them remain awake that night. In the morning a friend drops in to tell Will that Pinkerton guards have arrived at the mill. Will leaves for the mill; the women soon follow him. They fear that Buck will find out what happened and will kill Will.

Chaps. 17–18. The Horse Creek Valley men break down a fence and smash their way into the mill. They take their posts at the looms and wait for the power to be turned on by Will Thompson, who is hailed as the leader. Suddenly the power goes on, then some shots are heard. Will Thomson has been shot dead and the backbone of the town's resistance is broken. The girls weep

with agony. Pluto is frightened and Darling Jill comforts him with maternal love. They return home and when Ty Ty hears the news he moves God's little acre back under the house. Griselda tells Ty Ty that he has something in common with Will—they were both real men, as evidenced by their appreciation of her.

Chap. 19. A long, sleek car drives up and Jim Lesley steps out. He has come for Griselda. Ty Ty and Buck try to stop him from entering the house, but Jim Lesley is used to getting his own way. Buck finds him in the dining room with Griselda, with the other girls crouched behind a chair. Buck grabs a gun. Jim Lesley runs from the house, but Buck shoots him twice and he dies a few minutes later. Ty Ty is shattered. He

looks about at his dug-up land and wishes he could smooth it all out with a sweep of his arm. He warns Buck that the sheriff will come. Buck kisses Griselda goodbye and walks away into the distance. Ty Ty wills that God's little acre follow Buck and always be under him. He then picks up his shovel and begins to dig. Griselda asks what happened to the gun that Buck used and without raising his eyes Ty Ty tells her Buck took it with him. She runs away and Ty Ty goes on digging.

The Golden Ass of Lucius Apuleius

Novel by Lucius Apuleius, 2nd century A.D.

Published about 150. Various translations; translation from the Latin by Robert Graves published 1951 by Farrar, Straus, & Young, New York, © 1951 by Robert Graves. (PB, PL6)

THIS MAY BE the first extant novel, for it is a novel, though it is seldom so described. Within its structure as a novel *The Golden Ass* is a succession of tales, of which most were perhaps not original with the author and at least one certainly was not, the story of Cupid and Psyche. Some of the tales are bawdy and two or three might seem beyond the pale, but the book will disappoint anyone who has been led to expect pornography. It is the story of a man who was turned into an ass and of his adventures while in that form. Its title in Latin is literally "The Several Transformations of Lucius." It has had a tremendous effect on the novel through the ages and is good reading even today. Among other things it supports worship of the Egyptian gods Osiris and Isis, a pagan religion that appealed to a growing Roman minority at that time, and also Platonic philosophy; and it is refreshingly iconoclastic in its view of man as seen by his animal servants.

Chaps. 1–2. LUCIUS OF MADAURA is on his way to the town of Hypata in northern Greece. He meets a wholesale honey-buyer named ARISTOMENES who warns him not to go and tells him a story of a terrible occurrence in Hypata: Aristomenes and his friend SOCRATES went to an inn run by a witch, MEROE, who engaged in secret love rites and transformed into animals any men who refused to join in them. Socrates had offended her in this way, for that night two

witches came to his bed and cut out his heart. Despite the warning, Lucius goes on to Hypata. He stays with a niggardly moneylender, MILO, and Milo's wife PAMPHILE, who dabbles in magic. Though warned by his cousin BYRRHAENA to be careful, Lucius enters into a romance with Pamphile's slave girl, FOTIS.

Chaps. 3–4. On the eve of the Festival of Laughter, at a banquet in Byrrhaena's house, Lucius hears the terrible Tale of THELYPHRON. Thelyphron lost his nose and ears while trying to prevent witches from devouring those organs on a corpse. Returning to Milo's house, Lucius kills three brigands who seem to threaten the house. He is haled into court on the day of the festival and is tried for their murder. After much laughter, Lucius learns that the brigands were really hanging wine-skins that Pamphile had enchanted to make them seem like men. Confounded by these strange deeds, Lucius persuades Fotis to sneak him into Pamphile's magic rites.

Chaps. 5–6. Lucius watches Pamphile change herself into an owl, the bird of wisdom. He begs Fotis to take Pamphile's drugs and change him too. Feeling that the noble Lucius has merely used her, Fotis changes him instead into an ass, the goddess Isis's most despised creature. Fotis promises to restore him the next day by bringing him roses to eat; but before she can do this, Milo's house is invaded by thieves. They feel fortunate to find an ass available, and Lucius is laden with heavy spoils and driven away to a wild cave presided over by an old hag. In order to comfort a beautiful girl named CHARITE, who is taken there as a hostage, the hag tells the famous Tale of CUPID and PSYCHE.

Chaps. 7–9. Venus sent her son Cupid to destroy a beautiful girl, Psyche ("soul" in Greek), who rivaled her beauty. Instead Cupid fell in love with Psyche and took her to a secret palace where he visited her by night. Psyche, who had expected to be exposed to a monster, listened to her jealous sisters and lighted a candle to see who her lover was. Cupid abandoned his dis-

299

Fotis mischievously changes Lucius into an ass

trusting wife and Psyche wandered the world, at last coming to Venus's house and begging help, for she was soon to give birth to a child. Venus set various impossible tasks for the girl. She made Psyche sort a pile of grain, but some ants assisted Psyche. Venus made Psyche fleece some golden sheep, and brambles came to her aid. Venus sent her to the Underworld for a pitcher of water from the River Styx, and Jove's eagle did the work. With the help of a speaking tower, Psyche also brought back some of the beauty of Proserpina, the queen of Hades, in a jar. At last Venus relented and permitted Psyche to join her husband; so Love and Rational Soul were inextricably wed. [The story of Cupid and Psyche is told more fully in another volume.]

Chaps. 10–11. Lucius, trying to escape with the hostage Charite, kills the old hag but is caught and beaten. Charite's lover comes to the cave, disguised as a bandit, and leads her and the ass to safety. In gratitude Charite's family sends Lucius to a stud farm, where he waits for the spring roses to bloom. While Lucius is there he hears that Charite's lover has been killed by his best friend, who also hoped to marry the girl. Charite pretends to encourage the murderer until she gets him to her room and in her power. Then she puts his eyes out and everyone flees the cursed estate.

Chaps. 12–16. Lucius continues a life of drudgery while misfortunes plague his various lecherous, conniving owners. A band of eunuch priests buys him but they are imprisoned for stealing. His next owner, a miller, is killed by his adulterous wife, who then disappears. Lucius is next stolen from a poor farmer by a Roman soldier, who sells him to a nobleman. The nobleman, THYASUS, learns that Lucius is a talented jackass who acts surprisingly mortal. He decides to exhibit Lucius at some degrading gladiatorial shows in the spring.

Chaps. 17–19. Lucius escapes, bathes seven times in the sea and offers a beautiful prayer to the Blessed Queen of Heaven. The goddess Isis descends and leads him to her mystery rites. There, a year after his first transformation, Lucius is changed back into a man. After regaining his goods, Lucius goes to Rome and accepts Osiris as the Lord of all Gods and Isis as the Queen of all feminine deities. Thus he achieves the highest spiritual state possible to a mortal after his long suffering as a hated animal living among bestial men.

Goodbye, Mr. Chips

Novel by James Hilton, 1900-1954. Published 1934 by Little, Brown & Co.-Atlantic Monthly Press, Boston. © 1934 by James Hilton.

HILTON'S TRIBUTE to the familiar superannuated teacher was an unexpectedly successful tearjerker, producing not only a best-seller in the book stalls but also a successful play and motion picture. The book is very short, only about 25,000 words. It is very skillfully done and its record attests to the fact that it is one of the best things of its kind that have been written.

Chaps. 1–3. Mr. CHIPS—a nickname so time-honored that many think it is his real name—sits by the fire in Mrs. WICKETT's boarding house one late November afternoon in 1933. His mind is clouded with memories. He thinks of the first day he came to teach at Brookfield. That was in 1870, when Chips was only 23. He had taught for a while at another school, but he had not been successful because he had not been able to discipline the students. Smiling, old Chips recalls the first punishment he meted out at Brookfield; it was to a boy named COLLEY who had slammed the lid of his desk. After that, Chips had had no trouble with discipline at all. Still smiling, Chips remembers that Colley's son had been at Brookfield too—and his grandson. Three generations of Colleys, and Chips had taught Latin to them all. When Chips was new at Brookfield he was full of ambition and had hopes of being headmaster, but he learned he was only run-of-the-mill, like Brookfield itself. As the years passed, he learned to love "his boys," to remember every one of them by name. To everyone Chips seemed like a typical bachelor but they were wrong, for Chips had once been married.

Chaps. 4–8. Chips had been at Brookfield 25 years before he met KATHERINE BRIDGES, who was 25. He had never liked women; they had always seemed so strange and demanding. But Katherine was different. He met her on a walking tour of the Lake District. They were married, even though Chips was old enough to be her father. Katherine conquered Brookfield as wholly as she had conquered Chips. Everyone loved her and obeyed her. She was good for Chips and helped broaden his views and opinions. She taught him compassion. She taught Brookfield, too. Once Kathy convinced Chips that the school should play a soccer match with the boys from the London slum mission that Brookfield supported. The idea was revolutionary but the game was a huge success. When Kathy died in childbirth, only three years after they were married, Chips was desolate. She and the infant died on April 1, 1898—April Fool's Day. Chips did not even notice the little pranks the boys played that day.

Chaps. 9–13. Life at Brookfield had been good, but there had been some bad moments. Once a new headmaster had tried to make Chips resign. That was in 1908. The headmaster had called Chips old-fashioned because he refused to teach Latin by the "new" methods. But all the school rallied around Chips and he did not leave. The hardest years of all were the World War I years. Every day there was a new report of old Brookfieldians killed in action. Chips had retired when he was 65 but was called back to Brookfield for the "duration." The board of trustees asked him to act as headmaster and he agreed, his heart swelling with pride. Years later people still talked about Chips' courage during the German bombings and how one day he conducted his Latin class as though nothing were happening, while there were tremendous explosions all about.

Chaps. 14–18. Then the war was over and Chips moved back to Mrs. Wickett's. He was still a part of Brookfield—he prepared the school directory, attended Old Boys' dinners in London, and met visiting dignitaries. His reputation for "funny" sayings grew. He used to send boys into peals of laughter when he said he thought a Wurlitzer was a German sausage, or when he made some obscure Latin puns. Chips always tried to learn the names of new boys as they arrived, but this was becoming more and more difficult. Nevertheless, Chips still invited the boys to tea. Brookfield had been home for 63 years.

Reflecting about his past, this chilly November afternoon in 1933, Chips hears a rap at the door. Mrs. Wickett is out. He goes to the door and finds a little boy standing there, a new boy just arrived that week. The boy asks for "Mr. Chips," saying he was told that Chips had been looking for him. Chips smiles. It is an old schoolboy joke being played on the youngster. Chips says, "Yes, come in." He says he has wanted to have the boy to tea. They chat and at 5 o'clock promptly, Chips dismisses the boy in a gentle fashion. He dies quietly that night in his sleep. The boy will always remember that it was he who said goodbye to Mr. Chips.

The Good Companions

Novel by J. B. Priestley, 1894–
Published 1929.

THIS ONE NOVEL was sufficient to establish John Boynton Priestley as an important novelist, but he wrote several later novels that were as well received. In *The Good Companions* his characters won the sympathy of readers and critics and the adventures of those characters made the book continuously interesting.

Book I. Chaps. 1–3. JESS OAKROYD is a Yorkshireman 45 years of age, neither ugly nor handsome, with a nagging wife and a repulsive son. When he loses his job he decides to leave his unpleasant home and travel about England in search of adventure. On that same day, ELIZABETH TRANT, who has inherited several hundred pounds from her father and is considered an old maid, decides to leave her home. She is surfeited with reading. She buys her nephew's car and starts out on her journey. INIGO JOLLIFANT, a tall, thin youth of 26, an instructor at a school for boys, who is unhappy and has an urge to write fantastic tales, at his birthday party gets drunk and speaks his mind to the tyrannical wife of the headmaster. He is dismissed and leaves the school on that same day.

Chaps. 4–6. Jess Oakroyd dashes out of his house with no idea where he is going.

A passing lorry gives him a lift. When the driver and his helper stop at an inn for the night, Jess discovers the lorry is carrying stolen cloth. The next morning his companions are gone and with them all his money. Jess starts walking and comes upon a peddler in another lorry. The peddler's assistant does not show up for three days so Jess stays and helps the peddler. When it is time for him to leave, Jess comes upon Miss Trant's car, which has stalled. She appeals to Jess to fix it. It begins to rain and they take shelter under a tree. Miss Trant is drawn to the twinkling little man and they exchange stories. Miss Trant stopped at an inn for the night and next morning her car was driven off by mistake by ERIC TIPSTEAD and EFFIE, a barmaid with whom he was leaving his wife. Mrs. Tipstead and Miss Trant took Tipstead's car and caught the runaway couple. Tipstead chose to return with his wife, leaving Effie in tears with Miss Trant. A telegram arrived with the news that Miss ELSIE LONGSTAFF, sister of the sniffling Effie, was stranded with her theatrical troupe and needed money and her theatrical kit. Miss Trant was on her way with these things when her car stalled. The rain becomes a storm and Miss Trant and Jess go to a little tearoom, where they meet Inigo Jollifant and his banjo-playing friend, MORTON MITCHAM. So Miss Trant, Jess and Jollifant are brought together.

Book II. Chaps. 1–4. Elsie is younger and prettier than her sister Effie. She tells Miss Trant about the misfortunes of the "Dinky Doos," her theatrical troupe; the manager has left them stranded with four weeks' back pay due them. Impulsively Miss Trant decides to take over the company. She changes the name of the troupe to "The Good Companions" and invites both Jess and Jollifant to join them. The talent in the group consists of SUSIE DEAN, the young and pretty soubrette; JERRY JERNINGHAM, the handsome song-and-dance man; and Elsie, who dances and sings with music-hall gusto. Miss Trant is their manager, Jollifant the pianist, and Jess the man of odd jobs. The first appearance of The Good Companions is not very successful but their second engagement is and makes the entire cast happy. Just after this success Miss Trant is surprised by a visit from her sister, HILDA, who tries to get her to leave the troupe, but Miss Trant refuses. Jess Oakroyd is having the time of his life. Susie Dean is his favorite because she reminds him of his daughter LILY, who is married and living in Canada. Jess is disturbed when he receives a letter from his son, saying that a policeman has been looking for him, because Jess cannot think what he might have done. He remembers that the night he left home he helped a drunken man home. Then Jess meets an old neighbor in a pub and is relieved to learn that there are no charges against him.

Chaps. 5–7. The Good Companions travel by train from one town to another. One day Susie Dean misses the train and Jollifant jumps off to be with her while she

waits for the next train. Jollifant realizes that he is in love with her and he tells her so, but she is not yet interested in marriage. The morale of the troupe becomes low. Quarrels become frequent and even Miss Trant finds it difficult to hold on to her fraying temper. After a performance with only three people in the audience she calls a meeting and suggests closing the show, but Jess persuades them to take the bad luck with the good and they agree to go on.

Book III. Chaps. 1–3. The Good Companions are a hit in most of the towns they play, but Miss Trant is tired of show business. She has recouped most of her money and she is persuaded to make a last fling by hiring a large theater to give each of the players a chance to shine before visiting London producers. Jollifant, who has been composing gay songs for Susie, is tired of waiting for her to become a star. He goes to London, where a famous music publisher accepts his songs; but Jollifant refuses to sign a contract unless the publisher comes with him to hear Susie sing the songs. The publisher accompanies Jollifant but the evening's performance is a fiasco because the owner of the local movie houses has hired a gang to set fire to the hall. A riot ensues and Miss Trant is hurt. The publisher leaves after refusing to have anything further to do with Susie.

Chaps. 4–6. Elsie leaves the troupe to marry. Miss Trant is in the hospital under the care of Dr. HUGH MCFARLANE. It is not too long before they find themselves in love. Jerry Jerningham marries the rich Lady PARTLIT. She is about 30 years older than he and it is obvious that he has married her for her money and the three theaters she owns in London's West End. Jerry is true to his friends and they join the cast of his new revue. Susie is ecstatic, as she is to be the female star and Jollifant is to compose the music. Jess discovers the guilt of the movie operator who started the riot in the theater and the police free Miss Trant of any financial responsibility.

Jess Oakroyd receives a telegram from his son informing him that Mrs. Oakroyd is seriously ill. Shortly after Jess returns home, she dies. The morning of the funeral, he receives a letter from Miss Trant telling him of her marriage to Dr. McFarlane and asking him to come to them if he has no other plans. But Jess is going to Canada to visit his daughter Lily and, if he likes it there, to stay. Susie, who keeps postponing her marriage to Jollifant, sends Jess all the press clippings about the Good Companions. Jollifant sends him the recordings of his new songs. Jess proceeds to his new life, treasuring his theatrical experience.

The Good Earth

Novel by Pearl Buck, 1892–
Published 1931 by The John Day Co.,
New York. © 1931 by Pearl S. Buck.
(ML, 15; PB, C111)

NO ONE DISPUTES the place of *The Good Earth* as a classic of this century and it is considered to have contributed more to its author's winning the Nobel prize for literature (1938) than any other single title has done for any other Nobel-prize winner. A novel may have any of several main themes and *The Good Earth* superlatively answers to at least three. It is a timeless portrayal of timeless and universal human beings. It is a historical novel, giving the modern reader of English a better insight than any other book has given into the condition of the Chinese people in the early 1900s when the habits of a millenium persisted but were on the brink of being totally and suddenly overthrown. And it is a social and political sermon, though it never becomes unpalatable as a sermon might to one who is reading for relaxation only. The character O-lan is so great that an actress in motion pictures fell into an Academy Award just by being given the rôle.

Chaps. 1–4. WANG LUNG, a typical poor Chinese farmer who barely subsists on a small plot of land, is to be married. His aged father has arranged for him to be given a slave girl from the great House of HWANG in the nearest city. His father admonished him to take a girl who is strong but not good-looking (so that she would not have appealed to the young lords). Wang Lung washes himself all over, though there is a shortage of water, and dons clean and unpatched clothes. He spends most of his total hoard of six silver dollars for the wedding feast that night and the last dollar to tip the surly gatekeeper at the House of Hwang. He is overawed by the OLD MISTRESS, who calls in the big, ugly slave girl O-LAN and pronounces them man and wife between puffs on her opium pipe. The Old Mistress gives her slaves away when they are marriageable because she wants to win favor in heaven. O-lan follows her husband home, and on the way he pauses to light incense at the shrine to the two little gods he hates and fears. At once O-lan takes over all heavy duties in the house, serving Wang Lung and his father as a totally submissive slave, and also she works beside Wang Lung in the field all day. She leaves the field just long enough to enter the hut and have her first child, a son, unassisted; then she goes back to hoeing and plowing.

302

Chaps. 5–6. The great House of Hwang is running out of money. The OLD LORD and Old Mistress indulge themselves with new slave girls and opium, the Young Lords live extravagant lives in Chinese and foreign cities, and the daughters need big dowries. O-lan whispers this to Wang Lung and he buys a small piece of Hwang land with money from a good harvest. O-lan bears a second son. Wang Lung comes to be recognized as a prosperous citizen.

Chaps. 7–10. The next year O-lan gives birth to a daughter. Crows fly across the field. These are evil omens but Wang Lung defiantly sells his wheat—which is sparse, for there is a drought—and buys more land. Famine falls upon the land and there is little to eat in Wang Lung's house. O-lan is with child again. Her milk dries up and her baby daughter cries constantly from hunger. The little money that Wang Lung has hidden is of no use, for there is no food to buy. Wang Lung's UNCLE, his father's brother, comes to beg. The uncle and his family are idle and shiftless, and Wang Lung turns him away. The uncle spreads rumors that Wang Lung is a rich man with hoarded food, and at night the villagers come to take food by force. When they find nothing but a few dried beans and a handful of corn, they seize the furniture. O-lan stops them, and they listen to her because they are not evil men except when they are

Lotos in the teahouse

starving. CHING, Wang Lung's nearest neighbor, a small, silent man, is ashamed. He takes the beans he found and leaves, speechless. Wang Lung resolves to sell some land and take his family to the great city of the south, where there is food to buy. Grasping speculators come, seeking to buy land cheap. O-lan skillfully persuades Wang Lung not to sell land and sells their furniture instead. It seems almost impossible for them to make the long journey with the old father and the emaciated chil-

dren, but Ching brings them a handful of red beans and this puts heart into them. O-lan's child is born and she kills it; anyway, it was only a girl. As soon as she can walk they set out for the south.

Chaps. 11–14. Crowds of people ride the unfamiliar and feared "firewagons" to the great city and live there, like Wang Lung and his family, just outside the city's outer wall, in huts made of mats. Such people live in the greatest poverty in spite of the city's markets full of food and air of wealth. Wang Lung rents a riksha and draws passengers through the streets and O-lan and the children beg. There is never enough money, but with what there is one can buy food. Wang Lung hears young men on street corners shouting that if the rich would share there would be no poor people. Wang Lung does not quite understand. He thinks only of his lands. O-lan, who knows his longing, offers to sell their daughter, who is feeble-minded but pretty, into slavery so that they can return home. Wang Lung is tempted, but he loves his daughter and he will not sell her to be beaten or ravished in a great house. One night crowds break into the inner city where the great lords live. Wang Lung, borne along helplessly, finds himself in the inner court. A fat, soft lord, terrified, offers him money to spare him. Wang Lung takes all his money and takes his family north to his land.

Chaps. 15–17. One night Wang Lung finds a small, hard package between O-lan's breasts. In it are jewels. With her knowledge of great houses, she knew where to look for hiding places while the inner city was being looted. Wang Lung takes the jewels from her to buy more land, but she pleads for two little pearls and he lets her keep them, "just to feel at times." Wang Lung takes the jewels to the Great House. He finds there is no one there except the shabby Old Lord and a female servant, CUCKOO, who is in full control of the Old Lord and the few possessions he has left. She is happy to sell Wang Lung land in return for jewels. Wang Lung hires Ching as steward over the field hands now working for him. O-lan does not work in the fields any more, since she is the wife of a rich man. She bears twins, a boy and a girl, and both are healthy, but Wang Lung is still fondest of his "poor fool," his idiot oldest daughter. Wang Lung's only shame is that he cannot read, and businessmen laugh at him and cheat him. For this reason he sends his two older sons to school and neither of them works on the land.

Chaps. 18–24. Wang Lung becomes aware that O-lan is not comely, her feet were not bound, and she is too plain a wife for such an important man. At a teahouse in the town he finds Cuckoo in charge. She has let the ruined Great House. Cuckoo offers him his choice of the prostitutes and he chooses LOTUS, a beautiful, spoiled woman. He can think of nothing but Lotus. To make her happy he makes O-lan give back the two pearls. He makes Lotus his second wife and installs her in his house,

Pear Blossom likes old men because they are so kind

later bringing Cuckoo to be her attendant. On the day that Lotus comes, O-lan goes out and hoes the fields as she used to do. She will not go near the second wife. In spite of his prosperity Wang Lung is plagued with trouble. His uncle, who with his whole family has been living at Wang Lung's expense, reveals that he is leader of a troop of robbers, so that it is too dangerous for Wang Lung to put him out. Swarms of locusts descend on the fields and devour the crops. Wang Lung discovers that his eldest son, tired of waiting for his betrothed to grow old enough to marry, spends most of his time with Lotus. Wang Lung beats both of them and sends the boy south to study.

Chaps. 25–26. O-lan is in great pain with "a fire in her her vitals." The doctor says that she cannot live. Wang Lung sits besides her bed, neglecting Lotus and his land. O-lan will not die until she has seen her eldest son wed, so the boy is recalled from the south and is married to his betrothed. O-lan is content, and dies. Wang Lung's father, distraught, also dies in his sleep.

Chaps. 27–30. Although the worst famine Wang Lung can remember is on the land, Wang Lung's eldest son persuades him to buy the inner courts of the Great House of Hwang. The house is deserted now except for the poor who live in the outer courts. Wang Lung's first grandson is born, and his second son is betrothed. His eldest son insists that he buy the outer courts of the Great House. Wang Lung is now lord of the house he once feared to enter.

Chaps. 31–34. The wars have come close to the village. Wang Lung's uncle's son, a soldier, brings hordes of his friends to the house and there they stay, eating and drinking. In an attempt to placate the uncle's son, Wang Lung offers him a slave, PEAR BLOSSOM; but she is a delicate child who hates young men and Wang Lung is sorry for her and gives his uncle's son another slave instead. At last the soldiers leave, but there is no peace in the house. The wives of the sons quarrel and their children bicker. The youngest son wants to be a soldier and Wang Lung offers a slave if the boy will stay at home, but when the boy chooses Pear Blossom Wang Lung is suddenly angry and refuses. He is nearly 70 years old, but one night he calls Pear Blossom to him. She says she likes old men, because they are kind. He appeases Lotus with gifts. The youngest son, finding that his father has taken Pear Blossom, runs away. Pear Blossom serves Wang Lung well and is happy with him even when his lust is spent.

Now Wang Lung cannot think long on any subject. His grandsons grow and learn and they tell him there has been a revolution. One day, with Pear Blossom and his "poor fool" and a few servants, Wang Lung moves back to the earthen house on his own land. He hears his two older sons, who are now great and wealthy men in the town, discussing how they will divide his land after his death. Wang Lung cries out that they must not do this, that it is the end of a family when they begin to sell their land. His sons reassure him, swearing that they will never sell the land, but over his head they look at each other and smile.

The Good Soldier Schweik

Novel by Jaroslav Hasek, 1883–1923. Published 1929. Published in the U.S. 1930 by Doubleday & Co., New York, in a translation from the Czech by Paul Selver. © 1930 by Doubleday & Co.

THE DISARMING ARMED MAN, the eternal enigma to Army brass, has been a proper theme of every war. American readers met him during World War I in *Dere Mable* and during World War II in *See Here, Private Hargrove*, and *No Time for Sergeants*. But the most uproarious of them all, the true classic, is *The Good Soldier Schweik*. Hasek wrote nothing else that has contributed greatly to his reputation, perhaps because he died when he was 40. His short stories, published before and after *Schweik*, have been widely praised.

Book I. Chap. 1. JOSEF SCHWEIK, a stocky, round-faced citizen of Prague, earns a livelihood by the sale of mongrel dogs for which he forges pedigrees. Mrs. MULLER, the cleaning woman, tells him that Ferdinand has been shot and Schweik says he knows a Ferdinand the chemist and a Ferdinand the manure collector. Which one does she mean? She says it was the Archduke Ferdinand, the fat one, and Schweik says it's easier to shoot a fat one. He goes to his favorite café and gets into a discussion of the assassination with BRETSCHNEIDER, a plainsclothes policeman, who is not exactly sure he knows what Schweik has been talking about but arrests Schweik for high treason on general principles.

Chaps. 2–6. Schweik is taken to be cross-examined and greets his inquisitors affably. He is told to take the idiotic expression off his face, but he replies that he can't help it—he was discharged from the army as being officially weak-minded. He blandly admits to being guilty of a long list of preposterous charges. Schweik informs his cellmate that the cross-examination was fun—not like olden times when they made you walk on red-hot iron and drink molten lead. Schweik is again taken before the police commissioner and willingly signs a confession. The following morning Schweik is taken to court and asked if he signed the confession under pressure. He answers that everything was done in proper fashion. The judge decides Schweik must have a mental examination. He is sent to three serious medical authorities who question him and receive offhand and intriguing answers. They declare him an imbecile and he is taken to the lunatic asylum. Two other doctors test his reflexes and pronounce him a malingerer. The doctors order his discharge but Schweik says they can't do it until after lunch. He causes quite a scene and is arrested for disorderly behavior and taken to the commissariat of police. On a corner a crowd is reading the emperor's proclamation of war. Schweik shouts: "Long live Franz Josef! We'll win this war." This starts a riot. The baffled police cannot figure out charges against him and he is told to get out. At liberty again, he runs into Bret-

303

schneider, who has been told at headquarters to pretend he wants to buy a dog from Schweik and in this way observe Schweik's actions. Schweik proceeds to sell the detective a series of hideous freaks as full-blooded pedigreed animals and pockets a tidy sum for each of them.

Chaps. 7–9. The Austrian army is doing very badly and Schweik is drafted. He is in bed with rheumatism, but nothing daunted he puts on a military cap and has Mrs. Muller push him in a wheelchair to the medical board, where he brandishes a pair of crutches and shouts, "To Belgrade, to Belgrade!" He avows he will serve the emperor till he is hacked to pieces. The doctor calls him a malingerer and he is sent to military prison with men who have all kinds of malingering diseases—consumption, cancer, diabetes, kidney infections, and so on. Schweik receives the usual treatment, including swathing in cold wet sheets, large doses of aspirin and quinine, stomach-pumping twice a day, and a massive colonic irrigation. He takes it all cheerfully but complains that it really isn't helping his rheumatism. Schweik and almost all the other malingerers are declared fit for duty, including three in the last stages of consumption. A man with one leg and another with genuine cavities in his teeth are released. Schweik is taken to chapel to hear the chaplain, OTTO KATZ, preach a sermon. Schweik bursts into tears and the chaplain takes him aside and accuses him of shamming. Schweik readily admits it, but says he felt the sermon needed a reformed sinner. Katz takes a liking to Schweik and has him made his orderly.

Chaps. 10–11. Otto Katz, born a Jew, is overly fond of drinking and has the sacramental wine well laced with grog. Schweik often has to escort the babbling Katz home from a drinking party and put him to bed. The chaplain, out of funds, sends Schweik to borrow money from several officers and tells him to "pitch any yarn you please." Schweik returns with much more cash than Katz had expected and when Katz asks him how he managed it, Schweik says he merely told the officers that the chaplain was involved in a paternity case. The chaplain is so distressed that he drinks five bottles of brandy. Several days later Schweik assists the chaplain in a field mass, though he is unfamiliar with the routine. The chaplain is in a good mood, as he is using a large silver trophy cup, filled to the brim, as a substitute chalice.

Chaps. 12–13. Katz loses Schweik in a card game to Lt. LUKASH, an officer with a reputation for being hard on his batmen and soft on the ladies. Schweik ingratiates himself with his new master by procuring a bona fide Pomeranian for him, but the dog was stolen from an estimable booby of a colonel, who punishes Lukash by ordering him to the front. Lukash retaliates by taking Schweik with him, but Schweik merely says, "It'll be a good thing if you and me was to fall together fighting for the emperor."

304

Book II. 1–5. On the train, Schweik innocently asks a trainman how the alarm brake works and somehow the brake is pulled and the train is stopped. Schweik is ordered to report to the stationmaster at the next town. The train pulls away without him and Lukash heaves a sigh of relief. Schweik talks his way out of his troubles, but immediately is involved in new ones, since Lukash has his papers and his ticket. Schweik is ordered to buy a ticket and when he says he has no money the lieutenant tells him he can walk there for all he cares. Schweik starts his journey on foot, in the wrong direction. The next morning he is taken to the police station, where the sergeant is sure Schweik is a Russian spy. Schweik, not knowing he is under suspicion, readily agrees with every leading statement the sergeant makes. The sergeant sends Schweik, in the custody of a policeman, to headquarters in another town. The journey is cold and the two men, handcuffed together, stop for occasional drinks. They arrive in a happy state. The captain believes Schweik's story and puts him on a train. Schweik affably reports to Lukash, who turns pale and puts him in the guardhouse. The regiment is transferred to another town and Schweik is in the prisoners' car. A chaplain, deep in his cups, has mistakenly boarded the car and Schweik takes good care of him and puts him to bed. The next day the train stops at a town and the chaplain gives Schweik money to buy food and wine. Schweik gives it to Lukash and gets back in Lukash's good graces. Lukash goes to the theater in town, sees an attractive woman, and writes a note to her, which he instructs Schweik to deliver at 10 o'clock the next morning. Schweik gets to drinking with an old buddy and finally delivers the letter at noon, when the woman's husband is home for lunch. A

free-for-all follows and Schweik and his buddy are arrested. Schweik maintains he wrote the letter himself, and when asked to copy it for a handwriting comparison he claims that overnight he has forgotten how to write. But the colonel refuses to give official sanction to a civilian complaint and Schweik and his buddy are set free. The colonel appoints Schweik company orderly under Lt. Lukash, and Schweik takes a series of messages over the phone, and in his zeal he fouls up everything and makes Lukash late for a staff meeting. He receives one message in what may be code, decides the caller must have been an idiot, and throws it away.

Book III. Chaps. 1–4. The regiment receives new orders and entrains for the Russian front. En route, the captain gives the officers a new code based on page 161 of a novel. The other officers are completely bewildered because they have volume I of the novel and the captain has volume II. Schweik is the culprit—he has issued a copy of volume I to each officer because, as he subsequently explains, anyone reading a novel would naturally start with the first volume. At a small town, Lukash sends Schweik out to buy a bottle of brandy. A young lieutenant who has been trying to get something on Schweik finds the bottle on him, but Schweik tells him it is filled with a yellowish water from a nearby pump. The lieutenant cleverly orders Schweik to drink it all and Schweik coolly complies. Five minutes later Schweik reports to Lt. Lukash, tells him what has happened, and begs to report that he will soon be drunk as a lord. The train finally reaches its destination and Lukash sends Schweik and a couple of others ahead to arrange billets in the next town. The mayor of the town attempts to talk them into going on to the next town, but Schweik threatens to hang the mayor and when the company marches into town, there are plenty of beds available. Once again Lukash sends Schweik ahead to find quarters. Schweik's reaches a pond where an escaped Russian prisoner is bathing. Schweik wonders how he would look in a Rusian uniform and tries it on. An Austrian patrol comes by and he is arrested as a Russian fugitive and put in a labor gang.

Schweik reports to the lieutenant that he will soon be drunk as a lord

The Story of Gösta Berling

Novel by Selma Lagerlof, 1858–1940. Published 1894. Translation from the Swedish by Pauline Bancroft Flach published 1898 by Little, Brown & Co., Boston.

THE FIRST NOVEL by Selma Lagerlof is still rated high among her works. It is a skillful blending of Swedish folk superstitions with modern (19th century) life in Miss Lagerlof's native Värmland district of Sweden. Miss Lagerlof never actually reveals whether the superstitions are to be taken as an agency of the events of the novel or merely as coincidence. The characters are complex and most of them are developed fully. The novel is of moderate length, about 140,000 words.

Introduction. Young GÖSTA BERLING is the minister of a poor parish in the Western Värmland. Everybody in that cold, gloomy region drinks, but Gösta has overstepped the bounds and complaints are made to the bishop. The bishop comes to investigate and Gösta, on his first Sunday in church for many weeks, delivers an eloquent and impassioned sermon. The bishop is pleased and exonerates him. Captain CHRISTIAN, a drinking companion of Gösta, rudely warns the bishop to leave his friend alone. Gösta fears the bishop may think him responsible for the loutish Christian's threat and he flees from his home. He wanders through the snow-covered forests and over the icy roads and reaches the village of Bro in a disheveled, miserable condition. He steals some grain and sells it to buy brandy, then in drunken remorse he staggers out of town and throws himself in a snowbank to die. He is saved by a large, coarse woman who takes him to her estate at Ekeby. She tells him her name is MARGARETA and that she once loved a poor young man but was forced to marry the supposedly wealthy Major SAMZELIUS. Her husband turned out to have very little money, but her former lover returned a rich man. She had an affair with him and when he died he left her his seven estates to her and the major. She is now mistress of Ekeby, owner of iron mines, and the most powerful person in the region. But she cannot forget the curse her own mother put upon her for living in sin. Gösta Berling becomes a guest at Ekeby. He falls in love with EBBA DOHNA, the sister of a count, but she dies (perhaps having killed herself rather than marry a dismissed priest). Gösta feels he is doomed to suffer.

Part I. Chaps. 1–3. Seven years later Gösta is still living in the bachelor wing of Ekeby, with eleven other pensioners who are kept in comfort through the generosity of Margareta. Capt. Christian is one of the pensioners. They occupy their time in drinking, card-playing, and retelling stories of their past glories. On Christmas Eve they are carousing when SINTRAM, master of the local iron works, enters dressed as the devil. The men believe he actually is the Evil One. He tells them he has a contract with Margareta that allows her to continue as mistress of the seven estates in exchange for the soul of one of the pensioners every year. They are horrified and forget her many kindnesses to them. Gösta refuses to believe until Sintram tells him that Margareta told Ebba Dohna Gösta was a dismissed priest and Ebba killed herself. The "devil" agrees to cancel his contract with Margareta if the pensioners make a pact with him. They can have the seven estates in order to save their souls if they act like gentlemen for a year. If any one of them does something sensible, useful or effeminate during that time they will all lose their souls and the estates will go to someone else. The pensioners sign the contract in blood. The next day, at the great Christmas feast, Capt. Christian drunkenly denounces Margareta as an adulteress. Major Samzelius orders her from the estate, claiming he never knew he owed the seven estates to his wife's infidelities. Gösta does not defend Margareta because he blames her for the death of Ebba. Margareta feels that a judgment has been visited on her but she warns the other guests of dire things. She leaves and the major moves to his own little farm, placing the pensioners in charge of the seven estates in the hope that they will ruin the property.

Chaps. 4–7. Gösta goes to a ball at a neighboring estate and meets ANNA STJÄRNHÖK, a beautiful young woman who is engaged to be married. She falls in love with Gösta and his passion is aroused. He takes her for a sleigh ride and they are attacked by wolves and just manage to get back safely. Gösta believes the wolves are instruments of judgment upon him and he renounces Anna. At a ball at Ekeby the beautiful and sought-after MARIANNE SINCLAIR acts in a tableau with Gösta. They are attracted to each other and kiss, which seems to be part of the scene. During the ball Gösta plays cards with Marianne's father and wins his money, watch, and fur coat. Sintram, who is standing by, suggests that the old man stake his daughter against all that Gösta has won. Sinclair does and Gösta wins. While Gösta goes to dance with Marianne, Sintram tells Sinclair that the kiss was not part of the tableau. The old man leaves in a rage. Marianne walks home in the snow but when she arrives her father has locked her out. She pleads in vain and finally leaves the door and throws herself in a snowdrift. Gösta finds her half-frozen and takes her back to Ekeby. Later that night Margareta comes to Ekeby and commands the servants to oust the pensioners. Marianne overhears her and once again goes out into the frozen night, this time to summon Major Samzelius. The major takes his pack of muzzled bears to Ekeby with Marianne and frightens Margareta away. Margareta says she will go to seek release from her mother's curse.

Chaps. 8–9. Marianne is ill with smallpox at Ekeby. She loses her beauty but Gösta is faithful. Marianne's father, who is about to auction off all his belongings because he does not want Marianne to inherit them, relents when he hears of her illness, rushes to Ekeby, and takes her home. Now Gösta is angered because she went without leaving a message for him. He tells her he does not love her any more. She protests that she still loves him.

Chap. 10. Margareta has been arrested for trying to retake Ekeby and is a prisoner in the bailiff's house. The bailiff gives a party and the pensioners are among the guests. Count HENRIK DOHNA (Ebba's brother), an ugly, stupid man, is there with his young and beautiful wife ELIZABETH. Elizabeth asks Gösta to help Margareta but he refuses; then when Gösta asks her to dance, she refuses. Gösta broods, and as the party is breaking up he grabs Elizabeth and drives madly off with her in his sleigh with the others in hot pursuit. During the excitement two of the pensioners free Margareta. In the sleigh, Gösta forces his kisses on the struggling Elizabeth and then in sudden remorse takes her home. The stupid count berates his wife for refusing to dance with Gösta and orders her to kiss Gösta's hand. The proud Elizabeth obediently approaches Gösta but he is embarrassed and tells her she must not debase herself. To prevent her, Gösta puts his hands in the fire, but a friend pulls him away from the hearth.

Chaps. 11–12. Sintram tells Anna Stjärnhök that when she let Gösta go she sent his soul to the devil. Anna is frightened and is sure Sintram is the devil himself. She hears that Gösta and Elizabeth are in love and see each other often. Anna tells Elizabeth the story of Ebba Dohna. She does not tell Elizabeth that Gösta was the man, but Elizabeth hears a poem by Gösta that tells the same story she has just heard from Anna. She sends him away.

Part II. Chaps. 1–7. Gösta decides as penance to marry a poor, humble girl. He chooses a half-crazy peddler of brooms. Elizabeth goes on foot to beg Gösta not to marry this BROOM-GIRL. She is trapped on the breaking ice near Ekeby and the dam begins to give way. Gösta and others struggle to save the dam and prevent the raging waters from inundating the town. Gösta rescues Elizabeth and the two are joyous in their reunion. Countess MARTA, the mother of Henrik, tells her son that Elizabeth is unfaithful. Henrik makes Elizabeth wholly subject to his mother's commands. Marta humbles Elizabeth, making her do household chores and wait on guests, and tortures her. After a month Elizabeth runs away. She meets the pensioners on a river barge, loaded with iron from Ekeby on the way to market, and they hide her.

The pensioners lose their iron in a storm and one more disaster has befallen Ekeby. Henrik gets an annulment of his marriage to Elizabeth. A witch curses Countess Marta for not giving her food. She invokes a plague of magpies that almost drive the countess mad.

Chaps. 8–13. The pensioners hold a concert to distract the melancholy Gösta and they succeed in making him cheerful again. The pensioners will not let Henrik attend church, considering him unworthy to sit in the house of God. The count and his mother move to a faraway place. Capt. LENNART, who was falsely accused of theft by Sintram and sent to jail, comes back to town. The pensioners get him drunk, paint a horrible face on him, and take him home. His wife refuses to admit him and the captain, thinking it is God's will, devotes himself to helping the poor peasants. He wanders through the countryside giving aid and comfort and countering the evil wrought by Sintram.

Chaps. 14–18. Marianne Sinclair seeks to get away from her father, whom she fears and detests, by becoming engaged to her penniless cousin, Baron ADRIAN. Her father suffers a stroke and becomes more human, and Marianne is further pleased to learn that Adrian really loves her. Drought comes to the land and the people blame the hardhearted and miserly pastor of the parish. Gösta, remembering his own shame as a priest, counsels the pastor to change his ways and help the people. The next Sunday the pastor prays for rain and as a torrent comes down, he dies of happiness. Gösta is summoned by Elizabeth, who has been living with a peasant family. She has given birth to a son, and though Henrik is the father, he refuses to remarry Elizabeth. She wants the child to have a father and Gösta agrees to marry her, though he fears he will only bring ruin to Elizabeth. Their marriage makes Elizabeth the mistress of Ekeby. The child dies. Major Samzelius is severely bitten by one of his bears and dies just before Christmas.

The estate burns to the ground

Chaps. 19–22. The broom-girl disappears and the peasants think the pensioners have harmed her and storm Ekeby. The pensioners distract them by holding a great feast. Then the peasants mistake Elizabeth for the broom-girl and are about to carry her off, but the body of the broom-girl is found, dead from a fall in the forest. One of the pensioners becomes temporarily insane and believes Elizabeth is a witch. To get rid of her he sets fire to Ekeby. He recovers his senses, but the estate is burned to the ground. Lennart is killed by a brawler, and now the pensioners regret their prank that kept him from his wife and join in the mourning. Sintram tells Gösta he is going to destroy everyone. Gösta bargains with him and agrees to take his own life if Sintram will spare the others. He disappears but Elizabeth sends searchers into the forest and he is found and brought back. Elizabeth tells him that the pensioners have started to rebuild Ekeby, that he is needed as the leader, and that he must give up his bargain with Sintram.

Chap. 23. Margareta comes back to Ekeby, ill; but she has seen her aged mother and has been forgiven. The pensioners' year is up and they have won in their pact with Sintram—they have worked and they have acted sensibly. Since they have done this not for themselves but for others, Sintram —the force of evil—has lost. News comes that Sintram is dead. Margareta offers Ekeby to Gösta and Elizabeth, but they prefer to live simply and help others. Margareta dies. Gösta sums up how much has been learned during the year of joy and sorrow.

The Grapes of Wrath

Novel by John Steinbeck, 1900–
Published 1939 by Viking Press, New York. (ML, 148)

THIS IS ONE of the best examples of the propaganda novel in American literature, ranking with *Uncle Tom's Cabin* as an example of the art though not as a historical phenomenon. Steinbeck had tried straight propaganda once before (*In Dubious Battle,* 1936) and had not done it well. In *The Grapes of Wrath* he made virtually no mistakes. His characters are real, reasonable, and sympathetic, and he even permits an interlude of gaiety to break into their misery. The abuses he attacks—shameful treatment of itinerant agricultural workers in California—really existed. Ma Joad is widely considered the best character Steinbeck has created. The book is moderately long, approaching 200,000 words. The title is from the first stanza of "The Battle Hymn of the Republic."

Chaps. 1–6. Drought, duststorms and exhaustion of the soil have ruined the land in Oklahoma and parts of neighboring states. Sharecroppers can no longer raise enough to feed themselves and pay rent. Banks are foreclosing mortgages and the big land companies are evicting the farmers, and farming the land with "cats," giant tractors. The dispossessed farmers are migrating westward to California. TOM JOAD, just paroled from a prison term for killing a man in a fight, hears this from a truckdriver who gives him a ride. Walking the last stretch toward the Joad farm, Tom meets JIM CASY, a former preacher, and they share a bottle of whiskey. Casy has given up his calling, and now lives a derelict existence, because he can no longer see the difference between virtue and sin. Casy decides to accompany Tom. They find the Joad farm deserted. A neighbor, MULEY GRAVES, comes by and tells Tom that the Joads have been evicted and have moved to Tom's UNCLE JOHN's farm. Muley himself has been evicted but obstinately refuses to move. He hides near his old farm and lives on what he is able to catch for food; he has two scrawny cottontail rabbits, which he shares with Tom and Casy.

Chaps. 7–10. The next morning Tom and Casy walk the 8 miles to Uncle John's farm and find the family preparing to leave permanently in an old Hudson Super-Six sedan that they have converted to a truck. Throughout Oklahoma, predatory buyers are buying up farm equipment and furniture at distress prices, and heartless, dishonest used-car dealers are selling jalopies, at $50 to $100 each, that will hardly run; but Tom's 16-year-old brother AL is already a remarkably good mechanic and has bought a car in good condition for $75. The rest of the family are Tom's parents, PA and MA JOAD; his older brother NOAH; his sister ROSE OF SHARON, who is several months pregnant, and her husband CONNIE RIVERS; Tom's sister RUTHIE, 12, and brother WINFIELD, 10; GRAMPA, GRANMA, and Uncle John. They have $154 in all. Now, with Tom and Casy, there are twelve to go. They sell everything salable, but for almost nothing. They slaughter and pack as much meat as possible. They load the truck—overload it to the limit. Tom must break parole by crossing the state line, but this does not deter him. They pile into and onto the truck and go, with Muley waving goodbye.

Chaps. 11–13. The Joads join the long caravan of cars headed westward on Route 66. The journey is hot and uncomfortable, but there is little complaining. Stops are made along the roadside at night for cookfires and sleep. At one stop they meet a farm couple from Kansas, IVY WILSON and his wife SAIRY. At this stop Grampa has a stroke. Casy forces himself to pray for Grampa but the old man dies. The Joads decide to bury Grampa secretly; they have not enough money to live the extra days they would have to spend if they reported the death. Then the Joads join forces with the Wilsons, who have only $30 but whose 1925 Dodge will relieve some of the load on the truck. They travel on together.

Chaps. 14–17. In the Texas Panhandle the Wilson car breaks down. It seems most sensible to send part of the party on ahead, but Ma Joad refuses absolutely to let the family be split. At last everyone yields to the indomitable woman's will and Al and Tom go off in the truck to buy used parts. The family settles in a roadside camp where a bitter man, returning from California, informs them that the only jobs in California will not keep them alive because the market is flooded with emigrants like themselves and employers are paying starvation wages. The Joads refuse to be disheartened and when the Wilson car is ready they drive on into the mountains of New Mexico.

Chaps. 18–20. They cross the Painted Desert and finally reach California, but they still have the long desert to cross. They camp for a night, and while Ma is preparing dinner a state trooper tells her they can only spend the night because "Okies" are not wanted around those parts. Another returning emigrant tells the men that they will be exploited and treated like animals wherever they go in California. Grimly they head for the truck-farming section of the state. Noah abandons the party to stay by a river and fish. Sairy Wilson becomes too ill to continue and Ivy makes the Joads go on without them. Granma is all tuckered out and barely conscious. She dies the night before the Joads enter the lush San Joaquin Valley, but Ma keeps it a secret because any delay would prevent their making it. At Bakersfield they turn Granma's body over to the local coroner and pay what they can

Loading the truck

afford for her burial. They go to a camp outside of town, a collection of tents and shacks called, like all such camps, Hooverville. They are told how California farmowners keep the Okies starving—especially the Okies' children, so that the parents will work all day for one inadequate meal. Any attempt at organization by the Okies is met with beatings and jail for those deemed to be the leaders. The Joads learn this lesson personally when a brutal deputy sheriff comes to Hooverville with a contractor looking to hire cheap hands to pick his crops. The deputy threatens to burn down the camp so the people will have no shelter and must accept the low wage. There is an argument. The deputy tries to arrest a man and is knocked to the ground. He pulls his gun and shoots wildly, wounding a woman in the hand. Casy kicks the deputy into un-

consciousness. He warns Tom to run, and he stays behind. Four armed men arrive and Casy takes the blame for all that happened. They take him away to jail. Rose of Sharon's husband, Connie, deserts. Uncle John, fed up with all their troubles, spends some of their last money on whiskey, to get release from all the misery and hardship. The next day the Joads head southward to possible work.

Chaps. 21–26. The Joads are now part of the desperate horde who outbid one another for any work available, down to 15 cents an hour or less. They reach a government camp at Weedpatch and for the first time since they left Oklahoma they are given understanding and decent treatment. There are shower rooms, flush toilets, and other conveniences. The campers have a chance to voice their grievances and settle their problems through committee action. There is even a brief evening of fun, with dancing and music. Tom gets a job at 25 cents an hour digging ditches and laying pipes. The other Joad men find it impossible to obtain any work. Tom is laid off and the family, hungry and with no income at all, has to leave the government camp and look for work. They are directed to a ranch that is hiring peach pickers. When they reach the place they are escorted through the gate by state police, through lines of men and women shouting at them and brandishing their fists. Everybody except Rose of Sharon picks peaches for a nickel a pail and at the end of the day they have all picked enough to earn about $1.50. Ma buys food from the company store, is appalled by the prices, but buys what she can to feed the family. After dinner Tom goes for a walk but is stopped by a guard, who tells him a bunch of damned reds are picketing the ranch. Tom crawls under the fence and walks down the road. He meets Casy and some others who tell him they are striking be-

The deputy tries to arrest a man and is knocked to the ground

307

cause they had been promised 5 cents a pail, but were given 2½ cents—not enough to feed a family. The little group is suddenly attacked by the police or company men and Casy is clubbed to death. Tom goes berserk, grabs a club, and beats a man to the ground. He knows he has killed the man and runs, reaching the Joad shanty safely. The next morning the wages goes down to 2½ cents, yet hundreds of workers come to apply for it, nearly all with hungry children. That night the family hides Tom in the loaded truck and they leave to go back to Weedpatch. They reach a string of boxcars on a railroad embankment and see a sign saying "cotton pickers wanted." They take the jobs and live in a boxcar, and Tom goes into the woods to hide.

Chaps. 27–29. The boxcars make the best home the traveling Joads have had except for the government camp. Ma takes food to Tom every day. Ruthie, in a childish argument, tells some other children about Tom's being in hiding, and Tom has to leave. He plans to do what Casy was doing—lead the workers in a fight for a decent life. Al is now Pa's right hand but he is in love with a girl, AGGIE WAINWRIGHT, in another boxcar and wants to marry her and work in a city as a mechanic. Rose of Sharon goes out to pick cotton with the family; she gets a chill as rain begins to fall, and her labor pains begin. The rain comes down in torrents and swishing waters surround the boxcar. Ma and some neighbor women tend Rose of Sharon while the men frantically build levees, but the levees do not hold. Rose of Sharon's baby is born dead. The waters are over the floor of the boxcar and the family is forced to leave. The truck is under water and they walk until they reach a barn. Here they find a boy trying to comfort his father, who is dying of starvation. He is too weak to eat and must have milk. Ma looks at Rose of Sharon and she looks back with an understanding light in her eyes. The others go out. Rose of Sharon lies down beside the emaciated man and gives him the milk that was meant for her stillborn child.

Graustark

Novel by George Barr McCutcheon, 1866–1928.
Published 1901.

THE ROMANTIC NOVEL about the tiny Balkan or eastern European principality was all the rage around the turn of the century and Graustark deserves a place at the top of the list, along with *The Prisoner of Zenda*. In its time *Graustark* was McCutcheon's principal work, but now he is better remembered for *Brewster's Millions*.

Chaps. 1–2. GRENFALL LORRY, urbane, wealthy, not quite 30, and bored, is on a train out of Denver bound for the East. He becomes infatuated with a dark-haired, blue-eyed girl traveling with an elderly couple, as well as a maid and manservant. Lorry fails at a couple of elaborate stratagems calculated to effect an introduction to the girl. In West Virginia, the train stops at a small mining town. The girl strolls a short distance into town and Lorry follows her. The train pulls out unexpectedly without them. Lorry telegraphs ahead for the train to stop at a station four miles ahead. Then he hires a stagecoach, and after a wild and perilous chase along rough mountain roads they catch the train. Lorry still has not learned the girl's name but he does learn that she is from Graustark, a small European country whose capital is Edelweiss.

Chaps. 3–4. The girl's chaperones, who are her Aunt YVONNE and Uncle CASPAR, are grateful to Lorry and invite him to dinner, where he learns that the girl is Miss GUGGENSLOCKER. He is disappointed, because he is sure she must be the daughter of a butcher, a brewer, or a cobbler, but he is no less fascinated by her. In Washington he takes the girl and her aunt for a drive around the city, and he again is their guest at dinner. He has a moment alone with the girl, who invites him to come visit her in Graustark.

Chaps. 5–6. Lorry tries to do some work in his uncle's law office, but is unable to concentrate. He curses himself for a lovesick fool and takes the night train to New York. At the steamship offices he cannot find anyone named Guggenslocker on the passenger list, but on the pier he sees the girl at the ship's rail. He daringly throws her a kiss and when she throws a kiss back he is wafted to heaven. After pining all summer, he goes to Europe. In Paris he meets his Harvard classmate, HARRY ANGUISH, an art student. Anguish enthusiastically joins him in his search for Miss Guggenslocker. They arrive in Graustark and put up at the best hotel and make inquiries about the Guggenslockers. No one has heard of the name.

Chap. 7. Lorry and Anguish go to see Baron DANGLOSS, the chief of police, to inquire about the Guggenslockers. Dangloss is at first helpful, but as their story unfolds he becomes hostile and suggests that their search will be futile. On the way back to their hotel, the two men see Miss Guggenslocker and another young lady riding in a luxurious carriage. The eyes of Lorry and the girl meet. When the men return to their hotel, a groom hands Lorry an invitation from Miss Guggenslocker to accompany her messenger on the following afternoon, for a visit to her home.

Chaps. 8–10. After dinner, Lorry and Anguish take a stroll in the darkened town of Edelweiss. They lie down on the grass under a hedge to rest, and they overhear three men plotting to kidnap Princess YETIVE of Graustark. Lorry and Anguish decide to foil the plot themselves. They hide near the palace. The conspirators chloroform, bind and gag the guard, and substitute one of their own men. Lorry and Anguish knock out the false guard and go on to the castle. In the darkened halls, they become confused. Lorry enters the princess's antechamber, where her lady-in-waiting, Countess DAGMAR, sleeps. She wakes and calls for the guard, DANNOX, and she is incredulous when Lorry tells her that Dannox is in a plot to kidnap the princess, but he manages to convince her. She goes to warn the princess and Lorry sees in the light of the doorway that the princess is Miss Guggenslocker. Dannox runs in and hits Lorry on the head. As he is losing consciousness, he sees Anguish run in shooting. When he regains consciousness, he and Anguish are heroes, and that night eight plotters are caught and shot. But Lorry is angry because with these plotters dead there is no way of finding out who was behind the conspiracy.

Chap. 11. The princess visits Lorry in his sickroom. She tells him that he and Anguish will be royal guests in the castle. Lorry and the princess talk and he tells her he loves her. She admits that as a woman she loves him, but that as a princess she cannot and they must remain simply friends. He insists that he will find some solution.

Chaps. 12–13. From Count HALFONT, the elderly man of the train trip, and from Countess Dagmar, Lorry learns about local conditions. Graustark, 15 years before, lost a war to its neighbor Axphain. The peace treaty required Grustark to pay 20,000,000 gavvos plus interest. The payment is due in a few weeks. Graustark cannot raise more than half the money, and failure to pay means ceding to Axphain a ruinous amount of territory. Crown Prince LORENZ of Axphain is enamored of Princess Yetive, and so is GABRIEL, the Prince of Dawsbergen, Graustark's neighbor to the south. Gabriel, in return for her hand, will lend Graustark the needed money. Later that night, Yetive tells Lorry that she abhors both her royal suitors but that she is soon to be betrothed to Prince Lorenz. Lorry believes that the instigator of the kidnap plot was Prince Gabriel of Dawsbergen.

Chaps. 14–15. Lorry and Anguish return to the hotel. Several days later, Anguish bursts into their room to tell Lorry he is sure Gabriel was the leader of the kidnap attempt; he has just heard Gabriel speak, downstairs in the foyer, and it was the voice of the chief plotter. He and Lorry tell Baron Dangloss and they all go to the castle, but they cannot see the princess. Countess Dagmar tells them that Yetive has accepted Prince Lorenz, to save her country. They leave the castle in dejection.

Chaps. 16–17. Lorry and Anguish go to a café. Prince Lorenz and some of his officers are there, and Lorenz is toasting the princess and boasting of the kisses he

On the way to the dungeon

will have from her. Angered, Lorry knocks him under a table and challenges him to a duel. Prince Gabriel looks on with satisfaction. The seconds of Prince Lorenz arrive at the hotel and a duel is arranged for early the next morning. But the next morning Baron Dangloss has Lorry and Anguish taken to the tower of the royal dungeon. Prince Lorenz was found stabbed to death in his bed and a trail of blood led to Lorry's door. Captain QUINNOX, of the princess's bodyguard, arrives at the tower with an order, signed by the princess, for Lorry's arrest. Baron Dangloss reluctantly carries out the formal arrest—reluctantly because all Graustark is glad the hated betrothed of their beloved princess was killed.

Chaps. 18–19. Captain Quinnox brings Lorry a note from Yetive, saying that the way has been prepared for his escape. Lorry refuses to go without seeing the princess again. Late that night a guard brings another note from Yetive which seems to tell him she will see him again. He changes clothes with the guard and leaves the dungeon. A carriage is waiting outside to spirit him away through the stormy night. Lorry questions the young soldier who is riding with him and discovers his companion is the princess in a soldier's uniform. The princess tells Lorry he is to stay at a monastery high in the mountains until he can escape. She confesses her love for him, but refuses to leave Graustark with him.

Chaps. 20–21. Anguish, upon hearing of Lorry's escape, rushes to the castle and tells the princess and Countess Dagmar that since Lorry has disappeared from Graustark he, Anguish, has no excuse to remain. The two women acquaint him with Lorry's whereabouts and the princess says she will decree that Anguish is to remain in Graustark as a hostage. Prince BOLAROZ, the late Prince Lorenz's father, rages into Edelweiss

and says that if the murderer of his son is found and executed by the time the Graustarkian debt to Axphain is due, he will give Graustark a ten-year extension of time. Lorry chafes over his confinement and goes back to the castle with Quinnox.

Chaps. 22–24. On the day before Graustark must pay its debt, Gabriel offers the needed money in return for Yetive's hand. Both Count Halfont and the Princess angrily refuse the offer. That night Quinnox allows Lorry to go to see Yetive in her boudoir. Lorry is determined to give himself up for trial, in order to save Graustark, but Yetive persuades him to return to the monastery. As he is leaving, Gabriel appears at the door. In a jealous rage he accuses Yetive of having a lover. Quinnox appears, says he has been present all the time, and that Lorry is his prisoner. Gabriel says that if Lorry is in the tower dungeon the next day, he will believe the story.

Chaps. 25–26. The people of Edelweiss are in despair on the morning of the day the debt is due. With all the nobles in the throne room, Princess Yetive asks Prince Bolaroz for an extension of time. He refuses. Captain Quinnox and Lorry burst into the room; Lorry is determined to sacri-

fice himself. Yetive publicly declares her love for him. Anguish cries out that he knows the real murderer of Lorenz—that an accomplice has confessed the crime to him. Prince Gabriel turns savagely on one of his retinue, thereby giving away his guilt. Bolaroz is satisfied, gives Graustark a ten-year extension, and suggests a treaty of friendship. Lorry has a few minutes alone with Yetive, but leaves downcast because she will not promise to marry him. Anguish says that his accusation of Gabriel was pure bluff based on a shrewd guess.

Chaps. 27–28. Count Halfont tells Lorry he regrets that Lorry is not a prince but, since he is not, it is impossible for him to marry Yetive. The following day Princess Yetive assembles the nobles and tells them of her determination to marry Lorry. She asks them to revise the laws so that Lorry can become Prince Consort and their first male child, the Prince Regent. Thus Lorry could never become ruler of Graustark. The nobles finally consent.

Three months later, Lorry and Yetive and Anguish and Dagmar, two honeymooning couples, leave Graustark for a trip to America.

Great Expectations

Novel by Charles Dickens, 1812–1870. Published 1860–61. (PB, PL50)

GREAT EXPECTATIONS is one of Dickens' best novels, though for many years it was not very high in the popularity ranking of his works. Most of the characters are typical Dickens (which is by no means bad) and have their counterparts in some or all of his other novels, but Miss Havisham is an original creation. Left at the altar in her youth, she sat the rest of her life in her wedding dress, waiting for the bridegroom to arrive. Miss Havisham's ward Estella might have been equally effective, and the book would have been many times better, if Dickens had let her finally go the way of Miss Havisham. Dickens must have had this in mind, and almost to the end he left the way open for it. But then, as always, he bowed to the public taste and gave his book a happy ending.

Chaps. 1–6. PHILIP PIRRIP, called PIP, is in the churchyard near the marshes when he is accosted by an escaped convict in fetters, who makes him promise to bring food and a file. Pip, an orphan about 10 years old, lives with his sister and her husband, JOE GARGERY, the town blacksmith. When Pip takes the food and the file to the marshes he comes upon another escaped convict, whom he manages to avoid. He tells his acquaintance of the day before, who

seems to be infuriated. That day (Christmas), while Joe's family including Pip's Uncle PUMBLECHOOK are at dinner, a sergeant appears and asks Joe to fix a pair of handcuffs. Pip and his uncle follow the sergeant, who is seeking a pair of escaped convicts. The convicts are caught and Pip's man is careful to say that he stole the food and file from the blacksmith, so that Pip cannot be blamed.

Chaps. 7–9. About a year later, Pip has started his schooling at an institution run by Mr. WOPSLE'S great-aunt, where he is given considerable assistance by BIDDY, her granddaughter. Joe never had any schooling and is anxious for Pip to have it. Mrs. JOE (Pip's sister) is very excited when Miss HAVISHAM, an eccentric and mysteriously isolated lady in town, invites Pip to come to her house to play. Uncle Pumblechook takes Pip to Satis House, where Miss Havisham lives. Pip is admitted by a beautiful but insolent girl of about his own age, named ESTELLA, who takes him to a room where Miss Havisham sits, dressed as for a party, with candles about her. She tells him to play cards with Estella. When he is let out he is told to return in six days.

Chaps. 10–17. Pip has a curious adventure at a tavern called the *Three Brave Bargemen*, to which he takes a message to Joe. He sees Joe and Wopsle in a conversation with a stranger who stirs his rum with a file. The stranger gives Pip "a shilling"—wrapped in two £1 notes—with a cryptic message that Pip interprets as meaning they come from the convict he helped. Pip pays his second visit to Miss Havisham's. It is her birthday, and several relatives are visiting. Pip gets into a fight with a pale young gentleman, whom he soundly trounces. He is rewarded by a kiss from Estella. The visits to Miss Havisham go on for some time. She is always dressed in an elaborate white gown. At length it is time for Joe to put Pip on as his apprentice, and Miss Havisham pays Pip's fee. His visits to Satis House end, but his contact with Miss Havisham and Estella has made him conscious of his own lack of refinement and education. DODGE ORLICK, an assistant at the forge, makes uncomplimentary remarks about Mrs. Joe, for which Joe knocks him down. Pip calls on Miss Havisham and learns that Estella has gone to the continent to complete her education. Returning home, he meets Orlick. At the house his sister is lying on the floor, unconscious. Someone has struck her a savage blow. The officers who come from London cannot find the culprit and Mrs. Joe cannot speak. To help around the house, Joe calls on Biddy, who proves very quick in learning to interpret Mrs. Joe's wishes. Mrs. Joe seems to have most friendly feelings for Orlick, who soon becomes almost part of the family—to Biddy's distress, for Orlick has a strong affection for her and she does not reciprocate.

Chaps. 18–33. Pip visits Miss Havisham on his birthday each year, and each year she gives him a guinea. After four years of Pip's apprenticeship, a lawyer, Mr. JAGGERS, whom Pip has seen at Miss Havisham's house, tells Pip and Joe that a certain friend, who does not wish to be identified, has expressed the intention of leaving Pip a considerable fortune. In other words, Pip has "great expectations." Therefore Pip must leave his present life for London, to learn to live like a gentleman. Joe willingly relinquishes his rights in Pip, but Pip fails to recognize the great-hearted qualities of his brother-in-law and suddenly sees only the uncultured, rough-mannered laborer. Pip suspects that Miss Havisham is his benefactor, though he has no hint of any such thing from the lawyer. In London, Pip is turned over to Jaggers' clerk, young Mr. WEMMICK. Pip is to share lodgings at Barnard's Inn with young Mr. HERBERT POCKET, whose father, MATTHEW POCKET, is to be Pip's tutor. Mr. Pocket, Jr., turns out to be the pale young gentleman with whom Pip once fought. That does not prevent their getting on very well together now. Herbert teaches Pip polite behavior and also tells him Miss Havisham's story— the story of a faithless fiancé who failed to appear for the wedding, after which Miss Havisham became the recluse that Pip knows, always dressed for a wedding. The Pocket residence being quite an impossible place in which to live, because of Mrs. Pocket's dictatorial nature, Pip continues to make his quarters with Herbert Pocket. Pip becomes well acquainted with Wemmick and visits his home in Walworth, where Wemmick lives with his old, deaf father, whom he addresses as "Aged Parent." Pip dines with Mr. Jaggers and meets two

Pip meets young Mr. Pocket

of his fellow students, BENTLEY DRUMMLE and STARTOP. Joe Gargery brings news that Estella is back from the continent. Pip at once makes up his mind to go back and see her. Estella is now a grown woman, and a very beautiful one. Orlick is working for Miss Havisham as a porter. Pip returns to London madly in love with Estella. He confides this fact to Herbert, who reciprocates by confessing that he is in love with CLARA—but her father is a most difficult and unpleasant man. Pip has the honor of escorting Estella to Richmond, where she is to be introduced to society.

Chaps. 34–38. Pip and Herbert always spend more than their allowances and are constantly in debt. Pip's sister, Mrs. Joe, dies and Pip returns for the funeral. Shortly afterward, both he and Herbert come of age. Jaggers increases Pip's allowance most substantially and Pip is able to transfer a goodly sum to Herbert as a loan, without letting Herbert know the part he played. Wemmick, who arranges the matter, is falling in love with Miss SKIFFIN. Drummle is paying court to Estella and she seems to welcome his suit, which is painful to Pip, who still adores Estella.

Chaps. 39–46. Pip is 23 years old now, and the possessor of a considerable income, which he has always believed to come from Miss Havisham. He is alone at home one evening when a strange man calls on him.

The man is crude, roughly dressed and workworn. Pip learns, with a shock, that this man is his benefactor, not Miss Havisham. It is the convict whom Pip befriended so long ago, and he has returned to see the gentleman he has made of Pip, though he does it at the risk of his life, for the penalty of discovery is death. The man moves in as Pip's Uncle PROVIS. Herbert is sworn to secrecy, and the two young men agree that they must get Uncle Provis—or ABEL MAGWITCH, which is his real name— out of England as soon as possible. They hear his story and learn that he was victimized by one COMPEYSON, a gentlemanly swindler—the other convict Pip saw on the marsh. (Compeyson is also the faithless lover who jilted Miss Havisham.) Pip goes to see Miss Havisham and Estella once more, and learns that Estella is to marry Drummle. On his return to London he receives a note warning him not to go in his lodgings. They are being watched by someone. Magwitch has been secretly moved to a house on the shore of the river. Pip is to obtain a boat and row each day on the river, so that it will be a familiar sight and excite no suspicion when he rows Magwitch to a steamer later for his escape.

Chaps. 47–51. Pip learns that it is Compeyson who is watching him. Pip dines at Jaggers' house, and certain things about Jaggers' housekeeper convince Pip that she is Estella's mother. This is confirmed when Wemmick relates the woman's story. Estella marries. A fire at Satis House nearly results in Miss Havisham's death, but she is saved by Pip, whose hands are badly burned. On his return to London, Pip hears from Herbert a story that shows clearly that Magwitch is Estella's father.

Chaps. 52–59. The attempt to place Magwitch on the Hamburg steamer is a failure, due to Compeyson's espionage. Magwitch is captured, but before he is overpowered he deals Compeyson his death blow. Magwitch is held for trial, but he dies in prison before the trial takes place. Before he dies, he has the comfort of knowing that Pip has developed a real affection for him, and it also pleases him that Pip loves Estella deeply. After the death of his benefactor Pip suffers a long illness. When he returns to his old haunts, Miss Havisham has died and Joe is married to Biddy. Eleven years later he sees Estella. She is now a widow, but it is clear that she will now marry Pip.

310

The Great Galeoto

Play by José Echegaray, 1832–1916. Produced 1881.

THE TITLE of the first English translation was *The World and His Wife*. Echegaray was a Spanish Nobel Prize winner (1904). This has been his most popular play in the United States. The title is explained in the outline.

Prologue. Don JULIAN finds his young ward ERNEST trying to write a play but lacking a good idea. Don Julian advises a hunting trip, or at least a new plot. After Don Julian leaves inspiration comes to Ernest. He will write a play based on a story from Dante, the story of the violent and passionate love of Francesco and Paolo, and his play will be called "The Great Galeoto."

Act I. Julian tells TEODORA, his beautiful young wife, that he is worried about Ernest's future. Ernest feels that he lives on alms in Julian's house. Julian suggests that Ernest become his secretary and receive a salary. Ernest accepts. Don SEVERO, Julian's brother, and MERCEDES, Severo's wife, are certain that an affair is going on between Ernest and Teodora. "All Madrid" is gossiping about it. Severo tells Julian, who retorts that the story is a filthy lie but privately begins to entertain suspicions.

Act II. Having heard the rumors, Ernest moves out of Julian's house into a poorly furnished garret. Don Julian, filled with remorse, begs him to return. Julian is accompanied by Severo, who confesses that he foolishly gave credit to shabby innuendoes. Ernest challenges Viscount NEBREDA to a duel, for publicly voicing the slander, and Julian, too, wishes to challenge Nebreda. Severo's son asks Ernest who Galeoto was, and Ernest replies that he was a panderer who acted for Launcelot and Guinevere and who was used as a symbol of pandering in the romance of Francesco and Paolo. Ernest declares that all too often society as a whole is a Galeoto, forcing a man and woman together against their wills. Teodora comes to Ernest to prevent his duel with Nebreda. They hear a noise on the stairs and Teodora hides in Ernest's bedroom. Severo's son bursts in and reports that Julian has been severely wounded by Nebreda. A few seconds later Julian appears, supported by Don Severo. Despite Ernest's protests, Severo takes Julian into Ernest's bedroom. Teodora is discovered and Don Julian collapses.

Act III. Julian lies at home in grave condition. Ernest has fought and killed Nebreda. He comes to Julian's house to offer an explanation of what took place. Mercedes orders him turned away, but Ernest tells Mercedes that Teodora was in his rooms only to prevent a duel that would smudge Julian's honor. Mercedes dismisses this as a flimsy excuse. She goes to Teodora and tries to force her to confess love for Ernest. Teodora maintains that all her love is for Julian. Still unconvinced, Mercedes tries again to turn Ernest away but he persists and sees Teodora, who tells him they must never meet again. Ernest goes on his knees before her and Severo comes across them at this very instant. Severo seizes Teodora and drags her across the room, but Ernest intervenes and forces Severo to kneel before Teodora. Julian staggers into the room, half-delirious, and challenges Ernest to a duel. Severo and Mercedes carry Julian to his room. A cry of anguish is heard and Teodora hurries to Julian's room but Mercedes orders her out of the house. Julian has died without heirs, so the house belongs to Severo. Ernest protests again that Teodora is innocent. Severo screams that Ernest is a liar, then makes a menacing gesture toward Teodora. Ernest steps forward to protect her. He shouts that at last society has driven Teodora into his arms, against both their wills. Society, armed with stupidity and prejudice and gossip, has acted the panderer, the Galeoto, toward him and an innocent woman.

The Great Gatsby

Novel by F. Scott Fitzgerald, 1896–1940.
Published & © 1925 by Charles Scribner's Sons, New York.

EXCEPT FOR Hemingway and perhaps Faulkner, F. Scott Fitzgerald has probably influenced a greater number of young, talented novelists than any other modern writer. *The Great Gatsby* was the Fitzgerald novel that won them in the first place. The majority of readers will call it his best work. It is the book of the "lost generation" for which Fitzgerald was spokesman, and no one saw more keenly than he, or expressed so well, not only the things his generation did but why they did them. For a picture of the early postwar, early Prohibition era, *Gatsby* is the book.

Chap. 1. NICK CARRAWAY, 1915 Yale graduate, a member of a wealthy family, has come to New York in 1922 to learn the bond business. He rents a small house in the fashionable town of West Egg on Long Island. Next to his house is the sumptuous estate of the mysterious JAY GATSBY, who gives a big, open-house party every night. Nick is invited to dinner by his cousin DAISY BUCHANAN and her husband, TOM, both very rich, who live in the even more fashionable town of East Egg, which is visible across the bay. Also at dinner is Miss JORDON BAKER, an outstanding woman golfer. In Daisy, Tom, and Jordon Nick sees forced gaiety but actual boredom and discontent. Tom and Daisy have an argument, and Jordon tells Nick it is because Tom has a mistress. Upon returning from the Buchanans', Nick sees Gatsby for the first time, standing in front of his mansion and apparently disturbed.

Chap. 2. Tom introduces Nick to MYRTLE WILSON, his mistress, who lives in a little town halfway between West Egg and New York. She is the wife of the local garage mechanic, GEORGE WILSON. Tom maintains an apartment in New York to which she goes on the pretext that she is visiting her sister. At the apartment Nick also meets Myrtle's sister, Catherine. She tells Nick she has been to one of Gatsby's parties and that she is afraid of Gatsby. Catherine also says that Myrtle and Tom hate their respective mates but that Tom cannot get a divorce because Daisy is a Catholic. Nick knows this is not true.

Chap. 3. Throughout the summer Gatsby is host at parties attended by large crowds of people, most of whom do not even know Gatsby. There is plentiful food and liquor, a full orchestra, and lavish entertainment. On the evening that Nick attends his first party at Gatsby's, he believes he is one of the few guests to be formally invited. Jordan Baker is there. No one knows anything about Gatsby's background and there are many extravagant rumors about him—he is a murderer, a gangster, a former German spy. Gatsby tells Nick he was stationed in France during the war and seems to remember Nick from overseas. Gatsby tries to be friendly with Nick but Nick is not very sociable that summer. However, during the summer Nick sees Jordan a great deal.

Chap. 4. One July morning Gatsby calls on Nick at Nick's house. Gatsby is always restless and never has much to say. Nick privately has some doubts when Gatsby says he is from a wealthy Midwest family and was educated at Oxford. He shows Nick a picture taken at Oxford and a medal he won during World War I. Gatsby says he has traveled about to forget a sad thing that happened to him. Nick goes to lunch in New York with Gatsby, who introduces him to a gambler named WOLFSHEIM, who seems to be well acquainted with Gatsby. At tea, Jordan reveals that Daisy, as a popular girl in Louisville, was deeply in love with an army lieutenant stationed nearby. The lieutenant was sent overseas and Daisy married Tom, and Jordan believes that despite Daisy's love for the lieutenant Daisy was actually in love with Tom until he started seeing other women. It was not till six weeks ago that Daisy learned that the young army lieutenant had turned up as the fabulous Jay Gatsby across the Sound. Gatsby has told Jordan he bought his mansion just to be near Daisy. Across the bay between West Egg and East Egg he can see a green light that marks the Buchanans' place. Gatsby asks Nick to invite him and Daisy to tea so that he can meet her again.

Chap. 5. Daisy accepts Nick's invitation to tea. Gatsby, nervous and embarrassed, also comes. Nick leaves them alone together and when he reënters the room Gatsby seems like a new man. He takes Nick and Daisy on a tour of his elaborate mansion.

Chap. 6. Jay Gatsby's real name is James Gatz, and he is the son of poor, shiftless and unsuccessful farm people from North Dakota. He was haunted by fantastic conceits and dreams of glory. As a young man Gatsby worked for DAN CODY, a millionaire prospector who was growing old and slightly senile. Cody died and left Gatsby $25,000, but Gatsby never got the money. Gatsby became a gentleman legally when he was commissioned an officer in the U.S. Army. Gatsby is determined to repeat the past, not just erase it and start over. He wants Daisy to tell Tom she never loved him, and then marry Gatsby. Daisy and Tom attend one of Gatsby's parties, but Daisy does not enjoy the artificiality and Tom takes an instant dislike to Gatsby.

Chap. 7. Suddenly, and without explanation, Gatsby stops giving parties and fires all his servants, except a crew he has hired through the gambler Wolfsheim. Gatsby tells Nick he has taken these steps to prevent the servants from gossiping, as Daisy comes to visit him often. Nick and Gatsby are invited to lunch at Daisy's house, at which time Tom faces the realization that Daisy and Gatsby love each other. Daisy, Tom, Gatsby, Nick and Jordan decide to drive to New York. Gatsby and Daisy take Tom's coupé, and Tom drives Gatsby's large, expensive, yellow car. On the way to town, Tom stops for gas at the garage owned by George Wilson. George does not suspect that Tom is his wife's lover but he is aware that she is unfaithful to him. He tells Tom he is going to move out West with his wife. There is tension when the group arrives in New York. Tom confronts Gatsby with the knowledge of his relationship with Daisy, whereupon Gatsby tells Tom that Daisy never loved him. Daisy says that at one time she did love Tom, but now she is planning to leave him. Tom has had Gatsby investigated and reveals that Gatsby is associated with the bootlegging business. Gatsby and Daisy drive back to Long Island in his yellow car, the others following in Tom's coupé. On the way back to East Egg, Gatsby's car, driven by Daisy, is involved in an accident. Myrtle Wilson, thinking the yellow car is still being driven by Tom, runs out on the highway and the speeding car hits and kills her. Daisy does not stop.

Chap. 8. Nick advises Gatsby to leave town for a while, as the police are sure to trace the car to him. Gatsby refuses, still hoping that Daisy will leave her husband for him. Wilson, sure that the driver of the yellow car was Myrtle's lover, traces the car to Gatsby, goes to Gatsby's house, and shoots Gatsby in his swimming pool. Wilson then shoots himself. Both die.

Chap. 9. Nick attempts to find some of Gatsby's friends to attend his funeral, but there seems to be none. Daisy has gone away with Tom. Gatsby's father, HENRY G. GATZ, a tired old man, comes for the funeral. He speaks of Gatsby's youth and how he dreamed of a great future. There is no one at Gatsby's funeral but his father, Nick, and one other man who had been to a few of Gatsby's parties. After Gatsby's death, Nick feels that the East is haunted for him and decides to return to the Midwest. He and Jordan almost reached the point of marriage, but inexplicably they drifted apart. Before he leaves, he meets Tom once more. Tom confesses that he told Wilson it was Gatsby who drove the yellow car. Tom feels no guilt or remorse. Nick muses on the spoiled darlings of life, Tom and Daisy, who never suffer the consequences of their irresponsible acts, and on the dreamers such as Gatsby, who vainly pursue the future while time carries them inexorably back into the past.

The Green Bay Tree

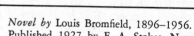

Novel by Louis Bromfield, 1896–1956. Published 1927 by F. A. Stokes, New York. (NAL, S1025; PB, 56)

CRITICAL OPINION of Louis Bromfield has been mixed, some critics considering him a major American novelist and some dismissing him as merely a popular one. This is not strange, since his novels ranged from quite poor to very good. The novel that was most successful, *The Rains Came* (1937), was very far from his best. *The Green Bay Tree*, his first novel, has best stood the test of time. Its interesting characters are women and when Bromfield based a play on it, in 1927, he called the play *The House of Women*. The theme of *The Green Bay Tree*, as of all of Bromfield's early novels, is the unrest and defiance of a new generation to the conservatism and tradition of an old family. The title occurs in the Bible, Psalm 37:35: "I have seen the wicked in great power and spreading himself like a green bay tree."

Chaps. 1–6. Mrs. JULIA SHANE, an old woman of wealth, position, and character, lives in a mansion in a provincial midwestern town. The mansion has lost its value and style since it has been surrounded by railroad yards, steel mills, and immigrant workers' homes, but Mrs. Shane refuses to move, because of sentiment. Mrs. Shane's younger daughter, IRENE, is shy and religious and seems unable to cope with the business of life. Mrs. Shane's older daughter, LILY, a warm, attractive girl of 24, is in love with the governor of the state, who is 20 years her senior. She is pregnant with his child but she refuses to marry him. Irene, delicate and neurotic, is haunted by an image of the governor opening the door of Lily's room.

Chaps. 7–13. Mrs. Shane wants to send Lily abroad before her condition can become known and cause a scandal. WILLIAM HARRISON (WILLIE), a businessman, asks Lily's hand in marriage, but she dislikes his cringing manner and decides to go to France. William's mother suspects the reason for the trip but there is little talk in the town. In Paris Lily lives well, and she

Tom stops for gas at the garage owned by George Wilson

decides to stay there. She sends a telegram to her mother, announcing the birth of her son, JEAN. Irene tells her mother that she wants to join the Catholic Church. Mrs. Shane, coming from a long line of Scottish Presbyterians, is appalled at the idea. She makes Irene promise not to be converted as long as she (Mrs. Shane) lives.

Chaps. 14–30. Four years later Lily comes home unexpectedly for a visit. Lily tells her mother that she has been baptized by the opportunistic but kind Mme. GIGON and has a respected position in French society. Lily gives parties in the old Shane mansion and for a while the gaiety of former days almost subdues the sound of the surrounding mills. William Harrison, now a mill owner, takes Lily and Irene on a tour of the mill and again asks Lily to marry him. She refuses, because he is neither exciting nor strong. Irene is teaching English to the millworkers and has an obsessive interest in their problems. She has made one friend among them, a handsome Russian, STEPHAN KRYLENKO. Lily meets her cousin, ELLEN TOLLIVER, who wants to study the piano in New York, and to get away from the drab life of her home. She idolizes Lily, because Lily has lived in Paris. Lily, catching some of Ellen's enthusiasm for France, longs to return and when she hears that her small son has measles she is only too glad to leave. Ellen Tolliver marries a New York salesman and escapes from the mill town.

Chaps. 31–48. Irene continues her work among the mill hands. Krylenko becomes a leader of the immigrant workmen. He reads Rousseau and Marx and becomes a revolutionary. Irene feels close to him and in her shy way even loves him. She has become righteous and smug and confesses to her mother that she hates Lily. Irene contends that of the two sisters only the younger is loved by God. Irene also tells her mother that she will never marry and that she wants Krylenko to remain pure and free of any woman. She wants him to be a saint. Krylenko organizes a strike at the mill and Irene is proud of his work. Mrs. Shane asks Lily to come back from France because she has only a few more months to live. Lily writes that she will return as soon as she has placed her son in a school in England. Lily comes home and finds her mother very weak. The town is up in arms and the strikers riot in the streets. Lily brings comfort to her mother and tells her charming stories about her grandson, Jean. Several days later Julia Shane dies in her sleep.

Chaps. 49–54. Irene gives the workers permission to meet on the grounds of her house. Lily listens to Krylenko speak to the crowd in several languages. She is moved by the passion of his words and when he is hurt by the police in a fight, Lily takes him into the house, binds his wounds, and promises to hide him from the police. The police come to the house, do not find the hidden Krylenko, and leave when Lily avows that she has not seen the strike leader. Afterwards Lily and Krylenko embrace. Irene breaks in on them and cries out in fury that Lily has ruined her saint and is damned forever. The next morning Lily leaves Krylenko a note saying that Irene has gone away and that she also is leaving. She wants him to remain in the house and tells him that she loves him. He stays in the great house, sending words of encouragement to the strikers, but the strike fails. Then he disappears.

Chaps. 55–67. Ellen Tolliver's husband dies and Ellen goes to Paris, where she becomes a successful, glamorous concert pianist, taking the name of LILLI BARR. Rumors of war stir Paris. Lily Shane takes a lover, Baron CESAIRE, a military man, who is kind and dignified. Irene has entered a convent at Lisieux. The shock of seeing Lily with Krylenko has shattered her faith in humanity and now she devotes herself entirely to God. Lily follows Krylenko's career as a strike leader and hopes for his ultimate success. She is frightened at the thought of becoming old and of losing her son, who is growing up and is attending a military academy.

Chaps. 68–70. Willie Harrison comes to Paris. His arrival awakens memories of Krylenko and Lily is sad. He tells her that he has quit the mill and come to Europe to lead his own life. The mill now belongs to a company that evicted the strikers from the company houses and blacklisted them, so that they find it impossible to find work anywhere else. Harrison's mother is dead and an epoch has come to an end in the midwestern town. Lily learns that her old home was burned and decides to sell the property to the town and forget that she ever lived there. After Willie's visit Lily writes to Irene, who has taken the name of Sister MONICA. This letter, like hundreds of others Lily has written to her sister, remains unanswered.

Chaps. 71–77. The Archduke of Austria is assassinated and war comes to Europe. The baron joins his regiment and Jean leaves his academy to fight for France. Lily moves to her house at Germigny on the Marne with Mme. Gigon. She is warned, by a friend in the War Ministry, to leave France, but she decides to stay. The Germans approach Germigny. Mme. Gigon suffers a fall and lies unconscious. Lily runs to the little church in the country town and brings the priest back to hear the confession of her friend and companion. Lily tells the priest the story of her own life and of the love she has for Krylenko. The baron briefly visits Lily and tells her a battle near Germigny is imminent. When he has left to rejoin his regiment, Lily weeps.

Chaps. 78–84. The battle goes badly for the French and the Germans take possession of the town. A German officer calls on Lily. He tells her he does not hate and does not want to kill but all men are caught in the war as flies in a spider's web. After he has gone, Lily looks through binoculars and sees that the Germans intend to blow up a bridge that the French must use in their retreat. She takes her revolver, hides in the brush, and kills the three Germans at the bridge. She is brought back to her house by some French soldiers and falls ill. When she recovers she is decorated by the French Government for her heroism. Cesaire is listed as missing in action and Jean is in the hospital, recovering from the amputation of his right leg. Lily moves back to Paris and becomes friendly with a French diplomat, RENÉ DE CYON. She uses some of her wealth to aid returning soldiers. She is becoming more and more like her mother in character.

Chap. 85. At a convention for American politicians in Paris, Lily meets her ex-lover, the governor, and finds him vulgar and the life he stands for repulsive. She is glad that she renounced the governor and that she is now married to René de Cyon. He appreciates her qualities and she makes a perfect wife for a man of politics. In 1920, a card from the convent at Lisieux informs Lily that Sister Monica has died, and in the newspapers Lily reads that Stephan Krylenko has died in Moscow.

The German officer tells Lily that he is a fly in a spider's web

Green Grow the Lilacs

Play by Lynn Riggs, 1899–1954. Produced in New York, 1931. Published 1931 by Samuel French, New York.

ON THIS PLAY was based the Rodgers and Hart operetta *Oklahoma!,* ensuring the lasting fame of the play. *Oklahoma!* was the most successful musical show that had been known up to its time (it was produced in 1943). *Green Grow the Lilacs* itself leaned heavily on its music—folk ballads of the West, chiefly those sung by the character Curly. But *Green Grow the Lilacs* is also a charming piece of writing and characterization. The title is from a line in a ballad sung by Curly.

Scene 1. Outside the Williams farmhouse in Indian Territory (later Oklahoma) on a June morning in 1900, a tall young cowboy, CURLY McCLAIN, is singing and Aunt ELLER asks him to come in. She says that if she wasn't an older woman and he wasn't so young and smart alecky, she'd marry him. Curly says he wouldn't marry her or any of her kinfolk, including Miss LAUREY WILLIAMS; but he gives himself away by asking where Laurey is. Aunt Eller taunts him with the fact that Laurey pays no attention to him. He boasts about his prowess as a bulldozer and she makes disparaging remarks about his being bowlegged. Curly says he wants to take Laurey to a party that Old Man PECK is giving across Dog Creek. Laurey overhears and comes in, saying she heard someone singing like a bullfrog. She asks Curly if he has a buggy with red wheels and a spanking team and Curly says he has a surrey with a fringe on the top, but then says he hasn't. Laurey flounces out of the room, but reappears and says she is going to the party with JEETER, the hired hand. Curly asks Aunt Eller to go to the party with him and tells her he really has hired the surrey. Then he goes out to look for Jeeter.

Scene 2. Laurey is in her bedroom preparing for the party. She acts very short with Aunt Eller, who surmises that she is in love. Laurey tells of once having seen a house burn to the ground and how sad it made her. She says she sometimes fears Jeeter may set their house on fire and she confesses that she is frightened by the hired hand. A wagon drives up with ALI HAKIM, a peddler, and ADO ANNIE CARNES. Aunt Eller buys an eggbeater and Laurey and Ado buy trinkets, garters, and face whitening. They hear shots from the smokehouse, where Curly has gone to find Jeeter, and they all rush out.

Scene 3. When Curly goes to the smokehouse to find Jeeter, the hired hand is looking at postcards. They exchange taunts.

Jeeter shows Curly his pictures and a pair of Colt .45 revolvers. They start playing cards. Jeeter starts musing about violent crimes, which he follows in detail, most of them having to do with men murdering young girls and trying to dispose of their bodies. When Curly admits that he comes to see Laurey, Jeeter becomes angry and forbids him to step foot on the place. Curly compares him to a scared rattlesnake and Jeeter snatches up a gun and pulls the trigger, splintering the wall. Curly points to a knot in a plank, picks up the other gun, and blows the knot out. Aunt Eller and Laurey arrive. Laurey is impressed by Curly's marksmanship. Ali Hakim comes in and Jeeter buys a wicked-looking knife. Curly counters by buying a pair of brass knuckles.

Scene 4. The party is in full swing at Old Man Peck's place. Jeeter asks Laurey why she doesn't like to be alone with him. He tells her how he tries to get her alone at the ranch and he suddenly seizes her in his arms. At first she is hysterical but suddenly her fears vanish and she tells him he is nothing but a mangy dog and someone might shoot him. Laurey finds Curly and tells him she is afraid. He holds her and kisses her and asks her to marry him.

Scene 5. Curly and Laurey have been married and are sneaking through a hayfield hoping to escape the shivaree, the post-wedding hazing ritual. The shivaree begins and all the neighboring men, who have been hiding in the fields, make suggestive remarks, manhandle Curly, and try to surround Laurey. In the midst of the uproar a haystack begins to burn and Jeeter appears, drunk, carrying a flaming torch, and threatening to burn the bride and groom to cracklings. He pulls out his knife and rushes at Curly. But he trips, and after groaning and whimpering he lies very still. The men persuade Curly to come with them and give himself up to the law.

Scene 6. Ado Annie and Aunt Eller, sewing in the living room, are worried because Laurey has not eaten or slept since Curly was taken away. They hear the dog barking outside and Curly appears. Laurey is thankful that they have let him off but he confesses that he broke out of the prison. Aunt Eller is wild, because she knows he will be followed. Curly tells Laurey not to worry, as he has heard that the hearing will be purely perfunctory. The posse arrives, but Aunt Eller gives the men a piece of her mind and they agree to leave Curly and Laurey alone until the next morning, when Curly will be freed at the hearing.

The Green Hat

Novel by Michael Arlen (Dikran Kouyoumdjian, 1895–1958). Published 1924. Play produced 1924 in New York.

AS A NOVEL The *Green Hat* was no work of art, perhaps because its Armenian author was not at home writing in English, but its story is a most dramatic one and the play based on the novel was a great success. It was one of Katharine Cornell's early triumphs. The basic theme is that the heroine Iris March, who affects flamboyant green hats as an act of bravado, married her brother's hero. The hero turned out to be unworthy while Iris herself was actually pure; but rather than disillusion her brother, Iris let her own reputation be smudged. Her brother became an alcoholic anyway, from shame that his sister had (as he thought) so betrayed his hero. While the play was running in 1924–25, most cities did not permit the word syphilis to be uttered on the stage and "a vile disease" was substituted.

Chap. 1. 1. The author lives in a flat in Shepherd's Green, London. Above him lives a misanthropic drunkard, GERALD MARCH. The author's bell rings and on the street he sees a green hat, the kind worn *pour le sport,* and a large yellow Hispano-Suiza. **2.** The girl in the green hat asks if Mr. March is in. He escorts her to Gerald's apartment. She is Gerald's twin sister, IRIS STORM, and has not seen her brother for ten years. They find him drunk. Iris explains that Gerald's youthful hero died and he never got over it. **3.** Iris has heard of the author from a mutual friend, HILARY TOWNSHEND. She has a drink of water in his flat and they talk. She calls herself "a house of men . . . of their desires and defeats and deaths" and tells him there is a curse on the Marches. He admires a ring on her finger. It was given her by her dead husband and she shows him how it falls off her finger; it is beautiful but loose. A policeman rings to inquire about the Hispano-Suiza. When the author returns to his flat he finds Iris asleep in his bed. **4.** In the morning Iris talks about the beast that comes to her in a dream. She says she is sorry they cannot be friends but she gives him a telephone number.

Chap. 2. 1. Gerald is described through the eyes of Hilary Townshend and GUY DE TRAVERT, both great friends of Barty March, father of Iris and Gerald. Gerald wrote a novel, then cut away from his friends, partly because his sister had become déclassé. Hilary describes Gerald as having been a "dark, diabolical schoolboy"; and Guy, who was his colonel in the Grenadiers during the war, calls him a "young, hellfire idiot." **2.** Proceeding with the description of Gerald: The author remembers his never having an overcoat and being a solitary drunkard. Gerald's novel *The Savage Device* was a story of adventure in which the hero plucks a wife from a San Francisco dive, the hero being obviously patterned on BOY FENWICK, Iris's husband and Gerald's hero, and the woman being inspired by Iris herself. Iris at 18 was in love with NAPIER HARPENDEN, but his father, Maj.-Gen. Sir MAURICE HARPENDEN, opposed any marriage. **3.** When Gerald is told of Iris's call he does not believe it, then he calls his sister a beast. The author moves to new lodgings and loses track of Gerald for two weeks. He calls Iris but finds she is on the continent. From there she sends him box of stationery.

Chap. 3. 1. The author meets Gerald at a newsstand. He offers Gerald money. Gerald counters by insisting that he himself accept a fiver, and sends his love to Iris. **2.** Hilary Townshend and Guy de Travert are described, as symbols of England. Guy has a wife who insists that he is cruel, and she threatens to take a lover but never does. **3.** The author talks to Hilary about Iris. Hilary says the Marches are cursed. The author discovers that Iris is very rich, having been left a fortune by her second husband, the steel magnate HECTOR STORM. Her first husband, Boy Fenwick, committed suicide on their wedding night. **4.** This happened in Deauville. The report was that Boy killed himself "for purity," after discovering that his wife was unchaste. Iris condoned the report, though it ruined her reputation. Hilary admits that Fenwick was not quite sane but says he acted in the depths of sudden despair and destroyed the girl by exalting himself. Hilary says that Iris was loved extravagantly by both her husbands.

Chap. 4. 1. The author goes with Hilary to a night club in Carlton House Terrace, where the aristocracy foregathers. There they see VENICE POLLEN, who is to marry Napier Harpenden. HUGO CYPRESS, dancing by with his wife, SHIRLEY, asks if they have seen the evening paper, about a friend of theirs. Hilary leaves the table and returns to say that Gerald is in an awful mess. Iris comes in with a colonel, then Guy comes in, most unsmiling. **2.** The author finds himself with Iris in the Hispano-Suiza. She insists on seeing Gerald before she goes abroad the next day. The author has learned Gerald has been fined for indecently annoying a woman in Hyde Park and is appealing the charge. They go to Shepherd's market and the author climbs to Gerald's flat. He comes back and tells Iris that her brother is drunk again, but actually he has blown his brains out.

Chap. 5. 1. Some months later the writer is in Paris. An acquaintance, CHERRY MARVEL, tells him that Iris is seriously ill at a nursing home; she has had an operation. The author has previously had a long letter from Iris, blaming him for some sort of

Gerald is a suicide

predicament in which Iris then found herself. Iris has admitted to Guy that she had a son by Storm before her second husband died but that the baby died. **2.** The author goes to the nursing home, but a nun tells him that Mrs. Storm is rather wild. The nun will not let him in.

Chap. 6. By tipping the lay sister (as she turns out to be) the author gets into the hospital. He has a talk with CONRAD MASTERS, a celebrated doctor, who explains that Iris is very ill with septic poisoning and has lost her desire to live. He finds that septic poisoning comes after one has had a baby or an abortion and that it is not necessarily fatal. Napier stops by the hos-

pital to inquire about Iris, not realizing the gravity of her illness. When Masters hears that Napier has been Iris's lover, he suggests a visit from Napier may inspire her to live, but Napier decides that he has to leave Paris with his wife, Venice.

Chap. 7. Napier is again urged to stay over and try to pull Iris through her crisis, but he refuses to upset his plans. Masters then decides that the author himself must make a second visit to Iris to persuade her to fight for her life.

Chaps. 8–10. The author sees Iris. She is very frightened and confesses that no one wants her, including God. She tells him that he has probably saved her life and seems satisfied when she learns that Napier does not suspect that he was the cause of her near brush with death. She assures the author that she will never again return to England. But later Hilary, Guy and the author see Napier and Iris together in a cab in London. Guy suggests that since it is very hot they should get up a swimming party. The author drives to Maidenhead with Iris and she buys a green hat on the way. When they go swimming Iris saves Venice from drowning, although it is obvious to everyone that Napier and Iris are contemplating an elopement.

Chap. 11. The principal characters meet at Sir Maurice Harpenden's, where they review the tangled threads of the romance between Napier and Iris. Iris accuses the old man of having wickedly broken up her girlhood romance with his son. For the first time it is revealed that Fenwick killed himself because he had syphilis while Iris, when she married him, was a virgin. Napier wants Iris to go away with him but Venice reveals that she is bearing Napier's child. Iris drives off in the Hispano-Suiza and intentionally kills herself in an accident.

Green Mansions

Novel by W. H. Hudson, 1841–1922. Published 1904; in U.S. published by Alfred A. Knopf, New York. (ML, 89)

As A NOVEL of nature, the supernatural, and romance, *Green Mansions* is an outstanding work of this century. William Henry Hudson was American by parentage, Argentine by birth, British by adopted nationality. He was a naturalist as well as a novelist and his novels are dependable as well as beautiful in their descriptions of natural life.

Prologue. The narrator of the prologue is the only person who knows the story of Mr. ABEL's sojourn in the desert. The only visible symbol of this sojourn was a flower-decorated urn filled with ashes in Abel's house. Abel was a Venezuelan who had

come into a fortune. People liked him well enough, and speculated about him, but none knew much about him. The narrator shared with Abel a great love of poetry, and the two became good friends, so that Abel consented to tell the narrator about his unusual experience.

Chap. 1. As a young man of 23, Abel is involved in a plot to overthrow the Venezuelan government. The plot fails and Abel is forced to flee. He decides to explore the wilderness region south of the Orinoco River, which is inhabited by tribes of primitive peoples. At Manapuri Abel falls ill of a fever, which keeps him incapacitated for six months. He meets a kindly trader, Don FANTA, who arranges for a group of friendly Indians to take Abel with them to a place where the climate is better. Abel is facile at learning the Indian dialects and as a result manages to get along with the natives. He is befriended by RUNI, the chief of an Indian tribe, and settles down to live among Runi's people.

Chaps. 2–3. Abel explores the lovely forest near the village, though the Indians warn that it is a dangerous place. Abel thinks their fears are merely superstition. In the wood he hears an exquisite melody that seems to resemble a human voice, but he fails to see the creature, be it human or not, that has made the sounds. One day he bribes one of the Indians, KUA-KO, to accompany him to the wood. Kua-Ko says that the Indians never kill any of the animals in the wood, for fear the daughter of DIDI would cause them to be killed. Abel infers that the Indians invented this superstition of a daughter of the water-spirit to explain the strange melodic voice. Kua-Ko runs from the wood in fear, leaving Abel behind. Abel hears the melodic voice again and becomes certain that it is a human voice.

Chaps. 4–5. Kua-Ko teaches Abel how to use the zabatana, a weapon for killing game. After several days, Abel revisits the wood. This time he does not hear the melodic voice but he has a strange adventure while watching a spider tracking its prey. The spider's maneuvers are so amusing that Abel feels like laughing, whereupon he hears a clear trill of merry laughter nearby. The next day he pushes farther into the wood and suddenly comes upon a girl, an exquisite, delicate creature, who is playing with a bird. She does not seem afraid, but she disappears. Abel goes back into the wood repeatedly and hears the voice in different places, but can see nothing. Kua-Ko offers Abel his sister in marriage if Abel will slay the mysterious girl with a poisoned arrow. The girl, says Kua-Ko, is the daughter of an evil being and prevents the Indian from hunting in the wood. Abel rejects the idea angrily.

Chap. 6. Abel is about to hit a poisonous coral snake with a rock when the girl boldly steps out of the forest. Immediately the snake seems to lose its anger and curls up about her foot. The girl is lovely, with a bright, luminous skin coloring and an ethereal appearance. When Abel moves to put his arm about her slender body to detain her, the snake bites him. Abel fears that he will die from the deadly bite, and implores the girl to help him. She appears grief-stricken but apparently has no knowledge of medical care. Abel tries to leave the wood but is lost. A storm has arisen and Abel, groping his way, goes over the edge of a precipice and loses consciousness.

Chaps. 7–8. Abel awakens in a hut occupied by an old man, NUFLO, and the girl, whose name is RIMA. Rima has saved Abel by having him brought to the hut. However, in the hut she seems to have lost the brighter aspect he saw in the wood. Nuflo reveals that they eat no meat, because Rima will not permit the killing of animals. When Abel has recovered somewhat, he goes walking in the wood. Rima seems to be once again the tantalizing, elusive creature he had first known. Rima speaks of her mother, who is dead, and tells Abel that they once lived in the village of Voa, but will tell him no more.

Chap. 9. As the days pass, Rima becomes silent and shy, and is only occasionally around. Nuflo goes off every day to a secret hiding place where he eats meat alone, so as not to offend Rima. He tells Abel that Rima's mother died young and that he took the child away to a better climate. Nuflo will not hunt in the wood, declaring that in that wood is one law, the law of Rima. Abel discovers that he loves Rima.

Chaps. 10–11. Abel returns to the Indian village for a short visit, but he returns to Rima the next day. A storm comes on and Abel gets lost again, but Rima leads him back to Nuflo's hut. Rima wishes Abel to tell her about the whole world, because she feels there must be people in the world who would understand her mysterious speech and thoughts and feelings. She asks Abel to go with her to seek her mother's people. Abel tells her it is impossible to cross the mountains of Riolama, and in a flash Rima knows that Riolama is her real name and also the name of the place her people are from.

Chaps. 12–13. Rima is angered that Nuflo never told her about Riolama and demands that he now take her there. She prays to her mother for revenge on Nuflo. Her prayer reveals that she loves Abel, though she does understand this emotion. Nuflo fears the curse and agrees to make the trip. While preparations are being made, Abel returns to spend a few days with Runi, who is now suspicious of him. Runi steals Abel's pistol and tries to keep him prisoner in the village, but Abel sneaks back to the forest of Rima.

Chaps. 14–15. Nuflo tells Abel Rima's story. About 17 years before, as a fugitive from the law, he went to Riolama and took shelter in a cave. Here he met a strange, wonderful-looking woman whose foot had been injured and who was about to give birth to a child. Nuflo took her to Voa, a village, where the child Rima was born. Mother and child would go into the wood and commune with each other in their wonderful language. Rima also learned Spanish from the villagers. The mother grew weak and on her deathbed implored

that Rima, who was also frail, be taken to a cooler mountainous region. Nuflo agreed to do so and built the hut where Abel had found them.

Chaps. 16–17. After an 18-day journey they arrive at Riolama, but Abel dissuades Rima from climbing the mountain to see her mother's country, telling her she might wander for years and that probably her people no longer exist. The brightness seems to go out of Rima and they fear she is dying, but gradually she seems to regain life. Abel holds her in his arms and kisses her. A radiance overspreads her face, and Abel explains that the emotion she has felt for him is love. Rima then insists on returning to her wood alone, because she has many things to do and can get there faster alone. Abel is against it, but Rima has her way. She will await his homecoming in rapturous expectation.

Chaps. 18–19. After another long, hard journey, Nuflo and Abel arrive in the wood of Rima. The hut is burned down and there is no sign of her. Abel comes upon some Indians of Runi's tribe in the wood, a place where they never would enter previously. He returns to the village and learns that the Indians found out Rima was gone and began hunting in the wood. Then one day Rima returned. The girl, frightened, climbed a tree, and to destroy her the Indians burned her in the tree. Abel is stunned and filled with rage. He leaves the Indians, killing Kua-Ko in his flight.

Chaps. 20–22. Abel seeks help from the tribe of Manango, a deadly enemy of Runi, and eventually this tribe kills Runi's tribe. Abel returns to the wood of Rima, where he lives in solitude in a small shelter he builds there. His health deteriorates, and he fears he is going mad. He still holds the hope that the Indians lied about Rima's death, but he finds the burnt tree and gathers up the ashes of Rima. Food becomes difficult to find, and he grows weaker. Finally he decides that Rima herself would prefer it if he left the wood. After a bad journey, Abel makes it to the coast. With him is the urn of sacred ashes that he has destined to mix with his own.

Abel comes upon some Indians of the Runi tribe

316

The Green Pastures

Play by Marc Connelly, 1890–
Produced Feb. 26, 1930, in New York.
Published and © 1930 by Rinehart
& Co., New York. (ML, G21)

THOUGH THE OUTLINE may make it appear a burlesque, this modern classic is a reverent retelling of the Book of Genesis. With its background music by a Negro choir, it is tremendously effective and touchingly beautiful. The play is based on stories (published in 1928 as *Ol' Man Adam an' His Chillum*) by Roark Bradford, who was an artist superior even to Joel Chandler Harris in this field of dialect stories.

Act I. 1. In a class of Sunday School children in a Negro church in Louisiana, the preacher, Mr. DESHEE, tells the children to listen to the story of Creation as he pictures it to them. The lights go down. **2.** The angels, all Negroes, are holding a fish fry in a typical picnic setting. The Angel GABRIEL enters and announces "de Lawd God Jehovah." The LORD enters, wearing a black Prince Albert coat, and exchanges greetings with the adoring angels. He tries some custard and says it needs more firmament. The Lord decrees the earth as a place to drain off the firmament and also decrees man. He decides to go down to inspect earth and leaves Gabriel in charge of heaven. **3.** The Lord sees that Adam is lonely so he creates Eve and tells the two to enjoy themselves in the garden, but not to eat the forbidden fruit. As the stage darkens, Mr. Deshee is heard asking a child what happened to Adam and Eve, and the girl replies that they ate the fruit and were driven out of the garden and that they had CAIN and ABEL. **4.** Cain is shown standing over the body of Abel. The Lord tells Cain that he'd better "git." **5.** Cain finds a young, enticing girl in the Parish of Nod and he decides to board with her folks. The Lord considers this bad business. **6.** In his private office in heaven, the Lord is going over affairs with Gabriel, who picks up his trumpet. The Lord warns him not to blow until the time comes. Gabriel reminds the Lord that he has not been down to earth in 400 years. The Lord decides to pay the earth a visit. **7.** The Lord, dressed as a preacher, walks down a country road on a Sunday morning. He finds the flashily dressed people violating the Sabbath, and men who seem to be kneeling in prayer turn out to be crapshooters. The Lord is about to wipe all people off the face of the earth when he meets NOAH, who mistakes the Lord for a fellow preacher and invites him to a chicken dinner at home. **8.** The Lord tells Noah of the coming rain. He tells Noah how to build an ark and instructs him to take his family and two of every kind of animal aboard. Noah asks to be allowed to take two kegs of liquor, but the Lord, causing a clap of thunder, insists on one keg. **9.** Noah and his sons, HAM, SETH and JAPETH, are building the ark while the people jeer and carry on scandalously. Thunder is heard and the rain comes down as the people scatter. The animals are led aboard the ark as the stage darkens, and a choir sings "De ol' Ark's a-moverin'." **10.** Noah is a little drunk; his wife scolds him and Noah sends a dove out with an olive branch. The Lord visits Noah and tells him to start making the earth bloom again. Gabriel doesn't think much of the possibilities, but the Lord hopes it will work out all right.

Act II. 1. The Lord is in his office with ABRAHAM, ISAAC, and JACOB, discussing a new plan to cure men of their continuing wickedness. He asks them to help him choose a leader and they suggest MOSES. The Lord agrees. **2.** The Lord appears to Moses and to overcome his skepticism causes a bush to burst into flame. He then calls in AARON to help Moses. He gives Moses a rod and teaches him some tricks to confound the wicked PHARAOH. **3.** Moses and Aaron appear before the Pharaoh in his palace and Moses turns the rod into a serpent, brings a plague of flies, and asks the Pharaoh to let his people go. The Pharaoh agrees but then changes his mind. Moses calls for the death of every firstborn Egyptian child and when the Pharaoh sees his dead son he allows the Hebrews to leave Egypt. **4.** The Hebrews are on the march with JOSHUA leading the army and Aaron leader of the priests. The Lord gives Moses the Ten Commandments and when Moses breaks the Tablets the Lord is displeased and says Moses cannot go on to the promised land, but he takes the old man to Heaven with him. The choir sings, "Joshua fit de battle of Jericho," and in the darkness Mr. Deshee is heard saying things didn't work out once again and the people of Israel were taken to Babylon in bondage. **5.** The King of Babylon enters a night club with several flashy girls, and the fat, corrupt High Priest of the Jews joins him. A prophet enters and reproaches them for their sinful conduct. He is shot by the king's guard. The high priest attempts to placate the Lord with an offering of silver, but the Lord appears and in a voice of doom says he has had enough of sinning. **6.** Abraham, Isaac and Jacob visit the Lord in his office and plead with him, as they have been doing every day for hundreds of years, to go back to their people. He refuses, but he sees the shadow of the prophet HOSEA and hears the voice of HEZDREL, a soldier guarding the temple in Jerusalem from the attacking Romans. The Lord decides to pay a visit to earth. **7.** The Lord, dressed as a country preacher, hears Hezdrel say they all must fight to the death for their God. The Lord asks Hezdrel why he has such faith, as God has abandoned man, and Hezdrel answers that God is no longer the Jehovah of wrath and vengeance but the God of Hosea, the God of mercy. The Lord asks if it isn't the same God, and Hezdrel says he doesn't know but that they have found Him through suffering. The Lord thanks Hezdrel for teaching him so much.

8. The Lord sits in heaven with the angels gathered around his chair. He tells Gabriel that mercy comes through suffering. Even God must suffer. A voice from below is heard forecasting the Crucifixion. The angels sing "Hallelujah, King Jesus!"

The Lord sits in Heaven with angels gathered around His chair

Grimm's Fairy Tales

Tales by Jakob Grimm, 1785–1863, and Wilhelm Grimm, 1786–1859. Published 1815.

THE BROTHERS GRIMM were great scholars in linguistics and lexicography. Their researches into language caused them to encounter many of the legends of medieval Europe and they collected them in what became the best-known book of fairy tales. As a result, any volume collecting the most famous fairy tales, such as Cinderella, Sleeping Beauty, Little Red Riding Hood, Snow White, and similar ones, is more than likely to be called "Grimm's Fairy Tales." Actually, it has long since been observed that the German versions of these stories are too cruel for children brought up by the accepted standards of today: The enemies of the "good" characters are far too likely to be put to death in some horrible way, or at the very least subjected to torture. Therefore the revised versions actually published for children are more likely to be based on the French versions of Charles Perrault (1628–1703) and even some of those have required considerable expurgation or revision to make them suitable for today's humanistic tastes.

HANSEL AND GRETEL

HANSEL and GRETEL are children of a poor woodchopper. There is not enough food for the family and their callous stepmother persuades their father to take them into the woods and abandon them. The first time the father does this, Hansel leaves a trail by dropping shiny pebbles all along the way, so the children find their way back home. The father tries again and this time Hansel tries to leave a trail by dropping crumbs from a slice of bread he has in his pocket, but birds eat the crumbs and the children are hopelessly lost, tired and hungry and frightened. A little bird guides them to a clearing in which there is a tiny cottage all made of gingerbread, cake, and candies. They eat their fill, but an old woman, a witch, who owns the cottage, catches them and makes them her prisoners. She plans to fatten up Hansel and eat him, and she makes Gretel her servant and treats her cruelly. The witch does not see very well, and each day she tells Hansel to put forth his arm so that she may feel it and see if he is fattening. He holds out a dry bone and makes her think he is too thin to eat. One day she decides to eat him anyway, and heats up the oven. She tells Gretel to put her head inside the oven and find out if it is hot enough. Gretel, warned by the bird, pretends she does not know how. The

angry witch puts her own head inside, to show how it is done, and Gretel pushes her in and slams the door. That is the end of the wicked witch. Gretel releases Hansel, and a great crowd of birds—the ones that ate the crumbs—repay the children by taking gems and pearls from the top of the cottage, where the witch had hidden them, and dropping them into aprons that the children hold. Now Hansel and Gretel are rich. The birds show them the way home, where their father is happy to see them.

THE SLEEPING BEAUTY

After many years of childlessness, a king and queen finally have a beautiful baby daughter. In honor of her birth the king gives a party to which he invites twelve out of the thirteen fairies in the kingdom. One by one, the fairies give presents to the little princess. Just as the twelfth fairy's turn comes, the uninvited fairy arrives, furious at the king for slighting her. She decrees that when the little princess is 15, she will prick her finger with a spindle and die. The twelfth fairy now steps forward to present her gift. She cannot undo the evil but she can soften it. The little princess will not die, but she and all in the palace will fall asleep for 100 years.

Hoping to avoid the misfortune altogether, the king has every spindle in the kingdom destroyed. But on her 15th birthday, the princess wanders into a strange room in the palace and finds an old woman spinning. She begs the woman to let her try, and as soon as she touches the spindle she pricks her finger and she and everyone in the palace fall asleep. A hedge of thorns grows up around the palace. Many princes try to break through it but no one succeeds

The sleeping beauty is rescued

until, 100 years later, a handsome, daring young prince manages to get through. He makes his way past all the sleeping people in the palace to the tower where the princess lies. He kisses her and she wakes. Instantly the spell is broken. Everyone in the palace wakes and everything is just as it was 100 years ago. The prince and princess are married and live happily ever after.

RAPUNZEL

A man and woman who have long wanted a child live next door to a beautiful garden that belongs to a witch. One day the wife is overcome with desire for a radish

from that garden and persuades her husband to get one for her. The witch catches him. She permits him to take the radishes but makes him promise to give her his firstborn child. A little daughter is born to the couple soon after. The witch claims her, names her RAPUNZEL, and takes her away. When Rapunzel is 12 years old she has long golden hair. The witch shuts her up in a tower without doors or stairs. When the witch wishes to enter the tower, she stands beneath its only window and calls: "Rapunzel, Rapunzel, let down your hair." Then Rapunzel lowers her beautiful gold braids and the witch climbs up. One day a prince happens by and sees the witch do this. When the witch has gone, he calls out to Rapunzel. She lowers her hair and he climbs up. They fall in love and decide to escape as soon as the prince has brought Rapunzel sufficient silk to make a ladder. But the witch learns of their plan. She cuts off Rapunzel's hair and carries the girl to a desert. Then she fastens Rapunzel's braids to the window latch and waits till the prince comes and climbs up. When he is told he will never see Rapunzel again, he leaps from the window and is blinded by a thorn bush into which he falls. For years he wanders through the land and at last he chances to come upon Rapunzel. She falls into his arms and weeps. Her tears moisten his eyes and cure his blindness. He takes her to his kingdom, where they live happily ever after.

THE FISHERMAN AND HIS WIFE

A fisherman lives with his wife in a ditch by the sea. One day the fisherman hooks a huge flounder. The flounder begs the fisherman to let him go, as he is not a real fish but an enchanted prince. The fisherman lets him swim away. That night he tells his wife the story and she orders him to return the following day and ask a favor of the enchanted fish. He must ask for a fine cottage in which to live. The fisherman goes back to the sea and tells the fish of his wife's demand. He is told to return home—the wish has already been granted. The wife is not content. She wants a fine stone mansion. This wish too is granted, but still she is not content. She wants her husband to be king, then emperor, and then Pope. Each new demand is granted, and each time the fisher-

The fisherman and the fish

318

man begs her to be happy with what she has, but she can never be satisfied. One morning, as she sees the sun rise without herself bidding it to do so, she decides she must be lord of the sun and moon. She tells her husband of this new wish, and trembling with fear he goes down to the sea, which is now rolling and roaring in anger. He tells the fish that his wife wishes to be lord of the sun and moon. "Go home to your ditch again," says the fish. And there they live to this very day.

RUMPELSTILTSKIN

A poor miller, wishing to impress the king, tells him he has a daughter who can spin straw into gold. The king, a greedy man, orders the girl brought to him and puts her in a room filled with straw. He tells her that if she has not spun it all into gold by the following morning she must die. As the girl sits alone, wondering how to save her life—for she knows nothing of how to spin straw into gold—a little man comes in. He asks what she will give if he spins all the straw into gold. She gives him her necklace and he spins the straw into gold in a twinkling. The next day the king puts the girl into a still larger straw-filled room, with the same command. Again the little man appears and this time the girl gives him her ring. On the third day she has nothing left to give the little man and he makes her promise to give him her first-born child. Then he spins the straw into gold. Soon after this, the girl marries the king and they have a baby. The little man appears to take the child, but the young queen pleads with him and he tells her if she can guess his name in three days she may keep her baby. For two days the girl guesses all the names she knows but none of them are right. On the morning of the third day her messenger tells her that while wandering in the woods he saw a little man dancing on one leg, shouting: "Today I stew, tomorrow bake, the next day I the queen's child take; how fortunate nobody knows my name is RUMPELSTILTSKIN." When the little man returns the queen calls him Rumpelstiltskin; he screams and stamps his foot so hard that it sticks in the ground. He cannot get it out and pulls so hard that it comes off. He goes hopping away, never to be heard from again.

The girl and Rumpelstiltskin

CINDERELLA

[*Note:* The Cinderella *of* The Brothers Grimm *differs from the French and English* Cinderella *stories. It does not include the Fairy Godmother or the pumpkin and rats and mice that become carriage, horses, and footmen. Also, in the Grimm version, the Grand Ball lasts three days. Cinderella's stepmother and sisters are finally punished with cruel deaths, not recited in most published versions today and not included in this outline.*]

A rich man loses his wife and is alone with his daughter. He marries a widow with two ugly daughters. These three hate the little girl because she is so beautiful, sweet, and kind. They clothe her in rags and make her do menial work; she has no bed and at night she huddles in the warm ashes on the hearth, so she is called CINDERELLA. The father goes to the fair and asks what the women wish him to bring back as presents. His two stepdaughters demand beautiful jewels and clothing, but Cinderella asks only for a green hazel twig. He brings it, and Cinderella plants it in the garden, where soon it becomes a tree. A dove makes its home in the tree and is Cinderella's friend.

A great ball, lasting three days, is to be held at the royal palace so that the prince may choose his bride. The ugly sisters make elaborate preparations. Cinderella begs to be allowed to go. Her stepmother agrees that Cinderella may go if she can sort out all the good peas that the stepmother drops in the ashes, and put them in a bowl within two hours. This is impossible, but Cinderella's friend the dove brings its friends and they do the job. Then the stepmother says that in one hour Cinderella must clean two pans full of peas. Once again the birds come and do the job. Still the stepmother will not let Cinderella go to the ball, for Cinderella has no dress to wear. The ugly stepsisters and their mother go off and Cinderella is left alone. She runs out to her hazel tree and begs it to shake down some fine party clothes on her. Her rags disappear and she is clad in lovely shining garments, with dainty gold slippers [in English versions, glass slippers; properly, fur slippers]. She goes to the ball and the prince is entranced with her. She has been warned by the hazel tree that she must be home by midnight, or else her finery will disappear. She slips away in time the first night, and the second. The prince tries to follow her, and once he thinks he sees her enter the yard of the house where she lives, but when he looks he sees only a shabby, ragged kitchen maid. On the third evening the prince has pitch placed on the grand staircase. When Cinderella slips out, one of her slippers is caught in the pitch. The prince determines to find the foot that fits the slipper. He goes to Cinderella's house and both of the ugly sisters are determined to make the shoe fit. The foot of one is too long, and she cuts off a bit of her big toe. The other's foot is too wide, and she snips off a bit of the side

of her foot. In each case the little dove whistles warnings to the prince to "see the blood on that shoe," and the prince finds he has been tricked. Cinderella finally comes out and puts on the slipper. It fits perfectly, and as she is standing there her rags disappear and she is once more dressed in her ballroom finery. The prince places her on his horse and they ride away to live happily ever after.

CINDERELLA (ENGLISH VERSION)

The wife of a rich man dies, leaving him with one daughter. He marries again, a widow with two ugly daughters. Jealous of their stepsister's beauty, they send her to live in the kitchen, where she must do the dirtiest work, wear rags, and tend the cinders. Because of this, they call her CINDERELLA. Several years later the king announces a ball, to last for three nights, at which his

son will choose a bride. The two ugly sisters spend weeks preparing themselves. The big night comes and they set out for the ball. Cinderella is left weeping by the grate. Magically an old woman appears before her and tells her she shall go to the ball. The old woman converts some mice and a pumpkin into a beautiful horse and carriage. Then she turns Cinderella's rags into the most beautiful gown in the world, and Cinderella has fur slippers [in traditional but incorrect English versions, glass slippers]. The old woman warns Cinderella that each midnight all her splendor will vanish and her dress will turn to rags. At the ball the prince is entranced with Cinderella and dances with no one else all evening. At midnight, remembering the old woman's warning, Cinderella hurries home. She does the same the next night. But on the third night she remains a few moments too long and as she runs away, at the first stroke of twelve, she drops one of her slippers. The prince finds the slipper and orders his heralds to search the kingdom for the maiden whose foot it fits. When the herald arrives at Cinderella's house, the two ugly sisters try desperately to squeeze their big feet into the slipper, but without success. Then Cinderella emerges from the kitchen and begs to try. The sisters laugh, but Cinderella puts the slipper on and it fits perfectly. Her rags turn into the beautiful ball dress again. The prince marries her amid much pomp and rejoicing.

SNOW WHITE AND ROSE RED

A poor widow lives in a hut by the side of the forest with her two daughters, who

319

are called Snow White and Rose Red. One wintry night a big black bear knocks at the door and begs to come in and warm himself. The widow lets him in and the girls play merrily with him. Every night after that, all winter long, the bear comes back to play with the children. When spring comes he tells them he must go to guard his treasures from the evil dwarfs who remain below ground all winter. Not long after the bear leaves, Snow White and Rose Red come upon a dwarf who is caught in the cleft of a log by the end of his beard. To release him, the girls are forced to cut off a piece of his beard. Instead of being grateful, he scolds them for ruining his beautiful beard. He picks up a sack of gold and runs off. A few days later they meet the dwarf again. This time he has caught his beard in a fishline. Once again they free him by snipping his beard, and once again he scolds them. Then he picks up a bag of pearls and runs away. A third time the girls free him, when a great eagle picks him up by the beard and is about to carry him off. Soon after this incident, the girls come upon a clearing in which they see the dwarf, surrounded by jewels and gold. The bear comes out of the forest and starts after the dwarf. The dwarf begs him to eat the girls instead,

The bear kills the dwarf

but the bear kills the dwarf with a single blow. The bear's rough coat falls off, revealing the shining golden clothes of a handsome prince. He explains that he was bewitched by the evil dwarf, who stole all his fortune. The dwarf's death has released him. He marries Snow White and his brother marries Rose Red and they all live happily ever after.

THE ADVENTURES OF TOM THUMB

Tom Thumb, the smallest boy in the world, is the son of a very poor woodcutter. When there is a famine in the land, the woodcutter is forced to take Tom and his six brothers out to the wood and abandon them. The first time he does this, Tom leaves a trail of pebbles and he and his brothers find their way back. The second time, Tom leaves a trail of breadcrumbs, but these are eaten by the birds and the little boys are lost. In the distance they see the lights of a cottage and they go to it. A woman opens the door and tells them this is the house of an ogre, who will surely eat them, but the boys would rather stay than

be torn by the wolves in the forest. When the ogre comes home he smells the boys and wants to kill them for tomorrow's lunch, but his wife persuades him to wait till morning. That night Tom and his brothers sleep in a room with the ogre's seven daughters, each of whom has a crown on her head. When the daughters fall asleep Tom takes their crowns and puts them on his brothers' heads and his own head. In the middle of the night the ogre comes into kill them, but when he feels the crowns on their heads he thinks they are his daughters and he ends up killing his daughters. Tom and his brothers escape as soon as the ogre leaves. The next morning the ogre puts on his 7-league boots and sets out after Tom and his brothers. He stops to rest and falls asleep. Tom, who is nearby, creeps up and steals the 7-league boots. Then he takes ten steps to the king's palace. There he is employed to carry messages to the king's army, which is a long way off but which Tom can reach in a short time because of the boots. He makes enough money to support his entire family for the rest of their lives. When the ogre wakes up he does not notice that his boots are missing. He comes to a bog that he could have crossed in one stride with the boots. He steps into it and sinks to the bottom, and that is the end of him.

LITTLE SNOW WHITE

A queen gives birth to a little girl as white as snow, with cheeks as red as blood and hair as black as ebony. She names her Snow White. Soon after, the queen dies and the king marries another wife, who is beautiful, proud, and haughty. She has a magic mirror and every day she asks her mirror, "Mirror, mirror, on the wall, who is the fairest in the land?"—and the mirror tells her she is. But Snow White grows prettier and one day the mirror says Snow White is

the fairest in the land. Outraged, the queen orders a huntsman to take Snow White into the woods and kill her. The huntsman takes pity on the little girl and lets her run away [a modified variety of charity, for he consoles himself with the thought that the wild beasts will kill her]. He kills a pig and shows the queen its heart as Snow White's. Snow White runs till she comes to a cottage that belongs to seven dwarfs. They agree to let her live with them and take care of the cottage. But the queen learns of this from her magic mirror and sets out to kill Snow White. Disguised as a peddler, she goes to the cottage while the dwarfs are away and shows Snow White a bodice, lacing the stays so tight that Snow White falls, breathless. Believing her dead, the queen goes home; but when the dwarfs return they unlace Snow White, who recovers. Again the queen, in disguise, calls on Snow White. This time she shows a poison comb, and when Snow White puts it in her hair she falls as though dead. But when the dwarfs return they take the comb out of her hair and she recovers. The next time the queen comes with a poisoned apple. Snow White takes one bite and falls dead. The dwarfs cannot revive her this time. They put her in a glass casket where they can see her all the time. The queen is delighted, for now the mirror tells her she is the fairest in the land. After many years, a handsome prince happens by and sees Snow White lying in the casket. Overcome by her beauty, he begs the dwarfs to let him take her. Seeing how much the prince loves her, they agree. When the prince moves Snow White, the piece of apple falls out of her throat and she comes to life. The prince takes her to his kingdom, where they are married. When the queen learns that Snow White is alive, she is so enraged that she rushes out of the castle and is never heard from again.

Growth of the Soil

Novel by Knut Hamsun, 1859–1952. Published 1917. Published 1921 by Alfred A. Knopf, New York.

KNUT HAMSUN WAS AWARDED the Nobel Prize in literature immediately after the publication of his *Growth of the Soil;* and, as has been noted before, the Nobel Prize is most likely to be awarded to an author immediately after the publication of a successful work. In this novel Hamsun took as his theme the time-honored one of a man's love of land and his reward from it. Pearl Buck's *The Good Earth* is similar in theme. Hamsun lost the respect he had enjoyed in Norway (and some other countries) when he proved to be a collaborationist with the Germans in their invasion of Norway in 1940.

Book I. Chaps. 1–2. ISAK, a sturdy rock of a Norwegian, with an iron beard, walks north. He is carrying a sack containing some food, and a few tools. At night he lies down on the heather, puts his head on his arm, and sleeps. Finally he halts at a range of pasture and woodland with a rich green hillside and a stream. He sets to work to build a hut of turf and stones. He strips birch trees of bark and carries a great load of the bark all the miles back to the village, where he exchanges it for food, more tools, and a cooking-pot. Isak later acquires three goats. He is seeking also a woman to help him, but he and his goats live through the winter alone.

In the late spring of that year a sturdy, brown-eyed, full-built, coarse young woman with large, strong hands appears at the hut, says vaguely she is on her way to see her kin, and remains with Isak. Her name is INGER. Isak is very happy with her. True, she speaks peculiarly because of a harelip; but Isak is no beauty himself. He now works twice as hard and begins to build a larger house. Inger makes a trip into the village and is gone so long that Isak believes she has deserted him, but she returns, leading a cow. Isak is delighted but fears she has stolen the cow.

Chaps. 3–4. Isak continues to work very hard, and his good fortune increases. The cow has a calf, and Isak buys a bull. On returning from a trip to the village he finds he has a son. The boy is named ELESEUS. A kinswoman of Inger, OLINE, comes to visit, and Isak is relieved to learn that the cow really is Inger's. Isak and Inger work as hard as ever and their goods increase; they survive a drought and a deluge. Inger has another son, named SIVERT for a wealthy uncle. One day a wandering Lapp, OS ANDERS, stops by to beg food. From his pack he takes a dead hare and this terribly frightens the pregnant Inger.

Chaps. 5–7. The local official or *Lensmand,* named GEISSLER, comes to survey Isak's farm, for it is on government land. Isak is told that for a small fee he can buy it. Geissler names the farm Sellanraa. He sees Eleseus playing with some heavy stones and takes a few along, thinking they may be ore samples. Inger gives birth to a girl with a harelip, and she strangles the infant and buries it. Oline, visiting again, snoops about and finds the grave. Inger accuses Oline of having sent the hare with Os Anders, to mark the unborn child, and she beats Oline with a heavy wooden spoon. Oline, obviously guilty, accuses Inger of murder and says she will inform the authorities. She does, and Inger is tried for her crime. The magistrate is sympathetic and Inger's sentence is only 8 years. Oline comes to Sellanraa to take care of the children.

Chaps. 8–9. Isak is very lonely without Inger and has endless troubles with nasty, clever, thieving Oline; but Oline is good to the children. Another family, that of BREDE OLSEN, takes up a homestead in the wilderness, between Sellanraa and the village. A telegraph line is strung over the land. Isak refuses the job of caretaker and it goes to Brede, who is an indifferent farmer.

Chaps. 10–11. Geissler, who has quit his post as Lensmand, obtains a pardon for Inger. Inger was pregnant when she left for prison and has given birth to another daughter, LEOPOLDINE, who is perfectly formed. Geissler buys from Isak the copper ore on his land for 200 daler and a share in the earnings. Isak goes to the boat to meet Inger and Leopoldine. Inger has had her harelip surgically repaired. She has learned city ways and is less simple and warm. She brings with her a sewing machine.

Chaps. 12–14. Isak works as hard as ever. He sets up a sawmill and puts up more buildings. Inger spends most of her time at her sewing machine, astounding the girls from the village with her skill and doing much work for them free. She asks Isak for a servant girl and a gold wedding ring and

she takes care not to have any more children.

Chaps. 15–16. Geissler, grayer, somewhat shabby, comes to visit. He shows Isak how to build irrigation sluices to save his parched crops. Then he wanders off on his way to Sweden. More settlers take up land between Sellanraa and the village. One, AXEL STROM, names his place Maaneland because it looks beautiful in the moonlight. Brede Olsen's oldest daughter, BARBRO, goes to Maaneland to do the woman's work. Inger becomes pregnant again and Isak gets the village smith's girl, JANSINA, as a servant for her. Inger gives birth to a girl and Isak names her REBECCA. The second son, Sivert, is now a young man and like his father is a hard worker and lover of the soil.

Chaps. 17–18. Eleseus comes home from school, quite dandified but a good sort. Oline reports that Uncle Sivert is on his deathbed and young Sivert goes to him and finds him feeble but up and about. Geissler brings a party of wealthy men, his wife's relatives, who buy Isak's mining property for 1,000 daler. Geissler, surveying Sellanraa, calls Isak a margrave, a landed squire. Uncle Sivert dies and it is found that he was not rich but actually penniless. Eleseus becomes enamored of Barbro, but she turns him down, preferring Axel. He pines for a while.

Chap. 19. Brede Olsen has let his farm, Breidablik, go to pot and now is forced to sell it. Isak wants to buy it for Eleseus but Inger wants Eleseus to have a professional career in the city.

Book II. Chap. 1. At the auction, Axel Strom buys Breidablik for his brother. Brede is about to lose his job as inspector of the telegraph lines because of neglect. Eleseus goes back to town to seek employment.

Chap. 2. One day Axel finds Barbro lying near a stream, dazed. She has just given birth to his child, which she has buried nearby. She recovers, but she quarrels constantly with Axel. She empty-headedly boasts that this was her second child; the first she threw into the harbor at Bergen. She returns Axel's engagement ring.

Chap. 3. Early in the winter, Barbro leaves Axel. One day when Axel is felling a tree it falls on him, pinning him to the ground. Brede Olsen comes along but he is angry because Axel is to have his telegraph inspection job and he simply walks away. It begins to snow. In one last effort, Axel shouts for help. Oline, wandering past, comes to his aid. Now aged and poverty-stricken, Oline installs herself in Axel's house as his servant. A new settler, ARONSEN, builds a general store, called Storborg.

Chaps. 4–7. The copper mine goes into production and Aronsen flourishes on the wages of the free-spending miners. Then, suddenly, the mine is shut down, the ore vein having played out. Geissler owns the tract of land to the south of the mine and the mine officials offer to buy it, but Geissler asks a price so high that the deal falls through. Barbro is arrested and tried in Bergen for the murder of her infant. At the trial, Axel is absolved of complicity; Barbro takes all the blame. She is given a suspended sentence and is remanded to the care of the wife of the Lensmand, HEYERDAHL.

Chaps. 8–9. Isak buys Aronsen's store, Storborg, for Eleseus. Geissler finally sells his mining land, but the mining engineers say they must work the lode from the far end, many miles away. Eleseus runs his store inefficiently and is in town on buying trips most of the time. ANDRESEN, who was Aronsen's chief clerk, keeps the store going.

Chaps. 10–12. Barbro comes back to Axel. The Lensmand's wife caught her sneaking out at two in the morning and dismissed her. Barbro seems chastened and wiser. She has marriage banns put up for herself and Axel. Oline puts off going away, on one excuse or another, until one night she dies quietly in her sleep. Eleseus admits failure at the store and leaves for America. He is never heard of again. The store goes to Andresen, who is to marry Leopoldine. Middle-aged, still sturdy, Isak and Inger are wealthy, respected, reasonably contented, for theirs is the strength of the soil.

Olive comes to the aid of Axel, pinned under a tree

Gulliver's Travels

Satire by Jonathan Swift, 1667–1745.
Published 1727. (ML, 100 & T32;
Viking, P37; RE, 10; PB, PL51)

JONATHAN SWIFT would probably
be quite amazed to learn that today
Gulliver's Travels is treated almost exclusively as a book for children. Swift
wrote the book as a satire on social and
political life of his times. The book
appeals to children, when it is somewhat bowdlerized, because it places its
hero Lemuel Gulliver in fantastic or
fairy-tale situations. *Gulliver's Travels*
consists of four parts, in which Gulliver travels to imaginary lands where
reside respectively tiny creatures,
giants, cloud-dwelling optimists, and
noble horses. In each case Gulliver can
contrast their society with the Europe
of his day. The noblest society was that
of the horses. They made Gulliver
ashamed to be a man. Some of Swift's
comparisons were echoed a century
and a half later by Mark Twain.

Part 1 (A Voyage to Lilliput). Chap. 1.
I, LEMUEL GULLIVER, was born in Notting-
hamshire, England, and after three years at
Cambridge and apprenticeship to a prominent London surgeon I signed aboard a
ship to serve as its doctor. I made several
trips to far-off corners of the world, then
settled down to marry MARY BURTON. But
I was not successful as a doctor and on May
4, 1699, I again signed aboard a ship, the
Antelope, bound for the East Indies. In
November a storm sank the ship. I escaped
in a lifeboat but high waves forced me to
abandon it and my friends. I swam to a previously undiscovered island called Lilliput,
where I collapsed with fatigue on the beach.
When I awoke, I found my whole body
fastened to the ground with threads. Hundreds of tiny creatures, not six inches high,
surrounded me on all sides. When I tried
to rise, they shot arrows at me that caused
my face and hands to smart. Afraid that
they might blind me, I decided to submit
to their will. A royal entourage approached
and the Lilliputians erected a stage so that
the EMPEROR could behold my huge frame.
The emperor had me fed some of their cattle, which were about the size of a lark's
wing. I devoured enormous quantities.
Then I was taken to the capital city of
Mildendo and housed outside the city gates
in a temple whose front portal was 4 feet
high. I was chained to the door and guarded
by hundreds of soldiers.

Chaps. 2–3. The emperor and his court
climbed a tower of the temple to observe
The Man Mountain, as they called me. The
emperor was a few inches taller than his
subjects. He wore European-Asiatic clothes.
We communicated by signs. The emperor

ordered two ministers to search me and remove harmful objects. They took my watch,
razor, and pistols, but promised to return
them later. I had won over the emperor and
he refused to have me shot with poisoned
arrows, as some of his counselors advised. I
became more beloved when I donated my
handkerchief to serve as a field for horseback skirmishes and stood with my legs
apart so the soldiers could parade through
them. After frequent petitions I was at last
loosened from my chains, but I was not
permitted to leave the kingdom. I was
promised enough food and drink every day
to satisfy 1,728 Lilliputians. Without any
provocation, I found a mortal enemy in the
Lilliputian admiral, SKYRESH BOLGOLAM.

Chaps. 4–5. I was finally allowed to see
the capital, with a special escort so that I
would not crush anyone. Shortly afterward
I became involved in politics. The emperor's
loyal subjects belonged to the Low-Heeled
faction and were opposed by courtiers who
wore high heels. Foreign affairs were troubling the emperor. Lilliput was endangered
by its traditional enemies from the nearby
island of Blefuscu. The two islands had
fought for centuries over the proper way to
break an egg. Now the Blefuscudians were
invading Lilliput. I swam to Blefuscu, terrified the enemy into leaving their ships, and
drew the fleet with me back to Lilliput. The
emperor conferred numerous honors upon
me. I refused to crush the Blefuscudians
completely, but they sued for peace and
thanked me for my generosity. I again
proved serviceable by saving the palace
from destruction by fire. I had drunk plenty
of wine and I urinated on the burning
buildings.

Chaps. 6–8. I was suspected of carrying
on a love affair with the Treasurer's wife.
This cost me the emperor's favor, though I
established my honor in the affair. My
enemy, the admiral Skyresh, had succeeded
in poisoning the emperor's mind, and
though the emperor refused to kill me he
agreed to blind me. I fled to Blefuscu, where
I was welcomed with great warmth; but
the Emperor of Blefuscu received word
from Lilliput that I must be blinded. Fortunately I found a small boat and escaped. I
was taken aboard an English ship and returned home in 1702.

Part II (A Voyage to Brobdingnag).
Chaps. 1–4. On my next voyage to the East,
in 1703, I left the main ship to gather
water from the unexplored land of Brobdingnag. I wandered away from my fellow
sailors and was picked up by a huge creature, taller than a church steeple. He carried me to his farmhouse, where his
enormous wife and children toyed with me.
I realized that they did not want to harm
me. I was put to bed in a handkerchief.
Two rats attacked me and I killed them
with my needlelike sword. I was protected
by the farmer's daughter, GLUMDALCLITCH
(or "little nurse"). She taught me her
language but could not persuade her father
to keep me at home. He put me in a cage
and exhibited me to other Brobdingnagians.

I was bought by the KING and QUEEN, who
allowed Glumdalclitch to take care of me
in a doll house in the Palace. Once I was attacked by bees, but I killed three of the
huge creatures and kept them as proof of
my experience. The queen's dwarf, who
measured about 30 feet high, took a dislike
to me. I traveled with Glumdalclitch
throughout the kingdom and saw the
Brobdingnag temple, which was 3,000 feet
high.

Chaps. 5–7. I continued to have adventures, such as getting caught in a hailstorm
in which the pellets were the size of tennis
balls. The king liked to talk with me about
the states of Europe and I delivered five
lectures. I was unable to persuade him that
Europeans are not "the most pernicious
race of little odious vermin that Nature
ever suffered to crawl upon the surface of
the earth." I tried to persuade the king to
manufacture cannon and gunpowder, but
he was horrified at the notion. I concluded
that the Brobdingnagians were not interested in progress.

Chap. 8. The king, after two years, took
me on a journey to the southern part of his
kingdom, near the sea. I traveled in a
special wooden crate, cradled in Glumdalclitch's lap. One afternoon the girl handed
me over to a page so that I could walk on
the beach. After enjoying a brisk walk, I
asked the page to put me back into my crate.
He did so, then went off to find some birds'
eggs. The tide swept my crate out to sea,
where I was rescued by an English merchant ship. I arrived home in 1706. I found
that my wife and children looked under-
nourished in comparison with the giants.

**Part III (A Voyage to Laputa, Balnibarbi,
Luggnagg, Glubbdubdrib, and Japan).**
Chaps. 1–4. In 1707 the ship on which I
was making my third great voyage was
seized by pirates and I was cast adrift in a
lifeboat. I landed on an island and saw
some men fishing on the shore. I was surprised to see the mountainous part of the
island rise up into the air above my head.
When I called to the people, they lifted me
up by pulleys into the strange land of
Laputa. The sky-dwellers, or Laputans,
were the royal and intellectual classes of the
island of Balnibarbi but had cut themselves
off from the common people below and the
Balnibarbarians had finally claimed their
independence. The Laputans spent so much
time in contemplation that their eyes turned
either inward or toward the heavens. Their
heads inclined either left or right. Nobody
except the women paid any attention to
me. The king did nothing but study geom-
etry and music. They had a very orderly
realm, but the houses were too symmetrical
and the food too unappealing. The poor
women wanted very much to return to the
earth. At my request, I was lowered to the
earthly land of Balnibarbi. There the neglect
of the inhabitants appalled me. The only
order in this country was maintained at
the Academy in the capital city of Lagado.

Gulliver is attacked by huge bees and kills three of them

The academicians had been trained above in Laputa.

Chaps. 5–6. I spent some time in the Academy debating with numerous professors. I was astounded by the things that these learned doctors were trying to do, such as to abolish all words. Their methods of teaching were also strange. They forced students to swallow wafers inscribed with ink so that the writing could penetrate their stomachs and brains. I listened attentively to their discussions of ways for uncovering government conspiracies.

Chaps. 7–11. I made a side journey to Glubbdubdrib, or the Land of Sorcerers. The governor of that island received me with great cordiality and summoned ghosts out of the past to entertain me. I saw many famous people, such as Julius Caesar, Pompey, and Alexander the Great. The Greek philosopher Aristotle told me that he was wrong in many of his deductions about natural philosophy and that thinkers such as Newton in our own time were making the same mistakes because logic can never yield absolute truth. I then proceeded to the island of Luggnagg. There I was received by the king with great hospitality, but I had to perform the usual ceremony of licking the dust beneath his throne. The most interesting people on this island were the Struldbrugs or Immortals, who are born with a red spot on the forehead and who live forever. Their lives were extremely miserable, for after the age of 30 they became morose. Although they were immortal, Struldbrugs were subject to old age and sickness. Therefore after the age of 90 they were exiled from the rest of society. The Luggnaggians offered to give me some Struldbrugs to take back to England but I refused. They might have taught Englishmen to welcome death, but they might also have monopolized our nation's highest positions. Next I visited Japan, where I was welcomed by the emperor, but I stayed for only a short time, then boarded a Dutch vessel for Amsterdam and returned to England in 1710.

Part IV (A Voyage to the Country of the Houyhnhnms). **Chaps. 1–4.** On my last great adventure I was made prisoner by mutinous sailors who put me out to sea in a boat. I arrived at an island where I saw some strange creatures known as Yahoos. These creatures resembled human beings except that they had pointed claws, hairy bodies, and mean faces. They tried to attack me, but I drove them away. Then I was found by a beautiful horse, who communicated with me by striking his hoof on the ground. I learned that the horses, called Houyhnhnms (pronounced *whinnums*), were masters of the filthy Yahoos. The horse invited me to his house, which resembled a simple stable, and there I dined on oats and milk. My host, whom I called MASTER, and his family taught me the horse language, which resembles Dutch. The Master was shocked to learn that in England the Yahoos control the horses, but on learning this he was not at all surprised that Englishmen are famous for their wars and corruption.

Chaps. 5–8. Although I tried very hard to explain how wars arose, my Master could see no logical reason for their taking place. He also asked why education did not bring about perfect justice such as existed in his own land. He did grant that England must produce some noble creatures, because I showed such wit and understanding. In the end, my Master showed his typical horse-sense by suggesting that a lack of reason was responsible for all English ills. Without reason there can be no virtue. He noted that most Yahoos in his land were governed by emotions and fancies that led to lewdness and laziness.

Chaps. 9–12. I heard a great debate among the horses as to whether they should exterminate the Yahoos entirely. Although the issue was decided negatively, I began to sympathize with the Houyhnhnms. I disliked the thought of going back to England, where people were so much like the Yahoos. My happiness was broken one day when the Houyhnhnms decided at their great debate that I was too Yahoolike to continue living there. My Master and his family provided me with a canoe and I left them with many tears and fond farewells. After a sea voyage and some further adventures, I arrived back in England in 1715. From that day to this, I have been unable to share the company of my family. I spend all of my time in the stable conversing with my horses.

Hamlet

Play by William Shakespeare, 1564–1616.
Produced about 1602.

FOR MORE THAN 300 years *Hamlet* has been accorded every evidence that it is the greatest work of both literature and drama in the English language. It is the most read, the best known, the most quoted, and the most often performed; its title rôle is the one every actor most wishes to play. Amid such general acclaim a self-respecting critic can hardly call *Hamlet* Shakespeare's greatest work for fear he be considered a sheep following the lead of others. Nearly anyone else is willing to admit it. ❡ There was probably a Danish or Juttish king named Hamlet (earlier spelled Amleth); legend sets his time around the year 700. Shakespeare does not follow the traditional stories very closely, and he gives most of his characters Latin names. The prince Amleth (junior) was a youth at school in the west (France or Belgium) when his father was killed by his uncle. He returned, feigned madness, and worked out an elaborate plan for revenge, which succeeded; but young Amleth himself did not die when he killed his uncle. He lived and became king of the land. The original versions imply an incestuous feeling between Hamlet and his mother, and most scholars have interpreted parts of Shakespeare's play to be an acceptance of this part of the story.

Act I. 1. On the ramparts of Elsinore Castle in Denmark HORATIO, friend of Prince HAMLET, joins MARCELLUS, an officer of the guard, to see a GHOST that appears nightly. The ghost resembles young Hamlet's father, King Hamlet, recently dead. **2.** Hamlet, recalled from school, pays his respects to the new king, his father's brother CLAUDIUS, who immediately married Hamlet's mother, Queen GERTRUDE. Claudius sends envoys to ask the king of Norway to stop the invasion of Denmark by his nephew Prince FORTINBRAS. LAERTES, son of the king's chief minister, POLONIUS, asks and is given leave to return to France. Left alone, Hamlet delivers his *first soliloquy*—"O! that this too too solid flesh would melt"—in which he regrets that suicide is forbidden by God and decries his mother's remarriage—"Frailty, thy name is woman!" Horatio and Marcellus tell Hamlet of the ghost. **3.** Laertes, leaving for France, warns his sister OPHELIA not to count on Hamlet's marrying her, because a prince does not have free choice. Polonius gives Laertes a series of famous "precepts," ending with "This above all: to thine own self be true." **4–5.** Hamlet, on the ramparts, meets his father's ghost and is told that Claudius murdered his father by dropping poison in his ear while he slept in the garden and that Gertrude was a party to the plot.

Act II. 1. Polonius sends his servant REYNALDO to France to observe the behavior of Laertes. Ophelia tells Polonius of Hamlet's strange behavior lately and Polonius concludes that Hamlet is mad with love of Ophelia. **2.** Claudius asks ROSENCRANTZ and GUILDENSTERN, courtiers and former companions of Hamlet, to attend Hamlet and keep him from doing mischief. The envoys return with a promise from Norway that Fortinbras will not attack. Polonius tells Claudius his theory of the reason for Hamlet's madness. Then Polonius talks to Hamlet, whose speech is cryptic and seems mad. It is the same when Hamlet talks to Rosencrantz and Guildenstern. Polonius brings in a company of strolling actors, who give a sample performance for Hamlet. Hamlet asks them to play, for the king and court, the *Murder of Gonzago,* with certain changes he will make. When they leave, Hamlet delivers his *second soliloquy,* beginning "O! what a rogue and peasant slave am I" and ending "The play's the thing/Wherein I'll catch the conscience of the king."

Act III. 1. The king and queen are worried about Hamlet's mental condition and the king is afflicted by conscience. Hamlet delivers his *third soliloquy,* "To be, or not to be; that is the question." He concludes that suicide would be a blessing if one could be sure of nothingness, but the fear of the unknown hereafter deters would-be suicides. Ophelia interrupts him and he rejects her, telling her to go to a nunnery. The king and Polonius, who were hidden, hear and are sure Hamlet is mad. **2.** The actors put on the play and, coached by Hamlet, duplicate the murder of Hamlet's father as Hamlet heard it from the ghost. The king is stricken by conscience, stops the performance, and leaves. Hamlet is now sure the ghost's story was true. Rosencrantz and Guildenstern, then Polonius, approach Hamlet but he talks

Hamlet and the Ghost

mad to them. He ends the scene with his *fourth soliloquy*: "'Tis now the very witching time of night/When churchyards yawn, and hell itself breathes out." **3.** The king is overcome and kneels alone to confess his guilt and pray. Hamlet sees him and delivers his *fifth soliloquy,* "Now might I do it pat, now he is praying"—but he will not kill Claudius because then Claudius, killed while praying, would go to heaven. **4.** Hamlet is summoned to his mother's room. Polonius is hiding behind the curtain. Hamlet accuses his mother of murder; then, detecting someone behind the curtain, stabs and kills Polonius, thinking it is Claudius. The ghost appears to Hamlet, but to Gertrude he is invisible.

Act IV. 1–3. Hamlet is being sent to England, attended by Rosencrantz and Guildenstern, ostensibly with messages to the English king. **4.** On their way, Hamlet, Rosencrantz and Guildenstern encounter Fortinbras at the head of an army. Left alone, Hamlet delivers his *sixth soliloquy,* beginning "How all occasions do inform against me" and ending "From this time forth,/My thoughts be bloody, or be nothing worth." **5.** At Elsinore, Ophelia goes mad from grief over Hamlet's madness and renunciation of her. Laertes returns in anger to kill Claudius, to avenge his father's death, but Claudius convinces him that it was Hamlet's doing. **6.** Horatio receives a letter from Hamlet that he is in Denmark. Horatio speeds to join him. **7.** Claudius receives a message from Hamlet, saying that he is returning to court, and Claudius promises to help Laertes revenge himself on Hamlet. Gertrude tells Laertes that Ophelia has drowned herself.

Act V. 1. Hamlet and Horatio walk through a graveyard. Hamlet muses upon the skull of YORICK, the king's jester, whom he knew and loved as a boy, and on the common fate of all things mortal. The funeral procession of Ophelia enters and Hamlet declares that his grief at her death is greater than anyone else's could be. He

challenges Laertes but they are not permitted to fight. **2.** Hamlet, back in the castle, tells Horatio how the treacherous king sent him to England bearing letters instructing the English king to put him to death; but Hamlet opened and changed the letters and sent Rosencrantz and Guildenstern on to their deaths. Hamlet is invited to give a fencing exhibition with Laertes. Claudius has poisoned Laertes' rapier, so when Hamlet is hit he is doomed, but in a scuffle the men change rapiers and Laertes is hit and poisoned. Claudius offers Hamlet a poisoned cup to drink, and Hamlet refuses it but Gertrude takes it and drinks before Claudius can stop her. Hamlet, aware what is going on, uses his last strength to stab and kill Claudius. All four die. As Hamlet is dying, Horatio proposes to kill himself too, but Hamlet urges him to stay alive so that the world may know the true story. Fortinbras enters with his army and assumes control of Denmark.

Hangman's House

Novel by Brian Donn Byrne, 1889–1928.

Published & © 1926 by Appleton-Century-Crofts, New York.

THIS EXCELLENT NOVEL by an excellent novelist is a story of adventure and intrigue in Ireland during the period (after World War I) when the Irish were struggling with England for independence. There is some contemporary Irish politics in it but not so much that the reader need understand it to enjoy the story. During the period covered by the novel, numerous Irish revolutionaries were gathered in New York as refugees and Donn Byrne, American-born, was personally familiar with them and their plotting.

Chap. 1. DERMOT McDERMOT of Dermotstown, not yet 25, stops to talk to the ancient lodgekeeper of his place in the Wicklow Hills in County Dublin and hears that his cousin JOHN D'ARCY is back from abroad and staying at "Jimmy the Hangman's," his name for Lord GLENMALURE, Lord Chief Justice of Ireland. The mission of the "twister," as D'Arcy is known unfavorably by the local folk, is to marry the lord's daughter, CONNAUGHT. Dermot visits with his mother, a Quaker lady, who came from Philadelphia to Ireland with her husband, now dead, and also lost her elder son, DESMOND, in the Boer War. Dermot tells his mother that he is going to ask Lord Glenmalure for his daughter's hand in marriage. She has misgivings.

Chap. 2. Connaught is a pretty girl who was educated in a convent and at 18 in-

Dermot visits the dying Lord Glenmalure and learns he was a rebel

herited a large fortune from her grandfather. She is interested in horseracing, in riding, and in the new sport of greyhound racing. Her father discovers that he is incurably ill and wishes Connaught to marry. The only young man she cares for is Dermot. Glenmalure says that Dermot's being the best gentleman rider in the county is not enough reason. He writes to ask John D'Arcy, son of an old schoolmate of his, to come to Glenmalure. D'Arcy, a member of the Irish rebel party, is a suave, burly man with a great reddish-brown beard (which Glenmalure forces him to shave off). Connaught becomes enamored of D'Arcy. Glenmalure interrogates D'Arcy about his connection with the rebels who are exiled in Paris, and specifically with PATRICK HOGAN and his sister MAEVE, with whom D'Arcy's name has been linked, but receives evasive answers.

Chap. 3. Dermot asks for Connaught's hand. Her father reminds him that Connaught wants a big career for her husband—adulation, position, luxury, and glamour. Dermot says he would not sell Dermotstown and get into politics, and Glenmalure tells him Connaught will marry D'Arcy.

Chap. 4. In New York a group of Irish rebels select Patrick Hogan to go back to lead the cause. He is the son of old DINNY HOGAN, the irreconcilable, known to the rebels as The Citizen.

Chap. 5. Connaught is badly neglected as Lord Glenmalure plans a political career for John D'Arcy. Politicians gather at the hall. Occasionally she plays tennis with her fiancé. She finds out that the servants do not think highly of D'Arcy. She also hears that Dermot is in love with her, though he has stayed away out of propriety. Her father tells her he has not long to live and she must marry D'Arcy within a week.

Chap. 6. Connaught seeks out Dermot and tells him she does not love D'Arcy. Dermot bravely answers that John is a fine man and everything will be all right. They hear a boy singing the old rebel song, "Shan Van Voght" (The Poor Old Woman, meaning Ireland). The boy says that he learned the song from a man in the mountains, a man called the Citizen. When John D'Arcy hears of the incident he turns pale and asks for a description of the Citizen. His knees sag and he staggers off for a drink.

Chap. 7. Dermot suffers when Connaught marries John but decides that she has made a wise choice. The couple leave on their honeymoon. Dermot visits Lord Glenmalure, who is dying, and learns from him that he was a rebel in his youth. The old man dies and Dermot sends a telegram to Waterford to intercept Connaught and John.

Chap. 8. Dermot finds Connaught a hard, white-faced woman since her marriage. Riding after the hounds, they see a stranger on a wild horse that tries to throw him until he croons to it a refrain from "Shan Van Voght." D'Arcy is turned down by the politicians, now that Glenmalure has died. The stranger on the wild horse asks D'Arcy if he was in Paris in '95 and D'Arcy replies that he was never in Paris in his life. Connaught asks why he lied and John answers that he doesn't want to be bothered with foreigners. Connaught finds out that John has informed on the stranger, who is being hunted by the constabulary.

Chap. 9. D'Arcy's estate becomes a meeting place for shady characters, gamblers, heavy drinkers, and crooked horse trainers and bookies. Connaught turns over her horses to a man named ROBINSON to train. After a greyhound race, Dermot meets a monk on the road, singing "Shan Van Voght." Dermot recognizes him as the man on the wild horse at the Tara Hunt but promises not to give him away.

Chaps. 10–11. The winter passes. Dermot learns that there is suspicion about a forthcoming horse race, the Dundrum Handicap, because John D'Arcy has laid heavy bets against Connaught's entry, the Bard. Connaught tells Dermot she is having trouble finding a jockey. On the day of the race

the horse is still riderless and Dermot volunteers to ride it but John forbids Connaught to accept. There is a near scene but Dermot rides anyway and wins the race. He and Connaught find John sobbing and learn that Dermot, by winning, has cost John £10,000, which he needed desperately. Connaught tells him she has money. Dermot turns away in disgust. A blind man with a quaint old overcoat compliments Dermot on his race. Dermot recognizes the Citizen.

Chaps. 12–14. John kills the horse, Bard. Dermot threatens to kill John but his Quaker mother restrains him and Connaught tells him her husband is only a poor crazy man. She leaves for England and John is reduced to entertaining bookmaker's touts, barmaids, and potboys. He tells Dermot he has only kissed Connaught once, on their wedding day, and he wants money to go to Florida or California. Dermot asks why he is afraid of the Citizen, and D'Arcy, in his cups, tells of having a long affair with Hogan's sister Maeve, whom he finally left, after they had had a child, to come to Ireland and marry Connaught. Dermot offers to lend him money if he will make a happy home for Connaught, and offers to intercede with the Citizen, but to his horror he learns that John is married to Maeve. He attacks him but is restrained. He tells D'Arcy to get out.

Chaps. 15–19. Connaught returns from England and Dermot tells her that John is gone for good. Dermot finds the Citizen and pleads with him for Connaught's sake to be quiet about D'Arcy. The Citizen agrees but says D'Arcy is marked for death. Connaught tells Dermot she was a wife in name only and she confesses her love for Dermot. Dermot seeks out the Citizen again, for D'Arcy's marriage to Maeve obviously made his marriage to Connaught illegal, but the Citizen says Maeve died before D'Arcy married Connaught. John returns to Glenmalure, having heard of Maeve's death. He accuses Dermot and Connaught of adultery but is convinced that everything has been circumspect. Connaught returns to England.

Chaps. 20–22. Dermot is left alone in Dermotstown. John is at Glenmalure, deserted by his servants. He has taken in tinkers, the Irish gypsies, to tend his house. Dermot hears from Connaught that she is coming to Ireland for a few days to attend the races. D'Arcy's tinkers tell him that a man is spying on the house and he suspects it is the Citizen. He finds the Citizen on the grounds and they enter the house together. D'Arcy has sprinkled the inside with kerosene. He shoots the Citizen and sets the house afire, but Dermot drags the Citizen out of the burning building. John, caught inside, jumps to his death. Dermot tends the Citizen's wound and helps him escape, then is united with his beloved Connaught.

325

Hedda Gabler

Play by Henrik Ibsen, 1828–1906.
Published 1890.

HEDDA GABLER does not have as general a social message as some of Ibsen's plays, though in its structure it is quite typical of them. It is a play about a neurotic woman who seeks compensation in running or influencing the lives of others, for the satisfaction or sense of power it gives her, and eventually plays out her neuroticism to its final stage by killing herself. For performance *Hedda Gabler* has been one of the two or three most popular Ibsen plays in the United States and it is regularly revived.

Act I. GEORGE TESMAN and his bride, the former HEDDA GABLER, are returning from their honeymoon. BERTE, the maid, is afraid she will not be able to please the grand new Mrs. Tesman, a general's daughter. Tesman tells his aunt, Miss JULIANA TESMAN, of the notes he made during the trip, which should aid him in getting a professorship at the university. Miss Tesman warns Tesman that Hedda may be too extravagant—she insisted on buying this elegant house in the suburbs of Oslo, and Miss Tesman mortgaged her annuity to give security for the fine furniture and carpets. Tesman's rival for the seat at the university is EJLERT LOVBORG. Lovborg has written a book, which may help him. Tesman is writing a book, but it will not be ready in time. Hedda comes in, the aunt leaves, and Tesman's friend Mrs. THEA ELVSTED calls. She says Lovborg, who was away, has returned to Oslo; and at Hedda's suggestion Tesman goes to write him a note and invite him to visit them. Mrs. Elvsted tells Hedda she has left her husband and wants only to be with Lovborg, but that there is another woman in Lovborg's life—a woman who actually threatened to shoot him when he left her. Mrs. Elvsted thinks it is a cabaret singer in town, and Hedda quickly agrees with her. As Mrs. Elvsted leaves, Judge BRACK comes to call. Tesman tells Brack that he has invited Lovborg to dinner, but Brack says he has Lovborg's promise to attend a stag party that night. Brack assures Tesman he will get the professorship. When Brack leaves, Hedda expresses her boredom at the thought of having a limited social life. She takes a pair of pistols that belonged to her father, General Gabler, and frightens Tesman by saying they are the only things she can amuse herself with.

Act II. Judge Brack visits Hedda and finds her toying with the pistols. While he is standing in the garden she makes a teasing shot that comes closer than he likes.

Hedda tells Brack she is bored with her husband and never loved him. Brack suggests an affair with her. She does not definitely refuse. Tesman returns. He is much impressed with Lovborg's new book but feels sure Lovborg will not stand in his way for the professorship. Lovborg calls. He tells Tesman he has written another, better book. Brack asks Lovborg to come to his party and read excerpts from the new book; but Hedda insists that Lovborg stay and have dinner with her and Mrs. Elvsted and he accepts. When Hedda and Lovborg are left alone, their conversation makes clear their former intimacy. Hedda was the woman who threatened to shoot him. Lovborg wonders why she did not shoot him when they broke up, and Hedda says it was because she dislikes scandal. Mrs. Elvsted arrives and there is a scene between the three with Hedda taunting the other two. Lovborg, torn between his liking for Mrs. Elvsted and his passion for Hedda, starts to drink. Hedda now prefers to have him go to Brack's party, and Lovborg leaves with Brack and Tesman. To Mrs. Elvsted, Hedda confesses she enjoys playing with the lives of others. She forces Mrs. Elvsted to join her at dinner, though Mrs. Elvsted is now frightened of her.

Act III. It is almost daylight. The women have waited up for the men. Hedda, who has been asleep on the sofa, wakes and sends Mrs. Elvsted to bed in the next room. Tesman returns. He says that Lovborg's new work is great and that Lovborg credits it to a woman's inspiration—probably Mrs. Elvsted. But Lovborg was drunk and on the way home he lost his manuscript. Tesman found it and he shows it to Hedda. There is

a message from Miss Tesman: Her sister is dying. Tesman goes to her at once. Hedda hides the manuscript. Brack comes to tell her that the drunken Lovborg went to the home of the cabaret singer, accused her of stealing his manuscript, and was arrested and jailed for creating a disturbance. Brack warns Hedda to have nothing to do with Lovborg and leaves. Lovborg enters in a disheveled state and asks for Mrs. Elvsted, who hears him and comes into the room. He tells her she is the woman who inspired him, but he has destroyed his work and his life and they must part. Distraught, Mrs. Elvsted goes out. Hedda expresses her amazement that this woman could have influenced Lovborg's life and work. He says he must end it all and Hedda gives him one of her pistols. When he has gone, she burns the manuscript.

Act IV. That evening, Tesman demands the manuscript. Hedda tells him she has burned it for his sake. He is shocked but overjoyed at what he considers an act of love for him. Mrs. Elvsted brings rumors that Lovborg has met with an accident, but Brack arrives to say that Lovborg is dying in a hospital after shooting himself. Mrs. Elvsted says she has the notes from which Lovborg's book was written and she and Tesman plan to recreate their friend's masterpiece. Brack tells Hedda that Lovborg is already dead and Hedda will be involved in the scandal if the pistol is traced to her, but that he is the only one who knows about it and will keep quiet about it. Hedda realizes she is in Brack's power. She remarks how well Tesman and Mrs. Elvsted get on together and she goes out. A shot is heard and Hedda is found dead.

Henry IV, V, VI

Six plays by William Shakespeare, 1564–1616.
Produced about 1596–1597.

SHAKESPEARE TOLD the story of the end of the Hundred Years War and of the Wars of the Roses—the background, progress, and conclusion in the establishment of the House of Tudor—in a series of eight plays beginning with *Richard II*, going through the six *Henrys*, and ending with *Richard III*. The Henrys comprised two plays for *Henry IV*, one play for *Henry V*, and three plays for *Henry VI*. Scholars have generally agreed that Shakespeare did not write the first part of *Henry VI*; he edited or revised the work of another playwright. Then, finding the subject popular and not completed, he wrote the remaining parts himself. The Henry plays in general are among the best work Shakespeare did and have always been popular. *Henry IV* introduced Shakespeare's most popular comic character, Sir John Falstaff. *Henry V* had an elaborate and distinguished motion-picture production in the 1950s with Sir Laurence Olivier playing the king. In *Henry V* there is a famous scene spoken in French (Act III, Scene 4) in which the Princess Katharine, daughter of the French king, receives a lesson in English from her maid; in this scene there are numerous double meanings and words that could not respectably be spoken in English. There is additional French dialogue in this play, some of it in the scene in which King Henry courts and wins the princess. ❡ A seventh "Henry" play by Shakespeare, *Henry VIII*, is not part of the series and is not accounted very good Shakespeare. It is not outlined below.

Henry IV, Part I

Act I. 1. King HENRY IV, unhappy over the late bloodshed that deposed Richard II, plans to lead an expedition to the Holy Land; but in Wales Lord MORTIMER, one of Henry's generals, is taken prisoner by GLENDOWER, the Welsh Chieftain, and the king defers his expedition. HOTSPUR, son of the Earl of NORTHUMBERLAND, has captured many Scottish prisoners but he refuses to surrender them to the king unless Henry ransoms Mortimer, who is Hotspur's brother-in-law. This the king will not do, because Mortimer has claims to the throne of England. 2. The madcap PRINCE OF WALES (HAL) and Sir JOHN FALSTAFF, with their companion POINS, plot a highway robbery as part of their adventures. 3. Northumberland's brother, the Earl of WORCESTER, is sent away by the king and called disobedient. Worcester joins Hotspur and Northumberland in plotting rebellion, in conjunction with the forces of Glendower and other dissident armies led by the Archbishop of YORK, and by DOUGLAS of Scotland.

Act II. 1. GADSHILL, a merchant at Rochester, is warned by his friend CHAMBERLAIN that there is a plot to rob travelers to Canterbury. 2. On a highway nearby, Prince Hal is planning to doublecross Falstaff in the robbery attempt. Falstaff and his men hold up the travelers, but are themselves overtaken and robbed by the disguised Prince Hal and Poins. 3. At Warworth Castle, Hotspur plans the union of the various forces fighting the king. 4. At the Boar's Head Tavern, Prince Hal and Poins discuss their recent adventure. Falstaff arrives and tells a hair-raising story of having been attacked by eleven men. The prince then reveals the practical joke. Good-naturedly, Falstaff laughs. The hostess, Mistress QUICKLY, interrupts the merrymaking when a nobleman arrives to summon Prince Hal to the king.

Act III. 1. At Bangor, the rebels plan how they will carve up the country into three parts. 2. In London the king berates his son Hal for his wild ways, as contrasted with young Hotspur, the rebel. Hal promises to redeem himself on the battlefield. 3. At the Boar's Head, Prince Hal picks up Falstaff to go to war with him.

Act IV. 1. In the rebel camp near Shrewsbury, Hotspur learns that Northumberland has deserted their cause, pleading illness. Glendower cannot draw any forces for 14 days because of an old prophecy. Nevertheless the rebels determine to meet the king's forces. 2. Falstaff sends his aide BARDOLPH ahead for a bottle of wine. WESTMORELAND, who leads one of the armies, and Prince Hal join him. 3. The rebel leaders argue about the time of the attack. 4. The Archbishop of York, sure that the rebels will be defeated, asks to see the king.

Act V. 1. The king meets with Worcester and VERNON, the rebel generals, and offers them generous terms. 2. Worcester

refuses to deliver the liberal surrender terms to his associates. He suspects the king of a trap. Therefore he and Vernon deliver to Hotspur and Douglas a call to battle. 3–4. The battle rages. Douglas first mistakes the injured BLUNT for the king, then finds the king and they fight. Prince Hal comes to his father's rescue, putting Douglas to flight. Hal then encounters Hotspur and kills him. 5. Worcester and Vernon are captured. The king has them executed at once. But Douglas, also a prisoner, is released. Prince Hal is sent against the Archbishop of York, after which the king and prince together will follow up the campaign against Wales.

Falstaff in a tavern

Henry IV, Part II

Act I. RUMOUR, in the prologue, summarizes the state of things at the end of the First Part of *Henry IV*. 1. Northumberland first hears a false report of rebel success but then is informed of the rebel failure and Hotspur's death, and the fact that the king's armies are approaching under the command of Henry's son, Prince JOHN OF LANCASTER, and the Earl of WESTMORELAND. Northumberland decides to join forces with the Archbishop of York. 2. Falstaff has been commissioned to enlist soldiers for the king's army but finds it difficult to leave the Boar's Head Tavern. The LORD CHIEF JUSTICE reprimands him for not coming when summoned. Falstaff tries to borrow money from him. 3. At York, the Archbishop worries for fear his forces are too weak to oppose the king's.

Act II. 1. Mistress Quickly has started legal action against Falstaff for his debts. Fang, on her behalf, arrests Falstaff. Falstaff is ready to fight, but the Chief Justice arrives and since Falstaff is in the king's service he escapes being sent to jail. 2. Bardolph brings a letter to Prince Hal from Falstaff, asking the prince to join him. 3. Northumberland's wife and Hotspur's widow ask the earl to break with the Archbishop of York and take temporary refuge in Scotland. 4. At the Boar's Head, Falstaff and his companions resume their merrymaking. Falstaff strikes up a romance with

DOLL TEARSHEET, a prostitute working for the Hostess. Then he manages to borrow even more money from the Hostess. Then Falstaff and Prince Hal are summoned to assume their duties in the campaign against the rebels.

Act III. 1. At Westminster, King Henry cannot sleep. He soliloquizes: His subjects sleep, but he cannot; "uneasy lies the head that wears a crown." His conscience brings his thoughts back to his deposing of Richard II. His counselors, WARWICK and SURREY, arrive. 2. In Gloucestershire, at the house of Justice SHALLOW, Falstaff is recruiting for the king's army. He allows suitable recruits to buy their way out of service, and he enlists unsuitable men.

Act IV. 1. The Archbishop of York, with MOWBRAY and HASTINGS, his fellow-conspirators, hear of the defection of Northumberland. Westmoreland offers to mediate their dispute with the Crown and they agree. 2–3. After promising on oath to give them redress if they will disband their armies, Lancaster breaks his word and has the rebel nobles executed. Lancaster informs London that the rebellion is ended. Falstaff is given permission to return via Gloucestershire, to settle accounts with Shallow. 4. At Westminster, the king is too ill to hear the good news about the rebellion's end. 5. Prince Hal is summoned to his father's bedside. He thinks the king dead and tries on the crown. The king wakes and accuses Hal of desiring his death, but Hal convinces his father this is not so. The king is carried off to die in a room called the Jerusalem Chamber. This fulfills an old prophecy that he will die in Jerusalem.

Act V. 1. Falstaff, staying with Shallow, boasts of his influence on Prince Hal. 2. At Westminster the Chief Justice reports the king's death. The princes assemble in mourning. Prince Hal is now King Henry V. 3. Falstaff hears of the king's death and Hal's ascendancy. 4. Mistress Quickly and Doll Tearsheet are arrested. The new king means to clean up things. 5. Falstaff is sadly disappointed: The new king banishes from his presence all the companions of his wild youth. The Justice sends Falstaff and his friends away to the Fleet. Henry V summons Parliament to discuss the planned invasion of France.

Henry V summons Parliament

Henry V

Act I. A CHORUS delivers the prologue. **1–2.** The Archbishop of CANTERBURY and the Bishop of ELY argue for King Henry's claims to the throne of France, on the theory that the Salic Law, which bars women and their descendants from the succession, cannot legally apply to him. French ambassadors from the DAUPHIN bring a reply to Henry's claim to certain lands in France. The Dauphin sends him tennis balls as a gesture of insult. Henry promises to turn the tennis balls into cannon balls and orders preparations for an invasion of France.

Act II. The Chorus tells of the conspiracy of three English nobles, the Earl of CAMBRIDGE, Lord SCROOP, and Sir THOMAS GREY, who are siding with France. **1.** At the Boar's Head Tavern, Falstaff's old friends are told by the HOSTESS (the former Mistress Quickly) that Falstaff has died of a broken heart. She blames the king for it. Her husband PISTOL, NYM, and BARDOLPH, the three cronies, decide to follow the king's army to France. **2.** King Henry discovers the plot of the three nobles and has them arrested and executed, just before he boards a ship for France. **3.** Pistol, Nym and Bardolph take leave of the Hostess. **4.** In his palace, King Charles of France sends his generals to fortify towns. Ambassadors from England arrive with Henry's demands. The Dauphin answers that he is looking forward to war with England, but King Charles requests that they wait overnight for his reply.

Act III. The Chorus tells how Henry's fleet approaches the French port of Harfleur. **1.** The English, led by Henry, assault Harfleur. Henry says, "Once more unto the breach, dear friends; once more!" **2.** Nym, Bardolph and Pistol have arrived on the scene. Henry's several loyal nations are represented by the Welsh captain FLUELLEN, the Scottish captain JAMY, and Captain MacMORRIS, an Irishman. **3.** On the walls of the town, the governor says that the Dauphin cannot send any help, therefore he will yield the town to the English. Henry puts his uncle EXETER in command of Harfleur. **4.** At the French king's palace, his young daughter KATHARINE is being taught English by her lady-in-waiting, ALICE, who has lived in England. [A scene famous for its coarse puns.] **5.** The French king and his nobles discuss Henry's progress and exhort one another to resist him. **6.** Though Henry's army is tired and badly fed, he blames MONTJOY, a French herald, that he is marching on Calais. **7.** At Agincourt, the large French army is set to do battle.

Act IV. The Chorus tells of Henry's walking around the camp at night, incognito, to listen to the conversation of the soldiers. **1.** Henry admits to GLOUCESTER that they are in great danger. He gets into a discussion with three common soldiers who do not know who he is. **2.** The French leaders

are confident and jeer at the English courage. **3.** In the English camp, the battle is being observed and discussed. The French outnumber them five to one. Montjoy comes and asks for ransom, because the English will surely be defeated. Henry refuses. **4.** Pistol and a French soldier, meeting on the battlefield, talk instead of fighting; neither understands the other's language, but Pistol outtalks the Frenchman and takes him prisoner. **5.** In another part of the field, the Dauphin and the French generals become aware of their defeat. **6.** Henry lauds his men for their valor, but the French are rallying and Henry orders all prisoners killed. **7–8.** The herald asks for permission to look for the French dead on the field and concedes that the English have won. The French have lost a great number, including many nobles; the English have only a few killed.

Act V. The Chorus tells of the great welcome given the king upon his return. **1.** Pistol and Fluellen get into an argument in which Pistol insults the Welshman; he is beaten by Fluellen. **2.** A peace meeting takes place in a French palace. Charles grants Henry the hand of Katharine in marriage and acknowledges him as heir to the French throne. Katharine does not yet speak English too well, but Henry expresses his love in words she can understand.

Henry VI, Part I

Act I. 1. As Henry V is being buried in Westminster Abbey, there is news from France that most of the territory he gained has again been lost. The DAUPHIN of France has been crowned King CHARLES of France, at Rheims. TALBOT, the English commander, has been taken prisoner. The Duke of BEDFORD, whom Henry V named regent of France, hastens to have young HENRY VI proclaimed king. **2.** Before Orleans, the Dauphin meets JOAN OF ARC (JOAN LA PUCELLE), who promises to guard him and help his cause. **3.** In London, the Duke of GLOUCESTER'S men get into a street fight with the servants of the Bishop of WINCHESTER. (Both are the king's uncles.) **4–5.** At Orleans, Talbot (who has been exchanged) and SALISBURY, the English generals, fight on against heavy odds. La Pucelle withdraws to supply Orleans with food. **6.** Orleans is delivered from the English, thanks to La Pucelle. She gains the respect of the Dauphin. Salisbury has been killed.

Act II. 1. While the French celebrate inside Orleans, the English, under Talbot, scale the walls and put the French to flight. **2–3.** The Duchess of AUVERGNE invites Talbot to visit her. She pretends to admire him but plans to assassinate him. He is suspicious and has the castle surrounded by troops. **4.** In London, RICHARD PLANTAGENET, head of the house of York, gets into an argument with the Lancaster heir, the Earl of SOMERSET. Richard asks his

followers to wear white roses to identify themselves, and Somerset, in turn, asks his men to wear red roses. **5.** In the Tower of London the imprisoned Mortimer is dying. He tells his nephew Richard, who visits him, that his father (executed by Henry V) was the true heir to the throne of King Richard II.

Act III. 1. Richard demands of Parliament the return of his titles and estates. Gloucester and Winchester are quarreling. Henry warns them that they are inviting civil war. Richard is granted his request and is created Duke of YORK. The king and court plan to set out for France and have Henry crowned King of France in Paris. **2.** La Pucelle manages to take the city of Rouen but loses it again to Talbot and the English. **3.** The Duke of BURGUNDY has been fighting on the English side but La Pucelle persuades him to join the French. **4.** In Paris, Henry creates Talbot Earl of SHREWSBURY.

Act IV. 1. The English king is crowned and the Governor of Paris swears allegiance to him. York and Somerset renew their quarrel and the king tries to make peace between them. He makes York regent of France and commander of foot soldiers and Somerset commander of the cavalry. **2–4.** Talbot is trying to take the city of Bordeaux, held by the Duke of Burgundy. York gets word in Gascony that Talbot needs reinforcements. The messenger, Sir WILLIAM LUCY, blames Somerset for Talbot's inevitable defeat. **5–7.** Talbot asks his son JOHN to avenge him, should he fall. In battle Talbot goes to the rescue of his son, but John is slain and his father dies of a broken heart. The Dauphin puts the blame for the English defeat on the dissension between York and Somerset.

Act V. 1–2. The Pope and the (Holy Roman) Emperor offer to make peace between England and France. The truce is to be followed by a marriage between Henry and the daughter of the Earl of Armagnac. Winchester has become a cardinal and Henry sends him to conclude the peace and bring back the bride. **3–4.** Before Angiers, York captures La Pucelle. The Earl of SUFFOLK captures MARGARET OF ANJOU. He falls in love with her, but since he is already married he plans to marry her to King Henry and so promises her father REIGNIER. York has La Pucelle burned at the stake as a sorceress, though she pretends she is pregnant. Charles of France is made Viceroy under Henry as part of the peace settlement. **5.** Henry, amazed by Suffolk's description of Margaret's beauty, decides to break his engagement to the daughter of Armagnac and marry Margaret. Suffolk remembers an old prophecy according to which he will rule both the new queen and the king.

Henry VI, Part II

Act I. 1. Margaret of Anjou arrives in London to marry King Henry VI. She

Margaret of Anjou arrives in London to marry King Henry VI

brings with her the treaty agreed upon by the Earl of Suffolk. Gloucester, the king's uncle and Protector, is dismayed that it requires the return of two of the richest French duchies, Anjou and Maine, to France, and there is no dowry. But the king is pleased with Margaret. The Duke of York is relieved of his post as French regent, and Suffolk is created a duke. York bides his time to seize the crown. 2. Gloucester's wife, ELEANOR, receives a priest named HUME, who offers by witchcraft to help her become queen. She does not know that Hume has been sent by Suffolk and Cardinal BEAUFORT (Bishop of Winchester) to embarrass her husband through her. 3. Queen Margaret suggests that Henry is old enough to do without a protector. Beaufort and Suffolk ask Gloucester to resign. The queen gets into a fight with Eleanor and slaps her. Eleanor swears she will not forget. 4. In Gloucester's garden, a spirit is raised by a witch and Hume for Eleanor. The spirit gives her a prophecy about the future of the crown. York and the Duke of BUCKINGHAM break into the circle and arrest the participants, including Eleanor.

Act II. 1. The queen continues to plot against Gloucester. A townsman who has been blind regains his sight by a miracle and the king is much impressed, being a simple and scholarly man. Buckingham brings word of Eleanor's arrest. The miracle turns out to be false. 2. In London, York convinces SALISBURY and WARWICK, two noblemen, that he is the rightful claimant to the throne. 3. Eleanor is tried for attending a witches' circle and is banished to the Isle of Man. Gloucester resigns his office in grief. The queen gloats. 4. Gloucester says goodbye to Eleanor. A herald summons him to Parliament.

Act III. 1. The king and his party arrive at Parliament. The queen and Suffolk do their

best to poison the king's mind against Gloucester. Somerset brings word that the remainder of the French possessions are lost. The king takes it calmly. Gloucester arrives and is arrested for treason. This causes the king such grief that after expressing faith in Gloucester's innocence he leaves Parliament and leaves decisions to his queen and the principal nobles. A messenger arrives with news of a revolt in Ireland and the Cardinal and Suffolk delegate York to go to Ireland and suppress it. 2. Two assassins kill Gloucester, on orders from the Cardinal and Suffolk. The king returns for Gloucester's trial. Warwick and Salisbury, as leaders of Parliament, demand Gloucester's freedom. They leave with his body instead. Suffolk is accused of the murder and the king banishes him. When he says goodbye to the queen she confesses her love for him and promises to have him recalled or to follow him into exile. Cardinal Beaufort is dying.

Act IV. 1. Suffolk is taken prisoner by pirates and WHITMORE, a sailor, kills him. 2–3. At Blackheath, a mob of rebels under the leadership of CADE plans to march on London. Cade claims to be a Mortimer and heir to the crown. Cade plans to open the prison gates and let the inmates out. 4. Suffolk's head is received by the queen in great grief. A messenger tells of the rebels' arrival in London. 5. Lord SCALES, governor of the Tower, tells citizens to resist Cade. 6–8. Cade is told an army is gathered at Smithfield to fight him. Lord SAY, a nobleman, is captured and pleads for his life, but Cade has him beheaded. Buckingham and Lord CLIFFORD speak to the rebels, promising pardon to anyone quitting Cade and going home. Clifford speaks to the mob of Henry V's valor and manages to turn them against Cade. 9. Cade flees, but York is on his way from Ireland to help Cade's

cause. The king sends Buckingham to promise York that Somerset will be held in the Tower. 10. Cade, now a fugitive, enters the garden of a country squire named IDEN, who kills him.

Act V. 1. York, pacified by Somerset's confinement, disbands his army. Iden arrives with Cade's head and is knighted by the king. Somerset is freed and the king asks that he be hidden before York can see him at liberty, but York has seen him and breaks into open rebellion. 2–3. At St. Albans, the houses of York and Lancaster fight in open battle. York is victorious. RICHARD, York's son, kills Somerset. The king and queen flee. York hurries to London before Henry can summon Parliament.

Henry VI, Part III

Act I. 1. At Parliament, the Duke of York takes the throne. Henry VI arrives and refuses to let York sit on it. There follows an argument that Henry VI is not lawful king because he is the descendant of the usurper, Henry IV. Most of the nobles support York. There is a compromise: Henry will be king for his own lifetime but will make York his heir. Some of the king's followers, notably Clifford, think this an outrage to Henry's son (Prince Edward). Queen Margaret denounces her husband and promises to raise an army herself against York. 2. EDWARD (afterwards King Edward IV) and RICHARD [King Richard III to be], York's sons, convince him that he should not wait Henry's death to become king. Margaret advances with any army. 3–4. In battle near Wakefield, Margaret is victorious. Clifford kills York, after jestingly crowning him with a paper crown. The queen orders York's head to be cut off and placed on the city gates of York.

Act II. 1. Edward and Richard carry on the fight. Warwick joins them. He has been defeated by the queen's army and craves revenge. 2–4. Henry's young son Prince Edward is knighted. There is a parley of the opposing leaders, which ends in defiance. Warwick and the two princes unite. Clifford is battled by Richard. 5. King Henry sits alone on a hill and bemoans his fate. He would rather be a commoner and unknown. In this unhappy civil war a father kills his son and a son his father. The queen's army is defeated. She and the young prince urge the king to flee with them and he agrees. 6. Clifford is captured and dies. York's son becomes King Edward IV. Warwick is sent to France to obtain the hand of BONA, sister-in-law of Louis XI, in marriage for Edward. His two brothers GEORGE and Richard are created Dukes of CLARENCE and GLOUCESTER.

Act III. 1. Two gamekeepers recognize the deposed Henry hiding in Scotland. The gamekeepers are loyal to Edward IV and arrest him. Henry is sent to London and imprisoned in the Tower. 2. At the London palace, Edward is visited by the widowed Lady GREY, whose husband fell at St. Albans. She has come to ask for restoration of her estates. The king asks her to become his mistress, but she refuses. He then offers to marry her and make her queen. 3. Margaret has found refuge at the French king's palace. She tries to influence France to support Henry's claim. Warwick arrives and Mar-

Lady Grey refuses to become the king's mistress

garet denounces him, but Louis and Bona agree to the marriage and alliance with Edward. Then word comes from England that Edward has married Lady Grey. Warwick, angered, denounces Edward and joins forces with Margaret. The French will help also. Warwick offers his daughter in marriage to young Prince Edward, Margaret's son, and Edward accepts.

Act IV. 1–2. Edward IV's brothers disagree and Clarence joins Warwick while Gloucester supports Edward. An invading army of French soldiers and English partisans prepares to battle Edward. 3. Edward is captured and sent to prison. The victors plan to march on London and restore Henry to power. 4–5. Edward is a prisoner in the hands of the Bishop of York, but escapes. 6. King Henry is released, but he is not really interested in government and has Clarence and Warwick run affairs for him. Edward has gone to Burgundy to raise a new army. Somerset, worried about further civil war, sends the young Earl of RICHMOND [afterwards Henry VII, the first Tudor king] out of the country, to save him for England. 7. Edward enters the city of York and proclaims himself king again. 8. At the London palace, Henry is seized by Edward and again deposed. Henry is sent to prison and Edward marches against Coventry, where Warwick waits.

Act V. 1–3. In the battle that follows, Clarence refuses to fight his own brothers. Warwick, wounded in battle, is left to die by Edward. Edward wins the battle, but Margaret is on the way with an army. 4. Queen Margaret exhorts her army to fight for the imprisoned Henry. 5. Prince Edward (Henry's son) fights the three

330

brothers and is stabbed to death. Margaret is defeated and taken prisoner. Richard (Gloucester) has run off to London to secure the Tower. 6. In the Tower of London, Richard kills King Henry. 7. Edward is restored to his throne. Queen Margaret has been ransomed by her father. Richard bides his time.

Henry Esmond

Novel by William Makepeace Thackeray, 1811–1863.
Published 1852. (ML, 80 & T34)

THACKERAY'S MOST POPULAR NOVEL is *Vanity Fair,* but probably *Henry Esmond* is his best. The difficulty with *Esmond* is that the reader must plow through long introductory pages of genealogy, in which an understanding requires some familiarity with the times from about 1680 on, when James II fell and when the Jacobite pretenders began their long conspiracy to regain the crown of England. After that, *Henry Esmond* is a fine romance with plenty of interesting intrigue and much love of beautiful women. At the end of the novel the happy Henry and his wife go to America and their experiences in Virginia are related in a sequel to *Henry Esmond,* called *The Virginians.*

Book I. Chaps. 1–4. HENRY ESMOND, reputed to be the illegitimate son of Lord

THOMAS ESMOND, Viscount of Castlewood, lives as a child in the humble home of French-speaking weavers. One day the viscount takes him from his poor surroundings and brings him to Castlewood to serve as a page to the Viscountess ISABELLA. Henry is put under the tutelage of Father HOLT, a Jesuit chaplain in the household, who educates the boy in Catholicism, in the classics, and in the use of the sword. Henry is an excellent scholar, but time often hangs heavy on his hands at Castlewood when the viscount and his household are in London.

Chaps. 5–9. The Catholic King James II is deposed and the Protestant King William of Orange and his wife Mary are crowned. Thomas Esmond and Father Holt join in the plot to restore James to the throne, and the viscount is killed in the battle of Boyne. Lady Isabella is taken prisoner and the 12-year-old Henry is left at Castlewood with the servants and a company of soldiers. Soon after, FRANCIS, a distant cousin of Thomas Esmond, arrives to claim the title and lands of Castlewood. He is accompanied by his wife RACHEL, a small daughter, BEATRIX, and an infant son, FRANK. Rachel is only 8 years older than Henry. The new viscount and his family give Henry attention and affection and the boy feels a part of the family. Rachel is devoted to her husband, but he spends much of his time hunting and carousing. Henry helps in the upbringing of Frank and Beatrix, becoming their tutor. Smallpox breaks out in the village and Henry, who has been exposed to it, brings the disease to Castlewood. Beatrix and Henry fall ill. The pockmarks mar Rachel's beauty and her husband neglects her completely and takes a mistress. This leads to bickering and unhappiness at Castlewood and Henry is in despair.

Chaps. 10–14. Henry leaves for Cambridge University after telling Rachel he will return at any time she or the children need him. His Catholic sympathies are forgotten in the anti-Catholic climate of England and he plans to become a clergyman in the Church of England. Henry lives alone at Cambridge, studying hard and reading widely in theology and philosophy. When he returns to Castlewood, he finds Beatrix has become an exceptionally beautiful girl. Rachel finds herself strangely attracted to Henry. She and her husband quarrel about Lord MOHUN, a visitor at Castlewood, who is a rake and a gambler. The viscount is heavily indebted to Mohun and when Beatrix innocently tells her father that Mohun is interested in Rachel and has written her several letters, the viscount flies into a jealous rage and determines to challenge Mohun to a duel. He goes off to London on a pretext and Henry, suspecting his reason, follows in the hope of dueling Mohun himself, to protect the life of his guardian. But the viscount insists on personally defending his honor and is fatally wounded. Before he dies, Francis confesses that Henry is not illegitimate but is the son of Thomas by an early marriage and is thus the rightful heir to Castlewood. Henry, out of loyalty to the family that befriended him, burns the confession and vows he will never claim the title and the estate.

Book II. Chaps. 1–4. Henry is imprisoned because of his part in the duel and Rachel comes to visit him. She is not aware of Henry's renunciation of his claim to Castlewood and she berates him for not preventing the duel and for not avenging the death of her husband. She forbids Henry ever to return to Castlewood. He resolves to make a name for himself and prove his worth to Rachael. When he is released from prison he visits the old viscountess, Isabella, and she aids him in securing a commission as ensign in the army.

Chaps. 5–9. Henry acquires his share of glory and wounds in the campaign against Spain led by the Duke of Marlborough. After the victory Henry returns to Castlewood in hopes of winning Rachel's forgiveness and he is welcomed by her. Beatrix has made her debut at court and is more radiant than ever. Rachel warns Henry not to become too fond of Beatrix, as the girl is basically cold and selfish. Henry returns to duty. He fights in the Battle of Blenheim in 1704 and wins new honors.

Chaps. 10–14. After recovering from a wound, Henry rejoins his family in London. He is greatly attached to Beatrix but she, being a coquette, toys with him. He is also aware of his love for Rachel, but he does not yet realize how much the older woman means to him. In London Henry is friendly with the famous wits Addison and Steele and he enjoys the pleasures of good talk and good drink. In 1706 he rejoins the army as a captain and takes Frank with him. Frank tells him that Beatrix is engaged to the Duke of HAMILTON and Henry despairs of ever winning her for himself. He meets Father Holt, who tells him that his father, Thomas, hastily married a poor Belgian weaver's daughter to legitimatize the unborn Henry, and then deserted the girl. Henry returns to Castlewood and Rachel tells him that she has learned of his parentage from Isabella and that she wants him to claim his rights. But he rejects his inheritance once again.

Book III. Chaps. 1–6. Back on the Continent, Henry is wounded in battle. He returns to London, where Rachel nurses him. Word comes that Frank has married a countess. Henry writes a satire about young women who torture their lovers, and the play is admired by Steele. Henry gives Beatrix a diamond necklace as an engagement present, but the duke refuses to allow her to accept such a gift from a man without a title. Rachel tells Beatrix and the duke that Henry is the real heir to Castlewood and the duke apologizes to Henry and asks him to be best man at the wedding. But the wedding never takes place. The duke is killed in a duel with Mohun, who also dies.

Chaps. 7–13. Rachel and Beatrix go back to Castlewood, where Beatrix devotes her time to nursing the sick in the village. She rejects Henry's proposal and plans to enter a convent. Henry becomes involved in a plot to place JAMES III, the Stuart pretender, on the throne of England when Queen Anne dies. James assumes the identity of Frank Esmond and is brought over from France. The pretender is a profligate and when he meets Beatrix in the London home of the Esmonds he finds her most attractive. She in turn begins to think in terms of being a queen rather than a nun and encourages James. Henry sends her to Castlewood and James angrily quarrels with him and disappears. The queen dies and James, not being in London, loses his chance to seize the throne. Henry and Frank find James with Beatrix at Castlewood, criticize his actions, and bring him back to London, where the people are acclaiming King George I. James returns to France to live out his dissolute life and Beatrix refuses to see her family. Henry, Rachel and Frank flee to France when their rôles in the plot to aid James become known. In France Henry realizes that he has always loved Rachel and he proposes to her. She accepts, as she has loved him for many years. They are finally pardoned and could return to England in safety, but they no longer care to live there. They obtain a grant to a large area of land in Virginia and sail for the colony. There they build a fine home and call it Castlewood. They raise a family and live a good life.

The Song of Hiawatha

Poem by Henry Wadsworth Longfellow, 1807–1882.
Published 1855.

THIS IS ONE of the best-known poems in the English language. Countless millions of schoolchildren have recited it and acted out various of its scenes. It has been translated into many languages. Hiawatha is not a faithful rendition of the legends of any particular Indian tribal or language group; Longfellow himself was most influenced by the Algonquian legends, but he read widely among other authorities on Indians (whose knowledge was not too great in those days, however). The meter of the poem is taken from the *Kalevala,* the great Finnish epic. Longfellow adopted this meter because he had found in the *Kalevala* certain legends similar to those of the American Indian. Some critics who had not read his notes accused him of plagiarism. The character of Hiawatha, a savior and peacemaker in a Christlike tradition, is found in various guises and by various names in the legends of many tribes.

I. The Peace-Pipe. GITCHE MANITO, the Master of Life, calls the nations together. He lights the Peace-Pipe and tells the nations he is weary of their quarrels. They have plenty. Only together will they be strong. He will send a prophet to them, and if they heed his teachings all will go well. If they do not, they will perish.

II. The Four Winds. Long ago MUDJE-KEEWIS performed a feat of great courage. He stole the Belt of Wampum from MISHE-MOKWA, the Great Bear, then he killed the Great Bear. As a reward, Mudjekeewis becomes the West Wind, Father of all the winds. Mudjekeewis gives the East Wind to WABUN, who is young and beautiful. SHAWONDASEE receives the South Wind, and the fierce KAIBONOKLA receives the cruel North Wind. Wabun falls in love with a beautiful and lonely earth maiden. He changes her into a star and now they are always together. Kaibonokla meets a diver, Shingebis, who defies him; they have a terrible wrestling match and the North Wind is defeated and retires to the land of the White Rabbit. Shawondasee loves a beautiful maiden but is too lazy and fat to do anything but sigh for her. One day he discovers that her lovely golden hair has turned white and he knows that his brother, the North Wind, has won her. The beautiful maiden is really the golden-headed dandelion that with the end of summer turns white and dies.

III. Hiawatha's Childhood. NOKOMIS warns her daughter WENONAH to beware of Mudjekeewis, the West Wind. Wenonah, like so many daughters, does not heed her mother. One day while she is lying in a meadow the West Wind comes and takes her. This is how HIAWATHA is born. The West Wind leaves Wenonah and she dies of a broken heart. The little Hiawatha is brought up by Nokomis, his grandmother. Nokomis teaches Hiawatha the wonders of nature and IAGOO, the great boaster, teaches him to hunt. Hiawatha kills his first deer and brings it proudly home.

IV. Hiawatha and Mudjekeewis. Hiawatha grows up to be a fine young man, handsome, strong, and brave. He has magic mittens that can crush rocks to powder and he has magic moccasins with which he can walk a mile with each step. Hiawatha must avenge his mother and goes to visit his father, the West Wind. After a terrible, indecisive battle between them, Mudjekeewis tells Hiawatha that he is proud of him and sends him back home to save the people. Then Mudjekeewis will share his great domain with Hiawatha. On his way home Hiawatha stops in the land of the Dacotahs, where he visits the old arrow-maker and meets his lovely daughter, MINNEHAHA, which means Laughing Water.

V. Hiawatha's Fasting. Hiawatha fasts for seven days and seven nights and prays for good to come to all the nations. He

Mudjekeewis sends his son Hiawatha back to bring peace to the nations

meets MONDAMIN, a young man dressed in green and yellow. Hiawatha wrestles three times with Mondamin, who tells him that the next time "You will conquer and overcome me;/Make a bed for me to lie in,/Where the rain may fall upon me." Hiawatha does this and before the summer is over maize begins to grow, a new gift of food for all the nations.

VI–VIII. Hiawatha's Friends; his Sailing; his Fishing. Hiathawa has two good friends, CHIBIABOS, a musician who sings so sweetly that the brook and the birds want to learn from him, and KWASIND, the strongest of all mortals, as good as he is strong. Hiawatha builds a wonderful canoe and sails it. Hiawatha meets the monster, MISHE-NAHMA, the great sturgeon, King of Fishes. There is a battle between them and the mighty Mishe-Nahma swallows Hiawatha and his canoe. The great sturgeon is washed up on the shore and Hiawatha's friends, the seagulls, come and peck at Mishe-Nahma until they free Hiawatha.

IX. Hiawatha and the Pearl-Feather. Old Nokomis tells Hiawatha to take his magic mittens and his magic moccasins and go to slay the wicked magician, PEARL FEATHER, who sends fever and disease and death to the tribes. Hiawatha and Pearl Feather have "the greatest battle/That the sun had ever looked on." Hiawatha's friend the woodpecker tells him that Pearl Feather's weak spot is his head. With this knowledge, Hiawatha defeats Pearl Feather. He rewards the woodpecker by staining the top of his head with bright red blood.

X–XI. Hiawatha's Wooing. Hiawatha cannot forget the lovely Minnehaha. Nokomis approves because their marriage will make peace with the Dacotahs. Hiawatha goes to the land of the Dacotahs and tells Minnehaha's father, the arrow-maker. Minnehaha loves Hiawatha and the lovers make the long journey back to Hiawatha's home. There is a great celebration, with feasting and songs and stories.

XII. The Son of the Evening Star. Iagoo tells the story: Long ago there was a hunter who had ten beautiful daughters. Nine of them married handsome warriors. The youngest daughter, OWEENEE, fell in love with OSSEO, an ugly old man, but a magician. All the other sisters and their husbands mocked Osseo. He changed himself into a handsome young man and made Oweenee old and feeble. The nine sisters and their husbands were changed into birds. Then Oweenee became young and lovely again. She and Osseo lived in peace and happiness on the evening star. Oweenee had a boy child who, with his bow and arrow, shot the birds. They fell to earth, like bright-colored autumn leaves, and returned to their mortal shapes; but instead of regaining their stature, they remained Puk-Wudjies, Little People, forever.

XIII. Blessing the Cornfields. Hiawatha tells Minnehaha that at night, when all are asleep, she must walk around the cornfields to bless them. KAHGAHGEE, King of the Ravens, calls all the crows and jays and other birds together and plans to ruin the corn, but the wise Hiawatha catches Kahgahgee and puts him in a cage.

XIV. Picture-Writing. Hiawatha teaches his people to draw a serpent to represent evil, a white circle to represent life, and a black circle to represent death, and to say many other things with pictures. The people begin to draw pictures.

XV. Hiawatha's Lamentation. Chibiabos falls through the ice of the frozen river and dies. Hiawatha mourns for his friend for seven weeks. When spring comes, medicine men visit Hiawatha. They bring healing roots and other things that can drive away disease. The medicine men work their magic and Chibiabos appears. They give him a hot coal and tell him he must light the fires that will guide all the dead who are to follow him. Chibiabos travels to the land of the dead. He sees many dead spirits along the way. All of them are weighed down with bows and arrows and other things their friends have buried with them. The dead spirits ask, "Why do the living lay such heavy burdens on us?" Hiawatha sets

out to teach men how to use the powders and roots that can heal wounds and drive away disease.

XVI–XVII. Pau-Puk-Keewis. PAU-PUK-KEEWIS, a handsome and mischievous youth who likes to make trouble, goes to the wigwam of Hiawatha and upsets everything. He then climbs high into the mountains and waits in glee for Hiawatha to discover what has happened. While he waits, he kills as many seagulls as he can, just to pass the time. The seagulls send word to Hiawatha to come and save them. Hiawatha pursues Pau-Puk-Keewis, who changes into a beaver and then a bird, but Hiawatha does not give up. Hiawatha finally bests the wicked Pau-Puk-Keewis and turns him into an eagle.

XVIII. The Death of Kwasind. The Puk-Wudjies, the Little People, hate the strong man, Kwasind. One day as he is sailing down the river, dozing in his canoe, they attack him with pine cones and he falls into the river and drowns.

XIX. The Ghosts. Two men come to the wigwam of Hiawatha. They are pale and silent. They tell Hiawatha they have come from the land of the dead to test him. He meets the tests and they instruct him to tell all the nations not to mourn for the dead and promise Hiawatha they will leave him forever.

XX. The Famine. There is a terrible famine and all the people are sick and sad. Hiawatha goes into the snowy forest, desperate for food for his beloved wife. When he returns empty-handed, Minnehaha is dead.

XXI. The White Man's Foot. A young man and an old man talk. The young man is Spring, the old man Winter. They boast of their adventures and debate which is stronger of the two. Spring wins, for warm sunshine melts the snow and ice. Iagoo tells the village that he has seen a great canoe with warriors whose faces are painted white. The villagers laugh, but Hiawatha knows Iagoo speaks the truth. In a vision Hiawatha has seen that these men are brothers and should be made welcome. In another vision, Hiawatha has seen the nations at war and scattered far and wide like the withered leaves of autumn.

XXII. Hiawatha's Departure. The Priest and his followers come to Hiawatha, who welcomes them. The Priest tells of the Virgin Mary and her blessed Son. Hiawatha knows that the time has come for him to depart. He says farewell to the faithful Nokomis and tells the warriors to listen to what the strangers say. The people stand on the shore and bid farewell to Hiawatha. The forests sigh, the waves sob, and the heron screams Farewell. Hiawatha sails away to the land of the Northwest wind, the Land of the Hereafter.

Horatio Hornblower

Trilogy (three novels) by Cecil Scott Forester, 1899–
Published 1937, 1938, 1939, by Little, Brown & Co., Boston. © by C. S. Forester.

C. S. FORESTER has carried his hero Horatio Hornblower from a midshipman to an admiral, with a title of nobility, in a long series of novels about the British Navy in the time of the Napoleonic Wars. *Captain Horatio Hornblower* comprises three novels of the finest adventure and seamanship. Forester's Hornblower stories are among the best of all sea stories and in modern times have been the most popular.

Beat to Quarters

Chaps. 1–5. Captain HORATIO HORNBLOWER, under secret orders from the British Admiralty, sails his frigate *Lydia* for seven months without making port, then lands on the Pacific Coast of Nicaragua. His orders are to aid the rebellion of Don JULIAN ALVARADO, known as EL SUPREMO, against Spain. He is met by General HERNANDEZ and taken to El Supremo. Hornblower is uneasy at the evidence of El Supremo's tyranny. His orders also are to capture or destroy the Spanish frigate *Natividad*. He is told that the *Natividad* is expected in the gulf momentarily and he awaits the enemy ship.

Chaps. 6–7. Hornblower decides on a surprise attack and swings the *Lydia* into position during the night. The Spaniards' resistance is short-lived and the British sailors seize the ship. According to the laws of the sea the *Natividad* is a British prize, but El Supremo demands it. Hornblower could insist on his rights, but the Admiralty's orders are to facilitate the rebellion against Spain. Hornblower allows El Supremo's men to take the *Natividad* and also takes El Supremo and 500 soldiers aboard the *Lydia*.

Chaps. 8–17. The rebels are carried to La Libertad, where they stage a successful rebellion against the Spanish rulers. Hornblower parts from El Supremo and sails away in the *Lydia*. Soon after, a Spanish frigate approaches with signal flags flying, for a parley. The captain of the frigate comes aboard the *Lydia* and gives Hornblower letters that announce an English treaty with Spain against the common enemy Napoleon, and orders Hornblower to proceed to Panama. There is also a letter from Lady BARBARA WELLESLEY, requesting passage from Panama to England. At Panama Hornblower receives orders from the Viceroy to seek out and destroy the *Natividad*. He takes Lady Barbara and her maid aboard and sails to find the enemy. The *Natividad* is engaged in battle and is finally sunk, but the Lydia suffers considerable damage and her losses in dead and wounded are heavy. The well-disciplined crew has fought with exceptional courage, and Hornblower is greatly impressed by Lady Barbara's quiet courage, uncomplaining acceptance of hardships, and nursing of the wounded.

Chaps. 19–21. The *Lydia* tries to limp back to port but another Spanish frigate brings Hornblower an order from the Viceroy forbidding him to enter any Spanish port. Though amazed, Hornblower manages to find an uninhabited island, where the ship is repaired. They set sail once more, bound round the Horn for England, and meet a Spanish lugger whose captain invites Hornblower aboard and shows him a raving El Supremo in chains. He is told the mad would-be conqueror will be hanged.

Chaps. 22–24. On the voyage home the captain is much in the company of Lady Barbara and they are mutually attracted. Hornblower is on the verge of declaring his love when he guiltily remembers his wife MARIA. He explains his timidity to Lady Barbara and her affection for him turns to cold rage. Soon after, the *Lydia* reaches St. Helena. Lady Barbara disembarks and Hornblower busies himself with taking aboard supplies.

Ships of the Line

Chaps. 1–4. Back in England, Hornblower is given command of the *Sutherland,* a 74-gun battleship, as a reward. His old crew immediately transfers and the ship's complement is rounded out with convicts and impressed sailors. Hornblower orders his master-at-arms not to treat the new men harshly, but to try to break them to discipline without the usual flogging. He receives an invitation from Lady Barbara, recently married to Admiral Sir PERCY LEIGHTON, to dine with them. He takes Maria, who is pregnant and dumpy-looking, and the contrast between the two women makes Hornblower miserable. He thinks of his audacity in loving the wife of his superior, and reflects ruefully on the low state of his finances.

Chaps. 5–8. Despite the greenness of many of the new crew, the *Sutherland* puts to sea and joins Admiral Leighton's flagship, *Pluto,* and another naval vessel in escorting a convoy of East Indiamen. The *Sutherland* encounters two French privateers, and despite his untrained crew Hornblower is skillful enough to sink one enemy vessel and drive off the other. Hornblower orders extra training and in ten days he has the crew in good discipline and the vessel in tiptop condition. A deputation from one of the East Indiamen brings a purse of £400 for the *Sutherland's* crew and Hornblower is invited to dine on the merchant ship. He refuses and makes a sudden decision to impress 20 men each from two merchant ships. This is flouting authority, but he needs the men, as he has orders to leave the convoy and sail into the Mediterranean for possible action.

Chaps. 9–14. The *Sutherland* is first to reach a rendezvous point with two other ships of the line. Another arrives and Hornblower dines with the captain and by the toss of a coin wins the right to proceed into the Mediterranean after French prizes. He sights a French brig and subdues it with a token shot. The brig is well loaded and *Sutherland's* share of the prize money figures to be a goodly sum. Hornblower takes his ship up the Spanish coast and sees a French shore battery guarding some small ships. He hoists French colors and deceives the French long enough to land a detachment of marines to destroy the battery. He then raids the port and personally leads a boarding party aboard a French ship. Hornblower feels he is at least £1,000 richer by his prizes and he thinks of the presents he can take Maria and the good clothes he can wear to see Lady Barbara. He leads his men in another raid on the coast. One day a small boat brings a Spanish cavalry officer, Colonel VILLENA, whose regiment has been routed by the French, who are marauding and plundering along the coast of Spain. Hornblower heads toward shore, where he sights a long column of soldiers. He gives the order to fire and the *Sutherland's* broadsides from 40 guns loaded with ball and grapeshot kill hundreds of French soldiers and scatter the rest. They also put a French coastal battery out of commission.

Chaps. 15–20. The *Sutherland* meets the *Pluto* and Hornblower reports his successes to the skeptical admiral, who would like to punish his brash captain but cannot because of the success of his bold ventures. Hornblower returns to his ship just as a storm breaks. The *Pluto* is seen out of control and being pounded on a reef. Hornblower brings his ship close and with superb seamanship pulls the *Pluto* off the reef and saves the ship and its crew from certain death. Leighton is now much better dis-

Pluto *is stranded on a reef*

posed toward Hornblower. The ships are refitted and Hornblower is ordered to lead the Spanish land forces against the French fortress at Rosas. But the Spanish have given the English an underestimate of the French strength, and the Spanish forces are poor in preparation and discipline. The attack fails and Hornblower retreats to the *Sutherland*. A British frigate, the *Cassandra*, approaches and signals that four French battleships have been sighted. Hornblower sends the frigate to find the *Pluto* and *Caligula*. The *Cassandra* returns and signals for the *Sutherland* to engage the enemy. Hornblower knows that Admiral Leighton must have initiated the order from the *Pluto*, out of sight. The *Sutherland* engages the French ships one by one and inflicts terrible damage on three of them, but in the end Hornblower is forced to surrender. He thinks of what the ignominy of surrender will mean to his career.

Flying Colours

Chaps. 1–2. Hornblower and the remnants of his crew are imprisoned by the French at Rosas. Hornblower is treated well, but he frets at the thought of his defeat, though it was honorable, and he tortures himself with alternate thoughts of Maria and Lady Barbara. He knows he will be tried by the French and executed before a firing squad. Hornblower is wakened one night by the sound of cannon; the *Pluto*, *Caligula* and three other British ships have engaged the one French ship that remained seaworthy after the battle with the *Sutherland*. The French ship blows up and the British ships sail away. A captured British sailor tells Hornblower that Admiral Leighton has been wounded. Hornblower's first thought is that if Leighton dies Lady Barbara will be free.

Chaps. 3–10. Hornblower and his wounded first lieutenant, BUSH, with BROWN, the bos'n, as their servant, are taken to Paris. The journey is long and tedious. One night the coach is stuck in the snow near Nevers. Col. CAILLARD, commanding the escort, sends men to town for help and directs the others to seek shelter in a snowbank. Hornblower sees a boat moored in the river nearby. He whispers to Brown to knock the colonel out and tie him up. This done, they carry Bush to the boat and start drifting with the current through the black night. The boat goes over a dam and upsets. The three men almost drown but they manage to get ashore and to a house, where they announce they are prisoners of war. They are taken in and cared for by the Comte de GRAÇAY. He shows them copies of French newspapers that revile Hornblower as a pirate who meekly surrendered. Hornblower is outraged, but de Graçay quickly assures him that not all Frenchmen believe this. He for one has

lost three sons and believes Napoleon is a perfidious tyrant. A soldier come to inquire about the three fugitives, and when de Graçay denies having seen them the soldier says they must have drowned. The count tells Hornblower he must wait for summer before going on. The winter passes. Hornblower is passionately attracted to MARIE, the count's widowed daughter-in-law, and has an affair with her. He and Brown build a boat. Napoleon has annexed Holland and de Graçay suggests that the three fugitives disguise themselves as Dutch customs officials. The count has uniforms made for them and gives Hornblower his late son's Legion of Honor medal as added protection.

Chaps. 11–15. The three men set out in their boat and pretend to fish as they go down the Loire. After a fairly pleasant trip, during which the usual separation of officers and men is forgotten, they reach Nantes. They see a captured British ship, the *Witch of Endor*, in the harbor, and a gang of prisoners loading other ships. Hornblower conceives the rash scheme of sailing the *Witch of Endor* to England. He has a harbor pilot take him to the ship and pretends to inspect it in his disguise as a Dutch customs officer. He has Brown and Bush tie up the French mate in his cabin and hold the pilot aboard. Then he goes to another dock and orders a sergeant in charge of a gang of prisoners to bring his men aboard the *Witch of Endor* to perform some work. Aboard the ship, the sergeant is disarmed and Hornblower promises to remove the prisoners' chains if they will crew the ship to England. They agree. Hornblower, now in his English uniform, orders the pilot to show the way out of the harbor. In the darkness the ship leaves harbor and at dawn it reaches the open sea. Some boats pursue them but Hornblower personally mans a gun and drives them off. During the voyage to England, Hornblower thinks of the possibility of his being court-martialed for surrendering the *Sutherland*. Hornblower learns from another British ship that Admiral Leighton is dead.

Chaps. 16–19. Hornblower reports to the Admiral of the Channel Fleet and tells his complete story. The Admiral approves and indicates that Hornblower, Bush and Brown will get the prize money for the *Witch of Endor*. But technically Hornblower is under arrest and awaiting court-martial, and he prepares a written report. He hears that his wife has died after giving birth to a son. He feels he has lost the only one who would stand by him and he regrets his unfaithfulness to her. The prize court awards £4,000 for the *Witch of Endor* and Hornblower is to receive two-thirds. A note from Lady Barbara informs him that she is caring for his son and asks him to call. The court-martial is held and Hornblower is not only exonerated but highly praised. He is cheered by all the men of the fleet and then is taken to London, where he is knighted and given an honorarium of £1,200 a year. He calls on Lady Barbara and sees his baby son. His eyes meet Lady Barbara's and their future together is assured.

The Horse's Mouth

Novel by Arthur Joyce Cary, 1888–1959.

Published 1945 by Harper & Bros., New York. © 1944 by Joyce Cary.

MOST AMERICAN READERS discovered the Anglo-Irish writer Joyce Cary very late. For example, the delightful novel *The Horse's Mouth* is the third volume of a trilogy, of which the first two passed almost without notice. There is no doubt, however, that *The Horse's Mouth* is the cream of the crop. It is completely zany and its hero Gulley Jimson is so completely honest in his dishonesty that the reader, like the old man, acquires singleness of purpose and wants only for the old man to be able to paint, just as that is all the old man wants. Some of the scenes will put anyone in a good humor for hours.

Chaps. 1–3. GULLEY JIMSON, 67 years old, is released from prison after a month. He is a penniless artist. Mr. HICKSON, an old, stingy but wealthy art-lover, has many of Jimson's pictures, but has given Jimson almost no money. Jimson adopted the habit of making many threatening calls to Hickson and it is for these calls that he was imprisoned. Now, trying to borrow money, Jimson goes to the bar where COKER works. Coker is an uneducated, roughspoken, but basically tender spinster. She is fond of Jimson but refuses to give him money because he already owes her too much. She does promise to go with him to his former wife, now named SARA MONDAY, who can give evidence that she sold Jimson's paintings to Hickson. Outside the bar Jimson meets NOSY, a stuttering schoolboy, who wants to be an artist. Jimson has no patience with Nosy and brushes him off. Jimson goes to his studio, which is an old, broken-down boathouse. He chases away some boys who are tearing down the boathouse to steal firewood, and he is relieved to find that his 15-foot-high painting of the Fall (of Adam and Eve) has not been badly damaged. Though some of Jimson's work sells for hundreds of pounds and hangs in fine museums, he is without brushes or paint. He calls Hickson, holding a pencil between his teeth to disguise his voice, and pretends to be the President of the Royal Academy soliciting aid for Jimson; but Hickson recognizes the voice and refuses to help. Jimson threatens to burn Hickson's house down. Jimson steals brushes from the oilman.

Chaps. 4–7. Jimson finds a man in Coker's bar who is willing to contribute to the William Blake Memorial Association, but Coker warns the man it is a swindle and Jimson goes back to the boathouse. Nosy brings Jimson coffee and a bun.

Gulley at work on The Fall

Chaps. 8–10. Jimson has started working again on his canvas when Coker comes to take him to Sara Monday's. Reluctantly he goes with her. Sara was a model and a voluptuous flirt. She is now gray and fat but she still has her charm and Jimson cannot resist pinching her several times. Coker insists that Sara sign a paper saying she gave 19 pictures to Hickson. Sara insists she gave Hickson only 17. One Sara gave away and the other, a picture of herself in the bath, she kept. Jimson is delighted to see Sara again. Looking at her gives him several ideas for painting Eve. Coker, though incensed, gives Jimson carfare home. Jimson has stolen a silver frame from Sara. He pawns it for enough money to buy more paints and some good brushes.

Chaps. 11–17. Jimson goes with Coker to visit Hickson. While Hickson's back is turned, Jimson puts some snuffboxes into his pocket. Hickson explains that the pictures merely paid off Jimson's debts. Coker realizes there can be no lawsuit. Hickson is willing to give Jimson a small allowance and £10 extra, but then the butler informs Hickson that the snuffboxes are gone. The police are summoned. Jimson tries to run but is captured and spends six months in jail.

Chaps. 18–20. Jail gives Jimson a chance to get over his winter cough. He receives a letter, forwarded by Coker, from a professor, A. W. ALABASTER, who wants to write a book about the masterpieces of Gulley Jimson. Gulley almost believes this, but is not very surprised when he is released and finds, at the address given on the letter, that no Mr. Alabaster exists. Coker is now 8 months pregnant, her fiancé WILLY has run away with a blonde, she has lost her job and her lodgings, and she and her mother have moved into Jimson's boathouse. Her mother keeps Jimson away.

Chaps. 21–24. Alabaster does exist, but he too is penniless and Jimson takes him to the lodging house where Jimson stays with his friend Mr. PLANT. Alabaster says

he has several friends who will buy Jimson's paintings. Gulley does not believe him and keeps referring to his would-be biographer as a cricket expert, his general opinion of all art critics. But Alabaster writes to Jimson that the millionaire Sir WILLIAM BEEDER and his wife, FLORA, would be interested in buying a Jimson painting. Alabaster is staying with the Beeders and asks Jimson to visit them. Jimson does so and shocks Lady Beeder by saying he would like to paint her in the nude. He drinks a great deal and stays to dinner. He suggests that the Beeders let him stay in their apartment and that he sleep with Lady Beeder. Instead Alabaster and Beeder carry Jimson out and he drunkenly makes his way back to his lodgings. He is ill that night and Nosy spends the night watching over him. The next day Nosy begs Jimson to go see his (Nosy's) mother and convince her that it is a good thing to be an artist. Jimson really agrees with Nosy's mother that only fools become artists, but he does as Nosy wishes and then is roundly scolded by Nosy's mother for his influence on her son. Jimson agrees to teach the boy everything he wants to know about art if Nosy will continue to work for his scholarship and keep the bourgeois life in mind. Jimson's own son, TOM, an illegitimate child by a model, ROSINA, has always hated art and has a good job in the civil service.

Chaps. 25–29. Jimson intends to sell his painting of the Fall to the Beeders, but he has to steal the painting from the Cokers, mother and daughter, who now have possession of his studio. When he gets there, with Nosy right behind him, he discovers that Mrs. Coker has cut up the canvas and patched the roof with it, covering it with tar. At first he is depressed, because he worked on that canvas for two years, but he cheers up when he sees Nosy weeping and he tells the boy he has an idea for an even better painting. Alabaster tells him the Beeders will not give him an advance on a

painting they have never seen but will buy his painting of Sara Monday in the nude for 300 guineas. Sara has kept that painting for herself. Jimson pays her a second visit and promises to give her £20 for the painting. She denies having it, but finally, when Jimson almost has found it in her box, she agrees to let him have it. She goes upstairs to wrap it for him. He kisses her goodbye but later, when he opens the package, he finds four rolls of toilet paper instead of his canvas. Sara is just too fond of looking at herself nude to give up the painting.

Chaps. 30–31. The next day Jimson goes to the Beeders' apartment to tell them that his agent is framing the picture they want. He hopes to get a little advance money. Alabaster tells Jimson he is too late: The Beeders have gone to America for three months. They will be glad to buy the painting when they come back. Jimson pawns Alabaster's coat and buys some good food, which they eat in high style in the luxurious apartment. Jimson invites himself for the night. The next morning Alabaster is called for by some wealthy friends who are taking him to the country for several months. Jimson persuades him to leave the key behind. Then Jimson gets an inspiration to paint a Lazarus mural on one big wall. He pawns several valuables in the house and buys paints and brushes. He hires a big Negro waiter to model for the feet he plans in the center. Jimson borrows a model from a sculptor named BISSON. The following day another sculptor, named ABEL, has a huge cement block lowered into the apartment and goes to work on a monument to Earth. Jimson tries to stop the invaders but cannot. The two artists pawn all the furniture in the room and become absorbed in their work. LOLIE, Abel's model and wife, keeps the two men company in their nightly round of pubs. She is a chunky girl and dresses in an 1890 style, which pleases Jimson. Nosy comes to find Jimson. He has lost his scholarship and is afraid to go home to his mother. Jimson gives him Sir William's bed. Abel finishes his work and has it placed on a lorry and carried off. He forgets Lolie, who faints—still holding her modeling pose—some hours later. Jimson and Nosy send her to the hospital.

Chaps. 32–34. When Jimson's work is half-finished the Beeders unexpectedly return. Jimson makes his escape just as they are calling the police to report a robbery. He and Nosy run away to the country. There Jimson tries to sell cards with cathedrals painted on them as dirty pictures. Someone gets angry and breaks his nose. In the hospital he writes to the Beeders, explaining that he was creating a mural for them and telling them where the pawn tickets are located. Alabaster writes back that all is forgiven but the Beeders are still only interested in the painting in Sara Monday's possession.

Chaps. 35–39. Back in London, Jimson returns to the boathouse. Coker's mother has gone but Coker is there with her baby. Jimson telephones Hickson to try to get some money and learns that Hickson has died and the Jimson paintings are now hanging in the Tate museum. Jimson is pleasantly surprised but he is still without money. He goes to his son's mother's (Rosina's) grave and there he meets Sara Monday, who was also a friend of the dead model. Sara wants money to have a nice funeral and almost gives Jimson the picture, but changes her mind. Jimson sneaks into her house and is trying to steal it when Sara finds him. He pushes her down the stairs. She calls for the police and he escapes through the kitchen. Nosy gives him the idea of doing a copy, which he does in 48 hours. Alabaster arranges for Sir William to buy it and Jimson gets enough money to live and work for a long time.

Chaps. 40–44. Jimson starts to do a Creation mural on a wall that is still precariously standing from a wrecked chapel. He gets many art students to help render the designs. Coker stirs the paint and keeps track of the finances. Sara Monday has been murdered and Jimson is afraid he will be suspected, but the description of the murderer eliminates him. The City Council wants to condemn the chapel as unsafe and tear it down. Jimson tries to get Sir William to prevent it but only succeeds in obtaining a commission to do a portrait of a duke. He goes ahead with his giant mural. The City Council comes to warn Jimson that they are going ahead with the demolition. He chooses to ignore them. They remove a few supports and while he is working on his whale the wall crumbles and falls on him. When he recovers consciousness he is being taken care of by a nun in a hospital. He laughs at the tricks life has played him and he is anxious to get back to work.

The House of the Seven Gables

Novel by Nathaniel Hawthorne, 1804–1864.
Published 1851. (PB, PL15; RE, 89)

THIS NOVEL RANKS as one of the two best Hawthorne wrote, the other being *The Scarlet Letter.* The majority of writers on American literature have placed *The Scarlet Letter* first, but *The House of the Seven Gables* was Hawthorne's favorite. Hawthorne was the first major novelist of the United States and his works have held up in critical judgment over the years. *The House of the Seven Gables* has strong and skillfully executed elements of suspense and mystery. The house itself actually existed; actually it stands today and is a standard place of interest to sightseers in Salem. They are invited to count the gables—seven of them—and to send postcard pictures of the house to their friends.

Chap. 1. The House of the Seven Gables is located on Pyncheon Street, in Salem, Mass., and standing before the door is a wide old elm tree called Pyncheon Elm. The street formerly bore the name of Maule's Lane, after the original occupant of the land, Matthew MAULE. After many years the location became desirable to Colonel PYNCHEON, a prominent and powerful resident. A controversy over the property arose between the two men, and Maule stubbornly defended his right to the land. During the Salem witchcraft trials, Maule was convicted of witchcraft and a leader in the accusations against him was Colonel Pyncheon. At the moment of his execution, Maule pointed a finger at Pyncheon and said, "God will give him blood to drink!" But Pyncheon got the land and set about building the house. While it was still under construction, the water in Maule's well, once delicious, turned hard and brackish. Many attributed this to Maule's curse. His house

Judge Pyncheon sees the shop

completed, Pyncheon planned a gala house-warming party, but on the day of the fête Pyncheon was found dead at his desk, his beard saturated with blood. The townspeople recalled Maule's curse, but the coroner's jury attributed it to natural causes. Pyncheon's family seemed destined for great wealth, having a claim to a large tract of land in what is now Maine, but Pyncheon's son and heir lacked his father's force of character and the legality of the claim could not be proved. Nevertheless, the claim persisted in the minds of the Pyncheon descendants for more than 100 years, contributing to their delusion of family importance. The family continued to occupy the house for the next two centuries, but nothing notable occurred except that 30 years before this story opens the nephew of a Pyncheon was convicted of

killing his uncle and was imprisoned. The House of the Seven Gables passed to another nephew, a cousin of the young man convicted of murder. The new heir was a dissipated youth who later reformed and became Judge PYNCHEON, a highly respected member of the community. Judge Pyncheon bought himself a country home and the judge's sister occupied the House of the Seven Gables. She was understood to be very poor, but refused to take any aid from her wealthy brother. The only other Pyncheons were the judge's son, who was in Europe, and a young country girl of 17, PHOEBE Pyncheon, the daughter of another of the Judge's cousins. There seemed no descendants of Matthew Maule left in the town. Many townspeople believed the Maules were possessed of mysterious and supernatural powers. The House of the Seven Gables was no longer in a fashionable part of town. In the front gable was a shop-door, cut by an earlier Pyncheon who

had suffered financial reverses and set up a shop—to the distress of the proud Pyncheons. After his death the shop door was locked and bolted, but all the old counters and fixtures remained.

Chap. 2. Miss HEPZIBAH Pyncheon, the present resident of the house, is an elderly spinster who has been a recluse for more than 25 years. She lacks grace or any semblance of beauty, and her nearsightedness seems to have molded her features into a permanent frown, though in truth she is not an ill-tempered woman. Miss Hepzibah is about to embark on a venture she is loath to undertake. Poverty has made it necessary for her to open the little shop in her house.

Chaps. 3–4. Hepzibah's first customer is Mr. HOLGRAVE, a young artist of 22 or so, who is the only other occupant of the house. He congratulates Hepzibah on her new venture. Customers filter in, but Hepzibah is not a good businesswoman and the profits are slight. One of the passers-by is Judge Pyncheon, and Hepzibah reveals her dislike of him. Another caller is an old man known in the neighborhood as Uncle VENNER, of whom Hepzibah is fond. Phoebe arrives to visit her aunt. She is a fresh, young and lovely girl who seems out of place in the gloomy surroundings.

Chaps. 5–6. Phoebe's mother having remarried, Phoebe wishes to live with Hepzibah. Hepzibah tries to dissuade her, adding that the master of the house will be returning and it will no longer be her place. Phoebe thinks Hepzibah means the judge, but Hepzibah vows he will never cross the threshold while she lives. She then shows the girl a picture of a handsome young man, her brother CLIFFORD. Hepzibah finally agrees to let Phoebe stay awhile and Phoebe makes herself extremely useful about the house and volunteers to be shopkeeper. Hepzibah becomes genuinely fond of the girl. In the garden Phoebe meets Holgrave. He is accustomed to tend the garden but suggests that she may prefer to do so. Phoebe is not sure she likes the young man but he seems to exercise a certain magnetic influence over her. The next morning Phoebe learns that Clifford has returned. Hepzibah is in a state of excitement and flutters about the kitchen to prepare a fine breakfast. Clifford seems but a shadow of the man he once must have been, and it is apparent that he is a man who has suffered. It is his nature to love beauty and refinement and he finds it hard to respond to Hepzibah's appearance, while he delights in the youth and beauty of Phoebe. While Phoebe is tending the shop, Judge Pyncheon comes to see Clifford. He tells Hepzibah how happy he is to hear of Clifford's homecoming, and offers assistance, but Hepzibah refuses his aid and will not permit him to see Clifford. Clifford calls out not to let the man in. The Judge finally gives up and leaves.

Chaps. 9–11. Clifford, in his youth a lover of poetry, art, and all refinements of life, retains his great love of beauty and of gaiety, loveliness, and grace. Years of confinement in prison, however, have taken their toll and Clifford is more child than man.

Chaps. 12–14. Phoebe sees Holgrave frequently. He reveals to her that he has undertaken many occupations during his young life. He seems quite interested in Hepzibah and her brother, but with curiosity not mixed with great affection. Phoebe sums him up as a cold person. Phoebe is curious to know why he chose the House of Seven Gables to live in, and Holgrave says it was to learn better how to hate the abominable past. Holgrave has put an incident of the Pyncheon family history into the form of a legend and plans to publish it. It is the story of ALICE Pyncheon, the lovely young daughter of GERVAYSE Pyncheon. She is hypnotized by a descendant of Matthew Maule and placed under his evil spell for the rest of her life. As he tells

the story, Holgrave is startled to observe that Phoebe seems to be falling into a hypnotic state herself. Holgrave realizes that with one wave of his hand he could have complete mastery over the girl, but his integrity prevents him from doing so. Phoebe is unaware of all this. A few days later Phoebe goes to visit her family in the country.

Chaps. 15–20. A gloom seems to settle over the house at Phoebe's departure, and this is intensified by stormy weather for several days. Judge Pyncheon returns, demanding to see Clifford to learn the secret of some hidden Pyncheon wealth he fancies Clifford knows about. He threatens to use his influence to have Clifford committed to an insane asylum. Hepzibah begs him to be kind, but knows she must give in. Hepzibah goes to Clifford's chamber but cannot find him. After searching for him for some time, she comes upon him in a state of excitement, a wild expression on his face. She is horrified upon returning to the parlor to find the Judge dead. Clifford bids Hepzibah get her cloak, as they are going to leave the house at once. Clifford and Hepzibah steal away in the stormy night. They board a train, and Clifford is in an unusual state of exhilaration. Meanwhile, the day and evening pass; the dead judge sits in the chair, as had his ancestor centuries before, his beard saturated with blood. Tradespeople and customers come by, but the house appears deserted. Phoebe returns from her visit and is met at the door by Holgrave, who has discovered the body. Holgrave is anxious to learn where Hepzibah and Clifford have gone. He feels the judge's death helps prove that Clifford did not kill his uncle, who died under similar circumstances. Holgrave points out that several Pyncheons have been stricken in the same way. It seems likely, adds Holgrave, that Judge Pyncheon himself made it appear that Clifford was guilty. Holgrave and Phoebe express their love for each other. At this moment, Hepzibah and Clifford return.

Chap. 21. As Holgrave had thought, the manner of the judge's death convinces many people that there was no murder committed in the case of Clifford's uncle years before. Apparently the judge had been in the act of stealing money from his uncle when the old man died. To protect himself, he framed his brother. By chance, the judge's son dies soon after his father, so Pyncheon's fortune passes to Hepzibah and Clifford. They decide to move into the judge's country house. Before their departure, Holgrave, who is to marry Phoebe, reveals that he is a descendant of Matthew Maule but said nothing because he was afraid of frightening Phoebe away. He also reveals a secret hiding-place behind the portrait of old Colonel Pyncheon, in which reposes the long-sought deed to the land in Maine. It is now, of course, useless.

Huckleberry Finn

Novel by Mark Twain (Samuel Langhorne Clemens, 1835–1910). Published 1885. (ML, G49; Viking, P20; RE, 11; PB, PL42).

IF MOBY DICK IS NOT the greatest novel written by an American of the 19th century, *Huckleberry Finn* is. The satire in *Huckleberry Finn* is matchless and sometimes is so subtle that it can be misunderstood. Witness a case in 1957 when it was moved to bar *Huckleberry Finn* from school reading because of its "anti-Negro" remarks. Certain passages were cited to support this motion. Far from being anti-Negro, these passages constitute the most devastating speech against slavery and against racial prejudice that any American has written. The superlative feature of *Huckleberry Finn* is that a child can read it (and it is most popular in the juvenile market) and understand *all* of it; then an intelligent adult can read it and understand ten times more.

Chaps. 1–3. A previous book [*Tom Sawyer*] tells how HUCK FINN and TOM SAWYER found some robbers' loot and each got $6,000. Huck's money is now in the care of Judge THATCHER. The Widow DOUGLAS has adopted Huck, and she and her sister, Miss WATSON, are trying to "civilize" him. He does not like it much. He sneaks out one night and joins Tom Sawyer and his gang in a cave. They form a blood bond to be robbers and murderers. Tom says it all has to be done just like it is in books. Anybody that tells secrets gets killed and his family too. They will take captives and keep the women in the cave and murder most of the victims they rob. Huck thinks it is all a big fake. He goes home and prays that his old drunken tramp of a father will not reappear. Miss Watson tells Huck he must pray or he will not go to paradise, but Huck thinks paradise sounds pretty dull. Rumor has it that his father has been drowned, but Huck does not believe it. The gang attacks the Arabs and their elephants and camels that Tom Sawyer told about, but they turn out to be part of a Sunday School picnic.

Chaps. 4–11. Huck's PAP appears, longhaired and dirty. He wants Huck's money and tells Huck he will "teach him for trying to live better" than his own father. He keeps getting drunk and raising a ruckus and finally he steals Huck and hides him in a cabin on an island. Huck does not mind going, except that his Pap beats him pretty often and one night he gets the D.T.'s and tries to kill Huck with a knife. So when Pap is off to town one day Huck saws a hole through the cabin wall and gets out. He then takes everything in the shack and loads a canoe he has found. Then with an ax and the blood of a pig he makes it look as if someone has broken into the cabin, killed him, and dumped the body in the river. Huck heads downriver and hides on an island near the town. A ferryboat passes with all his friends on board. They are shooting cannons off in an effort to locate Huck's drowned body. Huck comes upon a recent campfire, which scares him, but it turns out to belong to Miss Watson's slave, JIM, who has run away. Huck swears not to tell anyone. The river rises and floods and a house comes floating by. They paddle out to it and loot it, and Jim sees a dead man lying inside. Huck disguises himself as a girl and goes into town. A woman tells him about the murder of Huck Finn. Some people think an escaped slave named Jim did it. It is thought that Jim is hiding on the island and some men are about to go out to look. Huck rushes to the island and warns Jim, and they jump on a raft that they have acquired and just escape in time.

Chaps. 12–16. Huck and Jim build a wigwam on the raft. They shoot small game and borrow other food. Life is gloriously free. In the middle of a stormy night they come upon a wrecked steamboat. They go aboard and see three ruffians, who are threatening to murder one another for the loot they have stolen. Huck and Jim just miss getting caught. Later Huck takes the canoe to rescue the three men, but the steamboat wreck comes floating by with no one aboard. Huck and Jim are separated when the raft and canoe drift apart in the fog. Huck finally locates the raft and finds Jim asleep. Jim wakes up and Huck tells him it was all a dream. Jim is at first convinced, then is hurt that Huck could play such a joke on him after he had been "half sick to death" for fear Huck had drowned. Huck is sorry, then he begins to feel guilty that he is helping a slave to escape. But he saves Jim from being caught by some white men. Just after they discover that they have passed by the entrance to the Ohio River—Jim's road to freedom—during the night, they are hit by a steamboat. Both jump, and Huck swims to safety on the shore after having given up Jim as drowned.

Chaps. 17–18. Huck goes into a house, says that he fell off a steamboat, and is adopted by the GRANGERFORDS. They are a rich aristocratic family with many slaves and fine horses. Another such family, the SHEPHERDSONS, live nearby. The two families are feuding. Huck inadvertently aids the elopement of a Grangerford girl with a Shepherdson boy and the feud breaks out in full fury. Three of the Grangerfords get killed. Jim has meanwhile reappeared with the raft, and he and Huck shove off.

Chaps. 19–23. Huck and Jim come upon two men running along the bank, trying to escape pursuers, and take them aboard the raft. One claims to be the noble DUKE OF BRIDGEWATER and the other goes even further and says he is the DAUPHIN, the

The duke (left) and the king

rightful KING LOUIS XVII of France. Huck does not really believe them, but he goes along with their stories. The men are actually professional swindlers, specializing in "acting, phrenology, mesmerism, doctoring, or almost anything." Huck thinks that even if they are not real royalty, they act about the same as royalty has in history, so what is the difference? They stop at a backwater town and at a revival meeting the king pretends to be a reformed pirate who needs money to back and reform other pirates. He collects $87. The duke has meanwhile made a little money doing sly things with a printing press. They two then decide to do a Shakespearean revival at the next town, and practice outrageous histrionics on the raft. Shakespeare does not go over well, so the king and duke put on a fake burlesque, and on the third night they slyly escape an angry mob that is out to tar and feather them.

Chaps. 24–30. At the next town they meet a young man just leaving on a steamboat. He talks of the recent death in the town of one PETER WILKES. The king questions the young man and finds out all kinds of facts about the dead man, his family, and the town in general. The king discovers that two long-absent brothers of the deceased are due to arrive from England, one a preacher and the other a deaf-mute. The king and duke enter the town and play the rôles of the two brothers to the hilt. They endear themselves to the nieces of the deceased, and they get hold of $6,000 that Peter Wilkes left behind. They then stay around to sell Wilkes' slaves and property and to fleece the nieces out of every last cent. Huck, who is playing the part of their valet, feels bad about it and steals the gold from the two rogues to return it to the nieces. But he is almost caught and has to hide the sack of gold in Wilkes' coffin. Then the real set of brothers arrive and great argu-

ment rages as to which pair are the bona fide brothers. The king says that a certain mark is tattooed on the dead man's chest. The new arrivals contest this and half the town tramps off to the graveyard to dig up the body to examine it for the tattoo mark. They threaten to lynch the king and duke if their claim is false. When they open the coffin they find the gold on the dead man's chest. In the confusion, Huck gets to the raft, where Jim has been waiting, disguised as an Arab. To Huck's horror the king and duke also have escaped the mob and they climb aboard. They are enraged that they were about to be abandoned.

Chaps. 31–42. The king and duke turn Jim in for a reward, to Huck's great horror. After wrestling with his conscience and discovering that "you can't pray a lie," Huck decides to rescue Jim. He goes to the PHELPS family, who have Jim, and discovers that they are expecting their nephew, namely Tom Sawyer! They mistake Huck for Tom and Huck is pleased to carry out the deception. Tom arrives but Huck tells him what is going on and Tom pretends to be his own brother SID. About this time the king and duke are caught in one of their frauds and are tarred and feathered and run out of town on a rail. Tom and Huck discover Jim locked in a cabin behind the Phelps' house. Huck suggests that they pry the boards off the window to rescue Jim, but Tom says that would be too easy; prisoners have to be rescued "the proper way." They must dig Jim out and there must be rope ladders and secret messages and Jim must make inscriptions on the wall "like it says in the books." They do all this and it takes days. Tom insists that they put rats and spiders in the shack with Jim, because prisoners always have to deal with these. Jim good-naturedly puts up with everything. Finally Tom writes portentous notes to the family, saying that some ruffians are going to steal Jim at midnight, signed "Unknown Friend." The specified midnight approaches and many agitated farmers arrive with guns. Tom holds out until the very last minute, then he and Huck run off with Jim. The farmers shoot, but the three escape to the raft. Tom has been shot in the leg and Jim insists they get a doctor. Huck gets one and stays on shore, where the Phelpses find him. They are still unaware of his connection with the escape. Then Tom appears on a stretcher and Jim in chains. Jim stayed to help the doctor treat Tom and the doctor had Jim recaptured. Tom then gleefully tells his aunt the whole story and Huck discovers that Tom trumped up the whole adventure, knowing all along that Miss Watson had died and set Jim free. Huck learns that his money is still safe, but he fears his father will show up and try to take it. Jim tells him that the dead man he saw in the house on the river was Huck's father. Huckleberry Finn closes with the statement that he had better light out for new territory, as it looks as if his new Aunt Sally Phelps is going to adopt him and try to civilize him.

Hudibras

Poem by Samuel Butler, 1612–1680. Published 1663–1678.

HUDIBRAS IS a very long poem, about 10,000 lines. Its author is now called "Hudibras" Butler to distinguish him from the later Samuel Butler who wrote *The Way of All Flesh* and *Erewhon*. The poem *Hudibras* is a political satire in the form of a humorous epic. Taking its inspiration from *Don Quixote*, it describes the adventures of a pompous knight and his squire. Butler not only satirized political and religious wrangling but took a crack at hypocrisy and folly in many witty couplets that are still much quoted. The source of his name for his knight, Sir Hudibras, is not surely known but there was a Sir Hudibras in Spenser's *Faerie Queen* and he had "many rash adventures." The meter of *Hudibras* is conventional in one sense, because the lines have eight syllables each, but it is not straight iambic tetrameter. There is great variation in the placing of the stress. *Hudibras* was very popular—in fact it was "all the rage"—when it was published and remains one of the best satires in the English language.

Part I. Canto 1. Sir HUDIBRAS is a fat knight with a red beard. He knows logic, mathematics, and philosophy. He is fond of food and arguments. His man RALPHO, an adventurer and a vagabond, is very learned too, though his knowledge is of a different kind. He knows about medicine and the stars and is just as fond of argument as his master.

Hudibras and Ralpho set out on their adventures with some very odd equipment. Their arms are old and rusty; Hudibras rides on a broken-down, miserable, and half-starved horse. However, they carry with them much good food. They have heard that in a village not far off there is to be a bear-baiting and they decide to go and stop it. [Hudibras represents the Puritans, who were very much against this sport, not because it was cruel but mainly because it was entertainment.]

Canto 2. There is a terrible battle and the poor bear not only endures physical torture but, even worse, his feelings are deeply wounded. The bear escapes temporarily and Hudibras and Ralpho manage to capture one of the leaders of the bear-baiting. He is CROWDERO, a fiddler with one leg. They tie Crowdero up and drag him to an ancient castle, where they throw him into a dungeon.

Canto 3. The bear-baiters return and with renewed vigor begin a counterattack, led by TRULLA, a fierce Amazonian warrior. Hudibras and Ralpho are captured and Crowdero is released. In prison and having nothing else to occupy them, Hudibras and Ralpho have a long discussion about the comparative value of man and bears and other matters.

Part II. Canto 1. Love comes to the rescue of Hudibras. He has been interested in a wealthy widow, who now appears. Hudibras proclaims his love but the lady is suspicious. She says that if Hudibras is sincere he will prove his love by an act of good faith; if he submits to a whipping she will marry him. Hudibras agrees and the widow departs. Hudibras decides to postpone the ordeal of the whipping until morning.

Canto 2. Morning comes and Hudibras and Ralpho set out. Hudibras begins to think perhaps there is a way out of his promise to the widow, since he does not look forward to the whipping. Ralpho suggests that the whipping take place by proxy. Hudibras thinks this an excellent idea and he orders Ralpho to be his substitute. Ralpho does not like this plan and there is a heated argument. Hudibras and Ralpho are so angry that they draw their swords. At this point they are interrupted by a noisy procession of countryfolk, beating on pans and kettles and jeering angrily. It appears that they are punishing a wife who is a scold and her henpecked husband. Hudibras begins to make a speech. He is hit in the eye by a rotten egg. Ralpho receives the same treatment and the two make a speedy departure.

Canto 3. Hudibras, in consulation with Ralpho, decides to visit SIDROPHEL, an astrologer, who can tell him his fate with the widow. Hudibras and Ralpho approach the dwelling of Sidrophel and they meet WHACHUM, Sidrophel's right-hand man. Hudibras grows suspicious and sends Ralpho to fetch the police to expose the impostors, Sidrophel and Whachum. Ralpho departs and a fight begins. Sidrophel and Whachum pretend that they have been slain. Hudibras is frightened and flees. He realizes that when Ralpho returns everyone will think he is the murderer.

Part III. Canto 1. Hudibras decides to go to the widow and tell her he has submitted to the whipping, according to her command; but Ralpho has already gone to the widow and told her the truth. Therefore the widow knows Hudibras is lying. There is a loud knocking at the gate and Hudibras is sure that Sidrophel has sent evil spirits to punish him. Hudibras shows his cowardly nature and hides under a table. The spirits enter, drag the cowering Hudibras out of his hiding place, and force him to confess all. Then they give him a sound thrashing. Hudibras appeals to the good nature of one of the spirits. He reminds the spirit that mankind has aided him in many of his evil purposes. The spirit recognizes that this is true and to show his gratitude he helps Hudibras to escape.

Canto 2. [This canto interrupts the adventures of Hudibras and Ralpho and deals with political events of the period.]

Canto 3. Hudibras thinks he is being pursued by an evil spirit but discovers that it is Ralpho. They make up their quarrel and decide that Hudibras should consult a lawyer to see if he can force the widow to marry him. The lawyer thinks Hudibras has a good case. He advises him first to see that Sidrophel is properly punished. Meanwhile if Hudibras writes a letter to the widow, her reply may furnish some evidence. The lawyer also suggests that someone can be hired to imitate the widow's handwriting and add to her letter if necessary. Hudibras happily pays the lawyer for his excellent advice. Hudibras writes to the widow, excuses his misdeeds, and protests his love. The lady considers burning the letter without reading it, but decides it may at least amuse her, so she opens it and then writes her answer. She is not fooled by Hudibras. Her answer defends the rights of women and their powers and virtues.

Hudibras and Ralpho make a speedy departure

339

Humphry Clinker

Novel by Tobias Smollett, 1721–1771.
Published 1771. (ML, 159; RE, 48)

HUMPHRY CLINKER is the last novel of Smollett, who was a major English novelist of his century. The novel is the story of a trip, paralleling a coaching trip that Smollett himself had recently taken throughout Great Britain. It is a wonderful description of the places, people, customs and oddities of Great Britain in the late 18th century. The story is told in letters, a frequent device of novelists in those times. Thackeray said of the novel, "Humphry Clinker is the most laughable story that has ever been written since the goodly art of novel writing began."

A series of letters relate the adventures of a family—a bachelor, MATTHEW BRAMBLE; his spinster sister, Aunt TABITHA; and their niece and nephew, LYDIA (LIDDY) and JEREMIAH (JERRY) MEDFORD, on a trip by coach through England and Scotland.

Matthew's letters to his physician and dearest friend, Dr. RICHARD LEWIS, show him to be a man whose crusty exterior hides a kindly and generous heart. Tabitha's letters to Mrs. GWYLLIM, the housekeeper at Brambleton Hall, their ancestral home in Wales, show her to be penny-pinching, violently opinionated, and frantic at the thought of going husbandless. Jerry's letters to his friend Sir WATKINS PHILLIPS, at Jesus Hall, Oxford, are gay and amusing. Lydia's letters, most of them to LAETITIA WILLIS, her boarding-school chum at Gloucester, are touching confidences from an unspoiled personality. WINIFRED JENKINS, Tabitha's maid, writes letters to Mrs. MARY JONES, another maid at Brambleton Hall, which are quaintly spelled and frankly expressed accounts of the adventures that befall the group.

The first stop is to fetch Lydia from her boarding school. She is a sweet, simple girl When Tabitha learns this she refuses to go on. Matthew ignores her while Humphry rattles off his qualifications: He can read and write, take care of a stable, dress a horse, and shoe him, and bleed him, and rowel him. He can make hogs'-pudding and hobnails, mend kettles, dance a Welsh jig, and find a hare. Matthew calls him a complete fellow and tells him to make peace with Tabitha. They stop at an inn for dinner and in his anxiety to find favor with Tabitha Humphry attempts to serve the meal; but he is nervous and spills some custard on her shoulder. Aghast at what he has done, he steps back—onto the dog, Chowder. Tabitha accuses Humphry of trying to kill Chowder. Matthew grows angry and de-

livers an ultimatum to Tabitha: Either she gets rid of Chowder, or Matthew will leave her. Thoroughly chastened, Tabitha asks only that she be allowed to keep the dog as far as London.

In London their relative Lady GRISKIN shows them the sights and arranges introductions to important people. Tabitha gives Chowder to Lady Griskin. BARTON, a college friend of Jerry's, becomes enamored of Lydia, who gives him no encouragement. Tabitha, however, is quite interested in Barton. Barton takes Jerry to dinner with Mr. S——, a noted author who aids hack writers. Humphry preaches to a crowd on the evils of profane language and Tabitha and Lady Griskin encourage him. Barton goes to ask Tabitha and Matthew for Lydia's hand in marriage and Tabitha tries to construe it as a proposal to *her*. Barton leaves, but sends a note to say that much as he respects Tabitha, it is Lydia he wished to marry.

Clinker is suddenly clapped into Clerkenwell prison on false charges of robbery. He is saved by Mr. MARTIN, a Robin Hood character. Matthew gives Clinker a new horse and Jerry gets a new servant, DUTTON. They set out for Yorkshire and are held up by highwaymen. In the nick of time, Mr. Martin, the highwayman, saves them. At Harrowgate the travelers visit Squire BURDOCK, a relative, and meet Count DE MELVILLE and his family. During their stay at Burdock's, the Melvilles are saved from highwaymen by Grieve, a local apothecary, who is discovered to be their long-lost godson. There is a Scottish advocate of 17 and is infatuated with WILSON, a young actor. Jerry challenges Wilson to a duel, but the local constable intervenes. Uncle Matthew is told by the manager of Wilson's theatrical company that Wilson must be a gentleman, since he has refused to take any salary during the six months he has been with the troupe. Lydia is so upset that she takes to her bed for a week.

The group proceeds to Hot Well at Bristol. Matthew befriends a penniless widow, giving her £20 for the care of her invalid child. Tabitha is very angry with Matthew for "wasting" his money. They go to a hotel at Bath but move to a small house because the hotel is too noisy. Tabitha meets an Irish peer, Sir ULIC MACKILLIGUT, and encourages his attentions. When he finds that her fortune is less than he thought, he uses the excuse that her nasty little dog, Chowder, has bitten him and he disappears. Matthew meets an old friend, JAMES QUIN, and they have a general reunion with several others at a coffeehouse. Chowder bites Matthew's servant, JOHN THOMAS, who is so surly about the incident that he is dismissed.

Matthew hires a coach-and-four to take the group to London. One of the four horses falls, and while no one is hurt, Tabitha refuses to go on without a new postillion. A shabby country fellow is found to replace the postillion. When the carriage arrives at Marlborough, Tabitha begins to find fault

with the replacement for his shabbiness. The man says he is ashamed of his rags, but he has no other clothes and no friend or relation to help him. A long illness has taken all of his savings. Tabitha leaves the room in disgust, taking Lydia. Matthew asks if anyone will vouch for the poor fellow and the landlord identifies him as HUMPHRY CLINKER, who was an assistant to the inn's ostler. When Clinker became ill, the landlord made him leave. Matthew commends the landlord for his Christian charity and gives Humphry Clinker some money. The following day Tabitha is impressed by what she thinks is a new postillion, but it is the same Humphry Clinker in clothes redeemed from the pawnbroker. Harrowgate, Mr. MICKLEWHIMMEN. He is an invalid, confined to a wheelchair, but Tabitha has marital designs on him. There is a fire one night and Micklewhimmen forgets he is an invalid and rushes down the stairs, pushing everyone out of his way.

After stopping at Yorkshire to see the cathedral, they continue on their way to Scarborough. As they are fording a river, the carriage is overturned. Jerry rescues his sister and Dutton saves Tabitha. Humphry is carrying WINIFRED JENKINS, Tabitha's maid and his sweetheart, ashore when Jerry asks where Matthew is. Humphry promptly drops Winifred and turns back to the carriage. A miller comes to Winifred's rescue while Humphry dives underwater and drags Matthew ashore. When Matthew is revived he is very grateful and gives Humphry £30 a year for life.

They arrive at Stockton, where Martin appears again. Matthew gives him a letter to his lawyer, directing the lawyer to arrange for Martin to start a new life in the East Indies. Then they meet a Scottish lieutenant, OBADIAH LISMAHAGO, and Tabitha falls in love with him. He regales them with tales of his sojourn with the English army in America. He was captured by Indians and married an Indian princess, Squinkinacoosta, who died.

Dutton and Humphry contest for the hand of Winifred Jenkins. Dutton paints her face and has her dress like a lady, then takes her to a play. As they are returning home, the crowd ridicules them. The next day an Irishman, Leighlin Oneale, stops at the inn with his intended wife, a pawnbroker's daughter. They are looking for a parson to marry them. Dutton gives the pawnbroker's daughter a whirlwind courtship, and they leave early the next morning and are married.

The group arrives in Edinburgh. Tabitha goes to a summer ball in a heavy brocade gown and is miffed because none of the gentlemen pay any attention to her. They take a boat trip to the coast of Fife, and a storm comes up and they are almost drowned. Matthew and Jerry go to the Highlands while Tabitha, who has just parted from another prospective suitor, Mr. Moffat, over religious differences, takes Lydia for a rest at Cameron. The party reassembles and starts home. They meet Lis-

As the carriage is fording a river, it is overturned

mahago again and he asks Matthew if he has any objections to his marrying Tabitha. Matthew is relieved.

Matthew and Jerry go to dinner at Lord OXMINGTON'S. When the company is dismissed directly after dinner, Matthew is furious at the peer's rudeness and sends Lismahago to get an apology from Oxmington. Instead of apologizing, Oxmington insults Lismahago. Jerry decides to picket the gate of Oxmington's estate. Oxmington finally sends a man to apologize. Lismahago accepts the apology, then kicks the servant in the face.

On the way south Matthew visits an old friend, Mr. BAYNARD, who has an extravagant wife. She has forced Baynard to mortgage his estate and he is at his wit's end. Matthew tries to give him financial advice, but Baynard confesses that he loves his wife so much that he cannot try to make her change. After another coaching mishap, in the course of which Humphry again rescues Matthew, the party lodges at the house of a certain Mr. DENNISON until their coach is repaired. Matthew recognizes Dennison as an old college friend. Dennison speaks to Matthew as Matthew Lloyd of Glamorgan. When Humphry Clinker hears this name, he almost faints. He shows Matthew a cornelian seal and two scraps of paper that say he (Humphry Clinker) is Matthew Lloyd, Matthew's natural son. Clinker explains that his mother died and he took the name of the man to whom he was apprenticed. Matthew explains that he took his mother's name, which was Lloyd, as heir to her lands in Glamorgan. When he came of age, he sold her property to clear his paternal estate, and resumed his real name of Bramble.

As the group is having tea, Dennison's only son, GEORGE, comes in. He proves to be Lydia's love, Wilson. He left home to avoid marriage with a girl he did not love.

The girl married someone else and he returned home and told his parents of his love for Lydia. He and Lydia are betrothed. Tabitha and Lismahago decide to make it a double wedding.

Baynard's wife dies. Matthew spends three weeks helping Baynard to put his estate on a paying basis. Humphry asks Matthew's permission to wed Winifred Jenkins, Tabitha's maid. When Matthew agrees, a triple wedding is celebrated.

Hunger

Novel by Knut Hamsun, 1859–1952. Published 1890.

THIS IS THE DESCRIPTION of the actual hunger and misery of a penniless man. It is so well done that one is often acutely uncomfortable while reading it. Knut Hamsun, one of the principal Norwegian novelists, won the Nobel Prize in 1920 but lost much of the people's respect by being a collaborationist with the Germans during their occupation of Norway in World War II.

Part I. It was autumn, and I was in Christiania. All summer long I had been having trouble getting a job and had kept going by selling an occasional piece to a newspaper. My room was bare and shabby; the door had no workable latch, the wall was papered with old newspapers, and wind blew in through large cracks. Today was a beautiful sunny day and I felt that I could write something really worth while. I started out for the park. In front of me walked a crippled man carrying a heavy burden. He turned down just those streets I intended to walk, and since I was made somewhat lightheaded by hunger I got the idea he was following me. I tapped him on the shoulder and he whined for a little money, saying he was hungry. I told him to wait, pawned my waistcoat, and gave him some money. He looked at my shabby clothes and gave the money back to me. I cursed him and went to a delicatessen, where I bought bread and cheese for the whole of the sixpence I had. I went to the park to write, but found I had left my only pencil in my waistcoat pocket. I returned to the pawnshop and asked for the pencil, saying it had sentimental value to me, since with it I had written my dissertation in three volumes on philosophical cognition. On the way back to the park, I suddenly got the urge to annoy two women who were walking in front of me. I grimaced at them, cackled idiotically, said nonsense words to them, ran ahead of them, waited for them, and told them they had dropped objects I knew they were not carrying—and kept this up until they entered a house. One of them peeked out of the window at me, and I gave her the nonsense name of YLAJALI. In the park I became very depressed and asked God why he so grievously afflicted me. I tried to write but no ideas came to me. A man sat on the bench and I made up a fantastic story and told it to him. I tried again to write, but all I could do was write 1848 up and down and crossways on the paper. I returned home to find a note from my landlady telling me that I must pay my rent. I had seen a grocer's advertisement for a part-time bookkeeper, so I wrote an application. I went to bed, and suddenly ideas for a sketch flooded my mind. I wrote easily and well. I gave thanks to God. The next morning I took my blanket with me when I went to deliver the manuscript to an editor. Hunger gnawed and I started toward the pawnshop to get something on my blanket, but since I had borrowed it, I decided it was wrong to pawn it. I felt very proud of myself for this. I went to see the grocer but I had stupidly dated my application 1848, so he gave the job to someone else. Cursing myself, I wandered aimlessly. That night I slept in a field. I had six shaving tickets. I wrapped these and my necktie in a clean piece of writing paper and set out to peddle them, but upon approaching the first prospective buyer I became overwhelmed with shame and ran away, leaving the package in his hands. I went back to my room, hoping I might sneak in. On the table was a letter accepting my sketch, with payment of half-a-crown. I hurried out, and shouted, laughed, and cried, as I ran and jumped along the street.

Part II. One evening a few weeks later, I was sitting in a churchyard trying to write an article. It was not going well because I had not eaten for three days. I made a horn out of a sheet of paper and let the wind blow it away. I almost convinced myself it was full of coins. I looked at my belongings, which consisted of paper, a pencil, half a penknife, and a bunch of keys. I suddenly found myself in the palace of my beloved Princess Ylajali and all her beautiful and tender serving maidens. Then all this dissolved in a shower of stars as the policeman on the beat shook me awake. I started off without my hat and he asked me if I were drunk. I was very indignant but felt I had achieved revenge when he picked up the empty horn to see what was in it. I went to my room above a livery stable but I had lost my keys. I went back to the policeman, who told me to report myself to the police station as homeless. I did so and gave my name and occupation as ANDREAS TANGEN—*journalist*. At first I could not sleep; my heart beat wildly, and I was sure I was dying. In the morning, I was not given a meal, like other homeless men, because I was a journalist and they felt it might insult a professional man. I went to my room and was going to ask the stable-boy for the loan of a shilling, but he asked me first to lend him five shillings. I promised to get him the money that afternoon. I tried to find a friend, the theological student Hans Pauli Petterson, but could not. I found a piece of wood to chew on, and that helped a bit. I also found a pin and got the idea that if I used it to hold my coat together I could cut off my buttons and pawn them. I went to see an editor who had bought articles from me, but could not get an advance. I wanted to ask for the loan of a shilling but was too ashamed. I went to see a pastor but was too early for his office hours, which were 12 to 4. I suddenly remembered my blanket and rushed it to the pawnshop, but somehow I first tried to pawn my spectacles, for which "Uncle" would give me nothing because the frames were of steel. Nor would he take the worn blanket. I went back to the pastor's, but it was now after four and I had missed him. On a sudden unreasonable impulse, I went into the office of Cisler, the music seller, and asked for a loan. Of course, he refused me, for he had never seen me before. I went into several shops begging shamelessly, telling them how hungry I was, but no one would give me even a penny. A woman approached me; when she came close, she cried out, "Oh, what a face!" I felt sure I was dying. I hurried back to the pawnshop to pawn my buttons, but Uncle just laughed at me. I begged, but to no avail. As I was leaving, a friend of mine entered the pawnshop to borrow on his watch. He told me that if I would wait for him he would give me five shillings.

Part III. I had eaten something every day for a week, but now I had only a few pence left. I went to the editor of a popular journal with an article on Correggio. He told me kindly that it was too scholarly, that I should try something with an appeal to a wider audience. He offered me an advance on such an article, but I turned it down with thanks. Back at my room I tried to work on an article, but it grew dark and

I had no candle. I went out to walk. Near the Parliament House, I spoke to a girl. She was glad to walk with me, but I hastened to tell her I had not a penny. She would not believe me until she had turned all my pockets inside out. She asked me if my eyeglass frames were gold, and when I told her they were not, she told me to go to blazes. Then she came after me, and said I could come with her, anyway. I thanked her and gave her a lecture on morality, tell-

She told me to go to blazes

ing her I was Pastor So-and-so. I went to a store where I thought my credit might be good and asked a clerk, who knew me, for a candle. He was attending to a woman customer and told me to wait. When at last he gave me the candle, he also gave me change for a crown, thinking I had already paid. I became almost delirious but finally got hold of myself and gathered the coins into my hand to return them. I had walked away from the counter, and the clerk called to me that I had forgotten the candle. All I could think of was to run out of the store. It was my first theft. I went to a restaurant and ordered some beef; I told the waitress to keep the change. When I went out I became nauseated and vomited my meal. I asked a passer-by what one should do in such a case and he said warm milk was good. I went to a café and had some warm milk. When I neared home, I saw across the street from the livery stable a woman I had seen there before. I spoke to her and she let me walk with her. It turned out that she was Ylajali, one of the two women I had annoyed several weeks before. She had merely thought me a bit drunk. When we arrived at her home, she kissed me before she ran into her apartment. The next day it snowed hard. I went to the bazaar to see if I could pick up a second-hand waistcoat. I met a friend and had a glass of beer with him. It made me drunk. Suddenly, I feared that the police would arrest me for theft and that Ylajali would hear about it. I took all the money I had and gave it to a poor woman selling cakes. Then I felt pure again. I took a hansom cab to several ad-

dresses, looking for a wool dealer named Kierulf, who existed only in my imagination. I sneaked away from the cabbie, and walked and walked. I thought over my condition. I was gaunt, my hair was falling out, there was a bloody sore in the middle of my stomach, and my clothes were utterly filthy. I went into a butcher shop and begged a bone for a dog. It had a tiny piece of meat on it. I tried to suck on the bone, but its odor made me retch. I began to cry and hiccough and shout. Suddenly I remembered the ship *Nun* that had been in the harbor. Maybe I could get a berth. I hurried to the harbor but the *Nun* had sailed. Back in town, I ran into the editor, the "*Commandor,*" who had offered me an advance. He observed my condition and gave me half-a-sovereign. A few evenings later, I met Ylajali. Her mother was out and their maid had the evening off. We went to her apartment. I made amorous advances and terrified her. She wept and I desisted. I talked and talked until she asked me to go, fearing I was insane. But when I was about to leave, she let me kiss her.

Part IV. Deep winter had set in. I was living in a lodging house for travelers down in the Vaterland district. My money was long since exhausted. My rent was overdue, but my landlady had not said anything about it yet. I had tried to write, but ideas wouldn't come. My landlady asked me to add up some figures for her, since her accounts would not balance, but hunger made my head swim and I could not find the error. She became angry and said I could not go on living on credit. I tried again to write, but the landlady returned to tell me she had a traveler to put in my room and I would have to get out. A terrible fear of being out in the streets overcame me, and I begged to be allowed to stay downstairs for the night. I was allowed to sleep in an anteroom with no stove. Some good ideas for an allegorical drama came to me, and I worked at them. I managed to sleep on the floor of the anteroom for a few days. One day I saw Ylajali in the company of a famous gallant. I was shocked and heart-sick and I lost all further interest in Ylajali. I went to the provisioner's store and confessed I had stolen the change from a crown. The clerk asked me if I were not ashamed. I said I had given the money to the poor, and walked out indignantly. Finally my landlady made me leave. I went down to the harbor, where I saw a Russian barque discharging coal. Useful ideas came to me and I tried to write something, but the harbor noises distracted me. I went back to my former lodging house and sneaked up to my old room. I wrote furiously for a while. Then the landlady found me and ordered me out. Just as I was leaving, a messenger arrived with a letter for me. It was just an envelope with half-a-sovereign in it, no note. I asked the messenger who sent it. He said it was a lady. I knew it was from Ylajali and I was humiliated. I crumpled the envelope with the coin in it and threw it in the face of my landlady. Then I went out, so weak from hunger I could hardly walk. I wondered if there was a way to get the half-sovereign back. I remembered the cake seller to whom I had given the money I stole from the provisioner. I went to her and demanded cakes for the money. She whined and haggled but gave me several cakes. I walked around the market place eating the cakes, but my hunger´ was not assuaged. I went to the harbor and asked the captain of the Russian barque for a job, but I was indifferent about getting one. He talked to me kindly, and suddenly I wanted the berth more than anything in the world. I promised to work as hard as two men. At last he hired me. We were to sail to Leith in ballast and then fetch coal for Cadiz.

An Iceland Fisherman

Novel by Pierre Loti (Julien Viaud, 1850–1923).
Published 1888. Translation from the French by Frederick T. Chapman published 1946 by Alfred A. Knopf, New York.

"PIERRE LOTI" was a remarkably popular novelist in France and several of his novels were popular in translation. Perhaps the best liked is *An Iceland Fisherman*, a short novel (only about 60,000 words) about Breton sailors. Loti in his actual identity was a naval officer and wrote of the sea with affection and authority.

Part I. Chaps. 1–2. The French fishing boat *Marie* is in the cod-fishing waters off Iceland. SYLVESTRE MOAN, a manly looking boy of 17, is the youngest aboard. Another is YANN GAOS, whom Sylvestre regards as a brother because he is engaged to Yann's sister. Yann is huge in stature, quiet, and aloof. He is not married, though he is 27; he tells his shipmates he is going to marry the sea and invites them to the wedding. The sailors on the *Marie*, under Captain GUERMEUR, are all Frenchmen from around the towns of Paimpol and Treguier in Brittany. Each year at the end of the winter they sail to fish in the Arctic waters, leaving the homeland destitute of husbands and lovers. They return home briefly at the end of the summer, then go south to sell their fish, buy salt, and indulge in the pleasures of southern ports before returning home for the winter. Many never return from Iceland.

Chap. 3. Back in Paimpol, Sylvestre's old grandmother, YVONNE MOAN, is writing him a letter with the help of GAUD (Marguerite) MÉVEL, a comely young blonde. Gaud was cared for by Grandmother Moan when she was a motherless little girl years

before, while her father was in Iceland. Then her father made a lot of money by piratelike activities and Gaud lived in Paris and other cities. They have only recently returned to settle in Paimpol. Grandmother Moan thinks of Sylvestre, her only remaining grandson. All her other grandsons and sons have been swallowed by the Iceland sea. Now when Sylvestre returns he must go into military service for five years.

Chaps. 4–5. Gaud thinks of Yann, whom she secretly loves. She recalls how they first met, soon after her return to Paimpol at the age of 20. Yann was polite, but distant. Then one day she was to attend a wedding ceremony, and he was chosen as her partner. Afterwards, at the ball, he danced with her all evening. She found that he was not only fierce, handsome, and distant, as he appeared from the outside, but also gentle and sincere. He told her all about his life and the things he loved, and how he enjoyed being with her. She had expected to see him again soon, but she never did; he seemed to avoid her. She wonders why. Was it because of the city manners she acquired in Paris? Was it because she was richer than he?

Chap. 6 & Part II, Chap. 1. Off Iceland the *Marie* sights a mail and supply steamboat and makes toward it. Yann and Sylvestre read their letters from home. Sylvestre makes a complimentary reference to Gaud and Yann reacts with annoyance. A wind arises and the boats head for the open sea where they can better buck the storm. The wind becomes a furious gale and there are gigantic waves. Yann and Sylvestre, at the helm, laugh and sing as the boat rises and plunges.

Chaps. 2–4. The men are back home safely and Sylvestre has left for the service.

Gaud stops at the chapel

Gaud has not seen Yann, and she pines for him. She goes to his house at Ploubazlanic to aid in a business transaction between her

father and Yann's father. On the way she stops at a windy little chapel dedicated to sailors lost at sea. In it she sees plaques for many men of the Gaos family, lost in Iceland. Yann is not home, to Gaud's disappointment. That night Yann's parents tell him that he should marry. He says he never will.

Chaps. 5–10. Grandmother Moan receives a message that Sylvestre is to leave for China. She rushes off to see him at his base and they spend three days together, but part sadly. Sylvestre's trip takes many, many days and Sylvestre sees many strange new sights: The bright colors and bustling barter of Port Said, the silvery ribbon of the Suez Canal tapering across the sands, the blood-red water and burning sun of the Red Sea, the lush vegetation and exotic women of India, and finally the little yellow men of China.

Chaps. 11–13. Gaud has waited all winter but has not seen Yann. Then, on the day before the men are to leave for Iceland, Yann comes to her house on business with her father. Just as he is leaving she summons all her courage and rushes down to him, and asks him what she has done to incur his disfavor. He acts as if he is trapped, says that she is rich and he is poor, mumbles something else, then rushes off. She is left quivering with anguish and despair. The next day Yann leaves. The *Marie* runs onto a bar off the foggy coast of England, but late that night it washes clear. On the opposite side of the world, Sylvestre receives a note from his grandmother. It is not in Gaud's handwriting and Sylvestre worries. The letter tells him that Gaud's father has died. His fortune had been dissipated and Gaud is now penniless. Grandmother Moan concludes that Gaud and Yann will never get married.

Part III. Chaps. 1–7. Sylvestre is detailed for actual battle. The troops, marching through a rice field, are shot at, then charged. Sylvestre assumes leadership and with the butt of his rifle he bashes his way into the chargers and sends them spinning. But one turns and shoots him in the chest. Sylvestre is awarded a medal for bravery and is put on a hospital ship to be sent home. The ship is crowded, without ventilation, and sultry hot. Sylvestre pleads for more air, but he does not get enough and he dies. His body is buried in Singapore and his possessions auctioned off among the sailors. To Grandmother Moan the news is devastating. She staggers home from the commissioner's office and little children laugh at her, thinking she is drunk. The Moan family will be extinct when she dies. Gaud finds the old woman at home "whimpering plaintively like a child." Gaud goes to live with Grandmother Moan and take care of her.

Chaps. 8–11. When Yann in Iceland hears the news of Sylvestre's death he says nothing, but alone he weeps. The *Marie* is enveloped in fog for several days. In the fog it meets another boat from Paimpol and through the mist the sailors exchange hellos and information. Later it becomes known that the other boat has been wrecked.

Chaps. 12–17 & Part IV, Chaps. 1–8. The *Marie* returns home, but Gaud only sees Yann once, when they pass on the road. She is living in utter poverty with Grandmother Moan, doing needlework to stay alive. Grandmother Moan is out of her mind part of the time. There is not enough wood to keep the cottage warm. Then one day late in the winter, when Yann is on his way home with his pay from the last fishing season, he comes upon Grandmother Moan screaming at some boys in the street who have just stoned her cat to death. Gaud has just run up. Yann chases the boys away, then the three walk silently to Grandmother Moan's cottage. To Gaud's surprise, Yann enters and suddenly, hesitantly, asks her to marry him. She is overwhelmed, and weeps. The marriage is arranged for a short time later, before Yann leaves for Iceland. The two are deeply, passionately, in love, and spend many hours together. Gaud discovers to her relief that Yann's long avoidance of her was due only to stubbornness. Everybody had tried too hard to push him at her. He had been in love with her all along. On the day of the marriage a heavy storm arises and the sea roars ominously. Six days remain before Yann's departure, six days of tenderness and apprehension.

Part V. Chaps. 1–11. Yann and Gaud take a sad farewell of each other. Yann leaves on a new boat, the *Leopoldine*. Throughout the summer Gaud works hard and with her savings prepares the house for Yann's return. She also knits him a sweater. August comes and one of the boats comes in, then others. During the next weeks they all straggle in but two. Gaud tries to stay cheerful. Then the last boat, besides the *Leopoldine*, comes in. Lovers and husbands are greeted with gaiety. Gaud goes out each day and watches the sea from a rocky point guarded by bleak crucifixes. Day after day passes, and Guad beats her head against the wall. The long nights of winter finally come, but the *Leopoldine* never returns. Yann has finally married the sea forever, and all the sailors he invited years ago, except Sylvestre, were at the wedding.

I, Claudius

Novel by Robert Graves, 1895– Published 1934 by Random House, New York. (ML, 20)

THE VERY VERSATILE British author Robert Graves is a scholar as well as a poet and novelist. Because of the scholarship that prepared him for the writing, and the faith he had in his own interpretations of history, *I, Claudius* is an unusual historical novel. For example, Graves makes Livia, the wife of the emperor Augustus, one of the most powerful women of history and this is advanced as a serious interpretation, not as the usual device to make the novel easier to write. The novel is purported to be written in the first person by the emperor-to-be Claudius himself and if the book occasionally becomes a bit intricate in style and plot, Graves explains that this is consistent with the senile personality of Claudius. Many thousands of readers have found *I, Claudius* intensely interesting. Besides, it is a pleasant way to absorb some of the complex record of Roman history in those confused times.

Chaps. 1–4. CLAUDIUS, born in 10 B.C., is now 51 years old and Emperor of Rome. He was the son of the beloved general DRUSUS and ANTONIA, through whom he was related to the Caesars. His uncle was TIBERIUS, who reigned after AUGUSTUS, named URGULANIA, the daughter of one of Livia's closest confidantes. This was in 6 A.D. The next year, Germanicus was adopted as Tiberius's son into the Julian side of the Caesar family, and Claudius became head of the Claudian side. Postumus was trapped in an embarrassing situation in Livilla's room and was shipped away to an abandoned island. Livia had now made Tiberius Augustus's sole heir, with Germanicus and Castor after him.

Chaps. 12–13. Claudius compiled an Etruscan lexicon, yet everyone pitied him as a hopeless dunce. The Germanic wars met a disastrous turn for the worse but Germanicus managed to recover some of the lost territory by brilliant maneuvers, and his popularity soared—except with Livia. Germanicus persuaded Augustus that the exiled Postumus was innocent and the emperor brought Postumus back to Rome, masquerading as a servant, but Livia discovered the ruse and Postumus was stabbed one night in the street. In 14 A.D. Augustus fell sick. Livia fed him with her own hands, and a few days later he died. Tiberius became the second Caesar to rule the Roman Empire, though the people at large favored Germanicus.

Chaps. 14–16. A mutiny broke out among the Roman soldiers in the Rhine Valley when Tiberius was made emperor. Tiberius sent Castor to quell the riots, but Castor could not. Even the tough Lieutenant SEJANUS could not quiet the men, who were underpaid and brutally treated. As a last measure, Germanicus sped to Germany from France and won over the mutineers by his eloquence. The men wanted to make the general emperor, but Germanicus nobly refused. Germanicus's wife Agrippina gave birth to a beautiful baby boy named Gaius. This baby was popular with the troops, who gave him the nickname CALIGULA, or Little Boots, because he was often dressed as a soldier. Soon afterward Agrippina gave birth to a beautiful daughter, AGRIPPINILLA. Both of these children were fated to come to evil ends.

Chaps. 17–20. At the start of his reign Tiberius ruled moderately and well, despite the meddling of his mother Livia, but gradually he reduced freedom and he quartered a large Imperial Guard in the city, directed by the ambitious Sejanus. and Augustus died. His grandmother LIVIA, wife of Augustus, had an insatiable thirst for power and somehow managed to get rid of her enemies. Augustus adopted his young relative MARCELLUS as his heir, and Marcellus died suddenly after a banquet. General Agrippa proved popular with the people, and was quietly edged into retirement. Livia managed to marry her son by a previous marriage, Tiberius, to JULIA, Augustus's daughter through a previous marriage. Augustus and Livia had no children from their own marriage.

Chaps. 5–6. After his father's death, Claudius lived in a large mansion on the Palatine Hil in Rome, near the Imperial Palace. His mother, like everyone else, preferred Claudius's strong, handsome brother, GERMANICUS. Claudius's self-willed sister LIVILLA also treated him badly. Only Germanicus was kind to the stuttering, bumbling, half-crippled Claudius. Claudius plunged himself into historical studies of the Etruscans and Carthaginians. Tiberius also turned his mind toward meditation, for he was shocked by the flagrant misconduct of Julia, yet could not complain to Augustus about his own daughter. Tiberius got permission to retire to Rhodes, where he studied and debauched with equal intensity. Gaius and Lucius, Julia's sons by a previous marriage, themselves informed the emperor of their mother's immoral behavior. Livia quietly sentenced Julia to exile on the bleak island of Pandataria. Augustus never again to hear Julia's name. The two sons never reaped any reward; both died under mysterious circumstances.

Chaps. 7–11. Livia continued to plot so that her family would inherit the throne. The exiled Julia's last surviving son, POSTUMUS, was denied marriage with Claudius's sister Livilla, whom he loved. Instead, Livilla was betrothed to Tiberius's only son, CASTOR. Germanicus was married to one of Julia's daughters, AGRIPPINA. Germanicus and Tiberius were made generals of armies in Germany, but crippled Claudius was left in Rome, where he wrote histories until Livia forbade it. Claudius wanted to marry the lovely daughter of a famous general, but the girl died suddenly on the eve of the ceremony and Claudius was forced to wed a ferocious, manlike girl

Tiberias surrounds himself with philosophers and astronomers

Tiberius surrounded himself with philosophers and astronomers. In 16 A.D. Claudius deserted his wife and son DRUSILLUS to devote himself to scholarly pursuits at Capua, near Naples. Postumus, whom everyone believed dead, returned to Rome, expecting support from the rabble, but he was captured and quietly put to death. Germanicus won great successes in the north and in 17 A.D. Livia and Tiberius had to give him an extravagant triumphal parade.

Chaps. 20–21. The jealous Tiberius sent Germanicus and his wife to guard the eastern provinces, and dispatched a fawning nobleman named GNAEUS PISO and his wife PLANCINA to oversee Syria and counteract Germanicus's power. Germanicus and Piso haggled continually. Germanicus suddenly fell ill and died in the year 19. The Roman populace cried murder. Livia and Tiberius, to pacify the mobs, indicted Piso for murder, but Plancina stealthily produced letters from Livia urging Germanicus's death. Plancina's blackmail secured her own safety, but Piso died under circumstances judged to be suicide.

Chaps. 22–23. Again the Palace seethed with intrigue for determining Tiberius's heir. His only son, Castor, was hated by the people for his cowardice and drunkenness. Livilla plotted Castor's downfall with Sejanus, her new lover. Castor took sick suddenly and died in the year 23. The next struggle was between Livia and Sejanus. Sejanus proposed to marry his daughter to Claudius's son Drusillus, but Drusillus was found choked to death. Livia became increasingly fond of Caligula, who was now a thoroughly spoiled young man. Sejanus helped Claudius to divorce his monstrous wife Urgulania and marry Sejanus's adopted sister AELIA.

Chaps. 24–26. The rift between the 80-year-old Livia and her son Tiberius deepened. One night the old woman summoned Claudius to a dinner attended by Caligula. She revealed prophecies naming Caligula as Tiberius's successor and predicted that Claudius would avenge Caligula's death. She shamelessly confessed her poisonings. Then she gave Claudius a prophetic book that predicted that the fifth Caesar (including Julius, Augustus's predecessor) to enslave Rome would be "that idiot whom all despised." Livia died a natural death in the year 29, with Claudius at her side. Tiberius had taken to living on Capri, surrounded by hundreds of jaded companions. He left Rome in charge of his heir, Nero [not the one who became emperor], the eldest son of Agrippina, and Captain Sejanus. Tiberius had now become suspicious of Sejanus, because Sejanus had begged unsuccessfully to marry Livilla.

Chap. 27. With his mother dead, Tiberius lashed out unmercifully against his long-hated enemies. He used Sejanus to accuse Agrippina and her two eldest sons, Nero and Drusus, of moral turpitude. All three were exiled and slowly starved to death. To guard against a popular uprising the emperor spared Caligula, naming him the new imperial heir. Sejanus was preparing the way to seize control of the state, but in 31, Antonia found her daughter Livilla's treasonable love letters to Sejanus and dispatched them quickly to Capri. On Tiberius's order, Sejanus was executed; his body was dragged through the streets for three days and most of his friends and relatives were massacred, including Aelia. Antonia locked Livilla in a room in the palace and starved her to death.

Chap. 28. Tiberius appointed a crude guardsman named MACRO to replace Sejanus as captain. The emperor remained at Capri, often summoning Caligula to his depraved parties. At last, in 37, he started out for Rome but took sick and was carried to Misenum, near Naples. Caligula took the emperor's ring, believing him to be dead. Tiberius began to rise from a coma and Macro snuffed out his life with a pillow. Thus, at the age of 25, Caligula became the third emperor of Rome. The people hailed him, for he was Little Boots, sole surviving son of the great Germanicus.

Chaps. 29–31. Caligula began his reign auspiciously by denouncing Tiberius as a tyrant. He established his three sisters in the palace, DRUSILLA, Agrippinilla, and LESBIA. Caligula's good works came to an abrupt end the next year when he was seized with an epileptic attack. One night Caligula announced to Claudius that he was a god. From that time on, his reign was a nightmare. Caligula first eliminated his logical successor, Gemellus, son of Castor and Livilla. In protest against this crime, Antonia committed suicide. Caligula next condemned Macro to death and appointed the aged CASSIUS CHAEREA, a heroic soldier, to take his place. Despite his indiscriminate murders, the Roman people loved Caligula, for he was munificent with horse-shows and theater spectacles. His insanity showed itself more and more, especially when he nominated his horse Incitatus for a political office. Claudius was bankrupted from helping to pay off the emperor's debts. Caligula's sisters died or were banished. Claudius was spared because he was the butt of many of Caligula's cruel jokes.

Chaps. 32–34. Caligula showed one of his rare moments of good humor by betrothing Claudius to the beautiful but dangerous MESSALINA. At last, in 41, Captain Chaerea, along with two men named Cassius and Vitellius, struck down Caligula after a play. Claudius heard the uproar inside the palace and hid himself in his bedroom. As soldiers ransacked the palace, killing all of Caligula's friends and servants, they found Claudius quivering behind a tapestry. Recognizing him as Germanicus's brother, they raised him on their shoulders and bore him into the court, crying "Long live Emperor Claudius!" The cry spread, and without any formality or decree, Claudius became the fourth ruler of Rome, just as his grandmother Livia had predicted. His thoughts at that exciting time were not about glory and fame, but about the marvelous peace and leisure time he would have for completing his histories.

345

The Idiot

Novel by Feodor Mikhailovich Dostoevski, 1821–1881.
Published 1869. (ML, G60)

THE IDIOT IS ACCOUNTED among Dostoevski's greatest novels, though it is always placed behind *The Brothers Karamazov* and *Crime and Punishment*. Against the background of fashionable Russian society it tells the story of the deterioration of a man who begins as an eccentric and neurotic and inevitably achieves a hopeless end.

Part I. Chap. 1. On the train to St. Petersburg Prince MYSHKIN and PARFYON ROGOZHIN strike up an acquaintance. Myshkin is returning from Switzerland, where he was sent to be cured of epilepsy. He is penniless but is related to the wealthy Mme. EPANCHIN, the wife of a general. Rogozhin ran away from his home after quarreling with his father about a woman, NASTASYA FILIPPOVNA, whom Rogozhin loves; but now his father has died and he has inherited a large fortune. Rogozhin invites Myshkin to visit him, and promises to give him money and take him to see Nastasya. Myshkin confesses that he knows nothing of women, because of his illness, and Rogozhin is attracted by his new friend's innocence.

Chaps. 2–3. Myshkin calls on General Epanchin, his wife, and their three daughters, ALEXANDRA, ADELAIDA, and AGLAIA, 25, 23 and 20 years of age. They are all intelligent and beautiful, especially the youngest, and devoted to one another. Myshkin's good humor, frankness and childlike manner win the general's friendship. He gets the prince a small government job and arranges for a room for him at the home of his secretary, GANYA ARDALIN-OVITCH IVOLGIN. Myshkin is told that Ganya's family is too poor and that Ganya wants to marry Nastasya.

Chaps. 4–6. Nastasya was adopted as a small child by a gentleman of means and position, AFANASY TOTSKY. He educated her well and when she reached 16 he moved her into a house and made her his mistress. Now, at 55, Totsky wants to marry Alexandra. Nastasya has threatened to prevent his marriage. Totsky enlists Epanchin's help and they offer Ganya a large amount of money if he will marry Nastasya. Nastasya has not agreed to marry Ganya. She fears he may not respect her, because of her life with Totsky. On the evening of her birthday she plans to announce her decision. General Epanchin is himself in love with Nastasya and has bought her a string of pearls for her birthday. Myshkin tells Mme. Epanchin and her daughters of his experiences: how an execution he witnessed made him appreciate life; how in Switzerland he befriended a poor consumptive girl, MARIE, whom everyone mocked, and taught the children of the town to be kind to her.

Chaps. 7–9. Ganya gives Myshkin a note to take to Aglaia. She is the one he really loves, and if she will tell him to do so he will break off his relationship with Nastasya. Aglaia is not interested. Myshkin goes home with Ganya and meets his family: Ganya's long-suffering mother, NINA ALEXANDROVNA; his father, old General Ivolgin, who constantly tells boastful tales, most of them lies, and who drinks away the household money; and Ganya's sister, VARVARA, 25 years old, who is proud and stubborn. Ganya is frightened of her. Nina's younger son, KOLYA, quickly makes friends with Myshkin. Nina and Varvara strongly disapprove of Ganya's proposed marriage to Nastasya, calling it a disgrace to their honor. Nastasya comes to call, her first call, and Varvara and her mother are polite. Ganya is ashamed to have her meet his eccentric family, especially when his father tells her a charming anecdote, of which he is the hero, and she says she has read the same story in a magazine.

Chaps. 10–12. Rogozhin and a group of friends, half-drunk, burst into Ganya's apartment. Rogozhin has brought money to pay Ganya if he will abandon Nastasya. When Rogozhin sees Nastasya, he throws 80,000 rubles into her lap and begs her to accept him. Varvara insults Nastasya. Ganya starts to strike his sister but Myshkin interposes himself between them and receives the blow. Everyone is shocked. Myshkin goes to his room, Kolya follows to comfort him, and Ganya comes in to apologize. Ganya says General Epanchin has offered him a large sum to marry Nastasya and then let her become the general's mistress. Myshkin asks General Ivolgin to take him to Nastasya's birthday party, at which she will announce her decision, but the general is drunk and takes Myshkin instead to his mistress MARFA's flat. Kolya is there, visiting his friend, Marfa's son, IPPOLIT, who has consumption and is dying. Kolya's mother and sister help Marfa with money. Kolya takes Myshkin to Nastasya's house.

Chaps. 13–14. Myshkin, though he is not in evening clothes, is cordially welcomed by Nastasya. Epanchin, Totsky and Ganya are among the guests. There is a game in which each guest must tell the worst action of his life. Epanchin and Totsky tell harmless stories of youthful adventures. When it is Nastasya's turn she asks Myshkin whether she should marry Ganya and says she will abide by his decision. Myshkin is embarrassed but tells her she should not; Ganya has told him he will be cruel to her. In the turmoil that follows, Nastasya tells Totsky she will set him free and he does not have to pay for it. At this point Rogozhin arrives, with a dozen friends.

Chaps. 15–16. In a fever of passion Rogozhin puts 100,000 rubles before Nastasya. She becomes hysterical and says that she might just as well sell herself to the highest bidder. Myshkin tells Nastasya that he loves her and wants to marry her. He says he will work for her if they are poor, but he has a letter from a lawyer saying he has inherited a large fortune from an aunt. Epanchin knows the lawyer and says it must be true. Everyone congratulates Myshkin and Nastasya muses on becoming a princess—no longer the mistress of Totsky, but respected in society. Then she decides she is unwilling to ruin the prince. Also she is afraid of his goodness and afraid he will reproach her after they are married. She accepts Rogozhin's offer to run away with him, though it will ruin her for-

Ganya throws the money in the fire

ever. As for Ganya, she takes the 100,000 rubles, wrapped in paper, and throws them into the fire. She tells Ganya they are his if he will fetch them. His vanity prevents him from moving, but the strain is so great that he faints. The money, almost unharmed, is taken out of the fire, and Nastasya throws it near Ganya's unconscious body. Then, calling for wine and music, she leaves with Rogozhin and his troupe.

Part II. Chaps. 1–2. Prince Myshkin goes to Moscow to collect his inheritance. He is very popular in good society but after several months he leaves to chase Nastasya, who has left Rogozhin even though he offered to marry her. Totsky breaks off his engagement with Alexandra because he is infatuated with a French woman. Prince S., a man of the government, becomes engaged to Adelaida and his cousin, YEVGENY POVLOVITCH, pays court to Aglaia. Varvara marries a wealthy friend of Ganya's, PTITSYN, because Ganya is ill and cannot support the family. General Ivolgin is put into prison for debt, but he is happy telling stories to his fellow prisoners.

Chaps. 3–4. After six months Myshkin returns to Petersburg and goes to Rogozhin's house. Nastasya came to Myshkin in

Moscow after she left Rogozhin, but now she has run away from Myshkin and is planning to marry Rogozhin. Rogozhin tells Myshkin that Nastasya betrayed him several times with other men, and that she treats him badly and shames him in public, but his passion for her has only grown in intensity. Rogozhin knows Nastasya loves Myshkin—too much to marry him. Myshkin and Rogozhin pledge friendship and brotherhood, but this is marred by Rogozhin's ironic and mistrustful smile.

Chap. 5. Myshkin begins to feel absent-minded and confused, as he used to before an attack of epilepsy. He broods on Rogozhin's jealousy and he realizes that Nastasya shows symptoms of insanity. In his hotel, Myshkin sees Rogozhin come out of the shadows and raise a knife. He has an epileptic fit and falls down stairs. Rogozhin, frightened, runs away. When Myshkin recovers Kolya is taking care of him.

Chaps. 6–8. Myshkin goes to visit LEBEDYEV in the suburb of Pavlovsk. Lebedyev's other visitors include General Ivolgin, Kolya, Ptitsyn and Varvara, and Ganya. Mme. Epanchin and her daughters, along with Prince S., come to call. They too have a house in Pavlovsk. Aglaia recites a poem, directed to Myshkin, about a poor knight who suffers because of a lady and loses his reason. The prince realizes that Algaia is mocking him. Four young men, one of whom is Ippolit, come to see Myshkin on behalf of a young man named BURDOVSKY, who claims to be the illegitimate son of PAVLISHTCHEV, the man who adopted Myshkin and sent him to Switzerland. Burdovsky seeks to recover the money his supposed father spent on Myshkin, and he and his friends have published an article calling Myshkin an idiot (insane person) and demanding Myshkin's fortune for the real son. Myshkin says he is willing to give Burdovsky 10,000 rubles because Burdovsky is deceived in his claims by wicked friends. Myshkin has proof that Pavlistchev had no son, that he was abroad for one and a half years before Burdovsky's birth. Myshkin seeks the friendship of the young man who tried to take his fortune from him and he offers to give them money, but they are too proud to accept it. Mme. Epanchin is enraged not only by the young men but by Myshkin's attempt at Christian charity, which seems to her like an act of idiocy. Ippolit starts to cough blood and tells the gathering that the doctor has given him only two weeks to live. Delirious, he says he is now 18 and everything is over for him; he hates them all for pitying him; he hates Myshkin, because all Myshkin's good actions are misunderstood and ineffectual. He leaves with his friends. At this point Nastasya drives up to the house and calls out to Yevgeny that his I.O.U.s have been bought from the moneylender by Rogozhin and will be paid. Yevgeny protests that he has no I.O.U.s and is not on intimate terms with Nastasya. General Epanchin suspects that Nastasya is trying to spoil Aglaia's marriage as an act of revenge against him. Myshkin

is very depressed and does not understand the intrigues around him. Myshkin too now loves Aglaia.

Part III. Chaps. 1–3. Myshkin returns to Petersburg and has Ippolit come to stay with him. He tells the Epanchins that Ippolit caused trouble only because he wanted to give everyone his blessing and be blessed in return. Aglaia becomes hysterical, saying that Myshkin is too good to everyone; she is angry at him because he does not know that he is the most worthy of men. Aglaia often mocks Myshkin, because she really is very much in love with him. The Epanchins go to a public band concert in the park and Nastasya is there and loudly tells Yevgeny that his uncle, from whom he expected to inherit a fortune, has shot himself because he was suspected of taking money. A friend of Yevgeny's says that Nastasya should be whipped. She takes a whip and hits him across the face. In anger he tries to hit her but Myshkin prevents him. Rogozhin comes and takes Nastasya away. Aglaia slips the prince a note asking him to meet her in the park the next morning. Later Rogozhin tells him that Aglaia and Nastasya have been writing to each other; Nastasya wants Myshkin to marry Aglaia and will not marry Rogozhin until Myshkin and Aglaia are married. Myshkin says he believes Nastasya is out of her mind.

Chaps. 4–7. At Myshkin's villa his friends are waiting to celebrate his birthday. Ippolit begins to read his confession. He tells of experiences that have influenced him; he has come to believe that the universe is unjust and he would like to avenge himself and kill a dozen people. He has decided to shoot himself at sunrise, as a gesture of protest. When he is through reading most of the party mock him, and he runs into the garden and tries to shoot himself but the pistol does not go off. He falls unconscious and is taken to his room.

Chap. 8. Myshkin is unable to sleep and waits in the park until Aglaia meets him. Aglaia wants to run away from home; if he will not have her, she will marry Ganya. Myshkin tells Aglaia that he is no longer in love with Nastasya; his love has turned to pity. He explains that Nastasya tries to shame herself for revenge on Totsky, and that she cannot live with the love and respect Myshkin wanted to give her. But Aglaia believes that Myshkin loves Nastasya, and that Nastasya would kill herself if he married Aglaia. She says she will marry Ganya.

Chaps. 9–10. Nastasya sends three passionate love letters to Myshkin. She fears Rogozhin will kill her, but she will marry Rogozhin if it will help Myshkin find happiness. Myshkin asks her to stop writing to Aglaia. Nastasya catches Myshkin in the woods and asks him if he is happy. Myshkin does not answer and Rogozhin comes and takes Nastasya away.

Part IV. Chaps. 1–2. Myshkin is betrothed to Aglaia. Adelaida has postponed her wedding to have a double wedding with her sister. Ganya is bitter about the engage-

ment and also is worried about scandal: He believes his father has stolen 400 rubles to give to Marfa. Ippolit is now living with Ptitsyn and seems to be getting better. Ganya wanted Ippolit to live with the Ivolgin family, for Ippolit is now corresponding with Aglaia and Ganya wants him to influence her against Myshkin; but Ippolit dislikes Ganya and is unwilling to harm Myshkin.

Chaps. 3–4. General Ivolgin never really took the stolen money. He tells Myshkin a long, false story about his close friendship with Napoleon when he was a little boy, and Myshkin listens politely, but the general becomes angry anyway, suspecting Myshkin of pity rather than respect. The general runs from the house, raving, and has a stroke in the street.

Chap. 5–7. At a fashionable party at the Epanchins' Myshkin becomes excited while talking against the Roman Catholic Church. He is very anxious to please the company so as to impress Aglaia. In one of his gestures he breaks a valuable vase, and though Mme. Epanchin forgives him the strain is too much and he falls into an epileptic fit. This only makes Aglaia love him more.

Chaps. 8–12. Aglaia is still jealous of Nastasya and angry that she is receiving a man at another woman's command. She takes Myshkin with her to see Nastasya. The prince dreads the meeting, knowing that Aglaia wants him to prove that he loves her and not Nastasya. Actually he is afraid of Nastasya's insanity, but his compassion for her is so great that it is a form of love. He loves Aglaia, in a different way, and wants to build his life with her. The two women insult each other. Nastasya, her pride hurt, says Myshkin would leave Aglaia and marry her if she demanded it. Aglaia asks Myshkin to come to her. He hesitates, seeing Nastasya's desperate expression. His hesitation is too much for Aglaia; she runs from the house. Myshkin starts to follow but Nastasya faints and he stays with her. Aglaia becomes ill and is taken away by her parents. Nastasya sends Rogozhin away and prepares to marry Myshkin. There is a general scandal. General Ivolgin dies. The day set for Nastasya's wedding to Myshkin comes. As Nastasya walks down the aisle she sees Rogozhin. She begs him to take her away and he runs out of the church with her to Petersburg. Myshkin says he rather expected this to happen; he is quite calm. The next day he goes to Rogozhin's house. They tell him the master is not at home and Nastasya has not been there, but from the street he can see Rogozhin looking at him from behind a curtain. That night he returns and Rogozhin lets him in and shows him the body of Nastasya, still in her wedding dress, stabbed through the heart. Rogozhin is in a fever and begins to rave; Myshkin consoles him. When they are found the next day, Myshkin has again become an idiot. Rogozhin stands trial two months later and is sentenced to 15 years in Siberia. Yevgeny sends Myshkin back to Switzerland for treatment, but the doctor there is

347

afraid that he is now incurable. Aglaia marries an exiled Polish nobleman who has a false title, and refuses to have anything to do with her family.

Idylls of the King

Poem by Alfred, Lord Tennyson, 1809–1892.
Published 1859–1885.

TENNYSON MAY HAVE WRITTEN the *Idylls of the King* as part of a project that was intended from the start to tell the entire Arthurian legend, but he worked on the twelve idylls (scenes) for more than 40 years and not in the order in which they logically would be placed. Collected, the *Idylls of the King* have been one of the most widely read poems in English. The whole has a moral theme—that evil is never isolated but spreads far and wide, wherefore the unlawful love of Lancelot and Guinevere destroys the faith of all the knights, ends the effectiveness of the Round Table, and leaves King Arthur nothing to do but go to his supernatural end in Avilion (Avalon). Another strong moral is drawn when the knights of the Round Table go out on a wild search for the Holy Grail instead of fighting the evil that occurs at home. The poetry is very smooth, in blank verse that is easy to read and sounds good to the ear.

THE COMING OF ARTHUR

LEODOGRAN, King of Cameliard, calls on ARTHUR to help him drive out invaders and eliminate wild beasts. Arthur comes and for the first time sees Guinevere, Leodogran's only daughter, with whom he falls in love. Arthur sends three knights to ask for Guinevere's hand. Leodogran is uncertain about Arthur's birth and questions the knights. BEDIVERE tells how Arthur's father, King UTHER, fell in love with another man's wife, made war on him, and married the widow. Arthur was the child of this marriage. As a baby he was given into the magician MERLIN's care until Merlin judged the time had come to make Arthur's true identity known. Leodogran is still uncertain. BELLICENT, Queen of Orkney and Arthur's half-sister, tells Leodogran the story that was told to her by BLEYS, Merlin's master. The two magicians found a baby washed up on the shore. It was the night of King Uther's death and Merlin said the baby was Uther's heir. Leodogran decides that Arthur is truly of royal birth and gives his blessing to the marriage of Arthur and his daughter. LANCELOT, Arthur's bravest knight and dearest friend, comes to fetch Guinevere and she and Arthur are married.

GARETH AND LYNETTE

GARETH is the youngest son of Bellicent and Lot. Gareth's mother wants to keep him at home with her but he is eager to go to Court and become a knight. Finally his mother consents, on condition that for a year and a day he disguise himself as a lowly kitchen hand. Gareth agrees and after a month Bellicent releases him from his promise. Gareth begs Arthur to make him a knight. Arthur consents on condition that only Lancelot know of it.

LYNETTE comes to entreat Arthur to free her sister, LYONORS, who is held prisoner by a wicked knight and his three brothers. Gareth begs to undertake this mission. Lynette is insulted, thinking Gareth is only a kitchen hand, but Arthur gives permission and Gareth and Lynette set out. On the way Gareth endures the scorn and contempt of Lynette. Gareth fights and defeats the three brothers, Morning Star, Noonday Sun, and Star of Evening, and Lynette softens a bit. Lancelot appears and mistakes Gareth for Morning Star and fights him. Lancelot defeats him, but Gareth, when he learns who his conqueror is, does not feel ashamed. The last contest Gareth must wage is with Death. When he splits Death's skull, he discovers that Death is really a young boy whose wicked brothers have forced him so to disguise himself. Tennyson assures the reader that Gareth married Lynette, though the older legends say he married Lyonors.

THE MARRIAGE OF GERAINT
GERAINT AND ENID

GERAINT, one of Arthur's brave knights, falls in love with ENID, the daughter of YNIOL, who has come to poverty through the treachery of his enemies. Geraint brings Enid to Court. Guinevere dresses her in beautiful garments and everyone is happy. However, Geraint grows insanely jealous and spends all his days thinking about whether Enid is true to him, so that people "began to scoff and jeer and babble of him." Enid is grieved by this and while Geraint sleeps, she questions whether, as a loyal wife, she must tell her husband how foolish his behavior is. She murmurs, "I fear that I am no true wife." Geraint hears this and is sure that Enid is unfaithful. He then puts her through all sorts of humiliating tests, making her set out with him attired in old clothes, never speaking, and riding ahead in sorrowful silence. Enid proves her true love for Geraint in every encounter. Finally, when Geraint is wounded by the Earl of Doorm, and Enid's tears rain on his face, Geraint at last realizes that Enid is true and they are happy together again.

BALIN AND BALAN

BALIN and BALAN are twin brothers. Balin is a good knight but has a terrible temper. He worships the queen, Guinevere, and when he spies her walking with Lancelot in the garden and remembers the rumors he has heard about them, he grows mad with anger and pain and leaves the court in a rage. He meets the fair but wicked VIVIEN, who enflames his suspicions. When BALAN,

his brother, comes along and sees Balin, he mistakes him for a demon and there is a terrible battle between the brothers. Both are mortally wounded. Balan assures Balin that the queen is true and the brothers die in each other's arms.

MERLIN AND VIVIEN

Vivien is the mistress of MARK of Cornwall, Arthur's rival. She comes to Arthur's court and spreads evil rumors and scandal everywhere. Finally she departs with the mighty magician, Merlin. She uses every kind of strategy and cunning wile to persuade Merlin to tell her his secret charm. Merlin, though he is old and wise, cannot resist her charms and finally tells his secret. Then Vivien has the mighty Merlin in her power. She works the charm, "And in the hollow oak he lay as dead." Vivien exults.

LANCELOT AND ELAINE

Lancelot has left his shield with Elaine to guard in her tower at Astolat because he is to attend the last of Arthur's diamond jousts in disguise. For eight years Arthur has held a contest and to the victor has gone a diamond found long ago by Arthur in the crown of a murdered king. Lancelot has won all eight diamonds. Now he intends to win the last diamond and present it to the queen. Lancelot overcomes all contenders. However, since he is disguised, his loyal friends band together to attack the "stranger" and the mighty Lancelot is wounded. LAVAINE, Elaine's brother, takes him to a lonely cave and Elaine nurses him back to health. She falls deeply in love with Lancelot and begs to be his wife. Lancelot loves her with every kind of love except that of a man for a woman. He says had he met her before he knew the queen, it might have been different. He bids farewell to Elaine, who dies of a broken heart. When Lancelot returns to court, he presents the diamond to Guinevere. She, in a fit of jealousy, throws the diamond out the window into the river. As Lancelot sadly watches the diamond fall, he sees a barge coming down the river carrying Elaine's body. (She had made her family promise that when she died they would put her on a barge and send her down the river to Arthur's Court.) Arthur reads a letter in Elaine's hand, revealing her ill-fated love for Lancelot. Lancelot thinks to himself that he is unworthy of his great name.

THE HOLY GRAIL

PERCIVAL, known as "Percival the Pure," has become a monk. He tells AMBROSIUS, his fellow-monk, of the quest for the Holy Grail. Once when Arthur was away, all of the knights took a vow to follow the Holy Grail (the cup from which Jesus drank at the Last Supper). When Arthur hears what has happened he is grieved; for, he says, there is much work to be done in the world. Still, the knights have taken a vow and must go. Sir GALAHAD, of whom Arthur

Pelleas, when Ettarre betrays him, follows her to her castle

once said "God made thee good as thou art beautiful," succeeds and Percival and BORS have a vision of the grail. Lancelot makes a noble attempt but in him there is a sin which he cannot pluck out (his love for Guinevere) and so he fails. Most of the knights not only fail but die in the attempt. Arthur, seeing all the empty places at the Round Table, realizes in sorrow that in searching for the Holy Grail "and leaving human wrongs to right themselves" his knights have been untrue.

PELLEAS AND ETTARRE

PELLEAS, a brave young knight, falls in love with ETTARRE, who urges him to win a golden circlet for her in the tournament. She promises him her love as a reward. Pelleas performs this great feat and then the cruel Ettarre mocks him. Pelleas cannot believe this treachery and follows her to her castle. She turns him out and sends three knights to battle with him. Pelleas defeats them all. Then GAWAIN, another of Arthur's knights, comes along and promises to make the cold-hearted Ettarre relent. Instead, Gawain makes love to Ettarre himself. Pelleas discovers this betrayal and his love towards Ettarre dies. She, on the other hand, realizes that Pelleas is the one true knight and her only love. She pines for him the rest of her life. Pelleas learns from Percival that Lancelot and Guinevere are also false. He meets Lancelot and they fight and return together to the Court. The queen sees that something is wrong and there is a general feeling of impending doom.

THE LAST TOURNAMENT

Arthur's court is gloomy and sad. Everyone now knows about the love of Lancelot and the queen except Arthur, who leaves the Court and orders Lancelot to preside over the tournament. TRISTRAM, husband of ISOLT of Brittany, wins the tournament. He, however, is in love with another ISOLT, the wife of MARK. Tristram visits her and when Mark discovers the lovers he murders Tristram. Arthur returns to Court to find the queen's quarters dark and empty. She

has gone and only DAGONET, the fool, is there.

GUINEVERE

Sir MODRED spies on Lancelot and Guinevere. The lovers realize that their love must bring ruin to all and they must part. As they are saying their last farewell, Modred bursts in on them. Lancelot and Guinevere leave the Court in haste. Lancelot returns to his own land and Guinevere goes to a nunnery at Almesbury, where, in an agony of grief and repentence, she remains with only a young serving girl to comfort her. Arthur comes to her and forgives her and the queen finally understands that he is

really the man she wanted. But it is too late. Arthur leaves and Guinevere becomes an abbess in the nunnery. After three years she dies.

THE PASSING OF ARTHUR

Bedivere, now old, tells of the end of Arthur. On his way to put down Modred's rebellion, Bedivere hears Arthur lamenting that he has failed because he could not find God in men. Bedivere urges Arthur on and they go to fight Modred. There is a terrible battle in a dense fog "And friend slew friend not knowing whom he slew." Finally only Modred, Bedivere and Arthur remain and in a final combat Arthur slays the traitor Modred and is himself severely wounded. Arthur tells Bedivere to take Excalibur, his famous sword, and throw it into the lake and tell him what occurs. Twice Bedivere goes to perform Arthur's bidding and twice he hides the sword, thinking to save some token of the great king. Arthur is furious and threatens to slay Bedivere if he does not obey. Bedivere then does as Arthur commands and sees a ghostly arm clutch the sword, raise it high and disappear. Arthur knows that his time has come and orders Bedivere to carry him to the lake. A barge appears, crowded with dark figures. Three queens who have guarded over Arthur's life are there. Arthur says, "The old order changeth, yielding place to new,/And God fulfills himself in many ways." He asks Bedivere to pray for him and says that he will go now to Avilion.

If Winter Comes

Novel by A. S. M. Hutchinson, 1880–
Published 1921 by Little, Brown and
Co., Boston. © 1921, 1949 by A. S.
M. Hutchinson.

THIS NOVEL WAS tremendously popular when it was published in 1921. It is the story of a gentle man, spiritually wed to the ideals of beauty, generosity, and kindness, in life wed to a woman who neither understands nor would sympathize with his spirit and tries ruthlessly to mold him to her pattern. Later, his own innocence and unawareness of the evil minds of others lead him into a combination of circumstances that break his heart and almost destroy his body. But fortunately there are those who understand and love him and even more fortunately they include the woman he has always loved. The title is from the last line of Shelley's "Ode to the West Wind": "If winter comes, can spring be far behind?"

Chap. 1. Introduction. Year 1912. A garrulous solicitor, one HAPGOOD, is telling a friend about his recent meeting with an old schoolmate of theirs, MARK SABRE. They

used to call Sabre "puzzlehead" because he was always thinking, to try to see someone else's point of view. Sabre now has a plush job in Tidborough with the Fortune, East & Sabre Co., furnishers of ecclesiastic and scholastic goods. Sabre lives in Penny Green, a charming little village but rapidly changing under the hard-pushing hands of "garden suburb" promoters, particularly the vicar of Penny Green, the Venerable BOOM BAGSHAW. Sabre is married, but without children. His wife is pretty but Hapgood had lunch there and detected a suspicious stiffness between her and "old puzzlehead."

Chaps. 2–5. Penny Green is 7 miles from Tidborough. It is restful, old, quiet, green, and centuries away from the bustle of the modern world. Sabre lives in a big house, 250 years old. It is flawlessly managed by MABLE, his wife, whom he married in 1904. Early in their marriage Mable set aside for him a special room and called it his "den." He did not relish the stereotyped personality of old slippers, hunting togs, and pipes. Then Mable hired two maids, sisters named Jinks. Sabre called them "High Jinks" and "Low Jinks." She saw no humor in this and scolded Sabre for joking with "those sort of people." Mable and Sabre took separate bedrooms once when she was sick and never moved back together again. Sabre loves poetry and all forms of beauty, an appreciation Mable does not understand. Mable looks down on the "baser classes," people for whom Sabre feels compassion. But people consider Mable "refined, nice, and efficient." Every day Sabre rides his bicycle to and from work, 7 miles each way. During these rides he achieves a sense of detachment from the world and can think, view life philosophically. He also has a little game to see how far the bicycle will coast down the hill when he comes home each day. Mable has no patience with this, but the maids love it.

Chap. 6. The Fortune, East, and Sabre Co. has implacable dignity and a highly esteemed position. Mr. Fortune, the chief director, looks "like a stunted whale" and wears the expression "I have decided." Sabre is the founder and director of the department that publishes textbooks. He has great pride and love for the books, which have received wide acclaim, and he feels he is entitled to a partnership in the firm.

Chap. 7. Since Mable gives Sabre no sympathetic interest, he turns to what she thinks are "funny" friends. There is old Mr. FARGUS, who is harried by a wife and seven grown daughters. He plays chess and acrostics with Sabre. He feels that everybody has been put into life to fulfill a divine purpose. Then there are Sabre's friends the PERCHES. Mrs. Perch is a fragile old lady with a huge old house chockful of stuff accumulated over a lifetime. She lives with her bright, "birdlike" son.

Part II. Chap. 1. While riding his bicycle Sabre reflects that some of his marriage problem is his own fault in that he is capable of seeing his wife's point of view but won't, whereas she is incapable of seeing his. Just then he bumps into Lord TYBAR, debonair, carefree, and mocking, who is accompanied on horseback by his wife, NONA. An awkward conversation ensues, for Sabre was tremendously crushed ten years before when Nona chose Tybar instead of himself.

Chaps. 2–3. Sabre finds that the smooth-mannered, evil-tongued TWYNING, his associate, is going to be promoted to partnership. Sabre is keenly hurt. He decides he has not made enough effort at home, so he takes the afternoon off for a surprise holiday with his wife. She responds without enthusiasm, as her daily routine is upset, and snaps at him about a friendly note he has received from Nona. Then Bagshaw comes for lunch. Sabre disagrees with him about the virtues of the new Garden Home project. Mable is annoyed. Sabre's effort has been a failure.

Chaps. 4–7. Nona visits Sabre at his office. There are strong hints that she is unhappy. She responds warmly and excitedly to his ideas and enthusiasms, as no one else has done. His sympathy-starved soul leaps. Some indications that Lord Tybar has mistresses, to Nona's great distress, then appear. Sabre goes home and Mable dresses him down for always riding his bicycle to work. Some days later Sabre meets Nona

alone and she admits that she made the wrong choice for marriage. He groans, and walks away. His thoughts swing to his wife and the overwhelming sense of duty he feels toward her. He encounters a soldier named Otway, who warns him that there is going to be a war. Another scaremonger . . .

Part III. Chaps. 1–2. The year 1913 is bustling with debatable topics and no matter what the issue, Mark Sabre seems always to be on the wrong side both at business and at home. He will not go to Nona, but his mind desperately turns toward her.

Chaps. 3–9. Twyning is made a partner and brings his son, HAROLD, into the business. Mark receives a letter from Nona asking him to take her away. He writes to her to think it over and he will write again in one week. On the day he was to write to Nona war is declared. He becomes highly wrought emotionally and does not write. Instead he rushes home to tell his wife about the war, but she responds apathetically. Sabre tries to join up but is turned down because of his bad heart. Young Freddie Perch decides to join the army, but he must first find someone to take care of his mother. Sabre suggests EFFIE BRIGHT, the daughter of one of the men at his business, a loving, cheerful, pretty girl. The arrangement is made and Freddie goes off to war. Nona writes to Sabre and tells him Tybar has gone off to war, too, a gallant officer, and has been awarded a V.C. (Victoria Cross, the highest decoration for valor). Tybar has not written to Nona, however, only to other women. On New Year's Eve, when Sabre is relaxing with Mr. Fargus, he receives a note from Effie Bright that Freddie Perch has been killed. Sabre rushes over and finds Mrs. Perch dying. He and Effie sit up all night watching her die. When she dies, Sabre is torn apart, but when he tell Mable she merely finds it "funny" that he spent the whole night, and with Miss Bright there. So Sabre rushes off and this time manages to get into the army. He is overseas fighting for two years. He is delighted to hear that Mable has taken Effie Bright to live with her, but when he returns on leave he finds that Mable is bullying Effie, whose spark has dimmed. Sabre sticks up for her. Mable suspects something between them and abruptly fires Effie. Sabre returns to the

war, and in passing discovers that Tybar has been killed. Sabre is eventually knocked out of the war by a badly wounded knee.

Part IV. Chaps. 1–8. [Hapgood returns as narrator.] Hapgood made a recent visit to Sabre. Sabre was walking with a stick. Hapgood noticed a high tension between him and his wife. Sabre talked of his intense loneliness. He also spoke on how the modern god is a material god and will bring a fall. On Hapgood's next visit he finds Sabre alone with a young unmarried girl and her baby. The girl is Effie, who was turned from all doors and came to the Sabres for sanctuary. Mable objected, but Sabre refused to turn her out. So Mable left. Mr. Fortune heard about it and fired Sabre. Then the whole social world had ostracized and excommunicated him. Sabre was not bitter, but bewildered. He had not even thought that the baby might be thought to be his.

At Brighton one month later Hapgood meets Sabre, who is taking a short vacation to think. Sabre says he has finally found the key to life—that God is love! Sabre has also cut off communication with Nona. Then a divorce petition arrives from Mable, citing adultery. Sabre is torn with anguish and incredulity. To top everything off, he receives a message that Effie and her baby have been found dead, poisoned by oxalic acid. He had bought the acid for her; she said she wanted to clean his straw hat. The next day the inquest begins. Effie's father has hired a vicious, humpbacked lawyer who is prompted by the malicious Twyning. They proceed to attempt not only to pin the paternity of the child onto Sabre, but also to make a case that Sabre induced Effie to take her life. Sabre refuses to have a solicitor, and all evidence turns against him. The lawyer keeps turning his knife. Suddenly Nona enters, curses the court, and rushes to Sabre. He pushes her away. The jury finally judges high censure upon Sabre. Sabre has almost gone out of his mind with pain. He goes home and finds a note from Effie that says the father of the baby is Twyning's son, Harold. Sabre flies into a passion of fury and rushes to Twyning's office. He finds Twyning sobbing at his desk with a telegram that his son has been killed. Sabre throws Effie's note into the fire, rushes into his old office, and has a stroke. Nona and Hapgood take him to the hospital. He is in a coma for many days. Meanwhile the divorce proceedings go through. When Sabre finally regains consciousness Nona is beside him. He says he does not want to see her again. She hesitates, then takes him in her arms for the first time. He breaks down and cries "Beloved!"

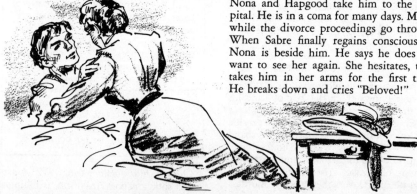

Sabre finally accepts the love of Nona

The Iliad

Epic poem by Homer, before 700 B.C.
Written perhaps 1000 B.C. Many translations and editions.

THE MAJORITY OF ALL the scholars
of all the lands of the Western world,
throughout history, have considered
the *Iliad* the greatest poem ever written. Perhaps a measure of its greatness
can be found in the excellence of so
many translations of it (Chapman's
translation sent John Keats into
ecstasies) and the stature of the poets
who have undertaken to translate it,
including Alexander Pope. The *Iliad*
is attributed to Homer, of course, but
no one knows who—or if—Homer
was. It must simply be assumed that
some great genius wrote or compiled
and edited the *Iliad,* and why not call
him Homer? The *Iliad* does not tell
the whole story of the Trojan War,
which is already in progress when the
poem opens, but nearly every event
leading up to the war is recalled in one
part or another of the *Iliad.* The *Iliad*
is the source of much of the standard
Greek mythology as it is known today.
The ancient name for Troy was Ilium
and *Iliad* means "about Ilium."

Books 1–10. The war of Troy was in its
ninth year and despite great and heroic
deeds on both sides it was a draw. Then
AGAMEMNON, commander of the Greeks
and brother to MENELAUS, quarreled with
ACHILLES, greatest of Greek heroes, because
Agamemnon kept the captured CHRYSEIS,
daughter of CHRYSES, priest of Apollo,
for himself. Apollo sent pestilence into the
Greek camp. Agamemnon consented to give
up the girl, but demanded that Achilles give
up BRISEIS, a beautiful captive maid.
Achilles agreed but declared that he would
withdraw his forces and return to Greece.

Among the gods and goddesses, Juno
and Minerva, hostile to Paris, sided with the
Achaians (Greeks); Venus backed the
Trojans, as did Mars, an admirer of Venus.
Neptune, due to Thetis's influence, supported the Greeks. Jove, though fond of
PRIAM, King of Troy, and Apollo were
impartial, siding sometimes with one and
then with the other. THETIS, mother of
Achilles, asked Jove to punish the Greeks
for the injury done to her son. Jove granted
her request and the Trojans won a battle,
driving the Greeks back to their ships.

Agamemnon heard NESTOR'S advice at
council: Yield Briseis and send gifts to
Achilles to atone for the wrong. Ulysses,
Ajax and Phoenix went to Achilles with
the penitent message, but Achilles refused
to return.

Books 10–20. The Greeks defended
themselves behind fortifications they built
around their ships, and the Trojans be-

sieged them. The Trojans broke through
and made ready to set the Greek ships afire.
In this emergency Neptune, in the form of
CALCHAS the prophet, appeared and inspired the Achaians to new effort and they
chased the Trojans back. AJAX, the huge
and heroic warrior, carried the day by meeting HECTOR, Priam's great son, the leader
of Troy's armies, in single combat. Ajax
hit Hector with a stone on the neck and
Hector fell. His bodyguard carried him off
the field.

Jupiter missed this phase of the battle
because Juno borrowed Venus's girdle,
which made the wearer irresistible, and
went to see him. Juno's wiles succeeded.
Jupiter found her so charming that he
forgot about battle, affairs of the world,
and everything. When Jupiter looked down
upon the scene of battle and saw the fallen
Hector, half dead, angrily he sent Juno
away and sumoned Apollo and Iris: Apollo
to heal Hector's bruises and revive his
heroic spirit, and Iris to tell Neptune to
return to the sea, his dominion. The stern
orders were carried out with the speed of
lightning and Hector, fully revived, returned to battle.

In this battle MACHAON, son of AESCU-
LAPIUS and inheritor of his father's art of
healing, was wounded by Paris's arrow.

Old Nestor with Machaon's body

Machaon was of great importance to the
Greeks, being their surgeon and also an
outstanding warrior. Old Nestor carried
Machaon past Achilles' ship on his chariot.
The hero recognized Nestor but not the
wounded chief, so he sent his companion
PATROCLUS to Nestor's tent to inquire.
When Patroclus wanted to return to Achilles' tent, Nestor held him back and told him
about the grave troubles of the Greeks. The
time had come for Patroclus to use his influence and win Achilles back to the Greek
cause; but if Achilles would not return, at
least let him send his soldiers into battle
with Patroclus, clad in Achilles' armor, the
sight of which alone might drive the Trojans back.

Patroclus told Achilles of how badly the
Greeks were faring: Diomedes, Ulysses,
Agamemnon and Machaon were wounded;
the Trojans were about to burn the ships,

and if so the Greeks' return would be cut
off. Just then one of the ships burst into
flames. Seeing this, Achilles relented partially. He allowed Patroclus to lead the
Myrmidons (Achilles' soldiers), wearing
his armor. Patroclus leading the Myrmidons
had a decisive effect. The Greeks attacked
with renewed heroism. The Trojans, seeing
the much-feared armor, retreated. The ships
were freed, the fires extinguished. Ajax,
Menelaus and Nestor pursued the fleeing
Trojans. Hector himself fled, leaving his
men to be slain by Patroclus.

Only SARPEDON, son of Jove, dared to
stand against Patroclus. Jupiter would have
intervened to save his offspring, but Juno
warned that if Jupiter interfered this time,
all dwellers on Olympus would act similarly
whenever their children were in danger.
Consequently Patroclus killed Sarpedon.
The Greeks succeeded in stripping the fallen hero's armor but Jove commanded
Apollo to carry the body away. Patroclus
won every point until he was confronted
by Hector, who killed Patroclus with his
spear. A bitter battle started for Patroclus's
body. Hector took Achilles' armor and put
it on in place of his own. Ajax and Menelaus
fought Hector and his foremost heroes and
Jove sent a cloud to cover the scene of battle. Ajax, wishing to send a messenger to
Achilles with the news of Patroclus's death,
prayed to Jove for daylight. When that
was granted, ANTILOCHUS was dispatched
to Achilles. The Greeks were able to take
the body to the ships, though pursued by
Hector and AENEAS at the head of the Trojans.

Achilles was beside himself from grief.
Thetis, deep in the sea, heard her son's
groans and hurried to his side. Achilles
blamed himself for Patroclus's death. Now
there was only one way to redeem himself:
revenge. He was ready to go out to find
Hector. His mother reminded him that he
had no armor. She went to Vulcan's place
and the god of fire and the forge started
work on a new suit of armor for Achilles,
and in one night the splendid new armor
was completed. Dressed in his new armor,
Achilles called a council of the chiefs. He
was reconciled with Agamemnon and urged
the Greeks to go to battle at once.

Books 20–24. Achilles threw himself into
battle with such ferocity that the men of
Troy either fell by his weapons or fled before him. Apollo kept Hector out of battle
but urged Aeneas to face the raging Achilles. Aeneas did not decline the combat,
though he thought himself unequal. Neptune, moved to admiration by the courage
of Aeneas, spread a cloud between the two
and lifted Aeneas from the ground and carried him to the rear of the battle. Achilles
attacked others with such force that the
Trojans fled in havoc. Priam ordered the
gates to be opened to let the fugitives in,
then shut in time to keep out the foe. Even
so Achilles would have penetrated the city
had not Apollo disguised himself as
AGENOR, one of Priam's sons, and stood up
before Achilles. The hero turned upon

him and he fled with haste, in this manner drawing Achilles far from the walls. Then Apollo disclosed himself to Achilles, who gave up the chase.

Hector was unhappy at the defeat of his men, and though Old Priam, his father, and HECUBA, his mother, pleaded with him, he was determined to face Achilles. He could not fail the heroic people who went to war on his command, and it was too late to offer Helen and all her treasures back to the Greeks. While he was so engrossed in his thoughts Achilles attacked him, and Hector fled. With Achilles in pursuit, they encircled the city walls three times. Minerva took the form of Hector's bravest brother, DEIPHOBUS, and appeared at Hector's side. With such support Hector dared to face Achilles. Hector threw his spear, which bounded back from Achilles's shield. Hector turned to Deiphobus for another spear, but there was no Deiphobus. Now Hector knew that his last battle had come. He rushed into the combat with drawn sword but was struck by Achilles' spear in the vulnerable part where the armor leaves the neck uncovered. Mortally wounded, Hector fell. He asked Achilles to spare his body to be ransomed, but Achilles granted no such honors to the dying hero, the dogs would feed on his carcass. He stripped Hector's body of its armor, fastened cords to the feet and tied them behind his chariot, and dragged the body of Hector to and fro before the city. Great weeping went up from the city of Troy. ANDROMACHE went to the wall and fainted from pain, foreseeing her country defeated and herself and her son living in the miseries of capitivity.

Meanwhile Achilles brought Hector's body to the Greek ships. Now that revenge was taken on Patroclus's killer, Patroclus's body was burned amidst due funeral rites and games. Achilles twice dragged Hector's body around Patroclus's tomb, then left it lying in the dust. Apollo, however, preserved the body free from all disfigurement.

Jupiter had had enough of Achilles' vengeance. He told Thetis to advise her son to give up Hector's body and he had Priam go to Achilles for the body of his son. Priam, with one follower, old Idaeus, the herald, and with rich treasures for a ransom, left Troy for the enemy camp. Jupiter assigned Mercury to guide and protect him. Mercury's wand put all guards to sleep. Old Priam kneeled before Achilles and reminded him of his own father, who may expect his son to return to him, and begged for Hector's body. Achilles was moved to pity by Priam's hoary locks and beard. He raised the old king and himself put Hector's body, safely covered, on a litter to be taken back to Troy. He pledged 12 days of truce for the funeral. Hector's ashes were placed in an urn of gold, which the Trojans buried in the earth; and they erected a massive pile of stones over the place.

The Importance of Being Earnest

Play by Oscar Wilde, 1854–1900. Published 1895. (Viking, P16)

THIS IS A FARCE, in that the characters do not act like sensible human beings; but apart from the few conceits that Oscar Wilde introduces to justify his plot, the dialogue is the standard conversation of a drawing-room comedy and the epigrammatic wit of Wilde is superb—it is always better than anyone else's. *The Importance of Being Earnest* was a dramatic success and it is also very amusing to read.

Act 1. In the morning room of ALGERNON MONCRIEFF'S London flat, LANE, Algernon's valet, is arranging tea. Algernon is expecting his aunt, Lady AUGUSTA BRACKNELL, and her daughter, GWENDOLEN FAIRFAX. JACK WORTHING, known to his town friends as ERNEST, arrives unexpectedly. He has come to town from his country estate expressly to propose to Gwendolen. Algernon, on behalf of his cousin, asks Jack who CECILY is. Jack explains that Cecily is the granddaughter of THOMAS CARDEW, a man who adopted Jack when he was a child. Cecily now lives at Jack's country place in the charge of her governess, MISS PRISM, and Jack is Cecily's guardian. Jack is known in town as Ernest so that Cecily will never hear of his gay adventures. He tells Cecily he has a wild young brother, Ernest. Algernon tells Jack he is an old "Bunburyist." Algernon has invented a friend named BUNBURY, who lives in the country and conveniently dies, requiring Algernon's presence at a funeral, whenever Algernon wants to avoid a boring dinner or any other embarrassing engagement. Lady Bracknell and Gwendolen enter and Algernon contrives to leave Jack and Gwendolen alone. Gwendolen tells Jack that she loves him primarily because his name is Ernest. He suggests that Jack is a good name too, but she finds that it lacks musical vibrations. Jack proposes marriage, going down on his knees. Gwendolen accepts, just as Lady Bracknell reënters. Lady Bracknell sends Gwendolen downstairs, then takes out a notebook and pen and begins to quiz Jack on his smoking habits, his age, his income, his property. She seems pleased with his answers until she discovers that Jack was found by the kind Mr. Thomas Cardew in a handbag in the cloakroom of Victoria station. He was named Worthing because Cardew had a ticket to Worthing, the seaside resort. Lady Bracknell refuses to consider Gwendolen's marrying someone so socially indiscreet as to be found in a handbag. She tells Jack his only hope is to find at least one parent before the London season is over. She sweeps out, but Gwendolen rushes back and says she will love her Ernest forever. She promises to write to him at his country house and Algernon secretly writes down the address, as he has developed a desire to meet Cecily.

Act II. In the garden of Jack's manor house, Miss Prism is trying to hold Cecily's attention but Cecily is wishing her Uncle Jack would bring his brother Ernest down. She finds her uncle too serious and proper. The Canon CHASUBLE comes and persuades Miss Prism to go for a walk with him. MERRIMAN, the butler, brings Cecily a card on a tray. It announces Mr. Ernest Worthing. Algernon enters and greets his "cousin Cecily." He praises her beauty and promises to try to reform that afternoon. Cecily invites him to lunch and they go in. Miss Prism and Dr. Chasuble return. Jack enters, dressed in mourning clothes, and tells Miss Prism and Chasuble that his brother Ernest has died. They offer him condolences. Jack asks Chasuble if he might be christened that afternoon; he wants to change his name to Ernest, the name that pleases Gwendolen. Cecily comes out and tells Jack his brother has arrived. He says this is nonsense, but Cecily goes back in and returns leading Algernon by the hand. Algernon, acting the repentant brother, asks Jack to forgive him, and Cecily makes Jack shake hands with Algernon. Ernest, according to Cecily, is not as bad as she had been led to believe; he often visits a sick friend named Bunbury. Algernon is left alone with Jack and tells him he has fallen in love with Cecily. Jack insists that Algernon leave on the next train. The dogcart is brought to take Algernon to the station but Cecily has it wait while she talks to Algernon. The next time Merriman announces the dogcart, Algernon sends it away for a week and asks Cecily to marry him. She consents and tells him that she has long been in love with him because she loves the name Ernest. He asks if she would marry someone named Algernon and she says she would not. So Algernon rushes off to find the vicar and have himself rechristened Ernest. Gwendolen arrives and she and Cecily talk. Cecily says she is engaged to Ernest Worthing and Gwendolen says there is some mistake, *she* is engaged to Ernset Worthing. The two women draw verbal swords, but Jack enters and Gwendolen discovers that her Ernest is also Jack. Then Algernon returns and is recognized as Ernest by Cecily. The girls put arms around each other and decide they have both been deceived. They go into the house to console each other.

Act III. Gwendolen and Cecily hear the explanations of Algernon and Jack. They agree to forgive everything, since both men plan to be christened Ernest. Lady Bracknell arrives, furious with her daughter for running away. She is told Algernon and Cecily are engaged, and she inquires about Cecily's family. Relieved to find the girl well-connected, she gives Algernon her consent. But Jack, as Cecily's guardian, refuses to give his consent. Cecily does not come of age until she is 35. Algernon promises to wait that long but Cecily is impatient. Jack says he will give his consent only if Lady Bracknell allows him to marry Gwendolen, and she refuses. Dr. Chasuble enters and announces it is time for the christenings; he is impatient, because Miss Prism is waiting for him. When Lady Bracknell hears the name Prism she becomes excited and asks to see the woman. Miss Prism comes in, seeking the canon, and when she sees Lady Bracknell she tries to hide. It seems Miss Prism once was the governess for Lord Bracknell's baby. In a moment of absentmindedness she placed the baby in her handbag and left the bag in the Victoria station. Jack runs to his room and brings back the bag in which he was found by Mr. Cardew. Miss Prism recognizes the bag as hers. Jack was the son of Mrs. Moncrieff, Lady Bracknell's dead sister, so Algernon and Jack are brothers. Jack's original name was Ernest. Jack and Gwendolen embrace. Chasuble and Miss Prism embrace. Algernon and Cecily embrace. Lady Bracknell says, "My nephew, you seem to be displaying signs of triviality." Jack replies, "On the contrary, Aunt Agatha, I've now realized for the first time in my life the vital importance of being earnest."

Independent People

Novel by Halldor Kiljan Laxness, 1902– Published 1945.

HALLDOR LAXNESS, the great modern Icelandic novelist who received the Nobel Prize in 1955, based this modern novel on ancient legends of Iceland. In general, however, it is a study of fierce pride, which most persons would call stubbornness but which Laxness, in the novel, treats with the greatest understanding. At the end, Laxness finds a means to introduce some of his socialistic ideas.

Chaps. 1–2. KULUMKILLI, the Irish sorcerer, sailed to Iceland in the early days of the papacy. Norsemen forced him to flee, but he cursed the land and lived on as an Evil Spirit. Later the Mistress GUNNVOR worshiped the fiend Kulumkilli and sacrificed her children, her husband and all travelers to his blood feast. The folk of ALBOGASTATHIR condemned her and her body was broken on the lich-gate of Rauthsmyri church and buried in a cairn. A traveler must throw a stone over her grave if he hopes to be free of her evil influence. But all men who lived on the land were haunted by spectres of Gunnvor and Kulumkilli.

Now, several centuries after the death

of the sorceress, BJARTUR comes to Albogastathir and claims the land. He throws no stone on the evil grave for he determines to be free of fear and to live as an independent man. He has worked 18 years in the employ of the Baliff at Rauthsmyri and has saved enough for a down payment on the farm he calls Summerhouses, and enough for some sheep and an old horse.

Chaps. 3–5. The wife of the Baliff, a poetess, lends Bjartur a tent for his marriage to ROSA, a servant girl in her house. Rosa wants to throw a stone on Gunnvor's grave but Bjartur refuses to allow it. Later he accuses her of infidelity with the Baliff, when he discovers that he was not her first man.

Chap. 6. Rosa had meat and milk when she was a servant, but her husband denies her these things because they are too expensive. He prefers to be independent and do without the luxuries a servant can have. Rosa becomes slatternly like an old woman. Bjartur grieves that after he has worked hard for 18 years his wife should bring him no happiness. He consoles himself with his dog, Titla, and his work. One night Rosa goes to throw a stone on Gunnvor's grave. She falls asleep on the road. When her husband finds her she becomes sick.

Chaps. 8–9. INGOLFUR, the son of the Baliff, comes to Bjartur's land with a party of friends. The men hunt while the girls pick berries. The master of Summerhouses is proud that the land is his and greets Ingolfur as an equal. The son of the Baliff is an Icelandic patriot and glad that men like Bjartur are farming the land and building the country.

Chaps. 10–14. The time for rounding up the sheep comes. Bjartur shaves off his beard and invites all the farmers to come to his house. Rosa's father is one of the men and she becomes a child again in her joy of seeing him. Bjartur leaves a little lamb to keep his wife company and goes off with the men. Rosa is frightened during the night and in anger the next morning she kills the lamb and feasts on its meat. When Bjartur returns he determines to go into the moors and find his lost sheep.

Chaps. 15–16. Bjartur sees a bull reindeer and jumps on its broad back, hoping to catch it and take it to Rosa for meat. The bull swims into the cold river and nearly drowns Bjartur. He jumps to safety on the opposite side of the river. Wet and cold, he must now detour 20 miles around the river to reach home. A snowstorm begins and he almost freezes. He recites poetry all night and the next day reaches a farmhouse. His lambs are out in the snow and he fears that they will be frozen.

Chaps. 17–23. When Bjartur arrives home he finds that Rosa has died in childbirth. The baby is alive. The dog has kept it warm with its own body. The child lives and Bjartur christens her ASTA SOLLILJA. The minister sends an old widowed woman and her daughter, FINNA, to live at the Summerhouses and take care of the baby and the house.

Chaps. 24–26. Fourteen years later, Bjartur of Summerhouses has married Finna and now there are four children, Asta, HELGI, GVENDUR, and little NONNI. Three others have died. Finna has dreamt that little Nonni will grow up to sing to all the world. The Baliff comes to offer a cow to Bjartur but Bjatur will not put himself in debt. Finna is always ill and in need of care. The Baliff offers to send medicine, and he wants his wife to educate Asta, but Bjartur will not accept anything from his former master.

Chaps. 27–29. Bjartur does buy the cow for his family. The Baliff and his son try to persuade Bjartur to join a coöperative venture for selling sheep, saying the merchant has been cheating the farmers. The merchant owes Bjartur money. But Bjartur refuses to join anything. He values his independence above profit.

Chap. 30. In the spring little Nonni and his mother go into the pasture each day to tend the cow. The mother teaches the boy to sing and tells him stories of the elves. He is happy with her. Bjartur takes his daughter with him to sell the sheep. He sleeps in the same bunk with Asta, holding her tightly. He suddenly disturbs the love they are feeling for each other by jumping out of bed. Asta feels that she has been guilty of something and is frightened. The cow gives birth to a calf. Despite the children's love for the animal, Bjartur kills the calf and takes its carcass to town. Finna becomes ill with grief.

Chaps. 34–38. A man on a vacation from the south obtains permission from Bjartur to hunt on his land. Asta is shy but happy with him and when he leaves she dreams about him. A blizzard kills many of the sheep. Times are hard at all the farms. Bjartur has to use the hay that was intended for the cow to keep alive his sick sheep. When the cow becomes so weak it cannot stand Bjartur kills it. Finna, who had loved the cow, dies too, of exhaustion and grief.

Chaps. 39–42. Several sheep die accidentally. Bjartur watches over his sheep each night but several other sheep are found with their throats cut. Helgi tells his father he has seen a strange person who changes shapes and sex lurking around the barn. Bjartur comes to believe that the evil spirit of Gunnvon is trying to lay waste his land. He goes to her grave and hurls defiant words at it, saying that he will not throw a propitiary stone in the cairn, but will stand alone against monster or moor.

Chap. 43–45. The neighborhood learns of the ghost at the Summerhouses and all the people arrive with the Priest to sing hymns to exorcise the evil spirit. Helgi runs away because he does not want them to harm the ghost, and he does not return. Bjartur tells the people to go home. He calls the sheriff to investigate the murder of his sheep. The sheriff is unable to find any evidence.

Chaps. 46–51. By Christmas time it is certain Helgi will not be found, and the other children grieve for him. Bjartur tells Asta he must leave them till Easter to earn

The Informer

Novel by Liam O'Flaherty, 1896–
Published 1929.

THIS IS A MOST EFFECTIVE study of
one harassed and harried. The character starts with the handicap of stupidity, succumbs to momentary greed or
fear, and suffers remorse mixed with
fear. The story is remarkably effective
as a novel and as a play and it made
one of the best of the early talking pictures (1934) with Victor McLaglen
in the part of Gypo Nolan.

Chaps. 1–2. FRANCIS JOSEPH MC-
PHILLIP (FRANKIE) runs into a slum
lodging house in Dublin in March, 192–.
He has been hiding in the mountains for
several months, since he killed the secretary of the Farmer's Union. At that time he
was a member of the Revolutionary Organization. In the lodging house he finds the
man he is looking for, GYPO NOLAN, a
giant of a man with huge muscles, a bulb-
ous nose, and thick lips. He and McPhillip,
close friends, were working together at the
time of the killing. He tells McPhillip they
have both been expelled from the Revolutionary Organization. Gypo was beaten by
the police and has since been wandering
around, homeless in the cold and half starving. The police are still out to get Mc-
Phillip, but McPhillip tells Gypo he is
going to sneak over to his father's house to
see his family. His speech is broken by a
wracking cough and he tells Gypo he is a
dying man. Gypo suddenly looks at him
intently, savagely. McPhillip leaves. Gypo
sits for a while, then slowly gets up and
walks down the street and into a police
station. He announces that he has come to
claim the reward of £20 offered by the
Farmer's Union for information concerning Francis Joseph McPhillip. Half an hour
later McPhillip is accidentally shot to death
while trying to escape from the police that
had surrounded his father's house.

Chaps. 3–5. Gypo, leaving the police
station, looks around suspiciously, fearfully;
then stifles the emotion and walks ahead
arrogantly. He goes to a pub to "make a
plan," but finds he is lost without McPhillip,
who always made the plans for the two of
them. KATIE FOX appears, a sharp-eyed,
degenerated slum girl who has often taken
care of Gypo in emergencies, and in her
sporadic way gives him affection. She gets
a drink off him, then asks suspiciously where
he got all the money. He panics, then tells
her he robbed an American sailor. She is
angry when he tries to get rid of her. Gypo
walks down the street, feeling that the
Revolutionary Organization must already
354

be out to murder him. The thought suddenly occurs to him that he will be suspected if he is not seen around the
McPhillips' house. He goes there and finds
many people there. Gypo blurts out in an
unnecessarily large shout to Mrs. McPhillip
that he is sorry for her trouble. Everybody
looks at him. The father, JACK MCPHILLIP,
a conservative socialist leader and hater of
the revolutionaries, attacks Gypo with a
tirade because Gypo was connected to the
revolutionary past that led to Francis's
death. Jack's daughter MARY, a girl who has
pushed herself into the middle class, shuts
him up. Gypo stands up and some silver
money falls out of his pocket. He is first
frozen with fear, then he rushes and gives
the money to Mrs. McPhillip and runs out.
BARTLEY MULHOLLAND and TOMMY
CONNOR, members of the Revolutionary
Organization, raise their eyebrows and follow Gypo. When Mulholland insinuates
his suspicion, Gypo almost strangles him to
death; then Gypo remembers fearfully that
they belong to the Organization. They take
Gypo to see the head of the Organization,
Commandant DAN GALLAGHER.

Chaps. 6–7. Gallagher is a dictator, intelligent, cold, intent, and seeking revolution by force and bloodshed. Gypo is at
first afraid, but Gallagher tells him they will
take him back into the Organization if
Gypo will help find the man who informed
on McPhillip. Gypo suddenly becomes

some money to replace the sheep. She
weeps. Several weeks later a stranger comes
to the Summerhouses, saying he is a teacher
sent for the children by Bjartur. The
stranger has a wooden foot and an air of
mystery. He recites poetry and tells the
story of the Bible. The children love him.
He tells Gvendur and Nonni that they can
have any wish come true. Gvendur wishes
prosperity for his father and Nonni wants
to go to a foreign country. The teacher
writes a letter and tells Nonni to send it
with the next traveler and his wish will
come true. When the boys have gone to
bed he takes Asta into his arms and she
becomes his mistress.

Chaps. 52–58. The merchant who owed
Bjartur money on his sheep is bankrupt.
Bjartur goes to the coöperative society
looking for work. They take him in and
promise to help him as they have helped
all the farmers. At Easter Bjartur comes
back and the teacher leaves. Asta cries for
love and wants to die for her sins and her
loneliness. A lady offers to take Nonni to
America and Bjartur's uncle there is willing to teach him a trade. Bjartur sends
Nonni away. Asta goes to the Baliff's house
to learn Christianity and be confirmed, but
the Baliff's wife discovers that Asta is pregnant and sends her home. When Bjartur
learns this he strikes Asta and sends her
away. She determines to find the teacher.
Bjartur doubts that Asta is really his daughter, since she was born long before his own
child was due.

Chaps. 59–62. World War I brings prosperity to the farming community in Ice-

land. It is called the blessed war by the
people. Bjartur hires several working men.
He has placed a headstone over Gunnvor's
grave. Gvendur, now 17 years old, who
loves the land, is held in respect because of
the considerable property he will inherit,
but he learns from Nonni that things are
good in America and he leaves his father to
go to the new country. Bjartur is proud to
be alone with the prosperity he has made
for himself.

Chaps. 63–71. On Gvendur's way to the
sea he visits Asta. She has been working as
a servant and supporting her little girl, who
is now 5. She tells Gvendur that she accepts
gifts from no one and is as independent as
Bjartur. She has become harder and less
beautiful. She tells her brother that the
Baliff came to her when she and her baby
were starving and told her that he had
seduced Rosa and was her father. He offered
her money but she would not take it. Gvendur wants to offer her his sheep but she
refuses and goes on washing her mistress's
clothes. Further on the road Gvendur meets
a lovely girl, Ingolfur's daughter, who is
the incarnation of the happy youth the
children of the Summerhouses never knew.
He falls in love with her and decides not
to go to America but to return to the Summerhouses and marry the girl.

Chaps. 72–73. Ingolfur has become an
important man in the government and exerts
his socialist influence on the land. Roads
are built and people's banks are established.
Bjartur takes out a loan to build a house.
The house proves to be cold and uninhabit-
able. Bjartur falls into debt and the coöperative stores will not extend further credit.
The world sheep market has fallen. Ingolfur's daughter refuses to speak to Gvendur
and he is miserable. Asta is living with a
drunken poet, whose child she bears. She
has consumption and her baby is ill. Gvendur often tries to get his father to go to
Asta but Bjartur refuses.

Chaps. 74–75. Finally Bjartur is so deeply
in debt that he must sell Summerhouses at
auction. He decides to move to the farm of
Finna's mother. The old woman is still alive.
Bjartur plans to turn her land at Urtharsel
into a fox farm, and start building again.
At the fjord there is a strike of men working on the waterways. Strikebreakers have
been hired and a fight is expected. Bjartur
and his son, on the way to town for supplies,
meet a striker who takes them to his comrades to share their bread. Among these
working people Bjartur and Gvendur learn
of the Russian Revolution and the fall of
the czar. Gvendur decides to stay with the
strikers and fight them the next day. Bjartur is proud of this decision. The next day
he goes to Asta, who is now coughing blood.
He tells her he is taking her and her children to Urtharsel, and she rejoices. Walking beside Bjartur, Asta falls down on a
grassy slope coughing. The Grandmother
looks at Asta and says that she will bury
another corpse, but Bjartur picks Asta up
and carries her the rest of the way. She
promises Bjartur that she will not die.

arrogant. He tells Gallagher that the "Rat MULLIGAN" did it—that he saw Mulligan sneak out after McPhillip at the lodging house, and that Mulligan had a grudge against McPhillip because McPhillip gave his sister a baby and refused to marry her. Gallagher tells Gypo to come to an inquest that night. Then Gallagher goes over to the McPhillips' house to ask a few questions. He meets Mary in the dark. They are drawn to each other, although she is frightened by his cruel face. He asks her to "join him"—the idea of marriage or even the admission of love being out of the question to a revolutionary. She asks him if he basically believes in anything or has pity for anybody. He answers no, a revolutionary cannot. He tells her to come to the inquest.

Chaps. 8–10. On leaving Gallagher, Gypo walks into the street and bellows an Irish war-cry, then picks a fight with a bystander and downs him. A policeman rushes up and Gypo with his great strength throws him over his head. Gypo runs away, but when the policeman has gone Gypo returns to retrieve his little hat, which somehow seems to protect him. A crowd has gathered, and Gypo impulsively proposes to feed all the rabble. They pile into a café with much excitement and Gypo pays for all. Gypo dominates the mob with his high stature and thundering voice— a moment of glory. Mulholland's sly face is seen in the crowd. Fierce political and religious arguments spring up on all sides. Gypo has for the moment forgotten the man who informed on Francis McPhillip. He then moves on, striding down stinking back streets, then wheels into a high-class brothel. It has been preëmpted for the night by a party of men, but Gypo barges in. His unwelcome reception changes tune when he flashes his money and buys drinks for all. He drinks heavily and a general orgy ensues. He then approaches an aloof woman in a corner of the room. She fights him off. She turns out to be an English officer's wife who has had her face disfigured and was deserted by her husband. Gypo, in a magnanimous gesture, gives her money to return to England. He chooses a blonde named CONNEMARA MAGGIE to take upstairs. Meanwhile Mulholland is sitting in Biddy Burke's pub, dejected because he has lost Gypo's trail. Katie Fox explodes into the pub, screaming with anger because she has seen Gypo with Connemara Maggie and because Gypo has been giving so much money away and has given her none. She insinuates that he is the informer. Mulholland rushes over and announces to Gypo that it is time for the inquest.

Chaps. 11–13. Gypo is taken to the "Bogey Hole," the wine cellars of an ancient nobleman's house. Several guards stand about with guns. Gypo is given a seat next to Mulligan. At first he is shocked to see Mulligan, a frail, yellowed, consumptive tailor. Then he sobers, becomes cunning, and jumps up cursing Mulligan as an in-

succumbs. After Gypo is thrown in the cell Mary McPhillip pleads with Gallagher not to kill Gypo. She tells him it would just be another murder. He is baffled by her outlook. Straws are drawn for the choice of the man to shoot Gypo, after they take him out to a lonely country road. The candidates are men drawn from the ordinary walks of life, not trained killers. They quake with apprehension.

Chaps. 14–15. Gypo in the cell sleeps like a dead man for ten minutes, then wakes and remembers something McPhillip once told him about this cell: It has an exit to the garden above. With incredible agility he climbs up on a ledge, swings his feet up, and forces an old trap door on the ceiling open. He just manages to scramble out of it before the guards rush in. Gypo dashes through the ruins above. Men shoot at him but miss. Gallagher, informed of the escape, is overwhelmed with fear that Gypo will now inform on the Organization and on himself. Mary sees his fear and weakness

Gypo finally is overcome

and loves him for it. They embrace passionately. He admits his great loneliness and tells her how he commands by fear, not by love. Yet basically he dispises all people.

Chaps. 16–18. Gypo runs toward the mountains, but at a bridge he spots Mul- Gypo falls to the floor groveling and screaming, without hope of mercy. All present feel pity except Gallagher. When they attempt to carry Gypo off to a cell he suddenly stiffens and puts up a tremendous fight before he former. The trial begins, and Mulligan accounts for his day. He proves he was three miles away from the lodging house at the hour when Gypo claims to have seen him there. Mulligan is released with good wishes. Gallagher proceeds to play verbally with Gypo as if he were a fish on a line, breaking Gypo's spirit coldly, without pity. Finally holland and another man standing guard. He turns back, is panicked by some policemen, and rushes hysterically and blindly through endless alleys. His need for rest becomes desperate and he remembers Katie Fox. He goes to her lodging and finds her at home with the old woman, LOUISA CUMMINS, with whom she lives. Katie is high on dope. Gypo gets into bed and cannot hold off his overwhelming need for sleep. Katie slips out to report to Gallagher, whose men sneak up Katie's stairs. Louisa Cummins warns Gypo. He leaps up and charges the men as they break through the door. They shoot and hit him in the thigh. He grapples them all with a roar and they fall over the banister to the next landing. Gypo gets away and runs through the door, bleeding. As he emerges several men shoot and hit. Gallagher is standing across the street coolly, with a faint smile. Gypo falls, gets up, and staggers across the street and into a church. Mrs. McPhillip is there and he falls at her feet and confesses his crime. She tells him that she forgives him, and with a last mighty effort he stands up to his full height and cries out toward the altar, "Frankie, yer mother has forgiven me." Then he falls to the floor, blood gushing from his mouth.

In His Steps

Novel by Charles Monroe Sheldon, 1857–1946.
Published 1896.

FOR A LONG TIME there was a general belief in the publishing industry that *In His Steps* had sold some 30,000,000 copies and was the best-selling novel of all time. Later researches have shown that the figure was vastly exaggerated—perhaps by ten times— but nevertheless *In His Steps* has been one of the outstanding best-sellers. It sold chiefly in "the Bible belt," where religious books have their biggest market. A true story connected with *In His Steps* is that the author or original publisher neglected to place the proper copyright notice in the first edition, with the result that every publisher was free to publish without payment of a royalty to the author. Many publishers did take advantage of this, but at least two gratuitously paid Sheldon his royalties despite the legal exemption they could have enjoyed.

Chap. 1. The Rev. HENRY MAXWELL is writing his next Sunday's sermon, on Atonement, when a tramp comes to his door and asks for work. Maxwell sends him away. On Sunday, in the First Church of Raymond, after the sermon, the tramp walks to the front of the church and addresses the congregation. There is a shocked silence. The tramp tells the people that he was a printer. He lost his job when new machines came in. He has tramped the country for ten months looking for a job. In Raymond no one was kind or charitable. Yet the preacher said in his sermon that we must follow in the steps of Christ. At the end of his speech, the tramp faints. A doctor says he has had a heart attack. The minister insists on taking the man into his house and nursing him alone. He sends for the man's little girl, who was staying with another printer. After five days the man dies, thanking Maxwell for his truly Christian care. The following Sunday he asks members of the parish to pledge to do nothing for a full year without asking what Jesus would do. He and fifty others make this pledge.

Chap. 2. One of those who made the pledge is EDWARD NORMAN, editor of the *Daily News*. He publishes his paper without a word about the prizefight and the paper does not sell. The men on the staff are afraid of going bankrupt. When Norman calls them together and announces his new policy they are confused, but they agree to stay with him. ALEXANDER POWERS, the director of the railroad, sets up a warm room where his workers can eat lunch and listen to lectures or music. Maxwell addresses the men of the railroad, his first contact with the working classes. Powers discovers that his company is cheating on a government tax law. He cannot make up his mind whether or not to report his company and tries to decide what Jesus would do.

Chaps. 3–4. VIRGINIA PAGE, a young millionairess, has her friend RACHEL WILSON over for lunch. Rachel, a singer, decides to turn down two offers of concert tours, because Jesus would not use his talents for money. Virginia cannot decide what to do with her wealth and is waiting for some future insight into Jesus before she acts. Virginia's brother ROLLIN is also at lunch. He is a playboy whose only serious passion is Rachel. She refuses to marry him because he does nothing useful. That night she tells her mother that she is giving up the stage and going to sing at Evangelical meetings held in Raymond's slum area, the Rectangle. Maxwell goes into the slums to preach. Rollin finds his way to the Rectangle to hear Rachel sing. Powers hands in his resignation to his company and turns state's witness. Norman writes an editorial praising the courage of Powers. His paper has eliminated scandal and undue crime details from its pages. A reporter who was fired from another paper for refusing to work on Sunday is given a job on the *Daily News*. MILTON WRIGHT, the owner of a large store, has met with his employees and has announced his intention of reorganizing his business on the basis of Christian love. At the next meeting in the Rectangle, the crowd is so moved that all the poor people kneel for Jesus.

Chap. 5. Rollin Page becomes a convert. JASPER CHASE, a young author, proposes to Rachel and is turned down. He has spoken too soon after the meeting; her thoughts are still with the people her voice reached. DONALD MARSH, the president of Lincolns College, organizes with Maxwell a political campaign to get rid of the present administration in the next election. They hope to stop the sale of liquor in the town.

Chap. 6. In the Rectangle Virginia finds a drunken girl, LOREEN, who had been at many of the evangelical meetings but fell back into sin. Learning that Loreen has no home, Virginia takes her to her own mansion. Her grandmother is furious and decides to leave the house rather than associate with the poor. Rollin comes in and comforts Virginia, saying that her choice was in the steps of Jesus. At the next meeting of those who took Maxwell's pledge, Norman confesses that his paper is rapidly losing money and soon will be unable to pay its operating expense. Virginia offers to lend half a million dollars to the *News*. They plan to develop a truly Christian paper. The election fight goes on. On the night of the election President Marsh, Rachel, Rollin, Virginia and Loreen, who follows Virginia everywhere, are in the Rectangle. The saloon-keepers stir up trouble and an angry crowd throws stones. Someone throws a bottle at Virginia. Loreen runs to shield her patroness. Loreen is hit on the head by the bottle and killed. Virginia kneels by her.

Chaps. 7–8. Raymond votes to continue liquor selling for another year. Rev. Maxwell instills into his congregation a new determination to rid the city of the curse of drink. During the summer, Maxwell forgoes his vacation and arranges instead a seaside trip for a poor family. Rachel continues singing and makes plans to teach music to the women of the slums. Virginia plans to build some nice lodgings and a recreation center. Rollin tries to convert his fashionable friends at the gay clubs he formerly frequented. The Rev. CALVIN BRUCE from Chicago visits Raymond and is deeply moved by the pledge to follow Jesus. He resolves to take the pledge himself and carry the idea to his own parish.

Chap. 9. FELICIA and ROSE STERLING are members of Bruce's church and cousins of Rachel Winslow. Felicia is receptive to the pledge of Jesus, while Rose prefers the luxuries of her frivolous life. Mrs. Sterling is an invalid. Mr. Sterling has been brooding for several days and on the Sunday Felicia takes the pledge of Jesus, Mr. Sterling shoots himself, and Mrs. Sterling, seeing her husband dead, dies also. Mr. Sterling had gone bankrupt and lost everything. Rose and Felicia, left penniless, move to Raymond to live with Rachel. Felicia, determined not to be dependent, undertakes the cooking for Rachel and Rachel's mother. She also teaches cooking in Virginia's new recreation center. She lives always with the thought "What would Jesus do?" and she becomes known in the Rectangle as the angel cook. The BISHOP OF CHICAGO, an old friend of Bruce's, decides after long thought that he will take the pledge. He decides he must give up his bishopric and work among the people as an humble servant of Christ. The two friends decide to move into the slums. Their decision, when announced, creates a furor in Chicago. In the worst part of the Chicago slums the Bishop comes across Felicia, who moved back to open a bakery shop for the poor. She plans to teach them ways of having good food cheaply. She goes to the settlement the Bishop is now running. There she meets a young man, STEPHEN CLYDE, who is working as a carpenter. His father also was once wealthy and lost his money. Clyde took the pledge for Jesus at the same time as Felicia.

Chap. 11. One night the Bishop is held up by two hoodlums. He prays for their souls and his wish is granted. One of the men he had taken into his house years before and obtained a job for him. The man had fallen back into drink. He recognizes the Bishop and refuses to allow anyone to rob him. He and his friend go back to the settlement with the Bishop and learn through prayer and love to give up drink and become friends of Christ. Bruce persuades one of his former parishioners to close the lease of a saloon-owner next door to the settlement. The building is then used for Felicia's cooking classes and for a school to teach girls housework, so they will have a means of earning a living as maids. A landlord comes to the Bishop and confesses his terrible sin in permitting houses to be such slums as those he owns in the settlement district. He plans to rebuild all the houses and in the meanwhile to give free coal and food to his starving tenants. Felicia and Stephen fall in love. They are both the children of God.

Chap. 12. Maxwell comes to Chicago to address a meeting of men who are out of work, hungry, and angry. They want to do what Jesus would do, but first they want jobs. Maxwell preaches at a fashionable church in Chicago and wins many new converts. He hopes to change the very fabric of the modern world to that of a Christian society. Maxwell thinks over the lives he has changed. He sees Rachel married to Rollin Page; Norman the owner of a successful and Christian paper; Milton Wright a Christian businessman. He sees Alexander Powers, who lost his job and social position but maintains his inner light and walks with Christ. Maxwell dreams of a future church, unblemished by hypocrisy, "following Him all the way, walking obediently in His Steps."

Mark Twain
1835–1910

Virgil
70–19 B.C.

The Invisible Man

Novel by Herbert George Wells, 1866–1946.
Published 1897. (PB, 1140)

PERHAPS BECAUSE EVERYONE daydreams at some time in his youth (and even later) of being invisible, this has proved to be one of the most popular of the books of fantasy and science fiction that Wells wrote. Actually it is inferior to most such Wells books because it has no rational scientific background. In 1958 *The Invisible Man* as created by Wells was made the subject of a series of television adventure films.

Chap. 1. On a stormy February day, a mysterious, heavily muffled man takes lodging at the Coach and Horses Inn. Mrs. HALL, the innkeeper's wife, welcomes him; guests are scarce during the winter. Her curiosity is aroused when she finds that his head is completely bandaged and his eyes are obscured by thick blue glasses. He snubs her efforts to draw him out as to the reason for the bandages.

Chap. 2. Mrs. Hall asks TEDDY HENFREY, the local clock-jobber, to look at the clock in her parlor. The mysterious lodger is in the parlor. He explains that he is an experimental investigator and requires quiet and solitude, but he allows Henfrey to fix the clock. While Henfrey is taking the clock apart, the lodger suddenly accuses him of humbugging and abruptly orders him to leave. Henfrey tells Mr. Hall of the suspicious visitor. That evening, after the guest has retired, Hall searches the parlor. He finds nothing but a piece of paper with some weird mathematical computations written on it.

Chap. 3. The visitor's luggage—a couple of trunks, a box of big, fat books, and a dozen crates containing glass bottles packed in straw—is delivered to the inn the next day by Mr. FEARENSIDE, whose dog bites the mysterious lodger on the hand and leg.

The lodger rushes up to his room and Hall goes to see if he can help him. Hall sees a handless arm and a shadowy face before he is abruptly pushed from the room. Later, the stranger unpacks his luggage and sets up his glass apparatus in the parlor. Fearenside confides to Teddy Henfrey that the stranger's leg appeared black when he caught a glimpse of it. Henfrey offers his opinion that the stranger is a piebald.

Chap. 4. Iping Village is alive with rumors about the mysterious stranger, who takes lonely walks at dusk. Dr. CUSS, curious about the stranger's bandages, fabricates an excuse to visit him. After a short visit, Dr. Cuss rushes out and calls on Mr. BUNTING, the vicar. He tells a strange tale of an apparently empty arm reaching up to his face and nipping his nose.

Chaps. 5–6. Early Whit-Monday morning, a burglary occurs at the vicarage. Mr. and Mrs. Bunting, hearing strange noises in the study, investigate and find a candle being lit, a door being opened and shut, but no sign of an intruder. All their savings are gone. Early the same morning, Hall finds the strange guest's bedroom door open. The room is empty, but the stranger's clothes and bandages are on the bed. He calls Mrs. Hall, and, as they are searching the room, they hear sneezes. Suddenly, several pieces of furniture start moving across the room, as if thrown. The Halls are pushed out of the room by an unknown force, and the door is shut violently. They call SANDY WADGERS, the blacksmith, to investigate. While Wadgers is questioning them in the downstairs hall, the stranger, completely dressed in hat, muffler, and overcoat, comes down the stairs from his previously empty bedroom and goes into the parlor.

Chap. 7. The stranger has not paid his bill. Mrs. Hall reminds him and he suddenly agrees to pay, though he did not have enough money the night before. Suspicious, Mrs. Hall asks him to explain how he entered the house that morning. He unwraps his head bandages and Mrs. Hall sees nothing where his head should be.

Taking his clothes off, he disappears before their eyes

She runs out to get BOBBY JAFFERS, the village constable. When Jaffers attempts to arrest the man, he explains that he is invisible. Then, taking his clothes off, he disappears before their eyes and escapes.

Chaps. 8–10. GIBBINS, the amateur naturalist of the district, while lying out on the open downs beyond the village, hears a series of sneezes and a cultivated voice muttering a rich variety of curses—but there is no one in sight. THOMAS MARVEL, a vagrant, is sitting by the roadside outside of Iping when the invisible man makes his presence known and scares the wits out of Marvel. The invisible man engages Marvel to aid him. Under the watchful eye of Mr. HUXTER, a storekeeper, the lone figure of Tom Marvel loiters outside the Coach and Horses. Marvel disappears suddenly but reappears with a big bundle and three books tied together. When Huxter chases him, some unknown force catches Huxter's legs and sends him flying.

Chaps. 11–12. In the meantime, Dr. Cuss and Mr. Bunting are investigating the books that the invisible man has left behind in his room at the Coach and Horses. A mysterious voice commands them to stop their search and asks their aid in getting clothing. In the bar at the Coach and Horses, Hall and Henfrey hear mysterious noises from the parlor. The parlor window is opened. Then their attention is diverted to Huxter across the road, who is shouting at the rapidly disappearing figure of Tom Marvel. All rush after him. Dr. Cuss and the vicar emerge from the parlor minus several articles of clothing. The invisible man causes a great deal of commotion, breaks all the windows of the inn, and disappears.

Chaps. 13–16. Tom Marvel tries to get out of his bargain with the invisible man, but to no avail. At the neighboring village of Port Stowe, Marvel starts to tell a mariner about the invisible man, when Marvel is suddenly made to stand and walk off. Dr. KEMP, in his house on a hill outside the town of Burdock, sees Marvel running as if someone were chasing him, breathlessly shouting, "The Invisible Man's coming!" Marvel rushes into the Jolly Cricketers Inn and explains his predicament. The bar man attempts to barricade the pub, but the invisible man finds Marvel and claims him.

Chaps. 17–18. Dr. Kemp works until very late on his experiments. When going to bed, he sees blood stains on his bed and a blood-stained bandage appears to be suspended in mid-air. The voice of the invisible man calmly explains. He identifies himself as GRIFFIN, a college acquaintance of Kemp's. Kemp gives him food and clothing. While the invisible man sleeps, Dr. Kemp writes a note to Col. ADYE, the chief of police.

Chaps. 19–23. At breakfast, the invisible man tells Dr. Kemp of his research on invisibility, and of how he caused his own father to commit suicide. After successfully making a white cat invisible, he, an albino, made himself invisible by the same process. He set fire to his lodgings to destroy any evidence. From a theatrical costume shop he procured a disguise of clothing and a false wig and nose, and made his way to Iping.

Chaps. 24–28. Col. Adye attempts to trap the invisible man in Kemp's rooms, but the man escapes. Under Kemp's directions, the entire village is alerted to the danger; all food and shelter is made secure; powdered glass is sprinkled on the roads so that the invisible man will cut himself and his blood will become visible. A mild-mannered man, Mr. WICKSTEED, is brutally murdered. Adye finds the invisible man but the man wrests Adye's revolver from him and wounds him. Two policemen chase the invisible man and manage to hit him several times. After a perilous escape from his own house, Kemp manages to gather the villagers into a cordon and surround the invisible man, who dies on the village street. As he dies, he becomes visible again.

Epilogue. Tom Marvel, now the owner of the pub, draws his blinds each night and reads from the strange books.

Ivanhoe

Novel by Sir Walter Scott, 1771–1832.
Published 1820. (PB, PL502)

AMONG THE Waverley novels (a series of historical novels that Scott began under the pseudonym Waverley) *Ivanhoe* has been the most popular. It is a wonderful romance of chivalry and if its pattern now seems to be stereotyped it is because it has so often been copied. The events are set in the year 1193 or 1194 when Richard Coeur-de-lion was returning from the Third Crusade. *Ivanhoe* has much less historical basis than most of the Waverley novels. Scott makes Richard the friend of the true Englishman and a champion of the former Saxon element in their struggle against the Norman robber barons. Much of the legend of Richard as a great knight and good man has persisted in English countries through *Ivanhoe*. Scott dictated *Ivanhoe*, during a period of serious illness when he was too weak to write. It is a very long book and in fact has never been published in its full original draft.

Chaps. 1–3. Sir BRIAN DE BOIS-GUILBERT, a Knight Templar, attended by squires and Saracen servants and riding in the company of the Prior AYMER, is headed for Rotherwood, the castle of CEDRIC the Saxon. They meet GURTH, a swineherd, and WAMBA, a jester, and ask the way. The jester answers in riddles and confuses them. They ride on and meet a PALMER, on a pilgrimage, who guides them to the castle.

Chaps. 4–6. Cedric is opposed to the ruling Normans in England but he makes his Norman guests comfortable and entertains them at dinner. His ward, Lady ROWENA, descendant of Saxon kings, enters and the Knight Templar looks at her with ill-concealed ardor. She draws her veil and Cedric rebukes the Crusader. A Jew, ISAAC of York, asks for shelter and Cedric bids him welcome, much to the annoyance of his other guests except the Palmer, who gives Isaac a place by the fire and serves him food. Cedric wants Rowena to wed ATHELSTANE, the principal Saxon candidate for the English throne. Cedric banished his own son, WILFRED OF IVANHOE, for falling in love with Rowena. Ivanhoe went to Palestine as a crusader with King RICHARD I (the Lion-Hearted). Rowena asks the Knight Templar which English knights acquitted themselves well at Jerusalem and the Palmer speaks up and says the English knights were all brave, but that six knights, including Ivanhoe, beat all comers in a tourney. Bois-Guilbert bridles and challenges Ivanhoe *in absentia*; Rowena pledges her name and fame that Ivanhoe will meet the challenge. Rowena takes the Palmer aside and asks for news of Ivanhoe, and he tells her Ivanhoe's happiness rests in her hands when he returns. The Palmer overhears a plot by Bois-Guilbert to seize Isaac and torture him to extort his wealth. The Palmer warns Isaac. Gurth the swineherd show them a secret exit and the Palmer escorts Isaac to Sheffield, where Isaac has relatives. Isaac offers payment but the Palmer declines. Isaac guesses that the Palmer is a knight in disguise and arranges to equip him with a horse and armor.

Chaps. 7–9. A great tournament is held at the town of Ashby. Spectators throng the place, among them Isaac and his beautiful daughter REBECCA. They attract the attention of the regent, Prince JOHN, who orders Athelstane to make room for them. Athelstane is reluctant and there is great commotion before Isaac and Rebecca are finally seated in the lower ring. John wishes to name Rebecca the Queen of Love and Beauty, but his counselor, WALDEMAR, dissuades him and it is decided to let the winning knight name the queen. Five knights appear through the barriers and designate the challengers they wish to oppose. The Norman challengers win in four encounters and Cedric is keenly disappointed. John is about to give the prize to Bois-Guilbert, who has overthrown two knights and foiled a third, when a new champion comes through the barrier and boldly designates Bois-Guilbert as his opponent. Bois-Guilbert tells him he will be dead before nightfall, but the knight unhorses him and the two have at it with swords until parted by the marshals. The strange knight drinks a toast to "all English heads and to the confusion of foreign tyrants." Then he vanquishes four other knights. John fears the victorious knight may be King Richard himself. John gives the winner a warhorse as the prize of the tourney and tells him to pick a queen. The mysterious knight chooses Rowena.

Chaps. 10–12. The strange knight has won rich prizes—the horses and armor of the vanquished challengers. He takes a portion of the ransom and distributes the remainder among the squires, heralds, and attendants. He tells Gurth, who is attending him, that they are playing their parts well; but the swineherd is worried lest Wamba recognize them. Gurth is sent to Isaac's house to pay off the knight's debt for his horse and armor. On his way out, Gurth is pulled aside by Rebecca, who refunds the money and gives him something extra. Returning from the village, Gurth is set upon by four of ROBIN HOOD'S men, who take away his money after he has fought bravely. When they discover that Gurth is against the Normans, they return his money. At the tourney the next day, the strange knight bests all comers until, at the very end, three challengers unite against him. An equally mysterious newcomer, the BLACK KNIGHT, comes to his aid and the two fight off the other three. Victorious but wounded, the strange knight totters to Rowena's feet to receive the chaplet from her. The marshals take off his helmet and she shrieks as she recognizes him as Ivanhoe. Ivanhoe faints and Isaac and Rebecca carry him off to nurse him back to health.

Chaps. 13–16. Prince John determines to have the Saxon heiress Rowena marry a Norman, DE BRACEY. John is handed a note by LOCKSLEY, an archer, which reads: "Take heed to yourself, for the Devil is unchained." (It means King Richard is free from his captivity in Europe.) John, much troubled, decides to have revenge on Locksley and matches him against his own champion, HUBERT. Locksley wins by splitting his opponent's arrow, which has already pierced the bull's eye. John asks Locksley to serve in his retinue but Locksley says he is pledged to Richard. There is a gala feast and when John proposes a toast to Ivanhoe, Cedric refuses to drink to his son, who has discarded the customs of the Saxons. Among various schemes of John's followers is that of Bracey to attack the Saxons and carry off Rowena, with Bois-Guilbert as his ally. The Black Knight, wandering in the woods, comes upon an ANCHORITE whom he discovers to be the Clerk of Copmanhurst. They dine sumptuously together on food that was hidden in the Anchorite's retreat and the Black Knight plays a harp and sings.

Chaps. 17–20. The Black Knight and Anchorite make merry until they are interrupted by Gurth. He seeks assistance for Cedric and Athelstane, who with Rebecca, are threatened by an ambushed armed band. Locksley also arrives and tells the Black Knight that it is a Norman knight, FRONT-DE-BOEUF, who is threatening Cedric and his party. The Black Knight is amazed that Front-de-Boeuf has turned thief and oppressor, but Locksley tells him he was always so.

Chaps. 21–24. Bois-Guilbert and Bracey capture Cedric, Athelstane, and the others, and they are imprisoned in Front-de-Boeuf's castle. In his dungeon, Isaac is told that Rebecca has been given to Bois-Guilbert as a handmaiden, since it was assumed that the girl was Isaac's concubine. Rowena is placed in an apartment of her own, where Bracey presses his suit. When she rejects him, he tells her that Cedric's fate depends on her acceptance. Rebecca has been placed in a distant turret, where ULRICA, a hag, tells her of the awful fate in store for her. Bois-Guilbert visits her and surprises her by asking her to change her religion and marry him. She leaps to the battlement and threatens to throw herself off. A clamor at the castle gates causes Bois-Guilbert to withdraw.

Chaps. 25–30. The Black Knight gathers

Rebecca leaps to the battlement and threatens to end her life

ransom. The Black Knight, who has proved himself the most formidable warrior anyone has ever seen, overcomes de Bracey, who humbly submits when the Black Knight whispers something to him. Isaac sets off to get the ransom for himself and Rebecca.

Chaps. 36–40. Rebecca is accused of sorcery by the Preceptor of the Templars and is taken before a tribunal, where evidence is brought against her concerning a spell she is supposed to have cast on Bois-Guilbert. There is a witness to the scene in which Rebecca threatened to throw herself from the battlement, and he embroiders the story by saying she floated around the castle three times. This convicts her. She

his forces for an assault on the castle of Front-de-Boeuf. He sends Wamba, disguised as a hermit, inside to ascertain the strength of the defenders. Wamba discovers that the wounded Ivanhoe is in the castle but the code of chivalry prevents Bracey from killing a defenseless knight. Front-de-Boeuf discovers the identity of Wamba by pulling aside his cape. Rebecca tends Ivanhoe and tells him of the battle being waged to deliver the Saxons. The attackers gain the advantage and the castle is set afire. Ulrica, a discarded former mistress of Front-de-Boeuf, takes revenge by locking him in a room to be burned alive. The bulwark of the Black Knight's forces is Locksley, revealed as an outlaw who leads a large party of men.

Chaps. 31–36. The prisoners are in dire peril. Ivanhoe begs Rebecca to flee the flames but she refuses, even when Bois-Guilbert offers to escort her to safety. Wamba cries out that the castle has been taken and the defenders lose heart. Athelstane is left for dead and Rowena, delivered from the flames, is carried off by Bois-Guilbert. Isaac is held for ransom. Torture has not made him reveal his wealth or its location, but when Rebecca's virtue is threatened he agrees to pay a large

can be saved only if a knight defends her cause and wins.

Chaps. 40–44. A grand tourney is held for the deliverance of Rebecca. Bois-Guilbert awaits the challenge of any knight who will defend her. Athelstane, who was thought dead, appears but relinquishes the defense of Rebecca to Ivanhoe, for he knows Ivanhoe is the man Rowena loves. Ivanhoe challenges Bois-Guilbert and they fight. They unhorse each other. Ivanhoe prevails but when he is about to kill his enemy with his sword, he finds that the Templar is already dead from an apopleptic fit. Ivanhoe is accepted by Cedric as a true son and true Englishman and he marries Rowena. The Black Knight turns out to be King Richard

I, and Locksley is revealed as Robin Hood, the King's devoted follower. Isaac and Rebecca leave England for a friendlier land.

Jalna

Novel by Mazo de la Roche, 1885–1961.

Published 1927 by Little, Brown & Co.-Atlantic Monthly Press, Boston. © 1927 by Little, Brown & Co., © 1955 by Mazo de la Roche.

THIS IS THE FIRST of a series of thirteen novels that Mazo de la Roche wrote about the Whiteoak family that lived at an estate called Jalna in Ontario. The series acquired such a faithful following that each considered the Whiteoaks part of his own family or himself part of theirs. After the first two or three Jalna books the critics tended to dismiss the steady flow, as they appeared one by one, with casual ho-hums; but the series contains a great deal of good writing and *Jalna* itself won the Atlantic Monthly prize the year it was published.

Chaps. 1–2. WAKEFIELD WHITEOAK, the youngest of the Whiteoak clan, saunters into the village for his daily lessons. He is thought to be too delicate to attend regular school. He dallies on the way and is so late that little Latin is learned that day. Wakefield saunters home to Jalna, the family estate, to find himself late for the family's one o'clock dinner. GRANDMA WHITEOAK, soon to be 100 years old, muses on her past life: Her marriage to Philip Whiteoak, captain in the British Army; their early life together in India; the birth of their daughter, AUGUSTA; their move to Canada; settlement in Quebec for a year, where their son, NICHOLAS, was born; the purchase of 1,000 acres in southern Ontario and the building of Jalna there; their other sons, ERNEST and PHILIP; Nicholas's marriage in England, his divorce from Millicent Hume, and his return to Jalna; Philip's marriage to the daughter of a Scottish physician and the birth of their daughter, MEG, and son, RENNY; the death of Philip's first wife and his remarriage to Mary Wakefield, who had been his children's nurse; the birth of their four sons, EDEN, PIERS, FINCH, and WAKEFIELD; Augusta's marriage to a baronet. At dinner, Eden confides that a book of his poetry is to be published.

Chaps. 3–5. Grandma returns to her downstairs bedroom to have a quiet hour with her pet parrot, Bonaparte, or "Boney." Ernest, a bachelor, retires to his room to annotate his Shakespeare and Eden visits him. Later, Ernest muses over the secret of his mother's will; she has never divulged who her heir is. Nicholas has returned to his room to rest his gouty leg, and Renny visits him. They discuss Eden's prospects; Renny is disturbed because Eden refused to take his final college exams. Renny thinks Eden should help on the farm, to put it on a better paying basis. Renny says Piers has been seeing PHEASANT, the illegitimate daughter of their close neighbor and friend, MAURICE VAUGHN (once betrothed to Meg). Piers and Pheasant hold a love tryst and plan to elope. Piers returns to Jalna and goes to the room he shares with Finch; Finch is trying to study and Piers obtains release from his frustrations by teasing him.

Chaps. 6–8. Pheasant wakes up on her wedding day and packs her few belongings. Her father tells her he wishes dinner at one o'clock instead of the usual 12:30. Since Pheasant is to meet Piers to elope at 2, she pleads a dentist appointment and says she will eat earlier. Piers and Pheasant are married at Stead and Piers sends telegrams to both families. They have dinner in the hotel dining room, where Pheasant is the focus of male attention. When they return to Jalna, Grandma Whiteoak is furious with Piers and insults Pheasant. Piers is so enraged that he throws Grandma's parrot to the floor and Grandma cracks Piers on the head with her cane. But Renny says Piers and Pheasant are to live at Jalna and the family concurs.

Chaps. 9–11. Eden goes to New York to see his publishers, Cory and Parsons, with a new book of poems; his first book has been well received. ALAYNE ARCHER, a poetry reader for the firm, congratulates him. Eden is invited to dine with Mr. CORY and Alayne is there. She is the only child of a professor, but both her parents died in the influenza epidemic. Cory was a friend of her father's. It was Alayne who first read Eden's poems and recommended them. Two weeks after they met, Eden asks her to marry him. She accepts, and Eden writes his news to Jalna. All at Jalna think her a rich American heiress. Alayne shows Eden New York City, and they visit her maiden aunts together. Eden asks Renny to be his best man, but Renny is needed at Jalna.

Chaps. 12–15. Wakefield, who shares a room with Renny, awakes to find Renny already up. Renny, a very little man, is naked. He amuses himself by adorning his small body with shaving cream, and Mrs. WRAGGE, the housekeeper, sees him and is frightened out of her wits. Renny dresses in his best, breakfasts on anchovies and stale toast, and goes to the village to meet Eden and his bride. While waiting he picks some daisies. He stops the bridal car, thrusts the daisies into Alayne's hand, and solemnly welcomes her to Jalna. Wakefield accompanies the bridal couple to Jalna, amusing them and Piers, who is driving, with his childish chatter. Meg makes Alayne welcome. A family dinner follows. Afterwards, Grandma takes Alayne to her room for a talk. Nicholas gives Alayne a silver bowl.

Grandma Whiteoak

Ernest and Alayne go over his Shakespearean annotations. Meg shows Alayne the gardens. Finch is disturbed over Alayne and cannot sleep. In the morning he dresses in his very best suit and tie for breakfast with Eden and Alayne. Eden asks Finch to show Alayne to the pine grove. Alayne is warm and friendly and Finch confides in her, telling her old stories of the family. They pass the orchard, where Piers is supervising the packing of apples for shipment. Piers, jealous because Eden and Alayne were welcomed while he and Pheasant were greeted coldly, is rude. Later Piers and Finch meet in the washroom and fight. Piers gives Finch a bloody nose, spoiling his best tie.

Chaps. 16–18. Each afternoon, Alayne, Eden, Ernest and Nicholas meet and discuss literature. Tea is served in Nicholas's room, and then he plays the piano. In the mornings, Eden writes. Alayne likes to take walks. One morning she and Renny are alone and he kisses her. Both promise to forget the incident. The Whiteoaks go to church, Grandma in a horse-drawn phaeton; the only motor vehicle she will ride in is the hearse at her funeral. At church, Renny reads part of the service. After supper Alayne asks Renny if Finch may have music lessons. He agrees, then whispers that they must not care for each other, as it is an impossible situation. Eden has become fascinated with Pheasant. He begins looking for a job. His poems are to be published in March and he is disturbed when Alayne seems to nag him about a novel he has mentioned writing.

Chaps. 19–21. Renny takes Eden and Alayne into the city, where Eden is applying for a job. Eden finds he must stay overnight and Renny and Alayne ride home alone. They discuss what to do about their love but come to no decision. Ernest and Nicholas suspect Renny and Alayne, but Eden is self-preoccupied and notices nothing. Lady BUCKLEY (Grandma's daughter Augusta) arrives from England. She encourages Finch with his music. This annoys Meg, who locks the piano, and Renny sends Finch to Vaughn's to practice. Eden is to start his new job after the New Year. After a jubilant Christmas, the family has a pillow fight. Ernest hits Eden with a pillow and Eden falls, breaking his leg. Alayne nurses Eden through his convalescence but sleeps in another room. Pheasant visits Eden and he confesses his love for her.

Chaps. 22–24. On his 10th birthday, Wakefield sounds reveille with the bugle Finch has given him. Renny gives him a pony. Finch accidentally comes upon Eden and Pheasant, kissing in a grove. He tells Piers, who goes after them. Pheasant, frightened, goes to her father's house, and Piers and Renny go after her. While Piers goes upstairs to Pheasant, Renny tells Vaughn about his love for Alayne. Piers takes Pheasant back to Jalna, and locks her in their room, telling her to stay there until he can bear the sight of her again.

Chaps. 25–26. All is in turmoil at Jalna. Eden has gone away. Meg has moved to the Fiddler's Hut, on the edge of Jalna, in rebellion against Piers' bringing Pheasant back. Alayne plans to return to New York right after the celebration of Gran's 100th birthday. Renny cannot persuade Meg to come back, but he tells Vaughn, who goes to the Fiddler's Hut and begs Meg to forget the past and marry him. She agrees. On Gran's 100th birthday, the family gives her 100 roses. The village church chimes 100 times. There are visits and gifts from everyone. Renny and Alayne kiss goodbye. Pheasant comforts Gran; she has been forgiven for her transgression with Eden.

Jane Eyre

Novel by Charlotte Brontë, 1816–1855. Published 1847. (PB, PL44; ML, 64 & T3; RE, Z4)

OF THE NOVELS written by the remarkable Brontë sisters, *Jane Eyre* was the greatest publishing success and for a long time was considered the best, though there now is a tendency to place *Wuthering Heights* ahead of it. Most of the material on which *Jane Eyre* is based comes from the experiences of Charlotte Brontë herself, her sisters, or their family. However, Charlotte did introduce into the novel an interesting mystery and many dramatic scenes and these contributed greatly to its contemporary popularity. *Jane Eyre* is still much read and is as interesting as ever. It is of only moderate length.

Jane helps Rochester

Chaps. 1–4. JANE EYRE is orphaned as an infant. Her mother's brother, Mr. REED, takes her but dies when she is a year old, exacting a deathbed promise from his wife that she will rear Jane as her child. Jane's life for her first 10 years is miserable; her aunt and her three cousins, JOHN, ELIZA, and GEORGIANA, taunt her on her poverty. John, a bully of 14, knocks her down and when she strikes back to protect herself Mrs. Reed punishes her by locking her up in the Red Room, where Mr. Reed died. Jane's horror makes her ill. BESSIE, the children's nurse, tends Jane, and Mr. LLOYD, the apothecary, is sympathetic to her. He suggests that Jane be sent away to school, and shortly thereafter she is sent to Lowood under the Rev. Mr. BROCKLEHURST. Lowood is a semi-charitable institution for orphaned girls. Mrs. Reed warns that Jane is deceitful and has generally wicked ways.

Chaps. 5–10. Jane is completely untaught, but her eagerness to learn quickly makes her equal to others of her own age. She becomes devoted to Miss MARIA TEMPLE, the headmistress. The food is scant and very poor. In the spring of Jane's second year at Lowood, a serious epidemic breaks out in the school, and many of the girls die. This brings a change in administration and great improvements, including vastly improved food. In all, Jane spends 8 years at Lowood, the last 2 as a teacher. When Miss Temple marries and goes away, Jane advertises for a position as a governess. She is hired to attend a little girl at a place called Thornfield, near the town of Millcote.

Chaps. 11–15. At Thornfield, Jane is warmly welcomed by Mrs. FAIRFAX, the housekeeper and manager. EDWARD ROCHESTER owns Thornfield. His ward, ADELE VARENS, is to be Jane's pupil. Walking through the house with Mrs. Fairfax, Jane is startled by a strange and terrifying laugh from a room on the third floor. Mrs. Fairfax says that a seamstress, GRACE POOLE, occupies that room. Jane is soon too busy with her young charge to think much more about the strange laugh. Adele has been brought up in France and speaks only a little English, but Jane is fluent in French. One winter day Jane walks to the village of

Hay and while she is walking home a horse slips on the icy road and its rider is tangled in the stirrups. Jane helps him to disengage himself and remount. He is Edward Rochester, her employer. He is not at all handsome but possesses a powerful personality, blunt and devoid of social smalltalk. Jane learns from him that Adele is the illegitimate daughter of Celine Varens, a Parisian opera dancer who at one time was Rochester's mistress and who abandoned her child. He is not Adele's father. Late one night Jane again hears the strange laughter; this time it is directly outside her own door. She sees no one in the hall but there is smoke coming from Mr. Rochester's door. The room is on fire and Rochester is unconscious. She extinguishes the fire with water from his washstand and in so doing drenches and arouses Rochester. He tells her to mention the fire to no one. He declares that he literally owes her his life, and he addresses her not as "Miss Eyre," which was his custom, but as "Jane." One more experienced than Jane might have recognized that he was in love with her. Jane knows only that she is in love with him.

Chaps. 16–22. Rochester leaves the house early next morning and remains away for three weeks. Mrs. Fairfax casually tells Jane that he is probably dancing attendance on a very beautiful young woman, BLANCHE INGRAM. Then Rochester has a house party and Jane remains in her quarters while gay festivities go on downstairs. Once, after dinner, Adele is allowed to appear to see the beautiful ladies and their beautiful dresses, and Jane is ordered to accompany her, which she does with great reluctance. Blanche Ingram is indescribably arrogant and haughty. One evening a gypsy fortune-teller comes to tell the fortunes of the young ladies. Blanche is the first to consult her and the other young women follow, until only Jane is left. The gypsy says there is one more young unmarried woman present and she too must see her. Jane goes, and gradually detects that the "gypsy woman" is Rochester, who has been playing the part. Jane recalls a message she must deliver to him, and tells him: A caller came to the door and claimed the right of an old friend to see Rochester; his name is

MASON and he is from the West Indies. This is obviously unwelcome news to Rochester. That night there are sounds of a scuffle in the room overhead, and wild cries for help. All the guests are aroused, but Rochester appears and reassures them. Jane is summoned by Rochester to help him. He says "she" flew at Mason with a knife and also bit him. Jane asks no questions, but helps Rochester dress the wounds and stays with Mason while Rochester goes to fetch a surgeon. The injured man is spirited out of the house and into a carriage very early in the morning. A day or so later ROBERT LEAVEN, the Reeds' coachman who is now married to Bessie, brings Jane sad news. John is dead, presumably by his own hand, after several years of dissipation. Mrs. Reed has had a stroke, and is not expected to recover. She has asked repeatedly to see Jane. Rochester gives Jane a leave of absence but makes her promise she will return. Jane finds that Mrs. Reed still hates her but has something on her conscience. Some three years before, Jane's uncle JOHN EYRE wrote to ascertain Jane's whereabouts; he wanted Jane to come and live with him in Madeira, and he intended to leave Jane his fortune. Mrs. Reed concealed the letter. Mrs. Reed dies, and after remaining a while to help Eliza and Georgiana, Jane returns to Thornfield, where she is warmly welcomed. The news of Rochester's pending marriage is an open secret. Jane cannot help feeling that Blanche Ingram will not make him a good wife, but she of course says nothing.

Chaps. 23–25. Jane meets Rochester in the garden, and after a long period of letting her think that his bride-to-be is Blanche, he suddenly tells her that she— Jane—is the one he loves. They happily plan to be married in four weeks. On the eve of their wedding day, Jane awakens to see a hag of unbelievable ugliness and evil appearance in her room, trying on Jane's bridal veil. She then tears it savagely in two. Jane faints, and when she recovers consciousness the woman is gone. Rochester soothes her next day by telling her that it was half dream and half true, for doubtless it was only Grace Poole.

Chaps. 26–27. The wedding ceremony is proceeding when a stranger enters and reads an affidavit from Richard Mason saying that Edward Rochester has a living wife. Rochester does not deny it, but he takes everyone to his house and shows them the maniac who lives hidden on the third floor, attended by Grace Poole. Heatedly, he asks if this can be considered a wife! But in spite of Rochester's pleas, Jane slips away.

Chaps. 28–33. Jane uses her last shillings to pay coach fare as far as she can go. She reaches a place called Whitcross and starts looking for work. She has no money for food and in the next three days eats only a slice of bread and some cold porridge, obtained by begging. At length she collapses on the doorsill of a cottage owned by a family named RIVERS. She gives her name as JANE ELLIOT. DIANA and MARY RIVERS are very thoughtful and considerate. Their brother, ST. JOHN, is a minister who is grimly determined to become a foreign missionary. As Jane's strength returns, she asks him to help her find work. He arranges for her to become a teacher in a small school that is to be opened in the village. She moves into the cottage provided for the schoolmistress. Shortly thereafter, St. John sees the name "Jane Eyre" scribbled on a piece of paper. From this he learns who she is. He tells Jane that John Eyre has died and she is his sole legatee. John Eyre was also the brother of St. John's mother, so Jane is a first cousin to the three who befriended her. Jane is happier to find a family of her own than she is about the money, which, to her amazement, is £20,-000. She insists upon dividing it equally among herself and her cousins.

Chaps. 34–38. At Christmas time Jane has left the school. She almost decides to marry St. John and help him in his missionary work, but she does not love him, nor he her. A strange feeling makes her seek Rochester once more. She journeys to Thornfield, only to find the house a crumbling, abandoned ruin, gutted by fire, which was set by the mad woman—who died that night, though Rochester tried to save her. In this act he was blinded and lost his left hand. Patiently she searches for Rochester and finds him at Ferndean, a small farm, where he now lives. Soon they are married. By some miracle he recovers the sight of one eye and can see his firstborn son.

Jean-Christophe

Novel by Romaine Rolland, 1866–1944. Published 1904–12. Translation from the French by Gilbert Cannan published 1910–13 and 1938–41 by Henry Holt & Co., N. Y. (ML, G38)

WITH NEARLY 1,600 pages and more than 600,000 words, *Jean-Christophe* qualifies as the longest novel in respectable world literature. It is in fact ten novels, and was so published originally. For its scope and its sustained excellence, *Jean-Christophe* has received lavish praise from critics. But it *is* awfully long.

BOOK I. JEAN-CHRISTOPHE

Part I. Dawn. Chaps. 1–3. JEAN-CHRISTOPHE KRAFFT is the son of MELCHIOR and LOUISA KRAFFT. Melchior is a violinist who had talent but allowed it to deteriorate through heavy drinking. Melchior's father, JEAN-MICHEL, is a competent musician also. Louisa is a dull, stupid peasant woman, the first nonmusician to marry a Krafft in 100 years. Jean-Christophe acquires a love of music at the age of 3 and shows such talent that Melchior forces him to devote more than six hours a day to piano practice. He greedily seeks to have a child-prodigy in the family. Jean-Christophe is compelled to write—at Melchior's dictation—an obsequious letter to the Grand Duke LEOPOLD, begging His Serene Highness to accept dedication of his album of compositions. The Grand Duke finds both letter and songs charming and sponsors and attends Jean-Christophe's first concert. Melchior calculatingly dresses Jean Christophe in a ludicrous outfit. Greeted by roars of laughter when he appears on stage, Jean-Christophe runs to the only apparent point of refuge—the piano. He plays, and the applause is deafening, but the ordeal makes him highly emotional.

Part II. Morning. Chap. 1. By the time Jean-Christophe is 11 he is earning his own living, playing second violin at the concert hall. He studies harmony and is informed that the harmonies so delightful to his ear are bad; he must follow the rules. Melchior has lost most of his students, and eventually loses all. Jean-Michel shares his small pension with the family, and Jean-Christophe has the allowance the grand duke awarded him after his first concert, but the family is poor. With Melchior's income as member of the Court orchestra, this constitutes the family's support. Jean-Michel dies and his pension ceases.

The Rhine River boat

Melchior does not work but remains self-indulgent and at last sells Jean-Michel's piano. Jean-Christophe is enraged and a dreadful scene ensues. Melchior is repentant and promises to stop drinking, but soon he reverts to drunkenness. Repeated absences from concerts eventually cost Melchior his job, and at 14 Jean-Christophe is the sole support of his family. He teaches, plays first violin in the orchestra, and composes music for special occasions at Royal Command.

Chap. 2. On a Rhine River boat, which is taking him to dinner with the director of the orchestra, Jean-Christophe meets OTTO DIENER, the son of a rich merchant, who admires Jean-Christophe as a violinist. Otto's hero-worship gives Jean-Christophe a pleasure he has never known before. They write impassioned letters to each other. Jean-Christophe's younger brothers misinterpret the letters from Otto and Jean-Christophe is shocked and disgusted. Otto has a similar experience, and as a result their friendship becomes self-conscious and gradually dies.

Chap. 3. After 15 years, a new chapter opens in Jean-Christophe's life. MINNA VON KERICH, a piano pupil of his, becomes his first love. From her mother, a young and attractive widow, Jean-Christophe learns a great deal about manners, speech, and deportment generally. Also, she teaches him to broaden his education by reading. Jean-Christophe begs Minna to wait until he becomes famous, and Minna declares her undying love for him, but Frau von Kerich adroitly persuades Minna that Jean-Christophe would make a most unsuitable husband. The romance dies and for a time Jean-Christophe is hurt and miserable. During this period, Melchior drowns himself.

Part III. Youth. Chap. 1. Jean-Christophe and his mother move to a small flat in the house of an old man, JUSTUS EULER. The orchestra, his pupils and his composing fill most of Christophe's time. Frau AMALIA VOGEL, Euler's married daughter, attempts to make a match between her daughter ROSA and Christophe, but he never even notices her machinations.

Chap. 2. Across a court from Christophe's apartment there is a shop run by SABINE, a young widow with a small daughter. Sabine's gentle beauty and serenity attract Christophe and he falls in love with her. Before he so much as kisses her, he leaves for a concert tour; and when he returns Sabine is dead of influenza.

Chap. 3. On one of his frequent strolls in the country, Christophe meets ADA, a rather crude and ignorant shop girl. Christophe is greatly attracted to her and they become lovers. His love turns to disgust when he learns that she has engaged in a casual affair with his brother, ERNEST, who has returned home after being discharged successively from a number of jobs. Christophe starts drinking heavily but is checked sharply when his uncle GOTTFRIED addresses him as "Melchior."

Part IV. Revolt. Chap. 1. Christophe throws himself into his music and is shocked to find fallacies in the works of his previous idols. He prepares an elaborate concert of his compositions, certain that the audience will acclaim the truth and honesty expressed in his music; but his defiance of familiar forms and classic harmonies bewilders and bores the audience, and his shame becomes fury as he realizes that he is rejected. A ray of hope appears in the person of FRANZ MANNHEIM, who is part-owner of a newspaper. He invites Christophe to become its music critic and guarantees full freedom. Christophe lashes out cruelly at performers, composers, and conductors. So bitter are his diatribes that they cease to trouble his victims, who merely laugh.

Chap. 2. A troupe of French actors comes to town and Christophe, seeing a young Frenchwoman who cannot obtain tickets, invites her to join him. She is very shy and self-conscious, but eventually accepts. Christophe learns afterward that her name is ANTOINETTE JEANNIN and that she is a governess. She loses her position for being seen in public with Christophe, whom her employers take to be her lover. She disappears and Christophe cannot find her. Shortly thereafter he loses his job on the paper and becomes the critic for a Socialist review. The grand duke is enraged and will no longer pay Christophe. This wipes out completely Christophe's income.

Chap. 3. Gottfried has died and Christophe now has no one except his mother, who understands nothing of his inner turmoil. He wants to leave Germany, but she pleads her age and infirmity. Christophe goes on a trip to Buir, where he becomes involved in a tavern brawl with some soldiers. One soldier is fatally injured. A young woman whom Christophe championed in the fight helps him to reach a train to Belgium, and Christophe is at last across the frontier and free from pursuit. He boards a train to Paris.

BOOK II. JEAN-CHRISTOPHE IN PARIS

Part I. The Marketplace. Chap. 1. The gaily lighted hotels in sight of the station in Paris seem too ostentatious and Christophe finds a dreary, dismal room in a side-street hotel. He seeks an old friend, SYLVAIN KOHN, who works for a publisher. Kohn has changed his name to Hamilton. He is glad to see Christophe and takes him to a music publisher, DANIEL HECHT, who insultingly offers Christophe a job writing piano scores. Christophe's furious rejection delights Kohn, who obtains several piano students for him. Among them is 18-year-old COLETTE STEVENS, a born coquette. Her attempts to charm Christophe meet with no reaction. At the Stevens house Christophe meets ACHILLE ROUSSIN, a Socialist deputy.

Chap. 2. Under the auspices of Kohn, Christophe is introduced to all the myriad forms of drama, music, opera, poetry and art in vogue during that period in Paris. There are decadence, immorality, and defiant violation of tradition, mixed with rigid adherence to old forms. In vain Christophe seeks honesty in the arts. This cannot be the France he has sought. Kohn only laughs, and Kohn is right.

Chap. 3. Christophe finds himself interested in the Old Testament story of David and Saul, and writes a musical interpretation of it. Roussin makes a stage production of it. The woman selected to sing the part of the boy David is quite wrong for the rôle and Christophe asks to have her removed. He learns that she is Roussin's mistress and that the entire production was undertaken for her sake. Christophe is dis-

at the theater.

Olivier fails his examination. Antoinette sustains them both for another year and Olivier finally passes, but Antoinette succumbs to tuberculosis and dies. Shortly after her funeral Olivier encounters Christophe at the Roussin home. Christophe and Olivier decide to take an apartment together.

Part III. The House. Chaps. 1–3. In the house where Christophe and Olivier take rooms, there are many different families. Christophe becomes acquainted with all of them and has an effect on all the lives in the house, and they are enriched by it. Guided by Olivier, he becomes acquainted with true French people, whom he had not met previously in Paris. Christophe and Olivier make very little money but they are happy together. Christophe's great vitality strengthens Olivier, and Olivier's similarity to Antoinette comforts Christophe. A kindly Jew, TADDÉE MOOCH, frequently obtains commissions for them. Through him, Hecht publishes Christophe's *David,* and its performance wins critical acclaim. Christophe's music is at last achieving recognition. He and Olivier collaborate on a Rabelaisian work. Christophe receives a brief note from Louisa, asking him to come to her. She dies a few minutes after he arrives. Olivier attends the funeral, but the German police are still seeking him and he gets away.

BOOK III. JEAN-CHRISTOPHE:
JOURNEY'S END

Part I. Love and Friendship. Chap. 1. Christophe and Olivier are poor even while Christophe's music is receiving great acclaim. Then unexpectedly a newspaper publisher decides to use his power to "make" Christophe. Reporters and writers besiege him, and in a short time Christophe is famous. He now makes money with less difficulty and more frequency. Olivier falls in love with JACQUELINE LANGEAIS, a shallow, selfish girl of wealthy parentage. Christophe encourages the romance, but after the marriage they shut themselves off from everyone—including Christophe. Then Jacqueline becomes bored, and the birth of a child does not draw her any closer to Olivier. She runs away with a writer and Olivier returns to Christophe. Soon after this, Christophe chances to meet Grazia again and regretfully learns that she is married and is going to the United States with her husband.

Part II. The Burning Bush. Chap. 1. Christophe becomes interested in the political unrest in Paris, taking hold in some quarters. There is to be a Communist rally on May 1, and there are rumors that the working classes are being mobilized. Christophe is outspoken in his championship of the working classes and Olivier cannot make him see the danger of this. Christophe insists upon attending the rally and takes Olivier with him. Unwittingly he becomes involved in a fight, and he is astonished to see a soldier bearing down on him with a

Colette's attempts to charm Jean-Christophe meet with no reaction

gusted, especially so when he finds that the Paris public is scoffing him. Little GRAZIA BUONTEMPI, Colette's cousin, to whom Christophe also gave piano lessons, grieves for him and yearns to comfort him, but she goes back to the countryside and woodlands she loves. Christophe does not suspect that one day she will fill an important part in his life. He is no longer welcome among Roussin's crowd of sycophants, and his small student enrollment dwindles to nothing. He takes a small garret room, which is miserably cold, and he becomes very ill. He is nursed by SIDONIE, who lives in the next apartment. When he recovers she tells him she is giving up her job and going away, and he does not suspect that it is because of her love for him. Roussin breaks with the singer who was his mistress and

again feels quite friendly toward Christophe. At Roussin's Christophe meets OLIVIER JEANNIN, a painfully shy young poet and artist who is almost a worshiper of Christophe's music. Christophe finds both the name and the young man's appearance familiar but cannot place them. However, Christophe knows he has found a real friend.

Part II. Antoinette. The Jeannin family had for centuries lived in the same town. When M. Jeannin, a banker, lost his money to a swindler he shot himself and left his wife and two children destitute. They moved to Paris, where Mme. Jeannin died shortly afterward. The daughter, Antoinette, worked as a governess to put her brother, Olivier, through school. It was at this time that she encountered Christophe bayonet. Christophe turns the blade against the soldier and kills him. Olivier has taken a bayonet thrust intended for another, and is dying. A friend tells Christophe to go quickly to Switzerland and Olivier will meet him there. Christophe goes, and Olivier dies without regaining consciousness.

Chaps. 2–3. In Switzerland Christophe goes to the place where his friends have arranged for him to stay. A letter the next day tells him of Olivier's death, and he walks madly for hours. He is near complete collapse when he reaches the house of his old friend, DR. ERICH BRAUN. When he recovers, his first thought is to obtain pupils and not be a burden on Braun and his wife, ANNA, but his notoriety hampers this. Anna and he find themselves enmeshed in an affair so powerful that neither has any control over it. The shame of their betrayal of Braun gnaws at them unmercifully, and at length Christophe slips away. In a lonely farmhouse in the Jura Mountains of Switzerland, Christophe makes his peace with himself and God and throws his energies into composition. His music is different now, and it satisfies him.

Part III. The New Dawn. Chap. 1. Years pass, and Christophe is famous everywhere. He is white-haired and aging. He is no longer a fugitive. In the mountains of Switzerland he meets Grazia again. She is a widow with two children. They find that they love each other deeply, but she will not marry him because she thinks marriage would destroy their beautiful companion-ship.

Chap. 2. Christophe goes back to Paris, after 20 years, to conduct a series of concerts. He finds many changes but still feels alternately fascinated and disgusted with the anthill that is Paris. Grazia comes to Paris and their love grows. LIONELLO, Grazia's son, dislikes Christophe and plays on his mother's weakness to prevent their marriage, feigning illness. But he becomes really ill, and Grazia also is ill, so that her doctor sends her to Egypt to avoid the northern winter. Christophe grieves for her.

Chap. 3. Olivier's son, GEORGES, has looked up Christophe, and they have become good friends. When there is a controversy over Christophe's work, George fights a duel to defend him. Grazia's son dies of tuberculosis, then Grazia dies. Colette break the news to Christophe. For a long time Christophe retires into himself, but eventually he is again at peace.

Chap. 4. Georges and AURORA, Grazia's daughter, meet through Christophe and fall in love. They are married, and though Christophe is ill he refuses to succumb until after the wedding. Then he collapses. As he lies in his bed, he asks himself whether it is better for him or his music to live on. He answers unhesitatingly that the music must live. Jean-Christophe dies.

Jean-Christophe throws all his energies into the work of composition

Jeeves

Novel by Pelham Grenville Wodehouse, 1881–
Published & © 1923 by Doubleday & Co., New York. (PB, 28)

JEEVES, THE PERFECT BUTLER, is the best-known creation of P. G. Wodehouse. No funnier writer than Wodehouse has existed in this century, if ever. It is true that Wodehouse too soon got the habit of using the same funny characters, scenes and devices over and over, but the original of any of them is worth anyone's reading time.

Chaps. 1–2. JEEVES, the perfect gentleman's gentleman, is advised by his master, BERTIE WOOSTER, that BINGO LITTLE, Bertie's friend, has a difficult problem. Bingo wants to marry MABEL, a waitress, but he fears that his rich old uncle will not approve. Jeeves suggests that Bingo read to his uncle some novels that depict the amours of upper-class gentlemen and working girls. Jeeves has been courting the uncle's cook and knows enough about the old codger to predict that romantic fiction will soften him up. Bingo gets laryngitis from reading to the old man, but the scheme works; the uncle gives his permission for Bingo to marry Mabel. However, the uncle cannot raise Bingo's allowance, as he himself has decided to marry his incomparable cook. Jeeves does not mind losing the cook, for he has come to know Mabel and she prefers him to Bingo.

Chaps. 3–4. Bertie's Aunt AGATHA is vacationing on the Riviera and invites Bertie to join her. He arrives and finds that she has selected a mate for him. Bertie meets the girl, ALINE HEMMINGWAY, and her brother SIDNEY, a curate. The girl is prim and plain and hardly to Bertie's taste. One day Sidney confesses to Bertie that he has indiscreetly gambled and lost more than he could afford and to cover his loss he made out a bad check. Aline and Sidney beg Bertie to lend them enough to make the check good. Bertie gives them the money and they give him a box supposedly containing a string of pearls. After they leave, Bertie discovers the box is empty. Jeeves tells him that the curate is Soapy Sid, a notorious jewel thief, and Aline is his accomplice. Jeeves then hands Bertie a duplicate box, which he lifted from the thief's overcoat. The box contains the pearls, which were stolen from Aunt Agatha.

Chaps. 5–8. Jeeves takes his annual holiday and leaves Bertie to his own devices. Aunt Agatha suggests another likely mate for Bertie, HONORIA GLOSSOP, an athletic type of girl. Bertie visits the Glossop estate, where Bingo, temporarily out of funds, is tutoring young OSWALD GLOSSOP. Bingo is in love with Honoria, and Bertie figures out what Jeeves might do in the situation. He tells Bingo to hide behind a bush near a bridge over a stream. Bertie will bring Honoria and Oswald and will slyly push Oswald into the water. Bingo will leap in and save the boy and become a hero in Honoria's eyes, and Bertie will be off the hook. Bertie does push Oswald into the water but Bingo is not there because he is chasing a more beautiful girl. Bertie has to jump in after the boy, who turns out to be a better swimmer than Bertie. Honoria is amused but touched and she decides to make a man of Bertie. Within two weeks Honoria has Bertie under control but he is shocked by her statement that Jeeves must go after they are married. Sir RODERICK, Honoria's father, is a nerve specialist, and he is concerned about Bertie because he pushed Oswald into the water. Jeeves returns and Bertie has him prepare lunch for the expected visit of Sir Roderick. Jeeves sets up a series of circumstances that convince Sir Roderick that Bertie is insane. The wedding is called off, and to avoid Aunt Agatha's wrath Jeeves suggests a trip to America.

Chaps. 9–10. Bertie is having a fine time in New York but longs for his old haunts in London. CYRIL BASSINGTON-BASSINGTON arrives, bearing a letter of introduction from Aunt Agatha. Bertie wants to make a favorable impression on Cyril, so that Cyril will send back a favorable report and Bertie can return to England. Cyril's love is the theater and he gets a small rôle in a musical comedy, just before word comes from Aunt Agatha that Bertie must by no means allow Cyril to have anything to do with the stage. Jeeves comes to the rescue by bribing the small son of the show's backer to insult Cyril, and Cyril quits the play.

Chaps. 11–12. Bertie and Jeeves return to England. Bingo is involved with another love, CHARLOTTE CORDAY ROWBOTHAM the daughter of a revolutionary, who has so intrigued Bingo that he wears a false beard to make her father think he is a Bolshevist. In this disguise Bingo makes a verbal attack on his uncle, Lord BRITTLE-SHAM, who has cut his allowance. He also sends his uncle a threatening letter. Then he gets £50 from the old man as expenses in tracking down the bearded culprit. Jeeves breaks up the affair with Charlotte by revealing Bingo's true identity to Charlotte's other suitor, who pulls his beard in front of all the comrades.

Chaps. 13–14. London is hot in August and Bertie goes to visit at Twing Hall in the country. His twin cousins are there, studying for an exam, and Bingo Little is tutor to the son of the family. Bertie and the others set up a sweepstakes in which the entries are all the pastors in the region. The one who preaches the longest sermon will be the winning entry. Bertie and the other members of the betting syndicate think they have a sure thing, but their man gets laryngitis and they switch their bets, only to lose because their parson hired another man to read his long-winded sermon. A few days later a fair is held with various events, such as a Choir Boys' Handicap Race, a Mother's Sash Race and a bird's Egg and Spoon Race. The first two races are lost by the syndicate choice because they have been deviously fixed by a local character. Jeeves saves them from ruin and recoups their fortunes on the last race by his own skullduggery.

Chaps. 15–16. Bertie, back in London, gets an urgent wire from Bingo at Twing Hall. Bingo is in love once more. Jeeves, who knows everything, says the girl this time is MARY BURGESS, the vicar's daughter. Bertie and Jeeves decide that Mary is the right girl for Bingo and they go to Twing Hall to help him win the girl. After they return to London they receive another urgent plea for help and Jeeves goes to counsel Bingo, who is losing ground to a rival suitor. Bingo takes Jeeves' advice to do good works, such as reading to the patients in the local hospital, but then ruins himself by putting on a musical revue in town. Mary marries the other suitor, but Jeeves has made a tidy sum by betting against Bingo.

Chaps. 17–18. Bertie's twin cousins fall in love with the same girl, who cares for neither one. Aunt Agatha, who thinks the twins are in Africa, is distressed because their father thinks he has seen them in London. She is considering packing the old

man off to an asylum. Jeeves induces the twins to go to Africa by telling their loved one has gone there. Bingo Little marries a waitress, who turns out to be ROSIE M. BANKS, the authoress of romantic novels Bingo once read to his uncle. For various reasons Bingo told his uncle that Bertie was the author of the books, and now Lord Brittlesham is furious at the hoax. Bingo faces a poor financial future, as his uncle threatens to cut off his allowance, but Jeeves comes to the rescue by telling Lord Brittlesham that Bertie is a looney and thinks he is Rosie M. Banks. Bertie is aghast, but he cannot contemplate getting along without his incomparable valet and Jeeves is forgiven.

Bingo's beard is pulled off

John Brown's Body

Poem by Stephen Vincent Benét, 1898–1943.
Published 1927 by Rinehart & Co., New York. © 1927, 1928 by Stephen Vincent Benét.

THIS LONG NARRATIVE POEM is novel length and actually is a novel in poetry, carrying the full stories of its various characters on both sides of the Civil War. As a historical novel it is interesting and educational, for Benét was diligent in his research and careful of his facts. Most of the poem is in blank verse but there are many beautiful lyric passages in rhyme. *John Brown's Body* won the Pulitzer Prize for poetry in 1928. It is the finest thing of its kind that has been written in America.

Prelude. The Yankee captain of a slave ship reads the Bible. Below in the hold is his cargo, a mass of chanting, groaning, terrified and miserable Negro slaves. The stench is formidable. The captain finds Biblical assurance that he is doing what the Lord bids. His young mate is not so sure.

Book I. JACK ELLYAT, a young man of

Connecticut, hunts in the autumn woods with his dog and has a premonition of war. He is not sure what is right but thinks he knows. CLAY WINGATE of Georgia, a member of one of the best Southern families, is handsome, spoiled and carefree; he is occupied with enjoying himself. In Maryland JOHN BROWN prays to the Lord and knows that he must fight to free the slaves. John Brown leads his 21 men in an attempt to capture the arsenal at Harper's Ferry, [West] Virginia. Two of John Brown's sons are killed and Brown is taken prisoner. In Georgia, the Wingates and their friends have a grand ball. Clay dances with SALLY DUPRÉ, who is very pretty but whose father was only a French dancing master. Sally is in love with Clay. Jack Ellyat and his family in Connecticut read the news of the raid on Harper's Ferry. John Brown is hanged after he makes an eloquent speech.

Book II. Fort Sumter falls and young men everywhere are going off to war. Clay Wingate is in the Black Horse Troop. He thinks of death and he thinks of Sally Dupré. The slaves wonder what it will be like to be free and big splayfooted SPADE thinks of escape. JAKE DEIFER, Pennsylvania farmer, hates to leave his farm and family to fight, but must. LUKE BRECKINRIDGE and his cousin, JIM, illiterate mountain men, enlist for the South chiefly because their hated neighbors, the Kelceys, are fighting for the North. Jack Ellyat is in the Northern Army. The First Battle of Bull Run is fought. Congressmen come out to see the show. Ellyat and Wingate are there, and so are Stonewall Jackson and Jefferson Davis. Walt Whitman reports the defeat and depression of the Union Army.

Book III. Jack Ellyat, wounded at Bull Run, is mustered out but reënlists and is with GRANT at Pittsburg Landing. He is taken prisoner but escapes and hides with a family of draft-dodgers. The daughter of the family, MELORA VILAS, who is 17 years old, is irresistibly drawn to Ellyat and goes to him where he sleeps outside. Ellyat loves her but feels compelled to rejoin the Union Army and again is taken prisoner.

Book IV. The South rejoices over its victories. Clay Wingate comes home to Wingate Hall. There is a grand ball—the dying gasp of Wingate's class—and Clay meets LUCY WEATHERBY, pretty, silly, and vain. Clay is fascinated, Sally Dupré is jealous. The tide of battle shifts; Grant's star rises. Spade escapes and makes his way through impossible obstacles to the North and supposed freedom.

Book V. Lincoln worries and wonders and asks God for guidance. Spade finds freedom is not what he thought; his blackness and his ignorance are exploited in the free North to the point of slavery. Melora Vilas is pregnant with Jack Ellyat's baby, and Jack suffers and starves in a prison camp. Jack plans to escape, but luck is with him and he is exchanged.

Book VI. The South begins to starve. Sally Dupré longs for Clay Wingate. In snowy New England Jack Ellyat recovers from his wounds and thinks of Melora. SHIPPY, a frightened little peddler who is acting as a spy only because he was too frightened to refuse, is caught and hanged on accusation of Luke Breckinridge—solely because Luke is Shippy's rival for the favor of SOPHY, a Richmond chambermaid. Lucy Weatherby in Richmond looks adoringly at her own reflection in the mirror and prepares to flee to safety. Stonewall Jackson dies.

Book VII. Lee makes his tremendous effort and the Battle of Gettysburg begins. Ellyat is there, now a seasoned veteran. The Union Army prevails; Appomattox is now inevitable. Ellyat is wounded again.

Book VIII. The Black Horse Troop is detailed to a desperate rear guard action but Clay Wingate is only wounded. The war ends with Lee's dignity matching Grant's generosity. Jake Deifer is back on his farm in Pennsylvania, minus an arm. Spade comes along and Jake hires him. Jack Ellyat is at home in Connecticut. Wingate Hall burns to the ground, but when Clay limps home Sally Dupré is waiting there for him. Melora sets out for the North with her father and her son, looking for Jack Ellyat, and finally she finds him. John Brown's body molders but from the fertilization of his moldering body grows a new nation.

Joseph and His Brothers

Tetralogy (four novels) by Thomas Mann, 1875–1955.
Published 1933–1944 by Alfred A. Knopf, New York. Translated from the German by H. T. Lowe-porter. © by Alfred A. Knopf.

THE STORY OF JOSEPH became a matter of consuming interest to Germany's greatest modern novelist and he told it in four novels published over the course of 11 years. Mann treated Joseph and the other ancients of his time as the spiritual and psychological ancestors of modern man. Most American critics have considered the Joseph epic Thomas Mann's greatest work.

Joseph and His Brothers

Prelude. Young JOSEPH, son of JACOB and RACHEL, is noted for his charm. He traces his physical and spiritual being back to a restless, brooding man [obviously ABRAHAM], who long before left Ur to wander like the moon, the deity of Ur. This wanderer, according to tradition, found a god whom he called provisionally by the plural Elohim, The Godhead. Elohim had promised him and his people everlasting possession of Canaan.

Chap. 1. Beside a well, handsome young Joseph, having washed and anointed himself, prays to the moon. His father, the aged Jacob, comes from the tents where they live, looking for him. Earlier, Joseph had planned to join his older brothers (of whom he has ten), but one of them, GAD, told him he was not wanted. Joseph, a compulsive prattler and talebearer, reports this to his father. As a result of Joseph's talebearing against REUBEN, the eldest brother and son of LEAH, Jacob plans to take from Reuben the rights of the first son and give them to his beloved Joseph, son of Jacob's favorite, Rachel. Jacob muses, recalling how the limp he has had for 12 years came from wrestling with a stranger (in the Bible, an angel) who gave him the name Israel, "God doeth battle," in which he takes great pride. Jacob tells Joseph he is worried about a drouth and Joseph tells of a dream in which he heard the Lord order rain. Jacob urges him not to tell his brothers of his gift of vision or they will be envious. But the next day, despite his promises, Joseph tells his brothers of his weather dreams. The brothers are annoyed, especially when a heavy rain comes.

Chap. 2. The story is told of ELIPHAZ, who set out to avenge his father, Jacob's twin brother ESAU, from whom Jacob tried to steal the inheritance from their father Isaac. Eliphaz pursued Jacob and with five or six armed men he overtook the fleeing Jacob in the desert. Jacob surrendered and blamed the trick on his mother, REBECCA. Eliphaz spared his

Jacob rides eastward

uncle's life, but he insisted on taking for Esau all the riches that Rebecca had given Jacob. Jacob had to continue eastward with nothing but his camel. Much later in time, after God had blessed Jacob and he had received the name Israel, Jacob and Esau were reconciled, but when Esau suggested

that they live together in brotherly fashion, Jacob politely refused, and they parted.

Chap. 3. Jacob and his family reach the city of Shechem in Canaan. Jacob's older sons suggest that they capture and plunder it, but Jacob refuses; they are not thieves but descendants of Abraham, a mighty prince. Jacob makes a compact with the Shechemites and settles in a tent community near the city. Some four years later, at a seven-day feast of the vintage, SICHEM, son of HAMOR, ruler of Shechem, falls in love with Jacob's 13-year-old daughter DINAH. Hamor suggests a marriage. First Jacob and his elder sons stipulate that Sichem must be circumcised, and this is done. Then the brothers hesitate because Sichem already has a wife and it is unfitting for Dinah to be merely a concubine. Jacob is distressed when Sichem abducts Dinah; he knows his sons have provoked this action to get an excuse to sack the city. Sichem asks them to fix the conditions of his marriage to Dinah and they insist that all the male citizens of Shechem be circumcised. When this is done, the crafty brothers attack and destroy the city while every man in it is suffering too much to fight. Jacob condemns his sons' act and removes his entire tribe to the sanctuary of Beth-el.

Chaps. 4–6. Jacob recalls how his mother told him that he, Jacob, was really the first-born son, but Isaac selected Jacob's twin, Esau. When the brothers were almost 30, Rebecca took advantage of Isaac's near-blindness to get the eldest son's blessing and inheritance for Jacob, when Isaac thought he was giving it to Esau. Though the hoax succeeded, Esau was so angry that Rebecca decided to send Jacob to her brother, LABAN, in far-off Aram. There Jacob met and loved Laban's daughter Rachel, but to win her he had to work for Laban 14 years and first marry Rachel's older sister, Leah. Then Jacob continued to live with Laban and became independently rich. He had sons by Leah, and by Leah's maid ZILPHA and by Rachel's maid BILHAH, but not by his beloved Rachel.

Chap. 7. In the 13th year of marriage and the 26th year of Jacob's sojourn, Rachel became pregnant. Before the child's birth, the joyful Jacob had already named it DUMUZI, the "true son." Leah, sick with jealousy, told her sons that if Rachel had a boy, Jacob would no longer be interested in them. Thus she planted the first seed of hatred in the brothers for Joseph. When at last the child was born, Jacob's 11th son, called Joseph, Jacob heard God's voice telling him to go with his family in the direction of the Mount of Gilead. They left during Laban's absence. Laban pursued but Jacob made a peaceful compact with him. It is Jacob's return journey that has taken him past Shechem. Now Rachel is pregnant again and Jacob is joyous but worried, for she had great trouble giving birth to Joseph. Rachel gives birth to another son, BENJAMIN, but dies. After she is buried, Jacob, now called Israel, continues on his journey.

Young Joseph

Chaps. 1–2. Joseph at 17 is an unusually handsome boy. He sometimes tends his father's flocks with his ten older brothers, but Jacob permits him to spend much free time in study, secretly hoping that this most-loved son will outstrip the others so that Jacob can give him the rights of the first-born. He also hopes it will give more stability to the boy, who is given to ecstatic states and prophetic seizures.

Chap. 3. Joseph tells his little 8-year-old brother, Benjamin, Rachel's other son and the only brother with any respect for him, of a dream. In the dream, Joseph is tending sheep when an eagle, representing an angel, snatches him up and takes him heavenward on a journey hours long. He sees God, who makes him a mighty prince. Joseph urges Benjamin not to tell the other brothers of the dream. The little boy points out that it is the talkative Joseph who can never resist telling.

Chap. 4. Joseph prods his father to give him a promised gift. Reluctantly Jacob discloses that it is the sumptuous wedding veil worn by Leah and Rachel, but he wants to defer giving it to avoid his other sons' jealousy. Joseph coaxes and is allowed to try it on. Wrapped in this coat of many colors he is so breathtakingly handsome, so like the beloved Rachel, that Jacob allows him to keep it. As Jacob feared, the gift arouses tremendous excitement and bitterness. Later, during the harvest season, Joseph insists on telling his brothers about one of his dreams. In this dream, he and his brothers are harvesting the grain, cutting the stalks, and binding the sheaves. Joseph's sheaf stands upright and the brothers' sheaves do obeisance to it. The brothers (except for Benjamin, who is not present) are enraged. Joseph provokes them further by relating another dream in which he is ruler of the world. The ten older brothers go to Shechem, to tend Jacob's flocks there.

Chap. 5. Jacob seeks to heal the breach by sending Joseph to Shechem with his greetings. On Joseph's arrival, his still resentful brothers fall upon him like wolves and rip off his prized many-colored veil and all his other clothing. Reuben, without fighting his brothers, tries to protect Joseph. When they wish to kill Joseph, Reuben dissuades them. Then they throw Joseph, bloody and bruised, down an old, dried-up well. They cover the well with the mossy well stone. Inside the pit, Joseph now knows that he has brought himself to this pass through his blissful conceit and the false assumption that everyone loves him.

Joseph remains in the pit for three days and three nights. Then he is rescued by Ishmaelite [Arab] traveling merchants looking for water at the well. The leader is impressed with him, especially when Joseph says he can read tablets and write cuneiform, and decides to take him along.

Reuben has decided to deceive the others

Potiphar's wife accuses Joseph

and rescue Joseph; but when he goes to the pit he finds it empty. Meanwhile, the others have learned of the Ishmaelites' presence. They sell Joseph to the Ishmaelites as a slave. Then they kill a lamb to honor the travelers and in its blood they dip the tattered bridal veil. Reuben, returning excitedly from the well, is not told of these happenings. They merely show him the bloody veil, explaining that they will let Jacob interpret from it that Joseph was killed by a lion.

When Jacob sees the bloody coat, he faints, laments, and even doubts God. Deep within him, perhaps not even consciously, he suspects the brothers of having a hand in murdering Joseph. In time, the brothers recall only vaguely what they did with Joseph. Because he is absent, their hatred for him ebbs. They can even grieve with Jacob for the absent one.

Joseph in Egypt

Chap. 1. Joseph is carried, a slave of the Ishmaelite merchants, across the desert to Egypt. He calls himself Usarsiph or Osarsiph ("the dead Joseph"); he is not unhappy but he views himself as one who is dead, a view reinforced by the journey to Egypt, the place always described by Jacob as the underworld—the kingdom of the dead.

Chaps. 2–4. In Egypt, at the city of Weset-per-Amun, Joseph is sold to MONT-KAW, steward in the house of Petepre, or POTIPHAR, a high official of the king. The steward is impressed by Joseph's looks, wit, and learning. His purchase of Joseph is favored by the kindly dwarf, SHEPSES-BES, while the household's other dwarf, DUDU, opposes it.

Through the efforts of Bes, Joseph gets a job as one of Potiphar's gardeners. One evening in the garden, he meets Potiphar and uses the opportunity to win his interest. Next day, Mont-kaw, eager to please his master, gives Joseph the task of waiting on Potiphar in the dining room and reading to him after meals. The steward also directs Joseph to understudy him in his work as overseer so that Joseph can be-

come his assistant. Mont-kaw then binds him in a pact to serve the master.

Chap. 5. Joseph gradually assumes the rôle of Potiphar's servant and spends considerable time reading to him, much to Potiphar's enjoyment. Mont-kaw marvels at the ease with which the youth grasps the problems of running the household. Soon Joseph is sent on business trips. He is popular and gets excellent prices for the estate's merchandise. Joseph retains the wisdom learned in the pit and makes great efforts to win good will. Only the dwarf Dudu, keeper of the robes, dislikes him, complaining about him to MUT-EM-ENET, who is Potiphar's wife, though in name only. Mut now begins to notice him. By the end of Joseph's 7th year the aging Mont-kaw has entrusted oversight of all the estate to him. Mont-kaw becomes ill and before he dies he blesses Joseph as his own son and makes over to him his office as steward.

Chap. 6. Mut becomes passionately attracted to Joseph. Afraid of her love for him, she asks her husband to send him away, but Potiphar refuses, despite her many false charges against him. Dudu, the troublemaker, seeks to fan the situation into an explosion. The good Bes warns Joseph. Joseph disregards the warning and meets Mut many times, for she pretends she is interested only in his practical talk of the household. When finally she reveals her love, Joseph wards off her advances. Not only is he loyal to his master, but he thinks of himself as betrothed to God; also, Mut to him represents the evil of Egypt that Jacob taught him to hate.

Chap. 7. Mut makes several unsuccessful attempts to seduce Joseph and even proposes that the two of them kill Potiphar. Dudu reports to Potiphar that the two are mutually infatuated. Mut loses all discretion, telling her friends of her love and seeking to win Joseph through hideous magic spells. On New Year's Day, Mut remains at home, telling Potiphar she will not participate in the public ceremonials. Joseph returns to the almost empty house a little ahead of the others and she tries once again to seduce him. He flees from her, leaving his jacket in her clutching hands. Half-demented, she screams out that she has been attacked. Joseph is seized by the returning members of the household. Potiphar spares him a severe punishment but sentences him to prison and slavery in the service of PHARAOH.

Joseph the Provider

Chap. 1. Joseph is sent by freight boat to the island prison fortress of Zawi-Re, in Lower Egypt. The governor, MAI-SACHME, a physician and amateur writer, is happy to have Joseph as an office assistant. Within six months Joseph has become the governor's right-hand man. Mai-Sachme enjoys both his conversation about literature and his stories of his past life. Two high officials of Pharaoh come to the prison, accused of conspiracy. Joseph, instructed by Mai-Sachme to make them comfortable, interprets their dreams for them, correctly foretelling that one will be pardoned, the other executed. The pardoned official promises to mention Joseph to Pharaoh but forgets to do so.

Chap. 2. The old Pharaoh dies and his young son ascends the throne. One day a messenger comes to take Joseph in haste to the new Pharaoh, to interpret two dreams. The pardoned official has at last remembered Joseph. The king, AMEN-HOTEP, a slender, sickly boy of 16, is subject to disabling headaches but explains his attacks as visitations from the god, Aton, whom he reveres.

Chap. 3. Joseph amuses and calms the emotional king. He declares that Amenhotep has dreamed only one dream but has dreamed it twice for emphasis. He suggests that the dream—seven fat cattle devoured by seven lean ones and seven fat ears of corn swallowed up by seven barren ears—represents God's prophecy of seven good crop years and seven bad. Joseph warns that grain must immediately be stored for the future famine and suggests that a "middleman" must be appointed to take over the task of husbanding food, setting prices, and educating the people to the needs of the time. Amenhotep appoints Joseph as the middleman, chief overseer over all.

Chaps. 4–5. Joseph initiates a system of taxation requiring the people to give the government a fifth of the grain harvest. He has many storehouses built to hold the surpluses. In the splendid house given him

by Pharaoh he installs his old friend, Mai-Sachme, as steward. Pharaoh even arranges Joseph's marriage to ASENATH, daughter of a high priest. During the fat years, Joseph's reputation grows and he becomes the father of two sons, MANASSEH and EPHRAIM.

In the first of the seven lean years, only Egypt has grain and cereal, and its power becomes greater. Joseph distributes supplies to all, demanding gold and silver for the government from those who can pay and giving it away to the poor. In the second lean year, his brothers come from Canaan to buy corn. He speaks to them through an interpreter, pretending unfamiliarity with their language, but he manages to learn that Jacob is alive. He pretends to think them spies and insists that they show good faith by bringing their youngest brother, Benjamin, on their next trip, and he holds one of them, SIMEON, as hostage. On the trip home they discover that the money they paid for the food has been returned to them.

Chap. 6. The brothers tell Jacob, now a patriarch of 90, their incredible story. At first he refuses to let them take Benjamin, only child of Rachel left to him; but after a year, when his tribe is again starving, he permits Benjamin, now almost 30, to go. In Egypt, Joseph showers attention on Benjamin, who begins to sense faint, intuitive stirrings of recognition. Joseph appears satisfied and allows the brothers to depart for home, but Mai-Sachme pursues them and accuses them of filching Joseph's valuable wine cup. They deny the charge, but the cup is found (as Joseph and his friend have arranged) in the sack of Benjamin. The brothers are taken back to Joseph, who decides he will hold Benjamin as his servant. Conscientious Judah, the fourth son, offers to remain instead, saying that thus he can expiate for all the brothers their sin in selling their 11th brother. Joseph is so overwhelmed with emotion that he reveals his identity. He sends them to bring Jacob to him.

Chap. 7. With his entire tribe the old

man journeys to Goshen, where Joseph comes to greet him. Pharaoh gives Joseph permission to settle his people in Goshen, and they become the overseers of Pharaoh's flocks. Jacob lives there in his tent for 17 years. Before dying, he hands on the blessing of Abraham to Judah. He believes that God has denied the blessing to Joseph as a punishment to him, Jacob, for his secret wish to give it to Joseph, but he exalts Joseph by taking Manasseh and Ephraim as his own sons. Joseph takes Jacob's body to be buried in Canaan, but Pharaoh will not risk either losing Joseph or hurting his feelings and directs that a huge entourage of Egyptians accompany Jacob's family on the journey. Joseph and his brothers are reconciled, Joseph declaring that they have no need to seek his forgiveness because all of them have merely enacted their rôles in God's play.

Joseph Vance

Novel by William De Morgan, 1839–1917.
Published 1906 by Henry Holt & Co., New York. © 1934 by Mary Beatrice De Morgan.

THE REMARKABLE THING about *Joseph Vance* is that it was the first novel De Morgan wrote and De Morgan was 65 when he wrote it. Despite his advanced starting age, he inaugurated with this novel a career as a quite prolific novelist. *Joseph Vance* is an excellent novel, rated as one of De Morgan's two or three best. It has special interest through being the first.

Chaps. 1–5. (The story is a reminiscence of JOSEPH VANCE, or JOE, who is now about 60.) Joe is 7 years old when his father, a warehouseman in London, is discharged for impertinence to a superior. Joe's mother suspects that her husband's weakness for drink is responsible. On the day the elder Vance receives notice, Joe accompanies him to a public house, where he becomes drunk, gets into a dispute, and is knocked unconscious and taken to a hospital. He takes his time about getting a new job. A second-hand dealer sells him a signboard inscribed "C. Dance. Builder. Repairs. Drains promptly attended to." Vance, christened Christopher, sees a chance to start his own business by repainting a single letter, so that the sign reads "C. Vance." The firm's first job comes from kindly Dr. RANDALL THORPE, a scholar. Joe goes with his father to Poplar Villa, the Thorpe home, and meets the doctor's younger daughter, LOSSIE, a young lady of

Joseph amuses and calms the emotional Pharaoh

Mr. Vance looks authoritative

15, and her 2-year-old brother, JOEY.

Chaps. 6–10. Through the magic of his signboard, Vance gets business. He soon develops the technique that brings him phenomenal success—he stands by and looks authoritative while others do the work. Joe meanwhile becomes popular with Lossie, who adopts him as her "other" brother. Thorpe is impressed by the untutored Joe's grasp of mathematics and sends him to the school attended by his son Oliver, called NOLLY.

Chaps. 11–15. Joe becomes an enthusiastic student of the classics. Later, he goes to St. Withold's, a public school, where he is appalled by the cruelty of masters to boys and of boys to each other. At the end of the first term, having reached the top of all his classes, he goes home to find his father so prosperous that the family is to move to a fine house, with servants and an office nearby for Mr. Vance. Joe sees Lossie, who, with Joey, is visiting at the house of Mr. SPENCER, Thorpe's legal advisor.

Chaps. 16–26. About two years later Mrs. Vance dies of tuberculosis. Joe worries about his father, who is turning to whiskey for solace. Lossie goes to Mr. Vance and sweetly begs him to stop drinking. He consents and pours a bottle's contents on the parlor fire to prove his good intentions. Joe is at Oxford when Dr. Thorpe visits him in distress to tell of Lossie's engagement to Gen. HUGH DESPREZ, a distinguished soldier. Thorpe approves the match but hates to think of Lossie's living in India. Joe realizes his own love for Lossie and that he has lost her. He knows she loves him only as her little brother. Hugh accepts Joe as a member of the Thorpe family. Lossie and Hugh are married and depart. Mr. Vance turns to whiskey again. Joe graduates from Oxford but without the top honors he and Lossie had dreamed of. He dabbles in engineering, his hobby, inventing a special engine. He meets JANE SPENCER, daughter of the solicitor Lossie visited.

Chaps. 27–29. Joe considers marriage, thinking a woman's influence might curb his father's drinking, though his love is reserved for Lossie. He makes an unromantic proposal to Jane and is refused. Dr. Thorpe suggests the use of a little more romance. Joe tries again and is accepted. Janey comes to think Joe merely wants a wife, not her, and breaks the engagement.

Chaps. 30–39. Several years later, Mr. Vance's drinking is still a problem. He decides to marry his faithful housemaid, PHEENER, with the approval of Joe. Joe meets Janey again and begs her to forgive him. Confessing that she broke the engagement because of his fondness for Lossie, she accepts him this time. They are married eight weeks later. On their return from their wedding trip, Mr. Vance, while drunk, accidentally sets fire to his factory and house and is rescued just in time. It turns out he has forgotten to mail the current fees due on his insurance and he is ruined. Some money is realized through the sale of a diamond tiara he bought for Pheener in a period of affluence. He dies soon afterward.

Chaps. 40–47. In the spring of 1874, Joe and Janey are shipwrecked on a voyage to Italy and Janey is lost. Joe decides to help Dr. Thorpe by taking Joey, now called by Lossie's pet name of BEPPINO, to Italy. Beppino goes from Milan to Tuscany, taking Joe's trunk and leaving his own to be fixed. He writes Joe that because of the name Vance on the trunk he is called Vance by everyone. Joe receives a love letter from a woman in Florence. Beppino explains it away as a joke. Dr. Thorpe dies.

Chaps. 48–53. Joe gets another letter from Florence just as Beppino is to marry an heiress. On his wedding journey, Beppino contracts typhoid fever and dies. A new letter from Italy reveals that Beppino made an illegal marriage, in the name of Giuseppe Vance, to an Italian girl. She has died, after the birth of a baby boy, CRISTOFORO VANCE, now 8 weeks old. To spare Lossie the truth about her rascally brother, Joe arranges to adopt the boy, telling everyone he has befriended an orphan. He goes to Brazil as a civil engineer, intending to stay six months, but he remains 20 years. Unable to tell the truth about the child, he breaks off writing to Lossie, who believes rumors that he is the boy's true father. Cristoforo goes to Harvard and Joe spends two years in London doing research but hiding from all who might know him. Lossie, now a widow with grown children, learns the truth in an old letter of Beppino's. She traces Joe and happily takes him back to Italy with her, where presumably they marry.

Jude the Obscure

Novel by Thomas Hardy, 1840–1928. Published 1894. (ML, 135)

WHEN IT WAS first published, *Jude the Obscure* was criticized as coarse and blasphemous. By today's standard it is neither, nor does such criticism necessarily color the appraisal of the artistic value of a work, so *Jude the Obscure* is now considered one of Hardy's best novels and by some is placed first among his novels. Like Hardy's other novels, it is set in the Wessex region of England. Also like Hardy's other novels, it shows a man powerless in the grip of the circumstances that control his life.

Part I. At Marygreen. Chaps. 1–5. The schoolmaster, RICHARD PHILLOTSON, is leaving the village to study for a university degree at Christminster, 20 miles away. He tells a boy of 11, JUDE FAWLEY, to look him up if Jude ever gets to Christminster. Jude, an orphan, lives with his great-aunt, DRUSILLA FAWLEY, in the little Wessex village of Marygreen, where she has a small bakery. Jude loves to read and a quack physician, Dr. VILBERT, offers to give Jude some Latin and Greek grammars but does not. Jude sends a note to Phillotson, who sends him the books he requires. Jude is crushed to learn how hard it is to learn, but he determines to learn the languages and studies while driving his aunt's bakery cart. He is 16 and still wants to live in Christminster, but he knows he must learn a trade and becomes an apprentice to a stonemason in the neighboring hamlet of Alderston.

Chaps. 6–11. Jude at 19 is still studying and has acquired a proficiency in the classics, particularly Latin. As Jude is walking along the road one day three girls coyly try to attract him and Jude, who has never bothered with girls before, singles out one of them, ARABELLA DONN, and promises to call on her the following Sunday. Arabella has been advertising the fact that she is enamored of Jude, and one of her friends advises her to become pregnant by Jude, for he is honorable and would marry her. Arabella takes the advice, seduces Jude and tells him that she is pregnant. He marries her and they settle in a cottage near Marygreen. Jude learns that Arabella is not expecting a baby but is compelled to accept her word that she made a mistake. From the start, the marriage is not a happy one. To forget his sorrows, Jude gets drunk. Upon returning to his cottage he finds that Arabella has gone, leaving a letter saying she is going with her parents to Australia. Jude has no objections and decides to seek a new home in Christminster.

Part II. At Christminster. Chaps. 1–5. Before his departure, Jude visits his great-aunt Drusilla, who tells him that his cousin, SUE BRIDEHEAD, lives at Christminster. Jude has seen a picture of the lovely Sue and is more determined than ever to go. At Christminster, Jude obtains a job with a stonemason. He learns that Sue is a designer for an ecclesiastical warehouse; but he is still a married man and does not call on her. Sue writes to him and the two meet. They walk to the village of Lumsdon, where Phillotson lives, still a schoolmaster. Jude loves Sue and is heartsick when she loses her job and plans to leave Christminster. He arranges for her to assist Phillotson at his school. Then Jude is distressed when Phillotson, though much older, seems to be romantically interested in the girl.

Chaps. 6–7. Jude wants to enter the university, but he cannot get a scholarship and the tuition would take him at least 15 years to earn. He feels he could bear this crushing blow with Sue by his side, but without her the disappointment seems too much to bear. Jude gets drunk and walks to Lumsdon to see Sue. He rattles on incoherently, and Sue insists that he spend the night at Phillotson's. Ashamed, he leaves the house the next morning before Sue has come downstairs to breakfast. Jude goes to his great-aunt's house at Marygreen and meets the curate, Mr. HIGHBRIDGE, who says Jude may enter the Church as a licentiate if he gives up strong drink.

Part III. At Melchester. Chaps. 1–4. Sue enters a college at Melchester to study teaching. Jude goes to a theological college in the same town to study while working at his trade during the days. His ulterior motive is to be near Sue, but he determines to try to love her as a friend and cousin only. Sue is happy to see him, but reveals that she has consented to marry Phillotson in two years, after she has finished her teacher's training. They agree that her engagement need not interfere with their friendship. Jude and Sue embark on a day's outing. They cannot catch the last train home and spend the night at a cottage, in separate rooms. On her return to the school, Sue is suspected of misbehavior and is punished. Resentfully, Sue leaves the school and goes to Jude. She says that the long-established traditions, such as the Church, are meaningless to her, and Jude is somewhat shocked. He wishes he could forget her sex, but he realizes that Sue is closer to him than any woman he has ever known.

Chaps. 5–7. Jude encounters Phillotson in Melchester and tells him that his relations with Sue have been completely innocent, but does not deny his love for the girl. Jude at last tells Sue the painful circumstances of his marriage. At first she is angry that he had not told her before, but they are still good friends. A few days later Sue writes that she plans to marry Phillotson soon and would like Jude, as her only near relation, to give the bride away, and Jude agrees. The marriage takes place. Sue seems frightened and tearful when the time comes for her to leave with her new husband. Jude senses that she would have liked to tell him of her love for him, but cannot express it.

Chaps. 8–10. Jude finds Arabella working as a barmaid in Christminster. He goes

372

Sue admits she is not married

with her to Aldbrickham, where they stay overnight in an inn. Arabella tells Jude she has committed bigamy by marrying another man in Australia and begs Jude not to tell her secret. Jude sees Sue at Marygreen and learns that her marriage is not going well. Arabella's second husband arrives in London to run a public house and Arabella lives there with him.

Part IV. At Shaston. Chaps. 1–4. Great-aunt Drusilla dies and Jude sees Sue in Marygreen. Sue respects and admires Phillotson but marriage to him is repugnant to her. She thinks that a person should be able to undo what has been done in ignorance, without the censure of society. At their parting the two embrace. Their kiss is a turning-point in Jude's life; he knows he cannot be a man of the Church while harboring such strong emotions for Sue. Sue begs Phillotson to let her leave him, so that she may go live with Jude, or at least to let her have a separate room. Phillotson first agrees to the latter proposal and then agrees to let Sue leave him, recognizing the extraordinary affinity Sue and Jude have for each other, not only physical.

Chaps. 5–6. Sue goes to Jude but begs him to keep their relationship above the physical level, and Jude agrees. Arabella wants a divorce, so that she may legally marry her second husband. Phillotson is condemned by the school authorities for allowing his wife to leave him, and he feels compelled to resign his post. He decides to grant Sue a divorce.

Part V. At Aldbrickham and Elsewhere. Chaps. 1–6. Some months later, Sue and Jude are living in Aldbrickham. Both are divorced and free to marry but Sue fears that such a binding agreement will destroy their relationship. Arabella visits Jude to ask his help; she is in financial distress and her second husband has refused to marry her legally. Sue is jealous, but Jude angrily tells her that he cannot refuse aid to Arabella. Now Sue agrees to marry Jude, but hesitantly postpones the marriage plans. Arabella writes again; her second husband has agreed to marry her after all. More important, she swears that Jude is the father of her child, born in Australia soon after she left him. Her parents have kept the boy in Australia but now want to send him to her. She begs Jude to take the boy. Jude

agrees, and Sue, feeling pity for the unwanted child, has no objections. The child arrives. He is known as Little Father Time because of his solemn nature. Sue and Jude have agreed to go through with their marriage, but Sue cannot overcome her fear that a permanent union will destroy their love. The townspeople begin to suspect that Sue and Jude are not really married. Jude and Sue decide to leave the town and settle elsewhere.

Chaps. 7–8. During the next three years, Sue, Jude and the boy travel to wherever Jude is able to find work. Jude becomes ill and Sue is selling cakes at a fair to make money when she meets Arabella, who is now a widow. Sue tells Arabella that she and Jude now have two children of their own and are expecting another. She also tells Arabella they are married, which is not true. Arabella still feels a strong attraction to Jude. She meets Phillotson, who is back at the little village school where he first knew Jude. Jude, somewhat recovered from his illness, decides to move his family back to Christminster.

Part VI. At Christminster Again. Chaps. 1–2. It is a university festival day when Jude and his family return to Christminster. They seek lodgings, but none of the innkeepers is willing to lodge children, and they are unable to find a room. Jude is at last able to find lodgings for the children and Sue, while he goes to an inn. After much probing, Sue finally admits to her landlady that she is not married, whereupon the woman tells her she must leave the next day. Little Father Time remarks that perhaps children ought not to be born into such a world. Sue, in a state of despondency, is prone to agree. The next morning Sue goes to tell Jude that they must move. When the couple return to her lodgings, they find that Little Father Time has hanged himself and the other children, leaving a note saying, "Done because we are too many."

Chaps. 3–5. The tragedy effects a deep change in Sue. She feels that they must conform to society and she begins to attend Church. She tells Jude that despite their divorces, in the eyes of the Church they are still married to their respective first husband and wife. Despite Jude's protests, Sue feels she must leave him and return to Phillotson, whom she does not love. Phillotson agrees to take Sue back, but knowing that she does not love him, he does not suggest that they resume the physical relations of a man and wife.

Chaps. 6–10. Arabella, having learned of Sue's leaving, is determined to resume relations with Jude. She succeeds in getting him drunk and taking him to her father's cottage, where, in a state of stupor, he agrees to marry her again. Their second marriage is no happier than the first. Longing to see Sue, Jude takes a train to visit her, though he is in poor health. Sue expresses her love for him but tells him to leave her. Jude returns home in a severe storm. He tells Arabella that he deliberately exposed himself to the weather in the hope it would lead to his death. Sue, meanwhile, is conscience-stricken because she did not resist Jude's attentions. She determines to humble herself to Phillotson by resuming physical re-

lations with him. Jude learns from Sue's housekeeper, Mrs. EDLIN, that Sue has again become Phillotson's wife in fact, and he is miserable.

Chap. 11. On festival day in Christminster the bells are pealing, but Jude is in a critical condition. Arabella, anxious to join in the fun, leaves Jude's bedside and goes out to join friends. She returns a while later to find Jude dead. But she has promised to rejoin her friends, so she leaves Jude's body and goes back to the festivities. Arabella wonders if Sue will come to Jude's funeral and reflects that Sue will never find peace until she too is dead.

Julius Caesar

Play by William Shakespeare, 1564–1616.
Produced about 1599.

JULIUS CAESAR had a long, active and eventful life and Shakespeare's play deals only with the closing days of it, then with the aftermath. Shakespeare took his history from Plutarch and his imagination, and the imagination created the greatest portions of the play—the meditative speeches on honor, ambition, and fate, and the pictures of the fickle masses, shown first as having shifted from Pompey to Caesar and next as being so easily subject to the sway of such orators as Brutus and Antony. Critics have never ranked *Julius Caesar* among Shakespeare's greatest plays, yet there must be some reason why it can be so much more easily read and enjoyed than the majority of those classed ahead of it in quality. More even than *Coriolanus*, this is Shakespeare's recognition of the sovereign force of public opinion and the natural laws by which that force may be controlled.

Act I. 1. The Roman crowds await the return of JULIUS CAESAR from his victory over Pompey. **2.** Caesar arrives, accompanied by his aide, MARK ANTONY. A SOOTHSAYER warns Caesar to beware the Ides of March. Caesar sees CASSIUS conversing with other nobles and tells Antony, "Yon Cassius has a lean and hungry look. He thinks too much; such men are dangerous." Cassius is indeed plotting against Caesar and he is asking BRUTUS, his brother-in-law, to join the conspirators. CASCA, one of the conspirators, goes to watch Caesar refuse the crown offered three times by Antony. The mob is angered by the refusal and Caesar suffers an epileptic fit. Brutus is persuaded that Caesar's great ambition is not good for Rome and he agrees to help in the plot to kill Caesar. **3.** The

conspirators meet to bind Brutus more firmly to their course. They need his honorable reputation as a cloak for their own selfish intentions.

Act II. 1. The conspirators meet at the home of Brutus. Cassius convinces him that Caesar must die. Brutus says the act must be regarded not as murder but as a sacrifice to the gods. Brutus does not tell his wife PORTIA of the plot. **2.** The priests announce unfavorable portents to Caesar. His wife, CALPURNIA, tells him she has had a horrible dream in which she saw the Romans bathing in blood running from Caesar's statue. She persuades him not to leave the house. DECIUS BRUTUS, one of the conspirators, calls on Caesar and reinterprets Calpurnia's dream in a favorable way. Caesar now decides to go to the Capitol. **3.** ARTEMIDORUS, a teacher, prepares a letter of warning to give to Caesar when he passes in the street. **4.** Portia senses that something dire is about to happen and sends a servant to the capitol to investigate. The soothsayer is on his way to warn Caesar again.

Act III. 1. Caesar passes the soothsayer, who reminds him that the Ides of March has come, but not yet gone. Artemidorus hands Caesar his letter of warning, but Caesar

does not open it. One of the conspirators hands Caesar a document in the capitol, and the other conspirators crowd around him. They stab him and as he dies, he cries, "Et tu, Brute" [You too, Brutus?] to Brutus, whom he had considered a friend. Antony pretends to approve of the murder and is told he may address the crowd at Caesar's funeral. **2.** Brutus explains to the crowd that Caesar has been killed for the good of Rome. He wins the people's support, but then Antony ("Friends, Romans, countrymen, lend me your ears") delivers a subtle funeral oration and turns the crowd against the conspirators. They howl for the death of the plotters. Antony goes to join OCTAVIUS and LEPIDUS to form the Triumvirate that will rule Rome. **3.** The conspirators flee Rome and the mob goes to burn their homes.

Act IV. 1. Antony, Octavius and Lepidus draw up a list of those to be executed. It includes Cicero. Lepidus goes to fetch Caesar's will. **2.** Brutus and Cassius are in camp at Sardis, where they expect an attack by the forces of Octavius and Antony. **3.** Brutus accuses Cassius of being a bribe-taker. News comes of Portia's suicide. Cassius, ashamed of himself, consoles the heart-broken Brutus. Against his better judgment, Cassius agrees to Brutus's suggestion that they meet the enemy at Philippi. The ghost of Caesar appears to Brutus and tells him they will meet again at Philippi.

Act V. 1. At Philippi a parley between the opponents comes to naught. **2.** Brutus sends his aide, MESSALA, to tell Cassius he has set back the forces of Octavius. **3.** Antony's forces drive back the army under Cassius. The latter sees troops approaching and sends TITINIUS to learn their identity. PINDARUS, the servant of Cassius, tells him that Titinius has been taken prisoner. Cassius, thinking he is being surrounded, has Pindarus kill him. Titinius comes back with Messala, whose troops Pindarus had mistaken for the enemy. Titinius, seeing Cassius dead, kills himself. **4.** Brutus is defeated and left with a few friends. He runs upon his sword and dies. Octavius and Antony find his body and Antony says, "This was the noblest Roman of them all."

Julius Caesar lies dead in the Forum

The Jungle

Novel by Upton Sinclair, 1878–
Published & © 1906 by Viking Press,
New York.

UPTON SINCLAIR had written several
novels before *The Jungle*, but they
created little or no stir. *The Jungle*
was a sensational success. It aroused
its readers by exposing unhealthful
conditions, for profit regardless of
honesty, in the Chicago stockyards and
also by exposing the shameful exploitation of the laborers there and their
resultant poverty. The novel strongly
espouses socialism (as Sinclair has)
but this did not hurt its popularity.

Chap. 1. The young immigrants, JURGIS
and ONA RUDKUS, have just been married.
They are celebrating with a typically Lithuanian *veselija* or free-for-all wedding festival in the back room of a saloon in
Chicago's meat-packing slum. According to
tradition no stranger is ever turned away
from the celebration, but most guests express their appreciation by dropping cash
contributions into a hat held by the bride's
mother. But this time TETA ELZBIETA,
Ona's stepmother, has been victimized by
unknown "Americanized" Lithuanians, who
have eaten and drunk without leaving a
single offering in her hat. Jurgis stolidly
asserts that he will take care of everything—
by working harder. He has the physique for
it, and this is his only response to any problem.

Chaps. 2–3. Jurgis first fell in love with
Ona, delicate and little more than a child,
in Lithuania a year and a half ago. The party
with which they came to America included
Jurgis and his ailing father, DEDE
ANTANAS; Ona and her stepmother,
Elzbieta; Elzbieta's brother JONAS, who
had instigated the whole venture; MARIJA,
Ona's 20-year old cousin; and Elzbieta's six
children. They made for the address of
Jonas's "rich" friend JOKUBAS, in Chicago,
and found themselves dumped in the midst
of Chicago's stockyard district with its sick-
ening slaughterhouse stench, its towering
chimneys belching forth clouds of oily,
black smoke, and its streets covered with
filth. Jokubas's "wealth" consisted of a
shabby Packingtown delicatessen. However,
Jokubas found lodgings for his compatriots
in the overcrowded slum, "back of the
yards," where squalid houses accommodate
6 to 14 "guests" to a room—provided they
furnish their own mattresses. Jurgis's native
optimism remained undampened. By the
next day he had a job at Brown's stockyards.

Chaps. 4–6. Jurgis's work is in the "killing beds" of the slaughterhouse. Broom in

374

hand, and wading to his ankles in blood, he
follows a man who pulls the steaming entrails out of each carcass. Jurgis sweeps
these entrails into a trap. They will eventually be converted into sausage casings. His
pay is 17½ cents an hour. Marija and Jonas
also soon find employment in the industry.
Dede Antanas, sickly and looking older than
his years, is turned down everywhere. With
Marija's and Antanas's little nesteggs from
the old country serving as a down payment,
the immigrants buy a house. They are swindled into investing their cash in a shoddy,
four-room shack that has been given a flimsy
paint-job and passed off on them as a "new"
house. Dede Antanas gets a job at the Durham packing house by agreeing to give the
foreman a third of his earnings. Elzbieta
learns that in addition to the $12-a-month
installments on their communal home they
must pay $7 a month in interest—not men-
tioned when they bought the house.
Elzbieta's eldest son, 13-year-old STAN-
ISLOVAS, whom Jurgis had planned to send
through school, goes to work at the Durham
plant to bring in a little extra money. Finally
Ona, too, against Jurgis's objections, takes
a job in the wrapping department of
Brown's.

Chaps. 7–10. The *veselija* has left Ona
and Jurgis $100 in debt. Winter brings
graver troubles. Dede Antanas is working
in the icy cellars of the Durham plant. All
day long he stands in pools of corrosive
pickling chemicals. These have already
eaten through his boots and attacked his
feet. Sooner or later, this happens to all
workers in the "pickle room," and when the
first foot sores appear they quit and seek
some other kind of work. But Antanas remembers how hard it was for him to get this
job, and he knows how much the money is
needed at home. He insists on ignoring his
physical condition until one day he keels
over, and a few weeks later he is buried—
another strain on the family's resources. The
smaller plants close down for their seasonal
slump and Marija loses her job. At Brown's
the men are required to report as usual at
7 A.M., but then they must hang around all
day, in below-zero temperatures, in hope
of a few hours' work in the afternoon. For
weeks at a time Jurgis earns no more than
35 cents a day. He begins to share the
workers' resentment of their bosses. He
joins the butcher-helpers' union and he attends night school to learn to speak and read
English. Summer comes and conditions are
better, though the oppressive heat of the
killing beds kills as many as three men a
day. Marija has found work again, thanks
to her oxlike strength; she has a male beef-
trimmer's job at half a man's pay. Ona is
delivered of a boy, named Antanas for his
grandfather. A week later Ona returns to
her job. She would lose it if she stayed away
longer.

Chaps. 11–14. Ona and Jurgis manage
to pay off almost all of their debts and even
start a bank account. Just before Christmas,
Jurgis catches his foot in the trap and
throws his ankle and leg out of joint. The

company doctor tells him he can expect to
be laid up for months. The plant, of course,
does not consider itself responsible. Jonas
disappears from Packingtown one payday,
and Elzbieta is obliged to take two more of
her sons out of school and put them in the
streets to sell papers. Jurgis's doctor finally
binds his ankle with a walking bandage and
tells him to go back to work, but Brown's
no longer has a job for him. Jurgis makes
the rounds and is turned down everywhere.
In desperation, he takes a job that the men
of the stockyard slums consider worse than
starving to death. He stands all day at the
vents of a mill where organic fertilizer is
ground up, dumping it by the shovelful
into waiting carts. The worker must keep
a sponge tied over his mouth to breathe.
After his first five minutes, Jurgis is brown
from hair to shoes, with the filth caking his
ears and eyelids. After half an hour he is
vomiting violently. But in the end he gets
used to it. Misfortune continues to dog the
family. Elzbieta's youngest child, a crippled
3-year old boy, dies, probably as the result
of eating a sausage made of tubercular
pork. Her two boys that sell papers are becoming corrupted by the prostitutes and
street life of the district. Jurgis decides they
must return to school. Elzbieta goes to work
herself, leaving her 13-year old daughter to
take care of a remaining younger brother
and little Antanas. Jurgis gradually takes to
drink, the occupational vice of most fertilizer workers. Ona is pregnant again and
she has developed a bad cough. Jurgis
knows that the life she is leading is slowly
killing her.

Chaps. 15–18. Ona's forelady, Miss
HENDERSON, runs a bawdyhouse on the
side, chiefly for the benefit of Mr. CONNOR,
the boss of the plant's loading-gang. She
refreshes her stock periodically from the
girls who work under her. One day Ona's
turn comes. First Ona refuses Connor, but
he threatens her and her entire family with
the loss of their jobs and she goes with him.
She has never spent the night away from
home before, and when her absence is repeated, just before the Christmas holiday,
Jurgis forces the truth out of her and then
sets out to kill Connor. He finds Connor at
the plant and almost tears him to pieces
before the police arrest him. Jurgis is sentenced to 30 days in jail for assault. They
almost starve at home, trying to live on the
few cents Elzbieta's children earn selling
newspapers. Marija, the only one whose job
was secure against Connor, has seriously
cut her hand at her work and is unemployed.
Ona even tried to return to Miss Henderson, but was turned away with a cursing.
On his release, Jurgis discovers that his people have lost their house for failure to keep
up the monthly payments. He traces them
to the cold, dingy boarding house where
they first stayed.

Chaps. 19–21. Ona has a premature birth
without benefit of a doctor or midwife, and
she and the child die. Jurgis has been blacklisted because of the Connor incident, but
he manages to get a job in a harvesting-

The police arrest and beat Jurgis for attacking the bartender

machine factory, built along model lines with many benefits for the worker. Its contrast to the stockyards is so marked that Jurgis, for the first time in months, feels some hope about the future. After nine days he loses his new job because of a seasonal slump. Another period of bitterness and starvation sets in. Then, through the interest of a settlement worker who came upon one of Elzbieta's boys foraging in a garbage dump for food, Jurgis gets a job in the steel mills of South Chicago. Jurgis sleeps on the floor, for 10¢ a night, at a Polish lodginghouse near the mill. Week-ends he goes home. Elzbieta and Marija are working, too, and the family is beginning to get back on its feet. But little Antanas drowns in a ditch filled with rainwater in the unpaved street.

Chaps. 22–25. Jurgis jumps a freight train and becomes a migratory worker. The freedom of working and wandering in the outdoors restores his health. In the fall he returns to Chicago and gets a job digging telephone tunnels. Jurgis is injured in an accident and while he is too disabled to work he takes to roaming the streets and begging. One evening a drunk gives him a $100 bill. When he goes to change it in a saloon, the bartender gives him change for $1. Jurgis attacks the bartender to get his money back. The police arrive and beat Jurgis across the face and head with their clubs. He is sentenced to 10 days and costs in the same jail as before, and here he runs into a safecracker, JACK DUANE, who briefly shared his cell the first time. As soon as he is released, he joins Duane in a life of crime and easy money. Then Jurgis takes advantage of his new underworld acquaintanceship with politicians and is assigned a job in Packingtown to line up the union vote for the Republican candidate for alderman.

Chaps. 26–31. Succeeding in this, Jurgis works in the plant as a scab during a strike. Jurgis runs into Connor in the yards and beats him nearly to death all over again. Connor turns out to be important in the political machine and Jurgis must clear out of Packingtown. He returns to downtown Chicago and is soon reduced to panhandling again. He finds Marija working

in a bordello to support Elzbieta and the children. Stanislovas has been killed by rats. Jurgis asks Marija for money and she gives him a quarter—not enough for drink. Jurgis wanders into a Socialist public meeting hall. Everything the speaker has to say about social injustices and the exploitation of the worker strikes Jurgis as truth. He becomes converted to Socialism almost on the spot. Glowing with new idealism, he finds work as a porter in a small hotel; his boss turns out to be the state organizer of the Socialist Party. Jurgis becomes more and more intensely absorbed by the party and his life takes on meaning and nobility again.

Juno and the Paycock

Play by Sean O'Casey, 1884–1964. Produced 1924. Published and © 1925. (ML, 30)

THIS PLAY was produced at the famous Abbey Theatre in Dublin. It is a comedy but provides occasion for some keen remarks on politics. O'Casey is ranked at the top among Irish playwrights. The title of the play contains a secondary allusion, for the goddess Juno herself had some dealings with a peacock. In 1959 there was an ambitious New York production of a musical version, called *Juno*, with music by Marc Blitzstein. It failed, closing in two weeks.

Act I. It is 1922 in Ireland. Political controversy has divided the people into two groups, those supporting the British-dominated Irish Free State, and those fighting for the Republic, an independent Ireland. The Boyle family live in two sparsely furnished rooms in a Dublin tenement. JUNO BOYLE and her daughter MARY discuss the recent killing of ROBBIE TANCRED, a neigh-

bor's son, who had fought against the Free State. Mrs. Boyle is thankful that her own son, JOHNNY, who has lost an arm for the Republic, no longer seems to be involved. JERRY DEVINE, Mary's one-time beau, comes in to tell Mary's father, "Captain" JACK BOYLE, about a job. The Captain, who struts around like a "paycock," comes in with his drinking companion JOXER DALY. Although jobs are scarce, the mere mention of one immediately brings pains to Boyle's legs. CHARLIE BENTHAM, a schoolteacher who has secretly been seeing Mary, comes in with good news. Bentham wrote the will for a cousin of Boyle's. Now the cousin has died, leaving Boyle almost £2,000.

Act II. Boyle is sitting in his newly decorated living room. Vulgar furniture and ornaments have been bought on credit. Bentham and Mary are engaged to be married and the Boyles are expecting a few neighbors in for a celebration. Bentham arrives and is given the seat of honor near the fire. He talks about his belief in theosophy and the ability of some people to see ghosts. Johnny leaves the room, but rushes back, pale and trembling. He saw the dead Robbie Tancred kneeling before the statue in his room. Bentham investigates and assures them there is no one there. Joxer and Mrs. Madigan, another neighbor, join the group and each has a turn at a song. Mrs. Tancred is heard in the hallway. The funeral procession passes in the street and all except Johnny go out to watch. A young man brings Johnny an order to attend a Battalion Staff meeting, saying it is believed he might know something about the betrayers of Tancred. Johnny says he will not go, that he has done enough for Ireland.

Act III. It is two months later. Mary is expecting a baby and Bentham, the father, has not been heard from in a month. Boyle reveals something he has known for some time: Because of a technical error in the will, he will not receive any money. He goes out to the pub. Two men come in to retrieve the furniture, which has not been paid for, and Juno goes out in search of her husband. Jerry Devine calls on Mary and tells her he has heard everything and still wants to marry her. When she refers to the baby, however, he is stunned and regretful, and leaves. Johnny berates Mary for the shame she has brought to the family and she rushes out. Johnny suddenly notices the votive light before the religious statue flickering. Terrified, he cries that he feels the pain of a bullet in his breast. Two men come in, accuse him of betraying Tancred, and drag him away. An hour later Mary and Juno are sitting in the darkened, almost empty room. Juno is summoned to identify a body believed to be her son's. In her grief Juno resolves never to return to the apartment or her husband again, but to work with Mary for the sake of the baby. When Mary cries that the child will have no father, Juno replies that it will be better off with two mothers. The women leave. Boyle and Joxer enter drunkenly and are blindly looking for the furniture as the curtain falls.

Jurgen

Novel by James Branch Cabell, 1879–1958.
Published 1919 by M. McBride & Co. (Sig, 601).

JURGEN DELIGHTED the sophisticated readers of the early 1920s and their conversation at any time was likely to include one or more allusions to or quotations from it. The conservative reading public was shocked, for the love affairs of Jurgen and various other unconventional attitudes expressed in the book were not then expected in novels that were sold openly over the counters. The attitude toward such matters having changed, *Jurgen* is no longer considered more than a pleasant fantasy, but neither is it read so much as it was. It still has devoted adherents who read into it many deep messages. The style is very formal but is saved by general good humor.

Jurgen rescues the lovely Dame Yolande from the monster

Chaps. 1–3. A legendary pawnbroker named JURGEN in the French town of Poictesme is married to a high-spirited, talkative woman, Dame LISA. One night on his way home, Jurgen justifies the good works of the Devil to a monk. Then Jurgen encounters a dark gentleman who thanks him for his defense. The gentleman inquires about his married life and Jurgen complains that Dame Lisa is not fond of his poetry. The dark man mutters that this is a shame and then disappears. When Jurgen arrives home, Lisa has vanished. Days later, Lisa's relatives report to Jurgen that Lisa is living in a cave. Jurgen works up the courage to visit the cave, where Lisa beckons him inside and Jurgen meets a centaur named NESSUS. Jurgen asks Nessus to restore his wife, and the centaur replies that the pawnbroker must first visit KOSHCHEI the Deathless, who made all things. Jurgen dons a splendid magic shirt and boards the centaur's back. They fly quickly to a beautiful garden. There men and women live happily under various delusions, such as the belief that they will never die.

Chaps. 4–5. In the garden Jurgen meets DOROTHY LA DÉSIRÉE, whom he loved but who married a man of noble ancestry. Dorothy appears just as she did in adolescence, and Jurgen very much desires her again, but Jurgen appears so much older that Dorothy is not interested. She is seeking the young Jurgen who first wrote love poems in her honor. Nessus explains, after Dorothy has wandered away, that the women men have loved dwell unchanged in this garden of illusions. Then suddenly Nessus transforms himself into a saddle horse.

Chaps. 6–7. Left to his own devices, Jurgen stops at the house of SEREDA, an aged woman who is patiently washing clothes. Sereda is actually a strong female deity. She offers Jurgen any day of the week to relive from his past life. Jurgen chooses Wednesday, and promptly encounters his mother, AZRA. Her nagging bores him. He then relives a youthful love affair with Dorothy. They are interrupted by her future husband, HEITMAN MICHAEL. Jurgen kills Michael, but the dream fades and Jurgen realizes that Michael, not he, actually won the beautiful Dorothy. Sereda then gives Jurgen the gift of perennial youth to speed him on his way to his wife.

Chaps. 8–11. Jurgen returns to the cave. There he sees recumbent marble statues of all the women he has loved. Jurgen then wanders into a hall, where he frees an enchanted princess, GUENEVERE, daughter of King GOGYRVAN, by kissing her motionless body. Guenevere has been enchanted by the evil THRAGNAR, whom Jurgen is pledged to fight. Calling himself duke of Logreus, Jurgen takes the magic sword, Caliburn, and rides away with Guenevere. They encounter Thragnar impersonating Jurgen's wife. Jurgen penetrates the disguise and decapitates the demon. Jurgen asks King Gogyrvan for Guenevere's hand. The king regrets that he cannot give his daughter to the self-styled duke, because she is pledged to the famous King ARTHUR.

Chaps. 12–14. While living at Gogyrvan's castle of Cameliard, Jurgen rescues the lovely Dame YOLANDE from a monster and wins Yolande's embraces, but returns to Cameliard and Guenevere. The king permits him to court the princess until Arthur arrives. Jurgen composes reams of chivalric poems but soon becomes disillusioned with the court. Everyone seems to have high ideals but is basically realistic and practical. Jurgen is also troubled by a shadow that seems to hover menacingly around him.

Chaps. 15–17. Guenevere finally consents to become Jurgen's mistress and they meet every night in the Hall of Judgment.

Then the magician MERLIN and ANAITIS, the Lady of the Lake, arrive to take the princess to King Arthur. One night Jurgen is visited by the ghosts of King SMOIT and Queen SYLVIA TEREU, members of the ruling dynasty of Cameliard. King Smoit tells Jurgen he is actually Jurgen's grandfather by a complicated relationship. Smoit asks Jurgen to haunt the White Turret of the castle that night, for Smoit must appear in Purgatory. Jurgen drinks a magic potion, becomes a ghost, and goes off with Queen Sylvia. Toward dawn Queen Sylvia becomes amorous toward Jurgen, but the two are interrupted by Anaitis. Queen Sylvia disappears but Jurgen is more attracted by the lovely, unmarried Anaitis. However, she tells him to stop carrying on with ghosts at night and goes abruptly back to bed.

Chaps. 18–21. Merlin tells Jurgen that the shadow is sent by the mother of small demons, ADÈRES, who will some day enlighten him. Jurgen and Guenevere part with tears. Jurgen encounters a brown man with queer feet, who unsuccessfully tries to persuade him to give up his poetic beliefs and surrender to reality. Guenevere rides off to London with Sir LANCELOT, and Anaitis, who likes Lancelot better than Arthur, whispers to Jurgen that she has given the two young people a magic love potion. Jurgen accepts the Lady of the Lake's invitation to her realm of wisdom, Cocaigne, and they ride there in a magic boat with an invisible crew.

Chaps. 22–25. Anaitis reveals that she is a moon-goddess. She dupes Jurgen into a secret wedding and for a while Jurgen languishes happily in the earthly paradise of Cocaigne. A Master Philologist decrees that they must part but he gives Jurgen 32 words to serve as his protection. Jurgen then tosses away the magic sword Caliburn, which Anaitis later gives to King Arthur.

Chaps. 26–28. Before they part, Anaitis allows Jurgen to visit the imaginary land of Leuke, ruled by Queen HELEN of Troy and King ACHILLES. Helen resembles Dorothy la Desirée. Jurgen is at first somewhat disappointed but after seeing Helen many times he is cured of passion for all other women. The mysterious shadow seems to disappear. Jurgen shuns the capital city of Pseudopolis, where Helen lives. He prefers the more natural life of woods and groves, where he meets and marries a simple nymph named CHLORIS. For a time Jurgen lives contentedly with his bride, but then he becomes restless.

Chaps. 29–33. Haunted by the recurring face of Helen, Jurgen creeps into her bedroom one night and watches her sleeping. When he leaves he feels he has put her behind him forever. The land of Leuke is attacked by the Realist forces of Philistia. King Achilles and his soldiers put up a brave fight, but imaginary people cannot defeat cold-blooded Realists. Chloris and Jurgen fall captive to the enemy. They are tried, judged to be illusions, and sentenced to doom in Limbo. Jurgen postpones exile by pretending love for DOLORES, queen of Philistia, to prove he is real. However, he makes the mistake of defending poetry and is banished. Even the 32 words of the Master Philologist cannot revoke this stern decree. Jurgen is sent to the Hell of his fathers.

Chaps. 34–39. In the underworld Jurgen meets his father, COTH OF THE ROCKS. They quarrel because each claims to be the more sinful. Everyone in Hell boasts about his sins on earth. Jurgen learns that Hell is the invention of one's ancestors, and the devils find it difficult to dole out the penalties demanded by the sufferers. Jurgen raises his social standing by calling himself the emperor of Noumaria. He meets a beautiful demon named FLORIMEL and accepts her proposal of marriage. Jurgen counsels Grandfather SATAN to quiet the pro-celestial factions of Hell by tearing apart any rebels. This advice is considered the wisest ever uttered, and Jurgen is a hero. At last thoughts of Dame Lisa return and Jurgen decides to seek his true wife in Heaven.

Chaps. 40–42. The Master Philologist's words move a boy at the white gates of Heaven to let Jurgen in. The boy turns out to be Jurgen's grandmother's notion of Jurgen himself. In Heaven, Jurgen represents himself as a deceased Pope. He finds that his own illusions of Heaven do not coincide with what others believe. God gives him permission to return to his own illusions. St. Peter sets Jurgen back down on the earth where his wanderings began.

Chaps. 43–44. Jurgen encounters Mother Sereda, who granted him his gift of youth. He complains that he has done nothing of importance; she disagrees, since he has met both God and Satan. She says Jurgen must not seek too deeply for meaning. Then she allows Jurgen to age rapidly. He proposes to find his beloved wife and descends a third time into the cave. Deep inside he finds a door marked "Manager's Office." The manager is Koshchei the Deathless, whom Jurgen was fated to meet. Jurgen complains again about his failure to see any meaning in the Universe. Koshchei merely states

that things are as they are. Jurgen asks for his wife, but Koshchei does not approve of Dame Lisa, because she stifles Jurgen's poetic expression, and he allows Jurgen to select a new mate.

Chaps. 45–50. The first candidate to appear is Guenevere, representing Faith. She does not recognize the aging Jurgen. Anaitis, or Desire, is next but no longer appeals to Jurgen. The third woman is Helen, or Vision of all things as they are. With great melancholy Jurgen also bids her farewell, thereby renouncing the art of poetry. At last Koshchei is forced to give Dame Lisa back to Jurgen. Lisa upbraids her husband harshly and Koshchei cannot understand why he wants her back. Jurgen insists, however, that Lisa and all women have poetry within them. He is satisfied with his plain wife. Jurgen suddenly suspects that this sorcerer is the dark gentleman and must be the Devil, whom he defended to the monk. Jurgen proceeds alone and meets Countess Dorothy, who wishes to pawn some jewels for her wastrel husband. Without a bit of emotion, Jurgen calculates their worth. Then, leaving his former mistress, he returns to the snug cosy fireplace and clacking tongue of Dame Lisa.

Justice

Poem by Sully Prudhomme, 1839–1908. Published 1878.

JUSTICE IS ONE of two long philosophical poems written by the French Nobel Prize winner (1901) and is considered his masterpiece. Like all poetry, it can hardly be judged unless it is read in the original, but its message survives in translation.

Watch I. The poet, called The SEEKER, is hungry for truth and anxious to discover the true nature of justice. A VOICE advises him to put aside the illusions of the senses and seek it with "humble science." Since earth is the region that is most accessible to him, the poet decides to search for justice there. The Voice tells him that science is vain; it reveals only a chain of phenomena.

Watch II. Science also does not show the Seeker any justice in the relationships among animals. They exist by devouring one another. The strong feed on the weak.

Watch III. The Seeker next turns from

creatures at large to individuals, and especially to a single man. Man is motivated by selfish instincts that preserve weak and strong alike. These instincts dominate the natural man so completely that his reasoning powers are impaired. After a time selfishness becomes the governing principle, stifling any inspiration toward true justice.

Watch IV. The Seeker next turns to communities of men, or states. He finds that nations at large act the same way toward one another as classes of animals do. The larger nations devour the smaller or keep them alive for purposes of exploitation. Man's reason allows him to be more cunning than beasts are, but his behavior is worse, for beasts kill only for food.

Watch V. The Seeker enters into a typical state to observe its operation. Within the state individual men are constantly struggling for power. They do not devour one another openly, for their selfish interests force them to coöperate to some extent. Nevertheless the great factories and offices are dens in which violent greeds are enacted. Human progress is certainly not a product of justice.

Watch VI. The Seeker concludes that science as apprehended by reason has not shown him any trace of just action or motivation. Therefore he consults the heavens. The sameness of matter throughout the universe forces him to conclude that all other worlds—if they exist—are as wicked as the earth. Furthermore the gravitation that holds the universe together leads one inevitably to fatalism. There is no true freedom anywhere, for all things are bound together. The Seeker considers the possibility of religion, but rejects it. Though deity exist, the brutal picture is unchanged.

Watches VII–VIII. Since reason has failed to disclose anything inspiring, the Seeker must appeal within himself. His conscience tells him that justice exists, that things are right or wrong. Therefore man must labor within to uncover moral laws. These laws will obviously not be found in the mind. Therefore the poet examines his heart.

Watches IX–X. The poet studies the theory of evolution, whereby successive changes of physical forms lead to an eventual perfection of those forms. He decides that the workings of conscience must resemble evolution. Every change in man's awareness leads to a richer existence. In this sense conscience or awareness of the good can almost be defined as consciousness or awareness of everything in nature. Since man has not yet accomplished full justice, he must not feel angry toward nature or God. The burden of being just rests on man, who is given the power to understand and achieve it on earth. This new knowledge of man's power gives the Seeker peace and joy.

Watch XI. The Seeker looks at the city, the highest product of the earth. In societies men must learn to trust their hearts, not their reason, for social life is basically instinctive. Justice among men asserts itself through love, and love is not possible without awareness. Only love can bring peace.

Kenilworth

Novel by Sir Walter Scott, 1771–1832.
Published 1821.

KENILWORTH is one of the Waverley
novels (see *Ivanhoe*) and has been one
of the most popular, chiefly because
the story is well told and is faster in action than that of many of the others.
Kenilworth is set at the time of Queen
Elizabeth I and concerns Leicester, one
of her chief ministers almost from the
time of her accession in 1558 until his
death, except the usual brief periods
when he was out of favor. His secret
marriage to Amy Robsart and her
mysterious death, as told in *Kenilworth,*
are based on actual history; the explanation of Amy's death as given in the
book is Scott's own, the actual cause
having been a mystery.

Chaps. 1–2. The village of Cumnor
boasted of an excellent inn, the Black Bear,
owned by GILES GOSLING. Gosling's
nephew MICHAEL LAMBOURNE, a ne'er-do-
well, appears at the inn unexpectedly, from
the European wars. All join in a reception
to welcome him except a solitary guest,
named TRESSILIAN. The revelers amuse
Michael with the latest village gossip. He
is especially interested in one TONY FOS-
TER, who has married well and become a
good Protestant, and who lives in the local
manor house, Cumnor Place. At news of
Foster, Tressilian suddenly becomes interested and makes an engagement with
Michael to visit Foster the following day.

Chaps. 3–5. Giles warns Tressilian of his
nephew's errant ways. However, Tressilian
sets out with Michael for Cumnor Place.
They find the path overgrown, the house
and surroundings dilapidated. Admitted to
the house, Tressilian is amazed at the ugly
mien of Foster. Michael leaves the room
with Foster. As Tressilian waits, a lovely
young woman, AMY, enters the room. She is
the object of Tressilian's visit. He informs
her that her father is very ill and is calling
for her. She tells him she will get permission
and come to her father within 12 hours.
Tressilian then leaves alone. While attempting to open the gate of the mansion park he
meets an old adversary, VARNEY. They
draw swords, but Michael comes upon them
in time to save Varney's life. Varney and
Foster discuss the matter of Amy, who is
secretly married to their lord, the Earl of
LEICESTER.

Chaps. 6–7. Amy is admiring a beautifully furnished room of the mansion that
has just been finished for the earl's imminent visit. Varney comes and asks her not to
mention Tressilian's visit to the earl. The
earl arrives and Amy begs him to proclaim

the fact of their marriage, but he refuses,
offering England's affairs of state as his excuse. In truth he is afraid that if Queen
Elizabeth learns that he is married, she will
be jealous and he will lose favor.

Chap. 8. Giles Gosling advises Tressilian
to leave that night. He is suspicious of his
nephew's designs on Tressilian. Tressilian
tells Giles of his search for his lost sweetheart, Amy Robsart, who he thinks is now

The encounter at the gate

Varney's paramour. With Giles' help, Tressilian leaves the inn by dark.

Chaps. 9–11. Tressilian takes the wrong
road, and his horse loses a shoe. He is
directed to the local blacksmith, WAYLAND
SMITH, who decides to accompany him.
They proceed to Lidcote Hall, Sir HUGH
ROBSART's home.

Chap. 12. Tressilian persuades Sir Hugh
that he (Tressilian) should inquire at the
Queen's Court regarding Amy's fate. Wayland Smith is to accompany him. A note
from the Earl of SUSSEX, asking him to
come to London, changes Tressilian's plans.

Chaps. 13–15. They arrive in London,
where Wayland Smith tours several chem-
ists, buying various secret medicines. Upon
arriving at Sussex's residence, Wayland
Smith administers a secret medicine to Sussex and cures him of his mysterious ailment.
Young RALEIGH, assistant to BLOUNT,
Sussex's Master of Horse, hastens to the
Queen's Court to explain why her physician
was not admitted to Sussex's bedside.
Raleigh gains the Queen's favor by spreading his cape so she will not have to walk in
a ditch. Elizabeth visits Sussex, taking
Raleigh with her when she leaves.

Chaps. 16–17. Sussex and Leicester meet
in the Queen's presence. The queen asks
about Amy and Varney tells the queen that
Amy is *his* wife. The queen closes the
audience by reminding Leicester that she is
to visit him at Kenilworth, and she invites
Sussex too. She orders Varney to bring Amy,
his supposed wife, as well. Tressilian sends
Wayland Smith back to Cumnor to watch
Foster and Varney closely.

Chaps. 18–20. Varney bids Lambourne
escort the alchemist, ALASCO, to Cumnor
Place. While Lambourne lures Tony Foster
down to the Black Bear, Wayland Smith
visits Amy, warning her against the
alchemist.

Chaps. 21–24. Leicester decides to send
Varney with a note requesting Amy to pose
as Varney's wife at Kenilworth. When Varney delivers the message to Amy, she is
furious and accuses him of deceit. She sets
out to meet her husband at Kenilworth,
accompanied by Wayland Smith. They are
pursued by Varney and Lambourne, but
disguise themselves as masquers traveling
with a troupe bound for Kenilworth, and so
escape.

Chaps. 25–29. They gain entrance to
Kenilworth. Amy gives Wayland a note to
deliver to Leicester, but Wayland, not
knowing of their marriage, takes it to Tressilian instead. Tressilian wants to inform the
queen of Amy's plight, but she will not
allow him to. As he leaves Amy's apartment
he meets Lambourne, who is suspicious.
When Wayland attempts to see Amy, Lambourne has him thrown out of Kenilworth.

Chaps. 30–32. Elizabeth enters Kenilworth. Tressilian tries to explain Amy's
plight but is repulsed. The queen confers
knighthood on Varney, Blount, and Raleigh,
but dismisses Tressilian as demented.

Chaps. 33–35. Amy escapes from her
tower room and waits in the palace garden.
The queen discovers her. Amy pleads to be
released from Varney's grasp. When the
queen questions her, she becomes distraught
and has to be taken away. Later that night,
Leicester and Varney try to persuade Amy
to visit her father's home in Varney's company, but she refuses.

Chaps. 36–37. Varney then tells Leicester
of a supposed tryst between Tressilian and
Amy. Stung by jealousy, the earl banishes
Amy. He gives Varney his signet ring and
tells him to take her to Cumnor Place. The
alchemist Alasco testifies to the queen that
Amy is mentally ill. Leicester sends Lambourne to warn Varney not to harm Amy.

Chap. 38. Tressilian asks Leicester to
meet him. Tressilian asks Leicester to explain Amy's plight.

Chap. 39. While the pageant is being
enacted, Tressilian and Leicester meet in a
grove. They duel, and Leicester is about to
stab Tressilian as Amy's seducer when the
lost message from Amy is brought. The note
establishes Tressilian's innocence and Var-
neys' treachery. Alarmed, Leicester prepares
to follow his wife and her faithless protector, Varney, to Cumnor.

Chap. 40. When Tressilian returns to the
castle, he is summoned to the queen's
presence. He tells all he knows of the affair
of Leicester and Amy, and Leicester acknowledges Amy as his bride before the
Queen. Elizabeth sends Tressilian and
Raleigh to fetch Amy from Cumnor so that
she can solemnize the marriage. On the trip,
Tressilian finds Lambourne dying, a victim
of Varney's wrath. His last warning concerns Amy.

Chap. 41. In the meantime, Varney and Foster uncover a trap outside Amy's chamber at Cumnor. Foster is dismayed at Varney's treachery, and warns Amy not to leave her rooms until she hears Leicester. A short while later, Varney goes to the outer court and imitates Leicester's signal to Amy. She runs from her chamber, falls into the trap, and dies. Almost immediately, Tressilian and Raleigh arrive, as Varney and Foster flee. Varney is apprehended, but takes poison. Foster is found many years later, in a secret chamber. Leicester retires to his estate, but is recalled to the court and serves the queen illustriously. Amy's father dies soon after his daughter, leaving his estate to Tressilian, who never recovers from Amy's death. He accompanies Raleigh on his Virginia expedition, and dies there.

Leicester acknowledges to the queen that Amy is his bride

The Keys of the Kingdom

Novel by Archibald Joseph Cronin, 1896–
Published & © 1941 by Little Brown & Co., Boston. (PB, F1474)

THIS WAS ONE of A. J. Cronin's most successful books and may have been his best. It is not about a doctor, but about a priest; but Cronin, a retired physician, does have his priest interested in medicine and an amateur practitioner. When Cronin wrote *The Keys of the Kingdom* he was at the peak of his popularity and was said to have a larger mass following in the United States than any other novelist.

Part I. In the year 1938 Father FRANCIS CHRISHOLM, aged 70, is pastor in Tweedside, the quiet village in Scotland where he was born. Monsignor SLEETH, secretary to Bishop ANSELM MEALEY, comes to look about. He sees that the priest is poor, his church affairs are not well organized, and some rather unorthodox statements have been made in his sermons. Sleeth, cold and efficient, announces that the Bishop thinks Father Chrisholm should retire and the boy Chrisholm has adopted, ANDREW, should be put in an orphange. Father Chrisholm, feeling rejected by man and God, muses on the history of his life.

Part II. Chap. 1. Francis Chrisholm is a boy in Tweedside. Each day he fishes with his father, ALEX CHRISHOLM, to help support the family. These are happy days. One day POLLY, Francis's aunt by marriage, a widow, brings NORA, her orphaned niece, to play with Francis, who is excited by Nora's charm and bright eyes. Anselm Mealey, a pious and unctious boy, comes to play. Francis and Nora play a trick on him, causing him to fall in the mud, and then run away. Alex Chrisholm does not appear. He has gone to Ettal, 4 miles away, where persecution of Catholics has been violent lately. Mrs. Chrisholm and Francis set out to find him. He is in a hut halfway home, severely beaten and bloody. Francis is sent off to get a doctor while his mother helps Alex home. They go over a footbridge across the swollen Tweed River. Alex slips, and both fall in and are drowned.

Chaps. 2–5. Francis is taken in by some relatives named GLENNIE, who treat him harshly and put him to work as a rivet boy. With the encouragement of his friend MALCOLM TULLOCH, an atheist doctor's son, Francis tries to run away but fails. He is eventually rescued from the Glennies by his Aunt Polly. She gives him loving care and good food, and he is infatuated with Nora. Then he is sent off to a Catholic school, Holywell. Here Francis is considered a somewhat wayward student by all the professors except "Rusty Mac" MACNABB, the headmaster, a bushy Highland gentleman with a great understanding of human nature. The two become friends over a fishing pole. Rusty Mac is also the only person in the school who does not admire the popular, efficient, busy, pious boy, Anselm Mealey. Francis gets a mysterious letter from home telling him not to return for vacation. Worried, he goes home anyway. Ned, his uncle by marriage, has given over the management of his tavern to THADDEUS GILFOYLE and sits about pale, blank-eyed. Aunt Polly is all nerves. Nora is wasted, cold, and bitter. Francis discovers that Nora has had a baby and indirect implications of fatherhood point to Ned. Francis tries to win Nora back to him, but she is too bitter. She throws herself under a train and Francis, shattered, decides to give himself to priesthood.

Chap. 6. Francis goes to train for the priesthood at an English seminary in San Morales, Spain. He goes off on a four-day escapade, which horrifies the priests until they discover that it was a kind of spiritual pilgrimage. Then Francis is honored.

Parts II & III. Francis becomes a curate at Shalesley, a poverty-stricken colliery town. The head priest, Father KEZER, is a fist-pounding, selfish, bombastic man. Francis sets out to bring a spark of life into the parish. His attempt to set up a community

Francis saves the merchant's son when Chinese doctoring has failed

recreation center is balked by Father Kezer. Then, while Father Kezer is away, Francis enlists the help of Sir GEORGE RENSHAW to build the recreation center. Father Kezer is speechless with fury but can do nothing, for Sir George is the greatest contributor to the church. Francis is transferred to Tyncastle and St. Dominic's Church. Here he again encounters Anselm Mealy, who is senior curate. Anselm is very popular and busy, and runs a number of organizations. Francis one day gives a somewhat unorthodox sermon concerning personal integrity. Father Fitzgerald is annoyed, and the sermon is countered the following week by a thunderous and successful oration by Anselm. About this time an amazing incident occurs. A spring that has been dry for years suddenly starts to flow, and a girl asserts that she was there and saw the Virgin Mary. She lies in bed for days, healthy and fresh without (apparently) taking any food. The church becomes wild with excitement. Father Fitzgerald is overjoyed that he will at last be in the limelight. But Francis inadvertently discovers that the whole thing has been a fraud. Then one day a patient who had a malignant growth is suddenly cured, after his mother bathes him in the spring. Francis suddenly realizes that it is faith that has power, not outside miracles. At this point the Bishop, his old friend MacNabb, appoints him to a missionary trip to China.

Part IV. Chaps. 1–2. Francis arrives at Pai-tan, China, in 1902. He was led to expect a flourishing mission there, but it proves to be a wrecked and deserted stable. Francis feels that God is chastising him for having been incompetent. At first Francis is chided by mobs, and no one will come to his masses. He opens a medical dispensary and a few people begin to come to that. Francis hears of an ancient Christian community lost somewhere in the mountains and a nine-day struggle by foot, alone, takes him to the ancient pastoral community. Here they practice a primitive form of Cathol-

icism brought to them by a wandering Portuguese priest in 1625. Francis is thrilled. A boy, JOSEPH, joins him as a follower when he leaves.

Chaps. 3–5. The medical dispensary begins to boom. One day the son of a rich merchant, CHIA, becomes very ill and the best Chinese doctoring seems to be of no help. Francis saves the boy and Chia gives him the deed to the most beautiful property in Pai-tan and men to help him build a mission. A beautiful mission springs up. Three English nuns come to care for the school Francis has organized. The head-nun, MARIA-VERONICA, takes violent exception to Father Chrisholm. She mistakes his kindness, humility, and spiritual honesty for crudeness and smallness. Her aristocratic pride is aroused. All three nuns stay distant. Francis feels hurt. At this time a plague sweeps down upon Pai-tan. Francis sets up a provisionary hospital and his old friend, Willie Tulloch, now a doctor, unexpectedly arrives to help. Maria-Veronica joins them and the three, with the help of Lieutenant Shon, fight a tireless battle against the disease. It is finally stemmed, but Willie Tulluch dies.

Chaps. 6–7. In the footsteps of the plague comes a great flood that washes away the mission's garden and crumbles the church. Canon Anselm Mealey, on a tour of inspection, arrives at this point and views the wreckage as a sign of failure. He reprimands Francis. When he leaves Maria-Veronica goes to Francis and tells him he has the finest spirit she has ever seen. She writes to her rich brother, who sends funds

to have the mission rebuilt. The mission flourishes. An American Methodist Mission is set up in the town and Francis befriends the new missionaries, Mr. and Mrs. WILBUR FISKE. Some time later Mrs. Fiske goes to England, and as a surprise she brings back Francis's Aunt Polly. The three nuns and Aunt Polly care for Francis with childish enthusiasm.

Chaps. 8–11. The war breaks out in Europe and two bandit war-lords begin a war for control of Pai-tan. Francis gives sanctuary in the mission compound to his Christian followers and forbids them to fight. General WAI has a big gun emplacement near the mission and he threatens to blow up the mission if food and men are not supplied to him. Francis plots a maneuver by which he blows up the gun. A number of Wai's men are killed and Francis finds difficulty in reconciling the horror of what he has done with the fact that he has saved those in the mission. In retreat Wai's soldiers burn the rice fields and there is a famine. Francis sends the children to the little lost Christian town he had discovered years before. Later he colonizes this town as his church grows. Maria-Veronica has returned to Europe. Joseph marries. The mission flourishes and Father Chrisholm's kindness and humility win the Chinese slowly.

Chaps. 12–23. Francis sets out to visit the little Christian village in the mountains with the Fiskes. They are captured by General Wai, whose men torture them by beating them and tying them in the icy river. Escape is finally made down the river in a sampan. Francis is shot in the jaw and has a broken leg. Dr. Fiske dies. Francis is now old and is recalled to England. At the last minute Chia, Francis's earliest friend, comes to have himself converted to Christianity. Francis is torn from the land he has made his own. The town provides a great show of love as they see him off.

Part V. In England Francis receives almost no attention or praise from Bishop Mealey. He rescues from the slums Andrew, the young son of Nora's illigitimate daughter.

Part VI. Monsignor Sleeth has written a highly negative report on Father Chrisholm and his little parish in Tweedside. Then people come to Sleeth and tell him what a "warm feeling" the town has had since Francis came. The gentleness and wisdom of Francis Chrisholm finally break through Sleeth's armor of pride and egotism. With a sudden gesture of humility and love, Sleeth tears up his report to the Bishop and spreads the fragments to the winds.

Kidnapped

Novel by Robert Louis Stevenson, 1850–1894.
Published 1886. (PB, PL34)

KIDNAPPED IS a standard among popular books for boys. Among Stevenson's books for boys it ranks second only to *Treasure Island*. It is a tale of high adventure on land and sea, in which the young hero is shanghaied (for which Stevenson used the word kidnapped). It is set in the mid-18th century when Scotland, the hero's country, was strongly partisan to the Jacobite pretenders to the British throne, the descendants of the deposed King James II.

Chap. 1. Mr. CAMPBELL, the minister of Essendean, bids DAVID, or DAVEY, BALFOUR goodbye. Davey's father's last letter instructed Davey to go to the SHAW'S, a house near Edinburgh. Campbell gives Davey a shilling, a Bible, and a recipe for "Lilly of the Valley water."

Chap. 2. Davey reaches Cramond, near Edinburgh, and inquires for the Shaws. The farm folk seem reluctant to talk about it. He finally is directed to it by a woman who curses it. The house is uncompleted and everything in disrepair.

Chaps. 3–4. Davey is allowed into the house by his uncle EBENEZER, a miser, who shares his porridge with Davey but acts as a jailer.

Ebenezer talks vaguely of a promise to his brother ALEXANDER, Davey's father, and gives Davey £40. Then he asks him to get a chest of papers in the tower. David starts up the tower stairs but a streak of lightning shows that the stairs are unfinished. Thoroughly angered by his uncle's treachery, David returns to the kitchen and asks for an explanation. Ebenezer has a slight heart attack but promises to explain everything in the morning.

Chaps. 5–7. The next morning Ebenezer does not explain his previous actions. A young seaman named RANSOME brings a message asking Ebenezer to met a Captain HOSEASON of the *Covenant* at Queensferry. Ebenezer and David set out together. Ebenezer speaks of taking David to meet his lawyer, a Mr. RANKEILLOR. While Ebenezer is closeted with Capt. Hoseason, Davey and Ransome go to an inn. The innkeeper tells them that Ebenezer is a wicked man and defrauded Alexander of his inheritance. Capt. Hoseason, by a show of friendliness, entices Davey on board the *Covenant*. Davey comes to in the brig of

the ship, bound hand and foot. He is rescued by Mr. RIACH, the first mate (second mate), a good seaman but a drunkard. From the sailors, Davey learns that he is to be sold into slavery in the Carolinas.

Chaps. 8–13. Capt. Hoseason orders Davey up to serve in the roundhouse. Davey discovers that Mr. SHUAN, the chief mate (first mate), while drunk, murdered Ransome, the former cabin boy. The *Covenant* picks up the sole survivor of a small boat and Davey hears the captain and mates scheming to obtain the man's money belt. He warns the man, who introduces himself as ALAN BRECK STEWART. Together, they make the roundhouse ready for attack and defend themselves against the attacks of the crew, killing six men including Shuan. Capt. Hoseason has a parley with Alan Breck and the captain agrees to land Alan in Scotland. Alan tells David of the Jacobite-Whig battles in Scotland, and how he seeks vengeance upon Colin Campbell, the Red Fox, for the injustices inflicted on the Stewarts. The ship is grounded on a reef and Davey is thrown overboard but manages to get ashore.

Chaps. 14–15. Davey is on a small island. For three days he lives on raw shellfish. It rains continually. On the third day a small fishing boat passes by but ignores Davey. The next day the fishermen return and tell him that at low tide he can walk from his island to the mainland.

Chaps. 15–17. Davey travels across the island of Mull. The sailors of the *Covenant* landed there and Alan left a message for Davey to meet him at Torosay. Davey gets directions from Alan's clansman, NEIL MACROB, and continues across the island of Marven. He meets a catechist named HENDERLAND, who shelters him for the night and finds a fisherman to take him across the bay to Appin. Davey is walking when he meets four men of the law. One turns out to be Colin Campbell, the Red Fox, Alan Breck's mortal enemy. Campbell is suddenly shot and dies in the road. Campbell's companions think that Davey is an accomplice to the murder and set out after him. He is hiding in the heather when he is joined by Alan Breck.

Chaps. 18–26. Davey and Alan plan to travel to the Lowlands together. Their first stop is the house of Alan's kinsman, James of the Glens, at Aucharn. The place is in an uproar. Since the murder of Colin Camp-

Alan and Davey hide

bell all Stewart homes are suspect, so James is busy hiding his ammunition and burning important papers. James tells them they are suspected of Colin's murder, and tells them to flee. Alan and Davey travel by night and find a hiding place atop a rock 20 feet high, close to an encampment of British soldiers. They escape at sundown and travel all night. Alan sends a message to James of the Glens, whose wife answers. She sends all the money she has and says that James is in prison and Alan and Davey are sought as Colin Campbell's suspected murderers. Alan and Davey travel across a waste of burned-out forest, narrowly escaping a group of British soldiers. They fall into an ambush, but the attackers are CLUNY MACPHERSON's men, friends of Alan, so they are taken to Cluny Macpherson's hideout on Ben Alder mountain. Davey becomes ill. While he is recovering, Alan and Cluny play cards. Alan loses all his money. He asks Davey to lend him his and loses that too. Cluny returns the money to them as they leave, but Alan and Davey quarrel over the money and Davey is tempted to leave Alan but decides against it. They travel through the land of the Campbells, Alan's arch-foes. Davey becomes ill again and Alan finds refuge for him in a friendly cottage. They are visited by ROBIN OIG, one of Rob Roy's sons. Alan and Robin have a piping contest, and Robin is much the better. After a month's rest they set out again. They try to cross the bridge at Sterling but it is closely guarded so they go up the river to Limekilns, where a friendly bar girl obtains a boat and rows them across.

Chaps. 27–30. In Queensferry they separate for the day. Davey makes his way to Mr. Rankeillor, who tells David the story of how Alexander and Ebenezer were in love with the same girl. Alexander won the girl and Ebenezer took the family estate. Mr. Rankeillor and Davey meet Alan and they go to the Shaws at night. Davey and Mr. Rankeillor conceal themselves in the bushes and Alan goes in. Alan leads Ebenezer to believe that he is in partnership with Capt. Hoseason. Ebenezer admits that he paid Hoseason £20 to sell Davey into slavery in the Carolinas. At that point, Mr. Rankeillor and Davey come into the open, and Ebenezer breaks down. He promises to give Davey two-thirds of the income from the estate, with the entire estate going to Davey after Ebenezer's death. Mr. Rankeillor advises Davey to go to the Advocate and make a clean breast of his part in the Highland murder. Davey then parts from Alan, who is bound for France.

Kim

Novel by Rudyard Kipling, 1865–1936.
Published 1901 by Doubleday & Co.,
New York. © 1927 by Rudyard Kipling. (ML, 99)

RUDYARD KIPLING was more successful with his stories and poems than with his novels, but *Kim* is both a good and a successful novel. It has been particularly popular with younger readers. It tells of cloak-and-dagger work for the British in India, with much intrigue and many interesting touches that tell the reader about life in India while Kipling was there. In the book Kim is also called "Kim of the Rishti (Irish)."

Chaps. 1–4. KIMBALL O'HARA, called KIM, is the orphaned son of an Irish soldier sent to India with the Maverick Regiment. His father died when Kim was only 4, and since then the boy has lived with a woman who sells trinkets. She is an opium addict. Kim spends his time avoiding persons who would send him to school, and doing errands for anyone who offers a small fee. He looks like any other urchin of the streets, and speaks the local dialects fluently. His English tends to be stilted. One day he meets a Red Lama from Tibet who is on a pilgrimage to the river that washes away all sin. Kim becomes *chela,* or disciple, to the old man and a deep affection springs up between them. Kim seeks MAHBUB ALI, a horse dealer, to beg train fare for them both and is given a mission, for which he is well paid. He is to deliver a message to a certain man in a certain house—and his shrewd mind perceives instantly that it is some kind of secret signal. He is not aware of it, but both Mahbub and Col. CREIGHTON, the man to whom he gives the message, are agents of the Secret Service. By careful listening, Kim learns that soldiers are coming to the area of Umballa. Later Kim uses this information to convince a priest that he has powers of divination. The priest in turn casts his horoscope and tells him that within three days he will come upon a red bull on a green field, and that this is important in his future life.

Chaps. 5–8. Kim is watching the installation of an army camp, and a flag with the red bull on a green field is raised. This is the symbol of the Mavericks, but to Kim it is the fulfillment of the prophecy. (About his neck he has always worn a leather amulet in which are sewn his birth certificate, his father's discharge certificate, and a bit of parchment with his father's signature that certifies his membership in the Masons.) Kim accidentally trips one of the chaplains and is taken inside for questioning. The amulet reveals that he is a sahib, though he looks like any dirty little native

boy. To his horror he must now go to school and be cared for by the Regiment or the Masons. A conversation with his Holy Man results in his being sent to St. Xavier, a Catholic school in Lucknow. To the astonishment of the chaplain and Creighton, the lama sends the money for his first year's schooling and guarantees the rest when it is due. Creighton is mightily impressed with the boy's subtlety, intelligence, and resourcefulness. Kim knows intuitively that he is some day to be used in the secret business that concerns Mahbub Ali, the horse dealer, and Col. Creighton. He is miserable in school but learns rapidly and thoroughly. On his first holiday, however, he goes out to roam his beloved countryside in the costume of a native, with brown dye on his skin. He overhears a plot to assassinate Mahbub Ali and saves his friend. This reaches Creighton's ears immediately, further convincing him that Kim will be valuable to the Secret Service. Dutifully, Kim returns to St. Xavier for the fall term. The next summer he proceeds again to live as he chooses. He tells the lama that the sahibs plan to make him a member of a surveying group. He has been taught mapmaking in great detail. Toward the middle of his holiday he meets Mahbub and is told that he must spend the remainder of his vacation in Simla with LURGAN SAHIB, a man who sells jewels and curios. Kim dislikes the order but senses that it is part of "the great game."

Chaps. 9–12. At Lurgan's shop Kim learns many things that are destined to prove useful in his future work in the Secret Service. Lurgan is entertained by Kim's versatile performance of the rôles of different local characters. His correct intonations, gestures and use of the proper vernacular in each case delight Lurgan, who asks Kim to maintain his final characterization as a customer enters the shop. The "customer" proves to be "one of us," as

Kim afterward phrases it. It is a Bengali named HURREE CHUNDER MOOKERJEE—a fat man with great talent for disguise. Hurree is most favorably impressed. Kim returns to school and continues to excel at his studies. After Kim has had three years of St. Xavier's, Mahbub convinces Creighton that the boy is ready to start his work with them. Kim is once more allowed to go with his holy man, who has unfailingly paid his school expenses throughout this time. Kim and the lama set out by train in a generally northerly direction, and en route Kim is able to save the life of another worker in "the game." The news of this reaches Hurree and Creighton and they decide to assign Kim to a project in the hill country, where Russian agents are working to undermine British control. Kim finds it easy to persuade the lama to go to the mountains to restore his failing strength, and they set out. They stop to visit an old woman of Kula and find there a peddler of drugs and charms who has won the confidence of the villagers. Kim is astounded when this man privately addresses him as "Mr. O'Hara." The peddler proves to be Hurree, the fat man, whose disguise was so expert that even his size had not given him away. A plan is adopted whereby Kim and the lama will travel by themselves some distance from Hurree, who will carry an umbrella as a signpost for Kim to follow. The old lama knows only that he is seeking his river and that Kim is his devoted *chela.*

Chaps. 13–15. The journey to the highest hills is arduous and long. Kim finds it difficult to keep up with the old lama, who is as agile as a youth in the hills. After many weeks, Kim's muscles have hardened and he is acclimated to the thin air of the high altitudes. They come upon Hurree, who has located the Russian pair they are seeking. He knows that the documents they want are in a certain case, but he cannot obtain them. He is disguised this time as a representative

They find a peddler of drugs and charms who has the people's confidence

382

of one of the hill rajahs, and the pair have accepted him as such. In their private conversations, which they assume cannot be understood, they openly scoff at the British. A stupid act by the Russian creates an opportunity to obtain the papers. One of the pair demands to buy an exquisite drawing of the Wheel of Life that the old lama—a fine artist—has made. The lama would never think of selling his picture, but the Russian does not understand this and seizes the sheet roughly, tearing it. The lama's instantaneous reaction of defense precipitates a violent fight. The lama is hurt, one of the Russians is seriously injured by Kim, and the bearers stampede. Hurree swiftly tells Kim how to get the important bag from the servants, who have run off with all the luggage. Then the fat man undertakes to guide the Russians to civilization. Kim gets the papers and descends with the lama to the house of the woman of Kula, where he succumbs to his exhaustion and falls ill. Hurree returns and Kim turns over the papers. The mission has succeeded admirably. While Kim was ill the old lama found his river and immersed himself in its cleansing waters; now he is ready, sinless, for his next step in eternity. Kim must also be cleansed in the River of the Arrow, and then, sure of Paradise, he will join the survey team. The lama is satisfied. He has found salvation for himself and his beloved *chela*.

King Lear

Play by William Shakespeare, 1564–1616.
Produced about 1607.

THE TRAGEDY of *Lear* is ranked very high among Shakespeare's work and is quite playable, being often revived. Lear, a king of Britain in ancient (pre-Roman) times, was the subject of standard legends that Shakespeare used as a basis for his play—particularly the story of his rewarding the two hypocritical daughters who were willing to flatter him and banishing the honest daughter who actually loved and respected him but would say no more. At the end Lear becomes a latter-day Job, beset by every imaginable misfortune, but he cannot take it so well as Job did and he dies. As for Cornelia, the dutiful daughter, who dies also to complete the tragedy, her lot was not too wholly undeserved. She knew she was the favorite daughter and her pride was hurt when her father put her to a public test, so she decided to assert herself and test wills with him. She lost.

Act I. 1. LEAR, king of Britain, decides to retire from the throne and divide his kingdom among his three daughters in proportion to the love that each of them has for him. GONERIL and REGAN, the two older daughters, express themselves hypocritically, but to his satisfaction. The youngest, CORDELIA, will not lie. She professes only dutiful devotion to her father. The king is enraged. To Goneril and her husband ALBANY, and to Regan and her husband CORNWALL, he gives all of his estates, leaving none to Cordelia, who is unmarried. He will live with each of the two married sisters in turn. He presents Cordelia to her suitor, the King of France, who is happy to have her even without a dowry. KENT, a loyal courtier, criticizes Lear for his actions and is banished. 2. GLOUCESTER, an old courtier, is deceived by a forged letter into thinking his son EDGAR plots to murder him. The letter was forged by Edgar's bastard brother, EDMUND. 3. OSWALD, steward to Goneril, reports that Lear, who lives with Goneril this month, has beaten one of her servants in anger. She authorizes Oswald to defy him. 4. Kent, disguised as a servant, offers himself to Lear, who does not recognize him and hires him. The FOOL and Lear make so much noise that Goneril protests the Fool's presence and suggests that Lear reduce his retinue. Lear denounces his daughter and decides to leave her. 5. Lear sends Kent to Gloucester with a letter and sends another letter to tell Regan of his coming.

Act II. 1. Edmund advances his father's belief that Edgar is a villain. Cornwall and Regan arrive for a visit. 2. In a minor argument, Kent strikes Oswald. Cornwall has Kent put into the stocks as punishment. Kent reminds him that he is the king's messenger, and Gloucester asks Cornwall not to offend the king, but Cornwall persists. 3. Edgar is a fugitive in the woods. He bemoans his fate, which he does not understand. 4. Lear and the Fool arrive before Gloucester's castle and find Kent in the stocks. Cornwall and Regan refuse to see Lear until he has apologized to Goneril. Goneril then arrives and Lear realizes that the sisters are united against him. Lear runs out into the night, although a storm is about to break. Only the Fool is with him.

Act III. 1. On the heath, Kent learns from a Gentleman that there is discord between Albany and Cornwall. Also, a French army is secretly on its way to England. 2. In another part of the heath, the storm is raging. Lear defies the elements. Kent finds him and persuades him to take refuge in a nearby hovel. 3. Gloucester tells Edmund he will seek out Lear. He asks Edmund not to let Cornwall know this, but Edmund can hardly wait to denounce his father. 4. On the heath, Lear, the Fool and Kent find the hovel. It is occupied by Edgar, who pretends to be Tom, a halfwit. Gloucester arrives but does not recognize his own son. Kent tells him Lear's mind has become unbalanced. 5. Cornwall and Edmund are plotting Gloucester's downfall. 6. In a farmhouse near the castle, Gloucester has found shelter for Lear and his friends. Here Lear holds a mock trial of his daughters, with the Fool and Tom the halfwit as judges. Gloucester warns Kent that he must take the king to Dover at once. Lear's life is now in danger. 7. Gloucester is arrested by Cornwall; who accuses him of treason. Cornwall puts out Gloucester's eyes and a servant of Gloucester's stabs Cornwall. Mortally wounded, Cornwall is led off by Regan.

Act IV. 1. Edgar finds his blind father in the heath. Gloucester confesses his mistakes and asks to be led to the cliffs of Dover to kill himself. 2. Albany berates his wife for the cruelty with which she and her sister have treated their father and Gloucester. A messenger reports that Cornwall has died. 3. The Gentleman tells Kent that the king of France has temporarily returned home to attend to affairs of state and that Cordelia is with the invading army. 4. Cordelia has found her mad father and asks her doctor to cure him. 5. Regan tells Oswald that she will marry Edmund, though she knows that her sister wants him too. 6. At Dover, Edgar fakes Gloucester's falling off the cliffs. The blind man thinks he has escaped death by a miracle. Lear, bedecked with flowers and quite mad, is being attacked by Oswald. Oswald is killed by Edgar. 7. Cordelia is caring for Lear in the French camp. He awakes cured and thinks he has escaped death by some miracle. He asks Cordelia to forgive him his errors.

Act V. 1. Albany joins forces with Edmund to fight off the French. Edgar leads his blind father between the battle lines. 2–3. The French army is defeated and Lear and Cordelia are taken prisoners. Edmund gives orders to have them executed in prison. Edgar steps forward and challenges Edmund to a duel. They fight and Edmund falls wounded. A messenger reports that Goneril has poisoned her sister and killed herself, when found out. Edmund tells of his order to have Lear and Cordelia executed. But it is too late to stop it. Lear enters with Cordelia dead in his arms. He then dies of a broken heart. Edmund dies of his wounds. Edgar, Albany and Kent are left to restore order in Britain.

Lear and the dead Cornelia

The King of the Golden River

Novel by John Ruskin, 1819–1900.
Published 1851.

THIS IS JUST A FAIRY TALE. It would not normally be expected to appear as a standard classic. But John Ruskin was a man of great eminence in the literary world, and he wrote chiefly essays and critical opinion of the kind that can hardly have a mass audience. This is the one book of his that can be generally read, so it is read. *The King of the Golden River* is an adaptation of an old legend and was written by Ruskin for children.

Chap. 1. There is a wonderfully fertile valley nestled among the mountains of Styria, called Treasure Valley. The valley belongs to three brothers, SCHWARTZ, HANS, and GLUCK. Schwartz and Hans are ugly, evil men, but Gluck, only 12 years old, is fair, blue-eyed, and kind to everyone.

There is a famine when all crops in the region, except those in Treasure Valley, are destroyed by hail and heavy rains. The brothers set their own prices and those who cannot afford to buy their corn starve. One day the two older brothers go out, leaving Gluck to mind the roast. Gluck takes pity on a poor little old man and lets him warm himself by the fire. He is about to cut a piece of meat for the old man when his brothers come home. They are angry with Gluck and order the old man to leave. The old man leaves but promises to return at midnight. It is a stormy night. The brothers shutter their windows and bar the door before going to bed, but as the clock strikes 12 the little old man returns, reclining on an enormous foamy globe. The roof has blown off the older brothers' rooms. The old man tells them to go into Gluck's room, where he had left the ceiling intact. The next morning Treasure Valley is a mass of ruin and desolation. The once fertile soil is a waste of red sand and gray mud. The storm has swept away all the food and money. The only thing left is the kitchen table, on which is the old man's card: SOUTH WEST WIND ESQUIRE.

Chap. 2. The brothers have nothing left but some curious old-fashioned pieces of gold plate. They decide to become goldsmiths and hire a furnace. Things do not go well because the two older brothers put a great deal of copper into the gold and people discover this. The older brothers occasionally leave Gluck to mind the furnace while they carouse at the alehouse. They are at last reduced to one drinking mug, which belongs to Gluck. The mug looks like the head of a little old man. The brothers tell Gluck to melt down the mug, and they go off to the alehouse. As Gluck is melting down the mug, he hears a voice singing and the face on the mug seems to say, "Pour me out." Gluck forces himself to take the crucible and pour out the gold, and a little golden dwarf, about a foot and a half high, emerges from the molten gold. The dwarf tells Gluck that he is the King of the Golden River at the top of the mountains that surround Treasure Valley. He was transformed to a mug by an evil king, but now Gluck has removed the spell. In gratitude the dwarf tells Gluck that whoever shall climb to the top of the mountain and cast three drops of holy water into the Golden River, for *him* and him only the river will turn to gold. But no one failing in his first attempt can succeed in a second attempt, and anyone who casts unholy water into the river will become a black stone. With this, the dwarf steps back into the fire and vanishes.

Chap. 3. When the two older brothers discover that their last piece of gold has disappeared, they beat poor Gluck until their arms are tired. But the next morning they begin to believe Gluck's strange story. They fight over which of them should first try his fortune at the Golden River. Neighbors call the constable; Hans hides but Schwartz is thrown into jail. Hans steals a cupful of holy water and sets off. As the sun grows hotter, Hans grows thirstier. He is about to quench his thirst from his flask when he notices a small dog, dying of thirst. He kicks the dog. Again, as Hans is about to quench his thirst, he sees a small child lying on a rock, its lips parched. He passes on. A third time he is about to use his flask when an old man calls to him for water. Hans passes him by also. As the sun sets Hans reaches the Golden River. He hurls the flask of holy water into the river. An icy chill shoots through his limbs; he staggers and falls. The water closes over his cry and the river gushes over the Black Stone.

Chap. 4. When Hans does not return Schwartz is pleased. Now he has a chance at the Golden River. Gluck has hired himself to a goldsmith and earns money to secure Schwartz's freedom. Schwartz takes the rest of Gluck's money and buys holy water from a bad priest. He trudges up the mountain, also ignoring the thirsting child and the old man. As Schwartz lifts the flask to his mouth a third time he thinks he sees the body of Hans lying beside the path, but he is so eager for the gold that he hurries on. Schwartz reaches the brink of the Golden River and casts the flask into the stream. Lightning glares in his eyes and the earth gives way beneath him. The river gushes over Two Black Stones.

Chap. 5. Gluck, worried about his brothers, sets out to find them. First he obtains some holy water from a good priest. Gluck is about to take a drink from his flask when he sees an old man coming down the path. The old man pleads with Gluck for water and Gluck gives him some. Later Gluck meets the little child and gives him all but a few drops of his water. When Gluck is about a few hundred yards from the Golden River he sees the panting dog on the path. Gluck decides to give the dog the rest of the water, for otherwise the dog will probably die. The dog evaporates and in its place stands the King of the Golden River. The king tells Gluck he turned the older brothers into stones because they threw unholy water into his river. When Gluck protests that they got the holy water from the church font, the king answers that water that is denied to the weary and dying is always unholy. He stoops and plucks a lily at his foot and shakes the dewdrops from it into Gluck's flask. Gluck is told to cast the flask into the river and then go back to Treasure Valley. The king disappears. Gluck does as he has been told and goes down into Treasure Valley, finding it a garden again. Gluck dwells in the valley and for him the river is a River of Gold. But to this day, at the top of the cataract of the Golden River, may be seen two black stones that everyone calls the Black Brothers.

In the Golden River stand two stones that everyone calls the Black Brothers

The King's Henchman

Novel by Edna St. Vincent Millay,
1892–1950.
Published 1927.

THIS IS THE LIBRETTO for an opera by
Deems Taylor, commissioned by the
Metropolitan Opera Company in New
York and performed by it in 1927.
The scene is England in the 10th century. *The King's Henchman* was widely
read in book form. It does not retain
throughout the excellence that made
Miss Millay the leading American
poetess of her times, but it does contain some of her best work and it is
well worth reading.

Act I. In his great hall at Winchester
King EADGAR, a handsome young man, not
quite 25, who has been king for 10 years,
sits with his lords around the banquet table.
It is 5 A.M. MACCUS, the harper, sings. The
women, not invited to the banquet, are
grouped at the back of the hall and gossip
among themselves. Eadgar plans to send
AETHELWOLD, his foster-brother and
closest friend, to Devon. ORDGAR, Thane
of Devon, has a daughter, ALFRIDA. If she
is fair, Aethelwold will bring her back to
be Eadgar's bride and queen. Everybody
knows that Aethelwold is very shy with
ladies, but he is fearless and is devoted to
Eadgar. At this point Aethelwold enters, a
fair, beardless young man, tall and graceful.
He tells Eadgar that he does not like this
mission to Devon. He is not capable of
judging beauty. Eadgar says that is the reason he can trust Aethelwold. After a farewell song Aethelwold and his men depart,
including Maccus, the harper.

Act II. The scene is a forest in Devonshire, one month later. It is All Hallow
Mass Eve. Aethelwold and Maccus grope
about in the darkness. Maccus goes off to
look for Aethelwold's men and Aethelwold
lies down to sleep. Alfrida, a tall, slender
girl of 17 years, with pale red hair falling
over her shoulders, enters with ASE, her
serving woman, who carries a torch. Alfrida
is frightened but Ase reassures her: Many
young maids are out this night, when spells
may reveal who their true loves will be.
Alfrida thinks it might still have been better
to remain by the cozy fire, even if it meant
she must marry the bumbling churl her
father has picked for her husband. Ase
leaves her and Alfrida discovers Aethelwold
asleep on the ground. He looks so beautiful
to her that she kisses him. He wakes and
sees Alfrida, who looks equally beautiful to
him. They embrace and Aethelwold wishes
they could hide themselves in the dark of
night forever. When Aethelwold hears that
his beloved's name is Alfrida he is filled

with dread and anguish. Alfrida and Ase
depart. When Maccus returns Aethelwold
explains his terrible plight. Aethelwold, in
despair, decides to leave at once. Alfrida and
Ase return and when they find that Aethelwold has gone, Alfrida falls to the ground,
sobbing bitterly. Offstage Maccus is heard
protesting that to return will mean disaster
for Aethelwold; but Aethelwold rushes
back and embraces Alfrida. He orders Maccus to return and tell Eadgar that Ordgar's
daughter is not beautiful or fine enough to
be Eadgar's queen and that Aethelwold desires the king's blessing on the marriage between himself and Alfrida. Maccus reluctantly agrees and departs.

Act III. The scene is Alfrida's father's
house, the following spring. Aethelwold
gazes listlessly out of the window. Alfrida
goes silently about her household chores.
Aethelwold complains sadly that he never
sees her alone; Alfrida protests that she is
too busy. Aethelwold asks if she loves him
and she replies that morning is no time for
him to be asking such questions; she is too
busy with her household chores. Alfrida
hates this dull life and wonders where is the
brave and glamorous Aethelwold, favorite
of the king—why does he not take her
away from here? Aethelwold promises to

take Alfrida away this very day. They will
go to Ghent, where Alfrida can buy all the
finery befitting a lady. Maccus announces
that Eadgar is at the gates. Aethelwold is
filled with fear. Now at last he tells Alfrida
of his betrayal and how, but for him, she
might have been Queen of England. Alfrida
must make herself look plain and coarse to
save Aethelwold. Alfrida promises to do
this. Ase whispers to her mistress that she
must not throw away her one great chance.
The women go out. Eadgar arrives with his
lords and greets his old friend Aethelwold
with joy. Aethelwold explains that Alfrida
is ill. Then Alfrida appears. She is dressed in
a gorgeous robe of embroidered silk and
looks more beautiful than ever before.

Eadgar realizes that Aethelwold has betrayed him and he exclaims that if he cannot trust his dearest friend than who in his
whole kingdom can be counted on? Aethelwold appeals to Eadgar, saying that the
misery each of them feels is too much for
one small room to bear. Eadgar and Alfrida
both remain cold and silent. Aethelwold
pulls out a small sword and stabs himself.
Alfrida weeps and Eadgar coldly tells her
that her heart is too narrow to grieve for
such a noble soul as Aethelwold. The lords
bear Aethelwold's body out and the villagers chant a sad song.

King Solomon's Mines

Novel by H. Rider Haggard, 1856–
1925.
Published 1886. (ML, 163)

HAGGARD was one of the most competent writers of adventure novels in
his period. His most successful novels
were set in South Africa, where he
lived for several years. *King Solomon's
Mines* was his first great success and,
with *She*, one of his two best books.
There is a sequel to it, *Allan Quarter-
main.*

Chaps. 1–5. ALLAN QUATERMAIN is an
exceptional elephant hunter. The span of
life of a commercial hunter is no more than
4 or 5 years, but at 55 Quatermain is still
the best in his profession. He is returning
by ship to his home in Natal when he meets
Sir HENRY CURTIS and Captain JOHN
GOOD, retired from the Royal Navy. Curtis
learns that Quatermain met a man named
NEVILLE in the Transvaal and tells him that
Neville is the assumed name of his younger
brother GEORGE, with whom he has
quarreled. Their parents died intestate and
though Sir Henry waited for his brother to
come to him for money, George left for
Africa instead, determined to make his fortune. No one has heard from him since.
Curtis's one aim now is to locate him.

Quatermain is sure Neville started for
King Solomon's mines. He tells them, in
confidence, the story of the mines. Ten
years before, Quatermain befriended a
Portuguese gentleman, JOSÉ SILVESTRE,
who died in his camp. Just before his death,
Silvestre told Quatermain the story of King
Solomon's mines, which an ancestor of Silvestre's had discovered 300 years ago. The
ancestor died trying to return to civilization, leaving a map of the mines etched in
his blood. Silvestre deciphered the map
and gave his life trying to rediscover the
mines. Curtis and Captain Good offer
Quatermain a large fee to take them to the
mines and Quatermain agrees. Quatermain
gets their equipment ready and hires two
Zula servants, VENTVOGEL and KHIVA. The
day they are ready to leave, a strange Zulu
named UMBOPA requests to go along without pay, saying he wishes to join his tribe
in the north. There is something about the
man that makes Quatermain uneasy, but
Curtis takes an instant liking to Umbopa.
They start their journey slowly, stopping to
hunt elephants. They lose Khiva when he
saves Good from a wounded bull elephant.
They come to the desert they must cross.
Here their enemies are heat, thirst, and
flies.

Chaps. 6–10. Water becomes the necessity of life. Quatermain insists that if they
follow the old Portuguese Don's map they
will find it. Ventvogel discovers a spring.

385

They can see their mountain destination, called Sheba's Left Breast; on its other side is King Solomon's road, which leads to the diamond mines. The climb up the mountain is hampered by extremely cold weather. Ventvogel freezes to death. In a cave they find the body of a white man, his body preserved by the freezing temperature. There seems no doubt that it is the ancestor of José Silvestre. They cross the mountaintop and the road built by King Solomon comes into view. At its end they come to a fertile valley. Game is plentiful and the food problem is solved. Good goes to a stream to shave and his scream attracts Quatermain. The captain is surrounded by a party of threatening natives. Quatermain speaks with them in Zulu. The leader, an old man with regal bearing, says they must die, but Quatermain says that he and his companions are magically descended from the stars. One of the natives catches sight of Captain Good replacing his false teeth, which fascinating spectacle lends verisimilitude to Quatermain's story. With theatrical timing Quatermain calls for his rifle, which he declares is a magic tube, and shoots an antelope passing on a near ridge. The natives fall back in wonder and INFADOOS, their leader, decides to lead them to TWALA, king of the Kukuanas. Quatermain notices that Umbopa resembles their captors. They reach Loo, where the one-eyed King Twala is holding his summer games. The king refuses to believe in their magical powers until Quatermain again demonstrates with his rifle. Twala is impressed and invites them to be present at his annual witch hunt. It is a horrible experience, with hundreds of men killed. The adviser to the king is an old witch named GAGOOL. She and her sister witches have devised this method for the king to rid himself of his enemies. One of the witches claims Umbopa for death but Quatermain claims divinity for him also, as their servant. Umbopa thanks Quatermain and reveals that he is the true King of the Kukuanas. Twala murdered his father when he was very young, and his mother fled with him over the mountains. His name

is IGNOSI, and to prove his right to the throne he displays the symbol of kingship, a large blue snake tattooed around his waist. Quatermain calls for Infadoos, who recognizes Umbopa and goes to spread the word among the chiefs.

Chaps. 11–14. Infadoos brings the chiefs, who ask for absolute proof. Umbopa shows them the snake symbol but they demand further proof from his white friends who practice magic. Good tells Quatermain that an eclipse of the sun is due at noon the following day and Quatermain tells the chiefs that he will darken the sun to prove Umbopa's right to be king. They say that if this is done, they will make him king. Curtis makes Ignosi promise that if he becomes king he will never put a man to death without trial. The next morning they are summoned by Twala to attend the dance of the maidens. It is the custom for the most beautiful girl among them to be sacrificed. Twala asks Quatermain to make the choice and Quatermain chooses a girl named FOULATA. When he discovers her fate, he and Good intervene to prevent her death. A dark ring begins to form around the sun. Fear grips the king and his followers, and Quatermain's party escapes, with Foulata and Infadoos. Outside the town the chiefs loyal to Ignosi have assembled their troops, about 20,000 men, to do battle for their rightful king. Twala's men attack the next morning. They are in the majority but the Englishmen use their guns and instill superstitious fear in the enemy, who are slaughtered in their flight. Ignosi and his white

friends enter the main square of the town. Twala is waiting for them with his only companion, the witch Gagool. It is his right as a defeated king to choose the instrument of his death. He chooses battle with Curtis, who wins by lopping off Twala's head with his axe.

Chaps. 15–20. Ignosi is proclaimed king. Good falls ill and is nursed by the grateful Foulata. The new king arranges for his white friends to go to King Solomon's mines. He forces old Gagool, under pain of death, to escort them to the secret place, which only she knows. Foulata accompanies them. They reach a large cave guarded by three huge stone figures. Gagool leads them through damp passages to a room she calls the Place of Death. Here all the kings of the Kukuanas are placed after death. The corpses are seated around a huge table, petrified in perfect condition by the mineral-laden water dripping from above. Gagool presses a lever, which lifts a massive stone. It reveals the treasure room of Solomon, filled with thousands of rare ivory tusks, great chests filled with diamonds, and goatskins full of gold coins. While the richest men in the world fill the air with their laughter, Gagool stabs Foulata. As she lies dying, Foulata calls out a warning that Gagool has pressed a secret lever and is escaping. The wounded girl clings to the witch and impedes her flight. Before the old woman can squeeze completely under the descending rock door, she is crushed to death by its weight. Foulata dies and Quatermain and his friends accept their own fate, that they are buried alive. They cannot find the hidden lever. For 24 hours they wait for death. Quatermain then wonders why the air inside their prison is still fresh and they follow a current of air and come to a subterranean passage. Before they proceed to explore it, Quatermain fills the pockets of his hunting coat and every available receptacle with diamonds. The passageway leads them to the outside and they are saved. A few weeks later they say goodbye to Ignosi and start back to Natal. Their guides take a different route and at an oasis they encounter George Curtis. He injured his leg two years before and could not proceed further on his travels. Quatermain insists that they divide the diamonds equally. Curtis refuses his share but is touched when Quatermain gives George the share meant for his brother.

The captain is surrounded by threatening natives

Kristin Lavransdatter

Novel by Sigrid Undset, 1882–1949.
Published 1922. © 1923, 1927 by
Sigrid Undset. Published 1923 by
Alfred A. Knopf, New York.

THE THREE NOVELS that make up the
trilogy *Kristin Lavransdatter* are
among the best work of the great Norwegian novelist Sigrid Undset, winner
of the Nobel Prize in 1928. It is a story
of Norway in the 14th century, built
around the central character, Kristin,
her experiences and family relationships, and her eventual disillusionment
and retirement to a convent. Shortly
after she brought her heroine Kristin
to ultimate peace in the convent,
Madame Undset herself became a convert to Catholicism.

The Bridal Wreath

Part I. Chap. 1. LAVRANS BJÖRGULFSÖN
marries RAGNFRID IVARSDATTER and they
go to live at his farm-manor, Skog, near
Oslo. Both come of distinguished Norse
stock and Lavrans' forebears also played a
part in the legendary past of Sweden.
Ragnfrid loses three sons, one after the
other, in their infancy, and withdraws
almost entirely from contact with the world.
Lavrans, having always felt that Ragnfrid
was not at home among the people of his
native south, decides to move to Ragnfrid's
family property, Jörundgaard, in the northern valley of Gudbrandsdal, which she inherited from her father in 1306. Lavrans,
Ragnfrid and the only child they have left,
a little girl named KRISTIN, take up life at
Jörundgaard. Ragnfrid remains as moody
and withdrawn as ever. As Kristin grows
up she spends more and more time with her
father, even going on hunting trips with
him. Among Lavrans' henchmen is a boy,
ARNE GYRDSÖN, who becomes Kristin's
best friend.

Chaps. 2–4. Lavrans makes it a practice
to travel south to Skog each summer. The
time comes for him to turn over this estate
to his younger brother, AASMUND, but
Lavrans wishes Kristin to see his father's
ancestral manor and the house where she
was born, so father and daughter visit Skog.
Ragnfrid gives birth to another daughter,
ULVHILD. At the age of 3, Ulvhild is crippled in an accident. Ragnfrid sends for
Lady AASHILD of Haugen to relieve the
child's pain. Lady Aashild is shunned
throughout the countryside as a "witch-
wife", but Ragnfrid is desperate. Lady
Aashild spends almost the entire summer
at Jörundgaard and saves the girl's life but
cannot restore the use of her legs.

Chaps. 5–7. Lavrans continues to prosper. He arranges Kristin's engagement, at
the age of 15, to SIMON ANDRESSÖN of the
powerful DRYFIN clan. Kristin's childhood
friend, Arne Gyrdsön, is preparing to leave
for the city of Hamar, where the bishop has
promised to sponsor his career. Arne and
Kristin exchange a tearful farewell. From
the start his family's genteel poverty has
rendered him ineligible as a match for
Lavrans' daughter. On her way home Kristin is assaulted by BENTEIN, grandson of
SIRA EIRIK, the parish priest. She fights
Bentein off and reports the incident. Bentein is sent to Hamar with letters from his
grandfather to the bishop. Kristin cannot
avoid feeling tainted by the encounter,
though she has come out of it unharmed,
and she sinks into complete melancholy
when Arne is killed in a fight with Bentein, provoked by Bentein's slurring references to Kristin. Kristin goes into a year's
retreat at the Convent of Nonneseter.

Part II. Chaps. 1–3. After her third week
at the cloister, Kristin and her "bedfellow,"
INGEBJÖRG FILIPPUSDATTER, are permitted
to go into Oslo on a shopping trip, accompanied by an old manservant named
HAAKON. On their way back the girls get
caught up in a crowd and are separated from
Haakon. Ingebjörg takes to her heels in
fright and Kristin follows. At an out-of-
the-way inn the girls engage two men,
foreigners by their speech, to guide them
back to the cloister. After taking them even
further out of their way, the men turn on
the girls and attempt to snatch their purses.
Kristin and Ingebjörg shriek at the top of
their lungs and attract a party of horsemen

Kristin and Erlend

to their rescue. A handsome and knightly
rider who comes to their assistance turns out
to be ERLEND NIKULAUSSÖN, nephew of
Lady Aashild. On St. Margaret's Day, in
July, the convent goes in a body to a special
mass at the church in Akar and Kristin spies
Erlend's tall figure in the congregation. That
evening, at the festival at the guild-hall,
Kristin and Erlend meet and pledge their
love. The next morning, Ingebjörg informs
Kristin that the Church only recently lifted
its ban against Erlend, for taking ELINE
ORMSDATTER away from her rightful husband, SIGURD, and of siring two illegitimate
children by her. Erlend tells Kristin that he
has been penalized by his father, the
Church, and the king, for his folly at 18,
when the affair with Eline began. But he
admits that Simon would make a far better
match. Kristin is determined to remain true
to her pledge to him.

Chaps. 4–8. In August Kristin visits her
uncle, Aasmund, at Skog. She meets Erlend
clandestinely and in secret their love is
consummated. Kristin returns to the convent convinced that she is with child, but
this is merely a guilty delusion. She confesses the relationship to the Minorite
Brother EDVIN, whom she knows from
home. She spends the following Yuletide
with the Dryfin clan but cannot bring herself to tell Simon of her desire to be freed
from her betrothal to him. After the holiday she returns to the convent and to her
assignations with Erlend. Simon's suspicions are aroused when he hears that Kristin
has been seen in the company of BRYNHILD
FLUGA, mistress of a local bawdy-house.
Kristin pacifies him and he agrees to release her from their betrothal. Lavrans
reluctantly agrees to terminate the betrothal.

Part III. Chaps. 1–3. Kristin's year of retreat comes to an end and she returns home.
The subject of her broken engagement is
tactfully avoided, except by Ulvhild, who
is preparing to enter a religious order. Ulvhild wishes she were not crippled and
could become Simon's wife. Ragnfrid warns
Kristin that Lavrans will never approve of
any suitor like Erlend. Erlend's closest male
kinsman, according to custom, presents Erlend's proposal to Lavrans, who rejects
Erlend as morally unfit to become Kristin's
husband. Erlend plans an elopement to
Sweden, where he has been promised the
protection of his kinswoman, Lady INGEB-
JÖRG, King Haakon's daughter. Lady
Aashild consents to help the lovers. She has
Kristin visit her at her manor, Haugen.
But Eline Ormsdatter bursts in, reproaches
and threatens Kristin and Erlend, and attempts to poison Kristin. Erlend catches
her and Eline kills herself with a dagger.
Erlend and Sir BJÖRN, Lady Aashild's hus-
band, spirit the dead body out of Haugen.

Chaps. 4–8. Kristin returns home, where
she is reminded daily of Lavran's hostility to
everything she loves. Ulvhild dies, and Kristin herself feels close to dying of a broken
heart. In the spring Erlend's kinsmen renew their proposal and this time Lavrans,
aware of Kristin's unhappiness, consents.
The berothal period is to last a year. Erlend
spends Whitsuntide at Jörundgaard and
Kristin becomes pregnant. A few months
later Lavrans, still drunk from the wedding
celebration, suddenly becomes aware of the
relationship between his daughter and Erlend. His bitterness is in no way alleviated
when Ragnfrid, to take the onus off Kristin,
confesses to Lavrans that he was not the
father of their short-lived, first-born son.

The Mistress of Husaby

Part I. Chaps. 1–4. Almost before the wedding festivities are over at Erlend's ancestral home of Husaby, where Kristin has been brought directly from Jörundgaard, she becomes aware of the deterioration of this former residence of kings. The walls behind the tapestries are black with dirt; the fur rugs and bed-throws are lice-infested; and a fortune in flax is rotting in store. Kristin takes in ORM, Erlend's bastard son, who since infancy has been the master of a farm-manor of his own. Kristin gives birth to the child she has been carrying since Whitsuntide. He is baptized NIKULAUS.

Chaps. 5–6. Erlend fetches Lavrans to visit Kristin. The new grandfather confirms his suspicions about his daughter's chastity before marriage. Kristin is also visited by Simon Andressön, who has married Lady HALFRID, an heiress 30 years his senior. He tells Kristin of the tragedy that has befallen his sister, SIGRID, who has brought a bastard into the world. Kristin is filled with a sense of her own sinfulness and she sets out on a pilgrimage of repentance.

Part II. Chaps. 1–4. Lavrans visits Husaby in the company of Sir ERLING VIDKUNSSÖN, a highly-placed court intriguer. Conspiracies both for and against Lady Ingebjörg and her 3-year old son, King MAGNUS VII of Norway and Sweden, are sweeping the country. Erlend and his cousin, Sir MUNAN, are involved in Sir Erling's plans in support of Lady Ingebjörg. Kristin has grown quite fond of Orm but can barely tolerate his arrogant sister, MARGARET. Her attachment to her own little Nikulaus is almost obsessive. She cannot bring herself, despite his age, to wean the child. When her second son, BJÖRGULT, is born she puts him straightaway in the care of a wet nurse. Her third, GAUTE, arrives when Björgult is 11 months old. Orm dies of a brain-sickness and at the same time Kristin has a miscarriage that endangers her life. Erlend is being drawn more deeply into the political situation. He has sold several valuable farmlands to finance the outfitting of two ships for use against the Russians. On his return from a trip in the northern waters, Kristin gives birth again. This time it is twins, IVAR and SKULE, bringing Kristin's productivity to five sons in five years. Erlend finds that child bearing has in no way diminished the radiance of Kristin's beauty.

Simon Andressön, now a widower, becomes engaged to Kristin's youngest sister, 14-year-old RAMBORG.

Chaps. 5–8. Simon had an illegitimate daughter, ARNJERD, by a servant-girl in his wife's house. Lady Halfrid insisted on taking the baby girl and was bringing her up properly, but Lady Halfrid became pregnant at too old an age and died. Simon's marriage to Ramborg is a big event and Erlend and Kristin visit Lavrans for the celebration. Kristin is amused to see Lavrans dote

388

on Erlend, the man he once considered unworthy to marry her. She takes pleasure in telling her father that Erlend used a bordello for their trysts when she was in the convent. That winter Kristin is heavy with child again. Erlend hears that Lavrans is dying and despite her expectant condition Kristin decides she must visit him. In April she is delivered of a sixth son, named Lavrans for his grandfather. A few days after the christening old Lavrans dies.

Part III. Chaps. 1–3. Not quite two years after the death of her husband, Ragnfrid dies too. Kristin's share of Ragnfrid's estate is Jörundgaard. She assigns its stewardship to Simon. Erlend becomes involved in a political contretemps. Lady Ingebjörg, whom Erlend and Sir Erling have both supported, has been long since discredited. Her son, King Magnus, after coming into his majority at 16, has been a power unto himself. Margaret, Erlend's daughter by Eline, has been caught in an indiscretion with a young man and is hastily married off to GERLAK, son of the German goldsmith TIEDEKEN. Nikulaus is now 12 and Kristin brings him a new brother, MUNAN. Magnus is ambitious to acquire the Danish province of Skane in southeastern Sweden and needs money but the Norse nobility, particularly Sir Erling and his followers, turn a deaf ear. Erlend tries to steer a discreet middle course but corresponds with Lady Ingebjörg in secret. He has domestic problems too. Kristin is burdened by the sinfulness of their early life together and has a way of reproaching him with resentments and guilt that have been storing up in her for 15 years. This results in Erlend's seeking consolation elsewhere. As a matter of course, Kristin hears of his infidelity.

Chaps. 4–7. Erlend and Kristin are reconciled after this adulterous interlude, but on an impersonal basis. Erlend has been plotting with Lady Ingebjörg to create an independent Kingdom of Norway and he is arrested for treason. He is sentenced to death and the confiscation of his lands. Then he is imprisoned for a year and tortured almost incessantly, but he refuses to expose his accomplices. Sir Erling, though concerned only with his own skin, finally yields to pressure from Simon Andressön and intercedes with the king on Erlend's behalf. Erlend's life is spared and he returns home.

The Cross

Part I. Chaps. 1–4. Kristin is aware that farm life is a strain on Erlend, who is accustomed to the more glamorous events of king-making and court intrigue. Yet she cannot help resenting his utter uselessness, which he has begun to communicate to their sons. Simon Andressön, in the meanwhile, has become the wealthiest man in the province. The two families, closely related by blood and marriage, are united even more when Kristin's gift for healing saves the life of the Andressön's only son.

Chaps. 5–6. During an Easter day alefeast at Simon's manor, Gaute is provoked by Simon's bastard daughter, Arngjerd, into defending his father's honor against her accusations of treachery. Just before Erlend's arrest, Gaute slipped certain incriminating papers out of Husaby. Gaute now announces that the guilty papers bore the Andressön family seal. Simon is overwhelmed. His efforts on Erlend's behalf were prompted by generous motives, but now Simon realizes that the Andressöns owe their affluence to Erlend's loyalty and silence under torture. Simon also admits to himself that his interest in Erlend's trial was really due to his interest in Kristin. Ramborg accuses Simon of loving Kristin and Simon replies that no matter what he feels for Kristin, he has never been untrue to Ramborg.

Part II. Chaps. 1–3. Unrest is spreading through Norway. The great lords are dissatisfied with the rule of King Magnus the Effeminate and openly threaten to take up arms to bring him to his senses. The alternative is to turn over the throne to the son of Lady Ingebjörg's sister. Kristin is worried about Erlend's influence on the political

Kristin cannot bring herself to wean her child

Kristin sees Erlend at the Parish church at Haugen

activity of 17-year old Nikulaus and she is worried about all three of her eldest sons, Nikulaus, Björgulf, and Gaute, because they are possessed of a dangerous way with women. Kristin's maternal protectiveness is aroused to a high pitch when she discovers that Erlend is planning to send the twins, Ivar and Skule, on a ship in the fleet owned by Margaret's rich husband, Gerlak. She angrily accuses Erlend of being unworthy to be lord of Jörundgaard and without another word Erlend takes himself off to Haugen. When Kristin finally realizes that Erlend intends to stay on at Haugen permanently, she asks the intervention of Sira Eirik, the priest. Eirik tells her that if she wants Erlend back she must fetch him herself. She goes to Haugen and sees Erlend at the parish church. He has been disquieted by reports of a disastrous flood in the Jörundgaard valley. Kristin rushes home without even waiting to speak to him after mass. Simon, shamed to think he might be disloyal to Erlend by loving Kristin, has forsworn any further contact with his in-laws; but now, with Erlend gone, Simon protests to Kristin against her aloofness to her sister Ramborg and her sister's family.

Chaps. 4–8. Shortly after Yule, Simon sets out for Dryfin with his wife and children. He ignores a slight knife wound in his forearm, accidentally dealt him in a taproom brawl, but the scratch becomes a dangerous infection. Simon asks to be taken home rather than to Dryfin, for his wife is pregnant and might react badly to shock. He also suggests that Kristin, with her healing powers, be sent for. Kristin goes but fails to effect a cure. Simon dies but exacts a deathbed promise from her to make her peace with Erlend for the sake of their children. Still Kristin cannot bring herself to go to Haugen. Ramborg returns home as a widow and informs Kristin that she will marry a wealthy man, Jammaelt Halvardssön, who has been secretly in love with her for years. The two sisters quarrel

and Ramborg tells Kristin that she knows well which of them Simon really loved. Kristin finally keeps her promise to Simon and visits Erlend at Haugen. She remains with him five days. Erlend refuses to return to Jörundgaard. Kristin discovers that she is with child again. She dispatches Nikulaus and Gaute to bring their father home, but Erlend will not go to Kristin nor Kristin to him. Kristin is delivered of another boy but he dies before he is three months old. Ulf, a distant kinsman of Erlend, who managed the property at Husaby and later at Jörundgaard, has become the innocent cause of dangerous gossip. Ulf's wife accuses him of the paternity of Kristin's dead child. Kristin, Ulf, and all of Kristin's sons but Lavrans are put under armed guard at Jörundgaard to await trial. Lavrans rides off to Haugen to fetch his father. Erlend returns almost at once. He sees Kristin in the courtyard of Jörundgaard, but when he attempts to speak to her two of her guards seize her to prevent her from answering. He strikes the nearest of these guards with his ax and, in retaliation, is pierced through his side and groin with a spear wielded by the general's son. The wounds prove fatal.

Part III. Chaps. 1–3. Lavrans is 15 but has become once again the youngest of Kristin's sons, Munan, his junior, having died.

Kristin's new brother-in-law, Jammaelt Halvardssön, persuades her to let Ivar and Skule take service with Inge Fluga, the natural son of Erlend's cousin Sir Munan and his long-standing mistress, the disreputable Brynhild Fluga. Nikulaus informs his mother that he and his nearly blind brother Björgulf plan to enter a holy order as soon as Gaute is old enough to look after Kristin and the others. King Magnus has decided to carry out the plan that cost Erlend his fortune and, indirectly, his life. Magnus is going to settle Norway as an individual kingdom on his younger son, Prince Haakon. The actual power behind this radical move is Bjarne, who more than his father, Sir Erling, was responsible for the King's clemency to Erlend. Bjarne has become Magnus's favorite, and Skule Bjarne's devoted follower. Ivar comes home to ask Nikulaus's permission to marry a wealthy young widow, Signe Gamalsdatter. After this wedding, Nikulaus and Björgulf enter the cloister at Tautra as novices. Gaute elopes with the daughter of a rich landowner, without her parents' consent. He brings her, Jofrid Helgesdatter, to live with him without benefit of matrimony at Jörundgaard. When their son is born in the spring he is christened Erlend Gautessön. That winter he wins her parents' consent to the marriage.

Chaps. 4–7. Kristin becomes aware that Jofrid resents her authority at Jörundgaard. She generously turns over the keys of the manor to her daughter-in-law, but after this grandiose gesture Kristin realizes that it is impossible for her to remain as a stranger in her own house. Besides, she is racked with memories of the past and an indefinable but everpresent sense of guilt. She decides to set out on a pilgrimage to the distant St. Olav's. Her need for peace is overwhelming, and she follows the example of her two monk sons and enters the Rein Convent at Nidaros as a commoner. After two years at the cloister, Kristin is preparing herself for the final step of taking the veil when Skule visits her and tells her that the dread Black Plague is sweeping the city of Niardos. The plague invades the cloisters and claims her two monk sons, Nikulaus and Björgulf. Skule is spared, but in time the plague catches up with Sister Kristin and at last she is permitted to join her cherished dead.

Robert Louis Stevenson
1850–1894

Louisa May Alcott
1832–1888

Lady Windermere's Fan

Play by Oscar Wilde, 1856–1900.
Produced 1892.

ALONG WITH *The Importance of Being Earnest,* this ranks as one of Oscar Wilde's two most successful plays. It is a more realistic story than *The Importance of Being Earnest*—a straight comedy of manners in which the reader's and viewer's credibility is not stretched too far. It does have the same witty, epigrammatic dialogue, in which field not even Shaw could outstrip Wilde. Such dialogue makes the play well worth reading for pleasure even if it is never seen.

Act I. Lord DARLINGTON calls on Lady WINDERMERE. He admires her fan, a birthday present from her husband. She is to give a ball that evening to celebrate her coming of age. She scolds Darlington for his flirtatious compliments. The Duchess of BERWICK and her daughter AGATHA call, and after Darlington goes the duchess sends her daughter out so she can talk privately to Lady Windermere about a Mrs. ERLYNNE. It seems Mrs. Erlynne came to London penniless only a few months ago but is now doing very well. This change coincides with her friendship with Lady Windermere's husband, who is seen almost daily at Mrs. Erlynne's house. The duchess says all London is talking about it and Lady Windermere had better take her husband abroad at once. When the duchess and Agatha leave, Lady Windermere recalls a remark by Darlington that a woman has a right to reciprocate her husband's infidelity. She looks through her husband's desk and finds a bankbook with payments entered in the name of Mrs. Erlynne. Windermere comes in and is faced with the evidence. He defends Mrs. Erlynne as a woman who was once well off and lost everything. She now wants to get back into society and Windermere asks his wife to invite her to the party. Lady Windermere refuses and Windermere himself sends off an invitation to Mrs. Erlynne. Lady Windermere threatens to insult her. Windermere cannot tell his wife who the woman really is.

Act II. The guests arrive for the dance. The Duchess of Berwick makes a big to-do over an Australian, HOPPER, who is rich and eligible. Lord AUGUSTUS, the black sheep brother of the duchess, asks Windermere about Mrs. Erlynne and cannot understand why the ladies hate her. Windermere again implores his wife to be polite to Mrs. Erlynne and again she refuses. In desperation Windermere is about to reveal Mrs. Erlynne's identity to his wife, but just then Mrs. Erlynne arrives. The men seem to know her and the women glare at her. She dances her first dance with Windermere. DUMBY, a gentleman of society, is scolded by Lady PLYMDALE for knowing Mrs. Erlynne. He promises never to see her again, but she wants him to introduce her husband to Mrs. Erlynne, so her husband will not bother her about her affair with Dumby. Darlington tells Lady Windermere he loves her and asks her to leave Windermere and go with him. She does not have the courage, and besides she hopes her husband will return to her; she turns Darlington down, and he tells her he will never see her again and leaves. The duchess has found Mrs. Erlynne quite the contrary of her reputation, and now recommends her highly. Hopper proposes to Agatha and is accepted. By the time the guests leave the women are full of praise for Mrs. Erlynne. Mrs. Erlynne and Windermere talk, oblivious to Lady Windermere's stares. Mrs. Erlynne tells Windermere she will accept Lord Augustus tomorrow. Windermere is to provide her with a sizable dowry. Lady Windermere changes her mind and decides to go to Darlington. She leaves a letter for her husband. Mrs. Erlynne, looking for her, sees and reads the letter. It is the same kind of letter she wrote many years ago to Lady Windermere's father. When Windermere returns, she crushes the letter and tells him his wife has gone to bed. As Lady Windermere's mother, she feels it her duty to save the situation. She summons Augustus and tells him to keep Windermere at his club all night.

Act III. Lady Windermere is at Darlington's house, waiting for him, very uncertain about what she has done. Mrs. Erlynne comes and asks her to go back home, but Lady Windermere thinks her husband has sent Mrs. Erlynne and refuses out of spite. Mrs. Erlynne burns the letter, but Lady Windermere does not believe it was her letter. As an inducement, Mrs. Erlynne promises never to see Windermere again. Mrs. Erlynne finally persuades her and they are about to leave when they hear Augustus, CECIL GRAHAM, Darlington and Dumby returning from the club. The two women hide. The men talk of morality and woman in general. Suddenly, Graham calls attention to Lady Windermere's fan on the sofa. Windermere demands an explanation from Darlington. Mrs. Erlynne lets herself be discovered behind the curtain while Lady Windermere slips out unnoticed. Mrs. Erlynne explains that she took the fan by mistake.

Act IV. Lady Windermere wonders if Mrs. Erlynne really covered for her, at the cost of her own honor. Windermere asks her to leave on a vacation with him at once (they are back together). Lady Windermere wants to see Mrs. Erlynne before leaving, to thank her. Now Windermere calls Mrs. Erlynne bad and Lady Windermere defends her. Mrs. Erlynne calls; she is going away too, but asks Lady Windermere for a picture of herself as a parting gift. Windermere berates her for her alleged misconduct and forbids her to see his wife again. Lady Windermere thinks her mother is dead; she does not know her mother is alive and is this divorcée of questionable repute. Lady Windermere goes to fetch the photograph and while she is gone Windermere threatens to reveal Mrs. Erlynne's identity to his wife. Mrs. Erlynne forbids it. Then while Windermere is out of the room Mrs. Erlynne makes Lady Windermere promise never to reveal the truth about last night. She asks for the fan as a memento. Augustus calls. At first he is cool toward Mrs. Erlynne, but she explains all to his satisfaction and they plan to marry.

Lady Windermere's fan is found on the sofa

Lassie Come-Home

Novel by Eric Knight, 1897–1943. Published 1940 by the John C. Winston Co., Philadelphia. © 1940 by Eric Knight.

"DOG STORIES" are traditionally the surest-fire publishing successes known, along with stories about doctors and Abraham Lincoln. *Lassie Come-Home* is perhaps the finest dog story ever written. It began as a short story in the *Saturday Evening Post.* An officer of the John C. Winston Company, a Philadelphia publisher, saw the possibilities in the story and arranged for Eric Knight to expand it to a full-length book. For years it was the best-selling book for children. It was also Eric Knight's most successful, though in the same year that *Lassie* was published Eric Knight had the top adult book, *This Above All.* Lassie also made a great motion picture—too good, in fact, for its success led to a shameful series of second-rate pictures and television shows based on the character Lassie. The title of the book and Lassie's name are seldom correctly understood. "Come-home" is part of the dog's name; in Eric Knight's Yorkshire, dogs are often trained as come-home dogs.

Chaps. 1–2. SAM CARRACLOUGH'S beautiful collie dog, LASSIE, is well known to all the villagers in Greenall Bridge in Yorkshire, England. Lassie, as sure as clockwork, meets her young master, JOE CARRACLOUGH, every day at 4 o'clock when school is over. The villagers also take pride in the fact that Sam has refused to sell Lassie despite many high offers. In this poor village many people have had to sell their fine dogs to meet their expenses. Leaving school one day, Joe is astonished to find no Lassie waiting for him. He rushes home and learns that since the coal mine is closed and there is no work, Lassie has been sold to the Duke of RUDLING, who has long wanted her. Joe is heartbroken.

Chaps. 3–5. The duke shows Lassie to his granddaughter, PRISCILLA, who comments on the sadness in Lassie's eyes. As 4 o'clock approaches, Lassie senses a stirring of desire within her; it is time to meet Joe. But she is caged in a kennel with a wire fence around it. Nevertheless, when Joe leaves school Lassie is waiting for him as if nothing were changed. Joe takes Lassie home but his mother says Lassie must be returned to the duke, the legal owner. The duke's kennelman, Mr. HYNES, comes looking for Lassie and rudely implies that Lassie is a "come-home" dog (trained to run back to her original owner). Hynes takes the dog, but the next day Lassie again is waiting for Joe outside the school. Sam Carraclough, being an honest man, makes Joe accompany him back to the duke's kennel with Lassie. Putting Lassie back in the kennel, Joe tells her half-heartedly not to come back again; she is no longer his, he no longer wants her.

Chap. 6. Hynes has carefully reinforced the wire fence so Lassie cannot dig out again. Lassie, with desperate effort, manages to get over the high fence and is at the school at 4 o'clock. This time Joe determines to run away with Lassie, and the boy and dog walk out on the moorland. Hynes accuses and threatens. Sam goes out on the moors and finds them. He is about to punish his son, but Mrs. Carraclough will not let him.

Chap. 7. To Joe, nothing is the same as it once was. His mother and father seem more impatient with each other; their supply of food is not what it once was. He is too young to know how bad conditions really are. The duke decides to take Lassie to his estate in Scotland, so far away that Lassie cannot return. Also, the duke plans to ready the dog for entry in several shows.

Chaps. 8–9. In Scotland, 400 miles north, Lassie retains her time sense and claws to get out of her pen each day at 4 o'clock. Hynes chains her in but Priscilla notices it and the duke is outraged. He orders Hynes to walk Lassie each day, to exercise her. One afternoon, toward 4 o'clock, Lassie balks

Lassie dashes away

and when Hynes tugs at the leash it slips over her head. She dashes away. Hynes is sure he can catch Lassie at the gate. By chance, Priscilla and the duke are standing by the gate, which is open. Hynes calls to the girl to close it (the duke being somewhat deaf), but Priscilla thinks of the forlorn boy and leaves the gate open. As Lassie flashes by, Priscilla waves goodbye.

Chap. 10. Lassie's instinct tells her which way is south. Two men recognize her as belonging to the duke and try but fail to capture her. This teaches Lassie that she must keep away from men. Through thunder and rain, Lassie moves steadily homeward. Her beautiful coat is now dirty and unkempt.

Chap. 11. Lassie travels steadily for four days. She is assailed by pangs of hunger on the fifth day, but instinct does not fail her. She learns the smell of rabbit and kills for food. Although she is leaner and her coat is torn, Lassie's rugged frame and strong muscles drive her along hour after hour.

Chap. 12. Lassie is observed by an artist and his friend. She approaches the edge of the lake; but never having been in deep water, she is afraid and decides to skirt the lake. This adds almost 100 miles to the distance. Lassie has come to the great lochs or lakes of Scotland, long bodies of water that cut the country almost in two.

Chap. 13. The pads of Lassie's feet are bruised and sore. Lassie comes to a fast-charging river, but leaps in. The current drives her against a rock, injuring her side, and a group of boys hurl stones at her, but at last she manages to reach shore. With a rib broken and her muscles badly bruised, Lassie falls ill and secretes herself in a den until the fever has passed. She remains there several days; then, though still weak, she feels compelled to move onward.

Chap. 14. Lassie, performing like a true thoroughbred, fights off two dogs that attack her on the commands of their owners, JOCK and ANDREW, who fear that Lassie wants to kill their sheep. Lassie's performance in battle so impresses Jock that he cannot bring himself to shoot her, and Lassie goes on her way.

Chaps. 15–16. Lassie has advanced steadily into the Lowlands of Scotland. A rabies scare in the area has led the authorities to capture all stray dogs. Lassie is caught and taken to the pound, but she escapes her jailers by making a fantastic 10-foot leap. Although momentarily stunned, Lassie wastes no time in moving on.

Chaps. 17–18. Progressing more slowly now because of weakness, Lassie swims the Tweed River and is in England at last. She is so weak that she just manages to reach shore. Lassie is saved by a kindhearted old couple, the FADDENS, who take her into their cottage and nurse her back to health. Mrs. Fadden wishes to keep Lassie; but once Lassie's health has come back, her time sense assails her again each day. Mrs. Fadden keeps Lassie indoors, but she sees that Lassie is anxious to be gone. Finally, with deep regret, Mrs. Fadden gives Lassie her freedom and Lassie continues homeward.

Chaps. 19–20. Lassie meets ROWLIE PALMER, a traveling peddler and a kindly, jovial man. Lassie travels with the peddler and his dog TOOTS, moving along behind their cart at a discreet distance. Rowlie is attacked by two bandits and Lassie comes to his rescue, fighting the thieves until they run away in fright. Toots, the little mongrel, is killed. At the crossroads Rowlie waits for Lassie, but she will go only south. Rowlie realizes that perhaps it is better to part, as this aristocratic animal could never fit in with his way of life. Winter is coming and the snow begins to fall on the moor. Lassie, lost and cold, travels onward.

Chap. 21. Joe cannot believe his eyes! There is Lassie waiting for him outside the school, a bedraggled Lassie, it is true. With all the obstacles and roundabout routes, Lassie must have traveled 1,000 miles, but she has made it home. However, Lassie is so sick she can hardly move. Joe bundles her up in his arms and runs home. There is only a little money left and Mrs. Carraclough was saving to pay her insurance, but she uses it to buy brandy and eggs for Lassie, who has pneumonia. The crisis passes and tender nursing brings Lassie back to health. Sam Carraclough, an honest man in spite of his sympathies, feels that the dog still must be returned to the duke, and Joe's worst fears are confirmed when the duke comes to see his father. Joe does not know the duke is unaware of his loss, and Joe blurts out enough to reveal the truth. However, Sam has outwrestled his conscience and by coping (disguising) Lassie he has made her look like another and a very unattractive dog. When asked if that is his dog, the wise old duke is not at all fooled by Sam's coping; he looks only at Lassie's pads, the record of her long journey. Then, with wonderment and incredulity, he says it is not his dog; that this dog never for one second belonged to him. The duke has come to offer Sam a job as head of his kennels, replacing Hynes. Sam accepts and the family goes to live in a cottage on the duke's estate. Inadvertently, the duke has Lassie back again.

Chap. 22. To Joe, it is just like old times again. There is one difference. Lassie has become the mother of seven collie pups.

Last Days of Pompeii

Novel by Edward Bulwer-Lytton, 1803–1873.
Published 1834.

THE ROMAN CITY and playground of Pompeii was destroyed in the year 79 but when Bulwer-Lytton wrote this novel the excavation of it had been going on less than a hundred years and new discoveries were still arousing excitement. (The excavation is still going on and discoveries are still being made). The novel about Pompeii proved to be the most popular of the many that Bulwer-Lytton wrote. It is a romantic historical novel of the type that seems always to be popular. Bulwer-Lytton did not miss much of being a major novelist in his period.

Book I. Chaps. 1–8. The two young men CLODIUS and GLAUCUS walk down the street of Pompeii. Their talk is trivial, concerning the various banquets. Glaucus is a Greek, immensely wealthy, while Clodius is a spendthrift Roman. Pompeii is the natural habitat of such young men. It is a miniature of the civilization of that age. Within its walls is contained every gift which luxury affords to power. In its glittering shops, its magnificent palaces, its theaters, its circus, all the energy and corruption and refinement of its people gives a model of the whole Roman Empire. Clodius and Glaucus are stopped by NYDIA, a blind flower girl, who is a Greek and has often been befriended by Glaucus. He greets her kindly, but with an absent mind, not realizing how the young girl idealizes him. Glaucus confides to Clodius that at last he has fallen in love, but he does not even know the name of the beautiful girl who has captured his heart. He saw her in the Athenian Temple while at his prayers, and he knew she also was Greek. As strangers from a far land they offered their devotions together and spoke to each other, but then they were separated by the crowd.

Ione, the Greek maiden

The two friends are interrupted by the Egyptian priest, ARBACES, an evil man who is supposed to possess the fatal gift of the evil eye. It is obvious from his greeting that he holds the young men, and Pompeii itself, in contempt.

Glaucus possesses every blessing a man should desire, but one. He has imagination, youth, fortune, and talents. But he was born in Athens and therefore is a subject of Rome. This deprives him of any ambition for glory and his greatest achievements are the luxurious banquets he provides for his many Roman friends. That evening he hears his friends discussing a beautiful and virtuous new arrival to their city. Her name is IONE. Glaucus insists that he be taken to meet her. She is the girl he has been seeking. Ione has a brother, APAECIDES, who is the ward of the evil Egyptian priest. Arbaces is training him in the mystic rites of the priesthood of Isis. The boy is confused by the deceptions of this cult. Arbaces is in love with Ione. He hopes to make Ione love him and despise the barbarian Romans.

The love of Glaucus and Ione is sudden and strong. When Arbaces discovers the extent of Ione's love for the young Greek, he tries by devious insinuations to destroy her feelings.

Book II. Chaps 1–9. Nydia goes about her flower-selling, singing the sad song of her heart. She realizes that her love for Glaucus will never be returned. She is a slave and in his kindness Glaucus buys her, planning to give her to Ione as a present. Glaucus has discovered the deception of Arbaces and writes to Ione denouncing the false accusations. Nydia delivers the letter. Ione is convinced but the habit of friendship with Arbaces is strong, and she goes to the temple to confront him with the letter. The wily Arbaces tries to beguile Ione with his eloquence and woos her for himself. Nydia returns to Glaucus and tells him of Ione's visit to the priest. He rushes to the temple and a violent quarrel ensues between the two men. It is interrupted by an earthquake.

Book III. Chaps. 1–11. Nydia has followed close behind her master and witnesses all that goes on. When the earthquake knocks the Egyptian priest unconscious, the two lovers escape, forgetting the slave girl. Nydia pushes her way out and reaches the house of Ione. The earthquake does little damage to the city. Glaucus and Ione remain together. Apaecides comes to visit them and tells them of his conversion to Christianity. Glaucus's attachment to Ione arouses the jealousy of JULIA, the daughter of one of the wealthiest men of Pompeii. She desires the Greek for herself and seeks the advice of Arbaces, who prepares a drug that is to be given to Glaucus.

Book IV. Chaps. 1–17. When Glaucus drinks the drugged liquid he loses his mind. In his madness he believes that Ione is in danger and he rushes out of his house to rescue her. Arbaces, not content with the mischief he has already perpetrated, meets Apaecides in a nearby cemetery and kills him. He then summons the passing crowd and accuses the mad Glaucus of committing the murder. Glaucus is arrested and taken before a magistrate. Hoping to win Glaucus for herself, Nydia has coöperated with Julia and the priest. She is terrified when she sees what has happened to her master, and she is determined to save him. The trial is held and Glaucus is condemned to the amphitheater. His only hope is that Ione believes in his innocence. But before Ione can do anything, Arbaces kidnaps her and takes her to his house. When Nydia discovers what has happened she tries to inform the magistrate, but the priest discovers her intention and she too is imprisoned. Still determined to rectify the wrong she has done, Nydia bribes a slave to carry a message to Glaucus's friend SALLUST. He is drunk and refuses to see the slave.

Book V. Chaps. 1–11. The day for Glaucus to appear in the amphitheater, as a guilty man facing wild beasts, arrives. It is a day of celebration for the entire city and unbeknownst to them it is also the last day of Pompeii. The crowd is in a demanding mood and is only pleased when the victims are quickly killed by the ferocious animals. When it is the turn of Glaucus, he faces his lion bravely; but the lion is not interested in killing him and returns to its cage without attacking. Sallust, when he becomes sober, reads the note Nydia sent him and hastens to help his friend. He arrives at the arena and demands the arrest of Arbaces. The presiding praetor listens to him and is convinced of the innocence of Glaucus. Not to be cheated of a kill, the waiting audience demands that Arbaces be thrown to the lions. Suddenly the eruption of Vesuvius begins and the milling mob riots in its efforts to escape. Pushing her way through the hysterical masses, Nydia reaches Glaucus and tells him of the abduction of Ione. Together they go to the palace of Arbaces. The sky is rapidly becoming black but Nydia's blindness has accustomed her to finding her way in darkness and she leads Glaucus safely to Ione. No one thinks of the evil Arbaces, awaiting his doom, and he is killed by the upheavals of the earthquake.

Glaucus and Ione are reunited and, with Nydia still leading them, they rush to the sea to escape the destruction and death of the city. They acquire a small boat and the three put out to the safety of the sea. Exhausted by their flight and fears, they fall asleep. In the middle of the night, Nydia quietly arises, gently kisses Glaucus and throws herself in the sea. The shadow of the last day of Pompeii fades as the two lovers go on to their future together.

The Last of the Mohicans

Novel by James Fenimore Cooper, 1789–1851.
Published 1826. Several editions available.

COOPER WROTE five novels called The Leatherstocking Tales. *The Last of the Mohicans* is the second of the series and has proved to be the most popular. The character Leatherstocking is known throughout the series by various names: Hawkeye, as in *The Last of the Mohicans*, but also the Deerslayer, the Pathfinder, and by his own name, Natty Bumppo. Cooper's novels are characterized by their author's ignorance and by most unnatural and unrealistic action and conversation, yet in Europe especially they were assumed to be authentic, they formed the European reader's notion of what the United States was like, and Cooper was rated a major novelist. In the United States their popularity has been chiefly among boys, whose critical standards are not too difficult to satisfy.

Chaps. 1–6. In the third year of the French and Indian War, a rich young officer of the Royal Americans, Major DUNCAN HEYWARD, is accompanying two sisters, ALICE and CORA, from Fort Edward to Fort William Henry, where their father, Col. MUNRO, is the commander. With them are DAVID GAMUT, a singing teacher, and the Indian runner, LE RENARD SUBTIL. They lose their way, and Heyward, going on ahead, meets the white scout HAWKEYE, Hawkeye's Mohican friend, CHINGACHGOOK, and the Indian's son, the brave young warrior, UNCAS. Hawkeye tells him that the runner, Le Renard Subtil, actually named MAGUA, is deceiving them and is probably leading them to the Iroquois, who are allies of the French. The scout and his Mohican friends try to capture Le Renard but he escapes. Hawkeye agrees to lead Heyward's party from the woods and takes them on a perilous canoe trip to a rocky cavern, where they rest for the night.

Chaps. 7–10. At dawn, as they prepare to resume their trip, they are attacked by Hurons, who wound Gamut. The attackers are beaten back, but one manages to steal Hawkeye's canoe. The scout and the Mohicans, regarding capture as certain, prepare to kill themselves, but at Cora's urging they decide to strike out for aid. Duncan insists on staying to guard the sisters. Waiting in the cavern, they are captured by the Hurons, their hiding place having been revealed when Duncan took a shot at Le Renard Subtil. The Hurons call Hawkeye "*La Longue Carabine*" (The Long Rifle) because of his skill with his rifle, which he calls "Killdeer." The Hurons depart to pursue Hawkeye, leaving the prisoners with a small band headed by Le Renard.

Chaps. 11–12. Leading the captives through the woods, Le Renard is promised by Duncan that Munro will reward him if he deceives the other Hurons and takes the sisters to him. Le Renard, or Magua, tells Cora that he was born a Huron chief but was cast out by his people because he became rascally after learning from the white Canadians to drink liquor. Adopted by the Mohawks as a warrior, eventually he fought against his own people under Munro's leadership, but ran afoul of Munro's strict edict against drunkenness and was severely punished. Cora defends her father's justice but urges the Huron to take his revenge by holding her and releasing Alice. Magua consents on condition that Cora become his bride to replace the Huron wife given away upon his expulsion from his tribe. When Cora indignantly refuses, he incites his comrades to tie the prisoners to trees and prepare to build a fire about them. Rescue appears in the shape of Hawkeye and the Mohicans, who exterminate all the Indians but the wily Le Renard Subtil, who plays dead, then escapes. Hawkeye discloses that he and his friends were hidden and followed along, witnessing much of what the Hurons did.

Chaps. 13–16. Hawkeye leads the party to the shelter of an old, crumbling blockhouse, where they rest until moonlight. Le Renard and a French scouting party approach but do not detect their presence, and the Indians in the party see a grave near the blockhouse and withdraw. Hawkeye then guides his party deep into the woods and through the bed of a brook to obscure their trail. By morning they have approached Fort William Henry. They are pursued by the French, who are besieging the fort, but are rescued by Munro himself. Some days later, Munro is shocked to discover that Duncan Heyward is in love with Alice and not with Cora, as he had supposed. The dark-haired Cora is the daughter of his first wife, who had West Indian blood, while Alice, fair and blue-eyed, is the daughter of his second wife, a Scot.

Munro confers with the French commander, MONTCALM, who displays an intercepted letter to Munro from General WEBB of Fort Edward. In the letter Webb advises Munro to surrender speedily, as it is impossible for him to send even a single reinforcement. Munro is dejected and bitter but agrees to the surrender when Montcalm pledges that the English can surrender with honor.

Chaps. 17–20. Next day, as the Anglo-American army prepares to depart, the Hurons, inflamed by the vindictive Magua, massacre them. Magua, again rejected by Cora, kidnaps the fainting Alice and is pursued by Cora. They are followed by David Gamut, charged by Duncan with looking after the girls. Munro and his friends look through the dead in search of the girls. Following Uncas's discovery of several clues leading to the woods, they decide to pursue the trail. Traveling in Hawkeye's birch canoe in the narrows of Lake George, they are chased by the Hurons but shake them off after a close race amidst volleys of rifle fire. After further travel and evasion of the enemy, they hide the canoe under brush and continue over land.

Chaps. 21–25. After a night deep in the wilderness, they follow a fresh trail discerned by Uncas, who finally scents the presence of the Hurons. Scouting the vicinity, Duncan and Hawkeye co...

David Gamut in Indian garb. He tells them Alice is with the Hurons, while Cora is held at another camp some two miles off. Gamut is allowed to wander freely because of the awe inspired by his singing. Deciding to pose as a friendly Canadian in Indian paint, Duncan accompanies David back to the Huron camp to rescue Alice. He is present when Uncas is brought in as a captive and sees the young warrior escape burning at the stake by a display of bravery; but then Uncas is recognized by Magua, who inflames his people against the Mohican. Uncas is condemned to death in public the next day. Posing as a physician, Duncan is taken by a chief to heal an ailing woman. A seemingly domesticated bear that follows them to the cave apartment of the sick woman is actually Hawkeye in an animal costume taken from a Huron conjuror. Hawkeye discovers Alice nearby, and as Duncan tells her all that has happened and speaks of his love for her, the malevolent Magua comes on them, gloating at the thought of burning Duncan at the stake. Duncan and the supposed bear overpower Magua and leave him bound and gagged. Duncan carries Alice, wrapped in Indian cloths, out of the cave. He announces to the sick woman's relatives, waiting outside the cave, that this is the sick woman and that he has rid her of the evil spirit that sickened her and is taking her to the woods to find strengthening roots. The counterfeit conjuror and his two friends are thus able to slip into the forest. Hawkeye takes them to a path that will lead them to the tribe holding Cora. He believes this tribe to be friendly Delawares. Hawkeye then returns to the Hurons to rescue Uncas.

Chaps. 26–33. At the Huron camp, Hawkeye meets David Gamut and tells him of the others' escape. David leads him to where Uncas is confined, getting in by pretending to take the conjuror-bear in to torment him. They cut Uncas's bonds. Uncas puts on the bear suit and Hawkeye dresses as David. David, grateful for all the protection given the white people by Uncas, takes his place as prisoner, and the two in disguise also pass safely into the forest. The Hurons discover this deception, then find the sick woman, now dead, and Magua in his bonds. Magua explains what has happened, and scouts are sent out and trace Hawkeye and Uncas to the Delaware camp. The next day Magua, heading 20 warriors, goes to the Delawares and tells them that Hawkeye, the enemy of Montcalm, is in their midst. This news causes a great stir among the Delawares, who have not taken up arms for the French but remain on good terms with them. Magua asks to be given the prisoners, and after much discussion among the Delawares, his request is granted by the revered sage of the tribe, TAMENUND. But Cora appeals eloquently to the old man and directs his attention to Uncas, who is received with great admiration when he displays the tortoise tattooed on his breast, signifying his high rank in the Delaware tribal system. Tamenund then agrees to let all the prisoners go, except Cora, who, he believes, is rightly Magua's. Hawkeye offers to remain in her place, but Magua scorns the offer and goes off with Cora.

Uncas leads an expedition against the Hurons and is united with all his friends in the course of it. The Hurons have been virtually defeated when Cora and Uncas are knifed in the last moments of battle. The cornered Magua kills himself falling down a mountainside while attempting to escape. A solemn funeral ceremony is held next day by the Indians for Cora and Uncas. Afterward, the white travelers leave the forest to return to civilization in charge of a French aide sent by Montcalm. Only Hawkeye stays, choosing to remain with his comrade, Chingachgook.

Duncan and the supposed bear overpower Magua and rescue Alice

The Late George Apley

Novel by John Phillips Marquand, 1893–1960.
Published 1937 by Little, Brown & Co., Boston. © 1936, 1937 by J. P. Marquand. (PB, 2258; ML, 182)

THE STYLE, the stories and the characters in the more serious novels of Marquand may, as critics have often averred, vary too little, but such an indictment cannot affect the right of any particular one of his novels to be ranked high and perhaps *The Late George Apley* deserves the highest place. The novel won the Pulitzer Prize for 1938. It made an excellent and very successful Broadway play (1944) which Marquand himself wrote in collaboration with George S. Kaufman. *The Late George Apley* is a novel in the form of a memoir or eulogy. It is highly ironic, often poking fun at the insular attitudes of families in Boston society and satirizing Bostonians who are unable to break the habit of congenital thinking-patterns.

Chap. 1. Mr. WILLING, an old friend and constant associate of the late GEORGE APLEY, is invited by JOHN APLEY, George's son, to write a memoir of his father. In his letter John requests Mr. Willing to be completely truthful and not gloss over any ugly details. From this point on, Mr. Willing acts as a narrator, deriving the facts from letters to and from George and excerpts from diaries and journals kept by friends and members of the Apley family.

Chaps. 2–3. George tells John and his sister, ELEANOR, not to laugh at the seeming stinginess of their great-uncle WILLIAM. The wealthy Apley family has never lived ostentatiously, but it has been generous in public and charitable work. He gives the family history from the arrival of the first Apley in Roxbury, Mass., in 1636. The family fortune was founded by his grandfather, a Boston sea captain. George's father, THOMAS, and his Uncle William nurtured it through textile mills and banking houses. Shortly before the Civil War Thomas was married to ELIZABETH HANCOCK. George's older sister, AMELIA, was born first, then George in 1866, and finally a younger sister, JANE. Thomas bought the family's country estate, Hillcrest, and the family's house on Beacon Street.

Chaps. 4–5. When George was a child, summers were spent at Hillcrest, where the children formed lifelong friendships. Their mother, who was a poet, taught them music and literature. During the winters on Beacon Street, George met other New England thinkers and industrialists like his father. When he was 9, George was sent to Hobson's School, where he indulged in the usual childish pranks. There were two groups of boys at the school, those whose families moved in the right circles, and those whose families did not. George was in the group whose families did. He formed a friendship with MIKE WALKER, who later had a lurid affair with a "Floradora" girl and whose name was never mentioned again in proper Boston society—but George remained his friend. At dancing school George first met his future wife, CATHERINE BOSWORTH.

Chap. 6. During his adolescence, George was exposed to the theater in New York and was entranced with the leading lady. Later, while spending the summer with Uncle HORATIO, he fell in love with his older cousin, HENRIETTA. This attachment was frowned on by his family, but George learned from it that there are two kinds of women in the world, good and bad. When George, like all Apleys, went to Harvard, Thomas admonished him to be moderate in drinking and to forego smoking; he promised to discuss the subject of women later.

Chaps. 7–8. Though George was to become disillusioned about Harvard 15 years later, while there he joined the proper clubs and was considered great fun (though not a "rake") by his friends. The new persons he met worried Thomas and Elizabeth, who felt some of them might not be quite suitable companions. George wrote a class composition on a visit to a bawdy house, defeated Harvard's boxing champion, and was elected to one of the college's select societies. George became interested in Catherine Bosworth, but his interest in girls spread in other directions, too. He wrote love letters to Miss Mary Monahan, a girl from the predominantly Irish and socially impossible South End of Boston. She was reluctant, since she knew what his background meant. He finally persuaded her to let him meet her family, who grudgingly approved of him and introduced him to the great boxer, John L. Sullivan. Thomas heard of the affairs and promptly shipped George off to Europe, to forget.

Chap. 9. George's trip was made with his aunt and uncle and cousin Henrietta. He had letters of introduction to some of the "best" people, and ample letters of credit. George was disappointed to discover that one could not lose one's identity in Europe, since all the people from home congregated no matter where they went.

Chap. 10. While attending Harvard Law School, George was invited to join the Board of Directors of the Boston Waifs Society, an old family charity, and to become a member of the Berkeley Club, a group of writers and musicians. The latter displeased Thomas, who proclaimed himself broadminded but still could not countenance the fact that George and other members of the Club had appeared on Tremont Street one evening dressed as Robin Hood and his Merry Men. Thomas sent George to the Apley Mills for a summer's training under Uncle William. Uncle William informed Thomas that George

was too easy-going and erratic to ever make a businessman.

Chaps. 11–12. In 1890, when George was 24, his engagement to Catherine was announced. The wedding was a great social event and presents poured in, including a house from Thomas and the long-overdue income from a trust George's grandmother had left him. The young couple had a two weeks' honeymoon at Rye Beach, N.H., where they were joined in several days by Catherine's parents. In Boston, George joined the real-estate firm of Reid and Smith (later Reid and Apley, and still later Apley and Reid). His searching of original property titles led him to write a paper called "Jonas Good of Cow Corner." The reading of this paper before the Browsers Club brought him a certain amount of local fame. Through this paper, George took his proper place in Boston's cultural scene and was invited to join the Boards of Directors of many of the city's oldest institutions.

Chap. 13. The birth of Catherine and George's first child brought on a family crisis; they could not agree to choose a name for the baby before it was born. They settled on John, a name common to both family trees. At about this time the question of flooding the mud flats behind Beacon Street arose. Thomas and George had opposing opinions. Thomas felt that making a lake of his backyard was infringing on his rights. George felt that it was for the common good and would be a city ornament. It was the first time George had ever opposed Thomas, then 70, who believed the younger generation was leading the country to disaster. Amelia married NEWCOMB SIMMINGS of the Simmings Mills, uniting two large textile holdings.

Chap. 14. Thomas died suddenly the following summer. His will was a great surprise to George, who had not realized how rich the family had become. Among his bequests were a million dollars to Harvard and a million dollars to the city of Boston. He left the rest of the money in trust because, he explained, he thought his son incapable of handling large sums of money. George felt that money placed people under certain obligations to the public; for instance, he had no real desire to collect Chinese bronzes but he had noted the lack of them in the Boston Museum and had started a collection to be willed to the Museum. Shortly after his father's death he received a letter from a New York lawyer stating that Thomas had had a mistress there for many years. A settlement was demanded and George, though disbelieving and shocked, paid rather than face any kind of scandal.

Chap. 15. George founded Pequod Island Camp, a rustic retreat where he and his men friends could hunt and fish, living a kind of primitive existence. This did not last for long, for Catherine and Amelia invaded the place and set up a regime to their own tastes.

Chap. 16. George was becoming the "Portrait of a Gentleman," just as Sargent

painted him. By 1902 he had become involved with different civic committees and was shocked to discover the patronage and laxness in city government. He wrote to HENRY SLATER, a civic crusader, that he was ready and willing to help on the "Save Boston Association." Amelia and Catherine joined the movement, urging more definite action from their husbands. George objected when a certain businessman was proposed for membership in the Providence Club, saying it was obvious that it was nothing more than a business transaction. These affairs led some acquaintances to say that George was becoming "radical."

Chap. 17. George confided his personal feelings and life only in letters to Mike Walker. Once he said that he had left the early rearing of the children to Catherine, but since John had reached middle childhood he hoped he could make his life happier than his own had been. He was coming home earlier from the office for talks with the boy, and reading to him the Waverley novels. John was sent to Groton School but did not adjust well to it, which disturbed George though he secretly understood the situation. He had made himself conform to the Boston pattern and he felt John should too, even though they both disliked it. George began to take long bird-watching walks in the woods at Hillcrest with his old playmate, CLARA GOODRICH. These raised ugly speculation in the minds of many people, including the old Unitarian pastor, NATHANIEL PETTINGILL.

Chap. 18. It was Mr. Pettingill who broke the news of George's mother's death to George, an hour after the family's traditional Thanksgiving dinner and parlor games. George went to New York to see Mike, who had married a former show girl, whom George liked and approved. While there he learned to do the turkey trot and other dance crazes.

Chap. 19. In 1910 John entered Harvard. George hoped his son's first objective would be to make "the Club" and that he should not try to throw off convention. George had sometimes wished he had, and had speculated on what would have happened if he had married Mary Monahan, but he had

Bird-watching with Clara

come to the conclusion it would never have worked.

Chaps. 20–21. In World War I George's attitude was "Germany is wrong and the Allies are right." He deplored the lack of action of President Wilson and the country at large. He became increasingly suspicious of the Irish Catholic element in Boston, alleging that they were pro-German. But the war gave him a new sense of democracy, since he was serving on many war committees with people of whom he had never heard. At the same time, as head of the Apley family, he could not countenance the divorce of a distant cousin. To avoid a scandal he put financial pressure on the offending parties and forced them to stay as they were. He deplored John's constant visits to New York, where he suspected a foreign philosophy. John joined the National Guard and was sent to the Mexican border. An English major had captured Eleanor's attention. John warned his father about the major and was right, for the Englishman turned out to be an impostor and left Boston with considerable debts.

Chaps. 22–23. Uncle William, who had been ailing, married his nurse. George at first felt shock and horror, but when financial matters were straightened out he was reconciled to the match. George was disturbed when Uncle William wished to leave his fortune in trust for John and Eleanor, which put a slight on George's ability to handle large sums. George advised John to think about doing something useful for the community, for example collecting tapestries. Another worry was Eleanor's lack of prudence, since she had gone to a "roadhouse" with a young man, unchaperoned.

Chaps. 24–25. John was sent to France. George could not imagine what would happen to his own life if John were killed in action, but when John was wounded George was proud and was sorry Uncle William and Uncle Horatio had not lived to see how well John had done. When John returned in 1919, George had difficulty understanding his new attitudes. John accepted a job in a New York law office and the blow sent George to bed for several ___s. He could only hope John would take ___ime to come to Boston frequently.

George at a night club

Chap. 26. Eleanor visited John and George was uneasy because she had been taken to a speakeasy, but he was broadminded, visited John, and was delighted with everything, including the Negro dancer in a grass skirt they saw in a night club. He was appalled when Eleanor began to discuss sex and Sigmund Freud, whose works he felt should be kept under lock and key.

Chap. 27. In the '20s George became increasingly active in the "Save Boston Association." He was aghast about the corruption on the police force and was ready to head a clean-up campaign. George grieved when John married a Mrs. LOUISE McCULLOUGH, a divorcée, but he and Catherine put up a brave front and told everyone how delighted they were. And they were, too, when they discovered Louise was a Hogarth from Connecticut and had a great deal of money.

Chap. 28. All of Boston was talking of the Apley-O'Reilly incident. O'Reilly was a currupt lawyer whom George had attacked in the course of honest government. In George's version of the events, he went to a hotel to meet a witness and was ushered into a room where a young lady in a negligee was seated. Before he could make his apologies, the door burst open and O'Reilly, with several policemen, appeared. O'Reilly, thinking George would do anything to avoid a scandal, was willing to trade silence for silence, but George insisted on being taken to the police station. The whole affair was reported in the papers. Many pleaded with George to drop the whole matter, but George was adamant. George did finally drop the case when his old love, Mary Monahan, asked him to. O'Reilly was a relative of hers by marriage.

Chaps. 29–30. In 1928, the news that he was to become a grandfather pleased George enormously, though he could not understand why Louise insisted on going to a hospital to have the baby when she could have had it at Hillcrest. He immediately entered the child at Groton. The next autumn George and Catherine made a trip to Europe. He did not really enjoy himself, feeling that Boston had skimmed the cream from European culture. Eleanor married a New York reporter named WILLIAM BUDD, who came from Lancaster, Pennsylvania. George and Catherine were not too happy about the match, since the couple were going to live on the Pacific coast, but they were broadminded about it.

Chap. 31. In his last letter to his son John, George Apley expressed all of his wishes for a quiet funeral, giving the details of who was to sit where and how each person was to be treated when the funeral was over. Though gloomy, he felt it was necessary to arrange everything. He expressed great joy that John and Louise and his grandson were at last coming back to Boston to live. He died two weeks after their return.

Les Miserables

Novel by Victor Hugo, 1802–1885. Published 1862. (ML, G3).

THE PRESTIGE of Victor Hugo was tremendous in his own country during his lifetime and his works are still better read in translation than those of any other serious French novelist. *Les Miserables,* a very long novel, is generally considered his masterpiece. He wrote it at a very mature age—almost 60—when he was in exile from the regime of Napoleon III. It is almost always presented by its untranslated title. Oddly enough, the principal character, Jean Valjean, is not developed by Hugo with any depth, while the secondary character Javert is a great creation in literature as the inexorable human bloodhound impelled by both duty and blind obedience to training. When Javert found these in conflict with a human emotion, he could not survive.

FANTINE

Book I. In October, 1815, a convict who has just been released from the galleys at Toulon stumbles into a provincial town in France. He is desperate for food and lodging, but nobody will receive him once he has shown his passport. The man is JEAN VALJEAN, a simple peasant from the town of Brie, who was sent to the galleys in 1796. His crime was the smashing of a baker's window and theft of a loaf of bread, which he used to feed his starving sister and her children. The original sentence was only five years, but his attempts to escape prolonged his term. At last, after being refused refuge at every inn, Jean is hospitably received by Bishop BIENVENU, who lives with his sister, Mme. MAGLOIRE. That night Jean steals out of the bishop's house with six silver plates and a pair of candlesticks. Mme. Magloire notifies the police the following morning, and Jean is caught and returned by the police; but the bishop says he gave the candlesticks to Jean and blesses him. Wandering down the highway, Jean sees a 40-sou piece escape from a small boy, PETIT GERVAIS. Unable to resist, he steps on the coin and refuses to return it. Petit Gervais runs away crying, and by the time Jean decides to give the coin back, it is too late.

Books II–III. An abandoned mother named FANTINE realizes that she must resort to prostitution to survive. Tearfully, she surrenders her beautiful baby daughter COSETTE to innkeepers named THÉNARDIER. Then, having agreed to pay them an exorbitant sum for Cosette's room and board, she goes off to a nearby town. The Thénardiers abuse Cosette and make her live in a manner befitting a beast. In the nearby town where Fantine lives in 1818, a mysterious gentleman has made a sudden fortune with a revolutionary process for manufacturing bead necklaces. He is a huge, strong man. He is called FATHER MADELEINE and is loved by the townspeople. But Inspector JAVERT of the police sees Father Madeleine perform an almost impossible feat of strength—lifting a huge cart to rescue a crushed man—and Javert reflects that the only man he ever knew who was so strong was an escaped convict named Valjean. The relentless Javert decides to investigate. Meanwhile he arrests a frowsy prostitute for disturbing the peace. The prostitute is Fantine.

Book IV. Father Madeleine, who has recently been elected mayor, saves Fantine from jail. Fantine is dying of tuberculosis and Madeleine plans to reunite her with her daughter. Javert confesses to the mayor that he suspected him of being Valjean, but now a man named Chapmathieu has been arrested and identified as Valjean.

Books V–VI. Father Madeleine cannot let an innocent man suffer. He goes to the trial at Arras and confesses that he is Valjean. He returns home long enough to order the town curé to distribute his wealth among the poor. Then he visits Fantine. Javert comes to make the arrest. Fantine dies. Valjean escapes.

COSETTE

Books I–III. Jean is caught and returned to the galleys. In 1823 he falls overboard from a ship at Toulon and is declared officially dead. Actually Jean survives. To redeem his promise to Fantine, he goes to the Thénardiers' inn to find Cosette. Appalled at the way the 8-year-old girl is forced to do heavy labor, he pays Thénardier 1,500 francs for the little girl.

Book IV. Jean and Cosette live in a poor quarter of Paris, but the landlady becomes suspicious because the old man (51 years old) has so much money. Then Jean notices a beggar who is often near the house and who resembles Javert. He and Cosette escape quickly.

Book V. They leave the rooming house, pursued by Javert and other detectives. Jean hoists Cosette over a wall and they take refuge in a dark garden. In the morning they spy a gardener, who turns out to be old FAUCHELEVENT, the man Jean rescued from the cart accident. They learn that they are in a convent.

Book VI. The gardener asks the Prioress if she will permit his brother and his brother's granddaughter to join him. The Prioress agrees, but makes a strange request. A recently deceased nun wishes to be entombed beneath the altar, in defiance of local law, so her casket must be buried empty. Fauchelevent agrees, for he can smuggle Valjean out of the convent in the casket; but the plot goes awry when another gravedigger is sent. In the nick of time Fauchelevent rescues Jean from asphyxiation. However, the Prioress accepts Jean as a gardener, believing him to be Fauchelevent's brother ULTIMUS, and enrolls Cosette in the convent school.

MARIUS

Books I–III. In 1831 the bankrupted Thénardiers move to Paris, where they live in the rooming house where formerly Cosette and Valjean lived. The father joins a gang of night prowlers. They change their family name from Thénardier to JONDRETTE. The only other tenant in the house is MARIUS PONTMERCY. He is the son of Baron Pontmercy, a hero killed at Water-

Jean steps on a coin

loo. Marius was brought up by his grandfather, a bourgeois, GILLENORMAND, and an elderly spinster aunt, Mlle. Gillenormand. For a long time the Gillenormands kept the boy away from his noble, haughty father, but when Pontmercy was dying Marius went to see him. Marius arrived too late but did receive a farewell note in which his dead father begged him to discover the whereabouts of a certain innkeeper named Thénardier, who saved Pontmercy's life at Waterloo. Marius quarreled with the staid Gillenormand and left home. He settled, unwittingly, near the very man whom he was searching, while he completed his law studies.

Books IV–VII. Marius joins a group of idealistic young revolutionaries called the Friends of the ABC. It is headed by the powerful intellectual, COURFEYRAC. In the Luxembourg Gardens Marius sees a beautiful girl in the company of a 60-year-old man. Every day he returns to watch the girl. It is Cosette.

Book VIII. Marius helps the Jondrettes

Marius sees a beautiful girl in the park with an elderly man

pay their rent, but he does not like them. One day, through a crack in the wall, he sees the family rehearsing an act to victimize a wealthy philanthropist. Their victim turns out to be Valjean (who now uses the name Fauchelevent) and Cosette is with him. Valjean gives the Jondrettes the money and leaves. Jondrette has recognized him as the man who took Cosette away, and the Jondrettes plot to kidnap Cosette. Marius determines to save the mysterious girl and old man. He tries to learn their address from Jondrette's daughter, EPONINE, but does not succeed. He learns that the trap will be set in the room next door and he informs the police. Unfortunately, the inspector he tells is Javert. On the night of the plot, Marius waits with a cocked pistol behind the wall crack. He sees Valjean enter the room, where he is overcome by Jondrette and three other burglars. Then he hears Jondrette confess that he is Thénardier, the man whom Marius is pledged to help. Torn with conflicting desires, Marius watches. The criminals decide to murder Valjean, but Javert breaks into the apartment. Javert's assistants apprehend the criminals, but Valjean escapes out a window. Javert suspects that the prisoner might have been more important than his captors.

SAINT DENIS

Book I–II. Marius moves away, averting a questioning by Javert. He moves in with his revolutionary friend Courfeyrac, who, along with ENJOLRAS and COMBEFERRE, is plotting an uprising to reëstablish the French Republic. Eponine gives Marius Cosette's address and Marius begins to spy on the mansion inhabited by Valjean, the girl, and an old servant named TOUSSAINT. (Valjean long since abandoned the convent, so that Cosette could live more comfortably. Often he disappears for brief periods and returns with money.)

Books III–IV. Marius leaves a love note in the garden of the house. Cosette finds it and knows it has come from the young man of the Luxembourg Gardens. Cosette also hears strange noises. When she tells Jean, he becomes suspicious and plans to flee to England. Revolution is brewing and he does not want to endanger his ward.

Books V–VI. Marius at last finds the courage to approach Cosette. Their love grows but they keep it hidden from Valjean. Marius returns to his grandfather Gillenormand for permission to marry, but the grandfather refuses and the two quarrel. Gillenormand repents, but too late; he does not know where Marius lives. Having no money, Marius abandons hope of marrying the apparently wealthy girl.

Book VIII–IX. By June 5, 1832, the revolutionary forces have gathered enough strength to strike. The rebels are a curious mixture of students, workers, criminals, and intellectuals. The tattered army assembles on the Left Bank and establishes a large barricade in the Rue de la Chanvrerie. Javert falls into their hands and Courfeyrac ties him up in a basement and orders

his eventual execution.

Book X–XI. Marius joins the rebels in their barricade. A street urchin named GAVROCHE is among the most valiant fighters. Marius saves Gavroche's life by a timely shot. Marius stumbles upon Eponine, who is dying. She gives Marius, whom she secretly loves, a letter from Cosette giving her new address. Cosette and Valjean are leaving within a week for England. Marius sends Gavroche with a despairing farewell letter to Cosette. Valjean has found out about Cosette's note by inspecting a blotter, and he is so disturbed that he rushes off to join the revolution. He intercepts the urchin with Marius's message and dupes the boy into giving it to him. He reads that Marius has abandoned all hope of gaining Cosette. This puts Jean at ease. Then, realizing his selfishness, Valjean calmly walks out of the house to join the fighting.

JEAN VALJEAN

Books I–II. The embattled rebels in the barricade face annihilation. By the morning of June 6 only a handful remain, Jean Valjean among them. Jean is entrusted with the duty of killing the hostage Javert. This is his opportunity to avenge himself on the man who has ruined his life, but he cannot do it; he sets Javert free. Javert does not want to accept this favor, but Valjean insists. The fighting continues and Enjolras and Marius are the only leaders that survive. Marius is wounded and falls; Jean Valjean picks him up but they are trapped in the barricade. The only exit is the sewer. Jean moves a heavy stone and carries the young man into the labyrinthine tunnels. Even this passage is blocked by soldiers and Jean must elude their lanterns and rifles. He bears Marius through the sea of slime. He reaches a locked outlet, but there is a criminal there, trying to pick the lock. It is Thénardier, who has escaped from prison and is sought by Javert. After picking the lock, Thénardier accepts Valjean's money as payment for allowing him to escape. Jean attains the upper air again, but Javert, searching for Thénardier, finds Valjean instead. Jean offers to surrender to the inspector, on condition that Marius be taken to the address of M. Gillenormand. They deposit the wounded grandson with the old man. Javert then permits Jean to make one

last visit to his home. When Jean looks outside the window, Javert has mysteriously disappeared.

Books III–IV. Javert cannot bring himself to arrest Valjean but neither can he betray his profession. His problem is insoluble and he commits suicide by plunging into the Seine. Marius recovers slowly and keeps calling for Cosette. At last his grandfather summons the girl and Jean. Marius does not know it was Jean who rescued him and Jean does not tell. The two lovers decide on immediate marriage, which is blessed by all concerned. Jean says that Cosette has somewhat less than 600,000 francs to bring to the marriage—a tremendous amount. It is the last of Jean's fortune as an industrialist, which has long been hidden in a forest near the Thénardiers' inn. Marius feels that he must repay two men: Thénardier, who saved his father, and the unknown man who saved Marius himself.

Books V–VII. The marriage takes place in 1833, and Jean finds himself alone again. One day Marius invites Valjean to live with them, but the old man confesses that he has been a robber and murderer. Marius, horrified, refuses to spend any more of Jean's money and gradually excludes his wife from Jean's company. The old man then makes a similar confession to Cosette, and he becomes a figure of mixed pity and resentment.

Book VIII. Soon afterward, Jean falls deathly sick. Thénardier comes to blackmail Marius by exposing his wife's lowly origin. Marius answers that he knows that Jean murdered a Monsieur Madeleine and Inspector Javert. He is pleasantly surprised when Thénardier disproves these statements. Thénardier insists, however, that Valjean murdered a young man in the sewers of Paris during the 1832 insurrection. Marius realizes that the alleged murdered man is himself. Relieved to have found his true savior at last, Marius dispatches his father's debt to Thénardier by giving the man 1,000 francs and expelling him from the house. Marius then takes Cosette quickly to see her dying guardian. At Jean Valjean's bedside, the lovers are forgiven. Jean tells them his money was earned through his powers of invention. Then the old man breathes his last.

Leviathan

Treatise by Thomas Hobbes, 1588–1679.
Published 1651.
THIS WORK of the philosopher Hobbes deserves to be as famous as *The Prince* of Machiavelli. Whereas Machiavelli treated the sovereign power as existing by right and fact, Hobbes treated it as existing in a State created by men for their own protection and convenience. Hobbes' definition of the nature and inevitable primary policy of any State is totally valid today, whereas Machiavelli's refers to a kind of State that no longer exists. As Hobbes sees it, man creates the State to protect and advance him, and the State must do precisely that without consideration of moral deterrents. Precisely so do all governments operate.

Introduction. That great LEVIATHAN called a COMMONWEALTH, or STATE, is but an artificial man, though of greater stature and strength than the natural man, for whose protection and defense it was intended; and in which *sovereignty* is an artificial soul, as giving life and motion to the whole body; *magistrates,* and other *officers* of the judiciary and executive, the joints; *reward* and *punishment,* the nerves; *wealth,* the strength; and so on through the whole body of this artificial man, Leviathan. Let us then examine and describe man in the single and in the aggregate.

Part I. of Man. Chap. 1. Of Sense. Concerning the thoughts of man; singly, they are every one a *representation* or *appearance* of some quality, or other accident of a body without us, which is commonly called an *object.* The cause of sense is the external body, or object, which presses the organ proper to each sense.

Chap. 2. Of Imagination. Just as water moved by wind continues to move in waves after the wind has ceased, so the motion made in the internal parts of man continues when the object no longer presses on the senses. Yet since our senses, once the object is removed from them, immediately are pressed upon by other objects which in their turn cause our main sensations, and the sensation of the first object is obscured, as the sun obscures the stars. The decaying first sensations become the matter of *imagination. Dreams* are the imaginations of our sleep.

Chap. 3. Of the Consequence or Train of Imaginations. By *consequence,* or train of thoughts, I understand that succession of one thought to another, which is called, to distinguish it from discourse in words, *mental discourse.* This discourse is of two sorts: first, *unguided, without design,* and inconstant; the second, regulated by some desire, and design, as when a man seeks causes and effects.

Chap. 4. Of Speech. The most noble and profitable invention of all other, was that of *speech,* consisting of names and *appellations,* and their connection; whereby men register their thoughts; recall them when they are past; and also declare them one to another for mutual utility and conversation; without which, there would have been among men neither commonwealth, nor society, nor contract, nor peace, no more than among lions, bears, and wolves.

Chap. 5. Of Reason and Science. *Reason* is nothing but *reckoning,* that is adding and subtracting, of the consequences of general names agreed upon for the *marking* and *signifying* of our thoughts. *Science* is the knowledge of consequences, and the dependence of one fact upon another; by which we can learn causes, and then, at a later time, knowing causes, produce like effects at will.

Chap. 6. There are in animals two sorts of motions peculiar to them: one is called *vital,* which includes breathing, the course of the blood, and other necessary and involuntary motions; the other is *animal,* or *voluntary,* motion, as to *go,* to *speak,* to *move* any of our limbs in such manner as is fancied in our minds. These two types of motion encompass our alternate succession of appetites, aversions, hopes and fears.

Chap. 7. Of all *discourse,* governed by desire of knowledge, there is at last an *end,* either by attaining, or by giving over. When we believe in any saying by reason of the authority and good opinion we have of him who says it, then it is not the argument of what he says but his person we honor by our faith. Thus, when we believe that the Scriptures are the word of God, having no immediate revelation from God himself, our belief, faith and trust is in the Church, whose word we take and acquiesce therein.

Chap. 8. Virtue consists in comparison, for if all things were equal in all men, nothing would be prized. Virtues are of two sorts: *natural* and *acquired.* By *natural,* I mean not that which is had from birth, but that *wit* which is gotten by use only, and experience, without method, culture, or instruction. Natural wit consists in *celerity of imagining,* and *steady direction* to some approved end. As for *acquired wit,* there is none but reason, which is grounded in the right use of speech and produceth the sciences.

Chap. 9. There are two kinds of knowledge: *knowledge of fact,* and *knowledge of the consequence of one affirmation to another.* The former is but sense and memory, is absolute knowledge, and its register is called *history.* The latter is conditional, is dependent on demonstrations, and is called *philosophy.*

Chap. 10. The *power of a man* is his present means to obtain some future apparent good. And is either *original* or *instrumental.* Original, or natural, power is the eminence of the faculties of body or mind, such as strength, form, prudence, eloquence, nobility. Instrumental powers are those which are acquired by natural powers, or by good fortune, and are used as instruments to acquire more, such as riches, reputation, friends, and the secret working of God which men call good luck.

Chap. 11. Manners, in the larger sense, are those qualities of mankind which concern their living together in peace and unity. Felicity consists not in repose of the mind satisfied, but in a continual progress of desire from one object to another.

Chap. 12. Religion is peculiar to mankind among all living creatures. It is peculiar to the nature of man to seek, first, the causes of events, especially causes of his own good and evil fortune; second, to seek beginnings among chains of causes; and thirdly, when he cannot assure himself of the true causes of things, but remembers antecedence and consequence, he looks to the authority and wisdom of others for such knowledge. Religion provides him with such knowledge of these matters as to satisfy him.

Chap. 13. Nature has made men equal insofar as there is not that which one man may have or covet that another man cannot aspire to it, and in some manner attain it. If nature makes one man physically stronger than another, the second may yet overcome the first by use of wiles. Thus, no man is safe from the attack of another. In the nature of man, we find three principal causes of quarrel: first, competition, which makes men invade for gain; second, diffidence, which makes men quarrel for safety; and third, glory, which makes men invade for reputation. Left to himself, man finds his state in nature solitary, poor, nasty, brutish, and short; a war of every man against every other man.

Chap. 14. Man has a natural right to liberty—a right to act to preserve his own life and property. But this liberty in man's state of nature results only in conflict. Therefore, man must accept, as a *first law of nature,* a deliberate quest for peace. Then, man will have to accept the *second law of nature:* a willingness to refrain from exercising his full right to liberty, and to be contented with only so much liberty against other men as he would allow himself. Such a mutual transferring of rights is what men call *contract.*

Chap. 15. If men enter into such a contract, they must bind themselves with other agreements, such as will achieve for them justice, gratitude, modesty, equity, mercy, and other moral virtues.

[In Chap. 16 Hobbes defined certain quasi-legal terms which seemed to him necessary to give his arguments a sound footing.]

Part II. Of Commonwealth. Chap. 17. The only really practical way that social contracts can be kept is to form a *commonwealth* headed by a single absolute ruler. In such a sovereign consists the essence of the commonwealth, that is, one person, of whose acts a great multitude, by mutual covenants with one another, have made themselves every one the author, to the end that he may use the strength and means of them all, as he shall think expedient, for their peace and common defense.

Chap. 18. The sovereign ruler must be truly sovereign in his possession of power. If it be argued that certain rulers possessing such power may abuse it and make certain of their subjects miserable, it should be remembered that the sovereign is only human, and that whatever unhappiness he may cause by his personal failings will not be so great as that which would exist in the chaos of the state of nature that would obtain if there were no ruler.

Chap. 19. There are three kinds of commonwealth. When the representative of all is one man, then the commonwealth is a *monarchy.* When there is an assembly of all in the commonwealth, it is a *democracy.* When only a part assemble, it is an *aristocracy.* Of these three, monarchy is best, for it is most likely to be free of internal conflict, and therefore, to offer the best hope of continuing peace.

Chap. 20. Besides sovereignty by institution, as that described above, there is *paternal* sovereignty, in which men, out of fear of each other but not of him who is to rule them, allow a ruler to have sovereign power over them. And there is *despotical* sovereignty, which is the result of conquest.

The rights and consequences of both paternal and despotical sovereignty are the same as those of sovereignty by institution; that is, it is the duty of him who is sovereign to prevent internal strife and to preserve peace.

Chap. 21. Since there cannot be enough laws to regulate all actions of men, the subjects of an absolute monarch have a large degree of freedom. They have no right to rebel against the monarch as long as he provides them with protection and peace; but if he fails in this duty, he has broken his part of the social contract, and his subjects have no obligations toward him.

[In Chaps. 22 to 30, Hobbes details the laws, crimes, excuses, punishments, rewards, and offices of a commonwealth that is an absolute sovereignty.]

Chap. 31. A commonwealth, being of the nature of one person—its ruler—should worship God as one person; that is, it should have an official form of public worship. If an individual wishes to worship differently, he may do so privately, but not publicly.

[Parts III and IV of *Leviathan* consists of Hobbes' opinions on certain questions of religious politics that concerned his times, and, to the modern reader who does not have the necessary historical background, are very little intelligible.]

Life With Father

Reminiscences by Clarence Day, Jr., 1874–1935.
Published 1935 by Alfred A. Knopf, Inc., New York. © 1920, 1935 by Clarence Day, Jr.

THIS IS A SERIES of sketches that appeared originally in *The New Yorker*. The work as a whole ranks very high as humorous writing. To a very large extent the stories are factual. Clarence Day was the son of a very well-to-do New York real-estate man, well placed in the New York social world. Within the sentimental and goodnatured structure of humor there is a very keen picture of life in New York City in the last quarter of the 19th century. A play, *Life With Father*, by Russel Crouse and Howard Lindsay, based on Clarence Day's stories, broke all previous records for long runs on Broadway; it was produced in 1939 and ran for some six years.

Chaps. 1–3. God and My Father. Father acknowledged the existence of churches and religion as he did banks, but he never permitted them to dictate to him. He took a distant attitude towards sects: He belonged to none. He disciplined himself quite firmly and saw no need for the Golden Rule. He thought the clergy a queer lot. Mother was devout, and even Father said God must see how lovely and good she was. It was understood that if there was any trouble about Father getting into Heaven, Mother would make it right. Father expected a good deal of God and never hesitated to call Him on the carpet, but his wrath never lasted long and if he didn't forgive, he forgot.

In spite of his independent behavior, father was one of the chiefs of our church. Mother had a sorrow that was always with her: Father had never been confirmed. He had picked the Episcopal Church when he was young because it served good cake in its Sunday School, but he could see no reason to carry the religion thing too far. But the worst was to come. Mother found out that Father had never even been baptized. When she asked Father to attend to this oversight immediately, he refused. He informed Mother he would be a Christian in his own way. Mother was desperate. Finally Father got the point in this baptism thing. He just wished to get it over. Mother was happy even as he continued to rage. One morning Father got up to find a cab waiting. Mother still had the job of convincing Father that the day for his baptism had been set, but her ally was Father's horror of wasting money on cabs. She just went and sat in the cab until Father could stand it no longer and finally gave in. All the way to the church Father looked like a caged lion. He announced this would be his last time and no diamond necklace for Mother either. Mother pointed out he was doing it for God, not her. Father just answered, "Pish." But Father still expected God to get him out of the whole affair. When the moment came to pour water on Father, Mr. MORLEY, the young minister, managed just to wet him a trifle. Father took it like a soldier but his soul boiled at the indignity.

"I'll take that one"

Chap. 4. Father hated sickness. Germs were nonsense. When people thought they were ill, it was a sign of their weak character. Since Father's constitution was iron, it was very difficult to persuade him he had pneumonia when he had; and as he recovered quickly, he was convinced that any illness could be conquered by firmness. He often proved his point when he had a headache. He would just lie down, shut his eyes tight, and yell until it went away.

Chap. 5. Father Hires A Cook. Mother was ill and our cook had walked out. As Mother was not able to go to an agency and knew nothing herself about cooking, Father took matters in his own hands. He went to the employment agency and demanded to know where the cooks were kept. The manager resisted but Father went into the room where the applicants were sitting, pointed his cane at one, and said "I'll take that one." It was Margaret, who didn't really wish to cook, but stayed with us for 26 years. Father reported to Mother that he couldn't understand why she made such a fuss about hiring servants.

Chap. 6. Father got great satisfaction from a well-balanced ledger. He tried to make Mother keep account of the household expenses but Mother was unsympathetic to figures. Charge accounts were invented for Mother. She bought for the moment, with the penalty of payment remote. She was always yielding to the temptation to buy a little piece of china, hoping that Father would not see it on the bill. Every time they had a financial conversation Father became exasperated with Mother's vague explanations. He made up his mind each month that he would start all over again next time. Father never gave up, but then neither did Mother.

Chap. 7. My name was the same as Father's, CLARENCE. I didn't like it but Father said it sounded just right. Having the same name caused great difficulties where letters were concerned. Father opened anything that came addressed to Clarence S. Day. He would never look to see if a Jr. was attached. When I was young, my mail consisted solely of bargain sales in false whiskers. Then as I grew older I began to get letters from girls. Father continued to open my mail and I got more embarrassed. I had a running war with my friends to please put Jr. on letters to me. Father and I were becoming too intimate with his reading of my letters.

Chap. 8. The telephone company sent us numerous circulars concerning their new invention but Father would have nothing to do with the telephone. Mother agreed with Father. She didn't like the telephone because machines made her nervous. It was nearly 15 years before our telephone was finally installed. Father treated it as if it was human, scolding and cursing when it rang. He had a running argument with "Central" and was always telling her how to run her business. Whenever the thing rang, Father assumed the call was for him. If the call was for one of us, he just couldn't believe it. He never stopped promising to have the confounded thing taken out.

Chap. 9. Father never permitted a party in his own house, though he always enjoyed himself when he attended them in other houses. Mother liked parties and knew that the only way to get invited was to give some of her own. She resorted to guile so that Father would not know until the very evening of her party. Father knew instantly what was afoot when he arrived home and found potted palms in the hall. As soon as Father saw the potted palms he knew he had lost another battle and he took JOHN, our butler pro tem, to the cellar for the right wines. He dressed carefully, muttering all the while. As soon as the guests arrived, especially the pretty women, Father began to enjoy himself. After the good dinner and excellent wine, there was no stopping him.

Liliom

Play by Ferenc Molnar, 1878–1952. Produced 1909. Available in various collections of plays.

THIS IS GENERALLY considered the finest work of the great Hungarian playwright Molnar. It is an excellent picture of the type—always potentially a criminal type—of man who is deficient in moral sense and kindness where his own interests or passions are concerned. The ending may be unnecessarily sentimental but does not spoil the play. Rodgers and Hammerstein fashioned a musical comedy, *Carousel* (1945), on *Liliom*. It was successful, though not to compare with their work *Oklahoma!,* which came just before it, and *South Pacific,* which came a few years later.

Prologue. LILIOM is a cocky carnival barker, working for Mrs. MUSKAT'S carousel. He is well liked by the girls, who enjoy his familiarities, and feared by their escorts, who resent them. **1.** Near the amusement park, Mrs. Muskat scolds two servant girls, JULIE and MARIE, for misbehaving on her carousel. She has seen Liliom put his arm around Julie's waist. Julie defies her. Liliom arrives, followed by four admiring servant girls. He dismisses them. Julie asks Liliom if Mrs. Muskat can make him throw her out. Mrs. Muskat repeats her jealous accusations and Liliom tells her to go back to the carousel. She tells him he is fired. He takes it very calmly. She wants to make up. He tells her to apologize to Julie but she refuses. Liliom tells her to go before he loses his temper and beats her up. Mrs. Muskat leaves. Liliom thinks Julie is sorry for him and he wants no one to feel pity for him. Liliom goes to fetch his things. Marie thinks he has fallen for Julie. She tells Julie that she is in love with a man named WOLF, who thinks he is a

soldier because he wears a uniform. Julie, who has been in the city longer, says Wolf must be a doorman. Liliom returns. He tells the girls one of them should go home, the other stay. Marie hesitates. Julie will lose her job if she is not back by 7. Liliom reminds her that he, too, has lost his job. Julie tells Marie to go and she will stay with Liliom. Liliom asks Julie if she has a sweetheart, and she says she has not but he does not believe her, since she is staying with him now after such short acquaintance. Two policemen interrupt them. They warn Julie against Liliom, who has a reputation for taking servant girls' money and deserting them after promising to marry them. She disregards their advice and stays with Liliom. Julie tells Liliom she would give him all the money she has, if she had any. She denies she loves him, and claims she will never marry, but she asks him not to go back to Mrs. Muskat. **2.** Julie and Liliom are married and have a room at Mrs. HOLLUNDER'S house. Mrs. Hollunder is Julie's aunt. Liliom has been in trouble with the police for fighting Mr. Hollunder. Marie brings Julie some money. Liliom cannot find a job; he knows only one thing, barking at carnivals. Julie ignores all attacks made by her aunt on Liliom. She has no interest in other men. Mrs. Muskat wants Liliom back; the business needs him. Liliom arrives with FICSUR. Mrs. Muskat warns Liliom of Ficsur's bad reputation. She tells him he should not beat Julie, he should leave her. She thinks Liliom looks awful. Liliom considers going back to the carousel but staying married to Julie, but Mrs. Muskat wants him, too. Julie tells Liliom she is to have a child. Liliom refuses Mrs. Muskat's money and tells her to go. He then discusses a robbery with Ficsur. He needs money in a hurry. **3.** Ficsur and Liliom plan to hold up the cashier of a leather factory, on his way to the bank. Liliom plans to go to America. He gets the kitchen knife and hides it in his coat. He is worried about what will hapen to him before God but Ficsur assures him that poor

people never get an even break up there anyway. Julie tries to keep Liliom home, but he pushes her aside and leaves. Mrs. Hollunder misses the kitchen knife. Marie brings her Wolf for a visit. He has a new job and they are planning the future together. **4.** Near the railroad tracks, Liliom and Ficsur nervously while the time away playing cards while waiting for the cashier. Liliom loses his share of the expected money to Ficsur. The cashier, LINZMAN, arrives and the two men try to hold him up, but he has a revolver. He captures them and summons the police. Rather than be taken prisoner, Liliom stabs himself with the kitchen knife. **5.** Liliom, dying, has a last talk with Julie. He tells her to remarry and not to tell the child how bad a father he was. Then he dies. Two messengers from the Beyond come and take Liliom away with them. **6.** Liliom, now in Heaven, is brought into a court for suicides. They have one more chance to go back to earth and complete unfinished business. Liliom pretends to the MAGISTRATE that he does not want to go back, but the Magistrate knows Liliom's heart. He sentences Liliom to 16 years of purification, after which Liliom will be sent back to earth to do one good deed for his child. **7.** Sixteen years later, Wolf is a prosperous man. He and Marie call on Julie and her daughter LOUISE. Liliom is brought to Julie's house by the heavenly policemen. Julie does not recognize him and thinks he is a beggar asking for food. He questions her about her husband. She tells him her husband died in America, and changes the subject. Liliom pretends he knew him and they talk about him. He then offers Louise a star, which he has brought from Heaven with him, as a gift. But Julie and Louise want him to leave. They are frightened of him. Liliom accidentally slaps Louise, but it does not seem to hurt her. Liliom thinks he has failed to do his good deed, and leaves. Julie is left with her memories. She compares the way the visitor slapped Louise with the way Liliom used to beat her; neither hurt.

Liliom, back on earth to do a good deed, brings Louise a star

Little Lord Fauntleroy

Novel by Frances Hodgson Burnett, 1849–1924.
Published 1886.

THIS TOO-SACCHARINE BOOK for children has generally offended the children, particularly the boys, but in the late Victorian world mothers loved it and made the poor children read it. The worst sufferers were boys who were actually made to wear "Little Lord Fauntleroy suits." Mrs. Burnett fashioned her hero on her own young son, who did actually call her Dearest. The times when mothers loved the book changed to times when they were revolted by it and now they can just laugh. But *Little Lord Fauntleroy* did give a name and an immortal juvenile character to the world.

Chap. 1. Capt. CEDRIC ERROL, the youngest son of the Earl of DORINCOURT, is sent by his father on a visit to America. He is the most intelligent and charming of the earl's three sons, and his father often wishes he were the oldest. After six months the earl longs for his favorite son and orders him back to England, but Cedric has simultaneously sent his father a letter informing him of his intended marriage to a pretty American girl. She is an orphan and is the companion to a difficult old woman. The earl disapproves the marriage and cuts Cedric off from the family, telling him he may never return home. Cedric marries his American girl and lives with her in genteel poverty. They have a beautiful son, also named CEDRIC, who is kind and intelligent. Cedric dies and little Cedric becomes the sole companion of his mother whom he calls "Dearest" as his father did. Cedric delights everyone in the neighborhood with his long curls and quaint manner. His particular friend is the grocer, Mr. HOBBES, who is a staunch democrat and enemy of aristocracy.

Chaps. 2–3. Cedric is not delighted when Mr. HAVISHAM, lawyer for the Earl of Dorincourt, comes to New York to tell Cedric that he is now Lord FAUNTLEROY, heir to the earldom. The older brothers have died. Cedric's grandfather has sent for him to come to England, but he never wants to see Dearest, since he hates Americans and imagines her as a mercenary creature. However, he has arranged for her to live near the castle so that her son may visit her. The earl is a selfish, unpopular man, but he suffers as much from loneliness as from gout. Havisham tells Cedric what it means to be an earl and asks what Cedric would do if he were rich. Cedric talks of the things he would do for people. He would buy the apple woman a shawl and his mother a new dress. He plans to help the bootblack and the cook's sister. Mr. Havisham is impressed. He gives Cedric $25 to give to a poor woman, and the new Lord Fauntleroy decides he will enjoy being an earl after all. Havisham arranges for Cedric to help all his friends.

Chap. 4. On the voyage Cedric makes friends with everybody aboard ship. His special friend is a seaman named JERRY, who tells him stories of Indians and pirates. Cedric is distressed that his mother will not be living with him and often sighs sadly. In England they are first driven to the lodge where his mother will stay. He is happy to see MARY, their former housekeeper, who was sent ahead to get things ready. He spends his first night with his mother. Havisham reports to the earl that Cedric's mother does not want to accept anything but the house from a man who hates her and that Cedric knows nothing of his grandfather's dislike for his mother. The earl thinks only that his son's wife is scheming against him.

Chap. 5. Cedric is amazed at the size and beauty of his new home. He goes into a huge room to see the earl and is met by a large mastiff, Dougal, with which he immediately makes friends. Cedric's grandfather is happy to see such a graceful, courageous and lovely child. He never paid at-

Fauntleroy and the mastiff

tention to his own children. The earl's foot is badly inflamed and he leans on the little lord on the way to dinner. He is pleased with the child's strength and persistence. Later he is proud of the way Cedric masters his homesickness. Havisham enters to find the gruff and selfish lord tenderly watching his grandchild sleeping beside Dougal.

Chap. 6. Lord Fauntleroy meets the housekeeper, Mrs. MELON, and his personal servant, DAWSON. There is a roomful of toys. When he goes to see his grandfather again he is overflowing with happiness. He teaches the earl to play a game with him. It is the first time the earl has ever played with a child. The rector, Mr. MORDAUNT, comes in and is amazed to find the earl in such a good temper. He reports that a tenant farmer, HIGGINS, has been ill and is unable to meet his bills. Ordinarily the earl would have ordered him off the land, but Fauntleroy asks that the tenant be given credit and the earl consents. The earl thinks back on his life of selfish deeds and is ashamed. In the afternoon not even a promise of seeing his new pony deters the little lord from going to see his mother.

Chap. 7. On Sunday the earl takes his grandson to church. All the people of the estate have come to look at the little lord. Tales of his goodness have spread and all the people bow to him. Fauntleroy can see his mother from the pew and is happy to be so near to her. After church Higgins comes to thank Fauntleroy, who assures him that it is only his grandfather's usual goodness. The earl is embarrassed.

Chap. 8. Every day Fauntleroy goes out riding with his groom, WILKINS. He talks with the village people and learns many of their names. He gives a crippled child a ride home and later takes him crutches. But he is puzzled that his mother never comes to the big house.

Chap. 9. The Earl of Dorincourt's health returns and he begins to go riding with Fauntleroy. The earl learns that his son's wife has been ministering to the poor and teaching sewing and cooking to the girls of the village. Dearest tells her son that there is a poor section of the land where the people are living in terrible houses and are often sick. The little lad assumes that his grandfather is ignorant of this and, if he knew, would build new cottages. The earl follows his grandchild's wish and goes to supervise the building.

Chap. 10. Lady LORRIDAILE, the earl's sister, has heard of Lord Fauntleroy, and the change he has brought about in her brother. She is anxious to meet the child and for the first time in years the earl gives a dinner party to show off the heir of Dorincourt. Lady Lorridaile is indignant that her brother has separated the child from his mother. At the dinner party the little lad talks freely to all the guests and delights them with stories of America. Havisham arrives late and tells the earl that the wife of his second son has come to England and demanded Lord Fauntleroy's position for her own son. The woman is described by Havisham as ignorant and mercenary, the very opposite of the youngest son's wife.

Chap. 11. In America Mr. Hobbes misses his young friend. He visits DICK, the bootblack, about whom Cedric had told him. The grocer and the bootblack become friends. When a letter arrives from England telling them that Cedric is no longer Lord Fauntleroy, as another boy has been found to whom the title belongs, the two friends feel that Cedric is being robbed.

Chap. 12. The story of Cedric's replacement is in all the newspapers. The tenants grieve that they will lose their favorite and his kind mother. Cedric is not at all worried, because his grandfather has promised to love him and keep him near, whether the title is his or not. The earl visits Mrs.

Errol for the first time. He is troubled because her son has lost the title. She receives him kindly and all the past rudeness is forgotten. He sees that many of the boy's fine qualities come from his mother. The earl asks permission to visit often and expresses his gratitude that she never told her son why he was not living with his mother.

Chap. 13. One morning Dick sees on the front page of a newspaper a picture of the woman who claims to be the real Lady Fauntleroy. Dick recognizes her as the wife of his older brother BEN, who took care of Dick when they were orphaned. Dick runs to Mr. Hobbes with his discovery. They go to a lawyer, who writes a letter to Havisham and another to Ben in California.

Chap. 14. The woman who calls herself the real Lady Fauntleroy thinks her claims should be fought. When the letter arrives from New York, the earl has his lawyer cable for Ben and Dick and Mr. Hobbes to come to England. Ben and Dick are taken to the woman and Ben identifies her as his wife, MINNA, and the little boy as his son, TOM. Dick confirms the identification. Ben takes the boy away with him and Minna disappears. The earl asks Lord Fauntleroy and his mother both to come and live at the castle.

Chap. 15. The earl buys Ben a cattle ranch of his own and plans to educate Dick. Mr. Hobbes stays in England and opens a grocery store near the castle.

Little Women

Novel by Louisa May Alcott, 1832–1888.
Published 1868.
FOR AT LEAST 75 years this was the most popular book for girls 12 to 15 and maybe it still is. (During much of that period, its "opposite number" among books for boys was *Treasure Island*.) *Little Women* is the story of a wife and her four daughters living in genteel poverty in the environs of Boston while the father is away as a chaplain in the Union Army during the Civil War. The characters are entirely natural and believable and the incidents, though never forced for dramatic device, are interesting. *Little Women* was not designed to be a great work of literature and in many respects it probably would not fit that definition, but in its way it is a great book. So natural are the action and the dialogue that even today *Little Women* is readable without a sense of Victorian stiffness and any year it can make a popular motion picture, as has been proved several times.

Chaps. 1–3. The approach of Christmas brings little cheer to the four March sisters in their modest but peaceful New England home. Not only are they poor but their father is far away, a chaplain in the Civil War. And their mother, Mrs. MARCH, whom the girls call MARMEE, has proposed that they spend no money on presents at a time when the men in military service are suffering. Each of the girls has a dollar and they decide to use their money to buy surprise gifts for their mother. Pretty, plump MEG, 16, the eldest, who works as a governess for four spoiled neighborhood children, chooses gloves. Tomboyish JO, 15, a bookworm, who works as companion to lame, rich AUNT MARCH, an irascible relative, selects slippers. BETH, 13, angelic and bashful, hems handkerchiefs, which she painstakingly embroiders with "Mother." AMY, the littlest, a curly-haired blonde who dreams of becoming an artist, affects fine manners, and uses big words she cannot pronounce, decides to buy her mother cologne; she gets a tiny bottle but at the last moment, ashamed of her stinginess, returns it and spends all her money on a big bottle. On Christmas morning the girls share their breakfast with the HUMMELS, a penniless family in the neighborhood. That evening their generosity is repaid when wealthy old Mr. LAURENCE, who lives with his young grandson in the stately house next door, sends over ice cream, cake, fruit, candy, and four bouquets of flowers. On New Year's Eve, Jo and Meg, making the best of their shabby clothes, attend a stylish dance, where bashful Jo meets Mr. Laurence's handsome grandson, Theodore, an orphan, called LAURIE. He and Jo get on well together, and he provides the use of his grandfather's carriage when Meg sprains her ankle.

Chaps. 4–6. Jo tosses a snowball at Laurie's window one day when he is recuperating from a cold, and he invites her in. Thereafter the sisters spend many happy times visiting Laurie. Even timid Beth goes, to practice on the fine piano. They in turn take the solitary boy into their humble home, where Mrs. March gives him a motherly welcome. Mr. Laurence becomes so fond of Beth that he gives her a small piano that belonged to a now dead granddaughter.

Chaps. 7–9. Jo will not let Amy go with her and Meg to the theater as Laurie's guests, and Amy angrily burns the manuscript of a book Jo is writing. Jo swears she will never forgive her. Next day when Amy follows Jo and Laurie to the river for ice-skating, Jo ignores her. Amy crashes through the ice and is saved only by Laurie's quick thinking. Amy recovers, but Jo reproaches herself. Mrs. March admonishes Jo to curb her hot temper.

Chaps. 10–14. In the spring the girls form a secret society, the Pickwick Club, of which Laurie is the only boy member. Jo is editor of the club's weekly newspaper, "The Pickwick Portfolio." Meg's charges and Aunt March depart for the summer and the girls play and rest. After a week they are thoroughly bored and adopt a regular schedule of duties. At a picnic, to which Laurie invites them, JOHN BROOKE, his tutor, is attentive to Meg. The Marches are thrilled when a newspaper publishes one of Jo's original stories.

Chaps. 15–19. In November a telegram requests Mrs. March to come immediately to Washington, where her husband is gravely ill. Some money for the trip is borrowed from Aunt March and Jo sells her chief beauty, her long, thick, brown hair, for $25. Mr. March's health improves. Beth catches scarlet fever after visiting the poor Hummels and grows so ill that though Mr. March has had a relapse, the doctor recommends sending for Mrs. March. Laurie is Jo's mainstay during these dark days, while she nurses Beth.

Chaps. 20–23. Christmastime is more joyous this year. Beth has recovered, Mr. March writes that he will soon be with them, and Meg daydreams of John Brooke, with whom she has fallen in love. At Christmas Mr. March returns. In the excitement John kisses Meg, as he says, "by mistake." The next day John proposes. She is happy but out of perverseness she sends him away. Aunt March urges her to make a rich match to help her family and says she will not leave her a penny if she marries John. Meg furiously replies she will marry whom she pleases, and her aunt departs in a rage. John, who has overheard this scene, embraces Meg, and she accepts him. Jo is resentful at the thought of losing Meg, but Laurie comforts her, saying "You've got me, anyhow. I'm not good for much, I know; but I'll stand by you."

Chaps. 24–26. In the three years that follow, Meg waits while John serves in the army, then takes a job in preparation for providing her with a home. Aunt March, who has taken a fancy to Amy, bribes her to become her companion with an offer of drawing lessons from a prominent teacher. Jo devotes herself to her writing, which is beginning to pay, and to Beth, who remains delicate. Laurie goes to college and is involved in many pranks and scrapes. After a quiet June wedding, Meg and John go to live in a little brown house nearby, called the Dovecote.

Chaps. 27–31. Jo wins a $100 prize for a story and uses the money to send Beth and Mrs. March to the seashore. She continues to earn money from what she calls her "rubbish." John and Meg become the parents of twins, a girl and a boy, DAISY and DEMI (short for Demijohn). Amy, who has become a polite young lady, is taken to Europe by an aunt, much to the disappointment of Jo, who has been passed over because of her blunt, independent manner.

Chaps. 32–34. Jo realizes that her

Jo meets the professor on a rainy day and they become engaged

"Teddy," as she calls Laurie, is beginning to care for her in a way she cannot reciprocate. She also wonders whether perhaps Beth is not in love with him. She determines to go to New York, where Mrs. KIRKE, a friend of her mother's, runs a large boardinghouse. Here she does the sewing and teaches the Kirke children. She secretly mends the socks of Professor FRIEDRICH BHAER, one of the boarders, a stout, bearded, kindly German. The professor supports himself and two orphaned nephews by giving lessons. When he discovers Jo's mending, he gives her German lessons in return. Jo writes sensational stories that sell readily to a trashy newspaper. She stops when the professor makes her feel she is poisoning the minds of young readers.

Chaps. 35–41. Laurie, who has settled down, is graduated from college with honors. The following day, he tells Jo that he has always loved her. Desperately unhappy at hurting him, she replies that they are unsuited to each other because of their quick tempers and strong wills. Mr. Laurence sends Laurie abroad on business. Laurie spends six months there, living frivolously, until Amy, whom he meets at Nice, reproaches him for wasting his time and he decides to go home. Meanwhile, Beth confides to Jo that she knows her life is ebbing away. Amy is in Switzerland when she gets news of Beth's death. Laurie, once

more abroad, goes to comfort her and decides she is the only woman who can take Jo's place in his heart. Amy says she will marry him.

Chaps. 41–47. Jo begins to write again. This time something of the spiritual crisis she has undergone finds its way into her work and she produces stories that are not only published but are much admired. When Laurie and Amy come home, married, Laurie tells Jo that he can never stop loving her but that the love is altered. They agree to resume their old footing, but as adults. Professor Bhaer comes to call. He is greeted cordially for Jo's sake but is soon liked for himself. He remains in the city and it is obvious that he is courting Jo. One rainy afternoon, Jo meets him while shopping and accepts the shelter of his umbrella. They become engaged in all the mud and rain, but Jo cries at the news that he has a teaching opportunity far off in the West. After a year of working and waiting they are able to marry, for Aunt March dies, leaving her home, Plumfield, to Jo. Here, Jo and the professor open a school for boys. Each year at apple-picking time the Marches, Laurences and Brookeses gather to help the Bhaers pick. When Marmee celebrates her 60th birthday, surrounded by children and grandchildren, she tells her girls that however long they live, "I never wish you a greater happiness than this."

Novel by Thomas Wolfe, 1900–1938. Published 1929 by Charles Scribner's Sons, New York. © 1929 by Thomas Wolfe; renewed 1957. (ML, G16)

HAVING ENDURED a boyhood and much preliminary education in North Carolina, and having virtually memorized the *Golden Treasury*, Thomas Wolfe journeyed North to write books. Around his books there grew a veritable cult that will still insist he is the greatest American novelist. Nonmembers may not be willing to subscribe to this view, but it must be granted that no novelist ever poured more of himself into a book than Thomas Wolfe did. He keenly felt every experience, every glimpse of life, and every phenomenon that came into his consciousness, and he wrote it all down. His manuscripts were rough and the great Scribner editor, the late Max Perkins, is credited with having given them the form to go with their substance. In fact, Wolfe died so young that much of his writing was incomplete and it was Perkins who constructed his later novels from the disorganized material Wolfe had left. *Look Homeward, Angel* is the first novel and is as good as the later ones, not necessarily better. The title is from *Lycidas*, Milton's elegy on the death of his college friend, in the line that reads "Look homeward, angel, now, and melt with ruth [pity]." Like Wolfe's other novels, and even more, *Look Homeward Angel* is autobiographical. His city of Altamont is Asheville, N.C.

Look Homeward, Angel

Part I. Chaps. 1–4. At the age of 15 OLIVER GANT became a stonecutter's apprentice in Baltimore, after which he went into business for himself in the Reconstruction South. A wild, romantic character, Gant had begun to drink during his apprenticeship and his own stonecutting business in the South was soon lost. His first wife died and Gant, at the age of 30, his health impaired by drinking, went west to the small mountain town of Altamont, in North Carolina. There he again set up a stonecutter's shop and he met and married

ELIZA PENTLAND, for whom he built a house on Woodson Street. There were basic conflicts between Eliza and Gant. Eliza had grown up in the depleted South after the Civil War and like all the Pentlands was property-mad. Gant's childhood had been one of plenty and he could not share her acquisitiveness, while Eliza could not understand his carefree ways, exuberance, and love of drinking.

In 11 years Eliza and Gant had nine children, of whom six lived. The oldest was STEVE; then DAISY, HELEN, the twins— GROVER and BEN—and LUKE. In 1900

the last child, EUGENE GANT, was born. This ended Eliza's child-bearing; and, sick of Gant's drinking and debauchery, she now hoped to concentrate on real estate.

Chaps. 5–7. In 1904, disregarding Gant's protests, Eliza left only Daisy at home and took the other children with her to the World's Fair in St. Louis, where she opened a boarding house. Grover died there of typhoid fever and in grief and guilt Eliza returned to the Woodson Street house to reëstablish the family's life together. But the old struggle between Eliza and Gant was soon resumed.

Chaps. 8–10. When Eugene was not quite 6 years old he insisted on going to school. He was an imaginative, brooding child and books soon constituted a vast inner life for him. Almost devoid of herd instinct, he did not mix well with his classmates but developed the habit of intense reading, which lasted throughout his life. At home his sisters and brothers had little time for him, except for their petty tormentings. Only Ben felt drawn to young Eugene; and in spite of Ben's gruffness of manner, a deep though secret affection grew between them. With almost an obsession for financial independence, Eliza had sent the boys to work after school hours when they were very young. Ben, rarely seen at home, got up at 3 a. m. and delivered papers. After the 8th grade he quit school, took on more work at the newspaper office, and lived with bitter pride in his financial independence. Under Eliza's tutelage Eugene's isolation in books and dreams could not last. At 6:30 in the morning he picked fruits and vegetables, which he sold throughout the neighborhood. Luke, who had a reputation for salesmanship, held the local agency for the *Saturday Evening Post* and soon Eugene was sent out to sell copies, an assignment that he approached with horror.

Chaps. 11–13. Eliza's knowledge of Altamont real estate was growing. The urge that had driven her to St. Louis led her to buy a large, poorly built boarding house called Dixieland. She and Gant separated when Eugene was not quite 8 years old. Eliza moved into Dixieland, taking Eugene with her. Helen remained on Woodson Street with her father. Ben and Luke drifted between the two houses. Daisy was getting married, and Steve, who led an erratic, wastrel's life, had been away from home most of the time since his 18th birthday. Eugene had essentially lost the warm, tumultuous home of his early childhood. He was ashamed of Dixieland and the loss of privacy. As the boarding house filled, the family's scale of living was steadily lowered. Eugene often spent mornings with Helen, who enjoyed mothering him but at the same time, resenting his inner world, sometimes attacked him physically or verbally.

Part II. Chaps. 14–17. The next four years brought Eugene relief from the bleakness of Dixieland. Having read a composition of his, MARGARET LEONARD insisted that he enter a private school that she and her husband, JOHN DORSEY LEONARD, were starting. She recognized Eugene's mounting quest of knowledge and a deep attachment grew between teacher and pupil. Eugene's years with the Leonards were rewarding.

Chaps. 18–21. There was a great deal of family battling among the Gants as each member sought to fulfill or forget ambitions. Helen began to travel around, singing with another girl in motion-picture theaters. Luke, a poor student, studied electrical engineering unsuccessfully and then held a variety of jobs until, World War I having begun, he went to work in a boiler factory. Gant was fearful of the disintegration that overtook him with age. His life had been one of riotous living. Now he was painfully dying of cancer. But his occasional huge debaucheries continued. He rented the upstairs of the Woodson Street house to a widow, which aggravated Eliza's bitterness, and his visits to Dixieland became less frequent. When Eliza told him the town was laughing he went on a typical, insanely drunken spree and the widow left Woodson Street.

Chaps. 22–27. Eliza grumbled incessantly at Eugene's apparent laziness while he was at the Leonards' school. When he was 14 Ben got him a job as a paper carrier. Margaret Leonard still fed his great love

for poetry and by the age of 15 he knew most of the major lyrics of the English language. Eliza went to Florida for her rheumatism and to look at properties and Eugene happily boarded at the Leonards for a while. The Leonards hoped to keep him for an extra year, but the Gant family, interested in saving a year's tuition, insisted that he leave for college.

Part III. Chaps. 28–29. Eugene was not yet 16 when he left for the state university at Pulpit Hill. Gant hoped Eugene's education would lead, through law and politics, to a life as a famous statesman. Eugene's first year was one of isolation and suffering and he was the butt of all of the traditional jokes. He changed lodgings several times and finally lived alone. He made one fairly close friend, JIM TRIVETT, who sponsored Eugene's first visit to a brothel. Eugene went home for a holiday vermin-ridden and burning with guilt. Ben took Eugene to a doctor, who assured Eugene that he would survive his experiences. Then Eugene felt his oncoming manhood with exultation. Helen, who had married HUGH BARTON, a cash-register salesman, lived within 35 miles of the university and Eugene often visited her there. Barton later got the Altamont Agency and when Eugene went home at the end of the year the Bartons were living with Gant on Woodson Street. Ben had tried to enlist but was rejected because of weak lungs.

Chaps. 30–32. Eugene met his first love, LAURA JAMES, who was 5 years older than he, early that summer at Dixieland. On a picnic he became her lover. Laura left Dixieland, saying she would return after a few days with her parents; but Eugene knew she would never come back. She married someone else and Eugene's summer was spent in frantic disbelief that he had

lost her. When he returned to school Eugene began to flourish in the university atmosphere. He felt a surge of brotherhood, joined everything, and became a leader in spite of his continued loneliness. He was happier than he had ever been before. Gant's illness had become much worse and he made a second trip to Johns Hopkins in Baltimore, but first he went on a gigantic spree. The doctor told Helen that Gant would soon die.

Chaps. 33–34. Eugene decided to go to Norfolk, Va., where Laura lived with her husband. There he had many adventures with jobs, spent money wildly, and once, penniless, nearly starved to death. After his near-death, Laura and the rest of his past seemed lost and he no longer tried to see her. He returned to the university. A telegram from his mother said Ben had pneumonia.

Chaps. 35–38. At Ben's bedside the family was turbulent, with the rancor and love among themselves and their guilt over neglecting Ben. Eliza had first summoned an ineffectual but cheap doctor and Ben's condition deteriorated rapidly. Ben died, severing Eugene's one strong tie to the family.

Chaps. 39–40. After Ben's death all family closeness was lost except for one final emotional interlude when Eliza and Gant went to Eugene's graduation. Their hopes were not realized, for Eugene still had no goals. He had only a great hunger for learning and travel. Gant awaited death; Eliza was deeply involved in her real estate projects; Helen, mentally affected by her childless state, tended Gant. When Gant neared death all of the children came home, concerned about his money. Eugene felt only their hatred and resentment of his schooling and before leaving for Harvard he gladly signed a statement, presented by Luke, by which he disclaimed any share of the inheritance. He intended to leave Altamont. On Eugene's last night there, outside his father's shop, he had a vision in which Ben told him that the past was lost forever. Eugene looked eagerly toward the world beyond Altamont.

On his last night before leaving, Eugene has a vision

407

Looking Backward

Novel by Edward Bellamy, 1850–1898. Published 1888. (ML, 22 & T42).

IN ONE RESPECT this is just another "Utopia" novel, but it is historic not only in publishing but in politics. It pictured a Socialist world according to the standards of the 1880s and much that it predicted for the year 2000 came true in American and British legislation of the 1930s. The book had a sensational sale when it was published and it is not unlikely that from its very remote period it still exerted influence on the governmental acts that made some of its dreams come true. As a novel it is just so-so.

Chaps. 1–2. I was born in Boston in 1857. My family was wealthy and lived well. In 1887, at the age of 30, I was engaged to EDITH BARTLETT, a beautiful girl, also of the best society. On Decoration Day, 1887, I left Edith in the early evening, to go home to retire early. I was much troubled with insomnia and when I had been sleepless for several nights, as I had now, it was my practice to have Dr. PILLSBURY, a "quack" who practiced mesmerism, put me to sleep. I had a special subterranean chamber, soundproof and solid, beneath my house, with an airpipe leading out. Dr. Pillsbury put me to sleep on Decoration Day night.

Chaps. 3–4. I was awakened and a man broke the news to me that it was Sept. 10, 2000. I had been in a trance for 113 years. He had been excavating for a new garden and had found me in the subterranean chamber and revived me. I could not believe this until he led me upstairs and showed me the modern city of Boston. I introduced myself as JULIAN WEST; he was Dr. LEETE. He had me meet his wife and his beautiful daughter, EDITH. The evidence seemed to show that my house of 1887 burned down the night I went to sleep and I was presumed dead in the fire.

Chaps. 5–7. Dr. Leete told me of vast changes in life and society that had taken place during my trance. The gradual growth of big business in trusts and cartels finally culminated in state socialism, with all the wealth and capital of the nation in the hands of The Great Trust. This was run for the good of the nation and the people. The change took place without bloodshed. Labor unrest ended. All citizens and labor took it as a matter of course that they had obligations of labor to the state, just as military service was an obligation in the 19th century. People were expected to work for 24 years, beginning at age 21, when education was completed, and ending at 45, when retirement begins. All men have a choice of what they want to do and are fitted for. No

one works harder than another. If work is harder, the hours are shorter. If any work is less popular, the reward is made greater. Professional and management personnel are chosen by aptitude and study.

Chaps. 8–10. I was disturbed by my present situation; Edith Leete comforted me. Dr. Leete continued his story. Money and banks no longer existed. No wages were paid. Everyone received an equal share of the nation's productivity and drew against a "credit card" for all purchases. No saving was necessary; people were expected to use their credits, which otherwise reverted to the state. Everyone's future was guaranteed by the state. All men were expected to do their best and were looked down upon if they didn't. Those who did extra well gained repute, distinction, and power.

Edith Leete took me shopping with her. No need to compare between stores. All merchandise available was the same everywhere. No sales pressure was needed. One bought what one wanted, and the merchandise was delivered later from a central warehouse, via pneumatic tubes. People lived in different types and sizes of houses and had various possessions, but not on the basis of differing levels of wealth, solely on the basis of choice.

Chaps. 11–12. Edith showed me how the finest music of all sorts was available in the home at the push of a button, via telephone and amplifier. There was no need for servants: Laundry and cooking were done centrally, with electricity providing fuel and power. Medical services were provided by the state doctors, all good, but allowing choice among them, and the doctor's fee was deducted from one's credit card.

Chaps. 13–15. I learned more about using transmitted music for night-time relaxation and for being awakened in the morning. Dr. Leete told me that most of the rest of the world was pretty much modeled after the American system. All world relationships were peaceful, wars were outmoded. There was no want; world trade was general, fair, equitable. Prices being general throughout the world, there was no need for profiteering. No money was needed, even for international trade. No nation had a monopoly of any product, and there was even a federal union of sorts in world relationships. It was expected that eventually there would be world unification into one nation. Already emigration from one country to another was freely permitted. Tourism went on as before.

Dr. Leete and Edith took me to dinner to the central community dining house, where all the cooking was done. It was raining heavily and the streets were protected by a waterproof covering that had been let down over the sidewalks. We ate in a private salon, rented annually by my host as an extension of his home, dining excellently. Meals were ordered in advance from anything on the market, as lavishly or as simply as one's tastes dictated. Afterward,

Dr. Leete explained how modern newspapers were no longer subservient to private interests. The newspapers were owned and run by their subscribers.

Chaps. 16–17. An early morning conversation with Edith Leete made me realize that I was becoming interested in her, and apparently she with me. I asked her about her family background, thinking I might be able to tell her something of her great-grandparents, but she put me off. Dr. Leete told me that I was already a celebrity, and that I was being awaited in society as a historian of the 19th century.

Production of the 20th century was regulated solely by demand and priced according to cost alone. The President of the United States was no longer elected by popular suffrage but was selected by the leaders and wisest men of the industrial army, from among retired men who had been top industrial leaders. I protested that men of 45, when retired from labor, as in his system, had many good years left in them. He assured me that the last half of people's lives were the best by far. With retirement came the opportunity for cultural enrichment.

Chaps. 19–21. There were no prisons now, little or no crime. With all men having what they needed, theft was practically unknown. The legal profession was largely unnecessary, but judges existed for certain needs. State governments no longer existed, as they were superfluous. There was no military establishment and no treasury department, there being no need for taxes. There were still police, but only minor need for them. Congress met infrequently and passed few laws. With no private property beyond personal possessions, few laws were needed. Education had become a universal privilege. Instead of only the wealthy or specially franchised getting a college education, everyone got it.

Chaps. 22–25. Dr. Leete explained the source of the greater national wealth. He pointed out the absence, and lack of need, of state and local governments with their expenses and debts. There was little civil service needed, no military establishments to maintain, no criminals to guard against or incarcerate. Financial operations and banking were outmoded. All these represented substantial savings. But the greatest savings came from centralized planning of all activities, doing away with periodic gluts and crises, the absence of irresponsible individuals working at cross purposes, competitively. The waste of labor in periods of unemployment was no longer a drain on the economy.

Edith Leete refused, for the present, to explain to me a remark I thought I remembered hearing her make to her father as I came out of my trance. Her father told me about the position of women in the 20th century. Women were, in almost every respect, the full equals of men. Each had her own full share in the national product. Each was educated as well as men and worked in the industrial army if she was not bearing children. With few or no household chores, they were free for careers and not dependent upon man for support. However, as always, marriage and love were looked upon as natural ends. Women freely told men of their feelings today.

Chaps. 26–28. On Sunday I listened, with the Leetes, to a fine sermon, largely based upon my arrival in this new world, about the vast difference in moral values between the 19th and 20th centuries. Later, somewhat depressed, I mused. I realized I was in love with Edith Leete. She sought me out in my depression, and I told her of my love. She reciprocated it, and confided that it had practically been her duty to love me. Edith Leete was, by strange coincidence, the great-granddaughter of my lost love, Edith Bartlett. When I was found, and Edith Bartlett's picture found in a locket about my neck, they at once knew who I was. Edith Leete did not want me to know until I was sure of my feelings. With the decided approval of the senior Leetes, Edith and I were betrothed.

When I awoke the next morning I was back in 1887, with my faithful personal servant beside me. I found everything in Boston as it had been. I saw the differences of condition of rich and poor; I saw the greed and fear in the faces that I had always taken for granted. I saw the competition and wastefulness of business. I saw the useless financial centers, which I had considered so perfect before my dream. All day I wandered throughout Boston, looking with newly opened eyes at all the familiar things which now seemed so wrong. I ended at Edith Bartlett's house. I tried to tell her and the people there something of the better world of my dream. They could not understand, and finally drove me out to cries of "Madman." I fought them, and, struggling, I awoke in Dr. Leete's house. The 20th century was real, the old Boston the dream.

Lord Jim

Novel by Joseph Conrad (Teodor Jozef Konrad Korzeniowski, 1857–1924). Published 1900. (ML, 186; RE, 85).

THIS IS ONE of the best-known works of Joseph Conrad, who was and by some still is considered a major novelist. It is a good adventure story and in part is a sensitive treatment of a tortured soul for whom the more modern word would be neurotic.

Chaps. 1–3. JIM is a seaman exiled from the sea, an outcast who wanders from seaport to seaport throughout the Orient, hiring himself out as a water-clerk to whoever will pay him and disappearing abruptly whenever the truth about his past is discovered. Originally from a parsonage, Jim felt his vocation for the sea early in life and obtained a berth on a training ship for officers of the mercantile marine. After two years he went to sea and in a short time he became chief mate of a fine ship. He was disabled by a falling spar and had a long convalescence. Then he took a berth as chief mate on the *Patna*, a battered old steamer bound for Mecca with 800 Malayan pilgrims. The ship collided with a floating object and began to go down.

Chaps. 4–14. About a month later, an investigation was gotten under way and Jim was brought in for questioning. During the inquiry he made the acquaintance of a man named MARLOW, who took a special interest in Jim because of his clean, forthright appearance and because he seemed to be suffering some kind of inner torment. Jim told Marlow what happened after the collision. It looked as though the ship would go down at any moment. The one thought in Jim's mind was that there were 800 persons and seven lifeboats. Nothing could save them. As the other members of the crew rushed back and forth in panic, helping to launch one of the lifeboats, Jim stood on the bridge, not knowing what to do. Suddenly he realized with horror that the other officers were lowering the boats for their own escape. He remained on the

Jim and Jewel

bridge, determined to stay with the ship, in spite of the jeers of the rest of the crew, who urged him to save his own skin. Then, just before the lifeboat shoved off, someone yelled "Jump," and he jumped. The minute he hit the boat he wished he could die, but there was no going back. He had deserted with the rest, and he despised himself as much as he despised them. Afterwards, he thought of killing himself, but that would have been the easy way out. To live was far greater torture.

They were picked up by a steamer and learned that the *Patna* did not sink after all. A French gunboat towed her into port. The news of the desertion spread and the inquiry was finally gotten under way. The other officers, a worthless lot, evaded trial, but Jim, determined to regain his lost morality, stayed to face the consequences. The court found that the officers had acted in utter disregard of their plain duty.

Chaps. 15–18. Marlow persuaded a friend of his, a rice-mill owner, to take Jim on. Jim did exceedingly well at his new job until about six months later one of the officers from the *Patna* turned up at the mill. His very presence was a torment to Jim, who left his job abruptly. Thus began Jim's endless running from one town to another.

Chaps. 19–23. Marlow keeps track of Jim, getting him jobs here and there. At last, to help Jim escape from the part of the world where his disgrace occurred, Marlow tells the story to his old friend STEIN, a wealthy and respected merchant who owns trading posts in the most out-of-the-way places. Stein concludes that Jim is a romantic. He punishes himself mercilessly for failing to live up to his high image of himself. Stein decides to appoint Jim manager of his trading post in Patusan, a remote island. He gives Jim a ring to present, as a sort of credential, to DORAMIN, an old native chief whom Stein knew in Patusan many years ago.

Chaps. 24–34. When Jim reaches Patusan he is taken prisoner by Rajah ALLANG, the Royal Governor of Patusan, and is held for three days while the rajah deliberates on his fate. Jim escapes and runs across the island to Doramin's house. He produces Stein's ring and is welcomed like a long-lost friend. Jim learns that the island is divided into two camps, that of Doramin and that of the rajah, who is a cruel and dishonest man who pretends to be the only trader in the country and who puts to death anyone foolish enough to challenge his monopoly. Another man, SHERIF ALI, has been terrorizing people all over the island. With the aid of Doramin's son DAIN WARIS, who becomes Jim's best friend, Jim attacks and defeats Sherif Ali. The beaten man flees the country and when the miserable, hunted villagers crawl out of the jungle back to their houses they appoint Jim head man and virtual ruler of the land. The rajah begins to tremble in fear of Jim. His triumph becomes legendary and supernatural powers are attributed to him. Jim falls in love with the daughter of a beautiful half-caste woman who died some time ago, leaving the girl to live with her brutal stepfather, CORNELIUS. Jim calls her JEWEL, because she is precious, and when he discovers an extraordinary gem—an emerald of enormous size and value—he gives it to her. Marlow visits Jim in Patusan and learns of Jim's success. The natives call him Tuan Jim, meaning Lord Jim. Jewel is instinctively afraid of Marlow, for she feels he has come to take Jim from her, but Jim assures her that he has no intention of leaving Patusan.

Chaps. 35–45. Marlow leaves Patusan, assured that Jim has got his confidence back but somehow feeling that they will never meet again. The end, a romantic end for a romantic youth, comes soon after. "Gentleman" BROWN, a roving cutthroat in need of money and food for himself and his crew, lands on Patusan while Jim is away and tries to plunder Jim's stronghold. Dain Waris takes over and forces Brown and his men up a hill, where they remain besieged but uncaptured until Jim arrives. After lengthy negotiations with Brown, Jim agrees to lift the siege on Brown's promise that he and his men will depart peacefully. Brown goes back on his word as soon as the natives, on Jim's order, withdraw. Egged on by the

evil old Cornelius (who has been filling their heads with promises of wealth) Brown and his men ambush the town. In the struggle that ensues, Dain Waris is killed. The natives (who had not wanted to free Brown) feel that Jim is responsible for his friend's death and will have to pay for it. Jim, having lost the confidence of his fellow men for the second time in his life, no longer wishes to live. He ignores Jewel's pleas to save himself and walks straight through town to offer himself to the father of Dain Waris, Doramin, who shoots him. Jim falls forward, dead. Jewel goes to live in Stein's house, a listless, pathetic figure. Marlow wonders if at last Jim found what he was looking for.

Lorna Doone

Novel by R. D. Blackmore, 1825–1900. Published 1869. (PB, PL508).

THIS WAS one of the most successful of 19th-century novels. It combines the usual appeal of historical fiction (it is set in the middle 17th century when the Stuart dynasty was in its declining years) and the equally natural appeal of a band of well-bred robbers.

Chaps. 1–8. JOHN RIDD, the narrator, a yeoman of the town of Oare, in Somerset, England, tells how, in November 1673, as a boy of 12, he is called back from boarding school to his home. At home, at Plover's Barrow farm, in Exmoor, a moorland region bordering both Somerset and Devon, John learns that his farmer father has been killed by the DOONES, an aristocratic family living as outlaws. Stripped of their lands through family feuds and trouble at Court, the Doones seek their revenge by sacking their immediate vicinity and killing all who resist them. John remains at home with his mother and two sisters, helping to run the farm. One day when he is 14 he wanders into Glen Doone, the outlaws' valley, where he saves himself from drowning in a deep pool and meets LORNA DOONE, a beautiful little girl of about 8, the granddaughter of old Sir ENSOR DOONE, head of the clan. Lorna helps John to escape capture by the outlaws.

Chaps. 9–15. The next year TOM FAGGUS, a cousin of the Ridds and a famous highwayman who has turned to robbery after losing his property in a lawsuit, visits the farm and a close friendship springs up between the cousins. Meanwhile John is growing into a plainspoken, brave young man, the tallest to be seen in Exmoor. When REUBEN HUCKABACK, John's wealthy shopkeeper great-uncle, is robbed by the Doones, he asks John to guide him to a spot where he can view Glen Doone and plan his revenge. John catches a glimpse of

Lorna, now 7 years older and "very light and white, nimble, smooth, and elegant."

Chaps. 16–22. John goes repeatedly to Glen Doone to meet Lorna. She tells him that she is said to be the daughter of Sir Ensor's eldest son but that she cannot recall her mother or father. She speaks of her horror at the violence and lawlessness amidst which she lives.

Chaps. 23–27. JEREMY STICKLES, a messenger in the service of King Charles II, arrives with a document calling upon John to testify in court at London concerning the Doones. John travels to London with Jeremy but is forced to cool his heels for two months before appearing before the Chief Justice, who questions him not only about the Doones but as to whether there is any sentiment against the king in Exmoor.

Chaps. 28–36. At home, John resumes his secret meetings with Lorna, who tells him she is resisting the attentions of her cousin, CARVER DOONE, who seeks to marry her. John confesses his own love for Lorna. She soon declares her love for him. Jeremy Stickles returns to the farm, making it his headquarters while he seeks to uncover a plot against the designation of the king's brother as heir to the throne.

Chaps. 37–44. Worried by Lorna's absence from their meeting place, John goes to Glen Doone at dusk in search of her. He finds that she is virtually the prisoner of Carver Doone, whose father, COUNSELLOR DOONE, is slated to succeed Sir Ensor, now near death, as head of the clan. Lorna promises to signal John if she is in peril. A short time after this, John is cutting saplings on his land when he overhears Carver and two companions waiting to ambush and kill the king's messenger, Jeremy Stickles. John saves Jeremy's life by running swiftly on ahead to warn him. The grateful Jeremy confides that he contemplates leading a band of musketeers against the Doones. John, sick with anxiety over Lorna's safety in the event of an attack, refuses to join in such a scheme. Lorna signals that she needs him and sends her maid,

GWENNY CARFAX, to tell John that the dying Sir Ensor has been told about him by Lorna and insists upon seeing him. He goes to the old man, who points out to him his lowly rank compared with that of Lorna. He asks John to pledge never to see or think of the girl again. But seeing the young people together, he realizes the intensity of their love and, though calling them foolish, does not insist on the pledge. Following Sir Ensor's death, Lorna is threatened by Carver with starvation unless she marries him. John rescues Lorna and Gwenny and carries them off through a deep winter snow across the moors to the farm, to be cared for by his mother.

Chaps. 45–58. Carver comes to the farm and threatens to kill Lorna unless she re-

John with Lorna and Gwenny

turns to the valley. When she refuses, he leads an outlaw force in an unsuccessful attack on the farm. His father, the Counsellor, also comes to the farm and attempts to separate the lovers by saying that John's father killed Carver's and that Lorna's father killed John's. This attempt fails but the Counsellor steals a valuable diamond necklace that has been Lorna's since childhood. Jeremy Stickles tells John of meeting an Italian woman, Lorna's old nurse, who reveals that Lorna is actually the Countess of Dugal, kidnapped by the outlaws in childhood from a wealthy family. The necklace had belonged to the child's true mother. Jeremy and John, with a raw local militia and a few army troopers, attack Glen Doone but fail to defeat the outlaws. Soon after this, John's sister, ANNIE, marries Tom Faggus, now a wealthy squire who has received a pardon from the King.

Chaps. 59–65. Lorna goes to London, where she has been called to appear before the Court of Chancery so that she may be placed in the care of a guardian. John hears nothing from her, while she becomes noted in London for her wealth and beauty. When Tom Faggus leaves home to join the rebel forces supporting the Duke of Monmouth against the new king, James II, Annie sends John to bring him home. John finds Tom wounded in battle and aids him but is himself captured by forces of the king, who believe him to be a rebel. They are about to hang him when he is rescued by Jeremy Stickles.

Chaps. 66–75. On reaching London, John visits Lorna, now a favorite at Court and the ward of her relative, Earl Brandir. When John complains that she has not written to him, it becomes known that Gwenny, the maid, has held back all of Lorna's letters to the farm in an effort to keep her mistress from making so lowly a marriage. Acutely conscious of his low rank, John does not press his suit, although Lorna declares that he must be her husband. He captures three burglars about to rob Earl Brandir, and when these same three men turn out to have been deeply involved in plotting against the king, John is brought before the king and queen and made Sir John Ridd. Returning to Exmoor, he discovers that the Doones, despite a pledge to refrain from robbery and violence during his absence, are again preying on the region. He goes to Carver Doone and asks him to make amends for the clan's recent depredations, but Carver refuses and orders his men to fire on John. John escapes being killed and now agrees to command a force marching against the outlaws. In the battle all the clan's dwellings are burned, and although John has seen to it that all the Doone women and children have been removed to safety, all of the Doone men are killed except the Counsellor and Carver. Carver manages to escape, and the Counsellor tells John that Carver was the slayer of the elder Ridd. John takes back from the Counsellor Lorna's precious diamond necklace but permits the old man to keep one diamond and to escape. Lorna returns to Plover's Barrow farm after the death of her guardian, free now to marry John. Immediately following the wedding, while still in the church, Lorna is shot by Carver. John, believing Lorna dead, rides furiously after Carver and overtakes him. In the terrible struggle which ensues, Carver is beaten and, exhausted, sinks from sight into a bog. Returning home, John discovers that Lorna is alive. They settle down to a placid, happy life on the farm.

Lost Horizon

Novel by James Hilton, 1900–1954. Published 1933 by William Morrow & Co., New York. © 1933 by James Hilton & William Morrow. (PB, 1)

IF NOTHING ELSE, *Lost Horizon* gave the world the name and concept of Shangri-La, the ideal retreat at which one cannot be touched by mundane cares and will have the added advantage of nearly endless youth. The literary world refused for a long time to admit that *Lost Horizon* was worth more than passing mention, but the public found its appeal irresistible. Eventually the book received a great deal of added publicity when President Franklin D. Roosevelt named his mountain hideaway Shangri-La. As literature, the novel is barely adequate to its popular and original treatment of the time-honored Utopia theme.

Prologue. The famous author RUTHERFORD relates to his old friend the incredible story of their schoolmate, HUGH CONWAY, whom he had discovered in a mission hospital in China suffering from shock and the loss of his memory. On the way home to England, Conway regained his memory and related the amazing story that follows, after which he returned "east."

Chaps. 1–2. The potential revolution in Baskul is approaching its climax and orders have been given to evacuate all the white residents. The Maharajah of Chandapore kindly assigns his private plane to four passengers: Miss ROBERTA BRINKLOW, an English missionary; HENRY BARNARD, an American; Hugh Conway, consul in the British consular service, and Hugh's assistant, young Capt. CHARLES MALLISON.

Conway, exhausted by his efforts in evacuating his people, is on his way to England for a brief vacation and reassignment to another post. He has been in the counsular service 10 years and is master of many oriental dialects, but he does not expect to receive any of the prize posts.

After they have been in the air several hours, Mallison notices that the pilot is not the one who originally was assigned to them. He and Conway also notice that they are flying in the opposite direction from their original course, over strange mountain ranges. The plane lands and is refueled by waiting tribesmen. The pilot, who is armed, takes off silently. The passengers are disturbed but Conway assures them that there is nothing they can do but wait.

The plane lurches suddenly and makes a landing on very dangerous terrain. When they go forward to question the pilot, he is unconscious. Miss Brinklow produces a flask of brandy and the pilot is brought around, with difficulty. Weakly, he answers a few questions put to him by Conway; then he dies. Conway tells the others that they have landed on a Tibetan plateau, high in the Himalaya Mountains. The pilot has informed them that they will find shelter and porters in a lamasery called Shangri-La.

Chaps. 3–4. A group of men approach. The leader of the group, a Chinese named CHANG, addresses them in perfect English and tells them that he will escort them to Shangri-La. The journey is hard and steep, with the altitude affecting their breathing. Mallison grumbles but Conway is enthralled by the scenic wonders. The lamasery finally comes into view, rising like petals of a flower with its graceful pavilions clinging to the cliffs. Once inside, the travelers are amazed at the comforts of the

West they find in such a remote corner of the world. Conway, after nearly a decade in China, likes the Chinese and feels at home with their ways. He dines with Chang and finds the atmosphere of the lamasery more Chinese than Tibetan. Chang explains the way of life in Shangri-La. There is moderation in everything and excess in nothing, including virtue. Conway finds himself drifting into the lap of contentment but Mallison challenges Chang about their way of departure. Chang assures him that in a few months porters will come to deliver supplies to the lamasery, and the party may return with these porters. Conway admits to himself that their presence here is not an accident but deliberately planned and they are prisoners, no matter how gently they are treated.

Chaps. 5–6. Conway is surprised at the ease with which Barnard and Miss Brinklow adjust to the two months' wait, and even Mallison stops arguing. They have a grand tour of the lamasery. Among the many treasures displayed is a piano, and a beautiful Manchu girl named LO-TSEN appears and plays for them with great artistry. The calm of Shangri-La lulls them all. Not even the revelation that Barnard is an embezzler, wanted for fraud in the United States, can disturb the peacefulness. After a week Chang tells Conway that he is to be received by the High Lama.

Chaps. 7–8. The High Lama is a very old man. He speaks clear and precise English. He tells Conway the story of a Capuchin monk, Father PERRAULT, who at the age of 34 was lost in the surrounding mountains and found his way to the lamasery. Passing his days reading about Buddhism, he was converted and chose to pass his life in the monastery. When at the age of 108 he lay dying, he miraculously recovered by the use of a narcotic drug, of local origin, with which he had experimented. The wonderful air also contributed greatly. When he was again well, the tribesmen of the valley helped him build Shangri-La and incorporate in it all the beauties of the world. As the story finishes, Conway knows for sure that the High Lama is Father Perrault, and says so. The High Lama tells Conway that he is 250 years old; for those who stay in Shangri-La have the secret of long life. The world, he continues, is running headlong towards destruction and wars, and his hopes are that this retreat will be overlooked until such time as tranquillity returns. He tells Conway that he and his companions were deliberately brought to the lamasery by their pilot. Now they cannot be permitted to leave, for their own safety. Once a visitor left after only a week and died when he returned to the outside world. Conway feels no regret at not returning to the outside world. He agrees not to say anything, for the time being, to his friends.

Chaps. 9–10. Mallison is disappointed that Conway did not ask the High Lama about the porters to lead them back to India, but neither Barnard nor Miss Brinklow seems anxious to leave. The weeks pass

First sight of Shangri-La

leisurely. Conway spends much time with BRIAC, who long ago was a pupil of Chopin. He is told the history of the beautiful Lo-Tsen, a Manchu princess, who was on the way to her wedding, many years before, when her bearers got lost and she was brought to the lamasery. While she appears about 18, she is really 65. After a month, Conway is sent for again by the High Lama. Thereafter they meet often. Conway begins to feel very quietly in love with the little Manchu princess. In one of their talks, the High Lama tells Conway that the time has come for him to die and that he does so gladly. He is leaving Conway in his place as ruler of the lamasery. His only instructions to Conway are to save what is best of civilization for the world when it is finished with wars. He is dead when Conway seeks to question him further.

Chap. 11. Mallison interrupts this solemn moment with the news that the porters have finally arrived. He has made all the arrangements with them through Lo-Tsen, who he says is going with them. Conway is shocked that she wants to leave, for he knows that once she leaves the rarefied atmosphere of the lamasery she will become old and die. As briefly as he can, he tells Mallison the story of Shangri-La as told him by the High Lama. Mallison refuses to believe him, choosing rather to think that Conway is mad. When Conway says he will remain, Mallison goes on alone with Lo-Tsen, with whom he too is in love. But Mallison becomes afraid to make the journey alone. He returns and pleads with Conway to come with them, so that he and Lo-Tsen will have a chance of happiness. Realizing that this boy and girl mean more to him than anything else, Conway goes with them, leaving his sanctuary of happiness.

Epilogue. Rutherford tries to trace Conway in the Orient but learns only that he was brought to the hospital by a very old Chinese woman, who died a short time afterward. Rutherford is convinced that Conway left to try to return to the lamasery. Secretly believing Conway's story, he hopes that Conway has reached Shangri-La.

Lysistrata

Play by Aristophanes, 448–385 B.C.
Produced 411 B.C.

THIS IS ONE of the cleverest ideas and best works of the greatest comic playwright of ancient Greece. It is one of the world's most compelling satires used as propaganda against violence. (When Aristophanes wrote the play there was civil strife within Athens and war against Sparta.) Far ahead of his times, since it was to be many centuries before women were considered capable of direct political influence, Aristophanes suggests that they contribute to peace by withholding their bodies from their husbands. In the name of the play and title of the heroine there is a play on words, since the Greek *lysis* means "I am cured (of disease)." A modern Belgian motion picture, *The Baker's Wife,* applied the same idea to war-prevention in modern times, but though the movie was a great success it did not cause the wives of the world to prevent World War II.

The play opens at the gate leading up to the main hill of Athens, the Acropolis. It is morning and LYSISTRATA (whose name means "Army-Disbander") is pacing, waiting for some women to assemble. Her friend CALONICE comes and Lysistrata says she has called this meeting of Athenian women in order to end the disastrous war with Sparta. Soon MYRRHINE, LAMPITO, and many other women come to learn Lysistrata's plan. Lysistrata learns that they, like herself, are miserable because their men are away. She says that the women of Greece must join together to end this male stupidity. They must all withhold their bodies from their husbands. At first the women are shocked by the proposal, but gradually they are struck by its ingenuity. They sacrifice wine into a large bowl, take an oath of continence, and pass through the gate to isolation on the Acropolis.

A CHORUS OF OLD MEN, who are the only men left at Athens, enters. They have heard about Lysistrata's plan and have come to burn down the gates. While they are kindling a fire, a CHORUS OF OLD WOMEN appears and douses it with water; then they douse the old men too. A pitched battle ensues and an Athenian MAGISTRATE enters with four Scythian (Russian) policemen. The policemen do not dare approach the vicious old women, for Lysistrata and the young women pelt them with eggs and garlic from the wall. Still the Magistrate is too vainly masculine to acknowledge Lysistrata's power. He says that women belong at home. Lysistrata shouts that men ought to use plain domestic sense. She speaks up for giving citizenship to foreigners and for consolidating Greek colonies and expanding the Athenian democracy. The Magistrate, bawling that war is men's business, is first dressed as a woman, then as a corpse, and finally is led off the stage. The old men and women resume their quarrel.

A few days pass. Some of the women try to make excuses to see their husbands. One hides a helmet under her dress and pretends to be pregnant. Lysistrata upbraids them for their weakness and they all go back through the gate. The old men and women return, singing insulting songs to each other. Myrrhine's husband, CINESIAS, appears, very distressed, with a slave who carries their baby. He begs his wife to come to him, using every sort of cajolery, and she slowly descends from the wall. After a brief kiss, however, Myrrhine insists that Cinesias sue for peace with the Spartans. He keeps agreeing, but Myrrhine goes back anyway. Cinesias moans tragically.

A Spartan HERALD enters, also much excited. He announces to the Magistrate that the women of Sparta are imitating the women of Athens. The Magistrate tells the Herald to send some ambassadors and they will discuss peace, for they cannot overcome the women. The choruses exchange insults. Groups of Spartan and Athenian AMBASSADORS enter. They are so eager to have their wives back that they are ready

412

to acknowledge Lysistrata's will. Lysistrata passes out through the gates, carrying a nude statue of the female goddess RECONCILIATION. She curses the men for killing the babies women bring into the world, and for slaying fellow Greeks while barbaric Persians lurk nearby. The men succumb to Lysistrata's beauty and conclude a hasty peace. The Ambassadors pass through the gates to the Acropolis, where a great banquet is held, and both Spartans and Athenians dance. Lysistrata urges them to forget their differences in the future and live in peace.

Macbeth

Play by William Shakespeare, 1564–1616.
Produced about 1605.

LITERATURE HARDLY CONTAINS a greater work than this. *Macbeth* dramatizes the power of suggestion on a man of ambition and imagination, the suggestion being supplied in two ways, first by the imagination itself (the significance of the witches who predict that Macbeth will be king), and then directly by the man's wife. Lady Macbeth is one of the finest parts Shakespeare wrote for a woman and it has been so recognized by the great English actresses. The sustained poetic excellence reaches a matchless height in Act V, Scene 3, when Lady Macbeth has died and Macbeth mourns in his speech "Tomorrow, and tomorrow, and tomorrow. . ." Of a piece with the general profundity of the play is the theme expressed in passing by the witches (called the "weird sisters" by Shakespeare), "Fair is foul and foul is fair."

Act I. 1. Three WITCHES meet in a thunderstorm. They agree to meet again on the heath, to prophesy to MACBETH, the thane of Glamis. **2.** King DUNCAN is told that Macbeth and BANQUO have defeated a rebellion by the thane of Cawdor, a Scottish nobleman. The king sends two noblemen to tell Macbeth he is the new thane of Cawdor. **3.** On the heath, the witches tell Macbeth that he will be thane of Cawdor, then king, and Banquo that his descendants will be kings. The two nobles arrive with the confirmation of part of the news. This makes Macbeth think that the rest of the prophecy may come true, too. **4.** Macbeth and Banquo return from their mission. The king makes his son MALCOLM Duke of Cumberland. Macbeth is conscious that Malcolm stands in the way of his becoming king. **5.** At Inverness, Lady Macbeth hears the king will stay at their castle that night. Macbeth comes home and together they plot the assassination of the king. **6–7.** Duncan arrives. Macbeth decides he cannot kill the king, being his host and kinsman. Lady Macbeth berates his cowardice. Macbeth gives in.

Act II. 1. On his way to Duncan's chamber Macbeth talks briefly with Banquo, then soliloquizes: "Is this a dagger which I see before me? . . . Come, let me grasp thee." **2.** Lady Macbeth has drugged the grooms attending Duncan's room. Macbeth returns and tells her he has committed the murder. He has stabbed Duncan in his sleep. But he reproaches himself already. **3.** MACDUFF, a nobleman, arrives at the castle to see the king. The murder is discovered and Macbeth pretends to be griefstricken. **4.** Duncan's sons MALCOLM and DONALBAIN fear they may be next, and flee abroad. Macbeth has the groom at the king's chamber put to death to divert suspicion from himself. The flight of the princes makes them suspects. Macbeth, as kinsman, becomes king.

Act III. 1. Macbeth is worried because the witches said Banquo's descendants, not his own, would be kings. He announces a state banquet in Banquo's honor and hires assassins to waylay Banquo and his son on their way to the feast. **2.** Lady Macbeth berates her husband for looking worried. He should forget the past and show his nobles a brighter face, lest they suspect his guilt. **3.** The murderers find Banquo and his son FLEANCE. They kill Banquo but the boy escapes. **4.** The banquet begins. The murderers report to Macbeth that Banquo is dead. Banquo's ghost appears and sits in Macbeth's chair. Macbeth talks to the ghost, whom no one else can see. The nobles become suspicious. Macbeth pretends it is an illness. Lady Macbeth breaks up the dinner to save her husband further embarrassment. **5.** HECATE, the chief witch, berates the three witches for having helped Macbeth. She considers him evil and wants him done away with. **6.** Malcolm has made overtures to Macduff to overthrow Macbeth. The English Earl of Northumberland may help them drive the tyrant out.

Act IV. 1. Macbeth goes to the witches for another prophecy. They tell him to beware of Macduff; to "be bloody, bold, and resolute," for none born of woman can harm him; and that he will be safe as long as Birnam Wood does not move to Dunsinane, his castle. But then he is shown eight descendants of Banquo who will be kings. LENNOX, one of Macbeth's nobles, brings the news that Macduff has fled to England to join Malcolm. **2.** Macbeth has Macduff's wife and children killed. **3.** In England, Malcolm and Macduff bemoan their misfortunes. Word of the murders reaches Macduff.

Act V. 1. At Dunsinane, Lady Macbeth is a subject of worry for her doctor. She walks in her sleep and talks of bloody deeds. **2.** Macbeth's nobles discuss the approaching English army. They decide to march toward Birnam Wood. **3.** Macbeth is not worried about the battle. One of his officers, SEYTON, brings him his armor. **6.** The attacking soldiers cut the branches behind which to hide as they advance. Birnam Wood is moving against Macbeth. **5.** Seyton reports that the queen is dead. Macbeth has time to grieve only briefly: "Tomorrow, and tomorrow, and tomorrow, creeps in this petty pace from day to day . . . Life is a tale told by an idiot, full of sound and fury, signifying nothing." **6.** The soldiers cut the branches down and the battle begins. Macduff and Macbeth meet face to face. Macduff informs him he was not born of a woman, but was cut out of the womb before his time. Macbeth is killed, and Malcom acclaimed King of Scotland.

Macbeth returns to the witches on the heath

413

Madame Bovary

Novel by Gustave Flaubert, 1821–1880. Published 1857. (ML, 28 & T17; RE, 2; PB, PL69).

UNIVERSALLY ACKNOWLEDGED to be one of the greatest novels of world literature, *Madame Bovary* may yet not be appreciated by an ' English reader of today who encounters one of the earlier and quite inept translations. Flaubert was a peerless stylist and in those translations the excellence of his style simply did not get through. In his picture of a bored wife who found natural but indefensible compensation in debt and adultery, and of a stupid husband who was too fond to observe and too insensitive to preclude the causes, Flaubert was a pioneer among novelists (in his day the novel was considered wicked). But such a theme has become commonplace and it is to the masterly treatment that *Madame Bovary* owes its continued high repute. The translation by Charlotte Underwood for Winston (Philadelphia) is an excellent one.

Part I. Chaps. 1–3. Thanks to his mother's determination to make a doctor of him, CHARLES BOVARY, a lazy and ungifted student, finally receives his medical degree. His mother is also responsible for his marriage to HELOISE DUBUC, an ugly widow, twice his age, but with a nice annual income. Heloise learns that Charles' frequent visits to a farm some 18 miles away are due chiefly to his interest in EMMA ROUAULT, the farmer's attractive daughter. Heloise badgers Charles until he swears he will never return to the Rouaults'. It is discovered that Heloise is not a woman of means but is nearly penniless. Charles' father rages at Heloise, and at his wife for arranging the match. But a week later Heloise has a stroke and dies. Charles gradually resumes his visits to the Rouaults. Emma's father, a self-indulgent peasant, is not averse to being relieved of a daughter who is of no use to him around the farm and he prompts Charles into proposing marriage to Emma.

Chaps. 4–6. Charles is completely enchanted with his young bride, but Emma is bored and depressed as a wife. Before marriage she imagined herself in love with Charles, but Charles is too commonplace, and too preoccupied with his work, to find time for the attentions that Emma fancies she needs.

Chaps. 7–9. The Marquis d' ANDERVILLIERS, who has great respect for Charles' skill as a doctor and is indebted to him for some cuttings from the superb cherry trees in the Bovary garden, has asked the young couple to a ball at his chateau. Emma is intoxicated by the glamour and elegance of this party and is more dissatisfied with the life she is doomed to lead with a country doctor. As time goes on the memory of the ball obsesses her. She neglects her obligations and household duties. When she finally realizes the ball will not have a sequel, her health becomes undermined and she develops palpitations and a dry chronic cough. Charles, who is more in love with Emma than ever, decides that a change of scene is indicated. He abandons the practice he has built up in four years, and they move to Yonville L'Abbaye, a large market town near Rouen. For the first time since their marriage, Emma is pregnant.

Part II. Chaps. 1–3. The Bovarys spend the night of their arrival in Yonville at an inn. A young law clerk, LEON DUPUIS, seeks them out. Dupuis and Emma enjoy each other's company and share many opinions. Emma gives birth to a little girl, whom she christens BERTHE, a name she heard at the chateau ball. She puts the baby out to nurse with the wife of a carpenter on the other side of town. Some six weeks later, Emma pays her first visit to little Berthe. She encounters Leon and they share the long walk back. There is an unspoken sympathy between them. After this, Leon, accompanied by Homais, the town apothecary, calls on the Bovarys several times.

Chaps. 4–8. At Homais' house, where Leon boards, Leon often sees Emma and Charles at little soirees and an odd, mute flirtation develops betwen Leon and Emma. He is shy and Emma seems inaccessibly virtuous. She, in turn, cannot quite make up her mind. His vague attitude disquiets her and keeps her in suspense. Leon decides to escape his conflicts by going to Paris to complete his legal studies. Emma curses herself for having driven him off by her own lack of demonstrativeness. Once again, Emma's spiritual ills assert themselves physically and she is seized with "spells" and "attacks." The arrival of RODOLPHE BOULANGER, the new owner of a chateau and farm near Yonville, ends her mooning for Leon. Rodolphe appears at Dr. Bovary's to have one of his men treated. He is taken with Emma at first sight, but unlike Leon he is accomplished in the art of seduction.

Chaps. 9–12. Rodolphe pays court to Emma in terms of her own romanticism and has little difficulty in overcoming her scruples. As the affair progresses through the winter, Rodolphe loses some of his ardor but Emma becomes more amorous. She also feels a mounting aversion to her husband. Charles has been collaborating with Homais on a machine to cure the deformity of a club-footed local stableman. When the experiments fail and gangrene sets in, Homais proclaims himself a mere observer and Charles suffers the censure of the community. Charles comes to Emma for consolation but she repulses his advances. She decides she must get out of his reach. Rodolphe, after attempting to discourage her, agrees to leave Yonville with Emma and little Berthe. They set their elopement for eight weeks in the future.

Chaps. 13–15. Rodolphe never seriously intends to go through with the plan. The night before their scheduled flight he writes Emma a farewell note. Emma's first impulse is suicidal, but circumstances prevent her from taking her life. She then has paroxysms and fainting spells and brain fever sets in. She is ill for months. Charles remains at her side, giving up his patients and all outside interests. By the time she is well, Charles is swamped by bills and is obliged to borrow a sizable sum from Yonville's unofficial moneylender, with whom Emma has already had secret dealings. Emma now becomes very active in charitable work. She and Charles go on a pleasure trip to Rouen. Emma is carried away by the opera *Lucia de Lammermoor*, thinking her own experience similar. At the opera they meet Leon Dupuis. Charles must return to his practice in Yonville but he suggests that Emma stay over in Rouen for the opera.

Part III. Chaps. 1–3. Leon has acquired polish and worldliness. He calls on Emma the next day and is no longer reticent. A new love affair brings a new docility to Emma. She returns to Yonville promptly on the date suggested by Charles. Charles has just received word of his father's sudden death. Emma's mother-in-law comes to Yonville to visit. The prospect of an inheritance brings the moneylender to Emma. He urges her to obtain her husband's power of attorney. Charles suggests that Emma consult Leon on legal aspects of the estate. She returns to Rouen and her reunion with Leon is like a honeymoon.

Chaps. 4–6. Emma arranges to take piano lessons again, so she can make a weekly visit to Rouen and see Leon. The love affair flourishes. Emma is often caught in contradictions or lies about her activities in the city, but Charles fails to suspect the truth. Emma squanders his money on finery and on costly gifts for Leon. She pays off her most pressing debts by using her power of attorney and selling a piece of Charles' recently inherited property. The transaction is handled by the moneylender and she signs notes and borrows more. Charles finally learns about this when it is time to meet the notes. He appeals to his mother to buy up the notes and he cancels Emma's power of attorney, as his mother has wished. Emma chafes at the enforced economy. Her relationship with Leon comes to be punctuated with quarrels and reproaches. When Emma is threatened with legal action by her creditors for a debt of 8,000 francs, and Leon is unable and not particularly anxious to help her, their relationship ends.

Chaps. 7–11. Emma's name is publicly posted in Yonville for the sum owed, as a preliminary to confiscating her property. She frantically turns to Rodolphe for help and when he, too, is unable to produce the money she needs, she abuses him. Emma knows that Charles, who is away on a trip, will return to find himself homeless and

Emma dies slowly from the arsenic she swallowed

bankrupt. Emma swallows a large dose of arsenic and dies slowly and agonizingly, to the lamentations of her husband, who has returned but too late to be of any help. Charles is tormented by grief. Hounded on every side by creditors, he goes even more deeply into debt to prevent anything that Emma ever owned from being sold.

Then one day he comes upon her love letters from Leon and Rodolphe. The actual evidence of Emma's adulteries is too much for him. Soon after this discovery, his daughter Berthe finds him dead. She is left to the tender mercies of her grandmother, with 12 francs that are her father's entire estate.

Mademoiselle de Maupin

Novel by Théophile Gautier, 1811–1872.
Published 1835.

GAUTIER WAS PRIMARILY a poet but his literary recognition cannot suffer from this novel. He was the earliest, or at least one of the earliest, of competent writers who recognized what modern novelists have been stressing for more than 30 years now—the extent to which sexual dreams and unfulfilled desires can monopolize the consciousness of the young man and woman. As an extravagant romance, *Mademoiselle de Maupin* can also be considered acceptable reading, though it is hard to believe that anyone ever took seriously the efforts of the writers of former ages (including Shakespeare) to have the same person double as an attractive man and an attractive woman.

Chaps. 1–3. D'ALBERT is 22 years old. Although he has had affairs with women, none satisfies his dreams. He would like to have a mistress but has not met anyone who meets with his standards of voluptuous perfection. His friend DE C——, a connoisseur of female beauty, on various occasions has offered to introduce D'Albert to his various female acquaintances. Now D'Albert accepts, but he is left cold by his first half-dozen encounters. De C—— calls D'Albert's attention to a lovely creature, in the house they are visiting, who has been inviting him with her handsome black eyes. D'Albert finds her provocative and alluring. Not too long afterwards, she becomes his mistress. D'Albert finds ROSETTE —he has named her after a rose dress she wore on their first meeting—satisfying in every way, yet after two months spent constantly in her company he feels curiously unfulfilled.

Chaps. 4–8. D'Albert's relationship with Rosette continues for five months. Rosette is aware that he is more in love with love than with her; but she finds him a perfect lover and lavishes affection on him. The lovers have moved to Rosette's chateau and Rosette, to give D'Albert some diversion, has begun to invite company. One of the guests is a young and handsome cavalier.

called THÉODORE DE SÉRANNES. D'Albert is beguiled by Théodore's beauty. In its blending of masculine and feminine perfection, it is the closest approximation of D'Albert's secret ideal that he has encountered. He finds himself wishing he were a woman. Rosette has nursed an unrequited passion for Théodore for years. She visits Théodore privately in his room and confesses to him that her love for him is as passionate as ever. Théodore reacts to her declaration of love tactfully but evasively. The next day Théodore's 14-year-old page boy, ISNABEL, is thrown from his horse and Rosette, the only one to witness the accident, tries to revive him. When she unbuttons his shirt, she discovers that the page actually is a girl. She is shocked, drawing the obvious conclusions. D'Albert, in the meantime, is compelled to admit to himself that he is in love with a man.

Chaps. 9–11. D'Albert now vacillates between believing that Théodore is a woman in disguise, and rationalizing his love for a member of his own sex. Théodore surely has the looks of a woman; yet at the hunt, mounting a horse or taking a jump, he displays an expertness that few men can equal. Théodore, who actually is a woman, explains her deception in a letter to her friend GRACIOSA. As a girl she determined to maintain her distance from the opposite sex until she had fathomed its secrets and could tell the base and evil from the good. Therefore she concealed her identity as MADELAINE DE MAUPIN and mastered the masculine arts of dueling, hunting, riding and such. When she is convinced she has met a man worthy of her, she will restore Mlle. de Maupin to life. D'Albert suggests to the company at the chateau that they stage a production of Shakespeare's *As You*

Rosette discovers that Théodore's page is a girl

415

Like It. Rosette's guests fall in eagerly with this idea. The part of Orlando goes to D'Albert, *Rosalind* to Rosette, and *Jaques* to Théodore. Rosette refuses her rôle when she discovers that Rosalind goes through two-thirds of the play dressed as a man. The part then falls to Théodore. At the rehearsal Théodore's beauty as a woman is so striking that the company is left breathless. D'Albert knows definitely now that his Théodore is a woman. He notices, too, that Rosette's reaction is almost as violent as his own; Rosette has suddenly realized why her love for Théodore has been, and will remain, unrequited. D'Albert decides, despite the fact that they are living under the same roof, to write Théodore a love letter.

Chaps. 12–14. Mlle. de Maupin, in another letter to Graciosa, tells of her past adventures as Théodore. She had to share a bed with a man at a crowded inn and her bedfellow, whose name was ALCIBIADES, invited her to visit the chateau of his aunt, a marchioness. As Théodore she made quite an impression on Alcibiades' sister, a lovely young widow (Rosette). Théodore, to render the masquerade more convincing, entered into a mild flirtation with Rosette. Rosette, unfortunately, fell madly in love with Théodore and the marchioness invited Théodore to be Rosette's suitor. Théodore declined gracefully, explaining that as a youngest son without any prospects of an inheritance he was planning to enter a monastic order. Théodore was surprised in his bedroom by a visit from Rosette, who began to make impassioned love to him. In this compromising position, Rosette and Théodore were discovered by Alcibiades. He suggested that the Chevalier de Sérannes marry his sister. When Théodore declined, Alcibiades was obliged to challenge him. They crossed swords on the spot, and Alcibiades was wounded. Almost fainting at the sight of the blood, Théodore quit the chateau, leaving Alcibiades for dead and Rosette in a swoon.

Chaps. 15–17. Théodore remained at an inn near the chateau long enough to ascertain that Alcibiades was not seriously wounded. At the inn, Théodore fell in with rowdy male company, with whom he traveled, learning to drink and swear like a trooper, to be tough and boisterous and crude. The only thing Théodore did not learn from his male associations is how to respect men. He acquired his young page, Isnabel, when he discovered the 14-year-old girl about to yield to the blandishments of a debauched and repulsive middle-aged prince. Despite her contempt for men, Madelaine de Maupin still wanted to have a lover and experience true sensual gratification. She received a beseeching letter from Rosette and accepted the young widow's request to visit her. She found Rosette with an "established lover," D'Albert. Madelaine found D'Albert attractive. Her revelation of her true sex, by playing Rosalind, was not entirely unintentional. And now, she

writes to Graciosa, since D'Albert is the first man to probe her disguise, he will also be the first man to instruct her in the ways of love. She will yield to him as soon as she hits on a way poetic enough to match his letter and his expectations.

For more than a fortnight, D'Albert is kept in suspense. Théodore gives him no indication that she received his letter. D'Albert has begun to doubt his own judgment; he may have been in error about Théodore's sex; or, if she is a woman, she can only be disregarding his eloquent declaration out of contempt. One afternoon,

he is standing at the window of his room considering a number of desperate alternatives, when Théodore enters, in all her womanly beauty. She spends the night with him, surrendering her whole being to him in her pent-up excitement and voluptuousness. Then she and her page ride out of the chateau, never to return. D'Albert receives a letter from her saying it is better this way than to face the boredom and disillusionment that come with overfamiliarity and the passing years. She has left fresh the memory of one ecstatic night of love, which they both can cherish now for eternity.

The Magic Mountain

Novel by Thomas Mann, 1875–1955. Published 1924. Published & © 1927 by Alfred A. Knopf, Inc.; © 1952 by Thomas Mann. Translated from the German by H. T. Lowe-Porter.

THIS IS ONE of the most respected works of a great and universally respected writer. Thomas Mann used this novel to ruminate on the knowledge and experience of the intellectual man, including many of the admitted imponderables. He used for a setting a sanatorium where the outer world is shut out, somewhat in the same way that Indian thinkers deliberately shut it out, and where time seems to stand still. A return to the less pleasant realities is skillfully engineered by the adventitious arrival of World War I and the conflicting emotions it arouses. Readers have read into *The Magic Mountain* much symbolism, including the idea that the tuberculosis of the sanatorium symbolizes the moral disease or disintegration of the 20th century. The ending of the novel leaves one vaguely unhappy; it might even be called tragic.

Chaps. 1–2. A quiet, unassuming young man named HANS CASTORP arrives at the Sanatorium Berghof in the Swiss Alps for a three week's visit to his cousin, JOACHIM ZIEMSSEN, who has tuberculosis. Castorp, an engineering student, is struck by the international flavor of the place, with its constant overtone of death and sickness. He enjoys the clean, wholesome life in the mountains as opposed to the crowded city of Hamburg where he was born. Hans' mother and father are dead and he was brought up by his kindly but stern grandfather, then lived with his uncle, Consul TIENAPPEL. His life up to this, his 23rd year, has been uneventful, and in every respect Hans seems a normal young man. His decision to visit his afflicted cousin proves to change his life.

Chap. 3. As Hans penetrates the Berghof society, he finds distinctions drawn between the "good" Russian table and the "bad." The good Russian table is frequented by a charming woman, Mme. CHAUCHAT, who married a Frenchman. Hans meets SETTEMBRINI, an Italian who resembles an organ-grinder. Settembrini, a political writer, tells Hans, "I am a humanist." After a time, Hans enjoys the Berghof but begins to acquire his cousin's fear of the two directing doctors, BEHRENS and KROKOWSKI. One day Hans coughs blood and feels dizzy. The almost satanic Settembrini suggests that he may not leave the sanatorium as soon as he planned.

Chap. 4. Hans still has not had an opportunity to speak with Madame Chauchat. Through a schoolteacher, Fräulein ENGELHART, he learns that Mme. Chauchat's first name is CLAVDIA. At the same time that Clavdia attracts him with her Asiatic features, Settembrini lectures Hans against the asceticism and violence of the East. Settembrini insists that all culture springs from a Western attention to rationalism, science, and coherent art. Hans is interested but not convinced. He attends Dr. Krokowski's lecture and hears that "all disease is only love transformed." A long walk in the mountains gives Hans a severe fainting and bleeding spell. Hans suspects that he is not free of the disease that plagues his new friends. On what was to be the last day of his stay, Fräulein VON MYLENDONK, the directress of the sanatorium, takes a temperature reading and discovers that Hans has a high fever. She sends him to Behrens and Krokowski, who agree that Hans is tubercular. Almost with a sense of relief, Hans takes his place among the patients.

Chap. 5. Time begins to assume new meaning for Hans, in the daily routine of the sanatorium. Three months pass more quickly than the first three weeks. As a new patient he finds himself among the lower class of the Berghof, but Joachim gives him constant companionship. One day Behrens permits Hans to examine Joachim's chest under X-ray, and Hans at last senses what it means to die. Death seems present

all around the sanatorium, even in the lovely Clavdia, whom he is afraid to approach. The mere thought of the Russian beauty causes his temperature to soar to a dangerous degree. Hans preserves his ideal love despite Settembrini's clever mockery and Doctor Behrens' cold analysis of human beauty, in which both life and death are processes of oxidation. Hans spends most of his time studying anatomy and chemistry. He acquires a thorough knowledge of animal forms, but the fundamental spirit of life cannot be defined in these terms. The Christmas season passes by with quiet frivolity, punctuated by the deaths of the hopeless cases in the secluded wings. Then at a Carnival Ball before the Lenten season, Hans at last works up enough courage to speak to Clavdia. Because he has drunk too much, he talks wildly and almost incoherently of his love. Clavdia answers cagily. The whole conversation, conducted in French, almost proves to be a non-sequitur. Eventually, however, Clavdia succumbs to Hans' drunken, poetic rhapsody.

Chap. 6. In the spring Clavdia returns to Russia. Behrens assures Hans that she will return, for she will never be wholly cured. Hans turns his attention to botany. Settembrini introduces him to a friend named NAPHTA, who lives in the nearby village. Naphta is a short, incredibly ugly teacher. Settembrini calls him "the scholastic" because he extols faith above reason. Hans hears the two men debate every aspect of human knowledge with intense perception.

Settembrini defends reason, science, and progress against faith, religion, and mystic communion with God. In August Joachim is given the startling news that he is cured. Joachim packs his bags and almost sadly bids farewell to Hans. Hans is visited by his uncle Tienappel, who insists that his nephew is well and must leave. He cannot persuade Hans to depart. As Hans moves into his second year of residence on the mountain, he considers Settembrini and Naphta two medieval adversaries who are struggling for his soul. Settembrini is the Devil and Naphta is a stereotyped God. One day, while walking alone in the mountains, Hans becomes lost in a snowstorm. There in the blinding flurries he has a vision in which he imagines an earthly paradise with groves, temples, and mother-goddesses. During this vision he decides that the issues of good and evil represented by his two friends do not present the whole story of life. Neither "mystic community" nor "windy individualism" offers an answer; "it is love, not reason, that is stronger than death." Poets with their magic dream of perfection, such as Castorp's vision, intuit the whole picture of moral endeavor. At this point Hans surpasses the limited logical knowledge of his eloquent friends. Unfortunately, on returning to the safety of the Berghof Hans finds the vision slipping away from his mind. News arrives that Joachim is returning to the sanatorium. Hans joyfully receives his cousin again. With Joachim is his mother, LOUISA ZIEMSSEN. Behrens confides to Hans that his cousin's condition is hopeless. Strangely, Joachim seems happier to be back on the mountain than he was on the plain. He soon dies.

Chap. 7. Eventually Clavdia returns. Soon afterward a 60-year-old, strong Dutch planter from Java arrives. He is called PIETER PEEPERKORN and is one of the most ebullient personalities in the sanatorium. Peeperkorn is suffering from a mysterious tropical fever but in no way resembles a sick man. His outgoing personality attracts everyone. Jealously Hans realizes that Clavdia is in love with the strange old man. One day, as a joke, Peeperkorn commands Hans to kiss Clavdia. When Hans refuses, he suspects that they have been in love with each other. Eventually Hans confesses their brief affair. The old man does not seem to be hurt by the news, but not long afterward he is found dead. After Peeperkorn's death, Hans is reunited with Clavdia. The love affair no longer has any magic, however, and Hans becomes depressed. His disillusionment is lightened somewhat by music, which he studies intensively. Hans also experiments briefly with seances, since a Danish girl named ELLY BRAND claims to have occult power. The girl manages to conjure some people into seeing Joachim's ghost, but Hans turns on the light in the room and the ghost disappears. As the years pass Settembrini and Naphta continue their endless debates. One day Naphta becomes so highly incensed at his humanist friend that he challenges him to a duel. At first everyone believes that the challenge is a joke, but Naphta issues it with deadly seriousness. Settembrini appears at the appointed place, but fires his shot into the air, refusing to aim at his friend. Naphta, enraged, shoots himself in the head and dies immediately.

Hans remains at the Berghof until the seventh year has passed. His only close companion during the last years is Settembrini. Hans comes to believe that only Settembrini's ideas of progress and humanity are tolerable. Then World War I begins. Settembrini rushes off to Italy to lead his nation's youth into the combat. The remainder of the cosmopolitan inhabitants of the Berghof scatter as enemies, Hans among them. His vision in the snow has long since disappeared, leaving only a vague sensation of its meaning. As Hans scrambles in and out of the foxholes of the battlefield, he hopes that love will one day prevail.

The two men debate every aspect of human knowledge

The Maid Silja

Novel by Frans Sillanpää, 1888–1964. Published 1931. Translation from the Finnish by Alexander Matson published and © 1933 by the Macmillan Co., New York.

THE FINNISH AUTHOR of this beautiful novel won the Nobel Prize in literature for 1939 and one who reads the novel, even with the disadvantage of reading it in translation, can readily understand why that honor went to him. It is not a happy novel and its ending makes it a tragic one, but like human life it has its happy moments mixed with its frustration and misfortunes. *The Maid Silja* well rewards the reading.

Chaps. 1–3. When death came to SILJA SALMELUS at 22, it was important because she was the last of her family. Her death was the end of a long chain of events that began 30 years before when her father, KUSTAA, inherited the Salmelus farm. Before Kustaa inherited the farm, he was a shy young man and very lonely after the death of his mother. In his longing for female softness and warmth he turned to HILMA, the servant girl of the household. She denied him nothing, and there grew between them an unbreakable closeness. Kustaa's father was not long in seeing what was passing between the girl and his son. He ordered her from the house, but Kustaa found her in her parents' home and continued to live with her.

Kustaa's father died and Hilma returned to the farm. She became pregnant and they married quietly. They were happy except that Hilma's family, the PLIHTARI, upset Kustaa. They were a whining, greedy lot, envious of Hilma's good fortune in getting a husband of substance. On a visit of Hilma and Kustaa to the Plihtari family, IIVARI, Hilma's brother, was drunk and insulted Hilma. Kustaa became furious and attacked Iivari. The next morning she began her labor pains and the child was born dead. The death made them closer and gradually they withdrew from contact with the outside world.

Chaps. 4–8. The years passed and a boy, TAAVETTI, and a girl, LAURA, were born to Hilma and Kustaa. They were sickly children. The days after their birth were hard ones for Kustaa. Hilma had been of little help in his struggle with the farm and he was forced to sign a note to the master of Roimalaa. Kustaa took to drinking. More notes were signed and it became a fight to retain the farm. Birth came for the fourth time, a girl, christened CECILIA but called SILJA. Her arrival brought the husband and wife together again, so it was not with great

regret that Kustaa sold the farm, paid his notes, and bought a smaller house and tract of land to the south. Before they could leave for their new home, Taavetti and Laura died. The grieving parents were not long settled in their new surroundings before Hilma died. Kustaa was left with his only child. Little Silja and her father lived together in complete companionship and joy. The child was Kustaa's only tie to life. As she grew to young womanhood, contact with the neighbors became more frequent. Silja became aware of restrictions of their life, but her love for her father, who was now an old man, was the pivot of her life.

Chaps. 9–12. Kustaa died alone while Silja was in the village preparing for her confirmation. The money she inherited was small and it was necessary for her to go to work as a maid at a farm, Nukari. She was quite content at the farm and as she reached her 17th birthday she began to go about steadily with her first "courter," OSKARI TONTTILA. Her innocence shone forth with such clarity that no one thought ill of their constant attachment. While Oskari was away for a year to work, a relative of the family came from America to visit. On his first night at the farm, he forced his way into Silja's bed against her wishes. This scandal soon got about the village and when Oskari returned, he avoided Silja. The mistress of Nukari, herself a comely woman, became jealous of the maid and made arrangements for her to go elsewhere. As Silja did not mind where she went, she went to another farm, Siiveri, which was bigger and more prosperous than the little, old-fashioned Nukari.

Chaps. 13–16. Silja did not stay long at Siiveri, for its master became involved in a prolonged strike of his workers. Because of her beauty, Silja was gossiped about unjustly, and it was with no regret that she left to go further south for her new position. She went to work at the Rantoo Villa

Silja gave in to grief

for Professor RANTOO and began the happiest days of her life, for her master was a kindly man. During her first summer there, Silja fell in love with ARMAS. They passed many romantic evenings together, quietly, without the knowledge of the Rantoo household, for the Professor's daughter, Miss LAURA, also found the young man attractive. Silja now had found a reason for living. She had no thoughts of the future, only for the enjoyment of the present. Silja's daydreams were cut short when Laura announced at breakfast one morning that Armas was leaving that day. He had told Silja nothing of his departure.

Chaps. 17–20. Armas came to the Rantoo Villa to say goodbye to Miss Laura and the Professor. He looked for Silja but did not find her, for she hid behind a door. Silja knew that life would never be the same again. She ran from the house to the woods, where in a state of semi-delirium she gave way to her grief. Her wish was to die. She was discovered in this state by her friend, SOPHIA, who carried her to her cottage. The Professor came to see her and told Sophia it would be a long time before she regained her health, for life no longer mattered to the little maid. For days and weeks, she lay with her mind wandering beyond earthly things. When life finally dragged her back to reality, the Professor was moving to another part of the country and she had to look elsewhere for work. With her mind filled only with thoughts of Armas, she went to the rundown farm, Kierikka, where the work was long and hard. World War I was continuing in the fighting between the Reds and the czarist forces of Russia and had a fresh outburst in the vicinity of Kierikka. Silja became involved when she unwittingly aided the escape of two White soldiers and the Reds held her for questioning. After a horror-filled night, she was released. Her lethargy fell away from her now, for the war brought a hope that Armas might be stationed in her parish. She heard that the death toll included Oskari Tonttila.

Chaps. 21–23. The next months of war were hard for Silja. She did all she could to help those around her. But her strength was small and she knew with a certainty that she had developed tuberculosis. The knowledge did not frighten her; rather, she was glad she would not have to spend many more summers with the pain in her heart for her lost love. She wanted chiefly to return to the neighborhood of Rantoo and obtained permission to go. The old Professor and Miss Laura both knew when they saw Silja that her days were numbered and pity for her shadowed their reunion. Armas had been seriously wounded, having lost a leg and the whole of one lung. The news comforted Silja in a strange way, for she no longer felt the need to fight to live. She went to bed in the bathhouse, never to get up again. Death was slow in coming but when it finally claimed her she felt complete unity with the spirit of her beloved Armas.

The Maid's Tragedy

Play by Francis Beaumont, 1584–1616, and John Fletcher, 1579–1625.
Produced 1610.

This was one of the most popular plays of England's best-known pair of collaborating playwrights and for more than 200 years it was regularly revived. The dialogue is bawdy (some have called it vulgar) but that was in the spirit of the times; and also the play seems at times unnecessarily melodramatic, but that also was in the spirit of the times. It contains a good story, some great poetry, and some beautiful lyrics for its songs.

Act I. 1. In the city of Rhodes, in the Palace of the King, MELANTIUS, a great soldier and loyal subject, has just returned from the wars. He comes to celebrate the marriage of his best friend, the noble AMINTOR. DIPHILUS, Melantius's brother, and LYSIPPUS, the king's brother, greet the returning warrior. The lovely maid, ASPATIA, enters and Melantius congratulates her on her marriage; then he learns that Amintor is not to marry Aspatia but is betrothed to Melantius's sister, EVADNE. This is a great shock, since the love of Amintor and Aspatia is well known. Amintor explains that the king himself has commanded his marriage to Evadne; and she is so beautiful that Amintor does not find the command difficult to obey. A messenger announces that a masque (play) to celebrate the marriage is about to begin. **2.** CALIANAX, old and feeble father of Aspatia, attends the masque. He is angry because Aspatia has been betrayed and he insults Melantius because he is Evadne's brother. The king and his attendants enter and the masque begins. The actors take the parts of Night, Cynthia (day), Neptune, and the wind. They all work together to make the wedding night long and peaceful for the lovers.

Act II. 1. Evadne's ladies are making her ready for her wedding night. All are merry except Aspatia, who declares that she will die and wishes Evadne joy. The ladies leave and Amintor enters. Evadne tells him she will never really be his wife. He is dumfounded. Evadne taunts him with the fact that she loves another. Amintor vows revenge, then discovers that Evadne's lover is the king, who arranged this marriage to protect Evadne's reputation as she is going to bear his child. Amintor's loyalty to the king is so great that he agrees to this marriage in name only, asking only that Evadne, before the world, pretend she is really his wife. Calianax and her ladies talk and weep. Calianax, seeing his daughter so woebegone, vows to right the wrong.

Act III. 1. In the antechamber to Evadne's bedroom her brother Diphilus and two lords, CLEON and STRATO, are joking about the wedding night. They are joined by Melantius and Amintor. Melantius senses that something is wrong with Amintor. Evadne enters and behaves in a properly loving way towards Amintor. When the King arrives Amintor thanks him with great irony for arranging the marriage. The king orders everyone except Evadne to leave, then accuses her of being false. Evadne denies this and to prove it she calls Amintor and admit that theirs is not a real marriage. Amintor is still loyal to the king and agrees to shield the lovers. **2.** Melantius forces Amintor to tell him the terrible truth. Melantius tells Diphilus and together they plan revenge. Melantius tries to make peace with old Calianax and orders him to give over the fortifications of the city to him. Calianax begs for time to think it over.

Act IV. 1. Melantius makes Evadne confess that she is the king's mistress. He threatens to kill her on the spot unless she agrees to kill the king herself. Evadne falls to her knees before Amintor and confesses how wicked she has been. Amintor forgives her but says they can never be together now. **2.** Calianax tells the king about Melantius's plot but Melantius brashly denies it and the king decides that old age has affected Calianax's mind. Amintor urges Melantius to go with him at once to kill the king, but Melantius appeals to Amintor's loyalty and dissuades him, since he has already made other plans for the king's murder.

Act V. 1. Evadne tells the king's gentleman that she is going to the king and they do not wish to be disturbed. **2.** The king is asleep. Evadne ties his arms and wakes him. She reproaches the king, then stabs him and he dies. The lords and the king's brother Lysippus discover what has happened. Strato brings word that Melantius has seized the fortifications. **3.** Melantius, Diphilus and Calianax stand on the walls of the fort. Below them are Lysippus and the lords. Melantius offers to acknowledge Lysippus as king. **4.** Aspatia enters Evadne's antechamber, disguised as a boy, and tells Amintor that she is Aspatia's brother, come to seek revenge. At first Amintor refuses to fight but finally he agrees and Aspatia is wounded. Evadne returns, bloody from the murder of the king. She begs Amintor to accept her as his true wife. Amintor says he cannot. Evadne kills herself, though Amintor tries to stop her. Aspatia tells Amintor her real identity and dies in his arms. Amintor then stabs himself. Melantius and Calianax and Lysippus enter. When they see the dead bodies Melantius tries to kill himself but Diphilus stops him. Melantius declares he will not eat or sleep or do anything to preserve his now worthless life.

Main Street

Novel by Sinclair Lewis, 1885–1951. Published & © 1920 by Harcourt, Brace & Co., New York. Renewal © 1948 by Sinclair Lewis.

SINCLAIR LEWIS produced *Main Street* at a time when he was becoming discouraged with his results as a writer and had almost resigned himself to a teaching career. The strong support of H. L. Mencken, who was then approaching the peak of his influence as an iconoclastic critic, helped greatly to spread the fame of *Main Street* and once people began reading it its success was assured. *Main Street* was not quite up to other of Lewis's novels (though it was better than several of them) but most importantly it established the style that his most important novels were to take, a baring of the smugness characteristic of American small towns and cities in particular and conservative society in general. *Main Street* is the story of a young wife who is aghast at the low level of cultural advancement in the Midwest and who tries unsuccessfully to effect an improvement in her own town. Essentially *Main Street* held up a mirror to some hundreds of thousands of Americans. They did not particularly like what they saw there, but they liked being scolded. Readers always do.

Chaps. 1–3. When CAROL MILFORD is graduated from Blodgett College on the edge of Minneapolis, she is filled with grandiose ideas of doing great things for dreary, depressed people. Exactly how one would go about this is somewhat vague in her mind. She settles, after graduation, for a job as librarian. She meets Dr. WILL KENNICOTT, general practitioner in Gopher Prairie, Minnesota, and after a year's conventional courtship they are married. The trip by train from Minneapolis to Gopher Prairie is dismal and depressing, but Carol is encouraged by Will's constant praise of the town where he lives. The people of Gopher Prairie, according to Will, are intelligent, modern, friendly, homey folks— and Carol will just love them, as they will just love her. She is uneasy on the train as she observes the stolid, blank-faced Scandinavian farmers and their wives, and the villages through which the train passes do not encourage her. Will says Gopher Prairie is far superior to any other of these towns, but when the train stops there the town looks every bit as ugly and dismal as the others and its only distinction is that Main Street is longer and there are more stores.

Chaps. 4–6. A group of villagers meet the train. Carol is confused by so many strange faces and strange names and knows that she is on exhibition before Will's friends. When she sees her new home she is horrified by the hideously ugly relics of former generations that her mother-in-law left as furnishings. Diffidently, Will says that Carol can do what she will with the house and its furnishings, but obviously he thinks that what was good enough for his mother—and has been good enough for him—should be good enough for anyone. They go to a welcoming party at the home of SAM CLARK and his wife. Carol meets again the crowd that had been merely a blur of faces at the railroad station. There are DAVE DYER, the druggist; HARRY HAYDOCK, owner of the Bon Ton department store, and his wife JUANITA; LUKE DAWSON, the richest man in town; NAT HICKS, the tailor; CHET DASHAWAY, furniture dealer and undertaker; GEORGE MOTT, superintendent of schools; and JACKSON ELDER, owner of a planing mill and the local hotel, as well as a good share in the Farmers' Naional Bank. Carol dutifully tries to place the names and their owners. Carol starts immediately to plan things for the improvement of the town—its appearance, its culture, its diversions. She is startled to discover that its inhabitants believe Gopher Prairie attractive as it is. Her redecoration of her own living room also produces mixed reactions. Carol is determined to bring something gay and beautiful to Gopher Prairie. She gives a house-warming party when the living room is completed. The party is somewhat unusual, there being none of the standard "stunts" that have been repeated for years at all Gopher Prairie parties. Even the refreshments are a departure from the standard salad, sandwiches, coffee, and angel-food cake. The local newspaper's society column reports the party favorably but Carol feels that she has even

Carol is horrified

further emphasized her strangeness.

Chaps. 7–10. Carol learns that she is expected to buy her groceries, clothing and supplies from persons who are likely to go to Will for medical care. Also she is mildly rebuked for buying things in Minneapolis or St. Paul rather than in Gopher Prairie. Will's life is of necessity centered upon Main Street, its shops, its suppliers, its diversions. The people are antagonistic to any life different from their own, thinking of other lives as necessarily depraved, immoral, or radical. Carol tries to enter into the social life of Gopher Prairie by joining the Jolly Seventeen, the elite group of the town, with its bridge parties and semi-annual dances. She also attempts participation in the Thanatopsis Club, an educational and "cultural" society, but the ludicrous and incredibly stupid imitations of learning that she encounters there are distressing. Carol herself is constantly criticized and watched by the gossips of the town. Her only friend —unknown to anyone—is MILES BJORN-STAM, called the "Red Swede," a rebel and nonconformist also.

Chaps. 11–14. At a meeting of the Thanatopsis Club, Carol tries vainly to steer the ladies away from a study of the Bible, superficial contemplation of china and furnishings, or a skimming of the more famous English writers and poets. China and furnishings wins out. Will accuses Carol of alienating his patients through her "idiotic" notions of remodeling the way of life in Gopher Prairie, where everything is exactly as everyone wants it.

Chaps. 15–16. Carol learns much about her husband that she has not suspected before. In the middle of the night he goes out to perform an appendectomy on a woman who is close to death, because of delay in summoning a doctor, and he saves her life, operating on a kitchen table in a Dutch farmhouse. While he is treating NELS ERDSTROM for jaundice, he is summoned to perform an emergency amputation. Carol is impressed into service as an anesthetist and manages to resist fainting until the operation is completed. She admires Will for his courage and professional excellence, but his absorption in real-estate deals, his car, hunting, and medicine soon makes her feel alien once again. Miles Bjornstam comes to the annual wood-cutting for their winter supply and Miles enters into a courtship of BEA SORENSON, Carol's maid-of-all-work.

Chaps. 17–18. A game of charades at Jake Elder's cottage, after a gay bobsled ride, inspires Carol to organize a dramatic society. It produces a dismal failure, after months of preparation and rehearsal. Carol is wholly discouraged. For the next three years the only interesting facets of her life are the Bjornstams, and her own baby.

Chaps. 19–22. Carol is appointed to a position on the library board and learns to her astonishment that several men in Gopher Prairie are very well-read. She serves with considerable humility and is happy enough to be out of it when her pregnancy makes it necessary. The advent of little HUGH places her in the group of all young mothers of Gopher Prairie. The Great War (World War I) has started in Europe, but it does not touch anyone about Carol. More close to home is the marriage of VIDA SHERWIN, a schoolteacher, and RAYMOND WUTHERSPOON, head of the shoe department in the Bon Ton.

Chaps. 23–25. Raymond Wutherspoon goes into the army and becomes a lieutenant. Two of the younger doctors enter the Medical Corps, leaving Will Kennicott to tend to Gopher Prairie. He wishes Carol would not constantly try to make him over into a combination poet and socialist, as he interprets it. Carol is told in a friendly fashion by the millionaire PERCY BRESNAHAN that it is no use to fight against things as they are. She likes him in spite of her irritation. Will keeps working hard, as usual. During the extremely hot weather Carol suggests that they move into the guest room for greater comfort and he makes no objection. When Will remarks that perhaps they ought to think of building a

Carol is pressed into service for the emergency operation

420

house, Carol is enthusiastic until she realizes that Will's idea of a house is a stark cube of utility, with no attention to the esthetic. She loses interest and at length Will stops talking of the idea. He sees Maud Dyer in his office one day, and after making certain that Dave, her husband, will be working until midnight, he goes to see her. Carol suspects nothing.

Chap. 26. Miles Bjornstam's little boy, OLAF, is a friend of Hugh's. Carol takes Hugh to the Bjornstam house one day to play and finds Bea and Olaf seriously ill. She calls Will, who pronounces the illness typhoid fever. Both mother and child die. None of the townspeople go to the double funeral.

Chaps. 27-30. Two new people come to Gopher Prairie: FERN MULLINS, the new teacher, and ERIK VALBORG, assistant to Nat Hicks, the tailor. Both appeal strongly to Carol, because of their total dissimilarity to the people of the village. She becomes aware that she feels more than casual friendship for Erik, and he is quite open in declaring that he loves and wants her. Gossip is inevitable, but Carol tries to ignore it. She has not heard any gossip about her husband and Maud Dyer. Erik wants to study design and Carol encourages him. One day he informs her that MYRTLE CASS's father will give him a fine position in the flour mill if he and Myrtle are married. Carol asks him if he wants to become like the rest of the pillars of Gopher Prairie.

Chaps. 31-36. One night when Will is out on a call, Erik comes to the house and there is a moment when Carol is tempted to let him make love to her, but the moment passes and she sends him away. The town is rocked by scandal next day. Old Mrs. Bogart accuses Fern Mullins of drunkenness and of corrupting Mrs. Bogart's son CY BOGART at a square dance. Actually Cy had become drunk and Fern drove the buggy home, fighting off the loutish young man's amorous attentions, but Cy has reported the situation in exact reverse. The school board accepts Fern's resignation. Will warns Carol that the town would be quite as willing to crucify her as the innocent Fern, and she must stop seeing Erik. Erik leaves for Minneapolis. Carol persuades Will to take her on a trip to the West Coast. They travel for three months. When they come back, a booster campaign starts touting the charm and merit of Gopher Prairie as an ideal spot for new industry, new homes, new shops. Carol fails to enter into the frantic spirit of the campaign. Eventually she reaches a showdown point with Will. She decides to take Hugh and go to Washington for an indefinite length of time.

Chaps. 37-39. In Washington it is not difficult to find office work. The Armistice comes a few weeks after Carol's arrival. She meets many kinds of people in Washington and her life is interesting. She meets Harry and Juanita Haydock in the street and they bring her up to date on news of Gopher Prairie. A few weeks later Will Kennicott comes to visit and they take a trip to Charleston that becomes almost a second honeymoon. Will returns to Gopher Prairie, leaving her the assurance that he wants her back, but only when she herself wants to go back. Five months later she returns to him, strangely pleased to be home, and expecting her second child. The town accepts her, and the baby, a girl, is born in August. Carol has at last become a woman of Main Street—but she will never concede that Gopher Prairie is the ideal place its inhabitants believe.

Man and Superman

Play by George Bernard Shaw, 1856–1950.

Produced 1903. © 1903, 1931 by George Bernard Shaw. Published 1903 by University Press, Cambridge, Mass. (PB, 8)

THOUGH THIS IS often rated among Shaw's most important plays, the justification of such high rank must rest on the famous scene of Don Juan in Hell, in Act III. This scene was selected as one of a group of readings given most successfully in American theaters by a distinguished group including Charles Laughton, Agnes Moorehead, Sir Cedric Hardwicke, Charles Boyer, and Tyrone Power.

Act I. ROEBUCK RAMSDEN has a visitor, a young man named OCTAVIUS ROBINSON, whose benefactor and friend, WHITEFIELD, has just died and wished Robinson to marry Whitefield's daughter ANN. Octavius doubts he will be acceptable, since he is not at all successful. Ramsden's chief objection is to Octavius's friendship with JOHN TANNER, who has just published a revolutionary handbook. Ramsden expects to be Ann's guardian. The MAID announces that Tanner, the widow Whitefield and Ann are all calling. Ramsden asks her to bring Tanner along to his study. Tanner has a copy of the Whitefield will, which appoints both him and Ramsden Ann's guardians. Tanner does not want the responsibility but Ann will not permit him to decline it. Ramsden is furious at the idea of sharing the guardianship with Tanner. Tanner suggests that Octavius marry Ann and take her off their hands. Ann and Mrs. Whitefield come in. Ann is asked her views of the guardianship matter but expertly throws the decision back to the two men, and in the end the terms of the will are accepted as they stand. Ann tells them that VIOLET, Octavius's sister, has had an affair with an unknown man and is expecting a child. All are shocked except Tanner, who intends to go to her and offer her help and money. Violet is already in Ramsden's house, in the housekeeper's room. The family council debates what to do about her. She will not divulge the name of the man. Ramsden wants her packed off abroad until the child is born. Left alone for a moment, Tanner and Ann talk of their schooldays together, when they had an understanding to share all their secrets. Tanner accuses her of now wanting to own his soul. Now that he is her guardian, he will concentrate only on improving her mind. He objects to her toying with the affections of Octavius. Ramsden, Octavius and SUSAN RAMSDEN, Roebuck's prim sister, return from a fruitless attempt to make Violet leave her man and London. Susan refuses to have anything further to do with her and Ramsden pleads with her for Violet, much to Tanner's surprise. Violet comes in and Tanner congratulates her on her courage. To everyone's surprise, she rejects his approval and discloses that she has been secretly married all along. Only Ann knows the truth. Violet will not disclose her husband's name. The family, embarrassed, apologizes to her.

Act II. Tanner's car has broken down near its destination, Richmond. The rest of the family are coming with an American friend, MALONE, in an American steam car. The class pride of the cockney is discussed briefly with Tanner's chauffeur, HENRY. Octavius has proposed to Ann and has been turned down. Octavius wants Tanner to intercede with Ann, for he cannot write without her as his inspiration. Tanner warns him that marriage will not provide continuous inspiration. Octavius gives Tanner a note from RHODA, Ann's younger sister. Rhoda was to come along in Tanner's car but Ann forbade her to ride with him. Ann excuses her interference on the grounds that her mother insisted on it. Tanner accuses Ann of lack of independence and dares her to go on a motor trip with him through Africa. Casually she accepts, much to his horror. Mrs. Whitefield arrives with Malone. Not only does Mrs. Whitefield approve of the

The Devil arrives and greets the statue politely

trip, she asks Tanner to take Rhoda out for a spin in his car sometime. Thus Tanner learns that Ann has been lying to him. When Malone and Violet are alone it becomes obvious that Malone is Violet's husband. The reason for the secrecy is that Malone's rich father would object to his son's marrying any Englishwoman without a title. Malone now wants to own up and be done with it. Henry tells Tanner that Ann is obviously not interested in Octavius but in him, Tanner. Struck as if by lightning, Tanner decides to run away from her. He tells Henry he will leave at once for darkest Africa.

Act III. In Spain, a group of bandits led by MENDOZA capture Tanner and Henry. (The bandits' political opinions reflect the diverse political views of contemporary England.) Tanner is quite prepared to pay a ransom. When Mendoza learns of Tanner's wealth, he provides them the best meal possible. A discussion of socialism follows. Mendoza tells them the story of his life. He ran off to be a bandit because a woman scorned him. The woman turns out to be Henry's sister LOUISA. While Tanner slowly falls asleep, Mendoza reads some of the poems he wrote for Louisa. Henry is fast asleep too. Gradually the scene turns into a simile of hell. DON JUAN and OLD WOMAN discuss the place; Don Juan is bored with hell and the old woman objects to being there. Don Juan accuses himself of being a murderer. He assures the old woman that only hell has justification: Since all the wickedness on earth is done in the name of various virtues, it follows that virtues must reside in hell. Don Juan has the unmistakable characteristics of Tanner. He advises the old woman to wish herself 27 years old. She does and turns into DOÑA ANA, who resembles Ann Whitefield. Juan

tells her her father is in heaven, and bored with it. The STATUE, which looks like Ramsden, arrives to visit his daughter. He horrifies his daughter by telling her he likes himself best as a statue and has no parental feelings toward her. He is convinced hell is a place to amuse yourself in. The DEVIL arrives and greets the statue politely. The Devil looks a lot like Mendoza. He pretends to be all for joy and happiness. Don Juan and the Devil are obviously not friends. The Devil hopes to persuade Don Juan to go to heaven, since he is obviously unsuited for life in hell. The Devil pictures heaven and hell as differing only in temperament, and accuses Juan of a lack of the faculty of enjoyment. Ana wants to go to heaven, but her father counsels against it. Heaven is full of Englishmen who do not actually like it but think they owe it to their position to be there. Juan tells Ana to stay in hell if she wants to find happiness; the reason Don Juan wants to go to heaven is to escape from the pursuit of happiness and spend eternity in solitary contemplation. He pleads for the equality of beliefs, which alone can bring salvation to man. It is ideas put into man's head that make his life bearable. The discussion turns to womanhood. Juan credits woman with the creation of all civilization, but it is the intellect in man that steers the life force into constructive channels. Art and beauty have led Juan to woman, but woman wants to possess him and rob him of his freedom. Juan confesses to having run away from all women except Ana. The statue thinks Juan is too clever for his own good. Juan calls marriage the most licentious of human institutions and a lifetime union between two persons essentially false and immoral. The Devil interjects that in his kingdom they can have all they desire. Juan decides to

leave for heaven at once, though the Devil warns him he will tire of it quickly. Juan is sure he will not be bored, because pursuit of the Life Force is never dull. Juan leaves, alone. Ana is annoyed. The Devil is depressed at losing Juan. Juan's pursuit of the Superman has made him oblivious to Man. In his pursuit of the Life Force, Juan has become a blind lunatic. The Devil assures Ana that the Superman has not yet been created. She vows to find a proper father so that the Superman may be given birth.

Back in Spain, the sleepers awake. Shots are heard. An expedition of soldiers is out to capture the bandits. Tanner promises not to testify against the bandits. Henry reluctantly agrees also, so his sister's name will not be dragged into court. Ann, Violet, Malone, and Ramsden arrive first. Then Octavius arrives. Tanner realizes he is trapped by the Life Force.

Act IV. Henry ushers old Mr. MALONE into a villa in Granada. Henry has given a note from Violet, addressed to the son, to the father by mistake. Violet sees Malone. She admits that young Malone wants to marry her. Old Malone says that in that case he will disinherit his son. He is able to buy two of England's most historic abbeys and insists that his son marry a woman with a title to match the purchase. Young Malone arrives and argues with his father; Violet manages to pacify them. The others in the party arrive and hear young Malone say he will marry Violet, regardless of his father's opposition. They think him mad, since they believe Violet is already married to someone else. Malone Jr. then has to admit he and Violet are married. Octavius congratulates Malone and he and Tanner offer Malone all the money he wants. Now the father asks his son's forgiveness, but the son ignores him. Violet sends Malone to the hotel to pack, then makes peace with Old Malone. Old Malone is now very happy with Violet. Ann tells Octavius that her mother wants her to marry Tanner. Octavius wonders if Tanner has been playing with him. Mrs. Whitefield assures Octavius that she never said anything to him about marrying Tanner; it is solely Ann's own decision. Tanner returns and Mrs. Whitefield tells him he should marry Ann. He alone would tell her the truth about herself. Violet leaves on her honeymoon. Ann is left alone with Tanner. He admits that he loves her, but fights for his freedom just the same. He embraces her violently, just as the others come back. She tells them she will marry Tanner, and faints. When she comes to, Tanner announces that there will be nothing sentimental about their wedding, but Ann, victorious, does not care.

422

Victor Hugo
1802–1885

Eugene O'Neill
1888–1958

Manon Lescaut

Novel by Abbé Prévost (Antoine François Prévost d'Exiles, 1697–1763). Published 1731.

THE CLAIM TO FAME of this 18th-century French book is that the great composers Massenet and Puccini both elected to write operas based on it. The principal feature of the novel is that it presents a woman irresistible because of her beauty—the same kind of woman that has appeared in some millions of pages of literature but that apparently is quite rare in life because so few men have met her or her sister. At least in this novel she succeeds in ruining her men, which seems to be the mission in life of such women.

Chaps. 1–4. The 17-year-old Chevalier DES GRIEUX is finishing his studies at Amiens. With his friend TIBERGE he watches the arrival of the coach from Arras. One of the passengers is a beautiful girl, MANON LESCAUT, about to enter a nearby convent. Des Grieux falls in love with her at sight, approaches her, and persuades her to meet him that night, when he declares his passion. Eager to escape the convent, Manon goes with him to Paris, where the two live together for three weeks in bliss. Then, since Manon continues affluent while his own money is running out, des Grieux suspects her of infidelity.

Under orders from des Grieux' father, three servants kidnap the young man and take him to his father's house. The father tells him that Manon is a harlot, having sold her favors to M. DE B—F. The grief-stricken son wishes to return to Manon, but his father keeps him locked up for six months. Tiberge visits him often, confirms that Manon is a harlot, and urges des Grieux to take holy orders. The Chevalier is persuaded to enroll at the Seminary of Saint-Supplice. He plunges into study to banish Manon from his mind. In two years he is ready for his public examination.

The outstanding ability of the candidate carries his name throughout Paris. Manon comes to hear him and is carried away by his fervor. She seeks him out after the ceremonies and des Grieux is again infatuated. He abandons his calling to go with Manon to Chaillot. Here they live happily but extravagantly on Manon's money. They also take quarters in Paris, where they are visited by Manon's brother, who presently moves in. LESCAUT is in the Royal Guards but is a gambler and a scoundrel. When the Chaillot house burns to the ground, Lescaut advises des Grieux to let Manon practice her profession to recoup their fortunes. Des Grieux refuses but accepts the alternative suggestion of becoming a professional gambler. His luck is good and he obtains money from Tiberge under

pretense of reform. The new period of extravagant luxury ends when a maid and a valet abscond with their money and jewelry. Manon then becomes the mistress of a wealthy eccentric, M. DE G—— M——. Des Grieux joins the household under pretense that he is a younger brother from whom Manon cannot bear to be separated.

Chaps. 5–7. The Chevalier is deeply depressed when Manon enters the house of her patron. Manon declares that she will remain true to des Grieux, and they plot to flee together after Manon has obtained money from old M. de G—— M—— that night. But their flight is quickly discovered. Police arrest the couple, return the booty to its owner, imprison Manon in the Magdalen, the Common Hospital for prostitutes, and send des Grieux to Saint-Lazare prison.

Des Grieux hopes to escape, and succeeds in ingratiating himself with the prison officers. Hearing of his good conduct, M. de G— M— visits him in the prison. The Chevalier hears for the first time that Manon has been committed to the Magdalen; incensed, he attacks the old man, and thus ruins his chance for a reprieve. He forms new plans of escape for both himself and Manon. Tiberge helps by smuggling a letter to Manon. Lescaut furnishes transportation and a pistol, and the Chevalier succeeds in escaping. Then Manon gets out by disguising herself in men's clothing. The lovers first take refuge in Lescaut's house, then leave for fear of detection. Lescaut is killed by a fellow gambler with a grudge, and the couple continue alone to the inn at Chaillot.

Chaps. 8–10. Financed again by the faithful Tiberge, the couple enjoy another idyllic period. Then young M. DE G—— M——, son of the old man, falls under Manon's spell, and presses her to become his mistress. Manon recounts this to des Grieux, and the two plan to dupe the son as they had

duped the father. For greater safety, Manon demands money and jewels in advance, and the gullible young man gives them to her. On his way to claim his reward, young M. de G— M— is waylaid by ruffians hired by des Grieux, but his servant escapes and hurries to the father. The old man calls the police, who again arrest the plotters and return them to their former prisons. The Chevalier soon obtains his freedom through intervention of his father. He then plans to obtain freedom for Manon by use of his meager inheritance.

Chaps. 11–13. Des Grieux learns from a prison guard that Manon has been sentenced to exile and will be sent to America on the next boat. Desperate for time, des Grieux tells the entire story of his love for Manon to his father, but his appeal for help is refused. Next he tries to arrange an attack on the guards who will accompany the convicts to the point of embarkation, but is frustrated. Finally he obtains passage to accompany Manon by posing as her husband.

In New Orleans the couple begin an exemplary life. The GOVERNOR befriends des Grieux with a minor appointment. Wishing to legalize their union, the Chevalier asks the Governor's permission to marry Manon, but is refused, because the Governor's nephew, M. SYNNELET, has fallen in love with her. Synnelet and des Grieux fight a duel. Des Grieux thinks he has killed his opponent; he and Manon flee, but fatigue combined with ill health overcome Manon and she dies in his arms. Des Grieux buries her and falls on the grave in a coma. He is found and brought back to New Orleans, where Synnelet is recovering. Tiberge arrives from France and escorts des Grieux back to his country and his family.

Manon, overcome with fatigue, dies in the arms of Des Grieux

The Man Without a Country

Story by Edward Everett Hale, 1822–1909.
Published 1863.

THIS IS ONE OF THE MOST famous and one of the best known of American short stories. (Today we might call it a novelette.) When it was written, patriotism was a far more active and personal emotion than it is today; but even by today's cynical standards the reader will probably find himself in sympathy with the idea of a man who in losing his identification with his country lost all he had.

FRED INGHAM, an American naval officer, reads of the death of PHILIP NOLAN aboard the U.S. Corvette *Levant*. Ingham then tells the story of "the man without a country," as Philip Nolan was known. (Official papers relating the case were probably destroyed when Washington was burned in the War of 1812, so that Ingham's reminiscences are probably the only remaining record.)

When Nolan was a young officer in the "Legion of the West" stationed near New Orleans, he met and was fascinated by AARON BURR. He was drawn into Burr's conspiracy to found a Western Empire. When Burr was exposed, Nolan also was brought to trial and was convicted of conspiracy. Asked if he wished to say anything before sentence was pronounced, Nolan cried out "Damn the United States! I wish I may never hear of the United States again."

The presiding judge, Colonel MORGAN, soon rendered the verdict, "The Court decides, subject to the approval of the President, that you may never hear the name of the United States again."

Nolan was taken to New Orleans and put aboard a government vessel bound on a long cruise. For the rest of his life he remained on ships at sea, being transferred to an outbound ship whenever necessary to keep him from entering an American port. He was not permitted to talk with the sailors unless an officer was present, and all personnel were instructed never to mention anything pertaining to the United States in his presence. He was allowed to read foreign newspapers, but only after all items mentioning the U.S. had been clipped out. He was also allowed books, and the most poignant of many incidents aggravating the hardship of his self-chosen lot grew out of a book.

With a group of officers, Nolan was reading aloud (Scott's) "The Lay of the Last Minstrel" when he came to the lines

Breathes there the man with soul so dead,
Who never to himself hath said—
This is my own, my native land!
Whose heart hath ne'er within him burned,
As home his footsteps he hath turned
From wandering on a foreign strand?—
If such there breathe, go, mark him well.
For him no minstrel raptures swell;
High though his titles, power, and pelf,
The wretch, concentred all in self . . .

At this juncture, Nolan stumbled to his feet and threw the book into the sea.

Ingham, the narrator, had many conversations with Nolan, and was hard put to conceal from Nolan that his native Texas had been taken into the Union. A letter to Ingham from his friend DANFORTH narrates Nolan's last illness and death. Nolan had made a shrine of his stateroom, draping it with American flags and patriotic symbols. He had drawn from memory a map of the United States, with the quaint old names— Indiana Territory, Mississippi Territory, and so on. He had even guessed that Texas was a state.

At Nolan's pleading, Danforth tells him much of what has happened in the United States during his exile of nearly 50 years. Nolan dies happy with his father's badge of the Society of the Cincinnati pressed to his lips. His will requests that he be buried at sea and that a monument be erected at Fort Adams bearing the legend "In memory of Philip Nolan, Lieutenant in the Army of the United States."

Man's Fate

Novel by André Malraux, 1895–
Published 1933. Translated from the French by Haakon M. Chevalier; © 1934 by Harrison Smith and Robert Haas, Inc. (ML, 33)

THERE WAS A TIME when André Malraux was the darling of international Communists and this novel had much to do with it. Despite its propagandistic aspects, *Man's Fate* is worth reading because Malraux knew his China, having lived there, and was a great writer who could interpret the sensations of a person drawn into such circumstances as afflicted his Chinese characters. *Man's Fate* won the Prix Goncourt despite the fact that it was undisguised propaganda. Malraux changed politics and when he did so he changed very radically, becoming a Gaullist.

Part I. 1. CH'EN TA ERH, a Chinese terrorist, is anguished at the thought of committing a murder for the sake of the revolutionary forces. Clutching a dagger and a razor, Ch'en approaches the sleeping victim. Convulsively, Ch'en stabs himself in the arm as if to prove that the resistance of the flesh is no obstacle. Finally, he draws the dagger and plunges it into his victim, then he steals the important paper for which he has committed the murder. The dead man had negotiated the sale of guns to the government. By obtaining the paper authorizing the sale, the Chinese insurrectionists will be able to commandeer the guns and thereby be in a better position to capture Shanghai. Ch'en feels his anguish subsiding as he leaves the murder scene. Hastening to the phonograph record shop of HEMMELREICH and his partner, LU YU HSUAN, Ch'en hands over the paper authorizing the delivery of the arms to KYO GISORS, one of the organizers of the Shanghai insurrection. Kyo reads that the arms have not yet been paid for, but he assures the others that he will be able to obtain them anyway. KATOV, a Russian organizer, questions Ch'en about the crime, but Ch'en cannot express in words the familiarity with death that has established itself in his being. Kyo advises Ch'en that the revolutionary troops will probably arrive in Shanghai the following day to touch off the insurrection. Making plans to take the arms from the ship *Shantung*, Kyo plots to have the ship's anchorage changed to thwart interference. After the failure of the February uprising, Kyo was authorized by the Chinese Communist Party to coördinate the insurrectionist forces. Kyo heads for a night club, the Black Cat, in search of the Baron de CLAPPIQUE, a Frenchman who deals in antiques, opium and smuggled wares. Clappique agrees to help Kyo's forces by using his influence to have the ship's anchorage moved. Meanwhile, Katov goes out to enlist volunteers to get the rifles.

2. Ch'en visits old GISORS, Kyo's father, a former professor of sociology at the University of Peking. Though dismissed because of his revolutionary teachings, old Gisors is not an active participant in the movement. Ch'en feels an attachment to the old man, who was once his teacher and like a father to him. Ch'en reveals that his victim of the previous evening was the first person he has ever killed. Gisors instinctively sees that terrorism is beginning to fascinate the young man. Ch'en states that he will soon die, and Gisors surmises that this is what Ch'en wishes above all things. Aspiring to no glory or happiness, Ch'en wants to give to death the meaning that others give to life by dying on what is for him the highest plane possible. Gisors perceive that Ch'en is a person incapable of living by an ideology that cannot immediately become transformed into action. After Ch'en's departure, Gisors thinks of his son Kyo, whose life is dedicated to helping the Chinese masses. For Kyo, this can be achieved only by Communism. 3. Katov and Kyo, accompanied by forces dressed as government soldiers, board the *Shantung*, where they overpower the ship's officers and succeed in unloading

the firearms. A truck awaits them at the wharf, and the firearms are distributed to the various insurrectionist posts.

Part II. 1. FERRAL, president of the French Chamber of Commerce and head of the Franco-Asiatic Consortium, is distressed because of the general strikes that have idled thousands of Chinese workers. The Consortium is a network of business enterprises throughout Asia. Ferral visits MARTIAL, head of the Shanghai police, who informs him that the government's last chance against the revolutionary forces approaching Shanghai is an armored train carrying White officers. Ferral surmises that once Shanghai falls to the revolutionary army the Kuomintang will have to choose between democracy and Communism. For Ferral, it is essential that democracy win, for if Communism takes a strong hold, the Consortium and all French trade in Shanghai will be destroyed. Ferral hopes to prevent the taking of the city before the army arrives. Martial discusses Gen. CHIANG KAI-SHEK's relations with the Communists. He tells Ferral of a rumor that Moscow has given orders to the political commissars to let their own troops be beaten before Shanghai; thus discredited, Chiang Kai-shek might be replaced by a Communist general.

2. Ch'en and his fellow insurgents overpower the police officers in the local precincts, stealing their firearms. Amid the gunfire, Ch'en's attention is drawn to an enemy whose leg has been torn off, his hands tied behind his back. Although there is danger of a grenade exploding in his face, Ch'en is overcome by a feeling much stronger than pity, a feeling that he himself is the man bound hand and foot. Ch'en cuts the cords; he then questions his own action, but decides that he could not have done otherwise. Nonetheless, he feels he has been foolish to suffer anguish over the man he murdered the night before.

3. The insurrection is seriously undermining Ferral's economic interests. He meets with Martial and an envoy sent by Chiang Kai-shek to question the police chief's intentions, should Chiang break with the Communists. The envoy asks Martial to guard Chiang, as there have been rumors of an assassination attempt. Ferral later confers with LIU TI YU, chief of the Shanghai Bankers' Association, to discuss Chiang's plans to break with the Communists, a step which he feels will benefit their economic interests. Ferral stresses the necessity of helping Chiang. The Communists are organizing the peasant unions in the rural districts; these organizations will attempt to nationalize the land and declare credits illegal, two measures that would strike a death blow to Ferral's economic interests. Ferral urges the necessity of an immediate decision, because all the governmental cantonments have fallen to the insurgents and the revolutionary army will be in Shanghai the following day. The chief danger lies in Hankow, where the Red Army was being formed. **4.** The army of

the Kuomintang is to reach Shanghai in a few hours. The assembly of delegates secretly united by the Kuomintang party before the insurrection has elected a central committee, the majority of whom are Communists. Kyo is disturbed to learn, however, that the Executive Committee formed to organize a new municipal government in Shanghai is not Communist-controlled. Kyo tells one of his soldiers that workers' militias will be organized in

Ch'en cuts the cords

Shanghai and that a new Red Army is being organized in Hankow to suppress the power of Chiang's Kuomintang. Upon learning later that the newly elected Shanghai Prefect is not a Communist, Kyo is angered and unable to understand why the Communist International seems to be following a line of leaving the power in Shanghai in the hands of the bourgeoisie. He resolves to visit Hankow to see the Communist leaders.

Part III. Kyo arrives in Hankow and tells VOLOGIN, a Communist official, that he believes the wrong policy is being pursued in Shanghai. Vologin disagrees, saying that by working within the framework of the Kuomintang, the Communists can undermine Chiang Kai-shek and ultimately gain power for the Party. Ch'en announces his plan to assassinate Chiang Kai-shek, but Vologin expresses firm disapproval of such a terrorist activity. He stresses obedience to the Party above all personal opinions and beliefs.

Part IV. 1. Clappique meets Count SHPILEVSKI in a bar. Because Clappique once saved the life of KÖNIG, the German who heads Chiang's police, König has sent Shpilevski with a warning that Chiang's police are planning to close in on the Communists and that Clappique is known to have aided them in getting arms from the *Shantung*. However, he is to be given a day of grace to escape. Clappique decides he must warn Kyo. **2.** Ch'en is ready to carry out his plan to assassinate Chiang Kai-shek. Holding a bomb in his briefcase, he encounters Pastor SMITHSON, his first teacher, who asks Ch'en what he has found

in place of the Christian faith he has abandoned. Ch'en replies that he has found another faith in Communism. Ch'en is to throw the bomb as Chiang's car passes on the street. Ch'en enters an antique shop to get a good vantage point. When Chiang's car appears, Ch'en rushes out in the street but the shopkeeper, following him to discuss a purchase, stands in his way and prevents him from throwing the bomb. Three thwarted assassins go to Hemmelreich's shop but Hemmelreich refuses to shelter them, fearing he might risk his child's safety. After their departure, Hemmelreich reproaches himself. Still anxious to murder Chiang, Ch'en decides that the assassins must throw themselves under the car with a bomb. This idea brings him a feeling of exaltation, but the others refuse to risk their lives in this manner. Meanwhile Clappique tells Kyo of Shpilevski's warning. Kyo refuses to leave Shanghai, but he offers Clappique money to escape and agrees to meet him at the Black Cat that night. Since his return from Hankow, Kyo has been secretly trying to organize combat groups against Chiang, but the Chinese Communist Party's propaganda of union with the Kuomintang has paralyzed his efforts. **3.** Katov visits Hemmelreich and tells him that if one believes in nothing, one is forced to believe in the virtues of the heart, which is what Hemmelreich has done in refusing shelter to Ch'en for the sake of his child. **4.** The political situation has made great trouble for Ferral. His American credits are about to be cut off and the industrial enterprises of the Consortium show a large deficit. Communism must be crushed in China if he is to win help from the French government. Ferral discusses fanaticism with Gisors. **5.** Ch'en, clutching the bomb, rushes with ecstatic joy at Chiang Kai-shek's car. An explosion follows, and Ch'en is killed.

Part V. 1. Clappique has learned that Chiang's special troops are planning to move in at 11 o'clock that night. He must warn Kyo to stay away from any meetings. Clappique decides to gamble what little money he has left in order to win enough to finance his department from Shanghai, in the event that Kyo is unable to help him. Intoxicated by the excitement of gambling, Clappique remains at the gambling tables long past the appointed hour of his meeting with Kyo, but loses all of his money. **2.** Kyo and his wife MAY wait at the Black Cat. Word comes that a bomb has been thrown at Chiang's car, but Chiang was not in the auto. Kyo realizes that if the Communists have to fight Chiang's forces tonight, they will be beaten for lack of firearms. When Clappique fails to appear, Kyo and May head for the committee headquarters. As they reach the street, May is knocked unconscious and left on the ground, while Kyo is knocked on the head and hauled away in a waiting automobile. **3.** Hemmelreich returns to his shop that evening to find that Chiang's soldiers have invaded it and have killed his wife and

The bomb explodes, killing Ch'en

child. Although he feels grief, he also feels the profound joy of liberation, for now he too can kill. He rushes to Communist headquarters and joins those preparing to fight despite the shortage of firearms. **4.** Clappique, remorseful at his failure to warn Kyo in time, promises Gisors that he will try to influence König to have Kyo released from prison—or at least to prevent the young man's being shot. However, König feels he has already repaid his obligation to Clappique, and refuses to release Kyo. **5.** After a vain struggle, the Communists are overpowered by the members of Chiang's Kuomintang.

Part VI. **1.** Kyo is placed in a prison cell. In the next cell, he hears a guard whipping another prisoner, a senseless idiot. Kyo offers the guard money to stop beating the wretch. König offers to spare Kyo's life if Kyo will work for him. Kyo refuses to enter the service of his enemies. **2.** Clappique, in disguise, boards a ship leaving Shanghai. Another passenger is Ferral, who is returning to France to seek financial support for the failing Consortium. **3.** In prison, Katov and Kyo have kept a vial of cyanide on their persons in order to kill themselves and thereby escape the executioner. From time to time prisoners are called out to be tortured to death. Kyo takes the poison and dies. In committing this act, he feels a sense of peace despite the present circumstances. During his life he has fought for something that had deep meaning for him. What, he asks himself before he dies, would have been the value of a life for which he would not have been willing to die? Kativ, feeling even more alone after Kyo dies, offers his cyanide to Suan, who takes it and dies, leaving Katov to a death by torture. **4.** Kyo's body is returned to his family for burial. For old Gisors the world no longer has any meaning.

Part VII. **1.** In Paris Ferral confers with the Minister of Finance and important French financiers but is unable to gain support for the Consortium, which is thus doomed to disintegrate. **2.** Gisors is now living in Kobe with a Japanese friend, an artist named KAMA. Gisors tells May, Kyo's widow, that he has decided to refuse a professorship in Moscow and plans to remain in Kobe. May, however, heads for Moscow to work in the Communist movement.

The Marble Faun

Novel by Nathaniel Hawthorne, 1804–1864.
Published 1860. (PB, PL59)

THIS NOVEL IS THE WORK of a great novelist in his later years. Hawthorne wrote *The Marble Faun* ten years after he had written the two works that are considered his masterpieces, *The Scarlet Letter* and *The House of the Seven Gables*. When he was appointed a United States consul in England he took the opportunity to tour the Continent. His travels in Italy suggested a novel set there and he wrote *The Marble Faun*. In this novel he turned to the occult but produced a novel quite agreeable to the modern taste.

Chaps. **1–5.** The mysterious, dark-eyed painter, MIRIAM SCHAEFER, and her two American friends, HILDA, a painter, and KENYON, a sculptor, note the striking resemblance of their young Italian friend, DONATELLO, to the sculpture of the marble faun by Praxiteles in the Capitol at Rome.

Many rumors circulate about the origins of Miriam, who appeared in Rome suddenly without any introduction. While touring the Catacombs, she loses her way and is guided back to her friends by a sepulchral stranger, who thereafter haunts her and is often used by her as a model.

Chaps. **6–11.** Miriam visits gentle Hilda and discloses that she is soon going away for the summer. She asks Hilda to deliver a small packet for her after four months, unless she hears otherwise, to the Cenci palace, once the home of Beatrice Cenci, who, in the 16th century, harassed by her father's cruel treatment, arranged his murder. Hilda shows Miriam an exquisite copy she has made of Guido Reni's famed portrait of Beatrice. Miriam keeps a date with the unsophisticated, childish Donatello, who tells her he loves her. She is charmed by his simplicity but warns him she is a dangerous person. "If you follow my footsteps they will lead you to no good. You ought to be afraid of me." Donatello swears that he will always love her. Miriam decides to be for an hour as he imagines her, and joins him in gay dancing with others in the woods to the music of a vagrant band. Her mood is shattered when she sees her strange model among the dancers. She insists that Donatello leave, though he offers to rid her of the model, whom he hates. Her persecutor tells Miriam she must leave Rome with him, leaving no trace of herself behind. He adds that he has the power to force her compliance. It seems that they have known each other before, as he speaks of the destiny they must fulfill together and of how he has tried to bury the past until their encounter in the Catacombs. He hints at Miriam's association with a dreadful crime in the past.

Chaps. **12–23.** Hilda learns from Kenyon that Donatello is the Count DI MONTE BENI, of a noble Tuscan family. The four friends take a moonlight stroll with other artists among the ruins of Rome. Miriam is disturbed by the appearance of her "shadow" and begs Donatello to flee the evil that hangs over her and that threatens him too. He insists on remaining, and when Miriam's dreadful persecutor reappears, Donatello throws him over a precipice. The deed is seen by Hilda, who on the following day does not keep her appointment to join the other three at the Church of the Capuchins. In the church the others see a dead monk in his bier. Donatello and Miriam are aghast to recognize him as the man Donatello killed. Miriam declares she and Donatello must part forever, and her despondent lover accepts her verdict. She calls on Hilda, who, horrified at the scene she witnessed, tells Miriam they can no longer be friends. Hilda confirms Donatello's claim that Miriam's eyes "bade" him do what he did.

Chaps. **24–30.** Kenyon, visiting Donatello at his gloomy old castle in Tuscany, finds him living alone with a few old servants, greatly changed from the playful youth his friend had compared with Praxiteles' faun. Kenyon notes that the brooding Donatello bears a horrifying emotional burden and that he has acquired a soul out of the grief and pain he has suffered. Kenyon models a bust of his host, but the work goes badly until by accident he achieves the expression Donatello wore when flinging his victim over the precipice. Still unaware of the murder, Kenyon is shocked. Donatello insists the bust must remain as it is, but the sympathetic sculptor alters it.

Chaps. 31–35. Miriam, wan and in mourning, comes to Monte Beni. Kenyon says he believes that Donatello still loves her, but with a depth attuned to his new maturity. He proposes to take Donatello to Perugia, where she can meet them as if by accident. At Perugia, she senses that the man of intellect who has replaced the faun still loves her. Donatello asks forgiveness for deserting her and declares that their lot lies together. Kenyon leaves them to seek Hilda in Rome.

Chaps. 36–45. In Rome, Hilda, wretched and alone, feels stained by the guilt of her secret. Though of Puritan heritage and unwilling to become a Catholic, she is moved to enter the confessional while in St. Peter's. With the burden of her secret lifted, she is serene when she meets Kenyon. Suddenly remembering Miriam's package, she delivers it to the Cenci palace and disappears.

Chaps. 46–50. Miriam and Donatello assure the worried Kenyon that Hilda is safe. Miriam discloses her own background: She is of strangely mixed parentage and connected with a wealthy, influential family of Southern Italy that was linked a few years back with a horrifying event. She was suspected of complicity but declares her innocence. The spectre of the catacomb was an evil figure that had haunted her life. Later, Hilda reappears, having been imprisoned in a convent because of her entanglement with Miriam and because of her confessor's hope that he might convert her. Donatello gives himself up for imprisonment, and Miriam disappears. Hilda and Kenyon decide to marry and return to their own country.

Marius in the temple

Marius the Epicurean

Novel by Walter Pater, 1839–1894. Published 1885. (ML, 90)

WALTER PATER WAS KNOWN chiefly as a critic and left only a few works of fiction. *Marius the Epicurean* is his one important novel and is a major work commensurate with the importance of its author. It has in it a great deal of the philosophical depth that had won its author an eminent position in the literary world of England, where in his day there were many other giants. The novel is interesting and quick in tempo.

Part I. Chaps. 1–7. Young MARIUS is a devout lad who takes much satisfaction in participating in the worship of the ancient Roman household gods. He enjoys fulfilling his obligation to the great populace of "little gods," dear to the Roman home, which the pontiffs have placed on the sacred list of the *Indigitamenta*, to be invoked on special occasion: Vatican, who causes the infant to utter the first cry; Fabulinus, who prompts the child's first word; Cuba, who keeps him quiet in his cot; and Marius's favorite, Domiduca, the goddess who watches over one's safe homecoming. Marius lives at the family home, White-Nights, a rural estate much shrunken in size due to the squandering of the family fortune by Marius's grandfather. Marius enjoys the simplicity of the farm life and loves the beauties of nature. He is strongly attached to his widowed mother, whose sorrowing at the loss of her husband seems to be ever fresh. Marius passes a peaceful boyhood, more given to contemplation than to action. He nourished a boyish ideal of priesthood, which has faded but left behind a sense of dedication that remains all through his life. In his teens, he is taken to a temple of Aesculapius, among the hills of Etruria, for the cure of an illness. Marius is pleasantly impressed by the beauty of the temple and he gladly enters into the solemnity of its rites. He returns home from the temple cured. His mother is seriously ill and dies soon afterward. Added to the sorrow of his loss is Marius's remorse at the childish anger he expressed at what was to be her last departure from home. Marius soon leaves White-Nights to live in the house of a guardian at Pisa. Here he attends a school modeled after the Academy of Plato. He becomes friendly with FLAVIAN, son of a freedman, who is a leader among the students. Together they eagerly read all the books they can get. Marius hopes to participate in a new school of literature, with Flavian at its head, which would revive the beauties of Latin; but

Flavian dies of the plague brought back from the Danube by the legions of Emperor MARCUS AURELIUS.

Part II. Chaps. 8–14. Heartbroken, Marius finds consolation in the philosophy of Heraclitus, which teaches that everything perceived by the senses is in continual flux and so is impermanent. Seeking further, Marius comes upon the writings of Aristippus, the Cyrenaic, who teaches that our direct sensations, whatever their shortcomings, are the only certain knowledge we possess. *Life,* he learns, *is the end of life.* Marius is eager to experience the richness of sensations offered by the golden age of Marcus Aurelius. However, he does not seek hedonism, whose excesses would be foreign to his nature. Not pleasure but fullness of life is the goal. *Be perfect in regard to what is here and now* is the precept that inspires him. At this time Marius is summoned to Rome by a friend of his father, who has recommended Marius to the emperor as a private scribe, or amanuensis. The Marius family owns a house on the Caelian hill in Rome and Marius goes there. At an inn he meets CORNELIUS, a young officer in the famed Twelfth Legion. The two young men become friends, and Cornelius undertakes to acquaint Marius with Rome. The city is giving Marcus Aurelius an ovation; Marius is happy at the colorful sights and new sounds, and particularly at the ceremonies. Marius is presented to the emperor. In the imperial chamber are the empress, FAUSTINA, and her children. It is the birthday of one of the children, and the emperor departs to make birthday offerings to the household gods. This act deeply touches Marius. Yet later, at the Coliseum, Marius sees the emperor sit passively through the bloody spectacle below, neither approving nor disapproving. Marius, in his clear disapproval, feels superior.

Part III. Chaps. 15–19. Marius listens to the lectures of the Stoic philosophers and many other views heard in Rome. He finds that he can no longer maintain his Cyrenaic beliefs, yet he is not clear as to what he now believes. A year from the time of his first summons to the imperial palace, he is called again. He is impressed anew by the peace and serenity in the countenance of Marcus Aurelius, as the emperor gives him an armful of scrolls to be edited. Later Marius is present at the death of one of the emperor's small sons, sees Aurelius take the dying boy in his arms, and feels keen sympathy for the ruler.

Part IV. Chaps. 20–28. Marius notices that Cornelius has friends of whom he never speaks; but after each visit with them Cornelius returns refreshed and invigorated. One day Cornelius takes Marius to the home of a matronly widow, CECILIA, whose house is a church of those who called themselves Christians. Marius, true to his Epicurean philosophy, sets about surrendering himself to the new doctrines heard here, in order to make a perfectly liberal inquiry into them. Later, Marius sees a Christian service. He is impressed by the expressions on the faces of the worshippers; he senses in their beliefs a dramatic action with a single appeal to eye and ear, which for him is the most beautiful thing in the world. He is drawn again and again to Cecilia's house, for though he cannot accept the Christian beliefs the poetry of their expression holds him strongly. Moreover, he feels that Cecilia may fulfill a need he has long felt, a desire for a woman to be a sister to him. Marius visits his old home, White-Nights, and finds it deserted and dust-covered. Melancholy induces him to have all family burial urns, which stand around the walls, buried. He looks upon himself sadly as the last of his race. Cornelius visits him at White-Nights. One morning Cornelius goes out of the house. Marius follows, knowing that because the plague is still abroad, the inhabitants of the region will not trust a stranger. Just as Marius finds

his friend, the hills of the district billow crazily in an earthquake. By the time the two friends reach the town, the populace is enraged at the Christians, whom they blame for the earthquake. Marius and Cornelius are arrested, but because of their rank they are able to demand trial in Rome. They begin a march with other captives to the great city. Rumor spreads that one of the captives is not a Christian. Out of love for his friend, and because he believes that Cornelius is to be Cecilia's husband, Marius tells the guards that Cornelius is the one not Christian and bribes them to release him. As the march wears on, day after day, Marius becomes utterly weary of life. The harshness of the march weakens him and he falls ill. Believing him unable to proceed, the guards leave him in care of some country folk, who care for him tenderly. In his last delirium, he thinks that Cornelius has gone on a mission to deliver him from death. As he sinks into death, the people utter Christian prayers over him, place between his lips a wafer, and anoint him with oil. They inter his remains in one of their secret burial places.

Martin Chuzzlewit

Novel by Charles Dickens, 1812–1870. Published 1844.

THE IMPORTANT THING about *Martin Chuzzlewit* is that in it Dickens revealed vicious antagonism toward the United States, an attitude that had not appeared in *The American Notes* that he wrote about his first visit to America in 1842. Except for this special feature, which made *Martin Chuzzlewit* one of the most discussed books of its time, the novel is just a Dickens novel, no better than most and not so good as some. *Martin Chuzzlewit* did introduce one of Dickens' most famous characters, Mr. Pecksniff.

Chaps. 1–2. Mr. PECKSNIFF, an architect and land surveyor, informs his two daughters, CHARITY and MERCY, that a new student is coming in place of JOHN WESTLOCK, who is leaving.

Chaps. 3–4. An old man lies desperately ill at the Blue Dragon Inn in the village. He is attended only by a girl of 17. The inn's landlady, Mrs. LUPIN, sends for Pecksniff, who recognizes MARTIN CHUZZLEWIT, the elder, a relation of his. Rumors about the old man's wealth keep Pecksniff interested in his health, and he haunts the inn—as do several other villagers. The village seems thickly populated with relatives of Chuzzlewit. They form a group for consultation as to how they may acquire his money. In the midst of their conniving, Chuzzlewit and the girl leave the village for parts unknown.

Chaps. 5–6. TOM PINCH, Pecksniff's

student and drudge, is sent to Salisbury to meet the new student, for whom he is instructed to ask as Mr. MARTIN. The new student proves to be another MARTIN CHUZZLEWIT, grandson of the old man. Pinch learns that Martin is in love with old Martin Chuzzlewit's young attendant, but she gives him no encouragement.

Chaps. 7–10. Pecksniff sets young Martin to work designing a grammar school, but they are interrupted by the appearance of MONTAGUE TIGG, on an errand to borrow from Tom Pinch; Tigg and CHEVY SLYME have run up a bill at the Blue Dragon. Martin recognizes Chevy Slyme's name as that of a disreputable kinsman. Mrs. Lupin

Mr. Pecksniff and Martin

accepts Tom as security for his friends. MARK TAPLEY, man-of-all-work at the inn, says he is going to leave the Blue Dragon in search of his fortune, after avowing his love for Mrs. Lupin. Pecksniff and his two daughters go to London, and they find that they have companions on their coach journey—ANTHONY CHUZZLEWIT, one of the disappointed kinsmen, and his son, JONAS. Pecksniff and his daughters go to the boarding-house of Mrs. TODGERS. One day they go out to seek RUTH PINCH, Tom's sister, to whom Pecksniff has a letter. Ruth is a governess with a family in Camberwell, and there they find her. Pecksniff greets the grateful sister of his grateful pupil, and keeps his eye on the daughter of the house. The business that brought Pecksniff to town appears when old Martin Chuzzlewit pays a visit. He is friendly to the Pecksniffs but insists upon the dismissal of his grandson from their house.

Chaps. 11–14. Young BAILEY, a servant at Todgers', announces a visitor for Miss Pecksniff. It is Jonas Chuzzlewit, who proposes to show the girls the town, after which they should dine with him and his father. The invitation is accepted. Jonas devotes himself to Charity, the older, but is really interested in Mercy. At dinner in the bachelor establishment of Anthony Chuzzlewit and his son appears the only other member of the household, an old clerk named CHUFFEY. Tom Pinch has meanwhile been in luck, for young Martin has said he will take care of Tom after coming into his fortune. Also, John Westlock has come into some property, and he invites Tom and Martin to dine with him. The conversation at the dinner shows the innocent character of Tom, the complete selfishness of Martin, and the generosity of John, who has paid Tigg's debt without Tom's knowledge. Next morning Mr. Pecksniff pointedly ignores Martin. When Martin demands an explanation, Pecksniff pretends to have uncovered some misdeed of Martin's, at which the young man scornfully departs, announcing his determination to seek his fortune in America. He has very little capital—a good suit of clothes, a watch, and a half sovereign that Tom Pinch surreptitiously gave him. He seeks in vain for some way of working his passage like a gentleman to the United States. When he is almost hopeless, he receives an envelope containing a £20 note but no message. He meets Mark Tapley, who offers his services as companion-valet and begins his duties by taking a letter to the girl companion of Martin's grandfather. She and Mark meet in the park, and she is instructed to use Tom Pinch as a go-between for letters thereafter. She gives Mark a diamond ring for her lover.

Chaps. 15–17. Martin and Mark set out for the United States and have a miserable steerage passage. The ship is boarded in New York by hordes of youngsters crying the papers—the *New York Sewer, Family Spy, Stabber, Peeper, Rowdy Journal,* and the like. A representative citizen of the new

Martin and Mark find that their Eden property is a swamp

country greets Martin. He is Col. DIVER, editor of the *Rowdy Journal,* and he introduces Martin to the war correspondent of his paper, JEFFERSON BRICK. The two take him to their boarding house, kept by Major PAWKINS, where Martin has an opportunity to learn something of American manners. Martin goes to bed somewhat disheartened.

Chaps. 18–20. In London Jonas Chuzzlewit is enjoying his wealth in anticipation, and one evening he stealthily digs out Anthony's will for a foretaste of pleasure. He is interrupted by Pecksniff and exits in panic. Anthony has sent for Pecksniff, perhaps to discuss Jason's probable intention of marrying Pecksniff's daughter. The next morning Anthony is dead, and Pecksniff calls in a professional nurse, Mrs. SAIREY GAMP, who helps Mr. MOULD, the undertaker. He escorts the late Anthony to his grave, the only real mourner apparently being Chuffey. The funeral over, Jonas goes to the country with Pecksniff. He asks Mercy to marry him, thereby angering Charity. The confusion is worse confounded by the unexpected appearance of old Martin Chuzzlewit and MARY GRAHAM, his attendant.

Chaps. 21–23. In New York, Martin sets out with Mark to Eden, recommended to him as one of the most promising investment spots in America. At the railway terminus they are introduced to the agent of Eden, ZEPHANIAH SCADDER. As a result of his claims, they sink nearly all of their savings into a choice lot in Eden. They reach Eden at last, only to find it a swamp, breeding malaria and miasma, with one solitary inhabitant. It is a bitter end to Martin's hopes.

Chaps. 24–29. Pecksniff is worried over having old Martin Chuzzlewit under the same roof as Jonas, and is surprised when the old man seems amenable. Mercy announces her intention of marrying Jonas; old Martin tries to dissuade her, but she pays no attention to him or the signs of evil that are becoming more and more apparent in Jonas himself. Jonas is often mentioned by a deliriously feverish man whom Sairey Gamp is tending at night, having been hired for the purpose by John Westlock. Daytimes she takes care of Chuffey. This daytime employment ceases,

however, when Jonas and his bride come home and Mercy takes over the housekeeping. POLL SWEEDLEPIPE, Mrs. Gamp's landlord, comes to take her home, accompanied by Bailey, who is now working for Tigg Montague. The latter, formerly known as Montague Tigg, has enjoyed a reversal of fortune; he is now chairman of the Anglo-Bengalee Disinterested Loan and Life Insurance Company, in which he is associated with DAVID CRIMPLE, formerly Crimp, the pawnbroker; Dr. JOBLING, who attended Anthony Chuzzlewit and is now the firm's medical officer; also a man named NADGETT, who makes inquiries for the office. They have considered Jonas as a possible policy buyer, but Tigg decides that he would be most useful in the company, as one of its directors. Jonas is told in some detail how the company operates. Mrs. Gamp's patient, Mr. LEWSOME, tries to tell John Westlock something, but whatever he says gives Westlock the impression that Lewsome is still delirious.

Chaps. 30–32. Charity, still bitterly angry at Jonas, vents her wrath on her father. Finally she leaves to live at Todgers'. Pecksniff is relieved, as he has some deep designs of his own. He has achieved some influence over old Martin and plans to clinch his position by marrying Mary, to whom he proposes. She rejects him flatly. She tells Tom Pinch the whole story, and his erroneous picture of Pecksniff crumbles. Pecksniff has been eavesdropping. In Tom's presence, he tells old Martin that he overheard Tom making love to Mary. Tom does not deny it, for fear the truth will anger Martin at both Mary and his grandson. Pecksniff thereupon discharges Tom, who goes off with the blessings of all the neighborhood. Charity, meanwhile, at Todgers' has succeeded in winning the affections of Mr. MODDLE, who at one time was in love with Mercy.

Chaps. 33–35. Young Martin Chuzzlewit falls in the dismal swamp of Eden. Mark tends him; but no sooner is Martin well than Mark becomes ill. In nursing his friend, Martin gains some idea of his own selfishness as well as Mark's fidelity and Mary's sacrifices. On Mark's recovery, they go back to New York. Mark hires out as

cook on a ship and thus pays their passage to England.

Chaps. 36–38. Tom Pinch and his sister Ruth—who has left her unpleasant situation as governess—take lodgings in Islington. John Westlock is as friendly and kind as ever, and is much taken with the pretty Ruth. Tom sees Charity and Mercy and learns of Mercy's dismal marital state. Although Tom does not know it, he passes Nadgett in the street. Nadgett is on his way to tell Tigg Montague something about Jonas that gives Tigg a formidable weapon to hold over Jonas's head.

Chaps. 39–42. As Tom is looking for a job, John Westlock brings the news that a Mr. FIPS has offered—in the name of an anonymous benefactor—a job as secretary and librarian at £100 a year. Tom goes to work, still uninformed as to his employer. Jonas and Mercy attempt to leave town, but a packet from Tigg Montague halts them. Tigg makes it clear that Jonas is in his power. Jonas goes off with Tigg on a trip for the purpose of hooking Pecksniff, but on the way the carriage overturns and young Bailey—who had accompanied the rascals—is left for dead.

Chaps. 43–47. Mark Tapley and young Martin arrive at the Blue Dragon. Martin is unable to see his grandfather alone, for Pecksniff stays in the room. Pecksniff, however, is properly bilked by Jonas and Tigg Montague, who take most of his property from him. It is now revealed that the man who gave Tom the packet for Jonas is none other than Nadgett, a man of mystery all round. At Jonas's house, a dismal gathering of friends and relations breaks up early. That night Tigg Montague is killed.

Chaps. 48–49. Tom goes with Mark and Martin to see John Westlock, who is talking with Lewsome. Lewsome says he supplied Jonas with a drug that doubtless caused Anthony's death. Tom recalls something Chuffey said that tends to confirm this, and they call on Mrs. Gamp to keep her eye on Chuffey. The landlord brings the news that Bailey is dead, Tigg has vanished, Crimple has absconded with the company's money, and Jonas has accused the firm of swindling him.

Chaps. 50–54. Next day Tom is visited in the library by old Martin Chuzzlewit, who is his secret benefactor. Now the old man is ready to expose Pecksniff. Jonas is about to murder Chuffey when he is confronted by old Martin, young Martin, Lewsome, Mark Tapley, Chevy Slyme, and Nadgett. Nadgett has traced the murder of Tigg to Jonas. Handcuffed, Jonas bribes Chevy Slyme to let him step into the next room, where he takes poison rather than face prison. Now old Martin can release his wrath at Pecksniff and his hypocrisy. Martin's fortune is distributed so that Mary and young Martin can marry; Mark marries Mrs. Lupin; John Westlock marries Ruth. Only Charity is still unwed. Mr. Moddle rebels at the last minute and runs away, determined never to be taken alive, as his farewell letter declares.

431

Medea

Play by Euripides, 480–406 B.C.
Produced 431 B.C. (NAL, MT241; RE, 29).

SCHOLARS CONSIDER the *Medea* of Euripides the high point in ancient Greek drama. The story of Medea is a standard in Greek legend. She helped Jason and the Argonauts to overcome her father and she fled with Jason and married him. In some legends, including the one Euripides follows, she was a powerful sorceress. After she had lived with Jason for some years, he put her aside for a more desirable wife, and she used her sorcery to avenge the wrong. The play covers this phase.

Medea rejects Jason's offer

The nurse of MEDEA'S children laments the series of events which have led to her mistress' cruel fate. She recounts Medea's despair since her unjust abandonment by JASON. Knowing Medea's strong will and dangerous nature, she fears the consequences. Medea is heard crying to the gods for her own death and for the destruction of Jason and his new bride. Medea enters and speaks to the CHORUS about the unhappiness of women and their unequal rights among men. CREON tells Medea that, because of threats she has made, she and her sons must leave Corinth immediately. He does not believe her promises of peace and ignores her pleas, but finally consents to let her stay one more day so that, for the sake of her children, she can plan the journey. He walks away and Medea reveals that before leaving Corinth she will murder the king, his daughter, and Jason, and she tries to decide on the best possible method.

Jason approaches and offers Medea any provisions she might need, saying her exile has been self-imposed by her angry threats. In bitter rage she recounts the help she gave him during his travels, killing his enemies and forfeiting her family and home. Now she is unjustly forsaken for a new bride. He explains that his decision to marry the king's daughter was made so that their sons might grow up with royal brothers and the whole family might live comfortably. He denounces women but renews his offer of help, which she rejects. AEGEUS, King of Athens, is passing through Corinth and Medea tells him of her misfortune. Ignorant of her evil plotting, he promises her a home and protection in his land while he lives. With this accomplished, Medea makes plans for revenge. She will apologize to her husband and beg him to allow their two sons to stay in Corinth. She will then send the children bearing gifts to the new bride, but these will be anointed with poison drugs; and the princess, and anyone who touches her, will die wretchedly. Before fleeing Corinth Medea will slay her children, partly to prevent their falling into

enemies' hands but also to pain her husband. The women of the chorus try to dissuade her.

Jason believes Medea's false words and agrees to intercede for her. The children are sent with the gifts, and the guardian reports that the two boys may stay in Corinth. Medea then almost relents in her treacherous plan, thinking of her love for the

children and her pain in bearing and nurturing them. But hatred overpowers her maternal feelings. With incongruous tenderness she kisses her sons, then unable to look at them any longer, sends them into the house. A messenger brings the news that the princess and the king are dead, describing in detail their ghastly and tortured ending. Medea is satisfied, but knows she must finish her job. She has one final moment of softness, then steels herself for what is ahead. Medea goes into the house, the children's cries are heard, and blood flows out beneath the door. Jason arrives, looking for his sons, afraid the king's kinsmen might try to avenge on them their mother's murder. The women of the chorus tell him, to his horror, what has happened. Just then Medea appears above the palace roof in a chariot drawn by dragons. In a fiery speech, Jason assails her for her treacherous deed. He realizes now the folly of marrying "a tigress" from a barbarian land who was a traitor to her father and home. Jason begs for a chance to touch once more the soft flesh of his children, and to give them proper burial. But Medea refuses, saying she will carry them away and bury them herself so that no one will be able to rifle their tomb. She predicts a horrible death for Jason, and says she will go, safe in the chariot given her by her grandfather, the Sun, to stay in Athens. Jason cries out to Zeus to witness his suffering.

The Merchant of Venice

Play by William Shakespeare, 1564–1616.
Produced about 1596. (PB, PL60)

THIS IS ONE of Shakespeare's most popular comedies. The main plot was apparently intended to be the one based on traditional Oriental stories in which the hero must solve a riddle to win the fair lady. After starting to write a play on this theme, Shakespeare apparently found that the story of Shylock and the pound of flesh was far more suited to his genius and he made it the main theme. *The Merchant of Venice* has been criticized and there have been many suggestions that it be omitted from school reading and from performance because the villain Shylock is a Jew, but in Shakespeare's times Jews and the entire Jewish people were customarily cast as villains and Shakespeare's play is outstanding because in it he develops an eloquent defense of the Jew's right to just treatment and freedom of worship. He fashioned the ending to suit his audiences' prejudice, but not before he had produced many speeches justifying or at least explaining Shylock's quest of vengeance.

Act I. 1. ANTONIO, a wealthy merchant of Venice, is approached by his friend, BASSANIO for a loan. Bassanio is in love with a rich widow, PORTIA, and needs funds to court her properly. Antonio is short of cash because his ships are at sea, but agrees to raise what money he can for Bassanio. 2. At Belmont, Portia discusses her many suitors with her maid, NERISSA. The maid prefers Bassanio to all others. 3. Bassanio calls on SHYLOCK, a money-lender, for a 3-month loan of 3,000 ducats. Shylock insists that Antonio stand surety for the loan. Shylock hates Antonio, who, he says, has "spit upon my Jewish gabardine." Antonio retorts that Shylock may lend the money as to an enemy, and Shylock agrees to make the loan in return for a bond entitling him to a pound of Antonio's flesh if the loan is not repaid on time. Antonio accepts, confident that his ships will come to port in ample time.

Act II. 1. The Prince of MOROCCO visits Portia and asks her to marry him. 2. LAUNCELOT, a servant who is quitting the service of Shylock, meets his blind father GOBBO, who does not recognize him: "It is a wise father that knows his own child." The son says that henceforth he will serve Bassanio. GRATIANO, known as a playboy, asks and is permitted to go with his friend Bassanio to Belmont. 3. Launcelot takes leave of Shylock's daughter JESSICA, who admits that her father's house is hell. 4. A masquerade is planned for that evening to celebrate Bassanio's departure to woo Portia. LORENZO, a friend of Bassanio, loves Jessica and plans to elope with her. 5. Shylock berates Launcelot for leaving him. Having to go out, Shylock turns his keys over to Jessica, warning her to keep the doors locked because of the masquerade revels. 6. Jessica, disguised as a page, elopes with Lorenzo, taking some of her father's money with her. 7. Portia explains that in conformance with her father's will she must test her suitors before choosing. The Prince of Morocco fails the test of selecting the proper one of three caskets shown him; Portia is happy to see him go. 8. Shylock is distraught to find his daughter and his ducats gone. 9. Another of Portia's suitors, the Prince of ARRAGON, selects the wrong casket and fails the test.

Act III. 1. Most of Antonio's ships have been lost. Shylock gloats; "Hath not a Jew eyes . . . hands . . . affections, passions?" Does he not crave revenge just as a Christian does? Shylock has sent TUBAL to search for Jessica. Tubal cannot find her. 2. Portia is attracted to Bassanio. She puts him to the test but aids him with a song containing clues to the answer, which he thereupon gives correctly. She gives him a ring and promises to marry him. Meanwhile, Gratiano has won Nerissa. Lorenzo arrives with Jessica. Bassanio receives bad news from Venice: Shylock demands repayment. Portia offers to pay the debt, and arranges a quick marriage so that Bassanio may then hurry to Venice to save Antonio. 3. Shylock has Antonio imprisoned. Friends assure Antonio that the Duke of Venice will not permit the bond to stand. 4. Portia bids Nerissa procure mens' clothing for Portia and herself, so that they may go to Venice in disguise of lawyer and law clerk. 5. Launcelot, in a comedy scene, tells Jessica that her conversion to Christianity is not a blessing because it might raise the price of pork.

Act IV. 1. The trial of Shylock against Antonio begins in Venice, the duke presiding. Bassanio offers Shylock twice the amount borrowed, but Shylock is adamant: he wants Antonio's life. Even the duke's plea cannot move him. Nerissa, in disguise of a law clerk, delivers to the Duke a letter from BELLARIO, a learned lawyer of Padua. Bellario recommends a "young doctor of Rome," who soon arrives—this "BALTHAZAR" is Portia in disguise. As Antonio's counsel, Portia offers three times the sum owed; Shylock refuses. Portia appeals to his mercy, to be freely granted—"The quality of mercy is not strained (forced)." Shylock refuses. Finally Portia grants that the bond entitles him to take a pound of flesh, but asserts that if he sheds a drop of Antonio's blood his property will, under the laws of Venice, be forfeit to the state. Thus checked, Shylock agrees to take instead the triple indemnity. Bassanio is ready to pay, but Portia stops him. Since Shylock has refused

this settlement in open court, he cannot have it now. And, since he has plotted against the life of a Venetian citizen, half his goods are forfeit to Antonio and the other half to the state. Antonio refuses to take his half, but requests that Shylock be compelled to will it to his son-in-law Lorenzo and also that Shylock be required to become a Christian immediately. The now abject Shylock agrees. Portia refuses a fee for her services. She requests only the ring Bassanio is wearing; he very reluctantly gives it to "Balthazar." 2. Nerissa likewise contrives to get her husband's ring away from him. The two women hurry back to Belmont.

Act V. Portia and Nerissa pretend to be incensed that their husbands have given away the rings they swore to cherish forever. Bassanio and Gratiano finally realize that the two women were "Balthazar" and the law clerk. Lorenzo and Jessica are given the signed document in which Shylock acknowledges them as his heirs. As a final cheerful note, word comes that the previous report was erroneous—Antonio's ships have come safely to harbor.

The Merry Wives of Windsor

Play by William Shakespeare, 1564–1616.
Produced about 1597.

SIR JOHN FALSTAFF was the most popular comic character Shakespeare created. He was so popular in *Henry VI* that Shakespeare catered to popular demand and wrote an entire play about him. (According to some accounts, he wrote *The Merry Wives* by the direct command of Queen Elizabeth.) Because of its contemporary popularity and its history, the play is one of the best known among Shakespeare's plays, but as a work of art it cannot be given high rank. It is simply a quite competent farce written for money-making purposes.

Act I. 1. SHALLOW, a country judge, and his cousin SLENDER complain to Sir Hugh EVANS, a Welsh parson, of the indignities they have suffered from Sir JOHN FALSTAFF. As they approach the house of Master PAGE, a Windsor gentlemen, Evans advises Slender to court his daughter, ANNE PAGE, for she has a substantial dowry. Page is entertaining Falstaff and his hangers-on, BARDOLPH, NYM, and PISTOL. Page and Evans effect a truce when the two parties met and begin to bicker. 2. Evans sends a letter to Mistress QUICKLY enlisting her influence with Anne Page on behalf of Slender. 3. Falstaff schemes to obtain money by wooing Mistress PAGE and Mistress FORD, both of whom hold their husbands' pursestrings. He writes amorous letters to both and asks Nym and Pistol to deliver the letters. When they refuse, he reviles them and entrusts the message to the boy ROBIN. For revenge, Nym and Pistol resolve to inform Page and Ford of the plot. 4. Dr. CAIUS, a French physician lodging with Mistress Quickly, asks her to intercede on his behalf with Anne Page. When he learns Evans has made the same request for Slender, he writes Evans a challenge to duel.

FENTON, a gentleman, also courts Anne Page.

Act II. 1. Mistress Page and Mistress Ford compare the letters sent them by Falstaff. Indignant, they resolve to trap Falstaff, and enlist the aid of Mistress Quickly. Meanwhile, Nym and Pistol inform Page and Ford. Page is merely amused, but Ford decides to take action. He asks the HOST of the Garter Inn to introduce him to Falstaff under the assumed name "BROOK." 2. Mistress Quickly carries pretended messages of encouragement from both women to Falstaff. Ford is introduced as Brook. He begs Falstaff's aid in procuring Mistress Ford, whom he has long coveted. Falstaff assures him he shall have her before the night is out. 3. Dr. Caius awaits Evans in a field near Windsor. Instead, Shallow appears; as a judge, he forbids the duel. The host persuades Dr. Caius to swallow his wrath and to call upon Anne Page.

Act III. 1. Evans awaits Dr. Caius in another field. The host has averted the duel by sending the two men to different fields. Shallow and Slender reconcile the foes. 2. Ford mets Mistress Page on the way to his house. He thinks she is really going to meet Falstaff, and resolves to catch the guilty pair. 3. Mistress Ford gives orders to have a big laundry basket full of dirty linen taken out of the house and emptied in a ditch. Falstaff arrives with amorous intent, which is interrupted when Mistress Page rushes in with the news that Ford is returning to the house. Falstaff hides in the laundry basket, which is carried out as Ford enters to search the house. 4. Anne Page indicates to Fenton that he is her choice, but her father favors Slender. The latter admits to Anne that he has little heart for the suit urged by Shallow and Page. 5. Falstaff returns to the inn wet and bedraggled. Mistress Quickly apologizes for the fiasco and promises that Falstaff shall have another opportunity to see Mistress Ford alone. "Brook" enters; Falstaff tells the story of his bad luck with Mistress Ford, but holds out the hope that Brook may still meet her.

Act IV. 1. Falstaff is at a second rendezvous with Mistress Ford while Mistress Page and Mistress Quickly plot his downfall. 2. Again Mistress Page interrupts the rendezvous to warn that Ford is returning. The two dames dress Falstaff in women's clothes, and also send out the laundry basket as a blind. Ford searches the basket furiously and finds nothing. Mistaking the disguised Falstaff for an old crone he hates, he cudgels "Mother Prat" out of the house. 3. The host agrees to furnish three horses to the German guests who have hired the Garter Inn for a week. 4. Mistress Page and Mistress

Falstaff is pursued by masquerade goblins, who pinch and beat him

Ford tell their husbands all about their jokes on Falstaff. New sport is plotted: Falstaff is to be induced to meet the ladies in the park, disguised as Herne the Hunter. —Page plans to let Anne elope with Slender, while his wife plans to let her elope with Dr. Caius. 5. Falstaff has returned to the inn. Mistress Quickly brings him the latest message from the ladies. The German guests have decamped with the horses. Dr. Caius says the duke they pretended to serve does not exist. 6. Fenton pays the host to help in confounding the other suitors of Anne Page.

Act V. 1. Falstaff tells "Brook" about the second fiasco. He urges Brook to accompany him to Windsor Park. 2. Page, Shallow and Slender are waiting in the park. 3. Mistress Page tells Dr. Caius he can find Anne in the park by her green costume. 4. Evans also is in the park, to aid Slender. 5. Falstaff is in the park, disguised as Herne the Hunter. The two ladies accost him but then flee on hearing a noise. Falstaff is engulfed by masquerade figures of fairies and hobgoblins, who pinch and beat him. All the friends and children of Page and Ford have joined in this prank. Dr. Caius elopes with a green-clad figure and Slender with another; both turn out to be pages, rather than Anne Page. The real Anne Page has been found by Fenton. They finally obtain her parents' consent to their union. Falstaff is finally told how he has been duped.

Merton of the Movies

Novel by Harry Leon Wilson, 1867–1939.
Published 1922 by Doubleday & Co.
© 1922 by Harry Leon Wilson.

HARRY LEON WILSON was never accorded his just position as a humorous novelist—nor, as a matter of fact, as a serious novelist, in which field he proved himself similarly capable. He is best remembered for one of his minor novels, *Merton of the Movies,* principally because it proved so successful when adapted for the Broadway stage and then for the motion pictures. Wilson wrote nostalgic and sentimental novels of somewhat earlier periods that were still within the recollection of his middleaged readers. *Merton,* however, is an exception; it is based on Wilson's experience when he first went to Hollywood to acquire some of the easy money available to authors. The novel is a satire on Hollywood customs and characters of the 1920s.

Chaps. 1–3. MERTON GILL is a clerk in the emporium of AMOS GASHWILER in Simsbury, Ill. He is ambitious to become a movie actor. He is abetted by his friend TESSIE KEARNS, who wants to write screenplays. Both have taken mail-order courses in their fields. Together they attend the local movie house, where they are revolted by low comedy but enthralled by the screen adventures of the glamorous star BEULAH BAXTER.

Chaps. 4–6. Having saved some money, Merton takes leave of absence from Gashwiler and goes to Hollywood. He rents a furnished room, assumes the stage name of CLIFFORD ARMYTAGE, and tries to get a job at the Holden lot. After a week of pavement-pounding, he catches the eye of the woman in charge of hiring extras. She is amused at his unsophistication and rusticity. She gives him a chance to see the inside of the movie lot, and he is entranced by the

bizarre sights and sounds—but the weeks go on without a job. Merton makes the acquaintance of some of the extras, among them the MONTAGUE family—the father and mother, old troupers, and the daughter FLIP. This girl has all the self-assurance that Merton lacks, and he shies away from her. He notices that others do not appear to resent her flippant, almost brazen, manner, and that she gets plenty of work. At last Merton is called for his first job—two days for $15. He appears in a cabaret scene in "The Blight of Broadway," as a diner bored by his pretty companion. Later he

434

gets a second bit, as a Bedouin walking the street of an Arabian town.

Chaps. 7–11. Merton's savings are almost exhausted. Rather than abandon his hopes, he gives up his room and takes lodging at night in the movie lot whenever he can find a set that includes a bed. One night in a huge tank built for an episode in the Beulah Baxter serial, he makes a shocking discovery. His idol is married; her husband is none other than the uncouth director SIG ROSENBLATT. Worst of all, during the filming of the perilous scene Beulah is not even on the lot—her part is played by Flip Montague. His admiration of Beulah and scorn for Flip undergo revulsion. On emerging from the tank, Flip sees Merton and notes the signs of destitution. She proposes to buy him a meal, but he stalks away in offended dignity. Later he wanders back to the deserted set and is surprised by Flip, who has returned to search for a lost pin. This time she succeeds in buying him a meal, lending him money, and persuading him to let her help him get a job. Next day she contacts JEFF BAIRD, the man who makes the low comedies that Merton despises. Baird is interested in her account of Merton as an actor who can play a scene "straight" no matter what absurdities are going on around him, and he agrees to give Merton a trial.

Chaps. 12–15. Flip takes Merton to see Baird. Though reluctant to be associated with slapstick, Merton hands over the stills he has had taken of himself registering various emotions. Baird is secretly convulsed with amusement; he signs Merton at $40 a week. After Merton has made some study of the films of HAROLD PARMALEE, he is considered ready for work. Skillfully guided by the director and writers, Merton plays his rôle with utmost seriousness, unaware that his over-acting is extremely funny on the screen. The ending, set in the old West, has Merton imitating BUCK BENSON, a cowboy hero of Hollywood. Lest Merton become aware of the hoax, Baird delays release of the first picture until a second is almost finished. Even then, difficulties arise. Merton objects to appearing in the same film with a cross-eyed man, one of the warhorses of the Baird productions. Baird persuades Merton that the cross-eyed man supports a large and sickly family and that to throw him out of work would be inhumane. In like manner Merton is reconciled to the circumstance that his film fiancée is a brawny six-foot woman weighing a couple of hundred pounds.

Chaps. 16–20. The new picture is a satire on another Hollywood idol, EDGAR WAYNE, who is always cast as a simple country boy with a heart of gold. Merton falls easily into the part, but begins to notice things. His own salary has been raised to $75, yet the cross-eyed man gets $1200 a week! Through intervention of Flip, Merton is signed to a 3-year contract at $250. Merton realizes he is falling in love with Flip. He buys her a watch to celebrate the première of his first film, but she tells him

to withhold the gift until after the event. She and Baird are now feeling anxiety and remorse at Merton's coming discovery that he has been duped. At the premier, Merton is' at first puzzled by the laughter; then he begins to perceive what an absurd figure he

cuts. He is outraged, but in the following days he is mollified by the storm of praise for this new-found comic talent and by the handsome offers that pour in. He accepts his fate, marries Flip, and settles down to the life of a famous comedy star.

A Message to García

Novel by Elbert Green Hubbard, 1856–1915.
Published 1899.

THIS SHORT TALE or essay is a piece of straight inspirational writing. It has a place in the history of American literature because of its tremendous popularity when it was published. Millions read it and talked about it and some corporations bought large quantities of copies to distribute free among their executives and friends. The book itself was quite decorative, that being Hubbard's primary business: he had founded the Roycrofters, a printing and publishing establishment dedicated to the making of better-looking books than were being produced by most publishing houses. Most of the Roycrofters' designs would seem corny to modern designers but they made an unquestionable contribution to the improvement of book design in the United States.

During the Spanish-American War, President McKinley wished to get an urgent

message to GARCÍA, leader of the insurgents. A man named ROWAN undertook to find García, and set off into the jungles of Cuba. Three weeks later he emerged on the other side of the island, having with great difficulty and perserverance traversed hostile country on foot and delivered the letter.

HUBBARD praises the man who can accept responsibility and, without stopping to ask questions, get the task done. He castigates others as falling short of this ideal, among them clock-watchers, gold-brickers, buck-passers, those whose sympathy is all for the "downtrodden worker" with none for the harassed employer who ages before his time trying to get "ne'er-do-wells to do intelligent work." Among workers, he says, indifferent and slipshod work is the rule. For this reason, socialism is far in the future. If men will not act for themselves, what will they do when they are asked to act for all? The man who never strikes or gets laid off "is wanted in every city, town and village—in every office, shop, store and factory. The world cries out for such: he is needed, and needed badly—the man who can CARRY A MESSAGE TO GARCÍA."

Rowan with great difficulty and perseverance traverses hostile country

Metamorphoses

Poems by Ovid, 43 B.C.–18 A.D. Published about 8 A.D. Translated from the Latin in 1567 by Arthur Golding. Other translations. (Everyman, 955)

OVID'S METAMORPHOSES was not a work intended primarily to recount the stories of the ancient Greek and Roman mythology; he used the mythology principally as illustrations of certain philosophical conclusions. Nevertheless, in the course of the work he managed to include nearly all the classical mythology and as a result the *Metamorphoses* have been used more than any other source for the standard versions of the stories. Bulfinch relied primarily on Ovid. Since the *Metamorphoses* is a Latin work, nearly all the gods and goddesses are better known to English readers by their Latin than their Greek names. The title, *Metamorphoses,* simply means changes or transformations. The work presents the philosophy that nothing is stable in the universe; gods change to men and animals, men to animals and plants, animals to stones and plants.

The poet says he will begin from the earliest times and recount events down to the period in which he lives. Out of primitive Chaos in which all matter was intertwined, some primary god separated the basic elements of fire, earth, air, and water. Out of the mixtures of these elements came primary forms. At last the nameless god desired "a living creature of finer stuff than these, more capable of lofty thought, one who could have dominion over all the rest." And thus man was born. This early time was the Age of Gold, when life was perfect. The prime god SATURN is exiled by his son JUPITER (or JOVE), and the Age of Silver follows, in which the seasons appear. Then, comes the Age of Bronze, filled with evil and violence. Jove calls a council of the Olympian gods and declares his intention to destroy most of mankind. A worldwide flood covers most of the earth. Only one man and woman survive, the chaste DEUCALION and PYRRHA. When the waters subside, Deucalion asks the ocean goddess THEMIS how to repopulate the earth. Themis tells him to throw his mother's bones over his back. Bewildered by this advice, Deucalion at last realizes that this "mother's bones" are the earth itself, mother of all men. He and his sister-wife Pyrrha then toss rocks over their shoulders, and a new race of men is born. Plants arise from various origins. For example, the manly god APOLLO loves a nymph named DAPHNE, who is too coy to return his passion. One day Apollo chases the girl through the woods and is about to catch her. Daphne prays to Apollo's sister DIANA, goddess of chastity, who changes the girl into a laurel tree. Thereafter Apollo uses the laurel wreath to signify victory in athletic contests.

The greatest of all transformers is Jupiter. Jupiter falls in love with the maiden IO and tries to hide the affair from his jealous wife, JUNO. Juno, however, sees through his protective clouds and watches her husband turn the nymph into a white heifer. Juno sets the many-eyed beast ARGUS to guard the heifer night and day. Taking pity on the girl, Jupiter sends his mischievous messenger son MERCURY to slay the beast. Mercury puts Argus to sleep with his magic cap and wand, freeing Io, who wanders about the world. Juno takes Argus's eyes and sets them in the tail of the peacock, her favorite bird. Eventually Jove changes Io back into a woman again. Jove also falls in love with a nymph, CALLISTO. Again Juno spies this infidelity and changes Callisto into a huge bear. One day this bear wanders in the woods and comes upon her son ARCAS, a hunter. Arcas prepares to shoot his own mother, but Jove intercedes by snatching them both up into the heavens. He makes them the Great and Little Bear. Juno, enraged by her husband's mercy, complains to FATHER OCEAN. As a result, neither constellation ever dips below the ocean's waters. Jove also becomes enamored of a princess of Sidon named EUROPA. He sends her a dream in which the girl realizes that some great honor awaits her. Then, transforming himself into a beautiful white bull, Jove approaches the princess on the sands of the Mediterranean coast. Europa climbs on his back for a ride, and Jove flies wildly away with her to the secluded island of Crete. Later the continent of Europe is named in her honor. Meanwhile Europa's father sends his son CADMUS to search for the missing girl. Cadmus wanders to Greece, where he decides to found a city. While preparing a sacrifice, his men are frightened by a golden snake that Cadmus later kills. To atone for this sacred snake's murder, Cadmus plants man-producing seed in the fields. An army of soldiers spring up, but they kill one another until only five remain. These five soldiers then aid Cadmus in building the city of Thebes.

One of the saddest victims of Juno is ECHO, a nymph who often helps Jove deceive his wife. In rage, Juno dooms Echo to repeat only the last phrases of words spoken to her. Poor Echo then falls in love with an arrogant young man, NARCISSUS, who refuses to accept any offer of love, preferring to sit on a riverbank and watch his reflection in the water. Slowly Narcissus pines away in fascination with his own image. Echo can do nothing but repeat his mournful words until the young man dies. Even in the underworld Narcissus contemplates himself, while Echo fades away until she is just a voice. Narcissus's memory remains as a beautiful yellow flower.

Another beautiful plant arises from the tragic love of PYRAMUS and THISBE. Great brick walls in the city of Babylon keep the two lovers apart. Still, they manage to communicate through a chink. They agree to meet at a deserted place in the forest. The girl Thisbe arrives early and is frightened away by a ferocious lion. In her flight, she loses her cloak, which the lion mauls and drops. Later Pyramus arrives and spies the torn cloak. Assuming that his beloved is dead, the young man drives his sword through his breast. Thisbe returns to the grove and sees her dead lover. She then commits suicide with the same sword. From that time on, the white-berried mulberry trees that grow in the grove change their color to red in memory of the lovers' unfortunate deaths.

One of the world's most significant changes, the seasons, is attributed to CERES, goddess of grain. Her lovely daughter PROSERPINE is playing on the island of Sicily when she is spied by PLUTO, god of

Narcissus at the river

436

the Underworld. The vengeful VENUS forces her son CUPID to wound the god. He thereby falls in love with Proserpine and carries her away to his dark palace. The grain goddess then begins to search the world for her daughter. Since she no longer cares for the crops, everything withers and becomes barren. At last Ceres comes upon the spring ARETHUSA, who tells her what has happened to her daughter. Ceres complains to Jupiter, who promises to return the girl if she has not eaten in Hell. Unfortunately Proserpine has already tasted Pluto's food. When Ceres refuses to accept this judgment and threatens to destroy fertility forever, Jupiter effects a compromise. Proserpine is allowed to spend half of the year on earth with her mother, and half of the year in Hades as its queen. When Proserpine is on earth, the seasons are spring and summer; when Proserpine is in the underworld, the seasons are fall and winter.

King TEREUS marries PROCNE, the daughter of King PANDION, and takes her to northern Greece. After a time, Tereus remembers Procne's sister, PHILOMELA, and contrives a way in which he can have her too. He begs his wife to allow him to bring the girl to live with them. His wife consents, and Tereus goes back to Pandion to escort the other daughter to his home. On the return journey, Tereus cannot restrain his passion and forces himself on the young girl. When Philomela threatens to reveal everything to his wife, Tereus cuts out her tongue and imprisons her in a tower. Philomela uses her cunning to weave a tapestry of the crime and send it to her sister. When Procne summons her to the palace, the two conspire revenge. Procne's son ITYS comes into the room and the sisters seize and kill the boy. They then boil his body and serve it to Tereus at a banquet. When Tereus demands to see his son, Procne hurls Itys' head at his father and suddenly Tereus grasps what his wife has done. He pursues the sisters, but Procne changes into a swallow and Philomela into a nightingale. Tereus himself changes into a hawk and he still pursues the two delicate birds throughout the world.

One of the most touching stories concerns the flight of the great artist DAEDALUS. Daedalus is called to Crete to build a great labyrinth to contain the half-bull, half-man MINOTAUR that terrorizes the countryside. After completing the immense edifice, however, he receives very bad treatment from King MINOS, who refuses to allow him to leave the island. Daedalus and his son ICARUS fashion wings of feathers and wax to fly over the ocean. The father cautions his son to strike a middle path. If they fly too high, the sun will melt the wax; if they fly too low, the salt spray will weigh the feathers down. Icarus, however, is exhilarated by the power of this new invention and soars higher and higher. He flies too near the sun and his wings disintegrate and he falls into the ocean and drowns. Daedalus successfully reaches the mainland. [The

myth is a parable of the "middle path" or "golden mean" expounded by ancient philosophers.]

Ovid recounts the external aspects of the Trojan War, the Quest of the Golden Fleece and Hercules' Labors. He does not dwell long on any of these events, because they are covered more thoroughly by other poets. At this point Ovid enters human history. He continues to repeat his theme: Nature

ever makes up forms from other forms. Nothing perishes in the whole universe. Birth is but the beginning of a new form, and death but cessation of a former one. Then, suddenly reversing his position at the end of the poem, he proclaims that the advent of Augustus Caesar will nullify all change by the stability of the Roman Empire. [This statement is assumed to be ironic.]

A Midsummer Night's Dream

Play by William Shakespeare, 1564–1616.
Produced about 1595. (PB, PL679)

THOUGH THIS PLAY contains some of Shakespeare's most beautiful early poetry (from a period when he was not quite so philosophical as he became in later years) and though Mendelssohn wrote beautiful music for it, the play is overcluttered with complications and is hard to read and hard to perform. It was produced in a spectacular and ambitious production by Max Reinhardt, both as a live performance and as a motion picture with a cast both famous and talented, in 1935. But the motion picture, like most motion-picture productions of Shakespeare, did not make money (there have been exceptions to this, principally the productions of Laurence Olivier, but they have been few).

Act I. 1. THESEUS, Duke of Athens, has decided to marry HIPPOLYTA, the queen of the Amazons, at the next new moon. PHILOSTRATE, the master of revels, is ordered to arrange festivities. EGEUS comes to court with his daughter HERMIA and her two suitors, LYSANDER and DEMETRIUS. Egeus wants her to marry Demetrius but she is in love with Lysander. The Athenian law provides the choice of death or a monastery for a disobedient child. The two lovers decide to escape from Athens rather than submit. Hermia is to meet Lysander in a forest outside of the city. HELENA, a friend of Hermia, is taken into their confidence. Helena is in love with Demetrius. He has spurned her advances but she hopes to change his mind by betraying the plot of Hermia and Lysander to him. 2. At QUINCE the carpenter's house in Athens, a group of craftsmen meet and decide to put on a play in honor of the Duke's wedding. After some bickering about the rôle each will get,

they decide to meet at the Duke's Oak for their first rehearsal.

Act II. 1. In the forest, PUCK and a FAIRY discuss the recent discord between OBERON, King of the Elves, and his queen TITANIA, over the possession of a little boy. Oberon and Titania accuse each other of love for Hippolyta and Theseus respectively. Oberon instructs Puck to pluck a certain flower, the juice of which makes a person fall in love with the first thing he sees on awaking. Puck is to drop this juice into the eyes of Titania, so that she may fall in love with some creature of the woods. Demetrius, followed by Helena, searches the same woods for Hermia. They quarrel and Demetrius tells her to leave him. Oberon, overhearing, now tells Puck to drop the liquid into the eyes of an Athenian youth who is in the forest and has refused his lady. Oberon himself will drop the liquid into Titania's eyes. 2. Oberon puts the drops into Titania's eyes but Puck puts his drops, intended for Demetrius, into the eyes of Lysander, the first Athenian youth he encounters. Helena, looking for Demetrius, chances to wake up Lysander and he falls madly in love with her. Lysander pursues Helena into the woods. Hermia goes to look for Lysander.

Act III. 1. The craftsmen meet near the spot where Titania lies asleep. BOTTOM gives stage directions for the play, which is "Pyramus and Thisby." Puck decides to play a prank on them by slipping a donkey's head over the shoulders of Bottom. The other workmen flee in terror, thinking Bottom has been bewitched. Bottom does not understand. He starts to sing to keep his courage up. This awakens Titania, who immediately falls in love with Bottom. Titania tells her Fairies to wait on her new lover and to bring him to her bower. 2. Puck reports his prank to Oberon. Hermia and Demetrius arrive, quarreling. She accuses him of having killed Lysander and she runs from his attentions. Lysander and Helena enter, while the exhausted Demetrius lies down to rest. Oberon puts the magic flower juice into his eyes. The noise of Helena's rejection of the amorous Lysander awakens the sleeping Demetrius. Since he sees Helena first on opening his eyes, he now falls madly in love with her and the two men compete for her favors. The noise brings back Hermia, who thinks Helena has stolen Lysander's love. The men decide to fight it out. The women run off into the woods. Oberon decides to straighten out the situation. He orders Puck to put the four lovers on the ground side by side and has him remove the spell from Lysander with the juice of another flower.

Act IV. 1. Titania is still under the spell and carries on her love affair with the donkey-headed Bottom. They finally fall asleep in each other's arms. Oberon has in the meantime gotten hold of the child, which was the object of his quarrels with Titania. He orders Puck to remove the donkey head from Bottom. He then awakens the queen, who is now free of the spell. She and Oberon fly away together. As the sun rises, Theseus and Hippolyta, with their followers, arrive in the woods to hunt. With them is Egeus, who sees his daughter asleep on the ground with her companions. Again he demands that Demetrius marry Hermia, but Demetrius tells him he loves Helena. Theseus is so pleased with this solution that he decides on a triple wedding. Bottom is the last one to wake up. He thinks he has had a rare vision. 2. The craftsmen are unhappy over the loss of Bottom, having no one to play his rôle. Bottom turns up just in time.

Act V. 1. In Theseus's palace, the craftsmen put on their play. Bottom is Pyramus the lover, and FLUTE is Thisby. At midnight the couples retire and leave the palace to Oberon, Titania, and their elves, to celebrate their reunion.

The Mill
on the Floss

Novel by George Eliot (Mary Ann Evans Cross, 1819–1880).. Published 1860. (PB, PL509)

IN AMERICA this is one of the best-known of George Eliot's novels, partly because excerpts from Book I were for many years used in "readers" in elementary schools. *The Mill on the Floss* was written in George Eliot's most fruitful period and was one of her best works. The novel (and River Floss) are set in Warwickshire, in central England.

Book I. Boy and Girl. 1–3. Mr. TULLIVER, his wife BESSY, his son TOM, 13, and his daughter MAGGIE, 9, live at Dorlcote Mill near the village of St. Ogg's on the River Floss. Although Mr. Tulliver has made a good living as a miller and farmer, he does not want Tom to follow in his footsteps. He decides to give Tom the best education money can buy. He laments only the fact that Maggie rather than Tom has inherited the brains in the family. Mr. Tulliver sends Tom to a boarding school run by a clergyman named STELLING. 4–5. Various incidents show how great is Maggie's love for Tom. Whenever she does something to make him angry, and he says he does not love her, she is very hurt. 6. After a quarrel with Maggie, Tom goes to play with his friend BOB JAKIN. Bob cheats at a game and the boys exchange blows, Tom exhibiting a keen sense of justice. 7. Mr. Tulliver's sisters, the former Misses DODSON, Aunt GLEGG, Aunt PULLET and Aunt DEANE, come to visit the Tullivers with their husbands. All three have married well; they believe Bessy has married below herself. They are critical of Mr. Tulliver and mock the Tulliver children, especially Maggie with her dark skin, unruly hair, and madcap ways, comparing her unfavorably with Mrs. Deane's daughter LUCY, who is blond, neat, and well-mannered. The relatives disapprove of the school Mr. Tulliver has chosen for Tom. Mrs. Glegg and Mr. Tulliver have a serious quarrel, as a result of which Mrs. Glegg threatens to call in a £500 note she holds on the Tullivers' property. 8. Mr. Tulliver decides he must pay Mrs. Glegg. His sister, Mrs. Moss, who has married badly, owes him £300. He goes to her, but the Mosses are in no position to repay him. 9–11. Lucy comes to stay with the Tullivers and Tom is kind to her and ignores Maggie because of her pranks. Maggie, in a fit of anger and jealousy, runs away to the gypsies, thinking that life among them will be pleasant; but she is soon disillusioned by their filth and their food and is happy to be returned to her home. Her father, who always takes Maggie's part, scolds his wife and son for mistreating her. 12–13. Mr. Glegg convinces his wife not to call in her money but Mr. Tulliver writes to her that he will pay her within a month and wants no more favors from her. The family breach grows and Mrs. Glegg does not visit the Tullivers until the night before Tom is to leave for school.

Book II. School Time. 1. Tom is unhappy at Mr. Stelling's; his ambition is to work at the Mill. Maggie visits him, the only bright spot of his first months at school. 2. When Tom is home for Christmas, his father is having legal troubles. Mr. Tulliver's pet peeve is lawyers—in particular Mr. WAKEM, who is representing the neighbor with whom he is feuding. 3–4. Tom returns to school and finds that Mr. Stelling has a second pupil, Mr. Wakem's crippled son PHILIP. Tom admires Philip's artistic talents and intelligence but is prejudiced because of his father and his deformity. However, the boys help each other. 5–6. Maggie, again visiting Tom at school, meets and takes a liking to Philip, especially when he is kind to Tom, who has injured his foot. Maggie and Philip kiss, promise to remember each other, and say they will kiss again whenever next they meet. Maggie goes away to school with Lucy but is called home when Tom is in his fifth and last half-year. She goes to school to get him, bringing the bad news that Mr. Tulliver has lost his legal case and stands to lose everything—his mill and his land. Tom and Maggie go home to their new life of sorrow; their childhood and their happiness are over.

Book III. The Downfall. 1. When Mr. Tulliver realizes he is ruined, he has a stroke. Tom tells Maggie she must never speak to Philip again. 2–4. Mrs. Tulliver's relatives show no real sympathy for the Tullivers. All the household goods are to be sold and they do not offer to help the family keep their most cherished possessions. Tom gets out his father's will, which states clearly that he wishes the Mosses' note destroyed. Tom insists that his father's will be honored, though this means losing everything. 5. Tom goes to Uncle Deane, in hope of getting a good position, but Mr. Deane says Tom should have learned bookkeeping rather than Latin. 6. Bob Jakin comes to see Tom for the first time since the boys fought and generously offers Tom a considerable sum of money. Tom appreciates the offer but feels he cannot accept it, even though all the household furnishings are sold. 7–9. Mrs. Tulliver begs Mr. Wakem not to buy their mill and their land; Uncle Deane's firm, Guest and Co., seems willing to buy it. But Mr. Wakem decides to buy the mill to humiliate Mr. Tulliver by letting him stay on and work for wages. Mr. Tulliver sadly agrees but has Tom write in the family Bible that he will never forget what Wakem has done and will seek revenge.

Book IV. The Valley of Humiliation. 1–2. The Tullivers are living economically; their creditors have been paid in part, and Mr. Tulliver strives to repay them in full before he dies. 3. Maggie feels hardest hit by the family misfortune, for she has lost not only her possessions and way of life but seemingly her father's and brother's love. One day she reads a passage by Thomas à Kempis that completely changes her outlook. She decides that her miseries have come from caring only about her own pleasures; from now on she will live only for others. Her life becomes one of self-renunciation.

Book V. Wheat and Tares. 1. In the Red Deeps, a favorite spot of hers near the mill on the River Floss, Maggie sees Philip for the first time in five years. He has followed her there. Philip expresses his love for her but Maggie says they must keep apart; seeing him has made her long once again for the full life she has forsworn. She tells Philip she is not free to love him, but she agrees to meet him again secretly by the river. 2. Tom, with his integrity, family regrets, pride, and personal ambition, is doing well in his job with Uncle Deane's firm. Still, he and his father are accumulat-

438

Maggie and Philip meet for the first time in five years

ing money only at a slow rate. Bob Jakin proposes a business partnership to Tom, and Tom and Bob succeed in borrowing money for their venture from the Gleggs, without the knowledge of Tulliver, who disapproves. **3–4.** Maggie and Philip see each other often. Philip tries unsuccessfully to convince Maggie that her resignation is willful and senseless. They declare their love for each other, but Maggie insists that it be kept secret, for she would never do anything to wound her father. **5.** Tom learns of their secret rendezvous and makes Maggie swear on the Bible never to see Philip again. She pleads that she be allowed to see him once more and Tom goes along. Tom is rude, questions Philip's intentions, and mocks his deformity. He drags Maggie away; sister and brother exchange harsh words. **6.** Tom surprises his father with the profits from his private enterprise: The creditors can be fully paid and honor restored to the Tulliver family after four years. **7.** After paying the creditors, Mr. Tulliver encounters Mr. Wakem on his way home. They have a fight, which brings on Mr. Tulliver's second stroke. Maggie asks her father to forgive the Wakems, but he refuses. He dies that night.

Book VI. The Great Temptation. 1. Aunt Deane has also passed away and Mrs. Tulliver has gone to manage her house at St. Ogg's. Lucy is home and expects Maggie to come for a long visit. Lucy and her beau, the very handsome and very wealthy STE-PHEN GUEST, hope Maggie will not object to seeing Philip Wakem, for Philip is one of their closest friends; they hope to be a happy foursome. **2–3.** Maggie finds life at the Deanes', with its daily round of boating, music, good food, and good books, a delightful change from her life at the third-rate school in which she had been teaching. Maggie and Stephen like each other from the very start. Maggie tells Lucy the story of her love for Philip. **4.** Maggie goes to see Tom, who is now boarding at the home of Bob Jakin and Bob's new bride, for she had promised never to see Philip again without his consent. Tom is displeased but agrees that she may see Philip as a friend

at the Deanes'. **5.** Uncle Deane compliments Tom on seven years of good work. Tom asks his uncle to have the firm buy his father's mill and land from Wakem, to satisfy one of Mr. Tulliver's dying wishes. Mr. Deane says the request will be considered. Even this business-loving man finds it sad that Tom cares only for business. **6.** Maggie is happy for the first time in years. She has been well-received in St. Ogg's society. She and Stephen care a great deal for each other. Lucy, though always with them, does not seem aware of their affection. On the night before Philip is to return, Stephen visits Maggie at a time when he knows Lucy will be out. **7.** Maggie tells Philip they can at least be friends. Lucy remains blind to the attraction between Mag-

gie and Stephen, to whom she is almost engaged, but Philip perceives the bond at once. **8.** Lucy suggests to Philip that he try to persuade his father to sell Dorlcote Mill to Mr. Deane, in the hope that Tom will then forget his hatred of the Wakems. Mr. Wakem is amenable to this idea; he will not agree to have any direct transactions with Tom, but he agrees to accept Maggie for his son's sake. **9.** Lucy tells Maggie that the mill and land will soon be Tom's again; she is surprised at Maggie's apparent lack of enthusiasm. Maggie plans to leave the Deanes and take a new situation. Lucy, distressed, asks Maggie if she does not love Philip enough to marry him. Maggie says she does but that to marry Philip would mean giving up Tom, which she cannot do. **10.** One night at a dance Stephen and Maggie step outside and he showers her with kisses. She is offended at the liberty he has taken. Later that evening she implies to Philip that she would marry him were it not for Tom. **11.** Maggie visits the Mosses and Stephen goes to see her there. He vows his love for her and finally she admits hers for him. **12.** Tom and Mrs. Tulliver now live at their old home once again. Lucy tells Tom how Philip persuaded his father to sell the mill to Guest & Co. and to accept Maggie as a daughter-in-law. This only makes Tom dislike the Wakems all the more. **13.** Philip, Lucy, Maggie and Stephen are to go on a boat ride but somehow Lucy and Philip have other plans and Maggie and Stephen go alone. The tide carries them farther than they had planned. Stephen wants to take Maggie away and marry her. They spend the night on a Dutch boat. **14.** They land at the

Stephen showers Maggie with kisses.

Maggie rescues Tom from the mill where he was stranded

town of Mudport the following morning and go to an inn. Though Stephen pleads, Maggie says she will not betray Lucy, who has been so good to her, nor will she hurt Philip. Stephen warns Maggie that she cannot return to St. Ogg's because of all the talk there will be, but Maggie is sure that Lucy will believe her and she leaves Stephen.

Book VII. The Final Rescue. 1. Five days after leaving with Stephen, Maggie returns to Dorlcote Mill. She plans to tell Tom everything but he will not listen. In his mind she has disgraced the family and betrayed her best friend. Mrs. Tulliver decides to go with Maggie. Bob Jakins will take them into his house. **2.** St. Ogg's "society" scorns Maggie although Stephen, now in Holland, has written a truthful letter to his father which completely exonerates her. Maggie now turns to Dr. KENN, the kindly parish priest, for counsel. **3.** Of all people, Aunt Glegg takes Maggie's part and invites her to stay at her house. Maggie receives a fond letter from Philip, who has gone abroad. He expresses his great love for her and trust in her. **4.** Maggie longs only for Lucy's forgiveness. Lucy, who has been ill, is going to the seashore with Stephen's sisters; the night before she leaves, she steals out of the house and goes to see Maggie. She assures Maggie that she believes she never meant to deceive her. **5.** Dr. Kenn, unable to find Maggie a position in St. Ogg's, has made her his own children's teacher; but he is recently widowed and soon there is gossip about Maggie and himself. He advises her to leave St. Ogg's; he will get her a good position in a nearby community. Maggie gets a letter from Stephen, in which he reproaches her for her perverted notion of right. He begs her to come to him. Maggie feels that for her there can never be love without pain; pain is her cross to bear in life and she hopes that death is not far off. The River Floss has flooded. Maggie must leave Bob's house when the water rises. The current takes her boat past the mill. Her mother is not at home but Tom is stranded there and Maggie rescues him.

Their boat capsizes and brother and sister are drowned together, united at last—in death.

Conclusion. Five years later, the flood's damages had been repaired. All the principals were alive but Tom and Maggie, whose bodies, found in close embrace, were buried together. Two men visited their tomb; both felt that their keenest joy and sorrow were forever buried there. One visited the tomb again years later with a sweet face by his side. The other always came alone and spent most of his time in the Red Deeps section by the River Floss, where the buried joy seemed to hover still.

Minna

Novel by Karl Gjellerup, 1857–1919. Published 1889. English translation from the Danish published 1913.

GJELLERUP, a winner of the Nobel Prize for Literature in 1917, was a Dane but lived in Dresden for many years and in this novel the principal setting is Saxony, along the Elbe River south of Dresden, in the resort area near the border of Czechoslovakia. The novel is very emotional. The author, in a note, professes to have received the manuscript from his friend Fenger; explains that Fenger died not long after Minna, of a combination of tuberculosis and a broken heart; and proposes a motto for the story, from Thomas More: "To live with them is far less sweet/than to remember thee."

Book I. Chaps. 1–10. At the end of a busy semester at the Dresden Polytechnic (college), I, HARALD FENGER, a Dane, decided to spend a whole month of my vaca-tion at Rathen, a small village on the Elbe. Aided by a local schoolmaster I finally found a room overlooking hills and the river. Below my pension was a sumptuous villa. The schoolmaster confided that a very attractive governess lived there. I went to Rathen by boat. I observed a pretty young lady (MINNA JAGEMANN) on board and managed to settle myself near her and the two little girls in her care. She wore an adorable little hat with a silver-grey veil. I glanced at her as unobtrusively as possible and decided I could easily fall in love with her type. I was sure she had noticed me, for at times she blushed over her book. I presumed it was a book of poetry, but it proved to be a German-Danish dictionary. When we reached Pirna I looked with some interest at its acropolis, Sonnenstein, earlier a fort and at present a large insane asylum. I had struck up enough acquaintance with the young lady to lend her my steamer rug, on account of the cold rain, and when the call came to disembark at Rathen we folded it together, our hands touching. "Thank you!" she said, and hurried off. I never expected to see her again.

I was exploring the country around my pension one day when I discovered a small grotto with a bench and small table in front. On the bench lay a small book, a German-Danish dictionary. After a while the owner, the girl I had met on the boat, appeared. She cried out, as she had not expected to see anyone. I asked why she was interested in Danish and she said she had known one of my countrymen. She vanished as soon as she could politely get away. At this second meeting she made a still deeper impression on me; she was the most beautiful girl I had ever seen. I went to see the schoolmaster. He told me the governess had been associated with a Danish painter who had jilted her. I felt very disturbed. Later one fine day I met her outside a cave; "Wotan's Cave" was painted on the rough stone wall. We talked about Wagner, literature, Faust, Marguerite. I went often again to Wotan's Cave, but in vain.

Every day about 1 P.M. I took dinner at the Erbgericht hotel. There I met an old German-Jewish couple whom I knew from Dresden; I had met their son, IMMANUEL HERTZ, at the polytechnic. The father had been a merchant in Königsberg. They had taken a house in Rathen near the river. They told me they had a relative, a girl, they wanted me to meet; she was a governess. I wondered if this was fate.

I met Minna on one of my walks and we agreed to pretend we had not met before. We were presented to each other by the Hertzes and it seemed that they thought we were well matched. I was happy, day after day, falling more and more in love.

Young Hans, the landlord's son, wanted to take us to his father's mine to watch blasting. While waiting for the workmen to arrange things, Minna told me about her home. It was simple but lacked happiness and was not homelike. Her father, until his death a year before, could not bear to have strangers come to the house. With the Hertz family she had found a real home. On our way home we picked blueberries, at first with our fingers, then with our mouths; and our lips met in a heavenly kiss. She said goodbye and hurried home, alone.

Book II. Chaps. 1–10. I walked in a dream along the bank, convincing myself that the story of the Danish painter was just gossip. As I walked along, Hans came running to bring me a letter he thought I had dropped while we watched the blasting, but it was Minna who had dropped it. In the dim light I made out the inscription on the envelope: To Artist Axel Stephensen, Denmark. I felt chills running up and down my spine. I knew the man. From what the schoolmaster had said, it must have been a couple of years since he saw her in Dresden, yet they still wrote to each other! I sent the letter to Minna.

A letter from Minna arrived in the morning. It told me more of her history. Her mother had six sisters. Their mother was busy in the house; the father occasionally beat them. With that sort of upbringing, five of them had babies before they were married. The other, Minna's mother, the youngest sister, did not; but Minna grew up with the idea that the more admirers a girl had, the more she rose in the opinion of others. A young musician moved in with them and she became attached to him in a childlike way. He asked Minna's mother for her hand but her mother said she was too young. The musician left and Stephensen came. He told Minna he had come only on account of her. One day the musician returned. He asked Minna for a kiss when he was leaving and it was given. Stephensen had overheard at the door and from then on he wanted Minna in his own way. A thousand times she wept because she had fallen so low in the opinion of one whom she later came to love, for she was really innocent. Stephenson became more and more demanding, but when Minna spoke of marriage he said an artist must be free. They parted with the understanding that they would correspond and be friends.

Minna also sent me a letter she had written to Stephensen: "I have made the acquaintance of a young student by the name of Fenger, a countryman of yours. I often meet him at the Hertzes'. He is very tall but stoops a little, and sometimes it seems to me that his chest is not very strong. I would be sorry if that were the case."

The Hertzes made a trip to Prague and invited Minna and me to accompany them part way. We went with them as far as Schandau. When we tried to get back to Rathen we found that there was no boat and there was nothing to do but go to a hotel. At the hotel we were given adjoining rooms (and the clerk leered). We gave each other a long goodnight kiss. Then we rapped another goodnight on the wall between our rooms. I was overcome with the feeling of not only loving, but being loved in return. We had reached an understanding.

The Hertzes returned frm Prague. We went to see them, arm in arm, and our health was drunk in Rhine wine. Hertz was ill from the cold and damp of Prague. Minna asked me to call on her mother in Dresden.

Book III. Chaps. 1–6. As soon as I could, I went to see my future mother-in-law, Minna's mother, in Dresden. If I had kept a diary, I would have written: "At ease—my mother-in-law is harmless." Two days later Minna arrived. She was depressed about something; it was a letter from Stephensen, which she showed me. He still expressed love. She did not understand; for he had urged her "to marry an honest man!" She played the piano for me. We explored Dresden and in the evening looked toward Rathen, our lost paradise. We went to the opera. The glance of love Minna gave me at the end I shall not forget till my dying day. But in the evening, at dinner in a little café, we encountered Stephensen!

Book IV. Chaps. 1–9. Stephensen began at once to remove the glove from his right hand, and Minna began to unfasten hers. She wore my ring. Stephensen stared at it morosely. She introduced me to him as her fiancé. We bowed almost too politely. He had come to town to copy Correggio's Magdalene. We left the café, and I took Minna home. I stole a last kiss at the street door. Then on the other side of the street I saw a dark figure. He crossed over to me; it was Stephensen. We went together to have a glass of beer. He touched on my financial position; could I support a family? I resented his acting as though he were Minna's guardian, but he said, "She will have to choose between us!" I replied, "She has chosen!" "No, she has not. She must be free to choose!"

The next evening I went to see Minna only to learn that it was possible for her to love two men. She said, "Perhaps I really love you best!" I felt as if I had received a blow! Finally I told her that I was the one who had severed the agreement. It was only the day before that we had exchanged rings! I left my purse, telling her to return it if she wanted me.

At home I found two letters. One was from my uncle in England, asking me to come to work for his firm within two weeks. The other was from Immanuel Hertz, congratulating me: He also had loved Minna and had been burnt. The purse was returned, and in a few minutes I was at the Jagemann door. Stephensen was there, talking to Mrs. Jagemann. Stephensen asked to sketch me. He also made a sketch of Minna and gave it to her, for her to give to the one who needed it most. Minna went to see an aunt at Meissen. A couple of evenings later I received a letter in Minna's handwriting.

Book V. Chaps. 1–8. My hand shook violently as I tried to open the letter. The first thing that I saw was the sketch of Minna, which she had sent me. The letter said, "It is all over; I must be his. I feel powerless to break with my first love to start all over with you." At first the loving tone soothed my pain. Then the reaction: Why hadn't I gone to her room at Schandau

and made her mine! I could gladly have changed places with old Hertz, who was dying. He died, and at his burial I saw Minna in mourning. I felt it was the burial of our love rather than of old Hertz. I heard from young Hertz that Stephensen had gone to Denmark to arrange matters. A week later I went to England.

Year after year passed in hard work. In the fourth year after I left Dresden I met a German musician who turned out to be the one who had lived with Mrs. Jagemann in Dresden and had been Minna's first half-childish lover. I became homesick, stopped visiting the house of a young lady I was half-courting, and a week later was in Copenhagen. After two weeks without seeing Minna, I heard Stephensen's voice in a café, effaced myself, and watched Minna. She looked tired. I listened to aesthetic conversation about the future of art. A smiling blonde at their table was near fainting with admiration for Stephensen: She was his model. He flung out clever sentences. A smile of cold disdain played on Minna's face. Then later I heard Minna laugh so loudly that it froze the whole party.

I made a business trip to Sweden and Russia for my uncle, and returning to Dresden made a visit to Rathen. There at the old grotto I met Minna and Stephensen; it seemed like a hallucination. "I saw you at the café," said Minna. I went with them as far as Pirna, then left for Dresden. On the evening train I saw Stephensen's face at a car window. He stepped out alone. He told me Minna was at Sonnenstein. I mumbled as if I did not grasp the meaning. He said Minna was not really insane, merely melancholy and upset. My skepticism gradually changed to fury and I shook my fist in his face. But he pulled away and was lost in the crowd. I went to Pirna, where the chief physician told me there was no immediate fear for Minna's mind but that she had an old heart lesion that might end with sudden death. He did not want me to see her at that time.

She sent me letters; I read them without tears until I came to a strangely crumpled and buckled one from me, which she had carried next to her heart. I pressed it to my lips and sobbed like a child. "Good night, Harald," she wrote, after telling me about Stephensen's infidelities—the blonde woman who posed as a model, and others—going back to the very first year. Her child had died. "I feel I belong to you. I never was his!"

I happened to see a portrait of her in an antique shop, Stephensen's pastel portrait of her. I bought it and let it slide into the river. When I reached my room that day there was a letter from the chief physician stating that Minna had died from coronary thrombosis that morning. I undertook to arrange for the funeral. I was able to obtain space near the resting place of Hertz and his wife, under one of the giant poplars. On the grave I ordered placed a broken column of the most exquisite Saxon Serpentine, without any inscription other than the name MINNA

The Misanthrope

Play by Molière (Jean Baptiste Poquelin, 1622–1673).
Produced 1666. (ML, T29)

MANY CRITICS HAVE CALLED this the masterpiece of Molière, a playwright acknowledged to be France's greatest. Molière was a satirical dramatist, poking fun at nearly all phases of fashionable society, and *The Misanthrope* falls into this pattern. The title part is that of Alceste. Molière undoubtedly intended through Alceste to express his scorn of the artificiality of French society, yet he made Alceste also a comic character—as evidenced by the fact that Molière originally played the part himself and Molière liked comic parts. The message seems to be that while it is stupid to conform entirely to social conventions, it is just as stupid to reject them entirely and be a rebel in one's own world.

Act I. 1. ALCESTE accuses his friend PHILINTE of bowing to the deceitful practices of the age in flattering everyone indiscriminately, even those unworthy of affection. Philinte replies that a little deception is often necessary to avoid hurting people's feelings. He advises Alceste to pay more attention to winning his lawsuit. The talk turns to CÉLIMÈNE, beloved of Alceste. In Philinte's opinion, she is a far less likely choice for Alceste and his high principles than someone like ÉLIANTE, Célimène's cousin, or even her friend, the prudish ARSINOÉ. Alceste agrees with Philinte but says that in matters of love good sense does not always rule. 2. ORONTE, also a suitor of Célimène, asks Alceste's opinion of a sonnet he has written. Alceste replies that it is poorly written. Oronte is deeply insulted. Philinte intercedes, praising the sonnet, and averts a quarrel. Philinte chides Alceste for not being more diplomatic, but Alceste refuses to listen.

Act II. 1. Alceste accuses Célimène of bestowing her interest on too many suitors. She replies that she cannot help her attractiveness, but she loves him alone. 2. The servant announces the arrival of ACASTE, a marquis. 3. Alceste accuses Célimène of giving her attention to everyone, regardless of worth. She replies that it is important to keep on the good side of such influential persons as Acaste. 4–5. Alceste warns Célimène that she must choose between her other suitors and him. Acaste and CLITANDRE arrive. Both are in love with Célimène. Célimène makes sarcastic, witty remarks about various persons. The marquises enjoy it; Alceste objects. 6. A guard, representing the Marshals of France, comes to summon Alceste, to settle the quarrel between him and Oronte over the sonnet.

Act III. 1. Clitandre and Acaste discuss their respective progress in winning Célimène. They agree that should either of them seem to be gaining the advantage, the other will withdraw. 2–3. Acaste discusses Arsinoé's reputation of being a prude. Célimène says that her prudishness merely hides her desire to have a lover, which her feeble charms have always prevented. 4. Célimène greets Arsinoé with a great show of fondness. 5. Arsinoé says she is compelled by friendship to tell Célimène that many people have begun to criticize her conduct. Célimène retorts that Arsinoé should pay less attention to the actions of others and concern herself more with her own. Arsinoé says she is not interested in the attentions of suitors; that such attentions are generally bought at too great a price. 6–7. Arsinoé tells Alceste that she can prove Célimène is untrue to him.

Act IV. 1. Philinte tells Éliante that Alceste would be far better off if he loved her rather than her fickle cousin. Éliante says she might welcome Alceste's attentions. Philinte declares that should Alceste succeed in his suit with Célimène, he would be happy to win Éliante for himself. 2. Arsinoé has given Alceste a letter written by Célimène and intended for Oronte. The letter indicates that Alceste is not the only man in Célimène's heart. Incensed, Alceste offers his love to Éliante. She replies that a spurned lover often turns to another out of revenge, but that later the lover's anger subsides and he returns to his beloved. Alceste declares that he will never relent. 3. Alceste confronts Célimène with the proof of her unfaithfulness, but artfully she makes him doubt its truth. He begs her to prove her innocence, but she replies that Alceste should not doubt her love. 4. Alceste learns that his lawsuit is proceeding badly and that he is threatened with arrest.

Act V. 1. Alceste has lost his lawsuit and regards this as proof that the world is corrupt and deceitful. He plans to withdraw from society and has asked Célimène to go away with him. 2. Oronte and Alceste tell Célimène that she must choose between them. She calls their demand unreasonable. 3–4. Acaste confronts Célimène with a letter she has written to Clitandre, in which she makes fun of all her suitors and professes her love for Clitandre. 5. Oronte says he will be made a fool of no longer, and tells Alceste he may have Célimène. 6. Arsinoé tries to console Alceste. Alceste asserts that he has no intention of seeking consolation in a new love with Arsinoé, and she indignantly denies any such intention. 7. Alceste tells Célimène he will forgive her if she will go away with him and retreat from the world. She expresses abhorrence of withdrawing from gay society.

Alceste and Célimène part

Alceste declares that he now loathes her. 8. Alceste tells Éliante that he is unworthy to pursue her, having only the remainder of a heart now. He has begun to feel he was not meant to marry, whereupon Philinte and Éliante pledge their love for each other. Alceste gives his good wishes to the union and announces his intention to seek a secluded spot on earth. Philinte tells Éliante they must persuade him to abandon this idea.

Mr. Britling Sees It Through

Novel by Herbert George Wells, 1866–1946.
Published 1916. © 1916, 1944 by H. G. Wells.

THIS WAS ONE of the most popular novels of World War I and perhaps the most popular that the prolific H. G. Wells wrote. It is not a war novel; rather it is a novel about Englishmen at home during the trying years and about their relationships with Americans and their attitudes toward Germans. Critics were surprised that Wells would take for his underlying theme such difficult topics. With his usual versatility, Wells did very well with them.

Book I. Chaps. 1–5. It is Mr. DIRECK's first trip to England. He is the overpaid secretary of the Massachusetts Society for the Study of Contemporary Thought and has come to persuade Mr. Britling, a famous writer, to deliver a series of lectures to the members of his society. Mr. Britling invites him for the week-end at his country home, Matching's Easy, in Essex. Direck finds England more charming than he expected, but Mr. Britling is another matter, not at all what the very American Mr. Direck expects of a Britisher. The casualness of his costume is a disappointment. There is none of the mildness expected of a country gentleman: Mr. Britling bristles with a naturally irritable mind. The two men like each other instantly. Direck looks forward to their drive to the house, but this is only the third time Mr. Britling has driven and it is a harrowing experience for both of them.

Direck is confused at the Britling household, which is thoroughly British. There are EDITH BRITLING, his charming preoccupied hostess, and two small barefooted boys who resemble her husband. There is HUGH, a lad of 17, a son by Britling's first marriage; also an old aunt, a German tutor, and Mr. Britling's secretary, TEDDY. Teddy lives in a cottage on the estate with his wife, LETTY, and her sister, CECILY CONNER. Cecily is a beautiful, lively girl of great intelligence; Direck quickly falls in love with her.

The week-end is a great success. Mr. Britling is inordinately proud of England, though he expresses it chiefly by abuse. Direck joins in all the pastimes and enjoys himself tremendously. He has several serious discussions with his host on the possibility of war with Germany. Mr. Britling believes war will never come. Even while they are talking, events are leading to the assassination of Archduke Francis Ferdinand of Austria.

On his last morning of the week-end, Direck goes for a drive with Mr. Britling. They collide with a motorcycle. Direck is injured, while Britling is only badly shaken. It pleases Direck that he has the monopoly of damage, for Cecily is very sympathetic and helpful. Mr. and Mrs. Britling insist that he must not leave until he is recovered, and he is delighted to prolong his visit.

Very different from the contentment of the bruised Direck is the agitation of Mr. Britling. He is sleepless and physically restless. The smashing of the car has upset certain plans he had for conducting his eighth love affair. Mr. Britling's first marriage was happy and passionate. His second is profoundly incompatible. Edith runs his house and children smoothly, but there is no excitement. This is now being provided by Mrs. HARROWDEAN, an attractive widow. The love affair does not run smoothly, for she is demanding and emotional. And there is OLIVER. Oliver is a staunch, dull admirer who stands ever ready to marry her at a moment's notice. The affair is a series of quarrels, recriminating letters, and joyful reconciliations.

Direck's wounds heal sooner than he wished. Before he leaves on a tour of Europe, he tells Cecily that he loves her and wishes to marry her. She asks for time to think it over, as she is confused in her own mind about the merits of marriage. She promises to give him an answer soon.

The clouds of war begin to gather. The German tutor is recalled to Germany and sadly leaves the Britlings to serve his country. Germany goes on the march. First France and Belgium are invaded, then Russia prepares to invade Germany. Mr. Britling tries to adapt his thinking to the horrible fact that war is here. He knows that Germany will never win, because Germany does not understand the spirit of man. On his way to see Mrs. Harrowdean, he thinks over the state of the world. His mind becomes absorbed with the present events and he decides that Oliver can have Mrs. Harrowdean. He hurries home to commit his thoughts to paper.

Book II. Chaps. 1–4. Upon the invasion of Belgium, Great Britain declares war. The Britling household organizes itself to be of the utmost use. Direck is in Germany; he immediately departs for England, anxious to be with Cecily at such a time. She welcomes him absent-mindedly and turns all her attention to England and the war. Direck feels like an outsider, for the United States stays neutral, but he is determined to stay near the girl he loves.

The members of the Britling household are drawn one by one into active service. Teddy, who laughs and jokes at all serious matters, is the first to join the armed forces. He is followed by Hugh Britling. Mrs. Britling applies her organizing ability in work for the Red Cross. Mr. Britling has difficulty finding his niche, but finally joins the local volunteers and is given the assignment of guarding public buildings and transportation. Matching's Easy is opened to Belgian refugees, and the unused barn is pressed into service as a billet for soldiers.

To a man of Mr. Britling's nature the war demands a great deal of thought. It is hard for him to realize just why the war happened. The German attitude is do or die with a vengeance, while the Englishman treats the whole affair as an honorable sport. The German campaign of hate is inconsistent, in Mr. Britling's mind, with the good Germans he has known. He realizes that there is good and evil on both sides; he foresees that as time goes on the English will become as embittered and cruel as the enemy. Wars are always the same and so are the people who fight them.

Hugh is sent to the front in Flanders, in the same regiment as Teddy. After a quick skirmish, Teddy is missing; this is the first worry to enter the Britling establishment. Letty grieves silently. Mr. Britling's uneasiness mounts. He finds he can no longer express in writing what he is thinking. Direck, to enhance himself in Cecily's eyes, leaves for Europe to find out what he can about her brother-in-law. While he is gone, Mr. Britling receives news that Hugh was killed in his first battle. Edith tries to comfort him, but loneliness for his son engulfs Britling. War now becomes a matter of revenge.

Book III. Chaps. 1–2. Letty remains firm in her belief that Teddy is alive, though Direck has found substantial evidence that he has been killed. Direck returns and tells Cecily that she must prepare her sister to accept her husband's death. Cecily finally convinces Letty that there is no further hope. Letty asks to be left alone. Everything in the house reminds her of her life with Teddy; she goes for a long walk to adjust herself to life alone. She meets Mr. Britling and recounts what Cecily has said. She is resentful that Teddy died for nothing and that the whole war is a mistake. Spurred by his own grief at the loss of Hugh, Mr. Britling has thought out the aims of the conflict. He tells Letty he does not believe that the war is being fought in vain. He believes that Hugh has died for a cause that is worth his life. The Germans are enforcing a way of life reprehensible to democratic peoples. When the Germans are defeated the world will be a better place to live in. Letty is comforted. She begins to accept Teddy's death, and returns home determined to carry on. She can hardly believe her eyes as she approaches her cottage —Teddy is there waiting for her. He is alive, discharged from service because he had lost a hand. In her joy at her husband's return, Letty does not notice that Cecily is strangely silent. Direck has joined the Canadian Army as a volunteer. Cecily realizes that she loves him.

Through his agent in New York, Mr. Britling learns that the German tutor was killed in the same battle as Hugh. He was a good boy and Mr. Britling realizes that his parents must be grieving for him just as Mr. Britling grieves for Hugh. He tries to write them of his feelings, but after a night of futile effort he destroys the letter. The war has claimed good from each side. Morning and the sunrise sweep across Matching's Easy and with it comes hope—hope for the better world.

The German tutor lies dead on a battlefield in France

443

Mr. Midshipman Easy

Novel by Frederick Marryat, 1792–1848. Published 1836.

PERHAPS THE OUTSTANDING feature of Captain Marryat's books is that the man had such a tremendous store of miscellaneous minor knowledge. It is impossible to read a Marryat book without learning a great many items of miscellaneous information that are interesting if nothing else. Among his adventure novels, this is the outstanding one. It is authoritative, for Captain Marryat was a sea captain; his store of miscellaneous information, in fact, came from the fact that he had sailed almost everywhere and had been a keen observer wherever he went. Marryat's books are no longer read, more's the pity.

Chaps. 1–3. NICODEMUS EASY is a wealthy gentleman philosopher. He believes that all men are born to inherit an equal share of the earth, to have equal rights. But no one agrees with him. Mrs. Easy bears a child, to Mr. Easy's delight. After long argument they decide to name him JOHN, or JACK by nickname. Dr. MIDDLETON brings in a wetnurse named SARAH for Jack. Mr. Easy examines her head, for he is interested in craniology. He finds that her bumps of benevolence, veneration, modesty and philoprogenitiveness are amply developed, so he is satisfied. Jack appears not to imbibe these qualities from Sarah's milk, however, for he snatches, scratches, and pulls hair.

Chaps. 4–5. Jack is spoiled by his doting mother. Dr. Middleton perceives this and suggests that the boy be sent away to school. Mr. Easy demurs because boys are flogged at school—inequality! One day in a moment of brattishness Jack spills boiling water on his father's legs, and then is sent off to school. The master, Mr. BONNY-CASTLE, does not flog his pupils—he canes them instead. Jack learns the meaning of discipline.

Chaps. 6–7. Jack becomes imbued with his father's ideas on equality. To test them he one day goes fishing in a private pond. Gamekeepers appear; Jack argues that it is only "might" that has brought about the distinction of property. The gamekeepers agree, and with all their "might" they throw Jack in the pond. Next Jack climbs a tree to steal apples. An outraged farmer sets a bulldog to guard the tree; a bull attacks the dog; Jack scrambles from the tree and is attacked by the bull; leaping over a hedge, he lands in a beehive; while running, he falls down a well. So much for equality! Jack decides to go to sea with Captain WILSON, a friend of the family who has borrowed £1,000 from Mr. Easy. Jack

444

thinks that at sea he will find a state of true equality.

Chaps. 8–12. Purseproud Jack insults the first lieutenant, Mr. SAWBRIDGE—on the grounds of equality. Captain Wilson treats Jack leniently because of his debt to Mr. Easy. He explains to Jack that some of the officers may act as if they are superior, but really it is all "zeal" in carrying out the obligations of His Majesty's navy, which are *equal* for all. Jack is violently seasick for the first few days of the voyage. He asks for some crumpets but gets only slop-soup from the steward, MESTY, a Negro ex-slave who was originally a prince in his own country. Later at the captain's table Jack voices his theories about equality, to the shock and amazement of the listeners. He gains some friends, however, among them the one-eyed Mr. JOLLIFFE, Mesty the Negro, and several of his midshipmen cabinmates after he soundly thrashes the bully of the cabin, named VIGORS. An officer named ASPERS attached himself to Jack because he knows that Jack has plenty of money. One day Jack sees the unpopular boatswain, BIGGS, punishing a sailor for being late for a summons because he was putting his pants on. "Duty before decency" roars Biggs. The next night, while Biggs is sleeping at an inn, Jack swipes his pants. Biggs is obliged to return to the ship pantless, to the great merriment of the crew. In a fit of rage, Jack one day kicks the purser's steward, an ex-pickpocket, EASTHUPP, down a hatchway. In another instance Jack is punished for not obeying a command with alacrity. He begins to learn "non-equality."

Chaps. 13–15. A Spanish merchant convoy is attacked by Jack's ship, the *Harpy*. Jack is given command of one of the small cruisers sent out for the attack. He captures one of the small Spanish boats. Instead of obeying orders to return, he with friend Mesty and the crew of eight, set out to catch something big. They sight a large Spanish gunboat; during the night they board it and overcome all the men aboard. The prisoners, with two gentleman and three lady passengers, are put aboard the smaller vessel and shoved off. Jack and his crew sail away. That night, while Jack sleeps, all the men get drunk and the ship buffets its way about the Mediterranean without a helmsman. Jack locks up the wine, but he is not a trained navigator and the boat is gale-driven upon an uninhabited island. The crewmen go ashore and presently plan a mutiny, but three of them, in trying to swim back to the boat, are eaten by sharks. After two months the crew's wine and provisions are exhausted and they beg Jack to take them aboard. Meanwhile Mesty has told the story of his life to Jack. He was once a prince and great warrior, with many wives, in Africa; he collected the skulls of his enemies; he was captured by slave-traders and taken to America; he escaped to England and shipped aboard the *Harpy*, where he was put into the degrading position of mess-steward.

Chaps. 16–21. Jack and his crew eventually encounter the *Harpy* battling a Spanish gunboat. They help the *Harpy* to win. Everyone is delighted to see the hero and his crew again and the prize they have brought. Mesty is made ship's corporal. Biggs and Easthupp insult Jack, and he challenges them to a duel. They meet on land for the fight; not knowing how three are supposed to duel, they form a triangle and each shoots at the next man. Easthupp is shot in the buttock and Biggs through the cheek, while Jack is unscratched. Jack and his friend GASCOIGNE hire a small boat to take them to Palermo. They shoot four pirates who attempt to board them at night. The boat is wrecked in a gale, but Jack and Gascoigne escape with their lives. They fall asleep in a hay wagon, which during the night is driven to a farm. They wake in time to stop two young men from killing an elderly man, Don REBIERA DE SILVA. One of the assailants is Don SILVIO, son of the Don's illegitimate half-brother. It is discovered that Don Rebiera's beautiful daughter, AGNES, is the girl who was aboard the Spanish ship captured by Jack. All are delighted, and Jack and Agnes fall in love. Jack and Gascoigne go on to Palermo, where they make friends with Agnes' two brothers. A captain discovers that Jack and Gascoigne are AWOL and claps them in irons. Agnes' brother kills the captain in a duel. Jack and Gascoigne are taken back to the *Harpy*. (Here the author inserts a polemic against the misuse of language by senior naval officers to their junior officers.)

Chaps. 22–24. Jack relates his adventures to the governor of Malta, Sir THOMAS, who is delighted. The *Harpy* goes off on another cruise and captures a large French vessel. The success is due partly to Jack's cleverness and partly to an explosion that kills many men. Next Jack and Gascoigne ship under Captain HOGGS to fetch some bullocks from Tetuan. Captain Hoggs falls in love with JULIA, sister of the Tetuan vice-consul, Mr. HICKS. Gascoigne falls in love with a beautiful Arabic girl, whom he courts in the disguise. Both he and Hoggs want to elope with their ladies. Jack arranges a trick whereby Hicks in disguise pretends to be both women. The boat pulls out, and in the morning all are infuriated, including Hicks, who is obliged to travel all the way to Malta and back in petticoats. Jack goes to a masquerade dressed as a devil. In this guise he scares off some monks from doing an evil deed, and rescues a rich old dowager from bandits, who prostrate themselves at the sight of the devil.

Chaps. 25–28. In pursuit of a frigate, the *Harpy* runs into a tremendous gale and is hit by lightning. A fire on board is smothered with wet blankets, Jack's bright idea. Captain Wilson receives a check for 1,000 gold dubloons from the estate of the dowager rescued by Jack. Jack at the time had given the captain's name as his own. Jack considers leaving the service to marry

The Harpy engages in battle with a Russian frigate

Agnes. Don Silvio appears and is arrested on Jack's identification.

Chaps. 29–33. The *Harpy* encounters a Russian frigate, and a furious broadside battle with guns ensues, which culminates in English victory. Upon return to Malta the *Harpy* sights a wrecked galley boat and takes time out to rescue the galley slaves and put them ashore. Among these men is Don Silvio. Jack is worried for Don Rebiera, and upon reaching Palermo he notifies the army of the prisoners on the loose. With Gascoigne, Mesty, and the Don's two sons, he forms a barricade around Don Rebiera's house in case of attack by Don Silvio and the galley slaves. The attack comes, and the defenders are driven back floor by floor. Don Silvio sets fire to the house but the defenders are saved by the arrival of troops. Jack now wishes to marry Agnes but Father THOMASO, the family priest will not approve. When Jack tries to bribe him through Mesty, the priest gives Mesty some powder with which to poison Jack. Mesty pretends to have done this and then flees with the priest. But en route Mesty poisons the Father with his own powder. On his return, Mesty is captured by Don Silvio, whom he kills.

Chaps. 34–41. Jack receives news that his mother is dead and his father has gone somewhat out of his mind. Jack quits the service and returns home with Mesty; he finds the household and estate in a mess due to his father's ideas on equality. Jack argues with his father that all men are not equal, and that it is fortunate that society is structured so that each may find his level. A few days later Mr. Easy is found dead in a formidable machine he had built to further the science of phrenology. Jack buys a frigate to fetch Agnes with style. In the Mediterranean the frigate aids a ship that turns out to be captained by Jack's old friend, Sawbridge. Later in the trip the frigate beats off an English warship bent on impressing her crew. Agnes is finally picked up and all return to England, where Jack becomes a happily married and highly respected country gentleman of conservative political outlook and much wealth. Mesty becomes his majordomo.

Moby Dick

Novel by Herman Melville, 1819–1891. Published 1851. (PB, PL28; RE, 6; NAL, D1229; ML, G64 & 119 & T26).

PERHAPS THE ONLY GROUNDS on which critics agree about this book is in placing it among the classics of world literature. In part it answers the classic definition of a novel, for it tells a connected story with a beginning, a middle, and an end; but it follows some 18th-century patterns in digressing frequently for essays and there are some parts that one can class only as poetry. Some critics, perhaps most, have considered *Moby Dick* an allegory in which the white whale represents the abstraction of evil, but could a writer so sensitive as Melville cast as evil an animal that simply defends itself against attack? The variety of the characters is great and Melville's portrayal of them is superb. At least some of the incident and character-casting must be considered allegorical or symbolic, including the name of the vengeful Captain Ahab, who like the Biblical Ahab pursued false gods. Contemporary critics simply did not know what to make of this book and Melville had great trouble getting it published. Now it has surpassed in esteem every other American work of its kind.

Chaps. 1–13. Call me ISHMAEL. Some years ago, having little money and nothing to interest me on shore, I decided to go to sea. Ordinarily when I go to sea, I go as a merchant sailor, but this time I took it into my head to go on a whaling voyage. I set out for Nantucket. I was forced to remain two nights, en route, in New Bedford. I stayed at a waterfront hotel, the Spouter Inn, where I was made to share my bed, very much against my will. Had I seen my bedfellow in advance, I do not think anything could have induced me to sleep with him. He was a huge, bald, tattooed black-skinned harpooner with strange habits of worship and a collection of shrunken heads. The fellow's name was QUEEQUEG. At first I thought he was a cannibal, but he showed himself to be a harmless and most affectionate sort. The next day being Sunday, I attended the whaleman's chapel. The sermon was on the sin of Jonah and his repentence in the belly of the whale. I returned to the Inn. Queequeg made me a present of an embalmed head, divided his $30 with me, swore to be my bosom friend, and invited me to join in the worship of his wooden idol. Then he told me he was a South Sea Islander, son of a native king, and that he ran away to Christendom early in life. As he, too, was anxious to go to sea again, we set out for Nantucket together.

Chaps. 14–27. I signed Queequeg and myself aboard the *Pequod,* a whaling vessel under command of Captain AHAB, who was described to me as a good swearing man, somewhat strange, never jolly, who had lost his leg to a whale on his previous voyage and was desperately moody and savage. Some said that his name, Ahab, that of the wicked king of old whose blood was licked by dogs after he was slain, was somehow prophetic. Queequeg and I were stopped by a strange sailor who hinted that anyone sailing with Captain Ahab was doomed, but we took no account of his veiled warnings. The *Pequod* sailed the following day and we were on board. Captain Ahab remained below deck for the first few days. The steering was left to the chief mate, STARBUCK, a steadfast man of action, courageous but superstitious, and to the second mate, STUBB, a happy-go-lucky fellow. These two, and FLASK, the third mate, were armed with whaling spears; in battle with the whale, they acted as a trio of lancers, just as their harpooners, Queequeg, TASHTEGO, and DAGGOO, were flingers of javelins.

Chaps. 28–46. Several mornings later,

Captain Ahab appeared on the quarterdeck for the first time. His whole high, broad form seemed to be made of solid bronze and shaped in an unalterable mould. A livid white scar threaded its way out from among his gray hairs and continued right down one side of his scorched face until it disappeared in his clothing. No allusion was made to this scar throughout the voyage, except once when it was said that Ahab had lived forty years before he had been branded thus and that he had gotten this mark at sea. In place of his lost limb, he wore a barbaric ivory leg fashioned from the polished bone of a sperm whale's jaw. The ship headed southward, looking for a school of whales. One morning the captain ordered everybody aft. He took out a Spanish gold piece and hammered it to the mainmast, shouting "Whosoever of ye raises me a white-headed whale with a wrinkled brow, a crooked jaw, and three holes punctured in his starboard fluke, shall have this gold ounce." It was this whale, MOBY DICK, that had chewed off Ahab's leg. Ahab vowed to chase him "round perdition's flames." "And this is what ye have shipped for, men," he cried, "to chase that white whale on both sides of land and over all sides of earth till he spouts black blood and rolls fin out." All the sailors cheered Ahab save Starbuck, who declared that he was game for the whale's jaw and game for the jaws of death, but that he had come to hunt whales and not his master's vengeance, and further, that it seemed madness, blasphemy in fact, to be so vengeful against a dumb brute. Ahab replied that he would strike the sun if it insulted him and that he saw in that white whale outrageous strength with an inscrutable malice sinewing it. With that, Ahab called for liquor and the crew drank a frantic toast to the death of Moby Dick. I, Ishmael, was one of that crew and my shouts went up with the rest, because Ahab's quenchless feud seemed mine. I learned the history of that murderous monster. From time to time, vessels reported they had encountered a Sperm Whale of uncommon magnitude and malignity, which after attacking assailants with great ferocity and cunning had always escaped them. Few hunters were willing to encounter the peril of its jaw. Some of the more superstitious said Moby Dick was both ubiquitous and immortal.

Chaps. 47–65. On a sultry afternoon we sighted our first school of sperm whales. Instantly all was commotion. Five crewmen, natives of Manila, were lowered in one of the three whaleboats. Their leader was FEDALLAH, a white-turbaned old man, who was to remain a muffled mystery to the last. My boat, commanded by Starbuck, was nearly swamped by a whale and we huddled in it, drenched through and shivering from cold, all night before the *Pequod* found us. Weeks later, as we were passing the Cape of Good Hope, we came across a whaler whose men told us that some time previously Moby Dick had killed one of their number.

"Thar she blows!"—The first school of whales is sighted

Chaps. 66–86. Near Java we came upon a sperm whale, and the boats were lowered into the water for the second time. Stubb went after the whale and killed it with Tashtego's aid. Then began the long process of hauling in the prize. When it was finally brought alongside the ship, we turned to the business of stripping it of its blubber, which yields more than 100 barrels of oil, and of beheading it and hanging its head from the side of the ship. The rest of the body was thrown back into the sea. As we were melting the blubber down into oil, we were hailed by another whaler, the *Jereboam*, whose captain told us that his first mate had been killed by Moby Dick.

Chaps. 87–99. As we were crossing the Straits of Sundra, we came upon a huge school of whales headed in the same direction. After a lengthy chase, Queequeg succeeded in harpooning only one of them. The others escaped, to be chased later by the *Rose-Bud.* Shortly afterward, PIP, the little Negro shipkeeper, was put into Stubb's whaleboat in place of the afteroarsman, who had sprained his hand. As they were paddling upon a whale, Pip leapt overboard and was left behind in the

Stubbs went after the whale

sea for several hours. By the time he was rescued, he had gone mad.

Chaps. 100–109. We met the *Samuel Enderby,* an English ship, and Ahab asked if it had seen the white whale. In answer, the captain held up an arm consisting of whalebone from the elbow down. Ahab boarded the *Samuel Enderby* to hear the story of the captain's encounter with Moby Dick. He was told that Moby Dick was heading East when last seen. In returning to the *Pequod,* Ahab broke his ivory leg and had to have another made.

Chaps. 110–115. Queequeg fell ill of fever. Thinking himself near death, he requested that a coffin-canoe be made to hold his remains. But he suddenly rallied and recovered. Thereafter he used the coffin as a sea-chest.

Chaps. 116–117. One night after we had slain four whales, Fedallah prophesied that before Ahab could die on this voyage, he must see two hearses on the sea, the first not made by mortal hands, and the second made of wood grown in America. Furthermore, Ahab could not die until Fedallah himself was dead, and only hemp could kill him.

Chaps. 118–132. Nearing the equator, Ahab decided he could do without his quadrant, a foolish toy that indicates only where it is not where it will be or where it is going. Thenceforth, Ahab would guide the ship only by compass and dead reckoning. That night we were caught in an electrical storm; lightning struck and set fire to the mast. The crew begged Ahab to change his course, but Ahab vowed again, before the burning pillar, to find and kill Moby Dick. Next day the compasses were awry. When the log was heaved, the line broke and the log slipped away. Next a man fell overboard; the dried-out lifebuoy sent after him sank, whereupon Queequeg offered his canoe-coffin as a substitute. On the following day we met a large ship, the *Rachel,* whose crew had seen Moby Dick only yesterday; the captain's son was lost chasing the white whale. The captain requested the *Pequod* to unite with the *Rachel* in the search for the missing whaleboat, but Ahab refused. Now that he was so close upon his prey, he did not want to lose a minute's time. And so began the chase, with Ahab remaining on the deck at all times.

133–135. At last Moby Dick was sighted by Ahab. The captain ordered the boats away and took the lead in the chase. As he neared Moby Dick, the whale shot his head under the boat and split it to pieces. The men were finally rescued, after the whale had been driven away. On the second day, the men managed to bury three harpoons in the white whale, but the whale turned and twisted so as to tangle the lines. Stubb's and Flask's boats were destroyed, though the men were rescued. Ahab managed to cut his own boat free, but Fedallah was killed. Starbuck tried without success to persuade

Ahab to give up the mad pursuit. On the third day, the boats quickly overtook Moby Dick, who this time seemed to be possessed by the devil himself. As Ahab drew near, he saw the remains of Fedallah bound to Moby Dick's back. This, then, was the first hearse. The boats were swamped by the whale; all but Ahab returned to the ship. Ahab still pursued the whale with his iron. In retaliation, Moby Dick bore down on the ship and smote its starboard bow, till men and timbers reeled and water poured through the breach. This was the second hearse—and the *Pequod's* wood was American. As the ship went down, Ahab hurled his harpoon at the whale, but the line ran foul and the hemp rope twisted around his neck, pulling him out of the boat. Everyone perished, except myself. I clung to Queequeg's canoe-coffin for two days before the *Rachel* picked me up.

A Modern Comedy
The White Monkey

Trilogy (*three novels*) by John Galsworthy, 1867–1933.
Published 1928 by Charles Scribner's Sons; © 1928 by John Galsworthy.
THIS SECOND TRILOGY, three full novels, on the Forsyte family, concludes Galsworthy's treatment of the process by which the English upper middle classes (the moneyed, principally the merchant classes) rose to social equality with the nobility and gentry—or near-equality, for among both there remained a slight and submerged consciousness of a difference. (See *Forsyte Saga*.) Galsworthy did not stop writing about the Forsytes here; there is a third trilogy, *End of the Chapter*, which includes the novels *Maid in Waiting, Flowering Wilderness*, and *One More River*; but they were not essential to the message. Nor were they quite such good reading. *A Modern Comedy* compares very favorably with the original Forsyte books.

Part I. Chaps. 1–3. Sir LAWRENCE MONT meets his son, MICHAEL, and Michael's best friend, WILFRED DESERT, a poet. Together they go to Michael's for tea with his young wife, FLEUR. Wilfred, who is in love with Fleur, asks her if there is any hope for him. She turns him down. That night, as Michael and Fleur prepare to leave a musicale they have attended, Wilfred comes up to Fleur and threatens to go East if she will not encourage him. She arranges to meet him the following Sunday. **4–6.** Michael and Fleur give a dinner party to celebrate their second wedding anniversary. Fleur meets Wilfred in an art gallery on a Sunday morning. She tells him that perhaps he may hope. As she

is leaving, she meets her father, SOAMES FORSYTE, and invites him home to dinner. **7–8.** Soames goes to a meeting of the P.P.-R.S. (Providential Premium Reassurance Society), which Sir Lawrence also attends. Soames demands that a full report on the society's foreign commitments be ready within a week. TONY BICKET, one of the packers in the publishing house of Danby and Winters (of which Michael Mont is a junior partner), is caught stealing books. Michael asks Wilfred to speak to Mr. DANBY in Bicket's behalf. Wilfred does, but Danby fires Bicket. **9–11.** Michael and Fleur attend a party at her Aunt ALLISON's. Wilfred tells Michael that he is in love with Fleur. Michael tells Fleur, who does not know what to say. Soames' cousin GEORGE FORSYTE is seriously ill and asks Soames to add a codicil to his will. Soames is especially taken with a picture of a strange white monkey hanging in George's bedroom. George dies. Bicket has not been able to find another job and is selling balloons on the street. Soames passes by and buys several balloons, tipping Bicket generously. **12–13.** The P.P.R.S. meets again and to Soames' gratification a full report of foreign interests is made. At Soames' club VAL DARTIE, his sister WINIFRED's son, asks if he can refuse the three horses left him by George, since Val cannot afford to pay the legacy tax on them. Soames advises him not to accept them. Soames goes to Fleur's for dinner and prods her about having a family. Soames blows up the balloons he bought from Bicket, and floats them out the window. Michael, who has been to the Labour candidates' meeting, catches the balloons and takes them to Fleur.

Part II. Chaps. 1–3. Soames is visited by a young Mr. BUTTERFIELD, from the P.P.R.S. office, who tells him that Mr. ELDERSON of the Board of Directors has been given great discretionary powers. VICTORINE BICKET,

Tony's wife, asks Michael to get Tony's job back. Michael cannot but he gives her a note to his friend, the artist AUBREY GREENE, asking him to use Victorine as a model. Greene consents to use her. **4–6.** Fleur visits Wilfred in his apartment. They see Michael in the street below. Frightened, Fleur departs and visits an art gallery across the street. Soames buys the picture of the white monkey from the estate of George Forsyte. Fleur is visited by HOLLY DARTIE, sister of Fleur's American cousin and old love, JON FORSYTE. Jon is not married and is raising peaches in South Carolina. JUNE FORSYTE, Fleur's cousin, tells Michael she saw Fleur entering Wilfred's apartment. Michael is heartsick. Soames tells Michael of Fleur's love affair with Jon Forsyte,

Victorine poses in the nude

emphasizing that it was over months before she married Michael. **7–9.** Victorine goes to Aubrey Greene's studio. She consents to pose for him in the nude, since she wants to earn money quickly for passage to Australia for herself and Tony. Soames confers with Sir Lawrence on the information given him by Butterfield. Together they visit Elderson, whose response is to dismiss Butterfield. Soames asks Michael to try to place Butterfield at Danby and Winters. **10–12.** Fleur is heartsick, lying on her rug. Hearing a slight noise, she goes to the window, and finds Wilfred's face staring in at her. Michael, returning home, sees Wilfred coming from his house. He asks Fleur if Wilfred has been with her. She tells Michael of seeing Wilfred's face at the window. Michael dashes over to Wilfred's apartment, jubilant with the news that Fleur is to become a mother, but Wilfred has left "for the East." Michael arives at Paddington Station in time to say farewell to Wilfred.

Part III. Chaps. 1–6. Tony sees a newspaper reproduction of Greene's painting of Victorine. He comments on the resemblance. Butterfield has made quite a success of his salesman's job at Danby and Winter's. Victorine asks Michael and Greene not to tell Tony that she was the model for Greene's picture. Soames is interested in buying the picture. But Tony does find out that Victorine was the model. He goes to Michael to find out more. Michael threatens to tell Victorine of Tony's theft of books if he makes any trouble for her about modeling. Tony returns home and is reconciled with Victorine. 7–9. Soames confronts Elderson with a demand that the stockholders be told of the loss of German insurance. Elderson is cool and calm. Later Soames receives a note from Elderson confessing his transgression and implying that he is going abroad. 10–14. Soames makes a post-nuptial settlement of £50,000 on Fleur. Soames advises the removal of the picture of the white monkey until after Fleur's baby arrives. Soames and Sir Lawrence attend the shareholders' meeting and Soames explains the Elderson affair but the stockholders are critical and Sir Lawrence and Soames resign. Soames then stops at his office and directs GRADMAN, his long-time chief clerk, to notify the family, with the exception of his sister, Winifred Dartie, that he will no longer handle their legal affairs. Fleur has a son and Fleur and Michael decide to make Aunt Allison and Wilfred Desert their son's godparents. Soames and Michael rehang the picture of the white monkey.

INTERLUDE: A SILENT WOOING

Jon Forsyte is recovering from a bout of flu at a hotel in South Carolina. He meets FRANCIS WILMOT and his sister ANNE. Anne and Jon go horseback riding together. Later, when Jon visits Anne at her home, they fall in love.

The Silver Spoon

Part I. Chaps. 1–5. FRANCIS WILMOT calls on Fleur, when he visits London, and is invited to be a house guest. Michael has given up publishing and is a member of Parliament. Soames has taken up golf. 6–7. Soames is disturbed over a bit of gossip about Fleur's "salon." He attends Fleur's "salon" and overhears MARJORIE FERRAR refer to Fleur as a "snob." He makes a scene and orders her out of Fleur's house. Fleur cries herself to sleep over the scene. Francis is fascinated with Marjorie and steals out in the middle of the night to locate her apartment. 8–9. Marjorie's father, Lord CHARLES FERRAR, demands that Soames write letters of apology to those who heard him call Marjorie a traitress. Soames refuses. He tells Sir Lawrence of the affair and Sir Lawrence goes to see the Marquess of SHROPSHIRE, Marjorie's grandfather. The Marquess informs Sir Lawrence that he has not spoken to his son, Lord Charles, in six years but if Marjorie comes by he will speak to her. Soames and Michael return home to find that Francis is leaving. Fleur is very angry with her father for his outburst. Francis meets Marjorie accidentally at a tea dance at his hotel. She invites him to her apartment for tea next afternoon. After the visit,

Francis goes to Fleur and tries to smooth over the affair, but Fleur is not at all interested. 11–14. Soames visits the newspaper that commented on Fleur's "salon." The editor gives him no satisfaction. Michael has embraced the political philosophy called Foggartism, which advocates a balance between city and farm workers; it recommends sending youths to farms in various parts of the Empire. Marjorie Ferrar brings action against Fleur for letters Fleur has written to her friends, calling Marjorie a "snake of the first water," and sues Soames for ordering her to leave Fleur's home. Soames, Michael and Fleur make plans for an out-of-court attack on Marjorie Ferrar.

Part II. Chaps. 1–2. Michael delivers his maiden speech, on Foggartism, in Parliament. Sir ALEXANDER MACGOWN, Marjorie Ferrar's fiancé, intimates that as a former publisher Michael has an interest in the sale of Sir JAMES FOGGART'S book, and the next day, MacGown and Michael exchange blows. 3–7. Marjorie is painting a portrait of Francis and MacGown is enraged. Michael visits Sir James Foggart, finding him to be an 84-year-old dreamer, out of touch with present-day reality. Michael is very depressed. Soames evolves a plan to trap Marjorie into defending an immoral book by writing a defense of it to a newspaper column. He enlists young Butterfield's help. Michael starts a small poultry farm on an unused portion of his father's land, in an effort to rehabilitate three down-and-out city workers he has met. He and Fleur go to a dinner where the ROYAL PRINCESS comments favorably on Michael's speech in Parliament. 8–9. Soames visits the offices of Marjorie's solicitor and offers £1,500 and a mutual apology to settle out of court. After a delay, he receives a letter saying that Marjorie will settle only for a full apology from Fleur. In the meantime, Soames has continued gathering evidence of Marjorie's lack of moral sense. Marjorie, carried away, promises to marry Francis, and MacGown warns Francis not to trespass. 10–12. Michael's agricultural experiment is temporarily halted by the suicide of one of his workers. Fleur sees Wilfred, just back from the East. A telegram summons her to Francis, who is ill at his hotel with pneumonia. She sees a note Marjorie has written him, asking him not to see her any more. In the evening paper, Fleur reads of Marjorie's engagement to MacGown. Marjorie goes to visit Francis at his hotel and Fleur lets her in, but Francis refuses to see her. He recovers from his pneumonia.

Part III. Chaps. 1–4. Soames and Michael confer with Sir JAMES FOSKISSON, their trial lawyer, after being rebuffed by MacGown on an offer to settle out of court. The Marquess of Shropshire promises Michael and Sir Lawrence that he will discuss the libel trial with Marjorie. Marjorie has breakfast with her grandfather and he advises her to settle out of court, but MacGown refuses to consider the idea. 5–8. At the trial, Foskisson questions Marjorie closely regarding her morals. When she refuses to answer his question as to whether

she has ever had a liaison, her attorney stops the trial and settles out of court. Francis Wilmot stops in to say goodbye to Fleur and Michael. 9–12. Fleur and Michael go to a party, at which Marjorie is present. Everything is strained. When they return home, Fleur asks Michael to take her on a trip around the world. Marjorie is despondent about her debts. Her grandfather agrees to pay them all if she will promise to reform. She agrees. Michael decides he cannot take Fleur on the round-the-world trip until Parliament closes in August. Soames offers to acompany Fleur on the trip, meeting Michael en route.

INTERLUDE: PASSERS BY

Soames is in Washington with Michael and Fleur. He catches a glimpse of Jon Forsyte and his young wife, Anne, and finds they are all staying at the same hotel. He goes to great lengths to make sure that Fleur does not meet Jon. That night he watches silently as IRENE FORSYTE, Jon's mother and Soames' first wife and only love, plays the piano in the hotel salon.

Swan Song

Part I. Chaps. 1–2. The General Strike of 1926 is on. Michael and Fleur organize a canteen to feed the volunteer railroad workers. They enlist NORAH CURFEW to help them. Winifred Dartie, Soames' sister, hears that her son Val, his wife Holly, and Holly's brother Jon Forsyte, are coming up to London to help in the strike. Winifred asks Fleur to let Holly help in the canteen. Soames plans to come up from Maplecurham, his country place. 3–6. Jon stays with Val and Holly. He has sold his Carolina peach farm and plans to buy a fruit farm in England. His wife, Anne, remains in Paris with Jon's mother, Irene. As Soames is being driven to London, a young chorus girl asks him for a ride. Soames is appalled at her nerve but gives her a ride. Val goes to work as a stoker during the strike. He eats at a canteen and discovers that his cousin, Fleur Mont, is running it. A college friend of Val's visits him to borrow money. After he leaves, Val's mother misses a valuable snuffbox. Soames tracks the man to his club and questions him about the snuffbox. He denies any knowledge of it. Then Soames tracks the man back to Winifred's door. Confronting him, he offers to buy the snuffbox back for £10. 7–10. The strike is over. Michael meets his uncle HILARY, a vicar, who has a slum-clearance project. Fleur is introduced to Anne, who has just come from Paris. All the while, she is planning an "accidental" meeting with Jon. Fleur goes early to Holly's. Only Jon is up. They chat, and she invites Anne and him to lunch the next day. Fleur's little boy, KIT, is introduced to Anne and Jon. 11–13. Soames, learning that Fleur has been talking to Jon alone, worries for fear Fleur and Jon will resume their love affair. Michael wonders about Jon and Fleur's old affair, and why they had parted. June Forsyte, Fleur's cousin and Jon's half-sister, tells him how Irene, Soames' first wife, left Soames and married JOLYON FORSYTE, Soames' cousin. Jon is the child of the Jolyon-Irene marriage.

Part II. Chaps. 1–6. Val decides to race his colt, RONDAVEL, at Ascot. Soames is determined to prevent Fleur from meeting Jon, but he is unsuccessful and during the races Fleur and Jon briefly disappear together. Val's horse wins his maiden race. Kit contracts measles and Fleur spends the days of his illness and convalescence dreaming of Jon. Michael and his father visit the Marquess of Shropshire and several other gentlemen to organize a committee for Uncle Hilary's slum-conversion project. 7–9. June Forsyte tries to persuade Fleur to have her portrait painted by June's newest protegé, HAROLD BLADE. Fleur arranges to take Kit to a summer cottage in a village not far from where Jon and Anne will be. She meets Jon on the train going down. Jon goes down to Wansdon, thinking of Fleur and Anne—double-hearted, he calls himself. 10–11. Val Dartie's college friend STAINFORD, the man who stole the snuffbox, brings Val information that SINNET, whom Val considers his best stable boy, is making the colt Rondavel ill. Reluctantly, Val pays Stainford £50 for the information. 12–13. Fleur is restless when she has been at the summer cottage a week and has not seen Jon and Anne. Impulsively, she returns to London and goes to June's, where Blade is painting Anne. Fleur watches Anne and Jon, as Anne is being painted. Soames goes down to take Fleur and Kit home. Arriving the night before, he goes to a hotel at which a costume party is being held. He sees Fleur and Jon dancing together, seeming lost in another world, as Anne watches them.

Part III. Chaps. 1–2. Soames and Michael talk of Fleur. Michael has noticed her preoccupation. Soames advises him not to do anything rash—merely wait. Michael tries to interest Fleur in the slum-conversion project. She decides to start a rest home for city girls. She asks her father for financial aid, buys an old house located an hour's drive away from Jon, furnishes and staffs the house, learns to drive a car—all with a view to being near Jon. Soames and Fleur arrange to have her portrait painted by Blade. 3–6. Fleur starts her sittings. Jon is also having his portrait painted by Blade. Fleur schemes to meet Jon. She forgets her purse after a sitting. Returning to June's to retrieve it, she meets Jon and drives him part of the way home. Later she again meets Jon and drives him out to see her rest home. Stainford forges a check in Val's name for £100. Soames exacts from Stainford a promise not to bilk Val again. Soames hires Butterfield as Gradman's assistant. 7–9. Fleur and Jon meet and go to Robin Hill, his boyhood home, the scene of their young romance. They walk to the coppice, their former trysting place. Fleur asks Jon to claim her, and he does. Afterwards, Fleur asks Jon when they will meet again. He

rushes off. She drives home, disconsolate. Jon writes a note to Fleur saying that it is all over. That evening Anne tells him that she is to have a child. Looking at him, she guesses what has happened between him and Fleur. He promises never to see Fleur again. 10–12. Fleur goes to meet Jon at Green Hills Farm, but he is not there. He has left a note telling her that Anne has guessed the situation, and that they must never see each other again. Soames drives to Sussex and spends a happy day tracking down his Forsyte ancestors and their lands. He stops at Fleur's rest home to take her to Mapledurham for the weekend. He is most

distressed over her appearance. 13–16. Fire breaks out in Soames' picture gallery. He rushes in to save the paintings and is severely injured. Fleur had been in the gallery smoking, shortly before, but she is so distraught she hardly remembers. She is at Soames' bedside as he dies and promises him that she will be "good." Michael is told by Holly that the affair is all over. Michael is much relieved.

Val has decided to race his colt at Ascot

Moll Flanders

Novel by Daniel Defoe, 1661–1731. Published 1722. (PB, C44; ML, 122 & T8; RE, 25).

THE FULL TITLE is *The Fortunes and Misfortunes of the Famous Moll Flanders.* A striking feature of the book is that the novelist Defoe obviously liked his heroine and condoned her immoralities and her crimes. The picture of the late 17th and early 18th centuries is justly famous and there is no moralizing to spoil the effect. Defoe's best-known book is *Robinson Crusoe* but it should be *Moll Flanders.*

The narrator does not divulge her true name, since she is too well known to the authorities at Newgate Prison and Old Bailey.

MOLL FLANDERS is the daughter of a convicted felon, who gave birth to her in Newgate prison while awaiting sentence. The mother was afterward transported to a plantation in America and was forced to leave the child in the hands of gypsies. Moll escapes from the gypsies at Colchester and is put in the charge of a good woman who runs a little children's school. Moll learns to read and write and to keep herself clean and neat. She becomes an excellent

needlewoman as well. When she is 12 years old, she is asked to live with a gentleman's family nearby. But her nurse cannot spare her for more than a month, so she returns to the school for the next two years. She becomes an assistant to the teacher and is very happy. When Moll is 14, the nurse dies and the school is disbanded.

Moll goes to live with the family she had visited two years before. She receives all the advantages of wealth—French, music, dancing, and vocal lessons—and she is treated as a member of the family. Her ripening beauty soon attracts the attention of the two young gentlemen of the house. The elder brother secretly courts her and plies her with golden coins, and she, truly in love for the first time, succumbs to his advances. He tells her he considers them married in each other's eyes and promises he will legally marry her when he receives his estate. In the meantime, the younger brother, ROBIN, falls in love with "Mrs. BETTY," as Moll refers to herself, and tells the family that he means to marry her. The elder brother, having tired of Mrs. Betty, tries to persuade her to marry his brother. Upset by the elder brother's infidelity, and not loving the younger brother, Moll falls into a decline. Eventually she recovers, and resolves to leave the family. But they are too fond of her, and she and Robin are married. They are happy enough for five years, but Robin dies, leaving her with two small children. At his death, she leaves the children with his parents. Moll marries a draper and they embark on an extravagant way of life. She has a child, but it dies. To escape prison for his debts, he is forced to flee to France. As he is leaving, he tells her where he has hidden his liquid assets and absolves her from the marriage. She never sees him again.

Next Moll marries a man who has a plantation in Virginia. They sail to America, where they meet the husband's mother. Moll gets along so well with her new mother-in-law that she asks her husband if his mother can live with them. The mother-in-law amuses Moll with the backgrounds of the leading citizens of the infant colony. Moll and her husband are very happy together and they have three children, two of whom die. One day, the mother-in-law tells Moll the background of her own life. She was a former Newgate prisoner, convicted of a felony, and branded on the palm of her hand. Moll questions her more closely and learns, to her horror, that her mother-in-law is, in reality, her true mother. This means that her husband is her brother! Moll does not know which way to turn. Finally, she tells her mother of their predicament. Together, they tell the brother. He is so shocked he offers to commit suicide as a way out. Moll dissuades him and leaves for England.

At the seaside resort of Bath, Moll becomes friendly with a gentleman whose wife has become mentally unbalanced. After several years' acquaintance, during which time Moll nurses him during a serious illness, they begin to live together as man and wife. She has three children by him, only one of which lives. After another serious illness, he repents of his sins and tells her he can see her no more. He offers to provide for her and their child. She asks for £50 more than he offers, knowing that this is the last money she will get from him. He takes the child, and she leaves for London.

Moll is now 42, and hardly wealthy. She meets a woman who is going to visit a sister and brother in Lancashire, near Liverpool. Moll is invited to accompany her on the trip and accepts. Before she leaves London, Moll goes to her bank for advice on how to handle her financial affairs. The banker, after a short acquaintance, becomes enamored of Moll and promises to marry her as soon as he is divorced from his erring wife. Moll puts him off gently, but not finally. Moll and her friend proceed to Lancashire where the brother, JAMES ("JEMMY"), and his sister meet them. After a short courtship Jemmy and Moll are married. They prepare to depart for his estate in Ireland. When Jemmy discovers that Moll is not the wealthy woman he had supposed, he confesses that he has no estate in Ireland. Though really in love, Moll and Jemmy part; Moll goes back to London, where she bears a baby boy. She writes to her old friend, the banker, who has now divorced his wife, and is most anxious to marry her.

Moll discovers that her supposed mother-in-law is actually her mother

They met at Brickhill and are married.

Moll lives for 5 years with her banker-husband, during which time she has two more children. He dies, and she spends the next 2 years in idleness, watching what money she has dwindle away. One day in an apothecary shop she steals a bundle left by a customer. This is the beginning of Moll's life as a thief in London.

Early in her career as a thief, she befriends a child on its way home from dancing school, and steals its gold necklace. Another time, she breaks a store window and steals two diamond rings. She does not know how to dispose of her ill-gotten goods. She resolves to return to her old "governess," the woman who took care of her when she bore Jemmy's child. The governess has turned pawnbroker. She disposes of Moll's stolen goods and Moll moves in with her. As Moll becomes well-known among the thieves, her governess advises her to try a few robberies dressed as a man. Moll follows her advice but gives up the plan after a narrow escape, during which she is encumbered by her disguise.

One evening at Bartholomew Fair, Moll meets a gentleman who is smitten with her. Under the influence of wine, he takes her to a hotel, where she yields to him. Afterwards, he takes her for a ride in his hired coach. When he falls asleep, Moll steals his gold watch and other valuables, and decamps. On hearing of Moll's adventure, the governess goes to the gentleman, returns his gold watch to him, and tells him that she is only acting for a good woman, who is overcome with remorse. The gentleman rewards the governess handsomely and asks to meet the charming thief. Moll and the gentleman are reconciled and enter into a liaison. He visits her once a month, providing for her handsomely, but his visits become less frequent, and Moll returns to stealing. This time she is caught, but she obtains a shrewd attorney, who proves her case to be one of mistaken identity. The accuser has to pay Moll £200 and provide her

with a new suit of black silk.

Moll then takes on another pursuit—that of "guiding" gentlemen at the gaming tables, pocketing some of their winnings for herself. She even travels to Harwich and relieves travelers of their luggage. Shortly after her return to London, she attempts to steal some brocade. Two maid-servants catch her. Moll is thrown into Newgate prison, miserable and remorseful. Her governess sends a minister to her and she repents of the sins of her past life. In the meantime, the governess is trying to obtain Moll's freedom. One day, a new prisoner is brought in, her Lancashire husband, Jemmy. The governess eventually obtains an excellent attorney for Moll and Jemmy. He succeeds in having their sentences transmuted from the death penalty to transportation to the colonies.

Moll and Jemmy find they have almost £500 with which to start their life in America. Moll also has £300 that the governess is to use to send them articles that may be scarce in America. In Virginia, Moll learns that her mother-brother has died and that her husband-brother, who is now senile, is living with their son, HUMPHREY, on the plantation. Moll's mother has left her a part-interest in the plantation, which Humphrey is managing. Humphrey is generous to his mother. Jemmy and Moll settle on a Maryland plantation they have bought and become successful farmers. For eight years their plantation thrives. Then they sell it at a nice profit, return to England, and settle down to a quiet life, repenting the wicked lives they once led.

Monsieur Beaucaire

Novelette by Booth Tarkington, 1869–1946.
Published 1900.

FOR ONE WHO WISHES to read something for sheer pleasure, not have to think too hard, and enjoy high romantic adventure, and who does not have too much time available at the moment, there is no story better worth recommending than *Monsieur Beaucaire*. Tarkington was a fine writer and he handled his romantic story very well. Anyone in a passing sentimental mood can be defied not to love it.

Chap. 1. VICTOR, quondam barber-hairdresser of the French Ambassador to the Court of St. James, has recently undergone a transformation into M. BEAUCAIRE, one of Bath's elusive and ambiguous "gentlemen of parts." Beaucaire has had occasion to observe the shady practices of the impoverished Duke of WINTERSET at the gaming tables, and he traps the duke in the act of cheating. Now Winterset must either face exposure or mollify this "greasy barber." Beaucaire demands merely that the duke present him to the beautiful and aloof Lady MARY CARLISLE at Lady MALBOURNE'S ball that evening. The duke agrees to take Beaucaire to the ball, under still another assumed identity, that of an improvised Duc de CHATEAURIEN. Winterset has a personal interest in Lady Mary, since his best chance to recoup the family fortunes is by marrying an heiress. Beaucaire laughingly warns him to give up all hope of such an alliance once the Duc de Chateaurien is on the scene.

Chaps. 2–4. At Lady Malbourne's ball the Duke of Chateaurien, resplendent in white satin court dress, has taken precedence over all of Lady Mary's other beaux and he is seeing her now to her sedan chair. He pleads for a rose from her corsage; she refuses. Mysteriously, just before her chair is carried off, a blood-red rose drops at his feet. Winterset warns him that roses last only till morning, and that this rose is an unlucky color. In the season that follows, Chateaurien becomes the pampered hero of fashionable Bath society. The only fault one can find with him is that he is a poor hand at gambling. Captain ROHRER, known for his skill as a duelist, provokes a quarrel with the French duke; Chateaurien ignores him until Rohrer makes insulting remarks about a member of the French Royal house, the Princess of BOURBON-CONTI. Then Chateaurien challenges the captain and, after casually running him through the left shoulder, sends a basket of blood-red roses to the Duke of Winterset. Another captain denounces the Duke of Chateaurien as an impostor and is wounded lightly by Chateaurien in a second duel. Chateaurien explains that he has fought the duel not in defense of his own honor, which is unassailable, but because he cannot overlook the reflection upon his sponsor, the Duke of Winterset. By this time Lady Mary holds Chateaurien in special favor. One night he escorts her return to Bath from a country mansion, riding horseback alongside the window of her carriage. Although the formidable Lady Rellerton shares the vehicle, Lady Mary is able to enjoy privacy with her admirer by putting her head out the carriage window. She has begun to commit herself romantically when a band of horsemen charges down the highway, scattering her outriders and storming the carriage. Masked, but with bared swords, they descend upon Chateaurien shouting "Kill the barber!" Chateaurien fights a losing battle against overwhelming odds; the Bath gentlemen in Lady Mary's escort stand by idly. The masked horsemen truss up Chateaurien and prepare to administer a lashing. But the wind finally carries the Frenchman's voice around the bend of the road, where his retainers have been posted. They make short work of their master's assailants, whose ringleader turns out to be the Duke of Winterset. Winterset explains to Lady Mary how he has been blackmailed by this M. Beaucaire, former barber to the French Ambassador. Beaucaire admits to Lady Mary that he originally came to London as a barber in the ambassador's suite. Winterset gives him 24 hours to leave Bath forever. Beaucaire jauntily replies that Winterset and his horsemen will find him in the Bath Assembly Room in exactly one week at 9 o'clock in the evening. Lady Mary drives off, scornful of the self-confessed barber.

Chaps. 5–6. The evening of Beaucaire's promised return to Bath finds BEAU NASH, the "King of Bath," promenading his crowded Assembly Room. The turnout is the celebrated mixture of wit, beauty, fashion and high aristocracy that characterizes his personal following. An added note of brilliance is the expected attendance of the Comte de BEAUJOLAIS, a young French Prince of the blood who just arrived from Paris that afternoon, accompanied by the Ambassador of Louis XV, the Marquis de MIREPOIX. Nash has taken the precaution of having the house and grounds surrounded by an armed guard, ready to seize Beaucaire should he show his face. The last Nash had heard of his whereabouts was that he disappeared a day ago from a neighboring farmhouse where he had been recovering from his highway "accident." The account of Winterset's encounter with the Frenchman has made the rounds of the Bath drawing-rooms and Winterset has become a hero. He has returned to Lady Mary's favor, too. As 9 o'clock strikes, Nash sends a footman out to see if the guards have caught Beaucaire on the grounds. There is a buzz of excitement and anticipation as the French Royal Prince and Ambassador are announced. The crowd rushes forward to catch a glimpse of the distinguished foreigners, and Lady Mary is caught in the crush. Winterset extricates her and goes to fetch her a glass of negus [hot wine punch]. Looking about her for a chair, she notices a small side salon and gratefully discovers that it is empty except for two men playing cards. The cardplayers turn out to be MOLYNEUX, a Bath dandy of her own set, and M. Beaucaire. She reviles Molyneux for keeping such low company, but offers him the opportunity to clear out before she spreads the alarm that Beaucaire is present. Beaucaire attempts to reason with her, but the Beauty of Bath is deaf to his plea. Winterset enters, accompanied by six friends. He has just been informed that Beaucaire entered the Assembly through a side door, accompanied by Molyneux. He has come now to eject the barber forcibly.

Beaucaire attempts to reason with Lady Mary but she scorns him

451

He offers to conduct Lady Mary to the door, but she prefers to wait. Winterset now notices that Beaucaire's chest is adorned with royal orders and decorations. He sneers at these as the fruits of robbery and commands his henchmen to rip them off Beaucaire's coat. Molyneux withdraws into the ballroom and returns with the young Count of Beaujolais and the French Ambassador. Beaujolais throws his arms around Beaucaire and addresses him as "Philippe" and "brother." The truth comes out: "M. Beaucaire" is indeed his older brother; Beaujolais has been sent to Bath to put an end to Beaucaire's masquerade and fetch him back to France. The man who slipped out of France disguised as M. de Mirepoix's hairdresser, Victor—the whilom gambler,

Beaucaire—the self-styled Duke of Castlenothing (Chateaurien)—is in reality His Royal Highness, Prince Louis-Philippe de Valois, the Duke of Chartres, Duke of Orleans, etc., etc., cousin to his most Christian Majesty Louis XV, King of France. He has been sulking in Bath to avoid making a marriage of the King's choice. Now that the King has relented and sent word that he is free to marry whom he pleases, Louis-Philippe has decided to return to his designated fiancée in France. He has discovered that he wants to marry her. She is loving and sweet, and what is more, he informs a contrite and humbled Lady Mary, she is the kind of woman who would go right on being loving and sweet to him even if he suddenly turned out to be a lackey.

The Moon and Sixpence

Novel by W. Somerset Maugham, 1874–1966.
Published 1919. © 1919 by W. S. Maugham & Doubleday & Co.
THOUGH THIS NOVEL is granted to be based on the life of Paul Gauguin, the French post-impressionist painter, it is a novel and not historical fiction. By common consent, Maugham's greatest novel is *Of Human Bondage*, but nearly everyone places *The Moon and Sixpence* second among his works. For convenience' sake Maugham made his fictional representation of Gauguin an Englishman, but Maugham was born in France and lived and studied much there and was quite capable of interpreting the French Gauguin as well as he could the English Charles Strickland.

1. The author of the book, SOMERSET MAUGHAM, reveals that when he first met CHARLES STRICKLAND he did not perceive anything extraordinary about him. However, time has proved the artist's greatness, and even those who do not like his art cannot help but be arrested by it. Much has been written about Strickland since he was acclaimed a great artist, not all of it true. Strickland lived in obscurity and was inclined to make enemies rather than friends. Strickland's son, glossing over his father's transgressions, described him as an excellent father and husband, whereas Dr. WEITBRECHT-ROTHOLZ, an art historian, went into detail about all the bizarre experiences in Strickland's life. 2–3. A trip to Tahiti led Maugham to write this book. As a young author who had achieved some success with his first book, Maugham lived in London and attended many literary teas. 4. At a tea at the home of ROSE WATERFORD, Maugham is introduced to Mrs. CHARLES STRICKLAND, a well-known hostess to all the literary figures in London. Rose Waterford tells Maugham that Mr. Strickland is

just a dull stockbroker who never attends his wife's literary fêtes and is not interested in the arts. 5–6. Mrs. Strickland invites Maugham to dinner but warns him that Charles, although she loves him, will probably bore him to death. The party is indeed tedious. 8. Maugham is astonished to learn from Rose Waterford that Strickland has run away from his wife. A long-standing appointment forces Maugham to visit Mrs. Strickland that day. Mrs. Strickland, in the company of her brother-in-law, Colonel MACANDREW, reveals her distress and says that Charles has run off to Paris with a woman, after 17 years of married life. 9. The colonel tells Maugham that the family never suspected anything. There had been no quarrels; Strickland simply sent a note to his wife that he was going to Paris and would never return to her. 10. Mrs. Strickland asks Maugham to go to Paris to see Charles. She will not give her husband a divorce and sends the message that she is waiting for him to return.

11–14. Maugham finds Strickland in a shabby hotel in Paris. He is unshaven and wearing old clothes, but seems more at ease than when he was a well-dressed broker in London. Maugham is astonished by the extraordinary callousness with which Strickland tells him that he never intends to see his wife again and does not care what happens to her. Neither does it matter to him what people think of him. At mention of another woman, Strickland laughs scornfully, saying he would never have done what he has for a woman. He reveals, to Maugham's increasing astonishment, that he wishes to paint and plans to learn even though he is in his forties. 15–16. Surprisingly, Mrs. Strickland is more enraged than if Charles had fallen in love with someone. She feels sure he will never return but she no longer cares because now she hates him. Left to make her own way, Mrs. Strickland establishes a shorthand and typing business.

17. Five years later, Maugham goes to Paris to live. Before he leaves London he stops to see Mrs. Strickland; her business

is doing well. 18–19. In Paris, Maugham meets an old friend, an artist named DIRK STROEVE. Although a bad painter, Stroeve has a great love of art. He is quick to discover talent and most generous to his fellow artists who, unfortunately, are inclined to take advantage of his good nature. Stroeve introduces Maugham to his wife, BLANCHE, with whom he is deeply in love. She is a tall, reserved woman and Maugham wonders why she married Stroeve. Maugham asks Dirk if he knows Strickland and Dirk does, adding that Strickland is a great painter. Blanche interjects that she dislikes him as he is rude. Dirk takes Maugham to see Strickland. 20–21. Strickland is more ragged in appearance and much thinner, yet he gives an impression of great strength. For five years he has worked tirelessly at his art but has sold no pictures. He has refused to accept help from anyone and so has lost much time in solving technical problems. Strickland seems to be aiming at something he does not perceive clearly, for he is never satisfied with his work. 22–23. During that winter, Maugham sees Strickland from time to time, but his pleasantest hours are spent in the company of Dirk Stroeve and his wife. 24–26. Dirk learns that Strickland is ill. Against Blanche's will Dirk takes Strickland to their apartment to care for him. Strickland is an extremely difficult patient, and behaves abominably. Blanche proves a capable nurse, and gives no evidence of the dismay she showed earlier. 27–31. After regaining his health, Strickland ejects Dirk from his own studio, saying he cannot work in the same room with him. A week later, Blanche leaves Dirk for Strickland. Maugham is sure Strickland does not love Blanche, as he seems incapable of love. 32–33. Dirk sends Blanche a note through Maugham, saying that if she is ever in trouble he will help her and bears her no ill feeling. 34–35. Strickland deserts Blanche and Blanche is in critical condition in the hospital, having taken poison. Dirk and Maugham visit the hospital, but Blanche refuses to see her husband. 36–38. Dirk, too tired to weep, tells Maugham that Blanche has died and that he is planning to return to his native Holland. 39. After Blanche's funeral, attended only by Maugham and himself, Dirk returns to the studio where they once lived. He finds a picture of Blanche painted by Strickland. In a fit of rage he is about to slash it to pieces, when something stops him. He realizes the painting is a work of art, and he is afraid to destroy it. To Maugham's astonishment, Dirk invites Strickland to Holland because they had both loved Blanche. Strickland refuses harshly, and Dirk leaves for Amsterdam. 40–42. Strickland invites Maugham to his studio to see his work. Although Maugham has a genuine horror of Strickland, he is also curious to discover the artist's motives. With inhuman callousness, Strickland reveals that he feels no remorse at Blanche's death. He tells Maugham that Blanche married Dirk after she had been seduced and become pregnant by the son of a wealthy Roman family in whose household she served as governess. Dirk found and married her after she attempted suicide. Strickland considers love a weakness and wants no woman's desires to dominate him. Maugham is disappointed in Strickland's paintings. However, he sees that here is a real power trying to express itself. A week afterward, Strickland goes to Marseilles, and Maugham never sees him again. **43–44.** Discussing Strickland's character, Maugham calls him an odious man but a great one, who cared nothing for fame or money and asked only of his fellow men that they leave him alone.

45–46. Visiting Tahiti many years later, Maugham meets Captain NICHOLS, who knew Strickland many years before in Marseilles and was the person who first suggested that Strickland go to Tahiti. **48–49.** Maugham meets several people who knew Strickland, including a merchant, COHEN, and Mrs. TIARE JOHNSON, the proprietress of a hotel in Tahiti. **50.** Maugham believes that some men, like Strickland, are born out of their proper surroundings and always long for a home they know not. He tells a story that illustrates this belief. **51–52.** Mrs. Johnson tells Maugham that she found a wife for Strickland because she felt sorry for him. The wife was a young Tahitian girl named ATA, who owned some property on the island. Strickland and Ata went to live in seclusion on her property, and Maugham believes these were probably the happiest years in the artist's life. They had two children. **53–54.** Maugham meets Captain BRUNOT, who also knew Strickland. Brunot says that what held Strickland was a passion to create beauty, which gave him no peace. **55–57.** Doctor COUTRAS, physician on the island, tells Maugham that he treated Strickland during his last illness—leprosy. Although the natives are horrified by this disease, Ata refused to leave him. When Doctor Coutras reached the hut in which they lived, he found Ata sobbing on the floor and Strickland dead. On the walls of the hut Strickland had painted a wonderful and elaborate composition, breathtaking in its magnificence. But Strickland had extracted a promise from Ata that she would set fire to the house, so this last mighty work was de-

The paintings are disappointing

stroyed. **58.** Upon returning to London, Maugham visits the first wife of Strickland, who is now living in modest comfort, having inherited some money from her sister. Maugham tells her what he learned about Strickland in Tahiti, omitting mention of Ata. With great ingenuity, she insinuates that her relations with Strickland had always been perfect. Maugham meets her son, ROBERT, now a grown man, and cannot help thinking of Strickland's Tahitian son.

The Moonstone

Novel by Wilkie Collins, 1824–1889. Published 1868. (ML, 27).

THIS IS CONSIDERED the first detective novel of the modern pattern written in the English language, although the other famous Collins mystery novel, *A Woman in White,* preceded it. *The Moonstone* so impressed Collins' friend Charles Dickens that Dickens began a mystery novel of his own, *The Mystery of Edwin Drood,* but unfortunately had not completed it at the time of his death.

Prologue. The Moonstone, a fabled yellow diamond of India, is acquired by JOHN HERNCASTLE at the storming of Seringapatam, 1799. The dying Indian from whom he takes it prophesies that the gem, once glowing in the forehead of an idol and now in a dagger, will have its vengeance on him and his people.

First Period. Chaps. 1–7. GABRIEL BETTEREDGE, the trusted house-steward of Lady (JULIA) VERINDER, tells how the diamond was brought to Lady Julia's Yorkshire home in 1848 by her nephew, FRANKLIN BLAKE. Franklin informs Gabriel that the gem has been left to John Herncastle's niece, Lady Verinder's daughter, RACHEL, on her 18th birthday. The conditions of the bequest are that Lady Verinder must be alive on that date and that Franklin's father serve as executor. The men speculate on whether Herncastle's motive is revenge on his sister, Lady Verinder, because she joined others in shunning him when there were rumors that he had gained the diamond by evil means.

Chaps. 8–11. During the four weeks before Rachel's birthday, Franklin falls in love with his cousin. No one can fathom Rachel's feelings. The housemaid, ROSANNA SPEARMAN, a rehabilitated convict, seems madly in love with Franklin. On Rachel's birthday, Franklin gives her the Moonstone. The famed gem casts a blight on the festivities, because of the recent appearance of three mysterious Indian jugglers in the vicinity. A guest, the celebrated traveler in India, Mr. MURTHWAITE, tells Betteredge and Franklin that the so-called jugglers are actually high-caste Brahmins in disguise and undoubtedly wish to steal the diamond to replace it in the idol's forehead. Next morning the diamond is gone from the unlocked drawer where Rachel put it. The police suspect the Indians but discover they were in town at the time of the theft. Rachel is distraught and refuses to coöperate with the investigation. Rosanna Spearman appears to know more about the jewel than she should.

Chaps. 12–13. Sergeant CUFF, a London police detective imported by Franklin, suspects that Rachel has stolen her own diamond with the aim of pawning it to pay debts, and has made Rosanna her confidante. His suspicions are raised by Rachel's insistence on departing to visit her aunt. Franklin is pained by her extreme hostility to him and arranges to go away. Rosanna disappears and is traced to the nearby quicksand, where it is obvious she committed suicide. Rachel, questioned by her mother, asserts she never spoke privately with Rosanna and never had the diamond after she put it away on her birthday. Lady Verinder takes Rachel to London to distract her.

Second Period. I. 1–6. As told by Miss DRUSILLA CLACK, a spinster cousin of the family, GODFREY ABLEWHITE, a handsome young barrister, philanthropist, and also a cousin, is set upon and searched. It is believed the Indians suspect him of having the diamond, since he was a guest in Verinder home during the birthday. The same day Mr. LUKER, a deal gems and a money-lender, ha perience and is robbed valuable jewel he ha bank. Godfrey pr She confesses "wretch." Verin h from her family attorney, MATHEW BRUFF, she breaks the engagement. Godfrey remains calm, but his insulted father refuses to remain as her guardian.

II. 1–3. Mr. Bruff recalls that under Lady Verinder's will Rachel is no heiress but has merely a life interest in her parent's property. It was Bruff's statement to Rachel that Godfrey was interested in her money that caused Rachel to jilt Godfrey.

III. Chaps. 1–10. Franklin tells of his return from traveling in the East because of his father's death and his own inheritance of a large fortune. He loves Rachel, though he has tried to forget her. Rachel is now living with a widowed aunt. Her new guardian refuses to see him. Resolved to unravel the mystery, he goes to Yorkshire, where Gabriel reveals that Rosanna left a letter addressed to him. Franklin reads her message, which directs him to go to the quicksand and pull out a certain chain. He does so and discovers a nightgown marked with his name and bearing paint smears from Rachel's bedroom door. The thief thus appears to be himself. An accompanying note from Rosanna explains that she discovered his paint-stained nightgown and hid it, fearing he would be revealed as the culprit. Her suicide resulted from despair at his departure. Returning to London, he reports this news to Bruff, who realizes that Rachel's coldness toward Franklin comes from her belief that he is the thief. When Franklin finally sees Rachel she scorns him, saying she herself saw him take the diamond. Seeking new clues, Franklin makes a fruitless visit to Mr. CANDY, the Verinder family doctor, who was a guest at the birthday party and has since been seriously ill, with a resulting loss of memory. Confiding in the doctor's assistant, EZRA JENNINGS, Franklin learns that Candy in delirium spoke of Franklin. Jennings displays his notes on the doctor's wanderings. They reveal that at the birthday dinner, in pique at Franklin's scorn of medicine for his sleeplessness, the doctor arranged to give him an opiate, intending to come by next day and explain his little trick. The doctor's illness and his loss of memory prevented the explanation. Jennings believes Franklin took the diamond in a trance induced by the drug and seeks to vindicate him by reproducing the event with a similar dose.

IV. Jenning's diary tells of the reopening of the Yorkshire house for the experiment. Rachel, who has returned, unknown to Franklin, places a crystal in the drawer where she had put the diamond. Franklin takes the opiate and soon rises from his bed in a trance, expressing worry that the Indians may still be in the house and will steal the diamond. He goes to Rachel's room and repeats his action by taking the crystal. He lets it fall to the floor, then falls into a deep sleep.

V. Franklin recalls awakening next day with no memory of these events. A quick reconciliation with Rachel, now aware of his innocence, follows. In London, Mr. Luker takes the diamond from the bank and gives it to a mysterious sailor, who next day is found murdered with an empty jewel box beside him. Sergeant Cuff discovers the sailor to be Godfrey Ablewhite in disguise.

VI. Epilogue. Sergeant Cuff writes to Franklin that evidence shows that the Indians murdered Godfrey. He reveals that Godfrey had lived a lavish existence, unknown to his family and friends, on wealth stolen from a trust fund of which he was a trustee. The money was due the heir soon after Rachel's birthday. Entrusted by Candy with putting the drug in Franklin's drink, Godfrey later saw his cousin take the diamond. He himself received the diamond from the dazed Franklin, who asked him to place it in the bank for safety. Seeing an answer to his financial needs, Godfrey kept the gem. He received a small loan on it from Luker to tide him over and later arranged to have it cut up into separate stones when he could redeem it.

Sergeant Cuff has the Indians traced to a ship bound for Bombay, from which they disappeared. In 1850 Mr. Bruff gets a letter from the traveler, Murthwaite, reporting that he has been in India and has seen the Moonstone once more in the forehead of the idol.

The Mother

Novel by Grazia Deledda, 1875–1936. Published 1923 by the Macmillan Co., New York. © 1920 by Grazia Deledda.

THE ITALIAN Nobel Prize winner Grazia Deledda (in private life Signora Madesani) was one of many upperclass women who elected to write about the peasantry. *The Mother* is a distinguished study of the conflict between the flesh and the spirit. It has been her most popular book in English translation.

Chaps. 1–2. In the little village of Aar, in Sardinia, a young priest, PAUL, has come to assume the parish, which has been without a pastor for several years. His mother, MARIA MADDELENA, keeps house for him. She has been aware for some months that he has more than a priestly interest in AGNES, a young woman living with only her servants in a large house not far from the presbytery. Paul goes to see the woman at night. His mother watches him go down the path to the orchard gate, and sees the gate open to receive him. The mother's heart is anguished, for this is the way to the darkest of sins. She yearns to be able to save him before he is lost—and her heart goes out also to the woman. The woman needs to be saved as well as Paul, for her sin also would be great.

Chaps. 3–4. Paul's mother speaks to him, tells him she knows where he has been, and begs him to stop before it is too late. Paul is angry and says he has been visiting with one who is ill. The mother is not deceived, and once again begs him not to do anything wrong. He angrily insists that he knows what is right and what is wrong for him. He goes to bed, and reviews his life—and his feelings for Agnes. He admits to himself that he loves her and he knows she loves him. He reflects on his life as a seminarist, when his mother worked as a kitchen drudge so that she might attend. During these years he met the prostitute, MARIA PASKA, and visited her several times. However, after he took his vows of chastity he never even entertained a thought of violating them—until he felt the mysterious, wonderful attraction of Agnes.

Chaps. 5–6. Paul's mother awakens him for morning mass. With grim determination he writes a note of farewell to Agnes, giving it to his mother to deliver. He goes to the Church, where his sacristan, ANTIOCHUS, awaits him. Antiochus wants to become a priest also. A message comes that an old hunter of the hills, NICODEMUS, is dy-

454

In a trance, he

and takes the crystal

ing, and the priest is needed. Antiochus returns to the presbytery with the priest's mother. Thinking of Agnes's wealth and her property, the mother almost unconsciously asks aloud why priests are not allowed to marry. Paul and Antiochus set out but when they reach the hunter's cabin he has disappeared.

Chaps. 7–8. Nicodemus has fled to his hut, halfway up the mountain. Before Paul sets out for there, a young widow comes in with her daughter, NINA MASIA. She says the girl is possessed by a demon and begs the priest to exorcize it. Paul does not believe in demons that inhabit human bodies, but he reads a passage that deals with the exorcizing of devils and the child calms quickly. He reflects that the only demon is the one in himself. He goes with Antiochus to the old hunter's hut and administers the final sacrament. Then Paul asks to be taken to see Antiochus's mother and Antiochus is excited at the thought of the honor Paul will do his mother's little wineshop by visiting it. Paul actually wants to ask Antiochus's parents if they are very sure he wants to become a priest. On the way back to the village, Paul notes signs of festivity. The villagers are celebrating his defeat of the devils in Nina Masia's body, which they consider a true miracle. There are fireworks and feasting, and the wine shop of Antiochus's mother does a fine business. Paul decides to ask some of the revelers home with him, so that he may be sure of keeping away from Agnes that night. He feels that he is saved if he can get through the night without seeing her.

Chaps. 9–10. The men who go back with the priest to his house leave early. Antiochus has waited because the priest wanted to see his mother, and together they go out. Maria Maddelena goes to bed, praying that her son will not go to the woman this night. She is filled with a premonition that he will, however. At the wine shop, Paul tries to tell Antiochus's mother how momentous a decision it is to set out for the priesthood. She speaks with some acerbity, and says that Antiochus can do as he wishes. Antiochus declares that he wants to be a priest, and thus his fate is decided. On leaving the shop, Paul sees one of Agnes's servants, who tells him that her mistress is ill. She fell, and they found her lying unconscious and bleeding from the nose. Will the priest not come and see her? Paul is tempted to go, but at length says that he will not. He bids the servant go home, and return if a serious need arises.

Chaps. 11–12. Paul tells his mother that Agnes is ill. He exaggerates her illness, because he so desperately wants to see his beloved again. His mother tells him to do as his conscience dictates, and he goes to Agnes. She asks him almost angrily why he has come, and refuses to believe that he has forsworn her because of his fear of God. It is his fear of man, and public opinion. And he has come back, not because she is pre-

Agnes and Paul

sumably ill, but because he loves her, as she loves him. Desperately, passionately, he falls into her arms and kisses her. She thinks that they will go away together, and the world will forgive them. Paul tries to explain that he offers her eternal spiritual love, but that they must not think of anything else. When she is convinced that he is in earnest, she tells him that he must then get out of the village that very night. He protests that he has to say mass the next morning, and cannot possibly go so soon. She then declares that if he does not, she will denounce him publicly in the church as a seducer of women. She is deadly serious, and he knows that she is. His only hope of appeasing her is to accede to her demand, or to enter into a life of darkest sin. He goes home.

Chaps. 13–14. Paul tells himself that Agnes will not carry out her threat, but by the time he wakes in the morning his conviction has reversed itself and he feels certain that Agnes will do as she threatened. He is tempted to feign illness, but this will only postpone the inevitable. He sets out for the church, but before he leaves he tells his mother of Agnes's threat. She too is terrified, but slowly she gathers her cloak and scarf about her and proceeds to the church. Paul hears the confessions of women who wish to take communion, and the scent of lavender on their clothing brings Agnes terribly near to him. He begins the Mass. His mother is there, stiff and pallid, suffering with him. Mother and son both look toward Agnes, waiting for the moment when she will rise and approach the altar rail to utter her denunciation. The suspense mounts, and with it the inner tensions of both mother and son. The communion is served, and Agnes thinks of what she is about to do. She is denouncing herself no less than the priest, and she knows that the people of this village have always respected her family—the nobles of the region. As she meditates, and as the mass drones on to its conclusion, she knows that she cannot do what she has planned, regardless of how bitter she may feel. The priest turns his eye in her direction frequently. Finally the mass is over and Agnes gets to her feet. The priest believes that she is about to utter her denunciation, and so does his mother. Both are transfixed. Agnes kneels, crosses herself, arises, and turns to leave the church. She has said nothing. A woman shrieks; Maria Maddelena is dead. Her son rushes to her side; he knows she has died of the suspense. In his misery and guilt, his eyes meet the eyes of Agnes, across the width of the church. There is nothing to say.

Sophocles
495–406 B.C.

Aeschylus
525–456 B.C.

Mourning Becomes Electra

Play by Eugene O'Neill, 1888–1953. Produced 1931. Published by Random House, New York. © 1931 by Eugene O'Neill.

BECAUSE IT IS actually three plays, which cannot conveniently be given in one continuous session, *Mourning Becomes Electra* is more valid as a work of literature than as a practical drama. It was inspired by the Electra story as told by the ancient Greek playwrights Sophocles and (in the *Oresteia*) Aeschylus. O'Neill agreed with Aeschylus and Sophocles that Electra was motivated principally by self-pity and that it was her neurotic expression of her resentment that caused her to inspire murder. O'Neill's character Lavinia is the equivalent of the classical Electra. The title *Mourning Becomes Electra* means that Lavinia thrives on tragedy. From the literary point of view this must be considered O'Neill's best work.

PART I. HOMECOMING

Act I. EZRA MANNON, a general in the Civil War, is expected home soon, as the war is over. The gardener, SETH, and a carpenter, AMES, discuss the celebration being held that night. They are fond of the general but dislike his wife, CHRISTINE. LAVINIA, the Mannons' daughter, learns of the war's ending from Seth just as PETER NILES and his sister HAZEL stop to visit. Hazel is anxious for news of Lavinia's brother, ORIN. Lavinia rejects Peter when he proposes to her; she feels her father will need her. Lavinia says she hates romance even when Peter questions her about a clipper captain who has been calling on her. As Peter goes, Christine enters; she berates Lavinia for permitting Seth's friends to roam the grounds and tells her that Captain BRANT is coming to call. Christine leaves. Seth warns Lavinia about Brant. He broadly hints Brant is really her cousin, the son of her disgraced Uncle DAVID. Brant arrives and regards Lavinia's coldness to him (due to Seth's news) as repayment for his once having said that he loved ships more than any woman. To test Brant, Lavinia insults his mother, a Canadian nurse. Brant, enraged, defends his mother and curses his Mannon blood. He says that Lavinia's grandfather disowned his father because he himself was also in love with Brant's mother. He is an orphan, for his father committed suicide and his mother died after being denied help by Lavinia's father. Lavinia accuses him of taking revenge by making love to Christine. He denies this, saying he loves only Lavinia.

Act II. Lavinia faces her mother and openly accuses her of having met Brant in New York. Finally Christine admits she loves Brant and says she hates the general. Lavinia tells her mother of Brant's relationship to the family, but she knows of it. Lavinia, to protect her father, promises Christine she will say nothing if Christine will stop seeing Brant. Christine accuses her of wanting Brant for herself and of wanting to take the general away from her. Christine finally gives in, saying she will see Brant for the last time. Christine then sends for Brant and extracts a promise from him that he will never give her up. She had hoped the general would not return but now she can only hope for his imminent death. Brant would rather face the general. Christine, however, tells Brant that the general has a bad heart and asks him to get a certain poison, which she will administer; the poison will make it appear that the general died of a heart attack. He hesitates and she calls him a coward. He agrees.

Act III. Lavinia finds Seth drunk after hearing the news of Lincoln's death. The general is due home that evening. Lavinia tries to tell Seth his suspicions of Brant are false, but he replies that Brant's mother even managed to get the general interested in her. This thought sends Lavinia to Christine, who assures her that she will never see Brant again. General Mannon returns and tells Lavinia that Orin has been wounded but will be home soon. Christine and Lavinia quarrel in front of the general, who stops them. Brant arrives and the general assumes he is a suitor of Lavinia's. The pair leave, and the general apologizes to his wife for any doubts he had had about Brant. He tells her he forgives her for hoping he would be killed so that she could devote all her attention to Orin. Christine denies this, but when the general reaffirms his love for her she rejects his embrace. Lavinia returns and in anger almost tells her father about Brant.

Act IV. In the middle of the night the general awakens and finds Christine also cannot sleep. He accuses her of not wanting him near her. Thinking of his heart condition, Christine goads him into a more heated argument by telling him of Brant and herself. He has a heart attack and asks for his medicine, and Christine gives him the poison. He takes it, then realizes it is not his medicine. Lavinia enters as the general dies, but with his last words he accuses Christine. Lavinia faces her mother, who tells the girl the truth about herself and Brant, and then falls to the floor in a faint, dropping the box of poison. Lavinia now knows her mother is a murderess.

PART II. THE HUNTED

Act I. BLAKE, the family doctor, and HILLS, the minister, and their wives are leaving the house after having paid their respects to the dead general. BORDON, the manager of the Mannon Shipping Company, stays on. Peter and Lavinia have gone to the station to meet Orin, who is coming home for the funeral. Hazel, in love with Orin, waits with Christine, who warns her that Lavinia will try to hold on to Orin. Orin arrives and his first words are for his mother, but before she has a chance to greet him Lavinia takes Orin aside and tells him about Brant. Orin swears Brant will not be allowed in the house. Lavinia tries to prepare Orin for Christine's lies but he thinks Lavinia is exaggerating. Christine finally greets him and when he enters the house Christine tells Lavinia that the box of poison she dropped was her own medicine. She asks her daughter what she has told Orin, but Lavinia does not answer.

Act II. In the sitting room Christine is making Orin comfortable. Hazel and Peter are there. Lavinia wants Orin to look at his father's body but Christine wants him to stay there. Peter and Hazel leave, and Orin wonders if Christine is pushing Hazel on him to get rid of him. He questions her about Brant and is told he is merely a beau of Lavinia's. Christine says that the late general hated Orin because of his closeness to her and that Lavinia is insane with jealousy. She tells him of her innocent trips to New York, but Orin is torn between suspicion and remorse for doubting her. Christine declares that Lavinia has accused her of murdering his father and pleads with Orin to protect her from Lavinia's madness. Orin assures her Lavinia will never go to the police but warns his mother that he will never forgive her if there is anything between her and Brant. He tells of a recurring dream of his in which he and his mother are in the South Sea Islands. She remembers that Brant has often mentioned the islands as a place for them. Orin assures his mother he will never marry and leave her. Indeed, he will try and get Lavinia to marry Peter so he and his mother can be alone. Lavinia now returns and insists he look at his father's body. He goes, and Christine defies Lavinia, saying that she has told Orin everything. Her defiance suddenly melts and she begs Lavinia not to tell Orin about Brant. Lavinia now knows her mother's weakness and decides to warn Brant that Orin may do him harm.

Act III. The general is laid out in state. Orin, looking at him, feels he really does not care much about his father's death. Lavinia enters and locks the door to talk to him without interruption. Orin is still filled with his war experiences but Lavinia tries to return to family matters. He tells her his wound was an accident and nothing heroic. She shows Orin the poison box. He says he will have it analyzed and prove she is wrong. Furious, Lavinia tells him about Brant and his mother. He demands proof and agrees that finding them together will be proof enough. Lavinia removes the poison box from his pocket and tells Orin to confront Christine with it. Christine enters when Orin unlocks the door and he tells her that he, too, thinks Lavinia is insane. Christine momentarily feels secure but shrinks when he confronts her with the poison box. Orin, now completely confused, leaves the room as Lavinia picks up the box in triumph.

458

Act IV. Brant's ship is at anchor in Boston harbor. His nerves are raw. He has almost killed a seaman whom he mistook for a burglar. He has been waiting for Christine with no means of getting a message to her. Christine arrives and tells him Orin and Lavinia have gone to visit cousins. As Brant and Christine go below deck, Orin and Lavinia, in disguise, come on board and listen through a transom. Brant and Christine agree that they must leave immediately. His own ship will not sail for a month but he will book passage on another. He vows to give up his ship and the sea for Christine. As they come on deck, Lavinia has to stop Orin from pulling his revolver on Brant. They hide and she makes Orin wait for Brant in his cabin; when he returns Orin kills him. Lavinia puts the cabin into great disorder to make it appear that a burglary and fatal struggle have taken place. Orin notices that the dead man resembles both the general and himself.

Act V. Hazel is with Christine, who cannot understand why Lavinia and Orin have not returned. Hazel leaves, and Orin shows his mother a newspaper account of Brant's death. Orin declares that Brant's influence made his mother kill his father but that he will forgive her if she will stay with him. Lavinia is horrified to see Orin still attached to their mother. Christine, completely overcome by Brant's death, shoots herself with the general's pistol. Orin breaks down and blames himself for her death. Unmoved, Lavinia sends Seth for the doctor and tells him Christine has killed herself for grief over her husband's death.

PART III. THE HAUNTED

Act I. 1. Seth and some friends arrive in front of the Mannon mansion. They have been drinking. SMALL, an elderly clerk, declares he does not believe in ghosts though there has been talk of Christine's ghost being seen in the house. Seth bets Small $10 he will not spend a night in the empty house. (Lavinia and Orin have gone to China.) Seth lets Small into the house. The other townspeople discuss ghosts with SILVA, a Portuguese fishing captain. Silva, MACKLE and Ames agree that ghosts do exist, but when they get curious about the general's death and Christine's suicide Seth silences them. Peter and Hazel arrive to tell Seth that Lavinia and Orin are coming home. Just then Small rushes out of the house and pays Seth the $10, swearing he has seen the general's ghost. Seth passes the incident off as a joke and tells Peter he had meant to discredit the talk of ghosts. However, he still believes the ghosts exist and suggests that Peter convince Lavinia and Orin not to live in the house. Peter does not believe in ghosts and wants to get the house ready for their return, but Hazel senses the evil that exists in the mansion. Orin and Lavinia arrive. Orin is in a kind of stupor, for Lavinia has replaced Christine as his mother and companion. She does not believe in ghosts, and she drags her brother inside. **2.** Orin is confused and wants to

look for his mother. Lavinia quiets him and reminds him that they came home so he could face the ghosts of the past and rid himself of his feeling of guilt. Peter greets Lavinia, whom he still loves. Orin tells Peter of their visit to the Islands. He says he did not like the native women but that Lavinia went wild over the men. Lavinia stops him and sends him to Hazel so she can be alone with Peter. She tells Peter that Orin is suffering from shock and she now can return Peter's love. Peter is too happy to examine her claims that the abandoned life of the islands has changed her feelings toward men. As they embrace, Orin and Hazel enter. The sight fills Orin with rage but he manages to congratulate them.

Act II. Orin has locked himself in his father's study and is busily writing when Lavinia knocks. He hastily conceals the manuscript and opens the door for her. She berates him for his brooding but he claims they never can escape from their guilt. Orin is engaged to Hazel but Lavinia is afraid to permit them to be alone for any length of time lest Orin tell her the whole truth. She wants to forget the past while Orin thinks only a full confession can free them. He tells her he has written a history of the Mannon family crimes and accuses her of having caused Brant's death because she wanted Brant for herself. Orin obviously is jealous of any man his sister loves. He tells her they now are in their parents' shoes, bound together by hatred, and they part weeping.

Act III. Lavinia now believes Orin would be better off dead. Seth comes to ask her to attend to a servant who is ill. Peter and Hazel arrive. Hazel wants to take Orin to her mother's house, believing his home and Lavinia are bad for him. Orin takes Hazel aside and gives her the manuscript he has written, asking her to keep it in a safe place. If he should die she is to read it, and on the day before Peter marries Lavinia she is to let him read it. He tells Hazel she is not to love him any more and, above all, not to let Peter marry Lavinia. Orin's strange

behavior shocks Hazel, but she knows Orin fears Lavinia. When Lavinia enters, Hazel tells her of her plan to take Orin home. Lavinia forbids it, they argue, and Hazel leaves in anger. At the door Lavinia sees the envelope containing the manuscript. She realizes its contents and pleads with Orin to give it to her. He takes the envelope from Hazel, telling her to leave and forget him, and gives it to Lavinia, declaring she must now give up Peter as he has given up Hazel. She agrees and he suggests she be his mistress, but suddenly he weakens and wants Lavinia to join him in confessing their guilt. Orin is going mad and imagines his mother is calling him. He goes into the study and Peter enters, looking for Hazel. Lavinia throws herself in Peter's arms as they hear a shot. They hurry into the study and find Orin dead. His death is passed off as an accident. Lavinia hides the manuscript but does not destroy it.

Act IV. Orin's funeral is over. Lavinia is setting flowers about the house to dispel the gloom. She is expecting Peter and hopes soon to marry and leave the house. With her marriage the name of Mannon will be no more. Hazel arrives, accuses Lavinia of being responsible for Orin's death, and pleads with her not to marry Peter. Lavinia's influence has caused her brother to move to a hotel. Lavinia tells Hazel to leave. Hazel says Peter knows about the manuscript. When Peter enters Hazel leaves, and Lavinia realizes that Peter's quarrel with his sister was about her. Lavinia is anxious to get married immediately and Peter wonders if there is something in the manuscript that would prevent the marriage. She begs him to make love to her, even though it is the day of Orin's funeral. Peter thinks her hysterical. She then tells him she can never marry him. Peter believes it is due to some affair she had in the islands, an idea she encourages, and he leaves in a rage. She then tells SETH to board up the windows, for she will live out her life with the ghosts as punishment for the misery she has caused.

At Lavinia's instigation Orin kills Brent

459

Baron Munchausen

Stories by Rudolf Raspe, 1737–1794.
Published 1785.

THE LIARS' CLUBS of various cities and states in the United States usually give their best prizes to stories that appeared nearly 200 years earlier in *Baron Munchausen's Miraculous Adventures on Land*. The book, the most famous of its kind ever published, is simply a collection of tall tales or Liars' Club items. It was written by an Englishman. The probability is that the English author selected the name Munchausen because he thought it would sound humorous—as German names so often do to English readers—and that the real Baron Munchausen accepted with delight the notoriety and identified himself with the book and the stories. Whatever the true history, the fact remains that the book was written in English and not by Baron Munchausen himself.

Chap. 1. I set off by horseback for Russia in midwinter. Going through Poland, I chanced upon an old man lying in the snow with barely anything on. I pitied the poor devil and, though my own blood was near frozen, I threw my mantle over him. A resounding voice from Heaven applauded the deed. That night I fastened my horse to something protruding from the snow and bedded myself nearby. I awoke next day in a village churchyard and found my steed fastened by his bridle to the steeple. The village had been snow-covered on my arrival, with only the steeple, to which I had tied my horse, piercing through. I shot the beast down and we rode on. I had procured a sled and was inside Russia when a hungry wolf bore down upon me. I laid myself flat in the sled. The wolf jumped over me, ate his way into the horse, and pushed right on into the harness. Thus, goaded by my whip, he drew me into St. Petersburg. There, while awaiting my commission in the army, I met an old general who had lost his pate in battle against the Turks and who could swallow prodigious quantities of liquor without effect. I finally deduced that the alcoholic vapors escaped through an aperture in the plate covering his skull. To prove it, I lit the fumes one night, producing an awesome column of fire above the gentleman's head.

Chap. 2. I suffered a fall one day on my way to hunt ducks and the blow made my eyes spark. I took no notice but hurried to the pond, there to discover that I had also sprung the bolt from my gun flint. Undismayed, I leveled the gun at the fowls, banged my fist against one of my eyes to produce the necessary flash, and brought down 16 birds. Another time, with but one shot left, I came upon several dozen wild ducks too widely dispersed to be got with a single shot. I took a piece of string, increased its length fourfold by unraveling it, tied a piece of bacon to one end, and threw the bacon on the water while I held the other end. The first duck swallowed the bacon and, the smooth morsel finding its exit unscathed, the next duck took it up, and so on until I had every bird neatly arrayed on the twine. The birds took to flight and, steering with my coattails, I was carried right to my house, where I landed safely by crushing their heads one by one. In a forest one day I met a marvelous black fox. So as not to harm its fur, I fired a spike instead of ball. The spike pinned him to a nearby tree and with my whip I flogged him nicely out of his handsome skin. And I once encountered in that same forest a wild pig guiding a blind sow by means of her holding his tail in her mouth. My shot severed the tail from the pig, which ran off. The sow, thinking that her guide had stopped, did not move. I took the tail in my hand and led the fierce beast docilely home. In a Polish forest, armed only with two flints, I was met by a terrible bear. The first flint I flung into the monster's open jaws and while he was recovering from that I threw the other up his rear portico. The two met in the middle, struck fire, and exploded the bear with a terrific bang. Another day a ferocious wolf rushed upon me, but instinctively I thrust my hand into his

Munchausen rides half a horse

mouth, grabbed his entrails, and turned him inside out like a glove.

Chap. 3. I have always been famed for my excellent dogs. One was a pointer, indefatigable, attentive, and courageous. On one hunting trip I rode ahead of my party to find game, and my dog, Dinah, quickly pointed at a flock of several hundred fowl. When my companions did not appear, I grew alarmed and turned back to find them. They had fallen, I discovered, into a coal mine shaft, and when at length they were rescued the hunt was postponed. I had to leave the next day on a business trip and did not remember until my return, a fortnight later, that I had forgotten Dinah. I returned to the fowls and there she was, still in point. She responded instantly to my order to charge, and with one shot I brought down 29 birds. But I had a greyhound that was even more remarkable. This dog ran so fast and was so long in my service that it actually ran off its legs and in later days could only be used as a dachshund, in which capacity it served me many more years. Another time, when my dog was heavy with young, we were coursing a hare when the dog disappeared. When I found her she had littered and her five pups had taken to the chase. They brought down the hare, which had also produced the same number of young ones—so I returned home with five more dogs and five more rabbits than I had anticipated.

I visited the Count Przobobowsky of Lithuania, who showed me a wild, unmanageable horse that inspired terror in all who had anything to do with him. I leaped atop the steed and in five minutes had tamed him to such an extent that I led him through the salon window and up on the tea table, where, without breaking a cup, I put him through his capers.

Chap. 4. The count was so pleased that he gave me the horse. In the battle of Oczakow I led the charge against the Turks, who were quickly routed. I then discovered to my amazement that I was alone on the battlefield, so I rode to the market place to await the rest of my troop. While there I led my horse to a trough for a well-deserved drink. His thirst was incredible; no amount of water would satisfy him. On turning my head, I discovered that his entire hindquarters were missing and the water was escaping as fast as he drank it in. We raced back to the pasture. Just as I had expected, we found his other half, which had been lopped off in battle, making sport with the mares. A farrier sewed the two parts together and the horse was as good as new. It was in that skirmish too that my arm got so worked up slicing down Turks that I could not stop its swinging and had to keep it in a sling for days to keep from injuring my own soldiers. And once during that siege I had the inspiration to get myself into the enemy fortification by hopping atop one of our balls as it left the cannon. Halfway there, however, I thought better of the notion. I jumped on one of their balls going the other way and arrived safely back in our own camp.

Chap. 5. Despite my bravery, I was taken prisoner. Every day I had to take the sultan's bees to pasture. One day I counted one bee missing and found it under attack by two great bears. I threw my ax at them, freeing the bee, but I had used such force that the weapon flew clear to the moon. I planted one of those Turkish beans that grow so fast and climbed up the stalk to recover my ax. By the time I reached the moon, the sun had burned through my ladder, so I had to cull straw to make a new rope and tied it to the end I was holding and so on to within a few miles of the earth, where the rope became threadbare from such treatment and broke. The impact of my fall gouged a hole about 9 rods deep into the earth, and I had to dig my way out with my fingernails. Finally, in the year of the great revolution in Russia when the Czar and his family were packed off to Siberia in weather so cold that the sun was frostbitten, peace was declared and I was free to return to my native Germany. I hired a stagecoach for the journey and once, rounding a bend, the postilion put his horn to mouth and blew himself purple, but not a note sounded. Alarmed because another coach could be heard coming the other way, I hoisted the stage, horses and all, upon my shoulders and jumped over a hedge to safety. The other vehicle gone, I jumped back to the road and we proceeded. At an inn a little later, the bugle suddenly sounded. The notes had frozen in the horn and now, to the infinite delight of all who heard, they thawed and tumbled out in several lively tunes.

Mutiny on the Bounty

Novel by Charles Nordhoff, 1887–1947, and James Norman Hall, 1887–1951. Published 1932 by Little, Brown & Co.-Atlantic Monthly Press, Boston; © 1932 by James Hall & Mrs. Laura Nordhoff. (PB, C34)

THE STORY of the ship *Bounty* and the mutiny of most of its crew including officers led by the chief mate, Fletcher Christian, is history. The official record of it is plentifully documented and the documents have been preserved. With the advantage of this research material, Nordhoff and Hall wrote one of the most distinguished quasi-histories, somewhat fictionalized, of a kind that has recently become very popular. Later books by the same authors cover the settlements that the mutineers established on South Sea islands and the remarkable return of Captain Bligh from midocean to land.

• **Chaps. 1–4.** In 1787, 17-year-old ROGER BYAM, who has a gift for languages, is asked by Sir JOSEPH BANKS to go to Tahiti and compile a dictionary of the Tahitian language. Banks introduces him to Lt. WILLIAM BLIGH of the British Navy, captain of the *Bounty,* which is to carry breadfruit plants from Tahiti to the West Indies for use as cheap food for slaves. Roger signs on as a midshipman for the two-year voyage. *Bounty* is a small vessel, with scant living space for her 45 men. FLETCHER CHRISTIAN, the mate, is a dark-haired, handsome

man of 24. Other officers are Mr. FRYER, a stout elderly man, and the surgeon, THOMAS HOGGAN, commonly referred to as "old Bacchus," a genial man with a wooden leg, who likes the bottle. Roger dines with Bligh aboard a man-of-war. Before dinner they watch a seaman, guilty of striking an officer, being flogged. When the man is cut down his back is bare to the bone and he is dead. Their host, the captain, complains that the interruption has caused his soup to get cold. The *Bounty* sails. JAMES MORRISON, the boatswain's mate, infuriates Bligh because he does not flog the men strongly enough. There are six midshipmen. Roger shares a berth with GEORGE STEWART, a young man of good family; EDWARD YOUNG, a pleasant fellow; and HAYWARD, a sulky 16-year-old bully. TINKLER, Fryer's 14-year-old brother-in-law, likeable and always up to mischief, shares a berth with HALLET, a weak, shifty-looking boy of 15. THOMAS ELLISON, youngest of the seamen and liked by all, serves the midshipmen as mess boy. Roger spends a good deal of time in the surgeon's cabin. Mr. NELSON, the botanist, and Mr. PICKOVER, the gunner, are usually there too. The food supply is scantier and of worse quality than on any other ship. Mr. SAMUEL, Bligh's clerk, issues rations to the messes without weighing them. When Bligh accuses the men of stealing two cheeses and is reminded he ordered them put ashore in England for his own use, the men realize he is lining his pockets at their expense. As a captain he is detested more for meanness than for harshness. Bligh curses the seamen and demands that they be flogged harder; Christian believes that kindness sometimes works better than beatings. Off the coast of Brazil JOHN MILLS, an old seaman, catches a large shark. Several men are dividing it for eating when Samuel demands a slice. Mills hurls it in his face and is given three dozen lashes. Poor Tinkler, for being up after hours, is sent by Bligh to the masthead to remain there in an icy wind all night. The carpenter, PURCELL, is put in irons for disagreeing with Bligh about the quality of some timber. Bligh has Young flogged for allowing one of the seamen to wander off from a foraging party. Just before landing at Tahiti, Bligh orders Fryer to sign the account book for provisions. Fryer refuses. Bligh calls all hands on deck and forces Fryer to sign in front of them.

Chap. 5–8. At Tahiti discontent vanishes. Roger goes to live ashore and study the natives' language for two months, while Nelson collects the breadfruit plants. On shore Roger is greeted by a tall chief, HITIHITI, who speaks English. He will be Roger's *taio,* or special friend. Christian pays a visit and is captivated by the beauty of MAIMITI, Hitihiti's niece. From then on, Christian visits Maimiti whenever possible. Roger gets to know and like him. Bligh causes discontent again when he orders Samuel to seize all the hogs and other gifts the men have been given by their taios.

Christian refuses to hand over two valuable pearls. The ship's corporal and two seamen desert and Roger is sent to find them. He and Hitihiti sail to another group of islands, where Roger sees TEHANI, a beautiful girl of noble birth, perform a ritual dance. When the deserters are found they are severely punished. The *Bounty* sails and a month later stops for wood and water at Namuka, where the natives are unfriendly. Bligh publicly insults Christian for suggesting a strong guard for the landing party; then, when the natives attack and Christian's inadequate party suffers losses, Bligh shouts that he is incompetent and cowardly. The next day Bligh accuses Christian of stealing some coconuts and reduces rations for all. That night Christian asks Roger to see his people in England should he not reach home. Roger says that Christian can count on him.

Chaps. 9–11. The next morning the men mutiny and take over the ship. Christian commands the mutineers. They cry to have Bligh killed on the spot, but Christian decides to send Bligh off with Fryer, Hayward, Hallet, and Samuel. Christian tells Roger and Nelson they may stay, but both choose to accompany Bligh. They go to collect their clothes and by the time they reach the deck the launch, overloaded with 19 men, is pulling away. Nine of the men left on board are not of Christian's party. Christian tells the men that they will never return to England but must settle on an island in the Pacific. The *Bounty* sails on. Christian runs the ship well, with strict discipline but not injustice. The *Bounty* picks up stores at Tahiti, but Christian does not allow Roger and his friends to go ashore. They plan to escape but a strong south wind blows day after day, making the escape impossible.

Chaps. 12–13. Christian wishes to settle on Tuphoi but the hostile natives prevent it and the *Bounty* returns to Tahiti once more. Eight of the men elect to remain on the *Bounty* with Christian. The rest disembark and Roger goes straight to Hitihiti's house. Christian takes Maimiti with him and the *Bounty* sails. Roger sets to work on his dictionary again. He again meets Tehani and falls in love with her. They are married and Hitihiti and his family act as Roger's relatives at the wedding ceremony. The seamen who were not part of the mutiny are building a ship to sail to England and they name her the *Resolution.* In 1790 Roger's daughter HELEN is born. The next spring, while Tehani is away on a visit, a British ship arrives.

Chaps. 14–19. Roger takes a canoe out to the British frigate, *Pandora.* He is immediately placed under guard. Captain EDWARDS refuses to believe that Roger is not one of the mutineers. Roger is put in irons, with Stewart and others. Roger learns from Dr. Hamilton, the surgeon, that Bligh has sworn he heard Roger say Christian could count on him. Bligh, untrue to his promise, has included those who stayed aboard unwillingly in his list of the muti-

neers. The men who planned to reach England in the *Resolution* are captured and made prisoners. Roger is allowed to see Tehani, who whispers to Roger that 300 men can attack the ship and free them, but he convinces her that the plan is hopeless. Tehani is griefstricken beyond tears. The *Pandora* leaves Tahiti in May, 1791. After searching for the *Bounty* for two months, the *Pandora* proceeds homeward. She hits a reef and sinks. The survivors assemble on a sandbar. The prisoners, stark naked, are refused the shelter of tents by Edwards and are forced to bury themselves in wet sand to escape the burning sun. On the rest of the trip back to England the prisoners are treated very humanely, against Edwards' will. After 4½ years, 15 months of which have been spent in irons, they see England again.

Chaps. 20–24. The prisoners are transferred to H.M.S. *Hector* in Portsmouth harbor to await court-martial. Their irons are removed and they receive decent food. Captain MONTAGUE summons Roger to his cabin and gives him a pack of letters. One, from Sir Joseph, tells him his mother died six weeks ago and that a cruel letter from Bligh was responsible for her death. Sir Joseph sees Roger and hears his story. Tinkler is Roger's best witness and Sir Joseph promises to find Tinkler if he is in England. But Tinkler is believed to have been lost in a hurricane. Some months later the prisoners are ordered to H.M.S. *Duke* for court-martial. Bligh's statement tells of Christian and Roger's conversation, but Fryer says that when he asked Roger if he was concerned with the mutiny Roger seemed horrified at the thought. Purcell, the carpenter, says that no more could have entered the launch without endangering the safety of all. Hayward and Hallett give malicious testimony against Roger. Fryer refutes this but testifies that in the launch Bligh frequently spoke of Roger as an ungrateful scoundrel and a mutineer. The next day the prisoners hear their sentences. Roger is sentenced to death by hanging. Some of the others, including Morrison, are condemned and some are acquitted. Sir Joseph brings Roger his dictionary and grammar, which he asks Roger to make ready for publication. Later Sir Joseph comes with the news that Tinkler is in London.

462

Roger is put in irons

Chaps. 25–27. One afternoon Morrison is reading aloud from the Bible to the other prisoners when a lieutenant and guard enter

and take away some of the men without even a chance for farewell. In the morning Capt. Montague brings word that Morrison and another man have been pardoned and Roger acquitted, as a result of Tinkler's testimony. Roger decides to return to Tehani and Tahiti for good. Sir Joseph and Captain Montague are stunned at the news. They remind him of his obligation to his name, which he must completely clear by continuing his career as a naval officer. War seems imminent and Montague invites him to serve on his ship. Roger returns to his family home and realizes his roots are there. The South Seas fade into unreality. He joins Montague's ship and serves in the wars against Napoleon. In 1809 he is sent to New South Wales, where Bligh, as governor, has been accused of tyranny and imprisoned. Roger hears Bligh shouting to the new governor to rule the depraved settlers with a hand of iron, and he knows that Bligh has not changed. Roger then sails to Tahiti, where he finds most of the population destroyed by war and disease. Tehani's brother tells him Tehani died shortly after Roger left. He then sees his daughter, married to a Tahitian of noble birth. He does not tell her who he is.

Nana

Novel by Émile Zola, 1840–1902. Published 1880. (PB, PL63; ML, 142)

THE LONG LIFE of this book—it is the best remembered novel of Émile Zola and the only one that is readily available in bookstores—is probably attributable to the fact that its title character is totally wicked and her allure and beauty are idealized by the author to the point of unreality. Undoubtedly there have been women of ill-fame who wreaked havoc among many admirers, but history does not record one who did it quite so thoroughly as Zola's Nana. The novel was condemned as wicked in its time. The principal reason for reading it now (a quite valid reason) is to see what all the fuss was about. The reader is likely to be puzzled, even after reading it.

Chaps. 1–2. LÉON FAUCHERY, a journalist on *Figaro,* takes his cousin HECTOR DE LA FALOISE, a newcomer to Paris, to the Théatre des Variétés for the debut of NANA, a theatrical unknown. BORDENAVE, the producer-manager of the Variétés, has been intimate with Nana and has decided to cast the theatrically unexperienced girl in the title role of *The Blonde Venus.* It is a typical Parisian first night and the audience includes STEINER, a banker who is the lover of ROSE MIGNON, a member of the cast;

Count DE VANDEUVRES, of distinguished ancestry but debauched; DAGUENET, Nana's "fancy man," who has run through his inheritance and now has nothing more to offer his women than an occasional bouquet or dinner; and the Count MUFFAT DE BEUVILLE, Chamberlain to the Empress. He owns a property near the Faloise estate in the country and Hector, it turns out, often visits him and his wife, the Countess SABINE, and her father, the Marquis DE CHOUARD, a Councillor of State. In the first act Nana comes on, awkwardly, and sings in a shrill, unmusical voice. The feelings of the house are about to turn against her when the 17-year-old GEORGES HUGON cries out in admiration at the sensuous movements of her body. The spontaneity of this outburst and Nana's good-natured reaction to it win over the audience. In the last act Nana makes her entrance in a diaphanous costume that reveals every ripe contour of her voluptuous body, which electrifies the Parisian first-nighters. The next day, in her furnished flat, Boulevard Haussman, Nana turns to her immediate problem of raising 300 francs to pay for the board of her little son, LOUIS, so that she can bring him back from the country. The flat is maintained for her by two "regular" visitors, one of whom, unfortunately, is irregular in his payments. She is determined to have her son back and arranges to go out in the afternoon on a date for 400 francs. When she comes home she is amazed to find her flat crowded with admirers. She orders her maid to send them all packing.

Chaps. 3–5. Fauchery and la Faloise attend one of Countess Sabine Muffat's regular Tuesday receptions. Fauchery has been delegated by Nana, as a reward for his ecstatic review in *Figaro*, to issue invitations to her midnight supper-party for the following evening. He has instructions to invite Count Muffat, to whom Nana seems especially attracted. Muffat declines firmly, as does his father-in-law, the marquis, though both had called on Nana the day after her theatrical debut on the pretext of soliciting funds for a local charity. Nana's party is a mixture of opulence, vulgarity, drunken confusion, and debauchery. At daybreak, when Nana is finally sure Count Muffat is not coming, she consents to become Steiner's mistress. This does not, of course, cause her to confine her favors exclusively to the banker.

Nana becomes the sensation of Paris. The Prince of Scots [an undisguised portrait of the actual Prince of Wales and future Edward VII of Great Britain] is taken backstage by Muffat and the marquis to meet the blonde beauty. Nana, taken by surprise in her dressing-room, almost without a stitch on, cavorts before the prince and his two French escorts. When she goes off with the prince for the night, the devout count is left burning with desire.

Chaps. 6–8. The Muffats and their unattractive 16-year-old daughter, ESTELLE, have gone to stay with Mme. HUGON at her country place, Les Fondettes, in Orleans. Young Georges is awaiting the visit of Fauchery and Daguenet. Even Vandeuvres, who has been promising to come for 5 years, is expected. The reason becomes apparent when Mme. Hugon innocently informs her guests that Steiner has recently bought a property, La Mignonette, about a league from Les Fondettes, for an actress friend of his. Nana has walked out on her theatrical contract and is expected momentarily at La Mignonette. Georges contrives to leave the house and arrive at La Mignonette, soaking wet, after falling into a water-hole. There are no masculine clothes in her house and Nana makes him change into a shift and petticoats. Carried away by the romantic setting and the perversity of being courted by this ardent young man who looks so much like a pretty girl in his improvised costume, Nana yields to Georges. She waxes sentimental over this new attachment, concealing Georges in her bedroom each night and keeping Steiner at a distance. This idyllic state is maintained for six days. Then Mme. Hugon catches sight of her son in Nana's victoria. When Georges returns home he is placed under what amounts to house arrest by his older brother, PHILIPPE, an army officer on leave. That same evening Nana accepts Count Muffat as a lover and the next day she returns to Paris. Three months later, despite her luxurious life, Nana is bored with her wealthy protectors, despite whom she is in debt. What she wants is love. She breaks off with Steiner. She informs Muffat that his countess is cuckolding him with

Fauchery, then she arranges things so that Muffat discovers her in bed with her new lover, FONTAN, the low comedian of the Variétés. She has been attracted by his particular type of ugliness and brutality. Nana lives with Fontan in a shabby two-room flat. Fontan's brutality increases until he beats her on the slightest pretext and reduces her to streetwalking to pay for his keep. She takes up with SATIN, a prostitute whom she befriended in earlier days. One evening she and Satin narrowly escape being arrested in a police raid. When she comes home, Fontan is in bed with another woman and throws Nana out.

Chaps. 9–11. Count Muffat, who has become Rose Mignon's protector, has never recovered from his obsession for Nana. Rose is to be starred in a new play, *La Petite Duchesse*, by Fauchery. Bordenave, after two failures, is badly in need of backing, which the count would be glad to provide if Nana were in the cast. Nana ousts Rose Mignon from the title role. Nana is a dismal failure at playing a "grand lady," but decides to become one in real life. Within a few months, Count Muffat has installed her in a lavishly decorated mansion, complete with a liveried domestic staff and five carriages. The relationship with the count has been resumed on the most explicit terms: 12,000 francs a month, gifts excepted, and Nana's pledge of absolute fidelity. The latter condition, however, is a matter of blind faith on the count's part, since Nana insists that his visits to her house be restricted to certain stated times. She loses little time in violating her promise to Muffat, whose generosity cannot meet her insatiable need for money. Making it clear to Vandeuvres that she is granting him no control over her personal freedom, she accepts the degenerate young aristocrat as a lover, adding another 10,000 francs to her month's "pin money." When Georges Hugon is finally released from his "captivity" at Les Fondettes, he turns up breathless at Nana's door and she occasionally bestows her favors upon him. Mme. Hugon hears of this and sends Philippe to Paris to rescue his brother. Philippe, too, falls under Nana's spell. One day, when she is out driving, she spots her friend Satin, dirty and bedraggled, and takes her home. Satin is installed as the prime favorite in the stately house and Nana's devotion to her is accepted by her retinue of lovers. Vandeuvres has been ruining himself for Nana's extravagances. He has two horses running in the Grand Prix at Longchamps, and he manipulates his bets to alter the odds against his filly, *Nana,* and for the favorite, *Lusignan,* which is also wearing his colors. When *Nana* wins the race, Vandeuvres is wiped out and he is warned off all tracks for his manipulations. That night he sets fire to his stables and destroys himself and his horses.

Chaps. 12–14. One morning Count Muffat sees a member of his own set at Court leaving Nana's bedroom and he confronts her with angry accusations. She informs the count that she goes to bed with

whom she chooses and she invites him to walk out of her life if he cannot reconcile himself to this state of affairs. Thereafter Nana takes on a procession of lovers to meet her constant need for money. Steiner is briefly reinstated until she has cost him whatever resources he has not tied up in shaky investments. La Faloise, who has come into a considerable fortune, also has all of his available funds dissipated in a matter of weeks. Muffat accepts all this with abject humility. To raise cash for Nana, he has begun to sell off valuable properties that belong jointly to the countess and himself. He receives a final shock one morning when he discovers his senile but depraved father-in-law, the Marquis de Chouard, in bed with Nana. He turns for consolation to religion, dedicating himself to a future of asceticism.

Georges Hugon, in the meantime, has happened upon Philippe and Nana making love. After overcoming his initial resentment of this intimacy, Georges proposes marriage to Nana. When she lightly dismisses his offer as a meaningless, childish fancy, he stabs himself with her scissors. Philippe is imprisoned for embezzling his army funds for Nana and Georges dies. Satin meets with an accident in the street and is taken to a hospital. Life once more has become unbearable to Nana. On a sudden impulse, she puts up her house, its furnishings and her personal jewelry for public sale. After realizing some 600,000 francs on the lot, she disappears from Paris. From time to time, travelers returning from distant countries bring back stories of Nana's fabulous diamonds and of her conquests in such places as Cairo, where she is installed in the viceregal palace, or Russia, where a grand duke is her slave. One day Nana returns to France to visit the sickbed of her son, Louis, who dies of smallpox the next day. Nana herself comes down with the ugly disease and is obliged to shut herself up in a room at the Grand Hotel. She dies alone, horribly disfigured by the infection.

Nana befriends Satin

463

The Nigger of the Narcissus

Novel by Joseph Conrad (Teodor Jozef Konrad Korzeniowski, 1857–1924). Published 1897. (ML, P44)

THROUGH SOME PROCESS that is not easy to explain, Joseph Conrad acquired a reputation as a great novelist. This is his one work that might justify such a reputation. In this novel Conrad sets a believable phenomenon of human relationships against a well-drawn background of the common sailor's life and the nature of the sea. Originally the title of the book was *The Children of the Sea.* Conrad spent his early years as a mariner and wrote sea stories from personal experience and with full authority.

Chap. 1. The big sailing ship, the *Narcissus,* is preparing for its voyage from Bombay to England. The forecastle is filled with excited sailors. There are the two Scandinavians, baby-faced giants. Old SINGLETON behind his white beard sits reading, with the wisdom and silence of 45 years at sea. A boy, CHARLEY, sits sulkily practicing knots. A little man named BELFAST is dancing about shouting of the injustices of the sailor's life. A new voice interrupts harshly and all look up. A ragged, beaky man stands impudently before them. His name is DONKIN. The sailors know his type. He has come aboard to eat, shirk work, cheat, cadge, wheedle, bully, and get paid for it all. The crew is called aft by the mate, Mr. BAKER, a gruff seaman who barks a lot but is basically warm-hearted. When roll is called, one sailor is missing. As the group begins to retire a booming voice calls "Wait!" A towering Negro appears and surveys the group coolly, condescendingly. It is JAMES WAIT. On the way to the forecastle he emits several ringing coughs.

Chap. 2. The *Narcissus* puts to sea in favorable winds. At sea the men become busy and peaceful, at first. One day when they are laughing and talking on the deck, they hear a rasping cough and James Wait emerges. He curses the men for their lack of consideration for him, a dying man, who needs sleep. Wait, or JIMMY, slowly comes to dominate the men with the specter of death he carries about. He scorns and criticizes the men for their every move; everything they do, he finds inconsiderate to himself. The men are cowed, angry, pitying, resentful. The concertina player no longer plays. The men begin to wait on black Jimmy with special favors. They steal from the kitchen for him and the Bible-thumping cook is outraged. But Donkin sniggers disbelievingly, and for some strange reason Jimmy responds almost warmly to Donkin for this, in comparison to the scorn he shows the others. Jimmy does little work on the ship, though the mate threatens and cajoles. The whole crew wonders if Jimmy is really dying—could it be a sham? Jimmy finally spends all his time in bed and is eventually given a little cabin to himself.

Chap. 3. The *Narcissus* approaches the rough waters near the Cape of Good Hope. The crew love their boat. They encourage, help, and pray for it on each wave. The men are constantly cold, wet, and sleepless. Captain ALLISTOUN never leaves the bridge. Finally, during a lull, the men prepare to relax. Suddenly a gigantic frothing sea rises in front of them, grabs the ship, raises it high, then viciously throws it over. Men scramble in all directions, clutching for handholds. They rope themselves to the deck. All are sick. Hours pass. Some show signs of hysteria. Someone suddenly shouts "Where's Jimmy?" Several men break free and crawl forward to find out. Jimmy is trapped in his cabin, still alive and bellowing in his watery near-coffin. The men risk their lives, fight their way through a pile of debris, chop their way through the planks, and Jimmy bursts out in hysterical fear. They drag him back to leeward while he curses them for their slowness and ineptness. They hate him passionately but handle him with utmost care. The men continue to pass the black, freezing hours in tortured silence. The next day they manage to raise the sails and right the ship.

Chap. 4. The men are near collapse but are immediately ordered to straighten up the ship. Donkin complains. Most of the men's belongings have been washed away and the bed mats are soaked. Calm waters are finally reached. The general unrest is fanned by the insidious Donkin. He tells the men that their pay is terrible and their food bad, and that the officers have unjustified benefits. The men despise him but listen. Men are always crowding in to visit Jimmy in his cabin now. One day Donkin privately accuses Jimmy of faking. Jimmy agrees that he is, and boastfully tells Donkin how he got away with the same ruse on his previous ship. Jimmy then coughs violently. Donkin eyes him carefully. Some time later the cook comes in alone and becomes thunderous with religious fanaticism. He tells Jimmy to repent, because he will soon die and go to hell. Jimmy screams in terror. Glassy-eyed with fear (mostly of death), he tells the captain he has been feeling better and will go to work again. The crew cheers, but the Captain says "No."

Looking at Jimmy's weakened, sweating form, he tells him that he has been shamming the whole trip and now he will *have* to stay in the cabin for the rest of the voyage. The crew is incensed. They do not realize that the Captain performed a great act of compassion, for he has seen that death, and fear of death, are actually written on Jimmy's face. Arguing and shouting, the men are incited to a rage by the ratlike Donkin. The violence culminates in Donkin's throwing a heavy metal pin at the captain's head. The audacity of this act quiets things for the night. Old Singleton authoritatively asserts that James Wait is going to die. The following morning the captain dresses down the crew and makes Donkin put the pin he threw back in its place. The crew is intimidated.

Chap. 5. The ship moves on, plagued by head winds and calms. Jimmy becomes more gaunt and deathlike. Belfast has become Jimmy's loving attendant and protector, while Donkin is ostracized by all except the cook. Singleton claims that a sick sailor will die when his boat comes in sight of land, and that is why the *Narcissus* is making such bad progress; James Wait does not want to see land. Finally, the Island of Flores is sighted and here the boat is becalmed. That night Donkin enters Jimmy's cabin. Jimmy is very sick. He tells Donkin of a girl in London. Donkin flames with peevish fury. That Jimmy has the love of a girl as well as of the crew is too much. Donkin curses him, tells him that he will never see London, that he is dying, dying, almost dead! Jimmy is torn with anguish. While he lies there gasping, Donkin opens his trunk and steals his money. Just as Donkin is leaving he turns and sees the last spark of Jimmy's life suddenly flare up, then ebb out. Next day, during the burying ceremony, Jimmy's body at first refuses to slide off the plank, as though clinging to the ship. Belfast, distraught with emotion, pushes the body off. The men become more distant to one another than at any previous time. A brisk, favorable wind springs up and the boat glides swiftly toward home. A week later it arrives in London. The men rush off for a farewell drink together, then slowly drift off in all directions, each knowing he will probably never see the others again.

Donkin robs the dying Jimmy

1984

Novel by George Orwell, 1903–1950. Published & © 1949 by Harcourt, Brace & Co., New York. (NAL, S798)

IT IS RATHER GRATIFYING that *1984* has been accepted as an important novel of this century. It would not have been surprising if the superficial defects of the novel had ruined it. The book is the brilliant George Orwell's dire prediction of a future world that has succumbed entirely to Communist propaganda, maneuverings, and subversion. Therefore this future world consists only of totalitarian states on the Soviet pattern. As a novel, *1984* is almost ludicrously bad. Orwell changed his mind in the course of writing it and did not bother to go back and make the early chapters consistent with the later ones. But Orwell's conception of a thoroughly developed Communist state and its inherent contradictions is so sound as to have convinced millions. His approach to Newspeak, a modification of English designed to fortify thought control, is a brilliant contribution. (The whole essay on Newspeak is contained in an appendix and is not part of the book proper.) And in addition to all this, the novel makes interesting reading even though in spots it offends one's sense of sequence and consistency. Very likely people will continue to read it with interest at least to the year 1983.

Book I. Chaps. 1–4. London is the chief city of Airstrip One, a province of Oceania, on April 4, 1984, when WINSTON SMITH starts his diary. Winston, 39, an Outer Party member, only vaguely remembers life before the revolution. He lives in a small, dreary room with the minimum of necessities and no comforts. Like every room in Oceania, his is equipped with a two-way television screen (telescreen), so there is virtually no privacy. Every moment of a person's life is planned and observed by the Party, and for the slightest deviation the culprit is immediately picked up and punished. Worst of all, the Thought Police are everywhere but no one knows their identity. Winston writes in an alcove out of sight of the telescreen. What he is doing is not necessarily illegal except that he is committing *thoughtcrime* by having thoughts not dictated by the Party. He writes his impression of some insidious propaganda films he had just seen, and then adds a threat to BIG BROTHER, the all-powerful Party leader, whose face is everywhere, staring from large posters that warn "Big Brother is Watching You!" Winston is employed at Minitrue, the Ministry of Truth, in the Records Department. Four huge pyramidal buildings, towering over the rest of London, house the four ministries that control the apparatus of government. The other three are the Ministry of Peace (*Minipax*), concerned with war; the Ministry of Love (*Miniluv*), which maintains order with iron discipline; the Ministry of Plenty (*Miniplent*), responsible for economic affairs. The names and peculiar meanings are part of Newspeak, the official language. The world now has only three nations and war is incessant. Every day all workers take a break for the Two Minute Hate Period. This day, on the telescreen appears the face of GOLDSTEIN, the "Enemy of the People," the former Party leader, who has turned against Big Brother and gone into hiding. Everyone yells abuse at Goldstein's picture. One day, at the height of the fury, Winston is aware of a girl who is looking at him boldly. He knows he hates her because he can never possess her. She is wearing the scarlet sash of the Anti-Sex League, aggressive symbol of chastity. The hate period ends, as always, with the Party slogan, "War is Peace, Freedom is Slavery, Ignorance is Strength," and the chanting of "B-B, B-B,-B-B." But Winston realizes he is hating not Goldstein but Big Brother, the Party, and his whole existence. Just then he glances at O'BRIEN and as their eyes meet he knows O'Brien shares his feelings. O'Brien is a powerful Inner Party member, who happened to be in the Records Department that day and stayed for the hate period. In the Records Department the past is adjusted to conform to Party dictates. Winston's specialty is to "rectify," i.e., falsify, the records. Here are deleted the names of *unpersons,* those who have been vaporized. When they are killed all records of their existence are wiped out. The Party wipes away any historical fact inimical to it by wiping out all reference to it and saying it never happened. By controlling the past the Party controls the future.

Chaps. 5–8. Winston sees the girl again in the canteen of the Ministry and desires her even more. No use; marriage of Party members has to be approved by a committee and permission is refused if the couple seems physically attracted to each other. The only purpose of marriage is to beget children for the Party. Winston thinks of his wife KATHARINE, who rigidly followed this belief. When their miserable marriage brought forth no children, she left him. The Party is insistent on eradicating the sexual impulse, because it takes energy away from Party work. The proletariat (called *proles* in Newspeak) are allowed to continue as before, since they are considered subservient blobs of no importance. Winston writes in his diary that hope lies in the proles. The thought of O'Brien's support gives him such strength and courage that he dedicates his diary to him. One day

Winston sees a document that proves that three old-time revolutionaries, who were executed 7 years before after confessing many crimes, were really innocent. To recapture the past, Winston one day goes for a walk in the prole district. This is punishable, as Party members must engage only in communal activities and not waste time in *ownlife*. Winston finds the antique shop run by kindly old Mr. CHARRINGTON, where he bought his diary. This time Charrington shows Winston a bedroom upstairs, preserved as it was before the revolution 40 years ago. The comfortable furnishings catch Winston's fancy. As he leaves the shop, he passes the girl on a side street and is convinced he is being followed and will be arrested.

Book II. Chaps. 1–5. Four days later in the office corridor the girl slips a note into his hand saying, "I love you." They meet in the country away from the omnipresent telescreen and become lovers. JULIA, 26, really hates the Party and the Anti-Sex League. Winston rents the bedroom above the antique shop for their meetings. They are there because they can speak freely to each other. It is inevitable that their love affair will be discovered sometime, but they have proved that the Party is not almighty.

Chaps. 6–10. One day the big, strong and strangely attractive O'Brien invites Winston to his house for a talk. Winston takes Julia. O'Brien lives luxuriously and is privileged to turn off his telescreen. He admits to being a leader of the Underground and Winston and Julia agree to join Goldstein's secret network, the Brotherhood, to destroy the Party. Later Winston gets a

Julia slips Winston a note

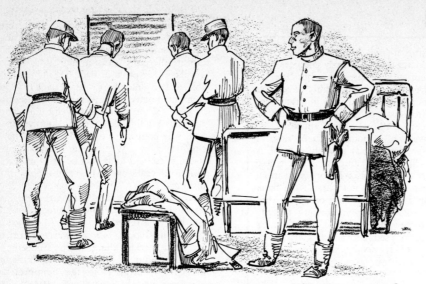

There was a telescreen behind the picture and Julia and Winston are arrested

copy of Goldstein's book from O'Brien but cannot read it at once because of a crisis. Oceania has been at war with Eurasia, but the Party line is suddenly switched and it is made clear that the enemy is really Eastasia, and never has been Eurasia. Winston has to work day and night changing all records that mention any conflict with Eurasia. He meets Julia above Charrington's shop and suddenly a voice challenges them from a loudspeaker. There has been a telescreen hidden in the room all the time. Guards burst in, led by Charrington, who is no old man but a 35-year-old member of the Thought Police. Julia and Winston are arrested and taken away separately.

Book III. Chaps. 1–2. O'Brien comes to Winston's cell and Winston suddenly realizes the man is not a prisoner and not a member of the underground. Winston is tortured. Then he gets a shave and a haircut, doctors give him sedatives, and intellectuals question him in relays for endless days and nights. Winston, dazed, confesses to anything they suggest. Through the blur he is conscious of O'Brien always at his side, seeming to direct everything, alternately tormentor and protector. Winston is strapped to a torturing machine and O'Brien operates the controls. O'Brien finally proves to Winston that the memory of the past does not exist, that documents Winston thought he had seen do not exist, that people can really control their memories. Winston is convinced. He even feels love for O'Brien, who is working so hard to purge him of his thinking so that he will never again commit thoughtcrime. But Winston must be washed clean of his love for Julia and his hate for Big Brother, so he can be shot. Winston might live, however, if he could be made truly incapable of human feelings. Finally O'Brien tells Winston that he has completed the first of the three stages of *integration*, which are *learning, understanding,* and *acceptance.* Having finished with learning, he was ready for understanding.

Chap. 3. With his hand ready on the dial of the machine, O'Brien starts by stating the aim of the Party—complete power over human beings, and above all their minds. In a state founded on hate there can be no emotions except hate, fear, rage, triumph and self-abasement. Links between friends, between children and their parents, and between man and wife have already been corrupted, so there is no longer any loyalty except to the Party, no love except

for Big Brother, no laughter except over a defeated enemy. O'Brien tells Winston to look at himself in the mirror and Winston sees an emaciated, disfigured, filthy skeleton —a mangled body with a mangled mind. But he retains his love for Julia. He is still human.

Chaps. 4–6. For a period Winston is treated well. He gains weight and even his mind becomes more active. He thinks only Party thoughts and feels completely subjugated. Now that he is completely clean, he wonders when he will be shot. But he still loves Julia and hates Big Brother, so he is taken to the dread room 101, the last resort.

O'Brien explains that everyone has some fear which is unendurable, and Room 101 is where this ultimate torture is applied.

Winston mortally fears rats. So they have put starved rats in a cage which will fit onto his face. Winston, to save himself at any cost, would rather have them do it to Julia. He is finally purged of love. They release Winston and give him a sinecure at the ministry. He spends much time drinking foul gin. Once he meets Julia, but she has been through the same process and they have no feeling for each other. The news of an important victory over the Eurasian army is blared out of the telescreen and Winston suddenly feels overwhelmingly grateful— he loves Big Brother.

Northwest Passage

Novel by Kenneth Roberts, 1885–1957. Published and © 1937 by Doubleday & Co., New York.

THE NOVELS OF Kenneth Roberts are first-class historical fiction and have been very popular in the United States despite the fact that Roberts has consistently refused to take the schoolbook view that in the Revolutionary War all American patriots were heroes and all Tories were villains. His major opus is *Northwest Passage,* which combines two ideal subjects for a historical novel, Rogers' Rangers, the original highly trained troup that inspired the British commandos and the later U.S. Rangers, and the long search for a Northwest passage that has never actually been realized though in 1955 —long after the Panama Canal had made the Northwest passage unnecessary—the goal was finally achieved. The Northwest passage was a projected route by which ships might sail from Europe to the Orient without rounding the Cape of Good Hope at the bottom of South America. ¶ Any novel written by Kenneth Roberts is skillfully constructed and a pleasure to read.

Chaps. 1–4. LANGDON TOWNE is encouraged in his early attempts to draw by his nearest friends, HUNKING MARRINER and CAP HUFF. His father enrolls him at Harvard College, and rumor goes around the town of Kittery, Maine, that Langdon is studying for the ministry, but Langdon has no desire for a ministerial career. Hunk and Cap visit Langdon at Harvard and eat some of the awful college food. Langdon makes a poster to protest the food served at the college. A young artist, JOHN SINGLETON COPLEY, advises Langdon on his poster. Langdon's tutor reprimands them and Langdon is placed on probation. His father sends him to his grandfather's farm for the summer. News of the British victory at Ticonderoga stimulates Langdon's father to recall him to help with the landslide of orders in the family rope industry.

Chaps. 5–9. Langdon visits ELIZABETH BROWNE at Portsmouth. Her sister JANE and Jane's fiancé, SAM LIVERMORE, are with her in the parlor, together with Copley. Mr. Browne expresses dismay over Langdon's artistic inclinations. Sam and Langdon leave together and meet Cap Huff, who is looking for Hunk. Sam and Langdon have dinner in a tavern and discuss Langdon's chances to be an artist. Langdon complains about the rich men that run the town, WYSEMAN CLAGGETT in particular. At that

Embarking to fight Indians

point, Claggett comes in and arrests Langdon for slander. He is rescued from prison by Cap and Hunk. Hunk gives him a letter, written by Sam, introducing him to Major ROBERT ROGERS at Ticonderoga.

Chaps. 10–14. Hunk and Langdon travel as far as Dunbarton, where they meet Sgt. McNOTT, one of Rogers' Rangers, and his Indian guide. They travel past Fort Number Four, where St. Francis Indians massacred many white men, and Langdon sketches it. Next day they arrive at Crown Point and Rogers accepts them as Rangers. That night they embark on a journey to attack the St. Francis Indians. Langdon goes in Rogers' boat as his secretary.

Chaps. 15–17. Langdon meets some of his boatmates: POMP WHIPPLE, a Negro, also from Kittery; Lt. CROFTON, whose brother was tortured and killed by the Indians; and Sgt. BRADLEY. Rogers introduces Langdon to Capt. OGDEN and Capt. WILLIAMS. He tells Langdon to keep an account of the expeditions. A scout brings news that Frenchmen and Indians are coming up the river and Rogers sends Stockbridge Indians to trail them and Mohawks to scout. The Rangers are masters of camouflage and the enemy passes by without discovering their boats. Rogers is very interested in a book Towne has read that speculates about finding a Northwest Passage. Langdon learns that a £20,000 reward is to be given to whoever finds one.

Chaps. 18–20. The Rangers take their boats to the shore of South Otter Bay, carry them across a spit of land, and launch them into North Otter Bay. Rogers is furious when the Mohawk scouts do not find the French ships and orders them back to Crown Point in disgrace. Capt. BUTTERFIELD sees a Mohawk stealing gunpowder and orders him to drop it; the Indian shoots his musket into the bag of powder and several men are burned, including Hunk Marriner. Rogers blames Butterfield for arousing the Indian and orders him back to Crown Point, with the wounded men.

Chaps. 21–23. The Rangers leave the boats to march 90 miles to St. Francis. Two Stockbridge Indians are left to watch the boats. The Rangers march two days through swamps. The two Indians report that the French have discovered and stolen the boats and provisions. Rogers sends a request to General AMHERST to send more provisions.

Chaps. 24–26. The Rangers march for nine days through a spruce bog. Several men fall out from fatigue. Finally they reach the St. Francis River. The Rangers form a human chain across the river, but several men are lost in the crossing. As they near St. Francis, 142 men are left of the 200 who started.

Chaps. 27–32. Lt. TURNER and Ensign AVERY reconnoiter with Rogers while the exhausted men sleep. The Rangers attack the town just before dawn, killing all male Indians and capturing the women and children. They set fire to all the houses, gather up food, and eat their first hot meal in three weeks. From the prisoners they learn that 200 Frenchmen are trailing them, with 300 more coming upstream. The Rangers leave in a hurry. Crofton secretly carries an Indian head in revenge for the torture and killing of his brother.

Chaps. 33–35. When they reach Memphremagog, the corn is rationed. They hold a council and decide to split up. Langdon makes maps for each group. He is assigned to Avery's detachment. A northeaster comes up. The captives are sent back to Crown Point. Langdon's group reaches a large ravine and he and Avery decide to cross it. The other detachments, Dunbar's, Turner's, and Jenkins', decide to camp at once. In the morning the French and Indians ambush the detachments that did not cross the ravine. Turning east to tell Rogers of the ambush, Avery and Langdon kill a moose. Avery sets the men to skinning the animal while he, Langdon, and two others go for firewood. Returning with the wood, they see that the others have been ambushed and captured.

Chaps. 36–37. They catch up to Rogers and report the bad news. They approach the Connecticut River, and Crofton goes crazy because Rogers has discovered the Indian head and taken it from him. Bradley takes off for his home in Concord. The men are starving, but Rogers' faith never wavers.

Chaps. 38–43. At the point where Rogers had asked General Amherst to store additional provisions, they find a warm campfire but no food. They hear troops going down river about a mile away and try unsuccessfully to attract them with shots. Rogers builds a raft to go downstream to get food for his men at Fort Number Four. Ogden, Langdon, and BILLY, an Indian boy, go with him in the freezing weather. Going over White River Falls, the raft breaks up. Ogden and Langdon hunt while Rogers and Billy build a fire to cut six spruces for a new raft—they are too weak to chop them down. Langdon kills a partridge and they divide it four ways. Still weak with hunger, they manage to build a raft. At Wattoquitchey Falls Rogers swims below the falls, the raft is eased over the falls, and Rogers, with superhuman effort, manages to hold it in the icy water and bring it ashore. They reach Fort Number Four.

Chaps. 44–46. Rogers leaves with food for the men they left behind. Odgen and Langdon start out for Crown Point. There they report to Gen. Amherst, who is astounded at their exploits. Langdon is made an ensign and is put under the command of Capt. TUTE and Capt. CARVER. He learns that Capt. Williams, badly burned when the Mohawk tried to steal the gunpowder, is now in New York, and that Sgt. McNott lost his leg. Of Hunk there is no news. Returning to Fort Number Four, Langdon picks up the Indian boy Billy. He returns to Durham, where he and Hunk left their canoe on their way to Crown Point. The canoe is there but Hunk is not. At last, home in Kittery, Langdon finds Hunk, but Hunk's shoulder is not healing.

Chaps. 47–49. Hunk dies the next morning. Langdon goes to visit Elizabeth and her family. They are cordial and invite him to dinner. He regales them with tales of Rogers and offers to do a portrait of him for Elizabeth. Langdon builds a shack and works at his painting. Copley visits his studio and advises him to get more training in London. Langdon obtains a commission for murals to amass the money for boat passage. The murals finished, Langdon goes for a week's fishing with Billy and his brother, ODIORNE. When he returns, he meets Rogers, who tells him he is to be married to Elizabeth and asks Langdon to be best man.

Book II. Chaps. 50–57. In London Langdon works hard, but realizes he must have a patron. He goes to Benjamin Franklin, who is Pennsylvania's representative. Franklin gives him a letter to the artist HOGARTH, who is so impressed with what Langdon has shown him that he returns to Langdon's rooms to see the rest of his work. Hogarth obtains a commission for Langdon to do a panel of Gen. Amherst at Crown Point. Langdon hears that Rogers is in London and visits him. Rogers seems discouraged about his marriage with Elizabeth, who is not with him. He is in London to get the king's consent to an expedition to find the Northwest Passage and he asks Langdon to go with him. Rogers cuts quite a figure in London society. His secretary, NATTY POTTER, invites Langdon to have dinner with Rogers at the home of Dr. JOHN CAMPBELL. Natty also asks Langdon to look up his daughter, ANN, by his divorced wife. Dr. Campbell has a group of distinguished dinner guests, including Sir JOSHUA REYNOLDS. Rogers talks of finding the Northwest Passage, showing Langdon's sketches. Reynolds advises a friend to buy the series of 40 sketches and the friend does, for 800 guineas. Next day, Langdon goes to the poorest slums of London and rescues Ann Potter from a life of begging. He takes Ann to his landlady, who takes care of her and obtains a good tutor for her. Langdon does a portrait of Ann and takes it to her father. Potter is badgering his former wife's solicitor for a settlement for Ann. He uses Langdon's portrait as proof that she is being cared for, obtains a large settlement, and then asks Towne to take care of Ann, since his debts are so high he cannot afford to. Rogers receives notice that he is to be the governor of the territory of Michilimackinac, in what is now northern Michigan. He has written two books of his exploits in America and writes a play about the Indian chief, Pontiac. Rogers tells Langdon he is receiving nagging letters from Elizabeth, whose London relatives have told her of the riotous life he is supposedly leading in London.

Chaps. 58–65. Rogers, Langdon, Ann and Potter sail for America. They find New York in a furor over the Stamp Tax. General GAGE gives Rogers his commission as governor of Michilimackinac. Langdon goes to Boston to visit Copley. Rogers arrives in Portsmouth and the party is joined by Elizabeth. They start for Michilimackinac, changing boats at Albany. At Oswego they meet Sgt. McNott, who tells Langdon that Gage is in cahoots with Gen. WILLIAM JOHNSON to put all power in the Northwest in the hands of the commissaries and that Rogers' title is an empty shell. Elizabeth takes over Ann, refusing to let Langdon take her with him when he sketches the Indians. Rogers holds council with Chief PONTIAC and eight other chiefs. Pontiac says Michilimackinac is different from other trading posts, as the Indians in the area are so far away from the post that the traders must go to them. Johnson arrives at Oswego, suspicious and jealous of Rogers' success with the Indians. Rogers and his party go to Michilimackinac and all but Rogers are disappointed with the site. Capt. Carver is there to greet them. Rogers tells the traders to visit the Indian camps, as Pontiac suggested. This is in defiance of Johnson, who has ordered that all Indians are to come to the trading posts. The traders depart in the huge laden canoes and Carver is sent with them to make maps for the Northwest expedition.

Chaps. 66–69. Letters arrive from Montreal authorizing Rogers to proceed with the exploration for the Northwest Passage, but there is no grant of money for supplies. Rogers sends most of the others ahead, including Langdon and Elizabeth, and says he will catch up with them as soon as he can. Langdon bids Ann goodbye. The party proceeds to the trading post at Prairie du Chien. Langdon spends the winter sketching, afterwards publishing his work as *Life Among the Dacotas*. He learns a secret Indian route to the Oregon River. When winter is over, they meet Carver and return to Prairie du

Chien. Disappointed when there is no letter from Ann, Langdon writes to her and realizes it is a love letter.

Chaps. 70–75. McNott, his wife and Langdon set out with Carver, Tute and Goddard for the Northwest Passage. McNott and Langdon are suspicious of the guides provided by Carver. They are local Indians, unfamiliar with much of the territory they plan to explore. At the headwaters of the Mississippi, the guides refuse to go farther. Carver and his cronies decide to go to Grand Portage and wait for supplies. McNott, his wife and Langdon go to the Falls of St. Anthony, where they learn Carver has abandoned the Northwest expedition because he has bought 100 square miles of land, which he intends to parcel off and sell to settlers. Letters arrive from Rogers and Ann. Rogers is waiting for the furs Carver is supposed to send him, to provide him with funds. Ann tells Langdon she misses him and asks for a portrait of himself. McNott is injured and they return to Michilimackinac, where they find that Rogers is in prison. Rogers and Potter fought over Rogers' attentions to Ann, and the Potters have gone. Langdon has a note from Ann, telling him to look for her in Montreal. Langdon and McNott start out for Montreal.

Chaps. 76–80. In June they reach Montreal but Potter and Ann have left for England. They see Rogers being hauled through Montreal, his leg almost broken from being in irons. McNott stays to help Rogers at his trial, but obtains free passage for Lang-

Hogarth sees Langdon's work

don to England and lends him £100 for his search. Langdon finds Ann in London and marries her. They read that Rogers is in London, acquitted of the Montreal charges and the darling of the king. Next, Rogers is in Fleet Prison for debt. Though bitter because of Rogers' actions toward Ann, at her request Langdon visits Rogers in prison. Rogers is now a drunken derelict. Langdon promises to write Rogers' brother to pay his debts. Ann and Langdon return to America with Sam Livermore and after the war they build a house near Kittery.

Notre Dame de Paris

Novel *by* Victor Hugo, 1802–1885. Published 1831. (ML, 35)

THIS NOVEL is usually called by its subtitle, "The Hunchback of Notre Dame," in translations and in motion pictures; so even among those who have read it, few can be expected to recognize it by any other name. Essentially it is a melodramatic story of adventure and suspense, but in the course of it Victor Hugo managed to interject descriptions of Paris and specifically of the Cathedral of Notre Dame. The book is important as one of the principal works of one of the principal French authors.

Book I. Chaps. 1–6. It is January of 1482 and the people of Paris are in a gay mood to celebrate a double holiday, the festival of the kings and the festival of the fools. As part of the festivities a mystery or morality play is to be performed in the Palais de Justice and the great hall is filled with a surging mob more interested in the comings and goings of noted personages than in the opening scenes of the play. The play's author, a poor poet named PIERRE GRINGOIRE, vainly tries to quiet the audience and attract its attention to the stage. A shout goes up for the selection of the Pope of the Fools and preparations are made while the morality play continues with few spectators. Each contestant is required to stick his head through a hole in a window and make an ugly grimace to the assembled mob. After several attempts have been made to win this grinning match, the crowd goes wild as an indescribably ugly face is thrust through the window. The owner of the face is QUASIMODO, the deformed bellringer of Notre Dame Cathedral. He has coarse red hair over his hunchbacked body, crooked limbs, one eye completely covered by a huge wart, a forked chin, and fanglike teeth. He is crowned Pope of the Fools, dressed in a robe, hoisted into a large portable chair, and carried away to be paraded through the streets. Gringoire, left with but a handful of spectators, attempts to continue with his play, but cries of "La Esmeralda, La Esmeralda," are heard and everyone rushes to the windows to look.

Book II. Chaps. 1–3. The penniless and hungry Gringoire leaves the Palais to find a place to sleep. He wanders into the Place de Greves, where a huge bonfire is burning and a large crowd is watching a beautiful gypsy girl dance. Gringoire learns that she is LA ESMERALDA. She dances sinuously and then exhibits a trained goat. Gringoire notices that two of the spectators are regarding her with ill will. One is Dom CLAUDE FROLLO, the Archdeacon of Notre Dame Cathedral, and the other is a woman known as THE SACHETTE, the recluse of the Tour-Rolland. The crowd is distracted when the parade honoring Quasimodo as Pope of the Fools comes into the square. The archdeacon sees Quasimodo and gets him off his throne. The hunchback grovels before him and the two discourse in sign language—for Quasimodo is totally deaf, from the terrible pounding in his ears from his years of ringing the great bells of Notre Dame. The crowd surges toward the strange pair to reclaim their Pope, but Quasimodo makes such threatening gestures that they retreat. The hunchback and the archdeacon leave.

Chaps. 4–7. Gringoire follows La Esmeralda through the dark and deserted streets. Suddenly he hears the girl scream and he sees two shadowy figures attempt to carry her off. Gringoire goes to help the girl, but Quasimodo, who is one of the kidnappers, hurls him heavily to the ground and leaves him stunned. Just then a troop of soldiers appear. They rescue the girl and capture Quasimodo, while his companion slinks away. Gringoire knows that the other man was Dom Claude Frollo. Esmeralda thanks her rescuers and learns their leader is Captain PHOEBUS DE CHATEAUPERS. The gypsy girl then darts off into the night. Gringoire continues his search for lodgings and is hemmed in by crippled beggars, who suddenly turn out to be sound of limb. They take him to their headquarters, the gathering place for all the miscreants and thieves in Paris, who are known as the Truands. They decide to hang the poor poet, but according to their law if a woman claims him as a husband his life will be spared. Not even any of the oldest hags want him, and Gringoire is about to swing when La Esmeralda claims him and they are declared man and wife. She takes him to her room and feeds him, but lets him know he is a husband in name only. She leaves and locks him in the room for the night.

Book III. Chaps. 1–2. Here the author gives a description of the great Cathedral of Notre Dame and the bird's-eye view of Paris to be had from its towers.

Book IV. Chaps. 1–6. Sixteen years earlier Quasimodo, a foundling, had been taken by the young priest, Claude Frollo, who felt pity for the misshapen and unwanted child. Frollo taught Quasimodo all he could and comforted him when he was mocked by normal children. When the boy was 14 and powerful, despite his grotesque body, he was made bellringer of Notre Dame. His outlook on life was as twisted as his body. He hated most men, but he dearly loved Frollo. He felt a part of the great cathedral and he dearly loved his bells. Frollo had by this time become an archdeacon with a cold and rigid attitude towards people. He particularly hated gypsies and secured an edict forbidding them to sing and dance near the cathedral. He also delighted in establishing them as witches and wizards working sorcery with goats.

Book V. Chap. 1. Quasimodo is brought to trial on the charge of disturbing the peace and offering violence to a woman. Being deaf, he does not understand the judge's questions and is deemed insolent. The poor wretch is sentenced to be publicly pilloried and flogged.

Chaps. 2–3. La Esmeralda passes the Tour-Rolland where some women are attempting to give something to the Sachette in her miserable hole under the tower. Sachette, some 20 years before, lost her mind when gypsies stole her little daughter and left one of her little shoes and the wretched Quasimodo in her place. The poor deserted woman screams when she sees La Esmeralda, and curses her as a gypsy.

Chaps. 4–5. Quasimodo is tied to the wheel of the pillory and brutally flogged until his back is raw. The crowd loves the spectacle and jeers his pleas for water. La Esmeralda comes along and gives him a drink. He tries to kiss her hand in gratitude, but she draws away in fright. The Sachette, viewing the spectacle from her hole, sees La Esmeralda and curses her. The girl turns pale and totters away.

Book VI. Chaps. 1–3. Not long after, La Esmeralda is dancing in sight of the cathedral and Dom Frollo glares down at her from one of the towers. Phoebus also sees her and invites her to entertain some guests. She is cruelly mocked by the fine ladies present. She takes heart when Phoebus defends her. Her goat spells out the captain's name in little wooden letters and La Esmeralda is called a sorceress as she is driven away. But Phoebus follows her. Dom Frollo, in the meantime, has left the tower to look for La Esmeralda in the square. He is perturbed by the fact that he saw Quasimodo intently staring at the girl. In the square he finds La Esmeralda gone but Gringoire is there, dressed as a clown. The poet tells the archdeacon he is the girl's husband but not her lover and adds that she has taught her goat to spell out the name Phoebus, which puzzles Dom Frollo. When Gringoire describes La Esmeralda's charms, Dom Frollo gives him a terrible look and rushes back into the cathedral. There the lonely Quasimodo has forgotten his beloved bells and thinks of La Esmeralda.

Chaps. 4–5. Dom Frollo's younger brother, JEHAN, visits him in his tower apartment in the cathedral and finds him engrossed in alchemy and a study of sorcery. Jehan makes reference to a Greek word for Fate scratched on a wall and the archdeacon turns pale. The king's attorney enters and asks whether he should arrest La Esmeralda as a sorceress. Dom Frollo watches a fly caught in a spider's web and says the girl will fall into his trap when the time is ripe.

Chaps. 6–8. Dom Frollo hears his brother call the name of Phoebus and he follows the two through the streets. He hears Phoe-bus make reference to a tryst with La Esmeralda and he shudders and stops to lean against a pillar like a drunkard. He disguises himself that evening and goes to a café, where he sees Jehan and Phoebus. When Phoebus leaves, he follows him and accosts him. Dom Frollo asks Phoebus whom he is going to meet, and when Phoebus gives the name of La Esmeralda the disguised archdeacon says he lies. Phoebus challenges him with his sword, but Dom Frollo says he will kill Phoebus some time hence. He then gives Phoebus some money on condition he can watch him meet the gypsy girl from a hiding place. Phoebus agrees and Dom Frollo watches them confess their love for each other. As they embrace he rushes upon the captain, stabs him several times in the back, and flees. La Esmeralda is horrorstruck by the evil face of the archdeacon and faints as she sees Phoebus fall. The gendarmes come, pick up the bleeding captain, and arrest the girl as a witch.

Book VII. Chaps. 1–5. La Esmeralda is tried as a witch, but she denies she bewitched Phoebus, who is dying, and says that an evil priest stabbed him. She is tortured until she cannot stand it any longer and confesses. She is sentenced to be hanged on the town gibbet before the great portal of Notre Dame. Dom Frollo visits her in her dungeon cell and she recognizes him as the priest who stabbed Phoebus. To her horror, Dom Frollo tells her he loves her and is tortured by his passion for her. She is distraught and keeps asking for Phoebus. Dom Frollo says he is dead. She curses the archdeacon, who leaves the cell. As he passes the Tour-Rolland, the Sachette calls from her hole and asks him who is to be hanged on the gibbet. He tells her it is a gypsy woman and she cackles hysterically.

Chap. 6. Phoebus is not dead. He has recovered from his wounds and becomes engaged to a young lady he was interested in before he met La Esmeralda. He stands beside his fiancée near the gibbet. La Esmeralda is driven up in a tumbrel and Dom Frollo approaches her to hear her confession. She denounces him and then sees Phoebus. The captain turns away from her and La Esmeralda faints. Quasimodo suddenly appears, snatches the unconscious girl, and carries her into the cathedral, claiming the ancient right of sanctuary. Minutes later Quasimodo appears on the summit of the bell tower with the girl, and his seldom-heard voice once more shouts "Sanctuary!"

Book VIII. Chaps. 1–6. Quasimodo makes La Esmeralda as comfortable as possible in a small room in one of the towers of Notre Dame. He brings her food and clothing, but sensing her fright at his aspect he does not set foot in her room. He sees her pet her little goat and he wishes he were either more of a beast or more of a man. La Esmeralda is grateful to the hunchback and tries to be pleasant to him. He gives her a little whistle, and tells her to blow it when she is in danger because the note it sounds is audible to him. She begs him to find Phoebus and bring him to her. The hunch-

469

Quasimodo grapples with his master and is saved by Esmeralda

back finds the captain but he refuses to go to the girl. Quasimodo goes back to La Esmeralda and tells her he could not find Phoebus. She censures him for not trying and the hunchback is heartbroken but suffers in silence. Dom Frollo learns that the girl is in the tower and he cannot still the torment of his desire for her. He goes to her room in the dark of night and tries to overwhelm her. She blows the whistle and Quasimodo comes and seizes the intruder. They grapple and Dom Frollo manages to pull a dagger out of his cloak just as the hunchback recognizes him as his master. La Esmeralda snatches the dagger from Dom Frollo and threatens to kill him. Quasimodo is abject because he has laid violent hands on his master and begs the archdeacon to kill him. Dom Frollo kicks him and goes back to his quarters.

Book IX. Chaps. 1–7. Dom Frollo goes out into the Paris streets and wanders around in his despair. He meets Gringoire and plots with him to spirit La Esmeralda out of Notre Dame and take her to a place where Dom Frollo can keep her for himself. The Truands hear that La Esmeralda may still be apprehended and hanged. They decide to storm the cathedral and rescue her. Quasimodo sees the mob trying to force entry and he thinks they intend harm to the gypsy girl. He hurls great stones and timber down on them, and heats up great caldrons of lead and pours the molten metal from a parapet onto the screaming Truands. The soldiers of the king arrive and rout the remaining besiegers. Jehan manages to get

into the tower but he is discovered by Quasimodo, who picks him up, swings him by one leg, and flings him to his death in the streets below. Quasimodo goes to La Esmeralda's cell and finds the girl gone. He weeps.

Book X. Chaps. 1–4. While the Truands are attempting to enter Notre Dame, La Esmeralda sees them far below and she too misunderstands their motives and is terrified. Gringoire and a hooded man appear and tell her they will help her make her escape. She leaves with them and Gringoire carries her little goat. They go down the river in a boat and then Gringoire leaves. The hooded man reveals himself as Dom Frollo and gives her a choice of himself or the gibbet. She chooses death. Dom Frollo is furious. He takes her to the Tour-Rolland, calls the Sachette to the bars of her hole, and leaves the gypsy girl with the demented hag while he goes to get soldiers to arrest her. The Sachette (also known to some as GODULE) reviles the girl. She flourishes the little shoe that is all she has to remind her of her lost daughter, and curses all gypsies. La Esmeralda tears open a little bag she wears around her neck and reveals the mate to the shoe. The two women are mother and daughter. When the soldiers come for La Esmeralda, the Sachette says she is not there, but the girl gives herself away when she sees Phoebus and calls to him. Her mother tells her tearful story to the leader of the soldiers and he sheds a tear at having to part the newly reunited pair. But duty is duty. The Sachette dies attempting to save her daughter and La Esmeralda is taken to the gibbet. From the towers of Notre Dame, Quasimodo and Dom Frollo watch the hanging. The hunchback pushes his now hated master over a parapet to his death, then disappears. About two years later his skeleton is found in the charnel house of Paris, holding in its twisted form the bones of his beloved.

The Odyssey

Poem by Homer, about 9th century B.C. Transcribed in 6th century B.C. (NAL, MD92; ML, 167 & T23).

THE ODYSSEY IS an epic poem that tells of the long, difficult and adventurous voyage of the Greek hero Odysseus (in Latin, Ulysses) on his way home from the Trojan War. A rambling voyage is called an odyssey because the original voyager's name was Odysseus and not vice versa. Because there is no real evidence that Homer (or a man it is convenient to call Homer) wrote the *Odyssey*, many scholars have insisted that it be classified as "author unknown" and that it be considered a collection of various legends by any number of different writers. The majority of the scholars, however, have insisted that the epic's unity of style and poetic magnificence could not have been created in a collection or by a compiler and that the poem must be attributed to a single and great poet, to wit Homer. Though only a scholar in Greek can comment authoritatively on the literary excellence of the *Odyssey*, the excellence of the many translations of it, and the fact that it can seriously be considered to be of the same authorship as the *Iliad*, combine to assure its rank among the greatest poems ever written.

Books I–IX. Fleet-footed ULYSSES sets sail with his warriors, returning from Troy to Ithaca, his kingdom, and to PENELOPE, his wife, and TELEMACHUS, his son. At Ismarus, the Ciconians' city, where they first land, Ulysses loses six men from each ship in a battle with natives. Then a storm drives them for nine days until they reach the land of the Lotus-eaters, who entertain three scouts of Ulysses and give them the lotus-plant to eat. All who taste this food lose their remembrance of home and the desire to return to it. Ulysses is forced to drag his men back to the ship.

Ulysses next reaches the island of the lawless Cyclopes, a pastoral people of giants who have only one eye each, in the middle of the forehead. Ulysses goes to the island with one ship, leaving the other ships at anchor. Ulysses and his men take a big jar of wine as a gift. They go into a large cave in which there are rich stores of food. The Cyclops who lives in the cave, POLYPHEMUS, returns and rolls an enormous rock over the cave's mouth, trapping the Greeks inside. Soon he discovers the strangers. Ulysses humbly tells the Cyclops that they are returning home and he begs hospitality in the name of the gods. Instead of answering, Polyphemus picks up two Greeks, throws them against the wall of the cave, then eats them. After this meal he lies down and sleeps. Ulysses wishes to kill him but realizes that if he does so they can never get out because they cannot budge the stone. Next morning, the Cyclops eats two more Greeks, moves the rock from the door, goes out, and replaces the rock behind him. Ulysses finds the way to escape. The Greeks sharpen to a fine point a massive bar of wood they find in the cave, then hide it under straw. Ulysses selects four of his most audacious companions to act with him when the time arrives. The giant returns at sunset, kills and eats two more Greeks, and is about to go to sleep. Ulysses offers him the wine, and Cyclops drinks it all. He promises, in return for the wine, to eat the offerer of the wine last. He asks his name, and Ulysses says, "My name is Noman."

When the giant is asleep, Ulysses and his four friends place the end of the stake into the fire until its end glows, then they thrust the hot point into the giant's eye, blinding him. The giant roars with pain and howls for help. Other giants come to his cave and the blinded Cyclops says, "I die and Noman kills me." The others answer, "If no man hurts thee, it is the stroke of Jove, and thou must bear it." And they leave.

Next morning, the Cyclops rolls the rock away to let out his flock, planting himself in the door. Ulysses harnesses the rams three abreast, and the Greeks suspend themselves under the rams. The Cyclops feels the backs and sides of the animals, not their bellies, and so the Greeks pass out safely; the last is Ulysses. The Greeks drive some of the flock to their ship, board it in a great hurry, and row away. Ulysses cannot resist yelling that his name is Ulysses. The Cyclops throws after them an enormous rock that almost capsizes the ship. And Polyphemus places a curse on Ulysses.

Books X–XII. Ulysses and his fleet come next to the island of AEOLUS, the king of winds. The monarch, after the friendliest reception, presents Ulysses at his departure with a leather bag bound by a silver string. Within the bag are all the contrary and harmful winds, while Aeolus orders fair winds to blow the ships toward Ithaca. On the ninth day of fair sailing Ulysses, sleepless for nine days, is overcome by fatigue and goes to sleep. Convinced that the mys-

Ulysses has himself lashed to the mast so the Sirens cannot lure him

terious bag contains treasures that Ulysses received from King Aeolus, the crew loosens the string of the bag and at once the winds blow out, driving the ship wildly back to the island of King Aeolus. King Aeolus, angered by their folly, refuses to help them, and the crew must work the oars to make headway.

In the harbor of the Laestrygonians, catastrophe overcomes all the ships but Ulysses' own. He has anchored his ship outside the harbor, while the others sail in to what seemed a fine port. There, the Laestrygonians break up the ships with huge rocks, capsize them and kill the warriors and seamen in the water. Ulysses and his crew escape by rowing away with all their might. They arrive at the isle of Aeaean, the realm of CIRCE, daughter of the sun. She is a powerful sorceress, who changes men into animals. Unwittingly, Ulysses sends half of his crew with EURYLOCHUS in command to investigate. At the center of the island they find Circe's house, and the goddess invites them in. Only Eurylochus suspects danger. Inside they are offered wine and fine food, and after feasting Circe touches them one by one with her wand and they change into swine though their intellects remain as before.

Eurylochus hurries back to report to Ulysses, who starts off to save his companions. On the way, MERCURY appears to Ulysses, warns him about Circe's magic, and gives him a sprig of moly that has wondrous qualities against sorceries. Circe treats Ulysses as she did the others, but when she touches him with the wand, Ulysses rushes at her with drawn sword. She falls to her knees and consents to restore Ulysses' companions to human form and not to try her sorcery against him or them. She not only keeps her oath but makes the lot of Ulysses and his men so pleasurable that Ulysses seems happy to stay. Some of his companions remind him of his duty, and at last Ulysses leaves. Circe tells them how to pass the coast of the Sirens safely and lets them go.

Books XII–XIV. The Sirens are sea nymphs whose songs so charm seamen that they dive into the sea and perish in it. Following Circe's advice Ulysses fills the ears of every man with wax, then orders them to tie him up to the mast and under no conditions, no matter what he tells them, to release him

until they have passed the island of the Sirens. And the warning is necessary, for Ulysses begs, threatens and curses to be released. Circe has warned Ulysses of still another danger, that of passing between the monsters SCYLLA and CHARYBDIS. Scylla, who was changed from a beautiful girl into a snaky, six-headed monster, by Circe herself, occupies a high cliff. She seizes one of the crew in each of her mouths, from any vessel passing within her reach. Charybdis, a gulf, three times a day draws water into her frightful chasm and three times disgorges it, causing a whirlpool. Ulysses hears the roar of the Charybdis and keeps his distance; in so doing he comes too close to Scylla, who catches six men.

Ulysses has been warned by Circe of one more danger, Trinakria, the pastureland of the cattle of HYPERION, the Sun, in charge of his daughters, LAMPETIA and PHAETHUSA. The cattle must not be touched or the offenders will be destroyed. Ulysses' companions swear solemnly to respect the desire of the sun god. However, hunger causes them, in the absence of Ulysses, to cut down some of the cattle. Ulysses notes the ominous signs: The skins creep on the ground, and the joints and meat low on the spits while roasting.

With the first fair wind, they sail from the island, but a fierce storm overtakes them. Lightning, winds and waves break up the ship. Ulysses makes a raft and reaches Calypso island. He is the sole survivor.

Calypso is a lovely sea nymph. She receives Ulysses with open arms and wants him to stay with her forever. Ulysses likes the nymph, but though immortality would be given him if he stayed, he resolutely plans to return to his wife and son. Jove commands Calypso to release Ulysses, and Calypso, though reluctantly, obeys the king of gods. On the well-provisioned raft that Calypso helps him build, Ulysses is in sight of land when a storm sweeps the raft back into the sea and threatens to break it up. A sea nymph, in the form of a cormorant, gives him a girdle, telling him to bind it around his chest when he must swim. The raft does break up, and the now naked Ulysses reaches the shore with great difficulty. This is the land of the Phaeacians, on the isle of Scheria, and their king is ALCINOUS, son of NAUSITHOUS. They are people akin to the gods. They live in peace, and their chief employment is navigation.

NAUSICAÄ, daughter of the king, goes

471

to the river with her attendants to wash her clothes. When the work is done, they eat their meal, then play with a ball. The ball falls in the river and the girls' screams awaken Ulysses. Ulysses realizes that without any clothes he cannot present himself before these girls. He uses some leaves to cover himself and approaches Nausicaä, whom he asks for help. She gives him clothing and orders him to come with her to her father's house. Ulysses, washed and clothed, presents himself at the palace of the king, where he is received with hospitality and a ship is promised him for his return to Ithaca. The next day, there is a feast at the palace. Ulysses surpasses everyone with throwing the weight. A blind bard is led in and he gives them the story of the Wooden Horse of Troy, which delights the hearers but moves Ulysses to tears. Now Ulysses reveals his identity and recounts his adventures since his departure from Troy. In recognition of the name of such a great hero the king and his chiefs present great treasures as gifts to the illustrious guest. Next day the Phaeacian vessel carries Ulysses away and this time he arrives safely at Ithaca, his own island. When the ship touches the shore Ulysses is asleep, so the Phaeacians carry him on shore, put the chest with the gifts at his side, then sail away. Neptune, however, is angered at the Phaeacians for rescuing Ulysses and punishes them by transforming the ship into a rock when it arrives at its port.

Books XIV–XXIV. Ulysses had been away from Ithaca for 20 years and on waking does not recognize his native land. MINERVA, in the form of a young shepherd, appears and tells him where he is and also that Penelope, imagining him dead, and without other support than Telemachus, has had to endure more than 100 nobles as suitors. The nobles behave as if they owned the palace and everything Ulysses owned. To take vengeance on them, Ulysses must not be recognized; so Minerva changes him into a poor beggar. EUMAEUS, his swineherd, a faithful servant, receives the beggar with hospitality.

Telemachus has sought his father in the lands of the kings who returned from the Trojan War. Now Minerva advises him to return to Ithaca. Telemachus goes first to Eumaeus. He meets the supposed beggar, whom he treats with courtesy. Telemachus sends Eumaeus to Penelope to tell her in secrecy that her son has returned. Caution is imperative because the suitors plan to assassinate him. As soon as Eumaeus is gone, Minerva directs Ulysses to reveal himself to his son, and touching him, Ulysses is changed back to his powerful self. Father and son plan the punishment of the suitors. Telemachus is to proceed to the palace. Ulysses will go as a beggar.

At the palace, the suitors behave outrageously, as usual. When Ulysses enters the courtyard of his palace, his old dog, Argus, recognizes him, but is too old to get up and greet his master, and dies. The old beggar is permitted to enter and is given a seat at

the table and some food. While Ulysses eats, the suitors single him out for their fun. When he dares to remonstrate, a suitor strikes him with a chair. Telemachus can hardly hold himself back.

Penelope has set this day to submit the question of her choice to a trial of skill among the suitors. The one who shoots arrows through 12 holes of axes arranged in a line will win the queen. Ulysses' old bow is brought out, but not one of the suitors can bend the bow to attach the string. At last, Ulysses takes the bow, adjusts the cord to its notch, and shoots 12 arrows through the 12 axe-rings. Then, aiming at the most insolent of the suitors, he shoots him through the neck. Telemachus, Eumaeus, and another faithful follower come to Ulysses' side, fully armed. Ulysses reveals himself as the long-lost king, whose hall they have outraged, whose goods they have squandered, and whose wife and son they had persecuted for 10 years. He slays every suitor, pardoning only MEDON, the herald, and PHEMIUS, the bard. Once more Ulysses is king in his own palace, ruler of his kingdom, and husband of his wife.

Oedipus Rex

Play by Sophocles, 495–406 B.C.
Produced about 429 B.C. (ML, 158; NAL, MT238; RE, 29).

THE OEDIPUS PLAYS by Sophocles constitute a trilogy, three separate plays. Two Oedipus plays are outlined here; the third play of the trilogy, *Antigone,* is separately outlined. Modern scholars believe that the three plays may have been written and performed separately, in three widely separated years, and not all at once as was the general custom in the Greek drama of the 5th century B.C. Almost surely the play *King Oedipus* (so titled below; more often called by its Latin name, *Oedipus Rex*) was the one first written. As literature and perhaps even in theme it was the grandest of the three. *Oedipus at Colonus* presents a relatively happy ending, for a tragedy, and has strong religious overtones. *Antigone* is best attuned to modern tastes because it displays a woman's strong will in rebellion against law repugnant to her principles.

OEDIPUS, King of Thebes, appears at the door of his palace. His subjects are mourning a pestilence. A priest begs Oedipus to determine the cause of their suffering, so that the gods may be placated. Oedipus is loved by his people. He came from nearby Corinth and slayed a Sphinx that had haunted Thebes, by answering the riddle of the Sphinx. He also won the throne, since the previous king, LAIUS, had been recently murdered, and he married Laius' widow, JOCASTA, and fathered two daughters, ANTIGONE and ISMENE. Oedipus tells the priest that his brother-in-law, CREON, has been sent to the oracle at Delphi to ask the god Apollo's advice. Creon returns with hopeful news. The oracle has warned Thebes that it is harboring the criminal who killed the former king, Laius. The city cannot be purified until this man is forced to leave. Oedipus rebukes the Thebans for not finding the king-killer. He vows the vengeance of all the gods upon the guilty man. Oedipus retires. The CHORUS prays to Apollo for redemption.

The king reappears and demands more information. The chorus says that details of the crime are scanty. Laius was killed at a deserted crossroads, attended only by litter-bearers who ran away. They bring in the blind prophet TIRESIAS for more clues. Tiresias says he knows the murderer but will not name him. When Oedipus insists, the old seer says that Oedipus himself is the murderer. Tiresias is ejected from the palace but predicts the king's downfall. Oedipus suspects that the prophet and Creon are in league against him. Creon protests his innocence. Queen Jocasta appears to say that Oedipus could not possibly be responsible for her first husband's death. She says that an oracle told Laius he would die by his own son's hand and that Oedipus is not Laius' son, but is the son of King POLYBUS of Corinth. But Oedipus remembers that while traveling once from Corinth to Delphi he killed a proud, wealthy old man who tried to drive him off the road. Jocasta recalls that a shepherd can attest to the death of her son, and Laius', and decides to call the shepherd for proof of the boy's death. A messenger informs Oedipus that Polybus has died and Oedipus is now ruler of Corinth.

Oedipus rejoices, because another oracle predicted that he would slay his own father and marry his own mother. It was to avert this dreadful crime that Oedipus was traveling to Delphi when he murdered the stranger on the highway. Oedipus exults in the fallibility of the gods; Polybus has died a natural death, and Oedipus vows that he will never marry Polybus' wife MEROPE. The messenger then sends shivers through his heart by informing Oedipus that he is not related by blood to Merope or Polybus. A shepherd took Oedipus from a mountainside and gave him to Polybus to be reared as his son. Sensing oncoming horror,

Oedipus insists upon seeing the shepherd. Jocasta runs into the palace.

The old SHEPHERD appears, first refuses to talk, and finally confesses that he gave Laius and Jocasta's son, whom he was supposed to destroy, to Polybus because he could not bear to kill the boy. The baby's ankles were bound tightly, in a way that might deform the feet. [Oedipus' name means "swollen-foot" in Greek.] With a cry, Oedipus dashes off, knowing that the words of the gods are true; he has killed his father and married his mother. As the Chorus laments the disaster that has fallen upon Thebes, an Attendant reports that Jocasta has hanged herself and Oedipus has blinded himself by tearing out his eyes. Oedipus returns, crying for the misery that has overtaken him. Everyone refuses to touch him until Creon, who has assumed control of the state, says that justice must be done. Creon will consult the gods to see if Oedipus may be exiled. The blind king fondles his daughters' heads for the last time and is then led away. The Chorus observes that no one can be finally called happy until he has died in peace.

OEDIPUS AT COLONUS

The lonely, blind Oedipus wanders about Greece in exile, attended only by his faithful daughter Antigone. The two come at last to the hamlet of Colonus, just one mile from Athens, where they sit in a sacred grove. A CHORUS of Colonus residents warns them both that the grove is sacred to certain spirits. When these people learn that the old man is the accursed Oedipus, they drive him away into barren ground. As Oedipus sits on a rock with Antigone, his other daughter, Ismene, rides up to them. Ismene tells her father that an oracle has told Thebes to receive Oedipus' body. The oracle warns that Thebes will never be powerful without their great ruler. Still, Oedipus is not permitted to reënter the city alive. Ismene continues to relate a terrible war that has split the city into two factions. Oedipus' two sons, POLYNICES and ETEOCLES, are wresting the power from King Creon. Eteocles has remained inside the city with his group, while Polynices has collected an army abroad. Oedipus curses his children for their vain ambitions and refuses to bless Thebes, since he is not welcomed there until after his death. Ismene rushes off to a spring to fetch water for her father.

King THESEUS, the great lawgiver of Athens, appears at the grove, for he has learned that it has been profaned by a stranger. When he learns who Oedipus is, Theseus is not the least bit horrified. Instead, he offers Oedipus his protection and help. As soon as Theseus rides off, Creon of Thebes approaches. Creon first demands that Oedipus return. Oedipus declines, because of the cruel way he was treated there. Furthermore, he knows that Thebes merely wants to use him to bind Athens to itself as an ally. Creon, angry at Oedipus' refusal, orders his soldiers to seize Ismene

and Antigone. Theseus returns; he rebukes Creon, whom he takes into his custody, and frees Oedipus' daughters. As they all proceed back to Athens, another rider ap-

Oedipus blind, with Antigone

proaches, Oedipus' rebellious son Polynices, who has also been warned by an oracle that Oedipus' blessing is essential for victory. Polynices tries to regain his father's benediction, but Oedipus is not betrayed by his false affection. Oedipus curses his son for splitting Thebes and also for neglect of his father. Polynices realizes that his cause against Thebes is lost. Despite Antigone's admonition to abandon warfare, he must lead his army against his native city and his brother Eteocles.

When Polynices departs, the air is filled with lightning and the sound of thunder. Oedipus knows his death is near. He calls Theseus to his side and tells him never to disclose his burial ground to anyone except successive kings of Athens. Then Oedipus' spirit will always guard the city. With his two daughters Oedipus departs to bathe before death. The girls return to tell of a miraculous event. After they bathed Oedipus he vanished. Only Theseus, who shielded his eyes as if blinded by a thunderbolt, knows what happened to his friend. He will not tell · the daughters but he promises to return them to Thebes, so that they may try to bring peace to their warring brothers.

Of Human Bondage

Novel by W. Somerset Maugham, 1874–1966.
Published and © 1915 by Doubleday & Co.; © 1942 by W. Somerset Maugham. (PB, C63; ML, 176 & P16).
CRITICS HAVE NOT treated W. Somerset Maugham too kindly on some of his many novels. He has been accused of using his facility at writing to produce too many incidental stories and novels for the almost unprecedentedly high prices that publishers pay him. But there is almost no dissent to the general opinion that his novel *Of Human Bondage* assures his immortality in the history of English literature and his rank as a major novelist of his times. The novel is about a man who is overpowered by his specific desire for a particular woman and about the woman's cruel exploitation of her indifference to a man she attracts. In writing this novel Maugham drew heavily on autobiographical material but there is no reason to think that the theme itself was suggested by any experience of his own.

Chaps. 1–10. Just before PHILIP CAREY'S mother dies, she arranges to leave the 9-year-old boy in the care of his late father's elder brother, WILLIAM CAREY. Philip, born club-footed, is a shy, lonely child, given to daydreams and solitary games. Life at his uncle's vicarage at Black-

stable is austere. His uncle and his Aunt LOUISA are well past middle age and inexperienced in dealing with children. Philip is sent away to school.

Chaps. 11–21. By the time Philip's classmates grow bored with tormenting him because of his clubfoot, he has become very self-conscious and ashamed of his deformity. He is determined not to go on to Oxford. His uncle finally consents to his going to Germany before he has completed his studies.

Chaps. 22–31. At Heidelberg, Philip stays at a *pension* run by Frau ERLIN, the wife of a teacher at the local high school, Professor Erlin, who teaches him Latin and German. Philip is taught French and mathematics by other tutors. He strikes up quite a warm relationship with an urbane English intellectual, HAYWARD, and with WEEKS, a young American scholar. Under their influence he turns agnostic, severing his last spiritual ties with the vicarage at Blackstable.

Chaps. 32–40. When Philip returns to Blackstable he meets Miss WILKINSON, whose father was his Uncle William's last rector. Miss Wilkinson has lived abroad, chiefly in France, supporting herself by working as a governess in wealthy but somewhat Bohemian households. Philip becomes involved with her in his first love affair. At first he is excited by his intimacy with the 40-year-old spinster, but after a time he becomes bored with her possessiveness and sentimentality. Secretly, he is relieved when they must part company. He begins his apprenticeship as an accountant in London.

After a year Philip throws up his job, wishing to go to Paris and become a painter, but he is only 20 and not in control of his small inheritance from his father. His uncle refuses to permit this latest whim, but Aunt Louisa comes to his rescue with £100, which Philip gratefully accepts, unaware that it is her entire savings.

Chaps. 41–51. Philip spends the next two years studying art in Paris. He acquires an exaggerated *avant garde* veneration for impressionism but learns that he will never achieve more than mediocrity as a painter. He is summoned back to Blackstable to attend his aunt's funeral.

Chaps. 52–63. When Philip sets forth from the vicarage for London, in full possession of his inheritance, he is determined to find some fixed place and meaning for himself. He is qualified to study medicine and decides to enter St. Luke's. Philip falls prey again to an old feeling of inadequacy. He finds an escape from loneliness by frequenting a tea shop and contemplating the attractions of a waitress named MILDRED ROGERS. Mildred, no beauty by conventional standards, thin and anemic, with ridiculously overdressed blonde hair, appeals to Philip, with his painter's eye, because of a classic Greek beauty in her profile. He tries to strike up acquaintance with her but is rebuffed. Wounded, he swears off waitresses and tea shops; but a few days later he returns to one of Mildred's tables. He finds her impersonal in serving him, though she maintains her usual coquetries with her "favorites" among the patrons. He becomes increasingly preoccupied with her. In time, a relationship of sorts develops between them, with Philip lovestruck and Mildred accepting his doglike devotion as her natural due but granting nothing in return. He recklessly strains his slender resources to gratify her vulgar notions of refinement. His obsessive lust for her undermines his work at school. He proposes marriage to her, realizing he will never achieve intimacy with her by any other means. After subjecting him to a thorough and unabashed sounding-out on the subject of his finances, she turns him down. A few weeks later, Mildred tells Philip that she is going to marry a middle-aged German named MILLER.

Chaps. 64–75. Philip buries his disappointment in cramming for an examination he previously failed. He is able to work well and easily at his studies again. When he meets NORAH NESBIT he takes to her at once. She is a plain-looking woman of 24 who is vivacious, talented, and intelligent. Philip becomes her lover and experiences the happiness of a forthright and comfortable intimacy. One day, without warning, Mildred turns up at Philip's flat. Miller, with a legal wife and three children of his own, never did get around to marrying Mildred. Now he has deserted her and she is pregnant. Penniless and with her baby three months off, she tells Philip with unaccustomed diffidence that she is ready to come back to him on any terms he desires. Philip has been aware, from the first mo-

Mildred is now a streetwalker

ment of seeing Mildred again, of still loving her as much as ever. He eagerly arranges to support Mildred in lodgings of her own and see her through the costs of her confinement. He breaks off with Norah, who is familiar with the unhappy story of his infatuation. The moment Philip takes over the responsibility, Mildred lapses into her characteristic treatment of him. Secretly hoping for a still-birth, she suggests going to Brighton for her confinement. Philip agrees and proposes a trip to France after her recovery and his exams—a romantic holiday for both of them. Mildred is delivered of a little girl at Brighton and promptly boards it out with a local housewife. Philip invites GRIFFITHS, the only friend he has made in all this time at St. Luke's, to meet Mildred at a supper party on their first evening out in London. A few days later, Mildred abruptly informs Philip that she is not going to France with him. She and Griffiths are completely taken with each other. She says she would rather starve in the streets than ever permit Philip to touch her.

Chaps. 76–90. Griffiths is without funds and in debt to almost everyone at St. Luke's, including Philip. Mildred comes to Philip in tears, and he takes perverse pleasure in financing her holiday with his best friend. Mildred assures Philip that on her return from Oxford she will resume their own platonic friendship. Within a week Griffiths is back at St. Luke's. He has been subjected to too large a dose of Mildred's banality and has no further interest in her. Mildred is heartbroken and disappears. This leaves a tragic gap in Philip's life. After several weeks of tormented brooding, and a rejected attempt to console himself with Norah, he returns to St. Luke's. He plunges into his school work with intensity and thinks of Mildred less and less often. In the next two years he advances in his profession and makes a new friend, THORPE ATHELNY, a patient. Athelny invites Philip to a Sunday dinner at his house. Athelny, a publicity man for a successful Regent Street firm, is erudite, sophisticated and a perfectionist in his tastes. Philip is warmly welcomed by Athelny's wife and their swarms of children and he soon becomes a regular guest. Then Philip spots Mildred on the street and from a distance he follows her

as she promenades back and forth. He realizes, to his dismay, that he has been observing the conventional progress of a streetwalker. When he greets her, Mildred tries to pretend that she is out on an innocent Sunday stroll. Although Philip's love for Mildred and the last traces of her power over him have long been dead, he is profoundly distressed by what life has reduced her to. He suggests that she and her baby come to stay with him in the spare room of his tiny flat. Philip makes it evident that he is motivated solely by pity and Mildred accepts his invitation.

Chaps. 91–104. Philip's work at the hospital keeps him away from the flat the greater part of the day and Mildred makes the most of her opportunities. She calmly informs the landlady that she is his wife. Later that same evening she insists to Philip that she has come only to cook and clean for him with the implicit understanding that their relationship would never stop there. Philip assures her that "there" is exactly where it had stopped and would remain. Mildred shrugs off this fact, assumes a marital authority over his life, and takes to wearing a wedding-ring and calling herself Mrs. Carey, with the most prudish pretentions to middle-class respectability. She continues, unsuccessfully, to attempt to trap him into erotic commitment to her. Failing in this, she takes her revenge by means of her little girl, to whom Philip has become attached. She has discovered that he cannot endure the sight of the child being treated roughly and she delights in watching him tremble when she slaps her daughter. She begins one evening to cajole Philip into making love to her and the more he maintains his strong indifference, the more incensed she becomes. Finally she breaks into the pettiest abuse and describes the vilest details of her sexual experiences. When she realizes that he has been witnessing her entire emotional eruption with clinical detachment, she spits out the word "cripple" at him and rushes out of the room. The next morning Philip wakes to find that Mildred and her baby have left his house and that she has literally destroyed its entire contents. The same week he receives word that he has been wiped out on the stock market, which he has lately been playing in an effort to raise his income to the level of Mildred's extravagances. His Uncle William, reproaching him for the life he is leading, refuses assistance. Philip pawns his

474

clothes, which are his only possession left undamaged by Mildred, and takes to roughing it around the countryside. A week of this sort of life is enough to overcome his embarrassment at confronting the Athelnys without a shilling to his name. They react to his poverty with their usual realism. The thing for him to do is to get a job at Lynn and Sedley's Department Store, where Athelny handles the publicity.

Chaps. 105–114. Philip is hired as a floorwalker. After three months he is promoted to window-dresser—chiefly because, as a gentleman, he can be relied upon for good taste. His next promotion is to costume designer, thanks to his training in art. One day he gets an urgent note from Mildred. Her baby has died. Mildred is ill and Philip, examining her, finds she is infected with a venereal disease. He cautions her against continuing her activities in the London streets and when he subsequently finds her still soliciting and indifferently passing on her infection, he gives her up for good. Uncle William dies the next summer. Philip returns to St. Luke's and finally qualifies as a doctor.

Chaps. 115–122. Philip is surprised at how SALLY, one of the Athelny daughters, has grown from girlhood into handsome maturity. At the age of almost 30 he receives his diploma as a surgeon. He has an affair with Sally, more a result of their mutual regard than of any grand passion. Ever since his childhood Philip has had the desire to travel. Now he is officially qualified to take on the part of ship's doctor and circumnavigate the earth. Sally suspects that she is pregnant. Philip resigns himself bitterly to the news, privately renouncing his dreams. Sally, however, finds out that she is not with child and eagerly she gives Philip the news of her freedom. But Philip has been reacting so intensely to the prospect of becoming a husband and father that he is disappointed at relinquishing the rôle. In the end, they agree there is no reason why he really should.

Lennie breaks the girl's neck

Of Mice and Men

Novel by John Steinbeck, 1902–
Published 1937 by The Viking Press, New York. © 1937 by John Steinbeck. (ML, 29).

CRITICS OFTEN COMMENT on the fact that this short novel became a play almost without change, but the fact is that the novel was never really a novel and was always a play, converted by punctuation and connective sentences into prose fiction. It is one of the most skillfully wrought miniatures in English literature. The title is from the familiar line in Burns' poem to a field-mouse, "The best-laid schemes of mice and men gang aft agley"; basically it alludes to the unquenchable dreaming of the hired hand for a place of his own and the fact that his schemes are seldom realized, but there is a play on words because the imbecilic giant Lenny in the story likes to fondle mice.

Chap. 1. GEORGE MILTON and LENNIE SMALL are on their way to a new ranch job in Southern California. They stop to eat a supper of canned beans and settle for the night. Lennie's innocent faculty for getting into trouble has kept them moving from ranch to ranch. Lennie is incredibly strong but very dull-witted. He has a compulsive desire to touch soft things, for example to stroke the soft coats of mice or rabbits, but he inevitably kills them by stroking too hard. They lost their last job because he wanted to feel the fabric of a girl's dress and had to be hit on the head before he would let her go. George, a small man, quick and alert, bitterly muses over the easy life he could have without Lennie. But Lennie is his charge; and Lennie, like a lost, obedient child, lovingly listens to and follows George.

Before they fall asleep, Lennie asks George to tell him once more about the farm they will have one day with a vegetable patch, and chickens, and rabbits—which Lennie will tend. Lennie knows the dream by heart. It is the dream of all itinerant ranch hands, a farm of their own.

Chap. 2. George and Lennie arrive at the ranch the next morning and are shown to the bunkhouse by the swamper, an old, stoop-shouldered man called CANDY. The boss assigns them to a grain team led by SLIM, the mule skinner (driver). George admits that Lennie is not very bright but says he is an exceptionally good worker. Next they meet CURLEY, the boss's son, who is small but handy with his fists and so immediately antagonistic to the huge Lennie. Curley has been especially difficult since his marriage two weeks before, Candy says, further reporting that Curley's wife is a "tart" and has been seen "giving the eye" to Slim and to CARLSON, a hand.

George reminds Lennie of the secret meeting place they have agreed on if there is trouble and they must leave.

Slim and Carlson come in to wash up for lunch. Slim has great dignity. He and George feel a kinship based on intelligences. Slim mentions his dog's nine new pups. George promises Lennie that he will ask Slim to give Lennie one of the pups.

Chap. 3. Slim has given Lennie a brown-and-white puppy, and cautions him to leave the pup in the barn with its mother and not pet it too much until it is a bit older. George, Lennie and Candy are sitting in the bunkhouse when Curley rushes in looking for his wife. Suspiciously, he goes out looking for Slim. Candy overhears George and Lennie pursuing their verbal dreams for a farm and asks for membership in their plans. With the money he can contribute, their dream can become a reality at the end of the month, and George agrees to take him in. At this moment Curley and Slim return, Slim angry and Curley apologetic, insisting he didn't mean anything but was just asking for his wife. Curley notices Lennie, still lost in his dream about the house, smiling to himself. Curley attacks Lennie, lashing one blow after another; Lennie does not fight back but cries to George to stop Curley. Slim decides to intercede but George finally gives Lennie permission to resist. Lennie grabs Curley's fist and crushes it in his hand. Curley wails. Slim warns Curley to say he caught his hand in a machine. Lennie is simply afraid he has done something bad again.

Chap. 4. On Saturday night most of the men have gone into town. CROOKS, the crippled Negro stable buck, is sitting in his shed, alone as always. Lennie enters, looking for company. Crooks is antagonistic at first but really wants company. Although Lennie doesn't understand, Crooks tells him about his loneliness. Lennie tells Crooks about the farm and the rabbits. Crooks says that every man he has known on a ranch has a piece of land in his head, but none ever gets it. Just like heaven. Candy comes in and talks about the house, and Crooks, forgetting his disbelief, offers to work on their land just for his keep and to invest his savings. Suddenly Curley's wife is standing in the doorway. The men try to get rid of her, afraid she will make trouble for them. But she, too, wants to talk to someone.

Chap. 5. The men are pitching horseshoes in the Sunday afternoon sun and Lennie is in the barn kneeling over his dead puppy. He is afraid that when George finds out he won't let him tend the rabbits. Curley's wife comes in and asks why he likes rabbits so much. He tells her he likes to pet soft things. She understands and lets him stroke her hair. But when she has had enough and wants to go, his fingers close on her hair and she screams. Lennie, frightened, grasps her. Then she is still, for Lennie has broken her neck. It takes him a few minutes to realize what has happened. Then he runs out to hide in the brush, the appointed meeting place. The men find the dead girl and Curley organizes a search party. Curley is raging with determination to kill Lennie on sight. George joins the party, with a pistol borrowed from Slim.

Chap. 6. Lennie is sitting on the bank of the river. George comes ahead of the other men. He promises Lennie he will not desert him and he makes Lennie turn his back to hear again the story of the farm and the rabbits. He shoots Lennie. The other men come and approve what George did, for Lennie was too big to capture. Slim understands and tells George he did the only thing he could.

The Old Wives' Tale

Novel by Arnold Bennett, 1867–1931. Published 1908 (England), 1911 by Doubleday & Co. New York. © 1938 by Marie Margaret Bennett. (ML, 184)

ARNOLD BENNETT was the most eminent historian of the Five Towns district of England and *The Old Wives' Tale* is the most noted of his works. Much of the background material that appeared in *The Old Wives' Tale* can be found in other Bennett stories and novels and for that reason the importance of *The Old Wives' Tale* is not unanimously acknowledged by today's critics, but Bennett was an important novelist and this is his important work and it should be read. *The Old Wives' Tale* has all the qualities of the great novel in its broad scope, keen examination of its characters, and logical plot.

Book I. Chaps. 1–3. The very special Five Towns are the center of the Staffordshire crockery manufacturing business. Bursley, oldest of the Five Towns, has as its center St. Luke's Square. Here are the draper, the chemist, the best bakery. Chief of the merchant aristocracy of the Square is JOHN BAINES, draper. To his store come people from the other Five Towns and from even further away. Baines has been a bedridden paralytic for the past ten years but still directs his business through his devoted wife and with the aid in times of crisis of his bitter-tongued but devoted friend CRITCHLOW, the leading chemist. Baines, his wife and two daughters, CONSTANCE and SOPHIA, live in a well-furnished, dark

and uncomfortable house which also contains the shop. There are communicating doors. The house has a dreadful, subterranean kitchen, from which the servant must climb steep stairs to bring food. Mr. Baines hates change, as does his wife. He refuses even to display a signboard over his store. This would be, he says, "puffing."

Sophia is the beauty, the lively one. Constance is quiet, uninterested in change, devoted to the store. One day the girls watch their servant MAGGIE crossing the Square on her day off. Sophia comments with contempt on Maggie's clothes. SAMUEL POVEY, who is first assistant in the store and lives in, is suffering from a bad toothache. In contrast to Sophia's mischief, Constance shows compassion, gets Mr. Povey down to the parlor, settles him in a chair by the fire, and brings him some laudanum in water to hold in his mouth. He swallows it, and it puts him to sleep. Sophia uses a pair of pliers to yank out a loose tooth from Mr. Povey's open mouth. When Mr. Povey wakes he thinks he has swallowed a tooth—but not the bad one. Sophia takes the tooth as a trophy. Constance gets it finally, after a real quarrel, and throws it out the window.

Sophia wants to be a teacher. Constance is perfectly content to work in the store. Sophia's teacher, Miss CHETWYND, is on Sophia's side, and finally Sophia's parents agree that Sophia shall continue her studies.

Chaps. 3–4. Once a year the Bursley Wakes are held, a festival like an old-fashioned fair, with circus animals and booths of trinkets, and goodies. This year, an elephant goes berserk and has to be shot. Everyone goes gleefully to view the dead elephant, but Sophia stays at home to watch over her paralyzed father. He must always be kept propped up with pillows to avoid strangulation. He seems in proper position, so Sophia runs down to the parlor to look out the window into the Square, hoping she will get a glimpse of GERALD SCALES, a flashy traveling salesman for whom she has fallen. When she returns, her father is half out of bed, his head nearly on the floor, his face and neck dark and congested. Realizing he is dead, she runs shrieking for Maggie, who runs for Critchlow. Critchlow accuses Sophia of gallivanting with Scales and of having killed her father. There is an elaborate funeral. Sophia, apparently anxious to please her mother, announces that she will forgo teaching and work in the shop.

Chaps. 5–7. Constance and Povey are absorbed in the shop. They are obviously in love. Two years have passed since the death of John Baines. Sophia is unhappy, for Scales has vanished. He reappears on New Year's Eve, and Sophia learns that he has spent two years in Paris and that he is college-educated and well connected with the owners of the firm he represents. He is her hero. Her mother warns that Scales has the reputation of being very "wild." Sophia meets Scales surreptitiously and is discovered and packed off to stay with an aunt. She elopes with Scales, just when

Constance becomes engaged. Sophia, knowing nothing of this, sends a telegram from London and later a note saying that she and Scales are going to live abroad.

Book II. Constance and Povey are married. Mrs. Baines turns over the house to them, going to live with her sister HARRIET in a nearby town. Maggie gives notice, to marry the fish-hawker. Constance has no particular problems, though she finds it hard to adapt herself to Povey's innovations—a magnificent signboard over the store, his cigars, and even a dog. A Christmas card comes from Sophia in Paris, addressed "Mrs. and Miss Baines."

Constance has a child, CYRIL, who becomes an unpleasant, sneaky, spoiled boy. Old Mrs. Baines dies, leaving her money to Cyril. When, Cyril is 13 he is caught stealing from the shop till, also selling tobacco and cigars to boys at his school. But the mild sensation of Cyril's bad behavior is overshadowed by the greatest sensation Bursley has ever known. Sam's cousin Daniel, the fine baker, finds his son Richard, on the stairs of his house, with a broken knee. Richard stumbled in the dark, calling for his mother to bring him some dinner. She is dead drunk, and Daniel strangles her. Sam Povey learns that the woman has become a drunkard during the past two years, and that the house is a pigsty. But Daniel is arrested.

Samuel devotes himself to the defense of his cousin. The citizens of the Five Towns rally to the cause. Samuel neglects his business and neglects his health. Everyone signs petitions, but to no avail. Daniel is condemned and hanged. Defeated, Samuel Povey dies. Cyril goes to art school. Constance sells the store to Critchlow. Cyril wins a national scholarship in art and goes to live in London. Constance remains alone in her uncomfortable house, now quite separate, with all entrances to the store blocked.

Book III. Sophia, after leaving her aunt's home, meets Scales in London. He has no intention of marrying her. Sophia shows her fury and pluck, forcing him to marry her. They settle in Paris, where Sophia learns sophistications and becomes disillusioned. Scales' money runs out, and after four years of marriage, during which he is constantly unfaithful, he deserts Sophia. She has the foresight to steal £200 from him when he comes home drunk.

When Sophia falls sick, Gerald's friend CHIRAC takes her to the apartment of an old courtesan, who nurses her through a long sickness. When Sophia is well she takes over this apartment from the old courtesan, buys the furniture, and starts renting rooms to respectable people. She makes money. She is only vaguely aware of the Franco-German War but is much more aware of the fact that money can be made during the long siege. With the help of a grocer-lodger, she accumulates quantities of food and charges exorbitant prices for the meals she serves. During the Commune she loses her only friend, Chirac. He goes up in

Sophia has the foresight to take Scales' money when he is drunk

one of the balloons sent up from Paris and is lost. Sophia, who seems incapable of any true emotions, gets over this loss easily enough. She drives a tough bargain with the English owners of the Pension Frensham, buys it cheap, runs it well, and becomes famous as a wonderful landlady. She is known as Mrs. Frensham. One day a young man from Bursley discovers Sophia's right name, recognizing her by her likeness to Cyril. He tells Cyril and Constance on his return to England, and Constance writes to Sophia. Sophia has a slight stroke, heeds the warning, sells her pension, and arrives in Bursley with her French poodle, Fossette. Sophia is very taken with her nephew but is critical of the old-fashioned way of life Constance has chosen. The servant gives notice and they find it hard to get a new one willing to face the dreadful old well of a kitchen and all the stairs. Sophia tries to persuade Constance to leave the house permanently and live in a hotel or modern apartment, but Constance is the stronger of the two and there the two old women stay, with their dying old dogs and their constant servant problem. Constance even dislikes taking a drive in Richard Povey's car. Though crippled for life, Richard is full of energy, has taken up cars, and deals in them and machinery.

Sophia is summoned to Manchester, where Gerald is dangerously ill. It is the first time she has heard of him in 26 years. Gerald Scales is dead by the time she arrives. The only paper they find on him shows he must have been living in South America. Sophia sees the dead man, a small, wizened old man with a tiny white goatee—not a trace left of the dashing lover she once knew. On the trip back to Bursley, Sophia has a stroke. She is carried into the house in Bursley and in a few hours, she too is dead. Cyril arrives and is unexpectedly helpful in making all funeral arrangements. He finds himself heir to Sophia's considerable fortune. But after two weeks he announces

that he must leave on a trip to Hungary. Constance is left completely alone except for some companionship from young Povey and his fiancé.

One more excitement occurs in the Square. Mrs. Critchlow attempts suicide by stabbing herself with scissors, because her business has failed. Some months later Constance receives notice to leave her house. She walks to the Town Hall with a petition, comes home in a downpour, is put to bed, and dies within a few days. Cyril cannot be reached. After the funeral, the servant returns to the house. No one is left except the half-blind, evil-smelling poodle Fossette, which Sophia brought from Paris.

Oliver Twist

> *Novel by* Charles Dickens, 1812–1870. Published 1839. (PB, PL514)
>
> THERE ARE MANY FLAWS in this novel, but it is secure in its place as one of the best-known novels of the English language because it embraces so many examples of the Dickens genius in characterization and incident. His character Fagin equals anything Shakespeare ever created by way of a villain. His descriptions of the lot of the underprivileged English classes and the callousness of their overseers, drawn exclusively from the lower classes, are eloquent and often dramatic. Beyond this, *Oliver Twist* is simply a commonplace thriller with incredible coincidences and exaggerated melodramatic scenes. Naturally, all of these defects help make *Oliver Twist* very readable.

Chaps. 1–3. OLIVER TWIST was born in a workhouse. His mother, ill, was rescued off the street just in time for this event.

She died at his birth, before she could tell her history. Little Oliver is a nameless orphan. He passes his first 9 years farmed out to Mrs. Mann (who handles many such orphans), cringing under cruel treatment, ill-fed, and unloved. The parish beadle, officious Mr. BUMBLE, the man who named him Oliver Twist (he named all orphans alphabetically), removes Oliver to the workhouse on his 9th birthday, to be taught a trade. The boys in the workhouse are fed one bowl of thin gruel, and are almost starved. They pick Oliver to ask the master for a second helping. He is frightened, but says, "Please, sir, I want some more." For this crime against propriety Oliver spends a week in solitary confinement. He barely escapes being given, plus £5, to a chimney sweep, Mr. Gamfield, who can beat a donkey or a child to death.

Chaps. 4–7. Oliver is taken by Mr. Bumble to be apprenticed to a Mr. SOWERBERRY, undertaker. Oliver immediately becomes the victim of Sowerberry's older, stronger charity boy, vicious, stupid NOAH CLAYPOLE, and a mean maid, CHARLOTTE, who is in love with Noah. Oliver endures Noah's brutality in meekness until Noah taunts him about his nameless birth. Oliver then finds the strength and passion to thrash the bigger, but cowardly, Claypole. Mr. Bumble thrashes Oliver and locks him in the workhouse, on bread and water. At night, Oliver escapes, saying goodbye only to LITTLE DICK, another orphan. Then he starts walking 70 miles to London. He has a crust of bread, a penny, and a pitiful bundle of clothes.

Chaps. 8–11. On the way to London Oliver meets a hardened lad of his own age, JACK DAWKINS, who is called the ARTFUL DODGER. He tells Oliver of a fine respectable old gentleman, FAGIN, in London. Fagin, a master thief, trains youngsters as pickpockets. Dawkins takes Oliver to Fagin, who sends Oliver out to learn the trade from the Artful Dodger and a lad named CHARLEY, Master BATES. Oliver sees them steal a handkerchief from a well-dressed old gentleman browsing at a bookstall. Oliver suddenly realizes they are thieves. The shout "Stop thief!" sends him running in a panic. His two companions escape, but he is seized. The old gentleman, a Mr. BROWNLOW, much struck by a familiar look about the boy, appears for Oliver before the harsh police-justice, Mr. FANG, and tells him that Oliver is innocent, saving Oliver from jail.

Chaps. 12–15. Mr. Brownlow takes Oliver to his own home in Pentonville, to care for him. Oliver begins to recover. He is strangely drawn toward a portrait in his room. Mr. Brownlow himself is struck by the likeness between the boy's face and the lady's in the portrait. Mr. Brownlow, ready to trace a possible connection, is unexpectedly thwarted. Fagin, fearing that Oliver might reveal the secret of his school of crime, tells one of his gang, a vicious man named BILL SIKES, to set his sweetheart, NANCY, a bad girl with a soft heart, on Oliver's trail. Mr. Brownlow has a guest, an irascible, warm-hearted old friend of his, Mr. GRIMWIG. Mr. Grimwig is suspicious of Oliver. Mr. Brownlow sends Oliver, who now is well fed and well dressed, on an errand back to the bookstall, carrying money. Nancy spies him there, claims him as her runaway brother, and carries him back to Fagin. At Brownlow's, the two old men wait in vain for Oliver to return.

Chaps. 16–22. Oliver must don rags again, instead of fine clothes. Fagin swears to teach him a lesson and make him a tool. Oliver is beaten and Sikes tries to set his fierce dog, Bull's-eye, on him, but Nancy fights to save Oliver. Meanwhile, Mr. Bumble goes to London on workhouse business. He sees an advertisement placed by Mr. Brownlow, offering a reward for aid in finding the missing Oliver Twist. He goes to see Brownlow, attempting to blacken Oliver's reputation, and succeeds only for the moment. Oliver is kept a prisoner by Fagin, with the Artful Dodger and Master Bates for companions. Fagin hatches a plan for a midnight robbery of a house at Chertsey. Oliver is to be used in the housebreaking, with three of Fagin's men, TOBY CRACKIT, Sikes, and BARNEY. Nancy plans to protect Oliver somehow. The three men and Oliver go to the house at Chertsey. Oliver is pushed through a small window and told to open the street door for the robbers. But the inmates of the house are alarmed. Oliver, who wanted to warn them, is shot in the arm. Sikes pulls him back through the window and the rest of the gang scatter.

Chaps. 23–31. Mr. Bumble is courting the workhouse matron, rich Mrs. CORNEY. She is told that old SALLY is dying and goes to see her. Sally, a workhouse inmate, was at Oliver's mother's deathbed. Sally is about to tell of some gold she had stolen from the dying mother, and also to tell the boy's real name, but Sally dies before she can. After his escape, Toby Crackit goes to Fagin, who already knows of the fiasco. Toby knows only that Sikes carried away the wounded boy and left him lying in a ditch. Fagin met a mysterious fellow at a public house, one MONKS, who seems to seek Oliver's safety but wants Fagin to make the boy a thief.

Mrs. Corney accepts Mr. Bumble's hand. He gloats over acquiring a woman of property.

Back at the scene of the crime, where Sikes carried the wounded Oliver on his back and Toby fled, pursuers with dogs appear. The angry Sikes has to drop Oliver into a ditch to escape with his own skin. The wounded boy crawls back to the house of the robbery. Found on the doorstep by servants, he is cared for by the occupants, Miss ROSE MAYLIE (an adopted orphan) and her aunt, Mrs. MAYLIE. They put him in the medical care of a surgeon, Mr. LOSBERNE. Though he is known as a member of a gang, Oliver is tenderly treated here. They even shield him from criminal guilt

Oliver is found on the doorstep

when the Bow Street officers (London police) made their investigation.

Chaps. 32–36. Improving slowly, Oliver, out with Mr. Losberne, chances to see Toby Crackit's house. They investigate, hoping to find the thieves. Failing, they go to see Mr. Brownlow. His house is closed. He has gone to the West Indies. Oliver returns to the Maylie house and lives there happily. Then Rose Maylie is taken ill, her life despaired of. Oliver is sent for Mr. Losberne. He runs into the stranger, Monks, and flees, frightened. Rose recovers and Mrs. Maylie's

son, HARRY, Rose's lover, returns home. From Harry's conversation with his mother, Oliver learns there is some mystery concerning Rose's birth. One evening Oliver sees Fagin and Monks looking at him through the window. He shouts for help, but the two men disappear and search proves vain. Harry pleads with Rose to marry him but she will not give her consent with a possible stain on her name.

Chaps. 37–40. Mr. Bumble, having married Mrs. Corney, resigns as beadle and becomes master of the workhouse. Mrs. Bumble dominates him, to his chagrin; after their first pitched battle he knows his place. Mr. Bumble, at a public house for comfort, falls in with Monks. Monks is trying to find the woman who was with Oliver's mother when she died. Bumble tells him of Sally's death and agrees to help Monks in his mysterious affairs. Bumble, Mrs. Bumble and Monks meet in an old mill near by. Mrs. Bumble tells all she knows—that old Sally died with a pawnbroker's ticket for a trinket. Mrs. Bumble redeemed the ticket, getting a locket with the name Agnes upon it. For this, and for her information, she receives £25 from Monks. He flings the trinket down a trap-door into the millstream. Monks returns to London and sees Fagin. Nancy overhears them and learns who Monk is and his plot against Oliver. Nancy carries the news to Rose Maylie, in a London hotel, that Monks is Oliver's evil brother. She tells of the identifying trinket in the millstream, and of Monk's desire to secure a fortune that belongs to Oliver and to keep Oliver a thief in Fagin's hands.

Sikes learns of Nancy's betrayal and beats her to death

478

Chap. 41. Nancy asks Rose not to reveal her part in the business. Living at the Maylies' house, Oliver sees Brownlow in the street and gets his address. Rose hires a carriage and drives there with Oliver. She finds Mr. Brownlow and Mr. Grimwig together and tells them what she has learned. Now all unite to bring Monks to justice and give Oliver his due.

Chaps. 42–48. Noah Claypole, with Charlotte's assistance, robs Sowerberry's till and they come to London. As luck would have it, they put up at The Three Cripples inn, one of Fagin's resorts. Fagin, overhearing their conversation, invites them to join his band. The Artful Dodger has just been caught at pocket-picking, and Noah Claypole, who now calls himself MORRIS BOLTER, is sent to the police court to learn the Dodger's fate. After this, Fagin sends Noah to dog Nancy's steps. Fagin fancies that she has a new attachment and seeks to escape from his power, and through her he wishes to get rid of the ruffian Bill Sikes, whom he fears. Nancy meets Mr. Brownlow and Rose Maylie under London Bridge, and Claypole hides and hears Nancy tell them where to find Monks. Learning of this, Fagin tells Sikes and Sikes beats Nancy to death. Then Sikes, dazed by his foul deed, wanders forth with his dog. He leaves London, then returns, resolved to flee the country. He tries to kill his dog, which inconveniences him, but the dog escapes.

Chaps. 49–50. Mr. Brownlow, on Nancy's information, gets help and captures Monks. He makes Monks sign a document restoring Oliver's rights; for Mr. Brownlow was a friend of Edward Leeford, the father of Monks and Oliver. Sikes comes to Fagin's, running from the police. His dog is already there. The boy Charley Bates, in a frenzied desire to deliver Sikes up, attacks him. While they are struggling, the officers arrive. Sikes wrenches himself from the boy, and with a rope tries to lower himself from the roof. Suddenly he seems to see the murdered Nancy in a vision. Unnerved, he throws up his arms and the rope forms a noose. He falls and strangles to death. His faithful dog leaps after him, dying with his master.

Chaps. 51–53. Two days later, Mr. Brownlow, Mrs. Maylie, Mr. Grimwig, Rose and Oliver go to Oliver's native town to face Monks and Mr. and Mrs. Bumble. From Monks they get the story of Oliver's birth: How Agnes Fleming, his mother, was suddenly widowed when her lover, Edward Leeford, died in Rome. The poor mother, under Monks' influence, ended by dying in the workhouse. Monks is Oliver's halfbrother. Rose proves to be the orphan child of the sister of Agnes Fleming, so she was Oliver's cousin. They learn of a will making Oliver an heir to his father's fortune. Mr. and Mrs. Bumble were parties to Monks' crime of throwing Agnes Fleming's identifying gold trinket into the millstream— Mrs. Bumble being party to the crime because she was supposed to obey her husband. Bumble makes a famous statement: "If the law supposes that, the law is a ass—a idiot . . . a bachelor." Oliver still needs certain papers that Monks deposited with Fagin for safekeeping. Oliver and Brownlow visit Fagin in his cell and from him force the secret of where to find the documents. And thus each character gets his deserts. Fagin is hanged. Rose and Harry are married. Monks flees to the new world, where he at last dies in prison. Mr. Brownlow adopts Oliver. Noah and Charlotte become degraded informants. And Mr. and Mrs. Bumble become paupers in the workhouse they once ruled.

The Ordeal of Richard Feverel

Novel by George Meredith, 1828–1909. Published 1859. (ML, 134 & T27)

CERTAINLY *The Ordeal of Richard Feverel* is the best-read Meredith novel, and why? The reason must be that the theme of the novel, the training of a young man to be wary of women and the attempt to select and train a wife for a man so brought up, has a basic appeal that cannot be matched by any ordinary novel of manners. Meredith may have been what today's youth would call a stuffed shirt, but apparently he did not approve of any such effort of one person to impose his will on another, and he took care that the experiment ended unsuccessfully. Like any other Meredith novel, *Richard Feverel* must be read with care but is good reading.

Chaps. 1–2. When Sir AUSTIN FEVEREL, Baronet, of Raynham Abbey, publishes *The Pilgrim's Script,* a book of aphorisms expressing his misogynistic point of view, he immediately becomes a celebrity and is pursued by women from all parts of England. This is in no way pleasing to him, for he is quite serious about his misogyny, so much so that he determines to shelter his son RICHARD from female society until the boy is 25. By raising Richard according to a strict system, Sir Austin feels he will save his son from his own experience: After 5 years of marriage, his wife ran off with his best friend, a poet.

Chaps. 3–6. Richard spends his early years at Raynham, with his father, his widowed aunt Mrs. DORIA FOREY, who acts as female head of the household, her little daughter CLARE, his cousin ADRIAN HARLEY, who superintends his education, and HEAVY BENSON, the butler, himself a taciturn hater of women. In his 14th year Richard begins to grow restless for want of companions his own age and on the advice of Adrian, Sir Austin brings RIPTON THOMPSON, his solicitor's son, to live with Richard. Richard and Rip unknowingly poach on the farm of GILES BLAIZE, who orders them off his land. When Richard becomes insolent, Blaize horsewhips them both. Feeling the blow to his pride more keenly than the blows on his back, Richard vows to get even with Blaize. Ripton suggests stoning him, but Richard rejects this as ungentlemanly. On the way home they meet TOM BLAKEWELL, a farm boy who has been ill-used by Blaize. Richard devises a way to take his revenge.

Chaps. 7–14. After dinner that night, Sir Austin overhears Richard and Rip talking mysteriously about setting something on fire. He watches as the two conspirators lean out of the window with a telescope and when he looks, too, he sees dense masses of smoke rising from the neighboring farm. The next morning, Sir Austin reads aloud the report of the extensive fire at Blaize's farm and watches the boys' reactions. The boys pretend innocence. The next day, Tom Blakewell is arrested on suspicion of arson. Tom does not reveal that Richard bribed him to commit the crime. Richard and Rip conceive a plan to help Tom escape from jail, but Tom refuses. At last Richard realizes he will have to do his duty, bitter as it is. He cannot permit Tom, a commoner, to sacrifice himself for him. Richard goes to Blaize to make a clean breast of the whole affair. When he gets there, he learns that his father has already paid Blaize £300 damages and has promised an apology from Richard. Richard announces that he is the one who set the fire. Blaize calls him a liar. He has a witness who saw Tom do it. Richard succeeds in confusing the witness, who is a dull-witted fellow anyway. Tom is acquitted. As a result of this, Tom becomes Richard's devoted servant.

Chaps. 15–18. As Richard passes into adolescence, he grows into a sober, thoughtful young man, tall, robust, and handsome, and secretly loved by his little cousin Clare. Sir Austin watches his progress under the System with pride, but when he discovers that Richard has taken to writing poetry he becomes disturbed and asks him to burn his manuscripts. Richard submits, but all confidence between father and son ceases from that time forth. When Richard approaches his 18th year, Sir Austin sets out for London to find a girl of excellent background and character who can be trained for seven years to be a suitable mate for so perfect a youth as Richard. Money and position will have no influence in his choice. But while rowing on the Thames one day Richard sees a beautiful golden-haired girl eating dewberries on the bank. He speaks to her and she tells him they have met before. She is LUCY DESBOROUGH, the orphan niece of farmer Blaize, and she was in the room the night Richard came to apologize. She does not tell him that she has been dreaming of him since then, but it is quite plain that they are falling in love.

Chaps. 19–28. In London, after much searching and many interviews, Sir Austin finds Richard's ideal future mate—a 13-year-old girl named CAROLA GRANDISON, one of eight sisters who have been brought up according to a System as rigid as Sir Austin's. Heavy Benson writes that Richard has been meeting Lucy, a farmer's niece and a Catholic, every day by the Thames. When Richard learns of Benson's treachery, he beats the butler mercilessly. The very next day he is summoned to London by his father, who lectures him soundly and tells him women are the ordeal of every man. Then he tries to make Richard confess to his affair with Lucy, but Richard says nothing. Richard is introduced to Carola, who delights him, but in a thoroughly unromantic way. During the first two weeks of his stay in London, Richard is sustained by notes from Lucy. These cease suddenly and he grows despondent. Upon his return, Richard learns that Lucy has been sent away to school at the request of Sir Austin, who has conceived a personal antagonism toward the girl—though he has received glowing reports about her from Lady BLANDISH, his friend. Richard sets out to find Lucy. On the way he becomes sick and is sent home. When he recovers, many weeks later, he is cold and despondent and he does not speak of Lucy at all.

Chaps. 29–34. Richard's dyspeptic Uncle HIPPIAS invites him to accompany him to London on a holiday, and Sir Austin consents to let the boy go, partly for the opportunity for him to see Carola Grandison. Tom, who has been selected by Sir Austin and Blaize as a fit husband for Lucy, goes to London by the same train. Richard tricks Tom into going to the wrong station and he meets Lucy instead. They fall into each others' arms and she agrees to marry him at once. Richard hurries her off to a lodging operated by his childhood nurse, Mrs. BERRY. With the aid of Mrs. Berry and Rip, who is working in London, Richard manages to deceive his uncle while he prepares for the wedding. He keeps up his visits to his London relatives, including Mrs. Doria and Clare. Walking in Kensington Gardens with them, Richard accidentally drops the wedding ring and it is picked up and kept by Clare. She did not see him drop it and she feels that finding a wedding ring while walking behind her true love is a good omen. Richard marries Lucy with a ring borrowed from Mrs. Berry.

Chaps. 35–37. Adrian, put on Richard's track by the jilted Tom, hurries to Mrs. Berry's house just after the departure of the newlyweds. He learns of the secret marriage. Sir Austin is forced to admit that his System has failed. Richard is not the perfect man after all, but simply a human being like the rest. He bears the blow of Richard's deception—which is to him far worse than the marriage—with philosophical resignation.

Chaps. 38–42. Anxious to effect a reconciliation, Adrian journeys to the Isle of Wight to see the honeymooners, incidentally bearing the news that Clare has consented to marry a man twice her age. Adrian remains a month, corresponding with Lady Blandish, who summons Richard to see her in London. Leaving Lucy in the charge of Lord MOUNTFALCON, a yachting acquaintance, Richard goes to London and arrives in time for Clare's marriage. His father makes no attempt to see him. Adrian is forced to invent all kinds of promises and

Richard speaks to the golden-haired girl on the bank

amusements to keep Richard from hurrying back to his bride. One night at a party Richard meets the glamorous Mrs. MOUNT, who wins his admiration and confidence. While Richard is waiting to see Sir Austin, he learns the true story of his mother and tracks her down to London, where she is living alone, having deserted her lover. Three months go by and there is still no word from his father. Richard decides to go back to Lucy, whose letters have grown sadder lately. That night he tells Mrs. Mount of his decision, whereupon she unlooses all her charms on him, and in spite of himself he succumbs in the privacy of her boudoir.

Chap. 43. Lucy has learned she is pregnant but has not told her husband. She does not hear from Richard for two weeks and assumes that he has gone in search of his father. Mrs. Berry, disturbed by the long separation between Richard and his wife, goes to fetch Lucy back to London. At the Isle of Wight she grows suspicious of Lord Mountfalcon's excessive interest in Lucy and persuades Lucy to leave immediately.

Chap 44. Sir Austin finally relents and comes to London to see Richard, who greets him with restrained calm. Richard has made no effort to see Lucy, who is in London with Mrs. Berry, for he is consumed with guilt for having made love to Mrs. Mount. Clare dies, wearing Richard's lost wedding ring, and the belated realization that she loved him all this time shocks and pains Richard deeply. Shattered by the events of the past six months, Richard goes off to the Continent.

Chaps. 45–49. Soon after Lucy gives birth, she is invited to Raynham, where Sir Austin receives her with fatherly warmth. He immediately writes to Richard, begging him to return, but Richard feels unworthy. At last he is told that he is a father and he hurries back to his wife and child. But their reunion is brief, for Richard has received a letter from Mrs. Mount telling him that her rogue of a husband, Lord Mountfalcon, paid her to keep Richard occupied in London so that he could seduce Lucy. Burning with anger, he challenges Mountfalcon to a duel to take place the following day. He does not reach Raynham until midnight. In tears, Richard confesses to Lucy that he broke the marriage vow by making love to Mrs. Mount. Lucy's reply is only that she loves him. She begs him never to leave her again, but he must go, though he cannot tell her why. Two days later Sir Austin receives a note telling him that Richard has been injured in a duel. He and Lucy rush to him, but the shock of the duel proves too much for Lucy. She falls ill of cerebral fever and dies without seeing Richard. Sir Austin breaks the tragic news to his son, who somehow manages to bear it and to survive. But if he survives, it is in body only, for his heart is broken. In spite of everything, Sir Austin still does not seem to perceive the error of his System and it seems quite possible that he will try to inflict it on his grandson should he ever get the chance.

The Oresteia and Electra

Trilogy of plays by Aeschylus, 525–456 B.C., and tragedy by Sophocles, 496–406 B.C.

Produced: *Oresteia,* 458 B.C.; *Electra,* 410 or 411 B.C.

THE STORY OF Agamemnon, and what happened to his family before and after his time, is a standard legend in the ancient Greek literature. Principally it is a trilogy, a series of three plays, by the great Greek dramatist Aeschylus. From his birth Agamemnon labored under a curse incurred by his father. Agamemnon became the commander of all the Greek forces in the Trojan Wars, but when he returned (not free of guilt, for he brought with him a new mistress acquired from Troy) he was murdered by the wife he left behind and her lover. This imposed upon his children the duty of killing his murderers and they did so. ¶ The story of one of these children, his daughter Electra, was used by all three of ancient Athens' great dramatists, Aeschylus, Euripides, and Sophocles. The Aeschylus version is the second part of the trilogy *Oresteia.* Euripides' *Electra,* presented in 413 B.C., was followed in 408 B.C. by his *Orestes,* which develops the psychological consequences of the matricide that is the culminating event in *Electra.* Sophocles' *Electra,* which is outlined below, may have been part of a trilogy, for such was the playwrighting custom of that age; but the other parts have not survived. ¶ Euripides and Sophocles similarly interpreted Electra's part in the tragedy: It was her resentment and self-pity that motivated her and caused her to impel Orestes to the act of revenge, when he himself had misgivings. O'Neill transposed this theme to a modern setting in his *Mourning Becomes Electra.*

Agamemnon

For 10 years CLYTEMNESTRA has been waiting for news from Troy, where her husband, AGAMEMNON, king of Argos, led the expedition of the united Greek forces to avenge the abduction of Helen by Paris, son of Ilium's (Troy's) king, Priam. Helen, most beautiful woman in the world, was the wife of Menelaus, Agamennon's brother. At last the long-awaited beacon signal, sent by Agamemnon out of Troy, flashes the news that the Greeks have taken Troy. When the HERALD delivers these tidings, there can be no more doubt: Paris and his Troy, and all sons of Priam, have paid double for their sin, as Zeus has willed, and Agamemnon, the victor, is on his way home. Over the general rejoicing ominous misgivings creep. The Herald cannot account for Menelaus's whereabouts. It is known that his fleet was destroyed at sea, and it is feared that the gods were angered by the desecration of their temples in conquered Troy. There are other old sins darkly mentioned.

Agamemnon arrives with rich spoils of war, among which is CASSANDRA, the seeress, now his concubine. Clytemnestra greets him, but Orestes, their son, lives with Atrophus the Phocian. Clytemnestra bids Cassandra enter and take her place among the slaves, but as Cassandra will not speak, nor move, Clytemnestra goes in. Now Cassandra foretells more crimes in the accursed house of the Atreidae (family of Agamemnon's father, King ATREUS): treacherous killing of a man by a woman; then her own, Cassandra's death; and more. So Cassandra enters the palace, though repulsed by the smell of dripping blood. The next moment Agamemnon's outcry is heard. The CHORUS OF OLD MEN are about to enter the palace to find out what has taken place when the doors are opened. Clytemnestra stands over the bodies of Agamemnon and Cassandra. She killed her husband to avenge her child, Iphigenia, whom Agamemnon slaughtered as a sacrifice so that the Greek fleet might

Clytemnestra beside the bodies

have fair winds to sail to Troy. Clytemnestra rejects the demon that haunts Atreus's house; vengeance has been done, therefore the house is now absolved from the madness of murder for murder.

Aegisthus, who is Clytemnestra's lover, comes out now and rejoices that a terrible deed was avenged. He is the surviving son of THYESTES, who seduced the wife of his brother Atreus. Atreus killed the children of Thyestes, excepting him, Aegisthus, and at a banquet Atreus served to the unsuspecting Thyestes the disguised flesh of his own children. When Thyestes divined the monstrous crime he cursed the house of Pelops, and so Atreus's sons, Agamemnon and Menelaus, inherited the curse. Aegisthus is now avenged. But the people of Argos are not satisfied with the prospect that Aegisthus, lover of Clytemnestra and plotter of Agamemnon's death, will go unpunished and be master of the kingdom. And though Clytemnestra tries to conciliate between Aegisthus and the people, a sharp clash in the future seems unavoidable.

The Libation Bearers

When ORESTES, son of Agamemnon and Clytemnestra, learns of the killing of his father, he returns from his exile in Phocis and arrives unnoticed at the royal palace in Argos. He is duty-bound to avenge the murder of his father. He discovers his sister ELECTRA at the tomb of Agamemnon, where she is with the LIBATION BEARERS to perform the sacred rites due to her father. Electra does not recognize her brother Orestes, and it takes some time and some proofs before they acknowledge each other. Once this is done, both know they have a sacred duty to perform: The murderers of their father must be killed. Yes, but the murderer is their own mother, Clytemnestra. Aegisthus only plotted the murder with her. But Aegisthus has to die too. Clytemnestra and Aegisthus are guarding themselves most carefully, expecting Orestes to come. Electra and Orestes agree that a ruse must be used: Orestes will go away, then will return disguised as a traveler.

And so he does. He returns and appears before Clytemnestra. He states that he has received a message for the queen from a foreigner, another traveler. Clytemnestra hears Orestes' message, and though she does not recognize her son she is uneasy and begins to suspect danger. She orders KILISSA, her maid, to go to warn Aegisthus and ask him to come to her. Now the Chorus interferes and argues with her not to send Kilissa. The Chorus prevails and she calls Kilissa back. Meanwhile Orestes is searching the palace for Aegisthus. They meet and Orestes kills Aegisthus. Now Orestes reveals himself to his mother, and while Electra urges him on, he forces Clytemnestra into the palace and kills her. And exactly as Agamemnon and Cassandra were laid out at the door of the palace, now Orestes and Electra place there the bodies of Clytemnestra and Aegisthus.

The Eumenides pursue Orestes

The Eumenides

The priestess or PYTHIA of Apollo's temple at Delphi says that a young man is lying at the altar begging for help from the horrid FURIES. The temple doors open and Apollo walks out, promising Orestes that he will protect him, for the gods demanded that Clytemnestra die for Agamemnon's murder. Apollo sends Orestes with the messenger god Hermes to Athens to beg for the help of Athena. The ghost of Clytemnestra appears, arousing the Furies from their sleep and demanding the corpse of her son as retribution. The Furies chant their desire for Orestes' blood, saying that "the hunted beast" has escaped their nets. Their howls stir Apollo's anger and he curses them, saying that they are not the shining gods of Olympus but dark evil forces out of the past. The Furies protest that they represent the tribal past, which demands the death of a son to repay the mother's spirit. Apollo says that the mother's death paid for the murder of her husband and that is more important. The Furies insist that it is worse for a son to kill a mother because they are of the same seed, but a husband and wife are not. Apollo refuses to acknowledge their claim of clan ties, and hurries off to defend his worshiper at Athens. The Furies also depart.

Orestes kneels at the foot of the statue of Athena at her temple, the Parthenon ("Virgin Shrine"), on the Acropolis at Athens. The Furies dash up to him but dare not touch him in the temple. The Furies howl louder, claiming authority to kill him, but Athena enters in a resplendent suit of armor. Athena demands an explanation of the turmoil in her sacred house, and the Furies try to incriminate Orestes. They then grant her full authority in deciding the case. Athena asks Orestes for his defense, and Orestes tells how his untrue mother murdered the great general in his bath. Learning who he is, Athena welcomes him to the city that is named for her but says that the old tribal gods cannot be swept aside for fear the earth will not be fertile. She says she will call a jury of twelve citizens and in the future this court will continue to judge cases.

Apollo enters the trial and the Furies protest because he is a god who can sway men's minds. Apollo confesses he told Orestes to slay his mother. Orestes and the Chorus of Furies exchange bitter words. Apollo testifies that Agamemnon was a great general who led Greece to victory over Troy, and says that the arts of men must take precedence over woman's fear of childbirth. Athena calls for the jury's decision and names the new court Areopagite, for it is situated on the Areopagus Hill, the hill of Ares, the god of war. Athena announces that the decision is split, with six votes for and against Orestes. Therefore she must cast the tie-breaking ballot. Athena votes for Orestes because "I am always for the male . . ." She cites her own motherless birth from Zeus's head as evidence of the unimportance of maternal ties. The overjoyed Apollo announces that the doomed house of Atreus is restored, and he leaves escorting Orestes home.

Athena is left with the embittered Furies, who threaten all sorts of dire punishment to crops. With the eloquent art of persuasion, the goddess of wisdom invites the Furies to come and live in Athens, where they shall have a temple on the Acropolis. She promises to change their names from the hated Furies to the EUMENIDES or bringers of good, who guard hearths and domestic life. The dark tribal gods of the country accept the offer of dwelling among civilized men in a shrine of justice. Thus Athena brings peace to Athens, salvation to Orestes, justice to the Greek world, and a quiet end to the primitive blood-feud religion that dominated the land. The play ends as Athena is led off the stage surrounded by a procession of Athenian women who lead a dance in honor of her, their patron goddess, and all-seeing Zeus.

Electra

The play opens in Mycenae, at the palace where ORESTES was born. Orestes has been led here by the PEDAGOGUE, or personal slave, into whose hands his sister ELECTRA placed him as an infant. Orestes says the oracle of Apollo has told him to be the sole avenger of his mother's crime (the killing of his father AGAMEMNON by his mother CLYTEMNESTRA). Orestes sends the pedagogue to spread a rumor that he has been killed in a chariot race at the Delphian games. Then, with his friend PYLADES, Orestes goes to present a tribute at the tomb of Agamemnon. Orestes prays he may somehow end the curse that has fallen on his house, the house of Atreus, since ancient days.

As Orestes leaves, Electra enters, in mourning. She curses her helplessness to destroy her evil mother Clytemnestra and her mother's paramour AEGISTHUS. The CHORUS, composed of neighbors, promises that some day her brother will return to seek revenge. Electra bewails her loneliness. She recounts the story of how Clytemnestra slew Agamemnon in his bath. The chorus warns that to dwell on ghastly details may twist her mind; Electra replies that to neglect the dead would be an even worse perversion. She tells the LEADER of the chorus how it pains her to see the foppish Aegisthus in Agamemnon's clothes. She tells of the insults she must bear for defending her father and for rescuing her infant brother Orestes from his would-be murderers. She concludes that there can be no moderation; one must fight evil with evil and kill too.

Electra's sister CHRYSOTHEMIS enters. She is clad in her finest clothes, preparing to offer a tribute at Agamemnon's tomb. She pauses long enough to rebuke Electra for being so moody and to counsel her to show obedience. Electra upbraids her sister for wickedly catering to the murderers of their father. Then Chrysothemis hints that when Aegisthus (who is away) returns home, Electra may be thrust into a dungeon. Electra warns her sister not to put Clytemnestra's offerings on Agamemnon's tomb, but Chrysothemis persists. Chrysothemis tells of a strange dream Clytemnestra had: She saw Agamemnon seize the scepter that Aegisthus has taken, and plant it; and from it a beautiful bough of fruit grew. Chrysothemis brushes away Electra's plea to join in a plot to kill the two murderers. She asks the chorus not to reveal Electra's words. Then she walks away toward her father's tomb, against the advice of the leader.

The chorus sings about the advent of Justice and the long mystery that has hung over the Atrean house. Queen Clytemnestra appears. She too rebukes Electra for sullenness. Clytemnestra defends her murder of Agamemnon by citing his sacrifice of their daughter IPHIGENIA. Electra defends her father's act: He was forced to sacrifice her sister, at the behest of the goddess Diana, so that the Greeks could win the Trojan War. Clytemnestra prays to Apollo that she may rule the house of Atreus in peace. The pedagogue arrives, disguised as an old man. He spreads the false rumor of Orestes' death in the horse races. Strangely enough, Clytemnestra does not revel in the death of her son, though she has long feared him. She says, "A mother may be wronged, but she never learns to hate her child." Electra's grief knows no limits. She contemplates suicide, despite encouraging words from the chorus. Chrysothemis returns joyfully from the tomb, saying Orestes must be in the vicinity; for she has found a milk offering on the tomb, along with a lock of hair. Electra tells her the sad news. Then she begs again that Chrysothemis help her kill Clytemnestra. Chrysothemis once more accuses Electra of lack of prudence but promises not to tell Clytemnestra. She rushes into the palace.

The chorus comforts Electra in her solitude. Orestes enters, with Pylades and some attendants. One of the attendants is carrying a burial urn. Orestes says he has come to find the home of Aegisthus, and Electra asks if the urn contains her brother's ashes. She again bewails the loss of "him whom I loved best on earth." Orestes can keep up the disguise no longer. He confesses his true identity and shows his sister his signet ring as proof. Electra and her brother embrace. Together they reaffirm their love for each other and their determination to carry out their dire plan. The pedagogue interrupts their speech; they discourse too lengthily in the midst of "deadly perils." Taking the pedagogue's advice, Orestes and Pylades enter the palace to kill Clytemnestra. Electra and the chorus wait to hear what will take place within. Together they tell how Orestes steals up on his mother, who is decking his funeral urn, and stabs her. They hear Clytemnestra's dying cries: "My son, my son . . . O, I am smitten!" Orestes returns to his sister to say that the ghastly deed has at last been done. The chorus warns them that Aegisthus is coming down the road and so the men hide. Aegisthus is joyful and asks Electra if the men have brought Orestes' corpse. Electra lures him to the house. When the corpse is revealed, it is that of Clytemnestra. Orestes then reveals

his true identity and with Pylades' help takes Aegisthus into the house to his death. As they leave the stage, the chorus announces that the long curse on the house of Atreus is ended.

Orestes leaves the dead bodies of Aegisthus and Clytemnestra

The Origin of Species and the Descent of Man

Treatise by Charles Robert Darwin, 1809–1882.
Published 1859. (NAL, MD222; ML, G27).

CHARLES DARWIN and Alfred Russel Wallace of England almost simultaneously published inescapable conclusions drawn from observation of natural life and millennia of selective breeding of domestic animals. Darwin's work was the one that became standard, so that his name is associated with the principle (Darwinism) that in certain ecological conditions animals well adapted to their environment tend to live, animals less well adapted tend to die, and the ultimate species must be those that are well adapted. Darwin anticipated opposition from those who would cling to not only the literal story but also the timetable based on the book of Genesis, but his anticipation did him no good. He was still made the devil, the serpent and the anti-Christ by tens of millions of good Christians who called themselves Fundamentalists, meaning that they accepted the Authorized Version of the Bible (that particular English translation) literally.

The Origin of Species

Chap. 1. The varieties and sub-varieties of the older cultivated plants and domesticated animals show greater differences than do the individuals of any one species or variety in a state of nature. Investigation shows that the main cause of the variation of the cultivated plants and animals is selective breeding practiced by man.

Chap. 2. In nature we find that the larger and more dominant genera tend to divide into the most species, and provide the greatest number of varieties. Thus, the larger genera tend to become larger, and throughout nature the dominant forms tend to become still more dominant by leaving many modified and dominant descendants.

Chap. 3. Throughout nature we find that there is a struggle for existence, that is, for the means of existence—food, breeding grounds, safety, etc. The struggle is not only one between species, but far more desperately between members of the same species. Witness the plant that drops a thousand seeds in an area that can support the growth of only one or two; the struggle among the seeds to germinate and grow is obvious.

Chap. 4. In the same way that man breeds his plants and animals by selecting those best fitted for preserving the characteristics of a breed or developing a new one, so does nature use a process of selection in maintaining or changing species. Nature's process I have named *Natural Selection*. In this process, those species, and consequently certain of the individuals within the species, that are selected are those which are best fitted by inherited characteristics to triumph in the struggle for existence. This triumph, which results in the continued existence of the species, is the *Survival of the Fittest*. As we look at the geological record we can see that certain species have continued to exist throughout the ages relatively unchanged, and that others have ceased to exist. Those selected to survive are the ones that have demonstrated their fitness.

Chaps. 5–7. Of greatest importance in survival of species is variation—variation to meet changed conditions of environment. That certain members of a species must vary widely to survive is shown by such anomalies as flightless birds, such as ostriches, penguins, loggerhead ducks. Yet under the conditions of their environment flightlessness is a distinct advantage, an adaptation to their struggle for existence which is responsible for their survival. The

483

change of the wings of penguins into swimming flippers is an example, for their only available food lives under the surface of the sea. The degeneration of a mole's eyes is to its advantage, since it has no use for the eyes, and if they were well-developed they would constantly be injured under the conditions of the mole's existence. It is absolutely essential for my theory that it can be demonstrated that every complex organ can be formed by numerous, successive, slight modifications of its simple ancestor. There is no known explanation for any alleged abrupt, profound change from simple to complex organ, whereas slight, long-continued adaptations to the conditions of the struggle for existence do provide the necessary explanation.

Chap. 8. It will not be disputed that instincts are of the highest importance to each animal. Under changing conditions of life, natural selection accumulates any slight modifications of instinct that are in any way useful. That canon of natural history, "Natura non facit saltum" [Nature makes no jump], is applicable to instincts as well as to corporeal structure. Instincts manifested in the young cuckoo's ejecting its foster-brothers from the nest, and ants making slaves, are not specially endowed or created but are small consequences of one general law leading to the advancement of all organic beings: multiply, vary, let the strongest live and the weakest die.

Chap. 9. The hybrids resulting from the mating of forms sufficiently distinct to be ranked as species are very generally, though not universally, sterile. This sterility has not been acquired through natural selection. The exact mechanism of the cause is not known.

Chaps. 10–11. The geological record is extremely imperfect; only a small portion of the globe has been geologically explored with care; only certain classes of organic beings have been largely preserved in a fossil state; the number both of specimens and of species preserved in our museum is absolutely as nothing compared with the number of generations that must have passed away even during a single geological formation. Therefore we do not find interminable varieties connecting together all extinct and existing forms by the finest graduated steps. Yet all the chief laws of paleontology plainly proclaim that species have been produced by ordinary generation; old forms having been supplanted by new and improved forms of life, the products of variation and the Survival of the Fittest.

Chaps. 11–13. If we make due allowance for our ignorance of the full effect of changes of climate and of level of land, which have certainly occurred with the recent geological period, and of other changes that have probably occurred; if we remember how ignorant we are with respect to the many curious means of occasional transport; if we bear in mind, and this is a very important consideration, how often a species may have ranged continuously over a wide area, and then have become extinct in the intermediate tracts—the difficulty is

not insuperable in believing that all the individuals of the same species, wherever found, are descended from common parents.

Chap. 14. The rules followed and the difficulties encountered by naturalists in arranging and classifying all organic beings in groups under groups, the wide opposition in value between analogical or adaptive characters, and characters of true affinity—all naturally follow if we admit the common parentage of allied forms, together with their modification through variation and natural selection, with the contingencies of extinction and divergence of character. If we extend the use of this element of descent—the certainly known cause of similarity in organic beings—we shall understand what is meant by the Natural System: It is genealogical in its attempted arrangement, with grade of acquired differences marked by the terms *varieties, species, genera, families, orders,* and *classes.* Finally, the several classes of facts that have been considered in this chapter seem to me to proclaim plainly that the innumerable species, genera and families with which this world is peopled are all descended from common parents and have all been modified in the course of descent.

Chap. 15. Of the material so far put forth, the truth of the following propositions cannot be disputed: that all parts of the organism and instincts offer, at least, individual differences; that there is a struggle for existence leading to the preservation of profitable deviations of structure or instinct; and that gradations in the state of perfection of each organ may have existed, each good of its kind.

I see no reason why the views given in this volume should shock the religious feelings of any one. It is satisfactory, as showing how tranistory such impressions are, to remember that the greatest discovery ever made by man, namely, the law of gravitation, was also attacked by Leibnitz, "as subversive of natural, and inferentially of revealed, religion." On the other hand, as a celebrated divine has written, "it is just as noble a conception of the Diety to believe that He created a few original forms capable of self-development into other and needful forms, as to believe that He required a fresh act of creation to supply the voids caused by the action of His laws."

One of the reasons that it has heretofore been believed that species were immutable productions was that the history of the world was thought to be of relatively short duration; and now that we have acquired some idea of the great lapse of time, and because we are slow in admitting great changes which we do not see in steps, we are too apt to assume, without proof, that the geological record is so perfect that it would have afforded us plain evidence of the mutation of species. The difficulty is the same as that felt by so many geologists when Charles Lyell first insisted that long lines of inland cliffs had been formed, and great valleys excavated, by the agencies we see still at work. The mind cannot possibly grasp the full meaning of the term of

even a million years; it cannot add up and perceive the full effects of many slight variations, accumulated during an almost infinite number of generations, as the agency giving birth to clear and distinct species.

When the views advanced by me, and by Mr. A. R. Wallace, are generally admitted, we can dimly forsee that there will be a considerable revolution in natural history. These views, as set forth in this volume, prove that, from the war of nature, from famine and death, the most exalted object of which we are capable of conceiving, namely, the production of the higher animals, directly follows.

The Descent of Man

THE DESCENT OR ORIGIN OF MAN

Chap. 1. It is well known that man is constructed on the same general type or model as other mammals. All the bones in his skeleton can be compared with corresponding bones in a monkey, bat, or seal. So it is with his muscles, nerves, blood vessels, and internal viscera; and also the structure of his brain. The likeness of the embryos of mammals, in their early stages, is also well known. All the higher animals bear some part or organ in a rudimentary condition. For instance, in man, the os coccyx together with certain other vertebrae, though functionless as a tail, plainly represent this part in other vertebrate animals. When we take these three sets of facts into consideration, and view them in the light of the whole animal series, considering the evidence derived from their affinities or classification, their geographical distribution and geological succession, we can understand how it came to pass that man and all other vertebrate animals have been constructed on the same general model, why they pass through the same early stages of development, and why they retain certain rudiments in common.

Chap. 2. Man at present is liable, like every other animal, to multiform individual differences or slight variations; so no doubt were his early progenitors. The variations were formerly induced by the same general causes, and the same laws, as at present; these were the struggle for existence and natural selection.

Chaps. 3–4. The difference between the mind of the lowest man and that of the highest ape is immense. Nevertheless, the difference in mind between man and the higher animals is certainly one of degree and not one of kind. The senses and intuitions, the various emotions and faculties, such as love, memory, attention, curiosity, imitation, reason, etc., may be found in an incipient, or even sometimes in a well-developed condition, in the lower animals. Our higher mental powers, such as the formation of general concepts, self-consciousness, etc., are developments and improvements on our inherited mental characteristics.

Chap. 5. Whereas animal species must have their structures modified by natural selection in order to meet changing conditions, man is enabled through his mental faculties to keep an unchanged body in harmony with a changing environment. He does this by inventing weapons, tools, stratagems, etc.—ways that are impossible to lower animals. All civilized peoples were originally primitive. In their struggle toward the civilized state, the law of the survival of the fittest acted on nations instead of on individual men.

Chap. 6. Man has a pedigree of prodigious length; the world appears as if it had been long preparing for the advent of man: and this, in one sense, is strictly true, for he owes the birth of his species to a long line of progenitors. If any single link in this chain had never existed, man would not be exactly what he is.

Chap. 7. The several races of man have all had a common progenitor. In their development, many races have suffered extinction along the way. We can see this process taking place today where civilized man has conquered the lands of primitive peoples, and the primitives, unable to meet the changed conditions of living imposed by civilized man, are dying out; e.g. the Tasmanians. Slight individual differences have been augmented during a long series of generation through natural selection.

SEXUAL SELECTION

Chap. 8. Secondary sexual characters are those which are of use in courtship and the rearing of the young. These play a direct part in the transmission of characteristics of the species. Secondary sexual characters which enable certain males to obtain more females will cause the characteristics of the males to be spread more widely throughout the species, and eventually to modify that species. For example, male birds with the brightest plumage will attract more females, and thereby will pass on their bright plumage to their male offspring.

Chap. 9. In animals belonging to the lower classes, the two sexes are often united in the same individual and therefore secondary sexual characteristics cannot be developed. However, in even so lowly a class as the *Crustacea*, secondary sexual characters are developed; for example, the fact that the males are usually larger than the females and have greatly enlarged fighting claws.

Chaps. 10–11. In insects the secondary sexual characters are well known: the organs possessed by the male for seizing the female; the brighter coloration of the males; the organs of the male for making clicking, humming, and other courtship sounds; the organs for doing battle for the female.

Chap. 12. Fishes, amphibians and reptiles all have highly developed secondary sexual characters. For example, the male stickleback's spines, a weapon used in his courtship battles; the bright colors of salamanders and newts, the large bladder that aids the bullfrog in his overwhelming croaking,

the rattles of the rattlesnake, the horns, spine ridges, and gular pouches of lizards.

Chaps. 13–16. Among birds are found the most varied and gaudiest secondary sexual characters. The ruffs, wattles, huge tailfeather developments, and bright colors, very few of which have any use in obtaining food or protection, are for the purpose of charming the female. Instinctual activities of certain species of the males during courtship, such as dancing before the females, are aided by the ability to expand and contract tail feathers and ruffs.

Chaps. 17–18. The law of battle for the possession of the female appears to prevail throughout the whole class of mammals. Therefore, highly-developed claws, horns, hoofs, and teeth are of great importance as secondary sexual characters of mammals. In certain species, the males' greater development of vocal organs, and their use during courtship, label such organs as secondary sexual characteristics.

In females of any class of animals those characters which attract the male are secondary sexual characteristics.

It is important to note that secondary sexual characteristics are passed on only to one sex; that is, male characteristics do not appear in female offspring, and vice versa.

SEXUAL SELECTION IN RELATION TO MAN

Chaps. 19–20. While there are obvious differences in the secondary sexual characteristics of human beings, yet the two sexes are less sharply differentiated than is the case in most species of animals. The law of battle for sexual favor prevails in man as among the males of other species of mammals. In mankind, both sexes attempt to add to their attractiveness by bodily adornment. The part that sexual selection has played in the history of man lacks scientific precision; however, man's elaborate courtship and marriage customs certainly seem to point to the fact that sexual selection has been responsible for the external differences in the races of man.

Chap. 21. The biological evidence for the descent—or ascent—of man from the lower animals is overwhelming. The process has taken place by means of natural selection, in which the particular mechanism of sexual selection has led to the survival of the fittest. The fact that man has risen from the lower animals by this process is good reason why the struggle for existence among men should not be abated by artificial means; better let it continue, and the fittest among men survive.

Othello

Play by William Shakespeare, 1564–1616.
Produced 1604. (PB, PL61; RE, 92).

IN OTHELLO Shakespeare produced his best drama and created his best villain. Also he wrote one of his most playable plots by the standards of the modern theater. The difficulty is that so seldom there is an actor good enough to play Othello and black enough to look the part. Some critics have called *Othello* Shakespeare's masterpiece and there is no higher praise imaginable.

Act I. 1. IAGO, an ensign in the service of the Moor OTHELLO, a Venetian general, complains to his wealthy friend RODERIGO that Othello has promoted CASSIO to lieutenant ahead of him. Spitefully, Iago and Roderigo arouse the sleeping Senator BRABANTIO and tell him his daughter DESDEMONA has eloped with Othello. Brabantio finds Desdemona gone and decides on a house-to-house search for her. 2. Iago converses with Othello. Cassio brings a summons from the Duke of Venice. Brabantio arrives to accuse Othello. But the duke's summons has priority for all and they leave together. 3. The DUKE of Venice discusses the impending attack of the Turkish fleet upon Cyprus and commissions Othello to lead the defense of Cyprus. Brabantio com-

plains that Othello has bewitched his daughter. Othello admits he has married her. Desdemona comes before the duke and says she loves Othello. Brabantio then blesses the union. Desdemona asks to accompany Othello to Cyprus. Othello plans to leave the next morning. Iago is to follow with Desdemona. Brabantio warns Othello to watch Desdemona, who deceived her father and may deceive her husband. Iago asks Roderigo, who is hopelessly in love with Desdemona, to accompany them.

Act II. 1. Off Cyprus, a violent storm has dispersed the approaching Turkish fleet and has delayed the arrival of the Venetian travelers. Finally Desdemona arrives, accompanied by her loyal companion EMILIA, wife of Iago. Cassio greets her as a matter of duty, but Iago plots to make Othello believe there is something between Cassio and Desdemona. Iago instructs the willing Roderigo in the details of his plot. 2. A herald proclaims general rejoicing in Cyprus for the deliverance from the Turks. 3. Iago gets Cassio drunk, and Roderigo picks a quarrel with him. The argument awakens Othello. Cassio is punished by being reduced to a common soldier. Iago then advises Cassio to ask Desdemona to intercede on his behalf with Othello.

Act III. 1. Cassio, on his way to see Desdemona, meets Iago. Iago promises him to keep Othello out of the way. Emilia arrives and takes Cassio to met her lady. 2. Othello asks Iago to join him in a walk on the fortifications. 3. Cassio is assured of Desdemona's help. Iago insinuates to

485

Desdemona pleads in vain for Othello's faith

Othello that Cassio's visit to Desdemona had an improper meaning. Desdemona intercedes for Cassio. Iago further hints that Cassio is in love with Desdemona and that he is finding favor with her. Emilia shows Iago a handkerchief that Desdemona lost. The handkerchief was given to her by Othello early in their courtship. Iago takes it and decides to plant it in Cassio's room. Othello returns and demands proof of the alleged infidelity of Desdemona. Iago tells Othello he has heard Cassio speak in his sleep of Desdemona. He then describes the handkerchief and tells Othello he has seen it in Cassio's possession. Othello is now fully convinced of Desdemona's guilt and asks Iago to help him carry out his revenge. 4. Desdemona is looking for Cassio to tell him of her talk with Othello. She runs into Othello, who asks her to show him the handkerchief he gave her long ago. She cannot produce it but cannot understand his anger over it. Cassio gives BIANCA, his mistress, the handkerchief, which he has found in his room. He wants her to make a copy of it. He does not know whose it is, but he wants a duplicate before someone claims it.

Act IV. 1. Iago works still further on Othello's jealousy. He arranges for Othello to listen in on a conversation between Cassio and Bianca. Bianca thinks the handkerchief belongs to another woman Cassio has been with, and berates him. She returns the handkerchief to him. Othello is convinced, and at Iago's suggestion he plans to strangle Desdemona. Iago himself will kill Cassio. LUDOVICO, a kinsman of Desdemona's, arrives from Venice with orders from the duke to recall Othello and appoint Cassio as his successor. Ludovico sees that there is dissension between Othello and Cassio. He also sees Othello strike his wife in anger at the mention of Cassio's name. 2. Emilia assures Othello that Desdemona is innocent. He does not believe her. Desdemona pleads with him in vain. He calls her vile names.

Desdemona then turns to Iago and asks him to help her win back Othello's love. Iago privately suggests to Roderigo that he waylay and kill Cassio. If this is not done, Othello will go to Africa with Desdemona and Roderigo will lose her forever.

3. Desdemona tells Emilia that Othello has ordered her to retire. She thinks he is less excited and hopes all will be well. She sings a sad song and then dismisses Emilia.

Act V. 1. Roderigo ambushes Cassio, but Cassio is only wounded. He wounds Roderigo in turn, and is stabbed in the leg by Iago. The noise brings Ludovico and some of the nobles. Iago quickly kills Roderigo to prevent him from disclosing the plot. Bianca arrives and Iago manages to throw suspicion on her as instigator of the attack. 2. Othello refuses to listen to Desdemona's plea of innocence, and smothers her. When Emilia returns to the chamber, he confesses the killing. Emilia had come to report the death of Roderigo and the wounding of Cassio. Her anguished cries bring on Ludovico and Iago. She reveals the truth about the handkerchief. Othello turns on Iago. Iago quickly kills Emilia to stop her from talking, then runs off. Othello, full of remorse now, wounds Iago, who is brought back as a prisoner by Ludovico. Letters implicating Iago have been found on Roderigo's body, but Iago refuses to explain his reasons for the plot. Othello then commits suicide. Iago is ordered executed.

Our Town

Play by Thornton Wilder, 1897– Produced 1938. Published and © 1938 by Coward McCann, New York.

THIS PLAY was a great departure in the American theater. Despite the prestige of its author, some observers despaired of it when it was projected; but it turned out to be one of the greatest successes in the history of the American theater. Thornton Wilder, in planning the play, drew on the traditions of the classical (ancient Greek and Roman) drama in having no established sets and in having an equivalent of the ancient chorus, the narrator who comments on the action and discourses with the actors. *Our Town* won the Pulitzer Prize in 1938. The innovational features of the play are self-evident in the outline.

Act 1. The STAGE MANAGER, the narrator of the play, enters. He describes the town of Grovers Corners, New Hampshire, on May 7, 1901. He points out the imaginary house of the Gibbs family on the right of the stage and that of the Webb family on the left. He explains that most of the people who are about to appear have since died. "DOC" GIBBS enters, on his way home after an early morning call, and stops to chat with the newsboy and the milkman. Mrs. WEBB enters her kitchen to prepare

breakfast. Mrs. GIBBS, after taking in the milk, chats briefly with her husband. Mrs. Webb rouses her children, WALLY and EMILY, while Mrs. Gibbs calls her children, GEORGE and REBECCA. The four children eat their food, talk of childhood desires, and dash off to school. Mrs. Gibbs, after feeding her chickens, crosses to help Mrs. Webb string some beans. They discuss Mrs. Gibb's desire to have a vacation in Paris, France, and her means of getting there. The Stage Manager thanks them, they retire, and he introduces Professor WILLARD, who reads a few stuffy statistics about Grovers Corners. After forcing the professor off, the Stage Manager brings on Mr. Webb, who is the editor of the local paper. He gives a few details on life in the town and is questioned by several people in the audience on matters of culture, drinking, etc. After thanking Mr. Webb, the Stage Manager sets the next scene. It is afternoon and children are getting out of school. George Gibbs and Emily Webb shyly discuss setting up a communication system between their windows, which are opposite each other, so George can get his homework done sooner. He leaves to play baseball and Mrs. Webb calls Emily to help her. Emily suffers qualms as to her prettiness and appeal to boys. As the scene ends, the Stage Manager sketches in the town's feeling of responsibility to the future and sets the scene for the end of the town's day. Off-stage sounds indicate that the choir is rehearsing. Emily and George, standing on two stepladders representing

Emily, dressed in white, looks around in childish wonder

their respective bedrooms, talk of homework and the brilliance of the moon. Dr. Gibbs calls George down to the kitchen, where they discuss George's allowance and his neglect of his chores. Mrs. SOAMES, Mrs. Webb and Mrs. Gibbs enter, comment on the brilliant moon and the choir director's drunkenness, and wish each other goodnight. Mr. Webb returns from his office, bids the constable goodnight, and goes into his house.

Act II. It is three years later. The Stage Manager sets the scene as he did in Act I. Mrs. Webb and Mrs. Gibbs enter their kitchens. The milkman, the constable and the newspaper boy meet and discuss the fact that George Gibbs is giving up baseball to marry Emily Webb. Dr. Gibbs enters the kitchen for breakfast. He and Mrs. Gibbs reminisce about how frightened they were on their wedding day and wondered what they would talk about for the rest of their lives. George clatters in briskly on his way over to the Webbs'. There he sits for a cup of coffee and some fatherly advice from Mr. Webb. The Stage Manager suggests showing the audience how George and Emily came to this fateful day and sets the scene by placing a board across two chairs to represent a counter. George and Emily enter, just out of school. After accepting George's offer to carry her books, Emily chastises him for having changed lately. He accepts her reprimand and suggests that they go to the drugstore for ice cream sodas. Emily is overcome with emotion and she enters the drugstore crying. The Stage Manager, acting as the druggist, comforts her with a glass of water and makes two sodas. George talks of his plan to go to the State Agricultural College, but suddenly declares that he might not go at all.

When he asks her to be his girl, Emily shyly confesses she always has been. George discovers he has no money to pay for the sodas. With much embarrassment he tells the druggist, who assures him that he will be trusted—for 10 years, if necessary. The Stage Manager reveals that the next scene will be the wedding. The stagehands set up chairs to represent pews in a church. Guests begin to fill the pews. Mrs. Webb enters, worrying about Emily's unpreparedness for marriage. George enters, suddenly terrified at the whole idea. Emily enters with her father, with an impulse to turn and run away. Snatches of the wedding ceremony are mixed with the comments of Mrs. Soames in the congregation. George and Emily turn and walk back, then run out through the theater. The Stage Manager says everyone can go out for a ten-minute intermission now.

Act III. Before the act starts ten chairs are placed toward the center of the stage. The scene is the cemetery and the chairs, occupied by characters in the play, represent graves. The Stage Manager tells of all the changes that have taken place in Grovers Corners in the last 9 years: fewer horses, more Fords. In a gentle speech he describes the cemetery and its occupants—Mrs. Gibbs, Mrs. Soames, and Emily's brother, Wally. Though not sitting stiffly, these actors do not move their heads when they occasionally speak to the "living" actors. Mr. Stoddard, the undertaker, enters and meets Sam Craig, who has returned to town for a funeral. Reading the different gravestones, they discuss the people who have died. The dead Mrs. Gibbs and Mrs. Soames talk of Emily, who has just died in childbirth. Men carrying an imaginary casket enter at the

rear, followed by mourners carrying umbrellas. From their midst Emily emerges. Dressed in white, she comes slowly down to the front of the stage, looking about in childlike wonder. She sits next to Mrs. Gibbs and tells her of all the wonderful things that she and George did to their farm and of her feeling of still being one of the living. Emily appeals to the Stage Manager to let her go back to the living for just one day, while all the other dead try to dissuade her. Though she wishes to choose an important day, they finally persuade her to pick an unimportant one and she chooses her 12th birthday. The Stage Manager sets the scene for her. Grovers Corners as it was in 1899. With wonderment and joy, Emily sees all the familiar sites of her childhood. The constable and the milkman enter on their daily rounds. Mrs. Webb, bustling in the kitchen, calls to the children. Emily, with effort, answers her. Mr. Webb enters, returning from a visit to his former college and bringing Emily a present. Emily is overcome with awe at how young her mother and father appear. She asks the Stage Manager if she can enter the house. When she does she appears to be 12 years old. Mrs. Webb gives her her birthday presents, Mr. Webb calls from offstage, and Emily suddenly cannot go on with the recreation of the scene. It moves too swiftly, she says, and no one realizes how wonderful life is every minute. She returns to her place in the graveyard. The various people in the cemetery talk about the stars that have just come out after the rain. George enters upstage and slowly comes toward the dead, finally sinking at Emily's feet. The Stage Manager enters, slowly drawing a dark curtain over the scene. He takes out his watch, remarking that almost everyone is asleep in Grovers Corners and wishing the audience goodnight.

Emily and George talk

487

The Overcoat

Novelette by Nikolai Vasilievich Gogol, 1809–1852.
Published 1842.

DESERVEDLY THIS is one of the most famous of all short stories (a long short story, which today would be called a novelette). There are passages in it so poignant that the reader is defied to resist weeping. The universal sympathy with the story and acclaim for it may be explained in the words of Jesus, "The poor we have always with us." It is probably unfortunate that Gogol felt impelled to give the story a supernatural ending.

The ghost demands his overcoat

AKAKY AKAKYEVICH is a poor civil servant in 19th-century Russia, a meek, lonely little man who is respected by no one and is constantly jeered at by his fellow workers. But he has a genius for copying letters and performs his work with the zeal and pleasure of one who lives for his job. He even takes work home with him to keep him company in his grim, barren flat, until it is time to go to bed.

One winter the terrible St. Petersburg frost sets in and penetrates to his back where his overcoat, an ancient, much-patched garment, has worn through. Akaky decides he will have to take the overcoat to PETROVICH, his tailor, to have the worn places patched. He expects Petrovich to demand an outrageous sum for the work and is prepared to bargain until the price is reasonable. He is totally unprepared for Petrovich's announcement that it is impossible to mend the overcoat, because there is nothing left of it. Akaky will have to get a new overcoat. The necessity for raising 80 rubles for it fills Akaky with despair. Actually he need raise only 40, for he has 40 saved up in a little box in his room. As for the needed 40, the only way to raise them is to cut down on his ordinary expenses for at least a year. He will give up his dinners several times a week, stop burning candles at night, walk only on the toes of his shoes to save leather, and in general do without everything he can possibly do without.

During all the months that Akaky lives under this strict economy, he is buoyed up by visions of what the overcoat will be like when he finally can buy it. At last Akaky has his 80 rubles and goes to see Petrovich, who makes him a finer overcoat than Akaky ever thought possible. The day the coat arrives is the happiest day in Akaky's life. He puts it on immediately and wears it to the office, where it is greeted with all the enthusiasm and excitement that Akaky could wish. Someone even suggests that they hold a celebration for it, and the assistant head clerk invites them all to come to his house that evening. At the party, a great fuss is made over Akaky and his overcoat for a few minutes, then everyone forgets about him and he is left alone, feeling awkward and uncomfortable. He finally leaves and starts down the deserted streets to his flat on the other side of town. Halfway home, he is attacked by two men who strip him of his overcoat and kick him into the icy gutter. Screaming in horror and desperation, Akaky rushes to a policeman who has been standing nearby and tells him what has happened right under his nose. The policeman denies having seen anything and advises Akaky to see the police commissioner the following morning if he has a complaint. The police commissioner seems far more interested in why Akaky was out so late than he does in the overcoat, and he makes no offer to help retrieve it. Someone in Akaky's office tells him of a Very Important Person who might help him. He goes to see this Very Important Person, who is not nearly so important as he likes people to think he is. He stamps his foot and shouts at Akaky, just to show how important he is. But Akaky becomes terrified and collapses with fright.

Somehow, Akaky finds himself out on the street in the middle of a howling blizzard. He makes his way home but that night he becomes sick and two days later he dies. Not long after, his ghost is seen by several people around St. Petersburg. The police are ordered to catch it and punish it in the most unmerciful manner, but the ghost remains at large. One cold night when the Very Important Person is on his way to his mistress's house, the ghost pulls him out of his carriage and demands his overcoat. Terrified, the Very Important Person throws off his overcoat, leaps into his carriage, and heads for home. The incident makes a deep impression on him and he stops stamping his foot at his subordinates and shouting at unimportant persons.

Pamela

Novel by Samuel Richardson, 1689–
1761.
Published 1741.

ON THE DEBIT SIDE of Richardson is
the too great length of his novels. On
the credit side is the fact that he explored his characters so thoroughly,
their thoughts and emotions, that he
gives them treatment in all dimen-
sions. Richardson was the pioneer in
the English novel presented as a series
of letters, a technique that has been
enormously popular from time to time
and is still employed now and then.
According to the story, he would not
have written *Pamela*, his first novel,
if he had not been asked to prepare a
guide to letter-writing. Writing sample
letters for his guide, he conceived the
idea of fashioning a novel from a
series of such letters. *Pamela* is very
long. Like *Clarissa*, Richardson's other
principal novel in letters, it is seldom
read today except in the course of
studying the English novel.

The novel is in the form of a series of
letters between GOODMAN ANDREWS, an
honest but poor teacher, and his daughter,
PAMELA, a 15-year-old servant. Pamela's
mistress dies, but her young master, Squire
B——, says he will take care of her. Her
parents caution her about the young master.
Lady DAVERS, the squire's sister, cautions
her not to let any young men get too near,
as she is very pretty. Mrs. JERVIS, the housekeeper, is like a mother to Pamela. She
suggests that perhaps Pamela is to be a
waiting maid to Lady Davers.

The squire kisses Pamela in the summer
house. She repulses him, but he charges her
with secrecy. Pamela asks Mrs. Jervis to
sleep with her, and tells her what has happened. Her parents caution her to come
home if this happens again. The squire
goes to Lincolnshire for three weeks. When
he returns he questions Pamela and Mrs.
Jervis. He kisses Pamela and she faints.
Mrs. Jervis explains how precious Pamela's
virtue is to Pamela. He says he will let her
go to her own home when she has finished
his waistcoat. Mrs. Jervis thinks he is in
love with Pamela. Pamela buys some home-
spun cloth and makes some simple clothes
to wear at home in place of the castoff silks
and linens the late mistress had given her.
The next day, the young master speaks
harshly to her within the hearing of JONA-
THAN, the butler. The other servants are
surprised to learn Pamela is leaving.

The squire entertains at a lavish dinner.
His guests are curious about Pamela and are
brought to see her, amusing themselves
with witty remarks in her hearing. Pamela

changes into her country clothes. The squire
sees her, and asks to be introduced, pretending he does not know her. He kisses
her and says she may stay a little longer;
perhaps she will be Lady Davers' maid.
Pamela is not receptive. She received a note
from Jonathan, warning her of the young
master. That night, as Pamela and Mrs.
Jervis are going to bed, the squire steps out
of the closet and tries to make love to
Pamela; she faints. The next morning Mrs.
Jervis resigns, and the squire apologizes.
Mrs. JEWKES, who is housekeeper at the
Squire's Lincolnshire home, will replace
Mrs. Jervis.

There is a rumor that the young squire is
to be made a lord. He calls for Pamela to
show her his court suit. Mr. LONGMAN,
the steward, begs that Mrs. Jervis be asked
to remain. The squire pleads with her, and
she agrees to stay. The squire tells Pamela
that he loves her and asks her to stay a fortnight. He promises to help her parents. She
wants to know what is required of her for
the 50 guineas he has promised to give her
father. He says perhaps he will get a husband for her—he knows of a nice young
clergyman, Mr. WILLIAMS. She refuses his
offer and asks to leave. He gives her 5
guineas and sends his carriage to her.

The squire has read all the letters Pamela
has written to her parents, through the dishonesty of the servant, JOHN ARNOLD, who

The lock has been changed!

carried them. His carriage takes her to his
Lincolnshire estate instead of to her own
home. He writes to her parents, saying that
she and the clergyman, Williams, plan to
marry. Goodman Andrews is suspicious
and walks all night to get to the squire's
Bedfordshire estate, where he is assured
that Pamela is safe. Pamela writes to
Mrs. Jervis of her journey to Lincolnshire. She is met by Mrs. Jewkes, who has
been instructed to call her madam. Pamela
is distraught. ROBERT, the coachman, begs
her pardon for his part in the intrigue; he

was only obeying his master's orders. Pamela
meets Williams, who has an apartment in
the squire's house. He asks her go to church
with him, but Mrs. Jewkes refuses to let
her go. John Arnold gives her a note confessing his perfidy and warning her of Mrs.
Jewkes. Pamela and Williams plan her
escape. He has a key to the garden door.
Pamela asks him to get her a duplicate key,
and to inform Lady Davers. Mrs. Jewkes
borrows Pamela's money from her, then
refuses to pay it back. A letter from the
squire asks her if he may come down to
visit her, saying that if Mrs. Jewkes is not
respectful he will send Mrs. Jervis down.
Pamela also receives a letter from Williams
saying that he has asked Lady JONES, Sir
SIMON DARNFORD and Mr. PETERS, the
local rector, to aid Pamela. All have refused.
He says he will help her escape if they hear
that the squire is coming. Pamela confers
with Mrs. Jewkes, who advises her to have
the squire visit her. Pamela ignores her
advice and refuses to see him.

Williams gets Pamela a duplicate key and
proposes to her. Pamela thanks him, but
refuses. The squire asks Williams to marry
Pamela and offers him the living (parish)
of the Rev. Mr. FOWNES, who has died. But
Pamela is to have complete freedom of
choice. Pamela resolves not to give Williams any encouragement until she receives
her parents' advice. Mrs. Jewkes promises
to return Pamela's money.

That night Williams is robbed and injured, but manages to save Pamela's letters
to her parents. Mrs. Jewkes goes to visit
him. While Mrs. Jewkes is gone, Pamela
attempts to escape, but a bull frightens her
and she returns. Williams confesses that
he tried to help Pamela escape. Pamela's
parents tell her to do as she wishes about
Williams. Pamela reads a letter from the
squire, intended for Mrs. Jewkes, saying he
will come in three weeks to decide Pamela's
fate, and that he is sending M. COLBRAND
to watch Pamela. The squire has Williams
put in jail for his debts.

Pamela plans to escape by night, leaving a petticoat in the pond so they will
think she has drowned. She is thwarted because Mrs. Jewkes has changed the lock in
the garden door. Pamela hides in the wood-
bin, but is discovered. She is very ill for
three days. She learns that all the servants
at the Bedfordshire house are in trouble
for speaking in her behalf. The squire arrives. He offers to make her his mistress and
settle money, jewels and servants on her
and to provide for her parents. At the end
of a year, he may decide to marry her. She
refuses. The squire leaves, supposedly for
Stamford. NAN, the maid, drinks too much
and Mrs. Jewkes sends her to bed. When
Mrs. Jewkes and Pamela go to bed, they
see Nan sitting in the chair asleep. Pamela
tells Mrs. Jewkes her life story, and goes
to bed. "Nan" turns out to be the squire
and he attempts to get into bed with Pamela,
who faints. Next day, he begs her forgiveness. He asks her if she loves anyone else;
Pamela says no.

Gypsies give Pamela a message warning her that the squire will try a sham marriage to her. The squire sends Pamela away to her parents' home. When her carriage arrives at an inn for the night, a letter is delivered from the squire, saying that he loves her and cannot bear to be separated from her. She returns to Lincolnshire and finds the squire ill. He gives her a letter from Lady Davers beseeching him not to marry Pamela, as she is beneath him. Next day, he is recovered and they go for a ride together. He confesses he considered a sham marriage but says he has reconsidered. Since he is the last male in his family, he must have a legitimate heir. He wants Pamela to meet the DARNFORDS, his neighbors, so they will know what she is like. He asks her to pardon Mrs. Jewkes. They make wedding plans and the squire readies the chapel. The squire is reconciled with Williams. The Darnfords come and Pamela delights them with her beauty and intelligence. Pamela's father also comes, as a surprise. Pamela and her father dine with the squire and his guests. All try to make Pamela set an early date for the wedding. The squire receives a nasty letter about his wedding from Lord Davers. He tears it up. Mrs. Jewkes warns the squire that Lady Davers is coming. The

wedding ceremony takes place secretly. Mrs. Jewkes attends Pamela, and Mr. Peters gives her away. Williams performs the ceremony. The bride and groom go for a ride in their carriage. On their return, Sir Charles Hargrove and two others come unexpectedly for dinner. They leave early, and the squire and Pamela spend their wedding night together.

Next day, the squire gives Pamela money to clear up her parents' debts. At Pamela's request, he reinstates the Bedfordshire servants. The squire is called away and tells Pamela he will meet her at the Darnfords' on Tuesday. As she is about to leave, Lady Davers comes with her nephew, JACKIE. She is very annoyed to see that Pamela is treated as the lady of the house. Pamela tries to ignore her insults, but she slaps Pamela. In desperation, Pamela tells Lady Davers of her marriage, then manages to escape to Darnfords', where she meets her husband. When they return to the house they have a long argument with Lady Davers but are finally reconciled. They go to Bedfordshire, where all welcome them. Pamela is reunited with Mrs. Jervis. John Arnold is to manage the farm in Kent which the squire has given to Pamela's parents. The squire gives Pamela his late mother's jewels.

Paradise Lost

Poem by John Milton, 1608–1674. Published 1667. (Viking, P44; RE, 35)

THE GREAT MAJORITY of critics throughout the history of modern English literature have considered Milton the greatest English poet (with Shakespeare excepted) and *Paradise Lost* the greatest epic poem in the English language. Milton, a stern Puritan, treated the Biblical account of the fall of Adam and Eve with faith, but he elaborated it from a vast store of knowledge of medieval angelology, ancient Jewish tradition, and apocryphal accounts. God, Satan, Adam and Christ are the principal characters. The poetic excursions into the philosophy and emotions of his men, and the descriptions of the great scenes that may be inferred from the Bible, are what make the poem great.

Book 1. Milton states his purpose in writing the poem: to "justify the ways of God to men." He then describes the flaming legions of SATAN, who has fallen into Hell with the sinful angels who contested God's power. Satan calls his most powerful underlords to a grand council at which they must decide how to avenge their lowly state. After he speaks, the palace of Pandemonium rises out of the fire and the infernal peers rush to the great debate.

Book 2. Satan first proposes another war against God, and is seconded by the fierce MOLOCH. BELIAL, however, suggests suing for peace. The devil MAMMON proposes that they make the best of what they have and explore the rumor that God has fashioned a new creature, whom they might seduce. Satan and most of the underlords agree that the seduction scheme seems wisest. Satan himself undertakes the task of flying out of Hell to the earth, God's newly-made land. At the gate of Hell, Satan sees his former lover, SIN, and their son, DEATH. Satan promises them that he will someday loose them upon the world. Then he flies toward the tiny planet of earth.

Book 3. God watches Satan's flight and tells his son CHRIST that man will fall prey to the devil's wiles. God pities man, but says that justice must be maintained; therefore man cannot be saved unless someone redeems his sins. Christ offers to assume mortal flesh and accomplish this task. God orders the angels to praise his Son and Heaven resounds with their hymns. Meanwhile Satan alights in the limbo of vanity around the earth. Assuming the form of a minor angel, he deceives URIEL into telling him where man lives. Then he moves on to Mount Niphates.

Book 4. Passing on to the Garden of Eden, Satan is torn by doubts about his mission. Resolving on evil, he then changes his shape to a cormorant and spies the happy life of ADAM and EVE. He hears Adam tell Eve that they must not eat from the Tree of Knowledge, and thereby invents a plan. Meanwhile Uriel, aware of Satan's deception, warns GABRIEL, who guards the Garden, that a devil is lurking among its fertile bowers. Despite the stationing of two angels near Adam and Eve, Satan changes into a cricket and whispers evil thoughts into Eve's sleeping ear. Gabriel and his angels apprehend Satan, but the arch-devil refuses to answer their questions and flies back to Hell.

Book 5. In the morning Eve relates her troubled dream to Adam, but he persuades her that such things have no meaning. God sends RAPHAEL to the Garden to explain to the first couple who they are and what force is trying to tempt them. Raphael finds Adam and Eve eating at an abundant table and then relates to them the War in Heaven, recently lost by Satan and his rebellious army. Only the angel ABDIEL, who joined Satan's ranks, saved himself by later devoting himself to God.

Book 6. Raphael then tells how MICHAEL and Gabriel marshalled God's forces for the first two days of the war. On the third day, God sent his Son into the battle, and Christ drove the rebellious angels into Hell. Christ then returned with triumph to his Father.

Book 7. Raphael then tells how God decided to create the earth and man to replace the fallen angels. He sent his Son and the angels to perform the work in six days.

Book 8. Adam asks Raphael about the movements of heavenly bodies, and is urged to turn his mind toward more worthwhile pursuits. Adam then describes his own impressions of the world after creation. He tells how he asked God for companionship and later, after falling asleep, awoke to find the beautiful Eve as his wife. Adam then relates the details of their wedding, their love and their promise to obey God's commands, particularly concerning the Tree of Knowledge. Raphael then returns, satisfied, to Heaven.

Book 9. The next morning Adam and Eve part to complete their daily routine of plucking fruit. Alone, Eve encounters Satan disguised as a serpent. Satan praises Eve above all other creatures and so completely fascinates the woman that she desires his knowledge and power of speech. Satan assures Eve that she can gain these faculties if she will eat from a certain tree. Eve recognizes the forbidden Tree of Knowledge, and refuses. At last, however, she falls victim to Satan and tastes an apple. Returning to Adam, Eve confesses her crime and the disgruntled husband also eats the fruit, fearing that he may lose his wife if he does not. The couple are overcome by lust, and later by violent dissension.

Book 10. When the crime is known in Heaven, God recalls the guardian angels, creates the seasons and sends Christ to earth. There the Son clothes the first couple, pronounces judgment upon them and returns to Heaven. Satan, meanwhile, having arrived once more in Hell, builds a grand highway to earth over which Sin and Death may pass into the world. He informs his rejoicing legions of his victory, but when a forbidden tree springs up in Hell, its fruit is nothing but dust and ashes. In Heaven God announces that the forces of good will eventually conquer the forces of evil. On earth, Eve wants to take drastic action against what she considers God's unkind action. Adam, however, remembers Christ's comforting but severe words and orders his wife to pray for their redemption.

Book 11. Christ informs God of the prayers of Adam and Eve, and repeats his desire to save them. God blesses the couple's act of repentance, but must enforce justice. Therefore he sends Michael and a band of angels to drive them out of Paradise. He also orders Michael to spread hope to men by revealing the future. Adam and Eve protest their explusion from the Garden, but to no avail. Michael calls Adam aside and takes him off to a high hill. There he shows Adam the world's history up to the great flood and Noah's ark.

Book 12. Michael then passes on to the time of Abraham and the coming of Christ. He tells Adam about Christ's death and resurrection, emphasizing that through this act the seed of men will be avenged against the serpent. Calm in mind, Adam returns to awaken his wife Eve, who also has grown more tranquil. As Michael leads them out of the Garden, a fiery sword waves behind the couple. Knowing that Paradise is lost but salvation can still be won, hand in hand they depart.

A Passage to India

Novel by E. M. Forster, 1879–
Published and © 1924 by Harcourt, Brace & Co., New York.

The purpose of Forster in writing this novel was partly, of course, to write a novel; but also it was to supply some protest against British insistence on retaining control of India. It is a good novel and was important when it was published because fictional descriptions of modern India and Indians were very rare. Since then the political situation has changed and there has been a great deal of very good writing, in novels and stories, about modern India. Therefore *A Passage to India* retains its importance chiefly in the history of the modern novel and as a story. It is a good story. Forster, like so many novelists whose works were highly praised in the second quarter of the 20th century, had strong socialist sympathies but they are only indirectly important to this book.

Chaps. 1–2. AZIZ, dining with his friends MAHMOUD ALI and HAMIDULLAH at the latter's house in Chandrapore, discuss whether it is possible to be friends with an Englishman. They agree that it is possible in England but not in India. Hamidullah asks Aziz to talk to his wife, a distant relative of Aziz. She asks why the doctor does not marry again and is told once is enough. He is a widower with three small children, who live with his mother-in-law. Aziz is summoned by his superior, Civil Surgeon CALLENDAR. Grumbling, Aziz goes but arrives after Callendar has left. Mrs. CALLENDAR and Mrs. LESLEY snub Aziz and take his carriage. Angry, he walks back, stopping at a mosque to pray. There he meet Mrs. MOORE, an elderly Englishwoman and mystic, to whom he is attracted. Mrs. Moore's son by a former marriage is RONNY HEASLOP, the City Magistrate. She tells Aziz of her younger children, RALPH and STELLA.

Chaps. 3–5. At the English club, tabu for natives, Mrs. Moore rejoins ADELA QUESTED, a young woman who has come to India to marry Ronny. Both women are eager to know more of the real India. Mrs. Moore mentions Dr. Aziz to her son, who takes a hostile attitude toward him. Collector TURTON has a "bridge" party (to bridge the gap between English and Indians). Among the guests are the two ladies; Nawab BAHADUR, a great proprietor and philanthropist; and Mr. GRAYSFORD and Mr. SORLEY, missionaries. RAM CHAND, a radical, refuses to attend. Mrs. Moore and Miss Quested try to meet the Indians on equal terms, ask Mrs. DAS and Mrs. BHATTACHARYA if they may call on them, and are baffled by Indian politeness. CYRIL FIELDING, principal of a small government college, is impressed by their kindness to Indians. Adela's attitude toward India distresses Ronny. He says the British are not in India to be pleasant. Mrs. Moore, a deeply religious woman, disagrees.

Chaps. 6–11. Fielding, who likes the Indians, entertains Aziz, the two ladies, and Professor GODBOLE, a Brahman, at tea. Aziz invites them to a picnic at the Marabar caves. Ronny arrives unexpectedly, disapproves of Adela's being with Indians, and is told by her that she cannot marry him. Later she changes her mind and agrees to marry him. Mrs. Moore feels her duty has been done and wants to return to England. Aziz finds Adela extremely unattractive.

Chaps. 12–14. After elaborate and expensive preparations, Dr. Aziz, Adela and Mrs. Moore board the dawn train for the Marabar caves. A huge retinue of servants and a mountain of provisions accompany them. Fielding and Godbole are supposed to come but miss the train. It is extremely hot when they reach the caves. An enormous breakfast is served because Aziz believes that English people eat all the time. Aziz entertains his guests with elaborate stories of ancient emperors. When they go into the caves, pitch dark, Mrs. Moore has a mystical impression of evil, loses Adela and Aziz, and comes out nearly fainting. She later mentions her queer impression to her son.

Chaps. 15–17. While Adela, Aziz and the guide examine the polished cave, Adela decides she cannot marry Ronny. She asks Aziz if he is married and inquires about his children. She shocks him by asking whether he has more than one wife. Adela is lost in the cave and a frantic search ensues. Then Aziz concludes that Adela is not lost but has gone to join her friends. He finds her field-glasses, the strap broken, beside the entrance to one of the caves. Later he thinks he sees her in the valley, talking to another woman. The car has brought Fielding and Miss DEREK, a friend of the police magistrate. The chauffeur says Miss Derek has driven back to Chandrapore "with the young lady." Fielding is troubled by this discourtesy to Aziz. On their return to Chandrapore, the police arrest Dr. Aziz. Collector Turton believes Adela was assaulted by Aziz in one of the caves. Fielding protests that Aziz is innocent.

Chaps. 18–21. Aziz in prison weeps and protests, but Adela's field-glasses are found on him. According to her story, he assaulted her in the cave and she hit him with the field-glasses and escaped. Miss Derek asserts that she saw Adela run toward the precipice and fall into a cactus patch; that she drove Adela back to town at Adela's request; and that Adela behaved strangely. Fielding is sure Aziz is innocent. Feeling runs high at the English Club. The Indians are near riot because Heaslop has refused bail to Aziz. Fielding insults Heaslop, is rebuked, and resigns from the club. The English regard him as a traitor.

Chaps. 22–23. Adela is recovering from shock, sun, and cactus spines. The case is to be tried by Das, who is Heaslop's Indian assistant. McBRYDE, the police superintendent, tells Adela that the defense has corrupted Fielding, who still insists that Aziz is innocent. Mrs. Moore is ill and seems unfriendly to Adela. Adela says she keeps hearing an echo; Mrs. Moore, alert for the first time, asks about it and, when Adela says she cannot get rid of it, remarks cryptically that she never will. To Ronny's dismay his mother refuses to appear at the trial. Adela has a sudden terrible feeling of doubt: Has she made a mistake? Mrs. Moore leaves suddenly for England.

Chap. 24. The trial opens with McBryde speaking for the prosecution. Everyone knows Aziz is guilty, he says. He not only assaulted Miss Quested but also crushed Mrs. Moore into a cave, to be rid of her. The Indians in the audience shout that Mrs. Moore was their friend, on their side. Mahmoud Ali, defending Aziz, accuses the opposition of abducting Mrs. Moore. Adela is called to testify. She suddenly has a mystical experience, relives the scene in the caves, and when McBryde asks her if Aziz followed her into the cave she says he did not. Pandemonium breaks out in the courtroom. Adela says she has made a mistake, Aziz is innocent; and she withdraws the charge.

Aziz finds Adela's field glasses

Chaps. 25–26. Adela escapes from the crowd, is plunged into a mass of Indians, and is flung against Fielding, who puts her into his carriage, calling to Aziz that he will come back. A mob of triumphant students pull the carriage off in a procession of victory. Adela and Fielding go into the college building. The police have struck, the college is closed, there is rioting all over town. Adela and Fielding discuss her strange behavior, deciding it was due to a hallucination. Heaslop arrives, refuses to come into the building because of his rift with Fielding, but tells them that his mother, Mrs. Moore, has died at sea. He came to get Adela but has nowhere to take her, since the British refuse to accept her. Fielding offers his place to her, saying he will be away for a few days.

Chaps. 27–30. Fielding tries to persuade Aziz not to demand heavy damages from Adela. He promises she will apologize. The English maintain that Aziz is guilty and that Adela simply could not face the court. Ronny, about to be transferred to another part of the province, thanks Fielding for helping Adela, whose passage Ronny has just arranged. But Adela tells him their engagement is broken. She agrees to write him from England.

Chaps. 31–32. Aziz repeats to Fielding the local gossip that Fielding has been having an affair with Adela. Aziz has decided not to ask for damages; he believes that Fielding intends to marry Adela. Fielding is conscious that Aziz is less friendly than before, and is puzzled. Business takes Fielding to Egypt, and he returns to England.

Chaps. 33–37. Two years later and hundreds of miles north of Chandrapore, Professor Godbole attends a religious ceremony at the palace of Rajah MAU. Godbole tells Aziz that Fielding has returned to India and is even now in the rajah's guest house. Aziz believes Fielding has married Adela Quested. After the trial, Aziz, vowing to have nothing more to do with the British, left Chandrapore to become the doctor of the rajah. He wanted to forget his English connections, so when he received a letter from Fielding beginning "I am married to someone you know" he threw the letter away unread. By chance he meets the English guests. The greeting between Aziz and Fielding is not friendly. When Fielding introduces his brother-in-law and Aziz addresses him as Mr. Quested, Fielding tells him that the name is Moore. Fielding has

married Stella Moore, not Adela. Later, at the religious procession, Aziz feels a mystic bond with Ralph Moore. They discuss Mrs. Moore and the fellowship of man. Friends again, Aziz and Fielding go for their last ride together. Aziz tells Fielding the British must leave India. "Whom do you want instead?" asks Fielding, "the Japanese?" Aziz says no, the Afghans, his own ancestors. In a burst of enthusiasm Aziz proclaims that, when the foreigners leave, Hindu and Moslem and Sikh will be all one and he and Fielding can be friends—but not yet.

Penguin Island

Novel by Anatole France (Jacques Anatole Thibault, 1844–1924). Published 1908. Published and © 1909 by Dodd, Mead, New York; © 1937 by A. W. Evans. Translated from the French by A. W. Evans. (ML, 210)

THE EARLY NOVELS of Anatole France were just novels. They carried no particular social or political message. Then, probably because he became interested in the Dreyfus case and was exposed to other writers and militant liberals who were overwhelmed by the injustices and abuses of the world's governments, Anatole France began to write novels designed to reform or at least improve the world. *Penguin Island* is a satire on the French and other modern governments. Like *Gulliver's Travels,* it is witty enough and imaginative enough (with a kingdom of penguins proposed as a parallel to European nations) to remain interesting reading even when many of the political allusions are no longer understandable except to a student of modern political history. In fact, *Penguin Island* is easier to read between the lines than *Gulliver's Travels* because the political system depicted is so much more modern.

Book I. 1–2. The Lord had sent MAËL, the governing monk of the Abbey of Yvern, a trough of stone, as an indication that his vocation is to convert the pagans on neighboring islands to Christianity. **3.** One day Maël learns that some of his first converts have returned to paganism. The DEVIL, disguised as a monk, persuades Maël to equip his trough with sails, so as to expedite the voyage to his faithless children. Maël hesitates, fearing the Lord's disapproval, but the Devil is an expert theologian! **4.** Maël cannot control his vessel and is transported to the polar regions. **5.** He lands on an island; there he mistakes the penguins for men and baptizes them. **6–7.** All paradise is upset by the situation. The saints assemble to determine the validity of the baptism. Can the birds be considered Christians? A solution is found: the Lord will change the penguins to men. **8.** The penguin people's island home, Alca, is moved to the Breton Coast.

Book II. 1–2. The Devil, again wearing monk's clothes, persuades Maël to clothe the penguins. And thus their troubles begin. **3.** The penguins set bounds to their fields. Property disputes cause fighting and killing. GREATAUK, a big penguin who murders an innocent little one, becomes a hero and

leader. **4.** The rich and powerful penguins in power vote against a just system of taxation; taxes should not be in proportion to wealth, for the rich must keep their wealth so that they may take care of the poor! **5.** KRAKEN, a shrewd penguin, marries ORBEROSIA, who had been the first clothed penguin woman. **6–8.** A dragon appears in Penguinia; he ravages property and carries off animals and children. Maël suggests that the dragon has been sent as a punishment for the wrongs committed by the people; history indicates that only a virgin will be able to deliver the island from the monster—but none can be found! **9.** Orberosia learns that the dragon is none other than her husband. **10.** The inhabitants organize a dragon defensive. **11–12.** Kraken no longer enjoys his dragonhood; he is frightened by the people who have joined forces to combat him. Orberosia tells him her plan: she will play the part of the pure virgin and will tame the dragon in front of the people. Kraken agrees to this plan. Orberosia tells Maël that the Penguin people will have to pay a huge annual tribute to her husband for their deliverance, else an even more terrible dragon will come. **13.** The plan is successful and Kraken becomes the richest and most powerful of the Pen-

492

guins. His son DRACO is the founder of the first royal dynasty of Penguins. At her death, Orberosia is adopted as the patron saint of Penguinia.

Book III. 1–2. A long line of powerful kings, including Draco the Great, issues from a cousin of BRIAN the Good. This unjust king transfers St. Orberosia's relics to Alca, where many miracles occur. **3.** The Penguins soon enter the Dark Ages. Unending wars take place between the Penguins and the Porpoises. Every Penguin who thinks differently from the others is immediately burned at the stake. **4.** The gruesome tragedies he sees at close range do not keep JOHANNES TALPA from recording these unhappy events and times. **5.** Art is no longer primitive and heaven-oriented, but becomes realistic and earth-centered. **6.** MARBODIUS, a 15th-century monk, leaves a record of his journey to visit the poet VIRGIL in hell. Virgil tells him that DANTE was incorrect in saying he believed in Christianity, for he believed only in his Greek gods. He also states that the dead have no life save that which the living lend them. **7.** Penguinia comes out of the Dark Ages into the light of the Renaissance, with its revival of learning.

Book IV. 1. The new rationalists doubt everything; they destroy St. Orberosia's tomb. **2.** The nobility and clergy are out of power; a Republic is established, but does not last long. TRINCO, a warrior, conquers half the world for Penguinia but then loses it, leaving the country with nothing but dubious glory to show for his battles. **3.** A new Republic is founded. In theory it is ruled by the people; in fact it is governed by a few of the rich, who care only for money and carry on wars for their own benefit.

Book V. 1. AGARIC, a monk, wants to overthrow the Republic and to restore Prince CRUCHO to the throne. He speaks of his plan to Father CORNEMUSE. The latter is against the project, believing it would be wiser to let the Republic die of its own vices; and besides, under the Republic, religion in general and Father Cornemuse in particular are very prosperous. **2.** Agaric ignores Cornemuse's advice and goes to see Prince Crucho, who is very willing to be restored. **3.** A cabal of royalists decides that the most prudent way to overthrow the Republic is to pretend that they want to do just the opposite. **4.** Emiral CHATILLON, commander of the Navy, is persuaded by the seductive royalist Vis-

countess OLIVE to be their Republican agent. **5.** Chatillon becomes the nation's hero. **6.** But the plan fails; the Republic survives, the royalists are defeated and Chatillon is shipped off to Porpoisia. **7.** Agaric goes to Cornemuse with new plans for restoration. The clergy is now being persecuted as a result of the attempt to overthrow the government; Cornemuse is now very poor; he will not listen to Agaric.

Book VI. 1. Eighty thousand trusses of hay are missing. Greatauk, the Minister of War, accuses a Jew named PYROT of the theft, though he has no evidence at all against him. **2.** Everyone believes what he wants to believe, so everyone believes in Pyrot's guilt. Rich Jews are hated; Pyrot is a rich Jew. **3.** Seven hundred Pyrotists (relatives of Pyrot) find evidence that Count de MAUBEC de la DENTDULYNX is the real culprit. The Pyrotists are sent to jail. General PANTHER, Chief of Staff, feels that proof must be found to convict Pyrot. Greatauk disagrees, believing that the best of proofs is none at all, for that is the only one which nobody discusses. **4.** COLOMBAN, a writer, posts bills throughout the land proclaiming that Pyrot is innocent and Maubec guilty. The populace is infuriated against him. **5.** But some people have listened to Colomban. Agaric goes to Cornemuse once more; the latter, his prosperity restored, furnishes money though still opposed to the restoration. **6–11.** The Pyrotists gradually increase to 30,000 in number. The Socialists enter the conflict, hoping that the governing classes will destroy each other and thus put forward by 10 years the growth of the Socialist party. The clergy enters and another of Cornemuse's predictions is fulfilled: the Republicans join together to turn against the clergy. Pyrot is saved.

Book VII. 1–4. EVELINE CLARENCE is anxious to marry but has no dowry. When she learns that one beau, the Viscount CLÉNA, has no money, she rejects him. She marries HIPPOLYTE CÉRÈS, a politician. **5.**

PAUL VISIRE becomes Prime Minister and makes Cérès a member of his cabinet. **6–8.** Eveline Cérès becomes the charm of the Ministry and Visire's mistress. Her husband catches the lovers in the act; but he must suffer quietly, for a Minister of Commerce cannot assault his own Prime Minister! **8–9.** His efforts to break up the romance are unsuccessful, but Cérès finally undermines Visire's ministry. On the day of Visire's fall, Penguinia goes to war with a neighboring and hostile land. Fifty years later, Mme. Cérès dies, leaving all her property to the Charity of St. Orberosia. Penguinia is now wealthy but lacks traditions, intellectual culture, and the arts. Money and ugliness reign.

Book VIII. 1–3. Although the present social order seems more firmly established than any seen thus far among mankind, the workmen revolt and anarchy reigns. Despite a temporary comeback, civilization continues to decline. **4.** Soon only animals are left in Penguinia. But then—enter the hunters, then the shepherds and we see history repeating itself in detail.

Penrod

Novel by Booth Tarkington, 1869–1946.
Published and © 1914 by Doubleday & Co., New York.

BOOTH TARKINGTON'S best-known work, *Penrod,* is a book about children but not a book for children. (Nevertheless, in its later years it came to be bought principally as a book for children and they seem to have read it, as they read almost anything they are given, with enjoyment.) *Penrod* deserves its great reputation. It is as funny as it can be and it is not really a distorted picture of a 12-year-old boy, his activities, and his friends. Booth Tarkington is almost sure to be longest remembered for *Penrod.*

Chap. 1. PENROD SCHOFIELD, dismayed at the idea of playing the Child Sir Launcelot in Mrs. REWBUSH'S pageant, climbs into his stronghold, the abandoned sawdust box in his father's barn. He helps his dog, Duke, into the sawdust box with the aid of an elaborately contrived "basket elevator." Taking out an old school notebook, he continues his work on a romantic tale called "Harold Ramorex, the Road Agent, or Wild Life among the Rocky Mts."

Chap. 2. Penrod lights a hayseed cigarette. He is scribbling furiously when his mother calls him to lunch. He is now in a much better frame of mind, better able to face the ordeal of the pageant. He pleads, cajoles, orders Duke into the basket elevator, but to no avail. Mrs. Schofield comes into the barn to hurry Penrod to lunch. He assures his mother that he will be right in.

The new king transfers St. Orberosia's relics to Alca

Penrod as Sir Launcelot

When she is safely out of sight, he dumps Duke unceremoniously into the basket and hoists him out of the sawdust box.

Chap. 3. Penrod's mother and sister, MARGARET, proceed to dress Penrod in their version of what a Child Sir Launcelot should look like. His costume is composed of tidbits such as the bodice of a salmon-pink satin dress his mother had before she was married; his sister's silk stockings, slightly gaping; his father's red flannel underwear, cut down and edged with silver braid; a borrowed Knights of Pythias sword; his sister's plaid golf cape; and powdered hair, colonial fashion. When Penrod sees himself in the mirror, he promptly throws a fit. Only by resorting to the threat of a telephone call to his father does Mrs. Schofield persuade Penrod to go to the pageant.

Chap. 4. Humiliated in front of the other boys and girls in the pageant, some of whom have elegant rented or tailormade costumes, Penrod seeks refuge in the janitor's closet. Mrs. Rewbush searches for him and finds him. As he is being dragged from the closet, Penrod feels a vital safety pin give way and hears the sound of a rip directly down the back of his costume.

Chap. 5. Penrod is persuaded by Mrs. Schofield to make his appearance in the pageant. When it comes his time to appear, he joins in a duet with MAURICE LEVY, one of his chief tormentors. He twists Maurice's wrist, causing him to writhe and moan in the middle of the duet. In Penrod's next appearance, he is supposed to kneel and take off his cape. This he does, revealing a huge pair of janitor's overalls, which he has donned to cover the split in his apparel. The sight of Penrod brings the audience to near hysteria, and the curtain comes down.

Chap. 6. Immediately after the curtain goes down, Penrod seizes Maurice Levy and gives him a sound thrashing. MARJORIE JONES, the apple of Penrod's eye, vows never to speak to Penrod again and goes

494

over to comfort Maurice. That evening Penrod is given a whipping by his father. Bruised in body and soul, Penrod retires to the sawdust box, accompanied by his faithful Duke. He continues his tale of Harold Ramorez. Strangely enough, the episode written that late evening had a marked resemblance to the indignities suffered by Penrod earlier in the day.

Chap. 7. Penrod manages not to part with the dime he has for Sunday School, by "losing" it at the proper moment. He goes to the Drug Emporium and buys a nickel sack of jawbreakers. The other nickel he squanders on the picture show, an impressive tale on the evils of drink. As he saunters home, he tries to think up a good excuse for the tardiness of his arrival home from Sunday school, musing upon the feasibility of a tale of rescuing a woman and baby from the outrages of a drunken man. When he arrives home, his lateness is not even noticed in the furor caused by the unexpected arrival of his Aunt CLARA and Cousin CLARA from Dayton. Penrod assumes that they are fleeing from the oppression of his Uncle JOHN, who *must* be a drunkard. Later, Margaret, explains to Penrod that there has been an epidemic of measles in Dayton and Cousin Clara's parents were afraid she might contract the disease.

Chap. 8. Penrod suffers from acute boredom in school. Spring has come, and Penrod is distracted by the sound of a hurdy-gurdy organ. He is inspired by the sight of VICTORINE RIORDAN, the girl in the seat in front of him. Her long braids are sweeping his desk. Unable to resist the impulse, he dips the braids into the purple ink of his inkwell. He carefully blots them, but still they make a few interesting marks on her plaid blouse. RUDOLPH KRAUSS, the boy across the aisle, inspired by Penrod, writes RATS in chalk on the back of the shirt of the boy in front of him.

Chap. 9. During the arithmetic lesson,

Penrod dreams that he has the power of self-levitation. He is soaring into the air, oblivious to Marjorie Jones, who is frantically pleading with him to come down, and then throwing wet kisses into the air. Miss SPENCE, the teacher, brings him down to earth with a jolt by asking him a question about fractions. Still in his dream, Penrod rudely demands that Miss Spence be quiet!

Chap. 10. Penrod is forced to sit on a stool in front of the class until lunch. After dismissing the rest of the class, Miss Spence demands to know why Penrod spoke as he did. Penrod makes up a story about his trouble at home. Curious, Miss Spence encourages him to elaborate. He divulges a frightful situation in which his mother and Aunt Clara are forced to sit up all night nursing little Cousin Clara, who is suffering from the bruises inflicted by her drunken father, while Penrod gives solace to a similarly bruised Aunt Clara and Mr. Schofield is at the railroad station anticipating the arrival of a wrathful, and drunken, Uncle John. Penrod finishes his tale by expressing a soulful desire to save Uncle John from the evils of drink. Miss Spence, carried away by Penrod's spirituality, kisses him.

Chap. 11. Aunt Clara meets Miss Spence, who is an old school friend. Miss Spence offers Aunt Clara condolences, murmuring that Penrod must be a great comfort to her in her hours of trial. Mrs. Schofield is so worried when she hears this that she cannot sleep. The next day she visits Miss Spence. Arriving home, she comes into the room where Penrod and his father are reading. Sensing what has occurred, Penrod disappears. Mrs. Schofield tells her husband what Penrod has done. In the meantime, Penrod has locked himself in the abandoned sawdust box. When Duke begs to be allowed into the box, Penrod throws a half can of old blue paint on him. Penrod's father deals with him appropriately.

Chap. 12. Professor BARTET conducts the Friday afternoon dancing class. For Penrod's benefit, he has Miss RINNSDALE, the youngest girl in the class, and GEORGIE BASSETT, the Best Boy in town, demonstrate a dance. Afterwards, the Professor announces a cotillion to be held the next afternoon. All the "ladies" are to go home directly from the class. Each "gentleman" will then make a formal call at a lady's home to invite her to the cotillion. Penrod runs all the way to Marjorie's home, only to be outdistanced by Maurice Levy in his chauffeur-driven limousine. Penrod finally calls on Miss Rinnsdale, the only girl who has not been visited. She accepts his invitation with tears of displeasure.

Chaps. 13–14. Penrod and SAM WILLIAMS, his best friend, set up an imaginary drug store with a collection of old bottles. They mix a concoction of the dregs of the bottles, call it "smallpox medicine," and feed it to long-suffering Duke. His reaction to the medicine makes them decide that it is potent to inflict on a human victim. At that moment, Maurice appears. Maurice drinks the whole bottle of medicine, thinking it is licorice water. He suffers no ill effects. Penrod and Sam go home to dress for the cotillion. Sam calls for Penrod and finds him up on the roof of his barn. Maurice and Marjorie Jones pass in Maurice's limousine. While waving to them, Penrod falls off the roof. Now he is exempt from attending the cotillion.

Chaps. 15–17. Penrod and Sam meet their new neighbors, an interesting Negro family; the father is in jail for putting a pitchfork through a man, and the big sister, Queenie, has a goiter the size of a melon. HERMAN, the older boy, has had a finger chopped off by his young brother, VERMAN, who has an interesting speech pattern, being tongue-tied. Penrod and Sam put on a side show to exhibit these interesting specimens, Herman and Verman. The show is a huge success at first. When business wanes, they are visited by RODERICK MAGSWORTH BITTS, who claims to be a nephew of Rena Magsworth, an infamous murderess. He is put on exhibition. Roderick's mother learns of the disgrace and informs the parents of Penrod and Sam. They are brought home in disgrace but later meet for sodas with funds provided by their parents, who have a sense of humor.

Chaps. 18–20. Penrod provokes BOB WILLIAMS, a suitor of his sister's, into giving him a dollar, which he promptly spends on a variety of circus foods and an accordion. He serenades Marjorie Jones and gives her brother a penny. After an acute case of indigestion, Penrod visits Marjorie. She is angry at him because her brother swallowed the penny.

Chaps. 21–23. RUPE COLLINS, a bully, attracts Penrod's fancy and Penrod begins to imitate him. One day Rupe tries his nasty tricks on both Penrod and Sam, and Herman and Verman attack him with scythe and lawn mower, permanently removing the threat of Rupe's presence.

Chaps. 24–25. The barber teases Penrod by calling him "little gentleman." Marjorie Jones continues this taunt. Enraged, Penrod turns to some tar in a cauldron, and the Great Tar Fight is on. That evening the minister, Mr. KINOSLING, comes to dinner. He inadvertently calls Penrod "little gentleman." As he is leaving, he finds his hat full of tar.

Chaps. 26–27. Herman gives an account of a Negro preacher climbing up a tree, "goin' to Heaven"; sliding down, "goin' to Hell." The boys go to Georgie's yard to practice this, within sight of Mrs. Bassett, the proud mother of the Best Boy, who is entertaining the minister at tea.

Chaps. 28–30. Penrod celebrates his 12th birthday by visiting his Aunt SARAH, who gives him a slingshot that once belonged to his father, and a penknife. Penrod's birthday party is sparked by the presence of FANCHON, a city girl, who teaches all the children the Bunny Hug. When the mothers discover this, Marjorie and Penrod are outside the tent. Marjorie, feeling snubbed because of Fanchon's popularity, holds Penrod personally responsible and has pulled him by the ear from the party. Mrs. Schofield is amazed that Penrod had no part in the dreadful display.

Chap. 31. Penrod breaks a window with the slingshot Aunt Sarah gave him. When Mr. Schofield finds out whose slingshot it was, he promptly forgives Penrod. As Penrod sits by the fence, stroking Duke, a note from Marjorie Jones flutters down. It states, "Your my Bow."

Père Goriot

Novel by Honoré de Balzac. 1799–1850.
Published 1835. Many translations.

BALZAC WROTE many great short novels but none greater and perhaps no other quite so good as *Père Goriot*. (Somerset Maugham placed it among the ten best novels of the world.) It is the story of a doting father who unduly sacrifices himself for his daughters, and very subtly Balzac develops the conclusion that the process has corrupted the daughters to the extent that they have been hurt even more than the father by his apparent indulgence. ❡ The problem of finding a proper English rendition of the French *père* has baffled all translators of this novel. Many have settled for the simplest literal translation, calling the old man "Father Goriot," but this is almost totally incorrect. *Père* is a familiar but condescending handle in addressing a person. Translators who have called the book "Old Goriot" or —better still—"Old Man Goriot" have come closer to the sense of the word but have not quite achieved it. The Englishman or American may speak even of a superior as "Old Man So-and-so" but would not dare so address him, whereas the Frenchman will speak not only about but also to a person as Père, father. The closest American equivalent is "Uncle," which cannot conveniently be used in translating because Uncle goes only with first names and Goriot is a last name. Since the problem has not been solved by many translators with their hours of study, no attempt will be made to solve it here.

In the year 1819, there are seven in residence at Mme. VAUQUER's boarding house in Paris. Among them are: Mlle. VICTORINE TAILLEFER, the daughter of a wealthy but heartless man who refuses to acknowledge her as his child and who has made his spoiled son his sole heir; EUGÈNE DE RASTIGNAC, an impoverished law student from the provinces, whose family has a title but little else; M. VAUTRIN, an inscrutable but jovial fellow; and "Père" GORIOT, a retired vermicelli manufacturer. Since his arrival at the boarding house six years ago, Goriot has sunk from apparent affluence to undeniable poverty. His fine clothes and his grand apartment on the first floor, which at one time caused Mme. Vauquer to regard him as a prospective husband, have long since given way to threadbare garments and the cheapest room in the house. He still receives visits from richly clad young women (who Goriot insists are his daughters, though of course no one believes him), but less and less frequently.

As his first year in Paris draws to a close, Eugène concludes that the study of law will never make him rich and that to be a success he must be accepted by fashionable society. Through his distant cousin, the celebrated Vicomtesse de BEAUSÉANT, he obtains an invitation to an exclusive ball. There he meets the beautiful Countess de RESTAUD, who invites him to call on her the following day. Returning late from the ball, Eugène peers through the keyhole of Goriot's room and sees the old man twisting a pair of silver lovebirds out of shape. The next morning Eugène learns that Vautrin has seen Goriot selling silver in the market place. Later, Goriot sends the houseboy, CHRISTOPHE, to Mme. de Restaud's house with a receipted bank-note. When Eugène calls on Mme. de Restaud he is astonished to see Goriot leaving. When he mentions his acquaintance with Goriot to the countess, he is coldly dismissed. He hurries to his cousin's house and asks for an explanation. She tells him that Mme. de

Restaud is one of Goriot's two daughters, both of whom married well because each received one-half of their father's fortune. Now they refuse to acknowledge Goriot or to tolerate anyone who knows of his shabby circumstances. Mme. de Restaud's door will be closed to Eugène forever; but he can still make his way into society through the other Goriot daughter, Mme. DE NUCINGEN, who has been eager for an introduction to Mme. de Beauseant for years and would do anything to obtain it. Eugène can promise to arrange it; in return, Mme. de Nucingen will idolize him, sponsor him and make him the most sought-after man in Paris.

Eugène learns that Goriot, after making his settlements on his daughters, kept enough for himself to live comfortably though simply; but the relatively little that he kept has gradually been bled out of him by these same selfish women, who continually get into debt and rely on their father for rescue. Horrified, Eugène befriends the old man and tries to bring him news of his daughters whenever he can. Vautrin, who has been watching Eugène's progress with interest, suggests that he make love to Mlle. Taillefer. Vautrin will have her brother murdered, so that she can become her father's heiress, whereupon she would certainly marry Eugène if he had loved her even in poverty. Eugène refuses to be party to such a crime.

As arranged by Mme. de Beauseant, Eugène meets Mme. de Nucingen at the theatre. She receives his attentions cordially and invites him to dinner the following night. Before dinner, however, Mme. de Nucingen asks Eugène to go to a gambling house for her and try to multiply her 100 francs into 6,000. Eugène succeeds in doing so. She tells him that she has a very important debt to pay and that her husband is a miser who never gives her any money, despite her luxurious surroundings. Eugène and Mme. de Nucingen grow closer, while Eugène is making a huge success in society. But before long he finds himself deeply in debt. Combined with uncertainty as to Mme. de Nucingen's affection, this leads him to renew attentions to Mlle. Taillefer, with whom he eventually exchanges vows. But when Vautrin congratulates him and promises that her brother will be killed the next day, Eugène begins to regret what he has done. His regret increases when he learns that Mme. de Nucingen has made Goriot sacrifice still more to set up elegant quarters for him in a fashionable part of town, so that she can meet him discreetly.

To prevent Eugène from warning Mlle. Taillefer's brother, Vautrin drugs him at dinner. When Eugène awakes the following morning, the brother has already been killed and Mlle. Taillefer has been named heiress to her father's millions. Shortly afterward the police arrive to arrest Vautrin, who turns out to be an escaped convict, known to the underworld as "Trompe-la-Mort." Next day, Goriot prepares to move into Eugène's new quarters. But both of Goriot's daughters come to him, again being

496

in financial difficulty. A terrible fight between the two women ensues, and this proves too much for old Goriot, who falls ill. Later, from struggling to the market place to sell his last few possessions, Goriot suffers a stroke. Ignoring his critical condition, his daughters attend a ball given by Mme. de Beauseant that evening. Mme. de Nucingen persuades Eugène to go, too, as she is at last going to receive the introduction she has craved so long. Goriot is worse the next day. He calls out desperately for his two daughters, but neither comes to see him. Goriot realizes that his daughters do not love him, and he dies. Mme. de Restaud does come, but too late.

The next day, Eugène tries to borrow money for a decent burial. The two daughters profess to be too grief-stricken to be seen. Goriot is buried in a pauper's grave. The daughters do not attend the funeral, but send their empty carriages to follow the coffin. Disillusioned at last, Eugène resolves to spend the rest of his life waging war against the heartless society of which he was once so anxious to become a part.

Peter Pan

Play by James M. Barrie, 1860–1937. Produced 1904. © 1938 by J. M. Barrie.

THE PLAYS of James M. Barrie have tremendous longevity and vitality and several of them are regularly revived, but the true perennial is *Peter Pan*. Many reviewers have read into *Peter Pan* all kinds of deep symbolic intents and perhaps they are right, but also there is the possibility that its author intended it simply as a clever fairy tale for children. The character of Peter Pan, the little boy who never grew up, is invariably played by a woman and usually by a middle-aged woman— Mary Martin first played it in her 50s. The most famous Peter Pan on the stage was Maude Adams, and quite likely the part was written for her. When she first played it she was barely more than 30 but she continued to play it all her long life on the stage.

Act I. At the DARLING household the

nurse NANA, a large Newfoundland dog, is getting the three Darling children ready for bed. They are WENDY, JOHN, and MICHAEL. Their mother comes into the nursery to say good-night. As she enters, she thinks she sees a strange little face in the window, but it vanishes quickly. Last week, on Nana's night out, she saw the same face in the room and screamed. Nana sprang at him and he leapt for the window and escaped, but his shadow did not have time to get out, and the window came down on it and cut it clean off. Mrs. Darling put the shadow in a drawer—she now shows it to her husband. Perhaps the little one has come back for his shadow.

Nana brings Michael's medicine; he objects to it. Mr. Darling promises to keep Michael company by swallowing a spoonful also. Thus coaxed, Michael takes his medicine, but Mr. Darling does not keep to the bargain: instead, he pours his own dose into Nana's bowl. The others cry that this is a terrible joke, and Mr. Darling, angered, chains Nana downstairs for the night. A few minutes after Mr. and Mrs. Darling leave, the nursery window blows open and in flies PETER PAN with the fairy TINKER BELL—a little ball of light with a bell for a voice. Tinker Bell flits here and there about the room and finally discovers the lost shadow in the drawer. Peter tries vainly to stick it on with soap. Suddenly Wendy wakes up. She introduces herself to Peter and sews on his shadow for him. He tells her that he ran away the day he was born, because he heard his parents talking of what he was to become when he was a man, and he preferred to remain a little boy. So he fled to Kensington Gardens and lived a long time among the fairies. Fairies, he tells her, began when the first baby laughed and the laugh broke into a thousand pieces and went skipping about. Now, every time a new baby is born its first laugh turns into a fairy; every time a child says "I don't believe in fairies," somewhere a fairy dies.

When Peter, who does not know any stories, learns that Wendy knows hundreds of them, he begs her to fly with him to Never Never Land, where he lives with the Lost Boys—the children who fall out of their prams while their nurses are looking the other way. She replies that she does not know how to fly and he says he will teach her. He also teaches John and Michael, who are awake now. The four of them fly off together through the window just as Mr. and Mrs. Darling return.

Act II. In Never Never Land, the Lost Boys eagerly await the return of Peter, for they are terrified of Captain HOOK and the pirates. Captain Hook is a sinister man with a hook for a right arm. He is awaiting his chance to get revenge on Peter, who cut off his arm and threw it to a crocodile. The crocodile liked his arm so much that he has been following Captain Hook from sea to sea, licking his chops for the rest of him. Were it not that the crocodile had swallowed an alarm clock, whose ticking warns everyone of its approach, Captain Hook would have been eaten long ago. Suddenly the ticking is heard. Captain Hook and his band flee, pursued by TIGER LILY, the Indian Princess, and her band of Piccaninny braves.

Wendy is seen flying overhead in her white nightgown. Tinker Bell, who is jealous of her, persuades the Lost Boys that she is a bird and they try to shoot her. But Wendy lands unhurt. Peter arrives and tells the boys that he has brought Wendy back to be a mother to them all. With the help of John and Michael, the Lost Boys quickly build a house around Wendy, and before she puts them to bed she tells them the story of Cinderella.

Act III. Peter takes Wendy to the Never Never Land Lagoon, where they try to catch mermaids. In the middle of the Lagoon is Marooner's Rock, where stranded sailors die. Peter and Wendy hide in the water and watch as the pirates drag in Tiger Lily, whom they tie to Marooner's Rock. Pretending to be Captain Hook, Peter orders the pirates to untie Tiger Lily immediately, and they obey. Just then the real Captain Hook arrives. A battle ensues between the pirates and the Lost Boys. Captain Hook and his men are defeated, but Peter is wounded and he and Wendy are left stranded on Marooner's Rock. Wendy escapes on the tail of a kite that has come to rescue her. Peter makes a boat from a bird's nest and sails to shore.

Act IV. As a bedtime story, Wendy tells all about the Darling family, whom John and Michael have completely forgotten. The story ends with a happy reunion between Mrs. Darling and her three children. Peter tells Wendy she is wrong about mothers. He used to feel as she does, but when he flew home one night he found the window barred and another little boy sleeping in his bed. The Darling children become frightened and decide to go home. The Lost Boys protest until Wendy tells them they can all come home with her. She is sure her parents will adopt them. Peter, who insists on remaining in Never Never Land, arranges for Tiger Lily to accompany them home. But their plans go awry when Captain Hook and his men attack the Piccaninny tribe and capture the children. Hook tries to poison Peter, but Tinker Bell intervenes in the nick of time and saves his life.

Act V. 1. Hook has brought the children to his pirate ship and is about to make them walk the plank when Peter comes to the rescue. At a word from him, the Lost Boys leap at the pirates and there is a battle. Hook gives the order to fire the powder magazine, but Peter catches the smoking bomb before it explodes and throws it overboard. Realizing that he has been defeated at last, Hook jumps into the mouth of the waiting crocodile. 2. Back at the nursery, Mrs. Darling waits with hopeful heart for her children's return. The nursery window is kept open for them day and night. Mr. Darling, sick with remorse for having tied up Nana, changes places with the dog. He lives in the kennel, while she

is treated as master of the house. Unseen, Peter flies through the window and slams it shut, so that Wendy will think her mother has forgotten her and will return to Never

Peter and Wendy hide in the water and watch the pirates

Never Land. But when Peter sees Mrs. Darling crying for her lost children, he decides to give Wendy up. He opens the window and flies away. A few minutes later, Wendy, John and Michael fly through the window and quietly creep into their beds. Finding them there, Mrs. Darling is overcome with joy. She and her husband agree to adopt the Lost Boys. Only Peter refuses to be adopted. He wants to be a little boy forever. Mrs.

Darling magnanimously offers to let Peter have Wendy once a year for Spring cleaning. But the following year, when Wendy arrives in Never Never Land, it is not the same. Peter has forgotten all their adventures together and he seems to resent the fact that she is a year older. She cannot see Peter so clearly this time and she realizes that soon she will be too old to see him at all.

Pickwick Papers

Novel by Charles Dickens, 1812–1870. Published 1837. (ML, 204)

PUBLICATION OF *The Pickwick Papers* (full title: *Posthumous Papers of the Pickwick Club*) made Dickens' reputation and could make any author's reputation. The book still has more of a following than any other single work of Dickens with the exception of *A Christmas Carol*. The Pickwick Papers are a work of genius and it is almost incredible that a writer who could have produced them before he was 25 years old could have gone on to write such immature novels as *Oliver Twist* and *Nicholas Nickleby* in his next few years. The great creations of *The Pickwick Papers* are the characters of Sam Weller, Mr. Pickwick's manservant, and Sam Weller's father. For today's readers *The Pickwick Papers* have the additional function of describing many aspects of English life in the 1830s more colorfully than anyone else has managed to describe them.

Chaps. 1–2. At a meeting of the Pickwick Club in London, four members are constituted a Corresponding Society, with the duty of travel, observation, and report to the club, each member being instructed to pay his own expenses. The four are SAMUEL PICKWICK, the founder of the Club; TRACY TUPMAN, AUGUSTUS SNODGRASS, and NATHANIEL WINKLE. They set out on the 18th of May, 1827. Their rendezvous is the Golden Cross. Pickwick has an altercation with his cab driver, which is broken up by ALFRED JINGLE, a strolling actor, who attaches himself to the party. At the Bull Inn, where they put up, there is to be a ball. After dinner, to which Jingle is invited, Tupman abstracts Winkle's coat, which he generously lends to Jingle. He explains that this is to be the official costume of the club, and that the large gilt button bears a bust in relief of Mr. Pickwick, in addition to the letters "P. C." They enter the hotel ballroom. Dr. SLAMMER, surgeon to the 97th, is paying great attention to the rich Widow BUDGER. This intrigues Jingle's sense of humor and he decides to cut out the pompous doctor. With no difficulty he arranges an introduction to

497

Mrs. Budger and proceeds to infuriate Dr. Slammer by monopolizing her attention—and her dances—and eventually seeing her to her carriage. This is too much for Dr. Slammer and he seeks satisfaction on the field of honor. Unfortunately, the description of his intended opponent given his second fits Winkle, and that bewildered man is duly challenged to a duel with a doctor he has never seen. Winkle dutifully selects Snodgrass as his second, and shudderingly presents himself on the dueling field at the prescribed hour. Dr. Slammer looks at him and shouts that this is not the man who offended him. The duel is off, much to Winkle's relief, and the two principals—and their two seconds—solemnly shake hands.

Chaps. 3–4. In the inn at dinner, a fresh quarrel is nearly precipitated when Dr. Slammer recognizes Jingle, but Jingle conveniently disappears. Next day Pickwick and his companions attend a military review. They get in the way and are rescued by a stout gentleman, Mr. WARDLE. He has come with his sister, Miss RACHEL WARDLE, and his two daughters, ISABELLA and EMILY. The two parties soon are on the best of terms.

Chaps. 5–6. On the following day, the Pickwickians set out for Manor Farm at Dingley Dell to visit Wardle. A carriage is brought to the door, a curious green box on wheels drawn by an immense brown horse. Another immense horse is saddled for Winkle. Tupman and Snodgrass insist that the honor of driving must go to Pickwick. The brown horse evinces a disconcerting inclination to back into the window behind the carriage. Pickwick loses the whip and unhappily asks Winkle to dismount and retrieve it. The horse evades Winkle's every attempt to remount. Further, it refuses to be led. When Pickwick descends to help his friend, the beast turns tail and gallops back to its stable. The carriage horse also runs away. Tupman throws himself into a hedge, followed by Snodgrass. The horse crashes the wagon against a wooden bridge, and thereafter is docile. Late in the afternoon the four men and one horse reach Manor Farm, tired, dusty, and footsore.

Chaps. 6–7. The first evening the Pickwickians meet a group of neighbors. Wardle takes them out for rook-shooting before breakfast, as a special compliment to Winkle, who is considered to be quite a sportsman. Winkle peppers Tupman instead of the rooks. Tupman has been struck by another marksman, Cupid, and aspires to the heart of Miss Rachel Wardle. Jingle reappears, and worms his way again into the Pickwick party.

Chaps. 8–10. Mr. Tupman makes rapid approaches but Miss Wardle is thrown into consternation by the realization that JOE, Wardle's fat servant, observes them. Jingle overhears Joe telling Mrs. Wardle of the romance. Jingle tells Rachel that Tupman is really making love to her niece, Emily. This wins Rachel's affections to

Jingle. He then tells Tupman that Rachel wants him to pretend to make love to Emily, to deceive the rest of the party. The farce continues for three days, then Jingle elopes with Miss Rachel. Wardle and Pickwick dash off in pursuit, but their carriage breaks to pieces within Jingle's sight. He laughs derisively and dashes on. Jingle puts up at the White Hart Inn, and early in the morning asks SAM WELLER, the boots, where the Doctors' Commons is located. Sam suspects a wish for a marriage license, and launches into a tale of his father's experience in that line—one that resulted in his marriage to his present wife. The pursuit party arrives, and Jingle is persuaded to give up his love for a round sum of money, whereupon Rachel returns with her father to Dingley Dell, bitterly disillusioned.

Chaps. 11–12. Tupman leaves Dingley Dell, but his friends discover where he is, and soon join him at the Leather Bottle, Cobham, Kent. The party soon returns to London, where Pickwick has lodgings with a widow, Mrs. BARDELL. Pickwick decides that he needs a manservant. He is so clumsy in explaining to Mrs. Bardell what he wants that she thinks she is receiving a proposal of marriage, and faints. Pickwick hires Sam Weller as his manservant.

Chaps. 13–16. The next journey of the Pickwickians is to Eatanswill, where they are invited by Mr. PERKER. The town is in the throes of a parliamentary election, and some of the Pickwickians are guests of Mr. POTT, editor of the paper that supports Perker's candidate. Those for whom Pott has no room stay at the inn. On their second day they attend a reception, at which they see Jingle, to their amazement. Jingle avoids them and soon departs. Sam makes friends with Jingle's servant, JOB TROTTER, who says that Jingle plans to elope with a student in a local girls' school. When Pickwick attempts to stand guard and is caught by the headmistress for his pains, they learn that this was merely a joke on Job's part.

Chaps. 17–19. Pickwick suffers an attack of rheumatism. Next he receives notice that Mrs. Bardell is suing him for breach of promise. He worries more about missing a shooting match than about the suit. To escape the process-servers, he hides in a large wheelbarrow, which Sam Weller trundles along behind the hunters. He has narrow escapes from Tupman's and Winkle's guns—which menace more than the game.

Chaps. 20–24. The lawsuit can no longer be ignored. Pickwick sets out to see Perker for legal advice. He meets Sam Weller's father en route, and although he does not immediately find Mr. Perker, he is entertained by the clerks. Pickwick, Sam, and PETER MAGNUS, who is on his way to propose to a woman, ride together in the Ipswich coach. Later, Pickwick loses his way in the unfamiliar corridors of the hotel and eventually reaches what he supposes to be his own room. He is already in one of the twin beds when a woman enters. He is obviously in the wrong room. After ill-re-

ceived explanations, Pickwick gets out. The next evening he meets the woman Peter Magnus wishes to marry, and discovers to his embarrassment that it is the woman of the wrong room, who recognizes him even without his nightcap.

Chaps. 25–31. Jingle is exposed in another matrimonial escapade, this time with the mayor's daughter. Pickwick returns to London to attend to the Bardell suit. He enjoys a brief respite at Christmas. Winkle falls desperately in love with ARABELLA ALLEN, a guest of the Wardles', where the Pickwickians spend the holiday. Immediately afterward, Pickwick is deeply enmeshed in the toils of the law.

Chaps. 32–35. Pickwick's case comes up in court on St. Valentine's Day. After proceedings verging on the farcical, Pickwick is ordered to pay £750 to the injured Mrs. Bardell. He stoutly declares he will never pay. Nothing more can be done for at least two months, and Pickwick philosophically decides to enjoy himself while he is still at liberty to do so. He spends the two months at Bath, with his friends.

Chaps. 36–40. Winkle learns to his delight that Arabella has chosen him. At the end of the second month, Pickwick returns to London and is immediately accosted by a sheriff's deputy. He refuses again to make any payment and is committed to debtors' prison.

Chaps. 41–48. In the debtors' prison Pickwick sees a side of life that is completely strange to him—a sordid, squalid side. He can release himself at will by paying the judgment, but he is stubborn for a long time. He is surprised to see Jingle and Job Trotter in the prison also. Sam Weller—faithful servitor—gets himself committed on a trumped-up complaint signed by his father, so that he can be with his master. In a final touch of absurdity, Mrs. Bardell too is put in the debtors' prison—for failing to pay her lawyers. Pickwick yields finally to the pleas of his friends, and pays his way out. Winkle is married to Arabella.

Chaps. 49–58. After his release from

Mr. Pickwick in prison

498

prison, Pickwick devotes some time to helping all his friends straighten out their various problems. His kindness even carries over to Jingle, for whom he obtains a post in Demerara, to which the faithful Job goes with him. With the marriage of Snodgrass to Emily Wardle, the Pickwickians have all been settled in spots of their own choosing. The Pickwick Club is quietly dissolved.

The Picture of Dorian Gray

Novel by Oscar Wilde, 1856–1900. Published 1891. (Viking, P16)

IN ADDITION TO BEING a very clever idea, *The Picture of Dorian Gray* was used by its clever author to exploit his own genius at witty conversation and aphorisms, so that the novel sparkles with slightly outrageous but never wholly untenable reflections on fashionable life. This is really an excellent novel in many respects.

Chaps. 1–2. Lord HENRY WOTTON arrives at the studio of his friend BASIL HALLWARD and gazes with rapt admiration at the unfinished portrait of a beautiful young man. Henry is witty, sophisticated, debonaire, and cynical. He inquires about the portrait, which he feels is the painter's finest to date. Where will it be exhibited? Basil replies that he is not going to exhibit it, that he has put too much of himself into it. Basil explains that from the first moment he laid eyes upon the subject, DORIAN GRAY, he felt a strange and passionate affinity for the exquisite young man. Henry is intrigued and desires to meet the magical Dorian. Basil says he will not allow such a meeting, lest Dorian become spoiled. At this moment Dorian arrives for a sitting. Basil cannot induce Henry to leave. Henry charms Dorian with his melodious and insidious flow of words, while Basil paints in oblivion. He tells Dorian that his beauty is astonishing, but that it will pass, for youth is fleeting. Basil finishes the painting. Henry is delighted with it, but Dorian flies into a petulant fit of annoyance and jealousy over it, for it will never age and lose its beauty, whereas he knows that he himself will; he would give his soul if only he could stay always young and let the portrait do the aging.

Chaps. 3–4. Henry investigates Dorian's parentage and discovers that he is the offspring of a romantic marriage between a beautiful noblewoman and a poverty-stricken unknown who was killed in a duel.

Dorian takes Basil to his private room and shows him the portrait

The girl died too, soon after Dorian's birth. Henry is entranced by his power to mold, influence and direct the development of the young man's character. He delights Dorian with his mastery of words. On a later occasion Dorian meets Henry's wife, an abrupt, flighty person. Dorian falls in love with an actress, SIBYL VANE. Henry tells him that he will have other loves, that people who only love once in their lives are shallow. The next day a telegram arrives announcing the engagement of Dorian to Sibyl.

Chaps. 5–8. Sibyl calls Dorian "Prince Charming" and is ecstatic with happiness, while her old mother scolds and asks whether the gentleman has money. Sibyl's young brother, JAMES, goes to sea. Just as he is leaving he learns that his mother was not married to his father—a "gentleman with connections." He is angry and suspicious of the new "gentleman" who is courting his sister and swears that if this gentleman ever does a wrong to his sister he will ferret him out and kill him. Basil Hallward is dismayed by the engagement. Dorian insists that Basil and Henry come to see Sibyl play Juliet. The three attend the play; to Dorian's horror and the audience's disgust, Sibyl plays Juliet stiffly and emotionlessly. Dorian tearfully apologizes to his companions. Backstage after the play, Sibyl tells Dorian that her love for him is the cause of her bad acting; this love is the first real thing that has come into her life. Dorian blurts out that she has killed his love for her. "You used to stir my imagination. Now you don't even stir my curiosity." Sibyl falls to the floor, distraught, and Dorian coldly walks out. At home he notices that Basil's portrait of him has altered. The mouth has become cruel. He remembers his wish that the portrait might alter rather than his own face. In trembling regret he decides that he must marry Sibyl. In the morning Henry informs him that Sibyl is dead, a suicide. With soothing words Henry declares that Dorian has had a "marvelous experience." Won over, Dorian decides to plunge into a life of sensuous abandonment

—the portrait will have to take the consequences.

Chaps. 9–11. Basil comes to commiserate with Dorian and is astounded to find Dorian coldly indifferent. Basil wants to borrow the painting to show it at an exhibition. Caught in a predicament, Dorian remembers that Basil, too, has a secret about the painting. He questions Basil and elicits a confession of Basil's infatuation with Dorian at the time the portrait was painted. Dorian uses this as a pretext not to permit Basil to see or borrow the portrait. Fearful that someone might see the face of his soul, Dorian hides the portrait in a room at the top of the house. Dorian receives as a present from Henry a book about the outlandish passions of a young Parisienne. Weird, poisonous, and profoundly corrupt, the book comes to dominate his development. Dorian begins to seek strange and sensuous pleasures—the strange rhythms and harmonies of little-known music, the voluptuousness of rare jewels, tapestries and supremely sheer silks, exotic perfumes, and the mysteries of Catholic ritual and Eastern religions. Rumor also has it that he indulges in esoteric vice in obscure parts of London. His face remains young and innocent, but his name becomes anathema in social circles. Often he looks upon the increasingly evil face of his portrait and compares it with his own, and trembles lest anyone else gain access to the room.

Chaps. 12–14. Before leaving for Paris, Basil Hallward stops in to see Dorian. He points out to Dorian the great corruption and disgrace all of Dorian's friends have fallen into, and asks him if the rumors of evil are true. He says he must see into Dorian's soul to know. Dorian takes him to the little room and there throws the cover off the portrait. Basil stands incredulous, horror-struck, and terrified. He cries out to Dorian to repent, to pray, that it is not too late to save himself. Dorian weeps that it is too late. Suddenly in rage and hatred, he seizes a knife and stabs Basil many times. Next day, Dorian summons ALAN CAMPBELL, a friend of former times. He tells Alan of the crime and begs him to dispose of the body. Alan refuses until Dorian threatens him with a blackmail letter of terrible import. Alan's laboratory tools are fetched—a burner and some acids—and Alan goes into the death-room. Hours later he emerges, white and speechless, and departs. Dorian goes to the room; there is a strong smell of acid, but no other trace of the corpse. To Dorian's unspeakable horror, he sees that the hand of his painted portrait is covered with painted blood!

Chaps. 15–18. The following night, Dorian attends a dinner party. The conversation is witty, but Dorian is distracted. He leaves early, overcome by a fit of terror. Dressed in common clothes, he takes a cab to a sordid quarter of London. He craves ugliness because it makes things real. Dorian knows that exculpation is impossible, but at least he can achieve forgetfulness through opium. He enters an opium den. At sight of an acquaintance whose downfall was Basil's doing, Dorian decides to go elsewhere. As he departs, a frowzy woman calls him "Prince Charming," and a sailor leaps up, follows him, seizes him, and prepares to shoot him. It is James Vane, Sibyl's brother. Dorian, terrified, saves himself by pointing to his own boylike face and insisting that it could not have been he who drove a girl to suicide 18 years ago. Soon afterward, however, James learns of Dorian's

perpetual youth and realizes that he has been duped. A week later, at a party in his own house, Dorian suddenly swoons; he has seen the face of James Vane pressed against a window. Some days later, at a shooting party, a friend of Dorian accidentally kills a man hidden in the bush. To Dorian's extreme relief, it turns out to be James Vane.

Chaps. 19–20. Dorian informs Henry that he is going to reform—that he has already done a good deed to a girl by not ruining her. They discuss the gossip about Basil Hallward's disappearance, about Alan Campbell's suicide, and about Henry's recent divorce after the elopement of his wife with another man. Henry urges Dorian not to spoil himself by renunciations. Dorian looks at his portrait, expecting to see it improved through his recent good deed. To his indignation he sees only new lines about the mouth that makes it appear hypocritical. He realizes that his "good deed" was impelled merely by vanity. Furious, Dorian decides to destroy the too-revealing portrait. He stabs the canvas with a knife. An agonizing cry rends the air. The servants enter to find on the wall the portrait of a young and beautiful Dorian Gray, while on the floor, a knife in its heart, lies a corpse "withered, wrinkled, and loathsome of visage."

Pilgrim's Progress

Novel by John Bunyan, 1628–1688. Published 1678. (PB, PL53)

NEXT TO THE Holy Bible, *Pilgrim's Progress* is the biggest-selling book in English history and perhaps in the history of any country. It is an allegory, abstractions being represented by persons. Bunyan wrote the book while in jail. He was not an educated man but he had read the Bible (the magnificent "King James" version) so much that his book not only resembled it in style and drew on it for content but in spots even approached it as literature.

The author, walking through the wilderness of the world, rests in a cave where he falls asleep. There suddenly appears to him the miraculous vision of a ragged man named CHRISTIAN. Christian senses that the City of Destruction in which he lives is doomed. He tries to persuade his wife, children and relatives to flee with him, but they will not heed his warning. Christian meets the EVANGELIST, who assures him that his premonition of destruction is true and advises him to seek salvation in death. As Christian runs out of the City of Destruction, he is pursued by OBSTINATE, who begs him to return. For a time another neighbor, PLIABLE, consents to follow Christian. Difficulty, however, Christian soon sheds these false companions. The hill is so steep that Christian falls into a weary sleep. By

Christian's path. When Christian tumbles into the Slough of Despond, Pliable rushes back to the city.

Christian is rescued from the swamp of despair by HELP. According to Help, every virtuous man who tries to save his soul sometimes falls into the mire of doubt. Continuing on his journey alone, Christian encounters Mr. WORLDLY WISEMAN. This elegant gentleman tries to persuade Christian to abandon his search for salvation and accept the honors of the world. Christian is overcome by the man's eloquence, and proceeds to follow his advice. The Evangelist appears again, however, and reproves Christian for his flagging spirit. Spurred on, Christian moves forward in search of the "straight gate" that leads toward eternal life. Approaching a wicket-gate, Christian sees an inscription: "Knock, and it shall be opened unto you." Then the porter GOOD WILL welcomes him to the true path to salvation. Good Will advises Christian never to resort to the help of Mr. LEGALITY, a smooth-tongued pleader of secular joy. He directs Christian onward to the house of the INTERPRETER, who shows him two young men named PASSION and PATIENCE. Passion wants to seize every honor immediately, but Patience is willing to wait. Deciding to follow the philosophy of Patience, Christian sings as he approaches the wall of Salvation. There he meets the FORMALIST and HYPOCRISY, who decide to accompany him. On reaching the Hill of

the time he reaches the top, he has forgotten a scroll containing Biblical quotations. After bewailing his sleep, Christian finds his scroll again, and proceeds to another gate guarded by lions. The PORTER allows him to enter, for Christian's destination is Mount Zion. The Porter also summons the maid DISCRETION and her sisters, PRUDENCE, PIETY and CHARITY, who invite the pilgrim to dinner. That night the sisters learn about Christian's journey and enforce his faith with sympathetic words. The next morning the sisters show him the distant Delectable Mountains that will mark the end of his journey.

Christian descends into the arduous Valley of Humiliation, where he encounters the monstrous fiend APOLLYON. Through his humility and faith, Christian drives the monster away. Then, taking out a sword, Christian moves through the Valley of the Shadow of Death. Despite pleas from retreating pilgrims, Christian refuses to turn aside. He soon learns that the monsters haunting the valley are imaginary. Then he overtakes a friend named FAITHFUL, from his own town, who was inspired by Christian's departure and decided to take the same road to Mount Zion. Faithful relates how he was pursued by SHAME, DISCONTENT, and TALKATIVENESS, and the two pilgrims journey on happily together. The Evangelist encounters them both and compliments them for their fine endurance. Then he cautions them to run forward to salvation, for they must not linger too long in talk. The Evangelist also warns them of the worldly temptations that lie ahead in Vanity Fair, the citadel of the wicked.

Entering Vanity Fair, neither pilgrim condescends to buy any of the magnificent wares nor to speak with the reveling people. Immediately they are suspected and interrogated. When the two pilgrims state their mission, they are not believed and are cast into a cage. Because the pilgrims almost persuade some of the revelers to join their cause, the men of Vanity Fair send them to trial before Lord HATE-GOOD. Faithful begins to defend himself in admirable terms, protesting his innocence, but is contended by ENVY and SUPERSTITION. The jury refuses to place any faith in the defendant's words, and therefore Faithful dies the death of a martyr at the stake. A chariot guided by angels carries Faithful's dead body away from the rabble. Christian soon escapes from prison and finds a new companion named HOPEFUL, who heard Faithful preach before his death. After rejecting the company of the timid Mr. BY-ENDS and the greedy MONEY-LOVE, the two pilgrims successfully pass by Lucre Hill. They are unattracted by its offer of great riches, expounded at great length by DEMAS. Looking back, they watch Money-love and By-ends fall into Demas' snare.

The two companions enter a beautiful meadow and cross a treacherous river. Eventually they fall asleep, unware that they are trespassing on the grounds of Giant DESPAIR, who lives in nearby Doubting

Castle. In the morning, Despair claims the pilgrims as his slaves and thrusts them into his dark dungeon. From Thursday through Saturday, Despair beats and torments his captives. For a time Christian's ardor flags, but his spirits are revived by Hopeful. At last, when Despair threatens them both with death, Christian remembers a key called Promise in his bosom. Using the key, he manages to escape with his friend. They offer prayers for their deliverance from the monster and move forward to the Delectable Mountains. There some simple shepherds welcome the pilgrims and instruct them on their future journey, warning them about the FLATTERER. On parting, the two pilgrims meet IGNORANCE, who lives in the land of Conceit. Ignorance says that he is not interested in saving his soul, for he is blissful in his lack of knowledge. Next they encounter LITTLE-FAITH, who has to beg his way to the end of his journey. Hopeful sympathizes greatly with Little-faith, but Christian justifies God's treatment of the man who had too many doubts to pursue a truly virtuous life.

Next the pilgrims meet a black man clothed in white, who compliments them for their courage but leads them into a net. The pilgrims realize too late that they have fallen victim to the Flatterer. The next morning they are freed from the net by a SHINING ONE, who reproves them sternly and sets them free. Somewhat sobered by this experience, the pilgrims are more cautious when they encounter the ATHEIST, who refuses to believe that Mount Zion exists. Christian pulls Hopeful away, for his friend begins to feel drowsy as he listens to the Atheist's clever words. Then Hopeful explains the great difficulty he experienced before receiving the illumination of conversion. Hopeful recounts how Faithful preached to him about Christ's way of life and the meaning of prayer. Christian agrees that prayers to Jesus are the keystone of true religious belief. Suddenly IGNORANCE appears again with stronger arguments against the zealous religious life. Ignorance professes to be a Christian, but not bound to prayers and an imitation of Christ's life. Christian and Hopeful allow Ignorance to stumble along the road behind them, as the poor man hopes in his own peculiar way to achieve salvation.

At last the two pilgrims enter the Blessed Land of Beulah, where they are greeted by the gardener of a fertile orchard. The gardener tells them to cross the huge River of Death to enter Paradise. At first Christian is fearful, but at last he and Hopeful swim across. On arriving at the other side of the river, they are greeted by angels. Hopeful and Christian have now put aside their mortality and are ready to enter Mount Zion. The two pilgrims are escorted by angels into the banquet hall of the KING, who welcomes them. There, in the midst of music and plentiful food, they experience the bliss that they have long awaited. At this time Ignorance approaches the River of Death, and tries to cross. He is received by

Christian is greeted by angels

a false ferryman named VAIN-HOPE, who carries the deluded man to Hell. The author remarks that a man can arrive very close to the gates of Heaven and still be carried to destruction. At this point the author exclaims: "I awoke, and behold it was a dream."

The Pit

Novel by Frank Norris, 1870–1902. Published 1903 by Doubleday & Co., New York.

THE OUTSTANDING FEATURE of this important American novel is its descriptions of the "pit," the floor of the Chicago Board of Trade, the greatest commodity exchange in the United States, where the traditional object of the speculator is to corner the wheat market. Frank Norris's description in Chapter 3 of a typical day's activity is considered the most lasting contribution of the novel. However, the novel is a worthy one apart from its topical significance.

Chap. 1. LAURA DEARBORN, her sister PAGE, and their aunt Mrs. WESSELS, are the guests of CHARLES CRESSLER, a friend of the girls' dead father, at the Chicago Grand Opera. They meet CURTIS JADWIN, a grain capitalist, who is attracted to Laura. SHELDON CORTHELL, an artist, who has asked Laura to marry him, is also present. LANDRY COURT squires Page. As they return home, they see lights on in the Grain Market. Everyone is working overtime on the Helmick market maneuver.

Chap. 2. Laura, Page, and Aunt Wess finish unpacking in their new home. Landry Court helps them. He confesses his love for Laura. Mrs. CRESSLER invites the girls to her home overnight and tells Laura that Curtis Jadwin is in love with her. She enlists Laura's aid in a charity play that Jadwin is sponsoring.

Chap. 3. Jadwin visits Gretry, Converse, and Company, grain brokers. GRETRY gives him secret information from the Paris grain market. Jadwin contracts for a million bushels of wheat, writing a check for $50,-000. Landry Court starts his day at the Board of Trade. There is excitement over a rumor of war between Britain and Turkey. Landry finds himself with a commission to sell, even though the market is going up. He uses all his ingenuity and manages to sell all his shares.

Chap. 4. Jadwin and Gretry have made $50,000 that day through the secret information from Paris, selling wheat at high and buying it at low. That night there is a rehearsal for the charity play at Cressler's home. Miss GRETRY, dull and awkward, has a nosebleed. Mr. GERARDY, the coach, is personally insulted by Miss Gretry's mishap. Rehearsal stops. Jadwin proposes to Laura. She is surprised. Sheldon orders hansoms and takes the Dearborns home. He proposes to Laura again. When she puts him off, he says he will go to Paris. Landry Court and Page are in the library. As Landry leaves for home, he steals a kiss from Laura. Appalled by the kiss and two proposals in one evening, Laura censures herself for being a flirt. She writes letters to Landry, Sheldon, and Curtis, telling them she will never marry them. They reply differently. Landry sends an incoherent note of apology. Sheldon sends delicate roses with a tender note enclosed. Jadwin comes to see her.

Chap. 5. Laura and Page visit the Cresslers on their front stoop in late spring. Landry Court is there, and Laura is formal with him. The charity play has been dropped, since Laura refused to play a romantic scene with Sheldon in it, and Sheldon went to Europe. Jadwin has been speculating again, with much success. Laura confides to Mrs. Cressler that she is to marry Jadwin in July. Jadwin has bought a country home at Geneva Lake. They are married in church, and Laura receives roses from Sheldon. After the ceremony, Laura returns to her room. Jadwin finds her there, praying on her knees. He lets her know that he understands. Tenderly, Laura gives him a voluntary kiss, which she had withheld before.

Chap. 6. Three years pass. The price of wheat declines. Jadwin speculates more and more, always successfully. Jadwin has Gretry to dinner and instructs him to buy September wheat, 500,000 bushels on margin, though Gretry disagrees. Jadwin shows him the art gallery in the new home, and the church organ with a player attachment.

Laura and Jadwin have a happy marriage. He is happiest when he is fishing or tinkering with his boat *Thetis*. They start a tour of Europe but Jadwin is so restless that they return home. Laura achieves a "grand manner." Page is living with them and Landry Court comes to call on her. Jadwin makes more and more money as the price of wheat rises. He buys a seat on the Board of Trade.

Chap. 7. Laura begs her husband to stop speculating. He explains the market to her briefly, telling her that he has bought 5 million bushels of wheat. Laura is apprehensive. She invites Sheldon Corthell to dinner and Jadwin is detained at the office so Sheldon and Laura dine alone. They indulge in a long discussion on philosophy, art, and literature, and then Sheldon plays the organ for her. Jadwin makes $500,000 on the market that day and promises Laura that he will stop speculating. But when there is activity in the grain market he is tempted to speculate again. He buys 10 million bushels of May wheat and he and Gretry realize that they have cornered the wheat market. The market talks of the mysterious, unknown buyer.

Jadwin loves to fish

Chap. 8. CALVIN CROOKES, the acknowledged leader of the bears of the Chicago grain market, tells Cressler that the price of wheat has reached 100—"Dollar Wheat." Crookes and his associates ask Cressler to join them in driving the unknown bull (who is Jadwin) out of the market. Cressler hesitates, since he has vowed never to speculate again, but he accepts. Crookes and his partners know their opponent is Jadwin but keep the knowledge from Cressler. Jadwin buys 20 million bushels of wheat. Engrossed with the grain market, he has no time for his wife. Sheldon Corthell begins to escort her to the theater. Their companionship grows, and Sheldon thinks Laura is unhappy in her marriage. However, when

Jadwin comes home unexpectedly, Laura completely forgets her appointment with Sheldon. Laura is uneasy and moody over her husband's speculations. One night, Sheldon is in Laura's private room, simply to give her some advice, and forgets his silver match box. Laura tells Aunt Wess that Sheldon and she were at the organ the entire evening but Page discovers the match box in Laura's sitting room, catching Laura in a foolish lie. When Sheldon calls, Laura tells him she can no longer see him. On an evening when Jadwin comes home for dinner, Gretry bursts in with the news that Crookes is to start his battle against Jadwin the next morning. The two men rush to their office and Laura is left alone.

Chap. 9. Jadwin has a recurrence of a dizziness he has been keeping secret from Laura. As the trading begins, Jadwin gives an order to sell bushel for bushel with Crookes. For four days, a titanic battle rages in the Board of Trade. Then Jadwin switches his tactics and starts to buy. Crookes holds tight. He has no wheat to cover his pledges, but to buy would push the price higher. He surmises that since there is no wheat for sale, someone has bought it all up. He begins to cover his own private losses. Cressler, who is near bankruptcy, learns that Jadwin is the unknown bull. The price of wheat goes to 120. Jadwin summons HARGUS, an old fellow who has been ruined in the "pit," together with SCANNELL, who was the cause of Hargus's ruin. Jadwin sells at 140 and 150 to Scannell and gives Scannell's check for $300,-000 to Hargus to repay what Hargus lost in 1878 and Scannell's check for $360,000 to Hargus as the interest on his money. The price of wheat is 160. Jadwin buys July wheat short; Gretry thinks he is crazy. Jadwin cannot sleep and suffers from dizzy spells and headaches. Laura is so lonely that she writes a letter to Sheldon, but she recalls it just in time. Jadwin inquires about Charles Cressler; Laura goes to see him and finds him at his desk with a bullet through his brain.

Chap. 10. Jadwin is having trouble supporting the high price of wheat. He has warehouses full of wheat costing him $6,-000 a day for insurance and storage. The minute he begins to sell, the price of wheat goes down. He mortgages his real estate. Meeting Hargus, he offers to borrow $100,-000 at 10% interest, but is refused. He cannot sell his wheat even below market price.

Page and Landry Court become engaged. Landry takes Page to the Board of Trade; the pit is a madhouse. Gretry delivers Jadwin's orders to buy, to support the price, but the effort fails. Jadwin goes into the pit himself, after striking Gretry and cursing him. The secretary of the Board of Trade announces that all trade with Gretry's company must close at once. Jadwin is beaten. Page reports to Laura that Jadwin has lost money, though she does not realize how much. Laura is unmoved; she is miffed because her husband has forgotten her birth-

day. Sheldon comes with violets. When he makes love to her, she promises to go away with him on the following evening. At that moment Jadwin, a beaten man, comes in.

Conclusion. Laura and Curtis sell their houses, furnishings, and yacht, to begin life anew out West. Page and Landry settle in New York. Jadwin says, "I didn't corner the wheat—it cornered me."

The Plague

Novel by Albert Camus, 1913–1961. Published 1947. Published 1948 by Alfred A. Knopf, New York. © 1948 by Albert Camus & Stuart Gilbert; translated from the French by Stuart Gilbert.

THE PLAGUE is the best-known novel, among English readers, of the French Nobel Prize winner of 1957. It is a parable, a profound study of human nature, and at the same time a novel of adventure. The novel is written in the first person, but the identity of the narrator is not revealed until nearly the end.

Part I. Oran is a port on the French coast of Algeria. The town is commercial, drab, unexciting. Dr. BERNARD RIEUX sees a dead rat on the landing of his staircase. He thinks nothing of it, but the concierge, M. MICHEL, is outraged. Rieux puts his ailing wife on a train to a sanatorium. His kind mother arrives to take care of him during his wife's absence. As Dr. Reiux makes his round of calls, he notices more and more dead rats. Soon they are virtually flowing out of all the cracks in the town and dying on the streets. Special sanitation trucks are sent out to collect them, and the town gasps in horror at the uncanny occurrence. Then one day the rats suddenly stop coming out, and the town sighs in relief. Rieux is called by the town clerk, JOSEPH GRAND, who has just rescued a man COTTARD from hanging himself. Cottard appears to fear a police inquiry. Another of Rieux's patients is M. Michel, who has taken to bed with a high fever and swollen ganglia. He becomes wracked with pain and dies horribly.

JEAN TARROU, a mysterious character, has recently come to Oran. He keeps a diary in which he records many detailed observations about the people around him and the town. He is intrigued by the mystery of the rats. Soon there are more cases of the new and curious fever, and more deaths like that of M. Michel. Somebody mentions the word "plague," but nobody takes it seriously. A little plague does not make an epidemic. Rieux thinks of the horrors of the historic plagues of the past, but such horrors seem remote, unlikely in such a tranquil town as Oran. Rieux comes into more contact with Grand, the obscure official living on a pittance, full of simple kindness and affection. He is trying to write a book in the evenings, but is strikingly unable to express himself. Grand tells Rieux more about Cottard—Cottard has always been aloof and mistrustful of people, but now suddenly has become very friendly to all. He has practically admitted that he wants to destroy the impression that he is "really a bad kind of man." Grand thinks that Cottard has something serious on his conscience. Rieux continues on his rounds and encounters more and more cases of plague. At first the authorities will not take drastic measures. The town grows uneasy as the number of deaths mounts to 30 per day. Then a telegram arrives from the Prefect, "Proclaim a state of plague stop close the town."

Part II. The gates of the town are closed and no one is permitted to leave. Thus the first great effect of the plague is to exile many of the inhabitants of the town. An emotional void opens up for them wherein the present is a frustration, the future an unknown, and the past merely a memory. Furthermore they cannot even receive sympathy from those around them because too many are in the same plight. Commerce begins to die of the plague also, as the passage of ships and trains ceases, goods become rationed, shops begin to close, and the streets become glutted with the unemployed.

RAYMOND RAMBERT, a visiting journalist from Paris, tries to obtain a health certificate so that he may leave the town. Rieux cannot grant it. Rieux soon is obliged to take police officials with him to compel families to relinquish their dying members to the isolation hospital.

The Catholic Father PANELOUX preaches a mighty sermon. He declares that the calamity of the plague has come as a punishment to sinners—to thresh the wheat from the chaff. He says that the plague is also an act of compassion by God, in that it points out the way to salvation. Some citizens become panicky and try violence to escape through the town's guarded gates. Rambert continues his endless struggles with officialdom to obtain release. Rieux discovers that the book that Grand is writing has never gotten beyond the first sentence. Grand hopes to perfect this sentence to such an extent that it will overwhelm the publishers. A "Plague Chronicle" is launched, in which the daily total of plague deaths is tallied. Some of the plague cases now become pneumonic. Early religious fervor gives way to passionate indulgence in pleasure, but fear holds the sceptre during the sultry summer days.

Tarrou volunteers to form a "sanitary squad" to help Rieux. He asks Rieux whether he believes in God. Rieux answers that no one can believe in the all-powerful God proposed by Paneloux. Why would such a God permit the plague? Tarrou forms sanitary squads of courageous volunteers, who work endlessly. Joseph Grand helps in his quiet way. Rambert is still trying desperately to leave the city. He comes in contact with Cottard, who is flourishing by black market activities. Cottard directs him to two gate guards who might be bribed, but the lead peters out. Tarrou finally persuades Rambert to join a sanitary squad.

Part III. The spectre of the plague spreads lawlessness and violence throughout the town. Bodies are at first buried separately, then in communal pits; finally the old crematorium on the edge of town is opened and trolly-cars deliver wholesale cargoes of corpses. Listless indifference sets in. The plague begins to kill off the faculty of love and of friendship. Rieux and others discover that "the habit of despair is worse than despair itself."

Part IV. The plague drags on into September and October. Rieux hears that the condition of his wife in the sanatorium is getting worse. He knows that she must be terribly lonely. In the meantime Cottard has become most genial and happy. He appears to thrive on the plague, and Tarrou feels that this is because the plague produces in the general population a condition similar to that which Cottard suffered for a long time. He feared arrest and the distrust of his fellow citizens. Now everybody suffers from fear of death and of contagion by his fellow citizens. Rambert has made arrangements for escape, and finally the prearranged day for his flight arrives. At the last moment he shrinks back; he declares to Rieux that he will remain and carry on his work with the sanitary squad. He has renounced his personal hopes to succor his fellow men.

A new antiplague serum is tried on a stricken child. Father Paneloux joins the doctors watching the case. The child dies before their eyes. Paneloux is torn by the sight; on the following Sunday he preaches a sermon dealing with the lesson of the plague. He says that the suffering of innocent children is beyond human comprehension. One cannot believe in God in one place and doubt him in another. It must be *all or nothing,* and who dares to utterly deny God? Therefore one must have complete faith in Him under *all* circumstances. Later Paneloux falls severely ill, but will not see a doctor. He has reached the conclusion that "it is illogical for a priest to call in a doctor." He dies.

Tarrou and Rieux have become close friends and one day Tarrou begins to talk of his life. He was alienated from his father at an early age, because his father, a lawyer, caused the court to condemn to death a human being. He soon discovered that his father had an indirect hand in the deaths of thousands of people, since he approved of the principles on which they were judged. Tarrou feels that all men nowadays in this respect have "the plague." There are plagues, victims of plagues, and "true healers"—men who have peace. Tarrou hopes to attain this third category through sympathy, not judgment. He wants to learn how to become a saint; but he does not believe in God. He wonders if one may be a saint if there is no God.

Christmas arrives and passes. Frosty weather sets in. Miraculously the great plague halts, weakens, and begins to ebb. The daily death toll subsides. The citizens rejoice—except for Cottard, who becomes petulant and surly. Finally a happy day arrives when officials declare that the plague is stemmed and that the town gates will be opened in two weeks. The city pulses with excitement. With a last flick of its tongue, the plague strikes Tarrou. Rieux watches his greatest friend die in agony. Immediately afterward, Rieux receives notice that his wife has died.

The gates of the town are thrown open. Jubilant crowds dance in the streets. Long-parted lovers are once again joined. At this point it is revealed that the narrator of the story is Rieux. In the midst of the rejoicing, Rieux and Grand witness a scene in a back street. Policemen are shooting at a house. A madman is on the loose there, firing at everybody in sight. He is finally subdued and dragged away. It is Cottard. Rieux goes to a balcony and watches fireworks against the cold sky. He reflects that "in a time of pestilence there are more things to admire in men than to despise." But the tale is not one of final victory. Plague is always imminent, and only the utmost vigilance can keep terror at bay. The world should strive to heal.

The priest joins the doctors in watching the care of the dying boy

Playboy of the Western World

Play by John Millington Synge, 1871–
1909.
Produced 1907. Published 1909. (ML,
30)

THIS IS A successful play that is also
noteworthy literature. Synge had the
knack of writing poetry in conversational prose. The charm of Irish dic-
tion, felt by nearly all Americans, adds
to the poetic effect. The play can occasionally be seen, for it is by no means
dead, and as a book it is an excellent
candidate for anyone's reading list.

Act I. CHRISTOPHER MAHON, a slight
young man, looking tired and dirty, walks
into the Flaherty public house on the wild
coast of Mayo. He tells MICHAEL FLAHERTY
and Flaherty's daughter, PEGEEN, that he
has been walking for 11 days and fears he
is being followed by the police because he
has killed his father, a cruel man. This admission of daring elevates him in the eyes
of the Flahertys, who hire him as an assistant. Pegeen is happy to have a protector,
since her father will be away all of that
night, attending a wake. Pegeen questions
Christy about the girls he has known. He
insists he has been lonely all his life and,
until the day he killed his father, lived
quietly. The Widow QUIN, the Flahertys'
only neighbor, is sent by SHAWN KEOGH,
to whom Pegeen is betrothed, to take the
stranger to her own house, for Pegeen's
protection. The women exchange angry
words, Pegeen accusing the other of wanting Christy for herself. Christopher refuses
to leave and Pegeen makes his bed on a
bench near the fireplace before she retires
to the other room. Christy, luxuriating in
the clean, soft quilt and the thought of two
fine women fighting over him, thinks as he
falls asleep that he was a foolish fellow not
to kill his father years before.

Act II. Early the next morning four
village girls come to see the new-found
hero. They invite him to join the sports
and races that afternoon. Shawn, afraid he
is losing his girl to Christy, tries to bribe
Christy to leave Mayo. This does not seem
to work and the Widow makes a bargain
with Shawn: She will marry Christy in exchange for several valuable gifts which she
names. As she is presenting her offer to
Christy, he sees "the walking spirit of my
murdered da" coming toward the house.
He darts behind the door. Old MAHON, his
head in a mass of bandages, comes in looking for his son, whom he describes as a
lazy, clumsy fool and afraid of women.
Widow Quin tells him Christy has gone
over the hills to catch a steamer and Mahon
dashes out after him. Taunting Christy as
the "walking Playboy of the Western
World," the Widow tells him Pegeen will
drive him away. But he rejects the Widow's
offer and, near tears, begs her to help him
win Pegeen, whom he loves. She finally
promises never to tell Pegeen that his
father still lives, in return for three gifts
when he marries.

Act III. Mahon, giving up his search for
Christy, returns to the public house. He and
Widow Quin watch the mule race from the
window and hear the crowds cheering
Christy, who has become the champion of
the day. Mahon recognizes his son, but the
Widow tells him he is a sniggering maniac
from the blow on his head, for this wonder
of the Western World could not possibly be
the fool of a boy he had described. Mahon
is finally convinced of his insanity and runs
off. Pegeen returns with the victorious
Christy and his many prizes. They reveal
their love for each other and make plans
for a wedding. Michael comes in with
Shawn and announces that Pegeen and
Shawn are to be married that day; he does
not want a son who is crusted with his
father's blood. He tries to get Shawn to
fight Christy, but Shawn flees. Convinced
again that "a daring fellow is the jewel of
the world," Michael gives his blessing to
Pegeen and Christy. Suddenly old Mahon
rushes in, followed by an excited crowd. He
knocks Christy down and begins to beat
him. Pegeen discovers Christy's lie and renounces him as he chases his father out.
There is a loud noise, then a dead silence,
and Christy comes back. The men slip a
rope around him and are dragging him out
to be hanged when they see old Mahon
crawling in and, startled, drop the rope.
Mahon unties his son and tries to take him
along. Christy tells his father he will go
"like a gallant captain with his heathen
slave." Walking out in front of his son,
Mahon murmers, "I am crazy again!"
Pegeen boxes Shawn on the ear and cries
wildly, "I've lost the only Playboy of the
Western World."

Poe's Stories

Short stories by Edgar Allan Poe, 1809–
1849.
Published 1839–1845. (ML, 82 & G40
& T58; Viking, 12; RE, 42; PB,
PL46).

POE WAS THE FIRST American who
was accepted by European critics as a
great figure in literature. He was a
hack, writing for subsistence and often
desperately dashing off a few words to
get his next meal or drink, so his work
is very uneven, but the fact remains
that he managed to write more truly
classic stories than anyone else, even
those who were similarly great and ten
times more prolific. The title of one
collection of Poe's stories, *Tales of the
Grotesque and Arabesque,* is a good
description for all of them. Among
other distinctions, Poe is credited by
those who ought to know with creating the modern type of detective story
and the modern type of amateur detective (his character C. Auguste Dupin). This character anticipated by
half a century the Sherlock Holmes of
Conan Doyle. Poe used very clever
themes for his short stories, perhaps
better than anyone else's, yet the quality of the stories is so much in the
writing that no outline can begin to do
them justice.

THE BLACK CAT

On the eve of his execution a murderer
pens an account of his life. From infancy
he was noted for his kindly disposition. He
was especially fond of animals and had
many pets. He married early. The happy
couple kept birds, goldfish, a dog, rabbits,
a monkey, and a totally black cat, named
PLUTO, which became his favorite and
playmate. Gradually, over a period of years,
Pluto's master became addicted to drink.
His disposition changed; he abused his
wife and ill-used his pets. Returning home
intoxicated one night, he seized the cat,
which bit his hand. Infuriated, he cut one
of the cat's eyes from its socket. The cat recovered but thereafter fled from its master,
whose short-lived remorse was succeeded
by a perverse impulse to destroy his pet.
With tears streaming down his face he
hanged the cat by its neck from the limb of
a tree outside his house. On the following
night the house caught fire and burned to
the ground. Only the white plaster wall behind the head of his bed remained standing.
As if graven in bas-relief on the wall was
the figure of a gigantic cat with a rope
around its neck. The image of the cat
haunted him. A longing for the animal
possessed him and he searched for another
to replace it. A one-eyed stray cat followed
him home to the decrepit building where
he lived. The cat was black and resembled
Pluto in all respects save that it had a
splotch of white on its breast. It showered
caresses on him, but disgusted him. The
white spot on its breast assumed the shape
of a gallows. He loathed and dreaded it,
and fled from it. He awoke from nightmares
to find it sitting on his heart. In the cellar
one day, in a fit of demoniacal fury, he
seized an ax to kill it. His wife intervened
and he drove the axe into her skull. Calmly
and carefully he enclosed his wife's body
upright in a cellar wall. He worked carefully and no trace of the murder remained.

When he looked for the cat to kill it too, it had vanished. For three days he lived in supreme happiness. On the fourth day the police came to search the house. Confidently he escorted them into the cellar. They found nothing. As they were leaving he called their attention to the solidity of the walls, striking with a cane the brickwork behind which he had immured his wife. Instantly he was answered by a muffled cry, like the sobbing of a child, which quickly swelled into a long, loud, continuing scream. The police tore down the wall to reveal the corpse, on its head with red mouth and fiery eye, the black cat.

THE MASQUE OF THE RED DEATH

A devastating plague afflicts the country ruled by Prince PROSPERO. Its victims suffer sharp pains, sudden dizziness, and bleeding at the pores. Within a half-hour of the onset of the disease death and dissolution take place. When half the population of his realm is destroyed, the prince gathers a thousand knights and ladies and retires to the seclusion of a magnificent abbey. Ample provisions have been provided. For the entertainment of his entourage the prince has summoned buffoons, actors, musicians, and ballet dancers. Toward the end of a half-year of isolation from the world, while the plague rages furiously outside, the prince and his followers hold a masked ball. The ballroom comprises seven irregularly shaped rooms, colored successively blue, purple, green, orange, white, violet, and black. In six rooms the stained-glass Gothic windows have the color of the room. The window panes in the black room are blood red. In the corridors outside the windows are braziers of fire. This flickering light, projected through the windows, provides the only illumination. In the black room everything appears ghastly and few revelers dare enter it. A gigantic ebony clock in that apartment strikes the hours with a peculiar brazen but musical clangor, causing the merrymakers to pause, disconcerted and trembling. The revelry is at its height when the clock strikes midnight and there appears among the company a tall gaunt figure attired in the vestments of the grave and with the blood-spattered countenance of a corpse. Prince Prospero is enraged. The revelers are terror-struck and shrink away as the newcomer moves deliberately through the rooms. Drawing his dagger, the prince rushes after the interloper into the black room. As he is about to strike, the figure turns to face him. The prince utters a cry and falls dead. A throng of revelers rushes forward and seizes the dread figure, only to find that it has no bodily substance. One by one they fall and die until all have perished, victims of the Red Death.

THE CASK OF AMONTILLADO

MONTRESOR, an Italian gentleman, has sworn to avenge the thousand injuries he has suffered at the hand of his friend FORTUNATO, a man generally respected, even feared, and like himself a connoisseur of wines. The two meet at dusk during the mad revelry of a carnival. Fortunato, wearing fool's motley, is tipsy. Montresor tells his friend he has received a cask purported to be amontillado sherry, but doubts its authenticity. Fortunato presses Montresor for a taste of it. Montresor pretends reluctance but finally yields. By flaring torchlight he leads Fortunato down a long winding staircase into the damp catacombs of the Montresors, where casks of wine are stored between walls of piled skeletons. Drops of moisture from the river far overhead trickle through the bones. They pass from vault to vault until at last, in a deep crypt at the farthest end of the catacombs, they reach a small recess. There Montresor chains Fortunato to the granite wall. Sadistically he begs his victim to leave. With stone and mortar prepared for the purpose Montresor begins to wall up the recess. He rests from time to time on a heap of bones to gloat over his helpless victim. When Fortunato screams in anguish Montresor yells back in savage exultation. The ghoulish duet continues while the fatal wall rises. As the final brick is put in place the last sound heard from the doomed man is the faint jingling of the bells on his fool's cap.

A DESCENT INTO THE MAELSTROM

Two Norwegian fishermen at sea in a hurricane face death when their craft is drawn into a fearful whirlpool. With dizzying speed the boat spins ever closer to the center of the maelstrom and destruction. The older man goes mad. The younger one notices that objects of cylindrical shape seem to whirl endlessly about the center of the whirlpool. He lashes himself to a cask and leaps into the eddying waters. Later, after the maelstrom has spent its force, he drifts to safety. Other fishermen rescue him. He knows them but they fail to recognize him and cannot believe his incredible tale. His awful experience has caused his hair to turn white and has altered entirely the expression of his face.

THE FALL OF THE HOUSE OF USHER

RODERICK and MADELINE USHER, brother and sister, sole survivors of their family, live in a gloomy and decaying mansion on the brink of a black and silent tarn (lake) in a noxious landscape of ghastly rotting tree trunks and gray sedge, reeking with pestilential vapors. A zigzag fissure traverses the entire front of the house and seems to descend into the tarn. Inside the house, all is old, comfortless, dilapidated. Brother and sister suffer from strange bodily and mental illnesses. Roderick has summoned a boyhood friend to aid him. The two men divert themselves with music and reading. Roderick informs his friend one evening that Madeline has died. Together they carry Madeline's body in a coffin to a place of temporary entombment in an underground vault. There follow days of bitter grief for Roderick. A week later,

The Usher mansion

during a violent storm, while Roderick's friend is reading to him a strange and horrifying tale to the accompaniment of frightening sounds outside their room, the door swings open and Madeline appears enshrouded in bloodstained white robes. With a cry she falls on Roderick and bears him to the floor. They expire simultaneously. The friend flees. Looking back, he sees amid the tempest the blood-red moon shining through the widening fissure in the house. The wind increases in fury, the walls of the mansion split asunder with a thunderous crash and disappear into the tarn.

THE GOLD BUG

WILLIAM LEGRAND, impoverished son of a once-wealthy Huguenot family of New Orleans, has settled in a small hut on Sullivan's Island opposite Charleston, S.C. There, attended by JUPITER, an old former slave, he fishes, hunts, and searches for rare shells and insects. Master and servant find a golden beetle marked with a death's head, and a scrap of old parchment. Legrand believes that the beetle is solid gold. The parchment, when heated, discloses a cipher [which is given in full]. Legrand solves the cipher and discovers it to be instructions for locating the buried treasure of the pirate, Captain Kidd. Accompanied by Jupiter and a friend, Legrand finds a human skull nailed to the seventh branch of a tulip tree. Jupiter climbs the tree and drops the golden beetle through the left eye of the skull. At a spot established by drawing a line 50 feet from the tree through the spot at which the beetle struck the ground, the three men uncover an enormously heavy chest containing heaps of gold and jewels. With this new-found wealth Legrand establishes himself in society.

MS. FOUND IN A BOTTLE

A manuscript found in a bottle tells the tragic story of a passenger on a voyage from Batavia to the Sunda Archipelago. A terrible storm springs up. The crew is swept overboard. Only the narrator and a Swedish sailor are spared. Several days later, during the height of the gale, a strange vessel of

The room on the Rue Morgue was in disorder, the woman brutally slain

enormous size bears down on them. The sailor perishes but the narrator is saved when he is thrown into the rigging of the mysterious ship. He stays long on board, but the crew do not see him. He spends the time in writing an account of his experience while a frightful current drives the vessel into Antarctic waters. Enclosing it in a bottle, he casts it into the sea as the ship goes down in a great whirlpool.

THE MURDERS IN THE RUE MORGUE

Madame L'ESPANAYE and her daughter CAMILLE have been murdered in a fourth-floor room of their house in the Rue Morgue in Paris. When the police and neighbors, alarmed by the women's screams, broke into the house, they found the door of the room locked with the key inside. As they struggled to reach the women they heard a guttural voice uttering unintelligible sounds. The violent disorder in the room and the brutal manner in which the women were slain indicated that the murderer possessed super-human strength. The police are unable to understand how the slayer got into and out of the room and the house, but have concluded that he must be extraordinarily agile. They cannot establish a motive for the crime. C. AUGUSTE DUPIN, amateur detective, undertakes to solve the mystery. With the permission of the police he examines the neighborhood and the house in the Rue Morgue. Minutely he scrutinizes the room on the fourth floor. Dupin concludes that the murderer is an ape, but says nothing. After leaving the Rue Morgue he places an advertisement in a daily newspaper. On the following day a Maltese sailor, responding to the advertisement, calls on Dupin and confesses that an orangutang escaped from his custody, that he followed it and saw it commit the murders. Later the ape is captured by its owner and sold at a profit to the Jardin des Plantes.

THE MYSTERY OF MARIE ROGET

[Originally sub-titled "A Sequel to the

Murders in the Rue Morgue," this story is based on the real-life murder of Mary Rogers in New York.]

MARIE, only daughter of the widow ESTELLE ROGET, beautiful and flirtatious, works as a perfumer's assistant outside Paris. She leaves home one day, saying she intends to visit her aunt. She disappears. Four days later her corpse is found floating in the river Seine. Her murder appears to be the outcome of a sexual attack. Suspicion falls on a number of her admirers, one is able to move only his head and enough of his left arm to feed himself with the oily spiced meat lying by his side. Enormous rats, attracted by the pungent odor of the meat, swarm over him. A dim light of mysterious origin now enables him to see that the sides and ceiling of his dungeon are made of jointed metal plates daubed whom commits suicide. The newspapers suggest that the corpse may not be that of Marie. The prefect of police of Paris is baffled. He offers a reward to Dupin, for a solution of the mystery. Dupin establishes the identity of the corpse as truly that of Marie Roget and proves the innocence of the dead suitor as well as of another suspected admirer. He concludes that Marie's dead body was cast into the river from a boat which was later set adrift after the murderer, a secret lover, reached shore. He suggests that the police find the boat and examine it for clues to the identity of the slayer. They do so and solve the mystery.

THE PIT AND THE PENDULUM

The only character is the narrator, who does not identify himself by name. On trial before the Inquisition in Toledo, Spain, he faints when he hears the sentence of death pronounced. He awakes to find himself in complete darkness lying on a slippery stone floor. Gropingly he explores his surroundings, stumbles, and falls at the edge of a deep pit. He retreats to the walls and sleeps. When he wakes again he discovers that he is strapped to a low wooden framework and

with hideous superstitious devices. From the ceiling directly overhead hangs a huge pendulum, its lower end being a crescent-shaped, razor-sharp steel blade. As the horrified victim watches, the pendulum, hissing as it sweeps back and forth at right angles to his length, slowly descends. He realizes that eventually it will pass through his heart. He smears his bonds with the remains of the meat, the rats bite through the straps, and he escapes. Immediately the pendulum is drawn up through the ceiling. Now the walls gleam with demons' eyes, become red hot, and, assuming the shape of a lozenge, slowly close in on him, forcing him toward the pit. As he totters, screaming, on the brink of the abyss, he hears trumpet blasts and human voices, the fiery walls rush back, and he is saved by General Lasalle. The French army has captured Toledo.

THE PURLOINED LETTER

Dupin is asked by the Paris prefect of police for aid in an important case. A cabinet minister has stolen a letter from the queen of France. He has been blackmailing the queen to his financial and political advantage. A elaborate and futile search of several months has convinced the prefect that the letter cannot be in the minister's house or on his person. The prefect is completely baffled. Dupin calls on the minister. The detective reasons that the minister, knowing the police search only for secret hiding places, must keep the letter in an obvious place. Dupin espies it in a cardrack hanging underneath the mantelpiece. On the following day, while the minister's attention is diverted by a disturbance arranged by the police in the street, Dupin recovers the letter. The queen is saved and Dupin receives a handsome reward.

THE TELL-TALE HEART

This story, written as from a prison cell, is a confession of murder. The guilty man

He sprang upon the old man

denies that he is mad but avows that he is dreadfully nervous, in consequence of which his senses have become extraordinarily acute. He lived with an old man whom he loved, who had never wronged him, and whose gold he did not covet. One of the old man's eyes, pale blue and covered with a film, resembled that of a vulture. Whenever the eye fell on the narrator his blood turned cold and the marrow in his bones froze. Gradually, an obsession to do away with the old man came over him. One night, listening at the door to the old man's room, he heard his heart beating with a sound like that of a watch enveloped in cotton. The sound, which seemed loud enough to wake their neighbors, frightened and infuriated him. He sprang upon the old man, who shrieked once loudly. He dragged the old man to the floor and pulled the heavy bed over him. Later he removed the bed and examined the corpse. The heart was still. He dismembered the body, pulled up three planks from the floor, deposited the remains between the scantlings, and replaced the planks leaving no trace of the grim deed. But the old man's shriek had been heard by a neighbor and the police came to investigate. Unperturbed, the murderer explained that the shriek was his own, uttered in a dream, and that the old man was absent in the country. With complete self-assurance he invited the police officers to make an inspection. They did so and, finding nothing amiss, remained to rest and talk. Murderer and police officers chatted easily. Suddenly, the murderer's head began to ache. He turned pale and heard a ringing in his ears. It seemed to be low, dull, and quick, like the beating of the old man's heart. He began to speak loudly and vehemently to cover the sound. The officers noticed nothing. The sound grew steadily louder. The murderer turned paler, became desperate. He grated his chair on the floor over the place where he had hidden the old man's dismembered corpse and from which the sound issued. He paced heavily across the floor. The policemen remained quietly in their chairs; they seemed to be mocking him in silent derision. Terrified by the still mounting sound and frightened and enraged by the attitude of the policemen, he suddenly cried, "I admit the deed."

Porgy

Novel by DuBose Heyward, 1885–1940.

Published 1925 by Doubleday & Co., New York. © 1925 by DuBose Heyward & Doubleday & Co.

THE NOVEL ITSELF is the masterpiece of a fine writer, but also it made a good play and finally an opera, *Porgy and Bess*, with music by George Gershwin, that has been played to acclaim around the world. The Negroes of the coastal cities and plantations of South Carolina are not exactly like any other people of the United States. They speak a language that at first sounds like gibberish and, even when one has accustomed himself to the intonations and the odd though English locutions, still contains many words that require language study. Surely much of their language stems directly from the African dialect of their ancestors. DuBose Heyward, a Charlestonian, was a sensitive observer of this Negro culture and society. The novel is set in a waterfront slum district of Charleston. How a white aristocrat got close enough to know this district as well as DuBose Heyward did must remain a mystery.

Parts 1–2. PORGY is a crippled beggar. He sits in a regular place each day, preoccupied and brooding. He has but one vice—gambling. At night, in Catfish Row, where he lives with his fellows, dice games flourish. One night, CROWN, a stevedore, has been drinking heavily. ROBBINS, another player, tries to cheat the slow-minded Crown, but is caught. Crown and Robbins have a terrific fight and Crown kills Robbins with his cargo hook. Crown escapes. The next day Porgy adds some money to the burial collection for Robbins and attends the funeral with the wailing mourners. The police come looking for Crown, and take away as a witness the old man, PETER, who used to drive Porgy to and from his beggar's stand. A white lawyer is finally induced to arrange for Peter's freedom. Porgy, in the meanwhile, has had to fend for himself. He builds a cart from an old packing case, with rough wheels, and gets a goat to pull it. When he first goes out to his regular place he causes much merriment, and much annoyance, too, from the goat's smell. He is now able to get about readily and sees much more of the city than before. He is also able to beg more money. BESS, Crown's woman, one day moves in with Porgy, unasked. Her company changes Porgy from a lonesome, introverted man into a happy one, friendly to others for the first time in his life.

Part 3. Bess is happy with Porgy. She takes care of him and spends his money wisely as she markets, bargaining shrewdly for fish down at the docks. She even squats behind Porgy at the dice games and holds his winnings for him. One night the game is joined by SPORTIN' LIFE, an octoroon, who has been to New York and dresses in flashy style. He loses money to Porgy, and slyly poisons the minds of the others by making them think that Porgy has been cheating. After Porgy departs, Sportin' Life plays up to Bess and gives her some dope (heroin, or "snow"). Bess gives him Porgy's winnings for more dope. A little later, though, when another woman accuses Porgy of cheating, Bess has a fight with her, which is only ended by the arrival of the police. They arrest Bess for fighting and for taking dope. Bess refuses to tell the court the source of the dope, and she is given 10 days in jail. As she is taken away, she is ashamed to look at Porgy, though he calls to her. Porgy retreats again into his lonesome shell.

MARIA, owner of the cook-shop in Catfish Row, is sent by Porgy to visit Bess in jail. Maria takes Bess food and a blanket from Porgy. She asks why Bess did not inform on Sportin' Life. Bess replies that she wants to go back to Porgy when she gets out of jail, and that she has to be "decent" about something. She will settle up with Sportin' Life herself when she catches up with him, but she will not inform on a Negro to "white folks." Maria praises her. Bess returns to Porgy sick and delirious, raving. The frightened Negroes will not let her be sent to a white man's hospital. Maria advises Porgy to have a "conjer" woman cast a spell to chase the devil out of Bess. Porgy gives $2 to a sailor to take to the conjure woman, and goes home happy. Bess recovers that night. The sailor, however, gets drunk and does not go to the woman. Maria finds this out, but hides it from Porgy.

Part 4. It is the day of the grand parade and picnic. All of Catfish Row is off for a boat ride. The boat leaves them all on an island in the bay. Bess goes into the woods to cut palmetto leaves for a tablecloth, while Porgy waits. In the woods Bess is accosted by Crown, who has been in hiding on the island. Bess tries to tell Crown she is a changed woman, but he laughs at her and forces her to come with him to his hut in the woods. At the end of the day, Crown releases Bess, but tells her he is coming back for her in the Fall. When Bess comes back to the picnic, Porgy guesses she has been with Crown and Bess admits it. She also tells Porgy what Crown has threatened, but indicates she does not want to leave Porgy. Robbins' widow and Maria also guess where Crown is and what has happened. SERENA, the widow, threatens to kill Crown if he returns. That night, Sportin' Life comes round again. Maria hits him in the head with a brick and chases him away for good.

Part 5. JAKE, part-owner of the *Seagull*, a fishing boat, encourages the fishing fleet to go out while the catch is good, despite threatening weather. The men have an excellent catch the first day, and the boats go out again the next day into the teeth of a hurricane. CLARA, Jake's wife, waits on shore with other women. Clara is terrified, as she was once told by a "conjer" woman that Jake will be drowned. The storm increases in intensity, and in the wharf-house the Negroes pray. At the height of the

507

Crown's body is found in the bay off Catfish Row

storm, the waiting people fight their way back to Catfish Row as roofs swirl off around them in the howling wind. Porgy and Bess cower together in their room until the wind-driven tide forces them to the second floor of the old building. There 40 refugees sing and pray through the night. In a lull in the storm, after daylight, Jake's foundered boat is seen in the harbor and Clara rushes out into the storm, leaving her baby in Bess' care. Clara does not return. When the storm is over, Bess voices her determination to keep the baby when others of the women want to take it from her.

Part 6. The arrival of wagons with bales of cotton signals the Fall. Porgy and Bess await Crown's threatened coming. Bess tells Porgy she wants to stay with him and the baby, but she is afraid that if Crown touches her she cannot resist him. Porgy enjoins her not to worry. Crown comes to the Row one night and Maria accosts him. She pleads with him to stay away from Bess, but Crown refuses. He leaves, threatening to return later. In the middle of the night Porgy is awakened by Crown entering through a window, and Porgy stabs Crown with his knife. Next morning Crown's body is found in the bay off Catfish Row. Police try to find the killer, but Serena has an alibi and nothing can be proved against Porgy. Catfish Row stands together. Bess is happy now with Porgy. Porgy is called to identify the body of Crown. Frightened, he runs away. He is caught and sent to jail for 5 days for contempt of court. When Porgy gets out and goes home, he finds Bess gone. Maria tells him that Bess, despondent over his jailing and not knowing how long he would be gone, fell in with some passing sailors.

They got her drunk, abducted her, and carried her off to Savannah. Porgy visibly shrinks. His summer of happiness is over; Porgy is now an old man.

Portrait of Jenny

Novel by Robert Nathan, 1894–
Published 1940 by Alfred A. Knopf, New York. © 1939 by Robert Nathan.

MOST OF Robert Nathan's novels are quite realistic in a sympathetic, gentle and whimsical way. His greatest success, however, and probably his longest lasting contribution to American literature, is this fantasy that invades the supernatural. Like all Nathan novels it is short and no one can go wrong by reading it.

1–3. EBEN ADAMS is a young artist whose landscapes reflect his New England ancestry. He has never sold a picture, and he is weeks behind in his rent. He has been trying desperately to raise money. Walking home through Central Park, he crosses the Mall, where he sees a little girl, JENNIE APPLETON, playing alone. She is friendly; they sit together and talk. Jennie tells him that her parents are on the stage at the Hammerstein Music Hall. Eben is puzzled, since the Hall

was torn down when he was a boy. At parting, Jennie expresses the wish that he will wait for her to grow up. The incident makes a great impression on Eben. He sketches a portrait of Jennie from memory. The sketch is bought by Mr. MATTHEWS, who promises to buy a finished portrait of the same subject. Luck has changed for the artist. He celebrates by having dinner with his friend, GUS MEYER, who persuades the restaurant-owner to commission Eben to paint a mural over the bar.

4–7. Three weeks later, Eben sees Jennie skating on the Central Park lake, and joins her. He tells her about Matthews, and she agrees to sit for a portrait. Seeking to solve the mystery of Jennie's identity, Eben questions her about CECILY, a friend whom Jennie had mentioned at their first meeting. Jennie replies that Cecily died two years ago. Eben makes some sketches of Jennie in skating costume. Matthews eagerly buys the sketches and reiterates his order for a finished portrait. Unfortunately Eben does not know where Jennie lives; he and Gus conduct a vain search. But Gus uncovers the startling fact that the APPLETONS, a couple who had played at Hammerstein's 20 years previously, had died in an accident. One afternoon Jennie appears at Eben's studio; she has come to pose. During their conversation, Eben mentions how lost he had been at the time they first met. Jennie seems upset at the word "lost." She says that they couldn't *both* have been lost. On returning to the room after a brief departure, Eben finds Jennie gone. He had not heard the hall door close. Too late he remembers that he has forgotten to ask Jennie where she lives.

8–11. During the winter, Eben is visited by a friend from New England, ARNE KUNSTLER. Eben shows him around New York. Arne departs, and solitude weighs on Eben as he waits for Jennie. At last she appears—pale, and clad in mourning. She says that her parents have died in an accident. Eben is not surprised; he has begun to perceive the pattern of events. Jennie poses as Eben begins the portrait of "Girl in a Black Dress" that is to make him famous. The long sitting is an ordeal; Jennie grows faint. She assures Eben that her aunt will take care of her. When Eben asks the address, Jennie explains that he cannot come to her—only she to him. Eben now understands the situation, and she knows that he knows. Jennie comes once more before the end of winter. She is gay; she is entering young womanhood. Eben realizes that he must finish the portrait quickly. Jennie gives a sprightly acount of her adventures in school. Eben feels that at last he has captured her animation on the canvas. Again Jennie departs while he is momentarily absent, leaving a note to say that she will return in the spring. Eben makes inquiry at the school named by Jennie, only to receive the expected reply that they have no pupil named Jennie Appleton. Eben postpones delivery of the finished portrait to Matthews; he cannot bear to part with it.

508

12–15. Spring is come, but not Jennie. Pressed for funds, Eben at last takes the portrait to Matthews, who declares it a masterpiece. Next day, Jennie comes to Eben. She is a young lady now. They have a whole day together; they accept the fact that they are in love. The idyll ends when Eben's landlady orders Jennie from the house. Jennie promises that she will return someday and remain with Eben forever. Eben knows the next event in the destined sequence: Jennie will go to a finishing school in Paris. It will be a long time before they will meet again. He joins Arne at Provincetown for the summer, to paint and to dream of Jennie.

16–18. The summer passes slowly, and by September Eben is too restless to paint. He and Arne set out in a small sailboat. They are caught in a hurricane, but manage to get back to shore. Eben sees Jennie on the beach, struggling against the gale. He rushes to rescue her, but a huge wave knocks him unconscious. Arne drags him to safety, but Jennie is gone. When Eben returns to New York, Gus shows him a newspaper clipping; it reports that Miss Jennie Appleton was washed overboard from the steamship on which she was returning from Europe after an absence of 8 years. Eben knows that, despite all adverse circumstance, Jennie will be with him always.

A Portrait of the Artist as a Young Man

Novel by James Joyce, 1882–1941. Published and © 1916 by B. W. Huebsch. © 1944 by Nora Joyce. (Compass, C9)

THE FIRST REAL BOOK by James Joyce is properly classed as a novel because it is told in the third person about fictionalized characters, but it is also an autobiography in which the protagonist is a representation of Joyce himself. One aspect of the book that makes it different is that it is also intended as a picture of any young man of original artistic nature. The style foreshadowed Joyce's later work in *Ulysses,* the center of action being placed "as much as possible inside the consciousness of the hero." Another distinctive feature of the book is that the style and viewpoints mature as the young hero matures. The first draft of this book, titled *Stephen Hero,* was published in 1944 by New Directions (a New York publishing house) as a posthumous work of Joyce's. The earlier version is similar except that it is more objective, that is, more conventional in treatment.

Chap. 1. The child STEPHEN DEDALUS experiences a kaleidoscope of infant sensations. He is told a bedtime story by his boastful, improvident father, SIMON, that "praiser of his own past." His mother plays a sailor's hornpipe on the piano. His grand-uncle CHARLES and his pious, fanatical aunt, Mrs. RIORDAN, clap when he dances. He calls Mrs. Riordan DANTE, which seems to be a nursery corruption of "aunty." EILEEN VANCE is his childhood sweetheart. Her white hands and golden hair later illuminate for him the meaning of "Tower of Ivory, House of Gold"—invocations from the Litany of the Virgin Mary. The boy Stephen goes to Clongowes Wood College, a Jesuit boarding school. He is puzzled by the conversation of older boys, stimulated by classroom competition, some-

times bullied, and sometimes homesick. He falls ill and goes to the infirmary in the care of Brother MICHAEL. There, fantasies of his own death mingle with thoughts of Parnell's death and with memories of political talk at home. Stephen goes home for Christmas. At Christmas dinner, Dante quarrels bitterly with Simon and Mr. JOHN CASEY over the dead Parnell and the priests who denounced him. Stephen's mother and uncle Charles attempt to pacify both sides. Back at Clongowes, Stephen is mystified by the expulsion of some older students for a nameless offense. He breaks his glasses and is unjustly punished by Father DOLAN, the prefect of studies. Stephen complains to the

He sees a lovely girl wading

rector, Father CONMEE, who accepts his plea. The boys praise Stephen's courage and Father Conmee's justice.

Chap. 2. During the summer in Black rock near Dublin, Stephen is much with his Uncle Charles. They go to the grocer's; to the park, where Charles chats with MIKE FLYNN; to the chapel, where Stephen is

respectfully unsympathetic with his uncle's piety; for Sunday walks with Stephen's father, when the two men talk politics and family legend. Stephen reads *The Count of Monte Cristo* in the evenings and imagines himself in the rôle. He has sham battles and rides the milkman's horse with his friend, AUBREY MILLS. The Dedalus family is in economic straits. Stephen cannot return to Clongowes. He begins vaguely to fear the future and to feel his difference from other children. Stephen's family moves to cheaper quarters, in Dublin. Stephen begins timidly to explore the city, resenting this new poverty. He is attracted to a girl at a children's party and writes a poem, *To E——C——.* [There are repeated allusions to her throughout the *Portrait,* although she is never named. But she is called EMMA CLERY in *Stephen Hero,* a partial first draft of the present novel, published in 1944 by New Directions.] Simon Dedalus encounters Father Conmee, now Jesuit provincial. The priest arranges a scholarship for Stephen and his younger brother, MAURICE, at Belvedere, the Jesuit school in Dublin. By the end of his second year at Belvedere, Stephen has a reputation for essay writing and a part in the school play. VINCENT HERON, his friend and rival, urges him to caricature the rector in the play. Heron taunts him about the charming girl (Emma) who comes with Simon, and playfully canes him, with the words, "Admit, admit." As Stephen mollifies his tormentor with a mocking "Confiteor," he remembers a similar scene in the recent past, when he was thus caned and bidden "admit" the fallacy of his preference for Byron over Tennyson. Stephen goes with his father by train to the father's birthplace, Cork, in connection with the sale of some property. He is embarrassed by Simon's sentimental nostalgia as they visit Queen's College, where Simon was once a medical student. Stephen wins £33 in school prizes. He spends it royally on delicacies and theater tickets for his family, presents and loans for everyone. Soon the money is gone, and he sees that it brought him no real communion with his family. The fierce sexual yearnings of puberty alternate with romantic visions of himself as the Count of Monte Cristo. A streetwalker takes him to her room and gives him his first knowledge of woman.

Chap. 3. Stephen spends his nights in Dublin brothels and his days in every sort of sensuality. With eyes and ears readily offended, he condemns his schoolfellows, and the pious. Meanwhile, as prefect of the sodality of the Blessed Virgin Mary, he is titillated by the irony of his position. He stills finds an arid pleasure in doctrinal discussion and notes that from lust all the other deadly sins have sprung, as St. James would indicate. At school, the rector announces a retreat in honor of St. Francis Xavier. Stephen is terrified at the prospect. Father ARNALL, the retreatmaster, preaches a series of sermons that fill Stephen with self-disgust, the fear of hell, and thoughts of the girl (Emma) of whom he is now unworthy. Stephen goes to confession—not in the college chapel, but as remotely as possible, to a Capuchin in the Church Street chapel. After confession, filled with peace and euphoria, he resolves to amend his life.

Chap. 4. Stephen now consecrates, in pious enthusiasm, each day of the week to a different image or mystery. He is a daily communicant, and carries a rosary in his trouser pocket. He mortifies his senses with fasting and self-denial, but the old desires recur. The director of the college discusses with him the possibility of his becoming a Jesuit, and once more Stephen imagines himself in a rôle he knows he will never fill. He goes home, where the younger children speak of another move for the Dedalus family, because the rent is unpaid. Stephen is now destined for the university, which worries his mother, who sees that his religious fervor is waning. Barefoot, walking along the strand of Dublin Bay, he sees a lovely young girl, wading, "like one whom magic had changed into the likeness of a strange and beautiful seabird." He is transfixed by the ecstatic knowledge of his poet's vocation.

Chap. 5. The Dedalus family is at very low water. A box of pawn tickets lies on the table as Stephen, now a university student, breakfasts on fried crusts and watery tea. He washes in an enamelled basin and hears his mother complain that the university has changed him. He begins, tardily, the walk across Dublin to his first lecture, thinking of the plays of Hauptmann, the prose of Newman, the songs of the Elizabethans, the metaphysics of Aristotle and Aquinas. He realizes that he has missed the English lecture. He thinks of his fellow students, especially CRANLY, to whom he has spoken of so many personal things, and DAVIN, the peasant student, that "dull-witted, loyal serf" to Irish myth and Roman Catholicism. Now late for his French class, he enters the physics theater, where the dean of studies, an English convert, is lighting a fire. They discuss aesthetics. The dean irritates Stephen by his polite surprise at Stephen's Irish word, "tundish," meaning funnel. Stephen, humiliated, reflects that this man is "a countryman of Ben Jonson." The class enters and the physics lecture begins, with whispered interruptions. After the lecture, a student named MACCANN solicits Stephen's signature to a petition for world peace. Cranly has given his, but Stephen refuses, and debates the issue with MacCann. Cranly leads Stephen and Stephen's naive admirer, TEMPLE, out of the crowd and away from the argument, inviting them in rough Latin to play handball. While the others play handball, Stephen explains to Davin why the Gaelic movement fails to interest him. Stephen leaves the handball court with LYNCH, expounding his Thomistic theory of aesthetics. Stephen defines pity and terror, which Aristotle did not define. They reach the library, where Stephen's "beloved" (Emma) is standing with other students. They do not speak, and Stephen thinks bitterly that "she has no

510

priest to flirt with." But he wonders if he has misjudged her. Stephen wakes on the morrow, the lines of a villanelle throbbing in his head. He finds only a cigarette package to write on. He thinks of his encounters with Emma over the past ten years. He finishes the poem. Stephen watches a bird on the library steps, while meditating on his mother's concern over his increasing agnosticism. He finds Cranly and DIXON in the library. They leave together and walk along chatting with other students. Stephen asks Cranly to come away for private conversation. He tells Cranly about a quarrel with his mother over his refusal to make his Easter duty. Cranly argues that Stephen should ease his mother's anxiety by receiving the sacraments, since the act should be a matter of indifference to an unbeliever. But Stephen, although he "will not serve," retains his dread of what would be, for a Catholic, sacrilege. Stephen says that he must leave Dublin, and Cranly agrees. The concluding pages are from Stephen's diary, immediately before his departure for Paris to learn to express his spirit freely.

Power

Novel by Leon Feuchtwanger, 1884–1958.
Published and © 1926 by The Viking Press, New York. Translated from the German by Willa and Edwin Muri.

THE LONG, carefully documented novels of Feuchtwanger were best when they described the historical position of the Jew in an alien government, for example Josephus in Rome. The protagonist of this, his best-known work, *Power*, was a Jew named Süss (the earlier translation of the German title is *Jew Süss*) who rose to great political importance. In addition to its good history, the novel has a good adventure story. It enjoyed great popularity when it was published and remains an item in the currently read literature of several countries.

Book I. The Princes. EBERHARD LUDWIG, Duke of Württemberg, has just departed from CHRISTL, his mistress for the past 30

years. He intended to cast her off, but the countess (Christl) has cleverly averted a definite break. Now, returning home, he is delighted by her cleverness in manipulating him, and feels that if the country has been bled by her exorbitant demands for money (as everybody complains), the money has been well spent. Also on the road are two Jews traveling to the spa of Wildbad. One is ISAAC LANDAUER, in his late sixties, wearing the caftan, earlocks, and even the badge prescribed for Jews. He is one of the most important men in Württemberg: Chief Minister of Finance and War for the Palatinate, and high in favor with the duke. He glories in the thought that he holds the real power of state, which rests on money, not titles. He does not understand the "younger generation" as represented by his 40-year-old companion, the rising financier JOSEPH OPPENHEIMER SÜSS. Süss is a dandy, spends his money on luxuries, wants to be accepted among the aristocracy. The two discuss the affairs of the countess, which are handled by Landauer, who benefits from her hold upon the duke.

The countryside is rife with tales of the Wandering Jew. The countess, a believer in Black Magic, commissions Landauer to bring this creature to her. Landauer appeals to Süss, for they both know that the prevalent description of the Wandering Jew fits Süss's Uncle GABRIEL. Süss is reluctant to become involved; he also knows that the upright Gabriel will not participate in shady doings. But Landauer offers Süss a partnership in the Countess' affairs; the bait is sufficient. Süss sends his secretary NICHOLAS PFAFFLE to fetch Gabriel. Pfaffle finds him a man of great seriousness, with three furrows on his brow forming the letter *shin,* which is the first letter of God's name, Shaddai.

Prince KARL ALEXANDER comes to Wildbad and petitions Parliament to increase his salary. He expects a favorable answer because he is a popular war hero. But two Jesuits influence the Protestant Parliament to refuse; they want the money to be furnished by a Catholic, so that Karl may be converted—thus giving the Catholics an entering wedge into the Protestant country. Süss ingratiates himself with Karl, who is his model of an aristocrat. Landauer laughs at Süss for wasting his time on a poor man.

Gabriel arrives in Wildbad, in charge of Süss's daughter NAEMI. Süss, so arrogant before everyone else, is shame-faced with Gabriel. Gabriel meets Karl, and under pressure to prophesy Karl's future says that he foresees two things. One he will not reveal; the other is the Ducal Crown. Karl laughs at the latter: Duke Eberhard is alive and hearty; there is one son already, and now that the duke is returning to his neglected wife, there may be other heirs. But Karl worries about the prophecy *not* told to him. His petition to Parliament denied, Karl's Catholic friends steer him to a wealthy Catholic princess, MARIE-AUGUSTE. Karl courts her; she agrees to marry him; he agrees to turn Catholic to irk the Protestants who refused him his due.

Meanwhile, Christl blunders by writing to a servant of the duke, asking for some of the duke's blood. Eberhard finds the note and concludes that the people, who have suspected her of witchcraft, are right. He gives her a large sum of money and gets her out of the country with Landauer's help. Süss take Naemi to a secluded place near Hirsau, telling Gabriel that he may visit her there. Karl and Marie-Auguste wed and depart on their honeymoon. Süss sends a courier after them with the news that the Crown Prince, Eberhard's son, is dead. Süss by this time is firmly fixed in Karl's entourage. Marie-Auguste likes him—she has never seen a Jew before, and finds Süss more refined than many Christians.

Book II. The People. Württemberg is a rich country coveted by foreign powers. When Eberhard dies suddenly, Karl becomes duke in accordance with Gabriel's prophecy. Süss rises with him and is made Privy Financial Councilor. Karl is loved by the people for his robust energy, but he is easily led. The Catholics plan to use him as a means to enter and then control the country. Keen only to the needs of military defense, Karl plans to build up the army. Parliament is reluctant to vote more taxes. Süss proposes to ignore Parliament and mulct the people in other ways. Karl agrees, for he is irked by the constitutional safeguards of popular rights—such as they are. The people begin to distrust Karl and hate Süss, who is recognized as the real power. Süss waxes wealthy, acquiring many mistresses, a palatial home, a luxurious table. Süss visits Naemi for three days. She is pure, simple, and adores her father. On the way back to town, Süss sees a beautiful girl and learns that she is MAGDALEN WEISSENSEE, of the illegal Pietist sect. Magdalen runs from Süss screaming, thinking he is the Devil. Nevertheless, she feels a mission to convert him. Another Pietist is young JAAKOB SCHOBER, who has seen Naemi and dreams of her.

Magdalen's father is one of the Committee of 11, comprising the leaders of Parliament. This Committee wants Karl to disband the army. Süss persuades Karl to pack the Committee with more members, favorable to him. The trick succeeds, and the Rump Parliament grants Karl greater power than any other ruler has had under the Constitution. Taxes are raised; the army is increased. The consequences are disastrous: the land lacks horses and men to work it; people are starving. Religion becomes their last refuge, and even religious freedom is imperiled.

Süss harrasses the domestic firm of SCHERTLIN on behalf of a competitor who wants to do business in Württemberg. WEISSENSEE brings his daughter to court at Süss's request. Magdalen faints when she recognizes Süss as her Devil. Actually, she is in love with him—but Karl sees her and takes her. Her father is appalled, but does not dare protest nor even refuse the honors

The horrified girl climbs to the roof and jumps to her death

paid him in consideration of Magdalen's becoming the duke's official mistress. The seduction occurs at a ball given for the nobility by Süss, the climax of his career. DOM PANCORBO, his chief rival in the jewel trade—one of his lucrative sidelines—is consumed with envy of the enormous solitaire Süss wears.

Book III. The Jews. Magdalen accepts Karl passively, as she does the friendship of his wife, Marie-Auguste. She hates Süss, for she realizes she could have been his had he not allowed Karl to take her. The people, too, hate Süss. Near Hirsau, Naemi sees flowers trained to spell the words "Süss—Pig—Jew." She faints; Jaakob Schober revives her and tries to explain matters. She calls him a slanderer and insists that her father is not a wicked man. Jaakob decides he has a mission to convert Naemi, and through her, Süss, and perhaps even Karl himself. Süss next reaches for a patent of nobility. He could get it easily by embracing Catholicism, but he balks. When he takes a long holiday, Karl discovers how dependent he is on Süss.

A peddler, KASPAR DIETERLE, goes to the fair at Esslingen with his much-abused mistress, BABETTE. In a drunken moment he beats Babette to death. He buries the body near the Jewish Inn and contrives to throw suspicion on JECHESKE SELIGMANN FREUDENTHAL, a Jew. This man is arrested; popular feeling runs high against him, as against all Jews because of Süss. Marie-Auguste is unfaithful to the duke and is caught. Her father obtains the aid of his Catholic friend, the Bishop of Wurzberg, to reconcile the couple. The event makes gains for the Catholic Church, and also lays the foundation for a "Catholic plot." Süss is elbowed aside by the Jesuit manipulators of Parliament. He visits Magdalen, who admits that she loves him. For the first time, he openly disparages the duke. He gloats over his new conquest. Weissensee, humiliated by his position, retires to Hirsau to work on a Bible study. He talks with Jaakob about Magdalen. Jaakob confides his love for Naemi. The older man wonders how Süss would feel had Naemi suffered Magdalen's fate.

Süss no longer enjoys unchallenged power, but Jews throughout the country look to him for protection against the anti-Semitism fanned by the Esslingen case. He refuses appeals to intervene in that case

from Landauer and a deputation of ten leading Jews. But when word comes through Gabriel that Naemi has begun to see him as he is, Süss decides he must rehabilitate himself in her eyes. He intervenes and obtains the release of Jecheske, to the plaudits of all Jews. Then Süss learns from his mother, MICAELE, that his father was not her Jewish husband but Baron GEORG EBERHARD VON HEYDERSDORFF—a once-renowned field marshal who fell into ignominy and turned monk. Süss contemplates telling the duke that he is Heydersdorff's bastard, to obtain the due honors of a Christian. Then he reflects that to have his power as a Christian is not so momentous as to have it as a Jew. Also, he cherishes his newfound popularity with the Jewish community.

Book IV. The Duke. Marie-Auguste bears a son, KARL EUGENE, baptised a Catholic to the dismay of the people, who have begun to resent the Catholic encroachment. Süss is a changed man. He withdraws from his sidelines, letting Dom Pancorbo take over. In Süss's absence at Hirsau to visit Naemi, Karl has his accounts audited. Karl has begun to fear the hold Süss has upon him. Süss stakes his future on a gamble: he asks for his demission, planning to retire if it is granted. The gamble works. Karl cannot do without Süss—yet. Back in power, Süss is less sympathetic, more imperious. He is no longer interested in Magdalen, who has changed into a prudent *hausfrau*, to the dismay of her father, who could forgive anything but this banality. Weissensee still plans retribution; he panders to Süss, and persuades the duke to visit Hirsau for a hunting trip. While the faithful Gabriel is away, Weissensee leads the duke to Naemi's cottage and incites the duke to seduce her. The horrified girl climbs to the roof and jumps to her death. Karl summons Süss, explains matters, apologizes, and regards the incident as closed. Süss conceals his fury and at once begins to devise revenge. Weissensee, too, is furious, for Süss has been made a martyr instead of a laughingstock. In the days that follow, Karl has to swallow many affronts from Süss. He issues an edict forbidding anyone to question Süss's financial transactions, past, present, or future. Süss is not bought off. Süss even sleeps with ELISABETH GOTZ, whom the duke has been courting.

Jaakob becomes Süss's secretary, still intent on converting him. When Süss dictates all the details of the Catholic plot, Jaakob is in a quandary. Shall he betray Süss and speak out to save Protestantism, or shall he stay quiet and let the Catholics take over? Karl dreams of ruling by Divine Right— thus getting rid of the hated Constitution. Süss plots a *coup d'etat:* The duke is to leave town, appointing a regency; a military group will seize power and proclaim Karl absolute sovereign; they will emasculate the Constitution and proclaim Protestant and Catholic equality. But secretly Süss orders Schober to deliver the details of the plot, and the password, to Parliament. Thus the attempted coup is frustrated. Karl collapses and dies when he hears the bad news. Süss is satisfied with his revenge. He offers himself to the leaders of the plot as a scapegoat.

Book V. The Others. Among the three regents named in Karl Alexander's will is 70-year-old KARL RUDOLPH, a just man. He refuses to act with the other regents,

Marie-Auguste and the Catholic Bishop. Parliament votes him a lone hand. Rudolph begins to clear up the mess; prosperity returns to Württemberg. Süss is in jail, but no charge can be found against him except under a long-dead law forbidding carnal intercourse between Christian and Jew. A packed jury convicts him. He resists all pleas to save himself by converting. His mother visits him in jail and is horrified to find that Süss has reverted to a Jew of the ghetto. But Gabriel approves the change. Jaakob proclaims Süss's part in saving the country from the Catholic plot, but is disbelieved. He returns to Hirsau to write poetry. Marie-Auguste leaves the country. Pfaffle and Landauer raise a fund to which Jews throughout the world contribute; the money is offered to Württemberg for Süss's life, but Rudolph refuses to set aside the sentence. Süss is hanged at Stuttgart and buried in Firth. On his brows appear the three furrows of the *shin.*

Pride and Prejudice

Novel by Jane Austen, 1775–1817. Published 1813. (PB, PL9; RE, 22; ML, 264 & T1)

SINCE JANE AUSTEN never wrote a novel that was not superlative, objectively there is little to choose among her six novels. *Pride and Prejudice* has been by far the most popular for the sole reason that its character Elizabeth Bennet is Jane Austen's best-loved heroine. Elizabeth also was probably the heroine that Jane Austen herself would most have liked to be, so she may be more of a self-portrait than similar characters in other Austen books. Like Jane Austen's other novels, *Pride and Prejudice* is a "drawing room comedy," witty and good-humored. Somerset Maugham selected *Pride and Prejudice,* from among Jane Austen's works, as one of the four best English novels and one of the ten best in the world.

Chaps. 1–5. Mr. BENNET's property in Meryton is entailed on a distant cousin, "in default of heirs male." His five dowerless daughters are: pretty, modest and sweet-tempered JANE; the novel's clever, spirited heroine, ELIZABETH; priggish, plain, bookish and rather stupid MARY, and the two youngest, CATHERINE and LYDIA, who are frivolous copies of their mother. Mrs. BENNET's principal interest is in finding husbands for her daughters. She is delighted that the nearby estate of Netherfield Park has been let, at last, to a young man of large fortune from the north of England. In the satiric opening words of the novel, "it is a truth universally acknowledged, that a single man in possession of a good fortune must be in want of a wife." Mr. Bennet, a man of cultivation and wry humor, has

little patience with his wife and little sympathy with any of his daughters but Elizabeth, who has inherited his temperament. He teases Mrs. Bennet by pretense of refusal to call on Netherfield's tenant, Mr. BINGLEY. In fact, the call is made, and the girls have the pleasure of dancing with their new neighbor at the next ball, where Bingley pays particular attention to Jane. But Elizabeth is enraged by the supercilious manner of Bingley's friend, DARCY, whose *pride* engenders her *prejudice* against him.

Chaps. 6–12. Bingley's interest in Jane flourishes, but Elizabeth remains skeptical of his merit and resents the haughtiness of his sister CAROLINE. Meanwhile, Darcy is secretly drawn to Elizabeth, and Catherine and Lydia are intrigued by the arrival of a regiment of militia in the neighborhood. Caroline Bingley invites Jane to spend the afternoon at Netherfield. Mrs. Bennet sends Jane on horseback, in hope that rain will enforce an overnight visit and foster the intimacy. The plan succeeds. The rain gives Jane such a bad cold that she must remain at Netherfield for several days, and Elizabeth goes there to nurse her. Bingley's devotion to Jane increases, as does Darcy's respect for Elizabeth. But Mrs. Bennet's vulgar and silly conversation embarrasses Elizabeth, delights the waspish Caroline, and horrifies Darcy, who is glad to see the young ladies return home, lest he be more attracted.

Chaps. 13–20. The Bennets are visited by Mr. COLLINS, the cousin who is heir to Mr. Bennet's property. Collins is a snobbish, pompous little clergyman. His patroness, Lady CATHERINE DE BOURGH, is aunt to Darcy. Collins suggests that he marry one of the Bennet girls in recompense for having deprived them of dowries. Mrs. Bennet replies coyly that her eldest daughter is soon to be engaged, but gives him permission to

court one of the younger girls. Collins accompanies the Bennet sisters to an evening at the home of their old friends, the LUCAS family. There Elizabeth meets a handsome young officer, WICKHAM. Wickham shocks her with a story of Darcy's alleged injustice to him. Wickham says he was Darcy's father's ward and Darcy deprived him of a legacy. Elizabeth's prejudice against Darcy increases. She is bitterly amused to hear that Darcy is unofficially engaged to the sickly daughter of Lady Catherine de Bourgh, because Caroline Bingley's designs on Darcy have been obvious to her. Elizabeth is somewhat charmed by Wickham. She is quite unaware that Collins is wooing her. He is merely a joke to her and her friend CHARLOTTE LUCAS. They look in vain for Wickham at the Netherfield ball. Elizabeth is disconcerted by the marked attentions of Darcy, whom she reproaches by ironic allusion to his supposed mistreatment of Wickham. The tension between Elizabeth and Darcy is increased when her mother outrages Darcy with idiotic conversation and arch references to his friend Bingley's approaching engagement to Jane. The odious Collins proposes marriage to Elizabeth and at first questions the sincerity of her refusal. Mrs. Bennet is angered by the girl's rejection of a perfectly good husband, but Mr. Bennet shares Elizabeth's opinion of Collins.

Chaps. 21–26. Jane receives a surprising letter from Caroline Bingley. Charles Bingley, whose love for Jane has been evident to all, has left for London on business. Caroline has decided to close Netherfield and follow him to London for the winter. The letter ends with a hint that Bingley will one day marry Darcy's sister, GEORGIANA. Heartbroken Jane sees only Caroline's wish to spare her disappointment, but Elizabeth suspects deceit. The Bennets are astounded to hear that Collins has proposed marriage to Charlotte Lucas and has been accepted. Elizabeth feels that she can never respect her friend again, because Charlotte is frankly marrying a man she despises for the sake of his fortune. Jane goes to spend some time in London with her aunt and uncle, the GARDINERS. The Bingleys do not even call on her there.

Chaps. 27–35. Elizabeth visits Charlotte, now married to Collins. At their home she meets Lady Catherine de Bourgh, whose "dignified impertinence" further buttresses Elizabeth's prejudice against Lady Catherine's nephew, Darcy. Elizabeth is wickedly amused to hear Lady Catherine's plans for the marriage of her frail, unattractive daughter to Darcy. Darcy is expected at Rosings, and Elizabeth anticipates observing his attentions to his cousin and thinking of Caroline Bingley's frustration. But when Darcy arrives, she is amazed to receive those attentions herself. She is simultaneously rather ambiguously courted by Darcy's cousin, Colonel FITZWILLIAM. Fitzwilliam unwittingly crowns her prejudice against Darcy with the casual information that Darcy was responsible for spiriting Bingley to London in time to prevent an unsuitable match—obviously with her sister Jane. At this peak of her dislike for Darcy, he surprises and enrages her with a condescending proposal of marriage. She refuses in terms which crush his pride. She accuses him of mistreating Wickham and interfering between Jane and Bingley. He writes a letter giving his version of both these stories: that Wickham had abused his father's trust, attempted to seduce Georgiana, and violated the conditions of the legacy; that Jane's natural modesty had concealed the strength of her attachment to Bingley, and convinced Darcy of her indifference. He apologizes for his cruel mistake.

Chaps. 36–42. Elizabeth is shamed by Darcy's letter, which convinces her of the injustice of her prejudice and evokes different emotions toward him. Concern for Jane is renewed by the knowledge that Bingley really valued her and is not the fickle lover Elizabeth had despised. She is further concerned for Catherine and Lydia, doubtless now flirting with the treacherous Wickham. She returns to her family's home, where Catherine and Lydia are desolate that the regiment is soon to depart. Lydia has been invited to visit the Colonel's wife, Mrs. FORSTER. But Elizabeth's anxiety for Lydia is forgotten in the pleasure of a trip through Derbyshire with the Gardiners. She is conscious that they may stop at Pemberley, the ancestral home of Darcy.

Chaps. 43–45. Elizabeth and the Gardiners call at Pemberley, in the presumed absence of its owner. They are impressed by its beauty and by the respectful affection of servants and tenants for Darcy. They are surprised by Darcy's return, and by his gracious deference to Elizabeth. The Bingleys and Georgiana Darcy appear. All but Caroline are most cordial.

Chaps. 46–51. The harmonious encounter is interrupted by a letter from Meryton with the dreadful news that Lydia has run off with Wickham. Elizabeth knows that he would never marry the dowerless girl. She cannot conceal her shock or its source from Darcy, who asks permission to search for the couple. Elizabeth returns to Meryton. Her uncle Gardiner hastens to assist Mr. Bennet in pursuing the runaways. Mr. Bennet returns in despair with the news that the couple are lost in London, but a few days later he receives a letter from Gardiner stating that Wickham and Lydia are found and that he will witness their wedding. Giddy Mrs. Bennet is overjoyed to have married off her youngest, but Mr. Bennet and Elizabeth fear that Gardiner cannot have enforced the marriage at less than ten thousand pounds, which they could never repay. Gardiner mysteriously begs them not to discuss it. Lydia and Wickham return to Meryton, brash, gay, not at all embarrassed.

Chaps. 52–61. Elizabeth writes privately to Gardiner for the true story of the Wickhams. Gardiner expresses astonishment at her ignorance that Lydia's dowry was Darcy's gift. Darcy had insisted on secrecy,

but the Gardiners naturally supposed that Elizabeth knew of this and that she and Darcy must be about to announce their engagement. Elizabeth's gratitude to Darcy and her appreciation of his delicacy increase her new love for him. Bingley arrives to reopen Netherfield and to woo Jane. Elizabeth suspects Darcy's influence here as well. But Darcy's manner is so stiff that Mrs. Bennet dislikes him more than ever. The engagement of Bingley and Jane is shortly followed by a call from Lady Catherine de Bourgh, who demands a private interview with Elizabeth. She tries imperiously to extort the girl's promise never to marry Darcy. Elizabeth, furious, refuses. Lady Catherine's call is promptly succeeded by another, from

Darcy. He once more proposes marriage to Elizabeth, but this time with humility and grace. She has lost her prejudice and he his pride. Mrs. Bennet's rapture at the marriage of three daughters overcomes her previous dislike of Darcy, whose fortune is even larger than Bingley's.

Bingley and Darcy woo Jane and Elizabeth

The Prince

Treatise by Niccolo Machiavelli, 1469–1527.
Published 1532. (NAL, MD69; ML, 65 & T25).

THIS IS ONE OF the best known works of all times yet not one in a thousand who quote it has ever read it. Because of one brief section of the book and a few miscellaneous statements advocating total cynicism and ruthlessness on the part of a ruler, *The Prince* has come to be considered solely as a work advocating unscrupulousness in international dealings and the term Machiavellian has become a common English word in the same sense. Actually *The Prince* is a careful study of good government in all its phases. In the introduction to the edition of *The Prince* published by Everyman's Library, W. K. Marriott writes, "*The Prince* was never published by [Machiavelli] and its text is still disputable." To Machiavelli must be credited the clearest statement of the concept of the relative and individual positions of the state and the citizen. The book has been castigated because so many tyrants and dictators seem to have conformed to its injunctions, but more objective analysis indicates that democratic governments have done precisely the same.

1. Principalities are either hereditary, or new. New principalities are either entirely new, or conquered and attached to the hereditary state of their prince. Of the latter, some are accustomed to the rule of a prince, some to live in freedom: some acquired by conquest by the prince himself, some by conquest of others, some through purchase, some through ability. 2. Hereditary states are easier to hold than new ones, for all a prince of average powers has to do to keep his rule is to follow the precedents set by his ancestors, and to meet with prudence whatever situations arise. True, the state may be wrested from him by superior force, but his chances of regaining it are good

513

whenever misfortune befalls his usurper. This is so because, as a rule, he is better loved by his subjects. 3. New principalities are more likely to be difficult. For one thing, when men change their rulers willingly, they do so because they hope to better themselves, but they are likely to find they have gone from bad to worse. A new prince usually burdens his newly-acquired state with soldiery and other hardships. He makes enemies of those he has displaced, and loses the friendship of those who supported him, by disappointing their expectations: nor can he take strong measures against the latter, since he has need of goodwill. This point is illustrated by the history of Louis the Twelfth of France and his connection with Milan. He occupied it quickly, and was quickly driven out by Duke Lodovico, having lost the support of those Milanese who at first had welcomed him and then were disappointed by his treatment of them. Then Louis took the city again, and this time he was less easily dislodged, because he had taken measures to secure a stronger hold. Just the same, he was driven out a second time, because he had failed to do what needed to be done, committing five errors: he helped to destroy the minor powers which bordered on Milan, by assisting Pope Alexander to occupy the Romagna; and by the same action increased the authority of the Church to a degree which endangered his own rule; he brought in the King of Spain, a foreign power; he did not settle in the country, to make his regime more secure; nor did he send in colonies, which are less offensive to the natives than troops. The injuries he inflicted were not of the heaviest, but this did not save his cause; for men ought either to be well-treated or crushed: a middle cause will displease enough to invite revenge, and inflict too little injury to deter such revenge.

4. How is it that the successors of Alexander the Great experienced so little difficulty in holding the empire he had conquered from Darius? I maintain the reason is, that he governed his principality with the help of servants who were beholden to him for their dignity; had he, like the King of France, been dependent upon barons of his realm, who hold their dignity by antiquity of blood and not by favor of their prince, he would have succeeded as little. Among modern governments, the closest in its resemblance to the empire of Alexander is the Turkish. 5. He who becomes master of a city accustomed to freedom must destroy it, or be himself destroyed, unless he chooses to reside there. 6. In keeping new principalities, those who have taken nothing from fortune but opportunity, who have seized and improved upon this opportunity through their own ability, have the best chance of succeeding (e.g., Moses, Cyrus, Theseus, Romulus). If unarmed, however, like Savonarola, they cannot maintain their rule. 7. Those who become princes solely through good fortune have a hard time maintaining their status (e.g., Cesare Borgia, in contrast to Francesco Sforza). They have to lay their

514

foundations *afterwards*. 8. A prince may acquire his station by wicked ways, like Agathocles, the Sicilian, who became King of Syracuse. Such methods may gain empire, but not glory. Oliverotto da Fermo is another example. Agathocles was wise enough to employ severity at once, and in sufficient strength, so it was not necessary to repeat it. 9. It is better, when one becomes prince by favour of his fellow-citizens, to owe one's elevation to the people generally, rather than to the nobles. For "it is necessary for a prince to have the people friendly, otherwise he has no security in adversity." 10. A prince who keeps his town well-fortified, and has the good will of his people, will not be easily dislodged. 11. Ecclesiastical principalities only are secure and happy. Alexander VI and Pope Julius have contributed greatly to the greatness of the Church that exists today under Pope Leo.

12. The chief foundations of all states are good laws and good arms. Mercenaries are not to be relied upon; armed citizenry are to be preferred. A republic with armed citizenry, like Rome, Sparta, Switzerland, keeps its freedom longer. Nations that employed mercenaries, and suffered therefrom, were the Carthaginians, the Thebans, the Milanese, and, most recently, the Florentines. Italy has been ruled for many years with mercenaries, with the result that they have brought the land to slavery and contempt, through their avoidance of both fatigue and dangers. 13. Auxiliaries are even more of a danger than mercenaries; the wise prince does not consider a victory gained with the arms of another a real one. Cesare Borgia, who employed in succession mercenaries, auxiliaries, and his own men, was most successful with the last. "The arms of others either fall from your back, or they weigh you down, or they bind you fast." No principality is secure that does not have its own forces. 14. A prince must study war, above all else: Those princes who have thought more of ease have lost their states. He should study war in peacetime especially; he should not only study it, he should train for it. He should study the actions of illustrious men in war, as Scipio studied the life of Cyrus, so he can follow suit if the occasion arises.

15. It is necessary for a prince wishing to hold his own to know how to do wrong, and to make use of it or not according to necessity. It would be best if a prince exhibited only good qualities: but since human conditions forbid this it is necessary for the prince to be prudent. 16. A reputation for liberality is good to have. However, it may prove too costly to attain. The great things done in our time have been accomplished by those who are accounted mean; in fact, meanness is one of those vices that enable a prince to govern. There is nothing that wastes so rapidly as liberality, nothing that is more likely to lead to a prince's being despised and hated. In sum: Since the attempt to gain a reputation for liberality may bring both reproach and hatred, while a reputation for meanness

brings only reproach, it is wiser to be reputed mean. 17. To be reproached for cruelty is better than to allow disorders to arise, through too much mercy. It is better to be feared than loved, since men have less scruple in offending one who is beloved than one who is feared. Nevertheless a prince ought to inspire fear in such a way that, if he does not win love, he avoids hatred. 18. It is praiseworthy in a prince to keep faith; but a wise lord cannot, ought not, keep faith when such observance may be turned against him. It is necessary to be a fox to discover the snares and a lion to terrify the wolves. Because men are bad, and will not keep faith with you, he who has known best how to play the fox has succeeded best. It is unnecessary for a prince to be altogether merciful, faithful, humane, upright, and religious, but it is important for him to appear so. 19. The prince who is highly esteemed is not easily conspired against; therefore one who would succeed must not incur hatred through rapacity, nor contempt through mean-spiritedness and irresolution; for then the prince must fear everything and everybody. So ought princes to leave affairs of reproach to the management of others, and keep those of grace.

20. Princes have employed various methods to secure their states: Some have disarmed their subjects, some have fostered factions, some have encouraged enemies to arise so that they may crush them and win greater renown, some have taken pains to win over those whom they distrusted at the beginning of their rule, some have built fortresses, some have overthrown and destroyed fortresses. All things considered, the best security is to avoid being hated by the people. 21. A prince can win esteem by great enterprises, as in the case of Ferdinand of Aragon, King of Spain; or by setting unusual examples in internal affairs which may be much spoken about, as related about Bernabo da Milano; by being either a true friend or a downright enemy, never by attempting to choose a perfectly safe course; by showing himself a patron of ability and of the arts; by entertaining the people with festivals and spectacles, and by showing esteem for the guilds or societies into which every city is divided. 22. The choice of servants is also important, and a guage of the prince's wisdom. The prince who chooses good servants, and treats them properly, will earn the general good opinion, and the loyalty of his servant. 23. A prince should be careful of flatterers; on the other hand, he should encourage only the wise men in his state to speak the truth to him, and then only of those things of which he inquires; outside of these, he should listen to no one, be steadfast in his resolutions. 24. States that have power enough to keep an army in the field cannot be lost, if the suggestions made here are followed, if the people have been won over, and if the loyalty of the nobles has been secured. 25. Fortune is the arbiter of half our actions, true, but we may still control the other half, or perhaps a little less than half, by setting up barriers and defenses against her forces.

The prince who relies entirely upon fortune is lost when it changes; fortune does not change when one changes his conduct to match the times. It is better to be adventurous than cautious, because fortune is a woman, and if you wish to keep her under it is necessary to beat and ill-use her. 26. There is no time more fit than the present to favor a new prince: Italy is now in such sore straits that she stands ready and willing to follow a banner if only someone will raise it. Let, therefore, the Medici take up this charge with that courage and hope with which all just enterprises are undertaken.

The Prince and the Pauper

Novel by Mark Twain (Samuel Clemens, 1835–1910).
Published 1882.

THIS IS A BETTER BOOK for children than Mark Twain's *Tom Sawyer* and is good reading for adults too, not only for the story but because the author introduced into the narrative the result of some interesting reading on 16th-century conditions, customs, and laws. The story concerns a young prince, based on the young son of Henry VIII of England, who ruled for a brief period as Edward VI (he became king when he was 10 and died when he was 16). Mark Twain says in his introduction to the book that "it could have happened."

Chaps. 1–2. Two boys are born on the same day in London in the second quarter of the 16th century. One is EDWARD, the longed-for son of King HENRY VIII. The other, TOM CANTY, is born in Offal Court in the slums. While the young Prince grows up, strictly trained and educated but in great luxury, Tom learns how to beg in the streets. He dislikes begging, and brings home only enough farthings to prevent his father, JOHN CANTY, from giving him one of his more extravagant beatings. Tom is taught to read by an old priest in the neighborhood, Father ANDREW, and his reading sets him daydreaming of princes and courts until he sometimes thinks himself a prince. Although the neighbors laugh at him at first, they soon discover that Tom is wise far beyond his years and come to him with their disputes. His mother, and his ignorant, good-hearted sisters, NAN and BET, love Tom and are good to him but they fear that his learning will turn his wits.

Chaps. 3–9. Tom wanders to Westminster, where the royal family is living. Inside the gates he sees the embodiment of his daydreams—a real prince in silk and satin, with a jeweled sword. As Tom draws close to the gates a soldier hurls him away. The Prince berates the guard and orders that Tom be let in. The two boys go to the Prince's quarters where Edward, sending his servants away so that Tom will not be embarrassed, hears about Tom's life and envies his freedom to play in the mud and swim in the river. Tom envies all that he can see of Edward's life. For a jest the boys change clothes and stand in front of the mirror, to discover that they are exactly alike in form, feature and carriage. The prince is now the pauper and the pauper the prince. When they recover from their astonishment, Edward realizes that the guard has hurt Tom's hand. He rushes away to make sure that the brutality is punished. As he hurries to the gate, Tom's rags fluttering around him, the guard seizes him and thrusts him out into a jeering mob, who shove and hustle him along until the Prince has no idea where he is. He tries to reach Offal Court, where he expects Tom's family to help him, but John Canty believes that he is Tom gone mad and hauls him in for a beating. Tom, left alone, grows worried by Edward's absence. He is sure that he will be hanged if he is found alone in the Prince's apartments, and when Lady JANE GREY is ushered in he falls on his knees to her. The young girl runs away in terror. The rumor runs through the palace that the Prince has gone mad. Presently Tom, almost paralyzed with fear, is ordered into the King's presence. The burly, tyrannous old King has always treated his son more kindly than anyone else and he is broken-hearted at the evidence that Tom's mind has gone astray. Tom cannot convince him that he is not the Prince, and is led away to begin his strange new life. He finds the reality very dreary in comparison with his daydreams; it is also embarrassing. He constantly tries to do things for himself that 3 servants are supposed to do. At a public banquet he drinks the rose water offered him to wash his hands. All his mistakes, however, are attributed to his malady.

Chaps. 10–13. John Canty in a fury kills Father Andrew and flees from Offal Court with his family. In the scramble, the Prince manages to get away from Canty, and makes his way to Guildhall, where Tom is being installed as Prince of Wales. While the real Prince stands at the gates the mock prince suddenly learns that his "father," King Henry, is dead and that he is king. Edward, as usual, tries to tell the crowds who he is and, as usual, is taunted and threatened. This time he is defended by MILES HENDON. Hendon is the son of a baronet. He left his home 7 years ago because his younger brother, HUGH, alleged that Miles intended to marry his cousin EDITH against his father's will. Miles has been a soldier and prisoner-of-war and is on his way home. Tickled by the Prince's spirit, though he thinks him mad, Hendon resolves to protect him and takes him to his room at an inn on London Bridge. Edward is grateful from the bottom of his heart, but he nevertheless expects Hendon to wait on him hand and foot. Hendon humors him in every way.

Chaps. 14–16. Tom at first finds being a king even drearier than being a prince. However, he discovers his "whipping-boy," HUMPHREY MARLOW, whose profession is to be beaten if his sovereign fails at his lessons. Humphrey is a gold mine of information about court people and customs. One thing Tom does not discover is the whereabouts of the Great Seal of England, which Henry VIII has given to Prince Edward, and which cannot be found. Tom saves a man from being boiled alive on a false accusation of poisoning and brings this punishment to an end in England. The people begin to feel that he is a sane and merciful ruler.

Chaps. 17–21. John Canty, unable to return home because of his murder of the priest, has joined a band of beggars. These men and women live in an old barn outside London and ply the streets during the day, using their real infirmities or feigning injuries and illness in order to get money from sympathizers. Canty lures Edward away from Hendon by a trick and tries to force him to beg, but Edward escapes. In his wandering through the woods he is kindly used by a peasant woman and nearly murdered by a mad hermit, but Canty finds him and takes him back to the beggars.

Chaps. 22–29. HUGO, a young ruffian Canty puts in charge of Edward, steals a package and deliberately thrusts it into Edward's hands. Miles Hendon appears as Edward is being taken to the justice of the peace, and manages to frighten a corrupt constable into letting the boy escape. He takes Edward to Hendon Hall. On their arrival Hendon finds that his father and his brother ARTHUR are dead. His brother Hugh has taken Miles' inheritance and has forced Edith to marry him. Hugh swears that Miles is not Miles Hendon but an impostor and, as his word is law in these parts, he is able to throw Hendon and Edward into jail. Edward hears much of the injustice of the laws and promises himself that he will change them when he is restored to his throne. To complete Hendon's punishment for being himself, he is set in the stocks for a day. Edward resists the officer in charge and is about to be whipped, but Hendon takes the stripes for him. Edward dubs him an earl, a "dreams and shadows" honor that touches Hendon as much as it amuses him. Edward learns that the coronation of the "King" is imminent and insists that he and Hendon return to London.

Chaps. 30–33. Tom is enjoying his kingship. He remains a champion of the oppressed but he thinks as little as possible of the lost King and of his own mother and sisters, for their memory makes him feel guilty and ashamed. All his pleasure in his great position ends during the triumphal "recognition procession" to the coronation, when his mother, recognizing him as he rides past, flings herself upon him and is torn away by Tom's attendants. Even when the crown is held above his head in Westminster Abbey, Tom feels nothing but remorse. Before the crown has touched Tom's head, the real King appears in the aisle, ragged but imperious, and claims the throne. Tom falls on his knees to welcome him, but the nobles refuse to believe the boys' story of how this strange thing came about. Their doubts vanish when Edward is able to tell them, as Tom never could, where the Great Seal is. It turns out that Tom in his ignorance has used the seal to crack nuts with. Edward finds that Tom has ruled mercifully and well and he endows him with the special title of King's Ward, which Tom bears honorably for the rest of his long life. Miles Hendon is found by Humphrey Marlow and is confirmed in the titles he thought were empty dreams. Hugh is sent to prison and, on his death a few years later, Edith and Miles are married. Edward's brief reign is a beneficent one, for he knows more about the troubles of his people than most kings ever learn.

The real King, ragged but imperious, arrives and claims the throne

The Prisoner of Zenda

Novel by Anthony Hope (Sir Anthony Hope Hawkins, 1863–1933). Published 1894.

NOVELS ABOUT small Balkan or eastern European kingdoms and principalities were all the rage at the turn of the century and this novel had much to do with creating their general popularity. It is the best of the lot and in fact it is very good. But the most significant thing about *The Prisoner of Zenda* is that it proves what no modern novelist seems to appreciate: That one can produce excellent romance without sending his hero and heroine to bed together.

Chaps. 1–3. RUDOLF RASSENDYLL is of good family, well-to-do, and idle. Rudolf differs from most other Rassendylls in that he has a long straight nose and bushy red hair. This, he claims, is the stamp of the ELPHBERGS, the royal family of Ruritania. Generations back an Elphberg prince visited England and had a certain hushed-up affair with a young and beautiful, though married, Rassendyll lady. This prince possessed bushy red hair and a long straight nose. Rudolf's sister-in-law chides him for his idleness, so he decides to take a journey. He tells her he is going for a ramble in the Tyrol, whereas actually he has decided to go to the famous Ruritania, as he has heard that the new king, RUDOLPH V, is soon to be crowned there. In Paris he discovers that a certain renowned lady, ANTOINETTE DE MAUBAN, is in love with the Duke of STRELSAU, brother of the new Ruritanian king-to-be, and she happens to ride on the same train with Rudolf all the way to Ruritania. Strelsau, town of the coronation, is overcrowded; Rudolf stops instead at Zenda, a village 50 miles distant. Here the castle of the Duke of Strelsau broods over the countryside, and inside the castle broods BLACK MICHAEL, the duke. Rudolf discovers that the king-to-be is staying in a hunting lodge nearby and that rivalry has existed between the king and his brother Michael both for the kingdom and for the hand of beautiful Princess FLAVIA. Rudolf wanders into the forest and meets two servants of the king, Colonel SAPT and FRITZ VON TARLENHEIM. They are astonished at his resemblance to their king. Suddenly the king himself appears and the two Rudolfs gaze at each other in amazement. Their looks are almost identical. The king knows the ancestral story also, and he laughs in delight. The four go off to have dinner together. It is the night before the coronation and much wine is consumed in jovial high spirits. The king drinks a special bottle of wine sent to him by his brother, Black Michael, and then falls asleep.

Chaps. 4–7. In the morning all awaken from their stupor except the king. No one can wake him, and they decide that the wine from Michael must have been drugged. A moment of panic ensues, for if Rudolph is not crowned that day he will probably never be; Michael will gain ascendancy. Suddenly Sapt brightens with an idea— Rudolf Rassendyll must impersonate the king for the coronation! They shave his beard and put the king in the wine cellar along with the maid, whom they tie and gag in case she has overheard anything. A trusted guard is left in the lodge. They then set out for Strelsau with pounding pulses, realizing that all their lives are in danger. Sapt begins hurriedly to acquaint Rudolf with the facts of the Ruritanian kingdom. In Strelsau the party is greeted by cheering crowds and stately personages. Rudolf is elated, plays the part to the hilt, and insists upon riding alone through the quarter of the town that is against him and in favor of Michael. Rudolf cuts a distinguished figure. The coronation in the cathedral proceeds flawlessly and Black Michael, attending, is astounded. He cannot expose the pretender, for then he would expose his own deception. Rudolf meets Princess Flavia and is highly charmed. The great day passes, then Rudolf has to prepare to flee the country. While von Tarlenheim guards the king's chamber, Rudolf and Sapt sneak out of the castle and ride away in the night. Rudolf is wrapped in a large cloak for disguise. They gallop 40 miles to the lodge and find strewn about the rags with which they had bound the maid. In the cellar they find the dead body of the man they left to guard the king, and find that the king has been taken away. The two stand shaken and aghast. They know that the king is merely kidnapped, not killed, for Michael would have nothing to gain by taking the king's life. They decide that the only thing to do is to go back to Strelsau and continue the impersonation. At this point several of Michael's men suddenly arrive to clean up the traces of their crime. Rudolf and Sapt attack and kill three of them.

Chaps. 8–10. Back in the capital, Rudolf now pays more attention to Princess Flavia, who is most receptive and finds him pleasantly changed since he has become king. Black Michael appears and introduces Rudolf to three of his six henchmen. Michael and Rudolf have to be congenial and fraternal toward each other in outward appearance, but their words have double meaning known to those in on the impersonation. Later in the day Rudolf receives a mysterious note from Antoinette, inviting him to meet her in an obscure place at midnight. Rudolf goes with trepidation. Antoinette warns him that Michael's men intend to kill him, and that this meeting has been planned for that purpose. Just then three of his antagonists arrive. He knocks them over with a tea table, wounds one with his pistol, then runs off laughing. The populace now begins to clamor for a furthering of the relationship between the king and Princess Flavia, and Sapt encourages this to insure Elphberg control of the crown. Rudolf is thrown into a very ticklish position. A great ball is given, and Rudolf courts Flavia and finds that he has really fallen in love with her and she with him. Afterwards he begs Sapt to take immediate action against Michael and to rescue the real king before his own position becomes untenable.

Chaps. 11–15. Rudolf tells the town marshal to have Princess Flavia carefully guarded while he goes to Zenda to seek out Michael. And if he does not return, then Flavia must be put on the throne and siege be laid to the castle of Zenda. Flavia gives Rudolf a passionate and loving farewell. Rudolf and some followers then set off for Zenda on the pretext of a boar hunt, and take lodging there in a chateau. A contingent from Michael, including the young, debonair and dangerous villain, RUPERT HENTZAU, greets them upon arrival. Rudolf soon acquires a spy, JOHANN, to inform him of activities within the castle of Zenda. Rupert Hentzau reappears and tries to bribe Rudolf into leaving the country. Upon Rudolf's refusal Rupert, with incredible audacity, tries to stab Rudolf to death in public, then escapes, leaving Rudolf only slightly wounded. Rudolf learns that the king is in a cell next to the moat of Michael's

The guard lies dead

castle, and that if the castle is attacked the king will be killed and his body sunk in the moat. The problem of rescue is thorny. When Flavia hears that Rudolf is hurt she comes to be near him, and their love grows even stronger. Rudolf now leads a stealthy night attack on Michael's castle. They find that the king cannot be rescued from the outside. The attacking party is discovered and a small battle ensues, with casualties on each side. Rupert escapes. The next day a messenger tells Rudolf that an English ambassador is searching for a lost Englishman named Rassendyll. Rudolf hides his alarm and has the man sent away.

Chaps. 16–19. Public pressure now forces Rudolf officially to declare the day on which he is to marry Princess Flavia; it is set for two weeks hence. At the same time he hears that the king is growing weaker and weaker in his cell, so the time has come for decisive action. Intelligence has it that Michael and Rupert are quarreling for the

favor of Antoinette de Mauban, who is trapped in the castle. So a plan of attack is formed about this bit of knowledge. At 2 A.M. Antoinette is to call "Help, help, Michael!" as if Rupert were attacking her. Michael will rush out into the hallway of the chateau (infiltrated by Rudolf's men) and be taken. His keys will open the adjoining castle, and his defenders will be taken one by one by Rudolf as they come out. Rudolf's men take their appointed positions before the hour of attack. But all does not go as scheduled, because Rupert actually does attack the fair Antoinette in her chamber. Michael breaks in and is slain by Rupert's sword. The fracas brings forth the castle's gate guard, whom Rudolf kills and from whom he gets keys to the king's cell. Rudolf then attacks the king's cell-guards and kills them both after a furious fight, during which the king is seriously wounded. Upon emerging from the cell Rudolf finds Rupert being shot at by the fiery Antoinette, and gives chase. Rudolf is weakened, however, by a wound received in the previous fight, and succeeds only in nicking the fleeing villain, who then escapes, laughing, into the forest.

Chaps. 20–21. Princess Flavia comes to find her loved one. Her guides mean to direct her to the king, but inadvertently she comes upon Rudolf. He, with great anguish, confesses his duplicity. She falls upon him in a faint. Rudolf then goes into hiding until his departure, while the real king assumes the crown. Rudolf sees Flavia once more before parting. The scene is passionate and tearful. Rudolf asks her to come away with him. She hesitates, then tells him that honor and faithfulness to her country must come first. Rudolf Rassendyll leaves Ruritania unobtrusively but showered with love and veneration by those who have known his closely. He first takes a rest in the Tyrol, then returns to England and settles down to a quiet country life. Once a year he has a rendevous with his old friend Fritz von Tarlenheim, and through him Princess Flavia and Rudolf Rassendyll send each other, each year, one red rose.

Rupert, leaving, is shot at by Antoinette

517

The Professor's House

Novel by Willa Cather, 1873–1947.
Published and © 1925 by Houghton
Mifflin Co., Boston.

ONE OF THE MOST ADMIRED of Miss
Cather's novels, *The Professor's House*
is essentially the musing of a man as
he adjusts to the ending of his middle
age and the onset of old age. Since the
man is a scholar and a quiet man, the
book is a quiet book; nothing exciting
happens but the mood is perfect
throughout. In this novel Miss Cather
first used material from her great interest in the Southwest, which became
the setting of her next novel, *Death
Comes for the Archbishop.*

Book I. The Family. 1. Prof. GODFREY ST.
PETER, a well-liked history professor at
Hamilton University in the Midwestern
U. S., is alone in the dismantled house
from which he and his wife LILLIAN are moving.
He muses upon the many happy hours he
has spent there, particularly those in his
private third-floor study. AUGUSTA APPEL-
HOFF, his landlord's spinster daughter, also
used it, during the daytime, to pursue her
occupation of sewing; but at night the study
was the professor's haven. There, working
at least four nights a week, he wrote his
Spanish Adventurers in North America, an
8-volume work that won for him the Oxford
Prize for history, a prize of $20,000, with
which he built the new house. But he has
no desire to move and abandon the study,
his haven. **2.** St. Peter and Lillian entertain
at dinner. Their guests include their two
daughters, KATHLEEN or KITTY (Mrs.
SCOTT McGREGOR) and ROSAMOND (Mrs.
LOUIE MARSELLUS), as well as Scott and
Louie. Mrs. St. Peter is fond of both her
sons-in-law, whereas the professor is highly
critical of both. Rosamond was once engaged to TOM OUTLAND, a brilliant scientist and inventor as well as the best pupil
St. Peter had ever had. Before his death in
World War I, Tom patented his inventions;
and he left everything to Rosamond. Louie,
an electrical engineer, has become rich as
a result of these patents, by carrying on
Tom's work. He and Rosamond have just
built a new country house and have named
it "Outland." **3.** St. Peter rents his former
house from Appelhoff so he can continue to
work in the third-floor study. **4.** Rosamond
offers to build the professor a study in her
new house, and offers also to settle an income on him so that he can devote all his
time to his writing and research. She insists that Tom would have wanted it that
way. But her father refuses the offer, insisting that there can be no question of
money between him and Tom, the one remarkable mind he has encountered in a
lifetime of teaching. He does not approve

of the way in which Rosamond and Louie
have commercialized Tom's genius. **5.** Scott
comes to the university just as the Professor
is winding up a brilliant lecture, and persuades him to go swimming. Scott criticizes
Louie but the professor will not discuss the
matter. The professor does have some sympathy for Scott, a newspaper writer, whom
he considers too talented for the writing he
is doing. **6.** Mrs. St. Peter likes Louie's idea
of surprising Rosamond with an emerald
necklace, but she is concerned that Louie,
a Jew and a newcomer in town, has let his
name be put up for an organization called
"The Arts and Letters." Scott is a member
and she plans to work on him to help Louie
get in. **7.** One day when St. Peter goes to
Kathleen's house he sees Rosamond leaving
in anger. Inside, he perceives Kathleen's
jealousy of Rosamond and her dislike of
Louie. The two sisters were once so close
that St. Peter wonders if it was for this that
the light in Tom's laboratory used to burn
so far into the night. **8.** The St. Peters go
to Chicago, where the professor has been
asked to lecture. Rosamond and Louie accompany them, and Louie makes them a
present of a suite at the fancy hotel where
he and Rosamond stay, in place of their
usual room at a more modest hotel. He also
gives them opera tickets. In Chicago the
professor has an intimate conversation with
Lillian and is amazed to learn that she would
rather have been picturesquely shipwrecked
with him while they were young than to
have had a family. He has had many similar thoughts. **9.** The professor spends
Christmas day working in his study. Augusta
stops in and explains the *Magnificat* to the
Professor; she is religious, he is not. He
reminisces and his thoughts take him back
to Paris, where he stayed as a student with
a French family. **10.** Scott complains to the
professor about Louie's practical attitude
toward Tom. Scott was a classmate of Tom's
whereas Louie never knew him. Later, in his
3rd-floor retreat, the professor thinks back
to the day he met Tom Outland.

Tom came to town knowing of Prof. St.
Peter, as he had read a pamphlet of his
about the Southwest. Tom wanted to go to
Hamilton, but though a priest in New Mexico had made him proficient in Latin and
Spanish, he had never had any mathematics.
The St. Peters asked the poor-looking boy
to stay for lunch. They expected to give him
something, but it was Tom who gave them
gifts—pottery and uncut turquoises he had
brought from New Mexico. He told them
about his fascinating early life as a "call
boy" for a railroad. They became good
friends and saw each other often that
summer. In four months Tom made up
three years of mathematics and entered the
university that fall. **11.** Kathleen visits her
father and tells him that Augusta has lost
$500, a small fortune for her, as a result of
a bad investment. She wishes to help
Augusta but Rosamond's help is necessary
and Rosamond is unwilling to contribute
because Louie advised Augusta against the
investment and Augusta should be taught

a lesson. The professor says he will handle
Rosamond. Kathleen and her father speak
of looking for RODNEY BLAKE (or
RODDY), a friend Tom often spoke of.
12. Mrs. CRANE, the wife of St. Peter's
closest colleague on the Hamilton faculty,
calls on the professor. Only Prof. Crane and
St. Peter have struggled to preserve university dignity, doing research work of an
uncommercial nature. Crane, a physics
professor, helped Tom to no small extent.
Now Crane is seriously ill and not well off,
and Mrs. Crane suddenly feels cheated out
of Tom's money by Rosamond. She is thinking of a legal battle with Louie. Though St.
Peter is convinced that the Cranes have no
legal right to the money and tells Mrs.
Crane this, he resolves to speak to his son-
in-law about the matter. **13.** That night he
goes to see Crane, hoping to persuade him
not to go to law, for he truly believes that
Louie if approached will very gladly give
him some money. He knows that the Cranes
would lose any legal action they might begin.
St. Peter questions Crane as to how much
he honestly believes he helped Tom, and is
saddened to see that money has corrupted
one who was once such an honest man. **14.**
St. Peter is even more disheartened by a
shopping trip to Chicago with Rosamond,
whose spree he compares to Napoleon's
looting of an Italian palace. This time he
insists on paying his own way in Chicago.
15. Louie brightens up the dull month of
March by inviting his in-laws to go with
him and Rosamond to France that coming
summer. Mrs. St. Peter accepts, the professor
does not; he gives his work as an excuse
but actually declines less because of Louie
than because of the way his wife and daughter have hardened since Rosamond's marriage. **16.** Louie wants to give Kathleen and
Scott some furniture from their house,
which they plan to sell before leaving for
Europe; Scott had admired it. But Rosamond becomes furious, partly because she
believes the rumor that it was Scott who
blackballed Louie for the Arts and Letters.
The professor apologizes to Louie for his
family's behavior; Louie could not be more
gracious. He believes that in time people
come around if you treat them well. **17.**
Lillian and the Marselluses are in France.
The professor is editing and annotating
Tom's diary for publication—a diary that
covered only six months of his life, his
summer on New Mexico's Blue Mesa.
Though the professor had gotten to know
Tom quite well, some things about the boy
were always a mystery to him. Why had he
come to Hamilton saying the only money
he had was in a bank in New Mexico and
that he could not touch it? Why did he hate
Washington, D.C., and the eastern sea-
board so much that he chose graduate work
with Crane at Hamilton over a Johns Hopkins instructorship he had been offered?
The professor learned the answers to these
questions one summer while he was working on his history and his wife and daughters were in Colorado.

Book II. Tom Outland's Story. 1. Tom

meets Rodney Blake while working as a call boy. It is his job to get the older railroad workers away from their poker games when they are suddenly needed for work, often late at night. Tom has to call Rodney, a gruff, unshaven man, when he is winning a lot of money in a poker game. Fearing that the men who have lost will try to steal their money back from Rodney, who is quite drunk, Tom takes him home. From then on the two are good friends. Tom gets Rodney to put all the money he won in a savings bank account that he cannot touch for a year. Tom is an orphan; Rodney, 10 years older, treats him like a younger brother. Tom has pneumonia and Rodney nurses him back to health, then takes him to work at a ranch job, for the sake of his health. **2.** The ranch foreman leaves Tom and Roddy in charge of some cattle near the Mesa. He warns them to stay away from the beautiful Mesa, but it has a strange appeal to them both. **3–5.** HENRY ATKINS, a poor, elderly man the foreman has taken pity on, joins Tom and Roddy at their cabin to cook and keep house. The three men get along well. Tom and Roddy can now go off together to explore the Mesa. When they begin to lose cattle to the Mesa, Tom goes to explore it. He sees there the remains of Old Indian civilization. He and Roddy begin to search for another entrance than the Cow Canyon to the Mesa, and after their ranch job is over they find it. The Cliff City is unbelievably beautiful and is pure and untouched. They work in the ruins, finding beautiful objects as well as bodies. The priest, Father DUCHENE, helps them study the civilization, its age and characteristics, and tells them they should report their findings to the government in Washington.

Tom uses $600 of Roddy's winnings for the trip. Henry has been killed by a rattlesnake; Roddy is left alone at the Mesa.

4. Tom has no luck at all in Washington. First he comes up against a vast amount of red tape. A kind secretary helps him, telling him that the only way to meet people is by inviting them out to expensive hotels for lunch. He does this but finds the people uninterested in his findings. Tom lives with a young couple he deems typical of Washington: They make themselves constantly miserable by trying to keep up with the Joneses. When his money is gone he returns to New Mexico. Roddy has sold all the beautiful relics to a German scientist to take to Mexico, for $4,000. Tom is angry, for money is of no interest to him. Roddy had not realized this and sees that the gulf between them can never be crossed. He sets out to leave, giving Tom his bankbook. Tom wants to stop him from going but cannot quite make himself do it.

5–6. Tom learns that Roddy sold the horse he set out on in a nearby town and bought a ticket to Arizona. Tom advertises for Roddy in many newspapers and decides to wait for him at the Mesa. Tom spends the summer studying Latin and reading; it is the high tide of his life. But the advertisements for Roddy are never answered, even when Tom offers a $1,000 reward for him. One year after his quarrel with Roddy Tom leaves the Mesa. That is when he shows up at the professor's house.

Book III. The Professor. 1–2. Professor St. Peter is spending a leisurely summer while his wife is away. He thinks a great deal about Tom. He spent two summers with the boy, one in Old Mexico, and one in New Mexico, where Tom got out his diary from the stone vault in which he had put it. It describes the Cliff City findings very beautifully; this is one of the only items Rodney did not sell. Reading Tom's diary makes the professor think of his own youth and then of death. **3.** The Professor becomes very sad. Suddenly he enjoys nothing at all. He goes to see a doctor; physically, at least, he is pronounced fit. **4.** In early fall the Professor gets a letter telling him that the Marselluses and his wife will soon be home: Rosamond is pregnant. Somehow the Professor wants only to be alone; he has fallen out of love, indeed he has fallen out of the human family altogether. He goes to his 3rd-floor room, lights the stove, lies down and soon is asleep. When he awakes, he finds the room is full of gas. Does he have to get up? How far is a man required to exert himself against an accident? **5.** When he next wakes up, Augusta is with him; she has rescued him. Augusta smelled smoke and when she heard a fall she knew the Professor was upstairs; he had tried to get to the door but he had not reached it. The professor feels lonely, all of a sudden, and is glad when Augusta offers to spend the night in the study with him. The professor realizes during the night that if he had thought sooner of Augusta, he would have gotten up from the couch sooner. Augusta has always had a remedial effect on him. He then looks back over his life, trying to see where he made his mistake. Perhaps his mistake was an attitude of mind; he never learned to live without delight. Though he is low in spirits, he has learned that he does not believe in suicide. He is apathetic and feels that his family does not need him nor he them, but he can face the future.

John Milton
1608–1674

James Joyce
1882–1941

Pygmalion

Play by George Bernard Shaw, 1856–1950.
Produced 1912. © 1913, 1941 by George Bernard Shaw. (RE, 90; ML, 19)

PYGMALION, in Greek legend, was the sculptor who made a statue of a woman, Galatea, and then fell in love with the statue. The legend suggested the title but not necessarily the story of Shaw's *Pygmalion,* one of his most popular plays—especially when it was converted to a musical, *My Fair Lady* (1957). The play ends on a strong presumption that Liza, the Galatea of the play, will marry Professor Higgins, the Pygmalion; and Higgins himself is sure of it. But Shaw, in an afterword, asserts that Liza's decision is a considered one and that she will not marry Higgins. She has observed him long enough to know the danger of marrying a confirmed bachelor.

Act I. It is a rainy evening in London. A crowd is waiting for cabs. A man stands by taking notes. A dirty, ragged girl hawks flowers with a pronounced Cockney accent. Someone warns her that a man is taking down what she says, but the notetaker assures everyone he is not a policeman and astonishes onlookers by telling each the section of England he comes from. To a gentleman by his side, who seems inordinately interested, the notetaker says that in six months he could pass the flower girl off as a duchess merely by correcting her speech. The gentleman introduces himself as Colonel Pickering. He has come to England to meet Professor HENRY HIGGINS, the phonetic expert. The notetaker replies that he is Henry Higgins and the two go off together.

Act II. The flower girl shows up at Higgins' house the next day, introduces herself as ELIZA DOOLITTLE, offers to pay Higgins to make her talk like a lady. Pickering bets Higgins that he cannot make good his boast and pass the flower girl off as a duchess in six months. Higgins accepts the bet. Over Eliza's protests, he has his housekeeper take the girl upstairs, scrub her down, burn her clothes, and send out for new clothes.

ALFRED DOOLITTLE, Eliza's father, is announced. He has heard that his daughter is here, and though he does not object to her staying with Higgins, he feels he is entitled to some compensation. Five pounds will do Higgins, delighted with Doolittle's unconventional morality, gladly pays him.

Act III. Having worked on Eliza intensively, Higgins takes her to a small gathering at his mother's house to test his progress. In her fashionable clothes, Eliza is quite a beauty. FREDDY, a young gentleman who is present, becomes infatuated with her. Eliza's pronunciation has improved noticeably. Her grammer is still atrocious and the subjects she chooses to discuss are shocking. Mrs. Higgins tells her son that if he means to pass Eliza off as a lady, she must be taught the art of conversation. Mrs. Higgins also expresses some concern about what will happen to Eliza when Higgins is through with her.

Act IV. The six months are up. Eliza, now

Eliza as a flower-girl

obviously a lady in speech and bearing, has been passed off as a duchess at a fashionable garden party and Higgins, satisfied that the experiment is a success, is ready to abandon Eliza to her own devices. But Eliza is furious. Along with her elegant speech and fine manners, she has developed a sense of human dignity and she objects to being cast off. What is to become of her? She cannot go back to selling flowers. Higgins is thoroughly insensitive and sees her only as an ungrateful girl. He is unmoved by Eliza's threat to leave his house immediately.

Act V. Higgins hurries to his mother's house in a terrible state the next morning. Eliza has vanished in the night, and as she keeps track of all his appointments and such, he is quite lost without her. Alfred Doolittle, dressed elegantly, rushes in and accuses Higgins of ruining him. Higgins wrote to some society in America that Alfred Doolittle was the most original moralist in England and now they want him to deliver lectures for quite a bit of money. It is not the lecturing Doolittle minds, it is the making a gentleman of a man who has prided himself on being one of the undeserving poor. Mrs. Higgins says the problem of Eliza is solved; Doolittle can provide for her. Higgins objects. He paid Doolittle £5 for Eliza and now she is his. At this point, Mrs. Higgins reveals that Eliza is upstairs. She fled from Higgins to his mother. Eliza enters the room. She has learned that the difference between a lady and a flower girl is not how she behaves, but how she is treated. Higgins will always treat her as a flower girl. But what she most objects to is his coldness, when she wants and deserves his affection. Higgins replies that he cannot help being the kind of person he is. Eliza considers marrying Freddy, who is wildly in love with her. Or, she may become a teacher of phonetics herself. Higgins admires her spunk and invites her to come and teach with himself and Pickering, but Eliza ignores his invitation. She is not yet certain just what she will do with her life. There is little doubt that she can do much with it.

Quo Vadis

Novel by Henryk Sienkiewicz, 1846–1916.
Published 1895. Translated from the Polish by Jeremiah Curtin.

IN WORLD LITERATURE *Quo Vadis* stands considerably above the many other historical-religious novels of the same kind, though in the United States (perhaps because of the quality of the available translations) it has not had nearly the popularity of Wallace's *Ben Hur* or Douglas's *The Robe.* Like those and so many other books, it is concerned with the events in the Roman world in the 1st century, contemporary or nearly so with the time when Jesus lived. Since two of its chief characters are the Emperor Nero and the celebrated Petronius Arbiter, and since its distinguished Polish author and Nobel Prize winner was careful as well as eloquent in his historical details, the book is educational as well as exciting. It has twice made highly spectacular motion pictures, in which the high point is the battle of the giant Ursus with the mad bull.

Chaps. 1–5. MARCUS VINICIUS asks the advice of his uncle, CAIUS PETRONIUS, about a most unusual problem: He fell in love with LYGIA, the daughter of the barbarian Lygian king, when visiting in the house of the famed old general, AULUS PLAUTIUS. Vinicius is a patrician and the girl is below his standing. Also, the one time Vinicius talked to Lygia she drew a fish in the sand, a sign that baffles not only Vicinius but his uncle. It is difficult to baffle Petronius, a brilliant man, the favorite of Emperor Nero as the "arbiter elegantiorum," dictator of taste. Petronius goes to Plautius's house with Vinicius. He finds Lygia extraordinarily beautiful and discovers that some members of the old general's household are Christians, among them POMPONIA, Plautius's wife. To get Lygia out of the general's house, Petronius has Nero claim her as a hostage of Rome. Out of the house, she is guarded by her gigantic Lygian servant, URSUS. To get Lygia back, Plautius begs for an audience with Nero. He does not get one, and even Seneca, Nero's old teacher, cannot help him. Plautius is relieved to learn that Vinicius is in love with Lygia and will probably protect her.

Chaps. 6–10. Petronius obtains Nero's word that Lygia will be given to Vinicius within a few days. In the palace she is under the care of ACTE, a Christian, a woman of charm and influence. Lygia and Vinicius are together at a festival in Nero's palace and fall more in love with each other, but Vinicius gets drunk and tells the frightened girl he will have her, as Nero has given her to him. Ursus carries her into Acte's apartment. There a plan is worked out to hide Lygia in Bishop LINUS's house. POPPAEA, Nero's wife, sees that Lygia is too dangerously beautiful to stay in the palace and promises that Lygia will be Vinicius's slave that very day. The penitent Vinicius begs Lygia's forgiveness and invites her to his house, saying he will be her slave. Lygia accepts.

Chaps. 10–15. Lygia starts for Vinicius's house but Christians attack the cortege, as planned, and disappear in the crowd with Lygia. Vinicius is beside himself. He cruelly punishes his servants and slaves, though Petronius tells him that this is the kind of behavior that antagonized Lygia. Vinicius searches for Lygia on the streets of Rome all night. At the palace Nero and Poppaea are at the bedside of their only daughter, baby AUGUSTA, who is ill. Acte tells Vinicius that Lygia does love him, but Poppaea thinks Lygia bewitched baby Augusta and if anything happens to the child Lygia will surely die. There is no trace of Lygia until EUNICE, Petronius's beautiful slave-girl, who is in love with her master, suggests that CHILO CHILONIDES, a 50-year-old Greek philosopher-pauper, can find Lygia. Chilo is engaged to seek her. Augusta dies.

Nero accuses Petronius, because he suggested that Lygia be brought to the palace. Petronius escapes by subtly flattering Nero but Petronius's position is precarious and TIGELLINUS, praetor of the palace and the other top court favorite, might gain the upper hand at any time. Chilo brings the first clue: Lygia's abductors are Christians, as the fish is their secret signal.

Chaps. 15–20. Chilo pretends to be a Christian. He runs into an obstacle in the person of a Christian, GLAUCUS, a physician, who knows Chilo and has reason to hate him. Chilo finds Ursus and talks the gullible giant into promising to kill Glaucus. Through Ursus there is a way to reach Lygia and Vinicius wants to go at once to her. Petronius advises Vinicius to hire CROTON, the strongest gladiator in Rome, as a bodyguard. Croton goes with Vinicius to a secret Christian meeting, where Vinicius hears the aged Apostle PETER's speech and at last sees Lygia.

Chaps. 21–25. After the meeting Vinicius, with Croton and Chilo, follow Lygia and Ursus to a house in Rome. Vinicius refuses to wait; he enters the house, certain that Croton will defeat Ursus and he will carry Lygia away. But Ursus kills Croton, and when Vinicius is about to carry Lygia off Ursus pushes Vinicius with such force that he falls with a bad head wound and a broken arm. When Vinicius regains consciousness he is surprised that his captors do not kill him. Glaucus sets his arm and treats his wound. Lygia, Glaucus, CRISPUS and MIRIAM assure him that Christians do not kill. To be near Lygia, Vinicius gives his word that he will not use force to have her, if they will only permit him to stay until he fully recovers. He sends Ursus for Chilo. Ursus brings the reluctant Chilo to the house. Glaucus recognizes Chilo and is about to avenge himself, but Peter stops him and makes him forgive Chilo.

Chaps. 25–30. During his slow recovery, Vinicius learns a great deal about Christianity from Peter, and his love for Lygia becomes much more profound. Ursus talks of her country and Vinicius realizes that if these powerful barbarians of the North were to unite, they might bring disaster to Rome. Lygia, the daughter of a strong tribe's king, is not a slave, and his first impulse to marry her was right. Lygia also falls more in love with Vinicius; but can she, a Christian, love a pagan? Lygia knows that Vinicius could not understand Christianity's doctrine that all human beings are equal before God. Lygia is tormented, believing that her love for Vinicius is sinful, until Peter and PAUL of Tarsus, who have recently come to Rome, calm her: Christ blessed love between man and woman. Vinicius does not know whether to accept: Christianity and Lygia or, as a Roman, to fight this destructive religion.

Chaps. 30–35. Petronius has a hard time with Nero. The emperor is furious that he has to stay in Rome to please the people, when he so much desires to go to Antium. Nero desires to see Rome destroyed, somehow, so he can show the world what a city he, Nero, would build. As Petronius's influence wanes, Tigellinus's influence grows. Nero gives a festival and Petronius advises Vinicius not to refuse. Vinicius is the handsomest man at the feast. He has to tell a story about the death of the famous Croton, how the gladiator attacked him and Vinicius had no choice but to kill him. During the feast Poppaea, to avenge herself on Nero for his desire for Rubria, a vestal virgin, practically offers herself to Vinicius, who refuses her. Luckily for Vinicius, he does not know that the veiled woman is the empress; otherwise such a refusal would have been fatal. Once more Chilo finds Lygia's hiding place. This time, however, Vinicius has Chilo flogged for spying on the Christians. The Greek swears vengeance against Vinicius. Vinicius does not go to Lygia. He goes and asks Peter and Paul to give him Lygia in marriage. Peter leads Vinicius to Lygia. Lygia declares that she will marry Vinicius and Peter blesses the couple and declares them engaged.

Chaps. 35–40. Vinicius celebrates his engagement to Lygia by freeing some slaves, giving money to others, and releasing those in prison. Vinicius, though he hates to be separated from Lygia, goes with Nero's court to Antium, accompanied by Paul of Tarsus, to be taught the teachings of Christ. Vinicius learns that the idea of setting Rome afire has been planted in Nero's mind.

Chaps. 40–50. In Antium, the seat of the arts and sciences, Petronius has such an advantage over the uncouth Tigellinus that he once more is the first favorite. To please Petronius, Nero orders Vinicius to go to Rome at once and marry the daughter of the Lygian king. Word comes that Rome is burning. Vinicius rides day and night to Rome, fearing for Lygia's life. In the raging conflagration he finds the house where Lygia used to stay, but not Lygia. Chilo leads Vinicius to Peter in the catacombs and Vinicius finds Lygia. By some miracle Petronius's house was spared by the flames and he takes Lygia there. Nero returns from Antium at the height of the burning of the city, and now everybody is convinced he ordered Rome set afire. Of the fourteen districts of Rome only four remain. Vinicius, fully converted, begs Peter to baptize him, which the Apostle does. The people of Rome hate Nero for their immeasurable loss, and Nero has to find someone who can be blamed for the fire. Tigellinus and Poppaea accuse the Christians. Nero grabs the idea. Petronius, to save his nephew, tries to interfere, but this time he loses. Chilo knows so much that is useful to Tigellinus that he is invited to stay in the palace. Chilo cheerfully betrays Vinicius. Nero orders the arrest of Lygia and the rounding up of all Christians.

Chaps. 50–60. Petronius sends Vinicius to save Lygia, but it is too late; Lygia has been caught and is in the Mamertine prison. Petronius advises Vinicius to pay a fortune to the prison guards to release Lygia. He is late again; the prison is surrounded by praetorian guards. Through fire-gutted Rome the shout is heard, "The Christians to the lions!" An immense amphitheater is built of wood, for the people of Rome to watch the Christians die, and hear Nero sing. Vinicius tries everything to free Lygia, but fails. Thousands of Christians are thrown in Rome's prisons. The first day of the circus spectacle arrives. Gladiator contests start the strictly formalized proceedings; then ferocious and hungry dogs are let loose on Christians; there are mass crucifixions; and the lions finish the bloody spectacle. The first day Lygia is not among the martyrs, but she and Ursus have been moved to the Esquiline dungeons. In the beginning, the Romans resent the way the Christians submit to death without any fight, but a strange feeling begins to overcome the Romans when they see the brave,

The great battle between Ursus and the bull

the unusual way the Christians await cruel death. Vinicius bribes the chief guard and is allowed to stay in the prison all night with Lygia, who is ill.

Chaps. 61–70. Lygia declares herself Vinicius's wife. They cling to each other, day after day, expecting any day her turn in the circus. But Nero has a special plan to enjoy Vinicius's suffering and Petronius's distress. One evening in the Imperial gardens thousands are soaked in tar and burned. Among them Chilo sees Glaucus, the physician, whom he betrayed. This so completely unnerves the Greek that he points at Nero and accuses him of setting Rome afire. Chilo refuses to retract, though Tigellinus has him tortured, his tongue torn out. Chilo, after being baptized by Paul, is crucified in the circus. Once more Petronius begs Nero to pardon Lygia. This time the tyrant grants the request; after tomorrow's games Lygia will be free. Now Petronius and Vinicius know that next day Lygia will be among the martyrs. Vinicius is near Nero, watching in agony the "games." Ursus is alone in the arena, and like a lamb he is awaiting his death, when an enormous German aurochs (wild ox) appears in the arena. Lygia is strapped to the head of the beast. Ursus grabs the aurochs by the horns and after a long and terrible struggle twists and breaks the animal's neck. At the wild acclamation of the spectators Nero, though reluctantly, must give the sign of mercy. Vinicius takes Lygia to Petronius's house, though Petronius, fearing Nero's vengeance, urges the young couple to go to the country as soon as Lygia is well enough to travel. Nero is in an especially vicious mood, as several Christians have been found in the palace among his own men. He orders the arrest of the Christian leaders, Peter and Paul. Vinicius and the other followers beg Peter to leave Rome. At last Peter gives in, and decides to leave. He is walking away from Rome, on the Appian Way, accompanied by Nazarus, one of his followers, when Christ appears to him. Peter asks,

524

"Quo vadis?" (Where art thou going?). Jesus answers, "If you desert my people, I am going to Rome to be crucified a second time." Peter turns and goes back to Rome, where he is arrested and crucified. The same evening Peter dies, Paul of Tarsus is beheaded.

Vinicius and Lygia leave Rome and live happily in the country. Petronius, also in the country, has his vein opened and dies, with Eunice, when Nero's order of death reaches him.

Rebecca

Novel by Daphne du Maurier, 1907– Published 1938 by Doubleday & Co., Inc.; © 1938 by Daphne du Maurier Browning. (PB, C53; ML, 227).

Rebecca is one of that small group of mystery stories that are not sold as mysteries. When one stops to think about it, he tends to rank *Rebecca* as a mystery novel and one of the finest. Daphne du Maurier has an odd way of writing, often lapsing into iambic pentameter as though she had suddenly decided to shift to poetry. She was very skillful in *Rebecca*, exploiting the many opportunities for suspense provided by her very adroit plot. *Rebecca* made a fine motion picture with Joan Fontaine winning acclaim as the second Mrs. de Winter. The story is a first-person narrative of the second Mrs. de Winter, who never names herself.

Chaps. 1–8. Manderley, the beautiful seaside home of the DE WINTER family, has

been destroyed by fire and it is certain that Mr. and Mrs. de Winter can never return. They begin their life again in a small hotel in Switzerland where they now share all things, thoughts and secrets. There are times, though, that Mrs. de Winter recalls the events that made MAXIM DE WINTER her husband.

As an orphan she was a traveling companion to Mrs. VAN HOPPER, a snob who frequented the resorts of southern Europe. There was often great embarrassment at the obvious social-climbing tactics of the rich American but at Monte Carlo it reached its height when she forced herself on the owner of Manderley, Maxim de Winter. He was recovering from the death of his wife, REBECCA, and was not inclined to be gracious. The shy orphan accompanying Mrs. Van Hopper interested him and when Mrs. Van Hopper became ill, he spent his days in her company. When she prepared to leave for America, de Winter asked her to marry him and she accepted, for she had fallen deeply in love with him.

They drove through Italy on a leisurely honeymoon and the second Mrs. de Winter was completely happy with her husband. She became nervous when they returned to England and Manderley. She was sure that a comparison between herself and Rebecca would not be to her advantage.

When they arrived at the magnificent estate, the entire staff was gathered to present their congratulations. Each was presented and Maxim helped his shy wife by returning their greetings for her. There was hostility in the attitude of Mrs. DANVERS, the housekeeper, towards her new mistress. Mrs. de Winter soon discovered that Mrs. Danvers' devotion to Rebecca had been so unusual that she would resent anyone who replaced Rebecca. Maxim and his wife never discussed Rebecca, but as the days went by the picture of the first Mrs. de Winter gradually unfolded. She was a beautiful, capricious woman who ran Manderley most efficiently. The second Mrs. de Winter could not hope to rival her social accomplishments.

Chaps. 9–15. Soon after their arrival, BEATRICE, Maxim's sister, came for lunch, with her husband. She was brusque but kind and Mrs. de Winter felt she had a friend and ally in the bewildering world haunted by Rebecca. Daily her feeling of inferiority to her predecessor grew. She seemed to lack all the qualities that Rebecca had possessed. One day she got lost in the maze of rooms of the big house and found herself in the room that Rebecca occupied. Mrs. Danvers suddenly appeared and insisted that Mrs. de Winter see all of Rebecca's possessions. The room was exactly as Rebecca left it the night she died.

Chaps. 16–20. Lady CROWAN suggested to Maxim that the traditional fancy dress ball at Manderley be revived. It was suggested that the ball be given in the honor of Mrs. de Winter, and Maxim consented. Determined to prove her worth as a hostess in the shade of Rebecca, Mrs. de Winter

Maxim shoots Rebecca: The event he confesses to his new wife

enlisted the help of the housekeeper in planning her costume. Mrs. Danvers suggested that she have her dress made the same as a portrait of one of the de Winters' ancestresses. The dress was in a beautiful portrait that hung so conspicuously in the hall that no one could miss the resemblance. The night of the ball, Mrs. de Winter felt that she looked beautiful. But as she descended the stairs, a hush fell over the assembled guests and Maxim did not even greet her. A sense of shock was in the air. Frightened by her reception, Mrs. de Winter fled to her room. Beatrice followed her and explained that at the last ball held at Manderley, Rebecca wore the same costume. Now Mrs. de Winter realized that Mrs. Danvers had tricked her. Beatrice persuaded her to dress in another gown and go down to her guests. Maxim did not speak to her the entire evening and for the second Mrs. de Winter the ball was a heartbreaking failure. She was sure she had lost her husband's love, if he ever loved her at all.

Shortly after the disastrous party, a boat was caught on the reefs in the bay of Manderley. A diving crew was sent to help the steamer and discovered Rebecca's boat and the remains of her body. This seemed unbelievable, as at the inquest Maxim had identified a body found washed up the river as his dead wife. Maxim became nervous and morose and his wife was distracted by his silences. She believed he was grieving for Rebecca. Her sadness finally reached Maxim and he confided the true story of Rebecca's death. Most people thought their marriage was a happy one, but to Maxim it was a long nightmare. Rebecca led a life that was dissolute and immoral and they finally made an agreement that if she behaved properly as the mistress of Manderley, he would not question what she did when she visited London. For a while this worked, but Rebecca became more sure of herself and began inviting her lovers to Manderley, where she would receive them in the boathouse. Gossip spread quickly about her and her cousin, JACK FAVELL,

who was often seen leaving the boathouse late at night. Maxim followed her to the boathouse one evening to bring their marriage to an end. Rebecca laughed at him. She told him he could prove nothing against her and that as long as it suited her she would remain married to him. She told Maxim that she was having a child that would bear his name and eventually inherit Manderley. To the world she would still appear the perfect wife and mother and he would have to accept it.

Horrified at this prospect, Maxim shot her. She died with a look of contempt on her face. He put her in the boat and sailed it down the river until he reached the widest point. Then he flooded the boat and left it to sink, giving the appearance of an accident.

Mrs. de Winter listened with growing horror, but at the same time a feeling of joy stole over her. Maxim had not loved Rebecca; he loved her. With this knowledge, she was able to face anything.

Chaps. 21–27. It was proved that the body in the boat was Rebecca and a coroner's inquest was held. It was proved that the boat could not have been sunk by a storm. The jury brought in a verdict of suicide, to the relief of the worried Mrs. de Winter. That same evening, Jack Favell appeared at Manderley. He was drunk and raving of his love for the dead Rebecca. He went into every detail of their love affair and tried to blackmail Maxim with the threat that he could prove that her death was murder by her husband. De Winter called Colonel JULYAN, who had acted as the magistrate at the inquest. Favell insisted that de Winter had killed his wife in a jealous rage when she asked for a divorce.

It had been learned from Rebecca's engagement book that just before her death she had visited in London a Doctor BAKER. Julyan decided that Baker might hold the key to the mystery. The de Winters drove with him and Favell to London to see Baker. Baker was coöperative and looked through his files for Rebecca's record. He could not find her name, but they found the name of

Mrs. Danvers and realized that Rebecca had assumed the housekeeper's name for the examination. It was shown by the examination that Rebecca had cancer that was incurable. Julyan considered this proof of suicide and closed the case.

Maxim was sure that Julyan had guessed the truth but that he had realized Rebecca's taunts of pregnancy had been to infuriate her husband so he would kill her. She wished to revenge herself even in death. Driving back to Manderley, Maxim telephoned that they were on their way. He was told that Mrs. Danvers had disappeared. As they approached their home, safe in their love, a blaze appeared. Manderley was in flames. Rebecca had had her vengeance through her devoted admirer, Mrs. Danvers.

The Red and the Black

Novel by Stendhal (Marie-Henri Beyle, 1783–1842).
Published 1830. (ML, 157)

THIS TREMENDOUSLY KEEN and dramatic portrait of an ambitious young man is generally acknowledged to rank among the greatest novels of world literature. The great character is the protagonist of the novel, Julien Sorel, who is neurotically obsessed with himself, the obsession leading both to his rise and to his fall in the world. The other characters are similarly real and are drawn with profound insight. There is an obvious similarity of the ending of this novel to the ending of *The Brothers Karamazov*, with the man awaiting his fate in the prison cell while the two women of his life vie for his approval or favor and he makes a distinct and heartless choice.

Book I. 1–5. JULIEN SOREL, a sawyer's son, despised by his father and brothers for his bookishness and delicate good looks, studies theology with the idea of eventually becoming a priest. Julien is not religious but he is practical. The Napoleonic period of glory, which Julien privately admires, is over. His secret hero Napoleon is dead and in disfavor. It is too late for one born poor and lowly as himself to gain fame and fortune as a soldier. But one can still rise to position and wealth through the increasingly powerful Church. Because of his assumed piety and his astonishing feat of having memorized the entire New Testament in Latin, Julien is hired as tutor to the children of the mayor of Verrières, one M. DE RENAL, an insensitive social climber who chiefly relishes the prestige conferred by having a tutor for his children.

6–8. Julien's careful behavior soon wins him the respect of everyone in Renal's household, but he deeply resents his lowly position. To bolster his self-respect, he decides he must seek to seduce the mayor's wife. She is a good and beautiful woman, but in spite of her desire to be loyal to her husband she is attracted to the handsome, brilliant tutor. When she learns that her maid, ELISA, has also fallen in love with Julien and is determined to marry him, Mme. de Renal trembles with anxiety. Not until she discovers that Julien has positively rejected Elisa will she agree to plead her maid's cause with him. She is thrilled when again Julien rejects Elisa. By now Mme. de Renal realizes that she is in love with Julien, but she still believes her love to be entirely spiritual. 9–11. Julien is still determined to seduce Mme. de Renal, chiefly because the mayor constantly offends Julien's sense of dignity. Every small concession that Julien wins from Mme. de Renal is equated in his mind with Napoleon's great triumphs on the field of battle. In a further challenge to the mayor's pride, Julien demands and obtains a three-day leave of absence to visit his friend FOUQUÉ. 12–14. When Julien tells Mme. de Renal he is going away for a few days, the poor woman (who has been feeling pangs of guilt, since she now realizes that her love for Julien is not entirely spiritual) is most unhappy, blaming her senseless virtue. Fouqué tries to persuade Julien to become his partner in a flourishing lumber business, but Julien, who feels he has a greater destiny than this, declines on the grounds of his vocation for the sacred ministry. Nevertheless, this handsome proposition haunts Julien and he determines to justify his refusal by becoming Mme. de Renal's lover at once. 15. Julien goes to her room when the house is asleep and obtains, at last, the favors he has sought so long. Julien is so busy playing the part of an experienced lover that he cannot relax and enjoy his first attempt. 16–17. On subsequent nights, Mme. de Renal's ardor reassures Julien and by the fourth rendezvous he is truly and madly in love.

18. It is announced that the King of —— will be visiting Verrières and that there will be a grand parade in his honor. Julien persuades Mme. de Renal to obtain a uniform and a horse for him. When the townspeople see him riding in the noblemen's guard they are outraged, for he is only a peasant. Since Mme. de Renal arranged this for him, he must be her lover. 19. Mme. de Renal's youngest child comes down with a fever and she seizes the idea that God is punishing her. Julien, who is himself enormously fond of the little boy, persuades Mme. de Renal not to put an end to their love affair. Together the lovers nurse the boy back to health, growing closer all the while. But this incident has made Mme. de Renal aware of the magnitude of her crime and she can never again be completely at peace with her soul. Soon after this, M. de Renal receives an anonymous letter that informs him in great detail of what is going on in his house. 20–23. Julien and his mistress learn about the letter. To make it look like the slander of a vicious rival, they compose a letter of accusation, addressed to Mme. de Renal. Mme. de Renal, pretending indignation, demands that Julien be sent back to his family immediately. M. de Renal is convinced of his wife's innocence, but it is deemed expedient for Julien to leave Verrières. Arrangements are made for him to enter the seminary at Besançon.

24–27. Julien is unhappy at the seminary. His fellow students are coarse, stupid peasants who care for nothing but food and bourgeois conforts. 28. One day when Julien goes to help decorate the Cathedral in town, he sees Mme. de Renal kneeling at the confessional. When she sees him he faints. Her companion warns Julien to go away immediately. Mme. de Renal has repented for her sins and is living a pious life. She must not see him again. 28–30. The Abbé PIRARD, a stern Jansenist who is under attack for his convictions, appreciates Julien's intellectual gifts. Julien receives an offer from the Marquis DE LA MOLE, a wealthy patron of Father Pirard, to be secretary to the marquis. Julien is overjoyed. On his way to Paris he pays a secret visit to Mme. de Renal, spends a night and a day in her quarters, and is finally forced to beat a hasty retreat through her window when M. de Renal suspects an intruder and organizes a search of the house.

Book II. 1–3. Julien is impressed and enthralled by Paris. He is keenly aware that he has much to learn about manners and the ways of the world. However, he manages to appear both educated and intelligent in society, for he has the gift of knowing when to keep silent and when to talk. 4.

The challenge to a duel

The marquis' daughter, MATHILDE, both fascinates and repels Julien. A coldly beautiful, willful girl, with great intelligence and too much pride, she seems to take most pleasure in humiliating those around her with her cruel wit. 5. Impressed with Julien's intelligence and discretion, the marquis begins to entrust him with the management of many important business affairs.

6. Julien is insulted by a stranger in a café one day and challenges him to a duel. The stranger throws his card in Julien's face and departs. Julien goes to the address shown on the card and is astonished to find that the card did not belong to the stranger who insulted him but to a gentleman, M. DE BEAUVOISIS—who is quite puzzled but graciously offers to fight the duel. Julien receives a slight shoulder wound and de Beauvoisis takes him home. He learns that Julien is merely a secretary and that it was his footman who insulted Julien. To cover up his humiliation at having fought with a secretary, de Beauvoisis circulates the rumor that Julien is, in reality, the illegitimate son of one of Marquis de la Mole's closest friends. 7–10. Mathilde is attracted to Julien because he seems indifferent to her and also because his intelligence is so far above that of all her silly Parisian friends. At a great ball she makes fools of all her dancing partners with her cutting remarks, trying to attract Julien's attention, but though she is the belle of the ball, Julien ignores her. He is deep in a political discussion. 11–16. As time goes on, it becomes clear that Mathilde is an incurable romantic. Her head is full of heroic tales and wild dreams and Julien is a part of them. She does everything she can to spend time in his company and constantly tries to win his affection. Julien does not trust her, suspecting that her desire is the conquest, not him. When at last he receives a note from her instructing him to climb up the ladder into her bedroom at one o'clock the following morning, he cannot decide whether to go with the joy of an expectant lover or prepared to be the butt of a terrible joke. But go he must, for to refrain would be cowardly. He decides to take a pistol with him, for he believes he may meet his death in her bedchamber. The precautions prove unnecessary. When he arrives he finds her alone, but her ardor has already cooled and she regrets her rashness. Their rendezvous is without passion. 17–31. A strange courtship follows, during which the fickle girl changes her mind about Julien a hundred times, loving him when she believes he does not love her, and scorning him when she believes he does. At last, in despair, Julien takes the advice of a friend and pays court to another young lady, to make Mathilde jealous. Now Mathilde realizes how much she adores Julien and she throws herself at his feet, but this time Julien keeps the reins. He continues to treat Mathilde with coldness, and her passion for him continues to grow. 32. Mathilde becomes pregnant and joyfully tells Julien. Now nothing can ever separate them. She will give up her place in society and marry Julien, and her father will give him his protection. Julien is not so sure and dreads having his benefactor hear. 33–34. The marquis is furious. Julien has betrayed him in the worst possible way. But he sees that the only way out of the difficulty is to make Julien rich, give him an Army commission, and have his name changed to the more aristocratic "DE LA VERNAYE." 35. The marquis is on the verge of consenting to their marriage when he receives a letter from Mme. de Renal, condemning Julien as a fortune-hunter and

526

seducer of women. The marquis refuses to consent to the marriage. His hopes crushed, Julien hurries to Verrières and arrives while the town is at mass. He stands at the back of the church until the ceremony is over, then fires a shot at Mme. de Renal, the authoress of his despair. She falls to the ground and Julien is arrested. **36.** Mme. de Renal suffers only a shoulder wound. She was forced to write the condemning letter by a stern, uncompromising father confessor. Julien instantly regrets what he has done and writes to Mme. de Renal to beg her forgiveness. He is ready to die for what he has done, for he realizes he still loves Mme. de Renal, that she is the only woman he has ever loved. **37.** Fouqué tries to arrange an escape for Julien, but Julien refuses. **38–40.** Mathilde tries to bribe jurors and authorities in Julien's behalf, but without success. She is passionately loyal, though Julien rejects her. **41–42.** Julien is found guilty and sentenced to death, though Mme. de Renal still lives. Her husband does not permit her to appear at the trial. **43–45.** Julien spends his last days on earth in the arms of Mme. de Renal, who comes to visit him in his prison cell every day. Their love reaches greater spiritual and emotional heights than ever before, and when, at last, his time comes, Julien goes calmly to his death. Mme. de Renal does not attend the funeral and, in keeping with a promise she has made to Julien, does not attempt to take her own life. But, with her children in her arms, she dies three days after Julien.

The Red Badge of Courage

Novel by Stephen Crane, 1871–1900. Published 1895. (PB, PL20; ML, 130; RE, 47).

THIS SHORT NOVEL, far more than many of its contemporary novels by much more distinguished authors, has held an enthusiastic following for nearly three-quarters of a century. Its adherents maintain that it is the finest fictional study every made of a soldier's true feelings under fire. One who reads it will indeed have great difficulty in thinking of a better. Strangely enough, when Stephen Crane wrote the book he had never seen a battle, yet the greatest admirers of his book are men who have. *The Red Badge of Courage* has only about 50,000 words. Stephen Crane died in his 29th year and left behind him little other literature of value except a few short stories.

Chap. 1. A regiment of Union soldiers, encamped by a river, discuss the rumor that after weeks of boredom they will finally see action. A tall soldier, JIM CONKLIN, spreads the news. Others, skeptical, argue that they will never move. HENRY FLEMING, a young private, listens to the rumors, then crawls into his hut to examine his feelings. Will he run in battle? He reviews his past ideas of glory, his enlistment, his mother's last words, his excitement when he left for Washington. He reflects that now he feels like a small part of a vast blue demonstration, his most important idea being personal comfort. He searches his soul, wondering if he is a coward. Jim Conklin enters his tent and Henry questions him about his feelings. Might he run? Jim says he might, but if others stand, he will stand too. Henry feels vaguely comforted.

Chap. 2. The rumor proves premature, and Henry is increasingly troubled about his reactions under fire. He is confused by his companions' attitudes, sometimes believing them heroes, sometimes suspecting them of being miserable like himself. The others are noisy, talkative, full of pranks, but Henry does not join them. WILSON, a loud soldier, accuses him of being blue and speaks with relish of the coming battle. Asked whether he will run, Wilson brags of his courage; and when Henry probes more deeply he becomes angry and stalks off. Henry lies in bed, imagining himself running while the others are cool and brave.

Chaps. 3–6. The next morning the troops move and Henry finds himself boxed in by hurrying men under fire. His feeling of panic and claustrophobia gives way first to curiosity about the aimlessness of the battle, then to rage against the stupidity of the generals. Gradually his anger is replaced by an unreal, detached feeling that he should not make so much fuss about getting killed, that it does not matter; in fact the best thing to do would be to get killed at once. As the

battle rages, Henry forgets his plans to get killed. He is surprised when Wilson, almost in tears, confesses that he expects to die and gives Henry a packet of letters for his family. Soon soldiers come running from the battle, but Henry has not seen the monster that caused their flight. He resolves to stay and get a view of it; then perhaps he will run. Moments of waiting follow, then a cry of "Here they come!" and Henry becomes a cog in the machine, loading, firing, reloading, conscious only of the work he has to do. He feels a red rage, not so much against the enemy as against the battle itself. He moves as in a dream, but as he wakes from his battle trance he regards himself with satisfaction, feeling that he has passed the test of courage and is a fine fellow. At that moment the attack is increased. Henry, seized by blind panic, turns and runs, growing more frightened as he runs, convinced that all is lost. He overhears a message that the line is holding after all.

Chaps. 7–9. Henry is horrified. He had convinced himself that the battle was lost, that only fools stood, and that he was superior. Now he feels resentment toward his comrades because he feels they have betrayed him. He hears sounds of firing and runs in a panic. In the woods he throws a pinecone at a squirrel and is reassured when the squirrel runs. That is nature's law, he tells himself; the wise man runs from danger. He plunges into a grove where the branches make a sort of chapel and confronts a long-dead corpse with ants crawling on its grey face. He plunges on until he comes to a road clogged with wounded men leaving the battle and joins the bloody band. A tattered soldier asks him where he is wounded. Guiltily, Henry flees, leaving the soldier astonished. He now meets Jim Conklin, terribly wounded. Jim tells him he is afraid he will fall and be run over, and implores Henry to stay with him. A moment later, changing his mind, he asks to be left alone. The tattered soldier, rejoining Henry,

Seized by blind panic, Henry turns and runs

advises him to get Jim out of the road, but before Henry can do so Jim breaks away and runs into the fields. He breaks into a paroxysm of death, performing "a sort of hideous hornpipe" before he falls dead. Henry, appalled, shakes his fist at the battlefield.

Chaps. 10–12. The tattered man muses on Conklin's death, wondering where his strength came from. Henry throws himself on the ground in horror and grief. Misunderstanding Henry's guilty flight before, the tattered man assures him he will take care of him. Again Henry rushes away, wishing in his agony of guilt that he too were dying. The road is choked with wagons and hurrying men, and Henry, thinking they are all running, ironically feels better. His guilt is not so great if it is shared by all. He tries to justify himself, but he imagines his regiment accusing him of cowardice and tortures himself imagining their jeers. In his anguish and fatigue he clutches the arm of a soldier, unable to speak. The man cries out and brings his rifle down on Henry's head. Henry, dazed and bleeding, is helped by a soldier who thinks he was wounded in battle. Henry explains that he has lost his regiment. His comrade points the way to the camp.

Chaps. 13–15. Henry is accepted with joy by his fellows, who thought him dead. They dress his wound and put him to bed, and when he wakes he is tenderly cared for by Wilson, the former braggart, now grown sober and reliant. Henry remembers the packet of letters and feels scornful and superior. Forgetting that he was ever afraid, Henry feels smug and superior, imagining himself back home, the conquering hero, admired for his brave deeds.

Chaps. 16–17. Next morning the regiment is moved into the trenches. Tired and bored, they again discuss the last battle. When a soldier suggests to Henry that he did not fight the whole battle, Henry is again terrified that his cowardice has been discovered. When the enemy advances and the battle begins, Henry loses all fear, caught up in an ecstasy of destruction. He is still firing after the enemy has ceased, and his furious, mindless courage rouses his companions' admiration.

Chaps. 18–19. In the confusion of battle the soldiers hear an officer remark that many of them will not return, and they realize they are making a hopeless stand. Henry observes that the delirium of war is heedless and blind, is a temporary but sublime absence of selfishness. There is no time to think of self. The regiment is halted, fights painfully onward, then stands indecisive. Henry, seeing the flag, runs toward it, and just as the color sergeant falls, he and a companion wrench the flag from him.

Chap. 20. The two soldiers scuffle for possession of the flag as the regiment retreats and advances. Henry is filled with an animal rage. Once again the advancing ranks find themselves in the midst of fury, panic-stricken. Henry feels choked and burning but does not share in the general panic. In

528

hand-to-hand fighting, the soldiers rally round the flag, and Henry feels proud that if they are to be defeated they will die fighting.

Chaps. 21–22. There is a lull in the battle and the soldiers return to their encampment. When Henry hears two officers praising the flag-bearers, and hears his name mentioned, he thrills with pride. When the soldiers emerge to pursue the enemy, Henry still carries the flag, resolved not to give it up.

Chap. 23. The colonel commands the regiment to charge, and Henry, with the flag, stays near the front, urging the men on. He sees the rival color-bearer wounded but fighting furiously. The Union soldiers attack, capture the flag, and take four prisoners.

Chap. 24. Slowly the soldiers realize that the fury has all but ceased. Henry wonders "What now?" as the regiment marches back along the corpse-strewn ground. Fate has been kind to Henry. He feels humble in the face of his triumph and his guilt, but the sky, he thinks, the sky will forget. He smiles as he sees the world as a world for him, now that he has rid himself of the red sickness of battle. He turns to images of tranquil skies, fresh meadows, cool brooks, peace.

Remembrance of Things Past

Novel by Marcel Proust, 1871–1922. Published 1913–27; in the U.S., 1918–1928. © 1918–1928 by Thomas Seltzer, Random House (New York), and others. Translations from the French by C. K. Scott-Moncrieff, except *The Past Recaptured* translated by Frederick A. Blossom. (ML, 120, 220, 213, 278, 59, 260, 172).

THIS TREMENDOUS WORK consists of seven full-length novels so unified that they must be treated as one novel—and the literature of the world hardly contains its superior. Proust wrote at a time when most novelists were still confining themselves to the upper classes, so that his masterpiece is a picture of fashionable French society and the people of it, but they are still human beings and he knew them well. Like the other great homosexual novelists, he was always attentive to the emotional relationships between man and man, but it did not lead him to undue distortion and perhaps it is just as well that he and the others were around to treat a phenomenon that undeniably exists and is almost always treated as nonexistent or taboo. The English title is from Shakespeare's 30th sonnet, "When in the sessions of sweet silent thought I summon up remembrance of things past . . ." In French it is *À la récherche du temps perdus* and the publication in French was in 16 volumes.

Swann's Way

Overture. Shifting and confused gusts of memory buffet the NARRATOR as he waits for sleep. He remembers time spent at his grandmother's house in Combray when he was a boy; how they were visited by M. SWANN, one of the most sought-after guests of Faubourg society; how his mother would come up after the guests' departure to kiss him goodnight; and how, one night, to soothe his excessive anguish and fears, his mother spent the entire night in his room. His memories remain diffuse until one winter day he has some tea with a "petite madeleine," which recalls Sunday mornings at Combray where a similar ritual was observed with his Aunt LEONIE.

Combray. The door to memory is opened wide and he remembers fully his days at Combray. He remembers incidents and people. Constant reading excited his imagination at that time and Swann introduced him to the works of the celebrated BERGOTTE. Saturdays at Combray were special: Lunch was an hour earlier to allow FRANÇOISE, the cook, to do her marketing, and in the evening the family went to Month of Mary Devotions and there would meet M. VINTEUIL, a composer, and his daughter, Mlle. Vinteuil. M. Vinteuil used to visit them, but no longer does for fear of meeting M. Swann, who has made a most unsuitable marriage. One day the Narrator has lunch with a M. LEGRANDIN, the local snob, who asks him if he knows any of the ladies of the GUERMANTES family. The name alone impresses the Narrator. The family has two choices when going for walks: the Guermantes way along the river, or the Meseglise way with its view of the plains. The Meseglise way was past Swann's home at Tansonville. "Swann's Way" is avoided by the ladies of the family since his marriage, but one day, with just his grandfather and father, the Narrator goes "Swann's Way." Everything about it impresses him. He sees the hawthorn; he sees Swann's 4-year-old daughter, GILBERTE. He falls in love with both the hawthorn and Gilberte. He also sees Swann's wife, ODETTE, and CHARLUS, a friend of the Swann family. A few years later, while on a walk himself, he chances to observe the lesbianism of Vinteuil's daughter. Also of significance to him is the day he catches his first glimpse of the beautiful Duchesse DE GUERMANTES. She has come to a wedding in Combray. All of what he has seen in Combray exposes the Narrator to later disillusionment.

Swann in Love. By an association of memories the Narrator pieces together the story of Swann's love affair, which took place before he was born. At the home of Mme. VERDURIN, a socially ambitious, vulgar and snobbish bourgeois, Swann meets ODETTE DE CRECY, a not really beautiful woman, a courtesan. He hears a sonata by Vinteuil, now dead, one phrase of which brings Odette to his mind when she is absent. At first it is Odette who seeks Swann, then, as Swann's affections grow, Odette is cool. This coolness drives Swann to passion. One evening at the home of the Verdurins, Swann defends his affections for his aristocratic friends of whom Mme. Verdurin is jealous. He breaks with the Verdurins. Odette is unfaithful with a nobleman, DE FORCHEVILLE. The only person Swann trusts with Odette is his friend Charlus. Charlus would always come to Swann with the details of his meetings with Odette. One evening Swann hears again the phrase from Vinteuil's sonata and his agony overcomes him. He receives a letter listing Odette's lovers, both men and women. Odette leaves on a cruise with the Verdurins, and in her absence Swann recovers. At the voyage's end, one of the Verdurin "faithful" tells Swann that Odette talked about him all the time with loyalty and affection. Thus learning that Odette is capable of normal feelings of friendship, Swann sees her again as a human being and is finally released from his passion for her.

Place-Names: The Name. Names of places and things have a great fascination in the imagination of the Narrator. Illness cancels a trip he was to have made to Italy and he must content himself with daily excursions to the Champs-Elysées. Still a child, here he sees Gilberte again, the daughter of Swann and Odette, who are now married. He falls in love with his playmate and with the very name of Swann. He wishes he looked like M. Swann, even to his baldness. He waits along the Allée des Acacias for glimpses of Mme. Swann. Revisiting, years later, the Allée des Acacias, he finds gone the realities he once knew there. All that remain are his memories.

Within a Budding Grove

Madame Swann at Home. The Narrator is allowed, though ill, to attend a matinee performance of BERMA, the great actress, in *Phedre*. The reality of the experience contradicts his imagination and he is disappointed even though the performance is critically a triumph for Berma. The Narrator's parents are concerned that he has not yet chosen a career for himself and he decides to pursue the literary life. He renews his acquaintance with Gilberte and becomes a close friend to the Swann family.

On one visit he hears Mme. Swann play the Vinteuil sonata. On another occasion Mme. Swann introduces him to the Napoleonic Princess MATHILDE. At the Swann home he meets Bergotte, the writer, whom he has long admired. Again he is disappointed. Bergotte seems quite a common person. Now that he is secure in his friendship with Gilberte's parents, the Narrator takes his relationship with her for granted. Then, on one occasion, he discovers that Gilberte does not really want his company, that her parents force her. There is a quarrel between him and Gilberte, which causes him acute pain. After unsuccessful attempts to woo Gilberte, he separates himself from her and finds pleasures in which she has no part. Finally his love subsides and all that remains of his intimacy with the Swanns are the walks he still takes in the Bois, on Sundays, with Mme. Swann; these he remembers more vividly than the pain of his love for Gilberte.

Place Names: The Place. Two years later, safely indifferent to Gilberte, the Narrator accompanies his grandmother to Balbec on the sea, where the elderly lady renews her acquaintance with Mme. DE VILLEPARISIS. After an attack of fever, he is entertained by being taken for drives with the women. He observes the charms of the girls they pass and wishes he were alone. He is introduced at this time to Mme. de Villeparisis' dashing young great-nephew, ROBERT DE SAINT-LOUP who is serving in the military nearby at Doncieres. They become fast friends. He also meets the Baron de Charlus, whom he had seen first at Combray and whose conduct toward him he finds enigmatic.

Seascapes With Frieze of Girls. The Narrator has seen, there on the shore, a band of happy, laughing girls, and he wishes he knew them. While visiting the painter, ELSTIR, he does meet one of them, ALBERTINE; and through her he makes friends with the entire little group. He contemplates the varied delights of each, but cannot decide whether to fix his love on ANDRÉE or Albertine. Finally, he picks Albertine, a girl of decidedly low social background. Then he decides he loves them all. The season at Balbec ends. Albertine is the first to leave; and shortly after, Françoise makes ready for the departure of the Narrator and his grandmother.

The Guermantes Way

Chap. 1. The house taken by the Narrator's family in Paris shares a courtyard with the Duc and Duchesse de Guermantes and the name loses for him the glamor that only distance could give it. However, he does, from a distance, fall in love with the Duchesse de Guermantes. She is to him the symbol of the Faubourg Saint-Germain society to which he aspires. He goes to visit his friend Saint-Loup at Doncieres. When the two of them are back in Paris, Saint-Loup introduces him to his mistress,

RACHEL, a former prostitute who has ambitions of becoming a great actress. At a tea party given by Mme. de Villeparisis the Narrator is finally introduced to the Duchesse de Guermantes. At this same party he hears the Dreyfus case discussed. When it is time to leave he is offered a ride by Charlus. Charlus offers to further him in society, but he makes nothing of the offer. His grandmother has been ill and while walking with him on the Champs-Elysées she suffers a stroke and later dies.

Chap. 2. His mother having gone to Combray after the grandmother's death, the Narrator is alone in the house under the care of Françoise. Albertine visits him and now permits him to kiss her. Another incident of note is an invitation from the Duc and Duchesse de Guermantes. He dines with them and they show him their paintings by Elstir. Also at this time he experiences the pain of disappointment. He had arranged an assignation with a Mme. de Stermaria in the Bois and the young lady never appeared. Again he repeats the patter of indifference to what is available and jealousy and pain to what is denied him. Later he receives an invitation from the Baron de Charlus. To his amazement, the baron spends the entire time upbraiding him; for what, he is not certain. One evening he is visiting the Duc and Duchesse de Guermantes. Swann comes to tell his old friends that he is dying and to give them an enlarged photograph of himself. But the duke and duchess are in a hurry to get to a party before news can reach them that they must go into mourning over the death of a relative. They have no time to talk to Swann. They do find the time, however, for the duchess to return to the house when it is discovered that she has worn the wrong color shoes.

Cities of the Plain

Chaps. 1–2. The Narrator is witness to the meeting of a young tailor, JUPIEN, with Charlus and the homosexuality of the baron is made apparent. Now the Narrator understands Charlus' unpredictable attitudes toward himself. The Princess DE GUERMANTES invites the Narrator to a party, where he renews his friendship with Saint-Loup. Saint-Loup intrigues him with the tale of a young woman, the maid of a Mme. Putbus, who formerly lived in a brothel and who also has a reputation of being a lesbian. The idea of the girl arouses his passion and he is not particularly interested when Albertine comes to visit him later that night. It is revealed at this time, at the princess's party, that both Swann and the Prince de Guermantes are Dreyfusards. Later, even the Duc de Guermantes is converted to the cause of Dreyfus.

In search of the maid mentioned by Saint-Loup, the Narrator returns to Balbec. He goes to the same hotel, the same room. While he is bending to unbutton his shoe, the door to memory is unlatched and an insurmountable grief for his dead grandmother overwhelms him. He does not meet the maid during his stay at Balbec, but he does meet Albertine, whom he takes with him to dine at the Verdurins'. On the train platform they meet Charlus, who is attracted by the handsome young violinist, MOREL, standing on the opposite platform. He falls in love with the young man instantly and it is through Morel that Charlus meets the Verdurins. While dining with the Verdurins the Narrator learns from Albertine that she knows the lesbian daughter of Vinteuil. He is tormented by suspicions that Albertine herself may be a lesbian.

Chaps. 3–4. Charlus keeps Morel and tries to advance him socially. This does not prevent Morel from spending a night in a brothel as the partner of the Prince de Guermantes, where he is discovered by the unbelieving Charlus. Meanwhile the Narrator is torn between a growing love for Albertine and his wish to be rid of her. His mother opposes a marriage to one beneath him socially, and he admits that the idea of becoming Albertine's husband is madness. He decides that he really loves Andrée, another member of the young group at Balbec. Andrée comes to visit him and from her he learns of a definite intimacy between Albertine and Vinteuil's daughter. The jealousy and anguish he feels at this knowledge forces him to admit that now he loves Albertine. He tells his mother it is absolutely necessary that he marry Albertine.

The Captive

Chap. 1. Albertine has moved into the Narrator's apartment while his parents are absent. Françoise, whose contempt for Albertine was never secret, is their only chaperone. Albertine occupies the Narrator's father's study just at the end of the hall and it is from there that she comes late at night to his room. He goes to the Duchesse de Guermantes for suggestions as to Albertine's clothes. Literally, he keeps Albertine captive. The only person he trusts her with is Andrée. After each outing, Andrée gives the Narrator the details of what happened and where they went. His

feelings alternate between satisfied indifference and passionate jealousy. Still, he does all he can to keep Albertine with him: presents, clothes, and the prospect of a possible marriage. She, on her part, invents complicated lies to get away and out of the house, if only for a short time. (It is at this point in the novel that the Narrator admits his name to be MARCEL, and it is by that name that he will be identified for the remainder of this synopsis.) Marcel is suspicious of all that Albertine does. He fears her assignations with Lea, a notorious actress, as well as with other women of varying social standings. Once Albertine comes home with a ring she claims to have bought herself. After the questioning, they are reconciled and go out for a drive together. Seeing Albertine out in the world, framed against the background of nature and the city, Marcel finds his sense of her beauty revived. In a later conversation, Albertine admits to Marcel that she has occasionally lied to him, but only about unimportant things. On the day of their drive, Marcel hears that Bergotte has died. The writer, though seriously ill, went to an art exhibit to see once more a painting by Vermeer of a street in Delft—in particular, the little yellow patch of wall in the picture. Seeing it, Bergotte wished he had written works the equal of that small patch of wall. It was then that he died. Marcel feels that Bergotte's surviving work is the symbol of his resurrection. It is also through the death of Bergotte that Marcel catches Albertine in a lie. She had reported that she had seen the great man that day. The man was already dead.

Chap. 2. The Verdurins, with the help of Charlus, give a large musical party to launch the musical and social career of the young Morel. The violinist is a tremendous success. All the fashionable and part of the less fashionable world is at the party. Charlus is ecstatic, and in this mood he makes brilliant fun of the rather pathetic Queen of Naples, who is present. Mme. Verdurin, forever jealous of Charlus' place in the world of fashion, warns Morel that the police are after the baron for his depraved sexual practices. Morel denounces Charlus before the assembly. Marcel looks on, holding back only because he looks

forward to the baron's blistering reply to the young upstart. But the reply never comes. Charlus is completely broken by this betrayal and it is the Queen of Naples, come back to collect her fan, who offers her arm to support the almost unconscious Charlus.

Chap. 3. Marcel confronts Albertine with his knowledge of her friendship and intimacy with Mlle. Vinteuil and Lea. When he fears that she might be planning to leave him he determines to dismiss her, but at a time of his own choosing. Finally he is convinced that he no longer needs Albertine and decides to take a trip to Venice. In the morning when he rings for Françoise to ask for a guide-book and timetable, the servant apologizes for not disturbing him sooner, because the fact is, Albertine has gone.

The Sweet Cheat Gone

Chap. 1. Marcel is overwhelmed with anguish. He asks Saint-Loup to help him get Albertine back. He writes to Albertine with the excuse of asking her advice: Should he arrange for Andrée to take her place with him? He is obsessed with jealousy and broods on the emotion constantly. Finally, in agony, he wires Albertine, begging her to return. The reply comes from the girl's aunt: Albertine is dead. She was killed in an accident while riding. Despite his grief, Marcel searches for the secrets of Albertine's life, the truth to all the lies she had told him. He questions everyone he knows who knew Albertine but receives no satisfactory information.

Chap. 2. Marcel begins to be relieved of his grief for Albertine. He sees a pretty red-haired young lady coming away from the home of the Duchesse de Guermantes and learns it was Gilberte, Swann's daughter, his first love. Gilberte is now received by the duchess because Swann is dead and Odette has married the Count de Forcheville, who has adopted the girl and given her his noble name. Swann himself is gone and forgotten. Further evidence of Marcel's new feeling toward Albertine is found in a short affair he has with Andrée. During the encounter Andrée admits to Marcel that she and Albertine were lovers. The news has no effect on Marcel.

Chap. 3. He journeys to Venice. He receives what appears to be a telegram from Albertine, saying she is not dead. Even this has little effect, beyond arousing his curiosity. The mistake in the telegram is finally discovered: It was from Gilberte and mistakes in the telegraph office produced a spelling that appeared to be Albertine.

Chap. 4. After leaving Venice, Marcel learns that Gilberte is to marry Saint-Loup. Some time after the wedding, Marcel visits Gilberte in Combray. Together they take long walks, many of them along paths known since his childhood. She tells him that Robert, her husband, has begun to

Albertine displays her ring and claims to have bought it herself

530

The baron is blind and old

practice homosexuality. Marcel reflects on his old love for Gilberte and all the pain it caused him. Both the love and the pain are gone.

The Past Recaptured

Chap. 1. Saint-Loup visits Marcel at Tansonville. Saint-Loup's new practices have made changes in him the opposite to those made in his uncle of similar tastes: He has grown more slender, quicker. It is in this period of his life that Marcel, coming across a section of the diary of the Goncourts, reflects on his earlier hopes for a literary career. Alternately he feels fresh hope for himself and deepening despair and disappointment.

Chap. 2. It is now the time of the first World War, 1916. Marcel returns to Paris, a different Paris from the one he knew so well. He learns that Saint-Loup has been killed in action. M. Verdurin too is dead, and Mme. Verdurin continues to advance herself despite the war. One night, lost in the blackout imposed on Paris by the war, Marcel chances on a hotel where he discovers the aging Charlus, with the help of the faithful Jupien, indulging in the most depraved sexual practices. Also at this time he takes note of the self-sacrifices of the lower classes in response to the war.

Chap. 3. Time passes. The war ends and sickness continues its advance in Marcel. He is now almost an invalid living in seclusion. He does, however, accept the invitation to a party being given by the Princesse de Guermantes. By this time the Princesse is Mme. Verdurin, who achieved the title by marriage after her husband's death. On the way to the party, Marcel comes across Charlus for the last time. The baron is old and blind, almost a depraved King Lear. Jupien still cares for him, trying to keep him out of trouble as best he can. Due to his blindness, Charlus once picked up a 10-year-old boy. Arriving in the courtyard of the Guermantes, Marcel accidentally hits his foot against two uneven stones. The sudden shock again opens the door to memory. Once inside, he continues his thoughts on his experience, evolving the

theory that a repeated sensation can bring the past to life, that art recovers all that is lost. He goes in to the party. It is a grotesque finale to all of his experience in society. Mme. Verdurin is the Princesse de Guermantes and Odette is the mistress of the Duc de Guermantes, now 83. Gilberte is growing old and he realizes, when she introduces him to her daughter, that he himself is aging. He witnesses the social humiliation of Berma, now old and dying, by Rachel, once the mistress of Saint-Loup, now become the great actress of her ambitions. He sees what time has done to all the people he has known; he is presented, as it were, with a summary of his life. He pays tribute in his thoughts to Swann, through whom he met, by a slender chain of events, all these people who gave him the experiences that in total constitute his life. He notes that "Swann's Way" has led finally to the "Guermantes Way." He vows to write then the work that will make his realizations regarding time and experience clear to everyone. He accepts the fact that he will have to impose upon himself a discipline almost monastic, but promises that if Time will grant him what is necessary to complete his work, he will bring to that work all the understanding he has received from the time that Time has given him.

The Republic

> *Treatise by* Plato, 427–347 B.C.
> Written about 390 B.C. The outline follows the translation of B. Jowett (Oxford University Press).

THE REPUBLIC is probably the work of Plato best known to the general reading public, chiefly because "Utopia" books have so universal an appeal. The *Republic* is one of the dialogues, the message being developed by questions, authoritative answers, and argument. The philosopher is Socrates and the presentation is as though Plato were simply reporting the words of his teacher Socrates, but no one doubts that the work is Plato's as naturally influenced by the ideas of Socrates his teacher. It has often been adduced as proof of the fixed nature and divine origin of the human mind that in all the centuries since Plato, no wisdom has shown his thinking to be inferior to what has come after, or fallacious in the light of later knowledge. Plato in the *Republic* does not describe the machinery or implementation of the ideal state. He contents himself with stating its philosophic foundation. Significantly, he remarks that whether or not it would work is irrelevant.

Book 1. Socrates and Glaucon, as they are returning from the Piraeus, are stopped by Polemarchus, Niceratus, and others, and are persuaded to visit the house of Cephalus, the father of Polemarchus. Cephalus is a very old man, and Socrates takes the opportunity of inquiring from him what he things of old age, is it a rough or easy path? Cephalus replies that he does not agree with the common complaints on the subject. Like Sophocles he finds it a time of peace and rest. Wealth may add to its comforts, but the great comfort of old age is the consciousness of a life well spent. The future retribution, which, though before treated with ridicule, has now become an object of serious thought, thus grows a source of hope, not of fear. Here again wealth has its advantages, as it diminishes the temptations to violate justice.

When Socrates hears the word justice, he says he would be glad to know what the word means. The popular definitions seem insufficient. Is it simply truth, or restoring a thing entrusted to one's care? A broader definition is needed. In the discussion that follows, justice is first defined as giving all their due, or benefitting our friends and injuring our enemies. But Socrates says we do not always know just who are our friends. Polemarchus then says that justice is benefitting the friend who is good, and injuring the enemy who is evil. Then, Thrasymachus, angry at what he thinks is quibbling, says that justice is the advantage of the stronger. When chided on this, he explains that he means that the laws of each state are made to secure the advantage of the governing, not the governed class. Thrasymachus then says that injustice is more profitable than justice, and injustice in its highest degree, tyranny, is the most profitable. Arguing this point, Socrates says that justice is a virtue, and injustice a vice of the soul. Consequently, the just soul will live well and be happy, and the unjust soul will be miserable. Since it is more profitable to be happy than unhappy, the just soul demonstrates that justice is more profitable than injustice.

Book II. Glaucon says men are just because they are not strong enough to be unjust. Adeimantus says that the common exhortations to justice show that it is the consequences of justice, not justice itself, that are desirable. Socrates says the subject is a difficult one and must be seen in the context of both the individual and of the state. Society arises from the wants of man. Each is not self-sufficient, but requires help from others. This involves divisions of labor. When any state prospers, there will be an increase in luxury, and luxury will lead to the danger of war. Therefore professional soldiers are needed. Consequently, we must seek guardians for our state, getting suitable natures and preparing them by education. We must be careful of the myths which we use in their education, careful to see that the myths are not simply lies.

Book III. The myths must stimulate the practice of various virtues, such as courage, truth, temperance, justice. Music and gymnastics must be pursued for both the cultivation of the soul and of the body. The rulers of the society we are planning must be chosen from the guardians and will be old men, whose only object will be the good of their country. They must be selected at an early age from the most promising part of the population, and exposed to every kind of test, to see whether they can retain the principle that "that is to be done which is best for the state." To secure the adhesion of the people to these rules it will be necessary to tell them a great lie: that while they seemed to be passing through their education, they were in reality being moulded below the earth.

Book IV. To any objection, Socrates goes on, that we do not secure the happiness of our guardians, our reply will be that our aim is not the happiness of any one class, but the good of the whole state. We believe this to be secured by each individual performing his work efficiently. The happiness of any class or of any individual we leave to nature. Our guardians have their trade like other artisans; to do it well they must have neither poverty nor riches. From these two we must guard the general body of our people, for one produces meanness, the other pride. Our state will have no money to fight for, and will gain allies by giving up its share of booty in war. The size of our state will be limited only by its unity. The greatest and noblest of our institutions will be those connected with our religion.

Our state is founded, but where is justice? Our state is perfectly good, and therefore will possess wisdom, courage, and temperance, and justice. If we discover the first three, the remainder will be justice. Wisdom is good counsel, courage is the valor of the state's soldiery, and temperance is harmony and agreement extending through all classes. The remainder, justice, is obtained when every citizen does that for which his nature has best fitted him. Then the state will be just when everyone performs his proper work. Justice in the individual will be similar to justice in the state, for the state is in every respect an exact copy of the individual. Now, we find the soul to be divided into three parts: the appetitive part, the reasoning part, and the spirited part. The harmonious working together of these parts makes a just individual; disharmony in them makes an unjust person.

Book V. Socrates is asked what will be the position of women and children in the state. Woman is simply a weaker man. Woman will have the same education as men. Each one will do the work for which she is best fitted. Wife and child of the guardians must be held in common. Even if this is not possible, it would be expedient,

as it would enable the uniting of the handsomest and healthiest couples. Marriage should be considered sacred, and should be in the hands of the authorities, who will arrange that the best are paired. Men and women will march together in battle. Socrates is asked if such a state is possible. He says this is not relevant but may be considered. The answer is that such a state will not be possible until philosophers are kings, or kings philosophers. To prove this, we must show what is meant by the term *philosopher*. The philosopher is a lover, and like other lovers loves the whole of his object—wisdom.

Book VI. The philosopher is not only a lover of truth, or real existence; he has besides in his character truth, temperance, liberality, magnanimity, courage, justice, aptness to learn, and elegance of mind. Adeimantus says that it is all very well for Socrates to say this about philosophers, and it is very hard to deny Socrates' arguments, but if we look about us in the world, we do not find philosophers to be so perfect. This is quite true, Socrates replies, but the fault is not with the philosophers, but with the state. The state is at present like a ship's company in mutiny, who have driven the pilot from the helm, and have undertaken to manage the vessel themselves. Philosophers are nowadays useless because no one will employ their talents. Also, because many who profess philosophy are of unworthy character. To get back to our perfect state, the guardians would have to have a good philosophical education, for they must know with certainty what the good is. Now just as in the physical world the sun is the source, not merely of light, but of birth, growth, and nutriment; so, in the intellectual, the good is the source, not merely of knowledge, but of truth and existence to the intelligible; the good itself not being existence, but stretching far beyond existence in dignity and power.

Book VII. The condition of mankind with regard to education, and the want of it, may be compared to that of men shut up from childhood in a cave, chained neck and legs, unable to turn their heads, seeing nothing but the shadows of things moved before a light, and hearing nothing but the voices of the men who moved them. In such a case they would consider the shadows to be realities, and would believe they spoke with the voices that are those of their manipulators. If one of the men in the cave were released and brought out into the world, he would have great difficulty in understanding what things really are. If when he finally learned about things in the upper world, he were returned to the cave, his companions would laugh at, and disbelieve the things he told them about the upper world. Thus it is with the philosopher; he seeks out and learns things that about which most men know nothing, and when he speaks of them, he is ridiculed. In his education, the philosopher will concern himself with (1) science, or dialectic, and (2) understanding, which together constitute intellect, which is concerned with real existence. He will also concern himself with

(1) belief, and (2) conjecture, which together constitute opinion, which is concerned with the apparent and the changing.

Book VIII. The foregoing are the institutions, the government, and the education of the perfect state. There are deviations from the perfect state, and these fall into four classes: timocracy, oligarchy, democracy, and tyranny. A timocracy is a kind of mean between aristocracy and oligarchy, resembling the former in the separation of the warrior class, and the latter in its love of wealth; and possessing a peculiar element of its own in the preponderance of party spirit and love of honors. The love of wealth in a timocracy leads to oligarchy, which is a political system in which the wealthy rule, and the poor have no share in the government Democracy arises out of oligarchy which becomes weak and corrupt, and is overthrown by the poor who throw open the public offices to all. Democracy is a pleasant form of government, because it lets a man say and do exactly as he pleases, but it does not fit our notions of the perfect state. Democracy falls from an excessive desire for liberty. The people soon become unwilling to obey any authority; the drones call in the aid of the rabble to help them plunder the rich. They choose a champion and furnish him with a bodyguard. Soon he consolidates his power for his own profit only, and in order to do so must subvert the constitution, and establish himself as an absolute governor. To maintain himself, he must get rid of all the best people in the state. A tyrant is little better than a parricide.

Book IX. If we ask which is the happiest among those who represent the different types of government, we are led to conclude that the just man in the just society is the happiest. This brings us to the fact that the pleasures of the philosophic life are the greatest. This is so because the intellect is the only real source of pleasure. To get back again to our original question concerning the advantages of justice over injustice, it is best for everyone to be ruled by what is good and prudent, best if he has it in himself, but if not, then from external authority. Since injustice is intemperance, how can one say that to be ruled by injustice is good? Thus, justice is the better ruler.

Book X. The imitative arts are concerned only with the inferior parts of the soul. Painting gives only the apparent bulk and form of things, and has nothing to do with the reasoning part, which gives real form and bulk. Imitative poetry has a similar fault. There is an old quarrel between poetry and philosophy, and the poets, with their imitative art, must excuse us if we exclude them from our state. The greatest rewards of virtue, rewards extending through all time, have not yet been mentioned. The soul is immortal, and that which is best for the soul leads to the greatest rewards. And that which corrupts the soul causes the greatest unhappiness. Injustice, intemperance, cowardice and ignorance corrupt the soul. Thus the just life will bring the greatest rewards.

The Return of the Native

Novel by Thomas Hardy, 1840–1928.
Published 1878. (PB, PL23; RE, 39).

IN MOST NOVELS by Thomas Hardy, little things are always happening but nothing much really happens. Yet there is a moral or a message in the whole. *The Return of the Native,* one of his most admired novels, is of this kind. Hardy was one of the earliest members of the school of the realistic novel and his works have had very great effect on novelists since. *The Return of The Native* is one of several Hardy novels that can be called important reading for the student of literature.

Book I. THOMASIN YEOBRIGHT, a pretty, gentle girl, has been brought up by her aunt, Mrs. YEOBRIGHT, in a cottage on Egdon Heath. It is Guy Fawkes day, and the villagers of Egdon have lighted a tremendous bonfire on a barrow of the heath in the evening. They are talking about Thomasin's marriage to DAMON WILDEVE, a former engineer turned innkeeper, on this day. As the bonfire dies down, they decide to go to the inn to treat the young couple to a serenade. Mrs. Yeobright finds Thomasin asleep in a van belonging to DIGGORY VENN. Diggory, the son of a small dairy farmer,

has loved Thomasin for years. Her refusal of him, more than a year before, broke his ambition and he became a reddleman, carting the red ocher used by farmers to mark their sheep. The product has smeared his good looks almost unrecognizably. Diggory tells Mrs. Yeobright that he found Thoma-

sin walking alone on the heath and that he offered to bring her closer to her aunt's house. Thomasin, waking, explains that something was wrong with the marriage license and that she and Wildeve are not married after all. She was frightened and angry when she learned this, and ran away. Mrs. Yeobright, who disapproves of the marriage so strongly that a year ago she forbade the banns, insists that Thomasin go with her to the inn to find out what Wildeve's intentions are now. Wildeve swears that he still wishes to marry Thomasin; but the girl cannot stay at the inn unmarried, so the women escape through a back window while the village serenaders crowd in to offer their compliments to Wildeve. As soon as he can get rid of his unwanted guests, Wildeve crosses the heath to a promontory where a single bonfire has burned all evening. EUSTACIA VYE is waiting for him. She is obliged to live in this (to her) dismal place with her grandfather, a retired naval captain. Eustacia is a dark, richly beautiful woman whose desire for romantic passion is almost impersonal. It is the emotion she craves rather than the specific man. In this place Wildeve is the only partially suitable man. He has courted her as well as Thomasin for months, and Eustacia is sure that he has given up his marriage for her sake. Although Wildeve insists that he intends to marry Thomasin, this does not happen. Diggory Venn spies on meetings between Wildeve and Eustacia and at last tries to reason Eustacia into giving up Wildeve, explaining that he loves Thomasin enough to want her to marry another man if this will make her happy. Eustacia will not agree to relinquish her power over Wildeve, but neither will she agree to go to America with Wildeve. CLYM YEOBRIGHT, Mrs. Yeobright's son and Thomasin's much-loved cousin, returns from Paris and Thomasin and her aunt resolve to tell him nothing about Thomasin's predicament.

Book II. The main topic of interest on the

Clym asks if she is a woman

heath is Clym Yeobright. There is a general opinion that Eustacia and Clym belong together, though they have never met. Eustacia herself, after once hearing Clym's voice, loses all interest in Wildeve and sees herself living in Paris with Clym. So as to see him without being seen, she joins a group of Egdon mummers who are giving the traditional play of *Saint George* at Christmastime at the Yeobrights' cottage. Eustacia buys the part of the Turkish Knight from a village boy, CHARLEY, at the price of his holding her hand for awhile. When the play is over, Clym asks if she is a woman but does not press for her name. Eustacia's chief feeling about the evening is that Thomasin is much too close to her cousin Clym. She makes it clear to Diggory that she would now be happy for Thomasin and Wildeve to marry and sends a letter breaking off with Wildeve. Wildeve, humiliated, immediately asks Thomasin to marry him and she agrees, although she is not very eager now. The marriage takes place on the day of Clym's return from a visit to a friend, and Mrs. Yeobright is obliged to tell him the whole story. Clym, deeply upset, plans to go to the church, but Venn meets him and says that the wedding is over and that Eustacia Vye gave Thomasin away. Wildeve is incredulous that Eustacia can be so happy he now belongs to Thomasin.

Book III. Clym Yeobright is much admired in Egdon Heath for his looks, his learning, and his glamor. Everyone knows he is connected with a diamond business in Paris. There is talk about why Clym is spending so long a time with his mother. The Egdon people do not care whether Clym's fate is happy or tragic so long as it is unusual. Clym tells them he disliked his life in Paris and that he plans to keep a school close to Egdon and have a night school in his mother's cottage. He wants to study for a few months to qualify himself. The Egdon people, including Clym's mother, are disappointed in him. Clym hears that one of the village women has stabbed Eustacia's arm with a knitting needle at church, believing Eustacia to be a witch, and he feels that he has not undertaken his project of educating the villagers too soon. He meets Eustacia, and his relations with his mother, who deeply resents the girl and her influence, grow colder. Clym persuades Eustacia to marry him and teach in his school. As she still longs for a wider kind of life, he promises to move to Budmouth after 6 months in a cottage on the heath. He tries to reconcile his mother to Eustacia but she quarrels bitterly with him and will not even meet her daughter-in-law.

Thomasin says that while Damon is a good husband, he gives her no money. Mrs. Yeobright decides to divide 100 guineas between Clym and Thomasin. She sends the money by CHRISTIAN CANTLE, a timid, stupid young man who works for her. Christian gambles all the money away to Wildeve, who has realized that it belongs to his wife. Wildeve feels insulted that the money was not entrusted to him in the first place. He is also heartsick because of Eustacia's marriage to Clym. When Diggory Venn comes in and offers to play, Wildeve accepts and gambles frantically. Venn plays coolly and wins the entire sum back. He does not know that 50 guineas belong to Clym and so delivers all the money to Thomasin.

Book IV. Mrs. Yeobright hears Christian's part of the story and decides to ask Eustacia if Wildeve delivered the money to Clym or Eustacia. Eustacia, already bitter with her mother-in-law, is insulted by the tone of the question. The two women quarrel violently and Eustacia tells Clym that she will never see his mother again. Clym tries to finish his studying so that he can take Eustacia away at once. He overstrains his eyes and is obliged to give up his studies entirely. He finds after some weeks that he can work as a furze-cutter on the heath, an occupation that will keep him busy and bring in a little money. Eustacia is in despair for himself and for her, especially because Clym seems to enjoy the work of a common laborer. She meets Wildeve at a village picnic and Wildeve is again enchanted by her. Diggory Venn sees that Wildeve goes to Eustacia's house at night and prevents him, by various ruses, from seeing her. Venn persuades Mrs. Yeobright to go to Eustacia and Clym and she takes the long walk across the hot, dusty heath. When she arrives, Clym is sleeping on the hearthrug. Eustacia is in back with Wildeve and dare not let Mrs. Yeobright in, but thinks she hears Clym get up. She sees Wildeve off. But Clym has not wakened, so no one received Mrs. Yeobright, who has started back feeling that she has been repulsed. Eustacia does not tell Clym of his mother's call but Clym has been dreaming about his mother and decides to go to see her. He finds her on the moor in a state of collapse. She has been bitten by an adder and overpowered by emotional and physical exhaustion. Eustacia, on her way to meet Clym, meets Wildeve. They saunter along, discussing Wildeve's inheritance from his uncle of £11,000 and the traveling he intends to do. Mrs. Yeobright is dying.

Book V. Clym has been seriously ill since his mother died, feeling that he caused her death. Eustacia waits for him to recover before she tells her part of the story, but Clym learns that Wildeve was with her and accuses her of his mother's murder and adultery with Wildeve. Eustacia breaks down and leaves the house. Thomasin's new baby has just been born and is to be named after Eustacia.

Eustacia goes to stay with her grandfather. The boy Charley tries to distract her from her suicidal thoughts and builds a bonfire on the spot where Eustacia's signal fires for Wildeve once burned. Wildeve comes at once and offers to send or to take Eustacia wherever she wishes to go. Clym repents of his harshness and, under Thomasin's urging, writes to ask Eustacia to return to him. The letter does not reach Eustacia in time. She has set out to run away with Wildeve.

Thomasin, suspicious of Eustacia and Wildeve, goes to tell Clym the story. She meets Diggory Venn and they continue together. Clym has found Wildeve and the two have gone together to look for Eustacia. In the darkness Eustacia loses her way and falls into the weir. Clym and Wildeve leap in to rescue her, but Wildeve founders and of the three only Clym is taken out alive. Clym feels that he has murdered Eustacia, as well as his mother.

Book VI. The suddenness of Thomasin's bereavement dulls her pain. She has not felt much love for Wildeve in the recent past, and her life is filled for awhile by her daughter, whom she takes to live at her aunt's old cottage. The inheritance of Wildeve's money makes her economically secure. Diggory Venn begins to make advances to Thomasin. They are obliged to wait for Clym's reluctant consent to the marriage, but there is no real objection to it since Venn has given up being a reddleman and has bought back his father's dairy. After the wedding, as Clym wanders about the heath, he meets Eustacia's young admirer, Charley. Charley begs for something that belonged to Eustacia and Clym gives the boy a lock of her hair.

On the following Sunday, Clym preaches a wise and simple sermon on the heath to anyone who will listen. After all his groping, he has found his vocation and knows that he has really returned as a native to the heath.

Richard II

Play by William Shakespeare, 1564–1616.

Produced about 1595.

WITH RICHARD II Shakespeare began his series of historical plays that carried the English kings successively through Henry IV, V and VI and Richard III. Richard II was a bad king, in the play called "England's landlord, not its king." But he was the legitimate king, and when he was deposed in favor of Henry IV the line of succession became a matter for dispute and the Wars of the Roses resulted. In Act II, Scene 1 occurs Shakespeare's most famous tribute to England, when the dying John of Gaunt calls it "this precious stone set in the silver sea" and other equally proud metaphors.

Act I. 1. JOHN OF GAUNT, Duke of Lancaster and uncle to RICHARD II, brings his son HENRY, called BOLINGBROKE, (and afterward King Henry IV) to court to make good his charges against Mowbray, the Duke of Norfolk. Henry accuses Mowbray of misappropriation of military funds and guilt in the death of the Duke of Gloucester, Richard's uncle. The king suggests a duel between the two adversaries on St. Lambert's Day at Coventry. **2.** The widowed Duchess of Gloucester asks John of Gaunt to help her obtain justice. **3.** At Coventry, Richard has changed his mind and does not permit the fight. He banishes Mowbray for life, and his cousin Henry for 6 years. He also makes them swear they will not plot against him. **4.** The Duke of AUMERLE, another cousin of Richard, reports the departure of Henry. Richard announces his intention to pursue the war against the Irish rebels. John of Gaunt is on his deathbed and Richard is anxious for Gaunt's death. He wants the inheritance to pay for the Irish campaign.

Act II. 1. Richard visits the dying Gaunt. Gaunt accuses the king of misrule and predicts that England will suffer for Richard's sins. Gaunt dies, and Richard orders all of Gaunt's property confiscated, depriving the banished Henry. The old Duke of YORK, uncle to Richard, protests in vain. The Earl of NORTHUMBERLAND reports to Henry's friends that Henry and a group of dissident nobles are on their way back to England by ship. **2.** At Windsor Castle, the Queen receives word of Henry's landing. The Duke of York is in charge, for Richard is in Ireland, but York is feeble and old. **3.** Henry is back and is with Northumberland, who has been proclaimed a traitor. Northumberland's son PERCY, called HOTSPUR, meets them. The Duke of York himself goes to meet Henry. He becomes convinced of Henry's just cause against the king. **4.** In Wales, the Earl of Salisbury cannot convince a Welsh captain that Richard is not dead and the army wishes to disband.

Act III. 1. BUSHY and GREEN, favorites of King Richard, are caught and executed by Henry. **2.** Richard decides to go to Flint Castle, now that he has no estate of his own. **3–4.** Henry arrives before Flint Castle. Percy defends it for Richard. Henry says he has returned from his exile solely to claim the title and property of his deceased father. Nevertheless, he insists that Richard accompany him to London. Richard is trapped in the castle.

Act IV. 1. At Westminster, Henry charges Richard with crimes against the State. Richard denies all guilt. Richard earlier sent word he was willing to resign but now wishes to hold onto his crown. But Henry takes the crown and sends Richard to prison in the Tower. Aumerle and the Bishop of CARLISLE plot in favor of Richard.

Act V. 1. The queen awaits Richard, who is being transferred to Pomfret Castle. The queen is to be sent to France. Richard and his queen sadly part. **2.** York and his wife decide to be loyal to Henry IV henceforth. Their son, Aumerle, arrives, and York questions him about a document he sees in Aumerle's coat. Aumerle refuses to show it. York takes it anyway and it is a treasonous document. York starts to report the plot to Henry. The duchess wishes him to forget it, to protect their son. Meanwhile,

Aumerle gets away. **3.** At the Palace, Aumerle seeks a private audience with his cousin. He plans to kill the new king, but his father arrives and sounds a warning. The duchess pleads with Henry for Aumerle's life. Henry pardons Aumerle. **4.** EXTON, a friend of Henry's, believes Henry wishes Richard killed. He decides to go to Pomfret and kill Richard. **5.** At Pomfret, Richard grows angry at his keepers, and kills one of the servants. Exton arrives just then and kills Richard. **6.** Henry receives the reports of the deaths of all his enemies in various parts of the country. Exton brings in the body of Richard. But Henry does not thank him for the deed. Instead, he banishes Exton from the court. He himself intends to do penitence for the murder of Richard by undertaking a pilgrimage to the Holy Land.

Richard III

Play by William Shakespeare, 1564–1616.
Produced about 1593.

RICHARD III RANKS VERY HIGH among Shakespeare's histories, chiefly because in it he created his most consummate villain, the hunchbacked Duke of Gloucester who became King Richard III. The part 'of Gloucester is so challenging but rewarding to an actor that the play is still frequently performed. The overthrow of the scheming and murdering Gloucester brought to the throne King Henry VII (in the play, the Earl of Richmond) who founded the House of Tudor and ended the Wars of the Roses. Since Elizabeth I, granddaughter of Henry VII, was reigning when Shakespeare wrote the play, Shakespeare had necessarily to glorify the first Tudor king, but he did not have to stray too far from English history to do so because the royal situation was untenable during the Wars of the Roses and stability was brought by the Tudors. Richard III opens with the famous lines, "Now is the winter of our discontent made glorious summer by this sun of York," and in the last scene of the play Richard III famously cries "My kingdom for a horse!"

Act I. 1. RICHARD, Duke of Gloucester and brother of King Edward IV, is ruthlessly determined to win the throne of England. He decides to revive an old prophecy that would cast suspicion on the loyalty of his brother the Duke of CLARENCE. Clarence is brought in under arrest. Richard falsely promises his brother to free him soon. He blames the queen for Clarence's imprisonment. HASTINGS, a supporter of the queen, informs Richard that King Edward is very ill. **2.** During the funeral procession of King Henry VI, Lady ANNE, the widowed daughter-in-law of Henry VI, accuses Richard of having caused the deaths of her father, her husband, and her king. Richard admits this, but says it was all done out of love for her. So convincing is he, that he gets her to ac-cept his ring as a symbol of their engagement. **3.** Queen ELIZABETH, formerly Lady Grey, and her brother, Earl RIVERS, discuss the precarious state of the king's health. Richard accuses Elizabeth of causing Clarence's downfall. This she denies. Old MARGARET, the widow of Henry VI, joins Elizabeth in cursing Richard but he shrugs them off. He convinces the nobles BUCKINGHAM, DERBY, and Hastings, that it was Elizabeth who poisoned the king's mind against Clarence. Then, secretly, Richard orders two murderers to do away with his brother. **4.** In the Tower, Clarence suffers remorse for his misdeeds. He thinks the king ungrateful. BRAKENBURY, the jailer, leaves the jail to protest at court. The murderers come and Clarence is killed.

Act II. 1. Edward, whose illness has grown worse, attempts to reconcile his wife Elizabeth and her friends with Richard. Peace is pledged by the two factions. Told of Clarence's death, the king blames himself. **2.** The Duchess of YORK, mother of Edward IV, hears from Queen Elizabeth that Edward has just died. Buckingham gives orders to fetch young EDWARD, Prince of Wales, to be crowned Edward V. Alone with Richard, Buckingham is revealed as loyal only to Richard. He plans to separate the boy from his mother. **3.** Two citizens of London bemoan the fact that England will have a child ruler. **4.** The Archbishop of York discusses preparations for the coronation with Queen Elizabeth and others. Word reaches them that the queen's supporters have been imprisoned by Richard. Now they fear for their own safety.

Act III. 1. Young Edward arrives in London. He hears from Hastings that his mother has taken sanctuary in a church. Richard suggests that young Edward and his younger brother, who is Duke of York, should stay at the Tower until coronation time. Both boys go off to the Tower. Richard sends CATESBY, his henchman, to order the execution of the imprisoned nobles. **2.** Catesby sounds out Hastings and finds him loyal to young Edward. **3.** The nobles are executed. **4.** Richard summons Hastings to discuss the coronation of young Edward. Suddenly he accuses Hastings of plotting against him and orders his immediate execution. **5.** Richard and Buckingham, in field armor, sound an alarm as if the city of London were in danger. They convince the Lord Mayor that Hastings' execution was necessary. Richard sends Buckingham to the Guildhall to tell the councilors that all of Edward's children are really illegitimate. **6.** Scrivener reads the belated indictment against Hastings. **7.** At Baynard's Castle, the citizens ask Richard to accept the crown. Richard pretends piety, appearing on the balcony, seemingly absorbed in a prayerbook, between two clerics. However, he accepts the offer.

Act IV. 1. Elizabeth, with the Duchess of York and Lady Anne, tries to enter the Tower to see the two young princes. They are refused and they learn of Richard's usurpation. Anne is summoned to Westminster to be crowned with Richard. Unhappily, she obeys. **2.** Richard becomes king, thanks to Buckingham's counsel. He immediately suggests to Buckingham the murder of the two young princes in the Tower, but Buckingham wants time to think it over. Richard summons TYRREL, a professional cutthroat. Promising him gold, he sends him to kill the two princes. The Earl of RICHMOND (afterwards King Henry VII) is approaching in order to dispute Richard the throne. Buckingham asks for his reward, the promised earldom of Hereford, but Richard ignores him. Buckingham realizes that he had better leave while he still can. **3.** Tyrrel reports the death

Richard condemns Hastings

of the two young princes. Buckingham goes over to Richmond. **4.** Margaret and Elizabeth recount Richard's evil deeds. When Richard passes, his mother asks a word with him. He refuses to listen. Anne has died, as Richard had arranged. Richard offers to marry Elizabeth, a daughter of Queen Elizabeth. The younger Elizabeth is the fiancée of Richmond. Richard persuades Queen Elizabeth to talk to her daughter about it. Meanwhile Richmond is advancing and many English nobles are joining him. Buckingham is taken prisoner. **5.** Derby sends word to Richmond that he is on his side but cannot say so openly since Richard holds his son George as a hostage.

Act V. 1. Buckingham is executed. **2.** Richard is confident of victory. **3.** Richard pitches his tent on Bosworth Field. But he cannot sleep. The ghosts of all the people Richard has murdered appear as good omens to the sleeping Richmond, but as symbols of doom to Richard. Both adversaries exhort their troops at the start of the battle. **4.** The battle begins, and Richard loses his horse. **5.** The battle is won by Richmond. Richard and Richmond engage in personal combat and Richard is killed. Richmond then promises to restore peace to strife-torn England and to marry Elizabeth, uniting the opposing York and Lancaster factions, the red and the white rose.

The Ring of the Lowenskolds

Novels by Selma Lagerlof, 1858–1940. Published 1931 by Doubleday & Co., New York.

CHARLOTTE LOWENSKOLD is the best-known name in a trilogy, or series of three novels, of which the official name is *The Ring of the Lowenskolds*. This is perhaps because it is the only novel of the three that bears the name of the family around which all the action centers. But *Charlotte Lowenskold* was not the first of the three novels. The trilogy began with *The General's Ring*, continued with *Charlotte Lowenskold*, and ended with *Anna Svard*. These novels are the acknowledged principal work of a novelist who won the Nobel Prize for literature in 1909.

The General's Ring

Chaps. 1–7. General BENGT LOWENSKOLD was a loyal and fearless soldier who served his king, Charles XII of Sweden, so well that the king rewarded him with the estate of Hedeby. Also, as a personal token of his esteem, the king gave the general a great signet ring. The general wishes to have the ring buried with him so that in Heaven the ring will win him the right to spend eternity at the side of the man he served most of his life. General Lowenskold dies in March 1741 and is laid to rest in the family vault with the great ring on his finger. A few months later his eldest son, Capt. GEORGE LOWENSKOLD, loses his little daughter and she is laid to rest in the vault. The people gathered round the open vault all remember the ring, and some have covetous thoughts. The captain neglects to have the vault closed that night and a farmer, BARD BARDSSON, and his wife steal the ring. As they leave the graveyard they see the sky red with flames and they are soon aware that their cottage is on fire. Bad luck follows them for years. Bard's wife drowns herself. When finally Bard is stricken, on his deathbed he sends for the RECTOR. Bard's son INGILBERT hears him confess the

theft of the ring and sees Bard give it to the rector to return to the captain. Ingilbert leads the rector through a bog, and when the rector sees that the young farmer is about to kill him he throws the little bag containing the ring to Ingilbert and flees. He reports the story of the original theft to Capt. Lowenskold and tells him of Ingilbert's new crime. The captain and his men search for Ingilbert and find that he has died and his body is being carried out of the woods by ERIC IVARSSON, his brother IVAR, and Eric's adopted son PAUL ELIASSON. Ingilbert's body is searched but the ring is not found on it. The Ivarssons and Paul are accused of taking it. They are tried and acquitted, but the verdict is reversed by another court. Finally the king decides they should be tried by ordeal—in this case a casting of dice. The one who casts the lowest number will be judged guilty. The whole town turns out for the ordeal, and sentiment towards the accused is varied. Eric, Ivar and Paul conduct themselves so well that everyone is won over and when each throws double sixes, the people feel all three are innocent. The king decides, however, that this could equally show all three to be guilty and they are all hanged.

Chaps. 8. Thirty years pass and MARIT, daughter of Eric Ivarsson, who had been betrothed to Paul Eliasson, finds an old woolen cap in a clothes chest. It has a colorful pattern and she remembers it as the cap Paul wore at the Ordeal. She starts to pull some strands of wool from the tassel to use in her knitting, when she suddenly sees the great signet ring concealed in the strands. Now she remembers Paul's telling her about the cap, which was worn by Ingilbert when they found his body; Paul was attracted by the pattern and took it. Her heart is heavy. For this small theft three men dear to her lost their lives. Marit believes with the other people of the region that the ghost of the old general is bringing evil to all who have the ring. She thinks she should go to the Rector, tell him how she found the ring, and give it to him. But she fears this will seem to justify the execution of her dear ones—after all, the ring was found in their possession and the story of the cap might

not be believed. At the moment of her indecision ADRIAN LOWENSKOLD, the grandson of the captain, is playing with another young boy who is the son of Marit's cousin. Adrian's cap is torn and Marit mends it and sews the ring into its tassel. She feels she can now strike back at the Lowenskolds for all the misery they have caused her. The ring will now bring them the curse of their own ancestor.

Chaps. 9–11. Several years pass and Adrian is now a young man. Since the time Marit sewed the ring in his cap the home of the Lowenskolds at Hedeby has been haunted by the ghost of the general. A new housekeeper, MALVINA SPAAK, sees the ghost but it does not threaten her. Malvina meets Marit, now old, in the fields and is warned by her that she should leave Hedeby because the ghost will not leave until he gets what he wants. Malvina tells Adrian of her meeting with Marit and asks if he knows what the ghost wants. He tells her that he does know and he wishes to find it and gain peace. The ghost appears to Adrian in the middle of the night and at first Adrian follows him without fear, but he is finally so terrified he falls to the ground in a coma. He is found the next morning close to death and the Lowenskolds do all they can to revive him, but he grows weaker and weaker. Malvina remembers Marit and has a feeling that Marit can help. She goes to the old woman and pleads with her to help Adrian if she can. Marit, though her heart is hardened to the Lowenskolds, sees that Malvina loves Adrian and consents to help. She comes to Hedeby and asks for a collection of Adrian's old clothes, and she insists that a little warm woolen cap be included. The old cap she mended years before is brought out. Marit tells Malvina that the clothes must be put in the general's grave. Malvina carries out the strange request and when she gets back to the house she finds Adrian recovered. He thanks her for what she has done, but her joy is shortlived as he tells her he is engaged to another woman.

Marit hides the ring

Charlotte Lowenskold

Chap. 1–7. About 40 years later the Baroness BEATA EKENSTEDT, born a Lowenskold, is the mistress of a fine house in Karlstedt. She is intelligent, graceful, and full of the accomplishments of her world. Her husband and her two plain daughters are relegated to the background while her son KARL ARTHUR is the center of her existence. The boy goes to college at Uppsala and decides to give up the life of ease and become a simple curate. He falls in love with CHARLOTTE LOWENSKOLD, a poor member of that proud family. She in turn is loved by a rich widower, SCHAGERSTROM, who proposes to her. She turns him down, feeling that Karl Arthur will some day be an important man in the Church. Karl Arthur meets THEA SUNDLER, the daughter of Malvina Spaak, who is married but secretly loves the curate. Thea tells him that Charlotte has great ambitions for him. Karl Arthur is greatly agitated and goes to Charlotte. They embrace but then quarrel and when Charlotte admits she wants him to become a bishop Karl is completely disillusioned and in his desire for a simple life he knows he cannot marry Charlotte. He leaves her and hurries down the country road, vowing to marry the one whom God chooses for him. He sees a lovely young girl who is carrying a bag of kitchen utensils. She is ANNA SVARD, a house-to-house peddler. Karl Arthur is suddenly smitten with her and feels that God has chosen for him. He immediately asks her to marry him. She sees he is in earnest and says she will see him later in the evening. He knows she will return, as she has been chosen for him by God. They do meet and spend several happy hours in talk. The next day he tells Charlotte about Anna and she is aghast at his marrying a peddler. She tries to dissuade him but he is adamant. She tries to beguile him and he almost succumbs to her charms, but then a servant brings in a bouquet sent by Schagerstrom. Karl Arthur leaves and soon after Charlotte receives a note from him saying that he had heard she wanted to marry Schagerstrom.

Chaps. 8–14. Charlotte knows that someone must have poisoned Karl Arthur's mind against her and she means to find out who it is and avenge herself. She knows she must take the blame for the breaking of her engagement to Karl Arthur, in order not to make him look bad in the eyes of his parents and others. She hears venomous gossip against her, and she realizes it could easily have been turned against Karl Arthur. She at least is comforted in the knowledge that she is protecting him. Charlotte knows Thea Sundler to be one of the worst gossips, but she does not yet know Thea to be the one who poisoned Karl Arthur's mind. Schagerstrom comes to offer Karl Arthur the post of chaplain in his community, but Karl Arthur accuses him of renewing his wooing of Charlotte. Schagerstrom protests, but he accuses the young man of treating Charlotte badly and he sends a note to Charlotte asking her to marry him. She accepts Schagerstrom's proposal and they arrange to publish the banns. Soon after this, the Baroness comes to see her son and visits with the relatives Charlotte lives with. Charlotte overhears the Baroness criticize her for her actions toward Karl Arthur; and though Charlotte is heartbroken, still she is pleased that the blame for the break-off has fallen on her. But when Thea Sundler comes to tea, Charlotte overhears her gossip to the Baroness and she realizes that Thea is the one who poisoned Karl Arthur's mind against her. The Baroness now understands what has happened. She forgives Charlotte and promises her that everything will turn out well.

Chaps. 15–23. Schagerstrom decides to have the banns published for his wedding to Charlotte. Karl Arthur preaches an extraordinarily beautiful sermon and when he finishes he turns to read the list of banns. He does not know that the names of Charlotte and Schagerstrom are on the list and when he comes to them he reads them in a low, agonized voice. Charlotte, too, did not know the banns were to be published and she is terribly distressed that people will think she actually planned to marry the rich ironmaster. Schagerstrom understands her distress and agrees to halt the banns. Karl Arthur's aunt dies and he goes home to the funeral. At his home he finds Anna Svard, to whom his mother has given work for a while. He announces to the family and guests that Anna is his fiancée. In the ensuing confusion, the Baroness falls and is injured. Anna runs out into the night and Karl Arthur follows her. He finds his parents have bribed Anna to leave him. He returns home in indignation and confronts his father with having tampered with the will of God, and he accuses his mother and Charlotte of being deceitful women. His father and Schagerstrom, who is present, tell him of his mother's devotion and Charlotte's self-sacrifice for him. But Karl Arthur refuses to listen to reason and he breaks with his parents. He goes to Charlotte and tells her what happened, and she begs him to make amends to his ailing mother. Karl Arthur refuses and Charlotte goes to Thea Sundler, hoping to persuade her to make Karl Arthur go to his mother. Thea says that Karl Arthur is afraid his mother will try to bring him together with Charlotte again. Charlotte loves the Baroness, and to relieve her pain and misery by bringing her son back, she agrees to Thea's sly proposition—namely that Thea will persuade Karl Arthur to reconcile with his mother if Charlotte will quickly marry Schagerstrom. Charlotte goes to care for her rich sister and overhears two maids discussing Karl Arthur's sermon, in which he told how he had wronged Charlotte and asked the congregation to pray for her because she was going to marry a rich man. Hearing this, Charlotte feels humiliation and suddenly knows that Karl Arthur has killed her love for him. She determines that no one shall have the satisfaction of seeing her unhappy in her marriage. She and Schagerstrom are married and he takes her to her new and beautiful home.

Anna Svard

Part I. Karl Arthur goes back to see his mother at Thea's instigation, but as he nears the house he changes his mind. He is about to leave when his sister sees him and he cannot help but go in. Mother and son are overjoyed at seeing each other, but Karl Arthur stubbornly demands that his mother ask his forgiveness for what he has done to him and Anna Svard. The Baroness suffers an attack and Karl Arthur, thinking her dead, goes to the Burgomaster and says he has killed his mother. The Burgomaster tells him he has just seen the doctor and that the Baroness is not dead. Karl Arthur returns to the estate and his sister tells him their mother has had a stroke and cannot speak. He leaves again and sees Charlotte and they both blame themselves for what has happened to the Baroness—Charlotte for being the one originally responsible for his going while he was still distraught; and he for his harshness to his mother. They part again but this time in sympathy and understanding. In the meantime Anne Svard has returned to her own home. She tells her family of the miracle—a well-born curate has asked her to marry him. Not all of her townsmen take her seriously, but she convinces most of them that she is not out of her mind. She receives a tender letter from Karl Arthur, and since she cannot read she goes to the sexton and he reads it to her. Several days later she has the sexton write a reply. On another occasion Anna asks the sexton to teach her to read and write. He agrees and she joins a group of young boys in their daily classes. Karl Arthur comes to Anna's town and they are married. Anna learns that her husband wants only to be married spiritually, not physically. They go to live in a humble little cottage with a tiny back room for Karl Arthur and a kitchen sofa for Anna. She is to be more a servant than a wife, but she finds another room behind a locked door, with a fine bed. Thea Sundler is visiting them, and it is she who has prepared the cottage. Anna cleverly gets Thea to openly admit the presence of the good bed, and she triumphantly sleeps in it—alone. Anna tries to make herself more attractive and gracious to Karl Arthur, and she almost succeeds, but in trying to thwart Thea she is not quite clever enough and she is made to look contemptible in his eyes.

Part II. Karl Arthur has been away for 18 months, serving in several parishes. He returns home to find that the old dean of his own parish has died and he is to fill the vacancy temporarily. He finds Anna caring for ten homeless children and the house noisy. He has some new feelings of love for Anna, but he does nothing about showing them. He meets Thea and she says she may arrange to place the children elsewhere. Anna is angry at this. When the children leave, the warmth and meaning go out of her life. An old peddler woman visits her and gives her 50 riksdollars for goods that Anna once left with her to be sold.

537

The Rise of Silas Lapham

Novel by William Dean Howells, 1837–1920.

Published 1885. (ML, G277 & T56; RE, 19)

HOWELLS ENJOYED the greatest prestige in his times. He was generally considered America's first man of letters. Little of his work is still actively read in the same sense that the work of his contemporary Mark Twain is still read, but *The Rise of Silas Lapham*, often considered his masterpiece, remains among living literature. There were numerous novels of upperclass Boston written in the same period, but Howells set a rising middle-class family in the upper-class society and showed two sides of the many-sided picture. Much of the writing concerns the emotional dilemmas of the characters, with pride or honor at stake, and these passages are admirably executed.

Chaps. 1–2. SILAS LAPHAM, born into a family of poor but hardworking farmers, is now, at 55, one of Boston's wealthiest businessmen. He owes this phenomenal success to his own determination and shrewdness and to a large deposit of mineral paint discovered on his father's farm 40 years ago. After the Civil War, on the encouragement of his wife, a good, sensible woman, Silas took a man named ROGERS as a partner. Rogers had the capital Silas needed at the time, but he knew nothing about paint and after about two years Silas bought Rogers out. Silas and his wife were of simple stock and never knew quite what to do with their wealth. They surrounded themselves with what luxuries they could think of, but they never thought of foreign travel or private schools for their daughters, PENELOPE and IRENE. It never occurred to them that their large, comfortable house was in an unfashionable section of town until Mrs. Lapham and Irene met the COREYS, one of Boston's leading families, and learned that the "best people" live on Beacon Hill. Now Tom Corey, the son, is showing an interest in Irene, who is a real beauty, and Mrs. Lapham begins to think about the future of her girls. As a first step, she and Silas decided to build a house on Beacon Hill.

Chaps. 3–4. A year later the house is in its first stages and the Laphams frequently ride to Beacon Hill to watch its progress. On one visit they meet Tom Corey. Silas likes the boy on sight. He eagerly shows Tom around, bragging, to the embarrassment of Irene.

Chaps. 5–9. Silas is overjoyed when Tom asks to come into the paint business. They agree that Tom should start out as a clerk, spend six months learning the business, and then strike out on his own to set up foreign offices and develop an international market. Silas takes Tom home with him that night to discuss the matter further. Mrs. Lapham first assumes that Tom is doing this because of his interest in Irene; but as weeks go by and Tom makes no effort to see Irene, Mrs. Lapham begins to feel that Tom is not in love with her daughter after all.

Chap. 10. Rogers turns up unexpectedly one day and asks Silas to lend him $20,000 for a business venture. Because he has always felt guilty about buying Rogers out of the business just as it was beginning to pay off big, Silas gives him the money and accepts stock in a milling property as security. Tom, at his own suggestion, comes home to dinner with Silas. The evening is a huge success, for Penelope is an intelligent, witty girl, and Irene makes a beautiful picture.

Chap. 11. Tom prevails on his father to call on Silas in his office, and Tom's visits to the Lapham house grow more and more frequent. But as he does not pay special attention to Irene, Mrs. Lapham is puzzled.

Chaps. 12–15. When Mrs. Corey returns from her summer vacation and learns of Tom's growing involvement with the Lapham family, she is distressed. She decides to call on Mrs. Lapham to find out for

Anna goes to order a large cupboard at the carpenter's. On the way she meets Thea and tells her of her good fortune. When Karl Arthur comes home he tells her that she should not spend money thusly, but use it for good deeds. She learns Thea has already told Karl Arthur of the 50 riksdollars and has gotten the money from him for treating her husband's gout. Anna now knows her husband has no real feeling for her and no power to help her. She leaves and Thea feels she now has Karl Arthur to herself. Charlotte meets Karl Arthur accidentally and comforts him in his distress. Schagerstrom has a serious accident in a sawmill and Charlotte thinks he may have tried to commit suicide because he suspects she still loves Karl Arthur. She tells her husband she really loves only him.

Anna, in the meantime, has gone to Karl Arthur's parents and she gets money from them to buy a farm. While looking for some likely land she sees Karl Arthur and Thea disguised and holding an evangelical meeting at a fair. She stifles her desire to denounce them as sinners. She then finds the ten children, whom she missed terribly, and is reconciled with them.

Part III. The second Baron Adrian Lowenskold has grown old, and has been married several times, but has no sons, only daughters. One snowy winter evening his vagabond brother GORAN comes with a child dressed in rags. He says the child is a son of his with a gypsy woman and begs Baron Adrian to take it. Goran leaves and is found frozen to death the next day. Much to his surprise Adrian finds the child is a girl, and he would send her back to her gypsy mother, but his wife takes pity on the child and contrives to have her catch the measles so she cannot be sent away. The Baroness remembers that Adrian's cousin Charlotte Lowenskold has expressed a desire to rear one of their first daughters, as she had no children of her own. Charlotte arrives at Hedeby and when she sees Goran's daughter she loves the child on sight. While Charlotte and the Baroness are out, Karl Arthur, dressed as a gypsy and accompanied by a gypsy woman, who claims to be the child's mother, come to the Baron for money. When he refuses them, they drive off but they see the child on the grounds and take her. The Baron and Charlotte pursue them. They see them trying to cross a frozen lake. Karl Arthur's sled goes through the ice and when the Baron rushes to the gaping hole he falls through and is lost. Karl Arthur, however, manages to climb out and is taken by Charlotte to a warm place. Thea appears to take him away, but Karl Arthur, contrite at last, appeals to Charlotte to save him from Thea. She rehabilitates him and sends for Anna. Anna is reluctant but comes to hear him preach and drops her wedding ring on the offering tray. She goes home, knowing he will come to her; and she knows not how she will receive him.

Karl Arthur's sled goes through the ice

herself how things stand. Irene is not home when she arrives. The hour Mrs. Corey spends with Mrs. Lapham and Penelope is unpleasant, because Mrs. Corey makes it clear that she considers the Laphams beneath her. Mrs. Corey decides that the best way to cure Tom of his infatuation will be to hold a dinner party and invite the Laphams, who are certain to appear vulgar and illbred beside her fashionable friends. With the exception of Penelope, who declines the invitation because of her dislike for Mrs. Corey, the Laphams accept, unaware of the real reason behind the dinner party. They eagerly anticipate the event and spend weeks in preparation for it. At last the big night arrives, and though the dinner goes off fairly well, Silas drinks too much wine and makes a fool of himself, talking excessively and bragging. The next day Silas is ashamed and denounces himself to Tom. Tom tells him he feels sure Silas is exaggerating what happened and that he and everyone else present realized the wine was responsible. Although Tom is aware of the difference between the Laphams and his own family, he resolves to give Silas ultimate proof of his faith and respect.

Chaps. 16–19. That evening, when Tom arrives at the Laphams', Silas is out and Penelope, the only one at home, receives him instead. They talk casually for awhile and then, casually, their conversation turns to the subject of love. Tom is in love with Penelope and has been for some time. That is what he came to see her father about tonight, to ask for her hand in marriage. Stunned by this unexpected turn of events because she realizes what a blow it will be to Irene, Penelope tells Tom he must go immediately and not try to see her again. Confused and distressed, Tom hurries out of the house without stopping to speak to Silas. The next morning, Silas mentions Tom's hasty departure to Mrs. Lapham, who hurries upstairs to Penelope. Penelope tells her mother about Tom's visit and then confesses that she has been in love with him from the beginning, but she is unwilling to hurt Irene. They seek the advice of their minister, who tells them what they have actually decided, that it would be foolish and cruel for Penelope to sacrifice a life of happiness with Tom just because Irene hoped to have him for herself.

Irene takes the news stoically but immediately makes plans to go away until she is over the shock. When Tom comes again to plead his suit with Penelope, she tells him about Irene's expectations and her own feeling of guilt. Tom reminds her gently that by forbidding him to love her, she cannot make him love Irene. Penelope realizes this but, feeling guilty as she does, cannot accept Tom now.

Chaps. 20–24. Silas begins to have financial difficulties. The paint market is slow. Creditors are pressing him and debtors are slow in paying. On top of this, Silas has discovered that Rogers is a scoundrel and the stocks he gave Silas as security for the $20,000 may prove to be worthless.

Silas finds himself in the most desperate situation of his career. A company in West Virginia has found a cheap way to manufacture paint and is cutting Silas's price by 50%. He will have to sell the unfinished house on Beacon Hill. Corey offers to invest $30,000 of his own in the business, but Silas rejects the offer, telling him that there is now more reason than ever not to take Tom in as a partner. The real-estate broker finds a customer for Silas and sets up an appointment for the following day. Now that he is actually on the point of selling the house, which represented his dreams for the future, Silas finds parting with it very hard. He goes there alone, lights a fire in the fireplace, and stays for several hours contemplating the turn his luck has taken. After he leaves, the house catches fire and burns to the ground. Silas rushes to examine his insurance policy and finds that it expired one week before.

Chap. 25. As a last stab at retrieving his failing fortunes, Silas decides to do business with his competitors, the West Virginia company. They agree to merge with him, on the condition that he raise the capital necessary to expand their business. They give him three days to do it. Silas can find nobody willing to lend him money on such short notice. However, just when things look their blackest, Rogers shows up and tells Silas a group of Englishmen are willing to buy their worthless property at an excellent price. Silas realizes that if he sells out to them, he will be duping the English-

men just as he was duped by Rogers. He spends a harrowing night trying to decide between dishonesty and certain financial ruin. He decides to reject Rogers' unethical offer.

Chap. 26. Silas does not come home the following night. Penelope, who has kept Tom away from the house during all their time of trouble, is finally forced to apply to Tom for information about her father. Tom tells her that Silas will be out of town for several days. Seeing her again, Tom is more in love with her than ever. The following day he asks his mother to call on the Laphams. Resigning herself to the unpleasant prospect of a match between her son and the Lapham girl, Mrs. Corey goes with her husband to call on Penelope, whom she dislikes as much on this second visit as she did on the first. Silas returns to Boston and tells his wife he is bankrupt. They sell everything to pay their debts and move back to the farm he came from. Tom enters the West Virginia paint company, on Silas's suggestion, and he persuades Penelope to marry him, though they both know that his family will never fully accept her and that she will never quite get over her guilt about Irene. Silas works on varieties of paint as hard as he ever did, though he has no illusions of recovering his lost prosperity. His one consolation in rare moments of despondency is that in spite of everything that happened, he never behaved dishonestly or unjustly to any man, and he has no regrets.

The Rivals

Play by Richard Brinsley Sheridan, 1751–1816.
Produced 1775.

THIS IS ONE of the best-known, perhaps *the* best-known, of the comedies of the late 18th century. Its preëminence stems from two of its remarkable characters: Bob Acres (or Akers) the fop and far more importantly Mrs. Malaprop, who has a genius for using the wrong word at the right time. Except that it must be condensed somewhat to conform to the time modern theater-goers are willing to devote to watching a play, *The Rivals* can be revived and enjoyed today.

Act I. 1. On the street at Bath, FAG, the servant of Capt. JACK ABSOLUTE, tells THOMAS, the coachman of Jack's father, Sir ANTHONY ABSOLUTE, that Jack has assumed the name of "Ensign BEVERLY" to woo the lovely and wealthy LYDIA LANGUISH, who, being very romantic, would not accept him on his own well-established merits. Thomas, in turn, reveals that JULIA, Sir Anthony's ward, is engaged to marry FAULKLAND, Jack's sighing and

melancholy friend. **2.** Lydia chides her maid, LUCY, for not having found her the latest sentimental novels. She is cheered by the arrival of her cousin Julia. Lydia's aunt, Mrs. MALAPROP, has intercepted her letters to "Beverly" and has been confined to her room as punishment. Mrs. Malaprop asks Lydia to 'illiterate' Beverly from her mind. Lydia says she cannot. Sir Anthony, calling on Mrs. Malaprop, proposes that his son Jack should become engaged to Lydia. Mrs. Malaprop accedes. Lucy assures Mrs. Malaprop that she has delivered the note to Sir LUCIUS O'TRIGGER. Lucy totes up the rich tips she has received from the various intrigues.

Act II. 1. Jack Absolute anticipates some fun teasing his friend Faulkland, who does not know that Julia has arrived. Faulkland is very melancholy because he has not heard from his beloved and becomes even more so when BOB ACRES arrives. Bob is a foppish young man who has been pursuing Lydia, but she cannot abide him. Bob tells Faulkland that Julia has been singing and dancing while Faulkland was away. Faulkland, in despair, rushes out to find Julia. Sir Anthony offers to raise Jack's allowance, but Jack is outraged to learn he must marry someone of his father's choosing. He is convinced she will be an old hag. Sir

539

Anthony leaves in a rage. Jack berates Fag and leaves in a rage. Fag berates an errand boy and leaves in a rage. 2. Lucy delivers another note from Mrs. Malaprop to Sir Lucius O'Trigger. Mrs. Malaprop signs the letters "DELIA" and O'Trigger thinks he is corresponding with Lydia. Lucy tells Fag it is Lydia Sir Anthony proposes for Jack. Fag rushes to tell Jack.

Act III. 1. Jack makes his peace with his father and promises to marry the person Sir Anthony has chosen, knowing it is Lydia. 2. Faulkland, downhearted because he thinks Julia has been too happy during his absence, chides her. She flees to her room in tears and he is overcome with remorse at his foolish jealousy. 3. Mrs. Malaprop shows Jack a note from the supposed Beverly, Lucy having passed it to Mrs. Malaprop instead of delivering it to Lydia. Jack is forced to read aloud its uncomplimentary remarks about Mrs. Malaprop. Jack suggests that Mrs. Malaprop allow Beverly and Lydia to plan an elopement; then Jack will arrive in the nick of time and carry off the girl himself. Lydia comes in and is shocked to see Beverly, but he assures her he has taken the disguise of Jack Absolute to fool Mrs. Malaprop. Delighted with the scheme, Lydia plays along. 4. After trying on some new foppish clothes, Bob Acres complains to O'Trigger that he has been snubbed by Lydia. Acres writes a note challenging him to a duel. O'Trigger plans to challenge Jack, who he feels is his rival for "Delia."

Act IV. 1. Acres and his servant, DAVID, discuss the impending duel. Both become more timid as the discussion goes on. Acres screws up his courage and asks Jack to deliver the challenge to Beverly. Jack declines to be Bob's second but promises to deliver the note. 2. Sir Anthony forces Jack to go to Mrs. Malaprop's with him. Lydia turns her face to the wall and refuses to meet Captain Absolute, but when he speaks she knows he is Beverly. Feeling cheated, she flings away a portrait of Jack and sweeps from the room declaring that she renounces Beverly forever. 3. Jack meets O'Trigger, who challenges him to a duel that evening, in the same place where Bob Acres is to meet Beverly. Jack persuades Faulkland to be his second. Faulkland, who has just received a note of forgiveness from Julia, decides to test her love by telling her he has become involved in a quarrel.

Act V. 1. On finding that Julia will go with him, if he must flee the country, Faulkland confesses that he was once again testing Julia's love by telling her a lie. She is hurt and tells him she does not wish to see him again. Lydia comes to ask Julia for advice but Julia is so taken up with her own unhappiness that she is unable to give Lydia any solace. They are interrupted by Mrs. Malaprop, accompanied by Fag and David, who ponderously relate that Jack, Faulkland and O'Trigger are involved in duels. There is great haste to get to the field before anything happens. 2. Jack, on his way to the dueling scene, meets his father. Jack tries to avoid his father but Sir Anthony recognizes him. Jack, after alluding to an assignation with Lydia, escapes. But David informs Sir Anthony of the duel and they pursue Jack. 3. At the dueling site O'Trigger instructs Bob Acres in the niceties of dueling. Acres' courage is ebbing fast. Jack and Faulkland appear. Acres greets Jack with enthusiasm, so O'Trigger assumes that Faulkland is Beverly. This misunderstanding is cleared up. Jack and O'Trigger draw but they are interrupted by the arrival of Sir Anthony and David, followed closely by Fag, Mrs. Malaprop, Lydia, and Julia. Jack, having confessed that he is Beverly, is forgiven by Lydia. She informs O'Trigger that Mrs. Malaprop is Delia. Bob Acres and O'Trigger give up all ideas of wives. Julia and Faulkland plan to marry immediately. Acres invites the whole company to a party within the hour.

Robinson Crusoe

Novel by Daniel Defoe, 1661–1731. Published 1719. (PB, PL510; ML, 92).

AN ENGLISH SAILOR, Alexander Selkirk, was cast ashore alone on an uninhabited Caribbean island in 1704 and survived there for five years, when he was rescued. On this experience Defoe fashioned his novel *Robinson Crusoe.* It was not written as a children's book but it has survived principally in the juvenile market, in which it is one of the "standard classics." Most of the details come from Defoe's imagination, but he was careful in his research and few flaws have been found in his account. Knowledge of the Robinson Crusoe story is part of an English-speaking person's fundamental education.

CRUSOE, born in 1632 to a family of good means, early shows an inclination to go to sea, despite his father's objections. At the age of 19 he sails with a friend from Hull to London, with no word to his parents. The ship is sunk in a storm and Crusoe lands at Yarmouth but does not take this as an omen. He next ships on a voyage to Africa, not as a sailor but as a gentleman adventurer. This trip brings him some small profit, but most of all a knowledge of navigation and trade. On a second voyage, Crusoe's ship is captured by Moorish pirates and he is made personal slave to the captain. He spends more than two years a captive, and finally is able to escape in a fishing boat. He sails south along the African coast and for several weeks gets food and water by landing occasionally and making friends with the natives. He finally meets a Portuguese ship, which takes him to Brazil. Crusoe reaches there with some small amount of money, buys a plantation, and settles down. After two years he is restless. He sends for his property in England and invests it wisely. His plantation prospers and he begins to get grand schemes of great wealth. He agrees to go with friends on a voyage to Africa to get slaves, and sets sail 8 years after first leaving home. They sail northward and run into a hurricane. They hope to reach a Caribbean island to refit the ship, but a second storm strikes and carries the ship upon a sandbar, part of an unknown island. The ship begins to break up. A small boat is launched but it overturns and Crusoe is the only one to swim ashore. He is stranded, with no resources.

The next morning, with the tide out, Crusoe swims to the stranded ship. He constructs a raft and ferries to shore food, liquor, tools, guns, clothes, and gunpowder. He finds a river's mouth and steers in there. Each day he brings in more supplies and everything of value is removed from the ship before it can break up in another storm. No sign of human life is seen on the island but Crusoe takes no chances. He builds a tent, surrounds it with high stakes, and moves everything within. He digs a cave into the hillside to protect his belongings. He shoots goats for meat. Crusoe figures he landed on September 20, 1659, and to keep track of the time he notches a post to mark each day. Gradually he enlarges his cave, builds furniture, and starts to keep a journal. Two cats and a dog from the ship are his only companions.

When Crusoe empties an old bag of grain a few seeds take root and some while later Crusoe finds barley and rice growing. (After a few years he harvests enough grain to make bread.) He is almost killed and his work undone by a great earthquake and storm. His home and cave are tumbled down. Fearing a recurrence, he determines to build a new house away from the hill. The ship's wreckage has been driven ashore and he gleans great sections of wood, plus iron bolts and fastenings. In mid-June Crusoe takes ill with fever, and for ten days is unable to move about. Without food or drink he almost dies. He looks in a chest for tobacco to try to use as a cure and finds some Bibles. He reads the Bible and finds consolation and strength.

After 10 months Crusoe begins to explore his island more fully. He finds fruits growing wild, which he gathers, and tobacco, which he dries. He builds a bower in the pleasant part of the woods. From mid-August to mid-October it is the rainy season and Crusoe is held close to his tent and cave. He begins to take note of the seasons and learns when to expect dry weather, when wet. He learns how to plant his little stock of grain to get seasonal crops. He builds a food reserve indoors so that he need not go out when it is wet. Crusoe goes all the way across the island and finds that he landed, by chance, on the poorer side. On the other side there is much pleasanter country, with great supplies of turtles for food, and fowl and goats. But being accustomed to his dwelling, he decides to stay there. He brings back a parrot and a young kid, which he tames. Thus a second year passes.

His grain crop is attacked by goats and hares; he has to fence in his small plot. Birds attack the grain and he makes scarecrows. But he gets a small crop. Tilling the soil has been a great job, nearly everything being done by hand, but he has time in plenty and uses it to make tools of wood. He experiments until he makes a few pots and dishes of clay and is able to cook. At the end of three years, Crusoe is able to have bread regularly.

In an effort to get off the island, Crusoe decides to build a canoe, a dugout hollowed from a tree. Without knowing how he will get it to the water, he works on it tirelessly for over half a year. When it is finished he cannot budge it in any way, and he gives up. The supplies brought to shore 4 years before are giving out. His ink is gone and his journal stops. His clothes wear out and he must make new garments of animal skins. He also makes an umbrella to shut off rain and sun. Five more years pass in the same uneventful fashion. He builds another canoe but it is too small to try to reach the mainland in it.

With his ammunition and gunpowder running low, Crusoe decides he must assure his meat supply by domesticating some goats. He traps several alive and fences them in an enclosure he has built. This is in the 11th year. Two years later he has 43 goats for food and a source of milk, from which he makes butter and cheese, after many experiments. He is now self-sufficient in all respects.

One day, walking on the beach, Crusoe sees the print of a bare foot. One single print, nothing more. In terror, he flees to his cave, fearful of savage cannibals. After three days he concludes it was his own footprint from his original landing; but the size is wrong, so it was more likely a native canoe visiting from the mainland. He fortifies his cave with a double wall, taking many months to do the job. He sets up muskets in the wall. More years pass, and it is now 17 years since his landing. He assures his food supply by hiding his herd of goats in the woods, in a new fenced enclosure. In the 18th year, he finds remnants on the beach of a cannibal feast, but on the side away from his dwelling. He knows now that people come to the island but do not stay and are not seeking him. He stays close to home for another two years, and does not leave the house without cutlass, pistol, and musket. In fear of revealing his presence, he does not fire a gun for 2 years. All the while he is perfecting his defenses. He finds a new cave in the center of the island and fortifies it. Crusoe enters the 23rd year of his residence.

Early one morning he sees the light of a fire. From the top of a hill he sees nine savages and two canoes. When they leave, he again finds the vestiges of a cannibal feast. In the 24th year he hears gun shots at night, and in the morning, after a storm subsides, he sees the wreck of a ship on the rocks offshore. No signs of life are seen, and Crusoe mourns the ship's crew. He sails his small canoe out to the wreck and removes from it everything of value.

After another year and a half, Crusoe sees five canoes and many savages come for another cannibal feast. He cannot attack so many. One of the captives escapes and runs toward Crusoe, who helps him kill two pursuers. The escaped native submits to

Robinson Crusoe sees a footprint in the sand

Crusoe, who names him FRIDAY, the day on which he had saved the man's life. The other natives leave the island. Crusoe feeds and dresses Friday, begins to teach him English, and at last has a companion. Friday is gentle and obedient. Crusoe teaches him to do everything needed for life on the island, and Friday relieves Crusoe of much of his work. Crusoe learns that Friday's island is off the mouth of the Orinoco River and he may yet be able to escape his island. Three years pass thus, during which Crusoe converts Friday to Christianity.

As Friday is also eager to leave the island and rejoin his people, they set about making another large canoe. Crusoe's original has rotted away. After four months they have a boat, furnished with mast and sails. Another party of natives comes to the island, and Friday reports to Crusoe that one of their intended victims is a white man. At this, despite the fact that there are 21 natives in the party, Crusoe and Friday attack. Their surprise with guns is so effective that only three natives escape and the white man, a Spaniard, is rescued. In a canoe left behind, another captive is found and this man turns out to be Friday's father. A great scene of joy takes place. The rescued men are cared for, fed, and housed, and now Crusoe is lord of an island with subjects.

Crusoe learns from the Spaniard that there are 15 other white men on the mainland. They would be willing to join Crusoe, to help sail northward. But for so great a number there is not enough food, and a half-year is allowed to pass while a great crop of grain is grown, many raisins cured, and goats bred. Friday and his father work on a boat. When food is sufficient, the Spaniard and Friday's father sail for the mainland in a small canoe to bring back any of the Europeans who wish to sail under Crusoe.

Before the men return, an English ship anchors off the island and a boat approaches shore. Crusoe is puzzled as to why it came. Eleven men land from the boat, of whom three are unarmed and seem to be prisoners. While the others roam the island, Crusoe and Friday approach the prisoners. They are the captain and officers, the crew having mutinied. The captain puts himself and his ship at Crusoe's service. Crusoe arms the Englishmen and they kill the two mutinous ringleaders. The other sailors yield and are bound. A second boat comes to shore to see what happened to the first. Seven men, all armed, land to seek their fellows, and three remain in the boat offshore. By stratagem the boat is brought to shore and captured by Crusoe and the captain. By nightfall all of the mutineers on shore are either killed or have yielded.

Taking the two boats, the captain and those of the surrendered crew he can trust, attack the ship at anchor during the night and capture it, killing the leader of the mutineers. The captain offers his ship and all aboard to Crusoe, as his savior. Crusoe proposes to leave the island. The three worst mutineers prefer to stay on the island rather than face trial and death in England, and Crusoe tells them everything about the island and how to fend for themselves. He also tells them to expect the returning Spaniards and to work with them in friendship. Crusoe sails from his island after being on it 28 years, 2 months, and 19 days.

In England, Crusoe's family are almost all gone, and having little money, Crusoe goes to London to find out about his plantation in Brazil. Despite the passage of time, with no proof of his death his estate has been kept intact; and after proper procedures are followed, Crusoe becomes master of a considerable fortune. He returns to England again, marries, and settles down.

Romeo and Juliet

Play by William Shakespeare, 1564–1616.
Produced about 1595.

THIS WAS SHAKESPEARE'S first tragedy and was written in his earlier period. In the play he employed much adornment, including rhyme; at one point (the last scene of Act I) the dialogue takes the form of a complete sonnet followed by a quatrain. Except for some portions, critics have not rated *Romeo and Juliet* among Shakespeare's greatest plays. Theater audiences, however, have perhaps liked it better than any other and it is one of the most often revived. This may be because of its surefire plot, that of "star-crossed lovers" who wish to marry despite the enmity of their families. At the time Shakespeare wrote *Romeo and Juliet* an Italian romance of this exact story was popular in England, but of course the theme had been a standard one long before that and it still is. Great actresses have aspired more to playing Juliet than any other Shakespearean part—in fact, more than any other woman's part ever written. Since actresses seldom consider themselves fully prepared for this supreme rôle until they are experienced, most of the famous Juliets have been middle-aged women trying to play a 14-year-old girl. Shakespeare has the character Mercutio express his own disapproval of family feuds: "A plague on both your houses!"

Act I. In the prologue it is learned that the two leading families of Verona are feuding and "a pair of star-crossed lovers" will die. **1.** Servants of these families, the CAPULETS and the MONTAGUES, fight in the streets of Verona. BENVOLIO, a Montague, tries to break up the fight. Old CAPULET, head of his family, wants to renew the fight. The Prince of Verona orders the two families to cease fighting. ROMEO, heir of the Montagues, is unhappy because his love for ROSALINE is not requited. **2.** Young County (Count) PARIS aspires to the hand of JULIET. Her father, Capulet, wonders if she is not too young to marry. Benvolio suggests that Romeo sneak into a masked ball to be given by the Capulets, to find a new

love. **3.** Lady Capulet, Juliet and Juliet's NURSE discuss Juliet's age. She is almost 14. Lady Capulet thinks she is old enough to marry. **4.** Romeo, with Benvolio and his friend MERCUTIO, is going to he masked ball. **5.** At the ball, Romeo meets Juliet. They fall in love. (Their first conversation is in the form of a full Shakespearean sonnet.) TYBALT, nephew of old Capulet, recognizes Romeo by his voice but his uncle orders him not to start a fight.

Act II. 1. Romeo's friends think he has gone home. **2.** But Romeo is in the garden of the Capulet house. He listens as Juliet, on her balcony (the celebrated "balcony scene"), confesses her love for Romeo despite their families' enmity: "What's in a name? That which we call a rose/By any other name would smell as sweet." Romeo shows himself and they have a love scene together. They decide to be married in secrecy. Juliet makes the nurse her confidante. **3.** Romeo asks his friend, Friar LAURENCE, to marry them at his cell. Laurence hopes that the marriage will reconcile the two warring families, and consents. **4.** Tybalt has challenged Romeo to a duel. The nurse helps make the arrangements for the wedding. **5.** Juliet sends the nurse to Friar Laurence to tell him she is ready. **6.** The wedding of Romeo and Juliet is performed by Friar Laurence.

Act III. 1. Mercutio and Benvolio encounter Tybalt; Romeo arrives and Tybalt challenges him. Romeo, remembering that Tybalt is now a relative, refuses to fight. Tybalt stabs Mercutio to death. Romeo then

fights Tybalt and kills him. Citizens gather around. The Prince of Verona comes and Romeo flees. The prince banishes him. **2.** Juliet is waiting for the evening, when Romeo will be with her. The nurse tells her of the fighting and that Romeo is hiding in Friar Laurence's cell. **3.** In the cell, Romeo hears of his banishment. The nurse comes to him, bringing him a ring from Juliet. He promises to visit her. **4.** Unaware of Juliet's marriage to Romeo, Lady Capulet assures Paris that her daughter will marry him quickly. **5.** Romeo visits Juliet, by climbing up to her room on a ladder. At dawn he escapes to Mantua. Lady Capulet reports to her husband that Juliet will not consent to marriage with Paris.

Act IV. 1. Paris asks Friar Laurence to marry him and Juliet on the next Thursday. Laurence tries his best to talk him out of it. Juliet arrives and confuses Paris with words of double meaning. When Paris leaves, Laurence suggests giving Juliet a sleeping potion that will make her appear dead. Then she will be taken to the Capulet burial vault. By the time she awakens, Romeo will return and together they can flee to Mantua. Juliet agrees to the scheme. **2.** The Capulets proceed with the arrangements for Juliet's wedding to Paris. **3.** Juliet takes the sleeping potion. **4–5.** It is the wedding day. Capulet orders Juliet awakened. The nurse reports her dead. Friar Laurence, arriving for the wedding, instead orders a burial service.

Act V. 1. In Mantua, Romeo hears from a stranger that Juliet is dead. Unfortunately, a letter Laurence has written him has been lost. The letter explained the plot. Romeo secures poison for himself and returns to Verona. **2.** Friar JOHN reports to Friar Laurence that he could not get to Mantua and deliver the letter. Laurence goes to wake Juliet. **3.** Paris brings flowers to Juliet's bier. Romeo arrives. They fight and Romeo kills Paris. Romeo then drinks the poison and dies. Friar Laurence arrives and wakes Juliet. When she sees Romeo dead, she snatches up his dagger and kills herself. The prince arrives on the scene with Montague and Capulet. The tragedy of the two young lovers unites the two warring families.

Romeo and Paris fight and Paris is killed

542

Confessions of Jean Jacques Rousseau

Autobiography by Jean Jacques Rousseau, 1712–1778.
Published 1765–70. Several translations.
(ML, 243; PB, PL56).

THERE ARE MANY famous autobiographies called "confessions," but none of them is more openly confessional than Rousseau's. He was undoubtedly insane when he wrote them and that probably helped. Rousseau influenced one of the most important centuries of radical thought and the influence of his writings still is great, but his reminiscence dwells on his inadequacies, his petty crimes, and the times when he was or was thought to be mediocre or inadequate. The *Confessions* carry his life only to the time of his uneventful exile in England, that is, to the year 1765. He returned to Paris in 1770 but did nothing more that was noteworthy.

Book I. I mean to present myself here as a man in all the integrity of nature. I know my own heart and have studied mankind; I am not made like anyone else of my acquaintance, perhaps like no one else in existence. In this book I claim the originality of exposing equally my laudable and my wicked thoughts and actions.

I was born in Geneva in 1712, the son of Isaac Rousseau and Susannah Bernard. My father was a watchmaker. My mother, a minister's daughter, did not survive my birth, and I was born so frail that I was not expected to live. But under the loving care of my father and his sister I grew from delicate infancy to childhood, my conscious thoughts gradually awakened by old romantic stories that my father read to me until I attained the age of 7, after which he directed my interest to Plutarch, Ovid, Bossuet, and Molière. From reading Plutarch's lives I conceived the liberal trend of free republican thought. My lifelong delight in music I owe to the songs my aunt sang to me.

My schooling began at Bossey, in the home of a Protestant clergyman, M. Lambercier, where my Uncle Bernard placed his son and me. At Bossey I learned to love country life. I left Bossey and spent some idle years in Geneva. My first employment, as a boy in a lawyer's office, was of short duration. I next became apprenticed to a scoundrelly engraver who tried to make a thief and liar of me. At 16 I stayed out too late one night. I knew my master would beat me and I decided to run away.

Book II. I walked the country roads and spent the nights with friendly villagers. At Confignon the priest, M. de Ponteverre, gave me an excellent dinner and letters of introduction to Mme. DE WARENS, a lady who lived in Annecy. My fate and my personality were settled by this contact. I was moderately good-looking, affectionately disposed, diffident, and altogether unworldly. Mme. de Warens, the daughter of a noble family at Vevey, was very young when she married. She fled her unhappy, childless marriage and went to Sardinia, where the King became her protector. He later sent her, with a modest pension, to a convent at Annecy. When I met her she was 28, a rather small person, radiant and gracious. I forever cherished her confidence. Arrangements were made for me to study at a divinity school in Turin, where I became a convert to Catholicism. I then sought to earn a living, but was unsuccessful until I found congenial employment in the household of Countess de Vercellis, who unfortunately died within a short time. During my brief stay in her service, I caused a young housemaid to be blamed for the theft of a silver ribbon, which I had stolen. For that cruel calumny my guilt has harrowed me ever since.

Book III. I was obsessed by lust and led a worthless life in Turin until a priest, M. Gaime, taught me that peace of mind derives only from wise conduct. The politically ambitious Count DE GOUVON engaged me as a footman, but sought to educate me for better duties. His son, a priest, started to teach me Latin, but I lost this opportunity when de Gouvon discharged me for insubordination. I started on foot for Geneva, and on the way I met a merry young man with whom I went into an unprofitable partnership exhibiting a mechanical toy fountain. I abandoned the partnership in Annecy and returned timorously to Mme. de Warens, who took me back into her care with the utmost good nature. Her scale of living, while far from palatial, ran to extravagances of entertainment; her debts were a constant worry, yet she made our home life serene. I called her "Mama," she called me "Baby." I was now 19. For some months she had me take Latin lessons from a rector, but he reported me incapable of learning. Madame then had me study under M. LeMAITRE, musical director of the cathedral. That was one of the happiest periods of my life. But Madame disapproved of my association with another musician, M. VENTURE, and to remove me from his influence she sent me to Lyons with M. LeMaitre, In Lyons M. LeMaitre suffered a sudden attack and fell unconscious on the street. I shamefully sneaked off, leaving him in the hands of casual passers-by. I returned to Annecy and lived for a while with M. Venture, for Mme. de Warens had gone to Paris.

Book IV. Soon I moved to Lausanne. I was penniless again, but had the impudence to take an assumed name and profess to be a music teacher. Somehow I persuaded a music-loving lawyer to finance the presentation of a symphony of mine, which I had not yet composed. I wrote it in two weeks and when it was played both the orchestra and the audience roared with laughter at the ridiculous jangle of noises. The next number won great applause and I claimed it was my own work, but in fact it was a minuet I had learned from M. Venture. The following winter I gave myself a sounder musical education by teaching music at Neufchatel. By chance I met a Greek monk from Jerusalem who was collecting money for the restoration of the Holy Sepulchre. He engaged me as his interpreter. He vanished after being investigated by the Marquis de Bonac, who questioned me also, then sent me to Paris to serve as tutor for the young nephew of Colonel GODARD, a wealthy Swiss attached to the French Army. I have never erased the disappointment I felt on first seeing Paris, with its dirty stinking streets and its poverty. Magnificent as I later found Paris to be, I cannot forget my first impression. Col. Godard wanted me to serve not as a tutor but as a valet, which I would not do. I set out for Chambéry, where Mme. de Warens now lived. She had me appointed to the ordnance survey as a secretary.

Book V. Madame had a faithful old friend, M. CLAUDE ANET, who guided her in money matters. In her garden the three of us formed a congenial company. My secretarial duties afforded me spare time and I soon had the pleasure of teaching music to a number of agreeable young ladies. These happy days ended with the sudden death of Claude Anet, after which Madame's financial status and my health both became alarming. I was nearly 21. Insomnia and heart trouble weakened me. Madame nursed me and I grew stronger. I turned to religion and Madame encouraged me in the study of philosophy, Latin, and natural history. We spent the summer at Charmettes, a lovely country place near Chambéry.

Book VI. My health required the attention of a certain doctor in Montpellier. On the way there I met a Mme. de Larnage and I became intimate with her. She was charming and I went on with her, entirely forgetting Madame de Warens. Two months later I realized the necessity of choosing between the two women—between real love or fascination. Reason dictated my choice. I wrote to "Mama," telling her I was coming home, but when I arrived I found someone else had taken my place. He was a tall, blond, vapid youth, a hairdresser, Vintzenried by name. Madame proposed the idea of continuing her intimacy with me as well as with the hairdresser, but this I could not endure. She hastened my departure by getting me a position as tutor to the children of M. MALBY, chief provost of Lyons. A year of tutoring convinced me I had not the patience needed. I thought I had outgrown my inclination for petty thievery, but I now took to stealing bottles of M. Malby's wine. M. Malby charitably refrained from prosecuting me and I fled back to Mme. de Warens. She received me coldly and I worked in solitude on a new system of musical notation I invented. I thought it would make my fortune and I raised sufficient funds to proceed to Paris. Thus ends the history of my early faults and errors.

Book VII. I arrived in Paris in the autumn of 1741 with my musical project, a comedy I had written, entitled *Narcissus,* and only 15 louis in my pocket. To demonstrate my notation system I gave free lessons to a young American lady, Mlle. des Roulins, and taught her in three months to read every kind of music. The French Academy refused to accept my system and so my project came to nothing. I became a close friend of the great scholar DIDEROT, then about my own age, 30. My knowledge of music won me patronage with the ladies of Parisian society, and I became smitten with Mme. DUPIN, a famous beauty of wealth and influence. She secured an appointment for me as secretary to M. DE MONTAIGU, French ambassador to Venice. Nothing could be easier than my work there, deciphering despatches. I attended diligently to business but the ambassador took a dislike to me and treated me brutally and disdainfully. An embassy colleague of mine, a young man named Carrio, persuaded me to join him in the purchase of a 12-year-old girl for us to share, but we found we could not have any sentiment other than paternal for the child, with whom we passed happy innocent hours. Men are truly more attached to women by the pleasure of living with them than by any kind of libertinism. De Montaigu accused me of selling our secret code and threatened to have his servants throw me out of the window. His accusation was unjustified, and I was exonerated by higher authority, but I left Venice after having been there only 18 months. Back in Paris, I lived at the old Hotel St. Quentin near the Luxembourg Garden. There I met a seamstress, THÉRÈSE, a simple country woman of 22, and my long affair with her began. I told her I would never marry her but would never abandon her. I lived with her in perfect agreement until her mother's knavish cunning spoiled the simplicity of our relationship.

I wrote an opera. The composer RAMEAU refused to examine it but the Duc de Richelieu had it sung by two full choruses at the king's expense. I was soon asked to help make some changes in a Voltaire play with music by Rameau. M. de Voltaire wrote me a cordial letter confirming the request, and I went ahead despite Rameau's animosity. Diderot and I planned to publish a periodical magazine, *le Persifleur,* aided by the encyclopedist, d'Alembert. Our plans were halted by Diderot's arrest and imprisonment on account of his books, *Lettre sur les Aveugles,* which contained some indiscreet attacks on privileged persons. I wrote to Mme. de Pompadour and beseeched her to get Diderot released. I received no answer but not long afterward he was freed.

Book VIII. Now begins the long chain of misfortunes I have suffered from the mistake of a moment. It came from reading in the *Mercure de France* this question: *Has the progress of sciences and arts corrupted morals or purified morals?* The moment I read this, I seemed to behold another world. All my little passions were stifled by enthusiasm for truth, liberty, and virtue. I told Diderot. He encouraged me to pursue my ideas and I clarified them in four letters to M. de Malesherbes. I dictated a discourse full of force and fire, though deficient in logic. I think I showed it to Baron Grimm, the noted literary critic, then I sent it off to be published. I was 42. My next undertaking was the preparation of a discourse on the *Origin of the Inequality of Mankind.* I then had an opportunity to settle advantageously in Geneva and I started for that city, taking Thérèse with me. On the road to Savoy I could not resist stopping off to see Mme. de Warens. Her looks, her vivacious charms and her prosperity all were gone. Her last jewel was a little diamond ring that she tried to give to Thérèse, who out of pity declined to take it. If I wished to be a citizen of Geneva, I would have to become a Protestant. This I resolved to do.

Book IX. I was the father of Thérèse's three babies and I had let them all be sent to an orphanage on the pretext that their upbringing was beyond my precarious means. I will not explain the reasoning that deceived me into thinking this was the act of an honest man. I have had five children and all were disposed of in the same manner. Through Mme. Dupin I had met M. DE FRANCUEIL, Receiver-General of Finance. He now appointed me cashier in his department. The amount of cash on hand never exceeded 30,000 livres, yet my anxiety over the care of the money kept me in such an upset state of mind that my delicate health broke down. I resigned and turned for livelihood to copying music manuscripts. My published views on the Origins of Inequality made enemies for me among men of letters, and I felt obliged to write indignant retorts refuting their attacks. Presently my success as the author of *Devin du Village* brought me into vogue. Thereafter there was not a man in Paris whose company was more popular than mine. The Duc D'AUMONT wanted to take me to the King to apply for a royal pension, but I dared not risk committing some absurdity at court, so I lost the pension. Now all my works were well-received, particularly *La Nouvelle Héloïse,* from which the state of my finances was a little improved. I next wrote *Institutions Politiques, Émile,* and *Contrat Social.* I lived contentedly in a small apartment with Thérèse and our dog and cat.

Book XI. In *Émile* I had written accounts of scenes I myself had witnessed, of the heartless abuse of peasants by aristocratic hunters devastating the countryside for the sake of sport. This caused such resentment among the nobility that I was warned of impending arrest. I decided to get out of France. I wanted to retire to Geneva, but realized that French influence would be able to torment me there. One of my dearest patronesses, Mme. de Boufflers, induced me to seek refuge in England. I dared not tell Thérèse where I was going, lest she be compelled to reveal my whereabouts.

Book XII. I had no natural inclination for England. Though David Hume, the Scottish historian, sent me word that I would be welcome, I went instead to Yverdon (fortunately not to Geneva, where my books were being burned). At Motiers, across the mountain from Yverdon, I found a convenient house and Thérèse joined me there; but knowing I would henceforth be a fugitive upon the earth, Thérèse lost her relish for my approaches, as had "Mama" de Warens before her. Let us not seek perfection, which nature never produces. All I thought of now was leading a quiet life. Although protected by the King of Prussia, I was exposed to the murmurs of the magistrates, the ministers, and the public. It became fashionable to insult me. One midnight a shower of stones crashed my door and windows. The Attorney-General urged me to retire to a place of better security. Again I was invited to England, this time by M. Horace Walpole, but I chose to try St. Peter Island in the middle of the lake of Bienne. Thérèse followed me to this asylum but we could not stay there. Finally I fled to England.

I have written the truth. For my part I declare that whoever shall examine my character, manners, pleasures and inclinations, and shall pronounce me a dishonest man, then it is himself who deserves the gibbet.

Rousseau arrives in Paris

Sanctuary and Requiem for a Nun

Novel by William Faulkner, 1897–1962.

Published 1931 and 1951 by Random House, New York; © 1931 and 1950, 1951 by William Faulkner. (NAL, D1486; ML, 61).

SANCTUARY HAS BEEN William Faulkner's best-selling book. Probably this is not entirely, as has been suggested, because the book has a sadistic sex crime as part of its plot. It is an interesting story and is easier for the general reader to follow than most Faulkner novels—that is, the reader does not have to read quite so carefully and think quite so hard. The sequel, *Requiem for a Nun,* followed nearly 20 years later and to a certain extent helps one to a full understanding of *Sanctuary.* Faulkner used the word "nun" in an old, obscure sense: prostitute. He divided *Requiem for a Nun* into acts and scenes and presented much of the dialogue as though it were a play, but it is not. There are long stretches of straight prose, some of it along stream-of-consciousness lines though told in the third person.

Sanctuary

1. Stopping to drink from a spring on his way to Jefferson, HORACE BENBOW, a lawyer from Kinston, is apprehended by POPEYE, who holds a gun on him and leads him to a ruined plantation house where RUBY LAMAR, a retired prostitute, lives. 2. The men at Ruby's include Ruby's man, LEE GOODWIN; Goodwin's blind, deaf old father; and TOMMY, an amiable fellow who tells Benbow they are moonshiners. They sell liquor to Popeye, a grotesque-looking but important gangster, of whom they are all afraid. Benbow gets a lift into Jefferson on Popeye's liquor truck. 3. At his sister's house in Jefferson, Benbow meets GOWAN STEVENS, a student from the University of Virginia, at which he has been taught chiefly "to drink like a gentleman." That evening Gowan has a date with 18-year-old TEMPLE DRAKE, a co-ed at State University, daughter of a judge in Jackson.

4. Gowan drives Temple back to the dormitory, having promised to take her to a ball game the next day. Gowan then picks up some hitchhikers and with them gets very drunk. He misses the train for the game but at the next station overtakes it in his car. Temple leaps off the train and joins him. Gowan is still drunk and stops frequently to drink. He is on his way to get more liquor from Goodwin when he crashes the car into a tree. He and Temple get out and find Popeye, shotgun in hand, standing over them.

5. Popeye leads Temple and Gowan to the old plantation house. 6. Gowan asks for liquor. Temple begs him to take her away; Ruby has warned her to leave before dark or something terrible will happen. Gowan refuses to ask to borrow a car. Temple offers to pay Popeye to drive her to town. He refuses and Temple runs back to Ruby in terror. 7. It grows dark. Temple becomes more frightened than ever. Gowan is dead drunk for the third time in one day. Ruby tells Temple that these men are not like her little boyfriends. Goodwin is an ex-convict who once was given a life sentence for murder. Ruby worked for years as a prostitute to get money to pay his lawyer. Ruby does not care what happens to Temple, but she does not want Goodwin hankering after some saucy little co-ed. 8–9. After Temple goes to bed that night, the men come into the room, one after the other, and stand over her staring. Ruby takes her to the barn and stays with her there until morning. 10. The next morning Gowan starts down the road to get a car; but he cannot face Temple after yesterday, so he makes arrangements for a farmer to pick up Temple. 11–14. Temple catches Goodwin staring at her at breakfast. She runs back to the barn for safety. Tommy promises to stand guard outside. Popeye crawls into the barn through the roof. He goes to the door, opens it, and shoots Tommy. Then he advances toward the ter-

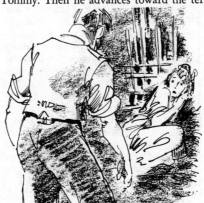

Temple in the corn crib

rified Temple, who is crouching in the corn crib. Goodwin discovers that Tommy has been shot and sends Ruby to call the sheriff.

15–17. Goodwin is arrested for Tommy's murder and Horace Benbow is retained as his lawyer. Goodwin refuses to say anything more than that he did not do it. This way he has a chance, because it is up to the court to prove him guilty and he is not guilty. If he told about Popeye (who speedily left the plantation, taking Temple), Goodwin would never get out of the courtroom alive. Popeye's men would take care of that. 18. Popeye drives Temple to Memphis. She is bleeding profusely. He takes her to Miss Reba's brothel in Memphis for medi-

cal attention. 19. Ruby tells Benbow about Gowan, Temple, and Popeye. Benbow goes to Temple's school to locate her but is told she left school about two weeks ago. Senator SNOPES tells him about an article in the paper saying that Temple's parents took her up North. 20–22. Several days later, Snopes offers to sell Benbow information. Benbow agrees, and Snopes tells him Temple Drake is being held prisoner at Miss Reba's brothel in Memphis. 23. Benbow hurries to Memphis and sees Temple. She is in a half-delirious state and he can make out little from what she tells him, except that she taunted Popeye and dared him to violate her. Benbow leaves. 24. After making a secret telephone call, Temple slips out of the brothel one night, but Popeye catches her in his car. As she refuses to go back to the brothel, Popeye drives her to a dance-hall where she has arranged to meet RED. He is a henchman of Popeye's whom Popeye has brought to make love to her several times while he watches. Temple begs Red to come away with her, but two of Popeye's men force her to leave. 25. An elaborate funeral is held at the dance hall for Red. It is believed he was killed by Popeye for fooling around with Temple.

26–27. The day before the Goodwin trial, Benbow is told that Temple and Popeye have disappeared from Miss Reba's brothel. The next morning Ruby takes the witness stand and tells the whole story of Tommy's murder, exactly as she told it to Benbow. Goodwin is sure now that Popeye will kill him. Benbow is certain that nothing will happen to Goodwin and that he will be acquitted. The following morning Temple, who has been located at last, is called to the stand. 28. Evidence is produced to prove that Temple was horribly violated (with a corncob) in the corn crib at the old plantation. But Temple testifies that it was Goodwin, not Popeye, who attacked her. 29–30. Goodwin is convicted. The townspeople, horrified by the grotesqueness of his supposed crime against Temple, lynch him.

30. Several months later, Popeye is arrested in Birmingham for the murder of a policeman in a small Alabama town. The murder took place on the night Popeye was at the dance hall with Temple. At the time of his arrest, Popeye was on the way to Pensacola to visit his mother. Popeye revealed his depravity early in life by cutting up live animals and birds with a pair of scissors, and spent five of his childhood years in a home for incorrigible children. He was always impotent. Popeye makes no effort to prove his innocence. He is convicted and hanged for a crime he did not commit. Temple is whisked off to Europe by her father.

Requiem for a Nun

Act I. The Courthouse. The records of Yoknapatawpha County were originally kept in an iron pirate's chest in the back room of the post office. They remained there for 30 years. Then, because of a jailbreak compounded by an ancient monster lock, transported 1,000 miles by horseback, the chest was moved to a lean-to built along one wall of the jail. This lean-to became the Yoknapatawpha Court house.

1. A Negress, NANCY MANNIGOE, 30, has been tried for smothering in its cradle a white infant of which she was nurse. The judge pronounces her guilty and sentences her to be hanged on March 13, four months from now.

2. A half-hour later, Temple and Gowan Stevens, now respectably married, the parents of the murdered child, return to their house with GAVIN STEVENS, Gowan's uncle and the Negress' lawyer. Gowan has not had a taste of liquor in the 8 years since he got drunk at the old plantation house. He is constantly haunted by the fact that he deserted Temple there, but the thing that most horrifies him, the thing he cannot forgive, is that Temple actually enjoyed her horrible experience.

3. Four months later, two days before the scheduled execution of Nancy Mannigoe, Gavin summons Temple from a visit in California. He is certain she knows something that would save Nancy.

Act II. 1. Having persuaded Temple to tell what she knows, Gavin takes her and Gowan to the Governor's house that night. Temple starts by telling the Governor that Nancy was a drug addict and prostitute whom she and Gowan took out of the gutter to nurse their children, not only to give Nancy another chance but because Temple, who could never be a sweet Southern lady again after her stay in the Memphis brothel, needed someone around who spoke her language. Temple relates in full everything that happened to her 8 years before, when Popeye violated and kidnaped her and held her prisoner until the time of Goodwin's trial, so that he could be sure she would lie in his behalf. Gowan interrupts Temple from time to time with self-accusations for having gotten drunk and abandoning Temple in the first place. To make up for this, Gowan married Temple the following winter in Europe. Eventually they moved back home, reëntered the town's chic social set, and behaved like a perfectly proper young couple, except when Temple relieved herself by talking to Nancy. From the beginning, Temple's and Gowan's marriage was troubled by their need to forgive and be forgiven by each other.

Now, while Temple was in the brothel she wrote certain love letters to a man named Red. Red's younger brother, PETE, a criminal, got hold of those letters and attempted to blackmail Temple; but Temple, wearied by her regimen of repentance and forgiveness and unhappy in her marriage, decided not only to give Pete money but also to run away with him, to be with a man who would not constantly be forgiving her. Also his brutality appealed to her. Nancy, the confidante, at first knew only of Temple's plan to pay her blackmailer.

Temple and Pete are caught

2. On a day in September, six months before, Nancy came into Temple's bedroom and found her there with Pete, preparing to run away. In the name of the two children, Nancy begged Temple not to run off. Temple rebuffed Nancy. Defeated, Nancy took a blanket and went into the nursery where the younger child was sleeping. A few minutes later she screamed.

3. Temple recounts what happened afterward—Nancy's arrest, the baby's funeral, and the trial, when Nancy put herself in the hands of God and did not even try to defend herself. When the account is finished, Gavin tells Temple that the Governor has refused a reprieve. He refused it before Gavin summoned Temple from California. Furious, Temple asks why she has been put through the anguish of confessing what has been torturing her for 8 years. Gavin replies that it was to affirm what Nancy is going to die for: that little children shall be intact, unanguished, untorn, and unterrified.

Act III. 1. The following morning Temple and Gavin go to visit Nancy in jail. Nancy does not seem disappointed that she has not received a pardon. She did not expect one. She has been prepared to die since the moment before she smothered the baby, and she is unafraid. God will take care of her. To Temple, who has none of Nancy's peace of mind, Nancy says: "Believe." Temple does not understand her. How can she believe anything except that we are put on earth to suffer? But Nancy, firm in her faith, can go to her death with an easy mind.

Sartor Resartus

Treatise by Thomas Carlyle, 1795–1881.
Published 1833–34.

THE SATIRE posing as a serious work is quite commonplace in literature; the serious work posing as a satire is extremely rare. Yet *Sartor Resartus,* which is presented with the original dressing of a satire, is actually a series of essays in which Carlyle makes a contribution to human thought, plus a brief biographical sketch that is partly a genuine autobiography of Carlyle. Thomas Carlyle was England's great sage at the time that Ralph Waldo Emerson was America's. It is hard to know whether to classify *Sartor Resartus* as a novel or as essays. The title means "the tailor retailored." *Weissnichtwo* means "Know not where."

Book I. Chaps. 1–4. Herr DIOGENES TEUFELSDRÖCKH of Weissnichtwo, Professor of Things in General, and his country's brightest intellectual light, has published the results of his life's work and wisdom in *Sartor Resartus,* his work on clothes. Unfortunately, the book has an almost total lack of arrangement. However, the editor has been able to discern that the work falls into two parts: a historical-descriptive and a philosophical-speculative.

Chap. 5. Neither in tailoring nor in legislating does man proceed by accident, but the hand that cuts the cloth is ever guided by an idea. The first purpose of clothes was not warmth and decency, but ornament. Among primitive people we find tattooing prior to clothes. Clothes, which began in love of ornament, gave rise to security, to heat, to shame; they gave us individuality, distinctions, social polity; they have made men of us; they threaten to make clothes-screens of us.

Chap. 6. Aprons are defenses; against injury to cleanliness, to safety, to modesty, sometimes to roguery. How much has been defended in aprons! Rightly considered, what is your whole military and police establishment but a huge iron-fastened apron, wherein society works, guarding itself from some soil and stithy-sparks, in this Devil's-smithy of a world?

Chap. 7. The Middle Ages in Europe, and down to the end of the 17th century, were the true era of extravagance in costume. Although women wore gowns scalloped out before and behind, with trains four or five ells long, with a flood of silver shell and buttons, and long mantles, skirts wide below and ending atop on a thick well-starched ruff—although women wore such rich clothes, men outdid them by their girdles of silver hung with silver bells, peaked caps an ell long, doublets of fustian, under which lie multiple ruffs of cloth, pasted together with batter, bushel breeches, and cornuted shoes.

Chap. 8. Man asks himself, Who am I; what is this ME? Pity all metaphysics that hitherto proved so inexpressibly unproductive. The secret of man's being is still like the sphinx's secret; a riddle that he cannot read, and for ignorance of which he suffers death, the worst death, a spiritual. Man is, and was always, much readier to feel and digest than to think and consider. Prejudice, which he pretends to hate, is his absolute lawgiver.

Chap. 9. First, *man is a spirit,* and bound by invisible bonds to *all men;* secondly, *he wears clothes,* which are visible emblems of that fact.

Chaps. 10–11. The beginning of all wisdom is to look fixedly on clothes, or even with armed eyesight, till they become *transparent.* All visible things are emblems; what thou seest is not there on its own account; it exists only spiritually, and to present some idea, and to body it forth. Whatsoever sensibly exists, whatsoever represents spirit to spirit, is properly a clothing.

Book II. Chaps. 1–3. Herr Professor Teufelsdröckh, turning to autobiography, tells us that one of the first things he learned was that obedience is our universal duty and destiny, wherein whoso will not bend must break. And that Nature alone is ancient, and man's oldest art but a mushroom. In contemplating Nature's antiquity may lie the beginning of those well-nigh unutterable meditations on the grandeur and mystery of TIME, and its relation to ETERNITY. Mind grows, not like a vegetable (by having its roots littered with etymological compost), but like a spirit, by mysterious contact of spirit, though kindling itself at the fire of living thought. First must the dead letter of religion own itself dead, if the living spirit of religion, freed from its charnel house, is to arise newborn.

Chaps. 4–6. Young Teufelsdröckh fell in love with a highborn young woman whom he identifies to us only as *Blumine*—his flower. When she chose, to wed another, Teufelsdröckh, in his sorrow, was given a shove along the path to philosophy; for, from then on, his only love was truth.

Chaps. 7–10. Teufelsdröckh became an unhappy wanderer. He came to feel that he was a fatherless outcast and that the Devil owned the universe. In despair he asked himself what he feared so much. Death? The Devil? Well, then, he asked himself, hast thou not a heart; canst thou not suffer whatsoever be? Then no longer need thou feel sorrow for thyself nor fear, but rather indignation and grim, fire-eyed defiance. Then the EVERLASTING NO pealed through the recesses of his being and he stood up in protest. Having cast out fear, he still did not feel free and happy. This period of his wanderings he calls his CENTER OF INDIFFERENCE. Finally, he came to believe that each man has allotted to himself God's infinite universe, and that if man will let love of God stream into his soul, then he will find his SELF annihilated, and his soul will be borne aloft to eternity on the roaring billows of time. This is the EVERLASTING YEA, wherein all contradiction is solved; wherein whoso walks and works, it is well with him. Having thus achieved wisdom, Teufelsdröckh saw that he must work while it is called today; for the night cometh, wherein no man can work.

Book III. Chaps. 1–2. According to Teufeldröckh, one of the most important events of modern history was the decision of George Fox, the Quaker shoemaker, to take up the clothes of the Church and to make for himself a single perennial suit of leather. Thus to him did the divine idea of the universe reveal itself. Church-clothes are the forms under which men have at various periods embodied and represented for themselves the religious principle. These are unspeakably the most important of all the vestures and garnitures of human Existence. They are first spun and woven by that wonder of wonders, SOCIETY, for it is only when two or three are gathered together that soul seeks to speak with soul, and religion, spiritually existent, seeks to be embodied in a visible communion and Church Militant.

Chaps. 3–5. Altars have been raised to silence and secrecy. Concealment, the kin of silence and secrecy, is connected with that wonderous agency, *symbols.* In a symbol there is concealment and yet revelation; here, by silence and by speech acting together, comes a double significance. In the symbol proper there is ever some embodiment and revelation of the infinite. The universe is but one vast symbol of God. The highest of all symbols are those wherein the artist or poet has risen to prophet, and all men can recognize a present God; that is, religious symbols.

Chaps. 6–8. Wondrous are the bonds that unite us one and all, whether by the soft binding of love or the iron chaining of necessity. Beautiful it is to understand and know that a thought did never yet die; that as the originator thereof did gather it and create it from the whole past, so will it be transmitted to the whole future. One of the most important organic filaments that bind us together is hero-worship. It is a manifestation of true religious loyalty in man's heart; it has always existed and will always exist among mankind, cornerstone of living rock, whereon all polities for the remotest time may stand secure. Custom makes dotards of us all. Philosophy is a continual battle against custom, and everrenewed effort to *transcend* the sphere of custom and so become transcendental. Space and time are thought-forms which are foremost in hiding reality. The earth is but dead and vision; can it resist spirits that have reality and live?

Chaps. 9–12. Let us turn our attention to two small divisions of mankind. These, like moths, may be regarded as clothes-animals, creatures that live, move, and have their being in cloth: we mean dandies and tailors. A dandy is a clothes-wearing man, a man whose trade, office and existence consist in the wearing of clothes; where others dress to live, he lives to dress. In Britain, dandyism has gone so far that there is a dandiacal sect, which indulges in that primeval superstition, *self-worship.* Tailors have long been looked down upon as being somehow subhuman. The truth, however, is that the tailor is not only a man but something of a creator or divinity. For is not a man by the tailor new-created into a nobleman, and clothed not only with wool but with dignity and a mystic dominion? What, too, are all poets and moral teachers, but a species of metaphorical tailors? Was it not a tailor-poet who first made gods for men; brought them down to us, and raised us up to them? When this is known widely, the world will recognize that the tailor is its hierophant and hierarch, or even its God.

The Scarlet Letter

Novel by Nathaniel Hawthorne, 1804–1864.
Published 1850. (PB, PL26; ML, 93 & T21; Viking, P38; RE, 1).

IN MOST REVIEWS of American literature, *The Scarlet Letter* is considered the first great American novel. It is still ranked with the best, ahead of Hawthorne's other principal classic, *The House of the Seven Gables,* which was published little more than a year later. There are few better studies of a tortured conscience than *The Scarlet Letter.* It has three major characters, the woman who must suffer publicly, the preacher who suffers only in his own conscience, and the vengeful enemy, and all are exceptional portraits. The educational value of the book is enhanced by its careful picture of early New England colonial life and for this reason it has always been a standard assignment for school reading.

Chaps. 1–2. A crowd has gathered outside the jail in 17th-century Boston to stare at a tall, handsome woman who emerges with a 3-months-old child in her arms and a large scarlet letter "A" elegantly embroidered on her blouse over her heart. They see this woman, HESTER PRYNNE, led to the center of the market place and made to ascend the scaffold, where she must stand for three hours with her child in her arms while the whole town witnesses her disgrace.

Chap. 3. As Hester stands there, she sees on the outskirts of the crowd an elderly man whom she seems to recognize, though he is a stranger to the town. This man asks his neighbor who this woman might be. He is told that Mistress Prynne has created a great scandal in the Rev. ARTHUR DIMMESDALE'S church. The wife of an Englishman, Hester was sent to America two years ago by her husband, who intended to follow her when he had put his affairs in order. But he did not arrive; and Hester, left to her own misguidance, has given birth to a child whose father is unknown. Ordinarily the

547

Hester on the scaffold

penalty for adultery is death; but in their mercy, the magistrates have doomed her only to stand on the scaffold and then wear the scarlet letter for the rest of her life. The ministers of the town, the most eloquent of whom is Dimmesdale, call on Hester to name her fellow-sinner, but she refuses. When her three-hour ordeal has ended she is led back to the jail with her lips still sealed.

Chap. 4. That night both Hester and her child are in need of medical attention, and ROGER CHILLINGWORTH, the stranger who asked about Hester, is brought in as physician to treat her. Chillingworth is Hester's husband, the scholar Prynne. His ship was wrecked and he has been a captive among the Indians. He begs Hester to tell him the name of the man who has dishonored them both. When she refuses, he warns her that though he seeks no vengeance against Hester, he will remain in Boston, practicing medicine, until he finds the scoundrel. He makes Hester promise not to reveal his true identity.

Chap. 5. When Hester's term of imprisonment comes to an end she goes to live with her child in a lonesome cottage on the outskirts of town. An outcast from society, she manages to support herself by needlework. She lives on the barest necessities and donates all her surplus earnings to charity, thereby winning a certain amount of admiration. She never ceases to suffer dreadful agony when a human eye is cast upon the scarlet symbol on her breast, but in time she comes to believe that this mark of shame gives her a sympathetic knowledge of hidden sin in other hearts.

Chap. 6. Her baby, whom she names PEARL, as being of great price, and whom she dresses in richly ornamented costumes, grows into a strange, spritelike creature, lovely to look at but capricious and undisciplined. Having no companions her own age, Pearl spends all her time with her mother whose scarlet letter fascinates her almost from infancy. From an early age Pearl badgers Hester to tell her whose child she really is.

Chaps. 7–8. The townsfolk start proceedings to take Pearl from her mother. Hester goes with her daughter to the governor's mansion to plead her case before a group that includes Dimmesdale and Chillingworth, now the town's leading physician. To test Hester's suitability as a religious instructor, the group asks Pearl if she knows who made her. Pearl has been told a hundred times that it is the Heavenly Father and knows the answer perfectly, but perversely Pearl replies that she was plucked from the rosebush that grows by the prison door. The group decides that Pearl cannot remain with her mother. Hester cries out in protest and her plea is so eloquent that Dimmesdale speaks for her, saying that Pearl may be able to lead her mother to heaven. His speech is persuasive and the governor decides in Hester's favor.

Chaps. 9–11. Dimmesdale's health has been failing gradually and he is placed in Chillingworth's care. The two men spend more and more time together and eventually arrange to live in the same house. But there is something almost evil in Chillingworth's persistent scrutiny of Dimmesdale, who comes to seem like someone haunted by Satan. Dimmesdale seems to be obsessed with the problem of hidden sin. One day while Dimmesdale is sleeping Chillingworth steals up on him and rips his shirt open. What he sees there causes him to shudder with horror and joy, the joy of a Satan who has discovered a fallen man. Time and again, Dimmesdale goes into the pulpit determined to bare his soul, but he always ends up speaking of his sinfulness in general terms and his congregation only reveres him the more for his humility.

Chap. 12. One night Dimmesdale goes to the scaffold where Hester stood in disgrace. After he has stood there in anguish for some time, Hester comes by with Pearl. Dimmesdale says that now all three stand on the scaffold. Pearl sees Chillingworth watching them from the shadows. Dimmesdale confesses his horror of the man; but Hester, bound by her promise, cannot tell him who Chillingworth really is.

Chaps. 13–14. Shocked by Dimmesdale's torment, and determined to free him of the evil influence of his secret enemy, Hester tells her former husband that she can keep his identity a secret no longer. Chillingworth still refuses to forgive and Hester bemoans the fact that hatred has transformed a wise and just man into a fiend.

Chaps. 15–19. Several days later, Hester encounters Dimmesdale in the woods. He asks her if she has found peace, for he has found nothing but despair. How much better to wear the scarlet letter openly, as she does, than to have it burn in secret like his own. Hester reveals Chillingworth's true identity and warns Dimmesdale against his evil influence. She does not think Dimmesdale will ever find peace here and she suggests that they return to the old world and seek a new life together, with Pearl, in England. As the first step towards their new freedom, she rips the scarlet letter off her breast and removes her cap, allowing her luxuriant dark hair to fall about her face for the first time in 7 years. Then she calls to Pearl, who is playing at a distance, for she wants the child to begin loving the minister at once. When Pearl sees her mother without the scarlet letter, she has a tantrum and refuses to draw near until Hester has replaced the sorrowful emblem on her breast. Hester declares that the child is right, she must bear the hateful token yet a little longer.

Chap. 20. With great secrecy, Hester books passage for three on a ship that is due to leave for England in four days. Dimmesdale feels as though he has been reborn, freed of his painful shackles. When Chillingworth sees Dimmesdale's peaceful, even joyful, countenance, he guesses that Hester has told all.

Chaps. 21–23. In celebration of a new governor's inauguration, the whole town takes a holiday and gathers in the market place to watch the elegant procession and to hear the speechmaking. Hester learns that Chillingworth has taken a berth on the same boat to England. Then Hester sees Dimmesdale marching in the procession and wonders at his altered countenance; he appears almost to be a stranger. After preliminary prayers are said, Dimmesdale delivers a sermon that is undoubtedly the most brilliant, the most inspired of his career. At its conclusion, Dimmesdale advances towards the scaffold and calls Hester and Pearl to him. At this point, Chillingworth rushes forward and beseeches him not to behave rashly. Dimmesdale replies that now at last, with God's help, he will escape Chillingworth. On the scaffold with Hester and Pearl, Dimmesdale confesses the terrible guilt that has haunted him. Hester's scarlet letter is but a shadow of what he bears on his own breast. He rips off the ministerial band and bares his breast. While the horror-stricken multitude stares at the ghastly miracle, Dimmesdale sinks, dying, on the scaffold. He dies peaceful in the knowledge that God has repaid him for his sins by giving him the burning torture to bear upon his breast and by sending the terrible Chillingworth to keep the torture always at red heat.

Chap. 24. Afterwards, most of the spectators testify to having seen a scarlet letter imprinted on the minister's flesh. Some say it was put there by his own hand; others that Chillingworth caused it to appear by using certain drugs; and still others that it was the result of remorse, gnawing from the heart outwards. And some deny that there was any mark at all and insist that his dying words admitted no guilt but were intended as a parable to show that we are all sinners. Within a year Chillingworth dies, leaving his considerable property to Pearl. Hester and Pearl disappear from the colony—to England, it is believed; but years later Hester returns alone, still wearing the scarlet letter, and passes the rest of her days in voluntary penance, doing charitable works. She receives letters from across the sea and when she is seen making a lavish baby-garment the townspeople conclude that Pearl is alive and married. Hester dies and is laid to rest in a grave whose tombstone bears the letter A.

The School for Scandal

Play by Richard Brinsley Sheridan, 1751–1816.
Produced 1777.

SHERIDAN WAS PROBABLY the greatest 18th-century English dramatist, and *The School for Scandal* was one of his two principal plays, the other being *The Rivals*. Both are usually listed among the four or five best plays of their period. In *The School for Scandal* Sheridan's gift of satire reached its highest point. It is still a playable and intensely readable comedy, in many parts sparkling and introducing two excellent female characters, Lady Sneerwell and Lady Teazle.

Act I. 1. Lady SNEERWELL, a target of scandal in her youth, has devoted all her energies since then to slandering others. Her latest plot concerns two brothers, CHARLES and JOSEPH SURFACE, both of whom are eager to marry the lovely MARIA, ward of the elderly Sir PETER TEAZLE. Charles, a pleasure-loving young man who has won a bad reputation for extravagance, is truly in love with Maria, who returns his affection. Joseph, an artful, selfish knave who passes for a youthful miracle of prudence, good sense, and benevolence, is interested in Maria only for her money. Lady Sneerwell, who wishes Charles for herself, conspires with Joseph to transfer Maria's affections from Charles to himself. Sir OLIVER SURFACE, Charles' and Joseph's wealthy uncle, who has been in the East Indies for many years, is soon to return to London. 2. Teazle, who only six months ago married a country girl less than half his age, is already mourning his lost bachelorhood. His young wife, who was undemanding and modest before their wedding, has in this short time become as extravagant and as much of a gossip as any lady in London. Act II. 1–2. Though he scorns Lady Sneerwell, Teazle goes with his wife to her house, where the worst gossips of London customarily gather. He listens with horror to the scandalous remarks and leaves abruptly. Joseph sees Maria alone and presses his suit, reminding her that her affection for Charles is contrary to the wishes of her guardian. He goes down on his knees to avow his love when Lady Teazle suddenly enters. Joseph has been making love to Lady Teazle for some time. Maria leaves and Joseph explains that Maria became suspicious of his relationship with Lady Teazle and he went down on his knees to reason with her. Actually, Joseph only intended to ingratiate himself with Lady Teazle so that she would help him win Maria, but now, somehow, he has become her serious lover. 3. Sir Oliver returns to London and consults his agent ROWLEY on the characters of his two nephews. Rowley believes that, contrary to popular opinion, Charles is the better of the two men. Teazle, on the other hand, extols Joseph's many virtues. Sir

Charles refuses to sell

Oliver concludes that Joseph clearly has too good a character to be an honest fellow.

Act III. 1. Sir Oliver, whom neither Charles nor Joseph has seen in 15 years, decides to visit each under an assumed identity. 2. Having learned that, as usual, Charles is desperately in need of money, Sir Oliver visits him first in the guise of "Mr. Premium," a banker who is willing to make a loan. Charles confesses that he is an extravagant young fellow who has converted all his possessions into cash except for a roomful of family portraits, which he offers for sale.

Act IV. 1. Though hurt by his nephew's callousness towards his ancestors, Sir Oliver, still in the guise of Mr. Premium, agrees to purchase the paintings for £300. There is one painting Charles refuses to part with, a portrait of Sir Oliver, even at a bid of £800. His uncle, he explains, has been very good to him and he will not part with his picture so long as he has a place to hang it. This convinces Sir Oliver that Charles is an honorable man who knows the meaning of gratitude. When Sir Oliver departs, Charles asks Rowley to take £100 to Mr. STANLEY, a poor relation whom he has never seen but who has asked him for help. 2. Rowley tells Sir Oliver of Charles' generosity. Sir Oliver decides to visit Joseph in the guise of the poor Mr. Stanley. 3. Lady Teazle tells Joseph that Teazle thinks she is having an affair with Charles. Joseph tells her that if her husband insists on being jealous, she must give him cause for jealousy. Teazle is heard in the hall and Lady Teazle barely manages to hide behind a screen before he enters. He tells Joseph of his suspicions and Joseph joins him in condemnation of his brother. Then Joseph reveals his own desire to wed Maria. Hearing this, Lady Teazle knows Joseph has been deceiving her. Charles is heard in the hall and Teazle asks Joseph to question Charles about his relations with Lady Teazle, while he hides in the closet. Joseph questions Charles, as directed, but Charles replies that he always thought Joseph was Lady Teazle's favorite and recounts the little incidents that led him to believe this. Embarrassed by this turn of events, Joseph tells Charles that Teazle is in the closet. Charles hauls him from the closet and the two compare notes on the now stained character of Joseph, who leaves the room to greet Lady Sneerwell. Teazle tells Charles that Joseph has a lady hidden behind his screen right now. They upset the screen, just as Joseph returns, and are astonished to find Lady Teazle, who now knows Joseph for the hypocrite he is. She refuses to back up his false explanations of her presence but admits she came to listen to Joseph's pretended passion. Now, having heard her husband express his tender sentiments toward her, she has recovered her senses and will be a model wife in the future.

Act V. 1. Sir Oliver, in the guise of Mr. Stanley, comes to Joseph for financial aid. Joseph tells him he would be delighted to help if he could but he has no money. His visitor says he has heard that Joseph receives large sums from a wealthy uncle in the East Indies. Joseph replies that Sir Oliver, though a worthy man, is old and that avarice is the vice of old age. When Sir Oliver hears this piece of ingratitude, he decides to make Charles his heir. 2–3. Sir Oliver reveals his true identity to his nephews, pronounces Charles his heir, and gives his blessing to the marriage of Charles and Maria, which will take place the next morning.

A Sentimental Journey

Novel by Laurence Sterne, 1713–1768. Published 1768.

LAURENCE STERNE is a writer whose works have been read with greatest appreciation by other writers and by contemplative readers in general. The full title of this one is *A Sentimental Journey to France and Italy*. It is narrated by Mr. Yorick, the clergyman who appears in Sterne's earlier work, *Tristram Shandy*. Whereas *Tristram Shandy* is full of pungent humor and often of iconoclasm (though Sterne was a clergyman), in *A Sentimental Journey* Sterne chiefly tells anecdotes that are sentimental and even inspirational. Yet he could not keep the humor out and the reader finds plenty to chuckle over. *A Sentimental Journey* is largely a sequel to *Tristram Shandy*, alluding often to other characters and to events in *Tristram Shandy*. It is quite short—about 50,000 words —compared to the long *Tristram Shandy*. It should be required reading for anyone who wishes to be well versed in English literature.

Calais. The Rev. Mr. YORICK (who is the narrator) packed a few necessaries in his portmanteau and caught the packet to Calais where, after dining sumptuously while briefly apostrophizing dear ELIZA, he declared peace on the world. A Franciscan MONK entered the inn, begging alms for his order. Yorick, predetermined to give him not a single sou, upbraided the fellow for seeking charity when he could work for his bread and the world overflows with truly desperate causes. The monk withdrew so piously, and with such resignation, that Yorick was abashed at his own unkindness. He shed a tear for his ill manners and left the inn in search of a carriage to accommodate his travels. He found one, but no one at hand to sell it; so he climbed in and set himself to writing the Preface, in which he delineated the several types, and their subdivisions, of travelers: Idle Travelers, Inquisitive, Proud, Vain, Splenetic Travelers (Travelers of Necessity, Delinquent & Felonious Travelers, Unfortunate and Innocent and Simple Travelers), concluding that he was a Sentimental Traveler as driven by necessity and *besoin de voyager* as any one of the class. His reflections were interrupted by two Englishmen (Inquisitive and Simple Travelers) inquiring astoundedly after the cause of the coach's exuberant motion. Later, when the hotel master gallantly dissuaded him from taking the aged coach, Yorick pursued his attempts to procure a coach. In front of the coach house, while the good innkeeper fumbled bravely with the wrong key and returned to find the right one, Yorick made the acquaintance and, in their mutual agitation, took the hand of an attractive, melancholy-looking lady of the better sort, probably a newly bereaved widow, who also was after a vehicle. He had seen her previously, discoursing with the monk. She inspired him to tender and compassionate musings, and they had established a mutual sympathy, when the monk returned. Apologies ensued, the monk and the lady protested the impossibility of Yorick's unkindness, tears and snuffboxes were exchanged, and Yorick and the world were set to rights again.

Eventually the inn-keeper came with the proper key and news that the lady's brother, the Count de L——, had arrived. Sadly, having hoped that the lady would accompany him as far as Amiens, her destination, Yorick bought a coach and proceeded to Paris, philosophizing en route over his special bugbears, Splenetic Travelers, specifically Smelfungus and Mundungus (Smollet and Dr. Samuel Sharp), both of whom had written ill-natured and ungenerous accounts of their Continental travels.

Montreuil. Muddy and exhausted from several mischances on the road, Yorick was favorably struck with the inn-keeper's inspiration: A servant? The very thing! And so LAFLEUR was hired; faithful, affectionate, simple LaFleur who, though his sole talents of drum-beating and splatterdash-making were of no great service, duly recompensed by the festivity of his temper. His only misfortune, claimed the landlord, was that he was always in love. But Yorick approved heartily; having been himself in love with one princess or another almost all his life and hoping to continue so until death, he was firmly convinced that if ever he did a mean action it would be between one passion and another, and he told the tale of the wicked town of Abdera, which was redeemed, through Euripides' *Andromache*, by love. As LaFleur and Yorick were about to leave, a small clan of "the sons and daughters of poverty" stopped them with heartrending pleas. Yorick apportioned his few extra sous among them.

Amiens. To LaFleur's extreme dissatisfaction, his horse balked at a dead ass in the road and flew straight back to Montruil. However, the reluctant beast was finally persuaded to return. Yorick alighted with much interest to hear the story of the ass's owner, who was bemoaning his loss piteously. The man had seen two of his sons sacrificed to smallpox; to prevent the loss of his third and last boy, he had vowed that he would make a pilgrimage to Spain (from his native Germany) if the lad were spared. Heaven had accepted his conditions and he had made the journey, suffering many hardships and misfortunes on the way. He was returning home when his faithful ass expired. Perhaps, he feared, he had overtaxed the creature and his selfishness caused the death. Yorick was much moved by such love and reflected that the world could profit from the man's story. In Amiens, Yorick found himself at the same hotel as the lady from Calais, Madame de L——, who requested that he deliver a letter to Mme. R—— in Paris and invited him to look her up if ever he should get to Brussels. To Brussels, then! thought Yorick, but was immediately reproached by memory of Eliza, to whom he had sworn eternal fidelity. Not to Brussels.

Paris. Alas, poor Yorick, he reflected; on the very first onset of all this glittering clatter thou art reduced to an atom. But recollection of his business with Mme. R—— prevented Yorick's escaping down some side street to seek solace in converse sweet with some kind *grisset* of a barber's wife. However, periwig problems prevented the business's conclusion that night. At the Opéra Comique Yorick was saddened by the sight of a poor dwarf trying to see over the head of a 7-foot brute, but a French officer in the next box (who reminded Yorick of his friend Tobias Shandy) brought the matter to a satisfactory end. After some conversation, the officer was inspired to remark that there is good and bad everywhere and the advantage of travel was that it taught us mutual toleration, which in turn taught us mutual love. Reminded by this of Polonius's advice to his son, Yorick stopped off at a bookstore to buy a Shakespeare. But the bookseller's only volumes had gone off that day to a Count de B—— of Versailles, who loved the English. Yorick was about to take his leave when his fancy was caught by a girl who he learned, after some talk of young hearts and girlish virtues, to be the maid of Mme. R——. So he paid his respects and promised to call on the lady in the morning. A police lieutenant had called at his hotel to learn if the gentleman called Yorick was properly attended by passport. He was not. In his hasty departure from England, Yorick had overlooked that matter; but he assured LaFleur, who feared that his master would spend his remaining years in the Bastille, that he would go directly to the Duc de C—— in Versailles and plead for the necessary papers.

The duke, however, was a busy and formidable gentleman. Yorick thought that the Anglophile, the Count of B——, might be sympathetic to his problem. And indeed he was. You are Yorick! he exclaimed delightedly on learning his visitor's identity; he embraced him tenderly and raced out of the house to return, two hours later, with a passport, readily granted by the duke, addressed to all lieutenant governors, governors, commandants of cities, generals of armies, justicians and all officers of justice to let Mr. Yorick, the king's jester, and his baggage travel quietly along. Further, through the count's intercessions, Yorick was introduced to and lionized by the brightest stars of Paris society. But soon he tired of the children of art and yearned for the children of nature; he ordered LaFleur to get the horses set for Italy.

Moulines. Having been much affected by his friend Mr. Shandy's account of his meeting with the poor, disordered maid, Maria, near Moulines, Yorick could not resist, when he found himself in that neighborhood, going to the village where her parents lived and inquiring after her. The old mother reported sadly that her husband had died about a month before of anguish for the loss of Maria's senses, and the poor girl, though brought to herself somewhat by the shock, was wandering about on the road—Yorick found her much as his friend had described her except that instead of the goat, which had proved as faithless as her lover, she now had a small dog. Yorick sat beside her and she allowed him to wipe away her tears, as they fell, with his handkerchief; which he then steeped in his own tears, concluding that he had a soul that not all the materialists in the world could argue out of him. Since her encounter with Mr. Shandy, Marie told Yorick, she had wandered as far as Rome, had found her way alone across the Apennines, and had traveled all over Lombardy without money and through the flinty roads of Savoy without shoes. How she had borne it, she could not tell; but God tempers the wind, she said, to the shorn lamb. The picture of Maria sitting pensive under her poplar clouded every festivity, and Yorick got almost to Lyons before he was able to cast a shade over her.

An adventure in the home of some simple, goodhearted peasants, where he saw *religion* in their jollity, further gladdened Yorick's heart, and he was inspired to reflect that a cheerful and contented mind is the best sort of thanks to Heaven that an illiterate peasant could pay. Or a learned prelate either.

After passing through Lyons, Yorick pursued his travels in more leisurely manner, with a pair of mules substituted for his horse in deference to the quieter, more gentle mood of that country, and headed toward Turin through Savoy. At a decent inn, one tempestuous night, Yorick was obliged to share his room with a young Piedmontese lady and her maid. This was mutually embarrassing, but they calmed their souls by making a treaty, and went to bed: Yorick in his black silk breeches was committed to nightlong silence, the lady having augmented her security by pinning the bed's hangings together. But alas, Yorick couldn't sleep and was forced finally to groan aloud. "You have broke the treaty," said the lady. A thousand apologies from Yorick, who unconsciously stretched out his hand in a supplicating gesture. The pins fell to the floor; the lady's maid rushed between the beds to forestall the hostilities she feared would ensue; and Yorick's hand grasped that of the maid——

Seven Against Thebes

Play by Aeschylus, 525–456 B.C.
Produced 467 B.C.

THE AESCHYLUS TRAGEDY of *The Seven Against Thebes* forms a convenient link between the two Oedipus plays and Antigone, which form a trilogy. Oedipus has been banished, his sons are contesting control of the city of Thebes, of which Oedipus was king, and the daughters of Oedipus have remained in the city. At the end of the play, the rebellious son is refused burial, the situation that exists at the start of Antigone. Aeschylus uses the play as a vehicle to deliver strong arguments against civil war. "The Seven" in the title are the generals of the attacking army and several of them appear in later Greek legends.

Prince ETEOCLES, who is defending Thebes against his brother POLYNICES' onslaught, prays to the gods to assist his cause. As the foreign army approaches, the Theban people, speaking as the CHORUS, express great fears about the outcome of the battle. A messenger arrives to warn Eteocles that Polynices' army has already created havoc in the suburbs. Eteocles calls his wailing subjects a "tribe of women" and urges them to show courage at this time of crisis. The Chorus refuses to be placated, however, until the prince demands silence. Eteocles prays for help; the Thebans continue to express their doubts. They know that their prince and his brother are the misbegotten sons of Oedipus, who killed his father and married his mother. Therefore the royal house of Thebes has a curse upon it and their own fates are bound up in this doom.

A Messenger tells of the arrangement of Polynices' army before Thebes' seven gates. He describes each of the seven main warriors with their shield designs: TYDEUS, with a full-moon crest; CAPANEUS, with a naked man carrying fire on his buckler; ETEOCLUS, with a man mounting a ladder to sack a town; HIPPOMEDON, with a serpent spouting fire; PARTHENOPAEUS, with the man-eating Sphinx; AMPHIARAUS, whose shield has no design; and Prince Polynices, who bears a picture of a woman called Justice guiding a man. Eteocles sends a prominent Theban to meet the attack of each. He is heartened by the fact that Amphiaraus has no design on his shield, since that man learned by an oracle that he would die in battle. Eteocles decides that he himself must resist the charge of his brother. For a time the Chorus tries to dissuade him from this, but Eteocles will not listen.

A messenger arrives to report the progress of the battle. Eteocles and Polynices have killed each other, and all the rebels are dead. The Chorus moans that Fate has run its dreaded course. Oedipus's daughters, ANTIGONE and ISMENE, enter beside the bodies of their two brothers. The sisters vent their grief, reproaching the brothers for inciting civil war. At last they take comfort in the hope that the curse of Oedipus has ended. A messenger arrives to tell the girls that the officials of Thebes have decreed that Polynices' body must go unburied. In Grecian times, this prohibition meant that the corpse's soul would wander homeless in the Underworld. Eteocles is to be honored with a splendid funeral.

Antigone cries out against the injustice of this decree. She contends that her rebellious brother Polynices was no more guilty than Eteocles. It is wrong for men to pass sudden judgments upon the lives of other men. Furthermore, as a sister, Antigone owes her brother the fulfillment of his last rite. The Herald tries to argue her out of her determined stand, but does not succeed. Antigone rushes away, repeating her vow, while the Herald warns her of the consequences. The Chorus bemoans Antigone's decision, for the curse may go on. They approve the decision of the state against Polynices, but they are subject to human feelings of kinship and love. As a last act, the Chorus divides into two halves. One half decides to accompany Antigone to the burial rite, while the other refuses to challenge the letter of the law.

The Seven That Were Hanged

Novelette by Leonid Andreyev, 1871–1919.

Published 1908; published 1937 by Harper & Bros., New York. Translated from the Russian by Eugenia Schimanshaya and Elizabeth Gow. (ML, P40)

THIS IS BOTH A NOVEL (or rather a novelette, for it is very short) and a play. As a play it ranks second in popularity, to *He Who Gets Slapped,* among Andreyev's plays. It is his most popular prose work, at least in its English translation. The novelette rather than the play is outlined below, for it is far more effective as a piece of writing. The author studies and compares a group of persons in the same predicament—a device used by many writers. Though anti-Bolshevist and exiled by the revolution, Andreyev was a liberal and was sympathetic to the terrorists in his story.

Chaps. 1–4. In Czarist Russia, early in the 20th century, a very fat Minister of State has been informed, with great care because of his physical infirmity, that a serious attempt upon his life has been plotted and that the seven conspirators are to be arrested at one o'clock the next afternoon. Imagining how a bomb would mangle him, the minister, tormented by asthma and insomnia, feels terrified of death; but he wonders logically why he, in his feeble condition, should be so horribly afraid of dying. His corpselike appearance alarms his household. His doctor is summoned.

In front of his house next day, four political conspirators are seized—three men and one woman. They are carrying loaded revolvers and a bomb. A second woman accomplice is arrested at her home, where the bomb was made and the assassination planned. All five prisoners are young, calm, thoughtful. They answer some questions readily; others they refuse to answer. One is SERGEY GOLOVIN, a former army officer and son of a retired colonel. The younger girl gives her name as MUSYA. Her attitude is disdainful. The police magistrates take an instant dislike to her. Next to Musya stands the prisoner named WERNER, showing cold, audacious valor. The police, with some respect, look upon him as the leader. VASILY KASHIRIN, standing beside Werner, is trying desperately to conceal his fear from the police. TANYA KOVALCHUK, the fifth terrorist, though still quite young, seems motherly toward the others. She smiles at Golovin and worries over Kashirin's obvious fright.

Two weeks before, a peasant, IVAN YANSON, was tried in the same court for robbery and murder, and was sentenced to be hanged. Like an imbecile Yanson has repeatedly cried out, "I must not be hanged!"

Another peasant murderer, sentenced at the same session with Yanson, when told he would be hanged, merely laughed and said, "Be sure to put on plenty of soap to grease the noose."

Chaps. 5–8. The five terrorists are condemned to hang but are not informed as to the date of execution. Tanya has no near relatives. Only Golovin and Kashirin are to see their families. Golovin's father, the retired colonel, tells his wife, Golovin's mother, how to behave at the last visit. "Kiss him and be silent," the colonel tells her. "Do not speak. Only kiss him. He has to die. Don't torture him." The visit saddens Golovin.

All her life Tanya had thought only of others, and now, in the fortress prison, it is for her comrades that she undergoes suffering and mental torture. For Musya she feels special pity, mistakenly believing Musya to be in love with Werner. But Musya is actually happy that she is to have the finest of martyr deaths. She is astonished that Kashirin fears it. She paces her cell vigorously. She has hallucinations, imagining she hears a military band. But now she really does hear martial music. Soldiers are drilling nearby. Exalted over her martyrdom, Musya falls happily asleep.

Golovin never thinks of death. He has always been a robust, capable man.

Chaps. 9–12. Under the same prison roof, Kashirin is finishing his life in an anguish of dread. From the first day of his imprisonment, people and life were transformed for him into a frightful world filled with unspeakable ills. When the soldiers and priest come for him his consciousness goes out like dying embers on the hearth. Then he asks for a cigarette and painfully begins to prepare himself.

The unknown, who calls himself Werner, is a man fatigued by struggle. He entertains a profound contempt for men. He knows no fear and his pity is cold, almost official. He plays games of chess in his mind. Toward the end, however, something happens that never has happened to Werner before. He weeps.

The first condemned prisoners are permitted to talk to one another just before they are taken out to be hanged. Only Tanya takes immediate advantage of this. The others merely touch icy hands. The cheeks and ears of Musya and Tanya are burning. Golovin is just a little pale. Kashirin looks extraordinarily dreadful. Werner asks them all to be quiet.

The two peasant murderers are taken to the place of execution along with the political prisoners. The peasant, Yanson, keeps protesting. At the place of execution, Kashirin complains and Tanya gives him her kerchief.

Yanson faints. A strong smell of ammonia emanates from him. A police doctor revives him. The condemned refuse the services of the priest. Quickly they kiss all around. Werner goes to the gallows with Yanson; Golovin with Kashirin. Two gallows are used. Tanya and Musya go together. The second peasant cries out against being hanged alone. Musya offers to go with him. All seven are hanged at dawn. Thus it is that they greet the rising sun.

All seven are hanged at dawn and so greet the rising sun

552

Marcel Proust
1871–1922

William Faulkner

The Sheik

Novel by Edith Maude Hull.
Published 1921 by A. L. Burt.

ONLY FOR HISTORICAL reasons can this novel be included. It has not yet been and will not be accused of being great literature. But its treatment of the independent woman subdued by her demon lover so captured the American imagination that "sheik" became a common noun to describe an irresistible lover. The popularity of the novel was greatly helped by a silent motion picture that starred Rudolph Valentino and, in fact, brought him his greatest fame. Thereafter he was forever identified with the sheik as a character as well as a lover.

Chaps. 1–2. Everyone in Biska is talking about DIANE MAYO. Her expedition alone into the desert with no chaperon and only native camel drivers and a guide is considered unconventional and improper. Her brother, Sir AUBREY MAYO, attributes the queer streak in Diane to her upbringing. As a small child she was left motherless and she has been brought up by her brother, who is nearly 20 years her senior. He treated her as a boy and she learned to ride and shoot and fish. Her upbringing was Spartan, with no allowances made for her sex, and Diane responded by becoming utterly fearless. Her present desert tour springs from a quarrel with Sir Aubrey. He wishes to go to America and find a wife to produce an heir, and Diane, who has just come of age, wishes to go off on her own. A compromise is reached by her promise to join him in New York in a month's time.

The night before her departure, a dance is given and Diane is surrounded by young men who interest her not at all. She has never been kissed in her young life and cannot imagine herself being subject to any man, in marriage or otherwise. The dance over, Diane is too excited about her expedition to sleep. She steps out on her balcony to see the full moon. She feels vaguely that she is being watched, and she even catches a glimpse of white drapery disappearing behind the shrubs. Puzzled, she dismisses the thought and goes to bed. Next morning Diane begins her trip with the guide, MUSTAFA ALI, who appears capable and efficient. Sir Aubrey accompanies her a short way and makes one more attempt to dissuade her. Diane makes it clear to him that she will never obey any will but her own. She goes on into the desert and in the great emptiness seems strangely at home, finding the realization infinitely greater than the anticipation. She does not envy Sir Aubrey his marriage plans, for the very idea of marriage is repugnant to her. She asks Mustafa Ali many questions about the country they are passing through, but he seems evasive in his answers. They stop for the midday meal and the guide assumes the prerogatives of head of the expedition. Diane is annoyed and, to teach him a lesson, she asserts her will. They are late in making their afternoon start because of this, and ride for many hours with no apparent camping place in sight. As dusk approaches, Diane sees black specks moving fast across the plain, which turn out to be a band of mounted men. They surround Mustafa's people and then circle around Diane. She is puzzled and impatient when the Arabs point their rifles at her and her attendants. As the seriousness of the attack dawns on her, her horse suddenly bolts and begins to run away. A solitary Arab rides after her. The sound of his amused laughter spurring her on, she tries in vain to escape her pursuer. Gaining her side, with a pair of powerful arms the Arab swings her clear of her saddle and on to his own horse in front of him. Diane struggles wildly but it is no use. Her fear grows. After a long and swift journey, she alights to find that she is in a rich tent. Her abductor is a tall man dressed in flowing white robes. His face is the handsomest and cruelest she has ever seen. He is Sheik AHMED BEN HASSAN. There is no mistaking the purpose for which he has brought her to his tent. Terror grips her as the full realization that she is a desirable woman takes hold. He kisses her roughly, robbing her of any power of resistance. He commands her to prepare herself for their night of love.

Chaps. 3–4. Next morning the lavish furnishings of the tent and the presence of her own baggage does not dispel her fear. The thought of seeing the Sheik again fills her with rage and humiliation, but she knows that she is helpless. She is served lunch by a French servant, GASTON, who informs her that Monseigneur dines at eight. Wandering about the tent, she catches unexpected glimpses of the personality of the Arab—evidences of education and unlooked-for taste in books. When the Sheik returns, it is to greet her with cool words. Diane threatens him with the authority of the French government but he laughs at her, for he recognizes no government but his own. He tells Diane that he paid Mustafa Ali to bring her to the desert because he wanted her. He will let her go when he is tired of her. Diane realizes that it is no use to fight any further for she has met a will stronger than hers. She is filled with hatred for the Arab and does not hestitate to tell him so.

A month passes and Diane is continually thinking of escape. Ahmed treats her well and there are many times when she finds him so interesting that she forgets he is an Arab. One evening he gives her a jade necklace, telling her he has given many jewels to many women. She refuses it and asks if he has a harem or wives. He tells her he has neither. Their wills clash often and Ahmed tells her coolly that he is determined to tame her and she can either obey him willingly or he will make her. Her fear overrules her mind and she tells him that she will obey.

Chaps. 5–6. Several weeks have passed since Diane's promise of obedience and her fear and hatred of the Sheik grow constantly. One day the absence of Ahmed gives her an opportunity to escape. She eludes Gaston on their daily ride and gallops to the north, hoping to meet friendly Arabs. After riding for several hours, she comes to an oasis where she and the horse refresh themselves. She rests for a while and her thoughts are crowded with recollection of the past months. As she continues on her way across the desert, a band of men approaches. Seeing with horror that their leader is Ahmed ben Hassan, Diane turns her horse and races the other way. He follows close behind and shoots her horse when she does not stop. He carries her back to their tent on his horse and quite suddenly she knows that she is glad he caught her. She knows she loves him. He is furious with her when they are alone. She had been in danger of capture by his enemy IBRAHEIM OMAIR. When two months have passed, Diane is happier than she has ever been. The desert, the tent and the Sheik become her natural settings. Hard though it is, she hides her love closely in her heart, for discovery of her feelings might make Ahmed tire of her.

The news that his friend RAOUL DE SAINT HUBERT is coming to visit Ahmed fills Diane with dismay. He is a famous French novelist and she resents his coming and is jealous of their friendship. Her pride is still a part of her and Diane cannot bear the thought of facing a European as the mistress of an Arab sheik. Raoul charms her and they become friends. He and Ahmed argue over Ahmed's holding on to Diane. Raoul shows Ahmed a newspaper with Diane's picture and an account of her mysterious disappearance. A great restlessness seizes Ahmed and he finds himself for the first time in his life jealous. He watches every move Diane makes towards his friend.

Chaps. 7–8. Saint Hubert discovers that he has fallen in love, with Diane. She regards him as a brother but is aware of Ahmed's constant jealous eyes. She begins to hope that at last he is beginning to love her. She takes her usual daily ride with Gaston and is captured by the men of Ibraheim Omair. It is a great prize for them to take prisoner the white woman of Ahmed ben Hassan. When the Sheik is informed of her disappearance he realizes how necessary she has become to him and how changed he is. He gathers his forces and, with Saint Hubert, rides to the tent of his enemy. He kills Omair in a fight but is himself seriously injured. Diane is saved from any indignity. The unconscious Sheik is carried back to his tent and Diane and Saint Hubert nurse him. In his delirium, he calls out his love for the English girl.

555

Chaps. 9–10. The vigil at the bedside reveals to Saint Hubert that Diane loves Ahmed. He tells her the strange story of this fascinating man. He is not an Arab but an Englishman. His mother was found wandering in the desert by the men of Ahmed ben Hassan the Elder and was brought to his tent as she was ready to bear a child. It was a boy. Even though, after his birth, she refused to give any account of herself, the old Sheik became passionately attached to her and adopted the boy as his own. When she was dying, she told him her story. She was a Spanish lady and her husband was the Earl of Glencaryll. He was older than she and was given to violent tempers and excesses in drink. No longer able to bear the situation when she was about to give birth, she slipped away in the middle of the night and ran off into the desert. She had been afraid to say who she was lest she be sent back to her husband. She made the old Sheik promise not to tell the boy of his heritage until he came of age. The boy grew up believing that Ahmed ben Hassan was his father. He was educated in Paris and London but the desert was his true home. When he was told the story of his mother, he cursed the English in Arabic and refused to meet his father. His hatred of the English became an obsession.

Diane finds it hard to think of the Sheik as an Englishman. She can only pray for

Diane tries to run away

his recovery. His great strength and splendid constitution stand him in good stead and his convalescence is rapid. With his recovery, Ahmed's attitude towards Diane reverts to a cold reserve. He sleeps in the outer room and Diane fears that he is now tired of her. When Saint Hubert leaves, she realizes that his going will bring matters to a head. She will now be alone and at Ahmed's mercy. He finally comes to her and tells her that he is sending her back to her people. In desperation, she tells him

that she loves him and does not want to go. Ahmed insists that she must, for, though he loves her, there is no future in the desert for her. His resolution is firm and she cannot change it. She goes to her room in the tent and tries to shoot herself. Ahmed, with his instinct for imminent danger, is able to prevent her suicide. Shaken by this demonstration of her love, Ahmed cannot face parting from her. Diane is no longer afraid of the desert or her future husband, and life again has meaning.

Sherlock Holmes
The Hound of the Baskervilles

Detective stories by Arthur Conan Doyle, 1859–1930.
Published 1887–1930.

THE FIRST book about Sherlock Holmes was *A Study in Scarlet*. Since Arthur Conan Doyle liked to be called not merely "Doyle" but "Conan Doyle," his full surname, he gave his hero a similar double surname and the great detective began as Mr. Sherlock Holmes. In later years Conan Doyle lost this prejudice and permitted Sherlock Holmes to be simply Holmes. Despite some inconsistencies and changes of plan, the Sherlock Holmes stories deserve their high prestige and have unquestionably contributed great-

ly to the development of modern police methods. Below are outlines of the first Sherlock Holmes novel and the one generally considered best, *The Hound of the Baskervilles*. Principally, of course, Conan Doyle's writing about Sherlock Holmes consisted of short stories, most notably collected as *The Adventures of Sherlock Holmes*. In some cases these stories made sequences almost equivalent to novels except for their episodic character— for example, the long record of Sherlock Holmes' struggle against the master criminal Moriarty and a lesser struggle against another master criminal, Moran.

Chaps. 1–4. SHERLOCK HOLMES and Dr. WATSON are discussing a walking stick. It bears initials and a date of presentation, and it looks like the kind carried by a country doctor. It proves to belong to JAMES MORTIMER, a physician of Grimpen, Devonshire, who appears almost immediately. He carries an ancient manuscript that describes a strange curse on the BASKERVILLE family in Devon. Many years before, an evil Baskerville kidnapped a young

woman and imprisoned her upstairs while he and his companions caroused on the lower floor. She escaped by climbing down the vines that grew on the side of the house. When HUGO BASKERVILLE found that she was gone he set out after her. Some friends trailed behind him, but when they overtook him he was dead, with his throat torn by a giant hound. The girl lay dead nearby. She apparently had died of fright. The name of the writer of the manuscript was

also Hugo Baskerville. In it he pleaded with his sons never to venture out on the moors at night, for many strange deaths had occurred in the family since the first appearance of the "Hound of Hell." Now, concludes Mortimer, after reading the manuscript aloud, another of the family has died a strange death. Sir CHARLES BASKERVILLE, a kindly, generous man, habitually took an evening walk. One night his walk became a death march. His footprints were normal at first but then it seemed he began to walk on tiptoes. His body was found near the end of a lane, the face contorted with emotion. The autopsy indicated death by heart failure, and it was known that Sir Charles had a long-standing heart ailment. Mortimer is doubtful, however, because he saw footprints of a giant hound some 20 feet from the body—something no one else seems to have noted. Holmes realizes that the tiptoe footprints signify a man running for his life. Mortimer is worried now because Sir HENRY BASKERVILLE, the heir to Sir Charles, is due in London within the hour. Holmes agrees to see both men next day. When they arrive, Sir Henry shows an anonymous letter, pasted together out of clips from the London *Times*. Sir Henry also reports the disappearance of one new tan shoe, which seems odd. They agree to meet at Sir Henry's hotel for lunch, and as Mortimer and Sir Henry leave, Holmes goes after them to see if they are being followed. He glimpses a man with a black beard, who is urging his driver to hurry. Holmes then calls on a young man and asks him to seek the copy of the *Times* from which the clips were taken. There is little chance of success but it is worth trying. In the note Sir Henry is warned not to go to Baskerville Hall.

Chaps. 5–9. The four men meet, as agreed, for lunch. Holmes learns that now an old black boot has disappeared. They find after lunch that the brown boot has been returned in the interim. The search for the newspaper proves fruitless, and there is only the cab number of the man with the black beard as a possible clue. The driver of the cab is located, but he can tell them only that his fare claimed to be Sherlock Holmes, proving to the real Holmes that his adversary is clever. Watson accompanies Sir Henry to the country to keep an eye on him and to report to Holmes. Watson and the baronet see a soldier silhouetted against the sky over the moor, and the coachman explains that a vicious criminal has escaped from Princetown gaol and is at large on the moor. Watson knows of the criminal— SELDEN—because of Holmes' former interest in the case. At Baskerville Hall, the butler, BARRYMORE, tells Sir Henry that he and his wife wish to leave as soon as possible. They were too fond of Sir Charles to remain there with another master. Watson goes to bed shortly after dinner, and hears the sound of a woman sobbing in the house somewhere. Next morning Mrs. Barrymore's eyes are red and swollen. Watson goes out walking and meets STAPLETON, a naturalist who lives nearby. Stapleton says he knows the moors well and can make his way safely between the pits of quicksand that trap the unwary. As if in proof of this, Watson sees a hapless pony sucked into the mire and hears its final despairing wail. Another sound reaches their ears. It is a strange sound, and Stapleton laughingly remarks that it is supposed to be the hound of the Baskervilles, howling for his prey. It is probably only some strange bird. When Stapleton dashes off after a moth, his sister BERYL appears. Believing Watson to be Sir Henry, she warns him to return to London if he values his life. She is very beautiful. Another of Baskerville's neighbors is Mr. FRANKLAND, of Lafter Hall, about 4 miles away. He has two hobbies: He brings lawsuits against anyone available, and he watches the moors through his telescope. He now hopes to spot the missing convict. Watson reports to Holmes that he has seen Barrymore prowling the halls at night with a candle, and then standing before a window, apparently waiting for something. Meanwhile, Sir Henry has fallen in love with Beryl Stapleton and wishes to marry her. She seems favorably disposed, but her brother forbids Sir Henry to see her. Later he apologizes by saying that his sister is all

he has in the world and he cannot bear the thought of losing her. Watson learns that Mrs. Barrymore's maiden name was Selden and the escaped convict is her brother. The Barrymores signal to him, and if he answers with another candle they take food to him. Watson and Sir Henry go out on the moor, where they see the convict and give chase, but he eludes them. They also hear the eerie howl again. Watson sees the silhouette of a tall man on a tor and wonders who it may be.

Chaps. 10–13. Barrymore tells Watson that on the night Sir Charles died, Sir Charles had gone out to meet a lady with the initials "L.L." Barrymore found in the grate the charred postscript of a letter, signed with those initials, which mentioned an appointment. Watson learns that the woman is LAURA LYONS, Frankland's married daughter, who lives in the nearby village of Coombes Tracey. When Watson confronts her, she says she had intended to ask Sir Charles to help her obtain a divorce, but that she had not kept the appointment. Watson next sees Frankland, who says he knows where the convict is hiding because he has seen a boy carrying bundles that probably contain food up to Black Tor. Watson knows that the silhouette he has seen there is not the convict, but he decides to go and investigate. To his amazement, Holmes' voice greets him. Holmes has found out several things. For one thing, Stapleton is Beryl's husband, not her brother. Also, Stapleton has a very bad record in a place where he once taught school and Holmes believes he is at the

The hound attacks Sir Henry

bottom of a fiendishly clever murder plot. Suddenly they hear the hound again, and the cries of a man in peril. They rush to the spot and find the body of a man dressed in Sir Henry's clothes. It is the escaped convict, Selden, to whom Barrymore had obviously given some of Sir Henry's discarded clothing. Selden did not die from a wound inflicted by the hound; while trying to escape, he fell and broke his neck. Stapleton appears and is startled when he finds that the dead man is Selden. However he covers

his confusion and returns home. Back at the hall, where Watson and Holmes go together, Holmes is electrified by one of the family portraits on the wall. It proves to be that of the original evil Sir Hugo, founder of the legend of the hound. With part of the face covered, it bears a startling resemblance to Stapleton. Holmes calls it a throwback in both appearance and character. He and Watson inform Sir Henry that they must go to London, but instead they visit Mrs. Lyons and she admits that she made the appointment—and later broke it—at Stapleton's urging. She has been in love with the naturalist, but when she learns that he is married and has deceived her she turns against him. Meanwhile, Holmes has sent for LESTRADE of Scotland Yard, who is on his way with a warrant.

Chaps. 14–15. Holmes, Lestrade, and Watson ambush themselves near Stapleton's house. Watson goes to look in the window, and sees Stapleton with Sir Henry. Stapleton gets up, goes to a small out-building, opens the door, shuts it again, and returns to the house. Sir Henry emerges, and a gigantic black hound with flaming jaws and eyes comes after him. Lestrade fires at it, and though its howl indicates that it is hurt, it continues to pursue Sir Henry. The hound grabs Sir Henry by the throat but is killed by five more shots. The flame effect was achieved by smearing the beast with phosphorus, to make it appear more terrifying. Sir Henry is unharmed, and Holmes, Lestrade and Watson go in search of Stapleton. They find Beryl bound and gagged upstairs, but Stapleton has fled across the moor toward a refuge he had prepared. However, a heavy fog that night hides his guide markers, and Stapleton never reaches the hiding place. Footprints are found leading part of the way, and then they disappear. He has sunk in the quagmire. Holmes then explains the resemblance between Stapleton and the first Hugo. Stapleton is the son of a Baskerville who went to South America and married there. He was third in line for the succession, and he used the family legend to eliminate the others. Holmes detected him first by negative evidence that no one else observed: *The hound did not bark* when Stapleton approached, therefore Stapleton was its master.

A Study in Scarlet

Chaps. 1–2. JOHN H. WATSON is in London after having been wounded in Afghanistan, where he served as an army surgeon. He has had a tropical fever, and is in a weakened condition. He is also short of money. An acquaintance suggests that he share lodgings with a man named SHERLOCK HOLMES. Watson meets Sherlock Holmes, who impresses him by telling him all about Watson—based on sheer observation. Watson and Sherlock Holmes are congenial and establish their residence at 32B Baker Street, London. Watson learns that Sherlock Holmes is a student solely of crime detection by observation and deductive reasoning and that he is most scornful of police methods in these respects.

Chaps. 3–4. Sherlock Holmes receives a request for help from TOBIAS GREGSON of Scotland Yard. A man has been found dead in an empty house. In his pocket are cards bearing the name of ENOCH J. DREBBER, of Cleveland, Ohio, U.S.A., and other cards with the name of JOSEPH STANGERSON. Sherlock Holmes and Watson go to the house and find the dead man with an expression of horror on his face. There are signs of a struggle, but no wound or weapon is visible. A woman's wedding band falls to the floor when the body is moved. Sherlock Holmes declares the death to be due to poison, and says that he will give further information when and if he is consulted further. The letters RACHE printed in blood on the wall indicate a woman's name to the police, but Holmes says it is merely the German word for revenge. With Watson, he goes to see JOHN RANCE, the constable who discovered the body. Rance says the only person he saw in the neighborhood was a drunken man. This information excites Sherlock Holmes, but he explains nothing.

Chaps. 5–6. Sherlock Holmes believes that the man seen by Rance was merely pretending to be drunk, and was actually returning to seek the wedding ring when he was accosted by Rance. An advertisement in the paper should bring him to claim the "found" ring that evidently is so important to him. Instead of the man, however, an old woman appears and accepts without question a substitute ring. Holmes follows her, but she escapes from her cab while it is moving, proving that "she" is really an agile youth. Gregson appears at the lodgings in Baker Street with the news that he has arrested the murderer. According to him, it is one Lieutenant CHARPENTIER, son of Drebber's landlady. The culprit is now safely in jail. To Gregson's chagrin, LESTRADE of the Yard appears and announces that Joseph Stangerson—Drebber's secretary and companion—has also been murdered, and at a time when the supposed murderer was in jail. Both killings were done by the same person, because the same word is printed by Stangerson's body—RACHE.

Chap. 7. Sherlock Holmes announces that he knows the name of the killer and it is merely a matter of picking up the man in question. He is certain of his facts, because he has deduced them in a logical manner. He has taken the trouble to make inquiries concerning Drebber in Cleveland, something that Scotland Yard had neglected to do. He therefore knows something that Gregson and Lestrade do not. However, he is willing to share his knowledge with them, and of course he expects them to take full credit in the newspapers. Sherlock Holmes pauses to show them a pair of handcuffs, which he praises highly. The two men from the Yard are not in the least interested. The conversation is interrupted by a boy who announces that the cab is waiting. Everyone is surprised when Sherlock Holmes asks

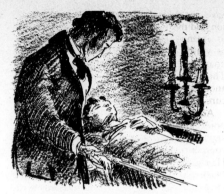

Hope removes Lucy's ring

the cabby help him with his box, since no one knew Sherlock Holmes planned a journey. As the driver bends over, Sherlock Holmes snaps on the handcuffs and presents JEFFERSON HOPE to the others as the murderer of Drebber and Stangerson. Hope smiles and seems quite willing to be arrested. He has a severe heart ailment, and cannot expect to live more than a few days at the most, but he tells his story.

Chaps. 8–13. Many years before, a man and a little girl were rescued from death on the desert of the western United States by a caravan of Mormons. They were the only surviving members of a party of 21. They traveled to Utah with the Mormons and settled there. The man, JOHN FERRIER, became a successful farmer, and LUCY, the daughter, grew to be a beautiful young woman. Two of the Mormon elders, Stangerson and Drebber, wanted to marry her, but she was in love with Jefferson Hope, a young adventurer, who had saved her from stampeding cattle. According to the rules of the encampment, no Mormon was allowed to marry outside the faith and a secret band of avengers swiftly punished any violation of the group's rules. The terror that the avengers inspired was genuine and was based substantially on fact. Lucy and her father were fearful, but John was determined that his daughter should not become part of the harem of either Stangerson or Drebber. Jefferson Hope returned and the three made their escape, eluding the rings of sentinels. Jefferson

Hope left them to search for game. Many days later he returned to find Lucy kidnapped and John murdered. Against her will, Lucy was married to Drebber. Jefferson Hope reached her too late. A few days after her wedding Lucy died, and Hope removed the wedding ring from her dead hand. Hope devoted the rest of his life to seeking Stangerson and Drebber, and at last in London he succeeded—as the police and Sherlock Holmes now know. He had followed them throughout the world, and somehow they had eluded him until now. As a cab driver, he was able to keep them in sight. At last he caught Drebber alone—a thing that rarely happened. Hope did not murder Drebber in cold blood, however. He had two pills in his possession—one harmless, and one a deadly poison. He gave Drebber his choice, and Drebber chose the lethal pill. He was well aware of his fate as he tremblingly selected his dose, and Jefferson Hope's revenge was half complete. The killing of Stangerson would have been done in the same fashion—with the choice between a harmless and a deadly pellet—had not Stangerson leaped out of bed and attacked Hope, with the result that Hope stabbed him in self-defense. Hope is now perfectly willing to die, as he knows he must.

Chap. 14. Sherlock Holmes explains how he knew the cabby's name, and how he knew that this was the killer. He communicated with the police in Cleveland and learned that at one time Drebber and Stangerson had asked for protection against one Jefferson Hope—an old rival in love, who was then in Europe. The woman's ring indicated a love story. The cab tracks indicated that the killer was working as a cabby. All that remained was to find a cab driver named Jefferson Hope. This mission was accomplished by the street urchins of the neighborhood, whom Holmes often used for errands where an older person would arouse suspicion. The magistrate's court to arraign Jefferson Hope never convened, because the overworked heart finally stopped beating just a day or two after the arrest was made. And, as Sherlock Holmes had predicted, all credit was given to Lestrade and Gregson.

She Stoops to Conquer

Play by Oliver Goldsmith, 1728–1774. Produced 1773.

THIS PLAY is almost invariably classed among the top four or five plays of the 18th century. Oliver Goldsmith was one of the leading wits of his times and could sustain fascinating dialogue through five acts. *She Stoops to Conquer* employed the time-honored theatrical technique of getting everything as confused as possible as early as possible and then working out the confusion as slowly as possible, preferably leaving it unresolved until the last minute of the last scene.

Act I. 1. Mr. and Mrs. HARDCASTLE engage in a long, frank debate about each other's weaknesses. Hardcastle criticizes his wife both for her age and her wastrel son, TONY LUMPKIN, the product of an earlier marriage. Mrs. Hardcastle counters by charging her husband with longwindedness. Miss KATE HARDCASTLE is told by her father that he has arranged a suitor for her, one MARLOW, son of his old friend Sir CHARLES MARLOW. Kate excitedly tells her cousin CONSTANCE NEVILLE. Miss Neville is pleased, because her own suitor, GEORGE HASTINGS, is a close friend of Marlow's. 2. Tony Lumpkin sings ribald songs at the nearby tavern. Hastings and Marlow arrive, seeking the Hardcastle house. Mischievously, Tony tells them that the house is far away and advises them to go to an inn, but actually directs them to the Hardcastle house.

Act II. Upon arriving at the house, Marlow and Hastings conduct themselves very arrogantly, treating all there as the staff of an inn. Mr. Hardcastle, who welcomes them hospitably, cannot understand their rudeness. Miss Neville appears and Hastings realizes that they have been tricked. He and Miss Neville secretly decide to fall in with the ruse by not telling Marlow. When the elegant Miss Hardcastle appears, the unsuspecting Marlow begins a staid, reserved courtship. Hastings learns from Mrs. Hardcastle herself that Tony is supposed to be courting Miss Neville. Tony quickly tells Hastings he will abandon the struggle.

Act III. Mr. Hardcastle finds Marlow too impudent to be his son-in-law, and Kate finds Marlow too cold. She decides to masquerade as a serving-girl and test his reaction. Miss Neville, who has misplaced her jewels, provokes Tony into stealing Mrs. Hardcastle's gems and presenting them to her. Mrs. Hardcastle discovers the theft and cries "Thief!" throughout the house. Kate approaches Marlow disguised as a barmaid. Marlow is fascinated by the "barmaid." Mr. Hardcastle interrupts the pair in the middle of a kiss, frightening Marlow away. Kate promises to show her father her suitor's modest side.

Act IV. Hastings and Miss Neville intend to use Mrs. Hardcastle's jewels to finance their elopement. Hastings gives them to Marlow, who is to arrange for a coach and horses. Marlow entrusts them to a servant and the servant hands them over to Mrs. Hardcastle for safekeeping, so the gems find their way back to their original owner. Mr. Hardcastle complains about Marlow's drunken servants. Marlow resents the "innkeeper's" impudence and demands his bill. Then at last he is made to realize that he has been a guest in his father's friend's house. Hardcastle demands his immediate departure. Marlow sees Kate, who affirms that the house belongs to the Hardcastle family but pretends to be a poor relative who acts as a servant. Marlow shows genuine pity for her poor condition and thereby insures her love. Kate vows that since she has "stooped to conquer," she is determined to have Marlow as her husband. A letter arrives for Tony, who has agreed to help in the elopement, from Hastings. Miss Neville tries to prevent Mrs. Hardcastle from seeing it, but Mrs. Hardcastle intercepts it and reads Hastings' message—that the horses

have not arrived. Enraged, she accuses her son and niece of deception, for she had tried to arrange their marriage. Tony promises to vindicate his failure by appearing two hours later in the garden with a new plan. Then he bundles Miss Neville off to another aunt, where she will be more secure.

Act V. 1. As Hastings leaves for his appointment with Tony, Sir Charles Marlow arrives to check up on his son's progress in courtship. On seeing his old friend, Mr. Hardcastle immediately forgets about young Marlow's impudence. Marlow comes to apologize sincerely to Mr. Hardcastle. When asked about his progress with Kate, Marlow says that they have not been intimate; for he still has not penetrated Kate's barmaid disguise. But Kate later gives the old gentlemen a different story and suggests that they hide behind a screen and learn who is telling the truth. 2. Tony has taken Mrs. Hardcastle and Miss Neville on

a whirlwind ride and then has deposited them in their own garden, making them think they are 40 miles from home. Mrs. Hardcastle struggles through the shrubbery in a state of exhaustion, while Hastings goes to claim his bride. Mr. Hardcastle rides by the garden, sees his wife, and informs her that she is home. Mrs. Hardcastle chases Tony off into the woods. 3. Mr. Hardcastle and Sir Charles hide behind a screen. Marlow confesses his passionate love for Kate. His father steps out and eventually Marlow learns that Kate has been posing as the barmaid. Marlow vows to leave the house in shame. Mrs. Hardcastle has accepted the elopement, but the elopers appear to ask her approval. Mr. Hardcastle reveals that Tony has been an adult for three months and can choose his own wife. Tony immediately relinquishes his hold upon Miss Neville, who becomes free to wed Hastings. Marlow has forgotten his shame and indignation and Kate consents to be his bride.

Showboat

Novel by Edna Ferber, 1887–1968. Published 1926 by Doubleday & Co., New York. © 1926 by Edna Ferber.

OF THE MANY novels and plays Edna Ferber has written, *Showboat* is the most logical candidate for immortality. Helped along by a great operetta based on it, with music by Jerome Kern and words by Oscar Hammerstein II, the novel retains its interest year after year. The setting is a colorful one, the characters are sympathetic, and the conclusion is a natural, not a forced one. It seems that for a novelist whom the higher-browed critics seldom mention, Edna Ferber has written an uncommon number of books with a broad American panorama not elsewhere adequately treated. *Showboat* is one of them.

Chaps. 1–4. MAGNOLIA RAVENAL, born Magnolia Hawks, grew up with the Mississippi river her backyard and the *Cotton Blossom,* the showboat of her father, Captain ANDY HAWKS, as her home. Between Magnolia and her father there is the strong bond of affection and mutual understanding that always exists between a henpecked husband and a harassed child of a shrew such as PARTHY ANN HAWKS. Parthy Ann wanted a proper life of bread bakings, Sunday prayer meetings, and white dimity curtains at the kitchen windows. The most serious quarrel of their married life is over the purchase of the *Cotton Blossom.* Belligerently Parthy Ann has defied the beauty and adventure of showboat life. But Magnolia has loved it all from the very beginning and she loves the people who form the little company of entertainers. There are

JULIE DOZIER, the finest actress on the river; ELLY CHIPLEY, the ingenue lead, who appears on the bills as LENORE LA VERNE; and DOC, who is their front man.

Chaps. 5–9. When April comes, the *Cotton Blossom* starts on its tour. To the farmers and villagers on the banks of the Mississippi it brings music, romance, gaiety. Mrs. Hawks and Magnolia spend most of their time aboard. Magnolia's schooling is attended to by her mother. Geography is her best subject, for she lives it. For the little girl, these are days of enchantment. For her mother, the life holds some compensation, for she has an entire boatload of people to boss. The *Cotton Blossom* gains a reputation as the sternest-disciplined, best managed and most generously provisioned boat in the business. Mrs. Andy Hawks is known as a holy terror.

Each day there are rehearsals and preparations. When evening comes, the showboat turns into a fairyland for Magnolia. She knows every part of every play in the repertoire. At 13, Magnolia has the theater in her blood. From Queenie, the Cotton Blossom's easy-going cook, she learns to sing Negro spirituals. But it is to Julie that she gives her heart. They spend long, lazy days together talking of nothing at all. Julie is in love with her tall, blond husband, STEVE, and they are rarely apart. Tragedy enters Magnolia's life when the showboat arrives at Lemoyne, Julie's birthplace, and it becomes known that Julie had a white father but colored mother. There is a law against miscegenation. Steve makes a cut in Julie's flesh and sucks blood from it before the entire troupe. When the sheriff arrives to arrest them, Captain Andy can now testify that Steve also has Negro blood in him. However, Julie and Steve leave the *Cotton Blossom* at the next port, and Magnolia's heart is broken.

Inevitably, when she is old enough Magnolia becomes an actress in the *Cotton Blossom Floating Theatre*. Elly runs away with a gambler in Mobile. Parthy Ann has hysterics and takes to her bed, but Magnolia simply takes Elly's place. Her mother finally accepts the fact that her daughter is an actress and a good one. A year later, Captain Andy loses his leading man. Desperate, with a performance the next day, he comes upon GAYLORD RAVENAL, a casual, elegant man with an air of distinction. A river gambler by profession, Ravenal is on notice to leave New Orleans. He has killed a man, and though it was in self-defense he must get out. He accepts Captain Andy's offer when he sees Magnolia—already a beauty at 18. Magnolia has never met a man like Ravenal. He is gentle and a little weak but with strong personal attractiveness. The showboat amuses and interests him, and with little effort he becomes the best juvenile lead on the river. Women have always adored him and Magnolia is no exception. There is little opportunity for them to be alone, for Mrs. Hawks is ever vigilant. Though Ravenal regards his life as an actor as temporary, he keeps putting off his departure because he has fallen in love with Magnolia.

Chaps. 10–14. Ravenal did not mean to fall in love, and most assuredly he never meant to marry, but he had never met a woman like Magnolia. Their romantic scenes together give them opportunity to express themselves. Captain Andy likes Ravenal and is not displeased when Magnolia runs off one afternoon and marries him, but Mrs. Hawks hates her son-in-law and treats him like a criminal. But Magnolia is in love, and even the knowledge that her husband is a professional gambler does not dim her happiness.

Magnolia dreads the idle winter months. The Hawks family has always returned to their little New England home, but this is impossible for Gaylord Ravenal. Magnolia lives the life of a gambler's wife. They move constantly. They rise at noon and retire in the morning. There are days when they are rich and other days when they are poor. With it all, she is a happy woman, beloved and in love.

Captain Andy builds a new *Cotton Blossom*. Magnolia has a daughter, who is named KIM because she is born at the Kentucky-Illinois-Missouri boundary. There follow four years of war and peace. Ravenal is content with his life except for his mother-in-law. The end of this period comes with Captain Andy's death. He is swept overboard in a dense fog. It surprises everyone that Mrs. Hawks wishes to continue on the river, but the Mississippi holds her as it did her husband and she appoints herself commander of the *Cotton Blossom Floating Palace Theatre*. Ravenal tries to accommodate himself to the new regime but finally he tells his wife to choose between her mother and him. She goes with him. Mrs. Hawks, at parting, wants Magnolia to retain her financial share in the

showboat, but Ravenal prefers to sell their share outright.

The money lasts about a year. After that, the ups and downs depend on Ravenal's gambling luck. It is remarkable that Mag-

Ravenal and Magnolia

nolia adapts to this life so easily, but she is interested, alert, eager, and in love with her husband. Her life on the river has accustomed her to the unusual. They often go from luxury to sordidness in a single day.

In such a life, Magnolia cannot make friends and her days are spent with Kim. She longs for the river and misses her mother, who she knows loves her and Kim.

Chaps. 15–19. There is the problem of Kim, her education and future. Magnolia wants security for her child. She asks Ravenal if she can return to the stage, but

he just laughs. She takes matters into her own hands and places Kim in a convent, where Kim appears to be happy. It is just in time, for Chicago is reformed and Ravenal's way of living is no more. Their fortunes are at lowest ebb but there is between them a curious and terrifying thing, a love bond that cannot be broken. At this bad time Mrs. Hawks decides to visit them. Magnolia has hidden their reverses from her mother and she is frightened at the coming visit. Ravenal leaves their small room to borrow money and returns many hours later, drunk and with $2,000. He borrowed $1,000 from Chicago's most notorious madam and with luck at the gaming tables, he doubled his stake. Magnolia repays the $1,000 loan and receives a receipt. For a fleeting second, the woman who writes the receipt for the owner of the brothel reminds Magnolia of her beloved Julie. It is only later that she realizes it really was Julie. With her courage still high, Magnolia goes to one of the variety houses to obtain a job in vaudeville. She sings the songs that old Queenie, the *Cotton Blossom* cook, taught her. She is hired. When she returns home, she finds a note from Ravenal. He has left her and she never sees him again. He dies in San Francisco before he can return to her. Magnolia Ravenal becomes famous for her Negro spirituals. Kim grows up to be an actress and a famous one. Her marriage with KENNETH CAMERON is happy and nice, but somehow Magnolia feels that her daughter is missing something. Mrs. Hawks dies in her 90th year and Magnolia returns to the showboat for her funeral. The river again grips her and, instead of returning to New York, she stays for the rest of the *Cotton Blossom's* tour. Kim and her husband come to persuade her to return but she refuses. Mrs. Hawks has left a great deal of money and Magnolia gives it to Kim. For herself she keeps the Mississippi.

Silas Marner

Novel by George Eliot (Mary Ann Evans Croft, 1819–1880). Published 1861. (PB, PL27)

NEARLY EVERY schoolboy and schoolgirl has to read *Silas Marner* at some time or other before getting out of high school. It is an ideal selection from the works of George Eliot, because it is not overlong, it is a real thriller, and it exploits the character of a miser, which is inexplicably one of those subjects of universal appeal. It has a happy ending and virtue triumphs. At the same time it is a novel by a major novelist with the expected authentic pictures of the time (early 19th century) and the country and people (rural England) depicted. One should not avoid reading it even if his school permits him to.

Part I. Chap. 1. In the early years of the 19th century, a linen weaver called SILAS MARNER lived in a stone cottage near the village of Raveloe. Silas had come to Raveloe 15 years before from a town farther north, but the simple and ignorant country folk still regarded him with suspicion, as they did all who were not native to the area. But he was the only linen weaver available to the district and all the housewives and cottagers brought him their little stocks of yarn to weave. At Raveloe Silas did not change outwardly but he changed within himself greatly. Before he came he was accustomed to the close fellowship of an artisan who is also a member of a narrow religious sect. He was very highly thought of in that world. At that time Silas was engaged to a young servant woman named SARAH and had a friend in his church named WILLIAM DANE. Silas had a trusting nature and did not perceive William's

The miser counts his gold

true character until it was too late. William turned the whole community against Silas by making it seem that he had murdered an old, ill deacon and stolen his money. Silas was judged guilty by the brethren of his community, but Silas knew that William was in fact the evildoer. He lost faith in his world and abandoned it, and Sarah had married William.

Chap. 2. So Silas came to Raveloe. He helped the cobbler's wife recover from a disease that had killed Silas's mother, so that he knew something about it. But the ignorant folk around him attributed his knowledge to occult powers and regarded him with fear—and with resentment when he refused to perform "charms" on other neighbors who fell ill. Silas came to be isolated except in his work, from which the money began to pile up. Gradually, for want of anything better, the accumulation of gold became Silas's absorbing passion. Now he keeps all his wealth hidden in the floor of his cottage. Each night he takes it out and counts his guineas.

Chap. 3. The greatest man in Raveloe is Squire CASS. He is a widower and lives in a large house with his sons, GODFREY, the elder, and DUNSTAN, or DUNSEY, the younger. They have turned out rather poorly. Godfrey wanted to marry a neighbor's daughter, Miss NANCY LAMMETER, but he entangled himself with a common woman, MOLLY FARREN, and as a result of some drunken goings-on he married her and had a child by her. His marriage is still a secret except to his unscrupulous younger brother, Dunsey, who takes every opportunity to blackmail Godfrey. Most recently he has forced Godfrey to give him his favorite hunter, Wildfire, to sell at the hunt meet.

Chap. 4. On his way to sell Wildfire, Dunstan passes Silas Marner's cottage and thinks it would be a good idea to have Godfrey force Silas to lend him some money. Then Dunsey could get it from Godfrey. Dunsey rides Wildfire to the hunt. He takes one jump too many and Wildfire is killed. Now Dunsey's desire for Marner's money becomes pressing. Dunstan walks by the cottage, finds Marner away, and steals the old man's money.

Chaps. 5–7. Silas returns from a brief errand to the village. When he goes to get out his gold it is gone. At first he cannot believe his eyes, but after fruitless searchings he realizes that he has been robbed. He rushes to the nearby inn, the Rainbow. He believes the thief must be JEM RODNEY, a poacher of the neighborhood. But Jem Rodney has been sitting in the inn all the time so it is obvious that Marner was mistaken. Silas goes to the constable's house.

Chap. 8. Marner's robbery is the talk of the village. The only clue is the discovery of a tinder box near Silas's house. Meanwhile Godfrey learns that Dunstan has disappeared and that Wildfire has been killed. He decides to tell everything to his father.

Chaps. 9–10. Godfrey tries, but unsuccessfully, to confess to his father. It seems quite likely that the squire will make a proposal of marriage to Nancy's father on Godfrey's behalf and Godfrey is appalled at the thought. Meanwhile Silas is utterly forlorn and lost without his gold. Yet the former antagonism of his neighbors is partly dissipated by their new sympathy for him. They try to be neighborly at Christmas and to persuade him to come to church and be more neighborly himself. Mrs. DOLLY WINTHROP in particular, and her little son of 7, AARON, visit Marner and try to sway him from his lonely sadness. But Silas cannot yet respond to people. Dunstan is still absent from the village. Godfrey looks forward to seeing Nancy over Christmas and New Year festivities but has no solution for his unfortunate situation.

Chaps. 11–13. On New Year's Eve Squire Cass gives a big party. Godfrey dances with Nancy and tries to find out if she might forgive him for past mistakes. She does not sound too reassuring. Meanwhile his wife Molly is making her way to Raveloe, with Godfrey's child in her arms. She plans exposure of the husband who had refused to acknowledge her. But she takes too much opium, which is her evil demon, and lies down to rest in the snow, with the child clutched to her. The place she chooses is near Silas's cottage. The child falls from its unconscious mother's grasp and crawls to the cottage, where it is discovered by Marner with amazement and pleasure. He then discovers the woman, who seems dead.

Carrying the child with him, he rushes off to Squire Cass's house to summon help. Godfrey recognizes the baby but is pleased when his wife is found to have died, for this leaves only Dunstan knowing of his marriage. He decides that while he will look out for the child, he will not acknowledge it. Silas Marner decides to keep the baby and take care of her. "It's a lone thing and I'm a lone thing," he declares.

Chaps. 14–15. Silas names the child HEPZIBAH and she is called EPPIE. The child leads Silas out of himself and back to becoming a social being. All the neighbors want to be helpful, Dolly Winthrop most of all. Godfrey is watchful of the child but plans to marry his Nancy, for as yet Dunsey has not reappeared.

Part II. Chaps. 16–17. It is 16 years since Silas Marner found Eppie. They are as close and affectionate a pair as could be found.

Marner is older and more feeble. His adopted daughter has become a very pretty young woman. She has plans to marry Aaron Winthrop, who has become a gardener, and live with him and Marner in Marner's cottage. She knows all about her past, except who her father was. She is a happy and lovely young woman and Marner's cottage has become a very cozy place. Much of its furniture was sent over from Godfrey Cass's house. Godfrey and Nancy are married but childless. Nancy has refused to adopt a child while Godfrey has always hoped to adopt Eppie, never fully realizing the deep affection between her and Silas.

Chap. 18. Godfrey comes home white and trembling to tell Nancy that his brother's skeleton has been found in the stone pit near Marner's cottage. With the body was Silas's money. At last the thief has been found. Godfrey now realizes that everything comes to light sometime and he tells Nancy of his former marriage and of Eppie's paternity. Nancy is sorry she did not know sooner, so that they could adopt Eppie. They go together to see Silas Marner.

Chaps. 19–20. Godfrey and Nancy ask Silas for Eppie. He lets the child make her choice. She has no desire to became "a lady" and would not for the world leave Silas and the future life she has planned. Silas is relieved. Godfrey resigns himself to not having a child. This is all that Nancy needs to feel happy, for the two love each other greatly.

Chap. 21. Silas and Eppie visit Silas's old home and he is amazed to see how ugly it looks to him. The old meeting place where Silas was the victim of injustice has been replaced by a factory. Silas goes back to Raveloe very happy. His trust in the goodness of the world has been restored. Eppie marries Aaron and everything ends very happily for all concerned.

Sister Carrie

Novel by Theodore Dreiser, 1871–1945.

Published 1900 by Doubleday & Co., New York. (ML, 8; RE, 86)

IN AMERICAN LITERATURE this is an important book, credited with influencing all modern American novelists. Among Dreiser's works it is not so famous as *An American Tragedy*, but it created much more of a stir when it was published. It was the start of the "realistic" school of the novel. In fact, it was considered so shocking that distribution was long held up by the unofficial censorship that controlled sales in those days. Today, *Sister Carrie* would be considered a run-of-the-mill kind of theme with a more-or-less happy ending, which statement is not intended to detract from the excellence of the work or its author.

Chaps. 1–5. On an August afternoon in 1889, CAROLINE (CARRIE) MEEBER, 18 years old, bright, timid, and full of the illusions of youth, boards the train for Chicago with a small trunk and a yellow snap-purse containing her ticket, a scrap of paper with her sister's address, and $4 in cash. On the train, she meets CHARLES DROUET, a dashing, somewhat flashy traveling salesman, a man who, in spite of his boldness, is quite a genial sort. She tells him she is going to try to find employment in Chicago, and when he offers to take her around the city she gives him her sister's address and accepts his card. When they arrive, Drouet bids her goodbye; then firm reality, in the form of her non-nonsense sister, MINNIE, grips her hand and leads her to a shabby flat. On the first evening, Carrie realizes that life here cannot be the gay wonderful existence of which she has dreamed. Minnie's life is a dreary, steady round of toil. Her husband is a grim, hard-working man who goes to bed and rises early. Carrie realizes that she cannot possibly allow Drouet to come there. Her sister would not approve of him or of Carrie's flirtation with him. So she writes him a note, telling him that the flat is too small for company and that he must wait to see her until he hears from her again. The next morning, Carrie sets out to find work as a shopgirl. After many rebuffs and disappointments she finds a job in a shoe factory at $4.50 a week. On her first day Carrie finds the work hard, the atmosphere unpleasant, and her fellow-workers quite different from the simple folk she has always known.

Chaps. 6–10. Of her $4.50, Carrie has to pay her sister $4 for room and board. The little she has left is not enough to buy a warm jacket, nor even to pay Carrie's carfare to and from work. On the first cold day Carrie catches cold. When she recovers three days later it is taken for granted that she has lost her job and she starts looking for another. Days go by and still she finds nothing. Her sister and brother-in-law, unwilling to keep her now that she cannot pay her way, suggest that she return home for the winter. And then, one day, while she is looking for work, Carrie runs into Drouet. He takes one look at her poor clothes and pale face and realizes that she is badly in need of money. He takes her to dinner and insists that she take $20 to buy new shoes and a warm jacket. Carrie hesitates but he prevails on her and the next day he accompanies her to the stores and buys her wonderful new clothes. She tells him of her troubles at her sister's flat and he urges her to let him provide a room for her. She finally agrees, for she cannot bear to spend any more time where she is so plainly unwanted. That night she leaves a note for her sister and goes to sleep alone in the little room Drouet has rented for her. In the days that follow, he takes her all around town, showing her the interesting sights and keeping her entertained. At last she goes to live with him in his comfortable flat on Chicago's West Side. Drouet promises to marry her as soon as he gets back from his Denver trip in January.

Then, one day, Drouet introduces her to a friend, G. W. HURSTWOOD, the manager of a large saloon. Hurstwood is charming, clever, and well-off. He is married, though not happily so, and has two grown children; but Carrie does not know this.

Chaps. 11–13. By imitating those about her, Carrie has begun to get the hang of the little things that the pretty woman who has vanity invariably adopts. In a short time her knowledge of the graces has doubled and her appearance has changed. She has become a girl of considerable taste. Therefore when Hurstwood meets her he finds a young woman who is much more than the Carrie that Drouet first met and he wonders how Drouet ever came to win her. Hurstwood becomes increasingly interested in Carrie and she is very much impressed by him. Once, when Carrie, Drouet and Hurstwood are at the theater, Hurstwood's son sees him and reports the incident to his mother. Mrs. HURSTWOOD questions Hurstwood and is not altogether satisfied with his reply that he was out with an old friend and his wife. When Drouet goes on the road, Hurstwood begins to pay court to Carrie, whose youth and beauty attract him enormously. Carrie, who feels she owes much to Drouet, though she does not love him, accepts Hurstwood's attentions with some misgiving at first, but when he tells her that he needs her love, that there is nothing pleasant in his life, which is all work and worry with people who are nothing to him, she yields to his persuasive ways and confesses her affection for him.

Chaps. 14–19. When Drouet comes back he gets Carrie a part in a production of *Gaslight*, which his lodge is planning to put on. Until now the idea of going into the theater has never occurred to Carrie. This opportunity suddenly fires her ambition and she takes the whole thing quite seriously. Hurstwood persuades many of his friends to attend the performance and is eager that Carrie should come off well. She gets off to a slow start and seems quite bad, but by the third scene she gets into the spirit of the part and turns out to be extraordinarily good. Both her lovers are

Carrie's career in the theater begins in a chorus line

astonished to find this additional quality in her and each longs to have her for himself.

Chaps. 20–23. The next day, Drouet learns from a chambermaid that Carrie has been seeing Hurstwood alone. At the same time, Mrs. Hurstwood learns that her husband has been out driving with another woman and that he and his friends attended Carrie's performance the previous night. She confronts her husband with this knowledge and tells him she intends to sue for divorce. Drouet tells Carrie that he knows she has been seeing Hurstwood and warns her not to have anything to do with him, for he is a married man. Shocked beyond belief, Carrie blames Drouet for not having told her before. She threatens to leave him, but he tells her to stay. He will leave instead. He doesn't want to be played for a sucker.

Chaps. 24–28. Hurstwood knows that a divorce will mean social and financial ruin for him, but he cannot bear the thought of giving Carrie up. When he does not hear from her for several days he surmises that she has been told about his married condition. He receives a note from his wife's lawyer informing him that divorce proceedings are under way. Meanwhile, Carrie who has decided to look for work in the theater, writes to Hurstwood telling him she knows of his deception and cannot see him any more. But Hurstwood takes this as an indication that she loves him still. That night he happens to find his employer's safe unlocked. It occurs to him that the $10,000 it contains would enable him to get rid of his wife by giving her a huge settlement and still have enough left over to live quietly with Carrie for years. The temptation is too much for him. He takes the money and hurries to Carrie's apartment. By telling her that Drouet has been hurt in an accident, he manages to get her on a train bound for Montreal. After they are safely out of Chicago he confesses that Drouet has not been hurt and that he has used a ruse to get her to come with him. He cannot live without her. He has left his wife forever. Carrie consents to stay with him.

Chaps. 29–33. In Montreal Hurstwood is approached by an agent of his former employer, who urges him to return the money. Hurstwood finally decides to return all but a small sum. Then he marries Carrie under the assumed name of Wheeler and the two of them go to New York. There Hurstwood enters into a partnership with a saloon-keeper. His situation is greatly reduced and he is forced to live in a style quite different from the one he has been used to. Carrie becomes friendly with Mrs. VANCE, a neighbor and a woman of great elegance and style, who brings Carrie into her wealthy circle of friends. Carrie starts to think seriously about going on the stage. One day Hurstwood confesses to her that he has lost all his money.

Chaps. 34–45. Hurstwood looks eagerly for a job for several weeks, but then he becomes discouraged and spends more and more time at home. The bills pile up and Hurstwood begins to let his appearance run down. He wears old clothes around the house, so as not to wear out his good ones, and he goes without a shave because he is loath to spend the money for one. As his self-respect diminishes, so does Carrie's respect for him. At last, when they are down to their last $50, Carrie gets a job in a chorus line. Still Hurstwood does not find a job, and Carrie begins to resent having to support him. Shortly after the show opens, she takes a flat with a friend and leaves Hurstwood to fend for himself. Carrie's success in the theater grows. At first she has only small parts, but she gets more and more important rôles until she becomes a well-known actress. Hurstwood, meanwhile, has been going from bad to worse. Before long he finds himself living in the flophouses on the Bowery and begging for change from passers-by.

Chaps. 46–47. One day, Drouet comes to see Carrie at the theater and tells her about Hurstwood's theft of the $10,000. She is shocked, but she realizes Hurstwood took it for her; so, when Hurstwood approaches her, in rags, the following night, she takes pity on him and gives him money. Though she is a rich and famous actress, Carrie has not found happiness and she is not sure how to find it. Hurstwood's former wife and their children come to New York, eager for amusement, which they can buy with the money obtained long ago through Mrs. Hurstwood's divorce settlement with her husband. He had given her everything. Hurstwood dies and is buried in Potter's field, unknown to anyone who was ever close to him, including Carrie.

Six Characters in Search of an Author

Play by Luigi Pirandello, 1867–1936. Produced 1921. Published and © 1922 by E. P. Dutton & Co. Translated from the Italian by Edward Storer.

THIS PLAY by the Italian winner of the 1934 Nobel Prize was as much of a departure in its day as Thornton Wilder's *Our Town*, with a similarly barren setting, proved to be a quarter-century later, and by the standard of its times it was almost as much of a success. Next to *As You Desire Me*, it has been Pirandello's most popular play in the United States. It is more dramatic and more easily understandable by an audience than might appear from an outline.

Act I. On an empty stage, the MANAGER, the Actors, and the Prompter gather to rehearse a Pirandello play, *Mixing It Up*. The Manager, himself considerably confused as to the meaning of Pirandello's symbolism, vainly attempts to explain the action of a scene to the company. They are interrupted by the Six Characters, who have unceremoniously followed the DOORKEEPER onto the stage. They are THE FATHER, THE MOTHER, THE STEPDAUGHTER, THE SON, THE BOY (14 years old), and THE CHILD (about 4). The Father introduces the family as CHARACTERS in search of an author, and, ignoring the protests of the incredulous and impatient Manager, goes on to explain that they were *born* Characters, who bring the theater a drama, although there is no book to contain it. The author who created them, he maintains, was no longer able or willing to put them into a work of art. Here they are, therefore, driven by their inner passion and their only reality as Characters, to seek self-fulfillment in acting out their story. The Manager understands as little of this explanation as he does of the play he was rehearsing, but when the Characters, in a lively discussion among themselves, reveal their drama, he recognizes, almost in spite of himself, the theater potential of the situation, and listens with interest.

It appears that the Father, driven by the Demon of Experiment, himself persuaded the Mother to go and live with another man, his secretary, to whom she was attracted. He had the Son raised by a wet-nurse in the country, to have him grow up healthy and strong. After the Mother has left him, on his own prompting, he continues to watch over her and her new family, the Stepdaughter, the Boy, and the Child, from afar, to observe the success of his "experiment." In the meantime he is reduced to seek female companionship wherever he can find it for sale. When the secretary dies, the Mother returns with her family to the city of her former abode, without, however, giving the Father news of their presence. She accepts work in Madame PACE's establishment, where the Stepdaughter, too, is employed, ostensibly to model clothes and hats. One day the Father finds his way to Madame Pace's salon and is on the point of enjoying the embraces of the Stepdaughter, whose services he has unwittingly purchased with a 100-lire note, when the Mother's accidental arrival on the scene leads to the timely discovery of the horror-fraught situation. The Characters are especially anxious to re-enact the scene at Madame Pace's, and the Manager, now greatly intrigued, rushes them backstage to outline the plot for a version sufficiently coherent for the company to follow later when they will be asked to act it in their turn.

Act II. The Characters enact their drama to "demonstrate" for the actors, who stand around watching, not yet sure whether to take this new and absurd situation seriously or not. The Manager has asked the PROPERTY MAN to set up on stage a reasonably plausible facsimile of Madame Pace's parlor, but the Characters are not satisfied with the effect of unreality that has been achieved. They feel that basically the theater over-simplifies and conventionalizes reality into a farce of transparent pretense, far removed from the reality of individual men engaged in momentarily real units of action. It soon becomes apparent that there is no Madame Pace among the Six Characters to do her part in the drama. The Father, by arranging cloaks and hats on pegs to re-create a more forcefully real atmosphere, succeeds in almost magnetically drawing Madame Pace into the theater, to the bewildered amazement of the company, who describe her appearance as a "trick." The LEADING MAN and the LEADING LADY, in their crude imitation of the Characters' heartfelt and intimately lived drama, reveal all the ineffective make-believe and remoteness from reality of the theater. The act ends with the scene at Madame Pace's once more acted out by the Characters themselves, and on the

agonized cry of the Mother as she discovers the Stepdaughter and the Father.

Act III. The Stepdaughter tries to explain the relationship between the Mother and the Son. The Son, who considers himself the only "legitimate" member of the family among "intruders," keeps studiously aloof from the proceedings and is the only one

of the Characters who does not want to take part in the action of the drama. Clearly he is an "unrealized" character, a failure of his author. The Manager shows increasing signs of irritation as the Father questions the "existence" of anyone except the Characters themselves, who have no other reality beyond illusion. The Manager nevertheless

proceeds to rehearse the Characters' drama in a different setting, a garden near a fountain. The Mother explains that she has gone to see the Son to make him understand her conduct. The Son leaves her, to avoid "a scene." A little later he comes upon her just in time to pull her out of the fountain. He sees with horror the body of the Child floating on the water. Soon after, a shot is heard, and, as the Manager and his company rush to the rear of the stage, they find the body of the Boy, who has shot himself, as it were, *in* the scene and *on* the scene. The Manager exclaims that illusion and reality can no longer be told apart. He has had enough. He has frittered away a whole day on these—"people!"

The Sketch Book of Geoffrey Crayon

Short stories by Washington Irving, 1783–1859.
Published 1819–1820.

IF NOTHING MORE could be said of it, the "*Sketchbook*" would still have unchallenged right to lasting fame because it has contributed to its country two peerless characters of folklore, Rip Van Winkle and the Headless Horseman. As was his custom in his early years, Washington Irving wrote these stories under a pseudonym. This time it was Geoffrey Crayon, Gent., and he acknowledged in the book contributions from his earlier pseudonymous author, Diedrich Knickerbocker. The stories are good stories, well told, and an essential part of Americana.

THE VOYAGE

The long ocean voyage that a traveler from America to Europe must make is a very good preparation for the excitement of new scenes. Suspended between two worlds, he may meditate on his past life and the future. "I delighted to loll over the quarter-railing, or climb to the main-top, of a calm day, and muse for hours together on the tranquil bosom of a summer's sea." Then there are sudden unexpected adventures, such as the sight of a distant sail or a drifting mast. What thoughts this mast can bring with it—a dreadful shipwreck, and all the dismal stories other travelers have to tell. Finally there is the great moment—arrival at the pier, thronged with eager waiting friends and relatives. With what joy a waiting wife spies her sailor husband! "I alone was solitary and idle. I had no friend to meet, no cheering to receive. I stepped upon the land of my forefathers, but felt that I was a stranger in the land."

THE WIFE

"Those disasters which break down the spirit of a man, and prostrate him in the dust, seem to call forth all the energies of

the softer sex, and give such intrepidity and elevation to their character that at times it approaches to sublimity." These thoughts have come to the author because of the experience of his intimate friend, LESLIE. Leslie married a beautiful girl with whom he was very much in love. She had no fortune, but Leslie was wealthy enough to indulge her every whim and desire. Then, through no fault of his own, Leslie's wealth was swept away. Now he cannot bear to think of his dear wife living a hard, unlovely life of poverty, and he is in despair. The author advises Leslie to confide in MARY, his wife, for should not those we love share our troubles as well as our joys. Leslie follows this advice and is overwhelmed by the strength and sweetness with which Mary accepts their reverses. She makes things so cheerful and agreeable that when his fortunes later improve, Leslie still considers this the happiest time of his life.

RIP VAN WINKLE

This tale was found among the papers of Diedrich Knickerbocker [a pen name Irving sometimes used]. At the foot of the

Mary accepts the reverses

Kaatskill mountains, in a little Dutch village, lives the good-natured RIP VAN WINKLE. All the children love him and "not a dog would bark at him"; he is "a kind neighbor, and an obedient henpecked husband." Rip does not like to work and would much rather fish and hunt. To escape his wife's constant nagging, he takes his dog, WOLF, and goes off into the woods. One day Rip climbs to the top of one of the highest of the Kaatskills hunting for squirrel. As he is about to return home he hears someone calling his name. He spies a short fellow with a grizzled beard and bushy hair, dressed in an old-fashioned Dutch costume. He is carrying a keg up the steep mountain. Rip helps this strange fellow and when they come to a hollow in the mountain Rip sees an odd-looking company playing ninepins. They look just like the figures in an old Flemish painting hanging on the wall in the village parson's parlor. As they roll the balls in their game, it sounds like thunder. Rip serves them wine from the keg, and soon he himself is tempted to take a sip. One sip follows another and Rip falls fast asleep.

When he wakes, Rip looks for his gun. To his surprise it is rusty and wormeaten. He calls for Wolf, but no dog comes. His joints are stiff as he begins to make his way home, worried about what his wife will say. As Rip approaches the village, he meets people he has never seen before. They are strangely dressed and they stare at him most curiously. Rip becomes aware that his beard is a foot long! His house is decayed and a strange dog snarls at him. In front of the inn there is a flag Rip has never seen before, with stars and stripes on it. On the sign where the face of King George used to gaze down on all, there is someone called General Washington, wearing a funny cocked hat.

Rip is bewildered. He inquires for his friends and finds they are all dead or gone away. He wonders if anyone knows Rip van Winkle, and a lazy, ragged man is pointed out to him: "That's Rip van Winkle yonder, leaning against the tree." Finally an old woman recognizes him and Rip tells his story. It seems that he has been asleep for 20 years and the man leaning against the tree is his son. Many people shake their heads and do not believe his tale. Old PETER VANDERDONK, however, recognizes Rip and says he knows for a fact that the Kaatskill mountains have always been haunted. Rip's daughter takes him to live with her and he soon makes friends with the young people of the village. He tells his story to one and all, and while there are some doubters, the old Dutch inhabitants believe him. "Even to this day they never hear a thunderstorm of a summer afternoon about the Kaatskill but they say Hendrik Hudson and his crew are at their game of ninepins; and it is a common wish of all henpecked husbands in the neighborhood, when life hangs heavy on their hands, that they might have a quieting draught out of Rip van Winkle's flagon."

THE LEGEND OF SLEEPY HOLLOW

Not far from Tarry Town there is a little valley "which is one of the quietest places in the whole world." It is called Sleepy Hollow. The people there seem to be under some kind of spell and believe all sorts of marvelous and strange stories having to do with visions and spirits. "The dominant spirit, however, that haunts this enchanted region, and seems to be commander-in-chief of all the powers of the air, is the apparition of a figure on horseback without a head."

In a remote time, "that is to say, some thirty years since" a man by the name of ICHABOD CRANE lived in Sleepy Hollow. He was the schoolteacher and also the singing master and also he helped the farmers with their work. Still Ichabod Crane was very poor. He believed in all the tales of ghosts and goblins, including the fearful tale of the Headless Horseman of Sleepy Hollow. Ichabod, who has "a soft and foolish heart," falls in love with his pretty pupil, KATRINA VAN TASSEL. Katrina's father is very well off and this adds to her attractions in the eyes of Ichabod. Unfortunately, BROM VAN BRUNT, a large and powerful fellow with a "waggish good humor," is also in love with Katrina. Brom BONES (as he is called) is very jealous of Ichabod. The rivals are invited to a quilting frolic at Katrina's house and Ichabod dances with Katrina while Brom Bones broods in a corner. Then everyone tells ghost stories and Brom boasts that he has met and challenged "the headless horseman" to a race.

As Ichabod returns home after the party he meets a silent horseman. He sees in the moonlight that the horseman is carrying his head on the pommel of the saddle in front of him. Ichabod flees in terror, wildly spurring on his old horse, Gunpowder. Then he sees the horseman fling the ghastly head after him. The head strikes poor Ichabod and sends him sprawling. After this, Ichabod disappears. Several years later an old farmer brings news that he is alive. Meantime, however, Brom Bones is safely married to Katrina and whenever the story is mentioned or anyone mentions "pumpkin" he is observed to laugh heartily. "The old country wives, however, who are the best judges of these matters, maintain to this day that Ichabod was spirited away by supernatural means; and it is a favorite story often told about the neighborhood round the winter evening fire."

THE SPECTER-BRIDEGROOM

On a wild and romantic mountain in Upper Germany stands the castle of Baron VON LANDSHORT. "The baron, though a small man, had a large soul, and it swelled with satisfaction at the consciousness of being the greatest man in the little world about him." The Baron has one beautiful and accomplished daughter. He has arranged a marriage for his daughter to Count VON ALTENBURG, and a glorious celebration is about to take place. Meanwhile the bridegroom and his friend, HERMAN VON STARKENFAUST, are traveling through a forest on their way to the castle and the

The horseman flings his head

bride. They are attacked by robbers and the bridegroom is mortally wounded. Before he dies he makes his friend von Starkenfaust swear that he will proceed to the castle to report the tragedy.

At the castle the feast is getting cold and everyone is anxious. A strange cavalier appears on a black steed and everyone rejoices because, naturally, they think the bridegroom has arrived. Before von Starkenfaust can explain who he is, he is carried off to the banquet. He meets the bride and is enchanted by her lovely face and sweet manner. Yet as the feast progresses the stranger maintains "a most singular and unseasonable gravity." To entertain the company, tales of the supernatural (of which the baron is especially fond) are told. The stranger makes ready to depart and the baron, protesting, follows him to the courtyard. The stranger tells the baron he must leave: "My engagement is with no bride—the worms! the worms expect me! I am a dead man—I have been slain by robbers—my body lies at Wurtzburg—at midnight I am to be buried—the grave is waiting for me—I must keep my appointment." The grief of the bride is great, as she loves the stranger. Two nights later from her chamber window she sees his figure and screams. Her aunt, who is sharing her chamber, learns what has occurred but is pledged to secrecy. One week later the baron's fair daughter disappears. Confusion and consternation reign in the castle until suddenly the baron's daughter gallops into the courtyard accompanied by the Specter Bridegroom, who is none other than Herman von Starkenfaust. He explains that he could not reveal the news of the true bridegroom's death and how he fell instantly in love with the fair maiden and how he wooed and won her and that they have been secretly married. The baron happily pardons the young couple and the festivities begin again, this time with a real bridegroom instead of a specter.

Soldiers of Fortune

> *Novel by* Richard Harding Davis, 1864–1916.
> Published 1897.
>
> RICHARD HARDING DAVIS was the most famous American war correspondent of his time. His assignments abroad, in and after the Spanish-American War, endowed his novels with special authority. In other respects they were just adventure novels such as any good magazine might buy at any time to serialize. *Soldiers of Fortune* was his best.

Chap. 1. At a dinner party at the home of some friends, ALICE LANGHAM meets a most interesting man, ROBERT CLAY, a westerner or "cowboy." Conversing with him, she learns that he is a civil and mining engineer and has been building an important railroad in Mexico. He confides that he knows about her, though this is their first meeting, because he has read of her début four years before and has carried her picture about with him and watched for news of her ever since. He tells her he is leaving the next day for South America. When Alice gets home she asks her father about Clay and learns that the job Clay is leaving to do is for a company her father owns.

Chaps. 2–3. A year earlier, Clay discovered a vast iron deposit in Olancho, a small republic on the northeast coast of South America. He interested Mr. LANGHAM in setting up a company to exploit the mine, and, the first man sent out having been unsuccessful, Clay, now free, has been

Clay defies Mendoza

commissioned, at a good fee, to take over the job. Overcoming the mismanagement and corruption, Clay placates the natives, both workers and politicians, and within six months has the mine in humming activity. Young TEDDY LANGHAM arrives to learn the mining business and look after his father's interests, and one day Teddy announces that his father and sisters are coming down to spend the winter in Valencia, the capital city nearby. As a surprise, the men build a beautiful house near the mines for the family. One night the leader of the opposition party, General MENDOZA, visits. He threatens to confiscate the mine on the grounds that the people are not satisfied with their share of the revenues, but he indicates willingness to take a bribe for his silence. Clay, who has had witnesses outside, defies him and drives him away. Mendoza vows he will engineer a revolution and take over the mines by force. The politicians in power all are quite friendly, however, and eager to welcome the Langham family. The day the Langhams arrive brings a big storm and the welcoming party is spoiled. But that evening, under the stars, Clay and Alice walk and talk, and she tells him she wants to be his friend. Clay realizes he is falling in love. Later in the evening they are startled to see entering the harbor the yacht of REGGIE KING, an old friend of Alice's and a potential suitor. Clay, at first upset by this arrival, soon realizes that he has his own intrinsic worth and need not be afraid of competition.

Chaps. 4–5. A few days later Clay takes the Langhams and King on a tour of the city and neighboring countryside. They visit the Presidential Palace, meet President and Mme. ÁLVAREZ, and are introduced to Captain STUART, an Englishman, who is commander of the President's household troops and responsible for his safety. At dinner that evening, Stuart and HOPE, Alice's younger sister, pair off, while Clay tries to turn his conversation with Alice to a personal vein. Alice, however, puts him off and tells him he must know far more about his feelings for her before he can talk so. Later, Hope tells Alice many interesting facts about Clay's background and exploits, which she has heard from Stuart; but Alice pretends lack of interest. Clay takes the visitors on an inspection trip through the mine workings, and despite Alice's attempt to attract his attention pays

little heed to her. Alice learns something of the local political background. The talk is that President Álvarez, incited by his ambitious wife, plans soon to proclaim himself dictator. The opposition, led by General Mendoza, may fight. Clay is trying to wean away from Mendoza a group of local soldiers who work at the mine, so that they will be available for protection in an emergency. Hope, who is a more vivacious girl than Alice, attracts Clay's attention at this time by her recognition of the tremendous job he has done in getting the mine into production. Alice is much more reserved and shows little appreciation.

Chaps. 6–7. Clay stays away from Alice for a week, but then she seeks him out. She chides him for paying little attention to her when she visited the mines and says he is more or less wasting his time in his present work. Clay resents this and tells her something of his earlier days, how he has risen from nothing to eminence in his profession. Later MACWILLIAMS, Clay's first assistant, remarks to Clay how different in temperament the two sisters are. That evening, when the Presidential Ball is scheduled, Alice insists that Hope is too young to go, particularly as she has not yet "come out." Hope is upset, but stays home. At the ball, Clay tells Alice he feels she was unjust to Hope and stuffy in her behavior. Alice insists that "society" abides by rules. She has left her fan at the Langham house and Clay, to get back into her good graces, rides off to get it. At the house he finds Hope still up. She is pleased when he confesses that he really came back to tell her he missed her at the ball and has brought her some favors. They talk for more than an hour in the moonlight, and Clay is much moved by her genuine interest in him and his activities, and her unfeigned enthusiasm for his past and its rewards.

Chaps. 8–9. As they leave the ball, Stuart tells Clay he must see him in secret that night. They meet and Stuart shows Clay a placard, one of many, that was posted during the ball, accusing Stuart of an affair with Mme. Álvarez and saying President Álvarez is a cuckold and a traitor. Clay advises Stuart to see Álvarez and tell him it is a lie, and to defy Mendoza and his men, who are undoubtedly responsible for the

placards. Clay will support Stuart. Next day Clay and Stuart are conferring in town when Clay recognizes a stranger as a notorious gunrunner. This man informs Clay and Stuart that he has supplied the Mendoza forces with arms and that trouble is imminent: Mendoza's revolution. President Álvarez can do little to prevent it, as he has looted the government, not paid his soldiers, and is uncertain as to the loyalty of the troops.

Chaps. 10–11. The Langham house is guarded by sailors from King's yacht. Hope asks Clay what is happening. He tells her everything and finds quick understanding. Clay minimizes himself when Hope asks him why he does not take control. He tells her what Alice said about him and his work. Hope disagrees, and she indicates that she loves him. Stuart and MacWilliams ride up and report that the trouble has started. Mendoza calls in the soldiers from the mines. Clay refuses to release them for the military review the next morning. He reproaches Langham for not having let him buy rifles two months before. MacWilliams and Stuart have learned that the revolutionists' arms have been hidden near the mines. Clay and MacWilliams gather some men, run a railroad locomotive near the spot, seize the guns and ammunition from the three revolutionists on guard, and lock them up in the mine. On the way back the train runs through a blockade of revolutionists seeking the guns, but they all return safely. The Langham girls greet them, Hope squeezing Clay's hand with special significance.

Chaps. 12–13. Clay, MacWilliams and young Langham join Stuart at the Presidential review the next morning. While they are sitting their horses amid the loyal "household" troops, MacWilliams points out Hope across the square. She has come in defiance of orders to remain at home under the guard of King's sailors. Clay brings her over and makes her get into Mme. Álvarez's carriage, just as Mendoza's men seize and carry off the President. Stuart is able to rescue Mme. Álvarez and Hope and get them back to the palace, followed by Clay and MacWilliams. While they all hurry Mme. Álvarez to flee the palace by the rear, she wants to stay till the President is found. Stuart tries to rally his guards to hold off the mob, but they revolt when they see Mme. Álvarez fleeing and they shoot Stuart down. The carriage containing Mme. Álvarez and Hope, guarded by Clay, MacWilliams, and Ted Langham, drives for the coast below the city, where King's yacht has been notified to be in waiting. They pass safely through an outpost, bribing their way with a jewel from Mme. Álvarez. They cut the telegraph wire to cut off any message that might be sent to head them off. When they finally reach the coastal city of Los Bocos in safety, they find King and the yacht waiting. But as Mme. Álvarez is being taken by boat to the yacht, firing breaks out and several men in the crew are hit. The boat gets away, however, as the three Americans return the fire. They, in turn, are rescued by Hope, who drives the carriage onto the beach so they can jump in. As they race away, Hope and Clay declare their love.

Chaps. 14–15. The travelers reach the Langham house by a circuitous route, to bypass the city of Valencia. Mr. Langham and Alice have been frantic with fear. They tell

the others that Álvarez was shot and Mendoza is in control. Mr. Langham is prepared to go away at once and relinquish his properties. Clay, however, says all is not lost. He confers with a group of loyal young officers who have sought his leadership for their men. These, plus his own mine soldiers, with the captured guns, are enough to put up a fight. Clay's army marches on the city and attacks the Palace, where Mendoza is

barricaded. After some fighting, the palace is captured, Mendoza is killed, and the rebel soldiers surrender. Although the people wish to proclaim Clay dictator, Clay liberates the popular and honest Vice-President and installs him as President. Then Clay turns over the mines to his subordinates, decides he will become an engineering consultant, and sails for the U.S. with Hope.

The Song of Bernadette

Novel by Franz Werfel, 1890–1945. Published 1941. Published and © 1942 by The Viking Press, New York. Translated from the German by Ludwig Lewisohn. (PB, C67; Compass, C12)

FRANZ WERFEL was an Austrian of Jewish ancestry, fleeing the Nazi terror and temporarily exiled in France, when in 1941 he asked the saints attending the shrine at Lourdes to help him escape. He vowed to write the story of the shrine. He escaped and *The Song of Bernadette* was published in 1942. Werfel was an emotional, sensitive writer whose work was best when he was describing the problems of persons in trouble, as in *The Forty Days of Musa Dagh. The Song of Bernadette,* probably because of its religious significance to the Christian market, has been the most successful of his works. It may also have been the best.

I. Chaps. 1–10. FRANÇOIS SOUBIROUS lives with his family in the Cachot, an abandoned jail. It is the poorest building in Lourdes, but, as the poverty of the Soubirous is chronic, it is all they can manage. The unhealthy dampness seeps through the walls and Mme. LOUISE SOUBIROUS worries about the oldest daughter, BERNADETTE, who is afflicted with asthma. Her other children, MARIE, JEAN MARIE, and little JUSTIN, are strong and hearty and can take care of themselves. François does odd jobs for the more prosperous citizens of the town, but there is never enough money. Louise takes in washing.

Bernadette is a backward child and at 14 is considered stupid even by the nuns who teach her. Her knowledge of religion is scanty. Marie, though younger, feels protective toward her and permits no one to make fun of her dull sister. She and JEANNE ABADIE take Bernadette with them to gather kindling near the grotto of Massabielle. They have to cross a cold stream to reach the firewood. Bernadette is afraid and the two girls go on without her. She is glad to be left alone and she sits quietly on a rock near the cave. There is not a shadow anywhere, for the rosy light of the sun

illuminates the entire spot except for a pointed niche in the inner grotto. Bernadette rubs her eyes, for she sees a vision standing in the niche surrounded by a golden light. It is no ghost, but a young lady, dainty and visibly of flesh and blood. She is dressed in a snow-white garment with a broad blue girdle. Most striking of all, her feet are bare, with two golden roses entwined in the slender toes. Bernadette cannot realize she is dealing with a heavenly thing. She kneels and, in a spirit of exaltation over the beauty of the lady, is about to make the sign of the cross; but she cannot, she cannot stir a finger. The lady in the niche raises her right hand and makes a great sign of the cross that seems to remain floating in the air. A mild power guides the girl's hand to make a similar sign. Bernadette would like to speak but she dare not. She takes her rosary and begins to say Hail Marys.

Marie and Jeanne return across the stream and find Bernadette kneeling in a rigid position, unaware of them. They throw pebbles at her and when a pebble hits her, the lady vanishes and Bernadette comes back to consciousness. The girls are angry at her for frightening them and demand to know what has happened. After making them promise not to tell anyone, she reports the vision. Marie breaks her word and tells their mother, who refuses to believe the story.

II. Chaps. 11–21. Almost immediately conditions become better for the Soubirous family. They are made a large gift of food, and François obtains steady work. Berna-

dette cannot fall asleep at night and begins to cry. Her mother comforts her but determines to get the opinion of the village priest concerning the matter of the Lady of Massabielle. The children at school discover Bernadette's secret and tease Mme. Soubirous to let Bernadette take them to the grotto. The priest, Father SEMPET, relieves Mme. Soubirous' mind. He regards the vision as a harmless phenomenon of childhood. Bernadette is given permission to go and her schoolmates are eager to see the vision. But when they reach the grotto, it is only Bernadette who sees the lady. She is so overwhelmed that a strange trance envelops her. It cannot be broken either by the frightened girls or by the neighboring peasants. A passing miller lifts Bernadette gently and carries her in this condition to his house. A small crowd follows, sure that she has lost her mind. Her rapture does not vanish gradually but comes to a sudden end and Bernadette is again herself. Her worried mother arrives and makes her promise never to go to Massabielle again without her permission. Mme. MILLET, for whom Louise does washing, expresses an interest in the vision. She persuades Mme. Soubirous to permit Bernadette to accompany her to the grotto. Afraid to lose her weekly wage, Louise allows her daughter to go. Bernadette sees the lady once more and is told to return to the grotto each day for 15 days. She speaks of her vision with a clarity and precision that is rare even among adults, and those who hear her begin to accompany her to the grotto each morning. Each day the crowd of mature and sober persons increases, but Bernadette pays no attention,

Bernadette kneels and finds she cannot move

567

salutes no one, and is wholly unconcerned as she hurries to greet her lady. The doctor of the town is sent by the governing council to observe her when she is in a trance. He finds her completely sane and not at all feeble-minded. The officials of the town of Lourdes suspect a plot of the Catholic Church, but when the Dean of Lourdes, MARIS DOMINIQUE PEYRAMALE, instructs the clergy not to set foot in the grotto, the people are nonplused. Bernadette is not troubled by the attempts of the police to frighten her, but she is upset by the disappearance of the old natural familiarity within her household. Her mother acts paralyzed, her father is subdued, and even Marie is affected. Bernadette's brothers simply avoid her.

One morning the lady asks Bernadette to tell the priests to build a chapel on the site of the grotto, and then to have the processions begin. With great fear, Bernadette goes to Dean Peyramale and repeats the request. He demands that he be given a sign from the lady that will prove she is a heaven-sent vision. He asks that she cause the rosebush to flower during the winter days. Bernadette delivers his reply to her lady, who smiles at the dean's message. She beckons to her favorite and instructs her to go drink from the spring. There is no spring in the direction that she points, so Bernadette begins digging with her hands. She reaches a trickle of water that is mixed with the sandy soil and scoops it in her hand and drinks. The sand makes her ill and, before the largest assembly that has thus far gathered around her, she vomits. They watch her actions in disgust, and, with no miracle of the roses to astound them, they depart, whispering that Bernadette is mad.

BOURIETTE, one of the villagers, who is nearly blind in his right eye, has a strange idea while watching Bernadette. When he returns home he sends his young daughter to fetch a small lump of the moist earth from the grotto and bring it to him. He places this on his bad eye. When it is removed, the eye has perfect vision. It is the first miracle of Lourdes.

III. Chaps. 22–30. Louise Soubirous has definitely decided to take Bernadette's part. She will no longer resist or entertain a doubt of the girl's sincerity. With the discovery that a spring of fresh water now gushes from the spot where Bernadette dug into the ground, the Soubirous family and pilgrims by the thousands feel the compassionate consolation that the lady brings to her child. They are a part of the miracle now. The Church and State feel otherwise. The State tries to trap the girl and her family by bribery, but without success. The Church watches carefully as the 15-day period draws to a close. Bernadette is unhappy as she approaches the grotto on the last day of her visitation. Her heart is filled with fear that this will be the last time she will see the lady. The lady appears quietly and assures her favorite that they will be together again. Bernadette is happy. She tells her mother that she will go to the grotto no more until she receives word that the lady will appear. Dean Peyramale is troubled. Events, and Bernadette herself, are beginning to convince him that something out of the ordinary has occurred. He consults with his bishop and learns that an episcopal commission of investigation will render a verdict on the visions. Meanwhile Bernadette is busy at home. She goes to school and waits patiently for a summons to the grotto. Many months pass and then it comes. Bernadette rushes to the grotto and kneels where she did the first day. The lady comes and stays longer than she ever has before. Bernadette knows this is her parting. As the lady gradually withdraws she waves to her favorite in farewell. Bernadette rises slowly to face the crowd that has gathered behind her. Not able to say a word, she sinks to the earth in a deep faint.

IV. Chaps. 31–40. Bernadette is seriously ill and is taken to the hospital. She recovers but the Dean arranges for her to stay there to protect her from curiosity-seekers. The State has barred the grotto from the public, but there is an uprising to rip away the fence. In Paris, the little son of the Empress Eugénie and Napoleon III is ill. His royal mother gives him the water of Lourdes to drink and vows that if it heals him she will cause the grotto to be opened. In the morning he is completely well. On her insistence, Napoleon III orders the grotto open to the public. In the midst of this stream of events, Bernadette lives as if it does not concern her. The bishop orders the Dean to find a suitable convent for Bernadette, for henceforth she is the ward of the Catholic Church.

Cures of miraculous import occur daily and people come from all over the world to see the place of miracles. The Dean arranges for Bernadette to enter her novitiate. He promises that her family will be established in the mill of François' dreams and that all will go well.

V. Chaps. 41–50. As a nun, Bernadette is cheerful and gay and wins the hearts of her sisters in the convent. She never likes to talk of her visions and the Mother Superior shields her from visitors. After many years of placid life, Bernadette is stricken with grief when her mother dies and for a while she too is thought to be dying. But her time is not yet. Her father comes to see her, looking well and prosperous, and her sister Marie also makes a visit. These contacts with the outside world tire Bernadette and it is with relief that she returns to the simple duties of her religious life. There is a tumor on her leg that develops into tuberculosis of the bone. It is a mortal illness of slow termination and Bernadette begins a death agony that is to last 7 years. When her time approaches, Bernadette sends for Dean Peyramale, who has cared for and guarded her so well. She tells him once more that she has never lied and that her visions were real. She does not know that after many years of thorough investigation the Church has finally verified them. The Dean comforts her in her last moments and death comes peacefully.

The fame of Bernadette spread over the face of the earth during her lifetime, but after her death her immortality was signalized by her canonization—the sweet, gay saint whose love for her lady, the Blessed Virgin Mary, brought forth one of the great miracles of the world, the water of Lourdes.

Sons and Lovers

Novel by D. H. Lawrence, 1885–1930. Published 1913. Published by Viking Press, New York. © 1913 by Mitchell Kennerley. (ML, 109; NAL, D1509).

MANY NOVELISTS can make one wonder if any normal human being actually feels as intensely as fictional characters do. D. H. Lawrence often employed his unquestioned genius to describe human emotions and relationships that one might readily feel are exaggerated. His best-known novel, because it employs so many taboo words, is *Lady Chatterley's Lover*. His most admired is *Sons and Lovers*. Some of his poetry is beautiful.

Part I. 1–3. GERTRUDE MOREL is a lady by birth and by inclination. Her husband, WALTER, a miner, first appealed to her because of his difference from the people she knew. He was soft, nonintellectual, warm, and fascinated with her. Their marriage was happy in its first months. Now begins the battle between husband and wife—a battle that will only end with the death of one. Walter's nature is purely sensuous and she is intent on making him moral and religious. He cannot endure this and leaves the house to drink. Having hurt his wife often in his drunkenness, he begins to hate her. A halt in the battle occurs with the birth of each of their four children; but each time Walter sees his wife as casting him off and turning for love and life to the children. Mrs. Morel is very proud of her first son, WILLIAM. He is ambitious but gives all his earnings to his mother. ANNIE, the only daughter, plans to be a teacher. PAUL, the second son, is clever and studies hard with his godfather, the clergyman. The youngest, ARTHUR, spoiled and good-looking, is trying for a scholarship for the High School in Nottingham. Mrs. Morel's children love and depend on her. William is the first to leave home. He goes to London, where he has a very good job. His departure brings grief to his mother.

4–6. All the children are antagonistic toward their father; Paul actually hates him. The children tell their mother everything,

Paul is inspired to paint

but shut their father out from family affairs. He responds by being surly. Mrs. Morel turns to Paul for companionship. She always feels a mixture of anguish in her love for him, for he was so delicate as a child that she did not expect him to live. Her intimacy with this second son is more subtle and fine, though not so passionate, as with the eldest. Paul loves to paint and his mother encourages him. William is the general favorite.

Morel is a man careless of danger and he has several accidents in the mine. One is very serious, arousing his wife's sympathy and making her feel guilty that she does not love him. The whole family is frightened until Morel begins to get better. Then they enjoy living in the peaceful house while he is in the hospital.

Paul gets his first job but Mrs. Morel clings to him. He is quiet and not brilliant. William becomes engaged and brings his fiancée home for the Christmas holidays. She is completely unsuited to him, with no thought for anyone but herself. She plays the great lady with the Morels. William is aware of her faults and talks endlessly with his mother about them, but he has given his word and feels that now he must marry her. William returns to London and his letters take on a feverish tone. One morning his landlady telegraphs that he is ill. Mrs. Morel leaves immediately for London and finds him delirious. He dies that night. Morel goes to London to help his wife and they bring William back with them to be buried near home. Mrs. Morel returns broken, with no interest in life. Paul does his best to cheer her with his accounts of the gay happenings of the day, but nothing stirs her. Then Paul becomes dangerously ill with pneumonia and Mrs. Morel realizes that her life is with the living and not with the dead. He recovers and his mother's life is now rooted in Paul. Morel is gentle with his wife for some time after the death of William and there is peace in the family.

II. 7–8. Paul goes often to visit the Leivers family on their farm. MIRIAM LEIVERS is a strange, brooding girl. She does not appeal to Mrs. Morel but Paul is stimulated by her. Miriam inspires an intensity in him to paint and he spends a great deal of time with her. Mrs. Morel can feel the girl drawing Paul away from her and she dislikes it. Paul insists that his family accept his friendship with Miriam, yet he finds at times that he himself hates her for her very absorption in him. He cannot bring himself to touch her, which infuriates him. He grows irritable and melancholic and Mrs. Morel hates Miriam increasingly. Mrs. Morel knows that Paul will be famous for his painting some day, though he is unaware of his powers.

Arthur, wild and restless, joins the army when he comes of age. Paul wins the first prize in an art exhibition and Mrs. Morel's pride in Paul keeps her from missing Arthur. On the last day of the exhibition, Paul meets Miriam there and she is accompanied by a friend, CLARA DAWES. His instinct about this woman is not at all spiritual, as in the case of Miriam. He recognizes her as a passionate woman and is drawn to her.

9–10. Paul is dissatisfied with himself and with everything. His deepest love belongs to his mother, but Miriam is a constant disturbance with her abnormal craving to be loved. In her simplicity, Miriam believes that Paul belongs to her no matter what happens. He acknowledges this, but still cannot bring himself to have physical contact with her. Finally, he tells her of this feeling and that he will never marry her. Life begins to change and Paul finds that the conditions of youth are gone. He no longer has any desire to be with Miriam. Clara Dawes becomes his interest. Mrs. Morel considers that this feeling at least is normal but Clara is married, though she is separated from her husband. Mrs. Morel wants Paul to climb out of his surroundings with the help of his painting and in the end marry a lady.

11–14. Paul's mother knows that his suffering is caused by his need for a woman and when he again returns to Miriam, she is silent. Paul persuades Miriam to have an affair with him, and for a while they find a fulfillment of their craving. Miriam is unresponsive and Paul realizes that he really does not want to marry her. They part and he turns to Clara, who is working in the same mill as he. Their relationship grows quickly, based on passion, but Paul feels no desire to marry her either. Miriam knows about their love affair but waits patiently for Paul to return to her. Paul's life is a conflict and his desire is to escape from it and go abroad to study painting. But he cannot leave his mother, and so he stays and continues his affair with Clara. Paul's paintings sell well and he is able to give his mother many luxuries. His father continues in the background, hardly part of the family at all. Annie marries and leaves home but lives nearby. Mrs. Morel gets cancer and doctors tell Paul she will slowly die. She lingers on, not wanting to leave her beloved son in his strange unhappiness. Finally, only morphine will relieve her suffering. Annie and Paul decide they must put an end to her pain. Paul decides to give her all the morphine at once in a glass of milk. They prepare it together and wait for the end. It comes quickly. Paul is numb, with nowhere to turn for comfort. Miriam has come to him but he still has no feeling for her. In desperation he again turns to Clara. Her husband, BAXTER DAWES, is in the hospital with typhoid fever and asks to see Paul. The two men find that they wish to be friends. Paul tells Dawes that he thinks Clara does not really want a divorce. He brings about a reconciliation between them.

This leaves Paul completely alone. Clara and Miriam have failed to bring him the answer of life without his mother. Paul and his father have lost their last bond in the death of Gertrude Morel. Paul wanders helplessly from day to day, trying to find some purpose in living. He is obsessed with the idea of dying so he can join his mother. He continues painting as his momentary release from his conflicts. In desperation, he asks Miriam to marry him, so that he will not be alone any longer. She asks him directly if he really wants to marry. He says he does not and Miriam refuses him. With this refusal comes release for Paul. He feels finally free of any regret for Miriam. He may not be happy but he knows it will be possible to live without his mother. There is no need to die, and he begins to paint with renewed vigor and courage.

So Red the Rose

Novel by Stark Young, 1881–1963. Published and © 1934 by Charles Scribner's Sons, New York.

STARK YOUNG'S best-selling novel came between one wave of Civil War romances at the end of the 19th century and a new wave that began with *Gone With The Wind* in 1936. Its stories and characters were 100% stereotyped but they were well treated and readers loved the book. The title is from Fitzgerald's translation of *The Rubaiyat*, "I sometimes think that never grows so red the rose as where some buried Caesar bled."

Chaps. 1–12. The subject of the Union and the South is uppermost in everybody's mind at Portobello in Mississippi. MALCOLM BEDFORD, owner of the great plantation, believes in slavery and states' rights. He is comfortable and happy in his home with his second wife, SARAH, their three children, an adopted daughter, VALETTE, and an orphaned nephew, MIDDLETON. He is loath to disturb this idyllic existence with talk of secession but it now seems inevitable, with the election of Lincoln. Sarah tries to turn his mind to plantation doings but both are thinking of their eldest son, DUNCAN, who is of military age. The Bedfords put aside such problems for a short while to go to the neighboring plantation, Montrose, for a birthday party. HUGH McGEHEE, the owner of Montrose, is married to Bedford's sister AGNES. He is a quiet man, not so jovial as his brother-in-law. He refuses to discuss the threatening war because he believes the existing Union is most practical and besides, though he is really against slavery, he does not know how to run his fields without slave labor. His son EDWARD arrives from college in time for the festivities and it is with him that McGehee talks of these matters. Edward expects to enlist if war comes. McGehee is proud of his son, though they differ in belief.

Chaps. 13–29. Valette is in love with Duncan but, as a true Southern belle, she must flirt with every man in sight. Duncan accused her of being fickle before he left for Virginia Military Academy and they parted angry. In the two months since then Valette has not received a letter. Whenever Duncan's mother receives a letter from him she shares it with Valette, who fears that Duncan will enlist without coming home.

Jefferson Davis has been elected President of the new Confederate States. Edward McGehee returns to Montrose to tell his family that he must now enlist. His cousin CHARLES TALIAFERRO, son of the eccentric but lovable SHELTON TALIAFERRO, comes to join Edward in his enlistment. LUCY, Edward's sister, is in love with Charles, but with no hope of being loved in return, for the young man is arrogant and willful and has no love for anyone but his father and Edward. Hs is an example of a certain Southern type, the planter's son who is a fine shot and has elegant manners and a certain code of his own, but has no education and has never done a day's work. This type will make up the majority of the lower officers of the Confederate army.

Valette finally receives a letter from Duncan. He has enlisted for the South and he is going to war loving her. Malcolm Bedford is proud but Sarah knows only fear. Valette is so thrilled to have her letter that not for several hours does she realize Duncan will not be coming home.

Chaps. 29–35. Heavy battles have been fought but the war is still far away from Natchez. Nearly a year has passed since Edward McGehee and Charles Taliaferro enlisted. Edward does not write often, but one morning his mother receives a long letter telling of a battle coming in three days. Agnes McGehee tells Lucy she is sure that Edward has been killed in that battle. Following this intuition, she leaves her daughter to go to the battlefield and bring home the body of her dead son. Lucy returns with Edward's body and those of two other boys of the neighborhood. There is no word at first about Charles Taliaferro, but then his body, too, is found. General Grant's army is pushing South. Malcolm Bedford has enlisted and is stationed at Vicksburg. Here he contracts dysentery and is given a leave of absence. The war is brought home when he arrives at Portobello. With the Emancipation Proclamation, the unrest among the Negroes becomes a matter of urgency to Sarah Bedford. She cannot run the plantation and also care for

The burning of Montrose

her husband without them. Malcolm's condition is so serious that when most of the slaves leave to join the Federal Army, she just closes her mind to the future. A week after Malcolm's return he is so weak that Sarah knows he is dying. The end comes on the morning Union forces occupy Natchez. The doom of the Confederacy is sealed. Sarah plans only to care for her children until Duncan comes home.

Chaps. 35–55. General Grant has given orders that everything should be done to avoid arousing hate among the Southerners, but at Montrose and Portobello life is greatly altered. At all hours of the night both plantations suffer indignities from the Federal troops. The escaped slaves begin to come back to their homes, asking forgiveness for their desertion. General Sherman makes temporary headquarters in Natchez. He is personally shocked at the behavoir of his men but powerless to stop the looting. He pays a visit to Montrose to present his sympathy to the McGehees. He had been the head of the military college Edward attended. He makes a good impression on both Hugh and Agnes for his kindness and concern for the South. He feels that the whole secession was unnecessary and now that Mississippi is in Federal hands it is time to think of peace. Shortly after the visit, Montrose is surrounded by Negro Union soldiers. They inform the McGehees that the house will be burned in 20 minutes and they may save what they can in that time. There is no way of appealing to these former slaves and the place is burnt to the ground with only a few of its treasures saved. The family moves to a small cottage on the plantation. Portobello encounters its own troubles with the Yankees. Sarah Bedford and Valette worry because there is no word from Duncan. Both think he is dead. One day, he walks in, with no warning. He has been in prison for striking a Union officer who spoke disparagingly of the South. After the end of the war, he was tried and set free. Valette blooms with love and Sarah begins to hope again for the future. Duncan is now the master of Portobello.

The assassination of Lincoln is a blow to the South, for it is well known that he favored a peaceful adjustment. Duncan is so much in love with Valette that he thinks he can conquer all the obstacles imposed by the vengeful North. He resolves that he will work the plantation without slave labor and pay the heavy taxes without selling any land. Sarah Bedford is worn out with the war and hard work. With Duncan assuming the plantation responsibilities, she again begins to think of matchmaking. She wants Valette and Duncan to marry as soon as possible, and her plans are helped by AMELIE BALFOUR and SACH McGEHEE. These two are to be married and they suggest that it be a double wedding, with Valette and Duncan. At first Valette demurs but is convinced by Duncan that waiting is pointless. It is a lovely wedding and Sarah knows it is the beginning of a new life at Portobello.

The Sound and the Fury

Novel by William Faulkner, 1897–1962.

Published 1929 by Random House, New York. © 1929 by William Faulkner. (ML, 187)

THE EUROPEAN literati were rhapsodic over *The Sound and the Fury,* which was Faulkner's fourth novel but his first great one. The stir created by *The Sound and the Fury* undoubtedly contributed to Faulkner's winning the Nobel Prize for literature in 1950. The novel is complex, as Faulkner novels are, and it is set in the fictitious town of Jefferson in the fictitious county of Yoknapatawpha, Mississippi, as Faulkner novels are. It is told from four points of view on four different days, in the first three of which it gives the first-person stories of the three sons of the decadent Compson family. The first part, the story of the idiot son Benjy, is a triumph of literary expression because Benjy cannot talk or think, he can only feel. Also there is elegance in the manner in which the four important female members of the cast are used to tie the story together though they are not among the narrators. One of the sons, Quentin, was the vehicle through whom Faulkner's later novel *Absalom, Absalom* was developed. *The Sound and the Fury* is historic in the annals of American literature. Not since *Moby Dick* had such distinguished writing been combined with such originality of style. The title is from Macbeth's celebrated speech on the death of Lady Macbeth—"Sound and fury, signifying nothing."

Part I. April 7, 1928. BENJAMIN COMPSON is 33 years old today. Originally named Maury after his mother's only brother, he was rechristened when she realized he had been born an idiot. He has loved three things: the pasture, his sister CANDACE (CADDY), and firelight. LUSTER, son of DILSEY, an old Negro woman who is the family servant, takes care of Benjy, trying to keep him from crying and disturbing his mother, who stays in her room most of the time. They go to the fence of what used to be the family pasture but was sold to give Caddy a fine wedding and Benjy's brother QUENTIN a year at Harvard. Benjy smells, hears, sees and feels acutely, but does not think. Everything he is aware of comes to him through these senses, which are associated somewhere in him with disjointed memories of other sensuous experiences. Standing at the fence he recalls going to the gate to meet Caddy when she came from school. Caddy always talked to him and gave him things. She smelled like trees. The children played together at the edge of the river. Benjy's brother JASON always kept his hands in his pockets. When they all got wet in the river Quentin tried to stop Caddy from taking her dress off. Benjy remembers the time he saw Caddy on the swing with a man, and how she washed her mouth with soap and said she would never do it again. And when their mother called Caddy into her room and she ran out crying. And then he saw her with flowers in her hair and a long veil like shining wind, and he cried inside of him, Caddy, Caddy. Sometimes when Benjy cries now Dilsey gives him the yellowing satin slipper and then Benjy stops. Every Sunday they take Benjy for a ride to the cemetery where Father and Quentin are.

Part II. June 2, 1910. Quentin has just completed his freshman year at Harvard. On this last day of his life he wanders through and around Cambridge, thinking and remembering. He has made a point of finishing the school year before committing suicide, because it was paid for with money from the sale of the pasture land, one of the three things in the world his brother, Benjy, loved. Before leaving his room he breaks the hands from the face of his watch and carries the watch, ticking, in his pocket. His reminiscences run on his mother, CAROLINE COMPSON, a proud but ineffectual woman trying to hold on to her dream of the family honor and dignity, and his father, JASON III, who is drinking himself to death. Quentin thinks mostly about his sister Caddy, who at an early age showed signs of sexual amorality and in April of this year, two months pregnant, was married to a man who was not the father of her child. Quentin begged her not to marry the man, and alternately tried to make a death pact with her and to persuade her to go away with him. Caddy knows she and her brother are doomed, and accepts it. Quentin loves his sister abnormally but does not commit incest, though he wants to. He believes or feels that by committing this greater sin Caddy would be absolved of all her other sins and they would be cast into Hell together. There, so terrible would be their sin, no one else could stay and the two of them would be alone, he protecting her and both of them protected by a white flame. Quentin leaves a note for his friend and one for his father and walks out in his best clothes to drown himself.

Part III. April 6, 1928. Jason is master of the house now. There is little left of the Compson property except the land on which stand the house and Dilsey's cabin. The year following Caddy's marriage, her husband divorced her and she sent her baby (a girl, but named QUENTIN after her brother) to her father's house. Periodically checks come for the child's support. Jason remembers bitterly that the divorce deprived him of an important job he had been promised by Caddy's husband. Later when Caddy asked for her baby back Jason refused, and in fact he made her pay him for an occasional surreptitious look at her. Mrs. Compson does not want the money Caddy sends, believing it is earned immorally. Jason pretends to destroy the checks each month, but cashes them and hoards the money in a box in his locked room. He also has kept money intended for the girl Quentin, who is now 17. He has saved $7,000, of which $4,000 belongs to Quentin. Jason, believing that Quentin has inherited what he considers her mother's sexual immorality, locks Quentin in her room at night and reminds her frequently that she never had a father. Quentin, deprived of any warmth or affection at home, except from Dilsey, spends more time with men who wander into town than she does in the house or at school. On this day she and Jason have had a vehement argument. He deposits her at school, but later sees her driving around in a Ford with a pitchman from a traveling street show.

Part IV. April 8, 1928. [This part is told in the third person by the author.] Dilsey, now old, seeming like a skeleton draped in unpadded skin, awakes at dawn and prepares breakfast for the family. She is called many times at the whim of Mrs. Compson, and with much labor she mounts the stairs to fill Mrs. Compson's requests. When Jason gets up he discovers that Quentin has not slept in her room. Then he finds the money box in his own room is empty. He rages out of the house, but the sheriff, whose help he asks, says that Jason drove Quentin away. Jason goes on to the next town where he knows the traveling show has moved, and there his suspicions are confirmed. Quentin has run off with the pitchman—who, however, has been fired, and their whereabouts are unknown. With a pounding headache Jason drives back to Jefferson, where he will be tortured for years by an unbearable fury based on his continuous consciousness of what has happened to him and his desire to murder his niece. In the meantime Dilsey has taken Benjy, for whom she cares with tenderness and understanding, and her own family to an Easter service at the church. Dilsey is the only member of the household who endures. She has the necessary combination of humanity and strength. Leaving the church she remarks that she saw the beginning and now she sees the ending. Later, rocking Benjy in her arms, she tells him that he is a child of the Lord—and so is she.

[The reader learns, from the author's preface, that Mrs. Compson dies in 1933 and Jason sends Benjy to the State Asylum in Jackson. Jason takes an apartment above the store where he works, and so he is free not only of the house and the idiot but of Dilsey, whom alone he has feared because she knows him too well.]

South Wind

Novel by Norman Douglas, 1868–
1952.
Published 1928 by Dodd, Mead & Co.,
New York. © 1917 by Norman
Douglas. (ML, 5)

ALMOST NO NOVEL of the 20th century is more highly esteemed than
South Wind. It is a *tour de force* of a
witty and facile writer who liked to
indulge himself on paper. It sparkles
with bright conversation such as no
one ever actually utters but is no less
enjoyable to read. Liberally sprinkled
throughout the novel are bits of Norman Douglas's vast store of knowledge
of unimportant but interesting items
of the world's culture. This is distinctly
among the novels that an educated
man is expected to have read.

Chaps. 1–6. THOMAS HEARD, Anglican
Bishop of Bampopo, in Africa, is delighted
with the island of Nepenthe, in the Mediterranean, near the Italian peninsula. There
is an air of contentment and opulence about
the place. Beautiful girls stroll in the bright
sunshine, or imbibe iced drinks; the gay
throng that gather at noon in the market
place talk and laugh and point. Nepenthe
is famous not only for its girls and lobsters,
but also for its south wind.

The reason for Mr. Heard's visit is to see
his cousin, Mrs. MEADOWS, who is awaiting
her husband from India. Before he can see
her, he is introduced to the Duchess of
SAN MARTINO, an imposing lady of mature
age who looks like a faded French beauty
but is an American. She is not a duchess, but
it is agreed that her husband should have
died a duke and that settles the matter. The
duchess invites Mr. Heard to her reception
after the festivities for the feast day of
Saint Dodekanus, the patron of Nepenthe.
Nothing very accurate is known about the
Saint, but the islanders are very fond of
him. Don FRANCESCO, the gay, worldly-
wise priest, always escorts the duchess when
he is on the island soliciting converts. He
is a thoroughgoing pagan but he loves converting people for the fun of it. Mr. Heard
takes a great fancy to the duchess and her
ecclesiastical escort and agrees to go to the
reception.

The next morning at 4 A.M. the festival
begins with an explosion similar to an
earthquake. The duchess has installed the
bishop in a small villa that she owns. Almost
immediately the villa is surrounded with
a flow of humanity that strikes him with a
sense of unreality. The south wind helps the
illusion. The procession deposits a caller for
the bishop. It is Mr. KEITH, a well-washed,
chubby individual who is older than the
Bishop but looks years younger. A man of

intelligence and wit, Keith appeals to Mr.
Heard as a guide to the island. At the
duchess's reception Mr. Heard meets more
inhabitants of this charmed isle. A many-
tongued conversation fills the air. There is
young DENIS PHIPPS, an Englishman, who
is in love for the first time in his life with
ANGELINA, a pretty brunette, the handmaiden of the duchess. Angelina has
another admirer in EDGAR MARTEN, a
scientist. Don Francesco is conversing with
the Commissioner, an expressive Italian,
who wishes to run the island like a Napoleon. His main target as Napoleon would be
Miss AMY WILBERFORCE. She is the town
drunkard and a thorn in the side of the
moral Commissioner.

Chaps. 7–15. Mr. Heard takes a carriage
to the Villa Mon Repos to call on his cousin,
Mrs. Meadows. She is not at home and he
looks around. It is a peaceful abode with a
strong sense of home and the bishop begins
to envy his cousin's happy married life. She
fails to return and Mr. Heard starts walking
home. He meets Count CALOVEGLIA, that
handsome soldierlike personality, who
passes for a dreamer but is in reality an extremely practical old man interested in
antiquities. Their conversation reminds the
bishop how charming a bit of small talk can
be when exchanged with an Italian gentleman of the caliber of the count.

Denis hears Marten's voice

At times Keith is a bore with his long
dissertations on various aspects of life, but
he can be a wonderful host. This happens
once a year at his annual bean-feast, a party
that is a real sacrifice to him—for he
is an egoist, solitary in his pleasures—
but that he gives because he feels a man
of his income owes certain duties to
society. All the elite come to his annual
party, including the MASTER and his contingent of Little White Cows. The Master
is an ex-monk named BAZHAKULOFF, who
formed a revised Church in Russia with a

limited number of disciples, 63, and called
them Little White Cows. After a series of
unpleasant incidents with the Russian government, he settled himself and his Sacred
Sixty-Three on Nepenthe, attracted by the
climate and the lobsters. Keith and Madame
STEYNLIN are the only ones on the island
who invite the Russians to their parties.
Mme. Steynlin, having given up marrying
after her fifth husband, is the great friend
of the Master's favorite disciple, young
PETER ARSENEIEVITCH KRASNOJABKIN.
It is quite a scandal, this association.

Denis Phipps is contemplative and sad
and he avoids the bean-feast. He decides to
climb down to the Cave of Mercury to
meditate. He wants to see Angelina but resists the temptation to search for the means
to be a man. Near the entrance of the cave
he pauses at the sound of human voices inside and he recognizes the voice of the
scientist Marten making love to Angelina.
It is a stab in the heart to Denis and he
walks away sadly. The next day, while Count
Caloveglia is listening to the tragedy of
Denis, news arrives that Mr. VAN KOPPEN,
the American millionaire, will soon come
to Nepenthe on his annual visit. The count
is joyous at the arrival of his old friend.
Denis feels the count is no longer interested
in talking and begins to walk to town. He
meets the bishop on the way and hears
about a robbery at the house of the duchess.
It would not have occurred if Angelina had
not been away from the house. Miss Wilberforce is also the victim of a robbery by the
same hand on the same evening. The robber
obviously took advantage of Keith's party.

After the Bishop leaves Denis, he proceeds to his cousin's house. Mrs. Meadows
is in and she greets him affectionately. Her
husband's leave from India has again been
canceled and she is thinking of traveling
back to England with Mr. Heard. She is extremely self-possessed though her eyes look
as if she had been weeping. Mr. Heard is
bothered by a feeling that she is holding
something back. Her last word to him before he leaves is a question about the English laws of illegitimacy. The meeting has
disturbed him.

In the days that follow nothing happens
in Nepenthe and the season is dull. The
atmosphere threatens mischief, for the people are bored. When the fountain of Saint
Elias ceases to flow everyone expects the
worst. The fountain is renowned for its
calming influence on lechers and alcoholics.
Only once before in the history of the island has the fountain behaved thus, and that
was on the eve of a great volcanic outbreak. This time the volcano looks harmless.
Van Koppen's yacht arrives and the old
man immediately seeks the company of
Caloveglia. They talk for hours at a time—
about what, no one seems able to find out.

Chaps. 16–24. There is trouble in the
marketplace and the militia is called out.
The Sacred Sixty-Three, irritated by the
Master's inactivity, have decided that it is
time for a new Revelation. A red cloud
hovers over the square and the muscular

Christians of the island interfere when the Russians start to preach the new law of their cult. A battle ensues; knives flash, and the number of wounded mount. The militia arrives and in ten minutes the marketplace is cleared and order again reigns in Nepenthe. While this is happening, Keith and the bishop are in a boat sailing over the sea drowsily.

Chaps. 25–40. Miss Wilberforce is again becoming a serious problem. For the 34th time she has been jailed for creating a drunken disturbance and Mr. Keith has bailed her out. Meetings and teas are held to discuss how to save her. The Count and van Koppen do not attend, for they are having a discussion about the value of an old statue of the Lori Faun that the count has

unearthed. Van Koppen knows the statue is a forgery by the old count himself, but his affection for his friend is so great that he buys it for a large sum, hoping the amount will suffice for the count's needs.

Mr. Heard is troubled about his cousin, who seems to be suffering greatly. Her husband and child command all her devotion, but something is wrong. The bishop and Denis walk one afternoon to the slope of a hill. The bishop takes his glasses and looks towards the Villa Mon Repos. He sees his cousin walking to the edge of the precipice in front of her house. Beside her is a man that he recognizes as her first husband. They seem to be enjoying each other when something unbelievable happens. Mrs. Meadows pushes the man over the precipice and walks

briskly back to her villa alone. Mr. Heard puts down his glasses, dazed. He lives with his hideous secret for two days and then comes to the conclusion that his cousin must have had a very good reason for the murder and, if so, he should let it go from his thoughts. The south wind has lulled his righteous conscience.

A cool north wind blows across the island 12 days after the arrival of the Bishop of Bampopo. As it arrives, that very reverend gentleman departs. His cousin's husband has at last received his leave and is arriving, and Denis Phipps is leaving to enter Parliament. The residents of Nepenthe find the recent events screamingly funny and they all join Miss Wilberforce in getting quite drunk.

The Spanish Tragedy

Play by Thomas Kyd, 1558–1594. Produced about 1586. (RE, 45)

AMONG THE FINEST PLAYS of the Elizabethan age, *The Spanish Tragedy* ranks very high. Since Kyd originally wrote it, many writers have modernized and added to it. The political events that are its background are current for its times, for Spain had just fought and won a war against Portugal. Tradition says that Thomas Kyd is the English dramatist who wrote an English *Hamlet* on which Shakespeare fashioned his own *Hamlet,* but no version of the reputed Kyd *Hamlet* survives.

Act I. 1. The GHOST OF ANDREA, a Spanish nobleman, asserts that he was slain in the recent war between Spain and Portugal. He has been permitted to return from the underworld to have the satisfaction of seeing the Spanish king's niece, BELLIMPERIA (whom he loved when alive), kill the Portuguese prince BALTHAZAR (who killed him, at disadvantage, during the last battle of the war). Between the acts of the play, REVENGE, a fury, assures the Ghost of this satisfaction. **2.** The KING OF SPAIN is informed that the wars have ended in a Spanish victory with the capture of Balthazar by HORATIO, a brave young gentleman, who is the son of HIERONIMO, the marshal of Spain. The honor of taking Balthazar prisoner is also claimed by LORENZO, nephew to the Spanish king and brother to Bellimperia. A compromise is reached, Lorenzo being awarded Balthazar's horse and armor, and Horatio being awarded Balthazar's ransom. **3.** There follows an episode, completed in Act III, Scene 1, in which the Portuguese VICEROY is deceived, by a treacherous nobleman, into believing that his son Balthazar has been killed through the negligence of another nobleman, whom he therefore condemns to death. (When the viceroy learns the truth he has the honest nobleman rewarded and the traitor executed.) **4.** Horatio tells Bellimperia how her lover Andrea was killed

by Balthazar. She resolves to love Horatio, partly to recompense his efforts to save Andrea and partly to spite Balthazar, whom she perceives to be in love with her. Her brother Lorenzo now enters, with Balthazar, who reveals his love for Bellimperia and his jealousy of Horatio. **5.** At a royal banquet to celebrate the peace, appropriate dumb shows are presented by Hieronimo as marshal.

Act II. 1–2. Lorenzo promises to help Balthazar court Bellimperia; he interrogates her servant PEDRINGANO, who reveals that Horatio is her favored lover and who agrees to betray their assignation, which is accordingly overheard by the conspirators. **3.** The Spanish king arranges with Bellimperia's father that she shall marry Balthazar. **4–5.** Horatio again meets Bellimperia, in his father's garden. Pedringano again fetches Lorenzo and Balthazar, with the latter's servant SERBERINE. Horatio is murdered and his body hung on a tree, where it is found by his father, Hieronimo, and his mother, ISABELLA. Hieronimo vows revenge.

Act III. 1. (See Act I. 3.) **2–3.** Hieronimo receives a letter in which Bellimperia denounces her brother and Balthazar as the murderers of Horatio. But caution dictates further investigation before revenge, and he asks Lorenzo for an interview with Bel-

limperia. Lorenzo refuses, and, suspecting that Serberine has betrayed the murderers, orders Pedringano to shoot him. He cunningly arranges for Pedringano to be captured after the murder. **4–6.** Lorenzo arranges also for Balthazar to revenge his servant's death by hastening the execution of Pedringano. Lorenzo sends Pedringano the promise of a last-moment reprieve. Believing this, Pedringano withholds his confession and is hanged in silence. **7.** Lorenzo has not reckoned on the discovery of an incriminating letter in Pedringano's pocket. The letter is brought to Hieronimo, who thus discovers that Bellimperia's letter was genuine and that his son was murdered by Balthazar and Lorenzo. He vows to have justice or revenge. **8.** His wife Isabella goes mad through grief at their son's death. **9.** Bellimperia, shut up by Lorenzo, refuses to receive Balthazar as a suitor, and abuses them both as murderers. **10–13.** Hieronimo, half-crazed with grief, contemplates suicide but rejects it in favor of revenge. He is on the point of calling on the king for justice when the presence of Lorenzo dissuades him, and he resolves instead on a cunning and private revenge. Hieronimo is himself petitioned for justice by an old man whose son, like his own, has been murdered. This further incenses Hieronimo and deranges his mind. **14.** Meanwhile preparations are

Horatio meets Bellimperia in her father's garden

going forward for Bellimperia's marriage to Balthazar, whose father has arrived from Portugal. Apparent reconciliations are made between Balthazar and Bellimperia, and between Lorenzo and Hieronimo.

Act IV. 1. Bellimperia joins with Hieronimo in a plan of revenge. He invites Lorenzo and Balthazar to act in a tragedy planned to celebrate the marriage day. He and Bellimperia also will act in the tragedy. **2.** Isabella, in her madness, stabs herself to death. **3–4.** Hieronimo's tragedy is performed before the entire Spanish court. In the course of it, Hieronimo stabs Lorenzo and Bellimperia stabs Balthazar and herself. Hieronimo, the sole survivor, reveals that the killings have been in earnest, and displays behind a back-curtain the body of Horatio, for whose death he and Bellimperia are now revenged. Threatened with torture, he reveals his fortitude by biting out his tongue, and then, pretending to have some explanation to write down, he requires a knife with which to mend his pen. It is brought, and with it he stabs Bellimperia's father and himself. **5.** The Ghost of Andrea declares himself satisfied and foretells the rewards and punishments of the good and evil characters in the next world.

[Additions to the play (printed in the edition of 1602) enlarge the part of Hieronimo, and further emphasize his madness, which had been popular in the original version.]

The Steppenwolf

Novel by Hermann Hesse, 1877-1962. Published 1927; in U.S., published 1929 by Henry Holt & Co., New York. © 1929 by Herman Hesse. Translated from the German by Basil Creighton.

THE STEPPENWOLF, or prairie wolf, is not a werewolf; but in this novel Hesse made it a symbol of the bestial nature of man and fashioned on this theme a fantasy that is no less real than most matter-of-fact novels. Hesse won the Nobel Prize for Literature in 1946, a great surprise to the American public, which had hardly heard of him. He is technically Swiss but was born in Germany and writes in German. *The Steppenwolf* has been his most widely read novel in the English-speaking countries.

PREFACE

The author introduces the manuscript left by HARRY HALLER, who also calls himself the STEPPENWOLF. Haller, a man of about 50, of prosperous and urbane appearance, rents a room in the flat of the author and his aunt. Here he spends his days in a clutter of books, pictures, and half-emptied wine bottles, all overlaid with cigar smoke. He eats irregularly, on some days not at all. He has been seen in the company of a pretty young woman, but after his meetings with her he seems even more distracted and morose than usual. Once the author finds the Steppenwolf seated on the top step of the staircase gazing down at the entrance hall of the flat below with its polished parquet floor and carefully tended plants. The Steppenwolf expresses his admiration for this vignette of cleanliness and order, so alien to him. In conclusion, the author states his conviction that although the Steppenwolf has disappeared, leaving the manuscript that follows, he has not committed suicide but is living out his tortured existence somewhere.

HARRY HALLER'S RECORDS

After a comfortable and uneventful day among his books, Haller feels impelled to escape the aura of bourgeois mediocrity. Most of his days are as dissatisfying as this one, but occasionally a few notes of music open to him the "golden track" to another world. On his walk through town he passes an old wall and sees, tonight for the first time, an archway in the middle of the wall. Above the archway flickering letters spell out MAGIC THEATER ENTRANCE NOT FOR EVERYBODY FOR MADMEN ONLY. Eagerly he rattles the door, but it remains locked. He spends the evening at an old tavern, and over his wine he recalls those notes that bring back again his blissful visions of art, music, and literature. On his way home he notes without surprise that the door in the wall is gone. But nearby he sees a man bearing a signboard advertising the magic theater. The man hands him a cheaply-bound book entitled *Treatise on the Steppenwolf—Not for Everybody.*

TREATISE ON THE STEPPENWOLF

The substance of the treatise is this: *Harry, the Steppenwolf, is outwardly a man and inwardly a beast. The conflict of the two usually torments him, yet he is uniquely happy when the two natures can act in concert. The solution is suicide and he once determined to defer this no later than his 50th birthday. He looks to the magic theater, and especially to humor, for the resolution of the conflict within him.*

Harry is amazed by the treatise, but reaffirms his decision to commit suicide. While watching a funeral procession and deploring the insincerity of the mourners, he notes that one of the mourners is the signboard carrier, who tells him to come to the Black Eagle for the magic show. Later Harry meets an acquaintance and with misgivings accepts an invitation to his house. There he is ill at ease and finally offends his hostess by commenting that her portrait of Goethe, his favorite writer, is an idealized rather than a true one. He leaves and wanders through the streets, trying to resist the urge to suicide. He enters a tavern called the Black Eagle, where he is attracted to a girl. She orders food and wine for him, makes light of his talk of suicide, and urges him to sleep. In his dream Goethe plays a schoolboy trick on him and disappears, laughing. The next day, in great anticipation, he keeps an appointment with the girl. She asks him to guess her name, and, reminded of his boyhood friend Herman, he calls her HERMINE. She tells him that he must return to the real world and insists that he learn to dance. Harry remarks that he enjoys obeying her commands, whereupon Hermine tells him that she will make him first fall in love with her and then obey her last command: to kill her. He tells her of the Steppenwolf treatise and finds that she is familiar with it. Hermine teaches him to dance, and at his first public dance she introduces him to the handsome musician PABLO. He dances with a beautiful girl named MARIA, whom Hermine advises him to pursue. Harry is sometimes disgusted by his new mode of life, but at the same time is enabled to see that the old Harry was as pedantically idealized as the portrait of Goethe he criticized. Once Harry meets Pablo and they talk of music. Pablo, who is a dealer in drugs as well as a saxophonist, thinks the dance tunes he plays are as much music as the works of Harry's beloved Mozart, because they are made and loved by ordinary living people.

The Steppenwolf returns home one night to find Maria in his bed. He realizes that she is another gift of life from Hermine. In his affair with Maria he is happier than he has been since his youth, though this is his first intimate association with one who cultivates the senses as avidly as he has cultivated the intellect. His friendship with Hermine remains close. She tells him that her life in the world of people has been as tortured as his in the world of ideas. She too has a "dimension too many": She cannot simply accept life but must seek its essence through suffering. But Hermine is sure that their dreams are right and life is wrong, and that there must be an eternity where they will meet the true Goethe, Mozart, the saints, and the Saviour. She invites him to meet her at a fancy-dress ball and he feels that this occasion will mark the climax of their relationship. He spends the night before the ball with Maria, his tenderness towards her increased by the foreknowledge that they will never meet again.

Reluctant and uneasy, Harry presents himself at the ball. For hours he wanders unhappily among the revelers. He sees Pablo in the band but cannot find Hermine. He decides to leave but at the cloakroom finds he has lost his ticket. A grinning devil hands him another. On it is scrawled TONIGHT AT THE MAGIC THEATER FOR MADMEN ONLY PRICE OF ADMITTANCE YOUR MIND HERMINE IS IN HELL. He hurries to the ballroom designated as Hell, meeting and embracing the disguised Maria on the way. There he finds Hermine, or rather Herman, for she is dressed as a young man. As comrades and rivals they dance with many women, and it is thus that she makes her conquest of the Steppenwolf. The orgiastic ball is ending when he takes as partner a girl freshly attired as a Pierrette and discovers that she is Hermine. They dance passionately. When everyone else has left, Pablo appears and leads them both upstairs to a bare circular room. Together they sip the sweet cordial and smoke the aromatic cigarettes Pablo offers them. Then Pablo invites Harry to his magic theater, where the show will be his own soul. In a mirror Pablo holds up, Harry sees his face intermingled with the image of a beautiful, shy wolf. Pablo leads the couple into a semicircular corridor with many doors. Before Harry can open any of them he must in a sense commit suicide, by casting aside the spectacles of his personality. In a gigantic mirror Harry sees his image fractured into innumerable Harrys, young, aged, solemn, merry, worthy, and comic. One, a good-looking boy, dashes madly for a door inscribed ALL THE GIRLS ARE YOURS ONE QUARTER IN THE SLOT. Harry opens a door marked JOLLY HUNTING GREAT HUNT IN AUTOMOBILES. There he sees automobiles running down pedestrians, and factories and towns afire. He and a school friend, now a professor of theology, declare war on machines and shoot at automobiles from a parapet. He falls from this height, to regain consciousness again in the corridor. He next opens a door marked BUILDING UP OF THE PERSONALITY, where a man teaches him to

play as at chess with the fractured images of his personality. Behind the door inscribed MARVELOUS TAMING OF THE STEPPEN-WOLF, he watches in horror as his double forces into submission a beautiful wolf; then the wolf takes the rôle of master. Entering the door the boy opened, he relives gratefully all the loves of his life and he leaves anxious to find Hermine, but the first door he sees reads HOW ONE KILLS FOR LOVE. Fleeing in terror, he meets Mozart, who laughs at his melancholic soul-searching. Bewildered, he wanders on to the last door. Inside he sees Hermine and Pablo asleep side by side, naked. He stabs Hermine. Mozart enters and tinkers with a wireless set, which emits a tinny rendition of the music of Handel. Harry bemoans the emasculated music; Mozart points out its eternal beauties. Mozart then bids the public prosecutor try him for misuse of the magic theater. He is sentenced to eternal life and is laughed out of court by a panel of immortals. Mozart, taking on the aspect of Pablo, takes up Hermine, turned doll-sized, and puts her in his pocket. With a glimmer of understanding, the Steppenwolf resolves to begin the game again, to learn humor, and to achieve the company of the Immortals.

Mozart picks up Hermine, who has turned doll-size

The Story of a Bad Boy

Chaps. 1–3. My name is TOM BAILEY and the bad boy of the story is myself. Though I am not very bad, I confess to being pretty bad. I was born in the New England town of Rivermouth and as an infant was taken by my parents to New Orleans. Now my father is sending me North to be educated. His plan upsets me at first, because not only do my friends

Novel by Thomas Bailey Aldrich, 1836–1907.
Published 1869–1870.

ALDRICH WAS a prolific, versatile and talented writer, leaving among other things some beautiful short lyrics. *The Story of a Bad Boy* is his best known work and is deservedly called an American classic. For many years it was on all lists of books to be read by children. It is no longer on so many lists, but then it is not actually a book for children. It is a book about children for adults to read. It is pretty much an autobiography, or the first section of one, though it is disguised as fiction.

scorn the Yankees but I myself, under the influence of our old Negro AUNT CHLOE, picture the North as a place abounding in log cabins and Indians who scalp women and children. I plan to keep my little brass pistol within reach till we get to Boston. Aboard the *Typhoon,* a sailing packet, I am dreadfully seasick. We are struck by a gale that lasts till we sight Massachusetts, and I keep to my berth until, one morning, the big cannon salutes Cape Cod and the ship stops rolling. I go about and soon make the acquaintance of a jovial sailor, BEN WATSON. He fascinates me because of the intriguing tattoos all over his body. At my request he is about to paint one on my chest when my father looks down the gangway and calls a halt.

Chaps. 4–5. No aborigines greet us at Boston, though I half expect them. After a train ride we reach Rivermouth and are greeted by Grandfather NUTTER, a rosy-faced old gentleman. I think the town, with its elm-lined streets and the harbor that was once a famous seaport for the West India trade, is the prettiest place in the world. The Nutter House has been in our family nearly 100 years. In my room are two oak shelves with books, including *Robinson Crusoe* and the *Arabian Nights,* that hold me enthralled. And at the foot of the bed hangs a single-barreled shotgun, placed there for a small boy's enjoyment by my grandfather, but quite safe, as the trigger is missing. The household consists of three. My grandfather, Captain Nutter, who captained militia in the War of 1812, is retired. Miss ABIGAIL NUTTER manages her brother as well as the household and believes "hot drops" cure all ills. The maid of all work is KITTY COLLINS, an immigrant from Ireland, regarded more as a friend than a servant, who grieves for a long-lost sailor husband who went to seek work one day and never returned.

Chap. 6. After my parents go, Captain Nutter wisely takes me at once to school. Here I meet Mr. GRIMSHAW and the 42 boys. The first day is notable for my receiving a burning tongue from cayenne pepper secreted in candy given me by another boy and for my making the acquaintance of the five boys who will become my constant companions. Soon my playmates make our barn their headquarters; but our efforts to amuse ourselves during wet weather by having a theater soon come to an end when, as William Tell, I shoot at the apple on the head of my son, played by PEPPER WHITCOMB, and the arrow enters Pepper's open mouth. He is not seriously hurt, but Captain Nutter insists on closing the theater. The only clouds on my horizon are CONWAY, who pesters me and whom I dream of fighting, and the gloominess of Sundays, when the old Puritan austerity takes over. Then even the reading of *Robinson Crusoe* is suppressed.

Chaps. 7–8. Plans for the Fourth of July rouse the town's entire juvenile population, myself included. I decide not to ask permission to attend the traditional midnight bonfire in the Square, so that if refused I will be breaking no orders. Instead, I let myself out the window down a piece of clothesline and, having forgotten to attach it, tumble into a rose bush. After the bonfire my friends and I burn an old mail coach and are taken to the local lockup, from which we escape by piling up benches and crawling through a window. Our parents learn we are the culprits and we must each contribute to the $15 owing to the owner, who, the week before, could not sell the coach for 75 cents. Later, CHARLEY MARDEN invites us to a round of ice cream, then sends me to order another round. Returning to the table, I find that he and the other boys have fled. Since I haven't a penny, I depart through the confectionery store window and start running. Unfortunately, I collide with a keg over some gunpowder fired with a slow match and am carried home insensible. As I return to consciousness, Miss Abigail, watching by my bed, hears me murmur, "Strawberry and verneller mixed!"

Chaps. 9–13. I am honored by membership in the Rivermouth Centipedes, a secret society at school. My long-awaited fight with Conway occurs, and thanks to my boxing practice he gets the beating he deserves for long months of persecuting me and BINNY WALLACE. Fighting is against the school rules and Mr. Grimshaw punishes both Conway and me, but Conway never bothers me again. We build and defend a wonderful snow fort against the South End boys. A number from each side are wounded before policemen arrive. The opposing generals agree, after a council of war in the hospital, to give up the fort to the police.

Chaps. 14–16. Tragedy comes when we buy the trim little boat *Dolphin*. A delightful day's trip to Sandpeep Island turns into a nightmare when the boat drifts out to angry seas with Binny Wallace in it. We others are rescued next morning, after the storm, and I become sick and delirious and do not regain my strength for many days. Binny Wallace's body is found later at the spot where we loved to swim.

It is more than two years since I have seen my parents, and my father's promised visit is cancelled because his banking house is not thriving. Homesick, I invite Pepper Whitcomb to accompany me to New Orleans, but my grandfather vetoes the scheme. Diversion comes with the arrival of a large ship in the harbor. Sailor Ben is a member of the crew and I invite him to meet Captain Nutter. Kitty recognizes the sailor as her lost husband, and he explains how he was shanghaied aboard a whaler bound on a three-year cruise. By the time he returned, all trace of Kitty had been lost. Now he decides to drop anchor in Rivermouth and buys a small cottage near us, painting portholes on the outside. Kitty returns there each night but remains in our service.

Chaps. 17–19. The Centipede Club alarms the town by setting off twelve old cannon on a deserted wharf. Joke-loving

Tom Bailey beats Conway

Sailor Ben helps by preparing fuses. I draw the task of firing the fuses at midnight, and soon the booming of Bailey's Battery routs all from sleep. Some think it is a bombardment, others believe it is Doomsday. The trick is so bold that the authorities never link us with it.

I have little luck with the "Primroses" at Miss Dorothy Gibbs Female Institute (their residence is Primrose Hall). But I am smitten with my grandfather's niece, NELLY GLENTWORTH, who visits us. At

least 5 years my senior, she wisely avoids being alone with me after I try to express my feelings. To my horror, after she goes, I learn she is engaged. My rôle for the next three weeks is that of a Blighted Being, which becomes quite enjoyable because it makes me an object of puzzlement to friends and family.

Chaps. 20–22. My father's business crashes and he must remain in New Orleans for an indefinite time. The longing to see my parents overwhelms me again, and I set off for Boston to apply for the post of cabin boy on a ship to New Orleans, as advertised in the Rivermouth *Barnacle*. To my amazement, the ADMIRAL (as Sailor Ben likes to be known) is on the same train. When he follows me through the city streets, I turn around and quiz him. He confesses that Captain Nutter has sent him to fetch me back. My grandfather greets me in a kindly manner and tries to read me the letter with a great black seal but cannot. I catch sight of my mother's handwriting and immediately understand that my father is dead of the cholera sweeping New Orleans.

To my great happiness, my mother soon comes North. There is not enough money to send me to college, but Uncle Snow in New York offers me a place in his counting-house, which I accept in the hope of working my way to independence. My mother and I go to New York to live. Miss Abigail, Kitty and Sailor Ben eventually pass away and my grandfather, still rosy and hale, divides his time between New York and Rivermouth.

Strange Interlude

Play by Eugene O'Neill, 1888–1953. Produced 1928. Published by Random House, New York. © 1928 by Eugene O'Neill.

IT MAY TURN OUT that America's greatest playwright, Eugene O'Neill, made his greatest contribution to the theater in *Strange Interlude*. In this play the characters reveal their thoughts by speaking them to the audience, not only in the "asides" of the typical melodrama but also in dialogue. Their unconscious as well as their conscious thoughts are expressed in this "interior dialogue." The play itself is dramatically magnificent. Its two parts were played together, so that playgoers arrived at 5 o'clock in the afternoon and satisfied their between-the-acts hunger with sausages and rolls, like German audiences at Wagnerian operas.

PART ONE

Act I. MARSDEN, about 35, a writer, enters the study of Professor HENRY LEEDS in a small college town in New England.

There Marsden is overcome by memories of his late father. He wonders why he has never fallen in love with NINA, the professor's daughter. His rambling is interrupted by the entrance of Leeds, who is glad to have Marsden back; he considers Marsden a good influence on his daughter. Nina's friend, GORDON, has been killed in the recent war (World War I) but she still dreams of him. Marsden has found the spot where Gordon's plane crashed but Leeds wants him not to remind Nina of it. Leeds thinks his daughter has come to hate him. He thinks it is because he prevented her marrying Gordon just before Gordon went off to the front. Nina did not definitely know that her father persuaded Gordon to wait, but Leeds thinks she knows it intuitively. Nina comes in, but almost ignores her old friend Marsden. She announces to her father that she is leaving home for good that evening. He reminds her that she is not over her nervous breakdown, she has no money, and she never finished her education. She replies she will study to be a nurse; a doctor friend of Gordon's has made the arrangements for her. She must make use of her life to help others, now that Gordon is dead. She cannot forgive herself for not having given herself to Gordon on that last night. Her father admits that he talked Gordon out of marrying her then, but defends his action as done for her sake. He also admits he did not want to lose her and be alone. Nina now forgives him. Marsden, very uncomfortable, joins the effort to make Nina stay, but the professor is now convinced that she should go. Marsden helps her pack. Leeds is almost relieved. Life will be easier for him now.

Act II. A year later, Leeds is on his deathbed in the upstairs room, while Marsden sits in the study. Nina comes in with Dr. DARRELL. She feels nothing; she lost all feeling when Gordon died. Marsden is jealous of Darrell. EVANS, a friend of Nina's whom Marsden has met at the hospital, comes in. He was a classmate of Gordon's. Evans hopes to marry Nina and he thinks his friend Darrell will help him. Evans tells Marsden of his love for Nina and Marsden somewhat sourly wishes him luck. Darrell returns to write a prescription for a sedative for Nina and Evans runs out to get it filled. Darrell asks Marsden to help cure Nina of her compulsions. It seems she is making love to every patient in the hospital that wants her. In this way she seeks to compensate for having denied herself to Gordon. Darrell wants Nina to marry Evans and not return to the hospital. Marsden accuses Darrell of loving her himself. Darrell assures him it is not so. He believes that Evans knows nothing about her promiscuity and therefore the match would be ideal. Nina joins them and sarcastically talks of her lack of emotion and inability to pray. Darrell goes out, to leave her alone with Marsden. Nina cries and Marsden comforts her. She tells him of her affairs with wartime cripples. He is in agony at the thought. She is now full of remorse and asks Marsden to punish her; for her, Marsden has taken the place of her father. In the same tone her father would use, Marsden advises her to marry Evans. Nina does not love Evans, but with an equivalent of obedience she consents to marry Evans. Slowly she passes out from emotional strain. Marsden, full of bitterness, then leaves for home to see his mother.

Act III. Seven months later, at Evans' mother's house, Nina writes to Darrell. She is happily expecting a baby but has not told anyone, not even her husband. They and Marsden are visiting Mrs. Evans. Marsden comes in and Nina tells him she is writing to Darrell. She seems much more herself now, but Marsden suspects that her old trouble is not all gone. Evans arrives with his mother. Mrs. Evans has detected Nina's pregnancy but sees that her son is unaware of it. She sends Evans to town with Marsden so she can speak to Nina alone. She tells Nina she must not have a child; insanity is hereditary in the Evans family. Her son does not know this. Nina is bitter and considers herself deceived. Now she hates Evans and she wants to kill the baby and leave Evans. But the mother pleads with her and Nina thinks that this may be the sacrifice Gordon intended for her. She

Gordon, himself unseen, sees Darrell kiss Nina goodbye

agrees to stay with her husband. Mrs. Evans then suggests that she have a healthy baby with another man, sometime, to give her husband the joy of a child without the curse.

Act IV. Again seven months have passed. Evans, working in the professor's old study, has difficulty concentrating; he cannot understand Nina's illness. Nina comes into the study. She wishes Evans would leave her. He is worried about losing the job. She reassures him. There is now compassion between them, if not love. She wants him to sleep with her again, after their months of separation. Darrell is expected. Marsden calls to return some manuscripts, part of Nina's biography of Gordon, and waits briefly to consult Darrell about his mother's illness. He leaves and Nina returns. Darrell thinks how he has always been physically attracted by her. He is still unmarried. Nina tells Darrell about the Evans' insanity background and asks him to father her baby. He feels guilty for having encouraged her marriage to Evans and he agrees, in the spirit of setting things right.

Act V. Nina is pregnant with Darrell's child. She has fallen in love with him. Evans enters, ready to tell her their marriage is no good. He is out of a job. Darrell is coming to bring a letter of introduction for another job. Marsden's mother has died. Darrell arrives and Nina flies into his arms. He is embarrassed. He knows he must not visit them again, yet he also loves her. At last she has forgotten Gordon. They confess love for each other. Marsden interrupts their embrace. He is broken up by his mother's death. Darrell tries to discourage marriage talk but Nina is set on divorcing Evans. When Darrell is alone with Evans for a moment, he says he has come to say goodbye before going abroad. Then he leaves before Nina returns. Crushed, Nina thinks Darrell does not love her after all.

But she keeps her secret and Evans is happy.

PART TWO

Act VI. A year later the Evanses have settled down to domesticity. Marsden is a visitor. He wonders what really went on that night a year ago, between Darrell and Nina. Evans has become a self-confident businessman. Marsden reports seeing Darrell in Munich in the company of a beautiful woman, with whom Darrell was living. Nina is startled and incredulous, thus giving herself away to Marsden. Darrell has not written to her. But Marsden says Darrell asked about the baby, and this gives Nina comfort. Marsden makes snide remarks, which disturb her, and she sets herself to retain his devotion—which is easy. Evans is proud of the baby GORDON. When Nina goes to feed the baby, Evans approaches Marsden about backing him so he can buy out the agency he works for. Marsden turns him down. Evans is not upset and asks Marsden to be his partner, investment or not. Marsden is not interested. Evans goes for a walk. Darrell arrives unexpectedly. He says he has come back to settle his father's estate, but Marsden is sure he has come to see Nina. Darrell admits having a mistress in Munich but is sure it makes no difference to Nina. Marsden tells Darrell how proud Evans is of the baby. Marsden goes out to fetch Evans and Darrell tells Nina how much he has suffered by their separation. He is now determined to tell Evans the truth. Evans must give Nina a divorce. But Nina wants no such thing. Evans must never know. But Darrell can be her lover again. He is furious at the suggestion and repeats that he will tell Evans the truth, but she is sure he will not dare. Evans returns and Darrell cannot bring himself to tell him about the baby. Nina triumphs in the thought that she now has four men: a husband, a lover, a father image in Marsden,

577

and her son. The arrangement suits her perfectly.

Act VII. The Evans household, now on Park Avenue, New York, celebrates young Gordon's 11th birthday. Darrell, aged considerably, is still Nina's lover; she almost wishes he would not hang around so much. Darrell, knowing he has made a mess of his own life, realizes that only Evans is normal among them, with no sign of insanity. Darrell is returning soon to his scientific studies in the West Indies. Gordon is glad to see him go. Darrell and Marsden both backed Evans and as a consequence become wealthy too. Darrell, bitter, speaks sarcastically of Evans. Gordon berates him for making fun of his father. The boy hates Darrell. Nina and Darrell speak of their continual ups and downs. Now and again he runs off, or she sends him away, but always they are soon reunited. Despite his son's hatred for him, Darrell is grateful to Nina for the only happiness he has ever known. Darrell is about to leave and kisses Nina goodbye. Gordon observes this, unseen himself. Marsden arrives and Darrell tells him he will be gone for two years. Marsden thinks he has gradually replaced Darrell in Nina's heart. Gordon brings his birthday gift from Darrell, a boat, into the room and destroys it before Darrell's eyes. Gordon threatens to tell Evans he saw Darrell kissing his mother. Darrell asks him to be a man of honor and keep silent. Gordon is less sure of his hatred for Darrell now. Just then Evans arrives and Darrell leaves hastily. Gordon at the end calls Darrell uncle. Nina tells Evans she is glad Darrell has left. To get rid of him, she had to kiss him. Gordon accepts the explanation, but when Nina then thinks of Darrell with remorse, Gordon seems to read her thoughts.

Act VIII. Ten years later, Nina, Evans, Darrell, Marsden and a young woman, MADELINE ARNOLD, are aboard Evans' yacht near Poughkeepsie, watching a boat race in which Gordon is taking part. Nina evidently is hostile to Madeline out of jealousy, but Evans is determined not to let her come between the young people. Darrell is completely over his love for Nina now. She is as neurotic as when he first knew her. Marsden would prefer to be elsewhere. His sister has just died. Nina insists that Gordon looks like Evans, but Evans thinks he looks more like his namesake. All go into the cabin for drinks except Nina and Darrell. Nina feels the present as a strange interlude, when all their debts to God have been paid and only the past and the future have reality. Now she and Darrell are just friends again. Nina is bitter about Evans' making their son entirely his. She does not care if the boy wins the race and she does not want him to marry Madeline. Darrell likes the girl, and when Nina asks him to use his influence against the marriage he refuses. Nina speaks cryptically of life and death. She will not let her Gordon leave her as the first Gordon did. Now she wants to tell Evans the truth about Gordon's paternity but Darrell refuses. Her hold over him is

gone. Marsden gets drunk and tells Nina he will marry her after Evans dies. Nina calls Madeline over to tell her she must not marry Gordon, but Darrell intercepts Madeline just in time and warns her that Nina is out of her mind. Nina tells the truth about Gordon and Darrell to Marsden, who is horrified. Evans and the others are rooting for Gordon's boat to win the race. Gordon wins and Evans has a stroke. Darrell and Nina pledge themselves to nurse him back to health.

Act IX. Evans has died, despite Nina's devotion. Gordon and Madeline discuss Darrell's position. Gordon is sure Nina fell in love with him after she married Evans. He expects them to marry now. Marsden is there too. Darrell joins them with Nina, and Gordon fights a feeling of dislike for

him. Gordon tells Darrell that Evans has left some money for Darrell's research. Darrell refuses to accept it. Rudely, Gordon advises him to accept and in the quarrel Gordon slaps Darrell. He immediately apologizes. He then tells Nina and Darrell to get married. Darrell is about to tell him the truth about himself, but Nina stops him. Gordon leaves with his image of his mother untouched. Nina then turns Darrell's proposal down. Darrell suggests she marry Marsden. She passes the suggestion on to Marsden, and Marsden, who would never have had the courage to ask her, agrees happily. Darrell goes. Now Nina and Marsden are alone again, just as they were before the first Gordon entered their lives. Marsden has become her husband as well as her father.

Studs Lonigan

Trilogy (three novels) by James T. Farrell, 1904–
Published 1932, 1933, 1935, and © by Vanguard Press, New York.

STUDS LONIGAN is a modern American classic. It is an epic-tragedy of the Chicago Irish but could apply to any society of any people anywhere for its human portraits and relationships. The work is a trilogy, three novels written and published at different times but following an original design—though it is not sure that the tragic ending was contemplated from the start. The same or similar backgrounds and characters run through the works of James T. Farrell and some of his other novels are as highly praised, but there can be little doubt that *Studs Lonigan* will be his best remembered and most lasting work.

Young Lonigan

Secs. I–IV. Chaps. 1–8. WILLIAM (STUDS) LONIGAN is first encountered on the day of his graduation from grammar school. He is sneaking a cigarette in the bathroom and tries frantically to clear the air with a towel when his sister's complaints bring his mother and father to the door. Beside sister FRANCES there is another sister, LORETTA, and a young brother, MARTIN. Studs' father is a painting contractor and he owns the apartment building they live in, in South Chicago. He is financially secure and wants his children to have benefits he did not have as a child. Studs and Frances are both graduating and the entire Lonigan family goes proudly off to the commencement exercises. At a party that night Studs is able to kiss his favorite girl, LUCY SCANLAN. One of his pals, WEARY REILLY, forces his attentions on one of the other girls and later takes her virginity behind a stairway. Summer begins and Studs' world revolves around sex, smok-

ing, and booze. Studs imagines himself a great athlete, a fine fighter, and a lady-killer. Early in the summer he gets into a fight with Weary Reilly, with Lucy watching, and wins the fight over his bigger opponent. He follows this with a one-day conquest of Lucy but he finds he cannot say the things he wishes and their few shy kisses are enjoyed in silence. The next day, much to his fury, his name and love for Lucy is chalked on sidewalks all over the neighborhood. His companionship for a tomboy, HELEN SHIRES, comes to a close when each feels awkward in the other's company, sensing for the first time the basic difference between male and female. In later life, Studs hears she has become a Lesbian. The summer is filled with braggadocio incidents: petty thievery, assaults on minority groups, practical jokes played on a moron, and constant fighting. The highlight of his summer is the loss of his virginity when he and seven of his pals are entertained by a 14-year-old nymphomaniac in her apartment during her mother's absence. Weary Reilly has earned the envy of his pals because he has run away from home and carries a pistol. Weary is later caught by the girl's mother and the girl is sent away to an institution. Reilly has no intention of going to high school and the others hopefully declare that they, too, have had enough school, though each boy knows his parents will have the final say in that decision. Another pal has contracted a venereal disease and he is a hero to the gang. The summer ends and Studs conceives a plan that might appeal to his father. He will tell him he wants to become an apprentice painter and begin to learn his father's business, which will some day pass on to Studs and his brother Martin. Studs' distorted values of himself and life have jelled during this summer. His mother and sisters are on pedestals and all other women are dirt. Studs even sneers at Lucy, though he truly believes he is in love with her. His mind is constantly filled with thoughts of sex in relation to himself and Lucy, and mental speculation of other men with Lucy (whereupon the scene would immediately shift to thoughts of his beating the other man to a pulp). In every situation he imagines himself invincible and he faces the coming year absolutely confident that life was invented for the sole enjoyment of Studs Lonigan.

The Young Manhood of Studs Lonigan

Sec. I. Chaps. 1–5. Studs Lonigan is enrolled at Loyola High School but has not attended classes in more than four months. His father hears of this and Studs leaves the house in an argument. The father finds him in the early hours of the morning. During that summer Studs gets a dollar a day while he looks for a job, but he never gets past the poolroom. At long last his father forces him to take a job as an apprentice painter and Studs likes the feeling of independence that working gives him. After his first payday he gets dressed in his Sunday best and joins the boys at the poolroom, getting drunk for the first time. His pal PAULIE HAGGERTY, married at 17, is now Studs' envy. The sexual fantasy of having a woman all the time is most appealing to Studs and he wistfully thinks of Lucy Scanlan, who was "his girl" the preceding summer. His daydreams burst into sordid reality when he meets a 14-year-old nymphomaniac and takes her into the bushes of Washington Park. On the way home her father ambushes him and beats him with a horsewhip and Studs escapes after being lashed severely three or four times.

Sec. II. Chaps. 6–12. Studs is reluctant to let his boyhood go and stubbornly plays football with a sandlot team. He celebrates the Armistice the same way and is sobered when his friend Paulie Haggerty dies on his 21st birthday. He is working steadily now and his Saturday nights become routine—poolroom, booze, and brothel. The family has moved to a new apartment in a house his father recently bought. He has a severe attack of flu but is up and around by Christmas Eve and gets very drunk, disgraces his sister, and stays out all night. He was at a roadhouse where various illicit entertainment was available and only Studs escaped when the place was raided. He jumped from a second-story window and sprained his ankle. On Christmas morning the whole family is shamefully waiting for him. He changes his clothes and resolves to mend his ways but in church he tries to pick up a girl and then upon leaving church he goes to the poolroom to tell the boys how he escaped.

Sec. III. Chaps. 13–19. Studs' friend Arnold Sheehan is killed in an accident and again this has a sobering effect on Studs. He stops drinking and resolves to join the "Y" to regain the bounce he once had and to improve his figure. PHILIP ROLFE, a Jewish boy, has become interested in Studs' sister Loretta but Studs does not know this yet. Studs joins the "Y" and his first swim strengthens his good intentions. Meanwhile his friends have gone to a dance hall catering to mixed crowds and all are busy drinking, dancing with Negro girls, and wondering what is wrong with Studs. Studs' reform continues. He joins a social club organized by the church and there sees a girl whom he saw once before in church and who has stayed in his mind ever since. She rebuffs him when he asks her to dance, so Studs leaves the church basement and gets drunk with his pals. Studs buys a ticket to his sister's sorority dance and decides to make a date with Lucy, who has long since moved out of the neighborhood. To get ready for this he decides to practice his dancing. He goes to a dance, meets a few girls, and then gets into a dice game in the men's room. There is a fight and Studs is triumphant. He leaves the dance with a young virgin who has made her dishonorable intentions plain. The virgin is misrepresented and Studs contracts a venereal disease. He has his date with Lucy and is thoroughly uncomfortable at the dance. On the way home he makes a violent pass at Lucy but she stalls him and then slips away from him. He goes home furious at the whole evening. His immature love for Lucy continues in his mind, for she refuses to go out with him the few times he calls. He boxes with a younger boy and is humiliated by the dexterity of his opponent. He gets drunk to forget Lucy and his aging body and fading muscles.

Sec. 4. Chaps. 20–25. Studs' mind is distorted with visions of Lucy contrasted with the realities he finds with prostitutes. His church has a mission and Studs and his friends attend it. Studs acquires a righteous feeling and a firmer resolution to do better in every way. The neighborhood is changing, with the Negro population rising, and Studs' father decides to sell the building and move. The move saddens Studs. Phil Rolfe, the Jewish boy courting Loretta, has converted to Catholicism and is accepted by the family, but Studs still takes a dim view of him. Rolfe helps them move. Martin, now in high school, is following in Studs' footsteps. He drinks bad prohibition whiskey and is hospitalized. Studs visits the old neighborhood and finds a few of his pals. He gets drunk on gin and does not get home until dawn. He and his friends decide to hold a reunion on New Year's Eve. It is a drunken brawl and Weary Reilly finally evens things with Studs by beating him insensible when Studs gets drunk. Reilly rapes a girl and the police arrest him. Studs is robbed on the street and is left lying in the gutter.

Judgment Day

Sec. I. Chaps. 1–16. Studs, returning from the funeral of his pal Shrimp Haggerty, is talking with his friends in the train bringing them home to Chicago from Terre Haute. Studs is counting the friends who have passed on and the thought of his own dying worries him. He drops out of the conversation and becomes silent with his personal worries. After the terrible New Year's Eve party, when Studs was found passed out in the gutter in below-freezing weather, pneumonia resulted and a heart condition developed. He has just about decided to marry and settle down. He wants to be married so he can use terms like ". . . my old lady" and hear people refer to his wife as "Studs' woman." Marriage to Studs means respectability and the right to all the sex enjoyment he wants. He has been going with a girl named CATHERINE BANAHAN and resolves to propose to her. He meets her for dinner and later, while walking in the park with her, he gives her an engagement ring. His world now seems to have righted itself. Studs' mother thinks Catherine is a little common and not good enough for Studs but he pays little attention to that. One night while Catherine is at her bridge club Studs goes downtown to a movie and encounters a friend, who introduces him to a man named IKE DUGAN. Dugan works for the SOLOMON UMBRAY empire, a vast utility holding company. Umbray is regarded as a financial genius. Listening to the profit picture described by Dugan, Studs decides to gamble all his savings of $2,000 in Umbray stock. He buys at 25 but the stock goes steadily down. He and Catherine quarrel over his manners. He has told no one of his investment. He stays away from Catherine and in the interim has a sordid sex adventure with a married woman he meets in his brother-in-law's bookie establishment. The woman has gambled away her household money. She picks up five men who have been betting and takes them to her apartment. One at a time they give her $2.50 and go to her bedroom, with her baby crying in the same room. Studs attempts to visit her again and is rebuffed. Indeed, he offers her $5.00 and she tells him he is repulsive as a lover. This enrages Studs and drives him back to Catherine. The joy of the reunion with Studs causes Catherine to throw discretion to the winds and she yields to his desires on the couch in her living room. Every time, Studs' expectations seem to result in clumsy, brutal disappointments; but their intimacy continues. Catherine's discovery of sex has made their romance a thing of passion. In hallways, parks and a taxicab Studs and Catherine continue their embraces. The dire shadow of a vengeful Catholic Church is cast upon them but they reassure each other by resolving each time is the last before they get married. Studs' stock drops lower and lower. His father needs a loan and Studs is forced to admit his folly. He has occasional heart spasms but still believes he is the tough Studs of yore. He joins some younger fellows in a game of sandlot baseball and is humiliated in his own mind at his lack of coördination and total lack of strength. His limitations

erine faints. The father, his money completely gone in a bank failure, is facing bankruptcy. It means the end of everything in one day; his business, his home, and his son. He revisits the scenes of his youth and is overcome with bitterness and sadness. He gets drunk and is taken home by two sympathetic men. He has watched a Communist parade and is puzzled by the cheerful faces of the marchers through a neighborhood ridden by poverty. A spare tire is stolen from his car and it is the last straw. The men drive him to his door and the mother wails at his condition with her son dying inside. The father goes to the kitchen and falls asleep at the table while the coffee he has put on the stove burns away. Studs' brother Martin arrives home as drunk as the father was, and the mother faints. Frances and Loretta discuss Catherine's problem and what to do if Studs dies. They decide to help; each of their husbands will contribute money. But they are moved to help Catherine more to save family face than for friendship. They agree with the mother that Catherine always was a bit common and the fact that she now has an unmarried pregnancy seems to verify this. And so, with the father drunk in the kitchen, the brother in a stupor, and the two sisters plotting Catherine's abortion, Studs dies and his mother's screams electrify them all.

The Sun Also Rises

Studs' father is ruined

are fast becoming apparent to him and when finally he has a fist fight with his younger brother, who beats him easily, it seems Studs' world is almost at an end. The stock reaches a new low of 6 points. Studs gets the crashing news that Catherine is pregnant. This means immediate marriage; but with the depression Studs' father's business has dwindled to practically nothing so Studs must perforce get a job. Both sets of parents are suspicious and Studs' sisters doubly so. Catherine and Studs see the priest and confess their situation. The priest is kindly and gives them advice. Feeling better, they resolve to marry immediately and Studs begins to look for work. One Sunday he and Catherine go swimming and Studs suffers a heart attack in the water. A doctor on the beach tells Catherine Studs' heart is in bad shape. She is quite worried but Studs shakes it off. He can no longer paint now, even if his father did have work, as it would be too strenuous. He begins to search for work in earnest and goes downtown on a rainy day. He walks from place to place in a dreary round of job-hunting, with discouragement mounting at each point of call. He is wet to the skin, miserable, and sick. He cannot wait to get home and almost does not make it. He collapses at the door of his apartment after dragging himself up the stairs on his hands and knees. He knocks at the door and falls unconscious in his mother's arms.

Sec. II. Chaps. 17–19. Studs is in a coma, his pneumonia and heart condition making his condition critical. The doctor approves of Studs' mother calling a priest for the last rites of the Church. Catherine arrives but is treated coldly by the mother, who strongly suspects that Catherine is pregnant and is the reason Studs was looking for work on a rainy day. She refuses to let Catherine see Studs but when the priest arrives Catherine and the mother pray in the room where Studs lies. The priest leaves and Studs' mother, with a false show of sympathy, elicits the truth from Catherine. The mother now turns on Catherine angrily and Cath-

Novel by Ernest Hemingway, 1898–1961.
Published and © 1926 by Charles Scribner's Sons, New York. © 1954 by Ernest Hemingway.
THE "LOST GENERATION" came out of the World War I years with an indefinable restlessness that seemed almost to burst their breasts and that unfitted them for the prosaic existence of simple work and gradual advancement. Many who could afford it went to Paris and tried to exorcise their demons by misbehavior to the point of bravado. Ernest Hemingway was there to write and this is what he wrote about them. He had not been very successful with his earlier writings but with the publication of *The Sun Also Rises* he was almost overnight recognized as an important novelist. The novel has held up through the subsequent decades of reëxamination and James T. Farrell is among those who have named it as Hemingway's best, though most critics prefer Hemingway's more mature work. ❡ The title is from the first chapter of Ecclesiastes: "One generation passeth away, and another generation cometh, but the earth abideth forever. The sun also ariseth, and the sun goeth down."

Book I. 1–2. JAKE BARNES is an American living in Paris, with a job as a newspaperman. He was wounded in World War I and the result was that he was emasculated. One of his close acquaintances is ROBERT COHN, who went to Princeton and there encountered just enough discrimination against Jews to affect nearly all his attitudes. Cohn's wife divorced him after 5 years of marriage and in Paris he is living with FRANCES, who wants to marry him. He has had one novel published, a bad one. Cohn asks Jake to go to South America with him but Jake refuses. 3–4. Jake meets a girl of the streets and takes her to dinner. They run into some friends of Jake's, one of whom is Cohn. The party goes to a dancing club. Lady BRETT ASHLEY comes in with several young men. Cohn is obviously taken with Brett, whose short-cropped hair, boyish figure, conversational bravado and British title answer his romantic yearnings. But Brett ignores him and leaves with Jake. In the taxi, she and Jake kiss. Jake jokes with her bitterly about his emasculation, and later, in his apartment, contemplates his frustration and Brett's as well. For he is aware that "she only wanted what she couldn't have." 5–6. Next day, Jake has lunch with Cohn. Cohn, who had been a boxer at Princeton, wants to fight Jake when Jake makes apparently unchivalrous comments about Brett. In the evening, Jake and Cohn meet again. This time, Frances is there. She tells Jake that Cohn wants to leave her. She creates a scene and Cohn takes her abuse without responding. 7. Jake returns to his apartment. Brett appears with a wealthy Greek count. She tells Jake she is going to leave Paris because she cannot stand being near him. The three go dancing. Suddenly Brett's inner misery breaks through her gay façade. Jake takes her home and bids her farewell.

Book II. 8–9. Several weeks later, Jake's friend BILL GORTON, a writer, returns to Paris from a binge that took him to Vienna and Budapest. The two plan to go fishing in Spain. Cohn, who has been away from Paris, has written that he would like to come along. Before they leave, Brett returns. She is to meet MIKE CAMPBELL, a Scottish bankrupt whom she intends to marry when her divorce from her present husband comes through. Bill expansively suggests that Brett and Mike come to Spain, too. Mike is enthusiastic, but Brett reveals to Jake that she has been away with Cohn. However, Jake writes to Cohn, who replies that having her and Mike come along is agreeable to him. 10. Bill and Jake meet Cohn in Bayonne; the three go to Pamplona in Spain. Cohn, not aware that Jake knows of his affair with Brett, says boastfully that he is

Romero is graceful and courageous in the ring

sure that Brett and Mike will not join them. Jake grows conscious of hatred for Cohn. When Brett and Mike are delayed, Cohn decides to wait for them. Jake and Bill go on, glad to be rid of Cohn. **11–12.** The bus trip to Burguete, for fishing, bodes well for the trip. The Basques are simple and earthy, contrasting with the two men's usual associates. There are five days of fair weather and good fishing. **13–14.** Somewhat reluctantly, Jake and Bill join their friends in Pamplona, where preparation for a fiesta and bullfights is under way. Cohn, a burden to them all, is taunted unmercifully by Mike. Of them all, only Jake has *afición*—passion—for bullfighting, but when the bulls are unloaded, Brett is deeply excited by them. They drink and argue and wait for the fiesta. **15.** On Sunday, the fiesta "explodes" and continues for seven days. The best of the matadors is PEDRO ROMERO, 19, graceful and courageous in the ring. Brett is fascinated by the boy. **16.** Jake converses with Romero, who is neither humble nor proud but looks on his skill as a fact. The others join Jake and Romero. Jake sees the danger for the bullfighter in associating with them. Mike, realizing that Brett has found another object for her affections, tries to insult the bullfighter and then turns on Cohn. Later, Brett persuades Jake to take her to Romero. They find him in a café, and Brett goes off with him. **17.** Jake rejoins the others. Cohn accuses him of pandering for Brett and the bullfighter. Jake swings at Cohn but is knocked out. When Jake returns to his hotel, he goes to Cohn's room. Cohn weeps and asks his forgiveness. In the morning it turns out that after their fight, Cohn went to Romero's room and beat up the bullfighter in front of Brett. Each time Cohn hit him Romero got up, only to be knocked down again. Brett is taking care of Romero. **18.** Despite the beating, Romero fights the bulls again next day and is superb. Romero's last bull of the day had killed a man in the morning; Romero seems in fighting it to be expiating his injuries from the beating by Cohn. That evening Bill, Mike and Jake are together. Cohn has left, probably to go back to Frances. Brett and Romero have gone off together. The fiesta is over.

Book III. 19. Bill, Mike and Jake separate. Bill is going back to the United States, Mike

to a resort where he can live on the cuff until money arrives from home. Jake decides to go to San Sebastian. In a few days he receives a telegram from Brett, asking him to come for her in Madrid; he goes. Brett tells him she has broken with Romero, because she knows she is not good for him. Such a sacrifice is "sort of what we have instead of God." In a taxi, Jake puts his arm around Brett. They grieve together that he could not have been her man and there are tears in their hearts but not in their eyes or their words.

The Swiss Family Robinson

Novel by Johann David Wyss, 1781–1830.
Published 1813. (PB, 22)

FOR MORE THAN a century and a half this has been classed among children's classics and in fact it was written by its author "for the instruction and amusement of my children" with the additional hope that "it may be useful to other young people, more especially to boys." The author's intention was to describe the antipodes, Australia or one of the nearby islands, stressing its plant and animal life and at the same time lecturing on the moral virtues. His purpose was admirable but his natural history was deplorable. Reference books often confuse the author of *The Swiss Family Robinson,* Johann David Wyss, with his father Johann Rudolf Wyss, who wrote the Swiss national anthem. The standard English translation is not a translation of the actual book (written in German) but is a retranslation from the French and the French translator was as much of an editor, altering the original ending and inserting numerous adventurous episodes.

Chap. 1. A ship of colonists, presumably bound for Tahiti, has been driven off course for six days by a terrible storm. On the seventh day the exhausted crew sight land. The ship strikes a large reef and they commit themselves to the sea in lifeboats. The Swiss pastor, ROBINSON, rushing on deck, sees the last of the boats departing and realizes that his family has been abandoned. The family group consists of himself, his frugal and practical wife, and their four sons: FRITZ, a youth of 15; ERNEST, a studious boy of 12; JACK, a 10-year-old; and FRANZ, 7. Constructing a raft of tubs when the storm has abated, the family succeeds in reaching the shore of the unknown island, on which they are to spend the following 11 years.
Chaps. 2–3. A preliminary search reveals no trace of other survivors. Setting up tents by the shore, the Robinsons apply themselves to bringing ashore the rich store of colonists' supplies which, fortunately, the stranded ship carries. In the following weeks they remove a vast quantity of tools, food, weapons, seeds, fruit trees—all that is needed for a thriving colony. Looking for survivors, with their two large mastiffs, Turk and Juno, the father and Fritz begin to discover the island's wonderful natural resources, among them coconuts, calabash gourds, and sugar cane. A monkey is de-

stroyed by Turk and its baby is adopted as a pet and named Knips. The dogs prove their value by valiantly protecting the family from a night attack by jackals. The livestock on the ship is helped to swim ashore. An attacking shark is shot by Fritz and it is agreed to call the island Shark Island.

Meanwhile the mother discovers a grove of great mangrove trees, in which she proposes the erection of a tree-house for both comfort and safety. With boards salvaged from the wreck a "roost" is built high in one tree, and the family sleeps without fear for the first time.
Chaps. 4–5. The original "home" by the shore is named Tentholm; the tree-house, Falconhurst. Potatoes are found near Falconhurst. The field, as it is dug, is resown with various grains. On a further trip to the wreck the father and boys discover the parts of a pinnace (little ship) ready for assembling. Ashore, the family increases its food supply with tropical fruits, fish, various wildlife including kangaroo and penguins, and cassava flour of manioc root. The pastor contentedly sees a flourishing colony growing about him.
Chaps. 6–8. The pinnace, assembled within the stranded wreck, is successfully launched by blowing out the side of the ship. Having removed everything of any value from the ship, the family prepares

A trip to the interior

for the rainy season by laying by quantities of food and supplies, the capture and taming of useful animals—especially notable are a buffalo and an onager—the construction of aqueducts, and the discovery of such commodities as flax.

Chaps. 9–10. In the spring of the second year a cave is carved in a rock cliff, to protect perishables from the next winter. In the course of the work they drive through into an enormous salt cave, which is fitted up as a winter home, named Rockburg. This year sees the addition of herring, seals and sturgeon to their stores; the capture of a platypus; and the making of birdlime, a material that proves useful in frustrating the ravages of monkeys upon one of their outposts. Wildfowl are added to their pigeon roosts. As the second rainy winter descends upon them, all turn to the study of languages.

Chaps. 11–13. The storms have stranded a whale on an outlying island, which becomes Whale Island. Valuable parts of the whale are salvaged and its oil procured and stored. The island is developed as a protected farm where, among other things, the raising of rabbits is possible without danger to cultivated fields. During this year Rockburg is attacked by an enormous boa constrictor, which is destroyed only after it has consumed an unlucky donkey, Grizzle. The growing boys are permitted more freedom on trips without parents and make constant discoveries among the amazing natural bounty of the island. An ostrich, named Hurricane (or "Hurry"), is captured and domesticated as a steed for Jack, and two marauding bears are killed, before the next winter season.

Chaps. 14–15. A cajack, built during the rainy season, gives Fritz the opportunity of further exploration. On one expedition he proceeds up a large river and finds elephants and hippopotamuses in the interior.

Chaps. 16–17. Ten years pass, with great development to the colony they call New Switzerland. Fritz discovers a large bay that is well stocked with pearl oysters. He ac-

cidentally wounds an albatross, on whose leg is tied a message: "Save an unfortunate Englishwoman from the smoking rock." He writes a return message and releases the bird. By agreement with his father, he sets off secretly to find her, rejoining his family only much later as they are on a pearl-fishing expedition to the bay. With Fritz is a stranger, introduced as EDWARD (but soon discovered to be JENNY) MONTROSE. She was shipwrecked 3 years before when the *Dorcas,* sailing from India to England, was destroyed by a tropical storm, and she found herself the lone survivor. Her father, a British colonel, was returning with his troops aboard a different ship. Jenny Montrose is welcomed into the family, as winter falls.

Chap. 18. The spring brings the final adventure when a British ship is discovered off the coast—searching, as it turns out, for Jenny Montrose. The choice of remaining in New Switzerland or returning to Europe is difficult, but it is agreed that Fritz, who has developed a mutual affection with Jenny, will accompany Jenny, and that Franz, the youngest, will also return, to attend school. Mother, Father, and the two middle sons are joined on their plantation by a family named WOLSTON, who, for reasons of health, desire the quiet life of the tropics. The sons, departing with great treasures accumulated during their island exile, set off to their new lives, promising to return in the future.

A Tale of Two Cities

Novel by Charles Dickens, 1812–1870. Published 1859. (ML, 189 & T9; PL, 522)

IT IS GENERALLY AGREED that this is the best-constructed novel that Dickens wrote. Also it is one of the best. The final chapter is perhaps Dickens' most dramatic scene, with the women of the proletariat watching the guillotine and knitting, counting off the victims, and so relentlessly demanding their victims that not even the dictatorial heads of the Revolution would have dared deny them. This chapter is a favorite of those who "read" in contests of declamation. The opening paragraph of the first chapter is a famous fragment of Dickens writing, and Sidney Carton's last speech, "It is a far, far better thing that I do than I have ever done," is among the most quoted speeches written by Dickens. The novel is one that nearly anyone can enjoy reading, even if it is a classic.

BOOK I. RECALLED TO LIFE

Chaps. 1–5. On a cold, wet night in November, 1775, JERRY CRUNCHER, a clerk in Tellson's Bank, stops the Dover Mail to give a message to JARVIS LORRY, one of the passengers. The message tells Lorry he will be joined at Dover by a young lady who will accompany him to Paris. Lorry's answer, given verbally, is "Recalled to life." At Dover Lorry meets LUCIE MANETTE, the young lady of Jerry Cruncher's message. She was brought to London from Paris in Lorry's arms 15 years before, and ever since then her father has been a prisoner in the Bastille. Recently he has been released and he is now in the care of a former servant, awaiting the arrival of his daughter and Lorry. Miss Manette, with MISS PROSS, her companion, and Lorry go to France. There, in the house of DEFARGE, a wineseller, they find Dr. MANETTE, white-haired, sitting on a stool busily making

shoes. He cannot realize that he is now free, nor does he recognize those about him. At last his daughter's presence awakens recollection in him, and—recalled to life—Dr. Manette is brought to London.

BOOK II. THE GOLDEN THREAD

Chaps. 1–4. Five years later, a young man is on trial for his life at the Old Bailey. He is charged with carrying messages between enemies of the King in London and in Paris, and among the unwilling witnesses against him are Dr. Manette and his daughter. They testify to having met CHARLES DARNAY (whose real name is Evrémonde) on the Dover packet on a certain night in November. Two spies, JOHN BARSAD and ROGER CLY, swear that Darnay was then carrying treasonable papers. Conviction seems certain, but one of the barristers, SIDNEY CARTON, draws the attention of the defendant's counsel to a startling resemblance between himself—Carton—and Darnay. With this resemblance as a basis, the defense attorney is able to create confusion in his cross-examination of the witnesses and to establish that the man seen may not have been Darnay. As a result, the prisoner is acquitted. That night Darnay and Sidney Carton dine together, and soon Carton declares that he is drunk. Further, he describes himself as a disappointed drudge for whom nobody cares and who cares for nobody.

Chaps. 5–9. Dr. Manette, Lucie and Miss Pross are living in London, and the doctor has returned to the practice of medicine. Lorry is a frequent visitor, and one night he, Charles Darnay and Sidney Carton all meet there—for the last time. On the morning after the gathering, a certain Monsieur le Marquis, uncle of Darnay, sets out from Paris for his chateau. His carriage strikes and kills a child, and he flings a gold piece at the bereaved father, driving on with no further thought to the tragedy. Just before dawn the next morning, however, a shadow slinks into the room where he is sleeping and plunges a knife into his heart.

Chaps. 10–13. Charles Darnay is the marquis's heir, but he renounces his inheritance and remains in London. He teaches French for a living and is a suitor for the hand of Miss Lucie Manette, upon whom he pays frequent calls. Sidney Carton is sometimes there also, and he too loves Lucie Manette, but he knows that his dissipated life has made him unfit to court her. She gives her sympathetic understanding and pity and regrets she cannot help him to be a happier and better man.

Chaps. 13–14. One day Jerry Cruncher, on his stool before Tellson's Bank, sees the funeral of Roger Cly, one of the spies who testified at Darnay's trial. Having a side business in providing corpses to surgeons, Jerry is naturally interested in funerals; so late that night he visits the cemetery, only to be disappointed. He finds no corpse to sell.

Chaps. 15–16. The other spy, John Barsad, appears in Paris at about this time and drops in at the wine shop of Defarge. Mme. DEFARGE places a rose in her hair, at which signal everyone leaves the shop. She knits the name "John" into her work and thinks to herself that if he stays long enough, "Barsad" will be there also. She then adds something that bodes no good for John Barsad.

Chaps. 17–24. Charles Darnay and Lucie have been married for two years and have a baby daughter. In mid-July of 1789, Lorry comes to their house late from the bank, remarking that great uneasiness in Paris has made all their customers transfer their funds to London. That same night the Bastille falls, with Defarge of the wineshop heading the mob. Outside of Paris the mobs rage also, and among the chateaus of the aristocracy that are burned is that of Charles Darnay. The postmaster of the village, M. GABELLE, is shortly thereafter taken prisoner, and he writes to Darnay begging for help. He says his only fault is having been true to Darnay, and Charles cannot resist this appeal. He sets out for Paris. Lorry, accompanied by Jerry Cruncher, has already gone there on business for the bank.

BOOK III. THE TRACK OF A STORM

Chaps. 1–3. Using Gabelle's letter as a passport, Darnay makes his way with difficulty toward Paris. One night he goes to bed in a small village still some distance from Paris. He is awakened at midnight by three armed patriots and a local official. He is put under arrest and is taken to La Force prison in Paris. Three days later, Lorry is seated in the bank in Paris, listening to the dreadful noises of riot and violence in the street, when the door bursts open and Dr. Manette and Lucie enter. Their errand is soon explained and Dr. Manette—feeling safe from the mob as a former Bastille prisoner—goes to seek Darnay. He does not return for three days, but meanwhile Lucie receives a note from Darnay, delivered by Defarge and his wife.

Chaps. 4–7. For a year and three months Darnay remains in prison. At last a day for his trial is fixed. Sidney Carton arrives in Paris to join the anxious group the night before the trial. Darnay is accused of being an emigré, but when it is told how he returned voluntarily to save a citizen's life, he is immediately and triumphantly acquitted. The family is happily united that evening, but four men carrying sabers appear at the door. They have come to arrest Darnay again. He has been denounced by Defarge, Mme. Defarge, and a third person whose name will not be revealed until the trial.

Chaps. 8–10. Sidney Carton sees the spy, Barsad, and convinces him that he—Carton —knows enough about him to have him guillotined. When asked about the other spy who swore falsely against Darnay in London, Barsad says that he is dead and is buried in London. Jerry Cruncher declares warmly that Roger Cly may be dead, but he certainly was not in the coffin that had ridden in Cly's so-called funeral. Carton whispers a parting admonition in Barsad's ear, knowing that the spy will have access to the prison where Darnay will be imprisoned if convicted. At the trial, the third person who has denounced Charles Darnay is revealed to be Dr. Manette. In his cell at the Bastille had been found a paper telling the circumstances that led to his imprisonment. He had tended two persons whom the Marquis of Evrémonde and his younger brother had brutally slain. He had later written a letter of protest to the Crown. In revenge, the two brutal nobles had caused him to be imprisoned. Now Dr. Manette's denunciation of them is extended to Charles Darnay, the present Marquis of Evrémonde, and he is doomed to death at the guillotine within 24 hours.

Chaps. 11–12. Dr. Manette does not return to his lodgings for several hours, and when he finally appears he is again the witless, pitiable creature that Lorry and Lucie found at Defarge's wine shop. Carton impresses upon Lorry the importance of immediate flight from Paris. He insists that at 2 o'clock the next afternoon Lucie, her child, her father and Lorry must be seated in their carriage and ready to leave, waiting for nothing save to have Carton's seat occupied.

Chap. 13. Early the next morning Carton is at the prison and Barsad, according to their agreement, admits him to Darnay's cell. He induces Darnay to change clothes with him. Darnay protests that it is impossible for him to escape in that manner—that Carton is only endangering his own life. Carton overpowers him with chloroform and Barsad carries him out, with the assistance of the turnkey, who believes the unconscious man to be Carton. Two hours later Carton is taken to the room where the day's condemned are gathered. A seamstress speaks to him, saying that she was in La Force with him. As she looks at him, she realizes that this is not Evrémonde—or Darnay—but a stranger who is to die in the place of the convicted man. She begs permission to hold the hand of the brave stranger to the very end, to give herself strength and courage.

Chaps. 14–15. Meanwhile, Carton's friends escape in their coach, and Miss Pross and Jerry Cruncher are left to follow them in a light carriage. Jerry goes for the coach and Miss Pross is ready to start when Mme. Defarge appears, demanding admittance. Miss Pross, to gain time for Jerry's return with the coach, refuses. There is a struggle and Mme. Defarge's pistol goes off. She falls dead on the threshold. Jerry returns with the carriage and the faithful Miss Pross locks up the apartment before she joins him. The sound of the shot is the last sound that Miss Pross ever hears. She has become stone deaf. After their carriage and the carriage bearing the other four are well out of the dangerous part of Paris, a group of tumbrils bearing the day's sacrifice to the guillotine rumbles through the streets. Below the guillotine women sit and knit and count the dead. Barsad looks anxiously to see if Carton is among the passengers, or if Carton has saved his own skin by betraying Barsad. He sees Carton there and Carton sees him. The tumbrils move on.

The Taming of the Shrew

Play by William Shakespeare, 1564–1616.
Produced about 1593.

HIGH ON THE LIST of Shakespeare's plays that are still played and playable for a general audience is *The Taming of the Shrew*—in fact, as recently as the 1950s it has made a successful musical comedy, *Kiss Me Kate*. Katherina, the shrew whom no man will have until one man recognizes her worth, is one of the best parts Shakespeare created for a woman. Obviously Shakespeare admired Kate very much, even loved her. She was a shrew only in protest against the silliness of her father and the bovine obedience of her sister. She merely wanted a strong man and when she found one she became the ideal wife.

Introduction. 1. A NOBLEMAN, returning from the chase, finds CHRISTOPHER SLY, a tinker, drunk in the street. As a practical joke he has the drunk tinker carried to his house and dressed in fancy clothes. A group of players is also spending the night with the nobleman. **2.** When Christopher wakes up, the nobleman's servants assure him that he is a nobleman too. They tell him he has been insane for 15 years and congratulate him on his coming to his senses. They dress a boy actor as a woman and present him to

583

Christopher as his wife. Also they tell Christopher that the itinerant players wish to present a play before him. Christopher believes all this and the players begin.

Act I. 1. Young LUCENTIO, a student from Pisa, has come to Padua, accompanied by his servant TRANIO. BAPTISTA, a rich merchant, firmly refuses to let anyone marry his young and sweet daughter BIANCA until his older, shrewish daughter KATHERINA (KATE) is married. GREMIO and HORTENSIO, rival suitors for Bianca, decide to collaborate in finding a husband for Katherina. Lucentio sees Bianca and immediately falls in love with her. He hears the father ask for a tutor for Bianca. Quickly changing clothes with his servant, Lucentio decides to offer himself as a tutor. **2.** Hortensio's old friend PETRUCHIO arrives from Verona to seek his fortune in Padua. When he hears that there is considerable dowry for Katherina he promises to woo her. Hortensio then asks Petruchio to offer him as a schoolmaster to old Baptista, so he can be near Bianca. He changes clothes with Petruchio's servant GRUMIO. The suitors for the hand of Bianca agree to pay the expenses of Petruchio's wooing of Katherina.

Act II. 1. Petruchio, Gremio and Tranio (disguised as Lucentio) arrive at Baptista's house. Petruchio presents his friend Hortensio, disguised as a music teacher. Gremio presents the disguised Lucentio as a teacher of languages, thinking Lucentio will read love books to Bianca on his (Gremio's) behalf. Tranio brings a lute. They leave the room to Petruchio and Katherina, who has just hit Hortensio over the head with the lute and is in a vile mood. There follows a biting exchange of remarks as Petruchio tries to praise her gentleness. He swears he will reduce her to a housewife. When Baptista returns, Petruchio announces he will marry Kate next Sunday. Kate says she will see him hanged first. Gremio and Tranio quarrel and Baptista restores peace by announcing he will give Bianca to the suitor with the larger income. The rivals argue about their respective estates. Baptista decides that on the Sunday after Katherina's wedding, the disguised Lucentio (actually Tranio) may wed Bianca, provided his father will vouchsafe a marriage agreement. Otherwise, Gremio will be the man. Tranio starts looking for someone to impersonate VINCENTIO, the father of his master Lucentio.

Act III. 1. In Baptista's house, while Hortensio tunes his lute Lucentio gives Bianca a Latin lesson. During the lesson he manages to reveal his true identity and purpose. He receives encouragement, while Hortensio is rebuffed. **2.** On the day of Katherina's and Petruchio's wedding, everybody is present but the groom. Finally Petruchio arrives, wearing dirty clothes. He misbehaves during the ceremony and refuses to stay for the wedding feast. Instead he takes Kate with him to his country place.

Act IV. 1. At Petruchio's country house, Grumio tells CURTIS, a servant, that Petruchio made the horses run so fast that they threw Kate into a ditch. Petruchio then beat Grumio so much that Katherina had to stop him. Petruchio and Kate appear. Petruchio continually berates the servants for bad service and each time Kate tries to take the servants' side. The servants are well aware of the purpose of Petruchio's tactics. Kate is broken down and ready to do anything to keep her husband quiet. **2.** At Baptista's house in Padua, Tranio and Hortensio reveal their identities to each other when they realize that Bianca loves only Lucentio. BIONDELLO, in Lucentio's service, tells Tranio he has seen an old man coming down the hill who will do fine to impersonate old Vincentio. The man turns out to be a PEDANT, and Tranio gets him to impersonate Lucentio's father. **3.** With Kate almost gentle, Petruchio decides to return with her to Padua. **4.** Tranio and the Pedant (disguised as Lucentio's father) meet with Baptista and Lucentio to complete the marriage arrangements for Bianca. **5.** On the road, Petruchio and Kate run into the real Vincentio, going to visit his son.

Act V. 1. At Padua, Vincentio is confronted by the impostors and worries about his son's safety. He calls for an officer to have them arrested. The impostors turn the law against the real Vincentio. Just in the nick of time, Lucentio appears with Bianca. They have eloped and he now gets his father's blessing. **2.** Hortensio has found a new love in the person of a widow. There is a triple wedding. During the banquet, Petruchio shows the others how obedient Katherina has become by having her lecture them on the duties of a good wife.

Tartarin of Tarascon

Novel by Alphonse Daudet, 1840–1897. Published 1872.

THIS FICTITIOUS BIOGRAPHY is an old favorite of French courses in school, for the writing is simple enough to be understandable to students. It is a very hilarious book, even in translation. When *Tartarin* was written, it was a custom, almost a tradition, among French writers, to make gentle, loving and somewhat admiring fun of the southern, or Provençal, French.

Episode I. 1–10. In Tarascon, a small township in the South of France, lives the fearless, the great, the incomparable TARTARIN, a man of around 45, short, on the stout side, ruddy-cheeked, brave, spirited, and kind. His comfortable house is famous for his rich collection of all sorts of weapons. In his native village everyone has two passions, hunting and singing songs. Tartarin excels in both. As there is no game whatever in the region, the hunters shoot at their own hats thrown up in the air. Tartarin's singing is limited to a single line, repeated many times, from Meyerbeer's opera *Robert the Devil;* but he does that very well and the good people of Tarascon look upon him as their most famous son and leader. Captain BRAVIDA calls him a "brick"; to LADEVÈZE, council president, he is a "character"; in the shops, in the tavern, at the market place, people say he has "double muscles." In spite of the general respect he enjoys Tartarin is not happy. He is bored, he craves real adventures. He reads every available adventure book and waits for *them* to come. No one ever comes to be received by the perfectly handled tomahawk, the deadly shot of poisoned arrow, or the efficient six-shooter. Fully armed, Tartarin goes out to tempt cannibals, enemy spies, opium smugglers; but not even a stray cat comes, or a drunk. Nothing. Ever. With all his pent-up yearning for adventure Tartarin has not slept one night away from Tarascon in his 45 years. He has not gone to Marseilles or across the Rhône to Beaucaire. He is the spirit of Don Quixote in the body of Sancho Panza, the Quixotic impulses being constantly checked by the realism of Sancho. Once Tartarin almost went to Shanghai. Ever since he has talked much of activities in Shanghai and his companions have listened, fascinated, to his reports. One day a lion comes to Tarascon, the star of a small menagerie; it is a real lion, and when Tartarin and his "hat-hunter" companions stand before the cage, the lion's roar frightens everybody away except Tartarin, who then utters some fatal words: "Yes, there will be lion-hunt." The news spreads that Tartarin will go to Africa to hunt lions.

11–14. When months pass and Tartarin still has not gone to Africa, his popularity fades. No one will believe him any longer. Capt. Bravida, unable to endure the defamation of his friend's character, calls on him, formally dressed, and tells him that he must go. Unfortunate Tartarin replies, "I shall go, my Captain." For months preparations for the lion hunt go on. Tartarin has two huge trunks labeled WEAPONS, plus every imaginable bit of equipment from bouillon cubes to a folding tent. The solemn day of departure arrives. The whole population of Tarascon is at his house to bid Godspeed to their hero. Tartarin, on his head an enormous red fez, his face half covered by huge blue spectacles, though pale, is as calm as Socrates before swallowing the hemlock. Thus he boards the train for Marseilles. Totally lost in the crowd at the port of Marseilles, Tartarin, dizzy, boards a ship for the land of lions.

Episode II. 1–7. The good ship *Zouave* runs into a gale, and though such new and interesting acquaintances are available as Prince GREGORY of Montenegro, and Capt. BARBASSOU, master of the ship, seasickness neutralizes Tartarin. When the ship reaches Algiers and black men invade the ship, Tartarin at last feels the thrill of adventure. He yells *Alarm! Pirates!* and goes for his weapons; but Barbassou stops him:

Those are porters, not pirates. So they are, and a couple of them conduct Tartarin to his hotel, where he arrives utterly confused by the Negroes, Arabs, Moors, Tunisians, Berbers. The moment he is in bed he falls asleep and sleeps for two solid days. Awakening, he goes to hunt lions. On the way out of the city he meets an Alsatian hunter who says he has a few rabbits in his bag. Tartarin thinks he is jesting. Tartarin walks for hours until it is pitch-dark. He is sure he was in the desert. To lure lions he imitates a kid. At last he sees a dark figure moving, shoots at it and is sure he has scored a hit. He goes to sleep and is awakened by the reveille of the nearby military barracks, to find himself in a vegetable garden. He follows the trail of blood and finds the wounded beast—a small donkey. The female owner of the wounded donkey makes such a fuss that Tartarin pays her 20 times more than he should. On the way back again he meets the Alsatian, who tells him there are no lions thereabouts; there may be some left further south. Tartarin makes up his mind to go south. For months, however, he stays in Algiers, for he chances upon Prince Gregory, who helps him rent a comfortable house and spend his money. Capt. Barbassou warns Tartarin about the "prince" and gives him a pack of French tobacco. In the pack Tartarin finds a clipping from a Provençal newspaper. It says that the people of Tarascon have had no news of Tartarin for months and all are worried about their hero's fate. Ashamed of himself, Tartarin goes south.

Episode III. 1–7. On the way south the old stagecoach in which Tartarin travels talks to him, having recognized him from the days when it used to ply between Tarascon and Nîmes. Now that the railroad has replaced stagecoaches in France, it has been deported to Africa. Tartarin brags about his lion-killing to an insignificant-looking man who turns out to be the famous big-game hunter, BOMBONNEL, with whom Tartarin has claimed to have hunted lions time and again. The big-game hunter advises Tartarin to return to Tarascon, as there were no lions left in this part of the world. When Tartarin gets off the coach in a town, he sees two Negroes with a rather obedient lion; Tartarin gets into a tumultuous argument over this blind, old, and very tame lion, and is rescued by Prince Gregory, who has followed along to hunt lions with Tartarin. They organize a caravan, but as the Negro carriers leave them for one reason or another, Tartarin buys a camel at an Arab market. The moment Tartarin and the prince are on the camel's back it bolts, and, chased by hundreds of laughing Arabs, gallops for miles with the captive riders. After a month's travel at last Tartarin hears the roar of a lion. He gives his billfold with all his papers and money to the prince for safekeeping while he stalks, alone, the king of beasts. After waiting for hours in the dark, he returns, tired, sleepy, and hungry, to the caravan. The camel is there, but not the Prince, who has disappeared with Tar-

tarin's money. Poor Tartarin, alone, deserted, penniless, doubting friendship, glory, even lions, breaks down and cries. Suddenly in front of him there appears a huge, roaring lion. Tartarin does not miss. He sends two bullets into the head of the lion. But what lion is it he has killed? The same old, blind and tame lion that once caused him trouble. This time there is no escape; he is arrested, taken to the nearby city, and fined 200,000 francs indemnity for killing the property of the two Negroes. He has to sell everything he has. He ships the lion's skin to Capt. Bravida in Tarascon. He tries to sell the camel but he cannot. It has developed a strange attachment for Tartarin; it will not leave him but follows him everywhere. In Algiers, Tartarin hides and the camel loses him. Tartarin boards the *S.S.*

Zouave to return to France. The camel comes rushing aboard, recognizing Tartarin with joy. As Tartarin disclaims the camel, the captain decides to take the animal to the Marseilles zoo. But at the Marseilles railway station, as the train starts, who appears and runs after it? The camel. The train stops at Tarascon and Tartarin has to get off, without a penny, very fearful. There on the station platform the whole township of Tarascon awaits him, roaring their welcome to their hero. The lion skin he sent to Capt. Bravida has done it. But the fantastic figure of the dust-covered, ever-faithful camel drives the good people of Tarascon into delirium. And Tartarin rises to the occasion, pointing at the melancholy animal and saying: "A noble beast. It was present every time I shot a lion."

Tartuffe

> *Play by* Molière (Jean Baptiste Poquelin, 1622–1673).
> Produced 1664. (ML, T29)
>
> MOLIÈRE WROTE *Tartuffe* as anti-Jansenist propaganda. Jansenism was a puritanical movement within the Roman Catholic church and was very strong in Molière's time. When Tartuffe was first produced, Molière played Orgon and his wife played Elmire.

Act I. 1–3. In the house of the wealthy ORGON, Orgon's mother, Mme. PERNELLE, is a strong supporter of TARTUFFE, a fat, pious Jansenist who lives with Orgon. DAMIS, Orgon's son, and DORINE, the bright maid of Orgon's daughter MARIANE, consider Tartuffe a hypocrite and deplore the great influence Tartuffe has over Orgon. Orgon's second wife, ELMIRE, and her brother CLÉANTE agree with Damis and Dorine. **4.** Damis is interested in the prospect of Mariane's marrying VALÈRE, because Damis likes Valère's sister. **5–6.** Orgon will not listen to complaints about Tartuffe and will not discuss Mariane's marriage, so that Cléante suspects that Orgon has unrevealed plans for Mariane.

Act II. 1–2. Orgon wants Mariane to marry Tartuffe; Mariane will not hear of it. Dorine, the saucy maid, argues with Orgon who has promised Mariane to Valère and wants some excuse to break his word. **3.** Dorine urges Mariane to oppose her father. Valère comes to see Mariane. They love each other but have a silly quarrel, which Dorine straightens out. All agree to save Mariane from Tartuffe.

Act III. 1. Dorine has to restrain Damis from attacking Tartuffe. Damis hides in a closet. **2–4.** Tartuffe comes in and pretends to be offended by Dorine's décolleté. When he is alone with Elmire (but Damis is listening to the conversation) Tartuffe offers his love to her. Elmire seeks only Tartuffe's support for Mariane's marriage to Valère. The impetuous Damis jumps out of his hiding place to tell his father he has caught Tartuffe making approaches to Elmire. Elmire cannot restrain Damis. **5–6.**

Orgon hears from Damis of Tartuffe's indecent offer to Elmire. Tartuffe on his knees confesses his unforgivable sin, and winds Orgon around his little finger—so much so that when Damis refuses to beg Tartuffe's pardon, Orgon sends Damis away and disinherits him. **7.** Orgon, out of remorse for the pain caused Tartuffe, plans to deed all his property to Tartuffe at once.

Act IV. 1. Cléante asks Tartuffe to intercede for Damis. Tartuffe refuses with pious excuses. **2.** Dorine begs Cléante to stop Mariane's marriage to Tartuffe, as Mariane is beside herself. **3–7.** Orgon is determined to hold the marriage at once. He agrees when Elmire asks him to observe her alone with Tartuffe, and hides under the table. Elmire, left alone with Tartuffe, manages to direct the conversation in such a manner that Tartuffe does declare himself: "sinning in secret is no sinning at all." Now Orgon begins to see the truth. Tartuffe wants to embrace Elmire, but Orgon stops him and orders him out of the house. Tartuffe goes, but warns Orgon that he will be back, as the house and all of Orgon's property now belong to him. **8.** Orgon is in trouble; Tartuffe has the deed of gift. And more—a certain box that holds important documents.

Act V. 1. The box is gone. Orgon kept in it the documents of a friend who had to flee for some grave reason. Now Orgon may be indicted. **2.** Damis is prevented by Cléante from going out to do violence to Tartuffe. **3.** Mme. Pernelle still does not believe that Tartuffe is a villain. **4.** Tartuffe sends an emissary with a writ to take over Orgon's house and property. **5.** Now at last Mme. Pernelle knows the truth about Tartuffe. **6–7.** Valère offers his coach and money to Orgon to escape. Tartuffe has accused Orgon of having kept the documents of a state criminal. Orgon is about to escape when Tartuffe comes with a police officer. Tartuffe makes the arrest in the name of the king and demands that the officer lead the prisoner away. But the officer arrests Tartuffe: The king has seen through the hypocrite because of his ingratitude to such a kind and good man as Orgon. The king annuls the deed of gift that Orgon gave Tartuffe. Tartuffe is led away.

Sir Thomas More
1478–1535

Emily Bronte
1818–1848

The Tempest

Play by William Shakespeare, 1564–1616.
Produced 1611 (RE, 51)

THIS MAY HAVE BEEN the last play Shakespeare wrote. It contains some of Shakespeare's best poetry and, as a lighter touch, some of his loveliest lyrics to be sung by the fairy Ariel. Nothing can be more impressive than the point in Act IV when Prospero is prosaically telling his guest Ferdinand that the show is over and unexpectedly one finds him launching into the speech that begins "Our revels now are ended" and ends "we are such stuff as dreams are made on, and our little life is rounded with a sleep." Apparently Shakespeare could open his mouth only slightly and poetry would drip out.

Act I. 1. On a ship at sea, battered by a storm, there is a group that includes ALONSO, the king of Naples; SEBASTIAN, his brother; ANTONIO, the usurping duke of Milan; FERDINAND, son of the king of Naples; and the king's counselor GONZALO. 2. On an enchanted island PROSPERO, who is the rightful duke of Milan and also a skilled magician whose magic storm has wrecked the ship, tells his daughter MIRANDA how his false brother Antonio seized power from him with the help of the king of Naples. Miranda urges him not to harm the voyagers. ARIEL, an air spirit, serves Prospero on the island, and CALIBAN (an anagram suggesting cannibal), the son of an evil witch, is Prospero's menial servant. Caliban complains that the island should be his, for it was his before Prospero came. The shipwrecked voyagers are ashore; Ariel leads Ferdinand towards Prospero's cave. Miranda falls in love with Ferdinand. Prospero decides to slow down the courtship lest it look too easy a victory for Ferdinand.

Act II. 1. In another part of the island, the rest of the shipwrecked party has found refuge. They think Ferdinand is dead. Ariel lulls them to sleep by magic music, except for Sebastian and Antonio, who stay awake and plot the death of the king and Gonzalo so that Sebastian will be king. Ariel awakens the others in time to save themselves. 2. Caliban meets TRINCULO, the king's jester, who is very drunk. They are joined by STEPHANO, the king's butler, who also is drunk. He brings along a bottle. Caliban likes the taste of liquor and swears he will serve Stephano forever.

Act III. 1. Ferdinand has been pressed into hard work, carrying logs, for Prospero wishes to judge the sincerity of his love for Miranda. He does not mind the hard work since Miranda is with him. 2. The three drunken companions, Caliban, Stephano, and Trinculo, are plotting to overthrow Prospero and take over the rule of the island. Ariel reports the plot to Prospero. 3. The shipwrecked party is tired and hungry. To mock and punish them, Prospero puts before them a banquet that disappears when they touch it. Antonio and Sebastian are still plotting the murder. Ariel, in the shape of a harpy, sings a song that reveals the plot against Prospero 12 years ago. Alonso is moved to remorse.

Act IV. 1. Prospero releases Ferdinand from his labors and accepts him as his future son-in-law. To celebrate the event, he presents a masquerade for Ferdinand and Miranda. Spirits in the guise of IRIS, CERES and JUNO perform various dances. Prospero curtails the festivities to command Ariel to punish the conspirators Caliban, Stephano, and Trinculo. Ariel hangs glittering garments to lure the conspirators, then Prospero sets on them a group of spirits in the shape of hunting dogs. The dogs drive them about the island.

Act V. 1. Prospero dons his magic robes and listens to a report from Ariel on the state of his enemies. Ariel recommends mercy, and Prospero agrees. Ariel, with his magic singing, then leads Alonso, Gonzalo and the others towards the cell. Prospero warmly welcomes his old friend Gonzalo. He is now dressed in the robes of a duke of Milan. Alonso asks forgiveness for his part in the plot. Prospero even forgives his wicked brother but reclaims his dukedom. Then he shows Alonso his son Ferdinand, well and alive, and informs him that Ferdinand is to marry Miranda. When Miranda sees that there are more persons like herself, Prospero, and Ferdinand, she is delighted: "O brave new world that has such people in it!" Alonso blesses their union. Ariel brings in two sailors, who report that the ship has been repaired. Prospero is so delighted that he promises to set Ariel free and asks Ariel to lift the spell from Caliban and his friends. Caliban, Stephano and Trinculo arrive, still drunk. Caliban sobers up and promises not to misbehave in the future and Prospero forgives him. Prospero promises not to use his magic any more, giving Ariel one last order—to calm the seas for the voyage home.

Tess of the D'Urbervilles

Novel by Thomas Hardy, 1840–1928.
Published 1891. (PB, PL525)

THIS HAS LASTED as the best-read of Hardy's novels. Superficially, it is just the story of an unfortunate girl in a series of interesting situations, and it appeased the Victorian moralists because Tess suffered death for her indiscretions; but also the novel has a motive typical of Hardy, the course of a helpless person toward a tragic but inescapable destiny. *Tess* is a major novel of a major novelist.

Phase I. Chaps. 1–11. JOHN DURBEYFIELD, a middle-aged traveling trader in the Vale of Blackmoor, Wessex, learns from casual conversation with an antiquarian parson that his real name is D'Urberville and that he is the legal head of that ancient decayed family. Durbeyfield's foolish head is turned by the news and he rides to the village proclaiming it loudly. His eldest daughter, TESS, 16 years old, going to an outdoor dance with other girls, is embarrassed by her father's conduct. A young gentleman, ANGEL CLARE, walking through the district with his two elder brothers, stops and joins the dance; he happens not to dance with Tess, but they notice each other. Tess's mother, JOAN, a shrewd coarse countrywoman, persuades herself that Tess will make a rich marriage and intends her to claim kinship with a rich family named D'Urberville living in the same county. Durbeyfield being too drunk to drive, Tess takes the cart, and by ill-luck the horse is killed in a road accident. To repair the loss, for which she blames herself, Tess agrees to visit her rich relations (as she supposes them, though they have merely taken the name to conceal their own plebeian origin). She makes her visit and meets ALEC D'URBERVILLE, a young gentleman, who compliments and flatters her. His mother is old and blind and he gets Tess employment as keeper of her poultry. Tess's family responsibilities force her to accept, though her fears are realized when Alec, while driving her to his home, forces his attentions on her. In four months, circumstances put her in his power: She is returning late from a fair with other countrywomen, when one of them (a discarded favourite of Alec's) quarrels with her. Alec appears, carries Tess off on his horse, and in the woods seduces the frightened and weary girl.

Phase II. Chaps. 12–15. Spurning Alec's offer to make her his mistress, Tess returns home. Her consciousness of sin is increased by her meeting a fanatic who daubs Biblical prohibitions of adultery in red paint on barns and stiles. She shrinks from the villagers as her pregnancy develops, but when her baby is born she reappears, works in the fields, and lovingly suckles the child there. The baby is sickly and dies. Tess improvises its baptism at home but cannot secure its burial in consecrated ground. After the winter, she decides to leave the village and be a milkmaid at a dairy farm some distance away.

Phase III. Chaps. 16–24. Tess is delighted

Angel proposes to Tess at milking time

by the rich country and hopes for a new and happier life. She begins work at the dairy and discovers that Angel Clare is learning dairy farming there. His father is a clergyman and his brothers also have entered the Church, but Angel has declined to do so because he has inflexible scruples about doctrine. Therefore he feels that he has no right to be supported by his father and he determines to be a farmer. Tess learns that his view of life is pessimistic and that he despises aristocratic families. He soon betrays an affection for Tess, which the other dairymaids are quick to notice because they themselves are hopelessly in love with him; but these girls—IZZ HUETT, RETTY PRIDDLE, and MARIAN—are good-natured and are very fond of Tess, in spite of their natural envy. Tess herself is in love with Angel; but feeling bound in conscience not to marry after her disgrace, she tries vainly to interest him in the other girls. Angel displays his love while carrying Tess over a flooded stream, and the other girls witness this with despair. Tess vows she will never stand in their way, but she is distressed to hear from them that Angel's family design him to marry a clergyman's daughter, MERCY CHANT. One day, however, while the cows are being milked, Angel declares his love, and though Tess weeps, he understands she loves him.

Phase IV. Chaps. 25–34. Angel, visiting his family, announces his intention of marrying Tess. His parents raise no objection. His father tells him of a fruitless effort he has made to convert Alec D'Urberville, who is otherwise unknown to both of them. Angel returns to the dairy and makes Tess a proposal of marriage, which she sadly declines. On several occasions he questions her about her refusal, and one day, as they are driving a load of milk to the railway station and pass one of the D'Urberville manor-houses, she tells him that she is a D'Urberville. Thinking that his known contempt for ancient families is her only reason for refusing him, he now proposes marriage so earnestly that Tess, carried away with delight, accepts him. She has never revealed her seduction by Alec, because of a promise to her mother. Consumed by her unrevealed secret, Tess delays naming the wedding-day; but at last she agrees to marry Angel on New Year's Eve. One day, when she is with Angel, a stranger makes an insulting remark about her past

life. Angel strikes the man, who then pretends he mistook Tess for another woman, but she resolves to tell Angel the truth and pushes a letter under his bedroom door. His unchanged behavior next day makes her think she is forgiven. Then she discovers that the letter went under the carpet and was unread, but the wedding-day is upon her and it is too late for confession. Though disturbed by premonitions, she marries Angel and they go to spend their honeymoon at a farmhouse that was formerly a D'Urberville manor-house. Tess puts on the jewels destined for Angel's wife and her descendants. Her feverish excitement turns to distress when a carrier, bringing their baggage, tells them that Retty has tried to drown herself and Marian has taken to drink. Evening comes on. Angel, recalling an agreement he made with Tess to confess their past indiscretions, admits that he once lay with a prostitute in London. Tess at once forgives him and encouraged by the similarity of their sins she recounts her experience with Alec.

Phase V. Chaps. 35–44. To her distress and horror, Angel declares that their marriage is ruined, because she is not the woman he took her for. He is agonized but inflexible, just as he had been earlier about not becoming a clergyman; though one night, while sleepwalking, he involuntarily reveals an unchanged love for her. After living miserably in the farmhouse together for some days, they decide to separate, and Tess returns to her parents. She does not stay there long, for her mother is unsympathetic, her father degenerating, the house overcrowded, and her story too well-known. Angel, on a sudden impulse, decides to accept a farming opportunity in Brazil. He happens to meet Izz Huett, and wildly invites her to go with him as his mistress. She passionately agrees, but generously lets drop a word about Tess's great love for him, and this sobers him into a withdrawal. He leaves for Brazil alone. Tess works first as a milkmaid, then she becomes a general farm-laborer for the man whom Angel struck for insulting her, and he is harsh and contemptuous. Tess suffers from misery, hard usage, and poverty, but she is too independent and self-reproachful to ask Angel's family for help and too honest to sell the jewels that are intended as a family heirloom. Also working at the farm are Marian and Izz, and Tess hears of Angel's offer to

Izz. Needing comfort of mind, she sets off to see Angel's father; but as she nears the end of the journey, she overhears Angel's brothers talking to Mercy Chant and feels from their words about Angel that they would all be unsympathetic toward her. She turns back and on her way passes a revivalist meeting in a barn. The preacher, to her astonishment, is Alec D'Urberville.

Phase VI. Chaps. 45–52. The words of Angel's father have converted Alec to fanatical zeal; but his passions remain as strong as ever and are reawakened by seeing Tess. He follows her, and visits at the farm, torn between his religion and his desire. Ironically, Angel's arguments against orthodox religion, some of which Alec hears from Tess when he asks her to pray for him, destroy his faith; and he now pursues Tess continually, in spite of her indignation. She writes to Angel, appealing to him to return and protect her from temptation. The letter reaches him just as he is returning to England after enduring hardship and sickness in Brazil. Meanwhile Tess's sister, 'LIZA LU, tells her to come home, as her mother is believed dying. Tess returns, still followed by Alec, and works to support her family. Her mother recovers but her father dies of a heart attack, and since the Durbeyfields' house is leased in his name they are turned out of it. Alec again appears and offers to help the family, but Tess, knowing his motives, refuses his help. She writes a bitter, desperate letter to Angel. The Durbeyfields travel to Kingsbere, a village anciently held by their ancestors, but the lodgings they engaged have been let to someone else. They are in despair. Alec renews his offer. Izz and Marian, who have observed Alec's attempts, write a letter to Angel and warn him to save Tess before it is too late.

Phase VII. Chaps. 53–59. Angel, who has received Tess's letters and is now at home, is anxious to trace her. The milkmaids' letter sharpens his anxiety. His views are now changed and he hopes to recover Tess's love, which her latest letter suggests that he has lost. He traces her to Kingsbere, where her mother directs him to Sandbourne, a coastal resort. He hurries there, and sees Tess, who, wild with grief, tells him that he is too late and that she is Alec's mistress. Angel, now reproaching himself bitterly, hurries away in horror. A short distance out of town he is overtaken by Tess, who has stabbed Alec to death. In love and pity he leads her into the country and they take refuge in an empty manor-house in the New Forest, where they live for a few tranquil days together. Sensing that they have been observed, Angel leads Tess away again, and they reach Stonehenge. Amid the pillars of the pagan temple, Tess urges Angel to love and marry 'Liza Lu when she is dead. They have no hope of meeting in a future life. Tess sleeps, and soon the police come to arrest her for the murder of Alec. In the last chapter, Angel and 'Liza Lu watch the black flag on Winchester Prison signal the death of Tess.

Thaïs

Novel by Anatole France (Jacques
Anatole Thibault, 1844–1924).
Published 1890.

ANATOLE FRANCE'S reputation was
made when *Thaïs* was published. It is
strongly-emotional and its story of the
carnal passions of an ascetic deals
with an age-old question. The story,
with music by Massenet, has made one
of the most popular of all grand
operas. Because of the opera, *Thaïs*
is one of the best read of Anatole France's
works and is likely to remain so.

Book I. The Lotus. In the cosmopolitan
city of Alexandria, in 3rd-century Egypt,
lives the actress THAÏS, a fascinating beauty
and voluptuous dancer. From the Christian
viewpoint she destroys her own soul and the
souls of others by being "kind" to the fine
young men and rich old men who seek her
love.

PAPHNUTIUS, a man of aristocratic birth,
was one of her admirers when he was a boy
of 15, but his youthful timidity prevented
him from asking her to grant him her
favors. His lascivious desire for her was
his adolescent "sin" and he has never forgotten her, though now, as a grown man,
he has become a fanatically religious ascetic
and anchorite monk. He has renounced all
pleasures of the flesh to live a life of complete self-denial as a recluse, dwelling in a
desert monastery of sun-baked huts, with 24
anchorite disciples. Devoted to penitence,
he fasts for days at a time and flagellates
himself twice a day for his bygone sins.

He has visions of Thaïs trapped by her
sinful career, condemned to eternal hell.
"With the help of God," he tells himself,
"I must save her." A holy hermit, PALEMON,
advises Paphnutius to stay away from Thaïs,
but his visions of her terrible fate will not
let Paphnutius abandon her to it. He goes
on foot to Alexandria, walking there in 20
days. From a wealthy Alexandrian friend of
his youth, NICIAS, Paphnutius borrows a
perfumed tunic, golden sandals, and scented
oil to anoint his beard. He also borrows
money and tells Nicias that he intends to
convert Thaïs and save her soul. Nicias, a
Greek pagan, warns him against offending
Venus, pagan goddess of love, whose powers
of revenge are merciless. Paphnutius scorns
such unchristian ideas and suspects that
Nicias is one of the lovers of Thaïs. Visions
of her still haunt Paphnutius as he goes to
the theater and watches her play the part
of a virgin in a Greek drama. After the performance Paphnutius goes to the stage door
and asks to speak to Thaïs.

Book II. The Papyrus. Thaïs is the daughter of a pagan who kept a waterfront tavern
frequented by sailors. Her mother is said
to have been a witch but Thaïs knows this
to be untrue. The only friend Thaïs had
during her unhappy girlhood was her
father's Negro slave, AHMES, a Christian.
Ahmes spoke to her of God and Jesus, and
had her baptized. Falsely accused by the
father of Thaïs, Ahmes was crucified for
theft. Thaïs knew he was innocent. After
that she feared she would suffer if she were
innocent and good. From the age of 11 she
took many lovers. Soon she worked for a
procuress who managed a troupe of dancers.
For six months Thaïs was the mistress of
LOLLIUS, son of a powerful proconsul. She
left him to join a theatrical company. She
had success on the stage and many more
lovers, Nicias among them. From him she
learned to read books of philosophy. She
yearned for a simple life but soon turned
to spendthrift pleasures.

In her dressing-room at the theater Thaïs
is admiring her reflection in her mirror
when suddenly Paphnutius appears. Dropping her mirror, Thaïs screams in fright.
"O God," exclaims Paphnutius, "grant that
this woman's face, instead of scandalizing,
may edify Thy servant!" He tells Thaïs who
he is. To himself he groans, "It is impossible
to approach her without staggering like a
drunken man."

She is angry at first but gradually feels
more tolerant toward him, sympathizing
with his austerities. Hearing that she has
been baptized, he kisses her on the forehead, saying, "Receive the kiss of peace,
sister. Take my hands, poor little wandering
sheep." He is enraptured by the idea that
he can save the soul of Thaïs. She laughs.
"What will people say," she asks, "when
they see I have this desert monk for a
lover?"

Paphnutius refuses to leave her and follows her to an elegant banquet where the
guests are rich and intelligent, though immoral. They show respect for the Christian
piety of Paphnutius. The banquet continues
all night, surfeiting the guests with witty
talk and heavy drinking. At daybreak the
monk seizes Thaïs by the hand and drags
her out, stepping over the drunken guests
and puddles of spilled wine on the floor.
Thaïs says, "I am weary to death of all this.
What must I do?" Paphnutius tells her she
must burn all her luxurious belongings,
then he will take her to a house of refuge
conducted by ALBINA, a Roman noblewoman who has become a holy woman.
Thaïs consents and Paphnutius takes her to
Albina's house, where Thaïs is voluntarily
confined in a bare tiny cell. Thaïs is sealed
in her cell by Paphnutius. He puts one of his
own hairs in the clay with which he seals
her door.

Book III. The Euphorbium. Paphnutius returns to his desert monastery, to the joy of
his disciples, who kiss his feet and sing
holy songs inspired by pious delirium, for
they have heard what he did in Alexandria.
Alone in his hut, Paphnutius realizes that
inwardly he has changed completely because of Thaïs. He no longer recognizes his
own sun-blackened face, nor the manuscripts he has written through the years.

With his forehead on the earth, he prays,
"Jesus, it is Thou who sendeth her to me. Do
not let her charms shine for others." Now
he has another vision, this time of a little
jackal laughing at him from the foot of his
bed. He has visions of Thaïs and of all her
luxurious possessions, which he has made
her destroy. He cries out, "Here are the
countless souls of the sins of Thaïs come to
me!" Paphnutius goes to the hermit Palemon, who advises him to regain his mental
balance by exercising his ability as a scribe.
That night Paphnutius dreams of a man
squatting on the top of a high stone column.
He finds such a column, obtains a ladder,
climbs to the top of the column, and sits
there cross-legged for days and nights. The
villagers are awed by his saintly endurance.
Boys bring him water and food. Pilgrims
come to look at him. He tells them, "I am
alone in a universe of evil thoughts." Barren
women, sick and blind and crippled pilgrims, seek him and he works miracles of
healing from the top of his column. But the
devil appears to him and he hurriedly
climbs down to the ground. For two days he
tramps the countryside, running away from
Satan. Now he has visions of a lute-playing
woman who keeps telling him, "Love me.
As long as you resist, I will torment you."

Wherever he goes, Paphnutius is crazed
by visions of women tempting him. From
a spiritualistic medium, a half-wit called
Paul the Simple, Paphnutius obtains visionary information that Thaïs is dying.
Paphnutius cries, "Fool that I was not to
possess Thaïs while there was yet time! I
must find an eternal hell in which to exhale
the rage that is in me."

He hastens back to Alexandria, to the
convent of Albina, where he left Thaïs in
the cell he himself sealed. He learns that
the seal broke without being touched by a
human hand. On a bed in the courtyard, in
the shade of a fig tree, Thaïs lies white and
near to death. "Father," she says, "wash from
me my wickedness, for my sin is ever before me." Paphnutius implores her, "Do
not die. I love you. Nothing is true but life
on earth and carnal love." She does not hear
him. She murmurs, "Heaven is opening. I
see the saints and angels. I see God." She
dies. Paphnutius throws himself upon her
corpse in a desperate embrace. Albina has
to drive him away from the dead body of
Thaïs. The nuns recoil from the sight of
him. He has become so hideous that with
his own hands he can feel the ugliness of
his face.

The Thousand and One Nights

Traditional stories, written and compiled in Arabic-speaking countries at various times in 5th to 16th centuries.
Published in various translations, 1839 to present day.

THE FIRST English translator called this work *Arabian Nights Entertainments* and the name has stuck to the near exclusion of others. The stories are about as miscellaneous a collection as one could imagine, some of Eastern and some of Western origin; no two texts agree entirely on what stories should be included. At no time has there been any full justification (such as exactly 1,000 stories) for the "thousand" in the title. The translation favored in English-speaking countries is that of R. F. Burton, published 1885 to 1889, but by far the widest sale has been of short, single-volume editions presenting a selection of the stories rewritten for reading by children. One other title is *The Thousand Nights and a Night.* Many of the stories are set in Persia, in the times and brilliant court of the caliph Haroun-al-Raschid in Baghdad, and are supposed to have resulted from the caliph's custom of walking the streets of the city in disguise, attended by his grand vizier, Giafar, and his chief of eunuchs and bodyguard, Mesrour.

A sultan of the Sassanidae (Moslem dynasty in Asia), named SCHAHRIAR, became so disillusioned when he found his beloved wife unfaithful that (after having her put to death) he adopted the practice of marrying a new wife every evening and having her beheaded the next morning. His grand vizier was required to obtain the women for him. After many young women had been sacrificed in this way, SCHEHERAZADE, the vizier's beautiful daughter, insisted that her father designate her as the sultan's next bride. Scheherazade took along her sister DINARZADE, who at the appropriate moment asked Scheherazade to tell the sultan one of her famous stories. By breaking off each story so as to arouse interest in what would come next, Scheherazade kept the sultan so intrigued that he postponed her execution day after day and year after year, saving the young womanhood of his realm.

THE FISHERMAN AND THE GENIE

A fisherman draws in a jar (or bottle) from the sea. When he opens it, a terrible genie emerges in a cloud of smoke. The genie, who was imprisoned long before for disobedience to the king of the genii, hates everyone and prepares to kill the fisherman. The fisherman saves himself by professing to doubt that so large a genie could ever have gotten into so small a jar. The genie furnishes proof by transforming himself again into smoke and reëntering the jar —which the fisherman quickly corks again.

ALI BABA AND THE FORTY THIEVES

ALI BABA, a poor woodcutter, happens upon a cave whose door is a great slab of rock. He sees a troop of forty robbers ride up. When their leader calls "Open, sesame!" the slab magically rolls aside and they enter the cave. Watching until they have all left the cave, Ali Baba uses the magic formula, enters the cave, and helps himself to the treasures inside. The words "Shut, sesame!" close the cave door again. The treasures he takes gradually from the cave make Ali Baba a rich man. Ali Baba's brother CASSIM cajoles the secret and the password from him and goes to the cave, but when inside the cave Cassim forgets the password and is found and killed by the robbers.

Through Cassim's death the robbers learn that it is Ali Baba who has been stealing their treasure. They plot to avenge themselves on Ali Baba, but Ali Baba's beautiful slave girl MORGIANA saves him. The forty thieves gain access to Ali Baba's house by hiding in large jars, and Morgiana kills them by pouring hot oil into the jars. Gratefully, Ali Baba gives her his son in marriage.

SINDBAD (OR SINBAD) THE SAILOR

A poor porter in Baghdad named HINDBAD envies the luxury in which the rich SINDBAD THE SAILOR lives. Sindbad has the porter brought into his great mansion and tells of the trials he had, in seven great voyages, to amass his wealth. [In these tales there are several similar to those of the *Odyssey.*]

First Voyage. Sindbad, a wealthy youth, squanders his money and, attempting to re-

The roc carries Sinbad

coup, buys a stock of merchandise and sails on a trading voyage. The ship stops at what seems to be a small island and Sindbad goes "ashore"; he is plunged into the sea when the island proves to be a sleeping whale. He reaches another island, where he is well treated by the king. He succeeds in reaching his ship in port, trades his merchandise, and returns to Baghdad rich again.

Second Voyage. Bored with his life of indolence, Sindbad embarks on another trading voyage. The ship stops for water at an island and Sindbad falls asleep and is left behind. He discovers a great white ball, about 50 feet in diameter; it is a roc's egg, and soon the roc comes to set. Sindbad ties himself to the roc's foot and when it flies away he is carried to the fabulous valley of diamonds—an unreachable chasm whose floor is covered with diamonds. Merchants throw lumps of meat from the cliffs above, and eagles pick them up—with diamonds sticking to them—and carry them to their nests, which the merchants can reach. Sindbad loads himself with diamonds, then rides out of the valley attached to a piece of meat. He returns to Baghdad richer than ever.

Third Voyage. Sindbad's ship is captured by savage dwarfs and is sailed to an island where a one-eyed giant ogre (equivalent to the Cyclops) devours the men one by one. Sindbad contrives to put out the giant's one eye and escape. He is then in danger from a gigantic man-eating snake, but he is rescued by a passing ship and again concludes a most profitable voyage.

Fourth Voyage. This time Sindbad is shipwrecked and cast ashore, with others, on an island where cannibals capture them and feed them well to fatten them. Sindbad saves himself by eating little and remaining lean. He escapes and reaches a kingdom where bridles and stirrups are unknown, and he makes himself rich and famous by "inventing" them. The king gives him a wife, but when she dies he finds that the surviving spouse is always buried alive with the dead one. Sindbad is so buried. He finds himself in an underground cavern full of jewels. He escapes, taking with him so many jewels that his riches are greatly increased.

Fifth Voyage. Sindbad and other merchants on his ship land on an island and find another roc's egg. Over Sindbad's protests, the other merchants destroy it. The roc then returns and destroys the ship. Only Sindbad escapes. Then he encounters the Old Man of the Sea, who fastens himself on Sindbad's back and uses Sindbad as a beast of burden. Sindbad rids himself of his burden by making wine and getting the Old Man drunk. A ship rescues Sindbad and on another island he acquires a stock of coconuts by throwing stones at monkeys, who retaliate by throwing back coconuts. Sindbad concludes his voyage with great profit.

Sixth Voyage. A storm drives Sindbad's ship ashore and breaks it up, but on the barren island Sindbad finds many precious stones and also an underground river, on which he rides a raft to the city of Serendib, where the king receives him well and sends him home with great wealth plus rich presents for the caliph Haroun-al-Raschid.

Seventh Voyage. The caliph sends Sindbad with return gifts to the king of Serendib. On the way back Sindbad is captured by pirates, who sell him as a slave to a merchant. The merchant gives him bow and arrows and makes him an elephant-hunter to kill elephants for ivory. Sindbad is so successful that the elephants eventually combine against him and carry him to their burial-ground, where he sees an almost limitless store of ivory. He returns with this news to the merchant, who rewards him with freedom and a stock of the ivory, with which Sindbad returns home.

ALADDIN AND THE WONDERFUL LAMP

The boy Aladdin is the indolent son of a poor tailor. He is accosted by a stranger, who introduces himself as Aladdin's rich uncle MUSTAPHA but is actually a magician. Mustapha takes him to a cave, gives him a ring to wear, and sends him in to bring back a certain lamp. A charm on the lamp makes it worthless to the magican unless he receives it from the hand of another. Aladdin, in stupid fear, does not obey instructions and the magician seals him in the cave and leaves. But when Aladdin rubs the ring a genie appears, the slave of the ring, and the genie delivers him from the cave. Aladdin takes the lamp home. When his mother begins to rub it, to polish it, another and more powerful genie appears, the slave of the lamp. This genie, summoned whenever Aladdin rubs the lamp, brings Aladdin wealth, the sultan's daughter as a wife, and a palace to live in. Aladdin becomes a great man in the kingdom. But the magician, disguising himself as a peddler and crying "New lamps for old!", tricks the princess into exchanging the magic lamp for a new one. Now the genie, obeying the magician, transports Aladdin's palace—with the princess in it—to Africa. The genie of the ring cannot help Aladdin except by transporting him to Africa, where the palace and princess are. The princess gets the lamp back from the magician and Aladdin is restored to his wealth and position. The magician's brother tries to obtain revenge but Aladdin is able to overcome him. When the sultan dies, Aladdin becomes sultan and reigns for many years.

THE HUNCHBACK

A tailor and his wife, seeing a hunchback singing before their door, invited him to dinner. The hunchback choked on a fishbone and died. Fearful of being charged with murder, they carried him to a Jewish physician and left him outside the physician's door. Coming out, the physician stumbled over the hunchback and thought he had killed him. Since it was sure death for an infidel to kill a Moslem, the physician stealthily placed the hunchback's body in the house of a rich neighbor, a Moslem. This neighbor, finding the hunchback in his house, took him for a thief and struck him. Then, frightened as the others had been, the neighbor put the body in the street. Here

a Christian merchant stumbled over him. A policeman arrested the Christian merchant, who was promptly sentenced to death.

But just as the merchant was to be hanged, one by one the Moslem, the physician and the tailor, all conscience-stricken, presented themselves and confessed. The curious matter came to the attention of the sultan. While he was making up his mind, a barber appeared and removed the fishbone from the throat of the hunchback, who promptly came back to life. All the accused men were freed and the barber became the sultan's personal barber.

Calling forth the genie

The Three Musketeers

Novel by Alexandre Dumas *père*, 1802–1870.
Published 1844. (ML, 143)

IT MAY NOT BE GOING TOO FAR to say that *The Three Musketeers* is the finest swashbuckling novel ever written; certainly it has been the most popular. Most translations of it are antiquated and stilted. Since *The Three Musketeers* is now generally published for boys to read, it appears almost entirely in cut versions, not so much because of any impropriety in the original text as because the novel is simply too long to publish at the low prices at which juvenile literature must be sold. The character d'Artagnan must appeal to anyone's romantic streak and it was probably the best rôle of the acrobatic motion-picture actor Douglas Fairbanks. D'Artagnan is not one of the three musketeers who appear in the title; after the earliest chapters there are four musketeers.

1. D'ARTAGNAN, a young Gascon, noble but impoverished, is en route to Paris with a letter of introduction to Capt. DE TREVILLE, commander of the King's Musketeers (private army or guard). In an innyard at Meung, d'Artagnan is drawn into swordplay with a dark stranger, of aristocratic appearance, who interrupts his conversation with a beautiful lady (addressed as "Milady") to make fun of d'Artagnan's sorry steed. The young Gascon is overcome when two friends of the stranger, together with the landlord, join forces against him. When he recovers he finds that his letter to de Treville has disappeared. 2. Arrived in Paris, d'Artagnan presents himself at the headquarters of the Musketeers. He overhears disparagement of the Cardinal, RICHELIEU; it seems the Musketeers frequently clash with the Cardinal's Guards. 3–4. Three musketeers, ARAMIS, PORTHOS, and ATHOS, are given a tongue-lashing by Capt.

de Treville for losing an encounter with the Cardinal's Guards. They correct the false accounts he has had of this matter, and he makes his peace with them. Then de Treville hears d'Artagnan's story. He promises to consider the young Gascon for the Musketeers—but at a future date. D'Artagnan suddenly catches a glimpse of his enemy of Meung from the window, and darts out of the building after him. He stumbles over Athos, then Porthos, and with each arranges to duel, with Athos at noon, Porthos at one. A third duel, with Aramis, is arranged when d'Artagnan ignorantly picks up a lady's handkerchief that Aramis has dropped. 5. D'Artagnan meets the three musketeers at the appointed place; but before they can cross swords, the Cardinal's Guards, led by DE JUSSAC, arrive and attempt to arrest the musketeers. D'Artagnan fights alongside the musketeers. He displays elegant swordsmanship and together the musketeers and d'Artagnan defeat the Guards. From this time on, they are fast friends. 6. De Treville defends the conduct of the three musketeers and their new friend when the King summons him for an explanation. The King recommends that d'Artagnan be enlisted in the Guard Company of des Essarts until there is a vacancy in the Musketeers. 7. D'Artagnan and the trio of Athos, Porthos, and Aramis see much of each other. Athos is a reserved type, rumored to have suffered a heartless betrayal at the hands of a woman he trusted. Porthos, a loquacious dandy, is a famous gallant with the ladies. Aramis' true vocation, he says is that of abbé, which he will assume at the proper time.

8–9. D'Artagnan's landlord, M. BONACIEUX, asks his help: His wife, CONSTANCE, seamstress to the Queen, has been abducted, for some reason connected with the Queen's reputed affair with the English Duke of BUCKINGHAM. At this moment, d'Artagnan spots the man of Meung from the window. Bonacieux names him as the abductor, and d'Artagnan dashes out after him, but his enemy has escaped him. The Cardinal's Guards burst in and arrest Bonacieux.

D'Artagnan and his friends feel they are enmeshed in a dangerous situation, likely to bring them into conflict with the Cardinal, who is the Queen's enemy. They swear a mutual oath: "All for one, one for all." 10. The Guards establish a "mousetrap" in Bonacieux's apartment and when Mme. Bonacieux returns the Guards seize her. D'Artagnan rushes downstairs, routs her assailants, and finds her charming. 11. On his way, later in the evening, to visit Aramis, d'Artagnan comes upon Mme. Bonacieux in the street. She declines to reveal what she is about, though he professes love. He promises not to spy on her. Later he runs across her again, with a man in musketeer's dress who turns out to be the Duke of Buckingham. D'Artagnan places himself at the duke's service and escorts both safely to the Louvre, where the Queen awaits them. 12. The Duke is in Paris at this difficult moment in history, when war between England and France is near, because of a trick of the Cardinal. He speaks words of love to the Queen. Though she reciprocates, she asks him to leave France at once. For pledge of her feelings towards him, she gives him a rosewood casket in which are twelve diamond studs, given to her by the King. 13–14. Bonacieux is put in the Bastille when he says he can recognize the man who abducted his wife. When he is removed from his cell he is convinced he is being taken to execution, but instead he is brought before the Cardinal, who pumps him for information. All he knows is that his wife, Constance, has been visiting linen-drapers much of late. He is removed. D'Artagnan's "man of Meung" tells the Cardinal of the Queen's gift of the diamond studs. The Cardinal exonerates Bonacieux, who becomes his man from then on. The Cardinal then dispatches a man to London, with a letter to Lady DE WINTER (the Milady of the inn at Meung), telling her to attend the first ball to which the duke goes and steal two of the diamond studs.

15–16. Treville denies to the King that Athos or d'Artagnan has engaged in any intrigue. The Cardinal tells the King that Buckingham has been in Paris and suggests it was for reasons of politics, not love. A letter taken from the Queen by the King's order confirms this: it is addressed to the King of Spain and carries a plan of attack against the Cardinal. Pretending friendship for the Queen despite this, the Cardinal suggests that the King give a ball for the Queen and she can wear the diamond studs he has given her. Eight days later the Cardinal hears from Milady that she has stolen two studs and will bring them to Paris.

17. When the Queen is told of the plan for the ball, she feels she is faced with ruin. Constance suggests sending her husband Bonacieux to the duke to bring back the studs. But Bonacieux refuses; he fears the Cardinal more than he fears Her Majesty. 18–19. D'Artagnan, having overheard, agrees to go for the studs. He gets a fortnight's leave for himself and for each of his three friends, who will go with him. "Four must start if one is to arrive."

20. At Chantilly, on the road to the Channel, a Cardinal's man picks a quarrel with Porthos. While Porthos fights, the other three go on. They run into an ambush near Beauvais. Aramis is wounded and is left at an inn at Crevecoeur. At Amiens, d'Artagnan and Athos run into another trap; only d'Artagnan escapes. At Calais, d'Artagnan obtains a pass to leave the country, by force, from the Count DE WARDES. When the young Gascon arrives in England he finds Buckingham and gives him the Queen's letter requesting the studs back. 21. Buckingham, having discovered two of the studs are gone, arranges for his jeweler to duplicate them. D'Artagnan leaves with them. 22. At the ball, the Cardinal calls the King's attention to the fact that the Queen is not wearing the diamond studs. When she says she left them at the Louvre, the King tells her to send for them. While she is out of the room, the Cardinal shows the King the two stolen studs. The King is bewildered, the Cardinal triumphant; then the Queen reappears, wearing twelve diamond studs! The Cardinal is defeated, and the Queen rewards d'Artagnan with a ring. 23. Treville warns d'Artagnan that the Cardinal will know who has thwarted him and try to square accounts.

24. D'Artagnan goes to a rendezvous with Constance and finds she has again been abducted by the dark man (whose name is DE ROCHFORT). 25–27. D'Artagnan rides out of Paris and finds Porthos recovering from his wound and Aramis preparing himself for ordination. When d'Artagnan gives Aramis a letter from his mistress, the Duchess de Chevreuse, Aramis becomes worldly again. In Amiens d'Artagnan finds Athos barricaded in the cellar of the inn, drunk. He learns Athos' story: When Athos was young, he fell in love with and married a beautiful girl. One day he discovered on her shoulder the brand of the fleur-de-lis, mark of a convicted thief. Enraged, he stripped her and hanged her to a tree. Since then he has been without faith in women. 28. Athos and d'Artagnan gamble their horses away. They find Aramis and Porthos also without horses. They have very little money. Back in Paris they are told that they must look to their equipment, since war is about to start. 29. Porthos makes up to a wealthy, mincing matron, Mme. Coquenard. 30. D'Artagnan, spotting Milady in church, decides to divert himself with a new heart interest. Besides, he thinks she may know something of the abduction of Mme. Bonacieux. He follows Milady but meets and quarrels with her brother-in-law, Lord de Winter, and arranges a duel—himself and the three musketeers on one side, Lord de Winter and three other Englishmen on the other. 31. The English are defeated. Lord de Winter, impressed by d'Artagnan's chivalry, courage, and skill, offers to introduce him to his sister-in-law. Milady, cold at first, accepts d'Artagnan's attentions. 32–37. D'Artagnan is madly in love with Milady, but she does not love him—she hates him, in fact, for sparing her brother-in-law's life (she expects an inheritance). D'Artagnan makes a conquest of KITTY, Milady's

maid, through whom he intercepts Milady's love notes to the Count de Wardes. The musketeers, each in his own way, manage to get their equipment together. D'Artagnan is taken for the Comte de Wardes, in the darkness, by Milady; she receives him warmly, and gives him a sapphire ring. He shows the ring to Athos, who recognizes it: It is one he gave to his false love. D'Artagnan spends the night with Milady. She accidentally reveals the brand on her shoulder. D'Artagnan and Athos decide both of them are in danger from Milady; fortunately, they will soon be at the siege of La Rochelle with the other Musketeers.

39. D'Artagnan receives two invitations: one to meet somebody, presumably a lady, on the road to Chaillot; the other, to go to the Cardinal's palace. He fails to find any lady waiting for him, though he catches a glimpse of Mme. Bonacieux in a passing carriage; and, escorted by his friends, he goes to the Cardinal. 40. The Cardinal offers d'Artagnan a commission in his Guards. D'Artagnan respectfully refuses. 41–43. The war has begun. D'Artagnan learns that Constance has been confined in a convent. D'Artagnan and his friends have several narrow escapes from dangers plotted by Milady.

44. The Cardinal asks Milady to go to Buckingham, bearing threats to ruin him unless he foregoes an attack on France. Milady agrees to go if the Cardinal will dispose of d'Artagnan for her. The three musketeers hear all this, through a stovepipe in the inn where Milady is staying. 45. Athos reveals himself to Milady as her husband, the Comte de la Fere, and warns her to let d'Artagnan alone or he himself will destroy her. The Cardinal has given her a letter of carte-blanche (unlimited freedom from arrest) and Athos compels her to surrender it to him. 46. The Musketeers tell d'Artagnan of the pact between the Cardinal and Milady. Before they finish breakfast they repel three attacks by the Rochelais. The Cardinal rewards them by making d'Artagnan a musketeer. 48. PLANCHET, d'Artagnan's lackey, and BAZIN, Aramis', are sent to warn the Queen and de Winter of the Cardinal's plot, and accomplish their missions.

49–50. Milady reaches England, where, against her will, she is conveyed to her brother-in-law's castle. Lord de Winter tells her he knows all about her activities and that she must remain his prisoner until she can be sent out of England to one of the colonies, never to return. He warns her jailor, Lt. FELTON, not to succumb to her blandishments. 51. The siege of La Rochelle continues. 52. In de Winter's castle-prison, Milady pretends a fainting-fit, deceiving Felton, but not Lord de Winter. She decides Felton, simple-minded and virtuous, can be corrupted. 53. Learning that Felton is a Puritan, Milady plays the Puritan lady, singing hymns, etc. 54. She half-persuades Felton that she is innocent of any dishonor. 55. Milady pretends to be on the point of suicide, by hanging, and asks Felton not to interfere. He wants to know the real truth about her. She asks him to come back later

—with a knife. **56.** Milady tells Felton a false story about being dishonored, by a great person, some years ago. **57.** It was her ravisher, she tells him, who had her branded, unjustly, and the man was none other than Buckingham. De Winter, already prejudiced against her because his family pride resented her marriage to his brother, has been further turned against her by Buckingham's false explanation of the branding. When de Winter interrupts this recital, she pretends to stab herself. **58.** Felton helps Milady escape from the castle and get aboard a ship bound for France; he will join her there, after avenging her dishonor by killing Buckingham. **59.** Felton visits Buckingham on a pretext, accuses him of seducing Milady, and stabs him to death. He is arrested and perceives that he has been betrayed. The ship with Milady on it has not waited for him but has set sail for France.

60. Aramis arranges to have Mme. Bonacieux released from the convent. **61.** Milady goes to the convent at Bethune. She finds Mme. Bonacieux there as a novice. Mme. Bonacieux tells her she is expecting d'Artagnan's arrival. **62.** The man of Meung arrives, to meet Milady. They arrange to meet later, at Armentières. **63.** Before Milady can spirit Mme. Bonacieux away, the musketeers arrive. As the next best thing, Milady poisons the young woman. D'Artagnan and his friends reach her too late; she is dying. Lord de Winter arrives. All are now united in purpose: to pursue and destroy Milady. **64.** They set off for Armentières, by different roads. Athos visits the Executioner of Lille, and persuades him to join them at their destination. **65.** Near Armentières, in a little house on the bank of the river Lys, they find Milady, alone. They accuse her, each in turn, of the crimes she has committed. The executioner, too: she has ruined his brother. Each in turn then passes sentence upon her: death. **66.** She makes a last stand by the river—but in vain. The executioner takes her across to the left bank; and before her judges, on the other bank, justice is done.

67 (Conclusion). The news of Buckingham's death reaches France; the King is overjoyed. The musketeers return to Paris. The man of Meung (de Rochfort), arrives to arrest d'Artagnan and bring him before the Cardinal, charged with treason. To the Cardinal, d'Artagnan denies the charge. He tells the story of Milady, her crimes and her punishment. The Cardinal, though affected, tells d'Artagnan he will be tried and even condemned. D'Artagnan then reveals he has a letter of *carte-blanche* from His Eminence himself (the letter originally prepared for Milady). The Cardinal alters purpose and hands d'Artagnan a blank commission in the Musketeers; Milady, after all, was too dangerous, and d'Artagnan can be a useful servant of the Cardinal. His Eminence tells Rochfort to make his peace with the young Gascon. For his part, d'Artagnan offers the commission to each of his friends in turn; when each in turn refuses it, Athos writes d'Artagnan's name in.

69. (Epilogue). La Rochelle surrenders. D'Artagnan assumes his rank. Porthos leaves the service and marries the rich widow Coquenard. Aramis takes holy orders. Athos remains a musketeer a while longer, then quits the service. D'Artagnan fights Rochfort three times; then they make up, for good.

Milady accidentally reveals her brand to d'Artagnan

594

The Time of Man

Novel by Elizabeth Madox Roberts, 1886–1941.
Published and © 1926 by Viking Press, New York. (NAL, S1133)

IN A PERIOD in which many novelists were reporting realistically and well on the poor whites of the South, and especially on the illiterate and semi-illiterate farming people of Kentucky and adjoining states, Elizabeth Madox Roberts wrote the best of the many. *The Time of Man* deserves high rank in American literature. It is sensitive, real, and in sum profound. Mrs. Roberts, a Kentuckian, knew her people from long personal observation. She wrote other worthy novels but this is her masterpiece and would be a masterpiece for almost any writer.

Chap. 1. ELLEN CHESSER and her parents NELLIE and HENRY, itinerant sharecroppers, leave the road to take up the offer of a likely job with farmer BODINE. Ellen is terribly sad that this means saying goodbye to their friends of the wagon trail, especially one woman, TESSIE WEST. Ellen achieves her 15th birthday and begins to mature. She longs for a place of her own, drawers to put things in, and pretty things. She decides to run away and find Tessie, who devoted time to her and shared many of her delights in the world. She walks and walks to the nearest town, expecting that the folk there will know where Tessie is. But she never finds Tessie and farmer Bodine's buggy, driven by her angry father, finally catches up with her and takes her home.

Chaps. 2–3. A year has passed. Ellen follows her mother in the tobacco fields. She is conscious now of men and particularly wants JOE TRENT, a farmer's son, to notice her. He only farms part of the time and is at college the rest. Henry Chesser moves to a new place, the Al Wakefield farm in another end of the county. He starts his crops. The Chessers like the new place. Ellen wonders about life. She is lonesome but loves being alive. By autumn Ellen knows many of the young people around her. She is asked to a party and sings there. Her singing is liked.

Chap. 4. The cow has a calf and the farmer gives it to Ellen. Also Ellen gets a new frock and her mother lets her choose the color. Ellen goes around with the young folk of the area and has a beau, JONAS PRATHER, whom she likes, and another, SEBE TOWNLEY, who does not attract her. She learns about infidelity when she sees SCOTT MACMURTRIE betray his wife CASSIE. Jonas asks Ellen to marry him. But he tells her he has an illegitimate baby by Jule Nestor, the local slut. He is wretched at the revelation, but Ellen bears it and tries to adjust herself to it because she loves him.

Chap. 5. Ellen and Jonas are engaged.

Tessie West in all these years. She thinks she might not know Tessie if she met her. And she thinks about life and herself, one, comprehensible and entire, without flaw. She feels great happiness and joy. But a barn in the neighborhood burns and Jasper's reputation of being a barn-burner has followed him, so he decides they must move. He says Ellen can stay, but she tells him she will always have to go where he has to go and they make their plans together. They do not know where they are going. Some better country, they hope. Their own land maybe, their own place maybe, a place to keep perhaps. So they leave, going their own way with the moon high and the sky blue, asking no questions of the way but taking their own turnings.

Jasper is acquitted but the Kents move again

Tobacco Road

Novel by Erskine Caldwell, 1903– Published 1932 by Duell, Sloan & Pearce, New York. © 1932 by Erskine Caldwell. (NAL, S627; ML, 249).

ERSKINE CALDWELL, who wrote the biggest-selling novel of all times (*God's Little Acre*), bade fair at one time to hold also the record for the longest-run play of all time, the dramatization of *Tobacco Road*. The longer run of the dramatization of *Life With Father* saved him from this double fate. As a novel, *Tobacco Road* is as readable and as shocking as *God's Little Acre*, perhaps more so. Readers who are gently bred, and even those bred not quite so gently, cannot help thinking that Caldwell's picture of the depth of poverty and reversion to human animality, as he depicts them in this book, *must* be exaggerated. Those who have traveled the backroads of the South know there is no exaggeration. That makes *Tobacco Road* and other Caldwell works sociologically important, for few other novelists have wished to write truly about such conditions and no other has done it so well. Like other Caldwell novels, *Tobacco Road* is set in the wornout farming region of central Georgia.

Then Jonas goes away to a job in another area but he promises faithfully to come back for Ellen. She writes to him and longs for him. She learns that Cassie has hanged herself.

Chap. 6. Ellen hears that Jonas has come back but is squiring SALLIE LOU, a girl more light of heart than Ellen. Ellen can hardly believe it. She dresses herself up and goes to find Jonas and get him back. After walking 10 miles to find him, she hears that he has left the neighborhood with Sallie Lou.

Chaps. 7–8. The Chessers move to another farm, the Orkeys' Place. It is a lonely place but Ellen meets JASPER KENT. They take to each other and Jasper tells her about his life. He asks her to be his wife and she agrees. Jasper is accused of barn-burning, and though the accusation is untrue Jasper has to go away. He promises to come back for Ellen and she knows he will. She has taken care, this time, not to have another girl steal him. Jasper comes back for Ellen and they go off and live on the place Jasper is working. They are very close and very happy. Ellen has her first child. Jasper is acquitted of the charge of barn-burning. Ellen has her second child, this time a girl. They move again. They are close to each other and happy with her children.

Chap. 9. Ellen notices a change in Jasper. She knows he has been unfaithful to her with HESTER SHUCK. Ellen feels as if her life has gone solid and stiff within her flesh. Yet still she tries to please Jasper. She takes care of her appearance so that she is noticed as a handsome woman. Ellen and Jasper fight each other. Jasper is jealous of his employer, JOE PHILLIPS, who finds Ellen attractive. Ellen, again pregnant, bears Jasper's accusations that she is not pregnant by him. She bears her child alone. He is not a healthy baby but Jasper and Ellen cherish him and the child brings them close again. It is a sad day when he dies, barely three years after his birth.

Chap. 10. Ellen watches her children grow and the country around her change. She wonders what might have become of

Chaps. 1–4. LOV BENSEY, on his way home with a bag of turnips he has just bought, stops on the road in front of the Lester place to complain to JEETER LESTER, the head of the family. Lov's wife, PEARL, is Jeeter's youngest child. She is 12 years old. She refuses to talk or sleep with her husband. Jeeter and the rest of the Lesters who live in the ramshackle three-room house are more interested in the turnips than in Lov's grievance; they have been close to starvation for some time. Jeeter's farm is not producing; he has no money or credit to buy seed-cotton and guano; he cannot (he says) get work as a sharecropper; and, besides, he is "sot." Nothing will satisfy him but to work his land; and since he cannot do that, he is waiting for the Lord to provide. Lov, unsympathetic, tells him he is simply lazy. Only two of the original seventeen children in the Lester family are in evidence; the others have all gone away and married. DUDE, the youngest son, is killing time throwing a baseball against the house and catching it on the rebound. But ELLIE MAY, Jeeter's harelipped daughter, has her eyes on Lov, not on his turnips. While talking to Jeeter, Lov begins to eat the turnips. Jeeter, his wife ADA and his old grandmother watch the turnips with hungry eyes. Ellie May watches Lov, edging closer and closer to him. Before long she has him forgetting about Pearl and about the turnips too. While Lov and Ellie May are "horsing," Jeeter makes a lunge for the bag of turnips. There is a scuffle, which ends with Jeeter in possession of the turnips and Lov entangled with Ellie May. Jeeter makes off with the turnips, but by this time Lov is past caring. Later he goes away, despairing of recovering them.

Chaps. 5–6. Gorged on stolen turnips, Jeeter comes back to the house and finds Sister BESSIE RICE, a woman preacher, sitting on the porch. The Lesters and Sister Bessie share what turnips are left, then Sister Bessie leads a prayer session, asking the Lord's pardon for each of the Lesters in turn. Bessie is a widow, and thinking of getting married again; she is interested in Dude, though she is close to 40 and he is only 16. He is enjoying her attentions. Bessie leaves to consult the Lord before deciding on a new marriage.

Chaps. 7–8. The story of Jeeter Lester is the story of a man with good intentions but not enough strength of will to carry them out. For 15 years he has had in mind an operation to correct Ellie May's harelip, but something has always stopped him from arranging it. But as for his land, he will never give it up willingly. Once it belonged

595

Sister Bessie performs her own marriage ceremony

to Jeeter's family. Since CAPTAIN JOHN, the landowner for whom he sharecropped, moved away to Augusta 7 years ago, Jeeter has had no luck making the soil yield again, but he still hopes. Jeeter, Ada and Jeeter's old mother are all wasting away from pellagra. Jeeter is sustained by the hope that his son TOM will give him some money. Ada would like to see her children and grandchildren and to get some money for a stylish dress to be buried in.

Chaps. 9–12. Bessie returns to tell Dude that the Lord has set His seal of approval on the marriage. Dude wants to marry—but not necessarily the woman preacher. He is repelled by her looks. Bessie wins him over with a promise to buy a new automobile, with a horn. They go to town, buy the automobile, and get a marriage license. Then they return to the Lester place, where Sister Bessie performs the marriage ceremony herself. After immediately consummating their marriage, the newlyweds take off for a ride in the new automobile. Jeeter begins talking to Ellie May about the advantages of marriage and is surprised to discover that she is crying.

Chaps. 13–14. The loan company in Augusta has refused Jeeter credit and the merchants in nearby Fuller have told him to forget about farming and go to work in the mills, but farming is in Jeeter's blood, especially at the spring plowing season. Each year that passes without sowing a crop hurts him more. Only dozing off eases the pain of these thoughts. At sunset, Dude and Sister Bessie return in their new automobile, whose right front fender and headlight are in bad shape, evidently from an accident. They explain that they hit a wagon with a Negro in it; the Negro is dead, apparently. Outside of deploring the damage to the new car, nobody is much upset.

Chaps. 15–16. Jeeter persuades Dude and Bessie to take him to Augusta with a load of firewood he hopes to sell. On the way some of the wood falls off and they have

to stop and load it on again. The engine overheats, then, after it cools off and they start off again, it comes to a second stop near a filling-station. They buy a gallon and a half of gasoline and start off again. Once in Augusta, Jeeter discovers he cannot sell his wood. Since the three of them have only a half dollar (Bessie's) as their total capital, they sell the spare tire on the automobile for $3. Flushed by this new wealth, Jeeter suggests they stay overnight at a hotel. They find one down the street. It turns out to be a strange sort of hotel;

Bessie is separated from her husband and sent from one room to another all night long. Before they return home Jeeter unloads the wood beside the road and burns it, as much as it will burn.

Chaps. 17–18. Dude and Bessie take the car into Burke County to see TOM, the Lester son who has made a success as a cross-tie contractor. They hope he will help his parents. They come back and report failure; Tom's sole contribution has been the suggestion that Jeeter and Ada go to the county poor-farm. Jeeter is warned away from the automobile by Bessie. The dispute turns to blows, with Jeeter and Ada against Bessie. In the end Bessie takes off, with Dude driving. Backing out, Dude runs over grandmother Lester, who has been watching the fight. The old woman dies; but Jeeter is too full of his hatred for Bessie to pay much attention. In any case, there is a new diversion: Lov comes racing down the road to tell the Lesters that Pearl has run off and left him. Jeeter's advice is to forget Pearl and take Ellie May in her place. As Lov turns away to go home, Ellie May makes ready to follow him.

Chap. 19. The time for spring plowing is over and once more Jeeter Lester has done nothing. There is still time, however, to prepare for next year's crop, by burning over the broom-sedge and the blackjack and pine on his land. So he starts it all burning in the late afternoon. When he goes to sleep, alone in the ramshackle house with Ada, it is still burning. They are both burned to death in the night, as they sleep.

Tom Jones

Novel by Henry Fielding, 1707–1754. Published 1749. (ML, 185 & T15)

SOME HISTORIANS of English literature have called *Tom Jones* the first real novel. Whether or not it was that, it was the first great novel. Because its author was almost as bitter as he was talented, *Tom Jones* is satirical, ironic, and often pessimistic, yet it is humorous to the point of broad farce and has a great amount of good humor in it. Fielding set out to write "a novel about a hero" and he made his hero a perfectly human being who made mistakes and did things he would later regret but who had the two qualities that to Fielding were the essence of the heroic, sincerity and generosity. *Tom Jones* is distinguished by the brief essays that precede the main sections of the book. In these essays Fielding chats with the reader as though they were observing the action together. The characters other than the hero Tom Jones are chiefly types that Fielding painted as broadly as possible. Critics may call them one-dimensional, a phrase that hardly anyone understands anyway, but there is no doubt that Fielding intended them to appear just as they do.

Book 1. The worthy and wealthy Squire ALLWORTHY, a childless widower whose estate is in Somersetshire with only his sister BRIDGET in his household, comes home from London to discover a newborn baby in his bed. Attempts are made to determine the identity of the child's mother; one JENNY JONES, who formerly worked in the Allworthy household, is accused. Neighborhood indignation forces Squire Allworthy to send Jenny away from the town, but he treats her kindly. The baby

he takes into his home. Miss Bridget suddenly marries Captain BLIFIL.

Book 2. Eight months later, the Blifils have a child. Though the captain objects, Allworthy has the Blifil boy brought up with the foundling, who has been named TOM JONES, and who thus is raised as a gentleman. A schoolmaster named PARTRIDGE, for whom Jenny had also worked, is made to leave the community because it is the popular belief that he is Tom's father. Captain Blifil, just when he was planning what to do with the wealth he would inherit from Allworthy, himself dies suddenly. By this somewhat drastic act he recaptures the love of his wife Bridget. It is the one and only sure way to do so.

Book 3. Tom and Master BLIFIL are educated by two tutors, SQUARE and THWACKUM. Both tutors like the sober Master Blifil, who appears virtuous; both persecute the carefree Tom, who shows a propensity to many vices. Tom's kinder nature is revealed when a gamekeeper named BLACK GEORGE is unfairly treated. Blifil clearly lacks the quality of mercy.

Book 4. Squire WESTERN, Allworthy's neighbor, a rough, hearty, hunting type, takes a liking to Tom, who like Western is a horseman. SOPHIA, the widowed Squire Western's dearly beloved daughter, long since took a liking to Tom, who was very kind to her when she was a child. She begins to fall in love with Tom. Tom's romantic interest at the time is MOLLY SEAGRIM, a local girl with a poor reputation. One day while out hunting with the Westerns, Tom rescues Sophia when her horse runs away. He is slightly injured and is taken into the Westerns' house to recuperate.

Book 5. One day Tom goes to visit Molly and finds her in bed with none other than Mr. Square. He promises not to betray his tutor. Shortly thereafter, Tom and Sophia declare their love for each other. Tom stays on in Western's house though he is fully recovered from his injury, for Western has become more and more fond of him. Allworthy is suddenly taken ill. He believes he is dying and reads his will. Generous sums are left to all the members of the household, the major part of the inheritance going to young Blifil. Only Tom is happy with his share; and while the others grumble about their lot, only Tom is concerned about the squire's health. Mrs. Blifil dies on her journey from London to her brother's sickbed. When Tom learns that Squire Allworthy will be well again, he becomes drunk while jubilantly toasting his health. Tom comes to blows with Blifil and Mr. Thwackum, who see him in the forest with Molly. Squire Allworthy is not informed of this tiff.

Book 6. Mrs. (Miss) WESTERN, Sophia's aunt, tells Squire Western that Sophia is in love with Tom. Squire Western, blind to the romance all along, is furious, though he likes Tom; it has no more occurred to him that his daughter might marry a poor man than that she might marry an animal of another species. He speaks with Allworthy about a match between Sophia and Blifil. Since the very unemotional Blifil believes the marriage will be to his financial advantage, he accepts it and a formal courtship is begun. Tom and Sophia continue to declare their mutual love in letters and at secret meetings. During one of these, Western surprises the couple and to his horror finds Sophia in Tom's arms. Enraged, he goes immediately to see Allworthy. Blifil chooses this opportune moment to tell Allworthy that Tom drank heavily and carried

The suspicious muff

on badly while he lay on his deathbed. Thwackum backs up this testimony. Allworthy believes Blifil. He gives Tom £500 and permanently turns him out of the house. Tom loses this £500. Black George, the gamekeeper Tom was once so good to, finds and keeps the money.

Books 7–8. Sophia makes plans to run away; her maid, Mrs. HONOUR, is persuaded to help her escape from her home. Tom sets out for Bristol to seek his fortune at sea. At a country inn he has a fight with a soldier and is wounded. The barber who treats Tom's wounds turns out to be Partridge, the man accused of being his father. The two take a liking to each other and decide to travel together. On their journey, they meet the MAN OF THE HILL, who tells them his life story.

Book 9. While walking with the Man of the Hill, Tom sees a woman being attacked by a ruffian. He saves her and takes her to an inn at nearby Upton. Because of their disheveled condition they are badly treated by the landlady until a soldier who sees them recognizes the woman as Captain WATERS' lady.

Book 10. A lady and her maid arrive at the inn, and later that evening comes a gentleman in search of his wife. The description he gives the chambermaid answers to Mrs. Waters' and he is led to her room. He bursts in and finds not only the lady but also Tom Jones. The man, a Mr. FITZPATRICK, sees his error and apologizes. Shortly thereafter, Sophia, who has succeeded in escaping, and Mrs. Honour come to the inn. Partridge indiscreetly reveals to Mrs. Honour Tom's relationship with Mrs. Waters. Sophia hears this and is very upset. She decides to leave the inn at once, but not before having the chambermaid place her muff, which Tom cannot fail to recognize, on his empty bed. Tom is angry with himself and with Partridge. Squire Western is the next to arrive. He finds Tom with Sophia's muff and concludes that Sophia must be with him. After a good deal of confusion, he is persuaded

that such is not the case. Tom leaves the inn.

Book 11. On the road, Sophia meets up with her cousin, Mrs. FITZPATRICK, who was at the inn, unbeknown to Sophia or to her pursuing husband. Mrs. Fitzpatrick confides her marital troubles to Sophia as the two ladies travel to London together. Once in the city, the cousins part. Sophia goes to stay with Lady BELLASTON, a friend of her aunt's. Lady Bellaston promises Sophia protection when she learns Sophia's reasons for fleeing home.

Book 12. Western gives up looking for Sophia shortly after leaving the inn and returns to his hunting. Tom and Partridge continue on their journey to London. They have many adventures and misfortunes on their travels. At one point Tom meets DOWLING, a lawyer and a friend of Allworthy's, to whom he tells his troubles.

Book 13. Upon their arrival in London, Tom and Partridge take lodgings with the widow Mrs. MILLER and her two daughters. Tom becomes friendly with another lodger, a Mr. NIGHTINGALE, who is in love with NANCY, Mrs. Miller's eldest daughter. Lady Bellaston meets Tom through Mrs. Fitzpatrick and becomes enamored of him. Her jealousy is aroused when she returns home one evening to find that Tom and Sophia have met, by chance, in her drawing room. Tom and Sophia are still in love.

Book 14. Tom has some difficulty handling the jealous Lady Bellaston. She comes to visit him in his room. He must conceal the fact from Sophia that Lady Bellaston has been supporting him. Nancy has been abandoned by Nightingale, whose father disapproves of such a marriage. Through Tom's efforts, Nightingale's father is persuaded to change his mind and the couple are to be married.

Book 15. Mrs. Fitzpatrick has written to Mrs. Western, telling her of Sophia's whereabouts, in the hope of regaining the Western family's favor, which she lost when she married Fitzpatrick against their consent. Squire Western comes to Lady Bellaston's house and takes Sophia with him. With Nightingale's help, Tom writes a letter extricating himself from his relationship with Lady Bellaston. Tom learns from Partridge the bad news that Allworthy is coming to London with Blifil, but also the good news that Black George is now a servant in Squire Western's household and will take a letter from Tom to Sophia.

Book 16. Lady Bellaston schemes against Tom. She shows Sophia a letter Tom wrote to break off his relationship with her. Sophia writes to Tom that she never wants to hear from him again. Mrs. Western hopes that Sophia will accept Lord FELLAMAR, who has been wooing her in London, since Sophia seems unrelenting in her refusal of Blifil. Tom goes to visit Mrs. Fitzpatrick, whose schemes to win back her family's favor have failed. Upon leaving her house he meets her jealous husband. Tom wounds

Fitzpatrick in a duel and is taken to prison.

Book 17. Things look bad for Tom, for it is believed that he has killed Fitzpatrick. Mrs. Miller tries to persuade both Allworthy and Sophia of Tom's goodness, giving examples of his kindnesses since he came to London. Mrs. Waters comes to prison to visit Tom. She has been traveling with Fitzpatrick since they met at the inn. Partridge recognizes Mrs. Waters as Jenny

Jones, who is supposedly Tom's mother. Now Tom seems guilty of an unforgivable relationship with his own mother.

Book 18. Squire Allworthy is almost ready to forgive Tom after hearing so many fine things about him from Mrs. Miller, Nightingale, and other friends Tom has made. He hears about Tom's relations with Mrs. Waters and almost changes his mind, but Mrs. Waters assures him that Tom is

not her child but the child of his sister Bridget by a student who once lived at the Squire's house. This student died before Tom's birth. Bridget put her infant on the Squire's bed and paid Jenny, who had taken care of her during her secret confinement, to let the suspicion fall on her. Soon the villany of Blifil is made known: He destroyed a letter Bridget had written, in which she admitted that Tom was her son; and he plotted to have Tom hanged for murder. Blifil is sent away, though Tom's attitude to him is forgiving. Fitzpatrick recovers and admits he started the duel, so Tom is set free. Allworthy makes Tom, his nephew, his heir; and Squire Western no longer has any objections to having Tom as a son-in-law. Tom and Sophia are at last together and marry shortly thereafter. All ends well for the worthy characters in the novel; all ends badly for the unworthy ones.

Tom Sawyer

Novel by Mark Twain (Samuel L. Clemens, 1835–1910).

Published 1876. (PB, PL39; ML, G49)

WHEN MARK TWAIN wrote *Tom Sawyer* there was no established market for children's books and *Tom Sawyer* was written to be read by adults. It has survived as one of the most popular books for juvenile readers and as a classic for adult readers. Nevertheless, despite its popularity and despite its occasional touches of the best Mark Twain style, its principal importance is as a preamble to Mark Twain's really great novel, the sequel to it, *Huckleberry Finn*.

Chap. 1. TOM SAWYER lives in a small Missouri town [Hannibal] on the Mississippi with his Aunt POLLY, sister MARY, and younger half-brother SID. He plays hookey from school to go swimming but is discovered because Sid tattles. Tom gets into a fight with a boy he does not know, gets home late, and is sentenced by his sweet-natured but long-suffering aunt to work on his Saturday holiday.

Chap. 2. Tom is set by his aunt to whitewash a fence. When other boys come along, Tom pretends that whitewashing the fence is a great privilege. The other boys are soon paying him to let them have turns at the job.

Chap. 3. There is a new girl in town. Tom tries to attract her attention but fails. At home he is chastized mistakenly by Aunt Polly for upsetting a sugar bowl, when Sid was the culprit. His aunt doesn't apologize but Tom knows she is sorry. He ends by standing below his new love's window, only to have a maid throw water on him.

Chap. 4. On Sunday Tom is sent out to wash. He dips the soap in the water and lays it down. Then he turns up his sleeves and pours the water on the ground. The maneuver fails and he is made to start washing all over. Sid, Mary and Tom set

off for Sabbath School and church service. The children are rewarded with tickets for the painful task of memorizing the Bible. Sufficient tickets win a Bible as a prize. Tom busily trades various items with the other children until he has amassed a sufficient number of tickets. His new love appears in the class and Tom is elated. The time for giving the Bible prize arrives and Tom, well-stocked with tickets, goes up to get it. It is a stunning surprise. Tom is asked to display his wonderful knowledge of the Bible. He is asked the names of the first two disciples and answers "David and Goliath."

Chap. 5. Tom, Sid, Mary and Aunt Polly stay for the sermon and Tom causes a great disturbance by accidentally letting loose a large black beetle. The insect interests a vagrant poodle, which causes a great disturbance in the church.

Chap. 6. On Monday Tom meets HUCKLEBERRY FINN, the juvenile delinquent of the village, of whom all the mothers disapprove. Of course Tom plays with Huck at every opportunity, as does every other boy. Tom trades a tooth he has just lost for a tick Huck Finn has. Tom arrives late at school and is made to sit with the girls. He finds himself next to his new love. Her name is BECKY THATCHER.

Chap. 7. Tom plays in school with his best friend, JOE HARPER, then at noon goes off with Becky, to whom he declares his love. He tells her they are engaged and kisses her, but inadvertently he reveals that he was previously engaged to AMY LAWRENCE. Becky is very miserable and refuses to make up.

Chaps. 8–9. Tom goes into the woods with Joe Harper and they play Robin Hood. That night Tom sneaks out to meet Huck Finn and go with him to bury a dead cat in the graveyard. There they see young Dr. ROBINSON body-snatching with the help of two disreputable men, MUFF POTTER and INJUN JOE. Injun Joe and Robinson get into a fight and Joe kills Robinson, robs his body, and puts his knife into Potter's

hand while Potter is still unconscious from a blow he received in the fight. The two boys run away. When Potter comes to, Injun Joe attributes the murder to him, telling him he was drunk. Injun Joe pretends to befriend Potter and promises to keep the secret.

Chap. 10. Tom and Huck are terrified. They sign a blood pact in which they agree never to reveal what they have seen. Injun Joe might kill them if he knew they had witnessed the scene at the graveyard. Next day Tom's aunt weeps over his general bad behavior. This upsets Tom still more, for he loves his aunt dearly. Then at school he is rebuffed by Becky and his misery is complete.

Chaps. 11–13. The village hears the news of the murder. Injun Joe accuses Muff Potter and Potter is put in jail. Tom begins to talk in his sleep, which makes Sid very suspicious, and Tom takes every opportunity to smuggle small comforts to Potter in jail. The villagers want to run Injun Joe out of town for body-snatching, but no one is quite brave enough to take the lead. Becky Thatcher stops coming to school and Tom is woebegone at her absence. His aunt thinks he is sick and doses him with medicines. Then Becky returns to school but continues to snub Tom. Tom and Joe and Huck Finn decide to become pirates and choose an island on the Mississippi River for their hangout. They steal a small log raft and make for the island, where they cook themselves a marvelous supper.

Chaps. 14–15. Their first day on the island they all have a wonderful time. Toward nightfall Tom and Joe begin to have misgivings but neither will admit it. Tom decides to sneak home secretly and leave a message for his aunt. At his aunt's house he peeks in and sees Aunt Polly, Sid, Mary and Joe Harper's mother grieving about their disappearance. Tom longs to reveal himself and relieve their unhappiness but he resists. They all think the boys were drowned while swimming. If there is no news before the week-end, the boys' funeral services are to be held. Tom is full of pity but still does not reveal himself. He makes his way back to the island.

Chaps. 16–17. After another day on the island the boys are homesick, but Tom has a stupendous plan. The boys agree it is a wonderful idea and they remain on the island another two nights. Back in town everyone is sad, even Becky Thatcher. On Sunday the funeral services are begun and there is much weeping. In the midst of all of this the three boys troup into the church. Tom feels it is his proudest moment. The whole congregation rejoices.

Chaps. 18–22. Tom has become a hero but Becky is still cold. She turns to another boy in school, but he realizes he is just a foil for Tom and blots Tom's copybook. Tom is whipped. He and Becky are reconciled at last. Then Tom has the measles.

Chaps. 23–24. The sleepy atmosphere of the town is stirred by Muff Potter's murder trial. Huck and Tom are still distressed about the whole business. They reswear each other to secrecy, but in vain, for just before the trial Tom can stand it no longer and tells all to Potter's lawyer. Potter is acquitted and though Tom is a hero by day, he goes in deathly fear of Injun Joe at night.

Chaps. 25–28. Tom and Huck go on a treasure hunt and detect Injun Joe hiding in a haunted house. Not only do Injun Joe and his companion have $600 of ill-gotten money on them but they also find a hidden treasure, thousands in gold coin left in the house by a previous gang of thieves. Both boys are terrified that Injun Joe will find them, but he goes away, taking the treasure. He explores the cave and finds a way out. Judge Thatcher, Becky's father, has the cave sealed. The sealing of the cave kills Injun Joe, who is found dead of suffocation. Tom and Huck return to the cave through the way Tom knows and find the gold treasure. They split it between them and the money is invested for them. Each is also allotted a generous weekly allowance. The widow Douglas gives Huck a home in return for his saving her life. Huck does not enjoy with him. They track him down and find out where he is hanging out but do not know where the treasure box is.

Chaps. 29–30. Becky Thatcher gives a picnic. Huck is watching Injun Joe's hideout. Joe and another man come out and Huck follows them. He learns that Injun Joe is planning to take revenge on the widow Douglas for an old grudge he has against her husband. Huck warns the widow and saves her. Tom and Becky are lost in a cave during the picnic. The town begins a search but after three dreadful days there is still no news.

Chaps. 31–35. Tom and Becky are left in the cave without light. Then, worst horror of all for Tom, he sees Injun Joe in the cave. Joe does not recognize Tom and flees. Tom gradually regains his courage. his new respectability but agrees on Tom's account to give it a try. Tom and Huck begin planning to start a gang of robbers.

They make for the island

Treasure Island

Novel by Robert Louis Stevenson, 1850–1894.

Published 1883. (PB, PL49)

ORIGINALLY STEVENSON called this story *The Sea Cook; Treasure Island* was only its subtitle. For at least 50 years it was the most popular of all books for boys, a position held among girls' books by *Little Women*. *Treasure Island* made popular as a quotation the old seaman's song, "Fifteen men on the Dead Man's Chest—Yo-ho-ho and a bottle of rum!", which the pirate sailors sing. However, the song is more often quoted than sung. An important "character," which however does not appear in the action and so is not outlined, is Long John Silver's parrot. *Treasure Island* is a perennial favorite of motion-picture producers.

Part I. Chap. 1. JIM HAWKINS begins his task of writing down all the particulars of Treasure Island from the beginning to the end, keeping nothing back save the bearings of the island and that only because there is still treasure there not yet lifted. He starts his tale in the year 17—, when he was a small boy. His father and mother kept the Admiral Benbow Inn on the coast and an old seaman with a sabre cut took up lodging there. He called himself the CAPTAIN. He took care to avoid any other seafaring men but asked Jim to look out for one—a man who had but a single leg.

Chap. 2. One frosty January day another man smacking of the sea, a man with two fingers missing on his left hand, appears looking for the captain. The captain gasps, calling the other "BLACK DOG." The two come to blows—Jim does not know about what—and then the captain has a stroke and is put to bed.

Chap. 3. Jim's father dies and Jim and his mother are left alone with the captain. The captain tells Jim that Black Dog and others even worse are after his sea-chest.

If these men put the black spot on him—a kind of summons—Jim is to call the magistrate and other lawful men. Then the captain is visited by a blind man who does give him the black spot. The captain jumps to his feet, planning to outdo his enemies, but has a fit and dies.

Chaps. 4–6. Jim and his mother are terrified to stay at the Inn. They go to the village for help but when the neighbors hear that one of the captain's enemies was Captain FLINT, they refuse to go to the Inn. Flint's reputation is too fearsome. Jim's mother refuses to lose the money the captain owed, and she and Jim go back alone and go through the captain's things in haste. They take some of the money due them and Jim also takes away an oilskin package that arouses his curiosity. They escape from the Inn just in time to miss the arrival of Black Dog, the blind man, and others, who thoroughly rifle the place. Jim's package is opened in the presence of Squire TRELAWNEY and Dr. LIVESY. It is found to contain a map of an island where a treasure is buried. The squire decides to charter a ship in Bristol and he, the doctor and Jim, as cabin-boy, will sail off to find the treasure. Meanwhile all must be on guard against the desperate buccaneers who attacked the inn.

Part II. Chaps. 7–12. After weeks the squire's boat, the *Hispaniola,* is ready. Jim takes leave of his mother and joins the ship's company in Bristol. The squire has employed LONG JOHN SILVER as sea cook. Silver has only one leg and Jim first fears he may be the captain's "one-legged man," but Silver is so kind that Jim's suspicions are overcome. The ship's captain, SMOLLETT, proves to know already what their plan is and where the treasure island lies; there has been too much talk. Nor does Capt. Smollett trust the crew hired by the squire. The ship sails. After several days at sea, Jim, hidden in an apple barrel, overhears a spine-chilling conversation: Silver tells one of the younger hands that he was one of Flint's men and that he is planning to take over the ship and the treasure. He plans to let Smollett find the treasure and navigate the ship almost back to port before he takes over. Jim tells the squire, the doctor, and Smollett. They realize that there is no one they can trust but one another and the squire's three servants. They must go on and must hope that later an opportunity will present itself for them to overcome the pirates, who number 19. The island is reached.

Part III. Chaps. 13–15. When John Silver and the men go ashore, Jim decides to go with them. He secretly sees Silver kill one of the more honest hands and hears another being murdered. Terrified, he runs off and meets BEN GUNN, a sailor who has been marooned on the island for 3 years and saw Flint and his men bury the treasure. Jim takes him into his confidence and Gunn, for assurance of his passage home, agrees to help them.

Part IV. Chaps. 16–21. On the ship the captain, squire and doctor hear the men being killed ashore. They decide to leave the ship and set themselves up in the stockade and log blockhouse they know to exist on the island. One of the ship's crew joins them, a seaman named GRAY. They attain the log cabin with some inadequate supplies and two guns. REDRUTH, one of the squire's

Silver offers a truce

men, is killed in the process. Jim Hawkins manages to join the others in the stockade. The next morning Silver offers truce terms but they are refused. Silver and his men attack the stockade. Five of them are killed, but the Captain is wounded and another of the squire's men is killed. Still, the odds against Jim and his company have improved.

Part V. Chaps 22–24. Jim sneaks out of the stockade and finds a small boat Ben Gunn told him he made. Jim decides to cut adrift the *Hispaniola* with the pirates still left aboard her. Instead, both the ship and Jim in his little boat start rapidly drifting out to sea. The next day, Jim manages to board the ship, which has no one at the wheel.

600

Chaps. 25–26. Two men were left aboard by the pirates but only one, the coxswain ISRAEL HANDS, is still alive. Jim succeeds in beaching the boat but just as he does so he is attacked by Hands. He overcomes Hands by a lucky accident but is pinned to the mast by a dirk thrown by Hands.

Chap. 27. Jim frees himself of the dirk and with the ship at hand to rescue the others he sets off for the blockhouse. When he gets there he finds not the kindly squire and company but John Silver and his men, who capture him.

Part VI. Chaps. 28–29. There are six buccaneers in the blockhouse and Silver is having a hard time keeping them under control. He knows they are ready to rebel against him, so he is anxious to save Hawkins from being murdered, in case he is forced to go over to the squire's side.

Chap. 30. Jim is awakened next morning by the doctor, who comes to treat the wounded buccaneers. With Silver's help, Jim is allowed a few minutes alone with the doctor and tells him where the ship is. The doctor refuses to tell Silver why they left the blockhouse and gave Silver the treasure chart, but the doctor promises that if Silver keeps Jim safe he will do his best for him

if they get back to England.

Chaps. 31–32. Jim is taken along when Silver and his men go off to find the treasure. At the hiding place they find the cache rifled and the treasure, £700,000, is gone.

Chap. 33. All the men turn on Long John Silver and Jim; but just as they are about to attack, three musket shots flash out. Two of the buccaneers die and three of them run off. Ben Gunn, the doctor and Gray appear and they, with Jim and Silver, go to the cave where Ben Gunn hid Flint's treasure. There Jim finds Smollett, recovering from his wound, and the squire, as well as the treasure, great heaps of coins and quadrilaterals built of bars of gold. Gray is stationed to guard the *Hispaniola*, which has been set afloat again by the tides.

Chap. 34. Next day all start work transporting the treasure to the ship. There are coins of every kind and country. It is decided that the three pirates on the island must be abandoned, as another mutiny cannot be risked. The *Hispaniola* sets sail for Bristol. Ben Gunn helps Silver to escape from the ship in the shore boat, for he did not feel anyone would be safe so long as Silver was aboard. They all reached Bristol safely and had ample share of the treasure.

The Tree of the Folkungs

Novel by Verner von Heidenstam, 1859–1940.
Published 1905–07. Published 1925 by Alfred A. Knopf, New York. Translated from the Swedish by Arthur J. Chuter.

THIS IS AN EPIC NOVEL of a Swedish hero who founded a noble family—which ultimately became royal—with the prestige and the booty of the Viking trips on which all young Norse warriors embarked in medieval times. The novel begins in the 11th century when Christianity is just making its way through the Scandinavian peninsula. The novel is set in Sweden, the homeland of Heidenstam, who won the Nobel Prize for Literature in 1916.

Part I. Chaps. 1–7. FOLKE FILBYTER, the chief of the Sveas, driven from his father's house, sails the seas to win his fortune. Weary of the sea, he takes his booty and turns inland. He carries his wealth of coins and gold bars in a sack on his back. In the woods he meets a Finnish dwarf, JORGRIMME. Folke drinks from the dwarf's horn with great thirst, unaware that the dwarf is cutting a slit in the sack. It is not until the next day that he sees the holes and realizes that he has lost many gold coins. He decides to remain where he is and build his home, to be called Folketuna, and make the Finnish dwarfs his thralls.

One day the dwarf Jorgrimme's daughter is found chained in a pit. The thralls want to kill her but Folke frees her and takes her to live with him at Folketuna. She gives birth to his three sons, INGEMUND, HALLSTEN, and INGEVALD. The youngest and weakest is required to stay at home and he will inherit all of Folketuna. The other two are given ships and sent to sea.

ULF ULFSSON, a wealthy neighbor, brings the news to Folke that there is a man in their vicinity begging for charity. Begging is unknown among the Sveas, whose custom it is to take, not to give. The man's name is JAKOB and he begs in the strange name of Jesus Christ. Folke asks Ulfsson for his eldest daughter's hand for Ingevald. Ulfsson is not eager for this marriage and announces that the decision remains with his grown sons.

Folke and Ingevald go to Ulfsson's house. They are received with great courtesy but the eldest daughter, HOLMDIS, looks with disfavor on Ingevald and refuses to marry him. Her two brothers agree that she is too good for the son of a dwarf woman. Folke is stunned and swears revenge. Ingevald is silent until they return home, then he vows to his father that no woman but Holmdis will come to Folketuna as his wife. He gathers the thralls to go with him to fetch her by force. They ride to Ulfsson's home, where all are asleep, and after pinning Ulfsson's hand to the bedpost with an arrow, Ingevald kidnaps the girl and returns with her to his house. Folke has little to say except that he would have preferred Ulf dead.

Chaps. 8–12. Holmdis never speaks a friendly word to her unwelcome husband. He falls more in love with her but cannot tame her. She bears Ingevald a son and then dies. Folke takes charge of the infant, for Ingevald grieves and loses interest in everything. The boy becomes very attached to his grandfather, who always refers to him as his son.

Shortly after Holmdis's death, the beggar Jakob appears again. Ingevald listens to him and pours out the story of his grief. He is converted to Christianity and in exchange for being saved gives Jakob his young son. When Folke discovers that the boy is gone, he searches unceasingly for him. In his desperation he even goes to his enemy Ulfsson for possible news. Jakob had stopped at Ulf's house with the child, but Ulf did not know it was his daughter's son.

There is no peace for the master of Folketuna. Ingevald dies and his father spends all his days searching for the child. He finds Jakob and puts him in chains but cannot make him talk. For Folke the weary years pass and he grows old but cannot die.

His two older sons, Ingemund and Hallsten, tire of their sea trips and decide to return home with their considerable booty. They meet Holmdis's sister ULFVA, who fled to the woods when the Christian king INGE killed her father because he refused conversion. Ulfva does not know the identity of the two brothers and tells them all that has happened since they went away. The brothers never wish to see their homestead again. They offer themselves to King Inge as body-guards and are accepted.

Chaps. 13–15. King Inge's EARL, a young cleric, is hard and ruthless in establishing the Christian faith and he wins converts by force. The king is weak in his religious practices and to strengthen him the earl causes his distracting mistress JULIA to be beheaded. Inge sorrows and with his sorrow come three years of famine. He is deposed, along with the earl, and their lives are saved by the old, wandering Folke, who feels a strange kinship with the forbidding young cleric. Folke discovers that the earl is his long-lost grandson. Folke is also reunited with his two older sons, who have become Christians. The two sons and the grandson are not happy about the old man's unchristian ways and try to convert him, but fail. Hallsten marries Ulfva. Folke has amassed great treasure and his heirs, the Folkungs, await his death, but ride off from Folketuna to seek their own fortunes.

Part II. Chaps. 1–10. Many years have passed. Ulfva is old and is devoted to her son EARL BIRGER. She is ruthless in her determination to wrest her full share of iron from the mines discovered by her late husband and his brother years ago. The Folkungs are now a powerful and wealthy family. Earl Birger is married to the king's sister and has a right to the throne when the king dies. The king dies and the earl vanquishes all his enemies and establishes himself firmly on the throne. He rules peacefully but his son, VALDEMAR, longs for his death

Ingevald listens to Jakob

as an end to the Folkungs' struggle for power. Valdemar reigns at Bellbo, the estate of the Folkungs, as the eldest son. His brother, MAGNUS, lives there with him. When their father strikes Valdemar in anger at his royal pretensions, Magnus instinctively goes to his brother's aid. Folke has a stroke, and while dying he manages to whisper to Magnus to take the kingdom, but Magnus refuses because it belongs to Valdemar. Valdemar, now king, discovers his wife SOFIA is unfaithful and turns to his sister-in-law, JUTTA. She spurns the king and desires only to enter a nunnery. Valdemar takes YRSA-LILL, a goat-girl, as a mistress. Jutta lives in fear that the king will conquer her and she goes to Magnus for advice. For the first time in his life, Magnus does not think of his brother first and agrees to help her flee. He asks her to be patient while he makes the plans. Valdemar discovers that Jutta plans to escape and stops her. Valdemar finds he really loves Jutta and asks to conduct her to the con-

vent himself.

Chaps. 11–22. Valdemar makes no secret of his love as he escorts Jutta to the convent. The journey takes many days and his love is shared by the young woman. Queen Sofia becomes jealous when she hears of this and she takes her vengeance on the goat-girl Yrsa-Lill, whom she imprisons and frightens with a swarm of snakes. The girl is rescued, but has lost the power of speech.

The years in the convent are long and monotonous for Jutta. She thinks not of Valdemar or of their son born in sin and longs to beg forgiveness of her sister, the queen. As she goes to a festival in the church with the other nuns, she sees her son, now a boy of 8, with Valdemar. The king does not recognize the nun, who embraces the child. Jutta is hurt by his forgetfulness. She goes to the palace and borrows a fine gown and appears before Valdemar. He is displeased. But Jutta leaves the convent permanently and receives the forgiveness of her sister and the custody of her son.

Valdemar goes on a mission to seek the Pope's aid in restoring part of his kingdom. Many of his followers have deserted him and have chosen Magnus as their king. The Pope tries to bring peace to the brothers, but fails. Magnus represents a new age and new laws and Valdemar is defeated. He receives a message that Jutta is dying and he goes to her. She dies giving him her last words of love.

The former king now lives in poverty and humiliation. His brother Magnus is acclaimed a great king, but Magnus is tormented and even religion is no solace to him. He is haunted by his betrayal of his brother. Valdemar comes to him, unarmed, to renew their kinship but Magnus imprisons him. Years later, when Magnus knows he is going to die, he goes to see his brother. He offers Valdemar his freedom to help atone for his misdeeds but the offer is refused. The former king is frightened of the world outside and prefers the security of imprisonment.

Trilby

Novel by George du Maurier, 1834–1896.
Published 1894.

IN TRILBY du Maurier gave the world one of its best-known villains, the hypnotist Svengali. The novel was tremendously popular in its day. It is seldom read now but its story is remembered and is important. Scientifically it is not sound the way du Maurier tells it; by hypnotism Svengali could not have turned a bad voice into a good one, though he might have relieved a psychological defect that prevented a good voice from being expressed. George du Maurier was the father of Daphne, the popular author of *Rebecca* and many other novels.

Parts 1–2. Three English artists share a large studio in the Latin Quarter of Paris. They call themselves TAFFY, THE LAIRD, and LITTLE BILLEE. They are devoted to art and to friendship, and the warmth of their personalities draws many friends to their studio. One of their frequent callers is a tall, bony individual of sinister aspect. His name is SVENGALI. He is usually accompanied by a little gypsy, GECKO, who plays the violin like an angel. Svengali, a brilliant pianist, and Gecko give an impromptu musicale. A tall, graceful girl of about 18 comes to the studio and introduces herself as TRILBY O'FERRALL, a model for the sculptor on the next floor. Svengali is enamored of the beautiful girl but her eyes look only at the Englishmen. Svengali asks her to sing and she does so in a voice so bad that her audience is embarrassed— except Svengali, who is able to hear the untrained quality of her tones.

Svengali is poor despite his talent, and he is not liked. He lives by borrowing and one morning he goes to get a few francs from the English artists. The Laird is in the studio with Trilby. She has neuralgia in her eyes and the pain is maddening. Svengali forgets his original errand and hypnotizes Trilby. The pain disappears and Svengali offers his services whenever she is in similar trouble; but there is something so sinister about him that she vows to endure the pain rather than see him again.

Trilby becomes a part of the Englishmen's lives, cooking, darning, and being generally so gay that they all love her as a respected sister. She makes soft eyes at all three indiscriminately but Little Billee is most effected. Trilby is happy except when Svengali comes to the studio. It is apparent that he comes only to see Trilby.

Parts 3–4. Little Billee is shocked when he finds Trilby posing nude in his art class. He is in love with her and he leaves Paris. Trilby suffers and writes a letter to the Laird confessing all her past misdemeanors. With this confession there comes to her a new feeling, that of self-respect. She begins to prepare herself for Little Billee's return and it is evident to Taffy and the Laird that she loves him.

Little Billee returns. Trilby is more beautiful than ever and is very happy. The only one who can mar this happiness is Svengali. He seems like a demon to Trilby, and she dreams of him in a series of nightmares. Christmas is celebrated with a great party and at its end Little Billee asks Trilby for the nineteenth time to marry him and she agrees.

Little Billee's mother and sister come to the studio accompanied by his uncle, a clergyman. Taffy sees them and tells Little Billee's mother of Trilby's fine qualities but she is not convinced that she would be a proper wife for her son. During the conversation Trilby arrives. She promises not to marry Little Billee, for she cannot bear to hurt him with his family. She disappears. When Little Billee finds out what has happened, he has an epileptic seizure that ends in brain fever. It is many weeks before he is out of danger and his very nature is changed. He is now languid and listless and he never mentions Trilby.

Five years pass and Little Billee is famous with the first showing of his paintings. Praise seems to mean nothing to him and it is as if a part of his brain is numbed.

Parts 5–6. Little Billee has a fine studio and a handsome suite of rooms in London. He works hard, for he loves to make money. He is the darling of society but tires of it

602

Death of Svengali

quickly. He has no close friends, and even for the Laird and Taffy he merely pretends to have the same deep feeling as before, though they are not aware of this. The three old friends hear of the magnificent voice of LA SVENGALI. She has never sung in England but is making her debut in Paris in a few months. They plan to go there together and hear her.

In Paris they visit the old studio, but the charm of their youth is gone. The fame of La Svengali spreads and the three Englishmen attend the opening performance in eager anticipation. They are surprised to see their old, dirty acquaintance, Svengali, in irreproachable evening dress, conducting the superb Hungarian orchestra. Their surprise becomes breathless when La Svengali appears and they discover that she is Trilby. They are amazed at her beautiful voice, since Trilby could hardly sing a note when they knew her. During the whole performance, Trilby's eyes never leave Svengali. Little Billee is so overcome with the beauty of the music and the sight of Trilby that he begins to sob. It is the first time in five years he has felt any emotion. For the three friends La Svengali is an unbelievable mystery. The Laird insists that no one could have taught Trilby to sing and they remember her loathing for Svengali. Little Billee finds that his old passion for her has returned.

Part 7. Little Billee, walking in Paris, sees the Svengalis in a magnificent open carriage. He sees Svengali speak to Trilby. He bows but both cut him dead. The next day, Little Billie encounters Svengali alone. There is a look of hate on the musician's face and he spits in Little Billee's face. Little Billee attacks Svengali. He is no match for the tall man but Taffy appears and makes the fight his own. He grasps Svengali's nose with one hand and uses the other to punch. The musician scuttles away as soon as he can free himself.

The Englishmen return to London. La Svengali is making her debut there and they buy tickets. There is great disappointment when the concert is canceled at the last minute. Gecko is still playing his fiddle for Svengali. His devotion to Trilby is greater than to Svengali and when the maestro strikes Trilby, in rehearsal, Gecko attacks him with a knife. During Svengali's recovery from the wound, Trilby is in a daze, so that she strikes the attending doctors as being imbecilic.

The concert is again announced but the doctors have forbidden Svengali to conduct because his heart is not sound. At the performance he is seated in a box, alone, directly facing Trilby on the stage. He sees the three friends enter and rises from his box to glare at them with unconcealed hatred. His wife moves forward on the stage with her eyes strained to join those of her husband. Svengali returns her look—but then he slumps forward in his chair. The orchestra begins but Trilby does not sing, staring all the while at the box. She has to be told to sing; and when finally she does so it is in the same tuneless, flat voice that the artists heard in the Paris studio. The conductor notices Svengali and ushers enter his box and find him dead. Trilby is led, terrified, from the stage. The three friends force their way to her dressing-room and take her to Little Billee's flat to care for her. Trilby is ill, weak, and strangely aged. She has no memory of her career as a singer. She remembers Svengali only as a kind man who took her in when she was griefstricken at leaving Little Billee. She tells them that Svengali has looked after her since then but did not marry her, for he had a wife and three children. She recalls that her headaches became worse and Svengali always cured them.

Trilby becomes weaker and weaker as the days pass and doctors can discover no cause. She is happy to be among her beloved Englishmen and in spite of her condition she listens and talks with much of her old gaiety.

Part 8. Svengali died of heart disease. He left no will and the money Trilby had earned went to his aged mother. Trilby has only her jewels, which are of great value. One day she receives a strange wooden box with no message. It contains a large photograph of Svengali. Trilby gazes at the picture for quite a while, then suddenly begins to sing in her beautiful voice. Once again she is the mistress of her art. When the song is ended, she falls asleep. A doctor is summoned and he finds her dead. Little Billee becomes ill again with brain fever and dies shortly after.

Many years later, Taffy and his wife, who was Little Billee's sister, are in Paris on a holiday. They meet Gecko, who is now an old man, and he tells them of the influence of Svengali over Trilby. Svengali was a magician and a madman. He could make her do anything or sing anything by controlling her with his eyes. She became two Trilbys, herself and the great singer created by Svengali. With Svengali's death the long spell was broken, but Trilby was too weak to live without her master.

Tristram Shandy

Novel by Laurence Sterne, 1713–1768.
Published 1760–67. (ML, 147 & T31;
PB, PL511; RE, 37)

THE FULL TITLE IS *The Life and Opinions of Tristram Shandy.* Nearly two centuries of those who write and those who read for pleasure have found the work one of the most delightful in English literature. Despite his clerical calling, the Rev. Laurence Sterne had a universal and broad sense of humor and *Tristram Shandy* is much less a novel than a long, rambling discourse upon everything in which Dr. Sterne found a quirk or a curious aspect. Both Tristram's father and Tristram's Uncle Toby are ranked among the greatest creations in English literature. The name Trismegistus, which was intended for Tristram instead of the name by which he was actually christened, means in Greek "the thrice greatest" and was an epithet of the encyclopedic writer Hermes, who is identified with an Egyptian divinity in ancient Greece. *Tristram Shandy* contains so many excursions into curious and comical aspects of life that they are far too numerous to outline, and to be appreciated at all the book must be read.

Book I. While my father and mother were engaged in begetting me, my mother remembered to ask if my father had remembered to wind the clock—"Good G—!" cried my father, "Did ever woman, since the creation of the world, interrupt a man with such a silly question?" I tremble to think what a foundation had been laid for a thousand weaknesses of body and mind, which no skill of the physician or the philosopher could ever afterwards set thoroughly to rights. I am indebted to my uncle Mr. TOBY SHANDY for the preceding anecdote. My father, WALTER SHANDY, who was an excellent natural philosopher, often complained of the incident. "Alas, my Tristram's misfortunes," said he, "begun nine months before ever he came into the world." I am able to set the date of my conception with exactitude because my father, a retired Turkey merchant, was one of the most regular men who ever lived; he wound up the clock on the first Sunday of every month. I, TRISTRAM SHANDY, Gent., was brought into this scurvy and disastrous world on November 5, 1718.

By the terms of her marriage settlement, my mother ELIZABETH MOLLINEUX SHANDY was entitled to lay in (have her child), if she wished, in London; but my father, after one annoyingly fruitless journey to that city, determined that she should have her next child at Shandy Hall in the country, to balance the matter. He had several well-reasoned arguments for doing so; and he argued as a Christian, as a heathen, a husband, a father, a patriot, and a man. As my mother could answer only as a woman, she was outnumbered seven to one and forced to concede.

Walter Shandy, as I have hinted, was a man of great good sense, knowing and curious in philosophy and wise in political reasoning; but he was unaccountably superstitious about the choice of Christian names, thinking that a great deal more depended on them than superficial minds were capable of conceiving. How many Caesars and Pompeys by the mere inspiration of their names have been rendered worthy of them, he would say, and how many, who might have done well in the world, have been Nicodemused into nothing?

He had the strongest liking and disliking for certain names, but to an equal number he was indifferent. (My elder brother BOBBY's name belongs to this neutral class. My father was away when it was bestowed and could only thank heaven that it was no worse.) But of all the names in the world, he had the most unconquerable aversion to Tristram.

My Uncle Toby was a gentleman who had not only all the virtues of a man of honor and rectitude but also a most extreme modesty of nature. This did not come from time spent in converse with the female sex, for Uncle Toby exchanged scarcely three words with that sex in as many years. It came from a blow from a stone, broken off by a cannon fire during the siege of Namur, which fell upon my uncle's groin. And my Uncle Toby's great modesty was combined with a little family pride: He could not bear to hear the story of Aunt Dinah who ran away with the coachman. He would remonstrate when my father brought the subject up. ("Dinah is only my aunt," my father would reply, "but Truth my sister.") Uncle Toby would answer this only by whistling a half dozen bars of the song *Lillibullero* [a ballad written about 1686], the usual channel through which his passions got vent.

The wound in Uncle Toby's groin making him unfit for service, he was sent to England and spent four years confined to his bed with great misery. Then he went to my father's house (at that time in London) to recuperate further.

Book II. Uncle Toby could not make his visitors comprehend what took place at the battle of Namur. He decided to purchase a map, lay out the citadel of Namur on it, and explain the siege move by move. This freed him from a world of sad explanations and provided him with a Hobby-horse. When his wound was nearly cured, he summoned Corporal TRIM, his man (himself disqualified by a wound in the knee), and embarked for his house near Shandy Hall. Trim soon was nearly as proficient as my uncle in military arts; and being of an inventive turn, he erected a scale model of the fortifications in the kitchen garden and the two devoted themselves to their campaigns.

(Returning to my birth.) The servant OBADIAH, having reported that Mrs. Shandy seemed to be in trouble, was sent to fetch Dr. SLOP, the man-midwife. Uncle Toby remarked that the doctor's coming put him in mind of Stevinus. My father, unable to see the connection between the great military engineer and the doctor's arrival, attacked my uncle's Hobby-horse. Uncle Toby, though a peaceful man, sent Trim for his book on Stevinus. A sermon fell out of the book, was read aloud to the delight of all by Trim, and was declared to have been written by none other than Mr. YORICK, the good parson (whose lack of gravity eventually brought about his murder).

Dr. Slop had invented a special kind of forceps, and so it was that I came into the world with a nose squashed against my face, as flat as a pancake.

Books III–IV. A sudden trampling upstairs reminded Dr. Slop that he had left his equipment at home. Obadiah was sent to get the bag. Dr. Slop wrestled and tugged and cursed and cut his thumb; and cursed, whereupon my father urged him to read Bishop Ernulphus's noble work, while Uncle Toby whistled Lillibullero. Dr. Slop demonstrated his new forceps on my uncle Toby's hands, cutting and bruising them expertly, and pshawed his way upstairs to my mother.

My father and Uncle Toby, having talked each other to sleep, were roused by Trim, who reported that Dr. Slop was in the kitchen making a bridge. (At this point I should introduce my Uncle Toby's amours with the delectable Widow WADMAN while Trim, ever loyal, followed suit with the widow's maid BRIDGET. Trim invited Bridget to view the battlements one evening in the kitchen garden, and that very same evening the Dutch drawbridge was mysteriously shattered. Toby naturally assumed—) But it was a bridge for my nose, which the doctor had crushed. He was making a bridge of cotton and a whalebone stay from the corset of my mother's maid SUSANNAH.

My father, as I have said, was a learned man. He read many curious books on all subjects and he was particularly distressed by the paucity of works of genius on great noses. However, he collected every pertinent volume he could find and had amassed a respectable library of nose-lore. He had taken the trouble to translate Slawkenbergius's vast work on the subject. The injury to my nose demoralized him. "To counteract the great injury done the child," he announced to my Uncle Toby, "I intend to do him the greatest good. He shall be christened Trismegistus."

At this, Susannah arrived to report that the child was having a fit and the curate was waiting in the dressing room for a name. "Trismegistus," my father told her and Susannah ran back. "'Tis Tris—, Tris—," she tried. "The only name in Christendom so starting is Tristram," said the curate.

"Tristram-gistus—," she tried. "No 'gistus'; Tristram is my own name," he said, and so was I christened.

After that my father became pensive. He sighed often and forbore to snap. Since my father thrived on argumentation he would certainly have died except that a fresh set of worries was left him, with a legacy of £1,000, by my Aunt Dinah. A new realm of possibilities was his, he would go to Rome, he would go to law, he would improve the house even, he would drain the Ox-moor, a bit of marshland belonging to the property, and he would especially set my brother Bobby off on his travels. But as he was planning the trip, Trim reported that Bobby had died.

Book V. My father, ever the philosopher, made a fine long speech, citing classical precedents in plenty, on the inevitability of death, stressing that one should be surprised not by the event of death but, rather, if it did not occur. Having lost all of Bobby and a good portion of me (my nose, my name), my father consoled himself with the writing of a Tristra-*paedia*, or a system of education. He was at this for three years. I was getting bigger. One day the chambermaid forgot to leave the ***** under the bed. "Cannot you contrive, my dear," said she, opening the window sash, "just this once?" But Susannah did not consider that nothing was well hung in our family, so slap came the sash down. "Nothing is left," cried Susannah, "nothing is left—for me, but to run to the country." My father called Dr. Slop, and consulted his library for works on circumcision.

Book VI. Dr. Slop, to exalt himself, debased me to death, so that in a week's time it was in everybody's mouth that poor Master Shandy ****** entirely.

"I'll put him, however, in breeches," said my father.

"Order the matter as you please, Mr. Shandy," my mother conceded, after a long argument.

It was about at this time that my uncle Toby, besieged by the widow Wadman, encouraged by Trim and Bridget, and advised and protected by my father, fell in love. But this matter should have a book to itself.

Book VII. In which I, accompanied by my father, my uncle Toby, Trim, and most of the male members of my family, make my Grand Tour on the Continent, describing monasteries, churches in Calais, Boulougne, and Montreuil, counting and classifying the streets of Paris, admiring the 30-volume history of China written in Chinese at Lyons, and occupying myself equally worthily through Fontainebleau, Sens, Joigny, et cetera, et cetera, and et cetera.

Book VIII. Widow Wadman had been, for several years, in love with my Uncle Toby, and my Uncle Toby had not been in love with the widow Wadman. In these circumstances, there was nothing for the widow to do but go on loving my Uncle Toby or let it alone. She would do neither. She stood ready harnessed and caparisoned at all

She opened the window

points to take advantage of opportunity.

Trim and Uncle Toby were campaigning one day on the bowling green and they came to an argument on the comparative distress of a wound of the knee and the groin. The good widow stood on her side of the hedge and listened. However, my Uncle Toby and Trim, gallants both, conceded the argument to each other, and Trim embarked on another tale. Widow Wadman grew impatient and, armed with a new plan, entered the garden with a "mote" in her eye and a plea for rescue. Uncle Toby could find nothing in the eye, but it was a gentle eye, soft and blue, and my Uncle Toby, unknowing in the ways of love, had no defenses.

My father, of course, was fascinated and discoursed long and well on love and procreation, citing many classical precedents. On the night that Uncle Toby, attired in full regalia, had set to sally forth and woo the lady, my father wrote an affectionate letter of advice, and he and my mother proceeded to deliver it in person and see . . .

Book IX. Trim and Toby went to the door of the widow's house, discoursed on love and liberty, marched once around the house, talked of honor, walked backwards and forwards, and let fall the rapper (doorknocker). My Uncle Toby whistled Lillibullero. Inside, Trim left for the kitchen to amuse Bridget and Toby prepared to present his suit. He professed his love, then letting it take care of itself, went on to some other matter. "But where, exactly," said the Widow Wadman, "did you receive your wound?" "I will show you the very place," my Uncle Toby replied. He pulled out his map.

At the time of all this, I was in Europe returning out of Italy, feeling the kindliest harmony vibrating within me.

—They were the sweetest notes I had ever heard, and I let down the fore-glass to hear them more distinctly. "'Tis MARIA," said the postilion. She was sitting upon a bank playing her vespers upon a pipe, with a little goat beside her. "Poor Maria, the love and pity of all the villages around us.

'Twas but three years ago the sun did not shine on so fair, quick-witted and amiable a maid, and better fate did Maria deserve than to have her banns forbid by the intrigues of the curate who published them—" As he said this, Maria began her song anew, ten times sweeter. But now, the postilion added, except for brief intervals, Maria was not mentally sound. When we came to the bank where Maria was sitting I sprang out of the coach to help her, and found myself sitting betwixt her and the goat. Maria looked wistfully for some time at me, then at her goat, then at me, then at her goat again, and so on alternately. "Well, Maria," said I softly, "what resemblance do you find?" I did not mean this jocularly but still I regretted the remark later.

Widow Wadman had tried all manner of ways to learn the extent of my Uncle Toby's injury. She had inquired of Dr. Slop, but he was the worst man alive at definitions. She consulted anatomy books but could make nothing of it.

My Uncle Toby asked Trim how often Bridget inquired about his knee injury. Trim replied that Bridget never inquired at all. That, my Uncle Toby pointed out, showed the difference between the woman and her maid: Mrs. Wadman was all compassion. Trim explained the different degrees of interest their respective injuries inspired.

By this time, through the combined agencies of my mother, who had been made a confidante of Mrs. Wadman; Susannah, whom my mother considered an adequate receptacle for family secrets; and Bridget, there was not a woman in the village who did not know of my Uncle Toby's siege and the secret articles which had delayed the surrender. My father, whose way was to force every event in nature into an hypothesis, had just heard of the report and was demonstrating to Yorick and Dr. Slop not only "That the devil was in women, and that the whole of the affair was lust" but that every evil and disorder of the world was owing in some way or other to the same unruly appetite.

Obadiah arrived in some distress. It seems that my father keeps a bull for the service of the parish, and one day or other the preceding summer (as chance would have it, it was the day upon which Obadiah married my father's housemaid) Obadiah had led his cow upon a visit to him. When Obadiah's wife was brought to bed, Obadiah thanked God— "Now," said Obadiah, "I shall have a calf." Obadiah went daily to visit his cow, but the cow did not calve, and after the sixth week of nonproduction, Obadiah cast his suspicions on the bull.

"But may not the cow be barren?" my father asked, turning to Dr. Slop.

"It never happens," said Dr. Slop, "but the man's wife may have come before her time naturally enough. Prithee has the child hair upon his head?"

"It is as hairy as I am," said Obadiah. Obadiah had not shaved for three weeks.

"Wheu—u—" cried my father, "and so, brother Toby, this poor Bull of mine might have been driven into Doctors Commons and lost his character—which to a Town Bull, brother Toby, is the very same thing as his life—"

"Lord!" said my mother, "what is this story all about?"

"A Cock and Bull," said Yorick—" And one of the best of its kind, I ever heard."

Twelfth Night

Play by William Shakespeare, 1564–1616.
Produced 1600. (RE, 92)

THIS PLAY IS good Shakespeare when read, though admittedly a bit confusing at times. Also it is still regularly produced but probably only because Malvolio is a fine part for a comic actor. The plot requires that one actor or actress be convincing both as a man and as a woman. Shakespeare used such plots often (others are Rosalind in *As You Like It* and Portia in *Merchant of Venice*), and of course in his days youths played the women's parts. Today it is too difficult to be done well.

Act I. 1. ORSINO, the Duke of Illyria, is in love with OLIVIA, a wealthy countess. His courtier VALENTINE tells him that Olivia is mourning the loss of a brother and is not now interested in suitors. 2. VIOLA, a young woman shipwrecked on the coast of Illyria, is unhappy at the thought of being separated from her brother SEBASTIAN. She does not know if he is alive. The ship's captain tells her about the duke and Olivia, and Viola decides to serve the duke, disguised as a boy. 3. At Olivia's house, Sir TOBY BELCH, Olivia's sponging uncle, and MARIA, Olivia's companion, discuss the somewhat foolish Sir ANDREW AGUECHEEK. Maria accuses Sir Toby of getting Sir Andrew drunk every night. Sir Andrew comes to ask Sir Toby's help in his suit to win Olivia. 4. Viola, disguised as the page CAESARIO, has found favor with the duke. He sends her to plead his cause with Olivia. But Viola is in love with the duke herself.

5. The CLOWN tries to talk Olivia out of her mourning. MALVOLIO, Olivia's ambitious steward, wants to impress his lady. Olivia sends word back to the duke by Caesario (Viola) that she cannot love him. But she finds Caesario interesting.

Act II. 1. Sebastian has also landed on the coast of Illyria. His captain, ANTONIO, sends him off to Orsino's court. 2. Malvolio, on Olivia's orders, follows Caesario (Viola) into the street. There he gives her a ring from Olivia. Viola is puzzled. 3. Malvolio

Olivia makes advances to Caesario (actually Viola)

berates Sir Toby, Maria and Sir Andrew for making too much noise at night. After he leaves, Maria suggests revenge on Malvolio. They will write a love note imitating the handwriting of Olivia. This note they will place in such a way that Malvolio must find it. 4. Viola reports to the duke, who again sends her to Olivia. 5. Malvolio finds the love letter, which identifies him by the yellow stockings he wears. Sir Andrew helps him identify the handwriting as Olivia's. The note asks Malvolio to smile always in the presence of his lady. Malvolio is sure it is from Olivia.

Act III. 1. Olivia makes advances to Caesario (Viola). Viola hints that she is not what Olivia thinks, but Olivia fails to understand. 2. Sir Andrew decides to leave Illyria because Olivia is more interested in Caesario than in him. Sir Toby has been getting money from Sir Andrew and does not want to lose his benefactor. He suggests that Sir Andrew challenge Caesario to a duel. 3. Sebastian and Antonio take leave of each other. Antonio gives Sebastian his purse. 4. While Olivia thinks only of entertaining Caesario, Malvolio arrives and speaks of the supposed love letter from Olivia. Olivia thinks Malvolio has gone mad. Maria and Sir Toby commit him to a dark room. Viola, as Caesario, is back at the countess' house. Viola remains loyal to the duke and asks again that Olivia love him. Sir Toby brings the challenge to the duel. Sir Andrew and Viola draw their swords. Just then Antonio arrives and mistakes Viola for her twin brother Sebastian. Antonio comes to his rescue. But there is an old suit against him pending in Illyria and he is arrested. He asks for his purse back, but Viola does not know of any purse. In fact, she denies having ever seen him before.

Act IV. 1. Before Olivia's house, the clown leads Sebastian towards the house. Sir Andrew mistakes him for Viola and wants to continue the duel. But to his astonishment the fight Sebastian gives him is different from the weak duel he had just fought with Viola. Sir Andrew and Sir Toby are wounded. The duel is stopped by Olivia. She takes Sebastian, whom she mistakes for Viola, into the house with her. He does not understand anything going on. 2. The Clown tells the imprisoned Malvolio that he is a parson arrived to cure him. 3. Olivia quickly summons a priest and marries the astonished Sebastian.

Act V. 1. The duke, accompanied by Viola as Caesario, arrives at Olivia's house. Viola pleads for Antonio. Antonio again demands his purse. Olivia arrives and calls Viola her husband. The priest is asked to confirm this fact. The duke turns against Viola. Sir Andrew arrives bleeding and accuses Viola of having wounded him. Finally, Sebastian arrives on the scene. Seeing the twins together unravels the mysteries. The duke marries Viola and Sir Toby decides to join hands with Maria. Only Malvolio is left. He is released from his prison, full of bitterness against them all.

20,000 Leagues Under the Sea

Novel by Jules Verne, 1828–1905.
Published 1870.

OF JULES VERNE's many remarkable pioneer novels in the science fiction field, this is the most accurate. Long before a practical submarine actually existed, Verne described it as it would eventually appear. Along with *Around the World in Eighty Days,* this is one of the two most popular of Verne's many books. Its continued appeal is evidenced by the fact that it has made several motion pictures, including a major production starring Kirk Douglas in the late 1950s. Captain Nemo and his submarine *Nautilus* have come to be among the best-known fictional proper names.

Part 1. Chaps. 1–7. In the year 1866 there appears in the world's seas an enormous and mysterious monster. Fast, elusive, tough, it is seen by many boats in different places. It was judged by most people to be an unknown species of marine monster. Professor PIERRE ARONNAX, famous French marine naturalist, while in America, is invited to join an expedition being sent out aboard an American frigate to find and destroy the monster. Aronnax joins the party, together with his servant, CONSEIL, aboard the *Abraham Lincoln.* An important member of the group is NED LAND, "prince of harpooners," who is to try at close range if guns fail to kill the monster. The boat sails from Brooklyn in early July, 1867, and rounds Cape Horn for the Pacific, where the monster was last seen. After four months of fruitless search the expedition is turning about for home when Ned Land spies the monster, shining electrically at a little distance. The frigate attacks, but the monster mocks it by staying at a fixed distance constantly. All the next day the same thing takes place. Shots bounce off the monster's back and it never tires. They lose the monster, then, near midnight, it shines in the distance. They sail up silently and Ned Land hurls his harpoon. A powerful waterspout washes over the frigate's bridge. Men are tumbled about, and Aronnax is thrown into the sea. As he is being pulled under by weariness and his sodden clothes, Conseil swims up; he jumped in after his master. They stay afloat for hours and meet Ned Land, also swept overboard. Ned has a footing on the floating monster and pulls them up on top of it. Aronnax finds it is made of metal and is a submarine. In the morning, the three men are pulled inside.

Chaps. 8–12. The castaways are brought before a strikingly handsome and distin-guished-looking man. He does not answer when they speak but has them fed. Next day the man introduces himself as Captain NEMO and tells them he speaks many languages and merely wanted to hear their stories before talking. He tells them they are his prisoners and will never be released, but they will have the freedom of the ship, the *Nautilus,* except on certain specific occasions. Nemo takes Aronnax for a tour of the ship; shows him a magnificent library and smoking room; a drawing-room, art gallery and museum combined; and an elegant bedroom for Aronnax. Nemo tells him everything on the boat is run by electricity; shows him the ship's engines, and says the boat can make 50 miles an hour. Nemo tells how the boat was constructed in secret on a deserted island in the ocean, from many parts ordered separately from all parts of the world. Nemo tells Aronnax he hates the land and loves the sea. On or in the sea, he is free of man's laws and is his own master.

Chaps. 13–18. Aronnax and the other two men are entertained by wonderful views of the underwater scene as panels draw back from windows and lights illuminate the water for vast distances. Nemo invites Aronnax to join in a hunting party the next day. They hunt under water, carrying their air supply with them in tanks on their backs, bearing their own light, and guns that shoot by air pressure. They leave the boat through an air lock, and walk about on the bottom of the sea. Months pass and the *Nautilus* cruises the Pacific, rising periodically to replenish the air supply but chiefly traveling below the surface.

Walking under the sea

Chaps. 19–21. Early in 1868 the *Nautilus* runs temporarily aground. They must wait for the full moon to bring a high tide and Captain Nemo permits a hunting expedition upon the nearby shore. The hunting party is attacked by savages but escapes to the *Nautilus.* The natives surround the *Nautilus* but cannot harm its metallic sides. As the submarine floats free Captain Nemo opens the hatches for air and

the savages leap forward; but they jump back, howling, as they touch an electrified cable.

Chaps. 22–23. A few days later, Aronnax sees Nemo much perturbed by something in the distance. Nemo tells him he and his companions must be locked up below for a while. They are fed and evidently the food is drugged, as they all fall into a deep sleep. No explanation is given. Nemo then asks Aronnax to tend a wounded sailor whose head has been shattered by a blow. Aronnax tells Nemo the man will soon be dead, but does not learn the cause of the wound. The dead sailor is interned in the underwater cemetery of the crew.

Part II. Chaps. 1–3. The cruise continues through January. Off Ceylon, Nemo takes Aronnax and his companions to visit a pearl fishery. In a hidden grotto Nemo shows Aronnax a gigantic oyster that Aronnax estimates to weigh 600 pounds. The captain props open its shells and inside can be seen a pearl the size of a cocoanut. It is being left to grow indefinitely. An Indian diver appears and is attacked by a huge shark. Nemo goes to the rescue with a knife and is helped by Ned Land, who dispatches the shark with his harpoon. Nemo carries the Indian to the fisherman's boat, revives him, and gives him a bag of pearls. Aronnax later remarks upon this kindness to a stranger and Nemo says it was because the man is an inhabitant of an oppressed land.

Chaps. 4–6. The *Nautilus* sails into the Red Sea. Nemo tells Aronnax they will be in the Mediterranean in a day or two. As the Suez Canal is not yet completed, Aronnax questions this. Nemo explains that he has discovered a subterranean passage between the Red Sea and the Mediterranean, beneath the Isthmus of Suez. The next night they are in the Mediterranean. Ned Land now proposes an attempt at escape. At first Aronnax demurs, wishing to continue his fascinating experiences; but realizing that Nemo can never dare release them voluntarily, and they may never again be so close to land, he agrees to try. The three men know they must succeed the first try, as there will never be a second chance. But Nemo, as if aware of the plans, surfaces infrequently thereafter. One night, while traveling under water near Crete, Aronnax and Nemo see a swimmer approach. Nemo goes to a chest and counts out a large number of gold ingots; Aronnax estimates there is £200,000. Some men of the crew carry out the chest, and the small boat is heard leaving the *Nautilus.* Again there is no explanation.

Chaps. 7–8. Two days later the *Nautilus* is in the Atlantic. Ned Land tells Aronnax that their only chance must come that night, when the *Nautilus* surfaces for air. Aronnax is unhappy, but realizes he must go too. Nemo tells him they are on the bottom of Vigo Bay, off Spain. Here in 1702 a Spanish fleet, laden with American gold, was sunk. The panels are drawn back and Aronnax sees the *Nautilus* crew loading gold from the sunken ships. Nemo explains that he uses this wealth for unfortunate people who are fighting oppression. Aronnax then realizes that the gold he saw near Crete was sent to fight the Turks.

Chaps. 9–15. Nemo takes Aronnax on a night expedition and they see the remains of lost Atlantis, lit by the glowing lava of a subterranean volcano. A day later, the *Nautilus* stops in a huge cavern hollowed by the sea in the base of an extinct volcano, and there Nemo shows Aronnax coal mines that he uses as the source of fuel to create electricity. The cruise continues through the Sargasso Sea. At one point they are blocked by a solid field of ice, but Nemo tells Aronnax he will pass under it and go on to the South Pole, which he himself has never been to before. Three days later they surface in open water at the Pole. The small boat carries them to nearby land and Nemo, the first man to set foot there, formally takes possession of the Pole in his own name. On the trip back, an iceberg above the *Nautilus* turns over, imprisoning the ship within a narrow pocket of ice. It cannot move in any direction.

Chaps. 16–19. The *Nautilus* is in great danger, both of being crushed and of using up all of its air. The crew try to chop their way out, but the water is freezing around them and their space gets constantly smaller. Jets of hot water are used to raise the temperature, and finally the *Nautilus* breaks out. All aboard are prostrate from lack of air and they reach a place to surface barely in time. They continue northward, staying in the Atlantic Ocean. A herd of manatees is attacked for meat, and the larders stocked. Now six months have passed and Ned Land is becoming more and more anxious to escape. They meet a school of gigantic cuttlefish and one becomes entangled in the ship's propeller. It becomes necessary to go out to kill it and free the ship, and a member of the *Nautilus* crew is lost. Nemo is very depressed and allows the ship to drift at random for 10 days. Then they sail northward with the Gulf Stream. Aronnax appeals to Nemo for freedom, but Nemo refuses. Nemo tells Aronnax that he has prepared a manuscript of his history, and the last survivor of the *Nautilus* will throw it overboard in a watertight case.

Chaps. 20–23. Nemo becomes a changed and saddened man and has none of his former contact with Aronnax. In June they surface and are attacked by a man-of-war of unknown nationality. The cannon balls bounce off the steel shell of the *Nautilus*. Ned Land tries to signal to the ship but is struck down by Nemo, who again sends the three men below. He prepares to ram and sink the naval vessel; he terms it an oppressor, through which he has lost all he loved: country, wife, and family. The three men plan to escape during the attack, but the *Nautilus* rams the other ship below the waterline. Nemo watches the death agony of the ship and its crew with terrible hatred. As Nemo returns to his cabin, Aronnax sees a portrait on its wall of a young woman and two small children. Nemo stretches his arms to them and bursts into sobs.

The *Nautilus* races rapidly northward for 15 or 20 days. One day Ned Land tells Aronnax the escape is planned for the next night. He has learned the shore is near, and they are not being guarded. The moment of the escape comes, and, as Aronnax passes Nemo in the dark, he hears Nemo murmur in despair, "Almighty God! enough! enough!" These are the last words he hears from Nemo. As the three friends try to release the small boat, the *Nautilus* begins to spin about. It has been drawn into a maelstrom off the coast of Norway. The *Nautilus* breaks up and Aronnax loses consciousness. He recovers in a hut on an island nearby, with Conseil and Ned Land.

No sign remains of Nemo, the *Nautilus*, or its crew. Aronnax wonders if Nemo's narrative will ever be found to tell what tormented Nemo and made of him a terrible avenger.

Two Years Before the Mast

Report by Richard Henry Dana, Jr., 1815–1882.
Published 1840. (ML, 236)

THIS IS CONSIDERED the best first-person account of a sailor's life on sailing vessels of the mid-19th century and when it was published it was especially sensational because of its descriptions of the brutality with which common sailors were treated. The author was a member of an aristocratic New England family and it was almost unheard-of for such a person to ship "before the mast"—that is, as a common sailor. Since the book assumes that the reader would be more or less familiar with common procedure on sailing ships—just as the modern reader would be familiar with the steamship—it is best read in an annotated edition.

Chaps. 1–3. At noon exactly on August 14 [1834] I board the brig *Pilgrim* in Boston harbor, she and I bound on a two-year voyage round Cape Horn to the California coast. Weak eyes have forced me to interrupt my studies at Harvard, but I can see I will not pass for a jack tar. My varnished black hat lacks a rakish tilt, my hands show a telltale white, I walk, I do not roll. I keep a log of my new experiences: the dizzying scramble up and down the rigging; standing watch in the awesome silence of night; the miseries of the airless, dark steerage to which we crewmen are assigned. My first storm brings on seasickness that lasts three days. When I go on deck again, I have my sea legs under me. A spell of good weather helps me learn my sea duties quickly: standing watch, steering, reefing, furling, bracing, making and setting sail; then tarring, greasing, oiling, varnishing, scraping and scrubbing. And if this seems too little for my $12 a month salary, I can always be set to picking oakum or scraping cable chain. It is a rule, I discover, that a sailor must be kept busy, and what he does is generally monotonous—or dangerous.

Chaps. 4–7. Real danger ahead now. We are nearing Cape Horn; for days, rain, hail, snow and sleet beat down on us. At the gale's height I do my trick at the helm for the first time. To my great relief, it goes well. A sailor learns to sleep anywhere in any weather, and a tin pot of tea sweetened with molasses cheers us morning and night after a freezing watch. We clear the Cape and head northward for Juan Fernandez, leaving behind the albatrosses that have been escorting us. We lose a man overboard; young BALLMER, the life of the crew, falls from the rigging. He cannot swim. We row about for an hour, without hope yet not wanting to give up. Death is different at sea, I feel. Suddenly a man is gone, and nothing is left but his *vacancy*. One early dawn, after 103 days at sea, Juan Fernandez lies like a deep blue cloud on the sea. To my joy I am one of the group ordered ashore to fill the water casks. We trade tobacco for melons, grapes, cherries, and enormous strawberries. This is our last treat until the traditional plum duff is set out for our Christmas dinner. Long-brewing trouble breaks out. We protest the cut in our small bread ration. Captain THOMPSON flies into a violent rage. I think there will be no peace or understanding between him and crew again.

Chaps. 7–8. We drop anchor at the mission port of Santa Barbara, to pick up our company agent who will buy all the cargo we will be transporting back home. It is January, but we wear our straw hats and duck trousers, our feet bare. A sudden gale sends us speeding on to Monterey.

Chap. 9. I find these Pacific ports colorful and fascinating, Monterey especially so. But these Californians are shiftless and make nothing themselves. They grow grapes in abundance, yet buy at great cost bad wine made in Boston and shipped out by us. The costumes are striking. The men wear broad-brimmed hats, with gilt bands and silk-lined rims, a short figured silk or calico jacket, open shirt, rich waistcoat, velveteen or broadcloth pantaloons slashed and laced at the knees. Their shoes are of deerskin, usually much ornamented. Scorning suspenders, they wear wide sashes, generally red, the quality of which sets their owners' social status (as does the color of the skin, varying from the clear olive of the pure-blooded Spaniard through graduated shades of dark to full-blooded Indian). Add to this the inevitable poncho or serape, which ranges from an elaborate broadcloth cloak to Indian blanket. The women, fond to excess of dress, favor European styles except that their sleeves are short and they wear neither corsets nor bonnets. They love bright colors and jewelry, especially earrings and necklaces. All the men ride horses, all the women have one or more servants. I am also struck by the fineness of their voices, the most ruffianish looking fellow speaking what sounds to me like elegant Spanish. Monterey I find the most civilized town in California—rigidly Catholic, too. A Protestant has no political rights, may not hold property, nor even remain on shore for more than a few weeks.

Chaps. 10–11. We work hard at loading hides, albeit all upset about the future. It now appears our two-year voyage may last four or more. This is bad enough for the rest, disastrous for me. I do not intend to be a sailor forever. Yet how can we appeal to owners in faraway Boston? Captain Thompson grows more surly and harsh. He brutally flogs SAM, a seaman, for no good cause, and JOHN THE SWEDE also, for daring to defend Sam. It is an experience I shall never forget, not because it is so rare but so common. The officers' cruelty and tyranny, the subhuman conditions in which crews must live, and the dangerous, grueling work they do—for a pittance—must someday arouse public opinion to protest. The sailor himself dare not; it would be mutiny.

Chaps. 12–13. A day of blessed liberty, spent with young SIMPSON: Lunch ashore, a veritable banquet, in a country monastery; a splendid ride along sand-packed beaches, and a lively hour with some Indians at their Sunday fiesta.

Chaps. 14–15. At San Diego I am assigned off ship to cure hides. With NICHOLAS, a Frenchman, and four Kanaka assistants, I learn a new trade. The work is disagreeable and fatiguing, but we are becoming hardened to it. Our evenings we often spend at the "Kanaka Hotel." These Kanakas, short for Sandwich Islanders [Hawaiians], are the finest people I have ever met—more gentle, generous and trustworthy than any countryman, any white man, I have known. One, a little fellow called HOPE, has adopted me for his *aikane,* the particular friend each Kanaka chooses, for whom he will do everything, even at great personal sacrifice. I am teaching Hope letters and numbers. We have time for fishing, crawfish being in good supply. Two of our Kanakas try barehanded for a shark, but it escapes.

Chaps. 16–18. I feel uneasy for having done it, but I have had pressure brought to bear from Boston on Captain Thompson to

permit my transfer to the *Alert.* This ship is sailing for home and with only hours to spare, I persuade a young sailor to take my place on the *Pilgrim.* My new ship is a great change, from Captain FAUCON down through crew to cook. It is clean and is efficiently and fairly run; food is good, crew content. Rumors of war between France and the U.S., of battles and a huge French fleet in the Pacific, remind us sharply that we are thousands of miles and two oceans from home. Later word scotches these tall tales.

Chaps. 18–21. After five days of fierce hurricanes, we reach San Francisco. The Bay is magnificent, and if ever California becomes a prosperous country this bay will be its center. We board a Russian brig, in from Sitka, in Russian America [Alaska]. Christmas is celebrated in San Francisco Bay. Our days are spent preparing the ship for the long voyage home. Off Monterey two incidents: A packet of letters from home, each man sharing his mail with the rest, and a boxing match between GEORGE, a slight Boston boy, and the ship's bully. George wins by sheer spirit. At San Diego we rejoin the *Pilgrim* to transfer the last load of hides. I manage to visit my Kanaka

friends and find Hope desperately ill. The captain says "the devil with him," but I secretly get medicines from the mate and before we leave he is much better.

Chaps. 22–27. Homeward bound we pass through the "doldrums," the variable weather that prevails near the Equator. We take advantage of heavy rains and stop the scuppers, let the deck flood, and with this improvised bath we soap, wash and scrub each other. We emerge shades lighter. The Fourth of July finds us cautiously sailing between icebergs and even ice fields that can suddenly heave up slabs 30 feet high. The *Alert* is now caked deep with ice, engulfed in fog, and heading into tremendous gales. For the men on deck it is terrible. Led by the carpenter, the crew nearly mutinies over the captain's management of our course.

The weather breaks and we sight barren but blessed land, round the tip of the Cape. With favoring winds we cover 2,000 miles in nine days. That's as good as steam! As we near home port all of us are electric with excitement. The familiar houses and steeples come into view, we leap to the rigging and, with a hearty chorus, for the last time we furl our sails.

Ulysses

Novel by James Joyce, 1882–1941. Published 1922 by Random House, New York. © 1914, 1946 by Nora Joseph Joyce. (ML, G52)

THIS IS ONE OF the most important novels ever written, and critics are increasingly drawn to the conclusion that it is one of the greatest, though there have been strong dissenting opinions. Ulysses carries on the experiences of the characters Stephen Dedalus and Buck Mulligan (patterned on Oliver St. John Gogarty) from *A Portrait of the Artist as a Young Man.* Also, like *A Portrait,* it contains some autobiographical material. To this extent *Ulysses* is a sequel to *A Portrait.* However, in *Ulysses* Joyce carries the techniques he used in *A Portrait* so much farther, and employs so many innovational techniques, that there can hardly be said to be comparison in style. The great contribution of *Ulysses* was in introducing the "stream of consciousness" writing into modern literature. ❡ The events of *Ulysses* take place in Dublin on a single day, June 16, 1904. (This date was during the week when Joyce first met his wife Nora.) The title *Ulysses* is significant in that the theme, structure and many events and characters have parallels in the *Odys-*

sey of Homer. For instance, the wandering, paternal Bloom corresponds to Ulysses; Stephen, the spiritual orphan, to Telemachus, the son of Ulysses; and there are so many parallel and cognate features that scholars have studied and analyzed *Ulysses* almost from before it was published and are still finding them. The plot of *Ulysses* is a mere shadow of the novel skeleton; the real substance of the novel is in the internal monologues of the chief characters in turn, commenting on the day's events. ❡ The legal history of Ulysses has been almost as significant in the literary world as the content of the book. At first it was generally banned on grounds of obscenity and it was published in Paris and smuggled to the United States. Publication in the United States became legal after an important court decision, in 1933, that obscenity in part is not necessarily ground for forbidding the sale of works that are as a whole genuine literature. ❡ It is impossible to dismiss the implications of the fact that the writing of James Joyce has attracted more students and has been studied with greater care and depth and devotion than the writing of any other English author since Shakespeare.

I. 1. It is 8 A.M. in the Martello tower, an abandoned fortification overlooking Dublin Bay. BUCK (MALACHI) MULLIGAN, a gay

and cynical medical student, prepares to shave on the roof of the tower, where he shares rough living quarters with STEPHEN

DEDALUS and HAINES, a young English literary tourist. [It is about a year since Stephen wrote the concluding journal entries of *A Portrait of the Artist as a Young Man.*] Stephen has had a taste of Paris, has been recalled to his mother's deathbed, and now teaches school for a living. Stephen joins Mulligan while the latter is shaving. Mulligan reproaches him for refusing to kneel and pray beside his dying mother. Stephen does not say so, but he is haunted by that memory, and suffers from his father's lack of understanding. They descend together, to breakfast with Haines. An old woman comes in to deliver milk. A symbol of Ireland, she does not understand the Gaelic in which Haines addresses her. After breakfast, the three men walk to the shore, where Mulligan swims while Haines sits on a rock, smoking. Stephen leaves for school, agreeing to meet them at 12:30.

2. It is 10 A.M. in the school of Mr. DEASY, where Stephen is reluctantly teaching history to a dull and inattentive class. The students rush out to play hockey, but one remains behind to make up his arithmetic lesson. At last the delinquent is released and Mr. Deasy calls Stephen to his study to be paid. Mr. Deasy discusses the virtues of economy, Anglo-Irish history, and the rôle of the Jew in that history. He writes a letter to the papers concerning an outbreak of hoof-and-mouth disease, and asks Stephen to arrange with his "literary friends" for its publication. (Later Buck Mulligan will call Stephen "the bullock-befriending bard" in allusion to this letter.) The old headmaster takes leave of Stephen at the school gate.

3. At 11 o'clock Stephen is walking along the Dublin strand. His thoughts range widely, from such fantasies as the idea of an umbilical telephone line to "Edenville," to such memories as that of his own boyish esthetic theories. [This internal monologue is virtually the only action of the episode, which alludes by complex means to the capture of "Proteus" as recounted by "Menelaus" in the Fourth Book of the *Odyssey.* Just as the *Odyssey's* prologue concerns "Telemachus," the son of "Ulysses" the wanderer, so these first three episodes of Joyce's novel focus on Stephen in search, as it were, of a father to replace the irresponsible and unsympathetic SIMON DEDALUS.]

II. 1. LEOPOLD BLOOM, the Jew whose son RUDY died in infancy, is the title character. At 8 A.M. (while Stephen is watching Mulligan shave), in his home at 7 Eccles Street, Mr. Bloom, thinking hungrily of kidneys, prepares a tray for his wife MOLLY (MARION) BLOOM, whose maiden name, TWEEDY, suggests one of her prototypes, "Penelope," the weaver of webs. Molly, the sensual, primitive and somewhat temperamental daughter of a Spanish Jewess and an Irish officer, is a popular soprano whose husband is most recently being cuckolded by her impresario, BLAZES BOYLAN. Significantly, her appearances in *Ulysses* are only in bed, where she is now about to breakfast. Mr. Bloom feeds his cat and goes

out to shop for kidneys, attended by his wandering thoughts. He returns to grill the only kidney he could find, talk with Molly while she drinks her tea, and think of their daughter MILLY, apprenticed to a provincial photographer. His interior monologue continues as he visits the privy at the back of his garden and there reads the prize story in an old magazine. He hears the bells of George's Church and remembers that he must attend a funeral this morning.

2. Mr. Bloom sets out for work, stopping at the Westland Row post office to pick up a letter from the typist with whom he corresponds flirtatiously under the pseudonym of Henry Flower. He meets and compares wry mental notes with Mr. McCOY, whose wife, like Bloom's, is a singer. A billboard announcing the play *Leah* opens a train of thought to Bloom's dead father. Bloom opens and reads the letter from the typist, MARTHA. He passes All Hallows Church, reads the notice of a sermon by the Very Rev. JOHN CONMEE, S.J., and reflects cynically on the practical advantages of Catholicism. He stops at a chemist's to order a special face lotion for Molly and to buy a cake of lemon soap. Outside the chemist's, Bloom encounters BANTAM LYONS and unwittingly gives him a racing tip. Inspired by the smell of lemon soap, Bloom strolls on to the public baths, where he luxuriates in a steaming tub.

3. It is 11 A.M. and the body of PATRICK DIGNAM is borne to the cemetery in a hearse, followed by an ancient cab containing Leopold Bloom, the extrovert Simon Dedalus, the sensible lawyer, MARTIN CUN-

Dilly is thin and ragged

NINGHAM, and debonair young Mr. POWER. The four men converse disjointedly until they reach Glasnevin cemetery, where Bloom's silent commentary accompanies the burial service and he has scattered words with the other mourners as they walk to the cemetery gate.

4. At noon, Bloom visits the premises of the *Freeman's Journal and National Press,* to place an advertisement for Alexander Keyes, tea, wine, and spirit merchant. [This, the so-called "Aeolus" episode, is presented in brief sections, with headlines suggestive of journalism.] In the newspaper office are the editor, MYLES CRAWFORD, and his cronies, Simon Dedalus, Professor MAC-HUGH, and NED LAMBERT. After some con-

versation [to which rhetoric is the key: this episode has been called "a thesaurus of rhetorical devices"] Bloom leaves, followed shortly by Simon, and thereupon by the entrance of Stephen Dedalus, bearing Mr. Deasy's "bullock-befriending" letter.

5. By one o'clock, Mr. Bloom, thinking hungrily of lunch, is pursuing his odyssey through the streets of Dublin, headed vaguely for the National Library, where he must trace an old advertisement for a client. He passes Stephen's sister, DILLY (DELIA) DEDALUS, outside Dillon's auction-rooms and sees how thin and ragged she is. He buys Banbury cakes to feed the gulls. He meets an old flame gone shabby-genteel, Mrs. BREEN, who tells him that their friend MINA PUREFOY has been in labor for three days at the lying-in hospital in Holles Street. He passes A.E. (GEORGE RUSSELL) chatting with a girl; and, rejecting his first choice of a restaurant, lunches on a cheese sandwich and a glass of burgundy in Davy Byrne's pub.

6. At 2 o'clock, in the National Library, Stephen Dedalus is engaged in a long discussion of Shakespeare and the personality of Hamlet, with Mr. BEST, JOHN EGLIN-TON, George Russell, and the librarian. [Their conversation is recorded in lyrics, in blank verse, and then in dramatic form—thus exemplifying the three forms of literature defined by Stephen in *A Portrait of the Artist as a Young Man.*] Buck Mulligan enters to complain that Stephen has neglected their appointment. He and Stephen go through the door with Bloom, who has finished his errand at the library. But Bloom and Stephen still do not meet face to face.

7. [This episode, in 18 sections, is a "labyrinthine small-scale model" of *Ulysses* as a whole. It takes place between 3 and 4 o'clock in the streets of Dublin and records the wanderings and chance encounters there of many characters.] The Very Rev. John Conmee, S.J., walks to Artane, greeting passers-by and later reading his breviary. Molly Bloom gives alms to a one-legged sailor. Blazes Boylan buys fruit for Molly. Haines and Mulligan converse in a tearoom. Stephen has a poignant meeting with his sister Dilly at a bookstall where she has bought a second-hand French primer. Each of these "wandering rocks" encounters one or more of the others on his way.

8. At 4 o'clock Simon Dedalus enters the bar of Ormond's restaurant, interrupting the talk of the "siren" barmaids, LYDIA DOUCE and MINA KENNEDY. Outside the bar, the jingle of Boylan's jaunting-car is heard, on his way to an assignation with Molly Bloom. [The successive entrances of LENEHAN, of Bloom, and of Boylan are presented as voices in a fugue, and the episode's entire structure imitates the structure of a fugue.] BEN DOLLARD and Dedalus, singing at the Ormond's piano, give further emphasis to the musical ambiance.

9. Shortly after 5, the anonymous Dubliner who narrates this, the "Cyclops" episode, enters Barney Kiernan's public house

609

Stephen with the prostitutes

with one JOE HYNES. There they talk with a fierce Sinn Feiner, THE CITIZEN, and the equally quarrelsome GARRYOWEN. Bloom approaches to inquire after Martin Cunningham, in order to arrange for the payment of Dignam's insurance to his widow. Bloom becomes reluctantly involved in a political argument, which touches at last on the position of Jews in Ireland. Bloom goes to look for Cunningham at court. In his absence someone gives a garbled report of his encounter earlier in the day with Bantam Lyons. Martin Cunningham arrives at the pub. By the time Bloom has returned, Cunningham sees that a small riot is brewing, which he tries unsuccessfully to forestall.

10. At sunset, three adolescent girl friends, CISSY CAFFREY, EDY BOARDMAN, and GERTY MacDOWELL, are seated on the rocky Sandymount shore of Dublin bay, in charge of Cissy's small brothers TOMMY and JACKY and the Boardman baby. Their silly conversation is reported with malicious accuracy, as is the internal monologue of Gerty, the vain, prudish "Nausicaä" of Bloom's odyssey. Gerty spies Leopold Bloom, who has come to the shore to recover from the verbal brawl of the previous episode. They are strangers, but their eyes meet flirtatiously. While Gerty sentimentally imagines an amorous relationship with the unknown Bloom, that "knight" is himself finding sexual release in more realistic thoughts of Gerty.

11. By 10 o'clock that evening, Bloom has decided to call at the lying-in hospital for news of Mina Purefoy, who is still in labor. He finds there a group of medical students in ribald obstetrical conversation with Stephen Dedalus, presently joined by Mulligan and Haines. When Mrs. Purefoy's delivery is announced, they adjourn to Burke's pub, where Stephen buys the drinks with his morning's pay. Bloom's half-conscious craving for paternity is aroused by the situation. He begins vaguely to associate Stephen with his dead son, Rudy. Stephen becomes

thoroughly intoxicated and the more sober Bloom watches over him.

12. At midnight, Bloom paternally follows Stephen to the border of Dublin's nighttown and thence into the brothel of Mrs. BELLA COHEN. There Stephen and LYNCH (an old friend from the *Portrait*) drunkenly discuss music with three prostitutes, while Stephen strums a piano. Bloom has a series of fantastic visions in which historical personages enter. He alternately thinks of himself as male and female and Mrs. Cohen as female and male. He conjures up fantasies of his father, his dead son, and his unfaithful wife. Mrs. Cohen demands her fees and the befuddled Stephen would overpay her, but Bloom intervenes. The young men dance with the prostitutes, and Stephen wildly breaks a chandelier, for which Bloom pays. Bloom then follows Stephen out of the brothel and attempts to rescue him from the wrath of two drunken soldiers, one of whom knocks Stephen unconscious. [This is the "Circe" episode, and its style reflects Stephen's drunken state of hallucination.]

III. 1. Bloom takes Stephen (now conscious but still less than sober) on foot to a cabman's shelter (the hut of "Eumaeus"), passing various Dubliners on the way. In the shelter, Bloom orders coffee and a bun for Stephen, and they converse with the sailors and stevedores loitering there. Bloom and Stephen have a serious, more or less philosophical dialogue. Bloom learns that Stephen has had no dinner and invites him home. On the way to Eccles Street they discuss music.

2. Long past midnight Stephen and Bloom arrive at the latter's house, where they drink cocoa and continue their talk. Bloom invites Stephen to stay the night but Stephen declines, proposing instead to take singing lessons from Mrs. Bloom and to have further intellectual dialogues with his host. The "father" and "son" have established a bond. Stephen departs. Bloom disrobes and goes to bed, where he narrates some of his day's adventures to Molly, who has been lying awake. [This minutely detailed episode is presented in the form of an impersonal catechism—perhaps to moderate the potency of its emotional content.]

3. [This last, the "Penelope" episode of *Ulysses,* is probably the most famous passage in the novel. It is the long unspoken monologue of Molly Bloom, sleepless in bed at the long day's end. According to Arnold Bennett, these are "forty difficult pages, some 25,000 words without any punctuation at all (which) might in (their) utterly convincing realism be an actual document, the magical record of inmost thought by a woman that existed."] Molly remembers her youth at Gibraltar, her earliest lovers, her father, Major TWEEDY, and the Rock itself. Her current lover, Boylan, and her husband, "Poldy," occur and recur among these thoughts. She is also titillated by the idea of the young Stephen Dedalus, whom Leopold proposes to have for a lodger. She recalls her afternoon's adultery with Boylan, thinks of her daughter Milly, and meditates such frivolities as shopping. The novel ends [on what Stuart Gilbert has called "a triple paean of affirmation"] as Molly relives the ecstasy of a long-forgotten embrace.

Uncle Tom's Cabin

Novel by Harriet Beecher Stowe, 1811–1896.
Published 1852. (ML, 261; PB, C231)

SIMPLY FROM THE standpoint of results, this book must be accounted the most effective piece of propaganda fiction that has been written in the English language. It has been criticized, and not only on sectional lines, because Mrs. Stowe did not know her subject from personal experience (having spent no more than two weeks of her life in slave territory, and that in an unrepresentative section, Kentucky near the Ohio border). And of course it may be criticized on the grounds that it is not very fine literature. Even its historic importance is subject to question, because the Civil War very likely would have been fought even if the book had never been published. But simply as propaganda the book must be highly admired. Mrs. Stowe observed all the rules for appealing to an intelligent audience. She gave the impression of being very fair, showing good slave-owners as well as bad ones and happy slaves as well as oppressed ones. Then, having done all this, she left her reader at the end with the unshakable impression that slavery is wrong and that since her hero intended to devote his life to fighting it, why shouldn't the reader too? ❡ As a publication, *Uncle Tom's Cabin* was the great success of the 19th century and, unlike many big-selling books, it brought its author wealth as well as fame. Also *Uncle Tom's Cabin* produced the longest continuous run ever accorded a play. For at least 75 years and probably for much longer, there was no time in which some "Tom show" somewhere was not putting on a performance of *Uncle Tom's Cabin.*

Chaps. 1–5. Over a bottle of wine Mr. SHELBY, a Kentucky landowner, tries to strike a bargain with HALEY, a coarse slave-trader. Haley agrees to buy "Uncle" TOM, a prime male Negro slave about 40 years old, but forces Shelby to include 5-year-old HARRY, whose beautiful young mother, ELIZA, is Mrs. Shelby's maid and favorite. Shelby is reluctant to sell either but faces financial ruin if he does not. Eliza's husband, GEORGE HARRIS, a slave on a neighboring estate, has been working at a factory and has invented a machine for cleaning hemp, but when his hard-hearted owner hears of his success he takes him from the factory and puts him to hard labor. George tells Eliza he may be driven to do something terrible under the cruel treatment. Eliza, a devout Christian, urges him to trust in the Lord, but George's heart is too full of bitterness to do so. He schemes to escape to Canada. Meanwhile, in the lowly cabin of Uncle Tom and Aunt CHLOE, young Master GEORGE, a boy in his early teens, is teaching Uncle Tom his letters while Chloe takes care of the household. Later a prayer meeting is held in the cabin; George reads aloud to the group of Negroes that assembles, and listens to the singing. Shelby. has now concluded the sale of Tom and Harry. Eliza overhears enough to suspect the worst. She tells Uncle Tom that she is leaving and urges him to join her. He refuses to leave, out of loyalty to his master.

Chaps. 6–10. Eliza and Harry are missing, and the Shelbys unwillingly help Haley collect a party to pursue them. The Shelbys' Negroes cleverly delay the start as long as possible. Eliza and Harry reach the Ohio River, but when they arrive the river is full of blocks of ice. A kindly innkeeper takes the fugitives in for the night. From the window Eliza sees Haley and his party arriving. Carrying Harry, she escapes through a side door, hurls herself down the bank of the river, and leaps from block to block of ice until she is across. Haley hires LOKAR and MARKS to pursue Eliza. On the free Ohio side, Senator BIRD and his wife are discussing the new "runaway slave law," which forbids giving food and shelter to a runaway slave. Mrs. Bird has condemned the law just as an old Negro servant asks her to come to the kitchen, where she finds Eliza and Harry. They are given food, shelter, and clothes and are passed along to JOHN VAN TROMPE, a former slave-owner who is now militantly anti-slavery and participates in the "Underground Railway."

Uncle Tom eats his last meal with his family before Haley carries him off. Mrs. Shelby promises to keep track of him and buy him back when she can. George castigates Haley for his evil trade and says he is now ashamed to be a Kentuckian. Haley puts fetters on Tom's legs, but in a hypocritical exhibition of kindness does not use handcuffs.

Chaps. 11–16. George Harris has escaped and $400 reward is offered for him. Mr. WILSON, owner of the factory where George worked, is in a tavern when a swarthy stranger asks to have a few words with him. In a locked room the stranger reveals himself as George Harris, his brown hair dyed black, his yellow skin browned with walnut bark. Wilson, kindly but con-

The slave auction

fused, warns George about the dangers of breaking the laws of slavery and urges him to trust in God, but George is still too bitter. He asks Wilson to give a brooch to Eliza.

Haley and Tom stop in Washington, Ky., to attend a slave sale. All the horrors of slavery are displayed—the anguish of parted families, the indignity of the slave block. Haley buys a young woman, Lucy, and her child, then sells the child while they are on the river boat. He seeks to console the heartbroken mother by promising her a new dress. Tom, sleeping on the deck, hears a splash and realizes Lucy has thrown herself overboard. Haley's only concern is for his loss of a valuable piece of property. Meanwhile, Eliza has reached a Quaker settlement in the North, where she is unexpectedly joined by George. The good Quaker SIMEON rebukes his little son for expressing hatred toward the slaveholders, explaining to him that a Quaker must help everyone. Tom, journeying down the Mississippi to be sold, notices a fellow passenger, AUGUSTINE ST. CLARE, a New Orleans aristocrat, and his small daughter EVA, age 5. Eva makes friends with Tom and promises him her papa will buy him. Tom rescues Eva when she falls overboard and out of gratitude St. Clare buys him and takes him to Louisiana. Living with the St. Clares is a cousin, Miss OPHELIA, a repressed spinster recently from Vermont, who is repelled by the Negroes. Miss Ophelia takes over the household duties which MARIE, St. Clare's wife, is too ailing or too indolent to handle. Marie, a selfish and heartless woman, feels that little Eva lacks the proper feeling of superiority toward the Negroes. Eva and Tom become fast friends.

Chaps. 17–20. PHINEAS FLETCHER, a Quaker, reports that a company of armed strangers are nearby, seeking runaway slaves. George and Eliza, with JIM, another runaway, and his old mother, are forced to flee. They are pursued by Haley's posse and are cornered on a rocky cliff. George calls to the pursuers that he is a free man and is armed. The posse moves in and shooting occurs; Haley and Marks flee, but Tom Lokar is wounded. The Quakers take him to DORCAS STEPHENS, who puts him to bed in her house and tends him. In Louisiana Miss Ophelia finds the St. Clare household in a shocking state, mismanaged by indolent Negroes. She tries to improve things, but actually despises the Negroes. Uncle Tom preaches to the servants and tries to make them Christians. He prays for St. Clare, who is intemperate. One morning St. Clare brings his daughter a present—a little 8-year-old Negro girl named TOPSY. She and Eva become fast friends. Topsy tells Miss Ophelia she was never born, she just "growed."

Chaps. 21–27. Eva and Tom spend a great deal of time together with the Bible and hymns. Eva spends more time in good works, and less time playing, but her health is failing. She dies surrounded by her heartbroken family and sincerely mourned by the slaves, with a bright, glorious smile on her face as she sees heaven at last.

Chaps. 27–29. Miss Ophelia, inspired by Eva's death, resolves to love and teach the incorrigible Topsy, who is so sad about Eva that she is tractable. St. Clare decides for Eva's sake to improve the lot of his own servants and to try to save his country from the disgrace of slavery. He intends to free Tom. But he is wounded in a stabbing affray in a tavern, where he was an innocent bystander, and he dies. His slaves are to be sold. Miss Ophelia writes to Mrs. Shelby, urging the Shelbys to repurchase Tom. The next day Tom and the rest of the servants are taken to a slave warehouse.

Chaps. 30–34. Tom again faces the horrors of the slave-block and the same heart-rending scenes occur. Tom himself is bought by the brutal SIMON LEGREE, who owns a cotton plantation on the Red River.

Tom and a female slave, EMMELINE, bought to be Legree's mistress, are loaded on a river boat, with chains on hands and feet. There are six other slaves, bought elsewhere. Legree takes Tom's good clothes and replaces them with rags. Tom manages to conceal his Bible, but Legree finds his hymnbook and warns him against praying and hymn-singing. He says that Tom no longer belongs to a church: "I'm your church now." Tom tries to comfort the frightened girl Emmeline, whom he had seen torn from her mother in the New Orleans warehouse. At Legree's plantation, Tom finds his overseers are two Negroes, QUIMBO and SAMBO, who have been trained in brutality by their master. Tom is put to work picking cotton. A newcomer in the field is a fierce, desperate woman of 35 named CASSY, who was Legree's mistress before Emmeline. The other pickers jeer at her. One slave woman, LUCY, is too ill to pick properly. Tom and Cassy secretly help her. At the weighing-in Legree calls Lucy a lazy beast and orders Tom to flog her. Tom refuses and is flogged himself. Cassy comes to tend him. She tells him he is wrong to trust in God, and relates the terrible story of her life. Tom tells her to believe in Christ and trust in the Lord.

Chaps. 35–36. Legree, drinking punch before his fire, is interrupted by Cassy, who disapproves his treatment of Tom. While they talk Sambo comes in with a "witch thing" he had taken from one of the hands. Legree, in superstitious terror, opens the paper and finds a silver dollar and a strand of hair. The hair reminds him of a lock of hair he received after his mother's death, together with a letter from her forgiving him for his brutality to her. Legree believes he is bewitched and is terrified. Cassy works on his fears, trying to frighten him into being kinder to Tom. Legree half assents but says Tom must apologize to him. Tom humbly protests that he did what he thought was right, and is beaten by Legree.

Chap. 37. At the Quaker settlement, Tom Lokar, tended by the gentle Quaker Aunt Dorcas, repents his former ways and tips her off that the slaves will be pursued to Sandusky by Marks. He suggests disguising them. On the last lap of the journey Eliza is disguised as a man, Harry as a little girl, and they slip through the fingers of the watchers and reach Canada safely.

Chaps. 38–44. Legree taunts Tom about his religion, saying God has deserted him, but Tom remains staunch. When Cassy tries to persuade him to escape, he says it is his duty to await the Lord's bidding. Cassy and Emmeline, pretending to escape, hide in the garret. Legree asks Tom where they are, and when Tom is silent, threatens to flog him to death. Sambo and Quimbo whip him, but are converted to Christ by Tom's forbearance. Meanwhile, Miss Ophelia's letter reaches the Shelbys after Mr. Shelby's death, and Mrs. Shelby and young George set off to rescue Tom. They reach Legree's plantation in time to hear Tom's dying words. George resolves to devote his life to the

abolition of slavery. Cassy, pretending to be the ghost of his mother, frightens Simon Legree into drinking himself to death. Two white-clad ghosts are seen near the house. In reality they are Cassy and Emmeline who escape to the river and board the same boat George Shelby has taken. They learn from him that George and Eliza are safe in Canada with their little son, and Cassy reveals

that Eliza is her long-lost daughter. A French woman on the same boat turns out to be George Harris's sister. She gives George money to go to France and educate himself, and he ultimately goes to Liberia with his family, to teach and preach to his own people. Miss Ophelia takes Topsy home to Vermont with her and trains her to be a missionary in Africa.

U. S. A.

Trilogy (three novels) by John Dos Passos, 1896–
Published 1930–33–36 by Houghton Mifflin Co., Boston. © 1930, 1937 by John Dos Passos. (ML, G44)

SOMEWHERE ALONG THE LINE John Dos Passos got sidetracked and did not turn out to be a major American novelist after all. The reason may range from bad luck to and through any number of rationalizations. For one thing, Dos Passos was an innovator and there is always danger in innovation. The public may go for it and may not. ❡ *U.S.A.* is three full novels constituting nearly 1,500 pages. In it the author uses many odd devices, such as newsreels, "the camera eye," and background color such as song lyrics and newspaper headlines. He makes his novels very complex, with separate sections on the multiplicity of characters. But the writing is often wonderful and the concept is grand.

The 42nd Parallel

Mac. MAC MCCREARY'S father (POP) loses his job when the Chadwick Mills in Middletown close because of a strike, and the family moves to Chicago to live with Uncle TIM, who says poverty is the fault of the system. Mac works in Tim's printing shop until it goes bankrupt. Mac goes on a book-selling tour with DOC BINGHAM, a smooth-talking swindler who carries both religious and salacious literature. Mac, left stranded with no money in Michigan, hikes to the railroad, where he and IKE HALL discover their common interest in socialism. They travel together for a time. Mac gets to San Francisco, where he works in a printshop owned by an Italian anarchist and joins the Industrial Workers of the World (IWW). He wants to go with FRED

HOFF to help the striking miners in Goldfield, Nev., but then he gets engaged to MAISIE SPENCER and he promises to stay and marry her. The next morning he feels he is selling out (betraying) the cause, and he leaves. In Goldfield BIG BILL HAYWOOD speaks on solidarity. Maisie keeps writing that she is pregnant and Mac goes back to Frisco. They marry and go to San Diego. Mac works at a job printer's and they have two children. They are estranged by Mac's political beliefs, and Maisie's extravagance keeps them in debt. Mac leaves her. He goes to Juarez, where he becomes involved with the Mexican revolutionists and lives with ENCARNACION, a Mexican girl.

Janey. JANEY WILLIAMS hates everything about her life in Georgetown but her brother JOE and his friend ALEC MCPHERSON. When Alec is killed in an accident she tells her best friend, ALICE DICK, that she will never love anyone else. Joe enlists in the Navy. Janey becomes secretary for a law firm and is friends with dissipated JERRY BURNHAM, who talks about marrying her. He gets angry when she will not make love to him and he leaves for the front as a war correspondent. Joe comes back and tells her that he had a fight with a petty officer and deserted. Janey becomes interested in politics and a business career.

J. Ward Moorehouse. JOHN WARD MOOREHOUSE (or J.W.), whose main assets are his blue eyes and his likable manner, grows up in Delaware wanting to be a songwriter. He goes to work for a real-estate company, which sends him to Ocean City, Md., on business. There his charm gets him a job with Col. WEDGEWOOD of the Ocean City Improvement and Realty Co., and he becomes engaged to wealthy, promiscuous socialite ANNABELLE MARIE STRANG. He goes ahead with the wedding even after he learns that she is carrying another man's child, because he cannot bring himself to give up her social and financial connections. They go to Europe and in Paris, Ward impresses Mr. MCGILL, who is manager of a steel plant in Pittsburgh.

The Ocean city real estate boom collapses and Ward and Annabelle have to return to get her father's affairs in order. Annabelle is unfaithful and Ward asks for a divorce.

Eleanor Stoddard. Fastidious ELEANOR STODDARD is revolted by her father, who works in the stockyards. She and a friend swear that if ever a boy touches them they will kill themselves. She works in a lace shop, where her artistic inclinations and her snobbish manners are exploited by her boss, who pays for her French lessons at Berlitz School. Eleanor's life really begins when she becomes friends with EVELINE HUTCHINS, the daughter of a Unitarian minister. Through Eveline her social life improves. She meets handsome ERIC EGSTROM. Eveline falls in love with him. Eleanor gets a job in the interior-decorating department at Marshall Field's. She spends all her free time with Miss PERKINS, a rich old maid, but when Miss Perkins dies and leaves all her money to a home for wayward girls, SALLY EMERSON, a wealthy patroness of the arts, backs Eleanor and Eveline in their own decorating business and they rent a house together. They do not make much money. When FREDDY SERGEANT, one of Eveline's beaux, wires them to come to New York to do the scenery and costumes for a play, they go.

J. Ward Moorehouse. Ward works on the *Times Reporter* until McGill gives him a job handling advertising and promotion. Ward meets GERTRUDE STAPLE, only daughter of HORACE STAPLE, owner of a large block of Standard Oil stock. Ward proposes to Gertrude, but her parents will not permit her to marry a man with a smaller income than hers. When public opinion is aroused against mine guards who kill several strikers, Ward suggests a new bureau to influence public opinion in favor of the corporations, and he is put in charge of it at $10,000 a year. Horace Staple dies and six months later Ward and Gertrude marry and go abroad for a year, but war talk in Europe cuts their trip short. Ward borrows $50,000 from Mrs. Staple and opens a lavish office, calling himself J. Ward Moorehouse, Public Relations Counsel. He hires EDGAR ROBBINS, an intemperate young reporter, to take over the copywriting. In Chicago he seeks out Judge BOWIE C. PLANET, a smalltime lawyer, and G. H. BARROW, an opportunist with labor connections, whom he wants to use to develop his contacts between capital and labor.

Eleanor Stoddard. Eleanor is dependent on Eveline until through Freddy she is accepted in the artistic and social life of New York. The scenery and costumes are a success, but the play fails after two weeks. Eveline returns to Chicago. Sally Emerson backs Eleanor in her own decorating business and helps her to get the commission to decorate the Moorehouse house in Great Neck. Ward admires her and they have a platonic friendship; Eleanor sympathizes with him because his wife is an invalid.

Janey. Janey is out of a job until she takes dictation for G. H. Barrow in Ward's suite. Ward hires her to replace his secretary, who has broken her hip, and she goes with him on a business trip to Mexico.

Mac. The Mexican rebels take Juarez; Huerta flees; Carranza is president. Mac wants to join Zapata and goes to Mexico City. Many of the Americans have fled and those remaining expect to be killed. Mac gets a job on the *Mexican Herald* and settles down to a real home life with CONCHA. Then he buys a bookstore. He and BEN STOWELL, a pro-Zapata oil promoter, show Barrow around, and Ben gives a party for Moorehouse, who has come to investigate Carranza's opposition to American investors. Carranza's government is defeated and the banks close; Mac takes Concha and her family to Vera Cruz.

Janey. G. H. Barrow is attentive to Janey on the trip up from Mexico. She goes to work in his New York office and rooms with GLADYS COMPTON, whose family is very good to her. Then Janey moves in with ELIZA TINGLEY and her brother and feels that she has come up in the world. Joe writes that he has been torpedoed but when he comes to see her she is ashamed of him and does not have her friends see him. Janey finds her work exciting and is completely devoted to J. W. Barrow proposes to Eleanor but she tells him they must remain just friends. Gertrude decides to divorce J. W. and Mrs. Staple is suing to recover her money. A new corporation is formed and Janey is to be made an officer.

Eleanor Stoddard. On her way to meet J.W., Eleanor is depressed about money and afraid she is losing her looks, but when she reads in a paper that war has been declared she feels elated and when J.W. tells her he is going to France she decides to join the Red Cross and go there too. When Mrs. Moorehouse learns that J.W. is going overseas she forgives him.

Charley Anderson. CHARLEY ANDERSON is happy to escape from the staid boarding house his mother keeps in Fargo, N. D., to work in his brother JIM's garage in Min-

neapolis in the summer. But when he smashes up a truck Jim sends him home. The summer he graduates from high school he becomes engaged to EMISCAH SVENSON. In the fall he gets a job in a machine shop and studies civil engineering. ED WALTERS, Charley's friend, gets Emiscah pregnant. Emiscah's family think it is Charley's fault and Charley permits the marriage to be announced. He is able to get some pills to make Emiscah miscarry. He breaks with Emiscah, gets involved with the I.W.W., goes to Chicago, and is arrested at a Wobbly meeting. He and an anarchist named GRASSI go to New Orleans for the Mardi Gras, then Charley goes to New York. He gets into a fight with some pacifists, and a week later is on his way to France to join the French ambulance corps.

1919

Joe Williams. Joe has a fight with an officer and deserts. He manages to get a forged Able Seaman certificate and signs on a merchant marine ship. Joe is defiant when they try to make him work in the stokehole, and he is thrown in irons. English officers board the ship and arrest him on charges of being a German spy. The American consul gets him out and gets a berth for him to Norfolk. Pretty, plump DELLA MATTHEWS promises to marry him if he gets a job in Norfolk, and Joe tries, but he does not have experience and finally has to sign on a coal barge. In Brooklyn he discovers he has contracted V.D. (a veneral disease). His landlady befriends him and he begins to study navigation, He ships as A.B. (able-bodied seaman) for Tampico and Bombay. When he gets back he is so glad to see his sister Janey he thinks he'll cry. But she is cold to him and when he leaves her he feels like a bum. Next he ships with Captain PERRY on the *North Star*. A German submarine forces them to abandon ship. Because Joe has the presence of mind to cut loose the lifeboats, all men are saved. Perry expresses his gratitude by helping Joe get his third mate's license, and he and Della are married. Della says she is

Charley Anderson is on his way to France

afraid to have a baby and Joe has to sail for France without having consummated his marriage.

Richard Ellsworth Savage. Dick remembers his comfortable life before his father went away and hates being poor and having his mother live in his aunt's boarding house. He works in a hotel. He inspires the patronage of HIRAM HALSEY COOPER, a lawyer and politician, who puts him through Harvard, where he makes the literary magazines and rooms with blasé NED WIGGLESWORTH, who gets tight nightly. When the Armed Ship Bill is passed, Dick learns he can get a degree without taking exams if he goes into war work. He enlists in the volunteer ambulance service and is sent to France. In Paris he eats well and makes love to as many French girls as he can.

Eveline Hutchins. Eveline lives a protected life in Chicago. She has some artistic talent and she becomes friends with exciting Sally Emerson, who encourages her to paint. She goes abroad and on the return trip falls in love with DIRK McARTHUR, who sees her often but does not propose. She decides she believes in free love, but when she comes back and offers herself to Dirk he is too interested in a chorus girl to accept. The next day she starts a decorating business with Eleanor and tries hard to fall in love with Freddy Sergeant. She accompanies her father to Santa Fe for his health, where she has an unsuccessful affair with a Spanish artist, who gives her up rather than lose the convenience of his Mexican wife. DON STEVENS, a communist writer, makes love to her and she forgets her fears about being pregnant. When war is declared she joins the Red Cross and goes to Paris as an assistant in a publicity office J.W. has secured for Eleanor.

Joe Williams. When Joe's ship reaches Bordeaux, America has just declared war on Germany. On the way back his ship is sunk. A fishing schooner picks up the survivors but Captain Perry dies of pneumonia. Joe's next ship is shot up and when Joe gets back home he is fed up with the sea and determined to settle down to married life. Della is disillusioned and goes to New York.

Richard Ellsworth Savage. Dick and his friends are moved up until they are within range of the guns. Then they are disbanded and enroll in the Red Cross for service in Italy. The censor objects when Dick writes a disillusioned letter home and Dick is sent back to the States. Going back home he is on the same ship with Ned Wigglesworth.

Eveline Hutchins lives with Eleanor in Paris and goes out a lot with Jerry Burnham. When J.W. arrives Eveline likes him at once and she is lonesome when he and Eleanor go to Italy to organize Red Cross publicity. Don Stevens is full of talk of the coming working-class rebellion. Eveline meets PAUL JOHNSON, a young soldier. Eleanor is very cool when she returns and Eveline looks for another apartment.

Joe Williams. Joe hangs around New York drinking until his landlady turns him out. He steadies down again for a while and applies for a second mate's license. Janey, overseas with the Red Cross, writes him patriotic letters. On Armistice night Joe is in St. Nazaire and the town is wild. He looks all over for a girl he knows and finds her dancing with a Senegalese. Joe gets into a fight with him and his skull is crushed.

Daughter. ANNE ELIZABETH TRENT is called Daughter. She is of a rich Texas family and has a horse and a Pierce-Arrow touring car and is the belle of her first dance. Somehow nothing comes of her love for JOE WASHBURN, a young lawyer in her father's office. She runs away from finishing school, then goes to Columbia University. She gets her name into the papers when she is arrested for interfering with a policeman who is kicking a woman striker in the face. Her father becomes sick and she returns to Texas to keep house for him. She takes it very hard when her brother BUD crashes in a defective plane. She goes overseas to Rome for the Near East Relief when the Armistice is declared.

Eveline Hutchins. Eveline begins celebrating the Armistice drinking champagne with Eleanor and J.W., but she loses them and dances in the streets, where Paul Johnson finds her. She and Eleanor go to Nice, and when J.W. shows up to see Eleanor off to Rome, Eveline and he have an affair and drive back to Paris together. She drops in unexpectedly on Eleanor, who is back from Rome, and sees J.W. in Eleanor's bed. Eveline has an affair with Paul Johnson. When she tells him she is going to have a baby he is disturbed because it changes his plans to study engineering, but they decide to be married.

Richard Ellsworth Savage. Through Mr. Cooper's influence Dick is commissioned a second lieutenant and is sent back to France, where his knowledge of French gets him assigned to the Post Dispatch Service with the rank of captain. When the Armistice is signed he is sent as a courier to the Peace Conference in Paris. Wilson is expected in Rome and when Dick is sent there he meets Anne Elizabeth, who falls in love with him. He makes love to her although

Daughter in a plane crash

she is a virgin, and when she gets back to Paris she writes that she is pregnant. He makes excuses to get out of marrying her. He takes a job with J.W. in his publicity office. Anne Elizabeth comes to him and begs him to marry her, but he says he just wants to be friends.

Daughter. Anne Elizabeth tears up the name of an abortionist Dick gives her. G. H. Barrow takes her to dinner and she sees Dick at the next table with Eleanor. She goes off with some French soldiers and gets drunk and persuades one of them to take her up in a plane. They crash.

Ben Compton. BEN COMPTON is studious and wants to grow up and make money to take care of his parents and his sister, but NICK GIGLI, a construction worker, teaches him about revolution and anarchy. After that Ben studies law with only one thought —to help the working class. He gets to be well known as a socialist agitator. He studies law in New York with a radical lawyer, MORRIS STEIN, but also has a job. When war is declared he registers as a conscientious objector and loses his job. Ben is arrested at a socialist meeting where he is speaking. Morris Stein gets him out on bail and he lives with FANYA, Morris's sister, who is in love with him. The court refuses to grant his appeal and at 23 he is sentenced to 10 years in jail.

Richard Ellsworth Savage. Dick goes to Eleanor's send-off party for Eveline and Paul, which Eleanor gives though she thinks the marriage is a mistake. The party is very stiff and J.W. is talking about a new era of international coöperation. Dick goes back to his hotel.

Big Money

Charley Anderson. Lt. Charley Anderson returns to New York a war hero. He goes to dinner at the lavish home of Wall Street broker NAT BENTON, where he immediately falls in love with DORIS HUMPHRIES. His brother Jim tries to get Charley to go into his business so he can capitalize on his war record. When their mother dies, Jim tries to get Charley's share of his money and gets nasty when Charley says he needs it to invest in airplane motors. Charley is running out of money waiting for JOE ASKEW to join him in New York to start the airplane business. He gets a job as a mechanic, plays high-stake poker, and drinks a lot. He and Eveline Johnson have an affair but he keeps proposing to Doris, and she refuses him. Joe and ANDY MERRITT form the Askew-Merritt company and Charley is made supervising engineer and given a percentage of the stock.

Mary French. MARY sympathizes with her father, Dr. FRENCH, who does much charity work in Trinidad, when her mother divorces him because he does not make money. Mary goes to Vassar and does settlement work in the summer. Her father dies of overwork in an influenza epidemic and she decides to dedicate her life to the underprivileged. She gets a job in a factory, works for strikers, and is heartbroken when her friend GUS MUSCOWSKI is arrested for distributing leaflets. She goes to work for G. H. Barrow on the Senatorial Investigating Commission but when Gus gets out of jail he says the senators sold the workers out. She has an affair with Barrow but she does not want to marry him and has an abortion.

Margo Dowling. When Margo's father FRED gets drunk more and more often, her stepmother AGNES leaves home. Margo is sent to a convent school until Agnes goes to live with FRANK MANDEVILLE. Then Margo lives in an old brownstone with them and Frank gives her singing and dancing lessons. Frank gets drunk and rapes her and she elopes with TONY GARRIDO, a Cuban guitarist, who takes her to Havana to live with his family.

Charley Anderson. Nat Benton involves Charley in the stock market. Doris returns from a trip to England with a wealthy Englishman, GEORGE DUQUESNE. Charley moves out of Joe's house into an apartment so he can have an affair with Doris. Doris writes him that she is going to marry George. Charley goes on a drinking spree. While he is drunk Nat Benton gets him to sign a contract swapping his shares of Askew-Merritt for Tern stock, and Charley leaves Joe to work in Detroit.

Margo Dowling. Margo discovers that Tony is effeminate. When she has his baby it is born blind and dies, because Tony has given Margo a venereal disease. She goes back to New York. Frank and Agnes marry and become respectable. Margo gets a few chorus jobs and Agnes is glad when TAD WHITTLESEA, a wealthy Yale halfback, falls in love with Margo. He gives her some pearls and she goes on a cruise on his yacht but takes another girl along. They meet Tony and when Tad learns he is her husband he loses all respect for her and leaves her. Tony steals her money and jewelry and runs away. She plans to hock her ring to get to Miami, where she has a job.

Charley Anderson. In Detroit Charley marries wealthy GLADYS WHEATLEY, who becomes frigid toward him after the birth of their second child. On a practice flight Charley's best friend is killed and Charley is seriously injured. He drinks heavily, neglects business, and plays the stock market. In Florida, where he goes to recuperate, he meets Margo Dowling. He falls in love with her and they have a good time together. Then Charley loses his money and his airplane stock, and his wife sues him for divorce.

Margo Dowling. Margo goes to work as a dress model. She meets SAM MARGOLIES, a photographer who takes pictures for *Vogue*. Her boss commits suicide and Margo is out of a job. She goes to bed with Charley and he promises to try to raise $1,000 for her.

Charley Anderson. Charley is unable to make a financial comeback and goes to Miami, where he and Margo live together and are happy for a while. But Charley starts drinking again and crashes a car. His brother Jim visits him in the hospital and, before Charley dies, asks him if he has made a will.

Margo Dowling. Agnes, who is in mourning for Frank, joins Margo in Miami after Charley's death. Margo, involved in real-estate speculation, loses all her money, and she and Agnes and Tony, who turns up and is put in chauffeur's uniform, drive to Los Angeles to get into the movies. They do badly, with only occasional jobs as an extra for Margo. She swaps their car for an old Rolls Royce and with the last of their money they go to Palm Springs. Sam Margolies, who has become a famous director, sees Margo and says she is the face he has been looking for. Tony, who has been blackmailing Margo, is killed at a drunken party. Sam makes a big star of Margo and she marries him.

Mary French. Mary does publicity for the garment workers in New York and hides Ben Compton in her apartment. They fall in love and she gives him all her money for the strikers. When she gets pregnant Ben feels they cannot spare the time to have a baby, and she has an abortion. She goes to Boston to work on the defense committee for Sacco and Vanzetti and is arrested for picketing the State House. Don Stevens bails her out.

Richard Ellsworth Savage. Dick works up a successful campaign to sell the idea of patent medicines to the public and gets a big contract for J.W. At this time J.W. is disappointed that Eleanor is marrying a titled Russian. When J.W. has a heart attack, Dick gets a raise and begins to step into J.W.'s job.

Mary French. Mary lives with Don and they both work for the strikers. When the party sends Don to Moscow, Mary goes to Pittsburgh to raise money for the miners and when Don returns married, Mary gets drunk and is sick. Eveline is overwhelmed by the uselessness of her life and dies of an overdose of sleeping pills. Mary goes back to her work with renewed ardor.

Utopia

Satire by Sir Thomas More, 1478–1535. Published 1516.

THIS IS THE MOST famous book ever written by a canonized saint. Literally hundreds of authors, and many of them great authors, have written about the ideal state, but it was St. (or Sir) Thomas More whose name *Utopia* became the generic term. More was a very great man. Henry VIII wooed him anxiously and was delighted when More was tractable enough to accept —what to many dukes and earls would have been an honor worth murdering for—the position of prime minister. But More never would knuckle down and eventually his unwillingness to compromise his principles led Henry to have him beheaded. As befits an English prime minister, Sir Thomas More was politically discreet. He had the description of his Utopia told by a man whose name means "nonsense-babbler," and the name Utopia itself means "noplace." *Utopia* was written in Latin and there are ample good translations. The political ideas expressed are almost incredibly advanced and profound when one considers that the book was written some 450 years ago.

Book I. More speaks of his visit, after the completion of an actual (1515) commission to Flanders, with PETER GILES, a citizen of Antwerp. At his house they listen to a learned Portuguese mariner, RAPHAEL HYTHLODAY, who was on three voyages with Amerigo Vespucci, going to South America, Ceylon, and the Far East. Left behind on one trip [some critics identify the place with Paraguay], Raphael reports that he was accepted by the natives and closely studied their ways. His hosts in Antwerp, who found the example of citizens ruled by good and wholesome laws a rarity, beg Raphael to serve as a king's counselor. The mariner refuses, holding that most monarchs are interested in war, not peace; in enlarging their territory and feeding on flattery, not in caring for their subjects and heeding sage advice. Raphael has been in England, at the home of More's own patron, the Archbishop of Canterbury, JOHN Cardinal MORTON, where he engaged in a long discussion on justice. During it, he says, he condemned the death penalty for theft; neglect of war veterans, particularly the wounded; raising of tenant farmers' rents; needless entourages of aristocrats and the general idleness of that class; and the cost and danger of standing armies. All of these work against the common good, Raphael maintains. Other causes of current unrest, he adds, are the changing of farmland into pasture to satisfy the wool monopolists; the eviction of families; the lack of a policy for diversifying industry; the concentration of wealth; the longwindedness of lawyers and the slowness of court procedure. More himself knew of all this at first hand, as lawyer, judge, and court official.

Asked for recommendations, since the state itself seems to provoke the situations in which starving men become thieves, then murderers, then victims of bad laws, Raphael tells of what he saw elsewhere. In Persia, among the Polylerites (Greek for "people of considerable nonsense"), thieves, of whatever social level, make exact restitution to their victims, either in goods or labor. Cruelty is avoided, reformation of the criminal is achieved, prisoners are restored to their original status in society as soon as possible. All except Raphael and Cardinal Morton agree that such a plan would never work in England. Again asked to consider the duty of becoming a royal adviser, Raphael says that as far back as Plato's time kings have been advised to seek wisdom and devote themselves to the study of philosophy, but few have heeded. Most kings are like the Achoriens ("people without place," without limitless empire) who seize kingdom after kingdom, plundering and despoiling, failing to govern and guide either the old or the new. They empty their treasury in the mad hope of gaining wealth elsewhere, then have to resort to devaluing their nation's currency, levying exorbitant taxes, finding moth-eaten laws that carry forgotten fines and penalties, and appointing blind judges who work only for the crown. This only creates a nation of beggars and grovelers. A king, Raphael insists, should be a shepherd, not a jailor; one who never does his subjects harm, but forever seeks to enrich them, like the ruler of the Macariens ("the happy race"). It is odd, he concludes ironically, that justice is widespread, prosperity flourishes, and men by working in common achieve considerable good order in Utopia, whereas in Christian Europe there is the sickness of craftiness, disorder, and selfishness.

Book II. After pausing for dinner, Raphael tells More and Giles about Utopia. It is an island shaped like a crescent moon, 200 miles at its widest point, with a shoreline of 500 miles. There are 24 cities, of 20 square miles each and at least 24 miles apart. The country is basically agricultural, the farmers living in units of no fewer than 40, plus 2 servants. Each unit is ruled by a wise man; each 30 units are supervised by a *Philarche* ("one fit to lead"); each 10 Philarches are under a superior called a *Tranibore*. There is an annual, ordered exchange of a proportion of the population between city and farm areas. Amaurote ("a place of vision, not easy to materialize"), the capital, is in the center of the country and looks somewhat like London. There are a river and bridge and walls; also block-long attached houses with glass windows and herb gardens. The citizens exchange houses every 10 years lest they become more attached to things than to ideas (a monastic touch).

Each year three wise men from each city come to Amaurote to discuss current problems. Laws are very few and are crystal clear in their wording. The prince rules for life but may be removed if he turns tyrannical. He is elected from four nominees of the people, voted on secretly by 200 *Syphograuntes* (stewards; another name for Philarches), who also elect the Tranibores. The Tranibores are chosen annually and are usually reëlected. They meet with the prince every three days. Major problems are always discussed at length so that rashness may be avoided. The people learn one trade each, besides farming; make their own clothes

(of identical style: another monastic touch); hate idleness; often study or attend lectures; listen to music; play games (but do not gamble); and enjoy conversational exchange.

Each city is limited to 6,000 persons; surpluses are moved to other city or country areas. In the center of each of four quarters of a city is a warehouse market. Here families obtain all that they need to live, and turn in what they have grown or made and do not need. No money is used; no greed is possible; no poverty exists. That which they lack, like iron, they obtain by barter. There is careful inspection of food. The sick are segregated according to illness; there are no plagues. Meals are enjoyed in common, with instructive reading (still another reference to monasticism) and music. The young, at table, learn from and with their elders. Travel is permitted to all, and many alien visitors come to Utopia. One group, the Anemolians ("windy boasters"), arrived in Utopia with elaborate apparel, jewelry, and pomp. The simple Utopians, who scorned gold, gems, feathers, and all display, could not understand their bondage to the material. The Utopians' formal learning is extensive: logic, music, mathematics, astronomy and meteorology have all been mastered. Raphael reports that when he introduced them to Greek culture and showed them how to make paper and print from type, they quickly became adept.

They believe in the immortality of the soul, reward and punishment after death, a divine purpose in life, and the brotherhood of man. Life is pleasant, for they never give displeasure to others. They cleave to virtue out of philosophical conviction. Those who refuse to act rationally, and persist in disturbing the way of life that most of the people have adopted through reason, are made servants. So are adulterers. Monogamy is the law, although divorce and remarriage are sometimes permitted. The incurably ill are allowed, after consultation, to starve themselves to death or to be dispatched by another. [More's remarks on divorce and euthanasia immediately precede a discussion of the Utopians' respect for their word—private promise or international treaty—in contrast to the dishonesty prevailing in Europe. Many hold that he was illustrating that reason alone can

lead men into what he considered errors, just as disregard of spiritual precepts had hurt the Europeans.]

Utopia approves defensive war or a compassionate invasion to aid an oppressed neighbor. It attempts to achieve victory without bloodshed and after negotiation, but offers a reward of gold (of no value) to anyone in another country who assassinates the causers of strife. It also employs mercenaries (*Zapoletes,* "willing sellers") rather than its own people, even though every man and woman in Utopia undergoes military training. No conquered city is ever sacked; captured soldiers are not slain but are made bondsmen, and the citizenry are spared. Wealth is distributed to those who need it, but those who caused the war are made to pay reparations.

In the final section, Raphael reports that in Utopia men worship God in many forms and in many ways. Such variety is permitted, but, since men have great reason, all strive to bring themselves to agree with the philosophers who believe in a Creator. (After Raphael told the Utopians about Christianity, many concluded that it was the wisest choice and adopted it. However, Utopians believe that religion should not be imposed by any force and those who sought to make everyone a Christian were condemned to exile.) Those who believe in no religion are tolerated, but, since it is expected that they will pursue philosophical study and that reason will lead them to acknowledge the existence of a Creator, they are not allowed to hold office while they are unbelievers. All priests are simple in their tastes, holy, devoted and learned men. Raphael finally warns his friends, and the reader, that the Utopians have merely begun to lay the foundations for a more perfect state. If modern man, he concludes, would labor to root out fraud, theft, pride, brawling, treachery, famine, poverty, and injustice, and seek more perfect concord, a better world would result. Imperfect as they are, the Utopians can still teach a world which, with more knowledge and a greater spiritual heritage, falls short in far too many ways. There are "many things" that call for further consideration, but the conversation of a single afternoon has not allowed him to cover everything fully nor his hosts to ask all the questions still in their minds.

Vanity Fair

Novel by William Makepeace Thackeray, 1811–1863.
Published 1847–48. (PB, 'PL750; ML, 131 & T33; RE, 76)

THE TITLE OF *Vanity Fair* comes from *Pilgrim's Progress,* in which there is a town called Vanity where a fair is in constant progress. The term came to be applied to fashionable London society, a constant fair or showplace where one's vanity is displayed. A long-lasting consensus has established *Vanity Fair* as the best of Thackeray's novels, and indeed it is a very fine novel that can hold its own in any company. The major character is the charming and seductive Becky Sharp who throughout her life knows "how to live on nothing a year" (without working). But the quality of *Vanity Fair* does not lie in its characters, even including Becky, or in its plot, of which there is little if any. The novel is great because of the manner in which Thackeray describes, usually with irony redeemed by good humor, the artificialities of the London and Continental society in which he set his rather unimportant characters.

Chaps. 1–7. When REBECCA (BECKY) SHARP and AMELIA SEDLEY, in the year 1814, leave the seminary where they have received their education—Amelia regretfully and Becky defiantly—Becky spends a month at the Sedleys' house in London. Becky is the sandy-haired, pretty, acute and scheming daughter of an improverished painter and an opera-dancer. She lays siege to JOSEPH (JOS) SEDLEY, Amelia's stout and wealthy brother from India. Amelia is courted, but not with much ardour, by Capt. GEORGE OSBORNE, whom she adores; she in her turn is adored by Osborne's gauche but good-hearted friend Capt. DOBBIN. Becky leaves to take up employment as governess in the household of Sir PITT CRAWLEY, a covetous and lecherous old man, at his country house, Queens Crawley.

Chaps. 8–11. Becky finds the house rundown by constant lawsuits and Sir Pitt brutal to his lowborn wife, who soon dies. Becky makes herself popular with both Sir Pitt and his elder son, also PITT CRAWLEY; she is intensely disliked by Sir Pitt's brother BUTE CRAWLEY, the rector of the parish, and by his wife. Becky is now laying claim to noble birth, which Mrs. Bute discovers to be false. Sir Pitt and both the Butes hope to inherit from their rich sister Miss CRAWLEY, a decrepit worldling whose favor Becky seeks. Becky also fascinates Miss Crawley's other favorite, her nephew Capt. RAWDON CRAWLEY, a large and rather stupid young dandy.

Chaps. 12–18. Becky returns to London with Miss Crawley and Rawdon, in high favor, and renews her acquaintance with Amelia. Sir Pitt proposes marriage to Becky and she is obliged to refuse, as she has already secretly married Rawdon. When the news is revealed Miss Crawley casts Becky off in a rage, falls ill, and is tended by Mrs. Bute. Meanwhile Amelia pines for George, who is in no hurry to propose. Amelia's father goes bankrupt and has to retire to a small house in the suburbs. Dobbin rescues Amelia's piano and sends it to her anonymously. George's snobbish and ambitious father forbids him to marry the now penniless Amelia and orders him to court the wealthy mulatto, Miss SWARTZ.

Chaps. 19–24. Mrs. Bute's attentions nearly kill Miss Crawley, who has to go to Brighton to recuperate, where also go Amelia and George on honeymoon, since George has defied his father and has married Amelia out of pity and duty. Here they meet Jos Sedley, and Becky and Rawdon, who have followed Miss Crawley. Dobbin discloses George's marriage and George's father disowns him.

Chaps. 25–32. George contracts gambling debts to Rawdon and flirts with Becky. Becky meets Miss Crawley's companion Miss BRIGGS, and, finding that Mrs. Bute has left, persuades Miss Briggs to intercede for them. Rawdon gains an interview with Miss Crawley but no material advantage. George and Amelia return to London, where George obtains what little money is his from his father. At regimental headquarters Amelia is wildly popular and Major O'DOWD's sister-in-law attempts to charm Dobbin. The regiment is ordered to Brussels for the French campaign against Napoleon, and Becky and Amelia and Jos Sedley go with them and join in the foolhardy revelry. They mingle with the aristocracy, among them Lord BAREACRES and his family. At the grand ball on the eve of the battle of Waterloo, Becky scores a social triumph and George invites her to elope with him. Immediately afterwards, the troops are summoned to the battlefield. Rawdon makes loving arrangements for his wife's safety, and Amelia, unhappily conscious of George's shortcomings, is left under Jos's care. Jos, when he hears rumors of defeat, deserts her, buys a horse at an exorbitant price from Becky, and flees to Ghent. Amelia remains with the eccentric but brave and kindly Mrs. O'Dowd. Becky goes to Paris.

Chaps. 33–34. Miss Crawley receives letters from Rawdon (now a colonel) and throws off Mrs. Bute's yoke. The younger Pitt Crawley comes to Brighton to court Lady JANE SHEEPSHANKS, a meek and devout young lady from a militant and devout family, and to toady to Miss Crawley, who becomes fond of Lady Jane but resists the influence of Lady SOUTHDOWN, Lady Jane's mother. Mrs. Bute attempts to regain influence over Miss Crawley by sending her

son JAMES CRAWLEY to visit her, but though his good looks make a good impression he mars it by smoking a cigar in the house and by running up a bill for the vulgar drink of gin-and-water. Meanwhile Becky in Paris is having a great social success, by her wit, beauty, and supposed noble birth, and by her sallies at the English aristocracy. When Becky's son is born, Miss Crawley in a rage makes young Pitt marry Lady Jane, gives them an annuity, and leaves her immense fortune to them in her will. Pitt, his wife and his wife's mother live with Miss Crawley and rule over her until her death.

Chap. 35. News of George Osborne's death is received by his family, and his father, griefstricken, visits his grave in Belgium, where he sees Amelia and hates her for causing the estrangement between himself and his son. He is unmoved when Dobbin pleads for Amelia and George's child, to be born to her. Amelia returns to her parents' house and devotes her life there to her baby son GEORGY.

Chaps. 36–41. Three years pass. Becky and Rawdon are living in London on Rawdon's gambling skill, in splendor and debt, since they had to quit their splendor and debts in Paris when Miss Crawley died and left them nothing. [Thackeray digresses to explain "how to live on nothing a year."] Becky deals with Miss Crawley's old tradespeople, who trust her, and since she never pays their bills she finally ruins them. Becky becomes fashionable and popular but cannot get herself admitted to the best society. She seeks the favor of the now wealthy Mr. Pitt, intending that Lady Jane shall sponsor her entry into aristocratic London society. Becky employs Miss Briggs as a companion and promptly borrows money from her. Becky is attempting to entrap the old and cynical *roué* Lord STEYNE into a liaison. Rawdon, ignored and eclipsed by his wife, lavishes his kindness and devotion on his son young RAWDON, whom Becky neglects. Old Sir Pitt grows more and more depraved; he lives with the butler's daughter and drinks himself into disintegration and eventual unmourned death. Young Pitt takes over the estate and the title, throws off the domination of his mother-in-law, and invites Rawdon and Becky to the funeral. Becky returns in triumph to Queens Crawley and by her wiles makes herself popular with Lady Jane, Sir Pitt, and even Lady Southdown.

Chaps. 42–45. George Osborne's sister MARIA BULLOCK has married a wealthy businessman, who in turn married her for her money; the other sister, JANE, is a spinster. Dobbin is in India, where GLORVINA O'DOWD is laying matrimonial siege to him, encouraged by her sister and the major, now Sir Michael O'Dowd. Dobbin is constant to Amelia and is distressed when he hears that she is about to marry. Becky uses her wiles on the new Sir Pitt and gains much influence over his affections but cannot induce him to settle Rawdon's debts. She grows more averse to her son, and

Becky becomes fashionable and popular

strikes him for listening to her singing to Lord Steyne, with whom she grows steadily more intimate. Lady Jane becomes secretly jealous of Becky.

Chaps. 46–49. Mr. Osborne is induced by his daughter's pleadings to see his grandson, and he offers to pay Amelia to allow him to take care of Georgy's upbringing. Amelia is miserable but fears she will be forced to agree for the sake of the money, as her allowance from Jos has mysteriously ceased and she is in utter poverty. [Thackeray in a digression describes the splendor of Lord Steyne's noble house and lineage and the sordid and disreputable history of both, including the present Lord Steyne.] Becky at last achieves one of her ambitions, being presented at court by Lady Jane. She is still very beautiful and she is exquisitely dressed, with jewels that she says are hired but that in fact are presents from admirers, especially Lord Steyne. She now intends to appear respectable and drops her unfashionable acquaintances. A second triumph follows when Lady Steyne, under Lord Steyne's orders, invites her to dinner. Becky incidentally gets Lord Steyne to give her money to pay her debt to Miss Briggs, then keeps most of it herself. At the Steynes' dinner Rawdon is uncomfortable, and the ladies will have nothing to do with Becky but she scores a triumph with the men.

Chaps. 50–51. Amelia, finding that Jos's allowance has not stopped but that her father has wasted it, finally gives up Georgy to his rich grandfather Osborne. Georgy is selfishly pleased. Becky lives in high society now, entertaining at great expense on mysterious supplies of money. Even royalty compliments her, and Lord Steyne is besotted. Rawdon is arrested for debt, for reasons that will be seen.

Chaps. 52–55. Lord Steyne, to get Becky to himself, has had young Rawdon sent to school. Becky's husband Rawdon becomes steadily more estranged from his fashionable wife. Steyne assumes that Rawdon knows of Becky's tricks, but Rawdon attempts to check his wife by never leaving her alone with Steyne. Hence Steyne has him arrested for debt. Becky does not pay him out. He appeals to Lady Jane and is successful. He hurries home to find Becky loaded with jewels, *tête-à-tête* with Lord Steyne. He strikes Lord Steyne down, seizes Becky's jewels and money to return them to the giver, and leaves her. He tells his brother Sir Pitt what has happened and begs him to take care of young Rawdon. He then makes plans for his duel with Steyne. But Rawdon is dissuaded from the duel and induced to accept an appointment abroad, which Steyne has contrived for him. Becky disappears from respectable society.

Chaps. 56–61. Georgy Osborne grows spoiled and domineering in the care of his doting grandfather. Old Mrs. Sedley dies, and Amelia, still only 30 years old, devotes herself to her father. Dobbin returns home and promptly goes to see Amelia, who is pleased to see him. But when he declares his love, she refuses, being still devoted to her husband's memory. Mr. Sedley dies, devotedly nursed by Amelia. Dobbin, as Georgy's guardian, comes to terms with old Mr. Osborne, who grows to respect Dobbin's courage and honesty and to feel kindly towards Amelia; but he dies suddenly. He leaves half his property to Georgy and an annuity to Amelia, who on the strength of this wealth is again received in polite society.

Chaps. 62–67. Dobbin, Jos, Amelia and Georgy go abroad and travel happily down the Rhine to the imaginary principality of Pumpernickel. They are presented at court, where Amelia is greatly admired. [Thackeray describes the geography, politics, and polite society of Pumpernickel; and the unaffected character of the aristocracy, who admire Amelia.] Jos falls in love with one of the young women. At a fête celebrating a royal wedding, Georgy gets caught up with a shabby woman gambler who makes him play for her before Dobbin can get him away. Jos discovers that the woman is Becky. [We hear Becky's past history: How she was forced to leave England on a small allowance from Rawdon, leaving young Rawdon with Sir Pitt, to become his heir when his son dies; how she went to Boulogne, where all the respectable English visitors ignored her and the vulgar were impertinent; how she took to drink and to gambling, and was forced out of one place after another by her reputation; and how at last, having fled from Rome in terror, fearing for her life at the hands of Lord Steyne, she has settled at Pumpernickel.] She captivates Jos and manages to arouse Amelia's sympathy because she has had to leave young Rawdon. Dobbin is not deceived, and when Amelia invites Becky to live with her, Dobbin leaves Amelia. Becky tries to be respectable but cannot give up drink. The family go to Ostend, where Amelia is importuned by Becky's disreputable friends. She writes to Dobbin for help. Becky also decides that Amelia must mourn for George no longer, but must be disillusioned and marry Dobbin; she therefore shows Amelia the note George Osborne wrote her on the eve of Waterloo inviting her to elope. Dobbin returns for the last time, to the delight of Amelia, Georgy, and himself. Becky goes to Bruges; Glorvina O'Dowd finally marries someone else; Dobbin, now a colonel, leaves the army and settles in Hampshire near Queens Crawley, where Amelia and Lady Jane, and Georgy and Rawdon, become close friends. But Jos becomes enslaved to Becky and dies after having insured his life in her favor. Young Rawdon eventually inherits Sir Pitt's title and estates and gives Becky an allowance, which enables her to live in England, apparently respectably.

Alexander Pope
1688–1744

Homer
About 10th Century B.C.

The Vicar of Wakefield

Novel by Oliver Goldsmith, 1728–1774.
Published 1766. (PB, PL54; ML, 291)

GOLDSMITH WROTE only this one novel. It was a great success in its time and is still rated among the best novels of its century. It is always called "charming" because of Goldsmith's light touch, his good-natured and gentle approach to life and people, and his wit and irony. Goldsmith calls his hero "simple in affluence and majestic in adversity," and much of his hero's benevolent and good nature are autobiographical of Goldsmith himself.

Chaps. 1–3. Dr. CHARLES PRIMROSE, a country minister, is the narrator. He tells of his family and of their life devoted to the care of parishioners, travelers from along the road, and parasitical relatives. He and his wife, DEBORAH, have six children: GEORGE, educated at Oxford and named after an uncle, who, therefore, willed the family £10,000; OLIVIA, 18, and SOPHIA, both beautiful and vivacious; MOSES, educated at home and destined for the business world; and RICHARD and WILLIAM, who are quite young. George is about to marry ARABELLA WILMOT, daughter of a neighboring clergyman with whom Dr. Primrose differs on theological matters. Word comes that the merchant having custody of the Primrose fortune has gone bankrupt. Dr. Primrose is now reduced to his clerical salary of £35 a year, and Arabella's father breaks off the wedding plans. After paying his debts, Dr. Primrose has only £400 left. He decides to move to Wakefield, 70 miles away, to take another church post. It pays only £15, but he can also manage a 20-acre farm for Squire THORNHILL. George is sent to London to seek work. Halfway to Wakefield, the Primroses stop at an inn, where they meet Mr. BURCHELL, apparently a wastrel. They pay his bill and he joins them on the road, saying he is related to their new landlord. Crossing a stream, Sophia is thrown from her horse and Burchell saves her from drowning.

Chaps. 4–11. At Wakefield, the new minister is greeted by a procession and a festive reception. Squire Thornhill, highly aristocratic in bearing, drops in during a hunt. Burchell also visits the house frequently, helping Sophia with her chores, although it is rumored that he is about to propose to Miss Wilmot. Thornhill also visits regularly and impresses Olivia. He arranges a dance and feast on the Primrose lawn, bringing with him Lady BLARNEY and Miss CAROLINE WILHELMINA AMELIA SKEGGS, who overwhelm all by their finery, polish, and conversational range. To complete the dancing party, the two daughters of a neighbor, SOLOMON FLAMBOROUGH, are invited.

Mrs. Primrose and the girls throw themselves into a frenzy of dressmaking and beauty treatments, seek news from a gypsy fortune-teller about possible marriage offers, and take to riding to church. They learn that the girls might earn a tidy sum as ladies' companions in London.

Chaps. 12–17. Moses is sent to a fair to sell the family colt. There he is tricked into spending the money on a gross of green spectacles. Flamborough is similarly bilked. The Primroses plan to sell their remaining horse to send the girls to the city. When the vicar goes to the fair, he sells the horse for a draft that proves worthless and again the trickster is EPHRAIM JENKINSON, the man who unloaded the two gross of spectacles. One of the younger sons finds a letter case and the family dishonorably reads an unsigned letter, seemingly from Burchell, warning the London ladies that Olivia and Sophia are not fit to be recommended as companions. Such "treachery" is thrown in Burchell's face. He counters by his anger at their reading of sealed correspondence and now he is banished from their lives. Mrs. Primrose, eager to marry Olivia to the squire, seeks to make the squire jealous by speaking of the amorous interest of a tenant farmer named WILLIAMS, including even plans for the wedding. Suddenly, the family is shocked to learn that Olivia has run away, weeping, with a man who came for her in a carriage.

Chaps. 18–20. The vicar goes angrily to Thornhill Castle, but the squire disclaims all knowledge of the affair. One of his servants tells the vicar that Olivia was at a race track with Burchell, and Dr. Primrose begins a long pursuit. However, he becomes ill on the way. Then, almost penniless, he joins a group of strolling players. While with them he meets a Mr. ARNOLD and discovers him to be an uncle of Miss Wilmot. Miss Wilmot inquires for George, with whom she seems still to be in love. All attend a theatrical performance for which an actor is imported especially from London. The actor turns out to be George. Later, George tells how he failed as a teacher and as a writer, then became companion to a NED THORNHILL and from him received a letter of recommendation to Sir WILLIAM THORNHILL, Ned's uncle. But nothing had come of this.

Chap. 21. Squire Thornhill calls on the Arnolds and finds Dr. Primrose there. Thornhill inquires about Olivia, arranges for George to get a commission in an army unit leaving for the West Indies, and sees the vicar off for home. Stopping at an inn, the vicar hears of a young lady who owes rent and is being evicted. It is Olivia. Her abductor was Squire Thornhill; the London ladies were actually prostitutes; and a marriage ceremony was performed by a "priest" who had previously married the squire to seven other women. Olivia tells how she escaped. She and her father start for home.

Chaps. 22–27. The vicar no sooner arrives in the village than he sees his house go up in flames. All are saved, but he is badly burned on the arm in rescuing the boys. The family is tearfully reunited, and they begin life again in one of the farm outbuildings. The squire proposes to Miss Wilmot and their wedding is announced. Dr. Primrose writes to her to expose Thornhill, but the letter is intercepted. The squire demands full rent from Dr. Primrose and, when he cannot pay, has him thrown into debtor's prison. The vicar prevents a riot by his parishioners, who are ready to tear him from the arms of officers. In prison, his companion is Ephraim Jenkinson. Mrs. Primrose and Sophia take a room nearby. Moses works as a laborer and lives in the prison with his younger brothers and their father. Dr. Primrose has some success in preaching to other prisoners.

Chaps. 28–29. Olivia, left behind because of illness, visits her father once; a few days later, Jenkinson reports that she has died. Mrs. Primrose brings news that Sophia has been kidnapped by a man who forced her into a passing carriage. George, whose regiment has not sailed, goes to challenge Squire Thornhill, kills one of four servants sent to attack him, and is brought, wounded and in chains, to the prison.

Chaps. 30–31. An 18th-century Job, the vicar has now suffered enough. Sophia comes to see him with Burchell, who has rescued her from her kidnapper. Burchell is now revealed to be the wealthy and virtuous Sir William Thornhill. Jenkinson identifies the villainous squire as the kidnapper. Miss Wilmot, passing through town, sees one of the Primrose boys in the street, learns of the family's distress, and visits the prison. There she hears of the squire's treachery. She breaks her engagement and is ready to marry George. Olivia is now brought in. Jenkinson lied about her "death" to bring matters to a climax. He also explains that her marriage was real, the clergyman honest, and the ceremony the only true one young Thornhill had gone through. The squire begs the forgiveness of all. Sir William, who always admired Sophia when he was "Mr. Burchell," now proposes to her.

Chap. 32. The vicar officiates at the ceremony that makes Sophia Lady Thornhill and Arabella Wilmot Mrs. George Thornhill. The Flamborough girls have been invited. The forgiven Jenkinson finds the elder attractive, and Moses takes a liking to the younger. The vicar even learns that the merchant who stole his fortune has been apprehended in Antwerp and much of the money recovered. The tale ends with the vicar's expression of gratitude for his complete good fortune.

Volpone

Play by Ben Jonson, 1572?–1637.
Produced 1605.

VOLPONE IS ONE of the best-remembered of Ben Jonson's plays, and by many is rated the best. It is not so often played by school groups as *The Alchemist*, because the lust of Volpone for another man's wife and the willingness of her husband to sacrifice her for money are considered too improper but cannot conveniently be expurgated. The names of the characters are Italian equivalents of their natures as depicted in the play: Volpone is the Fox, Mosca the fly, Voltore the vulture, and Corbaccio and Corvino the crow and/or the raven.

Act I. 1–5. VOLPONE, a Venetian magnifico, gloats over his wealth. To his parasite, MOSCA, he describes his novel way of enriching himself, namely by accepting presents from wealthy men who live in hopes of being his heir when he dies, and whose hopes he encourages by pretending to be very sick. After a song and dance by Volpone's entertainers, his first visitor, the lawyer VOLTORE, brings a present and is assured of the inheritance by Mosca, while Volpone lies in bed. The second visitor is CORBACCIO, an old man whom Mosca persuades to disinherit his son in favor of Volpone, so that Volpone will gratefully make Corbaccio his heir. The third is CORVINO, a merchant, who jealously guards his beautiful wife CELIA. Volpone, fired by Mosca's report of Celia's beauty, resolves to disguise himself and see her.

Act II. 1. Sir POLITICK WOULD-BE, a foolish English knight who affects to understand all the diplomatic secrets of Europe and keeps elaborate memoranda thereon, reveals his folly to PEREGRINE, a sensible traveler. They are standing by Corvino's house in Venice. **2–3.** Volpone enters, disguised as a mountebank (a peddler who puts on a show to attract customers), and demonstrates his art in front of the house. He asks for a handkerchief, and Celia throws one down from her window. Corvino sees this, and jealously chases away the supposed mountebank. **4.** Volpone, burning with lust for Celia, begs Mosca to procure her, at any expense. **5–7.** Meanwhile Corvino vents his jealous rage on Celia. Mosca tells Corvino that the physicians have prescribed for Volpone a young woman to sleep by him. Mosca's assurance that Volpone is impotent and Corvino's own covetous hope of reward persuade Corvino to offer Celia for the experiment. Ignorant of his intentions, she sets off with him for Volpone's house.

Act III. 1–2. Mosca meets old Corbaccio's son BONARIO, and reveals Corbaccio's plan of disinheriting him. **3–5.** Volpone endures a tedious visit from Lady WOULD-BE, who has a passion for displaying her learning. Mosca gets rid of her by pretending that he has seen her husband with a courtesan. **6–8.** Bonario arrives at Volpone's house and also (prematurely, from Mosca's point of view) Corvino and Celia. Mosca, having disposed of Bonario in another part of the house, returns to find Corvino fiercely insisting on Celia's wifely obedience, while she refuses to sacrifice her honor and his to his greed. She is left alone with Volpone, who boasts that his impotence is fictitious and offers her untold wealth and pleasure if she will be his mistress. When Celia refuses, Volpone attempts to ravish her but is prevented by Bonario, who rushes in, rescues Celia, and escapes with her, slightly wounding Mosca in the process. **9.** Corbaccio now arrives to sign the will making Volpone his heir. The lawyer Voltore also arrives. He suspects Mosca of duplicity, but he is persuaded to the contrary and is engaged as counsel in case Volpone is brought to trial on Bonario's evidence.

Act IV. 1. Sir Politick Would-be continues to exhibit his folly before Peregrine. **2–3.** Lady Would-be enters and mistakes Peregrine for the disguised courtesan of whom Mosca has told her, but discovers her mistake and acts the coquette with him. Peregrine resolves to make a fool of Sir Politick Would-be. **4–6.** At the Senate House, Volpone's trial is to begin. Voltore alleges that Celia is the notorious concubine of Bonario, whose father has disinherited him for his vice; that Bonario therefore intended to murder his father; and that, missing his opportunity he tried to murder his father's heir Volpone under pretense of saving Celia from him. Voltore's speech, the perjuries of his witnesses, and the enfeebled appearance of Volpone when he is brought in, delude the judges into convicting Bonario and Celia of perjury.

Act V. 1–3. Volpone, at home again, exults over his escape and invents a new stratagem. He has himself reported dead, so that when his dupes come to read his will he may conceal himself and enjoy their dismay on finding that the heir is Mosca. They all arrive, find Mosca derisive and triumphant, and depart in a rage. To anger them further, Mosca (dressed as a magnifico) and Volpone (disguised as an officer) pursue them. **4.** Peregrine warns Sir Politick that the officers suspect him of being a spy and intend to search his house. Sir Politic destroys his papers and hides under a large tortoise shell. Then he is ridiculed by Peregrine. **5–9.** Volpone and Mosca, in their disguises, mock the dupes. **10.** The judges meet again to sentence the supposed perjurers. Volpone is present in his disguise. To the amazement of all, Voltore confesses that his former accusations were false and his witnesses perjured. Corvino declares that the lawyer is acting out of mere anger because Mosca is Volpone's heir. The judges send for Mosca. They display new respect for him. **11–13.** Volpone, finding that Mosca is keeping up the fiction of his death, persuades Voltore that (since Mosca's master lives) it will pay him to resume his perjury. The lawyer does so, passing off his earlier confession as demoniac possession. But Volpone finds Mosca resolved to cheat him out of his own estate, and so, in despair, he confesses the truth. Volpone, Mosca and their dupes are all punished, and Bonario and Celia (who is freed from her jealous husband) are vindicated.

Walden

Treatise by Henry David Thoreau, 1817–1862.
Published 1854. (ML, T35 & 155; RE, 8; Viking, P31; NAL, MD176)

FROM JULY 4, 1845 to September 6, 1847 Thoreau lived alone in a hut he built himself on the shore of Walden Pond, near his home in Concord, Mass. From his experience he wrote one of the most famous of contemplative books. He argued the validity of the simple life and he described his feeling of kinship with all living and growing things of nature, which he loved. It was said of him that he "experienced nature as other men are said to experience religion." Walden is rather a series of essays than a straight account of a personal experience.

1. *Economy.* "The mass of men lead lives of quiet desperation." They are in such a hurry that they never stop to ask what is really necessary for their lives, whether they are spending their time foolishly or well. Some things are clearly necessary. The first of these is to keep the body warm. At the same time, the way people fuss over how they clothe their bodies is not necessary, for "A man who has at length found something to do will not need to get a new suit to do it in." Man also needs shelter but a shelter that requires all his energy simply to pay for it is not necessary. "We have built for this world a family mansion, and for the next a family tomb. The best works of art are the expression of man's struggle to free himself from this condition." The stay at Walden Pond is just this kind of an experiment. The work begins in March with the cutting of some tall white pines for tim-

622

ber. By the first of April, the house stands. It cost $28.12½. With farming, and with food to be found in the woods and the pond, $8.74 is the total cost for food for an eight-month period. A man can live on very little. But there are those who ask: Isn't this selfish; what about our obligations, our philanthropies? "As for Doing-good, that is one of the professions which are full." More important than doing good is to be so.

2. *Where I Lived, and What I Lived For.* About a mile and a half from Concord, with the birds for neighbors, the continually changing hills to observe and the lake to explore, it is possible to think as one wishes and to be wholly alive. "I went to the wood because I wished to live deliberately, to front only the essential facts of life, and see if I could not learn what it had to teach, and not, when I came to die, discover that I had not lived."

3–6. *Reading; Sounds; Solitude; Visitors.* Both the silent and the sociable aspects of life at Walden Pond are full of interest. Homer and the classics are fine companions, the kind we have "to stand on tiptoe to read." The trill of the sparrow, the whistle of a far-off train, the deep thump of the bullfrog all provide entertainment. "I rejoice that there are owls. Let them do the idiotic and maniacal hooting for men . . . They represent the stark twilight and unsatisfied thoughts which all have." Solitude itself is a good companion. "Every little pine needle expanded and swelled with sympathy and befriended me . . . Why should I feel lonely? is not our planet in the Milky Way?" Certainly it is not space between people that makes them feel lonely. What we want is to be near the source of life in ourselves. This should be our home. "The value of a man is not his skin, that we should touch him." When we are with nature, we are not alone, for are we not, after all, something of leaves and vegetable ourselves? This does not mean that good conversation and lively companions are not precious. "I have three chairs in my house; one for solitude, two for friendship, three for society." Guests come. Sometimes they seem timid and afraid, the kind of people who "would not go a-huckleberrying without a medicine chest." Children, philosophers, fishermen—all honest folk are welcome.

7–9. *The Bean-Field; The Village; The Ponds.* The summer is devoted to raising beans. "What shall I learn of beans or beans of me? I cherish them, I hoe them, early and late I have an eye to them." The determination to know beans is a passion that persists. It costs $14.72½ and yields $8.71½, plus many fruitful meditations on the meaning of harvest—of the soil no less than the soul.

Every day or two it is pleasant to walk into the village to hear the latest gossip. "As I walked in the woods to see the birds and squirrels, so I walked in the village to see the men and boys." It is delightful to set out through the deserted forest toward home after a day in the village. To be lost

Henry David Thoreau

in the woods is another valuable experience. Through being lost, we come to appreciate "the vastness and strangeness of nature"— and through being lost, we find ourselves.

Walden Pond is as various in its colors, moods, risings and fallings as any human being. Its water is pure, cool, and delicious. "A lake is the landscape's most beautiful and expressive feature. It is earth's eye; looking into which the beholder measures the depth of his own nature." There is nothing on earth more pure and fair than a lake—it is a mirror that no stone will ever crack.

10. *Baker's Farm.* A visit to Baker's Farm (a place considered by the author for the experiment at Walden Pond) makes for unexpected adventures. Seeking shelter from a sudden storm, the author discovers John Fields, an Irishman, his wife, and several children, ensconced in a long-deserted hut. They seem a sad and shiftless family. Yet they insist they are lucky to be in America "where you could get tea and coffee and meat everyday." The author, however, praises America because "you are at liberty to pursue such a mode of life as may enable you to do without these."

11. *Higher Laws.* There are two instincts in man: One towards the primitive, savage existence and another toward a life of spirit. "I reverence them both. I love the wild not less than the good." The life of the senses has definite attractions and equally definite dangers. "We are all sculptors and painters and our material is our own flesh and blood and bones. Any nobleness begins at once to refine a man's features, any meanness or sensuality to imbrute them."

12. *Brute Neighbors.* There are companions everywhere, the "retired otter," the phoebe, the clucking partridge. There are sometimes great dramas. After witnessing a battle between a red ant and a black one, "I felt for the rest of the day as if I had had my feelings excited by witnessing the struggle, the ferocity and carnage, of a human battle before my door."

13. *House-Warming.* With the coming of autumn, each morning there is a new and

more brilliant picture to enjoy. The chimney must be built and the house plastered for the winter will begin. "Every man looks at his woodpile with a kind of affection. I love to have mine before my window, and the more chips the better to remind me of my pleasing work." When the master is out for a walk in the snow, the house is not deserted. A "cheerful housekeeper," the fire takes care of things until the master returns.

14–16. *Former Inhabitants; and Winter Visitors; Winter Animals; The Pond in Winter.* The long, cold, white winter is not lonely. There are thoughts by the cozy fireside. Brister Freeman, a Negro and former slave, who once made his home nearby; Breed, the hired man who murdered a whole family; Hugh Quoil, the Irishman who fought at Waterloo—all these persons who once lived on this land are companions now. And there are a few hardy real-life visitors as well, especially a poet who seems not in the least deterred by the wind or snow. There are also the red squirrels, the jays, chickadees, and hares. And the pond, frozen thick, is as full of fascination as ever. To discover the lost bottom of Walden Pond is an ambition. "What if all ponds were shallow? Would it not react on the minds of men? I am thankful that this pond was made deep and pure for a symbol. While men believe in the infinite some ponds will be thought to be bottomless."

17. *Spring.* The coming of spring is a wonder. First, the ice begins to melt, and morning and evening the pond sends forth a booming sound. "Who would have suspected so large and cold and thick-skinned a thing to be so sensitive?" To observe the coming of spring was one of the reasons for coming to Walden Pond, and it is no disappointment. "The change from storm and winter to serene and mild weather, from dark and sluggish hours to bright and elastic ones, is a memorable crisis which all things proclaim." The first robin is heard as something heard thousands of years ago; "the same sweet and powerful song as of yore." Everything is new and old, familiar and strange and inevitably joyful. And the second year at Walden Pond is similar to the first.

18. "I left the wood for as good a reason as I went there. Perhaps it seemed to me that I had several more lives to live, and could not spare any more time for that one." How easily we grow accustomed to the paths we have made for ourselves. The path to the hut at Walden Pond is still visible five or six years later. "I learned this, at least, by my experiment; that if one advances confidently in the direction of his dreams, and endeavors to live the life which he has imagined, he will meet with a success unexpected in common hours."

The Wandering Jew

Novel by Eugene Sue, 1804–1857. Published 1844–45. (ML, G53)

EUGENE SUE was one of the first of the many physicians who have become novelists. He shifted to writing when he became rich, not in an effort to increase his wealth. *The Wandering Jew,* a major French novel of the mid-19th century, is his one work that has retained its place among current standard literature and perhaps its acceptance has been hindered by the fact that it is somewhat brazen anti-Jesuit propaganda. It is one of the longest novels of all time, approaching three quarters of a million words, nearly 1,500 big pages. It uses as background the traditional legend of the wandering Jew, who refused Christ rest on the way to the cross and was condemned never to die but to wander the earth eternally; and a similar legend attached to Herodias, the mother of Salome, who induced her daughter to have John the Baptist beheaded. These characters, however, are not a real part of the action of the novel. They hover over it and occasionally intercede as did the gods in ancient Greek works.

Prologue. On a late September day a tall man stands on the easternmost point of Siberia, separated from the westermost point of North America by the narrow Bering Strait. His shoe, with seven nails arranged in the form of a cross, has left a trail in the snow. For a brief instant the Aurora Borealis lights up the scene, revealing a woman of regal beauty standing on the American shore. The man stretches his arms imploringly to her and she responds by pointing to the heavens. Fog drifts in and they lose sight of each other. Who are these two who have seen each other for a brief moment and seem eternally separated?

PART I. THE TRANSGRESSION

Chaps. 1–16. In October, 1831, in the village of Mockern, Germany, MOROK, a lion-tamer, waits in the hostelry for the arrival of some travelers he has been ordered to detain. The orders come from the Abbé RODIN in Paris. The travelers, BLANCHE and ROSE, 15-year-old twin daughters of General SIMON, a hero under Napoleon, are accompanied by DAGOBERT, a trusted old guardist who has long served their father. They are on their way from Siberia to Paris, where they must be on February 13, 1832, a date engraved on a medal Rose wears on a chain around her neck. Dagobert tells the girls how their father met their mother, EVA, a Polish woman of French descent, while he was a prisoner of war in Warsaw. Because Simon had aided a friend involved in a military plot, he was banished from Poland, his wife was exiled to Siberia, and all their property was confiscated. Dagobert accompanied Eva to Siberia, where she gave birth to the twins three months later. The general has never heard of the birth and they have had news of him but once, when a tall, mysterious man brought the general's diary from India to Eva in Siberia. This same man had once saved the general's life in battle by suddenly stepping in front of a cannon, and another time by tending the general's wounds on the battlefield of Waterloo. Dagobert says that the stranger's eyebrows seemed to form one heavy black line across his forehead. The girls read parts of their father's diary and learn that in India his life was saved by a young prince, DJALMA, who had a French mother. They also read that Dagobert's adopted son, GABRIEL, became a priest. Morok plots to steal the old soldier's knapsack, containing his papers, and kill his horse, to prevent the travelers from reaching Paris on Feb. 13. Dagobert knows he must get the girls to Paris on that date, because their mother so instructed him on her deathbed. Dagobert recalls that the mysterious stranger in Siberia carried a replica of Rose's medal, and he remembers the imprint of the cross left by his shoe. The old soldier is startled by the terrified screams of his horse and he rushes out to find the beast killed. Morok accuses him of having left it untied. Morok has artfully spilled blood on his hand to make himself appear wounded in his attempt to save the horse. Dagobert asks indemnity for his horse, but the burgomaster decides against him and orders him detained, since he cannot find his knapsack containing his identity papers. Dagobert and the girls manage to escape. Morok feels sure they cannot travel without a horse and he sends off a report to the Abbé Rodin in Paris.

Chaps. 15–16. Rodin, secretary to the Provincial Head of the Jesuit Society, the Marquis D'AIGRIGNY, meets with his superior to discuss some correspondence relating to a certain group of identical medals, whose owners, though remotely related, are the last living descendants of the family of MARIUS DE RENNEPONT, French Protestant, who, 150 years ago, foresaw the revocation of the Edict of Nantes and went into voluntary exile. Seven descendants of the family remain. Rodin reads their dossiers. Rose and Blanche Simon, descended through their mother, are being escorted to Paris by a faithful guard, but Morok has reported their detention. FRANÇOIS HARDY, a wealthy manufacturer at Plessis, knows nothing of the significance of his medal, but he is being spied on by one of his closest friends. Prince Djalma, son of an Indian potentate, descended through his mother, has no idea of the value of his medal, and is reported in prison in India. JACQUES RENNEPONT is a drinker, idler, and profligate, whose mistress is being spied on by the Order. ADRIENNE RENNEPONT DE CARDOVILLE, a beautiful 21-year-old with a fine mind, can be controlled through her aunt, Princess SAINT-DIZIER, a Jesuit ally. GABRIEL RENNEPONT (adopted son of Dagobert), a Jesuit priest and missionary in America, does not know he is a member of the family, because as an orphaned foundling he was adopted by FRANCES BAUDOIN, the wife of Dagobert. She is entirely under Jesuit control and prevailed on Gabriel to become a member of the order despite the opposition of his adopted brother AGRICOLA, who works for François Hardy.

The seven descendants possess medals that bear on one side the inscription "Victim of L.C.D.J./Pray for me!/Paris/February 13, 1682," and on the other "At Paris/Rue St. François, No. 3/In a Century and a Half/you will be/February 13, 1832/Pray for me!" They must be in Paris on the given date, not by proxy, and whether minors, single, or married. But the Jesuit Order will do everything in its tremendous power to keep all except Gabriel, the Jesuit priest, away from the appointed rendezvous.

Rodin completes his report to his superior and two letters arrive for d'Aigrigny, one saying his dying mother calls for him and the other ordering him immediately to report to Rome. After a moment's anguish at the thought of leaving his mother to die in grief at his absence, d'Aigrigny sets out for Rome. Rodin sends a letter to a high Jesuit official in Rome, reporting d'Aigrigny's momentary hesitation.

Interlude. The tall, mysterious stranger is also concerned about the possessors of the medals, but he means to help them keep their appointment in Paris. He stands in an isolated spot, near where cholera has struck a town. Superstition has blamed him for bringing the plague to whatever region of the earth he visits. He thinks of the seven descendants of his sister, whom he must help. But he must go on, never stopping, never resting. He remembers the day the Saviour passed his shoemaker's shop, bearing his cross, and begged to be allowed to rest for an instant. He remembers refusing and telling the Saviour to "Go on!" and the Saviour's reply, "Thou shalt go on till the end of time." And through the long centuries he, AHASUERUS, has never paused. Not only does he suffer for himself, but he suffers doubly as he sees the weary, oppressed masses of humanity also going on without rest. Once in a century he meets another wanderer, HERODIAS, who must go on till the day of her redemption for having asked the death of St. John the Baptist. She, the only person on earth to share the WANDERING JEW'S destiny, has chosen to share his concern for the descendants of his sister who lived centuries ago when he was a shoemaker.

Ahasuerus, the tall, mysterious stranger

Chaps. 17–22. In Batavia, Djalma is expecting General Simon, who has booked passage for him on a ship soon to sail for France. While Djalma is asleep he is tattooed by a member of the Thuggee Society, a band of thieves and stranglers, with the mark of the Thug. This has been arranged by JOSHUA VAN DAEL, a Dutch merchant in the service of the Jesuits, who then has Djalma arrested by the authorities because he bears the incriminating tattoo. Van Dael sends a report of this to Rodin. The messenger he sends is killed and the letter stolen by FARINGHEA, a half-caste former chief of the Thuggees.

Chaps. 23–25. In the beginning of February, 1832, Rodin goes to visit the Princess Saint-Dizier at her castle on the coast of France. A storm arises and two ships are wrecked near the castle. To Rodin's amazement, the survivors include Blanche, Rose, and Dagobert, who were on one ship, and Gabriel and Djalma, who were on the other. Also among the survivors of the second ship is Faringhea. Dagobert and Gabriel are overjoyed at meeting. Rodin orders Gabriel to go to Paris, and Dagobert and the girls leave shortly after. Faringhea tends his countryman, Djalma, who is too weak to travel.

Chaps. 26–32. Dagobert takes the girls to the home of his wife, Frances, in Paris. Frances has worked hard through the 18 years of Dagobert's absence to bring up her family. Their son Agricola now supports his mother. A welcome guest in their house is MOTHER BUNCH, an 18-year-old hunchbacked girl of fine character. Rodin's spies have been watching the house, and Mother Bunch receives a warning that Agricola will be arrested for composing an incendiary song. Gabriel tells Agricola and Dagobert how he once faced certain death at the hands of American Indians but was rescued by a strange and beautiful woman, who then disappeared to the north.

Chaps. 33–35. Agricola, facing arrest, goes to seek the aid of Adrienne de Cardoville, for whom he has recently done a service. She consents to hide him and to support his mother, and she is overjoyed to learn that her relatives, the daughters of General Simon, are in Frances' house.

Adrienne has just received a letter from the steward of her aunt's castle informing her that Djalma, who she remembers is her cousin, is at the castle, without funds and clothing after being shipwrecked. Adrienne asks a friend to take clothing to Djalma and bring him back to her house in Paris.

Chaps. 36–45. In another wing of the house, Adrienne's aunt, Princess Saint-Dizier, is in conference with the Marquis d'Aigrigny, lately returned from Rome; Baron TRIPEAUD, Adrienne's guardian; and Dr. BALINIER, her physician. Adrienne is summoned and criticized for her way of life, and her aunt says she will be under constant observation in the future. Adrienne defies them, indicates that she knows something about their evil machinations, and confounds them by saying she is going to have Rose, Blanche and Djalma as her guests. She does not fully suspect the treachery of all three. When she learns that Agricola has been arrested, she relies on Dr. Balinier to help her release him, but he takes her to his asylum. He succeeds in convincing her that she is in danger of going mad and that he is helping her. She does not know he is part of the Jesuit plot.

Chaps. 46–53. Mother Bunch tells Frances of Agricola's imprisonment and Adrienne's incarceration in the asylum. Frances complies with a request sent by her priest to come for confession. In her confession she states that Rose and Blanche have never been baptized. The confessor insists that she bring the girls immediately so that they may be put in a convent, and warns her not to tell her husband or General Simon when Simon arrives in Paris. Frances hurries home and finds that an accomplice of the Princess has taken the twins, who are put in a convent next to Dr. Balinier's asylum. Dagobert returns home and is furious to learn the girls are gone. When he explains that they must be in Paris on the date inscribed on the medal, Frances reveals that Gabriel once wore a similar medal, which Abbé Rodin took years before. Dagobert now begins to suspect the Jesuits; and when Frances refuses to tell him where the girls are, he is sure that her confessor is responsi-

ble for the abduction. Dagobert takes Frances before a magistrate and accuses the priest. Frances refuses to answer the magistrate's inquires and is put in jail as an accomplice.

PART II. THE CHASTISEMENT

Chaps. 1–9. Mother Bunch tells her sister, the beautiful CEPHYSE, and her sister's lover, Jacques Rennepont, that his friend Agricola is in jail. Jacques gives Mother Bunch his last 500 francs to furnish bail for Agricola. Soon after Jacques himself is arrested and is put in debtor's prison. Mother Bunch goes to Adrienne's home with a letter from Agricola and learns that Adrienne is in an asylum. Adrienne's maid takes her to the Mother Superior of the convent where the twins are held. She offers Mother Bunch work as a spy, but Mother Bunch turns it down. On her way out, she sees one of the twins talking to Adrienne at the fence between the convent and the asylum and they give her a ring for Dagobert to take to a Count MONTBRON, who will know what to do. Dagobert wants to storm the convent and rescue the twins, but he is deterred by Agricola, who hurries to a magistrate to seek the legal release of the girls. Dagobert goes to the home of Count Montbron.

Chaps. 10–13. Dagobert comes home in dejection because Montbron is out of town. Agricola reports that the court cannot act in time. Frances begs them to go to d'Aigrigny, who has befriended Gabriel in the past. Dagobert remembers d'Aigrigny as a soldier before he became a Jesuit; he had loved Simon's wife, had been rejected by her, had turned against his country, had twice met Simon in battle, and had fought a duel with Simon which resulted in a wound for d'Aigrigny and exile for the General. Dagobert is sure d'Aigrigny is behind the kidnapping of the twins. Dagobert and Agricola go to the convent, break in, and almost succeed in freeing the twins, but they are discovered. They manage to escape capture.

Chaps. 14–16. Rodin gives d'Aigrigny information about the Renneponts that a priest learned in 1682 through a dying man's confession. Marius de Rennepont reverted to Catholicism when his properties were threatened with confiscation, but Louis XIV took the properties anyway and gave them to the Jesuits. But a house at No. 3 Rue Saint-François in Paris, and a sum of about 150,000 francs, had escaped confiscation. Marius entrusted the money to a friend and requested that the house be sealed, but he had medals coined charging his descendants alive 150 years later to meet at the house on the Rue Saint-François. Condemned to the galleys, Marius committed suicide. The man who distributed the medals was tall, had singular black eyebrows that joined, and was known as JOSEPH. Rodin and his master are convinced that the house and the money have always belonged to the Jesuits and that they

625

have been justified in their plot to recover them. They are interrupted by the arrival of Faringhea, who knows too much and now wishes to sell his silence. Rodin has him shown out and instructs Morok, now in Paris, to waylay him.

Chaps. 17–26. In the early morning of February 13, SAMUEL, the 82-year-old guardian of No. 3 Rue Saint-François, sits at home next door with his wife. He is the grandson of the man to whom Marius Rennepont entrusted the 150,000 francs. Samuel consults his ledger and tells his wife the sum has grown through the years and now amounts to more than 212,175,000 francs in securities. Rodin appears with Gabriel, a court clerk, and three masons, who follow Samuel's directions in breaking the seals on the house. D'Aigrigny arrives and Gabriel tells him he now feels the Jesuits are evil and he wants to break his ties with the Society. D'Aigrigny and Rodin accuse the young man of ingratitude and say he wants to renounce his oath because he knows he will inherit money. Gabriel, still unaware of the meaning of his medal, denies this and signs a paper giving all he may ever have to the Society. A notary attests the paper. Samuel opens the Red Room, where two portraits hang, one of the man with the heavy eyebrows, the other of a beautiful woman. Gabriel is awed by her resemblance to the woman who saved him from the Indians. At the stroke of noon, the notary declares Gabriel to be the sole Rennepont heir, and Rodin and d'Aigrigny exult in their triumph. Dagobert and Agricola enter and tell Gabriel how he has been deceived, but the notary says nothing can be done. Faringhea and General Simon's old father arrive and the notary hears how the other heirs have been detained. But still, despite all the evils committed by the Society, nothing can be done. Suddenly a woman appears, the woman of the portrait, and hands the notary a sealed envelope. He verifies it as a codicil to Marius Rennepont's will, extending the time for the appearance of the heirs to June 1, 1832.

Chaps. 27–31. Rodin and d'Aigrigny hurry to the Princess Saint-Dizier. Rodin informs them that they have failed and he is taking over; he has orders from the General of the Order in Rome to proceed with the affair. He goes to a small room he uses, in a poorer section, and writes some letters to Rome—he aspires to high power not only in the Order but in the whole Church. A neighbor, ROSE-POMPOM, comes to ask him to help Cephyse, the lover of Jacques Rennepont, who is in need. Rodin suddenly senses the key to the Rennepont fortune. He will be kind to the heirs, get in their good graces, and so confound them.

Chaps. 32–39. Rodin takes a magistrate to Dr. Balinier's asylum and accuses the doctor of having abducted Adrienne, in conspiracy with d'Aigrigny and the Princess. He charges the latter two with the abduction of the twins. Rodin, to win Adrienne's confidence, tells her of the whole intrigue

and puts the entire blame on d'Aigrigny. Rodin notes that Mother Bunch is in love with Agricola. Adrienne has plans to unite the Rennepont heirs and she provides Djalma with a house and money, but she does not want him to know she has done this. Dagobert comes to the convent just as Rodin is bringing Rose and Blanche out, and General (now restored to Marshal) Simon arrives a moment later. Both the father and the protector of the girls are grateful to Rodin.

Chaps. 40–52. Djalma believes that Rodin is his benefactor, but he longs to see Adrienne and she takes him out into Parisian society. Mother Bunch brings evidence that Rodin has met d'Aigrigny and later visited the Princess. Adrienne takes Mother Bunch's advice to eavesdrop on a meeting between Rodin and Djalma. She hears Rodin encourage Djalma in his love for her. Convinced of Rodin's decency, she reveals herself and Rodin leaves the blissful couple. Agricola tells Mother Bunch that a priest has incited the workers against his employer, François Hardy. He also tells her he has fallen in love with ANGELA, the daughter of a fellow-worker. The little hunchback suffers at this last news. Rodin tells Hardy of a friend's treachery, to win his confidence; but Rodin then exposes Hardy's mistress to her husband, and the woman flees without leaving a word for the sensitive Hardy.

PART III. THE REDEMPTION

Chap. 1. The Wandering Jew prays that the Lord will allow him to save the descendants of his sister and begs that Paris be spared the scourge of cholera.

Chaps. 2-14. The workers set Hardy's factory on fire and it is destroyed. Marshal

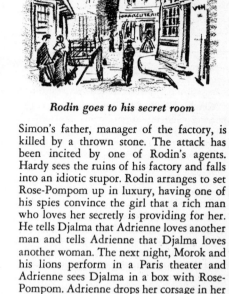

Rodin goes to his secret room

Simon's father, manager of the factory, is killed by a thrown stone. The attack has been incited by one of Rodin's agents. Hardy sees the ruins of his factory and falls into an idiotic stupor. Rodin arranges to set Rose-Pompom up in luxury, having one of his spies convince the girl that a rich man who loves her secretly is providing for her. He tells Djalma that Adrienne loves another man and tells Adrienne that Djalma loves another woman. The next night, Morok and his lions perform in a Paris theater and Adrienne sees Djalma in a box with Rose-Pompom. Adrienne drops her corsage in her agitation, and it falls in front of a black panther. Djalma leaps to the stage, kills the beast, and hands the corsage to Adrienne.

Chap. 15. The Wandering Jew pauses before the gates of Paris and pleads with the Lord that the city be spared, but inexorably rings the cry, "Go on, Go on," in his ears.

Chaps. 16–22. Rodin outlines his plan to the Belgian Cardinal MALIPIERI. Rodin says the Renneponts can be governed through their weaknesses and passions, and that he has Jacques now reduced to alcoholic impotence by Morok, and Hardy, the

Djalma kills the beast and hands the corsage to Adrienne

626

oversensitive, now placed under the guidance of the Church. Rodin suddenly staggers and falls. He is the first cholera victim in Paris. Jacques Rennepont dies in the arms of Cephyse a short time later, after engaging in a brandy-drinking duel with Morok.

Chaps. 17–30. Cephyse, desperate since the death of Jacques, and Mother Bunch are kept from suicide by Adrienne, who learns that Rose-Pompom means nothing to Djalma. She sends a letter to him and arranges to meet him. Faringhea, now in the service of Rodin, is plotting against them. The two lovers meet and clear up their misunderstanding. Hardy, in the meantime, has renounced life and entered a Jesuit retreat. Marshal Simon's mind has been poisoned by anonymous letters and he begins to doubt the loyalty of even his daughters and Dagobert. But the girls overcome his doubts, and Dagobert proves his loyalty.

Chaps. 50–51. The Wandering Jew and Herodias meet at the ruins of the Abbey of St. John the Baptist. For the first time in 18 centuries they appear older. Ahasuerus prays for their redemption and for the protection of his sister's descendants.

Chaps. 52–58. Rodin demands that d'Aigrigny find the opportunity to duel with Marshal Simon. Rodin tries to see the twins, but Dagobert stops him. Princess Saint-Dizier succeeds in winning the confidence of the girls and convinces them they should go to the hospital where their governess is a cholera victim. They are stricken by the disease and die. Morok, a victim of hydrophobia, attacks and bites Gabriel. Samuel, the keeper of the Rennepont inheritance, has a mysterious meeting with a gravedigger concerning the coffins of the twins. Rodin sends a note to the Marshal saying "You shall know who killed your daughters." The Princess tells Adrienne that her fortune has been eaten up and that her possessions will be sold on the morrow. Adrienne is not distressed at the thought of poverty.

Chap. 59. Adrienne and Djalma prepare for their marriage. A Father CABOCINNI arrives from Jesuit headquarters in Rome to assist Rodin, who suspects he has been sent to spy on him. Rodin is preparing a trap for Adrienne and Djalma.

Faringhea tricks Djalma into believing he is watching a love tryst between Adrienne and Agricola. In a jealous rage, Djalma kills the woman made up to look like Adrienne, and wounds Agricola, who had been lured there on a pretense. Djalma then takes poison, and Adrienne finds him and takes poison also. The two die on May 30. François Hardy is reported dead of extreme fasting, but his coffin has disappeared. On the evening of May 31, Marshal Simon comes to accuse d'Aigrigny of killing his daughters. They duel and both are killed, d'Aigrigny cursing Rodin with his last breath. Father Cabocinni gives Faringhea a message from Cardinal Malipieri, and on the next day Faringhea hands Rodin the

sprinkling brush from the font in the Jesuit chapel and Rodin makes the sign of the cross on his forehead with the brush. It is June 1, and Rodin goes to No. 3 Rue Saint-François to claim the inheritance, as Gabriel, the only remaining heir, turned it over to the Jesuits. Cabocinni gives Rodin a letter dated May 11 authorizing him to take over Rodin's power and send Rodin to a retreat. Rodin produces a letter dated May 18 appointing him General of the Order. The curtains at the end of the room part, and the bodies of the six dead heirs are revealed. Samuel says that the fortune cannot go to their murderer. Rodin reaches for the casket containing the treasure, but a fire breaks out inside the box and all the money and securities are turned to ashes. Rodin collapses in pain, and dying, remembers that Faringhea is a master of poisons— the sprinkling brush contained a lethal dose of a poison that works after being inhaled. Rodin dies. Princess Saint-Dizier, the third master plotter, loses her sanity completely.

Epilogue. 1. Four years later Gabriel is living with Dagobert's family on a farm bought with money Adrienne gave him. Agricola and Angela have several children and Mother Bunch helps Frances with the housework. Gabriel abominates the Order that brought death and misery to his family. **2.** A man and woman of extreme age sit on the slope of a hill. They sense that the end of their years of wandering is near. The Lord has forgiven them. Gabriel, the last of the aged man's family, lies dying. At the last moment the two weary wanderers bless their God and die.

War and Peace

Novel by Leo Tolstoy, 1828–1910. Published 1865–1869. Many translations, notably those of Nathan Haskins Dole and Aylmer Maude.

WAR AND PEACE has probably been called the world's greatest novel by more critics than all other novels put together. In its awesome length (more than 500,000 words) and complexity (some 500 characters) it combines as grand a design and as great a scope as any novelist has attempted, but the characters all become living persons to the reader and the interlocking of events almost never becomes confusing, so that nearly any person can read *War and Peace* with sustained interest and complete understanding. ❑ Tolstoy set his novel in the period that was history's most fascinating up to the present century, the Napoleonic Wars. The action begins in 1805 when those wars were well advanced and ends, substantially, in 1813, except for a brief closing picture of what became of the principal characters. Tolstoy combined his story with continuous development of his theory of history, which is that men do not make history but are made by it; that is, that they do not control events but are drawn along by the events themselves, which are inexorable. Among other features, *War and Peace* presents detailed descriptions of several major battles and much indirect treatment of the principal political events of the period. ❑ The characters in *War and Peace* occur in the original under so many different names—due to the Russian custom of using a multiplicity of diminutives and terms of endearment— that the reader of a full translation often finds difficulty in discerning which name applies to which character at any given point. In the outline below, only one name is used throughout for each character.

Part 1. At a soirée given by ANNA PAVLOVNA SCHERER in St. Petersburg, in 1805, many of the book's principal characters are present: Prince VASILI KURAGIN, an influential statesman, who is seeking good marriages for his dissolute son ANATOL and for his beautiful daughter ELENA (or HELENE). Prince ANDREI BOLKONSKY, son of a rich and famous but crotchety retired general; Andrei's attractive young wife, LISA, with whom he is bored; and Andrei's friend PIERRE, illegitimate but favored son of the old, fabulously rich Count BEZUKHOF. Princess ANNA DRUBETSKOY, well connected but impoverished, who persuades Vasili to get a good army commission for her son BORIS.

Pierre visits Andrei after the soirée, but Andrei and Lisa quarrel and Pierre goes on to a wild gathering of young men, including a young officer, DOLOKHOF, who lives chiefly by gambling. They indulge in mad pranks, are caught, and all are temporarily disgraced with their families.

Princess Drubetskoy goes to Moscow to visit her cousins the ROSTOFS, with whom Boris lives. Count ILYA ROSTOF, though rich, is too extravagant. The Rostofs' children are VERA, 21, who is being wooed by Lieut. BERG, a German in the Russian Army; NIKOLAI, who is about to enter the army; NATASHA (NATALYA), not quite 13; PETYA or PETRUSHA, the youngest. SONYA, a penniless niece of the countess, lives with them. She is 15 and in love with Boris. Prince Vasili has come to Moscow because old Count Bezukhof, his wife's cousin, is dying, and if the count can be persuaded not to legitimatize Pierre the Kuragins will inherit a great fortune. But after much intrigue, including an effort to steal the count's papers, the count dies leaving Pierre legitimate and making him the rich Count Bezukhof.

The duel between Pierre and Dolokhof

Andrei and Lisa go to the Bolkonsky estate, Lisiya Gori. Andrei's plain but kind, good and dutiful sister MARIA is dominated by the old general, who loves her but cannot show it; she finds consolation in religion and in correspondence with her friend JULIE, daughter of MARYA KARAGINA, a rich Moscow noblewoman. Andrei goes off to a new war against Napoleon, leaving at home Lisa, who is pregnant.

Part 2. Old Field Marshal Prince MIKHAIL KUTUZOF commands the Russian Army in the field. Dolokhof has been reduced to the ranks but is skillfully working his way up again. Nikolai is a cadet in the company of Capt. "VASKA" DENISOF, with whom he becomes close friends. Andrei is on Kutuzof's staff and participates in some of the principal events of the 1805 campaign, which will end in a great victory for Napoleon.

Part 3. Prince Vasili, having failed to cheat Pierre, now pretends to be his best friend and mentor and succeeds in making Pierre marry the beautiful Helene. Pierre forgives all and everyone, including his old maid sisters, who had hated him. Prince Vasili then takes Anatol to Lisiya Gori to arrange a marriage to Maria, but she refuses him to stay with her father, who she knows needs her and opposes the marriage. In the great Napoleonic victory at Austerlitz, in December 1805, Andrei fights gallantly and is badly wounded and captured.

Part 4. Nikolai takes Denisof home with him for a visit, early in 1806. There are rumors that Helene is having an affair with Dolokhof. Pierre and Dolokhof fight a duel and Dolokhof is wounded. Helene and Pierre separate. Andrei is reported dead and is mourned at home, but arrives home just before his son NIKOLUSHA (NIKOLAI) is born; the birth kills Lisa. Dolokhof proposes

to Sonya, who refuses him because she is in love with Nikolai. In revenge, Dolokhof wins from Nikolai 43,000 rubles, an amount huge enough almost to ruin Count Rostof, who is already heavily in debt. [The book implies that Dolokhof could cheat.] Denisof asks for Natasha's hand but her parents consider her too young and refuse. Count Rostof manages to raise the money to pay Nikolai's gambling debt, and Nikolai is overcome by remorse and resolves to be frugal and save it all.

Part 5. On a trip to St. Petersburg Pierre meets a Freemason, OSSIP BAZDAYEF, who impresses him so that he becomes a Freemason and it is an important part of his life from then on. Prince Vasili tries but fails to reconcile Pierre and Helene. Boris becomes a favorite of Helene's. Pierre plans ways to improve the lot of his serfs. The campaign of 1806–07 ends with peace and alliance made between NAPOLEON and Tsar ALEXANDER I, who meet at Tilsit; Boris and Nikolai are there.

Part 6. In 1809 Andrei visits Count Rostof, and meets and is greatly attracted to Natasha. Pierre has been persuaded to return to Helene. Berg marries Vera. Boris becomes interested in Natasha but Countess Rostof sends him away. At her first formal ball, Natasha meets Andrei again and he falls in love with her. His father persuades him to wait a year, but he proposes to Natasha, is accepted, and it is agreed that they will marry in a year. The betrothal is to be kept secret.

Part 7. Countess Rostof wants Nikolai to marry Julie, thinking partly of her fortune, but he refuses. Natasha is pining for Andrei, who has been away for months. Nikolai determines to marry Sonya, but the Rostofs' financial affairs are so bad that she refuses him, from a sense of obligation to his parents: He must marry money to save the

family.

Part 8. Pierre is engrossed in Freemasonry and dissatisfied with his life. Prince Bolkonsky and Maria go to live in Moscow; the old prince torments Maria by pretending affection for her companion, Mlle. BOURIENNE. Boris, seeking a rich wife, wins Julie. MARYA DMITRIEVNA, a rich friend of the Rostofs', noted for being outspoken but very fond of Natasha, takes the Rostofs to the opera, where Natasha meets Anatol. He resolves to seduce her and his sister Helene helps him. Anatol persuades Natasha to elope with him and plans a fake marriage to her (since, secretly, he is already married). Dolokhof helps Anatol plan the deception. Sonya learns Natasha's plans and tells Marya Dmitrievna, who prevents the elopement. She tells Pierre, who is enraged and forces Anatol to leave town. Natasha, in remorse, breaks her engagement to Andrei; and when he learns the facts he cannot forgive her. Natasha becomes very ill and finds only Pierre sympathetic.

Part 9. Napoleon and Alexander have drifted into antagonism and Napoleon resolves to invade Russia. The invasion begins in 1812. Andrei has been seeking Anatol, to challenge him, but now he goes to war. So does Nikolai. Pierre remains attentive to Natasha and loves her, but says nothing.

Part 10. The French invasion of Russia meets only ineffective opposition. As matters become desperate for Russia, Kutuzof is called from retirement and made commander-in-chief. As the French approach Lisiya Gori, old Prince Bolkonsky dies, after telling Maria that he loves her and repents of his tyranny. The serfs on a Bolkonsky estate, led by DRON, become unruly and will

Natasha as a girl

Andrei dies with Natasha at his bedside

not obey the overseer, ALPATITCH, or even Princess Maria. Nikolai's company arrives and he saves Maria and sends her off to safety. Denisof persuades Kutuzof to let him organize guerrillas to harass the advancing French. Pierre observes the great Battle of Borodino, where French losses are heavy but still they advance toward Moscow. Andrei again is seriously wounded.

Part 11. The French Army occupies Moscow; the Russians retreat 80 miles behind the city. Helene is wooed by a royal prince and plans to change religions so that she can get a divorce from Pierre and marry him. Pierre does not flee Moscow as most of the nobility do, including the Rostofs; but just before the Rostofs leave, among the wounded soldiers whom they are taking in to care for they find Andrei. Petya has gone off to war. The Rostofs take Andrei with them when they leave and Natasha nurses him day and night, but he is too sick to know her. Pierre resolves to assassinate Napoleon. The Russians who remain in Moscow set fire to the city. On the road away from Moscow, Andrei becomes conscious, recognizes Natasha, tells her he loves her, and forgives her. Pierre is arrested in Moscow, on suspicion, and is put in jail.

Part 12. The Russians wait while the French linger in Moscow. Nikolai is sent on a mission to Voronezh, where Maria has taken refuge, and he meets her again and wants to propose but has vowed that he will marry only Sonya; however, Sonya happens at this time to send him a letter insisting that he is free. However, he must now rejoin his regiment.

Pierre, in Moscow, thinks he is sentenced to death but is not. While imprisoned he meets a peasant, PLATON KARATAYEF, whose simple but wise philosophy has a lasting effect on him. He lives incognito, dirty and ill-fed, but happier than before.

Maria, learning that Andrei is with the Rostofs, finds him just before he dies. She and Natasha become friends.

Part 13. Napoleon wishes to make peace but the tsar will not—though Kutuzof's strategy is too deep for almost anyone in Russia, including the tsar, to understand.

The French Army begins its retreat from Moscow. Kutuzof restrains the Russian troops from attacking, as much as he can, but still many units attack the French and lose many men.

Part 14. The French retreat, harassed by guerrillas including Denisof's group, which Petya has joined, and also Dolokhof. The French have taken along with them many Russian prisoners. Denisof's force frees one group of prisoners and the group includes Pierre. The combination of cold, lack of supplies, and Russian action causes the French to lose men by the tens of thousands. But in one action Petya is killed.

Part 15. Maria returns to Moscow with Natasha to be with her, for Natasha is wholly despondent, thin and pale. News arrives that Petya has been killed. The

French Army is destroyed; Kutuzov, so greatly criticized in 1812 and 1813, is now a national hero. But his job is done and he dies.

Pierre is a changed man; though the war has cost him millions, he has learned to live soberly and his retrenchment makes him feel richer than ever. He learns that Helene has died. He returns to Moscow and calls on Maria; at Maria's he meets Natasha and knows definitely that he loves her. He sees Natasha regularly, and finally tells Maria, who assures him that Natasha will marry him.

Part 16. Pierre and Natasha marry in 1813. Natasha wishes Nikolai and Maria to marry, but Nikolai has taken a government job and is working to pay the debts of Count Rostof, who died bankrupt in 1813. Nikolai will not court Maria because she is so rich. But later that year he meets her by chance, she reproaches him for robbing her of happiness because of his pride, and he realizes his love for her and they marry.

Seven years later, in 1820, the Rostofs— Nikolai and Maria—and the Bezukhofs, Pierre and Natasha, are settled in lives of uneventful domesticity. Nikolai has become devoted to the efficient management of the estates of himself, his wife, and Andrei's son Nikolusha. Maria has three children, Natasha four. Sonya has not married. Natasha is interested only in her husband and children. Pierre's only outside interest is in Freemasonry. All of them have all but forgotten the war and their earlier lives in the social whirl of fashionable Moscow and St. Petersburg.

The War of the Worlds

Novelette by H. G. Wells, 1866–1946. Published 1898 by Harper & Bros., New York.

ONE OF THE MOST STARTLING phenomena in mass psychology since the migrations of the Middle Ages occurred when H. G. Wells' science-fiction story *The War of the Worlds* was presented in a radio dramatization in 1938. Orson Welles and his Mercury Players had prepared from the book a script made to resemble as nearly as possible on-the-spot reporting. Apparently some millions of persons tuned in just after the opening of the broadcast and believed that they were listening to an actual report of an invasion by Martians. Mass hysteria followed, telephone lines in the principal cities were tied up, panic-stricken families piled into their cars and began to run away. And, as a noteworthy minor point, it should be mentioned that the Mercury Theater was not the popular show at that hour; its audience was far exceeded by that of the week's most popular comedy show, which was on the air at the same time.

THE COMING OF THE MARTIANS

Chaps. 1–2. It is now six years since astronomers first detected an unusual series of flashes emanating from the planet Mars. We know now that these flashes signalized the beginning of the first attack from outer space upon our earth. What appears at first to be an ordinary shooting star, or meteorite, falls during the night and lands on Horsell Common. It turns out to be a cylinder, about thirty yards in diameter, apparently hollow, with somebody—or something— inside.

Chaps. 3–6. Crowds of curiosity-seekers gather around the cylinder, which is em-

Some escape the death ray

bedded in the ground. The Astronomer Royal arrives, with other scientists, and workmen under his direction try to unscrew the top of the cylinder. Without warning, the top of the cylinder is unscrewed from within. The horrified onlookers, after seeing creatures with tentacles begin to emerge, creatures "at once vital, intense, inhuman, crippled and monstrous," run for their lives. From a safe distance away, I see a group of men, waving a white flag, approach the cylinder. Before they can reach it, they are suddenly attacked and destroyed by a heat ray which leaps out of the pit at them. A crowd on the road from Chobham to Woking is nearly overtaken by the same fate, escaping death only because a hummock of heathery sand provides a shield from the ray.

Chaps. 7–11. I arrive, exhausted, at my home. The few people I encounter along the way simply laugh at my attempts to warn them. My wife, however, is so convinced of the danger that I find reasons to reassure her. The Martians, I say, will find it impossible to cope with earth's greater gravitational force. On Friday night, however, the second cylinder lands. The military authorities dispatch a body of troops to the vicinity. Before the soldiers can gather any impression of the invaders, the heat ray blasts them, destroys every other living thing within range, and sets fire to the countryside. After taking my wife to Leatherhead for safety, I make my way back to Maybury Hill, just in time to see the third falling star, and Martians mounted on high tripods striding about, dealing death and destruction. From a window of my home I see a swath of destruction. I am joined by an artilleryman, the only survivor of the military's ill-fated counter-attack.

Chaps. 12–17. A fresh detachment of troops scores a direct hit on one of the Martians, only to be heat-rayed out of existence soon after, together with all but a few of the inhabitants of two towns, Weybridge and Shepperton. Making my way toward London, I meet up with the curate of Weybridge, who is near mental collapse from the horror. In London, the news is received that Martians are on their way to the city, destroying everything in their path with a poisonous vapor. All London is in flight; there is din and indescribable confusion, violence and death everywhere. My brother and two traveling companions manage to escape on a steamboat bound for Ostend. The ironclad torpedo-ram "Thunder-Cloud" destroys two of the Martians, before it itself is destroyed.

THE EARTH UNDER THE MARTIANS

Chaps. 1–5. I am pinned down in my house with the curate for two days; the Martians are all about us. Shifting to a house in Sheen, we find ourselves prisoners for a fortnight, because a Martian cylinder landing hard by makes it impossible for us to leave. From our hiding-place in the ruined house, we observe the Martians at close hand. Their bodies are basically all head. From the mouths project tentacles, employed like hands. The Martians neither eat, nor digest, but derive their nourishment from the blood of other creatures, which they inject into their own veins. They do not sleep, do not reproduce sexually, have no emotions, and apparently communicate by telepathy. Their machines employ a complicated system of sliding parts, activated by electricity.

On the sixth day of imprisonment, the curate goes insane and makes for the door. I am compelled to fell him, and the Martians remove his body, but I escape notice. It is the fifteenth day and the Martians are gone. There is no sign of them.

Chaps. 6–10. Red weed, brought by the invaders from their planet, is everywhere. I see no living soul, nor Martians either, until on Putney Hill I meet with the artilleryman again. He has worked out an impracticable plan for survival under the Martians. London is a dead city. The only sound to be heard is an unearthly wailing from a Martian giant that stands unmoving. Then the wailing stops, and I realize the Martian is dead. They are all dead, killed by our earth's bacteria. England is coming back to life, but I hear that all at Leatherhead have perished. Back home, back at what I expect to be an empty house, I find my wife. We are both still alive and are together again. Will the Martians ever attempt another invasion? Who can tell? All that is certain now is that we can never view our planet and the future of our race in the same light again.

The Way of All Flesh

Novel by Samuel Butler, 1835–1902.
Published 1903. (RE, 7; ML, 13 & T5)

THIS SAMUEL BUTLER (there was another, the one who wrote *Hudibras*) was a most controversial man of letters. He had a large following that insisted that *The Way of All Flesh* is one of the greatest English novels, yet publishers did not think it worth their investment. It was not published until after Butler died. Modern criticism tends to agree with Butler's supporters (the most notable of whom was George Bernard Shaw). *The Way of All Flesh* is an important novel. It is largely autobiographical and very bitter. But it introduces characters that the reader does not forget and it introduces ideas that do not seem so startling today as when they were published.

Chaps. 1–16. EDWARD OVERTON, the narrator, is godfather to the book's hero, ERNEST PONTIFEX, and nominal friend to Ernest's father, THEOBALD. Overton, a successful playwright, is the son of the rector of Paleham. He records Ernest's ancestry in Paleham, beginning with the first Pontifex, a talented carpenter, and GEORGE PONTIFEX, spoiled and egocentric only son of the carpenter's old age. George becomes a prosperous London publisher. His children are the cowed and loveless Theobald; ELIZA, MARIA and JOHN, who inherit their father's bullying nature; and ALETHEA, the narrator's childhood sweetheart and the only attractive woman in the novel. Theobald's father tyrannizes him in his wretched boyhood, finally hounding him into the ministry against his will. Theobald becomes curate to Mr. ALLABY, a rector of small means, whose wife sees curates as potential husbands for her five unmarried daughters. The Allaby sisters quarrel and then play cards to determine which is to snare the oblivious Theobald. CHRISTINA ALLABY wins. She opens a campaign of flattery and trickery against woman-hating Theobald, who is trapped at last into a reluctant proposal and, when he falls heir to a college living, into matrimony. But on the honeymoon, he discovers to his satisfaction that it is possible to torment a wife as his father had tormented him. As rector of Battersby-on-the-Hill, he also discovers how much he hates every aspect of clerical life. He lacks the satisfaction of an avocation because he also hates hunting, fishing, cricket, art, literature, and politics.

Chaps. 17–26. Ernest Pontifex is born to Theobald and Christina. George's pompous pride in his first grandson, for whose christening he has preserved a bottle of Jordan water, contrasts with the dismay of John, who has produced only daughters thus far. George dies not long afterward, and Ernest's brother and sister, JOSEPH and CHARLOTTE, are born. Theobald's hatred of children poisons their infancy. Ernest is taught to kneel before he can walk, to pray when he can barely talk, to read English at 3 and Latin at 4. The narrator sees him beaten for babyish mispronunciation. Christina's vanity and self-deception are cruel traps for Ernest, who cannot fulfill her foolish hopes and must despise himself, therefore.

Chaps. 27–31. Ernest at 12 has read Virgil, Horace, Livy, and the Greek dramatists. He is sent to the Roughborough school of Dr. SKINNER, a smug and brutal hypocrite. Christina hopes that Ernest will make aristocratic friends, but his self-contempt increases because he hates school, fears the masters and the older boys, and cannot play cricket or football. Music, which Theobald dislikes, is Ernest's only comfort. In the absence of paternal beatings, Ernest fails in all his subjects and falls in with bad companions.

Chaps. 32–37. Ernest's witty, kind and tolerant godmother, Alethea, has been living alone in London, happy and vaguely literary. She avoids her family, but concern for Ernest brings her to visit him at Roughborough. Unmarried, she wants a worthy heir, and is charmed by Ernest's musical talent and touched by his unhappy life. She takes a house in the town of Roughborough on pretext of medical advice. She soothes relations between Ernest and his schoolmates by entertaining them at a festive tea, flatters Dr. Skinner and the masters into more kindness, encourages Ernest to learn organ-building as a substitute for cricket. A fatal attack of typhoid fever terminates this interlude, but Alethea's deathbed will leaves her fortune in secret trust with Overton, the narrator, for Ernest at 28. She dies without a message for Ernest, and Theobald viciously convinces the boy that Alethea cut him off without a word because of her disappointment in him. This new heartbreak undoes Alethea's good work. Ernest sells his schoolbooks to solace himself with cheap editions of the Handel

Miss Snow half seduces him

oratorios, falls into deep disgrace with masters and mates, and ends the term with a bad report.

Chaps. 38–44. During school holidays, ELLEN, a pretty, affectionate servant whom Ernest has always liked, is found pregnant. Theobald and Christina half suspect 14-year-old Ernest but discharge Ellen at once as a matter of course. Tender-hearted Ernest runs 5 miles after Ellen's coach to give her his watch, his knife, and his remaining pocket money, because he knows she has only £3 from his parents. He fabricates an excuse for the loss of the watch, but Theobald later finds it for sale in a shop and Ernest must tell the truth to protect Ellen from an accusation of theft. JOHN, the coachman who witnessed Ernest's generosity, prevents Theobald from beating Ernest and is himself discharged. Theobald cuts down Ernest's pocket money, but Ernest must confess that he is already illicitly in debt to shopkeepers near the school. Theobald blackmails him into naming the shopkeepers and the other boys who have contracted unlawful debts. Ultimately, Theobald worms from Ernest a list of further violations of school rules, with the names of the offenders. Ernest returns to school in worse disgrace than ever, because Theobald gives the list to Dr. Skinner and its source is obvious to everyone. Ernest finds some comfort when "Rev. Theobald Pontifex" is burned in effigy by the Roughborough boys on Guy Fawkes Day.

Chaps. 45–50. Ernest goes up to Cambridge, where he becomes less unpopular and life improves for him. He achieves notoriety for an undergraduate essay debunking the Greek drama and the Psalms. He comes of age and inherits his grandfather's legacy, but fails to realize his independence of his father and continues the hated classical studies even after taking a creditable degree. In awe of TOWNELEY, an urbanely charming fellow undergraduate, he makes friends among other divinity students, although he lacks enthusiasm for

ordination. Ernest is converted by GIDEON HAWKE, an evangelical preacher, to the Simeonite views of the ugly and bumptious BADCOCK. Now fervently religious, he even temporarily abandons smoking and is ordained a deacon at 23.

Chaps. 51–57. Ernest, now a junior curate in London, is converted anew, this time to the High Church opinions of PRYER, a handsome but effeminate fellow curate. Still in pursuit of sanctity, Ernest goes to live "among the poor" in the none-too-respectable lodging house of Mrs. JUPP. But an encounter with Towneley causes him to question these activities in the light of Towneley's pleasant worldliness. He reconsiders the prudence of having entrusted his grandfather's legacy to Pryer toward the foundation of a "College for Spiritual Pathology."

Chaps. 58–64. Ernest attempts the conversion of Mrs. Jupp's lodgers. But Mr. HOLT threatens and terrifies him, Mr. and Mrs. BAXTER nearly convert him to Methodism, and Mr. SHAW undermines his faith in the Resurrection. When he approaches the prostitute, Miss SNOW, she half seduces him. They are interrupted by the arrival of Towneley, to the embarrassment of all. Ernest flees to the room of the other female lodger, Miss MAITLAND, convinced that his state has only one remedy. Miss Maitland is, however, a reputable woman, and Ernest is jailed for indecent behavior. Towneley and the narrator come to Ernest's rescue, but he is sentenced to six months at hard labor. Ernest's money is lost to Pryer, he falls ill with brain fever, and his parents refuse to see him "forever." On recovery, he sees advantages in these misfortunes: He has lost his faith in religion and with it the hated rôle of clergyman, and he has lost Theobald's badgering interference.

Chaps. 65–70. Ernest is now disposed to preach his new agnosticism, but the kindly old prison chaplain, Mr. HUGHES, brushes this aside and will discuss only Ernest's practical problems. On his release, Ernest plans to abandon respectability and "kiss the soil" rather than "clutch onto a fag end of gentility at a starvation salary." To this end, he learns tailoring and becomes prison organist, so that his sentence passes pleasantly enough. The narrator suggests that Ernest has given up all for Christ's sake

631

and that his quarrel with Christianity is semantic. Christina and Theobald come to meet Ernest at the end of his prison term, despite their previous repudiation, but Ernest says that future communication will be impossible. Ernest calls on Overton and refuses his offer of a home. He takes cheap attic quarters and looks for work as a tailor, but discovers that he does not "belong" in a workshop full of tailors.

Chaps. 71–79. Ernest happens on Ellen, his mother's former servant, now an alcoholic shoplifter but still so pretty and friendly that Ernest falls in love with her and they are soon married. With Overton's help they buy a second-hand clothing shop, which prospers. Ernest has time for his music, and the marriage is temporarily successful. Ellen's secret drinking returns with pregnancy, and she is a hopeless drunkard by the time two children are born to them. Ernest is in despair until another accidental encounter, this time with John, the coachman, reveals that their marriage is invalid, because John married Ellen shortly after she left the house of Ernest's parents. Ellen is pensioned off by Overton; the children, ALICE and GEORGE, are farmed out with a happy, laboring-class family; and Ernest has been "inoculated" against matrimony. Overton offers Ernest £300 a year to manage what is his own estate—although Ernest is still unaware of this. Ernest has a nervous breakdown and is advised to go abroad.

Chaps. 80–85. Ernest and Overton tour Europe. Overton tries to foster the friendship with Towneley. On his 28th birthday, the incredulous Ernest receives Alethea's legacy, now a splendid fortune. Called to his mother's deathbed, he crushes Theobald with his lordly manner and obvious wealth and returns to a London life of quiet luxury. He becomes a successful essayist, travels often, and occasionally visits his grown children. It is said of him at 47 that Mr. Ernest Pontifex "hates not wisely but too well."

The Wealth of Nations

Treatise by Adam Smith, 1723–1790. Published 1776. (ML, G32)

THE FULL TITLE IS *An Inquiry into the Nature and Causes of the Wealth of Nations.* Among books on economics this is certainly the most famous with the sole exception of Karl Marx's *Capital.* One obvious reason is that the English ruling classes adopted Adam Smith's doctrine of governmental noninterference so devoutly that adherence to this dogma became almost essential to respectability. Adam Smith wrote another, less known but superior work, *A Theory of Moral Sentiments.* He was a great thinker in a century of great thinkers.

Introduction. The wealth of a nation consists of the annual produce of labor, or in what is purchased with that produce from other nations. The proportion of produce to consumer is regulated in every nation by (1) the skill, dexterity and judgment with which its labor is applied, and (2) by the proportion between those who are employed in useful labor and those who are not so employed.

Book I. Chaps. 1–3. The greatest improvement in the productive power of labor has come from the division of labor. It facilitates production in three ways: (1) by reducing every laborer's task to one simple operation, which he learns to perform with great dexterity; (2) by saving time that is commonly lost in passing from one sort of work to another; (3) by leading to the invention of a great number of machines which abridge labor and enable one man to do the work of many. The division of labor is a consequence of a human propensity to trade. Since this is so, the extent of the division must be limited by the extent of the power to trade, that is, by the market. This is why the first improvements of arts and industry have generally taken place among peoples who live close to the sea or to navigable rivers.

Chap. 4. Man originally had to bargain, using the products of his labor: grain, hides, salt, fruits, cattle, etc. This system of barter was replaced eventually by the use of metals in the form of money. Metals are (1) less perishable than most other commodities, and (2) can be divided into any number of parts, and reunited by fusion.

Chaps. 5–7. Every man is rich or poor in the degree to which he is able, directly or indirectly, to command the labor of others. Labor, therefore, is the real measure of the exchangeable value of all commodities; it was the first price, the original purchase money of all things. That is dear which costs much labor, and that is cheap which may be had with very little labor. The real price of a thing is expressed in terms of labor, the nominal price in money. The proportion between the quantities of labor necessary for acquiring different objects, seems to afford the only rule for exchanging them for one another. In every well-developed society, the price of any object may devolve on one or more of three things: wages, profit, and rent. The natural price of a commodity is that price which is just sufficient to pay the rent of the land, the wages of the labor, and the profits of the stock employed in raising, preparing, and bringing it to market. The actual price at which a commodity is sold, that is, the market price, is regulated by the proportion between the quantity which is actually brought to market, and the effectual demand for it, that is, the demand of those who are willing to pay the natural price of the commodity.

Chaps. 8–11. The produce of labor constitutes the natural recompense or wages of labor. Previous to the accumulation of stock and the appropriation of land, the whole produce belongs to the laborer. But as soon as land becomes private property, the landlord demands a share of the produce as rent. His rent makes deduction from the produce of labor. If the laborer employed upon the land must borrow to take care of his needs between harvests, he must pay the lender, that is, give a profit. This profit is the second deduction from the produce of the laborer.

The rate of profit in a country does not fall with the decline of wealth, but, on the contrary, it is naturally low in rich countries, and high in poor countries.

The whole annual produce of a country naturally divides into three parts, the rent of the land, the wages of labor, and the profits of stock. Therefore, landlords, laborers, and capitalists are the three great constituent orders of every civilized society, from whose revenue that of every other order is ultimately derived.

Book II. Introduction. Before division of labor can take place, a stock of goods must be stored up somewhere, sufficient to maintain the laborer and to supply him with the tools of his work.

Chaps. 1–2. The stock of a man who possesses more of it than is needed to satisfy his immediate wants, is divided into two parts: (1) The part from which he expects to draw revenue, which is called his capital; (2) the part which he reserves for the supply of his immediate wants. Capital is either circulating or fixed. Circulating capital consists of articles such as food, raw materials, and finished goods, which are continually passing to and fro between the capitalist and his workman customers. Fixed capital consists of such articles as remain continuously in the possession of the capitalist, such as machinery and tools. The stock of a country, too, is divided into that for consumption, and that which is fixed and circulating capital. The gross revenue of a country comprehends the whole annual produce of its land and labor, the net revenue comprehends what remains after maintaining (1) the fixed, and (2) the circulating capital. The real wealth of nations is in proportion not to their gross, but to the net revenue.

Chaps. 3–5. If labor adds to the value of the subject upon which it is bestowed, it is productive; if labor does not do this, it is unproductive. Capitals are increased by parsimony, diminished by prodigality. The annual produce of the land and labor of a country can be increased only by increasing either the number of its productive laborers, or the productive power of the laborers. Both these means require additional capital. Capital may be employed in four different ways: (1) in raising rude produce from the earth, (2) in manufacturing rude produce for immediate use, (3) in transporting rude or manufactured produce to places where they are most wanted, (4) in dividing particular portions of the produce into such small parcels as suit the occasional demands of those who want them.

Book III. Chaps. 1–4. The great commerce of every civilized society is that carried on between the inhabitants of the town and those of the country. It consists in the exchange of rude for manufactured produce, either immediately, or by means of money. In every period of every society, the surplus part both of the rude and manufactured produce, or that for which there is no demand at home, must be sent abroad, in order to be exchanged for something for which there is demand at home. According to the natural course of things, the greater part of capital of every growing society is, first, directed toward agriculture, afterward to manufactures, and last of all to foreign commerce. This sequence is clearly apparent in the history of Europe from the time of the fall of the Roman Empire.

Book IV. Introduction. Political economy, considered as a branch of statesmanship, proposes two distinct objects: (1) to enable the people of a country to provide a revenue or subsistence for themselves; (2) to supply the state or commonwealth with a revenue sufficient for the public services.

Chaps. 1–3. Acting on the belief that the wealth of a nation consists of the amount of money it possesses, certain statesmen have acted so as to prevent the exportation of gold and silver from their countries. By a system of restraints, sometimes called the "mercantile system," these statesmen have acted to increase the amount of gold and silver imported and kept in their countries, without at the same time acting to increase the uses of money within their countries. However, since money is an instrument of exchange, simply storing it up in a country does not increase the productive power, and therefore the real wealth of a nation. It was believed that one way to increase the wealth of a country was to restrain the import of such foreign goods as could be produced at home. Furthermore, there was imposed almost total restraint upon importation from countries with which an unfavorable balance of trade was believed to exist. The wrongness of this policy may be seen when it is understood that the importation of gold and silver is not the principle, much less the sole, benefit which a nation derives from its foreign trade. Between whatever places foreign trade is carried on, they all of them derive two distinct benefits from it: (1) it carries out that surplus part of the produce of their land and labor for which there is no demand among them, and (2) brings back in return for it something else for which there is a demand. By opening a more extensive market for whatever part of the produce of their labor may exceed the home consumption, it encourages them to improve its productive powers, and to augment its annual produce to the utmost, and thereby to increase the real revenue and wealth of society.

Chaps. 4–7. The methods used to encourage export and place restraints on import trade have been (1) to allow the merchant to draw back upon exportation, either the whole or a part of whatever excise or inland duty is imposed upon domestic industry, (2) the paying of bounties for exportation, (3) special restrictive treaties with other countries, (4) the establishment of colonies whose trade could be wholly controlled by means of chartered companies.

Chaps. 8–9. Consumption is the sole end and purpose of all production; and the interest of the producer ought to be attended to only insofar as it may be necessary for promoting that of the consumer. But in the mercantile system, the interest of the consumer is almost constantly sacrificed to that of the producer; and it seems to consider production, and not consumption, as the ultimate end and object of all industry and commerce. Clearly, the contrivers of the mercantile system have been the producers and not the consumers. Another unwise system has been the agricultural system which represents the produce of the land as being the sole source of revenue and wealth of a country. This system has never been put into practice, but since it is being considered, it is worthwhile pointing out that the special protection the producers in such a system would

need makes it akin to mercantilism, and predicts that it will suffer from the same difficulties.

Book V. Chap. 1. The expenses of a sovereign or a commonwealth include most importantly (1) those connected with the defense of society from violence and invasion by other societies, (2) the maintenance of justice, which includes protecting every member of the society from injustice or oppression; (3) the erection and maintenance of public institutions and public works.

Chap. 2. The money for public expenses should be raised by means of a system of taxes which should follow these four maxims: (1) payment should be according to the ability of taxpayer to pay; (2) the tax an individual must pay should be certain, not arbitrary; (3) taxes should be payable at a certain definite time, which should be set so as to be most convenient to the taxpayer; (4) the tax-collecting machinery should be efficient, so as to take as little out of the taxpayers' pockets over and above what is brought into the public treasury.

Chap. 3. A nation, like an individual, must live within the means of its income. A growing public debt will oppress and eventually ruin a nation.

The Weavers

Play by Gerhard Hauptmann, 1862–1946.
Produced 1892. (RE, 52)

THIS WAS HAUPTMANN'S most popular play in the United States and has consequently come to be his best-known work, though as literature it does not have the substance of several of his other plays. *The Weavers* is a straight documentary protest against the lot of pieceworkers in Germany (and in most other European countries). When it was produced in New York in 1905 it had a special appeal because the sweatshops of New York's garment industry were treating the workers almost as badly. As with *Tobacco Road,* the horrible appearance of the actors on the stage did much to create a shocked thrill and so draw in audiences. As always, Hauptmann was blatantly militant in calling for the workers of the world to unite.

Act I. It is pay day in the house of the fustian manufacturer, DREISSIGER, in Silesia. The weavers line up to deliver their packs of cloth. PFEIFER, Dreissiger's manager, examines the weaving through a magnifying glass. He has risen from the ranks of the weavers himself and now appears well-fed and elegantly clothed. He is

arrogant toward the weavers, deducts pay for any flaws in the cloth, and ignores those who appeal for a few pennies advance pay. His behavior is duplicated by NEUMANN, the cashier, and by TILGNER, the apprentice.

The weavers, men and women, are a miserable, half-starved, emaciated lot. Stories of bleakest poverty are exchanged among them. Old BAUMERT carries something carefully wrapped up in his cloth. It is the skinny carcass of his pet dog, which he went to have killed to afford the family a morsel of meat. BECKER, an unusually robust young weaver, differs markedly in his behavior from the rest. He is impudent as he talks to Pfeifer, who asks Dreissiger to intervene. Becker is discharged by the irate manufacturer, who recalls having seen the young weaver among a group of demonstrators singing an inflammatory and abusive song under his windows. During the exchange, a small boy faints with hunger. The act ends with a tirade by Dreissiger, guiltily on the defensive, who deplores the manufacturer's lot and extols his kindness in providing work for the weavers. He fails to mention that the pay is at a starvation rate. The pay rate is cut even further, as the curtain falls.

Act II. In a single room rented from old ANSORGE, an unemployed weaver, the Baumert family, including the crippled mother, an idiot son, two young daughters, and a grandchild, lives in dire and sordid misery. Father Baumert returns from the

The weavers, singly and in groups, ransack the house

factory with his small provisions. He is accompanied by MORITZ JAEGER, a reserve soldier, newly discharged, still flushed with abundant food, dressed in clean, new clothes. He also has enough money to provide a bottle of brandy. Jaeger, having acquired bravado and a hatred of the wealthy classes, prophesies better times to come if the weavers will take their fate into their own hands. He recites the "Dreissiger Song," which works strongly on the emotions of all present.

Act III. In the public house in the town of Peterswaldau the weavers' plight is discussed. Representatives of other trades—WIEGAND, the joiner; KUTSCHE, the policeman; the commercial traveler, and the peasant and forester, look down on the victims of Dreissiger's exploitation. HORNIG, the peddler, sympathizes with them. WITTIG, the smith, a revolutionary of the old stamp, is ready to give them all-out help. Groups of weavers gather in the public house. Under the leadership of Becker and Jaeger, they have banded together to demand higher wages and better working conditions.

Act IV. In the living room of Dreissiger's palatial residence, Pastor and Mrs. KITTELHAUS are guests as open rioting breaks out in front of the house. WEINHOLD, the young tutor of the manufacturer's children, is dismissed when he expresses sympathy for the workers. Dreissiger has Jaeger arrested, but the mob fights the police and releases him. Pastor Kittelhaus, unctuous and servile, tries to intercede on Dreissiger's behalf but fails. Pfeifer, in panic, seeks to save his own skin. Dreissiger and his family scramble into their coach to flee. The weavers, singly and in groups, invade the residence. At first they stand in awe, then incited by a few firebrands, they ransack the house.

Act V. The scene has shifted to Oberbielau, a neighboring village, where Old HILSE, despite poverty and privation, lives in piety and resignation to God's will. Hornig the peddler arrives with reports of the Peterswaldau rioting. It has spread to the factory and threatens to engulf Ober-

bielau in its turn. Old Hilse, at first in disbelief of what he is told, warns his family against having anything to do with violence and lawlessness. LUISE, his daughter-in-law, tired of a piety that has brought her nothing but misery, excitedly joins the marching rioters. She is reluctantly followed by her husband, GOTTLIEB. The first volleys are heard, fired by the regiment that has been sent to suppress the riots. Old Hilse stays at his loom, stubbornly remaining at work near the window, until a stray bullet kills him. He slumps over the loom. His blind and deaf wife calls out to him in agonized bewilderment.

Westward Ho!

Novel by Charles Kingsley, 1819–1875. Published 1855.

CHARLES KINGSLEY was a professor of history, so it may be taken that this novel of high adventure in the early years of the exploration of the Americas and in the time of the Spanish Armada is unusually authentic in detail. Partly for this reason, no doubt, it has been recommended reading for many generations of students. In addition, it is a real riproaring thriller in which the heroes are heroic and the villains villainous, the ladies beautiful and the coincidences incredible.

Chap. 1. AMYAS LEIGH, 15 years old in 1575, when the story opens, is the younger son of a gentleman of Bideford in Devonshire. His elder brother, FRANK, left home some time ago for travel in Europe and now, an accomplished scholar and a courtier, is living in London. Amyas also desires to travel, but he wants to go to sea with Drake

and other worthy men. One such sea captain, JOHN OXENHAM, fires his imagination with stirring tales of voyages to the Indies, and later (while supping with the Leighs and Sir RICHARD GRENVILLE, the famous mariner and Amyas's godfather) urges the boy's parents to let him sail with him, but they refuse. As he leaves the Leighs' house, Oxenham sees a white bird, an omen of death in his family.

Chaps. 2–6. Five years later, Amyas has returned home from his first voyage, which has taken him round the world with Drake. He was allowed to go to sea after his father's death. Sir Richard Grenville encouraged him, for Amyas had broken his schoolmaster's head and had fallen in love with the mayor's daughter, ROSE SALTERNE, and in all was too headstrong to be kept at home. Oxenham's ship has not returned and he and his crew are presumed lost. Amyas's cousin, EUSTACE LEIGH, a Roman Catholic who has been educated abroad by Jesuits, is courting Rose Salterne, with whom Amyas is still secretly in love. Eustace is encouraged by the Jesuits, because her money will benefit their cause, but Rose rejects him. Rose, who has many admirers, including Frank, visits LUCY PASSMORE, a "wise woman," and is told that if she will go down to the shore next evening with a mirror, she will see her future husband. The Leigh brothers, to avoid rivalry, agree to give up hopes of Rose. They intercept Eustace carrying a message announcing to the Jesuits (who are concealed at his father's house) that Spanish forces have landed in Ireland. Eustace wounds Frank, but Amyas rescues him. The brothers consult with Mr. CARY, a neighboring squire, and his son, WILL CARY, another admirer of Rose. They tell Grenville and he goes to Eustace's father's house but finds that the Jesuits have escaped. They have fled to the shore, where Rose awaits her vision. She sees them escape in a boat, taking with them Eustace, and she is terrified to think he is fated to be her husband. Lucy suggests that perhaps her husband will be a nobleman from over the sea.

Chap. 7. Amyas is at Grenville's house, preparing to leave for Ireland, and fight the Spaniards. An old seaman, SALVATION YEO, one of Oxenham's crew, tells how Oxenham, after many conquests, was destroyed by the Spaniards. One of them, Don FRANCISCO XARARTE, hated Oxenham for having a daughter by the Spaniard's wife. The wife and the daughter were with Oxenham at the time of his capture. The woman killed herself, but the fate of the "little maid" remains unknown. Yeo was captured and tortured by the Inquisition. He has vowed to find the girl if she is alive.

Chaps. 8–16. At a Bideford tavern, Frank, Amyas and Rose's other local admirers found the Brotherhood of the Rose, all pledging themselves to deeds of honor for her sake. JACK BRIMBLECOMBE, the schoolmaster's son, a fat, timorous Oxford graduate, now a clergyman, declares his own love for Rose and is initiated into the Brotherhood. Amyas, accompanied by Yeo, goes to Ireland. They serve under Lord Grey and Amyas meets Raleigh and Spenser. Amyas captures a Spaniard, Don GUZMAN DE SOTO, whose character is a strange compound of shrewdness and fanaticism, gentility and boastfulness. Don Guzman is known to Grenville, who invites him to stay with him in Bideford until his ransom arrives. There Don Guzman meets Rose; they are mutually attracted. Amyas and Yeo sail with Raleigh to Newfoundland in Sir Humphrey Gilbert's expedition. Eustace returns to Devon in disguise. Don Guzman continues to court the willing Rose and on her account fights a duel with Will Cary (of the Brotherhood). Rose, to avoid scandal, is packed off to the country by her father, while Don Guzman announces that his ransom has arrived and that he is departing to take up a governorship in the Spanish West Indies. However, when Amyas returns from the ill-fated expedition, in which Sir Humphrey Gilbert and his ship have been lost, Don Guzman has vanished, taking Rose with him. Traveling home to Bideford, Amyas and Yeo fall in with the GUBBINGS, wild folk of the moors, and Yeo kills their leader in a brawl. Eustace Leigh and one of the Jesuits are there, converting the Gubbings to Catholicism. Amyas learns that Eustace loved Rose, and made some agreement with Don Guzman, which the latter did not keep. At Bideford, Rose's father offers to provide the money for an expedition to find her and kill Don Guzman. Will Cary, Jack Brimblecombe and Frank are unanimously in favor of going in search of Rose. The ship *Rose* sails for the Indies, manned by Amyas, Frank, Will Cary, Brimblecombe, Yeo (who still seeks his "little maid"), and a crew of seasoned, honest mariners.

Chaps. 17–22. The *Rose* reaches the West Indies. At La Guayra, where Don Guzman has taken Rose, they learn that Don Guzman has anticipated their coming and has put to sea. Frank insists on going to see Rose, to discover whether she is the Spaniard's wife or his mistress and if possible to persuade her to return. Amyas is chosen by lot to go with Frank. They find Rose's house heavily guarded. Eustace Leigh (who has followed Don Guzman) is there and they hear him molesting Rose with offers of love, and (when she spurns him) with threats of handing her over to the Inquisition because she has not renounced her Protestantism. Frank reveals himself and appeals to Rose to save herself, but her passion for Don Guzman makes her refuse. The guards attack the brothers. Amyas escapes but Frank is captured. Amyas and his men defeat the Spaniards at sea and liberate English prisoners from a galley.

They put into a quiet bay for repairs. Don Guzman attacks them with an armed party, which they beat off. They march inland, hoping to find the legendary golden city of Manoa. Frank and Rose are in the hands of the Inquisition. Eustace, who betrayed them, is now distracted by remorse.

He abandons himself to Jesuitry and vanishes from the story.

Chaps. 23–27. Much reduced by disease and hardship, the English party gives up the search for Manoa. In the forests they meet AYACANORA, a girl wild as an Indian but of European appearance. She is known among the Indians as the Daughter of the Sun. Amyas grows fond of her and is almost tempted to remain, but he resists the desire. Ayacanora, secretly fond of Amyas, follows them. They reach the coast, and capture a

Ayacanora

galleon carrying great riches and a wicked Spanish bishop. Also in the galleon, as a prisoner, is Lucy Passmore, who fled from England with Rose. Lucy has been tortured by the Inquisition and Rose and Frank were burned to death. Amyas hangs the bishop and a monk, who were responsible for this. On the voyage home Ayacanora becomes gradually civilized, though she remains a creature of passionate moods. One day she recalls the words and tune of an English

sea song, and Yeo discovers with joy that she is his "little maid," John Oxenham's daughter.

Chaps. 28–33. Amyas returns home. His mother becomes a mother to Ayacanora. Salterne rejoices in the courage with which Rose died, and dies himself, that same day, leaving to Amyas a second ship, the *Vengeance,* in which to sail against the Spaniards. Amyas stays at home for a year, at his mother's desire. One day she tells him that Ayacanora loves him. He is unwilling to marry her because she has inherited from her mother the blood of the hated Spaniards. The approach of the Armada is announced and Amyas leaves for Plymouth. Drake and the other captains play at bowls before sailing against the Spaniards. Amyas is told that Don Guzman is aboard the *Santa Catherina,* and, forgetting England's cause in his private quarrel, he thinks only of revenge in spite of being knighted by Drake. The English fleet, by using fireships, disorganizes the enemy. The fleets engage. The *Vengeance* attacks the *Santa Catherina* and through a thunderstorm pursues her into the North Sea. The defeated Armada melts away in the storms. Amyas pursues Don Guzman around the north of Scotland and south through the Irish Sea, and in his rashness calls upon God to afford him vengeance, even though he be struck dead directly afterwards. At Lundy Island, the scene of Don Guzman's marriage with Rose, the *Santa Catherina* strikes the rock called the Shutter and vanishes forever. Amyas, mad with foiled vindictiveness, denounces God's injustice, hurls his sword into the sea, and is struck blind by lightning. The same flash kills old Yeo. Discovering that he is sightless, Amyas is in despair but at last is reconciled to God's will, repents his unchristian hatred, and forgives his enemies, even the dead Don Guzman. He returns to Bideford, where he speaks the funeral oration of Yeo. Ayacanora again declares her love for him and her desire to serve him; and Amyas, regenerate now and grateful to God, gladly accepts her.

Wild Animals I Have Known

Stories by Ernest Thompson Seton (Ernest Seton Thompson, 1860–1946).
Published 1898 by Charles Scribner's Sons, New York.

THIS BOOK IS A CLASSIC of its kind and has retained its popularity for more than 50 years. It was written for adults but became chiefly a favorite of boys. The author had great knowledge of woodsmanship and outdoor life and in addition had a pleasant style of writing and an ability to illustrate his work with charming pen-and-ink drawings that are authentic as well as decorative. The book was originally signed Ernest Seton Thompson, then Ernest Thompson Seton, and so much confusion arose that eventually no one was quite sure which was the man's real name.

The book is a collection of eight stories. Each deals with an animal closely observed by the author.

Lobo, the King of Currumpaw, tells of a

magnificent gray wolf that ranges over northern New Mexico and during its infamous career kills 6,000 head of cattle. The history of Lobo is followed by the author's account of how he traps and kills this wolf.

Silverspot centers about a crow that lives near the author's home. The crow, leader of its group, is well schooled in the art of survival and the training of the young crows is described in detail. Death to wild animals is always tragic, and Silverspot, after 20 years as leader, is finally killed by an owl. The crow's body is found by the author.

Raggylug, the story of a cottontail rabbit, relates the daily life of a baby rabbit in a swamp area as its mother teaches it the lore of the woods. Snakes, dogs, hawks, and man, the natural enemies of the rabbit, are constantly threatening but the greatest enemy arrives in the form of another, full-grown rabbit who invades Raggylug's swamp. Raggylug succeeds in duping this rabbit and lures it to its death by the farmer's dog. A fox causes the mother rabbit's death, but at the close of the story, Raggylug, now a veteran, is raising a family and imparting to them the knowledge that was passed on to him.

Bingo concerns the author's favorite dog. It is essentially an analysis of how a man's attachment for a dog can grow and grow until it is an obsession. Bingo, an ungainly and vigorous dog, has many adventures in the rugged country of Manitoba, but even after years of separation from the author the dog recognizes its old master and permits him to release its paw from the painful grip of a bear trap. Finally, after having eaten poisoned bait, the dog returns to the author's empty shanty to die on the doorstep of the only home it ever really knew.

The Springfield Fox describes a mother's love and mercy killing. A family of foxes takes residence near the author's house. He finds the lair and from a concealed vantage point observes the training of the young. The family consists of the father and mother and a brood of four. The father is shot by the author's uncle, and soon afterward the uncle discovers the whereabouts of the den. Three of the baby foxes are killed but the fourth is taken alive and chained in the barnyard. The mother makes many futile attempts to free the captive but fails. She finally gives the baby some poisoned bait, preferring to have it dead than a prisoner.

The Pacing Mustang is another account of an animal's striving for freedom. This mustang, an incredible horse, eludes capture though various schemes are attempted by men wise in the ways of the West. At last an old cook baits his personal trap with a brown mare and the lure of love leads the mustang to a rope. Then, having crudely branded his captive, the old-timer drives him towards his corral. Just short of the final indignity of a fenced-in existence, the horse, struggling against the hobbles on its forelegs, climbs a hill and leaps off a cliff to death on the rocks below.

Wully, the story of a yaller dog, has for its hero a mongrel dog trained as a sheep tender and owned by a drunken shepherd. The devotion of the dog to this kind, though befuddled, master becomes legend. The dog, separated from the master and flock at a

The mustang leaps off the cliff

ferry house, remains for more than two years, sniffing the feet of every passenger getting on or off the ferry. Since the ferry makes fifty trips a day, the number of people inspected by the dog is staggering. Finally a man arrives wearing articles of clothing that had belonged to the dog's former master, and the dog now attaches itself to this man and returns to the job of tending sheep in a different part of the country. The section has been bedeviled by a large fox that kills for sheer enjoyment. The flock tended by Wully escapes unscathed, for the yaller dog is more than a match for the wily, ferocious fox. But Wully, too, is vicious except to his flock, his new master, and the daughter of the house. After a particularly savage raid, the sheepmen of the neighborhood band together and follow the fox tracks through the snow. The tracks lead right to Wully. The dog is accused, over the strong denials of the master, but the men agree to watch it during the night and see if it can get out of the kitchen. The dog does so by cleverly raising a window. It is gone an hour or so and returns to the house in the same manner. Its muzzle is blood-specked, and the daughter accuses it. Realizing it has been caught, the dog pretends to grovel for forgiveness at the girl's feet, then suddenly lunges for her throat. She is almost killed before the master rushes in and destroys the animal. Wully, the finest sheep dog the master had ever known, was a savage killer of all sheep other than the home flock.

Redruff, the story of the Don Valley partridge, traces the life cycle of a partridge from its third day outside the shell to a cruel death by an attack from an owl, while it is caught in a snare. The life and times of the partridge are outlined in detail: Their enemies, friends, food, and family life, and the effect of the cycle of seasons.

William Tell

Play by Johann Christoph Friedrich von Schiller, 1759–1805.
Produced 1804.

WILLIAM TELL is the work most commonly read in English of the great German poet and playwright Schiller, partly because of the familiarity and appeal of its story, though some of Schiller's other plays have the advantage of translations into English by Coleridge. *William Tell* is a drama in poetry, designed to be acted as well as to be read.

Act I. 1. WILLIAM TELL, a Swiss hunter, helps a man sought by the tyrant GESSLER to escape across Lake Lucerne. Tell braves a storm to row the man to safety. 2. STAUFFACHER and his wife GERTRUDE, two peasants, discuss the rising tide of oppression engulfing Switzerland ever since Gessler was made governor by the Emperor. Stauffacher wants to discuss their grievances with other free men like himself, to see if they cannot do something about the situation. Tell delivers the rescued peasant to Stauffacher's house, though he does not enter himself. 3. Taskmasters drive the enslaved peasantry to build a new jail, so Gessler can imprison more of the rebellious Swiss. A procession arrives, carrying Gessler's hat on a pole. He has decreed that all must pay respects to the hat on the pole as though it were the governor himself. Anyone refusing will be put to death. Tell will not join the cause of the growing rebellion but keeps himself available if needed. 4. At the house of FUERST, the father-in-law of Tell, MELCHTHAL, another peasant, reports that his father has been blinded by Gessler. With Stauffacher and Fuerst, he plots a union of the free Swiss against the tyrant.

Act II. 1. ATTINGHAUSEN, a Swiss noble, is a friend of the peasants. His nephew and heir, ULRIC VON RUDENZ, has been impressed by the excitement of Gessler's court and decides to join the tyrant. Ulric is also in love with BERTHA, the tyrant's ward. Despite his uncle's warnings that the freedom movement will win out in the end, Ulric goes to join Gessler. 2. On the Ruetli, a meadow surrounded by high rocks, the conspirators meet at night. ROESSELMAN, a priest, suggests that perhaps a compromise can be found; but he is outvoted and the assembled men take an oath to destroy the tyrant.

Act III. 1. Tell prepares to visit Fuerst, who is a leader of the rebel movement. HEDWIG, Tell's wife, fearful for his safety, tries to keep him from going. But Tell assures her he is not one of the plotters and therefore has nothing to fear. Tell reveals

that he passed the governor some time ago in a desolate spot in the forest. The governor's fear evoked pity in him and he did not harm him then. Hedwig thinks Gessler will never forgive Tell for having seen him in a position of weakness. 2. Ulric is surprised to find Bertha's sentiments in favor of the rebels. She will not marry him unless he changes sides. Ulric is willing but not sure how he can extricate himself from his position with Gessler. 3. In the middle of a meadow, two soldiers are guarding the pole with Gessler's hat. Tell refuses to salute the cap and is seized by the guards. Gessler arrives with a hunting party. The peasants are in a mood to free Tell then and there. Tell asks the governor to forgive the oversight. Gessler remembers Tell's famed markmanship and commands Tell to shoot an apple off his son's head. The crowd is horrified, and Bertha pleads along with the others. Gessler insists. Ulric defies the governor and is about to draw his sword, when Tell shoots and hits the apple. Promising to spare Tell's life if he replies, the governor asks why Tell placed a second arrow in his quiver. Tell confesses that had he killed his son, the second arrow would have been for Gessler. Gessler then has Tell arrested and carried off.

Act IV. 1. The fishermen of Lake Lucerne are agitated by the report of Tell's escape. A storm has come up and Tell has been placed in charge of his captor's ship. Reaching land, Tell has jumped ashore, pushing the boat back into the waves. Tell himself arrives to confirm the story of his escape. He is now determined to take action and asks the fishermen the nearest road to Kuessnacht, toward which the governor's party is headed. **2.** Attinghausen is dying. The peasants gather around him. Ulric agrees to lead the uprising against Gessler. He tells the peasants to await a fiery signal from the mountaintops, then attack together. **3.** Meanwhile, however, Tell has arrived at a spot overlooking the hollow through which Gessler must pass on his way to Kuessnacht. While a Swiss woman stops the tyrant, asking for bread, Tell shoots him with a well-placed arrow. Gessler dies, and the woman shows the dead tyrant to her children, telling them this is how an oppressor must end his life.

Act V. 1. The conspirators are assembled to take further action. Word comes that the Emperor has been murdered by his own nephew, JOHN. The Swiss are horrified, for the Emperor had promised them their freedom charter. The peasants break open the prisons and liberate the prisoners. Among them is Bertha, who was placed there by Gessler. **2.** The murderer, John, comes to ask for food and is given aid by Tell, who takes pity on him. **3.** Bertha and Ulric join hands. Bertha is accepted into the freedom union, despite her aristocratic background, and Ulric immediately frees all his serfs.

The Wind in the Willows

Novel by Kenneth Grahame, 1859–1932.
Published and © 1908 by Charles Scribner's Sons, New York.

THIS BOOK ENJOYS a position among children's books of this century that is probably exceeded by nothing except A. A. Milne's Pooh books. The author casts small animals in the characters of upper-class Englishmen and combines a satire for adults with an adventure story for children. It is likely that the book will not appeal so much to American adult readers as to English readers. American children will like it no less.

Chaps. 1–5. The MOLE finds his spring cleaning suddenly interrupted by a divine discontent and longing. He flings down his broom, and pushing his way out into the meadow, goes down the lane, jeering at the rabbits, until he reaches the river, which he has never seen before. Before today he has been a stay-at-home animal. In a hole in the river bank he sees a bright eye looking at him, an eye that belongs to WATER RAT, a friendly animal, who loves nothing so much as "messing around in boats." In his little blue boat, Rat is introduced to the joys of river life and has the Wild Wood beyond pointed out to him. Rat intimates that although some friendly animals like BADGER live in the woods, others are not to be trusted entirely. As they reach the shore and unpack their delicious lunch-basket, OTTER appears. They speak of TOAD, a volatile animal, always pursuing a new hobby. Toad himself appears, rowing his new boat rather badly. Mole, entranced by boating, asks Rat if he may row, and though Rat urges caution he grabs the oars, tries to row, and lands in the river. Rat fishes him out and takes him home to live with him.

Mole learns to swim and row and asks Rat to take him to meet Toad. They go to Toad Hall, for Toad has inherited wealth, and find him in the garden studying a map. He has given up boating; he now has a yellow caravan and an old horse and persuades his friends to join him in a trip. Rat is unwilling to go but agrees because his friend, Mole, wants to. After two days of camping, during which Toad tries to avoid doing any work, the caravan is wrecked by an automobile. The animals are unhurt, but Toad has been seized by a passion for cars. The two friends decide to have nothing more to do with him. They live together happily, but Mole wants to call on Badger, and when Rat keeps putting him off, sneaks out one winter day when Rat is sleeping, goes to the Wild Wood, and gets lost and terribly frightened by glimpses of foxes. He creeps into a hole. Rat, waking and finding Mole missing, takes his pistols and follows the tracks of Mole's new overshoes until he finds the frightened animal. They are overtaken by a snowstorm and Mole cuts his leg on what turns out to be the bootscraper at Badger's front door. Badger comes grumbling to answer their knocks but is overjoyed to see his friends, warms them at his fire and gives them supper. Otter, who has heard that they were missing from the riverbank, drops in, followed by a pair of hedgehogs. Badger asks after Toad and learns he has had seven smash-ups and has been in the hospital three times. Rat is eager to be home, so Badger shows them through the long tunnel that runs to the edge of the Wild Wood, and accompanied by Otter, who knows the way, Mole and Rat head for the river bank. On the way, Mole smells his own home, forgotten for so long, and is wild with joy. Rat tries to persuade him to come home with him, but Mole longs for his own house. Good-natured Rat follows him into his hole and they prepare a cold supper. While they are eating they hear singing and find that a company of field mice are singing carols for them. They send out for provisions and have a feast with the mice, and next morning they return to Rat's home.

Chap. 6. Summer has returned, and Mole and Rat are interrupted by Badger, who tells them Toad's automobile has arrived and they must rescue him from his folly. They hasten to Toad Hall, drag Toad from the car, send it back to the shop, and imprison Toad. Feigning sickness, Toad escapes, eats dinner in an inn, and steals a car while its owners are dining. He is arrested and thrown into the dungeon of the stoutest castle in England.

Chaps. 7–8. Rat, returning from a day with Otter, reports to Mole that Otter's child, PORTLY, is missing. Although it is night, they decide to search for him by moonlight. Their boat reaches a silvery island where they have a vision of Pan with Portly in his arms. The vision fades, but they find Portly asleep, and as they take him to their boat they hear the heavenly music of Pan's great hymn. Toad repents and is helped to escape by the jailer's daughter. Disguised as a laundress, he reaches the railroad station and tries to buy a ticket, only to discover he has no money. A friendly engineer gives him a free ride, and when they are pursued by another train full of dungeon guards, police, and plainclothesmen, he slows down and allows Toad to jump out. Toad spends an uncomfortable night in a hollow tree.

Chap. 9. Rat falls under the spell of a wayfarer, SEA RAT, who tells him wonderful tales of far lands. Rat packs his bag to follow Sea Rat but is rescued by Mole, who cures him by suggesting he write poetry instead.

Chap. 10–11. Waking in the morning, Toad is given a ride by a stout woman on a barge, who asks him to wash some clothes. They are impossible to get clean, Toad's back aches, and worst of all, his hands are all crinkly. The woman jeers at him, saying she knew he was a braggart, and when he replies indignantly that he is Toad of Toad Hall, she throws him overboard. Furious, he steals her barge horse, rides it off, and sells it for six shillings six and breakfast. His old vanity returns, and he walks down the road singing a song of praise of himself. Attempting to flag down a ride, he stops the very car he stole from the inn, but the owners fail to penetrate his disguise. He tricks them into letting him drive and lands the car in a pond. Chased by the police, he leaps into the river, finds himself by Rat's hole, and is hauled in by his friend.

Warm and dry again, he starts to brag, but his friend silences him. He learns that, during his absence, the weasels, ferrets and stoats have taken over Toad Hall in spite of Badger's and Mole's brave attempts to save it. Toad tries to slip by the sentries but is turned back twice, the second time losing Rat's boat. He is scolded and, as usual, repents, but when Badger and Mole drop in he cannot resist boasting again. Badger rebukes him, then reveals that there is an underground passage from the river bank to the middle of Toad Hall. They plan an attack. While the usurpers are feasting unarmed at the birthday party of the Chief Weasel, they will sneak up on them through the tunnel. Donning Toad's washerwoman's

dress, Mole, pretending to be looking for work, remarks to the sentries that 100 blood-thirsty badgers, six boatloads of rats, armed to the teeth, and a picked body of toads are planning an attack, and that unless they clear out they will be slaughtered.

Chap. 12. At night the four friends, armed with pistols, sword, police truncheons, sandwiches, sticking plaster, and bandages, start down the tunnel to Toad Hall. They emerge in the dining room just as the Chief Weasel is singing a song ridiculing Toad. The weasels and ferrets, believing that hundreds of animals are attacking, flee in terror, and the four friends finish the birthday feast. Toad is chagrined be-

cause the animals were braver than he, but when Badger tells him he should have a banquet in honor of the homecoming, he begins to plan a program with himself as speaker, singer, and composer. He is told firmly that there are to be no songs or speeches in his own praise. At long last, Toad realizes that the others have done all the fighting and he is nothing but a braggart. The banquet is a great success; Toad is called on to speak, but he modestly refuses, and his friends see that this time he has really reformed. Toad sends presents to the jailer's daughter, the friendly train engineer, and even, with some prompting from the others, to the barge woman. The four animals settle down happily together in Toad Hall.

Winesburg, Ohio

Short stories by Sherwood Anderson, 1876–1941.
Published 1919 by B. W. Huebsch, New York. © 1947 by Eleanor Copenhaver Anderson. (NAL, 1304; ML, 104).

THIS COLLECTION OF STORIES was a sensational success when it was published and it is still the best-known work of Sherwood Anderson. In his later works Anderson strayed quite far from simple, straightforward writing (which is not to say that the quality of his work necessarily suffered) but in any case, he wrote *Winesburg, Ohio* before his style changed. It is quite easy to read and is yet very deep and penetrating in its study of the various types of person to be found in one small Ohio town. In his personal life Anderson was one of the most eccentric of all American writers. He suddenly gave up a prosaic but responsible job in a factory, deserted his wife and children, and went to Chicago to be a writer. He mixed with the fraternity of the best writers but assiduously avoided making any real friends.

The Book of the Grotesque. A writer, though an old man with a white mustache, has something young and visionary in him still. As he tries to go to sleep, the people he has known pass before him. They make such a deep impression on him that he writes a book that he calls "The Book of the Grotesque." In this book, he explains his philosophy. He believes that when things began in the world there were many thoughts but nothing like a truth. The truths were the putting together of many vague thoughts, and man made them himself. After that there were truths everywhere, and all of them were beautiful. The old man realizes that what people did with these beautiful truths made them "grotesque." This was very wrong and sad. What

happened was that as soon as anyone took a truth and possessed it and called it his own, and tried to make it his life, he became a grotesque, and the truth he tried to possess became a falsehood. This idea, the author says, had a tremendous effect on him, and he never forgot it, although the old writer never published his book, so it was only by chance that the author once saw "The Book of the Grotesque."

Hands. WING BIDDLEBAUM has not always been his name, and he has not always lived in Winesburg, Ohio. He got his name because of his hands. He is afraid of these hands and tries to keep them out of sight as much as he can. Wing Biddlebaum also seems to be afraid of people, but he likes the reporter, GEORGE WILLARD, and is able to talk to him. George senses that Wing's fear has to do with his hands, and he is correct. Wing used to be a schoolteacher in a Pennsylvania town, and his name was then Adolph Myers. He was a sensitive, gentle, kind person, and when he wanted to express himself he often used his hands. All his pupils loved him. Often he would stroke their shoulders or pat their heads. Then a half-witted boy began to think that he was in love with the kind teacher. At night, he imagined all sorts of strange things; then in the morning he told these things as if they had really happened. The parents of the pupils in Adolph Myers' class believed this half-witted boy, and they beat the teacher. They almost decided to hang him but instead drove him out of town. Wing Biddlebaum does not understand what really happened, but somehow he knows that his hands are the cause of the trouble, and he remembers the fathers of his pupils shouting about his hands and screaming at him to keep them to himself. Now Wing Biddlebaum's life is one of loneliness and fear, all because of his hands that never meant anybody any harm.

Mother. George Willard's mother, ELIZABETH, and his father, TOM, run an unprofitable "ghost" of a hotel in Winesburg. Tom Willard is one of those ordinary men who like to think they are big and important. He goes in for politics and shows off as much as he can. Elizabeth is a sad and defeated woman. She hoped that in her son, George, she would find her lost youth. When she was a girl, Elizabeth had many longings that she did not understand and without meaning to do anything wrong, got a reputation that was shaky. Her trouble was that she wanted to give something of herself to people and didn't know how to go about it. George feels a bond of sympathy with his mother, but they are uncomfortable with each other and cannot talk together. Elizabeth is determined that the creative thing in George must not be killed as it was in her. She feels that Tom will ruin him by constantly urging him to be a success. At last Elizabeth decides that to save her son she must kill her husband. Then one day George tells his mother that because of something his father said, George knows he must leave home. Elizabeth then understands that George will not be influenced by his father after all. She is filled with joy but she cannot tell George how she feels.

Godliness (Part I). The BENTLEY family have come to Ohio from New England. They are farmers. By the time the father and brothers of JESSE BENTLEY come into ownership of the Bentley property, most of the hard work of clearing the land has already been done, but the Bentleys still cling to old ways. They live a hard, brutal life. Jesse, however, who left home at 18 to become a scholar and a minister, is different. When Jesse's four brothers are killed in the Civil War and his mother dies, his father, old and discouraged, sends for Jesse. Jesse is so frail and sensitive that people smile at the idea of his handling the work done by his four strong brothers. Jesse surprises everybody. He is determined and drives everyone to work without mercy. The farm is successful, and Jesse gets the idea that he has been chosen by God. He prays to God to make him like the Jesse of the Bible so that he will rule other men and become the father of sons who will also rule other men. He has grown so greedy and arrogant that he cares for nobody. His wife wears herself out and dies giving birth to their daughter.

Godliness (Part II). Jesse Bentley's daughter, LOUISE, has a son, DAVID HARDY. David is not very happy at home, but he loves his grandfather's farm and goes to live there. Jesse is still torn between two desires: He wants to be a man of God and a leader of men, and he also wants to be rich, successful, and powerful. One day, Jesse and David drive through a forest, and Jesse remembers a night long ago when he prayed to God to give him a son. Jesse suddenly drops to his knees and begins to pray in a loud voice. David is terrified to see his grandfather behave in such a strange way. In his fright, the boy starts to run, falls, and strikes his head. As his grandfather drives David home he whispers to God, asking what it is that he has done that God does not approve of him.

Surrender (Part III). Louise Bentley Hardy was a lonely, moody, unhappy little girl, with no mother and a father who had wanted a son. She goes to live in town with the Hardy family. The Hardy girls are pretty and lively and have many beaux. This makes Louise feel lonelier than ever. She boldly writes a note to JOHN HARDY and tells him to meet her in the orchard at night, telling him she is lonely and wants to love and be loved. When Louise then finds she is going to have a child, she and John marry. Louise cannot talk to her husband and tell him what she feels, and gradually she becomes angry and bitter, especially with men. When her own baby turns out to be a boy, she refuses to nurse him and pushes him away from her. She tells her husband that because it is a man child it will get whatever it wants anyway.

Terror (Part IV). When David Hardy is 15 years old something happens that changes his entire life. Jesse, his grandfather, has a return of his religious fervor. He decides that he must go with David to the spot where long ago David hit his head on a rock while running in terror from Jesse. Together, Jesse and David must sacrifice a lamb to God. As Jesse prepares to butcher the lamb, David is suddenly filled with terror. He runs, and after him comes Jesse, knife in hand, prepared to slay the lamb. David picks up a stone, and, with his slingshot, he hits his grandfather, who falls to the ground. Thinking his grandfather is dead, David runs away. Nobody in Winesburg ever sees him again, and Jesse will never tell what happened. His only comment is that it happened because he was too greedy for glory.

Adventure. ALICE HINDMAN is 27 years old. She is a clerk in Winney's Dry Goods Store and lives with her mother and stepfather. Alice never thought she would be an old maid. When she was young she was deeply in love with NED CURRIE and he returned her love. Ned intends to rise in the world and to achieve his goal he must leave Winesburg. The night before he goes, he and Alice become lovers. A year passes, and Ned has forgotten Alice. She has not forgotten and still believes Ned will come back. She feels she could never marry anyone else, but still she is lonely. One dark, rainy night, Alice is seized with an irresistible desire. She feels that she must run naked through the streets with the rain on her body until she finds someone to love. She meets an old man and calls to him to wait, but he is so deaf he hardly hears her. In shame, Alice crawls home through the grass. Once more in her bed, she tries to face the fact that some people must live and die alone.

The Strength of God. The Rev. CURTIS HARTMAN has been pastor of the Presbyterian Church in Winesburg for ten years. He lives a good life, is married, does his work conscientiously, and does not think

Jesse falls to his knees

of other women. One Sunday, Hartman is at work on his sermon in the bell-tower room of the church. He sees a woman in the house next door. She is lying on a bed and she is smoking a cigarette. He is fascinated and shocked. Now begins a fierce struggle in the soul of Hartman—a struggle of the spirit and the flesh, of good and evil. Eventually one stormy night in January, Hartman endangers his health by going to the freezing bell-tower room to peep again. He sees a remarkable sight in the neighboring house. While he, who had come to watch and think sinful thoughts, looks on, he sees the woman weeping hysterically. She half rises and begins to pray. He is deeply affected and thinks that her figure is like that, on the leaded church window, of a boy in the presence of Christ. The Reverend Curtis Hartman feels that God has appeared to him through the woman and that he has seen the light.

The Untold Lie. RAY PEARSON and HAL WINTERS are farm hands. Ray is about 50 years old, with a wife (whose features have become sharp) and half a dozen thin children. Ray's life has not turned out as he planned. Hal is young, a hell-raiser, with his life before him. He becomes infatuated with a country schoolteacher and confides in Ray. The schoolteacher is going to have a baby and Hal wonders if he should marry her. Ray thinks of his own sad life and does not answer. Later, when his wife nags him, Ray decides he will tell Hal not to marry. On the way to town he meets Hal. Hal says he has decided he wants to marry the schoolteacher; he wants to have children and settle down. As Ray turns back toward home, he thinks of his own children and decides it is just as well he did not advise Hal. He feels that whatever he might have told him, either way, would have been untrue.

The Wizard of Oz

Novel by L. Frank Baum, 1856–1919. Published 1900.

THE FULL TITLE IS *The Wonderful Wizard of Oz*. Hardly a more popular children's book has ever been published and the book started a series that grew to 30 or more separate books about the adventures of the people of the Land of Oz. There are many good critics who cannot understand why librarians and school boards have almost unanimously refused to treat *The Wizard of Oz* and other Oz books as recommended reading for young children. The writing is good and the excellence of the story is attested by the fact that it made a great musical comedy (starring the famous Montgomery and Stone dancing pair) and at least one outstanding motion picture. The book is best for the age group of about 7 to 9.

Chaps. 1–4. DOROTHY, an orphan child who lives with her Uncle HENRY and Aunt EM on a bleak farm in Kansas, is standing at the door with her little dog, TOTO, when a cyclone begins. Instead of going to the cyclone hole, she goes to rescue Toto, who has run under the bed. The house, with child and dog in it, is carried off by the wind. For hours it sails through the air. Dorothy falls asleep, but wakes when the house is set down with a thump. She runs to the door and finds herself in a beautiful country. A delegation of queer little people greet her and thank her for killing the Wicked Witch of the East, on whom the house landed. Dorothy can see the witch's feet, shod in silver shoes, sticking out from below the house. The good Witch of the North, who is visiting, tells Dorothy to put on the silver shoes, which will protect her from harm. Dorothy asks how to get home to Kansas, and the good witch advises her to consult the Wizard of Oz. He lives in the Emerald City, which she can reach by following the yellow-brick road. On the road, Dorothy meets a Scarecrow, who accompanies her because he hopes the Wizard will give him some brains.

Chaps. 5–8. Dorothy and the Scarecrow come across an extraordinary man, made entirely of tin. He is rusted and cannot move until they oil his joints. When he can move his jaws, he tells them how the Wicked Witch of the East bewitched him, to prevent him from marrying his sweetheart, and he became a TIN WOODMAN. He has no heart now, and he asks if he can accompany Dorothy and the Scarecrow to the Wizard of Oz to get a heart. The three set off. The next morning, as they walk through the woods, a great lion leaps out. Dorothy, to protect Toto, slaps the lion on the nose. The lion explains that he is a

COWARDLY LION and would like to accompany them to Oz and ask the Wizard to give him courage. Soon they come to a great abyss, running across the road, and are pursued by fierce bear-bodied, tiger-headed animals called Kalidahs. The Cowardly Lion carries them over the ditch on his back. When they reach a river, the Tin Woodman makes a raft to take them across.

Chaps. 9–12. The raft leaves them at a great field of poppies; they start across. The heavy fumes put Toto and Dorothy to sleep. Realizing the danger, the Tin Woodman and the Scarecrow, immune to the fumes, carry Dorothy and Toto to safety but cannot carry the Lion. The Tin Woodman rescues a fieldmouse from a wildcat. It is the Queen of the Fieldmice. She summons so many fieldmice that they bring the Cowardly Lion to safety on a litter made by the Tin Woodman. The travelers stop at a farmhouse near the Emerald City. The farmer's wife tells them it is almost impossible to see the Wonderful Wizard of Oz. They reach the gates of the city, where they are given spectacles because the glory of the Emerald City will blind them unless their eyes are shielded. They arrive at the Palace, and each one sees the Wizard separately. To each he appears in a different form. He tells Dorothy if she will kill the Wicked Witch of the West he will grant all their petitions. They start out in search of the Wicked Witch, who rules the land of the Winkies. The Wicked Witch has only one eye but can see everywhere. Spying out the travelers, she sends a pack of wolves to devour them. The Tin Woodman kills all the wolves. Next, the Witch sends a flock of crows to peck out their eyes. The Scarecrow wrings the crows' necks. Finally the Witch uses her Golden Cap, which gives her power over the Winged Monkeys. The monkeys pick up the travelers and carry them to the Witch. She is frightened when she sees the Silver Shoes, for she cannot touch Dorothy as long as Dorothy is wearing them, but she sets Dorothy to work in her kitchen. When the Witch steals one of Dorothy's shoes, Dorothy throws a pail of water at her, and the Witch melts away. They are free at last.

Chaps. 13–16. The Witch had commanded the Winged Monkeys to drop the Tin Woodman on a rocky plain, where he now lies dented and disabled, to unstuff the Scarecrow, and to harness the Lion. The Winkies, grateful for being freed, rescue the friends, who start back to the Emerald City. Dorothy takes along the Golden Cap. Unable to find the way, Dorothy summons the Queen of the Fieldmice, who tells her to wish with the Golden Cap. Dorothy does and the Winged Monkeys appear and carry them to the Emerald City.

They are admitted to the Throne Room of the Wizard, and a great voice thunders, "I am Oz, the Great and Terrible. Why do you seek me?" Dorothy tells the voice the Witch has been destroyed. Toto, sniffing about, knocks over a screen, revealing a little man who admits that he is actually

not a wizard but a circus performer from Omaha. He was blown to Oz in a balloon. He gives the Lion a drink from a bottle labeled "Courage," and the Lion believes he is brave. A heart is supplied to the Tin Woodman, and a mixture of needles and pins, guaranteed to be brains, is put in the Scarecrow's head. The Wizard says the problem of getting Dorothy back to Kansas is not so easy, and that he must think about it.

Chaps. 17–20. The Wizard makes a balloon in which he and Dorothy can sail back home, but the balloon gets loose and leaves the ground with the Wizard in it before Dorothy can climb aboard. The Scarecrow becomes the ruler of the Emerald City. Dorothy summons the Winged Monkeys, but they cannot take her outside the magical country. A soldier suggests that Dorothy go to see GLINDA THE GOOD, Witch of the South. The friends start out next morning, are attacked by hostile trees, and travel through a country inhabited by Dresden china figurines, coming at last to a high china wall, over which they manage to climb.

Chaps. 21–24. They find themselves in a rough country full of bogs, forest, and underbrush. Dorothy is uneasy about the forest, but the Lion is delighted. He is made King of the Beasts by the animals there. Dorothy summons the Winged Monkeys for the last time, asking them to take her and her friends to Glinda's country. Glinda, the beautiful witch, receives them graciously and, after agreeing to return Dorothy to Kansas, asks the three others what they will do. The Scarecrow decides to return to Oz and rule there. The Tin Woodman wants to return to the country of the Winkies and rule there, and the Lion can hardly wait to return to the forest. Glinda kisses Dorothy goodbye and tells her to wish with her Silver Shoes. Before she knows it, Dorothy is safely back with Uncle Henry and Aunt Em. Somewhere on the journey home the Silver Shoes have dropped off.

The balloon leaves Dorothy

A Woman's Life

Novel by Guy de Maupassant, 1850–1893.
Published 1883.

THOUGH HE IS KNOWN chiefly for his short stories (and admittedly they are by far his best work), de Maupassant wrote numerous novels. *A Woman's Life* has been one of the two most popular in its English translation (the other being *Bel-Ami*). In French the title is *Une Vie, A Life*. This is a short novel, but it is written in de Maupassant's characteristic style in which much is expressed in few words.

Chaps. 1–3. It is the spring of the year 1819. JEANNE DES VAUDS is a girl of 17 who has been educated in a convent. Although her parents, Baron and Baroness des Vauds, were very wealthy, because of the baron's careless generosity and bad management the family is now forced to move to the Poplars, a chateau in Normandy. Jeanne looks forward eagerly to the freedom of life in the country that she loves. Jeanne meets a neighbor, the Vicomte JULIEN DE LAMARE. He is charming and very handsome. Julien soon becomes a frequent visitor at the Poplars and it is not long before he and Jeanne are betrothed.

Chaps. 4–5. After the marriage, the young couple start out on their wedding trip. Julien is poor but Jeanne's parents are eager only for their daughter's happiness and they do not mind. Jeanne before had only a girl's fancy for her husband but now she falls deeply and passionately in love with him. On their honeymoon trip she gives Julien her money, 2,000 francs, without giving the matter any thought. Later, when the couple are in Paris, Jeanne wishes to buy gifts for her parents. She asks Julien for her money. He returns only 100 francs. Jeanne is surprised but she says nothing.

Chaps. 6–7. The young couple returns home to Normandy. Jeanne begins to feel depressed and dull. She does not look forward to the routine of daily life; she misses the Mediterranean and feels miserable in the gray Normandy winter. Julien changes. His attitude toward money is greedy and miserly. He is cruel to the servants and this upsets Jeanne. He neglects his appearance and even sleeps apart from his wife. Jeanne grows more and more disillusioned. She is bored and hurt and angry with her husband. Then she makes a terrible discovery. Jeanne's illegitimate half-sister, ROSALIE, lives in the house as a servant. Rosalie is delivered of a child and Jeanne finds out that ever since he first came to the Poplars, Julien has been sleeping with the girl and it is Julien's baby that Rosalie bears. At first Julien denies everything. He even attempts to send Rosalie and the baby away. Jeanne, however, will not permit this. Finally Julien is forced to acknowledge the true facts when Rosalie wretchedly confesses everything before the Curé. Jeanne is now pregnant and for the sake of her child she agrees to remain with Julien. Rosalie is given a farm and the Baron des Vauds promises his daughter that he will help find a husband for Rosalie. A suitable peasant is bought to be Rosalie's husband and the father of Julien's child.

Chaps. 8–9. Rosalie leaves the Poplars and Jeanne and Julien continue their life together. They become friendly with the Count and Countess DE FOURVILLE and begin to spend much time with them. One day Jeanne is riding in the forest and comes upon the horses of Julien and the countess. She now knows that Julien and the countess are having an affair. She consoles herself with her little son, PAUL, and gives him all her love. Jeanne resolves never again will she allow herself to be disillusioned by the falseness and treacheries of people. She will in the future love only her child and her parents. Then Jeanne's mother dies. Among her mother's possessions Jeanne finds a letter that reveals that her mother had betrayed her father with the latter's best friend. Poor Jeanne is again disillusioned.

Chaps. 10–14. The Count de Fourville is very much in love with his beautiful wife. When he discovers that she has been unfaithful, he resolves to kill both her and Julien. Jeanne is pregnant again. The count carries out his resolve and the shock of Julien's death causes Jeanne's baby to be born dead. Now that Julien is dead, Jeanne thinks of him with love. She remembers only the happy days of their wedding trip. Paul is all she has left in life after her father dies. Paul grows up and it is plain to everyone but his mother that he is a worthless person. He spends all of Jeanne's money and becomes deeply involved with a scheming woman who keeps him apart from his mother. For many years Jeanne does not see her son, although she longs for him. At last, when Jeanne is ruined by Paul's extravagances and in poor health, the faithful Rosalie comes to her aid. Rosalie takes charge of everything. She insists that Jeanne sell the Poplars and she arranges for Jeanne to live in a comfortable little house. Rosalie looks after all of her affairs. Rosalie has never forgotten her half-sister's kindness of 25 years before. Things have gone well for Rosalie, while Jeanne is worn out and sick with loneliness for her son. After many weary months, she hears from Paul. His wife has died in childbirth and Paul has no one now to turn to but his mother. He begs her help. He wants Jeanne to take his child. The faithful Rosalie goes to fetch the baby and brings it back to Jeanne. Paul intends to follow after his wife's funeral. Jeanne is overwhelmed with emotion when she sees Paul's child. The practical Rosalie soothes her and comments that life is neither as good nor as bad as most people believe.

The World of the Thibaults

Novel by Roger Martin du Gard, 1881–1958.
Published 1922–40. © 1939 by Viking Press, New York. Translated from the French by Stuart Gilbert.

THIS VERY LONG NOVEL was published in eight parts over the course of 18 years. When it was nearly complete it won the Prix Goncourt and Martin du Gard was awarded the Nobel Prize in literature for 1937. The novel as a whole is the history of the disintegration of the entire cultural structure of the French middle class, culminating in World War I. Personal symbolism is used. The decay of one of the character's lungs is related to the decay of the body social; the emasculation of another character, through a war injury, is related to the emasculation of man in general. In the course of the novel Martin du Gard explores social standards and customs and shows the conflict of science and art and Catholicism and socialism. Like most novelists (and other artists) of his period, Martin du Gard was affected by the extravagant hopes for the new socialism that seemed to be making such progress until wars and authoritarian governments proved so better able to attract the allegiance of the proletariat.

Part I. Chaps. 1–9. OSCAR-MARIE THIBAULT has become a public figure through his welfare work and prominence in Catholic charities. He is a stern parent and disciplinarian. When his 13-year-old son JACQUES, who has been missing from home all day, fails to turn up by 9 o'clock in the evening, Thibault decides to undertake an investigation of Jacques' work at school, where he assumes the boy is being detained in punishment for some misconduct. From Abbé BINOT, the boy's master, he learns that Jacques has been missing from school all day. The Abbé suggests that whatever has happened has doubtless been due to the evil influence of another boy, DANIEL DE FONTANIN, a Protestant student at one of the city's boarding schools where corruption flourishes under every bench. The Abbé is quite certain that Jacques has run away with Daniel. Quite by accident, he has come across a secret copybook belonging to Jacques containing letters exchanged between the two boys, expressing sentiments more appropriate to members of opposite sexes. M. Thibault is horrified, even after he is assured that Jacques is the innocent dupe of Protestant depravity. Later when THÉRÈSE DE FONTANIN, Daniel's mother, comes to consult with M. Thibault and his eldest son, ANTOINE, about what action to take about the missing boys, she insists on the harmlessness of their friendship. The Abbé presents the letters as evidence and she reproaches him for prying into the secrets of children. Nevertheless, Mme. De Fontanin is worried. Daniel has been away from home for two days and his younger sister, JENNY, is bedridden with a fever. Her husband, JEROME, is away on "business," just when a man's authority is needed in the house. Thérèse goes to look for her husband at the home of his cousin and mistress, NOÉMIE PETIT-DUTREUIL, where she learns he has abandoned Noémie too and gone off on a holiday with her pretty maid. She writes him a note in care of the maid's address in Brittany and then sends for Pastor GREGORY, her minister. Jenny's illness has been diagnosed by Antoine Thibault, a successful physician, as meningitis, and the child's condition becomes hopeless. Pastor Gregory arrives and orders that doctors, nurses and medication be removed. Then by means of a strange combination of hypnotism and ecstatic religious exhortation, he effects a mystical cure.

Jacques and Daniel get as far as Marseilles, but lacking the proper papers they cannot ship out of the port. Their relationship, despite the Abbé's evil suspicions, is a chaste, typically adolescent compact against the hostility of their immediate environment. When they become separated in a quay brawl, Daniel spends the night with a motherly streetwalker and has his first sexual experience. He does not mention the episode to Jacques when they are reunited the next morning. The boys are thoroughly homesick by the time they are found by the police. Mme de Fontanin and Jenny welcome Daniel affectionately and without reproach. Antoine is relieved to see Jacques again and is sympathetic as always. But M. Thibault decides that his intractable son requires the sobering influence of a reformatory and Jacques is sent to an institution founded by his father.

Part II. Chaps. 1–12. Although M. Thibault has strictly forbidden it, Antoine undertakes a visit to the reformatory. He has heard stories about the brutality and neglect in such establishments and despite the false front that is put on for his benefit, and Jacques' stubborn refusal to complain, Antoine discovers his brother is being subjected to maltreatment. Antoine has promised to respect Jacques' secrecy and fear of reprisal, but he succeeds in gaining his

Antoine meets Rachel by chance and falls in love with her

father's consent to the boy's removal from the place. He assumes custody of his younger brother and takes a flat for this purpose. For the first time in his life, Jacques enjoys a liberal and intelligent home atmosphere. He begins to experience yearnings which must find their expression in love. His thoughts turn momentarily to GISÈLE, the niece of the Thibaults' housekeeper, who is a sort of an adoptive sister to him. Then one day, LISBETH, an Alsatian maid, turns up to take care of Antoine's flat and Jacques falls in love with her, unaware that she is going to bed with Antoine on the sly. On the basis of a few kisses, Jacques decides that he cannot live without Lisbeth and is determined to marry her and force her acceptance upon his father. M. Thibault has forbidden all communication between Jacques and Daniel but Jacques feels he must confide his new ecstasy in his friend. He persuades Antoine to lift the ban. Together they visit the de Fontanin household. Daniel seems changed, more mature but lacking his former intensity. He is so preoccupied with NICOLE PETIT-DUTREUIL that Jacques has no opportunity to tell him about his beautiful feeling for Lisbeth. Daniel is campaigning to seduce Nicole, who has been living with the de Fontanins since her mother, Noémie, went abroad to resume her affair with Jerome de Fontanin. Nicole rebuffs Daniel and Jacques is frustrated in his plans too, for Lisbeth goes off to marry a prosperous uncle in Strasbourg.

Part III. Chaps. 1–14. Jacques has passed his entrance exams for the École Normale with flying colors. He talks to Antoine about getting away from everything—from his fear of his father and from his memories of the reformatory. Antoine is accustomed to his brother's moodiness and scarcely listens. Jacques attempts to establish himself on a sentimental basis with Gisèle but the transition from comradeship to romance is difficult and he gives up. He next turns to Jenny, whose feelings toward men are not quite normal, after the conditioning she has received from her father's endless desertions and returns. Her object in life is to remain aloof from men entirely, avoiding her mother's kind of anguish. Deliberately she stifles the first signs of vulnerability that

Jacques succeeds in arousing in her.

Antoine, who is accustomed to taking his pleasure with women where he finds it, suddenly falls in love with RACHEL GOEPFERT, whom he meets by chance. Rachel is handsome, worldly, and unconventional. Early in her affair with Antoine she informs him that she is through with "established" relationships. All she values in life is the freedom to do as she pleases. Antoine is fascinated all the more with her. Most of her affairs center upon a lover, now in the Sudan, an international adventurer called HIRSCH, who emerges from Rachel's stories a fabulous and monstrous figure, perverse and perverted, rich and powerful. Hirsch has taken refuge in the Sudan to escape the French police, who suspect him of complicity in the death of his daughter and son-in-law during an incestuous honeymoon. Rachel protests that she hates Hirsch, but he has much the same power over her that only death could break for his daughter. When he cables her to join him, she finds herself incapable of resistance. She pretends to Antoine that she must go away to look after the oil interests that are the source of her income and she promises to return in a month or two. Antoine accompanies her to her boat at Le Havre and when he notices "R.H." on her luggage, he realizes the truth. Rachel does not deny it and they part tenderly.

Part IV. Chaps. 1–13. Gisèle has returned to Paris on a visit from London, where she has been going to school. Antoine, finding her in Jacques' deserted room in the Thibault house, tells her that M. Thibault is dying of cancer. No word is spoken about Jacques, who has disappeared and has been given up for dead by his father and brother for the past 3 years. Gisèle is convinced that Jacques is still alive. She received a private signal from him on her birthday, more than 2 years ago—an anonymous hamper of roses, sent from London, of a particular variety that has special reference to a romantic episode between Gisèle and Jacques. This was her reason for going to London to study.

Part V. Chaps. 1–12. M. Thibault's illness is in its final stage. His intervals of lucidity are punctuated by delusions of persecution and reversions to childhood memories. Antoine receives a letter addressed to Jacques, from a correspondent who apparently has never heard he is thought dead. It contains a personal literary comment, by Professor JALICOURT of the Academy, on a recently published story by Jacques. To Antoine it seems to be a definite indication that his brother is still alive. Through Jalicourt Antoine learns more about his brother's disappearance, which took place on a week-end Antoine spent with Rachel in her house. Jacques had quarreled with his father over his refusal to attend the École Normale and had run out of the house threatening to kill himself. Through Jalicourt and the Swiss magazine in which Jacques' story appeared, Antoine has little difficulty in tracing Jacques. He goes to Switzerland to fetch Jacques to their father's bedside. Jacques receives the news of his father's impending death with a callousness that surprises Antoine, but he does agree to return. Jacques' boyishness has gone and he behaves with a new determination and authority.

Part VI. Chaps. 1–14. During Antoine's absence, M. Thibault's suffering has become frightful. Due to complications, he can no longer have morphine. He is repeatedly thrown into coma by the sheer intensity of the pain. Jacques cannot tell if his father is aware of his presence in the room. M. Thibault lingers in agony, but both sons agree it must end and Antoine injects a fatal dose of morphine into his father's arm.

When Gisèle comes to Paris to pay her last respects, she sees Jacques again. He has no desire to accept her love or to return it. The roses merely referred to a moment of adolescent tenderness. After the funeral Jacques visits the reformatory and when he is ready to leave, he feels he has succeeded in purging himself of his past.

Summer 1914

Part I. Chaps. 1–2. Jacques is living and writing in Geneva. He has become an adherent of international socialism, the popular political philosophy of *avant garde* intellectuals who have come to Switzerland from all over Europe. The leader of this movement is MEYNESTREL, who owes his original fame to his identification with the pioneer days of aviation; in the Party he is still called "The Pilot." His political knowledge is profound and his revolutionary experience wide and varied. Jacques cannot bring himself to accept Meynestrel's incendiary views; he finds violence and brutality unjustifiable. Despite his dialectical difference with Meynestrel, he stays with the movement. He is in Vienna on a mission during the shooting of Archduke Francis Ferdinand at Sarajevo and he returns to Geneva with the news from the Austrian Socialist leadership that "if things are allowed to drift," the Pilot can expect Europe to be involved in a great war within months.

Chaps. 13–24. Jacques is sent to Paris to sound out the feelings and opinions of the French left wing on the possibility of war. He looks up Antoine, who has turned into merely a newer version of their father. Jacques admits to Antoine that he is a revolutionary and finds himself in the course of argument, unwittingly taking on Meynestrel's jargon. Antoine accuses him of Utopianism. They are interrupted by a servant announcing Jenny de Fontanin. She has come to fetch Antoine to Jerome de Fontanin, who has wounded himself in a suicide attempt. Jacques sees Jenny several times after this but while he is roused by old memories, she maintains the old hauteur.

Part II. Chaps. 1–13. Jacques shuttles back and forth between Geneva and Paris, with side trips to other cities. His Party missions are to seek the allegiance of minority and split parties to the growing socialist strength and to stem the momentum of the approaching cataclysm by persuading an organized proletariat to refuse to work on materials of war.

Chaps. 14–30. Jerome de Fontanin's wounds finally cause his death and Jacques arrives in Paris just as the funeral is taking place. He is thrown once more into Jenny's company and now he is determined to break down her resistance. After his experience in the political world and with his natural insight into human behavior and motivation, he understands what lies behind Jenny's frigidity. He overwhelms it by the sheer force of his own personality. His visits are welcomed by Jenny. Mme. de Fontanin, an impulsive woman, has decided to ignore the threat of war and put an end to the ugly rumors about her late husband's foreign peculations by investigating, in person, the state of his financial affairs in Vienna. The Socialist movement, which now numbers 12 million, has taken to holding meetings at which its followers are urged to wage revolution but *not* war.

Part III. Chaps. 1–31. In France preparation for mobilization has begun. Russia has blocked British efforts at mediation. The pacifist meetings go on in Paris, in a desperate attempt to postpone the inevitable. Jenny, who has accepted Jacques' ideology along with his love, attends these meetings. Jacques has been exempted from conscription because of a heart condition, but Antoine thinks it will be Jacques' duty to go into the army. Jacques asserts that he will fight against the war with revolution and sabotage, but will never wear a uniform. The next Sunday, Aug. 2, 1914, a general mobilization notice is posted in Paris. Returning to Paris on the last train from Vienna, Mme. de Fontanin finds Jenny and Jacques asleep in the same bed. Fleshly experience seems so remote from Jenny's character that at first Mme. de Fontanin almost believes the young couple have been murdered. The truth of the situation drives her out of the house and she does not return until days later. Then they are getting ready to leave for Switzerland, where Jenny plans to participate in Jacques' work. Mme. de Fontanin has no success in discouraging Jenny from her plans. Then, suddenly, at the last moment Jenny decides not to go. She must release Jacques for the sake of the future and in the name of civilization. He must be left free to carry out his world-shaking plans with Meynestrel. Jacques accompanies the Pilot on a flight to shower French and German soldiers with millions of leaflets, calling for them to lay down their arms. The plane is an old one and crashes behind the French lines. Meynestrel is burned to death. Jacques wakes up badly hurt and a prisoner of the French, who assume him to be a spy. He is shot to death by a gendarme.

Part IV. Chaps. 1–14. and Epilogue. Antoine, who has felt so moralistic about fighting in the war, is severely gassed. His knowledge of medicine is such that he knows the truth of his condition. In his detached scientific way, he reconciles himself to death. Mme. de Fontanin has found escape in the routine of running a hospital. She has also become a grandmother with the birth of JEAN-PAUL, Jenny's son by Jacques. The boy becomes Jenny's consuming interest in life and also provides a few pathetic responsibilities for Daniel de Fontanin, who has returned from the war a damaged man, emasculated by a shell splinter and left with the temperament of a nursery-maid. Antoine returns to the army hospital to which he has been retired from the field and continues to serve science and his profession. He keeps a diary in which he becomes his own case history, making a detailed study of the various stages in the decay-rate of his poisoned lungs. It is part of the essential irony of the disintegration of the world of the Thibaults, that Antoine must die without ever knowing that the Armistice has already been signed.

Wuthering Heights

Novel by Emily Brontë, 1818–1848. Published 1847. (PB, PL10; ML, 106 & T4; RE, 23)

SOMERSET MAUGHAM named *Wuthering Heights* one of the four best English novels and one of the world's ten best. It is a profound story, with interesting characters fully developed and with writing that endows the telling of the story with the mood of the dismal moors on which the action is set. Members of the very talented Brontë family never wrote anything bad, but *Wuthering Heights* has a distinction that places it in that rare class of great books that can still be set apart from other great books because they have something extra. *Wuthering Heights* was not a success at first; its hold on the reading public grew slowly before it eventually was established as a prime classic. Still it can capture a reader as few books can and one who starts it will not regret it.

Chaps. 1–3. The first narrator, Mr. LOCK-WOOD, an urbane young gentleman, tenant of Thrushcross Grange on the Yorkshire moors, pays a visit to his landlord, Mr. HEATHCLIFF, the novel's hero, at the lonely house at Wuthering Heights. He finds the house and its occupants uncouth and savage. Heathcliff himself gives him an inhospitable welcome. He also sees the old servant, JOSEPH, and the maid, ZILLAH, who rescues him from the savage dogs that molest him. On a second visit, however, he meets a beautiful and arrogant young woman, whom he mistakenly takes for Heathcliff's wife, and a young man of rough appearance and proud bearing, whom he takes for his son. Heathcliff reveals that the young woman, CATHERINE, is his daughter-in-law, that his son is dead, and that the young man is HARETON EARNSHAW, a name Lockwood has already observed carved over the porch of the house. Lockwood is refused either hospitality or a guide home through the snow, and, enraged by the preachings of the sanctimonious Joseph, and the brutal indifference of the others, seizes a lantern and departs. After being attacked by the dogs, however, he is finally given a room by Zillah. That night, he finds the names Catherine Earnshaw, Catherine Linton, and Catherine Heathcliff, scrawled on the windowpane, and diary notes by the same child, telling of alliances with Heathcliff and enmity with Catherine's brother, HINDLEY, his wife, and Joseph. Lockwood then falls into a nightmare and fancies he wakes to find this Catherine trying to enter the room. His cry of terror brings Heathcliff in in a rage, which changes mysteriously when he hears of Catherine. Lockwood retires to the kitchen until day, when he returns home.

Chaps. 4–5. Lockwood hears more of the family at Wuthering Heights from his housekeeper, ELLEN DEAN. She tells him that an EDGAR LINTON owned Thrushcross and married CATHERINE EARNSHAW (the CATHY of the dream), that Heathcliff married Edgar Linton's sister, ISABELLA; that in the next generation Cathy's daughter, the Catherine now living at Wuthering Heights, married Heathcliff's son, her cousin; and that Hareton Earnshaw is the nephew of the first Catherine and the son of her brother Hindley. Mrs. Dean then begins her story, telling how Cathy's and Hindley's father brings Heathcliff, a foundling, home from Liverpool when all three are children and how an immediate alliance grows up between Heathcliff and Cathy against Hindley.

Chaps. 6–10. On the father's death, Hindley inherits the property and devotes himself to his young wife. Cathy and Heathcliff, both uncontrollable, passionate, and courageous, run wild, and on one of their escapades Cathy is bitten by the bulldog at Thrushcross and taken in by the Linton family. During her convalescence, she becomes friendly with Edgar and Isabella, and through their flattery and example tries to act as a young lady, rather than as a tomboy. When she returns home she ridicules Heathcliff in front of Edgar. Heathcliff, who throws a bowl of hot apple sauce at him, is beaten by Hindley and vows revenge.

Soon after Hindley's son Hareton is born, his wife dies, and Hindley degenerates rapidly into a dipsomaniac. Heathcliff involuntarily saves Hareton from death, when Hindley in a drunken fury attacks his son and Mrs. Dean with a carving knife. Immediately afterward, he overhears Cathy say that, although she loves him, it would degrade her to marry him, and that she is going to marry Edgar Linton. When Cathy realizes Heathcliff has heard her, she searches wildly for him in a downpour of rain. She subsequently contracts a fever and is taken to convalesce at Thrushcross, where she is humored by all her relatives, and later marries Edgar. Heathcliff disappears.

Chaps. 10–16. Linton and Cathy are happily married for some months before Heathcliff returns to Wuthering Heights and reintroduces himself to Cathy at Thrushcross. She is ecstatic at his return and sees him often, as does Isabella, who falls in love with Heathcliff and is ridiculed for it by both of them. Nevertheless, Heathcliff pays her court because she is her brother's heir and to revenge himself on Cathy for marrying Linton. The situation provokes a quarrel between Heathcliff, Linton, and Cathy, and Cathy in her fury starves herself and brings on a second illness, this time becoming deranged. Meanwhile, Heathcliff elopes with Isabella. Cathy is ill for two months, but, devotedly nursed by Linton, makes a temporary recovery in the spring. Isabella, now living at Wuthering Heights,

tells in a letter to Mrs. Dean how Hindley has gambled his fortune into Heathcliff's hands; how the child, Hareton, is an uncared-for savage, tended only by the sanctimonious Joseph; that the house is unkempt; and that Heathcliff is brutal to her. Mrs. Dean goes to see her, and tells Heathcliff of Cathy's illness. He passionately demands to see Cathy, refuses to believe it will harm her, and forces Mrs. Dean by his threats to take a letter to her. Four days later Cathy receives the letter, and the name of Heathcliff restores her for the last time to reason and animation. Heathcliff arrives at the same time, and there follows a passionate scene of mutual upbraiding, when Heathcliff claims that Cathy has brought about their mutual misery and her own death by betraying their love and marrying Linton. Linton returns home to find Cathy unconscious; she dies in the night, in giving premature birth to her daughter, the younger Catherine. Heathcliff hears of her death from Mrs. Dean and in his agony curses Cathy and calls on her to haunt him. Cathy is buried in the churchyard, in neither the Linton nor the Earnshaw family vault.

Chap. 17. That same evening Isabella, though pregnant, runs away from Heathcliff and goes to Mrs. Dean, where she discloses the details of her life with him, recounting a fight between the drunken Hindley and the grief-crazed Heathcliff, in which Hindley receives a knife-wound. She goes to live near London, where she has a son, LINTON. Six months later Hindley dies and Mrs. Dean, fearing for his son Hareton under Heathcliff's care, finds that the Wuthering Heights estate is mortgaged to Heathcliff, who intends to bring up Hareton himself.

Chaps. 18–30. Young Catherine grows up under Mrs. Dean's care. At the age of 13, eager to go beyond the bounds of Thrushcross, she visits Wuthering Heights and encounters her cousin Hareton, now an uncouth and ignorant oaf, degraded by Heathcliff. Soon afterward Isabella dies and her son Linton, a sickly, sulky boy, a little younger than Catherine, comes to Thrushcross but is promptly claimed by his father, Heathcliff. At 16, Catherine again visits Wuthering Heights, encountering Heathcliff and her two cousins, Linton and Hareton. Her father is displeased and forbids her to go again, but Linton sends her secret love letters, which Ellen Dean discovers and forbids. Catherine again meets Heathcliff, who tells her that Linton is dying for love of her, and she visits the boy in secret and finds him consumptive but ill-humored, imperious, and quarrelsome. Hareton is violently jealous of this friendship. Mrs. Dean finds out about the visits and forbids them, but Catherine and Linton still meet on the moors. Though Linton is now mortally ill, Heathcliff forces him to pay court to Catherine. She is eventually tricked into going to Wuthering Heights, where she is kept a prisoner and forced to marry the dying and tyrannical Linton. She escapes only in time to see her father die. By this death and by

Catherine's marriage to Linton, Heathcliff is now master of Thrushcross as well as Wuthering Heights. He forces Catherine to return to Wuthering Heights (where she tends Linton until he too dies) and receives the first narrator, Mr. Lockwood, as tenant of Thrushcross, where Mrs. Dean is again housekeeper. Zillah, the maid at Wuthering Heights, tells how Catherine becomes proud and reserved and repels Hareton's clumsy attempts at friendship and sympathy.

Chaps. 30–34. Here, Mr. Lockwood resumes the narrative, and calls at Wuthering Heights, where he finds Catherine bored and miserable. Hareton is teaching himself to read, though angry at Catherine's scorn. Heathcliff shows himself distressed by the resemblance in both Catherine and Hareton to the dead Cathy and by the real power and worth of Hareton's character, despite the attempts Heathcliff has made to debase it.

A year later, Lockwood revisits Thrushcross and finds great changes at Wuthering Heights. Mrs. Dean has moved there, the house has been repaired, Catherine is teaching Hareton to read, and they are obviously in love, though Joseph laments their "wickedness" in being happy. Mrs. Dean tells Lockwood that she returned the previous year to find that Heathcliff's nature had spent its force, his hold on Catherine had weakened, and a friendship had begun between Catherine and Hareton. Heathcliff, observing it, and the likeness in both to Cathy, realized that his struggle to eradicate the taint of the Linton blood was over. His obsession with the dead Cathy grew so strong that he fancied her spirit was visible to him, he could take no food or rest, and finally he died in his sleep. He is buried beside Cathy in the churchyard, and their spirits are said to be seen on the moors.

Xenophon's Anabasis

History by Xenophon, 430–355 B.C. Written between 399 and 394 B.C.

THE GREEK WORD *anabasis* means "the going up." As used for the title of Xenophon's book, it probably refers to the fact that a Greek army went up from their homes into Persia to fight a war; but the fame and interest of the book derives far more from their going *back*—their retreat from Cunaxa near the Persian capital, Babylon, back to Europe and Grecian territory (then ruled by Sparta). ⓵ The Greek army was a collection of mercenaries from various Greek countries and colonies, each national group led by its own officers. Xenophon, an Athenian, was not originally one of the officers. He was a civilian who went along as an adviser. But when crisis came he showed his qualities of leadership and took effective though not official command. The Greek army is traditionally called "the Ten Thousand," but its actual numbers ranged from 13,000 at the peak to perhaps 8,000 at the end of the retreat. The campaign began in 401 B.C. The retreat began in the fall of 400 B.C., when Xenophon was 30 years old; it took the Greeks five months to cover about 500 miles, through cold and snow, and reach the Euxine or Black Sea; then the better part of another year to cover some 700 more miles to the straits of the Bosporus. ⓵ Xenophon's writing is more admired for its history than for its literary quality, but he had the gifts of simplicity and clarity and the *Anabasis* is easy to read —except, perhaps, for the generations of schoolboys for whom it was as traditional a Greek text as is Caesar in Latin.

Book I. 1. When Darius died, his elder son ARTAXERXES became king. His younger son CYRUS was falsely denounced for plotting by TISSAPHERNES (who Cyrus had thought was his friend) and was sentenced to death by Artaxerxes; but their mother, PARYSATIS, interceded and Cyrus was sent back to the Northwest, where he had been military commander in the time of Darius. Determined never again to be endangered by Artaxerxes, and to overthrow him, Cyrus built up a great army of Greeks (of various nations) in this secret way: Wherever an army was needed to keep order, or for a campaign, Cyrus raised a much larger army than was needed and overpaid the commanders to win their support. (All the soldiers were mercenaries.) There were various armies under CLEARCHUS, a Spartan exile; ARISTIPPUS of Thessaly; PROXENUS of Boeitia; SOPHAENETUS the Stymphalian; and SOCRATES the Achaean. Since there was good reason for each army, the King suspected nothing. 2. When his plans were complete, Cyrus assembled his armies, those named above and others under XENIAS the Arcadian, PASION the Megarian, SOSIS the Syracusan, and others. When the armies began to assemble, at Sardis in Asia Minor, Tissaphernes suspected Cyrus's plan and warned the King, who prepared to defend himself. Cyrus's army proceeded in marches of two or three days each. The army now numbered 11,000 hoplites (heavily armed infantrymen) and 2,000 peltasts (lightly armed). The queen of Cilicia, EPYAXA, supported Cyrus and gave him money. Her husband, King SYENNESIS, first opposed him but was won over by Epyaxa and he also gave Cyrus money. 3. But Cyrus was running out of money; the soldiers were unpaid and Clear-chus's large army mutinied—partly because they suspected that they were marching against the King, which was not in the terms of their enlistment. Clearchus supported his men. Cyrus pacified them with promises and a 50% pay increase. He still said they were not marching against the King and they accepted this but were still suspicious. 4. The march continued. After a few weeks Cyrus told the Greek generals that they were marching against the King. The soldiers refused to continue without higher pay, which Cyrus granted. They crossed the Euphrates, the first time it had been done on foot; ABROCOMAS, with one younger son CYRUS was falsely denounced for plotting by TISSAPHERNES (who Cyrus across the Arabian desert. A soldiers' quarrel almost caused a fight between Clearchus and Menon and their forces, but Cyrus reconciled them. 6. ORONTAS, a leader in Cyrus's Persian forces, wrote a letter to the King. It was intercepted and after a solemn trial Orontas was sentenced to death., but none of the Greeks saw him die. 7. In Babylonia, Cyrus's and the King's forces approached each other. Cyrus won over the doubtful Greeks by promising them more money and their leaders various satrapships after victory. Cyrus had 100,000 native troops plus the 13,000 Greeks. The King had 1,200,000 men in four armies of 300,-000 each, led by Abrocomas, Tissaphernes, GOBRYAS, and ARBACES; only 900,000 of these were at the battlefield, Abrocomas being five days' march away. Cyrus considered the Greek professional soldiers worth many times their number in native troops. The King's armies delayed fighting until Cyrus and his generals believed the King would not fight. 8. After some days the Battle of Cunaxa was fought. The Greeks were in the center and easily withstood vastly superior numbers. Cyrus saw the King and attacked him personally; he wounded the King but a javelin struck Cyrus under the eye and killed him. His faithful servant. ARTAPATAS leaped on Cyrus and died with him. 9. Cyrus's character is discussed: He was most kinglike of the Persians and most deserving of an empire. He was just and generous, but severe to evil-doers. He had many friends and no one was ever more generally beloved. 10. There was much looting by the King's forces but the Greeks guarded their baggage and fought on as though they were winning. They did not know Cyrus was dead.

Book II. 1. The following morning the Greeks learned that Cyrus was dead and that ARIAEUS, Cyrus's second in command, had fled. Cyrus sent word to Ariaeus that the Greeks would fight for him if he came to them, and would make him king. Then envoys arrived from the King, inviting the Greeks to surrender their arms and submit to the King. The Greeks refused to surrender their arms, but temporarily there was a truce. 2. Ariaeus sent word that he was going back (westward) and invited the Greeks to join him. Clearchus had become the leader of all the Greeks. For one

645

day the Greeks followed Ariaeus, but that night they found they had marched directly toward a camp of the King's army. The Greeks did not attack, for the men were tired and had no food, but they did not turn aside. They camped for the night. That night the King's army withdrew. 3. Apparently the King feared the Greeks, for the next morning he sent envoys to discuss terms. Clearchus refused to talk until the Greeks were fed, so the King's men led them to a village where they were well fed. Tissaphernes and the King's brother-in-law next came as envoys. Clearchus told them that the Greeks had not known they were marching against the King. Tissaphernes went to consult with the King, and after some days returned to say that the Greeks would be allowed to return home peaceably, if they would not plunder on the way, and that he would go with them. The Greeks accepted and it became a treaty. 4–5. The Greeks waited, suspicious both of Ariaeus, camped nearby, and the King, who might be waiting only until he could bring up a large army. After 20 days Tissaphernes arrived with his army, to go home, and with him Orontas, who had not been put to death by Cyrus. The armies began their march and despite various fears and rumors they marched for some weeks, crossing the Tigris. Clearchus saw Tissaphernes to try to clear up the suspicions. Tissaphernes assured Clearchus that he had no designs against the Greeks and asked Clearchus to bring all the generals and captains to hear for themselves. Clearchus brought 5 generals and 20 captains. Tissaphernes treacherously captured the generals and slaughtered the captains and soldiers who had come with them. When the Greeks heard this they sprang to arms, expecting an attack, but none came. They learned that Ariaeus had betrayed them, going over to the King. 6. The generals Clearchus, Proxenus, AGIAS and Socrates (the Achaean) were beheaded; MENON was punished more severely, being held prisoner for a year as a common criminal before dying.

Book III. 1–2. XENOPHON the Athenian had gone on the expedition not as an officer or soldier but as a friend of Proxenus. Now he took the lead in urging that the Greeks have no more dealings with the natives, who could not be trusted, but that they start home, fighting their way when necessary. The Greeks accepted Xenophon as a leader. He warned that discipline and bravery must be at the highest level if they were to have any chance of getting through. CHIRISOPHUS the Spartan was elected to lead the vanguard and TIMASION and Xenophon, the youngest generals, to command the rear. 3. Mithridates treacherously tried to parley as a friend, though he was actually sent by the King. Then Mithridates attacked, and because his archers had longer range than the Greek archers he did some damage to the Greeks but was driven back. 4. With a larger force he attacked again and this time there was a battle, the Greeks winning. The Greeks mutilated the dead

A soldier complains

left behind by Mithridates, to cause fear in the natives. The Greeks marched on, now pursued by Tissaphernes and his army, who harassed them from the rear. The Greeks came to a mountain and it was important to command the summit. Xenophon led a Greek detachment to take it. When a soldier complained that Xenophon was mounted while he had to carry a heavy shield, Xenophon leapt from his horse, took the soldier's shield, and led the advance on foot. The other soldiers forced the complainant to take back the shield and Xenophon to remount. The Greeks won the summit and the Persian army fled. 5. The Persians began to burn their own villages— something the Greeks had promised not to do. But now the Greeks did so also. At a conference, the Greek generals decided to take the difficult northern route over the mountains, through the territory of the Carduchi—a warlike people, enemies of the King, but not unfriendly to Greeks who came in peace—and thence into Armenia, a domain of Orontas.

Book IV. 1–2. The Carduchi resisted the Greek crossing of their territory, though the Greeks tried to be friendly. The Carduchis' only weapons were bows and slings, but their bows were 4 to 5 ft. long and their arrows, more than 3 ft. long, would pierce the Greek armor. The Greeks crossed the territory in 7 days, fighting all the way and losing more men than in all their previous engagements. 3. The Greeks camped on the river Cantrites, the border of Armenia. Armenian cavalry drew up on the other side to prevent their entrance. Xenophon had a dream that was taken as a good omen: He dreamed he was fettered but the fetters dropped off. Two soldiers found a new ford down the river. Chirisophus started across with the vanguard, while Xenophon pretended to lead the rear at high speed back to the regular ford so as to cut off the Armenian cavalry. The ruse worked. the Armenians rushed to the regular ford, and Xenophon returned to the new ford. The Carduchis attacked the rear but were frightened away by another ruse, when Xenophon's trumpeter sounded the attack. Xenophon then crossed after Chirisophus. 4. The Greeks march through

Armenia. In Western Armenia the governor, TIRIBAZUS, offered to let them pass if they would spare his villages. The Greek generals agreed. They marched on through the mountains, hampered by heavy snows. Learning from a scouting party and a captured prisoner that Tiribazus planned to attack them in a narrow pass, the only way through the mountains, they attacked first, put the natives to flight, and destroyed the camp of Tiribazus. 5. They continued through deep snow, crossing the Euphrates near its source. Xenophon had a hard time keeping men from dropping behind, from weariness and sickness. They reached a group of villages, where they were hospitably received and fed; in one village the dwellings were built underground, reached by ladder for men and tunnels for animals. 6. The Greeks continued through the mountains to the pass into the plains of the Chalybes. The pass was strongly held. Xenophon devised a plan to "steal" the mountain heights above the pass by night. He did so, and the enemy then abandoned the pass and the Greeks descended into the fertile plains with its rich villages. 7–8. In the land of the Taochi the natives had fortifications from which they rolled down heavy rocks on attackers. Xenophon's strategy was to have his men feint advance, then duck behind trees when the stones came down. So the Taochi used up their stones without doing much damage. Rather than be captured, the Taochi jumped from the heights; the women threw their children down before themselves. Marches through the lands of the friendly Macrones and the unfriendly Colchians brought the Greeks to Trapezus, on the Black Sea. The people here sold them food and made them gifts. The Greeks rejoiced and had athletic games, under Dracontius the Spartan, to celebrate.

Book V. 1–2. Some of the Greeks, tired of marching, proposed a return to Greece by sea. Chirisophus and others were delegated to seek ships. The others, in detachments led by officers, made plundering expeditions into enemy territory nearby, for food they would need whether they sailed or marched home. 3. Chirisophus did not return and the Greeks had only one ship, though it was a large one. They put on this the sick, the older men (over 40), and women and children. The rest began the march home. Account of them was taken: There were now 8,600, most of the others having died in battle, or of cold or sickness. They divided the money they had obtained by selling prisoners. Years later, Xenophon was to use part of this money to buy himself a large estate near Olympia [on the Peloponnesus]. 4–5. The Greeks were opposed by the Mossynoici, a barbarous people; so they allied themselves with another Mossynoici nation, which was at war with the first, and fought their way through. They marched through the countries of the Chalybes and Tibareni, meeting some friendly and some hostile peoples, until they came to Cotyora, a Greek city, a colony of the seaport Sinope. The city would not take them in, so they camped near it for 45 days, sacrificing to the gods and holding athletic games. They lived off the country-side, and ambassadors came from Sinope to protest this. Xenophon told them it was because Cotyora had shut its gates to them. After this the ambassadors assured them of friendship and the city of Cotyora sent gifts. 6–8. Wishing to go now by sea, the Greeks sent representatives to Sinope to ask for ships. Meanwhile Xenophon proposed founding a new city nearby. Merchants of the cities of Heraclea and Sinope, who were afraid to have such a powerful army quartered near them, offered the generals Timasion, Eurymachus and Thorax money to oppose Xenophon's plan and persuade all the Greeks to return. At a soldiers' meeting, however, Xenophon himself proposed that all the Greeks return home, and that any deserter be punished, and this was agreed. But the other generals still tried to stir up trouble for Xenophon, till he called all the soldiers together, spoke to them, and won their support. Some of the generals were deposed and Xenophon's right to discipline the men was confirmed.

Book VI. 1. The Greeks progressed through Paphlagonia, coming to terms with CORYLAS, the governor, and fraternizing with the natives. Having enough ships, they then sailed along the coast to Harmene, the port of Sinope, where Chirisophus joined them with a trireme obtained from his friend ANAXIBIUS the Spartan admiral. At this point the soldiers decided they would like to have one supreme commander—previously matters had been decided by a vote of the generals. They elected Xenophon, but he refused, saying the omens were not propitious. Then they elected Chirisophus, who accepted. 2. They sailed on to Heraclea, where the people sent gifts of food, but the soldiers decided to demand from the city 10,000 staters [gold coins, the total value demanded being at least $100,000]. Chirisophus and Xenophon opposed bringing pressure on a friendly city, but the soldiers sent representatives to the city anyway. The Heracleans promptly shut their gates and prepared for a siege. The soldiers blamed the generals and the Peloponnesians—Achaeans and Arcadians, about half the total men—formed an independent army. The Spartans and the Thracians stayed with Chirisophus, whose supreme command thus ended after six or seven days. The Peloponnesians sailed; then Xenophon sailed with the Athenians and others who stayed with him, and the third army, under Chirisophus, waited for some triremes he had been promised by CLEANDER, governor of Byzantium. 3. The Peloponnesians landed at Calpe in Chalcedon and went out to seek booty, but the natives won a victory and besieged their camp. Chirisophus and Xenophon landed safely in the same area. When Xenophon discovered the plight of the Peloponnesians he led his army to the camp and rescued them. 4. Another meeting was

held and the soldiers voted death to anyone who again proposed splitting the army. Chirisophus had died of a fever and NEON of Asine took his place. The army was reunited but was short of food and threatened by the enemy. 5. The enemy attacked but Xenophon's plan of battle was successful and the Greeks won. 6. The Greeks waited for the promised triremes. There was plenty of food. Cleander arrived with the triremes but no transports. Cleander became displeased with the Greeks and was going to withdraw his friendship, but Xenophon pacified him. Cleander sailed back to Byzantium, promising the Greeks a welcome there. The Greeks marched on.

Book VII. 1–2. The Greeks crossed the straits (Bosporus) to Byzantium (an outpost of Sparta). They were not welcome but had no money to go on. Xenophon wanted to leave them and go home, but Cleander and Anaxibius persuaded him to stay to keep peace until the Army was out of the city. The Greeks wanted to take over the city and make Xenophon king, but Xenophon convinced them that this would be unwise. Xenophon then sent to Anaxibius to ask for food and money for the men, but meanwhile a Theban named COIRATIDAS persuaded the Greeks to invade Thrace for booty, and they did so although their generals disagreed on what they should do next. ARISTARCHUS arrived in Byzantium to replace Cleander as governor, and Anaxibius was about to be replaced as admiral by POLUS. Anaxibius wanted Xenophon to lead the Greeks back into Asia Minor, but Aristarchus forbade this and Xenophon received an offer from the Thracian king, SEUTHES, who wanted the Greek army to

help him recover parts of his territory he had lost. Seuthes promised pay, a city, and refuge to the men; and to Xenophon he offered his daughter. 3–5. The Greeks decided to accept Seuthes' offer and fought a successful campaign for him; but discontent arose among the Greeks because they had not been paid. By this time Seuthes' army was bigger than the Greek army. 6–7. The Spartans decided to fight Tissaphernes and wanted the Greeks to join them. This seemed good for Seuthes because he no longer needed the Greeks. A meeting was held of Greeks, Spartan representatives, and Seuthes. Some of the Greek soldiers denounced Xenophon, thinking he had been paid when they had not, but he proved this was not so. The Greeks then proposed that the Spartans make Seuthes give them their back pay, as a price for joining the campaign against Tissaphernes. At this, Seuthes sneaked out of the meeting, but he sent word to Xenophon asking him to stay even if the Greek army went with the Spartans. However, the omens told Xenophon to go with the Greeks. Xenophon saw Seuthes and arranged for the Greeks to be paid; Seuthes gave 600 oxen, 4,000 sheep and 120 slaves, which were sold and the money divided. Xenophon wanted to leave the army then, but was begged to stay until it had crossed from Thrace to Thyron and had joined the Spartan command. 8. Xenophon sailed across to Lampsacus with the Greeks. He continued as leader of the Greeks until they joined the Spartans at Pergamon. Here the Spartans greeted him gratefully and offered him his pick of the booty. Xenophon then turned the army over to the Spartan commander Thibron and left.

You Can't Take It With You

Play by George S. Kaufman, 1889–1961 and Moss Hart, 1904–1961. Produced 1937. Published 1937 by Rinehart & Co., New York. © 1937 by George S. Kaufman. (ML, 276)

THIS IS THE MOST hilarious comedy ever written for a sophisticated audience and it should and probably will stand up with *Charley's Aunt* (a timeless comedy for the masses) in the history of the theater. *You Can't Take It With You* is a grand concept and furthermore (unlike *Charley's Aunt*) it includes some distinguished serious

writing when Grandpa expounds his philosophy—without in any way detracting from the happy mood of the audience. The Broadway performance was a triumph for Josephine Hull as Penny and Henry Travers as Grandpa. The motion picture was good too, though not as good. If this play has any hindrance in its sure course to immortality it is the fact that an amateur group cannot easily set up an ideal Vanderhof living room, but then again a group of amateurs on a determined treasure hunt might accomplish even that.

Act I. 1. In the living room of the house of MARTIN VANDERHOF (GRANDPA), near Columbia University, Grandpa's daughter, Mrs. PENELOPE (PENNY) SYCAMORE is writing a play. (She writes plays because some years before a delivery man left a typewriter at the house by mistake.) Previously Penny painted in the living room. In this same room meals are eaten,

served by RHEBA, the good-natured colored maid, or maybe by her boy friend, DONALD, if he happens to be around. Also in this room Grandpa keeps his snake collection, throws darts, and spends his time enjoying life, as he has ever since he suddenly decided, 35 years ago, to give up business; it is here that Penny's daughter ESSIE practices her ballet steps and takes lessons from the huge Russian Mr. KOLENKHOV; it is here Essie's husband, ED CARMICHAEL, plays the xylophone and prints the menu for the evening meal on his printing press; it is here Penny's husband, PAUL SYCAMORE, builds on the floor the Empire State Building or the Queen Mary or tries out the latest firecrackers he manufactures in the cellar with Mr. DE PINNA, the iceman who came 8 years ago and has stayed ever since, taking the place of CHARLIE, the milkman, who died after staying 5 years with the family and was then buried under the name of Martin Vanderhof because nobody had ever asked his name. Even ALICE SYCAMORE, Penny's other daughter, likes the living room, though she is the sole person who is in everyday contact with life, as she works for the Wall Street firm of Kirby & Co. Alice is devoted to her family, though she seems to have escaped the mild insanity of the rest of them. Alice has fallen in love with TONY KIRBY, the son of her boss, and has invited him to the house, though she can hardly dare hope he will understand her family. It is not Tony but Mr. HENDERSON of the Internal Revenue Department who comes. It seems that Martin Vanderhof has not paid income tax for 22 years. Grandpa gives his reason: He does not believe in income tax. Mr. Henderson leaves, threatening action for income-tax evasion. Tony arrives and Alice tries hard, but unsuccessfully, to make the family act conventionally before she escapes with Tony. 2. Tony and Alice are in love, but Alice is afraid that their case is hopeless, as how could his family and hers ever get along? To Tony their love is all that matters.

Act II. A week later GAY WELLINGTON, a middle-aged actress, is about to read Penny's latest play, but she drinks too much and passes out. Ed is disturbed because whenever he is delivering the candy that Essie makes, somebody follows him. Alice is anxious because the Kirbys, Tony's parents, are to come for dinner tomorrow. Everybody solemnly promises to coöperate. Grandpa is throwing darts. Kolenkhov is giving Essie a ballet lesson; but, he says, "Confidentially, she stinks." Essie is making fresh candy. Paul and Mr. De Pinna are preparing their Fourth of July line of firecrackers in the cellar. The Kirbys arrive. Consternation on both sides: They are one day ahead of time. Nothing is prepared and to Alice's distress everything goes wrong. Kolenkhov demonstrates wrestling on the dignified Mr. Kirby, throws him and breaks his glasses. The parlor game Penny suggests causes an argument between Mr. and Mrs. Kirby. When, against Tony's strong remonstrances, the Kirbys are about to leave, Department of Justice agents take possession of the house and arrest everyone, as they have found seditious printed matter in the candy that Essie makes and Ed delivers. Everybody, the indignant Kirbys included, is hustled into a patrol wagon.

Act III. The following day the papers are full of the arrest of the Kirbys and the Sycamores, though after spending a night in jail they were given suspended sentences for the manufacture of fireworks without a permit. But Alice decides to leave home and Tony, though Tony wants to marry her in spite of everything. Kolenkov brings the former Grand Duchess Olga Katrina for dinner. She makes herself at home, and as this is her evening off from Child's, where she is a waitress, she is glad to make some real blintzes for the family. Alice is just about to leave when Mr. Kirby comes to take Tony away. Grandpa and Kirby talk. Grandpa tells how he quit business suddenly, one day 35 years ago, because he was doing what he *had* to; since then, every day of his life, he has done only what he wants to. He asks Kirby, Why do you want to make so much money? You can't take it with you. Tony confesses that he purposely brought his parents on the wrong day. He does not want to make the mistake his father made, go into a business because he has to. He quits the vice-presidency in his father's firm and says he will do whatever pleases him and will marry Alice. The Grand Duchess brings in the blintzes, Kirby joins the Vanderhof family, and Alice stays, while Grandpa reads a letter from the Department of Internal Revenue: It seems Mr. Martin Vanderhoff died 8 years ago, so no back income tax is owed to the government.

Doctor Zhivago

Novel by Boris Pasternak, 1890–1960. Published 1957 in Italy; in U.S., published 1958 by Pantheon Books, New York. Translated from the Russian by Max Hayward and Manya Harari. ©1958 by Pantheon Books, Inc.

BOTH THIS NOVEL and its author aroused an international literary furore in 1958. Pasternak, perhaps the leading Russian poet of his generation, had long been out of favor with the Communist government but managed to stay alive, avoiding original works and winning praise with translations of Shakespeare's plays. In 1957 Pasternak submitted the manuscript of *Doctor Zhivago* for publication in Russia and at the same time sent a copy to an Italian publisher, Giangiacomo Feltrinelli Editore. The opposition of Soviet authorities precluded publication in Russia and also caused Pasternak to write to Italy and ask the return of the manuscript. The Italian publishers refused. Within two years *Doctor Zhivago* had been translated into eight languages. In 1958 Pasternak was awarded the Nobel Prize for literature. The Soviet government treated this as a national insult and Pasternak, after first joyously accepting, soon saw fit to refuse the prize and repudiate much of the message in the novel. What the Soviet government found objectionable is the objective and often condemnatory comments of Pasternak's character Zhivago on the practical workings of communism in Russia. The book is long—more than 200,000 words.

Part I. Chap. 1. YURII (YURA) ZHIVAGO is 10 years old in 1903 when his mother dies and he goes to live with his uncle NIKOLAI VEDENIAPIN, a newspaperman in a town on the Volga. Yura's father, a wastrel, squandered the family fortune and has not been heard from in several years. Nikolai takes Yura on several visits to the estate of LAURENTI KOLOGRIVOV, where Yura becomes friendly with NIKA DUDOROV, a boy 2 years older than himself, whose father is in prison for revolutionary activities. At about this time a young Jewish boy, MISHA GORDON, is on a train trip to Moscow with his father, who is a lawyer. A distraught man seeks information from his father about laws on fraud and bankruptcy and later commits suicide by leaping from the train. He is Yura's father.

Chap. 2. In 1905 Russia's war with Japan ends but waves of revolution are sweeping across the country. In Moscow the railway workers plan a strike. One of their leaders is KUPRIAN TIVERZIN, who lives with his mother and a young boy, PAVEL (PASHA) ANTIPOV, whose father is in exile in Siberia. Tiverzin befriends OSIP GALIULLIN, the janitor's young son. The railway workers strike and are severely beaten by the police and Cossack troops. Strikes break out everywhere, even in the small dressmaking establishment run by Mme. AMALIA GUISHAR, a widow of French extraction. Her daughter LARA is a schoolmate of NADIA, Kologrivov's daughter, and her son RODIA is a student in a military academy. Mme. Guishar's lawyer, KOMAROVSKY, is also her lover, but he seduces Lara and Mme. Guishar tries to commit suicide by drinking iodine. Yura and Misha Gordon happen to see a man and a girl with Mme. Guishar, and Yura cannot take his eyes off the girl. It is Lara. He does not meet her, but the memory of her haunts him. Yura's uncle has left him in Moscow at the home of the brothers GROMEKO, two cultured intellectuals. One of the brothers, ALEXANDER, has a daughter TONIA who is about the same age as Yura. Misha is also living at the Gromekos'. He tells Yura that Komarovsky was Yura's father's lawyer and drove him to drink and to his death.

Chap. 3. Nadia gets Lara a job as governess to her little sister and Lara goes to live at the Kologrivov estate. Her brother Rodia comes to beg her for money to replace a school fund he has gambled away. He threatens to shoot himself. Lara borrows the money from Kologrivov and sends her brother away with it. She wants to pay back the loan but she sends what little money she has to help Pasha Antipov's father in Siberia. Pasha is in love with Lara and is studying to be a teacher, at her suggestion. Lara also is taking university courses. In Moscow, Yura is studying medicine, Misha philosophy, and Tonia law. It is 1911. Yura has discovered he has a talent for writing and he composes poems. Nikolai now lives in Switzerland and has written some excellent books on history. Tonia's mother, ANNA IVANOVNA, falls ill with pneumonia and thinking she may die she calls Tonia and Yura to her bedside and urges them to marry. Lara comes to Moscow to get money from Komarovsky to pay her debt to Kologrivov. She intends to shoot Komarovsky if he refuses. Lara finds Komarovsky at a Christmas party and does shoot at him but her shot misses him and grazes KORNAKOV, the assistant public prosecutor. Everyone thinks Lara meant to kill Kornakov, who prosecuted the strikers, but Komarovsky knows he was the intended target. Yura is at the party and when Lara collapses he rushes to attend her, but an urgent message calls him and Tonia back to the Gromeko house. Once again Yura sees but does not meet Lara. He and Tonia rush home and find Anna Ivanovna dead.

Chap. 4. Komarovsky has Lara taken to a friend's house and sees to it that charges against the girl are dropped. Lara and Pasha marry and go off to the small town of Yuriatin, where both teach. A daughter is born to them, KATENKA. Yura, now Dr. ZHIVAGO, marries Tonia. They have a son and Zhivago prospers. World War I begins. The Russian armies are successful for a year, then suffer reverses. Pasha, wrongly believing Lara does not love him, enlists in the Army. Yura also joins the Army and is attached to a divisional hospital on the Austrian front. Misha Gordon is there and they have long discussions. Pasha's division is also on the Austrian front. He is bivouacked with his old friend Osip Galiullin, who is also a lieutenant. Pasha is taken prisoner. Lara is at the front as a nurse, at the same hospital as Zhivago. Zhivago is hit by a shell splinter and finds himself in the hospital with Galiullin in the next bed. They are both nursed by Lara. She is sure that Pasha is dead but Galiullin tells her Pasha is a prisoner, which is true although he thinks he is lying. Zhivago hears that Gordon and Nika Dudorov have published a book of his and that it was well received. News comes of the revolution in Petersburg.

Part II. Chap. 5. Russia is in turmoil. Zhivago, Galiullin and Lara are in a small town not far from the front; Yura and Lara work in the hospital. Yura writes to Tonia, describing the disintegration and anarchy in the army and telling Tonia he is working

with Lara. Tonia replies that some fate has kept bringing him and Lara together and that he should go off to the Urals with her rather than return to his family in Moscow. Yura reassures his wife immediately, saying he could not have gone on without his love for her. An independent republic is established in his locality, but falls two weeks later to loyal troops of the Provisional Government. A new commissar is killed and Galiullin is suspected of being involved; he disappears. Lara starts back to Yuriatin, where she lived with Pasha, and Zhivago starts for Moscow and home. The trains are crowded almost beyond belief.

Chap. 6. Zhivago arrives in Moscow and finds general disorder, with people bartering for crusts of bread. He and Tonia are lovingly reunited and Zhivago sees his son, SASHENKA, who is almost a stranger to him. Tonia gives a party to celebrate her husband's homecoming and Misha Gordon, Nika Dudorov and Uncle Nikolai are there. Zhivago feels close to no one except his wife and her father. Gordon is no longer a serious scholar but plays the merry fellow; Dudorov, formerly a carefree clown, is now a professor of history; Nikolai has not seen what is going on in Russia and is too optimistic and complacent about the future. Zhivago predicts that a sea of blood will engulf Russia before the world's first socialist state is established there. Zhivago resumes his duties at his former hospital. There is fighting in the streets of Moscow, The dictatorship of the proletariat is established in Russia. Zhivago goes out in a blizzard to buy a paper and a boy in a reindeer coat stops and stares at him. The boy has an aristocratic face.

The commissars take over in Moscow. To be a bourgeois is dangerous and Zhivago is careful. Life goes on for three years of strife and three terrible winters. The Zhivagos eat a thin gruel of millet boiled in water, soup made of herring heads, and kasha made of unground wheat. There is an epidemic of typhus and Zhivago works hard. Then Zhivago comes down with typhus. Tonia feeds him white bread and butter and sugared tea. His half-brother, EVGRAF brought them; he is the boy in the reindeer coat. The Zhivagos decide to leave Moscow and go to the former estate of Varykino near Yuriatin, far away in the Urals. The estate had belonged to Tonia's grandfather.

Chap. 7. The Zhivago family leaves Moscow in April of 1919. The train moves slowly past burned villages whose inhabitants had resisted the Red Army. There are rumors that White forces have occupied Yuriatin and that Osip Galiullin is one of the White leaders. Zhivago takes a walk while the train is stalled and is apprehended by a sentry, who takes him to the commander of the train, a zealous Red officer named STRELNIKOV. He lets Zhivago go but warns him to watch his step. Strelnikov is actually Lara's husband Pasha Antipov.

Chap. 8. The Zhivago family arrive at Varykino, and meet MIKULITSYN, who formerly managed the iron works owned by Tonia's grandfather, KRUEGER. Mikulitsyn is sorry they came, because their pres-

ence may bring harm to his family. His son LIBERIUS is the local leader of the Red Partisans, called the Forest Brotherhood. The brotherhood consists of former soldiers, deserters from the Austrian army, displaced peasants, and unfrocked priests.

Chap. 9. Zhivago gives up the practice of medicine, but since he is the only doctor in the area people still come to him. He keeps a notebook in which he jots down his thoughts and his criticisms of what is happening. The Zhivagos grow most of their food and store 20 sacks of potatoes, 2 barrels of salted cucumbers, 2 barrels of sauerkraut, and a good quantity of cabbages, carrots, beans, and turnips. Evgraf visits briefly the next year and Zhivago realizes that his brother has powerful connections. At the library in Yuriatin Zhivago sees Lara and finally he goes to see her. She is living in dreadful quarters with her daughter Katenka. Lara tells Zhivago she is sure Strelnikov is her husband and she feels he has done things to protect her and Katenka. She says Strelnikov is in Siberia leading his forces against White troops commanded by Galiullin. Zhivago thinks constantly of Lara. He returns to see her and they become lovers. Zhivago is torn between his love for Lara and his different but equal love for his wife, Tonia. One day when he is on his way to see Lara three members of the Forest Brotherhood stop him and force him to go to their camp. His services as a doctor are sorely needed by the Partisans.

Chaps. 10–12. Beyond the Urals and into Siberia the Partisans are the main defenders of the Bolshevik cause against the White armies. Comrade Liberius is an able leader, loved passionately by some and feared and hated by others. His forces are constantly being augmented by peasants and townspeople fleeing from the Whites. As the tides of battle sweep back and forth over the steppes, neighbor is set against neighbor and reprisals are taken for reprisals. Zhivago is constantly on the move with the Partisan group. He is not under guard and tries to escape on three different occasions. Each escape ends in his recapture, but he is not punished. Liberius likes Zhivago and shares his tent with him. Zhivago is up to his neck in work. In winter there is typhus, in summer dysentery, and there are always the hundreds of wounded men. Savagery is at its peak. Neither side bothers to take prisoners. They are killed and even the wounded are knifed in the field. Zhivago is struck by the fact that many men have a paper with the 91st Psalm written on it sewn into their clothing. [In Protestant Bibles the 90th, in Roman Catholic Bibles the 89th: "Lord, thou hast been our refuge in all generations."] Liberius tells him that Varykino has been sacked but that their families have escaped. The Partisans are surrounded, but winter sets in and the Whites cannot penetrate the dense undergrowth and deep snow. The Partisans break through to the rear and a stream of new refugees pours through the gap. The Whites close the gap. They chop an arm and a leg off a prisoner and send him crawling back through the

Trudging through the snow

snow to the Partisan camp as a warning. Liberius tells Zhivago that the Whites have been defeated in most other areas. Zhivago worries about his family and plans another escape. This time he is successful.

Chap. 13. Zhivago makes his way back to Yuriatin—weeks of trudging through the snow with hardly a scrap of food. He avoids everybody; the law of the jungle is in force. At Yuriatin he goes to Lara's house and finds a note telling him to wait for her. He does not notice something written on the back of the note. An old woman in the town tells Zhivago that his family is safe in Moscow. He goes back to Lara's house and this time sees the back part of the note, which says that Tonia gave birth to a daughter after he had been kidnapped. Zhivago is utterly fatigued and starved; he collapses. Lara nurses him back to health and they are deeply in love and confide in each other. She says that if Strelnikov were to resume his true identity as Pasha, she would crawl to him, and that it is likewise Zhivago's duty to return to his family.

Summer comes and goes and Zhivago is busy in the local hospital. He is worried about his family and heartsick over the difficulty of choosing between the two women he loves. He suggests to Lara that they go to Moscow, but she says she must stay where Pasha's fate will be decided. Tonia writes that the family is being deported, probably to Paris. Zhivago faints when he gets this news.

Chap. 14. Komarovsky appears during the winter and warns Lara and Zhivago that they are in danger because they have been flouting the local Communist line. He says that Zhivago's name is already on the list for destruction, but offers to use his influence to help the doctor escape. Komarovsky speaks of a new Red Republic about to be established in Far Eastern Siberia, in which he will be the Minister of Justice. He wants Lara, Katenka and Zhivago to accompany him to Vladivostok. Zhivago is skeptical and he and Lara argue with Komarovsky and throw him out. They go to Varykino, which is deserted and a shambles, but they stay in Mikulitsyn's house and try to make the best of things. Zhivago writes poetry at night while Lara is asleep. He fears he may go mad unless he can resolve his personal life. Komarovsky comes and says a train is waiting in Yuriatin to take them to Vladivostok. He privately

tells Zhivago that Strelnikov has been killed and that Lara and Katenka are in danger. Zhivago persuades Lara and Katenka to go off in the sleigh with Komarovsky and says he will soon follow on horseback. Lara does not know he does not plan to follow, and she leaves. Zhivago misses her terribly and drinks, neglects his writing, and is in despair. A man appears—Strelnikov. He has escaped from a trumped-up court-martial. Zhivago tells him that Lara thinks he is dead, that she knew he was her husband Pasha, and that she loves him dearly. Pasha seems overjoyed, but that night he shoots himself.

Chap. 15. Zhivago goes back to Moscow, making his way mostly on foot. He is once again depressed by the sight of burned and deserted villages and fields of unharvested grain. On the road he meets VASIA, a young boy who is homeless, and takes him to Moscow. They reach there in the spring of 1922. Zhivago writes pamphlets and Vasia prints them, but Vasia soon suspects Zhivago's political ideas and leaves him. Zhivago tries to have his family rehabilitated politically so that he may bring them home

from exile, and he also applies for a passport, but his efforts are half-hearted and bring no results. He goes to a poor section of town to see MARKEL, who had been the porter at the Gromeko home. Markel is manager of a dilapidated house and gives Zhivago a tiny room on the top floor. Zhivago lives here in poverty, gives up his career as a doctor, and does nothing other than write. He lives with Markel's daughter MARINA and accepts her devotion. They have two children. It is 1929. Gordon lives nearby. He moves among the cultured academicians, in the company of Dudorov, who was temporarily deported but is back in Moscow. Zhivago cannot bear their platitudes and their political mysticisms. Zhivago has been hearing from his family in Paris again, after a lapse of several years. He hopes that Tonia has found another man who will love and care for her. Zhivago disappears. He writes to Marina and sends her some money, but Gordon and Dudorov cannot find him. Zhivago runs into his brother Evgraf, who gets him a room, gives him money, and gets him a job in a hospital. Then Zhivago suffers a heart attack and dies in the street. Lara comes to the funeral. Then Lara leaves Moscow and is not heard from again.

Chap. 17. Gordon and Dudorov are officers in the Red Army in World War II. They were in a prison camp for several years but were released to serve in the front lines. They feel that war is a blessing compared to what they suffered as political prisoners. Evgraf is a general. He meets a girl, TANIA, who is a laundress for the troops. Tania tells Evgraf a strange story and when she is through he promises to care for her and to see that she receives an education. Gordon and Dudorov meet Tania and hear her story. She is the daughter of Lara and Zhivago, born when her mother was on her way to Vladivostok with Komarovsky. Lara gave the child to an old couple, but the old man was killed, the woman went mad, and Tania became a wanderer.

Some years later Gordon and Dudorov are looking through a book of Zhivago's writings that Evgraf collected. They feel that the spirit of freedom he expressed may yet prevail in Russia.

[To the novel are appended some poems of Zhivago's, written of course by Pasternak.]

Zuleika Dobson

Novel by Max Beerbohm, 1872–1956. Published 1911 by Dodd, Mead, New York. © 1911, 1938 by Max Beerbohm. (ML, 116)

THE CHARM OF *Zuleika Dobson*, which has made it from time to time a general favorite and especially (perhaps logically) in colleges, is that the author never makes any concessions to reality. He is writing a humorous fantasy and fantastic it will be. There are probably quite a few snatches of *Zuleika Dobson* that cannot be appreciated without some knowledge of Oxford, its customs and its terrain, but so far this has not been a sufficient disadvantage to prevent its appreciation by American readers.

Chaps. 1–3. A train arrives at Oxford station, bringing visitors to the colleges for Eights Week; among them is the irresistible ZULEIKA DOBSON, to whom all young men's eyes turn. She has come to see her grandfather, the Warden of Judas College. On Zuleika's ride to the college her landau passes an exquisite young man on horseback, the Duke of DORSET, who takes little notice of Zuleika, and a short, shabby young man named NOAKS, who sighs after her. Both are students of Judas College. As Zuleika passes the Sheldonian Theatre, the busts of the Roman emperors that adorn it sweat with prophetic agony at the havoc she will wreak in Oxford. While her maid MELISANDE unpacks Zuleika's exotic treasures, the beautiful Zuleika reviews her past career. She has risen, by the gift of a conjuring set from a young devotee, from a nursery governess to a performer at evening parties and finally to a figure that all the fashionable world adores. But although she delights in her power, Zuleika, in her innocence, is still hoping to meet a man that she can love and look up to, who will not abase himself before her. She hopes it may be the Duke of Dorset, whom she meets at dinner that night. He is as much a paragon as she, with illustrious heritage as well as talents, but his resistance to the passion she rouses in him keeps him haughty and remote (increasing her passion for him). He refuses her offer to turn the pages of his music during his coming concert, and he abruptly flees from her presence, only to find full proof of his love for her in a magical change of color of the pearl studs in his shirt.

Chaps. 3–8. By the following morning, the duke is reconciled to his love and attempts to confide in Noaks, only to find that he too adores Zuleika. Immediately afterward, Zuleika arrives to call on him. He confesses his love and by his self-abasement effectively extinguishes her love for him. After lunch the duke, undeterred, makes a long and formal proposal of marriage, describing the worldly advantages he can offer. She angrily rejects him but asks for the pearl studs as a memento of the love she once felt. He refuses to part with an heirloom but agrees to accompany her to the boat races. As they walk to the river, they meet a crowd of young men returning from the races, all of them enslaved by Zuleika's beauty. The Duke reveals to Zuleika his intention to drown himself as a warning to other men of her dangerous power. Zuleika is secretly delighted with the compliment but induces him to postpone his suicide until the next day. He agrees but refuses to dine with her that night, as he has a previous engagement with the Junta, a club of which he is president. At dinner, he refuses to toast the 18th-century beauty the club honors as "the fairest witch that ever was or will be," and Zuleika's name is unanimously substituted. He reveals his intention to die for her, and the other young men decide to follow his example.

Chaps. 9–10. At the concert, Zuleika's late arrival is so dazzling as to stop the per-

formance. The Duke plays Chopin's *Marche Funèbre* so brilliantly that the ghost of Chopin, tended by George Sand, comes to hear, and they look forward to meeting him on the morrow, when he will be dead also. During the intermission, Zuleika again begs for the pearl studs and again is refused. She hears from the Scotsman MCQUERN that all the young men in Oxford intend to die for her and she rewards them then and there with her conjuring act. In the course of it she manages to get the studs, giving the duke in return her earrings (which had undergone a similar change of color and have now turned black in mourning for him). The duke decides not to kill himself after all and attempts to kiss Zuleika, who runs indoors and empties a jug of water over him.

Chaps. 11–13. The author digresses to explain how he came to know the story. The Muse of History, Clio, becoming bored with historians, got leave of Zeus to have one notable event observed as it happened and recorded as in a novel. Zuleika's stay in Oxford is the event and the author, the chosen chronicler, is bound to observe and record every detail of the episode. He pities the duke for his humiliating wetting. He briefly observes the mundane Noaks making his will. Then he finds that the duke has caught cold, and now furiously despising Zuleika he is even more resolved not to die.

Chaps. 14–18. KATIE BATCH, the duke's landlady's daughter, who adores him, delivers a message to him from Zuleika. It is an apology, which amuses him but leaves him unmoved; but he also receives a telegram from his steward to say that the two owls that are omens of death in the duke's family have been seen and heard. He realizes that the gods have spoken and his doom is sealed. In his horror at the idea of meeting Zuleika, the duke flees from Melisande, whom he sees in the street and who slightly resembles her. He falls down and has to be tended by a pharmacist, both for his bruises and for his cold. He fears he may be prevented by accident from dying by drowning as he has planned. He tries to dissuade other undergraduates from sharing his fate but has no success. In his reformed mood he goes to the club and toasts the 18th-century beauty he spurned the night before. Returning home, he finds Zuleika waiting for him. She has perceived from the pearl studs, which have again changed color, that the duke no longer loves her, so her love for him has promptly returned. He tells her his death is inevitable, and she faints. When she recovers, he rejects her; she kills her love for him then and there, and thereby gets the better of him. The duke attempts to console himself with lunch and with Katie Batch. He offers her Zuleika's pearl earrings, which she at first spurns through pride and then accepts through cupidity. But when she assumes that he means to marry her he recoils and explains that he is going away. Mrs. Batch, the motherly landlady, is upset but partly consoled by payment of the bill and by a poem the duke writes in praise of the establishment. The

duke, now drinking and musing in solitude while comparing his fate with Byron's, suddenly resolves to die clothed in his magnificent robes as a Knight of the Order of the Garter.

Chap. 19. The duke's walk to the river in this costume creates a sensation among the crowds of visitors to the races, and when he pauses to warn two women of the dreadful thing about to happen at the river and tells them to go home, they think him not sane. He meets Zuleika and permits her to walk with him to the Judas barge, where she will stand to watch him (and all the other young men in Oxford) die. The duke decides to die immediately after the race between Judas and Magdalen colleges, but the onset of a thunderstorm, which would ruin his appearance in his fine robes, prompts him not to wait so long. He is followed in his death leap by all the undergraduates in Oxford, all of them dying, like him, with the name of Zuleika on their lips. The duke lives just long enough to see that Judas has won its race, and is now "head of the River." The older men, the other women, and Zuleika, in her hour of triumph, are left on the bank of the river in a downpour of rain.

Chaps. 20–22. CLARENCE BATCH, like the Messenger in classical tragedy, announces the dreadful news to his mother and Katie, who hears in a rage of jealousy that the duke called out Zuleika's name as he died. Mrs. Batch, in great distress, surmises that even the insignificant Noaks must be dead too. Zuleika does not drown herself in remorse but merely takes a bath and then dines with the Warden, who is mildly surprised to find no undergraduates present at what should be a supper of celebration. The 18th-century beauty and the Scholar Gipsy (of Matthew Arnold's poem) mourn the dead on the river banks. Katie Batch, tidying the lodgers' rooms, discovers the cowardly Noaks hiding behind the curtains; she adores him as the only man strong-minded enough (as she supposes) to resist Zuleika's beauty, and they become engaged, Noaks planning to set up a school on the proceeds from the pearl earrings. But Zuleika appears in the street below and now she adores Noaks. His feeble excuses to her for being still alive make Katie revile him. When the members of Katie's family appear and add their scorn, Noaks jumps out of the window in his cowardice and humiliation and he too is killed. Zuleika in her misery returns to Judas College and tells her grandfather how all the young men have died. She declares that she will spend the rest of her life in the seclusion of a convent. The Warden sympathizes with her and tells her that he also was irresistible as a young man, but that he is at last very contentedly married to a woman who withstood his fascination. Zuleika, relieved to find she is not unique, cheers up and changes her mind. She decides to leave Oxford, gives the pearl studs (last memento of the affair) to Melisande, and prepares for a visit to Cambridge.

651

INDEX OF AUTHORS

Authors of Works, Translators, Editors, Dramatists, Librettists and Composers

653

INDEX OF TITLES

Names and Subtitles or Alternative Titles
of Works in Literary Treasures, Including
Stories, Poems, Plays, Etc.

INDEX OF PROPER NAMES
Characters, Persons, and Places in Literary Treasures

To find a name, follow the usual customs of alphabetization, except that the first names of characters are grouped together in the index, regardless of the surnames following them, so that Al Grecco is alphabetized as AL and not as ALG and so precedes Alex; John Shaw appears with the other Johns and precedes Johnny. All names beginning with Mc- or Mac- are alphabetized as though they began with Mac-, so that McLean is alphabetized as though it were MacLean.

662

666

670

671

672

674

675

676

678